HARRAP'S
POCKET

French-English

DICTIONARY
DICTIONNAIRE

Anglais-Français

Michael Janes

HARRAP
London

Distributed in the United States by
PRENTICE HALL
New York

French Consultant
Fabrice Antoine

English Consultants
Hazel Curties
Stuart Fortey

First published in Great Britain 1988
by HARRAP BOOKS Ltd
Chelsea House, 26 Market Square, Bromley, Kent BR1 1NA

© *Harrap Books Limited, 1988*

In the United States, ISBN 0-13-382979-0

Library of Congress Cataloging-in-Publication Data

Harrap's pocket French-English dictionary =dictionnaire Anglais-
Français / [edited by] Michael Janes.
        p.   cm.
First published in Great Britain in 1988.
ISBN 0-13-382979-0 : $9.95 (U.S. : est.)
1. French language—Dictionaries—English.
2. English language—Dictionaries—French.
I. Janes, Michael. II. Title: Pocket French-English dictionary. III.
Title: Dictionnaire Anglais-Français.
PC2640.H29 1990   89-26636
443'.21—dc20   CIP

Dépôt légal pour cette édition : avril 1988

Printed in Great Britain by
Richard Clay Ltd, Bungay, Suffolk

Contents/Table des matières

Preface   iv
Préface   v

Grammar notes   vii
Notes sur la grammaire   viii

Abbreviations used in the text   ix
Abréviations employées dans le texte

Pronunciation of French   xi
Prononciation du français

Pronunciation of English   xii
Prononciation de l'anglais

FRENCH – ENGLISH   1
FRANÇAIS – ANGLAIS

French verb conjugations   (i)
Conjugaisons des verbes français

English irregular verbs   (vii)
Les verbes anglais irréguliers

Numerals   (x)
Les nombres

Days and months   (xii)
Les jours et les mois

ENGLISH – FRENCH   309
ANGLAIS – FRANÇAIS

iii

Preface

This dictionary is an entirely new publication designed to provide an up-to-date, practical and concise work of reference giving translations of the most useful French and English vocabulary.

The aim has been to achieve a work of great clarity of equal value to French and to English speakers, whether students, tourists, businessmen or -women or general readers, and to produce a text offering the maximum amount of guidance in pinpointing and understanding translations. Equal importance has been given to the presentation of French and English. Different translations of the same word or phrase are clearly labelled by means of bracketed context indicators and/or style and field labels. A single translation of a word is also often labelled as an additional aid to the user (e.g. **hedgehog** n (animal) hérisson m; **ungainly** a (clumsy) gauche; **béotien, -ienne** nmf (inculte) philistine). The user is helped by having indicators and labels in French in the French section and in English in the English section of the dictionary.

Style and field labels follow bracketed indicators (e.g. **grid** n . . . (system) El réseau m; **bidule** nm (chose) Fam thingummy). In the event of more than one translation within a grammatical category being qualified by the same style or field label, the label may then precede (see **calé, liquidizer, trucker**).

The user will find in the text important abbreviations, useful geographical information such as names of countries, and a wide coverage of American words and usage. The vocabulary treated includes French and English colloquialisms and slang, and important technical jargon. Comparatives and superlatives of English adjectives are also indicated.

In order to save space, derived words are usually included within the entry of a headword. All such words are highlighted by means of a lozenge. Derivatives may be written in full or abbreviated, as is usually the case for important derived forms (such as English **-ly** or French **-ment**).

An oblique stroke in bold is used to mark the stem of a headword at which point the derived ending is added. A bold dash stands for a headword or the portion of a headword to the left of the oblique stroke (e.g. **awkward** a . . . ◆—**ly** adv . . . ◆—**ness** n . . . ; **boulevers/er** vt . . . ◆—**ant** a . . . ◆—**ement** nm).

An oblique stroke within an entry is another space-saving device. It is used to separate non equivalent alternative parts of a phrase or expression matched exactly in French and English (e.g. **les basses/hautes classes** the lower/upper classes is to be understood as: **les basses classes** the lower classes and **les hautes classes** the upper classes; **to give s.o./sth a push** pousser qn/qch as: **to give s.o. a push** pousser qn and **to give sth a push** pousser qch).

A further typographical device, a filled square, may be used to introduce a string of English phrasal verbs (see **come, take**).

In common with other Harrap dictionaries, when a headword appears in an example in the same form, it is represented by its initial letter. This applies whether the headword starts a new line (e.g. **advance** n | in a. of s.o. avant qn) or appears within an entry, either in full form (e.g. ◆**arterial** a a. road route f principale), or in abbreviated form (e.g. (where ◆—**ed** stands for **advanced**) ◆—**ed** a a. in years âgé).

The pronunciation of both English and French is shown using the latest symbols of the International Phonetic Alphabet. Pronunciation is given for headwords at the start of an entry, and, as an additional help to the user, for a word within an entry where the correct pronunciation may be difficult to derive from the form of the word (e.g. ◆**aristocratie** [-asi]; ◆**aoûtien, -ienne** [ausjɛ̃, -jɛn]; ◆**rabid** ['ræbid]; ◆**prayer** [preə r]).

Stress in English is indicated for headwords and for derived words in which stress differs from that of a headword (e.g. **civilize** ['sɪvɪlaɪz] and ◆**civili'zation**). American English pronunciation is listed wherever it is considered to differ substantially from that of British English (e.g. **aristocrat** ['ærɪstəkræt, Am ə'rɪstəkræt], **quinine** ['kwɪniːn, Am 'kwaɪnaɪn]). American spelling is also given if considered sufficiently different (e.g. **tire** and **tyre, plow** and **plough**).

An original feature of this dictionary is its semantic approach to the order and arrangement of entries. An approach whereby the meaning of words is allowed to influence the structure of entries is felt to be of particular benefit to the user in his or her understanding of language.

Important semantic categories have been indicated by bold Arabic numerals within an entry (see **bolt**, **tail**, **général**) or have been entered as separate headwords (see **bug**[1] and **bug**[2], **draw**[1] and **draw**[2], **start**[1] and **start**[2]). Note that grammatical categories, apart from the first, have been marked by a dash.

Words are entered under the headword from which they are considered to derive (e.g. **approfondi**, abbreviated as ◆—i follows **approfond/ir**; ◆**astronomer** and ◆**astro′nomical** follow **astronomy**). Present and past participles (used adjectivally) are felt to be closely associated in meaning and form with the infinitive from which they derive. They are entered, usually in abbreviated form, within an entry immediately after the infinitive, any other derivatives there may be following in alphabetical order (e.g. **exalt/er** *vt* ... ◆—ant *a* ... ◆—é *a* ... ◆**exaltation** *nf*: **accommodat/e** *vt* ... ◆—ing *a* ... ◆**accommo′dation** *n*; **expir/e** *vi* ... ◆—ed *a* ... ◆**expi′ration** *n* ... ◆**expiry** *n*).

Derived words and compounds are felt to be semantically distinct and are, wherever possible, grouped together alphabetically and listed separately from each other (e.g. **base** *n* ... ◆—**less** *a* ... ◆—**ness** *n* ... ◆**baseball** *n* ... ◆**baseboard** *n*; **bouton** *nm* ... ◆**b.-d′or** *nm* ... ◆**b.-pression** *nm* ... ◆**boutonner** *vt* ... ◆**boutonneux, -euse** *a* ... ◆**boutonnière** *nf*). Compounds may be listed in the place within an entry where they are felt best to belong by virtue of meaning.

The author wishes to express his gratitude to Monsieur F. Antoine, Mrs H. Curties and Mr S. Fortey for their advice and help, to Mrs R. Hillmore for her assistance with proofreading, and to Mr J.-L. Barbanneau for his support and encouragement.

M. Janes
London, 1988

Préface

Ce dictionnaire entièrement nouveau a pour ambition d'être un ouvrage de référence moderne, pratique et compact, offrant les traductions des termes les plus courants du français comme de l'anglais.

Il veut être un ouvrage qui, par sa grande clarté, soit utile autant au francophone qu'à l'anglophone, pour les études, le tourisme, les affaires aussi bien que pour l'usage courant: il tente de fournir le plus d'indications possible pour aider l'utilisateur à cerner et à comprendre les traductions proposées. On a accordé la même importance à la présentation du français qu'à celle de l'anglais. Les différentes traductions d'un même mot ou d'une même expression sont clairement définies à l'aide d'indications de contexte entre parenthèses et/ou de symboles indiquant le niveau de langue et le domaine d'utilisation. Lorsqu'un mot est accompagné d'une seule traduction, celle-ci est également souvent précédée d'une indication destinée à fournir à l'utilisateur une aide supplémentaire (par exemple **hedgehog** *n* (*animal*) hérisson *m*; **ungainly** *a* (*clumsy*) gauche; **béotien, -ienne** *nmf* (*inculte*) philistine). L'accès à cet ouvrage est facilité par l'utilisation d'indications en français dans la partie français-anglais et en anglais dans la partie anglais-français.

Les indications de niveau de langue et de domaine d'utilisation viennent à la suite de celles entre parenthèses (par example **grid** ... (*system*) El réseau *m*; **bidule** *nm* (*chose*) *Fam* thingummy). Lorsque plusieurs traductions dans la même catégorie grammaticale sont définies par la même indication, celle-ci peut alors venir en tête (voir **calé**, **liquidizer**, **trucker**).

L'utilisateur trouvera dans cet ouvrage des abréviations importantes, de précieux éléments de géographie tels que des noms de pays, ainsi qu'une large sélection d'américanismes. Le lexique retenu comprend des mots et des expressions familiers et argotiques, tant en français qu'en anglais, et des termes techniques courants. De plus, les comparatifs et superlatifs des adjectifs anglais sont donnés.

Par souci de concision, les mots dérivés sont généralement donnés dans le corps des articles. Tous ces mots sont repérés par un losange. Les dérivés sont donnés soit sous leur forme complète, soit en abrégé, ce qui est généralement le cas pour les formes dérivées courantes (telles que celles en **-ly** en anglais ou en **-ment** en français).

On utilise une barre oblique pour indiquer le radical d'une entrée à la suite duquel la terminaison d'un dérivé sera ajoutée. Un tiret en gras remplace le mot d'entrée ou la partie de ce mot qui précède la barre oblique (par exemple **awkward** *a* . . . ◆—**ly** *adv* . . . ◆—**ness** *n* . . . ; **boulevers/er** *vt* . . . ◆—**ant** *a* . . . ◆—**ement** *nm*).

Toujours par souci de concision, une barre oblique est utilisée dans un article pour éviter la répétition d'un même élément de phrase (par exemple **les basses/hautes classes** the lower/upper classes se lira: **les basses classes** the lower classes et **les hautes classes** the upper classes; **to give s.o./sth a push** pousser qn/qch se lira: **to give s.o. a push** pousser qn et **to give sth a push** pousser qch).

Enfin, un carré plein peut être utilisé pour introduire une série de verbes à particule en anglais (voir **come**, **take**).

Comme il est d'usage dans les autres dictionnaires Harrap, lorsqu'un mot d'entrée est repris sous la même forme dans un exemple, il est remplacé par sa première lettre. Cela est le cas aussi bien lorsque le mot est au début d'un article (par exemple **advance** *n* in a. of s.o. avant qn) ou apparaît dans un article, sous sa forme complète (par exemple ◆**arterial** *a* **a. road** route *f* principale) ou en abrégé (par exemple ◆—**ed** remplaçant **advanced**) ◆—**ed** *a* **a. in years** âgé).

La prononciation de l'anglais comme du français est fournie; elle utilise la notation la plus moderne de l'Alphabet Phonétique International. La phonétique est donnée pour les mots d'entrée au début de l'article et, pour aider l'utilisateur, pour tout mot dans un article dont il pourrait être difficile de déduire la prononciation à partir de l'orthographe (par exemple ◆**aristocratie** [-asi]; ◆**aoûtien, -ienne** [ausje, -jɛn]; ◆**rabid** ['ræbɪd]; ◆**prayer** [preɔr]).

En anglais, l'accent tonique est indiqué pour les mots d'entrée et pour les dérivés chaque fois que l'accentuation diffère de celle de l'entrée (par exemple **civilize** et ◆**civili'zation**). Les prononciations américaines sont indiquées chaque fois qu'elles diffèrent de façon substantielle de celles de l'anglais britannique (par exemple **aristocrat** ['ærɪstəkræt, *Am* ə'rɪstəkræt], **quinine** ['kwɪniːn, *Am* 'kwaɪnaɪn]). On indique également l'orthographe américaine lorsqu'elle est suffisamment différente de celle de l'anglais britannique (par exemple **tire** et **tyre**, **plow** et **plough**).

Une des caractérisques originales de ce dictionnaire est son approche sémantique du classement et de l'organisation des articles. On a considéré que cette approche, où le sens des mots détermine pour une part l'organisation des articles, serait d'un grand secours à l'utilisateur en ce qui concerne sa compréhension de la langue.

Les catégories sémantiques importantes sont indiquées dans un article par des chiffres arabes en gras (voir **bolt**, **tail**, **général**) qui sont présentées comme des mots distincts (voir **bug**[1] et **bug**[2], **draw**[1] et **draw**[2], **start**[1] et **start**[2]). Les catégories grammaticales autres que la première traitée sont indiquées par un tiret.

Les mots apparaissent sous les mots d'entrée dont ils sont dérivés (par exemple **approfondi**, abrégé en ◆—**i** suit **approfond/ir**; ◆**astronomer** et ◆**astro'nomical** suivent **astronomy**). Les participes présents et passés (utilisés comme adjectifs) sont considérés comme étant étroitement associés par le sens et par la forme à l'infinitif dont ils sont dérivés. Ils sont placés dans l'article, généralement en abrégé, immédiatement après l'infinitif; tous les autres dérivés éventuels apparaissent ensuite par ordre alphabétique (par exemple **exalt/er** *vt* . . . ◆—**ant** *a* . . . ◆—**é** *a* . . . ◆**exaltation** *nf*; **accommodat/e** *vt* . . . ◆—**ing** *a* . . . ◆**accommo'dation** *n*; **expir/e** *vi* . . . ◆—**ed** *a* . . . ◆**expi'ration** *n* . . . ◆**expiry** *n*).

Les mots dérivés et les mots composés sont considérés comme étant distincts, du point de vue du sens, et sont, chaque fois que possible, regroupés séparément (par exemple **base** *n* . . . ◆—**less** *a* . . . ◆—**ness** *n* . . . ◆**baseball** *n* . . . ◆**baseboard** *n*; **bouton** *nm* . . . ◆**b.-d'or** *nm* . . . ◆**b.-pression** *nm* . . . ◆**boutonner** *vt* . . . ◆**boutonneux, -euse** *a* . . . ◆**boutonnière** *nf*). Les composés se trouvent placés dans les articles là où leur sens a semblé devoir les appeler.

L'auteur tient à exprimer sa gratitude à Monsieur F. Antoine, à Mrs H. Curties et à Mr S. Fortey pour leurs conseils et leur collaboration, à Mrs R. Hillmore qui a bien voulu nous aider à relire les épreuves, et à Monsieur J.-L. Barbanneau pour son soutien et ses encouragements.

M. Janes
Londres, 1988

Grammar notes

In French, the feminine of an adjective is formed as a rule by adding **e** to the masculine form (e.g. grand, grande; carré, carrée; chevalin, chevaline). If the masculine already ends in **e**, the feminine is the same as the masculine (e.g. utile). Irregular feminine forms of adjectives (e.g. généreux, généreuse; léger, légère; doux; douce) are given in the French-English side of the dictionary. In the English-French side, French adjectives are shown in the masculine form only. Irregular feminines of adjectives are listed in the following way: généreux, -euse; léger, -ère; doux, douce.

To form the plural of a French noun or adjective **s** is usually added to the singular (e.g. arbre, arbres; taxi, taxis; petit, petits). The plural form of a noun ending in **s**, **x** or **z** (e.g. pois, croix, nez) is the same as that of the singular. Plurals of nouns and adjectives which do not follow these general rules are listed in the French section, including the plurals of French compounds where the formation of the plural involves a change other than the addition of final **s** (e.g. arc-en-ciel, arcs-en-ciel). Those nouns and adjectives where **x** or **aux** is added in the plural are shown in the following way: cerveau, -x; général, -aux.

In English also, **s** is added to form the plural of a noun (e.g. cat, cats; taxi, taxis) but a noun ending in **ch**, **s**, **sh**, **x** or **z** forms its plural by the addition of **es** (e.g. glass, glasses; match, matches). (Note that when **ch** is pronounced [k], the plural is in **s**, e.g. monarch, monarchs.) When a noun ends in **y** preceded by a consonant, **y** is changed to **ies** to form the plural (e.g. army, armies). Irregular English plurals are given in the English-French side, including the plurals of English compounds where the formation of the plural involves a change other than the addition of final **s** (e.g. brother-in-law, brothers-in-law).

English nouns may be used as adjectives. When a French adjective is translated in this way, this use is made clear by the addition of a hyphen following the noun translation (e.g. farm- as a translation of **agricole**).

Most French verbs have regular conjugations though some display spelling anomalies (see French verb conjugations on p (i)). In the French section an asterisk is used to mark an irregular verb, and refers the user to the table of irregular verbs on p (ii).

Most English verbs form their past tense and past participle by adding **ed** to the infinitive (e.g. look, looked) or **d** to an infinitive already ending in **e** (e.g. love, loved). When a verb ends in **y** preceded by a consonant **y** becomes **ied** (e.g. satisfy, satisfied). To form the third person singular of a verb in the present tense **s** is added to the infinitive (e.g. know, knows) but an infinitive in **ch**, **s**, **sh**, **x** or **z** forms its third person singular by the addition of **es** (e.g. dash, dashes). When an infinitive ends in **y** preceded by a consonant, **y** is changed to **ies** to form the third person singular (e.g. satisfy, satisfies).

The English present participle is formed by the addition of **ing** to the infinitive (e.g. look, looking) but final **e** is omitted when an infinitive ends in **e** (e.g. love, loving). When the infinitive ends in a single consonant preceded by a vowel (e.g. tug), the final consonant is usually doubled in the past tense, past and present participles (e.g. tug, tugged, tugging).

Irregular English verb conjugations are given in the English headword list, and a summary of the most important irregular verbs may also be found on p (vii). The doubling of consonants in English verbs is indicated in the text. The latter is shown in the following way: **tug** . . . *vt* (**–gg–**).

Notes sur la grammaire

En français, le féminin d'un adjectif se forme en général en ajoutant **e** au masculin (par exemple grand, grande; carré, carrée; chevalin, chevaline). Lorsque le masculin se termine déjà par **e**, le féminin est identique (par exemple utile). Les féminins d'adjectifs qui ne se conforment pas à ces règles (par exemple généreux, généreuse; léger, légère; doux, douce) sont donnés dans la partie français-anglais où ils sont notés comme suit: généreux, -euse; léger, -ère; doux, douce. Dans la partie anglais-français, on ne donne que la forme masculine des adjectifs.

On forme en général le pluriel d'un nom ou d'un adjectif français en ajoutant **s** au singulier (par exemple arbre, arbres; taxi, taxis; petit, petits). Le pluriel d'un nom se terminant par **s**, **x** ou **z** (par exemple pois, croix, nez) est identique au singulier. Les pluriels des noms et adjectifs qui font exception à ces règles générales sont signalés dans la partie français-anglais, de même que les pluriels des mots composés français dont le passage au pluriel appelle une modification autre que le simple ajout d'un **s** final (par exemple arc-en-ciel, arcs-en-ciel). Les noms et adjectifs dont le pluriel se forme à l'aide d'un **x** ou de **aux** sont notés comme suit: cerveau, -x; général, -aux.

De la même façon, en anglais, on forme le pluriel des noms en ajoutant **s** (par exemple cat, cats; taxi, taxis) mais on ajoutera **es** aux noms qui se terminent par **ch**, **s**, **sh**, **x** ou **z** (par exemple glass, glasses; match, matches). (Noter cependant que lorsque **ch** se prononce [k], le pluriel est en **s**, comme dans monarch, monarchs.) Lorsqu'un nom se termine par un **y** précédé d'une consonne, ce **y** devient **ies** au pluriel (par exemple army, armies). Les pluriels irréguliers de l'anglais sont signalés dans la partie anglais-français, de même que les pluriels des mots composés anglais dont le passage au pluriel entraîne une modification autre que le simple ajout d'un **s** final (par exemple brother-in-law, brothers-in-law).

Les noms anglais peuvent s'utiliser comme adjectifs. Lorsqu'un adjectif français est traduit par un nom, cela est signalé par l'ajout d'un trait d'union à la suite de ce nom (par exemple farm- comme traduction de **agricole**).

La plupart des verbes français ont des conjugaisons régulières; cependant, certains subissent des variations orthographiques (voir: Conjugaisons des verbes français à la page (i)). Dans la partie français-anglais, un astérisque signale un verbe irrégulier et renvoie à la table des verbes irréguliers donnée en page (ii).

En anglais, le passé et le participe passé des verbes se forment dans la plupart des cas en ajoutant **ed** à l'infinitif (par exemple look, looked) ou seulement **d** lorsque l'infinitif se termine par un **e** (par exemple love, loved). Lorsqu'un verbe se termine par un **y** précédé d'une consonne, ce **y** devient **ied** (par exemple satisfy, satisfied). La troisième personne du singulier d'un verbe au présent se forme en ajoutant **s** à l'infinitif (par exemple know, knows), mais on ajoutera **es** aux infinitifs qui se terminent par **ch**, **s**, **sh**, **x** ou **z** (par exemple dash, dashes). Enfin, lorsqu'un verbe se termine par un **y** précédé d'une consonne, ce **y** devient **ies** à la troisième personne du singulier (par exemple satisfy, satisfies).

Le participe présent en anglais se forme en ajoutant la désinence **ing** à l'infinitif (par exemple look, looking); lorsqu'un infinitif comporte un **e** final, celui-ci disparaît (par exemple love, loving). Lorsque l'infinitif se termine par une seule consonne précédée d'une voyelle (par exemple tug), la consonne finale est le plus souvent doublée au passé et aux participes passé et présent (par exemple tug, tugged, tugging).

Les formes des verbes irréguliers anglais sont données dans la partie anglais-français et une liste récapitulative des verbes irréguliers usuels figure en page (vii). Le doublement des consonnes dans les verbes anglais est signalé dans le corps de l'ouvrage; il est noté comme suit: **tug** . . . *vt* (**–gg–**).

Abbreviations

Abréviations

adjective	*a*	adjectif
abbreviation	*abbr, abrév*	abréviation
adverb	*adv*	adverbe
agriculture	*Agr*	agriculture
American	*Am*	américain
anatomy	*Anat*	anatomie
architecture	*Archit*	architecture
slang	*Arg*	argot
article	*art*	article
cars, motoring	*Aut*	automobile
auxiliary	*aux*	auxiliaire
aviation, aircraft	*Av*	aviation
biology	*Biol*	biologie
botany	*Bot*	botanique
British	*Br*	britannique
Canadian	*Can*	canadien
carpentry	*Carp*	menuiserie
chemistry	*Ch*	chimie
cinema	*Cin*	cinéma
commerce	*Com*	commerce
conjunction	*conj*	conjonction
cookery	*Culin*	cuisine
definite	*def, déf*	défini
demonstrative	*dem, dém*	démonstratif
economics	*Econ, Écon*	économie
electricity	*El, Él*	électricité
et cetera	*etc*	et cetera
feminine	*f*	féminin
familiar	*Fam*	familier
football	*Fb*	football
figurative	*Fig*	figuré
finance	*Fin*	finance
feminine plural	*fpl*	féminin pluriel
French	*Fr*	français
geography	*Geog, Géog*	géographie
geology	*Geol, Géol*	géologie
geometry	*Geom, Géom*	géométrie
grammar	*Gram*	grammaire
history	*Hist*	histoire
humorous	*Hum*	humoristique
indefinite	*indef, indéf*	indéfini
indicative	*indic*	indicatif
infinitive	*inf*	infinitif
interjection	*int*	interjection
invariable	*inv*	invariable
ironic	*Iron*	ironique
journalism	*Journ*	journalisme
legal, law	*Jur*	juridique
linguistics	*Ling*	linguistique
literary	*Lit, Litt*	littéraire
literature	*Liter, Littér*	littérature

masculine	*m*	masculin
mathematics	*Math*	mathématique
medicine	*Med, Méd*	médecine
carpentry	*Menuis*	menuiserie
meteorology	*Met, Mét*	météorologie
military	*Mil*	militaire
masculine plural	*mpl*	masculin pluriel
music	*Mus*	musique
noun	*n*	nom
nautical	*Nau*	nautique
noun feminine	*nf*	nom féminin
noun masculine	*nm*	nom masculin
noun masculine and feminine	*nmf*	nom masculin et féminin
pejorative	*Pej, Péj*	péjoratif
philosophy	*Phil*	philosophie
photography	*Phot*	photographie
physics	*Phys*	physique
plural	*pl*	pluriel
politics	*Pol*	politique
possessive	*poss*	possessif
past participle	*pp*	participe passé
prefix	*pref, préf*	préfixe
preposition	*prep, prép*	préposition
present participle	*pres p*	participe présent
present tense	*pres t*	temps présent
pronoun	*pron*	pronom
psychology	*Psy*	psychologie
past tense	*pt*	prétérit
	qch	quelque chose
	qn	quelqu'un
registered trademark	®	marque déposée
radio	*Rad*	radio
railway, *Am* railroad	*Rail*	chemin de fer
relative	*rel*	relatif
religion	*Rel*	religion
school	*Sch, Scol*	école
singular	*sing*	singulier
slang	*Sl*	argot
someone	*s.o.*	
sport	*Sp*	sport
something	*sth*	
subjunctive	*sub*	subjonctif
technical	*Tech*	technique
telephone	*Tel, Tél*	téléphone
textiles	*Tex*	industrie textile
theatre	*Th*	théâtre
television	*TV*	télévision
typography, printing	*Typ*	typographie
university	*Univ*	université
United States	*US*	États-Unis
auxiliary verb	*v aux*	verbe auxiliaire
intransitive verb	*vi*	verbe intransitif
impersonal verb	*v imp*	verbe impersonnel
pronominal verb	*vpr*	verbe pronominal
transitive verb	*vt*	verbe transitif
transitive and intransitive verb	*vti*	verbe transitif et intransitif

Pronunciation of French

TABLE OF PHONETIC SYMBOLS

Vowels

[i]	vite, cygne	[y]	cru, sûr
[e]	été, donner	[ø]	feu, meule
[ɛ]	elle, mais	[œ]	œuf, jeune
[a]	chat, fameux	[ə]	le, refaire
[ɑ]	pas, âgé	[ɛ̃]	vin, plein, faim
[ɔ]	donne, fort	[ɑ̃]	enfant, temps
[o]	dos, chaud, peau	[ɔ̃]	mon, nombre
[u]	tout, cour	[œ̃]	lundi, humble

Consonants

[p]	pain, absolu	[z]	cousin, zéro
[b]	beau, abbé	[ʃ]	chose, schéma
[t]	table, nette	[ʒ]	gilet, jeter
[d]	donner, sud	[l]	lait, facile
[k]	camp, képi	[r]	rare, rhume
[g]	garde, second	[m]	mon, flamme
[f]	feu, phrase	[n]	né, canne
[v]	voir, wagon	[ɲ]	campagne
[s]	sou, cire	[ŋ]	jogging
		[']	hanche (*i.e. no liaison or elision*)

Semi-consonants

[j]	piano, voyage
[w]	ouest, noir
[ɥ]	muet, lui

Prononciation de l'anglais

TABLEAU DES SIGNES PHONÉTIQUES

Voyelles et diphtongues

[iː]	bee, police	[ɒ]	lot, what
[ɪə]	beer, real	[ɔː]	all, saw
[ɪ]	bit, added	[ɔɪ]	boil, toy
[e]	bet, said	[əʊ]	low, soap
[eɪ]	date, nail	[ʊ]	put, wool
[eə]	bear, air	[uː]	shoe, too
[æ]	bat, plan	[ʊə]	poor, sure
[aɪ]	fly, life	[ʌ]	cut, some
[ɑː]	art, ask	[ɜː]	burn, learn
[aʊ]	fowl, house	[ə]	china, annoy
		[(ə)]	relation

Consonnes

[p]	pat, top	[ð]	that, breathe
[b]	but, tab	[h]	hat, rehearse
[t]	tap, patter	[l]	lad, all
[d]	dab, sadder	[r]	red, barring
[k]	cat, kite	[ʳ]	better, here (*représente un r*
[g]	go, rogue		*final qui se prononce en*
[f]	fat, phrase		*liaison devant une voyelle,*
[v]	veal, rave		*par exemple* 'here is' [hɪəʳɪz])
[s]	sat, ace	[m]	mat, hammer
[z]	zero, houses	[n]	no, banner
[ʃ]	dish, pressure	[ŋ]	singing, link
[ʒ]	pleasure	[j]	yet, onion
[tʃ]	charm, rich	[w]	wall, quite
[dʒ]	judge, rage	[']	*marque l'accent tonique;*
[θ]	thatch, breath		*précède la syllable accentuée*

A

A, a [ɑ] *nm* A, a.

a [a] *voir* avoir.

à [a] *prép* (à + le = au [o], à + les = aux [o]) **1** (*direction*: *lieu*) to; (*temps*) till, to; **aller à Paris** to go to Paris; **de 3 à 4 h** from 3 till *ou* to 4 (o'clock). **2** (*position*: *lieu*) at, in; (*surface*) on; (*temps*) at; **être au bureau/à la ferme/au jardin/à Paris** to be at *ou* in the office/on *ou* at the farm/in the garden/in Paris; **à la maison** at home; **à l'horizon** on the horizon; **à 8 h** at 8 (o'clock); **à mon arrivée** on (my) arrival; **à lundi!** see you (on) Monday! **3** (*description*) **l'homme à la barbe** the man with the beard; **verre à liqueur** liqueur glass. **4** (*attribution*) **donner qch à qn** to give sth to s.o., give s.o. sth. **5** (*devant inf*) **apprendre à lire** to learn to read; **travail à faire** work to do; **maison à vendre** house for sale; **prêt à partir** ready to leave. **6** (*appartenance*) **c'est (son livre) à lui** it's his (book); **c'est à vous de** (*décider, protester etc*) it's up to you to; (*lire, jouer etc*) it's your turn to. **7** (*prix*) for; **pain à 2F** loaf for 2F. **8** (*poids*) by; **vendre au kilo** to sell by the kilo. **9** (*moyen, manière*) **à bicyclette** by bicycle; **à la main** by hand; **à pied** on foot; **au crayon** with a pencil, in pencil; **au galop** at a gallop; **à la française** in the French style *ou* way; **deux à deux** two by two. **10** (*appel*) **au voleur!** (stop) thief!

abaiss/er [abese] *vt* to lower; **a. qn** to humiliate s.o.; **— s'a.** *vpr* (*barrière*) to lower; (*température*) to drop; **s'a. à faire** to stoop to doing. **◆—ement** [-ɛsmɑ̃] *nm* (*chute*) drop.

abandon [abɑ̃dɔ̃] *nm* abandonment; surrender; desertion; *Sp* withdrawal; (*naturel*) abandon; (*confiance*) lack of restraint; **à l'a.** in a neglected state. **◆abandonner** *vt* (*renoncer à*) to give up, abandon; (*droit*) to surrender; (*quitter*) to desert, abandon; **—** *vi* to give up; *Sp* to withdraw; **— s'a.** *vpr* (*se détendre*) to let oneself go; (*se confier*) to open up; **s'a. à** to give oneself up to, abandon oneself to.

abasourdir [abazurdir] *vt* to stun, astound.

abat-jour [abaʒur] *nm inv* lampshade.

abats [aba] *nmpl* offal; (*de volaille*) giblets.

abattant [abatɑ̃] *nm* leaf, flap.

abattis. [abati] *nmpl* giblets.

abatt/re* [abatr] *vt* (*mur*) to knock down; (*arbre*) to cut down, fell; (*animal etc*) to slaughter; (*avion*) to shoot down; (*déprimer*) to demoralize; (*épuiser*) to exhaust; **— s'a.** *vpr* (*tomber*) to collapse; (*oiseau*) to swoop down; (*pluie*) to pour down. **◆—u** *a* (*triste*) dejected, demoralized; (*faible*) at a low ebb. **◆—age** *nm* felling; slaughter(ing). **◆—ement** *nm* (*faiblesse*) exhaustion; (*désespoir*) dejection. **◆abattoir** *nm* slaughterhouse.

abbaye [abei] *nf* abbey.

abbé [abe] *nm* (*chef d'abbaye*) abbot; (*prêtre*) priest. **◆abbesse** *nf* abbess.

abcès [apsɛ] *nm* abscess.

abdiquer [abdike] *vti* to abdicate. **◆abdication** *nf* abdication.

abdomen [abdɔmɛn] *nm* abdomen. **◆abdominal, -aux** *a* abdominal.

abeille [abɛj] *nf* bee.

aberrant [aberɑ̃] *a* (*idée etc*) ludicrous, absurd. **◆aberration** *nf* (*égarement*) aberration; (*idée*) ludicrous idea; **dire des aberrations** to talk sheer nonsense.

abhorrer [abɔre] *vt* to abhor, loathe.

abîme [abim] *nm* abyss, chasm, gulf.

abîmer [abime] *vt* to spoil, damage; **— s'a.** *vpr* to get spoilt; **s'a. dans ses pensées** *Litt* to lose oneself in one's thoughts.

abject [abʒɛkt] *a* abject, despicable.

abjurer [abʒyre] *vti* to abjure.

ablation [ablasjɔ̃] *nf* (*d'organe*) removal.

ablutions [ablysjɔ̃] *nfpl* ablutions.

abnégation [abnegasjɔ̃] *nf* self-sacrifice, abnegation.

abois (aux) [ozabwa] *adv* at bay.

abolir [abɔlir] *vt* to abolish. **◆abolition** *nf* abolition.

abominable [abɔminabl] *a* abominable, obnoxious. **◆abomination** *nf* abomination.

abondant [abɔ̃dɑ̃] *a* abundant, plentiful. **◆abondamment** *adv* abundantly. **◆abondance** *nf* abundance (**de** of); **en a.** in abundance; **années d'a.** years of plenty. **◆abonder** *vi* to abound (**en** in).

abonné, -ée [abɔne] *nmf* (*à un journal, au téléphone*) subscriber; *Rail Sp Th* season ticket holder; (*du gaz etc*) consumer.

◆**abonnement** *nm* subscription; (**carte d')a.** season ticket. ◆**s'abonner** *vpr* to subscribe (à to); to buy a season ticket.

abord [abɔr] **1** *nm* (*accès*) **d'un a. facile** easy to approach. **2** *nm* (*vue*) **au premier a.** at first sight. **3** *nmpl* (*environs*) surroundings; **aux abords de** around, nearby. ◆**abordable** *a* (*personne*) approachable; (*prix, marchandises*) affordable.

abord (d') [dabɔr] *adv* (*avant tout*) first; (*au début*) at first.

aborder [abɔrde] *vi* to land; − *vt* (*personne*) to approach, accost; (*lieu*) to approach, reach; (*problème*) to tackle, approach; (*attaquer*) Nau to board; (*heurter*) Nau to run foul of. ◆**abordage** *nm* (*assaut*) Nau boarding; (*accident*) Nau collision.

aborigène [abɔriʒɛn] *a & nm* aboriginal.

about/ir [abutir] *vi* to succeed; **a. à** to end at, lead to, end up in; **n'a. à rien** to come to nothing. ◆**—issants** *nmpl voir* tenants. ◆**—issement** *nm* (*résultat*) outcome; (*succès*) success.

aboyer [abwaje] *vi* to bark. ◆**aboiement** *nm* bark; *pl* barking.

abrasif, -ive [abrazif, -iv] *a & nm* abrasive.

abrég/er [abreʒe] *vt* (*récit*) to shorten, abridge; (*mot*) to abbreviate. ◆**—é** *nm* summary; **en a.** (*phrase*) in shortened form; (*mot*) in abbreviated form.

abreuver [abrœve] *vt* (*cheval*) to water; − **s'a.** *vpr* to drink. ◆**abreuvoir** *nm* (*récipient*) drinking trough; (*lieu*) watering place.

abréviation [abrevjasjɔ̃] *nf* abbreviation.

abri [abri] *nm* shelter; **à l'a. de** (*vent*) sheltered from; (*besoin*) safe from; **sans a.** homeless. ◆**abriter** *vt* (*protéger*) to shelter; (*loger*) to house; − **s'a.** *vpr* to (take) shelter.

abricot [abriko] *nm* apricot. ◆**abricotier** *nm* apricot tree.

abroger [abrɔʒe] *vt* to abrogate.

abrupt [abrypt] *a* (*versant*) sheer; (*sentier*) steep, abrupt; (*personne*) abrupt.

abrut/ir [abrytir] *vt* (*alcool*) to stupefy (*s.o.*); (*propagande*) to brutalize (*s.o.*); (*travail*) to leave (*s.o.*) dazed, wear (*s.o.*) out. ◆**—i, -ie** *nmf* idiot; − *a* idiotic.

absence [apsɑ̃s] *nf* absence. ◆**absent, -e** *a* (*personne*) absent, away; (*chose*) missing; **air a.** faraway look; − *nmf* absentee. ◆**absentéisme** *nm* absenteeism. ◆**s'absenter** *vpr* to go away.

abside [apsid] *nf* (*d'une église*) apse.

absolu [apsɔly] *a & nm* absolute. ◆**—ment** *adv* absolutely.

absolution [apsɔlysjɔ̃] *nf* absolution.

absorb/er [apsɔrbe] *vt* to absorb. ◆**—ant** *a* absorbent; **travail a.** absorbing job. ◆**absorption** *nf* absorption.

absoudre* [apsudr] *vt* to absolve.

abstenir* (**s'**) [sapstənir] *vpr* to abstain; **s'a. de** to refrain *ou* abstain from. ◆**abstention** *nf* abstention.

abstinence [apstinɑ̃s] *nf* abstinence.

abstraire* [apstrɛr] *vt* to abstract. ◆**abstrait** *a & nm* abstract. ◆**abstraction** *nf* abstraction; **faire a. de** to disregard, leave aside.

absurde [apsyrd] *a & nm* absurd. ◆**absurdité** *nf* absurdity; **dire des absurdités** to talk nonsense.

abus [aby] *nm* abuse, misuse; overindulgence; (*injustice*) abuse. ◆**abuser 1** *vi* to go too far; **a. de** (*situation, personne*) to take unfair advantage of; (*autorité*) to abuse, misuse; (*friandises*) to over-indulge in. **2 s'a.** *vpr* to be mistaken.

abusi/f, -ive [abyzif, -iv] *a* excessive; **emploi a.** Ling improper use, misuse. ◆**—vement** *adv* Ling improperly.

acabit [akabi] *nm* **de cet a.** Péj of that ilk *ou* sort.

acacia [akasja] *nm* (*arbre*) acacia.

académie [akademi] *nf* academy; Univ = (regional) education authority. ◆**académicien, -ienne** *nmf* academician. ◆**académique** *a* academic.

acajou [akaʒu] *nm* mahogany; **cheveux a.** auburn hair.

acariâtre [akarjɑtr] *a* cantankerous.

accabl/er [akable] *vt* to overwhelm, overcome; **a. d'injures** to heap insults upon; **accablé de dettes** (over)burdened with debt. ◆**—ement** *nm* dejection.

accalmie [akalmi] *nf* lull.

accaparer [akapare] *vt* to monopolize; (*personne*) Fam to take up all the time of.

accéder [aksede] *vi* **a. à** (*lieu*) to have access to, reach; (*pouvoir, trône, demande*) to accede to.

accélérer [akselere] *vi* Aut to accelerate; − *vt* (*travaux etc*) to speed up; (*allure, pas*) to quicken, speed up; − **s'a.** *vpr* to speed up. ◆**accélérateur** *nm* Aut accelerator. ◆**accélération** *nf* acceleration; speeding up.

accent [aksɑ̃] *nm* accent; (*sur une syllabe*) stress; **mettre l'a. sur** to stress. ◆**accentuation** *nf* accentuation. ◆**accentuer** *vt* to emphasize, accentuate, stress; − **s'a.** *vpr* to become more pronounced.

accepter [aksɛpte] *vt* to accept; **a. de faire**

to agree to do. ◆**acceptable** *a* acceptable.
◆**acceptation** *nf* acceptance.

acception [aksɛpsjɔ̃] *nf* sense, meaning.

accès [aksɛ] *nm* access (**à** to); (*de folie, colère, toux*) fit; (*de fièvre*) attack, bout; *pl* (*routes*) approaches. ◆**accessible** *a* accessible; (*personne*) approachable. ◆**accession** *nf* accession (**à** to); (*à un traité*) adherence; **a. à la propriété** home ownership.

accessoire [aksɛswar] *a* secondary; — *nmpl* Th props; (*de voiture etc*) accessories; **accessoires de toilette** toilet requisites.

accident [aksidɑ̃] *nm* accident; **a. d'avion/de train** plane/train crash; **par a.** by accident, by chance. ◆**accidenté, -ée** *a* (*terrain*) uneven; (*région*) hilly; (*voiture*) damaged (in an accident); — *nmf* accident victim, casualty. ◆**accidentel, -elle** *a* accidental. ◆**accidentellement** *adv* accidentally, unintentionally.

acclamer [aklame] *vt* to cheer, acclaim. ◆**acclamations** *nfpl* cheers, acclamations.

acclimater [aklimate] *vt*, — **s'a.** *vpr* to acclimatize, *Am* acclimate. ◆**acclimatation** *nf* acclimatization, *Am* acclimation.

accointances [akwɛ̃tɑ̃s] *nfpl* Péj contacts.

accolade [akɔlad] *nf* (*embrassade*) embrace; Typ brace, bracket.

accoler [akɔle] *vt* to place (side by side) (**à** against).

accommod/er [akɔmɔde] *vt* to adapt; Culin to prepare; **s'a. à** to adapt (oneself) to; **s'a. de** to make the best of. ◆**—ant** *a* accommodating, easy to please. ◆**—ement** *nm* arrangement, compromise.

accompagner [akɔ̃paɲe] *vt* (*personne*) to accompany, go *ou* come with, escort; (*chose*) & Mus to accompany; **s'a. de** to be accompanied by, go with. ◆**accompagnateur, -trice** *nmf* Mus accompanist; (*d'un groupe*) guide. ◆**accompagnement** *nm* Mus accompaniment.

accompl/ir [akɔ̃plir] *vt* to carry out, fulfil, accomplish. ◆**—i** *a* accomplished. ◆**—issement** *nm* fulfilment.

accord [akɔr] *nm* agreement; (*harmonie*) harmony; Mus chord; **être d'a.** to agree, be in agreement (**avec** with); **d'a.!** all right! ◆**accorder** *vt* (*donner*) to grant; Mus to tune; Gram to make agree; — **s'a.** *vpr* to agree; (*s'entendre*) to get along.

accordéon [akɔrdeɔ̃] *nm* accordion; **en a.** (*chaussette etc*) wrinkled.

accoster [akɔste] *vt* to accost; Nau to come alongside; — *vi* Nau to berth.

accotement [akɔtmɑ̃] *nm* roadside, verge.

accouch/er [akuʃe] *vi* to give birth (**de** to); — *vt* (*enfant*) to deliver. ◆**—ement** *nm* delivery. ◆**—eur** *nm* (**médecin**) a. obstetrician.

accouder (s') [sakude] *vpr* **s'a. à** *ou* **sur** to lean on (*with one's elbows*). ◆**accoudoir** *nm* armrest.

accoupl/er [akuple] *vt* to couple; — **s'a.** *vpr* (*animaux*) to mate (**à** with). ◆**—ement** *nm* coupling; mating.

accourir* [akurir] *vi* to come running, run over.

accoutrement [akutrəmɑ̃] *nm* Péj garb, dress.

accoutumer [akutyme] *vt* to accustom; — **s'a.** *vpr* to get accustomed (**à** to); **comme à l'accoutumée** as usual. ◆**accoutumance** *nf* familiarization (**à** with); Méd addiction.

accréditer [akredite] *vt* (*ambassadeur*) to accredit; (*rumeur*) to lend credence to.

accroc [akro] *nm* (*déchirure*) tear; (*difficulté*) hitch, snag.

accroch/er [akrɔʃe] *vt* (*déchirer*) to catch; (*fixer*) to hook; (*suspendre*) to hang up (**on** *a* hook); (*heurter*) to hit, knock; — *vi* (*affiche etc*) to grab one's attention; — **s'a.** *vpr* (*ne pas céder*) to persevere; (*se disputer*) Fam to clash; **s'a. à** (*se cramponner etc*) to cling to; (*s'écorcher*) to catch oneself on. ◆**—age** *nm* Aut knock, slight hit; (*friction*) Fam clash. ◆**—eur, -euse** *a* (*personne*) tenacious; (*affiche etc*) eyecatching, catchy.

accroître* [akrwatr] *vt* to increase; — **s'a.** *vpr* to increase, grow. ◆**accroissement** *nm* increase; growth.

accroup/ir (s') [sakrupir] *vpr* to squat *ou* crouch (down). ◆**—i** *a* squatting, crouching.

accueil [akœj] *nm* reception, welcome. ◆**accueill/ir*** *vt* to receive, welcome, greet. ◆**—ant** *a* welcoming.

acculer [akyle] *vt* **a. qn à qch** to drive s.o. to *ou* against sth.

accumuler [akymyle] *vt*, — **s'a.** *vpr* to pile up, accumulate. ◆**accumulateur** *nm* accumulator, battery. ◆**accumulation** *nf* accumulation.

accus/er [akyze] *vt* (*dénoncer*) to accuse; (*rendre responsable*) to blame (**de** for); (*révéler*) to show; (*faire ressortir*) to bring out; **a. réception** to acknowledge receipt (**de** of); **a. le coup** to stagger under the blow. ◆**—é, -ée 1** *nmf* accused; (*cour d'assises*) defendant. **2** *a* prominent. ◆**accusateur, -trice** *a* (*regard*) accusing;

(*document*) incriminating; − *nmf* accuser. ◆**accusation** *nf* accusation; *Jur* charge.

acerbe [asɛrb] *a* bitter, caustic.

acéré [asere] *a* sharp.

acétate [acetat] *nm* acetate. ◆**acétique** *a* acetic.

achalandé [aʃalɑ̃de] *a* **bien a.** (*magasin*) well-stocked.

acharn/er (s') [saʃarne] *vpr* **s'a. sur** (*attaquer*) to set upon, lay into; **s'a. contre** (*poursuivre*) to pursue (relentlessly); **s'a. à faire** to struggle to do, try desperately to do. ◆**−é, -ée** *a* relentless; − *nmf* (*du jeu etc*) fanatic. ◆**−ement** *nm* relentlessness.

achat [aʃa] *nm* purchase; *pl* shopping.

acheminer [aʃmine] *vt* to dispatch; − **s'a.** *vpr* to proceed (**vers** towards).

achet/er [aʃte] *vti* to buy, purchase; **a. à qn** (*vendeur*) to buy from s.o.; (*pour qn*) to buy for s.o. ◆**−eur, -euse** *nmf* buyer, purchaser; (*dans un magasin*) shopper.

achever [aʃve] *vt* to finish (off); **a. de faire qch** (*personne*) to finish doing sth; **a. qn** (*tuer*) to finish s.o. off; − **s'a.** *vpr* to end, finish. ◆**achèvement** *nm* completion.

achoppement [aʃɔpmɑ̃] *nm* **pierre d'a.** stumbling block.

acide [asid] *a* acid, sour; − *nm* acid. ◆**acidité** *nf* acidity.

acier [asje] *nm* steel. ◆**aciérie** *nf* steelworks.

acné [akne] *nf* acne.

acolyte [akɔlit] *nm* *Péj* confederate, associate.

acompte [akɔ̃t] *nm* part payment, deposit.

à-côté [akote] *nm* (*d'une question*) side issue; *pl* (*gains*) little extras.

à-coup [aku] *nm* jerk, jolt; **sans à-coups** smoothly; **par à-coups** in fits and starts.

acoustique [akustik] *a* acoustic; − *nf* acoustics.

acquérir* [akerir] *vt* to acquire, gain; (*par achat*) to purchase; **s'a. une réputation**/*etc* to win a reputation/*etc*; **être acquis à** (*idée, parti*) to be a supporter of. ◆**acquéreur** *nm* purchaser. ◆**acquis** *nm* experience. ◆**acquisition** *nf* acquisition; purchase.

acquiesc/er [akjese] *vi* to acquiesce (**à** to). ◆**−ement** *nm* acquiescence.

acquit [aki] *nm* receipt; **'pour a.'** 'paid'; **par a. de conscience** for conscience sake. ◆**acquitt/er** *vt* (*dette*) to clear, pay; (*accusé*) to acquit; **s'a. de** (*devoir, promesse*) to discharge; **s'a. envers qn** to repay s.o. ◆**−ement** *nm* payment; acquittal; discharge.

âcre [ɑkr] *a* bitter, acrid, pungent.

acrobate [akrɔbat] *nmf* acrobat. ◆**acrobatie(s)** *nf*(*pl*) acrobatics. ◆**acrobatique** *a* acrobatic.

acrylique [akrilik] *a & nm* acrylic.

acte [akt] *nm* act, deed; *Th* act; **un a. de** an act of; **a. de naissance** birth certificate; **prendre a. de** to take note of.

acteur, -trice [aktœr, -tris] *nmf* actor, actress.

actif, -ive [aktif, -iv] *a* active; − *nm* *Fin* assets; **à son a.** to one's credit; (*vols, meurtres*) *Hum* to one's name.

action [aksjɔ̃] *nf* action; *Fin* share. ◆**actionnaire** *nmf* shareholder. ◆**actionner** *vt* to set in motion, activate, actuate.

activer [aktive] *vt* to speed up; (*feu*) to boost; − **s'a.** *vpr* to bustle about; (*se dépêcher*) *Fam* to get a move on.

activiste [aktivist] *nmf* activist.

activité [aktivite] *nf* activity; **en a.** (*personne*) fully active; (*volcan*) active.

actuaire [aktɥɛr] *nmf* actuary.

actualité [aktɥalite] *nf* (*d'un problème*) topicality; (*événements*) current events; *pl* *TV Cin* news; **d'a.** topical.

actuel, -elle [aktɥɛl] *a* (*présent*) present; (*contemporain*) topical. ◆**actuellement** *adv* at present, at the present time.

acuité [akɥite] *nf* (*de douleur*) acuteness; (*de vision*) keenness.

acupuncture [akypɔ̃ktyr] *nf* acupuncture. ◆**acupuncteur, -trice** *nmf* acupuncturist.

adage [adaʒ] *nm* (*maxime*) adage.

adapter [adapte] *vt* to adapt; (*ajuster*) to fit (**à** to); **s'a. à** (*s'habituer*) to adapt to; (*tuyau etc*) to fit. ◆**adaptable** *a* adaptable. ◆**adaptateur, -trice** *nmf* adapter. ◆**adaptation** *nf* adaptation.

additif [aditif] *nm* additive.

addition [adisjɔ̃] *nf* addition; (*au restaurant*) bill, *Am* check. ◆**additionnel, -elle** *a* additional. ◆**additionner** *vt* to add (**à** to); (*nombres*) to add up.

adepte [adept] *nmf* follower.

adéquat [adekwa] *a* appropriate.

adhérer [adere] *vi* **a. à** (*coller*) to adhere ou stick to; (*s'inscrire*) to join; (*pneu*) to grip. ◆**adhérence** *nf* (*de pneu*) grip. ◆**adhérent, -ente** *nmf* member.

adhésif, -ive [adezif, -iv] *a & nm* adhesive. ◆**adhésion** *nf* membership; (*accord*) support.

adieu, -x [adjø] *int & nm* farewell, goodbye.

adipeux, -euse [adipø, -øz] *a* (*tissu*) fatty; (*visage*) fat.

adjacent [adʒasɑ̃] a (contigu) & Géom adjacent.

adjectif [adʒɛktif] nm adjective.

adjoindre* [adʒwɛ̃dr] vt (associer) to appoint (s.o.) as an assistant (à to); (ajouter) to add; **s'a. qn** to appoint s.o. ◆**adjoint, -ointe** nmf & a assistant; **a. au maire** deputy mayor.

adjudant [adʒydɑ̃] nm warrant officer.

adjuger [adʒyʒe] vt (accorder) to award; **s'a. qch** Fam to grab sth for oneself.

adjurer [adʒyre] vt to beseech, entreat.

admettre* [admɛtr] vt (laisser entrer, accueillir, reconnaître) to admit; (autoriser, tolérer) to allow; (supposer) to admit, grant; (candidat) to pass; **être admis à** (examen) to have passed.

administrer [administre] vt (gérer, donner) to administer. ◆**administrateur, -trice** nmf administrator. ◆**administratif, -ive** a administrative. ◆**administration** nf administration; **l'A.** (service public) government service, the Civil Service.

admirer [admire] vt to admire. ◆**admirable** a admirable. ◆**admirateur, -trice** nmf admirer. ◆**admiratif, -ive** a admiring. ◆**admiration** nf admiration.

admissible [admisibl] a acceptable, admissible; (après un concours) eligible (à for). ◆**admission** nf admission.

adolescent, -ente [adɔlesɑ̃, -ɑ̃t] nmf adolescent, teenager; — a teenage. ◆**adolescence** nf adolescence.

adonner (s') [sadɔne] vpr **s'a. à** (boisson) to take to; (étude) to devote oneself to.

adopter [adɔpte] vt to adopt. ◆**adoptif, -ive** a (fils, patrie) adopted. ◆**adoption** nf adoption; **suisse d'a.** Swiss by adoption.

adorer [adɔre] vt (personne) & Rel to worship, adore; (chose) Fam to adore, love; **a. faire** to adore ou love doing. ◆**adorable** a adorable. ◆**adoration** nf adoration, worship.

adosser [adose] vt **a. qch à** to lean sth back against; **s'a. à** to lean back against.

adouc/ir [adusir] vt (voix, traits etc) to soften; (boisson) to sweeten; (chagrin) to mitigate, ease; — **s'a.** vpr (temps) to turn milder; (caractère) to mellow. ◆**—issement** nm **a. de la température** milder weather.

adrénaline [adrenalin] nf adrenalin(e).

adresse [adrɛs] nf **1** (domicile) address. **2** (habileté) skill. ◆**adresser** vt (lettre) to send; (compliment, remarque etc) to address; (coup) to direct, aim; (personne) to direct (à to); **a. la parole à** to speak to;

s'a. à to speak to; (aller trouver) to go and see; (bureau) to enquire at; (être destiné à) to be aimed at.

Adriatique [adriatik] nf **l'A.** the Adriatic.

adroit [adrwa] a skilful, clever.

adulation [adylɑsjɔ̃] nf adulation.

adulte [adylt] a & nmf adult, grown-up.

adultère [adyltɛr] a adulterous; — nm adultery.

advenir [advənir] v imp to occur; **a. de** (devenir) to become of; **advienne que pourra** come what may.

adverbe [advɛrb] nm adverb. ◆**adverbial, -aux** a adverbial.

adversaire [advɛrsɛr] nmf opponent, adversary. ◆**adverse** a opposing.

adversité [adversite] nf adversity.

aérer [aere] vt (chambre) to air (out), ventilate; (lit) to air (out); — **s'a.** vpr Fam to get some air. ◆**aéré** a airy. ◆**aération** nf ventilation. ◆**aérien, -ienne** a (ligne, attaque etc) air-; (photo) aerial; (câble) overhead; (léger) airy.

aérobic [aerɔbik] nf aerobics.

aéro-club [aerɔklœb] nm flying club. ◆**aérodrome** nm aerodrome. ◆**aérodynamique** a streamlined, aerodynamic. ◆**aérogare** nf air terminal. ◆**aéroglisseur** nm hovercraft. ◆**aérogramme** nm air letter. ◆**aéromodélisme** nm model aircraft building and flying. ◆**aéronautique** nf aeronautics. ◆**aéronavale** nf = Br Fleet Air Arm; = Am Naval Air Force. ◆**aéroport** nm airport. ◆**aéroporté** a airborne. ◆**aérosol** nm aerosol.

affable [afabl] a affable.

affaiblir [afeblir] vt, — **s'a.** vpr to weaken.

affaire [afer] nf (question) matter, affair; (marché) deal; (firme) concern, business; (scandale) affair; (procès) Jur case; pl Com business; (d'intérêt public, personnel) affairs; (effets) belongings, things; **avoir a. à** to have to deal with; **c'est mon a.** that's my business ou affair ou concern; **faire une bonne a.** to get a good deal, get a bargain; **ça fera l'a.** that will do nicely; **toute une a.** (histoire) quite a business.

affair/er (s') [safere] vpr to busy oneself, run ou bustle about. ◆**—é** a busy. ◆**affairiste** nm (political) racketeer.

affaiss/er (s') [safese] vpr (personne) to collapse; (plancher) to cave in, give way; (sol) to subside, sink. ◆**—ement** [afesmɑ̃] nm (du sol) subsidence.

affaler (s') [safale] vpr to flop down, collapse.

affamé [afame] *a* starving; **a. de** *Fig* hungry for.

affect/er [afɛkte] *vt* (*destiner*) to earmark, assign; (*nommer à un poste*) to post; (*feindre, émouvoir*) to affect. **◆—é** *a* (*manières, personne*) affected. **◆affectation** *nf* assignment; posting; (*simulation*) affectation.

affectif, -ive [afɛktif, -iv] *a* emotional.

affection [afɛksjɔ̃] *nf* (*attachement*) affection; (*maladie*) ailment. **◆affectionn/er** *vt* to be fond of. **◆—é** *a* loving. **◆affectueux, -euse** *a* affectionate.

affermir [afɛrmir] *vt* (*autorité*) to strengthen; (*muscles*) to tone up; (*voix*) to steady.

affiche [afiʃ] *nf* poster; *Th* bill. **◆affich/er** *vt* (*affiche etc*) to post *ou* stick up; *Th* to bill; (*sentiment*) *Péj* to display; **a. qn** *Péj* to parade s.o., flaunt s.o. **◆—age** *nm* (bill-)posting; **panneau d'a.** hoarding, *Am* billboard.

affilée (d') [dafile] *adv* (*à la suite*) in a row, at a stretch.

affiler [afile] *vt* to sharpen.

affilier (s') [safilje] *vpr* **s'a. à** to join, become affiliated to. **◆affiliation** *nf* affiliation.

affiner [afine] *vt* to refine.

affinité [afinite] *nf* affinity.

affirmatif, -ive [afirmatif, -iv] *a* (*ton*) assertive, positive; (*proposition*) affirmative; **il a été a.** he was quite positive; — *nf* **répondre par l'affirmative** to reply in the affirmative.

affirmer [afirme] *vt* to assert; (*proclamer solennellement*) to affirm. **◆affirmation** *nf* assertion.

affleurer [aflœre] *vi* to appear on the surface.

affliger [afliʒe] *vt* to distress; **affligé de** stricken *ou* afflicted with.

affluence [aflyɑ̃s] *nf* crowd; **heures d'a.** rush hours.

affluent [aflyɑ̃] *nm* tributary.

affluer [aflye] *vi* (*sang*) to flow, rush; (*gens*) to flock. **◆afflux** *nm* flow; (*arrivée*) influx.

affol/er [afole] *vt* to drive out of one's mind; (*effrayer*) to terrify; — **s'a.** *vpr* to panic. **◆—ement** *nm* panic.

affranch/ir [afrɑ̃ʃir] *vt* (*timbrer*) to stamp; (*émanciper*) to free. **◆—issement** *nm* tarifs d'a. postage.

affréter [afrete] *vt* (*avion*) to charter; (*navire*) to freight.

affreux, -euse [afrø, -øz] *a* hideous, dreadful, ghastly. **◆affreusement** *adv* dreadfully.

affriolant [afriɔlɑ̃] *a* enticing.

affront [afrɔ̃] *nm* insult, affront; **faire un a. à** to insult.

affront/er [afrɔ̃te] *vt* to confront, face; (*mauvais temps, difficultés etc*) to brave. **◆—ement** *nm* confrontation.

affubler [afyble] *vt* *Péj* to dress, rig out (**de** in).

affût [afy] *nm* **à l'a. de** *Fig* on the look-out for.

affûter [afyte] *vt* (*outil*) to sharpen, grind.

Afghanistan [afganistɑ̃] *nm* Afghanistan.

afin [afɛ̃] *prép* **a. de** (+ *inf*) in order to; — *conj* **a. que** (+ *sub*) so that.

Afrique [afrik] *nf* Africa. **◆africain, -aine** *a* & *nmf* African.

agac/er [agase] *vt* (*personne*) to irritate, annoy. **◆—ement** *nm* irritation.

âge [ɑʒ] *nm* age; **quel â. as-tu?** how old are you?; **avant l'â.** before one's time; **d'un certain â.** middle-aged; **l'â. adulte** adulthood; **la force de l'â.** the prime of life; **le moyen â.** the Middle Ages. **◆âgé** *a* elderly; **â. de six ans** six years old; **un enfant â. de six ans** a six-year-old child.

agence [aʒɑ̃s] *nf* agency; (*succursale*) branch office; **a. immobilière** estate agent's office, *Am* real estate office.

agenc/er [aʒɑ̃se] *vt* to arrange; **bien agencé** (*maison etc*) well laid-out; (*phrase*) well put-together. **◆—ement** *nm* (*de maison etc*) lay-out.

agenda [aʒɛ̃da] *nm* diary, *Am* datebook.

agenouiller (s') [saʒnuje] *vpr* to kneel (down); **être agenouillé** to be kneeling (down).

agent [aʒɑ̃] *nm* agent; **a. (de police)** policeman; **a. de change** stockbroker; **a. immobilier** estate agent, *Am* real estate agent.

aggloméré [aglomere] *nm* & *a* (*bois*) chipboard, fibreboard.

agglomérer (s') [saglomere] *vpr* (*s'entasser*) to conglomerate. **◆agglomération** *nf* conglomeration; (*habitations*) built-up area; (*ville*) town.

aggraver [agrave] *vt* to worsen, aggravate; — **s'a.** *vpr* to worsen. **◆aggravation** *nf* worsening.

agile [aʒil] *a* agile, nimble. **◆agilité** *nf* agility, nimbleness.

agir [aʒir] **1** *vi* to act; **a. auprès de** to intercede with. **2 s'agir** *v imp* **il s'agit d'argent/etc** it's a question *ou* matter of money/etc, it concerns money/etc; **de quoi s'agit-il?** what is it?, what's it about?; **il s'agit de se dépêcher/etc** we have to

hurry/*etc.* ◆**agissant** *a* active, effective.
◆**agissements** *nmpl Péj* dealings.

agit/er [aʒite] *vt* (*remuer*) to stir; (*secouer*)
to shake; (*brandir*) to wave; (*troubler*) to
agitate; (*discuter*) to debate; — **s'a.** *vpr*
(*enfant*) to fidget; (*peuple*) to stir. ◆—**é** *a*
(*mer*) rough; (*malade*) restless, agitated;
(*enfant*) fidgety, restless. ◆**agitateur,
-trice** *nmf* (political) agitator. ◆**agitation**
nf (*de la mer*) roughness; (*d'un malade etc*)
restlessness; (*nervosité*) agitation; (*de la
rue*) bustle; *Pol* unrest.

agneau, -x [aɲo] *nm* lamb.

agonie [agoni] *nf* death throes; **être à l'a.** to
be suffering the pangs of death.
◆**agoniser** *vi* to be dying.

agrafe [agraf] *nf* hook; (*pour papiers*)
staple. ◆**agrafer** *vt* to fasten, hook, do up;
(*papiers*) to staple. ◆**agrafeuse** *nf*
stapler.

agrand/ir [agrɑ̃dir] *vt* to enlarge; (*grossir*)
to magnify; — **s'a.** *vpr* to expand, grow.
◆—**issement** *nm* (*de ville*) expansion; (*de
maison*) extension; (*de photo*) enlargement.

agréable [agreabl] *a* pleasant, agreeable,
nice. ◆—**ment** [-əmɑ̃] *adv* pleasantly.

agré/er [agree] *vt* to accept; **veuillez a. mes
salutations distinguées** (*dans une lettre*)
yours faithfully. ◆—**é** *a* (*fournisseur,
centre*) approved.

agrégation [agregasjɔ̃] *nf* competitive examination for recruitment of *lycée* teachers.
◆**agrégé, -ée** *nmf* teacher who has passed
the *agrégation*.

agrément [agremɑ̃] *nm* (*attrait*) charm;
(*accord*) assent; **voyage d'a.** pleasure trip.
◆**agrémenter** *vt* to embellish; **a. un récit
d'anecdotes** to pepper a story with anecdotes.

agrès [agrɛ] *nmpl Nau* tackle, rigging; (*de
gymnastique*) apparatus.

agresser [agrese] *vt* to attack. ◆**agresseur** *nm* attacker; (*dans la rue*) mugger;
(*dans un conflit*) aggressor. ◆**agressif,
-ive** *a* aggressive. ◆**agression** *nf* (*d'un
État*) aggression; (*d'un individu*) attack.
◆**agressivité** *nf* aggressiveness.

agricole [agrikɔl] *a* (*peuple*) agricultural,
farming; (*ouvrier, machine*) farm-.

agriculteur [agrikyltœr] *nm* farmer.
◆**agriculture** *nf* agriculture, farming.

agripper [agripe] *vt* to clutch, grip; **s'a. à** to
cling to, clutch, grip.

agronomie [agronomi] *nf* agronomics.

agrumes [agrym] *nmpl* citrus fruit(s).

aguerri [ageri] *a* seasoned, hardened.

aguets (aux) [ozagɛ] *adv* on the look-out.

aguich/er [agiʃe] *vt* to tease, excite.
◆—**ant** *a* enticing.

ah! [a] *int* ah!, oh!

ahur/ir [ayrir] *vt* to astound, bewilder.
◆—**i, -ie** *nmf* idiot.

ai [e] *voir* **avoir.**

aide [ɛd] *nf* help, assistance, aid; — *nmf*
(*personne*) assistant; **à l'a. de** with the help
ou aid of. ◆**a.-électricien** *nm* electrician's
mate. ◆**a.-familiale** *nf* home help.
◆**a.-mémoire** *nm inv Scol* handbook (*of
facts etc*).

aider [ede] *vt* to help, assist, aid (**à faire** to
do); **s'a. de** to make use of.

aïe! [aj] *int* ouch!, ow!

aïeul, -e [ajœl] *nmf* grandfather, grandmother.

aïeux [ajø] *nmpl* forefathers, forebears.

aigle [ɛgl] *nmf* eagle. ◆**aiglon** *nm* eaglet.

aiglefin [ɛgləfɛ̃] *nm* haddock.

aigre [ɛgr] *a* (*acide*) sour; (*voix, vent, parole*)
sharp, cutting. ◆**a.-doux, -douce** *a*
bitter-sweet. ◆**aigreur** *nf* sourness; (*de
ton*) sharpness; *pl* heartburn.

aigrette [ɛgrɛt] *nf* (*de plumes*) tuft.

aigr/ir (s') [segrir] *vpr* (*vin*) to turn sour;
(*caractère*) to sour. ◆—**i** [egri] *a* (*personne*)
embittered, bitter.

aigu, -uë [egy] *a* (*crise etc*) acute; (*dents*)
sharp, pointed; (*voix*) shrill.

aiguille [egɥij] *nf* (*à coudre, de pin*) needle;
(*de montre*) hand; (*de balance*) pointer; **a.
(rocheuse)** peak.

aiguill/er [egɥije] *vt* (*train*) to shunt, *Am*
switch; *Fig* to steer, direct. ◆—**age** *nm*
(*appareil*) *Rail* points, *Am* switches.
◆—**eur** *nm Rail* pointsman, *Am*
switchman; **a. du ciel** air traffic controller.

aiguillon [egɥijɔ̃] *nm* (*dard*) sting; (*stimulant*) spur. ◆**aiguillonner** *vt* to spur (on),
goad.

aiguiser [eg(ɥ)ize] *vt* (*affiler*) to sharpen;
(*appétit*) to whet.

ail [aj] *nm* garlic.

aile [ɛl] *nf* wing; (*de moulin à vent*) sail; *Am*
wing, *Am* fender; **battre de l'a.** to be in a
bad way; **d'un coup d'a.** (*avion*) in continuous flight. ◆**ailé** [ele] *a* winged. ◆**aileron**
nm (*de requin*) fin; (*d'avion*) aileron;
(*d'oiseau*) pinion. ◆**ailier** [elje] *nm Fb*
wing(er).

ailleurs [ajœr] *adv* somewhere else, elsewhere; **partout a.** everywhere else; **d'a.** (*du
reste*) besides, anyway; **par a.** (*en outre*)
moreover; (*autrement*) otherwise.

ailloli [ajɔli] *nm* garlic mayonnaise.

aimable [ɛmabl] *a* (*complaisant*) kind;

(*sympathique*) likeable, amiable; (*agréable*) pleasant. ◆**—ment** [-əmɑ̃] *adv* kindly.

aimant [ɛmɑ̃] **1** *nm* magnet. **2** *a* loving. ◆**aimanter** *vt* to magnetize.

aimer [eme] *vt* (*chérir*) to love; **a. (bien)** (*apprécier*) to like, be fond of; **a. faire** to like doing *ou* to do; **a. mieux** to prefer; **ils s'aiment** they're in love.

aine [ɛn] *nf* groin.

aîné, -e [ene] *a* (*de deux frères etc*) elder, older; (*de plus de deux*) eldest, oldest; – *nmf* (*enfant*) elder *ou* older (child); eldest *ou* oldest (child); **c'est mon a.** he's my senior.

ainsi [ɛ̃si] *adv* (*comme ça*) (in) this *ou* that way, thus; (*alors*) so; **a. que** as well as; **et a. de suite** and so on; **pour a. dire** so to speak.

air [ɛr] *nm* **1** air; **en plein a.** in the open (air), outdoors; **ficher** *ou* **flanquer en l'a.** *Fam* (*jeter*) to chuck away; (*gâcher*) to mess up, upset; **en l'a.** (*jeter*) (up) in the air; (*paroles, menaces*) empty; (*projets*) uncertain, (up) in the air; **dans l'a.** (*grippe, idées*) about, around. **2** (*expression*) look, appearance; **avoir l'a.** to look, seem; **avoir l'a. de** to look like; **a. de famille** family likeness. **3** (*mélodie*) tune; **a. d'opéra** aria.

aire [ɛr] *nf* (*de stationnement etc*) & *Math* area; (*d'oiseau*) eyrie; **a. de lancement** launching site.

airelle [ɛrɛl] *nf* bilberry, *Am* blueberry.

aisance [ɛzɑ̃s] *nf* (*facilité*) ease; (*prospérité*) easy circumstances, affluence.

aise [ɛz] *nf* **à l'a.** (*dans un vêtement etc*) comfortable; (*dans une situation*) at ease; (*fortuné*) comfortably off; **aimer ses aises** to like one's comforts; **mal à l'a.** uncomfortable, ill at ease. ◆**aisé** [eze] *a* (*fortuné*) comfortably off; (*naturel*) free and easy; (*facile*) easy. ◆**aisément** *adv* easily.

aisselle [ɛsɛl] *nf* armpit.

ait [ɛ] *voir* **avoir**.

ajonc(s) [aʒɔ̃] *nm(pl)* gorse, furze.

ajouré [aʒure] *a* (*dentelle etc*) openwork.

ajourn/er [aʒurne] *vt* to postpone, adjourn. ◆**—ement** *nm* postponement, adjournment.

ajout [aʒu] *nm* addition. ◆**ajouter** *vti* to add (à to); **s'a.** à to add to.

ajust/er [aʒyste] *vt* (*pièce, salaires*) to adjust; (*coiffure*) to arrange; (*coup*) to aim; **a. à** (*adapter*) to fit to. ◆**—é** *a* (*serré*) close-fitting. ◆**—ement** *nm* adjustment. ◆**—eur** *nm* (*ouvrier*) fitter.

alaise [alez] *nf* (waterproof) undersheet.

alambic [alɑ̃bik] *nm* still.

alambiqué [alɑ̃bike] *a* convoluted, over-subtle.

alanguir [alɑ̃gir] *vt* to make languid.

alarme [alarm] *nf* (*signal, inquiétude*) alarm; **jeter l'a.** to cause alarm. ◆**alarmer** *vt* to alarm; **s'a. de** to become alarmed at.

Albanie [albani] *nf* Albania. ◆**albanais, -aise** *a* & *nmf* Albanian.

albâtre [albɑtr] *nm* alabaster.

albatros [albatros] *nm* albatross.

albinos [albinos] *nmf* & *a inv* albino.

album [albɔm] *nm* (*de timbres etc*) album; (*de dessins*) sketchbook.

alcali [alkali] *nm* alkali. ◆**alcalin** *a* alkaline.

alchimie [alʃimi] *nf* alchemy.

alcool [alkɔl] *nm* alcohol; (*spiritueux*) spirits; **a. à brûler** methylated spirit(s); **lampe à a.** spirit lamp. ◆**alcoolique** *a* & *nmf* alcoholic. ◆**alcoolisé** *a* (*boisson*) alcoholic. ◆**alcoolisme** *nm* alcoholism. ◆**alcootest**® *nm* breath test; (*appareil*) breathalyzer.

alcôve [alkov] *nf* alcove.

aléas [alea] *nmpl* hazards, risks. ◆**aléatoire** *a* chancy, uncertain; (*sélection*) random.

alentour [alɑ̃tur] *adv* round about, around; **d'a.** surrounding; – *nmpl* surroundings, vicinity; **aux alentours de** in the vicinity of.

alerte [alɛrt] **1** *a* (*leste*) agile, spry; (*éveillé*) alert. **2** *nf* alarm; **en état d'a.** on the alert; **a. aérienne** air-raid warning. ◆**alerter** *vt* to warn, alert.

alezan, -ane [alzɑ̃ -an] *a* & *nmf* (*cheval*) chestnut.

algarade [algarad] *nf* (*dispute*) altercation.

algèbre [alʒɛbr] *nf* algebra. ◆**algébrique** *a* algebraic.

Alger [alʒe] *nm ou* *f* Algiers.

Algérie [alʒeri] *nf* Algeria. ◆**algérien, -ienne** *a* & *nmf* Algerian.

algue(s) [alg] *nf(pl)* seaweed.

alias [aljɑs] *adv* alias.

alibi [alibi] *nm* alibi.

alién/er [aljene] *vt* to alienate; **s'a. qn** to alienate s.o. ◆**—é, -ée** *nmf* insane person; *Péj* lunatic. ◆**aliénation** *nf* alienation; *Méd* derangement.

align/er [aliɲe] *vt* to align, line up; **les a.** *Arg* to fork out, pay up; **s'a.** (*personnes*) to fall into line, line up; *Pol* to align oneself (**sur** with). ◆**—ement** *nm* alignment.

aliment [alimɑ̃] *nm* food. ◆**alimentaire** *a* (*industrie, produit etc*) food-. ◆**alimentation** *nf* feeding; supply(ing); (*régime*) diet, nutrition; (*nourriture*) food; **magasin d'a.** grocer's, grocery store. ◆**alimenter** *vt* (*nourrir*) to feed; (*fournir*) to supply (**en** with); (*débat, feu*) to fuel.

alinéa [alinea] *nm* paragraph.

alité [alite] *a* bedridden.

allaiter [alete] *vti* to (breast)feed.

allant [alɑ̃] *nm* drive, energy, zest.

allécher [aleʃe] *vt* to tempt, entice.

allée [ale] *nf* path, walk, lane; (*de cinéma*) aisle; **allées et venues** comings and goings, running about.

allégation [alegasjɔ̃] *nf* allegation.

alléger [aleʒe] *vt* to alleviate, lighten.

allégorie [alegɔri] *nf* allegory.

allègre [alɛgr] *a* gay, lively, cheerful. ◆**allégresse** *nf* gladness, rejoicing.

alléguer [alege] *vt* (*excuse etc*) to put forward.

alléluia [aleluja] *nm* hallelujah.

Allemagne [almaɲ] *nf* Germany. ◆**allemand, -ande** *a* & *nmf* German; − *nm* (*langue*) German.

aller* [ale] **1** *vi* (*aux* **être**) to go; (*montre etc*) to work, go; **a. à** (*convenir à*) to suit; **a. avec** (*vêtement*) to go with, match; **a. bien/mieux** (*personne*) to be well/better; **il va savoir/venir/***etc* he'll know/come/*etc*, he's going to know/come/*etc*; **il va partir** he's about to leave, he's going to leave; **va voir!** go and see!; **comment vas-tu?**, (**comment**) **ça va?** how are you?; **ça va!** all right!, fine!; **ça va (comme ça)!** that's enough!; **allez-y** go on, go ahead; **j'y vais** I'm coming; **allons (donc)!** come on!, come off it!; **allez! au lit!** come on *ou* go on to bed!; **ça va de soi** that's obvious; − **s'en aller** *vpr* to go away; (*tache*) to come out. **2** *nm* outward journey; **a. (simple)** single (ticket), *Am* one-way (ticket); **a. (et) retour** return (ticket), *Am* round-trip (ticket).

allergie [alɛrʒi]·*nf* allergy. ◆**allergique** *a* allergic (**à** to).

alliage [aljaʒ] *nm* alloy.

alliance [aljɑ̃s] *nf* (*anneau*) wedding ring; *Pol* alliance; *Rel* covenant; (*mariage*) marriage.

alli/er [alje] *vt* (*associer*) to combine (**à** with); (*pays*) to ally (**à** with); − **s'a.** *vpr* (*couleurs*) to combine; (*pays*) to become allied (**à** with, to); **s'a. à** (*famille*) to ally oneself with. ◆**-é, -ée** *nmf* ally.

alligator [aligatɔr] *nm* alligator.

allô! [alo] *int Tél* hullo!, hallo!, hello!

allocation [alɔkasjɔ̃] *nf* (*somme*) allowance; **a. (de) chômage** unemployment benefit. ◆**allocataire** *nmf* claimant.

allocution [alɔkysjɔ̃] *nf* (short) speech, address.

allong/er [alɔ̃ʒe] *vt* (*bras*) to stretch out; (*jupe*) to lengthen; (*sauce*) to thin; − *vi* (*jours*) to get longer; − **s'a.** *vpr* to stretch out. ◆**-é** *a* (*oblong*) elongated.

allouer [alwe] *vt* to allocate.

allum/er [alyme] *vt* (*feu, pipe etc*) to light; (*électricité*) to turn *ou* switch on; (*désir, colère*) *Fig* to kindle; − **s'a.** *vpr* to light up; (*feu, guerre*) to flare up. ◆**-age** *nm* lighting; *Aut* ignition. ◆**allume-gaz** *nm inv* gas lighter. ◆**allumeuse** *nf* (*femme*) teaser.

allumette [alymɛt] *nf* match.

allure [alyr] *nf* (*vitesse*) pace; (*de véhicule*) speed; (*démarche*) gait, walk; (*maintien*) bearing; (*air*) look; *pl* (*conduite*) ways.

allusion [alyzjɔ̃] *nf* allusion; (*voilée*) hint; **faire a. à** to refer *ou* allude to; to hint at.

almanach [almana] *nm* almanac.

aloi [alwa] *nm* **de bon a.** genuine, worthy.

alors [alɔr] *adv* (*en ce temps-là*) then; (*en ce cas-là*) so, then; **a. que** (*lorsque*) when; (*tandis que*) whereas.

alouette [alwɛt] *nf* (sky)lark.

alourd/ir [alurdir] *vt* to weigh down; − **s'a.** *vpr* to become heavy *ou* heavier. ◆**-i** *a* heavy.

aloyau [alwajo] *nm* sirloin.

alpaga [alpaga] *nm* (*tissu*) alpaca.

alpage [alpaʒ] *nm* mountain pasture. ◆**Alpes** *nfpl* **les A.** the Alps. ◆**alpestre** *a*, ◆**alpin** *a* alpine. ◆**alpinisme** *nm* mountaineering. ◆**alpiniste** *nmf* mountaineer.

alphabet [alfabɛ] *nm* alphabet. ◆**alphabétique** *a* alphabetic(al). ◆**alphabétiser** *vt* to teach to read and write.

altercation [altɛrkasjɔ̃] *nf* altercation.

altérer [altere] *vt* (*denrée, santé*) to impair, spoil; (*voix, vérité*) to distort; (*monnaie, texte*) to falsify; (*donner soif à*) to make thirsty; − **s'a.** *vpr* (*santé, relations*) to deteriorate. ◆**altération** *nf* deterioration, change (**de** in); (*de visage*) distortion.

alternatif, -ive [altɛrnatif, -iv] *a* alternating. ◆**alternative** *nf* alternative; *pl* alternate periods. ◆**alternativement** *adv* alternately.

altern/er [altɛrne] *vti* to alternate. ◆**-é** *a* alternate. ◆**alternance** *nf* alternation.

altesse [altɛs] *nf* (*titre*) Highness.

altier, -ière [altje, -jɛr] *a* haughty.

altitude [altityd] *nf* altitude, height.

alto [alto] *nm* (*instrument*) viola.

aluminium [alyminjɔm] *nm* aluminium, *Am*

aluminum; **papier a.**, *Fam* **papier alu** tin foil.

alunir [alynir] *vi* to land on the moon.

alvéole [alveɔl] *nf* (*de ruche*) cell; (*dentaire*) socket. ◆**alvéolé** *a* honeycombed.

amabilité [amabilite] *nf* kindness; **faire des amabilités à** to show kindness to.

amadouer [amadwe] *vt* to coax, persuade.

amaigr/ir [amegrir] *vt* to make thin(ner). ◆**—i** *a* thin(ner). ◆**—issant** *a* (*régime*) slimming.

amalgame [amalgam] *nm* amalgam, mixture. ◆**amalgamer** *vt*, **— s'a.** *vpr* to blend, mix, amalgamate.

amande [amɑ̃d] *nf* almond.

amant [amɑ̃] *nm* lover.

amarre [amar] *nf* (mooring) rope, hawser; *pl* moorings. ◆**amarrer** *vt* to moor; *Fig* to tie down, make fast.

amas [amɑ] *nm* heap, pile. ◆**amasser** *vt* to pile up; (*richesse, preuves*) to amass, gather; **— s'a.** *vpr* to pile up; (*gens*) to gather.

amateur [amatœr] *nm* (*d'art etc*) lover; *Sp* amateur; (*acheteur*) *Fam* taker; **d'a.** (*talent*) amateur; (*travail*) *Péj* amateurish; **une équipe a.** an amateur team. ◆**amateurisme** *nm Sp* amateurism; *Péj* amateurishness.

amazone [amazɔn] *nf* horsewoman; **monter en a.** to ride sidesaddle.

ambages (sans) [sɑ̃zɑ̃baʒ] *adv* to the point, in plain language.

ambassade [ɑ̃basad] *nf* embassy. ◆**ambassadeur, -drice** *nmf* ambassador.

ambiance [ɑ̃bjɑ̃s] *nf* atmosphere. ◆**ambiant** *a* surrounding.

ambigu, -guë [ɑ̃bigy] *a* ambiguous. ◆**ambiguïté** [-gɥite] *nf* ambiguity.

ambitieux, -euse [ɑ̃bisjø, -øz] *a* ambitious. ◆**ambition** *nf* ambition. ◆**ambitionner** *vt* to aspire to; **il ambitionne de** his ambition is to.

ambre [ɑ̃br] *nm* (*jaune*) amber; (*gris*) ambergris.

ambulance [ɑ̃bylɑ̃s] *nf* ambulance. ◆**ambulancier, -ière** *nmf* ambulance driver.

ambulant [ɑ̃bylɑ̃] *a* itinerant, travelling.

âme [ɑm] *nf* soul; **â. qui vive** a living soul; **état d'â.** state of mind; **â. sœur** soul mate; **â. damnée** evil genius, henchman; **avoir charge d'âmes** to be responsible for human life.

améliorer [ameljɔre] *vt*, **— s'a.** *vpr* to improve. ◆**amélioration** *nf* improvement.

amen [amɛn] *adv* amen.

aménag/er [amenaʒe] *vt* (*arranger, installer*) to fit up, fit out (**en** as); (*bateau*) to fit out; (*transformer*) to convert (**en** into); (*construire*) to set up; (*ajuster*) to adjust. ◆**—ement** *nm* fitting up; fitting out; conversion; setting up; adjustment.

amende [amɑ̃d] *nf* fine; **frapper d'une a.** to impose a fine on; **faire a. honorable** to make an apology.

amender [amɑ̃de] *vt Pol* to amend; (*terre*) to improve; **— s'a.** *vpr* to mend *ou* improve one's ways.

amener [amne] *vt* to bring; (*causer*) to bring about; **— s'a.** *vpr Fam* to come along, turn up.

amenuiser (s') [sa|mənɥize] *vpr* to grow smaller, dwindle.

amer, -ère [amɛr] *a* bitter. ◆**amèrement** *adv* bitterly.

Amérique [amerik] *nf* America; **A. du Nord/du Sud** North/South America. ◆**américain, -aine** *a* & *nmf* American.

amerrir [amerir] *vi* to make a sea landing; (*cabine spatiale*) to splash down.

amertume [amɛrtym] *nf* bitterness.

améthyste [ametist] *nf* amethyst.

ameublement [amœbləmɑ̃] *nm* furniture.

ameuter [amøte] *vt* (*soulever*) to stir up; (*attrouper*) to gather, muster; (*voisins*) to bring out; **— s'a.** *vpr* to gather, muster.

ami, -e [ami] *nmf* friend; (*des livres, de la nature etc*) lover (**de** of); **petite amie** girlfriend; **— a** friendly.

amiable (à l') [alamjabl] *a* amicable; **— adv** amicably.

amiante [amjɑ̃t] *nm* asbestos.

amical, -aux [amikal, -o] *a* friendly. ◆**—ement** *adv* in a friendly manner.

amicale [amikal] *nf* association.

amidon [amidɔ̃] *nm* starch. ◆**amidonner** *vt* to starch.

amincir [amɛ̃sir] *vt* to make thin(ner); **— vi** (*personne*) to slim; **— s'a.** *vpr* to become thinner.

amiral, -aux [amiral, -o] *nm* admiral. ◆**amirauté** *nf* admiralty.

amitié [amitje] *nf* friendship; (*amabilité*) kindness; *pl* kind regrds; **prendre en a.** to take a liking to.

ammoniac [amɔnjak] *nm* (*gaz*) ammonia. ◆**ammoniaque** *nf* (*liquide*) ammonia.

amnésie [amnezi] *nf* amnesia.

amnistie [amnisti] *nf* amnesty.

amocher [amɔʃe] *vt Arg* to mess up, bash.

amoindrir [amwɛ̃drir] *vt*, **— s'a.** *vpr* to decrease, diminish.

amoll/ir [amɔlir] *vt* to soften; (*affaiblir*) to weaken. **◆—issant** *a* enervating.

amonceler [amɔ̃sle] *vt*, **— s'a.** *vpr* to pile up. **◆amoncellement** *nm* heap, pile.

amont (en) [ɑ̃namɔ̃] *adv* upstream.

amoral, -aux [amɔral, -o] *a* amoral.

amorce [amɔrs] *nf* (*début*) start; *Pêche* bait; (*détonateur*) fuse, detonator; (*de pistolet d'enfant*) cap. **◆amorcer** *vt* to start; (*hameçon*) to bait; (*pompe*) to prime; — **s'a.** *vpr* to start.

amorphe [amɔrf] *a* listless, apathetic.

amort/ir [amɔrtir] *vt* (*coup*) to cushion, absorb; (*bruit*) to deaden; (*dette*) to pay off; **il a vite amorti sa voiture** his car has been made to pay for itself quickly. **◆—issement** *nm* *Fin* redemption. **◆—isseur** *nm* shock absorber.

amour [amur] *nm* love; (*liaison*) romance, love; (*Cupidon*) Cupid; **pour l'a. de** for the sake of; **mon a.** my darling, my love. **◆a.-propre** *nm* self-respect, self-esteem. **◆s'amouracher** *vpr* *Péj* to become infatuated (**de** with). **◆amoureux, -euse** *nmf* lover; — *a* amorous, loving; **a. de** (*personne*) in love with; (*gloire*) *Fig* enamoured of.

amovible [amɔvibl] *a* removable, detachable.

ampère [ɑ̃per] *nm* *Él* amp(ere).

amphi [ɑ̃fi] *nm* *Univ Fam* lecture hall.

amphibie [ɑ̃fibi] *a* amphibious; — *nm* amphibian.

amphithéâtre [ɑ̃fiteatr] *nm* *Hist* amphitheatre; *Univ* lecture hall.

ample [ɑ̃pl] *a* (*vêtement*) ample, roomy; (*provision*) full; (*vues*) broad. **◆amplement** *adv* amply, fully; **a. suffisant** ample. **◆ampleur** *nf* (*de robe*) fullness; (*importance, étendue*) scale, extent; **prendre de l'a.** to grow.

amplifier [ɑ̃plifje] *vt* (*accroître*) to develop; (*exagérer*) to magnify; (*son, courant*) to amplify; — **s'a.** *vpr* to increase. **◆amplificateur** *nm* amplifier. **◆amplification** *nf* (*extension*) increase.

amplitude [ɑ̃plityd] *nf* *Fig* magnitude.

ampoule [ɑ̃pul] *nf* (*électrique*) (light) bulb; (*aux pieds etc*) blister; (*de médicament*) phial.

ampoulé [ɑ̃pule] *a* turgid.

amputer [ɑ̃pyte] *vt* **1** (*membre*) to amputate; **a. qn de la jambe** to amputate s.o.'s leg. **2** (*texte*) to curtail, cut (**de** by). **◆amputation** *nf* amputation; curtailment.

amuse-gueule [amyzɡœl] *nm inv* cocktail snack, appetizer.

amus/er [amyze] *vt* (*divertir*) to amuse, entertain; (*occuper*) to divert the attention of; — **s'a.** *vpr* to enjoy oneself, have fun; (*en chemin*) to dawdle, loiter; **s'a. avec** to play with; **s'a. à faire** to amuse oneself doing. **◆—ant** *a* amusing. **◆—ement** *nm* amusement; (*jeu*) game. **◆amusette** *nf* frivolous pursuit.

amygdale [amidal] *nf* tonsil.

an [ɑ̃] *nm* year; **il a dix ans** he's ten (years old); **par a.** per annum, per year; **bon a., mal a.** putting the good years and the bad together; **Nouvel a.** New Year.

anachronisme [anakrɔnism] *nm* anachronism.

anagramme [anagram] *nf* anagram.

analogie [analɔʒi] *nf* analogy. **◆analogue** *a* similar; — *nm* analogue.

analphabète [analfabet] *a* & *nmf* illiterate. **◆analphabétisme** *nm* illiteracy.

analyse [analiz] *nf* analysis; **a. grammaticale** parsing. **◆analyser** *vt* to analyse; (*phrase*) to parse. **◆analytique** *a* analytic(al).

ananas [anana(s)] *nm* pineapple.

anarchie [anarʃi] *nf* anarchy. **◆anarchique** *a* anarchic. **◆anarchiste** *nmf* anarchist; — *a* anarchistic.

anathème [anatɛm] *nm* *Rel* anathema.

anatomie [anatɔmi] *nf* anatomy. **◆anatomique** *a* anatomical.

ancestral, -aux [ɑ̃sestral, -o] *a* ancestral.

ancêtre [ɑ̃sɛtr] *nm* ancestor.

anche [ɑ̃ʃ] *nf* *Mus* reed.

anchois [ɑ̃ʃwa] *nm* anchovy.

ancien, -ienne [ɑ̃sjɛ̃, -jɛn] *a* (*vieux*) old; (*meuble*) antique; (*qui n'est plus*) former, ex-, old; (*antique*) ancient; (*dans une fonction*) senior; **a. élève** old boy, *Am* alumnus; **a. combattant** ex-serviceman, *Am* veteran; — *nmf* (*par l'âge*) elder; (*dans une fonction*) senior; **les anciens** (*auteurs, peuples*) the ancients. **◆anciennement** *adv* formerly. **◆ancienneté** *nf* age; (*dans une fonction*) seniority.

ancre [ɑ̃kr] *nf* anchor; **jeter l'a.** to (cast) anchor; **lever l'a.** to weigh anchor. **◆ancrer** *vt* *Nau* to anchor; (*idée*) *Fig* to root, fix; **ancré dans** rooted in.

andouille [ɑ̃duj] *nf* sausage (*made from chitterlings*); **espèce d'a.!** *Fam* (you) nitwit!

âne [ɑn] *nm* (*animal*) donkey, ass; (*personne*) *Péj* ass; **bonnet d'â.** dunce's cap; **dos d'â.** (*d'une route*) hump; **pont en dos d'â.** humpback bridge.

anéant/ir [aneɑ̃tir] *vt* to annihilate, wipe out, destroy; **— s'a.** *vpr* to vanish. **◆—i** *a* (*épuisé*) exhausted; (*stupéfait*) dismayed; (*accablé*) overwhelmed. **◆—issement** *nm* annihilation; (*abattement*) dejection.

anecdote [anɛkdɔt] *nf* anecdote. **◆anecdotique** *a* anecdotal.

anémie [anemi] *nf* an(a)emia. **◆anémique** *a* an(a)emic. **◆s'anémier** *vpr* to become an(a)emic.

anémone [anemɔn] *nf* anemone.

ânerie [ɑnri] *nf* stupidity; (*action etc*) stupid thing. **◆ânesse** *nf* she-ass.

anesthésie [anɛstezi] *nf* an(a)esthesia; **a. générale/locale** general/local an(a)esthetic. **◆anesthésier** *vt* to an(a)esthetize. **◆anesthésique** *nm* an(a)esthetic.

anfractuosité [ɑ̃fraktɥozite] *nf* crevice, cleft.

ange [ɑ̃ʒ] *nm* angel; **aux anges** in seventh heaven. **◆angélique** *a* angelic.

angélus [ɑ̃ʒelys] *nm Rel* angelus.

angine [ɑ̃ʒin] *nf* sore throat; **a. de poitrine** angina (pectoris).

anglais, -aise [ɑ̃glɛ, -ez] *a* English; **–** *nmf* Englishman, Englishwoman; **–** *nm* (*langue*) English; **filer à l'anglaise** to take French leave.

angle [ɑ̃gl] *nm* (*point de vue*) & *Géom* angle; (*coin*) corner.

Angleterre [ɑ̃glətɛr] *nf* England.

anglican, -ane [ɑ̃glikɑ̃, -an] *a* & *nmf* Anglican.

anglicisme [ɑ̃glisism] *nm* Anglicism. **◆angliciste** *nmf* English specialist.

anglo- [ɑ̃glo] *préf* Anglo-. **◆anglo-normand** *a* Anglo-Norman; **îles a.-normandes** Channel Islands. **◆anglophile** *a* & *nmf* anglophile. **◆anglophone** *a* English-speaking; **–** *nmf* English speaker. **◆anglo-saxon, -onne** *a* & *nmf* Anglo-Saxon.

angoisse [ɑ̃gwas] *nf* anguish. **◆angoissant** *a* distressing. **◆angoissé** *a* (*personne*) in anguish; (*geste*, *cri*) anguished.

angora [ɑ̃gɔra] *nm* (*laine*) angora.

anguille [ɑ̃gij] *nf* eel.

angulaire [ɑ̃gylɛr] *a* **pierre a.** cornerstone. **◆anguleux, -euse** *a* (*visage*) angular.

anicroche [anikrɔʃ] *nf* hitch, snag.

animal, -aux [animal, -o] *nm* animal; (*personne*) *Péj* brute, animal; **–** *a* animal.

animer [anime] *vt* (*inspirer*) to animate; (*encourager*) to spur on; (*débat, groupe*) to lead; (*soirée*) to enliven; (*regard*) to light up, brighten up; (*mécanisme*) to actuate, drive; **a. la course** *Sp* to set the pace; **animé de** (*sentiment*) prompted by; **— s'a.** *vpr* (*rue etc*) to come to life; (*yeux*) to light up, brighten up. **◆animé** *a* (*rue*) lively; (*conversation*) animated, lively; (*doué de vie*) animate. **◆animateur, -trice** *nmf TV* compere, *Am* master of ceremonies, emcee; (*de club*) leader, organizer; (*d'entreprise*) driving force, spirit. **◆animation** *nf* (*des rues*) activity; (*de réunion*) liveliness; (*de visage*) brightness; *Cin* animation.

animosité [animozite] *nf* animosity.

anis [ani(s)] *nm* (*boisson, parfum*) aniseed. **◆anisette** *nf* (*liqueur*) anisette.

ankylose [ɑ̃kiloz] *nf* stiffening. **◆s'ankylos/er** *vpr* to stiffen up. **◆—é** *a* stiff.

annales [anal] *nfpl* annals.

anneau, -x [ano] *nm* ring; (*de chaîne*) link.

année [ane] *nf* year; **bonne a.!** Happy New Year!

annexe [anɛks] *nf* (*bâtiment*) annex(e); **–** *a* (*pièces*) appended; **bâtiment a.** annex(e). **◆annexer** *vt* (*pays*) to annex; (*document*) to append. **◆annexion** *nf* annexation.

annihiler [aniile] *vt* to destroy, annihilate.

anniversaire [anivɛrsɛr] *nm* (*d'événement*) anniversary; (*de naissance*) birthday; **–** *a* anniversary.

annonce [anɔ̃s] *nf* (*avis*) announcement; (*publicitaire*) advertisement; (*indice*) sign; **petites annonces** classified advertisements, small ads. **◆annoncer** *vt* (*signaler*) to announce, report; (*être l'indice de*) to indicate; (*vente*) to advertise; **a. le printemps** to herald spring; **s'a. pluvieux/difficile/etc** to look like being rainy/difficult/etc. **◆annonceur** *nm* advertiser; *Rad TV* announcer.

annonciation [anɔ̃sjasjɔ̃] *nf* Annunciation.

annoter [anɔte] *vt* to annotate. **◆annotation** *nf* annotation.

annuaire [anɥɛr] *nm* yearbook; (*téléphonique*) directory, phone book.

annuel, -elle [anɥɛl] *a* annual, yearly. **◆annuellement** *adv* annually. **◆annuité** *nf* annual instalment.

annulaire [anɥlɛr] *nm* ring *ou* third finger.

annuler [anɥle] *vt* (*visite etc*) to cancel; (*mariage*) to annul; (*jugement*) to quash; **— s'a.** *vpr* to cancel each other out. **◆annulation** *nf* cancellation; annulment; quashing.

anoblir [anɔblir] *vt* to ennoble.

anodin [anɔdɛ̃] *a* harmless; (*remède*) ineffectual.

anomalie [anɔmali] *nf* (*irrégularité*) anomaly; (*difformité*) abnormality.

ânonner [ɑnɔne] *vt* (*en hésitant*) to stumble through; (*d'une voix monotone*) to drone out.

anonymat [anɔnima] *nm* anonymity; **garder l'a.** to remain anonymous. ◆**anonyme** *a* & *nmf* anonymous (person).

anorak [anɔrak] *nm* anorak.

anorexie [anɔrɛksi] *nf* anorexia.

anormal, -aux [anɔrmal, -o] *a* abnormal; (*enfant*) educationally subnormal.

anse [ɑ̃s] *nf* (*de tasse etc*) handle; (*baie*) cove.

antagonisme [ɑ̃tagɔnism] *nm* antagonism. ◆**antagoniste** *a* antagonistic; – *nmf* antagonist.

antan (d') [dɑ̃tɑ̃] *a Litt* of yesteryear.

antarctique [ɑ̃tarktik] *a* antarctic; – *nm* **l'A.** the Antarctic, Antarctica.

antécédent [ɑ̃tesedɑ̃] *nm Gram* antecedent; *pl* past history, antecedents.

antenne [ɑ̃tɛn] *nf TV Rad* aerial, *Am* antenna; (*station*) station; (*d'insecte*) antenna, feeler; **a. chirurgicale** surgical outpost; *Aut* emergency unit; **sur** *ou* **à l'a.** on the air.

antérieur [ɑ̃terjœr] *a* (*précédent*) former, previous, earlier; (*placé devant*) front; **membre a.** forelimb; **a. à** prior to. ◆**antérieurement** *adv* previously. ◆**antériorité** *nf* precedence.

anthologie [ɑ̃tɔlɔʒi] *nf* anthology.

anthropologie [ɑ̃trɔpɔlɔʒi] *nf* anthropology.

anthropophage [ɑ̃trɔpɔfaʒ] *nm* cannibal. ◆**anthropophagie** *nf* cannibalism.

antiaérien, -ienne [ɑ̃tiaerjɛ̃, -jɛn] *a* (*canon*) antiaircraft; (*abri*) air-raid.

antiatomique [ɑ̃tiatɔmik] *a* **abri a.** fallout shelter.

antibiotique [ɑ̃tibjɔtik] *a* & *nm* antibiotic.

antibrouillard [ɑ̃tibrujar] *a* & *nm* (**phare**) **a.** fog lamp.

anticancéreux, -euse [ɑ̃tikɑ̃serø, -øz] *a* **centre a.** cancer hospital.

antichambre [ɑ̃tiʃɑ̃br] *nf* antechamber, anteroom.

antichoc [ɑ̃tiʃɔk] *a inv* shockproof.

anticip/er [ɑ̃tisipe] *vti* **a. (sur)** to anticipate. ◆**-é** *a* (*retraite etc*) early; (*paiement*) advance; **avec mes remerciements anticipés** thanking you in advance. ◆**anticipation** *nf* anticipation; **par a.** in advance; **d'a.** (*roman etc*) science-fiction.

anticlérical, -aux [ɑ̃tiklerikal, -o] *a* anticlerical.

anticonformiste [ɑ̃tikɔ̃fɔrmist] *a* & *nmf* nonconformist.

anticonstitutionnel, -elle [ɑ̃tikɔ̃stitysjɔnɛl] *a* unconstitutional.

anticorps [ɑ̃tikɔr] *nm* antibody.

anticyclone [ɑ̃tisiklon] *nm* anticyclone.

antidater [ɑ̃tidate] *vt* to backdate, antedate.

antidémocratique [ɑ̃tidemɔkratik] *a* undemocratic.

antidérapant [ɑ̃tiderapɑ̃] *a* non-skid.

antidote [ɑ̃tidɔt] *nm* antidote.

antigel [ɑ̃tiʒɛl] *nm* antifreeze.

Antilles [ɑ̃tij] *nfpl* **les A.** the West Indies. ◆**antillais, -aise** *a* & *nmf* West Indian.

antilope [ɑ̃tilɔp] *nf* antelope.

antimite [ɑ̃timit] *a* mothproof; – *nm* mothproofing agent.

antiparasite [ɑ̃tiparazit] *a* **dispositif a.** *Rad* suppressor.

antipathie [ɑ̃tipati] *nf* antipathy. ◆**antipathique** *a* disagreeable.

antipodes [ɑ̃tipɔd] *nmpl* **aux a.** (*partir*) to the antipodes; **aux a. de** at the opposite end of the world from; *Fig* poles apart from.

antique [ɑ̃tik] *a* ancient. ◆**antiquaire** *nmf* antique dealer. ◆**antiquité** *nf* (*temps, ancienneté*) antiquity; (*objet ancien*) antique; *pl* (*monuments etc*) antiquities.

antirabique [ɑ̃tirabik] *a* (anti-)rabies.

antisémite [ɑ̃tisemit] *a* anti-Semitic. ◆**antisémitisme** *nm* anti-Semitism.

antiseptique [ɑ̃tisɛptik] *a* & *nm* antiseptic.

antisudoral, -aux [ɑ̃tisydɔral, -o] *nm* antiperspirant.

antithèse [ɑ̃titɛz] *nf* antithesis.

antivol [ɑ̃tivɔl] *nm* anti-theft lock *ou* device.

antonyme [ɑ̃tɔnim] *nm* antonym.

antre [ɑ̃tr] *nm* (*de lion etc*) den.

anus [anys] *nm* anus.

Anvers [ɑ̃vɛr(s)] *nm ou f* Antwerp.

anxiété [ɑ̃ksjete] *nf* anxiety. ◆**anxieux, -euse** *a* anxious; – *nmf* worrier.

août [u(t)] *nm* August. ◆**aoûtien, -ienne** [ausjɛ̃, -jɛn] *nmf* August holidaymaker *ou Am* vacationer.

apais/er [apeze] *vt* (*personne*) to appease, calm; (*scrupules, faim*) to appease; (*douleur*) to allay; – **s'a.** *vpr* (*personne*) to calm down. ◆**-ant** *a* soothing. ◆**-ements** *nmpl* reassurances.

apanage [apanaʒ] *nm* privilege, monopoly (**de** of).

aparté [aparte] *nm Th* aside; (*dans une réunion*) private exchange; **en a.** in private.

apartheid [aparted] *nm* apartheid.

apathie [apati] *nf* apathy. ◆**apathique** *a* apathetic, listless.

apatride [apatrid] *nmf* stateless person.

apercevoir* [apɛrsəvwar] *vt* to see, perceive; (*brièvement*) to catch a glimpse of; **s'a. de** to notice, realize. ◆**aperçu** *nm* overall view, general outline; (*intuition*) insight.

apéritif [aperitif] *nm* aperitif. ◆**apéro** *nm* Fam aperitif.

apesanteur [apəzɑ̃tœr] *nf* weightlessness.

à-peu-près [apøprɛ] *nm inv* vague approximation.

apeuré [apœre] *a* frightened, scared.

aphone [afɔn] *a* voiceless.

aphorisme [afɔrism] *nm* aphorism.

aphrodisiaque [afrɔdizjak] *a & nm* aphrodisiac.

aphte [aft] *nm* mouth ulcer. ◆**aphteuse** *af* **fièvre a.** foot-and-mouth disease.

apiculture [apikyltyr] *nf* beekeeping.

apit/oyer [apitwaje] *vt* to move (to pity); **s'a. sur** to pity. ◆**—oiement** *nm* pity, commiseration.

aplanir [aplanir] *vt* (*terrain*) to level; (*difficulté*) to iron out, smooth out.

aplat/ir [aplatir] *vt* to flatten (out); — **s'a.** *vpr* (*s'étendre*) to lie flat; (*s'humilier*) to grovel; (*tomber*) Fam to fall flat on one's face; **s'a. contre** to flatten oneself against. ◆**—i** *a* flat. ◆**—issement** *nm* (*état*) flatness.

aplomb [aplɔ̃] *nm* self-possession, self-assurance; Péj impudence; **d'a.** (*équilibré*) well-balanced; (*sur ses jambes*) steady; (*bien portant*) in good shape; **tomber d'a.** (*soleil*) to beat down.

apocalypse [apɔkalips] *nf* apocalypse; **d'a.** (*vision etc*) apocalyptic. ◆**apocalyptique** *a* apocalyptic.

apogée [apɔʒe] *nm* apogee; Fig peak, apogee.

apolitique [apɔlitik] *a* apolitical.

Apollon [apɔlɔ̃] *nm* Apollo.

apologie [apɔlɔʒi] *nf* defence, vindication. ◆**apologiste** *nmf* apologist.

apoplexie [apɔplɛksi] *nf* apoplexy. ◆**apoplectique** *a* apoplectic.

apostolat [apɔstɔla] *nm* (*prosélytisme*) proselytism; (*mission*) Fig calling. ◆**apostolique** *a* apostolic.

apostrophe [apɔstrɔf] *nf* **1** (*signe*) apostrophe. **2** (*interpellation*) sharp *ou* rude remark. ◆**apostropher** *vt* to shout at.

apothéose [apɔteoz] *nf* final triumph, apotheosis.

apôtre [apotr] *nm* apostle.

apparaître* [aparɛtr] *vi* (*se montrer, sembler*) to appear.

apparat [apara] *nm* pomp; **d'a.** (*tenue etc*) ceremonial, formal.

appareil [aparɛj] *nm* (*instrument etc*) apparatus; (*électrique*) appliance; Anat system; Tél telephone; (*avion*) aircraft; (*législatif etc*) Fig machinery; **a. (photo)** camera; **a. (auditif)** hearing aid; **a. (dentier)** brace; **qui est à l'a.?** Tél who's speaking?

appareiller [apareje] **1** *vi* Nau to get under way. **2** *vt* (*assortir*) to match (up).

apparence [aparɑ̃s] *nf* appearance; (*vestige*) semblance; **en a.** outwardly; **sous l'a. de** under the guise of; **sauver les apparences** to keep up appearances. ◆**apparemment** [-amɑ̃] *adv* apparently. ◆**apparent** *a* apparent; (*ostensible*) conspicuous.

apparent/er (s') [saparɑ̃te] *vpr* (*ressembler*) to be similar *ou* akin (à to). ◆**—é** *a* (*allié*) related; (*semblable*) similar.

appariteur [aparitœr] *nm* Univ porter.

apparition [aparisjɔ̃] *nf* appearance; (*spectre*) apparition.

appartement [apartəmɑ̃] *nm* flat, Am apartment.

appartenir* [apartənir] **1** *vi* to belong (à to); **il vous appartient de** it's your responsibility to. **2 s'a.** *vpr* to be one's own master. ◆**appartenance** *nf* membership (à of).

appât [apa] *nm* (*amorce*) bait; (*attrait*) lure. ◆**appâter** *vt* (*attirer*) to lure.

appauvrir [apovrir] *vt* to impoverish; — **s'a.** *vpr* to become impoverished *ou* poorer.

appel [apɛl] *nm* (*cri, attrait etc*) call; (*demande pressante*) & Jur appeal; Mil call-up; **faire l'a.** Scol to take the register; Mil to have a roll call; **faire a. à** to appeal to, call upon; (*requérir*) to call for.

appel/er [aple] *vt* (*personne, nom etc*) to call; (*en criant*) to call out to; Mil to call up; (*nécessiter*) to call for; **a. à l'aide** to call for help; **en a. à** to appeal to; **il est appelé à** (*de hautes fonctions*) he is marked out for; (*témoigner etc*) he is called upon to; — **s'a.** *vpr* to be called; **il s'appelle Paul** his name is Paul. ◆**—é** *nm* Mil conscript. ◆**appellation** *nf* (*nom*) term; **a. contrôlée** trade name guaranteeing quality of wine.

appendice [apɛ̃dis] *nm* appendix; (*d'animal*) appendage. ◆**appendicite** *nf* appendicitis.

appentis [apɑ̃ti] *nm* (*bâtiment*) lean-to.

appesantir (s') [sapəzɑ̃tir] *vpr* to become heavier; **s'a. sur** (*sujet*) to dwell upon.

appétit [apeti] *nm* appetite (**de** for); **mettre**

qn en a. to whet s.o.'s appetite; **bon a.!** enjoy your meal! ◆**appétissant** a appetizing.

applaud/ir [aplodir] vti to applaud, clap; a. à (approuver) to applaud. ◆**—issements** nmpl applause.

applique [aplik] nf wall lamp.

appliqu/er [aplike] vt to apply (**à** to); (surnom, baiser, gifle) to give; (loi, décision) to put into effect; **s'a. à** (un travail) to apply oneself to; (concerner) to apply to; **s'a. à faire** to take pains to do. ◆**—é** a (travailleur) painstaking; (sciences) applied. ◆**applicable** a applicable. ◆**application** nf application.

appoint [apwɛ̃] nm contribution; **faire l'a.** to give the correct money ou change.

appointements [apwɛ̃tmɑ̃] nmpl salary.

appontement [apɔ̃tmɑ̃] nm landing stage.

apport [apɔr] nm contribution.

apporter [apɔrte] vt to bring.

apposer [apoze] vt Jur to affix. ◆**apposition** nf Gram apposition.

apprécier [apresje] vt (évaluer) to appraise; (aimer, percevoir) to appreciate. ◆**appréciable** a appreciable. ◆**appréciation** nf appraisal; appreciation.

appréhender [apreɑ̃de] vt (craindre) to fear; (arrêter) to apprehend. ◆**appréhension** nf apprehension.

apprendre* [aprɑ̃dr] vti (étudier) to learn; (événement, fait) to hear of, learn of; (nouvelle) to hear; **a. à faire** to learn to do; **a. qch à qn** (enseigner) to teach s.o. sth; (informer) to tell s.o. sth; **a. à qn à faire** to teach s.o. to do; **a. que** to learn that; (être informé) to hear that.

apprenti, -ie [aprɑ̃ti] nmf apprentice; (débutant) novice. ◆**apprentissage** nm apprenticeship; **faire l'a. de** Fig to learn the experience of.

apprêt/er [aprete] vt, — **s'a.** vpr to prepare. ◆**—é** a Fig affected.

apprivois/er [aprivwaze] vt to tame; — **s'a.** vpr to become tame. ◆**—é** a tame.

approbation [aprobasjɔ̃] nf approval. ◆**approbateur, -trice** a approving.

approche [aprɔʃ] nf approach. ◆**approch/er** vt (chaise etc) to bring up, draw up (**de** to, close to); (personne) to approach, come close to; — vi to approach, draw near(er); **a. de, s'a. de** to approach, come close(r) ou near(er) to. ◆**—ant** a similar. ◆**—é** a approximate. ◆**—able** a approachable.

approfond/ir [aprofɔ̃dir] vt (trou etc) to deepen; (question) to go into thoroughly;

(mystère) to plumb the depths of. ◆**—i** a thorough. ◆**—issement** nm deepening; (examen) thorough examination.

approprié [aproprije] a appropriate.

approprier (s') [saproprije] vpr **s'a. qch** to appropriate sth.

approuver [apruve] vt (autoriser) to approve; (apprécier) to approve of.

approvisionn/er [aprovizjɔne] vt (ville etc) to supply (with provisions); (magasin) to stock; — **s'a.** vpr to stock up (**de** with), get one's supplies (**de** of). ◆**—ements** nmpl stocks, supplies.

approximat/if, -ive [aproksimatif, -iv] a approximate. ◆**—ivement** adv approximately. ◆**approximation** nf approximation.

appui [apɥi] nm support; (pour coude etc) rest; (de fenêtre) sill; **à hauteur d'a.** breast-high. ◆**appuie-tête** nm inv headrest. ◆**appuyer** vt (soutenir) to support; (accentuer) to stress; **a. qch sur** (poser) to lean ou rest sth on; (presser) to press sth on; — vi **a. sur** to rest on; (bouton etc) to press (on); (mot, élément etc) to stress; **s'a. sur** to lean on, rest on; (compter) to rely on; (se baser) to base oneself on.

âpre [ɑpr] a harsh, rough; **a. au gain** grasping.

après [aprɛ] prép (temps) after; (espace) beyond; **a. un an** after a year; **a. le pont** beyond the bridge; **a. coup** after the event; **a. avoir mangé** after eating; **a. qu'il t'a vu** after he saw you; **d'a.** (selon) according to, from; — adv after(wards); **l'année d'a.** the following year; **et a.?** and then what?

après-demain [apredmɛ̃] adv the day after tomorrow. ◆**a.-guerre** nm post-war period; **d'a.-guerre** post-war. ◆**a.-midi** nm ou f inv afternoon. ◆**a.-shampooing** nm (hair) conditioner. ◆**a.-ski** nm ankle boot, snow boot.

a priori [aprijɔri] adv at the very outset, without going into the matter; — nm inv premiss.

à-propos [apropo] nm timeliness, aptness.

apte [apt] a suited (**à** to), capable (**à** of). ◆**aptitude** nf aptitude, capacity (**à, pour** for).

aquarelle [akwarɛl] nf watercolour, aquarelle.

aquarium [akwarjɔm] nm aquarium.

aquatique [akwatik] a aquatic.

aqueduc [akdyk] nm aqueduct.

aquilin [akilɛ̃] a aquiline.

arabe [arab] a & nmf Arab; — a & nm (langue) Arabic; **chiffres arabes** Arabic

numerals; **désert a.** Arabian desert.
◆**Arabie** *nf* Arabia; **A. Séoudite** Saudi Arabia.
arabesque [arabɛsk] *nf* arabesque.
arable [arabl] *a* arable.
arachide [araʃid] *nf* peanut, groundnut.
araignée [areɲe] *nf* spider.
arbalète [arbalɛt] *nf* crossbow.
arbitraire [arbitrɛr] *a* arbitrary.
arbitre [arbitr] *nm* *Jur* arbitrator; (*maître absolu*) arbiter; *Fb* referee; *Tennis* umpire; **libre a.** free will. ◆**arbitr/er** *vt* to arbitrate; to referee; to umpire. ◆**—age** *nm* arbitration; refereeing; umpiring.
arborer [arbɔre] *vt* (*insigne, vêtement*) to sport, display.
arbre [arbr] *nm* tree; *Aut* shaft, axle. ◆**arbrisseau, -x** *nm* shrub. ◆**arbuste** *nm* (small) shrub, bush.
arc [ark] *nm* (*arme*) bow; (*voûte*) arch; *Math* arc; **tir à l'a.** archery. ◆**arcade** *nf* arch(way); *pl* arcade.
arc-boutant [arkbutɑ̃] *nm* (*pl* **arcs-boutants**) flying buttress. ◆**s'arc-bouter** *vpr* **s'a. à** *ou* **contre** to brace oneself against.
arceau, -x [arso] *nm* (*de voûte*) arch.
arc-en-ciel [arkɑ̃sjɛl] *nm* (*pl* **arcs-en-ciel**) rainbow.
archaïque [arkaik] *a* archaic.
archange [arkɑ̃ʒ] *nm* archangel.
arche [arʃ] *nf* (*voûte*) arch; **l'a. de Noé** Noah's ark.
archéologie [arkeɔlɔʒi] *nf* arch(a)eology. ◆**archéologue** *nmf* arch(a)eologist.
archer [arʃe] *nm* archer, bowman.
archet [arʃɛ] *nm* *Mus* bow.
archétype [arketip] *nm* archetype.
archevêque [arʃəvɛk] *nm* archbishop.
archicomble [arʃikɔbl] *a* jam-packed.
archipel [arʃipɛl] *nm* archipelago.
archiplein [arʃiplɛ̃] *a* chock-full, chock-a-block.
architecte [arʃitɛkt] *nm* architect. ◆**architecture** *nf* architecture.
archives [arʃiv] *nfpl* archives, records. ◆**archiviste** *nmf* archivist.
arctique [arktik] *a* arctic; **–** *nm* **l'A.** the Arctic.
ardent [ardɑ̃] *a* (*chaud*) burning, scorching; (*actif, passionné*) ardent, fervent; (*empressé*) eager. ◆**ardemment** [-amɑ̃] *adv* eagerly, fervently. ◆**ardeur** *nf* heat; (*énergie*) ardour, fervour.
ardoise [ardwaz] *nf* slate.
ardu [ardy] *a* arduous, difficult.
are [ar] *nm* (*mesure*) 100 square metres.

arène [arɛn] *nf* *Hist* arena; (*pour taureaux*) bullring; *pl* *Hist* amphitheatre; bullring.
arête [arɛt] *nf* (*de poisson*) bone; (*de cube etc*) & *Géog* ridge.
argent [arʒɑ̃] *nm* (*métal*) silver; (*monnaie*) money; **a. comptant** cash. ◆**argenté** *a* (*plaqué*) silver-plated; (*couleur*) silvery. ◆**argenterie** *nf* silverware.
Argentine [arʒɑ̃tin] *nf* Argentina. ◆**argentin, -ine** *a* & *nmf* Argentinian.
argile [arʒil] *nf* clay. ◆**argileux, -euse** *a* clayey.
argot [argo] *nm* slang. ◆**argotique** *a* (*terme*) slang.
arguer [argɥe] *vi* **a. de qch** to put forward sth as an argument; **a. que** (*protester*) to protest that. ◆**argumentation** *nf* argumentation, arguments. ◆**argumenter** *vi* to argue.
argument [argymɑ̃] *nm* argument.
argus [argys] *nm* guide to secondhand cars.
argutie [argysi] *nf* specious argument, quibble.
aride [arid] *a* arid, barren.
aristocrate [aristɔkrat] *nmf* aristocrat. ◆**aristocratie** [-asi] *nf* aristocracy. ◆**aristocratique** *a* aristocratic.
arithmétique [aritmetik] *nf* arithmetic; **–** *a* arithmetical.
arlequin [arləkɛ̃] *nm* harlequin.
armateur [armatœr] *nm* shipowner.
armature [armatyr] *nf* (*charpente*) framework; (*de lunettes, tente*) frame.
arme [arm] *nf* arm, weapon; **a. à feu** firearm; **carrière des armes** military career. ◆**arm/er** *vt* (*personne etc*) to arm (de with); (*fusil*) to cock; (*appareil photo*) to wind on; (*navire*) to equip; (*béton*) to reinforce; **– s'a.** *vpr* to arm oneself (de with). ◆**—ement(s)** *nm*(*pl*) arms.
armée [arme] *nf* army; **a. active/de métier** regular/professional army; **a. de l'air** air force.
armistice [armistis] *nm* armistice.
armoire [armwar] *nf* cupboard, *Am* closet; (*penderie*) wardrobe, *Am* closet; **a. à pharmacie** medicine cabinet.
armoiries [armwari] *nfpl* (coat of) arms.
armure [armyr] *nf* armour.
armurier [armyrje] *nm* gunsmith.
arôme [arom] *nm* aroma. ◆**aromate** *nm* spice. ◆**aromatique** *a* aromatic.
arpent/er [arpɑ̃te] *vt* (*terrain*) to survey; (*trottoir etc*) to pace up and down. ◆**—eur** *nm* (land) surveyor.
arqué [arke] *a* arched, curved; (*jambes*) bandy.

arrache-pied (d') [daraʃpje] *adv* unceasingly, relentlessly.

arrach/er [araʃe] *vt* (*clou, dent etc*) to pull out; (*cheveux, page*) to tear out, pull out; (*plante*) to pull up; (*masque*) to tear off, pull off; **a. qch à qn** to snatch sth from s.o.; (*aveu, argent*) to force sth out of s.o.; **a. un bras à qn** (*obus etc*) to blow s.o.'s arm off; **a. qn de son lit** to drag s.o. out of bed. ◆—**age** *nm* (*de plante*) pulling up.

arraisonner [arezɔne] *vt* (*navire*) to board and examine.

arrang/er [arɑ̃ʒe] *vt* (*chambre, visite etc*) to arrange, fix up; (*voiture, texte*) to put right; (*différend*) to settle; **a. qn** (*maltraiter*) *Fam* to fix s.o.; **ça m'arrange** that suits me (fine); — **s'a.** *vpr* (*se réparer*) to be put right; (*se mettre d'accord*) to come to an agreement *ou* arrangement; (*finir bien*) to turn out fine; **s'a. pour faire** to arrange to do, manage to do. ◆—**eant** *a* accommodating. ◆—**ement** *nm* arrangement.

arrestation [arestasjɔ̃] *nf* arrest.

arrêt [arɛ] *nm* (*halte, endroit*) stop; (*action*) stopping; *Méd* arrest; *Jur* decree; **temps d'a.** pause; **à l'a.** stationary; **a. de travail** (*grève*) stoppage; (*congé*) sick leave; **sans a.** constantly, non-stop.

arrêté [arete] *nm* order, decision.

arrêt/er [arete] *vt* to stop; (*appréhender*) to arrest; (*regard, jour*) to fix; (*plan*) to draw up; — *vi* to stop; **il n'arrête pas de critiquer**/*etc* he doesn't stop criticizing/*etc*, he's always criticizing/*etc*; — **s'a.** *vpr* to stop; **s'a. de faire** to stop doing. ◆—**é** *a* (*projet*) fixed; (*volonté*) firm.

arrhes [ar] *nfpl Fin* deposit.

arrière [arjɛr] *adv* **en a.** (*marcher*) backwards; (*rester*) behind; (*regarder*) back; **en a. de qn/qch** behind s.o./sth; — *nm & a inv* rear, back; (*joueur*) *Fb* (full) back; **faire marche a.** to reverse, back.

arrière-boutique [arjɛrbutik] *nm* back room (*of a shop*). ◆**a.-garde** *nf* rearguard. ◆**a.-goût** *nm* aftertaste. ◆**a.-grand-mère** *nf* great-grand-mother. ◆**a.-grand-père** *nm* (*pl* **arrière-grands-pères**) great-grand-father. ◆**a.-pays** *nm* hinterland. ◆**a.-pensée** *nf* ulterior motive. ◆**a.-plan** *nm* background. ◆**a.-saison** *nf* end of season, (late) autumn. ◆**a.-train** *nm* hindquarters.

arriéré [arjere] **1** *a* (*enfant*) (mentally) retarded; (*idée*) backward. **2** *nm* (*dette*) arrears.

arrimer [arime] *vt* (*fixer*) to rope down, secure.

arriv/er [arive] *vi* (*aux* **être**) (*venir*) to arrive, come; (*réussir*) to succeed; (*survenir*) to happen; **a. à** (*atteindre*) to reach; **a. à faire** to manage to do, succeed in doing; **a. à qn** to happen to s.o.; **il m'arrive d'oublier**/*etc* I happen (sometimes) to forget/*etc*, I (sometimes) forget/*etc*; **en a. à faire** to get to the point of doing. ◆—**ant, -ante** *nmf* new arrival. ◆—**ée** *nf* arrival; *Sp* (winning) post. ◆—**age** *nm* consignment. ◆**arriviste** *nmf Péj* social climber, self-seeker.

arrogant [arɔgɑ̃] *a* arrogant. ◆**arrogance** *nf* arrogance.

arroger (s') [sarɔʒe] *vpr* (*droit etc*) to assume (falsely).

arrond/ir [arɔ̃dir] *vt* to make round; (*somme, chiffre*) to round off. ◆—**i** *a* rounded.

arrondissement [arɔ̃dismɑ̃] *nm* (*d'une ville*) district.

arros/er [aroze] *vt* (*terre*) to water; (*repas*) to wash down; (*succès*) to drink to. ◆—**age** *nm* watering; *Fam* booze-up, celebration. ◆**arrosoir** *nm* watering can.

arsenal, -aux [arsənal, -o] *nm Nau* dockyard; *Mil* arsenal.

arsenic [arsənik] *nm* arsenic.

art [ar] *nm* art; **film/critique d'a.** art film/critic; **arts ménagers** domestic science.

artère [artɛr] *nf Anat* artery; *Aut* main road. ◆**artériel, -elle** *a* arterial.

artichaut [artiʃo] *nm* artichoke.

article [artikl] *nm* (*de presse, de commerce*) & *Gram* article; (*dans un contrat, catalogue*) item; **a. de fond** feature (article); **articles de toilette/de voyage** toilet/travel requisites; **à l'a. de la mort** at death's door.

articuler [artikyle] *vt* (*mot etc*) to articulate; — **s'a.** *vpr Anat* to articulate; *Fig* to connect. ◆**articulation** *nf Ling* articulation; *Anat* joint; **a. du doigt** knuckle.

artifice [artifis] *nm* trick, contrivance; **feu d'a.** (*spectacle*) fireworks, firework display.

artificiel, -elle [artifisjɛl] *a* artificial. ◆**artificiellement** *adv* artificially.

artillerie [artijri] *nf* artillery. ◆**artilleur** *nm* gunner.

artisan [artizɑ̃] *nm* craftsman, artisan. ◆**artisanal, -aux** *a* (*métier*) craftsman's. ◆**artisanat** *nm* (*métier*) craftsman's trade; (*classe*) artisan class.

artiste [artist] *nmf* artist; *Th Mus Cin* performer, artist. ◆**artistique** *a* artistic.

as [ɑs] *nm* (*carte, champion*) ace; **a. du volant** crack driver.

ascendant [asɑ̃dɑ̃] a ascending, upward; – nm ascendancy, power; pl ancestors. ◆**ascendance** nf ancestry.

ascenseur [asɑ̃sœr] nm lift, Am elevator.

ascension [asɑ̃sjɔ̃] nf ascent; **l'A.** Ascension Day.

ascète [asɛt] nmf ascetic. ◆**ascétique** a ascetic. ◆**ascétisme** nm asceticism.

Asie [azi] nf Asia. ◆**Asiate** nmf Asian. ◆**asiatique** a & nmf Asian, Asiatic.

asile [azil] nm (abri) refuge, shelter; (pour vieillards) home; Pol asylum; **a. (d'aliénés)** Péj (lunatic) asylum; **a. de paix** haven of peace.

aspect [aspɛ] nm (vue) sight; (air) appearance; (perspective) & Gram aspect.

asperge [aspɛrʒ] nf asparagus.

asperger [aspɛrʒe] vt to spray, sprinkle (**de** with).

aspérité [asperite] nf rugged edge, bump.

asphalte [asfalt] nm asphalt.

asphyxie [asfiksi] nf suffocation. ◆**asphyxier** vt to suffocate, asphyxiate.

aspic [aspik] nm (vipère) asp.

aspirant [aspirɑ̃] nm (candidat) candidate.

aspirateur [aspiratœr] nm vacuum cleaner, hoover®; **passer (à) l'a.** to vacuum, hoover.

aspir/er [aspire] vt (respirer) to breathe in, inhale; (liquide) to suck up; **a. à** to aspire to. ◆**–é** a Ling aspirate(d). ◆**aspiration** nf inhaling; suction; (ambition) aspiration.

aspirine [aspirin] nf aspirin.

assagir (s') [sasaʒir] vpr to sober (down), settle down.

assaill/ir [asajir] vt to assault, attack; **a. de** (questions etc) to assail with. ◆**–ant** nm assailant, attacker.

assainir [asenir] vt (purifier) to clean up; Fin to stabilize.

assaisonn/er [asɛzɔne] vt to season. ◆**–ement** nm seasoning.

assassin [asasɛ̃] nm murderer; assassin. ◆**assassinat** nm murder; assassination. ◆**assassiner** vt to murder; (homme politique etc) to assassinate.

assaut [aso] nm assault, onslaught; **prendre d'a.** to (take by) storm.

assécher [asefe] vt to drain.

assemblée [asɑ̃ble] nf (personnes réunies) gathering; (réunion) meeting; Pol Jur assembly; (de fidèles) Rel congregation.

assembl/er [asɑ̃ble] vt to assemble, put together; – **s'a.** vpr to assemble, gather. ◆**–age** nm (montage) assembly; (réunion d'objets) collection.

asséner [asene] vt (coup) to deal, strike.

assentiment [asɑ̃timɑ̃] nm assent, consent.

asseoir* [aswar] vt (personne) to sit (down), seat (**sur** on); (fondations) to lay; (autorité, réputation) to establish; **a. sur** (théorie etc) to base on; – **s'a.** vpr to sit (down).

assermenté [asɛrmɑ̃te] a sworn.

assertion [asɛrsjɔ̃] nf assertion.

asserv/ir [asɛrvir] vt to enslave. ◆**–issement** nm enslavement.

assez [ase] adv enough; **a. de pain/de gens** enough bread/people; **j'en ai a.** I've had enough; **a. grand/intelligent**/etc (suffisamment) big/clever/etc enough (**pour** to); **a. fatigué**/etc (plutôt) fairly ou rather ou quite tired/etc.

assidu [asidy] a (appliqué) assiduous, diligent; **a. auprès de** attentive to. ◆**assiduité** nf assiduousness, diligence; pl (empressement) attentiveness. ◆**assidûment** adv assiduously.

assiég/er [asjeʒe] vt (ville) to besiege; (guichet) to mob, crowd round; (importuner) to pester, harry; **assiégé de** (demandes) besieged with; (maux) beset by. ◆**–eant, -eante** nmf besieger.

assiette [asjɛt] nf 1 (récipient) plate; **a. anglaise** Culin (assorted) cold meats, Am cold cuts. 2 (à cheval) seat; **il n'est pas dans son a.** he's feeling out of sorts.

assigner [asiɲe] vt (attribuer) to assign; Jur to summon, subpoena. ◆**assignation** nf Jur subpoena, summons.

assimiler [asimile] vt to assimilate; – **s'a.** vpr (immigrants) to assimilate, become assimilated (**à** with). ◆**assimilation** nf assimilation.

assis [asi] a sitting (down), seated; (caractère) settled; (situation) stable, secure.

assise [asiz] nf (base) Fig foundation; pl Jur assizes; Pol congress; **cour d'assises** court of assizes.

assistance [asistɑ̃s] nf 1 (assemblée) audience; (nombre de personnes présentes) attendance, turn-out. 2 (aide) assistance; **l'A. (publique)** the child care service; **enfant de l'A.** child in care. ◆**assist/er 1** vt (aider) to assist, help. 2 vi **a. à** (réunion, cours etc) to attend, be present at; (accident) to witness. ◆**–ant, -ante** nmf assistant; – nmpl (spectateurs) members of the audience; (témoins) those present; **assistante sociale** social worker; **assistante maternelle** mother's help.

associ/er [asɔsje] vt to associate (**à** with); **a. qn à** (ses travaux, profits) to involve s.o. in; **s'a. à** (collaborer) to associate with, become associated with; (aux vues ou au chagrin de qn) to share; (s'harmoniser) to combine with. ◆—é, -ée *nmf* partner, associate; — *a* associate. ◆association *nf* association; (*amitié, alliance*) partnership, association.

assoiffé [aswafe] *a* thirsty (de for).

assombrir [asɔ̃brir] *vt* (*obscurcir*) to darken; (*attrister*) to cast a cloud over, fill with gloom; — s'a. *vpr* to darken; to cloud over.

assomm/er [asɔme] *vt* (*animal*) to stun, brain; (*personne*) to knock unconscious; (*ennuyer*) to bore stiff. ◆—ant *a* tiresome, boring.

assomption [asɔ̃psjɔ̃] *nf Rel* Assumption.

assort/ir [asɔrtir] *vt*, — s'a. *vpr* to match. ◆—i *a* bien a. (*magasin*) well-stocked; — *apl* (*objets semblables*) matching; (*fromages etc variés*) assorted; époux bien assortis well-matched couple. ◆—iment *nm* assortment.

assoup/ir [asupir] *vt* (*personne*) to make drowsy; (*douleur, sentiment etc*) Fig to dull; — s'a. *vpr* to doze off; Fig to subside. ◆—i *a* (*personne*) drowsy. ◆—issement *nm* drowsiness.

assoupl/ir [asuplir] *vt* (*étoffe, muscles*) to make supple; (*corps*) to limber up; (*caractère*) to soften; (*règles*) to ease, relax. ◆—issement *nm* exercices d'a. limbering up exercises.

assourd/ir [asurdir] *vt* (*personne*) to deafen; (*son*) to muffle. ◆—issant *a* deafening.

assouvir [asuvir] *vt* to appease, satisfy.

assujett/ir [asyʒetir] *vt* (*soumettre*) to subject (à to); (*peuple*) to subjugate; (*fixer*) to secure; s'a. à to subject oneself to, submit to. ◆—issant *a* (*travail*) constraining. ◆—issement *nm* subjection; (*contrainte*) constraint.

assumer [asyme] *vt* (*tâche, rôle*) to assume, take on; (*emploi*) to take up, assume; (*remplir*) to fill, hold.

assurance [asyrɑ̃s] *nf* (*aplomb*) (self-)assurance; (*promesse*) assurance; (*contrat*) insurance; a. au tiers/tous risques third-party/comprehensive insurance; assurances sociales = national insurance, *Am* = social security.

assur/er [asyre] *vt* (*rendre sûr*) to ensure, *Am* insure; (*par un contrat*) to insure; (*travail etc*) to carry out; (*fixer*) to secure; a. à qn que to assure s.o. that; a. qn de qch, a. qch à qn to assure s.o. of sth; — s'a. *vpr* (*se procurer*) to ensure, secure; (*par un contrat*) to insure oneself, get insured (contre against); s'a. que/de to make sure that/of. ◆—é, -ée *a* (*succès*) assured, certain; (*pas*) firm, secure; (*air*)

(self-)assured, (self-)confident; — *nmf* policyholder, insured person. ◆—ément *adv* certainly, assuredly. ◆assureur *nm* insurer.

astérisque [asterisk] *nm* asterisk.

asthme [asm] *nm* asthma. ◆asthmatique *a* & *nmf* asthmatic.

asticot [astiko] *nm* maggot, worm.

astiquer [astike] *vt* to polish.

astre [astr] *nm* star.

astreindre* [astrɛ̃dr] *vt* a. à (*discipline*) to compel to accept; a. à faire to compel to do. ◆astreignant *a* exacting ◆astreinte *nf* constraint.

astrologie [astrɔlɔʒi] *nf* astrology. ◆astrologue *nm* astrologer.

astronaute [astrɔnot] *nmf* astronaut. ◆astronautique *nf* space travel.

astronomie [astrɔnɔmi] *nf* astronomy. ◆astronome *nm* astronomer. ◆astronomique *a* astronomical.

astuce [astys] *nf* (*pour faire qch*) knack, trick; (*invention*) gadget; (*plaisanterie*) clever joke, wisecrack; (*finesse*) astuteness; les astuces du métier the tricks of the trade. ◆astucieux, -euse *a* clever, astute.

atelier [atəlje] *nm* (*d'ouvrier*) workshop; (*de peintre*) studio.

atermoyer [atermwaje] *vi* to procrastinate.

athée [ate] *a* atheistic; — *nmf* atheist. ◆athéisme *nm* atheism.

Athènes [atɛn] *nm ou f* Athens.

athlète [atlɛt] *nmf* athlete. ◆athlétique *a* athletic. ◆athlétisme *nm* athletics.

atlantique [atlɑ̃tik] *a* Atlantic; — *nm* l'A. the Atlantic.

atlas [atlas] *nm* atlas.

atmosphère [atmosfɛr] *nf* atmosphere. ◆atmosphérique *a* atmospheric.

atome [atom] *nm* atom. ◆atomique [atɔmik] *a* atomic; bombe a. atom *ou* atomic bomb.

atomis/er [atɔmize] *vt* (*liquide*) to spray; (*région*) to destroy (by *atomic weapons*). ◆—eur *nm* spray.

atone [atɔn] *a* (*personne*) lifeless; (*regard*) vacant.

atours [atur] *nmpl Hum* finery.

atout [atu] *nm* trump (card); (*avantage*) Fig trump card, asset; l'a. est cœur hearts are trumps.

âtre [ɑtr] *nm* (*foyer*) hearth.

atroce [atrɔs] *a* atrocious; (*crime*) heinous, atrocious. ◆atrocité *nf* atrociousness; *pl* (*actes*) atrocities.

atrophie [atrɔfi] *nf* atrophy. ◆atrophié *a* atrophied.

attabl/er (s') [satable] *vpr* to sit down at the table. ◆—**é** *a* (seated) at the table.

attache [ataʃ] *nf* (*objet*) attachment, fastening; *pl* (*liens*) links.

attach/er [ataʃe] *vt* (*lier*) to tie (up), attach (à to); (*boucler, fixer*) to fasten; **a. du prix/un sens à qch** to attach great value/a meaning to sth; **cette obligation m'attache à lui** this obligation binds me to him; **s'a. à** (*adhérer*) to stick to; (*se lier*) to become attached to; (*se consacrer*) to apply oneself to. ◆—**ant** *a* (*enfant etc*) engaging, appealing. ◆—**é, -ée** *nmf* (*personne*) Pol Mil attaché. ◆—**ement** *nm* attachment, affection.

attaque [atak] *nf* attack; **a. aérienne** air raid; **d'a.** in tip-top shape, on top form. ◆**attaqu/er** *vt*, **s'a. à** to attack; (*difficulté, sujet*) to tackle; – *vi* to attack. ◆—**ant, -ante** *nmf* attacker.

attard/er (s') [satarde] *vpr* (*chez qn*) to linger (on), stay on; (*en chemin*) to loiter, dawdle; **s'a. sur** *ou* **à** (*détails etc*) to linger over; **s'a. derrière qn** to lag behind s.o. ◆—**é** *a* (*enfant etc*) backward; (*passant*) late.

atteindre* [atɛdr] *vt* (*parvenir à*) to reach; (*idéal*) to attain; (*blesser*) to hit, wound; (*toucher*) to affect; (*offenser*) to hurt, wound; **être atteint de** (*maladie*) to be suffering from.

atteinte [atɛt] *nf* attack; **porter a. à** to attack, undermine; **a. à** (*honneur*) slur on; **hors d'a.** (*objet, personne*) out of reach; (*réputation*) unassailable.

attel/er [atle] *vt* (*bêtes*) to harness, hitch up; (*remorque*) to couple; **s'a. à** (*travail etc*) to apply oneself to. ◆—**age** *nm* harnessing; coupling; (*bêtes*) team.

attenant [atnã] *a* **a. (à)** adjoining.

attend/re [atãdr] *vt* to wait for, await; (*escompter*) to expect (**de** of, from); **elle attend un bébé** she's expecting a baby; – *vi* to wait; **s'a. à** to expect; **a. d'être informé** to wait to be informed; **a. que qn vienne** to wait for s.o. to come, wait until s.o. comes; **faire a. qn** to keep s.o. waiting; **se faire a.** (*réponse, personne*) to be a long time coming; **attends voir** Fam let me see; **en attendant** meanwhile; **en attendant que** (+ *sub*) until. ◆—**u** *a* (*avec joie*) eagerly-awaited; (*prévu*) expected; – *prép* considering; **a. que** considering that.

attendr/ir [atãdrir] *vt* (*émouvoir*), to move (to compassion); (*viande*) to tenderize; – **s'a.** *vpr* to be moved (**sur** by). ◆—**i** *a*

compassionate. ◆—**issant** *a* moving. ◆—**issement** *nm* compassion.

attentat [atãta] *nm* attempt (**on** s.o.'s life), murder attempt; Fig crime, outrage (à against); **a. (à la bombe)** (bomb) attack. ◆**attenter** *vi* **a. à** (*la vie de qn*) to make an attempt on; Fig to attack.

attente [atãt] *nf* (*temps*) wait(ing); (*espérance*) expectation(s); **une a. prolongée** a long wait; **être dans l'a. de** to be waiting for; **salle d'a.** waiting room.

attentif, -ive [atãtif, -iv] *a* (*personne*) attentive; (*travail, examen*) careful; **a. à** (*plaire etc*) anxious to; (*ses devoirs etc*) mindful of. ◆**attentivement** *adv* attentively.

attention [atãsjõ] *nf* attention; *pl* (*égards*) consideration; **faire ou prêter a. à** (*écouter, remarquer*) to pay attention to; **faire a. à/que** (*prendre garde*) to be careful of/that; **a.!** look out!, be careful!; **a. à la voiture!** mind *ou* watch the car! ◆**attentionné** *a* considerate.

atténu/er [atenɥe] *vt* to attenuate, mitigate; – **s'a.** *vpr* to subside. ◆—**antes** *afpl* **circonstances a.** extenuating circumstances.

atterrer [atere] *vt* to dismay.

atterr/ir [aterir] *vi* Av to land. ◆—**issage** *nm* Av landing; **a. forcé** crash *ou* emergency landing.

attester [ateste] *vt* to testify to; **a. que** to testify that. ◆**attestation** *nf* (*document*) declaration, certificate.

attifer [atife] *vt* Fam Péj to dress up, rig out.

attirail [atiraj] *nm* (*équipement*) Fam gear.

attir/er [atire] *vt* (*faire venir*) to attract, draw; (*plaire à*) to attract; (*attention*) to draw (**sur** on); **a. qch à qn** (*causer*) to bring s.o. sth; (*gloire etc*) to win *ou* earn s.o. sth; **a. dans** (*coin, guet-apens*) to draw into; – **s'a.** *vpr* (*ennuis etc*) to bring upon oneself; (*sympathie de qn*) to win; **a. sur soi** (*colère de qn*) to bring down upon oneself. ◆—**ant** *a* attractive. ◆**attirance** *nf* attraction.

attiser [atize] *vt* (*feu*) to poke; (*sentiment*) Fig to rouse.

attitré [atitre] *a* (*représentant*) appointed; (*marchand*) regular.

attitude [atityd] *nf* attitude; (*maintien*) bearing.

attraction [atraksjõ] *nf* attraction.

attrait [atrɛ] *nm* attraction.

attrape [atrap] *nf* trick. ◆**a.-nigaud** *nm* con, trick.

attraper [atrape] *vt* (*ballon, maladie, voleur, train etc*) to catch; (*accent, contravention etc*) to pick up; **se laisser a.** (*duper*) to get taken in *ou* tricked; **se faire a.** (*gronder*) *Fam* to get a telling off. ◆**attrapade** *nf* (*gronderie*) *Fam* telling off.

attrayant [atrejɑ̃] *a* attractive.

attribuer [atribɥe] *vt* (*donner*) to assign, allot (**à to**); (*imputer, reconnaître*) to attribute, ascribe (**à to**); (*décerner*) to grant, award (**à to**). ◆**attribuable** *a* attributable. ◆**attribution** *nf* assignment; attribution; (*de prix*) awarding; *pl* (*compétence*) powers.

attribut [atriby] *nm* attribute.

attrister [atriste] *vt* to sadden.

attroup/er [atrupe] *vt*, **— s'a.** *vpr* to gather. ◆**—ement** *nm* gathering, (disorderly) crowd.

au [o] *voir* **à**.

aubaine [oben] *nf* (**bonne**) **a.** stroke of good luck, godsend.

aube [ob] *nf* dawn; **dès l'a.** at the crack of dawn.

aubépine [obepin] *nf* hawthorn.

auberge [oberʒ] *nf* inn; **a. de jeunesse** youth hostel. ◆**aubergiste** *nmf* innkeeper.

aubergine [oberʒin] *nf* aubergine, eggplant.

aucun, -une [okœ̃, -yn] *a* no, not any; **il n'a a. talent** he has no talent, he doesn't have any talent; **a. professeur n'est venu** no teacher has come; — *pron* none, not any; **il n'en a a.** he has none (at all), he doesn't have any (at all); **plus qu'a.** more than any(one); **d'aucuns** some (people). ◆**aucunement** *adv* not at all.

audace [odas] *nf* (*courage*) daring, boldness; (*impudence*) audacity; *pl* daring innovations. ◆**audacieux, -euse** *a* daring, bold.

au-dedans, au-dehors, au-delà *voir* **dedans** *etc.*

au-dessous [odsu] *adv* (*en bas*) (down) below, underneath; (*moins*) below, under; (*à l'étage inférieur*) downstairs; — *prép* **au-d. de** (*arbre etc*) below, under, beneath; (*âge, prix*) under; (*température*) below; **au-d. de sa tâche** not up to *ou* unequal to one's task.

au-dessus [odsy] *adv* above; over; on top; (*à l'étage supérieur*) upstairs; — *prép* **au-d. de** above; (*âge, température, prix*) over; (*posé sur*) on top of.

au-devant de [odvɑ̃də] *prép* **aller au-d. de** (*personne*) to go to meet; (*danger*) to court; (*désirs de qn*) to anticipate.

audible [odibl] *a* audible.

audience [odjɑ̃s] *nf Jur* hearing; (*entretien*) audience.

audio [odjo] *a inv* (*cassette etc*) audio.

◆**audiophone** *nm* hearing aid. ◆**audio-visuel, -elle** *a* audio-visual.

auditeur, -trice [oditœr, -tris] *nmf Rad* listener; **les auditeurs** the audience; **a. libre** *Univ* auditor, *student allowed to attend classes but not to sit examinations.* ◆**auditif, -ive** *a* (*nerf*) auditory. ◆**audition** *nf* (*ouïe*) hearing; (*séance d'essai*) *Th* audition; (*séance musicale*) recital. ◆**auditionner** *vti* to audition. ◆**auditoire** *nm* audience. ◆**auditorium** *nm Rad* recording studio (*for recitals*).

auge [oʒ] *nf* (feeding) trough.

augmenter [ogmɑ̃te] *vt* to increase (**de by**); (*salaire, prix, impôt*) to raise, increase; **a. qn** to give s.o. a rise *ou Am* raise; — *vi* to increase (**de by**); (*prix, population*) to rise, go up. ◆**augmentation** *nf* increase (**de in, of**); **a. de salaire** (pay) rise, *Am* raise; **a. de prix** price rise *ou* increase.

augure [ogyr] *nm* (*présage*) omen; (*devin*) oracle; **être de bon/mauvais a.** to be a good/bad omen. ◆**augurer** *vt* to augur, predict.

auguste [ogyst] *a* august.

aujourd'hui [oʒurdɥi] *adv* today; (*actuellement*) nowadays, today; **a. en quinze** two weeks today.

aumône [omon] *nf* alms.

aumônier [omonje] *nm* chaplain.

auparavant [oparavɑ̃] *adv* (*avant*) before(hand); (*d'abord*) first.

auprès de [opredə] *prép* (*assis, situé etc*) by, close to, next to; (*en comparaison de*) compared to; **agir a. de** (*ministre etc*) to use one's influence with; **accès a. de qn** access to s.o.

auquel [okel] *voir* **lequel**.

aura, aurait [ora, orε] *voir* **avoir**.

auréole [oreol] *nf* (*de saint etc*) halo; (*trace*) ring.

auriculaire [orikyler] *nm* **l'a.** the little finger.

aurore [oror] *nf* dawn, daybreak.

ausculter [oskylte] *vt* (*malade*) to examine (*with a stethoscope*); (*cœur*) to listen to. ◆**auscultation** *nf Méd* auscultation.

auspices [ospis] *nmpl* **sous les a. de** under the auspices of.

aussi [osi] *adv* **1** (*comparaison*) as; **a. sage que** as wise as. **2** (*également*) too, also, as well; **moi a.** so do, can, am *etc* I; **a. bien que** as well as. **3** (*tellement*) so; **un repas a. délicieux** so delicious a meal, such a delicious meal. **4** *conj* (*donc*) therefore.

aussitôt [osito] *adv* immediately, at once; **a. que** as soon as; **a. levé, il partit** as soon as he was up, he left; **a. dit, a. fait** no sooner said than done.

austère [ɔster] *a* austere. ◆**austérité** *nf* austerity.

austral, *mpl* **-als** [ostral] *a* southern.

Australie [ostrali] *nf* Australia. ◆**australien, -ienne** *a* & *nmf* Australian.

autant [otɑ̃] *adv* **1 a. de** . . . **que** (*quantité*) as much . . . as; (*nombre*) as many . . . as; **il a a. d'argent/de pommes que vous** he has as much money/as many apples as you. **2 a. de** (*tant de*) so much; (*nombre*) so many; **je n'ai jamais vu a. d'argent/de pommes** I've never seen so much money/so many apples; **pourquoi manges-tu a.?** why are you eating so much? **3 a. que** (*souffrir, lire etc*) as much as; **il lit a. que vous/que possible** he reads as much as you/as possible; **il n'a jamais souffert a.** he's never suffered as *ou* so much; **a. que je sache** as far as I know; **d'a. (plus) que** all the more (so) since; **d'a. moins que** even less since; **d'a. avouer/*etc*** we, you *etc* might as well confess/*etc*; **en faire/dire a.** to do/say the same; **j'aimerais a. aller au cinéma** I'd just as soon go to the cinema.

autel [otel] *nm* altar.

auteur [otœr] *nm* (*de livre*) author, writer; (*de chanson*) composer; (*de procédé*) originator; (*de crime*) perpetrator; (*d'accident*) cause; **droit d'a.** copyright; **droits d'a.** royalties.

authenticité [otɑ̃tisite] *nf* authenticity. ◆**authentifier** *vt* to authenticate. ◆**authentique** *a* genuine, authentic.

autiste [otist] *a*, **autistique** *a* autistic.

auto [oto] *nf* car; **autos tamponneuses** bumper cars, dodgems.

auto- [oto] *préf* self-.

autobiographie [otobjɔgrafi] *nf* autobiography.

autobus [otobys] *nm* bus.

autocar [otokar] *nm* coach, bus.

autochtone [ɔtɔktɔn] *a* & *nmf* native.

autocollant [otokɔlɑ̃] *nm* sticker.

autocrate [otokrat] *nm* autocrat. ◆**autocratique** *a* autocratic.

autocuiseur [otokɥizœr] *nm* pressure cooker.

autodéfense [otodefɑ̃s] *nf* self-defence.

autodestruction [otodɛstryksjɔ̃] *nf* self-destruction.

autodidacte [otodidakt] *a* & *nmf* self-taught (person).

autodrome [otodrom] *nm* motor-racing track.

auto-école [otoekɔl] *nf* driving school, school of motoring.

autographe [otograf] *nm* autograph.

automate [ɔtɔmat] *nm* automaton. ◆**automation** *nf* automation. ◆**automatisation** *nf* automation. ◆**automatiser** *vt* to automate.

automatique [ɔtɔmatik] *a* automatic; – *nm* **l'a.** *Tél* direct dialling. ◆**—ment** *adv* automatically.

automne [otɔn] *nm* autumn, *Am* fall. ◆**automnal, -aux** *a* autumnal.

automobile [otomɔbil] *nf* & *a* (motor)car, *Am* automobile; **l'a.** *Sp* motoring; **Salon de l'a.** Motor Show; **canot a.** motor boat. ◆**automobiliste** *nmf* motorist.

autonome [otɔnɔm] *a* (*région etc*) autonomous, self-governing; (*personne*) *Fig* independent. ◆**autonomie** *nf* autonomy.

autopsie [ɔtɔpsi] *nf* autopsy, post-mortem.

autoradio [otoradjo] *nm* car radio.

autorail [ɔtɔrɑj] *nm* railcar.

autoris/er [ɔtɔrize] *vt* (*habiliter*) to authorize (à faire to do); (*permettre*) to permit (à faire to do). ◆**—é** *a* (*qualifié*) authoritative. ◆**autorisation** *nf* authorization; permission.

autorité [ɔtɔrite] *nf* authority. ◆**autoritaire** *a* authoritarian; (*homme, ton*) authoritative.

autoroute [otorut] *nf* motorway, *Am* highway, freeway.

auto-stop [otostɔp] *nm* hitchhiking; **faire de l'a.** to hitchhike. ◆**autostoppeur, -euse** *nmf* hitchhiker.

autour [otur] *adv* around; – *prép* **a. de** around.

autre [otr] *a* & *pron* other; **un a. livre** another book; **un a.** another (one); **d'autres** others; **as-tu d'autres questions?** have you any other *ou* further questions?; **qn/personne/rien d'a.** s.o./no one/nothing else; **a. chose/part** sth/somewhere else; **qui/quoi d'a.?** who/what else?; **l'un l'a., les uns les autres** each other; **l'un et l'a.** both (of them); **l'un ou l'a.** either (of them); **ni l'un ni l'a.** neither (of them); **les uns . . . les autres** some . . . others; **nous/vous autres Anglais** we/you English; **d'un moment à l'a.** any moment (now); **. . . et autres** . . . and so on. ◆**autrement** *adv* (*différemment*) differently; (*sinon*) otherwise; (*plus*) far more (**que** than); **pas a. satisfait/*etc*** not particularly satisfied/*etc*.

autrefois [otrǝfwa] *adv* in the past, in days gone by.

Autriche [otriʃ] *nf* Austria. ◆**autrichien, -ienne** *a* & *nmf* Austrian.

autruche [otryʃ] *nf* ostrich.

autrui [otrɥi] *pron* others, other people.

auvent [ovã] *nm* awning, canopy.

aux [o] *voir* à.

auxiliaire [ɔksiljɛr] *a* auxiliary; − *nm Gram* auxiliary; − *nmf* (*aide*) helper, auxiliary.

auxquels, -elles [okɛl] *voir* lequel.

avachir (s') [savaʃir] *vpr* (*soulier, personne*) to become flabby *ou* limp.

avait [avɛ] *voir* avoir.

aval (en) [ãnaval] *adv* downstream (**de** from).

avalanche [avalãʃ] *nf* avalanche; *Fig* flood, avalanche.

avaler [avale] *vt* to swallow; (*livre*) to devour; (*mots*) to mumble; − *vi* to swallow.

avance [avãs] *nf* (*marche, acompte*) advance; (*de coureur, chercheur etc*) lead; *pl* (*galantes*) advances; **à l'a., d'a., par a.** in advance; **en a.** (*arriver, partir*) early; (*avant l'horaire prévu*) ahead (of time); (*dans son développement*) ahead, in advance; (*montre etc*) fast; **en a. sur** (*qn, son époque etc*) ahead of, in advance of; **avoir une heure d'a.** (*train etc*) to be an hour early.

avanc/er [avãse] *vt* (*thèse, argent*) to advance; (*date*) to bring forward; (*main, chaise*) to move forward; (*travail*) to speed up; − *vi* to advance, move forward; (*montre*) to be fast; (*faire saillie*) to jut out (**sur** over); **a. en âge** to be getting on (in years); − **s'a.** *vpr* to advance, move forward; (*faire saillie*) to jut out. ◆**−é** *a* advanced; (*saison*) well advanced. ◆**−ée** *nf* projection, overhang. ◆**−ement** *nm* advancement.

avanie [avani] *nf* affront, insult.

avant [avã] *prép* before; **a. de voir** before seeing; **a. qu'il (ne) parte** before he leaves; **a. huit jours** within a week; **a. tout** above all; **a. toute chose** first and foremost; **a. peu** before long; − *adv* before; **en a.** (*mouvement*) forward; (*en tête*) ahead; **en a. de** in front of; **bien a. dans** (*creuser etc*) very deep(ly) into; **la nuit d'a.** the night before; − *nm* & *a inv* front; − *nm* (*joueur*) *Sp* forward.

avantage [avãtaʒ] *nm* advantage; (*bénéfice*) *Fin* benefit; **tu as a. à le faire** it's worth your while to do it; **tirer a. de** to benefit from. ◆**avantager** *vt* (*favoriser*) to favour; (*faire valoir*) to show off to advantage. ◆**avantageux, -euse** *a* worthwhile, attractive; (*flatteur*) flattering; *Péj* conceited; **a. pour qn** advantageous to s.o.

avant-bras [avãbra] *nm inv* forearm. ◆**a.-centre** *nm Sp* centre-forward. ◆**a.-coureur** *am* **a.-coureur de** (*signe*) heralding. ◆**a.-dernier, -ière** *a* & *nmf* last but one. ◆**a.-garde** *nf Mil* advance guard; **d'a.-garde** (*idée, film etc*) avant-garde. ◆**a.-goût** *nm* foretaste. ◆**a.-guerre** *nm ou f* pre-war period; **d'a.-guerre** pre-war. ◆**a.-hier** [avãtjɛr] *adv* the day before yesterday. ◆**a.-poste** *nm* outpost. ◆**a.-première** *nf* preview. ◆**a.-propos** *nm inv* foreword. ◆**a.-veille** *nf* **l'a.-veille (de)** two days before.

avare [avar] *a* miserly; **a. de** (*compliments etc*) sparing of; − *nmf* miser. ◆**avarice** *nf* avarice.

avarie(s) [avari] *nf* (*pl*) damage. ◆**avarié** *a* (*aliment*) spoiled, rotting.

avatar [avatar] *nm Péj Fam* misadventure.

avec [avɛk] *prép* with; (*envers*) to(wards); **et a. ça?** (*dans un magasin*) *Fam* anything else?; − *adv* **il est venu a.** (*son chapeau etc*) *Fam* he came with it.

avenant [avnã] *a* pleasing, attractive; **à l'a.** in keeping (**de** with).

avènement [avɛnmã] *nm* **l'a. de** the coming *ou* advent of; (*roi*) the accession of.

avenir [avnir] *nm* future; **d'a.** (*personne, métier*) with future prospects; **à l'a.** (*désormais*) in future.

aventure [avãtyr] *nf* adventure; (*en amour*) affair; **à l'a.** (*marcher etc*) aimlessly; **dire la bonne a. à qn** to tell s.o.'s fortune. ◆**aventur/er** *vt* to risk; (*remarque*) to venture; (*réputation*) to risk; − **s'a.** *vpr* to venture (**sur** on to, **à faire** to do). ◆**−é** *a* risky. ◆**aventureux, -euse** *a* (*personne, vie*) adventurous; (*risqué*) risky. ◆**aventurier, -ière** *nmf Péj* adventurer.

avenue [avny] *nf* avenue.

avér/er (s') [savere] *vpr* (*juste etc*) to prove (to be); **il s'avère que** it turns out that. ◆**−é** *a* established.

averse [avɛrs] *nf* shower, downpour.

aversion [avɛrsjɔ̃] *nf* aversion (**pour** to).

avert/ir [avɛrtir] *vt* (*mettre en garde, menacer*) to warn; (*informer*) to notify, inform. ◆**−i** *a* informed. ◆**−issement** *nm* warning; notification; (*dans un livre*) foreword. ◆**−isseur** *nm Aut* horn; **a. d'incendie** fire alarm.

aveu, -x [avø] *nm* confession; **de l'a. de** by the admission of.

aveugle [avœgl] *a* blind; − *nmf* blind man, blind woman; **les aveugles** the blind. ◆**aveuglément** [-emã] *adv* blindly.

◆**aveugl/er** *vt* to blind. ◆**—ement**
[-əmɑ̃] *nm* (*égarement*) blindness.
aveuglette (à l') [alavœglɛt] *adv* blindly;
chercher qch à l'a. to grope for sth.
aviateur, -trice [avjatœr, -tris] *nmf* airman,
airwoman. ◆**aviation** *nf* (*industrie,
science*) aviation; (*armée de l'air*) air force;
(*avions*) aircraft; **l'a.** *Sp* flying; **d'a.** (*terrain,
base*) air-.
avide [avid] *a* (*rapace*) greedy (**de** for); **a.
d'apprendre**/*etc* (*désireux*) eager to
learn/*etc*. ◆**—ment** *adv* greedily. ◆**avidité** *nf* greed.
avilir [avilir] *vt* to degrade, debase.
avion [avjɔ̃] *nm* aircraft, (aero)plane, *Am*
airplane; **a. à réaction** jet; **a. de ligne**
airliner; **par a.** (*lettre*) airmail; **en a., par a.**
(*voyager*) by plane, by air; **aller en a.** to fly.
aviron [avirɔ̃] *nm* oar; **faire de l'a.** to row,
practise rowing.
avis [avi] *nm* opinion; *Pol Jur* judgement;
(*communiqué*) notice; (*conseil*) & *Fin*
advice; **à mon a.** in my opinion, to my
mind; **changer d'a.** to change one's mind.
avis/er [avize] *vt* to advise, inform; (*voir*)
to notice; **s'a. de qch** to realize sth suddenly; **s'a. de faire** to venture to do.
◆**—é** *a* prudent, wise; **bien-/mal a.**
well-/ill-advised.
aviver [avive] *vt* (*couleur*) to bring out;
(*douleur*) to sharpen.
avocat, -ate [avɔka, -at] **1** *nmf* barrister,
counsel, *Am* attorney, counselor; (*d'une
cause*) *Fig* advocate. **2** *nm* (*fruit*) avocado
(pear).
avoine [avwan] *nf* oats; **farine d'a.** oatmeal.
avoir* [avwar] **1** *v aux* to have; **je l'ai vu** I've
seen him. **2** *vt* (*posséder*) to have; (*obtenir*)
to get; (*tromper*) *Fam* to take for a ride; **il a**
he has, he's got; **qu'est-ce que tu as?** what's
the matter with you?, what's wrong with
you?; **j'ai à lui parler** I have to speak

to her; **il n'a qu'à essayer** he only has to
try; **a. faim/chaud**/*etc* to feel
hungry/hot/*etc*; **a. cinq ans**/*etc* to be
five (years old)/*etc*; **en a. pour longtemps** to
be busy for quite a while; **j'en ai pour dix
minutes** this will take me ten minutes; (*ne
bougez pas*) I'll be with you in ten minutes;
en a. pour son argent to get *ou* have one's
money's worth; **en a. après** *ou* **contre** to
have a grudge against. **3** *v imp* **il y a** there is,
pl there are; **il y a six ans** six years ago; **il
n'y a pas de quoi!** don't mention it!;
qu'est-ce qu'il y a? what's the matter?,
what's wrong? **4** *nm* assets, property; (*d'un
compte*) *Fin* credit.
avoisin/er [avwazine] *vt* to border on.
◆**—ant** *a* neighbouring, nearby.
avort/er [avɔrte] *vi* (*projet etc*) *Fig* to
miscarry, fail; (**se faire**) **a.** (*femme*) to have
ou get an abortion. ◆**—ement** *nm* abortion; *Fig* failure. ◆**avorton** *nm Péj* runt,
puny shrimp.
avou/er [avwe] *vt* to confess, admit (**que**
that); **s'a. vaincu** to admit defeat; – *vi*
(*coupable*) to confess. ◆**—é** *a* (*ennemi, but*)
avowed; – *nm* solicitor, *Am* attorney.
avril [avril] *nm* April; **un poisson d'a.** (*farce*)
an April fool joke.
axe [aks] *nm Math* axis; (*essieu*) axle; (*d'une
politique*) broad direction; **grands axes**
(*routes*) main roads. ◆**axer** *vt* to centre; **il
est axé sur** his mind is drawn towards.
axiome [aksjom] *nm* axiom.
ayant [ɛjɑ̃] *voir* **avoir**.
azalée [azale] *nf* (*plante*) azalea.
azimuts [azimyt] *nmpl* **dans tous les a.** *Fam*
all over the place, here there and everywhere; **tous a.** (*guerre, publicité etc*) all-out.
azote [azot] *nm* nitrogen.
azur [azyr] *nm* azure, (sky) blue; **la Côte
d'A.** the (French) Riviera.
azyme [azim] *a* (*pain*) unleavened.

B

B, b [be] *nm* B, b.
babeurre [babœr] *nm* buttermilk.
babill/er [babije] *vi* to prattle, babble.
◆**—age** *nm* prattle, babble.
babines [babin] *nfpl* (*lèvres*) chops, chaps.
babiole [babjɔl] *nf* (*objet*) knick-knack;
(*futilité*) trifle.
bâbord [bɑbɔr] *nm Nau Av* port (side).

babouin [babwɛ̃] *nm* baboon.
baby-foot [babifut] *nm inv* table *ou* miniature football.
bac [bak] *nm* **1** (*bateau*) ferry(boat). **2** (*cuve*)
tank; **b. à glace** ice tray; **b. à laver** washtub.
3 *abrév* = **baccalauréat**.
baccalauréat [bakalɔrea] *nm* school leaving certificate.

bâche [baʃ] *nf* (*toile*) tarpaulin. ◆**bâcher** *vt* to cover over (*with a tarpaulin*).

bachelier, -ière [baʃəlje, -jɛr] *nmf* holder of the *baccalauréat*.

bachot [baʃo] *nm abrév* = **baccalauréat.** ◆**bachoter** *vi* to cram (*for an exam*).

bacille [basil] *nm* bacillus, germ.

bâcler [bɑkle] *vt* (*travail*) to dash off carelessly, botch (up).

bactéries [bakteri] *nfpl* bacteria. ◆**bactériologique** *a* bacteriological; **la guerre b.** germ warfare.

badaud, -aude [bado, -od] *nmf* (inquisitive) onlooker, bystander.

baderne [badɛrn] *nf* **vieille b.** *Péj* old fogey, old fuddy-duddy.

badigeon [badiʒɔ̃] *nm* whitewash. ◆**badigeonner** *vt* (*mur*) to whitewash, distemper; (*écorchure*) *Méd* to paint, coat.

badin [badɛ̃] *a* (*peu sérieux*) light-hearted, playful. ◆**badiner** *vi* to jest, joke; **b. avec** (*prendre à la légère*) to trifle with. ◆—**age** *nm* banter, jesting.

badine [badin] *nf* cane, switch.

bafouer [bafwe] *vt* to mock *ou* scoff at.

bafouiller [bafuje] *vti* to stammer, splutter.

bâfrer [bɑfre] *vi Fam* to stuff oneself (with food).

bagage [bagaʒ] *nm* (*valise etc*) piece of luggage *ou* baggage; (*connaissances*) *Fig* (fund of) knowledge; *pl* (*ensemble des valises*) luggage, baggage. ◆**bagagiste** *nm* baggage handler.

bagarre [bagar] *nf* brawl. ◆**bagarrer** *vi Fam* to fight, struggle; — **se b.** *vpr* to fight, brawl; (*se disputer*) to fight, quarrel.

bagatelle [bagatɛl] *nf* trifle, mere bagatelle; **la b. de** *Iron* the trifling sum of.

bagne [baɲ] *nm* convict prison; **c'est le b. ici** *Fig* this place is a real hell hole *ou* workhouse. ◆**bagnard** *nm* convict.

bagnole [baɲɔl] *nf Fam* car; **vieille b.** *Fam* old banger.

bagou(t) [bagu] *nm Fam* glibness; **avoir du b.** to have the gift of the gab.

bague [bag] *nf* (*anneau*) ring; (*de cigare*) band. ◆**bagué** *a* (*doigt*) ringed.

baguenauder [bagnode] *vi,* — **se b.** *vpr* to loaf around, saunter.

baguette [bagɛt] *nf* (*canne*) stick; (*de chef d'orchestre*) baton; (*pain*) (long thin) loaf, stick of bread; *pl* (*de tambour*) drumsticks; (*pour manger*) chopsticks; **b. (magique)** (magic) wand; **mener à la b.** to rule with an iron hand.

bah! [bɑ] *int* really!, bah!

bahut [bay] *nm* (*meuble*) chest, cabinet; (*lycée*) *Fam* school.

baie [bɛ] *nf* **1** *Géog* bay. **2** *Bot* berry. **3** (*fenêtre*) picture window.

baignade [bɛɲad] *nf* (*bain*) bathe, bathing; (*endroit*) bathing place. ◆**baign/er** *vt* (*immerger*) to bathe; (*enfant*) to bath, *Am* bathe; **b. les rivages** (*mer*) to wash the shores; **baigné de** (*sueur, lumière*) bathed in; (*sang*) soaked in; – *vi* **b. dans** (*tremper*) to soak in; (*être imprégné de*) to be steeped in; — **se b.** *vpr* to go swimming *ou* bathing; (*dans une baignoire*) to have *ou* take a bath. ◆—**eur, -euse 1** *nmf* bather. **2** *nm* (*poupée*) baby doll. ◆**baignoire** *nf* bath (tub).

bail, *pl* **baux** [baj, bo] *nm* lease. ◆**bailleur** *nm Jur* lessor; **b. de fonds** financial backer.

bâill/er [bɑje] *vi* to yawn; (*chemise etc*) to gape; (*porte*) to stand ajar. ◆—**ement** *nm* yawn; gaping.

bâillon [bɑjɔ̃] *nm* gag. ◆**bâillonner** *vt* (*victime, presse etc*) to gag.

bain [bɛ̃] *nm* bath; (*de mer*) swim, bathe; **salle de bain(s)** bathroom; **être dans le b.** (*au courant*) *Fam* to have got into the swing of things; **petit/grand b.** (*piscine*) shallow/deep end; **b. de bouche** mouthwash. ◆**b.-marie** *nm* (*pl* **bains-marie**) *Culin* double boiler.

baïonnette [bajɔnɛt] *nf* bayonet.

baiser [beze] **1** *vt* **b. au front/sur la joue** to kiss on the forehead/cheek; – *nm* kiss; **bons baisers** (*dans une lettre*) (with) love. **2** *vt* (*duper*) *Fam* to con.

baisse [bɛs] *nf* fall, drop (**de** in); **en b.** (*température*) falling.

baisser [bese] *vt* (*voix, prix etc*) to lower, drop; (*tête*) to bend; (*radio, chauffage*) to turn down; – *vi* (*prix, niveau etc*) to drop, go down; (*soleil*) to go down, sink; (*marée*) to go out, ebb; (*santé, popularité*) to decline; — **se b.** *vpr* to bend down, stoop.

bajoues [baʒu] *nfpl* (*d'animal, de personne*) chops.

bal, *pl* **bals** [bal] *nm* (*réunion de grand apparat*) ball; (*populaire*) dance; (*lieu*) dance hall.

balade [balad] *nf Fam* walk; (*en auto*) drive; (*excursion*) tour. ◆**balader** *vt* (*enfant etc*) to take for a walk *ou* drive; (*objet*) to trail around; — **se b.** *vpr* (*à pied*) to (go for a) walk; (*excursionner*) to tour (around); **se b. (en voiture)** to go for a drive. ◆**baladeur** *nm* Walkman®. ◆**baladeuse** *nf* inspection lamp.

balafre [balafr] *nf* (*blessure*) gash, slash;

(*cicatrice*) scar. ◆**balafrer** *vt* to gash, slash; to scar.

balai [balɛ] *nm* broom; **b. mécanique** carpet sweeper; **manche à b.** broomstick; *Av* joystick. ◆**b.-brosse** *nm* (*pl* **balais-brosses**) garden broom *ou* broom (*for scrubbing paving stones*).

balance [balɑ̃s] *nf* (*instrument*) (pair of) scales; (*équilibre*) *Pol Fin* balance; **la B.** (*signe*) Libra; **mettre en b.** to balance, weigh up.

balanc/er [balɑ̃se] *vt* (*bras*) to swing; (*hanches, tête, branches*) to sway; (*lancer*) *Fam* to chuck; (*se débarrasser de*) *Fam* to chuck out; **b. un compte** *Fin* to balance an account; **— se b.** *vpr* (*personne*) to swing (from side to side); (*arbre, bateau etc*) to sway; **je m'en balance!** I couldn't care less! ◆**—é** *a* **bien b.** (*phrase*) well-balanced; (*personne*) *Fam* well-built. ◆**—ement** *nm* swinging; swaying. ◆**balancier** *nm* (*d'horloge*) pendulum; (*de montre*) balance wheel. ◆**balançoire** *nf* (*escarpolette*) swing; (*bascule*) seesaw.

balayer [baleje] *vt* (*chambre, rue*) to sweep (out *ou* up); (*enlever, chasser*) to sweep away; **le vent balayait la plaine** the wind swept the plain. ◆**balayette** [balɛjɛt] *nf* (hand) brush; (*balai*) short-handled broom. ◆**balayeur, -euse** [balɛjœr, -øz] *nmf* roadsweeper.

balbutier [balbysje] *vti* to stammer.

balcon [balkɔ̃] *nm* balcony; *Th Cin* dress circle.

baldaquin [baldakɛ̃] *nm* (*de lit etc*) canopy.

baleine [balɛn] *nf* (*animal*) whale; (*fanon*) whalebone; (*de parapluie*) rib. ◆**baleinier** *nm* (*navire*) whaler. ◆**baleinière** *nf* whaleboat.

balise [baliz] *nf* *Nau* beacon; *Av* (ground) light; *Aut* road sign. ◆**balis/er** *vt* to mark with beacons *ou* lights; (*route*) to signpost. ◆**—age** *nm* *Nau* beacons; *Av* lighting; *Aut* signposting.

balistique [balistik] *a* ballistic.

balivernes [balivɛrn] *nfpl* balderdash, nonsense.

ballade [balad] *nf* (*légende*) ballad; (*poème court*) & *Mus* ballade.

ballant [balɑ̃] *a* (*bras, jambes*) dangling.

ballast [balast] *nm* ballast.

balle [bal] *nf* (*de tennis, golf etc*) ball; (*projectile*) bullet; (*paquet*) bale; *pl* (*francs*) *Fam* francs; **se renvoyer la b.** to pass the buck (to each other).

ballet [balɛ] *nm* ballet. ◆**ballerine** *nf* ballerina.

ballon [balɔ̃] *nm* (*jouet d'enfant*) & *Av* balloon; (*sport*) ball; **b. de football** football; **lancer un b. d'essai** *Fig* to put out a feeler. ◆**ballonné** *a* (*ventre*) bloated, swollen. ◆**ballot** *nm* (*paquet*) bundle; (*imbécile*) *Fam* idiot.

ballottage [balɔtaʒ] *nm* (*scrutin*) second ballot (*no candidate having achieved the required number of votes*).

ballotter [balɔte] *vti* to shake (about); **ballotté entre** (*sentiments contraires*) torn between.

balnéaire [balneɛr] *a* **station b.** seaside resort.

balourd, -ourde [balur, -urd] *nmf* (clumsy) oaf. ◆**balourdise** *nf* clumsiness, oafishness; (*gaffe*) blunder.

Baltique [baltik] *nf* **la B.** the Baltic.

balustrade [balystrad] *nf* (hand)rail, railing(s).

bambin [bɑ̃bɛ̃] *nm* tiny tot, toddler.

bambou [bɑ̃bu] *nm* bamboo.

ban [bɑ̃] *nm* (*de tambour*) roll; (*applaudissements*) round of applause; *pl* (*de mariage*) banns; **mettre qn au b. de** to cast s.o. out from, outlaw s.o. from; **un b. pour . . .** three cheers for . . .

banal, mpl -als [banal] *a* (*fait, accident etc*) commonplace, banal; (*idée, propos*) banal, trite. ◆**banalisé** *a* (*voiture de police*) unmarked. ◆**banalité** *nf* banality; *pl* (*propos*) banalities.

banane [banan] *nf* banana.

banc [bɑ̃] *nm* (*siège, établi*) bench; (*de poissons*) shoal; **b. d'église** pew; **b. d'essai** *Fig* testing ground; **b. de sable** sandbank; **b. des accusés** *Jur* dock.

bancaire [bɑ̃kɛr] *a* (*opération*) banking-; (*chèque*) bank-.

bancal, mpl -als [bɑ̃kal] *a* (*personne*) bandy, bow-legged; (*meuble*) wobbly; (*idée*) shaky.

bande [bɑ̃d] *nf* **1** (*de terrain, papier etc*) strip; (*de film*) reel; (*de journal*) wrapper; (*rayure*) stripe; (*de fréquences*) *Rad* band; (*pansement*) bandage; (*sur la chaussée*) line; **b. (magnétique)** tape; **b. vidéo** videotape; **b. sonore** sound track; **b. dessinée** comic strip, strip cartoon; **par la b.** indirectly. **2** (*groupe*) gang, troop, band; (*de chiens*) pack; (*d'oiseaux*) flock; **on a fait b. à part** we split into our own group; **b. d'idiots!** you load of idiots! ◆**bandeau, -x** *nm* (*sur les yeux*) blindfold; (*pour la tête*) headband; (*pansement*) head bandage. ◆**band/er** *vt* (*blessure etc*) to bandage; (*yeux*) to blindfold; (*arc*) to bend; (*muscle*) to tense. ◆—**age** nm (pansement) bandage.

banderole [bɑ̃drɔl] nf (sur mât) pennant, streamer; (sur montants) banner.

bandit [bɑ̃di] nm robber, bandit; (enfant) Fam rascal. ◆**banditisme** nm crime.

bandoulière [bɑ̃duljɛr] nf shoulder strap; **en b.** slung across the shoulder.

banjo [bɑ̃(d)ʒo] nm Mus banjo.

banlieue [bɑ̃ljø] nf suburbs, outskirts; **la grande b.** the outer suburbs; **de b.** (magasin etc) suburban; (train) commuter-. ◆**banlieusard, -arde** nmf (habitant) suburbanite; (voyageur) commuter.

banne [ban] nf (de magasin) awning.

bannière [banjɛr] nf banner.

bann/ir [banir] vt (exiler) to banish; (supprimer) to ban, outlaw. ◆—**issement** nm banishment.

banque [bɑ̃k] nf bank; (activité) banking.

banqueroute [bɑ̃krut] nf (fraudulent) bankruptcy.

banquet [bɑ̃kɛ] nm banquet.

banquette [bɑ̃kɛt] nf (bench) seat.

banquier [bɑ̃kje] nm banker.

banquise [bɑ̃kiz] nf ice floe ou field.

baptême [batɛm] nm christening, baptism; **b. du feu** baptism of fire; **b. de l'air** first flight. ◆**baptiser** vt (enfant) to christen, baptize; (appeler) Fig to christen.

baquet [bakɛ] nm tub, basin.

bar [bar] nm 1 (lieu, comptoir, meuble) bar. 2 (poisson marin) bass.

baragouin [baragwɛ̃] nm gibberish, gabble. ◆**baragouiner** vt (langue) to gabble (a few words of); — vi to gabble away.

baraque [barak] nf hut, shack; (maison) Fam house, place; Péj hovel; (de forain) stall. ◆—**ment** nm (makeshift) huts.

baratin [baratɛ̃] nm Fam sweet talk; Com patter. ◆**baratiner** vt to chat up; Am sweet-talk.

barbare [barbar] a (manières, crime) barbaric; (peuple, invasions) barbarian; — nmf barbarian. ◆**barbarie** nf (cruauté) barbarity. ◆**barbarisme** nm Gram barbarism.

barbe [barb] nf beard; **une b. de trois jours** three days' growth of beard; **se faire la b.** to shave; **à la b. de** under the nose(s) of; **rire dans sa b.** to laugh up one's sleeve; **la b.!** enough!; **quelle b.!** what a drag!; **b. à papa** candyfloss, Am cotton candy.

barbecue [barbəkju] nm barbecue.

barbelé [barbəle] a barbed; — nmpl barbed wire.

barb/er [barbe] vt Fam to bore (stiff); — **se**

b. vpr to be ou get bored (stiff). ◆—**ant** a Fam boring.

barbiche [barbiʃ] nf goatee (beard).

barbiturique [barbityrik] nm barbiturate.

barbot/er [barbɔte] 1 vi (s'agiter) to splash about, paddle. 2 vt (voler) Fam to filch. ◆—**euse** nf (de bébé) rompers.

barbouill/er [barbuje] vt (salir) to smear; (peindre) to daub; (gribouiller) to scribble; **avoir l'estomac barbouillé** Fam to feel queasy. ◆—**age** nm smear; daub; scribble.

barbu [barby] a bearded.

barda [barda] nm Fam gear; (de soldat) kit.

bardé [barde] a **b. de** (décorations etc) covered with.

barder [barde] v imp **ça va b.!** Fam there'll be fireworks!

barème [barɛm] nm (des tarifs) table; (des salaires) scale; (livre de comptes) ready reckoner.

baril [bari(l)] nm barrel; **b. de poudre** powder keg.

bariolé [barjɔle] a brightly-coloured.

barman, pl **-men** ou **-mans** [barman, -mɛn] nm barman, Am bartender.

baromètre [barɔmɛtr] nm barometer.

baron, -onne [barɔ̃, -ɔn] nm baron; — nf baroness.

baroque [barɔk] 1 a (idée etc) bizarre, weird. 2 a & nm Archit Mus etc baroque.

baroud [barud] nm **b. d'honneur** Arg gallant last fight.

barque [bark] nf (small) boat.

barre [bar] nf bar; (trait) line, stroke; Nau helm; **b. de soustraction** minus sign; **b. fixe** Sp horizontal bar. ◆**barreau, -x** nm (de fenêtre etc) & Jur bar; (d'échelle) rung.

barr/er [bare] 1 vt (route etc) to block (off), close (off); (porte) to bar; (chèque) to cross; (phrase) to cross out; Nau to steer; **b. la route à qn, b. qn** to bar s.o.'s way; 'rue barrée' 'road closed'. 2 **se b.** vpr Arg to hop it, make off. ◆—**age** nm (sur une route) roadblock; (barrière) barrier; (ouvrage hydraulique) dam; (de petite rivière) weir; **le b. d'une rue** the closure of a street; **tir de b.** barrage fire; **b. d'agents** cordon of police. ◆—**eur** nm Sp Nau cox.

barrette [barɛt] nf (pince) (hair)slide, Am barrette.

barricade [barikad] nf barricade. ◆**barricader** vt to barricade; — **se b.** vpr to barricade oneself.

barrière [barjɛr] nf (porte) gate; (clôture) fence; (obstacle, mur) barrier.

barrique [barik] nf (large) barrel.

baryton [baritɔ̃] *nm* baritone.
bas ¹, basse [ba, bas] *a* (*table, prix etc*) low; (*âme, action*) base, mean; (*partie de ville etc*) lower; (*origine*) lowly; **au b. mot** at the very least; **enfant en b. âge** young child; **avoir la vue basse** to be short-sighted; **le b. peuple** *Péj* the lower orders; **coup b.** *Boxe* blow below the belt; – *adv* low; (*parler*) in a whisper, softly; **mettre b.** (*animal*) to give birth; **mettre b. les armes** to lay down one's arms; **jeter b.** to overthrow; **plus b.** further *ou* lower down; **en b.** down (below); (*par l'escalier*) downstairs, down below; **en ou au b. de** at the foot *ou* bottom of; **de haut en b.** from top to bottom; **sauter à b. du lit** to jump out of bed; **à b. les dictateurs/etc!** down with dictators/etc!; – *nm* (*de côte, page etc*) bottom, foot; **du b.** (*tiroir, étagère*) bottom.
bas ² [ba] *nm* (*chaussette*) stocking; **b. de laine** *Fig* nest egg.
basané [bazane] *a* (*visage etc*) tanned.
bas-bleu [bablø] *nm Péj* bluestocking.
bas-côté [bakote] *nm* (*de route*) roadside, shoulder.
bascule [baskyl] *nf* (*jeu de*) **b.** (game of) seesaw; (*balance à*) **b.** weighing machine; **cheval/fauteuil à b.** rocking horse/chair. ◆**basculer** *vti* (*personne*) to topple over; (*benne*) to tip up.
base [baz] *nf* base; (*principe fondamental*) basis, foundation; **de b.** (*salaire etc*) basic; **produit à b. de lait** milk-based product; **militant de b.** rank-and-file militant. ◆**baser** *vt* to base; **se b. sur** to base oneself on.
bas-fond [bafɔ̃] *nm* (*eau*) shallows; (*terrain*) low ground; *pl* (*population*) *Péj* dregs.
basilic [bazilik] *nm Bot Culin* basil.
basilique [bazilik] *nf* basilica.
basket(-ball) [basket(bɔl)] *nm* basketball.
basque [bask] **1** *a & nmf* Basque. **2** *nfpl* (*pans de veste*) skirts.
basse [bas] **1** *voir* **bas ¹. 2** *nf Mus* bass.
basse-cour [baskur] *nf* (*pl* **basses-cours**) farmyard.
bassement [basmɑ̃] *adv* basely, meanly. ◆**bassesse** *nf* baseness, meanness; (*action*) base *ou* mean act.
bassin [basɛ̃] *nm* (*pièce d'eau*) pond; (*piscine*) pool; (*cuvette*) bowl, basin; (*rade*) dock; *Anat* pelvis; *Géog* basin; **b. houiller** coalfield. ◆**bassine** *nf* bowl.
basson [basɔ̃] *nm* (*instrument*) bassoon; (*musicien*) bassoonist.
bastingage [bastɛ̃gaʒ] *nm Nau* bulwarks, rail.

bastion [bastjɔ̃] *nm* bastion.
bastringue [bastrɛ̃g] *nm* (*bal*) *Fam* popular dance hall; (*tapage*) *Arg* shindig, din; (*attirail*) *Arg* paraphernalia.
bas-ventre [bavɑ̃tr] *nm* lower abdomen.
bat [ba] *voir* **battre**.
bât [ba] *nm* packsaddle.
bataclan [bataklɑ̃] *nm Fam* paraphernalia; **et tout le b.** *Fam* and the whole caboodle.
bataille [bataj] *nf* battle; *Cartes* beggar-my-neighbour. ◆**batailler** *vi* to fight, battle. ◆**—eur, -euse** *nmf* fighter; – *a* belligerent. ◆**bataillon** *nm* battalion.
bâtard, -arde [batar, -ard] *a & nmf* bastard; **chien b.** mongrel; **œuvre bâtarde** hybrid work.
bateau, -x [bato] *nm* boat; (*grand*) ship. ◆**b.-citerne** *nm* (*pl* **bateaux-citernes**) tanker. ◆**b.-mouche** *nm* (*pl* **bateaux-mouches**) (*sur la Seine*) pleasure boat.
batifoler [batifɔle] *vi Hum* to fool *ou* lark about.
bâtiment [batimɑ̃] *nm* (*édifice*) building; (*navire*) vessel; **le b., l'industrie du b.** the building trade; **ouvrier du b.** building worker. ◆**bât/ir** *vt* (*construire*) to build; (*coudre*) to baste, tack; **terrain à b.** building site. ◆**—i** *a* bien b. well-built; – *nm Menuis* frame, support. ◆**bâtisse** *nf Péj* building. ◆**bâtisseur, -euse** *nmf* builder (*de* of).
bâton [batɔ̃] *nm* (*canne*) stick; (*de maréchal, d'agent*) baton; **b. de rouge** lipstick; **donner des coups de b. à qn** to beat s.o. (with a stick); **parler à bâtons rompus** to ramble from one subject to another; **mettre des bâtons dans les roues à qn** to put obstacles in s.o.'s way.
batterie [batri] *nf Mil Aut* battery; **la b.** *Mus* the drums; **b. de cuisine** set of kitchen utensils.
batt/re* [batr] **1** *vt* (*frapper, vaincre*) to beat; (*blé*) to thresh; (*cartes*) to shuffle; (*pays, chemins*) to scour; (*à coups redoublés*) to batter, pound; **b. la mesure** to beat time; **b. à mort** to batter *ou* beat to death; **b. pavillon** to fly a flag; – *vi* to beat; (*porte*) to bang; **b. des mains** to clap (one's hands); **b. des paupières** to blink; **b. des ailes** (*oiseau*) to flap its wings; **le vent fait b. la porte** the wind bangs the door. **2 se b.** *vpr* to fight. ◆**—ant 1** *a* (*pluie*) driving; (*porte*) swing-. **2** *nm* (*de cloche*) tongue; (*vantail de porte etc*) flap; **porte à deux battants** double door. **3** *nm* (*personne*) fighter. ◆**—u** *a* **chemin** *ou* **sentier b.** beaten track. ◆**—age** *nm* (*du blé*) threshing; (*publicité*) *Fam*

publicity, hype, ballyhoo. ◆**—ement** *nm* (*de cœur, de tambour*) beat; (*délai*) interval; **battements de cœur** palpitations. ◆**—eur** *nm* (*musicien*) percussionist; **b. à œufs** egg beater.

baudet [bodɛ] *nm* donkey.

baume [bom] *nm* (*résine*) & *Fig* balm.

baux [bo] *voir* bail.

bavard, -arde [bavar, -ard] *a* (*loquace*) talkative; (*cancanier*) gossipy; – *nmf* chatterbox; gossip. ◆**bavard/er** *vi* to chat, chatter; (*papoter*) to gossip; (*divulguer*) to blab. ◆**—age** *nm* chatting, chatter(ing); gossip(ing).

bave [bav] *nf* dribble, slobber; foam; (*de limace*) slime. ◆**baver** *vi* to dribble, slobber; (*chien enragé*) to foam; (*encre*) to smudge; **en b.** *Fam* to have a rough time of it. ◆**bavette** *nf* bib. ◆**baveux, -euse** *a* (*bouche*) slobbery; (*omelette*) runny. ◆**bavoir** *nm* bib. ◆**bavure** *nf* smudge; (*erreur*) blunder; **sans b.** perfect(ly), flawless(ly).

bazar [bazar] *nm* (*magasin, marché*) bazaar; (*désordre*) mess, clutter; (*attirail*) *Fam* stuff, gear. ◆**bazarder** *vt* *Fam* to sell off, get rid of.

bazooka [bazuka] *nm* bazooka.

béant [beã] *a* (*plaie*) gaping; (*gouffre*) yawning.

béat [bea] *a* *Péj* smug; (*heureux*) *Hum* blissful. ◆**béatitude** *nf* *Hum* bliss.

beau (*or* **bel** *before vowel or mute h*), **belle**, *pl* **beaux, belles** [bo, bɛl] *a* (*femme, fleur etc*) beautiful, attractive; (*homme*) handsome, good-looking; (*voyage, temps etc*) fine, lovely; **au b. milieu** right in the middle; **j'ai b. crier/essayer/etc** it's no use (my) shouting/trying/*etc*; **un b. morceau** a good *or* sizeable bit; **de plus belle** (*recommencer etc*) worse than ever; **bel et bien** really; – *nm* **le b.** the beautiful; **faire le b.** (*chien*) to sit up and beg; **le plus b. de l'histoire** the best part of the story; – *nf* (*femme*) beauty; *Sp* deciding game.

beaucoup [boku] *adv* (*lire etc*) a lot, a great deal; **aimer b.** to like very much; **s'intéresser b. à** to be very interested in; **b. de** (*livres etc*) many, a lot *ou* a great deal of; (*courage etc*) a lot *ou* a great deal of, much; **pas b. d'argent**/*etc* not much money/*etc*; **j'en ai b.** (*quantité*) I have a lot; (*nombre*) I have many; **b. plus/moins** much more/less; many more/fewer; **b. trop** much too much; many too many; **de b.** by far; **b. sont** . . . many are . . .

beau-fils [bofis] *nm* (*pl* **beaux-fils**) (*d'un*

précédent *mariage*) stepson; (*gendre*) son-in-law. ◆**b.-frère** *nm* (*pl* **beaux-frères**) brother-in-law. ◆**b.-père** *nm* (*pl* **beaux-pères**) father-in-law; (*parâtre*) stepfather.

beauté [bote] *nf* beauty; **institut** *ou* **salon de b.** beauty parlour; **en b.** (*gagner etc*) magnificently; **être en b.** to look one's very best; **de toute b.** beautiful.

beaux-arts [bozar] *nmpl* fine arts. ◆**b.-parents** *nmpl* parents-in-law.

bébé [bebe] *nm* baby; **b.-lion**/*etc* (*pl* **bébés-lions**/*etc*) baby lion/*etc*.

bébête [bebɛt] *a* *Fam* silly.

bec [bɛk] *nm* (*d'oiseau*) beak, bill; (*de cruche*) lip, spout; (*de plume*) nib; (*bouche*) *Fam* mouth; *Mus* mouthpiece; **coup de b.** peck; **b. de gaz** gas lamp; **clouer le b. à qn** *Fam* to shut s.o. up; **tomber sur un b.** *Fam* to come up against a serious snag. ◆**b.-de-cane** *nm* (*pl* **becs-de-cane**) door handle.

bécane [bekan] *nf* *Fam* bike.

bécarre [bekar] *nm* *Mus* natural.

bécasse [bekas] *nf* (*oiseau*) woodcock; (*personne*) *Fam* simpleton.

bêche [bɛʃ] *nf* spade. ◆**bêcher** *vt* **1** (*cultiver*) to dig. **2** *Fig* to criticize; (*snober*) to snub. ◆**bêcheur, -euse** *nmf* snob.

bécot [beko] *nm* *Fam* kiss. ◆**bécoter** *vt*, **— se b.** *vpr* *Fam* to kiss.

becquée [beke] *nf* beakful; **donner la b. à** (*oiseau, enfant*) to feed. ◆**becqueter** *vt* (*picorer*) to peck (at); (*manger*) *Fam* to eat.

bedaine [bədɛn] *nf* *Fam* paunch, potbelly.

bedeau, -x [bədo] *nm* beadle, verger.

bedon [bədɔ̃] *nm* *Fam* paunch. ◆**bedonnant** *a* paunchy, potbellied.

bée [be] *a* **bouche b.** open-mouthed.

beffroi [befrwa] *nm* belfry.

bégayer [begeje] *vi* to stutter, stammer. ◆**bègue** [bɛg] *nmf* stutterer, stammerer; – *a* **être b.** to stutter, stammer.

bégueule [begœl] *a* prudish; – *nf* prude.

béguin [begɛ̃] *nm* **avoir le b. pour qn** *Fam* to have taken a fancy to s.o.

beige [bɛʒ] *a* & *nm* beige.

beignet [bɛɲɛ] *nm* *Culin* fritter.

bel [bɛl] *voir* beau.

bêler [bele] *vi* to bleat.

belette [bəlɛt] *nf* weasel.

Belgique [bɛlʒik] *nf* Belgium. ◆**belge** *a* & *nmf* Belgian.

bélier [belje] *nm* (*animal, machine*) ram; **le B.** (*signe*) Aries.

belle [bɛl] *voir* beau.

belle-fille [bɛlfij] *nf* (*pl* **belles-filles**) (*d'un* *précédent mariage*) stepdaughter; (*bru*) daughter-in-law. ◆**b.-mère** *nf* (*pl* **belles-mères**) mother-in-law; (*marâtre*) stepmother. ◆**b.-sœur** *nf* (*pl* **belles-sœurs**) sister-in-law.

belligérant [beliʒerɑ̃] *a* & *nm* belligerent.

belliqueux, -euse [belikø, -øz] *a* warlike; *Fig* aggressive.

belvédère [belvedɛr] *nm* (*sur une route*) viewpoint.

bémol [bemɔl] *nm* *Mus* flat.

bénédiction [benediksjɔ̃] *nf* blessing, benediction.

bénéfice [benefis] *nm* (*gain*) profit; (*avantage*) benefit; **b. (ecclésiastique)** living, benefice. ◆**bénéficiaire** *nmf* beneficiary; – *a* (*marge, solde*) profit-. ◆**bénéficier** *vi* **b. de** to benefit from, have the benefit of. ◆**bénéfique** *a* beneficial.

Bénélux [benelyks] *nm* Benelux.

benêt [bənɛ] *nm* simpleton; – *am* simple-minded.

bénévole [benevɔl] *a* voluntary, unpaid.

bénin, -igne [benɛ̃, -iɲ] *a* (*tumeur, critique*) benign; (*accident*) minor.

bénir [benir] *vt* to bless; (*exalter, remercier*) to give thanks to. ◆**bénit** *a* (*pain*) consecrated; **eau bénite** holy water. ◆**bénitier** [-itje] *nm* (holy-water) stoup.

benjamin, -ine [bɛ̃ʒamɛ̃, -in] *nmf* youngest child; *Sp* young junior.

benne [bɛn] *nf* (*de grue*) scoop; (*à charbon*) tub, skip; (*de téléphérique*) cable car; **camion à b. basculante** dump truck; **b. à ordures** skip.

béotien, -ienne [beɔsjɛ̃, -jɛn] *nmf* (*inculte*) philistine.

béquille [bekij] *nf* (*canne*) crutch; (*de moto*) stand.

bercail [bɛrkaj] *nm* (*famille etc*) *Hum* fold.

berceau, -x [bɛrso] *nm* cradle.

berc/er [bɛrse] *vt* (*balancer*) to rock; (*apaiser*) to lull; (*leurrer*) to delude (**de** with); **se b. d'illusions** to delude oneself. ◆**-euse** *nf* lullaby.

béret [berɛ] *nm* beret.

berge [bɛrʒ] *nm* (*rivage*) (raised) bank.

berger, -ère [bɛrʒe, -ɛr] **1** *nm* shepherd; **chien (de) b.** sheepdog; – *nf* shepherdess. **2** *nm* **b. allemand** Alsatian (dog), *Am* German shepherd. ◆**bergerie** *nf* sheepfold.

berline [bɛrlin] *nf* *Aut* (four-door) saloon, *Am* sedan.

berlingot [bɛrlɛ̃go] *nm* (*bonbon aux fruits*) boiled sweet; (*à la menthe*) mint; (*emballage*) (milk) carton.

berlue [bɛrly] *nf* **avoir la b.** to be seeing things.

berne (en) [ɑ̃bɛrn] *adv* at half-mast.

berner [bɛrne] *vt* to fool, hoodwink.

besogne [bəzɔɲ] *nf* work, job, task. ◆**besogneux, -euse** *a* needy.

besoin [bəzwɛ̃] *nm* need; **avoir b. de** to need; **au b.** if necessary, if need(s) be; **dans le b.** in need, needy.

bestial, -aux [bɛstjal, -o] *a* bestial, brutish. ◆**bestiaux** *nmpl* livestock; (*bovins*) cattle. ◆**bestiole** *nf* (*insecte*) creepy-crawly, bug.

bétail [betaj] *nm* livestock; (*bovins*) cattle.

bête[1] [bɛt] *nf* animal; (*bestiole*) bug, creature; **b. de somme** beast of burden; **b. à bon dieu** ladybird, *Am* ladybug; **b. noire** pet hate, pet peeve; **chercher la petite b.** (*critiquer*) to pick holes.

bête[2] [bɛt] *a* silly, stupid. ◆**bêtement** *adv* stupidly; **tout b.** quite simply. ◆**bêtise** [betiz] *nf* silliness, stupidity; (*action, parole*) silly *ou* stupid thing; (*bagatelle*) mere trifle.

béton [betɔ̃] *nm* concrete; **en b.** concrete-; **b. armé** reinforced concrete. ◆**bétonnière** *nf*, ◆**bétonneuse** *nf* cement *ou* concrete mixer.

betterave [bɛtrav] *nf* *Culin* beetroot, *Am* beet; **b. sucrière** *ou* **à sucre** sugar beet.

beugler [bøgle] *vi* (*taureau*) to bellow; (*vache*) to moo; (*radio*) to blare (out).

beurre [bœr] *nm* butter; **b. d'anchois** anchovy paste. ◆**beurrer** *vt* to butter. ◆**beurrier** *nm* butter dish.

beuverie [bøvri] *nf* drinking session, booze-up.

bévue [bevy] *nf* blunder, mistake.

biais [bjɛ] *nm* (*moyen détourné*) device, expedient; (*aspect*) angle; **regarder de b.** to look at sidelong; **traverser en b.** to cross at an angle. ◆**biaiser** [bjeze] *vi* to prevaricate, hedge.

bibelot [biblo] *nm* curio, trinket.

biberon [bibrɔ̃] *nm* (feeding) bottle.

bible [bibl] *nf* bible; **la B.** the Bible. ◆**biblique** *a* biblical.

bibliobus [biblijɔbys] *nm* mobile library.

bibliographie [biblijɔgrafi] *nf* bibliography.

bibliothèque [biblijɔtɛk] *nf* library; (*meuble*) bookcase; (*à la gare*) bookstall. ◆**bibliothécaire** *nmf* librarian.

bic® [bik] *nm* ballpoint, biro®.

bicarbonate [bikarbɔnat] *nm* bicarbonate.

bicentenaire [bisɑ̃tnɛr] *nm* bicentenary, bicentennial.

biceps [bisɛps] *nm* *Anat* biceps.

biche [biʃ] *nf* doe, hind; **ma b.** *Fig* my pet.

bichonner [biʃɔne] *vt* to doll up.

bicoque [bikɔk] *nf Péj* shack, hovel.

bicyclette [bisiklɛt] *nf* bicycle, cycle; **la b.** *Sp* cycling; **aller à b.** to cycle.

bide [bid] *nm* (*ventre*) *Fam* belly; **faire un b.** *Arg* to flop.

bidet [bidɛ] *nm* (*cuvette*) bidet.

bidon [bidɔ̃] **1** *nm* (*d'essence*) can; (*pour boissons*) canteen; (*ventre*) *Fam* belly. **2** *nm du* **b.** *Fam* rubbish, bluff; – *a inv* (*simulé*) *Fam* fake, phoney. **◆se bidonner** *vpr Fam* to have a good laugh.

bidonville [bidɔ̃vil] *nf* shantytown.

bidule [bidyl] *nm* (*chose*) *Fam* thingummy, whatsit.

bielle [bjɛl] *nf Aut* connecting rod.

bien [bjɛ̃] *adv* well; **il joue b.** he plays well; **je vais b.** I'm fine; *ou* well; **b. fatigué/ souvent**/*etc* (*très*) very tired/often/*etc*; **merci b.!** thanks very much!; **b.!** fine!, right!; **b. du courage**/*etc* a lot of courage/*etc*; **b. des fois/des gens**/*etc* lots *ou* many times/people/*etc*; **je l'ai b. dit** (*intensif*) I *did* say so; **c'est b. compris?** is that quite understood?; **c'est b. toi?** is it really you?; **tu as b. fait** you did right; **c'est b. fait (pour lui)** it serves him right; – *a inv* (*convenable*) all right, fine; (*agréable*) nice, fine; (*compétent, bon*) good, fine; (*à l'aise*) comfortable, fine; (*beau*) attractive; (*en forme*) well; (*moralement*) nice; **une fille b.** a nice *ou* respectable girl; – *nm* (*avantage*) good; (*capital*) possession; **ça te fera du b.** it will do you good; **le b. et le mal** good and evil; **biens de consommation** consumer goods. **◆b.-aimé, -ée** *a* & *nmf* beloved. **◆b.-être** *nm* wellbeing. **◆b.-fondé** *nm* validity, soundness.

bienfaisance [bjɛ̃fəzɑ̃s] *nf* benevolence, charity; **de b.** (*société etc*) benevolent, charitable. **◆bienfaisant** *a* beneficial.

bienfait [bjɛ̃fɛ] *nm* (*générosité*) favour; *pl* benefits, blessings. **◆bienfaiteur, -trice** *nmf* benefactor, benefactress.

bienheureux, -euse [bjɛ̃nœrø, -øz] *a* blessed, blissful.

biennal, -aux [bjenal, -o] *a* biennial.

bien que [bjɛ̃k(ə)] *conj* although.

bienséant [bjɛ̃seɑ̃] *a* proper. **◆bienséance** *nf* propriety.

bientôt [bjɛ̃to] *adv* soon; **à b.!** see you soon!; **il est b. dix heures**/*etc* it's nearly ten o'clock/*etc*.

bienveillant [bjɛ̃vejɑ̃] *a* kindly. **◆bienveillance** *nf* kindliness.

bienvenu, -ue [bjɛ̃vny] *a* welcome; – *nmf*

soyez le b.! welcome!; – *nf* welcome; **souhaiter la bienvenue à** to welcome.

bière [bjɛr] *nf* **1** (*boisson*) beer; **b. pression** draught beer. **2** (*cercueil*) coffin.

biffer [bife] *vt* to cross *ou* strike out.

bifteck [biftɛk] *nm* steak; **gagner son b.** *Fam* to earn one's (daily) bread.

bifurquer [bifyrke] *vi* to branch off, fork. **◆bifurcation** *nf* fork, junction.

bigame [bigam] *a* bigamous; – *nmf* bigamist. **◆bigamie** *nf* bigamy.

bigarré [bigare] *a* (*bariolé*) mottled; (*hétéroclite*) motley, mixed.

bigler [bigle] *vi* (*loucher*) *Fam* to squint; – *vti* **b. (sur)** (*lorgner*) *Fam* to leer at. **◆bigleux, -euse** *a Fam* cock-eyed.

bigorneau, -x [bigɔrno] *nm* (*coquillage*) winkle.

bigot, -ote [bigo, -ɔt] *nmf Péj* religious bigot; – *a* over-devout, fanatical.

bigoudi [bigudi] *nm* (hair)curler *ou* roller.

bigrement [bigrəmɑ̃] *adv Fam* awfully.

bijou, -x [biʒu] *nm* jewel; (*ouvrage élégant*) *Fig* gem. **◆bijouterie** *nf* (*commerce*) jeweller's shop; (*bijoux*) jewellery. **◆bijoutier, -ière** *nmf* jeweller.

bikini [bikini] *nm* bikini.

bilan [bilɑ̃] *nm Fin* balance sheet; (*résultat*) outcome; (*d'un accident*) (casualty) toll; **b. de santé** checkup; **faire le b.** to make an assessment (**de** of).

bilboquet [bilbɔkɛ] *nm* cup-and-ball (game).

bile [bil] *nf* bile; **se faire de la b.** *Fam* to worry, fret. **◆bilieux, -euse** *a* bilious.

bilingue [bilɛ̃g] *a* bilingual.

billard [bijar] *nm* (*jeu*) billiards; (*table*) billiard table; *Méd Fam* operating table; **c'est du b.** *Fam* it's a cinch.

bille [bij] *nf* (*d'un enfant*) marble; (*de billard*) billiard ball; **stylo à b.** ballpoint pen, biro®.

billet [bijɛ] *nm* ticket; **b. (de banque)** (bank)note, *Am* bill; **b. aller, b. simple** single ticket, *Am* one-way ticket; **b. (d')aller et retour** return ticket, *Am* round trip ticket; **b. doux** love letter.

billion [biljɔ̃] *nm* billion, *Am* trillion.

billot [bijo] *nm* (*de bois*) block.

bimensuel, -elle [bimɑ̃sɥɛl] *a* bimonthly, fortnightly.

bimoteur [bimɔtœr] *a* twin-engined.

binaire [biner] *a* binary.

biner [bine] *vt* to hoe. **◆binette** *nf* hoe; (*visage*) *Arg* mug, face.

biochimie [bjoʃimi] *nf* biochemistry.

biodégradable [bjɔdegradabl] a biodegradable.

biographie [bjɔgrafi] nf biography. ◆**biographe** nmf biographer.

biologie [bjɔlɔʒi] nf biology. ◆**biologique** a biological.

bip-bip [bipbip] nm bleeper.

bipède [bipɛd] nm biped.

bique [bik] nf Fam nanny-goat.

Birmanie [birmani] nf Burma. ◆**birman, -ane** a & nmf Burmese.

bis[1] [bis] adv (cri) Th encore; Mus repeat; **4 bis** (numéro) 4A; − nm Th encore.

bis[2], **bise** [bi, biz] a greyish-brown.

bisbille [bisbij] nf squabble; **en b. avec** Fam at loggerheads with.

biscornu [biskɔrny] a (objet) distorted, misshapen; (idée) cranky.

biscotte [biskɔt] nf (pain) Melba toast; (biscuit) rusk, Am zwieback.

biscuit [biskɥi] nm (salé) biscuit, Am cracker; (sucré) biscuit, Am cookie; **b. de Savoie** sponge (cake). ◆**biscuiterie** nf biscuit factory.

bise [biz] nf **1** (vent) north wind. **2** (baiser) Fam kiss.

biseau, -x [bizo] nm bevel.

bison [bizɔ̃] nm bison, (American) buffalo.

bisou [bizu] nm Fam kiss.

bisser [bise] vt (musicien, acteur) to encore.

bissextile [bisɛkstil] af **année b.** leap year.

bistouri [bisturi] nm scalpel, lancet.

bistre [bistr] a inv bistre, dark-brown.

bistro(t) [bistro] nm bar, café.

bitume [bitym] nm (revêtement) asphalt.

bivouac [bivwak] nm Mil bivouac.

bizarre [bizar] a peculiar, odd, bizarre. ◆−**ment** adv oddly. ◆**bizarrerie** nf peculiarity.

blabla(bla) [blabla(bla)] nm claptrap, bunkum.

blafard [blafar] a pale, pallid.

blague [blag] nf **1** (à tabac) pouch. **2** (plaisanterie, farce) Fam joke; pl (absurdités) Fam nonsense; **sans b.!** you're joking! ◆**blagu/er** vi to be joking; − vt to tease. ◆−**eur, -euse** nmf joker.

blair [blɛr] nm (nez) Arg snout, conk. ◆**blairer** vt Arg to stomach.

blaireau, -x [blɛro] nm **1** (animal) badger. **2** (brosse) (shaving) brush.

blâme [blɑm] nm (réprimande) rebuke; (reproche) blame. ◆**blâmable** a blameworthy. ◆**blâmer** vt to rebuke; to blame.

blanc, blanche [blɑ̃, blɑ̃ʃ] **1** a white; (page etc) blank; **nuit blanche** sleepless night; **voix blanche** expressionless voice; − nmf (personne) white (man ou woman); − nm (couleur) white; (de poulet) white meat, breast; (espace, interligne) blank; **b. (d'œuf)** (egg) white; **le b.** (linge) whites; **magasin de b.** linen shop; **laisser en b.** to leave blank; **chèque en b.** blank cheque; **cartouche à b.** blank (cartridge); **saigner à b.** to bleed white. **2** nf Mus minim, Am half-note. ◆**blanchâtre** a whitish. ◆**blancheur** nf whiteness.

blanchir [blɑ̃ʃir] vt to whiten; (draps) to launder; (mur) to whitewash; Culin to blanch; (argent) Fig to launder; **b. qn** (disculper) to clear s.o.; − vi to turn white, whiten. ◆**blanchissage** nm laundering. ◆**blanchisserie** nf (lieu) laundry. ◆**blanchisseur, -euse** nmf laundryman, laundrywoman.

blanquette [blɑ̃kɛt] nf **b. de veau** veal stew in white sauce.

blasé [blaze] a blasé.

blason [blazɔ̃] nm (écu) coat of arms; (science) heraldry.

blasphème [blasfɛm] nf blasphemy. ◆**blasphématoire** a (propos) blasphemous. ◆**blasphémer** vti to blaspheme.

blatte [blat] nf cockroach.

blazer [blazœr] nm blazer.

blé [ble] nm wheat; (argent) Arg bread.

bled [blɛd] nm Péj Fam (dump of a) village.

blême [blɛm] a sickly pale, wan; **b. de colère** livid with anger.

bless/er [blese] vt to injure, hurt; (avec un couteau, une balle etc) to wound; (offenser) to hurt, offend, wound; **se b. le** ou **au bras/etc** to hurt one's arm/etc. ◆−**ant** [blɛsɑ̃] a (parole, personne) hurtful. ◆−**é, -ée** nmf casualty, injured ou wounded person. ◆**blessure** nf injury; wound.

blet, blette [blɛ, blɛt] a (fruit) overripe.

bleu [blø] a blue; **b. de colère** blue in the face; **steak b.** Culin very rare steak; − nm (couleur) blue; (contusion) bruise; (vêtement) overalls; (conscrit) raw recruit; **bleus de travail** overalls. ◆**bleuir** vti to turn blue.

bleuet [bløɛ] nm cornflower.

blind/er [blɛ̃de] vt Mil to armour(-plate). ◆−**é** a (train etc) Mil armoured; **porte blindée** reinforced steel door; − nm Mil armoured vehicle.

bloc [blɔk] nm block; (de pierre) lump, block; (de papier) pad; (masse compacte) unit; Pol bloc; **en b.** all together; **à b.** (serrer etc) tight, hard; **travailler à b.** Fam to work flat out. ◆**b.-notes** nm (pl **blocs-notes**) writing pad.

blocage [blɔkaʒ] *nm* (*des roues*) locking; *Psy* mental block; **b. des prix** price freeze.

blocus [blɔkys] *nm* blockade.

blond, -onde [blɔ̃, -ɔ̃d] *a* fair(-haired), blond; − *nm* fair-haired man; (*couleur*) blond; − *nf* fair-haired woman, blonde; (**bière**) **blonde** lager, pale *ou* light ale. ◆**blondeur** *nf* fairness, blondness.

bloquer [blɔke] *vt* (*obstruer*) to block; (*coincer*) to jam; (*grouper*) to group together; (*ville*) to blockade; (*freins*) to slam *ou* jam on; (*roue*) to lock; (*salaires, prix*) to freeze; **bloqué par la neige/la glace** snowbound/icebound; **− se b.** *vpr* to stick, jam; (*roue*) to lock.

blottir (se) [səblɔtir] *vpr* (*dans un coin etc*) to crouch; (*dans son lit*) to snuggle down; **se b. contre** to huddle *ou* snuggle up to.

blouse [bluz] *nf* (*tablier*) overall, smock; (*corsage*) blouse. ◆**blouson** *nm* (waist-length) jacket.

blue-jean [bludʒin] *nm* jeans, denims.

bluff [blœf] *nm* bluff. ◆**bluffer** *vti* to bluff.

boa [bɔa] *nm* (*serpent, tour de cou*) boa.

bobard [bɔbar] *nm Fam* fib, yarn, tall story.

bobine [bɔbin] *nf* (*de fil, film etc*) reel, spool; (*pour machine à coudre*) bobbin, spool.

bobo [bobo] *nm* (*langage enfantin*) pain; **j'ai b., ça fait b.** it hurts.

bocage [bɔkaʒ] *nm* copse.

bocal, -aux [bɔkal, -o] *nm* glass jar; (*à poissons*) bowl.

bock [bɔk] *nm* (*récipient*) beer glass; (*contenu*) glass of beer.

bœuf, *pl* **-fs** [bœf, bø] *nm* (*animal*) ox (*pl* oxen), bullock; (*viande*) beef.

bohème [bɔɛm] *a* & *nmf* bohemian. ◆**bohémien, -ienne** *a* & *nmf* gipsy.

boire* [bwar] *vt* to drink; (*absorber*) to soak up; (*paroles*) *Fig* to take *ou* drink in; **b. un coup** to have a drink; **offrir à b. à qn** to offer s.o. a drink; **b. à petits coups** to sip; − *vi* to drink.

bois[1] [bwa] *voir* **boire**.

bois[2] [bwa] *nm* (*matière, forêt*) wood; (*de construction*) timber; (*gravure*) woodcut; *pl* (*de cerf*) antlers; *Mus* woodwind instruments; **en** *ou* **de b.** wooden; **b. de chauffage** firewood; **b. de lit** bedstead. ◆**boisé** *a* wooded. ◆**boiserie(s)** *nf*(*pl*) panelling.

boisson [bwasɔ̃] *nf* drink, beverage.

boit [bwa] *voir* **boire**.

boîte [bwat] *nf* box; (*de conserve*) tin, *Am* can; (*lieu de travail*) *Fam* firm; **b. aux** *ou* **à lettres** letterbox; **b. de nuit** nightclub; **mettre qn en b.** *Fam* to pull s.o.'s leg. ◆**boîtier** *nm* (*de montre etc*) case.

boiter [bwate] *vi* (*personne*) to limp. ◆**boiteux, -euse** *a* lame; (*meuble*) wobbly; (*projet etc*) *Fig* shaky.

bol [bɔl] *nm* (*récipient*) bowl; **prendre un b. d'air** to get a breath of fresh air; **avoir du b.** *Fam* to be lucky.

bolide [bɔlid] *nm* (*véhicule*) racing car.

Bolivie [bɔlivi] *nf* Bolivia. ◆**bolivien, -ienne** *a* & *nmf* Bolivian.

bombard/er [bɔ̃barde] *vt* (*ville etc*) to bomb; (*avec des obus*) to shell; **b. qn** *Fam* (*nommer*) to pitchfork s.o. (**à un poste** into a job); **b. de** (*questions*) to bombard with; (*objets*) to pelt with. ◆**−ement** *nm* bombing; shelling. ◆**bombardier** *nm* (*avion*) bomber.

bombe [bɔ̃b] *nf* (*projectile*) bomb; (*atomiseur*) spray; **tomber comme une b.** *Fig* to be a bombshell, be quite unexpected; **faire la b.** *Fam* to have a binge.

bomb/er [bɔ̃be] **1** *vi* (*gonfler*) to bulge; − *vt* **b. la poitrine** to throw out one's chest. **2** *vi* (*véhicule etc*) *Fam* to bomb *ou* belt along. ◆**−é** *a* (*verre etc*) rounded; (*route*) cambered.

bon[1], **bonne**[1] [bɔ̃, bɔn] *a* **1** (*satisfaisant etc*) good. **2** (*charitable*) kind, good. **3** (*agréable*) nice, good; **il fait b. se reposer** it's nice *ou* good to rest; **b. anniversaire!** happy birthday! **4** (*qui convient*) right; **c'est le b. clou** it's the right nail. **5** (*approprié, apte*) fit; **b. à manger** fit to eat; **b. pour le service** fit for service; **ce n'est b. à rien** it's useless; **comme te semble** as you think fit *ou* best; **c'est b. à savoir** it's worth knowing. **6** (*prudent*) wise, good; **croire b. de** to think it wise *ou* good to. **7** (*compétent*) good; **b. en français** good at French. **8** (*valable*) good; **ce billet est encore b.** this ticket's still good. **9** (*intensif*) **un b. moment** a good while. **10** **à quoi b.?** what's the use *ou* point *ou* good?; **pour de b.** in earnest; **tenir b.** to stand firm; **ah b.?** is that so? **11** *nm* **du b.** some good; **les bons** the good.

bon[2] [bɔ̃] *nm* (*billet*) coupon, voucher; (*titre*) *Fin* bond; (*formulaire*) slip.

bonasse [bɔnas] *a* feeble, soft.

bonbon [bɔ̃bɔ̃] *nm* sweet, *Am* candy. ◆**bonbonnière** *nf* sweet box, *Am* candy box.

bonbonne [bɔ̃bɔn] *nf* (*récipient*) demijohn.

bond [bɔ̃] *nm* leap, bound; (*de balle*) bounce; **faire faux b. à qn** to stand s.o. up, let s.o. down (*by not turning up*). ◆**bondir** *vi* to leap, bound.

bonde [bɔ̃d] *nf* (*bouchon*) plug; (*trou*) plughole.

bondé [bɔ̃de] *a* packed, crammed.

bonheur [bɔnœr] *nm* (*chance*) good luck, good fortune; (*félicité*) happiness; **par b.** luckily; **au petit b.** haphazardly.

bonhomie [bɔnɔmi] *nf* good-heartedness.

bonhomme, *pl* **bonshommes** [bɔnɔm, bɔ̃zɔm] **1** *nm* fellow, guy; **b. de neige** snowman; **aller son petit b. de chemin** to go on in one's own sweet way. **2** *a inv* good-hearted.

boniment(s) [bɔnimɑ̃] *nm*(*pl*) (*bobard*) claptrap; (*baratin*) patter.

bonjour [bɔ̃ʒur] *nm & int* good morning; (*après-midi*) good afternoon; **donner le b. à, dire b. à** to say hello to.

bonne² [bɔn] *nf* (*domestique*) maid; **b. d'enfants** nanny.

bonnement [bɔnmɑ̃] *adv* **tout b.** simply.

bonnet [bɔnɛ] *nm* cap; (*de femme, d'enfant*) bonnet; (*de soutien-gorge*) cup; **gros b.** *Fam* bigshot, bigwig. ◆**bonneterie** *nf* hosiery.

bonsoir [bɔ̃swar] *nm & int* (*en rencontrant qn*) good evening; (*en quittant qn*) goodbye; (*au coucher*) good night.

bonté [bɔ̃te] *nf* kindness, goodness.

bonus [bɔnys] *nm* no claims bonus.

bonze [bɔ̃z] *nm Péj Fam* bigwig.

boom [bum] *nm Écon* boom.

bord [bɔr] *nm* (*rebord*) edge; (*rive*) bank; (*de vêtement*) border; (*de chapeau*) brim; (*de verre*) rim, brim, edge; **au b. de la mer/route** at *ou* by the seaside/roadside; **b. du trottoir** kerb, *Am* curb; **au b. de** (*précipice*) on the brink of; **au b. des larmes** on the verge of tears; **à bord (de)** *Nau Av* on board; **jeter par-dessus b.** to throw overboard. ◆**border** *vt* (*vêtement*) to border, edge; (*lit, personne*) to tuck in; **b. la rue**/*etc* (*maisons, arbres etc*) to line the street/*etc*. ◆**bordure** *nf* border; **en b. de** bordering on.

bordeaux [bɔrdo] *a inv* maroon.

bordée [bɔrde] *nf* (*salve*) *Nau* broadside; (*d'injures*) *Fig* torrent, volley.

bordel [bɔrdɛl] *nm* **1** *Fam* brothel. **2** (*désordre*) *Fam* mess.

bordereau, -x [bɔrdəro] *nm* (*relevé*) docket, statement; (*formulaire*) note.

borgne [bɔrɲ] *a* (*personne*) one-eyed, blind in one eye; (*hôtel etc*) *Fig* shady.

borne [bɔrn] *nf* (*pierre*) boundary mark; *Él* terminal; *pl* (*limites*) *Fig* bounds; **b. kilométrique** = milestone; **dépasser** *ou* **franchir les bornes** to go too far. ◆**borner** *vt* (*limiter*) to confine; **se b. à** to confine oneself to. ◆**—é** *a* (*personne*) narrow-minded; (*intelligence*) narrow, limited.

bosquet [bɔskɛ] *nm* grove, thicket, copse.

bosse [bɔs] *nf* (*grosseur dorsale*) hump; (*enflure*) bump, lump; (*de terrain*) bump; **avoir la b. de** *Fam* to have a flair for; **rouler sa b.** *Fam* to knock about the world. ◆**bossu, -ue** *a* hunchbacked; **dos b.** hunchback; – *nmf* (*personne*) hunchback.

bosseler [bɔsle] *vt* (*orfèvrerie*) to emboss; (*déformer*) to dent.

bosser [bɔse] *vi Fam* to work (hard).

bot [bo] *nm* **pied b.** club foot.

botanique [bɔtanik] *a* botanical; – *nf* botany.

botte [bɔt] *nf* (*chaussure*) boot; ʼ(*faisceau*) bunch, bundle. ◆**botter** *vt* (*ballon etc*) *Fam* to boot. ◆**bottier** *nm* bootmaker. ◆**bottillon** *nm,* ◆**bottine** *nf* (ankle) boot.

Bottin® [bɔtɛ̃] *nm* telephone book.

bouc [buk] *nm* billy goat; (*barbe*) goatee; **b. émissaire** scapegoat.

boucan [bukɑ̃] *nm Fam* din, row, racket.

bouche [buʃ] *nf* mouth; **faire la petite** *ou* **fine b.** *Péj* to turn up one's nose; **une fine b.** a gourmet; **b. de métro** métro entrance; **b. d'égout** drain opening, manhole; **b. d'incendie** fire hydrant; **le b.-à-b.** the kiss of life. ◆**bouchée** *nf* mouthful.

bouch/er¹ [buʃe] **1** *vt* (*évier, nez etc*) to block (up), stop up; (*bouteille*) to close, cork; (*vue, rue etc*) to block; **se b. le nez** to hold one's nose. ◆**—é** *a* (*vin*) bottled; (*temps*) overcast; (*personne*) *Fig* stupid, dense. ◆**bouche-trou** *nm* stopgap. ◆**bouchon** *nm* stopper, top; (*de liège*) cork; (*de tube, bidon*) cap, top; *Pêche* float; (*embouteillage*) *Fig* traffic jam.

boucher² [buʃe] *nm* butcher. ◆**boucherie** *nf* butcher's (shop); (*carnage*) butchery.

boucle [bukl] *nf* **1** (*de ceinture*) buckle; (*de fleuve etc*) & *Av* loop; (*de ruban*) bow; **b. d'oreille** earring. **2 b.** (**de cheveux**) curl. ◆**boucl/er 1** *vt* to fasten, buckle; (*travail etc*) to finish off; (*enfermer, fermer*) *Fam* to lock up; (*budget*) to balance; (*circuit*) to lap; (*encercler*) to surround, cordon off; **b. la boucle** *Av* to loop the loop; **la b.** *Fam* to shut up. **2** *vt* (*cheveux*) to curl; – *vi* to be curly. ◆**—é** *a* (*cheveux*) curly.

bouclier [buklije] *nm* shield.

bouddhiste [budist] *a & nmf* Buddhist.

bouder [bude] *vi* to sulk; – *vt* (*personne, plaisirs etc*) to steer clear of. ◆**bouderie** *nf* sulkiness. ◆**boudeur, -euse** *a* sulky, moody.

boudin [budɛ̃] *nm* black pudding, *Am* blood pudding.

boue [bu] *nf* mud. ◆**boueux, -euse 1** *a*

muddy. **2** *nm* dustman, *Am* garbage collector.

bouée [bwe] *nf* buoy; **b. de sauvetage** life-buoy.

bouffe [buf] *nf Fam* food, grub, nosh.

bouffée [bufe] *nf* (*de fumée*) puff; (*de parfum*) whiff; (*d'orgueil*) fit; **b. de chaleur** *Méd* hot flush. ◆**bouff/er 1** *vi* to puff out. **2** *vti* (*manger*) *Fam* to eat. ◆**—ant** *a* (*manche*) puff(ed). ◆**bouffi** *a* puffy, bloated.

bouffon, -onne [bufɔ̃, -ɔn] *a* farcical; – *nm* buffoon. ◆**bouffonneries** *nfpl* antics, buffoonery.

bouge [buʒ] *nm* (*bar*) dive; (*taudis*) hovel.

bougeotte [buʒɔt] *nf* **avoir la b.** *Fam* to have the fidgets.

bouger [buʒe] *vi* to move; (*agir*) to stir; (*rétrécir*) to shrink; – *vt* to move; **— se b.** *vpr Fam* to move.

bougie [buʒi] *nf* candle; *Aut* spark(ing) plug. ◆**bougeoir** *nm* candlestick.

bougon, -onne [bugɔ̃, -ɔn] *a Fam* grumpy; – *nmf* grumbler, grouch. ◆**bougonner** *vi Fam* to grumble, grouch.

bougre [bugr] *nm* fellow, bloke; (*enfant*) *Péj* (little) devil. ◆**bougrement** *adv Arg* damned.

bouillabaisse [bujabɛs] *nf* fish soup.

bouillie [buji] *nf* porridge; **en b.** in a mush, mushy.

bouill/ir* [bujir] *vi* to boil; **b. à gros bouillons** to bubble, boil hard; **faire b. qch** to boil sth. ◆**—ant** *a* boiling; **b. de colère**/*etc* seething with anger/*etc.* ◆**bouilloire** *nf* kettle. ◆**bouillon** *nm* (*eau*) broth, stock; (*bulle*) bubble. ◆**bouillonner** *vi* to bubble. ◆**bouillotte** *nf* hot water bottle.

boulanger, -ère [bulɑ̃ʒe, -ɛr] *nmf* baker. ◆**boulangerie** *nf* baker's (shop).

boule [bul] *nf* (*sphère*) ball; *pl* (*jeu*) bowls; **b. de neige** snowball; **faire b. de neige** to snowball; **perdre la b.** *Fam* to go out of one's mind; **se mettre en b.** (*chat etc*) to curl up into a ball; **boules Quiès®** earplugs. ◆**boulet** *nm* (*de forçat*) ball and chain; **b. de canon** cannonball. ◆**boulette** *nf* (*de papier*) pellet; (*de viande*) meatball; (*gaffe*) *Fam* blunder.

bouleau, -x [bulo] *nm* (silver) birch.

bouledogue [buldɔg] *nm* bulldog.

boulevard [bulvar] *nm* boulevard.

boulevers/er [bulvɛrse] *vt* (*déranger*) to turn upside down; (*émouvoir*) to upset deeply, distress; (*vie de qn, pays*) to disrupt. ◆**—ant** *a* upsetting, distressing. ◆**—ement** *nm* upheaval.

boulon [bulɔ̃] *nm* bolt.

boulot, -otte [bulo, -ɔt] **1** *a* dumpy. **2** *nm* (*travail*) *Fam* work.

boum [bum] **1** *int & nm* bang. **2** *nf* (*surprise-partie*) *Fam* party.

bouquet [bukɛ] *nm* (*de fleurs*) bunch, bouquet; (*d'arbres*) clump; (*de vin*) bouquet; (*crevette*) prawn; **c'est le b.!** that's the last straw!

bouquin [bukɛ̃] *nm Fam* book. ◆**bouquiner** *vti Fam* to read. ◆**bouquiniste** *nmf* second-hand bookseller.

bourbeux, -euse [burbø, -øz] *a* muddy. ◆**bourbier** *nm* (*lieu, situation*) quagmire, morass.

bourde [burd] *nf* blunder, bloomer.

bourdon [burdɔ̃] *nm* (*insecte*) bumblebee. ◆**bourdonn/er** *vi* to buzz, hum. ◆**—ement** *nm* buzzing, humming.

bourg [bur] *nm* (small) market town. ◆**bourgade** *nf* (large) village.

bourgeois, -oise [burʒwa, -waz] *a & nmf* middle-class (person); *Péj* bourgeois. ◆**bourgeoisie** *nf* middle class, bourgeoisie.

bourgeon [burʒɔ̃] *nm* bud. ◆**bourgeonner** *vi* to bud; (*nez*) *Fam* to be pimply.

bourgmestre [burgmɛstr] *nm* (*en Belgique, Suisse*) burgomaster.

bourgogne [burgɔɲ] *nm* (*vin*) Burgundy.

bourlinguer [burlɛ̃ge] *vi* (*voyager*) *Fam* to knock about.

bourrade [burad] *nf* (*du coude*) poke.

bourrasque [burask] *nf* squall.

bourratif, -ive [buratif, -iv] *a* (*aliment*) *Fam* filling, stodgy.

bourreau, -x [buro] *nm* executioner; **b. d'enfants** child batterer; **b. de travail** workaholic.

bourrelet [burlɛ] *nm* weather strip; **b. de graisse** roll of fat, spare tyre.

bourr/er [bure] **1** *vt* to stuff, cram (full) (**de** with); (*pipe, coussin*) to fill; **b. de coups** to thrash; **b. le crâne à qn** to brainwash s.o. **2 se b.** *vpr* (*s'enivrer*) *Fam* to get plastered. ◆**—age** *nm* **b. de crâne** brainwashing.

bourrique [burik] *nf* ass.

bourru [bury] *a* surly, rough.

bourse [burs] *nf* (*sac*) purse; *Scol Univ* grant, scholarship; **la B.** the Stock Exchange; **sans b. délier** without spending a penny. ◆**boursier, -ière 1** *a* Stock Exchange-. **2** *nmf Scol Univ* grant holder, scholar.

boursouflé [bursufle] *a* (*visage etc*) puffy; (*style*) *Fig* inflated.

bousculer [buskyle] *vt* (*heurter, pousser*) to

jostle; (*presser*) to rush, push; **b. qch** (*renverser*) to knock sth over; **b. les habitudes/***etc* to turn one's habits/*etc* upside down. ◆**bousculade** *nf* rush, jostling.

bouse [buz] *nf* **b. de vache** cow dung.

bousiller [buzije] *vt Fam* to mess up, wreck.

boussole [busɔl] *nf* compass.

bout [bu] *nm* end; (*de langue, canne, doigt*) tip; (*de papier, pain, ficelle*) bit; **un b. de temps/chemin** a little while/way; **au b. d'un moment** after a moment; **à b.** exhausted; **à b. de souffle** out of breath; **à b. de bras** at arm's length; **venir à b. de** (*travail*) to get through; (*adversaire*) to get the better of; **à tout b. de champ** at every turn, every minute; **à b. portant** point-blank.

boutade [butad] *nf* (*plaisanterie*) quip, witticism.

boute-en-train [butɑ̃trɛ̃] *nm inv* (*personne*) live wire.

bouteille [butɛj] *nf* bottle; (*de gaz*) cylinder.

bouteur [butœr] *nm* bulldozer.

boutique [butik] *nf* shop; (*d'un grand couturier*) boutique. ◆**boutiquier, -ière** *nmf Péj* shopkeeper.

boutoir [butwar] *nm* **coup de b.** staggering blow.

bouton [butɔ̃] *nm* (*bourgeon*) bud; (*pustule*) pimple, spot; (*de vêtement*) button; (*poussoir*) (push-)button; (*de porte, de télévision*) knob; **b. de manchette** cuff link. ◆**b.-d'or** *nm* (*pl* **boutons-d'or**) buttercup. ◆**b.-pression** *nm* (*pl* **boutons-pression**) press-stud, *Am* snap. ◆**boutonner** *vt*, — **se b.** *vpr* to button (up). ◆**boutonneux, -euse** *a* pimply, spotty. ◆**boutonnière** *nf* buttonhole.

bouture [butyr] *nf* (*plante*) cutting.

bouvreuil [buvrœj] *nm* (*oiseau*) bullfinch.

bovin [bɔvɛ̃] *a* bovine; — *nmpl* cattle.

bowling [bolin] *nm* (tenpin) bowling; (*lieu*) bowling alley.

box, *pl* **boxes** [bɔks] *nm* (*d'écurie*) (loose) box; (*de dortoir*) cubicle; *Jur* dock; *Aut* lockup *ou* individual garage.

boxe [bɔks] *nf* boxing. ◆**boxer** *vi Sp* to box; — *vt Fam* to whack, punch. ◆**boxeur** *nm* boxer.

boyau, -x [bwajo] *nm Anat* gut; (*corde*) catgut; (*de bicyclette*) (racing) tyre *ou Am* tire.

boycott/er [bɔjkɔte] *vt* to boycott. ◆**—age** *nm* boycott.

BP [bepe] *abrév* (*boîte postale*) PO Box.

bracelet [braslɛ] *nm* bracelet, bangle; (*de montre*) strap.

braconner [brakɔne] *vi* to poach. ◆**braconnier** *nm* poacher.

brader [brade] *vt* to sell off cheaply. ◆**braderie** *nf* open-air (clearance) sale.

braguette [bragɛt] *nf* (*de pantalon*) fly, flies.

braille [braj] *nm* Braille.

brailler [braje] *vti* to bawl. ◆**braillard** *a* bawling.

braire* [brɛr] *vi* (*âne*) to bray.

braise(s) [brɛz] *nf*(*pl*) embers, live coals. ◆**braiser** [breze] *vt Culin* to braise.

brancard [brɑ̃kar] *nm* (*civière*) stretcher; (*de charrette*) shaft. ◆**brancardier** *nm* stretcher-bearer.

branche [brɑ̃ʃ] *nf* (*d'un arbre, d'une science etc*) branch; (*de compas*) leg; (*de lunettes*) side piece. ◆**branchages** *nmpl* (cut *ou* fallen) branches.

branch/er [brɑ̃ʃe] *vt Él* to plug in; (*installer*) to connect. ◆**—é** *a* (*informé*) *Fam* with it. ◆**—ement** *nm Él* connection.

brandir [brɑ̃dir] *vt* to brandish, flourish.

brandon [brɑ̃dɔ̃] *nm* (*paille, bois*) firebrand.

branle [brɑ̃l] *nm* impetus; **mettre en b.** to set in motion. ◆**b.-bas** *nm inv* turmoil. ◆**branl/er** *vi* to be shaky, shake. ◆**—ant** *a* shaky.

braqu/er [brake] **1** *vt* (*arme etc*) to point, aim; (*yeux*) to fix; **b. qn contre qn** to set *ou* turn s.o. against s.o. **2** *vti Aut* to steer, turn. ◆**—age** *nm Aut* steering; **rayon de b.** turning circle.

bras [bra] *nm* arm; **en b. de chemise** in one's shirtsleeves; **b. dessus, b. dessous** arm in arm; **sur les b.** *Fig* on one's hands; **son b. droit** *Fig* his right-hand man; **à b. ouverts** with open arms; **à tour de b.** with all one's might; **faire le b. d'honneur** *Fam* to make an obscene gesture; **à b.-le-corps** round the waist. ◆**brassard** *nm* armband. ◆**brassée** *nf* armful. ◆**brassière** *nf* (*de bébé*) vest, *Am* undershirt.

brasier [brazje] *nm* inferno, blaze.

brasse [bras] *nf* (*nage*) breaststroke; (*mesure*) fathom; **b. papillon** butterfly stroke.

brasser [brase] *vt* to mix; (*bière*) to brew. ◆**brassage** *nm* mixture; brewing. ◆**brasserie** *nf* (*usine*) brewery; (*café*) brasserie. ◆**brasseur** *nm* **b. d'affaires** *Péj* big businessman.

bravache [bravaʃ] *nm* braggart.

bravade [bravad] *nf* **par b.** out of bravado.

brave [brav] *a* & *nm* (*hardi*) brave (man); (*honnête*) good (man). ◆**bravement** *adv* bravely. ◆**braver** *vt* to defy; (*danger*) to brave. ◆**bravoure** *nf* bravery.

bravo [bravo] *int* well done, bravo, good show; – *nm* cheer.

break [brɛk] *nm* estate car, *Am* station wagon.

brebis [brɔbi] *nf* ewe; **b. galeuse** black sheep.

brèche [brɛʃ] *nf* breach, gap; **battre en b.** (*attaquer*) to attack (mercilessly).

bredouille [brɔduj] *a* **rentrer b.** to come back empty-handed.

bredouiller [brɔduje] *vti* to mumble.

bref, brève [brɛf, brɛv] *a* brief, short; – *adv* (**enfin**) **b.** in a word.

breloque [brɔlɔk] *nf* charm, trinket.

Brésil [brezil] *nm* Brazil. ◆**brésilien, -ienne** *a* & *nmf* Brazilian.

Bretagne [brɔtaɲ] *nf* Brittany. ◆**breton, -onne** *a* & *nmf* Breton.

bretelle [brɔtɛl] *nf* strap; (*voie de raccordement*) *Aut* access road; *pl* (*pour pantalon*) braces, *Am* suspenders.

breuvage [brœvaʒ] *nm* drink, brew.

brève [brɛv] *voir* **bref.**

brevet [brɔvɛ] *nm* diploma; **b. (d'invention)** patent. ◆**brevet/er** *vt* to patent. ◆**–é** *a* (*technicien*) qualified.

bréviaire [brevjɛr] *nm* breviary.

bribes [brib] *nfpl* scraps, bits.

bric-à-brac [brikabrak] *nm inv* bric-à-brac, jumble, junk.

brick [brik] *nm* (*de lait, jus d'orange etc*) carton.

bricole [brikɔl] *nf* (*objet, futilité*) trifle. ◆**bricol/er** *vi* to do odd jobs; – *vt* (*réparer*) to patch up; (*fabriquer*) to put together. ◆**–age** *nm* (*petits travaux*) odd jobs; (*passe-temps*) do-it-yourself; **salon/rayon du b.** do-it-yourself exhibition/department. ◆**–eur, -euse** *nmf* handyman, handywoman.

bride [brid] *nf* (*de cheval*) bridle; **à b. abattue** at full gallop. ◆**brider** *vt* (*cheval*) to bridle; (*personne, désir*) to curb; *Culin* to truss; **avoir les yeux bridés** to have slit eyes.

bridge [bridʒ] *nm* (*jeu*) bridge.

brièvement [brievmɑ̃] *adv* briefly. ◆**brièveté** *nf* brevity.

brigade [brigad] *nf* (*de gendarmerie*) squad; *Mil* brigade; **b. des mœurs** vice squad. ◆**brigadier** *nm* police sergeant; *Mil* corporal.

brigand [brigɑ̃] *nm* robber; (*enfant*) rascal.

briguer [brige] *vt* to covet; (*faveurs, suffrages*) to court.

brillant [brijɑ̃] *a* (*luisant*) shining; (*astiqué*) shiny; (*couleur*) bright; (*magnifique*) *Fig* brilliant; – *nm* shine; brightness; *Fig* brilliance; (*diamant*) diamond. ◆**brillamment** *adv* brilliantly.

briller [brije] *vi* to shine; **faire b.** (*meuble*) to polish (up).

brimer [brime] *vt* to bully. ◆**brimade** *nm* *Scol* bullying, ragging, *Am* hazing; *Fig* vexation.

brin [brɛ̃] *nm* (*d'herbe*) blade; (*de corde, fil*) strand; (*de muguet*) spray; **un b. de** *Fig* a bit of.

brindille [brɛ̃dij] *nf* twig.

bringue [brɛ̃g] *nf* **faire la b.** *Fam* to have a binge.

bringuebaler [brɛ̃gbale] *vi* to wobble about.

brio [brijo] *nm* (*virtuosité*) brilliance.

brioche [brijɔʃ] *nf* **1** brioche (*light sweet bun*). **2** (*ventre*) *Fam* paunch.

brique [brik] *nf* brick. ◆**briquette** *nf* (*aggloméré*) breezeblock.

briquer [brike] *vt* to polish (up).

briquet [brikɛ] *nm* (*cigarette*) lighter.

brise [briz] *nf* breeze.

bris/er [brize] *vt* to break; (*en morceaux*) to smash, break; (*espoir, carrière*) to shatter; (*fatiguer*) to exhaust; – **se b.** *vpr* to break. ◆**–ants** *nmpl* reefs. ◆**brise-lames** *nm inv* breakwater.

britannique [britanik] *a* British; – *nmf* Briton; **les Britanniques** the British.

broc [bro] *nm* pitcher, jug.

brocanteur, -euse [brɔkɑ̃tœr, -øz] *nmf* secondhand dealer (*in furniture etc*).

broche [brɔʃ] *nf* *Culin* spit; (*bijou*) brooch; *Méd* pin. ◆**brochette** *nf* (*tige*) skewer; (*plat*) kebab.

broché [brɔʃe] *a* **livre b.** paperback.

brochet [brɔʃɛ] *nm* (*poisson*) pike.

brochure [brɔʃyr] *nf* brochure, booklet, pamphlet.

broder [brɔde] *vt* to embroider (**de** with). ◆**broderie** *nf* embroidery.

broncher [brɔ̃ʃe] *vi* (*bouger*) to budge; (*reculer*) to flinch; (*regimber*) to balk.

bronches [brɔ̃ʃ] *nfpl* bronchial tubes. ◆**bronchite** *nf* bronchitis.

bronze [brɔ̃z] *nm* bronze.

bronz/er [brɔ̃ze] *vt* to tan; – *vi*, – **se b.** *vpr* to get (sun)tanned; **se (faire) b.** to sunbathe. ◆**–age** *nm* (sun)tan, sunburn.

brosse [brɔs] *nf* brush; **b. à dents** toothbrush; **cheveux en b.** crew cut. ◆**brosser** *vt* to brush; **b. un tableau de** to give an outline of; **se b. les dents/les cheveux** to brush one's teeth/one's hair.

brouette [bruɛt] *nf* wheelbarrow.

brouhaha [bruaa] *nm* hubbub.

brouillard [brujar] *nm* fog; **il fait du b.** it's foggy.

brouille [bruj] *nf* disagreement, quarrel. ◆**brouiller 1** *vt* (*papiers, idées etc*) to mix up; (*vue*) to blur; (*œufs*) to scramble; *Rad* to jam; — **se b.** *vpr* (*idées*) to be *ou* get confused; (*temps*) to cloud over; (*vue*) to blur. **2** *vt* (*amis*) to cause a split between; — **se b.** *vpr* to fall out (**avec** with). ◆**brouillon, -onne 1** *a* confused. **2** *nm* rough draft.

broussailles [brusaj] *nfpl* brushwood.

brousse [brus] *nf* **la b.** the bush.

brouter [brute] *vti* to graze.

broyer [brwaje] *vt* to grind; (*doigt, bras*) to crush; **b. du noir** to be (down) in the dumps.

bru [bry] *nf* daughter-in-law.

brugnon [bryɲɔ̃] *nm* (*fruit*) nectarine.

bruine [bruin] *nf* drizzle. ◆**bruiner** *v imp* to drizzle.

bruissement [bruismɑ̃] *nm* (*de feuilles*) rustle, rustling.

bruit [brui] *nm* noise, sound; (*nouvelle*) rumour; **faire du b.** to be noisy, make a noise. ◆**bruitage** *nm Cin* sound effects.

brûle-pourpoint (à) [abrylpurpwɛ̃] *adv* point-blank.

brûl/er [bryle] *vt* to burn; (*consommer*) to use up, burn; (*signal, station*) to go through (without stopping); **b. un feu (rouge)** to jump *ou* go through the lights; **ce désir le brûlait** this desire consumed him; – *vi* to burn; **b. (d'envie) de faire** to be burning to do; **ça brûle** (*temps*) it's baking *ou* scorching; — **se b.** *vpr* to burn oneself. ◆**—ant** *a* (*objet, soleil*) burning (hot); (*sujet*) *Fig* red-hot. ◆**—é 1** *nm* **odeur de b.** smell of burning. **2** *a* **cerveau b., tête brûlée** hothead. ◆**brûlure** *nf* burn; **brûlures d'estomac** heartburn.

brume [brym] *nf* mist, haze. ◆**brumeux, -euse** *a* misty, hazy; (*obscur*) *Fig* hazy.

brun, brune [brœ̃, bryn] *a* brown; (*cheveux*) dark, brown; (*personne*) dark-haired; – *nm* (*couleur*) brown; – *nmf* dark-haired person. ◆**brunette** *nf* brunette. ◆**brunir** *vt* (*peau*) to tan; – *vi* to turn brown; (*cheveux*) to go darker.

brushing [brœʃiŋ] *nm* blow-dry.

brusque [brysk] *a* (*manière etc*) abrupt, blunt; (*subit*) sudden, abrupt. ◆**brusquement** *adv* suddenly, abruptly. ◆**brusquer** *vt* to rush. ◆**brusquerie** *nf* abruptness, bluntness.

brut [bryt] *a* (*pétrole*) crude; (*diamant*) rough; (*sucre*) unrefined; (*soie*) raw; (*poids*) & *Fin* gross.

brutal, -aux [brytal, -o] *a* (*violent*) savage, brutal; (*franchise, réponse*) crude, blunt; (*fait*) stark. ◆**brutaliser** *vt* to ill-treat. ◆**brutalité** *nf* (*violence, acte*) brutality. ◆**brute** *nf* brute.

Bruxelles [brysɛl] *nm ou f* Brussels.

bruyant [bruijɑ̃] *a* noisy. ◆**bruyamment** *adv* noisily.

bruyère [bryjɛr] *nf* (*plante*) heather; (*terrain*) heath.

bu [by] *voir* **boire.**

buanderie [buɑ̃dri] *nf* (*lieu*) laundry.

bûche [byʃ] *nf* log; **ramasser une b.** *Fam* to come a cropper, *Am* take a spill. ◆**bûcher 1** *nm* (*local*) woodshed; (*supplice*) stake. **2** *vt* (*étudier*) *Fam* to slog away at. ◆**bûcheron** *nm* woodcutter, lumberjack.

budget [bydʒɛ] *nm* budget. ◆**budgétaire** *a* budgetary; (*année*) financial.

buée [bue] *nf* condensation, mist.

buffet [byfɛ] *nm* (*armoire*) sideboard; (*table, restaurant, repas*) buffet.

buffle [byfl] *nm* buffalo.

buis [bui] *nm* (*arbre*) box; (*bois*) boxwood.

buisson [buisɔ̃] *nm* bush.

buissonnière [buisɔnjɛr] *af* **faire l'école b.** to play truant *ou Am* hookey.

bulbe [bylb] *nm* bulb. ◆**bulbeux, -euse** *a* bulbous.

Bulgarie [bylgari] *nf* Bulgaria. ◆**bulgare** *a & nmf* Bulgarian.

bulldozer [byldozœr] *nm* bulldozer.

bulle [byl] *nf* **1** bubble; (*de bande dessinée*) balloon. **2** (*décret du pape*) bull.

bulletin [byltɛ̃] *nm* (*communiqué, revue*) bulletin; (*de la météo*) & *Scol* report; (*de bagages*) ticket, *Am* check; **b. de paie** pay slip; **b. de vote** ballot paper.

buraliste [byralist] *nmf* (*à la poste*) clerk; (*au tabac*) tobacconist.

bureau, -x [byro] *nm* **1** (*table*) desk. **2** (*lieu*) office; (*comité*) board; **b. de change** bureau de change; **b. de location** *Th Cin* box office; **b. de tabac** tobacconist's (shop). ◆**bureaucrate** *nmf* bureaucrat. ◆**bureaucratie** [-asi] *nf* bureaucracy. ◆**bureautique** *nf* office automation.

burette [byrɛt] *nf* oilcan; *Culin* cruet.

burlesque [byrlɛsk] *a* (*idée etc*) ludicrous; (*genre*) burlesque.

bus [bys] *nm Fam* bus.

bus [by] *voir* **boire.**

busqué [byske] *a* (*nez*) hooked.

buste [byst] *nm* (*torse, sculpture*) bust. ◆**bustier** *nm* long-line bra(ssiere).

but [by(t)] *nm* (*dessein, objectif*) aim, goal;

(*cible*) target; *Fb* goal; **de b. en blanc** point-blank; **aller droit au b.** to go straight to the point; **j'ai pour b. de ...** my aim is to ... .

but[2] [by] *voir* **boire**.

butane [bytan] *nm* (*gaz*) butane.

but/er [byte] **1** *vi* **b. contre** to stumble over; (*difficulté*) *Fig* to come up against. **2 se b.** *vpr* (*s'entêter*) to get obstinate. ◆—**é** *a* obstinate.

butin [bytɛ̃] *nm* loot, booty.

butiner [bytine] *vi* (*abeille*) to gather nectar.

butoir [bytwar] *nm* Rail buffer; (*de porte*) stop(per).

butor [bytɔr] *nm* Péj lout, oaf, boor.

butte [byt] *nf* hillock, mound; **en b. à** (*calomnie etc*) exposed to.

buvable [byvabl] *a* drinkable. ◆**buveur, -euse** *nmf* drinker.

buvard [byvar] *a & nm* (*papier*) **b.** blotting paper.

buvette [byvɛt] *nf* refreshment bar.

C

C, c [se] *nm* C, c

c *abrév* centime.

c' [s] *voir* **ce**[1].

ça [sa] *pron dém* (*abrév de* **cela**) (*pour désigner*) that; (*plus près*) this; (*sujet indéfini*) it, that; **ça m'amuse que ...** it amuses me that ... ; **où/quand/comment/etc ça?** where?/when?/how?/etc; **ça va (bien)?** how's it going?; **ça va!** fine!, OK!; **ça alors!** (*surprise, indignation*) well I never!, how about that!; **c'est ça** that's right; **et avec ça?** (*dans un magasin*) anything else?

çà [sa] *adv* **çà et là** here and there.

caban [kabɑ̃] *nm* (*veste*) reefer.

cabane [kaban] *nf* hut, cabin; (*à outils*) shed; (*à lapins*) hutch.

cabaret [kabarɛ] *nm* night club, cabaret.

cabas [kaba] *nm* shopping bag.

cabillaud [kabijo] *nm* (*fresh*) cod.

cabine [kabin] *nf Nau Av* cabin; *Tél* phone booth, phone box; (*de camion*) cab; (*d'ascenseur*) car, cage; **c. (de bain)** beach hut; (*à la piscine*) cubicle. **c. (de pilotage)** cockpit; (*d'un grand avion*) flight deck; **c. d'essayage** fitting room; **c. d'aiguillage** signal box.

cabinet [kabinɛ] *nm* (*local*) *Méd* surgery, *Am* office; (*d'avocat*) office, chambers; (*clientèle de médecin ou d'avocat*) practice; *Pol* cabinet; *pl* (*toilettes*) toilet; **c. de toilette** bathroom, toilet; **c. de travail** study.

câble [kabl] *nm* cable; (*cordage*) rope; **la télévision par c.** cable television; **le c.** *TV* cable. ◆**câbler** *vt* (*message*) to cable; **être câblé** *TV* to have cable.

caboche [kabɔʃ] *nf* (*tête*) *Fam* nut, noddle.

cabosser [kabɔse] *vt* to dent.

caboteur [kabɔtœr] *nm* (*bateau*) coaster.

cabotin, -ine [kabɔtɛ̃, -in] *nmf Th* ham actor, ham actress; *Fig* play-actor. ◆**cabotinage** *nm* histrionics, play-acting.

cabrer (se) [səkabre] *vpr* (*cheval*) to rear (up); (*personne*) to rebel.

cabri [kabri] *nm* (*chevreau*) kid.

cabrioles [kabriɔl] *nfpl* **faire des c.** (*sauts*) to cavort, caper.

cabriolet [kabriɔlɛ] *nm Aut* convertible.

cacah(o)uète [kakawɛt] *nf* peanut.

cacao [kakao] *nm* (*boisson*) cocoa.

cacatoès [kakatɔɛs] *nm* cockatoo.

cachalot [kaʃalo] *nm* sperm whale.

cache-cache [kaʃkaʃ] *nm inv* hide-and-seek. ◆**c.-col** *nm inv*, ◆**c.-nez** *nm inv* scarf, muffler. ◆**c.-sexe** *nm inv* G-string.

cachemire [kaʃmir] *nm* (*tissu*) cashmere.

cacher [kaʃe] *vt* to hide, conceal (à from); **je ne cache pas que ...** I don't hide the fact that ... ; **c. la lumière à qn** to stand in s.o.'s light; — **se c.** *vpr* to hide. ◆**cachette** *nf* hiding place; **en c.** in secret; **en c. de qn** without s.o. knowing.

cachet [kaʃɛ] *nm* (*sceau*) seal; (*de la poste*) postmark; (*comprimé*) tablet; (*d'acteur etc*) fee; *Fig* distinctive character. ◆**cacheter** *vt* to seal.

cachot [kaʃo] *nm* dungeon.

cachotteries [kaʃɔtri] *nfpl* secretiveness; (*petits secrets*) little mysteries. ◆**cachottier, -ière** *a & nmf* secretive (person).

cacophonie [kakɔfɔni] *nf* cacophony.

cactus [kaktys] *nm* cactus.

cadastre [kadastr] *nm* (*registre*) land register.

cadavre [kadɑvr] *nm* corpse. ◆**cadavéri-**

que *a* (*teint etc*) cadaverous; **rigidité c.** rigor mortis.

caddie® [kadi] *nm* supermarket trolly *ou Am* cart.

cadeau, -x [kado] *nm* present, gift.

cadenas [kadnɑ] *nm* padlock. ◆**cadenasser** *vt* to padlock.

cadence [kadɑ̃s] *nf* rhythm; *Mus* cadence; (*taux, vitesse*) rate; **en c.** in time. ◆**cadencé** *a* rhythmical.

cadet, -ette [kadɛ, -ɛt] *a* (*de deux frères etc*) younger; (*de plus de deux*) youngest; − *nmf* (*enfant*) younger (child); youngest (child); *Sp* junior; **c'est mon c.** he's my junior.

cadran [kadrɑ̃] *nm* (*de téléphone etc*) dial; (*de montre*) face; **c. solaire** sundial; **faire le tour du c.** to sleep round the clock.

cadre [kɑdr] *nm* **1** (*de photo, vélo etc*) frame; (*décor*) setting; (*sur un imprimé*) box; **dans le c. de** (*limites, contexte*) within the framework *ou* scope of, as part of. **2** (*chef*) *Com* executive, manager; *pl* (*personnel*) *Mil* officers; *Com* management, managers.

cadr/er [kɑdre] *vi* to tally (**avec** with); − *vt* (*image*) *Cin Phot* to centre. ◆**−eur** *nm* cameraman.

caduc, -uque [kadyk] *a* (*usage*) obsolete; *Bot* deciduous; *Jur* null and void.

cafard, -arde [kafar, -ard] **1** *nmf* (*espion*) sneak. **2** *nm* (*insecte*) cockroach; **avoir le c.** to be in the dumps; **ça me donne le c.** it depresses me. ◆**cafardeux, -euse** *a* (*personne*) in the dumps; (*qui donne le cafard*) depressing.

café [kafe] *nm* coffee; (*bar*) café; **c. au lait, c. crème** white coffee, coffee with milk; **c. noir, c. nature** black coffee; **tasse de c.** cup of black coffee. ◆**caféine** *nf* caffeine. ◆**cafétéria** *nf* cafeteria. ◆**cafetier** *nm* café owner. ◆**cafetière** *nf* percolator, coffeepot.

cafouiller [kafuje] *vi Fam* to make a mess (of things). ◆**cafouillage** *nm Fam* mess, muddle, snafu.

cage [kaʒ] *nf* cage; (*d'escalier*) well; (*d'ascenseur*) shaft; **c. des buts** *Fb* goal (area).

cageot [kaʒo] *nm* crate.

cagibi [kaʒibi] *nm* (storage) room, cubbyhole.

cagneux, -euse [kaɲø, -øz] *a* knock-kneed.

cagnotte [kaɲɔt] *nf* (*tirelire*) kitty.

cagoule [kagul] *nf* (*de bandit, pénitent*) hood.

cahier [kaje] *nm* (*carnet*) (note)book; *Scol* exercise book.

cahin-caha [kaɛ̃kaa] *adv* **aller c.-caha** to jog along (with ups and downs).

cahot [kao] *nm* jolt, bump. ◆**cahot/er** *vt* to jolt, bump; − *vi* (*véhicule*) to jolt along. ◆**−ant** *a*, ◆**cahoteux, -euse** *a* bumpy.

caïd [kaid] *nm Fam* big shot, leader.

caille [kɑj] *nf* (*oiseau*) quail.

cailler [kaje] *vti*, − **se c.** *vpr* (*sang*) to clot, congeal; (*lait*) to curdle; **faire c.** (*lait*) to curdle; **ça caille** *Fam* it's freezing cold. ◆**caillot** *nm* (blood) clot.

caillou, -x [kaju] *nm* stone; (*galet*) pebble. ◆**caillouté** *a* gravelled. ◆**caillouteux, -euse** *a* stony.

caisse [kɛs] *nf* (*boîte*) case, box; (*cageot*) crate; (*guichet*) cash desk, pay desk; (*de supermarché*) checkout; (*fonds*) fund; (*bureau*) (paying-in) office; *Mus* drum; *Aut* body; **c. (enregistreuse)** cash register, till; **c. d'épargne** savings bank; **de c.** (*livre, recettes*) cash-. ◆**caissier, -ière** *nmf* cashier; (*de supermarché*) checkout assistant.

caisson [kɛsɔ̃] *nm* (*de plongeur*) & *Mil* caisson.

cajoler [kaʒɔle] *vt* (*câliner*) to pamper, pet, cosset. ◆**cajolerie(s)** *nf*(*pl*) pampering.

cajou [kaʒu] *nm* (*noix*) cashew.

cake [kɛk] *nm* fruit cake.

calamité [kalamite] *nf* calamity.

calandre [kalɑ̃dr] *nf Aut* radiator grille.

calcaire [kalkɛr] *a* (*terrain*) chalky; (*eau*) hard; − *nm Géol* limestone.

calciné [kalsine] *a* charred, burnt to a cinder.

calcium [kalsjɔm] *nm* calcium.

calcul [kalkyl] *nm* **1** calculation; (*estimation*) calculation, reckoning; (*discipline*) arithmetic; (*différentiel*) calculus. **2** *Méd* stone. ◆**calcul/er** *vt* (*compter*) to calculate, reckon; (*évaluer, combiner*) to calculate. ◆**−é** *a* (*risque etc*) calculated. ◆**calculateur** *nm* calculator, computer. ◆**calculatrice** *nf* (*ordinateur*) calculator.

cale [kal] *nf* **1** (*pour maintenir*) wedge. **2** *Nau* hold; **c. sèche** dry dock.

calé [kale] *a Fam* (*instruit*) clever (**en qch** at sth); (*difficile*) tough.

caleçon [kalsɔ̃] *nm* underpants; **c. de bain** bathing trunks.

calembour [kalɑ̃bur] *nm* pun.

calendrier [kalɑ̃drije] *nm* (*mois et jours*) calendar; (*programme*) timetable.

cale-pied [kalpje] *nm* (*de bicyclette*) toe-clip.

calepin [kalpɛ̃] *nm* (pocket) notebook.

caler [kale] **1** *vt* (*meuble etc*) to wedge (up); (*appuyer*) to prop (up). **2** *vt* (*moteur*) to stall; – *vi* to stall; (*abandonner*) *Fam* give up.

calfeutrer [kalføtre] *vt* (*avec du bourrelet*) to draughtproof; **se c. (chez soi)** to shut oneself away, hole up.

calibre [kalibr] *nm* (*diamètre*) calibre; (*d'œuf*) grade; **de ce c.** (*bêtise etc*) of this degree. ◆**calibrer** *vt* (*œufs*) to grade.

calice [kalis] *nm* (*vase*) *Rel* chalice.

calicot [kaliko] *nm* (*tissu*) calico.

califourchon (à) [akalifurʃɔ̃] *adv* astride; **se mettre à c. sur** to straddle.

câlin [kalɛ̃] *a* endearing, cuddly. ◆**câliner** *vt* (*cajoler*) to make a fuss of; (*caresser*) to cuddle. ◆**câlineries** *nfpl* endearing ways.

calleux, -euse [kalø, -øz] *a* callous, horny.

calligraphie [kaligrafi] *nf* calligraphy.

calme [kalm] *a* calm; (*flegmatique*) calm, cool; (*journée etc*) quiet, calm; – *nm* calm(ness); **du c.!** keep quiet!; (*pas de panique*) keep calm!; **dans le c.** (*travailler, étudier*) in peace and quiet. ◆**calm/er** *vt* (*douleur*) to soothe; (*inquiétude*) to calm; (*ardeur*) to damp(en); **c. qn** to calm s.o. (down); – **se c.** *vpr* to calm down. ◆**—ant** *nm* sedative; **sous calmants** under sedation.

calomnie [kalɔmni] *nf* slander; (*par écrit*) libel. ◆**calomnier** *vt* to slander; to libel. ◆**calomnieux, -euse** *a* slanderous; libellous.

calorie [kalɔri] *nf* calorie.

calorifère [kalɔrifɛr] *nm* stove.

calorifuge [kalɔrifyʒ] *a* (heat-)insulating. ◆**calorifuger** *vt* to lag.

calot [kalo] *nm* *Mil* forage cap.

calotte [kalɔt] *nf* *Rel* skull cap; (*gifle*) *Fam* slap; **c. glaciaire** icecap.

calque [kalk] *nm* (*dessin*) tracing; (*imitation*) (exact *ou* carbon) copy; **(papier-)c.** tracing paper. ◆**calquer** *vt* to trace; to copy; **c. sur** to model on.

calumet [kalymɛ] *nm* **c. de la paix** peace pipe.

calvaire [kalvɛr] *nm* *Rel* calvary; *Fig* agony.

calvitie [kalvisi] *nf* baldness.

camarade [kamarad] *nmf* friend, chum; *Pol* comrade; **c. de jeu** playmate; **c. d'atelier** workmate. ◆**camaraderie** *nf* friendship, companionship.

cambouis [kãbwi] *nm* grease, (engine) oil.

cambrer [kãbre] *vt* to arch; **c. les reins** *ou* **le buste** to throw out one's chest; – **se c.** *vpr* to throw back one's shoulders. ◆**cambrure** *nf* curve; (*de pied*) arch, instep.

cambriol/er [kãbrijɔle] *vt* to burgle, *Am* burglarize. ◆**—age** *nm* burglary. ◆**—eur, -euse** *nmf* burglar.

came [kam] *nf* *Tech* cam; **arbre à cames** camshaft.

camée [kame] *nm* (*pierre*) cameo.

caméléon [kameleɔ̃] *nm* (*reptile*) chameleon.

camélia [kamelja] *nm* *Bot* camellia.

camelot [kamlo] *nm* street hawker. ◆**camelote** *nf* cheap goods, junk.

camembert [kamãbɛr] *nm* Camembert (cheese).

camer (se) [səkame] *vpr* *Fam* to get high (on drugs).

caméra [kamera] *nf* (TV *ou* film) camera. ◆**caméraman** *nm* (*pl* **-mans** *ou* **-men**) cameraman.

camion [kamjɔ̃] *nm* lorry, *Am* truck. ◆**c.-benne** *nm* (*pl* **camions-bennes**) dustcart, *Am* garbage truck. ◆**c.-citerne** *nm* (*pl* **camions-citernes**) tanker, *Am* tank truck. ◆**camionnage** *nm* (road) haulage, *Am* trucking. ◆**camionnette** *nf* van. ◆**camionneur** *nm* (*entrepreneur*) haulage contractor, *Am* trucker; (*conducteur*) lorry *ou* *Am* truck driver.

camisole [kamizɔl] *nf* **c. de force** straitjacket.

camomille [kamɔmij] *nf* *Bot* camomile; (*tisane*) camomile tea.

camoufl/er [kamufle] *vt* to camouflage. ◆**—age** *nm* camouflage.

camp [kã] *nm* camp; **feu de c.** campfire; **lit de c.** camp bed; **c. de concentration** concentration camp; **dans mon c.** (*jeu*) on my side; **ficher** *ou* **foutre le c.** *Arg* to clear off. ◆**camp/er** *vi* to camp; – *vt* (*personnage*) to portray (boldly); (*chapeau etc*) to plant boldly; – **se c.** *vpr* to plant oneself (boldly) (**devant** in front of). ◆**—ement** *nm* encampment, camp. ◆**—eur, -euse** *nmf* camper. ◆**camping** *nm* camping; (*terrain*) camp(ing) site. ◆**camping-car** *nm* camper.

campagne [kãpaɲ] *nf* **1** country(side); **à la c.** in the country. **2** (*électorale, militaire etc*) campaign. ◆**campagnard, -arde** *a* country-; – *nm* countryman; – *nf* countrywoman.

campanile [kãpanil] *nm* belltower.

camphre [kãfr] *nm* camphor.

campus [kãpys] *nm* *Univ* campus.

camus [kamy] *a* (*personne*) snub-nosed; **nez c.** snub nose.

Canada [kanada] *nm* Canada. ◆**canadien, -ienne** *a* & *nmf* Canadian; – *nf* fur-lined jacket.

canaille [kanɑj] *nf* rogue, scoundrel; – *a* vulgar, cheap.

canal, -aux [kanal, -o] *nm* (*artificiel*) canal; (*bras de mer*) & *TV* channel; (*conduite*) & *Anat* duct; **par le c. de** via, through. ◆**canalisation** *nf* (*de gaz etc*) mains. ◆**canaliser** *vt* (*rivière etc*) to canalize; (*diriger*) *Fig* to channel.

canapé [kanape] *nm* **1** (*siège*) sofa, couch, settee. **2** (*tranche de pain*) canapé.

canard [kanar] *nm* **1** duck; (*mâle*) drake. **2** *Mus* false note. **3** (*journal*) *Péj* rag. ◆**canarder** *vt* (*faire feu sur*) to fire at *ou* on.

canari [kanari] *nm* canary.

cancans [kɑ̃kɑ̃] *nmpl* (malicious) gossip. ◆**cancaner** *vi* to gossip. ◆**cancanier, -ière** *a* gossipy.

cancer [kɑ̃ser] *nm* cancer; **le C.** (*signe*) Cancer. ◆**cancéreux, -euse** *a* cancerous; – *nmf* cancer patient. ◆**cancérigène** *a* carcinogenic. ◆**cancérologue** *nmf* cancer specialist.

cancre [kɑ̃kr] *nm* *Scol Péj* dunce.

cancrelat [kɑ̃krəla] *nm* cockroach.

candélabre [kɑ̃delɑbr] *nm* candelabra.

candeur [kɑ̃dœr] *nf* innocence, artlessness. ◆**candide** *a* artless, innocent.

candidat, -ate [kɑ̃dida, -at] *nmf* candidate; (*à un poste*) applicant, candidate; **être** *ou* **se porter c. à** to apply for. ◆**candidature** *nf* application; *Pol* candidacy; **poser sa c.** to apply (à for).

cane [kan] *nf* (female) duck. ◆**caneton** *nm* duckling.

canette [kanet] *nf* **1** (*de bière*) (small) bottle. **2** (*bobine*) spool.

canevas [kanva] *nm* (*toile*) canvas; (*ébauche*) framework, outline.

caniche [kaniʃ] *nm* poodle.

canicule [kanikyl] *nf* scorching heat; (*période*) dog days.

canif [kanif] *nm* penknife.

canine [kanin] **1** *af* (*espèce, race*) canine; **exposition c.** dog show. **2** *nf* (*dent*) canine.

caniveau, -x [kanivo] *nm* gutter (*in street*).

canne [kan] *nf* (walking) stick; (*à sucre, de bambou*) cane; (*de roseau*) reed; **c. à pêche** fishing rod.

cannelle [kanel] *nf* *Bot Culin* cinnamon.

cannelure [kanlyr] *nf* groove; *Archit* flute.

cannette [kanet] *nf* = **canette**.

cannibale [kanibal] *nmf* & *a* cannibal. ◆**cannibalisme** *nm* cannibalism.

canoë [kanɔe] *nm* canoe; *Sp* canoeing. ◆**canoéiste** *nmf* canoeist.

canon [kanɔ̃] *nm* **1** (big) gun; *Hist* cannon; (*de fusil etc*) barrel; **c. lisse** smooth bore; **chair à c.** cannon fodder. **2** (*règle*) canon. ◆**canoniser** *vt* to canonize. ◆**canonnade** *nf* gunfire. ◆**canonnier** *nm* gunner.

cañon [kanɔ̃] *nm* canyon.

canot [kano] *nm* boat; **c. de sauvetage** lifeboat; **c. pneumatique** rubber dinghy. ◆**canot/er** *vi* to boat, go boating. ◆**—age** *nm* boating.

cantaloup [kɑ̃talu] *nm* (*melon*) cantaloup(e).

cantate [kɑ̃tat] *nf* *Mus* cantata.

cantatrice [kɑ̃tatris] *nf* opera singer.

cantine [kɑ̃tin] *nf* **1** (*réfectoire*) canteen; **manger à la c.** *Scol* to have school dinners. **2** (*coffre*) tin trunk.

cantique [kɑ̃tik] *nm* hymn.

canton [kɑ̃tɔ̃] *nm* (*en France*) district (*division d'arrondissement*); (*en Suisse*) canton. ◆**cantonal, -aux** *a* divisional; cantonal.

cantonade (à la) [alakɑ̃tɔnad] *adv* (*parler etc*) to all and sundry, to everyone in general.

cantonn/er [kɑ̃tɔne] *vt* *Mil* to billet; (*confiner*) to confine; – *vi* *Mil* to be billeted; **— se c.** *vpr* to confine oneself (**dans** to). ◆**—ement** *nm* (*lieu*) billet, quarters.

cantonnier [kɑ̃tɔnje] *nm* road mender.

canular [kanylar] *nm* practical joke, hoax.

canyon [kanɔ̃] *nm* canyon.

caoutchouc [kautʃu] *nm* rubber; (*élastique*) rubber band; *pl* (*chaussures*) galoshes; **en c.** (*balle etc*) rubber-; **c. mousse** foam. ◆**caoutchouter** *vt* to rubberize. ◆**caoutchouteux, -euse** *a* rubbery.

CAP [seape] *nm* *abrév* (*certificat d'aptitude professionnelle*) technical and vocational diploma.

cap [kap] *nm* *Géog* cape, headland; *Nau* course; **mettre le c. sur** to steer a course for; **franchir** *ou* **doubler le c. de** (*difficulté*) to get over the worst of; **franchir** *ou* **doubler le c. de la trentaine**/*etc* to turn thirty/*etc*.

capable [kapabl] *a* capable, able; **c. de faire** able to do, capable of doing. ◆**capacité** *nf* ability, capacity; (*contenance*) capacity.

cape [kap] *nf* cape; (*grande*) cloak.

CAPES [kapes] *nm* *abrév* (*certificat d'aptitude professionnelle à l'enseignement secondaire*) teaching diploma.

capillaire [kapiler] *a* (*huile, lotion*) hair-.

capitaine [kapiten] *nm* captain.

capital, -ale, -aux [kapital, -o] **1** *a* major, fundamental, capital; (*peine*) capital; (*péché*) deadly. **2** (*lettre*) capital; – *nf* (*lettre, ville*) capital. **3** *nm* & *nmpl* *Fin* capital. ◆**capitaliser** *vt* (*accumuler*) to build up; – *vi* to save up. ◆**capitalisme** *nm* capitalism. ◆**capitaliste** a & nmf capitalist.

capiteux, -euse [kapitø, -øz] a (vin, parfum) heady.

capitonn/er [kapitɔne] vt to pad, upholster. ◆**—age** nm (garniture) padding, upholstery.

capituler [kapityle] vi to surrender, capitulate. ◆**capitulation** nf surrender, capitulation.

caporal, -aux [kapɔral, -o] nm corporal.

capot [kapo] nm Aut bonnet, Am hood.

capote [kapɔt] nf Aut hood, Am (convertible) top; Mil greatcoat; **c. (anglaise)** (préservatif) Fam condom. ◆**capoter** vi Aut Av to overturn.

câpre [kɑpr] nf Bot Culin caper.

caprice [kapris] nm (passing) whim, caprice. ◆**capricieux, -euse** a capricious.

Capricorne [kaprikɔrn] nm **le C.** (signe) Capricorn.

capsule [kapsyl] nf (spatiale) & Méd etc capsule; (de bouteille, pistolet d'enfant) cap.

capter [kapte] vt (faveur etc) to win; (attention) to capture, win; (eau) to draw off; Rad to pick up.

captif, -ive [kaptif, -iv] a & nmf captive. ◆**captiver** vt to captivate, fascinate. ◆**captivité** nf captivity.

capture [kaptyr] nf capture; catch. ◆**capturer** vt (criminel, navire) to capture; (animal) to catch, capture.

capuche [kapyʃ] nf hood. ◆**capuchon** nm hood; (de moine) cowl; (pèlerine) hooded (rain)coat; (de stylo) cap, top.

capucine [kapysin] nf (plante) nasturtium.

caquet [kakɛ] nm (bavardage) cackle. ◆**caquet/er** vi (poule, personne) to cackle. ◆**—age** nm cackle.

car [kar] **1** conj because, for. **2** nm coach, bus, Am bus; **c. de police** police van.

carabine [karabin] nf rifle, carbine; **c. à air comprimé** airgun.

carabiné [karabine] a Fam violent; (punition, amende) very stiff.

caracoler [karakɔle] vi to prance, caper.

caractère [karaktɛr] nm **1** (lettre) Typ character; **en petits caractères** in small print; **caractères d'imprimerie** block capitals ou letters; **caractères gras** bold type ou characters. **2** (tempérament, nature) character, nature; (attribut) characteristic; **aucun c. de gravité** no serious element; **son c. inégal** his ou her uneven temper; **avoir bon c.** to be good-natured. ◆**caractériel, -ielle** a (trait, troubles) character-; — a & nmf disturbed (child). ◆**caractériser** vt to characterize; **se c. par** to be characterized by. ◆**caractéristique** a & nf characteristic.

carafe [karaf] nf decanter, carafe.

carambol/er [karãbɔle] vt Aut to smash into. ◆**—age** nm pileup, multiple smash-up.

caramel [karamɛl] nm caramel; (bonbon dur) toffee.

carapace [karapas] nf (de tortue etc) & Fig shell.

carat [kara] nm carat.

caravane [karavan] nf (dans le désert) caravan; Aut caravan, Am trailer; **c. publicitaire** publicity convoy. ◆**caravaning** n, ◆**caravanage** n caravanning.

carbone [karbɔn] nm carbon; **(papier) c.** carbon (paper). ◆**carboniser** vt to burn (to ashes), char; (substance) Ch to carbonize; **être mort carbonisé** to be burned to death.

carburant [karbyrã] nm Aut fuel. ◆**carburateur** nm carburettor, Am carburetor.

carcan [karkã] nm Hist iron collar; (contrainte) Fig yoke.

carcasse [karkas] nf Anat carcass; (d'immeuble etc) frame, shell.

cardiaque [kardjak] a (trouble etc) heart-; **crise c.** heart attack; **arrêt c.** cardiac arrest; — nmf heart patient.

cardinal, -aux [kardinal, -o] **1** a (nombre, point) cardinal. **2** nm Rel cardinal.

Carême [karɛm] nm Rel Lent.

carence [karãs] nf inadequacy, incompetence; Méd deficiency.

carène [karɛn] nf Nau hull. ◆**caréné** a Aut Av streamlined.

caresse [karɛs] nf caress. ◆**caress/er** [karese] vt (animal, enfant etc) to stroke, pat, fondle; (femme, homme) to caress; (espoir) to cherish. ◆**—ant** a endearing, loving.

cargaison [kargɛzɔ̃] nf cargo, freight. ◆**cargo** nm freighter, cargo boat.

caricature [karikatyr] nf caricature. ◆**caricatural, -aux** a ludicrous; **portrait c.** portrait in caricature. ◆**caricaturer** vt to caricature.

carie [kari] nf **la c. (dentaire)** tooth decay; **une c.** a cavity. ◆**carié** a (dent) decayed, bad.

carillon [karijɔ̃] nm (cloches) chimes, peal; (horloge) chiming clock. ◆**carillonner** vi to chime, peal.

carlingue [karlɛ̃g] nf (fuselage) Av cabin.

carnage [karnaʒ] *nm* carnage.
carnassier, -ière [karnasje, -jɛr] *a* carnivorous; — *nm* carnivore.
carnaval, *pl* **-als** [karnaval] *nm* carnival.
carné [karne] *a* (*régime*) meat-.
carnet [karnɛ] *nm* notebook; (*de timbres, chèques, adresses etc*) book; **c. de notes** school report; **c. de route** logbook; **c. de vol** *Av* logbook.
carnivore [karnivɔr] *a* carnivorous; — *nm* carnivore.
carotte [karɔt] *nf* carrot.
carotter [karɔte] *vt Arg* to wangle, cadge (à **qn** from s.o.).
carpe [karp] *nf* carp.
carpette [karpɛt] *nf* rug.
carquois [karkwa] *nm* (*étui*) quiver.
carré [kare] *a* square; (*en affaires*) *Fig* plain-dealing; — *nm* square; (*de jardin*) patch; *Nau* messroom; **c. de soie** (square) silk scarf.
carreau, -x [karo] *nm* (*vitre*) (window) pane; (*pavé*) tile; (*sol*) tiled floor; *Cartes* diamonds; **à carreaux** (*nappe etc*) check(ed); **se tenir à c.** to watch one's step; **rester sur le c.** to be left for dead; (*candidat*) *Fig* to be left out in the cold. **◆carrel/er** *vt* to tile. **◆—age** *nm* (*sol*) tiled floor; (*action*) tiling.
carrefour [karfur] *nm* crossroads.
carrelet [karlɛ] *nm* (*poisson*) plaice, *Am* flounder.
carrément [karemɑ̃] *adv* (*dire etc*) straight out, bluntly; (*complètement*) downright, well and truly.
carrer (se) [səkare] *vpr* to settle down firmly.
carrière [karjɛr] *nf* **1** (*terrain*) quarry. **2** (*métier*) career.
carrosse [karɔs] *nm Hist* (horse-drawn) carriage. **◆carrossable** *a* suitable for vehicles. **◆carrosserie** *nf Aut* body(work).
carrousel [karuzɛl] *nm* (*tourbillon*) *Fig* whirl, merry-go-round.
carrure [karyr] *nf* breadth of shoulders, build; *Fig* calibre.
cartable [kartabl] *nm Scol* satchel.
carte [kart] *nf* card; (*de lecteur*) ticket; *Géog* map; *Nau Mét* chart; *Culin* menu; *pl* (*jeu*) cards; **c. (postale)** (post)card; **c. à jouer** playing card; **c. de crédit** credit card; **c. des vins** wine list; **c. grise** *Aut* vehicle registration; **c. blanche** *Fig* free hand.
cartel [kartɛl] *nm Écon Pol* cartel.
carter [kartɛr] *nm* (*de moteur*) *Aut* crankcase; (*de bicyclette*) chain guard.

cartilage [kartilaʒ] *nm* cartilage.
carton [kartɔ̃] *nm* cardboard; (*boîte*) cardboard box, carton; **c. à dessin** portfolio; **en c.-pâte** (*faux*) *Péj* pasteboard; **faire un c. sur** *Fam* to take a potshot at. **◆cartonn/er** *vt* (*livre*) to case; **livre cartonné** hardback. **◆—age** *nm* (*emballage*) cardboard package.
cartouche [kartuʃ] *nf* cartridge; (*de cigarettes*) carton; *Phot* cassette. **◆cartouchière** *nf* (*ceinture*) cartridge belt.
cas [kɑ] *nm* case; **en tout c.** in any case *ou* event; **en aucun c.** on no account; **en c. de besoin** if need(s) be; **en c. d'accident** in the event of an accident; **en c. d'urgence** in (case of) an emergency; **faire c. de/peu de c. de** to set great/little store by; **au c. où elle tomberait** if she should fall; **pour le c. où il pleuvrait** in case it rains.
casanier, -ière [kazanje, -jɛr] *a* & *nmf* home-loving (person); (*pantouflard*) *Péj* stay-at-home (person).
casaque [kazak] *nf* (*de jockey*) shirt, blouse.
cascade [kaskad] *nf* **1** waterfall; (*série*) *Fig* spate; **en c.** in succession. **2** *Cin* stunt. **◆cascadeur, -euse** *nmf Cin* stunt man, stunt woman.
case [kɑz] *nf* **1** pigeonhole; (*de tiroir*) compartment; (*d'échiquier etc*) square; (*de formulaire*) box. **2** (*hutte*) hut, cabin.
caser [kaze] *vt Fam* (*ranger*) to park, place; **c. qn** (*dans un logement ou un travail*) to find a place for s.o.; (*marier*) to marry s.o. off; — **se c.** *vpr* to settle down.
caserne [kazɛrn] *nf Mil* barracks; **c. de pompiers** fire station.
casier [kazje] *nm* pigeonhole, compartment; (*meuble à clef*) filing cabinet; (*fermant à clef, à consigne automatique*) locker; **c. à bouteilles/à disques** bottle/record rack; **c. judiciaire** criminal record.
casino [kazino] *nm* casino.
casque [kask] *nm* helmet; (*pour cheveux*) (hair) dryer; **c. (à écouteurs)** headphones; **les Casques bleus** the UN peace-keeping force. **◆casqué** *a* helmeted, wearing a helmet.
casquer [kaske] *vi Fam* to pay up, cough up.
casquette [kaskɛt] *nf* (*coiffure*) cap.
cassation [kasasjɔ̃] *nf* **Cour de c.** supreme court of appeal.
casse¹ [kɑs] *nf* **1** (*action*) breakage; (*objets*) breakages; (*grabuge*) *Fam* trouble; **mettre à la c.** to scrap; **vendre à la c.** to sell for

scrap. **2** *Typ* case; **bas/haut de c.** lower/upper case.

casse² [kɑs] *nm* (*cambriolage*) *Arg* break-in.

casse-cou [kɑsku] *nmf inv* (*personne*) *Fam* daredevil. ◆**c.-croûte** *nm inv* snack. ◆**c.-gueule** *nm inv Fam* death trap; − *a inv* perilous. ◆**c.-noisettes** *nm inv*, ◆**c.-noix** *nm inv* nut-cracker(s). ◆**c.-pieds** *nmf inv* (*personne*) *Fam* pain in the neck. ◆**c.-tête** *nm inv* **1** (*massue*) club. **2** (*problème*) headache; (*jeu*) puzzle, brain teaser.

cass/er [kɑse] *vt* to break; (*noix*) to crack; (*annuler*) *Jur* to annul; (*dégrader*) *Mil* to cashier; − *vi*, − **se c.** *vpr* to break; **il me casse la tête** *Fam* he's giving me a headache; **elle me casse les pieds** *Fam* she's getting on my nerves; **se c. la tête** *Fam* to rack one's brains; **c. la figure à qn** *Fam* to smash s.o.'s face in; **se c. la figure** (*tomber*) *Fam* to come a cropper, *Am* take a spill; **ça ne casse rien** *Fam* it's nothing special; **ça vaut 50F à tout c.** *Fam* it's worth 50F at the very most; **il ne s'est pas cassé** *Iron Fam* he didn't bother himself *ou* exhaust himself. ◆**−ant** *a* (*fragile*) brittle; (*brusque*) curt, imperious; (*fatigant*) *Fam* exhausting. ◆**−eur** *nm Aut* breaker, scrap merchant; (*manifestant*) demonstrator who damages property.

casserole [kɑsrɔl] *nf* (sauce)pan.

cassette [kɑsɛt] *nf* (*pour magnétophone ou magnétoscope*) cassette; **sur c.** (*film*) on video; **faire une c. de** (*film*) to make a video of.

cassis 1 [kasis] *nm Bot* blackcurrant; (*boisson*) blackcurrant liqueur. **2** [kasi] *nm Aut* dip (*across road*).

cassoulet [kasulɛ] *nm* stew (*of meat and beans*).

cassure [kɑsyr] *nf* (*fissure, rupture*) break; *Géol* fault.

castagnettes [kastaɲɛt] *nfpl* castanets.

caste [kast] *nf* caste; **èsprit de c.** class consciousness.

castor [kastɔr] *nm* beaver.

castrer [kastre] *vt* to castrate. ◆**castration** *nf* castration.

cataclysme [kataklism] *nm* cataclysm.

catacombes [katakɔ̃b] *nfpl* catacombs.

catalogue [katalɔg] *nm* catalogue. ◆**cataloguer** *vt* (*livres etc*) to catalogue; **c. qn** *Péj* to categorize s.o.

catalyseur [katalizœr] *nm Ch & Fig* catalyst.

cataphote® [katafɔt] *nm Aut* reflector.

cataplasme [kataplasm] *nm Méd* poultice.

catapulte [katapylt] *nf Hist Av* catapult. ◆**catapulter** *vt* to catapult.

cataracte [katarakt] *nf* **1** *Méd* cataract. **2** (*cascade*) falls, cataract.

catastrophe [katastrɔf] *nf* disaster, catastrophe; **atterrir en c.** to make an emergency landing. ◆**catastrophique** *a* disastrous, catastrophic.

catch [katʃ] *nm* (all-in) wrestling. ◆**catcheur, -euse** *nmf* wrestler.

catéchisme [kateʃism] *nm Rel* catechism.

catégorie [kategɔri] *nf* category. ◆**catégorique** *a* categorical.

cathédrale [katedral] *nf* cathedral.

catholicisme [katɔlisism] *nm* Catholicism. ◆**catholique** *a* & *nmf* Catholic; **pas (très) c.** (*affaire, personne*) *Fig* shady, doubtful.

catimini (en) [ɑ̃katimini] *adv* on the sly.

cauchemar [koʃmar] *nm* nightmare.

cause [koz] *nf* cause; *Jur* case; **à c. de** because of, on account of; **et pour c.!** for a very good reason!; **pour c. de** on account of; **en connaissance de c.** in full knowledge of the facts; **mettre en c.** (*la bonne foi de qn etc*) to (call into) question; (*personne*) to implicate; **en c.** involved, in question.

caus/er [koze] **1** *vt* (*provoquer*) to cause. **2** *vi* (*bavarder*) to chat (**de** about); (*discourir*) to talk; (*jaser*) to blab. ◆**−ant** *a Fam* chatty, talkative. ◆**causerie** *nf* talk. ◆**causette** *nf* **faire la c.** *Fam* to have a little chat.

caustique [kostik] *a* (*substance, esprit*) caustic.

cauteleux, -euse [kotlø, -øz] *a* wily, sly.

cautériser [koterize] *vt Méd* to cauterize.

caution [kosjɔ̃] *nf* surety; (*pour libérer qn*) *Jur* bail; **sous c.** on bail; **sujet à c.** (*nouvelle etc*) very doubtful. ◆**cautionn/er** *vt* (*approuver*) to sanction. ◆**−ement** *nm* (*garantie*) surety.

cavalcade [kavalkad] *nf Fam* stampede; (*défilé*) cavalcade. ◆**cavale** *nf* **en c.** *Arg* on the run. ◆**cavaler** *vi Fam* to run, rush.

cavalerie [kavalri] *nf Mil* cavalry; (*de cirque*) horses. ◆**cavalier, -ière 1** *nmf* rider; − *nm Mil* trooper, cavalryman; *Échecs* knight; − *af* **allée cavalière** bridle path. **2** *nmf* (*pour danser*) partner, escort. **3** *a* (*insolent*) offhand.

cave [kav] **1** *nf* cellar, vault. **2** *a* sunken, hollow. ◆**caveau, -x** *nm* (*sépulture*) (burial) vault.

caverne [kavɛrn] *nf* cave, cavern; **homme**

des cavernes caveman. ◆**caverneux, -euse** a (voix, rire) hollow, deep-sounding.

caviar [kavjar] nm caviar(e).

cavité [kavite] nf cavity.

CCP [sesepe] nm abrév (Compte chèque postal) PO Giro account, Am Post Office checking account.

ce¹ [s(ə)] (c' before e and é) pron dém **1** it, that; **c'est toi/bon/demain**/etc it's ou that's you/good/tomorrow/etc; **c'est mon médecin** he's my doctor; **ce sont eux qui** ... they are the ones who ... ; **c'est à elle de jouer** it's her turn to play; **est-ce que tu viens?** are you coming?; **sur ce** at this point, thereupon. **2 ce que, ce qui** what; **je sais ce qui est bon/ce que tu veux** I know what is good/what you want; **ce que c'est beau!** how beautiful it is!

ce², **cette**, pl **ces** [s(ə), sɛt, se] (ce becomes cet before a vowel or mute h) a dém this, that, pl these, those; (+ -ci) this, pl these; (+ -là) that, pl those; **cet homme** this ou that man; **cet homme-ci** this man; **cet homme-là** that man.

ceci [səsi] pron dém this; **écoutez bien c.** listen to this.

cécité [sesite] nf blindness.

céder [sede] vt to give up (à to); Jur to transfer; **c. le pas à** to give way ou precedence to; – vi (personne) to give way, give in, yield (à to); (branche, chaise etc) to give way.

cédille [sedij] nf Gram cedilla.

cèdre [sɛdr] nm (arbre, bois) cedar.

CEE [seøø] nf abrév (Communauté économique européenne) EEC.

ceindre [sɛ̃dr] vt (épée) Lit to gird on.

ceinture [sɛ̃tyr] nf belt; (de robe de chambre) cord; (taille) Anat waist; (de remparts) Hist girdle; **petite/grande c.** Rail inner/outer circle; **c. de sécurité** Aut Av seatbelt; **c. de sauvetage** lifebelt. ◆**ceinturer** vt to seize round the waist; Rugby to tackle; (ville) to girdle, surround.

cela [s(ə)la] pron dém (pour désigner) that; (sujet indéfini) it, that; **c. m'attriste que** ... it saddens me that ... ; **quand/ comment/**etc **c.?** when?/how?/etc; **c'est c.** that is so.

célèbre [selɛbr] a famous. ◆**célébrité** nf fame; (personne) celebrity.

célébrer [selebre] vt to celebrate. ◆**célébration** nf celebration (de of).

céleri [sɛlri] nm (en branches) celery.

céleste [selɛst] a celestial, heavenly.

célibat [seliba] nm celibacy. ◆**célibataire** a (non marié) single, unmarried; (chaste) celibate; – nm bachelor; – nf unmarried woman, spinster.

celle voir **celui**.

cellier [selje] nm storeroom (for wine etc).

cellophane® [selɔfan] nf cellophane®.

cellule [selyl] nf cell. ◆**cellulaire** a (tissu etc) Biol cell-; **voiture c.** prison van.

celluloïd [selylɔid] nm celluloid.

cellulose [selyloz] nf cellulose.

celtique ou **celte** [sɛltik, sɛlt] a Celtic.

celui, celle, pl **ceux, celles** [səlɥi, sɛl, sø, sɛl] pron dém **1** the one, pl those, the ones; **c. de Jean** John's (one); **ceux de Jean** John's (ones), those of John. **2** (+ -ci) this one, pl these (ones); (dont on vient de parler) the latter; (+ -là) that one, pl those (ones); the former; **ceux-ci sont gros** these (ones) are big.

cendre [sɑ̃dr] nf ash. ◆**cendré** a ash(-coloured), ashen. ◆**cendrée** nf Sp cinder track.

Cendrillon [sɑ̃drijɔ̃] nm Cinderella.

censé [sɑ̃se] a supposed; **il n'est pas c. savoir** he's not supposed to know.

censeur [sɑ̃sœr] nm censor; Scol assistant headmaster, vice-principal. ◆**censure** nf **la c.** (examen) censorship; (comité, service) the censor; **motion de c.** Pol censure motion. ◆**censurer** vt (film etc) to censor; (critiquer) & Pol to censure.

cent [sɑ̃] ([sɑ̃t] pl [sɑ̃z] before vowel and mute h except un and onze) a & nm hundred; **c. pages** a ou une hundred pages; **deux cents pages** two hundred pages; **deux c. trois pages** two hundred and three pages; **cinq pour c.** five per cent. ◆**centaine** nf une c. a hundred (or so); **des centaines de** hundreds of. ◆**centenaire** a & nmf centenarian; – nm (anniversaire) centenary. ◆**centième** a & nmf hundredth; **un c.** a hundredth. ◆**centigrade** a centigrade. ◆**centime** nm centime. ◆**centimètre** nm centimetre; (ruban) tape measure.

central, -aux [sɑ̃tral, -o] **1** a central; **pouvoir c.** (power of) central government. **2** nm **c. (téléphonique)** (telephone) exchange. ◆**centrale** nf (usine) power station. ◆**centraliser** vt to centralize. ◆**centre** nm centre; **c. commercial** shopping centre. ◆**c.-ville** nm inv city ou town centre. ◆**centrer** vt to centre. ◆**centrifuge** a centrifugal. ◆**centrifugeuse** nf liquidizer, juice extractor.

centuple [sɑ̃typl] nm hundredfold; **au c.** a hundredfold. ◆**centupler** vti to increase a hundredfold.

cep [sɛp] *nm* vine stock. ◆**cépage** *nm* vine (plant).

cependant [səpɑ̃dɑ̃] *conj* however, yet.

céramique [seramik] *nf* (*art*) ceramics; (*matière*) ceramic; **de** *ou* **en c.** ceramic.

cerceau, -x [sɛrso] *nm* hoop.

cercle [sɛrkl] *nm* (*forme, groupe, étendue*) circle; **c. vicieux** vicious circle.

cercueil [sɛrkœj] *nm* coffin.

céréale [sereal] *nf* cereal.

cérébral, -aux [serebral, -o] *a* cerebral.

cérémonie [seremɔni] *nf* ceremony; **de c.** (*tenue etc*) ceremonial; **sans c.** (*inviter, manger*) informally; **faire des cérémonies** *Fam* to make a lot of fuss. ◆**cérémonial,** *pl* **-als** *nm* ceremonial. ◆**cérémonieux, -euse** *a* ceremonious.

cerf [sɛr] *nm* deer; (*mâle*) stag. ◆**cerf-volant** *nm* (*pl* **cerfs-volants**) (*jouet*) kite.

cerise [s(ə)riz] *nf* cherry. ◆**cerisier** *nm* cherry tree.

cerne [sɛrn] *nm* (*cercle, marque*) ring. ◆**cerner** *vt* to surround; (*problème*) to define; **les yeux cernés** with rings under one's eyes.

certain [sɛrtɛ̃] **1** *a* (*sûr*) certain, sure; **il est** *ou* **c'est c. que tu réussiras** you're certain *ou* sure to succeed; **je suis c. de réussir** I'm certain *ou* sure I'll succeed; **être c. de qch** to be certain *ou* sure of sth. **2** *a* (*imprécis, difficile à fixer*) certain; *pl* certain, some; **un c. temps** a certain (amount of) time; *– pron pl* some (people), certain people; (*choses*) some. ◆**certainement** *adv* certainly. ◆**certes** *adv* indeed.

certificat [sɛrtifika] *nm* certificate. ◆**certifi/er** *vt* to certify; **je vous certifie que** I assure you that. ◆**—é** *a* (*professeur*) qualified.

certitude [sɛrtityd] *nf* certainty; **avoir la c. que** to be certain that.

cerveau, -x [sɛrvo] *nm* (*organe*) brain; (*intelligence*) mind, brain(s); **rhume de c.** head cold; **fuite des cerveaux** brain drain.

cervelas [sɛrvəla] *nm* saveloy.

cervelle [sɛrvɛl] *nf* (*substance*) brain; *Culin* brains; **tête sans c.** scatterbrain.

ces *voir* **ce** [2].

CES [seəɛs] *nm abrév* (*collège d'enseignement secondaire*) comprehensive school, *Am* high school.

césarienne [sezarjɛn] *nf Méd* Caesarean (section).

cessation [sɛsasjɔ̃] *nf* (*arrêt, fin*) suspension.

cesse [sɛs] *nf* **sans c.** incessantly; **elle n'a (pas) eu de c. que je fasse . . .** she had no rest until I did . . . .

cesser [sese] *vti* to stop; **faire c.** to put a stop *ou* halt to; **il ne cesse (pas) de parler** he doesn't stop talking. ◆**cessez-le-feu** *nm inv* ceasefire.

cession [sɛsjɔ̃] *nf Jur* transfer.

c'est-à-dire [sɛtadir] *conj* that is (to say), in other words.

cet, cette *voir* **ce** [2].

ceux *voir* **celui**.

chacal, *pl* **-als** [ʃakal] *nm* jackal.

chacun, -une [ʃakœ̃, -yn] *pron* each (one), every one; (*tout le monde*) everyone.

chagrin [ʃagrɛ̃] **1** *nm* sorrow, grief; **avoir du c.** to be very upset. **2** *a Lit* doleful. ◆**chagriner** *vt* to upset, distress.

chahut [ʃay] *nm* racket, noisy disturbance. ◆**chahut/er** *vi* to create a racket *ou* a noisy disturbance; *– vt* (*professeur*) to be rowdy with, play up. ◆**—eur, -euse** *nmf* rowdy.

chai [ʃɛ] *nm* wine and spirits storehouse.

chaîne [ʃɛn] *nf* chain; *TV* channel, network; *Géog* chain, range; *Nau* cable; *Tex* warp; *pl* (*liens*) *Fig* shackles, chains; **c. de montage** assembly line; **travail à la c.** production-line work; **c. haute fidélité, c. hi-fi** hi-fi system; **c. de magasins** chain of shops *ou Am* stores; **collision en c.** *Aut* multiple collision; **réaction en c.** chain reaction. ◆**chaînette** *nf* (small) chain. ◆**chaînon** *nm* (*anneau, lien*) link.

chair [ʃɛr] *nf* flesh; (*couleur*) **c.** flesh-coloured; **en c. et en os** in the flesh; **la c. de poule** goose pimples, gooseflesh; **bien en c.** plump; **c. à saucisses** sausage meat.

chaire [ʃɛr] *nf Univ* chair; *Rel* pulpit.

chaise [ʃɛz] *nf* chair, seat; **c. longue** (*siège pliant*) deckchair; **c. d'enfant, c. haute** high-chair.

chaland [ʃalɑ̃] *nm* barge, lighter.

châle [ʃal] *nm* shawl.

chalet [ʃalɛ] *nm* chalet.

chaleur [ʃalœr] *nf* heat; (*douce*) warmth; (*d'un accueil, d'une voix etc*) warmth; (*des convictions*) ardour; (*d'une discussion*) heat. ◆**chaleureux, -euse** *a* warm.

challenge [ʃalɑ̃ʒ] *nm Sp* contest.

chaloupe [ʃalup] *nf* launch, long boat.

chalumeau, -x [ʃalymo] *nm* blowlamp, *Am* blowtorch; *Mus* pipe.

chalut [ʃaly] *nm* trawl net, drag net. ◆**chalutier** *nm* (*bateau*) trawler.

chamailler (se) [səʃamaje] *vpr* to squabble, bicker. ◆**chamailleries** *nfpl* squabbling, bickering.

chamarré [ʃamare] a (robe etc) richly coloured; **c. de** (décorations etc) Péj bedecked with.

chambard [ʃɑ̃bar] nm Fam (tapage) rumpus, row. ◆**chambarder** vt Fam to turn upside down; **il a tout chambardé dans** he's turned everything upside down in.

chambouler [ʃɑ̃bule] vt Fam to make topsy-turvy, turn upside down.

chambre [ʃɑ̃br] nf (bed)room; Pol Jur Tech Anat chamber; **c. à coucher** bedroom; (mobilier) bedroom suite; **c. à air** (de pneu) inner tube; **c. d'ami** guest ou spare room; **c. forte** strongroom; **c. noire** Phot darkroom; **garder la c.** to stay indoors. ◆**chambrée** nf Mil barrack room. ◆**chambrer** vt (vin) to bring to room temperature.

chameau, -x [ʃamo] nm camel.

chamois [ʃamwa] **1** nm (animal) chamois; **peau de c.** chamois (leather), shammy. **2** a inv buff(-coloured).

champ [ʃɑ̃] nm field; (domaine) Fig scope, range; **c. de bataille** battlefield; **c. de courses** racecourse, racetrack; **c. de foire** fairground; **c. de tir** (terrain) rifle range; **laisser le c. libre à qn** to leave the field open for s.o. ◆**champêtre** a rustic, rural.

champagne [ʃɑ̃paɲ] nm champagne; **c. brut** extra-dry champagne.

champignon [ʃɑ̃piɲɔ̃] nm **1** Bot mushroom; **c. vénéneux** toadstool, poisonous mushroom; **c. atomique** mushroom cloud. **2** Aut Fam accelerator pedal.

champion [ʃɑ̃pjɔ̃] nm champion. ◆**championnat** nm championship.

chance [ʃɑ̃s] nf luck; (probabilité de réussir, occasion) chance; **avoir de la c.** to be lucky; **tenter** ou **courir sa c.** to try one's luck; **c'est une c. que...** it's a stroke of luck that ...; **mes chances de succès** my chances of success. ◆**chanceux, -euse** a lucky.

chancel/er [ʃɑ̃sle] vi to stagger, totter; (courage) Fig to falter. ◆**—ant** a (pas, santé) faltering, shaky.

chancelier [ʃɑ̃səlje] nm chancellor. ◆**chancellerie** nf chancellery.

chancre [ʃɑ̃kr] nm Méd & Fig canker.

chandail [ʃɑ̃daj] nm (thick) sweater, jersey.

chandelier [ʃɑ̃dəlje] nm candlestick.

chandelle [ʃɑ̃dɛl] nf candle; **voir trente-six chandelles** Fig to see stars; **en c.** Av Sp straight into the air.

change [ʃɑ̃ʒ] nm Fin exchange; **le contrôle des changes** exchange control; **donner le c. à qn** to deceive s.o. ◆**chang/er** vt (modifier, remplacer, échanger) to change; **c. qn**

en to change s.o. into; **ça la changera de ne pas travailler** it'll be a change for her not to be working; **– vi** to change; **c. de voiture/d'adresse**/etc to change one's car/address/etc; **c. de train/de place** to change trains/places; **c. de vitesse/de cap** to change gear/course; **c. de sujet** to change the subject; **– se c.** vpr to change (one's clothes). ◆**—eant** a (temps) changeable; (humeur) fickle; (couleurs) changing. ◆**—ement** nm change; **aimer le c.** to like change. ◆**—eur** nm moneychanger; **c. de monnaie** change machine.

chanoine [ʃanwan] nm (personne) Rel canon.

chanson [ʃɑ̃sɔ̃] nf song. ◆**chant** nm singing; (chanson) song; (hymne) chant; **c. de Noël** Christmas carol. ◆**chant/er** vi to sing; (psalmodier) to chant; (coq) to crow; **si ça te chante** Fam if you feel like it; **faire c. qn** to blackmail s.o.; **– vt** to sing; (glorifier) to sing of; (dire) Fam to say. ◆**—ant** a (air, voix) melodious. ◆**—age** nm blackmail. ◆**—eur, -euse** nm singer.

chantier [ʃɑ̃tje] nm (building) site; (entrepôt) builder's yard; **c. naval** shipyard; **mettre un travail en c.** to get a task under way.

chantonner [ʃɑ̃tɔne] vti to hum.

chantre [ʃɑ̃tr] nm Rel cantor.

chanvre [ʃɑ̃vr] nm hemp; **c. indien** (plante) cannabis.

chaos [kao] nm chaos. ◆**chaotique** a chaotic.

chaparder [ʃaparde] vt Fam to filch, pinch (à from).

chapeau, -x [ʃapo] nm hat; (de champignon, roue) cap; **c.!** well done!; **donner un coup de c.** (pour saluer qn) to raise one's hat; **c. mou** trilby, Am fedora. ◆**chapelier** nm hatter.

chapelet [ʃaplɛ] nm rosary; **dire son c.** to tell one's beads; **un c. de** (saucisses, injures etc) a string of.

chapelle [ʃapɛl] nf chapel; **c. ardente** chapel of rest.

chaperon [ʃaprɔ̃] nm chaperon(e). ◆**chaperonner** vt to chaperon(e).

chapiteau, -x [ʃapito] nm (de cirque) big top; (pour expositions etc) marquee, tent; (de colonne) Archit capital.

chapitre [ʃapitr] nm chapter; **sur le c. de** on the subject of. ◆**chapitrer** vt to scold, lecture.

chaque [ʃak] a each, every.

char [ʃar] nm Hist chariot; (de carnaval)

float; *Can Fam* car; **c. à bœufs** oxcart; **c. (d'assaut)** *Mil* tank.

charabia [ʃarabja] *nm Fam* gibberish.

charade [ʃarad] *nf (énigme)* riddle; *(mimée)* charade.

charbon [ʃarbɔ̃] *nm* coal; *(fusain)* charcoal; **c. de bois** charcoal; **sur des charbons ardents** like a cat on hot bricks. ◆**charbonnages** *nmpl* coalmines, collieries. ◆**charbonnier, -ière** *a* coal-; – *nm* coal merchant.

charcuter [ʃarkyte] *vt (opérer) Fam Péj* to cut up (badly).

charcuterie [ʃarkytri] *nf* pork butcher's shop; *(aliment)* cooked (pork) meats. ◆**charcutier, -ière** *nmf* pork butcher.

chardon [ʃardɔ̃] *nm Bot* thistle.

chardonneret [ʃardɔnrɛ] *nm (oiseau)* goldfinch.

charge [ʃarʒ] *nf (poids)* load; *(fardeau)* burden; *Jur Él Mil* charge; *(fonction)* office; *pl Fin* financial obligations; *(dépenses)* expenses; *(de locataire)* (maintenance) charges; **charges sociales** national insurance contributions, *Am* Social Security contributions; **à c.** *(enfant, parent)* dependent; **être à c. à qn** to be a burden to s.o.; **à la c. de qn** *(personne)* dependent on s.o.; *(frais)* payable by s.o.; **prendre en c.** to take charge of, take responsibility for.

charg/er [ʃarʒe] *vt* to load; *Él Mil* to charge; *(passager) Fam* to pick up; **se c. de** *(enfant, tâche etc)* to take charge of; **c. qn de** *(impôts etc)* to burden s.o. with; *(paquets etc)* to load s.o. with; *(tâche etc)* to entrust s.o. with; **c. qn de faire** to instruct s.o. to do. ◆**-é, -ée** *a (personne, véhicule, arme)* loaded; *(journée etc)* heavy, busy; *(langue)* coated; **c. de** *(arbre, navire etc)* laden with; – *nmf* **c. de cours** *Univ* (temporary) lecturer. ◆**-ement** *nm (action)* loading; *(objet)* load. ◆**-eur** *nm (de piles)* charger.

chariot [ʃarjo] *nm (à bagages etc)* trolley, *Am* cart; *(de ferme)* waggon; *(de machine à écrire)* carriage.

charité [ʃarite] *nf (vertu, secours)* charity; *(acte)* act of charity; **faire la c.** to give to charity; **faire la c. à** *(mendiant)* to give to. ◆**charitable** *a* charitable.

charivari [ʃarivari] *nm Fam* hubbub, hullabaloo.

charlatan [ʃarlatɑ̃] *nm* charlatan, quack.

charme [ʃarm] *nm* **1** charm; *(magie)* spell. **2** *(arbre)* hornbeam. ◆**charm/er** *vt* to charm; **je suis charmé de vous voir** I'm delighted to see you. ◆**-ant** *a* charming.

◆**—eur, -euse** *nmf* charmer; – *a* engaging.

charnel, -elle [ʃarnɛl] *a* carnal.

charnier [ʃarnje] *nm* mass grave.

charnière [ʃarnjɛr] *nf* hinge; *Fig* meeting point *(de* between).

charnu [ʃarny] *a* fleshy.

charogne [ʃarɔɲ] *nf* carrion.

charpente [ʃarpɑ̃t] *nf* frame(work); *(de personne)* build. ◆**charpenté** *a* **bien c.** solidly built. ◆**charpenterie** *nf* carpentry. ◆**charpentier** *nm* carpenter.

charpie [ʃarpi] *nf* **mettre en c.** *(déchirer)* & *Fig* to tear to shreds.

charrette [ʃarɛt] *nf* cart. ◆**charretier** *nm* carter. ◆**charrier 1** *vt (transporter)* to cart; *(rivière)* to carry along, wash down *(sand etc)*. **2** *vti (taquiner) Fam* to tease.

charrue [ʃary] *nf* plough, *Am* plow.

charte [ʃart] *nf Pol* charter.

charter [ʃartɛr] *nm Av* charter (flight).

chas [ʃa] *nm* eye *(of a needle)*.

chasse [ʃas] *nf* **1** hunting, hunt; *(poursuite)* chase; *Av* fighter forces; **de c.** *(pilote, avion)* fighter-; **c. sous-marine** underwater (harpoon) fishing; **c. à courre** hunting; **tableau de c.** *(animaux abattus)* bag; **faire la c. à** to hunt down, hunt for; **donner la c. à** to give chase to; **c. à l'homme** manhunt. **2** **c. d'eau** toilet flush; **tirer la c.** to flush the toilet.

châsse [ʃas] *nf* shrine.

chassé-croisé [ʃasekrwaze] *nm (pl chassés-croisés) Fig* confused coming(s) and going(s).

chass/er [ʃase] *vt (animal)* to hunt; *(papillon)* to chase; *(faire partir)* to drive out *ou* off; *(employé)* to dismiss; *(mouche)* to brush away; *(odeur)* to get rid of; – *vi* to hunt; *Aut* to skid. ◆**—eur, -euse** *nmf* hunter; – *nm (domestique)* pageboy, bellboy; *Av* fighter; **c. à pied** infantryman. ◆**chasse-neige** *nm inv* snowplough, *Am* snowplow.

châssis [ʃasi] *nm* frame; *Aut* chassis.

chaste [ʃast] *a* chaste, pure. ◆**chasteté** *nf* chastity.

chat, chatte [ʃa, ʃat] *nmf* cat; **un c. dans la gorge** a frog in one's throat; **d'autres chats à fouetter** other fish to fry; **pas un c.** not a soul; **ma (petite) chatte** *Fam* my darling; **c. perché** *(jeu)* tag.

châtaigne [ʃatɛɲ] *nf* chestnut. ◆**châtaignier** *nm* chestnut tree. ◆**châtain** *a inv* (chestnut) brown.

château, -x [ʃato] *nm (forteresse)* castle; *(palais)* palace, stately home; **c. fort** fortified castle; **châteaux en Espagne** *Fig* castles in the air; **c. d'eau** water tower; **c. de cartes** house of cards. ◆**châtelain, -aine** *nmf* lord of the manor, lady of the manor.

châtier [ʃɑtje] *vt Litt* to chastise, castigate; (*style*) to refine.

châtiment [ʃɑtimɑ̃] *nm* punishment.

chaton [ʃatɔ̃] *nm* **1** (*chat*) kitten. **2** (*de bague*) setting, mounting. **3** *Bot* catkin.

chatouill/er [ʃatuje] *vt* (*pour faire rire*) to tickle; (*exciter, plaire à*) *Fig* to titillate. ◆**—ement** *nm* tickle; (*action*) tickling. ◆**chatouilleux, -euse** *a* ticklish; (*irritable*) touchy.

chatoyer [ʃatwaje] *vi* to glitter, sparkle.

châtrer [ʃɑtre] *vt* to castrate.

chatte [ʃat] *voir* **chat.**

chatteries [ʃatri] *nfpl* cuddles; (*friandises*) delicacies.

chatterton [ʃatɛrtɔn] *nm* adhesive insulating tape.

chaud [ʃo] *a* hot; (*doux*) warm; (*fervent*) *Fig* warm; **pleurer à chaudes larmes** to cry bitterly; *— nm* heat; warmth; **avoir c.** to be hot; to be warm; **il fait c.** it's hot; it's warm; **être au c.** to be in the warm(th); **ça ne me fait ni c. ni froid** it leaves me indifferent. ◆**chaudement** *adv* warmly; (*avec passion*) hotly.

chaudière [ʃodjɛr] *nf* boiler.

chaudron [ʃodrɔ̃] *nm* cauldron.

chauffard [ʃofar] *nm* road hog, reckless driver.

chauff/er [ʃofe] *vt* to heat up, warm up; (*métal etc*) *Tech* to heat; *— vi* to heat up, warm up; *Aut* to overheat; **ça va c.** *Fam* things are going to hot up; *— se c.* *vpr* to warm oneself up. ◆**—ant** *a* (*couverture*) electric; (*plaque*) hot-; (*surface*) heating. ◆**—age** *nm* heating. ◆**—eur** *nm* **1** (*de chaudière*) stoker. **2** *Aut* driver; (*employé, domestique*) chauffeur. ◆**chauffe-bain** *nm*, ◆**chauffe-eau** *nm inv* water heater. ◆**chauffe-plats** *nm inv* hotplate.

chaume [ʃom] *nm* (*tiges coupées*) stubble, straw; (*pour toiture*) thatch; **toit de c.** thatched roof. ◆**chaumière** *nf* thatched cottage.

chaussée [ʃose] *nf* road(way).

chausser [ʃose] *vt* (*chaussures*) to put on; (*fournir*) to supply in footwear; **c. qn** to put shoes on (to) s.o.; **c. du 40** to take a size 40 shoe; **ce soulier te chausse bien** this shoe fits (you) well; *— se c.* *vpr* to put on one's shoes. ◆**chausse-pied** *nm* shoehorn. ◆**chausson** *nm* slipper; (*de danse*) shoe; **c. (aux pommes)** apple turnover. ◆**chaus-**

sure *nf* shoe; *pl* shoes, footwear; **chaussures à semelles compensées** platform shoes.

chaussette [ʃosɛt] *nf* sock.

chauve [ʃov] *a & nmf* bald (person).

chauve-souris [ʃovsuri] *nf* (*pl* **chauves-souris**) (*animal*) bat.

chauvin, -ine [ʃovɛ̃, -in] *a & nmf* chauvinist.

chaux [ʃo] *nf* lime; **blanc de c.** whitewash.

chavirer [ʃavire] *vti Nau* to capsize.

chef [ʃɛf] *nm* **1 de son propre c.** on one's own authority. **2** leader, head; (*de tribu*) chief; *Culin* chef; **en c.** (*commandant, rédacteur*) in chief; **c'est un c.!** (*personne remarquable*) he's an ace!; **c. d'atelier** (shop) foreman; **c. de bande** ringleader, gang leader; **c. d'entreprise** company head; **c. d'équipe** foreman; **c. d'État** head of state; **c. d'état-major** chief of staff; **c. de famille** head of the family; **c. de file** leader; **c. de gare** stationmaster; **c. d'orchestre** conductor. ◆**chef-lieu** *nm* (*pl* **chefs-lieux**) chief town (*of a département*).

chef-d'œuvre [ʃɛdœvr] *nm* (*pl* **chefs-d'œuvre**) masterpiece.

chemin [ʃ(ə)mɛ̃] *nm* **1** road, path; (*trajet, direction*) way; **beaucoup de c. à faire** a long way to go; **dix minutes de c.** ten minutes' walk; **se mettre en c.** to start out, set out; **faire du c.** to come a long way; (*idée*) to make considerable headway; **c. faisant** on the way; **à mi-c.** half-way. **2 c. de fer** railway, *Am* railroad. ◆**chemin/er** *vi* to proceed; (*péniblement*) to trudge (along) on foot; (*évoluer*) *Fig* to progress. ◆**—ement** *nm Fig* progress. ◆**cheminot** *nm* railway *ou Am* railroad employee.

cheminée [ʃ(ə)mine] *nf* (*sur le toit*) chimney; (*de navire*) funnel; (*âtre*) fireplace; (*encadrement*) mantelpiece.

chemise [ʃ(ə)miz] *nf* shirt; (*couverture cartonnée*) folder; **c. de nuit** nightdress. ◆**chemiserie** *nf* men's shirt (and underwear) shop. ◆**chemisette** *nf* short-sleeved shirt. ◆**chemisier** *nm* (*vêtement*) blouse.

chenal, -aux [ʃənal, -o] *nm* channel.

chenapan [ʃ(ə)napɑ̃] *nm Hum* rogue, scoundrel.

chêne [ʃɛn] *nm* (*arbre, bois*) oak.

chenet [ʃ(ə)nɛ] *nm* firedog, andiron.

chenil [ʃ(ə)ni(l)] *nm* kennels.

chenille [ʃ(ə)nij] *nf* caterpillar; (*de char*) *Mil* caterpillar track.

cheptel [ʃɛptɛl] *nm* livestock.

chèque [ʃɛk] *nm* cheque, *Am* check; **c. de voyage** traveller's cheque, *Am* traveler's

check. ◆**c.-repas** nm (pl **chèques-repas**)
luncheon voucher. ◆**chéquier** nm cheque
book, Am checkbook.

cher, chère [ʃɛr] **1** a (aimé) dear (à to); –
nmf **mon c.** my dear fellow; **ma chère**
my dear (woman). **2** a (coûteux) dear,
expensive; (quartier, hôtel etc) expensive;
la vie chère the high cost of living;
payer c. (objet) to pay a lot for; (erreur etc)
Fig to pay dearly for. ◆**chèrement** adv
dearly.

cherch/er [ʃɛrʃe] vt to look for, search for;
(du secours, la paix etc) to seek; (dans un
dictionnaire) to look up; **c. ses mots** to
fumble for one's words; **aller c.** to (go and)
fetch ou get; **c. à faire** to attempt to do; **tu
l'as bien cherché!** it's your own fault!, you
asked for it! ◆**—eur, -euse** nmf research
worker; **c. d'or** gold-digger.

chér/ir [ʃerir] vt to cherish. ◆**—i, -ie** a
dearly loved, beloved; – nmf darling.

chérot [ʃero] am Fam pricey.

cherté [ʃɛrte] nf high cost, expensiveness.

chétif, -ive [ʃetif, -iv] a (puny) a (dérisoire)
wretched.

cheval, -aux [ʃ(ə)val, -o] nm horse; **c.
(vapeur)** Aut horsepower; **à c.** on horseback; **faire du c.** to go horse riding; **à c. sur**
straddling; **à c. sur les principes** a stickler
for principle; **monter sur ses grands
chevaux** to get excited; **c. à bascule** rocking horse; **c. d'arçons** Sp vaulting
horse; **c. de bataille** (dada) hobbyhorse;
chevaux de bois (manège) merry-go-
round. ◆**chevaleresque** a chivalrous.
◆**chevalier** nm knight. ◆**chevalin** a
equine; (boucherie) horse-.

chevalet [ʃ(ə)valε] nm easel; Menuis trestle.

chevalière [ʃ(ə)valjɛr] nf signet ring.

chevauchée [ʃ(ə)voʃe] nf (horse) ride.

chevaucher [ʃ(ə)voʃe] vt to straddle; – vi,
– se c. vpr to overlap.

chevet [ʃ(ə)vε] nm bedhead; **table/livre de
c.** bedside table/book; **au c. de** at the
bedside of.

cheveu, -x [ʃ(ə)vø] nm **un c.** a hair; **les
cheveux** hair; **couper les cheveux en quatre**
Fig to split hairs; **tiré par les cheveux**
(argument) far-fetched. ◆**chevelu** a hairy.
◆**chevelure** nf (head of) hair.

cheville [ʃ(ə)vij] nf Anat ankle; Menuis peg,
pin; (pour vis) (wall)plug; **c. ouvrière** Aut &
Fig linchpin; **en c. avec** Fam in cahoots
with. ◆**cheviller** vt Menuis to pin, peg.

chèvre [ʃɛvr] nf goat; (femelle) nanny-goat.
◆**chevreau, -x** nm kid.

chèvrefeuille [ʃɛvrəfœj] nm honeysuckle.

chevreuil [ʃəvrœj] nm roe deer; Culin venison.

chevron [ʃəvrɔ̃] nm (poutre) rafter; Mil
stripe, chevron; **à chevrons** (tissu, veste etc)
herringbone.

chevronné [ʃəvrəne] a seasoned, experienced.

chevroter [ʃəvrəte] vi to quaver, tremble.

chez [ʃe] prép **c. qn** at s.o.'s house, flat etc; **il
est c. Jean/c. l'épicier** he's at John's
(place)/at the grocer's; **il va c. Jean/c.
l'épicier** he's going to John's (place)/to the
grocer's; **c. moi, c. nous** at home; **je vais c.
moi** I'm going home; **c. les Suisses/les
jeunes** among the Swiss/the young; **c.
Camus** in Camus; **c. l'homme** in man; **une
habitude c. elle** a habit with her; **c. Mme
Dupont** (adresse) care of ou c/o Mme
Dupont. ◆**c.-soi** nm inv **un c.-soi** a home
(of one's own).

chialer [ʃjale] vi (pleurer) Fam to cry.

chic [ʃik] **1** a inv stylish, smart; (gentil) Fam
decent, nice; – int **c. (alors)!** great!; – nm
style, elegance. **2** nm **avoir le c. pour faire** to
have the knack of doing.

chicane [ʃikan] **1** nf (querelle) quibble. **2**
nfpl (obstacles) zigzag barriers. ◆**chicaner** vt to quibble with (s.o.); – vi to
quibble.

chiche [ʃiʃ] **1** a mean, niggardly; **c. de** sparing of. **2** int (défi) Fam I bet you I do, can
etc; **c. que je parte sans lui** I bet I leave
without him.

chichis [ʃiʃi] nmpl **faire des c.** to make a lot
of fuss.

chicorée [ʃikɔre] nf (à café) chicory; (pour
salade) endive.

chien [ʃjɛ̃] nm dog; **c. d'arrêt** pointer,
retriever; **un mal de c.** a hell of a job; **temps
de c.** filthy weather; **vie de c.** Fig dog's life;
entre c. et loup at dusk, in the gloaming.
◆**c.-loup** nm (pl **chiens-loups**) wolf-
hound. ◆**chienne** nf dog, bitch.

chiendent [ʃjɛ̃dɑ̃] nm Bot couch grass.

chiffon [ʃifɔ̃] nm rag; **c. (à poussière)** duster.
◆**chiffonner** vt to crumple; (ennuyer) Fig
to bother, distress. ◆**chiffonnier** nm
ragman.

chiffre [ʃifr] nm figure, number; (romain,
arabe) numeral; (code) cipher; **c. d'affaires**
Fin turnover. ◆**chiffrer** vt (montant) to
assess, work out; (message) to cipher,
code; – vi to mount up; **se c. à** to amount
to, work out at.

chignon [ʃiɲɔ̃] nm bun, chignon.

Chili [ʃili] nm Chile. ◆**chilien, -ienne** a &
nmf Chilean.

chimère [ʃimɛr] *nf* fantasy, (wild) dream. ◆**chimérique** *a* fanciful.

chimie [ʃimi] *nf* chemistry. ◆**chimique** *a* chemical. ◆**chimiste** *nmf* (research) chemist.

chimpanzé [ʃɛ̃pɑ̃ze] *nm* chimpanzee.

Chine [ʃin] *nf* China. ◆**chinois, -oise** *a* & *nmf* Chinese; – *nm* (*langue*) Chinese. ◆**chinoiser** *vi* to quibble. ◆**chinoiserie** *nf* (*objet*) Chinese curio; *pl* (*bizarreries*) *Fig* weird complications.

chiner [ʃine] *vi* (*brocanteur etc*) to hunt for bargains.

chiot [ʃjo] *nm* pup(py).

chiper [ʃipe] *vt Fam* to swipe, pinch (à from).

chipie [ʃipi] *nf* **vieille c.** (*femme*) *Péj* old crab.

chipoter [ʃipɔte] *vi* **1** (*manger*) to nibble. **2** (*chicaner*) to quibble.

chips [ʃips] *nmpl* (potato) crisps, *Am* chips.

chiquenaude [ʃiknod] *nf* flick (of the finger).

chiromancie [kirɔmɑ̃si] *nf* palmistry.

chirurgie [ʃiryrʒi] *nf* surgery. ◆**chirurgical, -aux** *a* surgical. ◆**chirurgien** *nm* surgeon.

chlore [klɔr] *nm* chlorine. ◆**chloroforme** *nm* chloroform. ◆**chlorure** *nm* chloride.

choc [ʃɔk] *nm* (*heurt*) impact, shock; (*émotion*) & *Méd* shock; (*collision*) crash; (*des opinions, entre manifestants etc*) clash.

chocolat [ʃɔkɔla] *nm* chocolate; **c. à croquer** plain *ou Am* bittersweet chocolate; **c. au lait** milk chocolate; **c. glacé** choc-ice; – *a inv* chocolate(-coloured). ◆**chocolaté** *a* chocolate-flavoured.

chœur [kœr] *nm* (*chanteurs, nef*) *Rel* choir; (*composition musicale*) & *Fig* chorus; **en c.** (all) together, in chorus.

choir [ʃwar] *vi* **laisser c. qn** *Fam* to turn one's back on s.o.

chois/ir [ʃwazir] *vt* to choose, pick, select. ◆**—i** *a* (*œuvres*) selected; (*terme, langage*) well-chosen; (*public*) select. ◆**choix** *nm* choice; (*assortiment*) selection; **morceau de c.** choice piece; **au c. du client** according to choice.

choléra [kɔlera] *nm* cholera.

cholestérol [kɔlesterɔl] *nm* cholesterol.

chôm/er [ʃome] *vi* (*ouvrier etc*) to be unemployed; **jour chômé** (public) holiday. ◆**—age** *nm* unemployment; **en** *ou* **au c.** unemployed; **mettre en c. technique** to lay off, dismiss.

chope [ʃɔp] *nf* beer mug, tankard; (*contenu*) pint.

choqu/er [ʃɔke] *vt* to offend, shock; (*verres*) to clink; (*commotionner*) to shake up. ◆**—ant** *a* shocking, offensive.

choral, -als [kɔral] *a* choral. ◆**chorale** *nf* choral society. ◆**choriste** *nmf* chorister.

chorégraphe [kɔregraf] *nmf* choreographer. ◆**chorégraphie** *nf* choreography.

chose [ʃoz] *nf* thing; **état de choses** state of affairs; **par la force des choses** through force of circumstance; **dis-lui bien des choses de ma part** remember me to him *ou* her; **ce monsieur C.** that Mr What's-his-name; **se sentir tout c.** *Fam* (*décontenancé*) to feel all funny; (*malade*) to feel out of sorts.

chou, -x [ʃu] *nm* cabbage; **choux de Bruxelles** Brussels sprouts; **mon c.!** my pet!; **c. à la crème** cream puff. ◆**c.-fleur** *nm* (*pl* **choux-fleurs**) cauliflower.

choucas [ʃuka] *nm* jackdaw.

chouchou, -oute [ʃuʃu, -ut] *nmf* (*favori*) *Fam* pet, darling. ◆**chouchouter** *vt* to pamper.

choucroute [ʃukrut] *nf* sauerkraut.

chouette [ʃwɛt] **1** *nf* (*oiseau*) owl. **2** *a* (*chic*) *Fam* super, great.

choyer [ʃwaye] *vt* to pet, pamper.

chrétien, -ienne [kretjɛ̃, -jɛn] *a* & *nmf* Christian. ◆**chrétienté** *nf* Christendom. ◆**Christ** [krist] *nm* Christ. ◆**christianisme** *nm* Christianity.

chrome [krom] *nm* chromium, chrome. ◆**chromé** *a* chromium-plated.

chromosome [krɔmozom] *nm* chromosome.

chronique [krɔnik] **1** *a* (*malade, chômage etc*) chronic. **2** *nf* (*annales*) chronicle; *Journ* report, news; (*rubrique*) column. ◆**chroniqueur** *nm* chronicler; *Journ* reporter, columnist.

chronologie [krɔnɔlɔʒi] *nf* chronology. ◆**chronologique** *a* chronological.

chronomètre [krɔnɔmɛtr] *nm* stopwatch. ◆**chronométr/er** *vt Sp* to time. ◆**—eur** *nm Sp* timekeeper.

chrysanthème [krizɑ̃tɛm] *nm* chrysanthemum.

chuchot/er [ʃyʃɔte] *vti* to whisper. ◆**—ement** *nm* whisper(ing). ◆**chuchoteries** *nfpl Fam* whispering.

chuinter [ʃwɛ̃te] *vi* (*vapeur*) to hiss.

chut! [ʃyt] *int* sh!, hush!

chute [ʃyt] *nf* fall; (*défaite*) (down)fall; **c. d'eau** waterfall; **c. de neige** snowfall; **c. de pluie** rainfall; **c. des cheveux** hair loss. ◆**chuter** *vi Fam* to fall.

Chypre [ʃipr] *nf* Cyprus. ◆**chypriote** *a* & *nmf* Cypriot.

ci [si] **1** *adv* **par-ci par-là** here and there. **2** *pron dém* **comme ci comme ça** so so. **3** *voir* **ce**[2]**, celui.**

ci-après [siaprɛ] *adv* below, hereafter. ◆**ci-contre** *adv* opposite. ◆**ci-dessous** *adv* below. ◆**ci-dessus** *adv* above. ◆**ci-gît** *adv* here lies (*on gravestones*). ◆**ci-inclus** *a*, ◆**ci-joint** *a* (*inv before n*) (*dans une lettre*) enclosed (herewith).

cible [sibl] *nf* target.

ciboulette [sibulɛt] *nf Culin* chives.

cicatrice [sikatris] *nf* scar. ◆**cicatriser** *vt*, **— se c.** *vpr* to heal up (*leaving a scar*).

cidre [sidr] *nm* cider.

Cie *abrév* (*compagnie*) Co.

ciel [sjɛl] *nm* **1** (*pl* **ciels**) sky; **à c. ouvert** (*piscine etc*) open-air; **c. de lit** canopy. **2** (*pl* **cieux** [sjø]) *Rel* heaven; **juste c.!** good heavens!; **sous d'autres cieux** *Hum* in other climes.

cierge [sjɛrʒ] *nm Rel* candle.

cigale [sigal] *nf* (*insecte*) cicada.

cigare [sigar] *nm* cigar. ◆**cigarette** *nf* cigarette.

cigogne [sigɔɲ] *nf* stork.

cil [sil] *nm* (eye)lash.

cime [sim] *nf* (*d'un arbre*) top; (*d'une montagne*) & *Fig* peak.

ciment [simã] *nm* cement. ◆**cimenter** *vt* to cement.

cimetière [simtjɛr] *nm* cemetery, graveyard; **c. de voitures** scrapyard, breaker's yard, *Am* auto graveyard.

ciné [sine] *nm Fam* cinema. ◆**c.-club** *nm* film society. ◆**cinéaste** *nm* film maker. ◆**cinéphile** *nmf* film buff.

cinéma [sinema] *nm* cinema; **faire du c.** to make films. ◆**cinémascope** *nm* cinemascope. ◆**cinémathèque** *nf* film library; (*salle*) film theatre. ◆**cinématographique** *a* cinema-.

cinglé [sɛ̃gle] *a Fam* crazy.

cingl/er [sɛ̃gle] *vt* to lash. ◆**—ant** *a* (*vent, remarque*) cutting, biting.

cinoche [sinɔʃ] *nm Fam* cinema.

cinq [sɛ̃k] *nm* five; — *a* ([sɛ̃] *before consonant*) five. ◆**cinquième** *a* & *nmf* fifth; **un c.** a fifth.

cinquante [sɛ̃kãt] *a* & *nm* fifty. ◆**cinquantaine** *nf* about fifty. ◆**cinquantenaire** *a* & *nmf* fifty-year-old (person); — *nm* fiftieth anniversary. ◆**cinquantième** *a* & *nmf* fiftieth.

cintre [sɛ̃tr] *nm* coathanger; *Archit* arch. ◆**cintré** *a* arched; (*veste etc*) tailored, slim-fitting.

cirage [siraʒ] *nm* (shoe) polish.

circoncis [sirkɔ̃si] *a* circumcised. ◆**circoncision** *nf* circumcision.

circonférence [sirkɔ̃ferɑ̃s] *nf* circumference.

circonflexe [sirkɔ̃flɛks] *a Gram* circumflex.

circonlocution [sirkɔ̃lɔkysjɔ̃] *nf* circumlocution.

circonscrire [sirkɔ̃skrir] *vt* to circumscribe. ◆**circonscription** *nf* division; **c. (électorale)** constituency.

circonspect, -ecte [sirkɔ̃spɛ(kt), -ɛkt] *a* cautious, circumspect. ◆**circonspection** *nf* caution.

circonstance [sirkɔ̃stɑ̃s] *nf* circumstance; **pour/en la c.** for/on this occasion; **de c.** (*habit, parole etc*) appropriate. ◆**circonstancié** *a* detailed. ◆**circonstanciel, -ielle** *a Gram* adverbial.

circonvenir [sirkɔ̃vnir] *vt* to circumvent.

circuit [sirkɥi] *nm Sp Él Fin* circuit; (*périple*) tour, trip; (*détour*) roundabout way; *pl Él* circuitry, circuits.

circulaire [sirkyler] *a* circular; — *nf* (*lettre*) circular. ◆**circulation** *nf* circulation; *Aut* traffic. ◆**circuler** *vi* to circulate; (*véhicule, train*) to move, travel; (*passant*) to walk about; (*rumeur*) to go round, circulate; **faire c.** to circulate; (*piétons etc*) to move on; **circulez!** keep moving!

cire [sir] *nf* wax; (*pour meubles*) polish, wax. ◆**cir/er** *vt* to polish, wax. ◆**—é** *nm* (*vêtement*) oilskin(s). ◆**—eur** *nm* bootblack. ◆**—euse** *nf* (*appareil*) floor polisher. ◆**cireux, -euse** *a* waxy.

cirque [sirk] *nm Th Hist* circus.

cirrhose [siroz] *nf Méd* cirrhosis.

cisaille(s) [sizaj] *nf*(*pl*) shears. ◆**ciseau, -x** *nm* chisel; *pl* scissors. ◆**ciseler** *vt* to chisel.

citadelle [sitadɛl] *nf* citadel.

cité [site] *nf* city; **c. (ouvrière)** housing estate (*for workers*), *Am* housing project *ou* development; **c. universitaire** (students') halls of residence. ◆**citadin, -ine** *nmf* city dweller; — *a* city-, urban.

citer [site] *vt* to quote; *Jur* to summon; *Mil* to mention, cite. ◆**citation** *nf* quotation; *Jur* summons; *Mil* mention, citation.

citerne [sitɛrn] *nf* (*réservoir*) tank.

cithare [sitar] *nf* zither.

citoyen, -enne [sitwajɛ̃, -ɛn] *nmf* citizen. ◆**citoyenneté** *nf* citizenship.

citron [sitrɔ̃] *nm* lemon; **c. pressé** (fresh)

lemon juice. ◆**citronnade** *nf* lemon drink, (still) lemonade.

citrouille [sitruj] *nf* pumpkin.

civet [sive] *nm* stew; **c. de lièvre** jugged hare.

civière [sivjɛr] *nf* stretcher.

civil [sivil] **1** *a* (*droits, guerre, mariage etc*) civil; (*non militaire*) civilian; (*courtois*) civil; **année civile** calendar year. **2** *nm* civilian; **dans le c.** in civilian life; **en c.** (*policier*) in plain clothes; (*soldat*) in civilian clothes. ◆**civilité** *nf* civility.

civiliser [sivilize] *vt* to civilize; **— se c.** *vpr* to become civilized. ◆**civilisation** *nf* civilization.

civique [sivik] *a* civic; **instruction c.** *Scol* civics. ◆**civisme** *nm* civic sense.

clair [klɛr] *a* (*distinct, limpide, évident*) clear; (*éclairé*) light; (*pâle*) light(-coloured); (*sauce, chevelure*) thin; **bleu/vert c.** light blue/green; **il fait c.** it's light *ou* bright; *— adv* (*voir*) clearly; *— nm* **c. de lune** moonlight; **le plus c. de** the major *ou* greater part of; **tirer au c.** (*question etc*) to clear up. ◆**—ement** *adv* clearly. ◆**claire-voie** *nf* à **c.-voie** (*barrière*) lattice-; (*caisse*) openwork; (*porte*) louvre(d).

clairière [klɛrjɛr] *nf* clearing, glade.

clairon [klɛrɔ̃] *nm* bugle; (*soldat*) bugler. ◆**claironner** *vt* (*annoncer*) to trumpet forth.

clairsemé [klɛrsəme] *a* sparse.

clairvoyant [klɛrvwajɑ̃] *a* (*perspicace*) clear-sighted. ◆**clairvoyance** *nf* clearsightedness.

clam/er [klame] *vt* to cry out. ◆**—eur** *nf* clamour, outcry.

clan [klɑ̃] *nm* clan, clique, set.

clandestin [klɑ̃dɛstɛ̃] *a* secret, clandestine; (*journal, mouvement*) underground; **passager c.** stowaway.

clapet [klapɛ] *nm* Tech valve; (*bouche*) Arg trap.

clapier [klapje] *nm* (rabbit) hutch.

clapot/er [klapɔte] *vi* (*vagues*) to lap. ◆**—ement** *nm*, ◆**clapotis** *nm* lap(ping).

claque [klak] *nf* smack, slap. ◆**claquer** *vt* (*porte*) to slam, bang; (*gifler*) to smack, slap; (*fouet*) to crack; (*fatiguer*) *Fam* to tire out; (*dépenser*) *Arg* to blow; **se c. un muscle** to tear a muscle; **faire c.** (*doigts*) to snap; (*langue*) to click; (*fouet*) to crack; *— vi* (*porte*) to slam, bang; (*drapeau*) to flap; (*coup de revolver*) to ring out; (*mourir*) *Fam* to die; (*tomber en panne*) *Fam* to break down; **c. des mains** to clap one's hands; **elle claque des dents** her teeth are chattering.

claquemurer (se) [səklakmyre] *vpr* to shut oneself up, hole up.

claquettes [klakɛt] *nfpl* tap dancing.

clarifier [klarifje] *vt* to clarify. ◆**clarification** *nf* clarification.

clarinette [klarinɛt] *nf* clarinet.

clarté [klarte] *nf* light, brightness; (*précision*) clarity, clearness.

classe [klɑs] *nf* class; **aller en c.** to go to school; **c. ouvrière/moyenne** working/middle class; **avoir de la c.** to have class.

class/er [klɑse] *vt* to classify, class; (*papiers*) to file; (*candidats*) to grade; (*affaire*) to close; **se c. parmi** to rank *ou* be classed among; **se c. premier** to come first. ◆**—ement** *nm* classification; filing; grading; (*rang*) place; *Sp* placing. ◆**—eur** *nm* (*meuble*) filing cabinet; (*portefeuille*) (loose leaf) file. ◆**classification** *nf* classification. ◆**classifier** *vt* to classify.

classique [klɑsik] *a* classical; (*typique*) classic; *— nm* (*œuvre, auteur*) classic. ◆**classicisme** *nm* classicism.

clause [kloz] *nf* clause.

claustrophobie [klostrɔfɔbi] *nf* claustrophobia. ◆**claustrophobe** *a* claustrophobic.

clavecin [klavsɛ̃] *nm* Mus harpsichord.

clavicule [klavikyl] *nf* collarbone.

clavier [klavje] *nm* keyboard.

clé, clef [kle] *nf* key; (*outil*) spanner, wrench; *Mus* clef; **fermer à c.** to lock; **sous c.** under lock and key; **c. de contact** ignition key; **c. de voûte** keystone; **poste/industrie c.** key post/industry; **clés en main** (*acheter une maison etc*) ready to move in; **prix clés en main** (*voiture*) on the road price.

clément [klemɑ̃] *a* (*temps*) mild, clement; (*juge*) lenient, clement. ◆**clémence** *nf* mildness; leniency; clemency.

clémentine [klemɑ̃tin] *nf* clementine.

clerc [klɛr] *nm* Rel cleric; (*de notaire*) clerk. ◆**clergé** *nm* clergy. ◆**clérical, -aux** *a* Rel clerical.

cliché [kliʃe] *nm* Phot negative; Typ plate; (*idée*) cliché.

client, -ente [klijɑ̃, -ɑ̃t] *nmf* (*de magasin etc*) customer; (*d'un avocat etc*) client; (*d'un médecin*) patient; (*d'hôtel*) guest. ◆**clientèle** *nf* customers, clientele; (*d'un avocat*) practice, clientele; (*d'un médecin*) practice, patients; **accorder sa c. à** to give one's custom to.

cligner [kliɲe] *vi* **c. des yeux** (*ouvrir et fermer*) to blink; (*fermer à demi*) to screw up one's eyes; **c. de l'œil** to wink.

◆**clignot/er** vi to blink; (*lumière*) to flicker; *Aut* to flash; (*étoile*) to twinkle. ◆**—ant** nm *Aut* indicator, *Am* directional signal.

climat [klima] nm *Mét & Fig* climate. ◆**climatique** a climatic. ◆**climatisation** nf air-conditioning. ◆**climatiser** vt to air-condition.

clin d'œil [klɛ̃dœj] nm wink; **en un c. d'œil** in the twinkling of an eye.

clinique [klinik] a clinical; – nf (*hôpital*) (private) clinic.

clinquant [klɛ̃kɑ̃] a tawdry.

clique [klik] nf *Péj* clique; *Mus Mil* (drum and bugle) band.

cliqueter [klikte] vi to clink. ◆**cliquetis** nm clink(ing).

clivage [klivaʒ] nm split, division (**de** in).

cloaque [klɔak] nm cesspool.

clochard, -arde [klɔʃar, -ard] nmf tramp, vagrant.

cloche [klɔʃ] nf **1** bell; **c. à fromage** cheese cover. **2** (*personne*) *Fam* idiot, oaf. ◆**clocher 1** nm bell tower; (*en pointe*) steeple; **de c.** *Fig* parochial; **esprit de c.** parochialism. **2** vi to be wrong *ou* amiss. ◆**clochette** nf (small) bell.

cloche-pied (à) [aklɔʃpje] adv **sauter à c.-pied** to hop on one foot.

cloison [klwazɔ̃] nf partition; *Fig* barrier. ◆**cloisonner** vt to partition; (*activités etc*) *Fig* to compartmentalize.

cloître [klwatr] nm cloister. ◆**se cloîtrer** vpr to shut oneself away, cloister oneself.

clopin-clopant [klɔpɛ̃klɔpɑ̃] adv **aller c.-clopant** to hobble.

cloque [klɔk] nf blister.

clore [klɔr] vt (*débat, lettre*) to close. ◆**clos** a (*incident etc*) closed; (*espace*) enclosed; – nm (*enclosed*) field.

clôture [klotyr] nf (*barrière*) enclosure, fence; (*fermeture*) closing. ◆**clôturer** vt to enclose; (*compte, séance etc*) to close.

clou [klu] nm nail; (*furoncle*) boil; **le c.** (**du spectacle**) *Fam* the star attraction; **les clous** (*passage*) pedestrian crossing; **des clous!** *Fam* nothing at all! ◆**clouer** vt to nail; **cloué au lit** confined to (one's) bed; **cloué sur place** nailed to the spot; **c. le bec à qn** *Fam* to shut s.o. up. ◆**clouté** a (*chaussures*) hobnailed; (*ceinture, pneus*) studded; **passage c.** pedestrian crossing, *Am* crosswalk.

clown [klun] nm clown.

club [klœb] nm (*association*) club.

cm *abrév* (*centimètre*) cm.

co- [kɔ] *préf* co-.

coaguler [kɔagyle] vti, **— se c.** vpr to coagulate.

coaliser (se) [səkɔalize] vpr to form a coalition, join forces. ◆**coalition** nf coalition.

coasser [kɔase] vi (*grenouille*) to croak.

cobaye [kɔbaj] nm (*animal*) & *Fig* guinea pig.

cobra [kɔbra] nm (*serpent*) cobra.

coca [kɔka] nm (*Coca-Cola*®) coke.

cocagne [kɔkaɲ] nf **pays de c.** dreamland, land of plenty.

cocaïne [kɔkain] nf cocain.

cocarde [kɔkard] nf rosette, cockade; *Av* roundel. ◆**cocardier, -ière** a *Péj* flag-waving.

cocasse [kɔkas] a droll, comical. ◆**cocasserie** nf drollery.

coccinelle [kɔksinel] nf ladybird, *Am* ladybug.

cocher¹ [kɔʃe] vt to tick (off), *Am* to check (off).

cocher² [kɔʃe] nm coachman. ◆**cochère** af **porte c.** main gateway.

cochon, -onne [kɔʃɔ̃, -ɔn] nm **1** pig; (*mâle*) hog; **c. d'Inde** guinea pig. **2** nmf (*personne sale*) (dirty) pig; (*salaud*) swine; – a (*histoire, film*) dirty, filthy. ◆**cochonnerie(s)** nf(pl) (*obscénité(s)*) filth; (*pacotille*) *Fam* rubbish.

cocktail [kɔktel] nm (*boisson*) cocktail; (*réunion*) cocktail party.

coco [kɔko] nm **noix de c.** coconut. ◆**cocotier** nm coconut palm.

cocon [kɔkɔ̃] nm cocoon.

cocorico [kɔkɔriko] int & nm cock-a-doodle-doo; **faire c.** (*crier victoire*) *Fam* to give three cheers for France, wave the flag.

cocotte [kɔkɔt] nf (*marmite*) casserole; **c. minute**® pressure cooker.

cocu [kɔky] nm *Fam* cuckold.

code [kɔd] nm code; **codes, phares c.** *Aut* dipped headlights, *Am* low beams; **C. de la route** Highway Code. ◆**coder** vt to code. ◆**codifier** vt to codify.

coefficient [kɔefisjɑ̃] nm *Math* coefficient; (*d'erreur, de sécurité*) *Fig* margin.

coéquipier, -ière [kɔekipje, -jɛr] nmf team mate.

cœur [kœr] nm heart; *Cartes* hearts; **au c. de** (*ville, hiver etc*) in the heart of; **par c.** by heart; **ça me (sou)lève le c.** that turns my stomach; **à c. ouvert** (*opération*) open-heart; (*parler*) freely; **avoir mal au c.** to feel sick; **avoir le c. gros** *ou* **serré** to have a heavy heart; **ça me tient à c.** that's close to my heart; **avoir bon c.** to be kind-hearted; **de bon c.** (*offrir*) with a good heart, willingly; (*rire*) heartily; **si le c. vous en dit** if you so desire.

coexister [kɔɛgziste] *vi* to coexist. ◆**coexistence** *nf* coexistence.

coffre [kɔfr] *nm* chest; (*de banque*) safe; (*de voiture*) boot, *Am* trunk; (*d'autocar*) luggage *ou Am* baggage compartment. ◆**c.-fort** *nm* (*pl* **coffres-forts**) safe. ◆**coffret** *nm* casket, box.

cogiter [kɔʒite] *vi Iron* to cogitate.

cognac [kɔɲak] *nm* cognac.

cogner [kɔɲe] *vti* to knock; **c. qn** *Arg* (*frapper*) to thump s.o.; (*tabasser*) to beat s.o. up; **se c. la tête**/*etc* to knock one's head/*etc*.

cohabiter [kɔabite] *vi* to live together. ◆**cohabitation** *nf* living together; *Pol Fam* power sharing.

cohérent [kɔerɑ̃] *a* coherent. ◆**cohérence** *nf* coherence. ◆**cohésion** *nf* cohesion, cohesiveness.

cohorte [kɔɔrt] *nf* (*groupe*) troop, band, cohort.

cohue [kɔy] *nf* crowd, mob.

coiffe [kwaf] *nf* headdress.

coiff/er [kwafe] *vt* (*chapeau*) to put on, wear; (*surmonter*) *Fig* to cap; (*être à la tête de*) to head; **c. qn** to do s.o.'s hair; **c. qn d'un chapeau** to put a hat on s.o.; — **se c.** *vpr* to do one's hair; **se c. d'un chapeau** to put on a hat. ◆**-eur, -euse**[1] *nmf* (*pour hommes*) barber, hairdresser; (*pour dames*) hairdresser. ◆**-euse**[2] *nf* dressing table. ◆**coiffure** *nf* headgear, hat; (*arrangement*) hairstyle; (*métier*) hairdressing.

coin [kwɛ̃] *nm* (*angle*) corner; (*endroit*) spot; (*de terre, de ciel*) patch; (*cale*) wedge; **du c.** (*magasin etc*) local; **dans le c.** in the (local) area; **au c. du feu** by the fireside; **petit c.** *Fam* loo, *Am* john.

coinc/er [kwɛ̃se] *vt* (*mécanisme, tiroir*) to jam; (*caler*) to wedge; **c. qn** *Fam* to catch s.o., corner s.o.; — **se c.** *vpr* (*mécanisme etc*) to get jammed *ou* stuck. ◆**-é** *a* (*tiroir etc*) stuck, jammed; (*personne*) *Fam* stuck.

coïncider [kɔɛ̃side] *vi* to coincide. ◆**coïncidence** *nf* coincidence.

coin-coin [kwɛ̃kwɛ̃] *nm inv* (*de canard*) quack.

coing [kwɛ̃] *nm* (*fruit*) quince.

coke [kɔk] *nm* (*combustible*) coke.

col [kɔl] *nm* (*de chemise*) collar; (*de bouteille*) & *Anat* neck; *Géog* pass; **c. roulé** polo neck, *Am* turtleneck.

colère [kɔlɛr] *nf* anger; **une c.** (*accès*) a fit of anger; **en c.** angry (**contre** with); **se mettre**

en c. to lose one's temper. ◆**coléreux, -euse** *a*, ◆**colérique** *a* quick-tempered.

colibri [kɔlibri] *nm* hummingbird.

colifichet [kɔlifiʃɛ] *nm* trinket.

colimaçon (en) [ɑ̃kɔlimasɔ̃] *adv* **escalier en c.** spiral staircase.

colin [kɔlɛ̃] *nm* (*poisson*) hake.

colique [kɔlik] *nf* diarrh(o)ea; (*douleur*) stomach pain, colic.

colis [kɔli] *nm* parcel, package.

collaborer [kɔlabɔre] *vi* collaborate (**avec** with, **à** on); **c. à** (*journal*) to contribute to. ◆**collaborateur, -trice** *nmf* collaborator; contributor. ◆**collaboration** *nf* collaboration; contribution.

collage [kɔlaʒ] *nm* (*œuvre*) collage.

collant [kɔlɑ̃] **1** *a* (*papier*) sticky; (*vêtement*) skin-tight; **être c.** (*importun*) *Fam* to be a pest. **2** *nm* (pair of) tights; (*de danse*) leotard.

collation [kɔlasjɔ̃] *nf* (*repas*) light meal.

colle [kɔl] *nf* (*transparente*) glue; (*blanche*) paste; (*question*) *Fam* poser, teaser; (*interrogation*) *Scol Arg* oral; (*retenue*) *Scol Arg* detention.

collecte [kɔlɛkt] *nf* (*quête*) collection. ◆**collect/er** *vt* to collect. ◆**-eur** *nm* collector; (**égout**) **c.** main sewer.

collectif, -ive [kɔlɛktif, -iv] *a* collective; (*hystérie, démission*) mass-; **billet c.** group ticket. ◆**collectivement** *adv* collectively. ◆**collectivisme** *nm* collectivism. ◆**collectivité** *nf* community, collectivity.

collection [kɔlɛksjɔ̃] *nf* collection. ◆**collectionn/er** *vt* (*timbres etc*) to collect. ◆**-eur, -euse** *nmf* collector.

collège [kɔlɛʒ] *nm* (secondary) school, *Am* (high) school; (*électoral, sacré*) college. ◆**collégien** *nm* schoolboy. ◆**collégienne** *nf* schoolgirl.

collègue [kɔlɛg] *nmf* colleague.

coller [kɔle] *vt* (*timbre etc*) to stick; (*à la colle transparente*) to glue; (*à la colle blanche*) to paste; (*affiche*) to stick up; (*papier peint*) to hang; (*mettre*) *Fam* to stick, shove; **c. contre** (*nez, oreille etc*) to press against; **c. qn** (*embarrasser*) *Fam* to stump s.o., catch s.o. out; (*consigner*) *Scol* to keep s.o. in; **être collé à** (*examen*) *Fam* to fail, flunk; **se c. contre** to cling (close) to; **se c. qn/qch** *Fam* to get stuck with s.o./sth.; — *vi* to stick, cling; **c. à** (*s'adapter*) to fit, correspond to; **ça colle!** *Fam* everything's just fine! ◆**colleur, -euse** *nmf* **c. d'affiches** billsticker.

collet [kɔlɛ] *nm* (*lacet*) snare; **prendre qn au c.** to grab s.o. by the scruff of the neck; **elle**

est/ils sont c. monté she is/they are prim and proper *ou* straight-laced.

collier [kɔlje] *nm* (*bijou*) necklace; (*de chien, cheval*) & *Tech* collar.

colline [kɔlin] *nf* hill.

collision [kɔlizjɔ̃] *nf* (*de véhicules*) collision; (*bagarre, conflit*) clash; **entrer en c. avec** to collide with.

colloque [kɔlɔk] *nm* symposium.

collusion [kɔlyzjɔ̃] *nf* collusion.

colmater [kɔlmate] *vt* (*fuite, fente*) to seal; (*trou*) to fill in; (*brèche*) *Mil* to close, seal.

colombe [kɔlɔ̃b] *nf* dove.

colon [kɔlɔ̃] *nm* settler, colonist; (*enfant*) *child taking part in a holiday camp.* ◆**colonial, -aux** *a* colonial. ◆**colonie** *nf* colony; **c. de vacances** (children's) holiday camp *ou Am* vacation camp.

coloniser [kɔlɔnize] *vt Pol* to colonize; (*peupler*) to settle. ◆**colonisateur, -trice** *a* colonizing; – *nmf* colonizer. ◆**colonisation** *nf* colonization.

côlon [kolɔ̃] *nm Anat* colon.

colonel [kɔlɔnɛl] *nm* colonel.

colonne [kɔlɔn] *nf* column; **c. vertébrale** spine. ◆**colonnade** *nf* colonnade.

color/er [kɔlɔre] *vt* to colour. ◆**—ant** *a* & *nm* colouring. ◆**—é** *a* (*verre etc*) coloured; (*teint*) ruddy; (*style, foule*) colourful. ◆**coloration** *nf* colouring, colour. ◆**coloriage** *nm* colouring; (*dessin*) coloured drawing. ◆**colorier** *vt* (*dessin etc*) to colour (in). ◆**coloris** *nm* (*effet*) colouring; (*nuance*) shade.

colosse [kɔlɔs] *nm* giant, colossus. ◆**colossal, -aux** *a* colossal, gigantic.

colporter [kɔlpɔrte] *vt* to peddle, hawk.

coltiner [kɔltine] *vt* (*objet lourd*) *Fam* to lug, haul; – **se c.** *vpr* (*tâche pénible*) *Fam* to take on, tackle.

coma [kɔma] *nm* coma; **dans le c.** in a coma.

combat [kɔ̃ba] *nm* fight; *Mil* combat. ◆**combatif, -ive** *a* (*personne*) eager to fight; (*instinct, esprit*) fighting. ◆**combatt/re*** *vt* to fight; (*maladie, inflation etc*) to combat, fight; – *vi* to fight. ◆**—ant** *nm Mil* combattant; (*bagarreur*) *Fam* brawler; – *a* (*unité*) fighting.

combien [kɔ̃bjɛ̃] **1** *adv* (*quantité*) how much; (*nombre*) how many; **c. de** (*temps, argent etc*) how much; (*gens, livres etc*) how many. **2** *adv* (*à quel point*) how; **tu verras c. il est bête** you'll see how silly he is. **3** *adv* (*distance*) **c. y a-t-il d'ici à . . . ?** how far is it to . . . ? **4** *nm inv* **le c. sommes-nous?** (*date*) *Fam* what date is it?; **tous les c.?** (*fréquence*) *Fam* how often?

combine [kɔ̃bin] *nf* (*truc, astuce*) *Fam* trick.

combin/er [kɔ̃bine] *vt* (*disposer*) to combine; (*calculer*) to devise, plan (out). ◆**—é** *nm* (*de téléphone*) receiver. ◆**combinaison** *nf* **1** combination; (*manœuvre*) scheme. **2** (*vêtement de femme*) slip; (*de mécanicien*) boiler suit, *Am* overalls; (*de pilote*) flying suit; **c. de ski** ski suit.

comble [kɔ̃bl] **1** *nm* **le c. de** (*la joie etc*) the height of; **pour c. (de malheur)** to crown *ou* cap it all; **c'est un *ou* le c.!** that's the limit! **2** *nmpl* (*mansarde*) attic, loft; **sous les combles** beneath the roof, in the loft *ou* attic. **3** *a* (*bondé*) packed, full.

combler [kɔ̃ble] *vt* (*trou, lacune etc*) to fill; (*retard, perte*) to make good; (*vœu*) to fulfil; **c. qn de** (*cadeaux etc*) to lavish on s.o.; (*joie*) to fill s.o. with; **je suis comblé** I'm completely satisfied; **vous me comblez!** you're too good to me!

combustible [kɔ̃bystibl] *nm* fuel; – *a* combustible. ◆**combustion** *nf* combustion.

comédie [kɔmedi] *nf* comedy; (*complication*) *Fam* fuss, palaver; **c. musicale** musical; **jouer la c.** *Fig* to put on an act, play-act; (*c'est de la c.* (*c'est faux*) it's a sham. ◆**comédien** *nm Th* & *Fig* actor. ◆**comédienne** *nf Th* & *Fig* actress.

comestible [kɔmɛstibl] *a* edible; – *nmpl* foods.

comète [kɔmɛt] *nf* comet.

comique [kɔmik] *a* (*style etc*) *Th* comic; (*amusant*) *Fig* comical, funny; **(auteur) c.** comedy writer; – *nm* comedy; (*acteur*) comic (actor); **le c.** (*genre*) comedy; *Fig* the comical side (**de** of).

comité [kɔmite] *nm* committee; **c. de gestion** board (of management); **en petit c.** in a small group.

commande [kɔmɑ̃d] **1** *nf* (*achat*) order; **sur c.** to order. **2** *nfpl* **les commandes** *Av Tech* the controls; **tenir les commandes** (*diriger*) *Fig* to have control.

command/er [kɔmɑ̃de] **1** *vt* (*diriger, exiger, dominer*) to command; (*faire fonctionner*) to control; – *vi* **c. à** (*ses passions etc*) to have control over; **c. à qn de faire** to command s.o. to do. **2** *vt* (*acheter*) to order. ◆**—ant** *nm Nau* captain; (*grade*) *Mil* major; (*grade*) *Av* squadron leader; **c. de bord** *Av* captain. ◆**—ement** *nm* (*autorité*) command; *Rel* commandment. ◆**commando** *nm* commando.

commanditaire [kɔmɑ̃diter] *nm Com* sleeping *ou* limited partner, *Am* silent partner.

comme [kɔm] **1** *adv* & *conj* as, like; **un peu**

c. a bit like; **c. moi** like me; **c. cela** like that; **blanc c. neige** (as) white as snow; **c. si** as if; **c. pour faire** as if to do; **c. par hasard** as if by chance; **joli c. tout** *Fam* ever so pretty; **c. ami** as a friend; **c. quoi** (*disant que*) to the effect that; (*ce qui prouve que*) so, which goes to show that; **qu'as-tu c. diplômes?** what do you have in the way of certificates? **2** *adv* (*exclamatif*) **regarde c. il pleut!** look how it's raining!; **c. c'est petit!** isn't it small! **3** *conj* (*temps*) as; (*cause*) as, since; **c. je pars** as I'm leaving; **c. elle entrait** (just) as she was coming in.

commémorer [kɔmemɔre] *vt* to commemorate. ◆**commémoratif, -ive** *a* commemorative. ◆**commémoration** *nf* commemoration.

commenc/er [kɔmɑ̃se] *vti* to begin, start (**à faire** to do, doing; **par** with; **par faire** by doing); **pour c.** to begin with. ◆**—ement** *nm* beginning, start.

comment [kɔmɑ̃] *adv* how; **c. le sais-tu?** how do you know?; **et c.!** and how!; **c.?** (*répétition, surprise*) what?; **c.!** (*indignation*) what!; **c. est-il?** what is he like?; **c. faire?** what's to be done?; **c. t'appelles-tu?** what's your name?; **c. allez-vous?** how are you?

commentaire [kɔmɑ̃tɛr] *nm* (*explications*) commentary; (*remarque*) comment. ◆**commentateur, -trice** *nmf* commentator. ◆**commenter** *vt* to comment (up)on.

commérage(s) [kɔmeraʒ] *nm(pl)* gossip.

commerce [kɔmɛrs] *nm* trade, commerce; (*magasin*) shop, business; **de c.** (*voyageur, maison, tribunal*) commercial; (*navire*) trading; **chambre de c.** chamber of commerce; **faire du c.** to trade; **dans le c.** (*objet*) (on sale) in the shops. ◆**commercer** *vi* to trade. ◆**commerçant, -ante** *nmf* shopkeeper; **c. en gros** wholesale dealer; – *a* (*nation*) trading, mercantile; (*rue, quartier*) shopping-; (*personne*) business-minded. ◆**commercial, -aux** *a* commercial, business-. ◆**commercialiser** *vt* to market.

commère [kɔmɛr] *nf* (*femme*) gossip.

commettre* [kɔmɛtr] *vt* (*délit etc*) to commit; (*erreur*) to make.

commis [kɔmi] *nm* (*de magasin*) assistant, *Am* clerk; (*de bureau*) clerk, *Am* clerical worker.

commissaire [kɔmisɛr] *nm Sp* steward; **c. (de police)** police superintendent *ou Am* chief; **c. aux comptes** auditor; **c. du bord** *Nau* purser. ◆**c.-priseur** *nm* (*pl* **commissaires-priseurs**) auctioneer. ◆**commis-**

sariat *nm* **c. (de police)** (central) police station.

commission [kɔmisjɔ̃] *nf* (*course*) errand; (*message*) message; (*réunion*) commission, committee; (*pourcentage*) *Com* commission (**sur** on); **faire les commissions** to do the shopping. ◆**commissionnaire** *nm* messenger; (*d'hôtel*) commissionaire; *Com* agent.

commod/e [kɔmɔd] **1** *a* (*pratique*) handy; (*simple*) easy; **il n'est pas c.** (*pas aimable*) he's unpleasant; (*difficile*) he's a tough one. **2** *nf* chest of drawers, *Am* dresser. ◆**—ément** *adv* comfortably. ◆**commodité** *nf* convenience.

commotion [kɔmosjɔ̃] *nf* shock; **c. (cérébrale)** concussion. ◆**commotionner** *vt* to shake up.

commuer [kɔmɥe] *vt* (*peine*) *Jur* to commute (**en** to).

commun [kɔmœ̃] **1** *a* (*collectif, comparable, habituel*) common; (*frais, cuisine etc*) shared; (*action, démarche etc*) joint; **ami c.** mutual friend; **peu c.** uncommon; **en c.** in common; **transports en c.** public transport; **avoir** *ou* **mettre en c.** to share; **vivre en c.** to live together; **il n'a rien de c. avec** he has nothing in common with. **2** *nm* **le c. des mortels** ordinary mortals. ◆**—ément** [kɔmynemɑ̃] *adv* commonly.

communauté [kɔmynote] *nf* community. ◆**communautaire** *a* community-.

commune [kɔmyn] *nf* (*municipalité française*) commune; **les Communes** *Br Pol* the Commons. ◆**communal, -aux** *a* communal, local, municipal.

communi/er [kɔmynje] *vi* to receive Holy Communion, communicate. ◆**—ant, -ante** *nmf Rel* communicant. ◆**communion** *nf* communion; *Rel* (Holy) Communion.

communiqu/er [kɔmynike] *vt* to communicate, pass on; (*mouvement*) to impart, communicate; **se c. à** (*feu, rire*) to spread to; – *vi* (*personne, pièces etc*) to communicate. ◆**—é** *nm* (*avis*) *Pol* communiqué; (*publicitaire*) message; **c. de presse** press release. ◆**communicatif, -ive** *a* communicative; (*contagieux*) infectious. ◆**communication** *nf* communication; **c. (téléphonique)** (telephone) call; **mauvaise c.** *Tél* bad line.

communisme [kɔmynism] *nm* communism. ◆**communiste** *a* & *nmf* communist.

communs [kɔmœ̃] *nmpl* (*bâtiments*) outbuildings.

commutateur [kɔmytatœr] *nm* (*bouton*) *Él* switch.

compact [kɔpakt] *a* dense; (*mécanisme, disque, véhicule*) compact.

compagne [kɔpaɲ] *nf* (*camarade*) friend; (*épouse, maîtresse*) companion. ◆**compagnie** *nf* (*présence, société*) & *Com Mil* company; **tenir c. à qn** to keep s.o. company. ◆**compagnon** *nm* companion; (*ouvrier*) workman; **c. de route** travelling companion, fellow traveller; **c. de jeu/de travail** playmate/workmate.

comparaître* [kɔparɛtr] *vi Jur* to appear (in court) (*devant* before).

compar/er [kɔpare] *vt* to compare; **— se c.** *vpr* to be compared (à to). ◆**—é** *a* (*science etc*) comparative. ◆**—able** *a* comparable. ◆**comparaison** *nf* comparison; *Littér* simile. ◆**comparatif, -ive** *a* (*méthode etc*) comparative; **—** *nm Gram* comparative.

comparse [kɔpars] *nmf Jur* minor accomplice, stooge.

compartiment [kɔpartimã] *nm* compartment. ◆**compartimenter** *vt* to compartmentalize, divide up.

comparution [kɔparysjɔ̃] *nf Jur* appearance (in court).

compas [kɔpa] *nm* **1** (*pour mesurer etc*) (pair of) compasses, *Am* compass. **2** (*boussole*) *Nau* compass.

compassé [kɔpase] *a* (*affecté*) starchy, stiff.

compassion [kɔpasjɔ̃] *nf* compassion.

compatible [kɔpatibl] *a* compatible. ◆**compatibilité** *nf* compatibility.

compat/ir [kɔpatir] *vi* to sympathize; **c. à** (*la douleur etc de qn*) to share in. ◆**—issant** *a* sympathetic.

compatriote [kɔpatrijɔt] *nmf* compatriot.

compenser [kɔpãse] *vt* to make up for, compensate for; **—** *vi* to compensate. ◆**compensation** *nf* compensation; **en c. de** in compensation for.

compère [kɔpɛr] *nm* accomplice.

compétent [kɔpetã] *a* competent. ◆**compétence** *nf* competence.

compétition [kɔpetisjɔ̃] *nf* competition; (*épreuve*) *Sp* event; **de c.** (*esprit, sport*) competitive. ◆**compétitif, -ive** *a* competitive. ◆**compétitivité** *nf* competitiveness.

compiler [kɔpile] *vt* (*documents*) to compile.

complainte [kɔplɛ̃t] *nf* (*chanson*) lament.

complaire (se) [səkɔplɛr] *vpr* **se c. dans qch/à faire** to delight in sth/in doing.

complaisant [kɔplɛzã] *a* kind, obliging; (*indulgent*) self-indulgent, complacent. ◆**complaisance** *nf* kindness, obligingness; self-indulgence, complacency.

complément [kɔplemã] *nm* complement; **le c.** (*le reste*) the rest; **un c. d'information** additional information. ◆**complémentaire** *a* complementary; (*détails*) additional.

complet, -ète [kɔplɛ, -ɛt] **1** *a* complete; (*train, hôtel, examen etc*) full; (*aliment*) whole; **au (grand) c.** in full strength. **2** *nm* (*costume*) suit. ◆**complètement** *adv* completely. ◆**compléter** *vt* to complete; (*ajouter à*) to complement; (*somme*) to make up; **— se c.** *vpr* (*caractères*) to complement each other.

complexe [kɔplɛks] **1** *a* complex. **2** *nm* (*sentiment, construction*) complex. ◆**complexé** *a Fam* hung up, inhibited. ◆**complexité** *nf* complexity.

complication [kɔplikasjɔ̃] *nf* complication; (*complexité*) complexity.

complice [kɔplis] *nm* accomplice; **—** *a* (*regard*) knowing; (*silence, attitude*) conniving; **c. de** *Jur* a party to. ◆**complicité** *nf* complicity.

compliment [kɔplimã] *nm* compliment; *pl* (*éloges*) compliments; (*félicitations*) congratulations. ◆**complimenter** *vt* to compliment (**sur, pour** on).

compliqu/er [kɔplike] *vt* to complicate; **— se c.** *vpr* (*situation*) to get complicated. ◆**—é** *a* complicated; (*mécanisme etc*) intricate; complicated; (*histoire, problème etc*) involved, complicated.

complot [kɔplo] *nm* plot, conspiracy. ◆**comploter** [kɔplɔte] *vti* to plot (**de faire** to do).

comport/er [kɔpɔrte] **1** *vt* (*impliquer*) to involve, contain; (*comprendre en soi, présenter*) to contain, comprise, have. **2 se c.** *vpr* to behave; (*joueur, voiture*) to perform. ◆**—ement** *nm* behaviour; (*de joueur etc*) performance.

compos/er [kɔpoze] *vt* (*former, constituer*) to compose, make up; (*musique, visage*) to compose; (*numéro*) *Tél* to dial; (*texte*) *Typ* to set (up); **se c. de, être composé de** to be composed of; **—** *vi Scol* to take an examination; **c. avec** to come to terms with. ◆**—ant** *nm* (*chimique, électronique*) component. ◆**—ante** *nf* (*d'une idée etc*) component. ◆**—é** *a* & *nm* compound. ◆**compositeur, -trice** *nmf Mus* composer; *Typ* typesetter. ◆**composition** *nf* (*action*) composing, making up; *Typ* typesetting; *Mus Littér Ch* composition; *Scol* test, class exam; **c. française** *Scol* French essay *ou* composition.

composter [kɔ̃pɔste] *vt* (*billet*) to cancel, punch.

compote [kɔ̃pɔt] *nf* stewed fruit; **c. de pommes** stewed apples, apple sauce. ◆**compotier** *nm* fruit dish.

compréhensible [kɔ̃preɑ̃sibl] *a* understandable, comprehensible. ◆**compréhensif, -ive** *a* (*personne*) understanding. ◆**compréhension** *nf* understanding, comprehension.

comprendre* [kɔ̃prɑ̃dr] *vt* to understand, comprehend; (*comporter*) to include, comprise; **je n'y comprends rien** I don't understand anything about it; **ça se comprend** that's understandable. ◆**compris** *a* (*inclus*) included (**dans** in); **frais c.** including expenses; **tout c.** (all) inclusive; **y c.** including; **c. entre** (situated) between; **(c'est) c.!** it's agreed!

compresse [kɔ̃pres] *nf* *Méd* compress.

compresseur [kɔ̃presœr] *a* **rouleau c.** steam roller.

comprim/er [kɔ̃prime] *vt* to compress; (*colère etc*) to repress; (*dépenses*) to reduce. ◆**—é** *nm* *Méd* tablet. ◆**compression** *nf* compression; (*du personnel etc*) reduction.

compromettre* [kɔ̃prɔmetr] *vt* to compromise. ◆**compromis** *nm* compromise. ◆**compromission** *nf* compromising action, compromise.

comptable [kɔ̃tabl] *a* (*règles etc*) book-keeping-; — *nmf* bookkeeper; (*expert*) accountant. ◆**comptabilité** *nf* (*comptes*) accounts; (*science*) bookkeeping, accountancy; (*service*) accounts department.

comptant [kɔ̃tɑ̃] *a* **argent c.** (hard) cash; — *adv* **payer c.** to pay (in) cash; **(au) c.** (*acheter, vendre*) for cash.

compte [kɔ̃t] *nm* (*comptabilité*) account; (*calcul*) count; (*nombre*) (right) number; **avoir un c. en banque** to have a bank(ing) account; **c. chèque** cheque account, *Am* checking account; **tenir c. de** to take into account; **c. tenu de** considering; **entrer en ligne de c.** to be taken into account; **se rendre c. de** to realize; **rendre c. de** (*exposer*) to report on; (*justifier*) to account for; **c. rendu** report; (*de livre, film*) review; **pour le c. de** on behalf of; **pour mon c.** for my part; **sur le c. de qn** about s.o.; **en fin de c.** all things considered; **à bon c.** (*acheter*) cheap(ly); **s'en tirer à bon c.** to get off lightly; **avoir un c. à régler avec qn** to have a score to settle with s.o.; **c. à rebours** countdown. ◆**c.-gouttes** *nm inv* *Méd* dropper; **au c.-gouttes** very sparingly. ◆**c.-tours** *nm inv* *Aut* rev counter.

compt/er [kɔ̃te] *vt* (*calculer*) to count; (*prévoir*) to reckon, allow; (*considérer*) to consider; (*payer*) to pay; **c. faire** to expect to do; (*avoir l'intention de*) to intend to do; **c. qch à qn** (*facturer*) to charge s.o. for sth; **il compte deux ans de service** he has two years' service; **ses jours sont comptés** his *ou* her days are numbered; — *vi* (*calculer, avoir de l'importance*) to count; **c. sur** to rely on; **c. avec** to reckon with; **c. parmi** to be (numbered) among. ◆**—eur** *nm* *Él* meter; **c. (de vitesse)** *Aut* speedometer; **c. (kilométrique)** milometer, clock; **c. Geiger** Geiger counter.

comptoir [kɔ̃twar] *nm* **1** (*de magasin*) counter; (*de café*) bar; (*de bureau*) (reception) desk. **2** *Com* branch, agency.

compulser [kɔ̃pylse] *vt* to examine.

comte [kɔ̃t] *nm* (*noble*) count; *Br* earl. ◆**comté** *nm* county. ◆**comtesse** *nf* countess.

con, conne [kɔ̃, kɔn] *a* (*idiot*) *Fam* stupid; — *nmf* *Fam* stupid fool.

concave [kɔ̃kav] *a* concave.

concéder [kɔ̃sede] *vt* to concede, grant (**à** to, **que** that).

concentr/er [kɔ̃sɑ̃tre] *vt* to concentrate; (*attention etc*) to focus, concentrate; — **se c.** *vpr* (*réfléchir*) to concentrate. ◆**—é** *a* (*solution*) concentrated; (*lait*) condensed; (*attentif*) in a state of concentration; — *nm* *Ch* concentrate; **c. de tomates** tomato purée. ◆**concentration** *nf* concentration.

concentrique [kɔ̃sɑ̃trik] *a* concentric.

concept [kɔ̃sept] *nm* concept. ◆**conception** *nf* (*idée*) & *Méd* conception.

concern/er [kɔ̃serne] *vt* to concern; **en ce qui me concerne** as far as I'm concerned. ◆**—ant** *prép* concerning.

concert [kɔ̃ser] *nm* *Mus* concert; (*de louanges*) chorus; **de c.** (*agir*) together, in concert.

concert/er [kɔ̃serte] *vt* to arrange, devise (*in agreement*); — **se c.** *vpr* to consult together. ◆**—é** *a* (*plan*) concerted. ◆**concertation** *nf* (*dialogue*) dialogue.

concession [kɔ̃sesjɔ̃] *nf* concession (**à** to); (*terrain*) plot (of land). ◆**concessionnaire** *nmf* *Com* (authorized) dealer, agent.

concev/oir* [kɔ̃səvwar] **1** *vt* (*imaginer, éprouver, engendrer*) to conceive; (*comprendre*) to understand; **ainsi conçu** (*dépêche etc*) worded as follows. **2** *vi* (*femme*) to conceive. ◆**—able** *a* conceivable.

concierge [kɔ̃sjɛrʒ] *nmf* caretaker, *Am* janitor.

concile [kɔ̃sil] *nm Rel* council.

concili/er [kɔ̃silje] *vt* (*choses*) to reconcile; **se c. l'amitié**/*etc* **de qn** to win (over) s.o.'s friendship/*etc*. ◆**—ant** *a* conciliatory. ◆**conciliateur, -trice** *nmf* conciliator. ◆**conciliation** *nf* conciliation.

concis [kɔ̃si] *a* concise, terse. ◆**concision** *nf* concision.

concitoyen, -enne [kɔ̃sitwajɛ̃, -ɛn] *nmf* fellow citizen.

conclu/re* [kɔ̃klyr] *vt* (*terminer, régler*) to conclude; **c. que** (*déduire*) to conclude that; – *vi* (*orateur etc*) to conclude; **c. à** to conclude in favour of. ◆**—ant** *a* conclusive. ◆**conclusion** *nf* conclusion.

concombre [kɔ̃kɔ̃br] *nm* cucumber.

concorde [kɔ̃kɔrd] *nf* concord, harmony. ◆**concord/er** *vi* (*faits etc*) to agree; (*caractères*) to match; **c. avec** to match. ◆**—ant** *a* in agreement. ◆**concordance** *nf* agreement; (*de situations, résultats*) similarity; **c. des temps** *Gram* sequence of tenses.

concourir* [kɔ̃kurir] *vi* (*candidat*) to compete (**pour** for); (*directions*) to converge; **c. à** (*un but*) to contribute to. ◆**concours** *nm Scol Univ* competitive examination; (*jeu*) competition; (*aide*) assistance; (*de circonstances*) combination; **c. hippique** horse show.

concret, -ète [kɔ̃krɛ, -ɛt] *a* concrete. ◆**concrétiser** *vt* to give concrete form to; **— se c.** *vpr* to materialize.

conçu [kɔ̃sy] *voir* **concevoir**; – *a* **c. pour faire** designed to do; **bien c.** (*maison etc*) well-designed.

concubine [kɔ̃kybin] *nf* (*maîtresse*) concubine. ◆**concubinage** *nm* cohabitation; **en c.** as husband and wife.

concurrent, -ente [kɔ̃kyrã, -ãt] *nmf* competitor; *Scol Univ* candidate. ◆**concurrence** *nf* competition; **faire c. à** to compete with; **jusqu'à c. de** up to the amount of. ◆**concurrencer** *vt* to compete with. ◆**concurrentiel, -ielle** *a* (*prix etc*) competitive.

condamn/er [kɔ̃dane] *vt* to condemn; *Jur* to sentence (**à** to); (*porte*) to block up, bar; (*pièce*) to keep locked; **c. à une amende** to fine. ◆**—é, -ée** *nmf Jur* condemned man, condemned woman; **être c.** (*malade*) to be doomed, be a hopeless case. ◆**condamnation** *nf Jur* sentence; (*censure*) condemnation.

condenser [kɔ̃dãse] *vt,* **— se c.** *vpr* to condense. ◆**condensateur** *nm Él* condenser. ◆**condensation** *nf* condensation.

condescendre [kɔ̃desãdr] *vi* to condescend (**à** to). ◆**condescendance** *nf* condescension.

condiment [kɔ̃dimã] *nm* condiment.

condisciple [kɔ̃disipl] *nm Scol* classmate, schoolfellow; *Univ* fellow student.

condition [kɔ̃disjɔ̃] *nf* (*état, stipulation, rang*) condition; *pl* (*clauses, tarifs*) *Com* terms; **à c. de faire, à c. que l'on fasse** providing *ou* provided (that) one does; **mettre en c.** (*endoctriner*) to condition; **sans c.** (*se rendre*) unconditionally. ◆**conditionnel, -elle** *a* conditional. ◆**conditionn/er** *vt* 1 (*influencer*) to condition. 2 (*article*) *Com* to package. ◆**—é** *a* (*réflexe*) conditioned; **à air c.** (*pièce etc*) air-conditioned. ◆**—ement** *nm* conditioning; packaging.

condoléances [kɔ̃dɔleãs] *nfpl* condolences.

conducteur, -trice [kɔ̃dyktœr, -tris] **1** *nmf Aut Rail* driver. **2** *a* & *nm* (*corps*) **c.** *Él* conductor; (**fil**) **c.** *Él* lead (wire).

conduire* [kɔ̃dɥir] **1** *vt* to lead; *Aut* to drive; (*affaire etc*) & *Él* to conduct; (*eau*) to carry; **c. qn à** (*accompagner*) to take s.o. to. **2 se c.** *vpr* to behave. ◆**conduit** *nm* duct. ◆**conduite** *nf* conduct, behaviour; *Aut* driving (**de** of); (*d'entreprise etc*) conduct; (*d'eau, de gaz*) main; **c. à gauche** (*volant*) left-hand drive; **faire un bout de c. à qn** to go with s.o. part of the way; **sous la c. de** under the guidance of.

cône [kon] *nm* cone.

confection [kɔ̃fɛksjɔ̃] *nf* making (**de** of); **vêtements de c.** ready-made clothes; **magasin de c.** ready-made clothing shop. ◆**confectionner** *vt* (*gâteau, robe*) to make.

confédération [kɔ̃federasjɔ̃] *nf* confederation. ◆**confédéré** *a* confederate.

conférence [kɔ̃ferãs] *nf* conference; (*exposé*) lecture. ◆**conférencier, -ière** *nmf* lecturer. ◆**conférer** *vt* (*attribuer, donner*) to confer (**à** on).

confess/er [kɔ̃fese] *vt* to confess; **— se c.** *vpr Rel* to confess (**à** to). ◆**—eur** *nm* (*prêtre*) confessor. ◆**confession** *nf* confession. ◆**confessionnal, -aux** *nm Rel* confessional. ◆**confessionnel, -elle** *a* (*école*) *Rel* denominational.

confettis [kɔ̃feti] *nmpl* confetti.

confiance [kɔ̃fjãs] *nf* trust, confidence; **faire c. à qn, avoir c. en qn** to trust s.o.; **c. en soi** (self-)confidence; **poste/abus de c.** position/breach of trust; **homme de c.** reliable man; **en toute c.** (*acheter*) quite confidently; **poser la question de c.** *Pol* to ask for a vote of confidence. ◆**confiant** *a* trusting; (*sûr de soi*) confident; **être c. en** *ou* **dans** to have confidence in.

confidence [kɔ̃fidɑ̃s] *nf* (*secret*) confidence; **en c.** in confidence; **il m'a fait une c.** he confided in me. ◆**confident** *nm* confidant. ◆**confidente** *nf* confidante. ◆**confidentiel, -ielle** *a* confidential.

confier [kɔ̃fje] *vt* **c. à qn** (*enfant, objet*) to give s.o. to look after, entrust s.o. with; **c. un secret/etc à qn** to confide a secret/etc to s.o.; **— se c.** *vpr* to confide (**à qn** in s.o.).

configuration [kɔ̃figyrasjɔ̃] *nf* configuration.

confin/er [kɔ̃fine] *vt* to confine; **– vi c. à** to border on; **— se c.** *vpr* to confine oneself (**dans** to). ◆**—é** *a* (*atmosphère*) stuffy.

confins [kɔ̃fɛ̃] *nmpl* confines.

confire [kɔ̃fir] *vt* (*cornichon*) to pickle; (*fruit*) to preserve.

confirmer [kɔ̃firme] *vt* to confirm (**que** that); **c. qn dans sa résolution** to confirm s.o.'s resolve. ◆**confirmation** *nf* confirmation.

confiserie [kɔ̃fizri] *nf* (*magasin*) sweet shop, *Am* candy store; *pl* (*produits*) confectionery, sweets, *Am* candy. ◆**confiseur, -euse** *nmf* confectioner.

confisquer [kɔ̃fiske] *vt* to confiscate (**à qn** from s.o.). ◆**confiscation** *nf* confiscation.

confit [kɔ̃fi] *a* **fruits confits** crystallized *ou* candied fruit. ◆**confiture** *nf* jam, preserves.

conflit [kɔ̃fli] *nm* conflict. ◆**conflictuel, -elle** *a Psy* conflict-provoking.

confluent [kɔ̃flyɑ̃] *nm* (*jonction*) confluence.

confondre [kɔ̃fɔ̃dr] *vt* (*choses, personnes*) to confuse, mix up; (*consterner, étonner*) to confound; (*amalgamer*) to fuse; **c. avec** to mistake for; **— se c.** *vpr* (*s'unir*) to merge; **se c. en excuses** to be very apologetic.

conforme [kɔ̃fɔrm] *a* **c. à** in accordance with; **c. (à l'original)** (*copie*) true (to the original). ◆**conform/er** *vt* to model, adapt; **— se c.** *vpr* to conform (**à** to). ◆**—ément** *adv* **c. à** in accordance with. ◆**conformisme** *nm* conformity, conformism. ◆**conformiste** *a* & *nmf* conformist. ◆**conformité** *nf* conformity.

confort [kɔ̃fɔr] *nm* comfort. ◆**confortable** *a* comfortable.

confrère [kɔ̃frɛr] *nm* colleague. ◆**confrérie** *nf Rel* brotherhood.

confronter [kɔ̃frɔ̃te] *vt Jur etc* to confront (**avec** with); (*textes*) to collate; **confronté à** confronted with. ◆**confrontation** *nf* confrontation; collation.

confus [kɔ̃fy] *a* (*esprit, situation, bruit*) confused; (*idée, style*) confused, jumbled, hazy; (*gêné*) embarrassed; **je suis c.!** (*désolé*) I'm terribly sorry!; (*comblé de bienfaits*) I'm overwhelmed! ◆**confusément** *adv* indistinctly, vaguely. ◆**confusion** *nf* confusion; (*gêne, honte*) embarrassment.

congé [kɔ̃ʒe] *nm* leave (of absence); (*avis pour locataire*) notice (to quit); (*pour salarié*) notice (of dismissal); (*vacances*) holiday, *Am* vacation; **c. de maladie** sick leave; **congés payés** holidays with pay, paid holidays; **donner son c. à** (*employé, locataire*) to give notice to; **prendre c. de** to take leave of. ◆**congédier** *vt* (*domestique etc*) to dismiss.

congeler [kɔ̃ʒle] *vt* to freeze. ◆**congélateur** *nm* freezer, deep-freeze. ◆**congélation** *nf* freezing.

congénère [kɔ̃ʒenɛr] *nmf* fellow creature. ◆**congénital, -aux** *a* congenital.

congère [kɔ̃ʒɛr] *nf* snowdrift.

congestion [kɔ̃ʒɛstjɔ̃] *nf* congestion; **c. cérébrale** *Méd* stroke. ◆**congestionn/er** *vt* to congest. ◆**—é** *a* (*visage*) flushed.

Congo [kɔ̃go] *nm* Congo. ◆**congolais, -aise** *a & nmf* Congolese.

congratuler [kɔ̃gratyle] *vt Iron* to congratulate.

congrégation [kɔ̃gregasjɔ̃] *nf* (*de prêtres etc*) congregation.

congrès [kɔ̃grɛ] *nm* congress. ◆**congressiste** *nmf* delegate (*to a congress*).

conifère [kɔnifɛr] *nm* conifer.

conique [kɔnik] *a* conic(al), cone-shaped.

conjecture [kɔ̃ʒɛktyr] *nf* conjecture. ◆**conjectural, -aux** *a* conjectural. ◆**conjecturer** *vt* to conjecture, surmise.

conjoint [kɔ̃ʒwɛ̃] **1** *a* (*problèmes, action etc*) joint. **2** *nm* spouse; *pl* husband and wife. ◆**conjointement** *adv* jointly.

conjonction [kɔ̃ʒɔ̃ksjɔ̃] *nf Gram* conjunction.

conjoncture [kɔ̃ʒɔ̃ktyr] *nf* circumstances; *Écon* economic situation. ◆**conjoncturel, -elle** *a* (*prévisions etc*) economic.

conjugal, -aux [kɔ̃ʒygal, -o] *a* conjugal.

conjuguer [kɔ̃ʒyge] *vt* (*verbe*) to conjugate; (*efforts*) to combine; **— se c.** *vpr* (*verbe*) to be conjugated. ◆**conjugaison** *nf Gram* conjugation.

conjur/er [kɔ̃ʒyre] *vt* (*danger*) to avert; (*mauvais sort*) to ward off; **c. qn** (*implorer*) to entreat s.o. (**de faire** to do). ◆**—é, -ée** *nmf* conspirator. ◆**conjuration** *nf* (*complot*) conspiracy.

connaissance [kɔnɛsɑ̃s] *nf* knowledge; (*personne*) acquaintance; *pl* (*science*) knowledge (**en** of); **faire la c. de qn, faire c. avec qn** to make s.o.'s acquaintance, meet s.o.; (*ami, époux etc*) to get to know s.o.; **à ma c.** as far as I know; **avoir c. de** to be aware of; **perdre c.** to lose consciousness, faint; **sans c.** unconscious. ◆**connaisseur** *nm* connoisseur.

connaître* [kɔnɛtr] *vt* to know; (*rencontrer*) to meet; (*un succès etc*) to have; (*un malheur etc*) to experience; **faire c.** to make known; **— se c.** *vpr* (*amis etc*) to get to know each other; **nous nous connaissons déjà** we've met before; **s'y c. à** *ou* **en qch** to know (all) about sth; **il ne se connaît plus** he's losing his cool.

connecter [kɔnɛkte] *vt* *Él* to connect. ◆**connexe** *a* (*matières*) allied. ◆**connexion** *nf* *Él* connection.

connerie [kɔnri] *nf* *Fam* (*bêtise*) stupidity; (*action*) stupid thing; *pl* (*paroles*) stupid nonsense.

connivence [kɔnivɑ̃s] *nf* connivance.

connotation [kɔnɔtasjɔ̃] *nf* connotation.

connu *voir* **connaître; — a** (*célèbre*) well-known.

conquér/ir* [kɔ̃kerir] *vt* (*pays, marché etc*) to conquer. ◆**—ant, -ante** *nmf* conqueror. ◆**conquête** *nf* conquest; **faire la c. de** (*pays, marché etc*) to conquer.

consacrer [kɔ̃sakre] *vt* (*temps, vie etc*) to devote (**à** to); (*église etc*) *Rel* to consecrate; (*coutume etc*) to establish, sanction, consecrate; **se c. à** to devote oneself to.

conscience [kɔ̃sjɑ̃s] *nf* **1** (*psychologique*) consciousness; **la c. de qch** the awareness *ou* consciousness of sth; **c. de soi** self-awareness; **avoir/prendre c. de** to be/become aware *ou* conscious of; **perdre c.** to lose consciousness. **2** (*morale*) conscience; **avoir mauvaise c.** to have a guilty conscience; **c. professionnelle** conscientiousness. ◆**consciemment** [kɔ̃sjamɑ̃] *adv* consciously. ◆**consciencieux, -euse** *a* conscientious. ◆**conscient** *a* conscious; **c. de** aware *ou* conscious of.

conscrit [kɔ̃skri] *nm* *Mil* conscript. ◆**conscription** *nf* conscription.

consécration [kɔ̃sekrasjɔ̃] *nf* *Rel* consecration; (*confirmation*) sanction, consecration.

consécuti/f, -ive [kɔ̃sekytif, -iv] *a* consecu-

tive; **c. à** following upon. ◆**—vement** *adv* consecutively.

conseil [kɔ̃sɛj] *nm* **1 un c.** a piece of advice, some advice; **des conseils** advice; (**expert-)c.** consultant. **2** (*assemblée*) council, committee; **c. d'administration** board of directors; **C. des ministres** *Pol* Cabinet; (*réunion*) Cabinet meeting. ◆**conseiller¹** *vt* (*guider, recommander*) to advise; **c. qch à qn** to recommend sth to s.o.; **c. à qn de faire** to advise s.o. to do. ◆**conseiller², -ère** *nmf* (*expert*) consultant; (*d'un conseil*) councillor.

consent/ir* [kɔ̃sɑ̃tir] *vi* **c. à** to consent to; **— vt** to grant (**à** to). ◆**—ement** *nm* consent.

conséquence [kɔ̃sekɑ̃s] *nf* consequence; (*conclusion*) conclusion; **en c.** accordingly; **sans c.** (*importance*) of no importance. ◆**conséquent** *a* logical; (*important*) *Fam* important; **par c.** consequently.

conservatoire [kɔ̃sɛrvatwar] *nm* academy, school (*of music, drama*).

conserve [kɔ̃sɛrv] *nf* **conserves** tinned *ou* canned food; **de** *ou* **en c.** tinned, canned; **mettre en c.** to tin, can.

conserv/er [kɔ̃sɛrve] *vt* (*ne pas perdre*) to retain, keep; (*fruits, vie, tradition etc*) to preserve; **— se c.** *vpr* (*aliment*) to keep. ◆**—é à bien c.** (*vieillard*) well-preserved. ◆**conservateur, -trice 1** *a & nmf* *Pol* Conservative. **2** *nm* (*de musée*) curator; (*de bibliothèque*) (*chief*) librarian. **3** *nm* (*produit*) *Culin* preservative. ◆**conservation** *nf* preservation; **instinct de c.** survival instinct. ◆**conservatisme** *nm* conservatism.

considér/er [kɔ̃sidere] *vt* to consider (**que** that); **c. qn** (*faire cas de*) to respect s.o.; **c. comme** to consider to be, regard as; **tout bien considéré** all things considered. ◆**—able** *a* considerable. ◆**considération** *nf* (*motif, examen*) consideration; (*respect*) regard, esteem; *pl* (*remarques*) observations; **prendre en c.** to take into consideration.

consigne [kɔ̃siɲ] *nf* (*instruction*) orders; *Rail* left-luggage office, *Am* baggage check-room; *Scol* detention; *Mil* confinement to barracks; (*somme*) deposit; **c. automatique** *Rail* luggage lockers, *Am* baggage lockers. ◆**consignation** *nf* (*somme*) deposit. ◆**consigner** *vt* (*écrire*) to record; (*bouteille etc*) to charge a deposit on; (*bagages*) to deposit in the left-luggage office, *Am* to check; (*élève*) *Scol* to keep in;

(*soldat*) *Mil* to confine (to barracks); (*salle*) to seal off, close.

consistant [kɔ̃sistɑ̃] *a* (*sauce, bouillie*) thick; (*argument, repas*) solid. ◆**consistance** *nf* (*de liquide*) consistency; **sans c.** (*rumeur*) unfounded; (*esprit*) irresolute.

consister [kɔ̃siste] *vi* **c. en/dans** to consist of/in; **c. à faire** to consist in doing.

consistoire [kɔ̃sistwar] *nm Rel* council.

console [kɔ̃sɔl] *nf Tech Él* console.

consoler [kɔ̃sɔle] *vt* to console, comfort (**de** for); **se c. de** (*la mort de qn etc*) to get over. ◆**consolation** *nf* consolation, comfort.

consolider [kɔ̃sɔlide] *vt* to strengthen, consolidate. ◆**consolidation** *nf* strengthening, consolidation.

consomm/er [kɔ̃sɔme] *vt* (*aliment, carburant etc*) to consume; (*crime, œuvre*) *Litt* to accomplish; − *vi* (*au café*) to drink; **c. beaucoup/peu** (*véhicule*) to be heavy/light on petrol *ou Am* gas. ◆**—é 1** *a* (*achevé*) consummate. **2** *nm* clear meat soup, consommé. ◆**consommateur, -trice** *nmf Com* consumer; (*au café*) customer. ◆**consommation** *nf* consumption; drink; **biens/société de c.** consumer goods/society.

consonance [kɔ̃sɔnɑ̃s] *nf Mus* consonance; *pl* (*sons*) sounds.

consonne [kɔ̃sɔn] *nf* consonant.

consortium [kɔ̃sɔrsjɔm] *nm Com* consortium.

consorts [kɔ̃sɔr] *nmpl* **et c.** *Péj* and people of that ilk.

conspirer [kɔ̃spire] *vi* **1** to conspire, plot (**contre** against). **2 c. à faire** (*concourir*) to conspire to do. ◆**conspirateur, -trice** *nmf* conspirator. ◆**conspiration** *nf* conspiracy.

conspuer [kɔ̃spɥe] *vt* (*orateur etc*) to boo.

constant, -ante [kɔ̃stɑ̃, -ɑ̃t] *a* constant; − *nf Math* constant. ◆**constamment** *adv* constantly. ◆**constance** *nf* constancy.

constat [kɔ̃sta] *nm* (official) report; **dresser un c. d'échec** to acknowledge one's failure.

constater [kɔ̃state] *vt* to note, observe (**que** that); (*vérifier*) to establish; (*enregistrer*) to record; **je ne fais que c.** I'm merely stating a fact. ◆**constatation** *nf* (*remarque*) observation.

constellation [kɔ̃stelasjɔ̃] *nf* constellation. ◆**constellé** *a* **c. de** (*étoiles, joyaux*) studded with.

consterner [kɔ̃stɛrne] *vt* to distress, dismay. ◆**consternation** *nf* distress, (profound) dismay.

constip/er [kɔ̃stipe] *vt* to constipate. ◆**—é**

a constipated; (*gêné*) *Fam* embarrassed, stiff. ◆**constipation** *nf* constipation.

constitu/er [kɔ̃stitɥe] *vt* (*composer*) to make up, constitute; (*être, représenter*) to constitute; (*organiser*) to form; (*instituer*) *Jur* to appoint; **constitué de** made up of; **se c. prisonnier** to give oneself up. ◆**—ant** *a* (*éléments*) component, constituent; (*assemblée*) *Pol* constituent. ◆**constitutif, -ive** *a* constituent. ◆**constitution** *nf* (*santé*) & *Pol* constitution; (*fondation*) formation (**de** of); (*composition*) composition. ◆**constitutionnel, -elle** *a* constitutional.

constructeur [kɔ̃stryktœr] *nm* builder; (*fabricant*) maker (**de** of). ◆**constructif, -ive** *a* constructive. ◆**construction** *nf* (*de pont etc*) building, construction (**de** of); (*édifice*) building, structure; (*de théorie etc*) & *Gram* construction; **de c.** (*matériaux, jeu*) building-.

construire* [kɔ̃strɥir] *vt* (*maison, route etc*) to build, construct; (*phrase, théorie etc*) to construct.

consul [kɔ̃syl] *nm* consul. ◆**consulaire** *a* consular. ◆**consulat** *nm* consulate.

consulter [kɔ̃sylte] **1** *vt* to consult; − **se c.** *vpr* to consult (each other), confer. **2** *vi* (*médecin*) to hold surgery, *Am* hold office hours. ◆**consultatif, -ive** *a* consultative, advisory. ◆**consultation** *nf* consultation; **cabinet de c.** *Méd* surgery, *Am* office; **heures de c.** *Méd* surgery hours, *Am* office hours.

consumer [kɔ̃syme] *vt* (*détruire, miner*) to consume.

contact [kɔ̃takt] *nm* contact; (*toucher*) touch; *Aut* ignition; **être en c. avec** to be in touch *ou* contact with; **prendre c.** to get in touch (**avec** with); **entrer en c. avec** to come into contact with; **prise de c.** first meeting; **mettre/couper le c.** *Aut* to switch on/off the ignition. ◆**contacter** *vt* to contact.

contagieux, -euse [kɔ̃taʒjø, -øz] *a* (*maladie, rire*) contagious, infectious; **c'est c.** it's catching *ou* contagious. ◆**contagion** *nf Méd* contagion, infection; (*de rire etc*) contagiousness.

contaminer [kɔ̃tamine] *vt* to contaminate. ◆**contamination** *nf* contamination.

conte [kɔ̃t] *nm* tale; **c. de fée** fairy tale.

contempler [kɔ̃tɑ̃ple] *vt* to contemplate, gaze at. ◆**contemplatif, -ive** *a* contemplative. ◆**contemplation** *nf* contemplation.

contemporain, -aine [kɔ̃tɑ̃pɔrɛ̃, -ɛn] *a* & *nmf* contemporary.

contenance [kɔ̃tnɑ̃s] *nf* **1** (*contenu*) capacity. **2** (*allure*) bearing; **perdre c.** to lose one's composure.

conten/ir* [kɔ̃tnir] *vt* (*renfermer*) to contain; (*avoir comme capacité*) to hold; (*contrôler*) to hold back, contain; **— se c.** *vpr* to contain oneself. ◆**—ant** *nm* container. ◆**—eur** *nm* (freight) container.

content [kɔ̃tɑ̃] **1** *a* pleased, happy, glad (**de faire** to do); **c. de qn/qch** pleased *ou* happy with s.o./sth; **c. de soi** self-satisfied; **non c. d'avoir fait** not content with having done. **2** *nm* **avoir son c.** to have had one's fill (**de** of). ◆**content/er** *vt* to satisfy, please; **se c. de** to be content with, content oneself with. ◆**—ement** *nm* contentment, satisfaction.

contentieux [kɔ̃tɑ̃sjø] *nm* (*affaires*) matters in dispute; (*service*) legal *ou* claims department.

contenu [kɔ̃tny] *nm* (*de récipient*) contents; (*de texte, film etc*) content.

cont/er [kɔ̃te] *vt* (*histoire etc*) to tell, relate. ◆**—eur, -euse** *nmf* storyteller.

conteste (sans) [sɑ̃kɔ̃tɛst] *adv* indisputably.

contest/er [kɔ̃tɛste] **1** *vt* (*fait etc*) to dispute, contest. **2** *vi* (*étudiants etc*) to protest; **– vt** to protest against. ◆**—é** *a* (*théorie etc*) controversial. ◆**—able** *a* debatable. ◆**contestataire** *a* **étudiant/ouvrier c.** student/worker protester; **–** *nmf* protester. ◆**contestation** *nf* (*discussion*) dispute; **faire de la c.** to protest (against the establishment).

contexte [kɔ̃tɛkst] *nm* context.

contigu, -uë [kɔ̃tigy] *a* **c. (à)** (*maisons etc*) adjoining. ◆**contiguïté** *nf* close proximity.

continent [kɔ̃tinɑ̃] *nm* continent; (*opposé à une île*) mainland. ◆**continental, -aux** *a* continental.

contingent [kɔ̃tɛ̃ʒɑ̃] **1** *a* (*accidentel*) contingent. **2** *nm* *Mil* contingent; (*part, quota*) quota. ◆**contingences** *nfpl* contingencies.

continu [kɔ̃tiny] *a* continuous. ◆**continuel, -elle** *a* continual, unceasing. ◆**continuellement** *adv* continually.

continuer [kɔ̃tinɥe] *vt* to continue, carry on (**à** *ou* **de faire** doing); (*prolonger*) to continue; **–** *vi* to continue, go on. ◆**continuation** *nf* continuation; **bonne c.!** *Fam* I hope the rest of it goes well, keep up the good work! ◆**continuité** *nf* continuity.

contondant [kɔ̃tɔ̃dɑ̃] *a* **instrument c.** *Jur* blunt instrument.

contorsion [kɔ̃tɔrsjɔ̃] *nf* contortion. ◆**se**

contorsionner *vpr* to contort oneself. ◆**contorsionniste** *nmf* contortionist.

contour [kɔ̃tur] *nm* outline, contour; *pl* (*de route, rivière*) twists, bends. ◆**contourn/er** *vt* (*colline etc*) to go round, skirt; (*difficulté, loi*) to get round. ◆**—é** *a* (*style*) convoluted, tortuous.

contraception [kɔ̃trasɛpsjɔ̃] *nf* contraception. ◆**contraceptif, -ive** *a* & *nm* contraceptive.

contract/er [kɔ̃trakte] *vt* (*muscle, habitude, dette etc*) to contract; **— se c.** *vpr* (*cœur etc*) to contract. ◆**—é** *a* (*inquiet*) tense. ◆**contraction** *nf* contraction.

contractuel, -elle [kɔ̃traktɥɛl] **1** *nmf* traffic warden; **–** *nf* *Am* meter maid. **2** *a* contractual.

contradicteur [kɔ̃tradiktœr] *nm* contradictor. ◆**contradiction** *nf* contradiction. ◆**contradictoire** *a* (*propos etc*) contradictory; (*rapports, théories*) conflicting; **débat c.** debate.

contraindre* [kɔ̃trɛ̃dr] *vt* to compel, force (**à faire** to do); **— se c.** *vpr* to compel *ou* force oneself; (*se gêner*) to restrain oneself. ◆**contraignant** *a* constraining, restricting. ◆**contraint** *a* (*air etc*) forced, constrained. ◆**contrainte** *nf* compulsion, constraint; (*gêne*) constraint, restraint.

contraire [kɔ̃trɛr] *a* opposite; (*défavorable*) contrary; **c. à** contrary to; **–** *nm* opposite; **(bien) au c.** on the contrary. ◆**—ment** *adv* **c. à** contrary to.

contrari/er [kɔ̃trarje] *vt* (*projet, action*) to thwart; (*personne*) to annoy. ◆**—ant** *a* (*action etc*) annoying; (*personne*) difficult, perverse. ◆**contrariété** *nf* annoyance.

contraste [kɔ̃trast] *nm* contrast. ◆**contraster** *v* to contrast (**avec** with); **faire c.** (*mettre en contraste*) to contrast.

contrat [kɔ̃tra] *nm* contract.

contravention [kɔ̃travɑ̃sjɔ̃] *nf* (*amende*) *Aut* fine; (*pour stationnement interdit*) (parking) ticket; **en c.** contravening the law; **en c. à** in contravention of.

contre [kɔ̃tr] **1** *prép* & *adv* against; (*en échange de*) (in exchange) for; **échanger qch c.** to exchange for; **fâché c.** angry with; **s'abriter c.** to shelter from; **il va s'appuyer c.** he's going to lean against it; **six voix c. deux** six votes to two; **Nîmes c. Arras** *Sp* Nîmes versus Arras; **un médicament c.** (*toux, grippe etc*) a medicine for; **par c.** on the other hand; **tout c.** close to *ou* by. **2** *nm* (*riposte*) *Sp* counter.

contre- [kɔ̃tr] *préf* counter-.

contre-attaque [kɔ̃tratak] *nf* counterattack. ◆**contre-attaquer** *vt* to counterattack.

contrebalancer [kɔ̃trəbalɑ̃se] *vt* to counterbalance.

contrebande [kɔ̃trəbɑ̃d] *nf* (*fraude*) smuggling, contraband; (*marchandise*) contraband; **de c.** (*tabac etc*) contraband, smuggled; **faire de la c.** to smuggle; **passer qch en c.** to smuggle sth. ◆**contrebandier, -ière** *nmf* smuggler.

contrebas (en) [ɑ̃kɔ̃trəba] *adv* & *prép* **en c. (de)** down below.

contrebasse [kɔ̃trəbas] *nf Mus* double-bass.

contrecarrer [kɔ̃trəkare] *vt* to thwart, frustrate.

contrecœur (à) [akɔ̃trəkœr] *adv* reluctantly.

contrecoup [kɔ̃trəku] *nm* (indirect) effect *ou* consequence; **par c.** as an indirect consequence.

contre-courant (à) [akɔ̃trəkurɑ̃] *adv* against the current.

contredanse [kɔ̃trədɑ̃s] *nf* (*amende*) *Aut Fam* ticket.

contredire* [kɔ̃trədir] *vt* to contradict; — **se c.** *vpr* to contradict oneself.

contrée [kɔ̃tre] *nf* region, land.

contre-espionnage [kɔ̃trɛspjɔnaʒ] *nm* counterespionage.

contrefaçon [kɔ̃trəfasɔ̃] *nf* counterfeiting, forgery; (*objet imité*) counterfeit, forgery. ◆**contrefaire** *vt* (*parodier*) to mimic; (*déguiser*) to disguise; (*monnaie etc*) to counterfeit, forge.

contreforts [kɔ̃trəfɔr] *nmpl Géog* foothills.

contre-indiqué [kɔ̃trɛ̃dike] *a* (*médicament*) dangerous, not recommended.

contre-jour (à) [akɔ̃trəʒur] *adv* against the (sun)light.

contremaître [kɔ̃trəmɛtr] *nm* foreman.

contre-offensive [kɔ̃trɔfɑ̃siv] *nf* counteroffensive.

contrepartie [kɔ̃trəparti] *nf* compensation; **en c.** in exchange.

contre-performance [kɔ̃trəperfɔrmɑ̃s] *nf Sp* bad performance.

contre-pied [kɔ̃trəpje] *nm* **le c.-pied d'une opinion/attitude** the (exact) opposite view/attitude; **à c.-pied** *Sp* on the wrong foot.

contre-plaqué [kɔ̃trəplake] *nm* plywood.

contrepoids [kɔ̃trəpwa] *nm Tech* & *Fig* counterbalance; **faire c. (à)** to counterbalance.

contrepoint [kɔ̃trəpwɛ̃] *nm Mus* counterpoint.

contrer [kɔ̃tre] *vt* (*personne, attaque*) to counter.

contre-révolution [kɔ̃trərevɔlysjɔ̃] *nf* counter-revolution.

contresens [kɔ̃trəsɑ̃s] *nm* misinterpretation; (*en traduisant*) mistranslation; (*non-sens*) absurdity; **à c.** the wrong way.

contresigner [kɔ̃trəsiɲe] *vt* to countersign.

contretemps [kɔ̃trətɑ̃] *nm* hitch, mishap; **à c.** (*arriver etc*) at the wrong moment.

contre-torpilleur [kɔ̃trətɔrpijœr] *nm* (*navire*) destroyer, torpedo boat.

contrevenir [kɔ̃trəvnir] *vi* **c. à** (*loi etc*) to contravene.

contre-vérité [kɔ̃trəverite] *nf* untruth.

contribu/er [kɔ̃tribɥe] *vi* to contribute (**à** to). ◆**—able** *nmf* taxpayer. ◆**contribution** *nf* contribution; (*impôt*) tax; *pl* (*administration*) tax office; **mettre qn à c.** to use s.o.'s services.

contrit [kɔ̃tri] *a* (*air etc*) contrite. ◆**contrition** *nf* contrition.

contrôle [kɔ̃trol] *nm* (*vérification*) inspection, check(ing) (**de** of); (*des prix, de la qualité*) control; (*maîtrise*) control; (*sur bijou*) hallmark; **un c.** (*examen*) a check (**sur** on); **le c. de soi(-même)** self-control; **le c. des naissances** birth control; **un c. d'identité** an identity check. ◆**contrôl/er** *vt* (*examiner*) to inspect, check; (*maîtriser, surveiller*) to control; — **se c.** *vpr* (*se maîtriser*) to control oneself. ◆**—eur, -euse** *nmf* (*de train*) (ticket) inspector; (*au quai*) ticket collector; (*de bus*) conductor, conductress.

contrordre [kɔ̃trɔrdr] *nm* change of orders.

controverse [kɔ̃trɔvers] *nf* controversy. ◆**controversé** *a* controversial.

contumace (par) [parkɔ̃tymas] *adv Jur* in one's absence, in absentia.

contusion [kɔ̃tyzjɔ̃] *nf* bruise. ◆**contusionner** *vt* to bruise.

convainc/re* [kɔ̃vɛ̃kr] *vt* to convince (**de** of); (*accusé*) to prove guilty (**de** of); **c. qn de faire** to persuade s.o. to do. ◆**—ant** *a* convincing. ◆**—u** *a* (*certain*) convinced (**de** of).

convalescent, -ente [kɔ̃valesɑ̃, -ɑ̃t] *nmf* convalescent; — *a* **être c.** to convalesce. ◆**convalescence** *nf* convalescence; **être en c.** to convalesce; **maison de c.** convalescent home.

conven/ir [kɔ̃vnir] *vi* **c. à** (*être approprié à*) to be suitable for; (*plaire à, aller à*) to suit; **ça convient** (*date etc*) that's suitable; **c. de** (*lieu etc*) to agree upon; (*erreur*) to admit; **c. que** to admit that; **il convient de** it's advisable to; (*selon les usages*) it is proper *ou* fitting to. ◆**—able** *a* (*approprié, acceptable*) suitable; (*correct*) decent, proper. ◆**—ablement** *adv* suitably; decently. ◆**convenance** *nf* **convenances** (*usages*) convention(s), proprieties; **à sa c.** to one's satisfaction *ou* taste.

convention [kɔ̃vɑ̃sjɔ̃] *nf* (*accord*) agreement, convention; (*règle*) & *Am Pol* convention; **c. collective** collective bargaining; **de c.** (*sentiment etc*) conventional. ◆**conventionné** *a* (*prix, tarif*) regulated (by voluntary agreement); **médecin c.** = National Health Service doctor (*bound by agreement with the State*). ◆**conventionnel, -elle** *a* conventional.

convergent [kɔ̃vɛrʒɑ̃] *a* converging, convergent. ◆**convergence** *nf* convergence. ◆**converger** *vi* to converge.

converser [kɔ̃vɛrse] *vi* to converse. ◆**conversation** *nf* conversation.

conversion [kɔ̃vɛrsjɔ̃] *nf* conversion. ◆**convert/ir** *vt* to convert (à to, en into); **— se c.** *vpr* to be converted, convert. ◆**—i, -ie** *nmf* convert. ◆**convertible** *a* convertible; **— nm** (*canapé*) **c.** bed settee.

convexe [kɔ̃vɛks] *a* convex.

conviction [kɔ̃viksjɔ̃] *nf* (*certitude, croyance*) conviction; **pièce à c.** *Jur* exhibit.

convier [kɔ̃vje] *vt* to invite (**à une soirée**/*etc* to a party/*etc*, **à faire** to do).

convive [kɔ̃viv] *nmf* guest (*at table*).

convoi [kɔ̃vwa] *nm* (*véhicules, personnes etc*) convoy; *Rail* train; **c.** (**funèbre**) funeral procession. ◆**convoy/er** *vt* to escort. ◆**—eur** *nm* *Nau* escort ship; **c. de fonds** security guard.

convoiter [kɔ̃vwate] *vt* to desire, envy, covet. ◆**convoitise** *nf* desire, envy.

convoquer [kɔ̃vɔke] *vt* (*candidats, membres etc*) to summon *ou* invite (to attend); (*assemblée*) to convene, summon; **c. à** to summon *ou* invite to. ◆**convocation** *nf* (*action*) summoning; convening; (*ordre*) summons (to attend); (*lettre*) (written) notice (to attend).

convulser [kɔ̃vylse] *vt* to convulse. ◆**convulsif, -ive** *a* convulsive. ◆**convulsion** *nf* convulsion.

coopérer [kɔɔpere] *vi* to co-operate (**à** in, **avec** with). ◆**coopératif, -ive** *a* co-operative; **— nf** co-operative (society). ◆**coopération** *nf* co-operation.

coopter [kɔɔpte] *vt* to co-opt.

coordonn/er [kɔɔrdɔne] *vt* to co-ordinate. ◆**—ées** *nfpl* *Math* co-ordinates; (*adresse,*

téléphone) *Fam* particulars, details. ◆**coordination** *nf* co-ordination.

copain [kɔpɛ̃] *nm* *Fam* (*camarade*) pal; (*petit ami*) boyfriend; **être c. avec** to be pals with.

copeau, -x [kɔpo] *nm* (*de bois*) shaving.

copie [kɔpi] *nf* copy; (*devoir, examen*) *Scol* paper. ◆**copier** *vti* to copy; *Scol* to copy, crib (**sur** from). ◆**copieur, -euse** *nmf* (*élève etc*) copycat, copier.

copieux, -euse [kɔpjø, -øz] *a* copious, plentiful.

copilote [kɔpilɔt] *nm* co-pilot.

copine [kɔpin] *nf* *Fam* (*camarade*) pal; (*petite amie*) girlfriend; **être c. avec** to be pals with.

copropriété [kɔprɔprijete] *nf* joint ownership; (**immeuble en) c.** block of flats in joint ownership, *Am* condominium.

copulation [kɔpylasjɔ̃] *nf* copulation.

coq [kɔk] *nm* cock, rooster; **c. au vin** coq au vin (*chicken cooked in wine*); **passer du c. à l'âne** to jump from one subject to another.

coque [kɔk] *nf* **1** (*de noix*) shell; (*mollusque*) cockle; **œuf à la c.** boiled egg. **2** *Nau* hull.

coquelicot [kɔkliko] *nm* poppy.

coqueluche [kɔklyʃ] *nf* *Méd* whooping-cough; **la c. de** *Fig* the darling of.

coquet, -ette [kɔkɛ, -ɛt] *a* (*chic*) smart; (*joli*) pretty; (*provocant*) coquettish, flirtatious; (*somme*) *Fam* tidy; **— nf** coquette, flirt. ◆**coquetterie** *nf* (*élégance*) smartness; (*goût de la toilette*) dress sense; (*galanterie*) coquetry.

coquetier [kɔktje] *nm* egg cup.

coquille [kɔkij] *nf* shell; *Typ* misprint; **c. Saint-Jacques** scallop. ◆**coquillage** *nm* (*mollusque*) shellfish; (*coquille*) shell.

coquin, -ine [kɔkɛ̃, -in] *nmf* rascal; **— a** mischievous, rascally; (*histoire etc*) naughty.

cor [kɔr] *nm* *Mus* horn; **c.** (**au pied**) corn; **réclamer** *ou* **demander à c. et à cri** to clamour for.

corail, -aux [kɔraj, -o] *nm* coral.

Coran [kɔrɑ̃] *nm* **le C.** the Koran.

corbeau, -x [kɔrbo] *nm* crow; (**grand) c.** raven.

corbeille [kɔrbɛj] *nf* basket; **c. à papier** waste paper basket.

corbillard [kɔrbijar] *nm* hearse.

corde [kɔrd] *nf* rope; (*plus mince*) (fine) cord; (*de raquette, violon etc*) string; **c.** (**raide**) (*d'acrobate*) tightrope; **instrument à cordes** *Mus* string(ed) instrument; **c. à linge** (washing *ou* clothes) line; **c. à sauter** skipping rope, *Am* jump rope; **usé jusqu'à**

la c. threadbare; **cordes vocales** vocal cords; **prendre un virage à la c.** *Aut* to hug a bend; **pas dans mes cordes** *Fam* not my line. ◆**cordage** *nm Nau* rope. ◆**cordée** *nf* roped (climbing) party. ◆**cordelette** *nf* (fine) cord. ◆**corder** *vt* (*raquette*) to string. ◆**cordon** *nm* (*de tablier, sac etc*) string; (*de soulier*) lace; (*de rideau*) cord, rope; (*d'agents de police*) cordon; (*décoration*) ribbon, sash; (*ombilical*) *Anat* cord. ◆**c.-bleu** *nm* (*pl* **cordons-bleus**) cordon bleu (cook), first-class cook.

cordial, -aux [kɔrdjal, -o] *a* cordial, warm; – *nm Méd* cordial. ◆**cordialité** *nf* cordiality.

cordonnier [kɔrdɔnje] *nm* shoe repairer, cobbler. ◆**cordonnerie** *nf* shoe repairer's shop.

Corée [kɔre] *nf* Korea. ◆**coréen, -enne** *a* & *nmf* Korean.

coriace [kɔrjas] *a* (*aliment, personne*) tough.

corne [kɔrn] *nf* (*de chèvre etc*) horn; (*de cerf*) antler; (*matière, instrument*) horn; (*angle, pli*) corner.

cornée [kɔrne] *nf Anat* cornea.

corneille [kɔrnej] *nf* crow.

cornemuse [kɔrnəmyz] *nf* bagpipes.

corner [kɔrne] **1** *vt* (*page*) to turn down the corner of, dog-ear. **2** *vi* (*véhicule*) to sound its horn. **3** [kɔrnɛr] *nm Fb* corner.

cornet [kɔrne] *nm* **1 c.** (**à pistons**) *Mus* cornet. **2** (*de glace*) cornet, cone; **c.** (**de papier**) (paper) cone.

corniaud [kɔrnjo] *nm* (*chien*) mongrel; (*imbécile*) *Fam* drip, twit.

corniche [kɔrniʃ] *nf Archit* cornice; (*route*) cliff road.

cornichon [kɔrniʃɔ̃] *nm* (*concombre*) gherkin; (*niais*) *Fam* clot, twit.

cornu [kɔrny] *a* (*diable etc*) horned.

corollaire [kɔrɔlɛr] *nm* corollary.

corporation [kɔrpɔrasjɔ̃] *nf* trade association, professional body.

corps [kɔr] *nm Anat Ch Fig etc* body; *Mil Pol* corps; **c. électoral** electorate; **c. enseignant** teaching profession; **c. d'armée** army corps; **garde du c.** bodyguard; **un c. de bâtiment** a main building; **c. et âme** body and soul; **lutter c. à c.** to fight hand-to-hand; **à son c. défendant** under protest; **prendre c.** (*projet*) to take shape; **donner c. à** (*rumeur, idée*) to give substance to; **faire c. avec** to form a part of, belong with; **perdu c. et biens** *Nau* lost with all hands; **esprit de c.** corporate spirit. ◆**corporel, -elle** *a* bodily; (*châtiment*) corporal.

corpulent [kɔrpylɑ̃] *a* stout, corpulent. ◆**corpulence** *nf* stoutness, corpulence.

corpus [kɔrpys] *nm Ling* corpus.

correct [kɔrɛkt] *a* (*exact*) correct; (*bienséant, honnête*) proper, correct; (*passable*) adequate. ◆**—ement** *adv* correctly; properly; adequately. ◆**correcteur, -trice 1** *a* (*verres*) corrective. **2** *nmf Scol* examiner; *Typ* proofreader. ◆**correctif, -ive** *a* & corrective.

correction [kɔrɛksjɔ̃] *nf* (*rectification etc*) correction; (*punition*) thrashing; (*exactitude, bienséance*) correctness; **la c. de** (*devoirs, examen*) the marking of; **c. d'épreuves** *Typ* proofreading. ◆**correctionnel, -elle** *a* **tribunal c.,** – *nf* magistrates' court, *Am* police court.

corrélation [kɔrelasjɔ̃] *nf* correlation.

correspond/re [kɔrɛspɔ̃dr] **1** *vi* (*s'accorder*) to correspond (**à** to, with); (*chambres etc*) to communicate; **c. avec** *Rail* to connect with; **— se c.** *vpr* (*idées etc*) to correspond; (*chambres etc*) to communicate. **2** *vi* (*écrire*) to correspond (**avec** with). ◆**—ant, -ante** *a* corresponding; – *nmf* correspondent; (*d'un élève, d'un adolescent*) pen friend; *Tél* caller. ◆**correspondance** *nf* correspondence; (*de train, d'autocar*) connection, *Am* transfer.

corrida [kɔrida] *nf* bullfight.

corridor [kɔridɔr] *nm* corridor.

corrig/er [kɔriʒe] *vt* (*texte, injustice etc*) to correct; (*épreuve*) *Typ* to read; (*devoir*) *Scol* to mark, correct; (*châtier*) to beat, punish; **c. qn de** (*défaut*) to cure s.o. of; **se c. de** to cure oneself of. ◆**—é** *nm Scol* model (answer), correct version, key.

corroborer [kɔrɔbɔre] *vt* to corroborate.

corroder [kɔrɔde] *vt* to corrode. ◆**corrosif, -ive** *a* corrosive. ◆**corrosion** *nf* corrosion.

corromp/re* [kɔrɔ̃pr] *vt* to corrupt; (*soudoyer*) to bribe; (*aliment, eau*) to taint. ◆**—u** *a* corrupt; (*altéré*) tainted. ◆**corruption** *nf* (*dépravation*) corruption; (*de juge etc*) bribery.

corsage [kɔrsaʒ] *nm* (*chemisier*) blouse; (*de robe*) bodice.

corsaire [kɔrsɛr] *nm* (*marin*) *Hist* privateer.

Corse [kɔrs] *nf* Corsica. ◆**corse** *a* & *nmf* Corsican.

cors/er [kɔrse] *vt* (*récit, action*) to heighten; **l'affaire se corse** things are hotting up. ◆**—é** *a* (*vin*) full-bodied; (*café*) strong; (*sauce, histoire*) spicy; (*problème*) tough; (*addition de restaurant*) steep.

corset [kɔrsɛ] *nm* corset.

cortège [kɔrtɛʒ] nm (défilé) procession; (suite) retinue; **c. officiel** (automobiles) motorcade.

corvée [kɔrve] nf chore, drudgery; Mil fatigue (duty).

cosaque [kɔzak] nm Cossack.

cosmopolite [kɔsmɔpɔlit] a cosmopolitan.

cosmos [kɔsmɔs] nm (univers) cosmos; (espace) outer space. ◆**cosmique** a cosmic. ◆**cosmonaute** nmf cosmonaut.

cosse [kɔs] nf (de pois etc) pod.

cossu [kɔsy] a (personne) well-to-do; (maison etc) opulent.

costaud [kɔsto] a Fam brawny, beefy; – nm Fam strong man.

costume [kɔstym] nm (pièces d'habillement) costume, dress; (complet) suit. ◆**costum/er** vt c. qn to dress s.o. up (en as). ◆**—é** a bal c. fancy-dress ball.

cote [kɔt] nf (marque de classement) mark, letter, number; (tableau des valeurs) (official) listing; (des valeurs boursières) quotation; (évaluation, popularité) rating; (de cheval) odds (de on); **c. d'alerte** danger level.

côte [kot] nf 1 Anat rib; (de mouton) chop; (de veau) cutlet; **à côtes** (étoffe) ribbed; **c. à c.** side by side; **se tenir les côtes** to split one's sides (laughing). 2 (montée) hill; (versant) hillside. 3 (littoral) coast.

côté [kote] nm side; (direction) way; **de l'autre c.** on the other side (**de** of); (direction) the other way; **de ce c.** (passer) this way; **du c. de** (vers, près de) towards; **de c.** (se jeter, mettre de l'argent etc) to one side; (regarder) sideways, to one side; **à c.** close by, nearby; (pièce) in the other room; (maison) next door; **la maison (d')à c.** the house next door; **à c. de** next to, beside; (comparaison) compared to; **passer à c.** (balle) to fall wide (**de** of); **venir de tous côtés** to come from all directions; **d'un c.** on the one hand; **de mon c.** for my part; **à mes côtés** by my side; **laisser de c.** (travail) to neglect; (**du**) **c.** argent/etc Fam as regards money/etc, moneywise/etc; **le bon c.** (d'une affaire) the bright side (**de** of).

coteau, -x [kɔto] nm (small) hill; (versant) hillside.

côtelé [kotle] a (étoffe) ribbed; **velours c.** cord(uroy).

côtelette [kotlɛt] nf (d'agneau, de porc) chop; (de veau) cutlet.

cot/er [kɔte] vt (valeur boursière) to quote. ◆**—é** a **bien c.** highly rated.

coterie [kɔtri] nf Péj set, clique.

côtier, -ière [kotje, -jɛr] a coastal; (pêche) inshore.

cotiser [kɔtize] vi to contribute (**à** to, **pour** towards); **c. (à)** (club) to subscribe (to); — **se c.** vpr to club together (**pour acheter** to buy). ◆**cotisation** nf (de club) dues, subscription; (de pension etc) contribution(s).

coton [kɔtɔ̃] nm cotton; **c. (hydrophile)** cottonwool, Am (absorbent) cotton. ◆**cotonnade** nf cotton (fabric). ◆**cotonnier, -ière** a (industrie) cotton-.

côtoyer [kotwaje] vt (route, rivière) to run along, skirt; (la misère, la folie etc) Fig to be ou come close to; **c. qn** (fréquenter) to rub shoulders with s.o.

cotte [kɔt] nf (de travail) overalls.

cou [ku] nm neck; **sauter au c. de qn** to throw one's arms around s.o.; **jusqu'au c.** Fig up to one's eyes ou ears.

couche [kuʃ] nf 1 (épaisseur) layer; (de peinture) coat; Géol stratum; **couches sociales** social strata. 2 (linge de bébé) nappy, Am diaper. 3 **faire une fausse c.** Méd to have a miscarriage; **les couches** Méd confinement.

couch/er [kuʃe] vt to put to bed; (héberger) to put up; (allonger) to lay (down ou out); (blé) to flatten; (par écrit) to put down (in writing); **c. qn en joue** to aim at s.o.; — vi to sleep (**avec** with); — **se c.** vpr to go to bed; (s'allonger) to lie flat ou down; (soleil) to set, go down; — nm (moment) bedtime; **c. de soleil** sunset. ◆**—ant** a (soleil) setting; — nm (aspect) sunset; **le c.** (ouest) west. ◆**—é** a **être c.** to be in bed; (étendu) to be lying (down). ◆**—age** nm sleeping (situation); (matériel) bedding; **sac de c.** sleeping bag. ◆**couchette** nf Rail sleeping berth, couchette; Nau bunk.

couci-couça [kusikusa] adv Fam so-so.

coucou [kuku] nm (oiseau) cuckoo; (pendule) cuckoo clock; Bot cowslip.

coude [kud] nm elbow; (de chemin, rivière) bend; **se serrer** ou **se tenir les coudes** to help one another, stick together; **c. à c.** side by side; **coup de c.** poke ou dig (with one's elbow), nudge; **pousser du c.** to nudge. ◆**coudoyer** vt to rub shoulders with.

cou-de-pied [kudpje] nm (pl cous-de-pied) instep.

coudre* [kudr] vti to sew.

couenne [kwan] nf (pork) crackling.

couette [kwɛt] nf (édredon) duvet, continental quilt.

couffin [kufɛ̃] nm (de bébé) Moses basket, Am bassinet.

couic! [kwik] *int* eek!, squeak! ◆**couiner** *vi Fam* to squeal; (*pleurer*) to whine.

couillon [kujɔ̃] *nm* (*idiot*) *Arg* drip, cretin.

coul/er[1] [kule] *vi* (*eau etc*) to flow; (*robinet, nez, sueur*) to run; (*fuir*) to leak; **c. de source** *Fig* to follow naturally; **faire c. le sang** to cause bloodshed; − *vt* (*métal, statue*) to cast; (*vie*) *Fig* to pass, lead; (*glisser*) to slip; **se c. dans** (*passer*) to slip into; **se la c. douce** to have things easy. ◆−**ant** *a* (*style*) flowing; (*caractère*) easygoing. ◆−**ée** *nf* (*de métal*) casting; **c. de lave** lava flow. ◆−**age** *nm* (*de métal, statue*) casting; (*gaspillage*) *Fam* wastage.

couler[2] [kule] *vi* (*bateau, nageur*) to sink; **c. à pic** to sink to the bottom; − *vt* to sink; (*discréditer*) *Fig* to discredit.

couleur [kulœr] *nf* colour; (*colorant*) paint; *Cartes* suit; *pl* (*teint, carnation*) colour; **c. chair** flesh-coloured; **de c.** (*homme, habit etc*) coloured; **en couleurs** (*photo, télévision*) colour-; **téléviseur c.** colour TV set; **haut en c.** colourful; **sous c. de faire** while pretending to do.

couleuvre [kulœvr] *nf* (grass) snake.

coulisse [kulis] *nf* **1** (*de porte*) runner; **à c.** (*porte etc*) sliding. **2 dans les coulisses** *Th* in the wings, backstage; **dans la c.** (*caché*) *Fig* behind the scenes. ◆**coulissant** *a* (*porte etc*) sliding.

couloir [kulwar] *nm* corridor; (*de circulation*) & *Sp* lane; (*dans un bus*) gangway.

coup [ku] *nm* blow, knock; (*léger*) tap, touch; (*choc moral*) blow; (*de fusil etc*) shot; (*de crayon, d'horloge*) & *Sp* stroke; (*aux échecs etc*) move; (*fois*) *Fam* time; **donner des coups à** to hit; **c. de brosse** brush(-up); **c. de chiffon** wipe (with a rag); **c. de sonnette** ring (on a bell); **c. de dents** bite; **c. de chance** stroke of luck; **c. d'État** coup; **c. dur** *Fam* nasty blow; **sale c.** dirty trick; **mauvais c.** piece of mischief; **c. franc** *Fb* free kick; **tenter le c.** *Fam* to have a go *ou* try; **réussir son c.** to bring it off; **faire les quatre cents coups** to get into all kinds of mischief; **tenir le c.** to hold out; **avoir/attraper le c.** to have/get the knack; **sous le c. de** (*émotion etc*) under the influence of; **il est dans le c.** *Fam* he's in the know; **après c.** after the event, afterwards; **sur le c. de midi** on the stroke of twelve; **sur le c.** (*alors*) at the time; **tué sur le c.** killed outright; **à c. sûr** for sure; **c. sur c.** (*à la suite*) one after the other, in quick succession; **tout à c.**, **tout d'un c.** suddenly; **à tout c.** at every go; **d'un seul c.** in one go; **du premier c.** *Fam* (at the) first go; **du c.**

suddenly; (*de ce fait*) as a result; **pour le c.** this time. ◆**c.-de-poing** *nm* (*pl* **coups-de-poing**) **c.-de-poing** (**américain**) knuckle-duster.

coupable [kupabl] *a* guilty (**de** of); (*plaisir, désir*) sinful; **déclarer c.** *Jur* to convict; − *nmf* guilty person, culprit.

coupe [kup] *nf* **1** *Sp* cup; (*à fruits*) dish; (*à boire*) goblet, glass. **2** (*de vêtement etc*) cut; *Géom* section; **c. de cheveux** haircut. ◆**coup/er** *vt* to cut; (*arbre*) to cut down; (*vivres etc*) & *Tél* to cut off; (*courant etc*) to switch off; (*voyage*) to break (off); (*faim, souffle etc*) to take away; (*vin*) to water down; (*morceler*) to cut up; (*croiser*) to cut across; **c. la parole à** to cut short; − *vi* to cut; **c. à** (*corvée*) *Fam* to get out of; **ne coupez pas!** *Tél* hold the line!; − **se c.** *vpr* (*routes*) to intersect; (*se trahir*) to give oneself away; **se c. au doigt** to cut one's finger. ◆−**ant** *a* sharp; − *nm* (cutting) edge. ◆−**é** *nm* *Aut* coupé.

coupe-circuit [kupsirkɥi] *nm inv* *Él* cutout, circuit breaker. ◆**c.-file** *nm inv* (*carte*) official pass. ◆**c.-gorge** *nm inv* cut-throat alley. ◆**c.-ongles** *nm inv* (finger nail) clippers. ◆**c.-papier** *nm inv* paper knife.

couperet [kuprɛ] *nm* (meat) chopper; (*de guillotine*) blade.

couperosé [kuproze] *a* (*visage*) blotchy.

couple [kupl] *nm* pair, couple. ◆**coupler** *vt* to couple, connect.

couplet [kuplɛ] *nm* verse.

coupole [kupɔl] *nf* dome.

coupon [kupɔ̃] *nm* (*tissu*) remnant, oddment; (*pour la confection d'un vêtement*) length; (*ticket, titre*) coupon; **c. réponse** reply coupon.

coupure [kupyr] *nf* cut; (*de journal*) cutting, *Am* clipping; (*billet*) banknote.

cour [kur] *nf* **1** court(yard); (*de gare*) forecourt; **c.** (**de récréation**) *Scol* playground. **2** (*de roi*) & *Jur* court. **3** (*de femme, d'homme*) courtship; **faire la c. à qn** to court s.o., woo s.o.

courage [kuraʒ] *nm* courage; (*zèle*) spirit; **perdre c.** to lose heart *ou* courage; **s'armer de c.** to pluck up courage; **bon c.!** keep your chin up! ◆**courageux, -euse** *a* courageous; (*énergique*) spirited.

couramment [kuramɑ̃] *adv* (*parler*) fluently; (*souvent*) frequently.

courant [kurɑ̃] **1** *a* (*fréquent*) common; (*compte, année, langage*) current; (*eau*) running; (*modèle, style*) standard; (*affaires*) routine; **le dix/etc c.** *Com* the tenth/etc inst(ant). **2** *nm* (*de l'eau, élec*-

trique) current; **c. d'air** draught; **coupure de c.** power cut; **dans le c. de** (*mois etc*) during the course of; **être/mettre au c.** to know/tell (**de** about); **au c.** (*à jour*) up to date.

courbature [kurbatyr] *nf* (muscular) ache. ◆**courbaturé** *a* aching (all over).

courbe [kurb] *a* curved; – *nf* curve. ◆**courber** *vti* to bend; – **se c.** *vpr* to bend (over).

courge [kurʒ] *nf* marrow, *Am* squash. ◆**courgette** *nf* courgette, *Am* zucchini.

cour/ir* [kurir] *vi* to run; (*se hâter*) to rush; (*à bicyclette, en auto*) to race; **en courant** (*vite*) in a rush; **le bruit court que** . . . there's a rumour going around that . . . ; **faire c.** (*nouvelle*) to spread; **il court encore** (*voleur*) he's still at large; – *vt* (*risque*) to run; (*épreuve sportive*) to run (in); (*danger*) to face, court; (*rues, monde*) to roam; (*magasins, cafés*) to go round; (*filles*) to run after. ◆**—eur** *nm Sp etc* runner; (*cycliste*) cyclist; *Aut* racing driver; (*galant*) *Péj* womanizer.

couronne [kurɔn] *nf* (*de roi, dent*) crown; (*funéraire*) wreath. ◆**couronn/er** *vt* to crown; (*auteur, ouvrage*) to award a prize to. ◆**—é** *a* (*tête*) crowned; (*ouvrage*) prize-. ◆**—ement** *nm* (*sacre*) coronation; *Fig* crowning achievement.

courrier [kurje] *nm* post, mail; (*transport*) postal *ou* mail service; (*article*) *Journ* column; **par retour du c.** by return of post, *Am* by return mail.

courroie [kurwa] *nf* (*attache*) strap; (*de transmission*) *Tech* belt.

courroux [kuru] *nm Litt* wrath.

cours [kur] *nm* **1** (*de maladie, rivière, astre, pensées etc*) course; (*cote*) rate, price; **c. d'eau** river, stream; **suivre son c.** (*déroulement*) to follow its course; **avoir c.** (*monnaie*) to be legal tender; (*théorie*) to be current; **en c.** (*travail*) in progress; (*année*) current; (*affaires*) outstanding; **en c. de route** on the way; **au c. de** during; **donner libre c. à** to give free rein to. **2** (*leçon*) class; (*série de leçons*) course; (*conférence*) lecture; (*établissement*) school; (*manuel*) textbook; **c. magistral** lecture. **3** (*allée*) avenue.

course [kurs] *nf* **1** (*action*) run(ning); (*épreuve de vitesse*) & *Fig* race; (*trajet*) journey, run; (*excursion*) hike; (*de projectile etc*) path, flight; *pl* (*de chevaux*) races; **il n'est plus dans la c.** *Fig* he's out of touch; **cheval de c.** racehorse; **voiture de c.** racing car. **2** (*commission*) errand; *pl* (*achats*)

shopping; **faire une c.** to run an errand; **faire les courses** to do the shopping.

coursier, -ière [kursje, -jɛr] *nmf* messenger.

court [kur] **1** *a* short; **c'est un peu c.** *Fam* that's not very much; – *adv* short; **couper c. à** (*entretien*) to cut short; **tout c.** quite simply; **à c. de** (*argent etc*) short of; **pris de c.** caught unawares. **2** *nm Tennis* court. ◆**c.-bouillon** *nm* (*pl* **courts-bouillons**) court-bouillon (*spiced water for cooking fish*). ◆**c.-circuit** *nm* (*pl* **courts-circuits**) *Él* short circuit. ◆**c.-circuiter** *vt* to short-circuit.

courtier, -ière [kurtje, -jɛr] *nmf* broker. ◆**courtage** *nm* brokerage.

courtisan [kurtizã] *nm Hist* courtier. ◆**courtisane** *nf Hist* courtesan. ◆**courtiser** *vt* to court.

courtois [kurtwa] *a* courteous. ◆**courtoisie** *nf* courtesy.

couru [kury] *a* (*spectacle, lieu*) popular; **c'est c.** (*d'avance*) *Fam* it's a sure thing.

couscous [kuskus] *nm Culin* couscous.

cousin, -ine [kuzɛ̃, -in] **1** *nmf* cousin. **2** *nm* (*insecte*) gnat, midge.

coussin [kusɛ̃] *nm* cushion.

cousu [kuzy] *a* sewn; **c. main** handsewn.

coût [ku] *nm* cost. ◆**coût/er** *vti* to cost; **ça coûte combien?** how much is it?, how much does it cost?; **ça lui en coûte de faire** it pains him *ou* her to do; **coûte que coûte** at all costs; **c. les yeux de la tête** to cost the earth. ◆**—ant** *a* **prix c.** cost price. ◆**coûteux, -euse** *a* costly, expensive.

couteau, -x [kuto] *nm* knife; **coup de c.** stab; **à couteaux tirés** at daggers drawn (**avec** with); **visage en lame de c.** hatchet face; **retourner le c. dans la plaie** *Fig* to rub it in.

coutume [kutym] *nf* custom; **avoir c. de faire** to be accustomed to doing; **comme de c.** as usual; **plus que de c.** more than is customary. ◆**coutumier, -ière** *a* customary.

couture [kutyr] *nf* sewing, needlework; (*métier*) dressmaking; (*raccord*) seam; **maison de c.** fashion house. ◆**couturier** *nm* fashion designer. ◆**couturière** *nf* dressmaker.

couvent [kuvã] *nm* (*pour religieuses*) convent; (*pour moines*) monastery; (*pensionnat*) convent school.

couv/er [kuve] *vt* (*œufs*) to sit on, hatch; (*projet*) *Fig* to hatch; (*rhume etc*) to be getting; **c. qn** to pamper s.o.; **c. des yeux** (*convoiter*) to look at enviously; – *vi* (*poule*) to brood; (*mal*) to be brewing;

(feu) to smoulder. ◆—**ée** *nf* (*petits*) brood; (*œufs*) clutch. ◆**couveuse** *nf* (*pour nouveaux-nés, œufs*) incubator.

couvercle [kuvɛrkl] *nm* lid, cover.

couvert [kuvɛr] **1** *nm* (*cuiller, fourchette, couteau*) (set of) cutlery; (*au restaurant*) cover charge; **mettre le c.** to lay the table; **table de cinq couverts** table set for five. **2** *nm* **sous (le) c. de** (*apparence*) under cover of; **se mettre à c.** to take cover. **3** *a* covered (*de* with, in); (*ciel*) overcast. ◆**couverture** *nf* (*de lit*) blanket, cover; (*de livre etc*) & *Fin Mil* cover; (*de toit*) roofing; **c. chauffante** electric blanket; **c. de voyage** travelling rug.

couvre-chef [kuvrəʃɛf] *nm Hum* headgear. ◆**c.-feu** *nm* (*pl* -**x**) curfew. ◆**c.-lit** *nm* bedspread. ◆**c.-pied** *nm* quilt.

couvr/ir* [kuvrir] *vt* to cover (**de** with); (*voix*) to drown; — **se c.** *vpr* (*se vêtir*) to cover up, wrap up; (*se coiffer*) to cover one's head; (*ciel*) to cloud over. ◆—**eur** *nm* roofer.

cow-boy [kɔbɔj] *nm* cowboy.

crabe [krab] *nm* crab.

crac! [krak] *int* (*rupture*) snap!; (*choc*) bang!, smash!

crach/er [kraʃe] *vi* to spit; (*stylo*) to splutter; (*radio*) to crackle; — *vt* to spit (out); **c. sur qch** *Fam* to turn one's nose up at sth. ◆—**é** **a c'est son portrait tout c.** *Fam* that's the spitting image of him *ou* her. ◆**crachat** *nm* spit, spittle.

crachin [kraʃɛ̃] *nm* (*fine*) drizzle.

crack [krak] *nm Fam* ace, wizard, real champ.

craie [krɛ] *nf* chalk.

craindre* [krɛ̃dr] *vt* (*personne, mort, douleur etc*) to be afraid of, fear, dread; (*chaleur etc*) to be sensitive to; **c. de faire** to be afraid of doing, dread doing; **je crains qu'elle ne vienne** I'm afraid *ou* I fear *ou* I dread (that) she might come; **c. pour qch** to fear for sth; **ne craignez rien** have no fear. ◆**crainte** *nf* fear, dread; **de c. de faire** for fear of doing; **de c. que** (+ *sub*) for fear that. ◆**craintif, -ive** *a* timid.

cramoisi [kramwazi] *a* crimson.

crampe [krɑ̃p] *nf Méd* cramp.

crampon [krɑ̃põ] **1** *nm* (*personne*) *Fam* leech, hanger-on. **2** *nmpl* (*de chaussures*) studs.

cramponner (se) [səkrɑ̃pɔne] *vpr* **se c. à** to hold on to, cling to.

cran [krɑ̃] *nm* **1** (*entaille*) notch; (*de ceinture*) hole; **c. d'arrêt** catch; **couteau à c. d'arrêt** flick-knife, *Am* switchblade; **c. de**

sûreté safety catch. **2** (*de cheveux*) wave. **3** (*audace*) *Fam* pluck, guts. **4 à c.** (*excédé*) *Fam* on edge.

crâne [krɑn] *nm* skull; (*tête*) *Fam* head. ◆**crânienne** *af* **boîte c.** cranium, brain pan.

crâner [krane] *vi Péj* to show off, swagger.

crapaud [krapo] *nm* toad.

crapule [krapyl] *nf* villain, (filthy) scoundrel. ◆**crapuleux, -euse** *a* vile, sordid.

craqueler [krakle] *vt*, — **se c.** *vpr* to crack.

craqu/er [krake] *vi* (*branche*) to snap; (*chaussure*) to creak; (*bois sec*) to crack; (*sous la dent*) to crunch; (*se déchirer*) to split, rip; (*projet, entreprise etc*) to come apart at the seams, crumble; (*personne*) to break down, reach breaking point; — *vt* (*faire*) **c.** (*allumette*) to strike. ◆—**ement** *nm* snapping *ou* creaking *ou* cracking (sound).

crasse [kras] **1** *a* (*ignorance*) crass. **2** *nf* filth. ◆**crasseux, -euse** *a* filthy.

cratère [kratɛr] *nm* crater.

cravache [kravaʃ] *nf* horsewhip, riding crop.

cravate [kravat] *nf* (*autour du cou*) tie. ◆**cravaté** *a* wearing a tie.

crawl [krol] *nm* (*nage*) crawl. ◆**crawlé** *a* **dos c.** backstroke.

crayeux, -euse [krɛjø, -øz] *a* chalky.

crayon [krɛjõ] *nm* (*en bois*) pencil; (*de couleur*) crayon; **c. à bille** ballpoint (pen). ◆**crayonner** *vt* to pencil.

créance [kreɑ̃s] *nf* **1** *Fin Jur* claim (*for money*). **2 lettres de c.** *Pol* credentials. ◆**créancier, -ière** *nmf* creditor.

créateur, -trice [kreatœr, -tris] *nmf* creator; — *a* creative; **esprit c.** creativeness. ◆**créatif, -ive** *a* creative. ◆**création** *nf* creation. ◆**créativité** *nf* creativity. ◆**créature** *nf* (*être*) creature.

crécelle [kresɛl] *nf* (*de supporter*) rattle.

crèche [krɛʃ] *nf* (*de Noël*) *Rel* crib, manger; *Scol* day nursery, crèche. ◆**crécher** *vi* (*loger*) *Arg* to bed down, hang out.

crédible [kredibl] *a* credible. ◆**crédibilité** *nf* credibility.

crédit [kredi] *nm* (*influence*) & *Fin* credit; *pl* (*sommes*) funds; **à c.** (*acheter*) on credit, on hire purchase; **faire c.** *Fin* to give credit (à to). ◆**créditer** *vt Fin* to credit (**de** with). ◆**créditeur, -euse** *a* (*solde, compte*) credit-; **son compte est c.** his account is in credit, he is in credit.

credo [kredo] *nm* creed.

crédule [kredyl] *a* credulous. ◆**crédulité** *nf* credulity.

créer [kree] *vt* to create.

crémaillère [kremajɛr] *nf* pendre la c. to have a house-warming (party).

crématoire [krematwar] *a* four c. crematorium. ◆**crémation** *nf* cremation.

crème [krɛm] *nf* cream; (*dessert*) cream dessert; **café c.** white coffee, coffee with cream *ou* milk; **c. Chantilly** whipped cream; **c. glacée** ice cream; **c. à raser** shaving cream; **c. anglaise** custard; *– a inv* cream(-coloured); *– nm* (*café*) white coffee. ◆**crémerie** *nf* (*magasin*) dairy (shop). ◆**crémeux, -euse** *a* creamy. ◆**crémier, -ière** *nmf* dairyman, dairywoman.

créneau, -x [kreno] *nm Hist* crenellation; (*trou*) Fig slot, gap; *Écon* market opportunity, niche; **faire un c.** *Aut* to park between two vehicles.

créole [kreɔl] *nmf* Creole; *– nm Ling* Creole.

crêpe [krɛp] **1** *nf Culin* pancake. **2** *nm* (*tissu*) crepe; (*caoutchouc*) crepe (rubber). ◆**crêperie** *nf* pancake bar.

crépi [krepi] *a & nm* roughcast.

crépit/er [krepite] *vi* to crackle. ◆**—ement** *nm* crackling (sound).

crépu [krepy] *a* (*cheveux, personne*) frizzy.

crépuscule [krepyskyl] *nm* twilight, dusk. ◆**crépusculaire** *a* (*lueur etc*) twilight-, dusk-.

crescendo [kreʃɛndo] *adv & nm inv* crescendo.

cresson [kresɔ̃] *nm* (water) cress.

crête [krɛt] *nf* (*d'oiseau, de vague, de montagne*) crest; **c. de coq** cockscomb.

Crète [krɛt] *nf* Crete.

crétin, -ine [kretɛ̃, -in] *nmf* cretin; *– a* cretinous.

creus/er [krøze] **1** *vt* (*terre, sol*) to dig (a hole *ou* holes in); (*trou, puits*) to dig; (*évider*) to hollow (out); (*idée*) Fig to go deeply into; **c. l'estomac** to whet the appetite. **2 se c.** *vpr* (*joues etc*) to become hollow; (*abîme*) Fig to form; **se c. la tête** *ou* **la cervelle** to rack one's brains. ◆**—é** *a* **c. de rides** (*visage*) furrowed with wrinkles.

creuset [krøzɛ] *nm* (*récipient*) crucible; (*lieu*) Fig melting pot.

creux, -euse [krø, -øz] *a* (*tube, joues, paroles etc*) hollow; (*estomac*) empty; (*sans activité*) slack; **assiette creuse** soup plate; *– nm* hollow; (*de l'estomac*) pit; (*moment*) slack period; **c. des reins** small of the back.

crevaison [krəvɛzɔ̃] *nf* puncture.

crevasse [krəvas] *nf* crevice, crack; (*de glacier*) crevasse; *pl* (*aux mains*) chaps.

◆**crevasser** *vt*, *– se c.* *vpr* to crack; (*peau*) to chap.

crève [krɛv] *nf* (*rhume*) Fam bad cold.

crev/er [krəve] *vi* (*bulle etc*) to burst; (*pneu*) to puncture, burst; (*mourir*) Fam to die, drop dead; **c. d'orgueil** to be bursting with pride; **c. de rire** Fam to split one's sides; **c. d'ennui/de froid** Fam to be bored/to freeze to death; **c. de faim** Fam to be starving; *– vt* to burst; (*œil*) to put *ou* knock out; **c. qn** Fam to wear *ou* knock s.o. out; **ça (vous) crève les yeux** Fam it's staring you in the face; **c. le cœur** to be heartbreaking. ◆**—ant** *a* (*fatigant*) Fam exhausting; (*drôle*) Arg hilarious, killing. ◆**—é** *a* (*fatigué*) Fam worn *ou* knocked out; (*mort*) Fam dead. ◆**crève-cœur** *nm inv* heartbreak.

crevette [krəvɛt] *nf* (*grise*) shrimp; (*rose*) prawn.

cri [kri] *nm* (*de joie, surprise*) cry, shout; (*de peur*) scream; (*de douleur, d'alarme*) cry; (*appel*) call, cry; **c. de guerre** war cry; **un chapeau/etc dernier c.** the latest hat/etc.

◆**criard** *a* (*enfant*) bawling; (*son*) screeching; (*couleur*) gaudy, showy.

criant [krijɑ̃] *a* (*injustice etc*) glaring.

crible [kribl] *nm* sieve, riddle. ◆**cribler** *vt* to sift; **criblé de** (*balles, dettes etc*) riddled with.

cric [krik] *nm* (*instrument*) Aut jack.

cricket [krikɛt] *nm Sp* cricket.

crier [krije] *vi* to shout (out), cry (out); (*de peur*) to scream; (*oiseau*) to chirp; (*grincer*) to creak, squeak; **c. au scandale**/etc to proclaim sth to be a scandal/etc; **c. après qn** Fam to shout at s.o.; *– vt* (*injure, ordre*) to shout (out); (*son innocence etc*) to proclaim; **c. vengeance** to cry out for vengeance. ◆**crieur, -euse** *nmf* **c. de journaux** newspaper seller.

crime [krim] *nm* crime; (*assassinat*) murder. ◆**criminalité** *nf* crime (in general), criminal practice. ◆**criminel, -elle** *a* criminal; *– nmf* criminal; (*assassin*) murderer.

crin [krɛ̃] *nm* horsehair; **c. végétal** vegetable fibre; **à tous crins** (*pacifiste etc*) out-and-out. ◆**crinière** *nf* mane.

crique [krik] *nf* creek, cove.

criquet [krikɛ] *nm* locust.

crise [kriz] *nf* crisis; (*accès*) attack; (*de colère etc*) fit; (*pénurie*) shortage; **c. de conscience** (moral) dilemma.

crisp/er [krispe] *vt* (*muscle*) to tense; (*visage*) to make tense; (*poing*) to clench; **c. qn** Fam to aggravate s.o.; **se c. sur** (*main*) to grip tightly. ◆**—ant** *a* aggravating. ◆**—é**

a (*personne*) tense. ◆**crispation** *nf* (*agacement*) aggravation.

crisser [krise] *vi* (*pneu, roue*) to screech; (*neige*) to crunch.

cristal, -aux [kristal, -o] *nm* crystal; *pl* (*objets*) crystal(ware); (*pour nettoyer*) washing soda. ◆**cristallin** *a* (*eau, son*) crystal-clear. ◆**cristalliser** *vti*, **— se c.** *vpr* to crystallize.

critère [kriter] *nm* criterion.

critérium [kriterjɔm] *nm* (*épreuve*) *Sp* eliminating heat.

critique [kritik] *a* critical; — *nf* (*reproche*) criticism; (*analyse de film, livre etc*) review; (*de texte*) critique; **faire la c. de** (*film etc*) to review; **affronter la c.** to confront the critics; — *nm* critic. ◆**critiqu/er** *vt* to criticize. ◆**—able** *a* open to criticism.

croasser [krɔase] *vi* (*corbeau*) to caw.

croc [kro] *nm* (*crochet*) hook; (*dent*) fang. ◆**c.-en-jambe** *nm* (*pl* **crocs-en-jambe**) = **croche-pied.**

croche [krɔʃ] *nf Mus* quaver, *Am* eighth (note).

croche-pied [krɔʃpje] *nm* **faire un c.-pied à qn** to trip s.o. up.

crochet [krɔʃɛ] *nm* (*pour accrocher*) & *Boxe* hook; (*aiguille*) crochet hook; (*travail*) crochet; (*clef*) picklock; *Typ* (*square*) bracket; **faire qch au c.** to crochet sth; **faire un c.** (*route*) to make a sudden turn; (*personne*) to make a detour *ou* side trip; (*pour éviter*) to swerve; **vivre aux crochets de qn** *Fam* to sponge off *ou* on s.o. ◆**crocheter** *vt* (*serrure*) to pick. ◆**crochu** *a* (*nez*) hooked.

crocodile [krɔkɔdil] *nm* crocodile.

crocus [krɔkys] *nm Bot* crocus.

croire* [krwar] *vt* to believe; (*estimer*) to think, believe (**que** that); **j'ai cru la voir** I thought I saw her; **je crois que oui** I think *ou* believe so; **je n'en crois pas mes yeux** I can't believe my eyes; **à l'en c.** according to him; **il se croit malin/quelque chose** he thinks he's smart/quite something; — *vi* to believe (**à, en** in).

croisé[1] [krwaze] *nm Hist* crusader. ◆**croisade** *nf* crusade.

crois/er [krwaze] *vt* to cross; (*bras*) to fold, cross; **c. qn** to pass *ou* meet s.o.; — *vi* (*veston*) to fold over; *Nau* to cruise; **— se c.** *vpr* (*voitures etc*) to pass *ou* meet (each other); (*routes*) to cross, intersect; (*lettres*) to cross in the post. ◆**—é[2], -ée** *a* (*bras*) folded, crossed; (*veston*) double-breasted; **mots croisés** crossword; **tirs croisés** crossfire; **race croisée** crossbreed; — *nf* (*fenêtre*)

casement; **croisée des chemins** crossroads. ◆**—ement** *nm* (*action*) crossing; (*de routes*) crossroads, intersection; (*de véhicules*) passing. ◆**—eur** *nm* (*navire de guerre*) cruiser. ◆**croisière** *nf* cruise; **vitesse de c.** *Nau Av* & *Fig* cruising speed.

croître* [krwatr] *vi* (*plante etc*) to grow; (*augmenter*) to grow, increase; (*lune*) to wax. ◆**croissant 1** *a* (*nombre etc*) growing. **2** *nm* crescent; (*pâtisserie*) croissant. ◆**croissance** *nf* growth.

croix [krwa] *nf* cross.

croque-mitaine [krɔkmiten] *nm* bogeyman. ◆**c.-monsieur** *nm inv* toasted cheese and ham sandwich. ◆**c.-mort** *nm Fam* undertaker's assistant.

croqu/er [krɔke] **1** *vt* (*manger*) to crunch; — *vi* (*fruit etc*) to be crunchy, crunch. **2** *vt* (*peindre*) to sketch; **joli à c.** pretty as a picture. ◆**—ant** *a* (*biscuit etc*) crunchy. ◆**croquette** *nf Culin* croquette.

croquet [krɔkɛ] *nm Sp* croquet.

croquis [krɔki] *nm* sketch.

crosse [krɔs] *nf* (*d'évêque*) crook; (*de fusil*) butt; (*de hockey*) stick.

crotte [krɔt] *nf* (*de lapin etc*) mess, droppings. ◆**crottin** *nm* (*horse*) dung.

crotté [krɔte] *a* (*bottes etc*) muddy.

croul/er [krule] *vi* (*édifice, projet etc*) to crumble, collapse; **c. sous une charge** (*porteur etc*) to totter beneath a burden; **faire c.** (*immeuble etc*) to bring down. ◆**—ant** *a* (*mur etc*) tottering; — *nm* (*vieux*) *Fam* old-timer.

croupe [krup] *nf* (*de cheval*) rump; **monter en c.** (*à cheval*) to ride pillion. ◆**croupion** *nm* (*de poulet*) parson's nose.

croupier [krupje] *nm* (*au casino*) croupier.

croupir [krupir] *vi* (*eau*) to stagnate, become foul; **c. dans** (*le vice etc*) to wallow in; **eau croupie** stagnant water.

croustill/er [krustije] *vi* to be crusty; to be crunchy. ◆**—ant** *a* (*pain*) crusty; (*biscuit*) crunchy; (*histoire*) *Fig* spicy, juicy.

croûte [krut] *nf* (*de pain etc*) crust; (*de fromage*) rind; (*de plaie*) scab; **casser la c.** *Fam* to have a snack; **gagner sa c.** *Fam* to earn one's bread and butter. ◆**croûton** *nm* crust (*at end of loaf*); *pl* (*avec soupe*) croûtons.

croyable [krwajabl] *a* credible, believable. ◆**croyance** *nf* belief (**à, en** in). ◆**croyant, -ante** *a* **être c.** to be a believer; — *nmf* believer.

CRS [seeres] *nmpl abrév* (*Compagnies républicaines de sécurité*) French state security police, riot police.

cru[1] [kry] *voir* **croire.**

cru[2] [kry] **1** *a* (*aliment etc*) raw; (*lumière*) glaring; (*propos*) crude; **monter à c.** to ride bareback. **2** *nm* (*vignoble*) vineyard; **un grand c.** (*vin*) a vintage wine; **vin du c.** local wine.

cruauté [kryote] *nf* cruelty (**envers** to).

cruche [kryʃ] *nf* pitcher, jug.

crucial, -aux [krysjal, -o] *a* crucial.

crucifier [krysifje] *vt* to crucify. ◆**crucifix** [krysifi] *nm* crucifix. ◆**crucifixion** *nf* crucifixion.

crudité [krydite] *nf* (*grossièreté*) crudeness; *pl Culin* assorted raw vegetables.

crue [kry] *nf* (*de cours d'eau*) swelling, flood; **en c.** in spate.

cruel, -elle [kryɛl] *a* cruel (**envers, avec** to).

crûment [krymɑ̃] *adv* crudely.

crustacés [krystase] *nmpl* shellfish, crustaceans.

crypte [kript] *nf* crypt.

Cuba [kyba] *nm* Cuba. ◆**cubain, -aine** *a* & *nmf* Cuban.

cube [kyb] *nm* cube; *pl* (*jeu*) building blocks; – *a* (*mètre etc*) cubic. ◆**cubique** *a* cubic.

cueillir* [kœjir] *vt* to gather, pick; (*baiser*) to snatch; (*voleur*) *Fam* to pick up, run in. ◆**cueillette** *nf* gathering, picking; (*fruits cueillis*) harvest.

cuiller, cuillère [kɥijɛr] *nf* spoon; **petite c., c. à café** teaspoon; **c. à soupe** table spoon. ◆**cuillerée** *nf* spoonful.

cuir [kɥir] *nm* leather; (*peau épaisse d'un animal vivant*) hide; **c. chevelu** scalp.

cuirasse [kɥiras] *nf Hist* breastplate. ◆**se cuirass/er** *vpr* to steel oneself (**contre** against). ◆**—é** *nm* battleship.

cuire* [kɥir] *vt* to cook; (*à l'eau*) to boil; (*porcelaine*) to bake, fire; **c. (au four)** to bake; (*viande*) to roast; – *vi* to cook; to boil; to bake; to roast; (*soleil*) to bake, boil; **faire c.** to cook. ◆**cuisant** *a* (*affront, blessure etc*) stinging. ◆**cuisson** *nm* cooking; (*de porcelaine*) baking, firing.

cuisine [kɥizin] *nf* (*pièce*) kitchen; (*art*) cooking, cuisine, cookery; (*aliments*) cooking; (*intrigues*) *Péj* scheming; **faire la c.** to cook, do the cooking; **livre de c.** cook(ery) book; **haute c.** high-class cooking. ◆**cuisiner** *vti* to cook; **c. qn** (*interroger*) *Fam* to grill s.o. ◆**cuisinier, -ière** *nmf* cook; – *nf* (*appareil*) cooker, stove, *Am* range.

cuisse [kɥis] *nf* thigh; (*de poulet, mouton*) leg.

cuit [kɥi] **1** *voir* **cuire;** – *a* cooked; **bien c.** well done *ou* cooked. **2** *a* (*pris*) *Fam* done for.

cuite [kɥit] *nf* **prendre une c.** *Fam* to get plastered *ou* drunk.

cuivre [kɥivr] *nm* (*rouge*) copper; (*jaune*) brass; *pl* (*ustensiles*) & *Mus* brass. ◆**cuivré** *a* copper-coloured, coppery.

cul [ky] *nm* (*derrière*) *Fam* backside; (*de bouteille etc*) bottom. ◆**c.-de-jatte** *nm* (*pl* **culs-de-jatte**) legless cripple. ◆**c.-de-sac** *nm* (*pl* **culs-de-sac**) dead end, cul-de-sac.

culasse [kylas] *nf Aut* cylinder head; (*d'une arme à feu*) breech.

culbute [kylbyt] *nf* (*cabriole*) sommersault; (*chute*) (backward) tumble; **faire une c.** to sommersault; to tumble. ◆**culbuter** *vi* to tumble over (backwards); – *vt* (*personne, chaise*) to knock over.

culinaire [kyliner] *a* (*art*) culinary; (*recette*) cooking.

culmin/er [kylmine] *vi* (*montagne*) to reach its highest point, peak (**à** at); (*colère*) *Fig* to reach a peak. ◆**—ant** *a* **point c.** (*de réussite, montagne etc*) peak.

culot [kylo] *nm* **1** (*aplomb*) *Fam* nerve, cheek. **2** (*d'ampoule, de lampe etc*) base. ◆**culotté** *a* **être c.** *Fam* to have plenty of nerve *ou* cheek.

culotte [kylɔt] *nf Sp* (pair of) shorts; (*de femme*) (pair of) knickers *ou Am* panties; **culottes (courtes)** (*de jeune garçon*) short trousers *ou Am* pants; **c. de cheval** riding breeches.

culpabilité [kylpabilite] *nf* guilt.

culte [kylt] *nm* (*hommage*) *Rel* worship, cult; (*pratique*) *Rel* religion; (*service protestant*) service; (*admiration*) *Fig* cult.

cultiv/er [kyltive] *vt* (*terre*) to farm, cultivate; (*plantes*) to grow, cultivate; (*goût, relations etc*) to cultivate; – **se c.** *vpr* to cultivate one's mind. ◆**—é** *a* (*esprit, personne*) cultured, cultivated. ◆**cultivateur, -trice** *nmf* farmer. ◆**culture** *nf* (*action*) farming, cultivation; (*agriculture*) farming; (*horticulture*) growing, cultivation; (*éducation, civilisation*) culture; *pl* (*terres*) fields (under cultivation); (*plantes*) crops; **c. générale** general knowledge. ◆**culturel, -elle** *a* cultural.

cumin [kymɛ̃] *nm Bot Culin* caraway.

cumul [kymyl] *nm* **c. de fonctions** plurality of offices. ◆**cumulatif, -ive** *a* cumulative. ◆**cumuler** *vt* **c. deux fonctions** to hold two offices (at the same time).

cupide [kypid] *a* avaricious. ◆**cupidité** *nf* avarice, cupidity.

Cupidon [kypidɔ̃] *nm* Cupid.

cure [kyr] *nf* **1** (course of) treatment, cure. **2** (*fonction*) office (of a parish priest); (*résidence*) presbytery. ◆**curable** *a* curable. ◆**curatif, -ive** *a* curative. ◆**curé** *nm* (parish) priest.

curer [kyre] *vt* to clean out; **se c. le nez/ les dents** to pick one's nose/teeth. ◆**curedent** *nm* toothpick. ◆**cure-ongles** *nm inv* nail cleaner. ◆**cure-pipe** *nm* pipe cleaner.

curieux, -euse [kyrjø, -øz] *a* (*bizarre*) curious; (*indiscret*) inquisitive, curious (**de** about); **c. de savoir** curious to know; – *nmf* inquisitive *ou* curious person; (*badaud*) onlooker. ◆**curieusement** *adv* curiously. ◆**curiosité** *nf* (*de personne, forme etc*) curiosity; (*chose*) curiosity; (*spectacle*) unusual sight.

curriculum (vitæ) [kyrikylɔm(vite)] *nm inv* curriculum (vitae), *Am* résumé.

curseur [kyrsœr] *nm* (*d'un ordinateur*) cursor.

cutané [kytane] *a* (*affection etc*) skin-. ◆**cuti(-réaction)** *nf* skin test.

cuve [kyv] *nf* vat; (*réservoir*) & *Phot* tank. ◆**cuvée** *nf* (*récolte de vin*) vintage.

◆**cuver** *vt* **c. son vin** *Fam* to sleep it off. ◆**cuvette** *nf* (*récipient*) & *Géog* basin, bowl; (*des cabinets*) pan, bowl.

cyanure [sjanyr] *nm* cyanide.

cybernétique [sibernetik] *nf* cybernetics.

cycle [sikl] *nm* **1** (*série, révolution*) cycle. **2** (*bicyclette*) cycle. ◆**cyclable** *a* (*piste*) cycle-. ◆**cyclique** *a* cyclic(al). ◆**cyclisme** *nm* *Sp* cycling. ◆**cycliste** *nmf* cyclist; – *a* (*course*) cycle-; (*champion*) cycling; **coureur c.** racing cyclist. ◆**cyclomoteur** *nm* moped.

cyclone [siklon] *nm* cyclone.

cygne [siɲ] *nm* swan; **chant du c.** *Fig* swan song.

cylindre [silɛ̃dr] *nm* cylinder; (*de rouleau compresseur*) roller. ◆**cylindrée** *nf* *Aut* (engine) capacity. ◆**cylindrique** *a* cylindrical.

cymbale [sɛ̃bal] *nf* cymbal.

cynique [sinik] *a* cynical; – *nmf* cynic. ◆**cynisme** *nm* cynicism.

cyprès [siprɛ] *nm* (*arbre*) cypress.

cypriote [siprijɔt] *a* & *nmf* Cypriot.

cytise [sitiz] *nf* *Bot* laburnum.

D

D, d [de] *nm* D, d.

d' [d] *voir de* **¹, ².**

d'abord [dabɔr] *adv* (*en premier lieu*) first; (*au début*) at first.

dactylo [daktilo] *nf* (*personne*) typist; (*action*) typing. ◆**dactylographie** *nf* typing. ◆**dactylographier** *vt* to type.

dada [dada] *nm* (*manie*) hobby horse, pet subject.

dadais [dadɛ] *nm* (**grand**) **d.** big oaf.

dahlia [dalja] *nm* dahlia.

daigner [deɲe] *vt* **d. faire** to condescend *ou* deign to do.

daim [dɛ̃] *nm* fallow deer; (*mâle*) buck; (*cuir*) suede.

dais [dɛ] *nm* (*de lit, feuillage etc*) canopy.

dalle [dal] *nf* paving stone; (*funèbre*) (flat) gravestone. ◆**dallage** *nm* (*action, surface*) paving. ◆**dallé** *a* (*pièce, cour etc*) paved.

daltonien, -ienne [daltɔnjɛ̃, -jɛn] *a & n* colour-blind (person). ◆**daltonisme** *nm* colour blindness.

dame [dam] *nf* **1** lady; (*mariée*) married lady. **2** *Échecs Cartes* queen; (*au jeu de dames*) king; (**jeu de**) **dames** draughts, *Am*

checkers. ◆**damer** *vt* (*au jeu de dames*) to crown; **d. le pion à qn** to outsmart s.o. ◆**damier** *nm* draughtboard, *Am* checkerboard.

damner [dane] *vt* to damn; **faire d.** *Fam* to torment, drive mad; – **se d.** *vpr* to be damned. ◆**damnation** *nf* damnation.

dancing [dɑ̃siŋ] *nm* dance hall.

dandiner (se) [sədɑ̃dine] *vpr* to waddle.

dandy [dɑ̃di] *nm* dandy.

Danemark [danmark] *nm* Denmark. ◆**danois, -oise** *a* Danish; – *nmf* Dane; – *nm* (*langue*) Danish.

danger [dɑ̃ʒe] *nm* danger; **en d.** in danger *ou* jeopardy; **mettre en d.** to endanger, jeopardize; **en cas de d.** in an emergency; **en d. de mort** in peril of death; **'d. de mort'** (*panneau*) 'danger'; **sans d.** (*se promener etc*) safely; **être sans d.** to be safe; **pas de d.!** *Fam* no way!, no fear! ◆**dangereux, -euse** *a* dangerous (**pour** to). ◆**dangereusement** *adv* dangerously.

dans [dɑ̃] *prép* in; (*changement de lieu*) into; (*à l'intérieur de*) inside, within; **entrer d.** to go in(to); **d. Paris** in Paris, within Paris;

d. un rayon de within (a radius of); **boire/prendre/etc d.** to drink/take/etc from *ou* out of; **marcher d. les rues** (*à travers*) to walk through *ou* about the streets; **d. ces circonstances** under *ou* in these circumstances; **d. deux jours/etc** (*temps futur*) in two days/etc, in two days'/etc time; **d. les dix francs/etc** (*quantité*) about ten francs/etc.

danse [dɑ̃s] *nf* dance; (*art*) dancing. ◆**dans/er** *vti* to dance; **faire d. l'anse du panier** (*domestique*) to fiddle on the shopping money. ◆**—eur, -euse** *nmf* dancer; **en danseuse** (*cycliste*) standing on the pedals.

dard [dar] *nm* (*d'abeille etc*) sting; (*de serpent*) tongue. ◆**darder** *vt Litt* (*flèche*) to shoot; (*regard*) to flash, dart; **le soleil dardait ses rayons** the sun cast down its burning rays.

dare-dare [dardar] *adv Fam* at *ou* on the double.

date [dat] *nf* date; **de vieille d.** (*amitié etc*) (of) long-standing; **faire d.** (*événement*) to mark an important date, be epoch-making; **en d. du ...** dated the ... ; **d. limite** deadline. ◆**datation** *nf* dating. ◆**dater** *vt* (*lettre etc*) to date; *– vi* (*être dépassé*) to date, be dated; **d. de** to date back to, date from; **à d. de** as from. ◆**dateur** *nm* (*de montre*) date indicator; *– a & nm* (*tampon*) d. date stamp.

datte [dat] *nf* (*fruit*) date. ◆**dattier** *nm* date palm.

daube [dob] *nf* **bœuf en d.** braised beef stew.

dauphin [dofɛ̃] *nm* (*mammifère marin*) dolphin.

davantage [davɑ̃taʒ] *adv* (*quantité*) more; (*temps*) longer; **d. de temps/etc** more time/etc; **d. que** more than; longer than.

de¹ [d(ə)] (**d'** *before a vowel or mute h*; **de + le = du, de + les = des**) *prép* 1 (*complément d'un nom*) of; **les rayons du soleil** the rays of the sun, the sun's rays; **la ville de Paris** the town of Paris; **le livre de Paul** Paul's book; **un pont de fer** an iron bridge; **le train de Londres** the London train; **une augmentation/diminution de** an increase/decrease in. 2 (*complément d'un adjectif*) **digne de** worthy of; **heureux de partir** happy to leave; **content de qch** pleased with sth. 3 (*complément d'un verbe*) **parler de** to speak of *ou* about; **se souvenir de** to remember; **décider de faire** to decide to do; **traiter de lâche** to call a coward. 4 (*provenance*: *lieu & temps*) from; **venir/dater de** to come/date from; **mes**

amis du village my friends from the village, my village friends; **le train de Londres** the train from London. 5 (*agent*) **accompagné de** accompanied by. 6 (*moyen*) **armé de** armed with; **se nourrir de** to live on. 7 (*manière*) **d'une voix douce** in *ou* with a gentle voice. 8 (*cause*) **puni de** punished for; **mourir de faim** to die of hunger. 9 (*temps*) **travailler de nuit** to work by night; **six heures du matin** six o'clock in the morning. 10 (*mesure*) **avoir six mètres de haut, être haut de six mètres** to be six metres high; **retarder de deux heures** to delay by two hours; **homme de trente ans** thirty-year-old man; **gagner cent francs de l'heure** to earn one hundred francs an hour.

de² [d(ə)] *art partitif* some; **elle boit du vin** she drinks (some) wine; **il ne boit pas de vin** (*négation*) he doesn't drink (any) wine; **des fleurs** (some) flowers; **de jolies fleurs** (some) pretty flowers; **d'agréables soirées** (some) pleasant evenings; **il y en a six de tués** (*avec un nombre*) there are six killed.

dé [de] *nm* (*à jouer*) dice; (*à coudre*) thimble; **les dés** the dice; (*jeu*) dice; **les dés sont jetés** *Fig* the die is cast; **couper en dés** *Culin* to dice.

déambuler [deɑ̃byle] *vi* to stroll, saunter.

débâcle [debɑkl] *nf Mil* rout; (*ruine*) *Fig* downfall; (*des glaces*) *Géog* breaking up.

déball/er [debale] *vt* to unpack; (*étaler*) to display. ◆**—age** *nm* unpacking; display.

débandade [debɑ̃dad] *nf* (mad) rush, stampede; *Mil* rout; **à la d.** in confusion; **tout va à la d.** everything's going to rack and ruin.

débaptiser [debatize] *vt* (*rue*) to rename.

débarbouiller [debarbuje] *vt* **d. qn** to wash s.o.'s face; **se d.** to wash one's face.

débarcadère [debarkader] *nm* landing stage, quay.

débardeur [debardœr] *nm* 1 (*docker*) stevedore. 2 (*vêtement*) slipover, *Am* (sweater) vest.

débarqu/er [debarke] *vt* (*passagers*) to land; (*marchandises*) to unload; **d. qn** (*congédier*) *Fam* to sack s.o.; *– vi* (*passagers*) to disembark, land; (*être naïf*) *Fam* not to be quite with it; **d. chez qn** *Fam* to turn up suddenly at s.o.'s place. ◆**—ement** *nm* landing; unloading; *Mil* landing.

débarras [debara] *nm* lumber room, *Am* storeroom; **bon d.!** *Fam* good riddance! ◆**débarrasser** *vt* (*voie, table etc*) to clear (**de** of); **d. qn de** (*ennemi, soucis etc*) to rid s.o. of; (*manteau etc*) to relieve s.o. of; **se d. de** to get rid of, rid oneself of.

débat [deba] *nm* discussion, debate; *pl Pol Jur* proceedings. ◆**débattre*** *vt* to discuss, debate; **— se d.** *vpr* to struggle *ou* fight (to get free), put up a fight.

débauche [deboʃ] *nf* debauchery; **une d. de** *Fig* a wealth *ou* profusion of. ◆**débauch/er** *vt* **d. qn** (*détourner*) *Fam* to entice s.o. away from his work; (*licencier*) to dismiss s.o., lay s.o. off. ◆**—é, -ée** *a* (*libertin*) debauched, profligate; **— nmf** debauchee, profligate.

débile [debil] *a* (*esprit, enfant etc*) weak, feeble; *Péj Fam* idiotic; **— nmf** *Péj Fam* idiot, moron. ◆**débilité** *nf* debility, weakness; *pl* (*niaiseries*) *Fam* sheer nonsense. ◆**débiliter** *vt* to debilitate, weaken.

débiner [debine] **1** *vt* (*décrier*) *Fam* to run down. **2 se d.** *vpr* (*s'enfuir*) *Arg* to hop it, bolt.

débit [debi] *nm* **1** (*vente*) turnover, sales; (*de fleuve*) (rate of) flow; (*d'un orateur*) delivery; **d. de tabac** tobacconist's shop, *Am* tobacco store; **d. de boissons** bar, café. **2** (*compte*) *Fin* debit. ◆**débiter** *vt* **1** (*découper*) to cut up, slice up (en into); (*vendre*) to sell; (*fournir*) to yield; (*dire*) *Péj* to utter, spout. **2** *Fin* to debit. ◆**débiteur, -trice** *nmf* debtor; **— a** (*solde, compte*) debit-; **son compte est d.** his account is in debit, he is in debit.

déblais [deble] *nmpl* (*terre*) earth; (*décombres*) rubble. ◆**déblayer** *vt* (*terrain, décombres*) to clear.

débloquer [debloke] **1** *vt* (*machine*) to unjam; (*crédits, freins, compte*) to release; (*prix*) to decontrol. **2** *vi* (*divaguer*) *Fam* to talk through one's hat, talk nonsense.

déboires [debwar] *nmpl* disappointments, setbacks.

déboît/er [debwate] **1** *vt* (*tuyau*) to disconnect; (*os*) *Méd* to dislocate. **2** *vi* *Aut* to pull out, change lanes. ◆**—ement** *nm Méd* dislocation.

débonnaire [deboner] *a* good-natured, easy-going.

débord/er [deborde] *vi* (*fleuve, liquide*) to overflow; (*en bouillant*) to boil over; **d. de** (*vie, joie etc*) *Fig* to be overflowing *ou* bubbling over with; **l'eau déborde du vase** the water is running over the top of the vase *ou* is overflowing the vase; **— vt** (*dépasser*) to go *ou* extend beyond; (*faire saillie*) to stick out from; *Mil Sp* to outflank; **débordé de travail/de visites** snowed under with work/visits. ◆**—ement** *nm* overflowing; (*de joie, activité*) outburst.

débouch/er [debuʃe] **1** *vt* (*bouteille*) to open, uncork; (*lavabo, tuyau*) to clear, unblock. **2** *vi* (*surgir*) to emerge, come out (**de** from); **d. sur** (*rue*) to lead out onto, lead into; *Fig* to lead up to. ◆**—é** *nm* (*carrière*) & *Géog* opening; (*de rue*) exit; (*marché*) *Com* outlet.

débouler [debule] *vi* (*arriver*) *Fam* to burst in, turn up.

déboulonner [debulone] *vt* to unbolt; **d. qn** *Fam* (*renvoyer*) to sack *ou* fire s.o.; (*discréditer*) to bring s.o. down.

débours [debur] *nmpl* expenses. ◆**débourser** *vt* to pay out.

debout [d(ə)bu] *adv* standing (up); **mettre d.** (*planche etc*) to stand up, put upright; **se mettre d.** to stand *ou* get up; **se tenir** *ou* **rester d.** (*personne*) to stand (up), remain standing (up); **rester d.** (*édifice etc*) to remain standing; **être d.** (*levé*) to be up (and about); **d.!** get up!; **ça ne tient pas d.** (*théorie etc*) that doesn't hold water *ou* make sense.

déboutonner [debutone] *vt* to unbutton, undo; **— se d.** *vpr* (*personne*) to undo one's buttons.

débraillé [debraje] *a* (*tenue etc*) slovenly, sloppy; **— nm** slovenliness, sloppiness.

débrancher [debrɑ̃ʃe] *vt El* to unplug, disconnect.

débrayer [debreje] *vi* **1** *Aut* to declutch, release the clutch. **2** (*se mettre en grève*) to stop work. ◆**débrayage** (*grève*) strike, walk-out.

débridé [debride] *a* (*effréné*) unbridled.

débris [debri] *nmpl* fragments, scraps; (*restes*) remains; (*détritus*) rubbish, debris.

débrouiller [debruje] **1** *vt* (*écheveau etc*) to unravel, disentangle; (*affaire*) to sort out. **2 se d.** *vpr* to manage, get by, make out; **se d. pour faire** to manage (somehow) to do. ◆**débrouillard** *a* smart, resourceful. ◆**débrouillardise** *nf* smartness, resourcefulness.

débroussailler [debrusaje] *vt* (*chemin*) to clear (of brushwood); (*problème*) *Fig* to clarify.

débusquer [debyske] *vt* (*gibier, personne*) to drive out, dislodge.

début [deby] *nm* start, beginning; **au d.** at the beginning; **faire ses débuts** (*sur la scène etc*) to make one's debut. ◆**début/er** *vi* to start, begin; (*dans une carrière*) to start out in life; (*sur la scène etc*) to make one's debut. ◆—ant, -ante *nmf* beginner; – *a* novice.

déca [deka] *nm Fam* decaffeinated coffee.

deçà (en) [ăd(ə)sa] *adv* (on) this side; – *prép* **en d. de** (on) this side of; (*succès, prix etc*) *Fig* short of.

décacheter [dekaʃte] *vt* (*lettre etc*) to open, unseal.

décade [dekad] *nf* (*dix jours*) period of ten days; (*décennie*) decade.

décadent [dekadă] *a* decadent. ◆**décadence** *nf* decay, decadence.

décaféiné [dekafeine] *a* decaffeinated.

décalaminer [dekalamine] *vt* (*moteur*) *Aut* to decoke, decarbonize.

décalcomanie [dekalkɔmani] *nf* (*image*) transfer, *Am* decal.

décal/er [dekale] *vt* **1** (*avancer*) to shift; (*départ, repas*) to shift (the time of). **2** (*ôter les cales de*) to unwedge. ◆—**age** *nm* (*écart*) gap, discrepancy; **d. horaire** time difference.

décalque [dekalk] *nm* tracing. ◆**décalquer** (*dessin*) to trace.

décamper [dekăpe] *vi* to make off, clear off.

décanter [dekăte] *vt* (*liquide*) to settle, clarify; **d. ses idées** to clarify one's ideas; **— se d.** *vpr* (*idées, situation*) to become clearer, settle.

décap/er [dekape] *vt* (*métal*) to clean, scrape down; (*surface peinte*) to strip. ◆—**ant** *nm* cleaning agent; (*pour enlever la peinture*) paint stripper. ◆—**eur** *nm* **d. thermique** hot-air paint stripper.

décapiter [dekapite] *vt* to decapitate, behead.

décapotable [dekapɔtabl] *a* (*voiture*) convertible.

décapsul/er [dekapsyle] *vt* **d. une bouteille** to take the cap *ou* top off a bottle. ◆—**eur** *nm* bottle-opener.

décarcasser (se) [sədekarkase] *vpr Fam* to flog oneself to death (**pour faire** doing).

décathlon [dekatlɔ̃] *nm Sp* decathlon.

décati [dekati] *a* worn out, decrepit.

décavé [dekave] *a Fam* ruined.

décéd/er [desede] *vi* to die. ◆—**é** *a* deceased.

déceler [desle] *vt* (*trouver*) to detect, uncover; (*révéler*) to reveal.

décembre [desăbr] *nm* December.

décennie [deseni] *nf* decade.

décent [desă] *a* (*bienséant, acceptable*) decent. ◆**décemment** [-amă] *adv* decently. ◆**décence** *nf* decency.

décentraliser [desătralize] *vt* to decentral-

ize. ◆**décentralisation** *nf* decentralization.

déception [desɛpsjɔ̃] *nf* disappointment. ◆**décevoir*** *vt* to disappoint. ◆**décevant** *a* disappointing.

décerner [desɛrne] *vt* (*prix etc*) to award; (*mandat d'arrêt etc*) *Jur* to issue.

décès [desɛ] *nm* death.

déchaîn/er [deʃene] *vt* (*colère, violence*) to unleash, let loose; **d. l'enthousiasme/les rires** to set off wild enthusiasm/a storm of laughter; **— se d.** *vpr* (*tempête, rires*) to break out; (*foule*) to run amok *ou* riot; (*colère, personne*) to explode. ◆—**é** *a* (*foule, flots*) wild, raging. ◆—**ement** [-ɛnmă] *nm* (*de rires, de haine etc*) outburst; (*de violence*) outbreak, eruption; **le d. de la tempête** the raging of the storm.

déchanter [deʃăte] *vi Fam* to become disillusioned; (*changer de ton*) to change one's tune.

décharge [deʃarʒ] *nf Jur* discharge; **d. (publique)** (*rubbish*) dump *ou* tip, *Am* (*garbage*) dump; **d. (électrique)** (electrical) discharge, shock; **recevoir une d. (électrique)** to get a shock; **à la d. de qn** in s.o.'s defence. ◆**décharg/er** *vt* to unload; (*batterie*) *Él* to discharge; (*accusé*) *Jur* to discharge, exonerate; **d. qn de** (*travail etc*) to relieve s.o. of; **d. sur qn** (*son arme*) to fire at s.o.; (*sa colère*) to vent on s.o.; **— se d.** *vpr* (*batterie*) to go flat; **se d. sur qn du soin de faire qch** to unload onto s.o. the job of doing sth. ◆—**ement** *nm* unloading.

décharné [deʃarne] *a* skinny, bony.

déchausser [deʃose] *vt* **d. qn** to take s.o.'s shoes off; **se d.** to take one's shoes off; (*dent*) to get loose.

dèche [deʃ] *nf* **être dans la d.** *Arg* to be flat broke.

déchéance [deʃeăs] *nf* (*déclin*) decline, decay, degradation.

déchet [deʃɛ] *nm* **déchets** (*résidus*) scraps, waste; **il y a du d.** there's some waste *ou* wastage.

déchiffrer [deʃifre] *vt* (*message*) to decipher; (*mauvaise écriture*) to make out, decipher.

déchiquet/er [deʃikte] *vt* to tear to shreds, cut to bits. ◆—**é** *a* (*drapeau etc*) (all) in shreds; (*côte*) jagged.

déchir/er [deʃire] *vt* to tear (up), rip (up); (*vêtement*) to tear, rip; (*ouvrir*) to tear *ou* rip open; (*pays, groupe*) to tear apart; **d. l'air** (*bruit*) to rend the air; **ce bruit me déchire les oreilles** this noise is ear-splitting; **— se d.** *vpr* (*robe etc*) to tear, rip. ◆—ant a (navrant) heart-breaking; (aigu) ear-splitting. ◆—ement nm (souffrance) heartbreak; pl (divisions) Pol deep rifts. ◆déchirure nf tear, rip; d. musculaire torn muscle.

déchoir [deʃwar] vi to lose prestige. ◆déchu a (ange) fallen; être d. de (ses droits etc) to have forfeited.

décibel [desibɛl] nm decibel.

décid/er [deside] vt (envoi, opération) to decide on; d. que to decide that; d. qn à faire to persuade s.o. to do; — vi d. de (destin de qn) to decide; (voyage etc) to decide on; d. de faire to decide to do; — se d. vpr (question) to be decided; se d. à faire to make up one's mind to do; se d. pour qch to decide on sth ou in favour of sth. ◆—é a (air, ton) determined, decided; (net, pas douteux) decided; c'est d. it's settled; être d. à faire to be decided about doing ou determined to do. ◆—ément adv undoubtedly.

décilitre [desilitr] nm decilitre.

décimal, -aux [desimal, -o] a decimal. ◆décimale nf decimal.

décimer [desime] vt to decimate.

décimètre [desimetr] nm decimetre; **double d.** ruler.

décisif, -ive [desizif, -iv] a decisive; (moment) crucial. ◆décision nf decision; (fermeté) determination.

déclamer [deklame] vt to declaim; Péj to spout. ◆déclamatoire a Péj bombastic.

déclarer [deklare] vt to declare (que that); (décès, vol etc) to notify; d. coupable to convict, find guilty; d. la guerre to declare war (à on); — se d. vpr (s'expliquer) to declare one's views; (incendie, maladie) to break out; se d. contre to come out against. ◆déclaration nf declaration; (de décès etc) notification; (commentaire) statement, comment; d. de revenus tax return.

déclasser [deklase] vt (livres etc) to put out of order; (hôtel etc) to downgrade; d. qn Sp to relegate s.o. (in the placing).

déclench/er [deklɑ̃ʃe] vt (mécanisme) to set ou trigger off, release; (attaque) to launch; (provoquer) to trigger off, spark off; d. le travail Méd to induce labour; — se d. vpr (sonnerie) to go off; (attaque, grève) to start. ◆—ement nm (d'un appareil) release.

déclic [deklik] nm (mécanisme) catch, trigger; (bruit) click.

déclin [deklɛ̃] nm decline; (du jour) close; (de la lune) wane. ◆décliner 1 vt (refuser) to decline. 2 vt (réciter) to state. 3 vi (forces etc) to decline, wane; (jour) to draw to a close.

déclivité [deklivite] nf slope.

décocher [dekɔʃe] vt (flèche) to shoot, fire; (coup) to let fly, aim; (regard) to flash.

décoder [dekɔde] vt (message) to decode.

décoiffer [dekwafe] vt d. qn to mess up s.o.'s hair.

décoincer [dekwɛse] vt (engrenage) to unjam.

décoll/er [dekɔle] **1** vi (avion etc) to take off; **elle ne décolle pas d'ici** Fam she won't leave ou budge. **2** vt (timbre etc) to unstick; — se d. vpr to come unstuck. ◆—age nm Av takeoff.

décolleté [dekɔlte] a (robe) low-cut; — nm (de robe) low neckline; (de femme) bare neck and shoulders.

décoloniser [dekɔlɔnize] vt to decolonize. ◆décolonisation nf decolonization.

décolor/er [dekɔlɔre] vt to discolour, fade; (cheveux) to bleach. ◆—ant nm bleach. ◆décoloration nf discolo(u)ration; bleaching.

décombres [dekɔ̃br] nmpl ruins, rubble, debris.

décommander [dekɔmɑ̃de] vt (marchandises, invitation) to cancel; (invités) to put off; — se d. vpr to cancel (one's appointment).

décomposer [dekɔ̃poze] vt to decompose; (visage) to distort; — se d. vpr (pourrir) to decompose; (visage) to become distorted. ◆décomposition nf decomposition.

décompresser [dekɔ̃prese] vi Psy Fam to unwind.

décompression [dekɔ̃presjɔ̃] nf decompression.

décompte [dekɔ̃t] nm deduction; (détail) breakdown. ◆décompter vt to deduct.

déconcerter [dekɔ̃sɛrte] vt to disconcert.

déconfit [dekɔ̃fi] a downcast. ◆déconfiture nf (state of) collapse ou defeat; (faillite) Fam financial ruin.

décongeler [dekɔ̃ʒle] vt (aliment) to thaw, defrost.

décongestionner [dekɔ̃ʒɛstjɔne] vt (rue) & Méd to relieve congestion in.

déconnecter [dekɔnɛkte] vt Él & Fig to disconnect.

déconner [dekɔne] vi (divaguer) Fam to talk nonsense.

déconseiller [dekɔ̃seje] vt d. qch à qn to advise s.o. against sth; d. à qn de faire to advise s.o. against doing; c'est déconseillé it is inadvisable.

déconsidérer [dekɔ̃sidere] vt to discredit.

décontaminer [dekɔ̃tamine] *vt* to decontaminate.

décontenancer [dekɔ̃tnɑ̃se] *vt* to disconcert; **— se d.** *vpr* to lose one's composure, become flustered.

décontracter [dekɔ̃trakte] *vt*, **— se d.** *vpr* to relax. ◆**décontraction** *nf* relaxation.

déconvenue [dekɔ̃vny] *nf* disappointment.

décor [dekɔr] *nm* Th scenery, decor; *Cin* set; (*paysage*) scenery; (*d'intérieur*) decoration; (*cadre, ambiance*) setting; **entrer dans le d.** (*véhicule*) *Fam* to run off the road.

décorer [dekɔre] *vt* (*maison, soldat etc*) to decorate (de with). ◆**décorateur, -trice** *nmf* (interior) decorator; *Th* stage designer; *Cin* set designer. ◆**décoratif, -ive** *a* decorative. ◆**décoration** *nf* decoration.

décortiquer [dekɔrtike] *vt* (*graine*) to husk; (*homard etc*) to shell; (*texte*) *Fam* to take to pieces, dissect.

découcher [dekuʃe] *vi* to stay out all night.

découdre [dekudr] *vt* to unstitch; **–** *vi* **en d.** *Fam* to fight it out; **— se d.** *vpr* to come unstitched.

découler [dekule] *vi* **d. de** to follow from.

découp/er [dekupe] *vt* (*poulet etc*) to carve; (*article etc*) *Journ* to cut out; **se d. sur** to stand out against. ◆**—é** *a* (*côte*) jagged. ◆**—age** *nm* carving; cutting out; (*image*) cut-out. ◆**découpure** *nf* (*contour*) jagged outline; (*morceau*) piece cut out, cut-out.

découplé [dekuple] *a* **bien d.** (*personne*) well-built, strapping.

décourag/er [dekuraʒe] *vt* (*dissuader*) to discourage (de from); (*démoraliser*) to dishearten, discourage; **— se d.** *vpr* to get discouraged *ou* disheartened. ◆**—ement** *nm* discouragement.

décousu [dekuzy] *a* (*propos, idées*) disconnected.

découvrir* [dekuvrir] *vt* (*trésor, terre etc*) to discover; (*secret, vérité etc*) to find out, discover; (*casserole etc*) to take the lid off; (*dévoiler*) to disclose (à to); (*dénuder*) to uncover, expose; (*voir*) to perceive; **d. que** to discover *ou* find out that; **— se d.** *vpr* (*se dénuder*) to uncover oneself; (*enlever son chapeau*) to take one's hat off; (*ciel*) to clear (up). ◆**découvert 1** *a* (*terrain*) open; (*tête etc*) bare; **à d.** exposed, unprotected; **agir à d.** to act openly. **2** *nm* (*d'un compte*) *Fin* overdraft. ◆**découverte** *nf* discovery; **partir** *ou* **aller à la d. de** to go in search of.

décrasser [dekrase] *vt* (*éduquer*) to take the rough edges off.

décrépit [dekrepi] *a* (*vieillard*) decrepit.

◆**décrépitude** *nf* (*des institutions etc*) decay.

décret [dekrɛ] *nm* decree. ◆**décréter** *vt* to order, decree.

décrier [dekrije] *vt* to run down, disparage.

décrire* [dekrir] *vt* to describe.

décroch/er [dekrɔʃe] **1** *vt* (*détacher*) to unhook; (*tableau*) to take down; (*obtenir*) *Fam* to get, land; **d. (le téléphone)** to pick up the phone. **2** *vi* *Fam* (*abandonner*) to give up; (*perdre le fil*) to be unable to follow, lose track. ◆**—é** *a* (*téléphone*) off the hook.

décroître* [dekrwatr] *vi* (*mortalité etc*) to decrease, decline; (*eaux*) to subside; (*jours*) to draw in. ◆**décroissance** *nf* decrease, decline (de in, of).

décrotter [dekrɔte] *vt* (*chaussures*) to clean *ou* scrape (the mud off). ◆**décrottoir** *nm* shoe scraper.

décrypter [dekripte] *vt* (*message*) to decipher, decode.

déçu [desy] *voir* **décevoir;** *– a* disappointed.

déculotter (se) [sədekylɔte] *vpr* to take off one's trousers *ou* *Am* pants. ◆**déculottée** *nf* *Fam* thrashing.

décupler [dekyple] *vti* to increase tenfold.

dédaigner [dedeɲe] *vt* (*personne, richesse etc*) to scorn, despise; (*repas*) to turn up one's nose at; (*offre*) to spurn; (*ne pas tenir compte de*) to disregard. ◆**dédaigneux, -euse** *a* scornful, disdainful (de of). ◆**dédain** *nm* scorn, disdain (pour, de for).

dédale [dedal] *nm* maze, labyrinth.

dedans [d(ə)dɑ̃] *adv* inside; **de d.** from (the) inside, from within; **en d.** on the inside; **au-d. (de), au d. (de)** inside; **au-d.** *ou* **au d. de lui-même** inwardly; **tomber d.** (*trou*) to fall in (it); **donner d.** (*être dupé*) *Fam* to fall in; **mettre d.** *Fam* (*en prison*) to put inside; (*tromper*) to take in; **je me suis fait rentrer d.** (*accident de voiture*) *Fam* someone went *ou* crashed into me; **–** *nm* **le d.** the inside.

dédicace [dedikas] *nf* dedication, inscription. ◆**dédicacer** *vt* (*livre etc*) to dedicate, inscribe (à to).

dédier [dedje] *vt* to dedicate.

dédire (se) [sədedir] *vpr* to go back on one's word; **se d. de** (*promesse etc*) to go back on. ◆**dédit** *nm* (*somme*) *Com* forfeit, penalty.

dédommag/er [dedɔmaʒe] *vt* to compensate (de for). ◆**—ement** *nm* compensation.

dédouaner [dedwane] *vt* (*marchandises*) to clear through customs; **d. qn** to restore s.o.'s prestige.

dédoubl/er [deduble] *vt (classe etc)* to split into two; **d. un train** to run an extra train; **— se d.** *vpr* to be in two places at once. **◆—ement** *nm* **d. de la personnalité** *Psy* split personality.

déduire* [deduir] *vt (retirer)* to deduct (**de** from); *(conclure)* to deduce (**de** from). **◆déductible** *a (frais)* deductible, allowable. **◆déduction** *nf (raisonnement)* & *Com* deduction.

déesse [deɛs] *nf* goddess.

défaill/ir* [defajir] *vi (s'évanouir)* to faint; *(forces)* to fail, flag; **sans d.** without flinching. **◆—ant** *a (personne)* faint; *(témoin)* *Jur* defaulting. **◆défaillance** *nf (évanouissement)* fainting fit; *(faiblesse)* weakness; *(panne)* fault; **une d. de mémoire** a lapse of memory.

défaire* [defɛr] *vt (nœud etc)* to undo, untie; *(bagages)* to unpack; *(installation)* to take down; *(coiffure)* to mess up; **d. qn de** to rid s.o. of; **— se d.** *vpr (nœud etc)* to come undone *ou* untied; **se d. de** to get rid of. **◆défait** *a (lit)* unmade; *(visage)* drawn; *(armée)* defeated. **◆défaite** *nf* defeat. **◆défaitisme** *nm* defeatism.

défalquer [defalke] *vt (frais etc)* to deduct (**de** from).

défaut [defo] *nm (faiblesse)* fault, shortcoming, failing, defect; *(de diamant etc)* flaw; *(désavantage)* drawback; *(contumace)* *Jur* default; **le d. de la cuirasse** the chink in the armour; **faire d.** to be lacking; **le temps me fait d.** I lack time; **à d. de** for want of; **en d.** at fault; **prendre qn en d.** to catch s.o. out; **ou, à d....** or, failing that....

défaveur [defavœr] *nf* disfavour. **◆défavorable** *a* unfavourable (**à** to). **◆défavoriser** *vt* to put at a disadvantage, be unfair to.

défection [defɛksjɔ̃] *nf* defection, desertion; **faire d.** to desert; *(ne pas venir)* to fail to turn up.

défectueux, -euse [defɛktɥø, -øz] *a* faulty, defective. **◆défectuosité** *nf* defectiveness; *(défaut)* defect (**de** in).

défendre [defɑ̃dr] **1** *vt (protéger)* to defend; **— se d.** *vpr* to defend oneself; **se d. de** *(pluie etc)* to protect oneself from; **se d. de faire** *(s'empêcher de)* to refrain from doing; **je me défends (bien)** *Fam* I can hold my own. **2** *vt* **d. à qn de faire** *(interdire)* to forbid s.o. to do, not allow s.o. to do; **d. qch à qn** to forbid s.o. sth. **◆défendable** *a* defensible.

défense [defɑ̃s] *nf* **1** *(protection)* defence, *Am* defense; **sans d.** defenceless. **2** *(interdiction)* **'d. de fumer'** 'no smoking'; **'d. d'entrer'** 'no entry', 'no admittance'. **3** *(d'éléphant)* tusk. **◆défenseur** *nm* defender; *(des faibles)* protector, defender. **◆défensif, -ive** *a* defensive; **— *nf* sur la défensive** on the defensive.

déférent [deferɑ̃] *a* deferential. **◆déférence** *nf* deference.

déférer [defere] **1** *vt (coupable)* *Jur* to refer (**à** to). **2** *vi* **d. à l'avis de qn** to defer to s.o.'s opinion.

déferler [defɛrle] *vi (vagues)* to break; *(haine etc)* to erupt; **d. dans** *ou* **sur** *(foule)* to surge *ou* sweep into.

défi [defi] *nm* challenge; **lancer un d. à qn** to challenge s.o.; **mettre qn au d. de faire** to defy *ou* dare *ou* challenge s.o. to do.

déficient [defisjɑ̃] *a* *Méd* deficient. **◆déficience** *nf* *Méd* deficiency.

déficit [defisit] *nm* deficit. **◆déficitaire** *a (budget etc)* in deficit; *(récolte etc)* *Fig* short, insufficient.

défier¹ [defje] *vt (provoquer)* to challenge (**à** to); *(braver)* to defy; **d. qn de faire** to defy *ou* challenge s.o. to do.

défier² (se) [sədefje] *vpr* **se d. de** *Litt* to distrust. **◆défiance** *nf* distrust (**de** of). **◆défiant** *a* distrustful (**à l'égard de** of).

défigur/er [defigyre] *vt (visage)* to disfigure; *(vérité etc)* to distort. **◆—ement** *nm* disfigurement; distortion.

défil/er [defile] *vi (manifestants)* to march *(devant* past); *Mil* to march *ou* file past; *(paysage, jours)* to pass by; *(visiteurs)* to keep coming and going, stream in and out; *(images)* *Cin* to flash by (on the screen); **— se d.** *vpr* *Fam* *(s'éloigner)* to sneak off; *(éviter d'agir)* to cop out. **◆—é** *nm* **1** *(cortège)* procession; *(de manifestants)* march; *Mil* parade, march past; *(de visiteurs)* stream, succession. **2** *Géog* gorge, pass.

défin/ir [definir] *vt* to define. **◆—i** *a (article)* *Gram* definite. **◆définition** *nf* definition; *(de mots croisés)* clue.

définitif, -ive [definitif, -iv] *a* final, definitive; **— *nf* en définitive** in the final analysis, finally. **◆définitivement** *adv (partir)* permanently, for good; *(exclure)* definitively.

déflagration [deflagrasjɔ̃] *nf* explosion.

déflation [deflasjɔ̃] *nf* *Écon* deflation.

déflorer [deflore] *vt (idée, sujet)* to spoil the freshness of.

défonc/er [defɔ̃se] **1** *vt (porte, mur etc)* to smash in *ou* down; *(trottoir, route etc)* to dig up, break up. **2 se d.** *vpr (drogué)* *Fam* to get high (à on). ◆—é a 1 (route) full of potholes, bumpy. 2 (drogué) Fam high.

déform/er [defɔrme] vt (objet) to put ou knock out of shape; (doigt, main) to deform; (faits, image etc) to distort; (goût) to corrupt; — se d. vpr to lose its shape. ◆—é a (objet) misshapen; (corps etc) deformed, misshapen; chaussée déformée uneven road surface. ◆déformation nf distortion; corruption; (de membre) deformity; c'est de la d. professionnelle it's an occupational hazard, it's a case of being conditioned by one's job.

défouler (se) [sədefule] vpr Fam to let off steam.

défraîchir (se) [sədefreʃir] vpr (étoffe etc) to lose its freshness, become faded.

défrayer [defreje] vt d. qn to pay ou defray s.o.'s expenses. d. la chronique to be the talk of the town.

défricher [defriʃe] vt (terrain) to clear (for cultivation); (sujet etc) Fig to open up.

défriser [defrize] vt (cheveux) to straighten; d. qn (contrarier) Fam to ruffle ou annoy s.o.

défroisser [defrwase] vt (papier) to smooth out.

défroqué [defrɔke] a (prêtre) defrocked.

défunt, -unte [defœ̃, -œ̃t] a (mort) departed; son d. mari her late husband; — nmf le d., la défunte the deceased, the departed.

dégag/er [degaʒe] vt (lieu, table) to clear (de of); (objet en gage) to redeem; (odeur) to give off; (chaleur) to give out; (responsabilité) to disclaim; (idée, conclusion) to bring out; d. qn de (promesse) to release s.o. from; (décombres) to free s.o. from, pull s.o. out of; cette robe dégage la taille this dress leaves the waist free and easy; — vi Fb to clear the ball (down the pitch); d.! clear the way!; — se d. vpr (rue, ciel) to clear; se d. de (personne) to release oneself from (promise); to get free from, free oneself from (rubble); se d. de (odeur) to issue ou emanate from; (vérité, impression) to emerge from. ◆—é a (ciel) clear; (ton, allure) easy-going, casual; (vue) open. ◆—ement nm 1 (action) clearing; redemption; (d'odeur) emanation; (de chaleur) emission; release; freeing; Fb clearance, kick; itinéraire de d. Aut relief road. 2 (espace libre) clearing; (de maison) passage.

dégainer [degene] vti (arme) to draw.

dégarn/ir [degarnir] vt to clear, empty; (arbre, compte) to strip; — se d. vpr (crâne) to go bald; (salle) to clear, empty. ◆—i a

(salle) empty, bare; (tête) balding; front d. receding hairline.

dégâts [dega] nmpl damage; limiter les d. Fig to prevent matters getting worse.

dégel [deʒɛl] nm thaw. ◆dégeler vt to thaw (out); (crédits) to unfreeze; — vi to thaw (out); — v imp to thaw; — se d. vpr (personne, situation) to thaw (out).

dégénér/er [deʒenere] vi to degenerate (en into). ◆—é, -ée a & nmf degenerate. ◆dégénérescence nf degeneration.

dégingandé [deʒɛ̃gɑ̃de] a gangling, lanky.

dégivrer [deʒivre] vt Aut Av to de-ice; (réfrigérateur) to defrost.

déglingu/er (se) [sədeglɛ̃ge] vpr Fam to fall to bits. ◆—é a falling to bits, in bits.

dégobiller [degɔbije] vt Fam to spew up.

dégonfl/er [degɔ̃fle] vt (pneu etc) to deflate, let down; — se d. vpr (flancher) Fam to chicken out, get cold feet. ◆—é, -ée a (pneu) flat; (lâche) Fam chicken, yellow; — nmf Fam yellow belly.

dégorger [degɔrʒe] vi (se déverser) to discharge (dans into); faire d. (escargots) Culin to cover with salt.

dégot(t)er [degɔte] vt Fam to find, turn up.

dégouliner [deguline] vi to trickle, drip, run.

dégourd/ir [degurdir] vt (doigts etc) to take the numbness out of; d. qn Fig to smarten ou wise s.o. up, sharpen s.o.'s wits; — se d. vpr to smarten up, wise up; se d. les jambes to stretch one's legs. ◆—i a (malin) smart, sharp.

dégoût [degu] nm disgust; le d. de (la vie, les gens etc) disgust for; avoir un ou du d. pour qch to have a (strong) dislike ou distaste for sth. ◆dégoût/er vt to disgust; d. qn de qch to put s.o. off sth; se d. de to take a (strong) dislike to, become disgusted with. ◆—ant a disgusting. ◆—é a disgusted; être d. de to be sick of ou disgusted with ou by ou at; elle est partie dégoûtée she left in disgust; il n'est pas d. (difficile) he's not too fussy; faire le d. to be fussy.

dégrad/er [degrade] 1 vt (avilir) to degrade; (mur etc) to deface, damage; — se d. vpr (s'avilir) to degrade oneself; (édifice, situation) to deteriorate. 2 vt (couleur) to shade off. ◆—ant a degrading. ◆—é nm (de couleur) shading off, gradation. ◆dégradation nf (de drogué etc) & Ch degradation; (de situation etc) deterioration; pl (dégâts) damage.

dégrafer [degrafe] vt (vêtement) to unfasten, unhook.

dégraisser [degrese] vt 1 (bœuf) to take the

fat off; (*bouillon*) to skim. **2** (*entreprise*) *Fam* to slim down, trim down the size of (*by laying off* workers).

degré [dəgre] *nm* **1** degree; **enseignement du premier/second d.** primary/secondary education; **au plus haut d.** (*avare etc*) extremely. **2** (*gradin*) *Litt* step.

dégrever [degrəve] *vt* (*contribuable*) to reduce the tax burden on.

dégriffé [degrife] *a* **vêtement d.** unlabelled designer garment.

dégringoler [degrɛ̃gɔle] *vi* to tumble (down); **faire d. qch** to topple sth over; — *vt* (*escalier*) to rush down. ◆**dégringolade** *nf* tumble.

dégriser [degrize] *vt* **d. qn** to sober s.o. (up).

dégrossir [degrosir] *vt* (*travail*) to rough out; **d. qn** to refine s.o.

déguerpir [degɛrpir] *vi* to clear off *ou* out.

dégueulasse [degœlas] *a Fam* lousy, disgusting.

dégueuler [degœle] *vi* (*vomir*) *Arg* to puke.

déguis/er [degize] *vt* (*pour tromper*) to disguise; **d. qn en** (*costumer*) to dress s.o. up as, disguise s.o. as; — **se d.** *vpr* to dress oneself up, disguise oneself (**en** as). ◆**—ement** *nm* disguise; (*de bal costumé etc*) fancy dress.

déguster [degyste] **1** *vt* (*goûter*) to taste, sample; (*apprécier*) to relish. **2** *vi* (*subir des coups*) *Fam* to cop it, get a good hiding. ◆**dégustation** *nf* tasting, sampling.

déhancher (se) [sədeɑ̃ʃe] *vpr* (*femme etc*) to sway *ou* wiggle one's hips; (*boiteux*) to walk lop-sided.

dehors [dəɔr] *adv* out(side); (*à l'air*) outdoors, outside; **en d.** on the outside; **en d. de** outside; (*excepté*) apart from; **en d. de la ville/fenêtre** out of town/the window; **au-d. (de), au d. (de)** outside; **déjeuner/jeter/etc d.** to lunch/throw/*etc* out; — *nm* (*extérieur*) outside; *pl* (*aspect*) outward appearance.

déjà [deʒa] *adv* already; **est-il d. parti?** has he left yet *ou* already?; **elle l'a d. vu** she's seen it before, she's already seen it; **c'est d. pas mal** that's not bad at all; **quand partez-vous, d.?** when are you leaving, again?

déjeuner [deʒœne] *vi* (*à midi*) to (have) lunch; (*le matin*) to (have) breakfast; — *nm* lunch; **petit d.** breakfast.

déjouer [deʒwe] *vt* (*intrigue etc*) to thwart, foil.

déjuger (se) [sədeʒyʒe] *vpr* to go back on one's opinion *ou* decision.

delà [d(ə)la] *adv* **au-d. (de), au d. (de), par-d.,**

par d. beyond; **au-d. du pont/*etc*** beyond *ou* past the bridge/*etc*; — *nm* **l'au-d.** the (world) beyond.

délabr/er (se) [sədelabre] *vpr* (*édifice*) to become dilapidated, fall into disrepair; (*santé*) to become impaired. ◆**—ement** *nm* dilapidation, disrepair; impaired state.

délacer [delase] *vt* (*chaussures*) to undo.

délai [delɛ] *nm* time limit; (*répit, sursis*) extra time, extension; **dans un d. de dix jours** within ten days; **sans d.** without delay; **à bref d.** at short notice; **dans les plus brefs délais** as soon as possible; **dernier d.** final date.

délaisser [delese] *vt* to forsake, desert, abandon; (*négliger*) to neglect.

délass/er [delase] *vt*, — **se d.** *vpr* to relax. ◆**—ement** *nm* relaxation, diversion.

délateur, -trice [delatœr, -tris] *nmf* informer.

délavé [delave] *a* (*tissu, jean*) faded; (*ciel*) watery; (*terre*) waterlogged.

délayer [deleje] *vt* (*mélanger*) to mix (with liquid); (*discours, texte*) *Fig* to pad out, drag out.

delco [dɛlko] *nm Aut* distributor.

délect/er (se) [sədelɛkte] *vpr* **se d. de qch/à faire** to (take) delight in sth/in doing. ◆**—able** *a* delectable. ◆**délectation** *nf* delight.

délégu/er [delege] *vt* to delegate (**à** to). ◆**—é, -ée** *nmf* delegate. ◆**délégation** *nf* delegation.

délest/er [deleste] *vt El* to cut the power from; **d. qn de** (*voler à qn*) *Fam* to relieve s.o. of. ◆**—age** *nm Aut* relief; **itinéraire de d.** alternative route (*to relieve congestion*).

délibér/er [delibere] *vi* (*réfléchir*) to deliberate (**sur** upon); (*se consulter*) to confer, deliberate (**de** about). ◆**—é** *a* (*résolu*) determined; (*intentionnel*) deliberate; **de propos d.** deliberately. ◆**—ément** *adv* (*à dessein*) deliberately. ◆**délibération** *nf* deliberation.

délicat [delika] *a* (*santé, travail etc*) delicate; (*question*) tricky, delicate; (*geste*) tactful; (*conscience*) scrupulous; (*exigeant*) particular. ◆**délicatement** *adv* delicately; tactfully. ◆**délicatesse** *nf* delicacy; tact(fulness); scrupulousness.

délice [delis] *nm* delight; — *nfpl* delights. ◆**délicieux, -euse** *a* (*mets, fruit etc*) delicious; (*endroit, parfum etc*) delightful.

délié [delje] **1** *a* (*esprit*) sharp; (*doigts*) nimble; (*mince*) slender. **2** *nm* (*d'une lettre*) (thin) upstroke.

délier [delje] *vt* to untie, undo; (*langue*) *Fig*

to loosen; **d. qn de** to release s.o. from; **— se d.** *vpr* (*paquet etc*) to come undone *ou* untied.

délimiter [delimite] *vt* to mark off, delimit; (*définir*) to define. ◆**délimitation** *nf* demarcation, delimitation; definition.

délinquant, -ante [delɛ̃kɑ̃, -ɑ̃t] *a & nmf* delinquent. ◆**délinquance** *nf* delinquency.

délire [delir] *nm Méd* delirium; (*exaltation*) *Fig* frenzy. ◆**délir/er** *vi Méd* to be delirious; (*dire n'importe quoi*) *Fig* to rave; **d. de** (*joie etc*) to be wild with. ◆**—ant** *a* (*malade*) delirious; (*joie*) frenzied, wild; (*déraisonnable*) utterly absurd.

délit [deli] *nm* offence, misdemeanour.

délivrer [delivre] *vt* **1** (*prisonnier*) to release, deliver; (*ville*) to deliver; **d. qn de** (*souci etc*) to rid s.o. of. **2** (*billet, diplôme etc*) to issue. ◆**délivrance** *nf* release; deliverance; issue; (*soulagement*) relief.

déloger [deloʒe] *vi* to move out; **—** *vt* to force *ou* drive out; *Mil* to dislodge.

déloyal, -aux [delwajal, -o] *a* disloyal; (*concurrence*) unfair. ◆**déloyauté** *nf* disloyalty; unfairness; (*action*) disloyal act.

delta [dɛlta] *nm* (*de fleuve*) delta.

deltaplane® [dɛltaplan] *nm* (*engin*) hang-glider; **faire du d.** to practise hang-gliding.

déluge [delyʒ] *nm* flood; (*de pluie*) downpour; (*de compliments, coups*) shower.

déluré [delyre] *a* (*malin*) smart, sharp; (*fille*) *Péj* brazen.

démagogie [demagoʒi] *nf* demagogy. ◆**démagogue** *nmf* demagogue.

demain [d(ə)mɛ̃] *adv* tomorrow; **à d.!** see you tomorrow!; **ce n'est pas d. la veille** *Fam* that won't happen for a while yet.

demande [d(ə)mɑ̃d] *nf* request; (*d'emploi*) application; (*de renseignements*) inquiry; *Écon* demand; (*question*) question; **d. (en mariage)** proposal (of marriage); **demandes d'emploi** *Journ* situations wanted. ◆**demander** *vt* to ask for; (*emploi*) to apply for; (*autorisation*) to request, ask for; (*charité*) to beg for; (*prix*) to charge; (*nécessiter, exiger*) to require; **d. un nom/le chemin/l'heure** to ask a name/the way/the time; **d. qch à qn** to ask s.o. for sth; **d. à qn de faire** to ask s.o. to do; **d. si/où** to ask *ou* inquire whether/where; **on te demande!** you're wanted!; **ça demande du temps/une heure** it takes time/an hour; **d. en mariage** to propose (marriage) to; **— se d.** *vpr* to wonder, ask oneself (**pourquoi** why, **si** if).

démanger [demɑ̃ʒe] *vti* to itch; **son bras le** *ou* **lui démange** his arm itches; **ça me démange de . . .** *Fig* I'm itching to . . . . ◆**démangeaison** *nf* itch; **avoir des démangeaisons** to be itching; **j'ai une d. au bras** my arm's itching.

démanteler [demɑ̃tle] *vt* (*bâtiment*) to demolish; (*organisation etc*) to break up.

démantibuler [demɑ̃tibyle] *vt* (*meuble etc*) *Fam* to pull to pieces.

démaquill/er (se) [sədemakije] *vpr* to take off one's make-up. ◆**—ant** *nm* make-up remover.

démarcation [demarkasjɔ̃] *nf* demarcation.

démarche [demarʃ] *nf* walk, step, gait; (*de pensée*) process; **faire des démarches** to take the necessary steps (**pour faire** to do).

démarcheur, -euse [demarʃœr, -øz] *nmf* *Pol* canvasser; *Com* door-to-door salesman *ou* saleswoman.

démarquer [demarke] *vt* (*prix*) to mark down; **se d. de** *Fig* to dissociate oneself from.

démarr/er [demare] *vi* (*moteur*) *Aut* to start (up); (*partir*) *Aut* to move *ou* drive off; (*entreprise etc*) *Fig* to get off the ground; **—** *vt* (*commencer*) *Fam* to start. ◆**—age** *nm* *Aut* start; **d. en côte** hill start. ◆**—eur** *nm* *Aut* starter.

démasquer [demaske] *vt* to unmask.

démêl/er [demele] *vt* to disentangle; (*discerner*) to fathom. ◆**—é** *nm* (*dispute*) squabble; *pl* (*ennuis*) trouble (**avec** with).

démembrer [demɑ̃bre] *vt* (*pays etc*) to dismember.

déménag/er [demenaʒe] *vi* to move (out), move house; **—** *vt* (*meubles*) to (re)move. ◆**—ement** *nm* move, moving (house); (*de meubles*) removal, moving (**de** of); **voiture de d.** removal van, *Am* moving van. ◆**—eur** *nm* removal man, *Am* (furniture) mover.

démener (se) [sədemne] *vpr* to fling oneself about; **se d. pour faire** to spare no effort to do.

dément, -ente [demɑ̃, -ɑ̃t] *a* insane; (*génial*) *Iron* fantastic; **—** *nmf* lunatic. ◆**démence** *nf* insanity. ◆**démentiel, -ielle** *a* insane.

dément/ir [demɑ̃tir] *vt* (*infirmer*) to belie; (*nouvelle, faits etc*) to deny; **d. qn** to give the lie to s.o. ◆**—i** *nm* denial.

démerder (se) [sədemɛrde] *vpr* (*se débrouiller*) *Arg* to manage (by oneself).

démesure [demzyr] *nf* excess. ◆**démesuré** *a* excessive, inordinate.

démettre [demɛtr] *vt* **1** (*os*) to dislocate; **se d. le pied** to dislocate one's foot. **2 d. qn de**

to dismiss s.o. from; **se d. de ses fonctions** to resign one's office.

demeurant (au) [odəmœrã] *adv* for all that, after all.

demeure [dəmœr] *nf* **1** dwelling (place), residence. **2 mettre qn en d. de faire** to summon *ou* instruct s.o. to do. ◆**demeur/er** *vi* **1** *(aux être)* *(rester)* to remain; **en d. là** *(affaire etc)* to rest there. **2** *(aux avoir)* *(habiter)* to live, reside. ◆**—é** *a Fam* (mentally) retarded.

demi, -ie [d(ə)mi] *a* half; **d.-journée** half-day; **une heure et demie** an hour and a half; *(horloge)* half past one; — *adv* **(à) d. plein** half-full; **à d. nu** half-naked; **ouvrir à d.** to open halfway; **faire les choses à d.** to do things by halves; — *nmf (moitié)* half; — *nm (verre)* (half-pint) glass of beer; *Fb* half-back; — *nf (à l'horloge)* half-hour.

demi-cercle [d(ə)miserkl] *nm* semicircle. ◆**d.-douzaine** *nf* **une d.-douzaine (de)** a half-dozen, half a dozen. ◆**d.-finale** *nf Sp* semifinal. ◆**d.-frère** *nm* step-brother. ◆**d.-heure** *nf* **une d.-heure** a half-hour, half an hour. ◆**d.-mesure** *nf* half-measure. ◆**d.-mot** *nm* **tu comprendras à d.-mot** you'll understand without my having to spell it out. ◆**d.-pension** *nf* half-board. ◆**d.-pensionnaire** *nmf* day boarder, *Am* day student. ◆**d.-saison** *nf* **de d.-saison** *(vêtement)* between seasons. ◆**d.-sel** *a inv (beurre)* slightly salted; *(fromage)* **d.-sel** cream cheese. ◆**d.-sœur** *nf* stepsister. ◆**d.-tarif** *nm & a inv (billet)* **(à) d.-tarif** half-price. ◆**d.-tour** *nm* about turn, *Am* about face; *Aut* U-turn; **faire d.-tour** to turn back.

démission [demisjɔ̃] *nf* resignation. ◆**démissionnaire** *a (ministre etc)* outgoing. ◆**démissionner** *vi* to resign.

démobiliser [demɔbilize] *vt* to demobilize. ◆**démobilisation** *nf* demobilization.

démocrate [demɔkrat] *nmf* democrat; — *a* democratic. ◆**démocratie** [-asi] *nf* democracy. ◆**démocratique** *a* democratic.

démod/er (se) [sədemɔde] *vpr* to go out of fashion. ◆**—é** *a* old-fashioned.

démographie [demɔgrafi] *nf* demography.

demoiselle [d(ə)mwazɛl] *nf (célibataire)* spinster, single woman; *(jeune fille)* young lady; **d. d'honneur** *(à un mariage)* bridesmaid; *(de reine)* maid of honour.

démolir [demɔlir] *vt (maison, jouet etc)* to demolish; *(projet etc)* to shatter; **d. qn** *(battre, discréditer)* *Fam* to tear s.o. to pieces. ◆**démolition** *nf* demolition; **en d.** being demolished.

démon [demɔ̃] *nm* demon; **petit d.** *(enfant)* little devil. ◆**démoniaque** *a* devilish, fiendish.

démonstrateur, -trice [demɔ̃stratœr, -tris] *nmf (dans un magasin etc)* demonstrator. ◆**démonstratif, -ive** *a* demonstrative. ◆**démonstration** *nf* demonstration; **d. de force** show of force.

démonter [demɔ̃te] *vt (assemblage)* to dismantle, take apart; *(installation)* to take down; **d. qn** *(troubler)* *Fig* to disconcert s.o.; **une mer démontée** a stormy sea; — **se d.** *vpr* to come apart; *(installation)* to come down; *(personne)* to be put out *ou* disconcerted.

démontrer [demɔ̃tre] *vt* to demonstrate, show.

démoraliser [demɔralize] *vt* to demoralize; — **se d.** *vpr* to become demoralized. ◆**démoralisation** *nf* demoralization.

démordre [demɔrdr] *vi* **il ne démordra pas de** *(son opinion etc)* he won't budge from.

démouler [demule] *vt (gâteau)* to turn out *(from its mould)*.

démunir [demynir] *vt* **d. qn de** to deprive s.o. of; **se d. de** to part with.

démystifier [demistifje] *vt (public etc)* to disabuse; *(idée etc)* to debunk.

dénationaliser [denasjɔnalize] *vt* to denationalize.

dénatur/er [denatyre] *vt (propos, faits etc)* to misrepresent, distort. ◆**—é** *(goût, père etc)* unnatural.

dénégation [denegasjɔ̃] *nf* denial.

déneiger [deneʒe] *vt* to clear of snow.

dénicher [denife] *vt (trouver)* to dig up, turn up; *(ennemi, fugitif)* to hunt out, flush out.

dénier [denje] *vt* to deny; *(responsabilité)* to disclaim, deny; **d. qch à qn** to deny s.o. sth.

dénigr/er [denigre] *vt* to denigrate, disparage. ◆**—ement** *nm* denigration, disparagement.

dénivellation [denivelasjɔ̃] *nf* unevenness; *(pente)* gradient; *pl (accidents)* bumps.

dénombrer [denɔ̃bre] *vt* to count, number.

dénomm/er [denɔme] *vt* to name. ◆**—é, -ée** *nmf* **un d. Dupont** a man named Dupont. ◆**dénomination** *nf* designation, name.

dénonc/er [denɔ̃se] *vt (injustice etc)* to denounce (à to); **d. qn** to inform on s.o., denounce s.o. (à to); *Scol* to tell on s.o. (à to); — **se d.** *vpr* to give oneself up (à to). ◆**dénonciateur, -trice** *nmf* informer. ◆**dénonciation** *nf* denunciation.

dénoter [denɔte] vt to denote.

dénouer [denwe] vt (nœud, corde) to undo, untie; (cheveux) to undo; (situation, intrigue) to unravel; (problème, crise) to clear up; — **se d.** vpr (nœud) to come undone ou untied; (cheveux) to come undone. ◆**dénouement** nm outcome, ending; Th dénouement.

dénoyauter [denwajote] vt (prune etc) to stone, Am to pit.

denrée [dɑ̃re] nf food(stuff); **denrées alimentaires** foodstuffs.

dense [dɑ̃s] a dense. ◆**densité** nf density.

dent [dɑ̃] nf tooth; (de roue) cog; (de fourche) prong; (de timbre-poste) perforation; **d. de sagesse** wisdom tooth; **rien à se mettre sous la d.** nothing to eat; **manger à belles dents/du bout des dents** to eat whole-heartedly/half-heartedly; **faire ses dents** (enfant) to be teething; **coup de d.** bite; **sur les dents** (surmené) exhausted; (énervé) on edge; **avoir une d. contre qn** to have it in for s.o. ◆**dentaire** a dental. ◆**dentée** af roue d. cogwheel. ◆**dentier** nm denture(s), (set of) false teeth. ◆**dentifrice** nm toothpaste. ◆**dentiste** nmf dentist; **chirurgien d.** dental surgeon. ◆**dentition** nf (dents) (set of) teeth.

dentelé [dɑ̃tle] a (côte) jagged; (feuille) serrated. ◆**dentelure** nf jagged outline ou edge.

dentelle [dɑ̃tɛl] nf lace.

dénud/er [denyde] vt to (lay) bare. ◆**-é** a bare.

dénué [denɥe] a **d. de** devoid of, without.

dénuement [denymɑ̃] nm destitution; **dans le d.** poverty-stricken.

déodorant [deɔdɔrɑ̃] nm deodorant.

dépann/er [depane] vt (mécanisme) to get going (again), repair; **d. qn** Fam to help s.o. out. ◆**-age** nm (emergency) repair; **voiture/service de d.** breakdown vehicle/service. ◆**-eur** nm repairman; Aut breakdown mechanic. ◆**-euse** nf (voiture) Aut breakdown lorry, Am wrecker, tow truck.

dépareillé [depareje] a (chaussure etc) odd, not matching; (collection) incomplete.

déparer [depare] vt to mar, spoil.

départ [depar] nm departure; (début) start, beginning; Sp start; **point/ligne de d.** starting point/post; **au d.** at the outset, at the start; **au d. de Paris/etc** (excursion etc) departing from Paris/etc.

départager [departaʒe] vt (concurrents) to decide between; **d. les votes** to give the casting vote.

département [departəmɑ̃] nm department.

◆**départemental, -aux** a departmental; **route départementale** secondary road.

départir (se) [sədepartir] vpr **se d. de** (attitude) to depart from, abandon.

dépass/er [depase] vt (durée, attente etc) to go beyond, exceed; (endroit) to go past, go beyond; (véhicule, bicyclette etc) to overtake, pass; (pouvoir) to go beyond, overstep; **d. qn** (en hauteur) to be taller than s.o.; (surclasser) to be ahead of s.o.; **ça me dépasse** Fig that's (quite) beyond me; — vi (jupon, clou etc) to stick out, show. ◆**-é** a (démodé) outdated; (incapable) unable to cope. ◆**-ement** nm Aut overtaking, passing.

dépays/er [depeize] vt to disorientate, Am disorient. ◆**-ement** nm disorientation; (changement) change of scenery.

dépecer [depase] vt (animal) to cut up, carve up.

dépêche [depɛʃ] nf telegram; (diplomatique) dispatch. ◆**dépêcher** vt to dispatch; — **se d.** vpr to hurry (up).

dépeign/er [depeɲe] vt **d. qn** to make s.o.'s hair untidy. ◆**-é** a **être d.** to have untidy hair; **sortir d.** to go out with untidy hair.

dépeindre* [depɛ̃dr] vt to depict, describe.

dépenaillé [depənaje] a in tatters ou rags.

dépend/re [depɑ̃dr] **1** vi to depend (de on); **d. de** (appartenir à) to belong to; (être soumis à) to be subject to; **ça dépend de toi** that depends on you, that's up to you. **2** vt (décrocher) to take down. ◆**-ant** a dependent (de on). ◆**dépendance 1** nf dependence; **sous la d. de qn** under s.o.'s domination. **2** nfpl (bâtiments) outbuildings.

dépens [depɑ̃] nmpl Jur costs; **aux d. de** at the expense of; **apprendre à ses d.** to learn to one's cost.

dépense [depɑ̃s] nf (action) spending; (frais) expense, expenditure; (d'électricité etc) consumption; (physique) exertion. ◆**dépenser** vt (argent) to spend; (électricité etc) to use; (forces) to exert; (énergie) to expend; — **se d.** vpr to exert oneself. ◆**dépensier, -ière** a wasteful, extravagant.

déperdition [deperdisjɔ̃] nf (de chaleur etc) loss.

dépér/ir [deperir] vi (personne) to waste away; (plante) to wither; (santé etc) to decline. ◆**-issement** nm (baisse) decline.

dépêtrer [depetre] vt to extricate; — **se d.** vpr to extricate oneself (de from).

dépeupl/er [depœple] vt to depopulate. ◆**-ement** nm depopulation.

dépilatoire [depilatwar] *nm* hair-remover.

dépist/er [depiste] *vt* (*criminel etc*) to track down; (*maladie, fraude*) to detect. ◆—**age** *nm* Méd detection.

dépit [depi] *nm* resentment, chagrin; **en d. de** in spite of. ◆**dépiter** *vt* to vex, chagrin; — **se d.** *vpr* to feel resentment *ou* chagrin.

déplac/er [deplase] *vt* to shift, move; (*fonctionnaire*) to transfer; — **se d.** *vpr* to move (about); (*voyager*) to get about, travel (about). ◆—**é** *a* (*mal à propos*) out of place; **personne déplacée** (*réfugié*) displaced person. ◆—**ement** *nm* (*voyage*) (business *ou* professional) trip; (*d'ouragan, de troupes*) movement; **les déplacements** (*voyages*) travel(ling); **frais de d.** travelling expenses.

déplaire* [depler] *vi* **d. à qn** to displease s.o.; **cet aliment lui déplaît** he *ou* she dislikes this food; **n'en déplaise à** Iron with all due respect to; — *v imp* **il me déplaît de faire** I dislike doing, it displeases me to do; — **se d.** *vpr* to dislike it. ◆**déplaisant** *a* unpleasant, displeasing. ◆**déplaisir** *nm* displeasure.

dépli/er [deplije] *vt* to open out, unfold. ◆—**ant** *nm* (*prospectus*) leaflet.

déplor/er [deplore] *vt* (*regretter*) to deplore; (*la mort de qn*) to mourn (over), lament (over); **d. qn** to mourn (for) s.o.; **d. que** (+ *sub*) to deplore the fact that, regret that. ◆—**able** *a* deplorable, lamentable.

déployer [deplwaje] *vt* (*ailes*) to spread; (*journal, carte etc*) to unfold, spread (out); (*objets, courage etc*) to display; (*troupes*) to deploy; — **se d.** *vpr* (*drapeau*) to unfurl. ◆**déploiement** *nm* (*démonstration*) display; Mil deployment.

dépoli [depoli] *a* **verre d.** frosted glass.

déport/er [deporte] *vt* **1** (*exiler*) Hist to deport (to a penal colony); (*dans un camp de concentration*) Hist to send to a concentration camp, deport. **2** (*dévier*) to veer *ou* carry (off course). ◆—**é, -ée** *nmf* deportee; (*concentration camp*) inmate. ◆**déportation** *nf* deportation; internment (in a concentration camp).

dépos/er [depoze] *vt* (*poser*) to put down; (*laisser*) to leave; (*argent, lie*) to deposit; (*plainte*) to lodge; (*armes*) to lay down; (*gerbe*) to lay; (*ordures*) to dump; (*marque de fabrique*) to register; (*projet de loi*) to introduce; (*souverain*) to depose; **d. qn** Aut to drop s.o. (off), put s.o. off; **d. son bilan** Fin to go into liquidation, file for bankruptcy; — *vi* Jur to testify; (*liquide*) to leave a deposit; — **se d.** *vpr* (*poussière, lie*) to settle. ◆**dépositaire** *nmf* Fin agent; (*de secret*) custodian. ◆**déposition** *nf* Jur statement; (*de souverain*) deposing.

déposséder [deposede] *vt* to deprive, dispossess (**de** of).

dépôt [depo] *nm* (*d'ordures etc*) dumping, (*lieu*) dump; (*de gerbe*) laying; (*d'autobus, de trains*) depot; (*entrepôt*) warehouse; (*argent*) deposit; (*de vin*) deposit, sediment; **d.** (*calcaire*) (*de chaudière etc*) deposit; **laisser qch à qn en d.** to give s.o. sth for safekeeping *ou* in trust.

dépotoir [depotwar] *nm* rubbish dump, Am garbage dump.

dépouille [depuj] *nf* hide, skin; (*de serpent*) slough; *pl* (*butin*) spoils; **d.** (**mortelle**) mortal remains. ◆**dépouill/er** *vt* (*animal*) to skin, flay; (*analyser*) to go through, analyse; **d. de** (*dégarnir*) to strip of; (*déposséder*) to deprive of; **se d. de** to divest oneself of, cast off; **d. un scrutin** to count votes. ◆—**é** *a* (*arbre*) bare; (*style*) austere, spare; **d. de** bereft of. ◆—**ement** *nm* (*de document etc*) analysis; (*privation*) deprivation; (*sobriété*) austerity; **d. du scrutin** counting of the votes.

dépourvu [depurvy] *a* **d. de** devoid of; **prendre qn au d.** to catch s.o. unawares *ou* off his guard.

dépraver [deprave] *vt* to deprave. ◆**dépravation** *nf* depravity.

dépréci/er [depresje] *vt* (*dénigrer*) to disparage; (*monnaie, immeuble etc*) to depreciate; — **se d.** *vpr* (*baisser*) to depreciate, lose (its) value. ◆**dépréciation** *nf* depreciation.

déprédations [depredasjɔ̃] *nfpl* damage, ravages.

dépression [depresjɔ̃] *nf* depression; **zone de d.** trough of low pressure; **d. nerveuse** nervous breakdown; **d. économique** slump. ◆**dépressif, -ive** *a* depressive. ◆**déprime** *nf* **la d.** (*dépression*) Fam the blues. ◆**déprim/er** *vt* to depress. ◆—**é** *a* depressed.

depuis [dəpɥi] *prép* since; **d. lundi** since Monday; **d. qu'elle est partie** since she left; **j'habite ici d. un mois** I've been living here for a month; **d. quand êtes-vous là?** how long have you been here?; **d. peu/longtemps** for a short/long time; **d. Paris jusqu'à Londres** from Paris to London; — *adv* since (then), ever since.

députation [depytasjɔ̃] *nf* (*groupe*) deputation, delegation; **candidat à la d.** parliamentary candidate. ◆**député** *nm* delegate, deputy; (*au parlement*) deputy, = *Br* MP, = *Am* congressman, congresswoman.

déracin/er [derasine] *vt* (*personne, arbre etc*) to uproot; (*préjugés etc*) to eradicate, root out. ◆**—ement** *nm* uprooting; eradication.

déraill/er [deraje] *vi* **1** (*train*) to jump the rails, be derailed; **faire d.** to derail. **2** (*divaguer*) *Fam* to drivel, talk through one's hat. ◆**—ement** *nm* (*de train*) derailment. ◆**—eur** *nm* (*de bicyclette*) derailleur (gear change).

déraisonnable [derezɔnabl] *a* unreasonable. ◆**déraisonner** *vi* to talk nonsense.

dérang/er [derɑ̃ʒe] *vt* (*affaires*) to disturb, upset; (*estomac*) to upset; (*projets*) to mess up, upset; (*vêtements*) to mess up; (*cerveau, esprit*) to derange; **d. qn** to disturb *ou* bother *ou* trouble s.o.; **je viendrai si ça ne te dérange pas** I'll come if that doesn't put you out *ou* if that's not imposing; **ça vous dérange si je fume?** do you mind if I smoke?; **— se d.** *vpr* to put oneself to a lot of trouble (**pour faire** to do), (*se déplacer*) to move; **ne te dérange pas!** don't trouble yourself!, don't bother! ◆**—ement** *nm* (*gêne*) bother, inconvenience; (*désordre*) disorder; **en d.** (*téléphone etc*) out of order.

dérap/er [derape] *vi* to skid. ◆**—age** *nm* skid; (*des prix, de l'inflation*) *Fig* loss of control (**de** over).

dératé [derate] *nm* **courir comme un d.** to run like mad.

dérégl/er [deregle] *vt* (*mécanisme*) to put out of order; (*estomac, habitudes*) to upset; (*esprit*) to unsettle; **— se d.** *vpr* (*montre, appareil*) to go wrong. ◆**—é** *a* out of order; (*vie, mœurs*) dissolute, wild; (*imagination*) wild. ◆**dérèglement** *nm* (*de mécanisme*) breakdown; (*d'esprit*) disorder; (*d'estomac*) upset.

dérider [deride] *vt*, **— se d.** *vpr* to cheer up.

dérision [derizjɔ̃] *nf* derision, mockery; **tourner en d.** to mock, deride; **par d.** derisively; **de d.** derisive. ◆**dérisoire** *a* ridiculous, derisory, derisive.

dérive [deriv] *nf* *Nau* drift; **partir à la d.** (*navire*) to drift out to sea; **aller à la d.** (*navire*) to go adrift; (*entreprise etc*) *Fig* to drift (towards ruin). ◆**dériv/er** *vi* *Nau Av* to drift; **d. de** (*venir*) to derive from, be derived from; **— vt** (*cours d'eau*) to divert; *Ling* to derive (**de** from). ◆**—é** *nm Ling Ch* derivative; (*produit*) by-product. ◆**dérivatif** *nm* distraction (**à** from). ◆**dérivation** *nf* (*de cours d'eau*) diversion; *Ling* derivation; (*déviation routière*) bypass.

dermatologie [dɛrmatɔlɔʒi] *nf* dermatology.

dernier -ière [dɛrnje, -jɛr] *a* last; (*nouvelles, mode*) latest; (*étage*) top; (*degré*) highest; (*qualité*) lowest; **le d. rang** the back *ou* last row; **ces derniers mois** these past few months, these last *ou* final months; **de la dernière importance** of (the) utmost importance; **en d.** last; **—** *nmf* last (person *ou* one); **ce d.** (*de deux*) the latter; (*de plusieurs*) the last-mentioned; **être le d. de la classe** to be (at the) bottom of the class; **le d. des derniers** the lowest of the low; **le d. de mes soucis** the least of my worries. ◆**d.-né**, ◆**dernière-née** *nmf* youngest (child). ◆**dernièrement** *adv* recently.

dérob/er [derɔbe] *vt* (*voler*) to steal (**à** from); (*cacher*) to hide (**à** from); **— se d.** *vpr* to get out of one's obligations; (*s'éloigner*) to slip away; (*éviter de répondre*) to dodge the issue; **se d. à** (*obligations*) to shirk, get out of; (*regards*) to hide from; **ses jambes se sont dérobées sous lui** his legs gave way beneath him. ◆**—é** *a* (*porte etc*) hidden, secret; **à la dérobée** *adv* on the sly, stealthily. ◆**dérobade** *nf* dodge, evasion.

déroger [derɔʒe] *vi* **d. à une règle/etc** to depart from a rule/etc. ◆**dérogation** *nf* exemption, (special) dispensation.

dérouiller [deruje] *vt* **d. qn** (*battre*) *Arg* to thrash *ou* thump s.o.; **se d. les jambes** *Fam* to stretch one's legs.

déroul/er [derule] *vt* (*carte etc*) to unroll; (*film*) to unwind; **— se d.** *vpr* (*événement*) to take place, pass off; (*paysage, souvenirs*) to unfold; (*récit*) to develop. ◆**—ement** *nm* (*d'une action*) unfolding, development; (*cours*) course.

dérouter [derute] *vt* (*avion, navire*) to divert, reroute; (*candidat etc*) to baffle; (*poursuivant*) to throw off the scent.

derrick [dɛrik] *nm* derrick.

derrière [dɛrjɛr] *prép & adv* behind; **d. moi** behind me, *Am* in back of me; **assis d.** (*dans une voiture*) sitting in the back; **de d.** (*roue*) back, rear; (*pattes*) hind; **par d.** (*attaquer*) from behind, from the rear; **—** *nm* (*de maison etc*) back, rear; (*fesses*) behind, bottom.

des [de] *voir* **de** [1,2], **le**.

dès [dɛ] *prép* from; **d. cette époque** (as) from that time, from that time on; **d. le début** (right) from the start; **d. son enfance** since *ou* from (his *ou* her) childhood; **d. le**

sixième siècle as early as *ou* as far back as the sixth century; **d. l'aube** at (the crack of) dawn; **d. qu'elle viendra** as soon as she comes.

désabusé [dezabyze] *a* disenchanted, disillusioned.

désaccord [dezakɔr] *nm* disagreement. ◆**désaccordé** *a Mus* out of tune.

désaccoutumer (se) [sədezakutyme] *vpr* **se d. de** to lose the habit of.

désaffecté [dezafɛkte] *a (école etc)* disused.

désaffection [dezafɛksjɔ̃] *nf* loss of affection, disaffection **(pour** for).

désagréable [dezagreabl] *a* unpleasant, disagreeable. ◆**—ment** [-əmã] *adv* unpleasantly.

désagréger [dezagreʒe] *vt*, **— se d.** *vpr* to disintegrate, break up. ◆**désagrégation** *nf* disintegration.

désagrément [dezagremã] *nm* annoyance, trouble.

désalter/er [dezaltere] *vt* **d. qn** to quench s.o.'s thirst; **se d.** to quench one's thirst. ◆**—ant** *a* thirst-quenching.

désamorcer [dezamɔrse] *vt (obus, situation)* to defuse.

désappointer [dezapwɛ̃te] *vt* to disappoint.

désapprouver [dezapruve] *vt* to disapprove of; **—** *vi* to disapprove. ◆**désapprobateur, -trice** *a* disapproving. ◆**désapprobation** *nf* disapproval.

désarçonner [dezarsɔne] *vt (jockey)* to throw, unseat; *(déconcerter) Fig* to nonpluss, throw.

désarm/er [dezarme] *vt (émouvoir) & Mil* to disarm; **—** *vi Mil* to disarm; *(céder)* to let up. ◆**—é** *a (charme etc)* disarming. ◆**—é** *a (sans défense)* unarmed; *Fig* helpless. ◆**—ement** *nm (de nation)* disarmament.

désarroi [dezarwa] *nm (angoisse)* distress.

désarticuler [dezartikyle] *vt (membre)* to dislocate.

désastre [dezastr] *nm* disaster. ◆**désastreux, -euse** *a* disastrous.

désavantage [dezavãtaʒ] *nm* disadvantage, handicap; *(inconvénient)* drawback, disadvantage. ◆**désavantager** *vt* to put at a disadvantage, handicap. ◆**désavantageux, -euse** *a* disadvantageous.

désaveu, -x [dezavø] *nm* repudiation. ◆**désavouer** *vt (livre, personne etc)* to disown, repudiate.

désaxé, -ée [dezakse] *a & nmf* unbalanced (person).

desceller [desele] *vt (pierre etc)* to loosen; **— se d.** *vpr* to come loose.

descend/re [desãdr] *vi (aux* **être**) to come *ou* go down, descend **(de** from); *(d'un train etc)* to get off *ou* out, alight **(de** from); *(d'un arbre)* to climb down **(de** from); *(nuit, thermomètre)* to fall; *(marée)* to go out; **d. à** *(une bassesse)* to stoop to; **d. à l'hôtel** to put up at a hotel; **d. de** *(être issu de)* to be descended from; **d. de cheval** to dismount; **d. en courant/flânant**/*etc* to run/stroll/*etc* down; **—** *vt (aux* **avoir**) *(escalier)* to come *ou* go down, descend; *(objets)* to bring *ou* take down; *(avion)* to bring *ou* shoot down; **d. qn** *(tuer) Fam* to bump s.o. off. ◆**—ant, -ante 1** *a* descending; *(marée)* outgoing. **2** *nmf (personne)* descendant. ◆**descendance** *nf (enfants)* descendants; *(origine)* descent.

descente [desãt] *nf (action)* descent; *(irruption)* raid **(dans** upon); *(en parachute)* drop; *(pente)* slope; **la d. des bagages** bringing *ou* taking down the luggage; **il fut accueilli à sa d. d'avion** he was met as he got off the plane; **d. à skis** downhill run; **d. de lit** *(tapis)* bedside rug.

descriptif, -ive [deskriptif, -iv] *a* descriptive. ◆**description** *nf* description.

déségrégation [desegregasjɔ̃] *nf* desegregation.

désemparé [dezãpare] *a* distraught, at a loss; *(navire)* crippled.

désemplir [dezãplir] *vi* **ce magasin**/*etc* **ne désemplit pas** this shop/*etc* is always crowded.

désenchant/er [dezãʃãte] *vt* to disenchant. ◆**—ement** *nm* disenchantment.

désencombrer [dezãkɔ̃bre] *vt (passage etc)* to clear.

désenfler [dezãfle] *vi* to go down, become less swollen.

déséquilibre [dezekilibr] *nm (inégalité)* imbalance; *(mental)* unbalance; **en d.** *(meuble etc)* unsteady. ◆**déséquilibrer** *vt* to throw off balance; *(esprit, personne) Fig* to unbalance.

désert [dezɛr] *a* deserted; **île déserte** desert island; **—** *nm* desert, wilderness. ◆**désertique** *a (région etc)* desert-.

déserter [dezɛrte] *vti* to desert. ◆**déserteur** *nm Mil* deserter. ◆**désertion** *nf* desertion.

désespér/er [dezɛspere] *vi* to despair **(de** of); **—** *vt* to drive to despair; **— se d.** *vpr* to (be in) despair. ◆**—ant** *a (enfant etc)* that drives one to despair, hopeless. ◆**—é, -ée** *a (personne)* in despair, despairing; *(cas, situation)* desperate, hopeless; *(efforts, cris)* desperate; **—** *nmf (suicidé)* person driven to despair *ou* desperation. ◆**—ément** *adv* desperately. ◆**désespoir** *nm* despair; **au d.** in despair; **en d. de cause** in desperation, as a (desperate) last resort.

déshabiller [dezabije] *vt* to undress, strip; **— se d.** *vpr* to get undressed, undress.

déshabituer [dezabitɥe] *vt* **d. qn de** to break s.o. of the habit of.

désherb/er [dezɛrbe] *vti* to weed. ◆**—ant** *nm* weed killer.

déshérit/er [dezerite] *vt* to disinherit. ◆**—é** *a* (*pauvre*) underprivileged; (*laid*) ill-favoured.

déshonneur [dezɔnœr] *nm* dishonour, disgrace. ◆**déshonor/er** *vt* to disgrace, dishonour. ◆**—ant** *a* dishonourable.

déshydrater [dezidrate] *vt* to dehydrate; **— se d.** *vpr* to become dehydrated.

désigner [dezine] *vt* (*montrer*) to point to, point out; (*élire*) to appoint, designate; (*signifier*) to indicate, designate; **ses qualités le désignent pour** his qualities mark him out for. ◆**désignation** *nf* designation.

désillusion [dezilyzjɔ̃] *nf* disillusion(ment). ◆**désillusionner** *vt* to disillusion.

désincarné [dezɛ̃karne] *a* (*esprit*) disembodied.

désinence [dezinɑ̃s] *nf Gram* ending.

désinfect/er [dezɛ̃fekte] *vt* to disinfect. ◆**—ant** *nm* & *a* disinfectant. ◆**désinfection** *nf* disinfection.

désinformation [dezɛ̃fɔrmasjɔ̃] *nf Pol* misinformation.

désintégrer (se) [sədezɛ̃tegre] *vpr* to disintegrate. ◆**désintégration** *nf* disintegration.

désintéress/er (se) [sədezɛ̃terese] *vpr* **se d. de** to lose interest in, take no further interest in. ◆**—é** *a* (*altruiste*) disinterested. ◆**—ement** [-ɛsmɑ̃] *nm* (*altruisme*) disinterestedness. ◆**désintérêt** *nm* lack of interest.

désintoxiquer [dezɛ̃tɔksike] *vt* (*alcoolique, drogué*) to cure.

désinvolte [dezɛ̃vɔlt] *a* (*dégagé*) easy-going, casual; (*insolent*) offhand, casual. ◆**désinvolture** *nf* casualness; offhandedness.

désir [dezir] *nm* desire, wish. ◆**désirable** *a* desirable. ◆**désirer** *vt* to want, desire; (*convoiter*) to desire; **je désire venir** I would like to come, I wish *ou* want to come; **je désire que tu viennes** I want you to come; **ça laisse à d.** it leaves something *ou* a lot to be desired. ◆**désireux, -euse** *a* **d. de faire** anxious *ou* eager to do, desirous of doing.

désist/er (se) [sədeziste] *vpr* (*candidat etc*) to withdraw. ◆**—ement** *nm* withdrawal.

désobé/ir [dezɔbeir] *vi* to disobey; **d. à qn** to disobey s.o. ◆**—issant** *a* disobedient. ◆**désobéissance** *nf* disobedience (à to).

désobligeant [dezɔbliʒɑ̃] *a* disagreeable, unkind.

désodorisant [dezɔdɔrizɑ̃] *nm* air freshener.

désœuvré [dezœvre] *a* idle, unoccupied. ◆**désœuvrement** *nm* idleness.

désol/er [dezɔle] *vt* to distress, upset (very much); **— se d.** *vpr* to be distressed *ou* upset (de at). ◆**—ant** *a* distressing, upsetting. ◆**—é** *a* (*région*) desolate; (*affligé*) distressed; **être d.** (*navré*) to be sorry (**que** (+ *sub*) that, **de faire** to do). ◆**désolation** *nf* (*peine*) distress, grief.

désolidariser (se) [sədesɔlidarize] *vpr* to dissociate oneself (**de** from).

désopilant [dezɔpilɑ̃] *a* hilarious, screamingly funny.

désordre [dezɔrdr] *nm* (*de papiers, affaires, idées*) mess, muddle, disorder; (*de cheveux, pièce*) untidiness; *Méd* disorder; *pl* (*émeutes*) disorder, unrest; **en d.** untidy, messy. ◆**désordonné** *a* (*personne, chambre*) untidy, messy.

désorganiser [dezɔrganize] *vt* to disorganize. ◆**désorganisation** *nf* disorganization.

désorienter [dezɔrjɑ̃te] *vt* **d. qn** to disorientate *ou Am* disorient s.o., make s.o. lose his bearings; (*déconcerter*) to bewilder s.o. ◆**désorientation** *nf* disorientation.

désormais [dezɔrme] *adv* from now on, in future, henceforth.

désosser [dezɔse] *vt* (*viande*) to bone.

despote [dɛspɔt] *nm* despot. ◆**despotique** *a* despotic. ◆**despotisme** *nm* despotism.

desquels, desquelles [dekɛl] *voir* **lequel**.

dessaisir (se) [sədesezir] *vpr* **se d. de qch** to part with sth, relinquish sth.

dessaler [desale] *vt* (*poisson etc*) to remove the salt from (*by smoking*).

dessécher [deseʃe] *vt* (*végétation*) to dry up, wither; (*gorge, bouche*) to dry, parch; (*fruits*) to desiccate, dry; (*cœur*) to harden; **— se d.** *vpr* (*plante*) to wither, dry up; (*peau*) to dry (up), get dry; (*maigrir*) to waste away.

dessein [desɛ̃] *nm* aim, design; **dans le d. de faire** with the aim of doing; **à d.** intentionally.

desserrer [desere] *vt* (*ceinture etc*) to loosen, slacken; (*poing*) to open, unclench;

(*frein*) to release; **il n'a pas desserré les dents** he didn't open his mouth; **— se d.** *vpr* to come loose.

dessert [desɛr] *nm* dessert, sweet.

desserte [desɛrt] *nf* **assurer la d. de** (*village etc*) to provide a (bus *ou* train) service to. ◆**desservir** *vt* **1** (*table*) to clear (away). **2 d. qn** to harm s.o., do s.o. a disservice. **3 l'autobus/*etc* dessert ce village** the bus/*etc* provides a service to *ou* stops at this village; **ce quartier est bien desservi** this district is well served by public transport.

dessin [desɛ̃] *nm* drawing; (*rapide*) sketch; (*motif*) design, pattern; (*contour*) outline; **d. animé** *Cin* cartoon; **d. humoristique** *Journ* cartoon; **école de d.** art school; **planche à d.** drawing board. ◆**dessinateur, -trice** *nmf* drawer; sketcher; **d. humoristique** cartoonist; **d. de modes** dress designer; **d. industriel** draughtsman, *Am* draftsman. ◆**dessiner** *vt* to draw; (*rapidement*) to sketch; (*meuble, robe etc*) to design; (*indiquer*) to outline, trace; **d. (bien) la taille** (*vêtement*) to show off the figure; **— se d.** *vpr* (*colline etc*) to stand out, be outlined; (*projet*) to take shape.

dessoûler [desule] *vti Fam* to sober up.

dessous [d(ə)su] *adv* under(neath), beneath, below; **en d.** (*sous*) under(neath); (*agir*) *Fig* in an underhand way; **vêtement de d.** undergarment; **drap de d.** bottom sheet; **— *nm* underneath**, *pl* (*vêtements*) underclothes; **d. de table** backhander, bribe; **les gens du d.** the people downstairs *ou* below; **avoir le d.** to be defeated, get the worst of it. ◆**d.-de-plat** *nm inv* table mat.

dessus [d(ə)sy] *adv* (*marcher, écrire*) on it; (*monter*) on top (of it), on it; (*lancer, passer*) over it; **de d. la table** off *ou* from the table; **vêtement de d.** outer garment; **drap de d.** top sheet; **par-d.** (*sauter etc*) over (it); **par-d. tout** above all; **— *nm* top**; (*de chaussure*) upper; **avoir le d.** to have the upper hand, get the best of it; **les gens du d.** the people upstairs *ou* above. ◆**d.-de-lit** *nm inv* bedspread.

déstabiliser [destabilize] *vt* to destabilize.

destin [destɛ̃] *nm* fate, destiny. ◆**destinée** *nf* fate, destiny (*of an individual*).

destin/er [destine] *vt* **d. qch à qn** to intend *ou* mean sth for s.o.; **d. qn à** (*carrière, fonction*) to intend *ou* destine s.o. for; **se d. à** (*carrière etc*) to intend *ou* mean to take up; **destiné à mourir/*etc* (*condamné*) destined *ou* fated to die/*etc*. ◆**destinataire** *nmf* addressee. ◆**destination** *nf* (*usage*)

purpose; (*lieu*) destination; **à d. de** (*train etc*) (going) to, (bound) for.

destituer [destitɥe] *vt* (*fonctionnaire etc*) to dismiss (from office). ◆**destitution** *nf* dismissal.

destructeur, -trice [destryktœr, -tris] *a* destructive; **— *nmf* (*personne*) destroyer. ◆**destructif, -ive** *a* destructive. ◆**destruction** *nf* destruction.

désuet, -ète [desɥe, -ɛt] *a* antiquated, obsolete.

désunir [dezynir] *vt* (*famille etc*) to divide, disunite. ◆**désunion** *nf* disunity, dissension.

détach/er¹ [detaʃe] *vt* (*ceinture, vêtement*) to undo; (*nœud*) to untie, undo; (*personne, mains*) to untie; (*ôter*) to take off, detach; (*mots*) to pronounce clearly; **d. qn** (*libérer*) to let s.o. loose; (*affecter*) to transfer s.o. (on assignment) (**à** to); **d. les yeux de qn/qch** to take one's eyes off s.o./sth; **— se d.** *vpr* (*chien, prisonnier*) to break loose; (*se dénouer*) to come undone; **se d. (de qch)** (*fragment*) to come off (sth); **se d. de** (*amis*) to break away from, grow apart from; **se d. (sur)** (*ressortir*) to stand out (against). ◆**—é a 1** (*nœud, main, etc*) loose, undone. **2** (*air, ton etc*) detached. ◆**—ement** *nm* **1** (*indifférence*) detachment. **2** (*de fonctionnaire*) (temporary) transfer; *Mil* detachment.

détach/er² [detaʃe] *vt* (*linge etc*) to remove the spots *ou* stains from. ◆**—ant** *nm* stain remover.

détail [detaj] *nm* **1** detail; **en d.** in detail; **le d. de** (*dépenses etc*) a detailing *ou* breakdown of. **2 de d.** (*magasin, prix*) retail; **vendre au d.** to sell retail; (*par petites quantités*) to sell separately; **faire le d.** to retail to the public. ◆**détaill/er** *vt* **1** (*vendre*) to sell in small quantities *ou* separately; (*au détail*) to (sell) retail. **2** (*énumérer*) to detail. ◆**—ant, -ante** *nmf* retailer. ◆**—é a** (*récit etc*) detailed.

détaler [detale] *vi Fam* to run off, make tracks.

détartrer [detartre] *vt* (*chaudière, dents etc*) to scale.

détaxer [detakse] *vt* (*denrée etc*) to reduce the tax on; (*supprimer*) to take the tax off; **produit détaxé** duty-free article.

détecter [detɛkte] *vt* to detect. ◆**détecteur** *nm* (*appareil*) detector. ◆**détection** *nf* detection.

détective [detɛktiv] *nm* **d. (privé)** (private) detective.

déteindre* [detɛ̃dr] *vi* (*couleur ou étoffe au lavage*) to run; (*au soleil*) to fade; **ton**

tablier bleu a déteint sur ma chemise the blue of your apron has come off on(to) my shirt; **d. sur qn** (*influencer*) to leave one's mark on s.o.

dételer [detle] *vt* (*chevaux*) to unhitch, unharness.

détend/re [detɑ̃dr] *vt* (*arc etc*) to slacken, relax; (*situation, atmosphère*) to ease; **d. qn** to relax s.o.; **— se d.** *vpr* to slacken, get slack; to ease; (*se reposer*) to relax; (*rapports*) to become less strained. **◆—u** *a* (*visage, atmosphère*) relaxed; (*ressort, câble*) slack. **◆détente** *nf* **1** (*d'arc*) slackening; (*de relations*) easing of tension, *Pol* détente; (*repos*) relaxation; (*saut*) leap, spring. **2** (*gâchette*) trigger.

déten/ir* [detnir] *vt* to hold; (*secret, objet volé*) to be in possession of; (*prisonnier*) to hold, detain. **◆—u, -ue** *nmf* prisoner. **◆détenteur, -trice** *nmf* (*de record etc*) holder. **◆détention** *nf* (*d'armes*) possession; (*captivité*) detention; **d. préventive** *Jur* custody.

détergent [deterʒɑ̃] *nm* detergent.

détériorer [deterjore] *vt* (*abîmer*) to damage; **— se d.** *vpr* (*empirer*) to deteriorate. **◆détérioration** *nf* damage (**de** to); (*d'une situation etc*) deterioration (**de** in).

détermin/er [determine] *vt* (*préciser*) to determine; (*causer*) to bring about; **d. qn à faire** to induce s.o. to do, make s.o. do; **se d. à faire** to resolve *ou* determine to do. **◆—ant** *a* (*motif*) determining, deciding; (*rôle*) decisive. **◆—é** *a* (*précis*) specific; (*résolu*) determined. **◆détermination** *nf* (*fermeté*) determination; (*résolution*) resolve.

déterrer [detere] *vt* to dig up, unearth.

détest/er [deteste] *vt* to hate, detest; **d. faire** to hate doing *ou* to do, detest doing. **◆—able** *a* awful, foul.

détonateur [detonatœr] *nm* detonator. **◆détonation** *nf* explosion, blast.

détonner [detone] *vi* (*contraster*) to jar, be out of place.

détour [detur] *nm* (*de route etc*) bend, curve; (*crochet*) detour; **sans d.** (*parler*) without beating about the bush; **faire des détours** (*route*) to wind.

détourn/er [deturne] *vt* (*fleuve, convoi etc*) to divert; (*tête*) to turn (away); (*coups*) to ward off; (*conversation, sens*) to change; (*fonds*) to embezzle, misappropriate; (*avion*) to hijack; **d. qn de** (*son devoir, ses amis*) to take *ou* turn s.o. away from; (*sa route*) to lead s.o. away from; (*projet*) to talk s.o. out of; **d. les yeux** to look away,

avert one's eyes; **— se d.** *vpr* to turn aside *ou* away; **se d. de** (*chemin*) to wander *ou* stray from. **◆—é** *a* (*chemin, moyen*) roundabout, indirect. **◆—ement** *nm* (*de cours d'eau*) diversion; **d.** (**d'avion**) hijack(ing); **d.** (**de fonds**) embezzlement.

détraqu/er [detrake] *vt* (*mécanisme*) to break, put out of order; **— se d.** *vpr* (*machine*) to go wrong; **se d. l'estomac** to upset one's stomach; **se d. la santé** to ruin one's health. **◆—é, -ée** *a* out of order; (*cerveau*) deranged; – *nmf* crazy *ou* deranged person.

détremper [detrɑ̃pe] *vt* to soak, saturate.

détresse [detrɛs] *nf* distress; **en d.** (*navire, âme*) in distress; **dans la d.** (*misère*) in (great) distress.

détriment de (au) [odetrimɑ̃də] *prép* to the detriment of.

détritus [detritys] *nmpl* refuse, rubbish.

détroit [detrwa] *nm Géog* strait(s), sound.

détromper [detrɔ̃pe] *vt* **d. qn** to undeceive s.o., put s.o. right; **détrompez-vous!** don't you believe it!

détrôner [detrone] *vt* (*souverain*) to dethrone; (*supplanter*) to supersede, oust.

détrousser [detruse] *vt* (*voyageur etc*) to rob.

détruire* [detrɥir] *vt* (*ravager, tuer*) to destroy; (*projet, santé*) to ruin, wreck, destroy.

dette [dɛt] *nf* debt; **faire des dettes** to run *ou* get into debt; **avoir des dettes** to be in debt.

deuil [dœj] *nm* (*affliction, vêtements*) mourning; (*mort de qn*) bereavement; **porter le d., être en d.** to be in mourning.

deux [dø] *a & nm* two; **d. fois** twice, two times; **tous** (**les**) **d.** both; **en moins de d.** *Fam* in no time. **◆d.-pièces** *nm inv* (*vêtement*) two-piece; (*appartement*) two-roomed flat *ou Am* apartment. **◆d.-points** *nm inv Gram* colon. **◆d.-roues** *nm inv* two-wheeled vehicle. **◆d.-temps** *nm inv* two-stroke (engine).

deuxième [døzjɛm] *a & nmf* second. **◆—ment** *adv* secondly.

dévaler [devale] *vt* (*escalier etc*) to hurtle *ou* race *ou* rush down; – *vi* (*tomber*) to tumble down, come tumbling down.

dévaliser [devalize] *vt* (*détrousser*) to clean out, strip, rob (of everything).

dévaloriser [devalɔrize] **1** *vt*, **— se d.** *vpr* (*monnaie*) to depreciate. **2** *vt* (*humilier etc*) to devalue, disparage. **◆dévalorisation** *nf* (*de monnaie*) depreciation.

dévaluer [devalɥe] *vt* (*monnaie*) & *Fig* to devalue. **◆dévaluation** *nf* devaluation.

devancer [d(ə)vɑ̃se] vt to get ou be ahead of; (question etc) to anticipate, forestall; (surpasser) to outstrip; **tu m'as devancé** (action) you did it before me; (lieu) you got there before me. ◆**devancier, -ière** nmf predecessor.

devant [d(ə)vɑ̃] prép & adv in front (of); **d.** (l'hôtel/etc) in front (of the hotel/etc); **marcher d. (qn)** to walk in front (of s.o.) ou ahead (of s.o.); **passer d. (l'église/etc)** to go past (the church/etc); **assis d.** (dans une voiture) sitting in the front; **l'avenir est d. toi** the future is ahead of you; **loin d.** a long way ahead ou in front; **d. le danger** (confronté à) in the face of danger; **d. mes yeux/la loi** before my eyes/the law; — nm front; **de d.** (roue, porte) front; **patte de d.** foreleg; **par d.** from ou at the front; **prendre les devants** (action) to take the initiative. ◆**devanture** nf (vitrine) shop window; (façade) shop front.

dévaster [devaste] vt (ruiner) to devastate. ◆**dévastation** nf devastation.

déveine [devɛn] nf Fam tough ou bad luck.

développ/er [devlɔpe] vt to develop; Phot to develop, process; — **se d.** vpr to develop. ◆**—ement** nm development; Phot developing, processing; **les pays en voie de d.** the developing countries.

devenir* [dəvnir] vi (aux être) to become; (vieux, difficile etc) to get, grow, become; (rouge, bleu etc) to turn, go, become; **d. un papillon/un homme/etc** to grow into a butterfly/a man/etc; **qu'est-il devenu?** what's become of him ou it?, where's he ou it got to?; **qu'est-ce que tu deviens?** Fam how are you doing?

dévergond/er (se) [sədevɛrgɔ̃de] vpr to fall into dissolute ways. ◆**—é** a dissolute, licentious.

déverser [devɛrse] vt (liquide, rancune) to pour out; (bombes, ordures) to dump; — **se d.** vpr (liquide) to empty, pour out (dans into).

dévêtir [devetir] vt, — **se d.** vpr Litt to undress.

dévier [devje] vt (circulation, conversation) to divert; (coup, rayons) to deflect; — vi (de ses principes etc) to deviate (de from); (de sa route) to veer (off course). ◆**déviation** nf deflection; deviation; (chemin) bypass; (itinéraire provisoire) diversion.

deviner [d(ə)vine] vt to guess (que that); (avenir) to predict; **d. (le jeu de) qn** to see through s.o. ◆**devinette** nf riddle.

devis [d(ə)vi] nm estimate (of cost of work to be done).

dévisager [devizaʒe] vt **d. qn** to stare at s.o.

devise [d(ə)viz] nf (légende) motto; pl (monnaie) (foreign) currency.

dévisser [devise] vt to unscrew, undo; — **se d.** vpr (bouchon etc) to come undone.

dévoiler [devwale] vt (révéler) to disclose; (statue) to unveil; — **se d.** vpr (mystère) to come to light.

devoir* [d(ə)vwar] v aux **1** (nécessité) **je dois refuser** I must refuse, I have (got) to refuse; **j'ai dû refuser** I had to refuse. **2** (forte probabilité) **il doit être tard** it must be late; **elle a dû oublier** she must have forgotten; **il ne doit pas être bête** he can't be stupid. **3** (obligation) **tu dois l'aider** you should help her, you ought to help her; **il aurait dû venir** he should have come, he ought to have come; **vous devriez rester** you should stay, you ought to stay. **4** (supposition) **elle doit venir** she should be coming, she's supposed to be coming, she's due to come; **le train devait arriver à midi** the train was due (to arrive) at noon; **je devais le voir** I was (due) to see him.

devoir* [d(ə)vwar] **1** vt to owe; **d. qch à qn** to owe s.o. sth, owe sth to s.o.; **l'argent qui m'est dû** the money due to ou owing to me, the money owed (to) me; **se d. à** to have to devote oneself to; **comme il se doit** as is proper. **2** nm duty; Scol exercise; **devoir(s)** (travail à faire à la maison) Scol homework; **présenter ses devoirs à qn** to pay one's respects to s.o.

dévolu [devɔly] **1** a **d. à qn** (pouvoirs, tâche) vested in s.o., allotted to s.o. **2** nm **jeter son d. sur** to set one's heart on.

dévor/er [devɔre] vt (manger) to gobble up, devour; (incendie) to engulf, devour; (tourmenter, lire) to devour. ◆**—ant** a (faim) ravenous; (passion) devouring.

dévot, -ote [devo, -ɔt] a & nmf devout ou pious (person). ◆**dévotion** nf devotion.

dévou/er (se) [sədevwe] vpr (à une tâche) to dedicate oneself, devote oneself (à to); **se d. (pour qn)** (se sacrifier) to sacrifice oneself (for s.o.). ◆**—é** a (ami, femme etc) devoted (à qn to s.o.); (domestique, soldat etc) dedicated. ◆**—ement** [-umɑ̃] nm devotion, dedication; (de héros) devotion to duty.

dévoyé, -ée [devwaje] a & nmf delinquent.

dextérité [dɛksterite] nf dexterity, skill.

diabète [djabɛt] nm Méd diabetes. ◆**diabétique** a & nmf diabetic.

diable [djɑbl] nm devil; **d.!** heavens!; **où/pourquoi/que d.?** where/why/what the devil?; **un bruit/vent/etc du d.** the devil of a noise/wind/*etc*; **à la d.** anyhow; **habiter au d.** to live miles from anywhere. ◆**diablerie** *nf* devilment, mischief. ◆**diablesse** *nf* **c'est une d.** *Fam* she's a devil. ◆**diablotin** *nm* (*enfant*) little devil. ◆**diabolique** *a* diabolical, devilish.

diabolo [djabɔlo] *nm* (*boisson*) lemonade *ou Am* lemon soda flavoured with syrup.

diacre [djakr] *nm Rel* deacon.

diadème [djadɛm] *nm* diadem.

diagnostic [djagnɔstik] *nm* diagnosis. ◆**diagnostiquer** *vt* to diagnose.

diagonal, -aux [djagɔnal, -o] *a* diagonal. ◆**diagonale** *nf* diagonal (line); **en d.** diagonally.

diagramme [djagram] *nm* (*schéma*) diagram; (*courbe*) graph.

dialecte [djalɛkt] *nm* dialect.

dialogue [djalɔg] *nm* conversation; *Pol Cin Th Littér* dialogue. ◆**dialoguer** *vi* to have a conversation *ou* dialogue.

dialyse [djaliz] *nf Méd* dialysis.

diamant [djamɑ̃] *nm* diamond.

diamètre [djamɛtr] *nm* diameter. ◆**diamétralement** *adv* **d. opposés** (*avis etc*) diametrically opposed, poles apart.

diapason [djapazɔ̃] *nm Mus* tuning fork; **être/se mettre au d. de** *Fig* to be/get in tune with.

diaphragme [djafragm] *nm* diaphragm.

diapositive, *Fam* **diapo** [djapozitiv, djapo] *nf* (colour) slide, transparency.

diarrhée [djare] *nf* diarrh(o)ea.

diatribe [djatrib] *nf* diatribe.

dictateur [diktatœr] *nm* dictator. ◆**dictatorial, -aux** *a* dictatorial. ◆**dictature** *nf* dictatorship.

dict/er [dikte] *vt* to dictate (à to). ◆**—ée** *nf* dictation. ◆**dictaphone**® *nm* dictaphone®.

diction [diksjɔ̃] *nf* diction, elocution.

dictionnaire [diksjɔnɛr] *nm* dictionary.

dicton [diktɔ̃] *nm* saying, adage, dictum.

didactique [didaktik] *a* didactic.

dièse [djez] *a* & *nm Mus* sharp.

diesel [djezɛl] *a* & *nm* (**moteur**) **d.** diesel (engine).

diète [djet] *nf* (*jeûne*) starvation diet; **à la d.** on a starvation diet. ◆**diététicien, -ienne** *nmf* dietician. ◆**diététique** *nf* dietetics; – *a* (*magasin etc*) health-; **aliment** *ou* **produit d.** health food.

dieu, -x [djø] *nm* god; **D.** God; **D. merci!** thank God!, thank goodness!

diffamer [difame] *vt* (*en paroles*) to slander; (*par écrit*) to libel. ◆**diffamation** *nf* defamation; (*en paroles*) slander; (*par écrit*)

libel; **campagne de d.** smear campaign. ◆**diffamatoire** *a* slanderous; libellous.

différent [diferɑ̃] *a* different; *pl* (*divers*) different, various; **d. de** different from *ou* to, unlike. ◆**différemment** [-amɑ̃] *adv* differently (**de** from, to). ◆**différence** *nf* difference (**de** in); **à la d. de** unlike; **faire la d. entre** to make a distinction between.

différencier [diferɑ̃sje] *vt* to differentiate (**de** from); **— se d.** *vpr* to differ (**de** from).

différend [diferɑ̃] *nm* difference (of opinion).

différentiel, -ielle [diferɑ̃sjɛl] *a* differential.

différ/er [difere] **1** *vi* to differ (**de** from). **2** *vt* (*remettre*) to postpone, defer. ◆**—é** *nm* **en d.** (*émission*) (pre)recorded.

difficile [difisil] *a* difficult; (*exigeant*) fussy, particular, hard *ou* difficult to please; **c'est d. à faire** it's hard *ou* difficult to do; **il (nous) est d. de faire ça** it's hard *ou* difficult (for us) to do that. ◆**—ment** *adv* with difficulty; **d. lisible** not easily read. ◆**difficulté** *nf* difficulty (**à faire** in doing); **en d.** in a difficult situation.

difforme [difɔrm] *a* deformed, misshapen. ◆**difformité** *nf* deformity.

diffus [dify] *a* (*lumière, style*) diffuse.

diffuser [difyze] *vt* (*émission, nouvelle etc*) to broadcast; (*lumière, chaleur*) *Phys* to diffuse; (*livre*) to distribute. ◆**diffusion** *nf* broadcasting; (*de connaissances*) & *Phys* diffusion; (*de livre*) distribution.

digérer [diʒere] *vt* to digest; (*endurer*) *Fam* to stomach; – *vi* to digest. ◆**digeste** *a*, ◆**digestible** *a* digestible. ◆**digestif, -ive** *a* digestive; – *nm* after-dinner liqueur. ◆**digestion** *nf* digestion.

digitale [diʒital] *af* **empreinte d.** fingerprint.

digne [diɲ] *a* (*fier*) dignified; (*honnête*) worthy; **d. de qn** worthy of s.o.; **d. d'admiration/etc** worthy of *ou* deserving of admiration/*etc*; **d. de foi** reliable. ◆**dignement** *adv* with dignity. ◆**dignitaire** *nm* dignitary. ◆**dignité** *nf* dignity.

digression [digresjɔ̃] *nf* digression.

digue [dig] *nf* dyke, dike.

dilapider [dilapide] *vt* to squander, waste.

dilater [dilate] *vt*, **— se d.** *vpr* to dilate, expand. ◆**dilatation** *nf* dilation, expansion.

dilatoire [dilatwar] *a* **manœuvre** *ou* **moyen d.** delaying tactic.

dilemme [dilɛm] *nm* dilemma.

dilettante [diletɑ̃t] *nmf Péj* dabbler, amateur.

diligent [diliʒɑ̃] *a* (*prompt*) speedy and efficient; (*soin*) diligent. ◆**diligence** *nf* **1** (*célérité*) speedy efficiency; **faire d.** to make haste. **2** (*véhicule*) *Hist* stagecoach.

diluer [dilɥe] *vt* to dilute. ◆**dilution** *nf* dilution.

diluvienne [dilyvjɛn] *af* **pluie d.** torrential rain.

dimanche [dimɑ̃ʃ] *nm* Sunday.

dimension [dimɑ̃sjɔ̃] *nf* dimension; **à deux dimensions** two-dimensional.

diminuer [diminɥe] *vt* to reduce, decrease; (*frais*) to cut down (on), reduce; (*mérite, forces*) to diminish, lessen, reduce; **d. qn** (*rabaisser*) to diminish s.o., lessen s.o.; – *vi* (*réserves, nombre*) to decrease, diminish; (*jours*) to get shorter, draw in; (*prix*) to drop, decrease. ◆**diminutif, -ive** *a* & *nm Gram* diminutive; – *nm* (*prénom*) nickname. ◆**diminution** *nf* reduction, decrease (**de in**).

dinde [dɛ̃d] *nf* turkey (hen), *Culin* turkey. ◆**dindon** *nm* turkey (cock).

dîner [dine] *vi* to have dinner, dine; (*au Canada, en Belgique etc*) to (have) lunch; – *nm* dinner; lunch; (*soirée*) dinner party. ◆**dînette** *nf* (*jouet*) doll's dinner service; (*jeu*) doll's dinner party. ◆**dîneur, -euse** *nmf* diner.

dingue [dɛ̃g] *a Fam* nuts, screwy, crazy; – *nmf Fam* nutcase.

dinosaure [dinozɔr] *nm* dinosaur.

diocèse [djɔsɛz] *nm Rel* diocese.

diphtérie [difteri] *nf* diphtheria.

diphtongue [diftɔ̃g] *nf Ling* diphthong.

diplomate [diplɔmat] *nm Pol* diplomat; – *nmf* (*négociateur*) diplomatist; – *a* (*habile, plein de tact*) diplomatic. ◆**diplomatie** [-asi] *nf* (*tact*) & *Pol* diplomacy; (*carrière*) diplomatic service. ◆**diplomatique** *a Pol* diplomatic.

diplôme [diplom] *nm* certificate, diploma; *Univ* degree. ◆**diplômé, -ée** *a* & *nmf* qualified (person); **être d. (de)** *Univ* to be a graduate (of).

dire* [dir] *vt* (*mot, avis etc*) to say; (*vérité, secret, heure etc*) to tell; (*penser*) to think (**de** of, about); **d. des bêtises** to talk nonsense; **elle dit que tu mens** she says (that) you're lying; **d. qch à qn** to tell s.o. sth, say sth to s.o.; **d. à qn que** to tell s.o. that, say to s.o. that; **d. à qn de faire** to tell s.o. to do; **dit-il** he said; **dit-on** they say; **d. que oui/non** to say yes/no; **d. du mal/du bien de** to speak ill/well of; **on dirait un château** it looks like a castle; **on dirait du Mozart** it sounds like Mozart; **on dirait du cabillaud** it tastes like cod; **on dirait que il**

would seem that; **ça ne me dit rien** (*envie*) I don't feel like *ou* fancy that; (*souvenir*) it doesn't ring a bell; **ça vous dit de rester?** do you feel like staying?; **dites donc!** I say!; **ça va sans d.** that goes without saying; **autrement dit** in other words; **c'est beaucoup d.** that's going too far; **à l'heure dite** at the agreed time; **à vrai d.** to tell the truth; **il se dit malade/etc** he says he's ill/etc; **ça ne se dit pas** that's not said; – *nm* **au d. de** according to; **les dires de** (*déclarations*) the statements of.

direct [dirɛkt] *a* direct; (*chemin*) straight, direct; (*manière*) straightforward, direct; **train d.** through train, non-stop train; – *nm* **en d.** (*émission*) live; **un d. du gauche** *Boxe* a straight left. ◆**—ement** *adv* directly; (*immédiatement*) straight (away), directly.

directeur, -trice [dirɛktœr, -tris] *nmf* director; (*d'entreprise*) manager(ess), director; (*de journal*) editor; *Scol* headmaster, headmistress; – *a* (*principe*) guiding; **idées** *ou* **lignes directrices** guidelines.

direction [dirɛksjɔ̃] *nf* **1** (*de société*) running, management; (*de club*) leadership, running; (*d'études*) supervision; (*mécanisme*) *Aut* steering; **avoir la d. de** to be in charge of; **sous la d. de** (*orchestre*) conducted by; **la d.** (*équipe dirigeante*) the management; **une d.** (*fonction*) *Com* a directorship; *Scol* a headmastership; *Journ* an editorship. **2** (*sens*) direction; **en d. de** (*train*) (going) to, for.

directive [dirɛktiv] *nf* directive, instruction.

dirig/er [diriʒe] *vt* (*société*) to run, manage, direct; (*débat, cheval*) to lead; (*véhicule*) to steer; (*orchestre*) to conduct; (*études*) to supervise, direct; (*conscience*) to guide; (*orienter*) to turn (**vers** towards); (*arme, lumière*) to point, direct (**vers** towards); **se d.** **vers** (*lieu, objet*) to make one's way towards, head *ou* make for; (*dans une carrière*) to turn towards. ◆**—eant** *a* (*classe*) ruling; – *nm* (*de pays, club*) leader; (*d'entreprise*) manager. ◆**—é** *a* (*économie*) planned. ◆**—eable** *a* & *nm* (**ballon**) **d.** airship. ◆**dirigisme** *nm Écon* state control.

dis [di] *voir* **dire.**

discern/er [disɛrne] *vt* (*voir*) to make out, discern; (*différencier*) to distinguish. ◆**—ement** *nm* discernment, discrimination.

disciple [disipl] *nm* disciple, follower.

discipline [disiplin] *nf* (*règle, matière*) discipline. ◆**disciplinaire** *a* disciplinary. ◆**disciplin/er** *vt* (*contrôler, éduquer*) to discipline; **— se d.** *vpr* to discipline oneself. **◆—é** *a* well-disciplined.

disco [disko] *nf Fam* disco; **aller en d.** to go to a disco.

discontinu [diskɔ̃tiny] *a* (*ligne*) discontinuous; (*bruit etc*) intermittent. **◆discontinuer** *vi* **sans d.** without stopping.

disconvenir [diskɔ̃vnir] *vi* **je n'en disconviens pas** I don't deny it.

discorde [diskɔrd] *nf* discord. **◆discordance** *nf* (*de caractères*) clash, conflict; (*de son*) discord. **◆discordant** *a* (*son*) discordant; (*témoignages*) conflicting; (*couleurs*) clashing.

discothèque [diskɔtɛk] *nf* record library; (*club*) discotheque.

discours [diskur] *nm* speech; (*écrit littéraire*) discourse. **◆discourir** *vi Péj* to speechify, ramble on.

discourtois [diskurtwa] *a* discourteous.

discrédit [diskredi] *nm* disrepute, discredit. **◆discréditer** *vt* to discredit, bring into disrepute; **— se d.** *vpr* (*personne*) to become discredited.

discret, -ète [diskrɛ, -ɛt] *a* (*personne, manière etc*) discreet; (*vêtement*) simple. **◆discrètement** *adv* discreetly; (*s'habiller*) simply. **◆discrétion** *nf* discretion; **vin/etc à d.** as much wine/etc as one wants. **◆discrétionnaire** *a* discretionary.

discrimination [diskriminasjɔ̃] *nf* (*ségrégation*) discrimination. **◆discriminatoire** *a* discriminatory.

disculper [diskylpe] *vt* to exonerate (**de** from).

discussion [diskysjɔ̃] *nf* discussion; (*conversation*) talk; (*querelle*) argument; **pas de d.!** no argument! **◆discut/er** *vt* to discuss; (*familièrement*) to talk over; (*contester*) to question; **ça peut se d., ça se discute** that's arguable; — *vi* (*parler*) to talk (**de** about, **avec** with); (*répliquer*) to argue; **d. de** *ou* **sur qch** to discuss sth. **◆—é** *a* (*auteur*) much discussed *ou* debated; (*théorie, question*) disputed, controversial. **◆—able** *a* arguable, debatable.

disette [dizɛt] *nf* food shortage.

diseuse [dizœz] *nf* **d. de bonne aventure** fortune-teller.

disgrâce [disgrɑs] *nf* disgrace, disfavour. **◆disgracier** *vt* to disgrace.

disgracieux, -euse [disgrasjø, -øz] *a* ungainly.

disjoindre [diszwɛ̃dr] *vt* (*questions*) to treat separately. **◆disjoint** *a* (*questions*) unconnected, separate. **◆disjoncteur** *nm Él* circuit breaker.

disloquer [dislɔke] *vt* (*membre*) to dislocate; (*meuble, machine*) to break; **— se d.** *vpr* (*cortège*) to break up; (*meuble etc*) to fall apart; **se d. le bras** to dislocate one's arm. **◆dislocation** *nf* (*de membre*) dislocation.

dispar/aître* [disparɛtr] *vi* to disappear; (*être porté manquant*) to be missing; (*mourir*) to die; **d. en mer** to be lost at sea; **faire d.** to remove, get rid of. **◆—u, -ue** *a* (*soldat etc*) missing, lost; — *nmf* (*absent*) missing person; (*mort*) departed; **être porté d.** to be reported missing. **◆disparition** *nf* disappearance; (*mort*) death.

disparate [disparat] *a* ill-assorted.

disparité [disparite] *nf* disparity (**entre, de** between).

dispendieux, -euse [dispɑ̃djø, -øz] *a* expensive, costly.

dispensaire [dispɑ̃sɛr] *nm* community health centre.

dispense [dispɑ̃s] *nf* exemption; **d. d'âge** waiving of the age limit. **◆dispenser** *vt* (*soins, bienfaits etc*) to dispense; **d. qn de** (*obligation*) to exempt *ou* excuse s.o. from; **je vous dispense de** (*vos réflexions etc*) I can dispense with; **se d. de faire** to spare oneself the bother of doing.

disperser [dispɛrse] *vt* to disperse, scatter; (*efforts*) to dissipate; **— se d.** *vpr* (*foule*) to disperse; **elle se disperse trop** she tries to do too many things at once. **◆dispersion** *nf* (*d'une armée etc*) dispersal, dispersion.

disponible [disponibl] *a* available; (*place*) spare, available; (*esprit*) alert. **◆disponibilité** *nf* availability; *pl Fin* available funds.

dispos [dispo] *a* fit, in fine fettle; **frais et d.** refreshed.

dispos/er [dispoze] *vt* to arrange; (*troupes*) *Mil* to dispose; **d. qn à** (*la bonne humeur etc*) to dispose *ou* incline s.o. towards; **se d. à faire** to prepare to do; — *vi* **d. de qch** to have sth at one's disposal; (*utiliser*) to make use of sth; **d. de qn** *Péj* to take advantage of s.o., abuse s.o. **◆—é** *a* **bien/mal d.** in a good/bad mood; **bien d. envers** well-disposed towards; **d. à faire** prepared *ou* disposed to do. **◆disposition** *nf* arrangement; (*de troupes*) disposition; (*de maison, page*) layout; (*humeur*) frame of mind; (*tendance*) tendency, (pre)disposition (**à** to); (*clause*) *Jur* provision; *pl* (*aptitudes*) ability, aptitude (**pour** for); **à la d. de qn** at s.o.'s disposal; **prendre ses** *ou* **des dispositions** (*préparatifs*) to make arrangements, prepare; (*pour l'avenir*) to

make provision; **dans de bonnes disposi-**
tions à l'égard de well-disposed towards.
dispositif [dispozitif] *nm* (*mécanisme*)
device; **d. de défense** *Mil* defence system;
d. antiparasite *Él* suppressor.
disproportion [disprɔpɔrsjɔ̃] *nf* disproportion. ◆**disproportionné** *a* disproportionate.
dispute [dispyt] *nf* quarrel. ◆**disputer** *vt*
(*match*) to play; (*terrain*, *droit etc*) to
contest, dispute; (*rallye*) to compete in; **d.**
qch à qn (*prix*, *première place etc*) to fight
with s.o. for *ou* over sth, contend with s.o.
for sth; **d. qn** (*gronder*) *Fam* to tell s.o. off;
— se d. *vpr* to quarrel (**avec** with); (*match*)
to take place; **se d. qch** to fight over sth.
disqualifier [diskalifje] *vt Sp* to disqualify;
— se d. *vpr Fig* to become discredited.
◆**disqualification** *nf Sp* disqualification.
disque [disk] *nm Mus* record; *Sp* discus;
(*cercle*) disc, *Am* disk; (*pour ordinateur*)
disk. ◆**disquaire** *nmf* record dealer.
◆**disquette** *nf* (*pour ordinateur*) floppy
disk.
dissection [disɛksjɔ̃] *nf* dissection.
dissemblable [disɑ̃blabl] *a* dissimilar (**à**
to).
disséminer [disemine] *vt* (*graines*, *mines*
etc) to scatter; (*idées*) *Fig* to disseminate.
◆**dissémination** *nf* scattering; (*d'idées*)
Fig dissemination.
dissension [disɑ̃sjɔ̃] *nf* dissension.
disséquer [diseke] *vt* to dissect.
disserter [diserte] *vi* **d. sur** to comment
upon, discuss. ◆**dissertation** *nf Scol*
essay.
dissident, -ente [disidɑ̃, -ɑ̃t] *a & nmf* dissident. ◆**dissidence** *nf* dissidence.
dissimul/er [disimyle] *vt* (*cacher*) to
conceal, hide (**à** from); — *vi* (*feindre*) to
pretend; **— se d.** *vpr* to hide, conceal
oneself. ◆**—é** *a* (*enfant*) *Péj* secretive.
◆**dissimulation** *nf* concealment; (*dupli-*
cité) deceit.
dissip/er [disipe] *vt* (*brouillard*, *craintes*) to
dispel; (*fortune*) to squander, dissipate; **d.**
qn to lead s.o. astray, distract s.o.; **— se d.**
vpr (*brume*) to clear, lift; (*craintes*) to
disappear; (*élève*) to misbehave. ◆**—é** *a*
(*élève*) unruly; (*vie*) dissipated. ◆**dissipa-**
tion *nf* (*de brouillard*) clearing; (*indis-*
cipline) misbehaviour; (*débauche*) *Litt*
dissipation.
dissocier [disɔsje] *vt* to dissociate (**de**
from).
dissolu [disɔly] *a* (*vie etc*) dissolute.
dissoudre* [disudr] *vt*, **— se d.** *vpr* to

dissolve. ◆**dissolution** *nf* dissolution.
◆**dissolvant** *a & nm* solvent; (*pour vernis*
à ongles) nail polish remover.
dissuader [disɥade] *vt* to dissuade, deter
(**de qch** from sth, **de faire** from doing).
◆**dissuasif, -ive** *a* (*effet*) deterrent; **être**
d. *Fig* to be a deterrent. ◆**dissuasion** *nf*
dissuasion; **force de d.** *Mil* deterrent.
distant [distɑ̃] *a* distant; (*personne*) aloof,
distant; **d. de dix kilomètres** (*éloigné*) ten
kilometres away; (*à intervalles*) ten kilometres apart. ◆**distance** *nf* distance; **à deux**
mètres de d. two metres apart; **à d.** at *ou*
from a distance; **garder ses distances** to
keep one's distance. ◆**distancer** *vt* to
leave behind, outstrip.
distendre [distɑ̃dr] *vt*, **— se d.** *vpr* to
distend.
distiller [distile] *vt* to distil. ◆**distillation**
nf distillation. ◆**distillerie** *nf* (*lieu*) distillery.
distinct, -incte [distɛ̃, -ɛ̃kt] *a* (*différent*)
distinct, separate (**de** from); (*net*) clear,
distinct. ◆**distinctement** *adv* distinctly,
clearly. ◆**distinctif, -ive** *a* distinctive.
◆**distinction** *nf* (*différence*, *raffinement*)
distinction.
distingu/er [distɛ̃ge] *vt* (*différencier*) to
distinguish; (*voir*) to make out; (*choisir*) to
single out; **d. le blé de l'orge** to tell wheat
from barley, distinguish between wheat
and barley; **— se d.** *vpr* (*s'illustrer*) to
distinguish oneself; **se d. de** (*différer*) to be
distinguishable from; **se d. par** (*sa gaieté*,
beauté etc) to be conspicuous for. ◆**—é** *a*
(*bien élevé*, *éminent*) distinguished; **senti-**
ments distingués (*formule épistolaire*) *Com*
yours faithfully.
distorsion [distɔrsjɔ̃] *nf* (*du corps*, *d'une*
image etc) distortion.
distraction [distraksjɔ̃] *nf* amusement,
distraction; (*étourderie*) (fit of)
absent-mindedness. ◆**distraire*** *vt* (*diver-*
tir) to entertain, amuse; **d. qn (de)**
(*détourner*) to distract s.o. (from); **— se d.**
vpr to amuse oneself, enjoy oneself. ◆**dis-**
trait *a* absent-minded. ◆**distraitement**
adv absent-mindedly. ◆**distrayant** *a*
entertaining.
distribuer [distribɥe] *vt* (*répartir*) to
distribute; (*donner*) to give *ou* hand out,
distribute; (*courrier*) to deliver; (*eau*) to
supply; (*cartes*) to deal; **bien distribué**
(*appartement*) well-arranged. ◆**distri-**
buteur *nm Aut Cin* distributor; **d. (automa-**
tique) vending machine; **d. de billets** *Rail*
ticket machine; (*de billets de banque*) cash

dispenser *ou* machine. ◆**distribution** *nf* distribution; (*du courrier*) delivery; (*de l'eau*) supply; (*acteurs*) *Th Cin* cast; **d. des prix** prize giving.

district [distrikt] *nm* district.

dit [di] *voir* **dire**; — *a* (*convenu*) agreed; (*surnommé*) called.

dites [dit] *voir* **dire**.

divaguer [divage] *vi* (*dérailler*) to rave, talk drivel. ◆**divagations** *nfpl* ravings.

divan [divã] *nm* divan, couch.

divergent [diverʒã] *a* diverging, divergent. ◆**divergence** *nf* divergence. ◆**diverger** *vi* to diverge (**de** from).

divers, -erses [diver, -ers] *apl* (*distincts*) varied, diverse; **d. groupes** (*plusieurs*) various *ou* sundry groups. ◆**diversement** *adv* in various ways. ◆**diversifier** *vt* to diversify; — **se d.** *vpr Écon* to diversify. ◆**diversité** *nf* diversity.

diversion [diversjõ] *nf* diversion.

divert/ir [divertir] *vt* to amuse, entertain; — **se d.** *vpr* to enjoy oneself, amuse oneself. ◆—**issement** *nm* amusement, entertainment.

dividende [dividãd] *nm Math Fin* dividend.

divin [divẽ] *a* divine. ◆**divinité** *nf* divinity.

diviser [divize] *vt*, — **se d.** *vpr* to divide (**en** into). ◆**divisible** *a* divisible. ◆**division** *nf* division.

divorce [divors] *nm* divorce. ◆**divorc/er** *vi* to get *ou* be divorced, divorce; **d. d'avec qn** to divorce s.o. ◆—**é, -ée** *a* divorced (**d'avec** from); — *nmf* divorcee.

divulguer [divylge] *vt* to divulge. ◆**divulgation** *nf* divulgence.

dix [dis] ([di] *before consonant*, [diz] *before vowel*) *a & nm* ten. ◆**dixième** [dizjɛm] *a & nmf* tenth; **un d.** a tenth. ◆**dix-huit** [dizɥit] *a & nm* eighteeen. ◆**dix-huitième** *a & nmf* eighteenth. ◆**dix-neuf** [diznœf] *a & nm* nineteen. ◆**dix-neuvième** *a & nmf* nineteenth. ◆**dix-sept** [dissɛt] *a & nm* seventeen. ◆**dix-septième** *a & nmf* seventeenth.

dizaine [dizɛn] *nf* about ten.

docile [dosil] *a* submissive, docile. ◆**docilité** *nf* submissiveness, docility.

dock [dok] *nm Nau* dock. ◆**docker** [dokɛr] *nm* docker.

docteur [doktœr] *nm Méd Univ* doctor (**ès, en** of). ◆**doctorat** *nm* doctorate, = PhD (**ès, en** in).

doctrine [doktrin] *nf* doctrine. ◆**doctrinaire** *a & nmf Péj* doctrinaire.

document [dokymã] *nm* document. ◆**documentaire** *a* documentary; — *nm*

(*film*) documentary. ◆**documentaliste** *nmf* information officer.

document/er [dokymãte] *vt* (*informer*) to document; — **se d.** *vpr* to collect material *ou* information. ◆—**é** *a* (**bien** *ou* **très**) **d.** (*personne*) well-informed. ◆**documentation** *nf* (*documents*) documentation, *Com* literature; (*renseignements*) information.

dodeliner [dodline] *vi* **d. de la tête** to nod (one's head).

dodo [dodo] *nm* (*langage enfantin*) **faire d.** to sleep; **aller au d.** to go to bye-byes.

dodu [dody] *a* chubby, plump.

dogme [dogm] *nm* dogma. ◆**dogmatique** *a* dogmatic. ◆**dogmatisme** *nm* dogmatism.

dogue [dog] *nm* (*chien*) mastiff.

doigt [dwa] *nm* finger; **d. de pied** toe; **à deux doigts de** within an ace of; **montrer du d.** to point (to); **savoir sur le bout du d.** to have at one's finger tips. ◆**doigté** *nm Mus* fingering, touch; (*savoir-faire*) tact, expertise. ◆**doigtier** *nm* fingerstall.

dois, doit [dwa] *voir* **devoir** ¹,².

doléances [doleãs] *nfpl* (*plaintes*) grievances.

dollar [dolar] *nm* dollar.

domaine [domɛn] *nm* (*terres*) estate, domain; (*sphère*) province, domain.

dôme [dom] *nm* dome.

domestique [domestik] *a* (*animal*) domestic(ated); (*de la famille*) family-, domestic; (*ménager*) domestic, household; — *nmf* servant. ◆**domestiquer** *vt* to domesticate.

domicile [domisil] *nm* home; *Jur* abode; **travailler à d.** to work at home; **livrer à d.** (*pain etc*) to deliver (to the house). ◆**domicilié** *a* resident (**à, chez** at).

domin/er [domine] *vt* to dominate; (*situation, sentiment*) to master, dominate; (*être supérieur à*) to surpass, outclass; (*tour, rocher*) to tower above, dominate (*valley, building etc*); — *vi* (*être le plus fort*) to be dominant, dominate; (*être le plus important*) to predominate; — **se d.** *vpr* to control oneself. ◆—**ant** *a* dominant. ◆—**ante** *a* dominant feature; *Mus* dominant. ◆**dominateur, -trice** *a* domineering. ◆**domination** *nf* domination.

dominicain, -aine [dominikẽ, -ɛn] *a & nmf Rel* Dominican.

dominical, -aux [dominikal, -o] *a* (*repos*) Sunday-.

domino [domino] *nm* domino; *pl* (*jeu*) dominoes.

dommage [domaʒ] *nm* **1** (**c'est**) **d.!** it's a

pity *ou* a shame! (**que** that); **quel d.!** what a pity *ou* a shame! **2** (*tort*) prejudice, harm; *pl* (*dégâts*) damage; **dommages-intérêts** *Jur* damages.

dompt/er [dɔ̃te] *vt* (*animal*) to tame; (*passions, rebelles*) to subdue. ◆**—eur, -euse** *nmf* (*de lions*) lion tamer.

don [dɔ̃] *nm* (*cadeau, aptitude*) gift; (*aumône*) donation; **le d. du sang**/*etc* (the) giving of blood/*etc*; **faire d. de** to give; **avoir le d. de** (*le chic pour*) to have the knack of. ◆**donateur, -trice** *nmf Jur* donor. ◆**donation** *nf Jur* donation.

donc [dɔ̃(k)] *conj* so, then; (*par conséquent*) so, therefore; **asseyez-vous d.!** (*intensif*) will you sit down!, sit down then!; **qui/quoi d.?** who?/what?; **allons d.!** come on!

donjon [dɔ̃ʒɔ̃] *nm* (*de château*) keep.

donne [dɔn] *nf Cartes* deal.

donner [dɔne] *vt* to give; (*récolte, résultat*) to produce; (*sa place*) to give up; (*pièce, film*) to put on; (*cartes*) to deal; **d. un coup à** to hit, give a blow to; **d. le bonjour à qn** to say hello to s.o.; **d. à réparer** to take (in) to be repaired; **d. raison à qn** to say s.o. is right; **ça donne soif/faim** it makes you thirsty/hungry; **je lui donne trente ans** I'd say *ou* guess he *ou* she was thirty; **ça n'a rien donné** (*efforts*) it hasn't got us anywhere; **c'est donné** *Fam* it's dirt cheap; **étant donné** (*la situation etc*) considering, in view of; **étant donné que** seeing (that), considering (that); **à un moment donné** at some stage; – *vi* **d. sur** (*fenêtre*) to look out onto, overlook; (*porte*) to open onto; **d. dans** (*piège*) to fall into; **d. de la tête contre** to hit one's head against; – **se d.** *vpr* (*se consacrer*) to devote oneself (**à** to); **se d. du mal** to go to a lot of trouble (**pour faire** to do); **s'en d. à cœur joie** to have a whale of a time, enjoy oneself to the full. ◆**données** *nfpl* (*information*) data; (*de problème*) (known) facts; (*d'un roman*) basic elements. ◆**donneur, -euse** *nmf* giver; (*de sang, d'organe*) donor; *Cartes* dealer.

dont [dɔ̃] *pron rel* (= **de qui, duquel, de quoi** *etc*) (*personne*) of whom; (*chose*) of which; (*appartenance: personne*) whose, of whom; (*appartenance: chose*) of which, whose; **une mère d. le fils est malade** a mother whose son is ill; **la fille d. il est fier** the daughter he is proud of *ou* whom he is proud; **les outils d. j'ai besoin** the tools I need; **la façon d. elle joue** the way (in which) she plays; **voici ce d. il s'agit** here's what it's about.

doper [dɔpe] *vt* (*cheval, sportif*) to dope; – **se d.** *vpr* to dope oneself. ◆**doping** *nm* (*action*) doping; (*substance*) dope.

dorénavant [dɔrenavɑ̃] *adv* henceforth.

dor/er [dɔre] *vt* (*objet*) to gild; **d. la pilule** *Fig* to sugar the pill; **se (faire) d. au soleil** to bask in the sun; – *vi Culin* to brown. ◆**—é** *a* (*objet*) gilt; (*couleur*) golden; – *nm* (*couche*) gilt. ◆**dorure** *nf* gilding.

dorloter [dɔrlɔte] *vt* to pamper, coddle.

dormir* [dɔrmir] *vi* to sleep; (*être endormi*) to be asleep; (*argent*) to lie idle; **histoire à d. debout** tall story, cock-and-bull story; **eau dormante** stagnant water. ◆**dortoir** *nm* dormitory.

dos [do] *nm* back; (*de nez*) bridge; (*de livre*) spine; **voir qn de d.** to have a back view of s.o.; **à d. de chameau** (riding) on a camel; **'voir au d.'** (*verso*) 'see over'; **j'en ai plein le d.** *Fam* I'm sick of it; **mettre qch sur le d. de qn** (*accusation*) to pin sth on s.o. ◆**dossard** *nm Sp* number (*fixed on back*). ◆**dossier** *nm* **1** (*de siège*) back. **2** (*papiers, compte rendu*) file, dossier; (*classeur*) folder, file.

dose [doz] *nf* dose; (*quantité administrée*) dosage. ◆**dos/er** *vt* (*remède*) to measure out the dose of; (*équilibrer*) to strike the correct balance between. ◆**—age** *nm* measuring out (*of dose*); (*équilibre*) balance; **faire le d. de** = **doser.** ◆**—eur** *nm* **bouchon d.** measuring cap.

dot [dɔt] *nf* dowry.

doter [dɔte] *vt* (*hôpital etc*) to endow; **d. de** (*matériel*) to equip with; (*qualité*) *Fig* to endow with. ◆**dotation** *nf* endowment; equipping.

douane [dwan] *nf* customs. ◆**douanier, -ière** *nm* customs officer; – *a* (*union etc*) customs-.

double [dubl] *a* double; (*rôle, avantage etc*) twofold, double; – *adv* double; (*de personne*) double; (*copie*) copy, duplicate; (*de timbre*) swap, duplicate; **le d. (de)** (*quantité*) twice as much (as). ◆**doublage** *nm* (*de film*) dubbing. ◆**doublement** *adv* doubly; – *nm* doubling. ◆**doubler 1** *vt* (*augmenter*) to double; (*vêtement*) to line; (*film*) to dub; (*acteur*) to stand in for; (*classe*) *Scol* to repeat; (*cap*) *Nau* to round; **se d. de** to be coupled with; – *vi* (*augmenter*) to double. **2** *vti Aut* to overtake, pass. ◆**doublure** *nf* (*étoffe*) lining; *Th* understudy; *Cin* stand-in, double.

douce [dus] *voir* **doux.** ◆**doucement** *adv* (*délicatement*) gently; (*à voix basse*) softly; (*sans bruit*) quietly; (*lentement*) slowly; (*sans à-coups*) smoothly; (*assez bien*) *Fam* so-so. ◆**douceur** *nf* (*de miel etc*) sweetness; (*de personne, pente etc*) gentleness; (*de peau etc*) softness; (*de temps*) mildness; *pl* (*sucreries*) sweets, *Am* candies; **en d.** (*démarrer etc*) smoothly.

douche [duʃ] *nf* shower. ◆**doucher** *vt* **d. qn** to give s.o. a shower; **— se d.** *vpr* to take *ou* have a shower.

doué [dwe] *a* gifted, talented (**en** at); (*intelligent*) clever; **d. de** gifted with; **il est d. pour** he has a gift *ou* talent for.

douille [duj] *nf* (*d'ampoule*) *Él* socket; (*de cartouche*) case.

douillet, -ette [dujɛ, -ɛt] *a* (*lit etc*) soft, cosy, snug; **il est d.** (*délicat*) *Péj* he's soft.

douleur [dulœr] *nf* (*mal*) pain; (*chagrin*) sorrow, grief. ◆**douloureux, -euse** *a* (*maladie, membre, décision, perte etc*) painful.

doute [dut] *nm* doubt; *pl* (*méfiance*) doubts, misgivings; **sans d.** no doubt, probably; **sans aucun d.** without (any *ou* a) doubt; **mettre en d.** to cast doubt on; **dans le d.** uncertain, doubtful; **ça ne fait pas de d.** there is no doubt about it. ◆**douter** *vi* to doubt; **d. de qch/qn** to doubt sth/s.o.; **d. que** (+ *sub*) to doubt whether *ou* that; **se d. de qch** to suspect sth; **je m'en doute** I suspect so, I would think so. ◆**douteux, -euse** *a* doubtful; (*louche, médiocre*) dubious; **il est d. que** (+ *sub*) it's doubtful whether *ou* that.

douve(s) [duv] *nf*(*pl*) (*de château*) moat.

Douvres [duvr] *nm ou f* Dover.

doux, douce [du, dus] *a* (*miel, son etc*) sweet; (*personne, pente etc*) gentle; (*peau, lumière, drogue etc*) soft; (*émotion, souvenir etc*) pleasant; (*temps, climat*) mild; **en douce** on the quiet.

douze [duz] *a & nm* twelve. ◆**douzaine** *nf* (*douze*) dozen; (*environ*) about twelve; **une d. d'œufs**/*etc* a dozen eggs/*etc.* ◆**douzième** *a & nmf* twelfth; **un d.** a twelfth.

doyen, -enne [dwajɛ̃, -ɛn] *nmf Rel Univ* dean; **d.** (**d'âge**) oldest person.

draconien, -ienne [drakɔnjɛ̃, -jɛn] *a* (*mesures*) drastic.

dragée [draʒe] *nf* sugared almond; **tenir la d. haute à qn** (*tenir tête à qn*) to stand up to s.o.

dragon [dragɔ̃] *nm* (*animal*) dragon; *Mil Hist* dragoon.

drague [drag] *nf* (*appareil*) dredge; (*filet*) drag net. ◆**draguer** *vt* **1** (*rivière etc*) to dredge. **2** *Arg* (*racoler*) to try and pick up;

(*faire du baratin à*) to chat up, *Am* smooth-talk.

drainer [drene] *vt* to drain.

drame [dram] *nm* drama; (*catastrophe*) tragedy. ◆**dramatique** *a* dramatic; **critique d.** drama critic; **auteur d.** playwright, dramatist; **film d.** drama. ◆**dramatiser** *vt* (*exagérer*) to dramatize. ◆**dramaturge** *nmf* dramatist.

drap [dra] *nm* (*de lit*) sheet; (*tissu*) cloth; **dans de beaux draps** *Fig* in a fine mess.

drapeau, -x [drapo] *nm* flag; **être sous les drapeaux** *Mil* to be in the services.

draper [drape] *vt* to drape (**de** with). ◆**draperie** *nf* (*étoffe*) drapery.

dresser [drese] **1** *vt* (*échelle, statue*) to put up, erect; (*piège*) to lay, set; (*oreille*) to prick up; (*liste*) to draw up, make out; **— se d.** *vpr* (*personne*) to stand up; (*statue, montagne*) to rise up, stand; **se d. contre** (*abus*) to stand up against. **2** *vt* (*animal*) to train; (*personne*) *Péj* to drill, teach. ◆**dressage** *nm* training. ◆**dresseur, -euse** *nmf* trainer.

dribbler [drible] *vti Fb* to dribble.

drogue [drɔg] *nf* (*médicament*) *Péj* drug; **une d.** (*stupéfiant*) a drug; **la d.** drugs, dope. ◆**drogu/er** *vt* (*victime*) to drug; (*malade*) to dose up; **— se d.** *vpr* to take drugs, be on drugs; (*malade*) to dose oneself up. ◆**—é, -ée** *nmf* drug addict.

droguerie [drɔgri] *nf* hardware shop *ou Am* store. ◆**droguiste** *nmf* owner of a *droguerie.*

droit¹ [drwa] *nm* (*privilège*) right; (*d'inscription etc*) fee(s), dues; *pl* (*de douane*) duty; **le d.** (*science juridique*) law; **avoir d. à** to be entitled to; **avoir le d. de faire** to be entitled to do, have the right to do; **à bon d.** rightly; **d. d'entrée** entrance fee.

droit² [drwa] *a* (*ligne, route etc*) straight; (*personne, mur etc*) upright, straight; (*angle*) right; (*veston*) single-breasted; (*honnête*) *Fig* upright; *— adv* straight; **tout d.** straight *ou* right ahead. ◆**droite¹** *nf* (*ligne*) straight line.

droit³ [drwa] *a* (*côté, bras etc*) right; *—* (*coup*) *Boxe* right. ◆**droite²** *nf* **la d.** (*côté*) the right (side); *Pol* the right (wing); **à d.** (*tourner*) (to the) right; (*rouler, se tenir*) on the right(-hand) side; **de d.** (*fenêtre etc*) right-hand; (*politique, candidat*) right-wing; **à d. de** on *ou* to the right of; **à d. et à gauche** (*voyager etc*) here, there and everywhere. ◆**droitier, -ière** *a & nmf* right-handed (person). ◆**droiture** *nf* uprightness.

drôle [drol] *a* funny; **d. d'air/de type** funny look/fellow. **◆—ment** *adv* funnily; (*extrêmement*) *Fam* dreadfully.

dromadaire [drɔmadɛr] *nm* dromedary.

dru [dry] *a* (*herbe etc*) thick, dense; – *adv* **tomber d.** (*pluie*) to pour down heavily; **pousser d.** to grow thick(ly).

du [dy] = **de** + **le**.

dû, due [dy] *a* **d. à** (*accident etc*) due to; – *nm* due; (*argent*) dues.

dualité [dɥalite] *nf* duality.

dubitatif, -ive [dybitatif, -iv] *a* (*regard etc*) dubious.

duc [dyk] *nm* duke. **◆duché** *nm* duchy. **◆duchesse** *nf* duchess.

duel [dɥɛl] *nm* duel.

dûment [dymã] *adv* duly.

dune [dyn] *nf* (sand) dune.

duo [dɥo] *nm Mus* duet; (*couple*) *Hum* duo.

dupe [dyp] *nf* dupe, fool; – *a* **d. de** duped by, fooled by. **◆duper** *vt* to fool, dupe.

duplex [dyplɛks] *nm* split-level flat, *Am* duplex; (*émission en*) **d.** *Tél* link-up.

duplicata [dyplikata] *nm inv* duplicate.

duplicateur [dyplikatœr] *nm* (*machine*) duplicator.

duplicité [dyplisite] *nf* duplicity, deceit.

dur [dyr] *a* (*substance*) hard; (*difficile*) hard, tough; (*viande*) tough; (*hiver, leçon, ton*) harsh; (*personne*) hard, harsh; (*brosse, carton*) stiff; (*œuf*) hard-boiled; **d. d'oreille** hard of hearing; **d. à cuire** *Fam* hard-bitten, tough; – *adv* (*travailler*) hard; – *nm Fam* tough guy. **◆durement** *adv* harshly. **◆dureté** *nf* hardness; harshness; toughness.

durant [dyrã] *prép* during.

durc/ir [dyrsir] *vti*, – **se d.** *vpr* to harden. **◆—issement** *nm* hardening.

durée [dyre] *nf* (*de film, événement etc*) length; (*période*) duration; (*de pile*) *Él* life; **de longue d.** (*disque*) long-playing. **◆dur/er** *vi* to last; **ça dure depuis . . .** it's been going on for . . . . **◆—able** *a* durable, lasting.

durillon [dyrijõ] *nm* callus.

duvet [dyvɛ] *nm* **1** (*d'oiseau, de visage*) down. **2** (*sac*) sleeping bag. **◆duveté** *a,* **◆duveteux, -euse** *a* downy.

dynamique [dinamik] *a* dynamic; – *nf* (*force*) *Fig* dynamic force, thrust. **◆dynamisme** *nm* dynamism.

dynamite [dinamit] *nf* dynamite. **◆dynamiter** *vt* to dynamite.

dynamo [dinamo] *nf* dynamo.

dynastie [dinasti] *nf* dynasty.

dysenterie [disãtri] *nf Méd* dysentery.

dyslexique [dislɛksik] *a & nmf* dyslexic.

E

E, e [ə, ø] *nm* E, e.

eau, -x [o] *nf* water; **il est tombé beaucoup d'e.** a lot of rain fell; **e. douce** (*non salée*) fresh water; (*du robinet*) soft water; **e. salée** salt water; **e. de Cologne** eau de Cologne; **e. de toilette** toilet water; **grandes eaux** (*d'un parc*) ornamental fountains; **tomber à l'e.** (*projet*) to fall through; **ça lui fait venir l'e. à la bouche** it makes his *ou* her mouth water; **tout en e.** sweating; **prendre l'e.** (*chaussure*) to take water, leak. **◆e.-de-vie** *nf* (*pl* **eaux-de-vie**) brandy. **◆e.-forte** *nf* (*pl* **eaux-fortes**) (*gravure*) etching.

ébah/ir [ebair] *vt* to astound, dumbfound, amaze. **◆—issement** *nm* amazement.

ébattre (s') [sebatr] *vpr* to frolic, frisk about. **◆ébats** *nmpl* frolics.

ébauche [eboʃ] *nf* (*esquisse*) (rough) outline, (rough) sketch; (*début*) beginnings. **◆ébaucher** *vt* (*projet, tableau, œuvre*) to sketch out, outline; **e. un sourire** to give a faint smile; – **s'é.** *vpr* to take shape.

ébène [ebɛn] *nf* (*bois*) ebony.

ébéniste [ebenist] *nm* cabinet-maker. **◆ébénisterie** *nf* cabinet-making.

éberlué [ebɛrlɥe] *a Fam* dumbfounded.

éblou/ir [ebluir] *vt* to dazzle. **◆—issement** *nm* (*aveuglement*) dazzling, dazzle; (*émerveillement*) feeling of wonder; (*malaise*) fit of dizziness.

éboueur [ebwœr] *nm* dustman, *Am* garbage collector.

ébouillanter [ebujãte] *vt* to scald; – **s'é.** *vpr* to scald oneself.

éboul/er (s') [sebule] *vpr* (*falaise etc*) to crumble; (*terre, roches*) to fall. **◆—ement** *nm* landslide. **◆éboulis** *nm* (mass of) fallen debris.

ébouriffant [eburifã] *a Fam* astounding.

ébouriffer [eburife] *vt* (*cheveux*) to dishevel, ruffle, tousle.

ébranl/er [ebrɑ̃le] vt (mur, confiance etc) to shake; (santé) to weaken, affect; (personne) to shake, shatter; **— s'é.** vpr (train, cortège etc) to move off. **◆—ement** nm (secousse) shaking, shock; (nerveux) shock.

ébrécher [ebreʃe] vt (assiette) to chip; (lame) to nick. **◆ébréchure** nf chip; nick.

ébriété [ebrijete] nf drunkenness.

ébrouer (s') [sebrue] vpr (cheval) to snort; (personne) to shake oneself (about).

ébruiter [ebrɥite] vt (nouvelle etc) to make known, divulge.

ébullition [ebylisjɔ̃] nf boiling; **être en é.** (eau) to be boiling; (ville) Fig to be in turmoil.

écaille [ekɑj] nf **1** (de poisson) scale; (de tortue, d'huître) shell; (résine synthétique) tortoise-shell. **2** (de peinture) flake. **◆écailler 1** vt (poisson) to scale; (huître) to shell. **2 s'é.** vpr (peinture) to flake (off), peel.

écarlate [ekarlat] a & nf scarlet.

écarquiller [ekarkije] vt **é. les yeux** to open one's eyes wide.

écart [ekar] nm (intervalle) gap, distance; (mouvement, embardée) swerve; (différence) difference (**de** in, **entre** between); **écarts de** (conduite, langage etc) lapses in; **le grand é.** (de gymnaste) the splits; **à l'é.** out of the way; **tenir qn à l'é.** Fig to keep s.o. out of things; **à l'é. de** away from, clear of. **◆écart/er** vt (objets) to move away from each other, move apart; (jambes) to spread, open; (rideaux) to draw (aside), open; (crainte, idée) to brush aside, dismiss; (carte) to discard; **é. qch de qch** to move sth away from sth; **é. qn de** (éloigner) to keep ou take s.o. away from; (exclure) to keep s.o. out of; **— s'é.** vpr (s'éloigner) to move away (**de** from); (se séparer) to move aside (**de** from); **s'é. de** (sujet, bonne route) to stray ou deviate from. **◆—é** a (endroit) remote; **les jambes écartées** with legs (wide) apart. **◆—ement** nm (espace) gap, distance (**de** between).

écartelé [ekartəle] a **é. entre** (tiraillé) torn between.

ecchymose [ekimoz] nf bruise.

ecclésiastique [eklezjastik] a ecclesiastical; — nm ecclesiastic, clergyman.

écervelé, -ée [esɛrvəle] a scatterbrained; — nmf scatterbrain.

échafaud [eʃafo] nm (pour exécution) scaffold.

échafaudage [eʃafodaʒ] nm (construction) scaffold(ing); (tas) heap; (système) Fig fabric. **◆échafauder** vi to put up scaffolding ou a scaffold; — vt (projet etc) to put together, think up.

échalas [eʃala] nm **grand é.** tall skinny person.

échalote [eʃalɔt] nf Bot Culin shallot, scallion.

échancré [eʃɑ̃kre] a (encolure) V-shaped, scooped. **◆échancrure** nf (de robe) opening.

échange [eʃɑ̃ʒ] nm exchange; **en é.** in exchange (**dé** for). **◆échanger** vt to exchange (**contre** for). **◆échangeur** nm (intersection) Aut interchange.

échantillon [eʃɑ̃tijɔ̃] nm sample. **◆échantillonnage** nm (collection) range (of samples).

échappatoire [eʃapatwar] nf evasion, way out.

échapp/er [eʃape] vi **é. à qn** to escape from s.o.; **é. à la mort/un danger/etc** to escape death/a danger/etc; **ce nom m'échappe** that name escapes me; **ça lui a échappé (des mains)** it slipped out of his ou her hands; **laisser é.** (cri) to let out; (objet, occasion) to let slip; **l'é. belle** to have a close shave; **ça m'a échappé** (je n'ai pas compris) I didn't catch it; **— s'é.** vpr (s'enfuir) to escape (**de** from); (s'éclipser) to slip away; Sp to break away; (gaz, eau) to escape, come out. **◆—é, -ée** nmf runaway. **◆—ée** nf Sp breakaway; (vue) vista. **◆—ement** nm **tuyau d'é.** Aut exhaust pipe; **pot d'é.** Aut silencer, Am muffler.

écharde [eʃard] nf (de bois) splinter.

écharpe [eʃarp] nf scarf; (de maire) sash; **en é.** (bras) in a sling; **prendre en é.** Aut to hit sideways.

écharper [eʃarpe] vt **é. qn** to cut s.o. to bits.

échasse [eʃas] nf (bâton) stilt. **◆échassier** nm wading bird.

échauder [eʃode] vt **être échaudé, se faire é.** (déçu) Fam to be taught a lesson.

échauffer [eʃofe] vt (moteur) to overheat; (esprit) to excite; **— s'é.** vpr (discussion) & Sp to warm up.

échauffourée [eʃofure] nf (bagarre) clash, brawl, skirmish.

échéance [eʃeɑ̃s] nf Com date (due), expiry ou Am expiration date; (paiement) payment (due); (obligation) commitment; **à brève/longue é.** (projet, emprunt) short-/long-term.

échéant (le cas) [ləkazeʃeɑ̃] adv if the occasion should arise, possibly.

échec [eʃɛk] nm **1** (insuccès) failure; **faire é. à** (inflation etc) to hold in check. **2 les**

échecs (*jeu*) chess; **en é.** in check; **é.!** check!; **é. et mat!** checkmate!

échelle [eʃɛl] *nf* 1 (*marches*) ladder; **faire la courte é. à qn** to give s.o. a leg up. 2 (*mesure, dimension*) scale; **à l'é. nationale** on a national scale. ◆**échelon** *nm* (*d'échelle*) rung; (*de fonctionnaire*) grade; (*dans une organisation*) echelon; **à l'é. régional/national** on a regional/national level. ◆**échelonner** *vt* (*paiements*) to spread out, space out; **— s'é.** *vpr* to be spread out.

écheveau, -x [eʃvo] *nm* (*de laine*) skein; *Fig* muddle, tangle.

échevelé [eʃəvle] *a* (*ébouriffé*) dishevelled; (*course, danse etc*) *Fig* wild.

échine [eʃin] *nf Anat* backbone, spine.

échiner (s') [eʃine] *vpr* (*s'évertuer*) *Fam* to knock oneself out (**à faire** doing).

échiquier [eʃikje] *nm* (*tableau*) chessboard.

écho [eko] *nm* (*d'un son*) echo; (*réponse*) response; *pl Journ* gossip (items), local news; **avoir des échos de** to hear some news about; **se faire l'é. de** (*opinions etc*) to echo. ◆**échotier, -ière** *nmf Journ* gossip columnist.

échographie [ekɔgrafi] *nf* (ultrasound) scan; **passer une é.** (*femme enceinte*) to have a scan.

échoir* [eʃwar] *vi* (*terme*) to expire; **é. à qn** (*part*) to fall to s.o.

échouer [eʃwe] 1 *vi* to fail; **é. à** (*examen*) to fail. 2 *vi*, **— s'é.** *vpr* (*navire*) to run aground.

éclabousser [eklabuse] *vt* to splash, spatter (**de** with); (*salir*) *Fig* to tarnish the image of. ◆**éclaboussure** *nf* splash, spatter.

éclair [eklɛr] 1 *nm* (*lumière*) flash; **un é.** *Mét* a flash of lightning. 2 *nm* (*gâteau*) éclair. 3 *a inv* (*visite, raid*) lightning.

éclaircir [eklɛrsir] *vt* (*couleur etc*) to lighten, make lighter; (*sauce*) to thin out; (*question, mystère*) to clear up, clarify; **— s'é.** *vpr* (*ciel*) to clear (up); (*idées*) to become clear(er); (*devenir moins dense*) to thin out; **s'é. la voix** to clear one's throat. ◆**—ie** *nf* (*dans le ciel*) clear patch; (*durée*) sunny spell. ◆**—issement** *nm* (*explication*) clarification.

éclairer [eklere] *vt* (*pièce etc*) to light (up); (*situation*) *Fig* to throw light on; **é. qn** (*avec une lampe etc*) to give s.o. some light; (*informer*) *Fig* to enlighten s.o.; **— vi** (*lampe*) to give light; **— s'é.** *vpr* (*visage*) to light up, brighten up; (*question*) *Fig* to become clear(er); **s'é. à la bougie** to use candlelight. ◆**—é** *a* (*averti*) enlightened; **bien/mal é.** (*illuminé*) well/badly lit.

◆**—age** *nm* (*de pièce etc*) light(ing); (*point de vue*) *Fig* light.

éclaireur, -euse [eklɛrœr, -øz] *nm Mil* scout; **— nmf** (boy) scout, (girl) guide.

éclat [ekla] *nm* 1 (*de la lumière*) brightness; (*de phare*) *Aut* glare; (*du feu*) blaze; (*splendeur*) brilliance, radiance; (*de la jeunesse*) bloom; (*de diamant*) glitter, sparkle. 2 (*fragment de verre ou de bois*) splinter; (*de rire, colère*) (out)burst; **é. d'obus** shrapnel; **éclats de voix** noisy outbursts, shouts. ◆**éclater** *vi* (*pneu, obus etc*) to burst; (*pétard, bombe*) to go off, explode; (*verre*) to shatter, break into pieces; (*guerre, incendie*) to break out; (*orage, scandale*) to break; (*parti*) to break up; **é. de rire** to burst out laughing; **é. en sanglots** to burst into tears. ◆**—ant** *a* (*lumière, couleur, succès*) brilliant; (*bruit*) thunderous; (*vérité*) blinding; (*beauté*) radiant. ◆**—ement** *nm* (*de pneu etc*) bursting; (*de bombe etc*) explosion; (*de parti*) break-up.

éclectique [eklɛktik] *a* eclectic.

éclipse [eklips] *nf* (*du soleil*) & *Fig* eclipse. ◆**éclipser** *vt* to eclipse; **— s'é.** *vpr* (*soleil*) to be eclipsed; (*partir*) *Fam* to slip away.

éclopé, -ée [eklɔpe] *a* & *nmf* limping *ou* lame (person).

éclore [eklɔr] *vi* (*œuf*) to hatch; (*fleur*) to open(out), blossom. ◆**éclosion** *nf* hatching; opening, blossoming.

écluse [eklyz] *nf Nau* lock.

écœurer [ekœre] *vt* (*aliment etc*) to make (s.o.) feel sick; (*au moral*) to sicken, nauseate. ◆**—ement** *nm* (*répugnance*) nausea, disgust.

école [ekɔl] *nf* school; (*militaire*) academy; **aller à l'é.** to go to school; **é. de danse/dessin** dancing/art school; **faire é.** to gain a following; **les grandes écoles** *university establishments giving high-level professional training*; **é. normale** teachers' training college. ◆**écolier, -ière** *nmf* schoolboy, schoolgirl.

écologie [ekɔlɔʒi] *nf* ecology. ◆**écologique** *a* ecological. ◆**écologiste** *nmf Pol* environmentalist.

éconduire [ekɔ̃dɥir] *vt* (*repousser*) to reject.

économe [ekɔnɔm] 1 *a* thrifty, economical. 2 *nmf* (*de collège etc*) bursar, steward. ◆**économie** *nf* (*activité économique, vertu*) economy; *pl* (*pécule*) savings; **une é. de** (*gain*) a saving of; **faire une é. de temps** to save time; **faire des économies** to save (up); **é. politique** economics. ◆**économique** *a* 1 (*doctrine etc*) economic; **science é.** economics. 2 (*bon marché*, *avantageux*) economical. ◆**économique-ment** *adv* economically. ◆**économiser** *vt* (*forces, argent, énergie etc*) to save; – *vi* to economize (**sur** on). ◆**économiste** *nmf* economist.

écoper [ekɔpe] **1** *vt* (*bateau*) to bail out, bale out. **2** *vi Fam* to cop it; **é. (de)** (*punition*) to cop, get.

écorce [ekɔrs] *nf* (*d'arbre*) bark; (*de fruit*) peel, skin; **l'é. terrestre** the earth's crust.

écorcher [ekɔrʃe] *vt* (*animal*) to skin, flay; (*érafler*) to graze; (*client*) *Fam* to fleece; (*langue étrangère*) *Fam* to murder; **é. les oreilles** to grate on one's ears; – **s'é.** *vpr* to graze oneself. ◆**écorchure** *nf* graze.

Écosse [ekɔs] *nf* Scotland. ◆**écossais, -aise** *a* Scottish; (*tissu*) tartan; (*whisky*) Scotch; – *nmf* Scot.

écosser [ekɔse] *vt* (*pois*) to shell.

écot [eko] *nm* (*quote-part*) share.

écoul/er [ekule] **1** *vt* (*se débarrasser de*) to dispose of; (*produits*) *Com* to sell (off), clear. **2 s'é.** *vpr* (*eau*) to flow out, run out; (*temps*) to pass, elapse; (*foule*) to disperse. ◆**-é** *a* (*années etc*) past. ◆**-ement** *nm* **1** (*de liquide, véhicules*) flow; (*de temps*) passage. **2** (*débit*) *Com* sale, selling.

écourter [ekurte] *vt* (*séjour, discours etc*) to cut short; (*texte, tige etc*) to shorten.

écoute [ekut] *nf* listening; **à l'é.** *Rad* tuned in, listening (**de** to); **être aux écoutes** (*attentif*) to keep one's ears open (**de** for). ◆**écout/er** *vt* to listen to; (*radio*) to listen (in) to; – *vi* to listen; (*aux portes etc*) to eavesdrop, listen; **si je m'écoutais** if I did what I wanted. ◆**-eur** *nm* (*de téléphone*) earpiece; *pl* (*casque*) headphones, earphones.

écrabouiller [ekrabuje] *vt Fam* to crush to a pulp.

écran [ekrɑ̃] *nm* screen; **le petit é.** television.

écras/er [ekraze] *vt* (*broyer*) to crush; (*fruit, insecte*) to squash, mash; (*cigarette*) to put out; (*tuer*) *Aut* to run over; (*vaincre*) to beat (hollow), crush; (*dominer*) to outstrip; **écrasé de** (*travail, douleur*) overwhelmed with; **se faire é.** *Aut* to get run over; – **s'é.** *vpr* (*avion, voiture*) to crash (**contre** into); **s'é. dans** (*foule*) to crush *ou* squash into. ◆**-ant** *a* (*victoire, nombre, chaleur*) overwhelming. ◆**-é** *a* (*nez*) snub. ◆**-ement** *nm* crushing.

écrémer [ekreme] *vt* (*lait*) to skim, cream; (*collection etc*) *Fig* to cream off the best from.

écrevisse [ekrəvis] *nf* (*crustacé*) crayfish.

écrier (s') [sekrije] *vpr* to cry out, exclaim (**que** that).

écrin [ekrɛ̃] *nm* (jewel) case.

écrire* [ekrir] *vt* to write; (*noter*) to write (down); (*orthographier*) to spell; **é. à la machine** to type; – *vi* to write; – **s'é.** *vpr* (*mot*) to be spelt. ◆**écrit** *nm* written document, paper; (*examen*) *Scol* written paper; *pl* (*œuvres*) writings; **par é.** in writing. ◆**écriteau, -x** *nm* notice, sign. ◆**écriture** *nf* (*système*) writing; (*personnelle*) (hand)writing; *pl Com* accounts; **l'É. Rel** the Scripture(s). ◆**écrivain** *nm* author, writer.

écrou [ekru] *nm Tech* nut.

écrouer [ekrue] *vt* to imprison.

écroul/er (s') [sekrule] *vpr* (*édifice, projet etc*) to collapse; (*blessé etc*) to slump down, collapse. ◆**-ement** *nm* collapse.

écru [ekry] *a* *f* **toile é.** unbleached linen; **soie é.** raw silk.

écueil [ekœj] *nm* (*rocher*) reef; (*obstacle*) *Fig* pitfall.

écuelle [ekɥel] *nf* (*bol*) bowl.

éculé [ekyle] *a* (*chaussure*) worn out at the heel; *Fig* hackneyed.

écume [ekym] *nf* (*de mer, bave d'animal etc*) foam; *Culin* scum. ◆**écumer** *vt Culin* to skim; (*piller*) to plunder; – *vi* to foam (**de rage** with anger). ◆**écumoire** *nf Culin* skimmer.

écureuil [ekyrœj] *nm* squirrel.

écurie [ekyri] *nf* stable.

écusson [ekysɔ̃] *nm* (*emblème d'étoffe*) badge.

écuyer, -ère [ekɥije, -er] *nmf* (*cavalier*) (horse) rider, equestrian.

eczéma [egzema] *nm Méd* eczema.

édenté [edɑ̃te] *a* toothless.

édicter [edikte] *vt* to enact, decree.

édifice [edifis] *nm* building, edifice; (*ensemble organisé*) *Fig* edifice. ◆**édification** *nf* construction; edification; enlightenment. ◆**édifier** *vt* (*bâtiment*) to construct, erect; (*théorie*) to construct; **é. qn** (*moralement*) to edify s.o.; (*détromper*) *Iron* to enlighten s.o.

Édimbourg [edɛ̃bur] *nm ou f* Edinburgh.

édit [edi] *nm Hist* edict.

éditer [edite] *vt* (*publier*) to publish; (*annoter*) to edit. ◆**éditeur, -trice** *nmf* publisher; editor. ◆**édition** *nf* (*livre, journal*) edition; (*diffusion, métier*) publishing. ◆**éditorial, -aux** *nm* (*article*) editorial.

édredon [edrədɔ̃] *nm* eiderdown.

éducation [edykasjɔ̃] *nf* (*enseignement*) education; (*façon d'élever*) upbringing, education; **avoir de l'é.** to have good manners, be well-bred. ◆**éducateur, -trice** *nmf* educator. ◆**éducatif, -ive** *a* educational. ◆**éduquer** *vt* (*à l'école*) to educate (*s.o.*); (*à la maison*) to bring (*s.o.*) up, educate (*s.o.*) (**à faire** to do); (*esprit*) to educate, train.

effac/er [efase] *vt* (*gommer*) to rub out, erase; (*en lavant*) to wash out; (*avec un chiffon*) to wipe away; (*souvenir*) *Fig* to blot out, erase; **— s'e.** *vpr* (*souvenir, couleur etc*) to fade; (*se placer en retrait*) to step ou draw aside. ◆**—é** *a* (*modeste*) self-effacing. ◆**—ement** *nm* (*modestie*) self-effacement. **effar/er** [efare] *vt* to scare, alarm. ◆**—ement** *nm* alarm.

effaroucher [efaruʃe] *vt* to scare away, frighten away.

effectif, -ive [efɛktif, -iv] **1** *a* (*réel*) effective, real. **2** *nm* (*nombre*) (total) strength; (*de classe*) *Scol* size, total number; *pl* (*employés*) & *Mil* manpower. ◆**effective-ment** *adv* (*en effet*) actually, effectively, indeed.

effectuer [efɛktɥe] *vt* (*expérience etc*) to carry out; (*paiement, trajet etc*) to make.

efféminé [efemine] *a* effeminate.

effervescent [efɛrvesɑ̃] *a* (*mélange, jeunesse*) effervescent. ◆**effervescence** *nf* (*exaltation*) excitement, effervescence; (*de liquide*) effervescence.

effet [efɛ] *nm* **1** (*résultat*) effect; (*impression*) impression, effect (**sur** on); **faire de l'e.** (*remède etc*) to be effective; **rester sans e.** to have no effect; **à cet e.** to this end, for this purpose; **en e.** indeed, in fact; **il me fait l'e. d'être fatigué** he seems to me to be tired; **sous l'e. de la colère** (*agir*) in anger, out of anger. **2 e. de commerce** bill, draft.

effets [efɛ] *nmpl* (*vêtements*) clothes, things.

efficace [efikas] *a* (*mesure etc*) effective; (*personne*) efficient. ◆**efficacité** *nf* effectiveness; efficiency.

effigie [efiʒi] *nf* effigy.

effilé [efile] *a* tapering, slender.

effilocher (s') [sefiloʃe] *vpr* to fray.

efflanqué [eflɑ̃ke] *a* emaciated.

effleurer [eflœre] *vt* (*frôler*) to skim, touch lightly; (*égratigner*) to graze; (*question*) *Fig* to touch on; **e. qn** (*pensée etc*) to cross s.o.'s mind.

effondr/er (s') [sefɔ̃dre] *vpr* (*projet, édifice, personne*) to collapse; (*toit*) to cave in, collapse. ◆**—ement** *nm* collapse; *Com* slump; (*abattement*) dejection.

efforcer (s') [seforse] *vpr* **s'e. de faire** to try (hard) ou endeavour ou strive to do.

effort [efɔr] *nm* effort; **sans e.** (*réussir etc*) effortlessly; (*réussite etc*) effortless.

effraction [efraksjɔ̃] *nf* **pénétrer par e.** (*cambrioleur*) to break in; **vol avec e.** housebreaking.

effranger (s') [sefrɑ̃ʒe] *vpr* to fray.

effray/er [efreje] *vt* to frighten, scare; **— s'e.** *vpr* to be frightened ou scared. ◆**—ant** *a* frightening, scary.

effréné [efrene] *a* unrestrained, wild.

effriter [efrite] *vt*, **— s'e.** *vpr* to crumble (away).

effroi [efrwa] *nm* (*frayeur*) dread. ◆**eff-royable** *a* dreadful, appalling. ◆**effroya-blement** *adv* dreadfully.

effronté [efrɔ̃te] *a* (*enfant etc*) cheeky, brazen; (*mensonge*) shameless. ◆**effronterie** *nf* effrontery.

effusion [efyzjɔ̃] *nf* **1 e. de sang** bloodshed. **2** (*manifestation*) effusion; **avec e.** effusively.

égailler (s') [segaje] *vpr* to disperse.

égal, -ale, -aux [egal, -o] *a* equal (**à** to); (*uniforme, régulier*) even; **ça m'est é.** I don't care, it's all the same to me; **— nmf** (*personne*) equal; **traiter qn d'é. à é.** ou **en é.** to treat s.o. as an equal; **sans é.** without match. ◆**—ement** *adv* (*au même degré*) equally; (*aussi*) also, as well. ◆**égaler** *vt* to equal, match (**en** in); (*en quantité*) *Math* to equal. ◆**égalisation** *nf* *Sp* equalization; levelling. ◆**égaliser** *vt* to equalize; (*terrain*) to level; **— vi** *Sp* to equalize. ◆**éga-litaire** *a* egalitarian. ◆**égalité** *nf* equality; (*régularité*) evenness; **à é. (de score)** *Sp* equal (on points); **signe d'é.** *Math* equals sign.

égard [egar] *nm* **à l'é. de** (*concernant*) with respect ou regard to; (*envers*) towards; **avoir des égards pour** to have respect ou consideration for; **à cet é.** in this respect; **à certains égards** in some respects.

égarer [egare] *vt* (*objet*) to mislay; **é. qn** (*dérouter*) to mislead s.o.; (*aveugler, troubler*) to lead s.o. astray, misguide s.o.; **— s'é.** *vpr* to lose one's way, get lost; (*objet*) to get mislaid, go astray; (*esprit*) to wander.

égayer [egeje] *vt* (*pièce*) to brighten up; **é. qn** (*réconforter, amuser*) to cheer s.o. up; **— s'é.** *vpr* (*par la moquerie*) to be amused.

égide [eʒid] *nf* **sous l'é. de** under the aegis of.

églantier [eglɑ̃tje] *nm* (*arbre*) wild rose. ◆**églantine** *nf* (*fleur*) wild rose.

église [egliz] *nf* church.

égocentrique [egɔsɑ̃trik] *a* egocentric.

égoïne [egɔin] *nf* (**scie**) é. hand saw.

égoïsme [egɔism] *nm* selfishness, egoism. ◆**égoïste** *a* selfish, egoistic(al); – *nmf* egoist.

égorger [egɔrʒe] *vt* to cut *ou* slit the throat of.

égosiller (s') [segɔzije] *vpr* to scream one's head off, bawl out.

égotisme [egɔtism] *nm* egotism.

égout [egu] *nm* sewer; **eaux d'é.** sewage.

égoutter [egute] *vt* (*vaisselle*) to drain; (*légumes*) to strain, drain; – *vi*, – **s'é.** *vpr* to drain; to strain; (*linge*) to drip. ◆**égouttoir** *nm* (*panier*) (dish) drainer.

égratigner [egratiɲe] *vt* to scratch. ◆**égratignure** *nf* scratch.

égrener [egrəne] *vt* (*raisins*) to pick off; (*épis*) to shell; **é. son chapelet** *Rel* to count one's beads.

Égypte [eʒipt] *nf* Egypt. ◆**égyptien, -ienne** [-sjɛ̃, -sjɛn] *a* & *nmf* Egyptian.

eh! [e] *int* hey!; **eh bien!** well!

éhonté [eɔ̃te] *a* shameless; **mensonge é.** barefaced lie.

éjecter [eʒɛkte] *vt* to eject. ◆**éjectable** *a* **siège é.** *Av* ejector seat. ◆**éjection** *nf* ejection.

élaborer [elabɔre] *vt* (*système etc*) to elaborate. ◆**élaboration** *nf* elaboration.

élaguer [elage] *vt* (*arbre, texte etc*) to prune.

élan [elɑ̃] *nm* **1** (*vitesse*) momentum, impetus; (*impulsion*) impulse; (*fougue*) fervour, spirit; **prendre son é.** *Sp* to take a run (up); **d'un seul é.** in one bound. **2** (*animal*) elk.

élanc/er [elɑ̃se] **1** *vi* (*dent etc*) to give shooting pains. **2 s'é.** *vpr* (*bondir*) to leap *ou* rush (forward); **s'é. vers le ciel** (*tour*) to soar up (high) into the sky. ◆—**é** *a* (*personne, taille etc*) slender. ◆—**ement** *nm* shooting pain.

élargir [elarʒir] **1** *vt* (*chemin*) to widen; (*esprit, débat*) to broaden; – **s'é.** *vpr* (*sentier etc*) to widen out. **2** *vt* (*prisonnier*) to free.

élastique [elastik] *a* (*objet, caractère*) elastic; (*règlement, notion*) flexible, supple; – *nm* (*tissu*) elastic; (*lien*) elastic *ou* rubber band. ◆**élasticité** *nf* elasticity.

élection [elɛksjɔ̃] *nf* election; **é. partielle** by-election. ◆**électeur, -trice** *nmf* voter, elector. ◆**électoral, -aux** *a* (*campagne, réunion*) election-; **collège é.** electoral college. ◆**électorat** *nm* (*électeurs*) electorate, voters.

électricien [elɛktrisjɛ̃] *nm* electrician. ◆**électricité** *nf* electricity; **coupure d'é.** power cut. ◆**électrifier** *vt Rail* to electrify. ◆**électrique** *a* (*pendule, décharge*) electric; (*courant, fil*) electric(al); (*phénomène, effet*) *Fig* electric. ◆**électriser** *vt* (*animer*) *Fig* to electrify. ◆**électrocuter** *vt* to electrocute.

électrode [elɛktrɔd] *nf Él* electrode.

électrogène [elɛktrɔʒɛn] *a* **groupe é.** *Él* generator.

électroménager [elɛktrɔmenaʒe] *am* **appareil é.** household electrical appliance.

électron [elɛktrɔ̃] *nm* electron. ◆**électronicien, -ienne** *nmf* electronics engineer. ◆**électronique** *a* electronic; (*microscope*) electron-; – *nf* electronics.

électrophone [elɛktrɔfɔn] *nm* record player.

élégant [elegɑ̃] *a* (*style, mobilier, solution etc*) elegant; (*bien habillé*) smart, elegant. ◆**élégamment** *adv* elegantly; smartly. ◆**élégance** *nf* elegance.

élégie [eleʒi] *nf* elegy.

élément [elemɑ̃] *nm* (*composante, personne*) & *Ch* element; (*de meuble*) unit; (*d'ensemble*) *Math* member; *pl* (*notions*) rudiments, elements; **dans son é.** (*milieu*) in one's element. ◆**élémentaire** *a* elementary.

éléphant [elefɑ̃] *nm* elephant. ◆**éléphantesque** *a* (*énorme*) *Fam* elephantine.

élévateur [elevatœr] *am* **chariot é.** forklift truck.

élévation [elevasjɔ̃] *nf* raising; *Géom* elevation; **é. de** (*hausse*) rise in.

élève [elɛv] *nmf Scol* pupil.

élev/er [elve] *vt* (*prix, objection, voix etc*) to raise; (*enfant*) to bring up, raise; (*animal*) to breed, rear; (*âme*) to uplift, raise; – **s'é.** *vpr* (*prix, montagne, ton, avion etc*) to rise; **s'é. à** (*prix etc*) to amount to; **s'é. contre** to rise up against. ◆—**é** *a* (*haut*) high; (*noble*) noble; **bien/mal é.** well-/bad-mannered. ◆—**age** *nm* (*de bovins*) cattle rearing; **l'é. de** the breeding *ou* rearing of. ◆—**eur, -euse** *nmf* breeder.

élider [elide] *vt Ling* to elide.

éligible [eliʒibl] *a Pol* eligible (à for).

élimé [elime] *a* (*tissu*) threadbare, worn thin.

éliminer [elimine] *vt* to eliminate. ◆**élimination** *nf* elimination. ◆**éliminatoire** *a* & *nf* (*épreuve*) *Sp* heat, qualifying round.

élire* [elir] *vt Pol* to elect (à to).

élision [elizjɔ̃] *nf Ling* elision.

élite [elit] *nf* elite (**de** of); **d'é.** (*chef, sujet etc*) top-notch.

elle [ɛl] *pron* **1** (*sujet*) she; (*chose, animal*) it;

pl they; **e. est** she is; it is; **elles sont** they are. **2** (*complément*) her; (*chose, animal*) it; *pl* them; **pour e.** for her; **pour elles** for them; **plus grande qu'e./qu'elles** taller than her/them. ◆**e.-même** *pron* herself; (*chose, animal*) itself; *pl* themselves.

ellipse [elips] *nf Géom* ellipse. ◆**elliptique** *a* elliptical.

élocution [elɔkysjɔ̃] *nf* diction; **défaut d'é.** speech defect.

éloge [elɔʒ] *nm* praise; (*panégyrique*) eulogy; **faire l'é. de** to praise. ◆**élogieux, -euse** *a* laudatory.

éloign/er [elwaɲe] *vt* (*chose, personne*) to move *ou* take away (**de** from); (*clients*) to keep away; (*crainte, idée*) to get rid of, banish; (*date*) to put off; **é. qn de** (*sujet, but*) to take *ou* get s.o. away from; — **s'é.** *vpr* (*partir*) to move *ou* go away (**de** from); (*dans le passé*) to become (more) remote; **s'é. de** (*sujet, but*) to get away from. ◆—**é** *a* far-off, remote, distant; (*parent*) distant; **é. de** (*village, maison etc*) far (away) from; (*très différent*) far removed from. ◆—**ement** *nm* remoteness, distance; (*absence*) separation (**de** from); **avec l'é.** (*avec le recul*) with time.

élongation [elɔ̃gasjɔ̃] *nf Méd* pulled muscle.

éloquent [elɔkã] *a* eloquent. ◆**éloquence** *nf* eloquence.

élu, -ue [ely] *voir* **élire**; — *nmf Pol* elected member *ou* representative; **les élus** *Rel* the chosen, the elect.

élucider [elyside] *vt* to elucidate. ◆**élucidation** *nf* elucidation.

éluder [elyde] *vt* to elude, evade.

émacié [emasje] *a* emaciated.

émail, -aux [emaj, -o] *nm* enamel; **en é.** enamel-. ◆**émailler** *vt* to enamel.

émaillé [emaje] *a* **é. de fautes**/*etc* (*texte*) peppered with errors/*etc*.

émanciper [emãsipe] *vt* (*femmes*) to emancipate; — **s'é.** *vpr* to become emancipated. ◆**émancipation** *nf* emancipation.

émaner [emane] *vt* to emanate. ◆**émanation** *nf* emanation; **une é. de** *Fig* a product of.

emball/er [ãbale] **1** *vt* (*dans une caisse etc*) to pack; (*dans du papier*) to wrap (up). **2** *vt* (*moteur*) to race; **e. qn** (*passionner*) *Fam* to enthuse s.o., thrill s.o.; — **s'e.** *vpr* (*personne*) *Fam* to get carried away; (*cheval*) to bolt; (*moteur*) to race. ◆—**é** *a Fam* enthusiastic. ◆—**age** *nm* (*action*) ⸬ packing; wrapping; (*caisse*) packaging; (*papier*) wrapping (paper). ◆—**ement** *nm Fam* (sudden) enthusiasm.

embarcadère [ãbarkadɛr] *nm* landing place, quay.

embarcation [ãbarkasjɔ̃] *nf* (small) boat.

embardée [ãbarde] *nf Aut* (sudden) swerve; **faire une e.** to swerve.

embargo [ãbargo] *nm* embargo.

embarqu/er [ãbarke] *vt* (*passagers*) to embark, take on board; (*marchandises*) to load (up); (*voler*) *Fam* to walk off with; (*prisonnier*) *Fam* to cart off; **e. qn dans** (*affaire*) *Fam* to involve s.o. in, launch s.o. into; — *vi*, — **s'e.** *vpr* to embark, (go on) board; **s'e. dans** (*aventure etc*) *Fam* to embark on. ◆—**ement** *nm* (*de passagers*) boarding.

embarras [ãbara] *nm* (*malaise, gêne*) embarrassment; (*difficulté*) difficulty, trouble; (*obstacle*) obstacle; **dans l'e.** in difficulty; **faire des e.** (*chichis*) to make a fuss. ◆**embarrass/er** *vt* (*obstruer*) to clutter, encumber; **e. qn** to be in s.o.'s way; (*déconcerter*) to embarrass s.o., bother s.o.; **s'e. de** to burden oneself with; (*se soucier*) to bother oneself about. ◆—**ant** *a* (*paquet*) cumbersome; (*question*) embarrassing.

embauche [ãboʃ] *nf* (*action*) hiring; (*travail*) work. ◆**embaucher** *vt* (*ouvrier*) to hire, take on.

embaumer [ãbome] **1** *vt* (*cadavre*) to embalm. **2** *vt* (*parfumer*) to give a sweet smell to; — *vi* to smell sweet.

embell/ir [ãbelir] *vt* (*texte, vérité*) to embellish; **e. qn** to make s.o. attractive. ◆—**issement** *nm* (*de ville etc*) improvement, embellishment.

embêt/er [ãbete] *vt Fam* (*contrarier, taquiner*) to annoy, bother; (*raser*) to bore; — **s'e.** *vpr Fam* to get bored. ◆—**ant** *a Fam* annoying; boring. ◆—**ement** [-ɛtmã] *nm Fam* **un e.** (some) trouble *ou* bother; **des embêtements** trouble(s), bother.

emblée (d') [dãble] *adv* right away.

emblème [ãblɛm] *nm* emblem.

embobiner [ãbɔbine] *vt* (*tromper*) *Fam* to hoodwink.

emboîter [ãbwate] *vt*, — **s'e.** *vpr* (*pièces*) to fit into each other, fit together; **e. le pas à qn** to follow on s.o.'s heels; (*imiter*) *Fig* to follow in s.o.'s footsteps.

embonpoint [ãbɔ̃pwɛ̃] *nm* plumpness.

embouchure [ãbuʃyr] *nf* (*de cours d'eau*) mouth; *Mus* mouthpiece.

embourber (s') [sãburbe] *vpr* (*véhicule*) & *Fig* to get bogged down.

embourgeoiser (s') [sãburʒwaze] *vpr* to become middle-class.

embout [ãbu] *nm* (*de canne*) tip, end piece; (*de seringue*) nozzle.

embouteill/er [ãbuteje] *vt Aut* to jam, congest. ◆**—age** *nm* traffic jam.

emboutir [ãbutir] *vt* (*voiture*) to bash *ou* crash into; (*métal*) to stamp, emboss.

embranch/er (s') [sãbrãʃe] *vpr* (*voie*) to branch off. ◆**—ement** *nm* (*de voie*) junction, fork; (*de règne animal*) branch.

embras/er [ãbraze] *vt* to set ablaze; **— s'e.** *vpr* (*prendre feu*) to flare up. ◆**—ement** *nm* (*troubles*) flare-up.

embrasser [ãbrase] *vt* (*adopter, contenir*) to embrace; **e. qn** to kiss s.o.; (*serrer*) to embrace *ou* hug s.o.; **— s'e.** *vpr* to kiss (each other). ◆**embrassade** *nf* embrace, hug.

embrasure [ãbrazyr] *nf* (*de fenêtre, porte*) opening.

embray/er [ãbreje] *vi* to let in *ou* engage the clutch. ◆**—age** *nm* (*mécanisme, pédale*) *Aut* clutch.

embrigader [ãbrigade] *vt* to recruit.

embrocher [ãbrɔʃe] *vt Culin & Fig* to skewer.

embrouiller [ãbruje] *vt* (*fils*) to tangle (up); (*papiers etc*) to muddle (up), mix up; **e. qn** to confuse s.o., get s.o. muddled; **— s'e.** *vpr* to get confused *ou* muddled (**dans** in, with). ◆**embrouillamini** *nm Fam* muddle, mix-up. ◆**embrouillement** *nm* confusion, muddle.

embroussaillé [ãbrusaje] *a* (*barbe, chemin*) bushy.

embruns [ãbrœ̃] *nmpl* (sea) spray.

embryon [ãbrijɔ̃] *nm* embryo. ◆**embryonnaire** *a Méd & Fig* embryonic.

embûches [ãbyʃ] *nfpl* (*difficultés*) traps, pitfalls.

embuer [ãbɥe] *vt* (*vitre, yeux*) to mist up.

embusquer (s') [sãbyske] *vpr* to lie in ambush. ◆**embuscade** *nf* ambush.

éméché [emeʃe] *a* (*ivre*) *Fam* tipsy.

émeraude [emrod] *nf* emerald.

émerger [emerʒe] *vi* to emerge (**de** from).

émeri [emri] *nm* **toile (d')é.** emery cloth.

émerveill/er [emerveje] *vt* to amaze; **— s'é.** *vpr* to marvel, be filled with wonder (**de** at). ◆**—ement** *nm* wonder, amazement.

émett/re* [emetr] *vt* (*lumière, son etc*) to give out, emit; *Rad* to transmit, broadcast; (*cri*) to utter; (*opinion, vœu*) to express; (*timbre-poste, monnaie*) to issue; (*chèque*) to draw; (*emprunt*) *Com* to float. ◆**—eur** *nm* (*poste*) é. *Rad* transmitter.

émeute [emøt] *nf* riot. ◆**émeutier, -ière** *nmf* rioter.

émietter [emjete] *vt*, **— s'é.** *vpr* (*pain etc*) to crumble.

émigr/er [emigre] *vi* (*personne*) to emigrate. ◆**—ant, -ante** *nmf* emigrant. ◆**—é, -ée** *nmf* exile, émigré. ◆**émigration** *nf* emigration.

éminent [eminã] *a* eminent. ◆**éminemment** [-amã] *adv* eminently. ◆**éminence** *nf* **1** (*colline*) hillock. **2** **son É.** *Rel* his Eminence.

émissaire [emiser] *nm* emissary.

émission [emisjɔ̃] *nf* (*programme*) *TV Rad* broadcast; (*action*) emission (**de** of); (*de programme*) *TV Rad* transmission; (*de timbre-poste, monnaie*) issue.

emmagasiner [ãmagazine] *vt* to store (up).

emmanchure [ãmãʃyr] *nf* (*de vêtement*) arm hole.

emmêler [ãmele] *vt* to tangle (up).

emménag/er [ãmenaʒe] *vi* (*dans un logement*) to move in; **e. dans** to move into. ◆**—ement** *nm* moving in.

emmener [ãmne] *vt* to take (à to); (*prisonnier*) to take away; **e. qn faire une promenade** to take s.o. for a walk.

emmerd/er [ãmerde] *vt Arg* to annoy, bug; (*raser*) to bore stiff; **— s'e.** *vpr Arg* to get bored stiff. ◆**—ement** *nm Arg* bother, trouble. ◆**—eur, -euse** *nmf* (*personne*) *Arg* pain in the neck.

emmitoufler (s') [sãmitufle] *vpr* to wrap (oneself) up.

emmurer [ãmyre] *vt* (*personne*) to wall in.

émoi [emwa] *nm* excitement; **en é.** agog, excited.

émoluments [emɔlymã] *nmpl* remuneration.

émotion [emosjɔ̃] *nf* (*trouble*) excitement; (*sentiment*) emotion; **une é.** (*peur*) a scare. ◆**émotif, -ive** *a* emotional. ◆**émotionné** *a Fam* upset.

émouss/er [emuse] *vt* (*pointe*) to blunt; (*sentiment*) to dull. ◆**—é** *a* (*pointe*) blunt; (*sentiment*) dulled.

émouv/oir* [emuvwar] *vt* (*affecter*) to move, touch; **— s'é.** *vpr* to be moved *ou* touched. ◆**—ant** *a* moving, touching.

empailler [ãpaje] *vt* (*animal*) to stuff.

empaler (s') [sãpale] *vpr* to impale oneself.

empaqueter [ãpakte] *vt* to pack(age).

emparer (s') [sãpare] *vpr* **s'e. de** to seize, take hold of.

empât/er (s') [sãpate] *vpr* to fill out, get fat(ter). ◆**—é** *a* fleshy, fat.

empêch/er [ãpeʃe] *vt* to prevent, stop; **e. qn de faire** to prevent *ou* stop s.o. (from) doing; **n'empêche qu'elle a raison** *Fam* all the same she's right; **n'empêche!** *Fam* all the same!; **elle ne peut pas s'e. de rire** she can't help laughing. ◆**—ement** [-ɛʃmɑ̃] *nm* difficulty, hitch; **avoir un e.** to be unavoidably detained.

empereur [ɑ̃prœr] *nm* emperor.

empeser [ɑ̃pəze] *vt* to starch.

empester [ɑ̃pɛste] *vt* (*pièce*) to make stink, stink out; (*tabac etc*) to stink of; **e. qn** to stink s.o. out; *— vi* to stink.

empêtrer (s') [sɑ̃petre] *vpr* to get entangled (**dans** in).

emphase [ɑ̃faz] *nf* pomposity. ◆**emphatique** *a* pompous.

empiéter [ɑ̃pjete] *vi* **e. sur** to encroach upon. ◆**empiétement** *nm* encroachment.

empiffrer (s') [sɑ̃pifre] *vpr Fam* to gorge *ou* stuff oneself (**de** with).

empil/er [ɑ̃pile] *vt*, **— s'e.** *vpr* to pile up (**sur** on); **s'e. dans** (*personnes*) to pile into (*building, car etc*). ◆**—ement** *nm* (*tas*) pile.

empire [ɑ̃pir] *nm* (*territoires*) empire; (*autorité*) hold, influence; **sous l'e. de** (*peur etc*) in the grip of.

empirer [ɑ̃pire] *vi* to worsen, get worse.

empirique [ɑ̃pirik] *a* empirical. ◆**empirisme** *nm* empiricism.

emplacement [ɑ̃plasmɑ̃] *nm* site, location; (*de stationnement*) place.

emplâtre [ɑ̃plɑtr] *nm* (*onguent*) *Méd* plaster.

emplette [ɑ̃plɛt] *nf* purchase; *pl* shopping.

emplir [ɑ̃plir] *vt*, **— s'e.** *vpr* to fill (**de** with).

emploi [ɑ̃plwa] *nm* **1** (*usage*) use; **e. du temps** timetable; **mode d'e.** directions (for use). **2** (*travail*) job, position, employment; **l'e.** (*travail*) *Écon Pol* employment; **sans e.** unemployed. ◆**employ/er** *vt* (*utiliser*) to use; **e. qn** (*occuper*) to employ s.o.; **— s'e.** *vpr* (*expression etc*) to be used; **s'e. à faire** to devote oneself to doing. ◆**—é, -ée** *nmf* employee; (*de bureau, banque*) clerk, employee; **e. des postes/etc** postal/etc worker; **e. de magasin** shop assistant, *Am* sales clerk. ◆**employeur, -euse** *nmf* employer.

empocher [ɑ̃pɔʃe] *vt* (*argent*) to pocket.

empoigner [ɑ̃pwaɲe] *vt* (*saisir*) to grab, grasp; **— s'e.** *vpr* to come to blows, fight. ◆**empoignade** *nf* (*querelle*) fight.

empoisonn/er [ɑ̃pwazɔne] *vt* (*personne, aliment, atmosphère*) to poison; (*empester*) to stink out; (*gâter, altérer*) to trouble, bedevil; **e. qn** (*embêter*) *Fam* to get on s.o.'s nerves; **— s'e.** *vpr* (*par accident*) to be poisoned; (*volontairement*) to poison oneself. ◆**—ant** *a* (*embêtant*) *Fam* irritating.

◆**—ement** *nm* poisoning; (*ennui*) *Fam* problem, trouble.

emport/er [ɑ̃pɔrte] *vt* (*prendre*) to take (away) (**avec soi** with one); (*enlever*) to take away; (*prix, trophée*) to carry off; (*décision*) to carry; (*entraîner*) to carry along *ou* away; (*par le vent*) to blow off *ou* away; (*par les vagues*) to sweep away; (*par la maladie*) to carry off; **l'e. sur qn** to get the upper hand over s.o.; **se laisser e.** *Fig* to get carried away (**par** by); **— s'e.** *vpr* to lose one's temper (**contre** with). ◆**—é** *a* (*caractère*) hot-tempered. ◆**—ement** *nm* anger; *pl* fits of anger.

empoté [ɑ̃pɔte] *a Fam* clumsy.

empourprer (s') [sɑ̃purpre] *vpr* to turn crimson.

empreint [ɑ̃prɛ̃] *a* **e. de** stamped with, heavy with.

empreinte [ɑ̃prɛ̃t] *nf* (*marque*) & *Fig* mark, stamp; **e. digitale** fingerprint; **e. des pas** footprint.

empress/er (s') [sɑ̃prese] *vpr* **s'e. de faire** to hasten to do; **s'e. auprès de qn** to busy oneself with s.o., be attentive to s.o.; **s'e. autour de qn** to rush around s.o. ◆**—é** *a* eager, attentive; **e. à faire** eager to do. ◆**—ement** [-ɛsmɑ̃] *nm* (*hâte*) eagerness; (*auprès de qn*) attentiveness.

emprise [ɑ̃priz] *nf* ascendancy, hold (**sur** over).

emprisonn/er [ɑ̃prizɔne] *vt Jur* to imprison; (*enfermer*) *Fig* to confine. ◆**—ement** *nm* imprisonment.

emprunt [ɑ̃prœ̃] *nm* (*argent*) *Com* loan; (*mot*) *Ling* borrowed word; **un e. à** *Ling* a borrowing from; **l'e. de qch** the borrowing of sth; **d'e.** borrowed; **nom d'e.** assumed name. ◆**emprunt/er** *vt* (*obtenir*) to borrow (**à qn** from s.o.); (*route etc*) to use; (*nom*) to assume; **e. à** (*tirer de*) to derive *ou* borrow from. ◆**—é** *a* (*gêné*) ill-at-ease.

empuantir [ɑ̃pɥɑtir] *vt* to make stink, stink out.

ému [emy] *voir* **émouvoir**; *— a* (*attendri*) moved; (*apeuré*) nervous; (*attristé*) upset; **une voix émue** a voice charged with emotion.

émulation [emylasjɔ̃] *nf* emulation.

émule [emyl] *nmf* imitator, follower.

en¹ [ɑ̃] *prép* **1** (*lieu*) in; (*direction*) to; **être en ville/en France** to be in town/in France; **aller en ville/en France** to go (in)to town/to France. **2** (*temps*) in; **en été** in summer; **en février** in February; **d'heure en heure** from hour to hour. **3** (*moyen, état etc*) by; in; at; on; **en avion** by plane; **en groupe**

in a group; **en mer** at sea; **en guerre** at war; **en fleur** in flower; **en congé** on leave; **en vain** in vain. **4** (*matière*) in; **en bois** wooden, in wood; **chemise en nylon** nylon shirt; **c'est en or** it's (made of) gold. **5** (*comme*) **en cadeau** as a present; **en ami** as a friend. **6** (+ *participe présent*) **en mangeant/chantant/etc** while eating/singing/etc; **en apprenant que** . . . on hearing that . . . ; **en souriant** smiling, with a smile; **en ne disant rien** by saying nothing; **sortir en courant** to run out. **7** (*transformation*) into; **traduire en** to translate into.

en² [ɑ̃] *pron & adv* **1** (= *de là*) from there; **j'en viens** I've just come from there. **2** (= *de ça, lui, eux etc*) **il en est content** he's pleased with it *ou* him *ou* them; **en parler** to talk about it; **en mourir** to die of *ou* from it; **elle m'en frappa** she struck me with it. **3** (*partitif*) some; **j'en ai** I have some; **en veux-tu?** do you want some *ou* any?; **je t'en supplie** I beg you (to).

encadr/er [ɑ̃kadre] *vt* (*tableau*) to frame; (*entourer d'un trait*) to box in; (*troupes, étudiants*) to supervise, train; (*prisonnier, accusé*) to flank. ◆**—ement** *nm* (*action*) framing; supervision; (*de porte, photo*) frame; (*décor*) setting; (*personnel*) training and supervisory staff.

encaissé [ɑ̃kese] *a* (*vallée*) deep.

encaisser [ɑ̃kese] *vt* (*argent, loyer etc*) to collect; (*effet, chèque*) *Com* to cash; (*coup*) *Fam* to take; **je ne peux pas l'e.** *Fam* I can't stand him *ou* her. ◆**encaissement** *nm* (*de loyer etc*) collection; (*de chèque*) cashing.

encapuchonné [ɑ̃kapyʃɔne] *a* hooded.

encart [ɑ̃kar] *nm* (*feuille*) insert. ◆**encarter** *vt* to insert.

en-cas [ɑ̃ka] *nm inv* (*repas*) snack.

encastrer [ɑ̃kastre] *vt* to build in (**dans** to), embed (**dans** into).

encaustique [ɑ̃kostik] *nf* (wax) polish. ◆**encaustiquer** *vt* to wax, polish.

enceinte [ɑ̃sɛ̃t] **1** *af* (*femme*) pregnant; **e. de six mois/etc** six months/etc pregnant. **2** *nf* (*muraille*) (surrounding) wall; (*espace*) enclosure; **e. acoustique** (loud)speakers.

encens [ɑ̃sɑ̃] *nm* incense. ◆**encensoir** *nm Rel* censer.

encercler [ɑ̃sɛrkle] *vt* to surround, encircle.

enchaîner [ɑ̃ʃene] *vt* (*animal*) to chain (up); (*prisonnier*) to put in chains, chain (up); (*assembler*) to link (up), connect; — *vi* (*continuer à parler*) to continue; — **s'e.** *vpr* (*idées etc*) to be linked (up). ◆**enchaînement** *nm* (*succession*) chain, series; (*liaison*) link(ing) (**de** between, of).

enchant/er [ɑ̃ʃɑ̃te] *vt* (*ravir*) to delight, enchant; (*ensorceler*) to bewitch, enchant. ◆**—é** *a* (*ravi*) delighted (**de** with, **que** (+ *sub*) that); **e. de faire votre connaissance!** pleased to meet you! ◆**—ement** *nm* delight; enchantment; **comme par e.** as if by magic. ◆**—eur** *a* delightful, enchanting; — *nm* (*sorcier*) magician.

enchâsser [ɑ̃ʃase] *vt* (*diamant*) to set, embed.

enchère [ɑ̃ʃɛr] *nf* (*offre*) bid; **vente aux enchères** auction; **mettre aux enchères** to (put up for) auction. ◆**enchér/ir** *vi* **e. sur qn** to outbid s.o. ◆**—isseur** *nm* bidder.

enchevêtrer [ɑ̃ʃvetre] *vt* to (en)tangle; — **s'e.** *vpr* to get entangled (**dans** in). ◆**enchevêtrement** *nm* tangle, entanglement.

enclave [ɑ̃klav] *nf* enclave. ◆**enclaver** *vt* to enclose (completely).

enclencher [ɑ̃klɑ̃ʃe] *vt Tech* to engage.

enclin [ɑ̃klɛ̃] *am* **e. à** inclined *ou* prone to.

enclore [ɑ̃klɔr] *vt* (*terrain*) to enclose. ◆**enclos** *nm* (*terrain, clôture*) enclosure.

enclume [ɑ̃klym] *nf* anvil.

encoche [ɑ̃kɔʃ] *nf* notch, nick (**à** in).

encoignure [ɑ̃kwaɲyr] *nf* corner.

encoller [ɑ̃kɔle] *vt* to paste.

encolure [ɑ̃kɔlyr] *nf* (*de cheval, vêtement*) neck; (*tour du cou*) collar (size).

encombre (sans) [sɑ̃zɑ̃kɔ̃br] *adv* without a hitch.

encombr/er [ɑ̃kɔ̃bre] *vt* (*couloir, pièce etc*) to clutter up (**de** with); (*rue*) to congest, clog (**de** with); **e. qn** to hamper s.o.; **s'e. de** to burden *ou* saddle oneself with. ◆**—ant** *a* (*paquet*) bulky, cumbersome; (*présence*) awkward. ◆**—é** *a* (*profession, marché*) overcrowded, saturated. ◆**—ement** *nm* (*embarras*) clutter; *Aut* traffic jam; (*volume*) bulk(iness).

encontre de (à l') [alɑ̃kɔ̃trədə] *adv* against; (*contrairement à*) contrary to.

encore [ɑ̃kɔr] *adv* **1** (*toujours*) still; **tu es e. là?** are you still here? **2** (*avec négation*) yet; **pas e.** not yet; **ne pars pas e.** don't go yet; **je ne suis pas e. prêt** I'm not ready yet, I'm still not ready. **3** (*de nouveau*) again; **essaie e.** try again. **4** (*de plus*) **e. un café** another coffee, one more coffee; **e. une fois** (once) again, once more; **e. un** another (one), one more; **e. du pain** (some) more bread; **que veut-il e.?** what else *ou* more does he want?; **e. quelque chose** something else; **qui/quoi e.?** who/what else?; **chante e.** sing some more. **5** (*avec comparatif*) even, still; **e. mieux** even better, better still. **6** (*aussi*) also. **7** si e. (*si seulement*) if only; **et e.!** (*à peine*) if that!, only just! **8** e. que (+ *sub*) although.

encourag/er [ãkuraʒe] *vt* to encourage (à faire to do). ◆**—eant** *a* encouraging. ◆**—ement** *nm* encouragement.

encourir* [ãkurir] *vt* (*amende etc*) to incur.

encrasser [ãkrase] *vt* to clog up (with dirt).

encre [ãkr] *nf* ink; **e. de Chine** Indian ink; **e. sympathique** invisible ink. ◆**encrier** *nm* inkwell, inkpot.

encroûter (s') [sãkrute] *vpr Péj* to get set in one's ways; **s'e. dans** (*habitude*) to get stuck in.

encyclique [ãsiklik] *nf Rel* encyclical.

encyclopédie [ãsiklɔpedi] *nf* encyclop(a)edia. ◆**encyclopédique** *a* encyclop(a)edic.

endémique [ãdemik] *a* endemic.

endetter [ãdete] *vt* **e. qn** to get s.o. into debt; **— s'e.** *vpr* to get into debt. ◆**endettement** *nm* (*dettes*) debts.

endeuiller [ãdœje] *vt* to plunge into mourning.

endiablé [ãdjable] *a* (*rythme etc*) frantic, wild.

endiguer [ãdige] *vt* (*fleuve*) to dam (up); (*réprimer*) *Fig* to stem.

endimanché [ãdimãʃe] *a* in one's Sunday best.

endive [ãdiv] *nf* chicory, endive.

endoctrin/er [ãdɔktrine] *vt* to indoctrinate. ◆**—ement** *nm* indoctrination.

endolori [ãdɔlɔri] *a* painful, aching.

endommager [ãdɔmaʒe] *vt* to damage.

endorm/ir* [ãdɔrmir] *vt* (*enfant, patient*) to put to sleep; (*ennuyer*) to send to sleep; (*soupçons etc*) to lull; (*douleur*) to deaden; **— s'e.** *vpr* to fall asleep, go to sleep. ◆**—i** *a* asleep, sleeping; (*indolent*) *Fam* sluggish.

endosser [ãdose] *vt* (*vêtement*) to put on, don; (*responsabilité*) to assume; (*chèque*) to endorse.

endroit [ãdrwa] *nm* **1** place, spot; (*de film, livre*) part, place. **2** (*de tissu*) right side; **à l'e.** (*vêtement*) right side out, the right way round.

enduire* [ãdɥir] *vt* to smear, coat (**de** with). ◆**enduit** *nm* coating; (*de mur*) plaster.

endurant [ãdyrã] *a* hardy, tough. ◆**endurance** *nf* endurance.

endurc/ir [ãdyrsir] *vt* to harden; **s'e. à** (*personne*) to become hardened to (*pain etc*). ◆**—i** *a* hardened; (*célibataire*) confirmed. ◆**—issement** *nm* hardening.

endurer [ãdyre] *vt* to endure, bear.

énergie [enɛrʒi] *nf* energy; **avec é.** (*protester etc*) forcefully. ◆**énergétique** *a* (*ressources etc*) energy-. ◆**énergique** *a* (*dynamique*) energetic; (*remède*) powerful; (*mesure, ton*) forceful. ◆**énergiquement** *adv* (*protester etc*) energetically.

énergumène [enɛrgymɛn] *nmf Péj* rowdy character.

énerv/er [enɛrve] *vt* **é. qn** (*irriter*) to get on s.o.'s nerves; (*rendre énervé*) to make s.o. nervous; **— s'é.** *vpr* to get worked up. ◆**—é** *a* on edge, irritated. ◆**—ement** *nm* irritation, nervousness.

enfant [ãfã] *nmf* child (*pl* children); **e. en bas âge** infant; **un e. de** (*originaire*) a native of; **attendre un e.** to expect a baby *ou* a child; **e. trouvé** foundling; **e. de chœur** *Rel* altar boy; **e. prodige** child prodigy; **e. prodigue** prodigal son; **bon e.** (*caractère*) good natured. ◆**enfance** *nf* childhood; **première e.** infancy, early childhood; **dans son e.** (*science etc*) in its infancy. ◆**enfanter** *vt* to give birth to; **—** *vi* to give birth. ◆**enfantillage** *nm* childishness. ◆**enfantin** *a* (*voix, joie*) childlike; (*langage, jeu*) children's; (*puéril*) childish; (*simple*) easy.

enfer [ãfɛr] *nm* hell; **d'e.** (*vision, bruit*) infernal; **feu d'e.** roaring fire; **à un train d'e.** at breakneck speed.

enfermer [ãfɛrme] *vt* (*personne etc*) to shut up, lock up; (*objet précieux*) to lock up, shut away; (*jardin*) to enclose; **s'e. dans** (*chambre etc*) to shut *ou* lock oneself (up) in; (*attitude etc*) *Fig* to maintain stubbornly.

enferrer (s') [sãfere] *vpr* **s'e. dans** to get caught up in.

enfiévré [ãfjevre] *a* (*surexcité*) feverish.

enfiler [ãfile] *vt* (*aiguille*) to thread; (*perles etc*) to string; (*vêtement*) *Fam* to slip on, pull on; (*rue, couloir*) to take; **s'e. dans** (*rue etc*) to take. ◆**enfilade** *nf* (*série*) row, string.

enfin [ãfɛ̃] *adv* (*à la fin*) finally, at last; (*en dernier lieu*) lastly; (*en somme*) in a word; (*conclusion résignée*) well; **e. bref** (*en somme*) *Fam* in a word; **il est grand, e. pas trop petit** he's tall — well, not too short anyhow; **mais e.** but; (*mais*) **e.!** for heaven's sake!

enflamm/er [ãflame] *vt* to set fire to, ignite; (*allumette*) to light; (*irriter*) *Méd* to inflame; (*imagination, colère*) to excite, inflame; **— s'e.** *vpr* to catch fire, ignite; **s'e. de colère** to flare up. ◆**—é** *a* (*discours*) fiery.

enfler [ɑ̃fle] *vt* to swell; (*voix*) to raise; – *vi* *Méd* to swell (up). ◆**enflure** *nf* swelling.

enfonc/er [ɑ̃fɔ̃se] *vt* (*clou etc*) to knock in, drive in; (*chapeau*) to push *ou* force down; (*porte, voiture*) to smash in; **e. dans** (*couteau, mains etc*) to plunge into; – *vi*, – **s'e.** *vpr* (*s'enliser*) to sink (**dans** into); **s'e. dans** (*pénétrer*) to plunge into, disappear (deep) into. ◆**–é** *a* (*yeux*) sunken.

enfouir [ɑ̃fwir] *vt* to bury.

enfourcher [ɑ̃furʃe] *vt* (*cheval etc*) to mount, bestride.

enfourner [ɑ̃furne] *vt* to put in the oven.

enfreindre* [ɑ̃frɛ̃dr] *vt* to infringe.

enfuir* (s') [sɑ̃fɥir] *vpr* to run away *ou* off, flee (**de** from).

enfumer [ɑ̃fyme] *vt* (*pièce*) to fill with smoke; (*personne*) to smoke out.

engag/er [ɑ̃gaʒe] *vt* (*bijou etc*) to pawn; (*parole*) to pledge; (*discussion, combat*) to start; (*clef etc*) to insert (**dans** into); (*capitaux*) to tie up, invest; **e. la bataille avec** to join battle with; **e. qn** (*lier*) to bind s.o., commit s.o.; (*embaucher*) to hire s.o., engage s.o.; **e. qn dans** (*affaire etc*) to involve s.o. in; **e. qn à faire** (*exhorter*) to urge s.o. to do; – **s'e.** *vpr* (*s'inscrire*) *Mil* to enlist; *Sp* to enter; (*au service d'une cause*) to commit oneself; (*action*) to start; **s'e. à faire** to commit oneself to doing, undertake to do; **s'e. dans** (*voie*) to enter; (*affaire etc*) to get involved in. ◆**–eant** *a* engaging, inviting. ◆**–é** *a* (*écrivain etc*) committed. ◆**–ement** *nm* (*promesse*) commitment; (*commencement*) start; (*de recrues*) *Mil* enlistment; (*inscription*) *Sp* entry; (*combat*) *Mil* engagement; **prendre l'e. de** to undertake to.

engelure [ɑ̃ʒlyr] *nf* chilblain.

engendrer [ɑ̃ʒɑ̃dre] *vt* (*procréer*) to beget; (*causer*) to generate, engender.

engin [ɑ̃ʒɛ̃] *nm* machine, device; (*projectile*) missile; **e. explosif** explosive device.

englober [ɑ̃glɔbe] *vt* to include, embrace.

engloutir [ɑ̃glutir] *vt* (*avaler*) to wolf (down), gobble (up); (*faire sombrer ou disparaître*) to engulf.

engorger [ɑ̃gɔrʒe] *vt* to block up, clog.

engouement [ɑ̃gumɑ̃] *nm* craze.

engouffrer [ɑ̃gufre] *vt* (*avaler*) to wolf (down); (*fortune*) to consume; **s'e. dans** to sweep *ou* rush into.

engourd/ir [ɑ̃gurdir] *vt* (*membre*) to numb; (*esprit*) to dull; – **s'e.** *vpr* to go numb, become dull. ◆**–issement** *nm* numbness; dullness.

engrais [ɑ̃grɛ] *nm* (*naturel*) manure; (*chimique*) fertilizer.

engraisser [ɑ̃grese] *vt* (*animal*) to fatten (up); – *vi*, – **s'e.** *vpr* to get fat, put on weight.

engrenage [ɑ̃grənaʒ] *nm* *Tech* gears; *Fig* mesh, chain, web.

engueuler [ɑ̃gœle] *vt* **e. qn** *Fam* to swear at s.o., give s.o. hell. ◆**engueulade** *nf* *Fam* (*réprimande*) dressing-down, severe talking-to; (*dispute*) slanging match, row.

enhardir [ɑ̃ardir] *vt* to make bolder; **s'e. à faire** to make bold to do.

énième [ɛnjɛm] *a* *Fam* umpteenth, nth.

énigme [enigm] *nf* enigma, riddle. ◆**énigmatique** *a* enigmatic.

enivrer [ɑ̃nivre] *vt* (*soûler, troubler*) to intoxicate; – **s'e.** *vpr* to get drunk (**de** on).

enjamber [ɑ̃ʒɑ̃be] *vt* to step over; (*pont etc*) to span (*river etc*). ◆**enjambée** *nf* stride.

enjeu, -x [ɑ̃ʒø] *nm* (*mise*) stake(s).

enjoindre [ɑ̃ʒwɛ̃dr] *vt* **e. à qn de faire** *Litt* to order s.o. to do.

enjôler [ɑ̃ʒole] *vt* to wheedle, coax.

enjoliv/er [ɑ̃ʒolive] *vt* to embellish. ◆**–eur** *nm* *Aut* hubcap.

enjoué [ɑ̃ʒwe] *a* playful. ◆**enjouement** *nm* playfulness.

enlacer [ɑ̃lase] *vt* to entwine; (*serrer dans ses bras*) to clasp.

enlaidir [ɑ̃ledir] *vt* to make ugly; – *vi* to grow ugly.

enlev/er [ɑ̃lve] *vt* to take away *ou* off, remove (**à qn** from s.o.); (*ordures*) to collect; (*vêtement*) to take off, remove; (*tache*) to take out, lift, remove; (*enfant etc*) to kidnap, abduct; – **s'e.** *vpr* (*tache*) to come out; (*vernis*) to come off. ◆**–é** *a* (*scène, danse etc*) well-rendered. ◆**enlèvement** *nm* kidnapping, abduction; (*d'un objet*) removal; (*des ordures*) collection.

enliser (s') [sɑ̃lize] *vpr* (*véhicule*) & *Fig* to get bogged down (**dans** in).

enneigé [ɑ̃neʒe] *a* snow-covered. ◆**enneigement** *nm* snow coverage; **bulletin d'e.** snow report.

ennemi, -ie [ɛnmi] *nmf* enemy; – *a* (*personne*) hostile (**de** to); (*pays etc*) enemy-.

ennui [ɑ̃nɥi] *nm* boredom; (*mélancolie*) weariness; **un e.** (*tracas*) (some) trouble *ou* bother; **des ennuis** trouble(s), bother; **l'e., c'est que ...** the annoying thing is that ....

ennuy/er [ɑ̃nɥije] *vt* (*agacer*) to annoy, bother; (*préoccuper*) to bother; (*fatiguer*) to bore; – **s'e.** *vpr* to get bored. ◆**–é**

a (*air*) bored; **je suis e.** that annoys *ou* bothers me. ◆**ennuyeux, -euse** *a* (*fastidieux*) boring; (*contrariant*) annoying.

énonc/er [enɔ̃se] *vt* to state, express. ◆**—é** *nm* (*de texte*) wording, terms; (*phrase*) Ling utterance.

enorgueillir [ɑ̃nɔrgœjir] *vt* to make proud; **s'e. de** to pride oneself on.

énorme [enɔrm] *a* enormous, huge, tremendous. ◆**énormément** *adv* enormously, tremendously; **e. de** an enormous *ou* tremendous amount of. ◆**énormité** *nf* (*dimension*) enormity; (*faute*) (enormous) blunder.

enquérir (s') [sɑ̃kerir] *vpr* **s'e. de** to inquire about.

enquête [ɑ̃kɛt] *nf* (*de police etc*) investigation; (*judiciaire, administrative*) inquiry; (*sondage*) survey. ◆**enquêter** *vi* (*police etc*) to investigate; **e. sur** (*crime*) to investigate. ◆**enquêteur, -euse** *nmf* investigator.

enquiquiner [ɑ̃kikine] *vt* Fam to annoy, bug.

enraciner (s') [sɑ̃rasine] *vpr* to take root; **enraciné dans** (*personne, souvenir*) rooted in; **bien enraciné** (*préjugé etc*) deep-rooted.

enrag/er [ɑ̃raʒe] *vi* **e. de faire** to be furious about doing; **faire e. qn** to get on s.o.'s nerves. ◆**—eant** *a* infuriating. ◆**—é** *a* (*chien*) rabid, mad; (*joueur etc*) Fam fanatical (**de** about); **rendre/devenir e.** (*furieux*) to make/become furious.

enrayer [ɑ̃reje] *vt* (*maladie etc*) to check; — **s'e.** *vpr* (*fusil*) to jam.

enregistr/er [ɑ̃rʒistre] *vt* **1** (*inscrire*) to record; (*sur registre*) to register; (*constater*) to note, register; (**faire**) **e.** (*bagages*) to register, *Am* check. **2** (*musique, émission etc*) to record. ◆**—ement** *nm* (*des bagages*) registration, *Am* checking; (*d'un acte*) registration; (*sur bande etc*) recording. ◆**—eur, -euse** *a* (*appareil*) recording-; **caisse enregistreuse** cash register.

enrhumer [ɑ̃ryme] *vt* **e. qn** to give s.o. a cold; **être enrhumé** to have a cold; — **s'e.** *vpr* to catch a cold.

enrich/ir [ɑ̃riʃir] *vt* to enrich (**de** with); — **s'e.** *vpr* (*personne*) to get rich. ◆**—issement** *nm* enrichment.

enrober [ɑ̃rɔbe] *vt* to coat (**de** in); **enrobé de chocolat** chocolate-coated.

enrôl/er [ɑ̃role] *vt*, — **s'e.** *vpr* to enlist. ◆**—ement** *nm* enlistment.

enrou/er (s') [sɑ̃rwe] *vpr* to get hoarse. ◆**—é** *a* hoarse. ◆**—ement** [ɑ̃rumɑ̃] *nm* hoarseness.

enrouler [ɑ̃rule] *vt* (*fil etc*) to wind; (*tapis, cordage*) to roll up; **s'e. dans** (*couvertures*) to roll *ou* wrap oneself up in; **s'e. sur** **autour de qch** to wind round sth.

ensabler [ɑ̃sable] *vt*, — **s'e.** *vpr* (*port*) to silt up.

ensanglanté [ɑ̃sɑ̃glɑ̃te] *a* bloodstained.

enseigne [ɑ̃sɛɲ] **1** *nf* (*de magasin etc*) sign; **e. lumineuse** neon sign; **logés à la même e.** *Fig* in the same boat. **2** *nm* **e. de vaisseau** lieutenant, *Am* ensign.

enseign/er [ɑ̃seɲe] *vt* to teach; **e. qch à qn** to teach s.o. sth; — *vi* to teach. ◆**—ant, -ante** [-ɛɲɑ̃, -ɑ̃t] *a* (*corps*) teaching-; — *nmf* teacher. ◆**—ement** [-ɛɲmɑ̃] *nm* education; (*action, métier*) teaching.

ensemble [ɑ̃sɑ̃bl] **1** *adv* together. **2** *nm* (*d'objets*) group, set; *Math* set; *Mus* ensemble; (*mobilier*) suite; (*vêtement féminin*) outfit; (*harmonie*) unity; **l'e. du personnel** (*totalité*) the whole (of the) staff; **l'e. des enseignants** all (of) the teachers; **dans l'e.** on the whole; **d'e.** (*vue etc*) general; **grand e.** (*quartier*) housing complex *ou* *Am* development; (*ville*) = new town, = *Am* planned community. ◆**ensemblier** *nm* (interior) decorator.

ensemencer [ɑ̃səmɑ̃se] *vt* (*terre*) to sow.

ensevelir [ɑ̃səvlir] *vt* to bury.

ensoleillé [ɑ̃sɔleje] *a* (*endroit, journée*) sunny.

ensommeillé [ɑ̃sɔmeje] *a* sleepy.

ensorceler [ɑ̃sɔrsəle] *vt* (*envoûter, séduire*) to bewitch. ◆**ensorcellement** *nm* (*séduction*) spell.

ensuite [ɑ̃sɥit] *adv* (*puis*) next, then; (*plus tard*) afterwards.

ensuivre* (s') [sɑ̃sɥivr] *vpr* to follow, ensue; — *v imp* **il s'ensuit que** it follows that.

entacher [ɑ̃taʃe] *vt* (*honneur etc*) to sully, taint.

entaille [ɑ̃taj] *nf* (*fente*) notch; (*blessure*) gash, slash. ◆**entailler** *vt* to notch; to gash, slash.

entame [ɑ̃tam] *nf* first slice.

entamer [ɑ̃tame] *vt* (*pain, peau etc*) to cut (into); (*bouteille, boîte etc*) to start (on); (*négociations etc*) to enter into, start; (*sujet*) to broach; (*capital*) to break *ou* eat into; (*métal, plastique*) to damage; (*résolution, réputation*) to shake.

entass/er [ɑ̃tase] *vt*, — **s'e.** *vpr* (*objets*) to pile up, heap up; (**s')e. dans** (*passagers etc*) to crowd *ou* pack *ou* pile into; **ils s'entassaient sur la plage** they were crowded *ou* packed (together) on the beach.

◆**—ement** *nm* (*tas*) pile, heap; (*de gens*) crowding.

entend/re [ãtãdr] *vt* to hear; (*comprendre*) to understand; (*vouloir*) to intend, mean; **e. parler de** to hear of; **e. dire que** to hear (it said) that; **e. raison** to listen to reason; **laisser e. à qn que** to give s.o. to understand that; **— s'e.** *vpr* (*être entendu*) to be heard; (*être compris*) to be understood; **s'e.** (**sur**) (*être d'accord*) to agree (on); **s'e.** (**avec qn**) (*s'accorder*) to get on (with s.o.); **on ne s'entend plus!** (*à cause du bruit etc*) we can't hear ourselves speak!; **il s'y entend** (*est expert*) he knows all about that. ◆**—u** *a* (*convenu*) agreed; (*compris*) understood; (*sourire*, *air*) knowing; **e.!** all right!; **bien e.** of course. ◆**—ement** *nm* (*faculté*) understanding. ◆**entente** *nf* (*accord*) agreement, understanding; (**bonne**) **e.** (*amitié*) good relationship, harmony.

entériner [ãterine] *vt* to ratify.

enterrer [ãtere] *vt* (*mettre en ou sous terre*) to bury; (*projet*) *Fig* to scrap. ◆**enterrement** *nm* burial; (*funérailles*) funeral.

entêtant [ãtetã] *a* (*enivrant*) heady.

en-tête [ãtɛt] *nm* (*de papier*) heading; **papier à en-tête** headed paper.

entêt/er (**s'**) [sãtete] *vpr* to persist (**à faire** in doing). ◆**—é** *a* (*têtu*) stubborn; (*persévérant*) persistent. ◆**—ement** [ãtɛtmã] *nm* stubbornness; (*à faire qch*) persistence.

enthousiasme [ãtuzjasm] *nm* enthusiasm. ◆**enthousiasmer** *vt* to fill with enthusiasm, enthuse; **s'e.** **pour** to be *ou* get enthusiastic over, enthuse over. ◆**enthousiaste** *a* enthusiastic.

enticher (**s'**) [sãtiʃe] *vpr* **s'e. de** to become infatuated with.

entier, -ière [ãtje, -jɛr] **1** *a* (*total*) whole, entire; (*absolu*) absolute, complete, entire; (*intact*) intact; **payer place entière** to pay full price; **le pays tout e.** the whole *ou* entire country; — *nm* (*unité*) whole; **en e., dans son e.** in its entirety, completely. **2** *a* (*caractère, personne*) unyielding. ◆**entièrement** *adv* entirely.

entité [ãtite] *nf* entity.

entonner [ãtɔne] *vt* (*air*) to start singing.

entonnoir [ãtɔnwar] *nm* (*ustensile*) funnel.

entorse [ãtɔrs] *nf Méd* sprain; **e. à** (*règlement*) infringement of.

entortill/er [ãtɔrtije] *vt* **e. qch autour de qch** (*papier etc*) to wrap sth around sth; **e. qn** *Fam* to dupe s.o., get round s.o.; — **s'e.** *vpr* (*lierre etc*) to wind, twist. ◆**—é** *a* (*phrase etc*) convoluted.

entour/er [ãture] *vt* to surround (**de** with);

(*envelopper*) to wrap (**de** in); **e. qn de ses bras** to put one's arms round s.o.; **s'e. de** to surround oneself with. ◆**—age** *nm* (*proches*) circle of family and friends.

entourloupette [ãturlupɛt] *nf Fam* nasty trick.

entracte [ãtrakt] *nm Th* interval, *Am* intermission.

entraide [ãtrɛd] *nf* mutual aid. ◆**s'entraider** [sãtrede] *vpr* to help each other.

entrailles [ãtraj] *nfpl* entrails.

entrain [ãtrɛ̃] *nm* spirit, liveliness; **plein d'e.** lively.

entraîn/er [ãtrene] **1** *vt* (*charrier*) to sweep *ou* carry away; (*roue*) *Tech* to drive; (*causer*) to bring about; (*impliquer*) to entail, involve; **e. qn** (*emmener*) to lead *ou* draw s.o. (away); (*de force*) to drag s.o. (away); (*attirer*) *Péj* to lure s.o.; (*charmer*) to carry s.o. away; **e. qn à faire** (*amener*) to lead s.o. to do. **2** *vt* (*athlète, cheval etc*) to train (**à** for); — **s'e.** *vpr* to train oneself; *Sp* to train. ◆**—ant** [-ãnã] *a* (*à musique*) captivating. ◆**—ement** [-ãnmã] *nm* **1** *Sp* training. **2** *Tech* drive; (*élan*) impulse. ◆**—eur** [-ãnœr] *nm* (*instructeur*) *Sp* trainer, coach; (*de cheval*) trainer.

entrave [ãtrav] *nf* (*obstacle*) *Fig* hindrance (**à** to). ◆**entraver** *vt* to hinder, hamper.

entre [ãtr(ə)] *prép* between; (*parmi*) among(st); **l'un d'e. vous** one of you; (*soit dit*) **e. nous** between you and me; **se dévorer e. eux** (*réciprocité*) to devour each other; **e. deux âges** middle-aged; **e. autres** among other things; **e. les mains de** in the hands of.

entrebâill/er [ãtrəbaje] *vt* (*porte*) to open slightly. ◆**—é** *a* ajar, slightly open. ◆**—eur** *nm* **e.** (**de porte**) door chain.

entrechoquer (**s'**) [sãtrəʃɔke] *vpr* (*bouteilles etc*) to knock against each other, chink.

entrecôte [ãtrəkot] *nf* (*boned*) rib steak.

entrecouper [ãtrəkupe] *vt* (*entremêler*) to punctuate (**de** with), intersperse (**de** with).

entrecroiser [ãtrəkrwaze] *vt*, — **s'e.** *vpr* (*fils*) to interlace; (*routes*) to intersect.

entre-deux-guerres [ãtrədøgɛr] *nm inv* inter-war period.

entrée [ãtre] *nf* (*action*) entry, entrance; (*porte*) entrance; (*accès*) entry, admission (**de** to); (*vestibule*) entrance hall, entry; (*billet*) ticket (of admission); *Culin* first course, entrée; (*mot dans un dictionnaire etc*) entry; (*processus informatique*) input; **à son e.** as he *ou* she came in; **'e. interdite'** 'no entry', 'no admittance'; **'e. libre'** 'admission free'; **e. en matière** (*d'un discours*) opening.

entrefaites (sur ces) [syrsezɑ̃trəfɛt] *adv* at that moment.

entrefilet [ɑ̃trəfilɛ] *nm Journ* (news) item.

entrejambes [ɑ̃trəʒɑ̃b] *nm inv* (*de pantalon*) crutch, crotch.

entrelacer [ɑ̃trəlase] *vt*, **— s'e.** *vpr* to intertwine.

entremêler [ɑ̃trəmele] *vt*, **— s'e.** *vpr* to intermingle.

entremets [ɑ̃trəmɛ] *nm* (*plat*) sweet, dessert.

entremetteur, -euse [ɑ̃trəmɛtœr, -øz] *nmf Péj* go-between.

entremise [ɑ̃trəmiz] *nf* intervention; **par l'e. de qn** through s.o.

entreposer [ɑ̃trəpoze] *vt* to store; *Jur* to bond. ◆**entrepôt** *nm* warehouse; (*de la douane*) *Jur* bonded warehouse.

entreprendre* [ɑ̃trəprɑ̃dr] *vt* (*travail, voyage etc*) to start on, undertake; **e. de faire** to undertake to do. ◆**entreprenant** *a* enterprising; (*galant*) brash, forward. ◆**entrepreneur** *nm* (*en bâtiment*) (building) contractor. ◆**entreprise** *nf* **1** (*opération*) undertaking. **2** (*firme*) company, firm.

entrer [ɑ̃tre] *vi* (*aux être*) (*aller*) to go in, enter; (*venir*) to come in, enter; **e. dans** to go into; (*carrière*) to enter, go into; (*club*) to join, enter; (*détail, question*) to go ou enter into; (*pièce*) to come ou go into, enter; (*arbre etc*) *Aut* to crash into; **e. en action** to go ou get into action; **e. en ébullition** to start boiling; **entrez!** come in!; **faire/laisser e. qn** to show/let s.o. in.

entresol [ɑ̃trəsɔl] *nm* mezzanine (floor).

entre-temps [ɑ̃trətɑ̃] *adv* meanwhile.

entreten/ir* [ɑ̃trətnir] *vt* **1** (*voiture, maison etc*) to maintain; (*relations, souvenir*) to keep up; (*famille*) to keep, maintain; (*sentiment*) to entertain; **e. sa forme/sa santé** to keep fit/healthy. **2 e. qn de** to talk to s.o. about; **s'e. de** to talk about (**avec** with). ◆**—u** *a* (*femme*) kept. ◆**entretien** *nm* **1** (*de route, maison etc*) maintenance, upkeep; (*subsistance*) keep. **2** (*dialogue*) conversation; (*entrevue*) interview.

entre-tuer (s') [sɑ̃trətɥe] *vpr* to kill each other.

entrevoir* [ɑ̃trəvwar] *vt* (*rapidement*) to catch a glimpse of; (*pressentir*) to (fore)see.

entrevue [ɑ̃trəvy] *nf* interview.

entrouvrir* [ɑ̃truvrir] *vt*, **— s'e.** *vpr* to half-open. ◆**entrouvert** *a* (*porte, fenêtre*) ajar, half-open.

énumérer [enymere] *vt* to enumerate, list. ◆**énumération** *nf* enumeration.

envah/ir [ɑ̃vair] *vt* to invade; (*herbe etc*) to overrun; **e. qn** (*doute, peur etc*) to overcome s.o. ◆**—issant** *a* (*voisin etc*) intrusive. ◆**—issement** *nm* invasion. ◆**—isseur** *nm* invader.

enveloppe [ɑ̃vlɔp] *nf* (*pli*) envelope; (*de colis*) wrapping; (*de pneu*) casing; (*d'oreiller*) cover; (*apparence*) *Fig* exterior; **mettre sous e.** to put into an envelope. ◆**envelopp/er** *vt* to wrap (up); **e. la ville** (*brouillard etc*) to envelop the town; **enveloppé de mystère** shrouded ou enveloped in mystery; **— s'e.** *vpr* to wrap oneself (up) (**dans** in). ◆**—ant** *a* (*séduisant*) captivating.

envenimer [ɑ̃vnime] *vt* (*plaie*) to make septic; (*querelle*) *Fig* to envenom; **— s'e.** *vpr* to turn septic; *Fig* to become envenomed.

envergure [ɑ̃vɛrgyr] *nf* **1** (*d'avion, d'oiseau*) wingspan. **2** (*de personne*) calibre; (*ampleur*) scope, importance; **de grande e.** wide-ranging, far-reaching.

envers [ɑ̃vɛr] **1** *prép* towards, *Am* toward(s). **2** *nm* (*de tissu*) wrong side; (*de médaille*) reverse side; **à l'e.** (*chaussette*) inside out; (*pantalon*) back to front; (*à contresens, de travers*) the wrong way; (*en désordre*) upside down.

envie [ɑ̃vi] *nf* **1** (*jalousie*) envy; (*désir*) longing, desire; **avoir e. de qch** to want sth; **j'ai e. de faire** I feel like doing, I would like to do; **elle meurt d'e. de faire** she's dying ou longing to do. **2** (*peau autour des ongles*) hangnail. ◆**envier** *vt* to envy (**qch à qn** s.o. sth). ◆**envieux, -euse** *a* & *nmf* envious (person); **faire des envieux** to cause envy.

environ [ɑ̃virɔ̃] *adv* (*à peu près*) about; **— nmpl** outskirts, surroundings; **aux environs de** (*Paris, Noël, dix francs etc*) around, in the vicinity of. ◆**environn/er** *vt* to surround. ◆**—ant** *a* surrounding. ◆**—ement** *nm* environment.

envisag/er [ɑ̃vizaʒe] *vt* to consider; (*imaginer comme possible*) to envisage, *Am* envision, consider; **e. de faire** to consider ou contemplate doing. ◆**—eable** *a* thinkable.

envoi [ɑ̃vwa] *nm* (*action*) dispatch, sending; (*paquet*) consignment; **coup d'e.** *Fb* kick-off.

envol [ɑ̃vɔl] *nm* (*d'oiseau*) taking flight; (*d'avion*) take-off; **piste d'e.** *Av* runway. ◆**s'envol/er** *vpr* (*oiseau*) to fly away; (*avion*) to take off; (*emporté par le vent*) to blow away; (*espoir*) *Fig* to vanish. ◆**—ée** *nf* (*élan*) *Fig* flight.

envoût/er [ãvute] *vt* to bewitch. ◆**—ement** *nm* bewitchment.

envoy/er* [ãvwaje] *vt* to send; (*pierre*) to throw; (*gifle*) to give; **e. chercher qn** to send for s.o.; **— s'e.** *vpr Fam* (*travail etc*) to take on, do; (*repas etc*) to put *ou* stash away. ◆**—é, -ée** *nmf* envoy; *Journ* correspondent. ◆**—eur** *nm* sender.

épagneul, -eule [epaɲœl] *nmf* spaniel.

épais, -aisse [epɛ, -ɛs] *a* thick; (*personne*) thick-set; (*esprit*) dull. ◆**épaisseur** *nf* thickness; (*dimension*) depth. ◆**épaissir** *vt* to thicken; — *vi*, — **s'é.** *vpr* to thicken; (*grossir*) to fill out; **le mystère s'épaissit** the mystery is deepening.

épanch/er [epãʃe] *vt* (*cœur*) *Fig* to pour out; — **s'é.** *vpr* (*parler*) to pour out one's heart, unbosom oneself. ◆**—ement** *nm* (*aveu*) outpouring; *Méd* effusion.

épanou/ir (s') [epanwir] *vpr* (*fleur*) to open out; (*personne*) *Fig* to fulfil oneself, blossom (out); (*visage*) to beam. ◆**—i** *a* (*fleur, personne*) in full bloom; (*visage*) beaming. ◆**—issement** *nm* (*éclat*) full bloom; (*de la personnalité*) fulfilment.

épargne [eparɲ] *nf* saving (**de** of); (*qualité, vertu*) thrift; (*sommes d'argent*) savings. ◆**épargn/er** *vt* (*ennemi etc*) to spare; (*denrée rare etc*) to be sparing with; (*argent, temps*) to save; **e. qch à qn** (*ennuis, chagrin etc*) to spare s.o. sth. ◆**—ant, -ante** *nmf* saver.

éparpiller [eparpije] *vt*, — **s'é.** *vpr* to scatter; (*efforts*) to dissipate. ◆**épars** *a* scattered.

épaté [epate] *a* (*nez*) flat. ◆**épatement** *nm* flatness.

épat/er [epate] *vt Fam* to stun, astound. ◆**—ant** *a Fam* stunning, marvellous.

épaule [epol] *nf* shoulder. ◆**épauler** *vt* (*fusil*) to raise (to one's shoulder); **é. qn** (*aider*) to back s.o. up.

épave [epav] *nf* (*bateau, personne*) wreck; *pl* (*débris*) *Nau* (pieces of) wreckage.

épée [epe] *nf* sword; **un coup d'é.** a sword thrust.

épeler [eple] *vt* (*mot*) to spell.

éperdu [eperdy] *a* frantic, wild (**de** with); (*regard*) distraught. ◆**—ment** *adv* (*aimer*) madly; **elle s'en moque e.** she couldn't care less.

éperon [eprɔ̃] *nm* (*de cavalier, coq*) spur. ◆**éperonner** (*cheval, personne*) to spur (on).

épervier [epɛrvje] *nm* sparrowhawk.

éphémère [efemer] *a* short-lived, ephemeral, transient.

épi [epi] *nm* (*de blé etc*) ear; (*mèche de cheveux*) tuft of hair.

épice [epis] *nf Culin* spice. ◆**épic/er** *vt* to spice. ◆**—é** *a* (*plat, récit etc*) spicy.

épicier, -ière [episje, -jɛr] *nmf* grocer. ◆**épicerie** *nf* (*magasin*) grocer's (shop); (*produits*) groceries.

épidémie [epidemi] *nf* epidemic. ◆**épidémique** *a* epidemic.

épiderme [epiderm] *nm Anat* skin.

épier [epje] *vt* (*observer*) to watch closely; (*occasion*) to watch out for; **é. qn** to spy on s.o.

épilepsie [epilepsi] *nf* epilepsy. ◆**épileptique** *a & nmf* epileptic.

épiler [epile] *vt* (*jambe*) to remove unwanted hair from; (*sourcil*) to pluck.

épilogue [epilɔg] *nm* epilogue.

épinard [epinar] *nm* (*plante*) spinach; *pl* (*feuilles*) *Culin* spinach.

épine [epin] *nf* **1** (*de buisson*) thorn; (*d'animal*) spine, prickle. **2 é. dorsale** *Anat* spine. ◆**épineux, -euse** *a* (*tige, question*) thorny.

épingle [epɛ̃gl] *nf* pin; **é. de nourrice, é. de sûreté** safety pin; **é. à linge** clothes peg, *Am* clothes pin; **virage en é. à cheveux** hairpin bend; **tiré à quatre épingles** very spruce. ◆**épingler** *vt* to pin; **é. qn** (*arrêter*) *Fam* to nab s.o.

épique [epik] *a* epic.

épiscopal, -aux [episkɔpal, -o] *a* episcopal.

épisode [epizɔd] *nm* episode; **film à épisodes** serial. ◆**épisodique** *a* occasional, episodic; (*accessoire*) minor.

épitaphe [epitaf] *nf* epitaph.

épithète [epitɛt] *nf* epithet; *Gram* attribute.

épître [epitr] *nf* epistle.

éploré [eplɔre] *a* (*personne, air*) tearful.

éplucher [eplyʃe] *vt* (*pommes de terre*) to peel; (*salade*) to clean, pare; (*texte*) *Fig* to dissect. ◆**épluchure** *nf* peeling.

éponge [epɔ̃ʒ] *nf* sponge. ◆**éponger** *vt* (*liquide*) to sponge up, mop up; (*carrelage*) to sponge (down), mop; (*dette etc*) *Fin* to absorb; **s'é. le front** to mop one's brow.

épopée [epɔpe] *nf* epic.

époque [epɔk] *nf* (*date*) time, period; (*historique*) age; **meubles d'é.** period furniture; **à l'é.** at the *ou* that time.

épouse [epuz] *nf* wife, *Jur* spouse.

épouser [epuze] *vt* **1 é. qn** to marry s.o. **2** (*opinion etc*) to espouse; (*forme*) to assume, adopt.

épousseter [epuste] *vt* to dust.

époustoufler [epustufle] vt Fam to astound.
épouvantail [epuvãtaj] nm (à oiseaux) scarecrow.
épouvante [epuvãt] nf (peur) terror; (appréhension) dread; **d'é.** (film etc) horror-. ◆**épouvanter/er** vt to terrify. ◆**—able** a terrifying; (très mauvais) appalling.
époux [epu] nm husband, Jur spouse; pl husband and wife.
éprendre* (s') [seprãdr] vpr **s'é. de qn** to fall in love with s.o. ◆**épris** a in love (de with).
épreuve [eprœv] nf (essai, examen) test; Sp event, heat; Phot print; Typ proof; (malheur) ordeal, trial; **mettre à l'é.** to put to the test.
éprouv/er [epruve] vt to test, try; (sentiment etc) to experience, feel; **é. qn** (mettre à l'épreuve) to put s.o. to the test; (faire souffrir) to distress s.o. ◆**—ant** a (pénible) trying. ◆**—é** a (sûr) well-tried.
éprouvette [epruvɛt] nf test tube; **bébé é.** test tube baby.
épuis/er [epɥize] vt (personne, provisions, sujet) to exhaust; **— s'é.** vpr (réserves, patience) to run out; **s'é. à faire** to exhaust oneself doing. ◆**—ant** a exhausting. ◆**—é** a exhausted; (édition) out of print; (marchandise) out of stock. ◆**—ement** nm exhaustion.
épuisette [epɥizɛt] nf fishing net (on pole).
épurer [epyre] vt to purify; (personnel etc) to purge; (goût) to refine. ◆**épuration** nf purification; purging; refining.
équateur [ekwatœr] nm equator; **sous l'é.** at ou on the equator. ◆**équatorial, -aux** a equatorial.
équation [ekwasjõ] nf Math equation.
équerre [ekɛr] nf **é.** (à dessiner) setsquare, Am triangle; **d'é.** straight, square.
équestre [ekɛstr] a (figure etc) equestrian; (exercices etc) horseriding-.
équilibre [ekilibr] nm balance; **tenir** ou **mettre en é.** to balance (**sur** on); **se tenir en é.** to (keep one's) balance; **perdre l'é.** to lose one's balance. ◆**équilibrer** vt (charge, budget etc) to balance; **— s'é.** vpr (équipes etc) to (counter)balance each other; (comptes) to balance.
équinoxe [ekinɔks] nm equinox.
équipage [ekipaʒ] nm Nau Av crew.
équipe [ekip] nf team; (d'ouvriers) gang; **é. de nuit** night shift; **é. de secours** search party; **faire é. avec** to team up with. ◆**équipier, -ière** nmf team member.
équipée [ekipe] nf escapade.
équip/er [ekipe] vt to equip (de with); **— s'é.** vpr to equip oneself. ◆**—ement** nm equipment; (de camping, ski etc) gear, equipment.
équitation [ekitasjõ] nf (horse) riding.
équité [ekite] nf fairness. ◆**équitable** a fair, equitable. ◆**équitablement** adv fairly.
équivalent [ekivalã] a & nm equivalent. ◆**équivalence** nf equivalence. ◆**équivaloir** vi é. à to be equivalent to.
équivoque [ekivɔk] a (ambigu) equivocal; (douteux) dubious; — nf ambiguity.
érable [erabl] nm (arbre, bois) maple.
érafler [erafle] vt to graze, scratch. ◆**éraflure** nf graze, scratch.
éraillée [eraje] af (voix) rasping.
ère [ɛr] nf era.
érection [erɛksjõ] nf (de monument etc) erection.
éreinter [erɛte] vt (fatiguer) to exhaust; (critiquer) to tear to pieces, slate, slam.
ergot [ergo] nm (de coq) spur.
ergoter [ergɔte] vi to quibble, cavil.
ériger [eriʒe] vt to erect; **s'é. en** to set oneself up as.
ermite [ermit] nm hermit.
érosion [erozjõ] nf erosion. ◆**éroder** vt to erode.
érotique [erɔtik] a erotic. ◆**érotisme** nm eroticism.
err/er [ere] vi to wander, roam. ◆**—ant** a wandering, roving; (animal) stray.
erreur [erœr] nf (faute) error, mistake; (action blâmable, opinion fausse) error; **par e.** by mistake, in error; **dans l'e.** mistaken. ◆**erroné** a erroneous.
ersatz [ɛrzats] nm substitute.
éructer [erykte] vi Litt to belch.
érudit, -ite [erydi, -it] a scholarly, erudite; — nmf scholar. ◆**érudition** nf scholarship, erudition.
éruption [erypsjõ] nf (de volcan, colère) eruption (de of); Méd rash.
es voir être.
ès [ɛs] prép of; **licencié/docteur ès lettres** = BA/PhD.
escabeau, -x [ɛskabo] nm stepladder, (pair of) steps; (tabouret) stool.
escadre [ɛskadr] nf Nau Av fleet, squadron. ◆**escadrille** nf (unité) Av flight. ◆**escadron** nm squadron.
escalade [ɛskalad] nf climbing; (de prix) & Mil escalation. ◆**escalader** vt to climb, scale.
escale [ɛskal] nf Av stop(over); Nau port of call; **faire e. à** Av to stop (over) at; Nau to put in at; **vol sans e.** non-stop flight.
escalier [ɛskalje] nm staircase, stairs; **e. mé-**

canique *ou* **roulant** escalator; **e. de secours** fire escape.

escalope [ɛskalɔp] *nf Culin* escalope.

escamot/er [ɛskamɔte] *vt* (*faire disparaître*) to make vanish; (*esquiver*) to dodge. ◆**—able** *a Av Tech* retractable.

escapade [ɛskapad] *nf* (*excursion*) jaunt; **faire une e.** to run off.

escargot [ɛskargo] *nm* snail.

escarmouche [ɛskarmuʃ] *nf* skirmish.

escarpé [ɛskarpe] *a* steep. ◆**escarpement** *nm* (*côte*) steep slope.

escarpin [ɛskarpɛ̃] *nm* (*soulier*) pump, court shoe.

escient [ɛsjɑ̃] *nm* **à bon e.** discerningly, wisely.

esclaffer (s') [sɛsklafe] *vpr* to roar with laughter.

esclandre [ɛsklɑ̃dr] *nm* (noisy) scene.

esclave [ɛsklav] *nmf* slave; **être l'e. de** to be a slave to. ◆**esclavage** *nm* slavery.

escompte [ɛskɔ̃t] *nm* discount; **taux d'e.** bank rate. ◆**escompter** *vt* 1 (*espérer*) to anticipate (**faire** doing), expect (**faire** to do). 2 *Com* to discount.

escorte [ɛskɔrt] *nf Mil Nau etc* escort. ◆**escorter** *vt* to escort.

escouade [ɛskwad] *nf* (*petite troupe*) squad.

escrime [ɛskrim] *nf Sp* fencing. ◆**escrimeur, -euse** *nmf* fencer.

escrimer (s') [sɛskrime] *vpr* to slave away (**à faire** at doing).

escroc [ɛskro] *nm* swindler, crook. ◆**escroquer** *vt* **e. qn** to swindle s.o.; **e. qch à qn** to swindle s.o. out of sth. ◆**escroquerie** *nf* swindling; **une e.** a swindle.

espace [ɛspas] *nm* space; **e. vert** garden, park. ◆**espacer** *vt* to space out; **espacés d'un mètre** (spaced out) one metre apart; — **s'e.** (*maisons, visites etc*) to become less frequent.

espadon [ɛspadɔ̃] *nm* swordfish.

espadrille [ɛspadrij] *nf* rope-soled sandal.

Espagne [ɛspaɲ] *nf* Spain. ◆**espagnol, -ole** *a* Spanish; — *nmf* Spaniard; — *nm* (*langue*) Spanish.

espèce [ɛspɛs] 1 *nf* (*race*) species; (*genre*) kind, sort; **c'est une e. d'idiot** he's a silly fool; **e. d'idiot!/de maladroit!/etc** (you) silly fool!/oaf!/etc. 2 *nfpl* (*argent*) **en espèces** in cash.

espérance [ɛsperɑ̃s] *nf* hope; **avoir des espérances** to have expectations; **e. de vie** life expectancy. ◆**espérer** *vt* to hope for; **e. que** to hope that; **e. faire** to hope to do; — *vi* to hope; **e. en qn/qch** to trust in s.o./sth.

espiègle [ɛspjɛgl] *a* mischievous. ◆**es-**

pièglerie *nf* mischievousness; (*farce*) mischievous trick.

espion, -onne [ɛspjɔ̃, -ɔn] *nmf* spy. ◆**espionnage** *nm* espionage, spying. ◆**espionner** *vt* to spy on; − *vi* to spy.

esplanade [ɛsplanad] *nf* esplanade.

espoir [ɛspwar] *nm* hope; **avoir de l'e.** to have hope(s); **sans e.** (*cas etc*) hopeless.

esprit [ɛspri] *nm* (*attitude, fantôme*) spirit; (*intellect*) mind; (*humour*) wit; (*être humain*) person; **avoir de l'e.** to be witty; **cette idée m'est venue à l'e.** this idea crossed my mind.

esquimau, -aude, -aux [ɛskimo, -od, -o] *a & nmf* Eskimo. 2 *nm* (*glace*) choc-ice (*on a stick*).

esquinter [ɛskɛ̃te] *vt Fam* (*voiture etc*) to damage, bash; (*critiquer*) to slam, pan (*author, film etc*); **s'e. la santé** to damage one's health; **s'e. à faire** (*se fatiguer*) to wear oneself out doing.

esquisse [ɛskis] *nf* (*croquis, plan*) sketch. ◆**esquisser** *vt* to sketch; **e. un geste** to make a (slight) gesture.

esquive [ɛskiv] *nf Boxe* dodge; **e. de** (*question*) dodging of, evasion of. ◆**esquiver** *vt* (*coup, problème*) to dodge; − **s'e.** *vpr* to slip away.

essai [ɛsɛ] *nm* (*épreuve*) test, trial; (*tentative*) try, attempt; *Rugby* try; *Littér* essay; **à l'e.** (*objet*) *Com* on trial, on approval; **pilote d'e.** test pilot; **période d'e.** trial period.

essaim [ɛsɛ̃] *nm* swarm (*of bees etc*).

essayer [eseje] *vt* to try (**de faire** to do); (*vêtement*) to try on; (*méthode*) to try (out); **s'e. à qch/à faire** to try one's hand at sth/at doing. ◆**essayage** *nm* (*de costume*) fitting.

essence [esɑ̃s] *nf* 1 (*extrait*) *Ch Culin* essence; *Aut* petrol, *Am* gas; **poste d'e.** filling station. 2 *Phil* essence. 3 (*d'arbres*) species. ◆**essentiel, -ielle** *a* essential (**à, pour** for); − *nm* **l'e.** the main thing *ou* point; (*quantité*) the main part (**de** of). ◆**essentiellement** *adv* essentially.

essieu, -x [esjø] *nm* axle.

essor [esɔr] *nm* (*de pays, d'entreprise etc*) development, rise, expansion; **en plein e.** (*industrie etc*) booming.

essor/er [esɔre] *vt* (*linge*) to wring; (*dans une essoreuse*) to spin-dry; (*dans une machine à laver*) to spin. ◆**—euse** *nf* (*à main*) wringer; (*électrique*) spin dryer.

essouffler [esufle] *vt* to make (*s.o.*) out of breath; − **s'e.** *vpr* to get out of breath.

essuyer [esɥije] 1 *vt* to wipe; − **s'e.** *vpr* to wipe oneself. 2 *vt* (*subir*) to suffer. ◆**es-**

suie-glace nm inv windscreen wiper, Am windshield wiper. ◆**essuie-mains** nm inv (hand) towel.

est[1] [ɛ] voir **être**.

est[2] [ɛst] nm east; — a inv (côte) east(ern); d'e. (vent) east(erly); de l'e. eastern; Allemagne de l'E. East Germany. ◆**e.-allemand, -ande** a & nmf East German.

estafilade [ɛstafilad] nf gash, slash.

estampe [ɛstɑ̃p] nf (gravure) print.

estamper [ɛstɑ̃pe] vt (rouler) Fam to swindle.

estampille [ɛstɑ̃pij] nf mark, stamp.

esthète [ɛstɛt] nmf aesthete, Am esthete. ◆**esthétique** a aesthetic, Am esthetic.

esthéticienne [ɛstetisjɛn] nf beautician.

estime [ɛstim] nf esteem, regard. ◆**estim/er** vt (objet) to value; (juger) to consider (que that); (calculer) to estimate; (apprécier) to appreciate; e. qn to have high regard for s.o., esteem s.o.; s'e. heureux/etc to consider oneself happy/etc. ◆—**able** a respectable. ◆**estimation** nf (de mobilier etc) valuation; (calcul) estimation.

estival, -aux [ɛstival, -o] a (période etc) summer-. ◆**estivant, -ante** nmf holidaymaker, Am vacationer.

estomac [ɛstɔma] nm stomach.

estomaquer [ɛstɔmake] vt Fam to flabbergast.

estomper [ɛstɔ̃pe] vt (rendre flou) to blur; — s'e. vpr to become blurred.

estrade [ɛstrad] nf (tribune) platform.

estropi/er [ɛstrɔpje] vt to cripple, maim. ◆—é, -ée nmf cripple.

estuaire [ɛstɥɛr] nm estuary.

esturgeon [ɛstyrʒɔ̃] nm (poisson) sturgeon.

et [e] conj and; vingt et un/etc twenty-one/etc.

étable [etabl] nf cowshed.

établi [etabli] nm Menuis (work)bench.

établ/ir [etablir] vt to establish; (installer) to set up; (plan, chèque, liste) to draw up; — s'é. vpr (habiter) to settle; (épicier etc) to set up shop as, set (oneself) up as. ◆—**issement** nm (action, bâtiment, institution) establishment; Com firm, establishment; é. scolaire school.

étage [etaʒ] nm (d'immeuble) floor, storey, Am story; (de fusée etc) stage; à l'é. upstairs; au premier é. on the first ou Am second floor. ◆**étager** vt, — s'é. vpr (rochers, maisons etc) to range above one another.

étagère [etaʒɛr] nf shelf; (meuble) shelving unit.

étai [etɛ] nm Tech prop, stay.

étain [etɛ̃] nm (métal) tin; (de gobelet etc) pewter.

était [etɛ] voir **être**.

étal, pl **étals** [etal] nm (au marché) stall.

étalage [etalaʒ] nm display; (vitrine) display window; faire é. de to make a show ou display of. ◆**étalagiste** nmf window dresser.

étaler [etale] vt (disposer) to lay out; (luxe etc) & Com to display; (crème, beurre etc) to spread; (vacances) to stagger; — s'é. vpr (s'affaler) to sprawl; (tomber) Fam to fall flat; s'é. sur (congés, paiements etc) to be spread over.

étalon [etalɔ̃] nm 1 (cheval) stallion. 2 (modèle) standard.

étanche [etɑ̃ʃ] a watertight; (montre) waterproof.

étancher [etɑ̃ʃe] vt (sang) to stop the flow of; (soif) to quench, slake.

étang [etɑ̃] nm pond.

étant [etɑ̃] voir **être**.

étape [etap] nf (de voyage etc) stage; (lieu) stop(over); faire é. à to stop off ou over at.

état [eta] nm 1 (condition, manière d'être) state; (registre, liste) statement, list; en bon é. in good condition; en é. de faire in a position to do; é. d'esprit state ou frame of mind; é. d'âme mood; é. civil civil status (birth, marriage, death etc); é. de choses situation, state of affairs; à l'é. brut in a raw state; de son é. (métier) by trade; faire é. de (mention) to mention, put forward. 2 É. (nation) State; homme d'É. statesman. ◆**étatisé** a state-controlled, state-owned.

état-major [etamaʒɔr] nm (pl états-majors) (d'un parti etc) senior staff.

États-Unis [etazyni] nmpl É.-Unis (d'Amérique) United States (of America).

étau, -x [eto] nm Tech vice, Am vise.

étayer [eteje] vt to prop up, support.

été[1] [ete] nm summer.

été[2] [ete] voir **être**.

éteindre* [etɛ̃dr] vt (feu, cigarette etc) to put out, extinguish; (lampe etc) to turn ou switch off; (dette, espoir) to extinguish; — vi to switch off; — s'é. vpr (feu) to go out; (personne) to pass away; (race) to die out. ◆**éteint** a (feu) out; (volcan, race, amour) extinct; (voix) faint.

étendard [etɑ̃dar] nm (drapeau) standard.

étend/re [etɑ̃dr] vt (nappe) to spread (out); (beurre) to spread; (linge) to hang out; (agrandir) to extend; é. le bras/etc to stretch out one's arm/etc; é. qn to stretch s.o. out; — s'é. vpr (personne) to stretch (oneself) out; (*plaine etc*) to stretch; (*feu*) to spread; (*pouvoir*) to extend; **s'é. sur** (*sujet*) to dwell on. ◆—**u** *a* (*forêt, vocabulaire etc*) extensive; (*personne*) stretched out. ◆—**ue** *nf* (*importance*) extent; (*surface*) area; (*d'eau*) expanse, stretch.

éternel, -elle [etɛrnɛl] *a* eternal. ◆**éternellement** *adv* eternally, for ever. ◆**éterniser** *vt* to perpetuate; — **s'é.** *vpr* (*débat etc*) to drag on endlessly; (*visiteur etc*) to stay for ever. ◆**éternité** *nf* eternity.

éternu/er [etɛrnɥe] *vi* to sneeze. ◆—**ement** [-ymɑ̃] *nm* sneeze.

êtes [ɛt] *voir* être.

éther [etɛr] *nm* ether.

Éthiopie [etjɔpi] *nf* Ethiopia. ◆**éthiopien, -ienne** *a & nmf* Ethiopian.

éthique [etik] *a* ethical; — *nf Phil* ethics; **l'é. puritaine**/*etc* the Puritan/*etc* ethic.

ethnie [etni] *nf* ethnic group. ◆**ethnique** *a* ethnic.

étinceler [etɛ̃sle] *vi* to sparkle. ◆**étincelle** *nf* spark. ◆**étincellement** *nm* sparkle.

étioler (s') [setjɔle] *vpr* to wilt, wither.

étiqueter [etikte] *vt* to label. ◆**étiquette** *nf* **1** (*marque*) label. **2** (*protocole*) (diplomatic *ou* court) etiquette.

étirer [etire] *vt* to stretch; — **s'é.** *vpr* to stretch (oneself).

étoffe [etɔf] *nf* material, cloth, fabric; (*de héros etc*) *Fig* stuff (**de** of).

étoffer [etɔfe] *vt*, — **s'é.** *vpr* to fill out.

étoile [etwal] *nf* **1** star; **à la belle é.** in the open. **2** é. de mer starfish. ◆**étoilé** *a* (*ciel, nuit*) starry; (*vitre*) cracked (*star-shaped*); **é. de** (*rubis etc*) studded with; **la bannière étoilée** *Am* the Star-Spangled Banner.

étonn/er [etɔne] *vt* to surprise, astonish; — **s'é.** *vpr* to be surprised *ou* astonished (**de qch** at sth, **que** (+ *sub*) that). ◆—**ant** *a* (*ahurissant*) surprising; (*remarquable*) amazing. ◆—**ement** *nm* surprise, astonishment.

étouff/er [etufe] *vt* (*tuer*) to suffocate, smother; (*bruit*) to muffle; (*feu*) to smother; (*révolte, sentiment*) to stifle; (*scandale*) to hush up; **é. qn** (*chaleur*) to stifle s.o.; (*aliment, colère*) to choke s.o.; — *vi* to suffocate; **on étouffe!** it's stifling!; **é. de colère** to choke with anger. — **s'é.** *vpr* (*en mangeant*) to choke, gag (**sur, avec** on); (*mourir*) to suffocate. ◆—**ant** *a* (*air*) stifling. ◆—**ement** *nm Méd* suffocation.

étourdi, -ie [eturdi] *a* thoughtless; — *nmf* scatterbrain. ◆**étourderie** *nf* thoughtlessness; **une é.** (*faute*) a thoughtless blunder.

étourd/ir [eturdir] *vt* to stun, daze; (*vertige,*

vin) to make dizzy; (*abrutir*) to deafen. ◆—**issant** *a* (*bruit*) deafening; (*remarquable*) stunning. ◆—**issement** *nm* dizziness; (*syncope*) dizzy spell.

étourneau, -x [eturno] *nm* starling.

étrange [etrɑ̃ʒ] *a* strange, odd. ◆—**ment** *adv* strangely, oddly. ◆**étrangeté** *nf* strangeness, oddness.

étranger, -ère [etrɑ̃ʒe, -ɛr] *a* (*d'un autre pays*) foreign; (*non familier*) strange (**à** to); **il m'est é.** he's unknown to me; — *nmf* foreigner; (*inconnu*) stranger; **à l'é.** abroad; **de l'é.** from abroad.

étrangl/er [etrɑ̃gle] *vt* **é. qn** (*tuer*) to strangle s.o.; (*col, aliment*) to choke s.o.; — **s'é.** *vpr* (*de colère, en mangeant etc*) to choke. ◆—**é** *a* (*voix*) choking; (*passage*) constricted. ◆—**ement** *nm* (*d'une victime*) strangulation. ◆—**eur, -euse** *nmf* strangler.

être* [ɛtr] **1** *vi* to be; **il est tailleur** he's a tailor; **est-ce qu'elle vient?** is she coming?; **il vient, n'est-ce pas?** he's coming, isn't he?; **est-ce qu'il aime le thé?** does he like tea?; **nous sommes dix** there are ten of us; **nous sommes le dix** today is the tenth (of the month); **où en es-tu?** how far have you got?; **il a été à Paris** (*est allé*) he's been to Paris; **elle est de Paris** she's from Paris; **elle est de la famille** she's one of the family; **c'est à faire tout de suite** it must be done straight away; **c'est à lui** it's his; **cela étant** that being so. **2** *v aux* (*avec venir, partir etc*) to have; **elle est déjà arrivée** she has already arrived. **3** *nm* (*personne*) being; **ê. humain** human being; **les êtres chers** the loved ones.

étreindre [etrɛ̃dr] *vt* to grip; (*ami*) to embrace. ◆**étreinte** *nf* grip; (*amoureuse etc*) embrace.

étrenner [etrene] *vt* to use *ou* wear for the first time.

étrennes [etrɛn] *nfpl* New Year gift; (*gratification*) = Christmas box *ou* tip.

étrier [etrije] *nm* stirrup.

étriper (s') [setripe] *vpr Fam* to fight (each other) to the kill.

étriqué [etrike] *a* (*vêtement*) tight, skimpy; (*esprit, vie*) narrow.

étroit [etrwa] *a* narrow; (*vêtement*) tight; (*parenté, collaboration etc*) close; (*discipline*) strict; **être à l'é.** to be cramped. ◆**étroitement** *adv* (*surveiller etc*) closely. ◆**étroitesse** *nf* narrowness; closeness; **é. d'esprit** narrow-mindedness.

étude [etyd] *nf* **1** (*action, ouvrage*) study; (*salle*) *Scol* study room; **à l'é.** (*projet*) under consideration; **faire des études de** (*médecine etc*) to study. **2** (*de notaire etc*) office. ◆**étudier** *vti* to study.

étui [etɥi] *nm* (*à lunettes, à cigarettes etc*) case; (*de revolver*) holster.

étymologie [etimɔlɔʒi] *nf* etymology.

eu, eue [y] *voir* **avoir**.

eucalyptus [økaliptys] *nm* (*arbre*) eucalyptus.

Eucharistie [økaristi] *nf Rel* Eucharist.

euh! [ø] *int* hem!, er!, well!

euphémisme [øfemism] *nm* euphemism.

euphorie [øfɔri] *nf* euphoria.

eurent [yr] *voir* **avoir**.

euro- [øro] *préf* Euro-.

Europe [ørɔp] *nf* Europe. ◆**européen, -enne** *a & nmf* European.

eut [y] *voir* **avoir**.

euthanasie [øtanazi] *nf* euthanasia.

eux [ø] *pron* (*sujet*) they; (*complément*) them; (*réfléchi, emphase*) themselves. ◆**eux-mêmes** *pron* themselves.

évacuer [evakɥe] *vt* to evacuate; (*liquide*) to drain off. ◆**évacuation** *nf* evacuation.

évad/er (s') [sevade] *vpr* to escape (*de* from). ◆**—é, -ée** *nmf* escaped prisoner.

évaluer [evalɥe] *vt* (*chiffre, foule etc*) to estimate; (*meuble etc*) to value. ◆**évaluation** *nf* estimation; valuation.

évangile [evɑ̃ʒil] *nm* gospel; É. Gospel. ◆**évangélique** *a* evangelical.

évanou/ir (s') [sevanwir] *vpr Méd* to black out, faint; (*espoir, crainte etc*) to vanish. ◆**—i** *a Méd* unconscious. ◆**—issement** *nm* (*syncope*) blackout, fainting fit; (*disparition*) vanishing.

évaporer (s') [sevapɔre] *vpr Ch* to evaporate; (*disparaître*) *Fam* to vanish into thin air. ◆**évaporation** *nf* evaporation.

évasif, -ive [evazif, -iv] *a* evasive.

évasion [evazjɔ̃] *nf* escape (**d'un lieu** from a place, **devant un danger**/*etc* from a danger/*etc*); (*hors de la réalité*) escapism; **é. fiscale** tax evasion.

évêché [eveʃe] *nm* (*territoire*) bishopric, see.

éveil [evɛj] *nm* awakening; **en é.** on the alert; **donner l'é.** à to alert.

éveill/er [eveje] *vt* (*susciter*) to arouse; **é. qn** to awake(n) s.o.; **— s'é.** *vpr* to awake(n) (**à** to); (*sentiment, idée*) to be aroused. ◆**—é** *a* awake; (*vif*) lively, alert.

événement [evɛnmɑ̃] *nm* event.

éventail [evɑ̃taj] *nm* **1** (*instrument portatif*) fan; **en é.** (*orteils*) spread out. **2** (*choix*) range.

évent/er [evɑ̃te] *vt* **1** (*secret*) to discover. **2**

é. qn to fan s.o. **3 s'é.** *vpr* (*bière, vin etc*) to turn stale. ◆**—é** *a* (*bière, vin etc*) stale.

éventrer [evɑ̃tre] *vt* (*animal etc*) to disembowel; (*sac*) to rip open.

éventuel, -elle [evɑ̃tɥel] *a* possible. ◆**éventuellement** *adv* possibly. ◆**éventualité** *nf* possibility; **dans l'é. de** in the event of.

évêque [evɛk] *nm* bishop.

évertuer (s') [severtɥe] *vpr* **s'é. à faire** to do one's utmost to do, struggle to do.

éviction [eviksjɔ̃] *nf* (*de concurrent etc*) & *Pol* ousting.

évident [evidɑ̃] *a* obvious, evident (**que** that). ◆**évidemment** [-amɑ̃] *adv* certainly, obviously. ◆**évidence** *nf* obviousness; **une é.** an obvious fact; **nier l'é.** to deny the obvious; **être en é.** to be conspicuous *ou* in evidence; **mettre en é.** (*fait*) to underline.

évider [evide] *vt* to hollow out.

évier [evje] *nm* (*kitchen*) sink.

évincer [evɛ̃se] *vt* (*concurrent etc*) & *Pol* to oust.

éviter [evite] *vt* to avoid (**de faire** doing); **é. qch à qn** to spare *ou* save s.o. sth.

évolu/er [evɔlɥe] *vi* **1** (*changer*) to develop, change; (*société, idée, situation*) to evolve. **2** (*se déplacer*) to move; *Mil* to manœuvre, *Am* maneuver. ◆**—é** *a* (*pays*) advanced; (*personne*) enlightened. ◆**évolution** *nf* **1** (*changement*) development; evolution. **2** (*d'un danseur etc*) & *Mil* movement.

évoquer [evɔke] *vt* to evoke, call to mind. ◆**évocateur, -trice** *a* evocative. ◆**évocation** *nf* evocation, recalling.

ex [ɛks] *nmf* (*mari, femme*) *Fam* ex.

ex- [ɛks] *préf* ex-; **ex-mari** ex-husband.

exacerber [ɛgzaserbe] *vt* (*douleur etc*) to exacerbate.

exact [ɛgzakt] *a* (*précis*) exact, accurate; (*juste, vrai*) correct, exact, right; (*ponctuel*) punctual. ◆**exactement** *adv* exactly. ◆**exactitude** *nf* exactness, accuracy; correctness; punctuality.

exaction [ɛgzaksjɔ̃] *nf* exaction.

ex aequo [ɛgzeko] *adv* **être classés ex ae.** *Sp* to tie, be equally placed.

exagér/er [ɛgzaʒere] *vt* to exaggerate; **— vi** (*parler*) to exaggerate; (*agir*) to overdo it, go too far. ◆**—é** *a* excessive. ◆**—ément** *adv* excessively. ◆**exagération** *nf* exaggeration; (*excès*) excessiveness.

exalt/er [ɛgzalte] *vt* (*glorifier*) to exalt; (*animer*) to fire, stir. ◆**—ant** *a* stirring. ◆**—é, -ée** *a* (*sentiment*) impassioned,

wild; − *nmf Péj* fanatic. ◆**exaltation** *nf*
(*délire*) elation, excitement.

examen [ɛgzamɛ̃] *nm* examination; *Scol* exam(ination); **e. blanc** *Scol* mock exam(ination). ◆**examinateur, -trice** *nmf*
Scol examiner. ◆**examiner** *vt* (*considérer,
regarder*) to examine.

exaspérer [ɛgzaspere] *vt* (*énerver*) to aggravate, exasperate. ◆**exaspération** *nf* exasperation, aggravation.

exaucer [ɛgzose] *vt* (*désir*) to grant; **e. qn** to
grant s.o.'s wish(es).

excavation [ɛkskavɑsjɔ̃] *nf* (*trou*) hollow.

excéder [ɛksede] *vt* **1** (*dépasser*) to exceed. **2**
é. qn (*fatiguer, énerver*) to exasperate s.o.
◆**excédent** *nm* surplus, excess; **e. de
bagages** excess luggage *ou Am* baggage.
◆**excédentaire** *a* (*poids etc*) excess-.

excellent [ɛkselɑ̃] *a* excellent. ◆**excellence** *nf* **1** excellence; **par e.** above all else
ou all others. **2 E.** (*titre*) Excellency.
◆**exceller** *vi* to excel (**en qch** in sth, **à faire**
in doing).

excentrique [ɛksɑ̃trik] **1** *a* & *nmf* (*original*)
eccentric. **2** *a* (*quartier*) remote. ◆**excentricité** *nf* (*bizarrerie*) eccentricity.

excepté [ɛksɛpte] *prép* except. ◆**excepter**
vt to except. ◆**exception** *nf* exception; **à
l'e. de** except (for), with the exception of;
faire e. to be an exception. ◆**exceptionnel, -elle** *a* exceptional. ◆**exceptionnellement** *adv* exceptionally.

excès [ɛksɛ] *nm* excess; (*de table*)
over-eating; **e. de vitesse** *Aut* speeding.
◆**excessif, -ive** *a* excessive. ◆**excessivement** *adv* excessively.

excit/er [ɛksite] *vt* (*faire naître*) to excite,
rouse, stir; **e. qn** (*mettre en colère*) to provoke s.o.; (*agacer*) to annoy s.o.; (*enthousiasmer*) to thrill s.o., excite s.o.; **e. qn à
faire** to incite s.o. to do; − **s'e.** *vpr*
(*nerveux, enthousiaste*) to get excited.
◆−**ant** *a* exciting; − *nm* stimulant. ◆−**é**
a excited. ◆−**able** *a* excitable. ◆**excitation** *nf* (*agitation*) excitement; **e. à** (*haine
etc*) incitement to.

exclamer (s') [ɛksklame] *vpr* to exclaim.
◆**exclamatif, -ive** *a* exclamatory. ◆**exclamation** *nf* exclamation.

excl/ure* [ɛksklyr] *vt* (*écarter*) to exclude
(**de** from); (*chasser*) to expel (**de** from); **e.
qch** (*rendre impossible*) to preclude sth.
◆−**u** *a* (*solution etc*) out of the question;
(*avec une date*) exclusive. ◆**exclusif, -ive**
a (*droit, modèle, préoccupation*) exclusive.
◆**exclusion** *nf* exclusion. ◆**exclusivement** *adv* exclusively. ◆**exclusivité** *nf*

Com exclusive rights; **en e.** (*film*) having an
exclusive showing (**à** at).

excommunier [ɛkskɔmynje] *vt* to excommunicate. ◆**excommunication** *nf* excommunication.

excrément(s) [ɛkskremɑ̃] *nm*(*pl*) excrement.

excroissance [ɛkskrwasɑ̃s] *nf* (out)growth.

excursion [ɛkskyrsjɔ̃] *nf* outing, excursion,
tour; (*à pied*) hike.

excuse [ɛkskyz] *nf* (*prétexte*) excuse; *pl* (*regrets*) apology; **des excuses** an apology;
faire des excuses to apologize (**à** to); **toutes
mes excuses** (my) sincere apologies.
◆**excuser** *vt* (*justifier, pardonner*) to excuse (**qn d'avoir fait, qn de faire** s.o. for doing); − **s'e.** *vpr* to apologize (**de** for, **auprès
de** to); **excusez-moi!, je m'excuse!** excuse
me!

exécrer [ɛgzekre] *vt* to loathe. ◆**exécrable**
a atrocious.

exécut/er [ɛgzekyte] *vt* **1** (*projet, tâche etc*)
to carry out, execute; (*statue, broderie etc*)
to produce; (*jouer*) *Mus* to perform. **2 e. qn**
(*tuer*) to execute s.o. **3 s'e.** *vpr* to comply.
◆−**ant, -ante** *nmf Mus* performer.
◆−**able** *a* practicable. ◆**exécutif** *am*
(*pouvoir*) executive; − *nm* **l'e.** *Pol* the executive. ◆**exécution** *nf* **1** carrying out, execution; production; performance. **2** (*mise
à mort*) execution.

exemple [ɛgzɑ̃pl] *nm* example; **par e.** for example, for instance; (*ça*) **par e.!** *Fam* good
heavens!; **donner l'e.** to set an example (**à**
to). ◆**exemplaire 1** *a* exemplary. **2** *nm*
(*livre etc*) copy.

exempt [ɛgzɑ̃] *a* **e. de** (*dispensé de*) exempt
from; (*sans*) free from. ◆**exempter** *vt* to
exempt (**de** from). ◆**exemption** *nf* exemption.

exercer [ɛgzɛrse] *vt* (*muscles, droits*) to exercise; (*autorité, influence*) to exert (**sur** over);
(*métier*) to carry on, work at; (*profession*)
to practise; **e. qn à** (*couture etc*) to train s.o.
in; **e. qn à faire** to train s.o. to do; − *vi*
(*médecin*) to practise; − **s'e.** *vpr* (*influence
etc*) to be exerted; **s'e.** (**à qch**) (*sportif etc*) to
practise (sth); **s'e. à faire** to practise doing.
◆**exercice** *nm* (*physique etc*) & *Scol* exercise; *Mil* drill, exercise; (*de métier*) practice; **l'e. de** (*pouvoir etc*) the exercise of; **en
e.** (*fonctionnaire*) in office; (*médecin*) in
practice; **faire de l'e., prendre de l'e.** to
(take) exercise.

exhaler [ɛgzale] *vt* (*odeur etc*) to give off.

exhaustif, -ive [ɛgzostif, -iv] *a* exhaustive.

exhiber [ɛgzibe] *vt* to exhibit, show.

◆**exhibition** nf exhibition. ◆**exhibition-niste** nmf exhibitionist.

exhorter [εgzɔrte] vt to urge, exhort (**à faire** to do).

exhumer [εgzyme] vt (cadavre) to exhume; (vestiges) to dig up.

exiger [εgziʒe] vt to demand, require (**de** from, **que** (+ sub) that). ◆**exigeant** a demanding, exacting. ◆**exigence** nf demand, requirement; **d'une grande e.** very demanding.

exigu, -uë [εgzigy] a (appartement etc) cramped, tiny. ◆**exiguïté** nf crampedness.

exil [εgzil] nm (expulsion) exile. ◆**exil/er** vt to exile; **– s'e.** vpr to go into exile. ◆**–é, -ée** nmf (personne) exile.

existence [εgzistɑ̃s] nf existence. ◆**existentialisme** nm existentialism. ◆**exist/er** vi to exist; **– v imp il existe . . .** (sing) there is . . . ; (pl) there are . . . . ◆**–ant** a existing.

exode [εgzɔd] nm exodus.

exonérer [εgzɔnere] vt to exempt (**de** from). ◆**exonération** nf exemption.

exorbitant [εgzɔrbitɑ̃] a exorbitant.

exorciser [εgzɔrsize] vt to exorcize. ◆**exorcisme** nm exorcism.

exotique [εgzɔtik] a exotic. ◆**exotisme** nm exoticism.

expansif, -ive [εkspɑ̃sif, -iv] a expansive, effusive.

expansion [εkspɑ̃sjɔ̃] nf Com Phys Pol expansion; **en (pleine) e.** (fast ou rapidly) expanding.

expatri/er (s') [sεkspatrije] vpr to leave one's country. ◆**–é, -ée** a & nmf expatriate.

expectative [εkspεktativ] nf **être dans l'e.** to be waiting to see what happens.

expédient [εkspedjɑ̃] nm (moyen) expedient.

expédier [εkspedje] vt 1 (envoyer) to send off. 2 (affaires, client) to dispose of quickly, dispatch. ◆**expéditeur, -trice** nmf sender. ◆**expéditif, -ive** a expeditious, quick. ◆**expédition** nf 1 (envoi) dispatch. 2 (voyage) expedition.

expérience [εksperjɑ̃s] nf (pratique, connaissance) experience; (scientifique) experiment; **faire l'e. de qch** to experience sth. ◆**expérimental, -aux** a experimental. ◆**expérimentation** nf experimentation. ◆**expériment/er** vt Phys Ch to try out, experiment with; **– vi** to experiment. ◆**–é** a experienced.

expert [εkspεr] a expert, skilled (**en** in); **–** nm expert; (d'assurances) valuer. ◆**e.-comptable** nm (pl **experts-comptables**) = chartered accountant, = Am certified public accountant. ◆**expertise** nf (évaluation) (expert) appraisal; (compétence) expertise.

expier [εkspje] vt (péchés, crime) to expiate, atone for. ◆**expiation** nf expiation (**de** of).

expir/er [εkspire] 1 vti to breathe out. 2 vi (mourir) to pass away; (finir, cesser) to expire. ◆**–ant** a dying. ◆**expiration** nf (échéance) expiry, Am expiration.

explicite [εksplisit] a explicit. ◆**–ment** adv explicitly.

expliquer [εksplike] vt to explain (**à** to); **– s'e.** vpr to explain oneself; (discuter) to talk things over, have it out (**avec** with); **s'e. qch** (comprendre) to understand sth; **ça s'explique** that is understandable. ◆**explicable** a understandable. ◆**explicatif, -ive** a explanatory. ◆**explication** nf explanation; (mise au point) discussion.

exploit [εksplwa] nm exploit, feat.

exploit/er [εksplwate] vt 1 (champs) to farm; (ferme, entreprise) to run; (mine) to work; (situation) Fig to exploit. 2 (abuser de) Péj to exploit (s.o.). ◆**–ant, -ante** nmf farmer. ◆**exploitation** nf 1 Péj exploitation. 2 farming; running; working; (entreprise) concern; (agricole) farm.

explorer [εksplɔre] vt to explore. ◆**explorateur, -trice** nmf explorer. ◆**exploration** nf exploration.

exploser [εksploze] vi (gaz etc) to explode; (bombe) to blow up, explode; **e. (de colère)** Fam to explode, blow up; **faire e.** (bombe) to explode. ◆**explosif, -ive** a & nm explosive. ◆**explosion** nf explosion; (de colère, joie) outburst.

exporter [εkspɔrte] vt to export (**vers** to, **de** from). ◆**exportateur, -trice** nmf exporter; **–** a exporting. ◆**exportation** nf (produit) export; (action) export(ation), exporting.

expos/er [εkspoze] vt (présenter, soumettre) & Phot to expose (**à** to); (marchandises) to display; (tableau etc) to exhibit; (idée, théorie) to set out; (vie, réputation) to risk, endanger; **s'e. à** to expose oneself to. ◆**–ant, -ante** nmf exhibitor. ◆**–é** a **bien e.** (édifice) having a good exposure; **e. au sud** facing south. 2 nm (compte rendu) account (**de** of); (discours) talk; Scol paper. ◆**exposition** nf (de marchandises etc) display; (salon) exhibition; (au danger etc) &

Phot exposure (à to); (*de maison etc*) aspect.

exprès [ɛksprɛ] *adv* on purpose, intentionally; (*spécialement*) specially.

exprès, **-esse** [ɛksprɛs] **1** *a* (*ordre, condition*) express. **2** *a inv* **lettre/colis e.** express letter/parcel. ◆**expressément** *adv* expressly.

express [ɛksprɛs] *a* & *nm inv* (*train*) express; (*café*) espresso.

expressif, **-ive** [ɛksprɛsif, -iv] *a* expressive. ◆**expression** *nf* (*phrase, mine etc*) expression. ◆**exprimer** *vt* to express; **— s'e.** *vpr* to express oneself.

exproprier [ɛksprɔprije] *vt* to seize the property of by compulsory purchase.

expulser [ɛkspylse] *vt* to expel (**de** from); (*joueur*) *Sp* to send off; (*locataire*) to evict. ◆**expulsion** *nf* expulsion; eviction; sending off.

expurger [ɛkspyrʒe] *vt* to expurgate.

exquis [ɛkski] *a* exquisite.

extase [ɛkstaz] *nf* ecstasy, rapture. ◆**s'extasi/er** *vpr* to be in raptures (**sur** over, about). ◆**—é** *a* ecstatic.

extensible [ɛkstãsibl] *a* expandable. ◆**extension** *nf* extension; (*essor*) expansion.

exténuer [ɛkstenɥe] *vt* (*fatiguer*) to exhaust. ◆**exténuation** *nf* exhaustion.

extérieur [ɛksterjœr] *a* (*monde etc*) outside; (*surface*) outer; (*signe*) outward, external; (*politique*) foreign; **e. à** external to; **— nm** outside, exterior; **à l'e.** (**de**) outside; **à l'e.** (*match*) away; **en e.** *Cin* on location. ◆**—ement** *adv* externally; (*en apparence*) outwardly. ◆**extérioriser** *vt* to express.

exterminer [ɛkstɛrmine] *vt* to exterminate,

wipe out. ◆**extermination** *nf* extermination.

externe [ɛkstɛrn] **1** *a* external. **2** *nmf Scol* day pupil; *Méd* non-resident hospital doctor, *Am* extern.

extincteur [ɛkstɛ̃ktœr] *nm* fire extinguisher. ◆**extinction** *nf* (*de feu*) extinguishing; (*de voix*) loss; (*de race*) extinction.

extirper [ɛkstirpe] *vt* to eradicate.

extorquer [ɛkstɔrke] *vt* to extort (**à** from). ◆**extorsion** *nf* extortion.

extra [ɛkstra] **1** *a inv* (*très bon*) *Fam* top-quality. **2** *nm inv Culin* (extra-special) treat; (*serviteur*) extra hand *ou* help.

extra- [ɛkstra] *préf* extra-. ◆**e.-fin** *a* extra-fine. ◆**e.-fort** *a* extra-strong.

extradition [ɛkstradisjɔ̃] *nf* extradition. ◆**extrader** *vt* to extradite.

extraire* [ɛkstrɛr] *vt* to extract (**de** from); (*charbon*) to mine. ◆**extraction** *nf* extraction. ◆**extrait** *nm* extract; **un e. de naissance** *a* (copy of one's) birth certificate.

extraordinaire [ɛkstraɔrdinɛr] *a* extraordinary. ◆**—ment** *adv* exceptionally; (*très, bizarrement*) extraordinarily.

extravagant [ɛkstravagã] *a* extravagant. ◆**extravagance** *nf* extravagance.

extrême [ɛkstrɛm] *a* extreme; **– nm** extreme; **pousser à l'e.** to take *ou* carry to extremes. ◆**—ment** *adv* extremely. ◆**extrémiste** *a* & *nmf* extremist. ◆**extrémité** *nf* (*bout*) extremity, end; *pl* (*excès*) extremes.

exubérant [ɛgzyberã] *a* exuberant. ◆**exubérance** *nf* exuberance.

exulter [ɛgzylte] *vi* to exult, rejoice. ◆**exultation** *nf* exultation.

F

F, f [ɛf] *nm* F, f.

F *abrév* franc(s).

fable [fabl] *nf* fable.

fabrique [fabrik] *nf* factory; **marque de f.** trade mark.

fabriquer [fabrike] *vt* (*objet*) to make; (*industriellement*) to manufacture; (*récit*) *Péj* to fabricate, make up; **qu'est-ce qu'il fabrique?** *Fam* what's he up to? ◆**fabricant**, **-ante** *nmf* manufacturer. ◆**fabrication** *nf* manufacture; (*artisanale*) making; **de f. française** of French make.

fabuleux, **-euse** [fabylø, -øz] *a* (*légendaire, incroyable*) fabulous.

fac [fak] *nf Univ Fam* = **faculté 2.**

façade [fasad] *nf* (*de bâtiment*) front, façade; (*apparence*) *Fig* pretence, façade; **de f.** (*luxe etc*) sham.

face [fas] *nf* face; (*de cube etc*) side;·(*de monnaie*) head; **de f.** (*photo*) full-face; (*vue*) front; **faire f. à** (*situation etc*) to face, face up to; **en f.** opposite; **en f. de** opposite, facing; (*en présence de*) in front of; **en f. d'un problème, f. à un problème** in the face of a

facétie [fasesi] *nf* joke, jest. ◆**facétieux, -euse** [-esjø, -øz] *a* (*personne*) facetious.

facette [faset] *nf* (*de diamant, problème etc*) facet.

fâch/er [faʃe] *vt* to anger; — **se f.** *vpr* to get angry *ou* annoyed (**contre** with); **se f. avec qn** (*se brouiller*) to fall out with s.o. ◆**—é** *a* (*air*) angry; (*amis*) on bad terms; **f. avec ou contre qn** angry *ou* annoyed with s.o.; **f. de qch** sorry about sth. ◆**fâcherie** *nf* quarrel. ◆**fâcheux, -euse** *a* (*nouvelle etc*) unfortunate.

facho [faʃo] *a* & *nmf Fam* fascist.

facile [fasil] *a* easy; (*caractère, humeur*) easygoing; (*banal*) *Péj* facile; **c'est f. à faire** it's easy to do; **il est f. de faire** ça it's easy to do that; **f. à vivre** easy to get along with, easygoing. ◆**—ment** *adv* easily. ◆**facilité** *nf* (*simplicité*) easiness; (*aisance*) ease; **facilités de paiement** *Com* easy terms; **avoir de la f.** to be gifted; **avoir toutes facilités pour** to have every facility *ou* opportunity to. ◆**faciliter** *vt* to facilitate, make easier.

façon [fasɔ̃] *nf* 1 way; **la f. dont elle parle** the way (in which) she talks; **f. (d'agir)** behaviour; **je n'aime pas ses façons** I don't like his *ou* her manners *ou* ways; **une f. de parler** a manner of speaking; **à la f. de** in the fashion of; **de toute f.** anyway, anyhow; **de f. à** so as to; **de f. générale** generally speaking; **à ma f.** my way, (in) my own way; **faire des façons** to make a fuss; **chêne imitation oak table.** 2 (*coupe de vêtement*) cut, style. ◆**façonner** *vt* (*travailler, former*) to fashion, shape; (*fabriquer*) to manufacture.

facteur [faktœr] *nm* 1 postman, *Am* mailman. 2 (*élément*) factor. ◆**factrice** *nf Fam* postwoman.

factice [faktis] *a* false, artificial; (*diamant*) imitation-.

faction [faksjɔ̃] *nf* 1 (*groupe*) *Pol* faction. 2 **de f.** *Mil* on guard (duty), on sentry duty.

facture [faktyr] *nf Com* invoice, bill. ◆**facturer** *vt* to invoice, bill.

facultatif, -ive [fakyltatif, -iv] *a* optional; **arrêt f.** request stop.

faculté [fakylte] *nf* 1 (*aptitude*) faculty; (*possibilité*) freedom (**de faire** to do); **une f. de travail** a capacity for work. 2 *Univ* faculty; **à la f.** *Fam* at university, *Am* at school.

fadaises [fadɛz] *nfpl* twaddle, nonsense.

fade [fad] *a* insipid. ◆**fadasse** *a Fam* wishy-washy.

fagot [fago] *nm* bundle (of firewood).

fagoter [fagɔte] *vt Péj* to dress, rig out.

faible [fɛbl] *a* weak, feeble; (*bruit, voix*) faint; (*vent, quantité, chances*) slight; (*revenus*) small; **f. en anglais/etc** poor at English/etc; — *nm* (*personne*) weakling; **les faibles** the weak; **avoir un f. pour** to have a weakness *ou* a soft spot for. ◆**faiblement** *adv* weakly; (*légèrement*) slightly; (*éclairer, parler*) faintly. ◆**faiblesse** *nf* weakness, feebleness; faintness; slightness; smallness; (*défaut, syncope*) weakness. ◆**faiblir** *vi* (*forces*) to weaken; (*courage, vue*) to fail; (*vent*) to slacken.

faïence [fajɑ̃s] *nf* (*matière*) earthenware; *pl* (*objets*) crockery, earthenware.

faille [faj] *nf Géol* fault; *Fig* flaw.

faillible [fajibl] *a* fallible.

faillir* [fajir] *vi* 1 **il a failli tomber** he almost *ou* nearly fell. 2 **f. à** (*devoir*) to fail in.

faillite [fajit] *nf Com* bankruptcy; *Fig* failure; **faire f.** to go bankrupt.

faim [fɛ̃] *nf* hunger; **avoir f.** to be hungry; **donner f. à qn** to make s.o. hungry; **manger à sa f.** to eat one's fill; **mourir de f.** to die of starvation; (*avoir très faim*) *Fig* to be starving.

fainéant, -ante [feneɑ̃, -ɑ̃t] *a* idle; — *nmf* idler. ◆**fainéanter** *vi* to idle. ◆**fainéantise** *nf* idleness.

faire* [fɛr] 1 *vt* (*bruit, pain, faute etc*) to make; (*devoir, dégâts, ménage etc*) to do; (*rêve, chute*) to have; (*sourire, grognement*) to give; (*promenade, sieste*) to have, take; (*guerre*) to wage, make; **ça fait dix mètres de large** (*mesure*) it's ten metres wide; **2 et 2 font 4** 2 and 2 are 4; **ça fait dix francs** that is *ou* comes to ten francs; **qu'a-t-il fait (de)?** what's he done (with)?; **que f.?** what's to be done?; **f. du tennis/du piano/etc** to play tennis/the piano/etc; **f. l'idiot** to act *ou* play the fool; **ça ne fait rien** that doesn't matter; **comment as-tu fait pour . . . ?** how did you manage to . . . ?; **il ne fait que travailler** he does nothing but work, he keeps on working; **je ne fais que d'arriver** I've just arrived; **oui, fit-elle** yes, she said. 2 *vi* (*agir*) to do; (*paraître*) to look; **il fait vieux** he looks old; **il fera un bon médecin** he'll be *ou* make a good doctor; **elle ferait bien de partir** she'd do well to leave. 3 *v imp* **il fait beau/froid/etc** it's fine/cold/etc; **quel temps fait-il?** what's the weather like?; **ça fait deux ans que je ne l'ai pas vu** I haven't seen him for two years, it's (been) two years since I saw him. **4** *v aux* (+ *inf*); **f. construire une maison** to have *ou* get a house built (**à qn, par qn** by s.o.); **f. crier/souffrir/***etc* **qn** to make s.o. shout/suffer/*etc*; **se f. couper les cheveux** to have one's hair cut; **se f. craindre/obéir/***etc* to make oneself feared/obeyed/*etc*; **se f. tuer/renverser/***etc* to get *ou* be killed/knocked down/*etc*. **5 se f.** *vpr* (*fabrication*) to be made; (*activité*) to be done; **se f. des illusions** to have illusions; **se f. des amis** to make friends; **se f. vieux/***etc* (*devenir*) to get old/*etc*; **il se fait tard** it's getting late; **comment se fait-il que?** how is it that?; **se f. à** to get used to, adjust to; **ne t'en fais pas!** don't worry!

faire-part [fɛrpar] *nm inv* (*de mariage etc*) announcement.

faisable [fəzabl] *a* feasible.

faisan [fəzɑ̃] *nm* (*oiseau*) pheasant.

faisandé [fəzɑ̃de] *a* (*gibier*) high.

faisceau, -x [fɛso] *nm* (*lumineux*) beam; (*de tiges etc*) bundle.

fait [fɛ] **1** *voir* **faire**; — *a* (*fromage*) ripe; (*homme*) grown; (*yeux*) made up; (*ongles*) polished; **tout f.** ready made; **bien f.** (*jambes, corps etc*) shapely; **c'est bien f.!** it serves you right! **2** *nm* event, occurrence; (*donnée, réalité*) fact; **prendre sur le f.** *Jur* to catch in the act; **du f. de** on account of; **f. divers** *Journ* (miscellaneous) news item; **au f.** (*à propos*) by the way; **aller au f.** to get to the point; **faits et gestes** actions; **en f.** in fact; **en f. de** in the matter of.

faîte [fɛt] *nm* (*haut*) top; (*apogée*) *Fig* height.

faites [fɛt] *voir* **faire**.

faitout [fɛtu] *nm* stewing pot, casserole.

falaise [falɛz] *nf* cliff.

falloir* [falwar] **1** *v imp* **il faut qch/qn** I, you, we *etc* need sth/s.o.; **il lui faut un stylo** he *ou* she needs a pen; **il faut partir/***etc* I, you, we *etc* have to go/*etc*; **il faut que je parte** I have to go; **il faudrait qu'elle reste** she ought to stay; **il faut un jour** it takes a day (**pour faire** to do); **comme il faut** proper(ly); **s'il le faut** if need be. **2 s'en f.** *v imp* **peu s'en est fallu qu'il ne pleure** he almost cried; **tant s'en faut** far from it.

falsifier [falsifje] *vt* (*texte etc*) to falsify. ◆**falsification** *nf* falsification.

famé (mal) [malfame] *a* of ill repute.

famélique [famelik] *a* ill-fed, starving.

fameux, -euse [famø, -øz] *a* famous; (*excellent*) *Fam* first-class; **pas f.** *Fam* not much good.

familial, -aux [familjal, -o] *a* family-.

familier, -ière [familje, -jɛr] *a* (*bien connu*) familiar (**à to**); (*amical*) friendly, informal; (*locution*) colloquial, familiar; **f. avec qn** (over)familiar with s.o.; — *nm* (*de club etc*) regular visitor. ◆**familiariser** *vt* to familiarize (**avec with**); — **se f.** *vpr* to familiarize oneself (**avec with**). ◆**familiarité** *nf* familiarity; *pl Péj* liberties. ◆**familièrement** *adv* familiarly; (*parler*) informally.

famille [famij] *nf* family; **en f.** (*dîner etc*) with one's family; **un père de f.** a family man.

famine [famin] *nf* famine.

fan [fɑ̃] *nm* (*admirateur*) *Fam* fan.

fana [fana] *nmf Fam* fan; **être f. de** to be crazy about.

fanal, -aux [fanal, -o] *nm* lantern, light.

fanatique [fanatik] *a* fanatical; — *nmf* fanatic. ◆**fanatisme** *nm* fanaticism.

fan/er (se) [səfane] *vpr* (*fleur, beauté*) to fade. ◆**-é** *a* faded.

fanfare [fɑ̃far] *nf* (*orchestre*) brass band; (*air, musique*) fanfare.

fanfaron, -onne [fɑ̃farɔ̃, -ɔn] *a* boastful; — *nmf* braggart.

fange [fɑ̃ʒ] *nf Litt* mud, mire.

fanion [fanjɔ̃] *nm* (*drapeau*) pennant.

fantaisie [fɑ̃tezi] *nf* (*caprice*) fancy, whim; (*imagination*) imagination, fantasy; (**de**) **f.** (*bouton etc*) fancy. ◆**fantaisiste** *a* (*pas sérieux*) fanciful; (*irrégulier*) unorthodox.

fantasme [fɑ̃tasm] *nm Psy* fantasy. ◆**fantasmer** *vi* to fantasize (**sur about**).

fantasque [fɑ̃task] *a* whimsical.

fantassin [fɑ̃tasɛ̃] *nm Mil* infantryman.

fantastique [fɑ̃tastik] *a* (*imaginaire, excellent*) fantastic.

fantoche [fɑ̃tɔʃ] *nm & a* puppet.

fantôme [fɑ̃tom] *nm* ghost, phantom; — *a* (*ville, train*) ghost-; (*firme*) bogus.

faon [fɑ̃] *nm* (*animal*) fawn.

faramineux, -euse [faraminø, -øz] *a Fam* fantastic.

farce¹ [fars] *nf* practical joke, prank; *Th* farce; **magasin de farces et attrapes** joke shop. ◆**farceur, -euse** *nmf* (*blagueur*) wag, joker.

farce² [fars] *nf Culin* stuffing. ◆**farcir** *vt* **1** *Culin* to stuff. **2 se f. qn/qch** *Fam* to put up with s.o./sth.

fard [far] *nm* make-up. ◆**farder** *vt* (*vérité*) to camouflage; — **se f.** *vpr* (*se maquiller*) to make up.

fardeau, -x [fardo] *nm* burden, load.

farfelu, -ue [farfəly] *a Fam* crazy, bizarre; — *nmf Fam* weirdo.

farine [farin] *nf* (*de blé*) flour; **f. d'avoine**

oatmeal. ◆**farineux, -euse** a Péj floury, powdery.

farouche [faruʃ] a **1** (timide) shy, unsociable; (animal) easily scared. **2** (violent, acharné) fierce. ◆**—ment** adv fiercely.

fart [far(t)] nm (ski) wax. ◆**farter** vt (skis) to wax.

fascicule [fasikyl] nm volume.

fasciner [fasine] vt to fascinate. ◆**fascination** nf fascination.

fascisme [faʃism] nm fascism. ◆**fasciste** a & nmf fascist.

fasse(nt) [fas] voir **faire**.

faste [fast] nm ostentation, display.

fastidieux, -euse [fastidj**ø**, -**ø**z] a tedious, dull.

fatal, mpl -als [fatal] a (mortel) fatal; (inévitable) inevitable; (moment, ton) fateful; **c'était f.!** it was bound to happen! ◆**—ement** adv inevitably. ◆**fataliste** a fatalistic; — nmf fatalist. ◆**fatalité** nf (destin) fate. ◆**fatidique** a (jour, date) fateful.

fatigue [fatig] nf tiredness, fatigue, weariness. ◆**fatigant** a (épuisant) tiring; (ennuyeux) tiresome. ◆**fatigu/er** vt to tire, fatigue; (yeux) to strain; (importuner) to annoy; (raser) to bore; — vi (moteur) to strain; — **se f.** vpr (se lasser) to get tired, tire (de of); (travailler) to tire oneself out (à faire doing). ◆**—é** a tired, weary (de of).

fatras [fatra] nm jumble, muddle.

faubourg [fobur] nm suburb. ◆**faubourien, -ienne** a (accent etc) suburban, common.

fauché [foʃe] a (sans argent) Fam broke.

fauch/er [foʃe] vt **1** (herbe) to mow; (blé) to reap; (abattre, renverser) Fig to mow down. **2** (voler) Fam to snatch, pinch. ◆**—euse** nf (machine) reaper.

faucille [fosij] nf (instrument) sickle.

faucon [fok**ɔ̃**] nm (oiseau) falcon, hawk; (personne) Fig hawk.

faudra, faudrait [fodra, fodrɛ] voir **falloir**.

faufiler (se) [s**ə**fofile] vpr to edge ou inch one's way (dans through, into; entre between).

faune [fon] nf wildlife, fauna; (gens) Péj set.

faussaire [fosɛr] nm (faux-monnayeur) forger.

fausse [fos] voir **faux** ¹. ◆**faussement** adv falsely.

fausser [fose] vt (sens, réalité etc) to distort; (clé etc) to buckle; **f. compagnie à qn** to give s.o. the slip.

fausseté [foste] nf (d'un raisonnement etc) falseness; (hypocrisie) duplicity.

faut [fo] voir **falloir**.

faute [fot] nf (erreur) mistake; (responsabilité) fault; (délit) offence; (péché) sin; Fb foul; **c'est ta f.** it's your fault, you're to blame; **f. de temps/etc** for lack of time/etc; **f. de mieux** for want of anything better; **en f.** at fault; **sans f.** without fail. ◆**fautif, -ive** a (personne) at fault; (erroné) faulty.

fauteuil [fot**œ**j] nm armchair; (de président) chair; (de théâtre) seat in the stalls; **f. roulant** wheelchair; **f. pivotant** swivel chair.

fauteur [fot**œ**r] nm **f. de troubles** troublemaker.

fauve [fov] **1** a & nm (couleur) fawn. **2** nm wild beast; **chasse aux fauves** big game hunting.

faux ¹, fausse [fo, fos] a (inauthentique) false; (pas vrai) untrue, false; (pas exact) wrong; (monnaie) counterfeit, forged; (bijou, marbre) imitation-, fake; (voix) out of tune; (col) detachable; — adv (chanter) out of tune; — nm (contrefaçon) forgery; **le f.** the false, the untrue. ◆**f.-filet** nm Culin sirloin. ◆**f.-fuyant** nm subterfuge. ◆**f.-monnayeur** nm counterfeiter.

faux ² [fo] nf (instrument) scythe.

faveur [fav**œ**r] nf favour; **en f. de** (au profit de) in favour of; **de f.** (billet) complimentary; (traitement, régime) preferential. ◆**favorable** a favourable (à to). ◆**favori, -ite** a & nmf favourite. ◆**favoriser** vt to favour. ◆**favoritisme** nm favouritism.

favoris [favori] nmpl sideburns, side whiskers.

fébrile [febril] a feverish. ◆**fébrilité** nf feverishness.

fécond [fek**ɔ̃**] a (femme, idée etc) fertile. ◆**féconder** vt to fertilize. ◆**fécondité** nf fertility.

fécule [fekyl] nf starch. ◆**féculents** nmpl (aliments) carbohydrates.

fédéral, -aux [federal, -o] a federal. ◆**fédération** nf federation. ◆**fédérer** vt to federate.

fée [fe] nf fairy. ◆**féerie** nf Th fantasy extravaganza; Fig fairy-like spectacle. ◆**féerique** a fairy(-like), magical.

feindre* [fɛdr] vt to feign, sham; **f. de faire** to pretend to do. ◆**feint** a feigned, sham. ◆**feinte** nf sham, pretence; Boxe Mil feint.

fêler [fele] vt, — **se f.** vpr (tasse) to crack. ◆**fêlure** nf crack.

félicité [felisite] nf bliss, felicity.

féliciter [felisite] vt to congratulate (qn de ou sur s.o. on); **se f. de** to congratulate oneself on. ◆**félicitations** *nfpl* congratulations (**pour** on).

félin [felɛ̃] *a* & *nm* feline.

femelle [fəmɛl] *a* & *nf* (*animal*) female.

féminin [feminɛ̃] *a* (*prénom, hormone etc*) female; (*trait, intuition etc*) & *Gram* feminine; (*mode, revue, équipe etc*) women's. ◆**féministe** *a* & *nmf* feminist. ◆**féminité** *nf* femininity.

femme [fam] *nf* woman; (*épouse*) wife; **f. médecin** woman doctor; **f. de chambre** (chamber)maid; **f. de ménage** cleaning lady, maid; **bonne f.** *Fam* woman.

fémur [femyr] *nm* thighbone, femur.

fendiller (se) [səfɑ̃dije] *vpr* to crack.

fendre [fɑ̃dr] *vt* (*bois etc*) to split; (*foule*) to force one's way through; (*onde, air*) to cleave; (*cœur*) *Fig* to break, rend; **— se f.** *vpr* (*se fissurer*) to crack.

fenêtre [f(ə)nɛtr] *nf* window.

fenouil [fənuj] *nm Bot Culin* fennel.

fente [fɑ̃t] *nf* (*de tirelire, palissade, jupe etc*) slit; (*de rocher*) split, crack.

féodal, -aux [feɔdal, -o] *a* feudal.

fer [fɛr] *nm* iron; (*partie métallique de qch*) metal (part); **de f., en f.** (*outil etc*) iron-; **fil de f.** wire; **f. à cheval** horseshoe; **f.** (**à repasser**) iron; **f. à friser** curling tongs; **f. de lance** *Fig* spearhead; **de f.** (*santé*) *Fig* cast-iron; (*main, volonté*) *Fig* iron-. ◆**fer-blanc** *nm* (*pl* **fers-blancs**) tin(-plate).

fera, ferait [fəra, fərɛ] *voir* **faire**.

férié [ferje] *a* **jour f.** (public) holiday.

ferme¹ [fɛrm] *nf* farm; (*maison*) farm(house).

ferme² [fɛrm] *a* (*beurre, décision etc*) firm; (*autoritaire*) firm (**avec** with); (*pas, voix*) steady; (*pâte*) stiff; **— adv** (*travailler, boire*) hard; (*discuter*) keenly; **tenir f.** to stand firm *ou* fast. ◆**—ment** [-əmɑ̃] *adv* firmly.

ferment [fɛrmɑ̃] *nm* ferment. ◆**fermentation** *nf* fermentation. ◆**fermenter** *vi* to ferment.

ferm/er [fɛrme] *vt* to close, shut; (*gaz, radio etc*) to turn *ou* switch off; (*passage*) to block; (*vêtement*) to do up; **f.** (**à clef**) to lock; **f. la marche** to bring up the rear; **— vi,** **— se f.** *vpr* to close, shut. ◆**—é** *a* (*porte, magasin etc*) closed, shut; (*route, circuit etc*) closed; (*gaz etc*) off. ◆**fermeture** *nf* closing, closure; (*heure*) closing time; (*mécanisme*) catch; **f. éclair**® zip (fastener), *Am* zipper. ◆**fermoir** *nm* clasp, (snap) fastener.

fermeté [fɛrməte] *nf* firmness; (*de geste, voix*) steadiness.

fermier, -ière [fɛrmje, -jɛr] *nmf* farmer; **— a** (*poulet, produit*) farm-.

féroce [ferɔs] *a* fierce, ferocious. ◆**férocité** *nf* ferocity, fierceness.

ferraille [fɛraj] *nf* scrap-iron; **mettre à la f.** to scrap. ◆**ferrailleur** *nm* scrap-iron merchant.

ferré [fɛre] *a* **1** (*canne*) metal-tipped; **voie ferrée** railway, *Am* road; (*rails*) track. **2** (*calé*) *Fam* well up (**en** in, **sur** on).

ferrer [fɛre] *vt* (*cheval*) to shoe.

ferronnerie [fɛrɔnri] *nf* ironwork.

ferroviaire [fɛrɔvjɛr] *a* (*compagnie etc*) railway-, *Am* railroad-.

ferry-boat [feribot] *nm* ferry.

fertile [fɛrtil] *a* (*terre, imagination*) fertile; **en incidents** eventful. ◆**fertiliser** *vt* to fertilize. ◆**fertilité** *nf* fertility.

fervent, -ente [fɛrvɑ̃, -ɑ̃t] *a* fervent; **— nmf** devotee (**de** of). ◆**ferveur** *nf* fervour.

fesse [fɛs] *nf* buttock; **les fesses** one's behind. ◆**fessée** *nf* spanking.

festin [fɛstɛ̃] *nm* (*banquet*) feast.

festival, pl -als [fɛstival] *nm Mus Cin* festival.

festivités [fɛstivite] *nfpl* festivities.

festoyer [fɛstwaje] *vi* to feast, carouse.

fête [fɛt] *nf* (*civile*) holiday; *Rel* festival, feast; (*entre amis*) party; **f. du village** village fair *ou* fête; **f. de famille** family celebration; **c'est sa f.** it's his *ou* her saint's day; **f. des Mères** Mother's Day; **jour de f.** (public) holiday; **faire la f.** to make merry, revel; **air de f.** festive air. ◆**fêter** *vt* (*événement*) to celebrate.

fétiche [fetiʃ] *nm* (*objet de culte*) fetish; (*mascotte*) *Fig* mascot.

fétide [fetid] *a* fetid, stinking.

feu¹, -x [fø] *nm* fire; (*lumière*) *Aut Nau Av* light; (*de réchaud*) burner; (*de dispute*) *Fig* heat; *pl* (*de signalisation*) traffic lights; **feux de position** *Aut* parking lights; **feux de croisement** *Aut* dipped headlights, *Am* low beams; **f. rouge** *Aut* (*lumière*) red light; (*objet*) traffic lights; **tous feux éteints** *Aut* without lights; **mettre le f. à** to set fire to; **en f.** on fire, ablaze; **avez-vous du f.?** have you got a light?; **donner le f. vert** to give the go-ahead (**à** to); **ne pas faire long f.** not to last very long; **à f. doux** *Culin* on a low light; **au f.!** (there's a) fire!; **f.! ** *Mil* fire!; **coup de f.** (*bruit*) gunshot; **feux croisés** *Mil* crossfire.

feu² [fø] *a inv* late; **f. ma tante** my late aunt.

feuille [fœj] *nf* leaf; (*de papier etc*) sheet; (*de température*) chart; *Journ* newssheet; **f. d'impôt** tax form *ou* return; **f. de paye** pay slip. ◆**feuillage** *nm* foliage. ◆**feuillet** *nm* (*de livre*) leaf. ◆**feuilleter** *vt* (*livre*) to flip *ou* leaf through; **pâte feuilletée** puff *ou* flaky pastry. ◆**feuilleton** *nm* (*roman, film etc*) serial. ◆**feuillu** *a* leafy.

feutre [føtr] *nm* felt; (*chapeau*) felt hat; **crayon f.** felt-tip(ped) pen. ◆**feutré** *a* (*bruit*) muffled; **à pas feutrés** silently.

fève [fɛv] *nf* bean.

février [fevrije] *nm* February.

fiable [fjabl] *a* reliable. ◆**fiabilité** *nf* reliability.

fiacre [fjakr] *nm* Hist hackney carriage.

fianc/er (se) [səfjãse] *vpr* to become engaged (**avec** to). ◆**—é** *nm* fiancé; *pl* engaged couple. ◆**—ée** *nf* fiancée. ◆**fiançailles** *nfpl* engagement.

fiasco [fjasko] *nm* fiasco; **faire f.** to be a fiasco.

fibre [fibr] *nf* fibre; **f.** (**alimentaire**) roughage, (*dietary*) fibre; **f. de verre** fibreglass.

ficelle [fisɛl] *nf* **1** string; **connaître les ficelles** (*d'un métier etc*) to known the ropes. **2** (*pain*) long thin loaf. ◆**ficeler** *vt* to tie up.

fiche [fiʃ] *nf* **1** (*carte*) index *ou* record card; (*papier*) slip, form; **f. technique** data record. **2** *Él* (*broche*) pin; (*prise*) plug. ◆**fichier** *nm* card index, file.

fiche(r) [fiʃ(e)] *vt* (*pp* **fichu**) *Fam* (*faire*) to do; (*donner*) to give; (*jeter*) to throw; (*mettre*) to put; **le camp** to shove off; **fiche-moi la paix!** leave me alone!; **se f. de qn** to make fun of s.o.; **je m'en fiche!** I don't give a damn!

ficher [fiʃe] *vt* **1** (*enfoncer*) to drive in. **2** (*renseignement, personne*) to put on file.

fichu [fiʃy] **1** *a Fam* (*mauvais*) lousy, rotten; (*capable*) able (**de faire** to do); **il est f.** he's had it, he's done for; **mal f.** (*malade*) not well. **2** *nm* (head) scarf.

fictif, -ive [fiktif, -iv] *a* fictitious. ◆**fiction** *nf* fiction.

fidèle [fidɛl] *a* faithful (**à** to); – *nmf* faithful supporter; (*client*) regular (customer); **les fidèles** (*croyants*) the faithful; (*à l'église*) the congregation. ◆**—ment** *adv* faithfully. ◆**fidélité** *nf* fidelity, faithfulness.

fief [fjɛf] *nm* (*spécialité, chasse gardée*) domain.

fiel [fjɛl] *nm* gall.

fier (se) [səfje] *vpr* **se f. à** to trust.

fier, fière [fjɛr] *a* proud (**de** of); **un f. culot** *Péj* a rare cheek. ◆**fièrement** *adv* proudly. ◆**fierté** *nf* pride.

fièvre [fjɛvr] *nf* (*maladie*) fever; (*agitation*) frenzy; **avoir de la f.** to have a temperature *ou* a fever. ◆**fiévreux, -euse** *a* feverish.

fig/er [fiʒe] *vt* (*sang, sauce etc*) to congeal; **f. qn** (*paralyser*) *Fig* to freeze s.o.; – *vi* (*liquide*) to congeal; — **se f.** *vpr* (*liquide*) to congeal; (*sourire, personne*) *Fig* to freeze. ◆**—é** *a* (*locution*) set, fixed; (*regard*) frozen; (*société*) petrified.

fignol/er [fiɲɔle] *vt Fam* to round off meticulously, refine. ◆**—é** *a Fam* meticulous.

figue [fig] *nf* fig; **mi-f., mi-raisin** (*accueil etc*) neither good nor bad, mixed. ◆**figuier** *nm* fig tree.

figurant, -ante [figyrã, -ãt] *nmf Cin Th* extra.

figure [figyr] *nf* **1** (*visage*) face. **2** (*personnage*) & *Géom* figure; (*de livre*) figure, illustration; **faire f. de riche/d'imbécile**/*etc* to look rich/a fool/*etc*. ◆**figurine** *nf* statuette.

figur/er [figyre] *vt* to represent; – *vi* to appear, figure; — **se f.** *vpr* to imagine; **figurez-vous que . . . ?** would you believe that . . . ? ◆**—é** *a* (*sens*) figurative; – *nm* **au f.** figuratively.

fil [fil] *nm* **1** (*de coton, pensée etc*) thread; (*lin*) linen; **f. dentaire** dental floss; **de f. en aiguille** bit by bit. **2** (*métallique*) wire; **f. de fer** wire; **f. à plomb** plumbline; **au bout du f.** *Tél* on the line; **passer un coup de f. à qn** *Tél* to give s.o. a ring *ou* a call. **3** (*de couteau*) edge. **4** **au f. de l'eau/des jours** with the current/the passing of time.

filament [filamã] *nm Él* filament.

filandreux, -euse [filãdrø, -øz] *a* (*phrase*) long-winded.

filante [filãt] *af* **étoile f.** shooting star.

file [fil] *nf* line; (*couloir*) *Aut* lane; **f. d'attente** queue, *Am* line; **en f.** (**indienne**) in single file; **chef de f.** leader; (**se**) **mettre en f.** to line up.

filer [file] **1** *vt* (*coton etc*) to spin. **2** *vt* **f. qn** (*suivre*) to shadow s.o., tail s.o. **3** *vt Fam* **f. qch à qn** (*objet*) to slip s.o. sth; **f. un coup de pied**/*etc* **à qn** to give s.o. a kick/*etc*. **4** *vi* (*partir*) to shoot off, bolt; (*aller vite*) to speed along; (*temps*) to fly; (*bas, collant*) to ladder, run; (*liquide*) to trickle, run; **filez!** hop it!; **f. entre les doigts de qn** to slip through s.o.'s fingers; **f. doux** to be obedient. ◆**filature** *nf* **1** (*usine*) textile mill. **2** (*de policiers etc*) shadowing; **prendre en f.** to shadow.

filet [filɛ] *nm* **1** (*de pêche*) & *Sp* net; (*à bagages*) *Rail* (luggage) rack; **f.** (**à provisions**) string *ou* net bag (*for shopping*). **2** (*d'eau*) trickle. **3** (*de poisson, viande*) fillet.

filial, -aux [filjal, -o] *a* filial.

filiale [filjal] *nf* subsidiary (company).

filiation [filjɑsjɔ̃] *nf* relationship.
filière [filjɛr] *nf* (*de drogue*) network; **suivre la f.** (*pour obtenir qch*) to go through the official channels; (*employé*) to work one's way up.
filigrane [filigran] *nm* (*de papier*) watermark.
filin [filɛ̃] *nm Nau* rope.
fille [fij] *nf* **1** girl; **petite f.** (little *ou* young) girl; **jeune f.** girl, young lady; **vieille f.** *Péj* old maid; **f. (publique)** *Péj* prostitute. **2** (*parenté*) daughter, girl. ◆**f.-mère** *nf* (*pl* **filles-mères**) *Péj* unmarried mother. ◆**fillette** *nf* little girl.
filleul [fijœl] *nm* godson. ◆**filleule** *nf* goddaughter.
film [film] *nm* film, movie; (*pellicule*) film; **f. muet/parlant** silent/talking film *ou* movie; **le f. des événements** the sequence of events. ◆**filmer** *vt* (*personne, scène*) to film.
filon [filɔ̃] *nm Géol* seam; **trouver le (bon) f.** to strike it lucky.
filou [filu] *nm* rogue, crook.
fils [fis] *nm* son; **Dupont f.** Dupont junior.
filtre [filtr] *nm* filter; **(à bout) f.** (*cigarette*) (filter-)tipped; **(bout) f.** filter tip. ◆**filtrer** *vt* to filter; (*personne, nouvelles*) to scrutinize; – *vi* to filter (through).
fin [fɛ̃] **1** *nf* end; (*but*) end, aim; **mettre f. à** to put an end *ou* a stop to; **prendre f.** to come to an end; **tirer à sa f.** to draw to an end *ou* a close; **sans f.** endless; **à la f.** in the end; **arrêtez, à la f.!** stop, for heaven's sake!; **f. de semaine** weekend; **f. mai** at the end of May; **à cette f.** to this end. **2** *a* (*pointe, travail, tissu etc*) fine; (*taille, tranche*) thin; (*plat*) delicate, choice; (*esprit, oreille*) sharp; (*observation*) sharp, fine; (*gourmet*) discerning; (*rusé*) shrewd; (*intelligent*) clever; **au f. fond de** in the depths of; – *adv* (*couper, moudre*) finely; (*écrire*) small.
final, -aux *ou* **-als** [final, -o] *a* final; – *nm Mus* finale. ◆**finale** *nf Sp* final; *Gram* final syllable; – *nm Mus* finale. ◆**finalement** *adv* finally; (*en somme*) after all. ◆**finaliste** *nmf Sp* finalist.
finance [finɑ̃s] *nf* finance. ◆**financ/er** *vt* to finance. ◆**—ement** *nm* financing. ◆**financier, -ière** *a* financial; – *nm* financier. ◆**financièrement** *adv* financially.
fine [fin] *nf* liqueur brandy.
finement [finmɑ̃] *adv* (*broder, couper etc*) finely; (*agir*) cleverly.
finesse [fines] *nf* (*de pointe etc*) fineness; (*de taille etc*) thinness; (*de plat*) delicacy; (*d'esprit, de goût*) finesse; *pl* (*de langue*) niceties.

fin/ir [finir] *vt* to finish; (*discours, vie*) to end, finish; – *vi* to finish, end; **f. de faire** to finish doing; (*cesser*) to stop doing; **f. par faire** to end up *ou* finish up doing; **f. par qch** to finish (up) *ou* end (up) with sth; **en f. avec** to put an end to, finish with; **elle n'en finit pas** there's no end to it, she goes on and on. ◆**—i** *a* (*produit*) finished; (*univers etc*) & *Math* finite; **c'est f.** it's over *ou* finished; **il est f.** (*fichu*) he's done for *ou* finished; – *nm* (*poli*) finish. ◆**—issant** *a* (*siècle*) declining. ◆**finish** *nm Sp* finish. ◆**finition** *nf* (*action*) *Tech* finishing; (*résultat*) finish.
Finlande [fɛ̃lɑ̃d] *nf* Finland. ◆**finlandais, -aise** *a* Finnish; – *nmf* Finn. ◆**finnois, -oise** *a* Finnish; – *nmf* Finn; – *nm* (*langue*) Finnish.
fiole [fjɔl] *nf* phial, flask.
firme [firm] *nf* (*entreprise*) *Com* firm.
fisc [fisk] *nm* tax authorities, = Inland Revenue, = *Am* Internal Revenue. ◆**fiscal, -aux** *a* fiscal, tax-. ◆**fiscalité** *nf* tax system; (*charges*) taxation.
fission [fisjɔ̃] *nf Phys* fission.
fissure [fisyr] *nf* split, crack, fissure. ◆**se fissurer** *vpr* to split, crack.
fiston [fistɔ̃] *nm Fam* son, sonny.
fixe [fiks] *a* fixed; (*prix, heure*) set, fixed; **idée f.** obsession; **regard f.** stare; **être au beau f.** *Mét* to be set fair; – *nm* (*paie*) fixed salary. ◆**—ment** [-əmɑ̃] *adv* **regarder f.** to stare at. ◆**fixer** *vt* (*attacher*) to fix (à to); (*choix*) to settle; (*règle, date etc*) to decide, fix; **f. (du regard)** to stare at; **f. qn sur** to inform s.o. clearly about; **être fixé** (*décidé*) to be decided; **comme ça on est fixé!** (*renseigné*) we've got the picture!; – **se f.** *vpr* (*regard*) to become fixed; (*s'établir*) to settle. ◆**fixateur** *nm Phot* fixer; (*pour cheveux*) setting lotion. ◆**fixation** *nf* (*action*) fixing; (*dispositif*) fastening, binding; *Psy* fixation.
flacon [flakɔ̃] *nm* bottle, flask.
flageoler [flaʒɔle] *vi* to shake, tremble.
flageolet [flaʒɔle] *nm Bot Culin* (dwarf) kidney bean.
flagrant [flagrɑ̃] *a* (*injustice etc*) flagrant, glaring; **pris en f. délit** caught in the act *ou* red-handed.
flair [flɛr] *nm* **1** (*d'un chien etc*) (sense of) smell, scent. **2** (*clairvoyance*) intuition, flair. ◆**flairer** *vt* to sniff at, smell; (*discerner*) *Fig* to smell, sense.
flamand, -ande [flamɑ̃, -ɑ̃d] *a* Flemish; – *nmf* Fleming; – *nm* (*langue*) Flemish.
flamant [flamɑ̃] *nm* (*oiseau*) flamingo.

flambant [flɑ̃bɑ̃] adv f. **neuf** brand new.
flambeau, -x [flɑ̃bo] nm torch.
flamb/er [flɑ̃be] **1** vi to burn, blaze; – vt (aiguille) Méd to sterilize; (poulet) to singe. **2** vi (jouer) Fam to gamble for big money. ◆**–é** a (ruiné) Fam done for. ◆**–ée** nf blaze; (de colère, des prix etc) Fig surge; (de violence) flare-up, eruption. ◆**–eur** nm Fam big gambler. ◆**flamboyer** vi to blaze, flame.
flamme [flam] nf flame; (ardeur) Fig fire; **en flammes** on fire. ◆**flammèche** nf spark.
flan [flɑ̃] nm **1** Culin custard tart ou pie. **2** au f. Fam on the off chance, on the spur of the moment.
flanc [flɑ̃] nm side; (d'une armée, d'un animal) flank; **tirer au f.** Arg to shirk, idle.
flancher [flɑ̃ʃe] vi Fam to give in, weaken.
Flandre(s) [flɑ̃dr] nf(pl) Flanders.
flanelle [flanɛl] nf (tissu) flannel.
flâner [flɑne] vi to stroll, dawdle. ◆**flânerie** nf (action) strolling; (promenade) stroll.
flanquer [flɑ̃ke] vt **1** to flank (de with). **2** Fam (jeter) to chuck; (donner) to give; **f. qn à la porte** to throw s.o. out.
flaque [flak] nf puddle, pool.
flash [flaʃ] nm, pl **flashes** [flaʃ] nm **1** Phot (éclair) flashlight; (dispositif) flash(gun). **2** TV Rad (news)flash.
flasque [flask] a flabby, floppy.
flatt/er [flɑte] vt to flatter; **se f. d'être malin/de réussir** to flatter oneself on being smart/on being able to succeed. ◆**–é** a flattered (de qch by sth, de faire to do, que that). ◆**flatterie** nf flattery. ◆**flatteur, -euse** nmf flatterer; – a flattering.
fléau, -x [fleo] nm **1** (calamité) scourge; (personne, chose) bane, plague. **2** Agr flail.
flèche [flɛʃ] nf arrow; (d'église) spire; **monter en f.** (prix) to (sky)rocket, shoot ahead. ◆**flécher** [fleʃe] vt to signpost (with arrows). ◆**fléchette** nf dart; pl (jeu) darts.
fléchir [fleʃir] vt (membre) to flex, bend; **f. qn** Fig to move s.o., persuade s.o.; – vi (membre) to bend; (poutre) to sag; (faiblir) to give way; (baisser) to fall off.
flegme [flɛgm] nm composure. ◆**flegmatique** a phlegmatic, stolid.
flemme [flɛm] nf Fam laziness; **il a la f.** he can't be bothered, he's just too lazy. ◆**flemmard, -arde** a Fam lazy; – nmf Fam lazybones.
flétrir [fletrir] **1** vt, – **se f.** vpr to wither. **2** vt (blâmer) to stigmatize, brand.
fleur [flœr] nf flower; (d'arbre, d'arbuste) blossom; **en f.** in flower, in bloom; in blos-

som; **à** ou **dans la f. de l'âge** in the prime of life; **à f. d'eau** just above the water; **à fleurs** (tissu) floral. ◆**fleur/ir** vi to flower, bloom; (arbre etc) to blossom; (art, commerce etc) Fig to flourish; – vt (table etc) to decorate with flowers. ◆**–i** a (fleur, jardin) in bloom; (tissu) flowered, floral; (teint) florid; (style) flowery, florid. ◆**fleuriste** nmf florist.
fleuve [flœv] nm river.
flexible [flɛksibl] a flexible, pliable. ◆**flexibilité** nf flexibility.
flexion [flɛksjɔ̃] nf **1** Anat flexion, flexing. **2** Gram inflexion.
flic [flik] nm Fam cop, policeman.
flinguer [flɛ̃ge] vt **f. qn** Arg to shoot s.o.
flipper [flipœr] nm (jeu) pinball.
flirt [flœrt] nm (rapports) flirtation; (personne) flirt. ◆**flirter** vi to flirt (avec with). ◆**flirteur, -euse** a flirtatious; – nmf flirt.
flocon [flɔkɔ̃] nm (de neige) flake; (de laine) flock; **flocons d'avoine** Culin porridge oats. ◆**floconneux, -euse** a fluffy.
floraison [flɔrɛzɔ̃] nf flowering; **en pleine f.** in full bloom. ◆**floral, -aux** a floral. ◆**floralies** nfpl flower show.
flore [flɔr] nf flora.
florissant [flɔrisɑ̃] a flourishing.
flot [flo] nm (de souvenirs, larmes) flood, stream; (marée) floodtide; pl (de mer) waves; (de lac) waters; **à flots** in abundance; **à f.** (bateau, personne) afloat; **mettre à f.** (bateau, firme) to launch; **remettre qn à f.** to restore s.o.'s fortunes.
flotte [flɔt] nf **1** Nau Av fleet. **2** Fam (pluie) rain; (eau) water. ◆**flottille** nf Nau flotilla.
flott/er [flɔte] vi to float; (drapeau) to fly; (cheveux) to flow; (pensées) to drift; (pleuvoir) Fam to rain. ◆**–ant** a **1** (bois, dette etc) floating; (vêtement) flowing, loose. **2** (esprit) indecisive. ◆**–ement** nm (hésitation) indecision. ◆**–eur** nm Pêche etc float.
flou [flu] a (photo) fuzzy, blurred; (idée) hazy, fuzzy; – nm fuzziness.
fluctuant [flyktɥɑ̃] a (prix, opinions) fluctuating. ◆**fluctuations** nfpl fluctuation(s) (de in).
fluet, -ette [flyɛ, -ɛt] a thin, slender.
fluide [flɥid] a (liquide) & Fig fluid; – nm (liquide) fluid. ◆**fluidité** nf fluidity.
fluorescent [flyɔresɑ̃] a fluorescent.
flûte [flyt] **1** nf Mus flute. **2** nf (verre) champagne glass. **3** int heck!, darn!, dash it! ◆**flûté** a (voix) piping. ◆**flûtiste** nmf flautist, Am flutist.
fluvial, -aux [flyvjal, -o] a river-, fluvial.

flux [fly] *nm* (*abondance*) flow; **f. et reflux** ebb and flow.

focal, -aux [fɔkal, -o] *a* focal. ◆**focaliser** *vt* (*intérêt etc*) to focus.

fœtus [fetys] *nm* foetus, *Am* fetus.

foi [fwa] *nf* faith; **sur la f. de** on the strength of; **agir de bonne/mauvaise f.** to act in good/bad faith; **ma f., oui!** yes, indeed!

foie [fwa] *nm* liver.

foin [fwɛ̃] *nm* hay; **faire du f.** (*scandale*) *Fam* to make a stink.

foire [fwar] *nf* fair; **faire la f.** *Fam* to go on a binge, have a ball.

fois [fwa] *nf* time; **une f.** once; **deux f.** twice, two times; **chaque f. que** each time (that), whenever; **une f. qu'il sera arrivé** (*dès que*) once he has arrived; **à la f.** at the same time, at once; **à la f. riche et heureux** both rich and happy; **une autre f.** (*elle fera attention etc*) next time; **des f.** *Fam* sometimes; **non mais des f.!** *Fam* you must be joking!; **une f. pour toutes, une bonne f.** once and for all.

foison [fwazɔ̃] *nf* **à f.** in plenty. ◆**foisonn/er** *vi* to abound (**de, en** in). ◆**—ement** *nm* abundance.

fol [fɔl] *voir* **fou**.

folâtre [fɔlɑtr] *a* playful. ◆**folâtrer** *vi* to romp, frolic.

folichon, -onne [fɔliʃɔ̃, -ɔn] *a* **pas f.** not very funny, not much fun.

folie [fɔli] *nf* madness, insanity; **faire une f.** to do a foolish thing; (*dépense*) to be wildly extravagant; **aimer qn à la f.** to be madly in love with s.o..

folklore [fɔlklɔr] *nm* folklore. ◆**folklorique** *a* (*danse etc*) folk-; (*pas sérieux*) *Fam* lightweight, trivial, silly.

folle [fɔl] *voir* **fou**. ◆**follement** *adv* madly.

fomenter [fɔmɑ̃te] *vt* (*révolte etc*) to foment.

foncé [fɔ̃se] *a* (*couleur*) dark.

foncer [fɔ̃se] **1** *vi* (*aller vite*) to tear *ou* charge along; **f. sur qn** to charge into *ou* at s.o. **2** *vti* (*couleur*) to darken.

foncier, -ière [fɔ̃sje, -jɛr] *a* **1** fundamental, basic. **2** (*propriété*) landed. ◆**foncièrement** *adv* fundamentally.

fonction [fɔ̃ksjɔ̃] *nf* (*rôle*) & *Math* function; (*emploi*) office, function, duty; **f. publique** civil service; **faire f. de** (*personne*) to act as; (*objet*) to serve *ou* act as; **en f. de** according to. ◆**fonctionnaire** *nmf* civil servant. ◆**fonctionnel, -elle** *a* functional. ◆**fonctionn/er** *vi* (*machine etc*) to work, operate, function; (*organisation*) to function; **faire f.** to operate, work. ◆**—ement** *nm* working.

fond [fɔ̃] *nm* (*de boîte, jardin, vallée etc*) bottom; (*de salle, armoire etc*) back; (*de culotte*) seat; (*de problème, débat etc*) essence; (*arrière-plan*) background; (*contenu*) content; (*du désespoir*) *Fig* depths; **au f. de** at the bottom of; at the back of; **fonds de verre** dregs; **f. de teint** foundation cream; **f. sonore** background music; **un f. de bon sens** a stock of good sense; **au f.** basically, in essence; **à f.** (*connaître etc*) thoroughly; **de f. en comble** from top to bottom; **de f.** (*course*) long-distance; (*bruit*) background-.

fondamental, -aux [fɔ̃damɑ̃tal, -o] *a* fundamental, basic.

fond/er [fɔ̃de] *vt* (*ville etc*) to found; (*commerce*) to set up; (*famille*) to start; **(se) f. sur** to base (oneself) on; **être fondé à croire/etc** to be justified in thinking/*etc*; **bien fondé** well-founded. ◆**—ement** *nm* foundation. ◆**fondateur, -trice** *nmf* founder; – *a* (*membre*) founding, founder-. ◆**fondation** *nf* (*création, œuvre*) foundation (**de** of).

fond/re [fɔ̃dr] *vt* to melt; (*métal*) to smelt; (*cloche*) to cast; (*amalgamer*) *Fig* to fuse (**avec** with); **faire f.** (*dissoudre*) to dissolve; – *vi* to melt; (*se dissoudre*) to dissolve; **f. en larmes** to burst into tears; **f. sur** to swoop on; – **se f.** *vpr* to merge, fuse. ◆**—ant** *a* (*fruit*) which melts in the mouth. ◆**—u f. enchaîné** *Cin* dissolve. ◆**—ue** *nf* *Culin* fondue. ◆**fonderie** *nf* (*usine*) smelting works, foundry.

fonds [fɔ̃] **1** *nm* **un f.** (*de commerce*) a business. **2** *nmpl* (*argent*) funds. **3** *nm* (*culturel etc*) *Fig* fund.

font [fɔ̃] *voir* **faire**.

fontaine [fɔ̃tɛn] *nf* (*construction*) fountain; (*source*) spring.

fonte [fɔ̃t] *nf* **1** (*des neiges*) melting; (*d'acier*) smelting. **2** (*fer*) cast iron; **en f.** (*poêle etc*) cast-iron.

fonts [fɔ̃] *nmpl* **f. baptismaux** *Rel* font.

football [futbol] *nm* football, soccer. ◆**footballeur, -euse** *nmf* footballer.

footing [futiŋ] *nm* *Sp* jogging, jog-trotting.

forage [fɔraʒ] *nm* drilling, boring.

forain [fɔrɛ̃] *a* (*marchand*) itinerant; **fête foraine** (fun)fair.

forçat [fɔrsa] *nm* (*prisonnier*) convict.

force [fɔrs] *nf* force; (*physique, morale*) strength; (*atomique etc*) power; **de toutes ses forces** with all one's strength; **les forces armées** the armed forces; **de f.** by force, forcibly; **en f.** (*attaquer, venir*) in force; **cas de f. majeure** circumstances beyond one's control; **dans la f. de l'âge** in the prime of life; **à f. de** through sheer force of, by dint of. ◆**forc/er** vt (*porte, fruits etc*) to force; (*attention*) to force, compel; (*voix*) to strain; (*sens*) to stretch; **f. qn à faire** to force *ou* compel s.o. to do; − vi (*y aller trop fort*) to overdo it; − **se f.** vpr to force oneself (**à faire** to do). ◆−**é** a forced (**de faire** to do); **un sourire f.** a forced smile; **c'est f.** *Fam* it's inevitable *ou* obvious. ◆−**ément** adv inevitably, obviously; **pas f.** not necessarily.

forcené, -ée [fɔrsəne] a frantic, frenzied; − nmf madman, madwoman.

forceps [fɔrsɛps] nm forceps.

forcir [fɔrsir] vi (*grossir*) to fill out.

forer [fɔre] vt to drill, bore. ◆**foret** nm drill.

forêt [fɔrɛ] nf forest. ◆**forestier, -ière** a forest-; − nm (*garde*) **f.** forester, *Am* (forest) ranger.

forfait [fɔrfɛ] nm **1** (*prix*) all-inclusive price; **travailler à f.** to work for a lump sum. **2** **déclarer f.** *Sp* to withdraw from the game. **3** (*crime*) *Litt* heinous crime. ◆**forfaitaire** a **prix f.** all-inclusive price.

forge [fɔrʒ] nf forge. ◆**forg/er** vt (*métal, liens etc*) to forge; (*inventer*) to make up. ◆−**é** a **fer f.** wrought iron. ◆**forgeron** nm (black)smith.

formaliser (se) [səfɔrmalize] vpr to take offence (**de** at).

formalité [fɔrmalite] nf formality.

format [fɔrma] nm format, size.

forme [fɔrm] nf (*contour*) shape, form; (*manière, genre*) form; pl (*de femme, d'homme*) figure; **en f. de** in the form of; **en f. d'aiguille/de poire/**etc needle-/pear-/etc shaped; **dans les formes** in due form; **en (pleine) f.** in good shape *ou* form, on form; **prendre f.** to take shape. ◆**formateur, -trice** a formative. ◆**formation** nf formation; (*éducation*) education, training. ◆**formel, -elle** a (*structure, logique etc*) formal; (*démenti*) categorical, formal; (*preuve*) positive, formal. ◆**formellement** adv (*interdire*) strictly. ◆**form/er** vt (*groupe, caractère etc*) to form; (*apprenti etc*) to train; − **se f.** vpr (*apparaître*) to form; (*institution*) to be formed. ◆−**é** a (*personne*) fully-formed.

formidable [fɔrmidabl] a tremendous.

formule [fɔrmyl] nf **1** formula; (*phrase*) (*set*) expression; (*méthode*) method; **f. de politesse** polite expression. **2** (*feuille*) form. ◆**formulaire** nm (*feuille*) form. ◆**formulation** nf formulation. ◆**formuler** vt to formulate.

fort¹ [fɔr] a strong; (*pluie, mer*) heavy; (*voix*) loud; (*fièvre*) high; (*femme, homme*) large; (*élève*) bright; (*pente*) steep; (*ville*) fortified; (*chances*) good; **f. en** (*maths etc*) good at; **c'est plus f. qu'elle** she can't help it; **c'est un peu f.** *Fam* that's a bit much; **à plus forte raison** all the more reason; − adv **1** (*frapper*) hard; (*pleuvoir*) hard, heavily; (*parler*) loud; (*serrer*) tight; **sentir f.** to have a strong smell. **2** (*très*) *Vieilli* very; (*beaucoup*) *Litt* very much; − nm **son f.** one's strong point; **les forts** the strong; **au plus f. de** in the thick of. ◆**fortement** adv greatly; (*frapper*) hard.

fort² [fɔr] nm *Hist Mil* fort. ◆**forteresse** nf fortress.

fortifi/er [fɔrtifje] vt to strengthen, fortify; − **se f.** vpr (*malade*) to fortify oneself. ◆−**ant** nm *Méd* tonic. ◆−**é** a (*ville, camp*) fortified. ◆**fortification** nf fortification.

fortuit [fɔrtɥi] a (*rencontre etc*) chance-, fortuitous. ◆**fortuitement** adv by chance.

fortune [fɔrtyn] nf (*argent, hasard*) fortune; **avoir de la f.** to have (private) means; **faire f.** to make one's fortune; **de f.** (*moyens etc*) makeshift; **dîner à la f. du pot** to take pot luck. ◆**fortuné** a (*riche*) well-to-do.

forum [fɔrɔm] nm forum.

fosse [fos] nf (*trou*) pit; (*tombe*) grave; **f. d'aisances** cesspool.

fossé [fose] nm ditch; (*douve*) moat; (*dissentiment*) *Fig* gulf, gap.

fossette [fosɛt] nf dimple.

fossile [fɔsil] nm & a fossil.

fossoyeur [fɔswajœr] nm gravedigger.

fou (*or* **fol** *before vowel or mute h*), **folle** [fu, fɔl] a (*personne, projet etc*) mad, insane, crazy; (*envie*) wild, mad; (*espoir*) foolish; (*rire*) uncontrollable; (*cheval, camion*) runaway; (*succès, temps*) tremendous; **f. à lier** raving mad; **f. de** (*musique, personne etc*) mad *ou* wild *ou* crazy about; **f. de joie** wild with joy; − nmf madman, madwoman; − nm (*bouffon*) jester; *Échecs* bishop; **faire le f.** to play the fool.

foudre [fudr] nf **la f.** lightning; **coup de f.** *Fig* love at first sight. ◆**foudroy/er** vt to strike by lightning; *Él* to electrocute; (*malheur etc*) *Fig* to strike (s.o.) down. ◆−**ant** a (*succès, vitesse etc*) staggering. ◆−**é** a (*stupéfait*) thunderstruck.

fouet [fwɛ] nm whip; *Culin* (egg) whisk. ◆**fouetter** vt to whip; (*œufs*) to whisk; (*pluie etc*) to lash (*face, windows etc*); **crème fouettée** whipped cream.

fougère [fuʒɛr] nf fern.

fougue [fug] *nf* fire, ardour. ◆**fougueux, -euse** *a* fiery, ardent.

fouille [fuj] *nf* **1** (*archéologique*) excavation, dig. **2** (*de personne, bagages etc*) search. ◆**fouiller 1** *vti* (*creuser*) to dig. **2** *vt* (*personne, maison etc*) to search; – *vi* **f. dans** (*tiroir etc*) to rummage *ou* search through.

fouillis [fuji] *nm* jumble.

fouine [fwin] *nf* (*animal*) stone marten.

fouin/er [fwine] *vi Fam* to nose about. ◆**—eur, -euse** *a Fam* nosy; – *nmf Fam* nosy parker.

foulard [fular] *nm* (*head*) scarf.

foule [ful] *nf* crowd; **en f.** in mass; **une f. de** (*objets etc*) a mass of; **un bain de f.** a walkabout.

foulée [fule] *nf Sp* stride; **dans la f.** *Fam* at one and the same time.

fouler [fule] *vt* to press; (*sol*) to tread; **f. aux pieds** to trample on; **se f. la cheville**/*etc* to sprain one's ankle/*etc*; **il ne se foule pas (la rate)** *Fam* he doesn't exactly exert himself. ◆**foulure** *nf* sprain.

four [fur] *nm* **1** oven; (*de potier etc*) kiln. **2 petit f.** (*gâteau*) (small) fancy cake. **3** *Th Cin* flop; **faire un f.** to flop.

fourbe [furb] *a* deceitful; – *nmf* cheat. ◆**fourberie** *nf* deceit.

fourbi [furbi] *nm* (*choses*) *Fam* stuff, gear, rubbish.

fourbu [furby] *a* (*fatigué*) dead beat.

fourche [furʃ] *nf* fork; **f. à foin** pitchfork. ◆**fourchette** *nf* **1** *Culin* fork. **2** (*de salaires etc*) *Écon* bracket. ◆**fourchu** *a* forked.

fourgon [furgɔ̃] *nm* (*camion*) van; (*mortuaire*) hearse; *Rail* luggage van, *Am* baggage car. ◆**fourgonnette** *nf* (small) van.

fourmi [furmi] *nf* **1** (*insecte*) ant. **2 avoir des fourmis** *Méd* to have pins and needles (**dans** in). ◆**fourmilière** *nf* anthill. ◆**fourmiller** *vi* **1** to teem, swarm (**de** with). **2** *Méd* to tingle.

fournaise [furnɛz] *nf* (*chambre etc*) *Fig* furnace.

fourneau, -x [furno] *nm* (*poêle*) stove; (*four*) furnace; **haut f.** blast furnace.

fournée [furne] *nf* (*de pain, gens*) batch.

fourn/ir [furnir] *vt* to supply, provide; (*effort*) to make; **f. qch à qn** to supply s.o. with sth; – *vi* **f. à** (*besoin etc*) to provide for; — **se f.** *vpr* to get one's supplies (**chez** from), shop (**chez** at). ◆**—i** *a* (*barbe*) bushy; **bien f.** (*boutique*) well-stocked. ◆**fournisseur** *nm* (*commerçant*) supplier. ◆**fourniture** *nf* (*action*) supply(ing) (**de** of); *pl* (*objets*) supplies.

fourrage [furaʒ] *nm* fodder.

fourrager [furaʒe] *vi Fam* to rummage (**dans** in, through).

fourreau, -x [furo] *nm* (*gaine*) sheath.

fourr/er [fure] **1** *vt Culin* to fill, stuff; (*vêtement*) to fur-line. **2** *vt Fam* (*mettre*) to stick; (*flanquer*) to chuck; **f. qch dans la tête de qn** to knock sth into s.o.'s head; **f. son nez dans** to poke one's nose into; — **se f.** *vpr* to put *ou* stick oneself (**dans** in). ◆**—é** *a* (*gant etc*) fur-lined; (*gâteau*) jam- *ou* cream-filled; **coup f.** (*traîtrise*) stab in the back. **2** *nm Bot* thicket. ◆**—eur** *nm* furrier. ◆**fourrure** *nf* (*pour vêtement etc, de chat etc*) fur.

fourre-tout [furtu] *nm inv* (*pièce*) junk room; (*sac*) holdall, *Am* carryall.

fourrière [furjɛr] *nf* (*lieu*) pound.

fourvoyer (se) [səfurvwaje] *vpr* to go astray.

foutre* [futr] *vt Arg* = **fiche(r)**. ◆**foutu** *a Arg* = **fichu 1**. ◆**foutaise** *nf Arg* rubbish, rot.

foyer [fwaje] *nm* (*domicile*) home; (*d'étudiants etc*) hostel; (*âtre*) hearth; (*lieu de réunion*) club; *Th* foyer; *Géom Phys* focus; **f. de** (*maladie etc*) seat of; (*énergie, lumière*) source of; **fonder un f.** to start a family.

fracas [fraka] *nm* din; (*d'un objet qui tombe*) crash. ◆**fracass/er** *vt*, — **se f.** *vpr* to smash. ◆**—ant** *a* (*nouvelle, film etc*) sensational.

fraction [fraksjɔ̃] *nf* fraction. ◆**fractionner** *vt*, — **se f.** *vpr* to split (up).

fracture [fraktyr] *nf* fracture; **se faire une f. au bras**/*etc* to fracture one's arm/*etc*. ◆**fracturer** *vt* (*porte etc*) to break (open); **se f. la jambe**/*etc* to fracture one's leg/*etc*.

fragile [fraʒil] *a* (*verre, santé etc*) fragile; (*enfant etc*) frail; (*équilibre*) shaky. ◆**fragilité** *nf* fragility; (*d'un enfant etc*) frailty.

fragment [fragmɑ̃] *nm* fragment. ◆**fragmentaire** *a* fragmentary, fragmented. ◆**fragmentation** *nf* fragmentation. ◆**fragmenter** *vt* to fragment, divide.

frais¹, fraîche [frɛ, frɛʃ] *a* (*poisson, souvenir etc*) fresh; (*temps*) cool, fresh, (*plutôt désagréable*) chilly; (*œufs*) new-laid, fresh; (*boisson*) cold, cool; (*peinture*) wet; (*date*) recent; **boire f.** to drink something cold *ou* cool; **servir f.** (*vin etc*) to serve chilled; – *nm* **prendre le f.** to get some fresh air; **il fait f.** it's cool; (*froid*) it's chilly; **mettre au f.** to put in a cool place. ◆**fraîchement** *adv* **1** (*récemment*) freshly. **2** (*accueillir etc*) coolly. ◆**fraîcheur** *nf* freshness; coolness;

chilliness. ◆**fraîchir** vi (temps) to get cooler ou chillier, freshen.

frais² [frɛ] nmpl expenses; (droits) fees; **à mes f.** at my expense; **faire des f.** to go to some expense; **faire les f.** to bear the cost (de of); **j'en ai été pour mes f.** I wasted my time and effort; **faux f.** incidental expenses; **f. généraux** running expenses, overheads.

fraise [frɛz] nf **1** (fruit) strawberry. **2** (de dentiste) drill. ◆**fraisier** nm (plante) strawberry plant.

framboise [frɑ̃bwaz] nf raspberry. ◆**framboisier** nm raspberry cane.

franc¹, franche [frɑ̃, frɑ̃ʃ] a **1** (personne, réponse etc) frank; (visage, gaieté) open; (net) clear; (cassure, coupe) clean; (vrai) Péj downright. **2** (zone) free; **coup f.** Fb free kick; **f. de port** carriage paid. ◆**franchement** adv (honnêtement) frankly; (sans ambiguïté) clearly; (vraiment) really. ◆**franchise** nf **1** frankness; openness; **en toute f.** quite frankly. **2** (exemption) Com exemption; **en f.** (produit) duty-free; '**f. postale**' 'official paid'. **3** (permis de vendre) Com franchise.

franc² [frɑ̃] nm (monnaie) franc.

France [frɑ̃s] nf France. ◆**français, -aise** a French; – nmf Frenchman, Frenchwoman; **les F.** the French; – nm (langue) French.

franch/ir [frɑ̃ʃir] vt (fossé) to jump (over), clear; (frontière, seuil etc) to cross; (porte) to go through; (distance) to cover; (limites) to exceed; (mur du son) to break (through), go through. ◆**—issable** a (rivière, col) passable.

franc-maçon [frɑ̃masɔ̃] nm (pl francs-maçons) Freemason. ◆**franc-maçonnerie** nf Freemasonry.

franco [frɑ̃ko] adv carriage paid.

franco- [frɑ̃ko] préf Franco-.

francophile [frɑ̃kɔfil] a & nmf francophile. ◆**francophone** a French-speaking; – nmf French speaker. ◆**francophonie** nf **la f.** the French-speaking community.

frange [frɑ̃ʒ] nf (de vêtement etc) fringe; (de cheveux) fringe, Am bangs.

frangin [frɑ̃ʒɛ̃] nm Fam brother. ◆**frangine** nf Fam sister.

franquette (à la bonne) [alabɔnfrɑ̃kɛt] adv without ceremony.

frappe [frap] nf **1** (dactylographie) typing; (de dactylo etc) touch; **faute de f.** typing error. **2** force de f. Mil strike force. ◆**frapp/er** vt (battre) to strike, hit; (monnaie) to mint; **f. qn** (surprendre, affecter) to strike s.o.; (impôt, mesure etc) to hit s.o.; **frappé de** (horreur etc) stricken with; **frappé de panique** panic-stricken; – vi (à la porte etc) to knock, bang (à at); **f. du pied** to stamp (one's foot); – **se f.** vpr (se tracasser) to worry. ◆**—ant** a striking. ◆**—é** a (vin) chilled.

frasque [frask] nf prank, escapade.

fraternel, -elle [fratɛrnɛl] a fraternal, brotherly. ◆**fraterniser** vi to fraternize (avec with). ◆**fraternité** nf fraternity, brotherhood.

fraude [frod] nf Jur fraud; (à un examen) cheating; **passer qch en f.** to smuggle sth; **prendre qn en f.** to catch s.o. cheating. ◆**fraud/er** vt to defraud; – vi Jur to commit fraud; (à un examen) to cheat (à in); **f. sur** (poids etc) to cheat on ou over. ◆**—eur, -euse** nmf Jur defrauder. ◆**frauduleux, -euse** a fraudulent.

frayer [freje] vt (voie etc) to clear; **se f. un passage** to clear a way, force one's way (à travers, dans through).

frayeur [frejœr] nf fear, fright.

fredaine [frədɛn] nf prank, escapade.

fredonner [frədɔne] vt to hum.

freezer [frizœr] nm (de réfrigérateur) freezer.

frégate [fregat] nf (navire) frigate.

frein [frɛ̃] nm brake; **donner un coup de f.** to brake; **mettre un f. à** Fig to put a curb on. ◆**frein/er** vi Aut to brake; – vt (gêner) Fig to check, curb. ◆**—age** nm Aut braking.

frelaté [frəlate] a (vin etc) & Fig adulterated.

frêle [frɛl] a frail, fragile.

frelon [frəlɔ̃] nm (guêpe) hornet.

frémir [fremir] vi to shake, shudder (de with); (feuille) to quiver; (eau chaude) to simmer.

frêne [frɛn] nm (arbre, bois) ash.

frénésie [frenezi] nf frenzy. ◆**frénétique** a frenzied, frantic.

fréquent [frekɑ̃] a frequent. ◆**fréquemment** [-amɑ̃] adv frequently. ◆**fréquence** nf frequency.

fréquent/er [frekɑ̃te] vt (lieu) to visit, frequent; (école, église) to attend; **f. qn** to see ou visit s.o.; – **se f.** vpr (fille et garçon) to see each other, go out together; (voisins) to see each other socially. ◆**—é** a très **f.** (lieu) very busy. ◆**fréquentable** a peu **f.** (personne, endroit) not very commendable. ◆**fréquentation** nf visiting; pl (personnes) company.

frère [frɛr] nm brother.

fresque [frɛsk] nf (œuvre peinte) fresco.

fret [frɛ] nm freight.

frétiller [fretije] vi (*poisson*) to wriggle; **f. de** (*impatience*) to quiver with; **f. de joie** to tingle with excitement.

fretin [frɔtɛ̃] nm **menu f.** small fry.

friable [frijabl] a crumbly.

friand [frijɑ̃] a **f. de** fond of, partial to. ◆**friandises** nfpl sweet stuff, sweets, *Am* candies.

fric [frik] nm (*argent*) *Fam* cash, dough.

fric-frac [frikfrak] nm (*cambriolage*) *Fam* break-in.

friche (en) [ɑ̃friʃ] adv fallow.

friction [friksjɔ̃] nf **1** massage, rub(-down); (*de cheveux*) friction. **2** (*désaccord*) friction. ◆**frictionner** vt to rub (down).

frigidaire® [friʒidɛr] nm fridge. ◆**frigo** nm *Fam* fridge. ◆**frigorifié** a (*personne*) *Fam* very cold. ◆**frigorifique** a (*vitrine*) refrigerated; (*wagon*) refrigerator-.

frigide [friʒid] a frigid. ◆**frigidité** nf frigidity.

frileux, -euse [fril∅, -∅z] a sensitive to cold, chilly.

frime [frim] nf *Fam* sham, show.

frimousse [frimus] nf *Fam* little face.

fringale [frɛ̃gal] nf *Fam* raging appetite.

fringant [frɛ̃gɑ̃] a (*allure etc*) dashing.

fringues [frɛ̃g] nfpl (*vêtements*) *Fam* togs, clothes.

frip/er [fripe] vt to crumple; **— se f.** vpr to get crumpled. ◆**—é** a (*visage*) crumpled, wrinkled.

fripier, -ière [fripje, -jɛr] nmf secondhand clothes dealer.

fripon, -onne [fripɔ̃, -ɔn] nmf rascal; *— a* rascally.

fripouille [fripuj] nf rogue, scoundrel.

frire* [frir] vti to fry; **faire f.** to fry.

frise [friz] nf *Archit* frieze.

fris/er [frize] **1** vti (*cheveux*) to curl, wave; **f. qn** to curl ou wave s.o.'s hair. **2** vt (*effleurer*) to skim; (*accident etc*) to be within an ace of; **f. la trentaine** to be close to thirty. ◆**—é** a curly. ◆**frisette** nf ringlet, little curl.

frisquet [friskɛ] am chilly, coldish.

frisson [frisɔ̃] nm shiver; shudder; **donner le f. à qn** to give s.o. the creeps ou shivers. ◆**frissonner** vi (*de froid*) to shiver; (*de peur etc*) to shudder (**de** with).

frit [fri] voir **frire**; *— a* (*poisson etc*) fried. ◆**frites** nfpl chips, *Am* French fries. ◆**friteuse** nf (deep) fryer. ◆**friture** nf (*matière*) (frying) oil ou fat; (*aliment*) fried fish; (*bruit*) *Rad Tél* crackling.

frivole [frivɔl] a frivolous. ◆**frivolité** nf frivolity.

froid [frwa] a cold; **garder la tête froide** to keep a cool head; *— nm* cold; **avoir/ prendre f.** to be/catch cold; **il fait f.** it's cold; **coup de f.** *Méd* chill; **jeter un f.** to cast a chill (**dans** over); **démarrer à f.** *Aut* to start (from) cold; **être en f.** to be on bad terms (**avec** with). ◆**froidement** adv coldly. ◆**froideur** nf (*de sentiment, personne etc*) coldness.

froisser [frwase] **1** vt, **— se f.** vpr (*tissu etc*) to crumple, rumple; **se f. un muscle** to strain a muscle. **2** vt **f. qn** to offend s.o.; **se f.** to take offence (**de** at).

frôler [frole] vt (*toucher*) to brush against, touch lightly; (*raser*) to skim; (*la mort etc*) to come within an ace of.

fromage [frɔmaʒ] nm cheese; **f. blanc** soft white cheese. ◆**fromager, -ère** a (*industrie*) cheese-; *— nm* (*fabricant*) cheesemaker. ◆**fromagerie** nf cheese dairy.

froment [frɔmɑ̃] nm wheat.

fronce [frɔ̃s] nf (*pli dans un tissu*) gather, fold. ◆**fronc/er** vt **1** (*étoffe*) to gather. **2 f. les sourcils** to frown. ◆**—ement** nm **f. de sourcils** frown.

fronde [frɔ̃d] nf **1** (*arme*) sling. **2** (*sédition*) revolt.

front [frɔ̃] nm forehead, brow; *Mil Pol* front; **de f.** (*heurter*) head-on; (*côte à côte*) abreast; (*à la fois*) (all) at once; **faire f. à** to face.

frontière [frɔ̃tjɛr] nf border, frontier; *— a inv* **ville**/*etc* **f.** border town/*etc*. ◆**frontalier, -ière** a border-, frontier-.

fronton [frɔ̃tɔ̃] nm *Archit* pediment.

frott/er [frɔte] vt to rub; (*astiquer*) to rub (up), shine; (*plancher*) to scrub; (*allumette*) to strike; **se f. à qn** (*défier*) to meddle with s.o., provoke s.o.; *— vi* to rub; (*nettoyer, laver*) to scrub. ◆**—ement** nm rubbing; *Tech* friction.

froufrou(s) [frufru] nm(pl) (*bruit*) rustling.

frousse [frus] nf *Fam* funk, fear; **avoir la f.** to be scared. ◆**froussard, -arde** nmf *Fam* coward.

fructifier [fryktifje] vi (*arbre, capital*) to bear fruit. ◆**fructueux, -euse** a (*profitable*) fruitful.

frugal, -aux [frygal, -o] a frugal. ◆**frugalité** nf frugality.

fruit [frɥi] nm fruit; **des fruits, les fruits** fruit; **porter f.** to bear fruit; **fruits de mer** seafood; **avec f.** fruitfully. ◆**fruité** a fruity. ◆**fruitier, -ière** a (*arbre*) fruit-; *— nmf* fruiterer.

frusques [frysk] nfpl (*vêtements*) *Fam* togs, clothes.

fruste [fryst] *a* (*personne*) rough.

frustr/er [frystre] *vt* **f. qn** to frustrate s.o.; **f. qn de** to deprive s.o. of. ◆**—é** *a* frustrated. ◆**frustration** *nf* frustration.

fuel [fjul] *nm* (fuel) oil.

fugace [fygas] *a* fleeting.

fugitif, -ive [fyʒitif, -iv] **1** *nmf* runaway, fugitive. **2** *a* (*passager*) fleeting.

fugue [fyg] *nf* **1** *Mus* fugue. **2** (*absence*) flight; **faire une f.** to run away.

fuir* [fɥir] *vi* to flee, run away; (*temps*) to fly; (*gaz, robinet, stylo etc*) to leak; **–** *vt* (*éviter*) to shun, avoid. ◆**fuite** *nf* (*évasion*) flight (**de** from); (*de gaz etc*) leak(age); (*de documents*) leak; **en f.** on the run; **prendre la f.** to take flight; **f. des cerveaux** brain drain; **délit de f.** *Aut* hit-and-run offence.

fulgurant [fylgyrɑ̃] *a* (*regard*) flashing; (*vitesse*) lightning-; (*idée*) spectacular, striking.

fulminer [fylmine] *vi* (*personne*) to thunder forth (**contre** against).

fumée [fyme] *nf* smoke; (*vapeur*) steam, fumes; *pl* (*de vin*) fumes. ◆**fum/er** *vi* to smoke; (*liquide brûlant*) to steam; (*rager*) *Fam* to fume; **–** *vt* to smoke. ◆**—é** *a* (*poisson, verre etc*) smoked. ◆**—eur, -euse** *nmf* smoker; **compartiment fumeurs** *Rail* smoking compartment. ◆**fume-cigarette** *nm inv* cigarette holder.

fumet [fymɛ] *nm* aroma, smell.

fumeux, -euse [fymø, -øz] *a* (*idée etc*) hazy, woolly.

fumier [fymje] *nm* manure, dung; (*tas*) dunghill.

fumigation [fymigasjɔ̃] *nf* fumigation.

fumigène [fymiʒɛn] *a* (*bombe, grenade etc*) smoke-.

fumiste [fymist] *nmf* (*étudiant etc*) time-waster, good-for-nothing. ◆**fumisterie** *nf Fam* farce, con.

funambule [fynɑ̃byl] *nmf* tightrope walker.

funèbre [fynɛbr] *a* (*service, marche etc*) funeral-; (*lugubre*) gloomy. ◆**funérailles** *nfpl* funeral. ◆**funéraire** *a* (*frais, salon etc*) funeral-.

funeste [fynɛst] *a* (*désastreux*) catastrophic.

funiculaire [fynikylɛr] *nm* funicular.

fur et à mesure (au) [ofyreamzyr] *adv* as one goes along, progressively; **au f. et à m. que** as.

furent [fyr] *voir* **être**.

furet [fyrɛ] *nm* (*animal*) ferret. ◆**furet/er** *vi* to pry *ou* ferret about. ◆**—eur, -euse** *a* inquisitive, prying; **–** *nmf* inquisitive person.

fureur [fyrœr] *nf* (*violence*) fury; (*colère*) rage, fury; (*passion*) passion (**de** for); **en f.** furious; **faire f.** (*mode etc*) to be all the rage. ◆**furibond** *a* furious. ◆**furie** *nf* (*colère, mégère*) fury. ◆**furieux, -euse** *a* (*violent, en colère*) furious (**contre** with, at); (*vent*) raging; (*coup*) *Fig* tremendous.

furoncle [fyrɔ̃kl] *nm Méd* boil.

furtif, -ive [fyrtif, -iv] *a* furtive, stealthy.

fusain [fyzɛ̃] *nm* **1** (*crayon, dessin*) charcoal. **2** *Bot* spindle tree.

fuseau, -x [fyzo] *nm* **1** *Tex* spindle; **en f.** (*jambes*) spindly. **2 f. horaire** time zone. **3** (*pantalon*) ski pants. ◆**fuselé** *a* slender.

fusée [fyze] *nf* rocket; (*d'obus*) fuse; **f. éclairante** flare.

fuselage [fyzlaʒ] *nm Av* fuselage.

fuser [fyze] *vi* (*rires etc*) to burst forth.

fusible [fyzibl] *nm Él* fuse.

fusil [fyzi] *nm* rifle, gun; (*de chasse*) shotgun; **coup de f.** gunshot, report; **un bon f.** (*personne*) a good shot. ◆**fusillade** *nf* (*tirs*) gunfire; (*exécution*) shooting. ◆**fusiller** *vt* (*exécuter*) to shoot; **f. qn du regard** to glare at s.o.

fusion [fyzjɔ̃] *nf* **1** melting; *Phys Biol* fusion; **point de f.** melting point; **en f.** (*métal*) molten. **2** (*union*) fusion; *Com* merger. ◆**fusionner** *vti Com* to merge.

fut [fy] *voir* **être**.

fût [fy] *nm* **1** (*tonneau*) barrel, cask. **2** (*d'arbre*) trunk. ◆**futaie** *nf* timber forest.

futé [fyte] *a* cunning, smart.

futile [fytil] *a* (*propos, prétexte etc*) frivolous, futile; (*personne*) frivolous; (*tentative, action*) futile. ◆**futilité** *nf* futility; *pl* (*bagatelles*) trifles.

futur, -ure [fytyr] *a* future; **future mère** mother-to-be; **–** *nmf* **f. (mari)** husband-to-be; **future (épouse)** wife-to-be; **–** *nm* future.

fuyant [fɥijɑ̃] *voir* **fuir**; **–** *a* (*front, ligne*) receding; (*personne*) evasive. ◆**fuyard** *nm* (*soldat*) runaway, deserter.

G

G, g [ʒe] *nm* G, g.

gabardine [gabardin] *nf* (*tissu, imperméable*) gabardine.

gabarit [gabari] *nm* (*de véhicule etc*) size, dimension.

gâcher [gɑʃe] *vt* **1** (*gâter*) to spoil; (*occasion, argent*) to waste; (*vie, travail*) to mess up. **2** (*plâtre*) to mix. ◆**gâchis** *nm* (*désordre*) mess; (*gaspillage*) waste.

gâchette [gɑʃɛt] *nf* (*d'arme à feu*) trigger; **une fine g.** (*personne*) *Fig* a marksman.

gadget [gadʒɛt] *nm* gadget.

gadoue [gadu] *nf* (*boue*) dirt, sludge; (*neige*) slush.

gaffe [gaf] *nf* (*bévue*) *Fam* blunder, gaffe. ◆**gaff/er** *vi* to blunder. ◆**—eur, -euse** *nmf* blunderer.

gag [gag] *nm* (*effet comique*) *Cin Th* (sight) gag.

gaga [gaga] *a Fam* senile, gaga.

gage [gaʒ] **1** *nm* (*promesse*) pledge; (*témoignage*) proof; (*caution*) security; **mettre en g.** to pawn. **2** *nmpl* (*salaire*) pay; **tueur à gages** hired killer, hitman.

gager [gaʒe] *vt* **que** *Litt* to wager that. ◆**gageure** [gaʒyr] *nf Litt* (impossible) wager.

gagn/er [gaɲe] **1** *vt* (*par le travail*) to earn; (*mériter*) *Fig* to earn. **2** *vt* (*par le jeu*) to win; (*réputation, estime etc*) *Fig* to win, gain; **g. qn** to win s.o. over (**à** to); **g. une heure**/*etc* (*économiser*) to save an hour/*etc*; **g. du temps** (*temporiser*) to gain time; **g. du terrain/du poids** to gain ground/weight; — *vi* (*être vainqueur*) to win; **g. à être connu** to be well worth getting to know. **3** *vt* (*atteindre*) to reach; **g. qn** (*sommeil, faim etc*) to overcome s.o.; − *vi* (*incendie etc*) to spread, gain. ◆**—ant, -ante** *a* (*billet, cheval*) winning; − *nmf* winner. ◆**gagne-pain** *nm inv* (*emploi*) job, livelihood.

gai [ge] *a* (*personne, air etc*) cheerful, gay, jolly; (*ivre*) merry, tipsy; (*couleur, pièce*) bright, cheerful. ◆**gaiement** *adv* cheerfully, gaily. ◆**gaieté** *nf* (*de personne etc*) gaiety, cheerfulness, jollity.

gaillard [gajar] *a* vigorous; (*grivois*) coarse; − *nm* (*robuste*) strapping fellow; (*type*) *Fam* fellow. ◆**gaillarde** *nf Péj* brazen wench.

gain [gɛ̃] *nm* (*profit*) gain, profit; (*avantage*) *Fig* advantage; *pl* (*salaire*) earnings; (*au jeu*) winnings; **un g. de temps** a saving of time.

gaine [gɛn] *nf* **1** (*sous-vêtement*) girdle. **2** (*étui*) sheath.

gala [gala] *nm* official reception, gala.

galant [galɑ̃] *a* (*homme*) gallant; (*ton, propos*) *Hum* amorous; − *nm* suitor. ◆**galanterie** *nf* (*courtoisie*) gallantry.

galaxie [galaksi] *nf* galaxy.

galbe [galb] *nm* curve, contour. ◆**galbé** *a* (*jambes*) shapely.

gale [gal] *nf* **la g.** *Méd* the itch, scabies; (*d'un chien*) mange; **une (mauvaise) g.** (*personne*) *Fam* a pest.

galère [galɛr] *nf* (*navire*) *Hist* galley. ◆**galérien** *nm Hist* & *Fig* galley slave.

galerie [galri] *nf* **1** (*passage, magasin etc*) gallery; *Th* balcony. **2** *Aut* roof rack.

galet [galɛ] *nm* pebble, stone; *pl* shingle, pebbles.

galette [galɛt] *nf* **1** round, flat, flaky cake; (*crêpe*) pancake. **2** (*argent*) *Fam* dough, money.

galeux, -euse [galø, -øz] *a* (*chien*) mangy.

galimatias [galimatja] *nm* gibberish.

Galles [gal] *nfpl* **pays de G.** Wales. ◆**gallois, -oise** *a* Welsh; − *nm* (*langue*) Welsh; − *nmf* Welshman, Welshwoman.

gallicisme [galisism] *nm* (*mot etc*) gallicism.

galon [galɔ̃] *nm* (*ruban*) braid; (*signe*) *Mil* stripe; **prendre du g.** *Mil* & *Fig* to get promoted.

galop [galo] *nm* gallop; **aller au g.** to gallop; **g. d'essai** *Fig* trial run. ◆**galopade** *nf* (*ruée*) stampede. ◆**galop/er** *vi* (*cheval*) to gallop; (*personne*) to rush. ◆**—ant** *a* (*inflation etc*) *Fig* galloping.

galopin [galɔpɛ̃] *nm* urchin, rascal.

galvaniser [galvanize] *vt* (*métal*) & *Fig* to galvanize.

galvauder [galvode] *vt* (*talent, avantage etc*) to debase, misuse.

gambade [gɑ̃bad] *nf* leap, caper. ◆**gambader** *vi* to leap *ou* frisk about.

gambas [gɑ̃bas] *nfpl* scampi.

gamelle [gamɛl] *nf* (*de soldat*) mess tin; (*de campeur*) billy(can).

gamin, -ine [gamɛ̃, -in] *nmf* (*enfant*) *Fam*

kid; — *a* playful, naughty. ◆**gaminerie** *nf* playfulness; (*acte*) naughty prank.

gamme [gam] *nf Mus* scale; (*série*) range.

gammée [game] *af* **croix g.** swastika.

gang [gɑ̃g] *nm* (*de malfaiteurs*) gang. ◆**gangster** *nm* gangster.

gangrène [gɑ̃grɛn] *nf* gangrene. ◆**se gangrener** [səgɑ̃grəne] *vpr Méd* to become gangrenous.

gangue [gɑ̃g] *nf* (*enveloppe*) *Fig Péj* outer crust.

gant [gɑ̃] *nm* glove; **g. de toilette** face cloth, cloth glove (*for washing*); **jeter/relever le g.** *Fig* to throw down/take up the gauntlet; **boîte à gants** glove compartment. ◆**ganté** *a* (*main*) gloved; (*personne*) wearing gloves.

garage [garaʒ] *nm Aut* garage; **voie de g.** *Rail* siding; *Fig* dead end. ◆**garagiste** *nmf* garage owner.

garant, -ante [garɑ̃, -ɑ̃t] *nmf* (*personne*) *Jur* guarantor; **se porter g. de** to guarantee, vouch for; — *nm* (*garantie*) guarantee. ◆**garantie** *nf* guarantee; (*caution*) security; (*protection*) *Fig* safeguard; **garantie(s)** (*de police d'assurance*) cover. ◆**garantir** *vt* to guarantee (**contre** against); **g. (à qn) que** to guarantee (s.o.) that; **g. de** (*protéger*) to protect from.

garce [gars] *nf Péj Fam* bitch.

garçon [garsɔ̃] *nm* boy, lad; (*jeune homme*) young man; (*célibataire*) bachelor; **g. (de café)** waiter; **g. d'honneur** (*d'un mariage*) best man; **g. manqué** tomboy; **de g.** (*comportement*) boyish. ◆**garçonnet** *nm* little boy. ◆**garçonnière** *nf* bachelor flat *ou Am* apartment.

garde [gard] **1** *nm* (*gardien*) guard; *Mil* guardsman; **g. champêtre** rural policeman; **g. du corps** bodyguard; **G. des Sceaux** Justice Minister. **2** *nf* (*d'enfants, de bagages etc*) care, custody (**de** of); **avoir la g. de** to be in charge of; **faire bonne g.** to keep a close watch; **prendre g.** to pay attention (**à qch** to sth), be careful (**à qch** of sth); **prendre g. de ne pas faire** to be careful not to do; **mettre en g.** to warn (**contre** against); **mise en g.** warning; **de g.** on duty; (*soldat*) on guard duty; **monter la g.** to stand *ou* mount guard; **sur ses gardes** on one's guard; **g. à vue** (*police*) custody; **chien de g.** watchdog. **3** *nf* (*escorte, soldats*) guard.

garde-à-vous [gardavu] *nm inv Mil* (position of) attention. ◆**g.-boue** *nm inv* mudguard, *Am* fender. ◆**g.-chasse** *nm* (*pl* **gardes-chasses**) gamekeeper. ◆**g.-côte** *nm* (*personne*) coastguard. ◆**g.-fou** *nm* railing(s), parapet. ◆**g.-malade** *nmf* (*pl*

gardes-malades) nurse. ◆**g.-manger** *nm inv* (*armoire*) food safe; (*pièce*) larder. ◆**g.-robe** *nf* (*habits, armoire*) wardrobe.

garder [garde] *vt* (*maintenir, conserver, mettre de côté*) to keep; (*vêtement*) to keep on; (*surveiller*) to watch (over); (*défendre*) to guard; (*enfant*) to look after, watch; (*habitude*) to keep up; **g. qn** (*retenir*) to keep s.o.; **g. la chambre** to keep to one's room; **g. le lit** to stay in bed; **— se g.** *vpr* (*aliment*) to keep; **se g. de qch** (*éviter*) to beware of sth; **se g. de faire** to take care not to do. ◆**garderie** *nf* day nursery. ◆**gardeuse** *nf* **g. d'enfants** babysitter.

gardien, -ienne [gardjɛ̃, -jɛn] *nmf* (*d'immeuble, d'hôtel*) caretaker; (*de prison*) (prison) guard, warder; (*de zoo, parc*) keeper; (*de musée*) attendant; **g. de but** *Fb* goalkeeper; **gardienne d'enfants** child minder; **g. de nuit** night watchman; **g. de la paix** policeman; **g. de** (*libertés etc*) *Fig* guardian of; — *am* **ange g.** guardian angel.

gare [gar] **1** *nf Rail* station; **g. routière** bus *ou* coach station. **2** *int* **g. à** watch *ou* look out for; **g. à toi!** watch *ou* look out!; **sans crier g.** without warning.

garer [gare] *vt* (*voiture etc*) to park; (*au garage*) to garage; — **se g.** *vpr* (*se protéger*) to get out of the way (**de** of); *Aut* to park.

gargariser (se) [səgargarize] *vpr* to gargle. ◆**gargarisme** *nm* gargle.

gargote [gargɔt] *nf* cheap eating house.

gargouille [garguj] *nf Archit* gargoyle.

gargouiller [garguje] *vi* (*fontaine, eau*) to gurgle; (*ventre*) to rumble. ◆**gargouillis** *nm* gurgling; rumbling.

garnement [garnəmɑ̃] *nm* rascal, urchin.

garn/ir [garnir] *vt* (*équiper*) to furnish, fit out (**de** with); (*magasin*) to stock; (*tissu*) to line; (*orner*) to adorn (**de** with); (*enjoliver*) to trim (**de** with); (*couvrir*) to cover; *Culin* to garnish; — **se g.** *vpr* (*lieu*) to fill (up) (**de** with). ◆**-i** *a* (*plat*) served with vegetables; **bien g.** (*portefeuille*) *Fig* well-lined. ◆**garniture** *nf Culin* garnish, trimmings; *pl Aut* fittings, upholstery; **g. de lit** bed linen.

garnison [garnizɔ̃] *nf Mil* garrison.

gars [gɑ] *nm Fam* fellow, guy.

gas-oil [gazwal] *nm* diesel (oil).

gaspill/er [gaspije] *vt* to waste. ◆**-age** *nm* waste.

gastrique [gastrik] *a* gastric. ◆**gastronome** *nmf* gourmet. ◆**gastronomie** *nf* gastronomy.

gâteau, -x [gɑto] *nm* cake; **g. de riz** rice pudding; **g. sec** (sweet) biscuit, *Am* cookie;

c'était du g. (*facile*) *Fam* it was a piece of cake.

gât/er [gɑte] *vt* to spoil; (*plaisir, vue*) to mar, spoil; **— se g.** *vpr* (*aliment, dent*) to go bad; (*temps, situation*) to get worse; (*relations*) to turn sour. ◆**—é** *a* (*dent, fruit etc*) bad. ◆**gâteries** *nfpl* (*cadeaux*) treats.

gâteux, -euse [gɑtø, -øz] *a* senile, soft in the head.

gauche¹ [goʃ] *a* (*côté, main etc*) left; **— nf la g.** (*côté*) the left (side); *Pol* the left (wing); **à g.** (*tourner etc*) (to the) left; (*marcher, se tenir*) on the left(-hand) side; **de g.** (*fenêtre etc*) left-hand; (*parti, politique etc*) left-wing; **à g. de** on *ou* to the left of. ◆**gaucher, -ère** *a* & *nmf* left-handed (person). ◆**gauchiste** *a* & *nmf Pol* (extreme) leftist.

gauche² [goʃ] *a* (*maladroit*) awkward. ◆**—ment** *adv* awkwardly. ◆**gaucherie** *nf* awkwardness; (*acte*) blunder.

gauchir [goʃir] *vti* to warp.

gaufre [gofr] *nf Culin* waffle. ◆**gaufrette** *nf* wafer (biscuit).

gaule [gol] *nf* long pole; *Pêche* fishing rod.

Gaule [gol] *nf* (*pays*) *Hist* Gaul. ◆**gaulois** *a* Gallic; (*propos etc*) *Fig* broad, earthy; **— nmpl les G.** *Hist* the Gauls. ◆**gauloiserie** *nf* broad joke.

gausser (se) [səgose] *vpr Litt* to poke fun (de at).

gaver [gave] *vt* (*animal*) to force-feed; (*personne*) *Fig* to cram (de with); **— se g.** *vpr* to gorge *ou* stuff oneself (de with).

gaz [gɑz] *nm inv* gas; **usine à g.** gasworks; **chambre/réchaud à g.** gas chamber/stove; **avoir des g.** to have wind *ou* flatulence.

gaze [gɑz] *nf* (*tissu*) gauze.

gazelle [gazɛl] *nf* (*animal*) gazelle.

gazer [gaze] **1** *vi Aut Fam* to whizz along; **ça gaze!** everything's just fine! **2** *vt Mil* to gas.

gazette [gazɛt] *nf Journ* newspaper.

gazeux, -euse [gɑzø, -øz] *a* (*état*) gaseous; (*boisson, eau*) fizzy. ◆**gazomètre** *nm* gasometer.

gazinière [gazinjɛr] *nf* gas cooker *ou* *Am* stove.

gazole [gɑzɔl] *nm* diesel (oil).

gazon [gɑzɔ̃] *nm* grass, lawn.

gazouiller [gazuje] *vi* (*oiseau*) to chirp; (*bébé, ruisseau*) to babble. ◆**gazouillis** *nm* chirping; babbling.

geai [ʒɛ] *nm* (*oiseau*) jay.

géant, -ante [ʒeɑ̃, -ɑ̃t] *a* & *nmf* giant.

Geiger [ʒɛʒɛr] *nm* **compteur G.** Geiger counter.

geindre [ʒɛ̃dr] *vi* to whine, whimper.

gel [ʒɛl] *nm* **1** (*temps, glace*) frost; (*de crédits*) *Écon* freezing. **2** (*substance*) gel. ◆**gel/er** *vti* to freeze; **on gèle ici** it's freezing here; **— v imp il gèle** it's freezing. ◆**—é** *a* frozen; (*doigts*) *Méd* frostbitten. ◆**—ée** *nf* frost; *Culin* jelly, *Am* jello; **g. blanche** ground frost.

gélatine [ʒelatin] *nf* gelatin(e).

gélule [ʒelyl] *nf* (*médicament*) capsule.

Gémeaux [ʒemo] *nmpl* **les G.** (*signe*) Gemini.

gém/ir [ʒemir] *vi* to groan, moan. ◆**—issement** *nm* groan, moan.

gencive [ʒɑ̃siv] *nf Anat* gum.

gendarme [ʒɑ̃darm] *nm* gendarme, policeman (*soldier performing police duties*). ◆**gendarmerie** *nf* police force; (*local*) police headquarters.

gendre [ʒɑ̃dr] *nm* son-in-law.

gène [ʒɛn] *nm Biol* gene.

gêne [ʒɛn] *nf* (*trouble physique*) discomfort; (*confusion*) embarrassment; (*dérangement*) bother, trouble; **dans la g.** *Fin* in financial difficulties. ◆**gên/er** *vt* (*déranger, irriter*) to bother, annoy; (*troubler*) to embarrass; (*mouvement, action*) to hamper, hinder; (*circulation*) *Aut* to hold up, block; **g. qn** (*vêtement*) to be uncomfortable on s.o.; (*par sa présence*) to be in s.o.'s way; **ça ne me gêne pas** I don't mind (**si** if); **— se g.** *vpr* (*se déranger*) to put oneself out; **ne te gêne pas pour moi!** don't mind me! ◆**—ant** *a* (*objet*) cumbersome; (*présence, situation*) awkward; (*personne*) annoying. ◆**—é** *a* (*intimidé*) embarrassed; (*mal à l'aise*) uneasy, awkward; (*silence, sourire*) awkward; (*sans argent*) short of money.

généalogie [ʒenealoʒi] *nf* genealogy. ◆**généalogique** *a* genealogical; **arbre g.** family tree.

général, -aux [ʒeneral, -o] **1** *a* (*global, commun*) general; **en g.** in general. **2** *nm* (*officier*) *Mil* general. ◆**générale** *nf Th* dress rehearsal. ◆**généralement** *adv* generally; **g. parlant** broadly *ou* generally speaking. ◆**généralisation** *nf* generalization. ◆**généraliser** *vti* to generalize; **— se g.** *vpr* to become general *ou* widespread. ◆**généraliste** *nmf Méd* general practitioner, GP. ◆**généralité** *nf* generality; **la g. de** the majority of.

générateur [ʒeneratœr] *nm*, ◆**génératrice** *nf Él* generator.

génération [ʒenerasjɔ̃] *nf* generation.

généreux, -euse [ʒenerø, -øz] *a* a generous (de with). ◆**généreusement** *adv* generously. ◆**générosité** *nf* generosity.

générique [ʒenerik] *nm Cin* credits.
genèse [ʒɔnɛz] *nf* genesis.
genêt [ʒɔnɛ] *nm* (*arbrisseau*) broom.
génétique [ʒenetik] *nf* genetics; − *a* genetic.
Genève [ʒɔnɛv] *nm ou f* Geneva.
génie [ʒeni] *nm* 1 (*aptitude, personne*) genius; **avoir le g. pour faire/de qch** to have a genius for doing/for sth. 2 (*lutin*) genie, spirit. 3 **g. civil** civil engineering; **g. militaire** engineering corps. ◆**génial, -aux** *a* (*personne, invention*) brilliant; (*formidable*) *Fam* fantastic.
génisse [ʒenis] *nf* (*vache*) heifer.
génital, -aux [ʒenital, -o] *a* genital; **organes génitaux** genitals.
génocide [ʒenɔsid] *nm* genocide.
genou, -x [ʒ(ɔ)nu] *nm* knee; **être à genoux** to be kneeling (down); **se mettre à genoux** to kneel (down); **prendre qn sur ses genoux** to take s.o. on one's lap *ou* knee. ◆**genouillère** *nf Fb etc* knee pad.
genre [ʒɑ̃r] *nm* 1 (*espèce*) kind, sort; (*attitude*) manner, way; **g. humain** mankind; **g. de vie** way of life. 2 *Littér Cin* genre; *Gram* gender; *Biol* genus.
gens [ʒɑ̃] *nmpl ou nfpl* people; **jeunes g.** young people; (*hommes*) young men.
gentil, -ille [ʒɑ̃ti, -ij] *a* (*agréable*) nice, pleasant; (*aimable*) kind, nice; (*mignon*) pretty; **g. avec qn** nice *ou* kind to s.o.; **sois g.** (*sage*) be good. ◆**gentillesse** *nf* kindness; **avoir la g. de faire** to be kind enough to do. ◆**gentiment** *adv* (*aimablement*) kindly; (*sagement*) nicely.
gentilhomme, *pl* **gentilshommes** [ʒɑ̃tijɔm, ʒɑ̃tizɔm] *nm* (*noble*) *Hist* gentleman.
géographie [ʒeɔgrafi] *nf* geography. ◆**géographique** *a* geographical.
geôlier, -ière [ʒolje, -jɛr] *nmf* jailer, gaoler.
géologie [ʒeɔlɔʒi] *nf* geology. ◆**géologique** *a* geological. ◆**géologue** *nmf* geologist.
géomètre [ʒeɔmɛtr] *nm* (*arpenteur*) surveyor.
géométrie [ʒeɔmetri] *nf* geometry. ◆**géométrique** *a* geometric(al).
géranium [ʒeranjɔm] *nm Bot* geranium.
gérant, -ante [ʒerɑ̃, -ɑ̃t] *nmf* manager, manageress; **g. d'immeubles** landlord's agent. ◆**gérance** *nf* (*gestion*) management.
gerbe [ʒɛrb] *nf* (*de blé*) sheaf; (*de fleurs*) bunch; (*d'eau*) spray; (*d'étincelles*) shower.
gercer [ʒɛrse] *vti*, **— se g.** *vpr* (*peau, lèvres*) to chap, crack. ◆**gerçure** *nf* chap, crack.

gérer [ʒere] *vt* (*fonds, commerce etc*) to manage.
germain [ʒɛrmɛ̃] *a* **cousin g.** first cousin.
germanique [ʒɛrmanik] *a* Germanic.
germe [ʒɛrm] *nm Méd Biol* germ; *Bot* shoot; (*d'une idée*) *Fig* seed, germ. ◆**germer** *vi Bot* & *Fig* to germinate.
gésir [ʒezir] *vi* (*être étendu*) *Litt* to be lying; **il gît/gisait** he is/was lying; **ci-gît** here lies.
gestation [ʒɛstasjɔ̃] *nf* gestation.
geste [ʒɛst] *nm* gesture; **ne pas faire un g.** (*ne pas bouger*) not to make a move. ◆**gesticuler** *vi* to gesticulate.
gestion [ʒɛstjɔ̃] *nf* (*action*) management, administration. ◆**gestionnaire** *nmf* administrator.
geyser [ʒɛzɛr] *nm Géol* geyser.
ghetto [gɛto] *nm* ghetto.
gibecière [ʒibsjɛr] *nf* shoulder bag.
gibier [ʒibje] *nm* (*animaux, oiseaux*) game.
giboulée [ʒibule] *nf* shower, downpour.
gicl/er [ʒikle] *vi* (*liquide*) to spurt, squirt; (*boue*) to splash; **faire g.** to spurt, squirt. ◆**−ée** *nf* spurt, squirt. ◆**−eur** *nm* (*de carburateur*) *Aut* jet.
gifle [ʒifl] *nf* slap (in the face). ◆**gifler** *vt* **g. qn** to slap s.o., slap s.o.'s face.
gigantesque [ʒigɑ̃tɛsk] *a* gigantic.
gigogne [ʒigɔɲ] *a* **table g.** nest of tables.
gigot [ʒigo] *nm* leg of mutton *ou* lamb.
gigoter [ʒigɔte] *vi Fam* to kick, wriggle.
gilet [ʒile] *nm* waistcoat, *Am* vest; (*cardigan*) cardigan; **g. (de corps)** vest, *Am* undershirt; **g. pare-balles** bulletproof jacket *ou Am* vest; **g. de sauvetage** life jacket.
gin [dʒin] *nm* (*eau-de-vie*) gin.
gingembre [ʒɛ̃ʒɑ̃br] *nm Bot Culin* ginger.
girafe [ʒiraf] *nf* giraffe.
giratoire [ʒiratwar] *a* **sens g.** *Aut* roundabout, *Am* traffic circle.
girl [gœrl] *nf* (*danseuse*) chorus girl.
girofle [ʒirɔfl] *nm* **clou de g.** *Bot* clove.
giroflée [ʒirɔfle] *nf Bot* wall flower.
girouette [ʒirwɛt] *nf* weathercock, weather vane.
gisement [ʒizmɑ̃] *nm* (*de minerai, pétrole*) *Géol* deposit.
gitan, -ane [ʒitɑ̃, -an] *nmf* (Spanish) gipsy.
gîte [ʒit] *nm* (*abri*) resting place.
gîter [ʒite] *vi* (*navire*) to list.
givre [ʒivr] *nm* (hoar)frost. ◆**se givrer** *vpr* (*pare-brise etc*) to ice up, frost up. ◆**givré** *a* frost-covered.
glabre [glabr] *a* (*visage*) smooth.
glace [glas] *nf* 1 (*eau gelée*) ice; (*crème glacée*) ice cream. 2 (*vitre*) window; (*miroir*) mirror; (*verre*) plate glass.

glacer [glase] **1** *vt* (*sang*) *Fig* to chill; **g. qn** (*transir, paralyser*) to chill s.o.; **– se g.** *vpr* (*eau*) to freeze. **2** *vt* (*gâteau*) to ice, (*au jus*) to glaze; (*papier*) to glaze. ◆**glaçant** *a* (*attitude etc*) chilling, icy. ◆**glacé** *a* **1** (*eau, main, pièce*) ice-cold, icy; (*vent*) freezing, icy; (*accueil*) *Fig* icy, chilly. **2** (*thé*) iced; (*fruit, marron*) candied; (*papier*) glazed. ◆**glaçage** *nm* (*de gâteau etc*) icing. ◆**glacial, -aux** *a* icy. ◆**glacier** *nm* **1** *Géol* glacier. **2** (*vendeur*) ice-cream man. ◆**glacière** *nf* (*boîte, endroit*) icebox. ◆**glaçon** *nm* *Culin* ice cube; *Géol* block of ice; (*sur le toit*) icicle.

glaïeul [glajœl] *nm* *Bot* gladiolus.

glaires [glɛr] *nfpl* *Méd* phlegm.

glaise [glɛz] *nf* clay.

gland [glɑ̃] *nm* **1** *Bot* acorn. **2** (*pompon*) *Tex* tassel.

glande [glɑ̃d] *nf* gland.

glander [glɑ̃de] *vi* *Arg* to fritter away one's time.

glaner [glane] *vt* (*blé, renseignement etc*) to glean.

glapir [glapir] *vi* to yelp, yap.

glas [glɑ] *nm* (*de cloche*) knell.

glauque [glok] *a* sea-green.

gliss/er [glise] *vi* (*involontairement*) to slip; (*patiner, coulisser*) to slide; (*sur l'eau*) to glide; **g. sur** (*sujet*) to slide *ou* gloss over; **ça glisse** it's slippery; **– vt** (*introduire*) to slip (**dans** into); (*murmurer*) to whisper; **se g. dans/sous** to slip into/under. ◆**–ant** *a* slippery. ◆**glissade** *nf* (*involontaire*) slip; (*volontaire*) slide. ◆**glissement** *nm* (*de sens*) *Ling* shift; **g. à gauche** *Pol* swing *ou* shift to the left; **g. de terrain** *Géol* landslide. ◆**glissière** *nf* groove; **porte à g.** sliding door; **fermeture à g.** zip (fastener), *Am* zipper.

global, -aux [glɔbal, -o] *a* total, global; **somme globale** lump sum. ◆**–ement** *adv* collectively, as a whole.

globe [glɔb] *nm* globe; **g. de l'œil** eyeball.

globule [glɔbyl] *nm* (*du sang*) corpuscle.

gloire [glwar] *nf* (*renommée, louange, mérite*) glory; (*personne célèbre*) celebrity; **se faire g. de** to glory in; **à la g. de** in praise of. ◆**glorieux, -euse** *a* (*plein de gloire*) glorious. ◆**glorifier** *vt* to glorify; **se g. de** to glory in.

glossaire [glɔsɛr] *nm* glossary.

glouglou [gluglu] *nm* (*de liquide*) gurgle. ◆**glouglouter** *vi* to gurgle.

glouss/er [gluse] *vi* (*poule*) to cluck; (*personne*) to chuckle. ◆**–ement** *nm* cluck; chuckle.

glouton, -onne [glutɔ̃, -ɔn] *a* greedy, gluttonous; **– nmf** glutton. ◆**gloutonnerie** *nf* gluttony.

gluant [glyɑ̃] *a* sticky.

glucose [glykoz] *nm* glucose.

glycérine [gliserin] *nf* glycerin(e).

glycine [glisin] *nf* *Bot* wisteria.

gnome [gnom] *nm* (*nain*) gnome.

gnon [ɲɔ̃] *nm* *Arg* blow, punch.

goal [gol] *nm* *Fb* goalkeeper.

gobelet [gɔblɛ] *nm* tumbler; (*de plastique, papier*) cup.

gober [gɔbe] *vt* (*œuf, mouche etc*) to swallow (whole); (*propos*) *Fig* to swallow.

godasse [gɔdas] *nf* *Fam* shoe.

godet [gɔdɛ] *nm* (*récipient*) pot; (*verre*) *Arg* drink.

goéland [gɔelɑ̃] *nm* (sea)gull.

gogo [gogo] *nm* (*homme naïf*) *Fam* sucker.

gogo (à) [agogo] *adv* *Fam* galore.

goguenard [gɔgnar] *a* mocking.

goguette (en) [ɑ̃gɔgɛt] *adv* *Fam* on the spree.

goinfre [gwɛ̃fr] *nm* (*glouton*) *Fam* pig, guzzler. ◆**se goinfrer** *vpr* *Fam* to stuff oneself (**de** with).

golf [gɔlf] *nm* golf; (*terrain*) golf course. ◆**golfeur, -euse** *nmf* golfer.

golfe [gɔlf] *nm* gulf, bay.

gomme [gɔm] *nf* **1** (*substance*) gum. **2** (*à effacer*) rubber, *Am* eraser. ◆**gommé** *a* (*papier*) gummed. ◆**gommer** *vt* (*effacer*) to rub out, erase.

gomme (à la) [alagɔm] *adv* *Fam* useless.

gond [gɔ̃] *nm* (*de porte etc*) hinge.

gondole [gɔ̃dɔl] *nf* (*bateau*) gondola. ◆**gondolier** *nm* gondolier.

gondoler [gɔ̃dɔle] **1** *vi*, **– se g.** *vpr* (*planche*) to warp. **2 se g.** *vpr* (*rire*) *Fam* to split one's sides.

gonfl/er [gɔ̃fle] *vt* to swell; (*pneu*) to inflate, pump up; (*en soufflant*) to blow up; (*poitrine*) to swell out; (*grossir*) *Fig* to inflate; **– vi**, **– se g.** *vpr* to swell; **se g. de** (*orgueil, émotion*) to swell with. ◆**–é** *a* swollen; **être g.** *Fam* (*courageux*) to have plenty of pluck; (*insolent*) to have plenty of nerve. ◆**–able** *a* inflatable. ◆**–ement** *nm* swelling. ◆**–eur** *nm* (air) pump.

gong [gɔ̃g] *nm* gong.

gorge [gɔrʒ] *nf* **1** throat; (*seins*) *Litt* bust. **2** *Géog* gorge. ◆**gorg/er** *vt* (*remplir*) to stuff (**de** with); **se g. de** to stuff *ou* gorge oneself with. ◆**–é** *a* (*saturé*) gorged with. ◆**–ée** *nf* mouthful; **petite g.** sip; **d'une seule g.** in *ou* at one gulp.

gorille [gɔrij] nm **1** (animal) gorilla. **2** (garde du corps) Fam bodyguard.

gosier [gozje] nm throat, windpipe.

gosse [gɔs] nmf (enfant) Fam kid, youngster.

gothique [gɔtik] a & nm Gothic.

gouache [gwaʃ] nf (peinture) gouache.

goudron [gudrɔ̃] nm tar. ◆**goudronner** vt to tar.

gouffre [gufr] nm gulf, chasm.

goujat [guʒa] nm churl, lout.

goulasch [gulaʃ] nf Culin goulash.

goulot [gulo] nm (de bouteille) neck; **boire au g.** to drink from the bottle.

goulu, -ue [guly] a greedy; — nmf glutton. ◆**goulûment** adv greedily.

goupille [gupij] nf (cheville) pin.

goupiller [gupije] vt (arranger) Fam to work out, arrange.

gourde [gurd] nf **1** (à eau) water bottle, flask. **2** (personne) Péj Fam chump, oaf.

gourdin [gurdɛ̃] nm club, cudgel.

gourer (se) [səgure] vpr Fam to make a mistake.

gourmand, -ande [gurmɑ̃, -ɑ̃d] a fond of eating, Péj greedy; **g. de** fond of; **être g. (de sucreries)** to have a sweet tooth; — nmf hearty eater, Péj glutton. ◆**gourmandise** nf good eating, Péj gluttony; pl (mets) delicacies.

gourmet [gurmɛ] nm gourmet, epicure.

gourmette [gurmɛt] nf chain ou identity bracelet.

gousse [gus] nf **g. d'ail** clove of garlic.

goût [gu] nm taste; **de bon g.** in good taste; **prendre g. à qch** to take a liking to sth; **par g.** from ou by choice; **sans g.** tasteless. ◆**goûter** vt (aliment) to taste; (apprécier) to relish, enjoy; **g. à qch** to taste (a little of) sth; **g. de** (pour la première fois) to try out, taste; — vi to have a snack, have tea; — nm snack, tea.

goutte [gut] nf **1** drop. **couler g. à g.** to drip. **2** (maladie) gout. ◆**g.-à-goutte** nm inv Méd drip. ◆**gouttelette** nf droplet. ◆**goutter** vi (eau, robinet, nez) to drip (de from).

gouttière [gutjɛr] nf (d'un toit) gutter.

gouvernail [guvɛrnaj] nm (pale) rudder; (barre) helm.

gouvernante [guvɛrnɑ̃t] nf governess.

gouvernement [guvɛrnəmɑ̃] nm government. ◆**gouvernemental, -aux** a (parti, politique etc) government-.

gouvern/er [guvɛrne] vti Pol & Fig to govern, rule. ◆**—ants** nmpl rulers. ◆**—eur** nm governor.

grabuge [grabyʒ] nm **du g.** (querelle) Fam a rumpus.

grâce [grɑs] **1** nf (charme) & Rel grace; (avantage) favour; (miséricorde) mercy; **crier g.** to cry for mercy; **de bonne/mauvaise g.** with good/bad grace; **donner le coup de g.** à to finish off; **faire g. de qch à qn** to spare s.o. sth. **2** prép **g. à** thanks to. ◆**gracier** vt (condamné) to pardon.

gracieux, -euse [grasjø, -øz] a **1** (élégant) graceful; (aimable) gracious. **2** (gratuit) gratuitous; **à titre g.** free (of charge). ◆**gracieusement** adv gracefully; graciously; free (of charge).

gracile [grasil] a Litt slender.

gradation [gradasjɔ̃] nf gradation.

grade [grad] nm Mil rank; **monter en g.** to be promoted. ◆**gradé** nm Mil non-commissioned officer.

gradin [gradɛ̃] nm Th etc row of seats, tier.

graduel, -elle [graduɛl] a gradual.

graduer [gradɥe] vt (règle) to graduate; (exercices) to grade, make gradually more difficult.

graffiti [grafiti] nmpl graffiti.

grain [grɛ̃] nm **1** (de blé etc) & Fig grain; (de café) bean; (de chapelet) bead; (de poussière) speck; pl (céréales) grain; **le g.** (de cuir, papier) the grain; **g. de beauté** mole; (sur le visage) beauty spot; **g. de raisin** grape. **2** Mét shower.

graine [grɛn] nf seed; **mauvaise g.** (enfant) Péj bad lot, rotten egg.

graisse [grɛs] nf fat; (lubrifiant) grease. ◆**graissage** nm Aut lubrication. ◆**graisser** vt to grease. ◆**graisseux, -euse** a (vêtement etc) greasy, oily; (bourrelets, tissu) fatty.

grammaire [gramɛr] nf grammar. ◆**grammatical, -aux** a grammatical.

gramme [gram] nm gram(me).

grand, grande [grɑ̃, grɑ̃d] a big, large; (en hauteur) tall; (mérite, âge, chaleur, ami etc) great; (bruit) loud, great; (différence) wide, great, big; (adulte, mûr, plus âgé) grown-up, big; (officier, maître) grand; (âme) noble; **g. frère/etc** (plus âgé) big brother/etc; **le g. air** the open air; **il est g. temps** it's high time (que that); — adv **g. ouvert** (yeux, fenêtre) wide-open; **ouvrir g.** to open wide; **en g.** on a grand ou large scale; — nm Scol senior; (adulte) grown-up; **les quatre Grands** Pol the Big Four. ◆**grandement** adv (beaucoup) greatly; (généreusement) grandly; **avoir g. de quoi vivre** to have plenty to live on. ◆**grandeur** nf (importance, gloire) greatness; (dimension) size, magnitude; (*majesté, splendeur*) grandeur; **g. na-ture** life-size; **g. d'âme** generosity.

grand-chose [grɑ̃ʃoz] *pron* **pas g.-chose** not much. ◆**g.-mère** *nf* (*pl* **grands-mères**) grandmother. ◆**grands-parents** *nmpl* grandparents. ◆**g.-père** *nm* (*pl* **grands-pères**) grandfather.

Grande-Bretagne [grɑ̃dbrətaɲ] *nf* Great Britain.

grandiose [grɑ̃djoz] *a* grandiose, grand.

grandir [grɑ̃dir] *vi* to grow; (*bruit*) to grow louder; – *vt* (*grossir*) to magnify; **g. qn** (*faire paraître plus grand*) to make s.o. seem taller.

grange [grɑ̃ʒ] *nf* barn.

granit(e) [granit] *nm* granite.

graphique [grafik] *a* (*signe, art*) graphic; – *nm* graph.

grappe [grap] *nf* (*de fruits etc*) cluster; **g. de raisin** bunch of grapes.

grappin [grapɛ̃] *nm* **mettre le g. sur** *Fam* to grab hold of.

gras, grasse [grɑ, grɑs] *a* (*personne, ventre etc*) fat; (*aliment*) fatty; (*graisseux*) greasy, oily; (*caractère*) *Typ* bold, heavy; (*plante, contour*) thick; (*rire*) throaty, deep; (*toux*) loose, phlegmy; (*récompense*) rich; **matières grasses** fat; **foie g.** *Culin* foie gras, fatted goose liver; – *nm* (*de viande*) fat. ◆**grassement** *adv* (*abondamment*) handsomely. ◆**grassouillet, -ette** *a* plump.

gratifier [gratifje] *vt* **g. qn de** to present *ou* favour s.o. with. ◆**gratification** *nf* (*prime*) bonus.

gratin [gratɛ̃] *nm* **1 au g.** *Culin* baked with breadcrumbs and grated cheese. **2** (*élite*) *Fam* upper crust.

gratis [gratis] *adv* *Fam* free (of charge), gratis.

gratitude [gratityd] *nf* gratitude.

gratte-ciel [gratsjɛl] *nm inv* skyscraper.

gratte-papier [gratpapje] *nm* (*employé*) *Péj* pen-pusher.

gratter [grate] *vt* (*avec un outil etc*) to scrape; (*avec les ongles, les griffes etc*) to scratch; (*boue*) to scrape off; (*effacer*) to scratch out; **ça me gratte** *Fam* it itches, I have an itch; – *vi* (*à la porte etc*) to scratch; (*tissu*) to be scratchy; **— se g.** *vpr* to scratch oneself. ◆**grattoir** *nm* scraper.

gratuit(e) [gratɥi] *a* (*billet etc*) free; (*hypothèse, acte*) gratuitous. ◆**gratuité** *nf* **la g. de l'enseignement**/*etc* free education/*etc*. ◆**gratuitement** *adv* free (of charge); gratuitously.

gravats [grava] *nmpl* rubble, debris.

grave [grav] *a* serious; (*juge, visage*) grave, solemn; (*voix*) deep, low; (*accent*) *Gram* grave; **ce n'est pas g.!** it's not important! ◆**—ment** *adv* (*malade, menacé*) seriously; (*dignement*) gravely.

graver [grave] *vt* (*sur métal etc*) to engrave; (*sur bois*) to carve; (*disque*) to cut; (*dans sa mémoire*) to imprint, engrave. ◆**—eur** *nm* engraver.

gravier [gravje] *nm* gravel. ◆**gravillon** *nm* gravel; *pl* gravel, (loose) chippings.

gravir [gravir] *vt* to climb (with effort).

gravité [gravite] *nf* **1** (*de situation etc*) seriousness; (*solennité*) gravity. **2** *Phys* gravity.

graviter [gravite] *vi* to revolve (**autour de** around). ◆**gravitation** *nf* gravitation.

gravure [gravyr] *nf* (*action, art*) engraving; (*à l'eau forte*) etching; (*estampe*) print; (*de disque*) recording; **g. sur bois** (*objet*) woodcut.

gré [gre] *nm* **à son g.** (*goût*) to his *ou* her taste; (*désir*) as he *ou* she pleases; **de bon g.** willingly; **contre le g. de** against the will of; **bon g. mal g.** willy-nilly; **au g. de** (*vent etc*) at the mercy of.

Grèce [grɛs] *nf* Greece. ◆**grec, grecque** *a* & *nmf* Greek; – *nm* (*langue*) Greek.

greffe [grɛf] **1** *nf* (*de peau*) & *Bot* graft; (*d'organe*) transplant. **2** *nm* *Jur* record office. ◆**greffer** *vt* (*peau etc*) & *Bot* to graft (**à** on to); (*organe*) to transplant. ◆**greffier** *nm* clerk (of the court). ◆**greffon** *nm* (*de peau*) & *Bot* graft.

grégaire [gregɛr] *a* (*instinct*) gregarious.

grêle [grɛl] **1** *nf* *Mét* & *Fig* hail. **2** *a* (*fin*) spindly, (very) slender *ou* thin. ◆**grêler** *v imp* to hail. ◆**grêlon** *nm* hailstone.

grêlé [grele] *a* (*visage*) pockmarked.

grelot [grəlo] *nm* (small round) bell.

grelotter [grələte] *vi* to shiver (**de** with).

grenade [grənad] *nf* **1** *Bot* pomegranate. **2** (*projectile*) *Mil* grenade. ◆**grenadine** *nf* pomegranate syrup, grenadine.

grenat [grəna] *a inv* (*couleur*) dark red.

grenier [grənje] *nm* attic; *Agr* granary.

grenouille [grənuj] *nf* frog.

grès [grɛ] *nm* (*roche*) sandstone; (*poterie*) stoneware.

grésiller [grezije] *vi* *Culin* to sizzle; *Rad* to crackle.

grève [grɛv] *nf* **1** strike; **g. de la faim** hunger strike; **g. du zèle** work-to-rule, *Am* rule-book slow-down; **g. perlée** go-slow, *Am* slow-down (strike); **g. sauvage/sur le tas** wildcat/sit-down strike; **g. tournante** strike by rota. **2** (*de mer*) shore; (*de rivière*) bank. ◆**gréviste** *nmf* striker.

gribouiller [gribuje] *vti* to scribble.
◆**gribouillis** *nm* scribble.

grief [grijɛf] *nm* (*plainte*) grievance.

grièvement [grijɛvmã] *adv* g. blessé seriously *ou* badly injured.

griffe [grif] *nf* **1** (*ongle*) claw; **sous la g. de qn** (*pouvoir*) in s.o.'s clutches. **2** (*de couturier*) (designer) label; (*tampon*) printed signature; (*d'auteur*) Fig mark, stamp. ◆**griffé** *a* (*vêtement*) designer-. ◆**griffer** *vt* to scratch, claw.

griffonn/er [grifɔne] *vt* to scrawl, scribble. ◆**—age** *nm* scrawl, scribble.

grignoter [griɲɔte] *vti* to nibble.

gril [gril] *nm* Culin grill, grid(iron). ◆**grillade** [grijad] *nf* (*viande*) grill. ◆**grille-pain** *nm inv* toaster. ◆**griller** *vt* (*viande*) to grill, broil; (*pain*) to toast; (*café*) to roast; (*ampoule*) El to blow; (*brûler*) to scorch; (*cigarette*) Fam to smoke; **g. un feu rouge** Aut Fam to drive through *ou* jump a red light; – *vi* **mettre à g.** to put on the grill; **on grille ici** Fam it's scorching. **g. de faire** to be itching to do.

grille [grij] *nf* (*clôture*) railings; (*porte*) (iron) gate; (*de fourneau, foyer*) grate; (*de radiateur*) Aut grid, grille; (*des salaires*) Fig scale; *pl* (*de fenêtre*) bars, grating; **g. (des horaires*) schedule. ◆**grillage** *nm* wire netting.

grillon [grijɔ̃] *nm* (*insecte*) cricket.

grimace [grimas] *nf* (*pour faire rire*) (funny) face, grimace; (*de dégoût, douleur*) grimace. ◆**grimacer** *vi* to grimace (with).

grimer [grime] *vt*, **— se g.** *vpr* (*acteur*) to make up.

grimp/er [grɛ̃pe] *vi* to climb (**à qch** up sth); (*prix*) Fam to rocket; – *vt* to climb. ◆**—ant** *a* (*plante*) climbing.

grinc/er [grɛ̃se] *vi* to grate, creak; **g. des dents** to grind *ou* gnash one's teeth. ◆**—ement** *nm* grating; grinding.

grincheux, -euse [grɛ̃ʃø, -øz] *a* grumpy, peevish.

gringalet [grɛ̃galɛ] *nm* (*homme*) Péj puny runt, weakling.

grippe [grip] *nf* **1** (*maladie*) flu, influenza. **2 prendre qch/qn en g.** to take a strong dislike to sth/s.o. ◆**grippé** *a* **être g.** to have (the) flu.

gripper [gripe] *vi*, **— se g.** *vpr* (*moteur*) to seize up.

grippe-sou [gripsu] *nm* skinflint, miser.

gris [gri] *a* grey, *Am* gray; (*temps*) grey; (*ivre*) tipsy; – *nm* grey. ◆**grisaille** *nf* (*de vie*) dullness, greyness, *Am* grayness. ◆**grisâtre** *a* greyish, *Am* grayish.

◆**griser** *vt* (*vin etc*) to make (s.o.) tipsy, intoxicate (s.o.); (*air vif, succès*) to exhilarate (s.o.). ◆**griserie** *nf* intoxication; exhilaration. ◆**grisonn/er** *vi* (*cheveux, personne*) to go grey. ◆**—ant** *a* greying.

grisou [grizu] *nm* (*gaz*) firedamp.

grive [griv] *nf* (*oiseau*) thrush.

grivois [grivwa] *a* bawdy. ◆**grivoiserie** *nf* (*propos*) bawdy talk.

Groenland [grɔɛnlãd] *nm* Greenland.

grog [grɔg] *nm* (*boisson*) grog, toddy.

grogn/er [grɔɲe] *vi* to growl, grumble (**contre** at); (*cochon*) to grunt. ◆**—ement** *nm* growl, grumble; grunt. ◆**grognon, -onne** *a* grumpy, peevish.

grommeler [grɔmle] *vti* to grumble, mutter.

gronder [grɔ̃de] *vi* (*chien*) to growl; (*tonnerre*) to rumble; – *vt* (*réprimander*) to scold. ◆**grondement** *nm* growl; rumble. ◆**gronderie** *nf* scolding.

gros, grosse [gro, gros] *a* big; (*gras*) fat; (*épais*) thick; (*effort, progrès*) great; (*fortune, somme*) large; (*bruit*) loud; (*averse, mer, rhume*) heavy; (*faute*) serious, gross; (*traits, laine, fil*) coarse; **g. mot** swear word; – *adv* **gagner g.** to earn big money; **risquer g.** to take a big risk; **en g.** (*globalement*) roughly; (*écrire*) in big letters; (*vendre*) in bulk, wholesale; – *nmf* (*personne*) fat man, fat woman; – *nm* **le g. de** the bulk of; **de g.** (*maison, prix*) wholesale.

groseille [grozɛj] *nf* (white *ou* red) currant; **g. à maquereau** gooseberry.

grossesse [grosɛs] *nf* pregnancy.

grosseur [grosœr] *nf* **1** (*volume*) size; (*obésité*) bigness. **2** (*tumeur*) Méd lump.

grossier, -ière [grosje, -jɛr] *a* (*matière, tissu, traits*) coarse, rough; (*idée, solution*) rough, crude; (*instrument*) crude; (*erreur*) gross; (*personne, manières*) coarse, uncouth, rude; **être g. envers** (*insolent*) to be rude to. ◆**grossièrement** *adv* (*calculer*) roughly; (*se tromper*) grossly; (*répondre*) coarsely, rudely. ◆**grossièreté** *nf* coarseness; roughness; (*insolence*) rudeness; (*mot*) rude word.

gross/ir [grosir] *vi* (*personne*) to put on weight; (*fleuve*) to swell; (*nombre, bosse, foule*) to swell, get bigger; (*bruit*) to get louder; – *vt* to swell; (*exagérer*) Fig to magnify; – *vti* (*verre, loupe etc*) to magnify; **verre grossissant** magnifying glass. ◆**—issement** *nm* increase in weight; swelling, increase in size; (*de microscope etc*) magnification.

grossiste [grosist] *nmf* Com wholesaler.

grosso modo [grosomɔdo] *adv* (*en gros*) roughly.

grotesque [grɔtɛsk] *a* (*risible*) ludicrous, grotesque.

grotte [grɔt] *nf* grotto.

grouill/er [gruje] **1** *vi* (*rue, fourmis, foule etc*) to be swarming (**de** with). **2 se g.** *vpr* (*se hâter*) *Arg* to step on it. ◆**—ant** *a* swarming (**de** with).

groupe [grup] *nm* group; **g. scolaire** (*bâtiments*) school block. ◆**groupement** *nm* (*action*) grouping; (*groupe*) group. ◆**grouper** *vt* to group (together); **— se g.** *vpr* to band together, group (together).

grue [gry] *nf* (*machine, oiseau*) crane.

grumeau, -x [grymo] *nm* (*dans une sauce etc*) lump. ◆**grumeleux, -euse** *a* lumpy.

gruyère [gryjɛr] *nm* gruyère (cheese).

gué [ge] *nm* ford; **passer à g.** to ford.

guenilles [gənij] *nfpl* rags (and tatters).

guenon [gənɔ̃] *nf* female monkey.

guépard [gepar] *nm* cheetah.

guêpe [gɛp] *nf* wasp. ◆**guêpier** *nm* (*nid*) wasp's nest; (*piège*) *Fig* trap.

guère [gɛr] *adv* (**ne**) **. . . g.** hardly, scarcely; **il ne sort g.** he hardly *ou* scarcely goes out.

guéridon [geridɔ̃] *nm* pedestal table.

guérilla [gerija] *nf* guerrilla warfare. ◆**guérillero** *nm* guerrilla.

guér/ir [gerir] *vt* (*personne, maladie*) to cure (**de** of); (*blessure*) to heal; **—** *vi* to recover; (*blessure*) to heal; (*rhume*) to get better; **g. de** (*fièvre etc*) to get over, recover from. ◆**—i** *a* cured, better, well. ◆**guérison** *nf* (*de personne*) recovery; (*de maladie*) cure; (*de blessure*) healing. ◆**guérisseur, -euse** *nmf* faith healer.

guérite [gerit] *nf Mil* sentry box.

guerre [gɛr] *nf* war; (*chimique etc*) warfare; **en g.** at war (**avec** with); **faire la g.** to wage *ou* make war (**à** on, against); **g. d'usure** war of attrition; **conseil de g.** court-martial. ◆**guerrier, -ière** *a* (*chant, danse*) war-; (*nation*) war-like; **—** *nmf* warrior. ◆**guerroyer** *vi Litt* to war.

guet [gɛ] *nm* **faire le g.** to be on the look-out. ◆**guett/er** *vt* to be on the look-out for,

watch (out) for; (*gibier*) to lie in wait for. ◆**—eur** *nm* (*soldat*) look-out.

guet-apens [gɛtapɑ̃] *nm inv* ambush.

guêtre [gɛtr] *nf* gaiter.

gueule [gœl] *nf* (*d'animal, de canon*) mouth; (*de personne*) *Fam* mouth; (*figure*) *Fam* face; **avoir la g. de bois** *Fam* to have a hangover; **faire la g.** *Fam* to sulk. ◆**gueuler** *vti* to bawl (out). ◆**gueuleton** *nm* (*repas*) *Fam* blow-out, feast.

gui [gi] *nm Bot* mistletoe.

guichet [giʃɛ] *nm* (*de gare, cinéma etc*) ticket office; (*de banque etc*) window; *Th* box office, ticket office; **à guichets fermés** *Th Sp* with all tickets sold in advance. ◆**guichetier, -ière** *nmf* (*à la poste etc*) counter clerk; (*à la gare*) ticket office clerk.

guide [gid] **1** *nm* (*personne, livre etc*) guide. **2** *nf* (*éclaireuse*) (girl) guide. **3** *nfpl* (*rênes*) reins. ◆**guider** *vt* to guide; **se g. sur** to guide oneself by.

guidon [gidɔ̃] *nm* (*de bicyclette etc*) handlebar(s).

guigne [giɲ] *nf* (*malchance*) *Fam* bad luck.

guignol [giɲɔl] *nm* (*spectacle*) = Punch and Judy show.

guillemets [gijmɛ] *nmpl Typ* inverted commas, quotation marks.

guilleret, -ette [gijrɛ, -ɛt] *a* lively, perky.

guillotine [gijɔtin] *nf* guillotine.

guimauve [gimov] *nf Bot Culin* marshmallow.

guimbarde [gɛ̃bard] *nf* (*voiture*) *Fam* old banger, *Am* (old) wreck.

guindé [gɛ̃de] *a* (*affecté*) stiff, stilted, stuck-up.

guingois (de) [dəgɛ̃gwa] *adv* askew.

guirlande [girlɑ̃d] *nf* garland, wreath.

guise [giz] *nf* **n'en faire qu'à sa g.** to do as one pleases; **en g. de** by way of.

guitare [gitar] *nf* guitar. ◆**guitariste** *nmf* guitarist.

guttural, -aux [gytyral, -o] *a* guttural.

gymnase [ʒimnaz] *nm* gymnasium. ◆**gymnaste** *nmf* gymnast. ◆**gymnastique** *nf* gymnastics.

gynécologie [ʒinekɔlɔʒi] *nf* gynaecology, *Am* gynecology. ◆**gynécologue** *nmf* gynaecologist, *Am* gynecologist.

H

H, h [aʃ] *nm* H, h; **l'heure H** zero hour; **bombe H** H-bomb.

ha! [ˈɑ] *int* ah!, oh!; **ha, ha!** (*rire*) ha-ha!

habile [abil] *a* clever, skilful (**à qch** at sth, **à faire** at doing). ◆**habilement** *adv* cleverly, skilfully. ◆**habileté** *nf* skill, ability.

habill/er [abije] *vt* to dress (**de** in); (*fournir en vêtements*) to clothe; (*couvrir*) to cover (**de** with); **h. qn en soldat**/*etc* (*déguiser*) to dress s.o. up as a soldier/*etc*; **— s'h.** *vpr* to dress (oneself), get dressed; (*avec élégance, se déguiser*) to dress up. ◆**—é** *a* dressed (**de** in); (*costume, robe*) smart, dressy. ◆**—ement** *nm* (*vêtements*) clothing, clothes.

habit [abi] *nm* costume, outfit; (*tenue de soi-rée*) evening dress, tails; *pl* (*vêtements*) clothes.

habit/er [abite] *vi* to live (**à, en, dans** in); — *vt* (*maison, région*) to live in; (*planète*) to inhabit. ◆**—ant, -ante** *nmf* (*de pays etc*) inhabitant; (*de maison*) resident, occupant. ◆**—é** *a* (*région*) inhabited; (*maison*) occu-pied. ◆**—able** *a* (in)habitable. ◆**habitat** *nm* (*d'animal, de plante*) habitat; (*condi-tions*) housing, living conditions. ◆**habitation** *nf* house, dwelling; (*action de résider*) living.

habitude [abityd] *nf* habit; **avoir l'h. de qch** to be used to sth; **avoir l'h. de faire** to be used to doing, be in the habit of doing; **prendre l'h. de faire** to get into the habit of doing; **d'h.** usually; **comme d'h.** as usual. ◆**habituel, -elle** *a* usual, customary. ◆**habituellement** *adv* usually. ◆**habi-tu/er** *vt* **h. qn à** to accustom s.o. to; **être habitué à** to be used ou accustomed to; **— s'h.** *vpr* to get accustomed (**à** to). ◆**—é, -ée** *nmf* regular (customer *ou* visitor).

hache [ˈaʃ] *nf* axe, *Am* ax. ◆**hachette** *nf* hatchet.

hach/er [ˈaʃe] *vt* (*au couteau*) to chop (up); (*avec un appareil*) to mince, *Am* grind; (*déchiqueter*) to cut to pieces. ◆**—é** *a* **1** (*viande*) minced, *Am* ground; chopped. **2** (*style*) staccato, broken. ◆**hachis** *nm* (*viande*) mince, minced *ou Am* ground meat. ◆**hachoir** *nm* (*couteau*) chopper; (*ap-pareil*) mincer, *Am* grinder.

hagard [ˈagar] *a* wild-looking, frantic.

haie [ˈɛ] *nf* (*clôture*) *Bot* hedge; (*rangée*) row; (*de coureur*) *Sp* hurdle; (*de chevaux*) *Sp* fence, hurdle; **course de haies** (*coureurs*) hurdle race; (*chevaux*) steeplechase.

haillons [ˈɑjɔ̃] *nmpl* rags (and tatters).

haine [ˈɛn] *nf* hatred, hate. ◆**haineux, -euse** *a* full of hatred.

haïr* [ˈair] *vt* to hate. ◆**haïssable** *a* hate-ful, detestable.

hâle [ˈɑl] *nm* suntan. ◆**hâlé** *a* (*par le soleil*) suntanned; (*par l'air*) weather-beaten.

haleine [alɛn] *nf* breath; **hors d'h.** out of breath; **perdre h.** to get out of breath; **reprendre h.** to get one's breath back, catch one's breath; **de longue h.** (*travail*) long-term; **tenir en h.** to hold in suspense.

hal/er [ˈale] *vt Nau* to tow. ◆**—age** *nm* towing; **chemin de h.** towpath.

halet/er [ˈalte] *vi* to pant, gasp. ◆**—ant** *a* panting, gasping.

hall [ˈol] *nm* (*de gare*) main hall, concourse; (*d'hôtel*) lobby, hall; (*de maison*) hall(way).

halle [ˈal] *nf* (covered) market; **les halles** the central food market.

hallucination [alysinɑsjɔ̃] *nf* hallucination. ◆**hallucinant** *a* extraordinary.

halo [ˈalo] *nm* (*auréole*) halo.

halte [ˈalt] *nf* (*arrêt*) stop, *Mil* halt; (*lieu*) stopping place, *Mil* halting place; **faire h.** to stop; **— *int* stop!**, *Mil* halt!

haltère [alter] *nm* (*poids*) *Sp* dumbbell. ◆**haltérophilie** *nf* weight lifting.

hamac [ˈamak] *nm* hammock.

hameau, -x [ˈamo] *nm* hamlet.

hameçon [amsɔ̃] *nm* (fish) hook; **mordre à l'h.** *Pêche & Fig* to rise to *ou* swallow the bait.

hamster [ˈamstɛr] *nm* hamster.

hanche [ˈɑ̃ʃ] *nf Anat* hip.

hand(-)ball [ˈadbal] *nm Sp* handball.

handicap [ˈadikap] *nm* (*désavantage*) & *Sp* handicap. ◆**handicap/er** *vt* to handicap. ◆**—é, -ée** *a* & *nmf* handicapped (person); **h. moteur** spastic.

hangar [ˈɑ̃gar] *nm* (*entrepôt*) shed; (*pour avions*) hangar.

hanneton [ˈantɔ̃] *nm* (*insecte*) cockchafer.

hanter [ˈɑ̃te] *vt* to haunt.

hantise [ˈɑ̃tiz] *nf* **la h. de** an obsession with.

happer ['ape] vt (*saisir*) to catch, snatch; (*par la gueule*) to snap up.

haras ['aʀɑ] nm stud farm.

harasser ['aʀase] vt to exhaust.

harceler ['aʀsəle] vt to harass, torment (de with). ◆**harcèlement** nm harassment.

hardi ['aʀdi] a bold, daring. ◆—**ment** adv boldly. ◆**hardiesse** nf boldness, daring; **une h.** (*action*) Litt an audacity.

harem ['aʀɛm] nm harem.

hareng ['aʀɑ̃] nm herring.

hargne ['aʀɲ] nf aggressive bad temper. ◆**hargneux, -euse** a bad-tempered, aggressive.

haricot ['aʀiko] nm (*blanc*) (haricot) bean; (*vert*) French bean, green bean.

harmonica [aʀmɔnika] nm harmonica, mouthorgan.

harmonie [aʀmɔni] nf harmony. ◆**harmonieux, -euse** a harmonious. ◆**harmonique** a & nm Mus harmonic. ◆**harmoniser** vt, — **s'h.** vpr to harmonize. ◆**harmonium** nm Mus harmonium.

harnacher ['aʀnaʃe] vt (*cheval etc*) to harness. ◆**harnais** nm (*de cheval, bébé*) harness.

harpe ['aʀp] nf harp. ◆**harpiste** nmf harpist.

harpon ['aʀpɔ̃] nm harpoon. ◆**harponner** vt (*baleine*) to harpoon; **h. qn** (*arrêter*) Fam to waylay s.o.

hasard ['azaʀ] nm **le h.** chance; **un h.** (*coïncidence*) a coincidence; **un heureux h.** a stroke of luck; **un malheureux h.** a rotten piece of luck; **par h.** by chance; **si par h.** if by any chance; **au h.** at random, haphazardly; **à tout h.** just in case; **les hasards de** (*risques*) the hazards of. ◆**hasard/er** vt (*remarque, démarche*) to venture, hazard; (*vie, réputation*) to risk; **se h. dans** to venture into; **se h. à faire** to risk doing, venture to do. ◆—**é** a, ◆**hasardeux, -euse** a risky, hazardous.

haschisch ['aʃiʃ] nm hashish.

hâte ['ɑt] nf haste, speed; (*impatience*) eagerness; **en h., à la h.** hurriedly, in a hurry, in haste; **avoir h. de faire** (*désireux*) to be eager to do, be in a hurry to do. ◆**hâter** vt (*pas, départ etc*) to hasten; — **se h.** vpr to hurry, make haste (**de faire** to do). ◆**hâtif, -ive** a hasty, hurried; (*développement*) precocious; (*fruit*) early.

hausse ['os] nf rise (**de** in); **en h.** rising. ◆**hausser** vt (*prix, voix etc*) to raise; (*épaules*) to shrug; **se h. sur la pointe des pieds** to stand on tip-toe.

haut ['o] a high; (*de taille*) tall; (*classes*) up-

per, higher; (*fonctionnaire etc*) high-ranking; **le h. Rhin** the upper Rhine; **la haute couture** high fashion; **à haute voix** aloud, in a loud voice; **h. de 5 mètres** 5 metres high ou tall; — adv (*voler, viser etc*) high (up); (*estimer*) highly; (*parler*) loud, loudly; **tout h.** (*lire, penser*) aloud, out loud; **h. placé** (*personne*) in a high position; **plus h.** (*dans un texte*) above, further back; — nm (*partie haute*) top; **en h. de** at the top of; **en h.** (*loger*) upstairs; (*regarder*) up; (*mettre*) on (the) top; **d'en h.** (*de la partie haute, du ciel etc*) from high up, from up above; **avoir 5 mètres de h.** to be 5 metres high ou tall; **des hauts et des bas** Fig ups and downs.

hautain ['otɛ̃] a haughty.

hautbois ['obwa] nm Mus oboe.

haut-de-forme ['odfɔʀm] nm (pl **hauts-de-forme**) top hat.

hautement ['otmɑ̃] adv (*tout à fait, très*) highly. ◆**hauteur** nf height; Géog hill; (*orgueil*) Péj haughtiness; Mus pitch; **à la h. de** (*objet*) level with; (*rue*) opposite; (*situation*) Fig equal to; **il n'est pas à la h.** he isn't up to it; **saut en h.** Sp high jump.

haut-le-cœur ['olkœʀ] nm inv **avoir des h.-le-cœur** to retch, gag.

haut-le-corps ['olkɔʀ] nm inv (*sursaut*) sudden start, jump.

haut-parleur ['opaʀlœʀ] nm loudspeaker.

hâve ['av] a gaunt, emaciated.

havre ['avʀ] nm (*refuge*) Litt haven.

Haye (La) [la'ɛ] nf The Hague.

hayon ['ɛjɔ̃] nm (*porte*) Aut tailgate, hatchback.

hé! [e] int hé (là) (*appel*) hey!; **hé! hé!** well, well!

hebdomadaire [ɛbdɔmadɛʀ] a weekly; — nm (*publication*) weekly.

héberg/er [ebɛʀʒe] vt to put up, accommodate. ◆—**ement** nm accommodation; **centre d'h.** shelter.

hébété [ebete] a dazed, stupefied.

hébreu, -x [ebʀø] am Hebrew; — nm (*langue*) Hebrew. ◆**hébraïque** a Hebrew.

hécatombe [ekatɔ̃b] nf (great) slaughter.

hectare [ɛktaʀ] nm hectare (= *2.47 acres*).

hégémonie [eʒemɔni] nf hegemony, supremacy.

hein! [ɛ̃] int (*surprise, interrogation etc*) eh!

hélas! ['elas] int alas!, unfortunately.

héler ['ele] vt (*taxi etc*) to hail.

hélice [elis] nf Av Nau propeller.

hélicoptère [elikɔptɛʀ] nm helicopter. ◆**héliport** nm heliport.

hellénique [elenik] a Hellenic, Greek.

helvétique [ɛlvetik] *a* Swiss.

hem! ['ɛm] *int* (a)hem!, hm!

hémicycle [emisikl] *nm* semicircle; *Pol Fig* French National Assembly.

hémisphère [emisfɛr] *nm* hemisphere.

hémorragie [emɔraʒi] *nf Méd* h(a)emorrhage; (*de capitaux*) *Com* outflow, drain.

hémorroïdes [emɔrɔid] *nfpl* piles, h(a)emorrhoids.

henn/ir ['enir] *vi* (*cheval*) to neigh. ◆**—issement** *nm* neigh.

hep! ['ɛp] *int* hey!, hey there!

hépatite [epatit] *nf* hepatitis.

herbe [ɛrb] *nf* grass; (*médicinale etc*) herb; **mauvaise h.** weed; **fines herbes** *Culin* herbs; **en h.** (*blés*) green; (*poète etc*) *Fig* budding. ◆**herbage** *nm* grassland. ◆**herbeux, -euse** *a* grassy. ◆**herbicide** *nm* weed killer. ◆**herbivore** *a* grass-eating, herbivorous. ◆**herbu** *a* grassy.

hercule [ɛrkyl] *nm* Hercules, strong man. ◆**herculéen, -enne** *a* herculean.

hérédité [eredite] *nf* heredity. ◆**héréditaire** *a* hereditary.

hérésie [erezi] *nf* heresy. ◆**hérétique** *a* heretical; – *nmf* heretic.

hériss/er ['erise] *vt* (*poils*) to bristle (up); **h. qn** (*irriter*) to ruffle s.o., ruffle s.o.'s feathers; – **se h.** *vpr* to bristle (up); to get ruffled. ◆**—é** *a* (*cheveux*) bristly; (*cactus*) prickly; **h. de** bristling with.

hérisson ['erisɔ̃] *nm* (*animal*) hedgehog.

hérit/er [erite] *vti* to inherit (**qch de qn** sth from s.o.); **h. de qch** to inherit sth. ◆**—age** *nm* (*biens*) inheritance; (*culturel, politique etc*) *Fig* heritage. ◆**héritier** *nm* heir. ◆**héritière** *nf* heiress.

hermétique [ɛrmetik] *a* hermetically sealed, airtight; (*obscur*) *Fig* impenetrable. ◆**—ment** *adv* hermetically.

hermine [ɛrmin] *nf* (*animal, fourrure*) ermine.

hernie ['ɛrni] *nf Méd* hernia, rupture; (*de pneu*) swelling.

héron ['erɔ̃] *nm* (*oiseau*) heron.

héros ['ero] *nm* hero. ◆**héroïne** [erɔin] *nf* **1** (*femme*) heroine. **2** (*stupéfiant*) heroin. ◆**héroïque** [erɔik] *a* heroic. ◆**héroïsme** [erɔism] *nm* heroism.

hésit/er [ezite] *vi* to hesitate (**sur** over, about; **à faire** to do); (*en parlant*) to falter, hesitate. ◆**—ant** *a* (*personne*) hesitating; (*pas, voix*) faltering, unsteady, wavering. ◆**hésitation** *nf* hesitation; **avec h.** hesitantly.

hétéroclite [eterɔklit] *a* (*disparate*) motley.

hétérogène [eterɔʒɛn] *a* heterogeneous.

hêtre ['ɛtr] *nm* (*arbre, bois*) beech.

heu! ['ø] *int* (*hésitation*) er!

heure [œr] *nf* (*mesure*) hour; (*moment*) time; **quelle h. est-il?** what time is it?; **il est six heures** it's six (o'clock); **six heures moins cinq** five to six; **six heures cinq** five past *ou Am* after six; **à l'h.** (*arriver*) on time; (*être payé*) by the hour; **dix kilomètres à l'h.** ten kilometers an hour; **à l'h. qu'il est** (by) now; **de dernière h.** (*nouvelle*) last minute; **de bonne h.** early; **à une h. avancée** at a late hour, late at night; **tout à l'h.** (*futur*) in a few moments, later; (*passé*) a moment ago; **à toute h.** (*continuellement*) at all hours; **faire des heures supplémentaires** to work *ou* do overtime; **heures creuses** off-peak *ou* slack periods; **l'h. d'affluence, l'h. de pointe** (*circulation etc*) rush hour; (*dans les magasins*) peak period; **l'h. de pointe** (*électricité etc*) peak period.

heureux, -euse [œrø, -øz] *a* happy; (*chanceux*) lucky, fortunate; (*issue, changement*) successful; (*expression, choix*) apt; **h. de qch/de voir qn** (*satisfait*) happy *ou* pleased *ou* glad about sth/to see s.o.; – *adv* (*vivre, mourir*) happily. ◆**heureusement** *adv* (*par chance*) fortunately, luckily, happily (**pour** for); (*avec succès*) successfully; (*exprimer*) aptly.

heurt ['œr] *nm* bump, knock; (*d'opinions etc*) *Fig* clash; **sans heurts** smoothly. ◆**heurt/er** *vt* (*cogner*) to knock, bump, hit (**contre** against); (*mur, piéton*) to bump into, hit; **h. qn** (*choquer*) to offend s.o., upset s.o.; – **se h. à** to bump into, hit; (*difficultés*) *Fig* to come up against. ◆**—é** *a* (*couleurs, tons*) clashing; (*style, rythme*) jerky. ◆**heurtoir** *nm* (door) knocker.

hexagone [ɛgzagɔn] *nm* hexagon; **l'H.** *Fig* France. ◆**hexagonal, -aux** *a* hexagonal; *Fig Fam* French.

hiatus [jatys] *nm Fig* hiatus, gap.

hiberner [ibɛrne] *vi* to hibernate. ◆**hibernation** *nf* hibernation.

hibou, -x ['ibu] *nm* owl.

hic ['ik] *nm* **voilà le h.** *Fam* that's the snag.

hideux, -euse ['idø, -øz] *a* hideous.

hier [(i)jɛr] *adv* & *nm* yesterday; **h. soir** last *ou* yesterday night, yesterday evening; **elle n'est pas née d'h.** *Fig* she wasn't born yesterday.

hiérarchie ['jerarʃi] *nf* hierarchy. ◆**hiérarchique** *a* (*ordre*) hierarchical; **par la voie h.** through (the) official channels. ◆**hiérarchiser** *vt* (*emploi, valeurs*) to grade.

hi-fi ['ifi] *a inv* & *nf inv Fam* hi-fi.

hilare [ilar] *a* merry. ◆**hilarant** *a* (*drôle*) hilarious. ◆**hilarité** *nf* (*sudden*) laughter.

hindou, -oue [ɛ̃du] *a* & *nmf* Hindu.

hippie ['ipi] *nmf* hippie.

hippique [ipik] *a* **un concours** *h.* a horse show, a show-jumping event. ◆**hippodrome** *nm* racecourse, racetrack (*for horses*).

hippopotame [ipɔpɔtam] *nm* hippopotamus.

hirondelle [irɔ̃dɛl] *nf* (*oiseau*) swallow.

hirsute [irsyt] *a* (*personne, barbe*) unkempt, shaggy.

hispanique [ispanik] *a* Spanish, Hispanic.

hisser ['ise] *vt* (*voile, fardeau etc*) to hoist, raise; **— se h.** *vpr* to raise oneself (up).

histoire [istwar] *nf* (*science, événements*) history; (*récit, mensonge*) story; (*affaire*) *Fam* business, matter; *pl* (*ennuis*) trouble; (*façons, chichis*) fuss; **toute une h.** (*problème*) quite a lot of trouble; (*chichis*) quite a lot of fuss; **h. de voir/etc** (so as) to see/*etc*; **h. de rire** for (the sake of) a laugh; **sans histoires** (*voyage etc*) uneventful. ◆**historien, -ienne** *nmf* historian. ◆**historique** *a* historical; (*lieu, événement*) historic; *— nm* **faire l'h. de** to give an historical account of.

hiver [ivɛr] *nm* winter. ◆**hivernal, -aux** *a* (*froid etc*) winter-.

HLM ['aʃɛlɛm] *nm ou f abrév* (*habitation à loyer modéré*) = council flats, *Am* = low-rent apartment building (*sponsored by government*).

hoch/er ['ɔʃe] *vt* **h. la tête** (*pour dire oui*) to nod one's head; (*pour dire non*) to shake one's head. ◆**—ement** *nm* **h. de tête** nod; shake of the head.

hochet ['ɔʃe] *nm* (*jouet*) rattle.

hockey ['ɔkɛ] *nm* hockey; **h. sur glace** ice hockey.

holà! ['ɔla] *int* (*arrêtez*) hold on!, stop!; (*pour appeler*) hallo!; *— nm inv* **mettre le h.** à to put a stop to.

hold-up ['ɔldœp] *nm inv* (*attaque*) holdup, stick-up.

Hollande ['ɔlɑ̃d] *nf* Holland. ◆**hollandais, -aise** *a* Dutch; *— nmf* Dutchman, Dutchwoman; *— nm* (*langue*) Dutch.

holocauste [ɔlɔkost] *nm* (*massacre*) holocaust.

homard ['ɔmar] *nm* lobster.

homélie [ɔmeli] *nf* homily.

homéopathie [ɔmeɔpati] *nf* hom(o)eopathy.

homicide [ɔmisid] *nm* murder, homicide; **h. involontaire** manslaughter.

hommage [ɔmaʒ] *nm* tribute, homage (à to); *pl* (*civilités*) respects; **rendre h. à** to pay (a) tribute to, pay homage to.

homme [ɔm] *nm* man; **l'h.** (*espèce*) man(kind); **des vêtements d'h.** men's clothes; **d'h. à h.** man to man; **l'h. de la rue** *Fig* the man in the street; **h. d'affaires** businessman. ◆**h.-grenouille** *nm* (*pl* **hommes-grenouilles**) frogman.

homogène [ɔmɔʒɛn] *a* homogeneous. ◆**homogénéité** *nf* homogeneity.

homologue [ɔmɔlɔg] *a* equivalent (**de** to); *— nmf* counterpart, opposite number.

homologuer [ɔmɔlɔge] *vt* to approve *ou* recognize officially, validate.

homonyme [ɔmɔnim] *nm* (*personne, lieu*) namesake.

homosexuel, -elle [ɔmɔsɛksɥɛl] *a* & *nmf* homosexual. ◆**homosexualité** *nf* homosexuality.

Hongrie ['ɔ̃gri] *nf* Hungary. ◆**hongrois, -oise** *a* & *nmf* Hungarian; *— nm* (*langue*) Hungarian.

honnête [ɔnɛt] *a* (*intègre*) honest; (*satisfaisant, passable*) decent, fair. ◆**honnêtement** *adv* honestly; decently. ◆**honnêteté** *nf* honesty.

honneur [ɔnœr] *nm* (*dignité, faveur*) honour; (*mérite*) credit; **en l'h. de** in honour of; **faire h. à** (*sa famille etc*) to be a credit to; (*par sa présence*) to do honour to; (*promesse etc*) to honour; (*repas*) to do justice to; **en h.** (*roman etc*) in vogue; **invité d'h.** guest of honour; **membre d'h.** honorary member; **avoir la place d'h.** to have pride of place *ou* the place of honour. ◆**honorabilité** *nf* respectability. ◆**honorable** *a* honourable; (*résultat, salaire etc*) *Fig* respectable. ◆**honoraire 1** *a* (*membre*) honorary. **2** *nmpl* (*d'avocat etc*) fees. ◆**honorer** *vt* to honour (**de** with); **h. qn** (*conduite etc*) to do credit to s.o.; **s'h. d'être** to pride oneself *ou* itself on being. ◆**honorifique** *a* (*titre*) honorary.

honte ['ɔ̃t] *nf* shame; **avoir h.** to be *ou* feel ashamed (**de qch/de faire** of sth/to do, of doing); **faire h. à** to put to shame; **fausse h.** self-consciousness. ◆**honteux, -euse** *a* (*déshonorant*) shameful; (*penaud*) ashamed, shamefaced; **être h. de** to be ashamed of. ◆**honteusement** *adv* shamefully.

hop! ['ɔp] *int* **allez, h.!** jump!, move!

hôpital, -aux [ɔpital, -o] *nm* hospital; **à l'h.** in hospital, *Am* in the hospital.

hoquet ['ɔkɛ] *nm* hiccup; **le h.** (the) hiccups. ◆**hoqueter** *vi* to hiccup.

horaire [ɔrer] a (salaire etc) hourly; (vitesse) per hour; − nm timetable, schedule.

horde ['ɔrd] nf (troupe) Péj horde.

horizon [ɔrizɔ̃] nm horizon; (vue, paysage) view; à l'h. on the horizon.

horizontal, -aux [ɔrizɔ̃tal, -o] a horizontal. ◆**−ement** adv horizontally.

horloge [ɔrlɔʒ] nf clock. ◆**horloger, -ère** nmf watchmaker. ◆**horlogerie** nf (magasin) watchmaker's (shop); (industrie) watchmaking.

hormis [ɔrmi] prép Litt save, except (for).

hormone [ɔrmɔn] nf hormone. ◆**hormonal, -aux** a (traitement etc) hormone-.

horoscope [ɔrɔskɔp] nm horoscope.

horreur [ɔrœr] nf horror; pl (propos) horrible things; **faire h. à** to disgust; **avoir h. de** to hate, loathe. ◆**horrible** a horrible, awful. ◆**horriblement** adv horribly. ◆**horrifiant** a horrifying, horrific. ◆**horrifié** a horrified.

horripiler [ɔripile] vt to exasperate.

hors ['ɔr] prép **h. de** (maison, boîte etc) outside, out of; (danger, haleine etc) Fig out of; **h. de doute** beyond doubt; **h. de soi** (furieux) beside oneself; **être h. jeu** Fb to be offside. ◆**h.-bord** nm inv speedboat; **moteur h.-bord** outboard motor. ◆**h.-concours** a inv non-competing. ◆**h.-d'œuvre** nm inv Culin starter, hors-d'œuvre. ◆**h.-jeu** nm inv Fb offside. ◆**h.-la-loi** nm inv outlaw. ◆**h.-taxe** a inv (magasin, objet) duty-free.

hortensia [ɔrtɑ̃sja] nm (arbrisseau) hydrangea.

horticole [ɔrtikɔl] a horticultural. ◆**horticulteur, -trice** nmf horticulturalist. ◆**horticulture** nf horticulture.

hospice [ɔspis] nm (pour vieillards) geriatric hospital.

hospitalier, -ière [ɔspitalje, -jɛr] a **1** (accueillant) hospitable. **2** (personnel etc) Méd hospital-. ◆**hospitaliser** vt to hospitalize. ◆**hospitalité** nf hospitality.

hostie [ɔsti] nf (pain) Rel host.

hostile [ɔstil] a hostile (à to, towards). ◆**hostilité** nf hostility (envers to, towards); pl Mil hostilities.

hôte [ot] **1** nm (maître) host. **2** nmf (invité) guest. ◆**hôtesse** nf hostess; **h. (de l'air)** (air) hostess.

hôtel [otɛl] nm hotel; **h. particulier** mansion, town house; **h. de ville** town hall; **h. des ventes** auction rooms. ◆**hôtelier, -ière** nmf hotel-keeper, hotelier; − a (industrie etc) hotel-. ◆**hôtellerie** nf **1** (auberge) inn, hostelry. **2** (métier) hotel trade.

hotte ['ɔt] nf **1** (panier) basket (carried on back). **2** (de cheminée etc) hood.

houblon ['ublɔ̃] nm **le h.** Bot hops.

houille ['uj] nf coal; **h. blanche** hydro-electric power. ◆**houiller, -ère** a (bassin, industrie) coal-; − nf coalmine, colliery.

houle ['ul] nf (de mer) swell, surge. ◆**houleux, -euse** a (mer) rough; (réunion etc) Fig stormy.

houppette ['upɛt] nf powder puff.

hourra ['ura] nm & int hurray, hurrah.

houspiller ['uspije] vt to scold, upbraid.

housse ['us] nf (protective) cover.

houx ['u] nm holly.

hublot ['yblo] nm Nau Av porthole.

huche ['yʃ] nf **h. à pain** bread box ou chest.

hue! ['y] int gee up! (to horse).

huer ['ɥe] vt to boo. ◆**huées** nfpl boos.

huile [ɥil] nf **1** oil; **peinture à l'h.** oil painting. **2** (personnage) Fam big shot. ◆**huiler** vt to oil. ◆**huileux, -euse** a oily.

huis [ɥi] nm **à h. clos** Jur in camera.

huissier [ɥisje] nm (introducteur) usher; (officier) Jur bailiff.

huit ['ɥit] a (['ɥi] before consonant) eight; **h. jours** a week; − nm eight. ◆**huitaine** nf (about) eight; (semaine) week. ◆**huitième** a & nmf eighth; **un h.** an eighth.

huître [ɥitr] nf oyster.

hululer ['ylyle] vi (hibou) to hoot.

humain [ymɛ̃] a human; (compatissant) humane; − nmpl humans. ◆**humainement** adv (possible etc) humanly; (avec humanité) humanely. ◆**humaniser** vt (prison, ville etc) to humanize, make more humane. ◆**humanitaire** a humanitarian. ◆**humanité** nf (genre humain, sentiment) humanity.

humble [œ̃bl] a humble. ◆**humblement** adv humbly.

humecter [ymɛkte] vt to moisten, damp(en).

humer ['yme] vt (respirer) to breathe in; (sentir) to smell.

humeur [ymœr] nf (caprice) mood, humour; (caractère) temperament; (irritation) bad temper; **bonne h.** (gaieté) good humour; **de bonne/mauvaise h.** in a good/bad mood ou humour; **égalité d'h.** evenness of temper.

humide [ymid] a damp, wet; (saison, route) wet; (main, yeux) moist; **climat/temps h.** (chaud) humid climate/weather; (froid, pluvieux) damp ou wet climate/weather. ◆**humidifier** vt to humidify. ◆**humidité** nf humidity; (plutôt froide) damp(ness); (vapeur) moisture.

humili/er [ymilje] vt to humiliate, humble.

◆—**ant** *a* humiliating. ◆**humiliation** *nf* humiliation. ◆**humilité** *nf* humility.

humour [ymur] *nm* humour; **avoir de l'h. ou beaucoup d'h. ou le sens de l'h.** to have a sense of humour. ◆**humoriste** *nmf* humorist. ◆**humoristique** *a* (*livre, ton etc*) humorous.

huppé ['ype] *a* (*riche*) *Fam* high-class, posh.

hurl/er ['yrle] *vi* (*loup, vent*) to howl; (*personne*) to scream, yell; – *vt* (*slogans, injures etc*) to scream. ◆—**ement** *nm* howl; scream, yell.

hurluberlu [yrlyberly] *nm* (*personne*) scatterbrain.

hutte ['yt] *nf* hut.

hybride [ibrid] *a* & *nm* hybrid.

hydrater [idrate] *vt* (*peau*) to moisturize; **crème hydratante** moisturizing cream.

hydraulique [idrolik] *a* hydraulic.

hydravion [idravjɔ̃] *nm* seaplane.

hydro-électrique [idroelektrik] *a* hydroelectric.

hydrogène [idrɔʒɛn] *nm Ch* hydrogen.

hydrophile [idrɔfil] *a* **coton h.** cotton wool, *Am* (*absorbent*) cotton.

hyène [jɛn] *nf* (*animal*) hyena.

hygiaphone [iʒjafɔn] *nm* (hygienic) grill.

hygiène [iʒjɛn] *nf* hygiene. ◆**hygiénique** *a* hygienic; (*promenade*) healthy; (*serviette, conditions*) sanitary; **papier h.** toilet paper.

hymne [imn] *nm Rel Littér* hymn; **h. national** national anthem.

hyper- [iper] *préf* hyper-.

hypermarché [ipermarʃe] *nm* hypermarket.

hypertension [ipɛrtɑ̃sjɔ̃] *nf* high blood pressure.

hypnose [ipnoz] *nf* hypnosis. ◆**hypnotique** *a* hypnotic. ◆**hypnotiser** *vt* to hypnotize. ◆**hypnotiseur** *nm* hypnotist. ◆**hypnotisme** *nm* hypnotism.

hypocrisie [ipɔkrizi] *nf* hypocrisy. ◆**hypocrite** *a* hypocritical; – *nmf* hypocrite.

hypodermique [ipɔdɛrmik] *a* hypodermic.

hypothèque [ipɔtɛk] *nf* mortgage. ◆**hypothéquer** (*maison, avenir*) to mortgage.

hypothèse [ipotez] *nf* assumption; (*en sciences*) hypothesis; **dans l'h. où . . .** supposing (that). . . . ◆**hypothétique** *a* hypothetical.

hystérie [isteri] *nf* hysteria. ◆**hystérique** *a* hysterical.

I

I, i [i] *nm* I, i.

iceberg [isberg] *nm* iceberg.

ici [isi] *adv* here; **par i.** (*passer*) this way; (*habiter*) around here, hereabouts; **jusqu'i.** (*temps*) up to now; (*lieu*) as far as this *ou* here; **d'i. à mardi** by Tuesday, between now and Tuesday; **d'i. à une semaine** within a week; **d'i. peu** before long; **i. Dupont** *Tél* this is Dupont, Dupont here; **je ne suis pas d'i.** I'm a stranger around here; **les gens d'i.** the people (from) around here, the locals. ◆**i.-bas** *adv* on earth.

icône [ikon] *nf Rel* icon.

idéal, -aux [ideal, -o] *a* & *nm* ideal; **l'i.** (*valeurs spirituelles*) ideals; **c'est l'i.** *Fam* that's the ideal thing. ◆**idéalement** *adv* ideally. ◆**idéaliser** *vt* to idealize. ◆**idéalisme** *nm* idealism. ◆**idéaliste** *a* idealistic; – *nmf* idealist.

idée [ide] *nf* idea (de of, que that); **changer d'i.** to change one's mind; **il m'est venu à l'i. que** it occurred to me that; **se faire une i. de** (*rêve*) to imagine; (*concept*) to get *ou* have

an idea of; **avoir dans l'i. de faire** to have it in mind to do; **i. fixe** obsession.

idem [idɛm] *adv* ditto.

identifier [idɑ̃tifje] *vt* to identify (**à, avec** with). ◆**identification** *nf* identification. ◆**identique** *a* identical (**à** to, with). ◆**identité** *nf* identity; **carte d'i** identity card.

idéologie [ideɔlɔʒi] *nf* ideology. ◆**idéologique** *a* ideological.

idiome [idjom] *nm* (*langue*) idiom. ◆**idiomatique** *a* idiomatic.

idiot, -ote [idjo, -ɔt] *a* idiotic, silly; – *nmf* idiot. ◆**idiotement** *adv* idiotically. ◆**idiotie** [-ɔsi] *nf* (*état*) idiocy; **une i.** an idiotic *ou* silly thing.

idole [idɔl] *nm* idol. ◆**idolâtrer** *vt* to idolize.

idylle [idil] *nf* (*amourette*) romance.

idyllique [idilik] *a* (*merveilleux*) idyllic.

if [if] *nm* yew (tree).

igloo [iglu] *nm* igloo.

ignare [iɲar] *a Péj* ignorant; – *nmf* ignoramus.

ignifugé [iɲifyʒe] *a* fireproof(ed).

ignoble [iɲɔbl] *a* vile, revolting.

ignorant [iɲɔrɑ̃] *a* ignorant (**de** of).
◆**ignorance** *nf* ignorance. ◆**ignor/er** *vt* not to know, be ignorant of; **j'ignore si I** don't know if; **i. qn** (*être indifférent à*) to ignore s.o., cold-shoulder s.o. ◆**—é** *a* (*inconnu*) unknown.

il [il] *pron* (*personne*) he; (*chose, animal*) it; **il est** he is; it is; **il pleut** it's raining; **il est vrai que** it's true that; **il y a** there is; *pl* there are; **il y a six ans** (*temps écoulé*) six years ago; **il y a une heure qu'il travaille** (*durée*) he's been working for an hour; **qu'est-ce qu'il y a?** what's the matter?, what's wrong?; **il n'y a pas de quoi!** don't mention it!; **il doit/peut y avoir** there must/may be.

île [il] *nf* island; **les îles Britanniques** the British Isles.

illégal, -aux [ilegal, -o] *a* illegal. ◆**illégalité** *nf* illegality.

illégitime [ileʒitim] *a* (*enfant, revendication*) illegitimate; (*non fondé*) unfounded.

illettré, -ée [iletre] *a* & *nmf* illiterate.

illicite [ilisit] *a* unlawful, illicit.

illico [iliko] *adv* **i.** (**presto**) *Fam* straightaway.

illimité [ilimite] *a* unlimited.

illisible [ilizibl] *a* (*écriture*) illegible; (*livre*) unreadable.

illogique [ilɔʒik] *a* illogical.

illumin/er [ilymine] *vt* to light up, illuminate; **— s'i.** *vpr* (*visage, personne, ciel*) to light up. ◆**—é** *a* (*monument*) floodlit, lit up. ◆**illumination** *nf* (*action, lumière*) illumination.

illusion [ilyzjɔ̃] *nf* illusion (**sur** about); **se faire des illusions** to delude oneself. ◆**s'illusionner** *vpr* to delude oneself (**sur** about). ◆**illusionniste** *nmf* conjurer. ◆**illusoire** *a* illusory, illusive.

illustre [ilystr] *a* famous, illustrious.

illustr/er [ilystre] *vt* (*d'images, par des exemples*) to illustrate (**de** with); **— s'i.** *vpr* to become famous. ◆**—é** *a* (*livre, magazine*) illustrated; **—** *nm* (*périodique*) comic. ◆**illustration** *nf* illustration.

îlot [ilo] *nm* **1** (*île*) small island. **2** (*maisons*) block.

ils [il] *pron* they; **ils sont** they are.

image [imaʒ] *nf* picture; (*ressemblance, symbole*) image; (*dans une glace*) reflection; **i. de marque** (*de firme etc*) (public) image. ◆**imagé** *a* (*style*) colourful, full of imagery.

imagination [imaʒinasjɔ̃] *nf* imagination; *pl* (*chimères*) imaginings.

imaginer [imaʒine] *vt* (*envisager, supposer*) to imagine; (*inventer*) to devise; **— s'i.** *vpr* (*se figurer*) to imagine (**que** that); (*se voir*) to imagine oneself. ◆**imaginable** *a* imaginable. ◆**imaginaire** *a* imaginary. ◆**imaginatif, -ive** *a* imaginative.

imbattable [ɛ̃batabl] *a* unbeatable.

imbécile [ɛ̃besil] *a* idiotic, — *nmf* imbecile, idiot. ◆**imbécillité** *nf* (*état*) imbecility; **une i.** (*action, parole*) an idiotic thing.

imbiber [ɛ̃bibe] *vt* to soak (**de** with, in); **— s'i.** *vpr* to become soaked.

imbriquer (s') [sɛ̃brike] *vpr* (*questions etc*) to overlap, be bound up with each other.

imbroglio [ɛ̃brɔljo] *nm* muddle, foul-up.

imbu [ɛ̃by] *a* **i. de** imbued with.

imbuvable [ɛ̃byvabl] *a* undrinkable; (*personne*) *Fig* insufferable.

imiter [imite] *vt* to imitate; (*contrefaire*) to forge; **i. qn** (*pour rire*) to mimic s.o., take s.o. off; (*faire comme*) to do the same as s.o., follow suit. ◆**imitateur, -trice** *nmf* imitator; (*artiste*) *Th* impersonator, mimic. ◆**imitatif, -ive** *a* imitative. ◆**imitation** *nf* imitation.

immaculé [imakyle] *a* (*sans tache, sans péché*) immaculate.

immangeable [ɛ̃mɑ̃ʒabl] *a* inedible.

immanquable [ɛ̃mɑ̃kabl] *a* inevitable.

immatriculer [imatrikyle] *vt* to register; **se faire i.** to register. ◆**immatriculation** *nf* registration.

immédiat [imedja] *a* immediate; — *nm* **dans l'i.** for the time being. ◆**immédiatement** *adv* immediately.

immense [imɑ̃s] *a* immense, vast. ◆**immensément** *adv* immensely. ◆**immensité** *nf* immensity, vastness.

immerger [imerʒe] *vt* to immerse, put under water; **— s'i.** *vpr* (*sous-marin*) to submerge. ◆**immersion** *nf* immersion; submersion.

immettable [ɛ̃metabl] *a* (*vêtement*) unfit to be worn.

immeuble [imœbl] *nm* building; (*d'habitation*) block of flats, *Am* apartment building; (*de bureaux*) office block.

immigr/er [imigre] *vi* to immigrate. ◆**—ant, -ante** *nmf* immigrant. ◆**—é, -ée** *a* & *nmf* immigrant. ◆**immigration** *nf* immigration.

imminent [iminɑ̃] *a* imminent. ◆**imminence** *nf* imminence.

immiscer (s') [simise] *vpr* to interfere (**dans** in).

immobile [imɔbil] *a* still, motionless. ◆**immobiliser** *vt* to immobilize; (*arrêter*) to stop; **— s'i.** *vpr* to stop, come to a standstill. ◆**immobilité** *nf* stillness; (*inactivité*) immobility.

immobilier, -ière [iməbilje, -jɛr] *a* (*vente*) property-; (*société*) construction-; **agent i.** estate agent, *Am* real estate agent.

immodéré [imɔdere] *a* immoderate.

immonde [imɔ̃d] *a* filthy. ◆**immondices** *nfpl* refuse, rubbish.

immoral, -aux [imɔral, -o] *a* immoral. ◆**immoralité** *nf* immorality.

immortel, -elle [imɔrtɛl] *a* immortal. ◆**immortaliser** *vt* to immortalize. ◆**immortalité** *nf* immortality.

immuable [imɥabl] *a* immutable, unchanging.

immuniser [imynize] *vt* to immunize (**contre** against); **immunisé contre** (*à l'abri de*) *Méd & Fig* immune to *ou* from. ◆**immunitaire** *a* (*déficience etc*) *Méd* immune. ◆**immunité** *nf* immunity.

impact [ɛ̃pakt] *nm* impact (**sur** on).

impair [ɛ̃pɛr] **1** *a* (*nombre*) odd, uneven. **2** *nm* (*gaffe*) blunder.

imparable [ɛ̃parabl] *a* (*coup etc*) unavoidable.

impardonnable [ɛ̃pardɔnabl] *a* unforgivable.

imparfait [ɛ̃parfɛ] **1** *a* (*connaissance etc*) imperfect. **2** *nm* (*temps*) *Gram* imperfect.

impartial, -aux [ɛ̃parsjal, -o] *a* impartial, unbiased. ◆**impartialité** *nf* impartiality.

impartir [ɛ̃partir] *vt* to grant (**à** to).

impasse [ɛ̃pas] *nf* (*rue*) dead end, blind alley; (*situation*) *Fig* impasse; **dans l'i.** (*négociations*) in deadlock.

impassible [ɛ̃pasibl] *a* impassive, unmoved. ◆**impassibilité** *nf* impassiveness.

impatient [ɛ̃pasjɑ̃] *a* impatient; **i. de faire** eager *ou* impatient to do. ◆**impatiemment** [-amɑ̃] *adv* impatiently. ◆**impatience** *nf* impatience. ◆**impatienter** *vt* to annoy, make impatient; **— s'i.** *vpr* to get impatient.

impayable [ɛ̃pɛjabl] *a* (*comique*) *Fam* hilarious, priceless.

impayé [ɛ̃peje] *a* unpaid.

impeccable [ɛ̃pekabl] *a* impeccable, immaculate. ◆**—ment** [-əmɑ̃] *adv* impeccably, immaculately.

impénétrable [ɛ̃penetrabl] *a* (*forêt, mystère etc*) impenetrable.

impénitent [ɛ̃penitɑ̃] *a* unrepentant.

impensable [ɛ̃pɑ̃sabl] *a* unthinkable.

imper [ɛ̃pɛr] *nm* *Fam* raincoat, mac.

impératif, -ive [ɛ̃peratif, -iv] *a* (*consigne,*

ton) imperative; **—** *nm* (*mode*) *Gram* imperative.

impératrice [ɛ̃peratris] *nf* empress.

imperceptible [ɛ̃persɛptibl] *a* imperceptible (**à** to).

imperfection [ɛ̃pɛrfɛksjɔ̃] *nf* imperfection.

impérial, -aux [ɛ̃perjal, -o] *a* imperial. ◆**impérialisme** *nm* imperialism.

impériale [ɛ̃perjal] *nf* (*d'autobus*) top deck.

impérieux, -euse [ɛ̃perjø, -øz] *a* (*autoritaire*) imperious; (*besoin*) pressing, imperative.

imperméable [ɛ̃pɛrmeabl] **1** *a* impervious (**à** to); (*manteau, tissu*) waterproof. **2** *nm* raincoat, mackintosh. ◆**imperméabilisé** *a* waterproof.

impersonnel, -elle [ɛ̃pɛrsɔnɛl] *a* impersonal.

impertinent [ɛ̃pɛrtinɑ̃] *a* impertinent (**envers** to). ◆**impertinence** *nf* impertinence.

imperturbable [ɛ̃pɛrtyrbabl] *a* unruffled, imperturbable.

impétueux, -euse [ɛ̃petɥø, -øz] *a* impetuous. ◆**impétuosité** *nf* impetuosity.

impitoyable [ɛ̃pitwajabl] *a* ruthless, pitiless, merciless.

implacable [ɛ̃plakabl] *a* implacable, relentless.

implanter [ɛ̃plɑ̃te] *vt* (*industrie, mode etc*) to establish; **— s'i.** *vpr* to become established. ◆**implantation** *nf* establishment.

implicite [ɛ̃plisit] *a* implicit. ◆**—ment** *adv* implicitly.

impliquer [ɛ̃plike] *vt* (*entraîner*) to imply; **i. que** (*supposer*) to imply that; **i. qn** (*engager*) to implicate s.o. (**dans** in). ◆**implication** *nf* (*conséquence, participation*) implication.

implorer [ɛ̃plɔre] *vt* to implore (**qn de faire** s.o. to do).

impoli [ɛ̃pɔli] *a* impolite, rude. ◆**impolitesse** *nf* impoliteness, rudeness; **une i.** an act of rudeness.

impopulaire [ɛ̃pɔpylɛr] *a* unpopular.

important [ɛ̃pɔrtɑ̃] *a* (*personnage, événement etc*) important; (*quantité, somme etc*) considerable, big, great; **—** *nm* **l'i., c'est de . . .** the important thing is to . . . ◆**importance** *nf* importance, significance; (*taille*) size; (*de dégâts*) extent; **ça n'a pas d'i.** it doesn't matter.

importer [ɛ̃pɔrte] **1** *v imp* to matter, be important (**à** to); **il importe de faire** it's important to do; **peu importe, n'importe** it doesn't matter; **n'importe qui/quoi/où/quand/comment** anyone/anything/anywhere/any time/anyhow. **2** *vt* (*marchandises etc*) to import (**de** from). ◆**im-**

portateur, -trice *nmf* importer; – *a* importing. ◆**importation** *nf* (*objet*) import; (*action*) import(ing), importation; **d'i.** (*article*) imported.

importun, -une [ɛ̃pɔrtœ̃, -yn] *a* troublesome, intrusive; – *nmf* nuisance, intruder. ◆**importuner** *vt* to inconvenience, trouble.

impos/er [ɛ̃poze] **1** *vt* to impose, enforce (à on); (*exiger*) to demand; (*respect*) to command; – *vi* **en i. à qn** to impress s.o., command respect from s.o.; – **s'i.** *vpr* (*chez qn*) *Péj* to impose; (*s'affirmer*) to assert oneself, compel recognition; (*aller de soi*) to stand out; (*être nécessaire*) to be essential. **2** *vt Fin* to tax. ◆**—ant** *a* imposing. ◆**—able** *a Fin* taxable. ◆**imposition** *nf Fin* taxation.

impossible [ɛ̃pɔsibl] *a* impossible (**à faire** to do); **il (nous) est i. de faire** it is impossible (for us) to do; **il est i. que** (+ *sub*) it is impossible that; **ça m'est i.** I cannot possibly; – *nm* **faire l'i.** to do the impossible. ◆**impossibilité** *nf* impossibility.

imposteur [ɛ̃pɔstœr] *nm* impostor. ◆**imposture** *nf* deception.

impôt [ɛ̃po] *nm* tax; *pl* (*contributions*) (income) tax, taxes; **i. sur le revenu** income tax.

impotent, -ente [ɛ̃pɔtɑ̃, -ɑ̃t] *a* crippled, disabled; – *nmf* cripple, invalid.

impraticable [ɛ̃pratikabl] *a* (*projet etc*) impracticable; (*chemin etc*) impassable.

imprécis [ɛ̃presi] *a* imprecise. ◆**imprécision** *nf* lack of precision.

imprégner [ɛ̃preɲe] *vt* to saturate, impregnate (**de** with); – **s'i.** *vpr* to become saturated *ou* impregnated (**de** with); **imprégné de** (*idées*) imbued *ou* infused with. ◆**imprégnation** *nf* saturation.

imprenable [ɛ̃prənabl] *a Mil* impregnable.

impresario [ɛ̃presarjo] *nm* (business) manager, impresario.

impression [ɛ̃presjɔ̃] *nf* **1** impression; **avoir l'i. que** to have the feeling *ou* impression that, be under the impression that; **faire une bonne i. à qn** to make a good impression on s.o. **2** *Typ* printing. ◆**impressionn/er** [ɛ̃presjɔne] *vt* (*influencer*) to impress; (*émouvoir, troubler*) to make a strong impression on. ◆**—ant** *a* impressive. ◆**—able** *a* impressionable.

imprévisible [ɛ̃previzibl] *a* unforeseeable. ◆**imprévoyance** *nf* lack of foresight. ◆**imprévoyant** *a* shortsighted. ◆**imprévu** *a* unexpected, unforeseen; – *nm* **en cas d'i.** in case of anything unexpected.

imprim/er [ɛ̃prime] *vt* **1** (*livre etc*) to print;

(*trace*) to impress (**dans** in); (*cachet*) to stamp. **2** (*communiquer*) *Tech* to impart (à to). ◆**—ante** *nf* (*d'ordinateur*) printer. ◆**—é** *nm* (*formulaire*) printed form; – *nm*(*pl*) (*par la poste*) printed matter. ◆**imprimerie** *nf* (*technique*) printing; (*lieu*) printing works. ◆**imprimeur** *nm* printer.

improbable [ɛ̃prɔbabl] *a* improbable, unlikely. ◆**improbabilité** *nf* improbability, unlikelihood.

impromptu [ɛ̃prɔ̃pty] *a* & *adv* impromptu.

impropre [ɛ̃prɔpr] *a* inappropriate; **i. à qch** unfit for sth. ◆**impropriété** *nf* (*incorrection*) *Ling* impropriety.

improviser [ɛ̃prɔvize] *vti* to improvise. ◆**improvisation** *nf* improvisation.

improviste (à l') [alɛ̃prɔvist] *adv* unexpectedly; **une visite à l'i.** an unexpected visit; **prendre qn à l'i.** to catch s.o. unawares.

imprudent [ɛ̃prydɑ̃] *a* (*personne, action*) careless, rash; **il est i. de** it is unwise to. ◆**imprudemment** [-amɑ̃] *adv* carelessly. ◆**imprudence** *nf* carelessness; **une i.** an act of carelessness.

impudent [ɛ̃pydɑ̃] *a* impudent ◆**impudence** *nf* impudence.

impudique [ɛ̃pydik] *a* lewd.

impuissant [ɛ̃pɥisɑ̃] *a* helpless; *Méd* impotent; **i. à faire** powerless to do. ◆**impuissance** *nf* helplessness; *Méd* impotence.

impulsif, -ive [ɛ̃pylsif, -iv] *a* impulsive. ◆**impulsion** *nf* impulse; **donner une i. à** (*élan*) *Fig* to give an impetus *ou* impulse to.

impunément [ɛ̃pynemɑ̃] *adv* with impunity. ◆**impuni** *a* unpunished.

impur [ɛ̃pyr] *a* impure. ◆**impureté** *nf* impurity.

imputer [ɛ̃pyte] *vt* to attribute, impute (à to); (*affecter*) *Fin* to charge (à to). ◆**imputable** *a* attributable (à to). ◆**imputation** *nf Jur* accusation.

inabordable [inabɔrdabl] *a* (*lieu*) inaccessible; (*personne*) unapproachable; (*prix*) prohibitive.

inacceptable [inaksɛptabl] *a* unacceptable.

inaccessible [inaksesibl] *a* inaccessible.

inaccoutumé [inakutyme] *a* unusual, unaccustomed.

inachevé [inaʃve] *a* unfinished.

inactif, -ive [inaktif, -iv] *a* inactive. ◆**inaction** *nf* inactivity, inaction. ◆**inactivité** *nf* inactivity.

inadapté, -ée [inadapte] *a* & *nmf* maladjusted (person). ◆**inadaptation** *nf* maladjustment.

inadmissible [inadmisibl] *a* unacceptable, inadmissible.

inadvertance (par) [parinadvɛrtɑ̃s] *adv* inadvertently.

inaltérable [inalterabl] *a* (*couleur*) fast; (*sentiment*) unchanging.

inamical, -aux [inamikal, -o] *a* unfriendly.

inanimé [inanime] *a* (*mort*) lifeless; (*évanoui*) unconscious; (*matière*) inanimate.

inanité [inanite] *nf* (*vanité*) futility.

inanition [inanisjɔ̃] *nf* **mourir d'i.** to die of starvation.

inaperçu [inapɛrsy] *a* **passer i.** to go unnoticed.

inapplicable [inaplikabl] *a* inapplicable (à to).

inappliqué [inaplike] *a* (*élève etc*) inattentive.

inappréciable [inapresjabl] *a* invaluable.

inapte [inapt] *a* unsuited (**à qch** to sth), inept (**à qch** at sth); *Mil* unfit ◆**inaptitude** *nf* ineptitude, incapacity.

inarticulé [inartikyle] *a* (*son*) inarticulate.

inattaquable [inatakabl] *a* unassailable.

inattendu [inatɑ̃dy] *a* unexpected.

inattentif, -ive [inatɑ̃tif, -iv] *a* inattentive, careless; **i. à** (*soucis, danger etc*) heedless of. ◆**inattention** *nf* lack of attention; **dans un moment d'i.** in a moment of distraction.

inaudible [inodibl] *a* inaudible.

inaugurer [inogyre] *vt* (*politique, édifice*) to inaugurate; (*école, congrès*) to open, inaugurate; (*statue*) to unveil. ◆**inaugural, -aux** *a* inaugural. ◆**inauguration** *nf* inauguration; opening; unveiling.

inauthentique [inotɑ̃tik] *a* not authentic.

inavouable [inavwabl] *a* shameful.

incalculable [ɛ̃kalkylabl] *a* incalculable.

incandescent [ɛ̃kɑ̃desɑ̃] *a* incandescent.

incapable [ɛ̃kapabl] *a* incapable; **i. de faire** unable to do, incapable of doing; — *nmf* (*personne*) incompetent. ◆**incapacité** *nf* incapacity, inability (**de faire** to do); *Méd* disability, incapacity.

incarcérer [ɛ̃karsere] *vt* to incarcerate. ◆**incarcération** *nf* incarceration.

incarné [ɛ̃karne] *a* (*ongle*) ingrown.

incarner [ɛ̃karne] *vt* to embody, incarnate. ◆**incarnation** *nf* embodiment, incarnation.

incartade [ɛ̃kartad] *nf* indiscretion, prank.

incassable [ɛ̃kasabl] *a* unbreakable.

incendie [ɛ̃sɑ̃di] *nm* fire; (*guerre*) *Fig* conflagration. ◆**incendiaire** *nmf* arsonist; — *a* (*bombe*) incendiary; (*discours*) inflammatory. ◆**incendier** *vt* to set fire to, set on fire.

incertain [ɛ̃sɛrtɛ̃] *a* uncertain; (*temps*) unsettled; (*entreprise*) chancy; (*contour*) indistinct. ◆**incertitude** *nf* uncertainty.

incessamment [ɛ̃sesamɑ̃] *adv* without delay, shortly.

incessant [ɛ̃sesɑ̃] *a* incessant.

inceste [ɛ̃sɛst] *nm* incest. ◆**incestueux, -euse** *a* incestuous.

inchangé [ɛ̃ʃɑ̃ʒe] *a* unchanged.

incidence [ɛ̃sidɑ̃s] *nf* (*influence*) effect.

incident [ɛ̃sidɑ̃] *nm* incident; (*accroc*) hitch.

incinérer [ɛ̃sinere] *vt* (*ordures*) to incinerate; (*cadavre*) to cremate. ◆**incinération** *nf* incineration; cremation.

inciser [ɛ̃size] *vt* to make an incision in. ◆**incision** *nf* (*entaille*) incision.

incisif, -ive[1] [ɛ̃sizif, -iv] *a* incisive, sharp.

incisive[2] [ɛ̃siziv] *nf* (*dent*) incisor.

inciter [ɛ̃site] *vt* to urge, incite (**à faire** to do). ◆**incitation** *nf* incitement (**à** to).

incliner [ɛ̃kline] *vt* (*courber*) to bend; (*pencher*) to tilt, incline; **i. la tête** (*approuver*) to nod one's head; (*révérence*) to bow (one's head); **i. qn à faire** to make s.o. inclined to do, incline s.o. to do; — *vi* **i. à** to be inclined towards; — **s'i.** *vpr* (*se courber*) to bow (down); (*s'avouer vaincu*) to admit defeat; (*chemin*) to slope down. ◆**inclinaison** *nf* incline, slope. ◆**inclination** *nf* (*goût*) inclination; (*de tête*) nod, (*révérence*) bow.

incl/ure* [ɛ̃klyr] *vt* to include; (*enfermer*) to enclose. ◆**-us** *a* inclusive; **du quatre jusqu'au dix mai i.** from the fourth to the tenth of May inclusive; **jusqu'à lundi i.** up to and including (next) Monday. ◆**inclusion** *nf* inclusion. ◆**inclusivement** *adv* inclusively.

incognito [ɛ̃kɔɲito] *adv* incognito.

incohérent [ɛ̃kɔerɑ̃] *a* incoherent. ◆**incohérence** *nf* incoherence.

incollable [ɛ̃kɔlabl] *a* *Fam* infallible, unable to be caught out.

incolore [ɛ̃kɔlɔr] *a* colourless; (*verre, vernis*) clear.

incomber [ɛ̃kɔ̃be] *vi* **i. à qn** (*devoir*) to fall to s.o.; **il lui incombe de faire** it's his *ou* her duty *ou* responsiblity to do.

incommode [ɛ̃kɔmɔd] *a* awkward. ◆**incommodité** *nf* awkwardness.

incommod/er [ɛ̃kɔmɔde] *vt* to bother, annoy. ◆**-ant** *a* annoying.

incomparable [ɛ̃kɔ̃parabl] *a* incomparable.

incompatible [ɛ̃kɔ̃patibl] *a* incompatible, inconsistent (**avec** with). ◆**incompatibilité** *nf* incompatibility, inconsistency.

incompétent [ɛ̃kɔ̃petɑ̃] *a* incompetent. ◆**incompétence** *nf* incompetence.

incomplet, -ète [ɛ̃kɔ̃plɛ, -ɛt] *a* incomplete; (*fragmentaire*) scrappy, sketchy.

incompréhensible [ɛ̃kɔ̃preɑ̃sibl] *a* incomprehensible. ◆**incompréhensif, -ive** *a* uncomprehending, lacking understanding. ◆**incompréhension** *nf* lack of understanding. ◆**incompris** *a* misunderstood.

inconcevable [ɛ̃kɔ̃svabl] *a* inconceivable.

inconciliable [ɛ̃kɔ̃siljabl] *a* irreconcilable.

inconditionnel, -elle [ɛ̃kɔ̃disjɔnɛl] *a* unconditional.

inconfort [ɛ̃kɔ̃fɔr] *nm* lack of comfort. ◆**inconfortable** *a* uncomfortable.

incongru [ɛ̃kɔ̃gry] *a* unseemly, incongruous.

inconnu, -ue [ɛ̃kɔny] *a* unknown (à to); — *nmf* (*étranger*) stranger; (*auteur*) unknown; — *nm* **l'i.** the unknown; — *nf* *Math* unknown (quantity).

inconscient [ɛ̃kɔ̃sjɑ̃] *a* unconscious (**de** of); (*irréfléchi*) thoughtless, senseless; — *nm* **l'i.** *Psy* the unconscious. ◆**inconsciemment** [-amɑ̃] *adv* unconsciously. ◆**inconscience** *nf* (*physique*) unconsciousness; (*irréflexion*) utter thoughtlessness.

inconséquence [ɛ̃kɔ̃sekɑ̃s] *nf* inconsistency.

inconsidéré [ɛ̃kɔ̃sidere] *a* thoughtless.

inconsolable [ɛ̃kɔ̃sɔlabl] *a* inconsolable.

inconstant [ɛ̃kɔ̃stɑ̃] *a* fickle. ◆**inconstance** *nf* fickleness.

incontestable [ɛ̃kɔ̃testabl] *a* undeniable, indisputable. ◆**incontesté** *a* undisputed.

incontinent [ɛ̃kɔ̃tinɑ̃] *a* incontinent.

incontrôlé [ɛ̃kɔ̃trole] *a* unchecked. ◆**incontrôlable** *a* unverifiable.

inconvenant [ɛ̃kɔ̃vnɑ̃] *a* improper. ◆**inconvenance** *nf* impropriety.

inconvénient [ɛ̃kɔ̃venjɑ̃] *nm* (*désavantage*) drawback; (*risque*) risk; (*objection*) objection.

incorporer [ɛ̃kɔrpɔre] *vt* (*introduire, admettre*) to incorporate (**dans** into); (*ingrédient*) to blend (à with); *Mil* to enrol. ◆**incorporation** *nf* incorporation (**de** of); *Mil* enrolment.

incorrect [ɛ̃kɔrɛkt] *a* (*inexact*) incorrect; (*inconvenant*) improper; (*grossier*) impolite. ◆**incorrection** *nf* (*faute*) impropriety, error; (*inconvenance*) impropriety; **une i.** (*grossièreté*) an impolite word *ou* act.

incorrigible [ɛ̃kɔriʒibl] *a* incorrigible.

incorruptible [ɛ̃kɔryptibl] *a* incorruptible.

incrédule [ɛ̃kredyl] *a* incredulous. ◆**incrédulité** *nf* disbelief, incredulity.

increvable [ɛ̃krəvabl] *a* (*robuste*) *Fam* tireless.

incriminer [ɛ̃krimine] *vt* to incriminate.

incroyable [ɛ̃krwajabl] *a* incredible, unbelievable. ◆**incroyablement** *adv* incredibly. ◆**incroyant, -ante** *a* unbelieving; — *nmf* unbeliever.

incrusté [ɛ̃kryste] *a* (*de tartre*) encrusted; **i. de** (*orné*) inlaid with. ◆**incrustation** *nf* (*ornement*) inlay; (*action*) inlaying.

incruster (s') [sɛ̃kryste] *vpr* (*chez qn*) *Fig* to dig oneself in, be difficult to get rid of.

incubation [ɛ̃kybasjɔ̃] *nf* incubation.

inculp/er [ɛ̃kylpe] *vt* *Jur* to charge (**de** with), indict (**de** for). ◆**-é, -ée** *nmf* **l'i.** the accused. ◆**inculpation** *nf* charge, indictment.

inculquer [ɛ̃kylke] *vt* to instil (à into).

inculte [ɛ̃kylt] *a* (*terre*) uncultivated; (*personne*) uneducated.

incurable [ɛ̃kyrabl] *a* incurable.

incursion [ɛ̃kyrsjɔ̃] *nf* incursion, inroad (**dans** into).

incurver [ɛ̃kyrve] *vt* to curve.

Inde [ɛ̃d] *nf* India.

indécent [ɛ̃desɑ̃] *a* indecent. ◆**indécemment** [-amɑ̃] *adv* indecently. ◆**indécence** *nf* indecency.

indéchiffrable [ɛ̃deʃifrabl] *a* undecipherable.

indécis [ɛ̃desi] *a* (*victoire, résultat*) undecided; (*indistinct*) vague; **être i.** (*hésiter*) to be undecided; (*de tempérament*) to be indecisive *ou* irresolute. ◆**indécision** *nf* indecisiveness, indecision.

indéfectible [ɛ̃defɛktibl] *a* unfailing.

indéfendable [ɛ̃defɑ̃dabl] *a* indefensible.

indéfini [ɛ̃defini] *a* (*indéterminé*) indefinite; (*imprécis*) undefined. ◆**indéfiniment** *adv* indefinitely. ◆**indéfinissable** *a* indefinable.

indéformable [ɛ̃defɔrmabl] *a* (*vêtement*) which keeps its shape.

indélébile [ɛ̃delebil] *a* (*encre, souvenir*) indelible.

indélicat [ɛ̃delika] *a* (*grossier*) indelicate; (*malhonnête*) unscrupulous.

indemne [ɛ̃dɛmn] *a* unhurt, unscathed.

indemniser [ɛ̃dɛmnize] *vt* to indemnify, compensate (**de** for). ◆**indemnisation** *nf* compensation. ◆**indemnité** *nf* (*dédommagement*) indemnity; (*allocation*) allowance.

indémontable [ɛ̃demɔ̃tabl] *a* that cannot be taken apart.

indéniable [ɛ̃denjabl] *a* undeniable.

indépendant [ɛ̃depɑ̃dɑ̃] *a* independent (**de**

of); (*chambre*) self-contained; (*journaliste*) freelance. ◆**indépendamment** *adv* independently (**de** of); **i. de** (*sans aucun égard à*) apart from. ◆**indépendance** *nf* independence.

indescriptible [ɛ̃dɛskriptibl] *a* indescribable.

indésirable [ɛ̃dezirabl] *a* & *nmf* undesirable.

indestructible [ɛ̃dɛstryktibl] *a* indestructible.

indéterminé [ɛ̃detɛrmine] *a* indeterminate. ◆**indétermination** *nf* (*doute*) indecision.

index [ɛ̃dɛks] *nm* (*liste*) index; *Anat* forefinger, index finger.

indexer [ɛ̃dɛkse] *vt* *Écon* to index-link, tie (**sur** to).

indicateur, -trice [ɛ̃dikatœr, -tris] **1** *nmf* (*espion*) (*police*) informer. **2** *nm* *Rail* guide, timetable; *Tech* indicator, gauge. **3** *a* **poteau i.** signpost. ◆**indicatif, -ive 1** *a* indicative (**de** of); – *nm* *Mus* signature tune; *Tél* dialling code, *Am* area code. **2** *nm* (*mode*) *Gram* indicative. ◆**indication** *nf* indication (**de** of); (*renseignement*) (piece of) information; (*directive*) instruction.

indice [ɛ̃dis] *nm* (*indication*) sign; (*dans une enquête*) *Jur* clue; (*des prix*) index; (*de salaire*) grade; **i. d'écoute** TV Rad rating.

indien, -ienne [ɛ̃djɛ̃, -jɛn] *a* & *nmf* Indian.

indifférent [ɛ̃diferɑ̃] *a* indifferent (**à** to); **ça m'est i.** that's all the same to me. ◆**indifféremment** [-amɑ̃] *adv* indifferently. ◆**indifférence** *nf* indifference (**à** to).

indigène [ɛ̃diʒɛn] *a* & *nmf* native.

indigent [ɛ̃diʒɑ̃] *a* (very) poor. ◆**indigence** *nf* poverty.

indigeste [ɛ̃diʒɛst] *a* indigestible. ◆**indigestion** *nf* (attack of) indigestion.

indigne [ɛ̃diɲ] *a* (*personne*) unworthy; (*chose*) shameful; **i. de qn/qch** unworthy of s.o./sth. ◆**indignité** *nf* unworthiness; **une i.** (*honte*) an indignity.

indigner [ɛ̃diɲe] *vt* **i. qn** to make s.o. indignant; — **s'i.** *vpr* to be or become indignant (**de** at). ◆**indignation** *nf* indignation.

indigo [ɛ̃digo] *nm* & *a inv* (*couleur*) indigo.

indiqu/er [ɛ̃dike] *vt* (*montrer*) to show, indicate; (*dire*) to point out, tell; (*recommander*) to recommend; **i. du doigt** to point to *ou* at. ◆**—é** *a* (*heure*) appointed; (*conseillé*) recommended; (*adéquat*) appropriate.

indirect [ɛ̃dirɛkt] *a* indirect. ◆**—ement** *adv* indirectly.

indiscipline [ɛ̃disiplin] *nf* lack of discipline. ◆**indiscipliné** *a* unruly.

indiscret, -ète [ɛ̃diskrɛ, -ɛt] *a* (*indélicat*) indiscreet, tactless; (*curieux*) *Péj* inquisitive, prying. ◆**indiscrétion** *nf* indiscretion.

indiscutable [ɛ̃diskytabl] *a* indisputable.

indispensable [ɛ̃dispɑ̃sabl] *a* indispensable, essential.

indispos/er [ɛ̃dispoze] *vt* (*incommoder*) to make unwell, upset; **i. qn (contre soi)** (*mécontenter*) to antagonize s.o. ◆**—é** *a* (*malade*) indisposed, unwell. ◆**indisposition** *nf* indisposition.

indissoluble [ɛ̃disɔlybl] *a* (*liens etc*) solid, indissoluble.

indistinct, -incte [ɛ̃distɛ̃(kt), -ɛ̃kt] *a* indistinct. ◆**—ement** [-ɛ̃ktəmɑ̃] *adv* indistinctly; (*également*) without distinction.

individu [ɛ̃dividy] *nm* individual. ◆**individualiser** *vt* to individualize. ◆**individualiste** *a* individualistic; – *nmf* individualist. ◆**individualité** *nf* (*originalité*) individuality. ◆**individuel, -elle** *a* individual. ◆**individuellement** *adv* individually.

indivisible [ɛ̃divizibl] *a* indivisible.

Indochine [ɛ̃dɔʃin] *nf* Indo-China.

indolent [ɛ̃dɔlɑ̃] *a* indolent. ◆**indolence** *nf* indolence.

indolore [ɛ̃dɔlɔr] *a* painless.

indomptable [ɛ̃dɔ̃tabl] *a* (*énergie, volonté*) indomitable. ◆**indompté** *a* (*animal*) untamed.

Indonésie [ɛ̃dɔnezi] *nf* Indonesia.

indubitable [ɛ̃dybitabl] *a* beyond doubt.

indue [ɛ̃dy] *af* **à une heure i.** at an ungodly hour.

induire* [ɛ̃dɥir] *vt* **i. qn en erreur** to lead s.o. astray.

indulgent [ɛ̃dylʒɑ̃] *a* indulgent (**envers** to, **avec** with). ◆**indulgence** *nf* indulgence.

industrie [ɛ̃dystri] *nf* industry. ◆**industrialisé** *a* industrialized. ◆**industriel, -elle** *a* industrial; – *nmf* industrialist.

inébranlable [inebrɑ̃labl] *a* (*certitude, personne*) unshakeable, unwavering.

inédit [inedi] *a* (*texte*) unpublished; (*nouveau*) *Fig* original.

ineffable [inefabl] *a* *Litt* inexpressible, ineffable.

inefficace [inefikas] *a* (*mesure, effort etc*) ineffective, ineffectual; (*personne*) inefficient. ◆**inefficacité** *nf* ineffectiveness; inefficiency.

inégal, -aux [inegal, -o] *a* unequal; (*sol, humeur*) uneven. ◆**inégalable** *a* incomparable. ◆**inégalé** *a* unequalled. ◆**inégalité** *nf* (*morale*) inequality; (*physique*) difference; (*irrégularité*) unevenness; *pl* (*bosses*) bumps.

inélégant [inelegɑ̃] *a* coarse, inelegant.

inéligible [ineliʒibl] *a* (*candidat*) ineligible.

inéluctable [inelyktabl] *a* inescapable.

inepte [inɛpt] *a* absurd, inept. ◆**ineptie** [-si] *nf* absurdity, ineptitude.

inépuisable [inepɥizabl] *a* inexhaustible.

inerte [inɛrt] *a* inert; (*corps*) lifeless. ◆**inertie** [-si] *nf* inertia.

inespéré [inespere] *a* unhoped-for.

inestimable [inɛstimabl] *a* priceless.

inévitable [inevitabl] *a* inevitable, unavoidable.

inexact [inɛgzakt] *a* (*erroné*) inaccurate, inexact; **c'est i.!** it's incorrect! ◆**inexactitude** *nf* inaccuracy, inexactitude; (*manque de ponctualité*) lack of punctuality.

inexcusable [inɛkskyzabl] *a* inexcusable.

inexistant [inɛgzistɑ̃] *a* non-existent.

inexorable [inɛgzɔrabl] *a* inexorable.

inexpérience [inɛksperjɑ̃s] *nf* inexperience. ◆**inexpérimenté** *a* (*personne*) inexperienced; (*machine, arme*) untested.

inexplicable [inɛksplikabl] *a* inexplicable. ◆**inexpliqué** *a* unexplained.

inexploré [inɛksplɔre] *a* unexplored.

inexpressif, -ive [inɛkspresif, -iv] *a* expressionless.

inexprimable [inɛksprimabl] *a* inexpressible.

inextricable [inɛkstrikabl] *a* inextricable.

infaillible [ɛ̃fajibl] *a* infallible. ◆**infaillibilité** *nf* infallibility.

infaisable [ɛ̃fəzabl] *a* (*travail etc*) that cannot be done.

infamant [ɛ̃famɑ̃] *a* ignominious.

infâme [ɛ̃fɑm] *a* (*odieux*) vile, infamous; (*taudis*) squalid. ◆**infamie** *nf* infamy.

infanterie [ɛ̃fɑ̃tri] *nf* infantry.

infantile [ɛ̃fɑ̃til] *a* (*maladie, réaction*) infantile.

infarctus [ɛ̃farktys] *nm* **un i.** *Méd* a coronary.

infatigable [ɛ̃fatigabl] *a* tireless, indefatigable.

infect [ɛ̃fɛkt] *a* (*puant*) foul; (*mauvais*) lousy, vile.

infecter [ɛ̃fɛkte] **1** *vt* (*air*) to contaminate, foul. **2** *vt Méd* to infect; — **s'i.** *vpr* to get infected. ◆**infectieux, -euse** *a* infectious. ◆**infection** *nf* **1** *Méd* infection. **2** (*odeur*) stench.

inférer [ɛ̃fere] *vt* (*conclure*) to infer (**de** from, **que** that).

inférieur, -eure [ɛ̃ferjœr] *a* (*partie*) lower; (*qualité, personne*) inferior; **à l'étage i.** on the floor below; **i. à** inferior to; (*plus petit que*) smaller than; — *nmf* (*personne*) *Péj* inferior. ◆**infériorité** *nf* inferiority.

infernal, -aux [ɛ̃fɛrnal, -o] *a* infernal.

infest/er [ɛ̃fɛste] *vt* to infest, overrun (**de** with). ◆**-é** *a* **i. de requins/de fourmis/***etc* shark-/ant-/*etc* infested.

infidèle [ɛ̃fidɛl] *a* unfaithful (**à** to). ◆**infidélité** *nf* unfaithfulness; **une i.** (*acte*) an infidelity.

infiltrer (s') [sɛ̃filtre] *vpr* (*liquide*) to seep *ou* percolate (through) (**dans** into); (*lumière*) to filter (through) (**dans** into); **s'i. dans** (*groupe, esprit*) *Fig* to infiltrate. ◆**infiltration** *nf* (*de personne, idée, liquide*) infiltration.

infime [ɛ̃fim] *a* (*très petit*) tiny; (*personne*) *Péj* lowly.

infini [ɛ̃fini] *a* infinite; — *nm Math Phot* infinity; *Phil* infinite; **à l'i.** (*beaucoup*) ad infinitum, endlessly; *Math* to infinity. ◆**infiniment** *adv* infinitely; (*regretter, remercier*) very much. ◆**infinité** *nf* **une i. de** an infinite amount of.

infinitif [ɛ̃finitif] *nm Gram* infinitive.

infirme [ɛ̃firm] *a* disabled, crippled; — *nmf* disabled person. ◆**infirmité** *nf* disability.

infirmer [ɛ̃firme] *vt* to invalidate.

infirmerie [ɛ̃firməri] *nf* infirmary, sickbay. ◆**infirmier** *nm* male nurse. ◆**infirmière** *nf* nurse.

inflammable [ɛ̃flamabl] *a* (in)flammable.

inflammation [ɛ̃flamɑsjɔ̃] *nf Méd* inflammation.

inflation [ɛ̃flɑsjɔ̃] *nf Écon* inflation. ◆**inflationniste** *a Écon* inflationary.

infléchir [ɛ̃fleʃir] *vt* (*courber*) to inflect, bend; (*modifier*) to shift. ◆**inflexion** *nf* bend; (*de voix*) tone, inflexion; **une i. de la tête** a nod.

inflexible [ɛ̃flɛksibl] *a* inflexible.

infliger [ɛ̃fliʒe] *vt* to inflict (**à** on); (*amende*) to impose (**à** on).

influence [ɛ̃flyɑ̃s] *nf* influence. ◆**influencer** *vt* to influence. ◆**influençable** *a* easily influenced. ◆**influent** *a* influential. ◆**influer** *vi* **i. sur** to influence.

information [ɛ̃fɔrmɑsjɔ̃] *nf* information; (*nouvelle*) piece of news; (*enquête*) *Jur* inquiry; *pl* information; *Journ Rad TV* news.

informatique [ɛ̃fɔrmatik] *nf* (*science*) computer science; (*technique*) data processing. ◆**informaticien, -ienne** *nmf* computer scientist. ◆**informatiser** *vt* to computerize.

informe [ɛ̃fɔrm] *a* shapeless.

informer [ɛ̃fɔrme] *vt* to inform (**de** of, about;

que that); — **s'i.** *vpr* to inquire (**de** about; **si** if, whether). ◆**informateur, -trice** *nmf* informant.
infortune [ɛ̃fɔrtyn] *nf* misfortune. ◆**infortuné** *a* ill-fated, hapless.
infraction [ɛ̃fraksjɔ̃] *nf* (*délit*) offence; **i. à** breach of, infringement of.
infranchissable [ɛ̃frɑ̃ʃisabl] *a* (*mur, fleuve*) impassable; (*difficulté*) *Fig* insuperable.
infrarouge [ɛ̃fraruʒ] *a* infrared.
infroissable [ɛ̃frwasabl] *a* crease-resistant.
infructueux, -euse [ɛ̃fryktɥø, -øz] *a* fruitless.
infuser [ɛ̃fyze] *vt* (**faire**) **i.** (*thé*) to infuse. ◆**infusion** *nf* (*tisane*) (herb *ou* herbal) tea, infusion.
ingénier (s') [sɛ̃ʒenje] *vpr* to exercise one's wits (**à faire** in order to do).
ingénieur [ɛ̃ʒenjœr] *nm* engineer. ◆**ingénierie** [-iri] *nf* engineering.
ingénieux, -euse [ɛ̃ʒenjø, -øz] *a* ingenious. ◆**ingéniosité** *nf* ingenuity.
ingénu [ɛ̃ʒeny] *a* artless, naïve.
ingérer (s') [sɛ̃ʒere] *vpr* to interfere (**dans** in). ◆**ingérence** *nf* interference.
ingrat [ɛ̃gra] *a* (*personne*) ungrateful (**envers** to); (*sol*) barren; (*tâche*) thankless; (*visage, physique*) unattractive; (*âge*) awkward. ◆**ingratitude** *nf* ingratitude.
ingrédient [ɛ̃gredjɑ̃] *nm* ingredient.
inguérissable [ɛ̃gerisabl] *a* incurable.
ingurgiter [ɛ̃gyrʒite] *vt* to gulp down.
inhabitable [inabitabl] *a* uninhabitable. ◆**inhabité** *a* uninhabited.
inhabituel, -elle [inabitɥɛl] *a* unusual.
inhalateur [inalatœr] *nm* *Méd* inhaler. ◆**inhalation** *nf* inhalation; **faire des inhalations** to inhale.
inhérent [inerɑ̃] *a* inherent (**à** in).
inhibé [inibe] *a* inhibited. ◆**inhibition** *nf* inhibition.
inhospitalier, -ière [inɔspitalje, -jɛr] *a* inhospitable.
inhumain [inymɛ̃] *a* (*cruel, terrible*) inhuman.
inhumer [inyme] *vt* to bury, inter. ◆**inhumation** *nf* burial.
inimaginable [inimaʒinabl] *a* unimaginable.
inimitable [inimitabl] *a* inimitable.
inimitié [inimitje] *nf* enmity.
ininflammable [inɛ̃flamabl] *a* (*tissu etc*) non-flammable.
inintelligent [inɛ̃teliʒɑ̃] *a* unintelligent.
inintelligible [inɛ̃teliʒibl] *a* unintelligible.
inintéressant [inɛ̃teresɑ̃] *a* uninteresting.

ininterrompu [inɛ̃terɔ̃py] *a* uninterrupted, continuous.
inique [inik] *a* iniquitous. ◆**iniquité** *nf* iniquity.
initial, -aux [inisjal, -o] *a* initial. ◆**initiale** *nf* (*lettre*) initial. ◆**initialement** *adv* initially.
initiative [inisjativ] *nf* **1** initiative. **2** syndicat **d'i.** tourist office.
initi/er [inisje] *vt* to initiate (**à** into); **s'i. à** (*art, science*) to become acquainted with *ou* initiated into. ◆**—é, -ée** *nmf* initiate; **les initiés** the initiated. ◆**initiateur, -trice** *nmf* initiator. ◆**initiation** *nf* initiation.
injecter [ɛ̃ʒɛkte] *vt* to inject; **injecté de sang** bloodshot. ◆**injection** *nf* injection.
injonction [ɛ̃ʒɔ̃ksjɔ̃] *nf* order, injunction.
injure [ɛ̃ʒyr] *nf* insult; *pl* abuse, insults. ◆**injurier** *vt* to abuse, insult, swear at. ◆**injurieux, -euse** *a* abusive, insulting (**pour** to).
injuste [ɛ̃ʒyst] *a* (*contraire à la justice*) unjust; (*partial*) unfair. ◆**injustice** *nf* injustice.
injustifiable [ɛ̃ʒystifjabl] *a* unjustifiable. ◆**injustifié** *a* unjustified.
inlassable [ɛ̃lɑsabl] *a* untiring.
inné [ine] *a* innate, inborn.
innocent, -ente [inɔsɑ̃, -ɑ̃t] *a* innocent (**de** of); — *nmf* *Jur* innocent person; (*idiot*) simpleton. ◆**innocemment** [-amɑ̃] *adv* innocently. ◆**innocence** *nf* innocence. ◆**innocenter** *vt* **i. qn** to clear s.o. (**de** of).
innombrable [inɔ̃brabl] *a* innumerable.
innommable [inɔmabl] *a* (*dégoûtant*) unspeakable, foul.
innover [inɔve] *vi* to innovate. ◆**innovateur, -trice** *nmf* innovator. ◆**innovation** *nf* innovation.
inoccupé [inɔkype] *a* unoccupied.
inoculer [inɔkyle] *vt* **i. qch à qn** to infect *ou* inoculate s.o. with sth. ◆**inoculation** *nf* (*vaccination*) inoculation.
inodore [inɔdɔr] *a* odourless.
inoffensif, -ive [inɔfɑ̃sif, -iv] *a* harmless, inoffensive.
inonder [inɔ̃de] *vt* to flood, inundate; (*mouiller*) to soak; **inondé de** (*envahi*) inundated with; **inondé de soleil** bathed in sunlight. ◆**inondable** *a* (*chaussée etc*) liable to flooding. ◆**inondation** *nf* flood; (*action*) flooding (**de** of).
inopérant [inɔperɑ̃] *a* inoperative.
inopiné [inɔpine] *a* unexpected.
inopportun [inɔpɔrtœ̃] *a* inopportune.
inoubliable [inublijabl] *a* unforgettable.
inouï [inwi] *a* incredible, extraordinary.

inox [inɔks] nm stainless steel; **en i.** (couteau etc) stainless-steel. ◆**inoxydable** a (couteau etc) stainless-steel; **acier i.** stainless steel.

inqualifiable [ɛ̃kalifjabl] a (indigne) unspeakable.

inquiet, -iète [ɛ̃kjɛ, -jɛt] a anxious, worried (**de** about). ◆**inquiéter** vt (préoccuper) to worry; (police) to bother, harass (suspect etc); — **s'i.** vpr to worry (**de** about). ◆**—ant** a worrying. ◆**inquiétude** nf anxiety, concern, worry.

inquisiteur, -trice [ɛ̃kizitœr, -tris] a (regard) Péj inquisitive. ◆**inquisition** nf inquisition.

insaisissable [ɛ̃sezisabl] a elusive.

insalubre [ɛ̃salybr] a unhealthy, insalubrious.

insanités [ɛ̃sanite] nfpl (idioties) absurdities.

insatiable [ɛ̃sasjabl] a insatiable.

insatisfait [ɛ̃satisfɛ] a unsatisfied, dissatisfied.

inscrire* [ɛ̃skrir] vt to write ou put down; (sur un registre) to register; (graver) to inscribe; **i. qn** to enrol s.o.; — **s'i.** vpr to enrol (**à** at); **s'i. à** (parti, club) to join, enrol in; (examen) to enter ou enrol ou register for; **s'i. dans (le cadre de)** to be part of; **s'i. en faux contre** to deny absolutely. ◆**inscription** nf writing down; enrolment; registration; (de médaille, sur écriteau etc) inscription; **frais d'i.** Univ tuition fees.

insecte [ɛ̃sɛkt] nm insect. ◆**insecticide** nm insecticide.

insécurité [ɛ̃sekyrite] nf insecurity.

insémination [ɛ̃seminasjɔ̃] nf Méd insemination.

insensé [ɛ̃sɑ̃se] a senseless, absurd.

insensible [ɛ̃sɑ̃sibl] a (indifférent) insensitive (à to); (graduel) imperceptible, very slight. ◆**insensiblement** adv imperceptibly. ◆**insensibilité** nf insensitivity.

inséparable [ɛ̃separabl] a inseparable (**de** from).

insérer [ɛ̃sere] vt to insert (**dans** into, in); **s'i. dans** (programme etc) to be part of. ◆**insertion** nf insertion.

insidieux, -euse [ɛ̃sidjø, -øz] a insidious.

insigne [ɛ̃siɲ] nm badge, emblem; pl (de maire etc) insignia.

insignifiant [ɛ̃siɲifjɑ̃] a insignificant, unimportant. ◆**insignifiance** nf insignificance.

insinuer [ɛ̃sinɥe] vt Péj to insinuate (**que** that); — **s'i.** vpr to insinuate oneself (**dans** into). ◆**insinuation** nf insinuation.

insipide [ɛ̃sipid] a insipid.

insist/er [ɛ̃siste] vi to insist (**pour faire** on doing); (continuer) Fam to persevere; **i. sur** (détail, syllabe etc) to stress; **i. pour que** (+ sub) to insist that. ◆**—ant** a insistent, persistent. ◆**insistance** nf insistence, persistence.

insolation [ɛ̃sɔlasjɔ̃] nf Méd sunstroke.

insolent [ɛ̃sɔlɑ̃] a (impoli) insolent; (luxe) indecent. ◆**insolence** nf insolence.

insolite [ɛ̃sɔlit] a unusual, strange.

insoluble [ɛ̃sɔlybl] a insoluble.

insolvable [ɛ̃sɔlvabl] a Fin insolvent.

insomnie [ɛ̃sɔmni] nf insomnia; pl (periods of) insomnia; **nuit d'i.** sleepless night. ◆**insomniaque** nmf insomniac.

insondable [ɛ̃sɔ̃dabl] a unfathomable.

insonoriser [ɛ̃sɔnɔrize] vt to soundproof, insulate. ◆**insonorisation** nf soundproofing, insulation.

insouciant [ɛ̃susjɑ̃] a carefree; **i. de** unconcerned about. ◆**insouciance** nf carefree attitude, lack of concern.

insoumis [ɛ̃sumi] a rebellious. ◆**insoumission** nf rebelliousness.

insoupçonnable [ɛ̃supsɔnabl] a beyond suspicion. ◆**insoupçonné** a unsuspected.

insoutenable [ɛ̃sutnabl] a unbearable; (théorie) untenable.

inspecter [ɛ̃spɛkte] vt to inspect. ◆**inspecteur, -trice** nmf inspector. ◆**inspection** nf inspection.

inspir/er [ɛ̃spire] **1** vt to inspire; **i. qch à qn** to inspire s.o. with sth; **s'i. de** to take one's inspiration from. **2** vi Méd to breathe in. ◆**—é** a inspired; **être bien i. de faire** to have the good idea to do. ◆**inspiration** nf **1** inspiration. **2** Méd breathing in.

instable [ɛ̃stabl] a (meuble) unsteady, shaky; (temps) unsettled; (caractère, situation) unstable. ◆**instabilité** nf unsteadiness; instability.

installer [ɛ̃stale] vt (équiper) to fit out, fix up; (appareil, meuble etc) to install, put in; (étagère) to put up; **i. qn** (dans une fonction, un logement) to install s.o. (**dans** in); — **s'i.** vpr (s'asseoir, s'établir) to settle (down); (médecin etc) to set oneself up; **s'i. dans** (maison, hôtel) to move into. ◆**installateur** nm fitter. ◆**installation** nf fitting out; installation; putting in; moving in; pl (appareils) fittings; (bâtiments) facilities.

instance [ɛ̃stɑ̃s] nf **1** (juridiction, autorité) authority; **tribunal de première i.** = magistrates' court; **en i. de** (divorce, départ) in the process of. **2** *nfpl* (*prières*) insistence, entreaties.

instant [ɛ̃stɑ̃] *nm* moment, instant; **à l'i.** a moment ago; **pour l'i.** for the moment. ◆**instantané** *a* instantaneous; **café i.** instant coffee; – *nm Phot* snapshot.

instaurer [ɛ̃stɔre] *vt* to found, set up.

instigateur, -trice [ɛ̃stigatœr, -tris] *nmf* instigator. ◆**instigation** *nf* instigation.

instinct [ɛ̃stɛ̃] *nm* instinct; **d'i.** instinctively, by instinct. ◆**instinctif, -ive** *a* instinctive.

instituer [ɛ̃stitɥe] *vt* (*règle, régime*) to establish, institute.

institut [ɛ̃stity] *nm* institute; **i. de beauté** beauty salon *ou* parlour; **i. universitaire de technologie** polytechnic, technical college. **instituteur, -trice** [ɛ̃stitytœr, -tris] *nmf* primary school teacher.

institution [ɛ̃stitysjɔ̃] *nf* (*règle, organisation, structure etc*) institution; *Scol* private school. ◆**institutionnel, -elle** *a* institutional.

instructif, -ive [ɛ̃stryktif, -iv] *a* instructive.

instruction [ɛ̃stryksjɔ̃] *nf* education, schooling; *Mil* training; *Jur* investigation; (*document*) directive; *pl* (*ordres*) instructions. ◆**instructeur** *nm* (*moniteur*) & *Mil* instructor.

instruire* [ɛ̃strɥir] *vt* to teach, educate; *Mil* to train; (*au courant*) *Jur* to investigate; **i. qn de** to inform *ou* instruct s.o. of; **– s'i.** *vpr* to educate oneself; **s'i. de** to inquire about. ◆**instruit** *a* educated.

instrument [ɛ̃strymɑ̃] *nm* instrument; (*outil*) implement, tool. ◆**instrumental, -aux** *a Mus* instrumental. ◆**instrumentiste** *nmf Mus* instrumentalist.

insu de (à l') [alɛ̃syd(ə)] *prép* without the knowledge of.

insuccès [ɛ̃syksɛ] *nm* failure.

insuffisant [ɛ̃syfizɑ̃] *a* (*en qualité*) inadequate; (*en quantité*) insufficient, inadequate. ◆**insuffisance** *nf* inadequacy.

insulaire [ɛ̃sylɛr] *a* insular; – *nmf* islander.

insuline [ɛ̃sylin] *nf Méd* insulin.

insulte [ɛ̃sylt] *nf* insult (à to). ◆**insulter** *vt* to insult.

insupportable [ɛ̃sypɔrtabl] *a* unbearable.

insurger (s') [sɛ̃syrʒe] *vpr* to rise (up), rebel (**contre** against). ◆**–é, -ée** *nmf* a insurgent, rebel. ◆**insurrection** *nf* insurrection, uprising.

insurmontable [ɛ̃syrmɔ̃tabl] *a* insurmountable, insuperable.

intact [ɛ̃takt] *a* intact.

intangible [ɛ̃tɑ̃ʒibl] *a* intangible.

intarissable [ɛ̃tarisabl] *a* inexhaustible.

intégral, -aux [ɛ̃tegral, -o] *a* full, complete; (*édition*) unabridged. ◆**intégralement** *adv* in full, fully. ◆**intégralité** *nf* whole (**de** of); **dans son i.** in full.

intègre [ɛ̃tɛgr] *a* upright, honest. ◆**intégrité** *nf* integrity.

intégr/er [ɛ̃tegre] *vt* to integrate (**dans** in); **– s'i.** *vpr* to become integrated, adapt. ◆**–ante** *af* **faire partie i. de** to be part and parcel of. ◆**intégration** *nf* integration.

intellectuel, -elle [ɛ̃telɛktɥel] *a & nmf* intellectual.

intelligent [ɛ̃teliʒɑ̃] *a* intelligent, clever. ◆**intelligemment** [-amɑ̃] *adv* intelligently. ◆**intelligence** *nf* (*faculté*) intelligence; *pl Mil Pol* secret relations; **avoir l'i. de qch** (*compréhension*) to have an understanding of sth; **d'i. avec qn** in complicity with s.o. ◆**intelligentsia** [-dʒɛntsja] *nf* intelligentsia.

intelligible [ɛ̃teliʒibl] *a* intelligible. ◆**intelligibilité** *nf* intelligibility.

intempérance [ɛ̃tɑ̃perɑ̃s] *nf* intemperance.

intempéries [ɛ̃tɑ̃peri] *nfpl* **les i.** the elements, bad weather.

intempestif, -ive [ɛ̃tɑ̃pɛstif, -iv] *a* untimely.

intenable [ɛ̃tnabl] *a* (*position*) untenable; (*enfant*) unruly, uncontrollable.

intendant, -ante [ɛ̃tɑ̃dɑ̃, -ɑ̃t] *nmf Scol* bursar. ◆**intendance** *nf Scol* bursar's office.

intense [ɛ̃tɑ̃s] *a* intense; (*circulation, trafic*) heavy. ◆**intensément** *adv* intensely. ◆**intensif, -ive** *a* intensive. ◆**intensifier** *vt*, **– s'i.** *vpr* to intensify. ◆**intensité** *nf* intensity.

intenter [ɛ̃tɑ̃te] *vt* **i. un procès à** *Jur* to institute proceedings against.

intention [ɛ̃tɑ̃sjɔ̃] *nf* intention; *Jur* intent; **avoir l'i. de faire** to intend to do; **à l'i. de qn** for s.o.; **à votre i.** for you. ◆**intentionné** *a* **bien i.** well-intentioned. ◆**intentionnel, -elle** *a* intentional, wilful. ◆**intentionnellement** *adv* intentionally.

inter- [ɛ̃ter] *préf* inter-.

interaction [ɛ̃teraksjɔ̃] *nf* interaction.

intercaler [ɛ̃terkale] *vt* to insert.

intercéder [ɛ̃tersede] *vt* to intercede (**auprès de** with).

intercepter [ɛ̃tersɛpte] *vt* to intercept. ◆**interception** *nf* interception.

interchangeable [ɛ̃terʃɑ̃ʒabl] *a* interchangeable.

interclasse [ɛ̃terklɑs] *nm Scol* break (between classes).

intercontinental, -aux [ɛ̃terkɔ̃tinɑ̃tal, -o] *a* intercontinental.

interdépendant [ɛ̃tɛrdepɑ̃dɑ̃] *a* interdependent.

interd/ire* [ɛ̃tɛrdir] *vt* to forbid, not to allow (**qch à qn** s.o. sth); (*meeting, film etc*) to ban; **i. à qn de faire** (*médecin, père etc*) not to allow s.o. to do, forbid s.o. to do; (*attitude, santé etc*) to prevent s.o. from doing, not allow s.o. to do. ◆**—it a 1** forbidden, not allowed; **il est i. de** it is forbidden to; **'stationnement i.'** 'no parking'. **2** (*étonné*) nonplussed. ◆**interdiction** *nf* ban (**de** on); **'i. de fumer'** 'no smoking'.

intéress/er [ɛ̃terese] *vt* to interest; (*concerner*) to concern; **s'i. à** to take an interest in, be interested in. ◆**—ant** *a* (*captivant*) interesting; (*affaire, prix etc*) attractive, worthwhile. ◆**—é, -ée** *a* (*avide*) self-interested; (*motif*) selfish; (*concerné*) concerned; *— nmf* **l'i.** the interested party.

intérêt [ɛ̃terɛ] *nm* interest; *Péj* self-interest; *pl Fin* interest; **tu as i. à faire** it would pay you to do, you'd do well to do; **des intérêts dans** *Com* an interest ou stake in.

interface [ɛ̃tɛrfas] *nf Tech* interface.

intérieur [ɛ̃terjœr] *a* (*cour, paroi*) inner, interior; (*poche*) inside; (*vie, sentiment*) inner, inward; (*mer*) inland; (*politique, vol*) internal, domestic; *— nm* (*de boîte etc*) inside (**de** of); (*de maison*) interior, inside; (*de pays*) interior; **à l'i. (de)** inside; **d'i.** (*vêtement, jeux*) indoor; **femme d'i.** home-loving woman; **ministère de l'I.** Home Office, *Am* Department of the Interior. ◆**—ement** *adv* (*dans le cœur*) inwardly.

intérim [ɛ̃terim] *nm* **pendant l'i.** in the interim; **assurer l'i.** to deputize (**de** for); **ministre/etc par i.** acting minister/etc. ◆**intérimaire** *a* temporary, interim; *— nmf* (*fonctionnaire*) deputy; (*secrétaire*) temporary.

interligne [ɛ̃tɛrliɲ] *nm Typ* space (between the lines).

interlocuteur, -trice [ɛ̃tɛrlɔkytœr, -tris] *nmf Pol* negotiator; **mon i.** the person I am, was *etc* speaking to.

interloqué [ɛ̃tɛrlɔke] *a* dumbfounded.

interlude [ɛ̃tɛrlyd] *nm Mus TV* interlude.

intermède [ɛ̃tɛrmɛd] *nm* (*interruption*) & *Th* interlude.

intermédiaire [ɛ̃tɛrmedjɛr] *a* intermediate; *— nmf* intermediary; **par l'i. de** through (the medium of).

interminable [ɛ̃tɛrminabl] *a* endless, interminable.

intermittent [ɛ̃tɛrmitɑ̃] *a* intermittent. ◆**intermittence** *nf* **par i.** intermittently.

international, -aux [ɛ̃tɛrnasjɔnal, -o] *a* international; *— nm* (*joueur*) *Sp* international.

interne [ɛ̃tɛrn] **1** *a* (*douleur etc*) internal; (*oreille*) inner. **2** *nmf Scol* boarder; **i. (des hôpitaux)** houseman, *Am* intern. ◆**internat** *nm* (*école*) boarding school.

intern/er [ɛ̃tɛrne] *vt* (*réfugié*) to intern; (*aliéné*) to confine. ◆**—ement** *nm* internment; confinement.

interpeller [ɛ̃tɛrpele] *vt* to shout at, address sharply; (*dans une réunion*) to question, (*interrompre*) to heckle; (*arrêter*) *Jur* to take in for questioning. ◆**interpellation** *nf* sharp address; questioning; heckling; (*de police*) arrest.

interphone [ɛ̃tɛrfɔn] *nm* intercom.

interplanétaire [ɛ̃tɛrplanetɛr] *a* interplanetary.

interpoler [ɛ̃tɛrpɔle] *vt* to interpolate.

interposer (s') [sɛ̃tɛrpoze] *vpr* (*dans une dispute etc*) to intervene (**dans** in); **s'i. entre** to come between.

interprète [ɛ̃tɛrprɛt] *nmf Ling* interpreter; (*chanteur*) singer; *Th Mus* performer; (*porte-parole*) spokesman, spokeswoman; **faire l'i.** *Ling* to interpret. ◆**interprétariat** *nm* (*métier*) *Ling* interpreting. ◆**interprétation** *nf* interpretation; *Th Mus* performance. ◆**interpréter** *vt* (*expliquer*) to interpret; (*chanter*) to sing; (*jouer*) *Th* to play, perform; (*exécuter*) *Mus* to perform.

interroger [ɛ̃terɔʒe] *vt* to question; *Jur* to interrogate; (*faits*) to examine. ◆**interrogateur, -trice** *a* (*air*) questioning; *— nmf Scol* examiner. ◆**interrogatif, -ive** *a & nm Gram* interrogative. ◆**interrogation** *nf* question; (*action*) questioning; (*épreuve*) *Scol* test. ◆**interrogatoire** *nm Jur* interrogation.

interrompre* [ɛ̃terɔ̃pr] *vt* to interrupt, break off; **i. qn** to interrupt s.o.; **— s'i.** *vpr* (*personne*) to break off, stop. ◆**interrupteur** *nm* (*bouton*) *Él* switch. ◆**interruption** *nf* interruption; (*des hostilités, du courant*) break (**de** in).

intersection [ɛ̃tɛrsɛksjɔ̃] *nf* intersection.

interstice [ɛ̃tɛrstis] *nm* crack, chink.

interurbain [ɛ̃tɛryrbɛ̃] *a & nm* (**téléphone**) **i.** long-distance telephone service.

intervalle [ɛ̃tɛrval] *nm* (*écart*) space, gap; (*temps*) interval; **dans l'i.** (*entretemps*) in the meantime.

intervenir* [ɛ̃tɛrvənir] *vi* (*s'interposer, agir*) to intervene; (*survenir*) to occur; (*opérer*) *Méd* to operate; **être intervenu** (*accord*) to be reached. ◆**intervention** *nf* intervention; **i. (chirurgicale)** operation.

intervertir [ɛ̃tɛrvɛrtir] *vt* to invert. ◆**interversion** *nf* inversion.
interview [ɛ̃tɛrvju] *nf Journ TV* interview. ◆**interviewer** [-vjuve] *vt* to interview.
intestin [ɛ̃tɛstɛ̃] *nm* intestine, bowel. ◆**intestinal, -aux** *a* intestinal, bowel-.
intime [ɛ̃tim] *a* intimate; (*ami*) close, intimate; (*vie, fête, journal*) private; (*pièce, coin*) cosy; (*cérémonie*) quiet; - *nmf* close *ou* intimate friend. ◆**—ment** *adv* intimately. ◆**intimité** *nf* intimacy; privacy; cosiness; **dans l'i.** (*mariage etc*) in private.
intimider [ɛ̃timide] *vt* to intimidate, frighten. ◆**intimidation** *nf* intimidation.
intituler [ɛ̃tityle] *vt* to entitle; — **s'i.** *vpr* to be entitled.
intolérable [ɛ̃tɔlerabl] *a* intolerable (**que** that). ◆**intolérance** *nf* intolerance. ◆**intolérant** *a* intolerant (**de** of).
intonation [ɛ̃tɔnasjɔ̃] *nf Ling* intonation; (*ton*) tone.
intoxiqu/er [ɛ̃tɔksike] *vt* (*empoisonner*) to poison; *Psy Pol* to brainwash; — **s'i.** *vpr* to be *ou* become poisoned. ◆**—é, -ée** *nmf* addict. ◆**intoxication** *nf* poisoning; *Psy Pol* brainwashing.
intra- [ɛ̃tra] *préf* intra-.
intraduisible [ɛ̃traduizibl] *a* untranslatable.
intraitable [ɛ̃trɛtabl] *a* uncompromising.
intransigeant [ɛ̃trɑ̃ziʒɑ̃] *a* intransigent. ◆**intransigeance** *nf* intransigence.
intransitif, -ive [ɛ̃trɑ̃zitif, -iv] *a & nm Gram* intransitive.
intraveineux, -euse [ɛ̃travɛnø, -øz] *a Méd* intravenous.
intrépide [ɛ̃trepid] *a* (*courageux*) fearless, intrepid; (*obstiné*) headstrong. ◆**intrépidité** *nf* fearlessness.
intrigue [ɛ̃trig] *nf* intrigue; *Th Cin Littér* plot. ◆**intrigant, -ante** *nmf* schemer. ◆**intriguer 1** *vi* to scheme, intrigue. **2** *vt* **i. qn** (*intéresser*) to intrigue s.o., puzzle s.o.
intrinsèque [ɛ̃trɛ̃sɛk] *a* intrinsic. ◆**—ment** *adv* intrinsically.
introduire* [ɛ̃trɔduir] *vt* (*présenter*) to introduce, bring in; (*insérer*) to insert (**dans** into), put in (**dans** to); (*faire entrer*) to show (*s.o.*) in; **s'i. dans** to get into. ◆**introduction** *nf* (*texte, action*) introduction.
introspectif, -ive [ɛ̃trɔspɛktif, -iv] *a* introspective. ◆**introspection** *nf* introspection.
introuvable [ɛ̃truvabl] *a* that cannot be found anywhere.
introverti, -ie [ɛ̃trɔvɛrti] *nmf* introvert.
intrus, -use [ɛ̃try, -yz] *nmf* intruder. ◆**intrusion** *nf* intrusion (**dans** into).

intuition [ɛ̃tɥisjɔ̃] *nf* intuition. ◆**intuitif, -ive** *a* intuitive.
inusable [inyzabl] *a Fam* hard-wearing.
inusité [inyzite] *a Gram* unused.
inutile [inytil] *a* unnecessary, useless; **c'est i. de crier** it's pointless *ou* useless to shout. ◆**inutilement** *adv* (*vainement*) needlessly. ◆**inutilité** *nf* uselessness.
inutilisable [inytilizabl] *a* unusable. ◆**inutilisé** *a* unused.
invalider [ɛ̃valide] *vt* to invalidate.
invariable [ɛ̃varjabl] *a* invariable. ◆**—ment** [-əmɑ̃] *adv* invariably.
invasion [ɛ̃vazjɔ̃] *nf* invasion.
invective [ɛ̃vɛktiv] *nf* invective. ◆**invectiver** *vt* to abuse; - *vi* **i. contre** to inveigh against.
invendable [ɛ̃vɑ̃dabl] *a* unsaleable. ◆**invendu** *a* unsold.
inventaire [ɛ̃vɑ̃tɛr] *nm* (*liste*) *Com* inventory; (*étude*) *Fig* survey; **faire l'i.** *Com* to do the stocktaking (**de** of).
inventer [ɛ̃vɑ̃te] *vt* (*découvrir*) to invent; (*imaginer*) to make up. ◆**inventeur, -trice** *nmf* inventor. ◆**inventif, -ive** *a* inventive. ◆**invention** *nf* invention.
inverse [ɛ̃vɛrs] *a* (*sens*) opposite; (*ordre*) reverse; *Math* inverse; - *nm* **l'i.** the reverse, the opposite. ◆**inversement** *adv* conversely. ◆**inverser** *vt* (*ordre*) to reverse. ◆**inversion** *nf Gram Anat etc* inversion.
investigation [ɛ̃vɛstigasjɔ̃] *nf* investigation.
invest/ir [ɛ̃vɛstir] **1** *vti Com* to invest (**dans** in). **2** *vt* **i. qn de** (*fonction etc*) to invest s.o. with. ◆**—issement** *nm Com* investment. ◆**investiture** *nf Pol* nomination.
invétéré [ɛ̃vetere] *a* inveterate.
invincible [ɛ̃vɛ̃sibl] *a* invincible.
invisible [ɛ̃vizibl] *a* invisible.
invit/er [ɛ̃vite] *vt* to invite; **i. qn à faire** to invite *ou* ask s.o. to do; (*inciter*) to tempt s.o. to do. ◆**—é, -ée** *nmf* guest. ◆**invitation** *nf* invitation.
invivable [ɛ̃vivabl] *a* unbearable.
involontaire [ɛ̃vɔlɔ̃tɛr] *a* involuntary. ◆**—ment** *adv* accidentally, involuntarily.
invoquer [ɛ̃vɔke] *vt* (*argument etc*) to put forward; (*appeler*) to invoke, call upon. ◆**invocation** *nf* invocation (**à** to).
invraisemblable [ɛ̃vrɛsɑ̃blabl] *a* incredible; (*improbable*) improbable. ◆**invraisemblance** *nf* improbability.
invulnérable [ɛ̃vylnerabl] *a* invulnerable.
iode [jɔd] *nm* **teinture d'i.** *Méd* iodine.
ira, irait [ira, irɛ] *voir* **aller 1.**
Irak [irak] *nm* Iraq. ◆**irakien, -ienne** *a & nmf* Iraqi.

Iran [irã] *nm* Iran. ◆**iranien, -ienne** *a* & *nmf* Iranian.

irascible [irasibl] *a* irascible.

iris [iris] *nm Anat Bot* iris.

Irlande [irlãd] *nf* Ireland. ◆**irlandais, -aise** *a* Irish; – *nmf* Irishman, Irishwoman; – *nm (langue)* Irish.

ironie [ironi] *nf* irony. ◆**ironique** *a* ironic(al).

irradier [iradje] *vt* to irradiate.

irraisonné [irezone] *a* irrational.

irréconciliable [irekõsiljabl] *a* irreconcilable.

irrécusable [irekyzabl] *a* irrefutable.

irréel, -elle [ireɛl] *a* unreal.

irréfléchi [irefleʃi] *a* thoughtless, unthinking.

irréfutable [irefytabl] *a* irrefutable.

irrégulier, -ière [iregylje, -jɛr] *a* irregular. ◆**irrégularité** *nf* irregularity.

irrémédiable [iremedjabl] *a* irreparable.

irremplaçable [irãplasabl] *a* irreplaceable.

irréparable [ireparabl] *a (véhicule etc)* beyond repair; *(tort, perte)* irreparable.

irrépressible [irepresibl] *a (rires etc)* irrepressible.

irréprochable [ireproʃabl] *a* beyond reproach, irreproachable.

irrésistible [irezistibl] *a (personne, charme etc)* irresistible.

irrésolu [irezoly] *a* irresolute.

irrespirable [irɛspirabl] *a* unbreathable; *Fig* stifling.

irresponsable [irɛspõsabl] *a (personne)* irresponsible.

irrévérencieux, -euse [ireverãsjø, -øz] *a* irreverent.

irréversible [ireversibl] *a* irreversible.

irrévocable [irevokabl] *a* irrevocable.

irriguer [irige] *vt* to irrigate. ◆**irrigation** *nf* irrigation.

irrit/er [irite] *vt* to irritate; – **s'i.** *vpr* to get angry **(de, contre** at). ◆**—ant** *a* irritating; – *nm* irritant. ◆**irritable** *a* irritable. ◆**irritation** *nf (colère)* & *Méd* irritation.

irruption [irypsjõ] *nf* faire i. dans to burst into.

islam [islam] *nm* Islam. ◆**islamique** *a* Islamic.

Islande [islãd] *nf* Iceland. ◆**islandais, -aise** *a* Icelandic.

isol/er [izole] *vt* to isolate **(de** from); *(contre le froid etc)* & *Él* to insulate; – **s'i.** *vpr* to cut oneself off, isolate oneself. ◆**—ant** *a* insulating; – *nm* insulating material. ◆**—é** *a* isolated; *(écarté)* remote, isolated; **i. de** cut off *ou* isolated from. ◆**isolation** *nf* insulation. ◆**isolement** *nm* isolation. ◆**isolément** *adv* in isolation, singly. ◆**isoloir** *nm* polling booth.

isorel® [izorɛl] *nm* hardboard.

Israël [israɛl] *nm* Israel. ◆**israélien, -ienne** *a* & *nmf* Israeli. ◆**israélite** *a* Jewish; – *nm* Jew; – *nf* Jewess.

issu [isy] *a* être i. de to come from.

issue [isy] *nf (sortie)* exit, way out; *(solution) Fig* way out; *(résultat)* outcome; **à l'i. de** at the close of; **rue etc sans i.** dead end; **situation etc sans i.** *Fig* dead end.

isthme [ism] *nm Géog* isthmus.

Italie [itali] *nf* Italy. ◆**italien, -ienne** *a* & *nmf* Italian. ◆**Italien** Italian; – *nm (langue)* Italian.

italique [italik] *a Typ* italic; – *nm* italics.

itinéraire [itinerɛr] *nm* itinerary, route.

itinérant [itinerã] *a* itinerant.

IVG [iveʒe] *nf abrév (interruption volontaire de grossesse)* (voluntary) abortion.

ivoire [ivwar] *nm* ivory.

ivre [ivr] *a* drunk **(de** with). ◆**ivresse** *nf* drunkenness; **en état d'i.** under the influence of drink. ◆**ivrogne** *nmf* drunk(ard).

J

J, j [ʒi] *nm* J, j; **le jour J.** D-day.

j' [ʒ] *voir* **je.**

jacasser [ʒakase] *vi (personne, pie)* to chatter.

jachère (en) [ãʒaʃɛr] *adv (champ etc)* fallow.

jacinthe [ʒasɛ̃t] *nf* hyacinth.

jacousi [ʒakuzi] *nm (baignoire, piscine)* jacuzzi.

jade [ʒad] *nm (pierre)* jade.

jadis [ʒadis] *adv* at one time, once.

jaguar [ʒagwar] *nm (animal)* jaguar.

jaill/ir [ʒajir] *vi (liquide)* to spurt (out), gush (out); *(lumière)* to flash, stream; *(cri)* to burst out; *(vérité)* to burst forth; *(étincelle)* to fly out. ◆**—issement** *nm (de liquide)* gush.

jais [ʒɛ] *nm (noir)* de j. jet-black.

jalon [ʒalɔ̃] *nm* (*piquet*) marker; **poser les jalons** *Fig* to prepare the way (**de** for). ◆**jalonner** *vt* to mark (out); (*border*) to line.

jaloux, -ouse [ʒalu, -uz] *a* jealous (**de** of). ◆**jalouser** *vt* to envy. ◆**jalousie** *nf* **1** jealousy. **2** (*persienne*) venetian blind.

Jamaïque [ʒamaik] *nf* Jamaica.

jamais [ʒamɛ] *adv* **1** (*négatif*) never; **sans j. sortir** without ever going out; **elle ne sort j.** she never goes out. **2** (*positif*) ever; **à (tout) j.** for ever; **si j.** if ever.

jambe [ʒɑ̃b] *nf* leg; **à toutes jambes** as fast as one can; **prendre ses jambes à son cou** to take to one's heels.

jambon [ʒɑ̃bɔ̃] *nm Culin* ham. ◆**jambonneau, -x** *nm* knuckle of ham.

jante [ʒɑ̃t] *nf* (*de roue*) rim.

janvier [ʒɑ̃vje] *nm* January.

Japon [ʒapɔ̃] *nm* Japan. ◆**japonais, -aise** *a nmf* Japanese; – & *nm* (*langue*) Japanese.

japp/er [ʒape] *vi* (*chien etc*) to yap, yelp. ◆**-ement** *nm* yap, yelp.

jaquette [ʒakɛt] *nf* (*d'homme*) tailcoat, morning coat; (*de femme, livre*) jacket.

jardin [ʒardɛ̃] *nm* garden; **j. d'enfants** kindergarten, playschool; **j. public** park; (*plus petit*) gardens. ◆**jardinage** *nm* gardening. ◆**jardiner** *vi* to do the garden, be gardening. ◆**jardinerie** *nf* garden centre. ◆**jardinier** *nm* gardener. ◆**jardinière** *nf* (*personne*) gardener; (*caisse à fleurs*) window box; **j. (de légumes)** *Culin* mixed vegetable dish; **j. d'enfants** kindergarten teacher.

jargon [ʒargɔ̃] *nm* jargon.

jarret [ʒarɛ] *nm Anat* back of the knee.

jarretelle [ʒartɛl] *nf* (*de gaine*) suspender, *Am* garter. ◆**jarretière** *nf* (*autour de la jambe*) garter.

jaser [ʒaze] *vi* (*bavarder*) to jabber.

jasmin [ʒasmɛ̃] *nm Bot* jasmine.

jatte [ʒat] *nf* (*bol*) bowl.

jauge [ʒoʒ] *nf* **1** (*instrument*) gauge. **2** (*capacité*) capacity; *Nau* tonnage. ◆**jauger** *vt* (*personne*) *Litt* to size up.

jaune [ʒon] **1** *a* yellow; – *nm* (*couleur*) yellow; **j. d'œuf** (egg) yolk. **2** *nm* (*ouvrier*) *Péj* blackleg, scab. ◆**jaunâtre** *a* yellowish. ◆**jaunir** *vti* to (turn) yellow. ◆**jaunisse** *nf Méd* jaundice.

Javel (eau de) [odʒavɛl] *nf* bleach. ◆**javelliser** *vt* to chlorinate.

javelot [ʒavlo] *nm* javelin.

jazz [dʒaz] *nm* jazz.

je [ʒ(ə)] *pron* (**j'** *before vowel or mute h*) I; **je suis** I am.

jean [dʒin] *nm* (pair of) jeans.

jeep [dʒip] *nf* jeep.

je-m'en-fichisme [ʒmɑ̃fiʃism] *nm inv Fam* couldn't-care-less attitude.

jérémiades [ʒeremjad] *nfpl Fam* lamentations.

jerrycan [(d)ʒerikan] *nm* jerry can.

jersey [ʒɛrzɛ] *nm* (*tissu*) jersey.

Jersey [ʒɛrzɛ] *nf* Jersey.

jésuite [ʒezɥit] *nm* Jesuit.

Jésus [ʒezy] *nm* Jesus; **J.-Christ** Jesus Christ.

jet [ʒɛ] *nm* throw; (*de vapeur*) burst, gush; (*de lumière*) flash; **j. d'eau** fountain; **premier j.** (*ébauche*) first draft; **d'un seul j.** in one go.

jetée [ʒ(ə)te] *nf* pier, jetty.

jeter [ʒ(ə)te] *vt* to throw (**à** to, **dans** into); (*mettre à la poubelle*) to throw away; (*ancre, regard, sort*) to cast; (*bases*) to lay; (*cri, son*) to let out, utter; (*éclat, lueur*) to throw out, give out; (*noter*) to jot down; **j. un coup d'œil sur** to have *ou* take a look at; (*rapidement*) to glance at; **– se j.** *vpr* to throw oneself; **se j. sur** to fall on, pounce on; **se j. contre** (*véhicule*) to crash into; **se j. dans** (*fleuve*) to flow into. ◆**jetable** *a* (*rasoir etc*) disposable.

jeton [ʒ(ə)tɔ̃] *nm* (*pièce*) token; (*pour compter*) counter; (*à la roulette*) chip.

jeu, -x [ʒø] *nm* **1** game; (*amusement*) play; (*d'argent*) gambling; *Th* acting; *Mus* playing; **j. de mots** play on words, pun; **jeux de société** parlour *ou* party games; **j. télévisé** television quiz; **maison de jeux** gambling club; **en j.** (*en cause*) at stake; (*forces etc*) at work; **entrer en j.** to come into play. **2** (*série complète*) set; (*de cartes*) pack, deck, *Am* deck; (*cartes en main*) hand; **j. d'échecs** (*boîte, pièces*) chess set. **3** (*de ressort, verrou*) *Tech* play.

jeudi [ʒødi] *nm* Thursday.

jeun (à) [aʒœ̃] *adv* on an empty stomach; **être à j.** to have eaten no food.

jeune [ʒœn] *a* young; (*inexpérimenté*) inexperienced; **Dupont j.** Dupont junior; **d'allure j.** young-looking; **jeunes gens** young people; – *nmf* young person; **les jeunes** young people. ◆**jeunesse** *nf* youth; (*apparence*) youthfulness; **la j.** (*jeunes*) the young, youth.

jeûne [ʒøn] *nm* fast; (*action*) fasting. ◆**jeûner** *vi* to fast.

joaillier, -ière [ʒɔaje, -jɛr] *nmf* jeweller.

◆**joaillerie** nf jewellery; (magasin) jewellery shop.

jockey [ʒɔkɛ] nm jockey.

jogging [dʒɔgiŋ] nm Sp jogging; (chaussure) running ou jogging shoe; **faire du j.** to jog.

joie [ʒwa] nf joy, delight; **feu de j.** bonfire.

joindre* [ʒwɛ̃dr] vt (mettre ensemble, relier) to join; (efforts) to combine; (insérer dans une enveloppe) to enclose (à with); (ajouter) to add (à to); **j. qn** (contacter) to get in touch with s.o.; **j. les deux bouts** Fig to make ends meet; **se j. à** (se mettre avec, participer à) to join. ◆**joint** a (efforts) joint, combined; **à pieds joints** with feet together; — nm Tech joint; (de robinet) washer. ◆**jointure** nf Anat joint.

joker [ʒɔkɛr] nm Cartes joker.

joli [ʒɔli] a nice, lovely; (femme, enfant) pretty. ◆—**ment** adv nicely; (très, beaucoup) awfully.

jonc [ʒɔ̃] nm Bot (bul)rush.

joncher [ʒɔ̃ʃe] vt to litter (de with); **jonché de** strewn ou littered with.

jonction [ʒɔ̃ksjɔ̃] nf (de tubes, routes etc) junction.

jongl/er [ʒɔ̃gle] vi to juggle. ◆—**eur, -euse** nmf juggler.

jonquille [ʒɔ̃kij] nf daffodil.

Jordanie [ʒɔrdani] nf Jordan.

joue [ʒu] nf Anat cheek; **coucher qn en j.** to aim (a gun) at s.o.

jouer [ʒwe] vi to play; Th to act; (au tiercé etc) to gamble, bet; (à la Bourse) to gamble; (entrer en jeu) to come into play; (être important) to count; (fonctionner) to work; **j. au tennis/aux cartes/etc** to play tennis/cards/etc; **j. du piano/du violon/etc** to play the piano/violin/etc; **j. des coudes** to use one's elbows; — vt (musique, tour, jeu) to play; (risquer) to gamble, bet (sur on); (cheval) to bet on; (personnage, rôle) Th to play; (pièce) Th to perform, put on; (film) to show, put on; **j. gros jeu** to play for high stakes; **se j. de** to scoff at; (difficultés) to make light of. ◆**jouet** nm toy; **le j. de qn** Fig s.o.'s plaything. ◆**joueur, -euse** nmf player; (au tiercé etc) gambler; **beau j., bon j.,** good loser.

joufflu [ʒufly] a (visage) chubby; (enfant) chubby-cheeked.

joug [ʒu] nm Agr & Fig yoke.

jouir [ʒwir] vi **1 j. de** (savourer, avoir) to enjoy. **2** (éprouver le plaisir sexuel) to come. ◆**jouissance** nf enjoyment; (usage) Jur use.

joujou, -x [ʒuʒu] nm Fam toy.

jour [ʒur] nm day; (lumière) (day)light; (ouverture) gap, opening; (aspect) Fig light; **il fait j.** it's (day)light; **grand j., plein j.** broad daylight; **de nos jours** nowadays, these days; **au j. le j.** from day to day; **du j. au lendemain** overnight; **mettre à j.** to bring up to date; **mettre au j.** to bring into the open; **se faire j.** to come to light; **donner le j. à** to give birth to; **le j. de l'An** New Year's day. ◆**journalier, -ière** a daily. ◆**journée** nf day; **pendant la j.** during the day(time); **toute la j.** all day (long). ◆**journellement** adv daily.

journal, -aux [ʒurnal, -o] nm (news)paper; (spécialisé) journal; (intime) diary; **j. (parlé)** Rad news bulletin; **j. de bord** Nau logbook. ◆**journalisme** nm journalism. ◆**journaliste** nmf journalist. ◆**journalistique** a (style etc) journalistic.

jovial, -aux [ʒɔvjal, -o] a jovial, jolly. ◆**jovialité** nf jollity.

joyau, -aux [ʒwajo] nm jewel.

joyeux, -euse [ʒwajø, -øz] a merry, happy, joyful; **j. anniversaire!** happy birthday!; **j. Noël!** merry ou happy Christmas!

jubilé [ʒybile] nm (golden) jubilee.

jubiler [ʒybile] vi to be jubilant. ◆**jubilation** nf jubilation.

jucher [ʒyʃe] vt, — **se j.** vpr to perch (sur on).

judaïque [ʒydaik] a Jewish. ◆**judaïsme** nm Judaism.

judas [ʒyda] nm (de porte) peephole, spy hole.

judiciaire [ʒydisjɛr] a judicial, legal.

judicieux, -euse [ʒydisjø, -øz] a sensible, judicious.

judo [ʒydo] nm judo. ◆**judoka** nmf judo expert.

juge [ʒyʒ] nm judge; Sp referee, umpire; **j. d'instruction** examining magistrate; **j. de paix** Justice of the Peace; **j. de touche** Fb linesman. ◆**juger** vt (personne, question etc) to judge; (affaire) Jur to try; (estimer) to consider (que that); **j. qn** Jur to try s.o.; — vi **j. de** to judge; **jugez de ma surprise/etc** imagine my surprise/etc. ◆**jugement** nm judg(e)ment; (verdict) Jur sentence; **passer en j.** Jur to stand trial. ◆**jugeote** nf Fam commonsense.

jugé (au) [oʒyʒe] adv by guesswork.

juguler [ʒygyle] vt to check, suppress.

juif, juive [ʒɥif, ʒɥiv] a Jewish; — nm Jew; — nf Jew(ess).

juillet [ʒɥijɛ] nm July.

juin [ʒɥɛ̃] nm June.

jumeau, -elle, pl **-eaux, -elles** [ʒymo, -ɛl] **1** a (frères, lits etc) twin; — nmf twin. **2** nfpl (*longue-vue*) binoculars; **jumelles de théâtre** opera glasses. ◆**jumel/er** *vt* (*villes*) to twin. ◆**-age** *nm* twinning.

jument [ʒymɑ̃] *nf* (*cheval*) mare.

jungle [ʒɶgl] *nf* jungle.

junior [ʒynjɔr] *nm & a* (*inv au sing*) *Sp* junior.

junte [ʒɶt] *nf Pol* junta.

jupe [ʒyp] *nf* skirt. ◆**jupon** *nm* petticoat.

jurer [ʒyre] **1** *vi* (*blasphémer*) to swear. **2** *vt* (*promettre*) to swear (**que** that, **de faire** to do); – *vi* **j. de qch** to swear to sth. **3** *vi* (*contraster*) to clash (**avec** with). ◆**juré** *a* (*ennemi*) sworn; – *nm Jur* juror. ◆**juron** *nm* swearword, oath.

juridiction [ʒyridiksjɔ̃] *nf* jurisdiction.

juridique [ʒyridik] *a* legal. ◆**juriste** *nmf* legal expert, jurist.

jury [ʒyri] *nm Jur* jury; (*de concours*) panel (of judges), jury.

jus [ʒy] *nm* (*des fruits etc*) juice; (*de viande*) gravy; (*café*) *Fam* coffee; (*électricité*) *Fam* power.

jusque [ʒysk] *prép* **jusqu'à** (*espace*) as far as, (right) up to; (*temps*) until, (up) till, to; (*même*) even; **jusqu'à dix francs/etc** (*limite*) up to ten francs/etc; **jusqu'en mai/etc** until May/etc; **jusqu'où?** how far?; **j. dans/sous/etc** right into/under/etc; **j. chez moi** as far as my place; **jusqu'ici** as far as this; (*temps*) up till now; **en avoir j.-là** *Fam* to be fed up; – *conj* **jusqu'à ce qu'il vienne** until he comes.

juste [ʒyst] *a* (*équitable*) fair, just; (*légitime*) just; (*calcul, heure, réponse*) correct, right, accurate; (*remarque*) sound; (*oreille*) good; (*voix*) *Mus* true; (*vêtement*) tight; **un peu j.** (*quantité, repas etc*) barely enough; **très j.!** quite so *ou* right!; **à 3 heures j.** on the stroke of 3; – *adv* (*deviner, compter*) correctly, right, accurately; (*chanter*) in tune; (*exactement, seulement*) just; **au j.** exactly; **tout j.** (*à peine, seulement*) only just; **c'était j.!** (*il était temps*) it was a near thing!; **un peu j.** (*mesurer, compter*) a bit on the short side; – *nm* (*homme*) just man. ◆**justement** *adv* precisely, exactly, just; (*avec justesse ou justice*) justly. ◆**justesse** *nf* (*exactitude*) accuracy; **de j.** (*éviter, gagner etc*) just.

justice [ʒystis] *nf* justice; (*organisation, autorités*) law; **en toute j.** in all fairness; **rendre j. à** to do justice to. ◆**justicier, -ière** *nmf* dispenser of justice.

justifier [ʒystifje] *vt* to justify; – *vi* **j. de** to prove; – **se j.** *vpr Jur* to clear oneself (**de** of); (*attitude etc*) to be justified. ◆**justifiable** *a* justifiable. ◆**justificatif, -ive** *a* **document j.** supporting document, proof. ◆**justification** *nf* justification; (*preuve*) proof.

jute [ʒyt] *nm* (*fibre*) jute.

juteux, -euse [ʒytø, -øz] *a* juicy.

juvénile [ʒyvenil] *a* youthful.

juxtaposer [ʒykstapoze] *vt* to juxtapose. ◆**juxtaposition** *nf* juxtaposition.

K

K, k [kɑ] *nm* K, k.

kaki [kaki] *a inv & nm* khaki.

kaléidoscope [kaleidɔskɔp] *nm* kaleidoscope.

kangourou [kɑ̃guru] *nm* **1** (*animal*) kangaroo. **2** ® (*porte-bébé*) baby sling.

karaté [karate] *nm Sp* karate.

kart [kart] *nm Sp* (go-)kart, go-cart. ◆**karting** [-iŋ] *nm Sp* (go-)karting.

kascher [kaʃer] *a inv Rel* kosher.

kayac [kajak] *nm* (*bateau*) *Sp* canoe.

képi [kepi] *nm* (*coiffure*) *Mil* kepi.

kermesse [kɛrmɛs] *nf* charity fête; (*en Belgique etc*) village fair.

kérosène [kerozɛn] *nm* kerosene, aviation fuel.

kibboutz [kibuts] *nm* kibbutz.

kidnapp/er [kidnape] *vt* to kidnap. ◆**-eur, -euse** *nmf* kidnapper.

kilo(gramme) [kilo, kilɔgram] *nm* kilo(gramme).

kilomètre [kilɔmetr] *nm* kilometre. ◆**kilométrage** *nm Aut* = mileage. ◆**kilométrique** *a* **borne k.** = milestone.

kilowatt [kilɔwat] *nm* kilowatt.

kimono [kimɔno] *nm* (*tunique*) kimono.

kinésithérapie [kineziterapi] *nf* physiotherapy. ◆**kinésithérapeute** *nmf* physiotherapist.

kiosque [kjɔsk] *nm* (*à journaux*) kiosk, stall; **k. à musique** bandstand.

kit [kit] *nm* (*meuble etc prêt à monter*) kit; **en k.** in kit form, ready to assemble.

klaxon® [klaksɔn] *nm Aut* horn. ◆**klaxonner** *vi* to hoot, *Am* honk.
km *abrév (kilomètre)* km.
k.-o. [kao] *a inv* **mettre k.-o.** *Boxe* to knock out.

kyrielle [kirjɛl] *nf* **une k. de** a long string of.
kyste [kist] *nm Méd* cyst.

L

L, l [ɛl] *nm* L, l.
l', la [l, la] *voir* **le**.
là [la] **1** *adv* there; *(chez soi)* in, home; **je reste là** I'll stay here; **c'est là que** *ou* **où** that's where; **c'est là ton erreur** that's *ou* there's your mistake; **là où il est** where he is; **à cinq mètres de là** five metres away; **de là son échec** *(cause)* hence his *ou* her failure; **jusque-là** *(lieu)* as far as that; **passe par là** go that way. **2** *adv (temps)* then; **jusque-là** up till then. **3** *int* **là, là!** *(pour rassurer)* there, there!; **alors là!** well!; **oh là là!** oh dear! **4** *voir* **ce²**, **celui**.
là-bas [laba] *adv* over there.
label [labɛl] *nm Com* label, mark *(of quality, origin etc)*.
labeur [labœr] *nm Litt* toil.
labo [labo] *nm Fam* lab. ◆**laboratoire** *nm* laboratory; **l. de langues** language laboratory.
laborieux, -euse [labɔrjø, -øz] *a (pénible)* laborious; *(personne)* industrious; **les classes laborieuses** the working classes.
labour [labur] *nm* ploughing, *Am* plowing, digging over. ◆**labour/er** *vt (avec charrue)* to plough, *Am* plow; *(avec bêche)* to dig over; *(visage etc) Fig* to furrow. ◆**—eur** *nm* ploughman, *Am* plowman.
labyrinthe [labirɛ̃t] *nm* maze, labyrinth.
lac [lak] *nm* lake.
lacer [lase] *vt* to lace (up). ◆**lacet** *nm* **1** *(shoe- ou boot-)*lace. **2** *(de route)* twist, zigzag; **route en l.** winding *ou* zigzag road.
lacérer [lasere] *vt (papier etc)* to tear; *(visage etc)* to lacerate.
lâche [lɑʃ] **1** *a* cowardly; — *nmf* coward. **2** *a (détendu)* loose, slack. ◆**lâchement** *adv* in a cowardly manner. ◆**lâcheté** *nf* cowardice; **une l.** *(action)* a cowardly act.
lâch/er [lɑʃe] *vt (main, objet etc)* to let go of; *(bombe, pigeon)* to release; *(place, études)* to give up; *(juron)* to utter, let slip; *(secret)* to let out; **l. qn** *(laisser tranquille)* to leave s.o. (alone); *(abandonner) Fam* to drop s.o.; **l. prise** to let go; — *vi (corde)* to give way; — *nm* release. ◆**—eur, -euse** *nmf Fam* deserter.
laconique [lakɔnik] *a* laconic.
lacrymogène [lakrimɔʒɛn] *a* **gaz l.** tear gas.
lacté [lakte] *a (régime)* milk-; **la Voie lactée** the Milky Way.
lacune [lakyn] *nf* gap, deficiency.
lad [lad] *nm* stable boy, groom.
là-dedans [lad(ə)dɑ̃] *adv (lieu)* in there, inside. ◆**là-dessous** *adv* underneath. ◆**là-dessus** *adv* on it, on that; *(monter)* on top; *(alors)* thereupon. ◆**là-haut** *adv* up there; *(à l'étage)* upstairs.
lagon [lagɔ̃] *nm (small)* lagoon. ◆**lagune** *nf* lagoon.
laid [lɛ] *a* ugly; *(ignoble)* wretched. ◆**laideur** *nf* ugliness.
laine [lɛn] *nf* wool; **de l., en l.** woollen. ◆**lainage** *nm (vêtement)* woollen garment, woolly; *(étoffe)* woollen material; *pl (vêtements, objets fabriqués)* woollens. ◆**laineux, -euse** *a* woolly.
laïque [laik] *a (vie)* secular; *(habit, tribunal)* lay; — *nmf (non-prêtre)* layman, laywoman.
laisse [lɛs] *nf* lead, leash; **en l.** on a lead *ou* leash.
laisser [lese] *vt* to leave; **l. qn partir/entrer/etc** *(permettre)* to let s.o. go/come in/etc; **l. qch à qn** *(confier, donner)* to let s.o. have sth, leave sth with s.o.; *(vendre)* to let s.o. have sth; **laissez-moi le temps de le faire** give me *ou* leave me time to do it; **se l. aller/faire** to let oneself go/be pushed around. ◆**laissé(e)-pour-compte** *nmf (personne)* misfit, reject. ◆**laisser-aller** *nm inv* carelessness, slovenliness; ◆**laissez-passer** *nm inv (sauf-conduit)* pass.
lait [lɛ] *nm* milk; **frère/sœur de l.** foster-brother/-sister; **dent de l.** milk tooth. ◆**laitage** *nm* milk product *ou* food. ◆**laiterie** *nf* dairy. ◆**laiteux, -euse** *a* milky. ◆**laitier, -ière** *a (produits)* dairy-; — *nm (livreur)* milkman; *(vendeur)* dairyman; — *nf* dairywoman.
laiton [lɛtɔ̃] *nm* brass.

laitue [lety] *nf* lettuce.

laïus [lajys] *nm Fam* speech.

lama [lama] *nm* (*animal*) llama.

lambeau, -x [lɑ̃bo] *nm* shred, bit; **mettre en lambeaux** to tear to shreds; **tomber en lambeaux** to fall to bits.

lambin, -ine [lɑ̃bɛ̃, -in] *nmf* dawdler. ◆**lambiner** *vi* to dawdle.

lambris [lɑ̃bri] *nm* panelling. ◆**lambrisser** *vt* to panel.

lame [lam] *nf* **1** (*de couteau, rasoir etc*) blade; (*de métal*) strip, plate; **l. de parquet** floorboard. **2** (*vague*) wave; **l. de fond** ground swell.

lamelle [lamel] *nf* thin strip; **l. de verre** (*pour microscope*) slide.

lamenter (se) [səlamɑ̃te] *vpr* to moan, lament; **se l. sur** to lament (over). ◆**lamentable** *a* (*mauvais*) deplorable; (*voix, cri*) mournful. ◆**lamentation** *nf* lament(ation).

laminé [lamine] *a* (*métal*) laminated.

lampadaire [lɑ̃pader] *nm* standard lamp; (*de rue*) street lamp.

lampe [lɑ̃p] *nf* lamp; (*au néon*) light; (*de vieille radio*) valve, *Am* (vacuum) tube; **l. de poche** torch, *Am* flashlight.

lampée [lɑ̃pe] *nf Fam* gulp.

lampion [lɑ̃pjɔ̃] *nm* Chinese lantern.

lance [lɑ̃s] *nf* spear; (*de tournoi*) *Hist* lance; (*extrémité de tuyau*) nozzle; **l. d'incendie** fire hose.

lance-flammes [lɑ̃sflam] *nm inv* flame thrower. ◆**l.-pierres** *nm inv* catapult. ◆**l.-roquettes** *nm inv* rocket launcher.

lanc/er [lɑ̃se] *vt* (*jeter*) to throw (**à** to); (*avec force*) to hurl; (*navire, mode, acteur, idée*) to launch; (*regard*) to cast (**à** at); (*moteur*) to start; (*ultimatum*) to issue; (*bombe*) to drop; (*gifle*) to give; (*cri*) to utter; **— se l.** *vpr* (*se précipiter*) to rush; **se l. dans** (*aventure, discussion*) to launch into; **— nm un l.** a throw; **le l. de** the throwing of. ◆**—ée** *nf* momentum. ◆**—ement** *nm Sp* throwing; (*de fusée, navire etc*) launch(ing).

lancinant [lɑ̃sinɑ̃] *a* (*douleur*) shooting; (*obsédant*) haunting.

landau [lɑ̃do] *nm* (*pl* **-s**) pram, *Am* baby carriage.

lande [lɑ̃d] *nf* moor, heath.

langage [lɑ̃gaʒ] *nm* (*système, faculté d'expression*) language; **l. machine** computer language.

lange [lɑ̃ʒ] *nm* (baby) blanket. ◆**langer** *vt* (*bébé*) to change.

langouste [lɑ̃gust] *nf* (spiny) lobster. ◆**langoustine** *nf* (Dublin) prawn, Norway lobster.

langue [lɑ̃g] *nf Anat* tongue; *Ling* language; **de l. anglaise/française** English-/French-speaking; **l. maternelle** mother tongue; **mauvaise l.** (*personne*) gossip. ◆**languette** *nf* (*patte*) tongue.

langueur [lɑ̃gœr] *nf* languor. ◆**langu/ir** *vi* to languish (**après** for, after); (*conversation*) to flag. ◆**—issant** *a* languid; (*conversation*) flagging.

lanière [lanjer] *nf* strap; (*d'étoffe*) strip.

lanterne [lɑ̃tern] *nf* lantern; (*électrique*) lamp; *pl Aut* sidelights.

lanterner [lɑ̃terne] *vi* to loiter.

lapalissade [lapalisad] *nf* statement of the obvious, truism.

laper [lape] *vt* (*boire*) to lap up; **—** *vi* to lap.

lapider [lapide] *vt* to stone.

lapin [lapɛ̃] *nm* rabbit; **mon (petit) l.!** my dear!; **poser un l. à qn** *Fam* to stand s.o. up.

laps [laps] *nm* **un l. de temps** a lapse of time.

lapsus [lapsys] *nm* slip (of the tongue).

laquais [lakɛ] *nm Hist & Fig* lackey.

laque [lak] *nf* lacquer; **l. à cheveux** hair spray, (hair) lacquer. ◆**laquer** *vt* to lacquer.

laquelle [lakɛl] *voir* **lequel**.

larbin [larbɛ̃] *nm Fam* flunkey.

lard [lar] *nm* (*fumé*) bacon; (*gras*) (pig's) fat. ◆**lardon** *nm Culin* strip of bacon *ou* fat.

large [larʒ] *a* wide, broad; (*vêtement*) loose; (*idées, esprit*) broad; (*grand*) large; (*généreux*) liberal; **l. d'esprit** broad-minded; **l. de six mètres** six metres wide; **—** *adv* (*calculer*) liberally, broadly; **— nm** breadth, width; **avoir six mètres de l.** to be six metres wide; **le l.** (*mer*) the open sea; **au l. de Cherbourg** *Nau* off Cherbourg; **être au l.** to have lots of room. ◆**—ment** *adv* widely; (*ouvrir*) wide; (*servir, payer*) liberally; (*au moins*) easily; **avoir l. le temps** to have plenty of time, have ample time. ◆**largesse** *nf* liberality. ◆**largeur** *nf* width, breadth; (*d'esprit*) breadth.

larguer [large] *vt* (*bombe, parachutiste*) to drop; **l. qn** (*se débarrasser de*) to drop s.o.; **l. les amarres** *Nau* to cast off.

larme [larm] *nf* tear; (*goutte*) *Fam* drop; **en larmes** in tears; **rire aux larmes** to laugh till one cries. ◆**larmoyer** *vi* (*yeux*) to water.

larve [larv] *nf* (*d'insecte*) larva, grub.

larvé [larve] *a* latent, underlying.

larynx [larɛ̃ks] *nm Anat* larynx ◆**laryngite** *nf Méd* laryngitis.

las, lasse [lɑ, lɑs] *a* tired, weary (**de** of).

◆**lasser** *vt* to tire, weary; **se l. de** to tire of.
◆**lassitude** *nf* tiredness, weariness.
lascar [laskar] *nm Fam* (clever) fellow.
lascif, -ive [lasif, -iv] *a* lascivious.
laser [lazɛr] *nm* laser.
lasso [laso] *nm* lasso.
latent [latɑ̃] *a* latent.
latéral, -aux [lateral, -o] *a* lateral, side-.
latin, -ine [latɛ̃, -in] *a* & *nmf* Latin; − *nm* (*langue*) Latin.
latitude [latityd] *nf Géog* & *Fig* latitude.
latrines [latrin] *nfpl* latrines.
latte [lat] *nf* slat, lath; (*de plancher*) board.
lauréat, -ate [lɔrea, -at] *nmf* (prize)winner; − *a* prize-winning.
laurier [lɔrje] *nm Bot* laurel, bay; **du l.** *Culin* bay leaves.
lavabo [lavabo] *nm* washbasin, sink; *pl* (*cabinet*) toilet(s), *Am* washroom.
lavande [lavɑ̃d] *nf* lavender.
lave [lav] *nf Géol* lava.
lave-auto [lavoto] *nm* car wash. ◆**l.-glace** *nm* windscreen *ou Am* windshield washer.
◆**l.-linge** *nm* washing machine.
◆**l.-vaisselle** *nm* dishwasher.
laver [lave] *vt* to wash; **l. qn de** (*soupçon etc*) to clear s.o. of; − **se l.** *vpr* to wash (oneself), *Am* wash up; **se l. les mains** to wash one's hands (*Fig* of of). ◆**lavable** *a* washable. ◆**lavage** *nm* washing; **l. de cerveau** *Psy* brainwashing. ◆**laverie** *nf* (*automatique*) launderette, *Am* laundromat.
◆**lavette** *nf* dish cloth; (*homme*) *Péj* drip.
◆**laveur** *nm* **l. de carreaux** window cleaner *ou Am* washer. ◆**lavoir** *nm* (*bâtiment*) washhouse.
laxatif, -ive [laksatif, -iv] *nm* & *a Méd* laxative.
laxisme [laksism] *nm* permissiveness, laxity. ◆**laxiste** *a* permissive, lax.
layette [lɛjɛt] *nf* baby clothes, layette.
le, la, *pl* **les** [l(ə), la, le] (**le** & **la** *become* **l'** *before a vowel or mute h*) **1** *art déf* (à + **le** = **au**, à + **les** = **aux**; **de** + **le** = **du**, **de** + **les** = **des**); **le garçon** the boy; **la fille** the girl; **venez, les enfants!** come children!; **les petits/rouges/***etc* the little ones/red ones/*etc*; **mon ami le plus intime** my closest friend. **2** (*généralisation, abstraction*) **la beauté** beauty; **la France** France; **les Français** the French; **les hommes** men; **aimer le café** to like coffee. **3** (*possession*) **il ouvrit la bouche** he opened his mouth; **se blesser au pied** to hurt one's foot; **avoir les cheveux blonds** to have blond hair. **4** (*mesure*) **dix francs le kilo** ten francs a kilo. **5** (*temps*) **elle vient le lundi** she comes on Monday(s);

elle passe le soir she comes over in the evening(s); **l'an prochain** next year; **une fois l'an** once a year. **6** *pron* (*homme*) him; (*femme*) her; (*chose, animal*) it; *pl* them; **je la vois** I see her; I see it; **je le vois** I see him; I see it; **je les vois** I see them; **es-tu fatigué? − je le suis** are you tired? − I am; **je le crois** I think so.
leader [lidœr] *nm Pol* leader.
lécher [leʃe] *vt* to lick; **se l. les doigts** to lick one's fingers. ◆**lèche-vitrines** *nm* **faire du l.-vitrines** to go window-shopping.
leçon [ləsɔ̃] *nf* lesson; **faire la l. à qn** to lecture s.o.
lecteur, -trice [lɛktœr, -tris] *nmf* reader; *Univ* (foreign language) assistant; **l. de cassettes** cassette player. ◆**lecture** *nf* reading; *pl* (*livres*) books; **faire de la l. à qn** to read to s.o.; **de la l.** some reading matter.
légal, -aux [legal, -o] *a* legal; (*médecine*) forensic. ◆**légalement** *adv* legally. ◆**légaliser** *vt* to legalize. ◆**légalité** *nf* legality (**de** of); **respecter la l.** to respect the law.
légation [legasjɔ̃] *nf Pol* legation.
légende [leʒɑ̃d] *nf* **1** (*histoire, fable*) legend. **2** (*de plan, carte*) key, legend; (*de photo*) caption. ◆**légendaire** *a* legendary.
léger, -ère [leʒe, -er] *a* light; (*bruit, faute, fièvre etc*) slight; (*café, thé, argument*) weak; (*bière, tabac*) mild; (*frivole*) frivolous; (*irréfléchi*) careless; **à la légère** (*agir*) rashly. ◆**légèrement** *adv* lightly; (*un peu*) slightly; (*à la légère*) rashly. ◆**légèreté** *nf* lightness; frivolity.
légiférer [leʒifere] *vi* to legislate.
légion [leʒjɔ̃] *nf Mil* & *Fig* legion. ◆**légionnaire** *nm* (*de la Légion étrangère*) legionnaire.
législatif, -ive [leʒislatif, -iv] *a* legislative; (*élections*) parliamentary. ◆**législation** *nf* legislation. ◆**législature** *nf* (*période*) *Pol* term of office.
légitime [leʒitim] *a* (*action, enfant etc*) legitimate; **en état de l. défense** acting in self-defence. ◆**légitimité** *nf* legitimacy.
legs [lɛg] *nm Jur* legacy, bequest; (*héritage*) *Fig* legacy. ◆**léguer** *vt* to bequeath (**à** to).
légume [legym] **1** *nm* vegetable. **2** *nf* **grosse l.** (*personne*) *Fam* bigwig.
lendemain [lɑ̃dmɛ̃] *nm* **le l.** the next day; (*avenir*) **le l.** the future; **le l. de** the day after; **le l. matin** the next morning.
lent [lɑ̃] *a* slow. ◆**lentement** *adv* slowly. ◆**lenteur** *nf* slowness.
lentille [lɑ̃tij] *nf* **1** *Bot Culin* lentil. **2** (*verre*) lens.
léopard [leɔpar] *nm* leopard.

lèpre [lɛpr] *nf* leprosy. ◆**lépreux, -euse** *a* leprous; − *nmf* leper.

lequel, laquelle, *pl* **lesquels, lesquelles** [ləkɛl, lakɛl, lekɛl] (+ à = **auquel, à laquelle, auxquel(le)s;** + de = **duquel, de laquelle, desquel(le)s**) *pron* (*chose, animal*) which; (*personne*) who, (*indirect*) whom; (*interrogatif*) which (one); **dans l.** in which; **parmi lesquels** (*choses, animaux*) among which; (*personnes*) among whom; **l. préférez-vous?** which (one) do you prefer?

les [le] *voir* **le.**

lesbienne [lɛsbjɛn] *nf* & *af* lesbian.

léser [leze] *vt* (*personne*) *Jur* to wrong.

lésiner [lezine] *vi* to be stingy (**sur** with).

lésion [lezjɔ̃] *nf* *Méd* lesion.

lessive [lesiv] *nf* (*produit*) washing powder; (*linge*) washing; **faire la l.** to do the wash(ing). ◆**lessiv/er** *vt* to scrub, wash. ◆**−é** *a* *Fam* (*fatigué*) washed-out; (*ruiné*) washed-up. ◆**−euse** *nf* (laundry) boiler.

lest [lɛst] *nm* ballast. ◆**lester** *vt* to ballast, weight down; (*remplir*) *Fam* to overload.

leste [lɛst] *a* (*agile*) nimble; (*grivois*) coarse.

léthargie [letarʒi] *nf* lethargy. ◆**léthargique** *a* lethargic.

lettre [lɛtr] *nf* (*missive, caractère*) letter; **en toutes lettres** (*mot*) in full; (*nombre*) in words; **les lettres** (*discipline*) *Univ* arts; **homme de lettres** man of letters. ◆**lettré, -ée** *a* well-read; − *nmf* scholar.

leucémie [løsemi] *nf* leuk(a)emia.

leur [lœr] **1** *a poss* their; **l. chat** their cat; **leurs voitures** their cars; − *pron poss* **le l., la l., les leurs** theirs. **2** *pron inv* (*indirect*) (to) them; **il l. est facile de . . .** it's easy for them to . . . .

leurre [lœr] *nm* illusion; (*tromperie*) trickery. ◆**leurrer** *vt* to delude.

lev/er [l(ə)ve] *vt* to lift (up), raise; (*blocus, interdiction*) to lift; (*séance*) to close; (*camp*) to strike; (*plan*) to draw up; (*impôts, armée*) to levy; **l. les yeux** to look up; − *vi* (*pâte*) to rise; (*blé*) to come up; − **se l.** *vpr* to get up; (*soleil, rideau*) (*jour*) to break; (*brume*) to clear, lift; − *nm* **le l. du soleil** sunrise; **le l. du rideau** *Th* the curtain. ◆**−ant** *a* (*soleil*) rising; − *nm* **le l.** the east. ◆**−é** *a* **être l.** (*debout*) to be up. ◆**−ée** *nf* (*d'interdiction*) lifting; (*d'impôts*) levying; (*du courrier*) collection; **l. de boucliers** public outcry.

levier [ləvje] *nm* lever; (*pour soulever*) crowbar.

lèvre [lɛvr] *nf* lip; **du bout des lèvres** half-heartedly, grudgingly.

lévrier [levrije] *nm* greyhound.

levure [ləvyr] *nf* yeast.

lexique [lɛksik] *nm* vocabulary, glossary.

lézard [lezar] *nm* lizard.

lézarde [lezard] *nf* crack, split. ◆**lézarder 1** *vi* *Fam* to bask in the sun. **2 se l.** *vpr* to crack, split.

liaison [ljɛzɔ̃] *nf* (*rapport*) connection; (*routière etc*) link; *Gram Mil* liaison; **l. (amoureuse)** love affair; **en l. avec qn** in contact with s.o.

liane [ljan] *nf* *Bot* jungle vine.

liant [ljɑ̃] *a* sociable.

liasse [ljas] *nf* bundle.

Liban [libɑ̃] *nm* Lebanon. ◆**libanais, -aise** *a* & *nmf* Lebanese.

libell/er [libele] *vt* (*contrat etc*) to word, draw up; (*chèque*) to make out. ◆**−é** *nm* wording.

libellule [libelyl] *nf* dragonfly.

libéral, -ale, -aux [liberal, -o] *a* & *nmf* liberal. ◆**libéraliser** *vt* to liberalize. ◆**libéralisme** *nm* liberalism. ◆**libéralité** *nf* liberality; (*don*) liberal gift.

libérer [libere] *vt* (*prisonnier etc*) to (set) free, release; (*pays, esprit*) to liberate (**de** from); **l. qn de** to free s.o. of *ou* from; − **se l.** *vpr* to get free, free oneself (**de** of, from). ◆**libérateur, -trice** *a* (*sentiment etc*) liberating; − *nmf* liberator. ◆**libération** *nf* freeing, release; liberation; **l. conditionnelle** *Jur* parole. ◆**liberté** *nf* freedom, liberty; **en l. provisoire** *Jur* on bail; **mettre en l.** to free, release; **mise en l.** release.

libraire [librɛr] *nmf* bookseller. ◆**librairie** *nf* (*magasin*) bookshop.

libre [libr] *a* free (**de qch** from sth, **de faire** to do); (*voie, route*) clear; (*place*) vacant, free; (*école*) private (and religious); **l. penseur** freethinker. ◆**l.-échange** *nm* *Écon* free trade. ◆**l.-service** *nm* (*pl* **libres-services**) (*système, magasin etc*) self-service. ◆**librement** *adv* freely.

Libye [libi] *nf* Libya. ◆**libyen, -enne** *a* & *nmf* Libyan.

licence [lisɑ̃s] *nf* *Sp Com Littér* licence; *Univ* (bachelor's) degree; **l. ès lettres/sciences** arts/science degree, = BA/BSc, = *Am* BA/BS. ◆**licencié, -ée** *a* & *nmf* graduate; **l. ès lettres/sciences** bachelor of arts/science, = BA/BSc = *Am* BA/BS.

licencier [lisɑ̃sje] *vt* (*ouvrier*) to lay off, dismiss. ◆**licenciement** *nm* dismissal.

licite [lisit] *a* licit, lawful.

licorne [likɔrn] *nf* unicorn.

lie [li] *nf* dregs.

liège [ljɛʒ] *nm* (*matériau*) cork.

lien [ljɛ̃] *nm* (*rapport*) link, connection; (*de*

parenté) tie, bond; (*attache, ficelle*) tie. ◆**lier** *vt* (*attacher*) to tie (up), bind; (*relier*) to link (up), connect; (*conversation, amitié*) to strike up; **l. qn** (*unir, engager*) to bind s.o.; **— se l.** *vpr* (*idées etc*) to connect, link together; **se l. avec qn** to make friends with s.o.; **amis très liés** very close friends.

lierre [ljɛr] *nm* ivy.

lieu, -x [ljø] *nm* place; (*d'un accident*) scene; **les lieux** (*locaux*) the premises; **sur les lieux** on the spot; **avoir l.** to take place, be held; **au l. de** instead of; **avoir l. de faire** (*des raisons*) to have good reason to do; **en premier l.** in the first place, firstly; **en dernier l.** lastly; **l. commun** commonplace. ◆**l.-dit** *nm* (*pl* **lieux-dits**) *Géog* locality.

lieue [ljø] *nf* (*mesure*) *Hist* league.

lieutenant [ljøtnā] *nm* lieutenant.

lièvre [ljɛvr] *nm* hare.

ligament [ligamā] *nm* ligament.

ligne [liɲ] *nf* (*trait, règle, contour, transport*) line; (*belle silhouette de femme etc*) figure; (*rangée*) row, line; **(se) mettre en l.** to line up; **en l.** *Tél* connected, through; **entrer en l. de compte** to be of consequence, count; **faire entrer en l. de compte** to take into account; **grande l.** *Rail* main line; **les grandes lignes** *Fig* the broad outline; **pilote de l.** airline pilot; **à la l.** *Gram* new paragraph.

lignée [liɲe] *nf* line, ancestry.

ligoter [ligɔte] *vt* to tie up.

ligue [lig] *nf* (*alliance*) league. ◆**se liguer** *vpr* to join together, gang up (**contre** against).

lilas [lila] *nm* lilac; *– a inv* (*couleur*) lilac.

limace [limas] *nf* (*mollusque*) slug.

limaille [limaj] *nf* filings.

limande [limād] *nf* (*poisson*) dab.

lime [lim] *nf* (*outil*) file. ◆**limer** *vt* to file.

limier [limje] *nm* (*chien*) bloodhound.

limite [limit] *nf* limit; (*de propriété, jardin etc*) boundary; *pl Fb* boundary lines; **dépasser la l.** to go beyond the bounds; *– a* (*cas*) extreme; (*vitesse, prix, âge etc*) maximum; **date l.** latest date, deadline; **date l. de vente** *Com* sell-by date. ◆**limitatif, -ive** *a* restrictive. ◆**limitation** *nf* limitation; (*de vitesse*) limit. ◆**limiter** *vt* to limit, restrict; (*délimiter*) to border; **se l. à faire** to limit *ou* restrict oneself to doing.

limoger [limɔʒe] *vt* (*destituer*) to dismiss.

limonade [limɔnad] *nf* (*fizzy*) lemonade.

limpide [lɛ̃pid] *a* (*eau, explication*) (crystal) clear. ◆**limpidité** *nf* clearness.

lin [lɛ̃] *nm Bot* flax; (*tissu*) linen; **huile de l.** linseed oil.

linceul [lɛ̃sœl] *nm* shroud.

linéaire [lineɛr] *a* linear.

linge [lɛ̃ʒ] *nm* (*pièces de tissu*) linen; (*à laver*) washing, linen; (*torchon*) cloth; **l.** (*de corps*) underwear. ◆**lingerie** *nf* (*de femmes*) underwear; (*local*) linen room.

lingot [lɛ̃go] *nm* ingot.

linguiste [lɛ̃gɥist] *nmf* linguist. ◆**linguistique** *a* linguistic; *– nf* linguistics.

lino [lino] *nm* lino. ◆**linoléum** *nm* linoleum.

linotte [linɔt] *nf* (*oiseau*) linnet; **tête de l.** *Fig* scatterbrain.

lion [ljɔ̃] *nm* lion. ◆**lionceau, -x** *nm* lion cub. ◆**lionne** *nf* lioness.

liquéfier [likefje] *vt*, **— se l.** *vpr* to liquefy.

liqueur [likœr] *nf* liqueur.

liquide [likid] *a* a liquid; **argent l.** ready cash; *– nm* liquid; **du l.** (*argent*) ready cash.

liquider [likide] *vt* (*dette, stock etc*) to liquidate; (*affaire, travail*) to wind up, finish off; **l. qn** (*tuer*) *Fam* to liquidate s.o. ◆**liquidation** *nf* liquidation; winding up; (*vente*) (clearance) sale.

lire[1] [lir] *vti* to read.

lire[2] [lir] *nf* (*monnaie*) lira.

lis[1] [lis] *nm* (*plante, fleur*) lily.

lis[2], **lisent** [li, liz] *voir* **lire**[1].

liseron [lizrɔ̃] *nm Bot* convolvulus.

lisible [lizibl] *a* (*écriture*) legible; (*livre*) readable. ◆**lisiblement** *adv* legibly.

lisière [lizjɛr] *nf* edge, border.

lisse [lis] *a* smooth. ◆**lisser** *vt* to smooth; (*plumes*) to preen.

liste [list] *nf* list; **l. électorale** register of electors, electoral roll; **sur la l. rouge** *Tél* ex-directory, *Am* unlisted.

lit[1] [li] *nm* bed; **l. d'enfant** cot, *Am* crib; **lits superposés** bunk beds; **garder le l.** to stay in bed. ◆**literie** *nf* bedding, bed clothes.

lit[2] [li] *voir* **lire**[1].

litanie [litani] **1** *nf* (*énumération*) long list (**de** of). **2** *nfpl* (*prière*) *Rel* litany.

litière [litjɛr] *nf* (*couche de paille*) litter.

litige [litiʒ] *nm* dispute; *Jur* litigation. ◆**litigieux, -euse** *a* contentious.

litre [litr] *nm* litre.

littéraire [literɛr] *a* literary. ◆**littérature** *nf* literature.

littéral, -aux [literal, -o] *a* literal. ◆**—ement** *adv* literally.

littoral, -aux [litɔral, -o] *a* coastal; *– nm* coast(line).

liturgie [lityrʒi] *nf* liturgy. ◆**liturgique** *a* liturgical.

livide [livid] *a* (*bleuâtre*) livid; (*pâle*) (ghastly) pale, pallid.

livre [livr] **1** *nm* book; **l. de bord** *Nau* log-

book; **l. de poche** paperback (book); **le l.,
l'industrie du l.** the book industry. **2** *nf*
(*monnaie, poids*) pound. ◆**livresque** *a*
(*savoir*) *Péj* bookish. ◆**livret** *nm* (*registre*)
book; *Mus* libretto; **l. scolaire** school report book; **l. de famille** family registration
book; **l. de caisse d'épargne** bankbook,
passbook.

livrée [livre] *nf* (*uniforme*) livery.

livrer [livre] *vt* (*marchandises*) to deliver (**à**
to); (*secret*) to give away; **l. qn à** (*la police
etc*) to give s.o. up *ou* over to; **l. bataille** to
do *ou* join battle; **— se l.** *vpr* (*se rendre*) to
give oneself up (**à** to); (*se confier*) to confide
(**à** in); **se l. à** (*habitude, excès etc*) to indulge
in; (*tâche*) to devote oneself to; (*désespoir,
destin*) to abandon oneself to. ◆**livraison**
nf delivery. ◆**livreur, -euse** *nmf* delivery
man, delivery woman.

lobe [lɔb] *nm Anat* lobe.

local, -aux [lɔkal, -o] **1** *a* local. **2** *nm & nmpl*
(*pièce, bâtiment*) premises. ◆**localement**
adv. locally. ◆**localiser** *vt* (*déterminer*) to
locate; (*limiter*) to localize. ◆**localité** *nf*
locality.

locataire [lɔkatɛr] *nmf* tenant; (*hôte payant*)
lodger.

location [lɔkasjɔ̃] *nf* (*de maison etc*) renting;
(*à bail*) leasing; (*de voiture*) hiring; (*réservation*) booking; (*par propriétaire*) renting
(out), letting; leasing (out); hiring (out);
(*loyer*) rental; (*bail*) lease; **bureau de l.**
booking office; **en l.** on hire.

lock-out [lɔkawt] *nm inv* (*industriel*) lock-
out.

locomotion [lɔkɔmosjɔ̃] *nf* locomotion.
◆**locomotive** *nf* locomotive, engine.

locuteur [lɔkytœr] *nm Ling* speaker.
◆**locution** *nf* phrase, idiom; *Gram*
phrase.

logarithme [lɔgaritm] *nm* logarithm.

loge [lɔʒ] *nf* (*de concierge*) lodge; (*d'acteur*)
dressing-room; (*de spectateur*) *Th* box.

log/er [lɔʒe] *vt* (*recevoir, mettre*) to accommodate, house; (*héberger*) to put up; **être
logé et nourri** to have board and lodging; **—
vi** (*à l'hôtel etc*) to put up, lodge; (*habiter*)
to live; (**trouver à**) **se l.** to find somewhere
to live; (*temporairement*) to find somewhere to stay; **se l. dans** (*balle*) to lodge
(itself) in. ◆**—eable** *a* habitable.
◆**—ement** *nm* accommodation, lodging;
(*habitat*) housing; (*appartement*) lodgings,
flat, *Am* apartment; (*maison*) dwelling.
◆**—eur, -euse** *nmf* landlord, landlady.

logiciel [lɔʒisjɛl] *nm* (*d'un ordinateur*) software *inv*.

logique [lɔʒik] *a* logical; **–** *nf* logic.
◆**—ment** *adv* logically.

logistique [lɔʒistik] *nf* logistics.

logo [lɔgo] *nm* logo.

loi [lwa] *nf* law; *Pol* act; **projet de l.** *Pol* bill;
faire la l. to lay down the law (**à** to).

loin [lwɛ̃] *adv* far (away *ou* off); **Boston est l.
(de Paris)** Boston is a long way away (from
Paris); **plus l.** further, farther; (*ci-après*)
further on; **l. de là** *Fig* far from it; **au l.** in
the distance, far away; **de l.** from a distance; (*de beaucoup*) by far; **de l. en l.** every
so often. ◆**lointain** *a* distant, far-off; **–**
nm **dans le l.** in the distance.

loir [lwar] *nm* (*animal*) dormouse.

loisir [lwazir] *nm* **le l. de faire** the time to do;
moment de l. moment of leisure; **loisirs**
(*temps libre*) spare time, leisure (time); (*dis-
tractions*) spare-time *ou* leisure activities.

Londres [lɔ̃dr] *nm ou f* London.
◆**londonien, -ienne** *a* London-; **–** *nmf*
Londoner.

long, longue [lɔ̃, lɔ̃g] *a* long; **être l. (à faire)**
to be a long time *ou* slow (in doing); **l. de
deux mètres** two metres long; **– nm avoir
deux mètres de l.** to be two metres long;
tomber de tout son l. to fall flat; (**tout**) **le l.
de** (*espace*) (all) along; **tout le l. de** (*temps*)
throughout; **de l. en large** (*marcher etc*) up
and down; **en l. et en large** thoroughly; **en
l.** lengthwise; **à la longue** in the long run.
◆**l.-courrier** *nm Av* long-distance airliner.
◆**longue-vue** *nf* (*pl* **longues-vues**) telescope.

longer [lɔ̃ʒe] *vt* to pass *ou* go along; (*forêt,
mer*) to skirt; (*mur*) to hug.

longévité [lɔ̃ʒevite] *nf* longevity.

longitude [lɔ̃ʒityd] *nf* longitude.

longtemps [lɔ̃tɑ̃] *adv* (for) a long time;
trop/avant l. too/before long; **aussi l. que**
as long as.

longue [lɔ̃g] *voir* **long.** ◆**longuement** *adv*
at length. ◆**longuet, -ette** *a Fam* (fairly)
lengthy. ◆**longueur** *nf* length; *pl* (*de
texte, film*) over-long passages; **saut en l.** *Sp*
long jump; **à l. de journée** all day long; **l.
d'onde** *Rad & Fig* wavelength.

lopin [lɔpɛ̃] *nm* **l. de terre** plot *ou* patch of
land.

loquace [lɔkas] *a* loquacious.

loque [lɔk] **1** *nfpl* rags. **2** *nf* **l. (humaine)**
(*personne*) human wreck.

loquet [lɔkɛ] *nm* latch.

lorgner [lɔrɲe] *vt* (*regarder, convoiter*) to
eye.

lors [lɔr] *adv* **l. de** at the time of; **depuis l.,**

dès l. from then on; **dès l. que** (*puisque*) since.

losange [lɔzɑ̃ʒ] *nm Géom* diamond, lozenge.

lot [lo] *nm* **1** (*de loterie*) prize; **gros l.** top prize, jackpot. **2** (*portion, destin*) lot. ◆**loterie** *nf* lottery, raffle. ◆**lotir** *vt* (*terrain*) to divide into lots; **bien loti** *Fig* favoured by fortune. ◆**lotissement** *nm* (*terrain*) building plot; (*habitations*) housing estate *ou* development.

lotion [losjɔ̃] *nf* lotion.

loto [lɔto] *nm* (*jeu*) lotto.

louche [luʃ] **1** *a* (*suspect*) shady, fishy. **2** *nf Culin* ladle.

loucher [luʃe] *vi* to squint; **l. sur** *Fam* to eye.

louer [lwe] *vt* **1** (*prendre en location*) to rent (*house, flat etc*); (*à bail*) to lease; (*voiture*) to hire, rent; (*réserver*) to book; (*donner en location*) to rent (out), let; to lease (out); to hire (out); **maison/chambre à l.** house/room to let. **2** (*exalter*) to praise (**de** for); **se l. de** to be highly satisfied with. ◆**louable** *a* praiseworthy, laudable. ◆**louange** *nf* praise; **à la l. de** in praise of.

loufoque [lufɔk] *a* (*fou*) *Fam* nutty, crazy.

loukoum [lukum] *nm* Turkish delight.

loup [lu] *nm* wolf; **avoir une faim de l.** to be ravenous. ◆**l.-garou** *nm* (*pl* **loups-garous**) werewolf.

loupe [lup] *nf* magnifying glass.

louper [lupe] *vt Fam* (*train etc*) to miss; (*examen*) to fail; (*travail*) to mess up.

lourd [lur] *a* heavy (*Fig* **de** with); (*temps, chaleur*) close, sultry; (*faute*) gross; (*tâche*) arduous; (*esprit*) dull; – *adv* **peser l.** (*malle etc*) to be heavy. ◆**lourdaud, -aude** *a* loutish, oafish; – *nmf* lout, oaf. ◆**lourdement** *adv* heavily. ◆**lourdeur** *nf* heaviness; (*de temps*) closeness; (*d'esprit*) dullness.

loutre [lutr] *nf* otter.

louve [luv] *nf* she-wolf. ◆**louveteau, -x** *nm* (*scout*) cub (scout).

louvoyer [luvwaje] *vi* (*tergiverser*) to hedge, be evasive.

loyal, -aux [lwajal, -o] *a* (*fidèle*) loyal (**envers** to); (*honnête*) honest, fair (**envers** to). ◆**loyalement** *adv* loyally; fairly. ◆**loyauté** *nf* loyalty; honesty, fairness.

loyer [lwaje] *nm* rent.

lu [ly] *voir* **lire** ¹.

lubie [lybi] *nf* whim.

lubrifi/er [lybrifje] *vt* to lubricate. ◆**—ant** *nm* lubricant.

lubrique [lybrik] *a* lewd, lustful.

lucarne [lykarn] *nf* (*ouverture*) skylight; (*fenêtre*) dormer window.

lucide [lysid] *a* lucid. ◆**lucidité** *nf* lucidity.

lucratif, -ive [lykratif, -iv] *a* lucrative.

lueur [lɥœr] *nf* (*lumière*) & *Fig* glimmer.

luge [lyʒ] *nf* toboggan, sledge.

lugubre [lygybr] *a* gloomy, lugubrious.

lui [lɥi] **1** *pron mf* (*complément indirect*) (to) him; (*femme*) (to) her; (*chose, animal*) (to) it; **je le lui ai montré** I showed it to him *ou* to her, I showed him it *ou* her it; **il lui est facile de . . .** it's easy for him *ou* her to . . . . **2** *pron m* (*complément direct*) him; (*chose, animal*) it; (*sujet emphatique*) he; **pour lui** for him; **plus grand que lui** taller than him; **il ne pense qu'à lui** he only thinks of himself. ◆**lui-même** *pron* himself; (*chose, animal*) itself.

luire* [lɥir] *vi* to shine, gleam. ◆**luisant** *a* (*métal etc*) shiny.

lumbago [lɔ̃bago] *nm* lumbago.

lumière [lymjɛr] *nf* light; **à la l. de** by the light of; (*grâce à*) *Fig* in the light of; **faire toute la l. sur** *Fig* to clear up; **mettre en l.** to bring to light. ◆**luminaire** *nm* (*appareil*) lighting appliance. ◆**lumineux, -euse** *a* (*idée, ciel etc*) bright, brilliant; (*ondes, source etc*) light-; (*cadran, corps etc*) *Tech* luminous.

lunaire [lynɛr] *a* lunar; **clarté l.** light *ou* brightness of the moon.

lunatique [lynatik] *a* temperamental.

lunch [lœ̃ʃ, lœntʃ] *nm* buffet lunch, snack.

lundi [lœ̃di] *nm* Monday.

lune [lyn] *nf* moon; **l. de miel** honeymoon.

lunette [lynɛt] *nf* **1** **lunettes** glasses, spectacles; (*de protection, de plongée*) goggles; **lunettes de soleil** sunglasses. **2** (*astronomique*) telescope; **l. arrière** *Aut* rear window.

lurette [lyrɛt] *nf* **il y a belle l.** a long time ago.

luron [lyrɔ̃] *nm* **gai l.** gay fellow.

lustre [lystr] *nm* (*éclairage*) chandelier; (*éclat*) lustre. ◆**lustré** *a* (*par l'usure*) shiny.

luth [lyt] *nm Mus* lute.

lutin [lytɛ̃] *nm* elf, imp, goblin.

lutte [lyt] *nf* fight, struggle; *Sp* wrestling; **l. des classes** class warfare *ou* struggle. ◆**lutter** *vi* to fight, struggle; *Sp* to wrestle. ◆**lutteur, -euse** *nmf* fighter; *Sp* wrestler.

luxe [lyks] *nm* luxury; **un l. de** a wealth of; **de l.** (*article*) luxury-; (*modèle*) de luxe. ◆**luxueux, -euse** *a* luxurious.

Luxembourg [lyksɑ̃bur] *nm* Luxembourg.

luxure [lyksyr] *nf* lewdness, lust.

luxuriant [lyksyrjɑ̃] *a* luxuriant.

luzerne [lyzɛrn] *nf Bot* lucerne, *Am* alfalfa.

lycée [lise] *nm* (secondary) school, *Am* high school. ◆**lycéen, -enne** *nmf* pupil (*at lycée*).

lymphathique [lɛ̃fatik] *a* (*apathique*) sluggish.

lynch/er [lɛ̃ʃe] *vt* to lynch. ◆—**age** *nm* lynching.

lynx [lɛ̃ks] *nm* (*animal*) lynx.

lyre [lir] *nf Mus Hist* lyre.

lyrique [lirik] *a* (*poème etc*) lyric; (*passionné*) *Fig* lyrical. ◆**lyrisme** *nm* lyricism.

lys [lis] *nm* (*plante, fleur*) lily.

M

M, m [ɛm] *nm* M, m.

m *abrév* (*mètre*) metre.

M [məsjø] *abrév* = **Monsieur.**

m' [m] *voir* me.

ma [ma] *voir* mon.

macabre [makabr] *a* macabre, gruesome.

macadam [makadam] *nm* (*goudron*) tarmac.

macaron [makarɔ̃] *nm* (*gâteau*) macaroon; (*insigne*) (round) badge.

macaroni(s) [makarɔni] *nm*(*pl*) macaroni.

macédoine [masedwan] *nf* **m. (de légumes)** mixed vegetables; **m. (de fruits)** fruit salad.

macérer [masere] *vti Culin* to soak. ◆**macération** *nf* soaking.

mâcher [mɑʃe] *vt* to chew; **il ne mâche pas ses mots** he doesn't mince matters *ou* his words.

machiavélique [makjavelik] *a* Machiavellian.

machin [maʃɛ̃] *nm Fam* (*chose*) thing, what's-it; (*personne*) what's-his-name.

machinal, -aux [maʃinal, -o] *a* (*involontaire*) unconscious, mechanical. ◆—**ement** *adv* unconsciously, mechanically.

machination [maʃinɑsjɔ̃] *nf* machination.

machine [maʃin] *nf* (*appareil, avion, système etc*) machine; (*locomotive, moteur*) engine; *pl Tech* machines, (heavy) machinery; **m. à coudre** sewing machine; **m. à écrire** typewriter; **m. à laver** washing machine. ◆**machinerie** *nf Nau* engine room. ◆**machiniste** *nm Th* stage-hand.

macho [matʃo] *nm* macho *m*; – *a* (*f inv*) (*attitude etc*) macho.

mâchoire [mɑʃwar] *nf* jaw.

mâchonner [mɑʃɔne] *vt* to chew, munch.

maçon [masɔ̃] *nm* builder; bricklayer; mason. ◆**maçonnerie** *nf* (*travaux*) building work; (*ouvrage de briques*) brickwork; (*de pierres*) masonry, stonework.

maculer [makyle] *vt* to stain (**de** with).

Madagascar [madagaskar] *nf* Madagascar.

madame, *pl* **mesdames** [madam, medam] *nf* madam; **oui m.** yes (madam); **bonjour mesdames** good morning (ladies); **Madame** *ou* **Mme Legras** Mrs Legras; **Madame** (*sur une lettre*) *Com* Dear Madam.

madeleine [madlɛn] *nf* (small) sponge cake.

mademoiselle, *pl* **mesdemoiselles** [madmwazɛl, medmwazɛl] *nf* miss; **oui m.** yes (miss); **bonjour mesdemoiselles** good morning (ladies); **Mademoiselle** *ou* **Mlle Legras** Miss Legras; **Mademoiselle** (*sur une lettre*) *Com* Dear Madam.

madère [madɛr] *nm* (*vin*) Madeira.

madone [madɔn] *nf Rel* madonna.

madrier [madrije] *nm* (*poutre*) beam.

maestro [maɛstro] *nm Mus* maestro.

maf(f)ia [mafja] *nf* Mafia.

magasin [magazɛ̃] *nm* shop, *Am* store; (*entrepôt*) warehouse; (*d'arme*) & *Phot* magazine; **grand m.** department store. ◆**magasinier** *nm* warehouseman.

magazine [magazin] *nm* (*revue*) magazine.

magie [maʒi] *nf* magic. ◆**magicien, -ienne** *nmf* magician. ◆**magique** *a* (*baguette, mot*) magic; (*mystérieux, enchanteur*) magical.

magistral, -aux [maʒistral, -o] *a* masterly, magnificent. ◆—**ement** *adv* magnificently.

magistrat [maʒistra] *nm* magistrate. ◆**magistrature** *nf* judiciary, magistracy.

magnanime [maɲanim] *a* magnanimous.

magnat [magna] *nm* tycoon, magnate.

magner (se) [səmaɲe] *vpr Fam* to hurry up.

magnésium [maɲezjɔm] *nm* magnesium.

magnétique [maɲetik] *a* magnetic. ◆**magnétiser** *vt* to magnetize. ◆**magnétisme** *nm* magnetism.

magnétophone [maɲetɔfɔn] *nm* (*Fam* **magnéto**) tape recorder; **m. à cassettes** cassette recorder. ◆**magnétoscope** *nm* video (cassette) recorder.

magnifique [maɲifik] *a* magnificent.
◆**magnificence** *nf* magnificence.
◆**magnifiquement** *adv* magnificently.

magnolia [maɲɔlja] *nm* (*arbre*) magnolia.

magot [mago] *nm* (*économies*) nest egg, hoard.

magouille(s) [maguj] *nf(pl) Pol Fam* fiddling, graft.

mai [mε] *nm* May.

maigre [mεgr] *a* thin, lean; (*viande*) lean; (*fromage, yaourt*) low-fat; (*repas, salaire, espoir*) meagre; **faire m.** to abstain from meat ◆**maigrement** *adv* (*chichement*) meagrely. ◆**maigreur** *nf* thinness; (*de viande*) leanness; (*médiocrité*) *Fig* meagreness. ◆**maigrichon, -onne** *a* & *nmf* skinny (person). ◆**maigrir** *vi* to get thin(ner); − *vt* to make thin(ner).

maille [maj] *nf* (*de tricot*) stitch; (*de filet*) mesh; **m. filée** (*de bas*) run, ladder. ◆**maillon** *nm* (*de chaîne*) link.

maillet [majε] *nm* (*outil*) mallet.

maillot [majo] *nm* (*de sportif*) jersey; (*de danseur*) leotard, tights; **m.** (**de corps**) vest, *Am* undershirt; **m.** (**de bain**) (*de femme*) swimsuit; (*d'homme*) (swimming) trunks.

main [mε̃] *nf* hand; **tenir à la m.** to hold in one's hand; **à la m.** (*livrer, faire etc*) by hand; **la m. dans la m.** hand in hand; **haut les mains!** hands up!; **donner un coup de m. à qn** to lend s.o. a (helping) hand; **coup de m.** (*habileté*) knack; **sous la m.** at hand, handy; **en venir aux mains** to come to blows; **avoir la m. heureuse** to be lucky, have a lucky streak; **mettre la dernière m. à** to put the finishing touches to; **en m. propre** (*remettre qch*) in person; **attaque/vol à m. armée** armed attack/ robbery; **homme de m.** henchman, hired man; **m. courante** handrail; **prêter m.-forte à** to lend assistance to. ◆**m.-d'œuvre** *nf* (*pl* **mains-d'œuvre**) (*travail*) manpower, labour; (*salariés*) labour *ou* work force.

maint [mε̃] *a Litt* many a; **maintes fois, à maintes reprises** many a time.

maintenant [mε̃tnɑ̃] *adv* now; (*de nos jours*) nowadays; **m. que** now that; **dès m.** from now on.

maintenir* [mε̃tnir] *vt* (*conserver*) to keep, maintain; (*retenir*) to hold, keep; (*affirmer*) to maintain (**que** that); − **se m.** *vpr* (*durer*) to be maintained; (*rester*) to keep; (*malade, vieillard*) to hold one's own. ◆**maintien** *nm* (*action*) maintenance (**de** of); (*allure*) bearing.

maire [mεr] *nm* mayor. ◆**mairie** *nf* town hall; (*administration*) town council.

mais [mε] *conj* but; **m. oui, m. si** yes of course; **m. non** definitely not.

maïs [mais] *nm* (*céréale*) maize, *Am* corn; **farine de m.** cornflour, *Am* cornstarch.

maison [mεzɔ̃] *nf* (*bâtiment*) house; (*immeuble*) building; (*chez-soi, asile*) home; *Com* firm; (*famille*) household; **à la m.** (*être*) at home; (*rentrer, aller*) home; − *a inv* (*pâté, tartes etc*) homemade; **m. de la culture** arts *ou* cultural centre; **m. d'étudiants** student hostel; **m. des jeunes** youth club; **m. de repos** rest home; **m. de retraite** old people's home. ◆**maisonnée** *nf* household. ◆**maisonnette** *nf* small house.

maître [mεtr] *nm* master; **se rendre m. de** (*incendie*) to master, control; (*pays*) to conquer; **être m. de** (*situation etc*) to be in control of, be master of; **m. de soi** in control of oneself; **m. d'école** teacher; **m. d'hôtel** (*restaurant*) head waiter; **m. de maison** host; **m. chanteur** blackmailer; **m. nageur** (**sauveteur**) swimming instructor (and lifeguard). ◆**maîtresse** *nf* mistress; **m. d'école** teacher; **m. de maison** hostess; (*ménagère*) housewife; **être m. de** (*situation etc*) to be in control of; − *af* (*idée, poutre*) main; (*carte*) master.

maîtrise [mεtriz] *nf* (*habileté, contrôle*) mastery (**de** of); (*grade*) *Univ* master's degree (**de** in); **m.** (**de soi**) self-control. ◆**maîtriser** *vt* (*émotion*) to master, control; (*sujet*) to master; (*incendie*) to bring under) control; **m. qn** to subdue s.o.; − **se m.** *vpr* to control oneself.

majesté [maʒεste] *nf* majesty; **Votre M.** (*titre*) Your Majesty. ◆**majestueux, -euse** *a* majestic, stately.

majeur [maʒœr] **1** *a* (*primordial*) & *Mus* major; **être m.** *Jur* to be of age; **la majeure partie de** most of; **en majeure partie** for the most part. **2** *nm* (*doigt*) middle finger.

majorer [maʒɔre] *vt* to raise, increase. ◆**majoration** *nf* (*hausse*) increase (**de** in).

majorette [maʒɔrεt] *nf* (*drum*) majorette.

majorité [maʒɔrite] *nf* majority (**de** of); (*âge*) *Jur* coming of age, majority; (*gouvernement*) party in office, government; **en m.** in the *ou* a majority; (*pour la plupart*) in the main. ◆**majoritaire** *a* (*vote etc*) majority-; **être m.** to be in the *ou* a majority; **être m. aux élections** to win the elections.

Majorque [maʒɔrk] *nf* Majorca.

majuscule [maʒyskyl] *a* capital; − *nf* capital letter.

mal, maux [mal, mo] **1** *nm Phil Rel* evil;

(*dommage*) harm; (*douleur*) pain; (*maladie*) illness; (*malheur*) misfortune; **dire du m.** de to speak ill of; **m. de dents** toothache; **m. de gorge** sore throat; **m. de tête** headache; **m. de ventre** stomachache; **m. de mer** seasickness; **m. du pays** homesickness; **avoir le m. du pays/etc** to be homesick/etc; **avoir m. à la tête/à la gorge/etc** to have a headache/sore throat/etc; **ça (me) fait m., j'ai m.** it hurts (me); **faire du m. à** to harm, hurt; **avoir du m. à faire** to have trouble (in) doing; **se donner du m. pour faire** to go to a lot of trouble to do. **2** *adv* (*travailler etc*) badly; (*entendre, comprendre*) not too well; **aller m.** (*projet etc*) to be going badly; (*personne*) *Méd* to be bad *or* ill; **m. (à l'aise)** uncomfortable; **se trouver m.** to (feel) faint; **(ce n'est) pas m.** (*mauvais*) (that's) not bad; **pas m.** (*beaucoup*) *Fam* quite a lot (de of); **c'est m. de jurer/etc** (*moralement*) it's wrong to swear/etc; **de m. en pis** from bad to worse; **m. renseigner/interpréter/** *etc* to misinform/misinterpret/*etc.*

malade [malad] *a* ill, sick; (*arbre, dent*) diseased; (*estomac, jambe*) bad; **être m. du foie/cœur** to have a bad liver/heart; – *nmf* sick person; (*à l'hôpital, d'un médecin*) patient; **les malades** the sick. ◆**maladie** *nf* illness, sickness, disease. ◆**maladif, -ive** *a* (*personne*) sickly; (*morbide*) morbid.

maladroit [maladrwa] *a* (*malhabile*) clumsy, awkward; (*indélicat*) tactless. ◆**maladresse** *nf* clumsiness, awkwardness; tactlessness; (*bévue*) blunder.

malaise [malɛz] *nm* (*angoisse*) uneasiness, malaise; (*indisposition*) faintness, dizziness; **avoir un m.** to feel faint *ou* dizzy.

malaisé [malɛze] *a* difficult.

Malaisie [malɛzi] *nf* Malaysia.

malaria [malarja] *nf* malaria.

malavisé [malavize] *a* ill-advised (**de faire** to do).

malax/er [malakse] *vt* (*pétrir*) to knead; (*mélanger*) to mix. ◆**—eur** *nm Tech* mixer.

malchance [malʃɑ̃s] *nf* bad luck; **une m.** (*mésaventure*) a mishap. ◆**malchanceux, -euse** *a* unlucky.

malcommode [malkɔmɔd] *a* awkward.

mâle [mal] *a* male; (*viril*) manly; – *nm* male.

malédiction [malediksjɔ̃] *nf* curse.

maléfice [malefis] *nm* evil spell. ◆**maléfique** *a* baleful, evil.

malencontreux, -euse [malɑ̃kɔ̃trø, -øz] *a* unfortunate.

malentendant, -ante [malɑ̃tɑ̃dɑ̃, -ɑ̃t] *nmf* person who is hard of hearing.

malentendu [malɑ̃tɑ̃dy] *nm* misunderstanding.

malfaçon [malfasɔ̃] *nf* defect.

malfaisant [malfəzɑ̃] *a* evil, harmful.

malfaiteur [malfɛtœr] *nm* criminal.

malformation [malfɔrmasjɔ̃] *nf* malformation.

malgré [malgre] *prép* in spite of; **m. tout** for all that, after all; **m. soi** (*à contrecœur*) reluctantly.

malhabile [malabil] *a* clumsy.

malheur [malœr] *nm* (*événement*) misfortune; (*accident*) mishap; (*malchance*) bad luck, misfortune; **par m.** unfortunately. ◆**malheureusement** *adv* unfortunately. ◆**malheureux, -euse** *a* (*misérable, insignifiant*) wretched, miserable; (*fâcheux*) unfortunate; (*malchanceux*) unlucky, unfortunate; – *nmf* (*infortuné*) (poor) wretch; (*indigent*) needy person.

malhonnête [malɔnɛt] *a* dishonest. ◆**malhonnêteté** *nf* dishonesty; **une m.** (*action*) a dishonest act.

malice [malis] *nf* mischievousness. ◆**malicieux, -euse** *a* mischievous.

malin, -igne [malɛ̃, -iɲ] *a* (*astucieux*) smart, clever; (*plaisir*) malicious; (*tumeur*) *Méd* malignant. ◆**malignité** *nf* (*méchanceté*) malignity; *Méd* malignancy.

malingre [malɛ̃gr] *a* puny, sickly.

malintentionné [malɛ̃tɑ̃sjɔne] *a* ill-intentioned (**à l'égard de** towards).

malle [mal] *nf* (*coffre*) trunk; (*de véhicule*) boot, *Am* trunk. ◆**mallette** *nf* small suitcase; (*pour documents*) attaché case.

malléable [maleabl] *a* malleable.

malmener [malməne] *vt* to manhandle, treat badly.

malodorant [malɔdɔrɑ̃] *a* smelly.

malotru, -ue [malɔtry] *nmf* boor, lout.

malpoli [malpɔli] *a* impolite.

malpropre [malprɔpr] *a* (*sale*) dirty. ◆**malpropreté** *nf* dirtiness.

malsain [malsɛ̃] *a* unhealthy, unwholesome.

malséant [malseɑ̃] *a* unseemly.

malt [malt] *nm* malt.

Malte [malt] *nf* Malta. ◆**maltais, -aise** *a* & *nmf* Maltese.

maltraiter [maltrete] *vt* to ill-treat.

malveillant [malvejɑ̃] *a* malevolent. ◆**malveillance** *nf* malevolence, ill will.

malvenu [malvəny] *a* (*déplacé*) uncalled-for.

maman [mamɑ̃] *nf* mum(my), *Am* mom(my).

mamelle [mamɛl] *nf* (*d'animal*) teat; (*de*

vache) udder. ◆**mamelon** *nm* **1** (*de femme*) nipple. **2** (*colline*) hillock.

mamie [mami] *nf Fam* granny, grandma.

mammifère [mamifɛr] *nm* mammal.

manche [mɑ̃ʃ] **1** *nf* (*de vêtement*) sleeve; *Sp Cartes* round; **la M.** *Géog* the Channel. **2** *nm* (*d'outil etc*) handle; **m. à balai** broomstick; (*d'avion, d'ordinateur*) joystick. ◆**manchette** *nf* **1** (*de chemise etc*) cuff. **2** *Journ* headline. ◆**manchon** *nm* (*fourrure*) muff.

manchot, -ote [mɑ̃ʃo, -ɔt] **1** *a* & *nmf* one-armed *ou* one-handed (person). **2** *nm* (*oiseau*) penguin.

mandarin [mɑ̃darɛ̃] *nm* (*lettré influent*) *Univ Péj* mandarin.

mandarine [mɑ̃darin] *nf* (*fruit*) tangerine, mandarin (orange).

mandat [mɑ̃da] *nm* **1** (*postal*) money order. **2** *Pol* mandate; *Jur* power of attorney; **m. d'arrêt** warrant (**contre qn** for s.o.'s arrest). ◆**mandataire** *nmf* (*délégué*) representative, proxy. ◆**mandater** *vt* to delegate; *Pol* to give a mandate to.

manège [manɛʒ] *nm* **1** (*à la foire*) merry-go-round, roundabout; (*lieu*) riding-school; (*piste*) ring, manège; (*exercice*) horsemanship. **2** (*intrigue*) wiles, trickery.

manette [manɛt] *nf* lever, handle.

manger [mɑ̃ʒe] *vt* to eat; (*essence, électricité*) *Fig* to guzzle; (*fortune*) to eat up; (*corroder*) to eat into; **donner à m.** to feed; — *vi* to eat; **on mange bien ici** the food is good here; **m. à sa faim** to have enough to eat; — *nm* food. ◆**mangeable** *a* eatable. ◆**mangeaille** *nf Péj* (bad) food. ◆**mangeoire** *nf* (feeding) trough. ◆**mangeur, -euse** *nmf* eater.

mangue [mɑ̃g] *nf* (*fruit*) mango.

manie [mani] *nf* mania, craze (**de** for). ◆**maniaque** *a* finicky, fussy; — *nmf* fusspot, *Am* fussbudget; **un m. de la propreté**/*etc* a maniac for cleanliness/*etc*.

manier [manje] *vt* to handle; **se m. bien** (*véhicule etc*) to handle well. ◆**maniabilité** *nf* (*de véhicule etc*) manoeuvrability. ◆**maniable** *a* easy to handle. ◆**maniement** *nm* handling; **m. d'armes** *Mil* drill.

manière [manjɛr] *nf* way, manner; *pl* (*politesse*) manners; **de toute m.** anyway, anyhow; **de m. à faire** so as to do; **à ma m.** my way, (in) my own way; **de cette m.** (in) this way; **la m. dont elle parle** the way (in which) she talks; **d'une m. générale** generally speaking; **faire des manières** (*chichis*) to make a fuss; (*être affecté*) to put on airs. ◆**maniéré** *a* affected; (*style*) mannered.

manif [manif] *nf Fam* demo.

manifeste [manifɛst] **1** *a* (*évident*) manifest, obvious. **2** *nm Pol* manifesto.

manifester [manifɛste] **1** *vt* to show, manifest; — **se m.** *vpr* (*apparaître*) to appear; (*sentiment, maladie etc*) to show *ou* manifest itself. **2** *vi Pol* to demonstrate. ◆**manifestant, -ante** *nmf* demonstrator. ◆**manifestation** *nf* **1** (*expression*) expression, manifestation; (*apparition*) appearance. **2** *Pol* demonstration; (*réunion, fête*) event.

manigance [manigɑ̃s] *nf* little scheme. ◆**manigancer** *vt* to plot.

manipuler [manipyle] *vt* (*manier*) to handle; (*faits, électeurs*) *Péj* to manipulate. ◆**manipulation** *nf* handling; *Péj* manipulation (**de** of); *pl Pol Péj* manipulation.

manivelle [manivɛl] *nf Aut* crank.

mannequin [manikɛ̃] *nm* (*femme, homme*) (fashion) model; (*statue*) dummy.

manœuvre [manœvr] **1** *nm* (*ouvrier*) labourer. **2** *nf* (*opération*) & *Mil* manoeuvre, *Am* maneuver; (*action*) manoeuvring; (*intrigue*) scheme. ◆**manœuvrer** *vt* (*véhicule, personne etc*) to manoeuvre, *Am* maneuver; (*machine*) to operate; — *vi* to manoeuvre, *Am* maneuver.

manoir [manwar] *nm* manor house.

manque [mɑ̃k] *nm* lack (**de** of); (*lacune*) gap; *pl* (*défauts*) shortcomings; **m. à gagner** loss of profit. ◆**manqu/er** *vt* (*chance, cible etc*) to miss; (*ne pas réussir*) to make a mess of, ruin; (*examen*) to fail; — *vi* (*faire défaut*) to be short *ou* lacking; (*être absent*) to be absent (**à from**); (*être en moins*) to be missing *ou* short; (*défaillir, échouer*) to fail; **m. de** (*pain, argent etc*) to be short of; (*attention, cohérence*) to lack; **ça manque de sel**/*etc* it lacks salt/*etc*, there isn't any salt/*etc*; **m. à** (*son devoir*) to fail in; (*sa parole*) to break; **le temps lui manque** he's short of time, he has no time; **elle/cela lui manque** he misses her/that; **je ne manquerai pas de venir** I won't fail to come; **ne manquez pas de venir** don't forget to come; **elle a manqué (de) tomber** (*faillir*) she nearly fell; — *v imp* **il manque/il nous manque dix tasses** there are/we are ten cups short. ◆**-ant** *a* missing. ◆**-é** *a* (*médecin, pilote etc*) failed; (*livre*) unsuccessful. ◆**-ement** *nm* breach (**à** of).

mansarde [mɑ̃sard] *nf* attic.

manteau, -x [mɑ̃to] *nm* coat.

manucure [manykyr] *nmf* manicurist. ◆**manucurer** *vt Fam* to manicure.

manuel, -elle [manɥɛl] **1** *a* (*travail etc*) manual. **2** *nm* (*livre*) handbook, manual.

manufacture [manyfaktyr] *nf* factory. ◆**manufacturé** *a* (*produit*) manufactured.

manuscrit [manyskri] *nm* manuscript; (*tapé à la machine*) typescript.

manutention [manytɑ̃sjɔ̃] *nf* Com handling (*of stores*). ◆**manutentionnaire** *nmf* packer.

mappemonde [mapmɔ̃d] *nf* map of the world; (*sphère*) Fam globe.

maquereau, -x [makro] *nm* (*poisson*) mackerel.

maquette [makɛt] *nf* (*scale*) model.

maquill/er [makije] *vt* (*visage*) to make up; (*voiture etc*) Péj to tamper with; (*vérité etc*) Péj to fake; **— se m.** to make (oneself) up. ◆**—age** *nm* (*fard*) make-up.

maquis [maki] *nm* Bot scrub, bush; Mil Hist maquis.

maraîcher, -ère [mareʃe, -ɛʃɛr] *nmf* market gardener, Am truck farmer.

marais [marɛ] *nm* marsh, bog; **m. salant** saltworks, saltern.

marasme [marasm] *nm* Écon stagnation.

marathon [maratɔ̃] *nm* marathon.

maraudeur, -euse [marodœr, -øz] *nmf* petty thief.

marbre [marbr] *nm* marble. ◆**marbrier** *nm* (*funéraire*) monumental mason.

marc [mar] *nm* (*eau-de-vie*) marc, brandy; **m. (de café)** coffee grounds.

marchand, -ande [marʃɑ̃, -ɑ̃d] *nmf* trader, shopkeeper; (*de vins, charbon*) merchant; (*de cycles, meubles*) dealer; **m. de bonbons** confectioner; **m. de couleurs** hardware merchant *ou* dealer; **m. de journaux** (*dans la rue*) newsvendor; (*dans un magasin*) newsagent, Am news dealer; **m. de légumes** greengrocer; **m. de poissons** fishmonger; **— *a* (*valeur*)** market; (*prix*) trade-. ◆**marchandise(s)** *nf*(*pl*) goods, merchandise.

marchand/er [marʃɑ̃de] *vi* to haggle, bargain; **— *vt* (*objet*)** to haggle over. ◆**—age** *nm* haggling, bargaining.

marche [marʃ] *nf* **1** (*d'escalier*) step, stair. **2** (*démarche, trajet*) walk; Mil Mus march; (*pas*) pace; (*de train, véhicule*) movement; (*de maladie, d'événement*) progress, course; **la m.** (*action*) Sp walking; **faire m. arrière** Aut to reverse; **la bonne m. de** (*opération, machine*) the smooth running of; **un train/véhicule en m.** a moving train/vehicle; **mettre qch en m.** to start sth (up). ◆**marcher** *vi* (*à pied*) to walk; Mil to

march; (*poser le pied*) to tread, step; (*train, véhicule etc*) to run, go, move; (*fonctionner*) to go, work, run; (*prospérer*) to go well; **faire m.** (*machine*) to work; (*entreprise*) to run; (*personne*) Fam to kid; **ça marche?** Fam how's it going?; **elle va m.** (*accepter*) Fam she'll go along (with it). ◆**marcheur, -euse** *nmf* walker.

marché [marʃe] *nm* (*lieu*) market; (*contrat*) deal; **faire son *ou* le m.** to do one's shopping (*in the market*); **être bon m.** to be cheap; **voiture(s)/etc bon m.** cheap car(s)/etc; **vendre (à) bon m.** to sell cheap(ly); **c'est meilleur m.** it's cheaper; **par-dessus le m.** Fig into the bargain; **au m. noir** on the black market; **le M. commun** the Common Market.

marchepied [marʃəpje] *nm* (*de train, bus*) step(s); (*de voiture*) running board.

mardi [mardi] *nm* Tuesday; **M. gras** Shrove Tuesday.

mare [mar] *nf* (*flaque*) pool; (*étang*) pond.

marécage [marekaʒ] *nm* swamp, marsh. ◆**marécageux, -euse** *a* marshy, swampy.

maréchal, -aux [mareʃal, -o] *nm* Fr Mil marshal. ◆**m.-ferrant** *nm* (*pl* maréchaux-ferrants*) blacksmith.

marée [mare] *nf* tide; (*poissons*) fresh (sea) fish; **m. noire** oil slick.

marelle [marɛl] *nf* (*jeu*) hopscotch.

margarine [margarin] *nf* margarine.

marge [marʒ] *nf* margin; **en m. de** (*en dehors de*) on the periphery of, on the fringe(s) of; **m. de sécurité** safety margin. ◆**marginal, -ale, -aux** *a* (*secondaire, asocial*) marginal; **— *nmf*** misfit, dropout; (*bizarre*) weirdo.

marguerite [margərit] *nf* (*fleur*) marguerite, daisy.

mari [mari] *nm* husband.

mariage [marjaʒ] *nm* marriage; (*cérémonie*) wedding; (*mélange*) Fig blend, marriage; **demande en m.** proposal (of marriage). ◆**mari/er** *vt* (*couleurs*) to blend; **m. qn** (*maire, prêtre etc*) to marry s.o.; **m. qn avec** to marry s.o. (off) to; **— se m.** *vpr* to get married, marry; **se m. avec qn** to marry s.o., get married to s.o. ◆**—é** *a* married; **—** *nm* (bride)groom; **les mariés** the bride and (bride)groom; **les jeunes mariés** the newly-weds. ◆**—ée** *nf* bride.

marijuana [mariʒyana] *nf* marijuana.

marin [marɛ̃] *a* (*air, sel etc*) sea-; (*flore*) marine; (*mille*) nautical; (*costume*) sailor-; **— *nm* seaman, sailor. ◆marine** *nf* **m. (de guerre)** navy; **m. marchande** merchant navy; **(bleu) m.** (*couleur*) navy (blue).

marina [marina] *nf* marina.
mariner [marine] *vti Culin* to marinate.
marionnette [marjɔnɛt] *nf* puppet; (*à fils*) marionnette.
maritalement [maritalmɑ̃] *adv* **vivre m.** to live together (as husband and wife).
maritime [maritim] *a* (*droit, province, climat etc*) maritime; (*port*) sea-; (*gare*) harbour-; (*chantier*) naval; (*agent*) shipping-.
marjolaine [marʒɔlɛn] *nf* (*aromate*) marjoram.
mark [mark] *nm* (*monnaie*) mark.
marmaille [marmɑj] *nf* (*enfants*) *Fam* kids.
marmelade [marmɔlad] *nf* **m. (de fruits)** stewed fruit; **en m.** *Culin Fig* in a mush.
marmite [marmit] *nf* (cooking) pot.
marmonner [marmɔne] *vti* to mutter.
marmot [marmo] *nm* (*enfant*) *Fam* kid.
marmotter [marmɔte] *vti* to mumble.
Maroc [marɔk] *nm* Morocco. ◆**marocain, -aine** *a* & *nmf* Moroccan.
maroquinerie [marɔkinri] *nf* (*magasin*) leather goods shop. ◆**maroquinier** *nm* leather dealer.
marotte [marɔt] *nf* (*dada*) *Fam* fad, craze.
marque [mark] *nf* (*trace, signe*) mark; (*de fabricant*) make, brand; (*points*) *Sp* score; **m. de fabrique** trademark; **m. déposée** registered trademark; **la m. de** (*preuve*) the stamp of; **de m.** (*hôte, visiteur*) distinguished; (*produit*) of quality. ◆**marqu/er** *vt* (*par une marque etc*) to mark; (*écrire*) to note down; (*indiquer*) to show, mark; (*point, but*) *Sp* to score; **m. qn** *Sp* to mark s.o.; **m. les points** *Sp* to keep (the) score; **m. le coup** to mark the event; − *vi* (*trace*) to leave a mark; (*date, événement*) to stand out; *Sp* to score. ◆**−ant** *a* (*remarquable*) outstanding. ◆**−é** *a* (*différence, accent etc*) marked, pronounced. ◆**−eur** *nm* (*crayon*) marker.
marquis [marki] *nm* marquis. ◆**marquise** *nf* **1** (*auvent*) marchioness. **2** (*auvent*) glass canopy.
marraine [marɛn] *nf* godmother.
marre [mar] *nf* **en avoir m.** *Fam* to be fed up (de with).
marr/er (se) [səmare] *vpr Fam* to have a good laugh. ◆**−ant** *a Fam* hilarious, funny.
marron¹ [marɔ̃] **1** *nm* chestnut; (*couleur*) (chestnut) brown; **m. (d'Inde)** horse chestnut; − *a inv* (*couleur*) (chestnut) brown. **2** *nm* (*coup*) *Fam* punch, clout. ◆**marronnier** *nm* (horse) chestnut tree.
marron², -onne [marɔ̃, -ɔn] *a* (*médecin etc*) bogus.
mars [mars] *nm* March.

marsouin [marswɛ̃] *nm* porpoise.
marteau, -x [marto] *nm* hammer; (*de porte*) (door)knocker; **m. piqueur, m. pneumatique** pneumatic drill. ◆**marteler** *vt* to hammer. ◆**martèlement** *nm* hammering.
martial, -aux [marsjal, -o] *a* martial; **cour martiale** court-martial; **loi martiale** martial law.
martien, -ienne [marsjɛ̃, -jɛn] *nmf* & *a* Martian.
martinet [martinɛ] *nm* (*fouet*) (small) whip.
martin-pêcheur [martɛ̃peʃœr] *nm* (*pl* **martins-pêcheurs**) (*oiseau*) kingfisher.
martyr, -yre¹ [martir] *nmf* (*personne*) martyr; **enfant m.** battered child. ◆**martyre²** *nm* (*souffrance*) martyrdom. ◆**martyriser** *vt* to torture; (*enfant*) to batter.
marxisme [marksism] *nm* Marxism. ◆**marxiste** *a* & *nmf* Marxist.
mascara [maskara] *nm* mascara.
mascarade [maskarad] *nf* masquerade.
mascotte [maskɔt] *nf* mascot.
masculin [maskylɛ̃] *a* male; (*viril*) masculine, manly; *Gram* masculine; (*vêtement, équipe*) men's; − *nm Gram* masculine. ◆**masculinité** *nf* masculinity.
masochisme [mazɔʃism] *nm* masochism. ◆**masochiste** *nmf* masochist; − *a* masochistic.
masque [mask] *nm* mask. ◆**masquer** *vt* (*dissimuler*) to mask (à from); (*cacher à la vue*) to block off.
massacre [masakr] *nm* massacre, slaughter. ◆**massacr/er** *vt* to massacre, slaughter; (*abîmer*) *Fam* to ruin. ◆**−ant** *a* (*humeur*) excruciating.
massage [masaʒ] *nm* massage.
masse [mas] *nf* **1** (*volume*) mass; (*gros morceau, majorité*) bulk (**de** of); **en m.** (*venir, vendre*) in large numbers; **départ en m.** mass *ou* wholesale departure; **manifestation de m.** mass demonstration; **la m.** (*foule*) the masses; **les masses** (*peuple*) the masses; **une m. de** (*tas*) a mass of; **des masses de** *Fam* masses of. **2** (*outil*) sledgehammer. **3** *Él* earth, *Am* ground. ◆**mass/er 1** *vt*, **− se m.** *vpr* (*gens*) to mass. **2** *vt* (*frotter*) to massage. ◆**−eur** *nm* masseur. ◆**−euse** *nf* masseuse.
massif, -ive [masif, -iv] **1** *a* massive; (*départs etc*) mass-; (*or, chêne etc*) solid. **2** *nm* (*d'arbres, de fleurs*) clump; *Géog* massif. ◆**massivement** *adv* (*en masse*) in large numbers.
massue [masy] *nf* (*bâton*) club.
mastic [mastik] *nm* (*pour vitres*) putty; (*pour bois*) filler; **m. (silicone)** mastic.

◆**mastiquer** vt **1** (vitre) to putty; (porte) to mastic; (bois) to fill. **2** (mâcher) to chew, masticate.

mastoc [mastɔk] a inv Péj Fam massive.

mastodonte [mastɔdɔ̃t] nm (personne) Péj monster; (véhicule) juggernaut.

masturber (se) [səmastyrbe] vpr to masturbate. ◆**masturbation** nf masturbation.

masure [mazyr] nf tumbledown house.

mat [mat] **1** a (papier, couleur) mat(t); (bruit) dull. **2** a inv & nm Échecs (check)mate; **faire** ou **mettre m.** to (check)mate.

mât [mɑ] nm (de navire) mast; (poteau) pole.

match [matʃ] nm Sp match, Am game; **m. nul** tie, draw.

matelas [matlɑ] nm mattress; **m. pneumatique** air bed. ◆**matelassé** a (meuble) padded; (tissu) quilted.

matelot [matlo] nm sailor, seaman.

mater [mate] vt (enfant, passion etc) to subdue.

matérialiser [materjalize] vt, **— se m.** vpr to materialize. ◆**matérialisation** nf materialization.

matérialisme [materjalism] nm materialism. ◆**matérialiste** a materialistic; – nmf materialist.

matériaux [materjo] nmpl (building) materials; (de roman, enquête etc) material.

matériel, -ielle [materjɛl] **1** a material; (personne) Péj materialistic; (financier) financial; (pratique) practical. **2** nm equipment, material(s); (d'un ordinateur) hardware inv. ◆**matériellement** adv materially; **m. impossible** physically impossible.

maternel, -elle [matɛrnɛl] a motherly, maternal; (parenté, réprimande) maternal; – nf (école) **maternelle** nursery school. ◆**materner** vt to mother. ◆**maternité** nf (état) motherhood, maternity; (hôpital) maternity hospital ou unit; (grossesse) pregnancy; **de m.** (congé, allocation) maternity-.

mathématique [matematik] a mathematical; – nfpl mathematics. ◆**mathématicien, -ienne** nmf mathematician. ◆**maths** [mat] nfpl Fam maths, Am math.

matière [matjɛr] nf (sujet) & Scol subject; (de livre) subject matter; **une m., la m., des matières** (substance(s)) matter; **m. première** raw material; **en m. d'art** /etc as regards art/etc, in art/etc; **s'y connaître en m. de** to be experienced in.

matin [matɛ̃] nm morning; **de grand m., de bon m., au petit m.** very early (in the morn-

ing); **le m.** (chaque matin) in the morning; **à sept heures du m.** at seven in the morning; **tous les mardis m.** every Tuesday morning. ◆**matinal, -aux** a (personne) early; (fleur, soleil etc) morning-. ◆**matinée** nf morning; Th matinée; **faire la grasse m.** to sleep late, lie in.

matou [matu] nm tomcat.

matraque [matrak] nf (de policier) truncheon, Am billy (club); (de malfaiteur) cosh, club. ◆**matraqu/er** vt (frapper) to club; (publicité etc) to plug (away) at. ◆**—age** nm. (publicitaire) plugging, publicity build-up.

matrice [matris] nf **1** Anat womb. **2** Tech matrix.

matricule [matrikyl] nm (registration) number; – a (livret, numéro) registration-.

matrimonial, -aux [matrimɔnjal, -o] a matrimonial.

mâture [mɑtyr] nf Nau masts.

maturité [matyrite] nf maturity. ◆**maturation** nf maturing.

maudire* [modir] vt to curse. ◆**maudit** a (sacré) (ac)cursed, damned.

maugréer [mogree] vi to growl, grumble (contre at).

mausolée [mozɔle] nm mausoleum.

maussade [mosad] a (personne etc) glum, sullen; (temps) gloomy.

mauvais [move] a bad; (méchant, malveillant) evil, wicked; (mal choisi) wrong; (mer) rough; **plus m.** worse; **le plus m.** the worst; **il fait m.** the weather's bad; **ça sent m.** it smells bad; **être m. en** (anglais etc) to be bad at; **mauvaise santé** ill ou bad ou poor health; – nm **le bon et le m.** the good and the bad.

mauve [mov] a & nm (couleur) mauve.

mauviette [movjɛt] nf personne) Péj weakling.

maux [mo] voir **mal.**

maxime [maksim] nf maxim.

maximum [maksimɔm] nm maximum; **le m. de** (force etc) the maximum (amount of); **au m.** as much as possible; (tout au plus) at most; – a maximum; **la température m.** maximum temperature. ◆**maximal, -aux** a maximum.

mayonnaise [majɔnɛz] nf mayonnaise.

mazout [mazut] nm (fuel) oil.

me [m(ə)] (m' before vowel or mute h) pron **1** (complément direct) me; **il me voit** he sees me. **2** (indirect) (to) me; **elle me parle** she speaks to me; **tu me l'as dit** you told me. **3** (réfléchi) myself; **je me lave** I wash myself.

méandres [meɑ̃dr] nmpl meander(ing)s.

mec [mɛk] *nm* (*individu*) *Arg* guy, bloke.
mécanique [mekanik] *a* mechanical; (*jouet*) clockwork-; – *nf* (*science*) mechanics; (*mécanisme*) mechanism. ◆**mécanicien** *nm* mechanic; *Rail* train driver. ◆**mécanisme** *nm* mechanism.
mécaniser [mekanize] *vt* to mechanize. ◆**mécanisation** *nf* mechanization.
mécène [mesɛn] *nm* patron (of the arts).
méchant [meʃɑ̃] *a* (*cruel*) malicious, wicked, evil; (*désagréable*) nasty; (*enfant*) naughty; (*chien*) vicious; **ce n'est pas m.** (*grave*) *Fam* it's nothing much. ◆**méchamment** *adv* (*cruellement*) maliciously; (*très*) *Fam* terribly. ◆**méchanceté** *nf* malice, wickedness; **une m.** (*acte*) a malicious act; (*parole*) a malicious word.
mèche [mɛʃ] *nf* **1** (*de cheveux*) lock; *pl* (*reflets*) highlights. **2** (*de bougie*) wick; (*de pétard*) fuse; (*de perceuse*) drill, bit. **3** de **m. avec qn** (*complicité*) *Fam* in collusion *ou* cahoots with s.o.
méconn/aître* [mekɔnɛtr] *vt* to ignore; (*méjuger*) to fail to appreciate. ◆**–u** *a* unrecognized. ◆**–aissable** *a* unrecognizable.
mécontent [mekɔ̃tɑ̃] *a* dissatisfied, discontented (**de** with). ◆**mécontent/er** *vt* to displease, dissatisfy. ◆**–ement** *nm* dissatisfaction, discontent.
médaille [medaj] *nf* (*décoration*) *Sp* medal; (*pieuse*) medallion; (*pour chien*) name tag; **être m. d'or/d'argent** *Sp* to be a gold/silver medallist. ◆**médaillé, -ée** *nmf* medal holder. ◆**médaillon** *nm* (*bijou*) locket, medallion; (*ornement*) *Archit* medallion.
médecin [medsɛ̃] *nm* doctor, physician. ◆**médecine** *nf* medicine; **étudiant en m.** medical student. ◆**médical, -aux** *a* medical. ◆**médicament** *nm* medicine. ◆**médicinal, -aux** *a* medicinal. ◆**médico-légal, -aux** *a* (*laboratoire*) forensic.
médias [medja] *nmpl* (mass) media. ◆**médiatique** *a* media-.
médiateur, -trice [medjatœr, -tris] *nmf* mediator; – *a* mediating. ◆**médiation** *nf* mediation.
médiéval, -aux [medjeval, -o] *a* medi(a)eval.
médiocre [medjɔkr] *a* mediocre, second-rate. ◆**médiocrement** *adv* (*pas très*) not very; (*pas très bien*) not very well. ◆**médiocrité** *nf* mediocrity.
médire* [medir] *vi* **m. de** to speak ill of, slander. ◆**médisance(s)** *nf*(*pl*) malicious gossip, slander; **une m.** a piece of malicious gossip.
méditer [medite] *vt* (*conseil etc*) to meditate on; **m. de faire** to consider doing; – *vi* to meditate (**sur** on). ◆**méditatif, -ive** *a* meditative. ◆**méditation** *nf* meditation.
Méditerranée [mediterane] *nf* **la M.** the Mediterranean. ◆**méditerranéen, -enne** *a* Mediterranean.
médium [medjɔm] *nm* (*spirite*) medium.
méduse [medyz] *nf* jellyfish.
méduser [medyze] *vt* to stun, dumbfound.
meeting [mitiŋ] *nm Pol Sp* meeting, rally.
méfait [mefɛ] *nm Jur* misdeed; *pl* (*dégâts*) ravages.
méfi/er (se) [səmefje] *vpr* **se m. de** to distrust, mistrust; (*faire attention à*) to watch out for, beware of; **méfie-toi!** watch out!, beware!; **je me méfie** I'm distrustful *ou* suspicious. ◆**–ant** *a* distrustful, suspicious. ◆**méfiance** *nf* distrust, mistrust.
mégalomane [megaloman] *nmf* megalomaniac. ◆**mégalomanie** *nf* megalomania.
mégaphone [megafon] *nm* loudhailer.
mégarde (par) [parmegard] *adv* inadvertently, by mistake.
mégère [meʒɛr] *nf* (*femme*) *Péj* shrew.
mégot [mego] *nm Fam* cigarette end *ou* butt.
meilleur, -eure [mejœr] *a* better (**que** than); **le m. moment/résultat**/*etc* the best moment/result/*etc*; – *nmf* **le m., la meilleure** the best (one).
mélancolie [melɑ̃kɔli] *nf* melancholy, gloom. ◆**mélancolique** *a* melancholy, gloomy.
mélange [melɑ̃ʒ] *nm* mixture, blend; (*opération*) mixing. ◆**mélanger** *vt* (*mêler*) to mix; (*brouiller*) to mix (up), muddle; **— se m.** *vpr* to mix; (*idées etc*) to get mixed (up) *ou* muddled.
mélasse [melas] *nf* treacle, *Am* molasses.
mêl/er [mele] *vt* to mix, mingle (**à** with); (*qualités, thèmes*) to combine; (*brouiller*) to mix (up), muddle; **m. qn à** (*impliquer*) to involve s.o. in; **— se m.** *vpr* to mix, mingle (**à** with); **se m. à** (*la foule etc*) to join; **se m. de** (*s'ingérer dans*) to meddle in; **mêle-toi de ce qui te regarde!** mind your own business! ◆**–é** *a* mixed (**de** with). ◆**–ée** *nf* (*bataille*) rough-and-tumble; *Rugby* scrum(mage).
méli-mélo [melimelo] *nm* (*pl* **mélis-mélos**) *Fam* muddle.
mélodie [melɔdi] *nf* melody. ◆**mélodieux, -euse** *a* melodious. ◆**mélodique** *a Mus* melodic. ◆**mélomane** *nmf* music lover.

mélodrame [melɔdram] *nm* melodrama. ◆**mélodramatique** *a* melodramatic.

melon [m(ə)lɔ̃] *nm* **1** (*fruit*) melon. **2** (**chapeau**) **m.** bowler (hat).

membrane [mɑ̃bran] *nf* membrane.

membre [mɑ̃br] *nm* **1** *Anat* limb. **2** (*d'un groupe*) member.

même [mɛm] **1** *a* (*identique*) same; **en m. temps** at the same time (**que** as); **ce livre/ etc m.** (*exact*) this very book/*etc*; **il est la bonté m.** he is kindness itself; **lui-m./vous-m./etc** himself/yourself/*etc*; – *pron* **le m., la m.** the same (one); **j'ai les mêmes** I have the same (ones). **2** *adv* (*y compris, aussi*) even; **m. si** even if; **tout de m., quand m.** all the same; **de m.** likewise; **de m. que** just as; **ici m.** in this very place; **à m. de** in a position to; **à m. le sol** on the ground; **à m. la bouteille** from the bottle.

mémento [memɛ̃to] *nm* (*aide-mémoire*) handbook; (*agenda*) notebook.

mémoire [memwar] **1** *nf* memory; **de m. d'homme** in living memory; **à la m. de** in memory of. **2** *nm* (*requête*) petition; *Univ* memoir; *pl Littér* memoirs. ◆**mémorable** *a* memorable. ◆**mémorandum** [memɔrɑ̃dɔm] *nm Pol Com* memorandum. ◆**mémorial, -aux** (*monument*) memorial.

menace [mənas] *nf* threat, menace. ◆**mena/cer** *vt* to threaten (**de faire** to do). ◆**—çant** *a* threatening.

ménage [menaʒ] *nm* (*entretien*) housekeeping; (*couple*) couple, household; **faire le m.** to do the housework; **faire bon m. avec** to get on happily with. ◆**ménager¹, -ère** *a* (*appareil*) domestic, household-; **travaux ménagers** housework; – *nf* (*femme*) housewife.

ménag/er² [menaʒe] *vt* (*arranger*) to prepare *ou* arrange (carefully); (*épargner*) to use sparingly, be careful with; (*fenêtre, escalier etc*) to build; **m. qn** to treat *ou* handle s.o. gently *ou* carefully. ◆**—ement** *nm* (*soin*) care.

ménagerie [menaʒri] *nf* menagerie.

mendier [mɑ̃dje] *vi* to beg; – *vt* to beg for. ◆**mendiant, -ante** *nmf* beggar. ◆**mendicité** *nf* begging.

menées [məne] *nfpl* schemings, intrigues.

men/er [məne] *vt* (*personne, vie etc*) to lead; (*lutte, enquête, tâche etc*) to carry out; (*affaires*) to run; (*bateau*) to command; **m. qn à** (*accompagner, transporter*) to take s.o. to; **m. à bien** *Fig* to carry through; – *vi Sp* to lead. ◆**—eur, -euse** *nmf* (*de révolte*) (ring)leader.

méningite [menɛ̃ʒit] *nf Méd* meningitis.

ménopause [menɔpoz] *nf* menopause.

menottes [mənɔt] *nfpl* handcuffs.

mensonge [mɑ̃sɔ̃ʒ] *nm* lie; (*action*) lying. ◆**mensonger, -ère** *a* untrue, false.

menstruation [mɑ̃stryasjɔ̃] *nf* menstruation.

mensuel, -elle [mɑ̃sɥɛl] *a* monthly; – *nm* (*revue*) monthly. ◆**mensualité** *nf* monthly payment. ◆**mensuellement** *adv* monthly.

mensurations [mɑ̃syrasjɔ̃] *nfpl* measurements.

mental, -aux [mɑ̃tal, -o] *a* mental. ◆**mentalité** *nf* mentality.

menthe [mɑ̃t] *nf* mint.

mention [mɑ̃sjɔ̃] *nf* mention, reference; (*annotation*) comment; **m. bien** *Scol Univ* distinction; **faire m. de** to mention. ◆**mentionner** *vt* to mention.

ment/ir* [mɑ̃tir] *vi* to lie, tell lies *ou* a lie (**à** to). ◆**—eur, -euse** *nmf* liar; – *a* lying.

menton [mɑ̃tɔ̃] *nm* chin.

menu [məny] **1** *a* (*petit*) tiny; (*mince*) slender, fine; (*peu important*) minor, petty; – *adv* (*hacher*) small, finely; – *nm* **par le m.** in detail. **2** *nm* (*carte*) *Culin* menu.

menuisier [mənɥizje] *nm* carpenter, joiner. ◆**menuiserie** *nf* carpentry, joinery; (*ouvrage*) woodwork.

méprendre (se) [səmeprɑ̃dr] *vpr* **se m. sur** to be mistaken about. ◆**méprise** *nf* mistake.

mépris [mepri] *nm* contempt (**de** of, for), scorn (**de** for); **au m. de** without regard to. ◆**mépris/er** *vt* to despise, scorn. ◆**—ant** *a* scornful, contemptuous. ◆**—able** *a* despicable.

mer [mɛr] *nf* sea; (*marée*) tide; **en m.** at sea; **par m.** by sea; **aller à la m.** to go to the seaside; **un homme à la m.!** man overboard!

mercantile [merkɑ̃til] *a Péj* money-grabbing.

mercenaire [mersəner] *a & nm* mercenary.

mercerie [mersəri] *nf* (*magasin*) haberdasher's, *Am* notions store. ◆**mercier, -ière** *nmf* haberdasher, *Am* notions merchant.

merci [mersi] **1** *int* thank you, thanks (**de, pour** for); (**non**) **m.!** no, thank you! **2** *nf* **à la m. de** at the mercy of.

mercredi [merkrədi] *nm* Wednesday.

mercure [merkyr] *nm* mercury.

merde! [merd] *int Fam* (bloody) hell!

mère [mɛr] *nf* mother; **m. de famille** mother (of a family); **la m. Dubois** *Fam* old Mrs Dubois; **maison m.** *Com* parent firm.

méridien [meridjɛ̃] *nm* meridian.

méridional, -ale, -aux [meridjɔnal, -o] *a* southern; − *nmf* southerner.

meringue [mərɛ̃g] *nf* (*gâteau*) meringue.

merisier [mərizje] *nm* (*bois*) cherry.

mérite [merit] *nm* merit; **homme de m.** (*valeur*) man of worth. ◆**mérit/er** *vt* (*être digne de*) to deserve; (*valoir*) to be worth; **m. de réussir**/*etc* to deserve to succeed/*etc*. ◆**−ant** *a* deserving. ◆**méritoire** *a* commendable.

merlan [mɛrlɑ̃] *nm* (*poisson*) whiting.

merle [mɛrl] *nm* blackbird.

merveille [mɛrvɛj] *nf* wonder, marvel; **à m.** wonderfully (well). ◆**merveilleusement** *adv* wonderfully. ◆**merveilleux, -euse** *a* wonderful, marvellous; − *nm* **le m.** (*surnaturel*) the supernatural.

mes [me] *voir* **mon.**

mésange [mezɑ̃ʒ] *nf* (*oiseau*) tit.

mésaventure [mezavɑ̃tyr] *nf* misfortune, misadventure.

mesdames [medam] *voir* **madame.**

mesdemoiselles [medmwazɛl] *voir* **mademoiselle.**

mésentente [mezɑ̃tɑ̃t] *nf* misunderstanding.

mesquin [mɛskɛ̃] *a* mean, petty. ◆**mesquinerie** *nf* meanness, pettiness; **une m.** an act of meanness.

mess [mes] *nm inv Mil* mess.

message [mesaʒ] *nm* message. ◆**messager, -ère** *nmf* messenger.

messageries [mesaʒri] *nfpl Com* courier service.

messe [mes] *nf Rel* mass.

Messie [mesi] *nm* Messiah.

messieurs [mesjø] *voir* **monsieur.**

mesure [məzyr] *nf* (*évaluation, dimension*) measurement; (*quantité, disposition*) measure; (*retenue*) moderation; (*cadence*) *Mus* time, beat; **fait sur m.** made to measure; **à m. que** as, as soon *ou* as fast as; **dans la m. où** in so far as; **dans une certaine m.** to a certain extent; **en m. de** able to, in a position to; **dépasser la m.** to exceed the bounds. ◆**mesur/er** *vt* to measure; (*juger, estimer*) to calculate, assess, measure; (*argent, temps*) to ration (out); **m. 1 mètre 83** (*personne*) to be six feet tall; (*objet*) to measure six feet; **se m. à** *ou* **avec qn** *Fig* to pit oneself against s.o. ◆**−é** *a* (*pas, ton*) measured; (*personne*) moderate.

met [me] *voir* **mettre.**

métal, -aux [metal, -o] *nm* metal. ◆**métallique** *a* (*objet*) metal-; (*éclat, reflet, couleur*) metallic. ◆**métallisé** *a* (*peinture*) metallic.

métallo [metalo] *nm Fam* steelworker. ◆**métallurgie** *nf* (*industrie*) steel industry; (*science*) metallurgy. ◆**métallurgique** *a* **usine m.** steelworks. ◆**métallurgiste** *a & nm* (*ouvrier*) m. steelworker.

métamorphose [metamɔrfoz] *nf* metamorphosis. ◆**métamorphoser** *vt,* **− se m.** *vpr* to transform (**en** into).

métaphore [metafɔr] *nf* metaphor. ◆**métaphorique** *a* metaphorical.

métaphysique [metafizik] *a* metaphysical.

météo [meteo] *nf* (*bulletin*) weather forecast.

météore [meteɔr] *nm* meteor. ◆**météorite** *nm* meteorite.

météorologie [meteɔrɔlɔʒi] *nf* (*science*) meteorology; (*service*) weather bureau. ◆**météorologique** *a* meteorological; (*bulletin, station, carte*) weather-.

méthode [metɔd] *nf* method; (*livre*) course. ◆**méthodique** *a* methodical.

méticuleux, -euse [metikylø, -øz] *a* meticulous.

métier [metje] *nm* **1** (*travail*) job; (*manuel*) trade; (*intellectuel*) profession; (*habileté*) professional skill; **homme de m.** specialist. **2 m.** (**à tisser**) loom.

métis, -isse [metis] *a & nmf* half-caste.

mètre [mɛtr] *nm* (*mesure*) metre; (*règle*) (metre) rule; **m.** (**à ruban**) tape measure. ◆**mètr/er** *vt* (*terrain*) to survey. ◆**−age** *nm* **1** surveying. **2** (*tissu*) length; (*de film*) footage; **long m.** (*film*) full length film; **court m.** (*film*) short (film). ◆**−eur** *nm* quantity surveyor. ◆**métrique** *a* metric.

métro [metro] *nm* underground, *Am* subway.

métropole [metrɔpɔl] *nf* (*ville*) metropolis; (*pays*) mother country. ◆**métropolitain** *a* metropolitan.

mets [me] *nm* (*aliment*) dish.

mett/re* [mɛtr] **1** *vt* to put; (*table*) to lay; (*vêtement, lunettes*) to put on, wear; (*chauffage, radio etc*) to put on, switch on; (*réveil*) to set (**à** for); (*dépenser*) to spend (**pour une robe**/*etc* on a dress/*etc*); **m. dix heures**/*etc* **à venir** (*consacrer*) to take ten hours/*etc* coming *ou* to come; **m. à l'aise** (*rassurer*) to put *ou* set at ease; (*dans un fauteuil etc*) to make comfortable; **m. en colère** to make angry; **m. en liberté** to free; **m. en bouteille(s)** to bottle; **m. du soin à faire** to take care to do; **mettons que** (+ *sub*) let's suppose that; **− se m.** *vpr* (*se placer*) to put oneself; (*debout*) to stand; (*assis*) to sit; (*objet*) to be put, go; **se m. en short**/**pyjama**/*etc* to get into one's shorts/pyjamas/*etc*; **se m. en rapport avec** to get in touch with; **se m. à** (*endroit*) to go to; (*travail*) to set oneself to, start; **se m. à faire** to start doing; **se m. à table** to sit (down) at the table; **se m. à l'aise** to make oneself comfortable; **se m. au beau/froid** (*temps*) to turn fine/cold. ◆**—able** *a* wearable. ◆**—eur** *nm* m. **en scène** *Th* producer; *Cin* director.

meuble [mœbl] *nm* piece of furniture; *pl* furniture. ◆**meubl/er** *vt* to furnish; (*remplir*) *Fig* to fill. ◆**—é** *nm* furnished flat *ou Am* apartment.

meugl/er [møgle] *vi* to moo, low. ◆**—ement(s)** *nm(pl)* mooing.

meule [møl] *nf* **1** (*de foin*) haystack. **2** (*pour moudre*) millstone.

meunier, -ière [mønje, -jɛr] *nmf* miller.

meurt [mœr] *voir* **mourir.**

meurtre [mœrtr] *nm* murder. ◆**meurtrier, -ière** *nmf* murderer; *– a* deadly, murderous.

meurtrir [mœrtrir] *vt* to bruise. ◆**meurtrissure** *nf* bruise.

meute [møt] *nf* (*de chiens, de créanciers etc*) pack.

Mexique [mɛksik] *nm* Mexico. ◆**mexicain, -aine** *a & nmf* Mexican.

mi- [mi] *préf* **la mi-mars**/*etc* mid March/*etc*; **à mi-distance** mid-distance, midway.

miaou [mjau] *int* (*cri du chat*) miaow. ◆**miaul/er** [mjole] *vi* to miaow, mew. ◆**—ement(s)** *nm(pl)* miaowing, mewing.

mi-bas [miba] *nm inv* knee sock.

miche [miʃ] *nf* round loaf.

mi-chemin (à) [amiʃmɛ̃] *adv* halfway.

mi-clos [miklo] *a* half-closed.

micmac [mikmak] *nm* (*manigance*) *Fam* intrigue.

mi-corps (à) [amikɔr] *adv* (up) to the waist.

mi-côte (à) [amikot] *adv* halfway up *ou* down (the hill).

micro [mikro] *nm* microphone, mike. ◆**microphone** *nm* microphone.

micro- [mikro] *préf* micro-.

microbe [mikrɔb] *nm* germ, microbe.

microcosme [mikrɔkɔsm] *nm* microcosm.

microfilm [mikrɔfilm] *nm* microfilm.

micro-onde [mikrɔɔ̃d] *nf* microwave; **four à micro-ondes** microwave oven.

microscope [mikrɔskɔp] *nm* microscope. ◆**microscopique** *a* microscopic.

midi [midi] *nm* **1** (*heure*) midday, noon, twelve o'clock; (*heure du déjeuner*) lunchtime. **2** (*sud*) south; **le M.** the south of France.

mie [mi] *nf* soft bread, crumb.

miel [mjɛl] *nm* honey. ◆**mielleux, -euse** *a* (*parole, personne*) unctuous.

mien, mienne [mjɛ̃, mjɛn] *pron poss* **le m., la mienne** mine, my one; **les miens, les miennes** mine, my ones; **les deux miens** my two; *– nmpl* **les miens** (*amis etc*) my (own) people.

miette [mjɛt] *nf* (*de pain, de bon sens etc*) crumb; **réduire en miettes** to smash to pieces.

mieux [mjø] *adv & a inv* better (**que** than); (*plus à l'aise*) more comfortable; (*plus beau*) better-looking; **la m., le m., les m.** (*convenir, être etc*) the best; (*de deux*) the better; **le m. serait de . . .** the best thing would be to . . . ; **de m. en m.** better and better; **tu ferais m. de partir** you had better leave; **je ne demande pas m.** there's nothing I'd like better (**que de faire** than to do); *– nm* (*amélioration*) improvement; **faire de son m.** to do one's best.

mièvre [mjɛvr] *a* (*doucereux*) *Péj* mannered, wishy-washy.

mignon, -onne [miɲɔ̃, -ɔn] *a* (*charmant*) cute; (*agréable*) nice.

migraine [migrɛn] *nf* headache; *Méd* migraine.

migration [migrɑsjɔ̃] *nf* migration. ◆**migrant, -ante** *a & nmf* (**travailleur**) **m.** migrant worker, migrant.

mijoter [miʒɔte] *vt* *Culin* to cook (lovingly); (*lentement*) to simmer; (*complot*) *Fig Fam* to brew; *– vi* to simmer.

mil [mil] *nm inv* (*dans les dates*) a *ou* one thousand; **l'an deux m.** the year two thousand.

milice [milis] *nf* militia. ◆**milicien** *nm* militiaman.

milieu, -x [miljø] *nm* (*centre*) middle; (*cadre, groupe social*) environment; (*entre extrêmes*) middle course; (*espace*) *Phys* medium; *pl* (*groupes, littéraires etc*) circles; **au m. de** in the middle of; **au m. du danger** in the midst of danger; **le juste m.** the happy medium; **le m.** (*de malfaiteurs*) the underworld.

militaire [militɛr] *a* military; *– nm* serviceman; (*dans l'armée de terre*) soldier.

milit/er [milite] *vi* (*personne*) to be a militant; (*arguments etc*) to militate (**pour** in favour of). ◆**—ant, -ante** *a & nmf* militant.

mille [mil] **1** *a & nm inv* thousand; **m. hommes**/*etc* a *ou* one thousand men/*etc*; **deux m.** two thousand; **mettre dans le m.** to hit the bull's-eye. **2** *nm* (*mesure*) mile. ◆**m.-pattes** *nm inv* (*insecte*) centipede.

◆**millième** *a* & *nmf* thousandth; **un m.** a thousandth. ◆**millier** *nm* thousand; **un m. (de)** a thousand or so.

millefeuille [milfœj] *nm* (*gâteau*) cream slice.

millénaire [milenɛr] *nm* millennium.

millésime [milezim] *nm* date (*on coins, wine etc*).

millet [mije] *nm Bot* millet.

milli- [mili] *préf* milli-.

milliard [miljar] *nm* thousand million, *Am* billion. ◆**milliardaire** *a* & *nmf* multimillionaire.

millimètre [milimɛtr] *nm* millimetre.

million [miljɔ̃] *nm* million; **un m. de livres/etc** a million pounds/*etc*; **deux millions** two million. ◆**millionième** *a* & *nmf* millionth. ◆**millionnaire** *nmf* millionaire.

mime [mim] *nmf* (*acteur*) mime; **le m.** (*art*) mime. ◆**mimer** *vti* to mime. ◆**mimique** *nf* (*mine*) (funny) face; (*gestes*) signs, sign language.

mimosa [mimoza] *nm* (*arbre, fleur*) mimosa.

minable [minabl] *a* (*médiocre*) pathetic; (*lieu, personne*) shabby.

minaret [minarɛ] *nm* (*de mosquée*) minaret.

minauder [minode] *vi* to simper, make a show of affectation.

mince [mɛ̃s] **1** *a* thin; (*élancé*) slim; (*insignifiant*) slim, paltry. **2** *int* **m. (alors)**! oh heck!, blast (it)! ◆**minceur** *nf* thinness; slimness. ◆**mincir** *vi* to grow slim.

mine [min] *nf* **1** appearance; (*physionomie*) look; **avoir bonne/mauvaise m.** (*santé*) to look well/ill; **faire m. de faire** to appear to do, make as if to do. **2** (*d'or, de charbon etc*) & *Fig* mine; **m. de charbon** coalmine. **3** (*de crayon*) lead. **4** (*engin explosif*) mine. ◆**miner** *vt* **1** (*saper*) to undermine. **2** (*garnir d'explosifs*) to mine.

minerai [minrɛ] *nm* ore.

minéral, -aux [mineral, -o] *a* & *nm* mineral.

minéralogique [mineralɔʒik] *a* **numéro m.** *Aut* registration *ou Am* license number.

minet, -ette [minɛ, -ɛt] *nmf* **1** (*chat*) puss. **2** (*personne*) *Fam* fashion-conscious young man *ou* woman.

mineur, -eure [minœr] *nm* **1** (*ouvrier*) miner. **2** *a* (*jeune, secondaire*) & *Mus* minor; – *nmf Jur* minor. ◆**minier, -ière** *a* (*industrie*) mining-.

mini- [mini] *préf* mini-.

miniature [minjatyr] *nf* miniature; – *a inv* (*train etc*) miniature-.

minibus [minibys] *nm* minibus.

minime [minim] *a* trifling, minor, minimal. ◆**minimiser** *vt* to minimize.

minimum [minimɔm] *nm* minimum; **le m. de** (*force etc*) the minimum (amount of); **au (grand) m.** at the very least; **la température m.** the minimum temperature. ◆**minimal, -aux** *a* minimum, minimal.

ministre [ministr] *nm Pol Rel* minister; **m. de l'Intérieur** = Home Secretary, *Am* Secretary of the Interior. ◆**ministère** *nm* ministry; (*gouvernement*) cabinet; **m. de l'Intérieur** = Home Office, *Am* Department of the Interior. ◆**ministériel, -ielle** *a* ministerial; (*crise, remaniement*) cabinet-.

minorer [minɔre] *vt* to reduce.

minorité [minɔrite] *nf* minority; **en m.** in the *ou* a minority. ◆**minoritaire** *a* (*parti etc*) minority-; **être m.** to be in the *ou* a minority.

Minorque [minɔrk] *nf* Minorca.

minuit [minɥi] *nm* midnight, twelve o'clock.

minus [minys] *nm* (*individu*) *Péj Fam* moron.

minuscule [minyskyl] **1** *a* (*petit*) tiny, minute. **2** *a* & *nf* (*lettre*) **m.** small letter.

minute [minyt] *nf* minute; **à la m.** (*tout de suite*) this (very) minute; **d'une m. à l'autre** any minute (now); – *a inv* **aliments** *ou* **plats m.** convenience food(s). ◆**minuter** *vt* to time. ◆**minuterie** *nf* time switch.

minutie [minysi] *nf* meticulousness. ◆**minutieux, -euse** *a* meticulous.

mioche [mjɔʃ] *nmf* (*enfant*) *Fam* kid, youngster.

miracle [mirakl] *nm* miracle; **par m.** miraculously. ◆**miraculeux, -euse** *a* miraculous.

mirador [miradɔr] *nm Mil* watchtower.

mirage [miraʒ] *nm* mirage.

mirifique [mirifik] *a Hum* fabulous.

mirobolant [mirɔbɔlɑ̃] *a Fam* fantastic.

miroir [mirwar] *nm* mirror. ◆**miroiter** *vi* to gleam, shimmer.

mis [mi] *voir* **mettre**; – *a* **bien m.** (*vêtu*) well dressed.

misanthrope [mizɑ̃trɔp] *nmf* misanthropist; – *a* misanthropic.

mise [miz] *nf* **1** (*action de mettre*) putting; **m. en service** putting into service; **m. en marche** starting up; **m. à la retraite** pensioning off; **m. à feu** (*de fusée*) blast-off; **m. en scène** *Th* production; *Cin* direction. **2** (*argent*) stake. **3** (*tenue*) attire. ◆**miser** *vt* (*argent*) to stake (**sur** on); – *vi* **m. sur** (*cheval*) to back; (*compter sur*) to bank on.

misère [mizɛr] *nf* (grinding) poverty; (*malheur*) misery; (*bagatelle*) trifle. ◆**mi-**

sérable a miserable, wretched; (*indigent*) poor, destitute; (*logement, quartier*) seedy, slummy; – *nmf* (poor) wretch; (*indigent*) pauper. ◆**miséreux, -euse** a destitute; – *nmf* pauper.

miséricorde [mizerikɔrd] *nf* mercy. ◆**miséricordieux, -euse** a merciful.

misogyne [mizɔʒin] *nmf* misogynist.

missile [misil] *nm* (*fusée*) missile.

mission [misjɔ̃] *nf* mission; (*tâche*) task. ◆**missionnaire** *nm* & a missionary.

missive [misiv] *nf* (*lettre*) missive.

mistral [mistral] *nm inv* (*vent*) mistral.

mite [mit] *nf* (*clothes*) moth; (*du fromage etc*) mite. ◆**mité** a moth-eaten.

mi-temps [mitɑ̃] *nf* (*pause*) *Sp* half-time; (*période*) *Sp* half; **à mi-t.** (*travailler etc*) part-time.

miteux, -euse [mitø, -øz] a shabby.

mitigé [mitiʒe] a (*zèle etc*) moderate, lukewarm; (*mêlé*) *Fam* mixed.

mitraille [mitraj] *nf* gunfire. ◆**mitrailler** *vt* to machinegun; (*photographier*) *Fam* to click *ou* snap away at. ◆**mitraillette** *nf* submachine gun. ◆**mitrailleur** a *fusil* m. machinegun. ◆**mitrailleuse** *nf* machinegun.

mi-voix (à) [amivwa] adv in an undertone.

mixe(u)r [miksœr] *nm* (*pour mélanger*) (food) mixer.

mixte [mikst] a mixed; (*école*) co-educational, mixed; (*tribunal*) joint.

mixture [mikstyr] *nf* (*boisson*) *Péj* mixture.

Mlle [madmwazɛl] *abrév* = **Mademoiselle**.

MM [mesjø] *abrév* = **Messieurs**.

mm *abrév* (*millimètre*) mm.

Mme [madam] *abrév* = **Madame**.

mobile [mɔbil] **1** a (*pièce etc*) moving; (*personne*) mobile; (*feuillets*) detachable, loose; (*reflets*) changing; **échelle m.** sliding scale; **fête m.** mov(e)able feast; – *nm* (*œuvre d'art*) mobile. **2** *nm* (*motif*) motive (de for). ◆**mobilité** *nf* mobility.

mobilier [mɔbilje] *nm* furniture.

mobiliser [mɔbilize] *vti* to mobilize. ◆**mobilisation** *nf* mobilization.

mobylette [mɔbilɛt] *nf* moped.

mocassin [mɔkasɛ̃] *nm* (*chaussure*) moccasin.

moche [mɔʃ] a *Fam* (*laid*) ugly; (*mauvais, peu gentil*) lousy, rotten.

modalité [mɔdalite] *nf* method (de of).

mode [mɔd] **1** *nf* fashion; (*industrie*) fashion trade; **à la m.** in fashion, fashionable; **passé de m.** out of fashion; **à la m. de** in the manner of. **2** *nm* mode, method; **m. d'emploi**

directions (for use); **m. de vie** way of life. **3** *nm Gram* mood.

modèle [mɔdɛl] *nm* (*schéma, exemple, personne*) model; **m. (réduit)** (scale) model; – a (*élève etc*) model-. ◆**model/er** *vt* to model (**sur** on); **se m. sur** to model oneself on. ◆**—age** *nm* (*de statue etc*) modelling. ◆**modéliste** *nmf Tex* stylist, designer.

modéré [mɔdere] a moderate. ◆**—ment** adv moderately.

modérer [mɔdere] *vt* to moderate, restrain; (*vitesse, allure*) to reduce; – **se m.** *vpr* to restrain oneself. ◆**modérateur, -trice** a moderating; – *nmf* moderator. ◆**modération** *nf* moderation, restraint; reduction; **avec m.** in moderation.

moderne [mɔdɛrn] a modern; – *nm* **le m.** (*mobilier*) modern furniture. ◆**modernisation** *nf* modernization. ◆**moderniser** *vt*, – **se m.** *vpr* to modernize. ◆**modernisme** *nm* modernism.

modeste [mɔdɛst] a modest. ◆**modestement** adv modestly. ◆**modestie** *nf* modesty.

modifier [mɔdifje] *vt* to modify, alter; – **se m.** *vpr* to alter. ◆**modification** *nf* modification, alteration.

modique [mɔdik] a (*salaire, prix*) modest. ◆**modicité** *nf* modesty.

module [mɔdyl] *nm* module.

moduler [mɔdyle] *vt* to modulate. ◆**modulation** *nf* modulation.

moelle [mwal] *nf Anat* marrow; **m. épinière** spinal cord.

moelleux, -euse [mwalø, -øz] a soft; (*voix, vin*) mellow.

mœurs [mœr(s)] *nfpl* (*morale*) morals; (*habitudes*) habits, customs.

mohair [mɔɛr] *nm* mohair.

moi [mwa] *pron* **1** (*complément direct*) me; **laissez-moi** leave me; **pour moi** for me. **2** (*indirect*) (to) me; **montrez-le-moi** show it to me, show me it. **3** (*sujet*) I; **moi, je veux** *I* want. **4** *nm inv Psy* self, ego. ◆**moi-même** *pron* myself.

moignon [mwaɲɔ̃] *nm* stump.

moindre [mwɛ̃dr] a **être m.** (*moins grand*) to be less; **le m. doute**/*etc* the slightest *ou* least doubt/*etc*; **le m.** (*de mes problèmes etc*) the least (**de** of); (*de deux problèmes etc*) the lesser (**de** of).

moine [mwan] *nm* monk, friar.

moineau, -x [mwano] *nm* sparrow.

moins [mwɛ̃] **1** adv ([mwɛz] before vowel) less (**que** than); **m. de** (*temps, zèle etc*) less (**que** than), not so much (**que** as); (*gens, livres etc*) fewer (**que** than), not so many (*que* as); (*cent francs etc*) less than; **m. froid/grand/etc** not as cold/big/etc (*que* as); **de m. en m.** less and less; **le m., la m., les m.** (*travailler etc*) the least; **le m. grand** the smallest; **au m., du m.** at least; **de m., en m.** (*qui manque*) missing; **dix ans/etc de m.** ten years/etc less; **en m.** (*personne, objet*) less; (*personnes, objets*) fewer; **les m. de vingt ans** those under twenty, the under-twenties; **à m. que** (+ *sub*) unless. **2** *prép Math* minus; **deux heures m. cinq** five to two; **il fait m. dix (degrés)** it's minus ten (degrees).

mois [mwa] *nm* month; **au m. de juin/etc** in (the month of) June/etc.

mois/ir [mwazir] *vi* to go mouldy; (*attendre*) *Fig* to hang about. ◆—**i** *a* mouldy; – *nm* mould, mildew; **sentir le m.** to smell musty. ◆**moisissure** *nf* mould, mildew.

moisson [mwasɔ̃] *nf* harvest. ◆**moissonner** *vt* to harvest. ◆**moissonneuse-batteuse** *nf* (*pl* **moissonneuses-batteuses**) combine-harvester.

moite [mwat] *a* sticky, moist. ◆**moiteur** *nf* stickiness, moistness.

moitié [mwatje] *nf* half; **la m. de la pomme/etc** half (of) the apple/etc; **à m.** (*remplir etc*) halfway; **à m. fermé/cru/etc** half closed/raw/etc; **à m. prix** (for *ou* at) half-price; **de m.** by half; **m.-moitié** *Fam* so-so; **partager m.-moitié** *Fam* to split fifty-fifty.

moka [mɔka] *nm* (*café*) mocha.

mol [mɔl] *voir* **mou.**

molaire [mɔlɛr] *nf* (*dent*) molar.

molécule [mɔlekyl] *nf* molecule.

moleskine [mɔlɛskin] *nf* imitation leather.

molester [mɔlɛste] *vt* to manhandle.

molette [mɔlɛt] *nf* **clé à m.** adjustable wrench *ou* spanner.

mollasse [mɔlas] *a Péj* flabby.

molle [mɔl] *voir* **mou.** ◆**mollement** *adv* feebly; (*paresseusement*) lazily. ◆**mollesse** *nf* softness; (*faiblesse*) feebleness. ◆**mollir** *vi* to go soft; (*courage*) to flag.

mollet [mɔlɛ] **1** *a* **œuf m.** soft-boiled egg. **2** *nm* (*de jambe*) calf.

mollusque [mɔlysk] *nm* mollusc.

môme [mom] *nmf* (*enfant*) *Fam* kid.

moment [mɔmɑ̃] *nm* (*instant*) moment; (*période*) time; **en ce m.** at the moment; **par moments** at times; **au m. de partir** when just about to leave; **au m. où** when, just as; **du m. que** (*puisque*) seeing that. ◆**momentané** *a* momentary. ◆**momentanément** *adv* temporarily, for the moment.

momie [mɔmi] *nf* (*cadavre*) mummy.

mon, ma, *pl* **mes** [mɔ̃, ma, me] (**ma** *becomes* **mon** [mɔ̃n] *before a vowel or mute h*) *a poss* my; **mon père** my father; **ma mère** my mother; **mon ami(e)** my friend.

Monaco [mɔnako] *nf* Monaco.

monarque [mɔnark] *nm* monarch. ◆**monarchie** *nf* monarchy. ◆**monarchique** *a* monarchic.

monastère [mɔnastɛr] *nm* monastery.

monceau, -x [mɔ̃so] *nm* heap, pile.

monde [mɔ̃d] *nm* world; (*milieu social*) set; **du m.** (*gens*) people; (*beaucoup*) a lot of people; **un m. fou** a tremendous crowd; **le (grand) m.** (high) society; **le m. entier** the whole world; **tout le m.** everybody; **mettre au m.** to give birth to; **pas le moins du m.!** not in the least *ou* slightest! ◆**mondain, -aine** *a* (*vie, réunion etc*) society-. ◆**mondanités** *nfpl* (*événements*) social events. ◆**mondial, -aux** *a* (*renommée etc*) world-; (*crise*) worldwide. ◆**mondialement** *adv* the (whole) world over.

monégasque [mɔnegask] *a & nmf* Monegasque.

monétaire [mɔnetɛr] *a* monetary.

mongolien, -ienne [mɔ̃gɔljɛ̃, -jɛn] *a & nmf Méd* mongol.

moniteur, -trice [mɔnitœr, -tris] *nmf* **1** instructor; (*de colonie de vacances*) assistant, *Am* camp counselor. **2** (*écran*) *Tech* monitor.

monnaie [mɔnɛ] *nf* (*devise*) currency, money; (*appoint, pièces*) change; **pièce de m.** coin; (**petite**) **m.** (small) change; **faire de la m.** to get change; **faire de la m. à qn** to give s.o. change (**sur un billet** for a note); **c'est m. courante** it's very frequent; **Hôtel de la M.** mint. ◆**monnayer** *vt* (*talent etc*) to cash in on; (*bien, titre*) *Com* to convert into cash.

mono [mɔno] *a inv* (*disque etc*) mono.

mono- [mɔno] *préf* mono-.

monocle [mɔnɔkl] *nm* monocle.

monologue [mɔnɔlɔg] *nm* monologue.

monoplace [mɔnɔplas] *a & nmf* (*avion, voiture*) single-seater.

monopole [mɔnɔpɔl] *nm* monopoly. ◆**monopoliser** *vt* to monopolize.

monosyllabe [mɔnɔsilab] *nm* monosyllable. ◆**monosyllabique** *a* monosyllabic.

monotone [mɔnɔtɔn] *a* monotonous. ◆**monotonie** *nf* monotony.

monseigneur [mɔ̃sɛɲœr] *nm* (*évêque*) His *ou* Your Grace; (*prince*) His *ou* Your Highness.

monsieur, *pl* **messieurs** [məsjø, mesjø] *nm* gentleman; **oui m.** yes; (*avec déférence*) yes sir; **oui messieurs** yes (gentlemen); **M. Legras** Mr Legras; **Messieurs** *ou* **MM Legras** Messrs Legras; **tu vois ce m.?** do you see that man *ou* gentleman?; **Monsieur** (*sur une lettre*) *Com* Dear Sir.

monstre [mɔ̃str] *nm* monster; *– a* (*énorme*) *Fam* colossal. ◆**monstrueux, -euse** *a* (*abominable, énorme*) monstrous. ◆**monstruosité** *nf* (*horreur*) monstrosity.

mont [mɔ̃] *nm* (*montagne*) mount.

montagne [mɔ̃taɲ] *nf* mountain; **la m.** (*zone*) the mountains; **montagnes russes** *Fig* roller coaster. ◆**montagnard, -arde** *nmf* mountain dweller; *– a* (*peuple*) mountain-. ◆**montagneux, -euse** *a* mountainous.

mont-de-piété [mɔ̃dpjete] *nm* (*pl* **monts-de-piété**) pawnshop.

monte-charge [mɔ̃tʃarʒ] *nm inv* service lift *ou* Am elevator.

mont/er [mɔ̃te] *vi* (*aux être*) (*personne*) to go *ou* come up; (*s'élever*) to go up; (*grimper*) to climb (up) (**sur** onto); (*prix*) to go up, rise; (*marée*) to come in; (*avion*) to climb; **m. dans un véhicule** to get in(to) a vehicle; **m. dans un train** to get on(to) a train; **m. sur** (*échelle etc*) to climb up; (*trône*) to ascend; **m. en courant**/*etc* to run/*etc* up; **m. (à cheval)** *Sp* to ride (a horse); **m. en graine** (*salade etc*) to go to seed; *– vt* (*aux avoir*) (*côte etc*) to climb (up); (*objets*) to bring *ou* take up; (*cheval*) to ride; (*tente, affaire*) to set up; (*machine*) to assemble; (*bijou*) to set, mount; (*complot, démonstration*) to mount; (*pièce*) *Th* to stage, mount; **m. l'escalier** to go *ou* come upstairs *ou* up the stairs; **faire m.** (*visiteur etc*) to show up; **m. qn contre qn** to set s.o. against s.o.; *– se m.* *vpr* (*s'irriter*) *Fam* to get angry; **se m. à** (*frais*) to amount to. ◆**—ant 1** *a* (*chemin*) uphill; (*mouvement*) upward; (*marée*) rising; (*col*) stand-up; (*robe*) high-necked; **chaussure montante** boot. **2** *nm* (*somme*) amount. **3** *nm* (*de barrière*) post; (*d'échelle*) upright. ◆**—é** *a* (*police*) mounted. ◆**—ée** *nf* ascent, climb; (*de prix, des eaux*) rise; (*chemin*) slope. ◆**—age** *nm* Tech assembling, assembly; *Cin* editing. ◆**—eur, -euse** *nmf* Tech fitter; *Cin* editor.

montre [mɔ̃tr] *nf* **1** watch; **course contre la m.** race against time. **2 faire m. de** to show. ◆**m.-bracelet** *nf* (*pl* **montres-bracelets**) wristwatch.

Montréal [mɔ̃real] *nm ou f* Montreal.

montrer [mɔ̃tre] *vt* to show (**à** to); **m. du doigt** to point to; **m. à qn à faire qch** to

show s.o. how to do sth; *– se m.* *vpr* to show oneself, appear; (*s'avérer*) to turn out to be; **se m. courageux**/*etc* (*être*) to be courageous/*etc.*

monture [mɔ̃tyr] *nf* **1** (*cheval*) mount. **2** (*de lunettes*) frame; (*de bijou*) setting.

monument [mɔnymɑ̃] *nm* monument; **m. aux morts** war memorial. ◆**monumental, -aux** *a* (*imposant, énorme etc*) monumental.

moquer (se) [səmɔke] *vpr* **se m. de** (*allure etc*) to make fun of; (*personne*) to make a fool of, make fun of; **je m'en moque!** *Fam* I couldn't care less! ◆**moquerie** *nf* mockery. ◆**moqueur, -euse** *a* mocking.

moquette [mɔket] *nf* fitted carpet(s), wall-to-wall carpeting.

moral, -aux [mɔral, -o] *a* moral; *– nm* **le m.** spirits, morale. ◆**morale** *nf* (*principes*) morals; (*code*) moral code; (*d'histoire etc*) moral; **faire la m. à qn** to lecture s.o. ◆**moralement** *adv* morally. ◆**moraliser** *vi* to moralize. ◆**moraliste** *nmf* moralist. ◆**moralité** *nf* (*mœurs*) morality; (*de fable, récit etc*) moral.

moratoire [mɔratwar] *nm* moratorium.

morbide [mɔrbid] *a* morbid.

morceau, -x [mɔrso] *nm* piece, bit; (*de sucre*) lump; (*de viande*) *Culin* cut; (*extrait*) *Littér* extract. ◆**morceler** *vt* (*terrain*) to divide up.

mordiller [mɔrdije] *vt* to nibble.

mord/re [mɔrdr] *vti* to bite; **ça mord** *Pêche* I have a bite. ◆**—ant 1** *a* (*voix, manière*) scathing; (*froid*) biting; (*personne, ironie*) caustic. **2** *nm* (*énergie*) punch. ◆**—u, -ue** *nmf* **un m. du jazz**/*etc* *Fam* a jazz/*etc* fan.

morfondre (se) [səmɔrfɔ̃dr] *vpr* to get bored (waiting), mope (about).

morgue [mɔrg] *nf* (*lieu*) mortuary, morgue.

moribond, -onde [mɔribɔ̃, -ɔ̃d] *a & nmf* dying *ou* moribund (person).

morne [mɔrn] *a* dismal, gloomy, dull.

morose [mɔroz] *a* morose, sullen.

morphine [mɔrfin] *nf* morphine.

mors [mɔr] *nm* (*de harnais*) bit.

morse [mɔrs] *nm* **1** Morse (code). **2** (*animal*) walrus.

morsure [mɔrsyr] *nf* bite.

mort¹ [mɔr] *nf* death; **mettre à m.** to put to death; **silence de m.** dead silence. ◆**mortalité** *nf* death rate, mortality. ◆**mortel, -elle** *a* (*hommes, ennemi, danger etc*) mortal; (*accident*) fatal; (*chaleur*) deadly; (*pâleur*) deadly; *– nmf* mortal. ◆**mortellement** *adv* (*blessé*) fatally.

mort², morte [mɔr, mɔrt] *a* (*personne, plante, ville etc*) dead; **m. de fatigue** dead tired; **m. de froid** numb with cold; **m. de peur** frightened to death; – *nmf* dead man, dead woman; **les morts** the dead; **de nombreux morts** (*victimes*) many deaths *ou* casualties; **le jour** *ou* **la fête des Morts** All Souls' Day. ◆**morte-saison** *nf* off season. ◆**mort-né** *a* (*enfant*) & *Fig* stillborn.

mortier [mɔrtje] *nm* mortar.

mortifier [mɔrtifje] *vt* to mortify.

mortuaire [mɔrtɥɛr] *a* (*avis, rites etc*) death-, funeral.

morue [mɔry] *nf* cod.

morve [mɔrv] *nf* (nasal) mucus. ◆**morveux, -euse** *a* (*enfant*) snotty (-nosed).

mosaïque [mɔzaik] *nf* mosaic.

Moscou [mɔsku] *nm ou f* Moscow.

mosquée [mɔske] *nf* mosque.

mot [mo] *nm* word; **envoyer un m. à** to drop a line to; **m. à** *ou* **pour m.** word for word; **bon m.** witticism; **mots croisés** crossword (puzzle); **m. d'ordre** *Pol* resolution, order; (*slogan*) watchword; **m. de passe** password.

motard [mɔtar] *nm Fam* motorcyclist.

motel [mɔtɛl] *nm* motel.

moteur[1] [mɔtœr] *nm* (*de véhicule etc*) engine, motor; *Él* motor.

moteur[2], **-trice** [mɔtœr, -tris] *a* (*force*) driving-; (*nerf, muscle*) motor.

motif [mɔtif] *nm* **1** reason, motive. **2** (*dessin*) pattern.

motion [mɔsjɔ̃] *nf Pol* motion; **on a voté une m. de censure** a vote of no confidence was given.

motiver [mɔtive] *vt* (*inciter, causer*) to motivate; (*justifier*) to justify. ◆**motivation** *nf* motivation.

moto [mɔto] *nf* motorcycle, motorbike. ◆**motocycliste** *nmf* motorcyclist.

motorisé [mɔtɔrize] *a* motorized.

motte [mɔt] *nf* (*de terre*) clod, lump; (*de beurre*) block.

mou (*or* **mol** before vowel or mute h), **molle** [mu, mɔl] *a* soft; (*faible, sans énergie*) feeble; – *nm* **avoir du m.** (*cordage*) to be slack.

mouchard, -arde [muʃar, -ard] *nmf Péj* informer. ◆**moucharder** *vt* **m. qn** *Fam* to inform on s.o.

mouche [muʃ] *nf* (*insecte*) fly; **prendre la m.** (*se fâcher*) to go into a huff; **faire m.** to hit the bull's-eye. ◆**moucheron** *nm* (*insecte*) midge.

moucher [muʃe] *vt* **m. qn** to wipe s.o.'s nose; **se m.** to blow one's nose.

moucheté [muʃte] *a* speckled, spotted.

mouchoir [muʃwar] *nm* handkerchief; (*en papier*) tissue.

moudre*** [mudr] *vt* (*café, blé*) to grind.

moue [mu] *nf* long face, pout; **faire la m.** to pout, pull a (long) face.

mouette [mwɛt] *nf* (sea)gull.

moufle [mufl] *nf* (*gant*) mitt(en).

mouill/er [muje] **1** *vt* to wet, make wet; **se faire m.** to get wet; – **se m.** *vpr* to get (oneself) wet; (*se compromettre*) *Fam* to get involved (*by taking risks*). **2** *vt* **m. l'ancre** *Nau* to (drop) anchor; – *vi* to anchor. ◆**—é** *a* wet (**de** with). ◆**—age** *nm* (*action*) *Nau* anchoring; (*lieu*) anchorage.

moule[1] [mul] *nm* mould, *Am* mold; **m. à gâteaux** cake tin. ◆**moul/er** *vt* to mould, *Am* mold; (*statue*) to cast; **m. qn** (*vêtement*) to fit s.o. tightly. ◆**—ant** *a* (*vêtement*) tight-fitting. ◆**—age** *nm* moulding; casting; (*objet*) cast. ◆**moulure** *nf Archit* moulding.

moule[2] [mul] *nf* (*mollusque*) mussel.

moulin [mulɛ̃] *nm* mill; (*moteur*) *Fam* engine; **m. à vent** windmill; **m. à café** coffee-grinder.

moulinet [mulinɛ] *nm* **1** (*de canne à pêche*) reel. **2** (*de bâton*) twirl.

moulu [muly] *voir* **moudre**; – *a* (*café*) ground; (*éreinté*) *Fam* dead tired.

mour/ir*** [murir] *vi* (*aux être*) to die (**de** of, from); **m. de froid** to die of exposure; **m. d'ennui/de fatigue** *Fig* to be dead bored/tired; **m. de peur** *Fig* to be frightened to death; **s'ennuyer à m.** to be bored to death; – **se m.** *vpr* to be dying. ◆**—ant, -ante** *a* dying; (*voix*) faint; – *nmf* dying person.

mousquetaire [muskətɛr] *nm Mil Hist* musketeeer.

mousse [mus] **1** *nf Bot* moss. **2** *nf* (*écume*) froth, foam; (*de bière*) froth; (*de savon*) lather; **m. à raser** shaving foam. **3** *nf Culin* mousse. **4** *nm Nau* ship's boy. ◆**mousser** *vi* (*bière etc*) to froth; (*savon*) to lather; (*eau savonneuse*) to foam. ◆**mousseux, -euse** *a* frothy; (*vin*) sparkling; – *nm* sparkling wine. ◆**moussu** *a* mossy.

mousseline [muslin] *nf* (*coton*) muslin.

mousson [musɔ̃] *nf* (*vent*) monsoon.

moustache [mustaʃ] *nf* moustache, *Am* mustache; *pl* (*de chat etc*) whiskers. ◆**moustachu** *a* wearing a moustache.

moustique [mustik] *nm* mosquito. ◆**moustiquaire** *nf* mosquito net; (*en métal*) screen.

moutard [mutar] *nm* (*enfant*) *Arg* kid.

moutarde [mutard] *nf* mustard.

mouton [mutɔ̃] *nm* sheep; (*viande*) mutton;

pl (sur la mer) white horses; (*poussière*) bits of dust; **peau de m.** sheepskin.

mouvement [muvmɑ̃] *nm* (*geste, déplacement, groupe etc*) & *Mus* movement; (*de colère*) outburst; (*impulsion*) impulse; **en m.** in motion. ◆**mouvementé** *a* (*animé*) lively, exciting; (*séance, vie etc*) eventful.

mouv/oir* [muvwar] *vi*, — **se m.** *vpr* to move; **mû par** (*mécanisme*) driven by. ◆**—ant** *a* (*changeant*) changing; **sables mouvants** quicksands.

moyen¹, -enne [mwajɛ̃, -ɛn] *a* average; (*format, entreprise etc*) medium(-sized); (*solution*) intermediate, middle; — *nf* average; (*dans un examen*) pass mark; (*dans un devoir*) half marks; **la moyenne d'âge** the average age; **en moyenne** on average. ◆**moyennement** *adv* averagely, moderately.

moyen² [mwajɛ̃] *nm* (*procédé, façon*) means, way (**de faire** of doing, to do); *pl* (*capacités*) ability, powers; (*argent, ressources*) means; **au m. de** by means of; **il n'y a pas m. de faire** it's not possible to do; **je n'ai pas les moyens** (*argent*) I can't afford it; **par mes propres moyens** under my own steam.

moyennant [mwajɛnɑ̃] *prép* (*pour*) (in return) for; (*avec*) with.

moyeu, -x [mwajø] *nm* (*de roue*) hub.

mucosités [mykozite] *nfpl* mucus.

mue [my] *nf* moulting; breaking of the voice. ◆**muer** [mɥe] *vi* (*animal*) to moult; (*voix*) to break; **se m. en** to become transformed into.

muet, -ette [mɥɛ, -ɛt] *a* (*infirme*) dumb; (*de surprise etc*) speechless; (*film, reproche etc*) silent; *Gram* mute; — *nmf* dumb person.

mufle [myfl] *nm* **1** (*d'animal*) nose, muzzle. **2** (*individu*) *Péj* lout.

mug/ir [myʒir] *vi* (*vache*) to moo; (*bœuf*) to bellow; (*vent*) *Fig* to roar. ◆**—issement(s)** *nm(pl)* moo(ing); bellow(ing); roar(ing).

muguet [mygɛ] *nm* lily of the valley.

mule [myl] *nf* **1** (*pantoufle*) mule. **2** (*animal*) (she-)mule. ◆**mulet¹** *nm* (he-)mule.

mulet² [mylɛ] *nm* (*poisson*) mullet.

multi- [mylti] *préf* multi-.

multicolore [myltikɔlɔr] *a* multicoloured.

multinationale [myltinasjɔnal] *nf* multinational.

multiple [myltipl] *a* (*nombreux*) numerous; (*ayant des formes variées*) multiple; — *nm Math* multiple. ◆**multiplication** *nf* multiplication; (*augmentation*) increase. ◆**multiplicité** *nf* multiplicity. ◆**multiplier** *vt* to

multiply; — **se m.** *vpr* to increase; (*se reproduire*) to multiply.

multitude [myltityd] *nf* multitude.

municipal, -aux [mynisipal, -o] *a* municipal; **conseil m.** town council. ◆**municipalité** *nf* (*corps*) town council; (*commune*) municipality.

munir [mynir] *vt* **m. de** to provide *ou* equip with; **se m. de** to provide oneself with; **muni de** (*papiers, arme etc*) in possession of.

munitions [mynisjɔ̃] *nfpl* ammunition.

muqueuse [mykøz] *nf* mucous membrane.

mur [myr] *nm* wall; **m. du son** sound barrier; **au pied du m.** *Fig* with one's back to the wall. ◆**muraille** *nf* (high) wall. ◆**mural, -aux** *a* (*carte etc*) wall-; **peinture murale** mural (painting). ◆**murer** *vt* (*porte*) to wall up; **m. qn** to wall s.o. in.

mûr [myr] *a* (*fruit, projet etc*) ripe; (*âge, homme*) mature. ◆**mûrement** *adv* (*réfléchir*) carefully. ◆**mûrir** *vti* (*fruit*) to ripen; (*personne, projet*) to mature.

muret [myrɛ] *nm* low wall.

murmure [myrmyr] *nm* murmur. ◆**murmurer** *vti* to murmur.

musc [mysk] *nm* (*parfum*) musk.

muscade [myskad] *nf* nutmeg.

muscle [myskl] *nm* muscle. ◆**musclé** *a* (*bras*) brawny, muscular. ◆**musculaire** *a* (*tissu, système etc*) muscular. ◆**musculature** *nf* muscles.

museau, -x [myzo] *nm* (*de chien etc*) muzzle; (*de porc*) snout. ◆**museler** *vt* (*animal, presse etc*) to muzzle. ◆**muselière** *nf* (*appareil*) muzzle.

musée [myze] *nm* museum; **m. de peinture** (public) art gallery. ◆**muséum** *nm* (natural history) museum.

musette [myzɛt] *nf* (*d'ouvrier*) duffel bag, kit bag.

music-hall [myzikol] *nm* variety theatre.

musique [myzik] *nf* music; (*fanfare*) *Mil* band. ◆**musical, -aux** *a* musical. ◆**musicien, -ienne** *nmf* musician; — *a* **être très/assez m.** to be very/quite musical.

musulman, -ane [myzylmɑ̃, -an] *a* & *nmf* Moslem, Muslim.

muter [myte] *vt* (*employé*) to transfer. ◆**mutation** *nf* **1** transfer. **2** *Biol* mutation.

mutil/er [mytile] *vt* to mutilate, maim; **être mutilé** to be disabled. ◆**—é, -ée** *nmf* **m. de guerre/du travail** disabled ex-serviceman/worker. ◆**mutilation** *nf* mutilation.

mutin [mytɛ̃] **1** *a* (*espiègle*) saucy. **2** *nm* (*rebelle*) mutineer. ◆**se mutin/er** *vpr* to mutiny. ◆**—é** *a* mutinous. ◆**mutinerie** *nf* mutiny.

mutisme [mytism] *nm* (stubborn) silence.
mutualité [mytyalite] *nf* mutual insurance. ◆**mutualiste** *nmf* member of a friendly *ou Am* benefit society. ◆**mutuelle**[1] *nf* friendly society, *Am* benefit society.
mutuel, -elle[2] [mytyɛl] *a* (*réciproque*) mutual. ◆**mutuellement** *adv* (*l'un l'autre*) each other (mutually).
myope [mjɔp] *a* & *nmf* shortsighted (person). ◆**myopie** *nf* shortsightedness.
myosotis [mjozɔtis] *nm Bot* forget-me-not.
myrtille [mirtij] *nf Bot* bilberry.

mystère [mistɛr] *nm* mystery. ◆**mystérieux, -euse** *a* mysterious.
mystifier [mistifje] *vt* to fool, deceive, hoax. ◆**mystification** *nf* hoax.
mystique [mistik] *a* mystic(al); – *nmf* (*personne*) mystic; – *nf* mystique (**de** of). ◆**mysticisme** *nm* mysticism.
mythe [mit] *nm* myth. ◆**mythique** *a* mythical. ◆**mythologie** *nf* mythology. ◆**mythologique** *a* mythological.
mythomane [mitɔman] *nmf* compulsive liar.

N

N, n [ɛn] *nm* N, n.
n' [n] *voir* ne.
nabot [nabo] *nm Péj* midget.
nacelle [nasɛl] *nf* (*de ballon*) car, gondola; (*de landau*) carriage, carrycot.
nacre [nakr] *nf* mother-of-pearl. ◆**nacré** *a* pearly.
nage [naʒ] *nf* (swimming) stroke; **n. libre** freestyle; **traverser à la n.** to swim across; **en n.** *Fig* sweating. ◆**nager** *vi* to swim; (*flotter*) to float; **je nage dans le bonheur** my happiness knows no bounds; **je nage complètement** (*je suis perdu*) *Fam* I'm all at sea; – *vt* (*crawl etc*) to swim. ◆**nageur, -euse** *nmf* swimmer.
nageoire [naʒwar] *nf* (*de poisson*) fin; (*de phoque*) flipper.
naguère [nagɛr] *adv Litt* not long ago.
naïf, -ïve [naif, -iv] *a* simple, naïve; – *nmf* (*jobard*) simpleton.
nain, naine [nɛ̃, nɛn] *nmf* dwarf; – *a* (*arbre, haricot*) dwarf-.
naissance [nesɑ̃s] *nf* birth; (*de bras, cou*) base; **donner n. à** *Fig* to give rise to; **de n.** from birth.
naître* [nɛtr] *vi* to be born; (*jour*) to dawn; (*sentiment, difficulté*) to arise (**de** from); **faire n.** (*soupçon, industrie etc*) to give rise to, create. ◆**naissant** *a* (*amitié etc*) incipient.
naïveté [naivte] *nf* simplicity, naïveté.
nant/ir [nɑ̃tir] *vt* **n. de** to provide with. ◆**—i** *a* & *nmpl* (*riche*) affluent.
naphtaline [naftalin] *nf* mothballs.
nappe [nap] *nf* **1** table cloth. **2** (*d'eau*) sheet; (*de gaz, pétrole*) layer; (*de brouillard*) blanket. ◆**napperon** *nm* (soft) table mat; (*pour vase etc*) (soft) mat, cloth.

narcotique [narkɔtik] *a* & *nm* narcotic.
narguer [narge] *vt* to flout, mock.
narine [narin] *nf* nostril.
narquois [narkwa] *a* sneering.
narration [narasjɔ̃] *nf* (*récit, acte, art*) narration. ◆**narrateur, -trice** *nmf* narrator.
nasal, -aux [nazal, -o] *a* nasal.
naseau, -x [nazo] *nm* (*de cheval*) nostril.
nasiller [nazije] *vi* (*personne*) to speak with a twang; (*micro, radio*) to crackle. ◆**nasillard** *a* (*voix*) nasal; (*micro etc*) crackling.
natal, mpl -als [natal] *a* (*pays etc*) native; **sa maison natale** the house where he *ou* she was born. ◆**natalité** *nf* birthrate.
natation [natasjɔ̃] *nf* swimming.
natif, -ive [natif, -iv] *a* & *nmf* native; **être n. de** to be a native of.
nation [nasjɔ̃] *nf* nation; **les Nations Unies** the United Nations. ◆**national, -aux** *a* national; ◆**nationale** *nf* (*route*) trunk road, *Am* highway. ◆**nationaliser** *vt* to nationalize. ◆**nationaliste** *a Péj* nationalistic; – *nmf* nationalist. ◆**nationalité** *nf* nationality.
nativité [nativite] *nf Rel* nativity.
natte [nat] *nf* **1** (*de cheveux*) plait, *Am* braid. **2** (*tapis*) mat, (piece of) matting. ◆**natt/er** *vt* to plait, *Am* braid. ◆**—age** *n* (*matière*) matting.
naturaliser [natyralize] *vt* (*personne*) *Pol* to naturalize. ◆**naturalisation** *nf* naturalization.
nature [natyr] *nf* (*monde naturel, caractère*) nature; **de toute n.** of every kind; **être de n. à** to be likely to; **payer en n.** *Fin* to pay in kind; **n. morte** (*tableau*) still life; **plus grand que n.** larger than life; – *a inv* (*omelette, yaourt etc*) plain; (*café*) black. ◆**natura-**

liste *nmf* naturalist. ◆**naturiste** *nmf* nudist, naturist.

naturel, -elle [natyrɛl] *a* natural; **mort naturelle** death from natural causes; – *nm* (*caractère*) nature; (*simplicité*) naturalness. ◆**naturellement** *adv* naturally.

naufrage [nofraʒ] *nm* (ship)wreck; (*ruine*) *Litt Fig* ruin; **faire n.** to be (ship)wrecked. ◆**naufragé, -ée** *a* & *nmf* shipwrecked (person).

nausée [noze] *nf* nausea, sickness. ◆**nauséabond** *a* nauseating, sickening.

nautique [notik] *a* nautical; (*sports, ski*) water-.

naval, mpl -als [naval] *a* naval; **constructions navales** shipbuilding.

navet [navɛ] *nm* **1** *Bot Culin* turnip. **2** (*film etc*) *Péj* flop, dud.

navette [navɛt] *nf* (*transport*) shuttle (service); **faire la n.** (*véhicule, personne etc*) to shuttle back and forth (**entre** between); **n. spatiale** space shuttle.

naviguer [navige] *vi* (*bateau*) to sail; (*piloter, voler*) to navigate. ◆**navigabilité** *nf* (*de bateau*) seaworthiness; (*d'avion*) airworthiness. ◆**navigable** *a* (*fleuve*) navigable. ◆**navigant** *a* **personnel n.** *Av Nau* crew. ◆**navigateur** *nm* *Av* navigator. ◆**navigation** *nf* (*pilotage*) navigation; (*trafic*) *Nau* shipping.

navire [navir] *nm* ship.

navr/er [navre] *vt* to upset (greatly), grieve. ◆**–ant** *a* upsetting. ◆**–é** *a* (*air*) grieved; **je suis n.** I'm (terribly) sorry (**de faire** to do).

nazi, -ie [nazi] *a* & *nmf* *Pol Hist* Nazi.

ne [n(ə)] (**n'** *before vowel or mute h; used to form negative verb with* **pas, jamais, que** *etc*) *adv* **1** (+ *pas*) not; **elle ne boit pas** she does not *ou* doesn't drink; **il n'ose (pas)** he doesn't dare; **n'importe** it doesn't matter. **2** (*with* **craindre, avoir peur** *etc*) **je crains qu'il ne parte** I'm afraid he'll leave.

né [ne] *a* born; **il est né** he was born; **née Dupont** née Dupont.

néanmoins [neɑ̃mwɛ̃] *adv* nevertheless, nonetheless.

néant [neɑ̃] *nm* nothingness, void; (*sur un formulaire*) = none.

nébuleux, -euse [nebylø, -øz] *a* hazy, nebulous.

nécessaire [neseser] *a* necessary; (*inéluctable*) inevitable; – *nm* **le n.** (*biens*) the necessities; **le strict n.** the bare necessities; **n. de couture** sewing box, workbox; **n. de toilette** sponge bag, dressing case; **faire le n.** to do what's necessary *ou* the necessary. ◆**né-**

cessairement *adv* necessarily; (*échouer etc*) inevitably. ◆**nécessité** *nf* necessity. ◆**nécessiter** *vt* to necessitate, require. ◆**nécessiteux, -euse** *a* needy.

nécrologie [nekrɔlɔʒi] *nf* obituary.

nectarine [nektarin] *nf* (*fruit*) nectarine.

néerlandais, -aise [neerlɑ̃dɛ, -ɛz] *a* Dutch; – *nmf* Dutchman, Dutchwoman; – *nm* (*langue*) Dutch.

nef [nɛf] *nf* (*d'église*) nave.

néfaste [nefast] *a* (*influence etc*) harmful (**à** to).

négatif, -ive [negatif, -iv] *a* negative; – *nm* *Phot* negative; – *nf* **répondre par la négative** to answer in the negative. ◆**négation** *nf* negation, denial (**de** of); *Gram* negation; (*mot*) negative.

négligeable [negliʒabl] *a* negligible.

négligent [negliʒɑ̃] *a* negligent, careless. ◆**négligemment** [-amɑ̃] *adv* negligently, carelessly. ◆**négligence** *nf* negligence, carelessness; (*faute*) (careless) error.

néglig/er [negliʒe] *vt* (*personne, conseil, travail etc*) to neglect; **n. de faire** to neglect to do; – **se n.** *vpr* (*négliger sa tenue ou sa santé*) to neglect oneself. ◆**–é** *a* (*tenue*) untidy, neglected; (*travail*) careless; – *nm* (*de tenue*) untidiness; (*vêtement*) negligee.

négoci/er [negɔsje] *vti* *Fin Pol* to negotiate. ◆**–ant, -ante** *nmf* merchant, trader. ◆**–able** *a* *Fin* negotiable. ◆**négociateur, -trice** *nmf* negotiator. ◆**négociation** *nf* negotiation.

nègre [nɛgr] **1** *a* (*art, sculpture etc*) Negro. **2** *nm* (*écrivain*) ghost writer.

neige [nɛʒ] *nf* snow; **n. fondue** sleet; **n. carbonique** dry ice. ◆**neiger** *v imp* to snow. ◆**neigeux, -euse** *a* snowy.

nénuphar [nenyfar] *nm* water lily.

néo [neo] *préf* neo-.

néon [neɔ̃] *nm* (*gaz*) neon; **au n.** (*éclairage etc*) neon-.

néophyte [neɔfit] *nmf* novice.

néo-zélandais, -aise [neozelɑ̃dɛ, -ɛz] *a* (*peuple etc*) New Zealand-; – *nmf* New Zealander.

nerf [nɛr] *nm* *Anat* nerve; **avoir du n.** (*vigueur*) *Fam* to have guts; **du n.!, un peu de n.!** buck up!; **ça me porte** *ou* **me tape sur les nerfs** it gets on my nerves; **être sur les nerfs** *Fig* to be keyed up *ou* het up. ◆**nerveux, -euse** *a* nervous; (*centre, cellule*) nerve-. ◆**nervosité** *nf* nervousness.

nervure [nɛrvyr] *nf* (*de feuille*) vein.

nescafé [nɛskafe] *nm* instant coffee.

n'est-ce pas? [nɛspɑ] *adv* isn't he?, don't

you? *etc*; **il fait beau, n'est-ce pas?** the weather's fine, isn't it?

net, nette [nɛt] **1** *a* (*conscience, idée, image, refus*) clear; (*coupure, linge*) clean; (*soigné*) neat; (*copie*) fair; − *adv* (*s'arrêter*) short, dead; (*tuer*) outright; (*parler*) plainly; (*refuser*) flat(ly); (*casser, couper*) clean. **2** *a* (*poids, prix etc*) Com net(t). ◆**nettement** *adv* clearly, plainly; (*sensiblement*) markedly. ◆**netteté** *nf* clearness; (*de travail*) neatness.

nettoyer [nɛtwaje] *vt* to clean (up); (*plaie*) to cleanse, clean (up); (*vider, ruiner*) Fam to clean out. ◆**nettoiement** *nm* cleaning; **service du n.** refuse *ou Am* garbage collection. ◆**nettoyage** *nm* cleaning; **n. à sec** dry cleaning.

neuf¹, neuve [nœf, nœv] *a* new; **quoi de n.?** what's new(s)?; − *nm* **il y a du n.** there's been something new; **remettre à n.** to make as good as new.

neuf² [nœf] *a* & *nm* [nœv] *before* **heures** & **ans**) nine. ◆**neuvième** *a* & *nmf* ninth.

neurasthénique [nørastenik] *a* depressed.

neutre [nøtr] **1** *a* (*pays, personne etc*) neutral; − *nm El* neutral. **2** *a* & *nm* Gram neuter. ◆**neutraliser** *vt* to neutralize. ◆**neutralité** *nf* neutrality.

neveu, -x [nəvø] *nm* nephew.

névralgie [nevralʒi] *nf* headache; Méd neuralgia. ◆**névralgique** *a* centre n. Fig nerve centre.

névrose [nevroz] *nf* neurosis. ◆**névrosé, -ée** *a* & *nmf* neurotic.

nez [ne] *nm* nose; **n. à n.** face to face (**avec** with); **au n. de qn** (*rire etc*) in s.o.'s face; **mettre le n. dehors** Fam to stick one's nose outside.

ni [ni] *conj* **ni . . . ni** (+ *ne*) neither . . . nor; **il n'a ni faim ni soif** he's neither hungry nor thirsty; **sans manger ni boire** without eating or drinking; **ni l'un(e) ni l'autre** neither (of them).

niais, -aise [njɛ, -ɛz] *a* silly, simple; − *nmf* simpleton. ◆**niaiserie** *nf* silliness; *pl* (*paroles*) nonsense.

niche [niʃ] *nf* (*de chien*) kennel; (*cavité*) niche, recess.

nich/er [niʃe] *vi* (*oiseau*) to nest; (*loger*) Fam to hang out; − **se n.** *vpr* (*oiseau*) to nest; (*se cacher*) to hide oneself. ◆**-ée** *nf* (*oiseaux, enfants*) brood; (*chiens*) litter.

nickel [nikɛl] *nm* (*métal*) nickel.

nicotine [nikɔtin] *nf* nicotine.

nid [ni] *nm* nest; **n. de poules** Aut pothole.

nièce [njɛs] *nf* niece.

nième [ɛnjɛm] *a* nth.

nier [nje] *vt* to deny (**que** that); − *vi Jur* to deny the charge.

nigaud, -aude [nigo, -od] *a* silly; − *nmf* silly fool.

Nigéria [niʒerja] *nm ou f* Nigeria.

n'importe [nɛ̃pɔrt] *voir* **importer 1**.

nippon, -one *ou* **-onne** [nipɔ̃, -ɔn] *a* Japanese.

niveau, -x [nivo] *nm* (*hauteur*) level; (*degré, compétence*) standard, level; **n. de vie** standard of living; **n. à bulle (d'air)** spirit level; **au n. de qn** (*élève etc*) up to s.o.'s standard. ◆**niveler** *vt* (*surface*) to level; (*fortunes etc*) to even (up).

noble [nɔbl] *a* noble; − *nmf* nobleman, noblewoman. ◆**noblement** *adv* nobly. ◆**noblesse** *nf* (*caractère, classe*) nobility.

noce(s) [nɔs] *nf(pl)* wedding; **faire la noce** Fam to have a good time, make merry; **noces d'argent/d'or** silver/golden wedding. ◆**noceur, -euse** *nmf Fam* fast liver, reveller.

nocif, -ive [nɔsif, -iv] *a* harmful. ◆**nocivité** *nf* harmfulness.

noctambule [nɔktɑ̃byl] *nmf* (*personne*) night bird *ou* prowler. ◆**nocturne** *a* nocturnal, night-; − *nm* (*de magasins etc*) late night opening; **(match en) n.** Sp floodlit match, *Am* night game.

Noël [nɔɛl] *nm* Christmas; **le père N.** Father Christmas, Santa Claus.

nœud [nø] *nm* **1** knot; (*ruban*) bow; **le n. du problème/etc** the crux of the problem/etc; **n. coulant** noose, slipknot; **n. papillon** bow tie. **2** (*mesure*) Nau knot.

noir, noire [nwar] *a* black; (*nuit, lunettes etc*) dark; (*idées*) gloomy; (*âme, crime*) vile; (*misère*) dire; **roman n.** thriller; **film n.** film noir; **il fait n.** it's dark; − *nm* (*couleur*) black; (*obscurité*) dark; **N.** (*homme*) black; **vendre au n.** to sell on the black market; − *nf Mus* crotchet, *Am* quarter note; **Noire** (*femme*) black. ◆**noirceur** *nf* blackness; (*d'une action etc*) vileness. ◆**noircir** *vt* to blacken; − *vi*, − **se n.** *vpr* to turn black.

noisette [nwazɛt] *nf* hazelnut. ◆**noisetier** *nm* hazel (tree).

noix [nwa] *nf* (*du noyer*) walnut; **n. de coco** coconut; **n. du Brésil** Brazil nut; **n. de beurre** knob of butter; **à la n.** Fam trashy, awful.

nom [nɔ̃] *nm* name; Gram noun; **n. de famille** surname; **n. de jeune fille** maiden name; **n. propre** Gram proper noun; **au n. de qn** on s.o.'s behalf; **sans n.** (*anonyme*) nameless; (*vil*) vile; **n. d'un chien!** Fam oh hell!

nomade [nɔmad] a nomadic; — nmf nomad.

nombre [nɔ̃br] nm number; **ils sont au** ou **du n. de** (parmi) they're among; **ils sont au n. de dix** there are ten of them; **elle est au n. de** she's one of them; **le plus grand n. de** the majority of. ◆**nombreux, -euse** a (amis, livres etc) numerous; (famille, collection etc) large; **peu n.** few; **venir n.** to come in large numbers.

nombril [nɔ̃bri] nm navel.

nominal, -aux [nɔminal, -o] a nominal. ◆**nomination** nf appointment, nomination.

nommer [nɔme] vt (appeler) to name; **n. qn** (désigner) to appoint s.o. (à un poste/etc to a post/etc); **n. qn président/lauréat** to nominate s.o. chairman/prizewinner; — **se n.** vpr (s'appeler) to be called. ◆**nommément** adv by name.

non [nɔ̃] adv & nm inv no; **n.!** no!; **tu viens ou n.?** are you coming or not?; **n. seulement** not only; **n. (pas) que** (+ sub) . . . not that . . . ; **c'est bien, n.?** Fam it's all right, isn't it?; **je crois que n.** I don't think so; **(ni) moi n. plus** neither do, am, can etc I; **une place n. réservée** an unreserved seat.

non- [nɔ̃] préf non-.

nonante [nɔnɑ̃t] a (en Belgique, en Suisse) ninety.

nonchalant [nɔ̃ʃalɑ̃] a nonchalant, apathetic. ◆**nonchalance** nf nonchalance, apathy.

non-conformiste [nɔ̃kɔ̃fɔrmist] a & nmf nonconformist.

non-fumeur, -euse [nɔ̃fymœr, -øz] nmf non-smoker.

non-sens [nɔ̃sɑ̃s] nm inv absurdity.

nord [nɔr] nm north; **au n. de** north of; **du n.** (vent, direction) northerly; (ville) northern; (gens) from ou in the north; **Amérique/Afrique du N.** North America/Africa; **l'Europe du N.** Northern Europe; — a inv (côte) north(ern). ◆**n.-africain, -aine** a & nmf North African. ◆**n.-américain, -aine** a & nmf North American. ◆**n.-est** nm & a inv north-east. ◆**n.-ouest** nm & a inv north-west.

nordique [nɔrdik] a & nmf Scandinavian.

normal, -aux [nɔrmal, -o] a normal. ◆**normale** nf norm, normality; **au-dessus de la n.** above normal. ◆**normalement** adv normally. ◆**normaliser** vt (uniformiser) to standardize; (relations etc) to normalize.

normand, -ande [nɔrmɑ̃, -ɑ̃d] a & nmf Norman. ◆**Normandie** nf Normandy.

norme [nɔrm] nf norm.

Norvège [nɔrvɛʒ] nf Norway. ◆**norvégien, -ienne** a & nmf Norwegian; — nm (langue) Norwegian.

nos [no] voir notre.

nostalgie [nɔstalʒi] nf nostalgia. ◆**nostalgique** a nostalgic.

notable [nɔtabl] a (fait etc) notable; — nm (personne) notable. ◆**—ment** [-əmɑ̃] adv (sensiblement) notably.

notaire [nɔtɛr] nm solicitor, notary.

notamment [nɔtamɑ̃] adv notably.

note [nɔt] nf (remarque etc) & Mus note; (chiffrée) Scol mark, Am grade; (compte, facture) bill, Am check; **prendre n. de** to make a note of. ◆**notation** nf notation; Scol marking. ◆**noter** vt (prendre note de) to note; (remarquer) to note, notice; (écrire) to note down; (devoir etc) Scol to mark, Am grade; **être bien noté** (personne) to be highly rated.

notice [nɔtis] nf (résumé, préface) note; (mode d'emploi) instructions.

notifier [nɔtifje] vt **n. qch à qn** to notify s.o. of sth.

notion [nɔsjɔ̃] nf notion, idea; pl (éléments) rudiments.

notoire [nɔtwar] a (criminel, bêtise) notorious; (fait) well-known. ◆**notoriété** nf (renom) fame; (de fait) general recognition.

notre, pl nos [nɔtr, no] a poss our. ◆**nôtre** pron poss **le** ou **la n., les nôtres** ours; — nmpl **les nôtres** (parents etc) our (own) people.

nouer [nwe] vt to tie, knot; (amitié, conversation) to strike up; **avoir la gorge nouée** to have a lump in one's throat. ◆**noueux, -euse** a (bois) knotty; (doigts) gnarled.

nougat [nuga] nm nougat.

nouille [nuj] nf (idiot) Fam drip.

nouilles [nuj] nfpl noodles.

nounours [nunurs] nm teddy bear.

nourrice [nuris] nf (assistante maternelle) child minder, nurse; (qui allaite) wet nurse; **mettre en n.** to put out to nurse.

nourr/ir [nurir] vt (alimenter, faire vivre) to feed; (espoir etc) Fig to nourish; (esprit) to enrich; **se n. de** to feed on; — vi (aliment) to be nourishing. ◆**—issant** a nourishing. ◆**nourriture** nf food.

nourrisson [nurisɔ̃] nm infant.

nous [nu] pron **1** (sujet) we; **n. sommes** we are. **2** (complément direct) us; **il n. connaît** he knows us. **3** (indirect) (to) us; **il n. l'a donné** he gave it to us, he gave us it. **4** (réfléchi) ourselves; **n. n. lavons** we wash ourselves. **5** (réciproque) each other;

n. n. **détestons** we hate each other. ◆**n.-mêmes** *pron* ourselves.

nouveau (*or* **nouvel** *before vowel or mute h*), **nouvelle** [1], *pl* **nouveaux, nouvelles** [nuvo, nuvɛl] *a* new; − *nmf Scol* new boy, new girl; − *nm* **du n.** something new; **de n.,** **à n.** again. ◆**n.-né, -ée** *a* & *nmf* new-born (baby). ◆**n.-venu** *nm*, ◆**nouvelle-venue** *nf* newcomer. ◆**nouveauté** *nf* newness, novelty; *pl* (*livres*) new books; (*disques*) new releases; (*vêtements*) new fashions; **une n.** (*objet*) a novelty.

nouvelle [2] [nuvɛl] *nf* **1** **nouvelle(s)** news; **une n.** a piece of news. **2** *Littér* short story.

Nouvelle-Zélande [nuvɛlzelɑ̃d] *nf* New Zealand.

novateur, -trice [nɔvatœr, -tris] *nmf* innovator.

novembre [nɔvɑ̃br] *nm* November.

novice [nɔvis] *nmf* novice; − *a* inexperienced.

noyau, -x [nwajo] *nm* (*de fruit*) stone, *Am* pit; (*d'atome, de cellule*) nucleus; (*groupe*) group; **un n. d'opposants** a hard core of opponents.

noyaut/er [nwajote] *vt Pol* to infiltrate. ◆**—age** *nm* infiltration.

noy/er [1] [nwaje] *vt* (*personne etc*) to drown; (*terres*) to flood; **— se n.** *vpr* to drown; (*se suicider*) to drown oneself; **se n. dans le détail** to get bogged down in details. ◆**—é, -ée** *nmf* (*mort*) drowned person; − *a* **être n.** (*perdu*) *Fig* to be out of one's depth. ◆**noyade** *nf* drowning.

noyer [2] [nwaje] *nm* (*arbre*) walnut tree.

nu [ny] *a* (*personne, vérité*) naked; (*mains, chambre*) bare; **tout nu** (*stark*) naked, (in the) nude; **voir à l'œil nu** to see with the naked eye; **mettre à nu** (*exposer*) to lay bare; **se mettre nu** to strip off; **tête nue,** **nu-tête** bare-headed; − *nm* (*femme, homme, œuvre*) nude.

nuage [nɥaʒ] *nm* cloud; **un n. de lait** *Fig* a dash of milk. ◆**nuageux, -euse** *a* (*ciel*) cloudy.

nuance [nɥɑ̃s] *nf* (*de sens*) nuance; (*de couleurs*) shade, nuance; (*de regret*) tinge, nuance. ◆**nuanc/er** *vt* (*teintes*) to blend, shade; (*pensée*) to qualify. ◆**—é** *a* (*jugement*) qualified.

nucléaire [nykleɛr] *a* nuclear.

nudisme [nydism] *nm* nudism. ◆**nudiste** *nmf* nudist. ◆**nudité** *nf* nudity, nakedness; (*de mur etc*) bareness.

nuée [nɥe] *nf* **une n. de** (*foule*) a host of; (*groupe compact*) a cloud of.

nues [ny] *nfpl* **porter qn aux n.** to praise s.o. to the skies.

nuire* [nɥir] *vi* **n. à** (*personne, intérêts etc*) to harm. ◆**nuisible** *a* harmful.

nuit [nɥi] *nf* night; (*obscurité*) dark(ness); **il fait n.** it's dark; **avant la n.** before nightfall; **la n.** (*se promener etc*) at night; **cette n.** (*aujourd'hui*) tonight; (*hier*) last night. ◆**nuitée** *nf* overnight stay (*in hotel etc*).

nul, nulle [nyl] **1** *a* (*risque etc*) non-existent, nil; (*médiocre*) useless, hopeless; (*non valable*) *Jur* null (and void); **faire match n.** *Sp* to tie, draw. **2** *a* (*aucun*) no; **de nulle importance** of no importance; **sans n. doute** without any doubt; **nulle part** nowhere; − *pron m* (*aucun*) no one. ◆**nullard, -arde** *nmf Fam* useless person. ◆**nullement** *adv* not at all. ◆**nullité** *nf* (*d'un élève etc*) uselessness; (*personne*) useless person.

numéraire [nymerɛr] *nm* cash, currency.

numéral, -aux [nymeral, -o] *a* & *nm* numeral. ◆**numérique** *a* numerical; (*montre etc*) digital.

numéro [nymero] *nm* number; (*de journal*) issue, number; (*au cirque*) act; **un n. de danse/de chant** a dance/song number; **quel n.!** (*personne*) *Fam* what a character!; **n. vert** *Tél* = Freefone®, = *Am* tollfree number. ◆**numérot/er** *vt* (*pages, sièges*) to number. ◆**—age** *nm* numbering.

nu-pieds [nypje] *nmpl* open sandals.

nuptial, -aux [nypsjal, -o] *a* (*chambre*) bridal; (*anneau, cérémonie*) wedding-.

nuque [nyk] *nf* back *ou* nape of the neck.

nurse [nœrs] *nf* nanny, (children's) nurse.

nutritif, -ive [nytritif, -iv] *a* nutritious, nutritive. ◆**nutrition** *nf* nutrition.

nylon [nilɔ̃] *nm* (*fibre*) nylon.

nymphe [nɛ̃f] *nf* nymph. ◆**nymphomane** *nf Péj* nymphomaniac.

O

O, o [o] *nm* O, o.

oasis [ɔazis] *nf* oasis.

obédience [ɔbedjɑ̃s] *nf Pol* allegiance.

obé/ir [ɔbeir] *vi* to obey; **o. à qn/qch** to obey s.o./sth; **être obéi** to be obeyed. **◆—issant** *a* obedient. **◆obéissance** *nf* obedience (à to).

obélisque [ɔbelisk] *nm* (*monument*) obelisk.

obèse [ɔbɛz] *a & nmf* obese (person). **◆obésité** *nf* obesity.

objecter [ɔbʒɛkte] *vt* (*prétexte*) to put forward, plead; **o. que** to object that; **on lui objecta son jeune âge** they objected that he *ou* she was too young. **◆objecteur** *nm* **o. de conscience** conscientious objector. **◆objection** *nf* objection.

objectif, -ive [ɔbʒɛktif, -iv] **1** *a* (*opinion etc*) objective. **2** *nm* (*but*) objective; *Phot* lens. **◆objectivement** *adv* objectively. **◆objectivité** *nf* objectivity.

objet [ɔbʒɛ] *nm* (*chose, sujet, but*) object; (*de toilette*) article; **faire l'o. de** (*étude, critiques etc*) to be the subject of; (*soins, surveillance*) to be given, receive; **objets trouvés** (*bureau*) lost property, *Am* lost and found.

obligation [ɔbligasjɔ̃] *nf* (*devoir, lieu, nécessité*) obligation; *Fin* bond. **◆obligatoire** *a* compulsory, obligatory; (*inévitable*) *Fam* inevitable. **◆obligatoirement** *adv* (*fatalement*) inevitably; **tu dois o. le faire** you have to do it.

oblig/er [ɔbliʒe] *vt* **1** (*contraindre*) to compel, oblige (à faire to do); (*engager*) to bind; **être obligé de faire** to have to do, be compelled *ou* obliged to do. **2** (*rendre service à*) to oblige; **être obligé à qn de qch** to be obliged to s.o. for sth. **◆—eant** *a* obliging, kind. **◆—é** *a* (*obligatoire*) necessary; (*fatal*) *Fam* inevitable. **◆obligeamment** [-amɑ̃] *adv* obligingly. **◆obligeance** *nf* kindness.

oblique [ɔblik] *a* oblique; **regard o.** sidelong glance; **en o.** at an (oblique) angle. **◆obliquer** *vi* (*véhicule etc*) to turn off.

oblitérer [ɔblitere] *vt* (*timbre*) to cancel; (*billet, carte*) to stamp; **timbre oblitéré** (*non neuf*) used stamp. **◆oblitération** *nf* cancellation; stamping.

oblong, -ongue [ɔblɔ̃, -ɔ̃g] *a* oblong.

obnubilé [ɔbnybile] *a* (*obsédé*) obsessed (**par** with).

obscène [ɔpsɛn] *a* obscene. **◆obscénité** *nf* obscenity.

obscur [ɔpskyr] *a* (*noir*) dark; (*peu clair, inconnu, humble*) obscure. **◆obscurcir** *vt* (*chambre etc*) to darken; (*rendre peu intelligible*) to obscure (*text, ideas etc*); **— s'o.** *vpr* (*ciel*) to cloud over, darken; (*vue*) to become dim. **◆obscurément** *adv* obscurely. **◆obscurité** *nf* dark(ness); (*de texte, d'acteur etc*) obscurity.

obséd/er [ɔpsede] *vt* to obsess, haunt. **◆—ant** *a* haunting, obsessive. **◆—é, -ée** *nmf* maniac (**de** for); **o. sexuel** sex maniac.

obsèques [ɔpsɛk] *nfpl* funeral.

obséquieux, -euse [ɔpsekjø, -øz] *a* obsequious.

observer [ɔpsɛrve] *vt* (*regarder*) to observe, watch; (*remarquer, respecter*) to observe; **faire o. qch à qn** (*signaler*) to point sth out to s.o. **◆observateur, -trice** *a* observant; *— nmf* observer. **◆observation** *nf* (*examen, remarque*) observation; (*reproche*) (critical) remark, rebuke; (*de règle etc*) observance; **en o.** (*malade*) under observation. **◆observatoire** *nm* observatory; (*colline etc*) *Fig & Mil* observation post.

obsession [ɔpsesjɔ̃] *nf* obsession. **◆obsessif, -ive** *a* (*peur etc*) obsessive. **◆obsessionnel, -elle** *a Psy* obsessive.

obstacle [ɔpstakl] *nm* obstacle; **faire o. à** to stand in the way of.

obstétrique [ɔpstetrik] *nf Méd* obstetrics.

obstin/er (s') [sɔpstine] *vpr* to be obstinate *ou* persistent; **s'o. à faire** to persist in doing. **◆—é** *a* stubborn, obstinate, persistent. **◆obstination** *nf* stubbornness, obstinacy, persistence.

obstruction [ɔpstryksjɔ̃] *nf Méd Pol Sp* obstruction; **faire de l'o.** *Pol Sp* to be obstructive. **◆obstruer** *vt* to obstruct.

obtempérer [ɔptɑ̃pere] *vi* to obey an injunction; **o. à** to obey.

obtenir* [ɔptənir] *vt* to get, obtain, secure. **◆obtention** *nf* obtaining, getting.

obturer [ɔptyre] *vt* (*trou etc*) to stop *ou* close up. **◆obturateur** *nm Phot* shutter; *Tech* valve.

obtus [ɔpty] *a* (*angle, esprit*) obtuse.

obus [ɔby] *nm Mil* shell.

occasion [ɔkazjɔ̃] *nf* **1** (*chance*) opportunity, chance (**de faire** to do); (*circonstance*) occasion; **à l'o.** on occasion, when the occasion arises; **à l'o. de** on the occasion of. **2** *Com* (*marché avantageux*) bargain; (*objet non neuf*) second-hand buy; **d'o.** second-hand, used. ◆**occasionner** *vt* to cause; **o. qch à qn** to cause s.o. sth.

occident [ɔksidɑ̃] *nm* **l'O.** *Pol* the West. ◆**occidental, -aux** *a Géog Pol* western; – *nmpl* **les occidentaux** *Pol* Westerners. ◆**occidentalisé** *a Pol* Westernized.

occulte [ɔkylt] *a* occult.

occup/er [ɔkype] *vt* (*maison, pays, usine etc*) to occupy; (*place, temps*) to take up, occupy; (*poste*) to hold, occupy; **o. qn** (*absorber*) to occupy s.o., keep s.o. busy; (*ouvrier etc*) to employ s.o.; **– s'o.** *vpr* to keep (oneself) busy (**à faire** doing); **s'o. de** (*affaire, problème etc*) to deal with; (*politique*) to be engaged in; **s'o. de qn** (*malade etc*) to take care of s.o.; (*client*) to see to s.o., deal with s.o.; **ne t'en occupe pas!** (*ne t'en fais pas*) don't worry!; (*ne t'en mêle pas*) mind your own business! **—ant, -ante** *a* (*armée*) occupying; – *nmf* (*habitant*) occupant; – *nm Mil* forces of occupation, occupier. ◆**—é** *a* busy (**à faire** doing); (*place, maison etc*) occupied; (*ligne*) *Tél* engaged, *Am* busy; (*taxi*) hired. ◆**occupation** *nf* (*activité, travail etc*) occupation; **l'o. de** (*action*) the occupation of.

occurrence [ɔkyrɑ̃s] *nf Ling* occurrence; **en l'o.** in the circumstances, as it happens *ou* happened.

océan [ɔseɑ̃] *nm* ocean. ◆**océanique** *a* oceanic.

ocre [ɔkr] *nm & a inv* (*couleur*) ochre.

octave [ɔktav] *nf Mus* octave.

octobre [ɔktɔbr] *nm* October.

octogénaire [ɔktɔʒenɛr] *nmf* octogenarian.

octogone [ɔktɔgɔn] *nm* octagon. ◆**octogonal, -aux** *a* octagonal.

octroi [ɔktrwa] *nm Litt* granting. ◆**octroyer** *vt Litt* to grant (**à** to).

oculaire [ɔkylɛr] *a* **témoin o.** eyewitness; **globe o.** eyeball. ◆**oculiste** *nmf* eye specialist.

ode [ɔd] *nf* (*poème*) ode.

odeur [ɔdœr] *nf* smell, odour; (*de fleur*) scent. ◆**odorant** *a* sweet-smelling. ◆**odorat** *nm* sense of smell.

odieux, -euse [ɔdjø, -øz] *a* odious, obnoxious.

œcuménique [ekymenik] *a Rel* (o)ecumenical.

œil, *pl* **yeux** [œj, jø] *nm* eye; **sous mes yeux** before my very eyes; **lever/baisser les yeux** to look up/down; **fermer l'o.** (*dormir*) to shut one's eyes; **fermer les yeux sur** to turn a blind eye to; **ouvre l'o.!** keep your eyes open!; **coup d'o.** (*regard*) glance, look; **jeter un coup d'o. sur** to (have a) look *ou* glance at; **à vue d'o.** visibly; **faire les gros yeux à** to scowl at; **avoir à l'o.** (*surveiller*) to keep an eye on; **à l'o.** (*gratuitement*) *Fam* free; **faire de l'o. à** *Fam* to make eyes at; **o. au beurre noir** *Fig* black eye; **mon o.!** *Fam* (*incrédulité*) my foot!; (*refus*) no way!, no chance!

œillade [œjad] *nf* (*clin d'œil*) wink.

œillères [œjɛr] *nfpl* (*de cheval*) & *Fig* blinkers, *Am* blinders.

œillet [œje] *nm* **1** *Bot* carnation. **2** (*trou de ceinture etc*) eyelet.

œuf, *pl* **œufs** [œf, ø] *nm* egg; *pl* (*de poisson*) (hard) roe; **o. sur le plat** fried egg; **étouffer qch dans l'o.** *Fig* to nip *ou* stifle sth in the bud.

œuvre [œvr] *nf* (*travail, acte, livre etc*) work; **o. (de charité)** (*organisation*) charity; **l'o. de** (*production artistique etc*) the works of; **mettre en o.** (*employer*) to make use of; **mettre tout en o.** to do everything possible (**pour faire** to do). ◆**œuvrer** *vi Litt* to work.

offense [ɔfɑ̃s] *nf* insult; *Rel* transgression. ◆**offens/er** *vt* to offend; **s'o. de** to take offence at. ◆**—ant** *a* offensive.

offensif, -ive [ɔfɑ̃sif, -iv] *a* offensive; – *nf* (*attaque*) offensive; (*du froid*) onslaught.

offert [ɔfɛr] *voir* **offrir**.

office [ɔfis] *nm* **1** (*fonction*) office; (*bureau*) office, bureau; **d'o.** (*être promu etc*) automatically; **faire o. de** to serve as; **ses bons offices** (*service*) one's good offices. **2** *nm Rel* service. **3** *nm ou f* (*pièce pour provisions*) pantry.

officiel, -ielle [ɔfisjɛl] *a* (*acte etc*) official; – *nm* (*personnage*) official. ◆**officiellement** *adv* officially. ◆**officieux, -euse** *a* unofficial.

officier [ɔfisje] **1** *vi Rel* to officiate. **2** *nm* (*dans l'armée etc*) officer.

offre [ɔfr] *nf* offer; (*aux enchères*) bid; **l'o. et la demande** *Écon* supply and demand; **offres d'emploi** *Journ* situations vacant. ◆**offrande** *nf* offering.

offr/ir* [ɔfrir] *vt* (*proposer, présenter*) to offer (**de faire** to do); (*donner en cadeau*) to give; (*démission*) to tender, offer; **je lui ai offert de le loger** I offered to put him up; **– s'o.** *vpr* (*cadeau etc*) to treat oneself to; (*se* *proposer*) to offer oneself (**comme** as); **s'o. à faire** to offer *ou* volunteer to do; **s'o.** (**aux yeux**) (*vue etc*) to present itself. ◆**—ant** *nm* **au plus o.** to the highest bidder.

offusquer [ɔfyske] *vt* to offend, shock; **s'o. de** to take offence at.

ogive [ɔʒiv] *nf* (*de fusée*) nose cone; **o. nucléaire** nuclear warhead.

ogre [ɔgr] *nm* ogre.

oh! [o] *int* oh!, o!

ohé! [ɔe] *int* hey (there)!

oie [wa] *nf* goose.

oignon [ɔɲɔ̃] *nm* (*légume*) onion; (*de tulipe, lis etc*) bulb; **occupe-toi de tes oignons!** *Fam* mind your own business!

oiseau, -x [wazo] *nm* bird; **à vol d'o.** as the crow flies; **drôle d'o.** (*individu*) *Péj* odd fish, *Am* oddball; **o. rare** (*personne étonnante*) *Iron* rare bird, perfect gem.

oiseux, -euse [wazø, -øz] *a* (*futile*) idle, vain.

oisif, -ive [wazif, -iv] *a* (*inactif*) idle; — *nmf* idler. ◆**oisiveté** *nf* idleness.

oléoduc [ɔleɔdyk] *nm* oil pipeline.

olive [ɔliv] *nf* (*fruit*) olive; **huile d'o.** olive oil; — *a inv* (*couleur*) (**vert**) **o.** olive (green). ◆**olivier** *nm* (*arbre*) olive tree.

olympique [ɔlɛ̃pik] *a* (*jeux, record etc*) Olympic.

ombilical, -aux [ɔ̃bilikal, -o] *a* (*cordon*) umbilical.

ombrage [ɔ̃braʒ] *nm* **1** (*ombre*) shade. **2 prendre o. de** (*jalousie, dépit*) to take umbrage at. ◆**ombrag/er** *vt* to give shade to. ◆**—é** *a* shady. ◆**ombrageux, -euse** *a* (*caractère, personne*) touchy.

ombre [ɔ̃br] *nf* (*d'arbre etc*) shade; (*de personne, objet*) shadow; **l'o. d'un doute** *Fig* the shadow of a doubt; **l'o. de** (*remords, reproche etc*) the trace of; **30° à l'o.** 30° in the shade; **dans l'o.** (*comploter, travailler etc*) in secret.

ombrelle [ɔ̃brɛl] *nf* sunshade, parasol.

omelette [ɔmlɛt] *nf* omelet(te); **o. au fromage/etc** cheese/*etc* omelet(te).

omettre* [ɔmɛtr] *vt* to omit (**de faire** to do). ◆**omission** *nf* omission.

omni- [ɔmni] *préf* omni-. ◆**omnipotent** *a* omnipotent.

omnibus [ɔmnibys] *a & nm* (*train*) **o.** slow train (*stopping at all stations*).

omoplate [ɔmɔplat] *nf* shoulder blade.

on [ɔ̃] (*sometimes* **l'on** [lɔ̃]) *pron* (*les gens*) they, people; (*nous*) we, one; (*vous*) you, one; **on dit** they say, people say, it is said; **on frappe** (*quelqu'un*) someone's knocking;

on me l'a donné it was given to me, I was given it.

once [ɔ̃s] *nf* (*mesure*) & *Fig* ounce.

oncle [ɔ̃kl] *nm* uncle.

onctueux, -euse [ɔ̃ktɥø, -øz] *a* (*liquide, crème*) creamy; (*manières, paroles*) *Fig* smooth.

onde [ɔ̃d] *nf* *Phys Rad* wave; **grandes ondes** long wave; **ondes courtes/moyennes** short/medium wave; **sur les ondes** (*sur l'antenne*) on the radio.

ondée [ɔ̃de] *nf* (*pluie*) (sudden) shower.

on-dit [ɔ̃di] *nm inv* rumour, hearsay.

ondoyer [ɔ̃dwaje] *vi* to undulate. ◆**ondulation** *nf* undulation; (*de cheveux*) wave. ◆**ondul/er** *vi* to undulate; (*cheveux*) to be wavy. ◆**—é** *a* wavy.

onéreux, -euse [ɔnerø, -øz] *a* costly.

ongle [ɔ̃gl] *nm* (finger) nail.

onglet [ɔ̃glɛ] *nm* (*entaille de canif etc*) (nail) groove.

ont [ɔ̃] *voir* **avoir.**

ONU [ɔny] *nf abrév* (*Organisation des nations unies*) UN.

onyx [ɔniks] *nm* (*pierre précieuse*) onyx.

onze [ɔ̃z] *a & nm* eleven. ◆**onzième** *a & nmf* eleventh.

opale [ɔpal] *nf* (*pierre*) opal.

opaque [ɔpak] *a* opaque. ◆**opacité** *nf* opacity.

opéra [ɔpera] *nm* (*ouvrage, art*) opera; (*édifice*) opera house. ◆**opérette** *nf* operetta.

opér/er [ɔpere] **1** *vt* (*exécuter*) to carry out; (*choix*) to make; — *vi* (*agir*) to work, act; (*procéder*) to proceed; — **s'o.** *vpr* (*se produire*) to take place. **2** *vt* (*personne, organe*) *Méd* to operate on (**de** for); (*tumeur*) to remove; **cela peut s'o.** this can be removed; **se faire o.** to have an operation; — *vi* (*chirurgien*) to operate. ◆**—ant** *a* (*efficace*) operative. ◆**—é, -ée** *nmf* *Méd* patient (*operated on*). ◆**opérateur, -trice** *nmf* (*de prise de vues*) *Cin* cameraman; (*sur machine*) operator. ◆**opération** *nf* (*acte*) & *Méd Mil Math etc* operation; *Fin* deal. ◆**opérationnel, -elle** *a* operational. ◆**opératoire** *a* *Méd* operative; **bloc o.** operating *ou* surgical wing.

opiner [ɔpine] *vi* **o.** (**de la tête** *ou* **du chef**) to nod assent.

opiniâtre [ɔpinjɑtr] *a* stubborn, obstinate. ◆**opiniâtreté** *nf* stubbornness, obstinacy.

opinion [ɔpinjɔ̃] *nf* opinion (**sur** about, on).

opium [ɔpjɔm] *nm* opium.

opportun [ɔpɔrtœ̃] *a* opportune, timely. ◆**opportunément** *adv* opportunely.

◆**opportunisme** *nm* opportunism. ◆**opportunité** *nf* timeliness.

oppos/er [ɔpoze] *vt* (*argument, résistance*) to put up (**à** against); (*équipes, rivaux*) to bring together, set against each other; (*objets*) to place opposite each other; (*couleurs*) to contrast; **o. qch à qch** (*objet*) to place sth opposite sth; **o. qn à qn** to set s.o. against s.o.; **match qui oppose . . .** match between . . . ; **— s'o.** *vpr* (*couleurs*) to contrast; (*équipes*) to confront each other; **s'o. à** (*mesure, personne etc*) to oppose, be opposed to; **je m'y oppose** I'm opposed to it, I oppose. ◆**—ant, -ante** *a* opposing; — *nmf* opponent. ◆**—é** *a* (*direction etc*) opposite; (*intérêts, équipe*) opposing; (*opinions*) opposite, opposing; (*couleurs*) contrasting; **être o. à** to be opposed to; — *nm* **l'o.** the opposite (**de** of); **à l'o.** (*côté*) on the opposite side (**de** from, to); **à l'o. de** (*contrairement à*) contrary to. ◆**opposition** *nf* opposition; **faire o. à** to oppose; **par o. à** as opposed to.

oppress/er [ɔprese] *vt* (*gêner*) to oppress. ◆**—ant** *a* oppressive. ◆**—eur** *nm Pol* oppressor. ◆**oppressif, -ive** *a* (*loi etc*) oppressive. ◆**oppression** *nf* oppression. ◆**opprim/er** *vt* (*tyranniser*) to oppress. ◆**—és** *nmpl* **les o.** the oppressed.

opter [ɔpte] *vi* **o. pour** to opt for.

opticien, -ienne [ɔptisjɛ̃, -jɛn] *nmf* optician.

optimisme [ɔptimism] *nm* optimism. ◆**optimiste** *a* optimistic; — *nmf* optimist.

optimum [ɔptimɔm] *nm & a* optimum; **la température o.** the optimum temperature. ◆**optimal, -aux** *a* optimal.

option [ɔpsjɔ̃] *nf* (*choix*) option; (*chose*) optional extra.

optique [ɔptik] *a* (*verre*) optical; — *nf* optics; (*aspect*) *Fig* perspective; **d'o.** (*illusion, instrument etc*) optical.

opulent [ɔpylɑ̃] *a* opulent. ◆**opulence** *nf* opulence.

or [ɔr] **1** *nm* gold; **en or** (*chaîne etc*) gold-; **d'or** (*cheveux, âge, règle*) golden; (*cœur*) of gold; **mine d'or** *Géol* goldmine; (*fortune*) *Fig* goldmine; **affaire en or** (*achat*) bargain; (*commerce*) *Fig* goldmine; **or noir** (*pétrole*) *Fig* black gold. **2** *conj* (*alors, cependant*) now, well.

oracle [ɔrakl] *nm* oracle.

orage [ɔraʒ] *nm* (*thunder*)storm. ◆**orageux, -euse** *a* stormy.

oraison [ɔrɛzɔ̃] *nf* prayer; **o. funèbre** funeral oration.

oral, -aux [ɔral, -o] *a* oral; — *nm* (*examen*) *Scol* oral.

orange [ɔrɑ̃ʒ] *nf* (*fruit*) orange; **o. pressée** (fresh) orange juice; — *a & nm inv* (*couleur*) orange. ◆**orangé** *a & nm* (*couleur*) orange. ◆**orangeade** *nf* orangeade. ◆**oranger** *nm* orange tree.

orang-outan(g) [ɔrɑ̃utɑ̃] *nm* (*pl* **orangs-outan(g)s**) orang-outang.

orateur [ɔratœr] *nm* speaker, orator.

orbite [ɔrbit] *nf* (*d'astre etc*) & *Fig* orbit; (*d'œil*) socket; **mettre sur o.** (*fusée etc*) to put into orbit.

orchestre [ɔrkɛstr] *nm* (*classique*) orchestra; (*moderne*) band; (*places*) *Th* stalls, *Am* orchestra. ◆**orchestrer** *vt* (*organiser*) & *Mus* to orchestrate.

orchidée [ɔrkide] *nf* orchid.

ordinaire [ɔrdinɛr] *a* (*habituel, normal*) ordinary, *Am* regular; (*médiocre*) ordinary, average; **d'o., à l'o.** usually; **comme d'o., comme à l'o.** as usual; **de l'essence o.** two-star (petrol), *Am* regular. ◆**—ment** *adv* usually.

ordinal, -aux [ɔrdinal, -o] *a* (*nombre*) ordinal.

ordinateur [ɔrdinatœr] *nm* computer.

ordination [ɔrdinasjɔ̃] *nf Rel* ordination.

ordonnance [ɔrdɔnɑ̃s] *nf* **1** (*de médecin*) prescription. **2** (*décret*) *Jur* order, ruling. **3** (*disposition*) arrangement. **4** (*soldat*) orderly.

ordonn/er [ɔrdɔne] *vt* **1** (*enjoindre*) to order (**que** (+ *sub*) that); **o. à qn de faire** to order s.o. to do. **2** (*agencer*) to arrange, order. **3** (*médicament etc*) to prescribe. **4** (*prêtre*) to ordain. ◆**—é** *a* (*personne, maison etc*) orderly.

ordre [ɔrdr] *nm* (*commandement, structure, association etc*) order; (*absence de désordre*) tidiness (*of room, person etc*); **en o.** (*chambre etc*) tidy; **mettre en o., mettre de l'o. dans** to tidy (up); **de premier o.** first-rate; **o.** (**public**) (law and) order; **par o. d'âge** in order of age; **à l'o. du jour** (*au programme*) on the agenda; (*d'actualité*) of topical interest; **les forces de l'o.** the police; **jusqu'à nouvel o.** until further notice; **de l'o. de** (*environ*) of the order of.

ordure [ɔrdyr] *nf* filth, muck; *pl* (*débris*) refuse, rubbish, *Am* garbage. ◆**ordurier, -ière** *a* (*plaisanterie etc*) lewd.

oreille [ɔrɛj] *nf* ear; **être tout oreilles** to be all ears; **faire la sourde o.** to turn a deaf ear; **casser les oreilles à qn** to deafen s.o.

oreiller [ɔreje] *nm* pillow.

oreillons [ɔrejɔ̃] *nmpl Méd* mumps.

ores (d') [ɔr] *adv* **d'ores et déjà** [ɔrzedeʒa] henceforth.

orfèvre [ɔrfɛvr] nm goldsmith, silversmith.
◆orfèvrerie nf (magasin) goldsmith's ou silversmith's shop; (objets) gold ou silver plate.

organe [ɔrgan] nm Anat & Fig organ; (porte-parole) mouthpiece. ◆organique a organic. ◆organisme nm 1 (corps) body; Anat Biol organism. 2 (bureaux etc) organization.

organisation [ɔrganizasjɔ̃] nf (arrangement, association) organization.

organis/er [ɔrganize] vt to organize; — s'o. vpr to organize oneself, get organized. ◆—é a (esprit, groupe etc) organized. ◆organisateur, -trice nmf organizer.

organiste [ɔrganist] nmf Mus organist.

orgasme [ɔrgasm] nm orgasm.

orge [ɔrʒ] nf barley.

orgie [ɔrʒi] nf orgy.

orgue [ɔrg] nm Mus organ; o. de Barbarie barrel organ; — nfpl organ; grandes orgues great organ.

orgueil [ɔrgœj] nm pride. ◆orgueilleux, -euse a proud.

orient [ɔrjɑ̃] nm l'O. the Orient, the East; Moyen-O., Proche-O. Middle East; Extrême-O. Far East. ◆oriental, -ale, -aux a eastern; (de l'Orient) oriental; — nmf oriental.

orient/er [ɔrjɑ̃te] vt (lampe, antenne etc) to position, direct; (voyageur, élève etc) to direct; (maison) to orientate, Am orient; — s'o. vpr to find one's bearings ou direction; s'o. vers (carrière etc) to move towards. ◆—é a (ouvrage, film etc) slanted. ◆orientable a (lampe etc) adjustable, flexible; (bras de machine) movable. ◆orientation nf direction; (action) positioning, directing; (de maison) aspect, orientation; (tendance) Pol Littér etc trend; o. professionnelle vocational guidance.

orifice [ɔrifis] nm opening, orifice.

originaire [ɔriʒinɛr] a être o. de (natif) to be a native of.

original, -ale, -aux [ɔriʒinal, -o] 1 a (idée, artiste, version etc) original; — nm (modèle) original. 2 a & nmf (bizarre) eccentric. ◆originalité nf originality; eccentricity.

origine [ɔriʒin] nf origin; à l'o. originally; d'o. (pneu etc) original; pays d'o. country of origin. ◆originel, -elle a (sens, péché, habitant etc) original.

orme [ɔrm] nm (arbre, bois) elm.

ornement [ɔrnəmɑ̃] nm ornament. ◆ornemental, -aux a ornamental. ◆ornementation nf ornamentation. ◆ornementé a

adorned, ornamented (de with). ◆orn/er vt to decorate, adorn (de with). ◆—é a (syle etc) ornate.

ornière [ɔrnjɛr] nf (sillon) & Fig rut.

orphelin, -ine [ɔrfəlɛ̃, -in] nmf orphan; — a orphaned. ◆orphelinat nm orphanage.

orteil [ɔrtej] nm toe; gros o. big toe.

orthodoxe [ɔrtɔdɔks] a orthodox; — nmpl les orthodoxes the orthodox. ◆orthodoxie [ɔrtɔdɔksi] nf orthodoxy.

orthographe [ɔrtɔgraf] nf spelling. ◆orthographier vt (mot) to spell.

orthopédie [ɔrtɔpedi] nf orthop(a)edics.

ortie [ɔrti] nf nettle.

os [ɔs, pl ɔ ou ɔs] nm bone; trempé jusqu'aux os soaked to the skin; tomber sur un os (difficulté) Fam to hit a snag.

OS [ɔɛs] abrév = ouvrier spécialisé.

oscar [ɔskar] nm Cin Oscar.

osciller [ɔsile] vi Tech to oscillate; (se balancer) to swing, sway; (hésiter) to waver; (varier) to fluctuate; (flamme) to flicker. ◆oscillation nf Tech oscillation; (de l'opinion) fluctuation.

oseille [ozɛj] nf 1 Bot Culin sorrel. 2 (argent) Arg dough.

os/er [oze] vti to dare; o. faire to dare (to) do. ◆—é a bold, daring.

osier [ozje] nm (branches) wicker.

ossature [ɔsatyr] nf (du corps) frame; (de bâtiment) & Fig framework. ◆osselets nmpl (jeu) jacks, knucklebones. ◆ossements nmpl (de cadavres) bones. ◆osseux, -euse a (tissu) bone-; (maigre) bony.

ostensible [ɔstɑ̃sibl] a conspicuous.

ostentation [ɔstɑ̃tasjɔ̃] nf ostentation.

otage [ɔtaʒ] nm hostage; prendre qn en o. to take s.o. hostage.

OTAN [ɔtɑ̃] nf abrév (Organisation du traité de l'Atlantique Nord) NATO.

otarie [ɔtari] nf (animal) sea lion.

ôter [ote] vt to remove, take away (à qn from s.o.); (vêtement) to take off, remove; (déduire) to take (away); ôte-toi de là! Fam get out of the way!

otite [ɔtit] nf ear infection.

oto-rhino [ɔtɔrino] nmf Méd Fam ear, nose and throat specialist.

ou [u] conj or; ou bien or else; ou elle ou moi either her or me.

où [u] adv & pron where; le jour où the day when, the day on which; la table où the table on which; l'état où the condition in which; par où? which way?; d'où? where from?; **d'où ma surprise**/*etc* (*conséquence*) hence my surprise/*etc*; **le pays d'où** the country from which; **où qu'il soit** wherever he may be.

ouate [wat] *nf Méd* cotton wool, *Am* absorbent cotton.

oubli [ubli] *nm* (*défaut*) forgetfulness; **l'o. de qch** forgetting sth; **un o.** a lapse of memory; (*omission*) an oversight; **tomber dans l'o.** to fall into oblivion. ◆**oublier** *vt* to forget (**de faire** to do); (*faute, problème*) to overlook; — **s'o.** *vpr* (*traditions etc*) to be forgotten; (*personne*) *Fig* to forget oneself. ◆**oublieux, -euse** *a* forgetful (**de** of).

oubliettes [ublijɛt] *nfpl* (*de château*) dungeon.

ouest [wɛst] *nm* west; **à l'o. de** west of; **d'o.** (*vent*) west(erly); **de l'o.** western; **Allemagne de l'O.** West Germany; **l'Europe de l'O.** Western Europe; — *a inv* (*côte*) west(ern). ◆**o.-allemand, -ande** *a* & *nmf* West German.

ouf! [uf] *int* (*soulagement*) ah!, phew!

oui [wi] *adv* & *nm inv* yes; **o.!** yes!; **les o.** (*votes*) the ayes; **tu viens, o.?** come on, will you?; **je crois que o.** I think so; **si o.** if so.

ouï-dire [widir] *nm inv* hearsay.

ouïe¹ [wi] *nf* hearing; **être tout o.** *Fam* to be all ears.

ouïe²! [uj] *int* ouch!

ouïes [wi] *nfpl* (*de poisson*) gills.

ouille! [uj] *int* ouch!

ouragan [uragɑ̃] *nm* hurricane.

ourler [urle] *vt* to hem. ◆**ourlet** *nm* hem.

ours [urs] *nm* bear; **o. blanc/gris** polar/grizzly bear.

oursin [ursɛ̃] *nm* (*animal*) sea urchin.

ouste! [ust] *int Fam* scram!

outil [uti] *nm* tool. ◆**outiller** *vt* to equip. ◆**—age** *nm* tools; (*d'une usine*) equipment.

outrage [utraʒ] *nm* insult (**à** to). ◆**outrager** *vt* to insult, offend. ◆**—eant** *a* insulting, offensive.

outrance [utrɑ̃s] *nf* (*excès*) excess; **à o.** (*travailler etc*) to excess; **guerre à o.** all-out war. ◆**outrancier, -ière** *a* excessive.

outre [utr] *prép* besides; — *adv* **en o.** besides, moreover; **o. mesure** inordinately; **passer o.** to take no notice (**à** of). ◆**o.-Manche** *adv* across the Channel. ◆**o.-mer** *adv* overseas; **d'o.-mer** (*peuple*) overseas.

outrepasser [utrəpase] *vt* (*limite etc*) to go beyond, exceed.

outr/er [utre] *vt* to exaggerate, overdo; **o. qn** (*indigner*) to outrage s.o. ◆**—é** *a* (*excessif*) exaggerated; (*révolté*) outraged.

outsider [awtsajdœr] *nm Sp* outsider.

ouvert [uvɛr] *voir* **ouvrir**; — *a* open; (*robinet, gaz etc*) on; **à bras ouverts** with open arms. ◆**ouvertement** *adv* openly. ◆**ouverture** *nf* opening; (*trou*) hole; (*avance*) & *Mus* overture; (*d'objectif*) *Phot* aperture; **o. d'esprit** open-mindedness.

ouvrable [uvrabl] *a* **jour o.** working day.

ouvrage [uvraʒ] *nm* (*travail, objet, livre*) work; (*couture*) (needle)work; — *a* (*travail*) a piece of work. ◆**ouvragé** *a* (*bijou etc*) finely worked.

ouvreuse [uvrøz] *nf Cin* usherette.

ouvrier, -ière [uvrije, -jɛr] *nmf* worker; **o. agricole** farm labourer; **o. qualifié/spécialisé** skilled/unskilled worker; — *a* (*législation etc*) industrial; (*quartier, éducation*) working-class; **classe ouvrière** working class.

ouvrir* [uvrir] *vt* to open (up); (*gaz, radio etc*) to turn on, switch on; (*inaugurer*) to open; (*hostilités*) to begin; (*appétit*) to whet; (*liste, procession*) to head; — *vi* to open; (*ouvrir la porte*) to open (up); — **s'o.** *vpr* (*porte, boîte etc*) to open (up); **s'o. la jambe** to cut one's leg open; **s'o. à qn** *Fig* to open one's heart to s.o. (**de qch** about sth). ◆**ouvre-boîtes** *nm inv* tin opener, *Am* can-opener. ◆**ouvre-bouteilles** *nm inv* bottle opener.

ovaire [ɔvɛr] *nm Anat* ovary.

ovale [ɔval] *a* & *nm* oval.

ovation [ɔvɑsjɔ̃] *nf* (standing) ovation.

OVNI [ɔvni] *nm abrév* (*objet volant non identifié*) UFO.

oxyde [ɔksid] *nm Ch* oxide; **o. de carbone** carbon monoxide. ◆**oxyder** *vt*, — **s'o.** *vpr* to oxidize.

oxygène [ɔksiʒɛn] *nm* oxygen; **à o.** (*masque, tente*) oxygen-. ◆**oxygén/er** *vt* (*cheveux*) to bleach; — **s'o.** *vpr Fam* to breathe *ou* get some fresh air. ◆**—ée** *af* **eau o.** (hydrogen) peroxide.

P

P, p [pe] *nm* P, p.

pachyderme [paʃidɛrm] *nm* elephant.

pacifier [pasifje] *vt* to pacify. ◆**pacification** *nf* pacification. ◆**pacifique 1** *a* (*non violent, non militaire*) peaceful; (*personne, peuple*) peace-loving. **2** *a* (*côte etc*) Pacific; **Océan P.** Pacific Ocean; – *nm* **le P.** the Pacific. ◆**pacifiste** *a* & *nmf* pacifist.

pack [pak] *nm* (*de lait etc*) carton.

pacotille [pakɔtij] *nf* (*camelote*) trash.

pacte [pakt] *nm* pact. ◆**pactiser** *vi* p. avec **qn** *Péj* to be in league with s.o.

paf! [paf] **1** *int* bang!, wallop! **2** *a inv* (*ivre*) *Fam* sozzled, plastered.

pagaie [pagɛ] *nf* paddle. ◆**pagayer** *vi* (*ramer*) to paddle.

pagaïe, pagaille [pagaj] *nf* (*désordre*) *Fam* mess, shambles; **en p.** *Fam* in a mess; **avoir des livres/etc en p.** *Fam* to have loads of books/*etc*.

paganisme [paganism] *nm* paganism.

page [paʒ] **1** *nf* (*de livre etc*) page; **à la p.** (*personne*) *Fig* up-to-date. **2** *nm* (*à la cour*) *Hist* page (boy).

pagne [paɲ] *nm* loincloth.

pagode [pagɔd] *nf* pagoda.

paie [pɛ] *nf* pay, wages. ◆**paiement** *nm* payment.

païen, -enne [pajɛ̃, -ɛn] *a* & *nmf* pagan, heathen.

paillasson [pajasɔ̃] *nm* (door)mat.

paille [paj] *nf* straw; (*pour boire*) (drinking) straw; **homme de p.** *Fig* stooge, man of straw; **tirer à la courte p.** to draw lots; **sur la p.** *Fig* penniless; **feu de p.** *Fig* flash in the pan. ◆**paillasse** *nf* **1** (*matelas*) straw mattress. **2** (*d'un évier*) draining-board.

paillette [pajɛt] *nf* (*d'habit*) sequin; *pl* (*de lessive, savon*) flakes; (*d'or*) *Géol* gold dust.

pain [pɛ̃] *nm* bread; **un p.** a loaf (of bread); **p. grillé** toast; **p. complet** wholemeal bread; **p. d'épice** gingerbread; **petit p.** roll; **p. de savon/de cire** bar of soap/wax; **avoir du p. sur la planche** (*travail*) *Fig* to have a lot on one's plate.

pair [pɛr] **1** *a* (*numéro*) even. **2** *nm* (*personne*) peer; **hors (de) p.** unrivalled, without equal; **aller de p.** to go hand in hand (**avec** with); **au p.** (*étudiante etc*) au pair; **travailler au p.** to work as an au pair.

paire [pɛr] *nf* pair (**de** of).

paisible [pezibl] *a* (*vie etc*) peaceful; (*caractère, personne*) peaceable.

paître* [pɛtr] *vi* to graze; **envoyer p.** *Fig* to send packing.

paix [pɛ] *nf* peace; (*traité*) *Pol* peace treaty; **en p.** in peace; (*avec sa conscience*) at peace (**avec** with); **avoir la p.** to have (some) peace and quiet.

Pakistan [pakistɑ̃] *nm* Pakistan. ◆**pakistanais, -aise** *a* & *nmf* Pakistani.

palabres [palabr] *nmpl* palaver.

palace [palas] *nm* luxury hotel.

palais [palɛ] *nm* **1** (*château*) palace; **P. de justice** law courts; **p. des sports** sports stadium *ou* centre. **2** *Anat* palate.

palan [palɑ̃] *nm* (*de navire etc*) hoist.

pâle [pɑl] *a* pale.

palet [palɛ] *nm* (*hockey sur glace*) puck.

paletot [palto] *nm* (knitted) cardigan.

palette [palɛt] *nf* **1** (*de peintre*) palette. **2** (*support pour marchandises*) pallet.

pâleur [palœr] *nf* paleness, pallor. ◆**pâlir** *vi* to go *ou* turn pale (**with**).

palier [palje] *nm* **1** (*d'escalier*) landing; **être voisins de p.** to live on the same floor. **2** (*niveau*) level; (*phase de stabilité*) plateau; **par paliers** (*étapes*) in stages.

palissade [palisad] *nf* fence (of stakes).

pallier [palje] *vt* (*difficultés etc*) to alleviate. ◆**palliatif** *nm* palliative.

palmarès [palmarɛs] *nm* prize list; (*des chansons*) hit-parade.

palme [palm] *nf* **1** palm (leaf); (*symbole*) *Fig* palm. **2** (*de nageur*) flipper. ◆**palmier** *nm* palm (tree).

palmé [palme] *a* (*patte, pied*) webbed.

palombe [palɔ̃b] *nf* wood pigeon.

pâlot, -otte [palo, -ɔt] *a* pale.

palourde [palurd] *nf* (*mollusque*) clam.

palp/er [palpe] *vt* to feel, finger. ◆**—able** *a* tangible.

palpit/er [palpite] *vi* (*frémir*) to quiver; (*cœur*) to palpitate, throb. ◆**—ant** *a* (*film etc*) thrilling. ◆**palpitations** *nfpl* quivering; palpitations.

pâmer (se) [səpame] *vpr* **se p. de** (*joie etc*) to be paralysed *ou* ecstatic with.

pamphlet [pɑ̃flɛ] *nm* lampoon.

pamplemousse [pɑ̃pləmus] *nm* grapefruit.

pan [pã] **1** *nm* (*de chemise*) tail; (*de ciel*) patch; (*de mur*) section of wall. **2** *int* bang!

pan- [pã, pan] *préf* Pan-.

panacée [panase] *nf* panacea.

panache [panaʃ] *nm* (*plumet*) plume; **avoir du p.** (*fière allure*) to have panache; **un p. de fumée** a plume of smoke.

panaché [panaʃe] **1** *a* (*bigarré, hétéroclite*) motley. **2** *a* & *nm* (**demi**) **p.** shandy; **bière panachée** shandy.

pancarte [pãkart] *nf* sign, notice; (*de manifestant*) placard.

pancréas [pãkreas] *nm Anat* pancreas.

panda [pãda] *nm* (*animal*) panda.

pané [pane] *a Culin* breaded.

panier [panje] *nm* (*ustensile, contenu*) basket; **p. à salade** salad basket; (*voiture*) *Fam* police van, prison van. ◆**p.-repas** *nm* (*pl* **paniers-repas**) packed lunch.

panique [panik] *nf* panic; **pris de p.** panic-stricken; – *a* **peur p.** panic fear. ◆**paniqu/er** *vi* to panic. ◆**–é** *a* panic-stricken.

panne [pan] *nf* breakdown; **tomber en p.** to break down; **être en p.** to have broken down; **p. d'électricité** power cut, blackout; **avoir une p. sèche** to run out of petrol *ou* *Am* gas.

panneau, -x [pano] *nm* **1** (*écriteau*) sign, notice, board; **p. (de signalisation)** traffic *ou* road sign; **p. (d'affichage)** (*publicité*) hoarding, *Am* billboard. **2** (*de porte etc*) panel. ◆**panonceau, -x** *nm* (*enseigne*) sign.

panoplie [panɔpli] *nf* **1** (*jouet*) outfit. **2** (*gamme, arsenal*) (wide) range, assortment.

panorama [panɔrama] *nm* panorama. ◆**panoramique** *a* panoramic.

panse [pãs] *nf Fam* paunch, belly. ◆**pansu** *a* potbellied.

pans/er [pãse] *vt* (*plaie, main etc*) to dress, bandage; (*personne*) to dress the wound(s) of, bandage (up); (*cheval*) to groom. ◆**–ement** *nm* (*bande*) bandage, dressing; **p. adhésif** sticking plaster, *Am* Band-Aid®.

pantalon [pãtalɔ̃] *nm* (pair of) trousers *ou* *Am* pants; **deux pantalons** two pairs of trousers *ou* *Am* pants; **en p.** in trousers, *Am* in pants.

pantelant [pãtlã] *a* gasping.

panthère [pãter] *nf* (*animal*) panther.

pantin [pãtɛ̃] *nm* (*jouet*) jumping jack; (*personne*) *Péj* puppet.

pantois [pãtwa] *a* flabbergasted.

pantoufle [pãtufl] *nf* slipper. ◆**pantou-**

flard, -arde *nmf Fam* stay-at-home, *Am* homebody.

paon [pã] *nm* peacock.

papa [papa] *nm* dad(dy); **de p.** (*désuet*) *Péj* outdated; **fils à p.** *Péj* rich man's son, daddy's boy.

pape [pap] *nm* pope. ◆**papauté** *nf* papacy.

paperasse(s) [papras] *nf*(*pl*) *Péj* (official) papers. ◆**paperasserie** *nf Péj* (official) papers; (*procédure*) red tape.

papeterie [papetri] *nf* (*magasin*) stationer's shop; (*articles*) stationery; (*fabrique*) paper mill. ◆**papetier, -ière** *nmf* stationer.

papi [papi] *nm Fam* grand(d)ad.

papier [papje] *nm* (*matière*) paper; **un p.** (*feuille*) a piece *ou* sheet of paper; (*formulaire*) a form; *Journ* an article; **en p.** (*sac etc*) paper-; **papiers (d'identité)** (identity) papers; **p. à lettres** writing paper; **du p. journal** (some) newspaper; **p. peint** wallpaper; **p. de verre** sandpaper.

papillon [papijɔ̃] *nm* **1** (*insecte*) butterfly; (*écrou*) butterfly nut, *Am* wing nut; **p. (de nuit)** moth. **2** (*contravention*) (parking) ticket.

papot/er [papɔte] *vi* to prattle. ◆**–age(s)** *nm*(*pl*) prattle.

paprika [paprika] *nm* (*poudre*) *Culin* paprika.

papy [papi] *nm Fam* grand(d)ad.

Pâque [pak] *nf* **la P.** *Rel* Passover.

paquebot [pakbo] *nm Nau* liner.

pâquerette [pakret] *nf* daisy.

Pâques [pak] *nm* & *nfpl* Easter.

paquet [pakɛ] *nm* (*de sucre, bonbons etc*) packet; (*colis*) package; (*de cigarettes*) pack(et); (*de cartes*) pack.

par [par] *prép* **1** (*agent, manière, moyen*) by; **choisi/frappé/etc** chosen/hit/etc by; **p. erreur** by mistake; **p. mer** by sea; **p. le train** by train; **p. la force/le travail/etc** by *ou* through force/work/etc; **apprendre p. un voisin** to learn from *ou* through a neighbour; **commencer/s'ouvrir p. qch** (*récit etc*) to begin/open with sth; **p. malchance** unfortunately. **2** (*lieu*) through; **p. la porte/le tunnel/etc** through *ou* by the door/tunnel/etc; **regarder/jeter p. la fenêtre** to look/throw out (of) the window; **p. les rues** through the streets; **p. ici/là** (*aller*) this/that way; (*habiter*) around here/there. **3** (*motif*) out of, from; **p. respect/pitié/etc** out of *ou* from respect/pity/etc. **4** (*temps*) on; **p. un jour d'hiver/etc** on a winter's day/etc; **p. le passé** in the past; **p. ce froid** in this cold. **5** (*distributif*) **dix fois p. an** ten times a *ou* per year; **deux p. deux** two by

two; **p. deux fois** twice. **6** (*trop*) **p. trop aimable**/*etc* far too kind/*etc.*

para [para] *nm Mil Fam* para(trooper).

para- [para] *préf* para-.

parabole [parabɔl] *nf* **1** (*récit*) parable. **2**
Math parabola.

parachever [paraʃve] *vt* to perfect.

parachute [paraʃyt] *nf* parachute.
◆**parachuter** *vt* to parachute; (*nommer*)
Fam to pitchfork (**à un poste** into a job).
◆**parachutisme** *nm* parachute jumping.
◆**parachutiste** *nmf* parachutist; *Mil* paratrooper.

parade [parad] *nf* **1** (*étalage*) show, parade;
(*spectacle*) & *Mil* parade. **2** *Boxe Escrime*
parry; (*riposte*) *Fig* reply. ◆**parader** *vi* to
parade, show off.

paradis [paradi] *nm* paradise, heaven.
◆**paradisiaque** *a* (*endroit etc*) *Fig* heavenly.

paradoxe [paradɔks] *nm* paradox.
◆**paradoxalement** *adv* paradoxically.

parafe [paraf] *voir* **paraphe.** ◆**parafer** *voir*
parapher.

paraffine [parafin] *nf* paraffin (wax).

parages [paraʒ] *nmpl* region, area (**de** of);
dans ces p. in these parts.

paragraphe [paragraf] *nm* paragraph.

paraître* [parɛtr] **1** *vi* (*se montrer*) to appear; (*sembler*) to seem, look, appear; *− v
imp* **il paraît qu'il va partir** it appears *ou*
seems (that) he's leaving. **2** *vi* (*livre*) to be
published, come out; **faire p.** to bring out.

parallèle [paralɛl] **1** *a* (*comparable*) & *Math*
parallel (**à** with, to); (*marché*) *Com* unofficial. **2** *nm* (*comparaison*) & *Géog* parallel.
◆**−ment** *adv* **p. à** parallel to.

paralyser [paralize] *vt* to paralyse, *Am* par-
alyze. ◆**paralysie** *nf* paralysis. ◆**paralytique** *a* & *nmf* paralytic.

paramètre [parametr] *nm* parameter.

paranoïa [paranɔja] *nf* paranoia. ◆**paranoïaque** *a* & *nmf* paranoid.

parapet [parapɛ] *nm* parapet.

paraphe [paraf] *nm* initials, signature;
(*traits*) flourish. ◆**parapher** *vt* to initial,
sign.

paraphrase [parafraz] *nf* paraphrase.
◆**paraphraser** *vt* to paraphrase.

parapluie [paraplɥi] *nm* umbrella.

parasite [parazit] *nm* (*personne, organisme*)
parasite; *pl Rad* interference; *− a* parasit-
ic(al).

parasol [parasɔl] *nm* parasol, sunshade.

paratonnerre [paratɔnɛr] *nm* lightning conductor *ou Am* rod.

paravent [paravã] *nm* (folding) screen.

parc [park] *nm* **1** park; (*de château*)
grounds. **2** (*de bébé*) (play) pen; (*à moutons, à bétail*) pen; **p.** (**de stationnement**)
car park, *Am* parking lot; **p. à huîtres** oyster bed.

parcelle [parsɛl] *nf* fragment, particle; (*terrain*) plot; (*de vérité*) *Fig* grain.

parce que [parskə] *conj* because.

parchemin [parʃəmɛ̃] *nm* parchment.

parcimonie [parsimɔni] *nf* **avec p.** parsimo-
niously. ◆**parcimonieux, -euse** *a* parsimonious.

par-ci par-là [parsiparla] *adv* here, there
and everywhere.

parcmètre [parkmɛtr] *nm* parking meter.

parcourir* [parkurir] *vt* (*région*) to travel
through, tour, scour; (*distance*) to cover;
(*texte*) to glance through. ◆**parcours** *nm*
(*itinéraire*) route; (*de fleuve*) & *Sp* course;
(*voyage*) trip, journey.

par-delà [pard(ə)la] *voir* **delà.**

par-derrière [pardɛrjɛr] *voir* **derrière.**

par-dessous [pard(ə)su] *prép* & *adv*
under(neath).

pardessus [pard(ə)sy] *nm* overcoat.

par-dessus [pard(ə)sy] *prép* & *adv* over (the
top of); **p.-dessus tout** above all.

par-devant [pard(ə)vã] *voir* **devant.**

pardon [pardɔ̃] *nm* forgiveness, pardon; **p.?**
(*pour demander*) excuse me?, *Am* pardon
me?; **p.!** (*je le regrette*) sorry!; **demander p.**
to apologize (**à** to). ◆**pardonn/er** *vt* to
forgive; **p. qch à qn/à qn d'avoir fait qch** to
forgive s.o. for sth/for doing sth. ◆**−able**
a forgivable.

pare-balles [parbal] *a inv* **gilet p.-balles** bulletproof jacket *ou Am* vest.

pare-brise [parbriz] *nm inv Aut* windscreen,
Am windshield.

pare-chocs [parʃɔk] *nm inv Aut* bumper.

pareil, -eille [parɛj] *a* similar; **p. à** the same
as, similar to; **être pareils** to be the same,
be similar *ou* alike; **un p. désordre**/*etc* such
a mess/*etc*; **en p. cas** in such a case; *− nmf*
(*personne*) equal; **rendre la pareille à qn** to
treat s.o. the same way; **sans p.** unparalleled, unique; *− adv Fam* the same.
◆**pareillement** *adv* in the same way;
(*aussi*) likewise.

parement [parmã] *nm* (*de pierre, de vêtement*) facing.

parent, -ente [parã, -ãt] *nmf* relation, relative; *− nmpl* (*père et mère*) parents; *− a*
related (**de** to). ◆**parenté** *nf* (*rapport*) relationship, kinship.

parenthèse [parãtɛz] *nf* (*signe*) bracket, parenthesis; (*digression*) digression.

parer [pare] **1** vt (coup) to parry, ward off; − vi **p. à** to be prepared for. **2** vt (orner) to adorn (**de** with).

paresse [pares] nf laziness, idleness. ◆**paresser** vi to laze (about). ◆**paresseux, -euse** a lazy, idle; − nmf lazybones.

parfaire [parfɛr] vt to perfect. ◆**parfait** a perfect; **p.!** excellent!; − nm Gram perfect (tense). ◆**parfaitement** adv perfectly; (certainement) certainly.

parfois [parfwa] adv sometimes.

parfum [parfœ̃] nm (odeur) fragrance, scent; (goût) flavour; (liquide) perfume, scent. ◆**parfum/er** vt to perfume, scent; (glace, crème etc) to flavour (**à** with); − **se p.** vpr to put on perfume; (habituellement) to wear perfume. ◆**−é** a (savon, mouchoir) scented; **p. au café**/etc coffee-/etc flavoured. ◆**parfumerie** nf (magasin) perfume shop.

pari [pari] nm bet, wager; pl Sp betting, bets; **p. mutuel urbain** = the tote, Am pari-mutuel. ◆**parier** vti to bet (**sur** on, **que** that). ◆**parieur, -euse** nmf Sp better, punter.

Paris [pari] nm ou f Paris. ◆**parisien, -ienne** a (accent etc) Parisian, Paris-; − nmf Parisian.

parité [parite] nf parity.

parjure [parʒyr] nm perjury; − nmf perjurer. ◆**se parjurer** vpr to perjure oneself.

parka [parka] nm parka.

parking [parkiŋ] nm (lieu) car park, Am parking lot.

par-là [parla] adv voir **par-ci.**

parlement [parləmɑ̃] nm parliament. ◆**parlementaire** a parliamentary; − nmf member of parliament.

parlementer [parləmɑ̃te] vi to parley, negotiate.

parl/er [parle] vi to talk, speak (**de** about, of; **à** to); **tu parles!** Fam you must be joking!; **sans p. de** . . . not to mention . . . ; − vt (langue) to speak; **p. affaires**/etc to talk business/etc; − **se p.** vpr (langue) to be spoken; − nm speech; (régional) dialect. ◆**−ant** a (film) talking; (regard etc) eloquent. ◆**−é** a (langue) spoken.

parloir [parlwar] nm (de couvent, prison) visiting room.

parmi [parmi] prép among(st).

parodie [parɔdi] nf parody. ◆**parodier** vt to parody.

paroi [parwa] nf wall; (de maison) inside wall; (de rocher) (rock) face.

paroisse [parwas] nf parish. ◆**paroissial,**

-aux a (registre, activité etc) parish-. ◆**paroissien, -ienne** nmf parishioner.

parole [parɔl] nf (mot, promesse) word; (faculté, langage) speech; **adresser la p. à** to speak to; **prendre la p.** to speak, make a speech; **demander la p.** to ask to speak; **perdre la p.** to lose one's tongue.

paroxysme [parɔksism] nm (de douleur etc) height.

parpaing [parpɛ̃] nm concrete block, breezeblock.

parquer [parke] vt (bœufs) to pen; (gens) to herd together, confine; (véhicule) to park; − **se p.** vpr Aut to park.

parquet [parkɛ] nm **1** (parquet) floor(ing). **2** Jur Public Prosecutor's office.

parrain [parɛ̃] nm Rel godfather; (répondant) sponsor. ◆**parrain/er** vt to sponsor. ◆**−age** nm sponsorship.

pars, part¹ [par] voir **partir.**

parsemer [parsəme] vt to strew, dot (**de** with).

part² [par] nf (portion) share, part; **prendre p. à** (activité) to take part in; (la joie etc de qn) to share; **de toutes parts** from ou on all sides; **de p. et d'autre** on both sides; **d'une p., . . . d'autre p.** on the one hand, . . . on the other hand; **d'autre p.** (d'ailleurs) moreover; **pour ma p.** as far as I'm concerned; **de la p. de** (provenance) from; **c'est de la p. de qui?** Tél who's speaking?; **faire p. de qch à qn** to inform s.o. of sth; **quelque p.** somewhere; **nulle p.** nowhere; **autre p.** somewhere else; **à p.** (séparément) apart; (mettre, prendre) aside; (excepté) apart from; **un cas/une place**/etc **à p.** a separate ou special case/place/etc; **membre à p. entière** full member.

partage [partaʒ] nm dividing (up), division; (participation) sharing; (distribution) sharing out; (sort) Fig lot. ◆**partag/er** vt (repas, frais, joie etc) to share (**avec** with); (diviser) to divide (up); (distribuer) to share out; − **se p.** vpr (bénéfices etc) to share (between themselves etc); **se p. entre** to divide one's time between. ◆**−é** a (avis etc) divided; **p. entre** (sentiments) torn between.

partance (en) [ɑ̃partɑ̃s] adv (train etc) about to depart (**pour** for).

partant [partɑ̃] nm (coureur, cheval) Sp starter.

partenaire [partənɛr] nmf (époux etc) & Sp Pol partner.

parterre [partɛr] nm **1** (de jardin etc) flower bed. **2** Th stalls, Am orchestra.

parti [parti] nm Pol party; (époux) match; **prendre un p.** to make a decision, follow a course; **prendre p. pour** to side with; **tirer p. de** to turn to (good) account; **p. pris** (*préjugé*) prejudice; **être de p. pris** to be prejudiced (**contre** against).

partial, -aux [parsjal, -o] *a* biased. ◆**partialité** *nf* bias.

participe [partisip] *nm Gram* participle.

particip/er [partisipe] *vi* **p. à** (*activité, jeu etc*) to take part in, participate in; (*frais, joie etc*) to share (in). ◆**—ant, -ante** *nmf* participant. ◆**participation** *nf* participation; sharing; (*d'un acteur*) appearance, collaboration; **p. (aux frais)** (*contribution*) share (in the expenses).

particule [partikyl] *nf* particle.

particulier, -ière [partikylje, -jɛr] *a* (*spécial, spécifique*) particular; (*privé*) private; (*bizarre*) peculiar; **p. à** peculiar to; **en p.** (*surtout*) in particular; (*à part*) in private; − *nm* private individual *ou* citizen. ◆**particularité** *nf* peculiarity. ◆**particulièrement** *adv* particularly; **tout p.** especially.

partie [parti] *nf* part; (*de cartes, de tennis etc*) game; (*de chasse, de plaisir*) & *Jur* party; (*métier*) line, field; *pl* parts; **en grande p.** mainly; **faire p. de** to be a part of; (*adhérer à*) to belong to; (*comité*) to be on. ◆**partiel, -ielle** *a* partial; − *nm* (**examen**) *m. Univ* term exam. ◆**partiellement** *adv* partially.

part/ir [partir] *vi* (*aux* **être**) (*aller, disparaître*) to go; (*s'en aller*) to leave, go (off); (*se mettre en route*) to set off; (*s'éloigner*) to go (away); (*moteur*) to start; (*fusil, coup de feu*) to go off; (*flèche*) to shoot off; (*bouton*) to come off; (*tache*) to come out; **p. de** (*commencer par*) to start (off) with; **ça part du cœur** it comes from the heart; **p. bien** to get off to a good start; **à p. de** (*date, prix*) from. ◆**—i** *a* **bien p.** off to a good start.

partisan [partizɑ̃] *nm* follower, supporter; *Mil* partisan; − *a* (*esprit*) *Péj* partisan; **être p. de qch/de faire** to be in favour of sth/of doing.

partition [partisjɔ̃] *nf Mus* score.

partout [partu] *adv* everywhere; **p. où tu vas** *ou* **iras** everywhere *ou* wherever you go; **p. sur la table**/*etc* all over the table/*etc*.

paru [pary] *voir* **paraître**. ◆**parution** *nf* (*de livre etc*) publication.

parure [paryr] *nf* (*toilette*) finery; (*bijoux*) jewellery.

parven/ir* [parvənir] *vi* (*aux* **être**) **p. à** (*lieu*) to reach; (*fortune, ses fins*) to achieve; **p. à faire** to manage to do. ◆**—u, -ue** *nmf Péj* upstart.

parvis [parvi] *nm* square (*in front of church etc*).

pas¹ [pɑ] *adv* (*négatif*) not; (**ne**) . . . **p.** not; **je ne sais p.** I do not *ou* don't know; **p. de pain/de café**/*etc* no bread/coffee/*etc*; **p. encore** not yet; **p. du tout** not at all.

pas² [pɑ] *nm* **1** step, pace; (*allure*) pace; (*bruit*) footstep; (*trace*) footprint; **à deux p. (de)** close by; **revenir sur ses p.** to go back on one's tracks; **au p.** at a walking pace; **rouler au p.** (*véhicule*) to go dead slow(ly); **au p. (cadencé)** in step; **faire les cent p.** to walk up and down; **faux p.** stumble; (*faute*) *Fig* blunder; **le p. de la porte** the doorstep. **2** (*de vis*) thread. **3** *Géog* straits; **le p. de Calais** the Straits of Dover.

pascal [paskal] *a* (*semaine, messe etc*) Easter-.

passable [pasabl] *a* acceptable, tolerable; mention **p.** *Scol Univ* pass. ◆**—ment** [-əmɑ̃] *adv* acceptably; (*beaucoup*) quite a lot.

passage [pasaʒ] *nm* (*action*) passing, passage; (*traversée*) *Nau* crossing, passage; (*extrait*) passage; (*couloir*) passage(way); (*droit*) right of way; (*venue*) arrival; (*chemin*) path; **p. clouté** *ou* **pour piétons** (pedestrian) crossing; **obstruer le p.** to block the way; **p. souterrain** subway, *Am* underpass; **p. à niveau** level crossing, *Am* grade crossing; **'p. interdit'** 'no thoroughfare'; **'cédez le p.'** *Aut* 'give way', *Am* 'yield'; **être de p.** to be passing through (**à Paris**/*etc* Paris/*etc*); **hôte de p.** passing guest. ◆**passager, -ère 1** *nmf* passenger; **p. clandestin** stowaway. **2** *a* (*de courte durée*) passing, temporary. ◆**passagèrement** *adv* temporarily.

passant, -ante [pasɑ̃, -ɑ̃t] **1** *a* (*rue*) busy; − *nmf* passer-by. **2** *nm* (*de ceinture etc*) loop.

passe [pas] *nf Sp* pass; **mot de p.** password; **en p. de faire** on the road to doing; **une mauvaise p.** *Fig* a bad patch.

passe-montagne [pasmɔ̃taɲ] *nm* balaclava.

passe-partout [paspartu] *nm inv* (*clé*) master key; − *a inv* (*compliment, phrase*) all-purpose.

passe-passe [paspas] *nm inv* **tour de p.-passe** conjuring trick.

passe-plat [paspla] *nm* service hatch.

passeport [paspɔr] *nm* passport.

passer [pase] *vi* (*aux* **être** *ou* **avoir**) (*aller, venir*) to pass (à to); (*facteur, laitier*) to come; (*temps*) to pass (by), go by; (*courant*) to flow; (*film, programme*) to be shown, be on; (*loi*) to be passed; (*douleur, mode*) to pass; (*couleur*) to fade; **p. devant** (*maison etc*) to go past *ou* by, pass (by); **p. à** *ou* **par Paris** to pass through Paris; **p. à la radio** to come *ou* go on the radio; **p. à l'ennemi/à la caisse** to go over to the enemy/the cash desk; **laisser p.** (*personne, lumière*) to let in *ou* through; (*occasion*) to let slip; **p. prendre** to pick up, fetch; **p. voir qn** to drop in on s.o.; **p. pour** (*riche etc*) to be taken for; **faire p. qn pour** to pass s.o. off as; **p. sur** (*détail etc*) to overlook, pass over; **p. capitaine/etc** to be promoted captain/*etc*; **p. en** (*seconde etc*) *Scol* to pass up into; *Aut* to change up to; **ça passe** (*c'est passable*) that'll do; **en passant** (*dire qch*) in passing; − *vt* (*aux avoir*) (*frontière etc*) to pass, cross; (*maison etc*) to pass, go past; (*donner*) to pass, hand (à to); (*mettre*) to put; (*omettre*) to overlook; (*temps*) to spend, pass (**à faire** doing); (*disque*) to play, put on; (*film, programme*) to show, put on; (*loi, motion*) to pass; (*chemise*) to slip on; (*examen*) to take, sit (for); (*thé*) to strain; (*café*) to filter; (*commande*) to place; (*accord*) to conclude; (*colère*) to vent (**sur** on); (*limites*) to go beyond; (*visite médicale*) to go through; **p.** (**son tour**) to pass; **p. qch à qn** (*caprice etc*) to grant s.o. sth; (*pardonner*) to excuse s.o. sth; **je vous passe . . .** *Tél* I'm putting you through to . . . ; **p. un coup d'éponge/etc à qch** to go over sth with a sponge/*etc*; − **se p.** *vpr* (*se produire*) to take place, happen; (*douleur*) to pass, go (away); **se p. de** to do *ou* go without; **se p. de commentaires** to need no comment; **ça s'est bien passé** it went off all right. ◆**passé 1** *a* (*temps etc*) past; (*couleur*) faded; **la semaine passée** last week; **dix heures passées** after *ou* gone ten (o'clock); **être passé** (*personne*) to have been (and gone); (*orage*) to be over; **avoir vingt ans passés** to be over twenty; − *nm* (*temps, vie passée*) past; *Gram* past (tense). **2** *prép* after; **p. huit heures** after eight (o'clock).

passerelle [pɑsrɛl] *nf* (*pont*) footbridge; (*voie d'accès*) *Nau Av* gangway.

passe-temps [pɑstɑ̃] *nm inv* pastime.

passeur, -euse [pɑsœr, -øz] *nmf* **1** *Nau* ferryman, ferrywoman. **2** (*contrebandier*) smuggler.

passible [pasibl] *a* **p. de** (*peine*) *Jur* liable to.

passif, -ive [pasif, -iv] **1** *a* (*rôle, personne etc*) passive; − *nm Gram* passive. **2** *nm Com* liabilities. ◆**passivité** *nf* passiveness, passivity.

passion [pɑsjɔ̃] *nf* passion; **avoir la p. des**

voitures/d'écrire/*etc* to have a passion *ou* a great love for cars/writing/*etc*. ◆**passionnel, -elle** *a* (*crime*) of passion. ◆**passionn/er** *vt* to thrill, fascinate; **se p. pour** to have a passion for. ◆**—ant** *a* thrilling. ◆**—é, -ée** *a* passionate; **p. de qch** passionately fond of sth; − *nmf* fan (**de** of). ◆**—ément** *adv* passionately.

passoire [pɑswar] *nf* (*pour liquides*) sieve; (*à thé*) strainer; (*à légumes*) colander.

pastel [pastɛl] *nm* pastel; **au p.** (*dessin*) pastel-; − *a inv* (*ton*) pastel-.

pastèque [pastɛk] *nf* watermelon.

pasteur [pastœr] *nm Rel* pastor.

pasteurisé [pastœrize] *a* (*lait, beurre etc*) pasteurized.

pastiche [pastiʃ] *nm* pastiche.

pastille [pastij] *nf* pastille, lozenge.

pastis [pastis] *nm* aniseed liqueur, pastis.

pastoral, -aux [pastɔral, -o] *a* pastoral.

patate [patat] *nf Fam* spud, potato.

patatras! [patatra] *int* crash!

pataud [pato] *a* clumsy, lumpish.

patauger [patoʒe] *vi* (*marcher*) to wade (**in** the mud etc); (*barboter*) to splash about; (*s'empêtrer*) *Fig* to flounder. ◆**pataugeoire** *nf* paddling pool.

patchwork [patʃwœrk] *nm* patchwork.

pâte [pɑt] *nf* (*substance*) paste; (*à pain, à gâteau*) dough; (*à tarte*) pastry; **pâtes** (*alimentaires*) pasta; **p. à modeler** plasticine®, modelling clay; **p. à frire** batter; **p. dentifrice** toothpaste.

pâté [pɑte] *nm* **1** (*charcuterie*) pâté; **p.** (**en croûte**) meat pie. **2 p.** (**de sable**) sand castle; **p. de maisons** block of houses. **3** (*tache d'encre*) (ink) blot.

pâtée [pɑte] *nf* (*pour chien, volaille etc*) mash.

patelin [patlɛ̃] *nm Fam* village.

patent [patɑ̃] *a* patent, obvious.

patère [pater] *nf* (coat) peg.

paternel, -elle [patɛrnɛl] *a* (*amour etc*) fatherly, paternal; (*parenté, réprimande*) paternal. ◆**paternité** *nf* (*état*) paternity, fatherhood; (*de livre*) authorship.

pâteux, -euse [pɑtø, -øz] *a* (*substance*) doughy, pasty; (*style*) woolly; **avoir la bouche** *ou* **la langue pâteuse** (*après s'être enivré*) to have a mouth full of cotton wool *ou* AM cotton.

pathétique [patetik] *a* moving; − *nm* pathos.

pathologie [patɔlɔʒi] *nf* pathology. ◆**pathologique** *a* pathological.

patient, -ente [pasjɑ̃, -ɑ̃t] **1** *a* patient. **2** *nmf Méd* patient. ◆**patiemment** [-amɑ̃] *adv* patiently. ◆**patience** *nf* patience; **prendre p.** to have patience; **perdre p.** to lose patience. ◆**patienter** *vi* to wait (patiently).

patin [patɛ̃] *nm* skate; (*pour le parquet*) cloth pad (*used for walking*); **p. à glace/à roulettes** ice/roller skate. ◆**patin/er** *vi Sp* to skate; (*véhicule, embrayage*) to slip. ◆**—age** *nm Sp* skating; **p. artistique** figure skating. ◆**—eur, -euse** *nmf Sp* skater. ◆**patinoire** *nf* (*piste*) & *Fig* skating rink, ice rink.

patine [patin] *nf* patina.

patio [patjo] *nm* patio.

pâtir [patir] *vi* **p. de** to suffer from.

pâtisserie [patisri] *nf* pastry, cake; (*magasin*) cake shop; (*art*) cake *ou* pastry making. ◆**pâtissier, -ière** *nmf* pastry-cook and cake shop owner.

patois [patwa] *nm Ling* patois.

patraque [patrak] *a* (*malade*) *Fam* under the weather.

patriarche [patrijarʃ] *nm* patriarch.

patrie [patri] *nf* (*native*) country; (*ville*) birth place. ◆**patriote** *nmf* patriot; – *a* (*personne*) patriotic. ◆**patriotique** *a* (*chant etc*) patriotic. ◆**patriotisme** *nm* patriotism.

patrimoine [patrimwan] *nm* (*biens*) & *Fig* heritage.

patron, -onne [patrɔ̃, -ɔn] **1** *nmf* (*chef*) employer, boss; (*propriétaire*) owner (**de** of); (*gérant*) manager, manageress; (*de bar*) landlord, landlady. **2** *nmf Rel* patron saint. **3** *nmf* (*modèle de papier*) *Tex* pattern. ◆**patronage** *nm* **1** (*protection*) patronage. **2** (*centre*) youth club. ◆**patronal, -aux** *a* (*syndicat etc*) employers'. ◆**patronat** *nm* employers. ◆**patronner** *vt* to sponsor.

patrouille [patruj] *nf* patrol. ◆**patrouill/er** *vi* to patrol. ◆**—eur** *nm* (*navire*) patrol boat.

patte [pat] *nf* **1** (*membre*) leg; (*de chat, chien*) paw; (*main*) *Fam* hand; **à quatre pattes** on all fours. **2** (*de poche*) flap; (*languette*) tongue.

pattes [pat] *nfpl* (*favoris*) sideboards, *Am* sideburns.

pâture [patyr] *nf* (*nourriture*) food; (*intellectuelle*) *Fig* fodder. ◆**pâturage** *nm* pasture.

paume [pom] *nf* (*de main*) palm.

paum/er [pome] *vt Fam* to lose; **un coin** *ou* **trou paumé** (*sans attrait*) a dump. ◆**—é, -ée** *nmf* (*malheureux*) *Fam* down-and-out, loser.

paupière [popjer] *nf* eyelid.

pause [poz] *nf* (*arrêt*) break; (*dans le discours etc*) pause.

pauvre [povr] *a* poor; (*terre*) impoverished, poor; **p. en** (*calories etc*) low in; (*ressources etc*) low on; – *nmf* (*indigent, malheureux*) poor man, poor woman; **les pauvres** the poor. ◆**pauvrement** *adv* poorly. ◆**pauvreté** *nf* (*besoin*) poverty; (*insuffisance*) poorness.

pavaner (se) [səpavane] *vpr* to strut (about).

pav/er [pave] *vt* to pave. ◆**—é** *nm* **un p.** a paving stone; (*rond, de vieille chaussée*) a cobblestone; **sur le p.** *Fig* on the streets. ◆**—age** *nm* (*travail, revêtement*) paving.

pavillon [pavijɔ̃] *nm* **1** (*maison*) house; (*de chasse*) lodge; (*d'hôpital*) ward; (*d'exposition*) pavilion. **2** (*drapeau*) flag.

pavoiser [pavwaze] *vt* to deck out with flags; – *vi* (*exulter*) *Fig* to rejoice.

pavot [pavo] *nm* (*cultivé*) poppy.

pay/er [peje] *vt* (*personne, somme*) to pay; (*service, objet, faute*) to pay for; (*récompenser*) to repay; **p. qch à qn** (*offrir en cadeau*) *Fam* to treat s.o. to sth; **p. qn pour faire** to pay s.o. to do *ou* for doing; – *vi* (*personne, métier, crime*) to pay; **se p. qch** (*s'acheter*) *Fam* to treat oneself to sth; **se p. la tête de qn** *Fam* to make fun of s.o. ◆**—ant** [pejɑ̃] *a* (*hôte, spectateur*) who pays, paying; (*place, entrée*) that one has to pay for; (*rentable*) worthwhile. ◆**payable** *a* payable. ◆**paye** *nf* pay, wages. ◆**payement** *nm* payment.

pays [pei] *nm* country; (*région*) region; (*village*) village; **p. des rêves/du soleil** land of dreams/sun; **du p.** (*vin, gens etc*) local.

paysage [peizaʒ] *nm* landscape, scenery.

paysan, -anne [peizɑ̃, -an] *nmf* (*small*) farmer; (*rustre*) *Péj* peasant; – *a* country-; (*monde*) farming.

Pays-Bas [peiba] *nmpl* **les P.-Bas** the Netherlands.

PCV [peseve] *abrév* (*paiement contre vérification*) **téléphoner en PCV** to reverse the charges, *Am* call collect.

PDG [pedeʒe] *abrév* = **président directeur général**.

péage [peaʒ] *nm* (*droit*) toll; (*lieu*) tollgate.

peau, -x [po] *nf* skin; (*de fruit*) peel, skin; (*cuir*) hide, skin; (*fourrure*) pelt; **dans la p. de qn** *Fig* in s.o.'s shoes; **faire p. neuve** *Fig* to turn over a new leaf. ◆**P.-Rouge** *nmf* (*pl* **Peaux-Rouges**) (Red) Indian.

pêche¹ [pɛʃ] *nf* (*activité*) fishing; (*poissons*) catch; (**à la ligne**) angling; **aller à la p.** to go fishing. ◆**pêcher¹** *vi* to fish; – *vt* (*chercher à prendre*) to fish for; (*attraper*) to catch; (*dénicher*) *Fam* to dig up. ◆**pêcheur** *nm* fisherman; angler.

pêche² [pɛʃ] *nf* (*fruit*) peach. ◆**pêcher²** *nm* (*arbre*) peach tree.

péché [peʃe] *nm* sin. ◆**péch/er** *vi* to sin; **p. par orgueil**/*etc* to be too proud/*etc*. ◆**—eur, -eresse** *nmf* sinner.

pectoraux [pɛktɔro] *nmpl* (*muscles*) chest muscles.

pécule [pekyl] *nm* **un p.** (*économies*) (some) savings, a nest egg.

pécuniaire [pekynjɛr] *a* monetary.

pédagogie [pedagɔʒi] *nf* (*science*) education, teaching methods. ◆**pédagogique** *a* educational. ◆**pédagogue** *nmf* teacher.

pédale [pedal] *nf* **1** pedal; **p. de frein** footbrake (pedal). **2** (*homosexuel*) *Péj* pansy, queer. ◆**pédaler** *vi* to pedal.

pédalo [pedalo] *nm* pedal boat, pedalo.

pédant, -ante [pedɑ̃, -ɑ̃t] *nmf* pedant; − *a* pedantic. ◆**pédantisme** *nm* pedantry.

pédé [pede] *nm* (*homosexuel*) *Péj Fam* queer.

pédiatre [pedjatr] *nmf Méd* p(a)ediatrician.

pédicure [pedikyr] *nmf* chiropodist.

pedigree [pedigre] *nm* (*de chien, cheval etc*) pedigree.

pègre [pɛgr] *nf* **la p.** the (criminal) underworld.

peigne [pɛɲ] *nm* comb; **passer au p. fin** *Fig* to go through with a fine toothcomb; **un coup de p.** (*action*) a comb. ◆**peigner** *vt* (*cheveux*) to comb; **p. qn** to comb s.o.'s hair; − **se p.** *vpr* to comb one's hair.

peignoir [pɛɲwar] *nm* dressing gown, *Am* bathrobe; **p. (de bain)** bathrobe.

peinard [pɛnar] *a Arg* quiet (and easy).

peindre* [pɛ̃dr] *vt* to paint; (*décrire*) *Fig* to depict, paint; **p. en bleu**/*etc* to paint blue/*etc*; − *vi* to paint.

peine [pɛn] *nf* **1** (*châtiment*) punishment; **p. de mort** death penalty *ou* sentence; **p. de prison** prison sentence; **'défense d'entrer sous p. d'amende'** 'trespassers will be fined'. **2** (*chagrin*) sorrow, grief; **avoir de la p.** to be upset *ou* sad; **faire de la p. à** to upset, cause pain *ou* sorrow to. **3** (*effort, difficulté*) trouble; **se donner de la p.** *ou* **beaucoup de p.** to go to a lot of trouble (**pour faire** to do); **avec p.** with difficulty; **ça vaut la p. d'attendre**/*etc* it's worth (while) waiting/*etc*; **ce n'est pas** *ou* **ça ne vaut pas la p.** it's not worth while *ou* worth it *ou* worth bothering. ◆**peiner 1** *vt* to upset, grieve. **2** *vi* to labour, struggle.

peine (à) [apɛn] *adv* hardly, scarcely.

peintre [pɛ̃tr] *nm* painter; **p. (en bâtiment)** (house) painter, (painter and) decorator. ◆**peinture** *nf* (*tableau, activité*) painting; (*couleur*) paint; **'p. fraîche'** 'wet paint'. ◆**peinturlurer** *vt Fam* to daub with colour; **se p. (le visage)** to paint one's face.

péjoratif, -ive [peʒɔratif, -iv] *a* pejorative, derogatory.

pékinois [pekinwa] *nm* (*chien*) pekin(g)ese.

pelage [pəlaʒ] *nm* (*d'animal*) coat, fur.

pelé [pəle] *a* bare.

pêle-mêle [pɛlmɛl] *adv* in disorder.

peler [pəle] *vt* (*fruit*) to peel; **se p. facilement** (*fruit*) to peel easily; − *vi* (*peau bronzée*) to peel.

pèlerin [pɛlrɛ̃] *nm* pilgrim. ◆**pèlerinage** *nm* pilgrimage.

pèlerine [pɛlrin] *nf* (*manteau*) cape.

pélican [pelikɑ̃] *nm* (*oiseau*) pelican.

pelisse [pəlis] *nf* fur-lined coat.

pelle [pɛl] *nf* shovel; (*d'enfant*) spade; **p. à poussière** dustpan; **ramasser** *ou* **prendre une p.** (*tomber*) *Fam* to come a cropper, *Am* take a spill; **à la p.** (*argent etc*) *Fam* galore. ◆**pelletée** *nf* shovelful. ◆**pelleteuse** *nf Tech* mechanical shovel, excavator.

pellicule [pelikyl] *nf Phot* film; (*couche*) film, layer; *pl Méd* dandruff.

pelote [pəlɔt] *nf* (*de laine*) ball; (*à épingles*) pincushion; **p. (basque)** *Sp* pelota.

peloter [pəlɔte] *vt* (*palper*) *Péj Fam* to paw.

peloton [pəlɔtɔ̃] *nm* **1** (*coureurs*) *Sp* pack, main body. **2** *Mil* squad; **p. d'exécution** firing squad. **3** (*de ficelle*) ball.

pelotonner (se) [səpəlɔtɔne] *vpr* to curl up (into a ball).

pelouse [pəluz] *nf* lawn; *Sp* enclosure.

peluche [pəlyʃ] *nf* (*tissu*) plush; *pl* (*flocons*) fluff, lint; **une p.** (*flocon*) a bit of fluff *ou* lint; **jouet en p.** soft toy; **chien**/*etc* **en p.** (*jouet*) furry dog/*etc*; **ours en p.** teddy bear. ◆**pelucher** *vi* to get fluffy *ou* linty. ◆**pelucheux, -euse** *a* fluffy, linty.

pelure [pəlyr] *nf* (*épluchure*) peeling; **une p.** a (piece of) peeling.

pénal, -aux [penal, -o] *a* (*droit, code etc*) penal. ◆**pénalisation** *nf Sp* penalty. ◆**pénaliser** *vt Sp Jur* to penalize (**pour** for). ◆**pénalité** *nf Jur Rugby* penalty.

penalty, pl -ties [penalti, -iz] *nm Fb* penalty.

penaud [pəno] *a* sheepish.

penchant [pɑ̃ʃɑ̃] *nm* (*goût*) liking (**pour** for); (*tendance*) inclination (**à qch** towards sth).

pench/er [pɑ̃ʃe] *vt* (*objet*) to tilt; (*tête*) to lean; − *vi* (*arbre etc*) to lean (over); **p. pour** *Fig* to be inclined towards; − **se p.** *vpr* to lean (forward); **se p. par** (*fenêtre*) to lean out of; **se p. sur** (*problème etc*) to examine. ◆**—é** *a* leaning.

pendaison [pɑ̃dɛzɔ̃] *nf* hanging.

pendant[1] [pɑ̃dɑ̃] *prép* (*au cours de*) during; **p. la nuit** during the night; **p. deux mois** (*pour une période de*) for two months; **p. que** while, whilst.

pendentif [pɑ̃dɑ̃tif] *nm* (*collier*) pendant.

penderie [pɑ̃dri] *nf* wardrobe.

pend/re [pɑ̃dr] *vti* to hang (à from); **— se p.** *vpr* (*se tuer*) to hang oneself; (*se suspendre*) to hang (à from). ◆**—ant**[2] [1] *a* hanging; (*langue*) hanging out; (*joues*) sagging; (*question*) *Fig* pending. **2** *nm* **p.** (*d'oreille*) drop earring. **3** *nm* **le p. de** the companion piece to. ◆**—u, -ue** *a* (*objet*) hanging (à from); **—** *nmf* hanged man, hanged woman.

pendule [pɑ̃dyl] **1** *nf* clock. **2** *nm* (*balancier*) & *Fig* pendulum. ◆**pendulette** *nf* small clock.

pénétr/er [penetre] *vi* **p. dans** to enter; (*profondément*) to penetrate (into); **—** *vt* (*substance, mystère etc*) to penetrate; **se p. de** (*idée*) to become convinced of. ◆**—ant** *a* (*esprit, froid etc*) penetrating, keen. ◆**pénétration** *nf* penetration.

pénible [penibl] *a* (*difficile*) difficult; (*douloureux*) painful, distressing; (*ennuyeux*) tiresome; (*agaçant*) annoying. ◆**—ment** [-əmɑ̃] *adv* with difficulty; (*avec douleur*) painfully.

péniche [peniʃ] *nf* barge; **p. de débarquement** *Mil* landing craft.

pénicilline [penisilin] *nf* penicillin.

péninsule [penɛ̃syl] *nf* peninsula. ◆**péninsulaire** *a* peninsular.

pénis [penis] *nm* penis.

pénitence [penitɑ̃s] *nf* (*punition*) punishment; (*peine*) *Rel* penance; (*regret*) penitence. ◆**pénitent, -ente** *nmf Rel* penitent.

pénitencier [penitɑ̃sje] *nm* prison. ◆**pénitentiaire** *a* (*régime etc*) prison-.

pénombre [penɔ̃br] *nf* half-light, darkness.

pensée [pɑ̃se] *nf* **1** thought. **2** (*fleur*) pansy. ◆**pens/er** *vi* to think (à of, about); **p. à qch/à faire qch** (*ne pas oublier*) to remember sth/to do sth; **p. à tout** (*prévoir*) to think of everything; **penses-tu!** you must be joking!, not at all!; **—** *vt* to think (**que** that); (*concevoir*) to think out; (*imaginer*) to imagine (**que** that); **je pensais rester** (*intention*) I was thinking of staying, I thought I'd stay; **je pense réussir** (*espoir*) I hope to succeed; **que pensez-vous de ... ?** what do you think of *ou* about . . . ?; **p. du bien de** to think highly of. ◆**—ant** *a* **bien p.** *Péj* or-

thodox. ◆**—eur** *nm* thinker. ◆**pensif, -ive** *a* thoughtful, pensive.

pension [pɑ̃sjɔ̃] *nf* **1** boarding school; (*somme, repas*) board; **être en p.** to board, be a boarder (**chez** with); **p.** (**de famille**) guesthouse, boarding house; **p. complète** full board. **2** (*allocation*) pension; **p. alimentaire** maintenance allowance. ◆**pensionnaire** (*élève*) boarder; (*d'hôtel*) resident; (*de famille*) lodger. ◆**pensionnat** *nm* boarding school; (*élèves*) boarders. ◆**pensionné, -ée** *nmf* pensioner.

pentagone [pɛ̃tagɔn] *nm* **le P.** *Am Pol* the Pentagon.

pentathlon [pɛ̃tatlɔ̃] *nm Sp* pentathlon.

pente [pɑ̃t] *nf* slope; **être en p.** to slope, be sloping.

Pentecôte [pɑ̃tkot] *nf* Whitsun, *Am* Pentecost.

pénurie [penyri] *nf* scarcity, shortage (**de** of).

pépère [pepɛr] **1** *nm Fam* grand(d)ad. **2** *a* (*tranquille*) *Fam* quiet (and easy).

pépier [pepje] *vi* (*oiseau*) to cheep, chirp.

pépin [pepɛ̃] *nm* **1** (*de fruit*) pip, *Am* pit. **2** (*ennui*) *Fam* hitch, bother. **3** (*parapluie*) *Fam* brolly.

pépinière [pepinjɛr] *nf Bot* nursery.

pépite [pepit] *nf* (gold) nugget.

péquenaud, -aude [pɛkno, -od] *nmf Péj Arg* peasant, bumpkin.

perçant [pɛrsɑ̃] *a* (*cri, froid*) piercing; (*yeux*) sharp, keen.

percée [pɛrse] *nf* (*dans une forêt*) opening; (*avance technologique, attaque militaire*) breakthrough.

perce-neige [pɛrsənɛʒ] *nm ou f inv Bot* snowdrop.

perce-oreille [pɛrsɔrɛj] *nm* (*insecte*) earwig.

percepteur [pɛrsɛptœr] *nm* tax collector. ◆**perceptible** *a* perceptible (à to), noticeable. ◆**perception** *nf* **1** (*bureau*) tax office; (*d'impôt*) collection. **2** (*sensation*) perception.

perc/er [pɛrse] *vt* (*trouer*) to pierce; (*avec perceuse*) to drill (a hole in); (*trou, ouverture*) to make, drill; (*mystère etc*) to uncover; **p. une dent** (*bébé*) to cut a tooth; **—** *vi* (*soleil, ennemi, sentiment*) to break *ou* come through; (*abcès*) to burst. ◆**—euse** *nf* drill.

percevoir* [pɛrsəvwar] *vt* **1** (*sensation*) to perceive; (*son*) to hear. **2** (*impôt*) to collect.

perche [pɛrʃ] *nf* **1** (*bâton*) pole; **saut à la p.** pole-vaulting. **2** (*poisson*) perch.

perch/er [pɛrʃe] *vi* (*oiseau*) to perch; (*volailles*) to roost; (*loger*) *Fam* to hang out; **—**

vt (*placer*) *Fam* to perch; **— se p.** *vpr* (*oiseau, personne*) to perch. ◆**—é** *a* perched. ◆**perchoir** *nm* perch; (*de volailles*) roost.

percolateur [pɛrkɔlatœr] *nm* (*de restaurant*) percolator.

percussion [pɛrkysjɔ̃] *nf Mus* percussion.

percutant [pɛrkytɑ̃] *a Fig* powerful.

percuter [pɛrkyte] *vt* (*véhicule*) to crash into; **— vi p. contre** to crash into.

perd/re [pɛrdr] *vt* to lose; (*gaspiller*) to waste; (*ruiner*) to ruin; (*habitude*) to get out of; **p. de vue** to lose sight of; **— vi** to lose; (*récipient, tuyau*) to leak; **j'y perds** I lose out, I lose on the deal; **— se p.** *vpr* (*s'égarer*) to get lost; (*dans les détails*) to lose oneself; (*disparaître*) to disappear; **je m'y perds** I'm lost *ou* confused. ◆**—ant, -ante** *a* (*billet*) losing; *– nmf* loser. ◆**—u** *a* lost; wasted; (*malade*) finished; (*lieu*) isolated, in the middle of nowhere; **à ses moments perdus** in one's spare time; **une balle perdue** a stray bullet; **c'est du temps p.** it's a waste of time. ◆**perdition (en)** *adv* (*navire*) in distress.

perdrix [pɛrdri] *nf* partridge. ◆**perdreau, -x** *nm* young partridge.

père [pɛr] *nm* father; **Dupont p.** Dupont senior; **le p. Jean** *Fam* old John.

péremptoire [perɑ̃ptwar] *a* peremptory.

perfection [pɛrfɛksjɔ̃] *nf* perfection. ◆**perfectionn/er** *vt* to improve, perfect; **se p. en anglais/***etc* to improve one's English/*etc.* ◆**—é** *a* (*machine etc*) advanced. ◆**—ement** *nm* improvement (**de** in, **par rapport à** on); **cours de p.** advanced *ou* refresher course. ◆**perfectionniste** *nmf* perfectionist.

perfide [pɛrfid] *a Litt* treacherous, perfidious. ◆**perfidie** *nf Litt* treachery.

perforer [pɛrfɔre] *vt* (*pneu, intestin etc*) to perforate; (*billet, carte*) to punch; **carte perforée** punch card. ◆**perforateur** *nm* (*appareil*) drill. ◆**perforation** *nf* perforation; (*trou*) punched hole. ◆**perforatrice** *nf* (*pour cartes*) *Tech* (card) punch. ◆**perforeuse** *nf* (paper) punch.

performance [pɛrfɔrmɑ̃s] *nf* (*d'athlète, de machine etc*) performance. ◆**performant** *a* (highly) efficient.

péricliter [periklite] *vi* to go to rack and ruin.

péril [peril] *nm* peril; **à tes risques et périls** at your own risk. ◆**périlleux, -euse** *a* perilous; **saut p.** somersault (*in mid air*).

périm/er [perime] *vi*, **— se p.** *vpr* laisser

(**se**) **p.** (*billet*) to allow to expire. ◆**—é** *a* expired; (*désuet*) outdated.

périmètre [perimɛtr] *nm* perimeter.

période [perjɔd] *nf* period. ◆**périodique** *a* periodic; *– nm* (*revue*) periodical.

péripétie [peripesi] *nf* (unexpected) event.

périphérie [periferi] *nf* (*limite*) periphery; (*banlieue*) outskirts. ◆**périphérique** *a* (*quartier*) outlying, peripheral; *– nm* (**boulevard**) **p.** (motorway) ring road, *Am* beltway.

périphrase [perifrɑz] *nf* circumlocution.

périple [peripl] *nm* trip, tour.

pér/ir [perir] *vi* to perish, die. ◆**—issable** *a* (*denrée*) perishable.

périscope [periskɔp] *nm* periscope.

perle [pɛrl] *nf* (*bijou*) pearl; (*de bois, verre etc*) bead; (*personne*) *Fig* gem, pearl; (*erreur*) *Iron* howler, gem. ◆**perler** *vi* (*sueur*) to form beads; **grève perlée** go-slow, *Am* slow-down strike.

permanent, -ente [pɛrmanɑ̃, -ɑ̃t] **1** *a* permanent; (*spectacle*) *Cin* continuous; (*comité*) standing. **2** *nf* (*coiffure*) perm. ◆**permanence** *nf* permanence; (*service, bureau*) duty office; (*salle*) *Scol* study room; **être de p.** to be on duty; **en p.** permanently.

perméable [pɛrmeabl] *a* permeable.

permettre* [pɛrmɛtr] *vt* to allow, permit; **p. à qn de faire** (*permission, possibilité*) to allow *ou* permit s.o. to do; **permettez!** excuse me!; **vous permettez?** may I?; **se p. de faire** to allow oneself to do, take the liberty to do; **se p. qch** (*se payer*) to afford sth. ◆**permis** *a* allowed, permitted; *– nm* (*autorisation*) permit, licence; **p. de conduire** (*carte*) driving licence, *Am* driver's license; **p. de travail** work permit. ◆**permission** *nf* permission; (*congé*) *Mil* leave; **demander la p.** to ask (for) permission (**de faire** to do).

permuter [pɛrmyte] *vt* to change round *ou* over, permutate. ◆**permutation** *nf* permutation.

pernicieux, -euse [pɛrnisjø, -øz] *a* (*nocif*) & *Méd* pernicious.

pérorer [perɔre] *vi Péj* to speechify.

Pérou [peru] *nm* Peru.

perpendiculaire [pɛrpɑ̃dikylɛr] *a* & *nf* perpendicular (**à** to).

perpétrer [pɛrpetre] *vt* (*crime*) to perpetrate.

perpétuel, -elle [pɛrpetɥɛl] *a* perpetual; (*fonction, rente*) for life. ◆**perpétuellement** *adv* perpetually. ◆**perpétuer** *vt* to

perpetuate. ◆**perpétuité (à)** adv in perpetuity; (condamné) for life.
perplexe [pɛrplɛks] a perplexed, puzzled. ◆**perplexité** nf perplexity.
perquisition [pɛrkizisjɔ̃] nf (house) search (by police). ◆**perquisitionner** vti to search.
perron [pɛrɔ̃] nm (front) steps.
perroquet [pɛrɔkɛ] nm parrot.
perruche [peryʃ] nf budgerigar, Am parakeet.
perruque [peryk] nf wig.
persan [pɛrsɑ̃] a (langue, tapis, chat) Persian; – nm (langue) Persian.
persécuter [pɛrsekyte] vt (tourmenter) to persecute; (importuner) to harass. ◆**persécuteur, -trice** nmf persecutor. ◆**persécution** nf persecution.
persévér/er [pɛrsevere] vi to persevere (dans in). ◆**—ant** a persevering. ◆**persévérance** nf perseverance.
persienne [pɛrsjɛn] nf (outside) shutter.
persil [pɛrsi] nm parsley.
persist/er [pɛrsiste] vi to persist (à faire in doing). ◆**—ant** a persistent; à feuilles persistantes (arbre etc) evergreen. ◆**persistance** nf persistence.
personnage [pɛrsɔnaʒ] nm (célébrité) (important) person; Th Littér character.
personnaliser [pɛrsɔnalize] vt to personalize; (voiture) to customize.
personnalité [pɛrsɔnalite] nf (individualité, personnage) personality.
personne [pɛrsɔn] 1 nf person; pl people; grande p. grown-up, adult; jolie p. pretty girl ou woman; en p. in person. 2 pron (négatif) nobody, no one; ne . . . p. nobody, no one; je ne vois p. I don't see anybody ou anyone; mieux que p. better than anybody ou anyone.
personnel, -elle [pɛrsɔnɛl] 1 a personal; (joueur, jeu) individualistic. 2 nm staff, personnel. ◆**personnellement** adv personally.
personnifier [pɛrsɔnifje] vt to personify. ◆**personnification** nf personification.
perspective [pɛrspɛktiv] nf (art) perspective; (point de vue) Fig viewpoint, perspective; (de paysage etc) view; (possibilité, espérance) prospect; en p. Fig in view, in prospect.
perspicace [pɛrspikas] a shrewd. ◆**perspicacité** nf shrewdness.
persuader [pɛrsɥade] vt to persuade (qn de faire s.o. to do); se p. que to be convinced that. ◆**persuasif, -ive** a persuasive.

◆**persuasion** nf persuasion; (croyance) conviction.
perte [pɛrt] nf loss; (gaspillage) waste (de temps/d'argent of time/money); (ruine) ruin; à p. de vue as far as the eye can see; vendre à p. to sell at a loss.
pertinent [pɛrtinɑ̃] a relevant, pertinent. ◆**pertinence** nf relevance.
perturb/er [pɛrtyrbe] vt (trafic, cérémonie etc) to disrupt; (ordre public, personne) to disturb. ◆**—é** a (troublé) Fam perturbed. ◆**perturbateur, -trice** a (élément) disruptive; – nmf trouble-maker. ◆**perturbation** nf disruption; (crise) upheaval.
péruvien, -ienne [peryvjɛ̃, -jɛn] a & nmf Peruvian.
pervenche [pɛrvɑ̃ʃ] nf Bot periwinkle.
pervers [pɛrvɛr] a wicked, perverse; (dépravé) perverted. ◆**perversion** nf perversion. ◆**perversité** nf perversity. ◆**pervert/ir** vt to pervert. ◆**—i, -ie** nmf pervert.
pesant [pəzɑ̃] a heavy, weighty; – nm valoir son p. d'or to be worth one's weight in gold. ◆**pesamment** adv heavily. ◆**pesanteur** nf heaviness; (force) Phys gravity.
pes/er [pəze] vt to weigh; – vi to weigh; p. lourd to be heavy; (argument etc) Fig to carry (a lot of) weight; p. sur (appuyer) to bear down upon; (influer) to bear upon; p. sur qn (menace) to hang over s.o.; p. sur l'estomac to lie (heavily) on the stomach. ◆**—ée** nf weighing; Boxe weigh-in; (effort) pressure. ◆**—age** nm weighing. ◆**pèse-bébé** nm (baby) scales. ◆**pèse-personne** nm (bathroom) scales.
pessimisme [pesimism] nm pessimism. ◆**pessimiste** a pessimistic; – nmf pessimist.
peste [pɛst] nf Méd plague; (personne, enfant) Fig pest.
pester [pɛste] vi to curse; p. contre qch/qn to curse sth/s.o.
pestilentiel, -ielle [pɛstilɑ̃sjɛl] a fetid, stinking.
pétale [petal] nm petal.
pétanque [petɑ̃k] nf (jeu) bowls.
pétarades [petarad] nfpl (de moto etc) backfiring. ◆**pétarader** vi to backfire.
pétard [petar] nm (explosif) firecracker, banger.
péter [pete] vi Fam (éclater) to go bang ou pop; (se rompre) to snap.
pétill/er [petije] vi (eau, champagne) to sparkle, fizz; (bois, feu) to crackle; (yeux) to sparkle. ◆**—ant** a (eau, vin, regard) sparkling.

petit, -ite [p(ə)ti, -it] *a* small, little; *(de taille)* short; *(bruit, espoir, coup)* slight; *(jeune)* young, small; *(mesquin, insignifiant)* petty; **tout p.** tiny; **un bon p. travail** a nice little job; **un p. Français** a (little) French boy; — *nmf* (little) boy, (little) girl; *(personne)* small person; *Scol* junior; *pl (d'animal)* young; *(de chien)* pups, young; *(de chat)* kittens, young; — *adv* **p. à p.** little by little. ◆**p.-bourgeois** *a Péj* middle-class. ◆**p.-suisse** *nm* soft cheese *(for dessert)*. ◆**petitement** *adv (chichement)* shabbily, poorly. ◆**petitesse** *nf (de taille)* smallness; *(mesquinerie)* pettiness.

petit-fils [p(ə)tifis] *nm (pl* **petits-fils)** grandson, grandchild. ◆**petite-fille** *nf (pl* **petites-filles)** granddaughter, grandchild. ◆**petits-enfants** *nmpl* grandchildren.

pétition [petisjɔ̃] *nf* petition.

pétrifier [petrifje] *vt (de peur, d'émoi etc)* to petrify.

pétrin [petrɛ̃] *nm (situation) Fam* fix; **dans le p.** in a fix.

pétrir [petrir] *vt* to knead.

pétrole [petrɔl] *nm* oil, petroleum; **p. (lampant)** paraffin, *Am* kerosene; **nappe de p.** *(sur la mer)* oil slick. ◆**pétrolier, -ière** *a (industrie)* oil-; — *nm (navire)* oil tanker. ◆**pétrolifère** *a* **gisement p.** oil field.

pétulant [petylɑ̃] *a* exuberant.

pétunia [petynja] *nm Bot* petunia.

peu [pø] *adv (lire, manger etc)* not much, little; **elle mange p.** she doesn't eat much, she eats little; **un p.** *(lire, surpris etc)* a little, a bit; **p. de sel/de temps/***etc* not much salt/time/*etc*, little salt/time/*etc*; **un p. de fromage/***etc* a little cheese/*etc*, a bit of cheese/*etc*; **le p. de fromage que j'ai** the little cheese I have; **p. de gens/de livres/***etc* few people/books/*etc*, not many people/books/*etc*; **p. sont...** few are...; **un (tout) petit p.** a (tiny) little bit; **p. intéressant/souvent/***etc* not very interesting/often/*etc*; **p. de chose** not much; **p. à p.** gradually, little by little; **à p. près** more or less; **p. après/avant** shortly after/before.

peuplade [pœplad] *nf* tribe.

peuple [pœpl] *nm (nation, masse)* people; **les gens du p.** the common people. ◆**peupl/er** *vt* to populate, people. ◆**—é** *a (quartier etc)* populated (**de** with).

peuplier [pøplije] *nm (arbre, bois)* poplar.

peur [pœr] *nf* fear; **avoir p.** to be afraid *ou* frightened *ou* scared (**de** of); **faire p. à** to frighten, scare; **de p. que** (+ *sub*) for fear that; **de p. de faire** for fear of doing.

◆**peureux, -euse** *a* fearful, easily frightened.

peut, peux [pø] *voir* pouvoir 1.

peut-être [pøtɛtr] *adv* perhaps, maybe; **p.-être qu'il viendra** perhaps *ou* maybe he'll come.

phallique [falik] *a* phallic. ◆**phallocrate** *nm Péj* male chauvinist.

phare [far] *nm Nau* lighthouse; *Aut* headlight, headlamp; **rouler pleins phares** *Aut* to drive on full headlights; **faire un appel de phares** *Aut* to flash one's lights.

pharmacie [farmasi] *nf* chemist's shop, *Am* drugstore; *(science)* pharmacy; *(armoire)* medicine cabinet. ◆**pharmaceutique** *a* pharmaceutical. ◆**pharmacien, -ienne** *nmf* chemist, pharmacist, *Am* druggist.

pharynx [farɛ̃ks] *nm Anat* pharynx.

phase [faz] *nf* phase.

phénomène [fenɔmɛn] *nm* phenomenon; *(personne) Fam* eccentric. ◆**phénoménal, -aux** *a* phenomenal.

philanthrope [filɑ̃trɔp] *nmf* philanthropist. ◆**philanthropique** *a* philanthropic.

philatélie [filateli] *nf* philately, stamp collecting. ◆**philatélique** *a* philatelic. ◆**philatéliste** *nmf* philatelist, stamp collector.

philharmonique [filarmɔnik] *a* philharmonic.

Philippines [filipin] *nfpl* **les P.** the Philippines.

philosophe [filɔzɔf] *nmf* philosopher; — *a (sage, résigné)* philosophical. ◆**philosopher** *vi* to philosophize (**sur** about). ◆**philosophie** *nf* philosophy. ◆**philosophique** *a* philosophical.

phobie [fɔbi] *nf* phobia.

phonétique [fɔnetik] *a* phonetic; — *nf* phonetics.

phonographe [fɔnɔɡraf] *nm* gramophone, *Am* phonograph.

phoque [fɔk] *nm (animal marin)* seal.

phosphate [fɔsfat] *nm Ch* phosphate.

phosphore [fɔsfɔr] *nm Ch* phosphorus.

photo [fɔto] *nf* photo; *(art)* photography; **prendre une p. de, prendre en p.** to take a photo of; — *a inv* **appareil p.** camera. ◆**photocopie** *nf* photocopy. ◆**photocopier** *vt* to photocopy. ◆**photocopieur** *nm*, ◆**photocopieuse** *nf (machine)* photocopier. ◆**photogénique** *a* photogenic. ◆**photographe** *nmf* photographer. ◆**photographie** *nf (art)* photography; *(image)* photograph. ◆**photographier** *vt* to photograph. ◆**photographique** *a* photographic. ◆**photomaton**® *nm* (*appareil*) photo booth.

phrase [frɑz] *nf* (*mots*) sentence.

physicien, -ienne [fizisjɛ̃, -jɛn] *nmf* physicist.

physiologie [fizjɔlɔʒi] *nf* physiology. ◆**physiologique** *a* physiological.

physionomie [fizjɔnɔmi] *nf* face.

physique [fizik] **1** *a* physical; − *nm* (*corps, aspect*) physique; **au p.** physically. **2** *nf* (*science*) physics. ◆**—ment** *adv* physically.

piaffer [pjafe] *vi* (*cheval*) to stamp; **p. d'impatience** Fig to fidget impatiently.

piailler [pjaje] *vi* (*oiseau*) to cheep; (*enfant*) Fam to squeal.

piano [pjano] *nm* piano; **p. droit/à queue** upright/grand piano. ◆**pianiste** *nmf* pianist.

piaule [pjol] *nf* (*chambre*) Arg room, pad.

pic [pik] *nm* **1** (*cime*) peak. **2** (*outil*) pick(axe); **p. à glace** ice pick. **3** (*oiseau*) woodpecker.

pic (à) [apik] *adv* (*verticalement*) sheer; **couler à p.** to sink to the bottom; **arriver à p.** Fig to arrive in the nick of time.

pichet [piʃɛ] *nm* jug, pitcher.

pickpocket [pikpɔkɛt] *nm* pickpocket.

pick-up [pikœp] *nm inv* (*camionnette*) pick-up truck.

picorer [pikɔre] *vti* to peck.

picoter [pikɔte] *vt* (*yeux*) to make smart; (*jambes*) to make tingle; **les yeux me picotent** my eyes are smarting.

pie [pi] **1** *nf* (*oiseau*) magpie. **2** *a inv* (*couleur*) piebald.

pièce [pjɛs] *nf* **1** (*de maison etc*) room. **2** (*morceau, objet etc*) piece; (*de pantalon*) patch; (*écrit*) & Jur document; **p. (de monnaie)** coin; **p. (de théâtre)** play; **p. (d'artillerie)** gun; **p. d'identité** proof of identity, identity card; **p. d'eau** pool, pond; **pièces détachées** *ou* **de rechange** (*de véhicule etc*) spare parts; **cinq dollars/etc (la)** p. five dollars/etc each; **travailler à la p.** to do piecework.

pied [pje] *nm* foot; (*de meuble*) leg; (*de verre, lampe*) base; Phot stand; **un p. de salade** a head of lettuce; **à p.** on foot; **aller à p.** to walk, go on foot; **au p. de** at the foot *ou* bottom of; **au p. de la lettre** Fig literally; **avoir p.** (*nageur*) to have a footing, touch the bottom; **coup de p.** kick; **donner un coup de p.** to kick (**à qn** s.o.); **sur p.** (*debout, levé*) up and about; **sur ses pieds** (*malade guéri*) up and about; **sur un p. d'égalité** on an equal footing; **comme un p.** (*mal*) Fam dreadfully; **faire un p. de nez** to thumb

one's nose (**à** at); **mettre sur p.** (*projet*) to set up. ◆**p.-noir** *nmf* (*pl* **pieds-noirs**) Algerian Frenchman *ou* Frenchwoman.

piédestal, -aux [pjedɛstal, -o] *nm* pedestal.

piège [pjɛʒ] *nm* (*pour animal*) & Fig trap. ◆**piéger** *vt* (*animal*) to trap; (*voiture etc*) to booby-trap; **engin piégé** booby trap; **lettre/colis/voiture piégé(e)** letter/parcel/car bomb.

pierre [pjɛr] *nf* stone; (*précieuse*) gem, stone; **p. à briquet** flint; **geler à p. fendre** to freeze (rock) hard. ◆**pierreries** *nfpl* gems, precious stones. ◆**pierreux, -euse** *a* stony.

piété [pjete] *nf* piety.

piétiner [pjetine] *vt* (*fouler aux pieds*) to trample (on); − *vi* to stamp (one's feet); (*marcher sur place*) to mark time; (*ne pas avancer*) Fig to make no headway.

piéton¹ [pjetɔ̃] *nm* pedestrian. ◆**piéton², -onne** *a*, ◆**piétonnier, -ière** *a* (*rue etc*) pedestrian-.

piètre [pjɛtr] *a* wretched, poor.

pieu, -x [pjø] *nm* **1** (*piquet*) post, stake. **2** (*lit*) Fam bed.

pieuvre [pjœvr] *nf* octopus.

pieux, -euse [pjø, -øz] *a* pious.

pif [pif] *nm* (*nez*) Fam nose. ◆**pifomètre (au)** *adv* (*sans calcul*) Fam at a rough guess.

pigeon [piʒɔ̃] *nm* pigeon; (*personne*) Fam dupe; **p. voyageur** carrier pigeon. ◆**pigeonner** *vt* (*voler*) Fam to rip off.

piger [piʒe] *vti* Fam to understand.

pigment [pigmɑ̃] *nm* pigment.

pignon [piɲɔ̃] *nm* (*de maison etc*) gable.

pile [pil] **1** *nf* Él battery; (*atomique*) pile; **radio à piles** battery radio. **2** *nf* (*tas*) pile; **en p.** in a pile. **3** *nf* (*de pont*) pier. **4** *nf* **p. (ou face)?** heads (or tails)?; **jouer à p. ou face** to toss up. **5** *adv* **s'arrêter p.** to stop short *ou* dead; **à deux heures p.** on the dot of two.

piler [pile] **1** *vt* (*amandes*) to grind; (*ail*) to crush. **2** *vi* (*en voiture*) to stop dead. ◆**pilonner** *vt* Mil to bombard, shell.

pilier [pilje] *nm* pillar.

pilon [pilɔ̃] *nm* (*de poulet*) drumstick.

piller [pije] *vti* to loot, pillage. ◆**pillage** *nm* looting, pillage. ◆**pillard, -arde** *nmf* looter.

pilori [pilɔri] *nm* **mettre au p.** Fig to pillory.

pilote [pilɔt] *nm* Av Nau pilot; (*de voiture, char*) driver; (*guide*) Fig guide; − *a* **usine(-)/projet(-)p.** pilot factory/plan. ◆**pilot/er** *vt* Av to fly, pilot; Nau to pilot; **p. qn** to show s.o. around. ◆**—age** *nm* piloting; **école de p.** flying school; **poste de p.** cockpit.

pilotis [pilɔti] *nm* (*pieux*) *Archit* piles.

pilule [pilyl] *nf* pill; **prendre la p.** (*femme*) to be on the pill; **se mettre à/arrêter la p.** to go on/off the pill.

piment [pimɑ̃] *nm* pimento, pepper. ◆**pimenté** *a Culin & Fig* spicy.

pimpant [pɛ̃pɑ̃] *a* pretty, spruce.

pin [pɛ̃] *nm* (*bois, arbre*) pine; **pomme de p.** pine cone.

pinailler [pinaje] *vi Fam* to quibble, split hairs.

pinard [pinar] *nm* (*vin*) *Fam* wine.

pince [pɛ̃s] *nf* (*outil*) pliers; *Méd* forceps; (*de cycliste*) clip; (*levier*) crowbar; *pl* (*de crabe*) pincers; **p. (à linge)** (clothes) peg *ou Am* pin; **p. (à épiler)** tweezers; **p. (à sucre)** sugar tongs; **p. à cheveux** hairgrip. ◆**pinc/er** *vt* to pinch; (*corde*) *Mus* to pluck; **p. qn** (*arrêter*) *Jur* to nab s.o., pinch s.o.; **se p. le doigt** to get one's finger caught (**dans** in). ◆**—é** *a* (*air*) stiff, constrained. ◆**—ée** *nf* (*de sel etc*) pinch (**de** of). ◆**pincettes** *nfpl* (fire) tongs; (*d'horloger*) tweezers. ◆**pinçon** *nm* pinch (mark).

pinceau, -x [pɛ̃so] *nm* (paint)brush.

pince-sans-rire [pɛ̃ssɑ̃rir] *nm inv* person of dry humour.

pinède [pined] *nf* pine forest.

pingouin [pɛ̃gwɛ̃] *nm* auk, penguin.

ping-pong [piŋpɔ̃g] *nm* ping-pong.

pingre [pɛ̃gr] *a* stingy; *– nmf* skinflint.

pinson [pɛ̃sɔ̃] *nm* (*oiseau*) chaffinch.

pintade [pɛ̃tad] *nf* guinea fowl.

pin-up [pinœp] *nf inv* (*fille*) pinup.

pioche [pjɔʃ] *nf* pick(axe). ◆**piocher** *vti* (*creuser*) to dig (with a pick).

pion [pjɔ̃] *nm* **1** (*au jeu de dames*) piece; *Échecs & Fig* pawn. **2** *Scol* master (in charge of discipline).

pionnier [pjɔnje] *nm* pioneer.

pipe [pip] *nf* (*de fumeur*) pipe; **fumer la p.** to smoke a pipe.

pipeau, -x [pipo] *nm* (*flûte*) pipe.

pipe-line [piplin] *nm* pipeline.

pipi [pipi] *nm* **faire p.** *Fam* to go for a pee.

pique [pik] **1** *nm* (*couleur*) *Cartes* spades. **2** *nf* (*arme*) pike. **3** *nf* (*allusion*) cutting remark.

pique-assiette [pikasjɛt] *nmf inv* scrounger.

pique-nique [piknik] *nm* picnic. ◆**pique-niquer** *vi* to picnic.

piqu/er [pike] *vt* (*entamer, percer*) to prick; (*langue, yeux*) to sting; (*curiosité*) to rouse; (*coudre*) to (machine-)stitch; (*édredon, couvre-lit*) to quilt; (*crise de nerfs*) to have;

(*maladie*) to get; **p. qn** (*abeille*) to sting s.o.; (*serpent*) to bite s.o.; *Méd* to give s.o. an injection; **p. qch dans** (*enfoncer*) to stick sth into; **p. qn** (*arrêter*) *Jur Fam* to nab s.o., pinch s.o.; **p. qch** (*voler*) *Fam* to pinch sth; **p. une colère** to fly into a rage; **p. une tête** to plunge headlong; *– vi* (*avion*) to dive; (*moutarde etc*) to be hot; *— se p. vpr* to prick oneself; **se p. de faire qch** to pride oneself on being able to do sth. ◆**—ant** *a* (*épine*) prickly; (*froid*) biting; (*sauce, goût*) pungent, piquant; (*mot*) cutting; (*détail*) spicy; *— nm Bot* prickle, thorn; (*d'animal*) spine, prickle. ◆**—é** *a* (*meuble*) worm-eaten; (*fou*) *Fam* crazy; *— nm Av* (nose)dive; **descente en p.** *Av* nosedive. ◆**—eur, -euse** *nmf* (*sur machine à coudre*) machinist. ◆**piqûre** *nf* (*d'épingle*) prick; (*d'abeille*) sting; (*de serpent*) bite; (*trou*) hole; *Méd* injection; (*point*) stitch.

piquet [pikɛ] *nm* **1** (*pieu*) stake, picket; (*de tente*) peg. **2 p. (de grève)** picket (line), strike picket. **3 au p.** *Scol* in the corner.

piqueté [pikte] *a* **p. de** dotted with.

pirate [pirat] *nm* pirate; **p. de l'air** hijacker; *– a* (*radio, bateau*) pirate-. ◆**piraterie** *nf* piracy; (*acte*) act of piracy; **p. (aérienne)** hijacking.

pire [pir] *a* worse (**que** than); **le p. moment/résultat/***etc* the worst moment/result/*etc*; *– nmf* **le** *ou* **la p.** the worst (one); **le p. de tout** the worst (thing) of all; **au p.** at (the very) worst; **s'attendre au p.** to expect the (very) worst.

pirogue [pirog] *nf* canoe, dugout.

pis [pi] **1** *nm* (*de vache*) udder. **2** *a inv & adv Litt* worse; **de mal en p.** from bad to worse; *– nm* **le p.** *Litt* the worst.

pis-aller [pizale] *nm inv* (*personne, solution*) stopgap.

piscine [pisin] *nf* swimming pool.

pissenlit [pisɑ̃li] *nm* dandelion.

pistache [pistaʃ] *nf* (*fruit, parfum*) pistachio.

piste [pist] *nf* (*trace de personne ou d'animal*) track, trail; *Sp* track, racetrack; (*de magnétophone*) track; *Av* runway; (*de cirque*) ring; (*de patinage*) rink; (*pour chevaux*) racecourse, racetrack; **p. cyclable** cycle track, *Am* bicycle path; **p. de danse** dance floor; **p. de ski** ski run; **tour de p.** *Sp* lap.

pistolet [pistolɛ] *nm* gun, pistol; (*de peintre*) spray gun.

piston [pistɔ̃] *nm* **1** *Aut* piston. **2 avoir du p.** (*appui*) to have connections. ◆**pistonner** *vt* (*appuyer*) to pull strings for.

pitié [pitje] *nf* pity; **j'ai p. de lui, il me fait p.** I pity him, I feel sorry for him. ◆**piteux, -euse** *a Iron* pitiful. ◆**pitoyable** *a* pitiful.

piton [pitɔ̃] *nm* **1** (*à crochet*) hook. **2** *Géog* peak.

pitre [pitr] *nm* clown. ◆**pitrerie(s)** *nf(pl)* clowning.

pittoresque [pitɔrɛsk] *a* picturesque.

pivert [pivɛr] *nm* (*oiseau*) woodpecker.

pivoine [pivwan] *nf Bot* peony.

pivot [pivo] *nm* pivot; (*personne*) *Fig* linchpin, mainspring. ◆**pivoter** *vi* (*personne*) to swing round; (*fauteuil*) to swivel; (*porte*) to revolve.

pizza [pidza] *nf* pizza. ◆**pizzeria** *nf* pizza parlour.

placage [plakaʒ] *nm* (*revêtement*) facing; (*en bois*) veneer.

placard [plakar] *nm* **1** (*armoire*) cupboard, *Am* closet. **2** (*pancarte*) poster. ◆**placarder** *vt* (*affiche*) to post (up); (*mur*) to cover with posters.

place [plas] *nf* (*endroit, rang*) & *Sp* place; (*occupée par qn ou qch*) room; (*lieu public*) square; (*siège*) seat, place; (*prix d'un trajet Aut* fare; (*emploi*) job, position; **p. (forte)** *Mil* fortress; **p. (de parking)** (parking) space; **p. (financière)** (money) market; **à la p.** (*échange*) instead (**de** of); **à votre p.** in your place; **sur p.** on the spot; **en p.** (*objet*) in place; **ne pas tenir en p.** to be unable to keep still; **mettre en p.** to install, set up; **faire p. à** to give way to; **changer qch de p.** to move sth.

plac/er [plase] *vt* (*mettre*) to put, place; (*situer*) to place, position; (*invité, spectateur*) to seat; (*argent*) to invest, place (**dans** in); (*vendre*) to place, sell; **p. un mot** to get a word in edgeways *ou Am* edgewise; **— se p.** *vpr* (*personne*) to take up a position, place oneself; (*objet*) to be put *ou* placed; (*cheval, coureur*) to be placed; **se p. troisième/etc** *Sp* to come *ou* be third/*etc*. ◆**—é** *a* (*objet*) & *Sp* placed; **bien/mal p. pour faire** in a good/bad position to do; **les gens haut placés** people in high places. ◆**—ement** *nm* (*d'argent*) investment.

placide [plasid] *a* placid.

plafond [plafɔ̃] *nm* ceiling. ◆**plafonnier** *nm Aut* roof light.

plage [plaʒ] *nf* **1** beach; (*ville*) (seaside) resort. **2** (*sur disque*) track. **3 p. arrière** *Aut* parcel shelf.

plagiat [plaʒja] *nm* plagiarism. ◆**plagier** *vt* to plagiarize.

plaid [plɛd] *nm* travelling rug.

plaider [plede] *vti Jur* to plead. ◆**plaideur, -euse** *nmf* litigant. ◆**plaidoirie** *nf Jur* speech (for the defence). ◆**plaidoyer** *nm* plea.

plaie [plɛ] *nf* (*blessure*) wound; (*coupure*) cut; (*corvée, personne*) *Fig* nuisance.

plaignant, -ante [plɛɲɑ̃, -ɑ̃t] *nmf Jur* plaintiff.

plaindre* [plɛ̃dr] **1** *vt* to feel sorry for, pity. **2 se p.** *vpr* (*protester*) to complain (**de** about, **que** that); **se p. de** (*maux de tête etc*) to complain of *ou* about. ◆**plainte** *nf* complaint; (*cri*) moan, groan. ◆**plaintif, -ive** *a* sorrowful, plaintive.

plaine [plɛn] *nf Géog* plain.

plaire* [plɛr] *vi* & *v imp* **p. à** to please; **elle lui plaît** he likes her, she pleases him; **ça me plaît** I like it; **il me plaît de faire** I like doing; **s'il vous** *ou* **te plaît** please; **— se p.** *vpr* (*à Paris etc*) to like *ou* enjoy it; (*l'un l'autre*) to like each other.

plaisance [plɛzɑ̃s] *nf* **bateau de p.** pleasure boat; **navigation de p.** yachting.

plaisant [plɛzɑ̃] *a* (*drôle*) amusing; (*agréable*) pleasing; **— *nm* mauvais p.** *Péj* joker. ◆**plaisanter** *vi* to joke, jest; **p. avec qch** to trifle with sth; **— *vt* to tease. ◆**plaisanterie** *nf* joke, jest; (*bagatelle*) trifle; **par p.** for a joke. ◆**plaisantin** *nm Péj* joker.

plaisir [plezir] *nm* pleasure; **faire p. à** to please; **faites-moi le p. de . . .** would you be good enough to . . . ; **pour le p.** for fun, for the fun of it; **au p. (de vous revoir)** see you again sometime.

plan [plɑ̃] **1** *nm* (*projet, dessin*) plan; (*de ville*) plan, map; (*niveau*) *Géom* plane; **au premier p.** in the foreground; **gros p.** *Phot Cin* close-up; **sur le p. politique/etc** from the political/*etc* viewpoint, politically/*etc*; **de premier p.** (*question etc*) major; **p. d'eau** stretch of water; **laisser en p.** (*abandonner*) to ditch. **2** *a* (*plat*) even, flat.

planche [plɑ̃ʃ] *nf* **1** board, plank; **p. à repasser/à dessin** ironing/drawing board; **p. (à roulettes)** skateboard; **p. (de surf)** surfboard; **p. (à voile)** sailboard; **faire de la p. (à voile)** to go windsurfing; **faire la p.** to float on one's back. **2** (*illustration*) plate. **3** (*de légumes*) bed, plot.

plancher [plɑ̃ʃe] *nm* floor.

plan/er [plane] *vi* (*oiseau*) to glide, hover; (*avion*) to glide; **p. sur qn** (*mystère, danger*) to hang over s.o.; **vol plané** glide. ◆**—eur** *nm* (*avion*) glider.

planète [planɛt] *nf* planet. ◆**planétaire** *a* planetary. ◆**planétarium** *nm* planetarium.

planifier [planifje] *vt Écon* to plan. ◆**pla-**

nification *nf* *Écon* planning. ◆**planning** *nm* (*industriel, commercial*) planning; **p familial** family planning.

planque [plɑ̃k] *nf* **1** (*travail*) *Fam* cushy job. **2** (*lieu*) *Fam* hideout. ◆**planquer** *vt,* **— se p.** *vpr Fam* to hide.

plant [plɑ̃] *nm* (*plante*) seedling; (*de légumes etc*) bed.

plante [plɑ̃t] *nf* **1** *Bot* plant; **p. d'appartement** house plant; **jardin des plantes** botanical gardens. **2 p. des pieds** sole (of the foot). ◆**plant/er** *vt* (*arbre, plante etc*) to plant; (*clou, couteau*) to drive in; (*tente, drapeau, échelle*) to put up; (*mettre*) to put (**sur** on; **contre** against); (*regard*) to fix (**sur** on); **p. là qn** to leave s.o. standing; **se p. devant qn** to plant oneself in front of. ◆**—é** *a* (*immobile*) standing; **bien p.** (*personne*) sturdy. ◆**plantation** *nf* (*action*) planting; (*terrain*) bed; (*de café, d'arbres etc*) plantation. ◆**planteur** *nm* plantation owner.

planton [plɑ̃tɔ̃] *nm* *Mil* orderly.

plantureux, -euse [plɑ̃tyrø, -øz] *a* (*repas etc*) abundant.

plaque [plak] *nf* plate; (*de verre, métal*) sheet, plate; (*de verglas*) sheet; (*de marbre*) slab; (*de chocolat*) bar; (*commémorative*) plaque; (*tache*) *Méd* blotch; **p. chauffante** *Culin* hotplate; **p. tournante** (*carrefour*) *Fig* centre; **p. minéralogique, p. d'immatriculation** *Aut* number *ou Am* license plate; **p. dentaire** (dental) plaque.

plaqu/er [plake] *vt* (*métal, bijou*) to plate; (*bois*) to veneer; (*cheveux*) to plaster (down); *Rugby* to tackle; (*aplatir*) to flatten (**contre** against); (*abandonner*) *Fam* to give (*sth*) up; **p. qn** *Fam* to ditch s.o.; **se p. contre** to flatten oneself against. ◆**—é** *a* (*bijou*) plated; **p. or** gold-plated; **— *nm* p. or** gold plate. ◆**—age** *nm* *Rugby* tackle.

plasma [plasma] *nm* *Méd* plasma.

plastic [plastik] *nm* plastic explosive. ◆**plastiquer** *vt* to blow up.

plastique [plastik] *a* (*art, substance*) plastic; **matière p.** plastic; **— *nm* (*matière*) plastic; **en p.** (*bouteille etc*) plastic.

plastron [plastrɔ̃] *nm* shirtfront.

plat [pla] **1** *a* flat; (*mer*) calm, smooth; (*fade*) flat, dull; **à fond p.** flat-bottomed; **à p. ventre** flat on one's face; **à p.** (*pneu, batterie*) flat; (*déprimé, épuisé*) *Fam* low; **poser à p.** to put *ou* lay (down) flat; **tomber à p.** to fall down flat; **assiette plate** dinner plate; **calme p.** dead calm; **— *nm* (*de la main*) flat. **2** *nm* (*récipient, mets*) dish; (*partie du repas*) course; **'p. du jour'** (*au restaurant*) 'today's special'.

platane [platan] *nm* plane tree.

plateau, -x [plato] *nm* (*pour servir*) tray; (*de balance*) pan; (*de tourne-disque*) turntable; (*plate-forme*) *Cin TV* set; *Th* stage; *Géog* plateau; **p. à fromages** cheeseboard.

plate-bande [platbɑ̃d] *nf* (*pl* **plates-bandes**) flower bed.

plate-forme [platfɔrm] *nf* (*pl* **plates-formes**) platform; **p.-forme pétrolière** oil rig.

platine [platin] **1** *nm* (*métal*) platinum. **2** *nf* (*d'électrophone*) deck. ◆**platiné** *a* (*cheveux*) platinum, platinum-blond(e).

platitude [platityd] *nf* platitude.

plâtre [plɑtr] *nm* (*matière*) plaster; **un p.** *Méd* a plaster cast; **dans le p.** *Méd* in plaster; **les plâtres** (*d'une maison etc*) the plasterwork; **p. à mouler** plaster of Paris. ◆**plâtr/er** *vt* (*mur*) to plaster; (*membre*) to put in plaster. ◆**—age** *nm* plastering. ◆**plâtrier** *nm* plasterer.

plausible [plozibl] *a* plausible.

plébiscite [plebisit] *nm* plebiscite.

plein [plɛ̃] *a* (*rempli, complet*) full; (*paroi*) solid; (*ivre*) *Fam* tight; **p. de** full of; **en pleine mer** on the open sea; **en p. visage**/*etc* right in the middle of the face/*etc*; **en p. jour** in broad daylight; **— *prép & adv* des billes p. les poches** pockets full of marbles; **du chocolat p. la figure** chocolate all over one's face; **p. de lettres/d'argent**/*etc* (*beaucoup de*) *Fam* lots of letters/money/*etc*; **à p.** (*travailler*) to full capacity; **— *nm* faire le p.** *Aut* to fill up (the tank); **battre son p.** (*fête*) to be in full swing. ◆**pleinement** *adv* fully.

pléonasme [pleonasm] *nm* (*expression*) redundancy.

pléthore [pletɔr] *nf* plethora.

pleurer [plœre] *vi* to cry, weep (**sur** over); **— *vt* (*regretter*) to mourn (for). ◆**pleureur** *a* **saule p.** weeping willow. ◆**pleurnicher** *vi* to snivel, grizzle. ◆**pleurs (en)** *adv* in tears.

pleurésie [plœrezi] *nf* *Méd* pleurisy.

pleuvoir* [pløvwar] *v imp* to rain; **il pleut** it's raining; **— *vi* (*coups etc*) to rain down (**sur** on).

pli [pli] *nm* **1** (*de papier etc*) fold; (*de jupe, robe*) pleat; (*de pantalon, de bouche*) crease; (*de bras*) bend; (**faux**) **p.** crease; **mise en plis** (*coiffure*) set. **2** (*enveloppe*) *Com* envelope, letter; **sous p. séparé** under separate cover. **3** *Cartes* trick. **4** (*habitude*) habit; **prendre le p. de faire** to get into the habit of doing. ◆**pli/er** *vt* to fold; (*courber*) to bend; **p. qn à** to submit s.o. to; **— *vi* (*branche*) to bend; **— se p.** *vpr* (*lit, chaise* *etc*) to fold (up); **se p. à** to submit to, give in to. ◆**—ant** *a* (*chaise etc*) folding; (*parapluie*) telescopic; — *nm* folding stool. ◆**—able** *a* pliable. ◆**—age** *nm* (*manière*) fold; (*action*) folding.

plinthe [plɛ̃t] *nf* skirting board, *Am* baseboard.

pliss/er [plise] *vt* (*jupe, robe*) to pleat; (*froisser*) to crease; (*lèvres*) to pucker; (*front*) to wrinkle, crease; (*yeux*) to screw up. ◆**—é** *nm* pleating, pleats.

plomb [plɔ̃] *nm* (*métal*) lead; (*fusible*) *Él* fuse; (*poids pour rideau etc*) lead weight; *pl* (*de chasse*) lead shot, buckshot; **de p.** (*tuyau etc*) lead-; (*sommeil*) *Fig* heavy; (*soleil*) blazing; (*ciel*) leaden. ◆**plomb/er** *vt* (*dent*) to fill; (*colis*) to seal (with lead). ◆**—é** *a* (*teint*) leaden. ◆**—age** *nm* (*de dent*) filling.

plombier [plɔ̃bje] *nm* plumber. ◆**plomberie** *nf* (*métier, installations*) plumbing.

plong/er [plɔ̃ʒe] *vi* (*personne, avion etc*) to dive, plunge; (*route, regard*) *Fig* to plunge; — *vt* (*mettre, enfoncer*) to plunge, thrust (**dans** into); **se p. dans** (*lecture etc*) to immerse oneself in. ◆**—eant** *a* (*décolleté*) plunging; (*vue*) bird's eye-. ◆**—é a p. dans** (*lecture etc*) immersed *ou* deep in. ◆**—ée** *nf* diving; (*de sous-marin*) submersion; **en p.** (*sous-marin*) submerged. ◆**plongeoir** *nm* diving board. ◆**plongeon** *nm* dive. ◆**plongeur, -euse** *nmf* diver; (*employé de restaurant*) dishwasher.

plouf [pluf] *nm & int* splash.

ployer [plwaje] *vti* to bend.

plu [ply] *voir* **plaire, pleuvoir.**

pluie [plɥi] *nf* rain; **une p.** (*averse*) & *Fig* a shower; **sous la p.** in the rain.

plume [plym] *nf* **1** (*d'oiseau*) feather. **2** (*pour écrire*) *Hist* quill (pen); (*pointe en acier*) (pen) nib; **stylo à p.** (fountain) pen; **vivre de sa p.** *Fig* to live by one's pen. ◆**plumage** *nm* plumage. ◆**plumeau, -x** *nm* feather duster. ◆**plumer** *vt* (*volaille*) to pluck; **p. qn** (*voler*) *Fig* to fleece s.o. ◆**plumet** *nm* plume. ◆**plumier** *nm* pencil box, pen box.

plupart (la) [laplypar] *nf* most; **la p. des cas/*etc*** most cases/*etc*; **la p. du temps** most of the time; **la p. d'entre eux** most of them; **pour la p.** mostly.

pluriel, -ielle [plyrjɛl] *a & nm Gram* plural; **au p.** (*nom*) plural, in the plural.

plus¹ [ply] ([plyz] *before vowel,* [plys] *in end position*) **1** *adv comparatif* (*travailler etc*) more (**que** than); **p. d'un kilo/de dix/*etc*** (*quantité, nombre*) more than a kilo/ten/

etc; **p. de thé/*etc*** (*davantage*) more tea/*etc*; **p. beau/rapidement/*etc*** more beautiful/rapidly/*etc* (**que** than). **p. tard** later; **p. petit** smaller; **de p. en p.** more and more; **de p. en p. vite** quicker and quicker; **p. il crie p. il s'enroue** the more he shouts the more hoarse he gets; **p. ou moins** more or less; **en p.** in addition (**de** to); **de p.** more (**que** than); (*en outre*) moreover; **les enfants (âgés) de p. de dix ans** children over ten; **j'ai dix ans de p. qu'elle** I'm ten years older than she is; **il est p. de cinq heures** it's after five (o'clock). **2** *adv superlatif* **le p.** (*travailler etc*) (the) most; **le p. beau/*etc*** the most beautiful/*etc*; (*de deux*) the more beautiful/*etc*; **le p. grand/*etc*** the biggest/*etc*; (*de deux*) the bigger/*etc*; **j'ai le p. de livres** I have (the) most books; **j'en ai le p.** I have (the) most; (*tout*) **au p.** at (the very) most.

plus² [ply] *adv de négation* **p. de** (*pain, argent etc*) no more; **il n'a p. de pain** he has no more bread, he doesn't have any more bread; **tu n'es p. jeune** you're no longer young, you're not young any more *ou* any longer; **elle ne le fait p.** she no longer does it, she doesn't do it any more *ou* any longer; **je ne la reverrai p.** I won't see her again.

plus³ [plys] *prép* plus; **deux p. deux font quatre** two plus two are four; **il fait p. deux (degrés)** it's two degrees above freezing; — *nm* **le signe p.** the plus sign.

plusieurs [plyzjœr] *a & pron* several.

plus-value [plyvaly] *nf* (*bénéfice*) profit.

plutonium [plytɔnjɔm] *nm* plutonium.

plutôt [plyto] *adv* rather (**que** than).

pluvieux, -euse [plyvjø, -øz] *a* rainy, wet.

PMU [peɛmy] *abrév* = **pari mutuel urbain.**

pneu [pnø] *nm* (*pl* **-s**) **1** (*de roue*) tyre, *Am* tire. **2** (*lettre*) express letter. ◆**pneumatique 1** *a* (*matelas etc*) inflatable; **marteau p.** pneumatic drill. **2** *nm* = **pneu.**

pneumonie [pnømɔni] *nf* pneumonia.

poche [pɔʃ] *nf* pocket; (*de kangourou etc*) pouch; (*sac en papier etc*) bag; *pl* (*sous les yeux*) bags; **livre de p.** paperback; **faire des poches** (*pantalon*) to be baggy; **j'ai un franc en p.** I have one franc on me. ◆**pochette** *nf* (*sac*) bag, envelope; (*d'allumettes*) book; (*de disque*) sleeve, jacket; (*mouchoir*) pocket handkerchief; (*sac à main*) (clutch) bag.

poch/er [pɔʃe] *vt* **1 p. l'œil à qn** to give s.o. a black eye. **2** (*œufs*) to poach. ◆**—é a œil p.** black eye.

podium [pɔdjɔm] *nm Sp* rostrum, podium.

poêle [pwal] **1** *nm* stove. **2** *nf* **p.** (**à frire**) frying pan.

poème [pɔɛm] *nm* poem. ◆**poésie** *nf* poet-

ry; **une p.** (*poème*) a piece of poetry.
◆**poète** *nm* poet; – *a* **femme p.** poetess.
◆**poétique** *a* poetic.

pognon [pɔɲɔ̃] *nm* (*argent*) *Fam* dough.

poids [pwa] *nm* weight; **au p.** by weight; **de p.** (*influent*) influential; **p. lourd** (heavy) lorry *ou Am* truck; **lancer le p.** *Sp* to put *ou* hurl the shot.

poignant [pwaɲɑ̃] *a* (*souvenir etc*) poignant.

poignard [pwaɲar] *nm* dagger; **coup de p.** stab. ◆**poignarder** *vt* to stab.

poigne [pwaɲ] *nf* (*étreinte*) grip.

poignée [pwaɲe] *nf* (*quantité*) handful (**de** of); (*de porte, casserole etc*) handle; (*d'épée*) hilt; **p. de main** handshake; **donner une p. de main à** to shake hands with.

poignet [pwaɲɛ] *nm* wrist; (*de chemise*) cuff.

poil [pwal] *nm* hair; (*pelage*) coat, fur; (*de brosse*) bristle; *pl* (*de tapis*) pile; (*d'étoffe*) nap; **à p.** (*nu*) *Arg* (stark) naked; **au p.** (*travail etc*) *Arg* top-rate; **de bon/mauvais p.** *Fam* in a good/bad mood; **de tout p.** *Fam* of all kinds. ◆**poilu** *a* hairy.

poinçon [pwɛ̃sɔ̃] *nm* (*outil*) awl, bradawl; (*marque de bijou etc*) hallmark. ◆**poinçonner** *vt* (*bijou*) to hallmark; (*billet*) to punch. ◆**poinçonneuse** *nf* (*machine*) punch.

poindre [pwɛ̃dr] *vi* (*jour*) *Litt* to dawn.

poing [pwɛ̃] *nm* fist; **coup de p.** punch.

point¹ [pwɛ̃] *nm* (*lieu, question, degré, score etc*) point; (*sur i, à l'horizon etc*) dot; (*tache*) spot; (*note*) *Scol* mark; (*de couture*) stitch; **sur le p. de faire** about to do, on the point of doing; **p. (final)** full stop, period; **p. d'exclamation** exclamation mark *ou Am* point; **p. d'interrogation** question mark; **p. de vue** point of view, viewpoint; (*endroit*) viewing point; **à p. (nommé)** (*arriver etc*) at the right moment; **à p.** (*rôti etc*) medium (cooked); (*steak*) medium rare; **mal en p.** in bad shape; **mettre au p.** *Phot* to focus; *Aut* to tune; (*technique etc*) to elaborate, perfect; (*éclaircir*) *Fig* to clarify, clear up; **mise au p.** focusing; tuning, tune-up; elaboration; *Fig* clarification; **faire le p.** *Fig* to take stock, sum up; **p. mort** *Aut* neutral; **au p. mort** *Fig* at a standstill; **p. noir** *Aut* (*accident*) black spot; **p. du jour** daybreak; **p. de côté** (*douleur*) stitch (in one's side). ◆**p.-virgule** *nm* (*pl* **points-virgules**) semicolon.

point² [pwɛ̃] *adv Litt* = **pas¹**.

pointe [pwɛ̃t] *nf* (*extrémité*) point, tip; (*pour grille*) spike; (*clou*) nail; *Géog* headland; (*maximum*) *Fig* peak; **une p. de** (*soupçon, nuance*) a touch of; **sur la p. des pieds** on

tiptoe; **en p.** pointed; **de p.** (*technique etc*) latest, most advanced; **à la p. de** (*progrès, etc*) *Fig* in *ou* at the forefront of.

point/er [pwɛ̃te] **1** *vt* (*cocher*) to tick (off), *Am* check (off). **2** *vt* (*braquer, diriger*) to point (**sur, vers** at). **3** *vti* (*employé*) to clock in, (*à la sortie*) to clock out; **— se p.** *vpr* (*arriver*) *Fam* to show up. **4** *vi* (*bourgeon etc*) to appear; **p. vers** to point upwards towards. ◆**—age** *nm* (*de personnel*) clocking in; clocking out.

pointillé [pwɛ̃tije] *nm* dotted line; – *a* dotted.

pointilleux, -euse [pwɛ̃tijø, -øz] *a* fussy, particular.

pointu [pwɛ̃ty] *a* (*en pointe*) pointed; (*voix*) shrill.

pointure [pwɛ̃tyr] *nf* (*de chaussure, gant*) size.

poire [pwar] *nf* **1** (*fruit*) pear. **2** (*figure*) *Fam* mug. **3** (*personne*) *Fam* sucker. ◆**poirier** *nm* pear tree.

poireau, -x [pwaro] *nm* leek.

poireauter [pwarote] *vi* (*attendre*) *Fam* to kick one's heels.

pois [pwa] *nm* (*légume*) pea; (*dessin*) (polka) dot; **petits p.** (garden) peas; **p. chiche** chickpea; **à p.** (*vêtement*) spotted, dotted.

poison [pwazɔ̃] *nm* (*substance*) poison.

poisse [pwas] *nf Fam* bad luck.

poisseux, -euse [pwasø, -øz] *a* sticky.

poisson [pwasɔ̃] *nm* fish; **p. rouge** goldfish; **les Poissons** (*signe*) Pisces. ◆**poissonnerie** *nf* fish shop. ◆**poissonnier, -ière** *nmf* fishmonger.

poitrine [pwatrin] *nf Anat* chest; (*seins*) breast, bosom; (*de veau, mouton*) *Culin* breast.

poivre [pwavr] *nm* pepper. ◆**poivr/er** *vt* to pepper. ◆**—é** *a Culin* peppery; (*plaisanterie*) *Fig* spicy. ◆**poivrier** *nm Bot* pepper plant; (*ustensile*) pepperpot. ◆**poivrière** *nf* pepperpot.

poivron [pwavrɔ̃] *nm* pepper, capsicum.

poivrot, -ote [pwavro, -ɔt] *nmf Fam* drunk(ard).

poker [pɔkɛr] *nm Cartes* poker.

polar [pɔlar] *nm* (*roman*) *Fam* whodunit.

polariser [pɔlarize] *vt* to polarize.

pôle [pol] *nm Géog* pole; **p. Nord/Sud** North/South Pole. ◆**polaire** *a* polar.

polémique [pɔlemik] *a* controversial, polemical; – *nf* controversy, polemic.

poli [pɔli] **1** *a* (*courtois*) polite (**avec** to, with). **2** *a* (*lisse, brillant*) polished; – *nm* (*aspect*) polish. ◆**—ment** *adv* politely.

police [pɔlis] *nf* **1** police; **faire** *ou* **assurer la**

p. to maintain order (**dans** in); **p. secours** emergency services; **p. mondaine** ou **des mœurs** = vice squad. **2 p.** (**d'assurance**) (insurance) policy. ◆**policier** a (enquête, état) police-; **roman p.** detective novel; — nm policeman, detective.

polichinelle [pɔliʃinɛl] nf **secret de p.** open secret.

polio [pɔljo] nf (maladie) polio; — nmf (personne) polio victim. ◆**poliomyélite** nf poliomyelitis.

polir [pɔlir] vt (substance dure, style) to polish.

polisson, -onne [pɔlisɔ̃, -ɔn] a naughty; — nmf rascal.

politesse [pɔlitɛs] nf politeness; **une p.** (parole) a polite word; (action) an act of politeness.

politique [pɔlitik] a political; **homme p.** politician; — nf (science, activité) politics; (mesures, manières de gouverner) Pol policies; **une p.** (tactique) a policy. ◆**politicien, -ienne** nmf Péj politician. ◆**politiser** vt to politicize.

pollen [pɔlɛn] nm pollen.

polluer [pɔlɥe] vt to pollute. ◆**polluant** nm pollutant. ◆**pollution** nf pollution.

polo [pɔlo] nm **1** (chemise) sweat shirt. **2** Sp polo.

polochon [pɔlɔʃɔ̃] nm (traversin) Fam bolster.

Pologne [pɔlɔɲ] nf Poland. ◆**polonais, -aise** a Polish; — nmf Pole; — nm (langue) Polish.

poltron, -onne [pɔltrɔ̃, -ɔn] a cowardly; — nmf coward.

polycopi/er [pɔlikɔpje] vt to mimeograph, duplicate. ◆**—é** nm Univ mimeographed copy (of lecture etc).

polyester [pɔliɛstɛr] nm polyester.

Polynésie [pɔlinezi] nf Polynesia.

polyvalent [pɔlivalɑ̃] a (rôle) multi-purpose, varied; (professeur, ouvrier) all-round; **école polyvalente, lycée p.** comprehensive school.

pommade [pɔmad] nf ointment.

pomme [pɔm] nf **1** apple; **p. d'Adam** Anat Adam's apple. **2** (d'arrosoir) rose. **3 p. de terre** potato; **pommes vapeur** steamed potatoes; **pommes frites** chips, Am French fries; **pommes chips** potato crisps ou Am chips. ◆**pommier** nm apple tree.

pommette [pɔmɛt] nf cheekbone.

pompe [pɔ̃p] **1** nf pump; **p. à essence** petrol ou Am gas station; **p. à incendie** fire engine; **coup de p.** Fam tired feeling. **2** nf (chaussure) Fam shoe. **3** nf (en gymnastique) press-up, Am push-up. **4** nfpl **pompes funèbres** undertaker's; **entrepreneur des pompes funèbres** undertaker. **5** nf **p. anti-sèche** Scol crib. **6** nf (splendeur) pomp. ◆**pomper** vt to pump; (évacuer) to pump out (**de** of); (absorber) to soak up; (épuiser) Fam to tire out; — vi to pump. ◆**pompeux, -euse** a pompous. ◆**pompier 1** nm fireman; **voiture des pompiers** fire engine. **2** a (emphatique) pompous. ◆**pompiste** nmf Aut pump attendant.

pompon [pɔ̃pɔ̃] nm (ornement) pompon.

pomponner [pɔ̃pɔne] vt to doll up.

ponce [pɔ̃s] nf (pierre) **p.** pumice (stone). ◆**poncer** vt to rub down, sand. ◆**ponceuse** nf (machine) sander.

ponctuation [pɔ̃ktɥasjɔ̃] nf punctuation. ◆**ponctuer** vt to punctuate (**de** with).

ponctuel, -elle [pɔ̃ktɥɛl] a (à l'heure) punctual; (unique) Fig one-off, Am one-of-a-kind. ◆**ponctualité** nf punctuality.

pondéré [pɔ̃dere] a level-headed. ◆**pondération** nf level-headedness.

pondre [pɔ̃dr] vt (œuf) to lay; (livre, discours) Péj Fam to produce; — vi (poule) to lay.

poney [pɔnɛ] nm pony.

pont [pɔ̃] nm bridge; (de bateau) deck; **p. (de graissage)** Aut ramp; **faire le p.** Fig to take the intervening day(s) off (between two holidays); **p. aérien** airlift. ◆**p.-levis** nm (pl **ponts-levis**) drawbridge.

ponte [pɔ̃t] **1** nf (d'œufs) laying. **2** nm (personne) Fam bigwig.

pontife [pɔ̃tif] nm **1** (souverain) **p.** pope. **2** (ponte) Fam bigshot. ◆**pontifical, -aux** a papal, pontifical.

pop [pɔp] nm & a inv Mus pop.

popote [pɔpɔt] nf (cuisine) Fam cooking.

populace [pɔpylas] nf Péj rabble.

populaire [pɔpylɛr] a (personne, tradition, gouvernement etc) popular; (quartier, milieu) lower-class; (expression) colloquial; (art) folk-. ◆**populariser** vt to popularize. ◆**popularité** nf popularity (**auprès de** with).

population [pɔpylasjɔ̃] nf population. ◆**populeux, -euse** a populous, crowded.

porc [pɔr] nm pig; (viande) pork; (personne) Péj swine.

porcelaine [pɔrsəlɛn] nf china, porcelain.

porc-épic [pɔrkepik] nm (pl **porcs-épics**) (animal) porcupine.

porche [pɔrʃ] nm porch.

porcherie [pɔrʃəri] nf pigsty.

pore [pɔr] nm pore. ◆**poreux, -euse** a porous.

pornographie [pɔrnɔgrafi] *nf* pornography. ◆**pornographique** *a* (*Fam* **porno**) pornographic.

port [pɔr] *nm* **1** port, harbour; **arriver à bon p.** to arrive safely. **2** (*d'armes*) carrying; (*de barbe*) wearing; (*prix*) carriage, postage; (*attitude*) bearing.

portable [pɔrtabl] *a* (*robe etc*) wearable; (*portatif*) portable.

portail [pɔrtaj] *nm* (*de cathédrale etc*) portal.

portant [pɔrtɑ̃] *a* **bien p.** in good health.

portatif, -ive [pɔrtatif, -iv] *a* portable.

porte [pɔrt] *nf* door, (*passage*) doorway; (*de jardin*) gate, (*passage*) gateway; (*de ville*) entrance, *Hist* gate; **p. (d'embarquement)** *Av* (departure) gate; **Alger, p. de . . .** Algiers, gateway to . . . ; **p. d'entrée** front door; **mettre à la p.** (*jeter dehors*) to throw out; (*renvoyer*) to sack. ◆**p.-fenêtre** *nf* (*pl* **portes-fenêtres**) French window.

porte-à-faux [pɔrtafo] *nm inv* **en p.-à-faux** (*en déséquilibre*) unstable.

porte-avions [pɔrtavjɔ̃] *nm inv* aircraft carrier. ◆**p.-bagages** *nm inv* luggage rack. ◆**p.-bébé** *nm* (*nacelle*) carrycot, *Am* baby basket; (*kangourou®*) baby sling. ◆**p.-bonheur** *nm* (*fétiche*) (lucky) charm. ◆**p.-cartes** *nm inv* card holder *ou* case. ◆**p.-clés** *nm inv* key ring. ◆**p.-documents** *nm inv* briefcase. ◆**p.-drapeau, -x** *nm Mil* standard bearer. ◆**p.-jarretelles** *nm inv* suspender *ou Am* garter belt. ◆**p.-monnaie** *nm inv* purse. ◆**p.-parapluie** *nm inv* umbrella stand. ◆**p.-plume** *nm inv* pen (*for dipping in ink*). ◆**p.-revues** *nm inv* newspaper rack. ◆**p.-savon** *nm* soapdish. ◆**p.-serviettes** *nm inv* towel rail. ◆**p.-voix** *nm inv* megaphone.

portée [pɔrte] *nf* **1** (*de fusil etc*) range; **à p. de qn** within reach of s.o.; (*richesse, plaisir etc*) *Fig* within s.o.'s grasp; **à p. de la main** within (easy) reach; **à p. de voix** within earshot; **hors de p.** out of reach. **2** (*animaux*) litter. **3** (*importance, effet*) significance, import. **4** *Mus* stave.

portefeuille [pɔrtəfœj] *nm* wallet; *Pol Com* portfolio.

portemanteau, -x [pɔrtmɑ̃to] *nm* (*sur pied*) hatstand; (*barre*) hat *ou* coat peg.

porte-parole [pɔrtparɔl] *nm inv* (*homme*) spokesman; (*femme*) spokeswoman (**de** for, of).

port/er [pɔrte] *vt* to carry; (*vêtement, lunettes, barbe etc*) to wear; (*trace, responsabilité, fruits etc*) to bear; (*regard*) to cast; (*attaque*) to make (**contre** against); (*coup*) to strike; (*sentiment*) to have (**à** for); (*inscrire*) to enter, write down; **p. qch à** (*amener*) to bring *ou* take sth to; **p. qn à faire** (*pousser*) to lead *ou* prompt s.o. to do; **p. bonheur/malheur** to bring good/bad luck; **se faire p. malade** to report sick; — *vi* (*voix*) to carry; (*canon*) to fire; (*vue*) to extend; **p. (juste)** (*coup*) to hit the mark; (*mot, reproche*) to hit home; **p. sur** (*reposer sur*) to rest on; (*concerner*) to bear on; (*accent*) to fall on; (*heurter*) to strike; — **se p.** *vpr* (*vêtement*) to be worn; **se p. bien/mal** to be well/ill; **comment te portes-tu?** how are you?; **se p. candidat** to stand as a candidate. ◆**—ant** *a* **bien p.** in good health. ◆**—é** *a* **p. à croire/etc** inclined to believe/*etc*; **p. sur qch** fond of sth. ◆**—eur, -euse** *nm Rail* porter; — *nmf Méd* carrier; (*de nouvelles, chèque*) bearer; **mère porteuse** surrogate mother.

portier [pɔrtje] *nm* doorkeeper, porter. ◆**portière** *nf* (*de véhicule, train*) door. ◆**portillon** *nm* gate.

portion [pɔrsjɔ̃] *nf* (*part, partie*) portion; (*de nourriture*) helping, portion.

portique [pɔrtik] *nm* **1** *Archit* portico. **2** (*de balançoire etc*) crossbar, frame.

porto [pɔrto] *nm* (*vin*) port.

portrait [pɔrtrɛ] *nm* portrait; **être le p. de** (*son père etc*) to be the image of; **faire un p.** to paint *ou* draw a portrait (**de** of); **p. en pied** full-length portrait. ◆**p.-robot** *nm* (*pl* **portraits-robots**) identikit (picture), photofit.

portuaire [pɔrtɥɛr] *a* (*installations etc*) harbour-.

Portugal [pɔrtygal] *nm* Portugal. ◆**portugais, -aise** *a & nmf* Portuguese; — *nm* (*langue*) Portuguese.

pose [poz] *nf* **1** (*installation*) putting up; putting in; laying. **2** (*attitude de modèle, affectation*) pose; (*temps*) *Phot* exposure. ◆**pos/er** *vt* to put (down); (*papier peint, rideaux*) to put up; (*sonnette, chauffage*) to put in; (*mine, moquette, fondations*) to lay; (*question*) to ask (**à qn** s.o.); (*principe, conditions*) to lay down; **p. sa candidature** to apply, put in one's application (**à** for); **ça pose la question de . . .** it poses the question of . . . ; — *vi* (*modèle etc*) to pose (**pour** for); — **se p.** *vpr* (*oiseau, avion*) to land; (*problème, question*) to arise; **se p. sur** (*yeux*) to fix on; **se p. en chef/etc** to set oneself up as *ou* pose as a leader/*etc*; **la question se pose!** this question should be asked! ◆**—é** *a* (*calme*) calm, staid.

◆**—ément** *adv* calmly. ◆**—eur, -euse** *nmf Péj* poseur.

positif, -ive [pozitif, -iv] *a* positive. ◆**positivement** *adv* positively.

position [pozisjɔ̃] *nf* (*attitude, emplacement, opinion etc*) position; **prendre p.** *Fig* to take a stand (**contre** against); **prise de p.** stand.

posologie [pozɔlɔʒi] *nf* (*de médicament*) dosage.

posséder [posede] *vt* to possess; (*maison etc*) to own, possess; (*bien connaître*) to master. ◆**possesseur** *nm* possessor; owner. ◆**possessif, -ive** *a* (*personne, adjectif etc*) possessive; — *nm Gram* possessive. ◆**possession** *nf* possession; **en p. de** in possession of; **prendre p. de** to take possession of.

possible [posibl] *a* possible (**à faire** to do); **il (nous) est p. de le faire** it is possible (for us) to do it; **il est p. que** (+ *sub*) it is possible that; **si p.** if possible; **le plus tôt/etc p.** as soon/*etc* as possible; **autant que p.** as much *ou* as many as possible; — *nm* **faire son p.** to do one's utmost (**pour faire** to do); **dans la mesure du p.** as far as possible. ◆**possibilité** *nf* possibility.

post- [pɔst] *préf* post-.

postdater [pɔstdate] *vt* to postdate.

poste [pɔst] **1** *nf* (*service*) post, mail; (*local*) post office; **bureau de p.** post office; **Postes (et Télécommunications)** (*administration*) Post Office; **par la p.** by post, by mail; **p. aérienne** airmail; **mettre à la p.** to post, mail. **2** *nm* (*lieu, emploi*) post; **p. de secours** first aid post; **p. de police** police station; **p. d'essence** petrol *ou Am* gas station; **p. d'incendie** fire hydrant; **p. d'aiguillage** signal box *ou Am* tower. **3** *nm* (*appareil*) *Rad TV* set; *Tél* extension (number). ◆**postal, -aux** *a* postal; **boîte postale** PO Box; **code p.** postcode, *Am* zip code. ◆**poster 1** *vt* **p. qn** (*placer*) *Mil* to post s.o. **2** *vt* (*lettre*) to post, mail. **3** [pɔster] *nm* poster.

postérieur [pɔsterjœr] **1** *a* (*document etc*) later; **p. à** after. **2** *nm* (*derrière*) *Fam* posterior.

postérité [pɔsterite] *nf* posterity.

posthume [pɔstym] *a* posthumous; **à titre p.** posthumously.

postiche [pɔstiʃ] *a* (*barbe etc*) false.

postier, -ière [pɔstje, -jɛr] *nmf* postal worker.

postillonner [pɔstijɔne] *vi* to sputter.

post-scriptum [pɔstskriptɔm] *nm inv* postscript.

postul/er [pɔstyle] *vt* **1** (*emploi*) to apply for. **2** (*poser*) *Math* to postulate. ◆**—ant, -ante** *nmf* applicant.

posture [pɔstyr] *nf* posture.

pot [po] *nm* **1** pot; (*à confiture*) jar, pot; (*à lait*) jug; (*à bière*) mug; (*de crème, yaourt*) carton; **p. de chambre** chamber pot; **p. de fleurs** flower pot; **prendre un p.** (*verre*) *Fam* to have a drink. **2** (*chance*) *Fam* luck; **avoir du p.** to be lucky.

potable [pɔtabl] *a* drinkable; (*passable*) *Fam* tolerable; **'eau p.'** 'drinking water'.

potage [pɔtaʒ] *nm* soup.

potager, -ère [pɔtaʒe, -ɛr] *a* (*jardin*) vegetable-; **plante potagère** vegetable; — *nm* vegetable garden.

potasser [pɔtase] *vt* (*examen*) to cram for; — *vi* to cram.

pot-au-feu [pɔtofø] *nm inv* (*plat*) beef stew.

pot-de-vin [podvɛ̃] *nm* (*pl* **pots-de-vin**) bribe.

pote [pɔt] *nm* (*ami*) *Fam* pal, buddy.

poteau, -x [pɔto] *nm* post; (*télégraphique*) pole; **p. d'arrivée** *Sp* winning post.

potelé [pɔtle] *a* plump, chubby.

potence [pɔtɑ̃s] *nf* (*gibet*) gallows.

potentiel, -ielle [pɔtɑ̃sjɛl] *a* & *nm* potential.

poterie [pɔtri] *nf* (*art*) pottery; **une p.** a piece of pottery; **des poteries** (*objets*) pottery. ◆**potier** *nm* potter.

potin [pɔtɛ̃] **1** *nmpl* (*cancans*) gossip. **2** *nm* (*bruit*) *Fam* row.

potion [posjɔ̃] *nf* potion.

potiron [pɔtirɔ̃] *nm* pumpkin.

pot-pourri [popuri] *nm* (*pl* **pots-pourris**) *Mus* medley.

pou, -x [pu] *nm* louse; **poux** lice.

poubelle [pubɛl] *nf* dustbin, *Am* garbage can.

pouce [pus] *nm* **1** thumb; **un coup de p.** *Fam* a helping hand. **2** (*mesure*) *Hist* & *Fig* inch.

poudre [pudr] *nf* powder; **p. (à canon)** (*explosif*) gunpowder; **en p.** (*lait*) powdered; (*chocolat*) drinking; **sucre en p.** castor *ou* caster sugar. ◆**poudrer** *vt* to powder; — **se p.** *vpr* (*femme*) to powder one's nose. ◆**poudreux, -euse** *a* powdery, dusty. ◆**poudrier** *nm* (powder) compact. ◆**poudrière** *nf* powder magazine; (*région*) *Fig* powder keg.

pouf [puf] **1** *int* thump! **2** *nm* (*siège*) pouf(fe).

pouffer [pufe] *vi* **p. (de rire)** to burst out laughing, guffaw.

pouilleux, -euse [pujø, -øz] *a* (*sordide*) miserable; (*mendiant*) lousy.

poulain [pulɛ̃] *nm* (*cheval*) foal; **le p. de qn** *Fig* s.o.'s protégé.

poule [pul] *nf* **1** hen, *Culin* fowl; **être p. mouillée** (*lâche*) to be chicken; **oui, ma p.!** *Fam* yes, my pet! **2** (*femme*) *Péj* tart. ◆**poulailler** *nm* **1** (hen) coop. **2 le p.** *Th Fam* the gods, the gallery. ◆**poulet** *nm* **1** (*poule, coq*) *Culin* chicken. **2** (*policier*) *Fam* cop.

pouliche [pulif] *nf* (*jument*) filly.

poulie [puli] *nf* pulley.

poulpe [pulp] *nm* octopus.

pouls [pu] *nm Méd* pulse.

poumon [pumɔ̃] *nm* lung; **à pleins poumons** (*respirer*) deeply; (*crier*) loudly; **p. d'acier** iron lung.

poupe [pup] *nf Nau* stern, poop.

poupée [pupe] *nf* doll.

poupin [pupɛ̃] *a* **visage p.** baby face.

poupon [pupɔ̃] *nm* (*bébé*) baby; (*poupée*) doll.

pour [pur] **1** *prép* for; **p. toi/moi/***etc* for you/me/*etc*; **faites-le p. lui** do it for him, do it for his sake; **partir p.** (*Paris etc*) to leave for; **elle va partir p. cinq ans** she's leaving for five years; **p. femme/base/***etc* as a wife/basis/*etc*; **p. moi, p. ma part** (*quant à moi*) as for me; **dix p. cent** ten per cent; **gentil p.** kind to; **elle est p.** she's in favour; **p. faire** (in order) to do, so as to do; **p. que tu saches** so (that) you may know; **p. quoi faire?** what for?; **trop petit/poli/***etc* **p. faire** too small/polite/*etc* to do; **assez grand/***etc* **p. faire** big/*etc* enough to do; **p. cela** for that reason; **jour p. jour/heure p. heure** to the day/hour; **p. intelligent/***etc* **qu'il soit** however clever/*etc* he may be; **ce n'est pas p. me plaire** it doesn't exactly please me; **acheter p. cinq francs de bonbons** to buy five francs' worth of sweets. **2** *nm* **le p. et le contre** the pros and cons.

pourboire [purbwar] *nm* (*argent*) tip.

pourcentage [pursɑ̃taʒ] *nm* percentage.

pourchasser [purfase] *vt* to pursue.

pourparlers [purparle] *nmpl* negotiations, talks.

pourpre [purpr] *a & nm* purple.

pourquoi [purkwa] *adv & conj* why; **p. pas?** why not?; – *nm inv* reason (**de** for); **le p. et le comment** the whys and wherefores.

pourra, pourrait [pura, purɛ] *voir* **pouvoir 1.**

pourrir [purir] *vi,* — **se p.** *vpr* to rot; – *vt* to rot; **p. qn** to corrupt s.o. ◆**pourri** *a* (*fruit, temps, personne etc*) rotten. ◆**pourriture** *nf* rot, rottenness; (*personne*) *Péj* swine.

poursuite [pursɥit] **1** *nf* chase, pursuit; (*du bonheur, de créancier*) pursuit (**de** of); (*continuation*) continuation; **se mettre à la p. de** to go in pursuit of. **2** *nfpl Jur* legal proceed-

ings (**contre** against). ◆**poursuiv/re* 1** *vt* (*courir après*) to chase, pursue; (*harceler, relancer*) to hound, pursue; (*obséder*) to haunt; (*but, idéal etc*) to pursue. **2** *vt* **p. qn** *Jur* (*au criminel*) to prosecute s.o.; (*au civil*) to sue s.o. **3** *vt* (*lecture, voyage etc*) to continue (with), carry on (with), pursue; – *vi,* — **se p.** *vpr* to continue, go on. ◆**—ant, -ante** *nmf* pursuer.

pourtant [purtɑ̃] *adv* yet, nevertheless.

pourtour [purtur] *nm* perimeter.

pourvoir* [purvwar] *vt* to provide (**de** with); **être pourvu de** to have, be provided with; – *vi* **p. à** (*besoins etc*) to provide for. ◆**pourvoyeur, -euse** *nmf* supplier.

pourvu que [purvyk(ə)] *conj* (*condition*) provided *ou* providing (that); **p. qu'elle soit là** (*souhait*) I only hope (that) she's there.

pousse [pus] *nf* **1** (*bourgeon*) shoot, sprout. **2** (*croissance*) growth.

pousse-café [puskafe] *nm inv* after-dinner liqueur.

pouss/er [puse] **1** *vt* to push; (*du coude*) to nudge, poke; (*véhicule, machine*) to drive hard; (*recherches*) to pursue; (*cri*) to utter; (*soupir*) to heave; **p. qn à faire** to urge s.o. to do; **p. qn à bout** to push s.o. to his limits; **p. trop loin** (*gentillesse etc*) to carry too far; **p. à la perfection** to bring to perfection; – *vi* to push; **p. jusqu'à Paris/***etc* to push on as far as Paris/*etc*; – **se p.** *vpr* (*se déplacer*) to move up *ou* over. **2** *vi* (*croître*) to grow; **faire p.** (*plante, barbe etc*) to grow. ◆**—é** *a* (*travail, études*) advanced. ◆**—ée** *nf* (*pression*) pressure; (*coup*) push; (*d'ennemi*) thrust, push; (*de fièvre etc*) outbreak; (*de l'inflation*) upsurge. ◆**poussette** *nf* pushchair, *Am* stroller; **p. canne** (baby) buggy, *Am* (collapsible) stroller; **p. de marché** shopping trolley *ou Am* cart. ◆**poussoir** *nm* (*bouton*) button.

poussière [pusjɛr] *nf* dust; **dix francs et des poussières** *Fam* a bit over ten francs. ◆**poussiéreux, -euse** *a* dusty.

poussif, -ive [pusif, -iv] *a* short-winded, puffing.

poussin [pusɛ̃] *nm* (*poulet*) chick.

poutre [putr] *nf* (*en bois*) beam; (*en acier*) girder. ◆**poutrelle** *nf* girder.

pouvoir* [puvwar] **1** *v aux* (*capacité*) to be able, can; (*permission, éventualité*) may, can; **je peux deviner** I can guess, I'm able to guess; **tu peux entrer** you may *ou* can come in; **il peut être malade** he may *ou* might be ill; **elle pourrait/pouvait venir** she might/could come; **j'ai pu l'obtenir** I managed to get it; **j'aurais pu l'obtenir** I could have got it *ou Am* gotten it; **je n'en peux plus** I'm utterly exhausted; *— v imp* **il peut neiger** it may snow; **— se p.** *vpr* **il se peut qu'elle parte** (it's possible that) she might leave. **2** *nm* (*capacité, autorité*) power; (*procuration*) power of attorney; **les pouvoirs publics** the authorities; **au p.** *Pol* in power; **en son p.** in one's power (**de faire** to do).

poux [pu] *voir* **pou.**

pragmatique [pragmatik] *a* pragmatic.

praire [prɛr] *nf* (*mollusque*) clam.

prairie [preri] *nf* meadow.

praline [pralin] *nf* sugared almond. ◆**praliné** *a* (*glace*) praline-flavoured.

praticable [pratikabl] *a* (*projet, chemin*) practicable.

praticien, -ienne [pratisjɛ̃, -jɛn] *nmf* practitioner.

pratique [pratik] **1** *a* (*connaissance, personne, instrument etc*) practical. **2** *nf* (*exercice, procédé*) practice; (*expérience*) practical experience; **la p. de la natation/du golf/etc** swimming/golfing/*etc*; **mettre en p.** to put into practice; **en p.** (*en réalité*) in practice. ◆**pratiqu/er** *vt* (*art etc*) to practise; (*football*) to play, practise; (*trou, route*) to make; (*opération*) to carry out; **p. la natation** to go swimming; *— vi* to practise. ◆**—ant, -ante** *a Rel* practising; *— nmf* churchgoer.

pratiquement [pratikmɑ̃] *adv* (*presque*) practically; (*en réalité*) in practice.

pré [pre] *nm* meadow.

pré- [pre] *préf* pre-.

préalable [prealabl] *a* previous, preliminary; **p. à** prior to; *— nm* precondition, prerequisite; **au p.** beforehand. ◆**—ment** [-əmɑ̃] *adv* beforehand.

préambule [preɑ̃byl] *nm* (*de loi*) preamble; *Fig* prelude (**à** to).

préau, -x [preo] *nm Scol* covered playground.

préavis [preavi] *nm* (*de congé etc*) (advance) notice (**de** of).

précaire [preker] *a* precarious.

précaution [prekosjɔ̃] *nf* (*mesure*) precaution; (*prudence*) caution; **par p.** as a precaution. ◆**précautionneux, -euse** *a* cautious.

précédent, -ente [presedɑ̃, -ɑ̃t] **1** *a* previous, preceding, earlier; *— nmf* previous one. **2** *nm* **un p.** (*fait, exemple*) a precedent; **sans p.** unprecedented. ◆**précédemment** [-amɑ̃] *adv* previously. ◆**précéder** *vti* to precede; **faire p. qch de qch** to precede sth by sth.

précepte [presept] *nm* precept.

précepteur, -trice [preseptœr, -tris] *nmf* (private) tutor.

prêcher [preʃe] *vti* to preach; **p. qn** *Rel* & *Fig* to preach to s.o.

précieux, -euse [presjø, -øz] *a* precious.

précipice [presipis] *nm* abyss, chasm.

précipit/er [presipite] *vt* (*jeter*) to throw, hurl; (*plonger*) to plunge (**dans** into); (*hâter*) to hasten; **— se p.** *vpr* (*se jeter*) to throw *ou* hurl oneself; (*foncer*) to rush (**à, sur** on to); (*s'accélérer*) to speed up. ◆**—é** *a* hasty. ◆**précipitamment** *adv* hastily. ◆**précipitation 1** *nf* haste. **2** *nfpl* (*pluie*) precipitation.

précis [presi] **1** *a* precise; (*idée, mécanisme*) accurate, precise; **à deux heures précises** at two o'clock sharp *ou* precisely. **2** *nm* (*résumé*) summary; (*manuel*) handbook. ◆**précisément** *adv* precisely. ◆**préciser** *vt* to specify (**que** that); **— se p.** *vpr* to become clear(er). ◆**précision** *nf* precision; accuracy; (*détail*) detail; (*explication*) explanation.

précoce [prekɔs] *a* (*fruit, mariage, mort etc*) early; (*personne*) precocious. ◆**précocité** *nf* precociousness; earliness.

préconçu [prekɔ̃sy] *a* preconceived.

préconiser [prekɔnize] *vt* to advocate (**que** that).

précurseur [prekyrsœr] *nm* forerunner, precursor; *— a* **un signe p. de qch** a sign heralding sth.

prédécesseur [predesesœr] *nm* predecessor.

prédestiné [predestine] *a* fated, predestined (**à faire** to do).

prédicateur [predikatœr] *nm* preacher.

prédilection [predileksjɔ̃] *nf* (special) liking; **de p.** favourite.

prédire* [predir] *vt* to predict (**que** that). ◆**prédiction** *nf* prediction.

prédisposer [predispoze] *vt* to predispose (**à qch** to sth, **à faire** to do). ◆**prédisposition** *nf* predisposition.

prédomin/er [predomine] *vi* to predominate. ◆**—ant** *a* predominant. ◆**prédominance** *nf* predominance.

préfabriqué [prefabrike] *a* prefabricated.

préface [prefas] *nf* preface. ◆**préfacer** *vt* to preface.

préfér/er [prefere] *vt* to prefer (**à** to); **p. faire** to prefer to do. ◆**—é, -ée** *a* & *nmf* favourite. ◆**—able** *a* preferable (**à** to). ◆**préférence** *nf* preference; **de p.** preferably; **de p. à** in preference to. ◆**préférentiel, -ielle** *a* preferential.

préfet [prefɛ] nm prefect, *chief administrator in a department*; **p. de police** prefect of police, Paris chief of police. ◆**préfecture** nf prefecture; **p. de police** Paris police headquarters.

préfixe [prefiks] nm prefix.

préhistoire [preistwar] nf prehistory. ◆**préhistorique** a prehistoric.

préjudice [preʒydis] nm Jur prejudice, harm; **porter p.** à to prejudice, harm. ◆**préjudiciable** a prejudicial (à to).

préjugé [preʒyʒe] nm (*parti pris*) prejudice; **avoir un p.** ou **des préjugés** to be prejudiced (**contre** against).

prélasser (se) [səprelase] vpr to loll (about), lounge (about).

prélat [prela] nm Rel prelate.

prélever [prelve] vt (*échantillon*) to take (**sur** from); (*somme*) to deduct (**sur** from). ◆**prélèvement** nm taking; deduction; **p. de sang** blood sample; **p. automatique** Fin standing order.

préliminaire [preliminɛr] a preliminary; — nmpl preliminaries.

prélude [prelyd] nm prelude (à to).

prématuré [prematyre] a premature; — nm (*bébé*) premature baby. ◆—**ment** adv prematurely, too soon.

préméditer [premedite] vt to premeditate. ◆**préméditation** nf Jur premeditation.

premier, -ière [prəmje, -jɛr] a first; (*enfance*) early; (*page*) Journ front, first; (*qualité, nécessité, importance*) prime; (*état*) original; (*notion, cause*) basic; (*danseuse, rôle*) leading; (*inférieur*) bottom; (*supérieur*) top; **nombre p.** Math prime number; **le p. rang** the front ou first row; **à la première occasion** at the earliest opportunity; **P. ministre** Prime Minister, Premier; — nmf first (one); **arriver le p.** ou **en p.** to arrive first; **être le p. de la classe** to be (at the top) of the class; — nm (*date*) first; (*étage*) first ou Am second floor; **le p. de l'an** New Year's Day; — nf Th Cin première; Rail first class; Scol = sixth form, Am = twelfth grade; Aut first (gear); (*événement historique*) first. ◆**premier-né** nm, ◆**première-née** nf first-born (child). ◆**premièrement** adv firstly.

prémisse [premis] nf premiss.

prémonition [premɔnisjɔ̃] nf premonition.

prémunir [premynir] vt to safeguard (**contre** against).

prénatal, mpl -als [prenatal] a antenatal, Am prenatal.

prendre* [prɑ̃dr] vt to take (**à qn** from s.o.); (*attraper*) to catch, get; (*voyager par*) to take, travel by; (*acheter*) to get; (*douche, bain*) to take, have; (*repas*) to have; (*nouvelles*) to get; (*temps, heure*) to take (up); (*pensionnaire*) to take (in); (*ton, air*) to put on; (*engager*) to take (s.o.) (on); (*chercher*) to pick up, get; **p. qn pour** (*un autre*) to (mis)take s.o. for; (*considérer*) to take s.o. for; **p. qn** (*doute etc*) to seize s.o.; **p. feu** to catch fire; **p. de la place** to take up room; **p. du poids/de la vitesse** to put on weight/speed; **à tout p.** on the whole; **qu'est-ce qui te prend?** what's got ou Am gotten into you?; — vi (*feu*) to catch; (*gelée, ciment*) to set; (*greffe, vaccin*) to take; (*mode*) to catch on; — **se p.** vpr (*objet*) to be taken; (*s'accrocher*) to get caught; (*eau*) to freeze; **se p. pour un génie/etc** to think one is a genius/etc; **s'y p.** to go ou set about it; **s'en p. à** (*critiquer, attaquer*) to attack; (*accuser*) to blame; **se p. à faire** to begin to do. ◆**prenant** a (*travail, film etc*) engrossing; (*voix*) engaging. ◆**preneur, -euse** nmf taker, buyer.

prénom [prenɔ̃] nm first name. ◆**prénommer** vt to name; **il se prénomme Louis** his first name is Louis.

préoccup/er [preɔkype] vt (*inquiéter*) to worry; (*absorber*) to preoccupy; **se p. de** to be worried about; to be preoccupied about. ◆—**ant** a worrying. ◆—**é** a worried. ◆**préoccupation** nf worry; (*idée, problème*) preoccupation.

préparer [prepare] vt to prepare; (*repas etc*) to get ready, prepare; (*examen*) to study for, prepare (for); **p. qch à qn** to prepare sth for s.o.; **p. qn à** (*examen*) to prepare ou coach s.o. for; — **se p.** vpr to get (oneself) ready, prepare oneself (à qch for sth); (*orage*) to brew, threaten. ◆**préparatifs** nmpl preparations (de for). ◆**préparation** nf preparation. ◆**préparatoire** a preparatory.

prépondérant [prepɔ̃derɑ̃] a dominant. ◆**prépondérance** nf dominance.

prépos/er [prepoze] vt **p. qn à** to put s.o. in charge of. ◆—**é, -ée** nmf employee; (*facteur*) postman, postwoman.

préposition [prepozisjɔ̃] nf preposition.

préretraite [prerətrɛt] nf early retirement.

prérogative [prerogativ] nf prerogative.

près [prɛ] adv **p. de** (*qn, qch*) near (to), close to; **p. de deux ans/etc** (*presque*) nearly two years/etc; **p. de partir/etc** about to leave/etc; **tout p.** nearby (**de qn/qch** s.o./sth), close by (**de qn/qch** s.o./sth); **de p.** (*lire, examiner, suivre*) closely; **à peu de chose p.** almost; **à cela p.** except that; **voici le**

chiffre à un franc p. here is the figure give or take a franc; **calculer au franc p.** to calculate to the nearest franc.

présage [prezaʒ] *nm* omen, foreboding. ◆**présager** *vt* to forebode.

presbyte [prɛsbit] *a* & *nmf* long-sighted (person). ◆**presbytie** [-bisi] *nf* long-sightedness.

presbytère [prɛsbitɛr] *nm Rel* presbytery.

préscolaire [preskɔlɛr] *a* (*âge etc*) pre-school.

prescrire* [prɛskrir] *vt* to prescribe. ◆**prescription** *nf* (*instruction*) & *Jur* prescription.

préséance [preseɑ̃s] *nf* precedence (**sur** over).

présent¹ [prezɑ̃] **1** *a* (*non absent*) present; **les personnes présentes** those present. **2** *a* (*actuel*) present; – *nm* (*temps*) present; *Gram* present (tense); **à p.** now, at present; **dès à p.** as from now. ◆**présence** *nf* presence; (*à l'école, au bureau etc*) attendance (**à** at); **feuille de p.** attendance sheet; **faire acte de p.** to put in an appearance; **en p.** (*personnes*) face to face; **en p. de** in the presence of; **p. d'esprit** presence of mind.

présent² [prezɑ̃] *nm* (*cadeau*) present.

présent/er [prezɑ̃te] *vt* (*offrir, exposer, animer etc*) to present; (*montrer*) to show, present; **p. qn à qn** to introduce *ou* present s.o. to s.o.; **— se p.** *vpr* to introduce *ou* present oneself (**à** to); (*chez qn*) to show up; (*occasion etc*) to arise; **se p. à** (*examen*) to sit for; (*élections*) to stand in *ou* at, run in; (*emploi*) to apply for; (*autorités*) to report to; **ça se présente bien** it looks promising. ◆**—able** *a* presentable. ◆**présentateur, -trice** *nmf TV* announcer, presenter. ◆**présentation** *nf* presentation; introduction. ◆**présentoir** *nm* (*étagère*) (display) stand.

préserver [prezɛrve] *vt* to protect, preserve (**de** from). ◆**préservatif** *nm* sheath, condom. ◆**préservation** *nf* protection, preservation.

présidence [prezidɑ̃s] *nf* (*de nation*) presidency; (*de firme etc*) chairmanship. ◆**président, -ente** *nmf* (*de nation*) president; (*de réunion, firme*) chairman, chairwoman; **p. directeur général** chairman and managing director, *Am* chief executive officer. ◆**présidentiel, -ielle** *a* presidential.

présider [prezide] *vt* (*réunion*) to preside at *ou* over, chair; – *vi* to preside.

présomption [prezɔ̃psjɔ̃] *nf* (*conjecture, suffisance*) presumption.

présomptueux, -euse [prezɔ̃ptɥø, -øz] *a* presumptuous.

presque [prɛsk(ə)] *adv* almost, nearly; **p. jamais/rien** hardly ever/anything.

presqu'île [prɛskil] *nf* peninsula.

presse [prɛs] *nf* (*journaux, appareil*) press; *Typ* (printing) press; **de p.** (*conférence, agence*) press-.

presse-citron [prɛssitrɔ̃] *nm inv* lemon squeezer. ◆**p.-papiers** *nm inv* paperweight. ◆**p.-purée** *nm inv* (potato) masher.

pressentir* [presɑ̃tir] *vt* (*deviner*) to sense (**que** that). ◆**pressentiment** *nm* foreboding, presentiment.

press/er [prese] *vt* (*serrer*) to squeeze, press; (*bouton*) to press; (*fruit*) to squeeze; (*départ etc*) to hasten; **p. qn** to hurry s.o. (**de faire** to do); (*assaillir*) to harass s.o. (**de questions** with questions); **p. le pas** to speed up; – *vi* (*temps*) to press; (*affaire*) to be pressing *ou* urgent; **rien ne presse** there's no hurry; **— se p.** *vpr* (*se grouper*) to crowd, swarm; (*se serrer*) to squeeze (together); (*se hâter*) to hurry (**de faire** to do); **presse-toi (de partir)** hurry up (and go). ◆**—ant** *a* pressing, urgent. ◆**—é** *a* (*personne*) in a hurry; (*air*) hurried; (*travail*) pressing, urgent. ◆**pressing** [-iŋ] *nm* (*magasin*) dry cleaner's. ◆**pressoir** *nm* (wine) press.

pression [presjɔ̃] *nf* pressure; **faire p. sur qn** to put pressure on s.o., pressurize s.o.; **bière (à la) p.** draught beer; – *nm* (**bouton-**)**p.** press-stud; *Am* snap.

pressuriser [presyrize] *vt Av* to pressurize.

prestance [prɛstɑ̃s] *nf* (imposing) presence.

prestation [prɛstasjɔ̃] *nf* **1** (*allocation*) allowance, benefit. **2** (*performance*) performance.

prestidigitateur, -trice [prɛstidiʒitatœr, -tris] *nmf* conjurer. ◆**prestidigitation** *nf* conjuring.

prestige [prɛstiʒ] *nm* prestige. ◆**prestigieux, -euse** *a* prestigious.

presto [prɛsto] *Fam voir* **illico**.

présumer [prezyme] *vt* to presume (**que** that).

présupposer [presypoze] *vt* to presuppose (**que** that).

prêt¹ [prɛ] *a* (*préparé, disposé*) ready (**à faire** to do, **à qch** for sth). ◆**p.-à-porter** [prɛtaporte] *nm inv* ready-to-wear clothes.

prêt² [prɛ] *nm* (*emprunt*) loan. ◆**p.-logement** *nm* (*pl* **prêts-logement**) mortgage.

prétend/re [pretɑ̃dr] *vt* to claim (**que** that); (*vouloir*) to intend (**faire** to do); **p.**

être/savoir to claim to be/to know; **elle se prétend riche** she claims to be rich; – *vi* **p. à** (*titre etc*) to lay claim to. ◆**—ant** *nm* (*amoureux*) suitor. ◆**—u** *a* so-called. ◆**—ument** *adv* supposedly.

prétentieux, -euse [pretãsjø, -øz] *a* & *nmf* pretentious (person). ◆**prétention** *nf* (*vanité*) pretension; (*revendication, ambition*) claim.

prêt/er [prete] *vt* (*argent, objet*) to lend (à to); (*aide, concours*) to give (à to); (*attribuer*) to attribute (à to); **p. attention** to pay attention (à to); **p. serment** to take an oath; – *vi* **p. à** (*phrase etc*) to lend itself to; **se p. à** (*consentir à*) to agree to; (*sujet etc*) to lend itself to. ◆**—eur, -euse** *nmf* (*d'argent*) lender; **p. sur gages** pawnbroker.

prétexte [pretɛkst] *nm* pretext, excuse; **sous p. de/que** on the pretext of/that. ◆**prétexter** *vt* to plead (**que** that).

prêtre [prɛtr] *nm* priest; **grand p.** high priest.

preuve [prœv] *nf* proof, evidence; **faire p. de** to show; **faire ses preuves** (*personne*) to prove oneself; (*méthode*) to prove itself.

prévaloir [prevalwar] *vi* to prevail (**contre** against, **sur** over).

prévenant [prevnã] *a* considerate. ◆**prévenance(s)** *nf*(*pl*) (*gentillesse*) consideration.

préven/ir* [prevnir] *vt* 1 (*avertir*) to warn (**que** that); (*aviser*) to tell, inform (**que** that). 2 (*désir, question*) to anticipate; (*malheur*) to avert. ◆**—u, -ue** 1 *nmf Jur* defendant, accused. 2 *a* prejudiced (**contre** against). ◆**préventif, -ive** *a* preventive. ◆**prévention** *nf* 1 prevention; **p. routière** road safety. 2 (*opinion*) prejudice.

prév/oir* [prevwar] *vt* (*anticiper*) to foresee (**que** that); (*prédire*) to forecast (**que** that); (*temps*) *Mét* to forecast; (*projeter, organiser*) to plan (for); (*réserver, préparer*) to allow, provide. ◆**—u** *a* (*conditions*) laid down; **un repas est p.** a meal is provided; **au moment p.** at the appointed time; **comme p.** as planned, as expected; **p. pour** (*véhicule, appareil etc*) designed for. ◆**prévisible** *a* foreseeable. ◆**prévision** *nf* (*opinion*) & *Mét* forecast; **en p. de** in expectation of.

prévoyant [prevwajã] *a* (*personne*) provident. ◆**prévoyance** *nf* foresight; **société de p.** provident society.

prier [prije] **1** *vi Rel* to pray; – *vt* **p. Dieu pour qu'il nous accorde** qch to pray (to God) for sth. **2** *vt* **p. qn de faire** to ask *ou* request s.o. to do; (*implorer*) to beg s.o. to do; **je vous en prie** (*faites donc, allez-y*)

please; (*en réponse à 'merci'*) don't mention it; **je vous prie** please; **se faire p.** to wait to be asked. ◆**prière** *nf Rel* prayer; (*demande*) request; **p. de répondre/etc** please answer/etc.

primaire [primer] *a* primary.

prime [prim] **1** *nf* (*d'employé*) bonus; (*d'État*) subsidy; (*cadeau*) *Com* free gift; **p. (d'assurance)** (insurance) premium. **2** *a* **de p. abord** at the very first glance.

primé [prime] *a* (*animal*) prize-winning.

primer [prime] *vi* to excel, prevail; – *vt* to prevail over.

primeurs [primœr] *nfpl* early fruit and vegetables.

primevère [primver] *nf* (*à fleurs jaunes*) primrose.

primitif, -ive [primitif, -iv] *a* (*art, société etc*) primitive; (*état, sens*) original; – *nm* (*artiste*) primitive. ◆**primitivement** *adv* originally.

primo [primo] *adv* first(ly).

primordial, -aux [primordjal, -o] *a* vital (**de faire** to do).

prince [prɛ̃s] *nm* prince. ◆**princesse** *nf* princess. ◆**princier, -ière** *a* princely. ◆**principauté** *nf* principality.

principal, -aux [prɛ̃sipal, -o] *a* main, chief, principal; – *nm* (*de collège*) *Scol* principal; **le p.** (*essentiel*) the main *ou* chief thing. ◆**—ement** *adv* mainly.

principe [prɛ̃sip] *nm* principle; **par p.** on principle; **en p.** theoretically, in principle; (*normalement*) as a rule.

printemps [prɛ̃tã] *nm* (*saison*) spring. ◆**printanier, -ière** *a* (*temps etc*) spring-, spring-like.

priorité [priorite] *nf* priority; **la p.** *Aut* the right of way; **la p. à droite** *Aut* right of way to traffic coming from the right; **'cédez la p.'** *Aut* 'give way'; *Am* 'yield'; **en p.** as a matter of priority. ◆**prioritaire** *a* (*industrie etc*) priority-; **être p.** to have priority; *Aut* to have the right of way.

pris [pri] *voir* **prendre**; – *a* (*place*) taken; (*crème, ciment*) set; (*eau*) frozen; (*gorge*) infected; (*nez*) congested; **être (très) p.** (*occupé*) to be (very) busy; **p. de** (*peur, panique*) stricken with.

prise [priz] *voir* **prendre**; – *nf* taking; (*manière d'empoigner*) grip, hold; (*de ville*) capture, taking; (*objet saisi*) catch; (*de tabac*) pinch; **p. (de courant)** *Él* (*mâle*) plug; (*femelle*) socket; **p. multiple** *Él* adaptor; **p. d'air** air vent; **p. de conscience** awareness; **p. de contact** first meeting; **p. de position** *Fig* stand; **p. de sang** blood test; **p.**

de son (sound) recording; **p. de vue(s)** *Cin Phot* (*action*) shooting; (*résultat*) shot; **aux prises avec** at grips with.

priser [prize] **1** *vt tabac* **à p.** snuff; − *vi* to take snuff. **2** *vt* (*estimer*) to prize.

prisme [prism] *nm* prism.

prison [prizɔ̃] *nf* prison, jail, gaol; (*réclusion*) imprisonment; **mettre en p.** to imprison, put in prison. ◆**prisonnier, -ière** *nmf* prisoner; **faire qn p.** to take s.o. prisoner.

privé [prive] *a* private; **en p.** (*seul à seul*) in private; − *nm* **dans le p.** in private life; *Com Fam* in the private sector.

priver [prive] *vt* to deprive (**de** of); **se p. de** to deprive oneself of, do without. ◆**privation** *nf* deprivation (**de** of); *pl* (*sacrifices*) hardships.

privilège [privileʒ] *nm* privilege. ◆**privilégié, -ée** *a* & *nmf* privileged (person).

prix [pri] *nm* **1** (*d'un objet, du succès etc*) price; **à tout p.** at all costs; **à aucun p.** on no account; **hors (de) p.** exorbitant; **attacher du p. à** to attach importance to; **menu à p. fixe** set price menu. **2** (*récompense*) prize.

pro- [pro] *préf* pro-.

probable [prɔbabl] *a* probable, likely; **peu p.** unlikely. ◆**probabilité** *nf* probability, likelihood; **selon toute p.** in all probability. ◆**probablement** *adv* probably.

probant [prɔbɑ̃] *a* conclusive.

probité [prɔbite] *nf* (*honnêteté*) integrity.

problème [prɔblɛm] *nm* problem. ◆**problématique** *a* doubtful, problematic.

procéd/er [prɔsede] *vi* (*agir*) to proceed; (*se conduire*) to behave; **p. à** (*enquête etc*) to carry out. ◆**—é** *nm* process; (*conduite*) behaviour. ◆**procédure** *nf* procedure; *Jur* proceedings.

procès [prɔsɛ] *nm* (*criminel*) trial; (*civil*) lawsuit; **faire un p. à** to take to court.

processeur [prɔsesœr] *nm* (*d'ordinateur*) processor.

procession [prɔsesjɔ̃] *nf* procession.

processus [prɔsesys] *nm* process.

procès-verbal, -aux [prɔsɛvɛrbal, -o] *nm* (*de réunion*) minutes; (*constat*) *Jur* report; (*contravention*) fine, ticket.

prochain, -aine [prɔʃɛ̃, -ɛn] **1** *a* next; (*avenir*) near; (*parent*) close; (*mort, arrivée*) impending; (*mariage*) forthcoming; **un jour p.** one day soon; − *nf* **à la prochaine!** *Fam* see you soon!; **à la prochaine (station)** at the next stop. **2** *nm* (*semblable*) fellow (man). ◆**prochainement** *adv* shortly, soon.

proche [prɔʃ] *a* (*espace*) near, close; (*temps*)

close (at hand); (*parent, ami*) close; (*avenir*) near; **p. de** near (to), close to; **une maison/etc p.** a house/etc nearby *ou* close by; − *nmpl* close relations.

proclamer [prɔklame] *vt* to proclaim, declare (**que** that); **p. roi** to proclaim king. ◆**proclamation** *nf* proclamation, declaration.

procréer [prɔkree] *vt* to procreate. ◆**procréation** *nf* procreation.

procuration [prɔkyrasjɔ̃] *nf* power of attorney; **par p.** (*voter*) by proxy.

procurer [prɔkyre] *vt* **p. qch à qn** (*personne*) to obtain sth for s.o.; (*occasion etc*) to afford s.o. sth; **se p. qch** to obtain sth.

procureur [prɔkyrœr] *nm* = *Br* public prosecutor, = *Am* district attorney.

prodige [prɔdiʒ] *nm* (*miracle*) wonder; (*personne*) prodigy. ◆**prodigieux, -euse** *a* prodigious, extraordinary.

prodigue [prɔdig] *a* (*dépensier*) wasteful, prodigal. ◆**prodiguer** *vt* to lavish (**à qn** on s.o.).

production [prɔdyksjɔ̃] *nf* production; (*de la terre*) yield. ◆**producteur, -trice** *nmf Com Cin* producer; − *a* producing; **pays p. de pétrole** oil-producing country. ◆**productif, -ive** *a* (*terre, réunion etc*) productive. ◆**productivité** *nf* productivity.

produire* [prɔdɥir] **1** *vt* (*fabriquer, présenter etc*) to produce; (*causer*) to bring about, produce. **2 se p.** *vpr* (*événement etc*) to happen, occur. ◆**produit** *nm* (*article etc*) product; (*pour la vaisselle*) liquid; (*d'une vente, d'une collecte*) proceeds; *pl* (*de la terre*) produce; **p. (chimique)** chemical; **p. de beauté** cosmetic.

proéminent [prɔeminɑ̃] *a* prominent.

prof [prɔf] *nm Fam* = **professeur**.

profane [prɔfan] **1** *nmf* lay person. **2** *a* (*art etc*) secular.

profaner [prɔfane] *vt* to profane, desecrate. ◆**profanation** *nf* profanation, desecration.

proférer [prɔfere] *vt* to utter.

professer [prɔfese] *vt* to profess (**que** that).

professeur [prɔfesœr] *nm* teacher; *Univ* lecturer, *Am* professor; (*titulaire d'une chaire*) *Univ* professor.

profession [prɔfesjɔ̃] *nf* **1** occupation, vocation; (*libérale*) profession; (*manuelle*) trade; **de p.** (*chanteur etc*) professional, by profession. **2 p. de foi** *Fig* declaration of principles. ◆**professionnel, -elle** *a* (*école*) vocational, trade-; − *nmf* (*non amateur*) professional.

profil [prɔfil] *nm* (*de personne, objet*) profile;

de p. in profile. ◆**profiler** *vt* to outline, profile; — **se p.** *vpr* to be outlined *ou* profiled (**sur** against).

profit [prɔfi] *nm* profit; (*avantage*) advantage, profit; **vendre à p.** to sell at a profit; **tirer p. de** to benefit by, profit by; **au p. de** for the benefit of. ◆**profitable** *a* profitable (**à** to). ◆**profiter** *vi* **p. de** to take advantage of; **p. à qn** to profit s.o.; **p. (bien)** (*enfant*) *Fam* to thrive. ◆**profiteur, -euse** *nmf Péj* profiteer.

profond [prɔfɔ̃] *a* deep; (*esprit, joie, erreur etc*) profound, great; (*cause*) underlying; **p. de deux mètres** two metres deep; — *adv* (*pénétrer etc*) deep; — *nm* **au plus p. de** in the depths of. ◆**profondément** *adv* deeply; (*dormir*) soundly; (*triste, souhaiter*) profoundly; (*extrêmement*) thoroughly. ◆**profondeur** *nf* depth; profoundness; *pl* depths (**de** of); **en p.** (*étudier etc*) in depth; **à six mètres de p.** at a depth of six metres.

profusion [prɔfyzjɔ̃] *nf* profusion; **à p.** in profusion.

progéniture [prɔʒenityr] *nf Hum* offspring.

progiciel [prɔʒisjɛl] *nm* (*pour ordinateur*) (software) package.

programme [prɔgram] *nm* programme, *Am* program; (*d'une matière*) *Scol* syllabus; (*d'ordinateur*) program; **p. (d'études)** (*d'une école*) curriculum. ◆**programmation** *nf* programming. ◆**programmer** *vt Cin Rad TV* to programme, *Am* program; (*ordinateur*) to program. ◆**programmeur, -euse** *nmf* (computer) programmer.

progrès [prɔgrɛ] *nm & nmpl* progress; **faire des p.** to make (good) progress. ◆**progresser** *vi* to progress. ◆**progressif, -ive** *a* progressive. ◆**progression** *nf* progression. ◆**progressiste** *a & nmf Pol* progressive. ◆**progressivement** *adv* progressively, gradually.

prohiber [prɔibe] *vt* to prohibit, forbid. ◆**prohibitif, -ive** *a* prohibitive. ◆**prohibition** *nf* prohibition.

proie [prwa] *nf* prey; **être en p. à** to be (a) prey to, be tortured by.

projecteur [prɔʒɛktœr] *nm* (*de monument*) floodlight; (*de prison*) & *Mil* searchlight; *Th* spot(light); *Cin* projector.

projectile [prɔʒɛktil] *nm* missile.

projet [prɔʒɛ] *nm* plan; (*ébauche*) draft; (*entreprise, étude*) project.

projeter [prɔʒte] *vt* **1** (*lancer*) to hurl, project. **2** (*film, ombre*) to project; (*lumière*) to flash. **3** (*voyage, fête etc*) to plan; **p. de faire** to plan to do. ◆**projection** *nf* (*lancement*) hurling, projection; (*de film, d'ombre*) projection; (*séance*) showing.

prolétaire [prɔleter] *nmf* proletarian. ◆**prolétariat** *nm* proletariat. ◆**prolétarien, -ienne** *a* proletarian.

proliférer [prɔlifere] *vi* to proliferate. ◆**prolifération** *nf* proliferation.

prolifique [prɔlifik] *a* prolific.

prolixe [prɔliks] *a* verbose, wordy.

prologue [prɔlɔg] *nm* prologue (**de, à** to).

prolonger [prɔlɔ̃ʒe] *vt* to prolong, extend; — **se p.** *vpr* (*séance, rue, effet*) to continue. ◆**prolongateur** *nm* (*rallonge*) *Él* extension cord. ◆**prolongation** *nf* extension; *pl Fb* extra time. ◆**prolongement** *nm* extension.

promenade [prɔmnad] *nf* (*à pied*) walk; (*en voiture*) ride, drive; (*en vélo, à cheval*) ride; (*action*) *Sp* walking; (*lieu*) walk, promenade; **faire une p.** = **se promener.** ◆**promener** *vt* to take for a walk *ou* ride; (*visiteur*) to take *ou* show around; **p. qch sur qch** (*main, regard*) to run sth over sth; **envoyer p.** *Fam* to send packing; — **se p.** *vpr* (*à pied*) to (go for a) walk; (*en voiture*) to (go for a) ride *ou* drive. ◆**promeneur, -euse** *nmf* walker, stroller.

promesse [prɔmɛs] *nf* promise. ◆**promett/re*** *vt* to promise (**qch à qn** s.o. sth); **p. de faire** to promise to do; **c'est promis** it's a promise; — *vi* **p. (beaucoup)** *Fig* to be promising; **se p. qch** to promise oneself sth; **se p. de faire** to resolve to do. ◆**—eur, -euse** *a* promising.

promontoire [prɔmɔ̃twar] *nm Géog* headland.

promoteur [prɔmɔtœr] *nm* **p. (immobilier)** property developer.

promotion [prɔmosjɔ̃] *nf* **1** promotion; **en p.** *Com* on (special) offer. **2** (*candidats*) *Univ* year. ◆**promouvoir*** *vt* (*personne, produit etc*) to promote; **être promu** (*employé*) to be promoted (**à** to).

prompt [prɔ̃] *a* swift, prompt, quick. ◆**promptitude** *nf* swiftness, promptness.

promulguer [prɔmylge] *vt* to promulgate.

prôner [prone] *vt* (*vanter*) to extol; (*préconiser*) to advocate.

pronom [prɔnɔ̃] *nm Gram* pronoun. ◆**pronominal, -aux** *a* pronominal.

prononc/er [prɔnɔ̃se] *vt* (*articuler*) to pronounce; (*dire*) to utter; (*discours*) to deliver; (*jugement*) *Jur* to pronounce, pass; — *vi Jur* Ling to pronounce; — **se p.** *vpr* (*mot*) to be pronounced; (*personne*) to reach a decision (**sur** about, on); **se p. pour** to come out in favour of. ◆**—é** *a* (*visible*) pronounced, marked. ◆**prononciation** *nf* pronunciation.

pronostic [prɔnɔstik] *nm* (*prévision*) & *Sp* forecast. ◆**pronostiquer** *vt* to forecast.

propagande [prɔpagɑ̃d] *nf* propaganda. ◆**propagandiste** *nmf* propagandist.

propager [prɔpaʒe] *vt*, **— se p.** *vpr* to spread. ◆**propagation** *nf* spread(ing).

propension [prɔpɑ̃sjɔ̃] *nf* propensity (à qch for sth, à faire to do).

prophète [prɔfɛt] *nm* prophet. ◆**prophétie** [-fesi] *nf* prophecy. ◆**prophétique** *a* prophetic. ◆**prophétiser** *vti* to prophesy.

propice [prɔpis] *a* favourable (à to).

proportion [prɔpɔrsjɔ̃] *nf* proportion; *Math* ratio; **en p.** de in proportion to; **hors de p.** out of proportion (**avec** to). ◆**proportionnel, -elle** *a* proportional (à to). ◆**proportionn/er** *vt* to proportion (à to). ◆**—é** *a* proportionate (à to); **bien p.** well *ou* nicely proportioned.

propos [prɔpo] **1** *nmpl* (*paroles*) remarks, utterances. **2** *nm* (*intention*) purpose. **3** *nm* (*sujet*) subject; **à p. de** about; **à p. de rien** for no reason; **à tout p.** for no reason, at every turn. **4** *adv* **à p.** (*arriver etc*) at the right time; **à p.!** by the way!; **juger à p. de faire** to consider it fit to do.

proposer [prɔpoze] *vt* (*suggérer*) to suggest, propose (**qch à qn** sth to s.o., **que** (+ *sub*) that); (*offrir*) to offer (**qch à qn** s.o. sth, **de faire** to do); (*candidat*) to put forward, propose; **je te propose de rester** I suggest (that) you stay; **se p. pour faire** to offer to do; **se p. de faire** to propose *ou* mean to do. ◆**proposition** *nf* suggestion, proposal; (*de paix*) proposal, (*affirmation*) proposition; *Gram* clause.

propre[1] [prɔpr] *a* clean; (*soigné*) neat; (*honnête*) decent; *— nm* **mettre qch au p.** to make a fair copy of sth. ◆**proprement**[1] *adv* (*avec propreté*) cleanly; (*avec netteté*) neatly; (*comme il faut*) decently. ◆**propreté** *nf* cleanliness; (*netteté*) neatness.

propre[2] [prɔpr] **1** *a* (à soi) own; **mon p. argent** my own money; **ses propres mots** his very *ou* his own words. **2** *a* (*qui convient*) right, proper; **p. à** (*attribut, coutume etc*) peculiar to; (*approprié*) well-suited to; **p. à faire** likely to do; **sens p.** literal meaning; **nom p.** proper noun; *— nm* **le p. de** (*qualité*) the distinctive quality of; **au p.** (*au sens propre*) literally. ◆**proprement**[2] *adv* (*strictement*) strictly; **à p. parler** strictly speaking; **le village/etc p. dit** the village/etc proper *ou* itself.

propriété [prɔprijete] *nf* **1** (*bien*) property; (*droit*) ownership, property. **2** (*qualité*) property. **3** (*de mot*) suitability. ◆**propriétaire** *nmf* owner; (*d'hôtel*) proprietor, owner; (*qui loue*) landlord, landlady; **p. foncier** landowner.

propulser [prɔpylse] *vt* (*faire avancer, projeter*) to propel. ◆**propulsion** *nf* propulsion.

prosaïque [prɔzaik] *a* prosaic, pedestrian.

proscrire* [prɔskrir] *vt* to proscribe, banish. ◆**proscrit, -ite** *nmf* (*personne*) exile. ◆**proscription** *nf* banishment.

prose [proz] *nf* prose.

prospecter [prɔspɛkte] *vt* (*sol*) to prospect; (*pétrole*) to prospect for; (*région*) *Com* to canvass. ◆**prospecteur, -trice** *nmf* prospector. ◆**prospection** *nf* prospecting; *Com* canvassing.

prospectus [prɔspɛktys] *nm* leaflet, prospectus.

prospère [prɔspɛr] *a* (*florissant*) thriving, prosperous; (*riche*) prosperous. ◆**prospérer** *vi* to thrive, flourish, prosper. ◆**prospérité** *nf* prosperity.

prostate [prɔstat] *nf* *Anat* prostate (gland).

prostern/er (se) [səprɔsterne] *vpr* to prostrate oneself (**devant** before). ◆**—é** *a* prostrate. ◆**—ement** *nm* prostration.

prostituer [prɔstitɥe] *vt* to prostitute; **— se p.** *vpr* to prostitute oneself. ◆**prostituée** *nf* prostitute. ◆**prostitution** *nf* prostitution.

prostré [prɔstre] *a* (*accablé*) prostrate. ◆**prostration** *nf* prostration.

protagoniste [prɔtagɔnist] *nmf* protagonist.

protecteur, -trice [prɔtɛktœr, -tris] *nmf* protector; (*mécène*) patron; *— a* (*geste etc*) & *Écon* protective; (*ton, air*) *Péj* patronizing. ◆**protection** *nf* protection; (*mécénat*) patronage; **de p.** (*écran etc*) protective. ◆**protectionnisme** *nm* *Écon* protectionism.

protég/er [prɔteʒe] *vt* to protect (**de** from, **contre** against); (*appuyer*) *Fig* to patronize; **— se p.** *vpr* to protect oneself. ◆**—é** *nm* protégé. ◆**—ée** *nf* protégée. ◆**protège-cahier** *nm* exercise book cover.

proteine [prɔtein] *nf* protein.

protestant, -ante [prɔtɛstɑ̃, -ɑ̃t] *a* & *nmf* Protestant. ◆**protestantisme** *nm* Protestantism.

protester [prɔteste] *vi* to protest (**contre** against); **p. de** (*son innocence etc*) to protest; *— vt* to protest (**que** that). ◆**protestation** *nf* protest (**contre** against); *pl* (*d'amitié*) protestations (**de** of).

prothèse [prɔtɛz] *nf* (**appareil de**) **p.** (*membre*) artificial limb; (*dents*) false teeth.

protocole [prɔtɔkɔl] *nm* protocol.

prototype [prɔtɔtip] *nm* prototype.

protubérance [prɔtyberɑ̃s] *nf* protuberance. ◆**protubérant** *a* (*yeux*) bulging; (*menton*) protruding.

proue [pru] *nf Nau* prow, bow(s).

prouesse [prues] *nf* feat, exploit.

prouver [pruve] *vt* to prove (**que** that).

Provence [prɔvɑ̃s] *nf* Provence. ◆**provençal, -ale, -aux** *a* & *nmf* Provençal.

provenir* [prɔvnir] *vi* **p. de** to come from. ◆**provenance** *nf* origin; **en p. de** from.

proverbe [prɔvɛrb] *nm* proverb. ◆**proverbial, -aux** *a* proverbial.

providence [prɔvidɑ̃s] *nf* providence. ◆**providentiel, -ielle** *a* providential.

province [prɔvɛ̃s] *nf* province; **la p.** the provinces; **en p.** in the provinces; **de p.** (*ville etc*) provincial. ◆**provincial, -ale, -aux** *a* & *nmf* provincial.

proviseur [prɔvizœr] *nm* (*de lycée*) headmaster.

provision [prɔvizjɔ̃] *nf* **1** (*réserve*) supply, stock; *pl* (*achats*) shopping; (*vivres*) provisions: **panier/sac à provisions** shopping basket/bag. **2** (*acompte*) advance payment; **chèque sans p.** dud cheque.

provisoire [prɔvizwar] *a* temporary, provisional. ◆**—ment** *adv* temporarily, provisionally.

provoquer [prɔvɔke] *vt* **1** (*causer*) to bring about, provoke; (*désir*) to arouse. **2** (*défier*) to provoke (*s.o.*). ◆**provocant** *a* provocative. ◆**provocateur** *nm* troublemaker. ◆**provocation** *nf* provocation.

proxénète [prɔksenɛt] *nm* pimp.

proximité [prɔksimite] *nf* closeness, proximity; **à p.** close by; **à p. de** close to.

prude [pryd] *a* prudish; *− nf* prude.

prudent [prydɑ̃] *a* (*circonspect*) cautious, careful; (*sage*) sensible. ◆**prudemment** [-amɑ̃] *adv* cautiously, carefully; (*sagement*) sensibly. ◆**prudence** *nf* caution, care, prudence; (*sagesse*) wisdom; **par p.** as a precaution.

prune [pryn] *nf* (*fruit*) plum. ◆**pruneau, -x** *nm* prune. ◆**prunelle** *nf* **1** (*fruit*) sloe. **2** (*de l'œil*) pupil. ◆**prunier** *nm* plum tree.

P.-S. [pees] *abrév* (*post-scriptum*) PS.

psaume [psom] *nm* psalm.

pseudo- [psødo] *préf* pseudo-.

pseudonyme [psødɔnim] *nm* pseudonym.

psychanalyse [psikanaliz] *nf* psychoanalysis. ◆**psychanalyste** *nmf* psychoanalyst.

psychiatre [psikjatr] *nmf* psychiatrist. ◆**psychiatrie** *nf* psychiatry. ◆**psychiatrique** *a* psychiatric.

psychique [psiʃik] *a* mental, psychic.

psycho [psiko] *préf* psycho-.

psychologie [psikɔlɔʒi] *nf* psychology. ◆**psychologique** *a* psychological. ◆**psychologue** *nmf* psychologist.

psychose [psikoz] *nf* psychosis.

PTT [petete] *nfpl* (*Postes, Télégraphes, Téléphones*) Post Office, = GPO.

pu [py] *voir* **pouvoir 1.**

puant [pɥɑ̃] *a* stinking. ◆**puanteur** *nf* stink, stench.

pub [pyb] *nf Fam* (*réclame*) advertising; (*annonce*) ad.

puberté [pybɛrte] *nf* puberty.

public, -ique [pyblik] *a* public; **dette publique** national debt; *− nm* public; (*de spectacle*) audience; **le grand p.** the general public; **en p.** in public. ◆**publiquement** *adv* publicly.

publication [pyblikasjɔ̃] *nf* (*action, livre etc*) publication. ◆**publier** *vt* to publish.

publicité [pyblisite] *nf* publicity (**pour** for); (*réclame*) advertising, publicity; (*annonce*) advertisement; *Rad TV* commercial. ◆**publicitaire** *a* (*agence, film*) publicity-, advertising-.

puce [pys] *nf* **1** flea; **le marché aux puces, les puces** the flea market. **2** (*d'un ordinateur*) chip, microchip.

puceron [pysrɔ̃] *nm* greenfly.

pudeur [pydœr] *nf* (*sense of*) modesty; **attentat à la p.** *Jur* indecency. ◆**pudibond** *a* prudish. ◆**pudique** *a* modest.

puer [pɥe] *vi* to stink; *− vt* to stink of.

puériculture [pɥerikyltyr] *nf* infant care, child care. ◆**puéricultrice** *nf* children's nurse.

puéril [pɥeril] *a* puerile. ◆**puérilité** *nf* puerility.

puis [pɥi] *adv* then; **et p. quoi?** and so what?

puiser [pɥize] *vt* to draw, take (**dans** from); *− vi* **p. dans** to dip into.

puisque [pɥisk(ə)] *conj* since, as.

puissant [pɥisɑ̃] *a* powerful. ◆**puissamment** *adv* powerfully. ◆**puissance** *nf* (*force, nation*) & *Math Tech* power; **en p.** (*talent, danger etc*) potential.

puits [pɥi] *nm* well; (*de mine*) shaft.

pull(-over) [pyl(ɔvɛr)] *nm* pullover, sweater.

pulluler [pylyle] *vi* (*Péj*) to swarm.

pulmonaire [pylmɔnɛr] *a* (*congestion, maladie*) of the lungs, lung-.

pulpe [pylp] *nf* (*de fruits*) pulp.

pulsation [pylsasjɔ̃] *nf* (heart)beat.

pulvériser [pylverize] *vt* (*broyer*) & *Fig* to pulverize; (*liquide*) to spray. ◆**pulvérisateur** *nm* spray, atomizer. ◆**pulvérisation** *nf* (*de liquide*) spraying.

punaise [pynɛz] *nf* **1** (*insecte*) bug. **2** (*clou*) drawing pin, *Am* thumbtack. ◆**punaiser** *vt* (*fixer*) to pin (up).

punch [pɔ̃ʃ] *nm* **1** (*boisson*) punch. **2** [pœnʃ] (*énergie*) punch.

punir [pynir] *vt* to punish. ◆**punissable** *a* punishable (**de** by). ◆**punition** *nf* punishment.

pupille [pypij] **1** *nf* (*de l'œil*) pupil. **2** *nmf* (*enfant sous tutelle*) ward.

pupitre [pypitr] *nm* (*d'écolier*) desk; (*d'orateur*) lectern; **p. à musique** music stand.

pur [pyr] *a* pure; (*alcool*) neat, straight. ◆**purement** *adv* purely. ◆**pureté** *nf* purity.

purée [pyre] *nf* purée; **p. (de pommes de terre)** mashed potatoes, mash.

purgatoire [pyrgatwar] *nm* purgatory.

purge [pyrʒ] *nf* *Pol Méd* purge.

purger [pyrʒe] *vt* **1** (*conduite*) *Tech* to drain, clear. **2** (*peine*) *Jur* to serve.

purifier [pyrifje] *vt* to purify. ◆**purification** *nf* purification.

purin [pyrɛ̃] *nm* liquid manure.

puriste [pyrist] *nmf Gram* purist.

puritain, -aine [pyritɛ̃, -ɛn] *a* & *nmf* puritan.

pur-sang [pyrsɑ̃] *nm inv* (*cheval*) thoroughbred.

pus¹ [py] *nm* (*liquide*) pus, matter.

pus², put [py] *voir* **pouvoir 1.**

putain [pytɛ̃] *nf Péj Fam* whore.

putois [pytwa] *nm* (*animal*) polecat.

putréfier [pytrefje] *vt*, **— se p.** *vpr* to putrefy. ◆**putréfaction** *nf* putrefaction.

puzzle [pœzl] *nm* (jigsaw) puzzle, jigsaw.

p.-v. [peve] *nm inv* (*procès-verbal*) (traffic) fine.

PVC [pevese] *nm* (*plastique*) PVC.

pygmée [pigme] *nm* pygmy.

pyjama [piʒama] *nm* pyjamas, *Am* pajamas; **un p.** a pair of pyjamas *ou Am* pajamas; **de p.** (*veste, pantalon*) pyjama-, *Am* pajama-.

pylône [pilon] *nm* pylon.

pyramide [piramid] *nf* pyramid.

Pyrénées [pirene] *nfpl* **les P.** the Pyrenees.

pyromane [pirɔman] *nmf* arsonist, firebug.

python [pitɔ̃] *nm* (*serpent*) python.

Q

Q, q [ky] *nm* Q, q.

QI [kyi] *nm inv abrév* (*quotient intellectuel*) IQ.

qu' [k] *voir* **que.**

quadrill/er [kadrije] *vt* (*troupes, police*) to be positioned throughout, comb, cover (*town etc*). ◆**—é** *a* (*papier*) squared. ◆**—age** *nm* (*lignes*) squares.

quadrupède [k(w)adryped] *nm* quadruped.

quadruple [k(w)adrypl] *a* **q. de** fourfold; — *nm* **le q. de** four times as much as. ◆**quadrupl/er** *vti* to quadruple. ◆**—és, -ées** *nmfpl* (*enfants*) quadruplets, quads.

quai [ke] *nm Nau* quay; (*pour marchandises*) wharf; (*de fleuve*) embankment, bank; *Rail* platform.

qualification [kalifikasjɔ̃] *nf* **1** description. **2** (*action*) *Sp* qualifying, qualification. ◆**qualificatif** *nm* (*mot*) term. ◆**qualifi/er 1** *vt* (*décrire*) to describe (**de** as); **se faire q. de menteur**/*etc* to be called a liar/*etc*. **2** *vt* (*rendre apte*) & *Sp* to qualify

(**pour qch** for sth, **pour faire** to do); **— se q.** *vpr Sp* to qualify (**pour** for). **3** *vt Gram* to qualify. ◆**—é** *a* qualified (**pour faire** to do); (*ouvrier, main-d'œuvre*) skilled.

qualité [kalite] *nf* quality; (*condition sociale etc*) occupation, status; **produit**/*etc* **de q.** high-quality product/*etc*; **en sa q. de** in one's capacity as. ◆**qualitatif, -ive** *a* qualitative.

quand [kɑ̃] *conj* & *adv* when; **q. je viendrai** when I come; **c'est pour q.?** (*réunion, mariage*) when is it?; **q. bien même vous le feriez** even if you did it; **q. même** all the same.

quant (à) [kɑ̃ta] *prép* as for.

quantité [kɑ̃tite] *nf* quantity; **une q., des quantités** (*beaucoup*) a lot (**de** of); **en q.** (*abondamment*) in plenty. ◆**quantifier** *vt* to quantify. ◆**quantitatif, -ive** *a* quantitative.

quarante [karɑ̃t] *a* & *nm* forty. ◆**quarantaine** *nf* **1** **une q. (de)** (*nombre*) (about) forty; **avoir la q.** (*âge*) to be about forty. **2** *Méd* quarantine; **mettre en q.** *Méd* to quarantine; *Fig* to send to Coventry, *Am* give the silent treatment to. ◆**quarantième** *a & nmf* fortieth.

quart [kar] *nm* **1** quarter; **q. (de litre)** quarter litre, quarter of a litre; **q. d'heure** quarter of an hour; **un mauvais q. d'heure** *Fig* a trying time; **il est une heure et q.** it's a quarter past *ou Am* after one; **une heure moins le q.** a quarter to one. **2** *Nau* watch; **de q.** on watch.

quartette [kwartɛt] *nm* (jazz) quartet(te).

quartier [kartje] **1** *nm* neighbourhood, district; (*chinois etc*) quarter; **de q.** (*cinéma etc*) local; **les gens du q.** the local people. **2** *nm* (*de pomme, lune*) quarter; (*d'orange*) segment. **3** *nm*(*pl*) **quartier(s)** *Mil* quarters; **q. général** headquarters.

quartz [kwarts] *nm* quartz; **montre**/*etc* **à q.** quartz watch/*etc*.

quasi [kazi] *adv* almost. ◆**quasi-** *préf* near; **q.-obscurité** near darkness. ◆**quasiment** *adv* almost.

quatorze [katɔrz] *a & nm* fourteen. ◆**quatorzième** *a & nmf* fourteenth.

quatre [katr] *a & nm* four; **se mettre en q.** to go out of one's way (**pour faire** to do); **son q. heures** (*goûter*) one's afternoon snack; **un de ces q.** *Fam* some day soon. ◆**quatrième** *a & nmf* fourth. ◆**quatrièmement** *adv* fourthly.

quatre-vingt(s) [katrəvɛ̃] *a & nm* eighty; **q.-vingts ans** eighty years; **q.-vingt-un** eighty-one. ◆**q.-vingt-dix** *a & nm* ninety.

quatuor [kwatɥɔr] *nm Mus* quartet(te).

que [k(ə)] (**qu'** before a vowel or mute h) **1** *conj* that; **je pense qu'elle restera** I think (that) she'll stay; **qu'elle vienne ou non** whether she comes or not; **qu'il s'en aille!** let him leave!; **ça fait un an q. je suis là** I've been here for a year; **ça fait un an q. je suis parti** I left a year ago. **2** (*ne*) . . . **q.** only; **tu n'as qu'un franc** you only have one franc. **3** (*comparaison*) than; (*avec aussi, même, tel, autant*) as; **plus/moins âgé q.** lui older/younger than him; **aussi sage**/*etc* **q.** as wise/*etc* as; **le même q.** the same as. **4** *adv* (**ce**) **qu'il est bête!** (*comme*) how silly he is!; **q. de gens!** (*combien*) what a lot of people! **5** *pron rel* (*chose*) that, which; (*personne*) that, whom; (*temps*) when; **le livre q. j'ai** the book (that *ou* which) I have; **l'ami q. j'ai** the friend (that *ou* whom) I have; **un jour/mois**/*etc* **q.** one day/month/*etc* when. **6** *pron interrogatif* what; **q. fait-il?**, **qu'est-ce qu'il fait?** what is he doing?; **qu'est-ce qui est dans ta poche?** what's in your pocket?; **q. préférez-vous?** which do you prefer?

Québec [kebɛk] *nm* **le Q.** Quebec.

quel, quelle [kɛl] **1** *a interrogatif* what, which; (*qui*) who; **q. livre/acteur?** what *ou* which book/actor?; **q. livre/acteur préférez-vous?** which *ou* what book/actor do you prefer?; **q. est cet homme?** who is that man?; **je sais q. est ton but** I know what your aim is; **q. qu'il soit** (*chose*) whatever it may be; (*personne*) whoever it *ou* he may be; – *pron interrogatif* which (one); **q. est le meilleur?** which (one) is the best? **2** *a exclamatif* **q. idiot!** what a fool!; **q. joli bébé!** what a pretty baby!

quelconque [kɛlkɔ̃k] *a* **1** any, some (or other); **une raison q.** any reason (whatever *ou* at all), some reason (or other). **2** (*banal*) ordinary.

quelque [kɛlk(ə)] **1** *a* some; **q. jour** some day; **quelques femmes** a few women, some women; **les quelques amies qu'elle a** the few friends she has. **2** *adv* (*environ*) about, some; **et q.** *Fam* and a bit; **q. grand qu'il soit** however tall he may be; **q. numéro qu'elle choisisse** whichever number she chooses; **q. peu** somewhat. **3** *pron* **q. chose** something; (*interrogation*) anything, something; **il a q. chose** *Fig* there's something the matter with him; **q. chose d'autre** something else; **q. chose de grand**/*etc* something big/*etc*. **4** *adv* **q. part** somewhere; (*interrogation*) anywhere, somewhere.

quelquefois [kɛlkəfwa] *adv* sometimes.

quelques-uns, -unes [kɛlkəzœ̃, -yn] *pron pl* some.

quelqu'un [kɛlkœ̃] *pron* someone, somebody; (*interrogation*) anyone, anybody, someone, somebody; **q. d'intelligent**/*etc* someone clever/*etc*.

quémander [kemɑ̃de] *vt* to beg for.

qu'en-dira-t-on [kɑ̃diratɔ̃] *nm inv* (*propos*) gossip.

quenelle [kənɛl] *nf Culin* quenelle, fish *ou* meat roll.

querelle [kərɛl] *nf* quarrel, dispute. ◆**se quereller** *vpr* to quarrel. ◆**querelleur, -euse** *a* quarrelsome.

question [kɛstjɔ̃] *nf* question; (*affaire, problème*) matter, issue, question; **il est q. de** it's a matter *ou* question of (**faire** doing); (*on projette de*) there's some question of (**faire** doing); **il n'en est pas q.** there's no question of it, it's out of the question; **en q.** in question; **hors de q.** out of the question;

(re)mettre en q. to (call in) question. ◆**questionner** *vt* to question (**sur** about).
quête [kɛt] *nf* **1** (*collecte*) collection. **2** (*recherche*) quest (**de** for); **en q. de** in quest *ou* search of. ◆**quêter** *vt* to seek, beg for; – *vi* to collect money.
queue [kø] *nf* **1** (*d'animal*) tail; (*de fleur*) stalk, stem; (*de fruit*) stalk; (*de poêle*) handle; (*de comète*) trail; (*de robe*) train; (*de cortège, train*) rear; **q. de cheval** (*coiffure*) ponytail; **faire une q. de poisson** *Aut* to cut in (**à qn** in front of s.o.); **à la q. de** (*classe*) at the bottom of; **à la q. leu leu** (*marcher*) in single file. **2** (*file*) queue, *Am* line; **faire la q.** to queue up, *Am* line up. **3** (*de billard*) cue. ◆**q.-de-pie** *nf* (*pl* queues-de-pie) (*habit*) tails.
qui [ki] *pron* (*personne*) who, that; (*interrogatif*) who; (*après prép*) whom; (*chose*) which, that; **l'homme q.** the man who *ou* that; **la maison q.** the house which *ou* that; **q.?** who?; **q. (est-ce q.) est là?** who's there?; **q. désirez-vous voir?, q. est-ce que vous désirez voir?** who(m) do you want to see?; **sans q.** without whom; **la femme de q. je parle** the woman I'm talking about *ou* about whom I'm talking; **l'ami sur l'aide de q. je compte** the friend on whose help I rely; **q. que vous soyez** whoever you are, whoever you may be; **q. que ce soit** anyone (at all); **à q. est ce livre?** whose book is this?
quiche [kiʃ] *nf* (*tarte*) quiche.
quiconque [kikɔ̃k] *pron* (*celui qui*) whoever; (*n'importe qui*) anyone.
quignon [kiɲɔ̃] *nm* chunk (of bread).
quille [kij] *nf* **1** (*de navire*) keel. **2** (*de jeu*) skittle; *pl* (*jeu*) skittles, ninepins. **3** (*jambe*) *Fam* leg.
quincaillier, -ière [kɛ̃kaje, -jɛr] *nmf* hardware dealer, ironmonger. ◆**quincaillerie** *nf* hardware; (*magasin*) hardware shop.
quinine [kinin] *nf* *Méd* quinine.
quinquennal, -aux [kɛ̃kenal, -o] *a* (*plan*) five-year.
quinte [kɛ̃t] *nf* *Méd* coughing fit.

quintessence [kɛ̃tesɑ̃s] *nf* quintessence.
quintette [kɛ̃tɛt] *nm* *Mus* quintet(te).
quintuple [kɛ̃typl] *a* **q. de** fivefold; – *nm* le **q. de** five times as much as. ◆**quintupl/er** *vti* to increase fivefold. ◆**-és, -ées** *nmfpl* (*enfants*) quintuplets, quins.
quinze [kɛ̃z] *a & nm* fifteen; **q. jours** two weeks, fortnight. ◆**quinzaine** *nf* **une q.** (**de**) (*nombre*) (about) fifteen; **q. (de jours)** two weeks, fortnight. ◆**quinzième** *a & nmf* fifteenth.
quiproquo [kiprɔko] *nm* misunderstanding.
quittance [kitɑ̃s] *nf* receipt.
quitte [kit] *a* quits, even (**envers** with); **q. à faire** even if it means doing; **en être q. pour une amende/etc** to (be lucky enough to) get off with a fine/etc.
quitter [kite] *vt* to leave; (*ôter*) to take off; – *vi* **ne quittez pas!** *Tél* hold the line!, hold on!; – **se q.** *vpr* (*se séparer*) to part.
qui-vive (sur le) [syrləkiviv] *adv* on the alert.
quoi [kwa] *pron* what; (*après prép*) which; **à q. penses-tu?** what are you thinking about?; **après q.** after which; **ce à q. je m'attendais** what I was expecting; **de q. manger/etc** (*assez*) enough to eat/etc; **de q. couper/écrire/etc** (*instrument*) something to cut/write/etc with; **q. que je dise** whatever I say; **q. que ce soit** anything (at all); **q. qu'il en soit** be that as it may; **il n'y a pas de q.!** (*en réponse à 'merci'*) don't mention it!; **q.? what?; c'est un idiot, q.!** (*non traduit*) *Fam* he's a fool!
quoique [kwak(ə)] *conj* (+ *sub*) (al)though.
quolibet [kɔlibe] *nm* *Litt* gibe.
quorum [k(w)ɔrɔm] *nm* quorum.
quota [k(w)ɔta] *nm* quota.
quote-part [kɔtpar] *nf* (*pl* quotes-parts) share.
quotidien, -ienne [kɔtidjɛ̃, -jɛn] *a* (*journalier*) daily; (*banal*) everyday; – *nm* daily (paper). ◆**quotidiennement** *adv* daily.
quotient [kɔsjɑ̃] *nm* quotient.

R

R, r [ɛr] *nm* R, r.
rabâch/er [rabaʃe] *vt* to repeat endlessly; – *vi* to repeat oneself ◆**–age** *nm* endless repetition.
rabais [rabɛ] *nm* (price) reduction, discount; **au r.** (*acheter*) cheap, at a reduction.
rabaisser [rabese] *vt* (*dénigrer*) to belittle, humble; **r. à** (*ravaler*) to reduce to.
rabat-joie [rabaʒwa] *nm inv* killjoy.

rabattre* [rabatr] vt (baisser) to put ou pull down; (refermer) to close (down); (replier) to fold down ou over; (déduire) to take off; **en r.** (prétentieux) Fig to climb down (from one's high horse); **— se r.** vpr (se refermer) to close; (après avoir doublé) Aut to cut in (**devant** in front of); **se r. sur** Fig to fall back on.

rabbin [rabɛ̃] nm rabbi; **grand r.** chief rabbi.

rabibocher [rabibɔʃe] vt (réconcilier) Fam to patch it up between; **— se r.** vpr Fam to patch it up.

rabiot [rabjo] nm (surplus) Fam extra (helping); **faire du r.** Fam to work extra time.

râblé [rɑble] a stocky, thickset.

rabot [rabo] nm (outil) plane. ◆**raboter** vt to plane.

raboteux, -euse [rabɔtø, -øz] a uneven, rough.

rabougri [rabugri] a (personne, plante) stunted.

rabrouer [rabrue] vt to snub, rebuff.

racaille [rakɑj] nf rabble, riffraff.

raccommod/er [rakɔmɔde] **1** vt to mend; (chaussette) to darn. **2** vt (réconcilier) Fam to reconcile; **— se r.** vpr Fam to make it up (**avec** with). ◆**—age** nm mending; darning.

raccompagner [rakɔ̃paɲe] vt to see ou take back (home); **r. à la porte** to see to the door, see out.

raccord [rakɔr] nm (dispositif) connection; (de papier peint) join; **r. (de peinture)** touch-up. ◆**raccord/er** vt, **— se r.** vpr to connect (up), join (up) (**à** with, to). ◆**—ement** nm (action, résultat) connection.

raccourc/ir [rakursir] vt to shorten; **—** vi to get shorter; (au lavage) to shrink. ◆**—i** nm **1** (chemin) short cut. **2 en r.** (histoire etc) in a nutshell.

raccroc (par) [parrakro] adv by (a lucky) chance.

raccrocher [rakrɔʃe] vt to hang back up; (récepteur) Tél to put down; (relier) to connect (**à** with, to); (client) to accost; **se r. à** to hold on to, cling to; (se rapporter à) to link (up) with; **—** vi Tél to hang up, ring off.

race [ras] nf (groupe ethnique) race; (animale) breed; (famille) stock; (engeance) Péj breed; **de r.** (chien) pedigree-; (cheval) thoroughbred. ◆**racé** a (chien) pedigree-; (cheval) thoroughbred; (personne) distinguished. ◆**racial, -aux** a racial. ◆**racisme** nm racism, racialism. ◆**raciste** a & nmf racist, racialist.

rachat [raʃa] nm Com repurchase; (de firme)

take-over; Rel redemption. ◆**racheter** vt to buy back; (objet d'occasion) to buy; (nouvel article) to buy another; (firme) to take over, buy out; (pêcheur, dette) to redeem; (compenser) to make up for; **r. des chaussettes/du pain/etc** to buy (some) more socks/bread/etc; **— se r.** vpr to make amends, redeem oneself.

racine [rasin] nf (de plante, personne etc) & Math root; **prendre r.** (plante) & Fig to take root.

racket [raket] nm (association) racket; (activité) racketeering.

raclée [rɑkle] nf Fam hiding, thrashing.

racler [rɑkle] vt to scrape; (enlever) to scrape off; **se r. la gorge** to clear one's throat. ◆**raclette** nf scraper; (à vitres) squeegee. ◆**racloir** nm scraper. ◆**raclures** nfpl (déchets) scrapings.

racol/er [rakɔle] vt (prostituée) to solicit (s.o.); (vendeur etc) to tout for (s.o.), solicit (s.o.). ◆**—age** nm soliciting; touting. ◆**—eur, -euse** nmf tout.

raconter [rakɔ̃te] vt (histoire) to tell, relate; (décrire) to describe; **r. qch à qn** (vacances etc) to tell s.o. about sth; **r. à qn que** to tell s.o. that, say to s.o. that. ◆**racontars** nmpl gossip, stories.

racornir [rakɔrnir] vt to harden; **— se r.** vpr to get hard.

radar [radar] nm radar; **contrôle r.** (pour véhicules etc) radar control. ◆**radariste** nmf radar operator.

rade [rad] nf **1** Nau (natural) harbour. **2 laisser en r.** to leave stranded, abandon; **rester en r.** to be left behind.

radeau, -x [rado] nm raft.

radiateur [radjatœr] nm (à eau) & Aut radiator; (électrique, à gaz) heater.

radiation [radjasjɔ̃] nf **1** Phys radiation. **2** (suppression) removal (**de** from).

radical, -ale, -aux [radikal, -o] a radical; **—** nm Ling stem; **—** nmf Pol radical.

radier [radje] vt to strike ou cross off (**de** from).

radieux, -euse [radjø, -øz] a (personne, visage) radiant, beaming; (soleil) brilliant; (temps) glorious.

radin, -ine [radɛ̃, -in] a Fam stingy; **—** nmf Fam skinflint.

radio [radjo] **1** nf radio; (poste) radio (set); **à la r.** on the radio. **2** nf (photo) Méd X-ray; **passer** ou **faire une r.** to be X-rayed, have an X-ray. **3** nm (opérateur) radio operator. ◆**radioactif, -ive** a radioactive. ◆**radioactivité** nf radioactivity. ◆**radiodiffuser** vt to broadcast (on the radio). ◆**radio-**

diffusion *nf* broadcasting. ◆**radiographie** *nf* (*photo*) X-ray; (*technique*) radiography. ◆**radiographier** *vt* to X-ray. ◆**radiologie** *nf* *Méd* radiology. ◆**radiologue** *nmf* (*technicien*) radiographer; (*médecin*) radiologist. ◆**radiophonique** *a* (*programme*) radio-. ◆**radiotélévisé** *a* broadcast on radio and television.

radis [radi] *nm* radish; **r. noir** horseradish.

radot/er [radɔte] *vi* to drivel (on), ramble (on). ◆**—age** *nm* (*propos*) drivel.

radouc/ir (se) [səradusir] *vpr* to calm down; (*temps*) to become milder. ◆**—issement** *nm* **r.** (**du temps**) milder weather.

rafale [rafal] *nf* (*vent*) gust, squall; (*de mitrailleuse*) burst; (*de balles*) hail.

raffermir [rafɛrmir] *vt* to strengthen; (*muscles etc*) to tone up; — **se r.** *vpr* to become stronger.

raffin/er [rafine] *vt* (*pétrole, sucre, manières*) to refine. ◆**—é** *a* refined. ◆**—age** *nm* (*du pétrole, sucre*) refining. ◆**—ement** *nm* (*de personne*) refinement. ◆**raffinerie** *nf* refinery.

raffoler [rafɔle] *vi* **r. de** (*aimer*) to be very fond of, be mad *ou* wild about.

raffut [rafy] *nm* *Fam* din, row.

rafiot [rafjo] *nm* (*bateau*) *Péj* (old) tub.

rafistoler [rafistɔle] *vt* *Fam* to patch up.

rafle [rafl] *nf* (*police*) raid.

rafler [rafle] *vt* (*enlever*) *Fam* to swipe, make off with.

rafraîch/ir [rafreʃir] *vt* to cool (down); (*remettre à neuf*) to brighten up; (*mémoire, personne*) to refresh; — *vi* **mettre à r.** *Culin* to chill; — **se r.** *vpr* (*boire*) to refresh oneself; (*se laver*) to freshen (oneself) up; (*temps*) to get cooler. ◆**—issant** *a* refreshing. ◆**—issement** *nm* **1** (*de température*) cooling. **2** (*boisson*) cold drink; *pl* (*fruits, glaces etc*) refreshments.

ragaillardir [ragajardir] *vt* to buck up.

rage [raʒ] *nf* **1** (*colère*) rage; **r. de dents** violent toothache; **faire r.** (*incendie, tempête*) to rage. **2** (*maladie*) rabies. ◆**rager** *vi* (*personne*) *Fam* to rage, fume. ◆**rageant** *a* *Fam* infuriating. ◆**rageur, -euse** *a* bad-tempered, furious.

ragots [rago] *nmpl* *Fam* gossip.

ragoût [ragu] *nm* *Culin* stew.

ragoûtant [ragutɑ̃] *a* **peu r.** (*mets, personne*) unsavory.

raid [rɛd] *nm* (*incursion, attaque*) *Mil Av* raid.

raide [rɛd] *a* (*rigide, guindé*) stiff; (*côte*) steep; (*cheveux*) straight; (*corde etc*) tight; **c'est r.!** (*exagéré*) *Fam* it's a bit stiff *ou*

much!; — *adv* (*grimper*) steeply; **tomber r. mort** to drop dead. ◆**raideur** *nf* stiffness; steepness. ◆**raidillon** *nm* (*pente*) short steep rise. ◆**raidir** *vt*, — **se r.** *vpr* to stiffen; (*corde*) to tighten; (*position*) to harden; **se r. contre** *Fig* to steel oneself against.

raie [rɛ] *nf* **1** (*trait*) line; (*de tissu, zèbre*) stripe; (*de cheveux*) parting, *Am* part. **2** (*poisson*) skate, ray.

rail [raj] *nm* (*barre*) rail; **le r.** (*transport*) rail.

railler [raje] *vt* to mock, make fun of. ◆**raillerie** *nf* gibe, mocking remark. ◆**railleur, -euse** *a* mocking.

rainure [renyr] *nf* groove.

raisin [rezɛ̃] *nm* raisin(s) grapes; **grain de r.** grape; **manger du r.** *ou* **des raisins** to eat grapes; **r. sec** raisin.

raison [rezɔ̃] *nf* **1** (*faculté, motif*) reason; **entendre r.** to listen to reason; **la r. pour laquelle je . . .** the reason (why *ou* that) I . . . ; **pour raisons de famille/de santé/etc** for family/health/*etc* reasons; **en r. de** (*cause*) on account of; **à r. de** (*proportion*) at the rate of; **avoir r. de qn/de qch** to get the better of s.o./sth; **mariage de r.** marriage of convenience; **à plus forte r.** all the more so; **r. de plus** all the more reason (**pour faire** to do, for doing). **2 avoir r.** to be right (**de faire** to do, in doing); **donner r. à qn** to agree with s.o.; (*événement etc*) to prove s.o. right; **avec r.** rightly. ◆**raisonnable** *a* reasonable. ◆**raisonnablement** *adv* reasonably.

raisonn/er [rezɔne] *vi* (*penser*) to reason; (*discuter*) to argue; — *vt* **r. qn** to reason with s.o. ◆**—é** *a* (*projet*) well-thought-out. ◆**—ement** *nm* (*faculté, activité*) reasoning; (*propositions*) argument. ◆**—eur, -euse** *a* *Péj* argumentative; — *nmf* *Péj* arguer.

rajeun/ir [raʒœnir] *vt* to make (feel *ou* look) younger; (*personnel*) to infuse new blood into; (*moderniser*) to modernize, update; (*personne âgée*) *Méd* to rejuvenate; — *vi* to get *ou* feel *ou* look younger. ◆**—issant** *a* *Méd* rejuvenating. ◆**—issement** *nm* *Méd* rejuvenation; **le r. de la population** the population getting younger.

rajout [raʒu] *nm* addition. ◆**rajouter** *vt* to add (à to); **en r.** *Fig* to overdo it.

rajuster [raʒyste] *vt* (*mécanisme*) to readjust; (*lunettes, vêtements*) to straighten, adjust; (*cheveux*) to rearrange; — **se r.** *vpr* to straighten up *ou* tidy oneself up.

râle [rɑl] *nm* (*de blessé*) groan; (*de mourant*) death rattle. ◆**râler** *vi* (*blessé*) to groan; (*mourant*) to give the death rattle; (*protes-*

er) *Fam* to grouse, moan. ◆**râleur, -euse** *nmf Fam* grouser, moaner.

ralent/ir [ralɑ̃tir] *vti*, **— se r.** *vpr* to slow down. ◆**—i** *nm Cin TV* slow motion; **au r.** (*filmer, travailler*) in slow motion; (*vivre*) at a slower pace; **tourner au r.** (*moteur, usine*) to idle, tick over, *Am* turn over.

rallier [ralje] *vt* (*rassembler*) to rally; (*rejoindre*) to rejoin; **r. qn à** (*convertir*) to win s.o. over to; **— se r.** *vpr* (*se regrouper*) to rally; **se r. à** (*point de vue*) to come over *ou* round to.

rallonge [ralɔ̃ʒ] *nf* (*de table*) extension; (*fil électrique*) extension (lead); (*de*) (*supplément*) *Fam* (some) extra. ◆**rallonger** *vti* to lengthen.

rallumer [ralyme] *vt* to light again, relight; (*lampe*) to switch on again; (*conflit, haine*) to rekindle; **— se r.** *vpr* (*guerre, incendie*) to flare up again.

rallye [rali] *nm Sp Aut* rally.

ramage [ramaʒ] **1** *nm* (*d'oiseaux*) song, warbling. **2** *nmpl* (*dessin*) foliage.

ramass/er [ramase] **1** *vt* (*prendre par terre, réunir*) to pick up; (*ordures, copies*) to collect, pick up; (*fruits, coquillages*) to gather; (*rhume, amende*) *Fam* to pick up, get; **r. une bûche** *ou* **une pelle** *Fam* to come a cropper, *Am* take a spill. **2 se r.** *vpr* (*se pelotonner*) to curl up. ◆**—é** *a* (*trapu*) squat, stocky; (*recroquevillé*) huddled; (*concis*) compact. ◆**—age** *nm* picking up; collection; gathering; **r. scolaire** school bus service.

ramassis [ramasi] *nm* **r. de** (*voyous etc*) *Péj* bunch of.

rambarde [rɑ̃bard] *nf* guardrail.

rame [ram] *nf* **1** (*aviron*) oar. **2** (*de métro*) train. **3** (*de papier*) ream. ◆**ramer** *vi* to row. ◆**rameur, -euse** *nmf* rower.

rameau, -x [ramo] *nm* branch; **les Rameaux** *Rel* Palm Sunday.

ramener [ramne] *vt* to bring *ou* take back; (*paix, calme, ordre etc*) to restore, bring back; (*remettre en place*) to put back; **r. à** (*réduire à*) to reduce to; **r. à la vie** to bring back to life; **— se r.** *vpr* (*arriver*) *Fam* to turn up; **se r. à** (*problème etc*) to boil down to.

ramier [ramje] *nm* (*pigeon*) **r.** wood pigeon.

ramification [ramifikasjɔ̃] *nf* ramification.

ramoll/ir [ramɔlir] *vt*, **— se r.** *vpr* to soften. ◆**—i** *a* soft; (*personne*) soft-headed.

ramon/er [ramone] *vt* (*cheminée*) to sweep. ◆**—age** *nm* (*chimney*) sweeping. ◆**—eur** *nm* (*chimney*)sweep.

rampe [rɑ̃p] *nf* **1** (*pente*) ramp, slope; **r. de lancement** (*de fusées etc*) launch(ing) pad. **2**

(*d'escalier*) banister(s). **3** (*projecteurs*) *Th* footlights.

ramper [rɑ̃pe] *vi* to crawl; (*plante*) to creep; **r. devant** *Fig* to cringe *ou* crawl to.

rancard [rɑ̃kar] *nm Fam* (*rendez-vous*) date; (*renseignement*) tip.

rancart [rɑ̃kar] *nm* **mettre au r.** *Fam* to throw out, scrap.

rance [rɑ̃s] *a* rancid. ◆**rancir** *vi* to turn rancid.

ranch [rɑ̃tʃ] *nm* ranch.

rancœur [rɑ̃kœr] *nf* rancour, resentment.

rançon [rɑ̃sɔ̃] *nf* ransom; **la r. de** (*inconvénient*) the price of (*success, fame etc*). ◆**rançonner** *vt* to hold to ransom.

rancune [rɑ̃kyn] *nf* grudge; **garder r. à qn** to bear s.o. a grudge; **sans r.!** no hard feelings! ◆**rancunier, -ière** *a* vindictive, resentful.

randonnée [rɑ̃dɔne] *nf* (*à pied*) walk, hike; (*en voiture*) drive, ride; (*en vélo*) ride.

rang [rɑ̃] *nm* (*rangée*) row, line; (*condition, grade, classement*) rank; **les rangs** (*hommes*) *Mil* the ranks (**de** of); **les rangs de ses ennemis** (*nombre*) *Fig* the ranks of his enemies; **se mettre en rang(s)** to line up (**par trois**/*etc* in threes/*etc*); **par r. de** in order of. ◆**rangée** *nf* row, line.

rang/er [rɑ̃ʒe] *vt* (*papiers, vaisselle etc*) to put away; (*chambre etc*) to tidy (up); (*chiffres, mots*) to arrange; (*voiture*) to park; **se r. parmi** (*auteur etc*) to rank among; **— se r.** *vpr* (*élèves etc*) to line up; (*s'écarter*) to stand aside; (*voiture*) to pull over; (*s'assagir*) to settle down; **se r. à** (*avis de qn*) to fall in with. ◆**—é** *a* (*chambre etc*) tidy; (*personne*) steady; (*bataille*) pitched. ◆**—ement** *nm* putting away; (*de chambre etc*) tidying (up); (*espace*) storage space.

ranimer [ranime] *vt* (*réanimer, revigorer*) to revive; (*encourager*) to spur on; (*feu, querelle*) to rekindle.

rapace [rapas] **1** *a* (*avide*) grasping. **2** *nm* (*oiseau*) bird of prey.

rapatrier [rapatrije] *vt* to repatriate. ◆**rapatriement** *nm* repatriation.

râpe [rɑp] *nf Culin* grater; shredder; (*lime*) rasp. ◆**râp/er** *vt* (*fromage*) to grate; (*carottes etc*) to shred, (*finement*) to grate; (*bois*) to rasp. ◆**—é 1** *a* (*fromage*) grated; **—** *nm* grated cheese. **2** *a* (*vêtement*) threadbare.

rapetisser [raptise] *vt* to make (look) smaller; (*vêtement*) to shorten; **—** *vi* to get smaller; (*au lavage*) to shrink; (*jours*) to get shorter.

râpeux, -euse [rɑpø, -øz] *a* rough.

raphia [rafja] *nm* raffia.

rapide [rapid] *a* fast, quick, rapid; (*pente*) steep; – *nm* (*train*) express (train); (*de fleuve*) rapid. ◆**—ment** *adv* fast, quickly, rapidly. ◆**rapidité** *nf* speed, rapidity.

rapiécer [rapjese] *vt* to patch (up).

rappel [rapɛl] *nm* (*de diplomate etc*) recall; (*évocation, souvenir*) reminder; (*paiement*) back pay; *pl Th* curtain calls; (**vaccination de**) **r.** *Méd* booster; **r. à l'ordre** call to order. ◆**rappeler** *vt* (*pour faire revenir*) & *Tél* to call back; (*diplomate, souvenir*) to recall; **r. qch à qn** (*redire*) to remind s.o. of sth; – *vi Tél* to call back; – **se r.** *vpr* (*histoire, personne etc*) to remember, recall, recollect.

rappliquer [raplike] *vi* (*arriver*) *Fam* to show up.

rapport [rapɔr] *nm* **1** (*lien*) connection, link; *pl* (*entre personnes*) relations; **rapports (sexuels)** (sexual) intercourse; **par r.** à compared to *ou* with; (*envers*) towards; **se mettre en r. avec qn** to get in touch with s.o.; **en r. avec** in keeping with; **sous le r. de** from the point of view of. **2** (*revenu*) *Com* return, yield. **3** (*récit*) report. ◆**rapporter 1** *vt* (*ramener*) to bring *ou* take back; (*ajouter*) to add; – *vi* (*chien*) to retrieve. **2** *vt* (*récit*) to report; (*mot célèbre*) to repeat; – *vi* (*moucharder*) *Fam* to tell tales. **3** *vt* (*profit*) *Com* to bring in, yield; – *vi* (*investissement*) *Com* to bring in a good return. **4** *vt* **r. qch à** (*rattacher*) to relate sth to; **se r. à** to relate to, be connected with; **s'en r. à** to rely on. ◆**rapporteur, -euse 1** *nmf* (*mouchard*) telltale. **2** *nm Jur* reporter. **3** *nm Géom* protractor.

rapproch/er [raprɔʃe] *vt* to bring closer (**de** to); (*chaise*) to pull up (**de** to); (*réconcilier*) to bring together; (*réunir*) to join; (*comparer*) to compare; – **se r.** *vpr* to come *ou* get closer (**de** to); (*se réconcilier*) to come together, be reconciled; (*ressembler*) to be close (**de** to). ◆**—é** *a* close, near; (*yeux*) close-set; (*fréquent*) frequent. ◆**—ement** *nm* (*réconciliation*) reconciliation; (*rapport*) connection; (*comparaison*) comparison.

rapt [rapt] *nm* (*d'enfant*) abduction.

raquette [rakɛt] *nf* (*de tennis*) racket; (*de ping-pong*) bat.

rare [rar] *a* rare; (*argent, main-d'œuvre etc*) scarce; (*barbe, herbe*) sparse; **il est r. que** (+ *sub*) it's seldom *ou* rare that. ◆**se raréfier** *vpr* (*denrées etc*) to get scarce. ◆**rarement** *adv* rarely, seldom. ◆**rareté** *nf* rarity; scarcity; **une r.** (*objet*) a rarity.

ras [rɑ] *a* (*cheveux*) close-cropped; (*herbe, poil*) short; (*mesure*) full; **en rase campagne** in (the) open country; **à r. de** very close to; **à r. bord** (*remplir*) to the brim; **en avoir r. le bol** *Fam* to be fed up (**de** with); **pull (au) r. du cou** *ou* **à col r.** crew-neck(ed) pullover; – *adv* short.

ras/er [rɑze] **1** *vt* (*menton, personne*) to shave; (*barbe, moustache*) to shave off; – **se r.** *vpr* to (have a) shave. **2** *vt* (*démolir*) to raze, knock down. **3** *vt* (*frôler*) to skim, brush. **4** *vt* (*ennuyer*) *Fam* to bore. ◆**—ant** *a Fam* boring. ◆**—é** *a* **bien r.** clean-shaven; **mal r.** unshaven. ◆**—age** *nm* shaving. ◆**—eur, -euse** *nmf Fam* bore. ◆**rasoir 1** *nm* shaver. **2** *a inv Fam* boring.

rassasier [rasazje] *vti* to satisfy; **être rassasié** to have had enough (**de** of).

rassembler [rasãble] *vt* to gather (together), assemble; (*courage*) to summon up, muster; – **se r.** *vpr* to gather, assemble. ◆**rassemblement** *nm* (*action, gens*) gathering.

rasseoir* **(se)** [səraswar] *vpr* to sit down again.

rassis, *f* **rassie** [rasi] *a* (*pain, brioche etc*) stale. ◆**rassir** *vti* to turn stale.

rassur/er [rasyre] *vt* to reassure; **rassure-toi** set your mind at rest, don't worry. ◆**—ant** *a* (*nouvelle*) reassuring, comforting.

rat [ra] *nm* rat; **r. de bibliothèque** *Fig* bookworm.

ratatiner (se) [səratatine] *vpr* to shrivel (up); (*vieillard*) to become wizened.

rate [rat] *nf Anat* spleen.

râteau, -x [rɑto] *nm* (*outil*) rake.

râtelier [rɑtəlje] *nm* **1** (*support pour outils, armes etc*) rack. **2** (*dentier*) *Fam* set of false teeth.

rat/er [rate] *vt* (*bus, cible, occasion etc*) to miss; (*gâcher*) to spoil, ruin; (*vie*) to waste; (*examen*) to fail; – *vi* (*projet etc*) to fail; (*pistolet*) to misfire. ◆**—é, -ée 1** *nmf* (*personne*) failure. **2** *nmpl* **avoir des ratés** *Aut* to backfire. ◆**—age** *nm* (*échec*) *Fam* failure.

ratifier [ratifje] *vt* to ratify. ◆**ratification** *nf* ratification.

ration [rasjɔ̃] *nf* ration; **r. de** *Fig* share of. ◆**rationn/er** *vt* (*vivres, personne*) to ration. ◆**—ement** *nm* rationing.

rationaliser [rasjonalize] *vt* to rationalize. ◆**rationalisation** *nf* rationalization.

rationnel, -elle [rasjonɛl] *a* (*pensée, méthode*) rational.

ratisser [ratise] *vt* **1** (*allée etc*) to rake; (*feuilles etc*) to rake up. **2** (*fouiller*) to comb. **3 r. qn** (*au jeu*) *Fam* to clean s.o. out.

raton [ratɔ̃] *nm* **r. laveur** rac(c)oon.

rattach/er [rataʃe] *vt* to tie up again; (*in-*

corporer, joindre) to join (**à** to); (*idée, question*) to bind s.o. to; **se r. à** (*son pays etc*) to be linked to. ◆**—ement** *nm* (*annexion*) joining (**à** to).

rattrap/er [ratrape] *vt* to catch; (*prisonnier etc*) to recapture; (*erreur, temps perdu*) to make up for; **r. qn** (*rejoindre*) to catch up with s.o., catch s.o. up; **— se r.** *vpr* to catch up; (*se dédommager, prendre une compensation*) to make up for it; **se r. à** (*branche etc*) to catch hold of. ◆**—age** *nm* **cours de r.** *Scol* remedial classes; **r. des prix/salaires** adjustment of prices/wages (*to the cost of living*).

rature [ratyr] *nf* deletion. ◆**raturer** *vt* to delete, cross out.

rauque [rok] *a* (*voix*) hoarse, raucous.

ravages [ravaʒ] *nmpl* devastation; (*de la maladie, du temps*) ravages; **faire des r.** to wreak havoc. ◆**ravager** *vt* to devastate, ravage.

raval/er [ravale] *vt* **1** (*façade etc*) to clean (and restore). **2** (*salive, sanglots*) to swallow. **3** (*avilir*) *Litt* to lower. ◆**—ement** *nm* (*de façade etc*) cleaning (and restoration).

ravi [ravi] *a* delighted (**de** with, **de faire** to do).

ravier [ravje] *nm* hors-d'œuvre dish.

ravigoter [ravigɔte] *vt Fam* to buck up.

ravin [ravɛ̃] *nm* ravine, gully.

ravioli [ravjɔli] *nmpl* ravioli.

rav/ir [ravir] *vt* **1** to delight; **à r.** (*chanter etc*) delightfully. **2** (*emporter*) to snatch (**à** from). ◆**—issant** *a* a delightful, lovely. ◆**ravisseur, -euse** *nmf* kidnapper.

raviser (se) [səravize] *vpr* to change one's mind.

ravitaill/er [ravitaje] *vt* to provide with supplies, supply; (*avion*) to refuel; **— se r.** *vpr* to stock up (with supplies). ◆**—ement** *nm* supplying; refuelling; (*denrées*) supplies; **aller au r.** (*faire des courses*) *Fam* to stock up, get stocks in.

raviver [ravive] *vt* (*feu, sentiment*) to revive; (*couleurs*) to brighten up.

ray/er [reje] *vt* (*érafler*) to scratch; (*mot etc*) to cross out; **r. qn de** (*liste*) to cross *ou* strike s.o. off. ◆**—é** *a* scratched; (*tissu*) striped; (*papier*) lined, ruled. ◆**rayure** *nf* scratch; (*bande*) stripe; **à rayures** striped.

rayon [rejɔ̃] *nm* **1** (*de lumière, soleil etc*) *Phys* ray; (*de cercle*) radius; (*de roue*) spoke; (*d'espoir*) *Fig* ray; **r. X** X-ray; **r. d'action** range; **dans un r.** de within a radius of. **2** (*planche*) shelf; (*de magasin*) department. **3** (*de ruche*) honeycomb. ◆**rayonnage** *nm* shelving, shelves.

rayonn/er [rejɔne] *vi* to radiate; (*dans une région*) to travel around (*from a central base*); **r. de joie** to beam with joy. ◆**—ant** *a* (*visage etc*) radiant, beaming (**de** with). ◆**—ement** *nm* (*éclat*) radiance; (*influence*) influence; (*radiation*) radiation.

raz-de-marée [radmare] *nm inv* tidal wave; (*bouleversement*) *Fig* upheaval; **r.-de-marée électoral** landslide.

razzia [ra(d)zja] *nf* **faire une r. sur** (*tout enlever sur*) *Fam* to raid.

re- [r(ə)] *préf* re-.

ré- [re] *préf* re-.

réabonn/er (se) [səreabɔne] *vpr* to renew one's subscription (**à** to). ◆**—ement** *nm* renewal of subscription.

réacteur [reaktœr] *nm* (*d'avion*) jet engine; (*nucléaire*) reactor.

réaction [reaksjɔ̃] *nf* reaction; **r. en chaîne** chain reaction; **avion à r.** jet (aircraft); **moteur à r.** jet engine. ◆**réactionnaire** *a* & *nmf* reactionary.

réadapter [readapte] *vt*, **— se r.** *vpr* to readjust (**à** to). ◆**réadaptation** *nf* readjustment.

réaffirmer [reafirme] *vt* to reaffirm.

réagir [reaʒir] *vi* to react (**contre** against, **à** to); (*se secouer*) *Fig* to shake oneself out of it.

réalis/er [realize] *vt* (*projet etc*) to carry out, realize; (*ambition, rêve*) to fulfil; (*achat, bénéfice, vente*) to make; (*film*) to direct; (*capital*) *Com* to realize; (*se rendre compte*) to realize (**que** that); **— se r.** *vpr* (*vœu*) to come true; (*projet*) to be carried out; (*personne*) to fulfil oneself. ◆**—able** *a* (*plan*) workable; (*rêve*) attainable. ◆**réalisateur, -trice** *nmf Cin TV* director. ◆**réalisation** *nf* realization; (*de rêve*) fulfilment; *Cin TV* direction; (*œuvre*) achievement.

réalisme [realism] *nm* realism. ◆**réaliste** *a* realistic; *– nmf* realist.

réalité [realite] *nf* reality; **en r.** in (actual) fact, in reality.

réanimer [reanime] *vt Méd* to resuscitate. ◆**réanimation** *nf* resuscitation; (**service de**) **r.** intensive care unit.

réapparaître [reaparɛtr] *vi* to reappear. ◆**réapparition** *nf* reappearance.

réarmer [rearme] *vt* (*fusil etc*) to reload; *– vi,* **— se r.** *vpr* (*pays*) to rearm. ◆**réarmement** *nm* rearmament.

rébarbatif, -ive [rebarbatif, -iv] *a* forbidding, off-putting.

rebâtir [r(ə)batir] *vt* to rebuild.

rebattu [r(ə)baty] *a* (*sujet*) hackneyed.

rebelle [rəbɛl] *a* rebellious; (*troupes*) rebel-; (*fièvre*) stubborn; (*mèche*) unruly; **r. à** resistant to; – *nmf* rebel. ◆**se rebeller** *vpr* to rebel (**contre** against). ◆**rébellion** *nf* rebellion.

rebiffer (se) [sər(ə)bife] *vpr Fam* to rebel.

rebond [r(ə)bɔ̃] *nm* bounce; (*par ricochet*) rebound. ◆**rebondir** *vi* to bounce; (*par ricochet*) to rebound; (*faire*) **r.** (*affaire, discussion etc*) to get going again. ◆**rebondissement** *nm* new development (**de** in).

rebondi [r(ə)bɔ̃di] *a* chubby, rounded.

rebord [r(ə)bɔr] *nm* edge; (*de plat etc*) rim; (*de vêtement*) hem; **r. de (la) fenêtre** windowsill, window ledge.

reboucher [r(ə)buʃe] *vt* (*flacon*) to put the top back on.

rebours (à) [ar(ə)bur] *adv* the wrong way.

rebrousse-poil (à) [arbruspwal] *adv* **prendre qn à r.-poil** *Fig* to rub s.o. up the wrong way.

rebrousser [r(ə)bruse] *vt* **r. chemin** to turn back.

rebuffade [rəbyfad] *nf Litt* rebuff.

rébus [rebys] *nm inv* (*jeu*) rebus.

rebut [rəby] *nm* **mettre au r.** to throw out, scrap; **le r. de la société** *Péj* the dregs of society.

rebut/er [r(ə)byte] *vt* (*décourager*) to put off; (*choquer*) to repel. ◆**-ant** *a* offputting; (*choquant*) repellent.

récalcitrant [rekalsitrɑ̃] *a* recalcitrant.

recaler [r(ə)kale] *vt* **r. qn** *Scol Fam* to fail s.o., flunk s.o.; **être recalé, se faire r.** *Scol Fam* to fail, flunk.

récapituler [rekapityle] *vti* to recapitulate. ◆**récapitulation** *nf* recapitulation.

recel [rəsɛl] *nm* receiving stolen goods, fencing; harbouring. ◆**receler** *vt* (*mystère, secret etc*) to contain; (*objet volé*) to receive; (*malfaiteur*) to harbour. ◆**receleur, -euse** *nmf* receiver (*of stolen goods*), fence.

recens/er [r(ə)sɑ̃se] *vt* (*population*) to take a census of; (*inventorier*) to make an inventory of. ◆**-ement** *nm* census; inventory.

récent [resɑ̃] *a* recent. ◆**récemment** [-amɑ̃] *adv* recently.

récépissé [resepise] *nm* (*reçu*) receipt.

récepteur [reseptœr] *nm Tél Rad* receiver. ◆**réceptif, -ive** *a* receptive (**à** to). ◆**réception** *nf* (*accueil, soirée*) & *Rad* reception; (*de lettre etc*) *Com* receipt; (*d'hôtel etc*) reception (desk). ◆**réceptionniste** *nmf* receptionist.

récession [resesjɔ̃] *nf Écon* recession.

recette [r(ə)sɛt] *nf* **1** *Culin* & *Fig* recipe. **2** (*argent, bénéfice*) takings; (*bureau*) tax office; **recettes** (*rentrées*) *Com* receipts; **faire r.** *Fig* to be a success.

recev/oir* [rəsvwar] *vt* to receive; (*obtenir*) to get, receive; (*accueillir*) to welcome; (*accepter*) to accept; **être reçu (à)** (*examen*) to pass; **être reçu premier** to come first; – *vi* to receive guests *ou* visitors *ou Méd* patients. ◆**-able** *a* (*excuse etc*) admissible. ◆**-eur, -euse** *nmf* (*d'autobus*) (bus) conductor, (bus) conductress; (*des impôts*) tax collector; (*des postes*) postmaster, postmistress.

rechange (de) [dər(ə)ʃɑ̃ʒ] *a* (*pièce, outil etc*) spare; (*solution etc*) alternative; **vêtements/chaussures de r.** a change of clothes/shoes.

rechapé [r(ə)ʃape] *a* **pneu r.** retread.

réchapper [reʃape] *vi* **r. de** *ou* **à** (*accident etc*) to come through.

recharge [r(ə)ʃarʒ] *nf* (*de stylo etc*) refill. ◆**recharger** *vt* (*camion, fusil*) to reload; (*briquet, stylo etc*) to refill; (*batterie*) to recharge.

réchaud [reʃo] *nm* (portable) stove.

réchauff/er [reʃofe] *vt* (*personne, aliment etc*) to warm up; – **se r.** *vpr* to warm oneself up; (*temps*) to get warmer. ◆**-é** *nm* **du r.** *Fig Péj* old hat. ◆**-ement** *nm* (*de température*) rise (**de** in).

rêche [rɛʃ] *a* rough, harsh.

recherche [r(ə)ʃɛrʃ] *nf* **1** search, quest (**de** for); **à la r. de** in search of. **2** **la r., des recherches** (*scientifique etc*) research (**sur** on, into); **faire des recherches** to research; (*enquête*) to make investigations. **3** (*raffinement*) studied elegance; *Péj* affectation. ◆**recherch/er** *vt* to search *ou* hunt for; (*cause, faveur, perfection*) to seek. ◆**-é** *a* **1** (*très demandé*) in great demand; (*rare*) much sought-after; **r. pour meurtre** wanted for murder. **2** (*élégant*) elegant; *Péj* affected.

rechigner [r(ə)ʃine] *vi* (*renâcler*) to jib (**à qch** at sth, **à faire** at doing).

rechute [r(ə)ʃyt] *nf Méd* relapse. ◆**rechuter** *vi Méd* to (have a) relapse.

récidive [residiv] *nf Jur* further offence; *Méd* recurrence (**de** of). ◆**récidiver** *vi Jur* to commit a further offence; (*maladie*) to recur. ◆**récidiviste** *nmf Jur* further offender.

récif [resif] *nm* reef.

récipient [resipjɑ̃] *nm* container, receptacle.

réciproque [resiprɔk] *a* mutual, reciprocal; – *nf* (*inverse*) opposite; **rendre la r. à qn** to get even with s.o. ◆**réciprocité** *nf* reciprocity. ◆**réciproquement** adv (l'un l'autre) each other; **et r.** and vice versa.

récit [resi] nm (compte rendu) account; (histoire) story.

récital, pl **-als** [resital] nm Mus recital.

réciter [resite] vt to recite. ◆**récitation** nf recitation.

réclame [reklam] nf advertising; (annonce) advertisement; **en r.** Com on (special) offer; **– a** inv **prix r.** (special) offer price; **vente r.** (bargain) sale.

réclamer [reklame] vt (demander, nécessiter) to demand, call for; (revendiquer) to claim; **– vi** to complain; **se r. de qn** to invoke s.o.'s authority. ◆**réclamation** nf complaint; pl (bureau) complaints department.

reclasser [r(ə)klase] vt (fiches etc) to reclassify.

reclus, -use [rəkly, -yz] a (vie) cloistered; **–** nmf recluse.

réclusion [reklyzjɔ̃] nf imprisonment (with hard labour); **r. à perpétuité** life imprisonment.

recoiffer (se) [sər(ə)kwafe] vpr (se peigner) to do ou comb one's hair.

recoin [rəkwɛ̃] nm nook, recess.

recoller [r(ə)kɔle] vt (objet cassé) to stick together again; (enveloppe) to stick back down.

récolte [rekɔlt] nf (action) harvest; (produits) crop, harvest; (collection) Fig crop. ◆**récolter** vt to harvest, gather (in); (recueillir) Fig to collect, gather; (coups) Fam to get.

recommand/er [r(ə)kɔmɑ̃de] **1** vt (appuyer, conseiller) to recommend; **r. à qn de faire** to recommend s.o. to do. **2** vt (lettre etc) to register. **3** vt **r. à** (âme) to commend to. **4 se r.** vpr **se r. de qn** to invoke s.o.'s authority. ◆**–é** nm **en r.** (envoyer) by registered post. ◆**–able** a **peu r.** not very commendable. ◆**recommandation** nf **1** (appui, conseil, louange) recommendation. **2** (de lettre etc) registration.

recommenc/er [r(ə)kɔmɑ̃se] vti to start ou begin again. ◆**–ement** nm (reprise) renewal (**de** of).

récompense [rekɔ̃pɑ̃s] nf reward (**de** for); (prix) award; **en r. de** in return for. ◆**récompenser** vt to reward (**de, pour** for).

réconcilier [rekɔ̃silje] vt to reconcile; **– se r.** vpr to become reconciled, make it up (**avec** with). ◆**réconciliation** nf reconciliation.

reconduire* [r(ə)kɔ̃dɥir] vt **1 r. qn** to see ou take s.o. back; (à la porte) to show s.o. out. **2** (mesures etc) to renew. ◆**reconduction** nf renewal.

réconfort [rekɔ̃fɔr] nm comfort. ◆**réconfort/er** vt to comfort; (revigorer) to fortify. ◆**–ant** a comforting; (boisson etc) fortifying.

reconnaissant [r(ə)kɔnɛsɑ̃] a grateful, thankful (**à qn de qch** to s.o. for sth). ◆**reconnaissance¹** nf (gratitude) gratitude.

reconnaître* [r(ə)kɔnɛtr] vt to recognize (**à qch** by sth); (admettre) to acknowledge, admit (**que** that); (terrain) Mil to reconnoitre; **être reconnu coupable** to be found guilty; **– se r.** vpr (s'orienter) to find one's bearings; **se r. coupable** to admit one's guilt. ◆**reconnu** a (chef, fait) acknowledged, recognized. ◆**reconnaissable** a recognizable (**à qch** by sth). ◆**reconnaissance²** nf recognition; (aveu) acknowledgement; Mil reconnaissance; **r. de dette** IOU.

reconsidérer [r(ə)kɔ̃sidere] vt to reconsider.

reconstituant [r(ə)kɔ̃stitɥɑ̃] adj (aliment, régime) restorative.

reconstituer [r(ə)kɔ̃stitɥe] vt (armée, parti) to reconstitute; (crime, quartier) to reconstruct; (faits) to piece together; (fortune) to build up again. ◆**reconstitution** nf reconstitution; reconstruction.

reconstruire* [r(ə)kɔ̃strɥir] vt (ville, fortune) to rebuild. ◆**reconstruction** nf rebuilding.

reconvertir [r(ə)kɔ̃vertir] **1** vt (bâtiment etc) to reconvert. **2 se r.** vpr to take up a new form of employment. ◆**reconversion** nf reconversion.

recopier [r(ə)kɔpje] vt to copy out.

record [r(ə)kɔr] nm & a inv Sp record.

recoucher (se) [sər(ə)kuʃe] vpr to go back to bed.

recoudre* [r(ə)kudr] vt (bouton) to sew back on.

recoup/er [r(ə)kupe] vt (témoignage etc) to tally with, confirm; **– se r.** vpr to tally, match ou tie up. ◆**–ement** nm cross-check(ing).

recourbé [r(ə)kurbe] a curved; (nez) hooked.

recours [r(ə)kur] nm recourse (**à** to); Jur appeal; **avoir r. à** to resort to; (personne) to turn to; **notre dernier r.** our last resort. ◆**recourir*** vi **r. à** to resort to; (personne) to turn to.

recouvrer [r(ə)kuvre] *vt* (*argent, santé*) to recover.

recouvrir* [r(ə)kuvrir] *vt* (*livre, meuble, sol etc*) to cover; (*de nouveau*) to recover; (*cacher*) *Fig* to conceal, mask.

récréation [rekreasjɔ̃] *nf* recreation; (*temps*) *Scol* break, playtime.

récriminer [rekrimine] *vi* to complain bitterly (**contre** about). ◆**récrimination** *nf* (bitter) complaint.

récrire [rekrir] *vt* (*lettre etc*) to rewrite.

recroqueviller (se) [sər(ə)krɔkvije] *vpr* (*papier, personne etc*) to curl up.

recrudescence [rəkrydesɑ̃s] *nf* new outbreak (**de** of).

recrue [rəkry] *nf* recruit. ◆**recrut/er** *vt* to recruit. ◆**—ement** *nm* recruitment.

rectangle [rɛktɑ̃gl] *nm* rectangle. ◆**rectangulaire** *a* rectangular.

rectifier [rɛktifje] *vt* (*erreur etc*) to correct, rectify; (*ajuster*) to adjust. ◆**rectificatif** *nm* (*document*) amendment, correction. ◆**rectification** *nf* correction, rectification.

recto [rɛkto] *nm* front (of the page).

reçu [r(ə)sy] *voir* **recevoir**; — *a* (*usages etc*) accepted; (*idée*) conventional, received; (*candidat*) successful; — *nm* (*écrit*) *Com* receipt.

recueil [r(ə)kœj] *nm* (*ouvrage*) collection (**de** of).

recueill/ir* [r(ə)kœjir] **1** *vt* to collect, gather; (*suffrages*) to win, get; (*prendre chez soi*) to take in. **2 se r.** *vpr* to meditate; (*devant un monument*) to stand in silence. ◆**—i** *a* (*air*) meditative. ◆**—ement** *nm* meditation.

recul [r(ə)kyl] *nm* (*d'armée, de négociateur, de maladie*) retreat; (*éloignement*) distance; (*déclin*) decline; (*mouvement de*) **r.** (*de véhicule*) backward movement; **avoir un mouvement de r.** (*personne*) to recoil; **phare de r.** *Aut* reversing light. ◆**reculade** *nf Péj* retreat. ◆**recul/er** *vi* to move *ou* step back; *Aut* to reverse; (*armée*) to retreat; (*épidémie, glacier*) to recede, retreat; (*renoncer*) to back down, retreat; (*diminuer*) to decline; **r. devant** *Fig* to recoil *ou* shrink from; — *vt* to move *ou* push back; (*différer*) to postpone. ◆**—é** *a* (*endroit, temps*) remote.

reculons (à) [arkylɔ̃] *adv* backwards.

récupérer [rekypere] *vt* to recover, get back; (*ferraille etc*) to salvage; (*heures*) to make up; (*mouvement, personne etc*) *Pol Péj* to take over, convert; — *vi* to recuperate, recover. ◆**récupération** *nf* recovery; salvage; recuperation.

récurer [rekyre] *vt* (*casserole etc*) to scour; **poudre à r.** scouring powder.

récuser [rekyze] *vt* to challenge; — **se r.** *vpr* to decline to give an opinion.

recycl/er [r(ə)sikle] *vt* (*reconvertir*) to retrain (*s.o.*); (*matériaux*) to recycle; — **se r.** *vpr* to retrain. ◆**—age** *nm* retraining; recycling.

rédacteur, -trice [redaktœr, -tris] *nmf* writer; (*de chronique*) *Journ* editor; (*de dictionnaire etc*) compiler; **r. en chef** *Journ* editor(-in-chief). ◆**rédaction** *nf* (*action*) writing; (*de contrat*) drawing up; (*devoir*) *Scol* essay, composition; (*rédacteurs*) *Journ* editorial staff; (*bureaux*) *Journ* editorial offices.

reddition [redisjɔ̃] *nf* surrender.

redemander [rədmɑ̃de] *vt* (*pain etc*) to ask for more; **r. qch à qn** to ask s.o. for sth back.

rédemption [redɑ̃psjɔ̃] *nf Rel* redemption.

redescendre [r(ə)desɑ̃dr] *vi* (*aux être*) to come *ou* go back down; — *vt* (*aux avoir*) (*objet*) to bring *ou* take back down.

redevable [rədvabl] *a* **être r. de qch à qn** (*argent*) to owe s.o. sth; *Fig* to be indebted to s.o. for sth.

redevance [rədvɑ̃s] *nf* (*taxe*) *TV* licence fee; *Tél* rental charge.

redevenir* [rədvənir] *vi* (*aux être*) to become again.

rédiger [rediʒe] *vt* to write; (*contrat*) to draw up; (*dictionnaire etc*) to compile.

redire* [r(ə)dir] **1** *vt* to repeat. **2** *vi* **avoir** *ou* **trouver à r. à qch** to find fault with sth. ◆**redite** *nf* (pointless) repetition.

redondant [r(ə)dɔ̃dɑ̃] *a* (*style*) redundant.

redonner [r(ə)dɔne] *vt* to give back; (*de nouveau*) to give more.

redoubl/er [r(ə)duble] *vti* **1** to increase; **r. de patience/etc** to be much more patient/*etc*; **à coups redoublés** (*frapper*) harder and harder. **2 r. (une classe)** *Scol* to repeat a year *ou Am* a grade. ◆**—ant, -ante** *nmf* pupil repeating a year *ou Am* a grade. ◆**—ement** *nm* increase (**de** in); repeating a year *ou Am* a grade.

redout/er [r(ə)dute] *vt* to dread (**de faire** doing). ◆**—able** *a* formidable, fearsome.

redress/er [r(ə)drese] *vt* to straighten (out); (*économie, mât, situation, tort*) to right; — **se r.** *vpr* (*se mettre assis*) to sit up; (*debout*) to stand up; (*pays, situation etc*) to right itself. ◆**—ement** [-ɛsmɑ̃] *nm* (*essor*) recovery.

réduction [redyksjɔ̃] *nf* reduction (**de** in); **en r.** (*copie, modèle etc*) small-scale.

réduire* [reduir] *vt* to reduce (**à** to, **de** by); **r. qn à** (*contraindre à*) to reduce s.o. to (*silence, inaction etc*); **se r. à** (*se ramener à*) to come down to, amount to; **se r. en cendres/etc** to be reduced to ashes/*etc*; – *vi* (*faire*) **r.** (*sauce*) to reduce, boil down. ◆**réduit 1** *a* (*prix, vitesse*) reduced; (*moyens*) limited; (*à petite échelle*) small-scale. **2** *nm* (*pièce*) *Péj* cubbyhole; (*recoin*) recess.

réécrire [reekrir] *vt* (*texte*) to rewrite.

rééduquer [reedyke] *vt* (*membre*) *Méd* to re-educate; **r. qn** to rehabilitate s.o., re-educate s.o. ◆**rééducation** *nf* re-education; rehabilitation.

réel, -elle [reɛl] *a* real; **le r.** reality. ◆**réellement** *adv* really.

réélire [reelir] *vt* to re-elect.

réexpédier [reɛkspedje] *vt* (*lettre etc*) to forward; (*à l'envoyeur*) to return.

refaire* [r(ə)fɛr] *vt* to do again, redo; (*erreur, voyage*) to make again; (*réparer*) to do up, redo; (*duper*) *Fam* to take in. ◆**réfection** *nf* repair(ing).

réfectoire [refɛktwar] *nm* refectory.

référendum [referɑ̃dɔm] *nm* referendum.

référer [refere] *vi* **en r. à** to refer the matter to; – **se r.** *vpr* **se r. à** to refer to. ◆**référence** *nf* reference.

refermer [r(ə)fɛrme] *vt*, – **se r.** *vpr* to close *ou* shut (again).

refiler [r(ə)file] *vt* (*donner*) *Fam* to palm off (**à** on).

réfléch/ir [refleʃir] **1** *vt* (*image*) to reflect; – **se r.** *vpr* to be reflected. **2** *vi* (*penser*) to think (**à, sur** about); – *vt* **r. que** to realize that. ◆**-i** *a* (*personne*) thoughtful, reflective; (*action, décision*) carefully thought-out; (*verbe*) *Gram* reflexive. ◆**réflecteur** *nm* reflector. ◆**réflexion** *nf* **1** (*de lumière etc*) reflection. **2** (*méditation*) thought, reflection; (*remarque*) remark; **à la r., r. faite** on second thoughts *ou* *Am* thought,on reflection.

reflet [r(ə)flɛ] *nm* (*image*) & *Fig* reflection; (*lumière*) glint; (*couleur*) tint. ◆**refléter** *vt* (*image, sentiment etc*) to reflect; – **se r.** *vpr* to be reflected.

réflexe [reflɛks] *nm* & *a* reflex.

refluer [r(ə)flye] *vi* (*eaux*) to ebb, flow back; (*foule*) to surge back. ◆**reflux** *nm* ebb; backward surge.

réforme *nf* **1** (*changement*) reform. **2** (*de soldat*) discharge. ◆**réformateur, -trice** *nmf* reformer. ◆**réformer 1** *vt* to reform;

– **se r.** *vpr* to mend one's ways. **2** *vt* (*soldat*) to invalid out, discharge.

refoul/er [r(ə)fule] *vt* to force *ou* drive back; (*sentiment*) to repress; (*larmes*) to hold back. ◆**-é** *a* (*personne*) *Psy* repressed. ◆**-ement** *nm Psy* repression.

réfractaire [refrakter] *a* **r. à** resisting to.

refrain [r(ə)frɛ̃] *nm* (*de chanson*) refrain, chorus; (*rengaine*) *Fig* tune.

refréner [r(ə)frene] *vt* to curb, check.

réfrigér/er [refriʒere] *vt* to refrigerate. ◆**-ant** *a* (*accueil, air*) *Fam* icy. ◆**réfrigérateur** *nm* refrigerator. ◆**réfrigération** *nf* refrigeration.

refroid/ir [r(ə)frwadir] *vt* to cool (down); (*décourager*) *Fig* to put off; (*ardeur*) to dampen, cool; – *vi* to get cold, cool down; – **se r.** *vpr Méd* to catch cold; (*temps*) to get cold; (*ardeur*) to cool (off). ◆**-issement** *nm* cooling; (*rhume*) chill; **r. de la température** fall in the temperature.

refuge [r(ə)fyʒ] *nm* refuge; (*pour piétons*) (traffic) island; (*de montagne*) (mountain) hut. ◆**se réfugi/er** *vpr* to take refuge. ◆**-é, -ée** *nmf* refugee.

refus [r(ə)fy] *nm* refusal; **ce n'est pas de r.** *Fam* I won't say no. ◆**refuser** *vt* to refuse (**qch à qn** s.o. sth, **de faire** to do); (*offre, invitation*) to turn down, refuse; (*client*) to turn away, refuse; (*candidat*) to fail; – **se r.** *vpr* (*plaisir etc*) to deny oneself; **se r. à** (*évidence etc*) to refuse to accept, reject; **se r. à croire/etc** to refuse to believe/*etc*.

réfuter [refyte] *vt* to refute.

regagner [r(ə)gaɲe] *vt* (*récupérer*) to regain; (*revenir à*) to get back to. ◆**regain** *nm* **r. de** (*retour*) renewal of.

régal, *pl* **-als** [regal] *nm* treat. ◆**régaler** *vt* to treat to a delicious meal; **r. de** to treat to; – **se r.** *vpr* to have a delicious meal.

regard *nm* **1** (*coup d'œil, expression*) look; (*fixe*) stare, gaze; **chercher du r.** to look (a)round for; **attirer les regards** to attract attention; **jeter un r. sur** to glance at. **2 au r. de** in regard to; **en r. de** compared with. ◆**regard/er 1** *vt* to look at; (*fixement*) to stare at, gaze at; (*observer*) to watch; (*considérer*) to consider, regard (**comme** as); **r. qn faire** to watch s.o. do; – *vi* to look; to stare, gaze; to watch; **r. à** (*dépense, qualité etc*) to pay attention to; **r. vers** (*maison etc*) to face; – **se r.** *vpr* (*personnes*) to look at each other. **2** *vt* (*concerner*) to concern. ◆**-ant** *a* (*économe*) careful (with money).

régates [regat] *nfpl* regatta.

régence [reʒɑ̃s] *nf* regency.

régénérer [reʒenere] *vt* to regenerate.

régenter [reʒɑ̃te] vt to rule over.

régie [reʒi] nf (entreprise) state-owned company; Th stage management; Cin TV production department.

regimber [r(ə)ʒɛ̃be] vi to balk (contre at).

régime [reʒim] nm 1 system; Pol régime. 2 Méd diet; se mettre au r. to go on a diet; suivre un r. to be on a diet. 3 (de moteur) speed; à ce r. Fig at this rate. 4 (de bananes, dattes) bunch.

régiment [reʒimɑ̃] nm Mil regiment; un r. de (quantité) Fig a host of.

région [reʒjɔ̃] nf region, area. ◆**régional, -aux** a regional.

régir [reʒir] vt (déterminer) to govern.

régisseur [reʒisœr] nm (de propriété) steward; Th stage manager; Cin assistant director.

registre [rəʒistr] nm register.

règle [rɛgl] 1 nf (principe) rule; en r. (papiers d'identité etc) in order; être/se mettre en r. avec qn to be/put oneself right with s.o.; en r. générale as a (general) rule. 2 nf (instrument) ruler; r. à calcul slide rule. 3 nfpl (menstruation) period.

règlement [rɛglɑ̃mɑ̃] nm 1 (arrêté) regulation; (règles) regulations. 2 (de conflit, problème etc) settling; (paiement) payment; r. de comptes Fig (violent) settling of scores. ◆**réglementaire** a in accordance with the regulations; (tenue) Mil regulation-. ◆**réglementation** nf 1 (action) regulation. 2 (règles) regulations. ◆**réglementer** vt to regulate.

régler [regle] 1 vt (conflit, problème etc) to settle; (mécanisme) to regulate, adjust; (moteur) to tune; (papier) to rule; se r. sur to model oneself on. 2 vti (payer) to pay; r. qn to settle up with s.o.; r. son compte à Fig to settle old scores with. ◆**réglé** a (vie) ordered; (papier) ruled. ◆**réglable** a (siège etc) adjustable. ◆**réglage** nm adjustment; (de moteur) tuning.

réglisse [reglis] nf liquorice, Am licorice.

règne [rɛɲ] nm reign; (animal, minéral, végétal) kingdom. ◆**régner** vi to reign; (prédominer) to prevail; faire r. l'ordre to maintain (law and) order.

regorger [r(ə)gɔrʒe] vi r. de to be overflowing with.

regresser [regrese] vi to regress. ◆**régression** nf regression; en r. on the decline.

regret [r(ə)grɛ] nm regret; à r. with regret; avoir le r. ou être au r. de faire to be sorry to do. ◆**regrett/er** vt to regret; r. qn to miss s.o.; je regrette I'm sorry; r. que (+ sub) to be sorry that, regret that. ◆—**able** a regrettable.

regrouper [r(ə)grupe] vt, — se r. vpr to gather together.

régulariser [regylarize] vt (situation) to regularize.

régulation [regylasjɔ̃] nf (action) regulation.

régulier, -ière [regylje, -jɛr] a regular; (progrès, vie, vitesse) steady; (légal) legal; (honnête) honest. ◆**régularité** nf regularity; steadiness; legality. ◆**régulièrement** adv regularly; (normalement) normally.

réhabiliter [reabilite] vt (dans l'estime publique) to rehabilitate.

réhabituer (se) [səreabitɥe] vpr se r. à qch/à faire qch to get used to sth/to doing sth again.

rehausser [rəose] vt to raise; (faire valoir) to enhance.

réimpression [reɛ̃presjɔ̃] nf (livre) reprint.

rein [rɛ̃] nm kidney; pl (dos) (small of the) back; r. artificiel Méd kidney machine.

reine [rɛn] nf queen.

reine-claude [rɛnklod] nf greengage.

réintégrer [reɛ̃tegre] vt 1 (fonctionnaire etc) to reinstate. 2 (lieu) to return to. ◆**réintégration** nf reinstatement.

réitérer [reitere] vt to repeat.

rejaillir [r(ə)ʒajir] vi to spurt (up ou out); r. sur Fig to rebound on.

rejet [r(ə)ʒɛ] nm 1 (refus) & Méd rejection. 2 Bot shoot. ◆**rejeter** vt to throw back; (épave) to cast up; (vomir) to bring up; (refuser) & Méd to reject; r. une erreur/etc sur qn to put the blame for a mistake/etc on s.o.

rejeton [rəʒtɔ̃] nm (enfant) Fam kid.

rejoindre* [r(ə)ʒwɛ̃dr] vt (famille, régiment) to rejoin, get ou go back to; (lieu) to get back to; (route, rue) to join; r. qn to join ou meet s.o.; (rattraper) to catch up with s.o.; — se r. vpr (personnes) to meet; (routes, rues) to join, meet.

réjou/ir [reʒwir] vt to delight; — se r. vpr to be delighted (de at, about; de faire to do). ◆—**i** a (air) joyful. ◆—**issant** a cheering. ◆**réjouissance** nf rejoicing; pl festivities, rejoicings.

relâche [r(ə)laʃ] nf Th Cin (temporary) closure; faire r. (théâtre, cinéma) to close; (bateau) to put in (dans un port at a port); sans r. without a break.

relâch/er [r(ə)laʃe] 1 vt to slacken; (discipline, étreinte) to relax; r. qn to release (s.o.); — se r. vpr to slacken; (discipline) to get lax. 2 vi (bateau) to put in. ◆—**é** a lax.

◆**—ement** *nm* (*de corde etc*) slackness; (*de discipline*) slackening.

relais [r(ə)lɛ] *nm* *Él Rad TV* relay; (**course de**) **r.** *Sp* relay (race); **r. routier** transport café, *Am* truck stop (café); **prendre le r.** to take over (**de** from).

relance [r(ə)lɑ̃s] *nf* (*reprise*) revival. ◆**relancer** *vt* to throw back; (*moteur*) to restart; (*industrie etc*) to put back on its feet; **r. qn** (*solliciter*) to pester s.o.

relater [r(ə)late] *vt* to relate (**que** that).

relatif, -ive [r(ə)latif, -iv] *a* relative (**à** to). ◆**relativement** *adv* relatively; **r. à** compared to, relative to.

relation [r(ə)lɑsjɔ̃] *nf* (*rapport*) relation(ship); (*ami*) acquaintance; **avoir des relations** (*amis influents*) to have connections; **entrer/être en relations avec** to come into/be in contact with; **relations internationales/***etc* international/*etc* relations.

relax(e) [rəlaks] *a Fam* relaxed, informal.

relaxer (se) [sər(ə)lakse] *vpr* to relax. ◆**relaxation** *nf* relaxation.

relayer [r(ə)leje] *vt* to relieve, take over from; (*émission*) to relay; **— se r.** *vpr* to take (it in) turns (**pour faire** to do); *Sp* to take over from one another.

reléguer [r(ə)lege] *vt* to relegate (**à** to).

relent [rəlɑ̃] *nm* stench, smell.

relève [r(ə)lɛv] *nf* (*remplacement*) relief; **prendre la r.** to take over (**de** from).

relev/er [rəlve] *vt* to raise; (*ramasser*) to pick up; (*chaise etc*) to put up straight; (*personne tombée*) to help up; (*col*) to turn up; (*manches*) to roll up; (*copier*) to note down; (*traces*) to find; (*relayer*) to relieve; (*rehausser*) to enhance; (*sauce*) to season; (*faute*) to pick *ou* point out; (*compteur*) to read; (*défi*) to accept; (*économie, pays*) to put back on its feet; (*mur*) to rebuild; **r. qn de** (*fonctions*) to relieve s.o. of; **— vi r. de** (*dépendre de*) to come under; (*maladie*) to get over; **— se r.** *vpr* (*personne*) to get up; **se r. de** (*malheur*) to recover from; (*ruines*) to rise from. ◆**—é** *nm* list; (*de dépenses*) statement; (*de compteur*) reading; **r. de compte** (bank) statement. ◆**relèvement** *nm* (*d'économie, de pays*) recovery.

relief [rəljɛf] **1** *nm* (*forme, ouvrage*) relief; **en r.** (*cinéma*) three-D; (*livre*) pop-up; **mettre en r.** *Fig* to highlight. **2** *nmpl* (*de repas*) remains.

relier [rəlje] *vt* to link, connect (**à** to); (*ensemble*) to link (together); (*livre*) to bind.

religion [r(ə)liʒjɔ̃] *nf* religion; (*foi*) faith. ◆**religieux, -euse 1** *a* religious; **mariage**

r. church wedding; **—** *nm* monk; **—** *nf* nun. **2** *nf Culin* cream bun.

reliquat [r(ə)lika] *nm* (*de dette etc*) remainder.

relique [r(ə)lik] *nf* relic.

relire* [r(ə)lir] *vt* to reread.

reliure [rəljyr] *nf* (*couverture de livre*) binding; (*art*) bookbinding.

reluire [r(ə)lɥir] *vi* to shine, gleam; **faire r.** (*polir*) to shine (up). ◆**reluisant** *a* shiny; **peu r.** *Fig* far from brilliant.

reluquer [r(ə)lyke] *vt Fig* to eye (up).

remâcher [r(ə)mɑʃe] *vt Fig* to brood over.

remanier [r(ə)manje] *vt* (*texte*) to revise; (*ministère*) to reshuffle. ◆**remaniement** *nm* revision; reshuffle.

remarier (se) [sər(ə)marje] *vpr* to remarry.

remarque [r(ə)mark] *nf* remark; (*annotation*) note; **je lui en ai fait la r.** I remarked on it to him *ou* her. ◆**remarquable** *a* remarkable (**par** for). ◆**remarquablement** *adv* remarkably. ◆**remarquer** *vt* **1** (*apercevoir*) to notice (**que** that); **faire r.** to point out (**à** to, **que** that); **se faire r.** to attract attention; **remarque!** mind (you)! **2** (*dire*) to remark (**que** that).

rembarrer [rɑ̃bare] *vt* to rebuff, snub.

remblai [rɑ̃blɛ] *nm* (*terres*) embankment. ◆**remblayer** *vt* (*route*) to bank up; (*trou*) to fill in.

rembourr/er [rɑ̃bure] *vt* (*matelas etc*) to stuff, pad; (*vêtement*) to pad. ◆**—age** *nm* (*action, matière*) stuffing; padding.

rembourser [rɑ̃burse] *vt* to pay back, repay; (*billet*) to refund. ◆**remboursement** *nm* repayment; refund; **envoi contre r.** cash on delivery.

remède [r(ə)mɛd] *nm* remedy, cure; (*médicament*) medicine. ◆**remédier** *vi* **r. à** to remedy.

remémorer (se) [sər(ə)memɔre] *vpr* (*histoire etc*) to recollect, recall.

remercier [r(ə)mɛrsje] *vt* **1** to thank (**de qch, pour qch**, for sth); **je vous remercie d'être venu** thank you for coming; **je vous remercie** (*non merci*) no thank you. **2** (*congédier*) to dismiss. ◆**remerciements** *nmpl* thanks.

remettre* [r(ə)mɛtr] *vt* to put back, replace; (*vêtement*) to put back on; (*donner*) to hand over (**à** to); (*restituer*) to give back (**à** to); (*démission, devoir*) to hand in; (*différer*) to postpone (**à** until); (*ajouter*) to add more *ou* another; (*peine*) *Jur* to remit; (*guérir*) to restore to health; (*reconnaître*) to place, remember; **r. en cause** *ou* **question** to call into question; **r. en état** to repair; **r. ça** *Fam* to start again; **se r. à** (*activité*) to go back to; **se r. à faire** to start to do again; **se r. de** (*chagrin, maladie*) to recover from, get over; **s'en r. à** to rely on. ◆**remise** *nf* **1** (*de lettre etc*) delivery; (*de peine*) *Jur* remission; (*ajournement*) postponement; **r. en cause** *ou* **question** calling into question; **r. en état** repair(ing). **2** (*rabais*) discount. **3** (*local*) shed; *Aut* garage. ◆**remiser** *vt* to put away.

réminiscences [reminisãs] *nfpl* (vague) recollections, reminiscences.

rémission [remisjõ] *nf Jur Rel Méd* remission; **sans r.** (*travailler etc*) relentlessly.

remmener [rãmne] *vt* to take back.

remonte-pente [r(ə)mõtpãt] *nm* ski lift.

remont/er [r(ə)mõte] *vi* (*aux* **être**) to come *ou* go back up; (*niveau, prix*) to rise again, go back up; (*dans le temps*) to go back (**à** to); **r. dans** (*voiture*) to go *ou* get back in(to); (*bus, train*) to go *ou* get back on(to); **r. sur** (*cheval, vélo*) to remount; – *vt* (*aux* **avoir**) (*escalier, pente*) to come *ou* go back up; (*porter*) to bring *ou* take back up; (*montre*) to wind up; (*relever*) to raise; (*col*) to turn up; (*objet démonté*) to reassemble; (*garde-robe etc*) to restock; **r. qn** (*ragaillardir*) to buck s.o. up; **r. le moral à qn** to cheer s.o. up. ◆**—ant** *a* (*boisson*) fortifying; – *nm Méd* tonic. ◆**—ée** *nf* **1** (*de pente etc*) ascent; (*d'eau, de prix*) rise. **2 r. mécanique** ski lift. ◆**remontoir** *nm* (*de mécanisme, montre*) button.

remontrance [r(ə)mõtrãs] *nf* reprimand; **faire des remontrances à** to reprimand, remonstrate with.

remontrer [r(ə)mõtre] *vi* **en r. à qn** to prove one's superiority over s.o.

remords [r(ə)mɔr] *nm & nmpl* remorse; **avoir des r.** to feel remorse.

remorque [r(ə)mɔrk] *nf Aut* trailer; (*câble de*) **r.** towrope; **prendre en r.** to tow; **en r.** on tow. ◆**remorquer** *vt* (*voiture, bateau*) to tow. ◆**remorqueur** *nm* tug(boat).

remous [r(ə)mu] *nm* eddy; (*de foule*) bustle; (*agitation*) *Fig* turmoil.

rempart [rãpar] *nm* rampart.

remplacer [rãplase] *vt* to replace (**par** with, by); (*succéder à*) to take over from; (*temporairement*) to stand in for. ◆**remplaçant, -ante** *nmf* (*personne*) replacement; (*enseignant*) supply teacher; *Sp* reserve. ◆**remplacement** *nm* (*action*) replacement; **assurer le r. de qn** to stand in for s.o.; **en r. de** in place of.

rempl/ir [rãplir] *vt* to fill (up) (**de** with); (*fiche etc*) to fill in *ou* out; (*condition, de-*

voir, tâche) to fulfil; (*fonctions*) to perform; – **se r.** *vpr* to fill (up). ◆**—i** *a* full (**de** of). ◆**remplissage** *nm* filling; (*verbiage*) *Péj* padding.

remporter [rãporte] *vt* **1** (*objet*) to take back. **2** (*prix, victoire*) to win; (*succès*) to achieve.

remu/er [r(ə)mɥe] *vt* (*déplacer, émouvoir*) to move; (*café etc*) to stir; (*terre*) to turn over; (*salade*) to toss; – *vi* to move; (*gigoter*) to fidget; (*se rebeller*) to stir; – **se r.** *vpr* to move; (*se démener*) to exert oneself. ◆**—ant** *a* (*enfant*) restless, fidgety. ◆**remue-ménage** *nm inv* commotion.

rémunérer [remynere] *vt* (*personne*) to pay; (*travail*) to pay for. ◆**rémunérateur, -trice** *a* remunerative. ◆**rémunération** *nf* payment (**de** for).

renâcler [r(ə)nɑkle] *vi* **1** (*cheval*) to snort. **2 r. à** to jib at, balk at.

renaître* [r(ə)nɛtr] *vi* (*fleur*) to grow again; (*espoir, industrie*) to revive. ◆**renaissance** *nf* rebirth, renaissance.

renard [r(ə)nar] *nm* fox.

renchérir [rãʃerir] *vi* **r. sur qn** *ou* **sur ce que qn dit**/*etc* to go further than s.o. in what one says/*etc*.

rencontre [rãkõtr] *nf* meeting; (*inattendue*) & *Mil* encounter; *Sp* match, *Am* game; (*de routes*) junction; **aller à la r. de** to go to meet. ◆**rencontrer** *vt* to meet; (*difficultés*) to come up against, encounter; (*trouver*) to come across, find; (*heurter*) to hit; (*équipe*) *Sp* to play; – **se r.** *vpr* to meet.

rendez-vous [rãdevu] *nm inv* appointment; (*d'amoureux*) date; (*lieu*) meeting place; **donner r.-vous à qn, prendre r.-vous avec qn** to make an appointment with s.o.

rendormir* (**se**) [sərãdɔrmir] *vpr* to go back to sleep.

rend/re [rãdr] *vt* (*restituer*) to give back, return; (*hommage*) to pay; (*invitation*) to return; (*santé*) to restore; (*monnaie, son*) to give; (*justice*) to dispense; (*jugement*) to pronounce, give; (*armes*) to surrender; (*exprimer, traduire*) to render; (*vomir*) to bring up; **r. célèbre**/**plus grand**/**possible**/*etc* to make famous/bigger/possible/*etc*; – *vi* (*arbre, terre*) to yield; (*vomir*) to be sick; – **se r.** *vpr* (*capituler*) to surrender (**à** to); (*aller*) to go (**à** to); **se r. à** (*évidence, ordres*) to submit to; **se r. malade**/**utile**/*etc* to make oneself ill/useful/*etc*. ◆**—u** *a* (*fatigué*) exhausted; **être r.** (*arrivé*) to have arrived. ◆**rendement** *nm Agr Fin* yield; (*de personne, machine*) output.

renégat, -ate [rənega, -at] *nmf* renegade.

rênes [rɛn] *nfpl* reins.

renferm/er [rɑ̃fɛrme] *vt* to contain; — **se r.** *vpr* **se r. (en soi-même)** to withdraw into oneself. ◆—**é 1** *a* (*personne*) withdrawn. **2** *nm* **sentir le r.** (*chambre etc*) to smell stuffy.

renflé [rɑ̃fle] *a* bulging. ◆**renflement** *nm* bulge.

renflouer [rɑ̃flue] *vt* (*navire*) & *Com* to refloat.

renfoncement [rɑ̃fɔ̃smɑ̃] *nm* recess; **dans le r. d'une porte** in a doorway.

renforcer [rɑ̃fɔrse] *vt* to reinforce, strengthen. ◆**renforcement** *nm* reinforcement, strengthening. ◆**renfort** *nm* **des renforts** *Mil* reinforcements; **de r.** (*armée, personnel*) back-up; **à grand r. de** *Fig* with a great deal of.

renfrogn/er (se) [sərɑ̃frɔɲe] *vpr* to scowl. ◆—**é** *a* scowling, sullen.

rengaine [rɑ̃gɛn] *nf* **la même r.** *Fig Péj* the same old song *ou* story.

rengorger (se) [sərɑ̃gɔrʒe] *vpr* to give oneself airs.

renier [rənje] *vt* (*ami, pays etc*) to disown; (*foi, opinion*) to renounce. ◆**reniement** *nm* disowning; renunciation.

renifler [r(ə)nifle] *vti* to sniff. ◆**reniflement** *nm* sniff.

renne [rɛn] *nm* reindeer.

renom [rənɔ̃] *nm* renown; (*réputation*) reputation (**de** for). ◆**renommé** *a* famous, renowned (**pour** for). ◆**renommée** *nf* fame, renown; (*réputation*) reputation.

renoncer [r(ə)nɔ̃se] *vi* **r. à** to give up, abandon; **r. à faire** to give up (the idea of) doing. ◆**renoncement** *nm*, ◆**renonciation** *nf* renunciation (**à** of).

renouer [rənwe] **1** *vt* (*lacet etc*) to retie. **2** *vt* (*reprendre*) to renew; — *vi* **r. avec qch** (*mode, tradition etc*) to revive sth; **r. avec qn** to take up with s.o. again.

renouveau, -x [r(ə)nuvo] *nm* revival.

renouveler [r(ə)nuvle] *vt* to renew; (*action, erreur, question*) to repeat; — **se r.** *vpr* (*incident*) to recur, happen again; (*cellules, sang*) to be renewed. ◆**renouvelable** *a* renewable. ◆**renouvellement** *nm* renewal.

rénover [renɔve] *vt* (*institution, méthode*) to reform; (*édifice, meuble etc*) to renovate. ◆**rénovation** *nf* reform; renovation.

renseign/er [rɑ̃sɛɲe] *vt* to inform, give information to (**sur** about); — **se r.** *vpr* to inquire, make inquiries, find out (**sur** about). ◆—**ement** *nm* (piece of) information; *pl* information; *Tél* directory inquiries, *Am* information; *Mil* intelligence;

prendre *ou* **demander des reseignements** to make inquiries.

rentable [rɑ̃tabl] *a* profitable. ◆**rentabilité** *nf* profitability.

rente [rɑ̃t] *nf* (private) income; (*pension*) pension; **avoir des rentes** to have private means. ◆**rentier, -ière** *nmf* person of private means.

rentr/er [rɑ̃tre] *vi* (*aux être*) to go *ou* come back, return; (*chez soi*) to go *ou* come (back) home; (*entrer*) to go *ou* come in; (*entrer de nouveau*) to go *ou* come back in; (*école*) to start again; (*argent*) to come in; **r. dans** (*entrer dans*) to go *ou* come into; (*entrer de nouveau dans*) to go *ou* come back into; (*famille, pays*) to return to; (*ses frais*) to get back; (*catégorie*) to come under; (*heurter*) to crash into; (*s'emboîter dans*) to fit into; **r. (en classe)** to start (school) again; **je lui suis rentré dedans** (*frapper*) *Fam* I laid into him *ou* her; — *vt* (*aux avoir*) to bring *ou* take in; (*voiture*) to put away; (*chemise*) to tuck in; (*griffes*) to draw in. ◆—**é** *a* (*colère*) suppressed; (*yeux*) sunken. ◆—**ée** *nf* **1** (*retour*) return; (*de parlement*) reassembly; (*d'acteur*) comeback; **r.** (**des classes**) beginning of term *ou* of the school year. **2** (*des foins etc*) bringing in; (*d'impôt*) collection; *pl* (*argent*) receipts.

renverse (à la) [alarɑ̃vɛrs] *adv* (*tomber*) backwards, on one's back.

renvers/er [rɑ̃vɛrse] *vt* (*mettre à l'envers*) to turn upside down; (*faire tomber*) to knock over *ou* down; (*piéton*) to knock down, run over; (*liquide*) to spill, knock over; (*courant, ordre*) to reverse; (*gouvernement*) to overturn, overthrow; (*projet*) to upset; (*tête*) to tip back; — **se r.** *vpr* (*en arrière*) to lean back; (*bouteille, vase etc*) to fall over. ◆—**ant** *a* (*nouvelle etc*) astounding. ◆—**ement** *nm* (*d'ordre, de situation*) reversal; (*de gouvernement*) overthrow.

renvoi [rɑ̃vwa] *nm* **1** return; dismissal; expulsion; postponement; (*dans un livre*) reference. **2** (*rot*) belch, burp. ◆**renvoyer*** *vt* to send back, return; (*importun*) to send away; (*employé*) to dismiss; (*élève*) to expel; (*balle etc*) to throw back; (*ajourner*) to postpone (**à** until); (*lumière, image etc*) to reflect; **r. qn à** (*adresser à*) to refer s.o. to.

réorganiser [reɔrganize] *vt* to reorganize.

réouverture [reuvɛrtyr] *nf* reopening.

repaire [r(ə)pɛr] *nm* den.

repaître (se) [sərəpɛtr] *vpr* **se r. de** (*sang*) *Fig* to wallow in.

répand/re [repɑ̃dr] *vt* (*liquide*) to spill;

(*idées, joie, nouvelle*) to spread; (*fumée, odeur*) to give off; (*chargement, lumière, larmes, sang*) to shed; (*gravillons etc*) to scatter; (*dons*) to lavish; — **se r.** *vpr* (*nouvelle, peur etc*) to spread; (*liquide*) to spill; **se r. dans** (*fumée, odeur*) to spread through; **se r. en louanges**/*etc* to pour forth praise/*etc*. ◆**—u** *a* (*opinion, usage*) widespread; (*épars*) scattered.

reparaître [r(ə)parɛtr] *vi* to reappear.

réparer [repare] *vt* to repair, mend; (*forces, santé*) to restore; (*faute*) to make amends for; (*perte*) to make good; (*erreur*) to put right. ◆**réparable** *a* (*montre etc*) repairable. ◆**réparateur, -trice** *nmf* repairer; — *a* (*sommeil*) refreshing. ◆**réparation** *nf* repairing; (*compensation*) amends, compensation (**de** for); *pl Mil Hist* reparations; **en r.** under repair.

reparler [r(ə)parle] *vi* **r. de** to talk about again.

repartie [reparti] *nf* (*réponse vive*) repartee.

repartir* [r(ə)partir] *vi* (*aux être*) to set off again; (*s'en retourner*) to go back; (*reprendre*) to start again; **r. à** *ou* **de zéro** to go back to square one.

répartir [repartir] *vt* to distribute; (*partager*) to share (out); (*classer*) to divide (up); (*étaler dans le temps*) to spread (out) (**sur** over). ◆**répartition** *nf* distribution; sharing; division.

repas [r(ə)pɑ] *nm* meal; **prendre un r.** to have *ou* eat a meal.

repass/er [r(ə)pɑse] **1** *vi* to come *ou* go back; — *vt* (*traverser*) to go back over; (*examen*) to resit; (*leçon, rôle*) to go over; (*film*) to show again; (*maladie, travail*) to pass on (**à** to). **2** *vt* (*linge*) to iron. **3** *vt* (*couteau*) to sharpen. ◆**—age** *nm* ironing.

repêcher [r(ə)peʃe] *vt* to fish out; (*candidat*) *Fam* to allow to pass.

repenser [r(ə)pɑse] *vt* to rethink.

repentir [r(ə)pɑtir] *nm* repentance. ◆**se repentir*** *vpr Rel* to repent (**de** of); **se r. de** (*regretter*) to regret, be sorry for. ◆**repentant** *a*, ◆**repenti** *a* repentant.

répercuter [reperkyte] *vt* (*son*) to echo; — **se r.** *vpr* to echo, reverberate; **se r. sur** *Fig* to have repercussions on. ◆**répercussion** *nf* repercussion.

repère [r(ə)pɛr] *nm* (*guide*) mark; (*jalon*) marker; **point de r.** (*espace, temps*) landmark, point of reference. ◆**repérer** *vt* to locate; (*personnne*) *Fam* to spot; — **se r.** *vpr* to get one's bearings.

répertoire [repɛrtwar] *nm* **1** index; (*carnet*) indexed notebook; **r. d'adresses** address

book. **2** *Th* repertoire. ◆**répertorier** *vt* to index.

répéter [repete] *vti* to repeat; *Th* to rehearse; — **se r.** *vpr* (*radoter*) to repeat oneself; (*se reproduire*) to repeat itself. ◆**répétitif, -ive** *a* repetitive. ◆**répétition** *nf* repetition; *Th* rehearsal; **r. générale** *Th* (final) dress rehearsal.

repiquer [r(ə)pike] *vt* **1** (*plante*) to plant out. **2** (*disque*) to tape, record (on tape).

répit [repi] *nm* rest, respite; **sans r.** ceaselessly.

replacer [r(ə)plase] *vt* to replace, put back.

repli [r(ə)pli] *nm* fold; withdrawal; *pl* (*de l'âme*) recesses. ◆**replier 1** *vt* to fold (up); (*siège*) to fold up; (*couteau, couverture*) to fold back; (*ailes, jambes*) to tuck in; — **se r.** *vpr* (*siège*) to fold up; (*couteau, couverture*) to fold back. **2** *vt*, — **se r.** *vpr Mil* to withdraw; **se r. sur soi-même** to withdraw into oneself.

réplique [replik] *nf* **1** (*réponse*) reply; (*riposte*) retort; *Th* lines; **pas de r.!** no answering back!; **sans r.** (*argument*) irrefutable. **2** (*copie*) replica. ◆**répliquer** *vt* to reply (**que** that); (*riposter*) to retort (**que** that); — *vi* (*être impertinent*) to answer back.

répond/re [repɔdr] *vi* to answer, reply; (*être impertinent*) to answer back; (*réagir*) to respond (**à** to); **r. à qn** to answer s.o., reply to s.o.; (*avec impertinence*) to answer s.o. back; **r. à** (*lettre, objection, question*) to answer, reply to; (*salut*) to return; (*besoin*) to meet, answer; (*correspondre à*) to correspond to; **r. de** (*garantir*) to answer for (*s.o., sth*); — *vt* (*remarque etc*) to answer *ou* reply with; **r. que** to answer *ou* reply that. ◆**—ant, -ante 1** *nmf* guarantor. **2** *nm* **avoir du r.** to have money behind one. ◆**—eur** *nm Tél* answering machine. ◆**réponse** *nf* answer, reply; (*réaction*) response (**à** to); **en r. à** in answer *ou* reply *ou* response to.

reporter¹ [r(ə)pɔrte] *vt* to take back; (*différer*) to postpone, put off (**à** until); (*transcrire, transférer*) to transfer (**sur** to); (*somme*) *Com* to carry forward (**sur** to); **se r. à** (*texte etc*) to refer to; (*en esprit*) to go *ou* think back to. ◆**report** *nm* postponement; transfer; *Com* carrying forward. ◆**reportage** *nm* (*news*) report, article; (*en direct*) commentary; (*métier*) reporting.

reporter² [r(ə)pɔrtɛr] *nm* reporter.

repos [r(ə)po] *nm* rest; (*tranquillité*) peace (and quiet); (*de l'esprit*) peace of mind; **r.!** *Mil* at ease!; **jour de r.** day off; **de tout r.** (*situation etc*) safe. ◆**repos/er 1** *vt* (*objet*) to put back down; (*problème, question*) to raise again. **2** *vt* (*délasser*) to rest, relax; **r. sa tête sur** (*appuyer*) to rest one's head on; **−** *vi* (*être enterré ou étendu*) to rest, lie; **r. sur** (*bâtiment*) to be built on; (*théorie etc*) to be based on, rest on; **laisser r.** (*vin*) to allow to settle; **— se r.** *vpr* to rest; **se r. sur qn** to rely on s.o. ◆**—ant** *a* relaxing, restful. ◆**—é** *a* rested, fresh.

repouss/er [r(ə)puse] **1** *vt* to push back; (*écarter*) to push away; (*attaque, ennemi*) to repulse; (*importun etc*) to turn away, repulse; (*dégoûter*) to repel; (*décliner*) to reject; (*différer*) to put off, postpone. **2** *vi* (*cheveux, feuilles*) to grow again. ◆**—ant** *a* repulsive, repellent.

répréhensible [repreɑ̃sibl] *a* reprehensible, blameworthy.

reprendre* [r(ə)prɑ̃dr] *vt* (*objet*) to take back; (*évadé, ville*) to recapture; (*passer prendre*) to pick up again; (*souffle*) to get back; (*activité*) to resume, take up again; (*texte*) to go back over; (*vêtement*) to alter; (*histoire, refrain*) to take up; (*pièce*) Th to put on again; (*blâmer*) to admonish; (*corriger*) to correct; **r. de la viande/un œuf/etc** to take (some) more meat/another egg/etc; **r. ses esprits** to come round; **r. des forces** to recover one's strength; **−** *vi* (*plante*) to take again; (*recommencer*) to resume, start (up) again; (*affaires*) to pick up; (*jour*) to go on, continue; **— se r.** *vpr* (*se ressaisir*) to take a hold on oneself; (*se corriger*) to correct oneself; **s'y r. à deux/plusieurs fois** to have another go/several goes (at it).

représailles [r(ə)prezaj] *nfpl* reprisals, retaliation.

représent/er [r(ə)prezɑ̃te] *vt* to represent; (*jouer*) Th to perform; **— se r.** *vpr* (*s'imaginer*) to imagine. ◆**—ant, -ante** *nmf* representative; ◆**r. de commerce** (travelling) salesman *ou* saleswoman, sales representative. ◆**représentatif, -ive** *a* representative (**de** of). ◆**représentation** *nf* representation; Th performance.

répression [represjɔ̃] *nf* suppression, repression; (*mesures de contrôle*) Pol repression. ◆**répressif, -ive** *a* repressive. ◆**réprimer** *vt* (*sentiment, révolte etc*) to suppress, repress.

réprimande [reprimɑ̃d] *nf* reprimand. ◆**réprimander** *vt* to reprimand.

repris [r(ə)pri] *nm* **r. de justice** hardened criminal.

reprise [r(ə)priz] *nf* (*de ville*) Mil recapture; (*recommencement*) resumption; (*de pièce de théâtre, de coutume*) revival; Rad TV repeat; (*de tissu*) mend, repair; Boxe round;

(*essor*) Com recovery, revival; (*d'un locataire*) money for fittings; (*de marchandise*) taking back; (*pour nouvel achat*) part exchange, trade-in; *pl* Aut acceleration; **à plusieurs reprises** on several occasions. ◆**repriser** *vt* (*chaussette etc*) to mend, darn.

réprobation [reprɔbasjɔ̃] *nf* disapproval. ◆**réprobateur, -trice** *a* disapproving.

reproche [r(ə)prɔʃ] *nm* reproach; **faire des reproches à qn** to reproach s.o.; **sans r.** beyond reproach. ◆**reprocher** *vt* **r. qch à qn** to reproach *ou* blame s.o. for sth; **r. qch à qch** to have sth against sth; **n'avoir rien à se r.** to have nothing to reproach *ou* blame oneself for.

reproduire* [r(ə)prɔduir] **1** *vt* (*son, modèle etc*) to reproduce; **— se r.** *vpr* Biol Bot to reproduce. **2 se r.** *vpr* (*incident etc*) to happen again, recur. ◆**reproducteur, -trice** *a* reproductive. ◆**reproduction** *nf* (*de son etc*) & Biol Bot reproduction.

réprouver [repruve] *vt* to disapprove of, condemn.

reptile [reptil] *nm* reptile.

repu [rəpy] *a* (*rassasié*) satiated.

république [repyblik] *nf* republic. ◆**républicain, -aine** *a* & *nmf* republican.

répudier [repydje] *vt* to repudiate.

répugnant [repyɲɑ̃] *a* repugnant, loathsome. ◆**répugnance** *nf* repugnance, loathing (**pour** for); (*manque d'enthousiasme*) reluctance. ◆**répugner** *vi* **r. à qn** to be repugnant to s.o.; **r. à faire** to be loath to do.

répulsion [repylsjɔ̃] *nf* repulsion.

réputation [repytasjɔ̃] *nf* reputation; **avoir la r. d'être franc** to have a reputation for frankness *ou* for being frank. ◆**réputé** *a* (*célèbre*) renowned (**pour** for); **r. pour être** (*considéré comme*) reputed to be.

requérir [rəkerir] *vt* (*nécessiter*) to demand, require; (*peine*) Jur to call for. ◆**requête** *nf* request; *Jur* petition. ◆**requis** *a* required, requisite.

requiem [rekɥijɛm] *nm inv* requiem.

requin [r(ə)kɛ̃] *nm* (*poisson*) & Fig shark.

réquisition [rekizisjɔ̃] *nf* requisition. ◆**réquisitionner** *vt* to requisition, commandeer.

réquisitoire [rekizitwar] *nm* (*critique*) indictment (**contre** of).

rescapé, -ée [rɛskape] *a* surviving; **−** *nmf* survivor.

rescousse (à la) [alarɛskus] *adv* to the rescue.

réseau, -x [rezo] *nm* network; **r. d'espionnage** spy ring *ou* network.

réserve [rezɛrv] *nf* **1** (*restriction, doute*) reservation; (*réticence*) reserve; **sans r.** (*admiration etc*) unqualified; **sous r. de** subject to; **sous toutes réserves** without guarantee. **2** (*provision*) reserve; (*entrepôt*) storeroom; (*de bibliothèque*) stacks; **la r.** *Mil* the reserve; **les réserves** (*soldats*) the reserves; **en r.** in reserve. **3** (*de chasse, pêche*) preserve; (*indienne*) reservation; **r. naturelle** nature reserve.

réserv/er [rezɛrve] *vt* to reserve; (*garder*) to keep, save; (*marchandises*) to put aside (à for); (*place, table*) to book, reserve; (*sort, surprise etc*) to hold in store (à for); **se r. pour** to save oneself for; **se r. de faire** to reserve the right to do. ◆**—é** *a* (*personne, place*) reserved; (*prudent*) guarded. ◆**réservation** *nf* reservation, booking. ◆**réservoir** *nm* (*lac*) reservoir; (*citerne, cuve*) tank; **r. d'essence** *Aut* petrol *ou* Am gas tank.

résidence [rezidɑ̃s] *nf* residence; **r. secondaire** second home; **r. universitaire** hall of residence. ◆**résident, -ente** *nmf* (foreign) resident. ◆**résidentiel, -ielle** *a* (*quartier*) residential. ◆**résider** *vi* to reside, be resident (à, en, dans in); **r. dans** (*consister dans*) to lie in.

résidu [rezidy] *nm* residue.

résigner (se) [səreziɲe] *vpr* to resign oneself (à qch to sth, à faire to doing). ◆**résignation** *nf* resignation.

résilier [rezilje] *vt* (*contrat*) to terminate. ◆**résiliation** *nf* termination.

résille [rezij] *nf* (*pour cheveux*) hairnet.

résine [rezin] *nf* resin.

résistance [rezistɑ̃s] *nf* resistance (à to); (*conducteur*) *Él* (heating) element; **plat de r.** main dish. ◆**résist/er** *vi* **r.** à to resist; (*chaleur, fatigue, souffrance*) to withstand; (*examen*) to stand up to. ◆**—ant, -ante** *a* tough, strong; **r. à la chaleur** heat-resistant; **r. au choc** shockproof; – *nmf Mil Hist* Resistance fighter.

résolu [rezɔly] *voir* **résoudre**; – *a* resolute, determined; **r. à faire** resolved *ou* determined to do. ◆**—ment** *adv* resolutely. ◆**résolution** *nf* (*décision*) resolution; (*fermeté*) determination.

résonance [rezɔnɑ̃s] *nf* resonance.

résonner [rezɔne] *vi* to resound (de with); (*salle, voix*) to echo.

résorber [rezɔrbe] *vt* (*chômage*) to reduce; (*excédent*) to absorb; – **se r.** *vpr* to be re-

duced; to be absorbed. ◆**résorption** *nf* reduction; absorption.

résoudre* [rezudr] *vt* (*problème*) to solve; (*difficulté*) to resolve; **r. de faire** to decide *ou* resolve to do; **se r. à faire** to decide *ou* resolve to do; (*se résigner*) to bring oneself to do.

respect [rɛspɛ] *nm* respect (**pour, de** for); **mes respects à** my regards *ou* respects to; **tenir qn en r.** to hold s.o. in check. ◆**respectabilité** *nf* respectability. ◆**respectable** *a* (*honorable, important*) respectable. ◆**respecter** *vt* to respect; **qui se respecte** self-respecting. ◆**respectueux, -euse** *a* respectful (**envers** to, **de** of).

respectif, -ive [rɛspɛktif, -iv] *a* respective. ◆**respectivement** *adv* respectively.

respirer [rɛspire] *vi* to breathe; (*reprendre haleine*) to get one's breath (back); (*être soulagé*) to breathe again; – *vt* to breathe (in); (*exprimer*) *Fig* to exude. ◆**respiration** *nf* breathing; (*haleine*) breath; **r. artificielle** *Méd* artificial respiration. ◆**respiratoire** *a* a breathing-, respiratory.

resplend/ir [rɛsplɑ̃dir] *vi* to shine; (*visage*) to glow (**de** with). ◆**—issant** *a* radiant.

responsable [rɛspɔ̃sabl] *a* responsible (**de qch** for sth, **devant qn** to s.o.); – *nmf* (*chef*) person in charge; (*dans une organisation*) official; (*coupable*) person responsible (**de** for). ◆**responsabilité** *nf* responsibility; (*légale*) liability.

resquiller [rɛskije] *vi* (*au cinéma, dans le métro etc*) to avoid paying; (*sans attendre*) to jump the queue, *Am* cut in (line).

ressaisir (se) [sər(ə)sezir] *vpr* to pull oneself together.

ressasser [r(ə)sase] *vt* (*ruminer*) to keep going over; (*répéter*) to keep trotting out.

ressemblance [r(ə)sɑ̃blɑ̃s] *nf* resemblance, likeness. ◆**ressembl/er** *vi* **r.** à to resemble, look *ou* be like; **cela ne lui ressemble pas** (*ce n'est pas son genre*) that's not like him *ou* her; – **se r.** *vpr* to look *ou* be alike. ◆**—ant** *a* portrait **r.** good likeness.

ressentiment [r(ə)sɑ̃timɑ̃] *nm* resentment.

ressentir* [r(ə)sɑ̃tir] *vt* to feel; **se r. de** to feel *ou* show the effects of.

resserre [r(ə)sɛr] *nf* storeroom; (*remise*) shed.

resserrer [r(ə)sere] *vt* (*nœud, boulon etc*) to tighten; (*contracter*) to close (up), contract; (*liens*) *Fig* to strengthen; – **se r.** *vpr* to tighten; (*amitié*) to become closer; (*se contracter*) to close (up), contract; (*route etc*) to narrow.

resservir [r(ə)sɛrvir] **1** *vi* (*outil etc*) to come

in useful (again). **2 se r.** *vpr* **se r. de** (*plat etc*) to have another helping of.

ressort [r(ə)sɔr] *nm* **1** *Tech* spring. **2** (*énergie*) spirit. **3 du r. de** within the competence of; **en dernier r.** (*décider etc*) in the last resort, as a last resort.

ressortir[1]* [r(ə)sɔrtir] *vi* (*aux* **être**) **1** to go *ou* come back out. **2** (*se voir*) to stand out; **faire r.** to bring out; **il ressort de** (*résulte*) it emerges that.

ressortir[2] [r(ə)sɔrtir] *vi* (*conjugated like* **finir**) **r. à** to fall within the scope of.

ressortissant, -ante [r(ə)sɔrtisɑ̃, -ɑ̃t] *nmf* (*citoyen*) national.

ressource [r(ə)surs] **1** *nfpl* (*moyens*) resources; (*argent*) means, resources. **2** *nf* (*recours*) recourse; (*possibilité*) possibility (**de faire** of doing); **dernière r.** last resort.

ressusciter [resysite] *vi* to rise from the dead; (*malade, pays*) to recover, revive; — *vt* (*mort*) to raise; (*malade, mode*) to revive.

restaurant [rɛstɔrɑ̃] *nm* restaurant.

restaurer [rɛstɔre] **1** *vt* (*réparer, rétablir*) to restore. **2 se r.** *vpr* to (have sth to) eat. ◆**restaurateur, -trice** *nmf* **1** (*de tableaux*) restorer. **2** (*hôtelier, hôtelière*) restaurant owner. ◆**restauration** *nf* **1** restoration. **2** (*hôtellerie*) catering.

reste [rɛst] *nm* rest, remainder (**de** of); *Math* remainder; *pl* remains (**de** of); (*de repas*) leftovers; **un r. de fromage**/*etc* some left-over cheese/*etc*; **au r., du r.** moreover, besides.

rester [rɛste] *vi* (*aux* **être**) to stay, remain; (*calme, jeune etc*) to keep, stay, remain; (*subsister*) to remain, be left; **il reste du pain**/*etc* there's some bread/*etc* left (over); **il me reste une minute**/*etc* I have one minute/*etc* left; **l'argent qui lui reste** the money he *ou* she has left; **reste à savoir** it remains to be seen; **il me reste deux choses à faire** I still have two things to do; **il me reste à vous remercier** it remains for me to thank you; **en r. à** to stop at; **restons-en là** let's leave it at that. ◆**restant** *a* remaining; **poste restante** poste restante, *Am* general delivery; — *nm* **le r.** the rest, the remainder; **un r. de viande**/*etc* some left-over meat/*etc*.

restituer [rɛstitɥe] *vt* **1** (*rendre*) to return, restore (**à** to). **2** (*son*) to reproduce; (*énergie*) to release. ◆**restitution** *nf* return.

restreindre* [rɛstrɛ̃dr] *vt* to restrict, limit (**à** to); — **se r.** *vpr* to decrease; '(*faire des économies*) to| cut back *ou* down. ◆**restreint** *a* limited, restricted (**à** to). ◆**restrictif, -ive**

a restrictive. ◆**restriction** *nf* restriction; **sans r.** unreservedly].

résultat [rezylta] *nm* result; (*conséquence*) outcome, result; **avoir qch pour r.** to result in sth. ◆**résulter** *vi* **r. de** to result from.

résum/er [rezyme] *vt* to summarize; (*récapituler*) to sum up; — **se r.** *vpr* (*orateur etc*) to sum up; **se r. à** (*se réduire à*) to boil down to. ◆**—é** *nm* summary; **en r.** in short; (*en récapitulant*) to sum up.

résurrection [rezyrɛksjɔ̃] *nf* resurrection.

rétabl/ir [retablir] *vt* to restore; (*fait, vérité*) to re-establish; (*malade*) to restore to health; (*employé*) to reinstate; — **se r.** *vpr* to be restored; (*malade*) to recover. ◆**—issement** *nm* restoring; re-establishment; *Méd* recovery.

retaper [r(ə)tape] *vt* (*maison, voiture etc*) to do up; (*lit*) to straighten; (*malade*) *Fam* to buck up.

retard [r(ə)tar] *nm* lateness; (*sur un programme etc*) delay; (*infériorité*) backwardness; **en r.** late; (*retardé*) backward; **en r. dans qch** behind in sth; **en r. sur qn/qch** behind s.o./sth; **rattraper** *ou* **combler son r.** to catch up; **avoir du r.** to be late; (*sur un programme*) to be behind (schedule); (*montre*) to be slow; **avoir une heure de r.** to be an hour late; **prendre du r.** (*montre*) to lose (time); **sans r.** without delay. ◆**retardataire** *a* (*arrivant*) late; **enfant r.** *Méd* slow learner; — *nmf* latecomer. ◆**retardement** *nm* **à r.** delayed-action-; **bombe à r.** time bomb.

retard/er [r(ə)tarde] *vt* to delay; (*date, départ, montre*) to put back; **r. qn** (*dans une activité*) to put s.o. behind; — *vi* (*montre*) to be slow; **r. de cinq minutes** to be five minutes slow; **r. (sur son temps)** (*personne*) to be behind the times. ◆**—é, -ée** *a* (*enfant*) backward; — *nmf* backward child.

retenir* [rətnir] *vt* (*empêcher d'agir, contenir*) to hold back; (*attention, souffle*) to hold; (*réserver*) to book; (*se souvenir de*) to remember; (*fixer*) to hold (in place), secure; (*déduire*) to take off; (*candidature, proposition*) to accept; (*chiffre*) *Math* to carry; (*chaleur, odeur*) to retain; (*invité, suspect etc*) to detain, keep; **r. qn prisonnier** to keep *ou* hold s.o. prisoner; **r. qn de faire** to stop s.o. (from) doing; — **se r.** *vpr* (*se contenir*) to restrain oneself; **se r. de faire** to stop oneself (from) doing; **se r. à** to cling to. ◆**retenue** *nf* **1** (*modération*) restraint. **2** (*de salaire*) deduction, stoppage; (*chiffre*) *Math* figure carried over. **3** *Scol* detention; **en r.** in detention.

retent/ir [r(ə)tɑ̃tir] *vi* to ring (out) (**de** with). ◆**—issant** *a* resounding; (*scandale*) major. ◆**—issement** *nm* (*effet*) effect; **avoir un grand r.** (*film etc*) to create a stir.

réticent [retisɑ̃] *a* (*réservé*) reticent; (*hésitant*) reluctant. ◆**réticence** *nf* reticence; reluctance.

rétine [retin] *nf Anat* retina.

retir/er [r(ə)tire] *vt* to withdraw; (*sortir*) to take out; (*ôter*) to take off; (*éloigner*) to take away; (*reprendre*) to pick up; (*offre, plainte*) to take back, withdraw; **r. qch à qn** (*permis etc*) to take sth away from s.o.; **r. qch de** (*gagner*) to derive sth from; **— se r.** *vpr* to withdraw, retire; (*mer*) to ebb. ◆**—é** *a* (*lieu, vie*) secluded.

retomber [r(ə)tɔ̃be] *vi* to fall; (*de nouveau*) to fall again; (*pendre*) to hang (down); (*après un saut etc*) to land; (*intérêt*) to slacken; **r. dans** (*erreur, situation*) to fall *ou* sink back into; **r. sur qn** (*frais, responsabilité*) to fall on s.o. ◆**retombées** *nfpl* (*radioactives*) fallout.

rétorquer [retorke] *vt* **r. que** to retort that.

retors [rətɔr] *a* wily, crafty.

rétorsion [retorsjɔ̃] *nf Pol* retaliation; **mesure de r.** reprisal.

retouche [r(ə)tuʃ] *nf* touching up; alteration. ◆**retoucher** *vt* (*photo, tableau*) to touch up, retouch; (*texte, vêtement*) to alter.

retour [r(ə)tur] *nm* return; (*de fortune*) reversal; **être de r.** to be back (**de** from); **en r.** (*en échange*) in return; **par r.** (**du courrier**) by return (of post), *Am* by return mail; **à mon retour** when I get *ou* got back (**de** from); **r. en arrière** flashback; **r. de flamme** *Fig* backlash; **match r.** return match *ou Am* game.

retourner [r(ə)turne] *vt* (*aux* **avoir**) (*tableau etc*) to turn round; (*matelas, steak etc*) to turn over; (*foin, terre etc*) to turn; (*vêtement, sac etc*) to turn inside out; (*maison*) to turn upside down; (*compliment, lettre*) to return; **r. qn** (*bouleverser*) *Fam* to upset s.o., shake s.o.; **r. contre qn** (*argument*) to turn against s.o.; (*arme*) to turn on s.o.; **de quoi il retourne** what it's about; **— vi** (*aux* **être**) to go back, return; **— se r.** *vpr* (*pour regarder*) to turn round, look back; (*sur le dos*) to turn over *ou* round; (*dans son lit*) to toss and turn; (*voiture*) to overturn; **s'en r.** to go back; **se r. contre** *Fig* to turn against.

retracer [r(ə)trase] *vt* (*histoire etc*) to retrace.

rétracter [retrakte] *vt*, **— se r.** *vpr* to retract. ◆**rétractation** *nf* (*désaveu*) retraction.

retrait [r(ə)trɛ] *nm* withdrawal; (*de bagages, billets*) collection; (*de mer*) ebb(ing); **en r.** (*maison etc*) set back.

retraite [r(ə)trɛt] *nf* **1** (*d'employé*) retirement; (*pension*) (retirement) pension; (*refuge*) retreat, refuge; **r. anticipée** early retirement; **prendre sa r.** to retire; **à la r.** retired; **mettre à la r.** to pension off. **2** *Mil* retreat; **r. aux flambeaux** torchlight tattoo. ◆**retraité, -ée** *a* retired; **—** *nmf* senior citizen, (old age) pensioner.

retrancher [r(ə)trɑ̃ʃe] **1** *vt* (*mot, passage etc*) to cut (**de** from); (*argent, quantité*) to deduct (**de** from). **2 se r.** *vpr* (*soldat, gangster etc*) to entrench oneself; **se r. dans/derrière** *Fig* to take refuge in/behind.

retransmettre [r(ə)trɑ̃smɛtr] *vt* to broadcast. ◆**retransmission** *nf* broadcast.

rétréc/ir [retresir] *vt* to narrow; (*vêtement*) to take in; **— vi, — se r.** *vpr* (*au lavage*) to shrink; (*rue etc*) to narrow. ◆**—i** *a* (*esprit, rue*) narrow.

rétribuer [retribɥe] *vt* to pay, remunerate; (*travail*) to pay for. ◆**rétribution** *nf* payment, remuneration.

rétro [retro] *a inv* (*mode etc*) which harks back to the past, retro.

rétro- [retro] *préf* retro-. ◆**rétroactif, -ive** *a* retroactive.

rétrograde [retrograd] *a* retrograde. ◆**rétrograder** *vi* (*reculer*) to move back; (*civilisation etc*) to go backwards; *Aut* to change down; **—** *vt* (*fonctionnaire, officier*) to demote.

rétrospectif, -ive [retrospɛktif, -iv] *a* (*sentiment etc*) retrospective; **—** *nf* (*de films, tableaux*) retrospective. ◆**rétrospectivement** *adv* in retrospect.

retrouss/er [r(ə)truse] *vt* (*jupe etc*) to hitch *ou* tuck up; (*manches*) to roll up ◆**—é** *a* (*nez*) snub, turned-up.

retrouver [r(ə)truve] *vt* to find (again); (*rejoindre*) to meet (again); (*forces, santé*) to regain; (*découvrir*) to rediscover; (*se rappeler*) to recall; **— se r.** *vpr* (*chose*) to be found (again); (*se trouver*) to find oneself (back); (*se rencontrer*) to meet (again); **s'y r.** (*s'orienter*) to find one's bearings *ou* way. ◆**retrouvailles** *nfpl* reunion.

rétroviseur [retrovizœr] *nm Aut* (rear-view) mirror.

réunion [reynjɔ̃] *nf* (*séance*) meeting; (*d'objets*) collection, gathering; (*d'éléments divers*) combination; (*jonction*) joining. ◆**réunir** *vt* to collect, gather; (*relier*) to join; (*convoquer*) to call together, assemble; (*rapprocher*) to bring together; (*qua-*

lités, tendances) to combine. ◆**réunis** *apl*
(*éléments*) combined.

réuss/ir [reysir] *vi* to succeed, be successful
(**à faire** in doing); (*plante*) to thrive; **r. à**
(*examen*) to pass; **r. à qn** to work (out) well
for s.o.; (*aliment, climat*) to agree with s.o.;
— *vt* to make a success of. ◆**—i** *a* successful. ◆**réussite** *nf* **1** success. **2 faire des**
réussites *Cartes* to play patience.

revaloir [r(ə)valwar] *vt* **je vous le revaudrai**
(*en bien ou en mal*) I'll pay you back.

revaloriser [r(ə)valɔrize] *vt* (*salaire*) to
raise. ◆**revalorisation** *nf* raising.

revanche [r(ə)vɑ̃ʃ] *nf* revenge; *Sp* return
game; **en r.** on the other hand.

rêve [rɛv] *nm* dream; **faire un r.** to have a
dream; **maison/voiture/etc de r.** dream
house/car/etc. ◆**rêvasser** *vi* to daydream.

revêche [rəvɛʃ] *a* bad-tempered, surly.

réveil [revɛj] *nm* waking (up); *Fig* awakening; (*pendule*) alarm (clock). ◆**réveill/er**
vt (*personne*) to wake (up); (*sentiment, souvenir*) *Fig* to revive, awaken; **— se r.** *vpr* to
wake (up); *Fig* to revive, awaken. ◆**—é** *a*
awake. ◆**réveille-matin** *nm inv* alarm
(clock).

réveillon [revɛjɔ̃] *nm* (*repas*) midnight supper (*on Christmas Eve or New Year's Eve*).
◆**réveillonner** *vi* to take part in a *réveillon.*

révéler [revele] *vt* to reveal (**que** that); **— se**
r. to be revealed; **se r. facile/etc** to turn out
to be easy/etc. ◆**révélateur, -trice** *a* re-
vealing; **r. de** indicative of. ◆**révélation**
nf revelation.

revenant [rəvnɑ̃] *nm* ghost.

revendiquer [r(ə)vɑ̃dike] *vt* to claim; (*exiger*) to demand. ◆**revendicatif, -ive** *a*
(*mouvement etc*) protest-. ◆**revendication** *nf* claim; demand; (*action*) claiming;
demanding.

revendre [r(ə)vɑ̃dr] *vt* to resell; **avoir (de)**
qch à r. to have sth to spare. ◆**revendeur,
-euse** *nmf* retailer; (*d'occasion*) second-
hand dealer; **r. (de drogue)** drug pusher; **r.**
de billets ticket tout. ◆**revente** *nf* resale.

revenir* [rəvnir] *vi* (*aux* être) to come back,
return; (*date*) to come round again; (*mot*)
to come *ou* crop up; (*coûter*) to cost (**à qn**
s.o.); **r. à** (*activité, sujet*) to go back to, return to; (*se résumer à*) to boil down to; **r. à**
qn (*forces, mémoire*) to come back to s.o.,
return to s.o.; (*honneur*) to fall to s.o.; **r. à**
soi to come to *ou* round; **r. de** (*maladie,
surprise*) to get over; **r. sur** (*décision,
promesse*) to go back on; (*passé, question*)

to go back over; **r. sur ses pas** to retrace
one's steps; **faire r.** (*aliment*) to brown.

revenu [rəvny] *nm* income (**de** from); (*d'un
État*) revenue (**de** from); **déclaration de
revenus** tax return.

rêv/er [reve] *vi* to dream (**de** of, **de faire** of
doing); — *vt* to dream (**que** that); (*désirer*)
to dream of. ◆**—é** *a* ideal.

réverbération [reverberasjɔ̃] *nf* (*de lumière*)
reflection; (*de son*) reverberation.

révérence [reverɑ̃s] *nf* reverence; (*salut
d'homme*) bow; (*salut de femme*) curts(e)y;
faire une r. to bow; to curts(e)y. ◆**révérer**
vt to revere.

révérend, -ende [reverɑ̃, -ɑ̃d] *a* & *nm* *Rel*
reverend.

rêverie [revri] *nf* daydream; (*activité*)
daydreaming.

revers [r(ə)ver] *nm* (*côté*) reverse; *Tennis*
backhand; (*de veste*) lapel; (*de pantalon*)
turn-up, *Am* cuff; (*d'étoffe*) wrong side;
(*coup du sort*) setback, reverse; **r. de main**
(*coup*) backhander; **le r. de la médaille** *Fig*
the other side of the coin.

réversible [reversibl] *a* reversible.

revêtir* [r(ə)vetir] *vt* to cover (**de** with);
(*habit*) to put on; (*caractère, forme*) to assume; (*route*) to surface; **r. qn** (*habiller*) to
dress s.o. (**de** in); **r. de** (*signature*) to provide with. ◆**revêtement** *nm* (*surface*) covering; (*de route*) surface.

rêveur, -euse [revœr, -øz] *a* dreamy; — *nmf*
dreamer.

revient [rəvjɛ̃] *nm* **prix de r.** cost price.

revigorer [r(ə)vigɔre] *vt* (*personne*) to revive.

revirement [r(ə)virmɑ̃] *nm* (*changement*)
about-turn, *Am* about-face; (*de situation,
d'opinion, de politique*) reversal.

réviser [revize] *vt* (*notes, texte*) to revise;
(*jugement, règlement etc*) to review; (*machine, voiture*) to overhaul, service. ◆**révision** *nf* revision; review; overhaul, service.

revivre* [r(ə)vivr] *vi* to live again; **faire r.** to
revive; — *vt* (*incident etc*) to relive.

révocation [revɔkasjɔ̃] *nf* **1** (*de contrat etc*)
revocation. **2** (*de fonctionnaire*) dismissal.

revoici [r(ə)vwasi] *prép* **me r.** here I am
again.

revoilà [r(ə)vwala] *prép* **la r.** there she is
again.

revoir* [r(ə)vwar] *vt* to see (again); (*texte*)
to revise; **au r.** goodbye.

révolte [revɔlt] *nf* revolt. ◆**révolt/er 1** to
revolt, incense. **2 se r.** *vpr* to revolt, rebel
(**contre** against). ◆**—ant** *a* (*honteux*) revolting. ◆**—é, -ée** *nmf* rebel.

révolu [revɔly] *a* (*époque*) past; **avoir trente ans révolus** to be over thirty (years of age).

révolution [revɔlysjɔ̃] *nf* (*changement, rotation*) revolution. ◆**révolutionnaire** *a* & *nmf* revolutionary. ◆**révolutionner** *vt* to revolutionize; (*émouvoir*) *Fig* to shake up.

revolver [revɔlver] *nm* revolver, gun.

révoquer [revɔke] *vt* **1** (*contrat etc*) to revoke. **2** (*fonctionnaire*) to dismiss.

revue [r(ə)vy] *nf* **1** (*examen*) & *Mil* review; **passer en r.** to review. **2** (*de music-hall*) variety show. **3** (*magazine*) magazine; (*spécialisée*) journal.

rez-de-chaussée [redʃose] *nm inv* ground floor, *Am* first floor.

rhabiller (se) [sərabije] *vpr* to get dressed again.

rhapsodie [rapsɔdi] *nf* rhapsody.

rhétorique [retɔrik] *nf* rhetoric.

Rhin [rɛ̃] *nm* **le R.** the Rhine.

rhinocéros [rinɔserɔs] *nm* rhinoceros.

rhododendron [rɔdɔdɛ̃drɔ̃] *nm* rhododendron.

rhubarbe [rybarb] *nf* rhubarb.

rhum [rɔm] *nm* rum.

rhumatisme [rymatism] *nm Méd* rheumatism; **avoir des rhumatismes** to have rheumatism. ◆**rhumatisant, -ante** *a* & *nmf* rheumatic. ◆**rhumatismal, -aux** *a* (*douleur*) rheumatic.

rhume [rym] *nm* cold; **r. de cerveau** head cold; **r. des foins** hay fever.

riant [rjɑ̃] *a* cheerful, smiling.

ricaner [rikane] *vi* (*sarcastiquement*) to snigger; (*bêtement*) to giggle.

riche [riʃ] *a* rich; (*personne, pays*) rich, wealthy; **r. en** (*minérai, vitamines etc*) rich in; — *nmf* rich ou wealthy person; **les riches** the rich. ◆**—ment** *a* (*vêtu, illustré etc*) richly. ◆**richesse** *nf* wealth; (*d'étoffe, de sol, vocabulaire*) richness; *pl* (*trésor*) riches; (*ressources*) wealth.

ricin [risɛ̃] *nm* **huile de r.** castor oil.

ricocher [rikɔʃe] *vi* to ricochet, rebound. ◆**ricochet** *nm* ricochet, rebound; **par r.** *Fig* as an indirect result.

rictus [riktys] *nm* grin, grimace.

ride [rid] *nf* wrinkle; ripple. ◆**rider** *vt* (*visage*) to wrinkle; (*eau*) to ripple; — **se r.** *vpr* to wrinkle.

rideau, -x [rido] *nm* curtain; (*métallique*) shutter; (*écran*) *Fig* screen (**de** of); **le r. de fer** *Pol* the Iron Curtain.

ridicule [ridikyl] *a* ridiculous, ludicrous; — *nm* (*moquerie*) ridicule; (*défaut*) absurdity; (*de situation etc*) ridiculousness; **tourner en r.** to ridicule. ◆**ridiculiser** *vt* to ridicule.

rien [rjɛ̃] *pron* nothing; **il ne sait r.** he knows nothing, he doesn't know anything; **r. du tout** nothing at all; **r. d'autre/de bon**/*etc* nothing else/good/*etc*; **r. de tel** nothing like it; **de r.!** (*je vous en prie*) don't mention it!; **ça ne fait r.** it doesn't matter; **en moins de r.** (*vite*) in no time; **trois fois r.** (*chose insignifiante*) next to nothing; **pour r.** (*à bas prix*) for next to nothing; **il n'en est r.** (*ce n'est pas vrai*) nothing of the kind; **r.** only, just; — *nm* trifle, (mere) nothing; **un r. de** a hint ou touch of; **en un r. de temps** (*vite*) in no time; **un r. trop petit**/*etc* just a bit too small/*etc*.

rieur, -euse [rijœr, -øz] *a* cheerful.

riflard [riflar] *nm Fam* brolly, umbrella.

rigide [riʒid] *a* rigid; (*carton, muscle*) stiff; (*personne*) *Fig* inflexible; (*éducation*) strict. ◆**rigidité** *nf* rigidity; stiffness; inflexibility; strictness.

rigole [rigɔl] *nf* (*conduit*) channel; (*filet d'eau*) rivulet.

rigoler [rigɔle] *vi Fam* to laugh; (*s'amuser*) to have fun ou a laugh; (*plaisanter*) to joke (**avec** about). ◆**rigolade** *nf Fam* fun; (*chose ridicule*) joke, farce; **prendre qch à la r.** to make a joke out of sth. ◆**rigolo, -ote** *a Fam* funny; — *nmf Fam* joker.

rigueur [rigœr] *nf* rigour; harshness; strictness; (*précision*) precision; **être de r.** to be the rule; **à la r.** if absolutely necessary, at ou *Am* in a pinch; **tenir r. à qn de qch** *Fig* to hold sth against s.o. ◆**rigoureux, -euse** *a* rigorous; (*climat, punition*) harsh; (*personne, morale, sens*) strict.

rillettes [rijɛt] *nfpl* potted minced pork.

rime [rim] *nf* rhyme. ◆**rimer** *vi* to rhyme (**avec** with); **ça ne rime à rien** it makes no sense.

rincer [rɛ̃se] *vt* to rinse (out). ◆**rinçage** *nm* rinsing; (*opération*) rinse.

ring [riŋ] *nm* (*boxing*) ring.

ringard [rɛ̃gar] *a* (*démodé*) *Fam* unfashionable, fuddy-duddy.

ripaille [ripaj] *nf Fam* feast.

riposte [ripɔst] *nf* (*réponse*) retort; (*attaque*) counter(attack). ◆**riposter** *vi* to retort; **r. à** (*attaque*) to counter; (*insulte*) to reply to; — *vt* **r. que** to retort that.

rire* [rir] *vi* to laugh (**de** at); (*s'amuser*) to have a good time; (*plaisanter*) to joke; **faire qch pour r.** to do sth for a laugh ou a joke; **se r. de qch** to laugh sth off; — *nm* laugh; *pl* laughter; **le r.** (*activité*) laughter. ◆**risée** *nf* mockery; **être la r. de** to be the laughing stock of. ◆**risible** *a* laughable.

ris [ri] *nm* **r. de veau** *Culin* (calf) sweetbread.

risque [risk] *nm* risk; **r. du métier** occupational hazard; **au r. de qch/de faire** at the risk of sth/of doing; **à vos risques et périls** at your own risk; **assurance tous risques** comprehensive insurance. ◆**risquer** *vt* to risk; (*question, regard*) to venture, hazard; **r. de faire** to stand a good chance of doing; **se r. à faire** to dare to do; **se r. dans** to venture into. ◆**risqué** *a* risky; (*plaisanterie*) daring, risqué.

ristourne [risturn] *nf* discount.

rite [rit] *nm* rite; (*habitude*) *Fig* ritual. ◆**rituel, -elle** *a* & *nm* ritual.

rivage [rivaʒ] *nm* shore.

rival, -ale, -aux [rival, -o] *a* & *nmf* rival. ◆**rivaliser** *vi* to compete (**avec** with, **de** in). ◆**rivalité** *nf* rivalry.

rive [riv] *nf* (*de fleuve*) bank; (*de lac*) shore.

rivé [rive] *a* **r. à** (*chaise etc*) *Fig* riveted to; **r. sur** *Fig* riveted on. ◆**rivet** *nm* (*tige*) rivet. ◆**riveter** *vt* to rivet (together).

riverain, -aine [rivrɛ̃, -ɛn] *a* riverside; lakeside; – *nmf* riverside resident; (*de lac*) lakeside resident; (*de rue*) resident.

rivière [rivjɛr] *nf* river.

rixe [riks] *nf* brawl, scuffle.

riz [ri] *nm* rice; **r. au lait** rice pudding. ◆**rizière** *nf* paddy (field), ricefield.

RN *abrév* = **route nationale**.

robe [rɔb] *nf* (*de femme*) dress; (*d'ecclésiastique, de juge*) robe; (*de professeur*) gown; (*pelage*) coat; **r. de soirée** *ou* **du soir** evening dress *ou* gown; **r. de grossesse/de mariée** maternity/wedding dress; **r. de chambre** dressing gown; **r. chasuble** pinafore (dress).

robinet [rɔbinɛ] *nm* tap, *Am* faucet; **eau du r.** tap water.

robot [rɔbo] *nm* robot; **r. ménager** food processor, liquidizer.

robuste [rɔbyst] *a* robust. ◆**robustesse** *nf* robustness.

roc [rɔk] *nm* rock.

rocaille [rɔkaj] *nf* (*terrain*) rocky ground; (*de jardin*) rockery. ◆**rocailleux, -euse** *a* rocky, stony; (*voix*) harsh.

rocambolesque [rɔkɑ̃bɔlɛsk] *a* (*aventure etc*) fantastic.

roche [rɔʃ] *nf*, **rocher** [rɔʃe] *nm* (*bloc, substance*) rock. ◆**rocheux, -euse** *a* rocky.

rock [rɔk] *nm* (*musique*) rock; – *a inv* (*chanteur etc*) rock-.

rod/er [rɔde] *vt* (*moteur, voiture*) to run in, *Am* break in; **être rodé** (*personne*) *Fig* to have got *ou Am* gotten the hang of things. ◆**—age** *nm* running in, *Am* breaking in.

rôd/er [rode] *vi* to roam (about); (*suspect*) to prowl (about). ◆**—eur, -euse** *nmf* prowler.

rogne [rɔɲ] *nf Fam* anger; **en r.** in a temper.

rogner [rɔɲe] *vt* to trim, clip; (*réduire*) to cut; – *vi* **r. sur** (*réduire*) to cut down on. ◆**rognures** *nfpl* clippings, trimmings.

rognon [rɔɲɔ̃] *nm Culin* kidney.

roi [rwa] *nm* king; **fête** *ou* **jour des rois** Twelfth Night.

roitelet [rwatlɛ] *nm* (*oiseau*) wren.

rôle [rol] *nm* role, part; **à tour de r.** in turn.

romain, -aine [rɔmɛ̃, -ɛn] **1** *a* & *nmf* Roman. **2** *nf* (*laitue*) cos (lettuce), *Am* romaine.

roman [rɔmɑ̃] **1** *nm* novel; (*histoire*) *Fig* story; **r.-fleuve** saga. **2** *a* (*langue*) Romance; *Archit* Romanesque. ◆**romancé** *a* (*histoire*) fictional. ◆**romancier, -ière** *nmf* novelist.

romanesque [rɔmanɛsk] *a* romantic; (*incroyable*) fantastic.

romanichel, -elle [rɔmaniʃɛl] *nmf* gipsy.

romantique [rɔmɑ̃tik] *a* romantic. ◆**romantisme** *nm* romanticism.

romarin [rɔmarɛ̃] *nm Bot Culin* rosemary.

romp/re* [rɔ̃pr] *vt* to break; (*pourparlers, relations*) to break off; (*digue*) to burst; – *vi* to break (*Fig* **avec** with); to burst; (*fiancés*) to break it off; – **se r.** *vpr* to break; to burst. ◆**—u** *a* **1** (*fatigué*) exhausted. **2 r. à** (*expérimenté*) experienced in.

romsteck [rɔmstɛk] *nm* rump steak.

ronces [rɔ̃s] *nfpl* (*branches*) brambles.

ronchonner [rɔ̃ʃɔne] *vi Fam* to grouse, grumble.

rond [rɔ̃] *a* round; (*gras*) plump; (*honnête*) straight; (*ivre*) *Fam* tight; **dix francs tout r.** ten francs exactly; – *adv* **tourner r.** (*machine etc*) to run smoothly; – *nm* (*objet*) ring; (*cercle*) circle; (*tranche*) slice; *pl* (*argent*) *Fam* money; **r. de serviette** napkin ring; **en r.** (*s'asseoir etc*) in a ring *ou* circle; **tourner en r.** (*toupie etc*) & *Fig* to go round and round. ◆**r.-de-cuir** *nm* (*pl* **ronds-de-cuir**) *Péj* pen pusher. ◆**r.-point** *nm* (*pl* **ronds-points**) *Aut* roundabout, *Am* traffic circle. ◆**ronde** *nf* (*tour de surveillance*) round; (*de policier*) beat; (*danse*) round (dance); (*note*) *Mus* semibreve, *Am* whole note; **à la r.** around; (*boire*) in turn. ◆**rondelet, -ette** *a* chubby; (*somme*) *Fig* tidy. ◆**rondelle** *nf* (*tranche*) slice; *Tech* washer. ◆**rondement** *adv* (*efficacement*) briskly; (*franchement*) straight. ◆**rondeur** *nf* roundness; (*du corps*) plumpness. ◆**rondin** *nm* log.

ronéotyper [rɔneɔtipe] *vt* to duplicate, roneo.

ronflant [rɔ̃flɑ̃] *a* (*langage etc*) *Péj* high-flown; (*feu*) roaring.

ronfler [rɔ̃fle] *vi* to snore; (*moteur*) to hum. ◆**ronflement** *nm* snore, snoring; hum(ming).

rong/er [rɔ̃ʒe] *vt* to gnaw (at); (*ver, mer, rouille*) to eat into (*sth*); (*chagrin, maladie*) to consume s.o.; **se r. les ongles** to bite one's nails; **se r. les sangs** (*s'inquiéter*) to worry oneself sick. ◆**—eur** *nm* (*animal*) rodent.

ronron [rɔ̃rɔ̃] *nm*, **ronronnement** [rɔ̃rɔnmɑ̃] *nm* purr(ing). ◆**ronronner** *vi* to purr.

roquette [rɔkɛt] *nf Mil* rocket.

rosbif [rɔsbif] *nm du r.* (*rôti*) roast beef; (*à rôtir*) roasting beef; **un r.** a joint of roast *ou* roasting beef.

rose [roz] **1** *nf* (*fleur*) rose. **2** *a* (*couleur*) pink; (*situation, teint*) rosy; — *nm* pink. ◆**rosé** *a* pinkish; & — *a* & *nm* (*vin*) rosé. ◆**rosette** *nf* (*d'un officier*) rosette; (*nœud*) bow. ◆**rosier** *nm* rose bush.

roseau, -x [rozo] *nm* (*plante*) reed.

rosée [roze] *nf* dew.

rosse [rɔs] *a* & *nf Fam* nasty (person).

ross/er [rɔse] *vt Fam* to thrash. ◆**—ée** *nf Fam* thrashing.

rossignol [rɔsiɲɔl] *nm* **1** (*oiseau*) nightingale. **2** (*crochet*) picklock.

rot [ro] *nm Fam* burp, belch. ◆**roter** *vi Fam* to burp, belch.

rotation [rɔtasjɔ̃] *nf* rotation; (*de stock*) turnover. ◆**rotatif, -ive** *a* rotary; — *nf* rotary press.

rotin [rɔtɛ̃] *nm* rattan, cane.

rôt/ir [rotir] *vti*, — **se r.** *vpr* to roast; **faire r.** to roast. ◆**—i** *nm du r.* roasting meat; (*cuit*) roast meat; **un r.** a joint; **r. de bœuf/de porc** (joint of) roast beef/pork. ◆**rôtissoire** *nf* (roasting) spit.

rotule [rɔtyl] *nf* kneecap.

roturier, -ière [rɔtyrje, -jɛr] *nmf* commoner.

rouage [rwaʒ] *nm* (*de montre etc*) (working) part; (*d'organisation etc*) *Fig* cog.

roublard [rublar] *a* wily, foxy.

rouble [rubl] *nm* (*monnaie*) r(o)uble.

roucouler [rukule] *vi* (*oiseau, amoureux*) to coo.

roue [ru] *nf* wheel; **r. (dentée)** cog(wheel); **faire la r.** (*paon*) to spread its tail; (*se pavaner*) *Fig* to strut; **faire r. libre** *Aut* to freewheel.

roué, -ée [rwe] *a* & *nmf* sly *ou* calculating (person).

rouer [rwe] *vt* **r. qn de coups** to beat s.o. black and blue.

rouet [rwe] *nm* spinning wheel.

rouge [ruʒ] *a* red; (*fer*) red-hot; — *nm* (*couleur*) red; (*vin*) *Fam* red wine; (à lèvres) lipstick; **r. (à joues)** rouge; **le feu est au r.** *Aut* the (traffic) lights are red; — *nmf* (*personne*) *Pol* Red. ◆**r.-gorge** *nm* (*pl* **rouges-gorges**) robin. ◆**rougeâtre** *a* reddish. ◆**rougeaud** *a* red-faced. ◆**rougeoyer** *vi* to glow (red). ◆**rougeur** *nf* redness; (*due à la gêne ou à la honte*) blush(ing); *pl Méd* red spots *ou* blotches. ◆**rougir** *vti* to redden, turn red; — *vi* (*de gêne, de honte*) to blush (**de** with); (*de colère, de joie*) to flush (**de** with).

rougeole [ruʒɔl] *nf* measles.

rouget [ruʒe] *nm* (*poisson*) mullet.

rouille [ruj] *nf* rust; — *a inv* (*couleur*) rust(-coloured). ◆**rouill/er** *vi* to rust; — **se r.** *vpr* to rust; (*esprit, sportif etc*) *Fig* to get rusty. ◆**—é** *a* rusty.

roul/er [rule] *vt* to roll; (*brouette, meuble*) to wheel, push; (*crêpe, ficelle, manches etc*) to roll up; **r. qn** (*duper*) *Fam* to cheat s.o.; — *vi* to roll; (*train, voiture*) to go, travel; (*conducteur*) to drive; **r. sur** (*conversation*) to turn on; **ça roule!** *Fam* everything's fine!; — **se r.** *vpr* to roll; **se r. dans** (*couverture etc*) to roll oneself (up) in. ◆**—ant** *a* (*escalier, trottoir*) moving; (*meuble*) on wheels. ◆**—é** *nm* (*gâteau*) Swiss roll. ◆**rouleau, -x** *nm* (*outil, vague*) roller; (*de papier, pellicule etc*) roll; **r. à pâtisserie** rolling pin; **r. compresseur** steamroller. ◆**roulement** *nm* (*bruit*) rumbling, rumble; (*de tambour, de tonnerre, d'yeux*) roll; (*ordre*) rotation; **par r.** in rotation; **r. à billes** *Tech* ball bearing. ◆**roulette** *nf* (*de meuble*) castor; (*de dentiste*) drill; (*jeu*) roulette. ◆**roulis** *nm* (*de navire*) roll(ing).

roulotte [rulɔt] *nf* (*de gitan*) caravan.

Roumanie [rumani] *nf* Romania. ◆**roumain, -aine** *a* & *nmf* Romanian; — *nm* (*langue*) Romanian.

round [rawnd, rund] *nm Boxe* round.

roupiller [rupije] *vi Fam* to kip, sleep.

rouquin, -ine [rukɛ̃, -in] *a Fam* red-haired; — *nmf Fam* redhead.

rouspét/er [ruspete] *vi Fam* to grumble, complain. ◆**—eur, -euse** *nmf* grumbler.

rousse [rus] *voir* **roux.**

rousseur [rusœr] *nf* redness; **tache de r.** freckle. ◆**roussir** *vt* (*brûler*) to singe, scorch; — *vi* (*feuilles*) to turn brown; **faire r.** *Culin* to brown.

route [rut] *nf* road (**de** to); (*itinéraire*) way,

route; (*aérienne, maritime*) route; (*chemin*) *Fig* path, way; **r. nationale/départementale** main/secondary road; **grande r., grand-r.** main road; **code de la r.** Highway Code; **en r.** on the way, en route; **en r.!** let's go!; **par la r.** by road; **sur la bonne r.** *Fig* on the right track; **mettre en r.** (*voiture etc*) to start (up); **se mettre en r.** to set out (**pour** for); **une heure de r.** *Aut* an hour's drive; **bonne r.!** *Aut* have a good trip! ◆**routier, -ière** *a* (*carte etc*) road-; − *nm* (*camionneur*) (long distance) lorry *ou Am* truck driver; (*restaurant*) transport café, *Am* truck stop.

routine [rutin] *nf* routine; **de r.** (*contrôle etc*) routine-. ◆**routinier, -ière** *a* (*travail etc*) routine-; (*personne*) addicted to routine.

rouvrir* [ruvrir] *vti*, − **se r.** *vpr* to reopen.

roux, rousse [ru, rus] *a* (*cheveux*) red, ginger; (*personne*) red-haired; − *nmf* redhead.

royal, -aux [rwajal, -o] *a* royal; (*cadeau, festin etc*) fit for a king; (*salaire*) princely. ◆**royalement** *adv* (*traiter*) royally. ◆**royaliste** *a* & *nmf* royalist. ◆**royaume** *nm* kingdom. ◆**Royaume-Uni** *nm* United Kingdom. ◆**royauté** *nf* (*monarchie*) monarchy.

ruade [rɥad] *nf* (*d'âne etc*) kick.

ruban [rybɑ̃] *nm* ribbon; (*d'acier, de chapeau*) band; **r. adhésif** adhesive *ou* sticky tape.

rubéole [rybeɔl] *nf* German measles, rubella.

rubis [rybi] *nm* (*pierre*) ruby; (*de montre*) jewel.

rubrique [rybrik] *nf* (*article*) *Journ* column; (*catégorie, titre*) heading.

ruche [ryʃ] *nf* (bee)hive.

rude [ryd] *a* (*grossier*) crude; (*rêche*) rough; (*pénible*) tough; (*hiver, voix*) harsh; (*remarquable*) tremendous. ◆**−ment** *adv* (*parler, traiter*) harshly; (*frapper, tomber*) hard; (*très*) *Fam* awfully. ◆**rudesse** *nf* harshness. ◆**rudoyer** *vt* to treat harshly.

rudiments [rydimɑ̃] *nmpl* rudiments. ◆**rudimentaire** *a* rudimentary.

rue [ry] *nf* street; **être à la r.** (*sans domicile*) to be on the streets. ◆**ruelle** *nf* alley(way).

ruer [rɥe] **1** *vi* (*cheval*) to kick (out). **2 se r.** *vpr* (*foncer*) to rush, fling oneself (**sur** at). ◆**ruée** *nf* rush.

rugby [rygbi] *nm* rugby. ◆**rugbyman,** *pl* **-men** [rygbiman, -mɛn] *nm* rugby player.

rug/ir [ryʒir] *vi* to roar. ◆**−issement** *nm* roar.

rugueux, -euse [rygø, -øz] *a* rough. ◆**rugosité** *nf* roughness; *pl* (*aspérités*) roughness.

ruine [rɥin] *nf* (*décombres*) & *Fig* ruin; **en r.** (*édifice*) in ruins; **tomber en r.** to fall into ruin. ◆**ruiner** *vt* to ruin; − **se r.** *vpr* (*en dépensant*) to ruin oneself. ◆**ruineux, -euse** *a* (*goûts, projet*) ruinously expensive; (*dépense*) ruinous.

ruisseau, -x [rɥiso] *nm* stream; (*caniveau*) gutter. ◆**ruisseler** *vi* to stream (**de** with).

rumeur [rymœr] *nf* (*protestation*) clamour; (*murmure*) murmur; (*nouvelle*) rumour.

ruminer [rymine] *vt* (*méditer*) to ponder on, ruminate over.

rumsteak [rɔmstɛk] *nm* rump steak.

rupture [ryptyr] *nf* break(ing); (*de fiançailles, relations*) breaking off; (*de pourparlers*) breakdown (**de** in); (*brouille*) break (up), split; (*de contrat*) breach; (*d'organe*) *Méd* rupture.

rural, -aux [ryral, -o] *a* rural, country-; − *nmpl* country people.

ruse [ryz] *nf* (*subterfuge*) trick; **la r.** (*habileté*) cunning; (*fourberie*) trickery. ◆**rusé, -ée** *a* & *nmf* crafty *ou* cunning (person). ◆**ruser** *vi* to resort to trickery.

Russie [rysi] *nf* Russia. ◆**russe** *a* & *nmf* Russian; − *nm* (*langue*) Russian.

rustique [rystik] *a* (*meuble*) rustic.

rustre [rystr] *nm* lout, churl.

rutabaga [rytabaga] *nm* (*racine*) swede, *Am* rutabaga.

rutilant [rytilɑ̃] *a* gleaming, glittering.

rythme [ritm] *nm* rhythm; (*de travail*) rate, tempo; (*de la vie*) pace; **au r. de trois par jour** at a *ou* the rate of three a day. ◆**rythmé** *a*, ◆**rythmique** *a* rhythmic(al).

S

S, s [ɛs] *nm* S, s.

s' [s] *voir* **se, si.**

sa [sa] *voir* **son²**.

SA *abrév* (*société anonyme*) *Com* plc, *Am* Inc.

sabbat [saba] *nm* (Jewish) Sabbath.

◆**sabbatique** *a* (*année etc*) *Univ* sabbatical.

sable [sabl] *nm* sand; **sables mouvants** quicksand(s). ◆**sabler** *vt* (*route*) to sand. ◆**sableux, -euse** *a* (*eau*) sandy. ◆**sablier** *nm* hourglass; *Culin* egg timer. ◆**sablière** *nf* (*carrière*) sandpit. ◆**sablonneux, -euse** *a* (*terrain*) sandy.

sablé [sable] *nm* shortbread biscuit *ou Am* cookie.

saborder [saborde] *vt* (*navire*) to scuttle; (*entreprise*) *Fig* to shut down.

sabot [sabo] *nm* **1** (*de cheval etc*) hoof. **2** (*chaussure*) clog. **3** (*de frein*) *Aut* shoe; **s. (de Denver)** *Aut* (wheel) clamp.

sabot/er [sabote] *vt* to sabotage; (*bâcler*) to botch. ◆—**age** *nm* sabotage; **un s.** an act of sabotage. ◆—**eur, -euse** *nmf* saboteur.

sabre [sabr] *nm* sabre, sword.

sabrer [sabre] *vt* (*élève, candidat*) *Fam* to give a thoroughly bad mark to.

sac [sak] *nm* **1** bag; (*grand et en toile*) sack; **s. (à main)** handbag; **s. à dos** rucksack. **2** **mettre à s.** (*ville*) *Mil* to sack.

saccade [sakad] *nf* jerk, jolt; **par saccades** jerkily, in fits and starts. ◆**saccadé** *a* (*geste, style*) jerky.

saccager [sakaʒe] *vt* (*ville, région*) *Mil* to sack; (*bouleverser*) *Fig* to turn upside down.

saccharine [sakarin] *nf* saccharin.

sacerdoce [sasɛrdɔs] *nm* (*fonction*) *Rel* priesthood; *Fig* vocation.

sachet [saʃɛ] *nm* (small) bag; (*de lavande etc*) sachet; **s. de thé** teabag.

sacoche [sakɔʃ] *nf* bag; (*de vélo, moto*) saddlebag; *Scol* satchel.

sacquer [sake] *vt Fam* (*renvoyer*) to sack; (*élève*) to give a thoroughly bad mark to.

sacre [sakr] *nm* (*d'évêque*) consecration; (*de roi*) coronation. ◆**sacrer** *vt* (*évêque*) to consecrate; (*roi*) to crown.

sacré [sakre] *a* (*saint*) sacred; (*maudit*) *Fam* damned. ◆—**ment** *adv Fam* (*très*) damn(ed); (*beaucoup*) a hell of a lot.

sacrement [sakrəmɑ̃] *nm Rel* sacrament.

sacrifice [sakrifis] *nm* sacrifice. ◆**sacrifier** *vt* to sacrifice (à to, **pour** for); – *vi* **s. à** (*mode etc*) to pander to; – **se s.** *vpr* to sacrifice oneself (à to, **pour** for).

sacrilège [sakrilɛʒ] *nm* sacrilege; – *a* sacrilegious.

sacristie [sakristi] *nf* vestry.

sacro-saint [sakrosɛ̃] *a Iron* sacrosanct.

sadisme [sadism] *nm* sadism. ◆**sadique** *a* sadistic; – *nmf* sadist.

safari [safari] *nm* safari; **faire un s.** to go on safari.

safran [safrɑ̃] *nm* saffron.

sagace [sagas] *a* shrewd, sagacious.

sage [saʒ] *a* wise; (*enfant*) well-behaved, good; (*modéré*) moderate; – *nm* wise man, sage. ◆**sagement** *adv* wisely; (*avec calme*) quietly. ◆**sagesse** *nf* wisdom; good behaviour; moderation.

sage-femme [saʒfam] *nf* (*pl* **sages-femmes**) midwife.

Sagittaire [saʒitɛr] *nm* **le S.** (*signe*) Sagittarius.

Sahara [saara] *nm* **le S.** the Sahara (desert).

saign/er [seɲe] *vti* to bleed. ◆—**ant** [seɲɑ̃] *a* (*viande*) *Culin* rare, underdone. ◆—**ée** *nf* **1** *Méd* bleeding, blood-letting; (*perte*) *Fig* heavy loss. **2** **la s. du bras** *Anat* the bend of the arm. ◆**saignement** *nm* bleeding; **s. de nez** nosebleed.

saillant [sajɑ̃] *a* projecting, jutting out; (*trait etc*) *Fig* salient. ◆**saillie** *nf* projection; **en s., faisant s.** projecting.

sain [sɛ̃] *a* healthy; (*moralement*) sane; (*jugement*) sound; (*nourriture*) wholesome, healthy; **s. et sauf** safe and sound, unhurt. ◆**sainement** *adv* (*vivre*) healthily; (*raisonner*) sanely.

saindoux [sɛ̃du] *nm* lard.

saint, sainte [sɛ̃, sɛ̃t] *a* holy; (*personne*) saintly; **s. Jean** Saint John; **sainte nitouche** *Iron* little innocent; **la Sainte Vierge** the Blessed Virgin; – *nmf* saint. ◆**s.-bernard** *nm* (*chien*) St Bernard. ◆**S.-Esprit** *nm* Holy Spirit. ◆**S.-Siège** *nm* Holy See. ◆**S.-Sylvestre** *nf* New Year's Eve.

sais [sɛ] *voir* **savoir.**

saisie [sezi] *nf Jur* seizure; **s. de données** data capture *ou* entry.

sais/ir [sezir] **1** *vt* to grab (hold of), seize; (*occasion*) & *Jur* to seize; (*comprendre*) to understand, grasp; (*frapper*) *Fig* to strike; **se s. de** to grab (hold of), seize. **2** *vt* (*viande*) *Culin* to fry briskly. ◆—**i** *a* **s. de** (*joie, peur etc*) overcome by. ◆—**issant** *a* (*film etc*) gripping; (*contraste, ressemblance*) striking. ◆—**issement** *nm* (*émotion*) shock.

saison [sɛzɔ̃] *nf* season; **en/hors s.** in/out of season; **en pleine** *ou* **haute s.** in (the) high season; **en basse s.** in the low season. ◆**saisonnier, -ière** *a* seasonal.

sait [sɛ] *voir* **savoir.**

salade [salad] **1** *nf* (*laitue*) lettuce; **s. (verte)** (green) salad; **s. de fruits/de tomates/***etc* fruit/tomato/*etc* salad. **2** *nf* (*désordre*) *Fam* mess. **3** *nfpl* (*mensonges*) *Fam* stories, nonsense. ◆**saladier** *nm* salad bowl.

salaire [salɛr] nm wage(s), salary.
salaison [salɛzɔ̃] nf Culin salting; pl (denrées) salt(ed) meat ou fish.
salamandre [salamɑ̃dr] nf (animal) salamander.
salami [salami] nm Culin salami.
salarial, -aux [salarjal, -o] a (accord etc) wage-. ◆**salarié, -ée** a wage-earning; — nmf wage earner.
salaud [salo] nm Arg Péj bastard, swine.
sale [sal] a dirty; (dégoûtant) filthy; (mauvais) nasty; (couleur) dingy. ◆**salement** adv (se conduire, manger) disgustingly. ◆**saleté** nf dirtiness; filthiness; (crasse) dirt, filth; (action) dirty trick; (camelote) Fam rubbish, junk; pl (détritus) mess, dirt; (obscénités) filth. ◆**salir** vt to (make) dirty; (réputation) Fig to sully, tarnish; — **se s.** vpr to get dirty. ◆**salissant** a (métier) dirty, messy; (étoffe) easily dirtied. ◆**salissure** nf (tache) dirty mark.
sal/er [sale] vt Culin to salt. ◆—**é** a 1 (eau) salt-; (saveur) salty; (denrées) salted; (grivois) Fig spicy. 2 (excessif) Fam steep. ◆**salière** nf saltcellar.
salive [saliv] nf saliva. ◆**saliver** vi to salivate.
salle [sal] nf room; (très grande, publique) hall; Th auditorium; (d'hôpital) ward; (public) Th house, audience; **s. à manger** dining room; **s. d'eau** washroom, shower room; **s. d'exposition** Com showroom; **s. de jeux** (pour enfants) games room; (avec machines à sous) amusement arcade; **s. d'opération** Méd operating theatre.
salon [salɔ̃] nm sitting room, lounge; (exposition) show; **s. de beauté/de coiffure** beauty/hairdressing salon; **s. de thé** tearoom(s).
salope [salɔp] nf (femme) Arg Péj bitch, cow. ◆**saloperie** nf Arg (action) dirty trick; (camelote) rubbish, junk; **des saloperies** (propos) filth.
salopette [salɔpɛt] nf dungarees; (d'ouvrier) overalls.
salsifis [salsifi] nf Bot Culin salsify.
saltimbanque [saltɛ̃bɑ̃k] nmf (travelling) acrobat.
salubre [salybr] a healthy, salubrious. ◆**salubrité** nf healthiness; **s. publique** public health.
saluer [salɥe] vt to greet; (en partant) to take one's leave; (de la main) to wave to; (de la tête) to nod to; Mil to salute; **s. qn comme** Fig to hail s.o. as. ◆**salut 1** nm greeting; wave; nod; Mil salute; — int Fam hello!, hi!; (au revoir) bye! **2** nm (de peuple

etc) salvation; (sauvegarde) safety. ◆**salutation** nf greeting.
salutaire [salytɛr] a salutary.
salve [salv] nf salvo.
samedi [samdi] nm Saturday.
SAMU [samy] nm abrév (service d'assistance médicale d'urgence) emergency medical service.
sanatorium [sanatɔrjɔm] nm sanatorium.
sanctifier [sɑ̃ktifje] vt to sanctify.
sanction [sɑ̃ksjɔ̃] nf (approbation, peine) sanction. ◆**sanctionner** vt (confirmer, approuver) to sanction; (punir) to punish.
sanctuaire [sɑ̃ktɥɛr] nm Rel sanctuary.
sandale [sɑ̃dal] nf sandal.
sandwich [sɑ̃dwitʃ] nm sandwich.
sang [sɑ̃] nm blood; **coup de s.** Méd stroke. ◆**sanglant** a bloody; (critique, reproche) scathing. ◆**sanguin, -ine 1** a (vaisseau etc) blood-; (tempérament) full-blooded. **2** nf (fruit) blood orange. ◆**sanguinaire** a blood-thirsty.
sang-froid [sɑ̃frwa] nm self-control, calm; **avec s.-froid** calmly; **de s.-froid** (tuer) in cold blood.
sangle [sɑ̃gl] nf (de selle, parachute) strap.
sanglier [sɑ̃glije] nm wild boar.
sanglot [sɑ̃glo] nm sob. ◆**sangloter** vi to sob.
sangsue [sɑ̃sy] nf leech.
sanitaire [sanitɛr] a health-; (conditions) sanitary; (personnel) medical; (appareils etc) bathroom-, sanitary.
sans [sɑ̃] ([sɑ̃z] before vowel and mute h) prép without; **s. faire** without doing; **ça va s. dire** that goes without saying; **s. qu'il le sache** without him ou his knowing; **s. cela, s. quoi** otherwise; **s. plus** (but) no more than that; **s. exception/faute** without exception/fail; **s. importance/travail** unimportant/unemployed; **s. argent/manches** penniless/sleeveless. ◆**s.-abri** nmf inv homeless person; **les s.-abri** the homeless. ◆**s.-gêne** a inv inconsiderate; — nm inv inconsiderateness. ◆**s.-travail** nmf inv unemployed person.
santé [sɑ̃te] nf health; **en bonne/mauvaise s.** in good/bad health, well/not well; **(à votre) s.!** (en trinquant) your health!, cheers!; **maison de s.** nursing home.
saoul [su] = **soûl.**
saper [sape] vt to undermine.
sapeur-pompier [sapœrpɔ̃pje] nm (pl sapeurs-pompiers) fireman.
saphir [safir] nm (pierre) sapphire; (d'électrophone) sapphire, stylus.

sapin [sapɛ̃] nm (arbre, bois) fir; **s. de Noël** Christmas tree.

sarbacane [sarbakan] nf (jouet) pea-shooter.

sarcasme [sarkasm] nm sarcasm; **un s.** a piece of sarcasm. ◆**sarcastique** a sarcastic.

sarcler [sarkle] vt (jardin etc) to weed.

Sardaigne [sardɛɲ] nf Sardinia.

sardine [sardin] nf sardine.

sardonique [sardɔnik] a sardonic.

SARL abrév (société à responsabilité limitée) Ltd, Am Inc.

sarment [sarmã] nm vine shoot.

sarrasin [sarazɛ̃] nm buckwheat.

sas [sɑ(s)] nm (pièce étanche) Nau Av air-lock.

Satan [satã] nm Satan. ◆**satané** a (maudit) blasted. ◆**satanique** a satanic.

satellite [satelit] nm satellite; **pays s.** Pol satellite (country).

satiété [sasjete] nf **à s.** (boire, manger) one's fill; (répéter) ad nauseam.

satin [satɛ̃] nm satin. ◆**satiné** a satiny, silky.

satire [satir] nf satire (**contre** on). ◆**satirique** a satiric(al).

satisfaction [satisfaksjɔ̃] nf satisfaction. ◆**satisfaire*** vt to satisfy; – vi **s. à** (conditions, engagement etc) to fulfil. ◆**satisfaisant** a (acceptable) satisfactory. ◆**satisfait** a satisfied, content (**de** with).

saturateur [satyratœr] nm (de radiateur) humidifier.

saturer [satyre] vt to saturate (**de** with).

satyre [satir] nm Fam sex fiend.

sauce [sos] nf sauce; (jus de viande) gravy; **s. tomate** tomato sauce. ◆**saucière** nf sauce boat; gravy boat.

saucisse [sosis] nf sausage. ◆**saucisson** nm (cold) sausage.

sauf¹ [sof] prép except (**que** that); **s. avis contraire** unless you hear otherwise; **s. erreur** barring error.

sauf², sauve [sof, sov] a (honneur) intact, saved; **avoir la vie sauve** to be unharmed. ◆**sauf-conduit** nm (document) safe-conduct.

sauge [soʒ] nf Bot Culin sage.

saugrenu [sogrəny] a preposterous.

saule [sol] nm willow; **s. pleureur** weeping willow.

saumâtre [somɑtr] a (eau) briny, brackish.

saumon [somɔ̃] nm salmon; – a inv (couleur) salmon (pink).

saumure [somyr] nf (pickling) brine.

sauna [sona] nm sauna.

saupoudrer [sopudre] vt (couvrir) to sprinkle (**de** with).

saur [sɔr] am **hareng s.** smoked herring, kip-per.

saut [so] nm jump, leap; **faire un s.** to jump, leap; **faire un s. chez qn** (visite) to pop round to s.o.; **au s. du lit** on getting out of bed; **s. à la corde** skipping, Am jumping rope. ◆**sauter** vi to jump, leap; (bombe) to go off, explode; (poudrière etc) to go up, blow up; (fusible) to blow; (se détacher) to come off; **faire s.** (détruire) to blow up; (arracher) to tear off; (casser) to break; (renvoyer) Fam to get rid of, fire; (fusible) to blow; Culin to sauté; **s. à la corde** to skip, Am jump rope; **ça saute aux yeux** it's obvious; – vt (franchir) to jump (over); (mot, classe, repas) to skip. ◆**saute-mouton** nm (jeu) leapfrog. ◆**sautiller** vi to hop. ◆**sautoir** nm Sp jumping area.

sauté [sote] a & nm Culin sauté. ◆**sauteuse** nf (shallow) pan.

sauterelle [sotrɛl] nf grasshopper.

sautes [sot] nfpl (d'humeur, de température) sudden changes (**de** in).

sauvage [sovaʒ] a wild; (primitif, cruel) savage; (farouche) unsociable, shy; (illégal) unauthorized; – nmf unsociable person; (brute) savage. ◆**sauvagerie** nf unsociability; (cruauté) savagery.

sauve [sov] a voir **sauf²**.

sauvegarde [sovgard] nf safeguard (**contre** against). ◆**sauvegarder** vt to safeguard.

sauver [sove] vt **1** to save; (d'un danger) to rescue (**de** from); (matériel) to salvage; **s. la vie à qn** to save s.o.'s life. **2 se s.** vpr (s'enfuir) to run away ou off; (partir) Fam to get off, go. ◆**sauve-qui-peut** nm inv stampede. ◆**sauvetage** nm rescue; **canot de s.** lifeboat; **ceinture de s.** life belt; **radeau de s.** life raft. ◆**sauveteur** nm rescuer. ◆**sauveur** nm saviour.

sauvette (à la) [alasovɛt] adv **vendre à la s.** to hawk illicitly (on the streets).

savant [savã] a learned, scholarly; (manœuvre etc) masterly, clever; – nm scientist. ◆**savamment** adv learnedly; (avec habileté) cleverly, skilfully.

savate [savat] nf old shoe ou slipper.

saveur [savœr] nf (goût) flavour; (piment) Fig savour.

savoir* [savwar] vt to know; (nouvelle) to know, have heard; **j'ai su la nouvelle** I heard ou got to know the news; **s. lire/nager/etc** (pouvoir) to know how to read/swim/etc; **faire s. à qn que** to inform ou tell s.o. that; **à s.** (c'est-à-dire) that is, namely; **je ne saurais pas** I could not, I cannot; **(pas) que je sache** (not) as far as I know; **je n'en sais rien** I have no idea, I don't know; **en s. long sur** to know a lot about; **un je ne sais quoi** a something or other; − *nm* (*culture*) learning, knowledge. ◆**s.-faire** *nm inv* know-how, ability. ◆**s.-vivre** *nm inv* good manners.

savon [savɔ̃] *nm* **1** soap; (*morceau*) bar of soap. **2 passer un s. à qn** (*réprimander*) *Fam* to give s.o. a dressing-down *ou* a talking-to. ◆**savonner** *vt* to soap. ◆**savonnette** *nf* bar of soap. ◆**savonneux, -euse** *a* soapy.

savourer [savure] *vt* to savour, relish. ◆**savoureux, -euse** *a* tasty; (*histoire etc*) *Fig* juicy.

saxophone [saksɔfɔn] *nm* saxophone.

sbire [sbir] *nm* (*homme de main*) *Péj* henchman.

scabreux, -euse [skabrø, -øz] *a* obscene.

scalpel [skalpɛl] *nm* scalpel.

scandale [skɑ̃dal] *nm* scandal; (*tapage*) uproar; **faire s.** (*livre etc*) to scandalize people; **faire un s.** to make a scene. ◆**scandaleux, -euse** *a* scandalous, outrageous. ◆**scandaleusement** *adv* outrageously. ◆**scandaliser** *vt* to scandalize, shock; **− se s.** *vpr* to be shocked *ou* scandalized (**de** by, **que** (+ *sub*) that).

scander [skɑ̃de] *vt* (*vers*) to scan; (*slogan*) to chant.

Scandinavie [skɑ̃dinavi] *nf* Scandinavia. ◆**scandinave** *a & nmf* Scandinavian.

scanner [skanɛr] *nm* (*appareil*) *Méd* scanner.

scaphandre [skafɑ̃dr] *nm* (*de plongeur*) diving suit; (*de cosmonaute*) spacesuit; **s. autonome** aqualung. ◆**scaphandrier** *nm* diver.

scarabée [skarabe] *nm* beetle.

scarlatine [skarlatin] *nf* scarlet fever.

scarole [skarɔl] *nf* endive.

sceau, -x [so] *nm* (*cachet, cire*) seal. ◆**scell/er** *vt* **1** (*document etc*) to seal. **2** (*fixer*) *Tech* to cement. ◆**−és** *nmpl* (*cachets de cire*) seals.

scélérat, -ate [selera, -at] *nmf* scoundrel.

scel-o-frais® [selɔfrɛ] *nm* clingfilm, *Am* plastic wrap.

scénario [senarjo] *nm* (*déroulement*) *Fig* scenario; (*esquisse*) *Cin* scenario; (*dialogues etc*) screenplay. ◆**scénariste** *nmf Cin* scriptwriter.

scène [sɛn] *nf* **1** *Th* scene; (*estrade, art*) stage; (*action*) action; **mettre en s.** (*pièce, film*) to direct. **2** (*dispute*) scene; **faire une s.** (à qn) to make *ou* create a scene; **s. de ménage** domestic quarrel.

scepticisme [sɛptisism] *nm* scepticism, *Am* skepticism. ◆**sceptique** *a* sceptical, *Am* skeptical; − *nmf* sceptic, *Am* skeptic.

scheik [ʃɛk] *nm* sheikh.

schéma [ʃema] *nm* diagram; *Fig* outline. ◆**schématique** *a* diagrammatic; (*succinct*) *Péj* sketchy. ◆**schématiser** *vt* to represent diagrammatically; (*simplifier*) *Péj* to oversimplify.

schizophrène [skizɔfrɛn] *a & nmf* schizophrenic.

sciatique [sjatik] *nf Méd* sciatica.

scie [si] *nf* (*outil*) saw. ◆**scier** *vt* to saw. ◆**scierie** *nf* sawmill.

sciemment [sjamɑ̃] *adv* knowingly.

science [sjɑ̃s] *nf* science; (*savoir*) knowledge; (*habileté*) skill; **sciences humaines** social science(s); **étudier les sciences** to study science. ◆**s.-fiction** *nf* science fiction. ◆**scientifique** *a* scientific; − *nmf* scientist.

scinder [sɛ̃de] *vt*, **− se s.** *vpr* to divide, split.

scintill/er [sɛ̃tije] *vi* to sparkle, glitter; (*étoiles*) to twinkle. ◆**−ement** *nm* sparkling; twinkling.

scission [sisjɔ̃] *nf* (*de parti etc*) split (**de** in).

sciure [sjyr] *nf* sawdust.

sclérose [skleroz] *nf Méd* sclerosis; *Fig* ossification; **s. en plaques** multiple sclerosis. ◆**sclérosé** *a* (*société etc*) *Fig* ossified.

scolaire [skɔlɛr] *a* school-. ◆**scolariser** *vt* (*pays*) to provide with schools; (*enfant*) to send to school, put in school. ◆**scolarité** *nf* schooling.

scooter [skutɛr] *nm* (motor) scooter.

score [skɔr] *nm Sp* score.

scories [skɔri] *nfpl* (*résidu*) slag.

scorpion [skɔrpjɔ̃] *nm* scorpion; **le S.** (*signe*) Scorpio.

scotch [skɔtʃ] *nm* **1** (*boisson*) Scotch, whisky. **2®** (*ruban adhésif*) sellotape®, *Am* scotch (tape)®. ◆**scotcher** *vt* to sellotape, *Am* to tape.

scout [skut] *a & nm* scout. ◆**scoutisme** *nm* scout movement, scouting.

script [skript] *nm* (*écriture*) printing.

scrupule [skrypyl] *nm* scruple; **sans scrupules** unscrupulous; (*agir*) unscrupulously. ◆**scrupuleux, -euse** *a* scrupulous. ◆**scrupuleusement** *adv* scrupulously.

scruter [skryte] *vt* to examine, scrutinize.

scrutin [skrytɛ̃] *nm* (*vote*) ballot; (*opérations électorales*) poll(ing).

sculpter [skylte] *vt* to sculpt(ure), carve.

◆**sculpteur** *nm* sculptor. ◆**sculptural, -aux** *a* (*beauté*) statuesque. ◆**sculpture** *nf* (*art, œuvre*) sculpture; **s. sur bois** wood-carving.

se [s(ə)] (**s'** *before vowel or mute h*) *pron* **1** (*complément direct*) himself; (*sujet femelle*) herself; (*non humain*) itself; (*indéfini*) oneself; *pl* themselves; **il se lave** he washes himself. **2** (*indirect*) to himself; to herself; to itself; to oneself; **se dire** to say to oneself; **elle se dit** she says to herself. **3** (*réciproque*) (to) each other, (to) one another; **ils s'aiment** they love each other *ou* one another; **ils** *ou* **elles se parlent** they speak to each other *ou* one another. **4** (*passif*) **ça se fait** that is done; **ça se vend bien** it sells well. **5** (*possessif*) **il se lave les mains** he washes his hands.

séance [seãs] *nf* **1** (*d'assemblée etc*) session, sitting; (*de travail etc*) session; **s.** (**de pose**) (*chez un peintre*) sitting. **2** *Cin Th* show, performance. **3 s. tenante** at once.

séant [seã] **1** *a* (*convenable*) seemly, proper. **2** *nm* **se mettre sur son s.** to sit up.

seau, -x [so] *nm* bucket, pail.

sec, sèche [sɛk, sɛʃ] *a* dry; (*fruits, légumes*) dried; (*ton*) curt, harsh; (*maigre*) spare; (*cœur*) *Fig* hard; **coup s.** sharp blow, tap; **bruit s.** (*rupture*) snap; − *adv* (*frapper, pleuvoir*) hard; (*boire*) neat, *Am* straight; − *nm* **à s.** dried up, dry; (*sans argent*) *Fam* broke; **au s.** in a dry place. ◆**séch/er** *vti* to dry; − **se s.** *vpr* to dry oneself. **2** *vt* (*cours*) *Scol Fam* to skip; − *vi* (*ignorer*) *Scol Fam* to be stumped. ◆**—age** *nm* drying. ◆**sécheresse** *nf* dryness; (*de ton*) curtness; *Mét* drought. ◆**séchoir** *nm* (*appareil*) drier; **s. à linge** clotheshorse.

sécateur [sekatœr] *nm* pruning shears, secateurs.

sécession [sesesjɔ̃] *nf* secession; **faire s.** to secede.

sèche [sɛʃ] *voir* **sec.** ◆**sèche-cheveux** *nm inv* hair drier. ◆**sèche-linge** *nm inv* tumble drier.

second, -onde[1] [sgɔ̃, -ɔ̃d] *a* & *nmf* second; **de seconde main** second-hand; − *nm* (*adjoint*) second in command; (*étage*) second floor, *Am* third floor; − *nf Rail* second class; *Scol* = fifth form, *Am* = eleventh grade; (*vitesse*) *Aut* second (gear). ◆**secondaire** *a* secondary.

seconde[2] [sgɔ̃d] *nf* (*instant*) second.

seconder [sgɔ̃de] *vt* to assist.

secouer [s(ə)kwe] *vt* to shake; (*paresse, poussière*) to shake off; **s. qn** (*maladie, nouvelle etc*) to shake s.o. up; **s. qch de qch**

(*enlever*) to shake sth out of sth; − **se s.** *vpr* (*faire un effort*) *Fam* to shake oneself out of it.

secour/ir [skurir] *vt* to assist, help. ◆**—able** *a* (*personne*) helpful. ◆**secourisme** *nm* first aid. ◆**secouriste** *nmf* first-aid worker.

secours [s(ə)kur] *nm* assistance, help; (*aux indigents*) aid, relief; **le s., les s.** *Mil* relief; (**premiers**) **s.** *Méd* first aid; **au s.!** help!; **porter s. à qn** to give s.o. assistance *ou* help; **de s.** (*sortie*) emergency-; (*équipe*) rescue-; (*roue*) spare.

secousse [s(ə)kus] *nf* jolt, jerk; (*psychologique*) shock; *Géol* tremor.

secret, -ète [səkrɛ, -ɛt] *a* secret; (*cachottier*) secretive; − *nm* (*discrétion*) secrecy; **en s.** in secret, secretly; **dans le s.** (*au courant*) in on the secret.

secrétaire [səkretɛr] **1** *nmf* secretary; **s. d'État** Secretary of State; **s. de mairie** town clerk; **s. de rédaction** subeditor. **2** *nm* (*meuble*) writing desk. ◆**secrétariat** *nm* (*bureau*) secretary's office; (*d'organisation internationale*) secretariat; (*métier*) secretarial work; **de s.** (*école, travail*) secretarial.

sécréter [sekrete] *vt Méd Biol* to secrete. ◆**sécrétion** *nf* secretion.

secte [sɛkt] *nf* sect. ◆**sectaire** *a* & *nmf Péj* sectarian.

secteur [sɛktœr] *nm Mil Com* sector; (*de ville*) district; (*domaine*) *Fig* area; (*de réseau*) *Él* supply area; (*ligne*) *Él* mains.

section [sɛksjɔ̃] *nf* section; (*de ligne d'autobus*) fare stage; *Mil* platoon. ◆**sectionner** *vt* to divide (into sections); (*artère, doigt*) to sever.

séculaire [sekylɛr] *a* (*tradition etc*) age-old.

secundo [s(ə)gɔ̃do] *adv* secondly.

sécurité [sekyrite] *nf* (*tranquillité*) security; (*matérielle*) safety; **s. routière** road safety; **s. sociale** = social services *ou* security; **de s.** (*dispositif, ceinture, marge etc*) safety-; **en s.** secure; safe. ◆**sécuriser** *vt* to reassure, make feel (emotionally) secure.

sédatif [sedatif] *nm* sedative.

sédentaire [sedãtɛr] *a* sedentary.

sédiment [sedimã] *nm* sediment.

séditieux, -euse [sedisjø, -øz] *a* seditious. ◆**sédition** *nf* sedition.

séduire* [sedɥir] *vt* to charm, attract; (*plaire à*) to appeal to; (*abuser de*) to seduce. ◆**séduisant** *a* attractive. ◆**séducteur, -trice** *a* seductive; − *nmf* seducer. ◆**séduction** *nf* attraction.

segment [sɛgmã] *nm* segment.

ségrégation [segregasjɔ̃] *nf* segregation.

seiche [sɛʃ] *nf* cuttlefish.

seigle [sɛgl] *nm* rye.

seigneur [sɛɲœr] *nm Hist* lord; **S.** *Rel* Lord.

sein [sɛ̃] *nm* (*mamelle, poitrine*) breast; *Fig* bosom; **bout de s.** nipple; **au s. de** (*parti etc*) within; (*bonheur etc*) in the midst of.

Seine [sɛn] *nf* **la S.** the Seine.

séisme [seism] *nm* earthquake.

seize [sɛz] *a & nm* sixteen. ◆**seizième** *a & nmf* sixteenth.

séjour [seʒur] *nm* stay; (*salle de*) **s.** living room. ◆**séjourner** *vi* to stay.

sel [sɛl] *nm* salt; (*piquant*) *Fig* spice; (*humour*) wit; *pl Méd* (smelling) salts; **sels de bain** bath salts.

sélect [selɛkt] *a Fam* select.

sélectif, -ive [selɛktif, -iv] *a* selective. ◆**sélection** *nf* selection. ◆**sélectionner** *vt* to select.

self(-service) [sɛlf(sɛrvis)] *nm* self-service restaurant *ou* shop.

selle [sɛl] **1** *nf* (*de cheval*) saddle. **2** *nfpl* **les selles** *Méd* bowel movements, stools. ◆**seller** *vt* (*cheval*) to saddle.

sellette [sɛlɛt] *nf* **sur la s.** (*personne*) under examination, in the hot seat.

selon [s(ə)lɔ̃] *prép* according to (**que** whether); **c'est s.** *Fam* it (all) depends.

Seltz (eau de) [odsɛls] *nf* soda (water).

semailles [s(ə)maj] *nfpl* (*travail*) sowing; (*période*) seedtime.

semaine [s(ə)mɛn] *nf* week; **en s.** (*opposé à week-end*) in the week.

sémantique [semɑ̃tik] *a* semantic; – *nf* semantics.

sémaphore [semafɔr] *nm* (*appareil*) *Rail Nau* semaphore.

semblable [sɑ̃blabl] *a* similar (**à** to); **être semblables** to be alike *ou* similar; **de semblables propos**/*etc* (*tels*) such remarks/*etc*; – *nm* fellow (creature); **toi et tes semblables** you and your kind.

semblant [sɑ̃blɑ̃] *nm* **faire s.** to pretend (**de faire** to do); **un s. de** a semblance of.

sembler [sɑ̃ble] *vi* to seem (**à** to); **il (me) semble vieux** he seems *ou* looks old (to me); **s. être/faire** to seem to be/to do; – *v imp* **il semble que** (+ *sub ou indic*) it seems that, it looks as if; **il me semble que** it seems to me that, I think.

semelle [s(ə)mɛl] *nf* (*de chaussure*) sole; (*intérieure*) insole.

semer [s(ə)me] *vt* **1** (*graines*) to sow; (*jeter*) *Fig* to strew; (*répandre*) to spread; **semé de** *Fig* strewn with, dotted with. **2** (*concurrent, poursuivant*) to shake off. ◆**semence** *nf*

seed; (*clou*) tack. ◆**semeur, -euse** *nmf* sower (**de** of).

semestre [s(ə)mɛstr] *nm* half-year; *Univ* semester. ◆**semestriel, -ielle** *a* half-yearly.

semi- [səmi] *préf* semi-.

séminaire [seminɛr] *nm* **1** *Univ* seminar. **2** *Rel* seminary.

semi-remorque [səmirəmɔrk] *nm* (*camion*) articulated lorry, *Am* semi(trailer).

semis [s(ə)mi] *nm* sowing; (*terrain*) seedbed; (*plant*) seedling.

sémite [semit] *a* Semitic; – *nmf* Semite. ◆**sémitique** *a* (*langue*) Semitic.

semonce [səmɔ̃s] *nf* reprimand; **coup de s.** *Nau* warning shot.

semoule [s(ə)mul] *nf* semolina.

sempiternel, -elle [sɑ̃pitɛrnɛl] *a* endless, ceaseless.

sénat [sena] *nm Pol* senate. ◆**sénateur** *nm Pol* senator.

sénile [senil] *a* senile. ◆**sénilité** *nf* senility.

sens [sɑ̃s] *nm* **1** (*faculté, raison*) sense; (*signification*) meaning, sense; **à mon s.** to my mind; **s. commun** commonsense; **s. de l'humour** sense of humour; **ça n'a pas de s.** that doesn't make sense. **2** (*direction*) direction; **s. giratoire** *Aut* roundabout, *Am* traffic circle, rotary; **s. interdit** *ou* **unique** (*rue*) one-way street; **'s. interdit**' 'no entry'; **à s. unique** (*rue*) one-way; **s. dessus dessous** [sɑ̃dsydsu] upside down; **dans le s./le s. inverse des aiguilles d'une montre** clockwise/anticlockwise, *Am* counterclockwise.

sensation [sɑ̃sasjɔ̃] *nf* sensation, feeling; **faire s.** to cause *ou* create a sensation; **à s.** (*film etc*) *Péj* sensational. ◆**sensationnel, -elle** *a Fig* sensational.

sensé [sɑ̃se] *a* sensible.

sensible [sɑ̃sibl] *a* sensitive (**à** to); (*douloureux*) tender, sore; (*perceptible*) perceptible; (*progrès etc*) appreciable. ◆**sensiblement** *adv* (*notablement*) appreciably; (*à peu près*) more or less. ◆**sensibiliser** *vt* **s. qn à** (*problème etc*) to make s.o. alive to *ou* aware of. ◆**sensibilité** *nf* sensitivity.

sensoriel, -ielle [sɑ̃sɔrjɛl] *a* sensory.

sensuel, -elle [sɑ̃syɛl] *a* (*sexuel*) sensual; (*musique, couleur etc*) sensuous. ◆**sensualité** *nf* sensuality; sensuousness.

sentence [sɑ̃tɑ̃s] *nf* **1** *Jur* sentence. **2** (*maxime*) maxim.

senteur [sɑ̃tœr] *nf* (*odeur*) scent.

sentier [sɑ̃tje] *nm* path.

sentiment [sɑ̃timɑ̃] *nm* feeling; **avoir le s. de** (*apprécier*) to be aware of; **faire du s.** to be sentimental. ◆**sentimental, -aux** *a* senti-

mental; (*amoureux*) love-. ◆**sentimenta-lité** *nf* sentimentality.
sentinelle [sɑ̃tinɛl] *nf* sentry.
sentir* [sɑ̃tir] *vt* to feel; (*odeur*) to smell; (*goût*) to taste; (*racisme etc*) to smack of; (*connaître*) to sense, be conscious of; **s. le moisi/le parfum/***etc* to smell musty/of perfume/*etc*; **s. le poisson/***etc* (*avoir le goût de*) to taste of fish/*etc*; **je ne peux pas le s.** (*supporter*) *Fam* I can't bear *ou* stand him; **se faire s.** (*effet etc*) to make itself felt; **se s. fatigué/humilié/***etc* to feel tired/humiliated/*etc*; *– vi* to smell.
séparation [separasjɔ̃] *nf* separation; (*en deux*) division, split; (*départ*) parting. ◆**séparer** *vt* to separate (**de** from); (*diviser en deux*) to divide, split (up); (*cheveux*) to part; *– se s.* *vpr* (*se quitter*) to part; (*adversaires, époux*) to separate; (*assemblée, cortège*) to disperse, break up; (*se détacher*) to split off; **se s. de** (*objet aimé, chien etc*) to part with. ◆**séparé** *a* (*distinct*) separate; (*époux*) separated (**de** from). ◆**séparément** *adv* separately.
sept [sɛt] *a & nm* seven. ◆**septième** *a & nmf* seventh; **un s.** a seventh.
septante [sɛptɑ̃t] *a & nm* (*en Belgique, Suisse*) seventy.
septembre [sɛptɑ̃br] *nm* September.
septennat [sɛptena] *nm Pol* seven-year term (of office).
septentrional, -aux [sɛptɑ̃trijɔnal, -o] *a* northern.
sépulcre [sepylkr] *nm Rel* sepulchre.
sépulture [sepyltyr] *nf* burial; (*lieu*) burial place.
séquelles [sekɛl] *nfpl* (*de maladie etc*) after-effects; (*de guerre*) aftermath.
séquence [sekɑ̃s] *nf Mus Cartes Cin* sequence.
séquestrer [sekɛstre] *vt* to confine (illegally), lock up.
sera, serait [s(ə)ra, s(ə)rɛ] *voir* **être**.
serein [sərɛ̃] *a* serene. ◆**sérénité** *nf* serenity.
sérénade [serenad] *nf* serenade.
sergent [sɛrʒɑ̃] *nm Mil* sergeant.
série [seri] *nf* series; (*ensemble*) set; **s. noire** *Fig* string *ou* series of disasters; **de s.** (*article etc*) standard; **fabrication en s.** mass production; **fins de s.** *Com* oddments; **hors s.** *Fig* outstanding.
sérieux, -euse [serjø, -øz] *a* (*personne, maladie, doute etc*) serious; (*de bonne foi*) genuine, serious; (*digne de foi, fiable*) reliable; (*bénéfices*) substantial; **de sérieuses chances de . . .** a good chance of . . . ; *–*

nm seriousness; (*fiabilité*) reliability; **prendre au s.** to take seriously; **garder son s.** to keep a straight face; **manquer de s.** (*travailleur*) to lack application. ◆**sérieusement** *adv* seriously; (*travailler*) conscientiously.
serin [s(ə)rɛ̃] *nm* canary.
seriner [s(ə)rine] *vt* **s. qch à qn** to repeat sth to s.o. over and over again.
seringue [s(ə)rɛ̃g] *nf* syringe.
serment [sɛrmɑ̃] *nm* (*affirmation solennelle*) oath; (*promesse*) pledge; **prêter s.** to take an oath; **faire le s. de faire** to swear to do; **sous s.** *Jur* *on ou* under oath.
sermon [sɛrmɔ̃] *nm Rel* sermon; (*discours*) *Péj* lecture. ◆**sermonner** *vt* (*faire la morale à*) to lecture.
serpe [sɛrp] *nf* bill(hook).
serpent [sɛrpɑ̃] *nm* snake; **s. à sonnette** rattlesnake.
serpenter [sɛrpɑ̃te] *vi* (*sentier etc*) to meander.
serpentin [sɛrpɑ̃tɛ̃] *nm* (*ruban*) streamer.
serpillière [sɛrpijɛr] *nf* floor cloth.
serre [sɛr] **1** *nf* greenhouse. **2** *nfpl* (*d'oiseau*) claws, talons.
serre-livres [sɛrlivr] *nm inv* bookend. ◆**s.-tête** *nm inv* (*bandeau*) headband.
serr/er [sere] *vt* (*saisir, tenir*) to grip, clasp; (*presser*) to squeeze, press; (*corde, nœud, vis*) to tighten; (*poing*) to clench; (*taille*) to hug; (*pieds*) to pinch; (*frein*) to apply, put on; (*rapprocher*) to close up; (*rangs*) *Mil* to close; **s. la main à** to shake hands with; **s. les dents** *Fig* to grit one's teeth; **s. qn** (*embrasser*) to hug s.o.; (*vêtement*) to be too tight for s.o.; **s. qn de près** (*talonner*) to be close behind s.o.; *– vi* **s. à droite** *Aut* to keep (to the) right; *– se s.* *vpr* (*se rapprocher*) to squeeze up *ou* together; **se s. contre** to squeeze up against. ◆**-é** *a* (*budget, nœud, vêtement*) tight; (*gens*) packed (together); (*mailles, lutte*) close; (*rangs*) serried; (*dense*) dense, thick; (*cœur*) *Fig* heavy; **avoir la gorge serrée** *Fig* to have a lump in one's throat.
serrure [seryr] *nf* lock. ◆**serrurier** *nm* locksmith.
sertir [sɛrtir] *vt* (*diamant etc*) to set.
sérum [serɔm] *nm* serum.
servante [sɛrvɑ̃t] *nf* (*maid*)servant.
serveur, -euse [sɛrvœr, -øz] *nmf* waiter, waitress; (*au bar*) barman, barmaid.
serviable [sɛrvjabl] *a* helpful, obliging. ◆**serviabilité** *nf* helpfulness.
service [sɛrvis] *nm* service; (*fonction, travail*) duty; (*pourboire*) service (charge); (*département*) *Com* department; *Tennis*

serve, service; **un s.** (*aide*) a favour; **rendre s.** to be of service (**à qn** to s.o.), help (**à qn** s.o.); **rendre un mauvais s. à qn** to do s.o. a disservice; **ça pourrait rendre s.** *Fam* that might come in useful; **s. (non) compris** service (not) included; **s. après-vente** *Com* aftersales (service); **s. d'ordre** (*policiers*) police; **être de s.** to be on duty; **s. à café/à thé** coffee/tea service *ou* set; **à votre s.!** at your service!

serviette [sɛrvjɛt] *nf* **1** towel; **s. de bain/de toilette** bath/hand towel; **s. hygiénique** sanitary towel; **s. (de table)** serviette, napkin. **2** (*sac*) briefcase.

servile [sɛrvil] *a* servile; (*imitation*) slavish. ◆**servilité** *nf* servility; slavishness.

servir* [sɛrvir] **1** *vt* to serve (**qch à qn** s.o. with sth, sth to s.o.); (*convive*) to wait on; – *vi* to serve; – **se s.** *vpr* (*à table*) to help oneself (**de** to). **2** *vi* (*être utile*) to be useful, serve; **s. à qch/à faire** (*objet*) to be used for sth/to do *ou* for doing; **ça ne sert à rien** it's useless, it's no good *ou* use (**de faire** doing); **à quoi ça sert de protester/***etc* what's the use *ou* good of protesting/*etc*; **s. de qch** (*objet*) to be used for sth, serve as sth; **ça me sert à faire/de qch** I use it to do *ou* for doing/as sth; **s. à qn de guide/***etc* to act as a guide/*etc* to s.o. **3 se s.** *vpr* **se s. de** (*utiliser*) to use.

serviteur [sɛrvitœr] *nm* servant. ◆**servitude** *nf* (*esclavage*) servitude; (*contrainte*) *Fig* constraint.

ses [se] *voir* **son²**.

session [sesjɔ̃] *nf* session.

set [sɛt] *nm* **1** *Tennis* set. **2 s. (de table)** (*napperon*) place mat.

seuil [sœj] *nm* doorstep; (*entrée*) doorway; (*limite*) *Fig* threshold; **au s. de** *Fig* on the threshold of.

seul, seule [sœl] **1** *a* (*sans compagnie*) alone; **tout s.** all alone, by oneself, on one's own; **se sentir s.** to feel lonely *ou* alone; – *adv* (**tout**) **s.** (*agir, vivre*) by oneself, alone, on one's own; (*parler*) to oneself; **s. à s.** (*parler*) in private. **2** *a* (*unique*) only; **la seule femme/***etc* the only *ou* sole woman/*etc*; **un s. chat/***etc* only one cat/*etc*; **une seule fois** only once; **pas un s. livre/***etc* not a single book/*etc*; **seuls les garçons . . . , les garçons seuls . . .** only the boys . . . ; – *nmf* **le s., la seule** the only one; **un s., une seule** only one, one only; **pas un s.** not (a single) one. ◆**seulement** *adv* only; **non s. . . . mais . . .** 'not only . . . but (also) . . . ; **pas s.** (*même*) not even; **sans s. faire** without even doing.

sève [sɛv] *nf Bot* & *Fig* sap.

sévère [sever] *a* severe; (*parents, professeur*) strict. ◆**—ment** *adv* severely; (*élever*) strictly. ◆**sévérité** *nf* severity; strictness.

sévices [sevis] *nmpl* brutality.

sévir [sevir] *vi* (*fléau*) *Fig* to rage; **s. contre** to deal severely with.

sevrer [səvre] *vt* (*enfant*) to wean; **s. de** (*priver*) *Fig* to deprive of.

sexe [sɛks] *nm* (*catégorie, sexualité*) sex; (*organes*) genitals; **l'autre s.** the opposite sex. ◆**sexiste** *a* & *nmf* sexist. ◆**sexualité** *nf* sexuality. ◆**sexuel, -elle** *a* sexual; (*éducation, acte etc*) sex-.

sextuor [sɛkstɥɔr] *nm* sextet.

seyant [sejɑ̃] *a* (*vêtement*) becoming.

shampooing [ʃɑ̃pwɛ̃] *nm* shampoo; **s. colorant** rinse; **faire un s. à qn** to shampoo s.o.'s hair.

shérif [ʃerif] *nm Am* sheriff.

shooter [ʃute] *vti Fb* to shoot.

short [ʃɔrt] *nm* (pair of) shorts.

si [si] **1** (= **s'** [s] *devant* **il, ils**) *conj* if; **s'il vient** if he comes; **si j'étais roi** if I were *ou* was king; **je me demande si** I wonder whether *ou* if; **si on restait?** (*suggestion*) what if we stayed?; **si je dis ça, c'est que . . .** I say this because . . . ; **si ce n'est** (*sinon*) if not; **si oui** if so. **2** *adv* (*tellement*) so; **pas si riche que toi/que tu crois** not as rich as you/as you think; **un si bon dîner** such a good dinner; **si grand qu'il soit** however big he may be; **si bien que** with the result that. **3** *adv* (*après négative*) yes; **tu ne viens pas? – si!** you're not coming? – yes (I am)!

siamois [sjamwa] *a* Siamese; **frères s., sœurs siamoises** Siamese twins.

Sicile [sisil] *nf* Sicily.

SIDA [sida] *nm Méd* AIDS. ◆**sidéen, -enne** *nmf* AIDS sufferer.

sidérer [sidere] *vt Fam* to flabbergast.

sidérurgie [sideryrʒi] *nf* iron and steel industry.

siècle [sjɛkl] *nm* century; (*époque*) age.

siège [sjɛʒ] *nm* **1** (*meuble, centre*) & *Pol* seat; (*d'autorité, de parti etc*) headquarters; **s. (social)** (*d'entreprise*) head office. **2** *Mil* siege; **mettre le s. devant** to lay siege to. ◆**siéger** *vi Pol* to sit.

sien, sienne [sjɛ̃, sjɛn] *pron poss* **le s., la sienne, les sien(ne)s** his; (*de femme*) hers; (*de chose*) its; **les deux siens** his *ou* her two; – *nmpl* **les siens** (*amis etc*) one's (own) people.

sieste [sjɛst] *nf* siesta; **faire la s.** to have *ou* take a nap.

siffler [sifle] *vi* to whistle; (*avec un sifflet*) to

blow one's whistle; (*gaz, serpent*) to hiss; (*en respirant*) to wheeze; − *vt* (*chanson*) to whistle; (*chien*) to whistle to; (*faute, fin de match*) *Sp* to blow one's whistle for; (*acteur, pièce*) to boo; (*boisson*) *Fam* to knock back. ◆**sifflement** *nm* whistling, whistle; hiss(ing). ◆**sifflet** *nm* (*instrument*) whistle; *pl Th* booing, boos; (**coup de**) **s.** (*son*) whistle. ◆**siffloter** *vti* to whistle.

sigle [sigl] *nm* (*initiales*) abbreviation; (*prononcé comme un mot*) acronym.

signal, -aux [siɲal, -o] *nm* signal; **s. d'alarme** *Rail* communication cord; **signaux routiers** road signs. ◆**signal/er 1** *vt* (*faire remarquer*) to point out (**à qn** to s.o., **que** that); (*annoncer, indiquer*) to indicate, signal; (*dénoncer à la police etc*) to report (**à** to). **2 se s.** *vpr* **se s. par** to distinguish oneself by. ◆**—ement** *nm* (*de personne*) description, particulars. ◆**signalisation** *nf* signalling; *Aut* signposting; **s. (routière)** (*signaux*) road signs.

signature [siɲatyr] *nf* signature; (*action*) signing. ◆**signataire** *nmf* signatory. ◆**signer 1** *vt* to sign. **2 se s.** *vpr Rel* to cross oneself.

signe [siɲ] *nm* (*indice*) sign, indication; **s. particulier/de ponctuation** distinguishing/punctuation mark; **faire s. à qn** (*geste*) to motion to *ou* beckon s.o. (**de faire** to do); (*contacter*) to get in touch with s.o.; **faire s. que oui** to nod (one's head); **faire s. que non** to shake one's head.

signet [siɲɛ] *nm* bookmark.

signification [siɲifikɑsjɔ̃] *nf* meaning. ◆**significatif, -ive** *a* significant, meaningful; **s. de** indicative of. ◆**signifier** *vt* to mean, signify (**que** that); **s. qch à qn** (*faire connaître*) to make sth known to s.o., signify sth to s.o.

silence [silɑ̃s] *nm* silence; *Mus* rest; **en s.** in silence; **garder le s.** to keep quiet *ou* silent (**sur** about). ◆**silencieux, -euse 1** *a* silent. **2** *nm Aut* silencer, *Am* muffler; (*d'arme*) silencer. ◆**silencieusement** *adv* silently.

silex [silɛks] *nm* (*roche*) flint.

silhouette [silwɛt] *nf* outline; (*en noir*) silhouette; (*ligne du corps*) figure.

silicium [silisjɔm] *nm* silicon. ◆**silicone** *nf* silicone.

sillage [sijaʒ] *nm* (*de bateau*) wake; **dans le s. de** *Fig* in the wake of.

sillon [sijɔ̃] *nm* furrow; (*de disque*) groove.

sillonner [sijɔne] *vt* (*traverser*) to cross; (*en tous sens*) to criss-cross.

silo [silo] *nm* silo.

simagrées [simagre] *nfpl* airs (and graces); (*cérémonies*) fuss.

similaire [similɛr] *a* similar. ◆**similitude** *nf* similarity.

similicuir [similikɥir] *nm* imitation leather.

simple [sɛ̃pl] *a* simple; (*non multiple*) single; (*employé, particulier*) ordinary; − *nmf* **s. d'esprit** simpleton; − *nm Tennis* singles. ◆**simplement** *adv* simply. ◆**simplet, -ette** *a* (*personne*) a bit simple. ◆**simplicité** *nf* simplicity. ◆**simplification** *nf* simplification. ◆**simplifier** *vt* to simplify. ◆**simpliste** *a* simplistic.

simulacre [simylakr] *nm* **un s. de** *Péj* a pretence of.

simuler [simyle] *vt* to simulate; (*feindre*) to feign. ◆**simulateur, -trice 1** *nmf* (*hypocrite*) shammer; (*tire-au-flanc*) & *Mil* malingerer. **2** *nm* (*appareil*) simulator. ◆**simulation** *nf* simulation; feigning.

simultané [simyltane] *a* simultaneous. ◆**—ment** *adv* simultaneously.

sincère [sɛ̃sɛr] *a* sincere. ◆**sincèrement** *adv* sincerely. ◆**sincérité** *nf* sincerity.

sinécure [sinekyr] *nf* sinecure.

singe [sɛ̃ʒ] *nm* monkey, ape. ◆**singer** *vt* (*imiter*) to ape, mimic. ◆**singeries** *nfpl* antics, clowning.

singulariser (se) [səsɛ̃gylarize] *vpr* to draw attention to oneself.

singulier, -ière [sɛ̃gylje, -jɛr] **1** *a* peculiar, odd. **2** *a* & *nm Gram* singular. ◆**singularité** *nf* peculiarity. ◆**singulièrement** *adv* (*notamment*) particularly; (*beaucoup*) extremely.

sinistre [sinistr] **1** *a* (*effrayant*) sinister. **2** *nm* disaster; (*incendie*) fire; (*dommage*) *Jur* damage. ◆**sinistré, -ée** *a* (*population, région*) disaster-stricken; − *nmf* disaster victim.

sinon [sinɔ̃] *conj* (*autrement*) otherwise, or else; (*sauf*) except (**que** that); (*si ce n'est*) if not.

sinueux, -euse [sinɥø, -øz] *a* winding. ◆**sinuosités** *nfpl* twists (and turns).

sinus [sinys] *nm inv Anat* sinus.

siphon [sifɔ̃] *nm* siphon; (*d'évier*) trap, U-bend.

sirène [sirɛn] *nf* **1** (*d'usine etc*) siren. **2** (*femme*) mermaid.

sirop [siro] *nm* syrup; (*à diluer, boisson*) (fruit) cordial; **s. contre la toux** cough mixture *ou* syrup.

siroter [sirɔte] *vt Fam* to sip (at).

sis [si] *a Jur* situated.

sismique [sismik] *a* seismic; **secousse s.** earth tremor.

site [sit] *nm* (*endroit*) site; (*environnement*) setting; (*pittoresque*) beauty spot; **s. (touristique)** (*monument etc*) place of interest.

sitôt [sito] *adv* **s. que** as soon as; **s. levée, elle partit** as soon as she was up, she left; **s. après** immediately after; **pas de s.** not for some time.

situation [situasjɔ̃] *nf* situation, position; (*emploi*) position; **s. de famille** marital status. ◆**situ/er** *vt* to situate, locate; **— se s.** *vpr* (*se trouver*) to be situated. ◆**-é** *a* (*maison etc*) situated.

six [sis] ([si] *before consonant*, [siz] *before vowel*) *a* & *nm* six. ◆**sixième** *a* & *nmf* sixth; **un s.** a sixth.

sketch [skɛtʃ] *nm* (*pl* **sketches**) *Th* sketch.

ski [ski] *nm* (*objet*) ski; (*sport*) skiing; **faire du s.** to ski; **s. nautique** water skiing. ◆**ski/er** *vi* to ski. ◆**-eur, -euse** *nmf* skier.

slalom [slalɔm] *nm* Sp slalom.

slave [slav] *a* Slav; (*langue*) Slavonic; *– nmf* Slav.

slip [slip] *nm* (*d'homme*) briefs, (under)pants; (*de femme*) panties, pants, knickers; **s. de bain** (swimming) trunks; (*d'un bikini*) briefs.

slogan [slɔgã] *nm* slogan.

SMIC [smik] *nm abrév* (*salaire minimum interprofessionnel de croissance*) minimum wage.

smoking [smɔkiŋ] *nm* (*veston, costume*) dinner jacket, *Am* tuxedo.

snack(-bar) [snak(bar)] *nm* snack bar.

SNCF [ɛsɛnseɛf] *nf abrév* (*Société nationale des Chemins de fer français*) French railways.

snob [snɔb] *nmf* snob; *– a* snobbish. ◆**snober** *vt* **s. qn** to snub s.o. ◆**snobisme** *nm* snobbery.

sobre [sɔbr] *a* sober. ◆**sobriété** *nf* sobriety.

sobriquet [sɔbrikɛ] *nm* nickname.

sociable [sɔsjabl] *a* sociable. ◆**sociabilité** *nf* sociability.

social, -aux [sɔsjal, -o] *a* social. ◆**socialisme** *nm* socialism. ◆**socialiste** *a* & *nmf* socialist.

société [sɔsjete] *nf* society; (*compagnie*) & *Com* company; **s. anonyme** *Com* (public) limited company, *Am* incorporated company. ◆**sociétaire** *nmf* (*d'une association*) member.

sociologie [sɔsjɔlɔʒi] *nf* sociology.

◆**sociologique** *a* sociological. ◆**sociologue** *nmf* sociologist.

socle [sɔkl] *nm* (*de statue, colonne*) plinth, pedestal; (*de lampe*) base.

socquette [sɔkɛt] *nf* ankle sock.

soda [sɔda] *nm* (*à l'orange etc*) fizzy drink, *Am* soda (pop).

sœur [sœr] *nf* sister; *Rel* nun, sister.

sofa [sɔfa] *nm* sofa, settee.

soi [swa] *pron* oneself; **chacun pour s.** every man for himself; **en s.** in itself; **cela va de s.** it's self-evident (**que** that); **amour/conscience de s.** self-love/-awareness. ◆**s.-même** *pron* oneself.

soi-disant [swadizã] *a inv* so-called; *– adv* supposedly.

soie [swa] *nf* **1** silk. **2** (*de porc etc*) bristle. ◆**soierie** *nf* (*tissu*) silk.

soif [swaf] *nf* thirst (*Fig* **de** for); **avoir s.** to be thirsty; **donner s. à qn** to make s.o. thirsty.

soign/er [swaɲe] *vt* to look after, take care of; (*malade*) to tend, nurse; (*maladie*) to treat; (*détails, présentation, travail*) to take care over; **se faire s.** to have (medical) treatment; **— se s.** *vpr* to take care of oneself, look after oneself. ◆**-é** *a* (*personne*) well-groomed; (*vêtement*) neat, tidy; (*travail*) careful. ◆**soigneux, -euse** *a* careful (**de** with); (*propre*) tidy, neat. ◆**soigneusement** *adv* carefully.

soin [swɛ̃] *nm* care; (*ordre*) tidiness, neatness; *pl* care; *Méd* treatment; **avoir** *ou* **prendre s. de qch/de faire** to take care of sth/to do; **les premiers soins** first aid; **soins de beauté** beauty care *ou* treatment; **aux bons soins de** (*sur lettre*) care of, c/o; **avec s.** carefully, with care.

soir [swar] *nm* evening; **le s.** (*chaque soir*) in the evening; **à neuf heures du s.** at nine in the evening; **du s.** (*repas, robe etc*) evening-. ◆**soirée** *nf* evening; (*réunion*) party; **s. dansante** dance.

soit 1 [swa] *voir* **être. 2** [swa] *conj* (*à savoir*) that is (to say); **s. . . . s. . . .** either . . . or . . . . **3** [swat] *adv* (*oui*) very well.

soixante [swasãt] *a* & *nm* sixty. ◆**soixantaine** *nf* **une s. (de)** (*nombre*) (about) sixty; **avoir la s.** (*âge*) to be about sixty. ◆**soixante-dix** *a* & *nm* seventy. ◆**soixante-dixième** *a* & *nmf* seventieth. ◆**soixantième** *a* & *nmf* sixtieth.

soja [sɔʒa] *nm* (*plante*) soya; **graine de s.** soya bean; **germes** *ou* **pousses de s.** beansprouts.

sol [sɔl] *nm* ground; (*plancher*) floor; (*matière, territoire*) soil.

solaire [sɔlɛr] *a* solar; (*chaleur, rayons*) sun's; (*crème, filtre*) sun-; (*lotion, huile*) suntan-.

soldat [sɔlda] *nm* soldier; **simple s.** private.

solde [sɔld] **1** *nm* (*de compte, à payer*) balance. **2** *nm* **en s.** (*acheter*) at sale price, *Am* on sale; *pl* (*marchandises*) sale goods; (*vente*) (clearance) sale(s). **3** *nf Mil* pay; **à la s. de** *Fig Péj* in s.o.'s pay. ◆**sold/er 1** *vt* (*articles*) to sell off, clear. **2** *vt* (*compte*) to pay the balance of. **3 se s.** *vpr* **se s. par** (*un échec, une défaite etc*) to end in. ◆**–é** *a* (*article etc*) reduced. ◆**solderie** *nf* discount *ou* reject shop.

sole [sɔl] *nf* (*poisson*) sole.

soleil [sɔlɛj] *nm* sun; (*chaleur, lumière*) sunshine; (*fleur*) sunflower; **au s.** in the sun; **il fait (du) s.** it's sunny, the sun's shining; **prendre un bain de s.** to sunbathe; **coup de s.** *Méd* sunburn.

solennel, -elle [sɔlanɛl] *a* solemn. ◆**solennellement** *adv* solemnly. ◆**solennité** [-anite] *nf* solemnity.

solex® [sɔlɛks] *nm* moped.

solfège [sɔlfɛʒ] *nm* rudiments of music.

solidaire [sɔlidɛr] *a* **être s.** (*ouvriers etc*) to be as one, show solidarity (**de** with); (*pièce de machine*) to be interdependent (**de** with). ◆**solidairement** *adv* jointly. ◆**se solidariser** *vpr* to show solidarity (**avec** with). ◆**solidarité** *nf* solidarity; (*d'éléments*) interdependence.

solide [sɔlid] *a* (*voiture, nourriture, caractère etc*) & *Ch* solid; (*argument, qualité, raison*) sound; (*vigoureux*) robust; – *nm Ch* solid. ◆**solidement** *adv* solidly. ◆**se solidifier** *vpr* to solidify. ◆**solidité** *nf* solidity; (*d'argument etc*) soundness.

soliste [sɔlist] *nmf Mus* soloist.

solitaire [sɔlitɛr] *a* solitary; – *nmf* loner; (*ermite*) recluse, hermit; **en s.** on one's own. ◆**solitude** *nf* solitude.

solive [sɔliv] *nf* joist, beam.

solliciter [sɔlisite] *vt* (*audience, emploi etc*) to seek; (*tenter*) to tempt, entice; **s. qn** (*faire appel à*) to appeal to s.o. (**de faire** to do); **être (très) sollicité** (*personne*) to be in (great) demand. ◆**sollicitation** *nf* (*demande*) appeal; (*tentation*) temptation.

sollicitude [sɔlisityd] *nf* solicitude, concern.

solo [sɔlo] *a inv* & *nm Mus* solo.

solstice [sɔlstis] *nm* solstice.

soluble [sɔlybl] *a* (*substance, problème*) soluble; **café s.** instant coffee. ◆**solution** *nf* (*d'un problème etc*) & *Ch* solution (**de** to).

solvable [sɔlvabl] *a Fin* solvent. ◆**solvabilité** *nf Fin* solvency.

solvant [sɔlvã] *nm Ch* solvent.

sombre [sɔ̃br] *a* dark; (*triste*) sombre, gloomy; **il fait s.** it's dark.

sombrer [sɔ̃bre] *vi* (*bateau*) to sink, founder; **s. dans** (*folie, sommeil etc*) to sink into.

sommaire [sɔmɛr] *a* summary; (*repas, tenue*) scant; – *nm* summary, synopsis.

sommation [sɔmasjɔ̃] *nf Jur* summons; (*de sentinelle etc*) warning.

somme [sɔm] **1** *nf* sum; **faire la s. de** to add up; **en s., s. toute** in short. **2** *nm* (*sommeil*) nap; **faire un s.** to have *ou* take a nap.

sommeil [sɔmɛj] *nm* sleep; (*envie de dormir*) sleepiness, drowsiness; **avoir s.** to be *ou* feel sleepy *ou* drowsy. ◆**sommeiller** *vi* to doze; (*faculté, qualité*) *Fig* to slumber.

sommelier [sɔməlje] *nm* wine waiter.

sommer [sɔme] *vt* **s. qn de faire** (*enjoindre*) & *Jur* to summon s.o. to do.

sommes [sɔm] *voir* **être**.

sommet [sɔmɛ] *nm* top; (*de montagne*) summit, top; (*de la gloire etc*) *Fig* height, summit; **conférence au s.** summit (conference).

sommier [sɔmje] *nm* (*de lit*) base; **s. à ressorts** spring base.

sommité [sɔmite] *nf* leading light, top person (**de** in).

somnambule [sɔmnãbyl] *nmf* sleepwalker; **être s.** to sleepwalk. ◆**somnambulisme** *nm* sleepwalking.

somnifère [sɔmnifɛr] *nm* sleeping pill.

somnolence [sɔmnɔlãs] *nf* drowsiness, sleepiness. ◆**somnolent** *a* drowsy, sleepy. ◆**somnoler** *vi* to doze, drowse.

somptueux, -euse [sɔ̃ptɥø, -øz] *a* sumptuous, magnificent. ◆**somptuosité** *nf* sumptuousness, magnificence.

son¹ [sɔ̃] *nm* **1** (*bruit*) sound. **2** (*de grains*) bran.

son², sa, *pl* **ses** [sɔ̃, sa, se] (*sa becomes* **son** [sɔn] *before a vowel or mute h*) *a poss* his; (*de femme*) her; (*de chose*) its; (*indéfini*) one's; **son père** his *ou* her *ou* one's father; **sa durée** its duration.

sonate [sɔnat] *nf Mus* sonata.

sonde [sɔ̃d] *nf Géol* drill; *Nau* sounding line; *Méd* probe; (*pour l'alimentation*) (feeding) tube; **s. spatiale** *Av* space probe. ◆**sondage** *nm* sounding; drilling; probing; **s. (d'opinion)** opinion poll. ◆**sonder** *vt* (*rivière etc*) to sound; (*terrain*) to drill; *Av* & *Méd* to probe; (*personne, l'opinion*) *Fig* to sound out.

songe [sɔ̃ʒ] *nm* dream.

song/er [sɔ̃ʒe] *vi* **s. à qch/à faire** to think of sth/of doing; – *vt* **s. que** to consider *ou* think that. ◆**—eur, -euse** *a* thoughtful, pensive.

sonner [sɔne] *vi* to ring; (*cor, cloches etc*) to sound; **midi a sonné** it has struck twelve; — *vt* to ring; (*domestique*) to ring for; (*cor etc*) to sound; (*l'heure*) to strike; (*assommer*) to knock out. ◆**sonnantes** *afpl* **à cinq/etc heures s.** on the stroke of five/*etc*. ◆**sonné** *a* **1 trois/etc heures sonnées** gone *ou* past three/*etc* o'clock. **2** (*fou*) crazy. ◆**sonnerie** *nf* (*son*) ring(ing); (*de cor etc*) sound; (*appareil*) bell. ◆**sonnette** *nf* bell; **s. d'alarme** alarm (bell); **coup de s.** ring.

sonnet [sɔnɛ] *nm* (*poème*) sonnet.

sonore [sɔnɔr] *a* (*rire*) loud; (*salle, voix*) resonant; (*effet, film, ondes etc*) sound-. ◆**sonorisation** *nf* (*matériel*) sound equipment *ou* system. ◆**sonoriser** *vt* (*film*) to add sound to; (*salle*) to wire for sound. ◆**sonorité** *nf* (*de salle*) acoustics, resonance; (*de violon etc*) tone.

sont [sɔ̃] *voir* **être**.

sophistiqué [sɔfistike] *a* sophisticated.

soporifique [sɔpɔrifik] *a* (*médicament, discours etc*) soporific.

soprano [sɔprano] *nmf* (*personne*) *Mus* soprano; — *nm* (*voix*) soprano.

sorbet [sɔrbɛ] *nm* *Culin* water ice, sorbet.

sorcellerie [sɔrsɛlri] *nf* witchcraft, sorcery. ◆**sorcier** *nm* sorcerer. ◆**sorcière** *nf* witch; **chasse aux sorcières** *Pol* witch-hunt.

sordide [sɔrdid] *a* (*acte, affaire etc*) sordid; (*maison etc*) squalid.

sornettes [sɔrnɛt] *nfpl* (*propos*) *Péj* twaddle.

sort [sɔr] *nm* **1** (*destin, hasard*) fate; (*condition*) lot. **2** (*maléfice*) spell.

sorte [sɔrt] *nf* sort, kind (**de** of); **en quelque s.** as it were, in a way; **de (telle) s. que** so that, in such a way that; **de la s.** (*de cette façon*) in that way; **faire en s. que** (+ *sub*) to see to it that.

sortie [sɔrti] *nf* **1** departure, exit; (*de scène*) exit; (*promenade*) walk; (*porte*) exit, way out; (*de livre, modèle*) *Com* appearance; (*de disque, film*) release; (*d'ordinateur*) output; *pl* (*argent*) outgoings; **à la s. de l'école** (*moment*) when school comes out; **l'heure de la s. de qn** the time at which s.o. leaves; **première s.** (*de convalescent etc*) first time out. **2 s. de bain** (*peignoir*) bathrobe.

sortilège [sɔrtilɛʒ] *nm* (*magic*) spell.

sort/ir* [sɔrtir] *vi* (*aux* **être**) to go out, leave; (*venir*) to come out; (*pour s'amuser*) to go out; (*film, modèle, bourgeon etc*) to come out; (*numéro gagnant*) to come up; **s. de** (*endroit*) to leave; (*sujet*) to stray from;

(*université*) to be a graduate of; (*famille, milieu*) to come from; (*légalité, limites*) to go beyond; (*compétence*) to be outside; (*gonds, rails*) to come off; **s. de l'ordinaire** to be out of the ordinary; **s. de table** to leave the table; **s. de terre** (*plante, fondations*) to come up; **s. indemne** to escape unhurt (**de** from); — *vt* (*aux* **avoir**) to take out (**de** of); (*film, modèle, livre etc*) *Com* to bring out; (*dire*) *Fam* to come out with; (*expulser*) *Fam* to throw out; **s'en s., se s. d'affaire** to pull *ou* come through, get out of trouble. ◆**—ant** *a* (*numéro*) winning; (*député etc*) *Pol* outgoing. ◆**—able** *a* (*personne*) presentable.

sosie [sozi] *nm* (*de personne*) double.

sot, sotte [so, sɔt] *a* foolish; — *nmf* fool. ◆**sottement** *adv* foolishly. ◆**sottise** *nf* foolishness; (*action, parole*) foolish thing; *pl* (*injures*) *Fam* insults; **faire des sottises** (*enfant*) to be naughty, misbehave.

sou [su] *nm* **sous** (*argent*) money; **elle n'a pas un** *ou* **le s.** she doesn't have a penny, she's penniless; **pas un s. de** (*bon sens etc*) not an ounce of; **appareil** *ou* **machine à sous** fruit machine, one-armed bandit.

soubresaut [subrəso] *nm* (*sursaut*) (sudden) start.

souche [suʃ] *nf* (*d'arbre*) stump; (*de carnet*) stub, counterfoil; (*famille, de vigne*) stock.

souci [susi] *nm* (*inquiétude*) worry, concern; (*préoccupation*) concern; **se faire du s.** to be worried, worry; **ça lui donne du s.** it worries him *ou* her. ◆**se soucier** *vpr* **se s. de** to be concerned *ou* worried about. ◆**soucieux, -euse** *a* concerned, worried (**de qch** about sth); **s. de plaire/etc** anxious to please/*etc*.

soucoupe [sukup] *nf* saucer; **s. volante** flying saucer.

soudain [sudɛ̃] *a* sudden; — *adv* suddenly. ◆**soudainement** *adv* suddenly. ◆**soudaineté** *nf* suddenness.

Soudan [sudã] *nm* Sudan.

soude [sud] *nf* *Ch* soda; **cristaux de s.** washing soda.

souder [sude] *vt* to solder; (*par soudure autogène*) to weld; (*groupes etc*) *Fig* to unite (closely); — **se s.** *vpr* (*os*) to knit (together). ◆**soudure** *nf* (*action*) soldering; (*métal*) solder; **s. (autogène)** welding.

soudoyer [sudwaje] *vt* to bribe.

souffle [sufl] *nm* puff, blow; (*haleine*) breath; (*respiration*) breathing; (*de bombe etc*) blast; (*inspiration*) *Fig* inspiration; **s. (d'air)** breath of air. ◆**souffler** *vi* to blow; (*haleter*) to puff; **laisser s. qn** (*reprendre haleine*) to let s.o. get his breath back; — *vt* (*bougie*) to blow out; (*fumée, poussière, verre*) to blow; (*par une explosion*) to blow down, blast; (*chuchoter*) to whisper; (*voler*) *Fam* to pinch (à from); (*étonner*) *Fam* to stagger; **s. son rôle à qn** *Th* to prompt s.o.; **ne pas s. mot** not to breathe a word. **3** *vt* (*exception*) to admit of. ◆**soufflet** *nm* **1** (*instrument*) bellows. **2** (*gifle*) *Litt* slap. ◆**souffleur, -euse** *nmf Th* prompter.

soufflé [sufle] *nm Culin* soufflé.

souffrance [sufrɑ̃s] *nf* **1** suffering. **2 en s.** (*colis etc*) unclaimed; (*affaire*) in abeyance.

souffreteux, -euse [sufrətø, -øz] *a* sickly.

souffr/ir* [sufrir] **1** *vi* to suffer; **s. de** to suffer from; (*gorge, pieds etc*) to have trouble with; **faire s. qn** (*physiquement*) to hurt s.o.; (*moralement*) to make s.o. suffer, hurt s.o. **2** *vt* (*endurer*) to suffer; **je ne peux pas le s.** I can't bear him. **3** *vt* (*exception*) to admit of. ◆**—ant** *a* unwell.

soufre [sufr] *nm* sulphur, *Am* sulfur.

souhait [swɛ] *nm* wish; **à vos souhaits!** (*après un éternuement*) bless you!; **à s.** perfectly. ◆**souhait/er** *vt* (*bonheur etc*) to wish for; **s. qch à qn** to wish s.o. sth; **s. faire** to hope to do; **s. que** (+ *sub*) to hope that. ◆**—able** *a* desirable.

souiller [suje] *vt* to soil, dirty; (*déshonorer*) *Fig* to sully.

soûl [su] **1** *a* drunk. **2** *nm* **tout son s.** (*boire etc*) to one's heart's content. ◆**soûler** *vt* to make drunk; **— se s.** *vpr* to get drunk.

soulager [sulaʒe] *vt* to relieve (**de** of). ◆**soulagement** *nm* relief.

soulever [sulve] *vt* to raise, lift (up); (*l'opinion, le peuple*) to stir up; (*poussière, question*) to raise; (*sentiment*) to arouse; **cela me soulève le cœur** it makes me feel sick, it turns my stomach; **— se s.** *vpr* (*malade etc*) to lift oneself (up); (*se révolter*) to rise (up). ◆**soulèvement** *nm* (*révolte*) (up)rising.

soulier [sulje] *nm* shoe.

souligner [suliɲe] *vt* (*d'un trait*) to underline; (*accentuer, faire remarquer*) to emphasize, underline; **s. que** to emphasize that.

soumettre* [sumɛtr] **1** *vt* (*pays, rebelles*) to subjugate, subdue; **s. à** (*assujettir*) to subject to; **— se s.** *vpr* to submit (à to). **2** *vt* (*présenter*) to submit (à to). ◆**soumis** *a* (*docile*) submissive; **s. à** subject to. ◆**soumission** *nf* **1** submission; (*docilité*) submissiveness. **2** (*offre*) *Com* tender.

soupape [supap] *nf* valve.

soupçon [supsɔ̃] *nm* suspicion; **un s. de** (*quantité*) *Fig* a hint *ou* touch of. ◆**soupçonner** *vt* to suspect (**de** of, **d'avoir fait** of

doing, **que** that). ◆**soupçonneux, -euse** *a* suspicious.

soupe [sup] *nf* soup. ◆**soupière** *nf* (*soup*) tureen.

soupente [supɑ̃t] *nf* (*sous le toit*) loft.

souper [supe] *nm* supper; — *vi* to have supper.

soupeser [supəze] *vt* (*objet dans la main*) to feel the weight of; (*arguments etc*) *Fig* to weigh up.

soupir [supir] *nm* sigh. ◆**soupir/er** *vi* to sigh; **s. après** to yearn for. ◆**—ant** *nm* (*amoureux*) suitor.

soupirail, -aux [supiraj, -o] *nm* basement window.

souple [supl] *a* (*personne, esprit, règlement*) flexible; (*cuir, membre, corps*) supple. ◆**souplesse** *nf* flexibility; suppleness.

source [surs] *nf* **1** (*point d'eau*) spring; **eau de s.** spring water; **prendre sa s.** (*rivière*) to rise (à at, **dans** in). **2** (*origine*) source; **de s. sûre** on good authority.

sourcil [sursi] *nm* eyebrow. ◆**sourciller** *vi* **ne pas s.** *Fig* not to bat an eyelid.

sourd, sourde [sur, surd] **1** *a* deaf (*Fig* **à** to); — *nmf* deaf person. **2** *a* (*bruit, douleur*) dull; (*caché*) secret. ◆**s.-muet** (*pl* **sourds-muets**), ◆**sourde-muette** (*pl* **sourdes-muettes**) *a* deaf and dumb; — *nmf* deaf mute.

sourdine [surdin] *nf* (*dispositif*) *Mus* mute; **en s.** *Fig* quietly, secretly.

souricière [surisjɛr] *nf* mousetrap; *Fig* trap.

sourire* [surir] *vi* to smile (**à** at); **s. à qn** (*fortune*) to smile on s.o.; — *nm* smile; **faire un s. à qn** to give s.o. a smile.

souris [suri] *nf* mouse.

sournois [surnwa] *a* sly, underhand. ◆**sournoisement** *adv* slyly. ◆**sournoiserie** *nf* slyness.

sous [su] *prép* (*position*) under(neath), beneath; (*rang*) under; **s. la pluie** in the rain; **s. cet angle** from that angle *ou* point of view; **s. le nom de** under the name of; **s. Charles X** under Charles X; **s. peu** (*bientôt*) shortly.

sous- [su] *préf* (*subordination, subdivision*) sub-; (*insuffisance*) under-.

sous-alimenté [suzalimɑ̃te] *a* undernourished. ◆**sous-alimentation** *nf* undernourishment.

sous-bois [subwa] *nm* undergrowth.

sous-chef [suʃɛf] *nmf* second-in-command.

souscrire* [suskrir] *vi* **s. à** (*payer, approuver*) to subscribe to. ◆**souscription** *nf* subscription.

sous-développé [sudevlɔpe] *a* (*pays*) underdeveloped.

sous-directeur, -trice [sudirektœr, -tris] *nmf* assistant manager, assistant manageress.

sous-entend/re [suzɑ̃tɑ̃dr] *vt* to imply. ◆**—u** *nm* insinuation.

sous-estimer [suzɛstime] *vt* to underestimate.

sous-jacent [suʒasɑ̃] *a* underlying.

sous-louer [sulwe] *vt* (*appartement*) to sublet.

sous-main [sumɛ̃] *nm inv* desk pad.

sous-marin [sumarɛ̃] *a* underwater; **plongée sous-marine** skin diving; – *nm* submarine.

sous-officier [suzɔfisje] *nm* noncommissioned officer.

sous-payer [supeje] *vt* (*ouvrier etc*) to underpay.

sous-produit [suprɔdɥi] *nm* by-product.

soussigné, -ée [susiɲe] *a* & *nmf* undersigned; **je s.** I the undersigned.

sous-sol [susɔl] *nm* basement; *Géol* subsoil.

sous-titre [sutitr] *nm* subtitle. ◆**sous-titrer** *vt* (*film*) to subtitle.

soustraire* [sustrɛr] *vt* to remove; *Math* to subtract, take away (**de** from); **s. qn à** (*danger etc*) to shield *ou* protect s.o. from; **se s. à** to escape from; (*devoir, obligation*) to avoid. ◆**soustraction** *nf Math* subtraction.

sous-trait/er [sutrete] *vi Com* to subcontract. ◆**—ant** *nm* subcontractor.

sous-verre [suvɛr] *nm inv* (*encadrement*) (frameless) glass mount.

sous-vêtement [suvɛtmɑ̃] *nm* undergarment; *pl* underwear.

soutane [sutan] *nf* (*de prêtre*) cassock.

soute [sut] *nf* (*magasin*) Nau hold.

souten/ir* [sutnir] *vt* to support, hold up; (*droits, opinion*) to uphold, maintain; (*candidat etc*) to back, support; (*malade*) to sustain; (*effort, intérêt*) to sustain, keep up; (*thèse*) to defend; (*résister à*) to withstand; **s. que** to maintain that; — **se s.** *vpr* (*blessé etc*) to hold oneself up; (*se maintenir, durer*) to be sustained. ◆**—u** *a* (*attention, effort*) sustained; (*style*) lofty. ◆**soutien** *nm* support; (*personne*) supporter; **s. de famille** breadwinner. ◆**soutien-gorge** *nm* (*pl* **soutiens-gorge**) bra.

souterrain [sutɛrɛ̃] *a* underground; – *nm* underground passage.

soutirer [sutire] *vt* **s. qch à qn** to extract *ou* get sth from s.o.

souvenir [suvnir] *nm* memory, recollection; (*objet*) memento; (*cadeau*) keepsake; (*pour touristes*) souvenir; **en s. de** in memory of; **mon bon s. à** (give) my regards to. ◆**se souvenir*** *vpr* **se s. de** to remember, recall; **se s. que** to remember *ou* recall that.

souvent [suvɑ̃] *adv* often; **peu s.** seldom; **le plus s.** more often than not, most often.

souverain, -aine [suvrɛ̃, -ɛn] *a* sovereign; (*extrême*) *Péj* supreme; – *nmf* sovereign. ◆**souveraineté** *nf* sovereignty.

soviétique [sɔvjetik] *a* Soviet; **l'Union s.** the Soviet Union; – *nmf* Soviet citizen.

soyeux, -euse [swajø, -øz] *a* silky.

spacieux, -euse [spasjø, -øz] *a* spacious, roomy.

spaghetti(s) [spageti] *nmpl* spaghetti.

sparadrap [sparadra] *nm Méd* sticking plaster, *Am* adhesive tape.

spasme [spasm] *nm* spasm. ◆**spasmodique** *a* spasmodic.

spatial, -aux [spasjal, -o] *a* (*vol etc*) space-; **engin s.** spaceship, spacecraft.

spatule [spatyl] *nf* spatula.

speaker [spikœr] *nm*, **speakerine** [spikrin] *nf Rad TV* announcer.

spécial, -aux [spesjal, -o] *a* special; (*bizarre*) peculiar. ◆**spécialement** *adv* especially, particularly; (*exprès*) specially.

spécialiser (se) [səspesjalize] *vpr* to specialize (**dans** in). ◆**spécialisation** *nf* specialization. ◆**spécialiste** *nmf* specialist. ◆**spécialité** *nf* speciality, *Am* specialty.

spécifier [spesifje] *vt* to specify (**que** that).

spécifique [spesifik] *a Phys Ch* specific.

spécimen [spesimɛn] *nm* specimen; (*livre etc*) specimen copy.

spectacle [spɛktakl] *nm* **1** (*vue*) spectacle, sight; **se donner en s.** *Péj* to make an exhibition of oneself. **2** (*représentation*) show; **le s.** (*industrie*) show business. ◆**spectateur, -trice** *nmf Sp* spectator; (*témoin*) onlooker, witness; *pl Th Cin* audience.

spectaculaire [spɛktakylɛr] *a* spectacular.

spectre [spɛktr] *nm* **1** (*fantôme*) spectre, ghost. **2** (*solaire*) spectrum.

spéculer [spekyle] *vi Fin Phil* to speculate; **s. sur** (*tabler sur*) to bank *ou* rely on. ◆**spéculateur, -trice** *nmf* speculator. ◆**spéculatif, -ive** *a Fin Phil* speculative. ◆**spéculation** *nf Fin Phil* speculation.

spéléologie [speleɔlɔʒi] *nf* (*activité*) potholing, caving, *Am* spelunking. ◆**spéléologue** *nmf* potholer, *Am* spelunker.

sperme [spɛrm] *nm* sperm, semen.

sphère [sfɛr] *nf* (*boule, domaine*) sphere. ◆**sphérique** *a* spherical.

sphinx [sfɛ̃ks] *nm* sphinx.

spirale [spiral] *nf* spiral.
spirite [spirit] *nmf* spiritualist. ◆**spiritisme** *nm* spiritualism.
spirituel, -elle [spiritɥɛl] *a* **1** (*amusant*) witty. **2** (*pouvoir, vie etc*) spiritual.
spiritueux [spiritɥø] *nmpl* (*boissons*) spirits.
splendide [splɑ̃did] *a* (*merveilleux, riche, beau*) splendid. ◆**splendeur** *nf* splendour.
spongieux, -euse [spɔ̃ʒjø, -øz] *a* spongy.
spontané [spɔ̃tane] *a* spontaneous. ◆**spontanéité** *nf* spontaneity. ◆**spontanément** *adv* spontaneously.
sporadique [spɔradik] *a* sporadic.
sport [spɔr] *nm* sport; **faire du s.** to play sport *ou* Am sports; **(de) s.** (*chaussures, vêtements*) casual, sports; **voiture/veste de s.** sports car/jacket. ◆**sportif, -ive** *a* (*attitude, personne*) sporting; (*association, journal, résultats*) sports, sporting; (*allure*) athletic; – *nmf* sportsman, sportswoman. ◆**sportivité** *nf* (*esprit*) sportsmanship.
spot [spɔt] *nm* **1** (*lampe*) spot(light). **2 s.** (**publicitaire**) Rad TV commercial.
sprint [sprint] *nm* Sp sprint. ◆**sprinter** *vt* to sprint; – *nm* [-œr] sprinter. ◆**-euse** *nf* sprinter.
square [skwar] *nm* public garden.
squelette [skəlɛt] *nm* skeleton. ◆**squelettique** *a* (*personne, maigreur*) skeleton-like; (*exposé*) sketchy.
stable [stabl] *a* stable. ◆**stabilisateur** *nm* stabilizer. ◆**stabiliser** *vt* to stabilize; – **se s.** *vpr* to stabilize. ◆**stabilité** *nf* stability.
stade [stad] *nm* **1** Sp stadium. **2** (*phase*) stage.
stage [staʒ] *nm* training period; (*cours*) (training) course. ◆**stagiaire** *a* & *nmf* trainee.
stagner [stagne] *vi* to stagnate. ◆**stagnant** *a* stagnant. ◆**stagnation** *nf* stagnation.
stalle [stal] *nf* (*box*) & Rel stall.
stand [stɑ̃d] *nm* (*d'exposition etc*) stand, stall; **s. de ravitaillement** Sp pit; **s. de tir** (*de foire*) shooting range; Mil firing range.
standard [stɑ̃dar] **1** *nm* Tél switchboard. **2** *a inv* (*modèle etc*) standard. ◆**standardiser** *vt* to standardize. ◆**standardiste** *nmf* (switchboard) operator.
standing [stɑ̃diŋ] *nm* standing, status; **de (grand) s.** (*immeuble*) luxury-.
starter [starter] *nm* **1** Aut choke. **2** Sp starter.
station [stasjɔ̃] *nf* (*de métro, d'observation etc*) & Rad station; (*de ski etc*) resort; (*d'autobus*) stop; **s. de taxis** taxi rank, Am

taxi stand; **s. debout** standing (position); **s. (thermale)** spa. ◆**s.-service** *nf* (*pl stations-service*) Aut service station.
stationnaire [stasjɔnɛr] *vi a* stationary.
stationner [stasjɔne] *vi* (*se garer*) to park; (*être garé*) to be parked. ◆**-ement** *nm* parking.
statique [statik] *a* static.
statistique [statistik] *nf* (*donnée*) statistic; **la s.** (*techniques*) statistics; – *a* statistical.
statue [staty] *nf* statue. ◆**statuette** *nf* statuette.
statuer [statɥe] *vi* **s. sur** Jur to rule on.
statu quo [statykwo] *nm inv* status quo.
stature [statyr] *nf* stature.
statut [staty] *nm* **1** (*position*) status. **2** *pl* (*règles*) statutes. ◆**statutaire** *a* statutory.
steak [stɛk] *nm* steak.
stencil [stɛnsil] *nm* stencil.
sténo [steno] *nf* (*personne*) stenographer; (*sténographie*) shorthand, stenography; **prendre en s.** to take down in shorthand. ◆**sténodactylo** *nf* shorthand typist, Am stenographer. ◆**sténographie** *nf* shorthand, stenography.
stéréo [stereo] *nf* stereo; – *a inv* (*disque etc*) stereo. ◆**stéréophonique** *a* stereophonic.
stéréotype [stereotip] *nm* stereotype. ◆**stéréotypé** *a* stereotyped.
stérile [steril] *a* sterile; (*terre*) barren. ◆**stérilisation** *nf* sterilization. ◆**stériliser** *vt* to sterilize. ◆**stérilité** *nf* sterility; (*de terre*) barrenness.
stérilet [sterilɛ] *nm* IUD, coil.
stéthoscope [stetɔskɔp] *nm* stethoscope.
steward [stiwart] *nm* Av Nau steward.
stigmate [stigmat] *nm* Fig mark, stigma (**de** of). ◆**stigmatiser** *vt* (*dénoncer*) to stigmatize.
stimul/er [stimyle] *vt* to stimulate. ◆**-ant** *nm* Fig stimulus; Méd stimulant. ◆**stimulateur** *nm* **s. cardiaque** pacemaker. ◆**stimulation** *nf* stimulation.
stimulus [stimylys] *nm* (*pl stimuli* [-li]) (*physiologique*) stimulus.
stipuler [stipyle] *vt* to stipulate (**que** that). ◆**stipulation** *nf* stipulation.
stock [stɔk] *nm* Com & Fig stock (**de** of). ◆**stock/er** *vt* to (keep in) stock. ◆**-age** *nm* stocking.
stoïque [stɔik] *a* stoic(al). ◆**stoïcisme** *nm* stoicism.
stop [stɔp] **1** *int* stop; – *nm* (*panneau*) Aut stop sign; (*feu arrière*) Aut brake light. **2** *nm* **faire du s.** Fam to hitchhike. ◆**stopp/er 1** *vti* to stop. **2** *vt* (*vêtement*) to

mend (invisibly). ◆**—age** *nm* (invisible) mending.

store [stɔr] *nm* blind, *Am* (window) shade; (*de magasin*) awning.

strabisme [strabism] *nm* squint.

strapontin [strapɔ̃tɛ̃] *nm* tip-up seat.

stratagème [strataʒɛm] *nm* stratagem, ploy.

stratège [strateʒ] *nm* strategist. ◆**stratégie** *nf* strategy. ◆**stratégique** *a* strategic.

stress [strɛs] *nm inv* *Méd* *Psy* stress. ◆**stressant** *a* stressful. ◆**stressé** *a* under stress.

strict [strikt] *a* strict; (*langue, tenue, vérité*) plain; (*droit*) basic; **le s. minimum/ nécessaire** the bare minimum/necessities. ◆**strictement** *adv* strictly; (*vêtu*) plainly.

strident [stridɑ̃] *a* strident, shrill.

strie [stri] *nf* streak; (*sillon*) groove. ◆**strier** *vt* to streak.

strip-tease [striptiz] *nm* striptease. ◆**strip-teaseuse** *nf* stripper.

strophe [strɔf] *nf* stanza, verse.

structure [stryktyr] *nf* structure. ◆**structural, -aux** *a* structural. ◆**structurer** *vt* to structure.

stuc [styk] *nm* stucco.

studieux, -euse [stydjø, -øz] *a* studious; (*vacances etc*) devoted to study.

studio [stydjo] *nm* (*de peintre*) & *Cin TV* studio; (*logement*) studio flat *ou Am* apartment.

stupéfait [stypefɛ] *a* amazed, astounded (**de** at, by). ◆**stupéfaction** *nf* amazement. ◆**stupéfi/er** *vt* to amaze, astound. ◆**—ant 1** *a* amazing, astounding. **2** *nm* drug, narcotic. ◆**stupeur** *nf* **1** (*étonnement*) amazement. **2** (*inertie*) stupor.

stupide [stypid] *a* stupid. ◆**stupidement** *adv* stupidly. ◆**stupidité** *nf* stupidity; (*action, parole*) stupid thing.

style [stil] *nm* style; **de s.** (*meuble*) period-. ◆**stylé** *a* stylized. ◆**styliste** *nmf* (*de mode etc*) designer. ◆**stylistique** *a* stylistic.

stylé [stile] *a* well-trained.

stylo [stilo] *nm* pen; **s. à bille** ballpoint (pen), biro®; **s. à encre** fountain pen.

su [sy] *voir* **savoir**.

suave [sɥav] *a* (*odeur, voix*) sweet.

subalterne [sybaltɛrn] *a & nmf* subordinate.

subconscient [sypkɔ̃sjɑ̃] *a & nm* subconscious.

subdiviser [sybdivize] *vt* to subdivide (**en** into). ◆**subdivision** *nf* subdivision.

subir [sybir] *vt* to undergo; (*conséquences, défaite, perte, tortures*) to suffer; (*influence*) to be under; **s. qn** (*supporter*) *Fam* to put up with s.o.

subit [sybi] *a* sudden. ◆**subitement** *adv* suddenly.

subjectif, -ive [sybʒektif, -iv] *a* subjective. ◆**subjectivement** *adv* subjectively. ◆**subjectivité** *nf* subjectivity.

subjonctif [sybʒɔ̃ktif] *nm Gram* subjunctive.

subjuguer [sybʒyge] *vt* to subjugate; (*envoûter*) to captivate.

sublime [syblim] *a & nm* sublime.

sublimer [syblime] *vt Psy* to sublimate.

submerger [sybmɛrʒe] *vt* to submerge; (*envahir*) *Fig* to overwhelm; **submergé de** (*travail etc*) overwhelmed with; **submergé par** (*ennemi, foule*) swamped by. ◆**submersible** *nm* submarine.

subordonn/er [sybɔrdɔne] *vt* to subordinate (**à** to). ◆**—é, -ée** *a* subordinate (**à** to); **être s. à** (*dépendre de*) to depend on; — *nmf* subordinate. ◆**subordination** *nf* subordination.

subreptice [sybrɛptis] *a* surreptitious.

subside [sypsid] *nm* grant, subsidy.

subsidiaire [sybsidjɛr] *a* subsidiary; **question s.** (*de concours*) deciding question.

subsister [sybziste] *vi* (*rester*) to remain; (*vivre*) to get by, subsist; (*doutes, souvenirs etc*) to linger (on), subsist. ◆**subsistance** *nf* subsistence.

substance [sypstɑ̃s] *nf* substance; **en s.** *Fig* in essence. ◆**substantiel, -ielle** *a* substantial.

substantif [sypstɑ̃tif] *nm Gram* noun, substantive.

substituer [sypstitɥe] *vt* to substitute (**à** for); **se s. à qn** to take the place of s.o., substitute for s.o.; (*représenter*) to substitute for s.o. ◆**substitution** *nf* substitution.

subterfuge [sypterfyʒ] *nm* subterfuge.

subtil [syptil] *a* subtle. ◆**subtilité** *nf* subtlety.

subtiliser [syptilize] *vt* (*dérober*) *Fam* to make off with.

subvenir* [sybvənir] *vi* **s. à** (*besoins, frais*) to meet.

subvention [sybvɑ̃sjɔ̃] *nf* subsidy. ◆**subventionner** *vt* to subsidize.

subversif, -ive [sybvɛrsif, -iv] *a* subversive. ◆**subversion** *nf* subversion.

suc [syk] *nm* (*gastrique, de fruit*) juice; (*de plante*) sap.

succédané [syksedane] *nm* substitute (de for).

succéder [syksede] *vi* s. à qn to succeed s.o.; s. à qch to follow sth, come after sth; **— se s.** *vpr* to succeed one another; to follow one another. ◆**successeur** *nm* successor. ◆**successif, -ive** *a* successive. ◆**successivement** *adv* successively. ◆**succession** *nf* 1 succession (de of, à to); **prendre la s. de** qn to succeed s.o. 2 (*patrimoine*) *Jur* inheritance, estate.

succès [syksɛ] *nm* success; **s. de librairie** (*livre*) best-seller; **avoir du s.** to be successful, be a success; **à s.** (*auteur, film etc*) successful; **avec s.** successfully.

succinct [syksɛ̃] *a* succinct, brief.

succion [sy(k)sjɔ̃] *nf* suction.

succomber [sykɔ̃be] *vi* 1 (*mourir*) to die. 2 **s. à** (*céder à*) to succumb to, give in to.

succulent [sykylɑ̃] *a* succulent.

succursale [sykyrsal] *nf* *Com* branch; **magasin à succursales multiples** chain *ou* multiple store.

sucer [syse] *vt* to suck. ◆**sucette** *nf* lollipop; (*tétine*) dummy, comforter, *Am* pacifier.

sucre [sykr] *nm* sugar; (*morceau*) sugar lump; **s. cristallisé** granulated sugar; **s. en morceaux** lump sugar; **s. en poudre, s. semoule** caster sugar, *Am* finely ground sugar; **s. d'orge** barley sugar. ◆**sucr/er** *vt* to sugar, sweeten. ◆**—é** *a* sweet, sugary; (*artificiellement*) sweetened; (*doucereux*) *Fig* sugary, syrupy. ◆**sucrerie 1** *nf* (*usine*) sugar refinery. 2 *nfpl* (*bonbons*) sweets, *Am* candy. ◆**sucrier, -ière** *a* (*industrie*) sugar-; **—** *nm* (*récipient*) sugar bowl.

sud [syd] *nm* south; **au s. de** south of; **du s.** (*vent, direction*) southerly; (*ville*) southern; (*gens*) from *ou* in the south; **Amérique/Afrique du S.** South America/Africa; **l'Europe du S.** Southern Europe; **—** *a inv* (*côte*) south(ern). ◆**s.-africain, -aine** *a* & *nmf* South African. ◆**s.-américain, -aine** *a* & *nmf* South American. ◆**s.-est** *nm* & *a inv* south-east. ◆**s.-ouest** *nm* & *a inv* south-west.

Suède [syɛd] *nf* Sweden. ◆**suédois, -oise** *a* Swedish; **—** *nmf* Swede; **—** *nm* (*langue*) Swedish.

suer [sɥe] *vi* (*personne, mur etc*) to sweat; **faire s. qn** *Fam* to get on s.o.'s nerves; **se faire s.** *Fam* to be bored stiff; **—** *vt* (*sang etc*) to sweat. ◆**sueur** *nf* sweat; **(tout) en s.** sweating.

suffire* [syfir] *vi* to be enough *ou* sufficient, suffice (à for); **ça suffit!** that's enough!; **il** **suffit de faire** one only has to do; **il suffit d'une goutte**/*etc* **pour faire** a drop/*etc* is enough to do; **il ne me suffit pas de faire** I'm not satisfied with doing; **— se s.** *vpr* **s. (à soi-même)** to be self-sufficient. ◆**suffisant** *a* 1 sufficient, adequate. 2 (*vaniteux*) conceited. ◆**suffisamment** *adv* sufficiently; **s. de** sufficient, enough. ◆**suffisance** *nf* (*vanité*) conceit.

suffixe [syfiks] *nm* *Gram* suffix.

suffoquer [syfɔke] *vti* to choke, suffocate. ◆**suffocant** *a* stifling, suffocating. ◆**suffocation** *nf* suffocation; (*sensation*) feeling of suffocation.

suffrage [syfraʒ] *nm* *Pol* (*voix*) vote; (*droit*) suffrage.

suggérer [sygʒere] *vt* (*proposer*) to suggest (**de faire** doing, **que** (+ *sub*) that); (*évoquer*) to suggest. ◆**suggestif, -ive** *a* suggestive. ◆**suggestion** *nf* suggestion.

suicide [sɥisid] *nm* suicide. ◆**suicidaire** *a* suicidal. ◆**se suicid/er** *vpr* to commit suicide. ◆**—é, -ée** *nmf* suicide (victim).

suie [sɥi] *nf* soot.

suif [sɥif] *nm* tallow.

suinter [sɥɛ̃te] *vi* to ooze, seep. ◆**suintement** *nm* oozing, seeping.

suis [sɥi] *voir* être, suivre.·

Suisse [sɥis] *nf* Switzerland. ◆**suisse** *a* & *nmf* Swiss. ◆**Suissesse** *nf* Swiss (woman *ou* girl).

suite [sɥit] *nf* (*reste*) rest; (*continuation*) continuation; (*de film, roman*) sequel; (*série*) series, sequence; (*appartement, escorte*) & *Mus* suite; (*cohérence*) order; *pl* (*résultats*) consequences; (*séquelles*) effects; **attendre la s.** to wait and see what happens next; **donner s. à** (*demande etc*) to follow up; **faire s. (à)** to follow; **prendre la s. de qn** to take over from s.o.; **par la s.** afterwards; **par s. de** as a result of; **à la s.** one after another; **à la s. de** (*derrière*) behind; (*événement, maladie etc*) as a result of; **de s.** in succession.

suiv/re* [sɥivr] *vt* to follow; (*accompagner*) to go with, accompany; (*classe*) *Scol* to attend, go to; (*malade*) to treat; **s. (des yeux ou du regard)** to watch; **s. son chemin** to go on one's way; **se s.** to follow each other; **—** *vi* to follow; **faire s.** (*courrier*) to forward; **'à s.'** 'to be continued'; **comme suit** as follows. ◆**—ant¹, -ante** *a* next, following; (*ci-après*) following; **—** *nmf* next (one); **au s.!** next!, the next person! ◆**—ant² prép** (*selon*) according to. ◆**—i** *a* (*régulier*) regular, steady; (*cohérent*) coherent; (*article*)

Com regularly on sale; **peu/très s.** (*cours*) poorly/well attended.

sujet¹, -ette [syʒɛ, -ɛt] *a* **s. à** (*maladie etc*) subject *ou* liable to; — *nmf* (*personne*) *Pol* subject.

sujet² [syʒɛ] *nm* **1** (*question*) & *Gram* subject; (*d'examen*) question; **au s. de** about; **à quel s.?** about what? **2** (*raison*) cause; **avoir s. de faire** to have (good) cause *ou* (good) reason to do. **3** *nm* (*individu*) subject; **un mauvais s.** (*garçon*) a rotten egg.

sulfurique [sylfyrik] *a* (*acide*) sulphuric, *Am* sulfuric.

sultan [syltã] *nm* sultan.

summum [sɔmɔm] *nm* (*comble*) *Fig* height.

super [sypɛr] **1** *a* (*bon*) *Fam* great. **2** *nm* (*supercarburant*) *Fam* four-star (petrol), *Am* premium *ou* hi-test gas.

superbe [sypɛrb] *a* superb.

supercarburant [sypɛrkarbyrã] *nm* high-octane petrol *ou Am* gasoline.

supercherie [sypɛrʃəri] *nf* deception.

superficie [sypɛrfisi] *nf* surface; (*dimensions*) area. ◆**superficiel, -ielle** *a* superficial. ◆**superficiellement** *adv* superficially.

superflu [sypɛrfly] *a* superfluous.

super-grand [sypɛrgrã] *nm* *Pol* *Fam* superpower.

supérieur, -eure [sypɛrjœr] *a* (*étages, partie etc*) upper; (*qualité, air, ton*) superior; (*études*) higher; **à l'étage s.** on the floor above; **s. à** (*meilleur que*) superior to, better than; (*plus grand que*) above, greater than; — *nmf* superior. ◆**supériorité** *nf* superiority.

superlatif, -ive [sypɛrlatif, -iv] *a* & *nm* *Gram* superlative.

supermarché [sypɛrmarʃe] *nm* supermarket.

superposer [sypɛrpoze] *vt* (*objets*) to put on top of each other; (*images etc*) to superimpose.

superproduction [sypɛrprɔdyksjɔ̃] *nf* (*film*) blockbuster.

superpuissance [sypɛrpɥisãs] *nf* *Pol* superpower.

supersonique [sypɛrsɔnik] *a* supersonic.

superstitieux, -euse [sypɛrstisjø, -øz] *a* superstitious. ◆**superstition** *nf* superstition.

superviser [sypɛrvize] *vt* to supervise.

supplanter [syplãte] *vt* to take the place of.

supplé/er [syplee] *vt* (*remplacer*) to replace; (*compenser*) to make up for; — *vi* **s. à** (*compenser*) to make up for. ◆**—ant, -ante**

a & *nmf* (*personne*) substitute, replacement; (*professeur*) **s.** supply teacher.

supplément [syplemã] *nm* (*argent*) extra charge, supplement; (*de livre, revue*) supplement; **en s.** extra; **un s. de** (*information, travail etc*) extra, additional. ◆**supplémentaire** *a* extra, additional.

supplice [syplis] *nm* torture; **au s.** *Fig* on the rack. ◆**supplicier** *vt* to torture.

suppli/er [syplije] *vt* **s. qn de faire** to beg *ou* implore s.o. to do; **je vous en supplie!** I beg *ou* implore you! ◆**—ant, -ante** *a* (*regard etc*) imploring. ◆**supplication** *nf* plea, entreaty.

support [sypɔr] *nm* **1** support; (*d'instrument etc*) stand. **2** (*moyen*) *Fig* medium; **s. audio-visuel** audio-visual aid.

support/er¹ [sypɔrte] *vt* to bear, endure; (*frais*) to bear; (*affront etc*) to suffer; (*résister à*) to withstand; (*soutenir*) to support. ◆**—able** *a* bearable; (*excusable, passable*) tolerable.

supporter² [sypɔrtɛr] *nm* *Sp* supporter.

supposer [sypoze] *vt* to suppose, assume (**que** that); (*impliquer*) to imply (**que** that); **à s.** *ou* **en supposant que** (+ *sub*) supposing (that). ◆**supposition** *nf* supposition, assumption.

suppositoire [sypozitwar] *nm* *Méd* suppository.

supprimer [syprime] *vt* to remove, get rid of; (*institution, loi*) to abolish; (*journal etc*) to suppress; (*mot, passage*) to cut, delete; (*train etc*) to cancel; (*tuer*) to do away with; **s. qch à qn** to take sth away from s.o. ◆**suppression** *nf* removal; abolition; suppression; cutting; cancellation.

suprématie [sypremasi] *nf* supremacy. ◆**suprême** *a* supreme.

sur [syr] *prép* on, upon; (*par-dessus*) over; (*au sujet de*) on, about; **s. les trois heures** at about three o'clock; **six s. dix** six out of ten; **un jour s. deux** every other day; **coup s. coup** blow after *ou* upon blow; **six mètres s. dix** six metres by ten; **mettre/monter/etc s.** to put/climb/etc on (to); **aller/tourner/etc s.** to go/turn/etc towards; **s. ce** after which, and then; (*maintenant*) and now.

sur- [syr] *préf* over-.

sûr [syr] *a* sure, certain (**de** of, **que** that); (*digne de confiance*) reliable; (*avenir*) secure; (*lieu*) safe; (*main*) steady; (*goût*) unerring; (*jugement*) sound; **s. de soi** self-assured; **bien s.!** of course!

surabondant [syrabɔ̃dã] *a* over-abundant.

suranné [syrane] *a* outmoded.

surboum [syrbum] *nf* *Fam* party.

surcharge [syrʃarʒ] *nf* **1** overloading; (*poids*) extra load; **s. de travail** extra work; **en s.** (*passagers etc*) extra. **2** (*correction de texte etc*) alteration; (*de timbre-poste*) surcharge. ◆**surcharger** *vt* (*voiture, personne etc*) to overload (**de** with).

surchauffer [syrʃofe] *vt* to overheat.

surchoix [syrʃwa] *a inv Com* top-quality.

surclasser [syrklase] *vt* to outclass.

surcroît [syrkrwa] *nm* increase (**de** in); **de s., par s.** in addition.

surdité [syrdite] *nf* deafness.

surdoué, -ée [syrdwe] *nmf* child who has a genius-level IQ.

surélever [syrelve] *vt* to raise (the height of).

sûrement [syrmã] *adv* certainly; (*sans danger*) safely.

surenchère [syrãʃer] *nf Com* higher bid; **s. électorale** *Fig* bidding for votes. ◆**surenchérir** *vi* to bid higher (**sur** than).

surestimer [syrestime] *vt* to overestimate; (*peinture etc*) to overvalue.

sûreté [syrte] *nf* safety; (*de l'état*) security; (*garantie*) surety; (*de geste*) sureness; (*de jugement*) soundness; **être en s.** to be safe; **mettre en s.** to put in a safe place; **de s.** (*épingle, soupape etc*) safety-.

surexcité [syreksite] *a* overexcited.

surf [sœrf] *nm Sp* surfing; **faire du s.** to surf, go surfing.

surface [syrfas] *nf* surface; (*dimensions*) (surface) area; **faire s.** (*sous-marin etc*) to surface; (**magasin à**) **grande s.** hypermarket.

surfait [syrfɛ] *a* overrated.

surgelé [syrʒəle] *a* (deep-)frozen; – *nmpl* (deep-)frozen foods.

surgir [syrʒir] *vi* to appear suddenly (**de** from); (*conflit, problème*) to arise.

surhomme [syrɔm] *nm* superman. ◆**surhumain** *a* superhuman.

sur-le-champ [syrləʃã] *adv* immediately.

surlendemain [syrlãdmɛ̃] *nm* **le s.** two days later; **le s. de** two days after.

surmen/er [syrməne] *vt*, **— se s.** *vpr* to overwork. ◆**—age** *nm* overwork.

surmonter [syrmɔ̃te] *vt* **1** (*obstacle, peur etc*) to overcome, get over. **2** (*être placé sur*) to be on top of, top.

surnager [syrnaʒe] *vi* to float.

surnaturel, -elle [syrnatyrel] *a & nm* supernatural.

surnom [syrnɔ̃] *nm* nickname. ◆**surnommer** *vt* to nickname.

surnombre [syrnɔ̃br] *nm* **en s.** too many; **je suis en s.** I am one too many.

surpasser [syrpase] *vt* to surpass (**en** in); **— se s.** *vpr* to surpass oneself.

surpeuplé [syrpœple] *a* overpopulated.

surplomb [syrplɔ̃] *nm* **en s.** overhanging. ◆**surplomber** *vti* to overhang.

surplus [syrply] *nm* surplus; *pl Com* surplus (stock).

surprendre* [syrprãdr] *vt* (*étonner, prendre sur le fait*) to surprise; (*secret*) to discover; (*conversation*) to overhear; **se s. à faire** to find oneself doing. ◆**surprenant** *a* surprising. ◆**surpris** *a* surprised (**de** at, **que** (+ *sub*) that). ◆**surprise** *nf* surprise. ◆**surprise-partie** *nf* (*pl* **surprises-parties**) party.

surréaliste [syrealist] *a* (*bizarre*) *Fam* surrealistic.

sursaut [syrso] *nm* (sudden) start *ou* jump; **en s.** with a start; **s. de** (*énergie etc*) burst of. ◆**sursauter** *vi* to start, jump.

sursis [syrsi] *nm Mil* deferment; (*répit*) *Fig* reprieve; **un an (de prison) avec s.** a one-year suspended sentence.

surtaxe [syrtaks] *nf* surcharge.

surtout [syrtu] *adv* especially; (*avant tout*) above all; **s. pas** certainly not; **s. que** especially as *ou* since.

surveill/er [syrveje] *vt* (*garder*) to watch, keep an eye on; (*épier*) to watch; (*contrôler*) to supervise; **s. son langage/sa santé** *Fig* to watch one's language/health; **— se s.** *vpr* to watch oneself. ◆**—ant, -ante** *nmf* (*de lycée*) supervisor (in charge of discipline); (*de prison*) warder; (*de chantier*) supervisor; **s. de plage** lifeguard. ◆**surveillance** *nf* watch (**sur** over); (*de travaux, d'ouvriers*) supervision; (*de la police*) surveillance, observation.

survenir* [syrvənir] *vi* to occur; (*personne*) to turn up.

survêtement [syrvetmã] *nm Sp* tracksuit.

survie [syrvi] *nf* survival. ◆**surviv/re*** *vi* to survive (**à qch** sth); **s. à qn** to outlive s.o., survive s.o. ◆**—ant, -ante** *nmf* survivor. ◆**survivance** *nf* (*chose*) survival, relic.

survol [syrvɔl] *nm* **le s. de** flying over; (*question*) *Fig* the overview of. ◆**survoler** *vt* (*en avion*) to fly over; (*question*) *Fig* to go over (quickly).

survolté [syrvɔlte] *a* (*surexcité*) worked up.

susceptible [syseptibl] *a* **1** (*ombrageux*) touchy, sensitive. **2 s. de** (*interprétations etc*) open to; **s. de faire** likely *ou* liable to do; (*capable*) able to do. ◆**susceptibilité** *nf* touchiness, sensitiveness.

susciter [sysite] *vt* (*sentiment*) to arouse; (*ennuis, obstacles etc*) to create.

suspect, -ecte [syspε(kt), -εkt] *a* suspicious, suspect; **s. de** suspected of; – *nmf* suspect. ◆**suspecter** *vt* to suspect (**de qch** of sth, **de faire** of doing); (*bonne foi etc*) to question, suspect, doubt.

suspend/re [syspɑ̃dr] *vt* **1** (*destituer, différer, interrompre*) to suspend. **2** (*fixer*) to hang (up) (**à** on); **se s. à** to hang from. ◆**–u** *a* s. **à** hanging from; **pont s.** suspension bridge. ◆**suspension** *nf* **1** (*d'hostilités, d'employé etc*) & *Aut* suspension; **points de s.** *Gram* dots, suspension points. **2** (*lustre*) hanging lamp.

suspens (en) [ɑ̃syspɑ̃] *adv* **1** (*affaire, travail*) in abeyance. **2** (*dans l'incertitude*) in suspense.

suspense [syspεns] *nm* suspense; **film à s.** thriller, suspense film.

suspicion [syspisjɔ̃] *nf* suspicion.

susurrer [sysyre] *vti* to murmur.

suture [sytyr] *nf Méd* stitching; **point de s.** stitch. ◆**suturer** *vt* to stitch up.

svelte [svεlt] *a* slender. ◆**sveltesse** *nf* slenderness.

SVP *abrév* (*s'il vous plaît*) please.

syllabe [silab] *nf* syllable.

symbole [sɛ̃bɔl] *nm* symbol. ◆**symbolique** *a* symbolic; (*salaire*) nominal. ◆**symboliser** *vt* to symbolize. ◆**symbolisme** *nm* symbolism.

symétrie [simetri] *nf* symmetry. ◆**symétrique** *a* symmetrical.

sympa [sɛ̃pa] *a inv Fam* = **sympathique.**

sympathie [sɛ̃pati] *nf* liking, affection; (*affinité*) affinity; (*condoléances*) sympathy; **avoir de la s. pour qn** to be fond of s.o. ◆**sympathique** *a* nice, pleasant; (*accueil, geste*) friendly. ◆**sympathis/er** *vi* to get

on well (**avec** with). ◆**–ant, -ante** *nmf Pol* sympathizer.

symphonie [sɛ̃fɔni] *nf* symphony. ◆**symphonique** *a* symphonic; (*orchestre*) symphony-.

symposium [sɛ̃pozjɔm] *nm* symposium.

symptôme [sɛ̃ptom] *nm* symptom. ◆**symptomatique** *a* symptomatic (**de** of).

synagogue [sinagɔg] *nf* synagogue.

synchroniser [sɛ̃krɔnize] *vt* to synchronize.

syncope [sɛ̃kɔp] *nf Méd* blackout; **tomber en s.** to black out.

syndicat [sɛ̃dika] *nm* **1** (*d'employés, d'ouvriers*) (trade) union; (*de patrons etc*) association. **2 s. d'initiative** tourist (information) office. ◆**syndical, -aux** *a* (*réunion etc*) (trade) union-. ◆**syndicalisme** *nm* trade unionism. ◆**syndicaliste** *nmf* trade unionist; – *a* (trade) union-. ◆**syndiqu/er** *vt* to unionize; – **se s.** *vpr* (*adhérer*) to join a (trade) union. ◆**–é, -ée** *nmf* (trade) union member.

syndrome [sɛ̃drom] *nm Méd* & *Fig* syndrome.

synode [sinɔd] *nm Rel* synod.

synonyme [sinɔnim] *a* synonymous (**de** with); – *nm* synonym.

syntaxe [sɛ̃taks] *nf Gram* syntax.

synthèse [sɛ̃tez] *nf* synthesis. ◆**synthétique** *a* synthetic.

syphilis [sifilis] *nf* syphilis.

Syrie [siri] *nf* Syria. ◆**syrien, -ienne** *a* & *nmf* Syrian.

système [sistεm] *nm* (*structure, réseau etc*) & *Anat* system; **le s. D** *Fam* resourcefulness. ◆**systématique** *a* systematic; (*soutien*) unconditional. ◆**systématiquement** *adv* systematically.

T

T, t [te] *nm* T, t.

t' [t] *voir* **te.**

ta [ta] *voir* **ton**[1].

tabac [taba] **1** *nm* tobacco; (*magasin*) tobacconist's (shop), *Am* tobacco store; **t. (à priser)** snuff. **2** *nm* **passer à t.** to beat up; **passage à t.** beating up. **3** *a inv* (*couleur*) buff. ◆**tabatière** *nf* (*boîte*) snuffbox.

tabasser [tabase] *vt Fam* to beat up.

table [tabl] *nf* **1** (*meuble*) table; (*nourriture*) fare; **t. de jeu/de nuit/d'opération** card/bedside/operating table; **t. basse** coffee

table; **t. à repasser** ironing board; **t. roulante** (tea) trolley, *Am* (serving) cart; **mettre/débarrasser la t.** to lay *ou* set/clear the table; **être à t.** to be sitting at the table; **à t.!** (food's) ready!; **faire t. rase** *Fig* to make a clean sweep (**de** of); **mettre sur t. d'écoute** (*téléphone*) to tap. **2** (*liste*) table; **t. des matières** table of contents.

tableau, -x [tablo] *nm* **1** (*peinture*) picture, painting; (*image, description*) picture; *Th* scene; **t. de maître** (*peinture*) old master. **2** (*panneau*) board; *Rail* train-indicator;

(liste) list; *(graphique)* chart; **t. (noir)** (b[l]ack)board; **t. d'affichage** notice board, *Am* bulletin board; **t. de bord** *Aut* dashboard; **t. de contrôle** *Tech* control panel.

tabler [table] *vi* **t. sur** to count *ou* rely on.

tablette [tablet] *nf* *(d'armoire, de lavabo)* shelf; *(de cheminée)* mantelpiece; *(de chocolat)* bar, slab.

tablier [tablije] *nm* **1** *(vêtement)* apron; *(d'écolier)* smock; **rendre son t.** *(démissionner)* to give notice. **2** *(de pont)* roadway.

tabou [tabu] *a* & *nm* taboo.

tabouret [taburɛ] *nm* stool.

tabulateur [tabylatœr] *nm* *(de machine à écrire etc)* tabulator.

tac [tak] *nm* **répondre du t. au t.** to give tit for tat.

tache [taʃ] *nf* spot, mark; *(salissure)* stain; **faire t.** *(détonner)* *Péj* to jar, stand out; **faire t. d'huile** *Fig* to spread. ◆**tacher** *vt*, **– se t.** *vpr* *(tissu etc)* to stain; **– vi** *(vin etc)* to stain. ◆**tacheté** *a* speckled, spotted.

tâche [taʃ] *nf* task, job; **travailler à la t.** to do piecework.

tâcher [taʃe] *vi* **t. de faire** to try *ou* endeavour to do.

tâcheron [taʃrɔ̃] *nm* drudge.

tacite [tasit] *a* tacit. ◆**–ment** *adv* tacitly.

taciturne [tasityrn] *a* taciturn.

tacot [tako] *nm* *(voiture)* *Fam* (old) wreck, banger.

tact [takt] *nm* tact.

tactile [taktil] *a* tactile.

tactique [taktik] *a* tactical; **– nf la t.** tactics; **une t.** a tactic.

Tahiti [taiti] *nm* Tahiti. ◆**tahitien, -ienne** [taisjɛ̃, -jɛn] *a* *nmf* Tahitian.

taie [tɛ] *nf* **t. d'oreiller** pillowcase, pillowslip.

taillade [tɑjad] *nf* gash, slash. ◆**taillader** *vt* to gash, slash.

taille¹ [tɑj] *nf* **1** *(stature)* height; *(dimension, mesure commerciale)* size; **de haute t.** *(personne)* tall; **de petite t.** short; **de t. moyenne** *(objet, personne)* medium-sized; **être de t. à faire** *Fig* to be capable of doing; **de t.** *(erreur, objet)* *Fam* enormous. **2** *Anat* waist; **tour de t.** waist measurement.

taille² [tɑj] *nf* cutting; cutting out; trimming; pruning; *(forme)* cut. ◆**taill/er** *vt* to cut; *(vêtement)* to cut out; *(haie, barbe)* to trim; *(arbre)* to prune; *(crayon)* to sharpen. **2 se t.** *vpr* *(partir)* *Arg* to clear off. ◆**–é** *a* **t. en athlète**/*etc* built like an athlete/*etc*; **t. pour faire** *Fig* cut out for doing.

taille-crayon(s) [tɑjkrɛjɔ̃] *nm inv* pencil-sharpener. ◆**t.-haies** *nm inv* (garden) shears; *(électrique)* hedge trimmer.

tailleur [tɑjœr] *nm* **1** *(personne)* tailor. **2** *(costume féminin)* suit.

taillis [tɑji] *nm* copse, coppice.

tain [tɛ̃] *nm* *(de glace)* silvering; **glace sans t.** two-way mirror.

taire* [tɛr] *vt* to say nothing about; **– vi faire t. qn** to silence s.o. **– se t.** *vpr* *(rester silencieux)* to keep quiet **(sur qch** about sth); *(cesser de parler)* to fall silent, shut up; **tais-toi!** be *ou* keep quiet!, shut up!

talc [talk] *nm* talcum powder.

talent [talɑ̃] *nm* talent; **avoir du t. pour** to have a talent for. ◆**talentueux, -euse** *a* talented.

taler [tale] *vt* *(fruit)* to bruise.

talion [taljɔ̃] *nm* **la loi du t.** *(vengeance)* an eye for an eye.

talisman [talismɑ̃] *nm* talisman.

talkie-walkie [talkiwalki] *nm* *(poste)* walkie-talkie.

taloche [talɔʃ] *nf* *(gifle)* *Fam* clout, smack.

talon [talɔ̃] *nm* **1** heel; **(chaussures à) talons hauts** high heels, high-heeled shoes. **2** *(de chèque, carnet)* stub, counterfoil; *(bout de pain)* crust; *(de jambon)* heel. ◆**talonner** *vt* *(fugitif etc)* to follow on the heels of; *(ballon)* *Rugby* to heel; *(harceler)* *Fig* to hound, dog.

talus [taly] *nm* slope, embankment.

tambour [tɑbur] *nm* **1** *(de machine etc)* & *Mus* drum; *(personne)* drummer. **2** *(porte)* revolving door. ◆**tambourin** *nm* tambourine. ◆**tambouriner** *vi* *(avec les doigts etc)* to drum **(sur** on).

tamis [tami] *nm* sieve. ◆**tamiser** *vt* to sift; *(lumière)* to filter, subdue.

Tamise [tamiz] *nf* **la T.** the Thames.

tampon [tɑpɔ̃] *nm* **1** *(bouchon)* plug, stopper; *(d'ouate)* wad, pad; *Méd* swab; **t. hygiénique** *ou* **périodique** tampon; **t. à récurer** scouring pad. **2** *(de train etc)* & *Fig* buffer; **état t.** buffer state. **3** *(marque, instrument)* stamp; **t. buvard** blotter; **t. encreur** ink(ing) pad. ◆**tamponn/er 1** *vt* *(visage etc)* to dab; *(plaie)* to swab. **2** *vt* *(train, voiture)* to crash into; **– se t.** *vpr* to crash into each other. **3** *vt* *(lettre, document)* to stamp. ◆**–euses** *afpl* **autos t.** dodgems, bumper cars.

tam-tam [tamtam] *nm* *(tambour)* tom-tom.

tandem [tɑdɛm] *nm* **1** *(bicyclette)* tandem. **2** *(duo)* *Fig* duo, pair; **en t.** *(travailler etc)* in tandem.

tandis que [tɑdik(ə)] *conj* *(pendant que)* while; *(contraste)* whereas, while.

tangent [tɑ̃ʒɑ̃] *a* **1** *Géom* tangential **(à** to).

2 (*juste*) *Fam* touch and go, close. ◆**tangente** *nf Géom* tangent.

tangible [tãʒibl] *a* tangible.

tango [tãgo] *nm* tango.

tang/uer [tãge] *vi* (*bateau, avion*) to pitch. ◆**—age** *nm* pitching.

tanière [tanjɛr] *nf* den, lair.

tank [tãk] *nm Mil* tank.

tanker [tãkɛr] *nm* (*navire*) tanker.

tann/er [tane] *vt* (*cuir*) to tan. ◆**—é** *a* (*visage*) weather-beaten, tanned.

tant [tã] *adv* so much (**que** that); **t. de** (*pain, temps etc*) so much (**que** that); (*gens, choses etc*) so many (**que** that); **t. de fois** so often, so many times; **t. que** (*autant que*) as much as; (*aussi fort que*) as hard as; (*aussi longtemps que*) as long as; **en t. que** (*considéré comme*) as; **t. mieux!** good!, I'm glad!; **t. pis!** too bad!, pity!; **t. soit peu** (even) remotely *ou* slightly; **un t. soit peu** somewhat; **t. s'en faut** far from it; **t. bien que mal** more or less, so-so.

tante [tãt] *nf* aunt.

tantinet [tãtinɛ] *nm & adv* **un t.** a tiny bit (**de** of).

tantôt [tãto] *adv* **1** . . . . **t.** sometimes . . . sometimes, now . . . now. **2** (*cet après-midi*) this afternoon.

taon [tã] *nm* horsefly, gadfly.

tapage [tapaʒ] *nm* din, uproar. ◆**tapageur, -euse** *a* **1** (*bruyant*) rowdy. **2** (*criard*) flashy.

tape [tap] *nf* slap. ◆**tap/er 1** *vt* (*enfant, cuisse*) to slap; (*table*) to bang; **t. qn** (*emprunter de l'argent à qn*) *Fam* to touch s.o., tap s.o. (**de** for); – *vi* (*soleil*) to beat down; **t. sur qch** to bang on sth; **t. à la porte** to bang on the door; **t. sur qn** (*critiquer*) *Fam* to run s.o. down, knock s.o.; **t. sur les nerfs de qn** *Fam* to get on s.o.'s nerves; **t. dans** (*provisions etc*) *Fam* to dig into; **t. du pied** to stamp one's foot; **t. dans l'œil à qn** *Fam* to take s.o.'s fancy; – **se t.** *vpr* (*travail*) *Fam* to do, take on; (*repas, vin*) *Fam* to put away. **2** *vti* (*écrire à la machine*) to type. ◆**—ant** *a* **à midi t.** at twelve sharp; **à huit heures tapant(es)** at eight sharp. ◆**—eur, -euse** *nmf Fam* person who borrows money.

tape-à-l'œil [tapalœj] *a inv* flashy, gaudy.

tapée [tape] *nf* **une t. de** *Fam* a load of.

tapioca [tapjɔka] *nm* tapioca.

tapir (se) [satapir] *vpr* to crouch (down). ◆**tapi** *a* crouching, crouched.

tapis [tapi] *nm* carpet; **t. de bain** bathmat; **t. roulant** (*pour marchandises*) conveyor belt; (*pour personnes*) moving pavement *ou Am*

sidewalk; **t. de sol** groundsheet; **t. de table** table cover; **envoyer qn au t.** (*abattre*) to floor s.o.; **mettre sur le t.** (*sujet*) to bring up for discussion. ◆**t.-brosse** *nm* doormat.

tapisser [tapise] *vt* (*mur*) to (wall)paper; to hang with tapestry; (*recouvrir*) *Fig* to cover. ◆**tapisserie** *nf* (*tenture*) tapestry; (*papier peint*) wallpaper. ◆**tapissier, -ière** *nmf* (*qui pose des tissus etc*) upholsterer; **t.(-décorateur)** interior decorator.

tapoter [tapɔte] *vt* to tap; (*joue*) to pat; – *vi* **t. sur** to tap (on).

taquin, -ine [takɛ̃, -in] *a* (*fond of*) teasing; – *nmf* tease(r). ◆**taquiner** *vt* to tease; (*inquiéter, agacer*) to bother. ◆**taquinerie(s)** *nf(pl)* teasing.

tarabiscoté [tarabiskɔte] *a* over-elaborate.

tarabuster [tarabyste] *vt* (*idée etc*) to trouble (*s.o.*).

tard [tar] *adv* late; **plus t.** later (on); **au plus t.** at the latest; **sur le t.** late in life. ◆**tarder** *vi* (*lettre, saison*) to be a long time coming; **t. à faire** to take one's time doing; (*différer*) to delay (in) doing; **ne tardez pas** (*agissez tout de suite*) don't delay; **elle ne va pas t.** she won't be long; **sans t.** without delay; **il me tarde de faire** I long to do. ◆**tardif, -ive** *a* late; (*regrets*) belated. ◆**tardivement** *adv* late.

tare [tar] *nf* **1** (*poids*) tare. **2** (*défaut*) *Fig* defect. ◆**taré** *a* (*corrompu*) corrupt; *Méd* defective; (*fou*) *Fam* mad, idiotic.

targuer (se) [satarge] *vpr* **se t. de qch/de faire** to boast about sth/about doing.

tarif [tarif] *nm* (*prix*) rate; *Aut Rail* fare; (*tableau*) price list, tariff. ◆**tarification** *nf* (*price*) fixing.

tarir [tarir] *vti*, – **se t.** *vpr* (*fleuve etc*) & *Fig* to dry up; **ne pas t. d'éloges sur qn** to rave about s.o.

tartare [tartar] *a* **sauce t.** tartar sauce.

tarte [tart] **1** *nf* tart, flan, *Am* (open) pie. **2** *a inv Fam* (*sot*) silly; (*laid*) ugly. ◆**tartelette** *nf* (small) tart.

tartine [tartin] *nf* slice of bread; **t. (de beurre/de confiture)** slice of bread and butter/jam. ◆**tartiner** *vt* (*beurre*) to spread; **fromage à t.** cheese spread.

tartre [tartr] *nm* (*de bouilloire*) scale, fur; (*de dents*) tartar.

tas [tã] *nm* pile, heap; **un** *ou* **des t. de** (*beaucoup*) *Fam* lots of; **mettre en t.** to pile *ou* heap up; **former qn sur le t.** (*au travail*) to train s.o. on the job.

tasse [tas] *nf* cup; **t. à café** coffee cup; **t. à thé** teacup; **boire la t.** *Fam* to swallow a mouthful (*when swimming*).

tasser [tɑse] vt to pack, squeeze (**dans** into); (*terre*) to pack down; **un café/etc bien tassé** (*fort*) a good strong coffee/*etc*; **— se t.** vpr (*se voûter*) to become bowed; (*se serrer*) to squeeze up; (*sol*) to sink, collapse; **ça va se t.** (*s'arranger*) Fam things will pan out (all right).

tâter [tɑte] vt to feel; (*sonder*) Fig to sound out; **— vi t. de** (*métier, prison*) to have a taste of, experience; **— se t.** vpr (*hésiter*) to be in **ou** of two minds. ◆**tâtonn/er** vi to grope about, feel one's way. ◆**—ement** nm **par t.** (*procéder*) by trial and error. ◆**tâtons (à)** adv **avancer à t.** to feel one's way (along); **chercher à t.** to grope for.

tatillon, -onne [tatijɔ̃, -ɔn] a finicky.

tatou/er [tatwe] vt (*corps, dessin*) to tattoo. ◆**—age** nm (*dessin*) tattoo; (*action*) tattooing.

taudis [todi] nm slum, hovel.

taule [tol] nf (*prison*) Fam nick, jug, Am can.

taupe [top] nf (*animal, espion*) mole. ◆**taupinière** nf molehill.

taureau, -x [tɔro] nm bull; **le T.** (*signe*) Taurus. ◆**tauromachie** nf bull-fighting.

taux [to] nm rate; **t. d'alcool/de cholestérol**/*etc* alcohol/cholesterol/*etc* level.

taverne [tavɛrn] nf tavern.

taxe [taks] nf (*prix*) official price; (*impôt*) tax; (*douanière*) duty; **t. de séjour** tourist tax; **t. à la valeur ajoutée** value-added tax. ◆**taxation** nf fixing of the price (**de** of); taxation (**de** of). ◆**taxer** vt **1** (*produit*) to fix the price of; (*objet de luxe etc*) to tax. **2 t. qn de** to accuse s.o. of.

taxi [taksi] nm taxi.

taxiphone [taksifɔn] nm pay phone.

Tchécoslovaquie [tʃekɔslɔvaki] nf Czechoslovakia. ◆**tchèque** a & nmf Czech; **—** nm (*langue*) Czech.

te [t(ə)] (**t'** before vowel or mute h) pron **1** (*complément direct*) you; **je te vois** I see you. **2** (*indirect*) (to) you; **il te parle** he speaks to you; **elle te l'a dit** she told you. **3** (*réfléchi*) yourself; **tu te laves** you wash yourself.

technicien, -ienne [tɛknisjɛ̃, -jɛn] nmf technician. ◆**technique** a technical; **—** nf technique. ◆**techniquement** adv technically. ◆**technocrate** nm technocrat. ◆**technologie** nf technology. ◆**technologique** a technological.

teck [tɛk] nm (*bois*) teak.

teckel [tekɛl] nm (*chien*) dachshund.

tee-shirt [tiʃœrt] nm tee-shirt.

teindre* [tɛ̃dr] vt to dye; **— se t.** vpr to dye one's hair. ◆**teinture** nf dyeing; (*produit*) dye. ◆**teinturerie** nf (*boutique*) (dry) cleaner's. ◆**teinturier, -ière** nmf dry cleaner.

teint [tɛ̃] nm **1** (*de visage*) complexion. **2 bon ou grand t.** (*tissu*) colourfast; **bon t.** (*catholique etc*) Fig staunch.

teinte [tɛ̃t] nf shade, tint; **une t. de** (*dose*) Fig a tinge of. ◆**teinter** vt to tint; (*bois*) to stain; **se t. de** (*remarque, ciel*) Fig to be tinged with.

tel, telle [tɛl] a such; **un t. homme/livre**/*etc* such a man/book/*etc*; **un t. intérêt**/*etc* such interest/*etc*; **de tels mots**/*etc* such words/*etc*; **t. que** such as, like; **t. que je l'ai laissé** just as I left it; **laissez-le t. quel** leave it just as it is; **en tant que t., comme t.** as such; **t. ou t.** such and such; **rien de t. que . . .** (there's) nothing like . . . ; **rien de t.** nothing like it; **Monsieur Un t.** Mr So-and-so; **t. père t. fils** like father like son.

télé [tele] nf (*téléviseur*) Fam TV, telly; **à la t.** on TV, on the telly; **regarder la t.** to watch TV ou the telly.

télé- [tele] préf tele-.

télébenne [telebɛn] nf, **télécabine** [telekabin] nf (*cabine, système*) cable car.

télécommande [telekɔmɑ̃d] nf remote control. ◆**télécommander** vt to operate by remote control.

télécommunications [telekɔmynikasjɔ̃] nfpl telecommunications.

téléfilm [telefilm] nm TV film.

télégramme [telegram] nm telegram.

télégraphe [telegraf] nm telegraph. ◆**télégraphie** nf telegraphy. ◆**télégraphier** vt (*message*) to wire, cable (**que** that). ◆**télégraphique** a (*fil, poteau*) telegraph-; (*style*) Fig telegraphic. ◆**télégraphiste** nm (*messager*) telegraph boy.

téléguid/er [telegide] vt to radio-control. ◆**—age** nm radio-control.

télématique [telematik] nf telematics, computer communications.

télépathie [telepati] nf telepathy.

téléphérique [teleferik] nm (*système*) cable car, cableway.

téléphone [telefɔn] nm (tele)phone; **coup de t.** (phone) call; **passer un coup de t. à qn** to give s.o. a call ou a ring; **au t.** on the (tele)phone; **avoir le t.** to be on the (tele)phone; **par le t. arabe** Fig on the grapevine. ◆**téléphoner** vt (*nouvelle etc*) to (tele)phone (**à** to); **—** vi to (tele)phone; **t. à qn** to (tele)phone s.o., call s.o. (up). ◆**téléphonique** a (*appel etc*) (tele)phone-. ◆**téléphoniste** nmf operator, telephonist.

télescope [telɛskɔp] *nm* telescope. ◆**télescopique** *a* telescopic.

télescop/er [telɛskɔpe] *vt Aut Rail* to smash into; **se t.** to smash into each other. ◆**—age** *nm* smash.

téléscripteur [teleskriptœr] *nm* (*appareil*) teleprinter.

télésiège [telesjɛʒ] *nm* chair lift.

téléski [teleski] *nm* ski tow.

téléspectateur, -trice [telespɛktatœr, -tris] *nmf* (television) viewer.

téléviser [televize] *vt* to televise; **journal télévisé** television news. ◆**téléviseur** *nm* television (set). ◆**télévision** *nf* television; **à la t.** on (the) television; **regarder la t.** to watch (the) television; **de t.** (*programme etc*) television-.

télex [telɛks] *nm* (*service, message*) telex.

telle [tɛl] *voir* **tel**.

tellement [tɛlmɑ̃] *adv* (*si*) so; (*tant*) so much; **t. grand/etc que** so big/etc that; **crier/etc t. que** to shout/etc so much that; **t. de** (*travail etc*) so much; (*soucis etc*) so many; **personne ne peut le supporter, il est bavard** nobody can stand him, he's so talkative; **tu aimes ça? - pas t.** do you like it? - not much *ou* a lot.

téméraire [temerɛr] *a* rash, reckless. ◆**témérité** *nf* rashness, recklessness.

témoign/er [temwaɲe] **1** *vi Jur* to testify (**contre** against); **t. de qch** (*personne, attitude etc*) to testify to sth; **- vt. que** *Jur* to testify that. **2** *vt* (*gratitude etc*) to show (**à qn** (to) s.o.). ◆**—age** *nm* **1** testimony, evidence; (*récit*) account; **faux t.** (*délit*) *Jur* perjury. **2** (*d'affection etc*) *Fig* token, sign (**de** of); **en t. de** as a token *ou* sign of.

témoin [temwɛ̃] **1** *nm* witness; **t. oculaire** eyewitness; **être t. de** (*accident etc*) to witness; **- a appartement t.** show flat *ou Am* apartment. **2** *nm Sp* baton.

tempe [tɑ̃p] *nf Anat* temple.

tempérament [tɑ̃peramɑ̃] *nm* **1** (*caractère*) temperament; (*physique*) constitution. **2** **acheter à t.** to buy on hire purchase *ou Am* on the installment plan.

tempérance [tɑ̃perɑ̃s] *nf* temperance.

température [tɑ̃peratyr] *nf* temperature; **avoir** *ou* **faire de la t.** *Méd* to have a temperature.

tempér/er [tɑ̃pere] *vt Litt* to temper. ◆**—é** *a* (*climat, zone*) temperate.

tempête [tɑ̃pɛt] *nf* storm; **t. de neige** snowstorm, blizzard.

tempêter [tɑ̃pete] *vi* (*crier*) to storm, rage (**contre** against).

temple [tɑ̃pl] *nm Rel* temple; (*protestant*) church.

tempo [tɛmpo] *nm* tempo.

temporaire [tɑ̃pɔrɛr] *a* temporary. ◆**—ment** *adv* temporarily.

temporel, -elle [tɑ̃pɔrɛl] *a* temporal.

temporiser [tɑ̃pɔrize] *vi* to procrastinate, play for time.

temps¹ [tɑ̃] *nm* (*durée, période, moment*) time; *Gram* tense; (*étape*) stage; **t. d'arrêt** pause, break; **en t. de guerre** in time of war, in wartime; **avoir/trouver le t.** to have/find (the) time (**de faire** to do); **il est t.** it is time (**de faire** to do); **il était t.!** it was about time (too)!; **pendant un t.** for a while *ou* time; **ces derniers t.** lately; **de t. en t.** [dətɑ̃zɑ̃tɑ̃], **de t. à autre** [dətɑ̃zaotr] from time to time, now and again; **en t. utile** [ɑ̃tɑ̃zytil] in good *ou* due time; **en même t.** at the same time (**que** as); **à t.** (*arriver*) in time; **à plein t.** (*travailler etc*) full-time; **à t. partiel** (*travailler etc*) part-time; **dans le t.** (*autrefois*) once, at one time; **avec le t.** (*à la longue*) in time; **tout le t.** all the time; **du t. de** in the time of; **de mon t.** in my time; **à quatre t.** (*moteur*) four-stroke.

temps² [tɑ̃] *nm* (*atmosphérique*) weather; **il fait beau/mauvais t.** the weather's fine/bad; **quel t. fait-il?** what's the weather like?

tenable [tənabl] *a* bearable.

tenace [tənas] *a* stubborn, tenacious. ◆**ténacité** *nf* stubbornness, tenacity.

tenailler [tənaje] *vt* (*faim, remords*) to rack, torture (*s.o.*).

tenailles [tənaj] *nfpl* (*outil*) pincers.

tenancier, -ière [tənɑ̃sje, -jɛr] *nmf* (*d'hôtel etc*) manager, manageress.

tenant, -ante [tənɑ̃, -ɑ̃t] *nmf* (*de titre*) *Sp* holder. **2** *nm* (*partisan*) supporter (**de** of).

tenants [tənɑ̃] *nmpl* **les t. et les aboutissants** (*d'une question etc*) the ins and outs (**de** of).

tendance [tɑ̃dɑ̃s] *nf* (*penchant*) tendency; (*évolution*) trend (**à** towards); **avoir t. à faire** to have a tendency to do, tend to do.

tendancieux, -euse [tɑ̃dɑ̃sjø, -øz] *a Péj* tendentious.

tendeur [tɑ̃dœr] *nm* (*pour arrimer des bagages*) elastic strap.

tendon [tɑ̃dɔ̃] *nm Anat* tendon, sinew.

tend/re¹ [tɑ̃dr] **1** *vt* to stretch; (*main*) to hold out (**à qn** to s.o.); (*bras, jambe*) to stretch out; (*cou*) to strain, crane; (*muscle*) to tense, flex; (*arc*) to bend; (*piège*) to lay, set; (*filet*) to spread; (*tapisserie*) to hang; **t. qch à qn** to hold out sth to s.o.; **t. l'oreille** *Fig* to prick up one's ears; **— se t.** *vpr* (*rap-*

ports) to become strained. **2** *vi* **t. à qch/à faire** to tend towards sth/to do. ◆**—u** *a* (corde) tight, taut; (personne, situation) tense; (rapports) strained; (main) outstretched.

tendre² [tɑ̃dr] *a* **1** (viande) tender; (peau) delicate, tender; (bois, couleur) soft. **2** (affectueux) loving, tender. ◆**—ment** [-əmɑ̃] *adv* lovingly, tenderly. ◆**tendresse** *nf* (affection) affection, tenderness. ◆**tendreté** *nf* (de viande) tenderness.

ténèbres [tenɛbr] *nfpl* darkness, gloom. ◆**ténébreux, -euse** *a* dark, gloomy; (mystérieux) mysterious.

teneur [tənœr] *nf* (de lettre etc) content; **t. en alcool**/etc alcohol/etc content (**de** of).

tenir* [tənir] *vt* (à la main etc) to hold; (pari, promesse) to keep; (hôtel) to run, keep; (comptes) Com to keep; (propos) to utter; (rôle) to play; **t. propre/chaud/**etc to keep clean/hot/etc; **je le tiens!** (je l'ai attrapé) I've got him!; **je le tiens de** (fait etc) I got it from; (caractère héréditaire) I get it from; **t. pour** to regard as; **t. sa droite** Aut to keep to the right; **t. la route** (voiture) to hold the road; – *vi* (nœud etc) to hold; (coiffure, neige) to last, hold; (offre) to stand; (résister) to hold out; **t. à** (personne, jouet etc) to be attached to, be fond of; (la vie) to value; (provenir) to stem from; **t. à faire** to be anxious to do; **t. dans qch** (être contenu) to fit into sth; **t. de qn** to take after s.o.; **tenez!** (prenez) here (you are)!; **tiens!** (surprise) hey!, well!; – *v imp* **il ne tient qu'à vous** it's up to you (**de faire** to do); — **se t.** *vpr* (rester) to keep, remain; (avoir lieu) to be held; **se t. (debout)** to stand (up); **se t. droit** to stand up *ou* sit up straight; **se t. par la main** to hold hands; **se t. à** to hold on to; **se t. bien** to behave oneself; **tout se tient** Fig it all hangs together; **s'en t. à** (se limiter à) to stick to; **savoir à quoi s'en t.** to know what's what.

tennis [tenis] *nm* tennis; (terrain) (tennis) court; **t. de table** table tennis; – *nfpl* (chaussures) plimsolls, pumps, Am sneakers.

ténor [tenɔr] *nm* Mus tenor.

tension [tɑ̃sjɔ̃] *nf* tension; **t. (artérielle)** blood pressure; **t. d'esprit** concentration; **avoir de la t.** Méd to have high blood pressure.

tentacule [tɑ̃takyl] *nm* tentacle.

tente [tɑ̃t] *nf* tent.

tenter¹ [tɑ̃te] *vt* (essayer) to try; **t. de faire** to try *ou* attempt to do. ◆**tentative** *nf* attempt; **t. de suicide** suicide attempt.

tent/er² [tɑ̃te] *vt* (allécher) to tempt; **tenté de faire** tempted to do. ◆**—ant** *a* tempting. ◆**tentation** *nf* temptation.

tenture [tɑ̃tyr] *nf* (wall) hanging; (de porte) drape, curtain.

tenu [təny] *voir* tenir; – *a* **t. de faire** obliged to do; **bien/mal t.** (maison etc) well/badly kept.

ténu [teny] *a* (fil etc) fine; (soupçon, différence) tenuous; (voix) thin.

tenue [təny] *nf* **1** (vêtements) clothes, outfit; (aspect) appearance; **t. de combat** Mil combat dress; **t. de soirée** (smoking) evening dress. **2** (conduite) (good) behaviour; (maintien) posture; **manquer de t.** to lack (good) manners. **3** (de maison, hôtel) running; (de comptes) Com keeping. **4 t. de route** Aut road-holding.

ter [tɛr] *a* **4 t.** (numéro) 4B.

térébenthine [terebɑ̃tin] *nf* turpentine.

tergal® [tɛrgal] *nm* Terylene®, Am Dacron®.

tergiverser [tɛrʒiverse] *vi* to procrastinate.

terme [tɛrm] *nm* **1** (mot) term. **2** (loyer) rent; (jour) rent day; (période) rental period. **3** (date limite) time (limit), date; (fin) end; **mettre un t. à** to put an end to; **à court/long t.** (projet etc) short-/long-term; **être né avant/à t.** to be born prematurely/at (full) term. **4 moyen t.** (solution) middle course. **5 en bons/mauvais termes** on good/bad terms (**avec qn** with s.o.).

terminer [tɛrmine] *vt* (achever) to finish, complete; (lettre, phrase, débat, soirée) to end; — **se t.** *vpr* to end (**par** with, **en** in). ◆**terminaison** *nf* Gram ending. ◆**terminal, -aux 1** *a* final; (phase) Méd terminal; – *a & nf* (classe) **terminale** Scol = sixth form, Am = twelfth grade. **2** *nm* (d'ordinateur, pétrolier) terminal.

terminologie [tɛrminɔlɔʒi] *nf* terminology.

terminus [tɛrminys] *nm* terminus.

termite [tɛrmit] *nm* (insecte) termite.

terne [tɛrn] *a* (couleur, journée etc) dull, drab; (personne) dull. ◆**ternir** *vt* (métal, réputation) to tarnish; (miroir, meuble) to dull; — **se t.** *vpr* (métal) to tarnish.

terrain [tɛrɛ̃] *nm* (sol) & Fig ground; (étendue) land; Mil Géol terrain; (à bâtir) plot, site; **un t.** a piece of land; **t. d'aviation** airfield; **t. de camping** campsite; **t. de football/rugby** football/rugby pitch; **t. de golf** golf course; **t. de jeu** playground; **t. de sport** sports ground, playing field; **t. vague** waste ground, Am vacant lot; **céder/gagner/perdre du t.** Mil & Fig to give/

lose ground; **tout t., tous terrains** (*véhicule*) all-purpose.

terrasse [tɛras] *nf* **1** terrace; (*toit*) terrace (roof). **2** (*de café*) pavement *ou Am* sidewalk area; **à la t.** outside.

terrassement [tɛrasmɑ̃] *nm* (*travail*) excavation.

terrasser [tɛrase] *vt* (*adversaire*) to floor, knock down; (*accabler*) *Fig* to overcome.

terrassier [tɛrasje] *nm* labourer, navvy.

terre [tɛr] *nf* (*matière*) earth; (*sol*) ground; (*opposé à mer, étendue*) land; *pl* (*domaine*) land, estate; *Él* earth, *Am* ground; **la t.** (*le monde*) the earth; **la T.** (*planète*) Earth; **à** *ou* **par t.** (*poser, tomber*) to the ground; **par t.** (*assis, couché*) on the ground; **aller à t.** *Nau* to go ashore; **sous t.** underground; **t. cuite** (baked) clay, earthenware; **en t. cuite** (*poterie*) clay-. ◆**t.-à-terre** *a inv* down-to-earth. ◆**t.-plein** *nm* (earth) platform; (*au milieu de la route*) central reservation, *Am* median strip. ◆**terrestre** *a* (*vie, joies*) earthly; (*animaux, transport*) land-; **la surface t.** the earth's surface; **globe t.** (terrestrial) globe. ◆**terreux, -euse** *a* (*goût*) earthy; (*sale*) grubby; (*couleur*) dull; (*teint*) ashen. ◆**terrien, -ienne** *a* land-owning; **propriétaire t.** landowner; – *nmf* (*habitant de la terre*) earth dweller, earthling.

terreau [tɛro] *nm* compost.

terrer (se) [sɛtɛre] *vpr* (*fugitif, animal*) to hide, go to ground *ou* earth.

terreur [tɛrœr] *nf* terror; **t. de** fear of. ◆**terrible** *a* terrible; (*formidable*) *Fam* terrific. ◆**terriblement** *adv* (*extrêmement*) terribly. ◆**terrifi/er** *vt* to terrify. ◆**—ant** *a* terrifying; (*extraordinaire*) incredible.

terrier [tɛrje] *nm* **1** (*de lapin etc*) burrow. **2** (*chien*) terrier.

terrine [tɛrin] *nf* (*récipient*) *Culin* terrine; (*pâté*) pâté.

territoire [tɛritwar] *nm* territory. ◆**territorial, -aux** *a* territorial.

terroir [tɛrwar] *nm* (*sol*) soil; (*région*) region; **du t.** (*accent etc*) rural.

terroriser [tɛrɔrize] *vt* to terrorize. ◆**terrorisme** *nm* terrorism. ◆**terroriste** *a & nmf* terrorist.

tertiaire [tɛrsjɛr] *a* tertiary.

tertre [tɛrtr] *nm* hillock, mound.

tes [te] *voir* **ton¹**.

tesson [tesɔ̃] *nm* **t. de bouteille** piece of broken bottle.

test [tɛst] *nm* test. ◆**tester** *vt* (*élève, produit*) to test.

testament [tɛstamɑ̃] *nm* **1** *Jur* will; (*œuvre*) *Fig* testament. **2** **Ancien/Nouveau T.** *Rel* Old/New Testament.

testicule [tɛstikyl] *nm Anat* testicle.

tétanos [tetanos] *nm Méd* tetanus.

têtard [tɛtar] *nm* tadpole.

tête [tɛt] *nf* head; (*figure*) face; (*cheveux*) (head of) hair; (*cerveau*) brain; (*cime*) top; (*de clou, cortège, lit*) head; (*de page, liste*) top, head; (*coup*) *Fb* header; **t. nucléaire** nuclear warhead; **tenir t. à** (*s'opposer à*) to stand up to; **t. nue** bare-headed; **tu n'as pas de t.!** you're a scatterbrain!; **faire la t.** (*bouder*) to sulk; **faire une t.** *Fb* to head the ball; **avoir/faire une drôle de t.** to have/give a funny look; **perdre la t.** *Fig* to lose one's head; **tomber la t. la première** to fall headlong *ou* head first; **calculer qch de t.** to work sth out in one's head; **se mettre dans la t. de faire** to get it into one's head to do; **à t. reposée** at one's leisure; **à la t. de** (*entreprise, parti*) at the head of; (*classe*) *Scol* at the top of; **de la t. aux pieds** from head *ou* top to toe; **en t.** *Sp* in the lead. ◆**t.-à-queue** *nm inv* **faire un t.-à-queue** *Aut* to spin right round. ◆**t.-à-tête** *adv* **(en) t.-à-tête** (*seul*) in private, alone together; – *nm inv* tête-à-tête. ◆**t.-bêche** *adv* head to tail.

têt/er [tete] *vt* (*lait, biberon etc*) to suck; **t. sa mère** (*bébé*) to suck, feed; – *vi* **donner à t.** to feed, suckle. ◆**—ée** *nf* (*de bébé*) feed. ◆**tétine** *nf* **1** (*de biberon*) teat, *Am* nipple; (*sucette*) dummy, *Am* pacifier. **2** (*de vache*) udder. ◆**téton** *nm Fam* breast.

têtu [tety] *a* stubborn, obstinate.

texte [tɛkst] *nm* text; *Th* lines, text; (*de devoir*) *Scol* subject; (*morceau choisi*) *Littér* passage. ◆**textuel, -elle** *a* (*traduction*) literal.

textile [tɛkstil] *a & nm* textile.

texture [tɛkstyr] *nf* texture.

TGV [teʒeve] *abrév* = **train à grande vitesse**.

Thaïlande [tailɑ̃d] *nf* Thailand. ◆**thaïlandais, -aise** *a & nmf* Thai.

thé [te] *nm* (*boisson, réunion*) tea. ◆**théière** *nf* teapot.

théâtre [teɑtr] *nm* (*art, lieu*) theatre; (*œuvres*) drama; (*d'un crime*) *Fig* scene; (*des opérations*) *Mil* theatre; **faire du t.** to act. ◆**théâtral, -aux** *a* theatrical.

thème [tɛm] *nm* theme; (*traduction*) *Scol* translation, prose.

théologie [teɔlɔʒi] *nf* theology. ◆**théologien** *nm* theologian. ◆**théologique** *a* theological.

théorème [teɔrɛm] *nm* theorem.

théorie [teɔri] *nf* theory; **en t.** in theory.

◆**théoricien, -ienne** *nmf* theorist, theoretician. ◆**théorique** *a* theoretical. ◆**théoriquement** *adv* theoretically.

thérapeutique [terapøtik] *a* therapeutic; – *nf* (*traitement*) therapy. ◆**thérapie** *nf Psy* therapy.

thermal, -aux [tɛrmal, -o] *a* **station thermale** spa; **eaux thermales** hot springs.

thermique [tɛrmik] *a* (*énergie, unité*) thermal.

thermomètre [tɛrmɔmɛtr] *nm* thermometer.

thermonucléaire [tɛrmɔnykleɛr] *a* thermonuclear.

thermos® [tɛrmɔs] *nm ou f* Thermos (flask)®, vacuum flask.

thermostat [tɛrmɔsta] *nm* thermostat.

thèse [tɛz] *nf* (*proposition, ouvrage*) thesis.

thon [tɔ̃] *nm* tuna (fish).

thorax [tɔraks] *nm Anat* thorax.

thym [tɛ̃] *nm Bot Culin* thyme.

thyroïde [tirɔid] *a & nf Anat* thyroid.

tibia [tibja] *nm* shin bone, tibia.

tic [tik] *nm* (*contraction*) tic, twitch; (*manie*) *Fig* mannerism.

ticket [tikɛ] *nm* ticket; **t. de quai** *Rail* platform ticket.

tic(-)tac [tiktak] *int & nm inv* tick-tock.

tiède [tjɛd] *a* (*luke*)warm, tepid; (*climat, vent*) mild; (*accueil, partisan*) half-hearted. ◆**tiédeur** *nf* (*luke*)warmness, tepidness; mildness; half-heartedness. ◆**tiédir** *vt* to cool (down); (*chauffer*) to warm (up); – *vi* to cool (down); to warm up.

tien, tienne [tjɛ̃, tjɛn] *pron poss* **le t., la tienne, les tien(ne)s** yours; **les deux tiens** your two; – *nmpl* **les tiens** (*amis etc*) your (own) people.

tiens, tient [tjɛ̃] *voir* tenir.

tiercé [tjɛrse] *nm* (*pari*) place betting (*on horses*); **gagner au t.** to win on the races.

tiers, tierce [tjɛr, tjɛrs] *a* third; – *nm* (*fraction*) third; (*personne*) third party; **assurance au t.** third-party insurance. ◆**T.-Monde** *nm* Third World.

tige [tiʒ] *nf* (*de plante*) stem, stalk; (*de botte*) leg; (*barre*) rod.

tignasse [tiɲas] *nf* mop (of hair).

tigre [tigr] *nm* tiger. ◆**tigresse** *nf* tigress.

tigré [tigre] *a* (*tacheté*) spotted; (*rayé*) striped.

tilleul [tijœl] *nm* lime (tree), linden (tree); (*infusion*) lime (blossom) tea.

timbale [tɛ̃bal] *nf* **1** (*gobelet*) (metal) tumbler. **2** *Mus* kettledrum.

timbre [tɛ̃br] *nm* **1** (*marque, tampon, vignette*) stamp; (*cachet de la poste*) postmark. **2** (*sonnette*) bell. **3** (*d'instrument, de voix*) tone (quality). ◆**t.-poste** *nm* (*pl* **timbres-poste**) (postage) stamp. ◆**timbrer** *vt* (*affranchir*) to stamp (*letter*); (*marquer*) to stamp (*document*). ◆—**é** *a* **1** (*voix*) sonorous. **2** (*fou*) *Fam* crazy.

timide [timid] *a* (*gêné*) shy, timid; (*timoré*) timid. ◆—**ment** *adv* shyly; timidly. ◆**timidité** *nf* shyness; timidity.

timonier [timɔnje] *nm Nau* helmsman.

timoré [timɔre] *a* timorous, fearful.

tintamarre [tɛ̃tamar] *nm* din, racket.

tinter [tɛ̃te] *vi* (*cloche*) to ring, toll; (*clés, monnaie*) to jingle; (*verres*) to chink. ◆—**ement(s)** *nm*(*pl*) ringing; jingling; chinking.

tique [tik] *nf* (*insecte*) tick.

tiquer [tike] *vi* (*personne*) to wince.

tir [tir] *nm* (*sport*) shooting; (*action*) firing, shooting; (*feu, rafale*) fire; *Fb* shot; **t. (forain), (stand de) t.** shooting *ou* rifle range; **t. à l'arc** archery; **ligne de t.** line of fire.

tirade [tirad] *nf Th & Fig* monologue.

tirailler [tiraje] **1** *vt* to pull (away) at; (*harceler*) *Fig* to pester, plague; **tiraillé entre** (*possibilités etc*) torn between. **2** *vi* (*au fusil*) to shoot wildly. ◆—**ement** *nm* **1** (*conflit*) conflict (**entre** between). **2** (*crampe*) *Méd* cramp.

tire [tir] *nf* **vol à la t.** *Fam* pickpocketing. ◆**tire-au-flanc** [tiroflɑ̃] *nm inv* (*paresseux*) shirker. ◆**t.-bouchon** *nm* corkscrew. ◆**t.-d'aile (à)** *adv* swiftly.

tirelire [tirlir] *nf* moneybox, *Am* coin bank.

tirer [tire] *vt* to pull; (*langue*) to stick out; (*trait, conclusion, rideaux*) to draw; (*chapeau*) to raise; (*balle, canon*) to fire, shoot; (*gibier*) to shoot; *Typ Phot* to print; **t. de** (*sortir*) to take *ou* pull *ou* draw out of; (*obtenir*) to get from; (*nom, origine*) to derive from; (*produit*) to extract from; **t. qn de** (*danger, lit*) to get s.o. out of; – *vi* to pull (**sur** on, at); (*faire feu*) to fire, shoot (**sur** at); *Fb* to shoot; (*cheminée*) to draw; **t. sur** (*couleur*) to verge on; **t. au sort** to draw lots; **t. à sa fin** to draw to a close; – **se t.** *vpr* (*partir*) *Fam* to beat it; **se t. de** (*problème, travail*) to cope with; (*danger, situation*) to get out of; **se t. d'affaire** to get out of trouble; **s'en t.** *Fam* (*en réchapper*) to come *ou* pull through; (*réussir*) to get along. ◆—**é** *a* (*traits, visage*) drawn; **t. par les cheveux** *Fig* far-fetched. ◆—**age** *nm* **1** (*action*) *Typ Phot* printing; (*édition*) edition; (*quantité*) (print) run; (*de journal*) circulation. **2** (*de loterie*) draw; **t. au sort**

drawing of lots. **3** (*de cheminée*) draught. ◆**—eur** *nm* gunman; **t. d'élite** marksman; **un bon/mauvais t.** a good/bad shot. ◆**—euse** *nf* **t. de cartes** fortune-teller.

tiret [tirɛ] *nm* (*trait*) dash.

tiroir [tirwar] *nm* (*de commode etc*) drawer. ◆**t.-caisse** *nm* (*pl* **tiroirs-caisses**) (cash) till.

tisane [tizan] *nf* herb(al) tea.

tison [tizɔ̃] *nm* (fire)brand, ember. ◆**tisonner** *vt* (*feu*) to poke. ◆**tisonnier** *nm* poker.

tiss/er [tise] *vt* to weave. ◆**—age** *nm* (*action*) weaving. ◆**tisserand, -ande** *nmf* weaver.

tissu [tisy] *nm* fabric, material, cloth; *Biol* tissue; **un t. de** (*mensonges etc*) a web of; **le t. social** the fabric of society, the social fabric; **du t.-éponge** (terry) towelling.

titre [titr] *nm* (*nom, qualité*) title; *Com* bond; (*diplôme*) qualification; *pl* (*droits*) claims (à to); (*gros*) **t.** *Journ* headline; **t. de propriété** title deed; **t. de transport** ticket; **à quel t.?** (*pour quelle raison*) on what grounds?; **à ce t.** (*en cette qualité*) as such; (*pour cette raison*) therefore; **à aucun t.** on no account; **au même t.** in the same way (**que** as); **à t. d'exemple/d'ami** as an example/friend; **à t. exceptionnel** exceptionally; **à t. privé** in a private capacity; **à juste t.** rightly. ◆**titr/er** *vt* (*film*) to title; *Journ* to run as a headline. ◆**—é** *a* (*personne*) titled. ◆**titulaire** *a* (*professeur*) staff-, full; **être t. de** (*permis etc*) to be the holder of; (*poste*) to hold; **—** *nmf* (*de permis, poste*) holder (**de** of). ◆**titulariser** *vt* (*fonctionnaire*) to give tenure to.

tituber [titybe] *vi* to reel, stagger.

toast [tost] *nm* **1** (*pain grillé*) piece *ou* slice of toast. **2** (*allocution*) toast; **porter un t. à** to drink (a toast) to.

toboggan [tɔbɔgɑ̃] *nm* **1** (*pente*) slide; (*traîneau*) toboggan. **2** *Aut* flyover, *Am* overpass.

toc [tɔk] **1** *int* **t. t.!** knock knock! **2** *nm* **du t.** (*camelote*) rubbish, trash; **en t.** (*bijou*) imitation-.

tocsin [tɔksɛ̃] *nm* alarm (bell).

tohu-bohu [tɔybɔy] *nm* (*bruit*) hubbub, commotion; (*confusion*) hurly-burly.

toi [twa] *pron* **1** (*complément*) you; **c'est t.** it's you; **avec t.** with you. **2** (*sujet*) you; **t., tu peux** you may. **3** (*réfléchi*) **assieds-t.** sit (yourself) down; **dépêche-t.** hurry up. ◆**t.-même** *pron* yourself.

toile [twal] *nf* **1** cloth; (*à voile*) canvas; (*à draps*) linen; **une t.** a piece of cloth *ou* canvas *ou* linen; **t. de jute** hessian; **drap de t.** linen sheet; **t. de fond** *Th* & *Fig* backcloth. **2** (*tableau*) canvas, painting. **3** **t. d'araignée** cobweb, (spider's) web.

toilette [twalɛt] *nf* (*action*) wash(ing); (*vêtements*) outfit, clothes; **articles de t.** toiletries; **cabinet de t.** washroom; **eau/savon/trousse de t.** toilet water/soap/bag; **table de t.** dressing table; **faire sa t.** to wash (and dress); **les toilettes** (*W-C*) the toilet(s); **aller aux toilettes** to go to the toilet.

toiser [twaze] *vt* to eye scornfully.

toison [twazɔ̃] *nf* (*de mouton*) fleece.

toit [twa] *nm* roof; **t. ouvrant** *Aut* sunroof. ◆**toiture** *nf* roof(ing).

tôle [tol] *nf* **la t.** sheet metal; **une t.** a steel *ou* metal sheet; **t. ondulée** corrugated iron.

tolér/er [tɔlere] *vt* (*permettre*) to tolerate, allow; (*supporter*) to tolerate, bear; (*à la douane*) to allow. ◆**—ant** *a* tolerant (**à l'égard de** of). ◆**—able** *a* tolerable. ◆**tolérance** *nf* tolerance; (*à la douane*) allowance.

tollé [tɔle] *nm* outcry.

tomate [tɔmat] *nf* tomato; **sauce t.** tomato sauce.

tombe [tɔ̃b] *nf* grave; (*avec monument*) tomb. ◆**tombale** *af* **pierre t.** gravestone, tombstone. ◆**tombeau, -x** *nm* tomb.

tomb/er [tɔ̃be] *vi* (*aux* **être**) to fall; (*température*) to drop, fall; (*vent*) to drop (off); (*cheveux, robe*) to hang down; **t. malade** to fall ill; **t.** (*par terre*) to fall (down); **faire t.** (*personne*) to knock over; (*gouvernement, prix*) to bring down; **laisser t.** (*objet*) to drop; (*personne, projet etc*) *Fig* to drop, give up; **tu m'as laissé t. hier** you let me down yesterday; **se laisser t. dans un fauteuil** to drop into an armchair; **tu tombes bien/mal** *Fig* you've come at the right/wrong time; **t. de fatigue** *ou* **de sommeil** to be ready to drop; **t. un lundi** to fall on a Monday; **t. sur** (*trouver*) to come across. ◆**—ée** *nf* **t. de la nuit** nightfall.

tombereau, -x [tɔ̃bro] *nm* (*charrette*) tip cart.

tombola [tɔ̃bɔla] *nf* raffle.

tome [tɔm] *nm* (*livre*) volume.

ton¹, ta, *pl* **tes** [tɔ̃, ta, te] (**ta** becomes **ton** [tɔ̃n] before a vowel or mute h) *a poss* your; **t. père** your father; **ta mère** your mother; **ton ami(e)** your friend.

ton² [tɔ̃] *nm* tone; (*de couleur*) shade, tone; (*gamme*) *Mus* key; (*hauteur de son*) & *Ling* pitch; **de bon t.** (*goût*) in good taste; **donner le t.** *Fig* to set the tone. ◆**tonalité** *nf* (*de* *radio etc*) tone; *Tél* dialling tone, *Am* dial tone.

tond/re [tɔ̃dr] *vt* **1** (*mouton*) to shear; (*cheveux*) to clip, crop; (*gazon*) to mow. **2 t. qn** (*escroquer*) *Fam* to fleece s.o. ◆**—euse** *nf* shears; (*à cheveux*) clippers; **t. (à gazon)** (lawn)mower.

tonifi/er [tɔnifje] *vt* (*muscles, peau*) to tone up; (*esprit, personne*) to invigorate. ◆**—ant** *a* (*activité, climat etc*) invigorating.

tonique [tɔnik] **1** *a* (*accent*) *Ling* tonic. **2** (*froid, effet, vin*) tonic, invigorating; *– nm Méd* tonic.

tonitruant [tɔnitryɑ̃] *a* (*voix*) *Fam* booming.

tonnage [tɔnaʒ] *nm Nau* tonnage.

tonne [tɔn] *nf* (*poids*) metric ton, tonne; **des tonnes de** (*beaucoup*) *Fam* tons of.

tonneau, -x [tɔno] *nm* **1** (*récipient*) barrel, cask. **2** (*manœuvre*) *Av* roll; **faire un t.** *Aut* to roll over. **3** (*poids*) *Nau* ton. ◆**tonnelet** *nm* keg.

tonnelle [tɔnɛl] *nf* arbour, bower.

tonner [tɔne] *vi* (*canons*) to thunder; (*crier*) *Fig* to thunder, rage (**contre** against); *– v imp* **il tonne** it's thundering. ◆**tonnerre** *nm* thunder; **coup de t.** thunderclap; *Fig* bombshell, thunderbolt; **du t.** (*excellent*) *Fam* terrific.

tonte [tɔ̃t] *nf* (*de moutons*) shearing; (*de gazon*) mowing.

tonton [tɔ̃tɔ̃] *nm Fam* uncle.

tonus [tɔnys] *nm* (*énergie*) energy, vitality.

top [tɔp] *nm* (*signal sonore*) *Rad* stroke.

topaze [tɔpaz] *nf* (*pierre*) topaz.

topinambour [tɔpinɑ̃bur] *nm* Jerusalem artichoke.

topo [tɔpo] *nm* (*exposé*) *Fam* talk, speech.

topographie [tɔpɔgrafi] *nf* topography.

toque [tɔk] *nf* (*de fourrure*) fur hat; (*de juge, jockey*) cap; (*de cuisinier*) hat.

toqu/er (se) [sɔtɔke] *vpr* **se t. de qn** *Fam* to become infatuated with s.o. ◆**—é** *a* (*fou*) *Fam* crazy. ◆**toquade** *nf Fam* (*pour qch*) craze (**pour** for); (*pour qn*) infatuation (**pour** with).

torche [tɔrʃ] *nf* (*flambeau*) torch; **t. électrique** torch, *Am* flashlight.

torcher [tɔrʃe] *vt* **1** (*travail*) to skimp. **2** (*essuyer*) *Fam* to wipe.

torchon [tɔrʃɔ̃] *nm* (*à vaisselle*) tea towel, *Am* dish towel; (*de ménage*) duster, cloth.

tord/re [tɔrdr] *vt* to twist; (*linge, cou*) to wring; (*barre*) to bend; **se t. la cheville/le pied/le dos** to twist *ou* sprain one's ankle/foot/back; *– se t. vpr* to twist; (*barre*) to bend; **se t. de douleur** to writhe with pain; **se t. (de rire)** to split one's sides

(laughing). ◆**—ant** *a* (*drôle*) *Fam* hilarious. ◆**—u** *a* (*esprit*) warped.

tornade [tɔrnad] *nf* tornado.

torpeur [tɔrpœr] *nf* lethargy, torpor.

torpille [tɔrpij] *nf* torpedo. ◆**torpill/er** *vt Mil & Fig* to torpedo. ◆**—eur** *nm* torpedo boat.

torréfier [tɔrefje] *vt* (*café*) to roast.

torrent [tɔrɑ̃] *nm* (*ruisseau*) torrent; **un t. de** (*injures, larmes*) a flood of; **il pleut à torrents** it's pouring (down). ◆**torrentiel, -ielle** *a* (*pluie*) torrential.

torride [tɔrid] *a* (*chaleur etc*) torrid, scorching.

torsade [tɔrsad] *nf* (*de cheveux*) twist, coil. ◆**torsader** *vt* to twist (together).

torse [tɔrs] *nm Anat* chest; (*statue*) torso.

torsion [tɔrsjɔ̃] *nf* twisting; *Phys Tech* torsion.

tort [tɔr] *nm* (*dommage*) wrong; (*défaut*) fault; **avoir t.** to be wrong (**de faire** to do, in doing); **tu as t. de fumer!** you shouldn't smoke!; **être dans son t.** *ou* **en t.** to be in the wrong; **donner t. à qn** (*accuser*) to blame s.o.; (*faits etc*) to prove s.o. wrong; **faire du t. à qn** to harm *ou* wrong s.o.; **à t.** wrongly; **à t. et à travers** wildly, indiscriminately; **à t. ou à raison** rightly or wrongly.

torticolis [tɔrtikɔli] *nm* stiff neck.

tortill/er [tɔrtije] *vt* to twist, twirl; (*moustache*) to twirl; (*tripoter*) to twiddle with; *– se t. vpr* (*ver, personne*) to wriggle; (*en dansant, des hanches*) to wiggle. ◆**—ement** *nm* wriggling, wiggling.

tortionnaire [tɔrsjɔner] *nm* torturer.

tortue [tɔrty] *nf* tortoise; (*marine*) turtle; **quelle t.!** *Fig* what a slowcoach *ou Am* slowpoke!

tortueux, -euse [tɔrtɥø, -øz] *a* tortuous.

torture [tɔrtyr] *nf* torture. ◆**torturer** *vt* to torture; **se t. les méninges** to rack one's brains.

tôt [to] *adv* early; **au plus t.** at the earliest; **le plus t. possible** as soon as possible; **t. ou tard** sooner or later; **je n'étais pas plus t. sorti que . . .** no sooner had I gone out than . . . .

total, -aux [tɔtal, -o] *a & nm* total; **au t.** all in all, in total; (*somme toute*) all in all. ◆**totalement** *adv* totally, completely. ◆**totaliser** *vt* to total. ◆**totalité** *nf* entirety; **la t. de** all of; **en t.** entirely, totally.

totalitaire [tɔtaliter] *a Pol* totalitarian.

toubib [tubib] *nm* (*médecin*) *Fam* doctor.

touche [tuʃ] *nf* (*de peintre*) touch; *Pêche* bite; (*clavier*) key; **une t. de** (*un peu de*) a touch *ou* hint of; **(ligne de) t.** *Fb Rugby* touchline.

touche-à-tout [tuʃatu] **1** *a* & *nmf inv* (*qui touche*) meddlesome (person). **2** *nmf inv* (*qui se disperse*) dabbler.

touch/er [tuʃe] *vt* to touch; (*paie*) to draw; (*chèque*) to cash; (*cible*) to hit; (*émouvoir*) to touch, move; (*concerner*) to affect; **t. qn** (*contacter*) to get in touch with s.o., reach s.o.; − *vi* **t. à** to touch; (*sujet*) to touch on; (*but, fin*) to approach; **− se t.** *vpr* (*lignes etc*) to touch; − *nm* (*sens*) touch; **au t.** to the touch. **◆−ant** *a* (*émouvant*) touching, moving.

touffe [tuf] *nf* (*de cheveux, d'herbe*) tuft; (*de plantes*) cluster. **◆touffu** *a* (*barbe, haie*) thick, bushy; (*livre*) *Fig* heavy.

toujours [tuʒur] *adv* always; (*encore*) still; **pour t.** for ever; **essaie t.!** (*quand même*) try anyhow!; **t. est-il que . . .** the fact remains that . . . .

toupet [tupɛ] *nm* (*audace*) *Fam* cheek, nerve.

toupie [tupi] *nf* (spinning) top.

tour[1] [tur] *nf* **1** *Archit* tower; (*immeuble*) tower block, high-rise. **2** *Échecs* rook, castle.

tour[2] [tur] *nm* **1** (*mouvement, ordre, tournure*) turn; (*artifice*) trick; (*excursion*) trip, outing; (*à pied*) stroll, walk; (*en voiture*) drive; **t. (de phrase)** turn of phrase; **t. (de piste)** *Sp* lap; **t. de cartes** card trick; **t. d'horizon** survey; **t. de poitrine/etc** chest/etc measurement *ou* size; **de dix mètres de t.** ten metres round; **faire le t. de** to go round; (*question, situation*) to review; **faire un t. (à pied)** to go for a stroll *ou* walk; (*en voiture*) to go for a drive; (*voyage*) to go on a trip; **faire** *ou* **jouer un t. à qn** to play a trick on s.o.; **c'est mon t.** it's my turn; **à qui le tour?** whose turn (is it)?; **à son t.** in (one's) turn; **à t. de rôle** in turn; **t. à t.** in turn, by turns. **2** *Tech* lathe; (*de potier*) wheel.

tourbe [turb] *nf* peat. **◆tourbière** *nf* peat bog.

tourbillon [turbijɔ̃] *nm* (*de vent*) whirlwind; (*d'eau*) whirlpool; (*de neige, sable*) eddy; (*tournoiement*) *Fig* whirl, swirl. **◆tourbillonner** *vi* to whirl, swirl; to eddy.

tourelle [turɛl] *nf* turret.

tourisme [turism] *nm* tourism; **faire du t.** to do some sightseeing *ou* touring; **agence/office de t.** tourist agency/office. **◆touriste** *nmf* tourist. **◆touristique** *a* (*guide, menu etc*) tourist-; **route t., circuit t.** scenic route.

tourment [turmã] *nm* torment. **◆tour-**

ment/er *vt* to torment; **− se t.** *vpr* to worry (oneself). **◆−é** *a* (*mer, vie*) turbulent, stormy; (*sol*) rough, uneven; (*expression, visage*) anguished.

tourmente [turmãt] *nf* (*troubles*) turmoil.

tourne-disque [turnədisk] *nm* record player.

tournée [turne] *nf* **1** (*de livreur etc*) round; (*théâtrale*) tour; **faire la t. de** (*magasins etc*) to make the rounds of, go round. **2** (*de boissons*) round.

tourn/er [turne] *vt* to turn; (*film*) to shoot, make; (*difficulté*) to get round; **t. en ridicule** to ridicule; − *vi* to turn; (*tête, toupie*) to spin; (*Terre*) to revolve, turn; (*moteur*) to run, go; (*usine*) to run; (*lait, viande*) to go off; *Cin* to shoot; **t. autour de** (*objet*) to go round; (*maison, personne*) to hang around; (*question*) to centre on; **t. bien/mal** (*évoluer*) to turn out well/badly; **t. au froid** (*temps*) to turn cold; **t. à l'aigre** (*ton, conversation etc*) to turn nasty *ou* sour; **t. de l'œil** *Fam* to faint; **− se t.** *vpr* to turn (**vers** to, towards). **◆−ant 1** *a* **pont t.** swing bridge. **2** *nm* (*virage*) bend, turning; (*moment*) *Fig* turning point. **◆−age** *nm* *Cin* shooting, filming. **◆−eur** *nm* (*ouvrier*) turner. **◆tournoyer** *vi* to spin (round), whirl. **◆tournure** *nf* (*expression*) turn of phrase; **t. d'esprit** way of thinking; **t. des événements** turn of events; **prendre t.** (*forme*) to take shape.

tournesol [turnəsɔl] *nm* sunflower.

tournevis [turnəvis] *nm* screwdriver.

tourniquet [turnikɛ] *nm* **1** (*barrière*) turnstile. **2** (*pour arroser*) sprinkler.

tournoi [turnwa] *nm* *Sp* & *Hist* tournament.

tourte [turt] *nf* pie.

tourterelle [turtərɛl] *nf* turtledove.

Toussaint [tusɛ̃] *nf* All Saints' Day.

tousser [tuse] *vi* to cough.

tout, toute, *pl* **tous, toutes** [tu, tut, tu, tut] **1** *a* all; **tous les livres/etc** all the books/etc; **t. l'argent/le village/etc** the whole (of the) money/village/etc, all the money/village/etc; **toute la nuit** all night, the whole (of the) night; **tous (les) deux** both; **tous (les) trois** all three; **t. un problème** quite a problem. **2** *a* (*chaque*) every, each; (*n'importe quel*) any; **tous les ans/jours/etc** every *ou* each year/day/etc; **tous les deux/trois mois/etc** every second/third month/etc; **tous les cinq mètres** every five metres; **t. homme** [tutɔm] every *ou* any man; **à toute heure** at any time. **3** *pron pl* (**tous** = [tus]) all; **ils sont tous là, tous sont là** they're all there. **4** *pron m sing* **tout** everything;

dépenser t. to spend everything, spend it all; **t. ce que** everything that, all that; **en t.** (*au total*) in all. **5** *adv* (*tout à fait*) quite; (*très*) very; **t. petit** very small; **t. neuf** brand new; **t. simplement** quite simply; **t. seul** all alone; **t. droit** straight ahead; **t. autour** all around, right round; **t. au début** right at the beginning; **le t. premier** the very first; **t. au moins/plus** at the very least/most; **t. en chantant/***etc* while singing/*etc*; **t. rusé qu'il est** however sly he may be; **t. à coup** suddenly, all of a sudden; **t. à fait** completely, quite; **t. de même** all the same; (*indignation*) really!; **t. de suite** at once. **6** *nm* **le t.** everything, the lot; **un t.** a whole; **le t. est** (*l'important*) the main thing is (**que** that, **de faire** to do); **pas du t.** not at all; **rien du t.** nothing at all; **du t. au t.** (*changer*) entirely, completely. ◆**t.-puissant, toute-puissante** *a* all-powerful.

tout-à-l'égout [tutalegu] *nm inv* mains drainage.

toutefois [tutfwa] *adv* nevertheless, however.

toutou [tutu] *nm* (*chien*) *Fam* doggie.

toux [tu] *nf* cough.

toxicomane [tɔksikɔman] *nmf* drug addict. ◆**toxicomanie** *nf* drug addiction. ◆**toxine** *nf* toxin. ◆**toxique** *a* toxic.

trac [trak] *nm* **le t.** (*peur*) the jitters; (*de candidat*) exam nerves; *Th* stage fright.

tracas [traka] *nm* worry. ◆**tracasser** *vt*, — **se t.** *vpr* to worry. ◆**tracasseries** *nfpl* annoyances. ◆**tracassier, -ière** *a* irksome.

trace [tras] *nf* (*quantité, tache, vestige*) trace; (*marque*) mark; (*de fugitif etc*) trail; *pl* (*de bête, de pneus*) tracks; **traces de pas** footprints; **suivre les traces de qn** *Fig* to follow in s.o.'s footsteps.

trac/er [trase] *vt* (*dessiner*) to draw; (*écrire*) to trace; **t. une route** to mark out a route; (*frayer*) to open up a route. ◆**—é** *nm* (*plan*) layout; (*ligne*) line.

trachée [trafe] *nf Anat* windpipe.

tract [trakt] *nm* leaflet.

tractations [traktasjɔ̃] *nfpl Péj* dealings.

tracter [trakte] *vt* (*caravane etc*) to tow. ◆**tracteur** *nm* (*véhicule*) tractor.

traction [traksjɔ̃] *nf Tech* traction; *Sp* pull-up; **t. arrière/avant** *Aut* rear-/front-wheel drive.

tradition [tradisjɔ̃] *nf* tradition. ◆**traditionnel, -elle** *a* traditional.

traduire* [tradɥir] *vt* **1** to translate (**de** from, **en** into); (*exprimer*) *Fig* to express. **2** **t. qn en justice** to bring s.o. before the

courts. ◆**traducteur, -trice** *nmf* translator. ◆**traduction** *nf* translation. ◆**traduisible** *a* translatable.

trafic [trafik] *nm* **1** *Aut Rail etc* traffic. **2** *Com Péj* traffic, trade; **faire du t.** to traffic, trade; **faire le t. de** to traffic in, trade in. ◆**trafiqu/er 1** *vi* to traffic, trade. **2** *vt* (*produit*) *Fam* to tamper with. ◆**—ant, -ante** *nmf* trafficker, dealer; **t. d'armes/de drogue** arms/drug trafficker *ou* dealer.

tragédie [traʒedi] *nf Th & Fig* tragedy. ◆**tragique** *a* tragic. ◆**tragiquement** *adv* tragically.

trahir [trair] *vt* to betray; (*secret etc*) to betray, give away; (*forces*) to fail (*s.o.*); — **se t.** *vpr* to give oneself away, betray oneself. ◆**trahison** *nf* betrayal; (*crime*) *Pol* treason.

train [trɛ̃] *nm* **1** (*locomotive, transport, jouet*) train; **t. à grande vitesse** high-speed train; **t. couchettes** sleeper; **t. auto-couchettes** (car) sleeper. **2** **en t.** (*forme*) on form; **se mettre en t.** to get (oneself) into shape. **3** **être en t. de faire** to be (busy) doing; **mettre qch en t.** to get sth going, start sth off. **4** (*allure*) pace; **t. de vie** life style. **5** (*de pneus*) set; (*de péniches, véhicules*) string. **6** **t. d'atterrissage** *Av* undercarriage.

traîne [trɛn] *nf* **1** (*de robe*) train. **2** **à la t.** (*en arrière*) lagging behind.

traîneau, -x [trɛno] *nm* sledge, sleigh, *Am* sled.

traînée [trene] *nf* **1** (*de substance*) trail, streak; (*bande*) streak; **se répandre comme une t. de poudre** (*vite*) to spread like wildfire. **2** (*prostituée*) *Arg* tart.

traîner [trene] *vt* to drag; (*mots*) to drawl; **(faire) t. en longueur** (*faire durer*) to drag out; — *vi* (*jouets, papiers etc*) to lie around; (*subsister*) to linger on; (*s'attarder*) to lag behind, dawdle; (*errer*) to hang around; **t. (par terre)** (*robe etc*) to trail (on the ground); **t. (en longueur)** (*durer*) to drag on; — **se t.** *vpr* (*avancer*) to drag oneself (along); (*par terre*) to crawl; (*durer*) to drag on. ◆**traînant** *a* (*voix*) drawling. ◆**traînailler** *vi Fam* = **traînasser**. ◆**traînard, -arde** *nmf* slowcoach, *Am* slowpoke. ◆**traînasser** *vi Fam* to dawdle; (*errer*) to hang around.

train-train [trɛ̃trɛ̃] *nm* routine.

traire* [trɛr] *vt* (*vache*) to milk.

trait [trɛ] *nm* **1** line; (*en dessinant*) stroke; (*caractéristique*) feature, trait; *pl* (*du visage*) features; **t. d'union** hyphen; (*intermédiaire*) *Fig* link; **d'un t.** (*boire*) in one gulp, in one go; **à grands traits** in outline; **t. de** (*esprit, génie*) flash of; (*bravoure*) act of; (*se rapporter à*) to relate to. **2 cheval de t.** draught horse.

traite [tret] *nf* **1** (*de vache*) milking. **2** *Com* bill, draft. **3 d'une (seule) t.** (*sans interruption*) in one go. **4 t. des Noirs** slave trade; **t. des blanches** white slave trade.

traité [trete] *nm* **1** *Pol* treaty. **2** (*ouvrage*) treatise (**sur** on).

trait/er [trete] *vt* (*se comporter envers*) & *Méd* to treat; (*problème, sujet*) to deal with; (*marché*) *Com* to negotiate; (*matériau, produit*) to treat, process; **t. qn de lâche/etc** to call s.o. a coward/etc; − *vi* to negotiate, deal (**avec** with); **t. de** (*sujet*) to deal with. ◆**—ant** [-etɑ̃] *a* **médecin t.** regular doctor. ◆**—ement** [-etmɑ̃] *nm* **1** treatment; **mauvais traitements** rough treatment; **t. de données/de texte** data/word processing; **machine de t. de texte** word processor. **2** (*gains*) salary.

traiteur [tretœr] *nm* (*fournisseur*) caterer; **chez le t.** (*magasin*) at the delicatessen.

traître [tretr] *nm* traitor; **en t.** treacherously; − *a* (*dangereux*) treacherous; **être t. à** to be a traitor to. ◆**traîtrise** *nf* treachery.

trajectoire [traʒɛktwar] *nf* path, trajectory.

trajet [traʒe] *nm* journey, trip; (*distance*) distance; (*itinéraire*) route.

trame [tram] *nf* **1** (*de récit etc*) framework. **2** (*de tissu*) weft.

tramer [trame] *vt* (*évasion etc*) to plot; (*complot*) to hatch.

trampoline [trɑ̃pɔlin] *nm* trampoline.

tram(way) [tram(wɛ)] *nm* tram, *Am* streetcar.

tranche [trɑ̃ʃ] *nf* (*morceau coupé*) slice; (*bord*) edge; (*partie*) portion; (*de salaire, impôts*) bracket; **t. d'âge** age bracket.

tranchée [trɑ̃ʃe] *nf* trench.

tranch/er [trɑ̃ʃe] **1** *vt* to cut. **2** *vt* (*difficulté, question*) to settle; − *vi* (*décider*) to decide. **3** *vi* (*contraster*) to contrast (**avec, sur** with). ◆**—ant 1** *a* (*couteau*) sharp; − *nm* (*cutting*) edge. **2** *a* (*péremptoire*) trenchant, cutting. ◆**—é** *a* (*couleurs*) distinct; (*opinion*) clear-cut.

tranquille [trɑ̃kil] *a* quiet; (*mer*) calm, still; (*conscience*) clear; (*esprit*) easy; (*certain*) *Fam* confident; **je suis t.** (*rassuré*) my mind is at rest; **soyez t.** don't worry; **laisser t.** to leave be *ou* alone. ◆**tranquillement** *adv* calmly. ◆**tranquillis/er** *vt* to reassure; **tranquillisez-vous** set your mind at rest. ◆**—ant** *nm* *Méd* tranquillizer. ◆**tranquillité** *nf* (peace and) quiet; (*d'esprit*) peace of mind.

trans- [trɑ̃z, trɑ̃s] *préf* trans-.

transaction [trɑ̃zaksjɔ̃] *nf* **1** (*compromis*) compromise. **2** *Com* transaction.

transatlantique [trɑ̃zatlɑ̃tik] *a* transatlantic; − *nm* (*paquebot*) transatlantic liner; (*chaise*) deckchair.

transcend/er [trɑ̃sɑ̃de] *vt* to transcend. ◆**—ant** *a* transcendent.

transcrire* [trɑ̃skrir] *vt* to transcribe. ◆**transcription** *nf* transcription; (*document*) transcript.

transe [trɑ̃s] *nf* **en t.** (*mystique*) in a trance; (*excité*) very exited.

transférer [trɑ̃sfere] *vt* to transfer (**à** to). ◆**transfert** *nm* transfer.

transfigurer [trɑ̃sfigyre] *vt* to transform, transfigure.

transformer [trɑ̃sfɔrme] *vt* to transform, change; (*maison, matière première*) to convert; (*robe etc*) to alter; (*essai*) *Rugby* to convert; **t. en** to turn into; − **se t.** *vpr* to change, be transformed (**en** into). ◆**transformateur** *nm* *Él* transformer. ◆**transformation** *nf* transformation, change; conversion.

transfuge [trɑ̃sfyʒ] *nm* *Mil* renegade; − *nmf* *Pol* renegade.

transfusion [trɑ̃sfyzjɔ̃] *nf* **t. (sanguine)** (blood) transfusion.

transgresser [trɑ̃sgrese] *vt* (*loi, ordre*) to disobey.

transi [trɑ̃zi] *a* (*personne*) numb with cold; **t. de peur** paralysed by fear.

transiger [trɑ̃ziʒe] *vi* to compromise.

transistor [trɑ̃zistɔr] *nm* (*dispositif, poste*) transistor. ◆**transistorisé** *a* (*téléviseur etc*) transistorized.

transit [trɑ̃zit] *nm* transit; **en t.** in transit. ◆**transiter** *vt* (**faire**) **t.** to send in transit; − *vi* to be in transit.

transitif, -ive [trɑ̃zitif, -iv] *a* *Gram* transitive.

transition [trɑ̃zisjɔ̃] *nf* transition. ◆**transitoire** *a* (*qui passe*) transient; (*provisoire*) transitional.

transmettre* [trɑ̃smetr] *vt* (*héritage, message etc*) to pass on (**à** to); *Phys Tech* to transmit; *Rad TV* to broadcast, transmit. ◆**transmetteur** *nm* (*appareil*) transmitter, transmitting device. ◆**transmission** *nf* transmission; passing on.

transparaître* [trɑ̃sparetr] *vi* to show (through).

transparent [trɑ̃sparɑ̃] *a* transparent. ◆**transparence** *nf* transparency.

transpercer [trɑ̃spɛrse] *vt* to pierce, go through.

transpirer [trɑ̃spire] *vi* (*suer*) to perspire; (*information*) *Fig* to leak out. ◆**transpiration** *nf* perspiration.

transplanter [trɑ̃splɑ̃te] *vt* (*organe, plante etc*) to transplant. ◆**transplantation** *nf* transplantation; (*greffe*) *Méd* transplant.

transport [trɑ̃spɔr] *nm* **1** (*action*) transport, transportation (**de** of); *pl* (*moyens*) transport; **moyen de t.** means of transport; **transports en commun** public transport. **2** (*émotion*) *Litt* rapture. ◆**transporter 1** *vt* (*véhicule, train*) to transport, convey; (*à la main*) to carry, take; **t. d'urgence à l'hôpital** to rush to hospital; **— se t.** *vpr* (*aller*) to take oneself (à to). **2** *vt Litt* to enrapture. ◆**transporteur** *nm* **t. (routier)** haulier, *Am* trucker.

transposer [trɑ̃spoze] *vt* to transpose. ◆**transposition** *nf* transposition.

transvaser [trɑ̃svɑze] *vt* (*vin*) to decant.

transversal, -aux [trɑ̃svɛrsal, -o] *a* (*barre, rue etc*) cross-, transverse.

trapèze [trapɛz] *nm* (*au cirque*) trapeze. ◆**trapéziste** *nmf* trapeze artist.

trappe [trap] *nf* (*dans le plancher*) trap door.

trappeur [trapœr] *nm* (*chasseur*) trapper.

trapu [trapy] *a* **1** (*personne*) stocky, thickset. **2** (*problème etc*) *Fam* tough.

traquenard [traknar] *nm* trap.

traquer [trake] *vt* to track *ou* hunt (down).

traumatiser [tromatize] *vt* to traumatize. ◆**—ant** *a* traumatic. ◆**traumatisme** *nm* (*choc*) trauma.

travail, -aux [travaj, -o] *nm* (*activité, lieu*) work; (*emploi, tâche*) job; (*façonnage*) working (**de** of); (*ouvrage, étude*) work, publication; *Écon Méd* labour; *pl* work; (*dans la rue*) roadworks; (*aménagement*) alterations; **travaux forcés** hard labour; **travaux ménagers** housework; **travaux pratiques** *Scol Univ* practical work; **travaux publics** public works; **t. au noir** moonlighting; **en t.** (*femme*) *Méd* in labour.

travailler [travaje] **1** *vi* to work (**à qch** at *ou* on sth); *— vt* (*discipline, rôle, style*) to work on; (*façonner*) to work; (*inquiéter*) to worry; **t. la terre** to work the land. **2** *vi* (*bois*) to warp. ◆**—é** *a* (*style*) elaborate. ◆**—eur, -euse** *a* hard-working; *— nmf* worker ◆**travailliste** *a Pol* Labour-; *— nmf Pol* member of the Labour party.

travers [travɛr] **1** *prép* **à** *ou* **à t.** through; **en t. (de)** across. **2** *adv* **de t.** (*chapeau, nez etc*) crooked; (*comprendre*) badly; (*regarder*) askance; **aller de t.** *Fig* to go wrong; **j'ai avalé de t.** it went down the wrong way. **3** *nm* (*défaut*) failing.

traverse [travɛrs] *nf* **1** *Rail* sleeper, *Am* tie. **2** **chemin de t.** short cut.

traverser [travɛrse] *vt* to cross, go across; (*foule, période, mur*) to go through. ◆**—ée** *nf* (*action, trajet*) crossing.

traversin [travɛrsɛ̃] *nm* (*coussin*) bolster.

travestir [travɛstir] *vt* to disguise; (*pensée, vérité*) to misrepresent. ◆**—i** *nm Th* female impersonator; (*homosexuel*) transvestite. ◆**—issement** *nm* disguise; misrepresentation.

trébucher [trebyʃe] *vi* to stumble (**sur** over); **faire t.** to trip (up).

trèfle [trɛfl] *nm* **1** (*plante*) clover. **2** (*couleur*) *Cartes* clubs.

treille [trɛj] *nf* climbing vine.

treillis [treji] *nm* **1** lattice(work); (*en métal*) wire mesh. **2** (*tenue militaire*) combat uniform.

treize [trɛz] *a* & *nm inv* thirteen. ◆**treizième** *a* & *nmf* thirteenth.

tréma [trema] *nm Gram* di(a)eresis.

trembler [trɑ̃ble] *vi* to tremble, shake; (*de froid, peur*) to tremble (**de** with); (*flamme, lumière*) to flicker; (*voix*) to tremble, quaver; (*avoir peur*) to be afraid (**que** (+ *sub*) that, **de faire** to do); **t. pour qn** to fear for s.o. ◆**—ement** *nm* (*action, frisson*) trembling; **t. de terre** earthquake. ◆**trembloter** *vi* to quiver.

trémousser (se) [sətremuse] *vpr* to wriggle (about).

trempe [trɑ̃p] *nf* (*caractère*) stamp; **un homme de sa t.** a man of his stamp.

tremper [trɑ̃pe] **1** *vt* to soak, drench; (*plonger*) to dip (**dans** in); *– vi* to soak; **faire t.** to soak; **— se t.** *vpr* (*se baigner*) to take a dip. **2** *vt* (*acier*) to temper. **3** *vi* **t. dans** (*participer*) *Péj* to be mixed up in. ◆**trempette** *nf* **faire t.** (*se baigner*) to take a dip.

tremplin [trɑ̃plɛ̃] *nm Natation* & *Fig* springboard.

trente [trɑ̃t] *a* & *nm* thirty; **un t.-trois tours** (*disque*) an LP. ◆**trentaine** *nf* **une t. (de)** (*nombre*) (about) thirty; **avoir la t.** (*âge*) to be about thirty. ◆**trentième** *a* & *nmf* thirtieth.

trépidant [trepidɑ̃] *a* (*vie etc*) hectic.

trépied [trepje] *nm* tripod.

trépigner [trepiɲe] *vi* to stamp (one's feet).

très [trɛ] *adv* (*before vowel or mute h*) very; **t. aimé/critiqué/***etc* much liked/criticized/*etc*.

trésor [trezɔr] *nm* treasure; **le T. (public)**

(*service*) public revenue (department); (*finances*) public funds; **des trésors de** *Fig* a treasure house of. ◆**trésorerie** *nf* (*bureaux d'un club etc*) accounts department; (*capitaux*) funds; (*gestion*) accounting. ◆**trésorier, -ière** *nmf* treasurer.

tressaill/ir* [tresajir] *vi* (*sursauter*) to jump, start; (*frémir*) to shake, quiver; (*de joie, peur*) to tremble (**de** with). ◆**—ement** *nm* start; quiver; trembling.

tressauter [tresote] *vi* (*sursauter*) to start, jump.

tresse [tres] *nf* (*cordon*) braid; (*cheveux*) plait, *Am* braid. ◆**tresser** *vt* to braid; to plait.

tréteau, -x [treto] *nm* trestle.

treuil [trœj] *nm* winch, windlass.

trêve [trev] *nf Mil* truce; (*répit*) *Fig* respite.

tri [tri] *nm* sorting (out); **faire le t. de** to sort (out); (**centre de**) **t.** (*des postes*) sorting office. ◆**triage** *nm* sorting (out).

triangle [trijɑ̃gl] *nm* triangle. ◆**triangulaire** *a* triangular.

tribord [tribɔr] *nm Nau Av* starboard.

tribu [triby] *nf* tribe. ◆**tribal, -aux** *a* tribal.

tribulations [tribylasjɔ̃] *nfpl* tribulations.

tribunal, -aux [tribynal, -o] *nm Jur* court; (*militaire*) tribunal.

tribune [tribyn] *nf* **1** (*de salle publique etc*) gallery; (*de stade*) (grand)stand; (*d'orateur*) rostrum. **2 t. libre** (*dans un journal*) open forum.

tribut [triby] *nm* tribute (**à** to).

tributaire [tribyter] *a* **t. de** *Fig* dependent on.

tricher [trife] *vi* to cheat. ◆**tricherie** *nf* cheating, trickery; **une t.** a piece of trickery. ◆**tricheur, -euse** *nmf* cheat, *Am* cheater.

tricolore [trikɔlɔr] *a* **1** (*cocarde etc*) red, white and blue; **le drapeau/l'équipe t.** the French flag/team. **2 feu t.** traffic lights.

tricot [triko] *nm* (*activité, ouvrage*) knitting; (*chandail*) jumper, sweater; **un t.** (*ouvrage*) a piece of knitting; **en t.** knitted; **t. de corps** vest, *Am* undershirt. ◆**tricoter** *vti* to knit.

tricycle [trisikl] *nm* tricycle.

trier [trije] *vt* (*séparer*) to sort (out); (*choisir*) to pick *ou* sort out.

trilogie [trilɔʒi] *nf* trilogy.

trimbal(l)er [trɛ̃bale] *vt Fam* to cart about, drag around; **— se t.** *vpr Fam* to trail around.

trimer [trime] *vi Fam* to slave (away), toil.

trimestre [trimestr] *nm* (*période*) *Com* quarter; *Scol* term. ◆**trimestriel, -ielle** *a* (*revue*) quarterly; (*bulletin*) *Scol* end-of-term.

tringle [trɛ̃gl] *nf* rail, rod; **t. à rideaux** curtain rail *ou* rod.

Trinité [trinite] *nf* **la T.** (*fête*) Trinity; (*dogme*) the Trinity.

trinquer [trɛ̃ke] *vi* to chink glasses; **t. à** to drink to.

trio [trijo] *nm* (*groupe*) & *Mus* trio.

triomphe [trijɔ̃f] *nm* triumph (**sur** over); **porter qn en t.** to carry s.o. shoulder-high. ◆**triomphal, -aux** *a* triumphal. ◆**triomph/er** *vi* to triumph (**de** over); (*jubiler*) to be jubilant. ◆**—ant** *a* triumphant.

tripes [trip] *nfpl* (*intestins*) *Fam* guts; *Culin* tripe. ◆**tripier, -ière** *nmf* tripe butcher.

triple [tripl] *a* treble, triple; **—** *nm* **le t.** three times as much (**de** as). ◆**tripl/er** *vti* to treble, triple. ◆**—és, -ées** *nmfpl* (*enfants*) triplets.

tripot [tripo] *nm* (*café etc*) *Péj* gambling den.

tripoter [tripote] *vt* to fiddle about *ou* mess about with; **—** *vi* to fiddle *ou* mess about.

trique [trik] *nf* cudgel, stick.

triste [trist] *a* sad; (*couleur, temps, rue*) gloomy, dreary; (*lamentable*) unfortunate, sorry. ◆**tristement** *adv* sadly. ◆**tristesse** *nf* sadness; gloom, dreariness.

triturer [trityre] *vt* (*manipuler*) to manipulate.

trivial, -aux [trivjal, -o] *a* coarse, vulgar. ◆**trivialité** *nf* coarseness, vulgarity.

troc [trɔk] *nm* exchange, barter.

troène [trɔen] *nm* (*arbuste*) privet.

trognon [trɔɲɔ̃] *nm* (*de pomme, poire*) core; (*de chou*) stump.

trois [trwa] *a* & *nm* three. ◆**troisième** *a* & *nmf* third. ◆**troisièmement** *adv* thirdly.

trolley(bus) [trɔle(bys)] *nm* trolley(bus).

trombe [trɔ̃b] *nf* **t. d'eau** (*pluie*) rainstorm, downpour; **en t.** (*entrer etc*) *Fig* like a whirlwind.

trombone [trɔ̃bɔn] *nm* **1** *Mus* trombone. **2** (*agrafe*) paper clip.

trompe [trɔ̃p] *nf* **1** (*d'éléphant*) trunk; (*d'insecte*) proboscis. **2** *Mus* horn.

tromper [trɔ̃pe] *vt* to deceive, mislead; (*escroquer*) to cheat; (*échapper à*) to elude; (*être infidèle à*) to be unfaithful to; **— se t.** *vpr* to be mistaken, make a mistake; **se t. de route/de train/etc** to take the wrong road/train/etc; **se t. de date/de jour/etc** to get the date/day/etc wrong. ◆**tromperie** *nf* deceit, deception. ◆**trompeur, -euse** *a* (*apparences etc*) deceptive, misleading; (*personne*) deceitful.

trompette [trɔ̃pet] *nf* trumpet. ◆**trompettiste** *nmf* trumpet player.

tronc [trɔ̃] nm **1** Bot Anat trunk. **2** Rel collection box.

tronçon [trɔ̃sɔ̃] nm section. **◆tronçonn/er** vt to cut (into sections). **◆—euse** nf chain saw.

trône [tron] nm throne. **◆trôner** vi (vase, personne etc) Fig to occupy the place of honour.

tronquer [trɔ̃ke] vt to truncate; (texte etc) to curtail.

trop [tro] adv too; too much; **t. dur/loin/**etc too hard/far/etc; **t. fatigué** too tired, overtired; **boire/lire/**etc **t.** to drink/read/etc too much; **t. de sel/**etc (quantité) too much salt/etc; **t. de gens/**etc (nombre) too many people/etc; **du fromage/**etc **de ou en t.** (quantité) too much cheese/etc; **des œufs/** etc **de ou en t.** (nombre) too many eggs/ etc; **un franc/verre/**etc **de t. ou en t.** one franc/glass/etc too many; **se sentir de t.** Fig to feel in the way.

trophée [trɔfe] nm trophy.

tropique [trɔpik] nm tropic. **◆tropical, -aux** a tropical.

trop-plein [trɔplɛ̃] nm (dispositif, liquide) overflow; (surabondance) Fig excess.

troquer [trɔke] vt to exchange (**contre** for).

trot [tro] nm trot; **aller au t.** to trot; **au t.** (sans traîner) Fam at the double. **◆trott/er** vi (cheval) to trot; (personne) Fig to scurry (along).

trotteuse [trɔtøz] nf (de montre) second hand.

trottiner [trɔtine] vi (personne) to patter (along).

trottinette [trɔtinet] nf (jouet) scooter.

trottoir [trɔtwar] nm pavement, Am sidewalk; **t. roulant** moving walkway, travolator.

trou [tru] nm hole; (d'aiguille) eye; (manque) Fig gap (**dans** in); (village) Péj hole, dump; **t. d'homme** (ouverture) manhole; **t. de (la) serrure** keyhole; **t. (de mémoire)** Fig lapse (of memory).

trouble [trubl] **1** a (liquide) cloudy; (image) blurred; (affaire) shady; **voir t.** to see blurred. **2** nm (émoi, émotion) agitation; (désarroi) distress; (désordre) confusion; pl Méd trouble; (révolte) disturbances, troubles. **◆troubl/er** vt to disturb; (liquide) to make cloudy; (projet) to upset; (esprit) to unsettle; (vue) to blur; (inquiéter) to trouble; **— se t.** vpr (liquide) to become cloudy; (candidat etc) to become flustered. **◆—ant** a (détail etc) disquieting. **◆trouble-fête** nmf inv killjoy, spoilsport.

trou/er [true] vt to make a hole ou holes in;

(silence, ténèbres) to cut through. **◆—ée** nf gap; (brèche) Mil breach.

trouille [truj] nf **avoir la t.** Fam to have the jitters, be scared. **◆trouillard** a (poltron) Fam chicken.

troupe [trup] nf Mil troop; (groupe) group; Th company, troupe; **la t., les troupes** (armée) the troops.

troupeau, -x [trupo] nm (de vaches) & Fig Péj herd; (de moutons, d'oies) flock.

trousse [trus] nf **1** (étui) case, kit; (d'écolier) pencil case; **t. à outils** toolkit; **t. à pharmacie** first-aid kit. **2** nfpl **aux trousses de qn** Fig on s.o.'s heels.

trousseau, -x [truso] nm **1** (de clés) bunch. **2** (de mariée) trousseau.

trouver [truve] vt to find; **aller/venir t. qn** to go/come and see s.o.; **je trouve que** (je pense que) I think that; **comment la trouvez-vous?** what do you think of her?; **— se t.** vpr to be; (être situé) to be situated; (se sentir) to feel; (dans une situation) to find oneself; **se t. mal** (s'évanouir) to faint; **il se trouve que** it happens that. **◆trouvaille** nf (lucky) find.

truand [tryɑ̃] nm crook.

truc [tryk] nm **1** (astuce) trick; (moyen) way; **avoir/trouver le t.** to have/get the knack (**pour faire** of doing). **2** (chose) Fam thing. **◆—age** nm = truquage.

truchement [tryʃmɑ̃] nm **par le t. de qn** through (the intermediary of) s.o.

truculent [trykylɑ̃] a (langage, personnage) colourful.

truelle [tryɛl] nf trowel.

truffe [tryf] nf **1** (champignon) truffle. **2** (de chien) nose.

truff/er [tryfe] vt (remplir) to stuff (**de** with). **◆—é** a (pâté etc) Culin with truffles.

truie [trɥi] nf (animal) sow.

truite [trɥit] nf trout.

truqu/er [tryke] vt (photo etc) to fake; (élections, match) to rig, fix. **◆—é** a (photo etc) fake-; (élections, match) rigged, fixed; (scène) Cin trick-. **◆—age** nm Cin (special) effect; (action) faking; rigging.

trust [trœst] nm Com (cartel) trust; (entreprise) corporation.

tsar [dzar] nm tsar, czar.

TSF [teɛsɛf] nf abrév (télégraphie sans fil) wireless, radio.

tsigane [tsigan] a & nmf (Hungarian) gipsy.

TSVP [teɛsvepe] abrév (tournez s'il vous plaît) PTO.

TTC [tetese] abrév (toutes taxes comprises) inclusive of tax.

tu [ty] pron you (familiar form of address).

tu² [ty] *voir* **taire.**

tuba [tyba] *nm* **1** *Mus* tuba. **2** *Sp* snorkel.

tube [tyb] *nm* **1** tube; (*de canalisation*) pipe. **2** (*chanson, disque*) *Fam* hit. ◆**tubulaire** *a* tubular.

tuberculeux, -euse [tybɛrkylø, -øz] *a* tubercular; **être t.** to have tuberculosis *ou* TB. ◆**tuberculose** *nf* tuberculosis, TB.

tue-mouches [tymuʃ] *a inv* **papier t.-mouches** flypaper. ◆**t.-tête (à)** *adv* at the top of one's voice.

tu/er [tɥe] *vt* to kill; (*d'un coup de feu*) to shoot (dead), kill; (*épuiser*) *Fig* to wear out; **— se t.** *vpr* to kill oneself; to shoot oneself; (*dans un accident*) to be killed; **se t. à faire** *Fig* to wear oneself out doing. ◆**—ant** *a* (*fatigant*) exhausting. ◆**tuerie** *nf* slaughter. ◆**tueur, -euse** *nmf* killer.

tuile [tɥil] *nf* **1** tile. **2** (*malchance*) *Fam* (stroke of) bad luck.

tulipe [tylip] *nf* tulip.

tuméfié [tymefje] *a* swollen.

tumeur [tymœr] *nf* tumour, growth.

tumulte [tymylt] *nm* commotion; (*désordre*) turmoil. ◆**tumultueux, -euse** *a* turbulent.

tunique [tynik] *nf* tunic.

Tunisie [tynizi] *nf* Tunisia. ◆**tunisien, -ienne** *a & nmf* Tunisian.

tunnel [tynɛl] *nm* tunnel.

turban [tyrbɑ̃] *nm* turban.

turbine [tyrbin] *nf* turbine.

turbulences [tyrbylɑ̃s] *nfpl Phys Av* turbulence.

turbulent [tyrbylɑ̃] *a* (*enfant etc*) boisterous, turbulent.

turfiste [tyrfist] *nmf* racegoer, punter.

Turquie [tyrki] *nf* Turkey. ◆**turc, turque** *a* Turkish; *— nmf* Turk; *— nm* (*langue*) Turkish.

turquoise [tyrkwaz] *a inv* turquoise.

tuteur, -trice [tytœr, -tris] **1** *nmf Jur* guardian. **2** *nm* (*bâton*) stake, prop. ◆**tutelle** *nf Jur* guardianship; *Fig* protection.

tutoyer [tytwaje] *vt* to address familiarly (*using tu*). ◆**tutoiement** *nm* familiar address, use of *tu*.

tutu [tyty] *nm* ballet skirt, tutu.

tuyau, -x [tɥijo] *nm* **1** pipe; **t. d'arrosage** hose(pipe); **t. de cheminée** flue; **t. d'échappement** *Aut* exhaust (pipe). **2** (*renseignement*) *Fam* tip. ◆**tuyauter** *vt* **t. qn** (*conseiller*) *Fam* to give s.o. a tip. ◆**tuyauterie** *nf* (*tuyaux*) piping.

TVA [tevea] *nf abrév* (*taxe à la valeur ajoutée*) VAT.

tympan [tɛ̃pɑ̃] *nm* eardrum.

type [tip] *nm* (*modèle*) type; (*traits*) features; (*individu*) *Fam* fellow, guy, bloke; **le t. même de** *Fig* the very model of; *— a inv* (*professeur etc*) typical. ◆**typique** *a* typical (**de** of). ◆**typiquement** *adv* typically.

typhoïde [tifɔid] *nf Méd* typhoid (fever).

typhon [tifɔ̃] *nm Mét* typhoon.

typographe [tipɔgraf] *nmf* typographer. ◆**typographie** *nf* typography, printing. ◆**typographique** *a* typographical, printing-.

tyran [tirɑ̃] *nm* tyrant. ◆**tyrannie** *nf* tyranny. ◆**tyrannique** *a* tyrannical. ◆**tyranniser** *vt* to tyrannize.

tzigane [dzigan] *a & nmf* (Hungarian) gipsy.

U

U, u [y] *nm* U, u.

ulcère [ylsɛr] *nm* ulcer, sore.

ulcérer [ylsere] *vt* (*blesser, irriter*) to embitter.

ultérieur [ylterjœr] *a* later. ◆**—ement** *adv* later.

ultimatum [yltimatɔm] *nm* ultimatum.

ultime [yltim] *a* final, last.

ultra- [yltra] *préf* ultra-. ◆**u.-secret, -ète** *a* (*document*) top-secret.

ultramoderne [yltramɔdɛrn] *a* ultramodern.

ultraviolet, -ette [yltravjɔle, -ɛt] *a* ultraviolet.

un, une [œ̃, yn] **1** *art indéf* a, (*devant voyelle*) an; **une page** a page; **un ange** [œ̃nɑ̃ʒ] an angel. **2** *a* one; **la page un** page one; **un kilo** one kilo; **un type** (*un quelconque*) some *ou* a fellow. **3** *pron & nmf* one; **l'un** one; **les uns** some; **le numéro un** number one; **j'en ai un** I have one; **l'un d'eux** one of them; **la une** *Journ* front page.

unanime [ynanim] *a* unanimous. ◆**unanimité** *nf* unanimity; **à l'u.** unanimously.

uni [yni] *a* united; (*famille etc*) close; (*surface*) smooth; (*couleur, étoffe*) plain.

unième [ynjɛm] *a* (*après un numéral*) (-)first; **trente et u.** thirty-first; **cent u.** hundred and first.

unifier [ynifje] *vt* to unify. ◆**unification** *nf* unification.

uniforme [ynifɔrm] **1** *a* (*régulier*) uniform. **2** *nm* (*vêtement*) uniform. ◆**uniformément** *adv* uniformly. ◆**uniformiser** *vt* to standardize. ◆**uniformité** *nf* uniformity.

unijambiste [yniʒɑ̃bist] *a* & *nmf* one-legged (man *ou* woman).

unilatéral, -aux [ynilateral, -o] *a* unilateral; (*stationnement*) on one side of the road only.

union [ynjɔ̃] *nf* union; (*association*) association; (*entente*) unity. ◆**unir** *vt* to unite, join (together); **u. la force au courage**/*etc* to combine strength with courage/*etc*; **— s'u.** *vpr* to unite; (*se marier*) to be joined together; (*se joindre*) to join (together).

unique [ynik] *a* **1** (*fille, fils*) only; (*espoir, souci etc*) only, sole; (*prix, salaire, voie*) single, one; **son seul et u. souci** his *ou* her one and only worry. **2** (*incomparable*) unique. ◆**uniquement** *adv* only, solely.

unisexe [ynisɛks] *a inv* (*vêtements etc*) unisex.

unisson (à l') [alynisɔ̃] *adv* in unison (de with).

unité [ynite] *nf* (*élément, grandeur*) & *Mil* unit; (*cohésion, harmonie*) unity. ◆**unitaire** *a* (*prix*) per unit.

univers [ynivɛr] *nm* universe.

universel, -elle [ynivɛrsɛl] *a* universal. ◆**universellement** *adv* universally. ◆**universalité** *nf* universality.

université [ynivɛrsite] *nf* university; **à l'u.** at university. ◆**universitaire** *a* university-; *– nmf* academic.

uranium [yranjɔm] *nm* uranium.

urbain [yrbɛ̃] *a* urban, town-, city-. ◆**urbaniser** *vt* to urbanize, build up. ◆**urbanisme** *nm* town planning, *Am* city planning. ◆**urbaniste** *nmf* town planner, *Am* city planner.

urgent [yrʒɑ̃] *a* urgent, pressing. ◆**urgence** *nf* (*cas*) emergency; (*de décision, tâche etc*) urgency; **d'u.** (*mesures etc*) emergency-; **état d'u.** *Pol* state of emergency; **faire qch d'u.** to do sth urgently.

urine [yrin] *nf* urine. ◆**uriner** *vi* to urinate. ◆**urinoir** *nm* (public) urinal.

urne [yrn] *nf* **1** (*électorale*) ballot box; **aller aux urnes** to go to the polls. **2** (*vase*) urn.

URSS [yrs] *nf abrév* (*Union des Républiques Socialistes Soviétiques*) USSR.

usage [yzaʒ] *nm* use; *Ling* usage; (*habitude*) custom; **faire u. de** to make use of; **faire de l'u.** (*vêtement etc*) to wear well; **d'u.** (*habituel*) customary; **à l'u. de** for (the use of); **hors d'u.** no longer usable. ◆**usagé** *a* worn, (*d'occasion*) used. ◆**usager** *nm* user. ◆**us/er** *vt* (*vêtement, personne*) to wear out; (*consommer*) to use (up); (*santé*) to ruin; *– vi* **u. de** to use; **— s'u.** *vpr* (*tissu, machine*) to wear out; (*personne*) to wear oneself out. ◆**—é** *a* (*tissu etc*) worn (out); (*sujet etc*) well-worn; (*personne*) worn out.

usine [yzin] *nf* factory; (*à gaz, de métallurgie*) works.

usiner [yzine] *vt* (*pièce*) *Tech* to machine.

usité [yzite] *a* commonly used.

ustensile [ystɑ̃sil] *nm* utensil.

usuel, -elle [yzɥɛl] *a* everyday, ordinary; *– nmpl* (*livres*) reference books.

usure [yzyr] *nf* (*détérioration*) wear (and tear); **avoir qn à l'u.** *Fig* to wear s.o. down (in the end).

usurier, -ière [yzyrje, -jɛr] *nmf* usurer.

usurper [yzyrpe] *vt* to usurp.

utérus [yterys] *nm Anat* womb, uterus.

utile [ytil] *a* useful (à to). ◆**utilement** *adv* usefully.

utiliser [ytilize] *vt* to use, utilize. ◆**utilisable** *a* usable. ◆**utilisateur, -trice** *nmf* user. ◆**utilisation** *nf* use. ◆**utilité** *nf* use(fulness); **d'une grande u.** very useful.

utilitaire [ytilitɛr] *a* utilitarian; (*véhicule*) utility-.

utopie [ytɔpi] *nf* (*idéal*) utopia; (*projet, idée*) utopian plan *ou* idea. ◆**utopique** *a* utopian.

V

V, v [ve] *nm* V, v.

va [va] *voir* **aller 1.**

vacances [vakɑ̃s] *nfpl* holiday(s), *Am* vacation; **en v.** on holiday, *Am* on vacation; **prendre ses v.** to take one's holiday(s) *ou Am* vacation; **les grandes v.** the summer

holidays *ou Am* vacation. ◆**vacancier, -ière** *nmf* holidaymaker, *Am* vacationer.
vacant [vakã] *a* vacant. ◆**vacance** *nf* (*poste*) vacancy.
vacarme [vakarm] *nm* din, uproar.
vaccin [vaksɛ̃] *nm* vaccine; **faire un v. à** to vaccinate. ◆**vaccination** *nf* vaccination. ◆**vacciner** *vt* to vaccinate.
vache [vaʃ] **1** *nf* cow; **v. laitière** dairy cow. **2** *nf* (**peau de**) **v.** (*personne*) *Fam* swine; — *a* (*méchant*) *Fam* nasty. ◆**vachement** *adv* *Fam* (*très*) damned; (*beaucoup*) a hell of a lot. ◆**vacherie** *nf* *Fam* (*action, parole*) nasty thing; (*caractère*) nastiness.
vacill/er [vasije] *vi* to sway, wobble; (*flamme, lumière*) to flicker; (*jugement, mémoire etc*) to falter, waver. ◆—**ant** *a* (*démarche, mémoire*) shaky; (*lumière etc*) flickering.
vadrouille [vadruj] *nf* **en v.** *Fam* roaming *ou* wandering about. ◆**vadrouiller** *vi* *Fam* to roam *ou* wander about.
va-et-vient [vaevjɛ̃] *nm inv* (*mouvement*) movement to and fro; (*de personnes*) comings and goings.
vagabond, -onde [vagabɔ̃, -ɔ̃d] *a* wandering; — *nmf* (*clochard*) vagrant, tramp. ◆**vagabond/er** *vi* to roam *ou* wander about; (*pensée*) to wander. ◆—**age** *nm* wandering; *Jur* vagrancy.
vagin [vaʒɛ̃] *nm* vagina.
vagir [vaʒir] *vi* (*bébé*) to cry, wail.
vague [vag] **1** *a* vague; (*regard*) vacant; (*souvenir*) dim, vague; — *nm* vagueness; **regarder dans le v.** to gaze into space, gaze vacantly; **rester dans le v.** (*être évasif*) to keep it vague. **2** *nf* (*de mer*) & *Fig* wave; **v. de chaleur** heat wave; **v. de froid** cold snap *ou* spell; **v. de fond** (*dans l'opinion*) *Fig* tidal wave. ◆**vaguement** *adv* vaguely.
vaillant [vajã] *a* brave, valiant; (*vigoureux*) healthy. ◆**vaillamment** *adv* bravely, valiantly. ◆**vaillance** *nf* bravery.
vain [vɛ̃] *a* **1** (*futile*) vain, futile; (*mots, promesse*) empty; **en v.** in vain, vainly. **2** (*vaniteux*) vain. ◆**vainement** *adv* in vain, vainly.
vainc/re* [vɛ̃kr] *vt* to defeat, beat; (*surmonter*) to overcome. ◆—**u, -ue** *nmf* defeated man *ou* woman; *Sp* loser. ◆**vainqueur** *nm* victor; *Sp* winner; — *am* victorious.
vaisseau, -x [vɛso] *nm* **1** *Anat Bot* vessel. **2** (*bateau*) ship, vessel; **v. spatial** spaceship.
vaisselle [vɛsɛl] *nf* crockery; (*à laver*) washing up; **faire la v.** to do the washing up, do *ou* wash the dishes.

val, *pl* **vals** *ou* **vaux** [val, vo] *nm* valley.
valable [valabl] *a* (*billet, motif etc*) valid; (*remarquable, rentable*) *Fam* worthwhile.
valet [valɛ] *nm* **1** *Cartes* jack. **2** **v. (de chambre)** valet, manservant; **v. de ferme** farmhand.
valeur [valœr] *nf* value; (*mérite*) worth; (*poids*) importance, weight; *pl* (*titres*) *Com* stocks and shares; **la v. de** (*quantité*) the equivalent of; **avoir de la v.** to be valuable; **mettre en v.** (*faire ressortir*) to highlight; **de v.** (*personne*) of merit, able; **objets de v.** valuables.
valide [valid] *a* **1** (*personne*) fit, able-bodied; (*population*) able-bodied. **2** (*billet etc*) valid. ◆**valider** *vt* to validate. ◆**validité** *nf* validity.
valise [valiz] *nf* (suit)case; **v. diplomatique** diplomatic bag *ou* *Am* pouch; **faire ses valises** to pack (one's bags).
vallée [vale] *nf* valley. ◆**vallon** *nm* (small) valley. ◆**vallonné** *a* (*région etc*) undulating.
valoir* [valwar] *vi* to be worth; (*s'appliquer*) to apply (**pour** to); **v. mille francs/cher/etc** to be worth a thousand francs/a lot/*etc*; **un vélo vaut bien une auto** a bicycle is as good as a car; **il vaut mieux rester** it's better to stay; **il vaut mieux que j'attende** I'd better wait; **ça ne vaut rien** it's worthless, it's no good; **ça vaut le coup** *Fam ou* **la peine** it's worthwhile (**de faire** doing); **faire v.** (*faire ressortir*) to highlight, set off; (*argument*) to put forward; (*droit*) to assert; — *vt* **v. qch à qn** to bring *ou* get s.o. sth; — **se v.** *vpr* (*objets, personnes*) to be as good as each other; **ça se vaut** *Fam* it's all the same.
valse [vals] *nf* waltz. ◆**valser** *vi* to waltz.
valve [valv] *nf* (*clapet*) valve. ◆**valvule** *nf* (*du cœur*) valve.
vampire [vɑ̃pir] *nm* vampire.
vandale [vɑ̃dal] *nmf* vandal. ◆**vandalisme** *nm* vandalism.
vanille [vanij] *nf* vanilla; **glace/etc à la v.** vanilla ice cream/*etc*. ◆**vanillé** *a* vanilla-flavoured.
vanité [vanite] *nf* vanity. ◆**vaniteux, -euse** *a* vain, conceited.
vanne [van] *nf* **1** (*d'écluse*) sluice (gate), floodgate. **2** (*remarque*) *Fam* dig, jibe.
vanné [vane] *a* (*fatigué*) *Fam* dead beat.
vannerie [vanri] *nf* (*fabrication, objets*) basketwork, basketry.
vantail, -aux [vɑ̃taj, -o] *nm* (*de porte*) leaf.
vanter [vɑ̃te] *vt* to praise; — **se v.** *vpr* to boast, brag (**de** about, of). ◆**vantard, -arde** *a* boastful; — *nmf* boaster, braggart.

◆**vantardise** *nf* boastfulness; (*propos*) boast.

va-nu-pieds [vanypje] *nmf inv* tramp, beggar.

vapeur [vapœr] *nf* (*brume, émanation*) vapour; **v. (d'eau)** steam; **cuire à la v.** to steam; **bateau à v.** steamship. ◆**vaporeux, -euse** *a* hazy, misty; (*tissu*) translucent, diaphanous.

vaporiser [vaporize] *vt* to spray. ◆**vaporisateur** *nm* (*appareil*) spray.

vaquer [vake] *vi* **v. à** to attend to.

varappe [varap] *nf* rock-climbing.

varech [varεk] *nm* wrack, seaweed.

vareuse [varøz] *nf* (*d'uniforme*) tunic.

varicelle [varisεl] *nf* chicken pox.

varices [varis] *nfpl* varicose veins.

vari/er [varje] *vti* to vary (**de** from). ◆**—é** *a* (*diversifié*) varied; (*divers*) various. ◆**—able** *a* variable; (*humeur, temps*) changeable. ◆**variante** *nf* variant. ◆**variation** *nf* variation. ◆**variété** *nf* variety; **spectacle de variétés** *Th* variety show.

variole [varjɔl] *nf* smallpox.

vas [va] *voir* **aller 1.**

vase [vaz] **1** *nm* vase. **2** *nf* (*boue*) silt, mud.

vaseline [vazlin] *nf* Vaseline®.

vaseux, -euse [vazø, -øz] *a* **1** (*boueux*) silty, muddy. **2** (*fatigué*) off colour. **3** (*idées etc*) woolly, hazy.

vasistas [vazistas] *nm* (*dans une porte ou une fenêtre*) hinged panel.

vaste [vast] *a* vast, huge.

Vatican [vatikã] *nm* Vatican.

va-tout [vatu] *nm inv* **jouer son v.-tout** to stake one's all.

vaudeville [vodvil] *nm Th* light comedy.

vau-l'eau (à) [avolo] *adv* **aller à v.-l'eau** to go to rack and ruin.

vaurien, -ienne [vorjε̃, -jεn] *nmf* good-for-nothing.

vautour [votur] *nm* vulture.

vautrer (se) [səvotre] *vpr* to sprawl; **se v. dans** (*boue, vice*) to wallow in.

va-vite (à la) [alavavit] *adv* in a hurry.

veau, -x [vo] *nm* (*animal*) calf; (*viande*) veal; (*cuir*) calf(skin).

vécu [veky] *voir* **vivre;** — *a* (*histoire etc*) real(-life), true.

vedette [vədεt] *nf* **1** *Cin Th* star; **avoir la v.** (*artiste*) to head the bill; **en v.** (*personne*) in the limelight; (*objet*) in a prominent position. **2** (*canot*) motor boat, launch.

végétal, -aux [veʒetal, -o] *a* (*huile, règne*) vegetable-; — *nm* plant. ◆**végétarien,** **-ienne** *a* & *nmf* vegetarian. ◆**végétation** **1** *nf* vegetation. **2** *nfpl Méd* adenoids.

végéter [veʒete] *vi* (*personne*) *Péj* to vegetate.

véhément [veemã] *a* vehement. ◆**véhémence** *nf* vehemence.

véhicule [veikyl] *nm* vehicle. ◆**véhiculer** *vt* to convey.

veille [vεj] *nf* **1 la v. (de)** (*jour précédent*) the day before; **à la v. de** (*événement*) on the eve of; **la v. de Noël** Christmas Eve. **2** (*état*) wakefulness; *pl* vigils.

veill/er [veje] *vi* to stay up *ou* awake; (*sentinelle etc*) to be on watch; **v. à qch** to attend to sth, see to sth; **v. à ce que** (+ *sub*) to make sure that; **v. sur qn** to watch over s.o.; — *vt* (*malade*) to sit with, watch over. ◆**—ée** *nf* (*soirée*) evening; (*réunion*) evening get-together; (*mortuaire*) vigil. ◆**—eur** *nm* **v. de nuit** night watchman. ◆**—euse** *nf* (*lampe*) night light; (*de voiture*) sidelight; (*de réchaud*) pilot light.

veine [vεn] *nf* **1** *Anat Bot Géol* vein. **2** (*chance*) *Fam* luck; **avoir de la v.** to be lucky; **une v.** a piece *ou* stroke of luck. ◆**veinard, -arde** *nmf Fam* lucky devil; — *a Fam* lucky.

vêler [vele] *vi* (*vache*) to calve.

vélin [velε̃] *nm* (*papier, peau*) vellum.

velléité [veleite] *nf* vague desire.

vélo [velo] *nm* bike, bicycle; (*activité*) cycling; **faire du v.** to cycle, go cycling. ◆**vélodrome** *nm Sp* velodrome, cycle track. ◆**vélomoteur** *nm* (lightweight) motorcycle.

velours [v(ə)lur] *nm* velvet; **v. côtelé** corduroy, cord. ◆**velouté** *a* soft, velvety; (*au goût*) mellow, smooth; — *nm* smoothness; **v. d'asperges**/*etc* (*potage*) cream of asparagus/*etc* soup.

velu [vəly] *a* hairy.

venaison [vənεzɔ̃] *nf* venison.

vénal, -aux [venal, -o] *a* mercenary, venal.

vendange(s) [vãdãʒ] *nf*(*pl*) grape harvest, vintage. ◆**vendanger** *vi* to pick the grapes. ◆**vendangeur, -euse** *nmf* grape-picker.

vendetta [vãdeta] *nf* vendetta.

vend/re [vãdr] *vt* to sell; **v. qch à qn** to sell s.o. sth, sell sth to s.o.; **v. qn** (*trahir*) to sell s.o. out; **à v.** (*maison etc*) for sale; — **se v.** *vpr* to be sold; **ça se vend bien** it sells well. ◆**—eur, -euse** *nmf* (*de magasin*) sales *ou* shop assistant, *Am* sales clerk; (*marchand*) salesman, saleswoman; *Jur* vendor, seller.

vendredi [vãdrədi] *nm* Friday; **V. saint** Good Friday.

vénéneux, -euse [venenø, -øz] *a* poisonous.

vénérable [venerabl] *a* venerable. ◆**vénérer** *vt* to venerate.

vénérien, -ienne [venerjɛ̃, -jɛn] *a Méd* venereal.

venger [vɑ̃ʒe] *vt* to avenge; **— se v.** *vpr* to take (one's) revenge, avenge oneself (**de qn** on s.o., **de qch** for sth). ◆**vengeance** *nf* revenge, vengeance. ◆**vengeur, -eresse** *a* vengeful; *− nmf* avenger.

venin [vanɛ̃] *nm* (*substance*) & *Fig* venom. ◆**venimeux, -euse** *a* poisonous, venomous; (*haineux*) *Fig* venomous.

venir* [v(ə)nir] *vi* (*aux* **être**) to come (**de** from); **v. faire** to come to do; **viens me voir** come and *ou* to see me; **je viens/venais d'arriver** I've/I'd just arrived; **en v. à** (*conclusion etc*) to come to; **où veux-tu en v.?** what are you driving *ou* getting at?; **d'où vient que...?** how is it that...?; **s'il venait à faire** (*éventualité*) if he happened to do; **les jours/etc qui viennent** the coming days/etc; **une idée m'est venue** an idea occurred to me; **faire v.** to send for, get.

vent [vɑ̃] *nm* wind; **il fait** *ou* **il y a du v.** it's windy; **coup de v.** gust of wind; **avoir v. de** (*connaissance de*) to get wind of; **dans le v.** (*à la mode*) *Fam* trendy, with it.

vente [vɑ̃t] *nf* sale; **v. (aux enchères)** auction (sale); **v. de charité** bazaar, charity sale; **en v.** (*disponible*) on sale; **point de v.** sales *ou* retail outlet; **prix de v.** selling price; **salle des ventes** auction room.

ventilateur [vɑ̃tilatœr] *nm* (*électrique*) & *Aut* fan; (*dans un mur*) ventilator. ◆**ventilation** *nf* ventilation. ◆**ventiler** *vt* to ventilate.

ventouse [vɑ̃tuz] *nf* (*pour fixer*) suction grip; **à v.** (*crochet, fléchette etc*) suction-.

ventre [vɑ̃tr] *nm* belly, stomach; (*utérus*) womb; (*de cruche etc*) bulge; **avoir/prendre du v.** to have/get a paunch; **à plat v.** flat on one's face. ◆**ventru** *a* (*personne*) pot-bellied; (*objet*) bulging.

ventriloque [vɑ̃trilɔk] *nmf* ventriloquist.

venu, -ue¹ [v(ə)ny] *voir* **venir**; *− nmf* **nouveau v., nouvelle venue** newcomer; **premier v.** anyone; *− a* **bien v.** (*à propos*) timely; **mal v.** untimely; **être bien/mal v. de faire** to have good grounds/no grounds for doing.

venue² [v(ə)ny] *nf* (*arrivée*) coming.

vêpres [vɛpr] *nfpl Rel* vespers.

ver [vɛr] *nm* worm; (*larve*) grub; (*de fruits, fromage etc*) maggot; **v. luisant** glow-worm;

v. à soie silkworm; **v. solitaire** tapeworm; **v. de terre** earthworm.

véracité [verasite] *nf* truthfulness, veracity.

véranda [verɑ̃da] *nf* veranda(h).

verbe [vɛrb] *nm Gram* verb. ◆**verbal, -aux** *a* (*promesse, expression etc*) verbal.

verbeux, -euse [vɛrbø, -øz] *a* verbose. ◆**verbiage** *nm* verbiage.

verdâtre [vɛrdɑtr] *a* greenish.

verdeur [vɛrdœr] *nf* (*de fruit, vin*) tartness; (*de vieillard*) sprightliness; (*de langage*) crudeness.

verdict [vɛrdikt] *nm* verdict.

verdir [vɛrdir] *vti* to turn green. ◆**verdoyant** *a* green, verdant. ◆**verdure** *nf* (*arbres etc*) greenery.

véreux, -euse [verø, -øz] *a* (*fruit etc*) wormy, maggoty; (*malhonnête*) *Fig* dubious, shady.

verge [vɛrʒ] *nf Anat* penis.

verger [vɛrʒe] *nm* orchard.

vergetures [vɛrʒətyr] *nfpl* stretch marks.

verglas [vɛrgla] *nm* (black) ice, *Am* sleet. ◆**verglacé** *a* (*route*) icy.

vergogne (sans) [sɑ̃vɛrgɔɲ] *a* shameless; *−* **adv** shamelessly.

véridique [veridik] *a* truthful.

vérifier [verifje] *vt* to check, verify; (*confirmer*) to confirm; (*comptes*) to audit. ◆**vérifiable** *a* verifiable. ◆**vérification** *nf* verification; confirmation; audit(ing).

vérité [verite] *nf* truth; (*de personnage, tableau etc*) trueness to life; (*sincérité*) sincerity; **en v.** in fact. ◆**véritable** *a* true, real; (*non imité*) real, genuine; (*exactement nommé*) veritable, real. ◆**véritablement** *adv* really.

vermeil, -eille [vɛrmɛj] *a* bright red, vermilion.

vermicelle(s) [vɛrmisɛl] *nm(pl) Culin* vermicelli.

vermine [vɛrmin] *nf* (*insectes, racaille*) vermine.

vermoulu [vɛrmuly] *a* worm-eaten.

vermouth [vɛrmut] *nm* vermouth.

verni [vɛrni] *a* (*chanceux*) *Fam* lucky.

vernir [vɛrnir] *vt* to varnish; (*poterie*) to glaze. ◆**vernis** *nm* varnish; glaze; (*apparence*) *Fig* veneer; **v. à ongles** nail polish *ou* varnish. ◆**vernissage** *nm* (*d'exposition de peinture*) first day. ◆**vernisser** *vt* (*poterie*) to glaze.

verra, verrait [vɛra, vɛrɛ] *voir* **voir**.

verre [vɛr] *nm* (*substance, récipient*) glass; **boire** *ou* **prendre un v.** to have a drink; **v. à bière/à vin** beer/wine glass; **v. de contact**

contact lens. ◆**verrerie** nf (objets) glass-ware. ◆**verrière** nf (toit) glass roof.

verrou [vɛru] nm bolt; **fermer au v.** to bolt; **sous les verrous** behind bars. ◆**verrouiller** vt to bolt.

verrue [vɛry] nf wart.

vers[1] [vɛr] prép (direction) towards, toward; (approximation) around, about.

vers[2] [vɛr] nm (d'un poème) line; pl (poésie) verse.

versant [vɛrsɑ̃] nm slope, side.

versatile [vɛrsatil] a fickle, volatile.

verse (à) [avɛrs] adv in torrents; **pleuvoir à v.** to pour (down).

versé [vɛrse] a **v. dans** (well-)versed in.

Verseau [vɛrso] nm **le V.** (signe) Aquarius.

vers/er [vɛrse] **1** vt to pour; (larmes, sang) to shed. **2** vt (argent) to pay. **3** vti (basculer) to overturn. ◆**—ement** nm payment. ◆**—eur** a bec v. spout.

verset [vɛrse] nm Rel verse.

version [vɛrsjɔ̃] nf version; (traduction) Scol translation, unseen.

verso [vɛrso] nm back (of the page); **'voir au v.'** 'see overleaf'.

vert [vɛr] a green; (pas mûr) unripe; (vin) young; (vieillard) Fig sprightly; − nm green.

vert-de-gris [vɛrdəgri] nm inv verdigris.

vertèbre [vɛrtɛbr] nf vertebra.

vertement [vɛrtəmɑ̃] adv (réprimander etc) sharply.

vertical, -ale, -aux [vɛrtikal, -o] a & nf vertical; **à la verticale** vertically. ◆**verticalement** adv vertically.

vertige [vɛrtiʒ] nm (feeling of) dizziness ou giddiness; (peur de tomber dans le vide) vertigo; pl dizzy spells; **avoir le v.** to feel dizzy ou giddy. ◆**vertigineux, -euse** a (hauteur) giddy, dizzy; (très grand) Fig staggering.

vertu [vɛrty] nf virtue; **en v. de** in accordance with. ◆**vertueux, -euse** a virtuous.

verve [vɛrv] nf (d'orateur etc) brilliance.

verveine [vɛrvɛn] nf (plante) verbena.

vésicule [vezikyl] nf **v. biliaire** gall bladder.

vessie [vesi] nf bladder.

veste [vɛst] nf jacket, coat.

vestiaire [vɛstjɛr] nm cloakroom, Am locker room; (meuble métallique) locker.

vestibule [vɛstibyl] nm (entrance) hall.

vestiges [vɛstiʒ] nmpl (restes, ruines) remains; (traces) traces, vestiges.

vestimentaire [vɛstimɑ̃tɛr] a (dépense) clothing-; (détail) of dress.

veston [vɛstɔ̃] nm (suit) jacket.

vêtement [vɛtmɑ̃] nm garment, article of clothing; pl clothes; **du v.** (industrie, commerce) clothing-; **vêtements de sport** sportswear.

vétéran [veterɑ̃] nm veteran.

vétérinaire [veterinɛr] a veterinary; − nmf vet, veterinary surgeon, Am veterinarian.

vétille [vetij] nf trifle, triviality.

vêt/ir* [vetir] vt, **− se v.** vpr to dress. ◆**—u** a dressed (**de** in).

veto [veto] nm inv veto; **mettre** ou **opposer son v. à** to veto.

vétuste [vetyst] a dilapidated.

veuf, veuve [vœf, vœv] a widowed; − nm widower; − nf widow.

veuille [vœj] voir **vouloir**.

veule [vøl] a feeble. ◆**veulerie** nf feebleness.

veut, veux [vø] voir **vouloir**.

vex/er [vɛkse] vt to upset, hurt; **− se v.** vpr to be ou get upset (**de** at). ◆**—ant** a hurtful; (contrariant) annoying. ◆**vexation** nf humiliation.

viable [vjabl] a (enfant, entreprise etc) viable. ◆**viabilité** nf viability.

viaduc [vjadyk] nm viaduct.

viager, -ère [vjaʒe, -ɛr] a **rente viagère** life annuity; − nm life annuity.

viande [vjɑ̃d] nf meat.

vibrer [vibre] vi to vibrate; (être ému) to thrill (**de** with); **faire v.** (auditoire etc) to thrill. ◆**vibrant** a (émouvant) emotional; (voix, son) resonant, vibrant. ◆**vibration** nf vibration. ◆**vibromasseur** nm (appareil) vibrator.

vicaire [vikɛr] nm curate.

vice [vis] nm vice; (défectuosité) defect.

vice- [vis] préf vice-.

vice versa [vis(e)vɛrsa] adv vice versa.

vicier [visje] vt to taint, pollute.

vicieux, -euse [visjø, -øz] **1** a depraved; − nmf pervert. **2** a **cercle v.** vicious circle.

vicinal, -aux [visinal, -o] a **chemin v.** by-road, minor road.

vicissitudes [visisityd] nfpl vicissitudes.

vicomte [vikɔ̃t] nm viscount. ◆**vicomtesse** nf viscountess.

victime [viktim] nf victim; (d'un accident) casualty; **être v. de** to be the victim of.

victoire [viktwar] nf victory; Sp win. ◆**victorieux, -euse** a victorious; (équipe) winning.

victuailles [viktɥaj] nfpl provisions.

vidange [vidɑ̃ʒ] nf emptying, draining; Aut oil change; (dispositif) waste outlet. ◆**vidanger** vt to empty, drain.

vide [vid] a empty; − nm emptiness, void; (absence d'air) vacuum; (gouffre etc) drop;

(*trou, manque*) gap; **regarder dans le v.** to stare into space; **emballé sous v.** vacuum-packed; **à v.** empty.

vidéo [video] *a inv* video. ◆**vidéocassette** *nf* video (cassette).

vide-ordures [vidɔrdyr] *nm inv* (refuse) chute. ◆**vide-poches** *nm inv Aut* glove compartment.

vid/er [vide] *vt* to empty; (*lieu*) to vacate; (*poisson, volaille*) Culin to gut; (*querelle*) to settle; **v. qn** Fam (*chasser*) to throw s.o. out; (*épuiser*) to tire s.o. out; — **se v.** *vpr* to empty. ◆**—é** *a* (*fatigué*) Fam exhausted. ◆**—eur** *nm* (*de boîte de nuit*) bouncer.

vie [vi] *nf* life; (*durée*) lifetime; **coût de la v.** cost of living; **gagner sa v.** to earn one's living *ou* livelihood; **en v.** living; **à v., pour la v.** for life; **donner la v. à** to give birth to; **avoir la v. dure** (*préjugés etc*) to die hard; **jamais de la v.!** not on your life!, never!

vieill/ir [vjejir] *vi* to grow old, (*changer*) to age; (*théorie, mot*) to become old-fashioned; — *vt* **v. qn** (*vêtement etc*) to age s.o. ◆**—i** *a* (*démodé*) old-fashioned. ◆**—issant** *a* ageing. ◆**—issement** *nm* ageing.

viens, vient [vjɛ̃] *voir* venir.

vierge [vjɛrʒ] *nf* virgin; **la V.** (*signe*) Virgo; — *a* (*femme, neige etc*) virgin; (*feuille de papier, film*) blank; **être v.** (*femme, homme*) to be a virgin.

Viêt-nam [vjɛtnam] *nm* Vietnam. ◆**viet-namien, -ienne** *a & nmf* Vietnamese.

vieux (*or* **vieil** before vowel or mute h), **vieille,** *pl* **vieux, vieilles** [vjø, vjɛj] *a* old; **être v. jeu** (*a inv*) to be old-fashioned; **v. garçon** bachelor; **vieille fille** Péj old maid; — *nm* old man; *pl* old people; **mon v.** (*mon cher*) Fam old boy, old man; — *nf* old woman; **ma vieille** (*ma chère*) Fam old girl. ◆**vieillard** *nm* old man; *pl* old people. ◆**vieillerie** *nf* (*objet*) old thing; (*idée*) old idea. ◆**vieillesse** *nf* old age. ◆**vieillot** *a* antiquated.

vif, vive [vif, viv] *a* (*enfant, mouvement*) lively; (*alerte*) quick, sharp; (*intelligence, intérêt, vent*) keen; (*couleur, lumière*) bright; (*froid*) biting; (*pas*) quick, brisk; (*impression, imagination, style*) vivid; (*parole*) sharp; (*regret, satisfaction, succès etc*) great; (*coléreux*) quick-tempered; **brûler/enterrer qn v.** to burn/bury s.o. alive; — *nm* **le v. du sujet** the heart of the matter; **à v.** (*plaie*) open; **piqué au v.** (*vexé*) cut to the quick.

vigie [viʒi] *nf* (*matelot*) lookout; (*poste*) lookout post.

vigilant [viʒilɑ̃] *a* vigilant. ◆**vigilance** *nf* vigilance.

vigile [viʒil] *nm* (*gardien*) watchman; (*de nuit*) night watchman.

vigne [viɲ] *nf* (*plante*) vine; (*plantation*) vineyard. ◆**vigneron, -onne** *nmf* wine grower. ◆**vignoble** *nm* vineyard; (*région*) vineyards.

vignette [viɲɛt] *nf* Aut road tax sticker; (*de médicament*) price label (*for reimbursement by Social Security*).

vigueur [vigœr] *nf* vigour; **entrer/être en v.** (*loi*) to come into/be in force. ◆**vigoureux, -euse** *a* (*personne, style etc*) vigorous; (*bras*) sturdy.

vilain [vilɛ̃] *a* (*laid*) ugly; (*mauvais*) nasty; (*enfant*) naughty.

villa [villa] *nf* (detached) house.

village [vilaʒ] *nm* village. ◆**villageois, -oise** *a* village-; — *nmf* villager.

ville [vil] *nf* town; (*grande*) city; **aller/être en v.** to go into/be in town; **v. d'eaux** spa (town).

villégiature [vileʒjatyr] *nf* **lieu de v.** (holiday) resort.

vin [vɛ̃] *nm* wine; **v. ordinaire** *ou* **de table** table wine; **v. d'honneur** reception (*in honour of s.o.*). ◆**vinicole** *a* (*région*) wine-growing; (*industrie*) wine-.

vinaigre [vinɛgr] *nm* vinegar. ◆**vinaigré** *a* seasoned with vinegar. ◆**vinaigrette** *nf* (*sauce*) vinaigrette, French dressing, *Am* Italian dressing.

vindicatif, -ive [vɛ̃dikatif, -iv] *a* vindictive.

vingt [vɛ̃] ([vɛ̃t] before vowel or mute h and in numbers 22–29) *a & nm* twenty; **v. et un** twenty-one. ◆**vingtaine** *nf* **une v. (de)** (*nombre*) about twenty; **avoir la v.** (*âge*) to be about twenty. ◆**vingtième** *a & nmf* twentieth.

vinyle [vinil] *nm* vinyl.

viol [vjɔl] *nm* rape; (*de loi, lieu*) violation. ◆**violation** *nf* violation. ◆**violenter** *vt* to rape. ◆**violer** *vt* (*femme*) to rape; (*loi, lieu*) to violate. ◆**violeur** *nm* rapist.

violent [vjɔlɑ̃] *a* violent; (*remède*) drastic. ◆**violemment** [-amɑ̃] *adv* violently. ◆**violence** *nf* violence; (*acte*) act of violence.

violet, -ette [vjɔlɛ, -ɛt] **1** *a & nm* (*couleur*) purple, violet. **2** *nf* (*fleur*) violet. ◆**violacé** *a* purplish.

violon [vjɔlɔ̃] *nm* violin. ◆**violoncelle** *nm* cello. ◆**violoncelliste** *nmf* cellist. ◆**violoniste** *nmf* violinist.

vipère [viper] *nf* viper, adder.

virage [viraʒ] *nm* (*de route*) bend; (*de véhicule*) turn; (*revirement*) Fig change of course. ◆**vir/er 1** vi to turn, veer; (sur soi) to turn round; **v. au bleu**/etc to turn blue/etc. **2** vt (expulser) Fam to throw out. **3** vt (somme) Fin to transfer (à to). ◆**—ement** nm Fin (bank ou credit) transfer.

virée [vire] nf Fam trip, outing.

virevolter [virvɔlte] vi to spin round.

virginité [virʒinite] nf virginity.

virgule [virgyl] nf Gram comma; Math (decimal) point; **2 v. 5** 2 point 5.

viril [viril] a virile, manly; (attribut, force) male. ◆**virilité** nf virility, manliness.

virtuel, -elle [virtɥɛl] a potential.

virtuose [virtɥoz] nmf virtuoso. ◆**virtuosité** nf virtuosity.

virulent [virylɑ̃] a virulent. ◆**virulence** nf virulence.

virus [virys] nm virus.

vis¹ [vi] voir **vivre, voir.**

vis² [vis] nf screw.

visa [viza] nm (timbre) stamp, stamped signature; (de passeport) visa; **v. de censure** (d'un film) certificate.

visage [vizaʒ] nm face.

vis-à-vis [vizavi] prép **v.-à-vis de** opposite; (à l'égard de) with respect to; (envers) towards; (comparé à) compared to; – nm inv (personne) person opposite; (bois, maison etc) opposite view.

viscères [visɛr] nmpl intestines. ◆**viscéral, -aux** a (haine etc) Fig deeply felt.

viscosité [viskozite] nf viscosity.

viser [vize] **1** vi to aim (à at); **v. à faire** to aim to do; – vt (cible) to aim at; (concerner) to be aimed at. **2** vt (passeport, document) to stamp. ◆**visées** nfpl (desseins) Fig aims; **avoir des visées sur** to have designs on. ◆**viseur** nm Phot viewfinder; (d'arme) sight.

visible [vizibl] a visible. ◆**visiblement** adv visibly. ◆**visibilité** nf visibility.

visière [vizjɛr] nf (de casquette) peak; (en plastique etc) eyeshade; (de casque) visor.

vision [vizjɔ̃] nf (conception, image) vision; (sens) (eye)sight, vision; **avoir des visions** Fam to be seeing things. ◆**visionnaire** a & nmf visionary. ◆**visionner** vt Cin to view. ◆**visionneuse** nf (pour diapositives) viewer.

visite [vizit] nf visit; (personne) visitor; (examen) inspection; **rendre v. à, faire une v. à** to visit; **v. (à domicile)** Méd call, visit; **v. (médicale)** medical examination; **v. guidée** guided tour; **de v.** (carte, heures) visiting-. ◆**visiter** vt to visit; (examiner) to inspect. ◆**visiteur, -euse** nmf visitor.

vison [vizɔ̃] nm mink.

visqueux, -euse [viskø, -øz] a viscous; (surface) sticky; (répugnant) Fig slimy.

visser [vise] vt to screw on.

visuel, -elle [vizɥɛl] a visual.

vit [vi] voir **vivre, voir.**

vital, -aux [vital, -o] a vital. ◆**vitalité** nf vitality.

vitamine [vitamin] nf vitamin. ◆**vitaminé** a (biscuits etc) vitamin-enriched.

vite [vit] adv quickly, fast; (tôt) soon; **v.!** quick(ly)! ◆**vitesse** nf speed; (régime) Aut gear; **boîte de vitesses** gearbox; **à toute v.** at top ou full speed; **v. de pointe** top speed; **en v.** quickly.

viticole [vitikɔl] a (région) wine-growing; (industrie) wine-. ◆**viticulteur** nm wine grower. ◆**viticulture** nf wine growing.

vitre [vitr] nf (window)pane; (de véhicule) window. ◆**vitrage** nm (vitres) windows. ◆**vitrail, -aux** nm stained-glass window. ◆**vitré** a glass-, glazed. ◆**vitreux, -euse** a (regard, yeux) Fig glassy. ◆**vitrier** nm glazier.

vitrine [vitrin] nf (de magasin) (shop) window; (meuble) showcase, display cabinet.

vitriol [vitrijɔl] nm Ch & Fig vitriol.

vivable [vivabl] a (personne) easy to live with; (endroit) fit to live in.

vivace [vivas] a (plante) perennial; (haine) Fig inveterate.

vivacité [vivasite] nf liveliness; (de l'air, d'émotion) keenness; (agilité) quickness; (de couleur, d'impression, de style) vividness; (emportement) petulance; **v. d'esprit** quick-wittedness.

vivant [vivɑ̃] a (en vie) alive, living; (être, matière, preuve) living; (conversation, enfant, récit, rue) lively; **langue vivante** modern language; – nm **de son v.** in one's lifetime; **bon v.** jovial fellow; **les vivants** the living.

vivats [viva] nmpl cheers.

vive¹ [viv] voir **vif.**

vive² [viv] int **v. le roi**/etc! long live the king/etc!; **v. les vacances!** hurray for the holidays!

vivement [vivmɑ̃] adv quickly, briskly; (répliquer) sharply; (sentir) keenly; (regretter) deeply; **v. demain!** roll on tomorrow!, I can hardly wait for tomorrow!; **v. que** (+ sub) I'll be glad when.

vivier [vivje] nm fish pond.

vivifier [vivifje] vt to invigorate.

vivisection [viviseksjɔ̃] nf vivisection.

vivre* [vivr] **1** vi to live; **elle vit encore** she's still alive ou living; **faire v.** (famille etc) to support; **v. vieux** to live to be old; **difficile/facile à** v. hard/easy to get on with; **manière de** v. way of life; **v. de** (*fruits etc*) to live on; (*travail etc*) to live by; **avoir de quoi** v. to have enough to live on; **vivent les vacances!** hurray for the holidays!; – *vt* (*vie*) to live; (*aventure, époque*) to live through; (*éprouver*) to experience. **2** *nmpl* food, supplies. ◆**vivoter** *vi* to jog along, get by.

vlan! [vlɑ̃] *int* bang!, wham!

vocable [vɔkabl] *nm* term, word.

vocabulaire [vɔkabylɛr] *nm* vocabulary.

vocal, -aux [vɔkal, -o] *a* (*cordes, musique*) vocal.

vocation [vɔkasjɔ̃] *nf* vocation, calling.

vociférer [vɔsifere] *vti* to shout angrily. ◆**vocifération** *nf* angry shout.

vodka [vɔdka] *nf* vodka.

vœu, -x [vø] *nm* (*souhait*) wish; (*promesse*) vow; **faire le** v. **de faire** to (make a) vow to do; **tous mes vœux!** (my) best wishes!

vogue [vɔg] *nf* fashion, vogue; **en** v. in fashion, in vogue.

voici [vwasi] *prép* here is, this is; *pl* here are, these are; **me** v. here I am; **me** v. **triste** I'm sad now; **v. dix ans/***etc* ten years/*etc* ago; **v. dix ans que** it's ten years since.

voie [vwa] *nf* (*route*) road; (*rails*) track, line; (*partie de route*) lane; (*chemin*) way; (*moyen*) means, way; (*de communication*) line; (*diplomatique*) channels; (*quai*) *Rail* platform; **en** v. **de** in the process of; **en** v. **de développement** (*pays*) developing; **v. publique** public highway; v. **navigable** waterway; **v. sans issue** cul-de-sac, dead end; **préparer la** v. *Fig* to pave the way; **sur la (bonne)** v. on the right track.

voilà [vwala] *prép* there is, that is; *pl* there are, those are; **les** v. there they are; **v., j'arrive!** all right, I'm coming!; **le** v. **parti** he has left now; **v. dix ans/***etc* ten years/*etc* ago; **v. dix ans que** it's ten years since.

voile[1] [vwal] *nm* (*étoffe qui cache, coiffure etc*) & *Fig* veil. ◆**voilage** *nm* net curtain. ◆**voil/er** *vt* (*visage, vérité etc*) to veil; – **se** v. *vpr* (*personne*) to wear a veil; (*ciel, regard*) to cloud over. ◆**–é** *a* (*femme, allusion*) veiled; (*terne*) dull; (*photo*) hazy.

voile[2] [vwal] *nf* (*de bateau*) sail; (*activité*) sailing; **bateau à voiles** sailing boat, *Am* sailboat; **faire de la** v. to sail, go sailing. ◆**voilier** *nm* sailing ship; (*de plaisance*) sailing boat, *Am* sailboat. ◆**voilure** *nf Nau* sails.

voiler[2] [vwale] *vt*, – **se** v. *vpr* (*roue*) to buckle.

voir* [vwar] *vti* to see; **faire** *ou* **laisser** v. **qch** to show sth; **fais** v. let me see, show me; **v. qn faire** to see s.o. do *ou* doing; **voyons!** (*sois raisonnable*) come on!; **y** v. **clair** (*comprendre*) to see clearly; **je ne peux pas la** v. (*supporter*) *Fam* I can't stand (the sight of) her; **v. venir** (*attendre*) to wait and see; **on verra bien** (*attendons*) we'll see; **ça n'a rien à** v. **avec** that's got nothing to do with; – **se** v. *vpr* to see oneself; (*se fréquenter*) to see each other; (*objet, attitude etc*) to be seen; (*reprise, tache*) to show; **ça se voit** that's obvious.

voire [vwar] *adv* indeed.

voirie [vwari] *nf* (*enlèvement des ordures*) refuse collection; (*routes*) public highways.

voisin, -ine [vwazɛ̃, -in] *a* (*pays, village etc*) neighbouring; (*maison, pièce*) next (**de** to); (*idée, état etc*) similar (**de** to); – *nmf* neighbour. ◆**voisinage** *nm* (*quartier, voisins*) neighbourhood; (*proximité*) proximity. ◆**voisiner** *vi* **avec** v. to be side by side with.

voiture [vwatyr] *nf Aut* car; *Rail* carriage, coach, *Am* car; (*charrette*) cart; v. **(à cheval)** (horse-drawn) carriage; **v. de course/ de tourisme** racing/private car; **v. d'enfant** pram, *Am* baby carriage; **en** v.! *Rail* all aboard!

voix [vwa] *nf* voice; (*suffrage*) vote; **à** v. **basse** in a whisper; **à portée de** v. within earshot; **avoir** v. **au chapitre** *Fig* to have a say.

vol [vɔl] *nm* **1** (*d'avion, d'oiseau*) flight; (*groupe d'oiseaux*) flock, flight; **v. libre** hang gliding; **v. à voile** gliding. **2** (*délit*) theft; (*hold-up*) robbery; **v. à l'étalage** shoplifting; **c'est du** v.! (*trop cher*) it's daylight robbery!

volage [vɔlaʒ] *a* flighty, fickle.

volaille [vɔlaj] *nf* **la** v. (*oiseaux*) poultry; **une** v. (*oiseau*) a fowl. ◆**volailler** *nm* poulterer.

volatile [vɔlatil] *nm* (*oiseau domestique*) fowl.

volatiliser (se) [səvɔlatilize] *vpr* (*disparaître*) to vanish (into thin air).

vol-au-vent [vɔlovɑ̃] *nm inv Culin* vol-au-vent.

volcan [vɔlkɑ̃] *nm* volcano. ◆**volcanique** *a* volcanic.

voler [vɔle] **1** *vi* (*oiseau, avion etc*) to fly; (*courir*) *Fig* to rush. **2** *vt* (*dérober*) to steal (**à** from); **v. qn** to rob s.o.; – *vi* to steal. ◆**volant 1** *a* (*tapis etc*) flying; **feuille volante** loose sheet. **2** *nm Aut* (steering) wheel; (*objet*) *Sp* shuttlecock; (*de jupe*) flounce. ◆**volée** *nf* flight; (*groupe d'oiseaux*) flock, flight; (*de coups, flèches etc*) volley; (*suite de* *coups*) thrashing; **lancer à toute v.** to throw as hard as one can; **sonner à toute v.** to peal *ou* ring out. ◆**voleter** *vi* to flutter. ◆**voleur, -euse** *nmf* thief; **au v.!** stop thief!; – *a* thieving.

volet [vɔlɛ] *nm* **1** (*de fenêtre*) shutter. **2** (*de programme, reportage etc*) section, part.

volière [vɔljɛr] *nf* aviary.

volley(-ball) [vɔlɛ(bɔl)] *nm* volleyball. ◆**volleyeur, -euse** *nmf* volleyball player.

volonté [vɔlɔ̃te] *nf* (*faculté, intention*) will; (*désir*) wish; *Phil Psy* free will; **elle a de la v.** she has willpower; **bonne v.** goodwill; **mauvaise v.** ill will; **à v.** at will; (*quantité*) as much as desired. ◆**volontaire** *a* (*délibéré, qui agit librement*) voluntary; (*opiniâtre*) wilful, *Am* willful; – *nmf* volunteer. ◆**volontairement** *adv* voluntarily; (*exprès*) deliberately. ◆**volontiers** [-ɔtje] *adv* willingly, gladly; (*habituellement*) readily; **v.!** (*oui*) I'd love to!

volt [vɔlt] *nm* *Él* volt. ◆**voltage** *nm* voltage.

volte-face [vɔltəfas] *nf inv* about turn, *Am* about face; **faire v.-face** to turn round.

voltige [vɔltiʒ] *nf* acrobatics.

voltiger [vɔltiʒe] *vi* to flutter.

volubile [vɔlybil] *a* (*bavard*) loquacious, voluble.

volume [vɔlym] *nm* (*capacité, intensité, tome*) volume. ◆**volumineux, -euse** *a* bulky, voluminous.

volupté [vɔlypte] *nf* sensual pleasure. ◆**voluptueux, -euse** *a* voluptuous.

vom/ir [vɔmir] *vt* to vomit, bring up; (*exécrer*) *Fig* to loathe; – *vi* to vomit, be sick. ◆**—i** *nm* *Fam* vomit. ◆**—issement** *nm* (*action*) vomiting. ◆**vomitif, -ive** *a* *Fam* nauseating.

vont [vɔ̃] *voir* **aller 1**.

vorace [vɔras] *a* (*appétit, lecteur etc*) voracious.

vos [vo] *voir* **votre**.

vote [vɔt] *nm* (*action*) vote, voting; (*suffrage*) vote; (*de loi*) passing; **bureau de v.** polling station. ◆**voter** *vi* to vote; – *vt* (*loi*) to pass; (*crédits*) to vote. ◆**votant, -ante** *nmf* voter.

votre, *pl* **vos** [vɔtr, vo] *a poss* your. ◆**vôtre** *pron poss* **le** *ou* **la v., les vôtres** yours; **à la v.!** (*toast*) cheers!; – *nmpl* **les vôtres** (*parents etc*) your (own) people.

vouer [vwe] *vt* (*promettre*) to vow (à to); (*consacrer*) to dedicate (à to); (*condamner*) to doom (à to); **se v. à** to dedicate oneself to.

vouloir* [vulwar] *vt* to want (**faire** to do); **je veux qu'il parte** I want him to go; **v. dire** to

mean (**que** that); **je voudrais rester** I'd like to stay; **je voudrais un pain** I'd like a loaf of bread; **voulez-vous me suivre** will you follow me; **si tu veux** if you like *ou* wish; **en v. à qn d'avoir fait qch** to hold it against s.o. for doing sth; **l'usage veut que . . .** (+ *sub*) custom requires that . . . ; **v. du bien à qn** to wish s.o. well; **je veux bien** I don't mind (**faire** doing); **que voulez-vous!** (*résignation*) what can you expect!; **sans le v.** unintentionally; **ça ne veut pas bouger** it won't move; **ne pas v. de qch/de qn** not to want sth/s.o.; **veuillez attendre** kindly wait. ◆**voulu** *a* (*requis*) required; (*délibéré*) deliberate, intentional.

vous [vu] *pron* **1** (*sujet, complément direct*) you; **v. êtes** you are; **il v. connaît** he knows you. **2** (*complément indirect*) (to) you; **il v. l'a donné** he gave it to you, he gave it you. **3** (*réfléchi*), *pl* **vous; v. v. lavez** you wash yourself; you wash yourselves. **4** (*réciproque*) each other; **v. v. aimez** you love each other. ◆**v.-même** *pron* yourself. ◆**v.-mêmes** *pron pl* yourselves.

voûte [vut] *nf* (*plafond*) vault; (*porche*) arch(way). ◆**voûté** *a* (*personne*) bent, stooped.

vouvoyer [vuvwaje] *vt* to address formally (*using vous*).

voyage [vwajaʒ] *nm* trip, journey; (*par mer*) voyage; **aimer les voyages** to like travelling; **faire un v., partir en v.** to go on a trip; **être en v.** to be (away) travelling; **de v.** (*compagnon etc*) travelling-; **bon v.!** have a pleasant trip!; **v. de noces** honeymoon; **v. organisé** (package) tour. ◆**voyager** *vi* to travel. ◆**voyageur, -euse** *nmf* traveller; (*passager*) passenger; **v. de commerce** commercial traveller. ◆**voyagiste** *nm* tour operator.

voyant [vwajɑ̃] **1** *a* gaudy, loud. **2** *nm* (*signal*) (warning) light; (*d'appareil électrique*) pilot light.

voyante [vwajɑ̃t] *nf* clairvoyant.

voyelle [vwajɛl] *nf* vowel.

voyeur, -euse [vwajœr, -øz] *nmf* peeping Tom, voyeur.

voyou [vwaju] *nm* hooligan, hoodlum.

vrac (en) [ɑ̃vrak] *adv* (*en désordre*) haphazardly; (*au poids*) loose, unpackaged.

vrai [vrɛ] *a* true; (*réel*) real; (*authentique*) genuine; – *adv* dire **v.** to be right (in what one says); – *nm* (*vérité*) truth. ◆**—ment** *adv* really.

vraisemblable [vrɛsɑ̃blabl] *a* (*probable*) likely, probable; (*plausible*) plausible. ◆**vraisemblablement** *adv* probably.

◆**vraisemblance** *nf* likelihood; plausibility.

vrille [vrij] *nf* **1** (*outil*) gimlet. **2** *Av* (tail)spin.

vromb/ir [vrɔ̃bir] *vi* to hum. ◆**—issement** *nm* hum(ming).

vu [vy] **1** *voir* **voir**; − *a* **bien vu** well thought of; **mal vu** frowned upon. **2** *prép* in view of; **vu que** seeing that.

vue [vy] *nf* (*spectacle*) sight; (*sens*) (eye)sight; (*panorama, photo, idée*) view; **en v.** (*proche*) in sight; (*en évidence*) on view; (*personne*) *Fig* in the public eye; **avoir en v.** to have in mind; **à v.** (*tirer*) on sight; (*payable*) at sight; **à première v.** at first sight; **de v.** (*connaître*) by sight; **en v. de faire** with a view to doing.

vulgaire [vylgɛr] *a* (*grossier*) vulgar, coarse; (*ordinaire*) common. ◆**—ment** *adv* vulgarly, coarsely; (*appeler*) commonly. ◆**vulgariser** *vt* to popularize. ◆**vulgarité** *nf* vulgarity, coarseness.

vulnérable [vylnerabl] *a* vulnerable. ◆**vulnérabilité** *nf* vulnerability.

W

W, w [dublǝve] *nm* W, w.

wagon [vagɔ̃] *nm* Rail (*de voyageurs*) carriage, coach, *Am* car; (*de marchandises*) wag(g)on, truck, *Am* freight car. ◆**w.-lit** *nm* (*pl* **wagons-lits**) sleeping car, sleeper. ◆**w.-restaurant** *nm* (*pl* **wagons-restaurants**) dining car, diner. ◆**wagonnet** *nm* (small) wagon *ou* truck.

wallon, -onne [walɔ̃, -ɔn] *a* & *nmf* Walloon.

waters [water] *nmpl* toilet.

watt [wat] *nm* *Él* watt.

w-c [(dublǝ)vese] *nmpl* toilet.

week-end [wikɛnd] *nm* weekend.

western [wɛstɛrn] *nm* Cin western.

whisky, *pl* **-ies** [wiski] *nm* whisky, *Am* whiskey.

X

X, x [iks] *nm* X, x; **rayon X** X-ray.

xénophobe [ksenɔfɔb] *a* xenophobic; − *nmf* xenophobe. ◆**xénophobie** *nf* xenophobia.

xérès [gzerɛs] *nm* sherry.

xylophone [ksilɔfɔn] *nm* xylophone.

Y

Y, y¹ [igrɛk] *nm* Y, y.

y² [i] **1** *adv* there; (*dedans*) in it; *pl* in them; (*dessus*) on it; *pl* on them; **elle y vivra** she'll live there; **j'y entrai** I entered (it); **allons-y** let's go; **j'y suis!** (*je comprends*) now I get it!; **je n'y suis pour rien** I have nothing to do with it, that's nothing to do with me. **2** *pron* (= *à cela*) **j'y pense** I think of it; **je m'y attendais** I was expecting it; **ça y est!** that's it!

yacht [jɔt] *nm* yacht.

yaourt [jaur(t)] *nm* yog(h)urt.

yeux [jø] *voir* **œil**.

yiddish [(j)idiʃ] *nm* & *a* Yiddish.

yoga [jɔga] *nm* yoga.

yog(h)ourt [jɔgur(t)] *voir* **yaourt**.

Yougoslavie [jugɔslavi] *nf* Yugoslavia. ◆**yougoslave** *a* & *nmf* Yugoslav(ian).

yo-yo [jojo] *nm inv* yoyo.

Z

Z, z [zɛd] *nm* Z, z.
zèbre [zɛbr] *nm* zebra. ◆**zébré** *a* striped, streaked (**de** with).
zèle [zɛl] *nm* zeal; **faire du z.** to overdo it. ◆**zélé** *a* zealous.
zénith [zenit] *nm* zenith.
zéro [zero] *nm* (*chiffre*) nought, zero; (*dans un numéro*) 0 [ʒʊ]; (*température*) zero; (*rien*) nothing; (*personne*) *Fig* nobody, nonentity; **deux buts à z.** *Fb* two nil, *Am* two zero; **partir de z.** to start from scratch.
zeste [zɛst] *nm* **un z. de citron** (a piece of) lemon peel.
zézayer [zezeje] *vi* to lisp.
zibeline [ziblin] *nf* (*animal*) sable.

zigzag [zigzag] *nm* zigzag; **en z.** (*route etc*) zigzag(ging); ◆**zigzaguer** *vi* to zigzag.
zinc [zɛ̃g] *nm* (*métal*) zinc; (*comptoir*) *Fam* bar.
zizanie [zizani] *nf* discord.
zodiaque [zɔdjak] *nm* zodiac.
zona [zona] *nm Méd* shingles.
zone [zon] *nf* zone, area; (*domaine*) *Fig* sphere; (*faubourgs misérables*) shanty town; **z. bleue** restricted parking zone; **z. industrielle** trading estate, *Am* industrial park.
zoo [zo(o)] *nm* zoo. ◆**zoologie** [zɔɔlɔʒi] *nf* zoology. ◆**zoologique** *a* zoological; **jardin** *ou* **parc z.** zoo.
zoom [zum] *nm* (*objectif*) zoom lens.
zut! [zyt] *int Fam* bother!, heck!

French verb conjugations

REGULAR VERBS

	-ER Verbs	-IR Verbs	-RE Verbs
Infinitive	*donn/er*	*fin/ir*	*vend/re*
1 Present	je donne	je finis	je vends
	tu donnes	tu finis	tu vends
	il donne	il finit	il vend
	nous donnons	nous finissons	nous vendons
	vous donnez	vous finissez	vous vendez
	ils donnent	ils finissent	ils vendent
2 Imperfect	je donnais	je finissais	je vendais
	tu donnais	tu finissais	tu vendais
	il donnait	il finissait	il vendait
	nous donnions	nous finissions	nous vendions
	vous donniez	vous finissiez	vous vendiez
	ils donnaient	ils finissaient	ils vendaient
3 Past historic	je donnai	je finis	je vendis
	tu donnas	tu finis	tu vendis
	il donna	il finit	il vendit
	nous donnâmes	nous finîmes	nous vendîmes
	vous donnâtes	vous finîtes	vous vendîtes
	ils donnèrent	ils finirent	ils vendirent
4 Future	je donnerai	je finirai	je vendrai
	tu donneras	tu finiras	tu vendras
	il donnera	il finira	il vendra
	nous donnerons	nous finirons	nous vendrons
	vous donnerez	vous finirez	vous vendrez
	ils donneront	ils finiront	ils vendront
5 Subjunctive	je donne	je finisse	je vende
	tu donnes	tu finisses	tu vendes
	il donne	il finisse	il vende
	nous donnions	nous finissions	nous vendions
	vous donniez	vous finissiez	vous vendiez
	ils donnent	ils finissent	ils vendent
6 Imperative	donne	finis	vends
	donnons	finissons	vendons
	donnez	finissez	vendez
7 Present participle	donnant	finissant	vendant
8 Past participle	donné	fini	vendu

SPELLING ANOMALIES OF -ER VERBS

Verbs in **-ger** (e.g. **manger**) take an extra **e** before endings beginning with **o** or **a**: *Present* je mange, nous mangeons; *Imperfect* je mangeais, nous mangions; *Past historic* je mangeai, nous mangeâmes; *Present participle* mangeant. Verbs in **-cer** (e.g. **commencer**) change **c** to **ç** before endings beginning with **o** or **a**: *Present* je commence, nous commençons; *Imperfect* je commençais, nous commencions; *Past historic* je commençai, nous commençâmes; *Present participle* commençant. Verbs containing mute **e** in their penultimate syllable fall into two groups. In the first (e.g. **mener**, **peser**, **lever**), **e** becomes **è** before an unpronounced syllable in the present and subjunctive, and in the future and conditional tenses (e.g. je mène, ils mèneront). The second group contains most verbs ending in **-eler** and **-eter** (e.g. **appeler**, **jeter**). These verbs change **l** to **ll** and **t** to **tt** before an unpronounced syllable (e.g. j'appelle, ils appelleront; je jette, ils jetteront). However, the following verbs in **-eler** and **-eter** fall into the first group in which **e** changes to **è** before mute **e** (e.g. je modèle, ils modèleront; j'achète, ils achèteront): **celer**, **ciseler**, **démanteler**, **geler**, **marteler**, **modeler**, **peler**; **acheter**, **crocheter**, **fureter**, **haleter**. Derived verbs (e.g. **dégeler**, **racheter**) are conjugated in the same way. Verbs containing **e** acute in their penultimate syllable change **é** to **è** before the unpronounced endings of the present and subjunctive only (e.g. je cède but je céderai). Verbs in **-yer** (e.g. **essuyer**) change **y** to **i** before an unpronounced syllable in the present and subjunctive, and in the future and conditional tenses (e.g. j'essuie, ils essuieront). In verbs in **-ayer** (e.g. **balayer**), **y** may be retained before mute **e** (e.g. je balaie or balaye, ils balaieront or balayeront).

IRREGULAR VERBS

Listed below are those verbs considered to be the most useful. Forms and tenses not given are fully derivable. Note that the endings of the past historic fall into three categories, the 'a' and 'i' categories shown at *donner*, and at *finir* and *vendre*, and the 'u' category which has the following endings: -us, -ut, -ûmes, -ûtes, -urent. Most of the verbs listed below form their past historic with 'u'. The imperfect may usually be formed by adding -ais, -ait, -ions, -iez, -aient to the stem of the first person plural of the present tense, e.g. 'je buvais' etc may be derived from 'nous buvons' (stem 'buv-' and ending '-ons'); similarly, the present participle may generally be formed by substituting -ant for -ons (e.g. buvant). The future may usually be formed by adding -ai, -as, -a, -ons, -ez, -ont to the infinitive or to an infinitive without final 'e' where the ending is -re (e.g. conduire). The imperative usually has the same forms as the second persons singular and plural and first person plural of the present tense.

1 = Present   2 = Imperfect   3 = Past historic   4 = Future
5 = Subjunctive   6 = Imperative   7 = Present participle
8 = Past participle   n = nous   v = vous   †verbs conjugated with **être** only.

abattre	*like* **battre**
absoudre	1 j'absous, n absolvons 2 j'absolvais
	3 j'absolus (*rarely used*) 5 j'absolve 7 absolvant
	8 absous, absoute
†s'abstenir	*like* **tenir**
abstraire	1 j'abstrais, n abstrayons 2 j'abstrayais 3 *none* 5 j'abstraie
	7 abstrayant 8 abstrait
accourir	*like* **courir**
accroître	*like* **croître** *except* 8 accru
accueillir	*like* **cueillir**
acquérir	1 j'acquiers, n acquérons 2 j'acquérais 3 j'acquis
	4 j'acquerrai 5 j'acquière 7 acquérant 8 acquis
adjoindre	*like* **atteindre**
admettre	*like* **mettre**
†aller	1 je vais, tu vas, il va, n allons, v allez, ils vont 4 j'irai
	5 j'aille, nous allions, ils aillent 6 va, allons, allez (*but note* vas-y)
apercevoir	*like* **recevoir**
apparaître	*like* **connaître**
appartenir	*like* **tenir**
apprendre	*like* **prendre**
asseoir	1 j'assieds, n asseyons, ils asseyent 2 j'asseyais 3 j'assis
	4 j'assiérai 5 j'asseye 7 asseyant 8 assis

astreindre	*like* **atteindre**
atteindre	1 j'atteins, n atteignons, ils atteignent 2 j'atteignais
	3 j'atteignis 4 j'atteindrai 5 j'atteigne 7 atteignant
	8 atteint
avoir	1 j'ai, tu as, il a, n avons, v avez, ils ont 2 j'avais 3 j'eus
	4 j'aurai 5 j'aie, il ait, n ayons, ils aient 6 aie, ayons, ayez
	7 ayant 8 eu
battre	1 je bats, n battons 5 je batte
boire	1 je bois, n buvons, ils boivent 2 je buvais 3 je bus
	5 je boive, n buvions 7 buvant 8 bu
bouillir	1 je bous, n bouillons, ils bouillent 2 je bouillais
	3 *not used* 5 je bouille 7 bouillant
braire	(*defective*) 1 il brait, ils braient 4 il braira, ils brairont
combattre	*like* **battre**
commettre	*like* **mettre**
comparaître	*like* **connaître**
comprendre	*like* **prendre**
compromettre	*like* **mettre**
concevoir	*like* **recevoir**
conclure	1 je conclus, n concluons, ils concluent 5 je conclue
concourir	*like* **courir**
conduire	1 je conduis, n conduisons 3 je conduisis 5 je conduise
	8 conduit
connaître	1 je connais, il connaît, n connaissons 3 je connus
	5 je connaisse 7 connaissant 8 connu
conquérir	*like* **acquérir**
consentir	*like* **mentir**
construire	*like* **conduire**
contenir	*like* **tenir**
contraindre	*like* **atteindre**
contredire	*like* **dire** *except* 1 v contredisez
convaincre	*like* **vaincre**
convenir	*like* **tenir**
corrompre	*like* **rompre**
coudre	1 je couds, n cousons, ils cousent 3 je cousis 5 je couse
	7 cousant 8 cousu
courir	1 je cours, n courons 3 je courus 4 je courrai 5 je coure
	8 couru
couvrir	1 je couvre, n couvrons 2 je couvrais 5 je couvre 8 couvert
craindre	*like* **atteindre**
croire	1 je crois, n croyons, ils croient 2 je croyais 3 je crus
	5 je croie, n croyions 7 croyant 8 cru
croître	1 je crois, il croît, n croissons 2 je croissais 3 je crûs
	5 je croisse 7 croissant 8 crû, crue
cueillir	1 je cueille, n cueillons 2 je cueillais 4 je cueillerai
	5 je cueille 7 cueillant
cuire	1 je cuis, n cuisons 2 je cuisais 3 je cuisis 5 je cuise
	7 cuisant 8 cuit
débattre	*like* **battre**
décevoir	*like* **recevoir**
découvrir	*like* **couvrir**
décrire	*like* **écrire**
décroître	*like* **croître** *except* 8 décru
déduire	*like* **conduire**
défaillir	1 je défaille, n défaillons 2 je défaillais 3 je défaillis
	5 je défaille 7 défaillant 8 défailli

défaire	*like* **faire**
dépeindre	*like* **atteindre**
déplaire	*like* **plaire**
déteindre	*like* **atteindre**
détenir	*like* **tenir**
détruire	*like* **conduire**
†devenir	*like* **tenir**
devoir	1 je dois, n devons, ils doivent 2 je devais 3 je dus 4 je devrai 5 je doive, n devions 6 *not used* 7 devant 8 dû, due, *pl* dus, dues
dire	1 je dis, n disons, v dites 2 je disais 3 je dis 5 je dise 7 disant 8 dit
disparaître	*like* **connaître**
dissoudre	*like* **absoudre**
distraire	*like* **abstraire**
dormir	*like* **mentir**
†échoir	(*defective*) 1 il échoit 3 il échut, ils échurent 4 il échoira 7 échéant 8 échu
écrire	1 j'écris, n écrivons 2 j'écrivais 3 j'écrivis 5 j'écrive 7 écrivant 8 écrit
élire	*like* **lire**
émettre	*like* **mettre**
émouvoir	*like* **mouvoir** *except* 8 ému
encourir	*like* **courir**
endormir	*like* **mentir**
enduire	*like* **conduire**
enfreindre	*like* **atteindre**
†s'enfuir	*like* **fuir**
†s'ensuivre	*like* **suivre** (*but third person only*)
entreprendre	*like* **prendre**
entretenir	*like* **tenir**
entrevoir	*like* **voir**
entrouvrir	*like* **couvrir**
envoyer	4 j'enverrai
†s'éprendre	*like* **prendre**
éteindre	*like* **atteindre**
être	1 je suis, tu es, il est, n sommes, v êtes, ils sont 2 j'étais 3 je fus 4 je serai 5 je sois, n soyons, ils soient 6 sois, soyons, soyez 7 étant 8 été
exclure	*like* **conclure**
extraire	*like* **abstraire**
faillir	(*defective*) 3 je faillis 4 je faillirai 8 failli
faire	1 je fais, n faisons, v faites, ils font 2 je faisais 3 je fis 4 je ferai 5 je fasse 7 faisant 8 fait
falloir	(*impersonal*) 1 il faut 2 il fallait 3 il fallut 4 il faudra 5 il faille 6 *none* 7 *none* 8 fallu
feindre	*like* **atteindre**
foutre	1 je fous, n foutons 2 je foutais 3 *none* 5 je foute 7 foutant 8 foutu
frire	(*defective*) 1 je fris, tu fris, il frit 4 je frirai (*rare*) 6 fris (*rare*) 8 frit (*for other persons and tenses use* faire frire)
fuir	1 je fuis, n fuyons, ils fuient 2 je fuyais 3 je fuis 5 je fuie 7 fuyant 8 fui
haïr	1 je hais, il hait, n haïssons
inclure	*like* **conclure**
induire	*like* **conduire**
inscrire	*like* **écrire**

instruire	*like* **conduire**
interdire	*like* **dire** *except* 1 v interdisez
interrompre	*like* **rompre**
intervenir	*like* **tenir**
introduire	*like* **conduire**
joindre	*like* **atteindre**
lire	1 je lis, n lisons 2 je lisais 3 je lus 5 je lise 7 lisant 8 lu
luire	*like* **nuire**
maintenir	*like* **tenir**
maudire	1 je maudis, n maudissons 2 je maudissais 3 je maudis 4 je maudirai 5 je maudisse 7 maudissant 8 maudit
méconnaître	*like* **connaître**
médire	*like* **dire** *except* 1 v médisez
mentir	1 je mens, n mentons 2 je mentais 5 je mente 7 mentant
mettre	1 je mets, n mettons 2 je mettais 3 je mis 5 je mette 7 mettant 8 mis
moudre	1 je mouds, n moulons 2 je moulais 3 je moulus 5 je moule 7 moulant 8 moulu
†mourir	1 je meurs, n mourons, ils meurent 2 je mourais 3 je mourus 4 je mourrai 5 je meure, n mourions 7 mourant 8 mort
mouvoir	1 je meus, n mouvons, ils meuvent 2 je mouvais 3 je mus (*rare*) 4 je mouvrai 5 je meuve, n mouvions 8 mû, mue, *pl* mus, mues
†naître	1 je nais, il naît, n naissons 2 je naissais 3 je naquis 4 je naîtrai 5 je naisse 7 naissant 8 né
nuire	1 je nuis, n nuisons 2 je nuisais 3 je nuisis 5 je nuise 7 nuisant 8 nui
obtenir	*like* **tenir**
offrir	*like* **couvrir**
omettre	*like* **mettre**
ouvrir	*like* **couvrir**
paître	(*defective*) 1 il paît 2 il paissait 3 *none* 4 il paîtra 5 il paisse 7 paissant 8 *none*
paraître	*like* **connaître**
parcourir	*like* **courir**
†partir	*like* **mentir**
†parvenir	*like* **tenir**
peindre	*like* **atteindre**
percevoir	*like* **recevoir**
permettre	*like* **mettre**
plaindre	*like* **atteindre**
plaire	1 je plais, n plaisons 2 je plaisais 3 je plus 5 je plaise 7 plaisant 8 plu
pleuvoir	(*impersonal*) 1 il pleut 2 il pleuvait 3 il plut 4 il pleuvra 5 il pleuve 6 *none* 7 pleuvant 8 plu
poursuivre	*like* **suivre**
pourvoir	*like* **voir** *except* 4 je pourvoirai
pouvoir	1 je peux *or* je puis, tu peux, il peut, n pouvons, ils peuvent 2 je pouvais 3 je pus 4 je pourrai 5 je puisse 6 *not used* 7 pouvant 8 pu
prédire	*like* **dire** *except* 1 v prédisez
prendre	1 je prends, n prenons, ils prennent 2 je prenais 3 je pris 5 je prenne 7 prenant 8 pris
prescrire	*like* **écrire**
pressentir	*like* **mentir**

prévenir	*like* tenir
prévoir	*like* voir *except* 4 je prévoirai
produire	*like* conduire
promettre	*like* mettre
promouvoir	*like* mouvoir *except* 8 promu
proscrire	*like* écrire
†provenir	*like* tenir
rabattre	*like* battre
rasseoir	*like* asseoir
recevoir	1 je reçois, n recevons, ils reçoivent 2 je recevais 3 je reçus 4 je recevrai 5 je reçoive, n recevions, ils reçoivent 7 recevant 8 reçu
reconnaître	*like* connaître
reconduire	*like* conduire
reconstruire	*like* conduire
recoudre	*like* coudre
recourir	*like* courir
recouvrir	*like* couvrir
recueillir	*like* cueillir
†redevenir	*like* tenir
redire	*like* dire
réduire	*like* conduire
refaire	*like* faire
rejoindre	*like* atteindre
relire	*like* lire
remettre	*like* mettre
†renaître	*like* naître
rendormir	*like* mentir
renvoyer	*like* envoyer
†repartir	*like* mentir
repentir	*like* mentir
reprendre	*like* prendre
reproduire	*like* conduire
résoudre	1 je résous, n résolvons 2 je résolvais 3 je résolus 5 je résolve 7 résolvant 8 résolu
ressentir	*like* mentir
ressortir	*like* mentir
restreindre	*like* atteindre
retenir	*like* tenir
†revenir	*like* tenir
revêtir	*like* vêtir
revivre	*like* vivre
revoir	*like* voir
rire	1 je ris, n rions 2 je riais 3 je ris 5 je rie, n riions 7 riant 8 ri
rompre	*regular except* 1 il rompt
rouvrir	*like* couvrir
satisfaire	*like* faire
savoir	1 je sais, n savons, il savent 2 je savais 3 je sus 4 je saurai 5 je sache 6 sache, sachons, sachez 7 sachant 8 su
séduire	*like* conduire
sentir	*like* mentir
servir	*like* mentir
sortir	*like* mentir
souffrir	*like* couvrir
soumettre	*like* mettre
sourire	*like* rire

souscrire	*like* **écrire**
soustraire	*like* **abstraire**
soutenir	*like* **tenir**
†se souvenir	*like* **tenir**
subvenir	*like* **tenir**
suffire	1 je suffis, n suffisons 2 je suffisais 3 je suffis 5 je suffise 7 suffisant 8 suffi
suivre	1 je suis, n suivons 2 je suivais 3 je suivis 5 je suive 7 suivant 8 suivi
surprendre	*like* **prendre**
†survenir	*like* **tenir**
survivre	*like* **vivre**
taire	1 je tais, n taisons 2 je taisais 3 je tus 5 je taise 7 taisant 8 tu
teindre	*like* **atteindre**
tenir	1 je tiens, n tenons, ils tiennent 2 je tenais 3 je tins, tu tins, il tint, n tînmes, v tîntes, ils tinrent 4 je tiendrai 5 je tienne 7 tenant 8 tenu
traduire	*like* **conduire**
traire	*like* **abstraire**
transcrire	*like* **écrire**
transmettre	*like* **mettre**
transparaître	*like* **connaître**
tressaillir	*like* **défaillir**
vaincre	1 je vaincs, il vainc, n vainquons 2 je vainquais 3 je vainquis 5 je vainque 7 vainquant 8 vaincu
valoir	1 je vaux, n valons 2 je valais 3 je valus 4 je vaudrai 5 je vaille 6 *not used* 7 valant 8 valu
†venir	*like* **tenir**
vêtir	1 je vêts, n vêtons 2 je vêtais 5 je vête 7 vêtant 8 vêtu
vivre	1 je vis, n vivons 2 je vivais 3 je vécus 5 je vive 7 vivant 8 vécu
voir	1 je vois, n voyons 2 je voyais 3 je vis 4 je verrai 5 je voie, n voyions 7 voyant 8 vu
vouloir	1 je veux, n voulons, ils veulent 2 je voulais 3 je voulus 4 je voudrai 5 je veuille 6 veuille, veuillons, veuillez 7 voulant 8 voulu.

Verbes anglais irréguliers

Infinitif	Prétérit	Participe passé
arise	arose	arisen
be	was, were	been
bear	bore	borne
beat	beat	beaten
become	became	become
begin	began	begun
bend	bent	bent
bet	bet, betted	bet, betted
bid	bade, bid	bidden, bid
bind	bound	bound
bite	bit	bitten
bleed	bled	bled
blow	blew	blown
break	broke	broken
breed	bred	bred

bring	brought	brought
broadcast	broadcast	broadcast
build	built	built
burn	burnt, burned	burnt, burned
burst	burst	burst
buy	bought	bought
cast	cast	cast
catch	caught	caught
choose	chose	chosen
cling	clung	clung
come	came	come
cost	cost	cost
creep	crept	crept
cut	cut	cut
deal	dealt	dealt
dig	dug	dug
dive	dived, *Am* dove	dived
do	did	done
draw	drew	drawn
dream	dreamed, dreamt	dreamed, dreamt
drink	drank	drunk
drive	drove	driven
dwell	dwelt	dwelt
eat	ate [et, *Am* eɪt]	eaten
fall	fell	fallen
feed	fed	fed
feel	felt	felt
fight	fought	fought
find	found	found
fling	flung	flung
fly	flew	flown
forbid	forbad(e)	forbidden
forecast	forecast	forecast
foresee	foresaw	foreseen
forget	forgot	forgotten
forgive	forgave	forgiven
forsake	forsook (*rare*)	forsaken
freeze	froze	frozen
get	got	got, *Am* gotten
give	gave	given
go	went	gone
grind	ground	ground
grow	grew	grown
hang	hung, hanged	hung, hanged
have	had	had
hear	heard	heard
hide	hid	hidden
hit	hit	hit
hold	held	held
hurt	hurt	hurt
keep	kept	kept
kneel	knelt, kneeled	knelt, kneeled
know	knew	known
lay	laid	laid
lead	led	led
lean	leant, leaned	leant, leaned
leap	leapt, leaped	leapt, leaped

learn	learnt, learned	learnt, learned.
leave	left	left
lend	lent	lent
let	let	let
lie	lay	lain
light	lit, lighted	lit, lighted
lose	lost	lost
make	made	made
mean	meant	meant
meet	met	met
mislay	mislaid	mislaid
mislead	misled	misled
misunderstand	misunderstood	misunderstood
mow	mowed	mown, mowed
overcome	overcame	overcome
pay	paid	paid
put	put	put
quit	quit, quitted	quit, quitted
read	read [red]	read [red]
rid	rid	rid
ride	rode	ridden
ring	rang	rung
rise	rose	risen
run	ran	run
saw	sawed	sawn, sawed
say	said	said
see	saw	seen
seek	sought	sought
sell	sold	sold
send	sent	sent
set	set	set
sew	sewed	sewn, sewed
shake	shook	shaken
shed	shed	shed
shine	shone ([ʃɒn, *Am* ʃəʊn])	shone ([ʃɒn, *Am* ʃəʊn])
shoot	shot	shot
show	showed	shown, showed
shrink	shrank	shrunk, shrunken
shut	shut	shut
sing	sang	sung
sink	sank	sunk
sit	sat	sat
sleep	slept	slept
slide	slid	slid
sling	slung	slung
slit	slit	slit
smell	smelt, smelled	smelt, smelled
sow	sowed	sown, sowed
speak	spoke	spoken
speed	sped, speeded	sped, speeded
spell	spelt, spelled	spelt, spelled
spend	spent	spent
spill	spilt, spilled	spilt, spilled
spin	spun	spun
spit	spat, spit	spat, spit
split	split	split
spoil	spoilt, spoiled	spoilt, spoiled

spread	spread	spread
spring	sprang	sprung
stand	stood	stood
steal	stole	stolen
stick	stuck	stuck
sting	stung	stung
stink	stank, stunk	stunk
stride	strode	stridden (*rare*)
strike	struck	struck
string	strung	strung
strive	strove	striven
swear	swore	sworn
sweep	swept	swept
swell	swelled	swollen, swelled
swim	swam	swum
swing	swung	swung
take	took	taken
teach	taught	taught
tear	tore	torn
tell	told	told
think	thought	thought
throw	threw	thrown
thrust	thrust	thrust
tread	trod	trodden
undergo	underwent	undergone
understand	understood	understood
undertake	undertook	undertaken
upset	upset	upset
wake	woke	woken
wear	wore	worn
weave	wove	woven
weep	wept	wept
win	won	won
wind	wound	wound
withdraw	withdrew	withdrawn
withhold	withheld	withheld
withstand	withstood	withstood
wring	wrung	wrung
write	wrote	written

Numerals

Cardinal numbers

nought	0
one	1
two	2
three	3
four	4
five	5
six	6
seven	7
eight	8
nine	9
ten	10

Les nombres

Les nombres cardinaux

zéro
un
deux
trois
quatre
cinq
six
sept
huit
neuf
dix

eleven	11	onze
twelve	12	douze
thirteen	13	treize
fourteen	14	quatorze
fifteen	15	quinze
sixteen	16	seize
seventeen	17	dix-sept
eighteen	18	dix-huit
nineteen	19	dix-neuf
twenty	20	vingt
twenty-one	21	vingt et un
twenty-two	22	vingt-deux
thirty	30	trente
forty	40	quarante
fifty	50	cinquante
sixty	60	soixante
seventy	70	soixante-dix
seventy-five	75	soixante-quinze
eighty	80	quatre-vingts
eighty-one	81	quatre-vingt-un
ninety	90	quatre-vingt-dix
ninety-one	91	quatre-vingt-onze
a *or* one hundred	100	cent
a hundred and one	101	cent un
a hundred and two	102	cent deux
a hundred and fifty	150	cent cinquante
two hundred	200	deux cents
two hundred and one	201	deux cent un
two hundred and two	202	deux cent deux
a *or* one thousand	1,000 (1 000)	mille
a thousand and one	1,001 (1 001)	mille un
a thousand and two	1,002 (1 002)	mille deux
two thousand	2,000 (2 000)	deux mille
a *or* one million	1,000,000 (1 000 000)	un million

Ordinal numbers

Les nombres ordinaux

first	1st	1er	premier
second	2nd	2e	deuxième
third	3rd	3e	troisième
fourth	4th	4e	quatrième
fifth	5th	5e	cinquième
sixth	6th	6e	sixième
seventh	7th	7e	septième
eighth	8th	8e	huitième
ninth	9th	9e	neuvième
tenth	10th	10e	dixième
eleventh	11th	11e	onzième
twelfth	12th	12e	douzième
thirteenth	13th	13e	treizième
fourteenth	14th	14e	quatorzième
fifteenth	15th	15e	quinzième
twentieth	20th	20e	vingtième
twenty-first	21st	21e	vingt et unième
twenty-second	22nd	22e	vingt deuxième
thirtieth	30th	30e	trentième

Examples of usage

three (times) out of ten — *trois (fois) sur dix*
ten at a time, in *or* by tens, ten by ten — *dix par dix, dix à dix*
the ten of us/you, we ten/you ten — *nous dix/vous dix*
all ten of them *or* us *or* you — *tous les dix, toutes les dix*
there are ten of us/them — *nous sommes dix/elles sont dix*
(between) the ten of them — *à eux dix, à elles dix*
ten of them came/were living together — *ils sont venus/ils vivaient à dix*
page ten — *page dix*
Charles the Tenth — *Charles Dix*
to live at number ten — *habiter au (numéro) dix*
to be the tenth to arrive/to leave — *arriver/partir le dixième*
to come tenth, be tenth *(in a race)* — *arriver dixième, être dixième*
it's the tenth (today) — *nous sommes le dix (aujourd'hui)*
the tenth of May, May the tenth, *Am* May tenth — *le dix mai*
to arrive/be paid/*etc* on the tenth — *arriver/être payé/etc le dix*
to arrive/be paid/*etc* on the tenth of May *or* on May the tenth *or Am* on May tenth — *arriver/être payé/etc le dix mai*
by the tenth, before the tenth — *avant le dix, pour le dix*
it's ten (o'clock) — *il est dix heures*
it's half past ten — *il est dix heures et demie*
ten past ten, *Am* ten after ten — *dix heures dix*
ten to ten — *dix heures moins dix*
by ten (o'clock), before ten (o'clock) — *pour dix heures, avant dix heures*
to be ten (years old) — *avoir dix ans*
a child of ten, a ten-year-old (child) — *un enfant de dix ans*

Days and months

Les jours et les mois

Monday *lundi*; Tuesday *mardi*; Wednesday *mercredi*; Thursday *jeudi*; Friday *vendredi*; Saturday *samedi*; Sunday *dimanche*

January *janvier*; February *février*; March *mars*; April *avril*; May *mai*; June *juin*; July *juillet*; August *août*; September *septembre*; October *octobre*; November *novembre*; December *décembre*

Examples of usage

Exemples d'emplois

on Monday (*e.g.* he arrives on Monday) — *lundi (par exemple il arrive lundi)*
(on) Mondays — *le lundi*
see you on Monday! — *à lundi!*
by Monday, before Monday — *avant lundi, pour lundi*
Monday morning/evening — *lundi matin/soir*
a week/two weeks on Monday, *Am* a week/two weeks from Monday — *lundi en huit/en quinze*
it's Monday (today) — *nous sommes (aujourd'hui) lundi*
Monday the tenth of May, Monday May the tenth, *Am* Monday May tenth — *(le) lundi dix mai*
on Monday the tenth of May, on Monday May the tenth *or Am* May tenth — *le lundi dix mai*
tomorrow is Tuesday — *demain c'est mardi*
in May — *en mai, au mois de mai*
every May, each May — *tous les ans en mai, chaque année en mai*
by May, before May — *avant mai, pour mai*

A

A, a [eɪ] *n* A, a *m*; **5A** (*number*) 5 bis; **A1** (*dinner etc*) *Fam* super, superbe; **to go from A to B** aller du point A au point B.

a [ə, *stressed* eɪ] (*before vowel or mute h* **an** [ən, *stressed* æn]) *indef art* **1** un, une; **a man** un homme; **an apple** une pomme. **2** (= *def art in Fr*) **six pence a kilo** six pence le kilo; **50 km an hour** 50 km à l'heure; **I have a broken arm** j'ai le bras cassé. **3** (*art omitted in Fr*) **he's a doctor** il est médecin; **Caen, a town in Normandy** Caen, ville de Normandie; **what a man!** quel homme! **4** (*a certain*) **a Mr Smith** un certain M. Smith. **5** (*time*) **twice a month** deux fois par mois. **6** (*some*) **to make a noise/a fuss** faire du bruit/des histoires.

aback [əˈbæk] *adv* **taken a.** déconcerté.

abandon [əˈbændən] **1** *vt* abandonner. **2** *n* (*freedom of manner*) laisser-aller *m*, abandon *m*. ◆**—ment** *n* abandon *m*.

abase [əˈbeɪs] *vt* **to a. oneself** s'humilier, s'abaisser.

abashed [əˈbæʃt] *a* confus, gêné.

abate [əˈbeɪt] *vi* (*of storm, pain*) se calmer; (*of flood*) baisser; — *vt* diminuer, réduire. ◆**—ment** *n* diminution *f*, réduction *f*.

abbey [ˈæbɪ] *n* abbaye *f*.

abbot [ˈæbət] *n* abbé *m*. ◆**abbess** *n* abbesse *f*.

abbreviate [əˈbriːvɪeɪt] *vt* abréger. ◆**abbreviˈation** *n* abréviation *f*.

abdicate [ˈæbdɪkeɪt] *vti* abdiquer. ◆**abdiˈcation** *n* abdication *f*.

abdomen [ˈæbdəmən] *n* abdomen *m*. ◆**abˈdominal** *a* abdominal.

abduct [æbˈdʌkt] *vt* *Jur* enlever. ◆**abduction** *n* enlèvement *m*, rapt *m*.

aberration [æbəˈreɪʃ(ə)n] *n* (*folly, lapse*) aberration *f*.

abet [əˈbet] *vt* (**-tt-**) **to aid and a. s.o.** *Jur* être le complice de qn.

abeyance [əˈbeɪəns] *n* **in a.** (*matter*) en suspens.

abhor [əbˈhɔːr] *vt* (**-rr-**) avoir horreur de, exécrer. ◆**abhorrent** *a* exécrable. ◆**abhorrence** *n* horreur *f*.

abide [əˈbaɪd] **1** *vi* **to a. by** (*promise etc*) rester fidèle à. **2** *vt* supporter; **I can't a. him** je ne peux pas le supporter.

ability [əˈbɪlətɪ] *n* capacité *f* (**to do** pour faire), aptitude *f* (**to do** à faire); **to the best of my a.** de mon mieux.

abject [ˈæbdʒekt] *a* abject; **a. poverty** la misère.

ablaze [əˈbleɪz] *a* en feu; **a. with** (*light*) resplendissant de; (*anger*) enflammé de.

able [ˈeɪb(ə)l] *a* (**-er, -est**) capable, compétent; **to be a. to do** être capable de faire, pouvoir faire; **to be a. to swim/drive** savoir nager/conduire. ◆**a.-ˈbodied** *a* robuste. ◆**ably** *adv* habilement.

ablutions [əˈbluːʃ(ə)nz] *npl* ablutions *fpl*.

abnormal [æbˈnɔːm(ə)l] *a* anormal. ◆**abnorˈmality** *n* anomalie *f*; (*of body*) difformité *f*. ◆**abnormally** *adv* *Fig* exceptionnellement.

aboard [əˈbɔːd] *adv* *Nau* à bord; **all a.** *Rail* en voiture; — *prep* **a. the ship** à bord du navire; **a. the train** dans le train.

abode [əˈbəʊd] *n* (*house*) *Lit* demeure *f*; *Jur* domicile *m*.

abolish [əˈbɒlɪʃ] *vt* supprimer, abolir. ◆**aboˈlition** *n* suppression *f*, abolition *f*.

abominable [əˈbɒmɪnəb(ə)l] *a* abominable. ◆**abomiˈnation** *n* abomination *f*.

aboriginal [æbəˈrɪdʒən(ə)l] *a* & *n* aborigène (*m*). ◆**aborigines** *npl* aborigènes *mpl*.

abort [əˈbɔːt] *vt* *Med* faire avorter; (*space flight, computer program*) abandonner; — *vi* *Med* & *Fig* avorter. ◆**abortion** *n* avortement *m*; **to have an a.** se faire avorter. ◆**abortive** *a* (*plan etc*) manqué, avorté.

abound [əˈbaʊnd] *vi* abonder (**in, with** en).

about [əˈbaʊt] *adv* **1** (*approximately*) à peu près, environ; (**at**) **a. two o'clock** vers deux heures. **2** (*here and there*) çà et là, ici et là; (*ideas, flu*) dans l'air; (*rumour*) en circulation; **to look a.** regarder autour; **to follow a.** suivre partout; **to bustle a.** s'affairer; **there are lots a.** il en existe beaucoup; (**out and**) **a.** (*after illness*) sur pied, guéri; (**up and**) **a.** (*out of bed*) levé, debout; **a. turn, a. face** *Mil* demi-tour *m*; *Fig* volte-face *f inv*; — *prep* **1** (*around*) **a. the garden** autour du jardin; **a. the streets** par *or* dans les rues. **2** (*near to*) **a. here** par ici. **3** (*concerning*) au sujet de; **to talk a.** parler de; **a book a. un** livre sur; **what's it (all) a.?** de quoi s'agit-il?; **while you're a. it** pendant que vous y êtes; **what** or **how a. me?** et moi alors?; **what** or **how a. a drink?** que dirais-tu de prendre un verre? **4** (+ *inf*) **a. to do** sur le point de faire; **I was a. to say** j'étais sur le point de dire, j'allais dire.

above [ə'bʌv] *adv* au-dessus; (*in book*) ci-dessus; **from a.** d'en haut; **floor a.** étage *m* supérieur or du dessus; – *prep* au-dessus de; **a. all** par-dessus tout, surtout; **a. the bridge** (*on river*) en amont du pont; **he's a. me** (*in rank*) c'est mon supérieur; **a. lying** incapable de mentir; **a. asking** trop fier pour demander. ◆**a.-'mentioned** *a* susmentionné. ◆**aboveboard** *a* ouvert, honnête; – *adv* sans tricherie, cartes sur table.

abrasion [ə'breɪʒ(ə)n] *n* frottement *m*; *Med* écorchure *f*. ◆**abrasive** *a* (*substance*) abrasif; (*rough*) *Fig* rude, dur; (*irritating*) agaçant; – *n* abrasif *m*.

abreast [ə'brest] *adv* côte à côte, de front; **four a.** par rangs de quatre; **to keep a. of** or **with** se tenir au courant de.

abridge [ə'brɪdʒ] *vt* (*book etc*) abréger. ◆**abridg(e)ment** *n* abrégement *m* (**of** de); (*abridged version*) abrégé *m*.

abroad [ə'brɔːd] *adv* **1** (*in or to a foreign country*) à l'étranger; **from a.** de l'étranger. **2** (*over a wide area*) de tous côtés; **rumour a.** bruit *m* qui court.

abrogate ['æbrəgeɪt] *vt* abroger.

abrupt [ə'brʌpt] *a* (*sudden*) brusque; (*person*) brusque, abrupt; (*slope, style*) abrupt. ◆**—ly** *adv* (*suddenly*) brusquement; (*rudely*) avec brusquerie.

abscess ['æbses] *n* abcès *m*.

abscond [əb'skɒnd] *vi* *Jur* s'enfuir.

absence ['æbsəns] *n* absence *f*; **in the a. of sth** à défaut de qch, faute de qch; **a. of mind** distraction *f*.

absent ['æbsənt] *a* absent (**from** de); (*look*) distrait; – [æb'sent] *vt* **to a. oneself** s'absenter. ◆**a.-'minded** *a* distrait. ◆**a.-'mindedness** *n* distraction *f*. ◆**absen'tee** *n* absent, -ente *mf*. ◆**absen'teeism** *n* absentéisme *m*.

absolute ['æbsəluːt] *a* absolu; (*proof etc*) indiscutable; (*coward etc*) parfait, véritable. ◆**—ly** *adv* absolument; (*forbidden*) formellement.

absolve [əb'zɒlv] *vt* *Rel* *Jur* absoudre; **to a. from** (*vow*) libérer de. ◆**absolution** [æbsə'luːʃ(ə)n] *n* absolution *f*.

absorb [əb'zɔːb] *vt* absorber; (*shock*) amortir; **to become absorbed in** (*work*) s'absorber dans. ◆**—ing** *a* (*work*)

absorbant; (*book, film*) prenant. ◆**absorbent** *a* & *n* absorbant (*m*); **a. cotton** *Am* coton *m* hydrophile. ◆**absorber** *n* **shock a.** *Aut* amortisseur *m*. ◆**absorption** *n* absorption *f*.

abstain [əb'steɪn] *vi* s'abstenir (**from** de). ◆**abstemious** *a* sobre, frugal. ◆**abstention** *n* abstention *f*. ◆**'abstinence** *n* abstinence *f*.

abstract ['æbstrækt] **1** *a* & *n* abstrait (*m*). **2** *n* (*summary*) résumé *m*. **3** [əb'strækt] *vt* (*remove*) retirer; (*notion*) abstraire. ◆**ab'straction** *n* (*idea*) abstraction *f*; (*absent-mindedness*) distraction *f*.

abstruse [əb'struːs] *a* obscur.

absurd [əb'sɜːd] *a* absurde, ridicule. ◆**absurdity** *n* absurdité *f*. ◆**absurdly** *adv* absurdement.

abundant [ə'bʌndənt] *a* abondant. ◆**abundance** *n* abondance *f*. ◆**abundantly** *adv* **a. clear** tout à fait clair.

abuse [ə'bjuːs] *n* (*abusing*) abus *m* (**of** de); (*curses*) injures *fpl*; – [ə'bjuːz] *vt* (*misuse*) abuser de; (*malign*) dire du mal de; (*insult*) injurier. ◆**abusive** [ə'bjuːsɪv] *a* injurieux.

abysmal [ə'bɪzm(ə)l] *a* (*bad*) *Fam* désastreux, exécrable.

abyss [ə'bɪs] *n* abîme *m*.

acacia [ə'keɪʃə] *n* (*tree*) acacia *m*.

academic [ækə'demɪk] *a* universitaire; (*scholarly*) érudit, intellectuel; (*issue etc*) *Pej* théorique; (*style, art*) académique; – *n* (*teacher*) *Univ* universitaire *mf*.

academy [ə'kædəmɪ] *n* (*society*) académie *f*; *Mil* *Mus* école *f*. ◆**acade'mician** *n* académicien, -ienne *mf*.

accede [ək'siːd] *vi* **to a. to** (*request, throne, position*) accéder à.

accelerate [ək'seləreɪt] *vt* accélérer; – *vi* s'accélérer; *Aut* accélérer. ◆**accele-'ration** *n* accélération *f*. ◆**accelerator** *n* *Aut* accélérateur *m*.

accent ['æksənt] *n* accent *m*; – [æk'sent] *vt* accentuer. ◆**accentuate** [æk'sentʃueɪt] *vt* accentuer.

accept [ək'sept] *vt* accepter. ◆**—ed** *a* (*opinion etc*) reçu, admis. ◆**acceptable** *a* (*worth accepting, tolerable*) acceptable. ◆**acceptance** *n* acceptation *f*; (*approval, favour*) accueil *m* favorable.

access ['ækses] *n* accès *m* (**to sth** à qch, **to s.o.** auprès de qn). ◆**ac'cessible** *a* accessible.

accession [æk'seʃ(ə)n] *n* accession *f* (**to** à); (*increase*) augmentation *f*; (*sth added*) nouvelle acquisition *f*.

accessory [ək'sesərɪ] **1** n (*person*) Jur complice mf. **2** npl (*objects*) accessoires mpl.

accident ['æksɪdənt] n accident m; **by a.** (*by chance*) par accident; (*unintentionally*) accidentellement, sans le vouloir. ◆**a.-prone** a prédisposé aux accidents. ◆**acci'dental** a accidentel, fortuit. ◆**acci'dentally** adv accidentellement, par mégarde; (*by chance*) par accident.

acclaim [ə'kleɪm] vt acclamer; **to a. king** proclamer roi. ◆**accla'mation** n acclamation(s) f(pl), louange(s) f(pl).

acclimate ['æklɪmeɪt] vti Am = **acclimatize**. ◆**a'cclimatize** vt acclimater; – vi s'acclimater. ◆**accli'mation** n Am, ◆**acclimati'zation** n acclimatisation f.

accolade ['ækəleɪd] n (*praise*) Fig louange f.

accommodat/e [ə'kɒmədeɪt] vt (*of house*) loger, recevoir; (*have room for*) avoir de la place pour (mettre); (*adapt*) adapter (**to** à); (*supply*) fournir (**s.o. with sth** qch à qn); (*oblige*) rendre service à; (*reconcile*) concilier; **to a. oneself to** s'accommoder à. ◆**—ing** a accommodant, obligeant. ◆**accommo'dation** n **1** (*lodging*) logement m; (*rented room or rooms*) chambre(s) f(pl); pl (*in hotel*) Am chambre(s) f(pl). **2** (*compromise*) compromis m, accommodement m.

accompany [ə'kʌmpənɪ] vt accompagner. ◆**accompaniment** n accompagnement m. ◆**accompanist** n Mus accompagnateur, -trice mf.

accomplice [ə'kʌmplɪs] n complice mf.

accomplish [ə'kʌmplɪʃ] vt (*task, duty*) accomplir; (*aim*) réaliser. ◆**—ed** a accompli. ◆**—ment** n accomplissement m; (*of aim*) réalisation f; (*thing achieved*) réalisation f; (*skills*) talents mpl.

accord [ə'kɔːd] **1** n accord m; **of my own a.** volontairement, de mon plein gré; – vi concorder. **2** vt (*grant*) accorder. ◆**accordance** n **in a. with** conformément à.

according to [ə'kɔːdɪŋtuː] prep selon, d'après, suivant. ◆**accordingly** adv en conséquence.

accordion [ə'kɔːdɪən] n accordéon m.

accost [ə'kɒst] vt accoster, aborder.

account [ə'kaʊnt] **1** n Com compte m; pl comptabilité f, comptes mpl; **accounts department** comptabilité f; **to take into a.** tenir compte de; **ten pounds on a.** un acompte de dix livres; **of some a.** d'une certaine importance; **on a. of** à cause de; **on**

no a. en aucun cas. **2** n (*report*) compte rendu m, récit m; (*explanation*) explication f; **by all accounts** au dire de tous; **to give a good a. of oneself** s'en tirer à son avantage; – vi **to a. for** (*explain*) expliquer; (*give reckoning of*) rendre compte de. **3** vt **to a. oneself lucky/etc** (*consider*) se considérer heureux/etc. ◆**accountable** a responsable (**for** de, **to** devant); (*explainable*) explicable.

accountant [ə'kaʊntənt] n comptable mf. ◆**accountancy** n comptabilité f.

accoutrements [ə'kuːtrəmənts] (*Am* **accouterments** [ə'kuːtəmənts]) npl équipement m.

accredit [ə'kredɪt] vt (*ambassador*) accréditer; **to a. s.o. with sth** attribuer qch à qn.

accrue [ə'kruː] vi (*of interest*) Fin s'accumuler; **to a. to** (*of advantage etc*) revenir à.

accumulate [ə'kjuːmjʊleɪt] vt accumuler, amasser; – vi s'accumuler. ◆**accumu'lation** n accumulation f; (*mass*) amas m. ◆**accumulator** n El accumulateur m.

accurate ['ækjʊrət] a exact, précis. ◆**accuracy** n exactitude f, précision f. ◆**accurately** adv avec précision.

accursed [ə'kɜːsɪd] a maudit, exécrable.

accus/e [ə'kjuːz] vt accuser (**of** de). ◆**—ed** n **the a.** Jur l'inculpé, -ée mf, l'accusé, -ée mf. ◆**—ing** a accusateur. ◆**accu'sation** n accusation f.

accustom [ə'kʌstəm] vt habituer, accoutumer. ◆**—ed** a habitué (**to sth** à qch, **to doing** à faire); **to get a. to** s'habituer à, s'accoutumer à.

ace [eɪs] n (*card, person*) as m.

acetate ['æsɪteɪt] n acétate m.

acetic [ə'siːtɪk] a acétique.

ache [eɪk] n douleur f, mal m; **to have an a. in one's arm** avoir mal au bras; – vi faire mal; **my head aches** ma tête me fait mal; **it makes my heart a.** cela me serre le cœur; **to be aching to do** brûler de faire. ◆**aching** a douloureux.

achieve [ə'tʃiːv] vt accomplir, réaliser; (*success, aim*) atteindre; (*victory*) remporter. ◆**—ment** n accomplissement m, réalisation f (**of** de); (*feat*) réalisation f, exploit m.

acid ['æsɪd] a & n acide (m). ◆**a'cidity** n acidité f.

acknowledge [ək'nɒlɪdʒ] vt reconnaître (**as** pour); (*greeting*) répondre à; **to a. (receipt of)** accuser réception de; **to a. defeat** s'avouer vaincu. ◆**—ment** n reconnaissance f; (*of letter*) accusé m de réception; (*receipt*) reçu m, récépissé m.

acme ['ækmɪ] *n* sommet *m*, comble *m*.

acne ['æknɪ] *n* acné *f*.

acorn ['eɪkɔːn] *n Bot* gland *m*.

acoustic [ə'kuːstɪk] *a* acoustique; – *npl* acoustique *f*.

acquaint [ə'kweɪnt] *vt* to a. s.o. with sth informer qn de qch; **to be acquainted with** (*person*) connaître; (*fact*) savoir; **we are acquainted** on se connaît. ◆**acquaintance** *n* (*person, knowledge*) connaissance *f*.

acquiesce [ækwɪ'es] *vi* acquiescer (**in** à). ◆**acquiescence** *n* acquiescement *m*.

acquire [ə'kwaɪər] *vt* acquérir; (*taste*) prendre (**for** à); (*friends*) se faire; **aquired taste** goût *m* qui s'acquiert. ◆**acqui'sition** *n* acquisition *f*. ◆**acquisitive** *a* avide, cupide.

acquit [ə'kwɪt] *vt* (**-tt-**) **to a. s.o.** (**of a crime**) acquitter qn. ◆**acquittal** *n* acquittement *m*.

acre ['eɪkər] *n* acre *f* (= 0,4 *hectare*). ◆**acreage** *n* superficie *f*.

acrid ['ækrɪd] *a* (*smell, manner etc*) âcre.

acrimonious [ækrɪ'məʊnɪəs] *a* acerbe.

acrobat ['ækrəbæt] *n* acrobate *mf*. ◆**acro-'batic** *a* acrobatique; – *npl* acrobatie(s) *f(pl)*.

acronym ['ækrənɪm] *n* sigle *m*.

across [ə'krɒs] *adv & prep* (*from side to side* (*of*)) d'un côté à l'autre (de); (*on the other side* (*of*)) de l'autre côté (de); (*crossways*) en travers (de); **to be a kilometre/etc a.** (*wide*) avoir un kilomètre/etc de large; **to walk** *or* **go a.** (*street etc*) traverser; **to come a.** (*person*) rencontrer (par hasard), tomber sur; (*thing*) trouver (par hasard); **to get sth a. to s.o.** faire comprendre qch à qn.

acrostic [ə'krɒstɪk] *n* acrostiche *m*.

acrylic [ə'krɪlɪk] *a & n* acrylique (*m*).

act [ækt] **1** *n* (*deed*) acte *m*; **a.** (**of parliament**) loi *f*; **caught in the a.** pris sur le fait; **a. of walking** action *f* de marcher; **an a. of folly** une folie. **2** *n* (*of play*) Th acte *m*; (*turn*) Th numéro *m*; **in on the a.** *Fam* dans le coup; **to put on an a.** *Fam* jouer la comédie; – *vt* (*part*) Th jouer; **to a. the fool** faire l'idiot; – *vi* Th Cin jouer; (*pretend*) jouer la comédie. **3** *vi* (*do sth, behave*) agir; (*function*) fonctionner; **to a. as** (*secretary etc*) faire office de; (*of object*) servir de; **to a.** (**up)on** (*affect*) agir sur; (*advice*) suivre; **to a. on behalf of** représenter; **to a. up** (*of person, machine*) *Fam* faire des siennes. ◆**—ing 1** *a* (*manager etc*) intérimaire, provisoire. **2** *n* (*of play*) représentation *f*; (*actor's art*) jeu *m*; (*career*) théâtre *m*.

action ['ækʃ(ə)n] *n* action *f*; *Mil* combat *m*; *Jur* procès *m*, action *f*; **to put into a.** (*plan*) exécuter; **out of a.** hors d'usage, hors (de) service; (*person*) hors de combat; **killed in a.** mort au champ d'honneur; **to take industrial a.** se mettre en grève.

active ['æktɪv] *a* actif; (*interest*) vif; (*volcano*) en activité. ◆**activate** *vt Ch* activer; (*mechanism*) actionner. ◆**activist** *n* activiste *mf*. ◆**ac'tivity** *n* activité *f*; (*in street*) mouvement *m*.

actor ['æktər] *n* acteur *m*. ◆**actress** *n* actrice *f*.

actual ['æktʃʊəl] *a* réel, véritable; (*example*) concret; **the a. book** le livre même; **in a. fact** en réalité, effectivement. ◆**—ly** *adv* (*truly*) réellement; (*in fact*) en réalité, en fait.

actuary ['æktʃʊərɪ] *n* actuaire *mf*.

actuate ['æktʃʊeɪt] *vt* (*person*) animer; (*machine*) actionner.

acumen ['ækjʊmen, *Am* ə'kjuːmən] *n* perspicacité *f*, finesse *f*.

acupuncture ['ækjʊpʌŋktʃər] *n* acupuncture *f*.

acute [ə'kjuːt] *a* aigu; (*anxiety, emotion*) vif, profond; (*observer*) perspicace; (*shortage*) grave. ◆**—ly** *adv* (*to suffer, feel*) vivement, profondément. ◆**—ness** *n* acuité *f*; perspicacité *f*.

ad [æd] *n Fam* pub *f*; (*private, in newspaper*) annonce *f*; **small ad** petite annonce.

AD [eɪ'diː] *abbr* (*anno Domini*) après Jésus-Christ.

adage ['ædɪdʒ] *n* adage *m*.

Adam ['ædəm] *n* **A.'s apple** pomme *f* d'Adam.

adamant ['ædəmənt] *a* inflexible.

adapt [ə'dæpt] *vt* adapter (**to** à); **to a.** (**oneself**) s'adapter. ◆**adaptable** *a* (*person*) capable de s'adapter, adaptable. ◆**adaptor** *n* (*device*) adaptateur *m*; (*plug*) prise *f* multiple. ◆**adap'tation** *n* adaptation *f*.

add [æd] *vt* ajouter (**to** à, **that** que); **to a.** (**up** *or* **together**) (*total*) additionner; **to a. in** inclure; – *vi* **to a. to** (*increase*) augmenter; **to a. up to** (*total*) s'élever à; (*mean*) signifier; **it all adds up** *Fam* ça s'explique. ◆**a'ddendum**, *pl* **-da** *n* supplément *m*. ◆**adding machine** *n* machine *f* à calculer. ◆**a'ddition** *n* addition *f*; augmentation *f*; **in a.** de plus; **in a. to** en plus de. ◆**a'dditional** *a* supplémentaire. ◆**a'dditionally** *adv* de plus. ◆**additive** *n* additif *m*.

adder ['ædər] *n* vipère *f*.

addict ['ædɪkt] n intoxiqué, -ée mf; **jazz/sport a.** fanatique mf du jazz/du sport; **drug a.** drogué, -ée mf. ◆**a'ddicted** a **to be a. to** (study, drink) s'adonner à; (music) se passionner pour; (to have the habit of) avoir la manie de; **a. to cigarettes** drogué par la cigarette. ◆**a'ddiction** n (habit) manie f; (dependency) Med dépendance f; **drug a.** toxicomanie f. ◆**a'ddictive** a qui crée une dépendance.

address [ə'dres, Am 'ædres] n (on letter etc) adresse f; (speech) allocution f; **form of a.** formule f de politesse; − [ə'dres] vt (person) s'adresser à; (audience) parler devant; (words, speech) adresser (**to** à); (letter) mettre l'adresse sur; **to a. to s.o.** (send, intend for) adresser à qn. ◆**addressee** [ædre'siː] n destinataire mf.

adenoids ['ædɪnɔɪdz] npl végétations fpl (adénoïdes).

adept ['ædept, Am ə'dept] a expert (**in, at** à).

adequate ['ædɪkwət] a (quantity) suffisant; (acceptable) convenable; (person, performance) compétent. ◆**adequacy** n (of person) compétence f; **to doubt the a. of sth** douter que qch soit suffisant. ◆**adequately** adv suffisamment; convenablement.

adhere [əd'hɪər] vi **to a. to** adhérer à; (decision) s'en tenir à; (rule) respecter. ◆**adherence** n, ◆**adhesion** n (grip) adhérence f; (support) Fig adhésion f. ◆**adhesive** a & n adhésif (m).

ad infinitum [ædɪnfɪ'naɪtəm] adv à l'infini.

adjacent [ə'dʒeɪsənt] a (house, angle etc) adjacent (**to** à).

adjective ['ædʒɪktɪv] n adjectif m.

adjoin [ə'dʒɔɪn] vt avoisiner. ◆**—ing** a avoisinant, voisin.

adjourn [ə'dʒɜːn] vt (postpone) adjourner; (session) lever, suspendre; − vi lever la séance; **to a. to** (go) passer à. ◆**—ment** n ajournement m; suspension f (de séance), levée f de séance.

adjudicate [ə'dʒuːdɪkeɪt] vti juger. ◆**adjudi'cation** n jugement m. ◆**adjudicator** n juge m, arbitre m.

adjust [ə'dʒʌst] vt Tech régler, ajuster; (prices) (r)ajuster; (arrange) arranger; **to a. (oneself) to** s'adapter à. ◆**—able** a réglable. ◆**—ment** n Tech réglage m; (of person) adaptation f; (of prices) (r)ajustement m.

ad-lib [æd'lɪb] vi (-bb-) improviser; − a (joke etc) improvisé.

administer [əd'mɪnɪstər] **1** vt (manage, dispense) administrer (**to** à). **2** vi **to a. to** pourvoir à. ◆**admini'stration** n administration f; (ministry) gouvernement m. ◆**administrative** a administratif. ◆**administrator** n administrateur, -trice mf.

admiral ['ædmərəl] n amiral m.

admir/e [əd'maɪər] vt admirer. ◆**—ing** a admiratif. ◆**—er** n admirateur, -trice mf. ◆**'admirable** a admirable. ◆**admi'ration** n admiration f.

admit [əd'mɪt] vt (-tt-) (let in) laisser entrer; (accept) admettre; (acknowledge) reconnaître, avouer; − vi **to a. to sth** (confess) avouer qch; **to a. of** permettre. ◆**admittedly** adv c'est vrai (que). ◆**admissible** a admissible. ◆**admission** n (entry to theatre etc) entrée f (**to** à, de); (to club, school) admission f; (acknowledgement) aveu m; **a. (charge)** (prix m d')entrée f. ◆**admittance** n entrée f; **'no a.'** 'entrée interdite'.

admonish [əd'mɒnɪʃ] vt (reprove) réprimander; (warn) avertir.

ado [ə'duː] n **without further a.** sans (faire) plus de façons.

adolescent [ædə'lesənt] n adolescent, -ente mf. ◆**adolescence** n adolescence f.

adopt [ə'dɒpt] vt (child, method, attitude etc) adopter; (candidate) Pol choisir. ◆**—ed** a (child) adoptif; (country) d'adoption. ◆**adoption** n adoption f. ◆**adoptive** a (parent) adoptif.

adore [ə'dɔːr] vt adorer; **he adores being flattered** il adore qu'on le flatte. ◆**adorable** a adorable. ◆**ado'ration** n adoration f.

adorn [ə'dɔːn] vt (room, book) orner; (person, dress) parer. ◆**—ment** n ornement m; parure f.

adrenalin(e) [ə'drenəlɪn] n adrénaline f.

Adriatic [eɪdrɪ'ætɪk] n **the A.** l'Adriatique f.

adrift [ə'drɪft] a & adv Nau à la dérive; **to come a.** (of rope, collar etc) se détacher; **to turn s.o. a.** Fig abandonner qn à son sort.

adroit [ə'drɔɪt] a adroit, habile.

adulation [ædjuː'leɪʃ(ə)n] n adulation f.

adult ['ædʌlt] a & n adulte (mf). ◆**adulthood** n âge m adulte.

adulterate [ə'dʌltəreɪt] vt (food) altérer.

adultery [ə'dʌltərɪ] n adultère m. ◆**adulterous** a adultère.

advanc/e [əd'vɑːns] n (movement, money) avance f; (of science) progrès mpl; pl (of friendship, love) avances fpl; **in a.** à l'avance, d'avance; (to arrive) en avance; **in a. of s.o.** avant qn; − a (payment) anticipé; **a. booking** réservation f; **a. guard** avant-garde f; − vt (put forward, lend) avancer; (*science, work*) faire avancer; – *vi* (*go forward, progress*) avancer; (*towards s.o.*) s'avancer, avancer. ◆—ed *a* avancé; (*studies*) supérieur; **a. in years** âgé. ◆—ement *n* (*progress, promotion*) avancement *m*.

advantage [əd'vɑːntɪdʒ] *n* avantage *m* (**over** sur); **to take a. of** profiter de; (*person*) tromper, exploiter; (*woman*) séduire; **to show (off) to a.** faire valoir. ◆**advan-'tageous** *a* avantageux (**to,** pour), profitable.

advent ['ædvent] *n* arrivée *f*, avènement *m*; **A.** *Rel* l'Avent *m*.

adventure [əd'ventʃər] *n* aventure *f*; – *a* (*film etc*) d'aventures. ◆**adventurer** *n* aventurier, -ière *mf*. ◆**adventurous** *a* aventureux.

adverb ['ædvɜːb] *n* adverbe *m*.

adversary ['ædvəsəri] *n* adversaire *mf*.

adverse ['ædvɜːs] *a* hostile, défavorable. ◆**ad'versity** *n* adversité *f*.

advert ['ædvɜːt] *n* *Fam* pub *f*; (*private, in newspaper*) annonce *f*.

advertis/e ['ædvətaɪz] *vt* (*goods*) faire de la publicité pour; (*make known*) annoncer; – *vi* faire de la publicité; **to a. (for s.o.)** mettre une annonce (pour chercher qn). ◆—**er** *n* annonceur *m*. ◆—**ement** [əd'vɜːtɪsmənt, *Am* ædvə'taɪzmənt] *n* publicité *f*; (*private or classified in newspaper*) annonce *f*; (*poster*) affiche *f*; **classified a.** petite annonce; **the advertisements** *TV* la publicité.

advice [əd'vaɪs] *n* conseil(s) *m(pl)*; *Com* avis *m*; **a piece of a.** un conseil.

advis/e [əd'vaɪz] *vt* (*counsel*) conseiller; (*recommend*) recommander; (*notify*) informer; **to a. s.o. to do** conseiller à qn de faire; **to a. against** déconseiller. ◆—**ed** *a* **well-. (***action***)** prudent. ◆—**able** *a* (*wise*) prudent (**to do** de faire); (*act*) à conseiller. ◆—**edly** [-ɪdlɪ] *adv* après réflexion. ◆—**er** *n* conseiller, -ère *mf*. ◆**advisory** *a* consultatif.

advocate 1 ['ædvəkət] *n* (*of cause*) défenseur *m*, avocat, -ate *mf*; *Jur* avocat *m*. **2** ['ædvəkeɪt] *vt* préconiser, recommander.

aegis ['iːdʒɪs] *n* **under the a. of** sous l'égide de.

aeon ['iːən] *n* éternité *f*.

aerial ['eərɪəl] *n* antenne *f*; – *a* aérien.

aerobatics [eərə'bætɪks] *npl* acrobatie *f* aérienne. ◆**ae'robics** *npl* aérobic *f*. ◆**'aerodrome** *n* aérodrome *m*. ◆**aero-dy'namic** *a* aérodynamique. ◆**aero-nautics** *npl* aéronautique *f*. ◆**'aeroplane** *n* avion *m*. ◆**'aerosol** *n* aérosol *m*. ◆**'aerospace** *a* (*industry*) aérospatial.

aesthetic [iːs'θetɪk, *Am* es'θetɪk] *a* esthétique.

afar [ə'fɑːr] *adv* **from a.** de loin.

affable ['æfəb(ə)l] *a* affable, aimable.

affair ['əfeər] *n* (*matter, concern*) affaire *f*; (**love) a.** liaison *f*; **state of affairs** état *m* de choses.

affect {ə'fekt] *vt* (*move, feign*) affecter; (*concern*) toucher, affecter; (*harm*) nuire à; (*be fond of*) affectionner. ◆—**ed** *a* (*manner*) affecté; (*by disease*) atteint. ◆**affec'tation** *n* affectation *f*.

affection [ə'fekʃ(ə)n] *n* affection *f* (**for** pour). ◆**affectionate** *a* affectueux, aimant. ◆**affectionately** *adv* affectueusement.

affiliate [ə'fɪlɪeɪt] *vt* affilier; **to be affiliated** s'affilier (**to** à); **affiliated company** filiale *f*. ◆**affili'ation** *n* affiliation *f*; *pl* (*political*) attaches *fpl*.

affinity [ə'fɪnɪtɪ] *n* affinité *f*.

affirm [ə'fɜːm] *vt* affirmer. ◆**affir'mation** *n* affirmation *f*. ◆**affirmative** *a* affirmatif; – *n* affirmative *f*.

affix [ə'fɪks] *vt* apposer.

afflict [ə'flɪkt] *vt* affliger (**with** de). ◆**afflic-tion** *n* (*misery*) affliction *f*; (*disorder*) infirmité *f*.

affluent ['æfluənt] *a* riche; **a. society** société *f* d'abondance. ◆**affluence** *n* richesse *f*.

afford [ə'fɔːd] *vt* **1** (*pay for*) avoir les moyens d'acheter, pouvoir se payer; (*time*) pouvoir trouver; **I can a. to wait** je peux me permettre d'attendre. **2** (*provide*) fournir, donner; **to a. s.o. sth** fournir qch à qn.

affray [ə'freɪ] *n* *Jur* rixe *f*, bagarre *f*.

affront [ə'frʌnt] *n* affront *m*; – *vt* faire un affront à.

Afghanistan [æf'gænɪstɑːn] *n* Afghanistan *m*. ◆**'Afghan** *a* & *n* afghan, -ane (*mf*).

afield [ə'fiːld] *adv* **further a.** plus loin; **too far a.** trop loin.

afloat [ə'fləʊt] *adv* (*ship, swimmer, business*) à flot; (*awash*) submergé; **life a.** la vie sur l'eau.

afoot [ə'fʊt] *adv* **there's sth a.** il se trame qch; **there's a plan a. to** on prépare un projet pour.

aforementioned [ə'fɔːmenʃənd] *a* susmentionné.

afraid [ə'freɪd] *a* **to be a.** avoir peur (**of, to** de; **that** que); **to make s.o. afraid** faire peur à qn; **he's a. (that) she may be ill** il a peur qu'elle (ne) soit malade; **I'm a. he's out** (*I regret to say*) je regrette, il est sorti.

afresh [əˈfreʃ] *adv* de nouveau.

Africa [ˈæfrɪkə] *n* Afrique *f*. ◆**African** *a & n* africain, -aine (*mf*).

after [ˈɑːftər] *adv* après; **the month a.** le mois suivant, le mois d'après; – *prep* après; **a. all** après tout; **a. eating** après avoir mangé; **day a. day** jour après jour; **page a.** page page sur page; **time a. time** bien des fois; **a. you!** je vous en prie!; **ten a. four** *Am* quatre heures dix; **to be a. sth/s.o.** (*seek*) chercher qch/qn; – *conj* après que; **a. he saw you** après qu'il t'a vu. ◆**aftercare** *n Med* soins *mpl* postopératoires; *Jur* surveillance *f*. ◆**aftereffects** *npl* suites *fpl*, séquelles *fpl*. ◆**afterlife** *n* vie *f* future. ◆**aftermath** [-mɑːθ] *n* suites *fpl*. ◆**after'noon** *n* après-midi *m or f inv*; **in the a.** l'après-midi; **good a.!** (*hello*) bonjour!; (*goodbye*) au revoir! ◆**after'noons** *adv Am* l'après-midi. ◆**aftersales (service)** *n* service *m* après-vente. ◆**aftershave (lotion)** *n* lotion *f* après-rasage. ◆**aftertaste** *n* arrière-goût *m*. ◆**afterthought** *n* réflexion *f* après coup. ◆**afterward(s)** *adv* après, plus tard.

afters [ˈɑːftəz] *npl Fam* dessert *m*.

again [əˈgen, əˈgeɪn] *adv* de nouveau, encore une fois; (*furthermore*) en outre; **to do a.** refaire; **to go down/up a.** redescendre/remonter; **never a.** plus jamais; **half as much a.** moitié plus; **a. and a., time and (time) a.** maintes fois; **what's his name a.?** comment s'appelle-t-il déjà?

against [əˈgenst, əˈgeɪnst] *prep* contre; **to go or be a.** s'opposer à; **a law a. drinking** une loi qui interdit de boire; **his age is a. him** son âge lui est défavorable; **a. a background of** sur (un) fond de; **a. the light** à contre-jour; **a. the law** illégal; **a. the rules** interdit, contraire aux règlements.

age [eɪdʒ] *n* (*lifespan, period*) âge *m*; (*old*) a. vieillesse *f*; **the Middle Ages** le moyen âge; **what a. are you?, what's your a.?** quel âge as-tu?; **five years of a.** âgé de cinq ans; **to be of a.** être majeur; **under a.** trop jeune, mineur; **to wait (for) ages** *Fam* attendre une éternité; **a. group** tranche *f* d'âge; – *vti* (*pres p* ag(e)ing) vieillir. ◆**a.-old** *a* séculaire. ◆**aged** *a* [eɪdʒd] **a. ten** âgé de dix ans; [ˈeɪdʒɪd] vieux, âgé; **the a.** les personnes *fpl* âgées. ◆**ageless** *a* toujours jeune.

agenda [əˈdʒendə] *n* ordre *m* du jour.

agent [ˈeɪdʒənt] *n* agent *m*; (*dealer*) *Com* concessionnaire *mf*. ◆**agency** *n* **1** (*office*) agence *f*. **2 through the a. of s.o.** par l'intermédiaire de qn.

agglomeration [əglɒməˈreɪʃ(ə)n] *n* agglomération *f*.

aggravate [ˈægrəveɪt] *vt* (*make worse*) aggraver; **to a. s.o.** *Fam* exaspérer qn. ◆**aggra'vation** *n* aggravation *f*; *Fam* exaspération *f*; (*bother*) *Fam* ennui(s) *m*(*pl*).

aggregate [ˈægrɪgət] *a* global; – *n* (*total*) ensemble *m*.

aggression [əˈgreʃ(ə)n] *n* agression *f*. ◆**aggressive** *a* agressif. ◆**aggressiveness** *n* agressivité *f*. ◆**agressor** *n* agresseur *m*.

aggrieved [əˈgriːvd] *a* (*offended*) blessé, froissé; (*tone*) peiné.

aghast [əˈgɑːst] *a* consterné, horrifié.

agile [ˈædʒaɪl, *Am* ˈædʒ(ə)l] *a* agile. ◆**a'gility** *n* agilité *f*.

agitate [ˈædʒɪteɪt] *vt* (*worry, shake*) agiter; – *vi* **to a. for** *Pol* faire campagne pour. ◆**agi'tation** *n* (*anxiety, unrest*) agitation *f*. ◆**agitator** *n* agitateur, -trice *mf*.

aglow [əˈgləʊ] *a* **to be a.** briller (**with** de).

agnostic [æɡˈnɒstɪk] *a & n* agnostique (*mf*).

ago [əˈgəʊ] *adv* **a year a.** il y a un an; **how long a.?** il y a combien de temps (de cela)?; **as long a. as 1800** (déjà) en 1800.

agog [əˈgɒg] *a* (*excited*) en émoi; (*eager*) impatient.

agony [ˈægənɪ] *n* (*pain*) douleur *f* atroce; (*anguish*) angoisse *f*; **to be in a.** souffrir horriblement; **a. column** *Journ* courrier *m* du cœur. ◆**agonize** *vi* se faire beaucoup de souci. ◆**agonized** *a* (*look*) angoissé; (*cry*) de douleur. ◆**agonizing** *a* (*pain*) atroce; (*situation*) angoissant.

agree [əˈgriː] *vi* (*come to terms*) se mettre d'accord; (*be in agreement*) être d'accord, s'accorder (**with** avec); (*of facts, dates etc*) concorder; *Gram* s'accorder; **to a. upon** (*decide*) convenir de; **to a. to sth/to doing** consentir à qch/à faire; **it doesn't a. with me** (*food, climate*) ça ne me réussit pas; – *vt* (*figures*) faire concorder; (*accounts*) *Com* approuver; **to a. to do** accepter de faire; **to a. that** (*admit*) admettre que. ◆**agreed** *a* (*time, place*) convenu; **we are a.** nous sommes d'accord; **a.!** entendu! ◆**agreeable** *a* **1** (*pleasant*) agréable. **2 to be a.** (*agree*) être d'accord; **to be a. to sth** consentir à qch. ◆**agreement** *n* accord *m*; *Pol Com* convention *f*, accord *m*; **in a. with** d'accord avec.

agriculture [ˈægrɪkʌltʃər] *n* agriculture *f*. ◆**agri'cultural** *a* agricole.

aground [əˈgraʊnd] *adv* **to run a.** *Nau* (s')échouer.

ah! [ɑː] *int* ah!

ahead [əˈhed] *adv* (*in space*) en avant; (*leading*) en tête; (*in the future*) dans l'avenir; **a. (of time *or* of schedule)** en avance (sur l'horaire); **one hour/*etc* a.** une heure/*etc* d'avance (of sur); **a. of** (*space*) devant; (*time, progress*) en avance sur; **to go a.** (*advance*) avancer; (*continue*) continuer; (*start*) commencer; **go a.!** allez-y!; **to go a. with** (*task*) prendre de l'avance; (*succeed*) réussir; **to think a.** penser à l'avenir; **straight a.** tout droit.

aid [eɪd] *n* (*help*) aide *f*; (*apparatus*) support *m*, moyen *m*; **with the a. of** (*a stick etc*) à l'aide de; **in a. of** (*charity etc*) au profit de; **what's this in a. of?** *Fam* quel est le but de tout ça?, ça sert à quoi?; – *vt* aider (**to do** à faire).

aide [eɪd] *n Pol* aide *mf*.

AIDS [eɪdz] *n Med* SIDA *m*.

ail [eɪl] *vt* **what ails you?** de quoi souffrez-vous? ◆**—ing** *a* souffrant, malade. ◆**—ment** *n* maladie *f*.

aim [eɪm] *n* but *m*; **to take a.** viser; **with the a. of** dans le but de; – *vt* (*gun*) braquer, diriger (**at** sur); (*lamp*) diriger (**at** vers); (*stone*) lancer (**at** à, vers); (*blow, remark*) décocher (**at** à); – *vi* viser; **to a. at s.o.** viser qn; **to a. to do** *or* **at doing** avoir l'intention de faire. ◆**—less** *a*, ◆**—lessly** *adv* sans but.

air [eər] **1** *n* air *m*; **in the open a.** en plein air; **by a.** (*to travel*) en *or* par avion; (*letter, freight*) par avion; **to be** *or* **go on the a.** (*person*) passer à l'antenne; (*programme*) être diffusé; **(up) in the a.** (*to throw*) en l'air; (*plan*) incertain, en l'air; **there's sth in the a.** *Fig* il se prépare qch; – *a* (*raid, base etc*) aérien; **a. force/hostess** armée *f*/hôtesse *f* de l'air; **a. terminal** aérogare *f*; – *vt* (*room*) aérer; (*views*) exposer; **airing cupboard** armoire *f* sèche-linge. **2** *n* (*appearance, tune*) air *m*; **to put on airs** se donner des airs; **with an a. of sadness/*etc*** d'un air triste/*etc*.

airborne [ˈeəbɔːn] *a* en (cours de) vol; (*troops*) aéroporté; **to become a.** (*of aircraft*) décoller. ◆**airbridge** *n* pont *m* aérien. ◆**air-conditioned** *a* climatisé. ◆**air-conditioner** *n* climatiseur *m*. ◆**aircraft** *n inv* avion(s) *m(pl)*; **a. carrier** porte-avions *m inv*. ◆**aircrew** *n Av* équipage *m*. ◆**airfield** *n* terrain *m* d'aviation. ◆**airgun** *n* carabine *f* à air comprimé. ◆**airletter** *n* aérogramme *m*. ◆**airlift** *n* pont *m* aérien; – *vt* transporter par avion. ◆**airline** *n* ligne *f* aérienne. ◆**airliner** *n* avion *m* de ligne. ◆**airlock** *n* (*chamber*) *Nau Av* sas *m*; (*in pipe*) bouchon *m*. ◆**airmail** *n* poste *f* aérienne; **by a.** par avion. ◆**airman** *n* (*pl* **-men**) aviateur *m*. ◆**airplane** *n Am* avion *m*. ◆**airpocket** *n* trou *m* d'air. ◆**airport** *n* aéroport *m*. ◆**airship** *n* dirigeable *m*. ◆**airsickness** *n* mal *m* de l'air. ◆**airstrip** *n* terrain *m* d'atterrissage. ◆**airtight** *a* hermétique. ◆**airway** *n* (*route*) couloir *m* aérien. ◆**airworthy** *a* en état de navigation.

airy [ˈeərɪ] *a* (**-ier, -iest**) (*room*) bien aéré; (*promise*) vain; (*step*) léger. ◆**a.-fairy** *a Fam* farfelu. ◆**airily** *adv* (*not seriously*) d'un ton léger.

aisle [aɪl] *n* couloir *m*; (*of church*) nef *f* latérale.

aitch [eɪtʃ] *n* (*letter*) h *m*.

ajar [əˈdʒɑːr] *a* & *adv* (*door*) entrouvert.

akin [əˈkɪn] *a* **a. (to)** apparenté (à).

alabaster [ˈæləbɑːstər] *n* albâtre *m*.

alacrity [əˈlækrɪtɪ] *n* empressement *m*.

à la mode [ælæˈməʊd] *a Culin Am* avec de la crème glacée.

alarm [əˈlɑːm] *n* (*warning, fear*) alarme *f*; (*apparatus*) sonnerie *f* (d'alarme); **false a.** fausse alerte *f*; **a. (clock)** réveil *m*, réveille-matin *m inv*; – *vt* (*frighten*) alarmer. ◆**alarmist** *n* alarmiste *mf*.

alas! [əˈlæs] *int* hélas!

albatross [ˈælbətrɒs] *n* albatros *m*.

albeit [ɔːlˈbiːt] *conj Lit* quoique.

albino [ælˈbiːnəʊ, *Am* ælˈbaɪnəʊ] *n* (*pl* **-os**) albinos *mf*.

album [ˈælbəm] *n* (*book, record*) album *m*.

alchemy [ˈælkəmɪ] *n* alchimie *f*. ◆**alchemist** *n* alchimiste *m*.

alcohol [ˈælkəhɒl] *n* alcool *m*. ◆**alco'holic** *a* (*person*) alcoolique; (*drink*) alcoolisé; – *n* (*person*) alcoolique *mf*. ◆**alcoholism** *n* alcoolisme *m*.

alcove [ˈælkəʊv] *n* alcôve *f*.

alderman [ˈɔːldəmən] *n* (*pl* **-men**) conseiller, -ère *mf* municipal(e).

ale [eɪl] *n* bière *f*.

alert [əˈlɜːt] *a* (*watchful*) vigilant; (*sharp, awake*) éveillé; – *n* alerte *f*; **on the a.** sur le qui-vive; – *vt* alerter. ◆**—ness** *n* vigilance *f*.

alfalfa [ælˈfælfə] *n Am* luzerne *f*.

algebra [ˈældʒɪbrə] *n* algèbre *f*. ◆**algeb-'raic** *a* algébrique.

Algeria [ælˈdʒɪərɪə] *n* Algérie *f*. ◆**Algerian** *a* & *n* algérien, -ienne (*mf*).

alias [ˈeɪlɪəs] *adv* alias; – *n* nom *m* d'emprunt.

alibi [ˈælɪbaɪ] *n* alibi *m*.

alien ['eɪlɪən] *a* étranger (**to** à); − *n* étranger, -ère *mf*. ◆**alienate** *vt* aliéner; **to a. s.o.** (*make unfriendly*) s'aliéner qn.

alight [ə'laɪt] **1** *a* (*fire*) allumé; (*building*) en feu; (*face*) éclairé; **to set a.** mettre le feu à. **2** *vi* descendre (**from** de); (*of bird*) se poser.

align [ə'laɪn] *vt* aligner. ◆**—ment** *n* alignement *m*.

alike [ə'laɪk] **1** *a* (*people, things*) semblables, pareils; **to look** *or* **be a.** se ressembler. **2** *adv* de la même manière; **summer and winter a.** été comme hiver.

alimony ['ælɪmənɪ, *Am* 'ælɪməʊnɪ] *n* Jur pension *f* alimentaire.

alive [ə'laɪv] *a* vivant, en vie; **a. to** conscient de; **a. with** grouillant de; **burnt a.** brûlé vif; **anyone a.** n'importe qui; **to keep a.** (*custom, memory*) entretenir, perpétuer; **a. and kicking** *Fam* plein de vie; **look a.!** *Fam* active-toi!

all [ɔːl] *a* tout, toute, *pl* tous, toutes; **a. day** toute la journée; **a. (the) men** tous les hommes; **with a. speed** à toute vitesse; **for a. her wealth** malgré toute sa fortune; − *pron* tous *mpl*, toutes *fpl*; (*everything*) tout; **a. will die** tous mourront; **my sisters are a. here** toutes mes sœurs sont ici; **he ate it a., he ate a. of it** il a tout mangé; **a. (that) he has** tout ce qu'il a; **a. in a.** à tout prendre; **in a., a. told** en tout; **a. but impossible/***etc* presque impossible/*etc*; **anything at a.** quoi que ce soit; **if he comes at a.** s'il vient effectivement; **if there's any wind at a.** s'il y a le moindre vent; **not at a.** pas du tout; (*after 'thank you'*) il n'y a pas de quoi; **a. of us** nous tous; **take a. of it** prends (le) tout; − *adv* tout; **a. alone** tout seul; **a. bad** entièrement; (*not at all*) mauvais; **a. over** (*everywhere*) partout; (*finished*) fini; **a. right** (très) bien; **he's a. right** (*not harmed*) il est sain et sauf; (*healthy*) il va bien; **a. too soon** bien trop tôt; **six a.** *Fb* six buts partout; **a. there** *Fam* éveillé, intelligent; **not a. there** *Fam* simple d'esprit; **a. in** *Fam* épuisé; **a.-in price** prix global; − *n* **my a.** tout ce que j'ai. ◆**a.-'clear** *n Mil* fin f d'alerte. ◆**a.-night** *a* (*party*) qui dure toute la nuit; (*shop*) ouvert toute la nuit. ◆**a.-out** *a* (*effort*) violent; (*war, strike*) tous azimuts. ◆**a.-'powerful** *a* tout-puissant. ◆**a.-purpose** *a* (*tool*) universel. ◆**a.-round** *a* complet. ◆**a.-'rounder** *n* personne f qui fait de tout. ◆**a.-time** *a* (*record*) jamais atteint; **to reach an a.-time low/high** arriver au point le plus bas/le plus haut.

allay [ə'leɪ] *vt* calmer, apaiser.

alleg/e [ə'ledʒ] *vt* prétendre. ◆**—ed** *a* (*so-called*) prétendu; (*author, culprit*) présumé; **he is a. to be** on prétend qu'il est. ◆**—edly** [-ɪdlɪ] *adv* d'après ce qu'on dit. ◆**alle'gation** *n* allégation f.

allegiance [ə'liːdʒəns] *n* fidélité f (**to** à).

allegory ['ælɪɡərɪ, *Am* 'æləɡɔːrɪ] *n* allégorie f. ◆**alle'gorical** *a* allégorique.

allergy ['ælədʒɪ] *n* allergie f. ◆**a'llergic** *a* allergique (**to** à).

alleviate [ə'liːvɪeɪt] *vt* alléger.

alley ['ælɪ] *n* ruelle f; (*in park*) allée f; **blind a.** impasse f; **that's up my a.** *Fam* c'est mon truc. ◆**alleyway** *n* ruelle f.

alliance [ə'laɪəns] *n* alliance f.

allied ['ælaɪd] *a* (*country*) allié; (*matters*) connexe.

alligator ['ælɪɡeɪtər] *n* alligator *m*.

allocate ['æləkeɪt] *vt* (*assign*) attribuer, allouer (**to** à); (*distribute*) répartir. ◆**allo'cation** *n* attribution f.

allot [ə'lɒt] *vt* (**-tt-**) (*assign*) attribuer; (*distribute*) répartir. ◆**—ment** *n* attribution f; (*share*) partage *m*; (*land*) lopin *m* de terre (*loué pour la culture*).

allow [ə'laʊ] **1** *vt* permettre; (*grant*) accorder; (*a request*) accéder à; (*deduct*) *Com* déduire; (*add*) *Com* ajouter; **to a. s.o. to do** permettre à qn de faire, autoriser qn à faire; **a. me!** permettez(-moi)!; **not allowed** interdit; **you're not allowed to go** on vous interdit de partir. **2** *vi* **to a. for** tenir compte de. ◆**—able** *a* (*acceptable*) admissible; (*expense*) déductible.

allowance [ə'laʊəns] *n* allocation f; (*for travel, housing, food*) indemnité f; (*for duty-free goods*) tolérance f; (*tax-free amount*) abattement *m*; **to make allowance(s) for** (*person*) être indulgent envers; (*thing*) tenir compte de.

alloy ['ælɔɪ] *n* alliage *m*.

allude [ə'luːd] *vi* **to a. to** faire allusion à. ◆**allusion** *n* allusion f.

allure [ə'lʊər] *vt* attirer.

ally ['ælaɪ] *n* allié, -ée *mf*; − [ə'laɪ] *vt* (*country, person*) allier.

almanac ['ɔːlmənæk] *n* almanach *m*.

almighty [ɔːl'maɪtɪ] **1** *a* tout-puissant; **the A.** le Tout-Puissant. **2** *a* (*great*) *Fam* terrible, formidable.

almond ['ɑːmənd] *n* amande f.

almost ['ɔːlməʊst] *adv* presque; **he fell/***etc* il a failli tomber/*etc*.

alms [ɑːmz] *npl* aumône f.

alone [ə'ləʊn] *a & adv* seul; **an expert a. can . . .** seul un expert peut . . . ; **I did it (all) a.** je l'ai fait à moi (tout) seul, je l'ai fait (tout) seul; **to leave** or **let a.** (*person*) laisser tranquille or en paix; (*thing*) ne pas toucher à.

along [ə'lɒŋ] *prep* (**all**) **a.** (tout) le long de; **to go** or **walk a.** (*street*) passer par; **a. here** par ici; **a. with** avec; – *adv* **all a.** d'un bout à l'autre; (*time*) dès le début; **come a.!** venez!; **move a.!** avancez!

alongside [əlɒŋ'saɪd] *prep* & *adv* à côté (de); **to come a.** *Nau* accoster; **a. the kerb** le long du trottoir.

aloof [ə'luːf] *a* distant; – *adv* à distance; **to keep a.** garder ses distances (**from** par rapport à). ◆**—ness** *n* réserve *f*.

aloud [ə'laʊd] *adv* à haute voix.

alphabet ['ælfəbet] *n* alphabet *m*. ◆**alpha-'betical** *a* alphabétique.

Alps [ælps] *npl* the **A.** les Alpes *fpl*. ◆**alpine** *a* (*club, range etc*) alpin; (*scenery*) alpestre.

already [ɔːl'redɪ] *adv* déjà.

alright [ɔːl'raɪt] *adv Fam* = **all right**.

Alsatian [æl'seɪʃ(ə)n] *n* (*dog*) berger *m* allemand, chien-loup *m*.

also ['ɔːlsəʊ] *adv* aussi, également. ◆**a.-ran** *n* (*person*) *Fig* perdant, -ante *mf*.

altar ['ɔːltər] *n* autel *m*.

alter ['ɔːltər] *vt* changer, modifier; (*clothing*) retoucher; – *vi* changer. ◆**alte'ration** *n* changement *m*, modification *f*; retouche *f*.

altercation [ɔːltə'keɪʃ(ə)n] *n* altercation *f*.

alternat/e [ɔːl'tɜːnət] *a* alterné; **on a. days** tous les deux jours; **a. laughter and tears** des rires et des larmes qui se succèdent; – ['ɔːltəneɪt] *vi* alterner (**with** avec); – *vt* faire alterner. ◆**—ing** *a* (*current*) *El* alternatif. ◆**—ely** *adv* alternativement. ◆**alter-'nation** *n* alternance *f*.

alternative [ɔːl'tɜːnətɪv] *a* **an a. way/etc** une autre façon/*etc*; **a. answers/etc** d'autres réponses/*etc* (différentes); – *n* (*choice*) alternative *f*. ◆**—ly** *adv* comme alternative; **or a.** (*or else*) ou bien.

although [ɔːl'ðəʊ] *adv* bien que, quoique (+ *sub*).

altitude ['æltɪtjuːd] *n* altitude *f*.

altogether [ɔːltə'geðər] *adv* (*completely*) tout à fait; (*on the whole*) somme toute; **how much a.?** combien en tout?

aluminium [ælju'mɪnjəm] (*Am* **aluminum** [ə'luːmɪnəm]) *n* aluminium *m*.

alumnus, pl -ni [ə'lʌmnəs, -naɪ] *n Am* ancien(ne) élève *mf*, ancien(ne) étudiant, -ante *mf*.

always ['ɔːlweɪz] *adv* toujours; **he's a. criticizing** il est toujours à critiquer.

am [æm, *unstressed* əm] *see* **be**.

a.m. [eɪ'em] *adv* du matin.

amalgam [ə'mælgəm] *n* amalgame *m*. ◆**a'malgamate** *vt* amalgamer; (*society*) *Com* fusionner; – *vi* s'amalgamer; fusionner.

amass [ə'mæs] *vt* (*riches*) amasser.

amateur ['æmətər] *n* amateur *m*; – *a* (*interest, sports*) d'amateur; **a. painter**/*etc* peintre/*etc* amateur. ◆**amateurish** *a* (*work*) *Pej* d'amateur; (*person*) *Pej* maladroit, malhabile. ◆**amateurism** *n* amateurisme *m*.

amaz/e [ə'meɪz] *vt* stupéfier, étonner. ◆**—ed** *a* stupéfait (**at sth** de qch), étonné (**at sth** par or de qch); **a. at seeing**/*etc* stupéfait or étonné de voir/*etc*. ◆**—ing** *a* stupéfiant; *Fam* extraordinaire. ◆**—ingly** *adv* extraordinairement; (*miraculously*) par miracle. ◆**amazement** *n* stupéfaction *f*.

ambassador [æm'bæsədər] *n* ambassadeur *m*; (*woman*) ambassadrice *f*.

amber ['æmbər] *n* ambre *m*; **a.** (**light**) *Aut* (feu *m*) orange *m*.

ambidextrous [æmbɪ'dekstrəs] *a* ambidextre.

ambiguous [æm'bɪgjʊəs] *a* ambigu. ◆**ambi'guity** *n* ambiguïté *f*.

ambition [æm'bɪʃ(ə)n] *n* ambition *f*. ◆**ambitious** *a* ambitieux.

ambivalent [æm'bɪvələnt] *a* ambigu, équivoque.

amble ['æmb(ə)l] *vi* marcher d'un pas tranquille.

ambulance ['æmbjʊləns] *n* ambulance *f*; **a. man** ambulancier *m*.

ambush ['æmbʊʃ] *n* guet-apens *m*, embuscade *f*; – *vt* prendre en embuscade.

amen [ɑː'men, eɪ'men] *int* amen.

amenable [ə'miːnəb(ə)l] *a* docile; **a. to** (*responsive to*) sensible à; **a. to reason** raisonnable.

amend [ə'mend] *vt* (*text*) modifier; (*conduct*) corriger; *Pol* amender. ◆**—ment** *n Pol* amendement *m*.

amends [ə'mendz] *npl* **to make a. for** réparer; **to make a.** réparer son erreur.

amenities [ə'miːnɪtɪz, *Am* ə'menɪtɪz] *npl* (*pleasant things*) agréments *mpl*; (*of sports club etc*) équipement *m*; (*of town*) aménagements *mpl*.

America [ə'merɪkə] *n* Amérique *f*; **North/South A.** Amérique du Nord/du Sud. ◆**American** *a* & *n* américain, -aine (*mf*). ◆**Americanism** *n* américanisme *m*.

amethyst ['æməθɪst] *n* améthyste *f*.

amiable ['eɪmɪəb(ə)l] *a* aimable.

amicab/le ['æmɪkəb(ə)l] *a* amical. ◆**—ly** *adv* amicalement; *Jur* à l'amiable.

amid(st) [ə'mɪd(st)] *prep* au milieu de, parmi.

amiss [ə'mɪs] *adv & a* mal (à propos); **sth is a.** (*wrong*) qch ne va pas; **that wouldn't come a.** ça ne ferait pas de mal; **to take a.** prendre en mauvaise part.

ammonia [ə'məʊnjə] *n* (*gas*) ammoniac *m*; (*liquid*) ammoniaque *f*.

ammunition [æmjʊ'nɪʃ(ə)n] *n* munitions *fpl*.

amnesia [æm'niːzjə] *n* amnésie *f*.

amnesty ['æmnəstɪ] *n* amnistie *f*.

amok [ə'mɒk] *adv* **to run a.** se déchaîner, s'emballer.

among(st) [ə'mʌŋ(st)] *prep* parmi, entre; **a. themselves/friends** entre eux/amis; **a. the French/**etc (*group*) chez les Français/etc; **a. the crowd** dans *or* parmi la foule.

amoral [eɪ'mɒrəl] *a* amoral.

amorous ['æmərəs] *a* amoureux.

amount [ə'maʊnt] **1** *n* quantité *f*; (*sum of money*) somme *f*; (*total of bill etc*) montant *m*; (*scope, size*) importance *f*. **2** *vi* **to a. to** s'élever à; (*mean*) *Fig* signifier; **it amounts to the same thing** ça revient au même.

amp(ere) ['æmp(eər)] *n El* ampère *m*.

amphibian [æm'fɪbɪən] *n & a* amphibie (*m*). ◆**amphibious** *a* amphibie.

amphitheatre ['æmfɪθɪətər] *n* amphithéâtre *m*.

ample ['æmp(ə)l] *a* (*roomy*) ample; (*enough*) largement assez de; (*reasons, means*) solides; **you have a. time** tu as largement le temps. ◆**amply** *adv* largement, amplement.

amplify ['æmplɪfaɪ] *vt* amplifier. ◆**amplifier** *n El* amplificateur *m*.

amputate ['æmpjuteɪt] *vt* amputer. ◆**ampu'tation** *n* amputation *f*.

amuck [ə'mʌk] *adv see* amok.

amulet ['æmjʊlət] *n* amulette *f*.

amus/e [ə'mjuːz] *vt* amuser, divertir; **to keep s.o. amused** amuser qn. ◆**—ing** *a* amusant. ◆**—ement** *n* amusement *m*, divertissement *m*; (*pastime*) distraction *f*; **a. arcade** salle *f* de jeux.

an [æn, *unstressed* ən] *see* **a.**

anachronism [ə'nækrənɪz(ə)m] *n* anachronisme *m*.

an(a)emia [ə'niːmɪə] *n* anémie *f*. ◆**an(a)emic** *a* anémique.

an(a)esthesia [ænɪs'θiːzɪə] *n* anesthésie *f*. ◆**an(a)esthetic** [ænɪs'θetɪk] *n* (*substance*) anesthésique *m*; **under the a.** sous anesthésie; **general/local a.** anesthésie *f* générale/locale. ◆**an(a)esthetize** [ə'niːsθɪtaɪz] *vt* anesthésier.

anagram ['ænəgræm] *n* anagramme *f*.

analogy [ə'nælədʒɪ] *n* analogie *f*. ◆**analogous** *a* analogue (**to** à).

analyse ['ænəlaɪz] *vt* analyser. ◆**analysis**, *pl* **-yses** [ə'næləsɪs, -ɪsiːz] *n* analyse *f*. ◆**analyst** *n* analyste *mf*. ◆**ana'lytical** *a* analytique.

anarchy ['ænəkɪ] *n* anarchie *f*. ◆**a'narchic** *a* anarchique. ◆**anarchist** *n* anarchiste *mf*.

anathema [ə'næθəmə] *n Rel* anathème *m*; **it is (an) a. to me** j'ai une sainte horreur de cela.

anatomy [ə'nætəmɪ] *n* anatomie *f*. ◆**ana'tomical** *a* anatomique.

ancestor ['ænsestər] *n* ancêtre *m*. ◆**an'cestral** *a* ancestral. ◆**ancestry** *n* (*lineage*) ascendance *f*; (*ancestors*) ancêtres *mpl*.

anchor ['æŋkər] *n* ancre *f*; **to weigh a.** lever l'ancre; – *vt* (*ship*) mettre à l'ancre; – *vi* jeter l'ancre, mouiller. ◆**—ed** *a* à l'ancre. ◆**—age** *n* mouillage *m*.

anchovy ['æntʃəvɪ, *Am* æn'tʃəʊvɪ] *n* anchois *m*.

ancient ['eɪnʃənt] *a* ancien; (*pre-medieval*) antique; (*person*) *Hum* vétuste.

ancillary [æn'sɪlərɪ] *a* auxiliaire.

and [ænd, *unstressed* ən(d)] *conj* et; **a knife a. fork** un couteau et une fourchette; **two hundred a. two** deux cent deux; **better a. better** de mieux en mieux; **go a. see** va voir.

anecdote ['ænɪkdəʊt] *n* anecdote *f*.

anemone [ə'nemənɪ] *n* anémone *f*.

anew [ə'njuː] *adv Lit* de *or* à nouveau.

angel ['eɪndʒəl] *n* ange *m*. ◆**an'gelic** *a* angélique.

anger ['æŋgər] *n* colère *f*; **in a., out of a.** sous le coup de la colère; – *vt* mettre en colère, fâcher.

angl/e ['æŋg(ə)l] **1** *n* angle *m*; **at an a.** en biais. **2** *vi* (*to fish*) pêcher à la ligne; **to a. for** *Fig* quêter. ◆**—er** *n* pêcheur, -euse *mf* à la ligne. ◆**—ing** *n* pêche *f* à la ligne.

Anglican ['æŋglɪkən] *a & n* anglican, -ane (*mf*).

anglicism ['æŋglɪsɪz(ə)m] *n* anglicisme *m*.

Anglo- ['æŋgləʊ] *pref* anglo-. ◆**Anglo-'Saxon** *a & n* anglo-saxon, -onne (*mf*).

angora [æŋ'gɔːrə] *n* (*wool*) angora *m*.

angry ['æŋgrɪ] *a* (**-ier, -iest**) (*person, look*) fâché; (*letter*) indigné; **to get a.** se fâcher, se mettre en colère (**with** contre). ◆**angrily** *adv* en colère; (*to speak*) avec colère.

anguish ['æŋgwɪʃ] *n* angoisse *f*. ◆**—ed** *a* angoissé.

angular ['æŋgjʊlər] *a* (*face*) anguleux.

animal ['ænɪməl] *a* animal; – *n* animal *m*, bête *f*.

animate ['ænɪmeɪt] *vt* animer; **to become animated** s'animer; – ['ænɪmət] *a* (*alive*) animé. ◆**ani'mation** *n* animation *f*.

animosity [ænɪ'mɒsɪtɪ] *n* animosité *f*.

aniseed ['ænɪsiːd] *n* Culin anis *m*.

ankle ['æŋk(ə)l] *n* cheville *f*; **a. sock** socquette *f*.

annals ['æn(ə)lz] *npl* annales *fpl*.

annex [ə'neks] *vt* annexer.

annex(e) ['æneks] *n* (*building*) annexe *f*. ◆**annex'ation** *n* annexion *f*.

annihilate [ə'naɪəleɪt] *vt* anéantir, annihiler. ◆**annihi'lation** *n* anéantissement *m*.

anniversary [ænɪ'vɜːsərɪ] *n* (*of event*) anniversaire *m*, commémoration *f*.

annotate ['ænəteɪt] *vt* annoter. ◆**anno-'tation** *n* annotation *f*.

announc/e [ə'naʊns] *vt* annoncer; (*birth, marriage*) faire part de. ◆**—ement** *n* annonce *f*; (*of birth, marriage*) avis *m*; (*private letter*) faire-part *m inv*. ◆**—er** *n* TV speaker *m*, speakerine *f*.

annoy [ə'nɔɪ] *vt* (*inconvenience*) ennuyer, gêner; (*irritate*) agacer, contrarier. ◆**—ed** *a* contrarié, fâché; **to get a.** se fâcher (**with** contre). ◆**—ing** *a* ennuyeux, contrariant. ◆**annoyance** *n* contrariété *f*, ennui *m*.

annual ['ænjʊəl] *a* annuel; – *n* (*book*) annuaire *m*. ◆**—ly** *adv* annuellement.

annuity [ə'njuːɪtɪ] *n* (*of retired person*) pension *f* viagère.

annul [ə'nʌl] *vt* (**-ll-**) annuler. ◆**—ment** *n* annulation *f*.

anoint [ə'nɔɪnt] *vt* oindre (**with** de). ◆**—ed** *a* oint.

anomalous [ə'nɒmələs] *a* anormal. ◆**anomaly** *n* anomalie *f*.

anon [ə'nɒn] *adv Hum* tout à l'heure.

anonymous [ə'nɒnɪməs] *a* anonyme; **to remain a.** garder l'anonymat. ◆**ano-'nymity** *n* anonymat *m*.

anorak ['ænəræk] *n* anorak *m*.

anorexia [ænə'reksɪə] *n* anorexie *f*.

another [ə'nʌðər] *a* & *pron* un(e) autre; **a. man** un autre homme; **a. month** (*additional*) encore un mois, un autre mois; **a. ten** encore dix; **one a.** l'un(e) l'autre, *pl* les un(e)s les autres; **they love one a.** ils s'aiment (l'un l'autre).

answer ['ɑːnsər] *n* réponse *f*; (*to problem*) solution *f* (**to** de); (*reason*) explication *f*; – *vt* (*person, question, phone etc*) répondre à; (*word*) répondre; (*problem*) résoudre; (*prayer, wish*) exaucer; **to a. the bell** *or* **the door** ouvrir la porte; – *vi* répondre; **to a.**

back répliquer, répondre; **to a. for** (*s.o., sth*) répondre de. ◆**—able** *a* responsable (**for** sth de qch, **to s.o.** devant qn).

ant [ænt] *n* fourmi *f*. ◆**anthill** *n* fourmilière *f*.

antagonism [æn'tægənɪz(ə)m] *n* antagonisme *m*; (*hostility*) hostilité *f*. ◆**antagonist** *n* antagoniste *mf*. ◆**antago'nistic** *a* antagoniste; (*hostile*) hostile. ◆**antagonize** *vt* provoquer (l'hostilité de).

antarctic [æn'tɑːktɪk] *a* antarctique; – *n* **the A.** l'Antarctique *m*.

antecedent [æntɪ'siːd(ə)nt] *n* antécédent *m*.

antechamber ['æntɪtʃeɪmbər] *n* antichambre *f*.

antedate ['æntɪdeɪt] *vt* (*letter*) antidater.

antelope ['æntɪləʊp] *n* antilope *f*.

antenatal [æntɪ'neɪt(ə)l] *a* prénatal.

antenna¹, *pl* **-ae** [æn'tenə, -iː] *n* (*of insect etc*) antenne *f*.

antenna² [æn'tenə] *n* (*pl* **-as**) (*aerial*) *Am* antenne *f*.

anteroom ['æntɪrʊm] *n* antichambre *f*.

anthem ['ænθəm] *n* **national a.** hymne *m* national.

anthology [æn'θɒlədʒɪ] *n* anthologie *f*.

anthropology [ænθrə'pɒlədʒɪ] *n* anthropologie *f*.

anti- ['ænti, *Am* 'æntaɪ] *pref* anti-; **to be against** **sth** *Fam* être contre qch. ◆**anti'aircraft** *a* antiaérien. ◆**antibi'otic** *a* & *n* antibiotique (*m*). ◆**antibody** *n* anticorps *m*. ◆**anti'climax** *n* chute *f* dans l'ordinaire; (*let-down*) déception *f*. ◆**anti'clockwise** *adv* dans le sens inverse des aiguilles d'une montre. ◆**anti'cyclone** *n* anticyclone *m*. ◆**antidote** *n* antidote *m*. ◆**antifreeze** *n Aut* antigel *m*. ◆**anti'histamine** *n Med* antihistaminique *m*. ◆**anti'perspirant** *n* antisudoral *m*. ◆**anti-Se'mitic** *a* antisémite. ◆**anti-'Semitism** *n* antisémitisme *m*. ◆**anti'septic** *a* & *n* antiseptique (*m*). ◆**anti'social** *a* (*misfit*) asocial; (*measure, principles*) antisocial; (*unsociable*) insociable.

anticipate [æn'tɪsɪpeɪt] *vt* (*foresee*) prévoir; (*forestall*) devancer; (*expect*) s'attendre à; (*the future*) anticiper sur. ◆**antici'pation** *n* prévision *f*; (*expectation*) attente *f*; **in a. of** en prévision de, dans l'attente de; **in a.** (*to thank s.o., pay etc*) d'avance.

antics ['æntɪks] *npl* bouffonneries *fpl*.

antipathy [æn'tɪpəθɪ] *n* antipathie *f*.

antipodes [æn'tɪpədiːz] *npl* antipodes *mpl*.

antiquarian [æntɪ'kweərɪən] *a* **a. bookseller**

libraire *mf* spécialisé(e) dans le livre ancien.

antiquated ['æntɪkweɪtɪd] *a* vieilli; (*person*) vieux jeu *inv*.

antique [æn'tiːk] *a* (*furniture etc*) ancien; (*of Greek etc antiquity*) antique; **a. dealer** antiquaire *mf*; **a. shop** magasin *m* d'antiquités; – *n* objet *m* ancien *or* d'époque, antiquité *f*. ◆**antiquity** *n* (*period etc*) antiquité *f*.

antithesis, *pl* **-eses** [æn'tɪθəsɪs, -ɪsiːz] *n* antithèse *f*.

antler ['æntlər] *n* (*tine*) andouiller *m*; *pl* bois *mpl*.

antonym ['æntənɪm] *n* antonyme *m*.

Antwerp ['æntwɜːp] *n* Anvers *m or f*.

anus ['eɪnəs] *n* anus *m*.

anvil ['ænvɪl] *n* enclume *f*.

anxiety [æŋ'zaɪətɪ] *n* (*worry*) inquiétude *f* (**about** au sujet de); (*fear*) anxiété *f*; (*eagerness*) impatience *f* (**for** de).

anxious ['æŋkʃəs] *a* (*worried*) inquiet (**about** de, pour); (*troubled*) anxieux; (*causing worry*) inquiétant; (*eager*) impatient (**to do** de faire); **I'm a. (that) he should go** je tiens beaucoup à ce qu'il parte. ◆**—ly** *adv* avec inquiétude; (*to wait etc*) impatiemment.

any ['enɪ] *a* 1 (*interrogative*) du, de la, des; **have you a. milk/tickets?** avez-vous du lait/des billets?; **is there a. man (at all) who . . . ?** y a-t-il un homme (quelconque) qui . . . ? 2 (*negative*) de; (*not any at all*) aucun; **he hasn't a. milk/tickets** il n'a pas de lait/de billets; **there isn't a. proof** il n'a aucune preuve. 3 (*no matter which*) n'importe quel. 4 (*every*) tout; **at a. hour** à toute heure; **in a. case, at a. rate** de toute façon; – *pron* 1 (*no matter which one*) n'importe lequel; (*somebody*) quelqu'un; **if a. of you** si l'un d'entre vous, si quelqu'un parmi vous; **more than a.** plus qu'aucun. 2 (*quantity*) en; **have you a.?** en as-tu?; **I don't see a.** je n'en vois pas; – *adv* (*usually not translated*) (**not**) **a. further/happier/etc** (pas) plus loin/plus heureux/*etc*; **I don't see her a. more** je ne la vois plus; **a. more tea?** (*a little*) encore du thé?, encore un peu de thé?; **a. better?** (un peu) mieux?

anybody ['enɪbɒdɪ] *pron* 1 (*somebody*) quelqu'un; **do you see a.?** vois-tu quelqu'un?; **more than a.** plus qu'aucun. 2 (*negative*) personne; **he doesn't know a.** il ne connaît personne. 3 (*no matter who*) n'importe qui; **a. would think that . . .** on croirait que . . .

anyhow ['enɪhaʊ] *adv* (*at any rate*) de toute façon; (*badly*) n'importe comment; **to**

leave sth a. (*in confusion*) laisser qch sens dessus dessous.

anyone ['enɪwʌn] *pron* = **anybody**.

anyplace ['enɪpleɪs] *adv Am* = **anywhere**.

anything ['enɪθɪŋ] *pron* 1 (*something*) quelque chose; **can you see a.?** voyez-vous quelque chose? 2 (*negative*) rien; **he doesn't do a.** il ne fait rien; **without a.** sans rien. 3 (*everything*) tout; **a. you like** (tout) ce que tu veux; **like a.** (*to work etc*) *Fam* comme un fou. 4 (*no matter what*) **a. (at all)** n'importe quoi.

anyway ['enɪweɪ] *adv* (*at any rate*) de toute façon.

anywhere ['enɪweər] *adv* 1 (*no matter where*) n'importe où. 2 (*everywhere*) partout; **a. you go** partout où vous allez, où que vous alliez; **a. you like** là où tu veux. 3 (*somewhere*) quelque part; **is he going a.?** va-t-il quelque part? 4 (*negative*) nulle part; **he doesn't go a.** il ne va nulle part; **without a. to put it** sans un endroit où le mettre.

apace [ə'peɪs] *adv* rapidement.

apart [ə'pɑːt] *adv* (*to or at one side*) à part; **to tear a.** (*to pieces*) mettre en pièces; **we kept them a.** (*separate*) on les tenait séparés; **with legs (wide) a.** les jambes écartées; **they are a metre a.** ils se trouvent à un mètre l'un de l'autre; **a. from** (*except for*) à part; **to take a.** démonter; **to come a.** (*of two objects*) se séparer; (*of knot etc*) se défaire; **to tell a.** distinguer entre; **worlds a.** (*very different*) diamétralement opposé.

apartheid [ə'pɑːteɪt] *n* apartheid *m*.

apartment [ə'pɑːtmənt] *n* (*flat*) *Am* appartement *m*; (*room*) chambre *f*; **a. house** *Am* immeuble *m* (d'habitation).

apathy ['æpəθɪ] *n* apathie *f*. ◆**apa'thetic** *a* apathique.

ape [eɪp] *n* singe *m*; – *vt* (*imitate*) singer.

aperitif [ə'perɪtɪf] *n* apéritif *m*.

aperture ['æpətʃʊər] *n* ouverture *f*.

apex ['eɪpeks] *n Geom & Fig* sommet *m*.

aphorism ['æfərɪz(ə)m] *n* aphorisme *m*.

aphrodisiac [æfrə'dɪzɪæk] *a & n* aphrodisiaque (*m*).

apiece [ə'piːs] *adv* chacun; **a pound a.** une livre (la) pièce *or* chacun.

apish ['eɪpɪʃ] *a* simiesque; (*imitative*) imitateur.

apocalypse [ə'pɒkəlɪps] *n* apocalypse *f*. ◆**apoca'lyptic** *a* apocalyptique.

apocryphal [ə'pɒkrɪfəl] *a* apocryphe.

apogee ['æpədʒiː] *n* apogée *m*.

apologetic [əpɒlə'dʒetɪk] *a* (*letter*) plein d'excuses; **to be a. about** s'excuser de. ◆**apologetically** *adv* en s'excusant.

apology [ə'pɒlədʒɪ] n excuses fpl; **an a. for a dinner** Fam Pej un dîner minable.
◆**apologist** n apologiste mf. ◆**apologize** vi s'excuser (**for** de); **to a. to s.o.** faire ses excuses à qn (**for** pour).

apoplexy ['æpəpleksɪ] n apoplexie f.
◆**apo'plectic** a & n apoplectique (mf).

apostle [ə'pɒs(ə)l] n apôtre m.

apostrophe [ə'pɒstrəfɪ] n apostrophe f.

appal [ə'pɔːl] (Am **appall**) vt (**-ll-**) épouvanter. ◆**appalling** a épouvantable.

apparatus [æpə'reɪtəs, Am -'rætəs] n (equipment, organization) appareil m; (in gym) agrès mpl.

apparel [ə'pærəl] n habit m, habillement m.

apparent [ə'pærənt] a (obvious, seeming) apparent; **it's a. that** il est évident que.
◆**—ly** adv apparemment.

apparition [æpə'rɪʃ(ə)n] n apparition f.

appeal [ə'piːl] n (call) appel m; (entreaty) supplication f; (charm) attrait m; (interest) intérêt m; Jur appel m; − vt **to a. to** (s.o., s.o.'s kindness) faire appel à; **to a. to s.o.** (attract) plaire à qn, séduire qn; (interest) intéresser qn; **to a. to s.o. for sth** demander qch à qn; **to a. to s.o. to do** supplier qn de faire; − vi Jur faire appel. ◆**—ing** a (begging) suppliant; (attractive) séduisant.

appear [ə'pɪər] vi (become visible) apparaître; (present oneself) se présenter; (seem, be published) paraître; (act) Th jouer; Jur comparaître; **it appears that** (it seems) il semble que (+ sub or indic); (it is rumoured) il paraîtrait que (+ indic).
◆**appearance** n (act) apparition f; (look) apparence f, aspect m; (of book) parution f; **to put in an a.** faire acte de présence.

appease [ə'piːz] vt apaiser; (curiosity) satisfaire.

append [ə'pend] vt joindre, ajouter (**to** à).
◆**—age** n Anat appendice m.

appendix, pl **-ixes** or **-ices** [ə'pendɪks, -ɪksiz, -ɪsiːz] n (of book) & Anat appendice m. ◆**appendicitis** [əpendɪ'saɪtɪs] n appendicite f.

appertain [æpə'teɪn] vi **to a. to** se rapporter à.

appetite ['æpɪtaɪt] n appétit m; **to take away s.o.'s a.** couper l'appétit à qn. ◆**appetizer** n (drink) apéritif m; (food) amuse-gueule m inv. ◆**appetizing** a appétissant.

applaud [ə'plɔːd] vt (clap) applaudir; (approve of) approuver, applaudir à; − vi applaudir. ◆**applause** n applaudissements mpl.

apple ['æp(ə)l] n pomme f; **stewed apples, a. sauce** compote f de pommes; **eating/**

cooking a. pomme f à couteau/à cuire; **a. pie** tarte f aux pommes; **a. core** trognon m de pomme; **a. tree** pommier m.

appliance [ə'plaɪəns] n appareil m.

apply [ə'plaɪ] **1** vt (put, carry out etc) appliquer; (brake) Aut appuyer sur; **to a. oneself to** s'appliquer à. **2** vi (be relevant) s'appliquer (**to** à); **to a. for** (job) poser sa candidature à, postuler; **to a. to s.o.** (ask) s'adresser à qn (**for** pour). ◆**applied** a (maths etc) appliqué. ◆**applicable** a applicable (**to** à). ◆**'applicant** n candidat, -ate mf (**for** à). ◆**appli'cation** n application f; (request) demande f; (for job) candidature f; (for membership) demande f d'adhésion or d'inscription; **a. (form)** (job) formulaire m de candidature; (club) formulaire m d'inscription or d'adhésion.

appoint [ə'pɔɪnt] vt (person) nommer (**to sth** à qch, **to do** pour faire); (time, date) désigner, fixer; **at the appointed time** à l'heure dite; **well-appointed** bien équipé. ◆**—ment** n nomination f; (meeting) rendez-vous m inv; (post) place f, situation f.

apportion [ə'pɔːʃ(ə)n] vt répartir.

apposite ['æpəzɪt] a juste, à propos.

appraise [ə'preɪz] vt évaluer. ◆**appraisal** n évaluation f.

appreciate [ə'priːʃɪeɪt] **1** vt (enjoy, value, assess) apprécier; (understand) comprendre; (be grateful for) être reconnaissant de. **2** vi prendre de la valeur. ◆**appreciable** a appréciable, sensible. ◆**appreci'ation** n **1** (judgement) appréciation f; (gratitude) reconnaissance f. **2** (rise in value) plus-value f. ◆**appreciative** a (grateful) reconnaissant (**of** de); (laudatory) élogieux; **to be a. of** (enjoy) apprécier.

apprehend [æprɪ'hend] vt (seize, arrest) appréhender. ◆**apprehension** n (fear) appréhension f. ◆**apprehensive** a inquiet (**about** de, au sujet de); **to be a. of** redouter.

apprentice [ə'prentɪs] n apprenti, -ie mf; − vt mettre en apprentissage (**to** chez). ◆**apprenticeship** n apprentissage m.

approach [ə'prəʊtʃ] vt (draw near to) s'approcher de (qn, feu, porte etc); (age, result, town) approcher de; (subject) aborder; (accost) aborder (qn); **to a. s.o. about** parler à qn de qn; − vi (of person, vehicle) s'approcher; (of date etc) approcher; − n approche f; (method) façon f de s'y prendre; (path) voie f d'accès m; **a. to** (question) manière f d'aborder; **to make approaches to** faire des avances à.

◆—**able** *a* (*place*) accessible; (*person*) abordable.

appropriate 1 [əˈprəʊprɪət] *a* (*place, tools, clothes etc*) approprié, adéquat; (*remark, time*) opportun; **a. to** *or* **for** propre à, approprié à. **2** [əˈprəʊprɪeɪt] *vt* (*set aside*) affecter; (*steal*) s'approprier. ◆—**ly** *adv* convenablement.

approv/e [əˈpruːv] *vt* approuver; **to a. of sth** approuver qch; **I don't a. of him** il ne me plaît pas, je ne l'apprécie pas; **I a. of his going** je trouve bon qu'il y aille; **I a. of her having accepted** je l'approuve d'avoir accepté. ◆—**ing** *a* approbateur. ◆**approval** *n* approbation *f*; **on a.** (*goods*) *Com* à l'essai.

approximate [əˈprɒksɪmət] *a* approximatif; – [əˈprɒksɪmeɪt] *vi* **to a. to** se rapprocher de. ◆—**ly** *adv* à peu près, approximativement. ◆**approxi'mation** *n* approximation *f*.

apricot [ˈeɪprɪkɒt] *n* abricot *m*.

April [ˈeɪprəl] *n* avril *m*; **to make an A. fool of** faire un poisson d'avril à.

apron [ˈeɪprən] *n* (*garment*) tablier *m*.

apse [æps] *n* (*of church*) abside *f*.

apt [æpt] *a* (*suitable*) convenable; (*remark, reply*) juste; (*word, name*) bien choisi; (*student*) doué, intelligent; **to be a. to** avoir tendance à; **a. at sth** habile à qch. ◆**aptitude** *n* aptitude *f* (**for** à, pour). ◆**aptly** *adv* convenablement; **a. named** qui porte bien son nom.

aqualung [ˈækwəlʌŋ] *n* scaphandre *m* autonome.

aquarium [əˈkweərɪəm] *n* aquarium *m*.

Aquarius [əˈkweərɪəs] *n* (*sign*) le Verseau.

aquatic [əˈkwætɪk] *a* (*plant etc*) aquatique; (*sport*) nautique.

aqueduct [ˈækwɪdʌkt] *n* aqueduc *m*.

aquiline [ˈækwɪlaɪn] *a* (*nose, profile*) aquilin.

Arab [ˈærəb] *a* & *n* arabe (*mf*). ◆**Arabian** [əˈreɪbɪən] *a* arabe. ◆**Arabic** *a* & *n* (*language*) arabe (*m*); **A. numerals** chiffres *mpl* arabes.

arabesque [ærəˈbesk] *n* (*decoration*) arabesque *f*.

arable [ˈærəb(ə)l] *a* (*land*) arable.

arbiter [ˈɑːbɪtər] *n* arbitre *m*. ◆**arbitrate** *vti* arbitrer. ◆**arbi'tration** *n* arbitrage *m*; **to go to a.** soumettre la question à l'arbitrage. ◆**arbitrator** *n* (*in dispute*) médiateur, -trice *mf*.

arbitrary [ˈɑːbɪtrərɪ] *a* arbitraire.

arbour [ˈɑːbər] *n* tonnelle *f*, charmille *f*.

arc [ɑːk] *n* (*of circle*) arc *m*.

arcade [ɑːˈkeɪd] *n* (*market*) passage *m* couvert.

arch [ɑːtʃ] *n* (*of bridge*) arche *f*; *Archit* voûte *f*, arc *m*; (*of foot*) cambrure *f*; – *vt* (*one's back etc*) arquer, courber. ◆**archway** *n* passage *m* voûté, voûte *f*.

arch- [ɑːtʃ] *pref* (*villain etc*) achevé; **a. enemy** ennemi *m* numéro un.

arch(a)eology [ɑːkɪˈɒlədʒɪ] *n* archéologie *f*. ◆**arch(a)eologist** *n* archéologue *mf*.

archaic [ɑːˈkeɪɪk] *a* archaïque.

archangel [ˈɑːkeɪndʒəl] *n* archange *m*.

archbishop [ɑːtʃˈbɪʃəp] *n* archevêque *m*.

archer [ˈɑːtʃər] *n* archer *m*. ◆**archery** *n* tir *m* à l'arc.

archetype [ˈɑːkɪtaɪp] *n* archétype *m*.

archipelago [ɑːkɪˈpeləgəʊ] *n* (*pl* -**oes** *or* -**os**) archipel *m*.

architect [ˈɑːkɪtekt] *n* architecte *m*. ◆**architecture** *n* architecture *f*.

archives [ˈɑːkaɪvz] *npl* archives *fpl*. ◆**archivist** *n* archiviste *mf*.

arctic [ˈɑːktɪk] *a* arctique; (*weather*) polaire, glacial; – *n* **the A.** l'Arctique *m*.

ardent [ˈɑːdənt] *a* ardent. ◆—**ly** *adv* ardemment. ◆**ardour** *n* ardeur *f*.

arduous [ˈɑːdjʊəs] *a* ardu.

are [ɑːr] *see* **be**.

area [ˈeərɪə] *n* *Math* superficie *f*; *Geog* région *f*; (*of town*) quartier *m*; *Mil* zone *f*; (*domain*) *Fig* domaine *m*, secteur *m*, terrain *m*; **built-up a.** agglomération *f*; **parking a.** aire *f* de stationnement; **a. code** *Tel Am* indicatif *m*.

arena [əˈriːnə] *n* *Hist* & *Fig* arène *f*.

Argentina [ɑːdʒənˈtiːnə] *n* Argentine *f*. ◆**Argentine** [ˈɑːdʒəntaɪn] *a* & *n*, ◆**Argentinian** *a* & *n* argentin, -ine (*mf*).

argu/e [ˈɑːgjuː] *vi* (*quarrel*) se disputer (**with** avec, **about** au sujet de); (*reason*) raisonner (**with** avec, **about** sur); **to a. in favour of** plaider pour; – *vt* (*matter*) discuter; **to a. that** (*maintain*) soutenir que. ◆—**able** [ˈɑːgʊəb(ə)l] *a* discutable. ◆—**ably** *adv* on pourrait soutenir que. ◆—**ment** *n* (*quarrel*) dispute *f*; (*reasoning*) argument *m*; (*debate*) discussion *f*; **to have an a.** se disputer. ◆**argu'mentative** *a* raisonneur.

aria [ˈɑːrɪə] *n* *Mus* air *m* (d'opéra).

arid [ˈærɪd] *a* aride.

Aries [ˈeərɪz] *n* (*sign*) le Bélier.

arise [əˈraɪz] *vi* (*pt* **arose**, *pp* **arisen**) (*of problem, opportunity etc*) se présenter; (*of cry, objection*) s'élever; (*result*) résulter (**from** de); (*get up*) *Lit* se lever.

aristocracy [ærɪˈstɒkrəsɪ] *n* aristocratie *f*. ◆**aristocrat** [ˈærɪstəkræt, *Am* əˈrɪstəkræt] *n* aristocrate *mf*. ◆**aristo'cratic** *a* aristocratique.

arithmetic [ə'rɪθmətɪk] *n* arithmétique *f*.

ark [ɑːk] *n* Noah's a. l'arche *f* de Noé.

arm [ɑːm] **1** *n* bras *m*; **a. in a.** bras dessus bras dessous; **with open arms** à bras ouverts. **2** *n* (*weapon*) arme *f*; **arms race** course *f* aux armements; – *vt* armer (**with** de). ◆**armament** *n* armement *m*. ◆**armband** *n* brassard *m*. ◆**armchair** *n* fauteuil *m*. ◆**armful** *n* brassée *f*. ◆**armhole** *n* emmanchure *f*. ◆**armpit** *n* aisselle *f*. ◆**armrest** *n* accoudoir *m*.

armadillo [ɑːmə'dɪləʊ] *n* (*pl* -**os**) tatou *m*.

armistice ['ɑːmɪstɪs] *n* armistice *m*.

armour ['ɑːmər] *n* (*of knight etc*) armure *f*; (*of tank etc*) blindage *m*. ◆**armoured** *a*, ◆**armour-plated** *a* blindé. ◆**armoury** *n* arsenal *m*.

army ['ɑːmɪ] *n* armée *f*; – *a* (*uniform etc*) militaire; **to join the a.** s'engager; **regular a.** armée *f* active.

aroma [ə'rəʊmə] *n* arôme *m*. ◆**aro'matic** *a* aromatique.

arose [ə'rəʊz] *see* **arise**.

around [ə'raʊnd] *prep* autour de; (*approximately*) environ, autour de; **to go a. the world** faire le tour du monde; – *adv* autour; **all a.** tout autour; **to follow a.** suivre partout; **to rush a.** courir çà et là; **a. here** par ici; **he's still a.** il est encore là; **there's a lot of flu a.** il y a pas mal de grippes dans l'air; **up and a.** (*after illness*) *Am* sur pied, guéri.

arouse [ə'raʊz] *vt* éveiller, susciter; (*sexually*) exciter; **to a. from sleep** tirer du sommeil.

arrange [ə'reɪndʒ] *vt* arranger; (*time, meeting*) fixer; **it was arranged that** il était convenu que; **to a. to do** s'arranger pour faire. ◆**—ment** *n* (*layout, agreement*) arrangement *m*; *pl* (*preparations*) préparatifs *mpl*; (*plans*) projets *mpl*; **to make arrangements to** s'arranger pour.

array [ə'reɪ] *n* (*display*) étalage *m*. ◆**arrayed** *a* (*dressed*) *Lit* (re)vêtu (**in** de).

arrears [ə'rɪəz] *npl* (*payment*) arriéré *m*; **to be in a.** avoir des arriérés.

arrest [ə'rest] *vt* arrêter; – *n Jur* arrestation *f*; **under a.** en état d'arrestation; **cardiac a.** arrêt *m* du cœur. ◆**—ing** *a* (*striking*) *Fig* frappant.

arrive [ə'raɪv] *vi* arriver. ◆**arrival** *n* arrivée *f*; **new a.** nouveau venu *m*, nouvelle venue *f*; (*baby*) nouveau-né, -ée *mf*.

arrogant ['ærəgənt] *a* arrogant. ◆**arro-**

gance *n* arrogance *f*. ◆**arrogantly** *adv* avec arrogance.

arrow ['ærəʊ] *n* flèche *f*.

arsenal ['ɑːsən(ə)l] *n* arsenal *m*.

arsenic ['ɑːsnɪk] *n* arsenic *m*.

arson ['ɑːs(ə)n] *n* incendie *m* volontaire. ◆**arsonist** *n* incendiaire *mf*.

art [ɑːt] *n* art *m*; (*cunning*) artifice *m*; **work of a.** œuvre *f* d'art; **fine arts** beaux-arts *mpl*; **faculty of arts** *Univ* faculté *f* des lettres; **a. school** école *f* des beaux-arts.

artefact ['ɑːtɪfækt] *n* objet *m* fabriqué.

artery ['ɑːtərɪ] *n Anat Aut* artère *f*. ◆**ar'terial** *a Anat* artériel; **a. road** route *f* principale.

artful ['ɑːtfəl] *a* rusé, astucieux. ◆**—ly** *adv* astucieusement.

arthritis [ɑː'θraɪtɪs] *n* arthrite *f*.

artichoke ['ɑːtɪtʃəʊk] *n* (globe) **a.** artichaut *m*; **Jerusalem a.** topinambour *m*.

article ['ɑːtɪk(ə)l] *n* (*object, clause*) & *Journ Gram* article *m*; **a. of clothing** vêtement *m*; **articles of value** objets *mpl* de valeur; **leading a.** *Journ* éditorial *m*.

articulat/e [ɑː'tɪkjʊlət] *a* (*sound*) net, distinct; (*person*) qui s'exprime clairement; – [ɑː'tɪkjʊleɪt] *vti* (*speak*) articuler. ◆**—ed** *a* **a. lorry** semi-remorque *m*. ◆**articu'lation** *n* articulation *f*.

artifact ['ɑːtɪfækt] *n* object *m* fabriqué.

artifice ['ɑːtɪfɪs] *n* artifice *m*.

artificial [ɑːtɪ'fɪʃ(ə)l] *a* artificiel. ◆**artifici'ality** *n* caractère *m* artificiel. ◆**artificially** *adv* artificiellement.

artillery [ɑː'tɪlərɪ] *n* artillerie *f*.

artisan ['ɑːtɪzæn] *n* artisan *m*.

artist ['ɑːtɪst] *n* (*actor, painter etc*) artiste *mf*. ◆**artiste** [ɑː'tiːst] *n Th Mus* artiste *m*. ◆**ar'tistic** *a* (*sense, treasure etc*) artistique; (*person*) artiste. ◆**artistry** *n* art *m*.

artless ['ɑːtləs] *a* naturel, naïf.

arty ['ɑːtɪ] *a Pej* du genre artiste.

as [æz, *unstressed* əz] *adv* & *conj* **1** (*manner etc*) comme; **as you like** comme tu veux; **such as** comme, tel que; **as much** *or* **as hard as I can** (au)tant que je peux; **as it is** (*this being the case*) les choses étant ainsi; (*to leave sth*) comme ça, tel quel; **it's late as it is** il est déjà tard; **as if, as though** comme si. **2** (*comparison*) **as tall as you** aussi grand que vous; **is he as tall as you?** est-il aussi *or* si grand que vous?; **as white as a sheet** blanc comme un linge; **as much** *or* **as hard as you** autant que vous; **the same as** le même que; **twice as big as** deux fois plus grand que. **3** (*concessive*) **(as) clever as he is** si *or* aussi intelligent qu'il soit. **4** (*capacity*) **as a**

teacher comme professeur, en tant que *or* en qualité de professeur; **to act as a father** agir en père. **5** (*reason*) puisque, comme; **as it's late** puisqu'il est tard, comme il est tard. **6** (*time*) **as I left** comme je partais; **as one grows older** à mesure que l'on vieillit; **as he slept** pendant qu'il dormait; **one day as . . .** un jour que . . . ; **as from, as of** (*time*) à partir de. **7** (*concerning*) **as for that, as to that** quant à cela. **8** (+ *inf*) **so as to** de manière à; **so stupid as to** assez bête pour.

asbestos [æs'bestəs] *n* amiante *f*.

ascend [ə'send] *vi* monter; – *vt* (*throne*) monter sur; (*stairs*) monter; (*mountain*) faire l'ascension de. ◆**ascent** *n* ascension *f* (of *also*); (*slope*) côte *f*.

ascertain [æsə'tein] *vt* (*discover*) découvrir; (*check*) s'assurer de.

ascetic [ə'setik] *a* ascétique; – *n* ascète *mf*.

ascribe [ə'skraib] *vt* attribuer (**to** à).

ash [æʃ] *n* **1** (*of cigarette etc*) cendre *f*; **A. Wednesday** mercredi *m* des Cendres. **2** (*tree*) frêne *m*. ◆**ashen** *a* (*pale grey*) cendré; (*face*) pâle. ◆**ashcan** *n* *Am* poubelle *f*. ◆**ashtray** *n* cendrier *m*.

ashamed [ə'feimd] *a* honteux; **to be a. of** avoir honte de; **to be a. (of oneself)** avoir honte.

ashore [ə'ʃɔːr] *adv* **to go a.** débarquer; **to put s.o. a.** débarquer qn.

Asia ['eiʃə] *n* Asie *f*. ◆**Asian** *a* asiatique; – *n* Asiatique *mf*, Asiate *mf*.

aside [ə'said] **1** *adv* de côté; **to draw a.** (*curtain*) écarter; **to take** *or* **draw s.o. a.** prendre qn à part; **to step a.** s'écarter; **a. from** en dehors de. **2** *n* *Th* aparté *m*.

asinine ['æsinain] *a* stupide, idiot.

ask [ɑːsk] *vt* demander; (*a question*) poser; (*invite*) inviter; **to a. s.o. (for) sth** demander qch à qn; **to a. s.o. to do** demander à qn de faire; – *vi* demander; **to a. for sth/s.o.** demander qch/qn; **to a. for sth back** redemander qch; **to a. about sth** se renseigner sur qch; **to a. after** *or* **about s.o.** demander des nouvelles de qn; **to a. s.o. about** interroger qn sur; **asking price** prix *m* demandé.

askance [ə'skɑːns] *adv* **to look a. at** regarder avec méfiance.

askew [ə'skjuː] *adv* de biais, de travers.

aslant [ə'slɑːnt] *adv* de travers.

asleep [ə'sliːp] *a* endormi; (*arm, leg*) engourdi; **to be a.** dormir; **to fall a.** s'endormir.

asp [æsp] *n* (*snake*) aspic *m*.

asparagus [ə'spærəgəs] *n* (*plant*) asperge *f*; (*shoots*) *Culin* asperges *fpl*.

aspect ['æspekt] *n* aspect *m*; (*of house*) orientation *f*.

aspersions [ə'spɜːʃ(ə)nz] *npl* **to cast a. on** dénigrer.

asphalt ['æsfælt, *Am* 'æsfɔːlt] *n* asphalte *m*; – *vt* asphalter.

asphyxia [əs'fiksiə] *n* asphyxie *f*. ◆**asphyxiate** *vt* asphyxier. ◆**asphyxi-'ation** *n* asphyxie *f*.

aspire [ə'spaiər] *vi* **to a. to** aspirer à. ◆**aspi-'ration** *n* aspiration *f*.

aspirin ['æsprin] *n* aspirine *f*.

ass [æs] *n* (*animal*) âne *m*; (*person*) *Fam* imbécile *mf*, âne *m*; **she-a.** ânesse *f*.

assail [ə'seil] *vt* assaillir (**with** de). ◆**assai-lant** *n* agresseur *m*.

assassin [ə'sæsin] *n* *Pol* assassin *m*. ◆**assassinate** *vt* *Pol* assassiner. ◆**assassi'nation** *n* *Pol* assassinat *m*.

assault [ə'sɔːlt] *n* *Mil* assaut *m*; *Jur* agression *f*; – *vt* *Jur* agresser; (*woman*) violenter.

assemble [ə'semb(ə)l] *vt* (*objects, ideas*) assembler; (*people*) rassembler; (*machine*) monter; – *vi* se rassembler. ◆**assembly** *n* (*meeting*) assemblée *f*; *Tech* montage *m*, assemblage *m*; *Sch* rassemblement *m*; **a. line** (*in factory*) chaîne *f* de montage.

assent [ə'sent] *n* assentiment *m*; – *vi* consentir (**to** à).

assert [ə'sɜːt] *vt* affirmer (**that** que); (*rights*) revendiquer; **to a. oneself** s'affirmer. ◆**assertion** *n* affirmation *f*; revendication *f*. ◆**assertive** *a* affirmatif; *Pej* autoritaire.

assess [ə'ses] *vt* (*estimate, evaluate*) évaluer; (*decide amount of*) fixer le montant de; (*person*) juger. ◆**—ment** *n* évaluation *f*; jugement *m*. ◆**assessor** *n* (*valuer*) expert *m*.

asset ['æset] *n* atout *m*, avantage *m*; *pl* *Com* biens *mpl*, avoir *m*.

assiduous [ə'sidjuəs] *a* assidu.

assign [ə'sain] *vt* (*allocate*) assigner; (*day etc*) fixer; (*appoint*) nommer (**to** à). ◆**—ment** *n* (*task*) mission *f*; *Sch* devoirs *mpl*.

assimilate [ə'simileit] *vt* assimiler; – *vi* s'assimiler. ◆**assimi'lation** *n* assimilation *f*.

assist [ə'sist] *vti* aider (**in doing, to do** à faire). ◆**assistance** *n* aide *f*; **to be of a. to s.o.** aider qn. ◆**assistant** *n* assistant, -ante *mf*; (*in shop*) vendeur, -euse *mf*; – *a* adjoint.

assizes [ə'saiziz] *npl* *Jur* assises *fpl*.

associate [ə'səufieit] *vt* associer (**with** à, avec); – *vi* **to a. with s.o.** fréquenter qn; **to**

a. (oneself) with (in business venture) s'associer à or avec; — [ə'səuʃiət] n & a associé, -ée (mf). ◆**associ'ation** n association f; pl (memories) souvenirs mpl.

assort/ed [ə'sɔːtɪd] a (different) variés; (foods) assortis; **well-a.** bien assorti. ◆**—ment** n assortiment m.

assuage [ə'sweɪdʒ] vt apaiser, adoucir.

assum/e [ə'sjuːm] vt **1** (take on) prendre; (responsibility, role) assumer; (attitude, name) adopter. **2** (suppose) présumer (that que). ◆**—ed** a (feigned) faux; **a. name** nom m d'emprunt. ◆**assumption** n (supposition) supposition f.

assur/e [ə'ʃuər] vt assurer. ◆**—edly** [-ɪdlɪ] adv assurément. ◆**assurance** n assurance f.

asterisk ['æstərɪsk] n astérisque m.

astern [ə'stɜːn] adv Nau à l'arrière.

asthma ['æsmə] n asthme m. ◆**asth'matic** a & n asthmatique (mf).

astir [ə'stɜːr] a (excited) en émoi; (out of bed) debout.

astonish [ə'stɒnɪʃ] vt étonner; **to be astonished** s'étonner (at sth de qch). ◆**—ing** a étonnant. ◆**—ingly** adv étonnamment. ◆**—ment** n étonnement m.

astound [ə'staund] vt stupéfier, étonner. ◆**—ing** a stupéfiant.

astray [ə'streɪ] adv **to go a.** s'égarer; **to lead a.** égarer.

astride [ə'straɪd] adv à califourchon; — prep à cheval sur.

astringent [ə'strɪndʒənt] a (harsh) sévère.

astrology [ə'strɒlədʒɪ] n astrologie f. ◆**astrologer** n astrologue mf.

astronaut ['æstrənɔːt] n astronaute mf.

astronomy [ə'strɒnəmɪ] n astronomie f. ◆**astronomer** n astronome m. ◆**astro'nomical** a astronomique.

astute [ə'stjuːt] a (crafty) rusé; (clever) astucieux.

asunder [ə'sʌndər] adv (to pieces) en pièces; (in two) en deux.

asylum [ə'saɪləm] n asile m; **lunatic a.** Pej maison f de fous, asile m d'aliénés.

at [æt, unstressed ət] prep **1** à; **at the end** à la fin; **at work** au travail; **at six (o'clock)** à six heures. **2** chez; **at the doctor's** chez le médecin; **at home** chez soi, à la maison. ◆**at-home** n réception f. **3** en; **at sea** en mer; **at war** en guerre; **good at** (geography etc) fort en. **4** contre; **angry at** fâché contre. **5** sur; **to shoot at** tirer sur; **at my request** sur ma demande. **6** de; **to laugh at** rire de; **surprised at** surpris de. **7** (au)près de; **at the window** (au)près de la fenêtre. **8** par; **to**

come in at the door entrer par la porte; **six at a time** six par six. **9** at night la nuit; **to look at** regarder; **not at all** pas du tout; (after 'thank you') pas de quoi!; **nothing at all** rien du tout; **to be (hard) at it** être très occupé, travailler dur; **he's always (on) at me** Fam il est toujours après moi.

ate [et, Am eɪt] see eat.

atheism ['eɪθɪz(ə)m] n athéisme m. ◆**atheist** n athée mf.

Athens ['æθɪnz] n Athènes m or f.

athlete ['æθliːt] n athlète mf; **a.'s foot** Med mycose f. ◆**ath'letic** a athlétique; **a. meeting** réunion f sportive. ◆**ath'letics** npl athlétisme m.

atishoo! [ə'tɪʃuː] (Am atchoo [ə'tʃuː]) int atchoum!

Atlantic [ət'læntɪk] a atlantique; — n the A. l'Atlantique m.

atlas ['ætləs] n atlas m.

atmosphere ['ætməsfɪər] n atmosphère f. ◆**atmos'pheric** a atmosphérique.

atom ['ætəm] n atome m; **a. bomb** bombe f atomique. ◆**a'tomic** a atomique. ◆**atomizer** n atomiseur m.

atone [ə'təun] vi **to a. for** expier. ◆**—ment** n expiation f (for de).

atrocious [ə'trəuʃəs] a atroce. ◆**atrocity** n atrocité f.

atrophy ['ætrəfɪ] vi s'atrophier.

attach [ə'tætʃ] vt attacher (to à); (document) joindre (to à); **attached to** (fond of) attaché à. ◆**—ment** n (affection) attachement m; (fastener) attache f; (tool) accessoire m.

attaché [ə'tæʃeɪ] n **1** Pol attaché, -ée mf. **2 a. case** attaché-case m.

attack [ə'tæk] n Mil Med & Fig attaque f; (of fever) accès m; (on s.o.'s life) attentat m; **heart a.** crise f cardiaque; — vt attaquer; (problem, plan) s'attaquer à; — vi attaquer. ◆**—er** n agresseur m.

attain [ə'teɪn] vt parvenir à, atteindre, réaliser. ◆**—able** a accessible. ◆**—ment** n (of ambition, aim etc) réalisation f (of de); pl (skills) talents mpl.

attempt [ə'tempt] n tentative f; **to make an a. to** essayer or tenter de; **a. on** (record) tentative pour battre; **a. on s.o.'s life** attentat m contre qn; — vt tenter; (task) entreprendre; **to a. to do** essayer or tenter de faire; **attempted murder** tentative de meurtre.

attend [ə'tend] vt (match etc) assister à; (course) suivre; (school, church) aller à; (wait on, serve) servir; (escort) accompagner; (patient) soigner; — vi assister; **to a. to** (pay attention to) prêter attention à;

(*take care of*) s'occuper de. ◆**—ed** *a*
well-a. (*course*) très suivi; (*meeting*) où il y a
du monde. ◆**attendance** *n* présence *f* (**at**
à); (*people*) assistance *f*; **school a.** scolarité
f; **in a.** de service. ◆**attendant 1** *n*
employé, -ée *mf*; (*in museum*) gardien,
-ienne *mf*; *pl* (*of prince, king etc*) suite *f*. **2** *a*
(*fact*) concomitant.

attention [ə'tenʃ(ə)n] *n* attention *f*; **to pay a.**
prêter *or* faire attention (**to** à); **a.!** *Mil*
garde-à-vous!; **to stand at a.** *Mil* être au
garde-à-vous; **a. to detail** minutie *f*.
◆**attentive** *a* (*heedful*) attentif (**to** à);
(*thoughtful*) attentionné (**to** pour).
◆**attentively** *adv* avec attention, attentivement.

attenuate [ə'tenjυeɪt] *vt* atténuer.

attest [ə'test] *vti* **to a. (to)** témoigner de.

attic ['ætɪk] *n* grenier *m*.

attire [ə'taɪər] *n Lit* vêtements *mpl*.

attitude ['ætɪtjuːd] *n* attitude *f*.

attorney [ə'tɜːnɪ] *n* (*lawyer*) *Am* avocat *m*;
district a. *Am* = procureur *m* (de la République).

attract [ə'trækt] *vt* attirer. ◆**attraction** *n*
attraction *f*; (*charm, appeal*) attrait *m*.
◆**attractive** *a* (*price etc*) intéressant; (*girl*)
belle, jolie; (*boy*) beau; (*manners*)
attrayant.

attribut/e 1 ['ætrɪbjuːt] *n* (*quality*) attribut
m. **2** [ə'trɪbjuːt] *vt* (*ascribe*) attribuer (**to** à).
◆**—able** *a* attribuable (**to** à).

attrition [ə'trɪʃ(ə)n] *n* **war of a.** guerre *f*
d'usure.

attuned [ə'tjuːnd] *a* **a. to** (*of ideas, trends etc*)
en accord avec; (*used to*) habitué à.

atypical [eɪ'tɪpɪk(ə)l] *a* peu typique.

aubergine ['əʊbəʒiːn] *n* aubergine *f*.

auburn ['ɔːbən] *a* (*hair*) châtain roux.

auction ['ɔːkʃən] *n* vente *f* (aux enchères); —
vt **to a. (off)** vendre (aux enchères).
◆**auctio'neer** *n* commissaire-priseur *m*,
adjudicateur, -trice *m*.

audacious [ɔː'deɪʃəs] *a* audacieux.
◆**audacity** *n* audace *f*.

audib/le ['ɔːdɪb(ə)l] *a* perceptible, audible.
◆**—ly** *adv* distinctement.

audience ['ɔːdɪəns] *n* assistance *f*, public *m*;
(*of speaker, musician*) auditoire *m*; *Th Cin*
spectateurs *mpl*; *Rad* auditeurs *mpl*; (*interview*) audience *f*.

audio ['ɔːdɪəʊ] *a* (*cassette, system etc*) audio
inv. ◆**audiotypist** *n* dactylo *f* au
magnétophone, audiotypiste   *mf*.
◆**audio-'visual** *a* audio-visuel.

audit ['ɔːdɪt] *vt* (*accounts*) vérifier; — *n* vérifi-

cation *f* (des comptes). ◆**auditor** *n*
commissaire *m* aux comptes.

audition [ɔː'dɪʃ(ə)n] *n* audition *f*; — *vti* auditionner.

auditorium [ɔːdɪ'tɔːrɪəm] *n* salle *f* (*de spectacle, concert etc*).

augment [ɔːg'ment] *vt* augmenter (**with, by**
de).

augur ['ɔːgər] *vt* présager; — *vi* **to a. well** être
de bon augure.

august [ɔː'gʌst] *a* auguste.

August ['ɔːgəst] *n* août *m*.

aunt [ɑːnt] *n* tante *f*. ◆**auntie** *or* **aunty** *n*
Fam tata *f*.

au pair [əʊ'peər] *adv* au pair; — *n* **au p. (girl)**
jeune fille *f* au pair.

aura ['ɔːrə] *n* émanation *f*, aura *f*; (*of place*)
atmosphère *f*.

auspices ['ɔːspɪsɪz] *npl* auspices *mpl*.

auspicious [ɔː'spɪʃəs] *a* favorable.

austere [ɔː'stɪər] *a* austère. ◆**austerity** *n*
austérité *f*.

Australia [ɒ'streɪlɪə] *n* Australie *f*. ◆**Australian** *a* & *n* australien, -ienne (*mf*).

Austria ['ɒstrɪə] *n* Autriche *f*. ◆**Austrian** *a*
& *n* autrichien, -ienne (*mf*).

authentic [ɔː'θentɪk]   *a*   authentique.
◆**authenticate**   *vt*   authentifier.
◆**authen'ticity** *n* authenticité *f*.

author ['ɔːθər] *n* auteur *m*. ◆**authoress** *n*
femme *f* auteur. ◆**authorship** *n* (*of book
etc*) paternité *f*.

authority [ɔː'θɒrɪtɪ] *n* autorité *f*; (*permission*)
autorisation *f* (**to do** de faire); **to be in a.** (*in
charge*) être responsable. ◆**authori-
'tarian** *a* & *n* autoritaire (*mf*).
◆**authoritative** *a* (*report*) autorisé; (*tone,
person*) autoritaire.

authorize ['ɔːθəraɪz] *vt* autoriser (**to do** à
faire). ◆**authori'zation** *n* autorisation *f*.

autistic [ɔː'tɪstɪk] *a* autiste, autistique.

autobiography [ɔːtəυbaɪ'ɒgrefɪ] *n* autobiographie *f*.

autocrat ['ɔːtəkræt] *n* autocrate *m*. ◆**auto-
'cratic** *a* autocratique.

autograph ['ɔːtəɡrɑːf] *n* autographe *m*; — *vt*
dédicacer (**for** à).

automat ['ɔːtəmæt] *n Am* cafétéria *f* à
distributeurs automatiques.

automate ['ɔːtəmeɪt]   *vt*   automatiser.
◆**auto'mation** *n* automatisation *f*, automation *f*.

automatic [ɔːtə'mætɪk]   *a*   automatique.
◆**automatically** *adv* automatiquement.

automaton [ɔː'tɒmətən] *n* automate *m*.

automobile ['ɔːtəməbiːl] *n Am* auto(mobile)
f.

autonomous [ɔː'tɒnəməs] *a* autonome. ◆**autonomy** *n* autonomie *f.*

autopsy ['ɔːtɒpsɪ] *n* autopsie *f.*

autumn ['ɔːtəm] *n* automne *m.* ◆**autumnal** [ɔː'tʌmnəl] *a* automnal.

auxiliary [ɔːg'zɪljərɪ] *a & n* auxiliaire (*mf*); **a. (verb)** (verbe *m*) auxiliaire *m.*

avail [ə'veɪl] **1** *vt* **to a. oneself of** profiter de, tirer parti de. **2** *n* **to no a.** en vain; **of no a.** inutile.

available [ə'veɪləb(ə)l] *a* (*thing, means etc*) disponible; (*person*) libre, disponible; (*valid*) valable; **a. to all** (*goal etc*) accessible à tous. ◆**availa'bility** *n* disponibilité *f*; validité *f*; accessibilité *f.*

avalanche ['ævəlɑːnʃ] *n* avalanche *f.*

avarice ['ævərɪs] *n* avarice *f.* ◆**ava'ricious** *a* avare.

avenge [ə'vendʒ] *vt* venger; **to a. oneself** se venger (**on** de).

avenue ['ævənjuː] *n* avenue *f*; (*way to a result*) *Fig* voie *f.*

average ['ævərɪdʒ] *n* moyenne *f*; **on a.** en moyenne; – *a* moyen; – *vt* (*do*) faire en moyenne; (*reach*) atteindre la moyenne de; (*figures*) faire la moyenne de.

averse [ə'vɜːs] *a* **to be a. to doing** répugner à faire. ◆**aversion** *n* (*dislike*) aversion *f*, répugnance *f.*

avert [ə'vɜːt] *vt* (*prevent*) éviter; (*turn away*) détourner (**from** de).

aviary ['eɪvɪərɪ] *n* volière *f.*

aviation [eɪvɪ'eɪʃ(ə)n] *n* aviation *f.* ◆**'aviator** *n* aviateur, -trice *mf.*

avid ['ævɪd] *a* avide (**for** de).

avocado [ævə'kɑːdəʊ] *n* (*pl* -os) **a. (pear)** avocat *m.*

avoid [ə'vɔɪd] *vt* éviter; **to a. doing** éviter de faire. ◆**—able** *a* évitable. ◆**avoidance** *n* **his a. of** (*danger etc*) son désir *m* d'éviter; **tax a.** évasion *f* fiscale.

avowed [ə'vaʊd] *a* (*enemy*) déclaré, avoué.

await [ə'weɪt] *vt* attendre.

awake [ə'weɪk] *vi* (*pt* **awoke**, *pp* **awoken**) s'éveiller; – *vt* (*person, hope etc*) éveiller; – *a* réveillé, éveillé; **(wide-)a.** éveillé; **to keep s.o. a.** empêcher de dormir, tenir qn éveillé; **he's (still) a.** il ne dort pas (encore); **a. to** (*conscious of*) conscient de. ◆**awaken 1** *vti* = **awake.** **2** *vt* **to a. s.o. to sth** faire prendre conscience de qch à qn. ◆**awakening** *n* réveil *m.*

award [ə'wɔːd] *vt* (*money*) attribuer; (*prize*) décerner, attribuer; (*damages*) accorder; – *n* (*prize*) prix *m*, récompense *f*; (*scholarship*) bourse *f.*

aware [ə'weər] *a* avisé, informé; **a. of** (*conscious*) conscient de; (*informed*) au courant de; **to become a. of** prendre conscience de. ◆**—ness** *n* conscience *f.*

awash [ə'wɒʃ] *a* inondé (**with** de).

away [ə'weɪ] *adv* **1** (*distant*) loin; (*far*) **a.** au loin, très loin; **5 km a.** à 5 km (de distance). **2** (*absent*) parti, absent; **a. with you!** va-t-en!; **to drive a.** partir (en voiture); **to look a.** détourner les yeux; **to work/talk/** *etc* **a.** travailler/parler/*etc* sans relâche; **to fade/melt a.** disparaître/fondre complètement. **3 to play a.** *Sp* jouer à l'extérieur.

awe [ɔː] *n* crainte *f* (*mêlée de respect*); **to be in a. of s.o.** éprouver de la crainte envers qn. ◆**a.-inspiring** *a*, ◆**awesome** *a* (*impressive*) imposant; (*frightening*) effrayant.

awful ['ɔːfəl] *a* affreux; (*terrifying*) épouvantable; (*ill*) malade; **an a. lot of** *Fam* un nombre incroyable de; **I feel a. (about it)** j'ai vraiment honte. ◆**—ly** *adv* affreusement; (*very*) *Fam* terriblement; **thanks a.** merci infiniment.

awhile [ə'waɪl] *adv* quelque temps; (*to stay, wait*) un peu.

awkward ['ɔːkwəd] *a* **1** (*clumsy*) maladroit; (*age*) ingrat. **2** (*difficult*) difficile; (*cumbersome*) gênant; (*tool*) peu commode; (*time*) inopportun; (*silence*) gêné. ◆**—ly** *adv* maladroitement; (*speak*) d'un ton gêné; (*placed*) à un endroit difficile. ◆**—ness** *n* maladresse *f*; difficulté *f*; (*discomfort*) gêne *f.*

awning ['ɔːnɪŋ] *n* auvent *m*; (*over shop*) store *m*; (*glass canopy*) marquise *f.*

awoke(n) [ə'wəʊk(ən)] *see* **awake.**

awry [ə'raɪ] *adv* **to go a.** (*of plan etc*) mal tourner.

axe [æks] (*Am* **ax**) *n* hache *f*; (*reduction*) *Fig* coupe *f* sombre; – *vt* réduire; (*eliminate*) supprimer.

axiom ['æksɪəm] *n* axiome *m.*

axis, *pl* **axes** ['æksɪs, 'æksiːz] *n* axe *m.*

axle ['æks(ə)l] *n* essieu *m.*

ay(e) [aɪ] **1** *adv* oui. **2** *n* **the ayes** (*votes*) les voix *fpl* pour.

azalea [ə'zeɪlɪə] *n* (*plant*) azalée *f.*

B

B, b [biː] *n* B, b *m*; **2B** (*number*) 2 ter.
BA *abbr* = Bachelor of Arts.
babble ['bæb(ə)l] *vi* (*of baby, stream*) gazouiller; (*mumble*) bredouiller; – *vt* **to b. (out)** bredouiller; – *n inv* gazouillement *m*, gazouillis *m*; (*of voices*) rumeur *f*.
babe [beɪb] *n* **1** petit(e) enfant *mf*, bébé *m*. **2** (*girl*) *Sl* pépée *f*.
baboon [bə'buːn] *n* babouin *m*.
baby ['beɪbɪ] *n* bébé *m*; – *a* (*clothes etc*) de bébé; **b. boy** petit garçon *m*; **b. girl** petite fille *f*; **b. carriage** *Am* voiture *f* d'enfant; **b. sling** kangourou® *m*, porte-bébé *m*; **b. tiger/etc** bébé-tigre/*etc m*; **b. face** visage *m* poupin. **2** *n Sl* (*girl*) pépée *f*; (*girlfriend*) copine *f*. **3** *vt Fam* dorloter. ◆**b.-batterer** *n* bourreau *m* d'enfants. ◆**b.-minder** *n* gardien, -ienne *mf* d'enfants. ◆**b.-sit** *vi* (*pt & pp* **-sat**, *pres p* **-sitting**) garder les enfants, faire du baby-sitting. ◆**b.-sitter** *n* baby-sitter *mf*. ◆**b.-snatching** *n* rapt *m* d'enfant. ◆**b.-walker** *n* trotteur *m*, youpala® *m*.
babyish ['beɪbɪʃ] *a Pej* de bébé; (*puerile*) enfantin.
bachelor ['bætʃələr] *n* **1** célibataire *m*; **b. flat** garçonnière *f*. **2 B. of Arts/of Science** licencié -ée *mf* ès lettres/ès sciences.
back [bæk] *n* (*of person, animal*) dos *m*; (*of chair*) dossier *m*; (*of hand*) revers *m*; (*of house*) derrière *m*, arrière *m*; (*of room*) fond *m*; (*of page*) verso *m*,(*of fabric*) envers *m*; *Fb* arrière *m*; **at the b. of** (*book*) à la fin de; (*car*) à l'arrière de; **at the b. of one's mind** derrière la tête; **b. to front** devant derrière, à l'envers; **to get s.o.'s b. up** *Fam* irriter qn; **in b. of** *Am* derrière; – *a* arrière *inv*, de derrière; (*taxes*) arriéré; **b. door** porte *f* de derrière; **b. room** pièce *f* du fond; **b. end** (*of bus*) arrière *m*; **b. street** rue *f* écartée; **b. number** vieux numéro *m*; **b. pay** rappel *m* de salaire; **b. tooth** molaire *f*; – *adv* en arrière; **far b.** loin derrière; **far b. in the past** à une époque reculée; **to stand b.** (*of house*) être en retrait (*from* par rapport à); **to go b. and forth** aller et venir; **to come b.** revenir; **he's b.** il est de retour, il est rentré *or* revenu; **a month b.** il y a un mois; **the trip there and b.** le voyage aller et retour; – *vt Com* financer; (*horse etc*) parier sur, jouer;

(*car*) faire reculer; (*wall*) renforcer; **to b. s.o (up)** (*support*) appuyer qn; – *vi* (*move backwards*) reculer; **to b. down** se dégonfler; **to b. out** (*withdraw*) se retirer; *Aut* sortir en marche arrière; **to b. on to** (*of window etc*) donner par derrière sur; **to b. up** *Aut* faire marche arrière. ◆**—ing** *n* (*aid*) soutien *m*; (*material*) support *m*, renfort *m*. ◆**—er** *n* (*supporter*) partisan *m*; *Sp* parieur, -euse *mf*; *Fin* bailleur *m* de fonds.
backache ['bækeɪk] *n* mal *m* aux reins. ◆**back'bencher** *n Pol* membre *m* sans portefeuille. ◆**backbiting** *n* médisance *f*. ◆**backbreaking** *a* éreintant. ◆**backcloth** *n* toile *f* de fond. ◆**backchat** *n* impertinence *f*. ◆**back'date** *vt* (*cheque*) antidater. ◆**back'handed** *a* (*compliment*) équivoque. ◆**backhander** *n* revers *m*; (*bribe*) *Fam* pot-de-vin *m*. ◆**backrest** *n* dossier *m*. ◆**backside** *n* (*buttocks*) *Fam* derrière *m*. ◆**back'stage** *adv* dans les coulisses. ◆**backstroke** *n Sp* dos *m* crawlé. ◆**backtrack** *vi* rebrousser chemin. ◆**backup** *n* appui *m*; (*tailback*) *Am* embouteillage *m*; **b. lights** *Aut* feux *mpl* de recul. ◆**backwater** *n* (*place*) trou *m* perdu. ◆**backwoods** *npl* forêts *f* vierges. ◆**back'yard** *n* arrière-cour *f*; *Am* jardin *m* (à l'arrière d'une maison).
backbone ['bækbəʊn] *n* colonne *f* vertébrale; (*of fish*) grande arête *f*; (*main support*) pivot *m*.
backfire [bæk'faɪər] *vi Aut* pétarader; (*of plot etc*) *Fig* échouer.
backgammon ['bækgæmən] *n* trictrac *m*.
background ['bækgraʊnd] *n* fond *m*, arrière-plan *m*; (*events*) *Fig* antécédents *mpl*; (*education*) formation *f*; (*environment*) milieu *m*; (*conditions*) *Pol* climat *m*, contexte *m*; **to keep s.o. in the b.** tenir qn à l'écart; **b. music** musique *f* de fond.
backlash ['bæklæʃ] *n* choc *m* en retour, retour *m* de flamme.
backlog ['bæklɒg] *n* (*of work*) arriéré *m*.
backward ['bækwəd] *a* (*glance etc*) en arrière; (*retarded*) arriéré; **b. in doing** lent à faire; – *adv* = **backwards**. ◆**—ness** *n* (*of country etc*) retard *m*. ◆**backwards** *adv* en arrière; (*to walk*) à reculons; (*to fall*) à la

renverse; **to move b.** reculer; **to go b. and forwards** aller et venir.

bacon ['beɪkən] n lard m; (in rashers) bacon m; **b. and eggs** œufs mpl au jambon.

bacteria [bæk'tɪərɪə] npl bactéries fpl.

bad [bæd] a (**worse, worst**) mauvais; (wicked) méchant; (sad) triste; (accident, wound etc) grave; (tooth) carié; (arm, leg) malade; (pain) violent; (air) vicié; **b. language** gros mots mpl; **it's b. to think that** . . . ce n'est pas bien de penser que . . . ; **to feel b.** Med se sentir mal; **I feel b. about it** ça m'a chagriné; **things are b.** ça va mal; **she's not b.!** elle n'est pas mal!; **to go b.** se gâter; (of milk) tourner; **in a b. way** mal en point; (ill) très mal; (in trouble) dans le pétrin; **too b.!** tant pis! ◆**b.-'mannered** a mal élevé. ◆**b.-'tempered** a grincheux. ◆**badly** adv mal; (hurt) grièvement; **b. affected/shaken** très touché/bouleversé; **to be b. mistaken** se tromper lourdement; **b. off** dans la gêne; **to be b. off for** manquer de; **to want b.** avoir grande envie de.

badge [bædʒ] n insigne m; (of postman etc) plaque f; (bearing slogan or joke) badge m.

badger ['bædʒər] **1** n (animal) blaireau m. **2** vt importuner.

badminton ['bædmɪntən] n badminton m.

baffle ['bæf(ə)l] vt (person) déconcerter, dérouter.

bag [bæg] **1** n sac m; pl (luggage) valises fpl, bagages mpl; (under the eyes) poches fpl; **bags of** Fam (lots of) beaucoup de; **an old b.** une vieille taupe; **in the b.** Fam dans la poche. **2** vt (-gg-) (take, steal) Fam piquer, s'adjuger; (animal) Sp tuer.

baggage ['bægɪdʒ] n bagages mpl; Mil équipement m; **b. car** Am fourgon m; **b. room** Am consigne f.

baggy ['bægɪ] a (-ier, -iest) (clothing) trop ample; (trousers) faisant des poches.

bagpipes ['bægpaɪps] npl cornemuse f.

Bahamas [bə'hɑːməz] npl **the B.** les Bahamas fpl.

bail [beɪl] **1** n Jur caution f; **on b.** en liberté provisoire; – vt **to b. (out)** fournir une caution pour; **to b. out** (ship) écoper; (person, company) Fig tirer d'embarras. **2** vi **to b. out** Am Av sauter (en parachute).

bailiff ['beɪlɪf] n Jur huissier m; (of landowner) régisseur m.

bait [beɪt] **1** n amorce f, appât m; – vt (fishing hook) amorcer. **2** vt (annoy) asticoter, tourmenter.

baize [beɪz] n **green b.** (on card table etc) tapis m vert.

bak/e [beɪk] vt (faire) cuire (au four); – vi (of cook) faire de la pâtisserie or du pain; (of cake etc) cuire (au four); **we're** or **it's baking (hot)** Fam on cuit. ◆**—ed** a (potatoes) au four; **b. beans** haricots mpl blancs (à la tomate). ◆**—ing** n cuisson f; **b. powder** levure f (chimique). ◆**—er** n boulanger, -ère mf. ◆**bakery** n boulangerie f.

balaclava [bælə'klɑːvə] n **b. (helmet)** passe-montagne m.

balance ['bæləns] n (scales) & Econ Pol Com balance f; (equilibrium) équilibre m; (of account) Com solde m; (remainder) reste m; **to strike a b.** trouver le juste milieu; **sense of b.** sens m de la mesure; **in the b.** incertain; **on b.** à tout prendre; **b. sheet** bilan m; – vt tenir or mettre en équilibre (on sur); (budget, account) équilibrer; (compare) mettre en balance, peser; **to b. (out)** (compensate for) compenser; **to b. (oneself)** se tenir en équilibre; – vi (of accounts) être en équilibre, s'équilibrer.

balcony ['bælkənɪ] n balcon m.

bald [bɔːld] a (-er, -est) chauve; (statement) brutal; (tyre) lisse; **b. patch** or **spot** tonsure f. ◆**b.-'headed** a chauve. ◆**balding** a **to be b.** perdre ses cheveux. ◆**baldness** n calvitie f.

balderdash ['bɔːldədæʃ] n balivernes fpl.

bale [beɪl] **1** n (of cotton etc) balle f. **2** vi **to b. out** Av sauter (en parachute).

baleful ['beɪlfʊl] a sinistre, funeste.

balk [bɔːk] vi reculer (**at** devant), regimber (**at** contre).

ball [bɔːl] n balle f; (inflated) Fb Rugby etc ballon m; Billiards bille f; (of string, wool) pelote f; (sphere) boule f; (of meat or fish) Culin boulette f; **on the b.** (alert) Fam éveillé; **he's on the b.** (efficient, knowledgeable) Fam il connaît son affaire, il est au point; **b. bearing** roulement m à billes; **b. game** Am partie f de baseball; **it's a whole new b. game** or **a different b. game** Am Fig c'est une tout autre affaire. ◆**ballcock** n robinet m à flotteur. ◆**ballpoint** n stylo m à bille.

ball[2] [bɔːl] n (dance) bal m. ◆**ballroom** n salle f de danse.

ballad ['bæləd] n Liter ballade f; Mus romance f.

ballast ['bæləst] n lest m; – vt lester.

ballet ['bæleɪ] n ballet m. ◆**balle'rina** n ballerine f.

ballistic [bə'lɪstɪk] a **b. missile** engin m balistique.

balloon [bə'luːn] n ballon m; Met ballon-sonde m.

ballot ['bælət] *n* (*voting*) scrutin *m*; **b. (paper)** bulletin *m* de vote; **b. box** urne *f*; – *vt* (*members*) consulter (par un scrutin).

ballyhoo [bælɪ'huɪ] *n Fam* battage *m* (publicitaire).

balm [baɪm] *n* (*liquid, comfort*) baume *m*. ◆**balmy** *a* (-ier, -iest) **1** (*air*) *Lit* embaumé. **2** (*crazy*) *Fam* dingue, timbré.

baloney [bə'ləʊnɪ] *n Sl* foutaises *fpl*.

Baltic ['bɔɪltɪk] *n* the **B.** la Baltique.

balustrade ['bæləstreɪd] *n* balustrade *f*.

bamboo [bæm'buɪ] *n* bambou *m*.

bamboozle [bæm'buɪz(ə)l] *vt* (*cheat*) *Fam* emboîner.

ban [bæn] *n* interdiction *f*; – *vt* (-nn-) interdire; **to b. from** (*club etc*) exclure de; **to ban s.o. from doing** interdire à qn de faire.

banal [bə'nɑɪl, *Am* 'beɪn(ə)l] *a* banal. ◆**ba'nality** *n* banalité *f*.

banana [bə'nɑɪmə] *n* banane *f*.

band [bænd] **1** *n* (*strip*) bande *f*; (*of hat*) ruban *m*; **rubber** *or* **elastic b.** élastique *m*. **2** *n* (*group*) bande *f*; *Mus* (petit) orchestre *m*; *Mil* fanfare *f*; – *vi* **to b. together** former une bande, se grouper. ◆**bandstand** *n* kiosque *m* à musique. ◆**bandwagon** *n* to **jump on the b.** Fig suivre le mouvement.

bandage ['bændɪdʒ] *n* (*strip*) bande *f*; (*for wound*) pansement *m*; (*for holding in place*) bandage *m*; – *vt* **to b. (up)** (*arm, leg*) bander; (*wound*) mettre un pansement sur.

Band-Aid® ['bændeɪd] *n* pansement *m* adhésif.

bandit ['bændɪt] *n* bandit *m*. ◆**banditry** *n* banditisme *m*.

bandy ['bændɪ] **1** *a* (-ier, -iest) (*person*) bancal; (*legs*) arqué. ◆**b.-'legged** *a* bancal. **2'** *vt* **to b. about** (*story etc*) faire circuler, propager.

bane [beɪn] *n Lit* fléau *m*. ◆**baneful** *a* funeste.

bang [bæŋ] **1** *n* (*hit, noise*) coup *m* (violent); (*of gun etc*) détonation *f*; (*of door*) claquement *m*; – *vt* cogner, frapper; (*door*) (faire) claquer; **to b. one's head** se cogner la tête; – *vi* cogner, frapper; (*of door*) claquer; (*of gun*) détoner; (*of firework*) éclater; **to b. down** (*lid*) rabattre (violemment); **to b. into sth** heurter qch; – *int* vlan!, pan!; **to go (off) b.** éclater. **2** *adv* (*exactly*) *Fam* exactement; **b. in the middle** en plein milieu; **b. on six** à six heures tapantes.

banger ['bæŋər] *n* **1** *Culin Fam* saucisse *f*. **2** (*firecracker*) pétard *m*. **3** old **b.** (*car*) *Fam* tacot *m*, guimbarde *f*.

bangle ['bæŋg(ə)l] *n* bracelet *m* (rigide).

bangs [bæŋz] *npl* (*of hair*) *Am* frange *f*.

banish ['bænɪʃ] *vt* bannir.

banister ['bænɪstər] *n* **banister(s)** rampe *f* (d'escalier).

banjo ['bændʒəʊ] *n* (*pl* -os *or* -oes) banjo *m*.

bank [bæŋk] **1** *n* (*of river*) bord *m*, rive *f*; (*raised*) berge *f*; (*of earth*) talus *m*; (*of sand*) banc *m*; **the Left B.** (*in Paris*) la Rive gauche; – *vt* **to b. (up)** (*earth etc*) amonceler; (*fire*) couvrir. **2** *n Com* banque *f*; **b. account** compte *m* en banque; **b. card** carte *f* d'identité bancaire; **b. holiday** jour *m* férié; **b. note** billet *m* de banque; **b. rate** taux *m* d'escompte; – *vt* (*money*) *Com* mettre en banque; – *vi* avoir un compte en banque (**with** à). **3** *vi Av* virer. **4** *vi* **to b. on s.o./sth** (*rely on*) compter sur qn/qch. ◆**—ing** *a* bancaire; – *n* (*activity, profession*) la banque. ◆**—er** *n* banquier *m*.

bankrupt ['bæŋkrʌpt] *a* **to go b.** faire faillite; **b. of** (*ideas*) *Fig* dénué de; – *vt* mettre en faillite. ◆**bankruptcy** *n* faillite *f*.

banner ['bænər] *n* (*at rallies etc*) banderole *f*; (*flag*) & *Fig* bannière *f*.

banns [bænz] *npl* bans *mpl*.

banquet ['bæŋkwɪt] *n* banquet *m*.

banter ['bæntər] *vti* plaisanter; – *n* plaisanterie *f*. ◆**—ing** *a* (*tone, air*) plaisantin.

baptism ['bæptɪzəm] *n* baptême *m*. ◆**baptize** *vt* baptiser.

bar [bɑɪr] **1** *n* barre *f*; (*of gold*) lingot *m*; (*of chocolate*) tablette *f*; (*on window*) & *Jur* barreau *m*; **b. of soap** savonnette *f*; **behind bars** *Jur* sous les verrous; **to b. to** *Fig* faire obstacle à. **2** *n* (*pub*) bar *m*; (*counter*) comptoir *m*. **3** *n* (*group of notes*) *Mus* mesure *f*. **4** *vt* (-rr-) (*way etc*) bloquer, barrer; (*window*) griller. **5** *vt* (*prohibit*) interdire (**s.o. from doing** à qn de faire); (*exclude*) exclure (**from** à). **6** *prep* sauf. ◆**barmaid** *n* serveuse *f* de bar. ◆**barman** *n*, ◆**bartender** *n* barman *m*.

Barbados [bɑɪ'beɪdɒs] *n* Barbade *f*.

barbarian [bɑɪ'beərɪən] *n* barbare *mf*. ◆**barbaric** *a* barbare. ◆**barbarity** *n* barbarie *f*.

barbecue ['bɑɪbɪkjuɪ] *n* barbecue *m*; – *vt* griller au barbecue.

barbed [bɑɪbd] *a* **b. wire** fil *m* de fer barbelé; (*fence*) barbelés *mpl*.

barber ['bɑɪbər] *n* coiffeur *m* (*pour hommes*).

barbiturate [bɑɪ'bɪtjʊrət] *n* barbiturique *m*.

bare [beər] *a* (-er, -est) nu; (*tree, hill etc*) dénudé; (*cupboard*) vide; (*mere*) simple; **the b. necessities** le strict nécessaire; **with his b. hands** à mains nues; – *vt* mettre à nu.

◆**—ness** n (*of person*) nudité f.
◆**bareback** adv **to ride b.** monter à cru.
◆**barefaced** a (*lie*) éhonté. ◆**barefoot**
adv nu-pieds; – a aux pieds nus. ◆**bare-**
'headed a & adv nu-tête inv.

barely ['beəlɪ] adv (*scarcely*) à peine, tout
juste.

bargain ['bɑːgɪn] n (*deal*) marché m, affaire
f; **a (good) b.** (*cheap buy*) une occasion, une
bonne affaire; **it's a b.!** (*agreed*) c'est
entendu!; **into the b.** par-dessus le marché;
b. price prix m exceptionnel; **b. counter**
rayon m des soldes; – vi (*negotiate*)
négocier; (*haggle*) marchander; **to b. for** or
on sth Fig s'attendre à qch. ◆**—ing** n
négociations fpl; marchandage m.

barge [bɑːdʒ] **1** n chaland m, péniche f. **2** vi
to b. in (*enter a room*) faire irruption;
(*interrupt*) interrompre; **to b. into** (*hit*) se
cogner contre.

baritone ['bærɪtəʊn] n (*voice, singer*)
baryton m.

bark [bɑːk] **1** n (*of tree*) écorce f. **2** vi (*of dog*
etc) aboyer; – n aboiement m. ◆**—ing** n
aboiements mpl.

barley ['bɑːlɪ] n orge f; **b. sugar** sucre m
d'orge.

barmy ['bɑːmɪ] a (**-ier, -iest**) Fam dingue,
timbré.

barn [bɑːn] n (*for crops etc*) grange f; (*for*
horses) écurie f; (*for cattle*) étable f.
◆**barnyard** n basse-cour f.

barometer [bə'rɒmɪtər] n baromètre m.

baron ['bærən] n baron m; (*industrialist*) Fig
magnat m. ◆**baroness** n baronne f.

baroque [bə'rɒk, Am bə'rəʊk] a & n Archit
Mus etc baroque (m).

barracks ['bærəks] npl caserne f.

barrage ['bærɑːʒ, Am bə'rɑːʒ] n (*barrier*)
barrage m; **a b. of** (*questions etc*) un feu
roulant de.

barrel ['bærəl] n **1** (*cask*) tonneau m; (*of oil*)
baril m. **2** (*of gun*) canon m. **3 b. organ**
orgue m de Barbarie.

barren ['bærən] a stérile; (*style*) Fig aride.

barrette [bə'ret] n (*hair slide*) Am barrette f.

barricade ['bærɪkeɪd] n barricade f; – vt
barricader; **to b. oneself (in)** se barricader.

barrier ['bærɪər] n barrière f; Fig obstacle m,
barrière f; (**ticket**) **b.** Rail portillon m;
sound b. mur m du son.

barring ['bɑːrɪŋ] prep sauf, excepté.

barrister ['bærɪstər] n avocat m.

barrow ['bærəʊ] n charrette f or voiture f à
bras; (*wheelbarrow*) brouette f.

barter ['bɑːtər] vt troquer, échanger (**for**
contre); – n troc m, échange m.

base [beɪs] **1** n (*bottom, main ingredient*)
base f; (*of tree, lamp*) pied m. **2** n Mil base f.
3 vt baser, fonder (**on** sur); **based in** or **on**
London basé à Londres. **4** a (*dishonourable*)
bas, ignoble; (*metal*) vil. ◆**—less** a sans
fondement. ◆**—ness** n bassesse f.
◆**baseball** n base-ball m. ◆**baseboard**
n Am plinthe f.

basement ['beɪsmənt] n sous-sol m.

bash [bæʃ] n Fam (*bang*) coup m; **to have a**
b. (*try*) essayer un coup; – vt Fam (*hit*)
cogner; **to b. up** (*ill-treat*) malmener;
to b. s.o. up tabasser qn; **to b. in** or **down**
(*door etc*) défoncer. ◆**—ing** n (*thrashing*)
Fam raclée f.

bashful ['bæʃfəl] a timide.

basic ['beɪsɪk] a fondamental; (*pay etc*) de
base; – n **the basics** Fam l'essentiel m.
◆**—ally** [-klɪ] adv au fond.

basil ['bæz(ə)l] n Bot Culin basilic m.

basilica [bə'zɪlɪkə] n basilique f.

basin ['beɪs(ə)n] n bassin m, bassine f; (*for*
soup, food) bol m; (*of river*) bassin m;
(*portable washbasin*) cuvette f; (*sink*)
lavabo m.

basis, pl **-ses** ['beɪsɪs, -siːz] n base f; **on the**
b. of d'après; **on that b.** dans ces conditions; **on a weekly/etc b.** chaque
semaine/etc.

bask [bɑːsk] vi se chauffer.

basket ['bɑːskɪt] n panier m; (*for bread,*
laundry, litter) corbeille f. ◆**basketball** n
basket(-ball) m.

Basque [bæsk] a & n basque (mf).

bass[1] [beɪs] n Mus basse f; – a (*note, voice*)
bas.

bass[2] [bæs] n (*sea fish*) bar m; (*fresh-water*)
perche f.

bassinet [bæsɪ'net] n (*cradle*) Am couffin m.

bastard ['bɑːstəd] **1** n & a bâtard, -arde
(mf). **2** n Pej Sl salaud m, salope f.

baste [beɪst] vt **1** (*fabric*) bâtir. **2** Culin
arroser.

bastion ['bæstɪən] n bastion m.

bat [bæt] **1** n (*animal*) chauve-souris f. **2** n
Cricket batte f; Table Tennis raquette f; **off**
my own b. de ma propre initiative; – vt
(**-tt-**) (*ball*) frapper. **3** vt **she didn't b. an**
eyelid elle n'a pas sourcillé.

batch [bætʃ] n (*of people*) groupe m; (*of*
letters) paquet m; (*of books*) lot m; (*of*
loaves) fournée f; (*of papers*) liasse f.

bated ['beɪtɪd] a **with b. breath** en retenant
son souffle.

bath [bɑːθ] n (pl **-s** [bɑːðz]) bain m; (*tub*)
baignoire f; **swimming baths** piscine f; – vt
baigner; – vi prendre un bain.

◆**bathrobe** n peignoir m (de bain); Am robe f de chambre. ◆**bathroom** n salle f de bain(s); (toilet) Am toilettes fpl. ◆**bathtub** n baignoire f.

bath/e [beɪð] vt baigner; (wound) laver; – vi se baigner; Am prendre un bain; – n bain m (de mer), baignade f. ◆**—ing** n baignade(s) f(pl); **b. costume** or **suit** maillot m de bain.

baton ['bætən, Am bə'tɒn] n Mus Mil bâton m; (truncheon) matraque f.

battalion [bə'tæljən] n bataillon m.

batter ['bætər] **1** n pâte f à frire. **2** vt battre, frapper; (baby) martyriser; Mil pilonner; **to b. down** (door) défoncer. ◆**—ed** a (car, hat) cabossé; (house) délabré; (face) meurtri; (wife) battu. ◆**—ing** n **to take a b.** souffrir beaucoup.

battery ['bætəri] n Mil Aut Agr batterie f; (in radio etc) pile f.

battle ['bæt(ə)l] n bataille f; (struggle) Fig lutte f; **that's half the b.** Fam c'est ça le secret de la victoire; **b. dress** tenue f de campagne; – vi se battre, lutter. ◆**battlefield** n champ m de bataille. ◆**battleship** n cuirassé m.

battlements ['bæt(ə)lmənts] npl (indentations) créneaux mpl; (wall) remparts mpl.

batty ['bætɪ] a (-ier, -iest) Sl dingue, toqué.

baulk [bɔːk] vi reculer (**at** devant), regimber (**at** contre).

bawdy ['bɔːdɪ] a (-ier, -iest) paillard, grossier.

bawl [bɔːl] vti **to b. (out)** beugler, brailler; **to b. s.o. out** Am Sl engueuler qn.

bay [beɪ] **1** n Geog Archit baie f. **2** n Bot laurier m. **3** n (for loading etc) aire f. **4** n (of dog) aboiement m; **at b.** aux abois; **to hold at b.** tenir à distance; – vi aboyer. **5** a (horse) bai.

bayonet ['beɪənɪt] n baïonnette f.

bazaar [bə'zɑːr] n (market, shop) bazar m; (charity sale) vente f de charité.

bazooka [bə'zuːkə] n bazooka m.

BC [biː'siː] abbr (before Christ) avant Jésus-Christ.

be [biː] vi (pres t **am, are, is**; pt **was, were**; pp **been**; pres p **being**) **1** être; **it is green/small** c'est vert/petit; **she's a doctor** elle est médecin; **he's an Englishman** c'est un Anglais; **it's 3 (o'clock)** il est trois heures; **it's the sixth of May** c'est or nous sommes le six mai. **2** avoir; **to be hot/right/lucky** avoir chaud/raison/de la chance; **my feet are cold** j'ai froid aux pieds; **he's 20** (age) il a 20 ans; **to be 2 metres high** avoir 2 mètres de haut; **to be 6 feet tall** mesurer 1,80 m. **3**

(health) aller; **how are you?** comment vas-tu? **4** (place, situation) se trouver, être; **she's in York** elle se trouve or elle est à York. **5** (exist) être; **the best painter there is** le meilleur peintre qui soit; **leave me be** laissez-moi (tranquille); **that may be** cela se peut. **6** (go, come) **I've been to see her** je suis allé or j'ai été la voir; **he's (already) been** il est (déjà) venu. **7** (weather) & Math faire; **it's fine** il fait beau; **2 and 2 are 4** 2 et 2 font 4. **8** (cost) coûter, faire; **it's 20 pence** ça coûte 20 pence; **how much is it?** ça fait combien?, c'est combien? **9** (auxiliary) **I am/was doing** je fais/faisais; **I'm listening to the radio** (in the process of) je suis en train d'écouter la radio; **she's been there some time** elle est là depuis longtemps; **he was killed** il a été tué, on l'a tué; **I've been waiting (for) two hours** j'attends depuis deux heures; **it is said** on dit; **to be pitied** à plaindre; **isn't it?, aren't you?** etc n'est-ce pas?, non?; **I am!, he is!** etc oui! **10** (+ inf) **he is to come** (must) il doit venir; **he's shortly to go** (intends to) il va bientôt partir. **11** **there is** or **are** il y a; (pointing) voilà; **here is** or **are** voici.

beach [biːtʃ] n plage f. ◆**beachcomber** n (person) ramasseur, -euse mf d'épaves.

beacon ['biːkən] n Nau Av balise f; (lighthouse) phare m.

bead [biːd] n (small sphere, drop of liquid) perle f; (of rosary) grain m; (of sweat) goutte f; (string of) **beads** collier m.

beak [biːk] n bec m.

beaker ['biːkər] n gobelet m.

beam [biːm] **1** n (of wood) poutre f. **2** n (of light) rayon m; (of headlight, torch) faisceau m (lumineux); – vi rayonner; (of person) Fig sourire largement. **3** vt Rad diffuser. ◆**—ing** a (radiant) radieux.

bean [biːn] n haricot m; (of coffee) grain m; (broad) **b.** fève f; **to be full of beans** Fam déborder d'entrain. ◆**beanshoots** npl, ◆**beansprouts** npl germes mpl de soja.

bear[1] [beər] n (animal) ours m.

bear[2] [beər] vt (pt **bore**, pp **borne**) (carry, show) porter; (endure) supporter; (resemblance) offrir; (comparison) soutenir; (responsibility) assumer; (child) donner naissance à; **to b. in mind** tenir compte de; **to b. out** corroborer; – vi **to b. left**/etc (turn) tourner à gauche/etc; **to b. north**/etc (go) aller en direction du nord/etc; **to b. (up)on** (relate to) se rapporter à; **to b. heavily on** (of burden) Fig peser sur; **to b. with** être indulgent envers, être patient avec; **to bring to b.** (one's energies) consacrer (**on** à);

(*pressure*) exercer (**on** sur); **to b. up** ne pas se décourager, tenir le coup; **b. up!** du courage! ◆**—ing** n (*posture, conduct*) maintien m; (*relationship, relevance*) relation f (**on** avec); *Nau Av* position f; **to get one's bearings** s'orienter. ◆**—able** a supportable. ◆**—er** n porteur, -euse mf.

beard [bɪəd] n barbe f. ◆**bearded** a barbu.

beast [biːst] n bête f, animal m; (*person*) *Pej* brute f. ◆**beastly** a *Fam* (*bad*) vilain, infect; (*spiteful*) méchant; — adv *Fam* terriblement.

beat [biːt] n (*of heart, drum*) battement m; (*of policeman*) ronde f; *Mus* mesure f, rythme m; — vt (pt **beat**, pp **beaten**) battre; (*defeat*) vaincre, battre; **to b. a drum** battre du tambour; **that beats me** *Fam* ça me dépasse; **to b. s.o. to it** devancer qn; **b. it!** *Sl* fichez le camp!; **to b. back** or **off** repousser; **to b. down** (*price*) faire baisser; **to b. in** or **down** (*door*) défoncer; **to b. out** (*rhythm*) marquer; (*tune*) jouer; **to b. s.o. up** tabasser qn; — vi battre; (*at door*) frapper (**at** à); **to b. about** or **around the bush** *Fam* tourner autour du pot; **to b. down** (*of rain*) tomber à verse; (*of sun*) taper. ◆**—ing** n (*blows, defeat*) raclée f. ◆**—er** n (*for eggs*) batteur m.

beauty ['bjuːtɪ] n (*quality, woman*) beauté f; **it's a b.!** c'est une merveille!; **the b. of it is ...** le plus beau, c'est que ... ; **b. parlour** institut m de beauté; **b. spot** (*on skin*) grain m de beauté; (*in countryside*) site m pittoresque. ◆**beau'tician** n esthéticienne f. ◆**beautiful** a (*très*) beau; (*superb*) merveilleux. ◆**beautifully** adv merveilleusement.

beaver ['biːvər] n castor m; — vi **to b. away** travailler dur (**at sth** à qch).

because [bɪˈkɒz] conj parce que; **b. of** à cause de.

beck [bek] n **at s.o.'s b. and call** aux ordres de qn.

beckon ['bekən] vti **to b. (to) s.o.** faire signe à qn (**to do** de faire).

becom/e [bɪˈkʌm] **1** vi (pt **became**, pp **become**) devenir; **to b. a painter** devenir peintre; **to b. thin** maigrir; **to b. worried** commencer à s'inquiéter; **what has b. of her?** qu'est-elle devenue? **2** vt **that hat becomes her** ce chapeau lui sied or lui va. ◆**—ing** a (*clothes*) seyant; (*modesty*) bienséant.

bed [bed] n lit m; *Geol* couche f; (*of vegetables*) carré m; (*of sea*) fond m; (*flower bed*) parterre m; **to go to b.** (aller) se coucher; **in b.** couché; **to get out of b.** se lever; **b. and**

breakfast (*in hotel etc*) chambre f avec petit déjeuner; **b. settee** (canapé m) convertible m; **air b.** matelas m pneumatique; — vt (**-dd-**) **to b. (out)** (*plant*) repiquer; — vi **to b. down** se coucher. ◆**bedding** n literie f. ◆**bedbug** n punaise f. ◆**bedclothes** npl couvertures fpl et draps mpl. ◆**bedridden** a alité. ◆**bedroom** n chambre f à coucher. ◆**bedside** n chevet m; — a (*lamp, book, table*) de chevet. ◆**bed'sitter** n, *Fam* ◆**bedsit** n chambre f meublée. ◆**bedspread** n dessus-de-lit m inv. ◆**bedtime** n heure f du coucher.

bedeck [bɪˈdek] vt orner (**with** de).

bedevil [bɪˈdev(ə)l] vt (**-ll-**, *Am* **-l-**) (*plague*) tourmenter; (*confuse*) embrouiller; **bedevilled by** (*problems etc*) perturbé par, empoisonné par.

bedlam ['bedləm] n (*noise*) *Fam* chahut m.

bedraggled [bɪˈdræg(ə)ld] a (*clothes, person*) débraillé.

bee [biː] n abeille f. ◆**beehive** n ruche f. ◆**beekeeping** n apiculture f. ◆**beeline** n **to make a b. for** aller droit vers.

beech [biːtʃ] n (*tree, wood*) hêtre m.

beef [biːf] **1** n bœuf m. **2** vi (*complain*) *Sl* rouspéter. ◆**beefburger** n hamburger m. ◆**beefy** a (**-ier**, **-iest**) *Fam* musclé, costaud.

beer [bɪər] n bière f; **b. glass** chope f. ◆**beery** a (*room, person*) qui sent la bière.

beet [biːt] n betterave f (à sucre); *Am* = **beetroot**. ◆**beetroot** n betterave f (potagère).

beetle ['biːt(ə)l] **1** n cafard m, scarabée m. **2** vi **to b. off** *Fam* se sauver.

befall [bɪˈfɔːl] vt (pt **befell**, pp **befallen**) arriver à.

befit [bɪˈfɪt] vt (**-tt-**) convenir à.

before [bɪˈfɔːr] adv avant; (*already*) déjà; (*in front*) devant; **the month b.** le mois d'avant or précédent; **the day b.** la veille; **I've never done it b.** je ne l'ai jamais (encore) fait; — prep (*time*) avant; (*place*) devant; **the year b. last** il y a deux ans; — conj avant que (+ ne + sub), avant de (+ inf); **b. he goes** avant qu'il (ne) parte; **b. going** avant de partir. ◆**beforehand** adv à l'avance, avant.

befriend [bɪˈfrend] vt offrir son amitié à, aider.

befuddled [bɪˈfʌd(ə)ld] a (*drunk*) ivre.

beg [beg] vt (**-gg-**) **to b. (for)** solliciter, demander; (*bread, money*) mendier; **to b. s.o. to do** prier or supplier qn de faire; **I b. to** je me permets de; **to b. the question** esquiver la question; — vi mendier;

(*entreat*) supplier; **to go begging** (*of food, articles*) ne pas trouver d'amateurs. ◆**beggar** *n* mendiant, -ante *mf*; (*person*) *Sl* individu *m*; **lucky b.** veinard, -arde *mf*. ◆**beggarly** *a* misérable.

beget [bɪ'get] *vt* (*pt* begot, *pp* begotten, *pres p* begetting) engendrer.

begin [bɪ'gɪn] *vt* (*pt* began, *pp* begun, *pres p* beginning) commencer; (*fashion, campaign*) lancer; (*bottle, sandwich*) entamer; (*conversation*) engager; **to b. doing** *or* **to do** commencer *or* se mettre à faire; — *vi* commencer (**with** par, **by doing** par faire); **to b. on sth** commencer qch; **beginning from** à partir de; **to b. with** (*first*) d'abord. ◆**—ning** *n* commencement *m*, début *m*. ◆**—ner** *n* débutant, -ante *mf*.

begrudge [bɪ'grʌdʒ] *vt* (*give unwillingly*) donner à contrecœur; (*envy*) envier (**s.o. sth** qch à qn); (*reproach*) reprocher (**s.o. sth** qch à qn); **to b. doing** faire à contrecœur.

behalf [bɪ'hɑːf] *n* **on b. of** pour, au nom de, de la part de; (*in the interest of*) en faveur de, pour.

behave [bɪ'heɪv] *vi* se conduire; (*of machine*) fonctionner; **to b. (oneself)** se tenir bien; (*of child*) être sage. ◆**behaviour** *n* conduite *f*, comportement *m*; **to be on one's best b.** se conduire de son mieux.

behead [bɪ'hed] *vt* décapiter.

behest [bɪ'hest] *n* *Lit* ordre *m*.

behind [bɪ'haɪnd] **1** *prep* derrière; (*more backward than, late according to*) en retard sur; — *adv* derrière; (*late*) en retard (**with, in** dans). **2** *n* (*buttocks*) *Fam* derrière *m*. ◆**behindhand** *adv* en retard.

beholden [bɪ'həʊldən] *a* redevable (**to** à, **for** de).

beige [beɪʒ] *a* & *n* beige (*m*).

being ['biːɪŋ] *n* (*person, life*) être *m*; **to come into b.** naître, être créé.

belated [bɪ'leɪtɪd] *a* tardif.

belch [beltʃ] **1** *vi* (*of person*) faire un renvoi, éructer; — *n* renvoi *m*. **2** *vt* **to b. (out)** (*smoke*) vomir.

beleaguered [bɪ'liːgəd] *a* (*besieged*) assiégé.

belfry ['belfrɪ] *n* beffroi *m*, clocher *m*.

Belgium ['beldʒəm] *n* Belgique *f*. ◆**Belgian** ['beldʒən] *a* & *n* belge (*mf*).

belie [bɪ'laɪ] *vt* démentir.

belief [bɪ'liːf] *n* (*believing, thing believed*) croyance *f* (**in s.o.** en qn, **in sth** à *or* en qch); (*trust*) confiance *f*, foi *f*; (*faith*) *Rel* foi *f* (**in** en).

believ/e [bɪ'liːv] *vti* croire (**in sth** à qch, **in God/s.o.** en Dieu/qn); **I b. so** je crois que oui; **I b. I'm right** je crois avoir raison; **to b.**

in doing croire qu'il faut faire; **he doesn't b. in smoking** il désapprouve que l'on fume. ◆**—able** *a* croyable. ◆**—er** *n* *Rel* croyant, -ante *mf*; **b. in** (*supporter*) partisan, -ane *mf* de.

belittle [bɪ'lɪt(ə)l] *vt* déprécier.

bell [bel] *n* cloche *f*; (*small*) clochette *f*; (*in phone*) sonnerie *f*; (*on door, bicycle*) sonnette *f*; (*on dog*) grelot *m*. ◆**bellboy** *n*, ◆**bellhop** *n* *Am* groom *m*.

belle [bel] *n* (*woman*) beauté *f*, belle *f*.

belligerent [bɪ'lɪdʒərənt] *a* & *n* belligérant, -ante (*mf*).

bellow ['beləʊ] *vi* beugler, mugir.

bellows ['beləʊz] *npl* (**pair of**) **b.** soufflet *m*.

belly ['belɪ] *n* ventre *m*; **b. button** *Sl* nombril *m*. ◆**bellyache** *n* mal *m* au ventre; — *vi* *Sl* rouspéter. ◆**bellyful** *n* **to have a b.** *Sl* en avoir plein le dos.

belong [bɪ'lɒŋ] *vi* appartenir (**to** à); **to b. to** (*club*) être membre de; **the cup belongs here** la tasse se range ici. ◆**—ings** *npl* affaires *fpl*.

beloved [bɪ'lʌvɪd] *a* & *n* bien-aimé, -ée (*mf*).

below [bɪ'ləʊ] *prep* (*lower than*) au-dessous de; (*under*) sous, au-dessous de; (*unworthy of*) *Fig* indigne de; — *adv* en dessous; **see b.** (*in book etc*) voir ci-dessous.

belt [belt] **1** *n* ceinture *f*; (*area*) zone *f*, région *f*; *Tech* courroie *f*. **2** *vt* (*hit*) *Sl* rosser. **3** *vi* **to b. (along)** (*rush*) *Sl* filer à toute allure; **b. up!** (*shut up*) *Sl* boucle-la!

bemoan [bɪ'məʊn] *vt* déplorer.

bench [bentʃ] *n* (*seat*) banc *m*; (*work table*) établi *m*, banc *m*; **the B.** *Jur* la magistrature (assise); (*court*) le tribunal.

bend [bend] *n* courbe *f*; (*in river, pipe*) coude *m*; (*in road*) *Aut* virage *m*; (*of arm, knee*) pli *m*; **round the b.** (*mad*) *Sl* tordu; — *vt* (*pt* & *pp* bent) courber; (*leg, arm*) plier; (*direct*) diriger; **to b. the rules** faire une entorse au règlement; — *vi* (*of branch*) plier, être courbé; (*of road*) tourner; **to b. (down)** se courber; **to b. (over** *or* **forward)** se pencher; **to b. to** (*s.o.'s will*) se soumettre à.

beneath [bɪ'niːθ] *prep* au-dessous de, sous; (*unworthy of*) indigne de; — *adv* (au-)dessous.

benediction [benɪ'dɪkʃ(ə)n] *n* bénédiction *f*.

benefactor ['benɪfæktər] *n* bienfaiteur *m*. ◆**benefactress** *n* bienfaitrice *f*.

beneficial [benɪ'fɪʃəl] *a* bénéfique.

beneficiary [benɪ'fɪʃərɪ] *n* bénéficiaire *mf*.

benefit ['benɪfɪt] *n* (*advantage*) avantage *m*; (*money*) allocation *f*; *pl* (*of science, education etc*) bienfaits *mpl*; **to s.o.'s b.** dans l'intérêt de qn; **for your (own) b.** pour vous, pour votre bien; **to be of b.** faire du bien (to à); **to give s.o. the b. of the doubt** accorder à qn le bénéfice du doute; **b. concert**/etc concert/etc m de bienfaisance; — vt faire du bien à; (be useful to) profiter à; — vi gagner (**from doing** à faire); **you'll b. from** or **by the rest** le repos vous fera du bien.

Benelux ['benɪlʌks] n Bénélux m.

benevolent [bɪ'nevələnt] a bienveillant. ◆**benevolence** n bienveillance f.

benign [bɪ'naɪn] a bienveillant, bénin; (climate) doux; (tumour) bénin.

bent [bent] **1** a (nail, mind) tordu; (dishonest) Sl corrompu; **b. on doing** résolu à faire. **2** n (talent) aptitude f (**for** pour); (inclination, liking) penchant m, goût m (**for** pour).

bequeath [bɪ'kwiːð] vt léguer (**to** à). ◆**bequest** n legs m.

bereaved [bɪ'riːvd] a endeuillé; — n **the b.** la famille, la femme etc du disparu. ◆**bereavement** n deuil m.

bereft [bɪ'reft] a **b. of** dénué de.

beret ['bereɪ, Am bə'reɪ] n béret m.

berk [bɜːk] n Sl imbécile mf.

Bermuda [bə'mjuːdə] n Bermudes fpl.

berry ['berɪ] n baie f.

berserk [bə'zɜːk] a **to go b.** devenir fou, se déchaîner.

berth [bɜːθ] n (in ship, train) couchette f; (anchorage) mouillage m; — vi (of ship) mouiller.

beseech [bɪ'siːtʃ] vt (pt & pp besought or beseeched) Lit implorer (**to do** de faire).

beset [bɪ'set] vt (pt & pp beset, pres p besetting) assaillir (qn); **b. with obstacles**/etc semé or hérissé d'obstacles/etc.

beside [bɪ'saɪd] prep à côté de; **that's b. the point** ça n'a rien à voir; **b. oneself** (angry, excited) hors de soi.

besides [bɪ'saɪdz] prep (in addition to) en plus de; (except) excepté; **there are ten of us b.** Paul nous sommes dix sans compter Paul; — adv (in addition) de plus; (moreover) d'ailleurs.

besiege [bɪ'siːdʒ] vt (of soldiers, crowd) assiéger; (annoy) Fig assaillir (**with** de).

besotted [bɪ'sɒtɪd] a (drunk) abruti; **b. with** (infatuated) entiché de.

bespatter [bɪ'spætər] vt éclabousser (**with** de).

bespectacled [bɪ'spektɪk(ə)ld] a à lunettes.

bespoke [bɪ'spəʊk] a (tailor) à façon.

best [best] a meilleur; **the b. page in the book** la meilleure page du livre; **the b. part of** (most) la plus grande partie de; **the b. thing** le mieux; **b. man** (at wedding) témoin m, garçon m d'honneur; — n **the b. (one)** le

meilleur, la meilleure; **it's for the b.** c'est pour le mieux; **at b.** au mieux; **to do one's b.** faire de son mieux; **to look one's b., be at one's best** être à son avantage; **to the b. of my knowledge** autant que je sache; **to make the b. of** (accept) s'accommoder de; **to get the b. of it** avoir le dessus; **in one's Sunday b.** endimanché; **all the b.!** portez-vous bien!; (in letter) amicalement; — adv (**the**) **b.** (to play etc) le mieux; **the b. loved** le plus aimé; **to think it b. to** juger prudent de ◆**b.-'seller** n (book) best-seller m.

bestow [bɪ'stəʊ] vt accorder, conférer (**on** à).

bet [bet] n pari m; — vti (pt & pp bet or betted, pres p betting) parier (**on** sur, **that** que); **you b.!** Fam (of course) tu parles! ◆**betting** n pari(s) m(pl); **b. shop** or **office** bureau m du pari mutuel.

betoken [bɪ'təʊkən] vt Lit annoncer.

betray [bɪ'treɪ] vt trahir; **to b. to s.o.** (give away to) livrer à qn. ◆**betrayal** n (disloyalty) trahison f; (disclosure) révélation f.

better ['betər] a meilleur (**than** que); **she's (much) b.** Med elle va (bien) mieux; **he's b. than** (at games) il joue mieux que; (at maths etc) il est plus fort que; **that's b.** c'est mieux; **to get b.** (recover) se remettre; (improve) s'améliorer; **it's b. to go** il vaut mieux partir; **the b. part of** (most) la plus grande partie de; — adv mieux; **I had b. go** il vaut mieux que je parte; **so much the b., all the b.** tant mieux (**for** pour); — n **to get the b. of** s.o. l'emporter sur qn; **change for the b.** amélioration f; **one's betters** ses supérieurs mpl; — vt (improve) améliorer; (outdo) dépasser; **to b. oneself** améliorer sa condition. ◆**—ment** n amélioration f.

between [bɪ'twiːn] prep entre; **we did it b. (the two of) us** nous l'avons fait à nous deux; **b. you and me** entre nous; **in b.** entre; — adv **in b.** (space) au milieu, entre les deux; (time) dans l'intervalle.

bevel ['bevəl] n (edge) biseau m.

beverage ['bevərɪdʒ] n boisson f.

bevy ['bevɪ] n (of girls) essaim m, bande f.

beware [bɪ'weər] vi to **b. of** (s.o., sth) se méfier de, prendre garde à; **b.!** méfiez-vous!, prenez garde!; **b. of falling**/etc prenez garde de (ne pas) tomber/etc; **'b. of the trains'** 'attention aux trains'.

bewilder [bɪ'wɪldər] vt dérouter, rendre perplexe. ◆**—ment** n confusion f.

bewitch [bɪ'wɪtʃ] vt enchanter. ◆**—ing** a enchanteur.

beyond [bɪ'jɒnd] prep (further than) au-delà

de; (*reach, doubt*) hors de; (*except*) sauf; **b. a year**/*etc* (*longer than*) plus d'un an/*etc*; **b. belief** incroyable; **b. his** *or* **her means** au-dessus de ses moyens; **it's b. me** ça me dépasse; – *adv* (*further*) au-delà.

bias ['baɪəs] **1** *n* penchant *m* (**towards** pour); (*prejudice*) préjugé *m*, parti pris *m*; – *vt* (-**ss**- *or* -**s**-) influencer. **2** *n* **cut on the b.** (*fabric*) coupé dans le biais. ◆**bias(s)ed** *a* partial; **to be b. against** avoir des préjugés contre.

bib [bɪb] *n* (*baby's*) bavoir *m*.

bible ['baɪb(ə)l] *n* bible *f*; **the B.** la Bible. ◆**biblical** ['bɪblɪk(ə)l] *a* biblique.

bibliography [bɪblɪ'ɒɡrəfɪ] *n* bibliographie *f*.

bicarbonate [baɪ'kɑːbənət] *n* bicarbonate *m*.

bicentenary [baɪsen'tiːnərɪ] *n*, ◆**bicentennial** *n* bicentenaire *m*.

biceps ['baɪseps] *n* *Anat* biceps *m*.

bicker ['bɪkər] *vi* se chamailler. ◆**—ing** *n* chamailleries *fpl*.

bicycle ['baɪsɪk(ə)l] *n* bicyclette *f*; – *vi* faire de la bicyclette.

bid[1] [bɪd] *vt* (*pt & pp* **bid**, *pres p* **bidding**) offrir, faire une offre de; – *vi* faire une offre (**for** pour); **to b. for** *Fig* tenter d'obtenir; – *n* (*at auction*) offre *f*, enchère *f*; (*tender*) *Com* soumission *f*; (*attempt*) tentative *f*. ◆**—ding**[1] *n* enchères *fpl*. ◆**—der** *n* enchérisseur *m*; soumissionnaire *mf*; **to the highest b.** au plus offrant.

bid[2] [bɪd] *vt* (*pt* **bade** [bæd], *pp* **bidden** *or* **bid**, *pres p* **bidding**) (*command*) commander (**s.o. to do** à qn de faire); (*say*) dire. ◆**—ding**[2] *n* ordre(s) *m(pl)*.

bide [baɪd] *vt* **to b. one's time** attendre le bon moment.

bier [bɪər] *n* (*for coffin*) brancards *mpl*.

bifocals [baɪ'fəʊkəlz] *npl* verres *mpl* à double foyer.

big [bɪɡ] *a* (**bigger, biggest**) grand, gros; (*in age, generous*) grand; (*in bulk, amount*) gros; **b. deal!** *Am Fam* (bon) et alors!; **b. mouth** *Fam* grande gueule *f*; **b. toe** gros orteil *m*; – *adv* **to do things b.** *Fam* faire grand; **to talk b.** fanfaronner. ◆**bighead** *n*, ◆**big'headed** *a* *Fam* prétentieux, -euse (*mf*). ◆**big-'hearted** *a* généreux. ◆**big-shot** *n*, ◆**bigwig** *n* *Fam* gros bonnet *m*. ◆**big-time** *a* *Fam* important.

bigamy ['bɪɡəmɪ] *n* bigamie *f*. ◆**bigamist** *n* bigame *mf*. ◆**bigamous** *a* bigame.

bigot ['bɪɡət] *n* fanatique *mf*; *Rel* bigot, -ote *mf*. ◆**bigoted** *a* fanatique; *Rel* bigot.

bike [baɪk] *n* *Fam* vélo *m*; – *vi* *Fam* aller à vélo.

bikini [bɪ'kiːnɪ] *n* bikini *m*.

bilberry ['bɪlbərɪ] *n* myrtille *f*.

bile [baɪl] *n* bile *f*. ◆**bilious** ['bɪlɪəs] *a* bilieux.

bilge [bɪldʒ] *n* (*nonsense*) *Sl* foutaises *fpl*.

bilingual [baɪ'lɪŋɡwəl] *a* bilingue.

bill [bɪl] **1** *n* (*of bird*) bec *m*. **2** *n* (*invoice*) facture *f*, note *f*; (*in restaurant*) addition *f*; (*in hotel*) note *f*; (*draft*) *Com* effet *m*; (*of sale*) acte *m*; (*banknote*) *Am* billet *m*; (*law*) *Pol* projet *m* de loi; (*poster*) affiche *f*; **b. of fare** menu *m*; **b. of rights** déclaration *f* des droits; – *vt* *Th* mettre à l'affiche, annoncer; **to b. s.o.** *Com* envoyer la facture à qn. ◆**billboard** *n* panneau *m* d'affichage. ◆**billfold** *n* *Am* portefeuille *m*.

billet ['bɪlɪt] *vt* *Mil* cantonner; – *n* cantonnement *m*.

billiard ['bɪljəd] *a* (*table etc*) de billard. ◆**billiards** *npl* (jeu *m* de) billard *m*.

billion ['bɪljən] *n* billion *m*; *Am* milliard *m*.

billow ['bɪləʊ] *n* flot *m*; – *vi* (*of sea*) se soulever; (*of smoke*) tourbillonner.

billy-goat ['bɪlɪɡəʊt] *n* bouc *m*.

bimonthly [baɪ'mʌnθlɪ] *a* (*fortnightly*) bimensuel; (*every two months*) bimestriel.

bin [bɪn] *n* boîte *f*; (*for bread*) coffre *m*, huche *f*; (*for litter*) boîte *f* à ordures, poubelle *f*.

binary ['baɪnərɪ] *a* binaire.

bind [baɪnd] **1** *vt* (*pt & pp* **bound**) lier; (*fasten*) attacher, lier; (*book*) relier; (*fabric, hem*) border; **to b. s.o. to do** *Jur* obliger *or* astreindre qn à faire. **2** *n* (*bore*) *Fam* plaie *f*. ◆**—ing 1** *a* (*contract*) irrévocable; **to be b. on s.o.** *Jur* lier qn. **2** *n* (*of book*) reliure *f*. ◆**—er** *n* (*for papers*) classeur *m*.

binge [bɪndʒ] *n* **to go on a b.** *Sl* faire la bringue.

bingo ['bɪŋɡəʊ] *n* loto *m*.

binoculars [bɪ'nɒkjʊləz] *npl* jumelles *fpl*.

biochemistry [baɪəʊ'kemɪstrɪ] *n* biochimie *f*.

biodegradable [baɪəʊdɪ'ɡreɪdəb(ə)l] *a* biodégradable.

biography [baɪ'ɒɡrəfɪ] *n* biographie *f*. ◆**biographer** *n* biographe *mf*.

biology [baɪ'ɒlədʒɪ] *n* biologie *f*. ◆**biological** *a* biologique.

biped ['baɪped] *n* bipède *m*.

birch [bɜːtʃ] *n* **1** (*tree*) bouleau *m*. **2** (*whip*) verge *f*; – *vt* fouetter.

bird [bɜːd] *n* oiseau *m*; (*fowl*) *Culin* volaille *f*; (*girl*) *Sl* poulette *f*, nana *f*; **b.'s-eye view**

perspective *f* à vol d'oiseau; *Fig* vue *f* d'ensemble. ◆**birdseed** *n* grains *mpl* de millet.

biro® ['baɪərəʊ] *n* (*pl* **-os**) stylo *m* à bille, bic® *m*.

birth [bɜːθ] *n* naissance *f*; **to give b. to** donner naissance à; **b. certificate** acte *m* de naissance; **b. control** limitation *f* des naissances. ◆**birthday** *n* anniversaire *n*; **happy b.!** bon anniversaire! ◆**birthplace** *n* lieu *m* de naissance; (*house*) maison *f* natale. ◆**birthrate** *n* (taux *m* de) natalité *f*. ◆**birthright** *n* droit *m* (*qu'on a dès sa naissance*), patrimoine *m*.

biscuit ['bɪskɪt] *n* biscuit *m*, gâteau *m* sec; *Am* petit pain *m* au lait.

bishop ['bɪʃəp] *n* évêque *m*; (*in chess*) fou *m*.

bison ['baɪs(ə)n] *n inv* bison *m*.

bit[1] [bɪt] *n* **1** morceau *m*; (*of string, time*) bout *m*; **a b.** (*a little*) un peu; **a tiny b.** un tout petit peu; **quite a b.** (*very*) très; (*much*) beaucoup; **not a b.** pas du tout; **a b. of luck** une chance; **b. by b.** petit à petit; **in bits (and pieces)** en morceaux; **to come to bits** se démonter. **2** (*coin*) pièce *f*. **3** (*of horse*) mors *m*. **4** (*of drill*) mèche *f*. **5** (*computer information*) bit *m*.

bit[2] [bɪt] *see* **bite.**

bitch [bɪtʃ] **1** *n* chienne *f*; (*woman*) *Pej Fam* garce *f*. **2** *vi* (*complain*) *Fam* râler. ◆**bitchy** *a* (**-ier, -iest**) *Fam* vache.

bit/e [baɪt] *n* (*wound*) morsure *f*; (*from insect*) piqûre *f*; *Fishing* touche *f*; (*mouthful*) bouchée *f*; (*of style etc*) *Fig* mordant *m*; **a b. to eat** un morceau à manger; – *vti* (*pt* **bit**, *pp* **bitten**) mordre; (*of insect*) piquer, mordre; **to b. one's nails** se ronger les ongles; **to b. on sth** mordre qch; **to b. sth off** arracher qch d'un coup de dent(s). ◆**—ing** *a* mordant; (*wind*) cinglant.

bitter ['bɪtər] **1** *a* (*person, taste, irony etc*) amer; (*cold, wind*) glacial, âpre; (*criticism*) acerbe; (*shock, fate*) cruel; (*conflict*) violent. **2** *n* bière *f* (pression). ◆**—ness** *n* amertume *f*; âpreté *f*; violence *f*. ◆**bitter-'sweet** *a* aigre-doux.

bivouac ['bɪvʊæk] *n Mil* bivouac *m*; – *vi* (**-ck-**) bivouaquer.

bizarre [bɪ'zɑːr] *a* bizarre.

blab [blæb] *vi* (**-bb-**) jaser. ◆**blabber** *vi* jaser. ◆**blabbermouth** *n* jaseur, -euse *mf*.

black [blæk] *a* (**-er, -est**) noir; **b. eye** œil *m* au beurre noir; **to give s.o. a b. eye** pocher l'œil à qn; **b. and blue** (*bruised*) couvert de bleus; **b. sheep** *Fig* brebis *f* galeuse; **b. ice** verglas *m*; **b. pudding** boudin *m*; – *n* (*colour*) noir *m*; (*Negro*) Noir, -e *mf*; – *vt*

noircir; (*refuse to deal with*) boycotter; – *vi* **to b. out** (*faint*) s'évanouir. ◆**blacken** *vti* noircir. ◆**blackish** *a* noirâtre. ◆**blackness** *n* noirceur *f*; (*of night*) obscurité *f*.

blackberry ['blækbərɪ] *n* mûre *f*. ◆**blackbird** ['blækbɜːd] *n* merle *m*. ◆**blackboard** *n* tableau *m* (noir). ◆**black'currant** *n* cassis *m*. ◆**blackleg** *n* (*strike breaker*) jaune *m*. ◆**blacklist** *n* liste *f* noire; – *vt* mettre sur la liste noire. ◆**blackmail** *n* chantage *m*; – *vt* faire chanter. ◆**blackmailer** *n* maître chanteur *m*. ◆**blackout** *n* panne *f* d'électricité; (*during war*) *Mil* black-out *m*; *Med* syncope *f*; (*news*) **b.** black-out *m*. ◆**blacksmith** *n* forgeron *m*.

blackguard ['blægɑːd, -gəd] *n* canaille *f*.

bladder ['blædər] *n* vessie *f*.

blade [bleɪd] *n* lame *f*; (*of grass*) brin *m*; (*of windscreen wiper*) caoutchouc *m*.

blame [bleɪm] *vt* accuser; (*censure*) blâmer; **to b. sth on s.o.** *or* **s.o. for sth** rejeter la responsabilité de qch sur qn; **to b. s.o. for sth** (*reproach*) reprocher qch à qn; **you're to b.** c'est ta faute; – *n* faute *f*; (*censure*) blâme *m*. ◆**—less** *a* irréprochable.

blanch [blɑːntʃ] *vt* (*vegetables*) blanchir; – *vi* (*turn pale with fear etc*) blêmir.

blancmange [blə'mɒnʒ] *n* blanc-manger *m*.

bland [blænd] *a* (**-er, -est**) doux; (*food*) fade.

blank [blæŋk] *a* (*paper, page*) blanc, vierge; (*cheque*) en blanc; (*look, mind*) vide; (*puzzled*) ébahi; (*refusal*) absolu; – *a & n* **b. (space)** blanc *m*; **b. (cartridge)** cartouche *f* à blanc; **my mind's a b.** j'ai la tête vide. ◆**blankly** *adv* sans expression.

blanket ['blæŋkɪt] **1** *n* couverture *f*; (*of snow etc*) *Fig* couche *f*; – *vt* (*cover*) *Fig* recouvrir. **2** *a* (*term etc*) général. ◆**—ing** *n* (*blankets*) couvertures *fpl*.

blare [bleər] *n* (*noise*) beuglement *m*; (*of trumpet*) sonnerie *f*; – *vi* **to b. (out)** (*of radio*) beugler; (*of music, car horn*) retentir.

blarney ['blɑːnɪ] *n Fam* boniment(s) *m(pl)*.

blasé ['blɑːzeɪ] *a* blasé.

blaspheme [blæs'fiːm] *vti* blasphémer. ◆**'blasphemous** *a* blasphématoire; (*person*) blasphémateur. ◆**'blasphemy** *n* blasphème *m*.

blast [blɑːst] **1** *n* explosion *f*; (*air from explosion*) souffle *m*; (*of wind*) rafale *f*, coup *m*; (*of trumpet*) sonnerie *f*; **(at) full b.** (*loud*) à plein volume; (*fast*) à pleine vitesse; **b. furnace** haut fourneau *m*; – *vt* (*blow up*) faire sauter; (*hopes*) *Fig* détruire; **to b. s.o.** *Fam* réprimander qn. **2** *int* zut!, merde! ◆—**ed** a Fam fichu. ◆**blast-off** n (of spacecraft) mise f à feu.

blatant ['bleɪtənt] a (obvious) flagrant, criant; (shameless) éhonté.

blaz/e [bleɪz] **1** n (fire) flamme f, feu m; (conflagration) incendie m; (splendour) Fig éclat m; **b. of light** torrent m de lumière; − vi (of fire) flamber; (of sun, colour, eyes) flamboyer. **2** vt **to b. a trail** marquer la voie. ◆—**ing** a (burning) en feu; (sun) brûlant; (argument) Fig violent.

blazer ['bleɪzər] n blazer m.

bleach [bliːtʃ] n décolorant m; (household detergent) eau f de Javel; − vt (hair) décolorer, oxygéner; (linen) blanchir.

bleak [bliːk] a (-er, -est) (appearance, future etc) morne; (countryside) désolé.

bleary ['blɪərɪ] a (eyes) troubles, voilés.

bleat [bliːt] vi bêler.

bleed [bliːd] vti (pt & pp bled) saigner; **to b. to death** perdre tout son sang. ◆—**ing** a (wound) saignant; (bloody) Sl foutu.

bleep [bliːp] n signal m, bip m; − vt appeler au bip-bip. ◆**bleeper** n bip-bip m.

blemish ['blemɪʃ] n (fault) défaut m; (on fruit, reputation) tache f; − vt (reputation) ternir.

blend [blend] n mélange m; − vt mélanger; − vi se mélanger; (go together) se marier (with avec). ◆—**er** n Culin mixer m.

bless [bles] vt bénir; **to be blessed with** avoir le bonheur de posséder; **b. you!** (sneezing) à vos souhaits! ◆—**ed** [-ɪd] a saint, béni; (happy) Rel bienheureux; (blasted) Fam fichu, sacré. ◆—**ing** n bénédiction f; (divine favour) grâce f; (benefit) bienfait m; **what a b. that . . .** quelle chance que . . . .

blew [bluː] see **blow** [1].

blight [blaɪt] n (on plants) rouille f; (scourge) Fig fléau m; **to be** or **cast a b. on** avoir une influence néfaste sur; **urban b.** (area) quartier m délabré; (condition) délabrement m (de quartier). ◆**blighter** n Pej Fam type m.

blimey! ['blaɪmɪ] int Fam zut!, mince!

blimp [blɪmp] n dirigeable m.

blind [blaɪnd] **1** a aveugle; **b. person** mf; **b. in one eye** borgne; **he's b. to** (fault) il ne voit pas; **to turn a b. eye to** fermer les yeux sur; **b. alley** impasse f; − n **the b.** les aveugles mpl; − vt aveugler. **2** n (on window) store m; (deception) feinte f. ◆—**ly** adv aveuglément. ◆—**ness** n cécité f; Fig aveuglement m. ◆**blinders** npl Am œillères fpl. ◆**blindfold** n bandeau m; − vt bander les yeux à; − adv les yeux bandés.

blink [blɪŋk] vi cligner des yeux; (of eyes)

cligner; (of light) clignoter; − vt **to b. one's eyes** cligner des yeux; − n clignement m; **on the b.** (machine) Fam détraqué. ◆—**ing** a (bloody) Fam sacré. ◆**blinkers** npl (for horse) œillères fpl; (indicators) Aut clignotants mpl.

bliss [blɪs] n félicité f. ◆**blissful** a (happy) très joyeux; (wonderful) merveilleux. ◆**blissfully** adv (happy, unaware) parfaitement.

blister ['blɪstər] n (on skin) ampoule f; − vi se couvrir d'ampoules.

blithe [blaɪð] a joyeux.

blitz [blɪts] n (attack) Av raid m éclair; (bombing) bombardement m aérien; Fig Fam offensive f; − vt bombarder.

blizzard ['blɪzəd] n tempête f de neige.

bloat [bləʊt] vt gonfler.

bloater ['bləʊtər] n hareng m saur.

blob [blɒb] n (of water) (grosse) goutte f; (of ink, colour) tache f.

bloc [blɒk] n Pol bloc m.

block [blɒk] **1** n (of stone etc) bloc m; (of buildings) pâté m (de maisons); (in pipe) obstruction f; (mental) blocage m; **b. of flats** immeuble m; **a b. away** Am une rue plus loin; **school b.** groupe m scolaire; **b. capitals** or **letters** majuscules fpl. **2** vt (obstruct) bloquer; (pipe) boucher, bloquer; (one's view) boucher; **to b. off** (road) barrer; (light) intercepter; **to b. up** (pipe, hole) bloquer. ◆**blo'ckade** n blocus m; − vt bloquer. ◆**blockage** n obstruction f. ◆**blockbuster** n Cin superproduction f, film m à grand spectacle. ◆**blockhead** n imbécile mf.

bloke [bləʊk] n Fam type m.

blond [blɒnd] a & n blond (m). ◆**blonde** a & n blonde (f).

blood [blʌd] n sang m; − a (group, orange etc) sanguin; (donor, bath etc) de sang; (poisoning etc) du sang; **b. pressure** tension f (artérielle); **high b. pressure** (hyper)tension f. ◆**bloodcurdling** a à vous tourner le sang. ◆**bloodhound** n (dog, detective) limier m. ◆**bloodletting** n saignée f. ◆**bloodshed** n effusion f de sang. ◆**bloodshot** a (eye) injecté de sang. ◆**bloodsucker** n (insect, person) sangsue f. ◆**bloodthirsty** a sanguinaire.

bloody ['blʌdɪ] **1** a (-ier, -iest) sanglant. **2** a (blasted) Fam sacré; − adv Fam vachement. ◆**b.-'minded** a hargneux, pas commode.

bloom [bluːm] n fleur f; **in b.** en fleur(s); − vi fleurir; (of person) Fig s'épanouir. ◆—**ing**

a **1** (*in bloom*) en fleur(s); (*thriving*) florissant. **2** (*blinking*) *Fam* fichu.

bloomer ['bluːmər] *n Fam* (*mistake*) gaffe *f*.

blossom ['blɒsəm] *n* fleur(s) *f*(*pl*); – *vi* fleurir; **to b. (out)** (*of person*) s'épanouir; **to b. (out) into** devenir.

blot [blɒt] *n* tache *f*; – *vt* (*-tt-*) tacher; (*dry*) sécher; **to b. out** (*word*) rayer; (*memory*) effacer. ◆**blotting** *a* **b. paper** (papier *m*) buvard *m*. ◆**blotter** *n* buvard *m*.

blotch [blɒtʃ] *n* tache *f*. ◆**blotchy** *a* (*-ier, -iest*) couvert de taches; (*face*) marbré.

blouse [blauz, *Am* blaus] *n* chemisier *m*.

blow¹ [bləu] *vt* (*pt* **blew**, *pp* **blown**) (*of wind*) pousser (*un navire etc*), chasser (*la pluie etc*); (*smoke, glass*) souffler; (*bubbles*) faire; (*trumpet*) souffler dans; (*fuse*) faire sauter; (*kiss*) envoyer (**to** à); (*money*) *Fam* claquer; **to b. one's nose** se moucher; **to b. a whistle** siffler; **to b. away** (*of wind*) emporter; **to b. down** (*chimney etc*) faire tomber; **to b. off** (*hat etc*) emporter; (*arm*) arracher; **to b. out** (*candle*) souffler; (*cheeks*) gonfler; **to b. up** (*building etc*) faire sauter; (*tyre*) gonfler; (*photo*) agrandir; – *vi* (*of wind, person*) souffler; (*of fuse*) sauter; (*of papers etc*) s'éparpiller; **b.!** *Fam* zut!; **to b. down** (*fall*) tomber; **to b. off** *or* **away** s'envoler; **to b. out** (*of light*) s'éteindre; **to b. over** (*pass*) passer; **to b. up** (*explode*) exploser. ◆**—er** *n* (*telephone*) *Fam* bigophone *m*. ◆**blow-dry** *n* brushing *m*. ◆**blowlamp** *n* chalumeau *m*. ◆**blowout** *n* (*of tyre*) éclatement *m*; (*meal*) *Sl* gueuleton *m*. ◆**blowtorch** *n Am* chalumeau *m*. ◆**blow-up** *n Phot* agrandissement *m*.

blow² [bləu] *n* coup *m*; **to come to blows** en venir aux mains.

blowy ['bləuɪ] *a* **it's b.** *Fam* il y a du vent.

blowzy ['blauzɪ] *a* **b. woman** (*slovenly*) *Fam* femme *f* débraillée.

blubber ['blʌbər] *n* graisse *f* (de baleine).

bludgeon ['blʌdʒən] *n* gourdin *m*; – *vt* matraquer.

blue [bluː] *a* (**bluer, bluest**) bleu; **to feel b.** *Fam* avoir le cafard; **b. film** *Fam* film *m* porno; – *n* bleu *m*; **the blues** (*depression*) *Fam* le cafard; *Mus* le blues. ◆**bluebell** *n* jacinthe *f* des bois. ◆**blueberry** *n* airelle *f*. ◆**bluebottle** *n* mouche *f* à viande. ◆**blueprint** *n Fig* plan *m* (de travail).

bluff [blʌf] **1** *a* (*person*) brusque, direct. **2** *vti* bluffer; – *n* bluff *m*.

blunder ['blʌndər] **1** *n* (*mistake*) bévue *f*, gaffe *f*; – *vi* faire une bévue. **2** *vi* (*move awkwardly*) avancer à tâtons. ◆**—ing** *a* maladroit; – *n* maladresse *f*.

blunt [blʌnt] *a* (*-er, -est*) (*edge*) émoussé; (*pencil*) épointé; (*person*) brusque; (*speech*) franc; – *vt* émousser; épointer. ◆**—ly** *adv* carrément. ◆**—ness** *n Fig* brusquerie *f*; (*of speech*) franchise *f*.

blur [blɜːr] *n* tache *f* floue, contour *m* imprécis; – *vt* (*-rr-*) estomper, rendre flou; (*judgment*) *Fig* troubler. ◆**blurred** *a* (*image*) flou, estompé.

blurb [blɜːb] *n Fam* résumé *m* publicitaire, laïus *m*.

blurt [blɜːt] *vt* **to b. (out)** laisser échapper, lâcher.

blush [blʌʃ] *vi* rougir (**at, with** de); – *n* rougeur *f*; **with a b.** en rougissant.

bluster ['blʌstər] *vi* (*of person*) tempêter; (*of wind*) faire rage. ◆**blustery** *a* (*weather*) de grand vent, à bourrasques.

boa ['bəuə] *n* (*snake*) boa *m*.

boar [bɔːr] *n* (*wild*) **b.** sanglier *m*.

board¹ [bɔːd] **1** *n* (*piece of wood*) planche *f*; (*for notices, games etc*) tableau *m*; (*cardboard*) carton *m*; (*committee*) conseil *m*, commission *f*; **b. (of directors)** conseil *m* d'administration; **on b.** *Nau Av* à bord (de); **B. of Trade** *Br Pol* ministère *m* du Commerce; **across the b.** (*pay rise*) général; **to go by the b.** (*of plan*) être abandonné. **2** *vt Nau Av* monter à bord de; (*bus, train*) monter dans; **to b. up** (*door*) boucher. ◆**—ing** *n Nau Av* embarquement *m*. ◆**boardwalk** *n Am* promenade *f*.

board² [bɔːd] *n* (*food*) pension *f*; **b. and lodging, bed and b.** (chambre *f* avec) pension *f*; – *vi* (*lodge*) être en pension (**with** chez); **boarding house** pension *f* (de famille); **boarding school** pensionnat *m*. ◆**—er** *n* pensionnaire *mf*.

boast [bəust] *vi* se vanter (**about, of** de); – *vt* se glorifier de; **to b. that one can do . . .** se vanter de (pouvoir) faire . . . ; – *n* vantardise *f*. ◆**—ing** *n* vantardise *f*. ◆**boastful** *a* vantard. ◆**boastfully** *adv* en se vantant.

boat [bəut] *n* bateau *m*; (*small*) barque *f*, canot *m*; (*liner*) paquebot *m*; **in the same b.** *Fig* logé à la même enseigne; **b. race** course *f* d'aviron. ◆**—ing** *n* canotage *m*; **b. trip** excursion *f* en bateau.

boatswain ['bəusən] *n* maître *m* d'équipage.

bob [bɒb] *vi* (*-bb-*) **to b. (up and down)** (*on water*) danser sur l'eau.

bobbin ['bɒbɪn] *n* bobine *f*.

bobby ['bɒbɪ] *n* **1** (*policeman*) *Fam* flic *m*, agent *m*. **2 b. pin** *Am* pince *f* à cheveux.

bode [bəʊd] *vi* **to b. well/ill** être de bon/mauvais augure.

bodice ['bɒdɪs] *n* corsage *m*.

body ['bɒdɪ] *n* corps *m*; (*of vehicle*) carrosserie *f*; (*quantity*) masse *f*; (*institution*) organisme *m*; **the main b.** of le gros de; **b. building** culturisme *m*. ◆**bodily** *a* physique; (*need*) matériel; − *adv* physiquement; (*as a whole*) tout entier. ◆**bodyguard** *n* garde *m* du corps, gorille *m*. ◆**bodywork** *n* carrosserie *f*.

boffin ['bɒfɪn] *n* *Fam* chercheur, -euse *mf* scientifique.

bog [bɒg] *n* marécage *m*; − *vt* **to get bogged down** s'enliser. ◆**boggy** *a* (-ier, -iest) marécageux.

bogey ['bəʊgɪ] *n* spectre *m*; **b. man** croque-mitaine *m*.

boggle ['bɒg(ə)l] *vi* **the mind boggles** cela confond l'imagination.

bogus ['bəʊgəs] *a* faux.

bohemian [bəʊ'hiːmɪən] *a* & *n* (*artist etc*) bohème (*mf*).

boil [bɔɪl] **1** *n* *Med* furoncle *m*, clou *m*. **2** *vi* bouillir; **to b. away** (*until dry*) s'évaporer; (*on and on*) bouillir sans arrêt; **to b. down to** *Fig* se ramener à; **to b. over** (*of milk, emotions etc*) déborder; − *vt* **to b. (up)** faire bouillir; − *n* **to be on the b., come to the b.** bouillir; **to bring to the b.** amener à ébullition. ◆**—ed** *a* (*beef*) bouilli; (*potato*) (*cuit*) à l'eau; **b. egg** œuf *m* à la coque. ◆**—ing** *n* ébullition *f*; **at b. point** à ébullition; − *a* & *adv* **(hot)** bouillant; **it's b. (hot)** (*weather*) il fait une chaleur infernale. ◆**—er** *n* chaudière *f*; **b. suit** bleu *m* (de travail).

boisterous ['bɔɪstərəs] *a* (*noisy*) tapageur; (*child*) turbulent; (*meeting*) houleux.

bold [bəʊld] *a* (-er, -est) hardi; **b. type** caractères *mpl* gras. ◆**—ness** *n* hardiesse *f*.

Bolivia [bə'lɪvɪə] *n* Bolivie *f*. ◆**Bolivian** *a* & *n* bolivien, -ienne (*mf*).

bollard ['bɒləd, 'bɒlɑːd] *n* *Aut* borne *f*.

boloney [bə'ləʊnɪ] *n* *Sl* foutaises *fpl*.

bolster ['bəʊlstər] **1** *n* (*pillow*) traversin *m*, polochon *m*. **2** *vt* **to b. (up)** (*support*) soutenir.

bolt [bəʊlt] **1** *n* (*on door etc*) verrou *m*; (*for nut*) boulon *m*; − *vt* (*door*) verrouiller. **2** *n* (*dash*) fuite *f*, ruée *f*; − *vi* (*dash*) se précipiter; (*flee*) détaler; (*of horse*) s'emballer. **3** *n* **b. (of lightning)** éclair *m*. **4** *vt* (*food*) engloutir. **5** *adv* **b. upright** tout droit.

bomb [bɒm] *n* bombe *f*; **letter b.** lettre *f* piégée; **b. disposal** désamorçage *m*; − *vt* bombarder. ◆**—ing** *n* bombardement *m*.
◆**—er** *n* (*aircraft*) bombardier *m*; (*terrorist*) plastiqueur *m*. ◆**bombshell** *n* **to come as a b.** tomber comme une bombe. ◆**bombsite** *n* terrain *m* vague, lieu *m* bombardé.

bombard [bɒm'bɑːd] *vt* bombarder (**with** de). ◆**—ment** *n* bombardement *m*.

bona fide [bəʊnə'faɪdɪ, *Am* -'faɪd] *a* sérieux, de bonne foi.

bonanza [bə'nænzə] *n* *Fig* mine *f* d'or.

bond [bɒnd] **1** *n* (*agreement, promise*) engagement *m*; (*link*) lien *m*; *Com* bon *m*, obligation *f*; (*adhesion*) adhérence *f*. **2** *vt* (*goods*) entreposer.

bondage ['bɒndɪdʒ] *n* esclavage *m*.

bone [bəʊn] **1** *n* os *m*; (*of fish*) arête *f*; **b. of contention** pomme *f* de discorde; **b. china** porcelaine *f* tendre; − *vt* (*meat etc*) désosser. **2** *vi* **to b. up on** (*subject*) *Am Fam* bûcher. ◆**bony** *a* (-ier, -iest) (*thin*) osseux, maigre; (*fish*) plein d'arêtes.

bone-dry [bəʊn'draɪ] *a* tout à fait sec.
◆**b.-idle** *a* paresseux comme une couleuvre.

bonfire ['bɒnfaɪər] *n* (*for celebration*) feu *m* de joie; (*for dead leaves*) feu *m* (de jardin).

bonkers ['bɒŋkəz] *a* (*crazy*) *Fam* dingue.

bonnet ['bɒnɪt] *n* (*hat*) bonnet *m*; *Aut* capot *m*.

bonus ['bəʊnəs] *n* prime *f*; **no claims b.** *Aut* bonus *m*.

boo [buː] **1** *int* hou! **2** *vti* huer; − *npl* huées *fpl*.

boob [buːb] *n* (*mistake*) gaffe *f*; − *vi* *Sl* gaffer.

booby-trap ['buːbɪtræp] *n* engin *m* piégé; − *vt* (-pp-) piéger.

book [bʊk] *n* livre *m*; (*of tickets*) carnet *m*; (*record*) registre *m*; *pl* (*accounts*) comptes *mpl*; **(excercise) b.** cahier *m*. **2** *vt* **to b. (up)** (*seat etc*) réserver, retenir; **to b. s.o.** *Jur* donner un procès-verbal à qn; **to b. (down)** inscrire; **(fully) booked (up)** (*hotel, concert*) complet; (*person*) pris; − *vi* **to b. (up)** réserver des places; **to b. in** (*in hotel*) signer le registre. ◆**—ing** *n* réservation *f*; **b. clerk** guichetier, -ière *mf*; **b. office** bureau *m* de location, guichet *m*. ◆**—able** *a* (*seat*) qu'on peut réserver. ◆**bookish** *a* (*word, theory*) livresque; (*person*) studieux.

bookbinding ['bʊkbaɪndɪŋ] *n* reliure *f*. ◆**bookcase** *n* bibliothèque *f*. ◆**book-end** *n* serre-livres *m inv*. ◆**bookkeeper** *n* comptable *mf*. ◆**bookkeeping** *n* comptabilité *f*. ◆**booklet** *n* brochure *f*. ◆**book-lover** *n* bibliophile *mf*. ◆**bookmaker** *n* bookmaker *m*. ◆**bookmark** *n*

marque *f*. ◆**bookseller** *n* libraire *mf*.
◆**bookshelf** *n* rayon *m*. ◆**bookshop** *n*,
Am ◆**bookstore** *n* librairie *f*. ◆**bookstall** *n* kiosque *m* (à journaux). ◆**bookworm** *n* rat *m* de bibliothèque.

boom [buːm] **1** *vi* (*of thunder, gun etc*)
gronder; – *n* grondement *m*; **sonic b.** bang
m. **2** *n Econ* expansion *f*, essor *m*, boom *m*.

boomerang ['buːməræŋ] *n* boomerang *m*.

boon [buːn] *n* aubaine *f*, avantage *m*.

boor [buər] *n* rustre *m*. ◆**boorish** *a* rustre.

boost [buːst] *vt* (*push*) donner une poussée
à; (*increase*) augmenter; (*product*) faire de
la réclame pour; (*economy*) stimuler;
(*morale*) remonter; – *n* to give a b. to = to
boost. ◆**—er** *n* **b.** (**injection**) piqûre *f* de
rappel.

boot [buːt] **1** *n* (*shoe*) botte *f*; (**ankle**) **b.**
bottillon *m*; (**knee**) **b.** bottine *f*; **to get the b.**
Fam être mis à la porte; **b. polish** cirage *m*;
– *vt* (*kick*) donner un coup *or* des coups de
pied à; **to b. out** mettre à la porte. **2** *n Aut*
coffre *m*. **3** *n* **to b. en plus.** ◆**bootblack** *n*
cireur *m*. ◆**boo'tee** *n* (*of baby*) chausson
m.

booth [buːð, buːθ] *n Tel* cabine *f*; (*at fair*)
baraque *f*.

booty ['buːtɪ] *n* (*stolen goods*) butin *m*.

booz/e [buːz] *n Fam* alcool *m*, boisson(s)
f(pl); (*drinking bout*) beuverie *f*; – *vi Fam*
boire (beaucoup). ◆**—er** *n Fam* (*person*)
buveur, -euse *mf*; (*place*) bistrot *m*.

border ['bɔːdər] *n* (*of country*) & *Fig*
frontière *f*; (*edge*) bord *m*; (*of garden etc*)
bordure *f*; – *a* (*town*) frontière *inv*; (*incident*) de frontière; – *vt* (*street*) border; **to b.
(on)** (*country*) toucher à; **to b. (up)on**
(*resemble*) être voisin de. ◆**borderland** *n*
pays *m* frontière. ◆**borderline** *n* frontière
f; **b. case** cas *m* limite.

bor/e[1] [bɔːr] **1** *vt* (*weary*) ennuyer; **to be
bored** s'ennuyer; – *n* (*person*) raseur, -euse
mf; (*thing*) ennui *m*. **2** *vt Tech* forer,
creuser; (*hole*) percer; – *vi* forer. **3** *n* (*of
gun*) calibre *m*. ◆**—ing** *a* ennuyeux.
◆**boredom** *n* ennui *m*.

bore[2] [bɔːr] *see* **bear**[2].

born [bɔːn] *a* né; **to be b.** naître; **he was b.** il
est né.

borne [bɔːn] *see* **bear**[2].

borough ['bʌrə] *n* (*town*) municipalité *f*;
(*part of town*) arrondissement *m*.

borrow ['bɒrəʊ] *vt* emprunter (**from** à).
◆**—ing** *n* emprunt *m*.

Borstal ['bɔːst(ə)l] *n* maison *f* d'éducation
surveillée.

bosom ['buzəm] *n* (*chest*) & *Fig* sein *m*; **b.
friend** ami, -ie *mf* intime.

boss [bɒs] *n Fam* patron, -onne *mf*, chef *m*;
– *vt Fam* diriger; **to b. s.o. around** *or* **about**
régenter qn. ◆**bossy** *a* (**-ier, -iest**) *Fam*
autoritaire.

boss-eyed ['bɒsaɪd] *a* **to be b.-eyed** loucher.

bosun ['bəʊs(ə)n] *n* maître *m* d'équipage.

botany ['bɒtənɪ] *n* botanique *f*. ◆**bo'tanical** *a* botanique. ◆**botanist** *n* botaniste
mf.

botch [bɒtʃ] *vt* **to b. (up)** (*spoil*) bâcler;
(*repair*) rafistoler.

both [bəʊθ] *a* les deux, l'un(e) et l'autre; –
pron tous *or* toutes (les) deux, l'un(e) et
l'autre; **b. of us** nous deux; – *adv* (*at the
same time*) à la fois; **b. you and I** vous et
moi.

bother ['bɒðər] *vt* (*annoy, worry*) ennuyer;
(*disturb*) déranger; (*pester*) importuner; **I
can't be bothered!** je n'en ai pas envie!, ça
m'embête!; – *vi* **to b. about** (*worry about*) se
préoccuper de; (*deal with*) s'occuper de; **to
b. doing** *or* **to do** se donner la peine de faire;
– *n* (*trouble*) ennui *m*; (*effort*) peine *f*;
(*inconvenience*) dérangement *m*; (**oh**) **b.!**
zut alors!

bottle ['bɒt(ə)l] *n* bouteille *f*; (*small*) flacon
m; (*wide-mouthed*) bocal *m*; (*for baby*)
biberon *m*; (**hot-water**) **b.** bouillotte *f*; **b.
opener** ouvre-bouteilles *m inv*; – *vt* mettre
en bouteille; **to b. up** (*feeling*) contenir.
◆**b.-feed** *vt* (*pt & pp* **-fed**) nourrir au
biberon. ◆**bottleneck** *n* (*in road*) goulot
m d'étranglement; (*traffic holdup*) bouchon
m.

bottom ['bɒtəm] *n* (*of sea, box, etc*) fond *m*;
(*of page, hill etc*) bas *m*; (*buttocks*) *Fam*
derrière *m*; (*of class*) bout *m*; **to be (at the)
b. of the class** être le dernier de la classe; –
a (*part, shelf*) inférieur, du bas; **b. floor**
rez-de-chaussée *m*; **b. gear** première vitesse
f. ◆**—less** *a* insondable.

bough [baʊ] *n Lit* rameau *m*.

bought [bɔːt] *see* **buy**.

boulder ['bəʊldər] *n* rocher *m*.

boulevard ['buːləvaːd] *n* boulevard *m*.

bounc/e [baʊns] **1** *vi* (*of ball*) rebondir; (*of
person*) faire des bonds; **to b. into** bondir
dans; – *vt* faire rebondir; – *n* (re)bond *m*.
2 *vi* (*of cheque*) *Fam* être sans provision,
être en bois. ◆**—ing** *a* (*baby*) robuste.
◆**—er** *n* (*at club etc*) *Fam* videur *m*.

bound[1] [baʊnd] **1 a b. to do** (*obliged*) obligé
de faire; (*certain*) sûr de faire; **it's b. to
happen** ça arrivera sûrement; **to be b. for**

être en route pour. **2** *n* (*leap*) bond *m*; — *vi* bondir.

bound² [baʊnd] *see* **bind 1**; — *a* b. up with (*connected*) lié à.

bounds [baʊndz] *npl* limites *fpl*; out of b. (*place*) interdit. ◆**boundary** *n* limite *f*. ◆**bounded** *a* b. by limité par. ◆**boundless** *a* sans bornes.

bountiful ['baʊntɪfʊl] *a* généreux.

bounty ['baʊntɪ] *n* (*reward*) prime *f*.

bouquet [bəʊ'keɪ] *n* (*of flowers, wine*) bouquet *m*.

bourbon ['bɜːbən] *n* (*whisky*) *Am* bourbon *m*.

bout [baʊt] *n* période *f*; *Med* accès *m*, crise *f*; *Boxing* combat *m*; (*session*) séance *f*.

boutique [buː'tiːk] *n* boutique *f* (de mode).

bow¹ [bəʊ] *n* (*weapon*) arc *m*; *Mus* archet *m*; (*knot*) nœud *m*; b. tie nœud *m* papillon. ◆b.-'legged *a* aux jambes arquées.

bow² [baʊ] **1** *n* révérence *f*; (*nod*) salut *m*; — *vt* courber, incliner; — *vi* s'incliner (to devant); (*nod*) incliner la tête; to b. down (*submit*) s'incliner. **2** *n* *Nau* proue *f*.

bowels ['baʊəlz] *npl* intestins *mpl*; (*of earth*) *Fig* entrailles *fpl*.

bowl [bəʊl] **1** *n* (*for food*) bol *m*; (*basin*) & *Geog* cuvette *f*; (*for sugar*) sucrier *m*; (*for salad*) saladier *m*; (*for fruit*) corbeille *f*, coupe *f*. **2** *npl* *Sp* boules *fpl*. **3** *vi* *Cricket* lancer la balle; to b. along *Aut* rouler vite; — *vt* (*ball*) *Cricket* servir; to b. s.o. over (*knock down*) renverser qn; (*astound*) bouleverser qn. ◆—ing *n* (*tenpin*) *Sp* bowling *m*; b. alley bowling *m*. ◆—er¹ *n* *Cricket* lanceur, -euse *mf*.

bowler² ['bəʊlər] *n* b. (hat) (chapeau *m*) melon *m*.

box [bɒks] **1** *n* boîte *f*; (*large*) caisse *f*; (*of cardboard*) carton *m*; *Th* loge *f*; *Jur* barre *f*, banc *m*; (*for horse*) box *m*; *TV Fam* télé *f*; b. office bureau *m* de location, guichet *m*; b. room (*lumber room*) débarras *m*; (*bedroom*) petite chambre *f* (carrée); — *vt* to b. (up) mettre en boîte; to b. in (*enclose*) enfermer. **2** *vti Boxing* boxer; to b. s.o.'s ears gifler qn. ◆—ing *n* **1** boxe *f*; b. ring ring *m*. **2** B. Day le lendemain de Noël. ◆—er *n* boxeur *m*. ◆**boxcar** *n* *Rail Am* wagon *m* couvert. ◆**boxwood** *n* buis *m*.

boy [bɔɪ] *n* garçon *m*; English b. jeune Anglais *m*; old b. *Sch* ancien élève *m*; yes, old b.! oui, mon vieux!; the boys (*pals*) *Fam* les copains *mpl*; my dear b. mon cher ami; oh b.! *Am* mon Dieu! ◆**boyfriend** *n* petit ami *m*. ◆**boyhood** *n* enfance *f*. ◆**boyish** *a* de garçon; *Pej* puéril.

boycott ['bɔɪkɒt] *vt* boycotter; — *n* boycottage *m*.

bra [brɑː] *n* soutien-gorge *m*.

brac/e [breɪs] *n* (*for fastening*) attache *f*; (*dental*) appareil *m*; *pl* (*trouser straps*) bretelles *fpl*; — *vt* (*fix*) attacher; (*press*) appuyer; to b. oneself for (*news, shock*) se préparer à. ◆—ing *a* (*air etc*) fortifiant.

bracelet ['breɪslɪt] *n* bracelet *m*.

bracken ['brækən] *n* fougère *f*.

bracket ['brækɪt] *n* *Tech* support *m*, tasseau *m*; (*round sign*) *Typ* parenthèse *f*; (*square*) *Typ* crochet *m*; *Fig* groupe *m*, tranche *f*; — *vt* mettre entre parenthèses *or* crochets; to b. together *Fig* mettre dans le même groupe.

bradawl ['brædɔːl] *n* poinçon *m*.

brag [bræg] *vi* (-gg-) se vanter (about, of de). ◆—ging *n* vantardise *f*. ◆**braggart** *n* vantard, -arde *mf*.

braid [breɪd] *vt* (*hair*) tresser; (*trim*) galonner; — *n* tresse *f*; galon *m*.

Braille [breɪl] *n* braille *m*.

brain [breɪn] *n* cerveau *m*; (*of bird etc*) & *Pej* cervelle *f*; — *a* (*operation, death*) cérébral; — *vt Fam* assommer; to have brains (*sense*) avoir de l'intelligence; b. drain fuite *f* des cerveaux. ◆**brainchild** *n* invention *f* personnelle. ◆**brainstorm** *n* *Psy Fig* aberration *f*; *Am* idée *f* géniale. ◆**brainwash** *vt* faire un lavage de cerveau à. ◆**brainwave** *n* idée *f* géniale.

brainy ['breɪnɪ] *a* (-ier, -iest) *Fam* intelligent.

braise [breɪz] *vt Culin* braiser.

brak/e [breɪk] *vi* freiner; — *n* frein *m*; b. light *Aut* stop *m*. ◆—ing *n* freinage *m*.

bramble ['bræmb(ə)l] *n* ronce *f*.

bran [bræn] *n* *Bot* son *m*.

branch [brɑːntʃ] *n* branche *f*; (*of road*) embranchement *m*; (*of store etc*) succursale *f*; b. office succursale *f*; — *vi* to b. off (*of road*) bifurquer; to b. out (*of family, tree*) se ramifier; *Fig* étendre ses activités.

brand [brænd] *n* (*trademark, stigma & on cattle*) marque *f*; — *vt* (*mark*) marquer; (*stigmatize*) flétrir; to be branded as avoir la réputation de.

brandish ['brændɪʃ] *vt* brandir.

brand-new [brænd'njuː] *a* tout neuf, flambant neuf.

brandy ['brændɪ] *n* cognac *m*; (*made with pears etc*) eau-de-vie *f*.

brash [bræʃ] *a* effronté, fougueux.

brass [brɑːs] *n* cuivre *m*; (*instruments*) *Mus* cuivres *mpl*; the top b. (*officers, executives*) *Fam* les huiles *fpl*; b. band fanfare *f*.

brassiere ['bræzɪər, *Am* brə'zɪər] *n* soutien-gorge *m*.

brat [bræt] *n Pej* môme *mf*, gosse *mf*; (*badly behaved*) galopin *m*.

bravado [brə'vɑɪdəʊ] *n* bravade *f*.

brave [breɪv] *a* (**-er, -est**) courageux, brave; – *n* (*Red Indian*) guerrier *m* (indien), brave *m*; – *vt* braver. ◆**bravery** *n* courage *m*.

bravo! ['brɑɪvəʊ] *int* bravo!

brawl [brɔɪl] *n* (*fight*) bagarre *f*; – *vi* se bagarrer. ◆**—ing** *a* bagarreur.

brawn [brɔɪn] *n* muscles *mpl*. ◆**brawny** *a* (**-ier, -iest**) musclé.

bray [breɪ] *vi* (*of ass*) braire.

brazen ['breɪz(ə)n] *a* (*shameless*) effronté; – *vt* **to b. it out** payer d'audace, faire front.

Brazil [brə'zɪl] *n* Brésil *m*. ◆**Brazilian** *a* & *n* brésilien, -ienne (*mf*).

breach [briɪtʃ] **1** *n* violation *f*, infraction *f*; (*of contract*) rupture *f*; (*of trust*) abus *m*; – *vt* (*law, code*) violer. **2** *n* (*gap*) brèche *f*; – *vt* (*wall etc*) ouvrir une brèche dans.

bread [bred] *n inv* pain *m*; (*money*) *Sl* blé *m*, fric *m*; **loaf of b.** pain *m*; (*slice* or *piece of*) **b. and butter** tartine *f*; **b. and butter** (*job*) *Fig* gagne-pain *m*. ◆**breadbin** *n, Am* ◆**breadbox** *n* coffre *m* à pain. ◆**breadboard** *n* planche *f* à pain. ◆**breadcrumb** *n* miette *f* (de pain); *pl Culin* chapelure *f*. ◆**breadline** *n* **on the b.** indigent. ◆**breadwinner** *n* soutien *m* de famille.

breadth [bretθ] *n* largeur *f*.

break [breɪk] *vt* (*pt* **broke**, *pp* **broken**) casser; (*into pieces*) briser; (*silence, vow etc*) rompre; (*strike, heart, ice etc*) briser; (*record*) *Sp* battre; (*law*) violer; (*one's word*) manquer à; (*journey*) interrompre; (*sound barrier*) franchir; (*a fall*) amortir; (*news*) révéler (**to** à); **to b.** (**oneself of**) (*habit*) se débarrasser de; **to b. open** (*safe*) forcer; – *vi* (*of voice*) casser; se briser; se rompre; (*of voice*) s'altérer; (*of boy's voice*) muer; (*of weather*) se gâter; (*of news*) éclater; (*of day*) se lever; (*of wave*) déferler; **to b. free** se libérer; **to b. loose** s'échapper; **to b. with s.o.** rompre avec qn; – *n* cassure *f*; (*in relationship, continuity etc*) rupture *f*; (*in journey*) interruption *f*; (*rest*) repos *m*; (*for tea*) pause *f*; *Sch* récréation *f*; (*change*) *Met* changement *m*; **a lucky b.** *Fam* une chance. ◆**—ing** *a* **b. point** *Tech* point *m* de rupture; **at b. point** (*patience*) à bout; (*person*) sur le point de craquer, à bout. ◆**—able** *a* cassable. ◆**—age** *n* casse *f*; *pl* (*things broken*) la casse. ◆**—er** *n* (*wave*) brisant *m*; (*dealer*)

Aut casseur *m*. ◾ **to b. away** *vi* se détacher; – *vt* détacher. ◆**breakaway** *a* (*group*) dissident; **to b. down** *vt* (*door*) enfoncer; (*resistance*) briser; (*analyse*) analyser; – *vi Aut Tech* tomber en panne; (*of negotiations etc*) échouer; (*collapse*) s'effondrer. ◆**breakdown** *n* panne *f*; analyse *f*; (*in talks*) rupture *f*; (*nervous*) dépression *f*; – *a* (*service*) *Aut* de dépannage; **b. lorry** dépanneuse *f*; **to b. in** *vi* interrompre; (*of burglar*) entrer par effraction; – *vt* (*door*) enfoncer; (*horse*) dresser; (*vehicle*) *Am* roder. ◆**break-in** *n* cambriolage *m*; **to b. into** *vt* (*safe*) forcer; (*start*) entamer; **to b. off** *vt* détacher; (*relations*) rompre; – *vi* se détacher; (*stop*) s'arrêter; **to b. off with** rompre avec; **to b. out** *vi* éclater; (*escape*) s'échapper; **to b. out in** (*pimples*) avoir une poussée de; **to b. through** *vi* (*of sun*) & *Mil* percer; – *vt* (*defences*) percer. ◆**breakthrough** *n Fig* percée *f*, découverte *f*; **to b. up** *vt* mettre en morceaux; (*marriage*) briser; (*fight*) mettre fin à; – *vi* (*end*) prendre fin; (*of group*) se disperser; (*of marriage*) se briser; *Sch* partir en vacances. ◆**breakup** *n* fin *f*; (*in friendship, marriage*) rupture *f*.

breakfast ['brekfəst] *n* petit déjeuner *m*.

breakwater ['breɪkwɔːtər] *n* brise-lames *m inv*.

breast [brest] *n* sein *m*; (*chest*) poitrine *f*. ◆**b.-feed** *vt* (*pt* & *pp* **-fed**) allaiter. ◆**breaststroke** *n* (*swimming*) brasse *f*.

breath [breθ] *n* haleine *f*, souffle *m*; (*of air*) souffle *m*; **under one's b.** tout bas; **one's last b.** son dernier soupir; **out of b.** à bout de souffle; **to get a b. of air** prendre l'air; **to take a deep b.** respirer profondément. ◆**breathalyser**® *n* alcootest® *m*. ◆**breathless** *a* haletant. ◆**breathtaking** *a* sensationnel.

breath/e [briːð] *vti* respirer; **to b. in** aspirer; **to b. out** expirer; **to b. air into sth** souffler dans qch; – *vt* (*a sigh*) pousser; (*a word*) dire. ◆**—ing** *n* respiration *f*; **b. space** moment *m* de repos. ◆**—er** *n Fam* moment *m* de repos; **to go for a b.** sortir prendre l'air.

bred [bred] *see* **breed** 1; – *a* **well-b.** bien élevé.

breeches ['brɪtʃɪz] *npl* culotte *f*.

breed [briːd] **1** *vt* (*pt* & *pp* **bred**) (*animals*) élever; (*cause*) *Fig* engendrer; – *vi* (*of animals*) se reproduire. **2** *n* race *f*, espèce *f*. ◆**—ing** *n* élevage *m*; reproduction *f*; *Fig* éducation *f*. ◆**—er** *n* éleveur, -euse *mf*.

breeze [briːz] *n* brise *f*. ◆**breezy** *a* (**-ier,**

-iest) 1 (*weather, day*) frais, venteux. **2** (*cheerful*) jovial; (*relaxed*) décontracté.

breezeblock ['briːzblɒk] *n* parpaing *m*, briquette *f*.

brevity ['brevɪtɪ] *n* brièveté *f*.

brew [bruː] *vt* (*beer*) brasser; (*trouble, plot*) préparer; **to b. tea** préparer du thé; (*infuse*) (faire) infuser du thé; – *vi* (*of beer*) fermenter; (*of tea*) infuser; (*of storm, trouble*) se préparer; – *n* (*drink*) breuvage *m*; (*of tea*) infusion *f*. ◆**-er** *n* brasseur *m*. ◆**brewery** *n* brasserie *f*.

bribe [braɪb] *n* pot-de-vin *m*; – *vt* soudoyer, corrompre. ◆**bribery** *n* corruption *f*.

brick [brɪk] *n* brique *f*; (*child's*) cube *m*; **to drop a b.** *Fam* faire une gaffe; – *vt* **to b. up** (*gap, door*) murer. ◆**bricklayer** *n* maçon *m*. ◆**brickwork** *n* ouvrage *m* en briques; (*bricks*) briques *fpl*.

bridal ['braɪd(ə)l] *a* (*ceremony*) nuptial; **b. gown** robe *f* de mariée.

bride [braɪd] *n* mariée *f*; **the b. and groom** les mariés *mpl*. ◆**bridegroom** *n* marié *m*. ◆**bridesmaid** *n* demoiselle *f* d'honneur.

bridge [brɪdʒ] **1** *n* pont *m*; (*on ship*) passerelle *f*; (*of nose*) arête *f*; (*false tooth*) bridge *m*; – *vt* **to b. a gap** combler une lacune. **2** *n* *Cards* bridge *m*.

bridle ['braɪd(ə)l] *n* (*for horse*) bride *f*; – *vt* (*horse, instinct etc*) brider; **b. path** allée *f* cavalière.

brief [briːf] **1** *a* (**-er, -est**) bref; **in b.** en résumé. **2** *n* *Jur* dossier *m*; (*instructions*) *Mil Pol* instructions *fpl*; *Fig* tâche *f*, fonctions *fpl*; – *vt* donner des instructions à; (*inform*) mettre au courant (**on** de). **3** *npl* (*underpants*) slip *m*. ◆**-ing** *n* *Mil Pol* instructions *fpl*; *Av* briefing *m*. ◆**-ly** *adv* (*quickly*) en vitesse; (*to say*) brièvement.

brigade [brɪ'ɡeɪd] *n* brigade *f*. ◆**briga'dier** *n* général *m* de brigade.

bright [braɪt] *a* (**-er, -est**) brillant, vif; (*weather, room*) clair; (*clever*) intelligent; (*happy*) joyeux; (*future*) brillant, prometteur; (*idea*) génial; **b. interval** *Met* éclaircie *f*; – *adv* **b. and early** (*to get up*) de bonne heure. ◆**-ly** *adv* brillamment. ◆**-ness** *n* éclat *m*; (*of person*) intelligence *f*. ◆**brighten** *vt* **to b. (up)** (*person, room*) égayer; – *vi* **to b. (up)** (*of weather*) s'éclaircir; (*of face*) s'éclairer.

brilliant ['brɪljənt] *a* (*light*) éclatant; (*very clever*) brillant. ◆**brilliance** *n* éclat *m*; (*of person*) grande intelligence *f*.

brim [brɪm] *n* bord *m*; – *vi* (**-mm-**) **to b. over** déborder (**with** de).

brine [braɪn] *n* *Culin* saumure *f*.

bring [brɪŋ] *vt* (*pt & pp* **brought**) (*person, vehicle etc*) amener; (*thing*) apporter; (*to cause*) amener; (*action*) *Jur* intenter; **to b. along** *or* **over** *or* **round** amener; apporter; **to b. back** ramener; rapporter; (*memories*) rappeler; **to b. sth up/down** monter/descendre qch; **to b. sth in/out** rentrer/sortir qch; **to b. sth to** (*perfection, a peak etc*) porter qch à; **to b. to an end** mettre fin à; **to b. to mind** rappeler; **to b. sth on oneself** s'attirer qch; **to b. oneself to do** se résoudre à faire; **to b. about** provoquer, amener; **to b. down** (*overthrow*) faire tomber; (*reduce*) réduire; (*shoot down*) abattre; **to b. forward** (*in time or space*) avancer; (*witness*) produire; **to b. in** (*person*) faire entrer *or* venir; (*introduce*) introduire; (*income*) *Com* rapporter; **to b. off** (*task*) mener à bien; **to b. out** (*person*) faire sortir; (*meaning*) faire ressortir; (*book*) publier; (*product*) lancer; **to b. over to** (*convert to*) convertir à; **to b. round** *Med* ranimer; (*convert*) convertir (**to** à); **to b. s.o. to** *Med* ranimer qn; **to b. together** mettre en contact; (*reconcile*) réconcilier; **to b. up** (*child etc*) élever; (*question*) soulever; (*subject*) mentionner; (*vomit*) vomir.

brink [brɪŋk] *n* bord *m*.

brisk [brɪsk] *a* (**-er, -est**) vif; (*trade*) actif; **at a b. pace** d'un bon pas. ◆**-ly** *adv* vivement; (*to walk*) d'un bon pas. ◆**-ness** *n* vivacité *f*.

bristl/e ['brɪs(ə)l] *n* poil *m*; – *vi* se hérisser. ◆**-ing** *a* **b. with** (*difficulties*) hérissé de.

Britain ['brɪt(ə)n] *n* Grande-Bretagne *f*. ◆**British** *a* britannique; – *n* **the B.** les Britanniques *mpl*. ◆**Briton** *n* Britannique *mf*.

Brittany ['brɪtənɪ] *n* Bretagne *f*.

brittle ['brɪt(ə)l] *a* cassant, fragile.

broach [brəʊtʃ] *vt* (*topic*) entamer.

broad¹ [brɔːd] *a* (**-er, -est**) (*wide*) large; (*outline*) grand, général; (*accent*) prononcé; **in b. daylight** au grand jour; **b. bean** fève *f*; **b. jump** *Sp Am* saut *m* en longueur. ◆**b.-'minded** *a* à l'esprit large. ◆**b.-'shouldered** *a* large d'épaules. ◆**broaden** *vt* élargir; – *vi* s'élargir. ◆**broadly** *adv* **b. (speaking)** en gros, grosso modo.

broad² [brɔːd] *n* (*woman*) *Am Sl* nana *f*.

broadcast ['brɔːdkɑːst] *vt* (*pt & pp* **broadcast**) *Rad & Fig* diffuser; *TV* téléviser; – *vi* (*of station*) émettre; (*of person*) parler à la radio *or* à la télévision; – *a* (*radio*) diffusé; télévisé; – *n* émission *f*. ◆**-ing** *n* radio-diffusion *f*; télévision *f*.

broccoli ['brɒkəlɪ] n inv brocoli m.
brochure ['brəʊʃər] n brochure f, dépliant m.
brogue [brəʊg] n Ling accent m irlandais.
broil [brɔɪl] vti griller. ◆**—er** n poulet m (à rôtir); (apparatus) gril m.
broke [brəʊk] 1 see **break**. 2 a (penniless) fauché. ◆**broken** see **break**; – a (ground) accidenté; (spirit) abattu; (man, voice, line) brisé; **b. English** mauvais anglais m; **b. home** foyer m brisé. ◆**broken-'down** a (machine etc) (tout) déglingué, détraqué.
brolly ['brɒlɪ] n (umbrella) Fam pépin m.
bronchitis [brɒŋ'kaɪtɪs] n bronchite f.
bronze [brɒnz] n bronze m; – a (statue etc) en bronze.
brooch [brəʊtʃ] n (ornament) broche f.
brood [bruɪd] 1 n couvée f, nichée f; – vi (of bird) couver. 2 vi méditer tristement (**over**, **on** sur); **to b. over** (a plan) ruminer. ◆**broody** a (-ier, -iest) (person) maussade, rêveur; (woman) Fam qui a envie d'avoir un enfant.
brook [brʊk] 1 n ruisseau m. 2 vt souffrir, tolérer.
broom [bruːm] n 1 (for sweeping) balai m. 2 Bot genêt m. ◆**broomstick** n manche m à balai.
Bros abbr (Brothers) Frères mpl.
broth [brɒθ] n bouillon m.
brothel ['brɒθ(ə)l] n maison f close, bordel m.
brother ['brʌðər] n frère m. ◆**b.-in-law** n (pl **brothers-in-law**) beau-frère m. ◆**brotherhood** n fraternité f. ◆**brotherly** a fraternel.
brow [braʊ] n (forehead) front m; (of hill) sommet m.
browbeat ['braʊbiːt] vt (pt **-beat**, pp **-beaten**) intimider.
brown [braʊn] a (-er, -est) brun; (reddish) marron; (hair) châtain; (tanned) bronzé; – n brun m; marron m; – vt brunir; Culin faire dorer; **to be browned off** Fam en avoir marre. ◆**brownish** a brunâtre.
Brownie ['braʊnɪ] n 1 (girl scout) jeannette f. 2 **b.** Culin Am petit gâteau m au chocolat.
browse [braʊz] vi (in shop) regarder; (in bookshop) feuilleter des livres; (of animal) brouter; – vt (book) feuilleter.
bruis/e [bruːz] vt contusionner, meurtrir; (fruit, heart) meurtrir; – n bleu m, contusion f. ◆**—ed** a couvert de bleus.
brunch [brʌntʃ] n repas m mixte (petit déjeuner pris comme déjeuner).
brunette [bruː'net] n brunette f.

brunt [brʌnt] n **to bear the b. of** (attack etc) subir le plus gros de.
brush [brʌʃ] n brosse f; (for shaving) blaireau m; (little broom) balayette f; (action) coup m de brosse; (fight) accrochage m; – vt (teeth, hair etc) brosser; (clothes) donner un coup de brosse à; **to b. aside** écarter; **to b. away** or **off** enlever; **to b. up (on)** (language) se remettre à; – vi **to b. against** effleurer. ◆**b.-off** n Fam to give s.o. **the b.-off** envoyer promener qn. ◆**b.-up** n coup m de brosse. ◆**brushwood** n broussailles fpl.
brusque [bruːsk] a brusque.
Brussels ['brʌs(ə)lz] n Bruxelles m or f; **B. sprouts** choux mpl de Bruxelles.
brutal ['bruːt(ə)l] a brutal. ◆**bru'tality** n brutalité f.
brute [bruːt] n (animal, person) brute f; – a **by b. force** par la force.
BSc, Am **BS** abbr = **Bachelor of Science**.
bubble ['bʌb(ə)l] n (of air, soap etc) bulle f; (in boiling liquid) bouillon m; **b. and squeak** Fam friture f de purée et de viande réchauffées; **b. bath** bain m moussant; **b. gum** chewing-gum m; – vi bouillonner; **to b. over** déborder (**with** de). ◆**bubbly** n Hum Fam champagne m.
buck [bʌk] 1 n Am Fam dollar m. 2 n (animal) mâle m. 3 vt **to b. up** remonter le moral à; – vi **to b. up** prendre courage; (hurry) se grouiller. ◆**buckshot** n inv du gros plomb m. ◆**buck'tooth** n (pl **-teeth**) dent f saillante.
bucket ['bʌkɪt] n seau m.
buckle ['bʌk(ə)l] 1 n boucle f; – vt boucler. 2 vti (warp) voiler, gauchir. 3 vi **to b. down to** (task) s'atteler à.
bud [bʌd] n (of tree) bourgeon m; (of flower) bouton m; – vi (-dd-) bourgeonner; pousser des boutons. ◆**budding** a (talent) naissant; (doctor etc) en herbe.
Buddhist ['bʊdɪst] a & n bouddhiste (mf).
buddy ['bʌdɪ] n Am Fam copain m, pote m.
budge [bʌdʒ] vi bouger; – vt faire bouger.
budgerigar ['bʌdʒərɪgɑːr] n perruche f.
budget ['bʌdʒɪt] n budget m; – vi dresser un budget; **to b. for** inscrire au budget. ◆**budgetary** a budgétaire.
budgie ['bʌdʒɪ] n Fam perruche f.
buff [bʌf] 1 a **b.(-coloured)** chamois inv. 2 n jazz/etc **b.** Fam fana(tique) mf du jazz/etc. 3 n **in the b.** Fam tout nu.
buffalo ['bʌfələʊ] n (pl **-oes** or **-o**) buffle m; (American) **b.** bison m.
buffer ['bʌfər] n (on train) tampon m; (at end of track) butoir m; **b. state** état m tampon.

buffet 1 ['bʌfɪt] *vt* frapper; (*of waves*) battre; (*of wind, rain*) cingler (*qn*). **2** ['bʊfeɪ] *n* (*table, meal, café*) buffet *m*; **cold b.** viandes *fpl* froides.

buffoon [bə'fuːn] *n* bouffon *m*.

bug[1] [bʌg] **1** *n* punaise *f*; (*any insect*) *Fam* bestiole *f*; *Med Fam* microbe *m*, virus *m*; **the travel b.** (*urge*) le désir de voyager. **2** *n* *Fam* (*in machine*) défaut *m*; (*in computer program*) erreur *f*. **3** *n* (*apparatus*) *Fam* micro *m*; − *vt* (**-gg-**) (*room*) *Fam* installer des micros dans.

bug[2] [bʌg] *vt* (**-gg-**) (*annoy*) *Am Fam* embêter.

bugbear ['bʌgbeər] *n* (*worry*) cauchemar *m*.

buggy ['bʌgɪ] *n* (**baby**) **b.** (*pushchair*) poussette *f*; (*folding*) poussette-canne *f*; (*pram*) *Am* landau *m*.

bugle ['bjuːg(ə)l] *n* clairon *m*. ◆**bugler** *n* (*person*) clairon *m*.

build [bɪld] **1** *n* (*of person*) carrure *f*. **2** *vt* (*pt & pp* **built**) construire; (*house, town*) construire, bâtir; **to b. in** (*cupboard etc*) encastrer; − *vi* bâtir, construire. ◆**built-in** *a* (*cupboard etc*) encastré; (*element of machine etc*) incorporé; (*innate*) *Fig* inné. **3 to b. up** *vt* (*reputation*) bâtir; (*increase*) augmenter; (*accumulate*) accumuler; (*business*) monter; (*speed, one's strength*) prendre; − *vi* augmenter, monter; s'accumuler. ◆**build-up** *n* montée *f*; accumulation *f*; *Mil* concentration *f*; *Journ* publicité *f*. ◆**built-up** *a* urbanisé; **b.-up area** agglomération *f*.

builder ['bɪldər] *n* maçon *m*; (*contractor*) entrepreneur *m*; (*of cars etc*) constructeur *m*; (*labourer*) ouvrier *m*.

building ['bɪldɪŋ] *n* bâtiment *m*; (*flats, offices*) immeuble *m*; (*action*) construction *f*; **b. society** caisse *f* d'épargne-logement, = société *f* de crédit immobilier.

bulb [bʌlb] *n* *Bot* bulbe *m*, oignon *m*; *El* ampoule *f*. ◆**bulbous** *a* bulbeux.

Bulgaria [bʌl'geərɪə] *n* Bulgarie *f*. ◆**Bulgarian** *a* & *n* bulgare (*mf*).

bulge ['bʌldʒ] *vi* **to b.** (**out**) se renfler, bomber; (*of eyes*) sortir de la tête; − *n* renflement *m*; (*increase*) *Fam* augmentation *f*. ◆**—ing** *a* renflé, bombé; (*eyes*) protubérant; (*bag*) gonflé (**with** de).

bulk [bʌlk] *n inv* grosseur *f*, volume *m*; **the b. of** (*most*) la majeure partie de; **in b.** (*to buy, sell*) en gros. ◆**bulky** *a* (**-ier, -iest**) gros, volumineux.

bull [bʊl] *n* **1** taureau *m*. **2** (*nonsense*) *Fam* foutaises *fpl*. ◆**bullfight** *n* corrida *f*.

◆**bullfighter** *n* matador *m*. ◆**bullring** *n* arène *f*.

bulldog ['bʊldɒg] *n* bouledogue *m*; **b. clip** pince *f* (à dessin).

bulldoz/e ['bʊldəʊz] *vt* passer au bull-dozer. ◆**—er** *n* bulldozer *m*, bouteur *m*.

bullet ['bʊlɪt] *n* balle *f*. ◆**bulletproof** *a* (*jacket, Am vest*) pare-balles *inv*; (*car*) blindé.

bulletin ['bʊlətɪn] *n* bulletin *m*.

bullion ['bʊljən] *n* or *m* or argent *m* en lingots.

bullock ['bʊlək] *n* bœuf *m*.

bull's-eye ['bʊlzaɪ] *n* (*of target*) centre *m*; **to hit the b.-eye** faire mouche.

bully ['bʊlɪ] *n* (*grosse*) brute *f*, tyran *m*; − *vt* brutaliser; (*persecute*) tyranniser; **to b. into doing** forcer à faire.

bulwark ['bʊlwək] *n* rempart *m*.

bum [bʌm] **1** *n* (*loafer*) *Am Fam* clochard *m*; − *vi* (**-mm-**) **to b.** (**around**) se balader. **2** *vt* (**-mm-**) **to b. sth off s.o.** (*cadge*) *Am Fam* taper qn de qch. **3** *n* (*buttocks*) *Fam* derrière *m*.

bumblebee ['bʌmb(ə)lbiː] *n* bourdon *m*.

bumf [bʌmf] *n* *Pej Sl* paperasses *fpl*.

bump [bʌmp] *vt* (*of car etc*) heurter; **to b. one's head/knee** se cogner la tête/le genou; **to b. into** se cogner contre; (*of car*) rentrer dans; (*meet*) *Fam* tomber sur; **to b. off** (*kill*) *Sl* liquider; **to b. up** *Fam* augmenter; − *vi* **to b. along** (*on rough road*) *Aut* cahoter; − *n* (*impact*) choc *m*; (*jerk*) cahot *m*; (*on road, body*) bosse *f*. ◆**—er** *n* (*of car etc*) pare-chocs *m inv*; − *a* (*crop etc*) exceptionnel; **b. cars** autos *fpl* tamponneuses. ◆**bumpy** *a* (**-ier, -iest**) (*road, ride*) cahoteux.

bumpkin ['bʌmpkɪn] *n* rustre *m*.

bumptious ['bʌmpʃəs] *a* prétentieux.

bun [bʌn] *n* **1** *Culin* petit pain *m* au lait. **2** (*of hair*) chignon *m*.

bunch [bʌntʃ] *n* (*of flowers*) bouquet *m*; (*of keys*) trousseau *m*; (*of bananas*) régime *m*; (*of people*) bande *f*; **b. of grapes** grappe *f* de raisin; **a b. of** (*mass*) *Fam* un tas de.

bundle ['bʌnd(ə)l] **1** *n* paquet *m*; (*of papers*) liasse *f*; (*of firewood*) fagot *m*. **2** *vt* (*put*) fourrer; (*push*) pousser (**into** dans); **to b.** (**up**) mettre en paquet; **to b. s.o. off** expédier qn; − *vi* **to b.** (**oneself**) **up** se couvrir (bien).

bung [bʌŋ] **1** *n* (*stopper*) bonde *f*; − *vt* **to b. up** (*stop up*) boucher. **2** *vt* (*toss*) *Fam* balancer, jeter.

bungalow ['bʌŋgələʊ] *n* bungalow *m*.

bungl/e ['bʌŋg(ə)l] *vt* gâcher; − *vi* travailler

mal. ◆**—ing** n gâchis m; – a (clumsy) maladroit.

bunion ['bʌnjən] n (on toe) oignon m.

bunk [bʌŋk] n **1** Rail Nau couchette f; **b. beds** lits mpl superposés. **2** Sl = **bunkum**. ◆**bunkum** n Sl foutaises fpl.

bunker ['bʌŋkər] n Mil Golf bunker m; (coalstore in garden) coffre m.

bunny ['bʌnɪ] n Fam Jeannot m lapin.

buoy [bɔɪ] n bouée f; – vt to **b. up** (support) Fig soutenir.

buoyant ['bɔɪənt] a Fig gai, optimiste; (market) ferme. Fin

burden ['bɜːd(ə)n] n fardeau m; (of tax) poids m; – vt charger, accabler (with de).

bureau, pl **-eaux** ['bjʊərəʊ, -əʊz] n (office) bureau m; (desk) secrétaire m. ◆**bureaucracy** [bjʊə'rɒkrəsɪ] n bureaucratie f. ◆**bureaucrat** ['bjʊərəkræt] n bureaucrate mf.

burger ['bɜːgər] n Fam hamburger m.

burglar ['bɜːglər] n cambrioleur, -euse mf; **b. alarm** sonnerie f d'alarme. ◆**burglarize** vt Am cambrioler. ◆**burglary** n cambriolage m. ◆**burgle** vt cambrioler.

burial ['berɪəl] n enterrement m; – a (service) funèbre; **b. ground** cimetière m.

burlap ['bɜːlæp] n (sacking) Am toile f à sac.

burlesque [bɜː'lesk] n parodie f; Th Am revue f.

burly ['bɜːlɪ] a (-ier, -iest) costaud.

Burma ['bɜːmə] n Birmanie f. ◆**Bur'mese** a & n birman, -ane (mf).

burn [bɜːn] n brûlure f; – vt (pt & pp burned or burnt) brûler; to **b. down** or **off** or **up** brûler; **burnt alive** brûlé vif; – vi brûler; to **b. down** (of house) brûler (complètement), être réduit en cendres; to **b. out** (of fire) s'éteindre; (of fuse) sauter. ◆**—ing** a en feu; (fire) allumé; (topic, fever etc) Fig brûlant; – n smell of **b.** odeur f de brûlé. ◆**—er** n (of stove) brûleur m.

burp [bɜːp] n Fam rot m; – vi Fam roter.

burrow ['bʌrəʊ] n (hole) terrier m; – vti creuser.

bursar ['bɜːsər] n (in school) intendant, -ante mf.

bursary ['bɜːsərɪ] n (grant) bourse f.

burst [bɜːst] n éclatement m, explosion f; (of laughter) éclat m; (of applause) salve f; (of thunder) coup m; (surge) élan m; (fit) accès m; (burst water pipe) Fam tuyau m crevé; – vi (pt & pp burst) (of bomb etc) éclater; (of bubble, tyre, cloud etc) crever; to **b. into** (room) faire irruption dans; to **b. into tears** fondre en larmes; to **b. into flames** prendre feu, s'embraser; to **b. open** s'ouvrir avec

force; to **b. out laughing** éclater de rire; – vt crever, faire éclater; (rupture) rompre; to **b. open** ouvrir avec force. ◆**—ing** a (full) plein à craquer (with de); **b. with** (joy) débordant de; to be **b. to do** mourir d'envie de faire.

bury ['berɪ] vt (dead person) enterrer; (hide) enfouir; (plunge, absorb) plonger.

bus [bʌs] n (auto)bus m; (long-distance) (auto)car m; – a (driver, ticket etc) d'autobus; d'autocar; **b. shelter** abribus m; **b. station** gare f routière; **b. stop** arrêt m d'autobus; – vt (-ss-) (children) transporter (en bus) à l'école. ◆**bussing** n Sch ramassage m scolaire.

bush [bʊʃ] n buisson m; (of hair) tignasse f; **the b.** (land) la brousse. ◆**bushy** a (-ier, -iest) (hair, tail etc) broussailleux.

bushed [bʊʃt] a (tired) Fam crevé.

business ['bɪznɪs] n affaires fpl, commerce m; (shop) commerce m; (task, concern, matter) affaire f; **the textile b.** le textile; **big b.** Fam les grosses entreprises fpl commerciales; **on b.** (to travel) pour affaires; **it's your b. to** . . . c'est à vous de . . . ; **you have no b. to** . . . vous n'avez pas le droit de . . . ; **that's none of your b.!** ça ne vous regarde pas!; to **mean b.** Fam ne pas plaisanter; – a commercial; (meeting, trip) d'affaires; **b. hours** (office) heures fpl de travail; (shop) heures fpl d'ouverture. ◆**businesslike** a sérieux, pratique. ◆**businessman** n (pl -men) homme m d'affaires. ◆**businesswoman** n (pl -women) femme f d'affaires.

busker ['bʌskər] n musicien, -ienne mf des rues.

bust [bʌst] **1** n (sculpture) buste m; (woman's breasts) poitrine f. **2** a (broken) Fam fichu; to **go b.** (bankrupt) faire faillite; – vti (pt & pp bust or busted) Fam = to **burst** & to **break.** ◆**b.-up** n Fam (quarrel) engueulade f; (breakup) rupture f.

bustl/e ['bʌs(ə)l] vi to **b. (about)** s'affairer; – n activité f, branle-bas m. ◆**—ing** a (street) bruyant.

bus/y ['bɪzɪ] a (-ier, -iest) occupé (doing à faire); (active) actif; (day) chargé; (street) animé; (line) Tel Am occupé; to be **b. doing** (in the process of) être en train de faire; – vt to **b. oneself** s'occuper (with à qch, doing à faire). ◆**—ily** adv activement. ◆**busybody** n to be a **b.** faire la mouche du coche.

but [bʌt, unstressed bət] **1** conj mais. **2** prep (except) sauf; **b. for that** sans cela; **b. for him** sans lui; **no one b. you** personne d'autre que toi. **3** *adv* (*only*) ne . . . que, seulement.

butane ['bjuːteɪn] *n* (*gas*) butane *m*.

butcher ['butʃər] *n* boucher *m*; **b.'s shop** boucherie *f*; – *vt* (*people*) massacrer; (*animal*) abattre. ◆**butchery** *n* massacre *m* (**of** de).

butler ['bʌtlər] *n* maître *m* d'hôtel.

butt [bʌt] **1** *n* (*of cigarette*) mégot *m*; (*of gun*) crosse *f*; (*buttocks*) *Am Fam* derrière *m*; **b. for ridicule** objet *m* de risée. **2** *vi* **to b. in** interrompre, intervenir.

butter ['bʌtər] *n* beurre *m*; **b. bean** haricot *m* blanc; **b. dish** beurrier *m*; – *vt* beurrer; **to b. s.o. up** *Fam* flatter qn. ◆**buttercup** *n* bouton-d'or *m*. ◆**buttermilk** *n* lait *m* de beurre.

butterfly ['bʌtəflaɪ] *n* papillon *m*; **to have butterflies** *Fam* avoir le trac; **b. stroke** *Swimming* brasse *f* papillon.

buttock ['bʌtək] *n* fesse *f*.

button ['bʌtən] *n* bouton *m*; – *vt* **to b. (up)** boutonner; – *vi* **to b. up** (*of garment*) se boutonner. ◆**buttonhole 1** *n* boutonnière *f*; (*flower*) fleur *f*. **2** *vt* (*person*) *Fam* accrocher.

buttress ['bʌtrɪs] *n Archit* contrefort *m*; *Fig* soutien *m*; **flying b.** arc-boutant *m*; – *vt* (*support*) *Archit & Fig* soutenir.

buxom ['bʌksəm] *a* (*woman*) bien en chair.

buy [baɪ] *vt* (*pt & pp* **bought**) acheter (**from s.o.** à qn, **for s.o.** à *or* pour qn); (*story etc*) *Am Fam* avaler, croire; **to b. back** racheter; **to b. over** (*bribe*) corrompre; **to b. up** acheter en bloc; – *n* **a good b.** une bonne affaire. ◆**—er** *n* acheteur, -euse *mf*.

buzz [bʌz] **1** *vi* bourdonner; **to b. off** *Fam* décamper; – *n* bourdonnement *m*. **2** *vt* (*building etc*) *Av* raser. **3** *vt* **to b. s.o.** *Tel* appeler qn; – *n Tel Fam* coup *m* de fil. ◆**—er** *n* interphone *m*; (*of bell, clock*) sonnerie *f*; (*hooter*) sirène *f*.

by [baɪ] *prep* **1** (*agent, manner*) par; **hit/chosen/etc by** frappé/choisi/*etc* par; **surrounded/followed/etc by** entouré/suivi/ *etc* de; **by doing** en faisant; **by sea** par mer; **by mistake** par erreur; **by car** en voiture; **by bicycle** à bicyclette; **by moonlight** au clair de lune; **one by one** un à un; **day by day** de jour en jour; **by sight/day/far** de vue/ jour/loin; **by the door** (*through*) par la porte; **(all) by oneself** tout seul. **2** (*next to*) à côté de; (*near*) près de; **by the lake/sea** au bord du lac/de la mer; **to pass by the bank** passer devant la banque. **3** (*before in time*) avant; **by Monday** avant lundi, d'ici lundi; **by now** à cette heure-ci, déjà; **by yesterday** (dès) hier. **4** (*amount, measurement*) à; **by the kilo** au kilo; **taller by a metre** plus grand d'un mètre; **paid by the hour** payé à l'heure. **5** (*according to*) d'après; – *adv* **close by** tout près; **to go by, pass by** passer; **to put by** mettre de côté; **by and by** bientôt; **by and large** en gros. ◆**by-election** *n* élection *f* partielle. ◆**by-law** *n* arrêté *m*; (*of organization*) *Am* statut *m*. ◆**by-product** *n* sous-produit *m*. ◆**by-road** *n* chemin *m* de traverse.

bye(-bye)! [baɪ('baɪ)] *int Fam* salut!, au revoir!

bygone ['baɪgɒn] *a* **in b. days** jadis.

bypass ['baɪpɑːs] *n* déviation *f* (routière), dérivation *f*; – *vt* contourner; (*ignore*) *Fig* éviter de passer par.

bystander ['baɪstændər] *n* spectateur, -trice *mf*; (*in street*) badaud, -aude *mf*.

byword ['baɪwɜːd] *n* **a b. for** *Pej* un synonyme de.

C

C, c [siː] *n* C, c *m*.

c *abbr* = **cent**.

cab [kæb] *n* taxi *m*; (*horse-drawn*) *Hist* fiacre *m*; (*of train driver etc*) cabine *f*. ◆**cabby** *n Fam* (*chauffeur m de*) taxi *m*; *Hist* cocher *m*.

cabaret ['kæbəreɪ] *n* (*show*) spectacle *m*; (*place*) cabaret *m*.

cabbage ['kæbɪdʒ] *n* chou *m*.

cabin ['kæbɪn] *n Nau Rail* cabine *f*; (*hut*) cabane *f*, case *f*; **c. boy** mousse *m*.

cabinet ['kæbɪnɪt] **1** *n* (*cupboard*) armoire *f*; (*for display*) vitrine *f*; (**filing**) **c.** classeur *m* (de bureau). **2** *n Pol* cabinet *m*; – *a* ministériel; **c. minister** ministre *m*. ◆**c.-maker** *n* ébéniste *m*.

cable ['keɪb(ə)l] *n* câble *m*; **c. car** (*with overhead cable*) téléphérique *m*; *Rail* funiculaire *m*; **c. television** la télévision par câble; **to have c.** *Fam* avoir le câble; – *vt* (*message etc*) câbler (**to** à).

caboose [kə'buːs] *n Rail Am* fourgon *m* (de queue).

cache [kæʃ] *n* (*place*) cachette *f*; **an arms' c.** des armes cachées, une cache d'armes.

cachet ['kæʃeɪ] *n* (*mark, character etc*) cachet *m*.

cackle ['kæk(ə)l] *vi* (*of hen*) caqueter; (*laugh*) glousser; – *n* caquet *m*; glousse-ment *m*.

cacophony [kə'kɒfənɪ] *n* cacophonie *f*.

cactus, *pl* -**ti** *or* -**tuses** ['kæktəs, -taɪ, -təsɪz] *n* cactus *m*.

cad [kæd] *n Old-fashioned Pej* goujat *m*.

cadaverous [kə'dævərəs] *a* cadavérique.

caddie ['kædɪ] *n Golf* caddie *m*.

caddy ['kædɪ] *n* (*tea*) **c.** boîte *f* à thé.

cadence ['keɪdəns] *n Mus* cadence *f*.

cadet [kə'det] *n Mil* élève *m* officier.

cadge [kædʒ] *vi* (*beg*) *Pej* quémander; – *vt* (*meal*) se faire payer (**off s.o.** par qn); **to c. money from** *or* **off s.o.** taper qn.

Caesarean [sɪ'zeərɪən] *n* **c. (section)** *Med* césarienne *f*.

café ['kæfeɪ] *n* café(-restaurant) *m*. ◆**cafe-teria** [kæfɪ'tɪərɪə] *n* cafétéria *f*.

caffeine ['kæfiːn] *n* caféine *f*.

cage [keɪdʒ] *n* cage *f*; – *vt* **to c. (up)** mettre en cage.

cagey ['keɪdʒɪ] *a Fam* peu communicatif (**about** à l'égard de).

cahoots [kə'huːts] *n* **in c.** *Sl* de mèche, en cheville (**with** avec).

cajole [kə'dʒəʊl] *vt* amadouer, enjôler.

cak/e [keɪk] **1** *n* gâteau *m*; (*small*) pâtisse-rie *f*; **c. of soap** savonnette *f*. **2** *vi* (*harden*) durcir; – *vt* (*cover*) couvrir (**with** de). ◆**—ed** *a* (*mud*) séché.

calamine ['kæləmaɪn] *n* **c. (lotion)** lotion *f* apaisante (à la calamine).

calamity [kə'læmɪtɪ] *n* calamité *f*. ◆**calamitous** *a* désastreux.

calcium ['kælsɪəm] *n* calcium *m*.

calculat/e ['kælkjʊleɪt] *vti* calculer; **to c. that** *Fam* supposer que; **to c. on** compter sur. ◆**—ing** *a* (*shrewd*) calculateur. ◆**calcu'lation** *n* calcul *m*. ◆**calculator** *n* (*desk computer*) calculatrice *f*; (*pocket*) **c.** calculatrice (de poche). ◆**calculus** *n Math Med* calcul *m*.

calendar ['kælɪndər] *n* calendrier *m*; (*direc-tory*) annuaire *m*.

calf [kɑːf] *n* (*pl* **calves**) **1** (*animal*) veau *m*. **2** *Anat* mollet *m*.

calibre ['kælɪbər] *n* calibre *m*. ◆**calibrate** *vt* calibrer.

calico ['kælɪkəʊ] *n* (*pl* -**oes** *or* -**os**) (*fabric*) calicot *m*; (*printed*) *Am* indienne *f*.

call [kɔːl] *n* appel *m*; (*shout*) cri *m*; (*vocation*) vocation *f*; (*visit*) visite *f*; (**telephone**) **c.** communication *f*, appel *m* téléphonique; **to make a c.** *Tel* téléphoner (**to** à); **on c.** de garde; **no c. to do** aucune raison de faire; **there's no c. for that article** *Com* cet article n'est pas très demandé; **c. box** cabine *f* (téléphonique); – *vt* appeler; (*wake up*) réveiller; (*person to meeting*) convoquer (**to** à); (*attention*) attirer (**to** sur); (*truce*) demander; (*consider*) considérer; **he's called David** il s'appelle David; **to c. a meeting** convoquer une assemblée; **to c. s.o. a liar/etc** qualifier *or* traiter qn de menteur/etc; **to c. into question** mettre en question; **let's c. it a day** *Fam* on va s'arrêter là, ça suffit; **to c. sth (out)** (*shout*) crier qch; – *vi* appeler; **to c. (out)** (*cry out*) crier; **to c. (in** *or* **round** *or* **by** *or* **over)** (*visit*) passer. ■ **to c. back** *vti*; **to c. for** *vt* (*require*) demander; (*summon*) appeler; (*collect*) passer prendre; **to c. in** *vt* faire venir *or* entrer; (*police*) appeler; (*recall*) rappeler, faire rentrer; – *vi* **to c. in on s.o.** passer chez qn. ◆**call-in** *a* (*programme*) *Rad* à ligne ouverte; **to c. off** *vt* (*cancel*) annuler; (*dog*) rappeler; **to c. out** *vt* (*doctor*) appeler; (*workers*) donner une consigne de grève à; – *vi* **to c. out for** demander à haute voix; **to c. up** *vt Mil Tel* appeler; (*memories*) évoquer. ◆**call-up** *n Mil* appel *m*, mobilisation *f*; **to c. (up)on** *vi* (*visit*) passer voir, passer chez; (*invoke*) invoquer; **to c. (up)on s.o. to do** inviter qn à faire; (*urge*) sommer qn de faire. ◆**calling** *n* vocation *f*; **c. card** *Am* carte *f* de visite. ◆**caller** *n* visiteur, -euse *mf*; *Tel* correspondant, -ante *mf*.

calligraphy [kə'lɪgrəfɪ] *n* calligraphie *f*.

callous ['kæləs] *a* **1** cruel, insensible. **2** (*skin*) calleux. ◆**callus** *n* durillon *m*, cal *m*.

callow ['kæləʊ] *a* inexpérimenté.

calm [kɑːm] *a* (-er, -est) calme, tranquille; **keep c.!** (*don't panic*) du calme!; – *n* calme *m*; – *vt* **to c. (down)** calmer; – *vi* **to c. down** se calmer. ◆**—ly** *adv* calmement. ◆**—ness** *n* calme *m*.

calorie ['kælərɪ] *n* calorie *f*.

calumny ['kæləmnɪ] *n* calomnie *f*.

calvary ['kælvərɪ] *n Rel* calvaire *m*.

calve [kɑːv] *vi* (*of cow*) vêler.

camber ['kæmbər] *n* (*in road*) bombement *m*.

came [keɪm] *see* come.

camel ['kæməl] *n* chameau *m*.

camellia [kə'miːlɪə] *n Bot* camélia *m*.

cameo ['kæmiəu] n camée m.

camera ['kæmrə] n appareil(-photo) m; *TV Cin* caméra f. ◆**cameraman** n (pl -men) caméraman m.

camomile ['kæməmaɪl] n Bot camomille f.

camouflage ['kæməflɑːʒ] n camouflage m; – vt camoufler.

camp 1 [kæmp] n camp m, campement m; **c. bed** lit m de camp; – vi **to c. (out)** camper. ◆—**ing** n Sp camping m; **c. site** (terrain m de) camping m. ◆—**er** n (person) campeur, -euse mf; (vehicle) camping-car m. ◆**campfire** n feu m de camp. ◆**camp-site** n camping m.

camp 2 [kæmp] a (affected) affecté, exagéré (de façon à provoquer le rire).

campaign [kæm'peɪn] n Pol Mil Journ etc campagne f; – vi faire campagne. ◆—**er** n militant, -ante mf (for pour).

campus ['kæmpəs] n Univ campus m.

can 1 [kæn, unstressed kən] v aux (pres t **can**; pt **could**) (be able to) pouvoir; (know how to) savoir; **if I c.** si je peux; **she c. swim** elle sait nager; **if I could** si je savais nager; **he could do it tomorrow** il pourrait le faire demain; **he couldn't help me** il ne pouvait pas m'aider; **he could have done it** il aurait pu le faire; **you could be wrong** (possibility) tu as peut-être tort; **he can't be old** (probability) il ne doit pas être vieux; **c. I come in?** (permission) puis-je entrer?; **you can't** or **c. not come** tu ne peux pas venir; **I c. see** je vois.

can 2 [kæn] n (for water etc) bidon m; (tin for food) boîte f; – vt (**-nn-**) mettre en boîte. ◆**canned** a en boîte, en conserve; **c. food** conserves fpl. ◆**can-opener** n ouvre-boîtes m inv.

Canada ['kænədə] n Canada m. ◆**Canadian** [kə'neɪdɪən] a & n canadien, -ienne (mf).

canal [kə'næl] n canal m.

canary [kə'neərɪ] n canari m, serin m.

cancan ['kænkæn] n french-cancan m.

cancel ['kænsəl] vt (**-ll-**, Am **-l-**) annuler; (goods, taxi, appointment) décommander; (word, paragraph etc) biffer; (train) supprimer; (stamp) oblitérer; **to c. a ticket** (with date) composter un billet; (punch) poinçonner un billet; **to c. each other out** s'annuler. ◆**cance'llation** n annulation f; suppression f; oblitération f.

cancer ['kænsər] n cancer m; **C.** (sign) le Cancer; **c. patient** cancéreux, -euse mf. ◆**cancerous** a cancéreux.

candelabra [kændɪ'lɑːbrə] n candélabre m.

candid ['kændɪd] a franc, sincère. ◆**candour** n franchise f, sincérité f.

candidate ['kændɪdeɪt] n candidat, -ate mf. ◆**candidacy** n, ◆**candidature** n candidature f.

candle ['kænd(ə)l] n bougie f; (tallow) chandelle f; Rel cierge m; **c. grease** suif m. ◆**candlelight** n **by c.** à la (lueur d'une) bougie; **to have dinner by c.** dîner aux chandelles. ◆**candlestick** n bougeoir m; (tall) chandelier m.

candy ['kændɪ] n Am bonbon(s) m(pl); (sugar) sucre m candi; **c. store** Am confiserie f. ◆**candied** a (fruit) confit, glacé. ◆**candyfloss** n barbe f à papa.

cane [keɪn] n canne f; (for basket) rotin m; Sch baguette f; – vt (punish) Sch fouetter.

canine ['keɪnaɪn] **1** a canin. **2** n (tooth) canine f.

canister ['kænɪstər] n boîte f (en métal).

canker ['kæŋkər] n (in disease) & Fig chancre m.

cannabis ['kænəbɪs] n (plant) chanvre m indien; (drug) haschisch m.

cannibal ['kænɪbəl] n & a cannibale (mf).

cannon ['kænən] n (pl **-s** or inv) canon m. ◆**cannonball** n boulet m (de canon).

cannot ['kænɒt] = **can not**.

canny ['kænɪ] a (**-ier, -iest**) rusé, malin.

canoe [kə'nuː] n canoë m, kayak m; – vi faire du canoë or du kayak. ◆—**ing** n **to go c.** Sp faire du canoë or du kayak. ◆**canoeist** n canoëiste mf.

canon ['kænən] n (law) canon m; (clergyman) chanoine m. ◆**canonize** vt Rel canoniser.

canopy ['kænəpɪ] n (over bed, altar etc) dais m; (hood of pram) capote f; (awning) auvent m; (made of glass) marquise f; (of sky) Fig voûte f.

cant [kænt] n (jargon) jargon m.

can't [kɑːnt] = **can not**.

cantaloup(e) ['kæntəluːp, Am -ləup] n (melon) cantaloup m.

cantankerous [kæn'tæŋkərəs] a grincheux, acariâtre.

cantata [kæn'tɑːtə] n Mus cantate f.

canteen [kæn'tiːn] n (place) cantine f; (flask) gourde f; **c. of cutlery** ménagère f.

canter ['kæntər] n petit galop m; – vi aller au petit galop.

cantor ['kæntər] n Rel chantre m, maître m de chapelle.

canvas ['kænvəs] n (grosse) toile f; (for embroidery) canevas m.

canvass ['kænvəs] vt (an area) faire du démarchage dans; (opinions) sonder; **to c.**

s.o. *Pol* solliciter des voix de qn; *Com* solliciter des commandes de qn. ◆**—ing** *n* *Com* démarchage *m*, prospection *f*; *Pol* démarchage *m* (électoral). ◆**—er** *n* *Pol* agent *m* électoral; *Com* démarcheur, -euse *mf*.

canyon ['kænjən] *n* cañon *m*, canyon *m*.

cap¹ [kæp] *n* **1** (*hat*) casquette *f*; (*for shower etc*) & *Nau* bonnet *m*; *Mil* képi *m*. **2** (*of bottle, tube, valve*) bouchon *m*; (*of milk or beer bottle*) capsule *f*; (*of pen*) capuchon *m*. **3** (*of child's gun*) amorce *f*, capsule *f*. **4** (**Dutch**) **c.** (*contraceptive*) diaphragme *m*.

cap² [kæp] *vt* (**-pp-**) (*outdo*) surpasser; **to c. it all** pour comble; **capped with** (*covered*) coiffé de.

capable ['keɪpəb(ə)l] *a* (*person*) capable (**of** sth de qch, **of doing** de faire), compétent; **c. of** (*thing*) susceptible de. ◆**capa'bility** *n* capacité *f*. ◆**capably** *adv* avec compétence.

capacity [kə'pæsɪtɪ] *n* (*of container*) capacité *f*, contenance *f*; (*ability*) aptitude *f*, capacité *f*; (*output*) rendement *m*; **in my c. as** en ma qualité de; **in an advisory**/*etc* **c.** à titre consultatif/*etc*; **filled to c.** absolument plein, comble; **c. audience** salle *f* comble.

cape [keɪp] *n* **1** (*cloak*) cape *f*; (*of cyclist*) pèlerine *f*. **2** *Geog* cap *m*; **C. Town** Le Cap.

caper ['keɪpər] **1** *vi* (*jump about*) gambader. **2** *n* (*activity*) *Sl* affaire *f*; (*prank*) *Fam* farce *f*; (*trip*) *Fam* virée *f*. **3** *n* *Bot Culin* câpre *f*.

capital ['kæpɪtəl] **1** *a* (*punishment, letter, importance*) capital; — *n* **c.** (*city*) capitale *f*; **c.** (**letter**) majuscule *f*, capitale *f*. **2** *n* (*money*) capital *m*, capitaux *mpl*. ◆**capitalism** *n* capitalisme *m*. ◆**capitalist** *a* & *n* capitaliste (*mf*). ◆**capitalize** *vi* **to c.** on tirer parti de.

capitulate [kə'pɪtʃuleɪt] *vi* capituler. ◆**capitu'lation** *n* capitulation *f*.

caprice [kə'priːs] *n* caprice *m*. ◆**capricious** [kə'prɪʃəs] *a* capricieux.

Capricorn ['kæprɪkɔːn] *n* (*sign*) le Capricorne.

capsize [kæp'saɪz] *vi* *Nau* chavirer; — *vt* (*faire*) chavirer.

capsule ['kæpsəl, 'kæpsjuːl] *n* (*medicine, of spaceship etc*) capsule *f*.

captain ['kæptɪn] *n* capitaine *m*; — *vt* *Nau* commander; *Sp* être le capitaine de.

caption ['kæpʃ(ə)n] *n* *Cin Journ* sous-titre *m*; (*under illustration*) légende *f*.

captivate ['kæptɪveɪt] *vt* captiver.

captive ['kæptɪv] *n* captif, -ive *mf*, prisonnier, -ière *mf*. ◆**cap'tivity** *n* captivité *f*.

capture ['kæptʃər] *n* capture *f*; — *vt* (*person, animal*) prendre, capturer; (*town*) prendre; (*attention*) capter; (*represent in words, on film etc*) rendre, reproduire.

car [kɑːr] *n* voiture *f*, auto(mobile) *f*; *Rail* wagon *m*; — *a* (*industry*) automobile; **c. ferry** ferry-boat *m*; **c. park** parking *m*; **c. radio** autoradio *m*; **c. wash** (*action*) lavage *m* automatique; (*machine*) lave-auto *m*. ◆**carfare** *n* *Am* frais *mpl* de voyage. ◆**carport** *n* auvent *m* (pour voiture). ◆**carsick** *a* **to be c.** être malade en voiture.

carafe [kə'ræf] *n* carafe *f*.

caramel ['kærəməl] *n* (*flavouring, toffee*) caramel *m*.

carat ['kærət] *n* carat *m*.

caravan ['kærəvæn] *n* (*in desert*) & *Aut* caravane *f*; (*horse-drawn*) roulotte *f*; **c. site** camping *m* pour caravanes.

caraway ['kærəweɪ] *n* *Bot Culin* cumin *m*, carvi *m*.

carbohydrates [kɑːbəʊ'haɪdreɪts] *npl* (*in diet*) féculents *mpl*.

carbon ['kɑːbən] *n* carbone *m*; **c. copy** double *m* (au carbone); *Fig* réplique *f*, double *m*; **c. paper** (papier *m*) carbone *m*.

carbuncle ['kɑːbʌŋk(ə)l] *n* *Med* furoncle *m*, clou *m*.

carburettor [kɑːbjʊ'retər] (*Am* **carburetor** ['kɑːbəreɪtər]) *n* carburateur *m*.

carcass ['kɑːkəs] *n* (*body, framework*) carcasse *f*.

carcinogenic [kɑːsɪnə'dʒenɪk] *a* cancérigène.

card [kɑːd] *n* carte *f*; (*cardboard*) carton *m*; (*index*) **c.** fiche *f*; **c. index** fichier *m*; **c. table** table *f* de jeu; **to play cards** jouer aux cartes; **on** *or Am* **in the cards** *Fam* très vraisemblable; **to get one's cards** (*be dismissed*) *Fam* être renvoyé. ◆**cardboard** *n* carton *m*. ◆**cardsharp** *n* tricheur, -euse *mf*.

cardiac ['kɑːdɪæk] *a* cardiaque.

cardigan ['kɑːdɪɡən] *n* cardigan *m*, gilet *m*.

cardinal ['kɑːdɪn(ə)l] **1** *a* (*number etc*) cardinal. **2** *n* (*priest*) cardinal *m*.

care [keər] **1** *vi* **to c. about** (*feel concern about*) se soucier de, s'intéresser à; **I don't c.** ça m'est égal; **I couldn't c. less** *Fam* je m'en fiche; **who cares?** qu'est-ce que ça fait? **2** *vi* (*like*) aimer, vouloir; **would you c. to try?** voulez-vous essayer?, aimeriez-vous essayer?; **I don't c. for it** (*music etc*) je n'aime pas tellement ça; **to c. for** (*a drink, a change etc*) avoir envie de; **to c. about** *or* **for s.o.** avoir de la sympathie pour qn; **to c. for**

(*look after*) s'occuper de; (*sick person*) soigner. **3** *n* (*application, heed*) soin(s) *m*(*pl*), attention *f*; (*charge, protection*) garde *f*, soin *m*; (*anxiety*) souci *m*; **to take c. not to do** faire attention à ne pas faire; **take c. to put everything back** veillez à tout ranger; **to take c. of** s'occuper de; **to take c. of itself** (*of matter*) s'arranger; **to take c. of oneself** (*manage*) se débrouiller; (*keep healthy*) faire attention à sa santé. ◆**carefree** *a* insouciant. ◆**caretaker** *n* gardien, -ienne *mf*, concierge *mf*.

career [kəˈrɪər] **1** *n* carrière *f*; – *a* (*diplomat etc*) de carrière. **2** *vi* **to c. along** aller à toute vitesse.

careful [ˈkeəf(ə)l] *a* (*diligent*) soigneux (**about, of** de); (*cautious*) prudent; **c. (with money)** regardant; **to be c. of** or **with** (*heed*) faire attention à. ◆**—ly** *adv* avec soin; prudemment. ◆**careless** *a* négligent; (*thoughtless*) irréfléchi; (*inattentive*) inattentif (**of** à). ◆**carelessness** *n* négligence *f*, manque *m* de soin.

caress [kəˈres] *n* caresse *f*; – *vt* (*stroke*) caresser; (*kiss*) embrasser.

cargo [ˈkɑːɡəʊ] *n* (*pl* **-oes**, *Am* **-os**) cargaison *f*; **c. boat** cargo *m*.

Caribbean [kærɪˈbiːən, *Am* kəˈrɪbɪən] *a* caraïbe *f*; – *n* **the C. (Islands)** les Antilles *fpl*.

caricature [ˈkærɪkətʃʊər] *n* caricature *f*; – *vt* caricaturer.

caring [ˈkeərɪŋ] *a* (*loving*) aimant; (*understanding*) compréhensif; – *n* affection *f*.

carnage [ˈkɑːnɪdʒ] *n* carnage *m*.

carnal [ˈkɑːnəl] *a* charnel, sexuel.

carnation [kɑːˈneɪʃən] *n* œillet *m*.

carnival [ˈkɑːnɪvəl] *n* carnaval *m*.

carnivore [ˈkɑːnɪvɔːr] *n* carnivore *m*. ◆**car-ˈnivorous** *a* carnivore.

carol [ˈkærəl] *n* chant *m* (de Noël).

carouse [kəˈrauz] *vi* faire la fête.

carp [kɑːp] **1** *n* (*fish*) carpe *f*. **2** *vi* critiquer; **to c. at** critiquer.

carpenter [ˈkɑːpɪntər] *n* (*for house building*) charpentier *m*; (*light woodwork*) menuisier *m*. ◆**carpentry** *n* charpenterie *f*; menuiserie *f*.

carpet [ˈkɑːpɪt] *n* tapis *m*; (*fitted*) moquette *f*; **c. sweeper** balai *m* mécanique; – *vt* recouvrir d'un tapis *or* d'une moquette; (*of snow etc*) *Fig* tapisser. ◆**—ing** *n* (*carpets*) tapis *mpl*; moquette *f*.

carriage [ˈkærɪdʒ] *n* (*horse-drawn*) voiture *f*, équipage *m*; *Rail* voiture *f*; *Com* transport *m*; (*bearing of person*) port *m*; (*of typewriter*) chariot *m*; **c. paid** port payé. ◆**car-riageway** *n* (*of road*) chaussée *f*.

carrier [ˈkærɪər] *n* *Com* entreprise *f* de transports; *Med* porteur, -euse *mf*; **c. (bag)** sac *m* (en plastique); **c. pigeon** pigeon *m* voyageur.

carrion [ˈkærɪən] *n* charogne *f*.

carrot [ˈkærət] *n* carotte *f*.

carry [ˈkærɪ] *vt* porter; (*goods*) transporter; (*by wind*) emporter; (*involve*) comporter; (*interest*) *Com* produire; (*extend*) faire passer; (*win*) remporter; (*authority*) avoir; (*child*) *Med* attendre; (*motion*) *Pol* faire passer, voter; (*sell*) stocker; *Math* retenir; **to c. too far** pousser trop loin; **to c. oneself** se comporter; – *vi* (*of sound*) porter. ■ **to c. away** *vt* emporter; *Fig* transporter; **to be** or **get carried away** (*excited*) s'emballer; **to c. back** *vt* (*thing*) rapporter; (*person*) ramener; (*in thought*) reporter; **to c. off** *vt* emporter; (*kidnap*) enlever; (*prize*) remporter; **to c. it off** réussir; **to c. on** *vt* continuer; (*conduct*) diriger, mener; (*sustain*) soutenir; – *vi* continuer (**doing** à faire); (*behave*) *Pej* se conduire (mal); (*complain*) se plaindre; **to c. on with sth** continuer qch; **to c. on about** (*talk*) causer de. ◆**carryings-'on** *npl Pej* activités *fpl*; (*behaviour*) *Pej* façons *fpl*; **to c. out** (*plan etc*) exécuter, réaliser; (*repair etc*) effectuer; (*duty*) accomplir; (*meal*) *Am* emporter; **to c. through** *vt* (*plan etc*) mener à bonne fin.

carryall [ˈkærɪɔːl] *n Am* fourre-tout *m inv*. ◆**carrycot** *n* (nacelle *f*) porte-bébé *m*.

cart [kɑːt] **1** *n* charrette *f*; (*handcart*) voiture *f* à bras. **2** *vt* (*goods, people*) transporter; **to c. (around)** *Fam* trimbal(l)er; **to c. away** emporter. ◆**carthorse** *n* cheval *m* de trait.

cartel [kɑːˈtel] *n Econ Pol* cartel *m*.

cartilage [ˈkɑːtɪlɪdʒ] *n* cartilage *m*.

carton [ˈkɑːtən] *n* (*box*) carton *m*; (*of milk, fruit juice etc*) brick *m*, pack *m*; (*of cigarettes*) cartouche *f*; (*of cream*) pot *m*.

cartoon [kɑːˈtuːn] *n Journ* dessin *m* (humoristique); *Cin* dessin *m* animé; **(strip) c.** bande *f* dessinée. ◆**cartoonist** *n Journ* dessinateur, -trice *mf* (humoristique).

cartridge [ˈkɑːtrɪdʒ] *n* (*of firearm, pen, camera, tape deck*) cartouche *f*; (*of record player*) cellule *f*; **c. belt** cartouchière *f*.

carv/e [kɑːv] *vt* (*cut*) tailler (**out of** dans); (*sculpt*) sculpter; (*initials etc*) graver; **to c. (up)** (*meat*) découper; **to c. up** (*country*) dépecer, morceler; **to c. out sth for oneself** (*career etc*) se tailler qch. ◆**—ing** *n* (*wood*) **c.** sculpture *f* (sur bois).

cascade [kæsˈkeɪd] *n* (*of rocks*) chute *f*; (*of*

blows) déluge *m*; (*of lace*) flot *m*; − *vi* tomber; (*hang*) pendre.

case [keɪs] *n* **1** (*instance*) & *Med* cas *m*; *Jur* affaire *f*; *Phil* arguments *mpl*; **in any c.** en tout cas; **in c. it rains** au cas où il pleuvrait; **in c. of** en cas de; (**just**) **in c.** à tout hasard. **2** (*bag*) valise *f*; (*crate*) caisse *f*; (*for pen, glasses, camera, violin, cigarettes*) étui *m*; (*for jewels*) coffret *m*. ◆**casing** *n* (*covering*) enveloppe *f*.

cash [kæʃ] *n* argent *m*; **to pay (in) c.** (*not by cheque*) payer en espèces *or* en liquide; **to pay c.** (**down**) payer comptant; **c. price** prix *m* (au) comptant; **c. box** caisse *f*; **c. desk** caisse *f*; **c. register** caisse *f* enregistreuse; − *vt* (*banknote*) changer; **to c. a cheque** (*of person*) encaisser un chèque; (*of bank*) payer un chèque; **to c. in on** *Fam* profiter de. ◆**ca'shier 1** *n* caissier, -ière *mf*. **2** *vt* (*dismiss*) *Mil* casser.

cashew [ˈkæʃuː] *n* (*nut*) cajou *m*.

cashmere [ˈkæʃmɪər] *n* cachemire *m*.

casino [kəˈsiːnəu] *n* (*pl* -os) casino *m*.

cask [kɑːsk] *n* fût *m*, tonneau *m*. ◆**casket** *n* (*box*) coffret *m*; (*coffin*) cercueil *m*.

casserole [ˈkæsərəul] *n* (*covered dish*) cocotte *f*; (*stew*) ragoût *m* en cocotte.

cassette [kəˈset] *n* cassette *f*; *Phot* cartouche *f*; **c. player** lecteur *m* de cassettes; **c. recorder** magnétophone *m* à cassettes.

cassock [ˈkæsək] *n* soutane *f*.

cast [kɑːst] **1** *n* *Th* acteurs *mpl*; (*list*) *Th* distribution *f*; (*mould*) moulage *m*; (*of dice*) coup *m*; *Med* plâtre *m*; (*squint*) léger strabisme *m*; **c. of mind** tournure *f* d'esprit. **2** *vt* (*pt* & *pp* **cast**) (*throw*) jeter; (*light, shadow*) projeter; (*blame*) rejeter; (*glance*) jeter; (*doubt*) exprimer; (*lose*) perdre; (*metal*) couler; (*role*) *Th* distribuer; (*actor*) donner un rôle à; **to c. one's mind back** se reporter en arrière; **to c. a vote** voter; **to c. aside** rejeter; **to c. off** (*chains etc*) se libérer de; (*shed, lose*) se dépouiller de; *Fig* abandonner. **3** *vi* **to c. off** *Nau* appareiller. **4** *n* **c. iron** fonte *f*. ◆**c.-'iron** *a* (*pan etc*) en fonte; (*will etc*) *Fig* de fer, solide.

castaway [ˈkɑːstəweɪ] *n* naufragé, -ée *mf*.

caste [kɑːst] *n* caste *f*.

caster [ˈkɑːstər] *n* (*wheel*) roulette *f*; **c. sugar** sucre *m* en poudre.

castle [ˈkɑːs(ə)l] *n* château *m*; (*in chess*) tour *f*.

castoffs [ˈkɑːstɒfs] *npl* vieux vêtements *mpl*.

castor [ˈkɑːstər] *n* (*wheel*) roulette *f*; **c. oil** huile *f* de ricin; **c. sugar** sucre *m* en poudre.

castrate [kæˈstreɪt] *vt* châtrer. ◆**castration** *n* castration *f*.

casual [ˈkæʒuəl] *a* (*meeting*) fortuit; (*remark*) fait en passant; (*stroll*) sans but; (*offhand*) désinvolte, insouciant; (*worker*) temporaire; (*work*) irrégulier; **c. clothes** vêtements *mpl* sport; **a c. acquaintance** quelqu'un que l'on connaît un peu. ◆**—ly** *adv* par hasard; (*informally*) avec désinvolture; (*to remark*) en passant.

casualty [ˈkæʒuəltɪ] *n* (*dead*) mort *m*, morte *f*; (*wounded*) blessé, -ée *mf*; (*accident victim*) accidenté, -ée *mf*; **casualties** morts et blessés *mpl*; **c. department** *Med* service *m* des accidentés.

cat [kæt] *n* chat *m*, chatte *f*; **c. burglar** monte-en-l'air *m* *inv*; **c.'s eyes**® cataphotes® *mpl*, clous *mpl*. ◆**catcall** *n* sifflet *m*, huée *f*.

cataclysm [ˈkætəklɪzəm] *n* cataclysme *m*.

catalogue [ˈkætəlɒg] (*Am* **catalog**) *n* catalogue *m*; − *vt* cataloguer.

catalyst [ˈkætəlɪst] *n* *Ch* & *Fig* catalyseur *m*.

catapult [ˈkætəpʌlt] *n* lance-pierres *m* *inv*; *Hist* *Av* catapulte *f*; − *vt* catapulter.

cataract [ˈkætərækt] *n* (*waterfall*) & *Med* cataracte *f*.

catarrh [kəˈtɑːr] *n* catarrhe *m*, rhume *m*.

catastrophe [kəˈtæstrəfɪ] *n* catastrophe *f*. ◆**cata'strophic** *a* catastrophique.

catch [kætʃ] *vt* (*pt* & *pp* **caught**) (*ball, thief, illness etc*) attraper; (*grab*) prendre, saisir; (*surprise*) (sur)prendre; (*understand*) saisir; (*train etc*) attraper, (*réussir à*) prendre; (*attention*) attirer; (*of nail etc*) accrocher; (*finger etc*) se prendre (**in** dans); **to c. sight of** apercevoir; **to c. fire** prendre feu; **to c. s.o. (in)** *Fam* trouver qn (chez soi); **to c. one's breath** (*rest a while*) reprendre haleine; (*stop breathing*) retenir son souffle; **I didn't c. the train/etc** j'ai manqué le train/etc; **to c. s.o. out** prendre qn en défaut; **to c. s.o. up** rattraper qn; − *vi* (*of fire*) prendre; **her skirt (got) caught in the door** sa jupe s'est prise *or* coincée dans la porte; **to c. on** prendre, devenir populaire; (*understand*) saisir; **to c. up** se rattraper; **to c. up with s.o.** rattraper qn; − *n* capture *f*, prise *f*; (*trick, snare*) piège *m*; (*on door*) loquet *m*. ◆**—ing** *a* contagieux. ◆**catch-phrase** *n*, ◆**catchword** *n* slogan *m*.

catchy [ˈkætʃɪ] *a* (**-ier, -iest**) (*tune*) *Fam* facile à retenir.

catechism [ˈkætɪkɪzəm] *n* *Rel* catéchisme *m*.

category [ˈkætɪgərɪ] *n* catégorie *f*. ◆**cate-**

'gorical *a* catégorique. ◆**categorize** *vt*
classer (par catégories).
cater ['keɪtər] *vi* s'occuper de la nourriture;
to c. for *or* **to** (*need, taste*) satisfaire; (*readership*) *Journ* s'adresser à. ◆**—ing** *n*
restauration *f*. ◆**—er** *n* traiteur *m*.
caterpillar ['kætəpɪlər] *n* chenille *f*.
catgut ['kætgʌt] *n* (*cord*) boyau *m*.
cathedral [kə'θiːdrəl] *n* cathédrale *f*.
catholic ['kæθlɪk] **1** *a* & *n* **C.** catholique
(*mf*). **2** *a* (*taste*) universel; (*view*) libéral.
◆**Ca'tholicism** *n* catholicisme *m*.
cattle ['kæt(ə)l] *npl* bétail *m*, bestiaux *mpl*.
catty ['kætɪ] *a* (**-ier, -iest**) *Fam* rosse,
méchant.
caucus ['kɔːkəs] *n* *Pol Am* comité *m* électoral.
caught [kɔːt] *see* **catch.**
cauldron ['kɔːldrən] *n* chaudron *m*.
cauliflower ['kɒlɪflaʊər] *n* chou-fleur *m*.
cause [kɔːz] *n* cause *f*; (*reason*) raison *f*; **c.
for complaint** sujet *m* de plainte; – *vt*
causer, occasionner; (*trouble*) créer, causer
(**for** à); **to c. sth to move**/*etc* faire
bouger/*etc* qch.
causeway ['kɔːzweɪ] *n* chaussée *f*.
caustic ['kɔːstɪk] *a* (*remark, substance*) caustique.
cauterize ['kɔːtəraɪz] *vt* *Med* cautériser.
caution ['kɔːʃ(ə)n] *n* (*care*) prudence *f*,
précaution *f*; (*warning*) avertissement *m*; –
vt (*warn*) avertir; **to c. s.o. against sth**
mettre qn en garde contre qch. ◆**caution-
ary** *a* (*tale*) moral. ◆**cautious** *a* prudent,
circonspect. ◆**cautiously** *adv* prudemment.
cavalcade ['kævəlkeɪd] *n* (*procession*)
cavalcade *f*.
cavalier [kævə'lɪər] **1** *a* (*selfish*) cavalier. **2** *n*
(*horseman, knight*) *Hist* cavalier *m*.
cavalry ['kævəlrɪ] *n* cavalerie *f*.
cave [keɪv] **1** *n* caverne *f*, grotte *f*. **2** *vi* **to c. in**
(*fall in*) s'effondrer. ◆**caveman** *n* (*pl*
-men) homme *m* des cavernes. ◆**cavern**
['kævən] *n* caverne *f*.
caviar(e) ['kævɪɑːr] *n* caviar *m*.
cavity ['kævɪtɪ] *n* cavité *f*.
cavort [kæ'vɔːt] *vi* *Fam* cabrioler; **to c.
naked**/*etc* se balader tout nu/*etc*.
cease [siːs] *vti* cesser (**doing** de faire).
◆**c.-fire** *n* cessez-le-feu *m* *inv*. ◆**ceaseless** *a* incessant. ◆**ceaselessly** *adv* sans
cesse.
cedar ['siːdər] *n* (*tree, wood*) cèdre *m*.
cedilla [sɪ'dɪlə] *n* *Gram* cédille *f*.
ceiling ['siːlɪŋ] *n* (*of room, on wages etc*)
plafond *m*.

celebrat/e ['selɪbreɪt] *vt* (*event*) fêter; (*mass,
s.o.'s merits etc*) célébrer; – *vi* faire la fête;
we should c. (that)! il faut fêter ça! ◆**—ed**
a célèbre. ◆**cele'bration** *n* fête *f*; **the c. of**
(*marriage etc*) la célébration de.
◆**ce'lebrity** *n* (*person*) célébrité *f*.
celery ['selərɪ] *n* céleri *m*.
celibate ['selɪbət] *a* (*abstaining from sex*)
célibataire; (*monk etc*) abstinent. ◆**celibacy** *n* (*of young person etc*) célibat *m*; (*of
monk etc*) abstinence *f*.
cell [sel] *n* cellule *f*; *El* élément *m*. ◆**cellular** *a* cellulaire; **c. blanket** couverture *f* en
cellular.
cellar ['selər] *n* cave *f*.
cello ['tʃeləʊ] *n* (*pl* **-os**) violoncelle *m*.
◆**cellist** *n* violoncelliste *mf*.
cellophane® ['seləfeɪn] *n* cellophane® *f*.
celluloid ['seljʊlɔɪd] *n* celluloïd *m*.
cellulose ['seljʊləʊs] *n* cellulose *f*.
Celsius ['selsɪəs] *a* Celsius *inv*.
Celt [kelt] *n* Celte *mf*. ◆**Celtic** *a* celtique,
celte.
cement [sɪ'ment] *n* ciment *m*; **c. mixer**
bétonnière *f*; – *vt* cimenter.
cemetery ['semətrɪ, *Am* 'seməterɪ] *n* cimetière *m*.
cenotaph ['senətɑːf] *n* cénotaphe *m*.
censor ['sensər] *n* censeur *m*; – *vt* (*film etc*)
censurer. ◆**censorship** *n* censure *f*.
censure ['senʃər] *vt* blâmer; *Pol* censurer; –
n blâme *m*; **c. motion, vote of c.** motion *f* de
censure.
census ['sensəs] *n* recensement *m*.
cent [sent] *n* (*coin*) cent *m*; **per c.** pour cent.
centenary [sen'tiːnərɪ, *Am* sen'tenərɪ] *n*
centenaire *m*.
centigrade ['sentɪgreɪd] *a* centigrade.
centimetre ['sentɪmiːtər] *n* centimètre *m*.
centipede ['sentɪpiːd] *n* mille-pattes *m* *inv*.
centre ['sentər] *n* centre *m*; **c. forward** *Fb*
avant-centre *m*; – *vt* centrer; – *vi* **to c. on**
(*of thoughts*) se concentrer sur; (*of question*)
tourner autour de. ◆**central** *a* central.
◆**centralize** *vt* centraliser. ◆**centrifugal**
[sen'trɪfjʊgəl] *a* centrifuge.
century ['sentʃərɪ] *n* siècle *m*; (*score*) *Sp* cent
points *mpl*.
ceramic [sə'ræmɪk] *a* (*tile etc*) de *or* en
céramique; – *npl* (*objects*) céramiques *fpl*;
(*art*) céramique *f*.
cereal ['sɪərɪəl] *n* céréale *f*.
cerebral ['serɪbrəl, *Am* sə'riːbrəl] *a* cérébral.
ceremony ['serɪmənɪ] *n* (*event*) cérémonie *f*;
to stand on c. faire des cérémonies *or* des
façons. ◆**cere'monial** *a* de cérémonie; –

n cérémonial *m.* ◆**cere'monious** *a* cérémonieux.

certain ['sɜːtən] *a* (*particular, some*) certain; (*sure*) sûr, certain; **she's c. to come, she'll come for c.** c'est certain *or* sûr qu'elle viendra; **I'm not c. what to do** je ne sais pas très bien ce qu'il faut faire; **to be c. of sth/that** être certain de qch/que; **for c.** (*to say, know*) avec certitude; **be c. to go!** vas-y sans faute!; **to make c. of** (*fact*) s'assurer de; (*seat etc*) s'assurer. ◆**—ly** *adv* certainement; (*yes*) bien sûr; (*without fail*) sans faute; (*without any doubt*) sans aucun doute. ◆**certainty** *n* certitude *f.*

certificate [sə'tɪfɪkɪt] *n* certificat *m*; *Univ* diplôme *m.*

certify ['sɜːtɪfaɪ] *vt* certifier; **to c. (insane)** déclarer dément; – *vi* **to c. to sth** attester qch.

cervix ['sɜːvɪks] *n* col *m* de l'utérus.

cesspool ['sespuːl] *n* fosse *f* d'aisances; *Fig* cloaque *f.*

chafe [tʃeɪf] *vt* (*skin*) *Lit* frotter.

chaff [tʃæf] *vt* (*tease*) taquiner.

chaffinch ['tʃæfɪntʃ] *n* (*bird*) pinson *m.*

chagrin ['ʃægrɪn, *Am* ʃə'grɪn] *n* contrariété *f*; – *vt* contrarier.

chain [tʃeɪn] *n* (*of rings, mountains*) chaîne *f*; (*of ideas, events*) enchaînement *m*, suite *f*; (*of lavatory*) chasse *f* d'eau; **c. reaction** réaction *f* en chaîne; **to be a c.-smoker, to c.-smoke** fumer cigarette sur cigarette, fumer comme un pompier; **c. saw** tronçonneuse *f*; **c. store** magasin *m* à succursales multiples; – *vt* **to c. (down)** enchaîner; **to c. (up)** (*dog*) mettre à l'attache.

chair [tʃeər] *n* chaise *f*; (*armchair*) fauteuil *m*; *Univ* chaire *f*; **the c.** (*office*) la présidence; **c. lift** télésiège *m*; – *vt* (*meeting*) présider. ◆**chairman** *n* (*pl* **-men**) président, -ente *mf.* ◆**chairmanship** *n* présidence *f.*

chalet ['ʃæleɪ] *n* chalet *m.*

chalk [tʃɔːk] *n* craie *f*; **not by a long c.** loin de là, tant s'en faut; – *vt* marquer *or* écrire à la craie; **to c. up** (*success*) *Fig* remporter. ◆**chalky** *a* (**-ier, -iest**) crayeux.

challeng/e ['tʃælɪndʒ] *n* défi *m*; (*task*) gageure *f*; *Mil* sommation *f*; **c. for** (*bid*) tentative *f* d'obtenir; – *vt* défier (**s.o. to do** qn de faire); (*dispute*) contester; **to c. s.o. to a game** inviter qn à jouer; **to c. s.o. to a duel** provoquer qn en duel. ◆**—ing** *a* (*job*) exigeant; (*book*) stimulant. ◆**—er** *n Sp* challenger *m.*

chamber ['tʃeɪmbər] *n* chambre *f*; (*of judge*) cabinet *m*; – *a* (*music, orchestra*) de cham-

bre; **c. pot** pot *m* de chambre. ◆**chambermaid** *n* femme *f* de chambre.

chameleon [kə'miːlɪən] *n* (*reptile*) caméléon *m.*

chamois ['ʃæmɪ] *n* **c. (leather)** peau *f* de chamois.

champagne [ʃæm'peɪn] *n* champagne *m.*

champion ['tʃæmpɪən] *n* champion, -onne *mf*; **c. skier** champion, -onne du ski; – *vt* (*support*) se faire le champion de. ◆**championship** *n Sp* championnat *m.*

chance [tʃɑːns] *n* (*luck*) hasard *m*; (*possibility*) chances *fpl*, possibilité *f*; (*opportunity*) occasion *f*; (*risk*) risque *m*; **by c.** par hasard; **by any c.** (*possibly*) par hasard; **on the off c. (that)** you could help me au cas où tu pourrais m'aider; – *a* (*remark*) fait au hasard; (*occurrence*) accidentel; – *vt* **to c. doing** prendre le risque de faire; **to c. to find**/*etc* trouver/*etc* par hasard; **to c. it** risquer le coup; – *v imp* **it chanced that** (*happened*) il s'est trouvé que.

chancel ['tʃɑːnsəl] *n* (*in church*) chœur *m.*

chancellor ['tʃɑːnsələr] *n Pol Jur* chancelier *m.* ◆**chancellery** *n* chancellerie *f.*

chandelier [ʃændə'lɪər] *n* lustre *m.*

chang/e [tʃeɪndʒ] *n* changement *m*; (*money*) monnaie *f*; **for a c.** pour changer; **it makes a c. from** ça change de; **to have a c. of heart** changer d'avis; **a c. of clothes** des vêtements de rechange; – *vt* (*modify*) changer; (*exchange*) échanger (**for** contre); (*money*) changer; (*transform*) transformer (**into** en); **to c. trains/one's skirt**/*etc* changer de train/de jupe/*etc*; **to c. gear** *Aut* changer de vitesse; **to c. the subject** changer de sujet; – *vi* (*alter*) changer; (*change clothes*) se changer; **to c. over** passer. ◆**—ing** *n* (*of guard*) relève *f*; **c. room** vestiaire *m.* ◆**changeable** *a* (*weather, mood etc*) changeant, variable. ◆**changeless** *a* immuable. ◆**changeover** *n* passage *m* (**from** de, **to** à).

channel ['tʃænəl] *n* (*navigable*) chenal *m*; *TV* chaîne *f*, canal *m*; (*groove*) rainure *f*; *Fig* direction *f*; **through the c. of** par le canal de; **the C.** *Geog* la Manche; **the C. Islands** les îles anglo-normandes; – *vt* (**-ll-,** *Am* **-l-**) (*energies, crowd etc*) canaliser (**into** vers).

chant [tʃɑːnt] *n* (*of demonstrators*) chant *m* scandé; *Rel* psalmodie *f*; – *vt* (*slogan*) scander; – *vi* scander des slogans.

chaos ['keɪɒs] *n* chaos *m.* ◆**cha'otic** *a* chaotique.

chap [tʃæp] **1** *n* (*fellow*) *Fam* type *m*; **old c.!**

mon vieux! **2** *n* (*on skin*) gerçure *f*; – *vi*
(**-pp-**) se gercer; – *vt* gercer.

chapel ['tʃæp(ə)l] *n* chapelle *f*; (*non-conformist church*) temple *m*.

chaperon(e) ['ʃæpərəʊn] *n* chaperon *m*; – *vt* chaperonner.

chaplain ['tʃæplɪn] *n* aumônier *m*.

chapter ['tʃæptər] *n* chapitre *m*.

char [tʃɑːr] **1** *vt* (**-rr-**) (*convert to carbon*) carboniser; (*scorch*) brûler légèrement. **2** *n Fam* femme *f* de ménage; – *vi* to go char-ring *Fam* faire des ménages. **3** *n* (*tea*) *Sl* thé *m*.

character ['kærɪktər] *n* (*of person, place etc*) & *Typ* caractère *m*; (*in book, film*) person-nage *m*; (*strange person*) numéro *m*; **c. actor** acteur *m* de genre. ◆**characte-'ristic** *a* & *n* caractéristique (*f*). ◆**characte'ristically** *adv* typiquement. ◆**characterize** *vt* caractériser.

charade [ʃə'rɑːd] *n* (*game*) charade *f* (mimée); (*travesty*) parodie *f*, comédie *f*.

charcoal ['tʃɑːkəʊl] *n* charbon *m* (de bois); (*crayon*) fusain *m*, charbon *m*.

charge [tʃɑːdʒ] *n* (*in battle*) *Mil* charge *f*; *Jur* accusation *f*; (*cost*) prix *m*; (*responsibil-ity*) responsabilité *f*, charge *f*; (*care*) garde *f*; *pl* (*expenses*) frais *mpl*; **there's a c.** (**for it**) c'est payant; **free of c.** gratuit; **extra c.** supplément *m*; **to take c. of** prendre en charge; **to be in c. of** (*child etc*) avoir la garde de; (*office etc*) être responsable de; **the person in c.** le *or* la responsable; **who's in c. here?** qui commande ici?; – *vt Mil El* charger; *Jur* accuser, inculper; **to c. s.o.** *Com* faire payer qn; **to c. (up) to** *Com* mettre sur le compte de; **how much do you c.?** combien demandez-vous?; – *vi* (*rush*) se précipiter; **c.!** *Mil* chargez! ◆—**able** *a* **c. to** aux frais de. ◆**charger** *n* (*for battery*) chargeur *m*.

chariot ['tʃærɪət] *n Mil* char *m*.

charisma [kə'rɪzmə] *n* magnétisme *m*.

charity ['tʃærɪtɪ] *n* (*kindness, alms*) charité *f*; (*society*) fondation *f or* œuvre *f* charitable; **to give to c.** faire la charité. ◆**charitable** *a* charitable.

charlady ['tʃɑːleɪdɪ] *n* femme *f* de ménage.

charlatan ['ʃɑːlətən] *n* charlatan *m*.

charm [tʃɑːm] *n* (*attractiveness, spell*) charme *m*; (*trinket*) amulette *f*; – *vt* charmer. ◆—**ing** *a* charmant. ◆—**ingly** *adv* d'une façon charmante.

chart [tʃɑːt] *n* (*map*) carte *f*; (*graph*) graphique *m*, tableau *m*; (**pop**) **charts** hit-parade *m*; **flow c.** organigramme *m*; –

vt (*route*) porter sur la carte; (*figures*) faire le graphique de; (*of graph*) montrer.

charter ['tʃɑːtər] *n* (*document*) charte *f*; (*aircraft*) charter *m*; **the c. of** (*hiring*) l'affrètement *m* de; **c. flight** charter *m*; – *vt* (*aircraft etc*) affréter. ◆—**ed** *a* **c. accoun-tant** expert-comptable *m*.

charwoman ['tʃɑːwʊmən] *n* (*pl* -**women**) femme *f* de ménage.

chary ['tʃeərɪ] *a* (-**ier**, -**iest**) (*cautious*) pru-dent.

chase [tʃeɪs] *n* poursuite *f*, chasse *f*; **to give c.** se lancer à la poursuite (**to de**); – *vt* poursuivre; **to c. away** *or* **off** chasser; **to c. sth up** *Fam* essayer d'obtenir qch, rechercher qch; – *vi* **to c. after** courir après.

chasm ['kæzəm] *n* abîme *m*, gouffre *m*.

chassis ['ʃæsɪ, *Am* 'tʃæsɪ] *n Aut* châssis *m*.

chaste [tʃeɪst] *a* chaste. ◆**chastity** *n* chas-teté *f*.

chasten ['tʃeɪs(ə)n] *vt* (*punish*) châtier; (*cause to improve*) faire se corriger, assagir. ◆—**ing** *a* (*experience*) instructif.

chastise [tʃæ'staɪz] *vt* punir.

chat [tʃæt] *n* causette *f*; **to have a c.** bavarder; – *vi* (-**tt-**) causer, bavarder; – *vt* **to c. up** *Fam* baratiner, draguer. ◆**chatty** *a* (-**ier**, -**iest**) (*person*) bavard; (*style*) familier; (*text*) plein de bavardages.

chatter ['tʃætər] *vi* bavarder; (*of birds, monkeys*) jacasser; **his teeth are chattering** il claque des dents; – *n* bavardage *m*; jacassement *m*. ◆**chatterbox** *n* bavard, -arde *mf*.

chauffeur ['ʃəʊfər] *n* chauffeur *m* (de maître).

chauvinist ['ʃəʊvɪnɪst] *n* & *a* chauvin, -ine (*mf*); **male c.** *Pej* phallocrate *m*.

cheap [tʃiːp] *a* (-**er**, -**est**) bon marché *inv*, pas cher; (*rate etc*) réduit; (*worthless*) sans valeur; (*superficial*) facile; (*mean, petty*) mesquin; **cheaper** moins cher, meilleur marché; – *adv* (*to buy*) (à) bon marché, au rabais; (*to feel*) humilié. ◆**cheapen** *vt Fig* déprécier. ◆**cheaply** *adv* (à) bon marché. ◆**cheapness** *n* bas prix *m*; *Fig* mesquinerie *f*.

cheat [tʃiːt] *vt* (*deceive*) tromper; (*defraud*) frauder; **to c. s.o. out of sth** escroquer qch à qn; **to c. on** (*wife, husband*) faire une infidé-lité *or* des infidélités à; – *vi* tricher; (*defraud*) frauder; – *n* (*at games etc*) tricheur, -euse *mf*; (*crook*) escroc *m*. ◆—**ing** *n* (*deceit*) tromperie *f*; (*trickery*) tricherie *f*. ◆—**er** *n Am* = **cheat**.

check[1] [tʃek] *vt* (*examine*) vérifier; (*inspect*) contrôler; (*tick*) cocher, pointer; (*stop*) arrêter, enrayer; (*restrain*) contenir, maîtriser; (*rebuke*) réprimander; (*baggage*) *Am* mettre à la consigne; **to c. in** (*luggage*) *Av* enregistrer; **to c. sth out** confirmer qch; – *vi* vérifier; **to c. in** (*at hotel etc*) signer le registre; (*arrive at hotel*) arriver; (*at airport*) se présenter (à l'enregistrement), enregistrer ses bagages; **to c. on sth** vérifier qch; **to c. out** (*at hotel etc*) régler sa note; **to c. up** vérifier, se renseigner; – *n* vérification *f*; contrôle *m*; (*halt*) arrêt *m*; *Chess* échec *m*; (*curb*) frein *m*; (*tick*) = croix *f*; (*receipt*) *Am* reçu *m*; (*bill in restaurant etc*) *Am* addition *f*; (*cheque*) *Am* chèque *m*. ◆**c.-in** *n Av* enregistrement *m* (des bagages). ◆**checking account** *n Am* compte *m* courant. ◆**checkmate** *n Chess* échec et mat *m*. ◆**checkout** *n* (*in supermarket*) caisse *f*. ◆**checkpoint** *n* contrôle *m*. ◆**checkroom** *n Am* vestiaire *m*; (*left-luggage office*) *Am* consigne *f*. ◆**checkup** *n* bilan *m* de santé.

check² [tʃek] *n* (*pattern*) carreaux *mpl*; – *a* à carreaux. ◆**checked** *a* à carreaux.

checkered ['tʃekəd] *a Am* = **chequered**.

checkers ['tʃekəz] *npl Am* jeu *m* de dames.

cheddar ['tʃedər] *n* (*cheese*) cheddar *m*.

cheek [tʃiːk] *n* joue *f*; (*impudence*) *Fig* culot *m*. ◆**cheekbone** *n* pommette *f*. ◆**cheeky** *a* (*-ier, -iest*) (*person, reply etc*) effronté.

cheep [tʃiːp] *vi* (*of bird*) piauler.

cheer¹ [tʃiər] *n* **cheers** (*shouts*) acclamations *fpl*; **cheers!** *Fam* à votre santé! – *vt* (*applaud*) acclamer; **to c. on** encourager; **to c. (up)** donner du courage à; (*amuse*) égayer; – *vi* applaudir; **to c. up** prendre courage, s'égayer; **c. up!** (du) courage! ◆**—ing** *n* (*shouts*) acclamations *fpl*; – *a* (*encouraging*) réjouissant.

cheer² [tʃiər] *n* (*gaiety*) joie *f*; **good c.** (*food*) la bonne chère. ◆**cheerful** *a* gai. ◆**cheerfully** *adv* gaiement. ◆**cheerless** *a* morne.

cheerio! [tʃiəri'əu] *int* salut!, au revoir!

cheese [tʃiːz] *n* fromage *m*. ◆**cheeseburger** *n* cheeseburger *m*. ◆**cheesecake** *n* tarte *f* au fromage blanc. ◆**cheesed** *a* **to be c. (off)** *Fam* en avoir marre (**with** de). ◆**cheesy** *a* (*-ier, -iest*) (*shabby, bad*) *Am Fam* miteux.

cheetah ['tʃiːtə] *n* guépard *m*.

chef [ʃef] *n Culin* chef *m*.

chemistry ['kemistri] *n* chimie *f*. ◆**chemical** *a* chimique; – *n* produit *m* chimique. ◆**chemist** *n* (*dispensing*) pharmacien,

-ienne *mf*; (*scientist*) chimiste *mf*; **chemist('s)** (*shop*) pharmacie *f*.

cheque [tʃek] *n* chèque *m*. ◆**chequebook** *n* carnet *m* de chèques.

chequered ['tʃekəd] *a* (*pattern*) à carreaux; (*career etc*) qui connaît des hauts et des bas.

cherish ['tʃeriʃ] *vt* (*person*) chérir; (*hope*) nourrir, caresser.

cherry ['tʃeri] *n* cerise *f*; – *a* cerise *inv*; **c. brandy** cherry *m*.

chess [tʃes] *n* échecs *mpl*. ◆**chessboard** *n* échiquier *m*.

chest [tʃest] *n* **1** *Anat* poitrine *f*. **2** (*box*) coffre *m*; **c. of drawers** commode *f*.

chestnut ['tʃestnʌt] *n* châtaigne *f*, marron *m*; – *a* (*hair*) châtain; **c. tree** châtaignier *m*.

chew [tʃuː] *vt* **to c. (up)** mâcher; **to c. over** *Fig* ruminer; – *vi* mastiquer; **chewing gum** chewing-gum *m*.

chick [tʃik] *n* poussin *m*; (*girl*) *Fam* nana *f*. ◆**chicken 1** *n* poulet *m*; *pl* (*poultry*) volaille *f*; **it's c. feed** *Fam* c'est deux fois rien, c'est une bagatelle. **2** *a Fam* froussard; – *vi* **to c. out** *Fam* se dégonfler. ◆**chickenpox** *n* varicelle *f*.

chickpea ['tʃikpiː] *n* pois *m* chiche.

chicory ['tʃikəri] *n* (*in coffee etc*) chicorée *f*; (*for salad*) endive *f*.

chide [tʃaid] *vt* gronder.

chief [tʃiːf] *n* chef *m*; (*boss*) *Fam* patron *m*, chef *m*; **in c.** (*commander, editor*) en chef; – *a* (*main, highest in rank*) principal. ◆**—ly** *adv* principalement, surtout. ◆**chieftain** *n* (*of clan etc*) chef *m*.

chilblain ['tʃilblein] *n* engelure *f*.

child, *pl* **children** ['tʃaild, 'tʃildrən] *n* enfant *mf*; **c. care** *or* **welfare** protection *f* de l'enfance; **child's play** *Fig* jeu *m* d'enfant; **c. minder** gardien, -ienne *mf* d'enfants. ◆**childbearing** *n* (*act*) accouchement *m*; (*motherhood*) maternité *f*. ◆**childbirth** *n* accouchement *m*, couches *fpl*. ◆**childhood** *n* enfance *f*. ◆**childish** *a* puéril, enfantin. ◆**childishness** *n* puérilité *f*. ◆**childlike** *a* naïf, innocent.

chill [tʃil] *n* froid *m*; (*coldness in feelings*) froideur *f*; *Med* refroidissement *m*; **to catch a c.** prendre froid; – *vt* (*wine, melon*) faire rafraîchir; (*meat, food*) réfrigérer; **to c. s.o.** (*with fear, cold etc*) faire frissonner qn (**with** de); **to be chilled to the bone** être transi. ◆**—ed** *a* (*wine*) frais. ◆**chilly** *a* (*-ier, -iest*) froid; (*sensitive to cold*) frileux; **it's c.** il fait (un peu) froid.

chilli ['tʃili] *n* (*pl* **-ies**) piment *m* (de Cayenne).

chime [tʃaɪm] vi (of bell) carillonner; (of clock) sonner; **to c. in** (interrupt) interrompre; – n carillon m; sonnerie f.

chimney ['tʃɪmnɪ] n cheminée f. ◆**chimneypot** n tuyau m de cheminée. ◆**chimneysweep** n ramoneur m.

chimpanzee [tʃɪmpæn'zɪ] n chimpanzé m.

chin [tʃɪn] n menton m.

china ['tʃaɪnə] n inv porcelaine f; – a en porcelaine. ◆**chinaware** n (objects) porcelaine f.

China ['tʃaɪnə] n Chine f. ◆**Chi'nese** a & n chinois, -oise (mf); – n (language) chinois m.

chink [tʃɪŋk] **1** n (slit) fente f. **2** vi tinter; – vt faire tinter; – n tintement m.

chip [tʃɪp] vt (-pp-) (cup etc) ébrécher; (table etc) écorner; (paint) écailler; (cut) tailler; – vi **to c. in** Fam contribuer; – n (splinter) éclat m; (break) ébréchure f; écornure f; (microchip) puce f; (counter) jeton m; pl (French fries) frites fpl; (crisps) Am chips mpl. ◆**chipboard** n (bois m) aggloméré m. ◆**chippings** npl road or loose c. gravillons mpl.

chiropodist [kɪ'rɒpədɪst] n pédicure mf.

chirp [tʃɜːp] vi (of bird) pépier; – n pépiement m.

chirpy ['tʃɜːpɪ] a (-ier, -iest) gai, plein d'entrain.

chisel ['tʃɪz(ə)l] n ciseau m; – vt (-ll-, Am -l-) ciseler.

chit [tʃɪt] n (paper) note f, billet m.

chitchat ['tʃɪttʃæt] n bavardage m.

chivalry ['ʃɪvəlrɪ] n (practices etc) chevalerie f; (courtesy) galanterie f. ◆**chivalrous** a (man) galant.

chives [tʃaɪvz] npl ciboulette f.

chloride ['klɔːraɪd] n chlorure m. ◆**chlorine** n chlore m. ◆**chloroform** n chloroforme m.

choc-ice ['tʃɒkaɪs] n (ice cream) esquimau m.

chock [tʃɒk] n (wedge) cale f; – vt caler.

chock-a-block [tʃɒkə'blɒk] a, ◆**c.-'full** a Fam archiplein.

chocolate ['tʃɒklɪt] n chocolat m; milk c. chocolat au lait; plain or Am bittersweet c. chocolat à croquer; – a (cake) au chocolat; (colour) chocolat inv.

choice [tʃɔɪs] n choix m; from c., out of c. de son propre choix; – a (goods) de choix.

choir ['kwaɪər] n chœur m. ◆**choirboy** n jeune choriste m.

chok/e [tʃəʊk] **1** vt (person) étrangler, étouffer; (clog) boucher, engorger; **to c. back** (sobs etc) étouffer; – vi s'étrangler, étouffer; **to c. on** (fish bone etc) s'étrangler avec. **2** n Aut starter m. ◆**-er** n (scarf) foulard m; (necklace) collier m (de chien).

cholera ['kɒlərə] n choléra m.

cholesterol [kə'lestərɒl] n cholestérol m.

choose [tʃuːz] vt (pt chose, pp chosen) choisir (**to do** de faire); **to c. to do** (decide) juger bon de faire; – vi choisir; **as I/you/etc c.** comme il me/vous/etc plaît. ◆**choos(e)y** a (-sier, -siest) difficile (**about** sur).

chop [tʃɒp] **1** n (of lamb, pork) côtelette f; **to lick one's chops** Fig s'en lécher les babines; **to get the c.** Sl être flanqué à la porte. **2** vt (-pp-) couper (à la hache); (food) hacher; **to c. down** (tree) abattre; **to c. off** trancher; **to c. up** hacher. **3** vti **to c. and change** changer constamment d'idées, de projets etc. ◆**chopper** n hachoir m; Sl hélicoptère m. ◆**choppy** a (sea) agité.

chopsticks ['tʃɒpstɪks] npl Culin baguettes fpl.

choral ['kɔːrəl] a choral; c. **society** chorale f. ◆**chorister** ['kɒrɪstər] n choriste mf.

chord [kɔːd] n Mus accord m.

chore [tʃɔːr] n travail m (routinier); (unpleasant) corvée f; pl (domestic) travaux mpl du ménage.

choreographer [kɒrɪ'ɒgrəfər] n chorégraphe mf.

chortle ['tʃɔːt(ə)l] vi glousser; – n gloussement m.

chorus ['kɔːrəs] n chœur m; (dancers) Th troupe f; (of song) refrain m; c. **girl** girl f.

chose, chosen [tʃəʊz, 'tʃəʊz(ə)n] see choose.

chowder ['tʃaʊdər] n Am soupe f aux poissons.

Christ [kraɪst] n Christ m. ◆**Christian** ['krɪstʃən] a & n chrétien, -ienne (mf); C. **name** prénom m. ◆**Christi'anity** n christianisme m.

christen ['krɪs(ə)n] vt (name) & Rel baptiser. ◆**-ing** n baptême m.

Christmas ['krɪsməs] n Noël m; at C. (time) à (la) Noël; Merry C. Joyeux Noël; Father C. le père Noël; – a (tree, card, day, party etc) de Noël; C. **box** étrennes fpl.

chrome [krəʊm] n, ◆**chromium** n chrome m.

chromosome ['krəʊməsəʊm] n chromosome m.

chronic ['krɒnɪk] a (disease, state etc) chronique; (bad) Sl atroce.

chronicle ['krɒnɪk(ə)l] n chronique f; – vt faire la chronique de.

chronology [krə'nɒlədʒɪ] n chronologie f.
◆**chrono'logical** a chronologique.
chronometer [krə'nɒmɪtər] n chronomètre m.
chrysanthemum [krɪ'sænθəməm] n chrysanthème m.
chubby ['tʃʌbɪ] a (-ier, -iest) (body) dodu; (cheeks) rebondi. ◆**c.-'cheeked** a joufflu.
chuck [tʃʌk] vt Fam jeter, lancer; **to c. (in)** or **(up)** (give up) Fam laisser tomber; **to c. away** Fam balancer; (money) gaspiller; **to c. out** Fam balancer.
chuckle ['tʃʌk(ə)l] vi glousser, rire; – n gloussement m.
chuffed [tʃʌft] a Sl bien content; (displeased) Iron Sl pas heureux.
chug [tʃʌg] vi (-gg-) **to c. along** (of vehicle) avancer lentement (en faisant teuf-teuf).
chum [tʃʌm] n Fam copain m. ◆**chummy** a (-ier, -iest) Fam amical; **c. with** copain avec.
chump [tʃʌmp] n (fool) crétin, -ine mf.
chunk [tʃʌŋk] n (gros) morceau m. ◆**chunky** a (-ier, -iest) (person) Fam trapu; (coat, material etc) de grosse laine.
church [tʃɜːtʃ] n église f; (service) office m; (Catholic) messe f; **c. hall** salle f paroissiale. ◆**churchgoer** n pratiquant, -ante mf. ◆**churchyard** n cimetière m.
churlish ['tʃɜːlɪʃ] a (rude) grossier; (bad-tempered) hargneux.
churn [tʃɜːn] **1** n (for making butter) baratte f; (milk can) bidon m. **2** vt **to c. out** Pej produire (en série).
chute [ʃuːt] n glissière f; (in playground, pool) toboggan m; (for refuse) vide-ordures m inv.
chutney ['tʃʌtnɪ] n condiment m épicé (à base de fruits).
cider ['saɪdər] n cidre m.
cigar [sɪ'gɑːr] n cigare m. ◆**ciga'rette** n cigarette f; **c. end** mégot m; **c. holder** fume-cigarette m inv; **c. lighter** briquet m.
cinch [sɪntʃ] n **it's a c.** Fam (easy) c'est facile; (sure) c'est (sûr et) certain.
cinder ['sɪndər] n cendre f; **c. track** Sp cendrée f.
Cinderella [sɪndə'relə] n Liter Cendrillon f; Fig parent m pauvre.
cine-camera ['sɪnɪkæmrə] n caméra f.
cinema ['sɪnəmə] n cinéma m. ◆**cinema-goer** n cinéphile mf. ◆**cinemascope** n cinémascope m.
cinnamon ['sɪnəmən] n Bot Culin cannelle f.
cipher ['saɪfər] n (code, number) chiffre m; (zero, person) Fig zéro m.
circle ['sɜːk(ə)l] n (shape, group, range etc)

cercle m; (around eyes) cerne m; Th balcon m; pl (milieux) milieux mpl; – vt (move round) faire le tour de; (word etc) entourer d'un cercle; – vi (of aircraft, bird) décrire des cercles. ◆**circular** a circulaire; – n (letter) circulaire f; (advertisement) prospectus m. ◆**circulate** vi circuler; – vt faire circuler. ◆**circu'lation** n circulation f; Journ tirage m; **in c.** (person) Fam dans le circuit.
circuit ['sɜːkɪt] n circuit m; Jur Th tournée f; **c. breaker** El disjoncteur m. ◆**circuitous** [sɜː'kjuːɪtəs] a (route, means) indirect. ◆**circuitry** n El circuits mpl.
circumcised ['sɜːkəmsaɪzd] a circoncis. ◆**circum'cision** n circoncision f.
circumference [sɜː'kʌmfərəns] n circonférence f.
circumflex ['sɜːkəmfleks] n circonflexe m.
circumscribe ['sɜːkəmskraɪb] vt circonscrire.
circumspect ['sɜːkəmspekt] a circonspect.
circumstance ['sɜːkəmstæns] n circonstance f; pl Com situation f financière; **in** or **under no circumstances** en aucun cas. ◆**circum'stantial** a (evidence) Jur indirect.
circus ['sɜːkəs] n Th Hist cirque m.
cirrhosis [sɪ'rəʊsɪs] n Med cirrhose f.
cistern ['sɪstən] n (in house) réservoir m (d'eau).
citadel ['sɪtəd(ə)l] n citadelle f.
cite [saɪt] vt citer. ◆**citation** [saɪ'teɪʃ(ə)n] n citation f.
citizen ['sɪtɪz(ə)n] n Pol Jur citoyen, -enne mf; (of town) habitant, -ante mf; **Citizens' Band** Rad la CB. ◆**citizenship** n citoyenneté f.
citrus ['sɪtrəs] a **c. fruit(s)** agrumes mpl.
city ['sɪtɪ] n (grande) ville f, cité f; **c. dweller** citadin, -ine mf; **c. centre** centre-ville m inv; **c. hall** Am hôtel m de ville; **c. page** Journ rubrique f financière.
civic ['sɪvɪk] a (duty) civique; (centre) administratif; (authorities) municipal; – npl (social science) instruction f civique.
civil ['sɪv(ə)l] a **1** (rights, war, marriage etc) civil; **c. defence** défense f passive; **c. servant** fonctionnaire mf; **c. service** fonction f publique. **2** (polite) civil. ◆**ci'vilian** a & n civil, -ile (mf). ◆**ci'vility** n civilité f. **civilize** ['sɪvɪlaɪz] vt civiliser. ◆**civili'zation** n civilisation f.
civvies ['sɪvɪz] npl **in c.** Sl (habillé) en civil.
clad [klæd] a vêtu (**in de**).
claim [kleɪm] vt (one's due etc) revendiquer, réclamer; (require) réclamer; **to c. that**

(*assert*) prétendre que; − *n* (*demand*) prétention *f*, revendication *f*; (*statement*) affirmation *f*; (*complaint*) réclamation *f*; (*right*) droit *m*; (*land*) concession *f*; (*insurance*) c. demande *f* d'indemnité; **to lay c. to** prétendre à. ◆**claimant** *n* allocataire *mf*.

clairvoyant [kleə'vɔɪənt] *n* voyant, -ante *mf*.

clam [klæm] *n* (*shellfish*) praire *f*.

clamber ['klæmbər] *vi* **to c. (up)** grimper; **to c. up** (*stairs*) grimper; (*mountain*) gravir.

clammy ['klæmɪ] *a* (*hands etc*) moite (et froid).

clamour ['klæmər] *n* clameur *f*; − *vi* vociférer (**against** contre); **to c. for** demander à grands cris.

clamp [klæmp] *n* crampon *m*; *Carp* serre-joint(s) *m*; (*wheel*) c. *Aut* sabot *m* (de Denver); − *vt* serrer; − *vi* **to c. down** *Fam* sévir (**on** contre). ◆**clampdown** *n* (*limitation*) *Fam* coup *m* d'arrêt, restriction *f*.

clan [klæn] *n* clan *m*.

clandestine [klæn'destɪn] *a* clandestin.

clang [klæŋ] *n* son *m* métallique. ◆**clanger** *n* *Sl* gaffe *f*; **to drop a c.** faire une gaffe.

clap [klæp] **1** *vti* (**-pp-**) (*applaud*) applaudir; **to c. (one's hands)** battre des mains; − *n* battement *m* (des mains); (*on back*) tape *f*; (*of thunder*) coup *m*. **2** (**-pp-**) (*put*) *Fam* fourrer. ◆**clapped-'out** *a* (*car, person*) *Sl* crevé. ◆**clapping** *n* applaudissements *mpl*. ◆**claptrap** *n* (*nonsense*) *Fam* boniment *m*.

claret ['klærət] *n* (*wine*) bordeaux *m* rouge.

clarify ['klærɪfaɪ] *vt* clarifier. ◆**clarifi-'cation** *n* clarification *f*.

clarinet [klærɪ'net] *n* clarinette *f*.

clarity ['klærətɪ] *n* (*of water, expression etc*) clarté *f*.

clash [klæʃ] *vi* (*of plates, pans*) s'entrechoquer; (*of interests, armies*) se heurter; (*of colours*) jurer (**with** avec); (*of people*) se bagarrer; (*coincide*) tomber en même temps (**with** que); − *n* (*noise, of armies*) choc *m*, heurt *m*; (*of interests*) conflit *m*; (*of events*) coïncidence *f*.

clasp [klɑːsp] *vt* (*hold*) serrer; **to c. one's hands** joindre les mains; − *n* (*fastener*) fermoir *m*; (*of belt*) boucle *f*.

class [klɑːs] *n* classe *f*; (*lesson*) cours *m*; (*grade*) *Univ* mention *f*; **the c. of 1987** *Am* la promotion de 1987; − *vt* classer. ◆**classmate** *n* camarade *mf* de classe. ◆**classroom** *n* (*salle f* de) classe *f*.

classic ['klæsɪk] *a* classique; − *n* (*writer, work etc*) classique *m*; **to study classics** étudier les humanités *fpl*. ◆**classical** *a* classique. ◆**classicism** *n* classicisme *m*.

classif/y ['klæsɪfaɪ] *vt* classer, classifier. ◆**—ied** *a* (*information*) secret. ◆**classifi-'cation** *n* classification *f*.

classy ['klɑːsɪ] *a* (**-ier, -iest**) *Fam* chic *inv*.

clatter ['klætər] *n* bruit *m*, fracas *m*.

clause [klɔːz] *n* *Jur* clause *f*; *Gram* proposition *f*.

claustrophobia [klɔːstrə'fəʊbɪə] *n* claustrophobie *f*. ◆**claustrophobic** *a* claustrophobe.

claw [klɔː] *n* (*of cat, sparrow etc*) griffe *f*; (*of eagle*) serre *f*; (*of lobster*) pince *f*; − *vt* (*scratch*) griffer; **to c. back** (*money etc*) *Pej Fam* repiquer, récupérer.

clay [kleɪ] *n* argile *f*.

clean [kliːn] *a* (**-er, -est**) propre; (*clear-cut*) net; (*fair*) *Sp* loyal; (*joke*) non paillard; (*record*) *Jur* vierge; **c. living** vie *f* saine; **to make a c. breast of it** tout avouer; − *adv* (*utterly*) complètement, carrément; **to break a c.** se casser net; **to cut c.** couper net; − *n* **to give sth a c.** nettoyer qch; − *vt* nettoyer; (*wash*) laver; (*wipe*) essuyer; **to c. one's teeth** se brosser *or* se laver les dents; **to c. out** nettoyer; (*empty*) *Fig* vider; **to c. up** nettoyer; (*reform*) *Fig* épurer; − *vi* **to c. (up)** faire le nettoyage. ◆**—ing** *n* nettoyage *m*; (*housework*) ménage *m*; **c. woman** femme *f* de ménage. ◆**—er** *n* (*woman*) femme *f* de ménage; (*dry*) c. teinturier, -ière *mf*. ◆**—ly** *adv* (*to break, cut*) net. ◆**—ness** *n* propreté *f*. ◆**clean-'cut** *a* net. ◆**clean-'living** *a* honnête, chaste. ◆**clean-'shaven** *a* rasé (de près). ◆**clean-up** *n* *Fig* épuration *f*.

cleanliness ['klenlɪnɪs] *n* propreté *f*.

cleans/e [klenz] *vt* nettoyer; (*soul, person etc*) *Fig* purifier. ◆**—ing** a **c. cream** crème *f* démaquillante. ◆**—er** *n* (*cream, lotion*) démaquillant *m*.

clear [klɪər] *a* (**-er, -est**) (*water, sound etc*) clair; (*glass*) transparent; (*outline, photo*) net, clair; (*mind*) lucide; (*road*) libre, dégagé; (*profit*) net; (*obvious*) évident, clair; (*certain*) certain; (*complete*) entier; **to be c. of** (*free of*) être libre de; (*out of*) être hors de; **to make oneself c.** se faire comprendre; **c. conscience** conscience *f* nette *or* tranquille; − *adv* (*quite*) complètement; **c. of** (*away from*) à l'écart de; **to keep** *or* **steer c. of** se tenir à l'écart de; **to get c. of** (*away from*) s'éloigner de; − *vt* (*path, place, table*) débarrasser, dégager; (*land*) défricher; (*fence*) franchir (sans toucher); (*obstacle*) éviter; (*person*) *Jur* disculper;

(*cheque*) compenser; (*goods, debts*) liquider; (*through customs*) dédouaner; (*for security etc*) autoriser; **to c. s.o. of** (*suspicion*) laver qn de; **to c. one's throat** s'éclaircir la gorge; – *vi* **to c. (up)** (*of weather*) s'éclaircir; (*of fog*) se dissiper. ■ **to c. away** *vt* (*remove*) enlever; – *vi* (*of fog*) se dissiper; **to c. off** *vi* (*leave*) *Fam* filer; – *vt* (*table*) débarrasser; **to c. out** *vt* (*empty*) vider; (*clean*) nettoyer; (*remove*) enlever; **to c. up** *vt* (*mystery etc*) éclaircir; – *vti* (*tidy*) ranger. ◆**–ing** *n* (*in woods*) clairière *f*. ◆**–ly** *adv* clairement; (*to understand*) bien, clairement; (*obviously*) évidemment. ◆**–ness** *n* (*of sound*) clarté *f*, netteté *f*; (*of mind*) lucidité *f*. ◆**clearance** *n* (*sale*) soldes *mpl*; (*space*) dégagement *m*; (*permission*) autorisation *f*; (*of cheque*) compensation *f*. ◆**clear-'cut** *a* net. ◆**clear-'headed** *a* lucide.

clearway ['klɪəweɪ] *n* route *f* à stationnement interdit.

cleavage ['kliːvɪdʒ] *n* (*split*) clivage *m*; (*of woman*) *Fam* naissance *f* des seins.

cleft [kleft] *a* (*palate*) fendu; (*stick*) fourchu; – *n* fissure *f*.

clement ['klemənt] *a* clément. ◆**clemency** *n* clémence *f*.

clementine ['kleməntaɪn] *n* clémentine *f*.

clench [klentʃ] *vt* (*press*) serrer.

clergy ['klɜːdʒɪ] *n* clergé *m*. ◆**clergyman** *n* (*pl* -men) ecclésiastique *m*.

cleric ['klerɪk] *n* Rel clerc *m*. ◆**clerical** *a* (*job*) d'employé; (*work*) de bureau; (*error*) d'écriture; Rel clérical.

clerk [klɑːk, *Am* klɜːk] *n* employé, -ée *mf* (de bureau); *Jur* clerc *m*; (*in store*) *Am* vendeur, -euse *mf*; **c. of the court** *Jur* greffier *m*.

clever ['klevər] *a* (-er, -est) intelligent; (*smart, shrewd*) astucieux; (*skilful*) habile (**at sth** à qch, **at doing** à faire); (*ingenious*) ingénieux; (*gifted*) doué; **c. at** (*English etc*) fort en; **c. with one's hands** habile or adroit de ses mains. ◆**–ly** *adv* intelligemment; astucieusement; habilement. ◆**–ness** *n* intelligence *f*; astuce *f*; habileté *f*.

cliché ['kliːʃeɪ] *n* (*idea*) cliché *m*.

click [klɪk] **1** *n* déclic *m*, bruit *m* sec; – *vi* faire un déclic; (*of lovers etc*) *Fam* se plaire du premier coup; **it clicked** (*I realized*) *Fam* j'ai compris tout à coup. **2** *vt* **to c. one's heels** *Mil* claquer des talons.

client ['klaɪənt] *n* client, -ente *mf*. ◆**clientele** [kliːɑnˈtel] *n* clientèle *f*.

cliff [klɪf] *n* falaise *f*.

climate ['klaɪmɪt] *n* Met & Fig climat *m*; **c.**

of opinion opinion *f* générale. ◆**cli'matic** *a* climatique.

climax ['klaɪmæks] *n* point *m* culminant; (*sexual*) orgasme *m*; – *vi* atteindre son point culminant.

climb [klaɪm] *vt* **to c. (up)** (*steps*) monter, gravir; (*hill, mountain*) gravir, faire l'ascension de; (*tree, ladder*) monter à, grimper à; **to c. (over)** (*wall*) escalader; **to c. down (from)** descendre de; – *vi* **to c. (up)** monter; (*of plant*) grimper; **to c. down** descendre; (*back down*) Fig en rabattre; – *n* montée *f*. ◆**–ing** *n* montée *f*; (*mountain*) **c.** alpinisme *m*. ◆**–er** *n* grimpeur, -euse *mf*; Sp alpiniste *mf*; Bot plante *f* grimpante; **social c.** arriviste *mf*.

clinch [klɪntʃ] *vt* (*deal, bargain*) conclure; (*argument*) consolider.

cling [klɪŋ] *vi* (*pt & pp* clung) se cramponner, s'accrocher (**to** à); (*stick*) adhérer (**to** à). ◆**–ing** *a* (*clothes*) collant. ◆**clingfilm** *n* scel-o-frais®*m*, film *m* étirable.

clinic ['klɪnɪk] *n* (*private*) clinique *f*; (*health centre*) centre *m* médical. ◆**clinical** *a* Med clinique; Fig scientifique, objectif.

clink [klɪŋk] *vi* tinter; – *vt* faire tinter; – *n* tintement *m*.

clip [klɪp] **1** *vt* (-pp-) (*cut*) couper; (*sheep*) tondre; (*hedge*) tailler; (*ticket*) poinçonner; **to c. sth out of** (*newspaper etc*) découper qch dans. **2** *n* (*for paper*) attache *f*, trombone *m*; (*of brooch, of cyclist, for hair*) pince *f*; – *vt* (-pp-) **to c. (on)** attacher. **3** *n* (*of film*) extrait *m*; (*blow*) *Fam* taloche *f*. ◆**clipping** *n* Journ coupure *f*. ◆**clippers** *npl* (*for hair*) tondeuse *f*; (*for nails*) pince *f* à ongles; (*pocket-sized, for finger nails*) coupe-ongles *m inv*.

clique [kliːk] *n* Pej clique *f*. ◆**cliquey** *a* Pej exclusif.

cloak [kləʊk] *n* (grande) cape *f*; Fig manteau *m*; **c. and dagger** (*film etc*) d'espionnage. ◆**cloakroom** *n* vestiaire *m*; (*for luggage*) Rail consigne *f*; (*lavatory*) toilettes *fpl*.

clobber ['klɒbər] **1** *vt* (*hit*) Sl rosser. **2** *n* (*clothes*) Sl affaires *fpl*.

clock [klɒk] *n* (*large*) horloge *f*; (*small*) pendule *f*; Aut compteur *m*; **against the c.** Fig contre la montre; **round the c.** Fig vingt-quatre heures sur vingt-quatre; **c. tower** clocher *m*; – *vt* Sp chronométrer; **to c. up** (*miles*) Aut Fam faire; – *vi* **to c. in** or **out** (*of worker*) pointer. ◆**clockwise** *adv* dans le sens des aiguilles d'une montre. ◆**clockwork** *a* mécanique; Fig régulier;

− *n* **to go like c.** aller comme sur des roulettes.

clod [klɒd] *n* **1** (*of earth*) motte *f*. **2** (*oaf*) *Fam* balourd, -ourde *mf*.

clog [klɒg] **1** *n* (*shoe*) sabot *m*. **2** *vt* (**-gg-**) **to c.** (**up**) (*obstruct*) boucher.

cloister ['klɔɪstər] *n* cloître *m*; − *vt* cloîtrer.

close[1] [kləus] *a* (**-er, -est**) (*place, relative etc*) proche (**to** de); (*collaboration, resemblance, connection*) étroit; (*friend etc*) intime; (*order, contest*) serré; (*study*) rigoureux; (*atmosphere*) *Met* lourd; (*vowel*) fermé; **c. to** (*near*) près de, proche de; **c. to tears** au bord des larmes; **to have a c. shave** *or* **call** l'échapper belle; − *adv* **c. (by)**, **c. at hand** (tout) près; **c. to** près de; **c. behind** juste derrière; **c. on** (*almost*) *Fam* pas loin de; **c. together** (*to stand*) serrés; **to follow c.** suivre de près; − *n* (*enclosed area*) enceinte *f*. ◆**c.-'cropped** *a* (*hair*) (coupé) ras. ◆**c.-'knit** *a* très uni. ◆**c.-up** *n* gros plan *m*.

close[2] [kləuz] *n* fin *f*, conclusion *f*; **to bring to a c.** mettre fin à; **to draw to a c.** tirer à sa fin; − *vt* fermer; (*discussion*) terminer, clore; (*opening*) boucher; (*road*) barrer; (*gap*) réduire; (*deal*) conclure; **to c. the meeting** lever la séance; **to c. ranks** serrer les rangs; **to c. in** (*enclose*) enfermer; **to c. up** fermer; − *vi* se fermer; (*end*) (se) terminer; **to c. (up)** (*of shop*) fermer; (*of wound*) se refermer; **to c. in** (*approach*) approcher; **to c. in on s.o.** se rapprocher de qn. ■ **to c. down** *vti* (*close for good*) fermer (définitivement); − *vi* *TV* terminer les émissions. ◆**c.-down** *n* fermeture *f* (définitive); *TV* fin *f* (des émissions). ◆**closing** *n* fermeture *f*; (*of session*) clôture *f*; − *a* final; **c. time** heure *f* de fermeture. ◆**closure** ['kləuʒər] *n* fermeture *f*.

closely ['kləusli] *adv* (*to link, guard*) étroitement; (*to follow*) de près; (*to listen*) attentivement; **c. contested** très disputé; **to hold s.o. c.** tenir qn contre soi. ◆**closeness** *n* proximité *f*; (*of collaboration etc*) étroitesse *f*; (*of friendship*) intimité *f*; (*of weather*) lourdeur *f*.

closet ['klɒzɪt] *n* (*cupboard*) *Am* placard *m*; (*wardrobe*) *Am* penderie *f*.

clot [klɒt] **1** *n* (*of blood*) caillot *m*; − *vt* (**-tt-**) (*blood*) coaguler; − *vi* (*of blood*) se coaguler. **2** *n* (*person*) *Fam* imbécile *mf*.

cloth [klɒθ] *n* tissu *m*, étoffe *f*; (*of linen*) toile *f*; (*of wool*) drap *m*; (*for dusting*) chiffon *m*; (*for dishes*) torchon *m*; (*tablecloth*) nappe *f*.

cloth/e [kləuð] *vt* habiller, vêtir (**in** de).

◆**—ing** *n* habillement *m*; (*clothes*) vêtements *mpl*; **an article of c.** un vêtement.

clothes [kləuðz] *npl* vêtements *mpl*; **to put one's c. on** s'habiller; **c. shop** magasin *m* d'habillement; **c. brush** brosse *f* à habits; **c. peg**, *Am* **c. pin** pince *f* à linge; **c. line** corde *f* à linge.

cloud [klaud] *n* nuage *m*; (*of arrows, insects*) *Fig* nuée *f*; − *vt* (*mind, issue*) obscurcir; (*window*) embuer; − *vi* **to c. (over)** (*of sky*) se couvrir. ◆**cloudburst** *n* averse *f*. ◆**cloudy** *a* (**-ier, -iest**) (*weather*) couvert, nuageux; (*liquid*) trouble.

clout [klaut] **1** *n* (*blow*) *Fam* taloche *f*; − *vt* *Fam* flanquer une taloche à, talocher. **2** *n* *Pol Fam* influence *f*, pouvoir *m*.

clove [kləuv] *n* clou *m* de girofle; **c. of garlic** gousse *f* d'ail.

clover ['kləuvər] *n* trèfle *m*.

clown [klaun] *n* clown *m*; − *vi* **to c. (around)** faire le clown.

cloying ['klɔɪɪŋ] *a* écœurant.

club [klʌb] **1** *n* (*weapon*) matraque *f*, massue *f*; (*golf*) **c.** (*stick*) club *m*; − *vt* (**-bb-**) matraquer. **2** *n* (*society*) club *m*, cercle *m*; − *vi* (**-bb-**) **to c. together** se cotiser (**to buy** pour acheter). **3** *n* & *npl* *Cards* trèfle *m*. ◆**clubhouse** *n* pavillon *m*.

clubfoot ['klʌbfut] *n* pied *m* bot. ◆**club-'footed** *a* pied bot *inv*.

cluck [klʌk] *vi* (*of hen*) glousser.

clue [klu:] *n* indice *m*; (*of crossword*) définition *f*; (*to mystery*) clef *f*; **I don't have a c.** *Fam* je n'en ai pas la moindre idée. ◆**clueless** *a* *Fam* stupide.

clump [klʌmp] *n* (*of flowers, trees*) massif *m*.

clumsy ['klʌmzi] *a* (**-ier, -iest**) maladroit; (*shape*) lourd; (*tool*) peu commode. ◆**clumsily** *adv* maladroitement. ◆**clumsiness** *n* maladresse *f*.

clung [klʌŋ] *see* **cling**.

cluster ['klʌstər] *n* groupe *m*; (*of flowers*) grappe *f*; (*of stars*) amas *m*; − *vi* se grouper.

clutch [klʌtʃ] **1** *vt* (*hold tight*) serrer, étreindre; (*cling to*) se cramponner à; (*grasp*) saisir; − *vi* **to c. at** essayer de saisir; − *n* étreinte *f*. **2** *n* (*apparatus*) *Aut* embrayage *m*; (*pedal*) pédale *f* d'embrayage. **3** *npl* **s.o.'s clutches** (*power*) les griffes *fpl* de qn.

clutter ['klʌtər] *n* (*objects*) fouillis *m*, désordre *m*; − *vt* **to c. (up)** encombrer (**with** de).

cm *abbr* (*centimetre*) cm.

co- [kəu] *prep* co-.

Co *abbr* (*company*) Cie.

coach [kəutʃ] **1** *n* (*horse-drawn*) carrosse *m*; *Rail* voiture *f*, wagon *m*; *Aut* autocar *m*. **2** *n* (*person*) *Sch* répétiteur, -trice *mf*; *Sp* entraîneur *m*; − *vt* (*pupil*) donner des leçons (particulières) à; (*sportsman etc*) entraîner; **to c. s.o. for** (*exam*) préparer qn à. ◆**coachman** *n* (*pl* **-men**) cocher *m*.

coagulate [kəʊˈægjʊleɪt] *vi* (*of blood*) se coaguler; − *vt* coaguler.

coal [kəʊl] *n* charbon *m*; *Geol* houille *f*; − *a* (*basin etc*) houiller; (*merchant, fire*) de charbon; (*cellar, bucket*) à charbon. ◆**coalfield** *n* bassin *m* houiller. ◆**coalmine** *n* mine *f* de charbon.

coalition [kəʊəˈlɪʃ(ə)n] *n* coalition *f*.

coarse [kɔɪs] *a* (**-er, -est**) (*person, manners*) grossier, vulgaire; (*surface*) rude; (*fabric*) grossier; (*salt*) gros; (*accent*) commun, vulgaire. ◆**−ness** *n* grossièreté *f*; vulgarité *f*.

coast [kəʊst] **1** *n* côte *f*. **2** *vi* **to c.** (**down** *or* **along**) (*of vehicle etc*) descendre en roue libre. ◆**coastal** *a* côtier. ◆**coaster** *n* (*ship*) caboteur *m*; (*for glass etc*) dessous *m* de verre, rond *m*. ◆**coastguard** *n* (*person*) garde *m* maritime, garde-côte *m*. ◆**coastline** *n* littoral *m*.

coat [kəʊt] *n* manteau *m*; (*overcoat*) pardessus *m*; (*jacket*) veste *f*; (*of animal*) pelage *m*; (*of paint*) couche *f*; **c. of arms** blason *m*, armoiries *fpl*; **c. hanger** cintre *m*; − *vt* couvrir, enduire (**with** de); (*with chocolate*) enrober (**with** de). ◆**−ed** *a* **c. tongue** langue *f* chargée. ◆**−ing** *n* couche *f*.

coax [kəʊks] *vt* amadouer, cajoler; **to c. s.o. to do** *or* **into doing** amadouer qn pour qu'il fasse. ◆**−ing** *n* cajoleries *fpl*.

cob [kɒb] *n* **corn on the c.** épi *m* de maïs.

cobble [ˈkɒb(ə)l] *n* pavé *m*; − *vt* **to c. together** (*text etc*) *Fam* bricoler. ◆**cobbled** *a* pavé. ◆**cobblestone** *n* pavé *m*.

cobbler [ˈkɒblər] *n* cordonnier *m*.

cobra [ˈkəʊbrə] *n* (*snake*) cobra *m*.

cobweb [ˈkɒbweb] *n* toile *f* d'araignée.

cocaine [kəʊˈkeɪn] *n* cocaïne *f*.

cock [kɒk] **1** *n* (*rooster*) coq *m*; (*male bird*) (*oiseau m*) mâle *m*. **2** *vt* (*gun*) armer; **to c.** (**up**) (*ears*) dresser. ◆**c.-a-doodle-'doo** *n* & *int* cocorico (*m*). ◆**c.-and-'bull story** *n* histoire *f* à dormir debout.

cockatoo [kɒkəˈtuː] *n* (*bird*) cacatoès *m*.

cocker [ˈkɒkər] *n* **c. (spaniel)** cocker *m*.

cockerel [ˈkɒkərəl] *n* jeune coq *m*, coquelet *m*.

cock-eyed [kɒkˈaɪd] *a Fam* **1** (*cross-eyed*) bigleux. **2** (*crooked*) de travers. **3** (*crazy*) absurde, stupide.

cockle [ˈkɒk(ə)l] *n* (*shellfish*) coque *f*.

cockney [ˈkɒknɪ] *a* & *n* cockney (*mf*).

cockpit [ˈkɒkpɪt] *n Av* poste *m* de pilotage.

cockroach [ˈkɒkrəʊtʃ] *n* (*beetle*) cafard *m*.

cocksure [kɒkˈʃʊər] *a Fam* trop sûr de soi.

cocktail [ˈkɒkteɪl] *n* (*drink*) cocktail *m*; (*fruit*) **c.** macédoine *f* (de fruits); **c. party** cocktail *m*; **prawn c.** crevettes *fpl* à la mayonnaise.

cocky [ˈkɒkɪ] *a* (**-ier, -iest**) *Fam* trop sûr de soi, arrogant.

cocoa [ˈkəʊkəʊ] *n* cacao *m*.

coconut [ˈkəʊkənʌt] *n* noix *f* de coco; **c. palm** cocotier *m*.

cocoon [kəˈkuːn] *n* cocon *m*.

cod [kɒd] *n* morue *f*; (*bought fresh*) cabillaud *m*. ◆**c.-liver 'oil** *n* huile *f* de foie de morue.

COD [siːəʊˈdiː] *abbr* (*cash on delivery*) livraison *f* contre remboursement.

coddle [ˈkɒd(ə)l] *vt* dorloter.

cod/e [kəʊd] *n* code *m*; − *vt* coder. ◆**−ing** *n* codage *m*. ◆**codify** *vt* codifier.

co-educational [kəʊedjʊˈkeɪʃən(ə)l] *a* (*school, teaching*) mixte.

coefficient [kəʊɪˈfɪʃənt] *n Math* coefficient *m*.

coerce [kəʊˈɜɪs] *vt* contraindre. ◆**coercion** *n* contrainte *f*.

coexist [kəʊɪgˈzɪst] *vi* coexister. ◆**coexistence** *n* coexistence *f*.

coffee [ˈkɒfɪ] *n* café *m*; **white c.** café *m* au lait; (*ordered in restaurant etc*) (café *m*) crème *m*; **black c.** café *m* noir, café nature; **c. bar, c. house** café *m*, cafétéria *f*; **c. break** pause-café *f*; **c. table** table *f* basse. ◆**coffeepot** *n* cafetière *f*.

coffers [ˈkɒfəz] *npl* (*funds*) coffres *mpl*.

coffin [ˈkɒfɪn] *n* cercueil *m*.

cog [kɒg] *n Tech* dent *f*; (*person*) *Fig* rouage *m*.

cogent [ˈkəʊdʒənt] *a* (*reason, argument*) puissant, convaincant.

cogitate [ˈkɒdʒɪteɪt] *vi Iron* cogiter.

cognac [ˈkɒnjæk] *n* cognac *m*.

cohabit [kəʊˈhæbɪt] *vi* (*of unmarried people*) vivre en concubinage.

coherent [kəʊˈhɪərənt] *a* cohérent; (*speech*) compréhensible. ◆**cohesion** *n* cohésion *f*. ◆**cohesive** *a* cohésif.

cohort [ˈkəʊhɔɪt] *n* (*group*) cohorte *f*.

coil [kɔɪl] *n* (*of wire etc*) rouleau *m*; *El* bobine *f*; (*contraceptive*) stérilet *m*; − *vt* (*rope, hair*) enrouler; − *vi* (*of snake etc*) s'enrouler.

coin [kɔɪn] *n* pièce *f* (de monnaie); (*currency*) monnaie *f*; − *vt* (*money*) frapper; (*word*) *Fig* inventer, forger; **to c. a phrase** pour ainsi dire. ◆**c.-operated** *a* automatique. ◆**coinage** n (coins) monnaie f; Fig invention f.

coincide [kəʊɪn'saɪd] vi coïncider (**with** avec). ◆**co'incidence** n coïncidence f. ◆**coinci'dental** a fortuit; **it's c.** c'est une coïncidence.

coke [kəʊk] n **1** (fuel) coke m. **2** (Coca-Cola®) coca m.

colander ['kʌləndər] n (for vegetables etc) passoire f.

cold [kəʊld] n froid m; Med rhume m; **to catch c.** prendre froid; **out in the c.** Fig abandonné, en carafe; – a (**-er, -est**) froid; **to be** or **feel c.** (of person) avoir froid; **my hands are c.** j'ai les mains froides; **it's c.** (of weather) il fait froid; **to get c.** (of weather) se refroidir; (of food) refroidir; **to get c. feet** Fam se dégonfler; **in c. blood** de sang-froid; **c. cream** crème f de beauté; **c. meats,** Am **c. cuts** Culin assiette f anglaise. ◆**c.-'blooded** a (person) cruel, insensible; (act) de sang-froid. ◆**c.-'shoulder** vt snober. ◆**coldly** adv avec froideur. ◆**coldness** n froideur f.

coleslaw ['kəʊlslɔː] n salade f de chou cru.

colic ['kɒlɪk] n Med coliques fpl.

collaborate [kə'læbəreɪt] vi collaborer (**on** à). ◆**collabo'ration** n collaboration f. ◆**collaborator** n collaborateur, -trice mf.

collage ['kɒlɑːʒ] n (picture) collage m.

collapse [kə'læps] vi (fall) s'effondrer, s'écrouler; (of government) tomber; (faint) Med se trouver mal; – n effondrement m, écroulement m; (of government) chute f. ◆**collapsible** a (chair etc) pliant.

collar ['kɒlər] n (on garment) col m; (of dog) collier m; **to seize by the c.** saisir au collet; – vt Fam saisir (qn) au collet; Fig Fam retenir (qn); (take, steal) Sl piquer. ◆**collarbone** n clavicule f.

collate [kə'leɪt] vt collationner, comparer (**with** avec).

colleague ['kɒliːg] n collègue mf, confrère m.

collect [kə'lekt] vt (pick up) ramasser; (gather) rassembler, recueillir; (taxes) percevoir; (rent, money) encaisser; (stamps etc as hobby) collectionner; (fetch, call for) (passer) prendre; – vi (of dust) s'accumuler; (of people) se rassembler; **to c. for** (in street, church) quêter pour; – adv **to call** or **phone c.** Am téléphoner en PCV. ◆**collection** [kə'lekʃ(ə)n] n ramassage m; (of taxes) perception f; (of objects) collection f; (of poems etc) recueil m; (of money in church etc) quête f; (of mail) levée f. ◆**collective** a collectif. ◆**collectively** adv

collectivement. ◆**collector** n (of stamps etc) collectionneur, -euse mf.

college ['kɒlɪdʒ] n Pol Rel Sch collège m; (university) université f; Mus conservatoire m; **teachers' training c.** école f normale; **art c.** école f des beaux-arts; **agricultural c.** institut m d'agronomie, lycée m agricole.

collide [kə'laɪd] vi entrer en collision (**with** avec), se heurter (**with** à). ◆**collision** n collision f; Fig conflit m, collision f.

colliery ['kɒlɪərɪ] n houillère f.

colloquial [kə'ləʊkwɪəl] a (word etc) familier. ◆**colloquialism** n expression f familière.

collusion [kə'luːʒ(ə)n] n collusion f.

collywobbles ['kɒlɪwɒb(ə)lz] npl **to have the c.** (feel nervous) Fam avoir la frousse.

cologne [kə'ləʊn] n eau f de Cologne.

colon ['kəʊlən] n **1** Gram deux-points m inv. **2** Anat côlon m.

colonel ['kɜːn(ə)l] n colonel m.

colony ['kɒlənɪ] n colonie f. ◆**colonial** [kə'ləʊnɪəl] a colonial. ◆**coloni'zation** n colonisation f. ◆**colonize** vt coloniser.

colossal [kə'lɒs(ə)l] a colossal.

colour ['kʌlər] n couleur f; – a (photo, television) en couleurs; (television set) couleur inv; (problem) racial; **c. supplement** Journ supplément m illustré; **off c.** (not well) mal fichu; (improper) scabreux; – vt colorer; **to c. (in)** (drawing) colorier. ◆**-ed** a (person, pencil) de couleur; (glass, water) coloré. ◆**-ing** n coloration f; (with crayons) coloriage m; (hue, effect) coloris m; (matter) colorant m. ◆**colour-blind** a daltonien. ◆**colourful** a (crowd, story) coloré; (person) pittoresque.

colt [kəʊlt] n (horse) poulain m.

column ['kɒləm] n colonne f. ◆**columnist** n Journ chroniqueur m; **gossip c.** échotier, -ière mf.

coma ['kəʊmə] n coma m; **in a c.** dans le coma.

comb [kəʊm] n peigne m; – vt peigner; (search) Fig ratisser; **to c. one's hair** se peigner; **to c. out** (hair) démêler.

combat ['kɒmbæt] n combat m; – vti combattre (**for** pour). ◆**'combatant** n combattant, -ante mf.

combine [kəm'baɪn] vt unir, joindre (**with** à); (elements, sounds) combiner; (qualities, efforts) allier, joindre; – vi s'unir; **everything combined to . . .** tout s'est ligué pour . . . . ◆**-ed** a (effort) conjugué; **c. wealth**/etc (put together) richesses/etc fpl réunies; **c. forces** Mil forces fpl alliées. ◆**combi'nation** n combinaison f; (of *qualities*) réunion *f*; (*of events*) concours *m*; **in c. with** en association avec.

combine² ['kɒmbaɪn] *n Com* cartel *m*; **c. harvester** *Agr* moissonneuse-batteuse *f*.

combustion [kəm'bʌstʃ(ə)n] *n* combustion *f*.

come [kʌm] *vi* (*pt* came, *pp* come) venir (**from** de, **to** à); (*arrive*) arriver, venir; (*happen*) arriver; **c. and see me** viens me voir; **I've just c. from** j'arrive de; **to c. for** venir chercher; **to c. home** rentrer; **coming!** j'arrive!; **c. now!** voyons!; **to c. as a surprise (to)** surprendre; **to c. near** *or* **close to doing** faillir faire; **to c. on page 2** se trouver à la page 2; **nothing came of it** ça n'a abouti à rien; **to c. to** (*understand etc*) en venir à; (*a decision*) parvenir à; **to c. to an end** toucher à sa fin; **to c. true** se réaliser; **c. May/etc** *Fam* en mai/etc; **the life to c.** la vie future; **how c. that . . . ?** *Fam* comment se fait-il que . . . ? ■ **to c. about** *vi* (*happen*) se faire, arriver; **to c. across** *vi* (*of speech*) faire de l'effet; (*of feelings*) se montrer; – *vt* (*thing, person*) tomber sur; **to c. along** *vi* venir (**with** avec); (*progress*) avancer; **c. along!** allons!; **to c. at** *vt* (*attack*) attaquer; **to c. away** *vi* (*leave, come off*) partir; **to c. back** *vi* revenir; (*return home*) rentrer. ◆**comeback** *n* retour *m*; *Th Pol* rentrée *f*; (*retort*) réplique *f*; **to c. by** *vi* (*obtain*) obtenir; (*find*) trouver; **to c. down** *vi* descendre; (*of rain, price*) tomber. ◆**comedown** *n Fam* humiliation *f*; **to c. forward** *vi* (*make oneself known, volunteer*) se présenter; **to c. forward with** offrir, suggérer; **to c. in** *vi* entrer; (*of tide*) monter; (*of train, athlete*) arriver; *Pol* arriver au pouvoir; (*of clothes*) devenir à la mode, se faire beaucoup; (*of money*) rentrer; **to c. in for** recevoir; **to c. into** (*money*) hériter de; **to c. off** *vi* se détacher, partir; (*succeed*) réussir; (*happen*) avoir lieu; (*fare, manage*) s'en tirer; – *vt* (*fall from*) tomber de; (*get down from*) descendre de; **to c. on** *vi* (*follow*) suivre; (*progress*) avancer; (*start*) commencer; (*arrive*) arriver; (*of play*) être joué; **c. on!** allez!; **to c. out** *vi* sortir; (*of sun, book*) paraître; (*of stain*) s'enlever, partir; (*of secret*) être révélé; (*of photo*) réussir; **to c. out (on strike)** se mettre en grève; **to c. over** *vi* (*visit*) venir, passer; **to c. over funny** *or* **peculiar** se trouver mal; – *vt* (*take hold of*) saisir (*qn*), prendre (*qn*); **to c. round** *vi* (*visit*) venir, passer; (*recur*) revenir; (*regain consciousness*) revenir à soi; **to c. through** *vi* (*survive*) s'en tirer; – *vt* se tirer indemne de; **to c. to** *vi* (*regain consciousness*) revenir

à soi; (*amount to*) *Com* revenir à, faire; **to c. under** *vi* être classé sous; (*s.o.'s influence*) tomber sous; **to c. up** *vi* (*rise*) monter; (*of plant*) sortir; (*of question, job*) se présenter; **to c. up against** (*wall, problem*) se heurter à; **to c. up to** (*reach*) arriver jusqu'à; (*one's hopes*) répondre à; **to c. up with** (*idea, money*) trouver; **to c. upon** *vt* (*book, reference etc*) tomber sur. ◆**coming** *a* (*future*) à venir; – *n Rel* avènement *m*; **comings and goings** allées *fpl* et venues.

comedy ['kɒmɪdɪ] *n* comédie *f*. ◆**co'median** *n* (acteur *m*) comique *m*, actrice *f* comique.

comet ['kɒmɪt] *n* comète *f*.

comeuppance [kʌm'ʌpəns] *n* **he got his c.** *Pej Fam* il n'a eu que ce qu'il mérite.

comfort ['kʌmfət] *n* confort *m*; (*consolation*) réconfort *m*, consolation *f*; (*peace of mind*) tranquillité *f* d'esprit; **to like one's comforts** aimer ses aises *fpl*; **c. station** *Am* toilettes *fpl*; – *vt* consoler; (*cheer*) réconforter. ◆**—able** *a* (*chair, house etc*) confortable; (*person*) à l'aise; **he's c.** (*in chair etc*) il est à l'aise, il est bien; **make yourself c.** mets-toi à l'aise. ◆**—ably** *adv* **c. off** (*rich*) à l'aise. ◆**—er** *n* (*baby's dummy*) sucette *f*; (*quilt*) *Am* édredon *m*. ◆**comfy** *a* (-**ier**, -**iest**) (*chair etc*) *Fam* confortable; **I'm c.** je suis bien.

comic ['kɒmɪk] *a* comique; – *n* (*actor*) comique *m*; (*actress*) actrice *f* comique; (*magazine*) illustré *m*; **c. strip** bande *f* dessinée. ◆**comical** *a* comique, drôle.

comma ['kɒmə] *n Gram* virgule *f*.

command [kə'mɑːnd] *vt* (*order*) commander (**s.o. to do** à qn de faire); (*control, dominate*) commander (*régiment, vallée etc*); (*be able to use*) disposer de; (*respect*) imposer (**from** à); (*require*) exiger; – *vi* commander; – *n* ordre *m*; (*power*) commandement *m*; (*troops*) troupes *fpl*; (*mastery*) maîtrise *f* (**of** de); **at one's c.** (*disposal*) à sa disposition; **to be in c. (of)** (*ship, army etc*) commander; (*situation*) être maître (de). ◆**—ing** *a* (*authoritative*) imposant; (*position*) dominant; **c. officer** commandant *m*. ◆**—er** *n* chef *m*; *Mil* commandant *m*. ◆**—ment** *n Rel* commandement *m*.

commandant ['kɒməndænt] *n Mil* commandant *m* (*of un camp etc*). ◆**comman'deer** *vt* réquisitionner.

commando [kə'mɑːndəu] *n* (*pl* -**os** *or* -**oes**) *Mil* commando *m*.

commemorate [kə'meməreɪt] *vt* commémorer. ◆**commemo'ration** *n* commémoration f. ◆**commemorative** a commémoratif.

commence [kə'mens] vti commencer (**doing** à faire). ◆**—ment** n commencement m; Univ Am remise f des diplômes.

commend [kə'mend] vt (praise) louer; (recommend) recommander; (entrust) confier (**to** à). ◆**—able** a louable. ◆**commen'dation** n éloge m.

commensurate [kə'menʃərət] a proportionné (**to, with** à).

comment ['kɒment] n commentaire m, remarque f; — vi faire des commentaires or des remarques (**on** sur); **to c. on** (text, event, news item) commenter; **to c. that** remarquer que. ◆**commentary** n commentaire m; (live) c. TV Rad reportage m. ◆**commentate** vi TV Rad faire un reportage (**on** sur). ◆**commentator** n TV Rad reporter m, commentateur, -trice mf.

commerce ['kɒmɜːs] n commerce m. ◆**co'mmercial 1** a commercial; (street) commerçant; (traveller) de commerce. **2** n (advertisement) TV publicité f; **the commercials** TV la publicité. ◆**co'mmercialize** vt (event) Pej transformer en une affaire de gros sous.

commiserate [kə'mɪzəreɪt] vi **to c. with s.o.** s'apitoyer sur (le sort de) qn. ◆**commise-'ration** n commisération f.

commission [kə'mɪʃ(ə)n] n (fee, group) commission f; (order for work) commande f; **out of c.** hors service; **to get one's c.** Mil être nommé officier; — vt (artist) passer une commande à; (book) commander; Mil nommer (qn) officier; **to c. to do** charger de faire. ◆**commissio'naire** n (in hotel etc) commissionnaire m. ◆**commissioner** n Pol commissaire m; (police) c. préfet m (de police).

commit [kə'mɪt] vt (-tt-) (crime) commettre; (entrust) confier (**to** à); **to c. suicide** se suicider; **to c. to memory** apprendre par cœur; **to c. to prison** incarcérer; **to c. oneself** s'engager (**to** à); (compromise oneself) se compromettre. ◆**—ment** n obligation f; (promise) engagement m.

committee [kə'mɪtɪ] n comité m.

commodity [kə'mɒdɪtɪ] n produit m, article m.

common ['kɒmən] **1** a (-er, -est) (shared, vulgar) commun; (frequent) courant, fréquent, commun; **the c. man** l'homme m du commun; **in c.** (shared) en commun (**with** avec); **to have nothing in c.** n'avoir rien de commun (**with** avec); **in c. with** (like) comme; **c. law** droit m coutumier; **C.**

Market Marché m commun; **c. room** salle f commune; **c. or garden** ordinaire. **2** n (land) terrain m communal; **House of Commons** Pol Chambre f des Communes; **the Commons** Pol les Communes fpl. ◆**—er** n roturier, -ière mf. ◆**—ly** adv (generally) communément; (vulgarly) d'une façon commune. ◆**—ness** n fréquence f; (vulgarity) vulgarité f. ◆**commonplace** a banal; — n banalité f. ◆**common'sense** n sens m commun; — a sensé.

Commonwealth ['kɒmənwelθ] n **the C.** le Commonwealth.

commotion [kə'məʊʃ(ə)n] n agitation f.

communal [kə'mjuːn(ə)l] a (of the community) communautaire; (shared) commun. ◆**—ly** adv en commun; (to live) en communauté.

commune 1 ['kɒmjuːn] n (district) commune f; (group) communauté f. **2** [kə'mjuːn] vi Rel & Fig communier (**with** avec). ◆**co'mmunion** n communion f; (Holy) C. communion f.

communicate [kə'mjuːnɪkeɪt] vt communiquer; (illness) transmettre; — vi (of person, rooms etc) communiquer. ◆**communi-'cation** n communication f; **c. cord** Rail signal m d'alarme. ◆**communicative** a communicatif. ◆**communiqué** n Pol communiqué m.

communism ['kɒmjuːnɪz(ə)m] n communisme m. ◆**communist** a & n communiste (mf).

community [kə'mjuːnɪtɪ] n communauté f; — a (rights, life etc) communautaire; **the student c.** les étudiants mpl; **c. centre** centre m socio-culturel; **c. worker** animateur, -trice mf socio-culturel(le).

commut/e [kə'mjuːt] **1** vt Jur commuer (**to** en). **2** vi (travel) faire la navette (**to work** pour se rendre à son travail). ◆**—ing** n trajets mpl journaliers. ◆**—er** n banlieusard, -arde mf; **c. train** train m de banlieue.

compact 1 [kəm'pækt] a (car, crowd, substance) compact; (style) condensé; **c. disc** ['kɒmpækt] disque m compact. **2** ['kɒmpækt] n (for face powder) poudrier m.

companion [kəm'pænjən] n (person) compagnon m, compagne f; (handbook) manuel m. ◆**companionship** n camaraderie f.

company ['kʌmpənɪ] n (fellowship, firm) compagnie f; (guests) invités, -ées mfpl; **to keep s.o. c.** tenir compagnie à qn; **to keep good c.** avoir de bonnes fréquentations; **he's good c.** c'est un bon compagnon.

compar/e [kəmˈpeər] *vt* comparer; **compared to** *or* **with** en comparaison de; – *vi* être comparable, se comparer (**with** à). ◆**—able** [ˈkɒmpərəb(ə)l] *a* comparable. ◆**comparative** *a* comparatif; (*relative*) relatif. ◆**comparatively** *adv* relativement. ◆**comparison** *n* comparaison *f* (**between** entre; **with** à, avec).

compartment [kəmˈpɑːtmənt] *n* compartiment *m*. ◆**compart'mentalize** *vt* compartimenter.

compass [ˈkʌmpəs] *n* **1** (*for navigation*) boussole *f*; *Nau* compas *m*; (*range*) *Fig* portée *f*. **2** (*for measuring etc*) *Am* compas *m*; (**pair of**) **compasses** compas *m*.

compassion [kəmˈpæʃ(ə)n] *n* compassion *f*. ◆**compassionate** *a* compatissant; **on c. grounds** pour raisons de famille.

compatible [kəmˈpætɪb(ə)l] *a* compatible. ◆**compati'bility** *n* compatibilité *f*.

compatriot [kəmˈpætrɪət, kəmˈpeɪtrɪət] *n* compatriote *mf*.

compel [kəmˈpel] *vt* (**-ll-**) contraindre (**to do** à faire); (*respect etc*) imposer (**from** à); **compelled to do** contraint de faire. ◆**compelling** *a* irrésistible.

compendium [kəmˈpendɪəm] *n* abrégé *m*.

compensate [ˈkɒmpənseɪt] *vt* **to c. s.o.** (*with payment, recompense*) dédommager qn (**for** de); **to c. for sth** (*make up for*) compenser qch; – *vi* compenser. ◆**compen'sation** *n* (*financial*) dédommagement *m*; (*consolation*) compensation *f*, dédommagement *m*; **in c. for** en compensation de.

compère [ˈkɒmpeər] *n* *TV Rad* animateur, -trice *mf*, présentateur, -trice *mf*; – *vt* (*a show*) animer, présenter.

compete [kəmˈpiːt] *vi* prendre part (**in** à), concourir (**in** à); (*vie*) rivaliser (**with** avec); *Com* faire concurrence (**with** à); **to c. for** (*prize etc*) concourir pour; **to c. in a rally** courir dans un rallye.

competent [ˈkɒmpɪtənt] *a* (*capable*) compétent (**to do** pour faire); (*sufficient*) suffisant. ◆**—ly** *adv* avec compétence. ◆**competence** *n* compétence *f*.

competition [kɒmpəˈtɪʃ(ə)n] *n* (*rivalry*) compétition *f*, concurrence *f*; **a c.** (*contest*) un concours; *Sp* une compétition. ◆**com'petitive** *a* (*price, market*) compétitif; (*selection*) par concours; (*person*) aimant la compétition; **c. exam(ination)** concours *m*. ◆**com'petitor** *n* concurrent, -ente *mf*.

compil/e [kəmˈpaɪl] *vt* (*dictionary*) rédiger; (*list*) dresser; (*documents*) compiler. ◆**—er** *n* rédacteur, -trice *mf*.

complacent [kəmˈpleɪsənt] *a* content de

soi. ◆**complacence** *n*, ◆**complacency** *n* autosatisfaction *f*, contentement *m* de soi.

complain [kəmˈpleɪn] *vi* se plaindre (**of, about** de; **that** que). ◆**complaint** *n* plainte *f*; *Com* réclamation *f*; *Med* maladie *f*; (**cause for**) **c.** sujet *m* de plainte.

complement [ˈkɒmplɪmənt] *n* complément *m*; – [ˈkɒmplɪment] *vt* compléter. ◆**comple'mentary** *a* complémentaire.

complete [kəmˈpliːt] *a* (*total*) complet; (*finished*) achevé; (*downright*) *Pej* parfait; – *vt* (*add sth missing*) compléter; (*finish*) achever; (*a form*) remplir. ◆**—ly** *adv* complètement. ◆**completion** *n* achèvement *m*, réalisation *f*.

complex [ˈkɒmpleks] **1** *a* complexe. **2** *n* (*feeling, buildings*) complexe *m*; **housing c.** grand ensemble *m*. ◆**com'plexity** *n* complexité *f*.

complexion [kəmˈplekʃ(ə)n] *n* (*of the face*) teint *m*; *Fig* caractère *m*.

compliance [kəmˈplaɪəns] *n* (*agreement*) conformité *f* (**with** avec).

complicat/e [ˈkɒmplɪkeɪt] *vt* compliquer. ◆**—ed** *a* compliqué. ◆**compli'cation** *n* complication *f*.

complicity [kəmˈplɪsɪtɪ] *n* complicité *f*.

compliment [ˈkɒmplɪmənt] *n* compliment *m*; *pl* (*of author*) hommages *mpl*; **compliments of the season** meilleurs vœux pour Noël et la nouvelle année; – [ˈkɒmplɪment] *vt* complimenter. ◆**compli'mentary** *a* **1** (*flattering*) flatteur. **2** (*free*) à titre gracieux; (*ticket*) de faveur.

comply [kəmˈplaɪ] *vi* obéir (**with** à); (*request*) accéder à.

component [kəmˈpəʊnənt] *a* (*part*) constituant; – *n* (*chemical, electronic*) composant *m*; *Tech* pièce *f*; (*element*) *Fig* composante *f*.

compos/e [kəmˈpəʊz] *vt* composer; **to c. oneself** se calmer. ◆**—ed** *a* calme. ◆**—er** *n* *Mus* compositeur, -trice *mf*. ◆**compo-'sition** *n* *Mus Liter Ch* composition *f*; *Sch* rédaction *f*. ◆**composure** *n* calme *m*, sang-froid *m*.

compost [ˈkɒmpɒst, *Am* ˈkɒmpəʊst] *n* compost *m*.

compound 1 [ˈkɒmpaʊnd] *n* (*substance, word*) composé *m*; (*area*) enclos *m*; – *a* *Ch* composé; (*sentence, number*) complexe. **2** [kəmˈpaʊnd] *vt* *Ch* composer; (*increase*) *Fig* aggraver.

comprehend [kɒmprɪˈhend] *vt* comprendre. ◆**comprehensible** *a* compréhensible. ◆**comprehension** *n* compréhension *f.* ◆**comprehensive** *a* complet; (*knowledge*) étendu; (*view, measure*) d'ensemble; (*insurance*) tous-risques *inv*; – *a* & *n* **c.** (**school**) = collège *m* d'enseignement secondaire.

compress [kəm'pres] *vt* comprimer; (*ideas etc*) *Fig* condenser. ◆**compression** *n* compression *f*; condensation *f*.

comprise [kəm'praɪz] *vt* comprendre, englober.

compromise ['kɒmprəmaɪz] *vt* compromettre; – *vi* accepter un compromis; – *n* compromis *m*; – *a* (*solution*) de compromis.

compulsion [kəm'pʌlʃ(ə)n] *n* contrainte *f*. ◆**compulsive** *a* (*behaviour*) *Psy* compulsif; (*smoker, gambler*) invétéré; **c. liar** mythomane *mf*.

compulsory [kəm'pʌlsərɪ] *a* obligatoire.

compunction [kəm'pʌŋkʃ(ə)n] *n* scrupule *m*.

comput/e [kəm'pjuːt] *vt* calculer. ◆–**ing** *n* informatique *f*. ◆**computer** *n* ordinateur *m*; – *a* (*system*) informatique; (*course*) d'informatique; **c. operator** opérateur, -trice *mf* sur ordinateur; **c. science** informatique *f*; **c. scientist** informaticien, -ienne *mf*. ◆**computerize** *vt* informatiser.

comrade ['kɒmreɪd] *n* camarade *mf*. ◆**comradeship** *n* camaraderie *f*.

con [kɒn] *vt* (**-nn-**) *Sl* rouler, escroquer; **to be conned** se faire avoir *or* rouler; – *n Sl* escroquerie *f*; **c. man** escroc *m*.

concave ['kɒnkeɪv] *a* concave.

conceal [kən'siːl] *vt* (*hide*) dissimuler (**from s.o.** à qn); (*plan etc*) tenir secret. ◆–**ment** *n* dissimulation *f*.

concede [kən'siːd] *vt* concéder (**to** à, **that** que); – *vi* céder.

conceit [kən'siːt] *n* vanité *f*. ◆**conceited** *a* vaniteux. ◆**conceitedly** *adv* avec vanité.

conceiv/e [kən'siːv] *vt* (*idea, child etc*) concevoir; – *vi* (*of woman*) concevoir; **to c. of** concevoir. ◆–**able** *a* concevable, envisageable. ◆–**ably** *adv* **yes, c.** oui, c'est concevable.

concentrate ['kɒnsəntreɪt] *vt* concentrer; – *vi* se concentrer (**on** sur); **to c. on doing** s'appliquer à faire. ◆**concen'tration** *n* concentration *f*; **c. camp** camp *m* de concentration.

concentric [kən'sentrɪk] *a* concentrique.

concept ['kɒnsept] *n* concept *m*. ◆**con'ception** *n* (*idea*) & *Med* conception *f*.

concern [kən'sɜːn] *vt* concerner; **to c. oneself with, be concerned with** s'occuper de; **to be concerned about** s'inquiéter de; –

n (*matter*) affaire *f*; (*anxiety*) inquiétude *f*; (*share*) *Com* intérêt(s) *m*(*pl*) (**in** dans); (**business**) **c.** entreprise *f*. ◆–**ed** *a* (*anxious*) inquiet; **the department c.** le service compétent; **the main person c.** le principal intéressé. ◆–**ing** *prep* en ce qui concerne.

concert ['kɒnsət] *n* concert *m*; **in c.** (*together*) de concert (**with** avec). ◆**c.-goer** *n* habitué, -ée *mf* des concerts. ◆**con'certed** *a* (*effort*) concerté.

concertina [kɒnsə'tiːnə] *n* concertina *m*; **c. crash** *Aut* carambolage *m*.

concession [kən'seʃ(ə)n] *n* concession *f* (**to** à).

conciliate [kən'sɪlɪeɪt] *vt* **to c. s.o.** (*win over*) se concilier qn; (*soothe*) apaiser qn. ◆**concili'ation** *n* conciliation *f*; apaisement *m*. ◆**conciliatory** [kən'sɪlɪətərɪ, *Am* -tɔːrɪ] *a* conciliant.

concise [kən'saɪs] *a* concis. ◆–**ly** *adv* avec concision. ◆–**ness** *n*, ◆**concision** *n* concision *f*.

conclud/e [kən'kluːd] *vt* (*end, settle*) conclure; **to c. that** (*infer*) conclure que; – *vi* (*of event etc*) se terminer (**with** par); (*of speaker*) conclure. ◆–**ing** *a* final. ◆**conclusion** *n* conclusion *f*; **in c.** pour conclure. ◆**conclusive** *a* concluant. ◆**conclusively** *adv* de manière concluante.

concoct [kən'kɒkt] *vt* *Culin Pej* concocter, confectionner; (*scheme*) *Fig* combiner. ◆**concoction** *n* (*substance*) *Pej* mixture *f*; (*act*) confection *f*; *Fig* combinaison *f*.

concord ['kɒnkɔːd] *n* concorde *f*.

concourse ['kɒnkɔːs] *n* (*hall*) *Am* hall *m*; *Rail* hall *m*, salle *f* des pas perdus.

concrete ['kɒnkriːt] **1** *a* (*real, positive*) concret. **2** *n* béton *m*; – *a* en béton; **c. mixer** bétonnière *f*, bétonneuse *f*.

concur [kən'kɜːr] *vi* (**-rr-**) **1** (*agree*) être d'accord (**with** avec). **2 to c. to** (*contribute*) concourir à.

concurrent [kən'kʌrənt] *a* simultané. ◆–**ly** *adv* simultanément.

concussion [kən'kʌʃ(ə)n] *n Med* commotion *f* (cérébrale).

condemn [kən'dem] *vt* condamner; (*building*) déclarer inhabitable. ◆**condem'nation** *n* condamnation *f*.

condense [kən'dens] *vt* condenser; – *vi* se condenser. ◆**conden'sation** *n* condensation *f* (**of** de); (*mist*) buée *f*.

condescend [kɒndɪ'send] *vi* condescendre (**to do** à faire). ◆**condescension** *n* condescendance *f*.

condiment ['kɒndɪmənt] *n* condiment *m*.

condition ['kɒndɪʃ(ə)n] **1** *n* (*stipulation, circumstance, rank*) condition *f*; (*state*) état *m*, condition *f*; **on c. that one does** à condition de faire, à condition que l'on fasse; **in/out of c.** en bonne/mauvaise forme. **2** *vt* (*action etc*) déterminer, conditionner; **to c. s.o.** *Psy* conditionner qn (**into doing** à faire). ◆**conditional** *a* conditionnel; **to be c. upon** dépendre de. ◆**conditioner** *n* (*hair*) **c.** après-shampooing *m*.

condo ['kɒndəʊ] *n abbr* (*pl* -os) *Am* = **condominium**.

condolences [kən'dəʊlənsɪz] *npl* condoléances *fpl*.

condom ['kɒndəm] *n* préservatif *m*, capote *f* (anglaise).

condominium [kɒndə'mɪnɪəm] *n Am* (*building*) (immeuble *m* en) copropriété *f*; (*apartment*) appartement *m* dans une copropriété.

condone [kən'dəʊn] *vt* (*forgive*) pardonner; (*overlook*) fermer les yeux sur.

conducive [kən'djuːsɪv] *a* **c. to favorable** à.

conduct ['kɒndʌkt] *n* (*behaviour, directing*) conduite *f*; – [kən'dʌkt] *vt* (*lead*) conduire, mener; (*orchestra*) diriger; (*electricity etc*) conduire; **to c. oneself** se conduire. ◆**—ed** *a* (*visit*) guidé; **c. tour** excursion *f* accompagnée. ◆**conductor** *n Mus* chef *m* d'orchestre; (*on bus*) receveur *m*; *Rail Am* chef *m* de train; (*metal, cable etc*) conducteur *m*. ◆**conductress** *n* (*on bus*) receveuse *f*.

cone [kəʊn] *n* cône *m*; (*of ice cream*) cornet *m*; (*paper*) **c.** cornet *m* (de papier); **traffic c.** cône *m* de chantier.

confectioner [kən'fekʃənər] *n* (*of sweets*) confiseur, -euse *mf*; (*of cakes*) pâtissier, -ière *mf*. ◆**confectionery** *n* (*sweets*) confiserie *f*; (*cakes*) pâtisserie *f*.

confederate [kən'fedərət] *a* confédéré; – *n* (*accomplice*) complice *mf*, acolyte *m*. ◆**confederacy** *n*, ◆**confede'ration** *n* confédération *f*.

confer [kən'fɜːr] **1** *vt* (-rr-) (*grant*) conférer (**on** à); (*degree*) *Univ* remettre. **2** *vi* (-rr-) (*talk together*) conférer, se consulter.

conference ['kɒnfərəns] *n* conférence *f*; (*scientific etc*) congrès *m*.

confess [kən'fes] **1** *vt* avouer, confesser (**that** que, **to** à); – *vi* avouer; **to c. to** (*crime etc*) avouer, confesser. **2** *vt Rel* confesser; – *vi* se confesser. ◆**confession** *n* aveu *m*, confession *f*; *Rel* confession *f*. ◆**confessional** *n Rel* confessionnal *m*.

confetti [kən'fetɪ] *n* confettis *mpl*.

confide [kən'faɪd] *vt* confier (**to** à, **that** que);

– *vi* **to c. in** (*talk to*) se confier à. ◆**'confidant, -ante** [-ænt] *n* confident, -ente *mf*. ◆**'confidence** *n* (*trust*) confiance *f*; (*secret*) confidence *f*; (*self-*)**c.** confiance *f* en soi; **in c.** en confidence; **motion of no c.** *Pol* motion *f* de censure; **c. trick** escroquerie *f*; **c. trickster** escroc *m*. ◆**'confident** *a* sûr, assuré; (*self-*)**c.** sûr de soi. ◆**confi'dential** *a* confidentiel; (*secretary*) particulier. ◆**confi'dentially** *adv* en confidence. ◆**'confidently** *adv* avec confiance.

configuration [kənfɪgjʊ'reɪʃ(ə)n] *n* configuration *f*.

confin/e [kən'faɪn] *vt* enfermer, confiner (**to, in** dans); (*limit*) limiter (**to** à); **to c. oneself to doing** se limiter à faire. ◆**—ed** *a* (*atmosphere*) confiné; (*space*) réduit; **c. to bed** obligé de garder le lit. ◆**—ement** *n Med* couches *fpl*; *Jur* emprisonnement *m*. ◆**'confines** *npl* limites *fpl*, confins *mpl*.

confirm [kən'fɜːm] *vt* confirmer (**that** que); (*strengthen*) raffermir. ◆**—ed** *a* (*bachelor*) endurci; (*smoker, habit*) invétéré. ◆**confir'mation** *n* confirmation *f*; raffermissement *m*.

confiscate ['kɒnfɪskeɪt] *vt* confisquer (**from s.o.** à qn). ◆**confis'cation** *n* confiscation *f*.

conflagration [kɒnflə'greɪʃ(ə)n] *n* (*grand*) incendie *m*, brasier *m*.

conflict ['kɒnflɪkt] *n* conflit *m*; – [kən'flɪkt] *vi* être en contradiction, être incompatible (**with** avec); (*of dates, events, TV programmes*) tomber en même temps (**with** que). ◆**—ing** *a* (*views, theories etc*) contradictoires; (*dates*) incompatibles.

confluence ['kɒnfluəns] *n* (*of rivers*) confluent *m*.

conform [kən'fɔːm] *vi* se conformer (**to, with** à); (*of ideas etc*) être en conformité. ◆**conformist** *a* & *n* conformiste (*mf*). ◆**conformity** *n* (*likeness*) conformité *f*; *Pej* conformisme *m*.

confound [kən'faʊnd] *vt* confondre; **c. him!** que le diable l'emporte! ◆**—ed** *a* (*damned*) *Fam* sacré.

confront [kən'frʌnt] *vt* (*danger*) affronter; (*problems*) faire face à; **to c. s.o.** (*be face to face with*) se trouver en face de qn; (*oppose*) s'opposer à qn; **to c. s.o. with** (*person*) confronter qn avec; (*thing*) mettre qn en présence de. ◆**confron'tation** *n* confrontation *f*.

confus/e [kən'fjuːz] *vt* (*perplex*) confondre; (*muddle*) embrouiller; **to c. with** (*mistake for*) confondre avec. ◆**—ed** *a* (*situation,* *noises etc*) confus; **to be c.** (*of person*) s'y perdre; **to get c.** s'embrouiller. ◆**—ing** *a* difficile à comprendre, déroutant. ◆**confusion** *n* confusion *f*; **in c.** en désordre.

congeal [kən'dʒiːl] *vt* figer; − *vi* (se) figer.

congenial [kən'dʒiːnɪəl] *a* sympathique.

congenital [kən'dʒenɪtəl] *a* congénital.

congested [kən'dʒestɪd] *a* (*street*) encombré; (*town*) surpeuplé; *Med* congestionné. ◆**congestion** *n* (*traffic*) encombrement(s) *m*(*pl*); (*overcrowding*) surpeuplement *m*; *Med* congestion *f*.

Congo ['kɒŋgəu] *n* Congo *m*.

congratulate [kən'grætʃuleɪt] *vt* féliciter (**s.o. on sth** qn de qch). ◆**congratu-'lations** *npl* félicitations *fpl* (**on** pour). ◆**congratu'latory** *a* (*telegram etc*) de félicitations.

congregate ['kɒŋgrɪgeɪt] *vi* se rassembler. ◆**congre'gation** *n* (*worshippers*) assemblée *f*, fidèles *mfpl*.

congress ['kɒŋgres] *n* congrès *m*; **C.** *Pol Am* le Congrès. ◆**Congressman** *n* (*pl -men*) *Am* membre *m* du Congrès. ◆**Con-'gressional** *a Am* du Congrès.

conic(al) ['kɒnɪk(ə)l] *a* conique.

conifer ['kɒnɪfər] *n* (*tree*) conifère *m*.

conjecture [kən'dʒektʃər] *n* conjecture *f*; − *vt* conjecturer; − *vi* faire des conjectures. ◆**conjectural** *a* conjectural.

conjugal ['kɒndʒugəl] *a* conjugal.

conjugate ['kɒndʒugeɪt] *vt* (*verb*) conjuguer. ◆**conju'gation** *n Gram* conjugaison *f*.

conjunction [kən'dʒʌŋkʃ(ə)n] *n Gram* conjonction *f*; **in c. with** conjointement avec.

conjur/e ['kʌndʒər] *vt* **to c. (up)** (*by magic*) faire apparaître; **to c. up** (*memories etc*) *Fig* évoquer. ◆**—ing** *n* prestidigitation *f*. ◆**—er** *n* prestidigitateur, -trice *mf*.

conk [kɒŋk] **1** *n* (*nose*) *Sl* pif *m*. **2** *vi* **to c. out** (*break down*) *Fam* claquer, tomber en panne.

conker ['kɒŋkər] *n* (*horse-chestnut fruit*) *Fam* marron *m* (d'Inde).

connect [kə'nekt] *vt* relier (**with, to** à); (*telephone, stove etc*) brancher; **to c. with** *Tel* mettre en communication avec; (*in memory*) associer avec; − *vi* (*be connected*) être relié; **to c. with** (*of train, bus*) assurer la correspondance avec. ◆**—ed** *a* (*facts etc*) lié, connexe; (*speech*) suivi; **to be c. with** (*have dealings with*) être lié à; (*have to do with, relate to*) avoir rapport à; (*by marriage*) être allié à. ◆**connection** *n* (*link*) rapport *m*, relation *f* (**with** avec);

(*train, bus etc*) correspondance *f*; (*phone call*) communication *f*; (*between pipes etc*) *Tech* raccord *m*; *pl* (*contacts*) relations *fpl*; **in c. with** à propos de.

connive [kə'naɪv] *vi* **to c. at** fermer les yeux sur; **to c. to do** se mettre de connivence pour faire (**with** avec); **to c. together** agir en complicité. ◆**connivance** *n* connivence *f*.

connoisseur [kɒnə'sɜːr] *n* connaisseur *m*.

connotation [kɒnə'teɪʃ(ə)n] *n* connotation *f*.

conquer ['kɒŋkər] *vt* (*country, freedom etc*) conquérir; (*enemy, habit*) vaincre. ◆**—ing** *a* victorieux. ◆**conqueror** *n* conquérant, -ante *mf*, vainqueur *m*. ◆**conquest** *n* conquête *f*.

cons [kɒnz] *npl* **the pros and (the) c.** le pour et le contre.

conscience ['kɒnʃəns] *n* conscience *f*. ◆**c.-stricken** *a* pris de remords.

conscientious [kɒnʃɪ'enʃəs] *a* consciencieux; **c. objector** objecteur *m* de conscience. ◆**—ness** *n* application *f*, sérieux *m*.

conscious ['kɒnʃəs] *a* conscient (**of sth** de qch); (*intentional*) délibéré; *Med* conscient; **to be c. of doing** avoir conscience de faire. ◆**—ly** *adv* (*knowingly*) consciemment. ◆**—ness** *n* conscience *f* (**of** de); *Med* connaissance *f*.

conscript ['kɒnskrɪpt] *n Mil* conscrit *m*; − [kən'skrɪpt] *vt* enrôler (par conscription). ◆**con'scription** *n* conscription *f*.

consecrate ['kɒnsɪkreɪt] *vt* (*church etc*) *Rel* consacrer. ◆**conse'cration** *n* consécration *f*.

consecutive [kən'sekjutɪv] *a* consécutif. ◆**—ly** *adv* consécutivement.

consensus [kən'sensəs] *n* consensus *m*, accord *m* (général).

consent [kən'sent] *vi* consentir (**to** à); − *n* consentement *m*; **by common c.** de l'aveu de tous; **by mutual c.** d'un commun accord.

consequence ['kɒnsɪkwəns] *n* (*result*) conséquence *f*; (*importance*) importance *f*, conséquence *f*. ◆**consequently** *adv* par conséquent.

conservative [kən'sɜːvətɪv] **1** *a* (*estimate*) modeste; (*view*) traditionnel. **2** *a* & *n* **C.** *Pol* conservateur, -trice (*mf*). ◆**conservatism** *n* (*in behaviour*) & *Pol Rel* conservatisme *m*.

conservatoire [kən'sɜːvətwɑːr] *n Mus* conservatoire *m*.

conservatory [kən'sɜːvətrɪ] *n* (*greenhouse*) serre *f*.

conserve [kən'sɜːv] *vt* préserver, conserver;

(*one's strength*) ménager; **to c. energy** faire des économies d'énergie. ◆**conser-'vation** n (*energy-saving*) économies *fpl* d'énergie; (*of nature*) protection *f* de l'environnement; *Phys* conservation *f*.

consider [kən'sɪdər] *vt* considérer; (*take into account*) tenir compte de; **I'll c. it** j'y réfléchirai; **to c. doing** envisager de faire; **to c. that** estimer *or* considérer que; **he's** *or* **she's being considered (for the job)** sa candidature est à l'étude; **all things considered** en fin de compte. ◆**—ing** *prep* étant donné, vu. ◆**—able** *a* (*large*) considérable; (*much*) beaucoup de. ◆**—ably** *adv* beaucoup, considérablement. ◆**conside-'ration** n (*thought, thoughtfulness, reason*) considération *f*; **under c.** à l'étude; **out of c. for** par égard pour; **to take into c.** prendre en considération.

considerate [kən'sɪdərət] *a* plein d'égards (**to** pour), attentionné (**to** à l'égard de).

consign [kən'saɪn] *vt* (*send*) expédier; (*give, entrust*) confier (**to** à). ◆**—ment** n (*act*) expédition *f*; (*goods*) arrivage *m*.

consist [kən'sɪst] *vi* consister (**of** en, **in** dans, **in doing** à faire).

consistent [kən'sɪstənt] *a* logique, conséquent; (*coherent*) cohérent; (*friend*) fidèle; **c. with** compatible avec, conforme à. ◆**—ly** *adv* (*logically*) avec logique; (*always*) constamment. ◆**consistency** n **1** logique *f*; cohérence *f*. **2** (*of liquid etc*) consistance *f*.

console[1] [kən'səʊl] *vt* consoler. ◆**conso-'lation** n consolation *f*; **c. prize** prix *m* de consolation.

console[2] ['kɒnsəʊl] n (*control desk*) *Tech* console *f*.

consolidate [kən'sɒlɪdeɪt] *vt* consolider; — *vi* se consolider. ◆**consoli'dation** n consolidation *f*.

consonant ['kɒnsənənt] n consonne *f*.

consort 1 ['kɒnsɔːt] n époux *m*, épouse *f*; **prince c.** prince *m* consort. **2** [kən'sɔːt] *vi* **to c. with** *Pej* fréquenter.

consortium [kən'sɔːtɪəm] n *Com* consortium *m*.

conspicuous [kən'spɪkjʊəs] *a* visible, en évidence; (*striking*) remarquable, manifeste; (*showy*) voyant; **to be c. by one's absence** briller par son absence; **to make oneself c.** se faire remarquer. ◆**—ly** *adv* visiblement.

conspire [kən'spaɪər] **1** *vi* (*plot*) conspirer (**against** contre); **to c. to do** comploter de faire. **2** *vt* **to c. to do** (*of events*) conspirer à faire. ◆**conspiracy** n conspiration *f*.

constable ['kʌnstəb(ə)l] n (*police*) **c.** agent *m* (de police). ◆**con'stabulary** n la police.

constant ['kɒnstənt] *a* (*frequent*) incessant; (*unchanging*) constant; (*faithful*) fidèle. ◆**constancy** n constance *f*. ◆**constantly** *adv* constamment, sans cesse.

constellation [kɒnstə'leɪʃ(ə)n] n constellation *f*.

consternation [kɒnstə'neɪʃ(ə)n] n consternation *f*.

constipate ['kɒnstɪpeɪt] *vt* constiper. ◆**consti'pation** n constipation *f*.

constituent [kən'stɪtjʊənt] **1** *a* (*element etc*) constituant, constitutif. **2** n *Pol* électeur, -trice *mf*. ◆**constituency** n circonscription *f* électorale; (*voters*) électeurs *mpl*.

constitute ['kɒnstɪtjuːt] *vt* constituer. ◆**consti'tution** n (*of person etc*) & *Pol* constitution *f*. ◆**consti'tutional** *a* *Pol* constitutionnel.

constrain [kən'streɪn] *vt* contraindre.

constrict [kən'strɪkt] *vt* (*tighten, narrow*) resserrer; (*movement*) gêner. ◆**con-'striction** n resserrement *m*.

construct [kən'strʌkt] *vt* construire. ◆**con-struction** n construction *f*; **under c.** en construction. ◆**constructive** *a* constructif.

construe [kən'struː] *vt* interpréter, comprendre.

consul ['kɒnsəl] n consul *m*. ◆**consular** *a* consulaire. ◆**consulate** n consulat *m*.

consult [kən'sʌlt] *vt* consulter; — *vi* **to c. with** discuter avec, conférer avec. ◆**—ing** *a* (*room*) *Med* de consultation; (*physician*) consultant. ◆**consultancy** n **c. (firm)** *Com* cabinet *m* d'experts-conseils; **c. fee** honoraires *mpl* de conseils. ◆**consultant** n conseiller, -ère *mf*; *Med* spécialiste *mf*; (*financial, legal*) conseil *m*, expert-conseil *m*; — *a* (*engineer etc*) consultant. ◆**consul'tation** n consultation *f*. ◆**con-sultative** *a* consultatif.

consum/e [kən'sjuːm] *vt* (*food, supplies etc*) consommer; (*of fire, grief, hate*) consumer. ◆**—ing** *a* (*ambition*) brûlant. ◆**—er** n consommateur, -trice *mf*; **c. goods/society** biens *mpl*/société *f* de consommation. ◆**con'sumption** n consommation *f* (**of** de).

consummate ['kɒnsəmət] *a* (*perfect*) consommé.

contact ['kɒntækt] n contact *m*; (*person*) relation *f*; **in c. with** en contact avec; **c. lenses** lentilles *fpl or* verres *mpl* de contact; — *vt* se mettre en contact avec, contacter.

contagious [kən'teɪdʒəs] *a* contagieux.
contain [kən'teɪn] *vt* (*enclose, hold back*) contenir; **to c. oneself** se contenir. ◆**—er** *n* récipient *m*; (*for transporting freight*) conteneur *m*, container *m*.
contaminate [kən'tæmɪneɪt] *vt* contaminer. ◆**contami'nation** *n* contamination *f*.
contemplate ['kɒntəmpleɪt] *vt* (*look at*) contempler; (*consider*) envisager (**doing** de faire). ◆**contem'plation** *n* contemplation *f*; **in c. of** en prévision de.
contemporary [kən'tempərərɪ] *a* contemporain (**with** de); – *n* (*person*) contemporain, -aine *mf*.
contempt [kən'tempt] *n* mépris *m*; **to hold in c.** mépriser. ◆**contemptible** *a* méprisable. ◆**contemptuous** *a* dédaigneux (**of** de).
contend [kən'tend] **1** *vi* **to c. with** (*problem*) faire face à; (*person*) avoir affaire à; (*compete*) rivaliser avec; (*struggle*) se battre avec. **2** *vt* **to c. that** (*claim*) soutenir que. ◆**—er** *n* concurrent, -ente *mf*. ◆**contention** *n* **1** (*argument*) dispute *f*. **2** (*claim*) affirmation *f*. ◆**contentious** *a* (*issue*) litigieux.
content[1] [kən'tent] *a* satisfait (**with** de); **he's c. to do** il ne demande pas mieux que de faire. ◆**—ed** *a* satisfait. ◆**—ment** *n* contentement *m*.
content[2] ['kɒntent] *n* (*of text, film etc*) contenu *m*; *pl* (*of container*) contenu *m*; (**table of**) **contents** (*of book*) table *f* des matières; **alcoholic/iron/***etc* **c.** teneur *f* en alcool/fer/*etc*.
contest [kən'test] *vt* (*dispute*) contester; (*fight for*) disputer; – ['kɒntest] *n* (*competition*) concours *m*, (*fight*) lutte *f*; *Boxing* combat *m*. ◆**con'testant** *n* concurrent, -ente *mf*; (*in fight*) adversaire *mf*.
context ['kɒntekst] *n* contexte *m*.
continent ['kɒntɪnənt] *n* continent *m*; **the C.** l'Europe *f* (continentale). ◆**conti'nental** *a* continental; européen; **c. breakfast** petit déjeuner *m* à la française.
contingent [kən'tɪndʒənt] **1** *a* (*accidental*) contingent; **to be c. upon** dépendre de. **2** *nm Mil* contingent *m*. ◆**contingency** *n* éventualité *f*; **c. plan** plan *m* d'urgence.
continu/e [kən'tɪnjuː] *vt* continuer (**to do** *or* **doing** à *or* de faire); (*resume*) reprendre; **to c.** (**with**) (*work, speech etc*) poursuivre, continuer; – *vi* continuer; (*resume*) reprendre; **to c. in** (*job*) garder. ◆**—ed** *a* (*interest, attention etc*) soutenu, assidu; (*presence*) continu(el); **to be c.** (*of story*) à suivre. ◆**continual** *a* continuel. ◆**continually**

adv continuellement. ◆**continuance** *n* continuation *f*. ◆**continu'ation** *n* continuation *f*; (*resumption*) reprise *f*; (*new episode*) suite *f*. ◆**continuity** [kɒntɪ'njuːɪtɪ] *n* continuité *f*. ◆**continuous** *a* continu; **c. performance** *Cin* spectacle *m* permanent. ◆**continuously** *adv* sans interruption.
contort [kən'tɔːt] *vt* (*twist*) tordre; **to c. oneself** se contorsionner. ◆**contortion** *n* contorsion *f*. ◆**contortionist** *n* (*acrobat*) contorsionniste *mf*.
contour ['kɒntuər] *n* contour *m*.
contraband ['kɒntrəbænd] *n* contrebande *f*.
contraception [kɒntrə'sepʃ(ə)n] *n* contraception *f*. ◆**contraceptive** *a* & *n* contraceptif (*m*).
contract 1 ['kɒntrækt] *n* contrat *m*; **c. work** travail *m* en sous-traitance; – *vi* **to c. out of** (*agreement etc*) se dégager de. **2** [kən'trækt] *vt* (*habit, debt, muscle etc*) contracter; – *vi* (*of heart etc*) se contracter. ◆**con'traction** *n* (*of muscle, word*) contraction *f*. ◆**con'tractor** *n* entrepreneur *m*.
contradict [kɒntrə'dɪkt] *vt* contredire; (*belie*) démentir. ◆**contradiction** *n* contradiction *f*. ◆**contradictory** *a* contradictoire.
contralto [kən'træltəʊ] *n* (*pl* **-os**) contralto *m*.
contraption [kən'træpʃ(ə)n] *n Fam* machin *m*, engin *m*.
contrary 1 ['kɒntrərɪ] *a* contraire (**to** à); – *adv* **c. to** contrairement à; – *n* contraire *m*; **on the c.** au contraire; **unless you, I** *etc* **hear to the c.** sauf avis contraire; **she said nothing to the c.** elle n'a rien dit contre. **2** [kən'treərɪ] *a* (*obstinate*) entêté, difficile.
contrast 1 ['kɒntrɑːst] *n* contraste *m*; **in c. to** par opposition à. **2** [kən'trɑːst] *vi* contraster (**with** avec); – *vt* faire contraster, mettre en contraste. ◆**—ing** *a* (*colours etc*) opposés.
contravene [kɒntrə'viːn] *vt* (*law*) enfreindre. ◆**contravention** *n* **in c. of** en contravention de.
contribute [kən'trɪbjuːt] *vt* donner, fournir (**to** à); (*article*) écrire (**to** pour); **to c. money to** contribuer à, verser de l'argent à; – *vi* **to c. to** contribuer à; (*publication*) collaborer à. ◆**contri'bution** *n* contribution *f*; (*to pension fund etc*) cotisation(s) *f*(*pl*); *Journ* article *m*. ◆**contributor** *n Journ* collaborateur, -trice *mf*; (*of money*) donateur, -trice *mf*. ◆**contributory** *a* **a c. factor** un facteur qui a contribué (**in** à).
contrite [kən'traɪt] *a* contrit. ◆**contrition** *n* contrition *f*.
contriv/e [kən'traɪv] *vt* inventer; **to c. to do**

trouver moyen de faire. ◆**—ed** a artificiel. ◆**contrivance** n (device) dispositif m; (scheme) invention f.

control [kən'trəʊl] vt (-ll-) (business, organization) diriger; (traffic) régler; (prices, quality) contrôler; (emotion, reaction) maîtriser, contrôler; (disease) enrayer; (situation) être maître de; **to c. oneself** se contrôler; – n (authority) autorité f (**over** sur); (of traffic) réglementation f; (of prices etc) contrôle m; (of emotion etc) maîtrise f; pl (of train etc) commandes fpl; (knobs) TV Rad boutons mpl; (**self-**)**c.** le contrôle de soi-même; **to keep s.o. under c.** tenir qn; **everything is under c.** tout est en ordre; **in c. of** maître de; **to lose c. of** (situation, vehicle) perdre le contrôle de; **out of c.** (situation, crowd) difficilement maîtrisable; **c. tower** Av tour f de contrôle. ◆**controller** n air traffic **c.** aiguilleur m du ciel.

controversy ['kɒntrəvɜːsɪ] n controverse f. ◆**contro'versial** a (book, author) contesté, discuté; (doubtful) discutable.

conundrum [kə'nʌndrəm] n devinette f, énigme f; (mystery) énigme f.

conurbation [kɒnɜː'beɪʃ(ə)n] n agglomération f, conurbation f.

convalesce [kɒnvə'les] vi être en convalescence. ◆**convalescence** n convalescence f. ◆**convalescent** n convalescent, -ente mf; **c. home** maison f de convalescence.

convector [kən'vektər] n radiateur m à convection.

convene [kən'viːn] vt convoquer; – vi se réunir.

convenient [kən'viːnɪənt] a commode, pratique; (well-situated) bien situé (**for the shops/**etc par rapport aux magasins/etc); (moment) convenable, opportun; **to be c. (for)** (suit) convenir (à). ◆**—ly** adv (to arrive) à propos; **c. situated** bien situé. ◆**convenience** n commodité f; (comfort) confort m; (advantage) avantage m; **to or at one's c.** à sa convenance; **c. food(s)** plats mpl or aliments mpl minute; (**public**) **conveniences** toilettes fpl.

convent ['kɒnvənt] n couvent m.

convention [kən'venʃ(ə)n] n (agreement) & Am Pol convention f; (custom) usage m, convention f; (meeting) Pol assemblée f. ◆**conventional** a conventionnel.

converg/e [kən'vɜːdʒ] vi converger. ◆**—ing** a convergent. ◆**convergence** n convergence f.

conversant [kən'vɜːsənt] a **to be c. with**

(custom etc) connaître; (fact) savoir; (cars etc) s'y connaître en.

conversation [kɒnvə'seɪʃ(ə)n] n conversation f. ◆**conversational** a (tone) de la conversation; (person) loquace. ◆**conversationalist** n causeur, -euse mf.

converse 1 [kən'vɜːs] vi s'entretenir (**with** avec). **2** ['kɒnvɜːs] a & n inverse (m). ◆**con'versely** adv inversement.

convert [kən'vɜːt] vt (change) convertir (**into** en); (building) aménager (**into** en); **to c. s.o.** convertir qn (**to** à); – ['kɒnvɜːt] n converti, -ie mf. ◆**con'version** n conversion f; aménagement m. ◆**con'vertible** a convertible; – n (car) (voiture f) décapotable f.

convex ['kɒnveks] a convexe.

convey [kən'veɪ] vt (goods, people) transporter; (sound, message, order) transmettre; (idea) communiquer; (evoke) évoquer; (water etc through pipes) amener. ◆**conveyance** n transport m; Aut véhicule m. ◆**conveyor** n transport m; Aut véhicule m.

convict ['kɒnvɪkt] n forçat m; – [kən'vɪkt] vt déclarer coupable, condamner. ◆**con'viction** n Jur condamnation f; (belief) conviction f; **to carry c.** (of argument etc) être convaincant.

convinc/e [kən'vɪns] vt convaincre, persuader. ◆**—ing** a convaincant. ◆**—ingly** adv de façon convaincante.

convivial [kən'vɪvɪəl] a joyeux, gai; (person) bon vivant.

convoke [kən'vəʊk] vt (meeting etc) convoquer.

convoluted [kɒnvə'luːtɪd] a (argument, style) compliqué, tarabiscoté.

convoy ['kɒnvɔɪ] n (ships, cars, people) convoi m.

convulse [kən'vʌls] vt bouleverser, ébranler; (face) convulser. ◆**convulsion** n convulsion f. ◆**convulsive** a convulsif.

coo [kuː] vi (of dove) roucouler.

cook [kʊk] vt (faire) cuire; (accounts) Fam truquer; **to c. up** Fam inventer; – vi (of food) cuire; (of person) faire la cuisine; **what's cooking?** Fam qu'est-ce qui se passe?; – n (person) cuisinier, -ière mf. ◆**—ing** n cuisine f; **c. apple** pomme f à cuire. ◆**—er** n (stove) cuisinière f; (apple) pomme f à cuire. ◆**cookbook** n livre m de cuisine. ◆**cookery** n cuisine f; **c. book** livre m de cuisine.

cookie ['kʊkɪ] n Am biscuit m, gâteau m sec.

cool [kuːl] a (-er, -est) (weather, place etc) frais; (manner, person) calme; (reception etc) froid; (impertinent) Fam effronté; **I feel**

c. j'ai (un peu) froid; **a c. drink** une boisson fraîche; **a c. £50** la coquette somme de 50 livres; − *n* (*of evening*) fraîcheur *f*; **to keep (in the) c.** tenir au frais; **to keep/lose one's c.** garder/perdre son sang-froid; − *vt* **to c. (down)** refroidir, rafraîchir; − *vi* **to c. (down** *or* **off)** (*of enthusiasm*) se refroidir; (*of anger, angry person*) se calmer; (*of hot liquid*) refroidir; **to c. off** (*refresh oneself by drinking, bathing etc*) se rafraîchir; **to c. off towards s.o.** se refroidir envers qn. ◆**—ing** *n* (*of air, passion etc*) refroidissement *m*. ◆**—er** *n* (*for food*) glacière *f*. ◆**—ly** *adv* calmement; (*to welcome*) froidement; (*boldly*) effrontément. ◆**—ness** *n* fraîcheur *f*; (*unfriendliness*) froideur *f*. ◆**cool-'headed** *a* calme.

coop [kuːp] **1** *n* (*for chickens*) poulailler *m*. **2** *vt* **to c. up** (*person*) enfermer.

co-op ['kəʊɒp] *n Am* appartement *m* en copropriété.

co-operate [kəʊ'ɒpəreɪt] *vi* coopérer (**in** à, **with** avec). ◆**co-ope'ration** *n* coopération *f*. ◆**co-operative** *a* coopératif; − *n* coopérative *f*.

co-opt [kəʊ'ɒpt] *vt* coopter.

co-ordinate [kəʊ'ɔːdɪneɪt] *vt* coordonner. ◆**co-ordinates** [kəʊ'ɔːdɪnəts] *npl Math* coordonnées *fpl*; (*clothes*) coordonnés *mpl*. ◆**co-ordi'nation** *n* coordination *f*.

cop [kɒp] **1** *n* (*policeman*) *Fam* flic *m*. **2** *vt* (**-pp-**) (*catch*) *Sl* piquer. **3** *vi* (**-pp-**) **to c. out** *Sl* se défiler, éviter ses responsabilités.

cope [kəʊp] *vi* **to c. with** s'occuper de; (*problem*) faire face à; (**to be able to**) **to c.** (*savoir*) se débrouiller.

co-pilot ['kəʊpaɪlət] *n* copilote *m*.

copious ['kəʊpɪəs] *a* copieux.

copper ['kɒpər] *n* **1** cuivre *m*; *pl* (*coins*) petite monnaie *f*. **2** (*policeman*) *Fam* flic *m*.

coppice ['kɒpɪs] *n*, ◆**copse** [kɒps] *n* taillis *m*.

copulate ['kɒpjʊleɪt] *vi* s'accoupler. ◆**copu'lation** *n* copulation *f*.

copy ['kɒpɪ] *n* copie *f*; (*of book etc*) exemplaire *m*; *Phot* épreuve *f*; − *vti* copier; − *vt* **to c. out** *or* **down** (re)copier. ◆**copyright** *n* copyright *m*.

coral ['kɒrəl] *n* corail *m*; **c. reef** récif *m* de corail.

cord [kɔːd] **1** *n* (*of curtain, pyjamas etc*) cordon *m*; *El* cordon *m* électrique; **vocal cords** cordes *fpl* vocales. **2** *npl Fam* velours *m*, pantalon *m* en velours (côtelé).

cordial ['kɔːdɪəl] **1** *a* (*friendly*) cordial. **2** *n* (*fruit*) **c.** sirop *m*.

cordon ['kɔːdən] *n* cordon *m*; − *vt* **to c. off** (*place*) boucler, interdire l'accès à.

corduroy ['kɔːdərɔɪ] *n* (*fabric*) velours *m* côtelé; *pl* pantalon *m* en velours (côtelé), velours *m*.

core [kɔːr] *n* (*of fruit*) trognon *m*; (*of problem*) cœur *m*; (*group of people*) & *Geol* El noyau *m*; − *vt* (*apple*) vider. ◆**corer** *n* vide-pomme *m*.

cork [kɔːk] *n* liège *m*; (*for bottle*) bouchon *m*; − *vt* **to c. (up)** (*bottle*) boucher. ◆**corkscrew** *n* tire-bouchon *m*.

corn [kɔːn] *n* **1** (*wheat*) blé *m*; (*maize*) *Am* maïs *m*; (*seed*) grain *m*; **c. on the cob** épi *m* de maïs. **2** (*hard skin*) cor *m*. ◆**corned** *a* **c. beef** corned-beef *m*, singe *m*. ◆**cornflakes** *npl* céréales *fpl*. ◆**cornflour** *n* farine *f* de maïs, maïzena® *f*. ◆**cornflower** *n* bleuet *m*. ◆**cornstarch** *n Am* = **cornflour**.

cornea ['kɔːnɪə] *n Anat* cornée *f*.

corner ['kɔːnər] **1** *n* coin *m*; (*of street, room*) coin *m*, angle *m*; (*bend in road*) virage *m*; *Fb* corner *m*; **in a (tight) c.** dans une situation difficile. **2** *vt* (*animal, enemy etc*) acculer; (*person in corridor etc*) *Fig* coincer, accrocher; (*market*) *Com* accaparer; − *vi Aut* prendre un virage. ◆**cornerstone** *n* pierre *f* angulaire.

cornet ['kɔːnɪt] *n* (*of ice cream etc*) & *Mus* cornet *m*.

Cornwall ['kɔːnwəl] *n* Cornouailles *fpl*. ◆**Cornish** *a* de Cornouailles.

corny ['kɔːnɪ] *a* (**-ier, -iest**) (*joke etc*) rebattu.

corollary [kə'rɒlərɪ, *Am* 'kɒrələrɪ] *n* corollaire *m*.

coronary ['kɒrənərɪ] *n Med* infarctus *m*.

coronation [kɒrə'neɪʃ(ə)n] *n* couronnement *m*, sacre *m*.

coroner ['kɒrənər] *n Jur* coroner *m*.

corporal ['kɔːpərəl] **1** *n Mil* caporal(-chef) *m*. **2** *a* **c. punishment** châtiment *m* corporel.

corporation [kɔːpə'reɪʃ(ə)n] *n* (*business*) société *f* commerciale; (*of town*) conseil *m* municipal. ◆**'corporate** *a* collectif; **c. body** corps *m* constitué.

corps [kɔːr, *pl* kɔːz] *n Mil Pol* corps *m*.

corpse [kɔːps] *n* cadavre *m*.

corpulent ['kɔːpjʊlənt] *a* corpulent. ◆**corpulence** *n* corpulence *f*.

corpus ['kɔːpəs] *n Ling* corpus *m*.

corpuscle ['kɔːpʌs(ə)l] *n Med* globule *m*.

corral [kə'ræl] *n Am* corral *m*.

correct [kə'rekt] *a* (*right, accurate*) exact, correct; (*proper*) correct; **he's c.** il a raison; − *vt* corriger. ◆**—ly** *adv* correctement.

◆**—ness** n (*accuracy, propriety*) correction f. ◆**correction** n correction f. ◆**corrective** a (*act, measure*) rectificatif.

correlate ['kɒrəleɪt] vi correspondre (**with** à); – vt faire correspondre. ◆**corre'lation** n corrélation f.

correspond [kɒrɪ'spɒnd] vi **1** (*agree, be similar*) correspondre (**to** à, **with** avec). **2** (*by letter*) correspondre (**with** avec). ◆**—ing** a (*matching*) correspondant; (*similar*) semblable. ◆**correspondence** n correspondance f; **c. course** cours m par correspondance. ◆**correspondent** n correspondant, -ante mf; *Journ* envoyé, -ée mf.

corridor ['kɒrɪdɔːr] n couloir m, corridor m.

corroborate [kə'rɒbəreɪt] vt corroborer.

corrode [kə'rəʊd] vt ronger, corroder; – vi se corroder. ◆**corrosion** n corrosion f. ◆**corrosive** a corrosif.

corrugated ['kɒrəgeɪtɪd] a (*cardboard*) ondulé; **c. iron** tôle f ondulée.

corrupt [kə'rʌpt] vt corrompre; – a corrompu. ◆**corruption** n corruption f.

corset ['kɔːsɪt] n (*boned*) corset m; (*elasticated*) gaine f.

Corsica ['kɔːsɪkə] n Corse f.

cos [kɒs] n **c.** (*lettuce*) (laitue f) romaine f.

cosh [kɒʃ] n matraque f; – vt matraquer.

cosiness ['kəʊzɪnəs] n intimité f, confort m.

cosmetic [kɒz'metɪk] n produit m de beauté; – a esthétique; *Fig* superficiel.

cosmopolitan [kɒzmə'pɒlɪtən] a & n cosmopolite (mf).

cosmos ['kɒzmɒs] n cosmos m. ◆**cosmic** a cosmique. ◆**cosmonaut** n cosmonaute mf.

Cossack ['kɒsæk] n cosaque m.

cosset ['kɒsɪt] vt choyer.

cost [kɒst] vti (*pt & pp* cost) coûter; **how much does it c.?** ça coûte or ça vaut combien?; **to c. the earth** *Fam* coûter les yeux de la tête; – n coût m, prix m; **at great c.** à grands frais; **to my c.** à mes dépens; **at any c., at all costs** à tout prix; **at c. price** au prix coûtant. ◆**c.-effective** a rentable. ◆**costly** a (-ier, -iest) (*expensive*) coûteux; (*valuable*) précieux.

co-star ['kəʊstɑːr] n *Cin Th* partenaire mf.

costume ['kɒstjuːm] n costume m; (*woman's suit*) tailleur m; (*swimming*) **c.** maillot m (de bain); **c. jewellery** bijoux mpl de fantaisie.

cosy ['kəʊzɪ] **1** a (-ier, -iest) douillet, intime; **make yourself nice (and) c.** mets-toi à l'aise; **we're c.** on est bien ici. **2** n (tea) **c.** couvre-théière m.

cot [kɒt] n lit m d'enfant; (*camp bed*) *Am* lit m de camp.

cottage ['kɒtɪdʒ] n petite maison f de campagne; (*thatched*) **c.** chaumière f; **c. cheese** fromage m blanc (maigre); **c. industry** travail m à domicile (*activité artisanale*).

cotton ['kɒtən] **1** n coton m; (*yarn*) fil m (de coton); **absorbent c.** *Am*, **c. wool** coton m hydrophile, ouate f; (*candy Am* barbe f à papa. **2** vi **to c. on (to)** *Sl* piger.

couch [kaʊtʃ] **1** n canapé m. **2** vt (*express*) formuler.

couchette [kuː'ʃet] n *Rail* couchette f.

cough [kɒf] **1** n toux f; **c. mixture** sirop m contre la toux; – vi tousser; – vt **to c. up** (*blood*) cracher. **2** vt **to c. up** (*money*) *Sl* cracher; – vi **to c. up** *Sl* payer, casquer.

could [kʊd, *unstressed* kəd] *see* can[1].

couldn't ['kʊd(ə)nt] = **could not.**

council ['kaʊns(ə)l] n conseil m; **c. flat/house** appartement m/maison f loué(e) à la municipalité, HLM m or f. ◆**councillor** n conseiller, -ère mf; (**town**) **c.** conseiller m municipal.

counsel ['kaʊnsəl] n (*advice*) conseil m; *Jur* avocat, -ate mf; – vt (**-ll-**, *Am* **-l-**) conseiller (**s.o. to do** à qn de faire). ◆**counsellor** n conseiller, -ère mf.

count[1] [kaʊnt] vt (*find number of, include*) compter; (*deem*) considérer; **not counting Paul** sans compter Paul; **to c. in** (*include*) inclure; **to c. out** exclure; (*money*) compter; – vi (*calculate, be important*) compter; **to c. against s.o.** être un désavantage pour qn, jouer contre qn; **to c. on s.o.** (*rely on*) compter sur qn; **to c. on doing** compter faire; – n compte m; *Jur* chef m (d'accusation); **he's lost c. of the books he has** il ne sait plus combien il a de livres. ◆**countdown** n compte m à rebours.

count[2] [kaʊnt] n (*title*) comte m.

countenance ['kaʊntɪnəns] **1** n (*face*) mine f, expression f. **2** vt (*allow*) tolérer; (*approve*) approuver.

counter ['kaʊntər] **1** n (*in shop, bar etc*) comptoir m; (*in bank etc*) guichet m; **under the c.** *Fig* clandestinement, au marché noir; **over the c.** (*to obtain medicine*) sans ordonnance. **2** n (*in games*) jeton m. **3** n *Tech* compteur m. **4** adv **c. to** à l'encontre de. **5** vt (*plan*) contrarier; (*insult*) riposter à; (*blow*) parer; – vi riposter (**with** par).

counter- ['kaʊntər] pref contre-.

counterattack ['kaʊntərətæk] n contre-attaque f; – vt contre-attaquer.

counterbalance ['kaʊntəbæləns] n contrepoids m; – vt contrebalancer.

counterclockwise [kauntə'klɒkwaɪz] *a* & *adv Am* dans le sens inverse des aiguilles d'une montre.

counterfeit ['kauntəfɪt] *a* faux; − *n* contrefaçon *f*, faux *m*; − *vt* contrefaire.

counterfoil ['kauntəfɔɪl] *n* souche *f*.

counterpart ['kauntəpɑːt] *n* (*thing*) équivalent *m*; (*person*) homologue *mf*.

counterpoint ['kauntəpɔɪnt] *n Mus* contrepoint *m*.

counterproductive [kauntəprə'dʌktɪv] *a* (*action*) inefficace, qui produit l'effet contraire.

countersign ['kauntəsaɪn] *vt* contresigner.

countess ['kauntes] *n* comtesse *f*.

countless ['kauntləs] *a* innombrable.

countrified ['kʌntrɪfaɪd] *a* rustique.

country ['kʌntrɪ] *n* pays *m*; (*region*) région *f*, pays *m*; (*homeland*) patrie *f*; (*opposed to town*) campagne *f*; − *a* (*house etc*) de campagne; **c. dancing** la danse folklorique. ◆**countryman** *n* (*pl* **-men**) (*fellow*) **c.** compatriote *m*. ◆**countryside** *n* campagne *f*.

county ['kauntɪ] *n* comté *m*; **c. seat** *Am*, **c. town** chef-lieu *m*.

coup [kuː, *pl* kuːz] *n Pol* coup *m* d'État.

couple ['kʌp(ə)l] **1** *n* (*of people, animals*) couple *m*; **a c. of** deux ou trois; (*a few*) quelques. **2** *vt* (*connect*) accoupler. **3** *vi* (*mate*) s'accoupler.

coupon ['kuːpɒn] *n* (*voucher*) bon *m*; (*ticket*) coupon *m*.

courage ['kʌrɪdʒ] *n* courage *m*. ◆**courageous** [kə'reɪdʒəs] *a* courageux.

courgette [kuə'ʒet] *n* courgette *f*.

courier ['kurɪər] *n* (*for tourists*) guide *m*; (*messenger*) messager *m*; **c. service** service *m* de messagerie.

course [kɔːs] **1** *n* (*duration, movement*) cours *m*; (*of ship*) route *f*; (*of river*) cours *m*; (*way*) *Fig* route *f*, chemin *m*; (*means*) moyen *m*; **c.** (*of action*) ligne *f* de conduite; (*option*) parti *m*; **your best c. is to** . . . le mieux c'est de . . . ; **as a matter of c.** normalement; **in (the) c. of time** avec le temps, à la longue; **in due c.** en temps utile. **2** *n Sch Univ* cours *m*; **c. of lectures** série *f* de conférences; **c.** (*of treatment*) *Med* traitement *m*. **3** *n Culin* plat *m*; **first c.** entrée *f*. **4** *n* (*racecourse*) champ *m* de courses; (*golf*) **c.** terrain *m* (de golf). **5** *adv* **of c.!** bien sûr!, mais oui!; **of c. not!** bien sûr que non!

court [kɔːt] **1** *n* (*of monarch*) cour *f*; *Jur* cour *f*, tribunal *m*; *Tennis* court *m*; **c. of enquiry** commission *f* d'enquête; **high c.** cour *f* suprême; **to take to c.** poursuivre en justice; **c. shoe** escarpin *m*. **2** *vt* (*woman*) faire la cour à; (*danger, support*) rechercher. ◆**-ing** *a* (*couple*) d'amoureux; **they are c.** ils sortent ensemble. ◆**courthouse** *n* palais *m* de justice. ◆**courtier** *n Hist* courtisan *m*. ◆**courtroom** *n* salle *f* du tribunal. ◆**courtship** *n* (*act, period of time*) cour *f*. ◆**courtyard** *n* cour *f*.

courteous ['kɜːtɪəs] *a* poli, courtois. ◆**courtesy** *n* politesse *f*, courtoisie *f*.

court-martial [kɔːt'mɑːʃəl] *n* conseil *m* de guerre; − *vt* (**-ll-**) faire passer en conseil de guerre.

cousin ['kʌz(ə)n] *n* cousin, -ine *mf*.

cove [kəuv] *n* (*bay*) *Geog* anse *f*.

covenant ['kʌvənənt] *n Jur* convention *f*; *Rel* alliance *f*.

Coventry ['kɒvəntrɪ] *n* **to send s.o. to C.** *Fig* mettre qn en quarantaine.

cover ['kʌvər] *n* (*lid*) couvercle *m*; (*of book*) & *Fin* couverture *f*; (*for furniture, typewriter*) housse *f*; (*bedspread*) dessus-de-lit *m*; **the covers** (*blankets*) les couvertures *fpl*; **to take c.** se mettre à l'abri; (*in restaurant*) couvert *m*; **c. charge** (*in restaurant*) couvert *m*; **c. note** certificat *m* provisoire d'assurance; **under separate c.** (*letter*) sous pli séparé; − *vt* couvrir; (*protect*) protéger, couvrir; (*distance*) parcourir, couvrir; (*include*) englober, recouvrir; (*treat*) traiter; (*event*) *Journ TV Rad* couvrir, faire le reportage de; (*aim gun at*) tenir en joue; (*insure*) assurer; **to c. over** recouvrir; **to c. up** recouvrir; (*truth, tracks*) dissimuler; (*scandal*) étouffer, camoufler; − *vi* **to c. (oneself) up** se couvrir; **to c. up for s.o.** couvrir qn. ◆**c.-up** *n* tentative *f* pour étouffer *or* camoufler une affaire. ◆**covering** *n* (*wrapping*) enveloppe *f*; (*layer*) couche *f*; **c. letter** lettre *f* jointe (*à un document*).

coveralls ['kʌvərɔːlz] *npl Am* bleus *mpl* de travail.

covert ['kəuvət, 'kʌvət] *a* secret.

covet ['kʌvɪt] *vt* convoiter. ◆**covetous** *a* avide.

cow [kau] **1** *n* vache *f*; (*of elephant etc*) femelle *f*; (*nasty woman*) *Fam* chameau *m*. **2** *vt* (*person*) intimider. ◆**cowboy** *n* cow-boy *m*. ◆**cowhand** *n* vacher, -ère *mf*. ◆**cowshed** *n* étable *f*.

coward ['kauəd] *n* lâche *mf*. ◆**-ly** *a* lâche. ◆**cowardice** *n* lâcheté *f*.

cower ['kauər] *vi* (*crouch*) se tapir; (*with fear*) *Fig* reculer (par peur).

cowslip ['kauslɪp] *n Bot* coucou *m*.

cox [kɒks] *vt Nau* barrer; − *n* barreur, -euse *mf*.

coy [kɔɪ] *a* (**-er, -est**) qui fait son *or* sa timide. ◆**coyness** *n* timidité *f* feinte.

coyote [kaɪˈəʊtɪ] *n* (*wolf*) *Am* coyote *m*.

cozy [ˈkəʊzɪ] *Am* = **cosy**.

crab [kræb] **1** *n* crabe *m*. **2** *n* **c. apple** pomme *f* sauvage. **3** *vi* (**-bb-**) (*complain*) *Fam* rouspéter. ◆**crabbed** *a* (*person*) grincheux.

crack[1] [kræk] *n* (*fissure*) fente *f*; (*in glass etc*) fêlure *f*; (*in skin*) crevasse *f*; (*snapping noise*) craquement *m*; (*of whip*) claquement *m*; (*blow*) coup *m*; (*joke*) *Fam* plaisanterie *f* (**at** aux dépens de); **to have a c. at doing** *Fam* essayer de faire; **at the c. of dawn** au point du jour; − *vt* (*glass, ice*) fêler; (*nut*) casser; (*ground, skin*) crevasser; (*whip*) faire claquer; (*joke*) lancer; (*problem*) résoudre; (*code*) déchiffrer; (*safe*) percer; **it's not as hard as it's cracked up to be** ce n'est pas aussi dur qu'on le dit; − *vi* se fêler; se crevasser; (*of branch, wood*) craquer; **to get cracking** (*get to work*) *Fam* s'y mettre; (*hurry*) se grouiller; **to c. down on** sévir contre; **to c. up** (*mentally*) *Fam* craquer. ◆**c.-up** *n Fam* dépression *f* nerveuse; (*crash*) *Am Fam* accident *m*. ◆**cracked** *a* (*crazy*) *Fam* fou. ◆**cracker** *n* **1** (*cake*) biscuit *m* (salé). **2** (*firework*) pétard *m*; **Christmas c.** diablotin *m*. **3 she's a c.** *Fam* elle est sensationnelle. ◆**crackers** *a* (*mad*) *Sl* cinglé. ◆**crackpot** *a Fam* fou; − *n* fou *m*, folle *f*.

crack[2] [kræk] *a* (*first-rate*) de premier ordre; **c. shot** tireur *m* d'élite.

crackle [ˈkræk(ə)l] *vi* crépiter; (*of sth frying*) *Culin* grésiller; − *n* crépitement *m*; grésillement *m*.

cradle [ˈkreɪd(ə)l] *n* berceau *m*; − *vt* bercer.

craft [krɑːft] **1** *n* (*skill*) art *m*; (*job*) métier *m* (artisanal); − *vt* façonner. **2** *n* (*cunning*) ruse *f*. **3** *n inv* (*boat*) bateau *m*. ◆**craftsman** *n* (*pl* **-men**) artisan *m*. ◆**craftsmanship** *n* (*skill*) art *m*; **a piece of c.** un beau travail, une belle pièce. ◆**crafty** *a* (**-ier, -iest**) *Pej* rusé.

crag [kræg] *n* rocher *m* à pic. ◆**craggy** *a* (*rock*) à pic; (*face*) rude.

cram [kræm] *vt* (**-mm-**) **to c. into** (*force*) fourrer dans; **to c. with** (*fill*) bourrer de; − *vi* **to c. into** (*of people*) s'entasser dans; **to c. (for an exam)** bachoter.

cramp [kræmp] *n Med* crampe *f* (**in** à). ◆**cramped** *a* (*in a room or one's clothes*) à l'étroit; **in c. conditions** à l'étroit.

cranberry [ˈkrænbərɪ] *n Bot* canneberge *f*.

crane [kreɪn] **1** *n* (*bird*) & *Tech* grue *f*. **2** *vt* **to c. one's neck** tendre le cou.

crank [kræŋk] **1** *n* (*person*) *Fam* excentrique *mf*; (*fanatic*) fanatique *mf*. **2** *n* (*handle*) *Tech* manivelle *f*; − *vt* **to c. (up)** (*vehicle*) faire démarrer à la manivelle. ◆**cranky** *a* (**-ier, -iest**) excentrique; (*bad-tempered*) *Am* grincheux.

crannies [ˈkrænɪz] *npl* **nooks and c.** coins et recoins *mpl*.

craps [kræps] *n* **to shoot c.** *Am* jouer aux dés.

crash [kræʃ] *n* accident *m*; (*of firm*) faillite *f*; (*noise*) fracas *m*; (*of thunder*) coup *m*; **c. course/diet** cours *m*/régime *m* intensif; **c. helmet** casque *m* (anti-choc); **c. landing** atterrissage *m* en catastrophe; − *int* (*of fallen object*) patatras!; − *vt* (*car*) avoir un accident avec; **to c. one's car into** faire rentrer sa voiture dans; − *vi Aut Av* s'écraser; **to c. into** rentrer dans; **the cars crashed (into each other)** les voitures se sont percutées *or* carambolées; **to c. (down)** tomber; (*break*) se casser; (*of roof*) s'effondrer. ◆**c.-land** *vi* atterrir en catastrophe.

crass [kræs] *a* grossier; (*stupidity*) crasse.

crate [kreɪt] *n* caisse *f*, cageot *m*.

crater [ˈkreɪtər] *n* cratère *m*; (*bomb*) **c.** entonnoir *m*.

cravat [krəˈvæt] *n* foulard *m* (*autour du cou*).

crav/e [kreɪv] *vt* **to c. (for)** éprouver un grand besoin de; (*mercy*) implorer. ◆**—ing** *n* désir *m*, grand besoin *m* (**for** de).

craven [ˈkreɪvən] *a Pej* lâche.

crawl [krɔːl] *vi* ramper; (*of child*) se traîner (à quatre pattes); *Aut* avancer au pas; **to be crawling with** grouiller de; − *n Swimming* crawl *m*; **to move at a c.** *Aut* avancer au pas.

crayfish [ˈkreɪfɪʃ] *n inv* écrevisse *f*.

crayon [ˈkreɪən] *n* crayon *m*, pastel *m*.

craze [kreɪz] *n* manie *f* (**for** de), engouement *m* (**for** pour). ◆**crazed** *a* affolé.

crazy [ˈkreɪzɪ] *a* (**-ier, -iest**) fou; **c. about sth** fana de qch; **c. about s.o.** fou de qn; **c. paving** dallage *m* irrégulier. ◆**craziness** *n* folie *f*.

creak [kriːk] *vi* (*of hinge*) grincer; (*of timber*) craquer. ◆**creaky** *a* grinçant; qui craque.

cream [kriːm] *n* crème *f*; (*élite*) *Fig* crème *f*, gratin *m*; − *a* (*cake*) crème *f*; **c.(-coloured)** crème *inv*; **c. cheese** fromage *m* blanc; − *vt* (*milk*) écrémer; **to c. off** *Fig* écrémer. ◆**creamy** *a* (**-ier, -iest**) crémeux.

crease [kriːs] *vt* froisser, plisser; − *vi* se froisser; − *n* pli *m*; (*accidental*) (faux) pli *m*. ◆**c.-resistant** *a* infroissable.

create [kriː'eɪt] *vt* créer; (*impression, noise*) faire. ◆**creation** *n* création *f*. ◆**creative** *a* créateur, créatif. ◆**creativeness** *n* créativité *f*. ◆**crea'tivity** *n* créativité *f*. ◆**creator** *n* créateur, -trice *mf*.

creature ['kriːtʃər] *n* animal *m*, bête *f*; (*person*) créature *f*; **one's c. comforts** ses aises *fpl*.

crèche [kreʃ] *n* (*nursery*) crèche *f*; (*manger*) *Rel Am* crèche *f*.

credence ['kriːdəns] *n* **to give** *or* **lend c. to** ajouter foi à.

credentials [krɪ'denʃəlz] *npl* références *fpl*; (*identity*) pièces *fpl* d'identité; (*of diplomat*) lettres *fpl* de créance.

credible ['kredɪb(ə)l] *a* croyable; (*politician, information*) crédible. ◆**credi'bility** *n* crédibilité *f*.

credit ['kredɪt] *n* (*influence, belief*) & *Fin* crédit *m*; (*merit*) mérite *m*; *Univ* unité *f* de valeur; *pl* Cin générique *m*; **to give c. to** (*person*) *Fin* faire crédit à; *Fig* reconnaître le mérite de; (*statement*) ajouter foi à; **to be a c. to** faire honneur à; **on c.** à crédit; **in c.** (*account*) créditeur; **to one's c.** *Fig* à son actif; – *a* (*balance*) créditeur; **c. card** carte *f* de crédit; **c. facilities** facilités *fpl* de paiement; – *vt* (*believe*) croire; *Fin* créditer (**s.o. with sth** qn de qch); **to c. s.o. with** (*qualities*) attribuer à qn. ◆**creditable** *a* honorable. ◆**creditor** *n* créancier, -ière *mf*. ◆**creditworthy** *a* solvable.

credulous ['kredjʊləs] *a* crédule.

creed [kriːd] *n* credo *m*.

creek [kriːk] *n* (*bay*) crique *f*; (*stream*) *Am* ruisseau *m*; **up the c.** (*in trouble*) *Sl* dans le pétrin.

creep [kriːp] **1** *vi* (*pt & pp* crept) ramper; (*silently*) se glisser (furtivement); (*slowly*) avancer lentement; **it makes my flesh c.** ça me donne la chair de poule. **2** *n* (*person*) *Sl* salaud *m*; **it gives me the creeps** *Fam* ça me fait froid dans le dos. ◆**creepy** *a* (-**ier**, -**iest**) *Fam* terrifiant; (*nasty*) *Fam* vilain. ◆**creepy-'crawly** *n* *Fam*, *Am* ◆**creepy-'crawler** *n* *Fam* bestiole *f*.

cremate [krɪ'meɪt] *vt* incinérer. ◆**cremation** *n* crémation *f*. ◆**crema'torium** *n* crématorium *m*. ◆**'crematory** *n* *Am* crématorium *m*.

Creole ['kriːəʊl] *n* créole *mf*; *Ling* créole *m*.

crêpe [kreɪp] *n* (*fabric*) crêpe *m*; **c. (rubber)** crêpe *m*; **c. paper** papier *m* crêpon.

crept [krept] *see* **creep 1**.

crescendo [krɪ'ʃendəʊ] *n* (*pl* -**os**) crescendo *m inv*.

crescent ['kres(ə)nt] *n* croissant *m*; (*street*) *Fig* rue *f* (en demi-lune).

cress [kres] *n* cresson *m*.

crest [krest] *n* (*of bird, wave, mountain*) crête *f*; (*of hill*) sommet *m*; (*on seal, letters etc*) armoiries *fpl*.

Crete [kriːt] *n* Crète *f*.

cretin ['kretɪn, *Am* 'kriːt(ə)n] *n* crétin, -ine *mf*. ◆**cretinous** *a* crétin.

crevasse [krɪ'væs] *n* (*in ice*) *Geol* crevasse *f*.

crevice ['krevɪs] *n* (*crack*) crevasse *f*, fente *f*.

crew [kruː] *n* *Nau Av* équipage *m*; (*gang*) équipe *f*; **c. cut** (coupe *f* en) brosse *f*. ◆**c.-neck(ed)** *a* à col ras.

crib [krɪb] **1** *n* (*cradle*) berceau *m*; (*cot*) *Am* lit *m* d'enfant; *Rel* crèche *f*. **2** *n* (*copy*) plagiat *m*; *Sch* traduction *f*; (*list of answers*) *Sch* pompe *f* anti-sèche; – *vti* (-**bb-**) copier.

crick [krɪk] *n* **c. in the neck** torticolis *m*; **c. in the back** tour *m* de reins.

cricket ['krɪkɪt] *n* **1** (*game*) cricket *m*. **2** (*insect*) grillon *m*. ◆**cricketer** *n* joueur, -euse *mf* de cricket.

crikey! ['kraɪkɪ] *int Sl* zut (alors)!

crime [kraɪm] *n* crime *m*; (*not serious*) délit *m*; (*criminal practice*) criminalité *f*. ◆**criminal** *a* & *n* criminel, -elle (*mf*).

crimson ['krɪmz(ə)n] *a* & *n* cramoisi (*m*).

cring/e [krɪndʒ] *vi* reculer (**from** devant); *Fig* s'humilier (**to, before** devant). ◆**—ing** *a* *Fig* servile.

crinkle ['krɪŋk(ə)l] *vt* froisser; – *vi* se froisser; – *n* fronce *f*. ◆**crinkly** *a* froissé; (*hair*) frisé.

crippl/e ['krɪpəl] *n* (*lame*) estropié, -ée *mf*; (*disabled*) infirme *mf*; – *vt* estropier; (*disable*) rendre infirme; (*nation etc*) *Fig* paralyser. ◆**—ed** *a* estropié; infirme; (*ship*) désemparé; **c. with** (*rheumatism, pains*) perclus de. ◆**—ing** *a* (*tax*) écrasant.

crisis, *pl* -**ses** ['kraɪsɪs, -siːz] *n* crise *f*.

crisp [krɪsp] **1** *a* (-**er**, -**est**) (*biscuit*) croustillant; (*apple etc*) croquant; (*snow*) craquant; (*air, style*) vif. **2** *npl* (*potato*) **crisps** (pommes *fpl*) chips *mpl*. ◆**crispbread** *n* pain *m* suédois.

criss-cross ['krɪskrɒs] *a* (*lines*) entrecroisés; (*muddled*) enchevêtrés; – *vi* s'entrecroiser; – *vt* sillonner (en tous sens).

criterion, *pl* -**ia** [kraɪ'tɪərɪən, -ɪə] *n* critère *m*.

critic ['krɪtɪk] *n* critique *m*. ◆**critical** *a* critique. ◆**critically** *adv* (*to examine etc*) en critique; (*harshly*) sévèrement; (*ill*) gravement. ◆**criticism** *n* critique *f*. ◆**criticize** *vti* critiquer. ◆**cri'tique** *n* (*essay etc*) critique *f*.

croak [krəʊk] *vi* (*of frog*) croasser; – *n* croassement *m*.

crochet ['krəʊʃeɪ] *vt* faire au crochet; – *vi* faire du crochet; – *n* (travail *m* au) crochet *m*; **c. hook** crochet *m*.

crock [krɒk] *n* **a c., an (old) c.** *Fam* (*person*) un croulant; (*car*) un tacot.

crockery ['krɒkərɪ] *n* (*cups etc*) vaisselle *f*.

crocodile ['krɒkədaɪl] *n* crocodile *m*.

crocus ['krəʊkəs] *n* crocus *m*.

crony ['krəʊnɪ] *n Pej Fam* copain *m*, copine *f*.

crook [krʊk] *n* **1** (*thief*) escroc *m*. **2** (*shepherd's stick*) houlette *f*.

crooked ['krʊkɪd] *a* courbé; (*path*) tortueux; (*hat, picture*) de travers; (*deal, person*) malhonnête; – *adv* de travers. ◆—**ly** *adv* de travers.

croon [kruːn] *vti* chanter (à voix basse).

crop [krɒp] **1** *n* (*harvest*) récolte *f*; (*produce*) culture *f*; (*of questions etc*) *Fig* série *f*; (*of people*) groupe *m*. **2** *vt* (**-pp-**) (*hair*) couper (ras); – *n* **c. of hair** chevelure *f*. **3** *vi* (**-pp-**) **to c. up** se présenter, survenir. ◆**cropper** *n* **to come a c.** *Sl* (*fall*) ramasser une pelle; (*fail*) échouer.

croquet ['krəʊkeɪ] *n* (*game*) croquet *m*.

croquette [krəʊ'ket] *n Culin* croquette *f*.

cross¹ [krɒs] **1** *n* croix *f*; **a c. between** (*animal*) un croisement entre *or* de. **2** *vt* traverser; (*threshold, barrier*) franchir; (*legs, animals*) croiser; (*thwart*) contrecarrer; (*cheque*) barrer; **to c. off** *or* **out** rayer; **it never crossed my mind that . . .** il ne m'est pas venu à l'esprit que . . . ; **crossed lines** *Tel* lignes *fpl* embrouillées; – *vi* (*of paths*) se croiser; **to c. (over)** traverser. ◆—**ing** *n Nau* traversée *f*; (*pedestrian*) **c.** passage *m* clouté. ◆**cross-breed** *n* métis, -isse *mf*, hybride *m*. ◆**c.-'country** *a* à travers champs; **c.-country race** cross(-country) *m*. ◆**c.-exami'nation** *n* contre-interrogatoire *m*. ◆**c.-e'xamine** *vt* interroger. ◆**c.-eyed** *a* qui louche. ◆**c.-'legged** *a* & *adv* les jambes croisées. ◆**c.-'purposes** *npl* **to be at c.-purposes** se comprendre mal. ◆**c.-'reference** *n* renvoi *m*. ◆**c.-section** *n* coupe *f* transversale; *Fig* échantillon *m*.

cross² [krɒs] *a* (*angry*) fâché (**with** contre). ◆—**ly** *adv* d'un air fâché.

crossbow ['krɒsbəʊ] *n* arbalète *f*.

crosscheck [krɒs'tʃek] *n* contre-épreuve *f*; – *vt* vérifier.

crossfire ['krɒsfaɪər] *n* feux *mpl* croisés.

crossroads ['krɒsrəʊdz] *n* carrefour *m*.

crosswalk ['krɒswɔːk] *n Am* passage *m* clouté.

crossword ['krɒswɜːd] *n* **c. (puzzle)** mots *mpl* croisés.

crotch [krɒtʃ] *n* (*of garment*) entre-jambes *m inv.*

crotchet ['krɒtʃɪt] *n Mus* noire *f.*

crotchety ['krɒtʃɪtɪ] *a* grincheux.

crouch [kraʊtʃ] *vi* **to c. (down)** s'accroupir, se tapir. ◆—**ing** *a* accroupi, tapi.

croupier ['kruːpɪər] *n* (*in casino*) croupier *m*.

crow [krəʊ] **1** *n* corbeau *m*, corneille *f*; **as the c. flies** à vol d'oiseau; **c.'s nest** *Nau* nid *m* de pie. **2** *vi* (*of cock*) chanter; (*boast*) *Fig* se vanter (**about** de). ◆**crowbar** *n* levier *m*.

crowd [kraʊd] *n* foule *f*; (*particular group*) bande *f*; (*of things*) *Fam* masse *f*; **quite a c.** beaucoup de monde; – *vi* **to c. into** (*of people*) s'entasser dans; **to c. round s.o.** se presser autour de qn; **to c. together** se serrer; – *vt* (*fill*) remplir; **to c. into** (*press*) entasser dans; **don't c. me!** *Fam* ne me bouscule pas! ◆—**ed** *a* plein (**with** de); (*train etc*) bondé, plein; (*city*) encombré; **it's very c.!** il y a beaucoup de monde!

crown [kraʊn] *n* (*of king, tooth*) couronne *f*; (*of head, hill*) sommet *m*; **c. court** cour *f* d'assises; **C. jewels**, joyaux *mpl* de la Couronne; – *vt* couronner. ◆—**ing** *a* (*glory etc*) suprême; **c. achievement** couronnement *m*.

crucial ['kruːʃəl] *a* crucial.

crucify ['kruːsɪfaɪ] *vt* crucifier. ◆**crucifix** ['kruːsɪfɪks] *n* crucifix *m*. ◆**cruci'fixion** *n* crucifixion *f*.

crude [kruːd] *a* (**-er, -est**) (*oil, fact*) brut; (*manners, person*) grossier; (*language, light*) cru; (*painting, work*) rudimentaire. ◆—**ly** *adv* (*to say, order etc*) crûment. ◆—**ness** *n* grossièreté *f*; crudité *f*; état *m* rudimentaire.

cruel [krʊəl] *a* (**crueller, cruellest**) cruel. ◆**cruelty** *n* cruauté *f*; **an act of c.** une cruauté.

cruet ['kruːɪt] *n* **c. (stand)** salière *f*, poivrière *f* et huilier *m*.

cruis/e [kruːz] *vi Nau* croiser; *Aut* rouler; *Av* voler; (*of taxi*) marauder; (*of tourists*) faire une croisière; – *n* croisière *f*. ◆—**ing** *a* **c. speed** *Nau Av* & *Fig* vitesse *f* de croisière. ◆—**er** *n Nau* croiseur *m*.

crumb [krʌm] *n* miette *f*; (*of comfort*) *Fig* brin *m*; **crumbs!** *Hum Fam* zut!

crumble ['krʌmb(ə)l] *vt* (*bread*) émietter; – *vi* (*collapse*) s'effondrer; **to c. (away)** (*in small pieces*) & *Fig* s'effriter. ◆**crumbly** *a* friable.

crummy ['krʌmɪ] *a* (**-ier, -iest**) *Fam* moche, minable.

crumpet ['krʌmpɪt] *n Culin* petite crêpe *f* grillée (*servie beurrée*).

crumple ['krʌmp(ə)l] *vt* froisser; – *vi* se froisser.

crunch [krʌntʃ] **1** *vt* (*food*) croquer; – *vi* (*of snow*) craquer. **2** *n* **the c.** *Fam* le moment critique. ◆**crunchy** *a* (**-ier, -iest**) (*apple etc*) croquant.

crusade [kruːˈseɪd] *n Hist & Fig* croisade *f*; – *vi* faire une croisade. ◆**crusader** *n Hist* croisé *m*; *Fig* militant, -ante *mf*.

crush [krʌʃ] **1** *n* (*crowd*) cohue *f*; (*rush*) bousculade *f*; **to have a c. on s.o.** *Fam* avoir le béguin pour qn. **2** *vt* écraser; (*hope*) détruire; (*clothes*) froisser; (*cram*) entasser (**into** dans). ◆**—ing** *a* (*defeat*) écrasant.

crust [krʌst] *n* croûte *f*. ◆**crusty** *a* (**-ier, -iest**) (*bread*) croustillant.

crutch [krʌtʃ] *n* **1** *Med* béquille *f*. **2** (*crotch*) entre-jambes *m inv*.

crux [krʌks] *n* **the c. of** (*problem, matter*) le nœud de.

cry [kraɪ] *n* (*shout*) cri *m*; **to have a c.** *Fam* pleurer; – *vi* (*weep*) pleurer; **to c. (out)** pousser un cri, crier; (*exclaim*) s'écrier; **to c. (out) for** demander (à grands cris); **to be crying out for** avoir grand besoin de; **to c. off** (*withdraw*) abandonner; **to c. off (sth)** se désintéresser (de qch); **to c. over** pleurer (**sur**); – *vt* (*shout*) crier. ◆**—ing** *a* (*need etc*) très grand; **a c. shame** une véritable honte; – *n* cris *mpl*; (*weeping*) pleurs *mpl*.

crypt [krɪpt] *n* crypte *f*.

cryptic ['krɪptɪk] *a* secret, énigmatique.

crystal ['krɪst(ə)l] *n* cristal *m*. ◆**c.-'clear** *a* (*water, sound*) cristallin; *Fig* clair comme le jour *or* l'eau de roche. ◆**crystallize** *vt* cristalliser; – *vi* (se) cristalliser.

cub [kʌb] *n* **1** (*of animal*) petit *m*. **2** (*scout*) louveteau *m*.

Cuba ['kjuːbə] *n* Cuba *m*. ◆**Cuban** *a & n* cubain, -aine (*mf*).

cubbyhole ['kʌbɪhəʊl] *n* cagibi *m*.

cube [kjuːb] *n* cube *m*; (*of meat etc*) dé *m*. ◆**cubic** *a* (*shape*) cubique; (*metre etc*) cube; **c. capacity** volume *m*; *Aut* cylindrée *f*.

cubicle ['kjuːbɪk(ə)l] *n* (*for changing*) cabine *f*; (*in hospital*) box *m*.

cuckoo ['kʊkuː] **1** *n* (*bird*) coucou *m*; **c. clock** coucou *m*. **2** *a* (*stupid*) *Sl* cinglé.

cucumber ['kjuːkʌmbər] *n* concombre *m*.

cuddle ['kʌd(ə)l] *vt* (*hug*) serrer (dans ses bras); (*caress*) câliner; – *vi* (*of lovers*) se serrer; **to (kiss and) c.** s'embrasser; **to c. up to** (*huddle*) se serrer *or* se blottir contre; – *n*

caresse *f*. ◆**cuddly** *a* (**-ier, -iest**) *a* câlin, caressant; (*toy*) doux, en peluche.

cudgel ['kʌdʒəl] *n* trique *f*, gourdin *m*.

cue [kjuː] *n* **1** *Th* réplique *f*; (*signal*) signal *m*. **2** (**billiard**) **c.** queue *f* (de billard).

cuff [kʌf] **1** *n* (*of shirt etc*) poignet *m*, manchette *f*; (*of trousers*) *Am* revers *m*; **off the c.** *Fig* impromptu; **c. link** bouton *m* de manchette. **2** *vt* (*strike*) gifler.

cul-de-sac ['kʌldəsæk] *n* impasse *f*, cul-de-sac *m*.

culinary ['kʌlɪnərɪ] *a* culinaire.

cull [kʌl] *vt* choisir; (*animals*) abattre sélectivement.

culminate ['kʌlmɪneɪt] *vi* **to c. in** finir par. ◆**culmi'nation** *n* point *m* culminant.

culprit ['kʌlprɪt] *n* coupable *mf*.

cult [kʌlt] *n* culte *m*.

cultivat/e ['kʌltɪveɪt] *vt* (*land, mind etc*) cultiver. ◆**—ed** *a* cultivé. ◆**culti'vation** *n* culture *f*; **land** *or* **fields under c.** cultures *fpl*.

culture ['kʌltʃər] *n* culture *f*. ◆**cultural** *a* culturel. ◆**cultured** *a* cultivé.

cumbersome ['kʌmbəsəm] *a* encombrant.

cumulative ['kjuːmjʊlətɪv] *a* cumulatif; **c. effect** (*long-term*) effet *m* or résultat *m* à long terme.

cunning ['kʌnɪŋ] *a* astucieux; *Pej* rusé; – *n* astuce *f*; ruse *f*. ◆**—ly** *adv* avec astuce; avec ruse.

cup [kʌp] *n* tasse *f*; (*goblet, prize*) coupe *f*; **that's my c. of tea** *Fam* c'est à mon goût; **c. final** *Fb* finale *f* de la coupe. ◆**c.-tie** *n Fb* match *m* éliminatoire. ◆**cupful** *n* tasse *f*.

cupboard ['kʌbəd] *n* armoire *f*; (*built-in*) placard *m*.

Cupid ['kjuːpɪd] *n* Cupidon *m*.

cupola ['kjuːpələ] *n Archit* coupole *f*.

cuppa ['kʌpə] *n Fam* tasse *f* de thé.

curate ['kjuərɪt] *n* vicaire *m*.

curator [kjuəˈreɪtər] *n* (*of museum*) conservateur *m*.

curb [kɜːb] **1** *n* (*kerb*) *Am* bord *m* du trottoir. **2** *vt* (*feelings*) refréner, freiner; (*ambitions*) modérer; (*expenses*) limiter; – *n* frein *m*; **to put a c. on** mettre un frein à.

curdle ['kɜːd(ə)l] *vt* cailler; – *vi* se cailler; (*of blood*) *Fig* se figer.

curds [kɜːdz] *npl* lait *m* caillé. ◆**curd cheese** *n* fromage *m* blanc (maigre).

cure [kjuər] **1** *vt* guérir (**of** de); (*poverty*) *Fig* éliminer; – *n* remède *m* (**for** contre); (*recovery*) guérison *f*; **rest c.** cure *f* de repos. **2** *vt Culin* (*smoke*) fumer; (*salt*) saler; (*dry*) sécher. ◆**curable** *a* guérissable, curable. ◆**curative** *a* curatif.

curfew ['kɜːfjuː] *n* couvre-feu *m*.

curio ['kjuərıəu] n (pl -os) bibelot m, curiosité f.

curious ['kjuərıəs] a (odd) curieux; (inquisitive) curieux (about de); **c. to know** curieux de savoir. ◆—**ly** adv (oddly) curieusement. ◆**curi'osity** n curiosité f.

curl [kɜːl] **1** vti (hair) boucler, friser; — n boucle f; (of smoke) Fig spirale f. **2** vi **to c. up** (shrivel) se racornir; **to c. oneself up** (into a ball) se pelotonner. ◆—**er** n bigoudi m. ◆**curly** a (-ier, -iest) bouclé, frisé.

currant ['kʌrənt] n (fruit) groseille f; (dried grape) raisin m de Corinthe.

currency ['kʌrənsı] n (money) monnaie f; (acceptance) Fig cours m; **(foreign) c.** devises fpl (étrangères).

current ['kʌrənt] **1** a (fashion, trend etc) actuel; (opinion, use, phrase) courant; (year, month) en cours, courant; **c. affairs** questions fpl d'actualité; **c. events** actualité f; **the c. issue** (of magazine etc) le dernier numéro. **2** n (of river, air) & El courant m. ◆—**ly** adv actuellement, à présent.

curriculum, pl **-la** [kə'rıkjuləm, -lə] n programme m (scolaire); **c. (vitae)** curriculum (vitae) m inv.

curry ['kʌrı] **1** n Culin curry m, cari m. **2** vt to **c. favour with** s'insinuer dans les bonnes grâces de.

curs/e [kɜːs] n malédiction f; (swearword) juron m; (bane) Fig fléau m; — vt maudire; **cursed with** (blindness etc) affligé de; — vi (swear) jurer. ◆—**ed** [-ıd] a Fam maudit.

cursor ['kɜːsər] n (on computer screen) curseur m.

cursory ['kɜːsərı] a (trop) rapide, superficiel.

curt [kɜːt] a brusque. ◆—**ly** adv d'un ton brusque. ◆—**ness** n brusquerie f.

curtail [kɜː'teıl] vt écourter, raccourcir; (expenses) réduire. ◆—**ment** n raccourcissement m; réduction f.

curtain ['kɜːt(ə)n] n rideau m; **c. call** Th rappel m.

curts(e)y ['kɜːtsı] n révérence f; — vi faire une révérence.

curve [kɜːv] n courbe f; (in road) Am virage m; pl (of woman) Fam rondeurs fpl; — vt courber; — vi se courber; (of road) tourner, faire une courbe.

cushion ['kuʃən] n coussin m; — vt (shock) Fig amortir. ◆**cushioned** a (seat) rembourré; **c. against** Fig protégé contre.

cushy ['kuʃı] a (-ier, -iest) (job, life) Fam pépère, facile.

custard ['kʌstəd] n crème f anglaise; (when set) crème f renversée.

custodian [kʌ'stəudıən] n gardien, -ienne mf.

custody ['kʌstədı] n (care) garde f; **to take into c.** Jur mettre en détention préventive. ◆**cu'stodial** a **c. sentence** peine f de prison.

custom ['kʌstəm] n coutume f; (patronage) Com clientèle f. ◆**customary** a habituel, coutumier; **it is c.** to il est d'usage de. ◆**custom-built** a, ◆**customized** a (car etc) (fait) sur commande.

customer ['kʌstəmər] n client, -ente mf; Pej individu m.

customs ['kʌstəmz] n & npl **(the) c.** la douane; **c. (duties)** droits mpl de douane; **c. officer** douanier m; **c. union** union f douanière.

cut [kʌt] n coupure f; (stroke) coup m; (of clothes, hair) coupe f; (in salary) réduction f; (of meat) morceau m; — vt (pt & pp cut, pres p cutting) couper; (meat) découper; (glass, tree) tailler; (record) graver; (hay) faucher; (profits, prices etc) réduire; (tooth) percer; (corner) Aut prendre à la corde; **to c. open** ouvrir (au couteau etc); **to c. short** (visit) abréger; — vi (of person, scissors) couper; (of material) se couper; **to c. into** (cake) entamer. ■ **to c. away** vt (remove) enlever; **to c. back (on)** vti réduire. ◆**cutback** n réduction f; **to c. down** vt (tree) abattre, couper; **to c. down (on)** vti réduire; **to c. in** vi interrompre; Aut faire une queue de poisson (**on s.o.** à qn); **to c. off** vt couper; (isolate) isoler; **to c. out** vi (of engine) Aut caler; — vt (article) découper; (garment) tailler; (remove) enlever; (leave out, get rid of) Fam supprimer; **to c. out drinking** (stop) Fam s'arrêter de boire; **c. it out!** Fam ça suffit!; **c. out to be a doctor**/etc fait pour être médecin/etc. ◆**cutout** n (picture) découpage m; El coupe-circuit m inv; **to c. up** vt couper (en morceaux); (meat) découper; **c. up about** démoralisé par. ◆**cutting** n coupe f; (of diamond) taille f; (article) Journ coupure f; (plant) bouture f; Cin montage m; — a (wind, word) cinglant; **c. edge** tranchant m.

cute [kjuːt] a (-er, -est) Fam (pretty) mignon; (shrewd) astucieux.

cuticle ['kjuːtık(ə)l] n petites peaux fpl (de l'ongle).

cutlery ['kʌtlərı] n couverts mpl.

cutlet ['kʌtlıt] n (of veal etc) côtelette f.

cut-price [kʌt'praıs] a à prix réduit.

cutthroat ['kʌtθrəut] n assassin m; — a (competition) impitoyable.

cv [siː'viː] n abbr curriculum (vitae) m inv.

cyanide ['saɪənaɪd] n cyanure m.

cybernetics [saɪbə'netɪks] n cybernétique f.

cycle ['saɪk(ə)l] **1** n bicyclette f, vélo m; – a (path, track) cyclable; (race) cycliste; – vi aller à bicyclette (**to** à); Sp faire de la bicyclette. **2** n (series, period) cycle m. ◆**cycling** n cyclisme m; – a (champion) cycliste. ◆**cyclist** n cycliste mf. ◆**cyclic(al)** ['sɪklɪk(əl)] a cyclique.

cyclone ['saɪkləʊn] n cyclone m.

cylinder ['sɪlɪndər] n cylindre m. ◆**cy-'lindrical** a cylindrique.

cymbal ['sɪmbəl] n cymbale f.

cynic ['sɪnɪk] n cynique mf. ◆**cynical** a cynique. ◆**cynicism** n cynisme m.

cypress ['saɪprəs] n (tree) cyprès m.

Cyprus ['saɪprəs] n Chypre f. ◆**Cypriot** ['sɪprɪət] a & n cypriote (mf).

cyst [sɪst] n Med kyste m.

czar [zɑːr] n tsar m.

Czech [tʃek] a & n tchèque (mf). ◆**Czecho'slovak** a & n tchécoslovaque (mf). ◆**Czechoslo'vakia** n Tchécoslovaquie f. ◆**Czechoslo'vakian** a & n tchécoslovaque (mf).

D

D, d [diː] n D, d m. ◆**D.-day** n le jour J.

dab [dæb] n a **d. of** un petit peu de; – vt (-bb-) (wound, brow etc) tamponner; **to d. sth on sth** appliquer qch (à petits coups) sur qch.

dabble ['dæb(ə)l] vi **to d. in** s'occuper or se mêler un peu de.

dad [dæd] n Fam papa m. ◆**daddy** n Fam papa m; **d. longlegs** (cranefly) tipule f; (spider) Am faucheur m.

daffodil ['dæfədɪl] n jonquille f.

daft [dɑːft] a (-er, -est) Fam idiot, bête.

dagger ['dægər] n poignard m; **at daggers drawn** à couteaux tirés (**with** avec).

dahlia ['deɪljə, Am 'dæljə] n dahlia m.

daily ['deɪlɪ] a quotidien, journalier; (wage) journalier; – adv quotidiennement; – n d. (paper) quotidien m; **d. (help)** (cleaning woman) femme f de ménage.

dainty ['deɪntɪ] a (-ier, -iest) délicat; (pretty) mignon; (tasteful) élégant. ◆**daintily** adv délicatement; élégamment.

dairy ['deərɪ] n (on farm) laiterie f; (shop) crémerie f; – a (produce, cow etc) laitier. ◆**dairyman** n (pl -men) (dealer) laitier m. ◆**dairywoman** n (pl -women) laitière f.

daisy ['deɪzɪ] n pâquerette f.

dale [deɪl] n Geog Lit vallée f.

dally ['dælɪ] vi musarder, lanterner.

dam [dæm] n (wall) barrage m; – vt (-mm-) (river) barrer.

damag/e ['dæmɪdʒ] n dégâts mpl, dommages mpl; (harm) Fig préjudice m; pl Jur dommages-intérêts mpl; – vt (spoil) abîmer; (material object) endommager, abîmer; (harm) Fig nuire à. ◆**—ing** a préjudiciable (**to** à).

dame [deɪm] n Lit dame f; Am Sl nana f, fille f.

damn [dæm] vt (condemn, doom) condamner; Rel damner; (curse) maudire; **d. him!** Fam qu'il aille au diable!; – int **d. (it)!** Fam zut!, merde!; – n **he doesn't care a d.** Fam il s'en fiche pas mal; – a Fam fichu, sacré; – adv Fam sacrément; **d. all** rien du tout. ◆**—ed 1** a (soul) damné. **2** Fam = **damn** a & adv. ◆**—ing** a (evidence etc) accablant. ◆**dam'nation** n damnation f.

damp [dæmp] a (-er, -est) humide; (skin) moite; – n humidité f. ◆**damp(en)** vt humecter; **to d. (down)** (zeal) refroidir; (ambition) étouffer. ◆**damper** n **to put a d. on** jeter un froid sur. ◆**dampness** n humidité f.

damsel ['dæmzəl] n Lit & Hum demoiselle f.

damson ['dæmzən] n prune f de Damas.

danc/e [dɑːns] n danse f; (social event) bal m; **d. hall** dancing m; – vi danser; **to d. for joy** sauter de joie; – vt (polka etc) danser. ◆**—ing** n danse f; **d. partner** cavalier, -ière mf. ◆**—er** n danseur, -euse mf.

dandelion ['dændɪlaɪən] n pissenlit m.

dandruff ['dændrʌf] n pellicules fpl.

dandy ['dændɪ] **1** n dandy m. **2** a (very good) Am Fam formidable.

Dane [deɪn] n Danois, -oise mf.

danger ['deɪndʒər] n (peril) danger m (**to** pour); (risk) risque m; **in d.** en danger; **in d. of** (threatened by) menacé de; **to be in d. of falling**/etc risquer de tomber/etc; **on the d. list** Med dans un état critique; **d. signal** signal m d'alarme; **d. zone** zone f dangereuse. ◆**dangerous** a (place, illness, *person etc*) dangereux (**to** pour). ◆**dangerously** *adv* dangereusement; (*ill*) gravement.

dangle ['dæŋg(ə)l] *vt* balancer; (*prospect*) *Fig* faire miroiter (**before s.o.** aux yeux de qn); – *vi* (*hang*) pendre; (*swing*) se balancer.

Danish ['deɪnɪʃ] *a* danois; – *n* (*language*) danois *m*.

dank [dæŋk] *a* (**-er, -est**) humide (et froid).

dapper ['dæpər] *a* pimpant, fringant.

dappled ['dæp(ə)ld] *a* pommelé, tacheté.

dar/e [deər] *vt* oser (**do** faire); **she d. not come** elle n'ose pas venir; **he doesn't d. (to) go** il n'ose pas y aller; **if you d.** si tu l'oses, si tu oses le faire; **I d. say he tried** il a sans doute essayé, je suppose qu'il a essayé; **to d. s.o. to do** défier qn de faire. ◆**—ing** *a* audacieux; – *n* audace *f*. ◆**daredevil** *n* casse-cou *m inv*, risque-tout *m inv*.

dark [dɑːk] *a* (**-er, -est**) obscur, noir, sombre; (*colour*) foncé, sombre; (*skin*) brun, foncé; (*hair*) brun, noir, foncé; (*eyes*) foncé; (*gloomy*) sombre; **it's d.** il fait nuit *or* noir; **to keep sth d.** tenir qch secret; **d. glasses** lunettes *fpl* noires; – *n* noir *m*, obscurité *f*; **after d.** après la tombée de la nuit; **to keep s.o. in the d.** laisser qn dans l'ignorance (**about** de). ◆**d.-'haired** *a* aux cheveux bruns. ◆**d.-'skinned** *a* brun; (*race*) de couleur. ◆**darken** *vt* assombrir, obscurcir; (*colour*) foncer; – *vi* s'assombrir; (*of colour*) foncer. ◆**darkness** *n* obscurité *f*, noir *m*.

darkroom ['dɑːkruːm] *n* *Phot* chambre *f* noire.

darling ['dɑːlɪŋ] *n* (*favourite*) chouchou, -oute *mf*; (**my**) **d.** (mon) chéri, (ma) chérie; **he's a d.** c'est un amour; **be a d.!** sois un ange!; – *a* chéri; (*delightful*) *Fam* adorable.

darn [dɑːn] **1** *vt* (*socks*) repriser. **2** *int* **d. it!** bon sang! ◆**—ing** *n* reprise *f*; – *a* (*needle, wool*) à repriser.

dart [dɑːt] **1** *vi* se précipiter, s'élancer (**for** vers); – *n* **to make a d.** se précipiter (**for** vers). **2** *n* *Sp* fléchette *f*; *pl* (*game*) fléchettes *fpl*. ◆**dartboard** *n* *Sp* cible *f*.

dash [dæʃ] **1** *n* (*run, rush*) ruée *f*; **to make a d.** se précipiter (**for** vers); – *vi* se précipiter; (*of waves*) se briser (**against** contre); **to d. off** *or* **away** partir *or* filer en vitesse; – *vt* jeter (**with** force); (*shatter*) briser; **d. (it)!** *Fam* zut!; **to d. off** (*letter*) faire en vitesse. **2** *n* **a d. of** un (petit) peu de; **a d. of milk** une goutte *or* un nuage de lait. **3** *n* (*stroke*) trait

m; *Typ* tiret *m*. ◆**—ing** *a* (*person*) sémillant.

dashboard ['dæʃbɔːd] *n* *Aut* tableau *m* de bord.

data ['deɪtə] *npl* données *fpl*; **d. processing** informatique *f*.

date[1] [deɪt] *n* date *f*; (*on coin*) millésime *m*; (*meeting*) *Fam* rendez-vous *m inv*; (*person*) *Fam* copain, -ine *mf* (*avec qui on a un rendez-vous*); **up to d.** moderne; (*information*) à jour; (*well-informed*) au courant (**on** de); **out of d.** (*old-fashioned*) démodé; (*expired*) périmé; **to d.** à ce jour, jusqu'ici; **d. stamp** (*object*) (tampon *m*) dateur *m*; (*mark*) cachet *m*; – *vt* (*letter etc*) dater; (*girl, boy*) *Fam* sortir avec; – *vi* (*become out of date*) dater; **to d. back to, d. from** dater de. ◆**dated** *a* démodé.

date[2] [deɪt] *n* *Bot* datte *f*.

datebook ['deɪtbuk] *n* *Am* agenda *m*.

daub [dɔːb] *vt* barbouiller (**with** de).

daughter ['dɔːtər] *n* fille *f*. ◆**d.-in-law** *n* (*pl* daughters-in-law) belle-fille *f*, bru *f*.

daunt [dɔːnt] *vt* décourager, rebuter. ◆**—less** *a* intrépide.

dawdl/e ['dɔːd(ə)l] *vi* traîner, lambiner. ◆**—er** *n* traînard, -arde *mf*.

dawn [dɔːn] *n* aube *f*, aurore *f*; – *vi* (*of day*) poindre; (*of new era, idea*) naître, voir le jour; **it dawned upon him that . . .** il lui est venu à l'esprit que . . . . ◆**—ing** *a* naissant.

day [deɪ] *n* jour *m*; (*working period, whole day long*) journée *f*; *pl* (*period*) époque *f*, temps *mpl*; **all d. (long)** toute la journée; **what d. is it?** quel jour sommes-nous?; **the following** *or* **next d.** le lendemain; **the d. before** la veille; **the d. before yesterday** avant-hier; **the d. after tomorrow** après-demain; **to the d.** jour pour jour; **d. boarder** demi-pensionnaire *mf*; **d. nursery** crèche *f*; **d. return** *Rail* aller et retour *m* (*pour une journée*); **d. tripper** excursionniste *mf*. ◆**d.-to-'d.** *a* journalier; **on a d.-to-day basis** (*every day*) journellement. ◆**daybreak** *n* point *m* du jour. ◆**daydream** *n* rêverie *f*; – *vi* rêvasser. ◆**daylight** *n* (lumière *f* du) jour *m*; (*dawn*) point *m* du jour; **it's d.** il fait jour. ◆**daytime** *n* journée *f*.

daze [deɪz] *vt* (*with drugs etc*) hébéter; (*by blow*) étourdir; – *n* **in a d.** étourdi; hébété.

dazzle ['dæz(ə)l] *vt* éblouir; – *n* éblouissement *m*.

deacon ['diːkən] *n* *Rel* diacre *m*.

dead [ded] *a* mort; (*numb*) engourdi; (*party etc*) qui manque de vie, mortel; (*telephone*) sans tonalité; **in (the) d. centre** au beau milieu; **to be a d. loss** (*person*) *Fam* n'être bon à rien; **it's a d. loss** *Fam* ça ne vaut rien; **d. silence** un silence de mort; **a d. stop** un arrêt complet; **d. end** (*street*) & *Fig* impasse *f*; **a d.-end job** un travail sans avenir; − *adv* (*completely*) absolument; (*very*) très; **d. beat** *Fam* éreinté; **d. drunk** *Fam* ivre mort; **to stop d.** s'arrêter net; − *n* **the d.** les morts *mpl*; **in the d. of** (*night, winter*) au cœur de. ◆**—ly** a (-ier, -iest) (*enemy, silence, paleness*) mortel; (*weapon*) meurtrier; **d. sins** péchés *mpl* capitaux; − *adv* mortellement. ◆**deadbeat** *n Am Fam* parasite *m*. ◆**deadline** *n* date *f* limite; (*hour*) heure *f* limite. ◆**deadlock** *n Fig* impasse *f*. ◆**deadpan** a (*face*) figé, impassible.

deaden ['ded(ə)n] *vt* (*shock*) amortir; (*pain*) calmer; (*feeling*) émousser.

deaf [def] a sourd (**to** à); **d. and dumb** sourd-muet; **d. in one ear** sourd d'une oreille; − *n* **the d.** les sourds *mpl*. ◆**d.-aid** *n* audiophone *m*, prothèse *f* auditive. ◆**deafen** *vt* assourdir. ◆**deafness** *n* surdité *f*.

deal¹ [diːl] **1** *n* **a good** or **great d.** beaucoup (**of** de). **2** *n Com* marché *m*, affaire *f*; *Cards* donne *f*; **fair d.** traitement *m* or arrangement *m* équitable; **it's a d.** d'accord; **big d.!** *Iron* la belle affaire! **3** *vt* (*pt* & *pp* **dealt** [delt]) (*blow*) porter; **to d. (out)** (*cards*) donner; (*money*) distribuer. **4** *vi* (*trade*) traiter (**with s.o.** avec qn); **to d. in** faire le commerce de; **to d. with** (*take care of*) s'occuper de; (*concern*) traiter de, parler de; **I can d. with him** (*handle*) je sais m'y prendre avec lui. ◆**—ings** *npl* relations *fpl* (**with** avec); *Com* transactions *fpl*. ◆**—er** *n* marchand, -ande *mf* (**in** de); (*agent*) dépositaire *mf*; (*for cars*) concessionnaire *mf*; (*in drugs*) *Sl* revendeur, -euse *mf* de drogues; *Cards* donneur, -euse *mf*.

deal² [diːl] *n* (*wood*) sapin *m*.

dean [diːn] *n Rel Univ* doyen *m*.

dear [diər] a (-er, -est) (*loved, precious, expensive*) cher; (*price*) élevé; **D. Sir** (*in letter*) *Com* Monsieur; **D. Uncle** (mon) cher oncle; **oh d.!** oh là là!, oh mon Dieu!; − *n* (**my**) **d.** (*darling*) (mon) chéri, (ma) chérie; (*friend*) mon cher, ma chère; **she's a d.** c'est un amour; **be a d.!** sois un ange!; − *adv* (*to cost, pay*) cher. ◆**—ly** *adv* tendrement; (*very much*) beaucoup; **to pay d. for sth** payer qch cher.

dearth [dɜːθ] *n* manque *m*, pénurie *f*.

death [deθ] *n* mort *f*; **to put to d.** mettre à mort; **to be bored to d.** s'ennuyer à mourir;

to be burnt to d. mourir carbonisé; **to be sick to d.** en avoir vraiment marre; **many deaths** (*people killed*) de nombreux morts *mpl*; − a (*march*) funèbre; (*mask*) mortuaire; **d. certificate** acte *m* de décès; **d. duty** droits *mpl* de succession; **d. penalty** or **sentence** peine *f* de mort; **d. rate** mortalité *f*; **it's a d. trap** il y a danger de mort. ◆**deathbed** *n* lit *m* de mort. ◆**deathblow** *n* coup *m* mortel. ◆**deathly** a mortel, de mort; − *adv* **d. pale** d'une pâleur mortelle.

debar [dɪ'bɑːr] *vt* (-rr-) exclure; **to d. from doing** interdire de faire.

debase [dɪ'beɪs] *vt* (*person*) avilir; (*reputation, talents*) galvauder; (*coinage*) altérer.

debat/e [dɪ'beɪt] *vti* discuter; **to d. (with oneself) whether to leave/etc** se demander si on doit partir/*etc*; − *n* débat *m*, discussion *f*. ◆**—able** a discutable, contestable.

debauch [dɪ'bɔːtʃ] *vt* corrompre, débaucher. ◆**debauchery** *n* débauche *f*.

debilitate [dɪ'bɪlɪteɪt] *vt* débiliter. ◆**debility** *n* faiblesse *f*, débilité *f*.

debit ['debɪt] *n* débit *m*; **in d.** (*account*) débiteur; − a (*balance*) *Fin* débiteur; − *vt* débiter (**s.o. with sth** qn de qch).

debonair [debə'neər] a jovial; (*charming*) charmant; (*polite*) poli.

debris ['debriː] *n* débris *mpl*.

debt [det] *n* dette *f*; **to be in d.** avoir des dettes; **to be £50 in d.** devoir 50 livres; **to run** or **get into d.** faire des dettes. ◆**debtor** *n* débiteur, -trice *mf*.

debunk [diː'bʌŋk] *vt Fam* démystifier.

debut ['deɪbjuː] *n Th* début *m*.

decade ['dekeɪd] *n* décennie *f*.

decadent ['dekədənt] a décadent. ◆**decadence** *n* décadence *f*.

decaffeinated [diː'kæfɪneɪtɪd] a décaféiné.

decal ['diːkæl] *n Am* décalcomanie *f*.

decant [dɪ'kænt] *vt* (*wine*) décanter. ◆**—er** *n* carafe *f*.

decapitate [dɪ'kæpɪteɪt] *vt* décapiter.

decathlon [dɪ'kæθlɒn] *n Sp* décathlon *m*.

decay [dɪ'keɪ] *vi* (*go bad*) se gâter; (*rot*) pourrir; (*of tooth*) se carier, se gâter; (*of building*) tomber en ruine; (*decline*) *Fig* décliner; − *n* pourriture *f*; *Archit* délabrement *m*; (*of tooth*) carie(s) *f*(*pl*); (*of nation*) décadence *f*; **to fall into d.** (*of building*) tomber en ruine. ◆**—ing** a (*nation*) décadent; (*meat, fruit etc*) pourrissant.

deceased [dɪ'siːst] a décédé, défunt; − *n* **the d.** le défunt, la défunte; *pl* les défunt(e)s.

deceit [dɪ'siːt] *n* tromperie *f*. ◆**deceitful** a

trompeur. ◆**deceitfully** *adv* avec duplicité.

deceive [dɪ'siːv] *vti* tromper; **to d. oneself** se faire des illusions.

December [dɪ'sembər] *n* décembre *m*.

decent ['diːsənt] *a* (*respectable*) convenable, décent; (*good*) *Fam* bon; (*kind*) *Fam* gentil; **that was d. (of you)** c'était chic de ta part. ◆**decency** *n* décence *f*; (*kindness*) *Fam* gentillesse *f*. ◆**decently** *adv* décemment.

decentralize [diː'sentrəlaɪz] *vt* décentraliser. ◆**decentrali'zation** *n* décentralisation *f*.

deception [dɪ'sepʃ(ə)n] *n* tromperie *f*. ◆**deceptive** *a* trompeur.

decibel ['desɪbel] *n* décibel *m*.

decid/e [dɪ'saɪd] *vt* (*question etc*) régler, décider; (*s.o.'s career, fate etc*) décider de; **to d. to do** décider de faire; **to d. that** décider que; **to d. s.o. to do** décider qn à faire; – *vi* (*make decisions*) décider; (*make up one's mind*) se décider (**on doing** à faire); **to d. on sth** décider de qch, se décider à qch; (*choose*) se décider pour qch. ◆—**ed** *a* (*firm*) décidé, résolu; (*clear*) net. ◆—**edly** *adv* résolument; nettement. ◆—**ing** *a* (*factor etc*) décisif.

decimal ['desɪməl] *a* décimal; **d. point** virgule *f*; – *n* décimale *f*. ◆**decimali-'zation** *n* décimalisation *f*.

decimate ['desɪmeɪt] *vt* décimer.

decipher [dɪ'saɪfər] *vt* déchiffrer.

decision [dɪ'sɪʒ(ə)n] *n* décision *f*. ◆**decisive** [dɪ'saɪsɪv] *a* (*defeat, tone etc*) décisif; (*victory*) net, incontestable. ◆**decisively** *adv* (*to state*) avec décision; (*to win*) nettement, incontestablement.

deck [dek] **1** *n* Nau pont *m*; **top d.** (*of bus*) impériale *f*. **2** *n* **d. of cards** jeu *m* de cartes. **3** *n* (*of record player*) platine *f*. **4** *vt* **to d. (out)** (*adorn*) orner. ◆**deckchair** *n* chaise *f* longue.

declare [dɪ'kleər] *vt* déclarer (**that** que); (*verdict, result*) proclamer. ◆**decla'ration** *n* déclaration *f*; proclamation *f*.

declin/e [dɪ'klaɪn] **1** *vi* (*deteriorate*) décliner; (*of birthrate, price etc*) baisser; **to d. in importance** perdre de l'importance; – *n* déclin *m*; (*fall*) baisse *f*. **2** *vt* refuser, décliner; **to d. to do** refuser de faire. ◆—**ing** *a* one's **d.** years ses dernières années.

decode [diː'kəʊd] *vt* (*message*) décoder.

decompose [diːkəm'pəʊz] *vt* décomposer; – *vi* se décomposer. ◆**decompo'sition** *n* décomposition *f*.

decompression [diːkəm'preʃ(ə)n] *n* décompression *f*.

decontaminate [diːkən'tæmɪneɪt] *vt* décontaminer.

decor ['deɪkɔːr] *n* décor *m*.

decorat/e ['dekəreɪt] *vt* (*cake, house, soldier*) décorer (**with** de); (*paint etc*) peindre (et tapisser); (*hat, skirt etc*) orner (**with** de). ◆—**ing** *n* **interior d.** décoration *f* d'intérieurs. ◆**deco'ration** *n* décoration *f*. ◆**decorative** *a* décoratif. ◆**decorator** *n* (*house painter etc*) peintre *m* décorateur; (**interior**) **d.** ensemblier *m*, décorateur, -trice *mf*.

decorum [dɪ'kɔːrəm] *n* bienséances *fpl*.

decoy ['diːkɔɪ] *n* (*artificial bird*) appeau *m*; (**police**) **d.** policier *m* en civil.

decreas/e [dɪ'kriːs] *vti* diminuer; – ['diːkriːs] *n* diminution *f* (**in** de). ◆—**ing** *a* (*number etc*) décroissant. ◆—**ingly** *adv* de moins en moins.

decree [dɪ'kriː] *n* Pol Rel décret *m*; Jur jugement *m*; (*municipal*) arrêté *m*; – *vt* (*pt* & *pp* **decreed**) décréter.

decrepit [dɪ'krepɪt] *a* (*building*) en ruine; (*person*) décrépit.

decry [dɪ'kraɪ] *vt* décrier.

dedicat/e ['dedɪkeɪt] *vt* (*devote*) consacrer (**to** à); (*book*) dédier (**to** à); **to d. oneself to** se consacrer à. ◆**dedi'cation** *n* (*in book*) dédicace *f*; (*devotion*) dévouement *m*.

deduce [dɪ'djuːs] *vt* (*conclude*) déduire (**from** de, **that** que).

deduct [dɪ'dʌkt] *vt* (*subtract*) déduire, retrancher (**from** de); (*from wage, account*) prélever (**from** sur). ◆**deductible** *a* à déduire (**from** de); (*expenses*) déductible. ◆**deduction** *n* (*inference*) & Com déduction *f*.

deed [diːd] *n* action *f*, acte *m*; (*feat*) exploit *m*; Jur acte *m* (notarié).

deem [diːm] *vt* juger, estimer.

deep [diːp] *a* (**-er, -est**) profond; (*snow*) épais; (*voice*) grave; (*note*) Mus bas; (*person*) insondable; **to be six metres/etc d.** avoir six mètres/etc de profondeur; **d. in thought** absorbé *or* plongé dans ses pensées; **the d. end** (*in swimming pool*) le grand bain; **d. red** rouge foncé; – *adv* (*to breathe*) profondément; **d. into the night** tard dans la nuit; – *n* **the d.** l'océan *m*. ◆—**ly** *adv* (*grateful, to regret etc*) profondément. ◆**deep-'freeze** *vt* surgeler; – *n* congélateur *m*. ◆**d.-'fryer** *n* friteuse *f*. ◆**d.-'rooted** *a*, ◆**d.-'seated** *a* bien ancré, profond. ◆**d.-'set** *a* (*eyes*) enfoncés.

deepen ['diːpən] vt approfondir; (increase) augmenter; − vi devenir plus profond; (of mystery) s'épaissir. ◆**—ing** a grandissant.

deer [dɪər] n inv cerf m.

deface [dɪ'feɪs] vt (damage) dégrader; (daub) barbouiller.

defamation [defə'meɪʃ(ə)n] n diffamation f. ◆**de'famatory** a diffamatoire.

default [dɪ'fɔːlt] n by d. Jur par défaut; **to win by d.** gagner par forfait; − vi Jur faire défaut; **to d. on one's payments** Fin être en rupture de paiement.

defeat [dɪ'fiːt] vt battre, vaincre; (plan) faire échouer; − n défaite f; (of plan) échec m. ◆**defeatism** n défaitisme m.

defect 1 [dɪ'fekt] n défaut m. **2** [dɪ'fekt] vi Pol déserter, faire défection; **to d. to** (the West, the enemy) passer à. ◆**de'fection** n défection f. ◆**de'fective** a défectueux; Med déficient. ◆**de'fector** n transfuge mf.

defence [dɪ'fens] (Am defense) n défense f; **the body's defences** la défense de l'organisme (against contre); **in his d.** Jur à sa décharge, pour le défendre. ◆**defenceless** a sans défense. ◆**defensible** a défendable. ◆**defensive** a défensif; − n **on the d.** sur la défensive.

defend [dɪ'fend] vt défendre. ◆**defendant** n (accused) Jur prévenu, -ue mf. ◆**defender** n défenseur m; (of title) Sp détenteur, -trice mf.

defer [dɪ'fɜːr] **1** vt (-rr-) (postpone) différer, reporter. **2** vi (-rr-) **to d. to** (yield) déférer à. ◆**—ment** n report m.

deference ['defərəns] n déférence f. ◆**defe'rential** a déférent, plein de déférence.

defiant [dɪ'faɪənt] a (tone etc) de défi; (person) rebelle. ◆**defiance** n (resistance) défi m (of à); **in d. of** (contempt) au mépris de. ◆**defiantly** adv d'un air de défi.

deficient [dɪ'fɪʃənt] a insuffisant; Med déficient; **to be d. in** manquer de. ◆**deficiency** n manque m; (flaw) défaut m; Med carence f; (mental) déficience f.

deficit ['defɪsɪt] n déficit m.

defile [dɪ'faɪl] vt souiller, salir.

define [dɪ'faɪn] vt définir. ◆**defi'nition** n définition f.

definite ['defɪnɪt] a (date, plan) précis, déterminé; (obvious) net, évident; (firm) ferme; (certain) certain; **d. article** Gram article m défini. ◆**—ly** adv certainement; (appreciably) nettement; (to say) catégoriquement.

definitive [dɪ'fɪnɪtɪv] a définitif.

deflate [dɪ'fleɪt] vt (tyre) dégonfler. ◆**deflation** n dégonflement m; Econ déflation f.

deflect [dɪ'flekt] vt faire dévier; − vi dévier.

deform [dɪ'fɔːm] vt déformer. ◆**—ed** a (body) difforme. ◆**deformity** n difformité f.

defraud [dɪ'frɔːd] vt (customs, State etc) frauder; **to d. s.o. of sth** escroquer qch à qn.

defray [dɪ'freɪ] vt (expenses) payer.

defrost [diː'frɒst] vt (fridge) dégivrer; (food) décongeler.

deft [deft] a adroit (with de). ◆**—ness** n adresse f.

defunct [dɪ'fʌŋkt] a défunt.

defuse [diː'fjuːz] vt (bomb, conflict) désamorcer.

defy [dɪ'faɪ] vt (person, death etc) défier; (effort, description) résister à; **to d. s.o. to do** défier qn de faire.

degenerate [dɪ'dʒenəreɪt] vi dégénérer (into en); − [dɪ'dʒenərət] a & n dégénéré, -ée (mf). ◆**degene'ration** n dégénérescence f.

degrade [dɪ'greɪd] vt dégrader. ◆**degradation** [degrə'deɪʃ(ə)n] n Mil Ch dégradation f; (of person) déchéance f.

degree [dɪ'griː] n **1** degré m; **not in the slightest d.** pas du tout; **to such a d.** à tel point (that que). **2** Univ diplôme m; (Bachelor's) licence f; (Master's) maîtrise f; (PhD) doctorat m.

dehumanize [diː'hjuːmənaɪz] vt déshumaniser.

dehydrate [diːhaɪ'dreɪt] vt déshydrater.

de-ice [diː'aɪs] vt Av Aut dégivrer.

deign [deɪn] vt daigner (**to do** faire).

deity ['diːɪtɪ] n dieu m.

dejected [dɪ'dʒektɪd] a abattu, découragé. ◆**dejection** n abattement m.

dekko ['dekəʊ] n Sl coup m d'œil.

delay [dɪ'leɪ] vt retarder; (payment) différer; − vi (be slow) tarder (**doing** à faire); (linger) s'attarder; − n (lateness) retard m; (waiting period) délai m; **without d.** sans tarder. ◆**delayed-'action** a (bomb) à retardement. ◆**delaying** a **d. tactics** moyens mpl dilatoires.

delectable [dɪ'lektəb(ə)l] a délectable.

delegate 1 ['delɪgeɪt] vt déléguer (**to** à). **2** ['delɪgət] n délégué, -ée mf. ◆**dele'gation** n délégation f.

delete [dɪ'liːt] vt rayer, supprimer. ◆**deletion** n (thing deleted) rature f; (act) suppression f.

deleterious [delɪ'tɪərɪəs] a néfaste.

deliberate¹ [dɪ'lɪbəreɪt] vi délibérer; − vt délibérer sur.

deliberate² [dɪ'lɪbərət] a (intentional) délibéré; (cautious) réfléchi; (slow) mesuré.

◆**—ly** adv (intentionally) exprès, délibéré-
ment; (to walk) avec mesure. ◆**delibe-
'ration** n délibération f.
delicate ['delɪkət] a délicat. ◆**delicacy** n
délicatesse f; Culin mets m délicat, gourmandise f. ◆**delicately** adv délicatement.
◆**delica'tessen** n (shop) épicerie f fine,
traiteur m.
delicious [dɪ'lɪʃəs] a délicieux.
delight [dɪ'laɪt] n délice m, grand plaisir m,
joie f; pl (pleasures, things) délices fpl; **to be
the d. of** faire les délices de; **to take d. in
sth/in doing** se délecter de qch/à faire; — vt
réjouir; — vi se délecter (**in doing** à faire).
◆**—ed** a ravi, enchanté (**with sth** de qch, **to
do** de faire, **that** que). ◆**delightful** a
charmant; (meal, perfume, sensation)
délicieux. ◆**delightfully** adv avec
beaucoup de charme; (wonderfully)
merveilleusement.
delineate [dɪ'lɪnɪeɪt] vt (outline) esquisser;
(portray) décrire.
delinquent [dɪ'lɪŋkwənt] a & n délinquant,
-ante (mf). ◆**delinquency** n délinquance
f.
delirious [dɪ'lɪərɪəs] a délirant; **to be d.**
avoir le délire, délirer. ◆**delirium** n Med
délire m.
deliver [dɪ'lɪvər] vt **1** (goods, milk etc) livrer;
(letters) distribuer; (hand over) remettre (**to**
à). **2** (rescue) délivrer (**from** de). **3** (give
birth to) mettre au monde, accoucher de; **to
d. a woman('s baby)** accoucher une femme.
4 (speech) prononcer; (ultimatum, warning)
lancer; (blow) porter. ◆**deliverance** n
délivrance f. ◆**delivery** n **1** livraison f;
distribution f; remise f. **2** Med accouchement m. **3** (speaking) débit m. ◆**deliver-
yman** n (pl **-men**) livreur m.
delta ['deltə] n (of river) delta m.
delude [dɪ'lu:d] vt tromper; **to d. oneself** se
faire des illusions. ◆**delusion** n illusion f;
Psy aberration f mentale.
deluge ['delju:dʒ] n (of water, questions etc)
déluge m; — vt inonder (**with** de).
de luxe [dɪ'lʌks] a de luxe.
delve [delv] vi **to d. into** (question, past)
fouiller; (books) fouiller dans.
demagogue ['deməgɒg] n démagogue mf.
demand [dɪ'mɑːnd] vt exiger (**sth from s.o.**
qch de qn), réclamer (**sth from s.o.** qch à
qn); (rights, more pay) revendiquer; **to d.
that** exiger que; **to d. to know** insister pour
savoir; — n exigence f; (claim) revendication f, réclamation f; (request) & Econ
demande f; **in great d.** très demandé; **to**

make demands on s.o. exiger beaucoup de
qn. ◆**—ing** a exigeant.
demarcation [diːmɑː'keɪʃ(ə)n] n démarcation f.
demean [dɪ'miːn] vt **to d. oneself** s'abaisser,
s'avilir.
demeanour [dɪ'miːnər] n (behaviour)
comportement m.
demented [dɪ'mentɪd] a dément.
demerara [demə'reərə] n **d. (sugar)**
cassonade f, sucre m roux.
demise [dɪ'maɪz] n (death) décès m; Fig
disparition f.
demo ['deməʊ] n (pl **-os**) (demonstration)
Fam manif f.
demobilize [diː'məʊbɪlaɪz] vt démobiliser.
democracy [dɪ'mɒkrəsɪ] n démocratie f.
◆**democrat** ['deməkræt] n démocrate mf.
◆**demo'cratic** a démocratique; (person)
démocrate.
demography [dɪ'mɒgrəfɪ] n démographie f.
demolish [dɪ'mɒlɪʃ] vt démolir. ◆**demo-
'lition** n démolition f.
demon ['diːmən] n démon m.
demonstrate ['demənstreɪt] vt démontrer;
(machine) faire une démonstration de; — vi
Pol manifester. ◆**demon'stration** n
démonstration f; Pol manifestation f.
◆**de'monstrative** a démonstratif.
◆**demonstrator** n Pol manifestant, -ante
mf; (in shop etc) démonstrateur, -trice mf.
demoralize [dɪ'mɒrəlaɪz] vt démoraliser.
demote [dɪ'məʊt] vt rétrograder.
demure [dɪ'mjʊər] a sage, réservé.
den [den] n antre m, tanière f.
denationalize [diː'næʃ(ə)nəlaɪz] vt dénationaliser.
denial [dɪ'naɪəl] n (of truth etc) dénégation f;
(of rumour) démenti m; (of authority) rejet
m; **to issue a d.** publier un démenti.
denigrate ['denɪgreɪt] vt dénigrer.
denim ['denɪm] n (toile f de) coton m; pl
(jeans) (blue-)jean m.
denizen ['denɪz(ə)n] n habitant, -ante mf.
Denmark ['denmɑːk] n Danemark m.
denomination [dɪnɒmɪ'neɪʃ(ə)n] n confession f, religion f; (sect) secte m; (of coin,
banknote) valeur f; Math unité f.
◆**denominational** a (school) confessionnel.
denote [dɪ'nəʊt] vt dénoter.
denounce [dɪ'naʊns] vt (person, injustice
etc) dénoncer (**to** à); **to d. s.o. as a spy/etc**
accuser qn publiquement d'être un
espion/etc. ◆**denunci'ation** n dénonciation f; accusation f publique.
dense [dens] a (**-er, -est**) dense; (stupid)

Fam lourd, bête. ◆**—ly** *adv* **d.** **popu-lated**/*etc* très peuplé/*etc*. ◆**density** *n* densité *f.*

dent [dent] *n* (*in metal*) bosselure *f*; (*in car*) bosse *f*, gnon *m*; **full of dents** (*car*) cabossé; **to make a d. in** one's savings taper dans ses économies; *− vt* cabosser, bosseler.

dental ['dent(ə)l] *a* dentaire; **d. surgeon** chirurgien *m* dentiste. ◆**dentist** *n* dentiste *mf.* ◆**dentistry** *n* médecine *f* dentaire; **school of d.** école *f* dentaire. ◆**dentures** *npl* dentier *m.*

deny [dɪ'naɪ] *vt* nier (**doing** avoir fait, **that** que); (*rumour*) démentir; (*authority*) rejeter; (*disown*) renier; **to d. s.o. sth** refuser qch à qn.

deodorant [diː'əʊdərənt] *n* déodorant *m.*

depart [dɪ'pɑːt] *vi* partir; (*deviate*) s'écarter (**from** de); *− vt* **to d. this world** *Lit* quitter ce monde. ◆**—ed** *a & n* (*dead*) défunt, -unte (*mf*). ◆**departure** *n* départ *m*; **a d. from** (*custom, rule*) un écart par rapport à, une entorse à; **to be a new d. for** constituer une nouvelle voie pour.

department [dɪ'pɑːtmənt] *n* département *m*; (*in office*) service *m*; (*in shop*) rayon *m*; *Univ* section *f*, département *m*; **that's your d.** (*sphere*) c'est ton rayon; **d. store** grand magasin *m.* ◆**depart'mental** *a* **d.** **manager** (*office*) chef *m* de service; (*shop*) chef *m* de rayon.

depend [dɪ'pend] *vi* dépendre (**on, upon** de); **to d. (up)on** (*rely on*) compter sur (**for sth** pour qch); **you can d. on it!** tu peux en être sûr! ◆**—able** *a* (*person, information etc*) sûr; (*machine*) fiable, sûr. ◆**dependant** *n* personne *f* à charge. ◆**dependence** *n* dépendance *f.* ◆**dependency** *n* (*country*) dépendance *f.* ◆**dependent** *a* dépendant (**on, upon** de); (*relative*) à charge; **to be d. (up)on** dépendre de.

depict [dɪ'pɪkt] *vt* (*describe*) dépeindre; (*pictorially*) représenter. ◆**depiction** *n* peinture *f*; représentation *f.*

deplete [dɪ'pliːt] *vt* (*use up*) épuiser; (*reduce*) réduire. ◆**depletion** *n* épuisement *m*; réduction *f.*

deplor/e [dɪ'plɔːr] *vt* déplorer. ◆**—able** *a* déplorable.

deploy [dɪ'plɔɪ] *vt* (*troops etc*) déployer.

depopulate [diː'pɒpjʊleɪt] *vt* dépeupler. ◆**depopu'lation** *n* dépeuplement *m.*

deport [dɪ'pɔːt] *vt* *Pol Jur* expulser; (*to concentration camp etc*) *Hist* déporter. ◆**depor'tation** *n* expulsion *f*; déportation *f.*

deportment [dɪ'pɔːtmənt] *n* maintien *m.*

depose [dɪ'pəʊz] *vt* (*king etc*) déposer.

deposit [dɪ'pɒzɪt] *vt* (*object, money etc*) déposer; *− n* (*in bank, wine*) & *Ch* dépôt *m*; (*part payment*) acompte *m*; (*against damage*) caution *f*; (*on bottle*) consigne *f*; **d. account** *Fin* compte *m* d'épargne. ◆**—or** *n* déposant, -ante *mf*, épargnant, -ante *mf.*

depot ['depəʊ, *Am* 'diːpəʊ] *n* dépôt *m*; (*station*) *Rail Am* gare *f*; (**bus**) **d.** *Am* gare *f* routière.

deprave [dɪ'preɪv] *vt* dépraver. ◆**depravity** *n* dépravation *f.*

deprecate ['deprɪkeɪt] *vt* désapprouver.

depreciate [dɪ'priːʃɪeɪt] *vt* (*reduce in value*) déprécier; *− vi* se déprécier. ◆**depreci-'ation** *n* dépréciation *f.*

depress [dɪ'pres] *vt* (*discourage*) déprimer; (*push down*) appuyer sur. ◆**—ed** *a* déprimé; (*in decline*) en déclin; (*in crisis*) en crise; **to get d.** se décourager. ◆**depression** *n* dépression *f.*

depriv/e [dɪ'praɪv] *vt* priver (**of** de). ◆**—ed** *a* (*child etc*) déshérité. ◆**depri'vation** *n* privation *f*; (*loss*) perte *f.*

depth [depθ] *n* profondeur *f*; (*of snow*) épaisseur *f*; (*of interest*) intensité *f*; **in the depths of** (*forest, despair*) au plus profond de; (*winter*) au cœur de; **to get out of one's d.** *Fig* perdre pied, nager; **in d.** en profondeur.

deputize ['depjʊtaɪz] *vi* assurer l'intérim (**for** de); *− vt* députer (**s.o. to do** qn pour faire). ◆**depu'tation** *n* députation *f.* ◆**deputy** *n* (*replacement*) suppléant, -ante *mf*; (*assistant*) adjoint, -ointe *mf*; **d. (sheriff)** *Am* shérif *m* adjoint; **d. chairman** vice-président, -ente *mf.*

derailed [dɪ'reɪld] *a* **to be d.** (*of train*) dérailler. ◆**derailment** *n* déraillement *m.*

deranged [dɪ'reɪndʒd] *a* (*person, mind*) dérangé.

derelict ['derɪlɪkt] *a* à l'abandon, abandonné.

deride [dɪ'raɪd] *vt* tourner en dérision. ◆**derision** *n* dérision *f.* ◆**derisive** *a* (*laughter etc*) moqueur; (*amount*) dérisoire. ◆**derisory** *a* dérisoire.

derive [dɪ'raɪv] *vt* **to d. from** (*pleasure, profit etc*) tirer de; *Ling* dériver de; **to be derived from** dériver de, provenir de; *− vi* **to d. from** dériver de. ◆**deri'vation** *n* *Ling* dérivation *f.* ◆**derivative** *a & n* *Ling Ch* dérivé (*m*).

dermatology [dɜːmə'tɒlədʒɪ] *n* dermatologie *f.*

derogatory [dɪ'rɒgət(ə)rɪ] *a* (*word*) péjoratif; (*remark*) désobligeant (**to** pour).

derrick ['derɪk] n (*over oil well*) derrick m.
derv [dɜːv] n gazole m, gas-oil m.
descend [dɪ'send] vi descendre (**from** de);
(*of rain*) tomber; **to d. upon** (*attack*) faire
une descente sur, tomber sur; (*of tourists*)
envahir; – vt (*stairs*) descendre; **to be
descended from** descendre de. ◆—**ing** a
(*order*) décroissant. ◆**descendant** n
descendant, -ante mf. ◆**descent** n 1
descente f; (*into crime*) chute f. 2 (*ancestry*)
souche f, origine f.
describe [dɪ'skraɪb] vt décrire. ◆**description** n description f; (*on passport*) signalement m; **of every d.** de toutes sortes.
◆**descriptive** a descriptif.
desecrate ['desɪkreɪt] vt profaner. ◆**dese-
'cration** n profanation f.
desegregate [diː'segrɪgeɪt] vt supprimer la
ségrégation raciale dans. ◆**desegre-
'gation** n déségrégation f.
desert[1] ['dezət] n désert m; – a désertique;
d. island île f déserte.
desert[2] [dɪ'zɜːt] vt déserter, abandonner; **to
d. s.o.** (*of luck etc*) abandonner qn; – vi Mil
déserter. ◆—**ed** a (*place*) désert. ◆—**er** n
Mil déserteur m. ◆**desertion** n désertion
f; (*by spouse*) abandon m (du domicile
conjugal).
deserts [dɪ'zɜːts] n one's just **d.** ce qu'on
mérite.
deserv/e [dɪ'zɜːv] vt mériter (**to do** de faire).
◆—**ing** a (*person*) méritant; (*act, cause*)
louable, méritoire; **d. of** digne de. ◆—**edly**
[-ɪdlɪ] adv à juste titre.
desiccated ['desɪkeɪtɪd] a (des)séché.
design [dɪ'zaɪn] vt (*car, furniture etc*)
dessiner; (*dress*) créer, dessiner; (*devise*)
concevoir (**for s.o.** pour qn, **to do** pour
faire); **well designed** bien conçu; – n (*aim*)
dessein m, intention f; (*sketch*) plan m,
dessin m; (*of dress, car*) modèle m; (*planning*) conception f, création f; (*pattern*)
motif m, dessin m; **industrial d.** dessin m
industriel; **by d.** intentionnellement; **to have
designs on** avoir des desseins sur. ◆—**er** n
dessinateur, -trice mf; **d. clothes** vêtements
mpl griffés.
designate ['dezɪgneɪt] vt désigner. ◆**desig-
'nation** n désignation f.
desir/e [dɪ'zaɪər] n désir m; **I've no d. to** je
n'ai aucune envie de; – vt désirer (**to do**
faire). ◆—**able** a désirable; **d. property**/*etc* (*in advertising*) (très) belle
propriété/*etc*.
desk [desk] n Sch pupitre m; (*in office*)
bureau m; (*in shop*) caisse f; (**reception**) **d.**
réception f; **the news d.** Journ le service des

informations; – a (*job*) de bureau; **d. clerk**
(*in hotel*) Am réceptionniste mf.
desolate ['desələt] a (*deserted*) désolé; (*in
ruins*) dévasté; (*dreary, bleak*) morne,
triste. ◆**deso'lation** n (*ruin*) dévastation
f; (*emptiness*) solitude f.
despair [dɪ'speər] n désespoir m; **to drive
s.o. to d.** désespérer qn; **in d.** au désespoir;
– vi désespérer (**of s.o.** de qn, **of doing** de
faire). ◆—**ing** a désespéré; (*criminal*) capable de tout;
(*serious*) grave; **to be d. for** (*money, love etc*)
avoir désespérément besoin de; (*a cigarette, baby etc*) mourir d'envie d'avoir.
◆'**desperately** adv (*ill*) gravement; (*in
love*) éperdument. ◆**despe'ration** n
désespoir m; **in d.** (*as a last resort*) en désespoir de cause.
despatch [dɪ'spætʃ] see dispatch.
desperado [despə'rɑːdəu] n (*pl* -*oes* or -*os*)
criminel m.
despise [dɪ'spaɪz] vt mépriser. ◆**despicable** a ignoble, méprisable.
despite [dɪ'spaɪt] prep malgré.
despondent [dɪ'spɒndənt] a découragé.
◆**despondency** n découragement m.
despot ['despɒt] n despote m. ◆**despotism** n despotisme m.
dessert [dɪ'zɜːt] n dessert m. ◆**dessert-
spoon** n cuiller f à dessert.
destabilize [diː'steɪbəlaɪz] vt déstabiliser.
destination [destɪ'neɪʃ(ə)n] n destination f.
destine ['destɪn] vt destiner (**for** à, **to do** à
faire); **it was destined to happen** ça devait
arriver. ◆**destiny** n destin m; (*fate of individual*) destinée f.
destitute ['destɪtjuːt] a (*poor*) indigent; **d. of**
(*lacking in*) dénué de. ◆**desti'tution** n
dénuement m.
destroy [dɪ'strɔɪ] vt détruire; (*horse etc*)
abattre. ◆—**er** n (*person*) destructeur,
-trice mf; (*ship*) contre-torpilleur m.
◆**destruct** vt Mil détruire. ◆**destruction**
n destruction f. ◆**destructive** a (*person,
war*) destructeur; (*power*) destructif.
detach [dɪ'tætʃ] vt détacher (**from** de).
◆—**ed** a (*indifferent*) détaché; (*view*)
désintéressé; **d. house** maison f
individuelle. ◆—**able** a (*lining*) amovible.
◆—**ment** n (*attitude*) & Mil détachement
m; **the d. of** (*action*) la séparation de.
detail ['diːteɪl, Am dɪ'teɪl] **1** n détail m; **in d.**
en détail; – vt raconter or exposer en détail
or par le menu, détailler. **2** vt Mil détacher
(**to do** pour faire); – n détachement m.
◆—**ed** a (*account etc*) détaillé.
detain [dɪ'teɪn] vt retenir; (*imprison*) détenir.

◆**detai'nee** n Pol Jur détenu, -ue mf.
◆**detention** n Jur détention f; Sch retenue f.

detect [dɪ'tekt] vt découvrir; (perceive) distinguer; (identify) identifier; (mine) détecter; (illness) dépister. ◆**detection** n découverte f; identification f; détection f; dépistage m. ◆**detector** n détecteur m.

detective [dɪ'tektɪv] n agent m de la Sûreté, policier m (en civil); (private) détective m; – a (film etc) policier; **d. story** roman m policier; **d. constable** = inspecteur m de police.

deter [dɪ'tɜɪr] vt (-rr-) to **d. s.o.** dissuader or décourager qn (**from doing** de faire, **from sth** de qch).

detergent [dɪ'tɜɪdʒənt] n détergent m.

deteriorate [dɪ'tɪərɪəreɪt] vi se détériorer; (of morals) dégénérer. ◆**deterio'ration** n détérioration f; dégénérescence f.

determin/e [dɪ'tɜɪmɪn] vt déterminer; (price) fixer; to **d. s.o. to do** décider qn à faire; to **d. that** décider que; to **d. to do** se déterminer à faire. ◆**—ed** a (look, quantity) déterminé; **d. to do** or **on doing** décidé à faire; **I'm d. she'll succeed** je suis bien décidé à ce qu'elle réussisse.

deterrent [dɪ'terənt, Am dɪ'tɜɪrənt] n Mil force f de dissuasion; **to be a d.** Fig être dissuasif.

detest [dɪ'test] vt détester (**doing** faire). ◆**—able** a détestable.

detonate ['detəneɪt] vt faire détoner or exploser; – vi détoner. ◆**deto'nation** n détonation f. ◆**detonator** n détonateur m.

detour ['diːtuər] n détour m.

detract [dɪ'trækt] vi **to d. from** (make less) diminuer. ◆**detractor** n détracteur, -trice mf.

detriment ['detrɪmənt] n détriment m. ◆**detri'mental** a préjudiciable (**to** à).

devalue [diː'væljuː] vt (money) & Fig dévaluer. ◆**devalu'ation** n dévaluation f.

devastat/e ['devəsteɪt] vt (lay waste) dévaster; (opponent) anéantir; (person) Fig foudroyer. ◆**—ing** a (storm etc) dévastateur; (overwhelming) confondant, accablant; (charm) irrésistible.

develop [dɪ'veləp] vt développer; (area, land) mettre en valeur; (habit, illness) contracter; (talent) manifester; Phot développer; to **d. a liking for** prendre goût à; – vi se développer; (of event) se produire; **to d. into** devenir. ◆**—ing** a (country) en voie de développement; – n Phot développement m. ◆**—er** n (property) **d.** promoteur m (de construction).

◆**—ment** n développement m; (of land) mise f en valeur; (housing) **d.** lotissement m; (large) grand ensemble m; **a (new) d.** (in situation) un fait nouveau.

deviate ['diːvɪeɪt] vi dévier (**from** de); **to d. from the norm** s'écarter de la norme. ◆**deviant** a anormal. ◆**devi'ation** n déviation f.

device [dɪ'vaɪs] n dispositif m, engin m; (scheme) procédé m; **left to one's own devices** livré à soi-même.

devil ['dev(ə)l] n diable m; **a** or **the d. of a problem** Fam un problème épouvantable; **a** or **the d. of a noise** Fam un bruit infernal; **I had a** or **the d. of a job** Fam j'ai eu un mal fou (**doing, to do** à faire); **what/where/why the d.?** Fam que/où/pourquoi diable?; **like the d.** (to run etc) comme un fou. ◆**devilish** a diabolique. ◆**devilry** n (mischief) diablerie f.

devious ['diːvɪəs] a (mind, behaviour) tortueux; **he's d.** il a l'esprit tortueux. ◆**—ness** n (of person) esprit m tortueux.

devise [dɪ'vaɪz] vt (plan) combiner; (plot) tramer; (invent) inventer.

devitalize [diː'vaɪtəlaɪz] vt rendre exsangue, affaiblir.

devoid [dɪ'vɔɪd] a **d. of** dénué or dépourvu de; (guilt) exempt de.

devolution [diːvə'luːʃ(ə)n] n Pol décentralisation f; **the d. of** (power) la délégation de.

devolve [dɪ'vɒlv] vi **to d. upon** incomber à.

devot/e [dɪ'vəut] vt consacrer (**to** à). ◆**—ed** a (devoted; admirer) fervent. ◆**—edly** adv avec dévouement. ◆**devo'tee** n Sp Mus passionné, -ée mf. ◆**devotion** n dévouement m; (religious) dévotion f; pl (prayers) dévotions fpl.

devour [dɪ'vauər] vt (eat, engulf, read etc) dévorer.

devout [dɪ'vaut] a dévot, pieux; (supporter, prayer) fervent.

dew [djuː] n rosée f. ◆**dewdrop** n goutte f de rosée.

dext(e)rous ['dekst(ə)rəs] a adroit, habile. ◆**dex'terity** n adresse f, dextérité f.

diabetes [daɪə'biːtiːz] n Med diabète m. ◆**diabetic** a & n diabétique (mf).

diabolical [daɪə'bɒlɪk(ə)l] a diabolique; (bad) épouvantable.

diadem ['daɪədem] n diadème m.

diagnosis, pl **-oses** [daɪəg'nəusɪs, -əusiːz] n diagnostic m. ◆**'diagnose** vt diagnostiquer.

diagonal [daɪ'æɡən(ə)l] a diagonal; – n (line) diagonale f. ◆**—ly** adv en diagonale.

diagram ['daɪəɡræm] n schéma m,

diagramme *m*; *Geom* figure *f*. ◆**diagra'mmatic** *a* schématique.

dial ['daɪəl] *n* cadran *m*; − *vt* (-ll-, *Am* -l-) (*number*) *Tel* faire, composer; (*person*) appeler; **to d. s.o. direct** appeler qn par l'automatique; **d. tone** *Am* tonalité *f*. ◆**dialling** *a* **d. code** indicatif *m*; **d. tone** tonalité *f*.

dialect ['daɪəlekt] *n* (*regional*) dialecte *m*; (*rural*) patois *m*.

dialogue ['daɪəlɒɡ] (*Am* **dialog**) *n* dialogue *m*.

dialysis, *pl* **-yses** [daɪˈælɪsɪs, -ɪsiːz] *n Med* dialyse *f*.

diameter [daɪˈæmɪtər] *n* diamètre *m*. ◆**dia'metrically** *adv* (*opposed*) diamétralement.

diamond ['daɪəmənd] **1** *n* (*stone*) diamant *m*; (*shape*) losange *m*; (*baseball*) **d.** *Am* terrain *m* (de baseball); **d. necklace**/*etc* rivière *f*/*etc* de diamants. **2** *n & npl Cards* carreau *m*.

diaper ['daɪəpər] *n* (*for baby*) *Am* couche *f*.

diaphragm ['daɪəfræm] *n* diaphragme *m*.

diarrh(o)ea [daɪəˈrɪə] *n* diarrhée *f*.

diary ['daɪərɪ] *n* (*calendar*) agenda *m*; (*private*) journal *m* (intime).

dice [daɪs] *n inv* dé *m* (à jouer); − *vt Culin* couper en dés.

dicey ['daɪsɪ] *a* (-ier, -iest) *Fam* risqué.

dichotomy [daɪˈkɒtəmɪ] *n* dichotomie *f*.

dickens ['dɪkɪnz] *n* **where/why/what the d.?** *Fam* où/pourquoi/que diable?

dictate [dɪkˈteɪt] *vt* dicter (**to** à); − *vi* dicter; **to d. to s.o.** (*order around*) régenter qn. ◆**dictation** *n* dictée *f*. ◆**'dictaphone®** *n* dictaphone® *m*.

dictates ['dɪkteɪts] *npl* préceptes *mpl*; **the d. of conscience** la voix de la conscience.

dictator [dɪkˈteɪtər] *n* dictateur *m*. ◆**dicta-'torial** *a* dictatorial. ◆**dictatorship** *n* dictature *f*.

diction ['dɪkʃ(ə)n] *n* langage *m*; (*way of speaking*) diction *f*.

dictionary ['dɪkʃənərɪ] *n* dictionnaire *m*.

dictum ['dɪktəm] *n* dicton *m*.

did [dɪd] *see* **do.**

diddle ['dɪd(ə)l] *vt Sl* rouler; **to d. s.o. out of sth** carotter qch à qn; **to get diddled out of sth** se faire refaire de qch.

die [daɪ] **1** *vi* (*pt & pp* **died,** *pres p* **dying**) mourir (**of, from** de); **to be dying to do** *Fam* mourir d'envie de faire; **to be dying for sth** *Fam* avoir une envie folle de qch; **to d. away** (*of noise*) mourir; **to d. down** (*of fire*) mourir; (*of storm*) se calmer; **to d. off** mourir (les uns après les autres); **to d. out** (*of custom*) mourir. **2** *n* (*in engraving*) coin

m; *Tech* matrice *f*; **the d. is cast** *Fig* les dés sont jetés.

diehard ['daɪhɑːd] *n* réactionnaire *mf*.

diesel ['diːzəl] *a & n* **d. (engine)** (moteur *m*) diesel *m*; **d. (oil)** gazole *m*.

diet ['daɪət] *n* (*for slimming etc*) régime *m*; (*usual food*) alimentation *f*; **to go on a d.** faire un régime; − *vi* suivre un régime. ◆**dietary** *a* diététique; **d. fibre** fibre(s) *f*(*pl*) alimentaire(s). ◆**die'tician** *n* diététicien, -ienne *mf*.

differ ['dɪfər] *vi* différer (**from** de); (*disagree*) ne pas être d'accord (**from** avec). ◆**difference** *n* différence *f* (**in** de); (*in age, weight etc*) écart *m*, différence *f*; **d. (of opinion)** différend *m*; **it makes no d.** ça n'a pas d'importance; **it makes no d. to me** ça m'est égal; **to make a d. in sth** changer qch. ◆**different** *a* différent (**from, to** de); (*another*) autre; (*various*) différents, divers. ◆**diffe-'rential** *a* différentiel; − *npl Econ* écarts *mpl* salariaux. ◆**diffe'rentiate** *vt* différencier (**from** de); **to d. (between)** faire la différence entre. ◆**differently** *adv* différemment (**from, to** de), autrement (**from, to** que).

difficult ['dɪfɪkəlt] *a* difficile (**to do** à faire); **it's d. for us to ...** il nous est difficile de ... ; **the d. thing is to ...** le plus difficile est de .... ◆**difficulty** *n* difficulté *f*; **to have d. doing** avoir du mal à faire; **to be in d.** avoir des difficultés; **d. with** des ennuis *mpl* avec.

diffident ['dɪfɪdənt] *a* (*person*) qui manque d'assurance; (*smile, tone*) mal assuré. ◆**diffidence** *n* manque *m* d'assurance.

diffuse [dɪˈfjuːz] *vt* (*spread*) diffuser; − [dɪˈfjuːs] *a* (*spread out, wordy*) diffus. ◆**diffusion** *n* diffusion *f*.

dig [dɪɡ] *vt* (*pt & pp* **dug,** *pres p* **digging**) (*ground*) bêcher; (*hole, grave etc*) creuser; (*understand*) *Sl* piger; (*appreciate*) *Sl* aimer; **to d. sth into** (*thrust*) enfoncer qch dans; **to d. out** (*animal, fact*) déterrer; (*accident victim*) dégager; (*find*) *Fam* dénicher; **to d. up** déterrer; (*weed*) arracher; (*earth*) retourner; (*street*) piocher; − *vi* creuser; (*of pig*) fouiller; **to d. (oneself) in** *Mil* se retrancher; **to d. in** (*eat*) *Fam* manger; **to d. into** (*s.o.'s food*) fouiller dans; (*meal*) *Fam* attaquer; − *n* (*with spade*) coup *m* de bêche; (*push*) coup *m* de poing *or* de coude; (*remark*) *Fam* coup *m* de griffe. ◆**digger** *n* (*machine*) pelleteuse *f*.

digest [daɪˈdʒest] *vti* digérer; − ['daɪdʒest] *n* *Journ* condensé *m*. ◆**digestible** *a* digeste.

◆**digestion** *n* digestion *f.* ◆**digestive** *a* digestif.

digit ['dɪdʒɪt] *n* (*number*) chiffre *m.* ◆**digital** *a* (*watch, keyboard etc*) numérique.

dignified ['dɪgnɪfaɪd] *a* digne, qui a de la dignité. ◆**dignify** *vt* donner de la dignité à; **to d. with the name of** honorer du nom de. ◆**dignitary** *n* dignitaire *m.* ◆**dignity** *n* dignité *f.*

digress [daɪ'gres] *vi* faire une digression; **to d. from** s'écarter de. ◆**digression** *n* digression *f.*

digs [dɪgz] *npl Fam* chambre *f* (meublée), logement *m.*

dilapidated [dɪ'læpɪdeɪtɪd] *a* (*house*) délabré. ◆**dilapi'dation** *n* délabrement *m.*

dilate [daɪ'leɪt] *vt* dilater; – *vi* se dilater. ◆**dilation** *n* dilatation *f.*

dilemma [daɪ'lemə] *n* dilemme *m.*

dilettante [dɪlɪ'tæntɪ] *n* dilettante *mf.*

diligent ['dɪlɪdʒənt] *a* assidu, appliqué; **to be d. in doing sth** faire qch avec zèle. ◆**diligence** *n* zèle *m*, assiduité *f.*

dilly-dally [dɪlɪ'dælɪ] *vi Fam* (*dawdle*) lambiner, lanterner; (*hesitate*) tergiverser.

dilute [daɪ'luːt] *vt* diluer; – *a* dilué.

dim [dɪm] *a* (**dimmer, dimmest**) (*feeble*) faible; (*colour*) terne; (*room*) sombre; (*memory, outline*) vague; (*person*) stupide; – *vt* (**-mm-**) (*light*) baisser, réduire; (*glory*) ternir; (*memory*) estomper. ◆**-ly** *adv* faiblement; (*vaguely*) vaguement. ◆**-ness** *n* faiblesse *f*; (*of memory etc*) vague *m*; (*of room*) pénombre *f.* ◆**dimwit** *n* idiot, -ote *mf.* ◆**dim'witted** *a* idiot.

dime [daɪm] *n* (*US & Can coin*) (pièce *f* de) dix cents *mpl*; **a d. store** = un Prisunic®, un Monoprix®.

dimension [daɪ'menʃ(ə)n] *n* dimension *f*; (*extent*) *Fig* étendue *f.* ◆**dimensional** *a* **two-d.** à deux dimensions.

diminish [dɪ'mɪnɪʃ] *vti* diminuer. ◆**-ing** *a* qui diminue.

diminutive [dɪ'mɪnjʊtɪv] **1** *a* (*tiny*) minuscule. **2** *a & n Gram* diminutif (*m*).

dimple ['dɪmp(ə)l] *n* fossette *f.* ◆**dimpled** *a* (*chin, cheek*) à fossettes.

din [dɪn] **1** *n* (*noise*) vacarme *m.* **2** *vt* (**-nn-**) **to d. into s.o. that** rabâcher à qn que.

din/e [daɪn] *vi* dîner (**off, on** de); **to d. out** dîner en ville. ◆**-ing** *a* **d. car** *Rail* wagon-restaurant *m*; **d. room** salle *f* à manger. ◆**-er** *n* dîneur, -euse *mf*; *Rail* wagon-restaurant *m*; (*short-order restaurant*) *Am* petit restaurant *m.*

ding(dong)! ['dɪŋ(dɒŋ)] *int* (*of bell*) dring!, ding (dong)!

dinghy ['dɪŋgɪ] *n* petit canot *m*, youyou *m*; (**rubber**) **d.** canot *m* pneumatique.

dingy ['dɪndʒɪ] *a* (**-ier, -iest**) (*dirty*) malpropre; (*colour*) terne. ◆**dinginess** *n* malpropreté *f.*

dinner ['dɪnər] *n* (*evening meal*) dîner *m*; (*lunch*) déjeuner *m*; (*for dog, cat*) pâtée *f*; **to have d.** dîner; **to have s.o. to d.** avoir qn à dîner; **d. dance** dîner-dansant *m*; **d. jacket** smoking *m*; **d. party** dîner *m* (à la maison); **d. plate** grande assiette *f*; **d. service, d. set** service *m* de table.

dinosaur ['daɪnəsɔːr] *n* dinosaure *m.*

dint [dɪnt] *n* **by d. of** à force de.

diocese ['daɪəsɪs] *n Rel* diocèse *m.*

dip [dɪp] *vt* (**-pp-**) plonger; (*into liquid*) tremper, plonger; **to d. one's headlights** se mettre en code; – *vi* (*of sun etc*) baisser; (*of road*) plonger; **to d. into** (*pocket, savings*) puiser dans; (*book*) feuilleter; – *n* (*in road*) déclivité *f*; **to go for a d.** faire trempette.

diphtheria [dɪp'θɪərɪə] *n* diphtérie *f.*

diphthong ['dɪfθɒŋ] *n Ling* diphtongue *f.*

diploma [dɪ'pləʊmə] *n* diplôme *m.*

diplomacy [dɪ'pləʊməsɪ] *n* (*tact*) & *Pol* diplomatie *f.* ◆**'diplomat** *n* diplomate *mf.* ◆**diplo'matic** *a* diplomatique; **to be d.** (*tactful*) *Fig* être diplomate.

dipper ['dɪpər] *n* **the big d.** (*at fairground*) les montagnes *fpl* russes.

dire ['daɪər] *a* affreux; (*poverty, need*) extrême.

direct [daɪ'rekt] **1** *a* (*result, flight, person etc*) direct; (*danger*) immédiat; – *adv* directement. **2** *vt* (*work, one's steps, one's attention*) diriger; (*letter, remark*) adresser (**to** à); (*efforts*) orienter (**to, towards** vers); (*film*) réaliser; (*play*) mettre en scène; **to d. s.o. to** (*place*) indiquer à qn le chemin de; **to d. s.o. to do** charger qn de faire. ◆**direction** *n* direction *f*, sens *m*; (*management*) direction *f*; (*of film*) réalisation *f*; (*of play*) mise *f* en scène; *pl* (*orders*) indications *fpl*; **directions** (*for use*) mode *m* d'emploi; **in the opposite d.** en sens inverse. ◆**directive** [dɪ'rektɪv] *n* directive *f.* ◆**directly** *adv* (*without detour*) directement; (*at once*) tout de suite; (*to speak*) franchement; – *conj Fam* aussitôt que. ◆**directness** *n* (*of reply*) franchise *f.* ◆**director** *n* directeur, -trice *mf*; (*of film*) réalisateur, -trice *mf*; (*of play*) metteur *m* en scène. ◆**directorship** *n Com* poste *m* de directeur.

directory [daɪ'rektərɪ] *n Tel* annuaire *m*; (*of*

streets) guide *m*; (*of addresses*) répertoire *m*; **d. enquiries** *Tel* renseignements *mpl.*
dirge [dɜːdʒ] *n* chant *m* funèbre.
dirt [dɜːt] *n* saleté *f*; (*filth*) ordure *f*; (*mud*) boue *f*; (*earth*) terre *f*; (*talk*) *Fig* obscénité(s) *f*(*pl*); **d. cheap** *Fam* très bon marché; **d. road** chemin *m* de terre; **d. track** *Sp* cendrée *f*. ◆**dirty** *a* (**-ier, -iest**) sale; (*job*) salissant; (*obscene, unpleasant*) sale; (*word*) grossier, obscène; **to get d.** se salir; **to get sth d.** salir qch; **a d. joke** une histoire cochonne; **a d. trick** un sale tour; **a d. old man** un vieux cochon; − *adv* (*to fight*) déloyalement; − *vt* salir; (*machine*) encrasser; − *vi* se salir.
disabl/e [dɪˈseɪb(ə)l] *vt* rendre infirme; (*maim*) mutiler. ◆**−ed** *a* infirme, handicapé; (*maimed*) mutilé; − *n* **the d.** les infirmes *mpl*, les handicapés *mpl.* ◆**disa-'bility** *n* infirmité *f*; *Fig* désavantage *m.*
disadvantage [dɪsədˈvɑːntɪdʒ] *n* désavantage *m*; − *vt* désavantager.
disaffected [dɪsəˈfektɪd] *a* mécontent. ◆**disaffection** *n* désaffection *f* (**for** pour).
disagree [dɪsəˈɡriː] *vi* ne pas être d'accord, être en désaccord (**with** avec); (*of figures*) ne pas concorder; **to d. with** (*of food etc*) ne pas réussir à. ◆**−able** *a* désagréable. ◆**−ment** *n* désaccord *m*; (*quarrel*) différend *m.*
disallow [dɪsəˈlaʊ] *vt* rejeter.
disappear [dɪsəˈpɪər] *vi* disparaître. ◆**disappearance** *n* disparition *f.*
disappoint [dɪsəˈpɔɪnt] *vt* décevoir; **I'm disappointed with it** ça m'a déçu. ◆**−ing** *a* décevant. ◆**−ment** *n* déception *f.*
disapprov/e [dɪsəˈpruːv] *vi* **to d. of s.o./sth** désapprouver qn/qch; **I d.** je suis contre. ◆**−ing** *a* (*look etc*) désapprobateur. ◆**disapproval** *n* désapprobation *f.*
disarm [dɪsˈɑːm] *vti* désarmer. ◆**disarmament** *n* désarmement *m.*
disarray [dɪsəˈreɪ] *n* (*disorder*) désordre *m*; (*distress*) désarroi *m.*
disaster [dɪˈzɑːstər] *n* désastre *m*, catastrophe *f*; **d. area** région *f* sinistrée. ◆**d.-stricken** *a* sinistré. ◆**disastrous** *a* désastreux.
disband [dɪsˈbænd] *vt* disperser; − *vi* se disperser.
disbelief [dɪsbəˈliːf] *n* incrédulité *f.*
disc [dɪsk] (*Am* **disk**) *n* disque *m*; **identity d.** plaque *f* d'identité; **d. jockey** animateur, -trice *mf* (de variétés *etc*), disc-jockey *m.*
discard [dɪsˈkɑːd] *vt* (*get rid of*) se débarrasser de; (*plan, hope etc*) *Fig* abandonner.
discern [dɪˈsɜːn] *vt* discerner. ◆**−ing** *a*

(*person*) averti, sagace. ◆**−ible** *a* perceptible. ◆**−ment** *n* discernement *m.*
discharge [dɪsˈtʃɑːdʒ] *vt* (*gun, accused person*) décharger; (*liquid*) déverser; (*patient, employee*) renvoyer; (*soldier*) libérer; (*unfit soldier*) réformer; (*one's duty*) accomplir; − *vi* (*of wound*) suppurer; − [ˈdɪstʃɑːdʒ] *n* (*of gun*) & *El* décharge *f*; (*of liquid*) & *Med* écoulement *m*; (*dismissal*) renvoi *m*; (*freeing*) libération *f*; (*of unfit soldier*) réforme *f.*
disciple [dɪˈsaɪp(ə)l] *n* disciple *m.*
discipline [ˈdɪsɪplɪn] *n* (*behaviour, subject*) discipline *f*; − *vt* (*control*) discipliner; (*punish*) punir. ◆**discipli'narian** *n* partisan, -ane *mf* de la discipline; **to be a (strict) d.** être très à cheval sur la discipline. ◆**disci'plinary** *a* disciplinaire.
disclaim [dɪsˈkleɪm] *vt* désavouer; (*responsibility*) (dé)nier.
disclose [dɪsˈkləʊz] *vt* révéler, divulguer. ◆**disclosure** *n* révélation *f.*
disco [ˈdɪskəʊ] *n* (*pl* **-os**) *Fam* disco(thèque) *f.*
discolour [dɪsˈkʌlər] *vt* décolorer; (*teeth*) jaunir; − *vi* se décolorer; jaunir. ◆**disco-lo(u)'ration** *n* décoloration *f*; jaunissement *m.*
discomfort [dɪsˈkʌmfət] *n* (*physical, mental*) malaise *m*, gêne *f*; (*hardship*) inconvénient *m.*
disconcert [dɪskənˈsɜːt] *vt* déconcerter.
disconnect [dɪskəˈnekt] *vt* (*unfasten etc*) détacher; (*unplug*) débrancher; (*wires*) *El* déconnecter; (*gas, telephone etc*) couper. ◆**−ed** *a* (*speech*) décousu.
discontent [dɪskənˈtent] *n* mécontentement *m.* ◆**discontented** *a* mécontent.
discontinu/e [dɪskənˈtɪnjuː] *vt* cesser, interrompre. ◆**−ed** *a* (*article*) *Com* qui ne se fait plus.
discord [ˈdɪskɔːd] *n* discorde *f*; *Mus* dissonance *f.*
discotheque [ˈdɪskətek] *n* (*club*) discothèque *f.*
discount 1 [ˈdɪskaʊnt] *n* (*on article*) remise *f*; (*on account paid early*) escompte *m*; **at à d.** (*to buy, sell*) au rabais; **d. store** solderie *f.* **2** [dɪsˈkaʊnt] *vt* (*story etc*) ne pas tenir compte de.
discourage [dɪsˈkʌrɪdʒ] *vt* décourager; **to get discouraged** se décourager. ◆**−ment** *n* découragement *m.*
discourse [ˈdɪskɔːs] *n* discours *m.*
discourteous [dɪsˈkɜːtɪəs] *a* impoli, discourtois. ◆**discourtesy** *n* impolitesse *f.*
discover [dɪsˈkʌvər] *vt* découvrir. ◆**discovery** *n* découverte *f.*

discredit [dɪs'kredɪt] vt (cast slur on) discréditer; (refuse to believe) ne pas croire; – n discrédit m. ◆**—able** a indigne.

discreet [dɪ'skriːt] a (careful) prudent, avisé; (unassuming, reserved etc) discret. ◆**discretion** n prudence f; discrétion f; **I'll use my own d.** je ferai comme bon me semblera. ◆**discretionary** a discrétionnaire.

discrepancy [dɪ'skrepənsɪ] n divergence f, contradiction f (**between** entre).

discriminat/e [dɪ'skrɪmɪneɪt] vi **to d. between** distinguer entre; **to d. against** établir une discrimination contre; – vt **to d. sth/s.o. from** distinguer qch/qn de. ◆**—ing** a (person) averti, sagace; (ear) fin. ◆**discrimi'nation** n (judgement) discernement m; (distinction) distinction f; (partiality) discrimination f. ◆**discriminatory** [-ətərɪ] a discriminatoire.

discus ['dɪskəs] n Sp disque m.

discuss [dɪ'skʌs] vt (talk about) discuter de; (examine in detail) discuter. ◆**discussion** n discussion f; **under d.** (matter etc) en question, en discussion.

disdain [dɪs'deɪn] vt dédaigner; – n dédain m. ◆**disdainful** a dédaigneux; **to be d. of** dédaigner.

disease [dɪ'ziːz] n maladie f. ◆**diseased** a malade.

disembark [dɪsɪm'bɑːk] vti débarquer. ◆**disembar'kation** n débarquement m.

disembodied [dɪsɪm'bɒdɪd] a désincarné.

disembowel [dɪsɪm'bauəl] vt (-ll-, Am -l-) éventrer.

disenchant [dɪsɪn'tʃɑːnt] vt désenchanter. ◆**—ment** n désenchantement m.

disengage [dɪsɪn'geɪdʒ] vt (object) dégager; (troops) désengager.

disentangle [dɪsɪn'tæŋg(ə)l] vt démêler; **to d. oneself from** se dégager de.

disfavour [dɪs'feɪvər] n défaveur f.

disfigure [dɪs'fɪgər] vt défigurer. ◆**—ment** n défigurement m.

disgorge [dɪs'gɔːdʒ] vt (food) vomir.

disgrac/e [dɪs'greɪs] n (shame) honte f (**to** à); (disfavour) disgrâce f; – vt déshonorer, faire honte à. ◆**—ed** a (politician etc) disgracié. ◆**disgraceful** a honteux (**of s.o.** de la part de qn). ◆**disgracefully** adv honteusement.

disgruntled [dɪs'grʌnt(ə)ld] a mécontent.

disguise [dɪs'gaɪz] vt déguiser (**as** en); – n déguisement m; **in d.** déguisé.

disgust [dɪs'gʌst] n dégoût m (**for, at, with** de); in d. dégoûté; – vt dégoûter, écœurer. ◆**—ed** a dégoûté (**at, by, with** de); **to be d. with s.o.** (annoyed) être fâché contre qn; **d.**

to hear that . . . indigné d'apprendre que . . . . ◆**—ing** a dégoûtant, écœurant. ◆**—ingly** adv d'une façon dégoûtante.

dish [dɪʃ] 1 n (container) plat m; (food) mets m, plat m; **the dishes** la vaisselle; **she's a (real) d.** Sl c'est un beau brin de fille. 2 vt **to d. out** distribuer; **to d. out** or **up** (food) servir. ◆**dishcloth** n (for washing) lavette f; (for drying) torchon m. ◆**dishpan** n Am bassine f (à vaisselle). ◆**dishwasher** n lave-vaisselle m inv.

disharmony [dɪs'hɑːmənɪ] n désaccord m; Mus dissonance f.

dishearten [dɪs'hɑːt(ə)n] vt décourager.

dishevelled [dɪ'ʃev(ə)ld] a hirsute, échevelé.

dishonest [dɪs'ɒnɪst] a malhonnête; (insincere) de mauvaise foi. ◆**dishonesty** n malhonnêteté f; mauvaise foi f.

dishonour [dɪs'ɒnər] n déshonneur m; – vt déshonorer; (cheque) refuser d'honorer. ◆**—able** a peu honorable. ◆**—ably** adv avec déshonneur.

dishy ['dɪʃɪ] a (-ier, -iest) (woman, man) Sl beau, sexy, qui a du chien.

disillusion [dɪsɪ'luːʒ(ə)n] vt désillusionner; – n désillusion f. ◆**—ment** n désillusion f.

disincentive [dɪsɪn'sentɪv] n mesure f dissuasive; **to be a d. to s.o.** décourager qn; **it's a d. to work/invest/etc** cela n'encourage pas à travailler/investir/etc.

disinclined [dɪsɪn'klaɪnd] a peu disposé (**to** à). ◆**disincli'nation** n répugnance f.

disinfect [dɪsɪn'fekt] vt désinfecter. ◆**disinfectant** a & n désinfectant (m). ◆**disinfection** n désinfection f.

disinherit [dɪsɪn'herɪt] vt déshériter.

disintegrate [dɪs'ɪntɪgreɪt] vi se désintégrer; – vt désintégrer. ◆**disinte'gration** n désintégration f.

disinterested [dɪs'ɪntrɪstɪd] a (impartial) désintéressé; (uninterested) Fam indifférent (**in** à).

disjointed [dɪs'dʒɔɪntɪd] a décousu.

disk [dɪsk] n 1 Am = disc. 2 (magnetic) d. (of computer) disque m (magnétique).

dislike [dɪs'laɪk] vt ne pas aimer (**doing** faire); **he doesn't d. it** ça ne lui déplaît pas; – n aversion f (**for, of** pour); **to take a d. to** (person, thing) prendre en grippe; **our likes and dislikes** nos goûts et dégoûts mpl.

dislocate ['dɪsləkeɪt] vt (limb) disloquer; Fig désorganiser; (enemy) déloger. ◆**dislo'cation** n dislocation f.

dislodge [dɪs'lɒdʒ] vt faire bouger, déplacer; (enemy) déloger.

disloyal [dɪs'lɔɪəl] a déloyal. ◆**disloyalty** n déloyauté f.

dismal ['dɪzməl] *a* morne, triste. ◆**—ly** *adv* (*to fail, behave*) lamentablement.

dismantle [dɪs'mænt(ə)l] *vt* (*machine etc*) démonter; (*organization*) démanteler.

dismay [dɪs'meɪ] *vt* consterner; – *n* consternation *f*.

dismember [dɪs'membər] *vt* (*country etc*) démembrer.

dismiss [dɪs'mɪs] *vt* congédier, renvoyer (**from** de); (*official*) destituer; (*appeal*) *Jur* rejeter; (*thought etc*) *Fig* écarter; **d.!** *Mil* rompez!; (*class*) **d.!** *Sch* vous pouvez partir. ◆**dismissal** *n* renvoi *m*; destitution *f*.

dismount [dɪs'maunt] *vi* descendre (**from** de); – *vt* (*rider*) démonter, désarçonner.

disobey [dɪsə'beɪ] *vt* désobéir à; – *vi* désobéir. ◆**disobedience** *n* désobéissance *f*. ◆**disobedient** *a* désobéissant.

disorder [dɪs'ɔːdər] *n* (*confusion*) désordre *m*; (*riots*) désordres *mpl*; **disorder(s)** *Med* troubles *mpl*. ◆**disorderly** *a* (*meeting etc*) désordonné.

disorganize [dɪs'ɔːɡənaɪz] *vt* désorganiser.

disorientate [dɪs'ɔːrɪənteɪt] (*Am* **disorient** [dɪs'ɔːrɪənt]) *vt* désorienter.

disown [dɪs'əun] *vt* désavouer, renier.

disparag/e [dɪs'pærɪdʒ] *vt* dénigrer. ◆**-ing** *a* peu flatteur.

disparate [dɪs'pærət] *a* disparate. ◆**disparity** *n* disparité *f* (**between** entre, de).

dispassionate [dɪs'pæʃənət] *a* (*unemotional*) calme; (*not biased*) impartial.

dispatch [dɪs'pætʃ] *vt* (*letter, work*) expédier; (*troops, messenger*) envoyer; – *n* expédition *f* (**of** de); *Journ Mil* dépêche *f*; **d. rider** *Mil etc* courrier *m*.

dispel [dɪs'pel] *vt* (**-ll-**) dissiper.

dispensary [dɪs'pensərɪ] *n* (*in hospital*) pharmacie *f*; (*in chemist's shop*) officine *f*.

dispense [dɪs'pens] **1** *vt* (*give out*) distribuer; (*justice*) administrer; (*medicine*) préparer. **2** *vi* **to d. with** (*do without*) se passer de; **to d. with the need for** rendre superflu. ◆**dispensation** *n* distribution *f*; **special d.** (*exemption*) dérogation *f*. ◆**dispenser** *n* (*device*) distributeur *m*; **cash d.** distributeur *m* de billets.

disperse [dɪ'spɜːs] *vt* disperser; – *vi* se disperser. ◆**dispersal** *n*, ◆**dispersion** *n* dispersion *f*.

dispirited [dɪ'spɪrɪtɪd] *a* découragé.

displace [dɪs'pleɪs] *vt* (*bone, furniture, refugees*) déplacer; (*replace*) supplanter.

display [dɪs'pleɪ] *vt* montrer; (*notice, electronic data etc*) afficher; (*painting, goods*) exposer; (*courage etc*) faire preuve de; – *n* (*in shop*) étalage *m*; (*of force*) déploiement *m*; (*of anger etc*) manifestation *f*; (*of paintings*) exposition *f*; (*of luxury*) étalage *m*; *Mil* parade *f*; (*of electronic data*) affichage *m*; **d. (unit)** (*of computer*) moniteur *m*; **on d.** exposé; **air d.** fête *f* aéronautique.

displeas/e [dɪs'pliːz] *vt* déplaire à. ◆**-ed** *a* mécontent (**with** de). ◆**-ing** *a* désagréable. ◆**displeasure** *n* mécontentement *m*.

dispos/e [dɪs'pəuz] *vt* disposer (**s.o. to do** qn à faire); – *vi* **to d. of** (*get rid of*) se débarrasser de; (*one's time, money*) disposer de; (*sell*) vendre; (*matter*) expédier, liquider; (*kill*) liquider. ◆**-ed** *a* disposé (**to do** à faire); **well-d. towards** bien disposé envers. ◆**-able** *a* (*plate etc*) à jeter, jetable; (*income*) disponible. ◆**disposal** *n* (*sale*) vente *f*; (*of waste*) évacuation *f*; **at the d. of** à la disposition de. ◆**dispo'sition** *n* (*placing*) disposition *f*; (*character*) naturel *m*; (*readiness*) inclination *f*.

dispossess [dɪspə'zes] *vt* déposséder (**of** de).

disproportion [dɪsprə'pɔːʃ(ə)n] *n* disproportion *f*. ◆**disproportionate** *a* disproportionné.

disprove [dɪs'pruːv] *vt* réfuter.

dispute [dɪs'pjuːt] *n* discussion *f*; (*quarrel*) dispute *f*; *Pol* conflit *m*; *Jur* litige *m*; **beyond d.** incontestable; **in d.** (*matter*) en litige; (*territory*) contesté; – *vt* (*claim etc*) contester; (*discuss*) discuter.

disqualify [dɪs'kwɒlɪfaɪ] *vt* (*make unfit*) rendre inapte (**from** à); *Sp* disqualifier; **to d. from driving** retirer le permis à. ◆**disquali'fication** *n* *Sp* disqualification *f*.

disquiet [dɪs'kwaɪət] *n* inquiétude *f*; – *vt* inquiéter.

disregard [dɪsrɪ'ɡɑːd] *vt* ne tenir aucun compte de; – *n* indifférence *f* (**for** à); (*law*) désobéissance *f* (**for** à).

disrepair [dɪsrɪ'peər] *n* **in (a state of) d.** en mauvais état.

disreputable [dɪs'repjutəb(ə)l] *a* peu recommandable; (*behaviour*) honteux.

disrepute [dɪsrɪ'pjuːt] *n* discrédit *m*; **to bring into d.** jeter le discrédit sur.

disrespect [dɪsrɪ'spekt] *n* manque *m* de respect. ◆**disrespectful** *a* irrespectueux (**to** envers).

disrupt [dɪs'rʌpt] *vt* perturber; (*communications*) interrompre; (*plan*) déranger. ◆**disruption** *n* perturbation *f*; interruption *f*;

dérangement *m*. ◆**disruptive** *a* (*element etc*) perturbateur.

dissatisfied [dɪˈsætɪsfaɪd] *a* mécontent (**with** de). ◆**dissatis'faction** *n* mécontentement *m*.

dissect [darˈsekt] *vt* disséquer. ◆**dissection** *n* dissection *f*.

disseminate [dɪˈsemɪneɪt] *vt* disséminer.

dissension [dɪˈsenʃ(ə)n] *n* dissension *f*.

dissent [dɪˈsent] *vi* différer (d'opinion) (**from sth** à l'égard de qch); – *n* dissentiment *m*. ◆**—ing** *a* dissident.

dissertation [dɪsəˈteɪʃ(ə)n] *n Univ* mémoire *m*.

dissident [ˈdɪsɪdənt] *a & n* dissident, -ente (*mf*). ◆**dissidence** *n* dissidence *f*.

dissimilar [dɪˈsɪmɪlər] *a* dissemblable (**to** à).

dissipate [ˈdɪsɪpeɪt] *vt* dissiper; (*energy*) gaspiller. ◆**dissi'pation** *n* dissipation *f*; gaspillage *m*.

dissociate [dɪˈsəʊʃɪeɪt] *vt* dissocier (**from** de).

dissolute [ˈdɪsəluːt] *a* (*life, person*) dissolu.

dissolve [dɪˈzɒlv] *vt* dissoudre; – *vi* se dissoudre. ◆**disso'lution** *n* dissolution *f*.

dissuade [dɪˈsweɪd] *vt* dissuader (**from doing** de faire); **to d. s.o. from sth** détourner qn de qch. ◆**dissuasion** *n* dissuasion *f*.

distance [ˈdɪstəns] *n* distance *f*; **in the d.** au loin; **from a d.** de loin; **at a d.** à quelque distance; **it's within walking d.** on peut y aller à pied; **to keep one's d.** garder ses distances. ◆**distant** *a* éloigné, lointain; (*relative*) éloigné; (*reserved*) distant; **5 km d. from** à (une distance de) 5 km de. ◆**distantly** *adv* **we're d. related** nous sommes parents éloignés.

distaste [dɪsˈteɪst] *n* aversion *f* (**for** pour). ◆**distasteful** *a* désagréable, déplaisant.

distemper [dɪˈstempər] **1** *n* (*paint*) badigeon *m*; – *vt* badigeonner. **2** *n* (*in dogs*) maladie *f*.

distend [dɪˈstend] *vt* distendre; – *vi* se distendre.

distil [dɪˈstɪl] *vt* (**-ll-**) distiller. ◆**distil-'lation** *n* distillation *f*. ◆**distillery** *n* distillerie *f*.

distinct [dɪˈstɪŋkt] *a* **1** (*voice, light etc*) distinct; (*definite, marked*) net, marqué; (*promise*) formel. **2** (*different*) distinct (**from** de). ◆**distinction** *n* distinction *f*; *Univ* mention *f* très bien; **of d.** (*singer, writer etc*) de marque. ◆**distinctive** *a* distinctif. ◆**distinctively** *adv* distinctement; (*to stipulate, forbid*) formellement; (*noticeably*) nettement, sensiblement; **d. possible** tout à fait possible.

distinguish [dɪˈstɪŋgwɪʃ] *vti* distinguer (**from**, **between** entre); **to d. oneself** se distinguer (**as** en tant que). ◆**—ed** *a* distingué. ◆**—ing** *a* **d. mark** signe *m* particulier; (*discernible*) visible. ◆**—able** *a* qu'on peut distinguer; (*discernible*) visible.

distort [dɪˈstɔːt] *vt* déformer. ◆**—ed** *a* (*false*) faux. ◆**distortion** *n El Med* distorsion *f*; (*of truth*) déformation *f*.

distract [dɪˈstrækt] *vt* distraire (**from** de). ◆**—ed** *a* (*troubled*) préoccupé; (*mad with worry*) éperdu. ◆**—ing** *a* (*noise etc*) gênant. ◆**distraction** *n* (*lack of attention, amusement*) distraction *f*; **to drive to d.** rendre fou.

distraught [dɪˈstrɔːt] *a* éperdu, affolé.

distress [dɪˈstres] *n* (*pain*) douleur *f*; (*anguish*) chagrin *m*; (*misfortune, danger*) détresse *f*; **in d.** (*ship, soul*) en détresse; **in (great) d.** (*poverty*) dans la détresse; – *vt* affliger, peiner. ◆**—ing** *a* affligeant, pénible.

distribute [dɪˈstrɪbjuːt] *vt* distribuer; (*spread evenly*) répartir. ◆**distri'bution** *n* distribution *f*; répartition *f*. ◆**distributor** *n Aut Cin* distributeur *m*; (*of goods*) *Com* concessionnaire *mf*.

district [ˈdɪstrɪkt] *n* région *f*; (*of town*) quartier *m*; (*administrative*) arrondissement *m*; **d. attorney** *Am* = procureur *m* (de la République); **d. nurse** infirmière *f* visiteuse.

distrust [dɪsˈtrʌst] *vt* se méfier de; – *n* méfiance *f* (**of** de). ◆**distrustful** *a* méfiant; **to be d. of** se méfier de.

disturb [dɪˈstɜːb] *vt* (*sleep, water*) troubler; (*papers, belongings*) déranger; **to d. s.o.** (*bother*) déranger qn; (*alarm, worry*) troubler qn. ◆**—ed** *a* (*person etc*) *Psy* troublé. ◆**—ing** *a* (*worrying*) inquiétant; (*annoying, irksome*) gênant. ◆**disturbance** *n* (*noise*) tapage *m*; *pl Pol* troubles *mpl*.

disunity [dɪsˈjuːnɪtɪ] *n* désunion *f*.

disuse [dɪsˈjuːs] *n* **to fall into d.** tomber en désuétude. ◆**disused** [-ˈjuːzd] *a* désaffecté.

ditch [dɪtʃ] **1** *n* fossé *m*. **2** *vt Fam* se débarrasser de.

dither [ˈdɪðər] *vi Fam* hésiter, tergiverser; **to d. (around)** (*waste time*) tourner en rond.

ditto [ˈdɪtəʊ] *adv* idem.

divan [dɪˈvæn] *n* divan *m*.

div/e [daɪv] **1** *vi* (*pt* **dived**, *Am* **dove** [dəʊv]) plonger; (*rush*) se précipiter, se jeter; **to d. for** (*pearls*) pêcher; – *n* plongeon *m*; (*of submarine*) plongée *f*; (*of aircraft*) piqué *m*. **2** *n* (*bar, club*) *Pej* boui-boui *m*. ◆**—ing** *n* (*underwater*) plongée *f* sous-marine; **d. suit** scaphandre *m*; **d. board** plongeoir *m*. ◆**—er** *n* plongeur, -euse *mf*; (*in suit*) scaphandrier *m*.

diverge [daɪ'vɜːdʒ] *vi* diverger (**from** de). ◆**divergence** *n* divergence *f*. ◆**divergent** *a* divergent.

diverse [daɪ'vɜːs] *a* divers. ◆**diversify** *vt* diversifier; — *vi Econ* se diversifier. ◆**diversity** *n* diversité *f*.

divert [daɪ'vɜːt] *vt* détourner (**from** de); (*traffic*) dévier; (*aircraft*) dérouter; (*amuse*) divertir. ◆**diversion** *n Aut* déviation *f*; (*amusement*) divertissement *m*; *Mil* diversion *f*.

divest [daɪ'vest] *vt* **to d. of** (*power, rights*) priver de.

divid/e [dɪ'vaɪd] *vt* diviser (**into** en); **to d. (off) from** séparer de; **to d. up** (*money*) partager; **to d. one's time between** partager son temps entre; — *vi* se diviser. ◆**—ed** *a* (*opinion*) partagé. ◆**—ing** *a* **d. line** ligne *f* de démarcation.

dividend ['dɪvɪdənd] *n Math Fin* dividende *m*.

divine [dɪ'vaɪn] *a* divin. ◆**divinity** *n* (*quality, deity*) divinité *f*; (*study*) théologie *f*.

division [dɪ'vɪʒ(ə)n] *n* division *f*; (*dividing object*) séparation *f*. ◆**divisible** *a* divisible. ◆**divisive** [-'vaɪsɪv] *a* qui sème la zizanie.

divorc/e [dɪ'vɔːs] *n* divorce *m*; — *vt* (*spouse*) divorcer d'avec; *Fig* séparer; — *vi* divorcer. ◆**—ed** *a* divorcé (**from** d'avec); **to get d.** divorcer. ◆**divorcee** [dɪvɔː'siː, *Am* dɪvɔː'seɪ] *n* divorcé, -ée *mf*.

divulge [dɪ'vʌldʒ] *vt* divulguer.

DIY [diːaɪ'waɪ] *n abbr* (*do-it-yourself*) bricolage *m*.

dizzy ['dɪzɪ] *a* (**-ier, -iest**) (*heights*) vertigineux; **to feel d.** avoir le vertige; **to make s.o. (feel) d.** donner le vertige à qn. ◆**dizziness** *n* vertige *m*.

DJ [diː'dʒeɪ] *abbr* = **disc jockey**.

do [duː] **1** *v aux* (*3rd person sing pres t* **does**; *pt* **did**; *pp* **done**; *pres p* **doing**) **do you know?** savez-vous?, est-ce que vous savez?; **I do not** or **don't see** je ne vois pas; **he did say so** (*emphasis*) il l'a bien dit; **do stay** reste donc; **you know him, don't you?** tu le connais, n'est-ce pas?; **better than I do** mieux que je ne le fais; **neither do I** moi non plus; **so do I** moi aussi; **oh, does he?** (*surprise*) ah oui?; **don't!** non! **2** *vt* faire; **to do nothing but sleep** ne faire que dormir; **what does she do?** (*in general*), **what is she doing?** (*now*) qu'est-ce qu'elle fait?, que

fait-elle?; **what have you done (with)** . . . ? qu'as-tu fait (de) . . . ?; **well done** (*congratulations*) bravo!; *Culin* bien cuit; **it's over and done (with)** c'est fini; **that'll do me** (*suit*) ça fera mon affaire; **I've been done** (*cheated*) *Fam* je me suis fait avoir; **I'll do you!** *Fam* je t'aurai!; **to do s.o. out of sth** escroquer qch à qn; **he's hard done by** on le traite durement; **I'm done (in)** (*tired*) *Sl* je suis claqué *or* vanné; **he's done for** *Fam* il est fichu; **to do in** (*kill*) *Sl* supprimer; **to do out** (*clean*) nettoyer; **to do over** (*redecorate*) refaire; **to do up** (*coat, button*) boutonner; (*zip*) fermer; (*house*) refaire; (*goods*) emballer; **do yourself up (well)!** (*wrap up*) couvre-toi (bien)! **3** *vi* (*get along*) aller, marcher; (*suit*) faire l'affaire, convenir; (*be enough*) suffire; (*finish*) finir; **how do you do?** (*introduction*) enchanté; — (*greeting*) bonjour; **he did well** or **right to leave** il a bien fait de partir; **do as I do** fais comme moi; **to make do** se débrouiller; **to do away with sth/s.o.** supprimer qch/qn; **I could do with** (*need, want*) j'aimerais bien (avoir *or* prendre); **to do without sth/s.o.** se passer de qch/qn; **to have to do with** (*relate to*) avoir à voir avec; (*concern*) concerner; **anything doing?** *Fam* est-ce qu'il se passe quelque chose? **4** *n* (*pl* **dos** *or* **do's**) (*party*) soirée *f*, fête *f*; **the do's and don'ts** ce qu'il faut faire ou ne pas faire.

docile ['dəʊsaɪl] *a* docile.

dock [dɒk] **1** *n Nau* dock *m*; — *vi* (*in port*) relâcher; (*at quayside*) se mettre à quai; (*of spacecraft*) s'arrimer. **2** *n Jur* banc *m* des accusés. **3** *vt* (*wages*) rogner; **to d. sth from** (*wages*) retenir qch sur. ◆**—er** *n* docker *m*. ◆**dockyard** *n* chantier *m* naval.

docket ['dɒkɪt] *n* fiche *f*, bordereau *m*.

doctor ['dɒktər] **1** *n Med* médecin *m*, docteur *m*; *Univ* docteur *m*. **2** *vt* (*text, food*) altérer; (*cat*) *Fam* châtrer. ◆**doctorate** *n* doctorat *m* (**in** ès, en).

doctrine ['dɒktrɪn] *n* doctrine *f*. ◆**doctrinaire** *a & n Pej* doctrinaire (*mf*).

document ['dɒkjʊmənt] *n* document *m*; — ['dɒkjʊment] *vt* (*inform*) documenter; (*report in detail*) *TV Journ* accorder une large place à. ◆**docu'mentary** *a & n* documentaire (*m*).

doddering ['dɒdərɪŋ] *a* (*senile*) gâteux; (*shaky*) branlant.

dodge [dɒdʒ] *vt* (*question, acquaintance etc*) esquiver; (*pursuer*) échapper à; (*tax*) éviter de payer; — *vi* faire un saut (de côté); **to d. out of sight** s'esquiver; **to d. through**

(*crowd*) se faufiler dans; – *n* mouvement *m* de côté; (*trick*) *Fig* truc *m*, tour *m*.

dodgems ['dɒdʒəmz] *npl* autos *fpl* tamponneuses.

dodgy ['dɒdʒɪ] *a* (**-ier, -iest**) *Fam* (*tricky*) délicat; (*dubious*) douteux; (*unreliable*) peu sûr.

doe [dəʊ] *n* (*deer*) biche *f*.

doer ['duːər] *n Fam* personne *f* dynamique.

does [dʌz] *see* do.

dog [dɒg] **1** *n* chien *m*; (*person*) *Pej* type *m*; **d. biscuit** biscuit *m or* croquette *f* pour chien; **d. collar** *Fam* col *m* de pasteur; **d. days** canicule *f*. **2** *vt* (**-gg-**) (*follow*) poursuivre. ◆**d.-eared** *a* (*page etc*) écorné. ◆**d.-'tired** *a Fam* claqué, crevé. ◆**doggy** *n Fam* toutou *m*; **d. bag** (*in restaurant*) *Am* petit sac *m* pour emporter les restes.

dogged ['dɒgɪd] *a* obstiné. ◆—**ly** *adv* obstinément.

dogma ['dɒgmə] *n* dogme *m*. ◆**dog'matic** *a* dogmatique. ◆**dogmatism** *n* dogmatisme *m*.

dogsbody ['dɒgzbɒdɪ] *n Pej* factotum *m*, sous-fifre *m*.

doily ['dɔɪlɪ] *n* napperon *m*.

doing ['duːɪŋ] *n* **that's your d.** c'est toi qui as fait ça; **doings** *Fam* activités *fpl*, occupations *fpl*.

do-it-yourself [duːɪtjə'self] *n* bricolage *m*; – *a* (*store, book*) de bricolage.

doldrums ['dɒldrəmz] *npl* **to be in the d.** (*of person*) avoir le cafard; (*of business*) être en plein marasme.

dole [dəʊl] **1** *n* **d. (money)** allocation *f* de chômage; **to go on the d.** s'inscrire au chômage. **2** *vt* **to d. out** distribuer au compte-gouttes.

doleful ['dəʊlful] *a* morne, triste.

doll [dɒl] **1** *n* poupée *f*; (*girl*) *Fam* nana *f*; **doll's house,** *Am* **dollhouse** maison *f* de poupée. **2** *vt* **to d. up** bichonner.

dollar ['dɒlər] *n* dollar *m*.

dollop ['dɒləp] *n* (*of food*) *Pej* gros morceau *m*.

dolphin ['dɒlfɪn] *n* (*sea animal*) dauphin *m*.

domain [dəʊ'meɪn] *n* (*land, sphere*) domaine *m*.

dome [dəʊm] *n* dôme *m*, coupole *f*.

domestic [də'mestɪk] *a* familial, domestique; (*animal*) domestique; (*trade, flight*) intérieur; (*product*) national; **d. science** arts *mpl* ménagers; **d. servant** domestique *mf*. ◆**domesticated** *a* habitué à la vie du foyer; (*animal*) domestique.

domicile ['dɒmɪsaɪl] *n* domicile *m*.

dominant ['dɒmɪnənt] *a* dominant;

(*person*) dominateur. ◆**dominance** *n* prédominance *f*. ◆**dominate** *vti* dominer. ◆**domi'nation** *n* domination *f*. ◆**domi'neering** *a* dominateur.

dominion [də'mɪnjən] *n* domination *f*; (*land*) territoire *m*; *Br Pol* dominion *m*.

domino ['dɒmɪnəʊ] *n* (*pl* **-oes**) domino *m*; *pl* (*game*) dominos *mpl*.

don [dɒn] **1** *n Br Univ* professeur *m*. **2** *vt* (**-nn-**) revêtir.

donate [dəʊ'neɪt] *vt* faire don de; (*blood*) donner; – *vi* donner. ◆**donation** *n* don *m*.

done [dʌn] *see* do.

donkey ['dɒŋkɪ] *n* âne *m*; **for d.'s years** *Fam* depuis belle lurette, depuis un siècle; **d. work** travail *m* ingrat.

donor ['dəʊnər] *n* (*of blood, organ*) donneur, -euse *mf*.

doodle ['duːd(ə)l] *vi* griffonner.

doom [duːm] *n* ruine *f*; (*fate*) destin *m*; (*gloom*) *Fam* tristesse *f*; – *vt* condamner, destiner (**to** à); **to be doomed (to failure)** être voué à l'échec.

door [dɔːr] *n* porte *f*; (*of vehicle, train*) portière *f*, porte *f*; **out of doors** dehors; **d.-to-door salesman** démarcheur *m*. ◆**doorbell** *n* sonnette *f*. ◆**doorknob** *n* poignée *f* de porte. ◆**doorknocker** *n* marteau *m*. ◆**doorman** *n* (*pl* **-men**) (*of hotel etc*) portier *m*, concierge *m*. ◆**doormat** *n* paillasson *m*. ◆**doorstep** *n* seuil *m*. ◆**doorstop(per)** *n* butoir *m* (de porte). ◆**doorway** *n* **in the d.** dans l'encadrement de la porte.

dope [dəʊp] **1** *n Fam* drogue *f*; (*for horse, athlete*) doping *m*; – *vt* doper. **2** *n* (*information*) *Fam* tuyaux *mpl*. **3** *n* (*idiot*) *Fam* imbécile *mf*. ◆**dopey** *a* (**-ier, -iest**) *Fam* (*stupid*) abruti; (*sleepy*) endormi; (*drugged*) drogué, camé.

dormant ['dɔːmənt] *a* (*volcano, matter*) en sommeil; (*passion*) endormi.

dormer ['dɔːmər] *n* **d. (window)** lucarne *f*.

dormitory ['dɔːmɪtrɪ, *Am* 'dɔːmɪtɔːrɪ] *n* dortoir *m*; *Am* résidence *f* (universitaire).

dormouse, *pl* **-mice** ['dɔːmaʊs, -maɪs] *n* loir *m*.

dos/e [dəʊs] *n* dose *f*; (*of hard work*) *Fig* période *f*; (*of illness*) attaque *f*; – *vt* **to d. oneself (up)** se bourrer de médicaments. ◆—**age** *n* (*amount*) dose *f*.

dosshouse ['dɒshaʊs] *n Sl* asile *m* (de nuit).

dossier ['dɒsɪeɪ] *n* (*papers*) dossier *m*.

dot [dɒt] *n* point *m*; **polka d.** pois *m*; **on the d.** *Fam* à l'heure pile; – *vt* (**-tt-**) (*an i*) mettre un point sur. ◆**dotted** *a* d. **line** pointillé *m*; d. **with** parsemé de.

dot/e [dəʊt] *vt* **to d. on** être gaga de. ◆—**ing** *a* affectueux; **her d. husband/father** son mari/père qui lui passe tout.

dotty ['dɒtɪ] *a* (**-ier, -iest**) *Fam* cinglé, toqué.

double ['dʌb(ə)l] *a* double; **a d. bed** un grand lit; **a d. room** une chambre pour deux personnes; **d. 's'** deux 's'; **d. six** deux fois six; **d. three four two** (*phone number*) trente-trois quarante-deux; – *adv* deux fois; (*to fold*) en deux; **he earns it I earn** il gagne le double de moi *or* deux fois plus que moi; **to see d.** voir double; – *n* double *m*; (*person*) double *m*, sosie *m*; (*stand-in*) *Cin* doublure *f*; **on** *or* **at the d.** au pas de course; – *vt* doubler; **to d. back** *or* **over** replier; – *vi* doubler; **to d. back** (*of person*) revenir en arrière; **to d. up** (*with pain, laughter*) être plié en deux. ◆**d.-'barrelled** *a* (*gun*) à deux canons; (*name*) à rallonges. ◆**d.-'bass** *n Mus* contrebasse *f*. ◆**d.-'breasted** *a* (*jacket*) croisé. ◆**d.-'cross** *vt* tromper. ◆**d.-'dealing** *n* double jeu *m*. ◆**d.-'decker (bus)** *n* autobus *m* à impériale. ◆**d.-'door** *n* porte *f* à deux battants. ◆**d.-'dutch** *n Fam* baragouin *m*. ◆**d.-'glazing** *n* (*window*) double vitrage *m*, double(s) fenêtre(s) *f(pl)*. ◆**d.-'parking** *n* stationnement *m* en double file. ◆**d.-'quick** *adv* en vitesse.

doubly ['dʌblɪ] *adv* doublement.

doubt [daʊt] *n* doute *m*; **to be in d. about** avoir des doutes sur; **I have no d. about it** je n'en doute pas; **no d.** (*probably*) sans doute; **in d.** (*result, career etc*) dans la balance; – *vt* douter de; **to d. whether** *or* **that** *or* **if** douter que (+ *sub*). ◆**doubtful** *a* douteux; **to be d. about sth** avoir des doutes sur qch; **it's d. whether** *or* **that** il est douteux que (+ *sub*). ◆**doubtless** *adv* sans doute.

dough [dəʊ] *n* pâte *f*; (*money*) *Fam* fric *m*, blé *m*. ◆**doughnut** *n* beignet *m* (rond).

dour ['dʊər] *a* austère.

douse [daʊs] *vt* arroser, tremper; (*light*) *Fam* éteindre.

dove[1] [dʌv] *n* colombe *f*. ◆**dovecote** [-kɒt] *n* colombier *m*.

dove[2] [dəʊv] *Am see* **dive 1**.

Dover ['dəʊvər] *n* Douvres *m or f*.

dovetail ['dʌvteɪl] **1** *n Carp* queue *f* d'aronde. **2** *vi* (*fit*) *Fig* concorder.

dowdy ['daʊdɪ] *a* (**-ier, -iest**) peu élégant, sans chic.

down[1] [daʊn] *adv* en bas; (*to the ground*) par terre, à terre; (*of sun*) couché; (*of blind,* *temperature*) baissé; (*out of bed*) descendu; (*of tyre*) dégonflé, (*worn*) usé; **d. (in writing)** inscrit; (*lie*) **d.!** (*to dog*) couché!; **to come** *or* **go d.** descendre; **to come d. from** (*place*) arriver de; **to fall d.** tomber (par terre); **d. there** *or* **here** en bas; **d. with traitors/etc!** à bas les traîtres/etc!; **d. with (the) flu** grippé; **to feel d.** (*depressed*) *Fam* avoir le cafard; **d. to** (*in series, numbers, dates etc*) jusqu'à; **d. payment** acompte *m*; **d. under** aux antipodes, en Australie; **d. at heel,** *Am* **d. at the heels** miteux; – *prep* (*at bottom of*) en bas de; (*from top to bottom of*) du haut en bas de; (*along*) le long de; **to go d.** (*hill etc*) descendre; **to live d. the street** habiter plus loin dans la rue; – *vt* (*shoot down*) abattre; (*knock down*) terrasser; **to d. a drink** vider un verre. ◆**down-and-'out** *a* sur le pavé; – *n* clochard, -arde *mf*. ◆**downbeat** *a* (*gloomy*) *Fam* pessimiste. ◆**downcast** *a* découragé. ◆**downfall** *n* chute *f*. ◆**downgrade** *vt* (*job etc*) déclasser; (*person*) rétrograder. ◆**down'hearted** *a* découragé. ◆**down'hill** *adv* en pente; **to go d.** descendre; *Fig* être sur le déclin. ◆**downmarket** *a Com* bas de gamme. ◆**downpour** *n* averse *f*, pluie *f* torrentielle. ◆**downright** *a* (*rogue etc*) véritable; (*refusal etc*) catégorique; **a d. nerve** *or* **cheek** un sacré culot; – *adv* (*rude etc*) franchement. ◆**'downstairs** *a* (*room, neighbours*) d'en bas; (*on the ground floor*) du rez-de-chaussée; – [daʊn'steəz] *adv* en bas; au rez-de-chaussée; **to come** *or* **go d.** descendre l'escalier. ◆**down'stream** *adv* en aval. ◆**down-to-'earth** *a* terre-à-terre *inv*. ◆**down'town** *adv* en ville; **d. Chicago/etc** le centre de Chicago/etc. ◆**downtrodden** *a* opprimé. ◆**downward** *a* vers le bas; (*path*) qui descend; (*trend*) à la baisse. ◆**downward(s)** *adv* vers le bas.

down[2] [daʊn] *n* (*on bird, person etc*) duvet *m*.

downs [daʊnz] *npl* collines *fpl*.

dowry ['daʊərɪ] *n* dot *f*.

doze [dəʊz] *n* petit somme *m*; – *vi* sommeiller; **to d. off** s'assoupir. ◆**dozy** *a* (**-ier, -iest**) assoupi; (*silly*) *Fam* bête, gourde.

dozen ['dʌz(ə)n] *n* douzaine *f*; **a d.** (*eggs, books etc*) une douzaine de; **dozens of** *Fig* des dizaines de.

Dr *abbr* (*Doctor*) Docteur.

drab [dræb] *a* terne; (*weather*) gris. ◆—**ness** *n* caractère *m* terne; (*of weather*) grisaille *f*.

draconian [drə'kəʊnɪən] *a* draconien.

draft [drɑːft] **1** n (*outline*) ébauche f; (*of letter etc*) brouillon m; (*bill*) Com traite f; − vt **to d. (out)** (*sketch out*) faire le brouillon de; (*write out*) rédiger. **2** n Mil Am conscription f; (*men*) contingent m; − vt (*conscript*) appeler (sous les drapeaux). **3** n Am = **draught.**

draftsman ['drɑːftsmən] n = **draughtsman.**

drag [dræg] vt (**-gg-**) traîner, tirer; (*river*) draguer; **to d. sth from s.o.** (*confession etc*) arracher qch à qn; **to d. along** (en)traîner; **to d. s.o. away from** arracher qn à; **to d. s.o. into** entraîner qn dans; − vi traîner; **to d. on** or **out** (*last a long time*) se prolonger; − n Fam (*tedium*) corvée f; (*person*) raseur, -euse mf; (*on cigarette*) bouffée f (**on** de); **in d.** (*clothing*) en travesti.

dragon ['drægən] n dragon m. ◆**dragonfly** n libellule f.

drain [dreɪn] n (*sewer*) égout m; (*pipe, channel*) canal m; (*outside house*) puisard m; (*in street*) bouche f d'égout; **it's (gone) down the d.** (*wasted*) Fam c'est fichu; **to be a d. on** (*resources, patience*) épuiser; − vt (*land*) drainer; (*glass, tank*) vider; (*vegetables*) égoutter; (*resources*) épuiser; **to d. (off)** (*liquid*) faire écouler; **to d. of** (*deprive of*) priver de; − vi **to d. (off)** (*of liquid*) s'écouler; **to d. away** (*of strength*) s'épuiser; **draining board** paillasse f. ◆**—age** n (*act*) drainage m; (*sewers*) système m d'égouts. ◆**—er** n (*board*) paillasse f; (*rack, basket*) égouttoir m. ◆**drainboard** n Am paillasse f. ◆**drainpipe** n tuyau m d'évacuation.

drake [dreɪk] n canard m (mâle).

dram [dræm] n (*drink*) Fam goutte f.

drama ['drɑːmə] n (*event*) drame m; (*dramatic art*) théâtre m; **d. critic** critique m dramatique. ◆**dra'matic** a dramatique; (*very great, striking*) spectaculaire. ◆**dra'matically** adv (*to change, drop etc*) de façon spectaculaire. ◆**dra'matics** n théâtre m. ◆**dramatist** ['dræmətɪst] n dramaturge m. ◆**dramatize** vt (*exaggerate*) dramatiser; (*novel etc*) adapter (pour la scène or l'écran).

drank [dræŋk] see **drink.**

drap/e [dreɪp] vt draper (**with** de); (*wall*) tapisser (de tentures); − npl tentures fpl; (*heavy curtains*) Am rideaux mpl. ◆**—er** n marchand, -ande mf de nouveautés.

drastic ['dræstɪk] a radical, sévère; (*reduction*) massif. ◆**drastically** adv radicalement.

draught [drɑːft] n courant m d'air; (*for fire*) tirage m; pl (*game*) dames fpl; − a (*horse*) de trait; (*beer*) (à la) pression; **d. excluder**

bourrelet m (*de porte, de fenêtre*). ◆**draughtboard** n damier m. ◆**draughty** a (**-ier, -iest**) (*room*) plein de courants d'air.

draughtsman ['drɑːftsmən] n (pl **-men**) dessinateur, -trice mf (industriel(le) or technique).

draw[1] [drɔː] n (*of lottery*) tirage m au sort; Sp match m nul; (*attraction*) attraction f; − vt (pt **drew**, pp **drawn**) (*pull*) tirer; (*pass*) passer (**over** sur, **into** dans); (*prize*) gagner; (*applause*) provoquer; (*money from bank*) retirer (**from, out of** de); (*salary*) toucher; (*attract*) attirer; (*well-water, comfort*) puiser (**from** dans); **to d. a smile** faire sourire (**from s.o.** qn); **to d. a bath** faire couler un bain; **to d. sth to a close** mettre fin à qch; **to d. a match** Sp faire match nul; **to d. in** (*claws*) rentrer; **to d. out** (*money*) retirer; (*meeting*) prolonger; **to d. up** (*chair*) approcher; (*contract, list, plan*) dresser, rédiger; **to d. (up)on** (*savings*) puiser dans; − vi (*enter*) entrer (**into** dans); (*arrive*) arriver; **to d. near (to)** s'approcher (de); (*of time*) approcher (de); **to d. to a close** tirer à sa fin; **to d. aside** (*step aside*) s'écarter; **to d. away** (*go away*) s'éloigner; **to d. back** (*recoil*) reculer; **to d. in** (*of days*) diminuer; **to d. on** (*of time*) s'avancer; **to d. up** (*of vehicle*) s'arrêter. ◆**drawback** n inconvénient m. ◆**drawbridge** n pont-levis m.

draw[2] [drɔː] vt (pt **drew**, pp **drawn**) (*picture*) dessiner; (*circle*) tracer; (*parallel, distinction*) Fig faire (**between** entre); − vi (*as artist*) dessiner. ◆**—ing** n dessin m; **d. board** planche f à dessin; **d. pin** punaise f; **d. room** salon m.

drawer [drɔːr] **1** n (*in furniture*) tiroir m. **2** npl (*women's knickers*) culotte f.

drawl [drɔːl] vi parler d'une voix traînante; − n voix f traînante.

drawn [drɔːn] see **draw**[1,2]; − a (*face*) tiré, crispé; **d. match** or **game** match m nul.

dread [dred] vt redouter (**doing de faire**); − n crainte f, terreur f. ◆**dreadful** a épouvantable; (*child*) insupportable; (*ill*) malade; **I feel d. (about it)** j'ai vraiment honte. ◆**dreadfully** adv terriblement; **to be** or **feel d. sorry** regretter infiniment.

dream [driːm] vti (pt & pp **dreamed** or **dreamt** [dremt]) rêver; (*imagine*) songer (**of** à, **that** que); **I wouldn't d. of it!** (il n'en est pas question!; **to d. sth up** imaginer qch; − n rêve m; (*wonderful thing or person*) Fam merveille f; **to have a d.** faire un rêve (**about** de); **to have dreams of** rêver de; **a d. house/etc** une maison/etc de rêve; **a d.**

world un monde imaginaire. ◆**—er** n rêveur, -euse mf. ◆**dreamy** a (-ier, -iest) rêveur.

dreary ['drɪərɪ] a (-ier, -iest) (gloomy) morne; (monotonous) monotone; (boring) ennuyeux.

dredg/e [dredʒ] vt (river etc) draguer; — n drague f. ◆**—er** n 1 (ship) dragueur m. 2 Culin saupoudreuse f.

dregs [dregz] npl **the d.** (in liquid, of society) la lie.

drench [drentʃ] vt tremper; **to get drenched** se faire tremper (jusqu'aux os).

dress [dres] **1** n (woman's garment) robe f; (style of dressing) tenue f; **d. circle** Th (premier) balcon m; **d. designer** dessinateur, -trice mf de mode; (well-known) couturier m; **d. rehearsal** (répétition f) générale f; **d. shirt** chemise f de soirée. **2** vt (clothe) habiller; (adorn) orner; (salad) assaisonner; (wound) panser; (skins, chicken) préparer; **to get dressed** s'habiller; **dressed for tennis/etc** en tenue de tennis/etc; — vi s'habiller; **to d. up** (smartly) bien s'habiller; (in disguise) se déguiser (as en). ◆**—ing** n Med pansement m; (seasoning) Culin assaisonnement m; **to give s.o. a d.-down** passer un savon à qn; **d. gown** robe f de chambre; (of boxer) peignoir m; **d. room** Th loge f; **d. table** coiffeuse f. ◆**—er** n 1 (furniture) vaisselier m; Am coiffeuse f. **2 she's a good d.** elle s'habille toujours bien. ◆**dressmaker** n couturière f. ◆**dressmaking** n couture f.

dressy ['dresɪ] a (-ier, -iest) (smart) chic inv; (too) d. trop habillé.

drew [druː] see draw 1,2.

dribble ['drɪb(ə)l] vi (of baby) baver; (of liquid) tomber goutte à goutte; Sp dribbler; — vt laisser tomber goutte à goutte; (ball) Sp dribbler.

dribs [drɪbz] npl in **d. and drabs** par petites quantités; (to arrive) par petits groupes.

dried [draɪd] a (fruit) sec; (milk) en poudre; (flowers) séché.

drier ['draɪər] n = dryer.

drift [drɪft] vi être emporté par le vent or le courant; (of ship) dériver; Fig aller à la dérive; (of snow) s'amonceler; **to d. about** (aimlessly) se promener sans but, traînailler; **to d. apart** (of husband and wife) devenir des étrangers l'un pour l'autre; **to d. into/towards** glisser dans/vers; — n mouvement m; (direction) sens m; (of events) cours m; (of snow) amoncellement m, congère f; (meaning) sens m général.

◆**—er** n (aimless person) paumé, -ée mf. ◆**driftwood** n bois m flotté.

drill [drɪl] **1** n (tool) perceuse f; (bit) mèche f; (for rock) foreuse f; (for tooth) fraise f; (pneumatic) marteau m pneumatique; — vt percer; (tooth) fraiser; (oil well) forer; — vi **to d. for oil** faire de la recherche pétrolière. **2** n Mil Sch exercice(s) m(pl); (procedure) Fig marche f à suivre; — vi faire l'exercice; — vt faire faire l'exercice à.

drink [drɪŋk] n boisson f; (glass of sth) verre m; **to give s.o. a d.** donner (quelque chose) à boire à qn; — vt (pt drank, pp drunk) boire; **to d. oneself to death** se tuer à force de boire; **to d. down** or **up** boire; — vi boire (out of dans); **to d. up** finir son verre; **to d. to** boire à la santé de. ◆**—ing** a (water) potable; (song) à boire; **d. bout** beuverie f; **d. fountain** fontaine f publique, borne-fontaine f; **d. trough** abreuvoir m. ◆**—able** a (fit for drinking) potable; (palatable) buvable. ◆**—er** n buveur, -euse mf.

drip [drɪp] vi (-pp-) dégouliner, dégoutter; (of washing, vegetables) s'égoutter; (of tap) fuir; — vt (paint etc) laisser couler; — n (drop) goutte f; (sound) bruit m (de goutte); (fool) Fam nouille f. ◆**d.-dry** a (shirt etc) sans repassage. ◆**dripping** n (Am drippings) Culin graisse f; — a & adv **d.** (wet) dégoulinant.

driv/e [draɪv] n promenade f en voiture; (energy) énergie f; Psy instinct m; Pol campagne f; (road to private house) allée f; **an hour's d.** une heure de voiture; **left-hand d.** Aut (véhicule m à) conduite f à gauche; **front-wheel d.** Aut traction f avant; — vt (pt drove, pp driven) (vehicle, train, passenger) conduire; (machine) actionner; **to d. (away** or **out)** (chase away) chasser; **to d. s.o. to do** pousser qn à faire; **to d. to despair** réduire au désespoir; **to d. mad** or **crazy** rendre fou; **to d. the rain/smoke against** (of wind) rabattre la pluie/fumée contre; **to d. back** (enemy etc) repousser; (passenger) Aut ramener (en voiture); **to d. in** (thrust) enfoncer; **to d. s.o. hard** surmener qn; **he drives a Ford** il a une Ford; — vi (drive a car) conduire; **to d. (along)** (go, run) Aut rouler; **to d. on the left** rouler à gauche; **to d. away** or **off** Aut partir; **to d. back** Aut revenir; **to d. on** Aut continuer; **to d. to** Aut aller (en voiture) à; **to d. up** Aut arriver; **what are you driving at?** Fig où veux-tu en venir? ◆**—ing** n conduite f; **d. lesson** leçon f de conduite; **d. licence, d. test** permis m de conduire; **d. school** auto-école *f.* **2** *a* (*forceful*) **d. force** force *f* agissante; **d. rain** pluie *f* battante. ◆**—er** *n* (*of car*) conducteur, -trice *mf*; (*of taxi, lorry*) chauffeur *m*, conducteur, -trice *mf*; (**train**) **d.** mécanicien *m*; **she's a good d.** elle conduit bien; **driver's license** *Am* permis *m* de conduire.

drivel ['drɪv(ə)l] *vi* (**-ll-**, *Am* **-l-**) radoter; — *n* radotage *m*.

drizzle ['drɪz(ə)l] *n* bruine *f*, crachin *m*; — *vi* bruiner. ◆**drizzly** *a* (*weather*) de bruine; **it's d.** il bruine.

droll [drəʊl] *a* drôle, comique.

dromedary ['drɒmədərɪ, *Am* 'drɒmɪderɪ] *n* dromadaire *m*.

drone [drəʊn] **1** *n* (*bee*) abeille *f* mâle. **2** *n* (*hum*) bourdonnement *m*; (*purr*) ronronnement *m*; *Fig* débit *m* monotone; — *vi* (*of bee*) bourdonner; (*of engine*) ronronner; **to d. (on)** *Fig* parler d'une voix monotone.

drool [druːl] *vi* (*slaver*) baver; *Fig* radoter; **to d. over** *Fig* s'extasier devant.

droop [druːp] *vi* (*of head*) pencher; (*of eyelid*) tomber; (*of flower*) se faner.

drop [drɒp] **1** *n* (*of liquid*) goutte *f*. **2** *n* (*fall*) baisse *f*, chute *f* (**in** de); (*slope*) descente *f*; (*distance of fall*) hauteur *f* (de chute); (*jump*) *Av* saut *m*; — *vt* (**-pp-**) laisser tomber; (*price, voice*) baisser; (*bomb*) larguer; (*passenger, goods*) *Aut* déposer; *Nau* débarquer; (*letter*) envoyer (**to** à); (*put*) mettre; (*omit*) omettre; (*remark*) laisser échapper; (*get rid of*) supprimer; (*habit*) abandonner; (*team member*) *Sp* écarter; **to d. s.o. off** *Aut* déposer qn; **to d. a line** écrire un petit mot (**to** à); **to d. a hint** faire une allusion; **to d. a hint that** laisser entendre que; **to d. one's h's** ne pas aspirer les h; **to d. a word in s.o.'s ear** glisser un mot à l'oreille de qn; — *vi* (*fall*) tomber; (*of person*) (se laisser) tomber; (*of price*) baisser; (*of conversation*) cesser; **he's ready to d.** *Fam* il tombe de fatigue; **let it d.!** *Fam* laisse tomber!; **to d. across** *or* **in** passer (**chez** qn); **to d. away** (*diminish*) diminuer; **to d. back** *or* **behind** rester en arrière, se laisser distancer; **to d. off** (*fall asleep*) s'endormir; (*fall off*) tomber; (*of interest, sales etc*) diminuer. ◆**d.-off** *n* (*decrease*) diminution *f* (**in** de); **to d. out** (*fall out*) tomber; (*withdraw*) se retirer; (*socially*) se mettre en marge de la société; *Sch Univ* laisser tomber ses études. ◆**d.-out** *n* marginal, -ale *mf*; *Univ* étudiant, -ante *mf* qui abandonne ses études. ◆**droppings** *npl* (*of animal*) crottes *fpl*; (*of bird*) fiente *f.*

dross [drɒs] *n* déchets *mpl.*

drought [draʊt] *n* sécheresse *f.*

drove [drəʊv] *see* **drive.**

droves [drəʊvz] *npl* (*of people*) foules *fpl*; **in d.** en foule.

drown [draʊn] *vi* se noyer; — *vt* noyer; **to d. oneself, be drowned** se noyer. ◆**—ing** *a* qui se noie; — *n* (*death*) noyade *f.*

drowse [draʊz] *vi* somnoler. ◆**drows/y** *a* (**-ier, -iest**) somnolent; **to feel d.** avoir sommeil; **to make s.o. (feel) d.** assoupir qn. ◆**—ily** *adv* d'un air somnolent. ◆**—iness** *n* somnolence *f.*

drubbing ['drʌbɪŋ] *n* (*beating*) raclée *f.*

drudge [drʌdʒ] *n* bête *f* de somme, esclave *mf* du travail; — *vi* trimer. ◆**drudgery** *n* corvée(s) *f*(*pl*), travail *m* ingrat.

drug [drʌg] *n Med* médicament *m*, drogue *f*; (*narcotic*) stupéfiant *m*, drogue *f*; *Fig* drogue *f*; **drugs** (*dope in general*) la drogue; **to be on drugs, take drugs** se droguer; **d. addict** drogué, -ée *mf*; **d. addiction** toxicomanie *f*; **d. taking** usage *m* de la drogue; — *vt* (**-gg-**) droguer; (*drink*) mêler un somnifère à. ◆**druggist** *n Am* pharmacien, -ienne *mf*, droguiste *mf*. ◆**drugstore** *n Am* drugstore *m.*

drum [drʌm] *n Mus* tambour *m*; (*for oil*) bidon *m*; **the big d.** *Mus* la grosse caisse; **the drums** *Mus* la batterie; — *vi* (**-mm-**) *Mil* battre du tambour; (*with fingers*) tambouriner; — *vt* **to d. sth into s.o.** *Fig* rabâcher qch à qn; **to d. up** (*support, interest*) susciter; **to d. up business** *or* **custom** attirer les clients. ◆**drummer** *n* (joueur, -euse *mf* de) tambour *m*; (*in pop or jazz group*) batteur *m*. ◆**drumstick** *n Mus* baguette *f* de tambour; (*of chicken*) pilon *m*, cuisse *f.*

drunk [drʌŋk] *see* **drink**; — *a* ivre; **d. with** *Fig* ivre de; **to get d.** s'enivrer; — *n* ivrogne *mf*, pochard, -arde *mf*. ◆**drunkard** *n* ivrogne *mf*. ◆**drunken** *a* (*quarrel*) d'ivrogne; (*person*) ivrogne; (*driver*) ivre; **d. driving** conduite *f* en état d'ivresse. ◆**drunkenness** *n* (*state*) ivresse *f*; (*habit*) ivrognerie *f.*

dry [draɪ] *a* (**drier, driest**) sec; (*well, river*) à sec; (*day*) sans pluie; (*toast*) sans beurre; (*wit*) caustique; (*subject, book*) aride; **on d. land** sur la terre ferme; **to keep sth d.** tenir qch au sec; **to wipe d.** essuyer; **to run d.** se tarir; **to feel** *or* **be d.** *Fam* avoir soif; **d. dock** cale *f* sèche; **d. goods store** *Am* magasin *m* de nouveautés; — *vt* sécher; (*dishes etc*) essuyer; **to d. off** *or* **up** sécher; — *vi* sécher; **to d. off** sécher; **to d. up** sécher; (*run dry*) se tarir; **d. up!** *Fam* tais-toi! ◆**—ing** *n* séchage *m*; essuyage *m*. ◆**—er** *n* (*for hair,* *clothes*) sécher *m*; (*helmet-style for hair*) casque *m*. ◆**—ness** *n* sécheresse *f*; (*of wit*) causticité *f*; (*of book etc*) aridité *f*. ◆**dry-'clean** *vt* nettoyer à sec. ◆**dry-'cleaner** *n* teinturier, -ière *mf*.

dual ['djuːəl] *a* double; **d. carriageway** route *f* à deux voies (séparées). ◆**du'ality** *n* dualité *f*.

dub [dʌb] *vt* (**-bb-**) **1** (*film*) doubler. **2** (*nickname*) surnommer. ◆**dubbing** *n* *Cin* doublage *m*.

dubious ['djuːbɪəs] *a* (*offer, person etc*) douteux; **I'm d. about going** *or* **whether to go** je me demande si je dois y aller; **to be d. about sth** douter de qch.

duchess ['dʌtʃɪs] *n* duchesse *f*. ◆**duchy** *n* duché *m*.

duck [dʌk] **1** *n* canard *m*. **2** *vi* se baisser (vivement); – *vt* (*head*) baisser; **to d. s.o.** plonger qn dans l'eau. ◆**—ing** *n* bain *m* forcé. ◆**duckling** *n* caneton *m*.

duct [dʌkt] *n* *Anat Tech* conduit *m*.

dud [dʌd] *a* *Fam* (*bomb*) non éclaté; (*coin*) faux; (*cheque*) en bois; (*watch etc*) qui ne marche pas; – *n* (*person*) zéro *m*, type *m* nul.

dude [duːd] *n* *Am Fam* dandy *m*; **d. ranch** ranch(-hôtel) *m*.

due[1] [djuː] *a* (*money, sum*) dû (**to** à); (*rent, bill*) à payer; (*respect*) qu'on doit (**to** à); (*fitting*) qui convient; **to fall d.** échoir; **she's d. for** (*a rise etc*) elle doit *or* devrait recevoir; **he's d. to** (*to arrive*) (*is awaited*) il doit arriver, il est attendu; **I'm d. there** je dois être là-bas; **in d. course** (*at proper time*) en temps utile; (*finally*) à la longue; **d. to** (*attributable to*) dû à; (*because of*) à cause de; (*thanks to*) grâce à; – *n* dû *m*; *pl* (*of club*) cotisation *f*; (*official charges*) droits *mpl*; **to give s.o. his d.** admettre que qn a raison.

due[2] [djuː] *adv* (tout) droit; **d. north/south** plein nord/sud.

duel ['djuːəl] *n* duel *m*; – *vi* (**-ll-**, *Am* **-l-**) se battre en duel.

duet [djuː'et] *n* duo *m*.

duffel, duffle ['dʌf(ə)l] *a* **d. bag** sac *m* de marin; **d. coat** duffel-coat *m*.

dug [dʌg] *see* **dig**. ◆**dugout** *n* **1** *Mil* abri *m* souterrain. **2** (*canoe*) pirogue *f*.

duke [djuːk] *n* duc *m*.

dull [dʌl] *a* (**-er, -est**) (*boring*) ennuyeux; (*colour, character*) terne; (*weather*) maussade; (*mind*) lourd, borné; (*sound, ache*) sourd; (*edge, blade*) émoussé; (*hearing, sight*) faible; – *vt* (*senses*) émousser; (*sound, pain*) amortir; (*colour*) ternir;

(*mind*) engourdir. ◆**—ness** *n* (*of mind*) lourdeur *f* d'esprit; (*tedium*) monotonie *f*; (*of colour*) manque *m* d'éclat.

duly ['djuːlɪ] *adv* (*properly*) comme il convient (convenait etc); (*in fact*) en effet; (*in due time*) en temps utile.

dumb [dʌm] *a* (**-er, -est**) muet; (*stupid*) *Fam* idiot, bête. ◆**—ness** *n* mutisme *m*; bêtise *f*. ◆**dumbbell** *n* (*weight*) haltère *m*. ◆**dumb'waiter** *n* (*lift for food*) monte-plats *m inv*.

dumbfound [dʌm'faʊnd] *vt* sidérer, ahurir.

dummy ['dʌmɪ] **1** *n* (*of baby*) sucette *f*; (*of dressmaker*) mannequin *m*; (*of book*) maquette *f*; (*of ventriloquist*) pantin *m*; (*fool*) *Fam* idiot, -ote *mf*. **2** *a* factice, faux; **d. run** (*on car etc*) essai *m*.

dump [dʌmp] *vt* (*rubbish*) déposer; **to d.** (**down**) déposer; **to d. s.o.** (*ditch*) *Fam* plaquer qn; – *n* (*for ammunition*) *Mil* dépôt *m*; (*dirty or dull town*) *Fam* trou *m*; (*house, slum*) *Fam* baraque *f*; (*rubbish*) **d.** tas *m* d'ordures; (*place*) dépôt *m* d'ordures, décharge *f*; **to be** (**down**) **in the dumps** *Fam* avoir le cafard; **d. truck = dumper.** ◆**—er** *n* **d.** (**truck**) camion *m* à benne basculante.

dumpling ['dʌmplɪŋ] *n* *Culin* boulette *f* (de pâte).

dumpy ['dʌmpɪ] *a* (**-ier, -iest**) (*person*) boulot, gros et court.

dunce [dʌns] *n* cancre *m*, âne *m*.

dune [djuːn] *n* dune *f*.

dung [dʌŋ] *n* crotte *f*; (*of cattle*) bouse *f*; (*manure*) fumier *m*.

dungarees [dʌŋgə'riːz] *npl* (*of child, workman*) salopette *f*; (*jeans*) *Am* jean *m*.

dungeon ['dʌndʒən] *n* cachot *m*.

dunk [dʌŋk] *vt* (*bread, biscuit etc*) tremper.

dupe [djuːp] *vt* duper; – *n* dupe *f*.

duplex ['djuːpleks] *n* (*apartment*) *Am* duplex *m*.

duplicate ['djuːplɪkeɪt] *vt* (*key, map*) faire un double de; (*on machine*) polycopier; – ['djuːplɪkət] *n* double *m*; **in d.** en deux exemplaires; **a d. copy**/*etc* une copie/*etc* en double; **a d. key** un double de la clef. ◆**dupli'cation** *n* (*on machine*) polycopie *f*; (*of effort*) répétition *f*. ◆**duplicator** *n* duplicateur *m*.

duplicity [djuː'plɪsɪtɪ] *n* duplicité *f*.

durable ['djuːərəb(ə)l] *a* (*shoes etc*) résistant; (*friendship, love*) durable. ◆**dura'bility** *n* résistance *f*; durabilité *f*.

duration [djuə'reɪʃ(ə)n] *n* durée *f*.

duress [djuː'res] *n* **under d.** sous la contrainte.

during ['djuərɪŋ] *prep* pendant, durant.

dusk [dʌsk] n (twilight) crépuscule m.

dusky ['dʌskɪ] a (-ier, -iest) (complexion) foncé.

dust [dʌst] n poussière f; d. cover (for furniture) housse f; (for book) jaquette f; d. jacket jaquette f; − vt épousseter; (sprinkle) saupoudrer (with de). ◆—er n chiffon m. ◆dustbin n poubelle f. ◆dustcart n camion-benne m. ◆dustman n (pl -men) éboueur m, boueux m. ◆dustpan n petite pelle f (à poussière).

dusty ['dʌstɪ] a (-ier, -iest) poussiéreux.

Dutch [dʌtʃ] a néerlandais, hollandais; D. cheese hollande m; to go D. partager les frais (with avec); − n (language) hollandais m. ◆Dutchman n (pl -men) Hollandais m. ◆Dutchwoman n (pl -women) Hollandaise f.

duty ['djuːtɪ] n devoir m; (tax) droit m; pl (responsibilities) fonctions fpl; on d. Mil de service; (doctor etc) de garde; Sch de permanence; off d. libre. ◆d.-'free a (goods, shop) hors-taxe inv. ◆dutiful a respectueux, obéissant; (worker) conscien- cieux.

dwarf [dwɔːf] n nain m, naine f; − vt (of building, person etc) rapetisser, écraser.

dwell [dwel] vi (pt & pp dwelt) demeurer; to d. (up)on (think about) penser sans cesse à; (speak about) parler sans cesse de, s'étendre sur; (insist on) appuyer sur. ◆—ing n habitation f. ◆—er n habitant, -ante mf.

dwindl/e ['dwɪnd(ə)l] vi diminuer (peu à peu). ◆—ing a (interest etc) décroissant.

dye [daɪ] n teinture f; − vt teindre; to d. green/etc teindre en vert/etc. ◆dyeing n teinture f; (industry) teinturerie f. ◆dyer n teinturier, -ière mf.

dying ['daɪɪŋ] see die 1; − a mourant, moribond; (custom) qui se perd; (day, words) dernier; − n (death) mort f.

dyke [daɪk] n (wall) digue f; (ditch) fossé m.

dynamic [daɪ'næmɪk] a dynamique. ◆'dynamism n dynamisme m.

dynamite ['daɪnəmaɪt] n dynamite f; − vt dynamiter.

dynamo ['daɪnəməʊ] n (pl -os) dynamo f.

dynasty ['dɪnəstɪ, Am 'daɪnəstɪ] n dynastie f.

dysentery ['dɪsəntrɪ] n Med dysenterie f.

dyslexic [dɪs'leksɪk] a & n dyslexique (mf).

E

E, e [iː] n E, e m.

each [iːtʃ] a chaque; − pron chacun, -une; e. one chacun, -une; e. other l'un(e) l'autre, pl les un(e)s les autres; to see e. other se voir (l'un(e) l'autre); e. of us chacun, -une d'entre nous.

eager ['iːgər] a impatient (to do de faire); (enthusiastic) ardent, passionné; to be e. for désirer vivement; e. for (money) avide de; e. to help empressé (à aider); to be e. to do (want) avoir envie de faire. ◆—ly adv (to await) avec impatience; (to work, serve) avec empressement. ◆—ness n impa- tience f (to do de faire); (zeal) empresse- ment m (to do à faire); (greed) avidité f.

eagle ['iːg(ə)l] n aigle m. ◆e.-'eyed a au regard d'aigle.

ear ¹ [ɪər] n oreille f; all ears Fam tout ouïe; up to one's ears in work débordé de travail; to play it by e. Fam agir selon la situation; thick e. Fam gifle f. ◆earache n mal m d'oreille. ◆eardrum n tympan m. ◆earmuffs npl serre-tête m inv (pour protéger les oreilles), protège-oreilles m inv. ◆earphones npl casque m. ◆earpiece n écouteur m. ◆earplug n (to keep out noise) boule f Quiès®. ◆earring n boucle f d'oreille. ◆earshot n within e. à portée de voix. ◆ear-splitting a assourdissant.

ear ² [ɪər] n (of corn) épi m.

earl [ɜːl] n comte m.

early ['ɜːlɪ] a (-ier, -iest) (first) premier; (fruit, season) précoce; (death) prématuré; (age) jeune; (painting, work) de jeunesse; (reply) rapide; (return, retirement) anticipé; (ancient) ancien; it's e. (looking at time) il est tôt; it's too e. to get up/etc il est trop tôt pour se lever/etc; to be e. (ahead of time) arriver de bonne heure or tôt, être en avance; (in getting up) être matinal; in e. times jadis; in e. summer au début de l'été; one's e. life sa jeunesse; − adv tôt, de bonne heure; (ahead of time) en avance; (to die) prématurément; as e. as possible le plus tôt possible; earlier (on) plus tôt; at the earliest au plus tôt; **as e. as yesterday** déjà hier. ◆**e.-'warning system** n dispositif m de première alerte.

earmark ['ɪəmɑːk] vt (funds) assigner (**for** à).

earn [ɜːn] vt gagner; (interest) Fin rapporter. ◆**—ings** npl (wages) rémunérations fpl; (profits) bénéfices mpl.

earnest ['ɜːnɪst] a sérieux; (sincere) sincère; – n **in e.** sérieusement; **it's raining in e.** il pleut pour de bon; **he's in e.** il est sérieux. ◆**—ness** n sérieux m; sincérité f.

earth [ɜːθ] n (world, ground) terre f; El terre f, masse f; **to fall to e.** tomber à or par terre; **nothing/nobody on e.** rien/personne au monde; **where/what on e.?** où/que diable? ◆**earthly** a (possessions etc) terrestre; **not an e. chance** Fam pas la moindre chance; **for no e. reason** Fam sans la moindre raison. ◆**earthy** a terreux; (person) Fig terre-à-terre inv. ◆**earthquake** n tremblement m de terre. ◆**earthworks** npl (excavations) terrassements mpl. ◆**earthworm** n ver m de terre.

earthenware ['ɜːθənwɛər] n faïence f; – a en faïence.

earwig ['ɪəwɪg] n (insect) perce-oreille m.

ease [iːz] **1** n (physical) bien-être m; (mental) tranquillité f; (facility) facilité f; **(ill) at e.** (in situation) (mal) à l'aise; **at e. (of mind)** tranquille; **(stand) at e.!** Mil repos!; **with e.** facilement; **2** vt (pain) soulager; (mind) calmer; (tension) diminuer; (loosen) relâcher; **to e. off/along** enlever/déplacer doucement; **to e. oneself through** se glisser par; – vi **to e. (off or up)** (of situation) se détendre; (of pressure) diminuer; (of demand) baisser; (of pain) se calmer; (not work so hard) se relâcher. ◆**easily** adv facilement; **e. the best/etc** de loin le meilleur/etc; **that could e. be** ça pourrait bien être. ◆**easiness** n aisance f.

easel ['iːz(ə)l] n chevalet m.

east [iːst] n est m; **Middle/Far E.** Moyen-/Extrême-Orient m; – a (coast) est inv; (wind) d'est; **E. Africa** Afrique f orientale; **E. Germany** Allemagne f de l'Est; – adv à l'est, vers l'est. ◆**eastbound** a (carriageway) est inv; (traffic) en direction de l'est. ◆**easterly** a (point) est inv; (direction) de l'est; (wind) d'est. ◆**eastern** a (coast) est inv; **E. France** l'Est m de la France; **E. Europe** Europe f de l'Est. ◆**easterner** n habitant, -ante mf de l'Est. ◆**eastward(s)** a & adv vers l'est.

Easter ['iːstər] n Pâques m sing or fpl; **E. week** semaine f pascale; **Happy E.!** joyeuses Pâques!

easy ['iːzɪ] a (-ier, -iest) facile; (manners) naturel; (life) tranquille; (pace) modéré; **to feel e. in one's mind** être tranquille; **to be an e. first** Sp être bon premier; **I'm e.** Fam ça m'est égal; **e. chair** fauteuil m (rembourré); – adv doucement; **go e. on** (sugar etc) vas-y doucement or mollo avec; (person) ne sois pas trop dur avec or envers; **take it e.** (rest) repose-toi; (work less) ne te fatigue pas; (calm down) calme-toi; (go slow) ne te presse pas. ◆**easy'going** a (carefree) insouciant; (easy to get on with) traitable.

eat [iːt] vt (pt **ate** [et, Am eɪt], pp **eaten** ['iːt(ə)n]) manger; (meal) prendre; (one's words) Fig ravaler; **to e. breakfast** or **lunch** déjeuner; **what's eating you?** Sl qu'est-ce qui te tracasse?; **to e. up** (finish) finir; **eaten up with** (envy) dévoré de; – vi manger; **to e. into** (of acid) ronger; **to e. out** (lunch) déjeuner dehors; (dinner) dîner dehors. ◆**—ing** a **e. apple** pomme f à couteau; **e. place** restaurant m. ◆**—able** a mangeable. ◆**—er** n **big e.** gros mangeur m, grosse mangeuse f.

eau de Cologne [əʊdəkə'ləʊn] n eau f de Cologne.

eaves [iːvz] npl avant-toit m. ◆**eavesdrop** vt (-pp-) **to e. (on)** écouter (de façon indiscrète). ◆**eavesdropper** n oreille f indiscrète.

ebb [eb] n reflux m; **e. and flow** le flux et le reflux; **e. tide** marée f descendante; **at a low e.** Fig très bas; – vi refluer; **to e. (away)** (of strength etc) Fig décliner.

ebony ['ebənɪ] n (wood) ébène f.

ebullient [ɪ'bʌlɪənt] a exubérant.

eccentric [ɪk'sentrɪk] a & n excentrique (mf). ◆**eccen'tricity** n excentricité f.

ecclesiastic [ɪkliːzɪ'æstɪk] a & n ecclésiastique (m). ◆**ecclesiastical** a ecclésiastique.

echelon ['eʃəlɒn] n (of organization) échelon m.

echo ['ekəʊ] n (pl -oes) écho m; – vt (sound) répercuter; (repeat) Fig répéter; – vi **the explosion/etc echoed** l'écho de l'explosion/etc se répercuta; **to e. with the sound of** résonner de l'écho de.

éclair [eɪ'kleər] n (cake) éclair m.

eclectic [ɪ'klektɪk] a éclectique.

eclipse [ɪ'klɪps] n (of sun etc) & Fig éclipse f; – vt éclipser.

ecology [ɪ'kɒlədʒɪ] n écologie f. ◆**eco-'logical** a écologique.

economic [iːkə'nɒmɪk] a économique; (profitable) rentable. ◆**economical** a économique; (*thrifty*) économe. ◆**economically** *adv* économiquement. ◆**economics** *n* (science *f*) économique *f*; (*profitability*) aspect *m* financier.

economy [ɪˈkɒnəmɪ] *n* (*saving, system, thrift*) économie *f*; **e. class** *Av* classe *f* touriste. ◆**economist** *n* économiste *mf*. ◆**economize** *vti* économiser (**on** sur).

ecstasy [ˈekstəsɪ] *n* extase *f*. ◆**ec'static** *a* extasié; **to be e. about** s'extasier sur. ◆**ec'statically** *adv* avec extase.

ecumenical [iːkjuːˈmenɪk(ə)l] *a* œcuménique.

eczema [ˈeksɪmə] *n Med* eczéma *m*.

eddy [ˈedɪ] *n* tourbillon *m*, remous *m*.

edg/e [edʒ] *n* bord *m*; (*of forest*) lisière *f*; (*of town*) abords *mpl*; (*of page*) marge *f*; (*of knife etc*) tranchant *m*, fil *m*; **on e.** (*person*) énervé; (*nerves*) tendu; **to set s.o.'s teeth on e.** (*irritate s.o.*) crisper qn, faire grincer les dents à qn; **to have the e.** *or* **a slight e.** *Fig* être légèrement supérieur (**over, on** à); − *vt* (*clothing etc*) border (**with** de); − *vti* **to e.** (*oneself*) **into** (*move*) se glisser dans; **to e.** (*oneself*) **forward** avancer doucement. ◆**─ing** *n* (*border*) bordure *f*. ◆**edgeways** *adv* de côté; **to get a word in e.** *Fam* placer un mot.

edgy [ˈedʒɪ] *a* (**-ier, -iest**) énervé. ◆**edginess** *n* nervosité *f*.

edible [ˈedɪb(ə)l] *a* (*mushroom, berry etc*) comestible; (*meal, food*) mangeable.

edict [ˈiːdɪkt] *n* décret *m*; *Hist* édit *m*.

edifice [ˈedɪfɪs] *n* (*building, organization*) édifice *m*.

edify [ˈedɪfaɪ] *vt* (*improve the mind of*) édifier.

Edinburgh [ˈedɪnb(ə)rə] *n* Édimbourg *m* or *f*.

edit [ˈedɪt] *vt* (*newspaper etc*) diriger; (*article etc*) mettre au point; (*film*) monter; (*annotate*) éditer; (*compile*) rédiger; **to e.** (**out**) (*cut out*) couper. ◆**editor** *n* (*of review*) directeur, -trice *mf*; (*compiler*) rédacteur, -trice *mf*; *TV Rad* réalisateur, -trice *mf*; **sports e.** *Journ* rédacteur *m* sportif, rédactrice *f* sportive; **the e. (in chief)** (*of newspaper*) le rédacteur *m* en chef. ◆**edi'torial** *a* de la rédaction; **e. staff** rédaction *f*; − *n* éditorial *m*.

edition [ɪˈdɪʃ(ə)n] *n* édition *f*.

educat/e [ˈedjʊkeɪt] *vt* (*family, children*) éduquer; (*pupil*) instruire; (*mind*) former, éduquer; **to be educated at** faire ses études à. ◆**─ed** *a* (*voice*) cultivé; (**well-**)**e.** (*person*) instruit. ◆**edu'cation** *n* éducation *f*; (*teaching*) instruction *f*, enseigne-

ment *m*; (*training*) formation *f*; (*subject*) *Univ* pédagogie *f*. ◆**edu'cational** *a* (*establishment*) d'enseignement; (*method*) pédagogique; (*game*) éducatif; (*supplies*) scolaire. ◆**edu'cationally** *adv* du point de vue de l'éducation. ◆**educator** *n* éducateur, -trice *mf*.

EEC [iːiːˈsiː] *n abbr* (*European Economic Community*) CEE *f*.

eel [iːl] *n* anguille *f*.

eerie [ˈɪərɪ] *a* (**-ier, -iest**) sinistre, étrange.

efface [ɪˈfeɪs] *vt* effacer.

effect [ɪˈfekt] **1** *n* (*result, impression*) effet *m* (**on** sur); *pl* (*goods*) biens *mpl*; **to no e.** en vain; **in e.** en fait; **to put into e.** mettre en application, faire entrer en vigueur; **to come into e., take e.** entrer en vigueur; **to take e.** (*of drug etc*) agir; **to have an e.** (*of medicine etc*) faire de l'effet; **to have no e.** rester sans effet; **to this e.** (*in this meaning*) dans ce sens; **to the e. that** (*saying that*) comme quoi. **2** *vt* (*carry out*) effectuer, réaliser.

effective [ɪˈfektɪv] *a* (*efficient*) efficace; (*actual*) effectif; (*striking*) frappant; **to become e.** (*of law*) prendre effet. ◆**─ly** *adv* efficacement; (*in effect*) effectivement. ◆**─ness** *n* efficacité *f*; (*quality*) effet *m* frappant.

effeminate [ɪˈfemɪnɪt] *a* efféminé.

effervescent [efəˈves(ə)nt] *a* (*mixture, youth*) effervescent; (*drink*) gazeux. ◆**effervesce** *vi* (*of drink*) pétiller. ◆**effervescence** *n* (*excitement*) & *Ch* effervescence *f*; pétillement *m*.

effete [ɪˈfiːt] *a* (*feeble*) mou, faible; (*decadent*) décadent.

efficient [ɪˈfɪʃ(ə)nt] *a* (*method*) efficace; (*person*) compétent, efficace; (*organization*) efficace, performant; (*machine*) performant, à haut rendement. ◆**efficiency** *n* efficacité *f*; compétence *f*; performances *fpl*. ◆**efficiently** *adv* efficacement; avec compétence; **to work e.** (*of machine*) bien fonctionner.

effigy [ˈefɪdʒɪ] *n* effigie *f*.

effort [ˈefət] *n* effort *m*; **to make an e.** faire un effort (**to** pour); **it isn't worth the e.** ça ne *or* n'en vaut pas la peine; **his** *or* **her latest e.** *Fam* ses dernières tentatives. ◆**─less** *a* (*victory etc*) facile. ◆**─lessly** *adv* facilement, sans effort.

effrontery [ɪˈfrʌntərɪ] *n* effronterie *f*.

effusive [ɪˈfjuːsɪv] *a* (*person*) expansif; (*thanks, excuses*) sans fin. ◆**─ly** *adv* avec effusion.

e.g. [iː'dʒiː] *abbr* (*exempli gratia*) par exemple.

egalitarian [ˌɪgælɪ'teərɪən] *a* (*society etc*) égalitaire.

egg [eg] *n* œuf *m*; **e. timer** sablier *m*; **e. whisk** fouet *m* (à œufs). ◆**eggcup** *n* coquetier *m*. ◆**egghead** *n Pej* intellectuel, -elle *mf*. ◆**eggplant** *n* aubergine *f*. ◆**eggshell** *n* coquille *f*.

egg [eg] *vt* **to e. on** (*encourage*) inciter (**to do** à faire).

ego [ˈiːgəʊ] *n* (*pl* -os) **the e.** *Psy* le moi. ◆**ego'centric** *a* égocentrique. ◆**egoism** *n* égoïsme *m*. ◆**egoist** *n* égoïste *mf*. ◆**ego'istic(al)** *a* égoïste. ◆**egotism** *n* égotisme *m*.

Egypt [ˈiːdʒɪpt] *n* Égypte *f*. ◆**E'gyptian** *a & n* égyptien, -ienne (*mf*).

eh? [eɪ] *int Fam* hein?

eiderdown [ˈaɪdədaʊn] *n* édredon *m*.

eight [eɪt] *a & n* huit (*m*). ◆**eigh'teen** *a & n* dix-huit (*m*). ◆**eigh'teenth** *a & n* dix-huitième (*mf*). ◆**eighth** *a & n* huitième (*mf*); **an e.** un huitième. ◆**eightieth** *a & n* quatre-vingtième (*mf*). ◆**eighty** *a & n* quatre-vingts (*m*); **e.-one** quatre-vingt-un.

Eire [ˈeərə] *n* République *f* d'Irlande.

either [ˈaɪðər] **1** *a & pron* (*one or other*) l'un(e) ou l'autre; (*with negative*) ni l'un(e) ni l'autre; (*each*) chaque; **on e.** side de chaque côté, des deux côtés. **2** *adv* **she can't swim e.** elle ne sait pas nager non plus; **I don't e.** (ni) moi non plus; **not so far off e.** (*moreover*) pas si loin d'ailleurs. **3** *conj* **e. ... or** ou (bien) ... ou (bien), soit ... soit; (*with negative*) ni ... ni ...

eject [ɪ'dʒekt] *vt* expulser; *Tech* éjecter. ◆**ejector** *a* **e. seat** *Av* siège *m* éjectable.

eke [iːk] *vt* **to e. out** (*income etc*) faire durer; **to e. out a living** gagner (difficilement) sa vie.

elaborate [ɪ'læbərət] *a* compliqué, détaillé; (*preparation*) minutieux; (*style*) recherché; (*meal*) raffiné; – [ɪ'læbəreɪt] *vt* (*theory etc*) élaborer; – *vi* entrer dans les détails (**on** de). ◆**—ly** *adv* (*to plan*) minutieusement; (*to decorate*) avec recherche. ◆**elabo'ration** *n* élaboration *f*.

elapse [ɪ'læps] *vi* s'écouler.

elastic [ɪ'læstɪk] *a* (*object, character*) élastique; **e. band** élastique *m*; – *n* (*fabric*) élastique *m*. ◆**ela'sticity** *n* élasticité *f*.

elated [ɪ'leɪtɪd] *a* transporté de joie. ◆**elation** *n* exaltation *f*.

elbow [ˈelbəʊ] *n* coude *m*; **e. grease** *Fam* huile *f* de coude; **to have enough e. room**

avoir assez de place; – *vt* **to e. one's way** se frayer un chemin (à coups de coude) (**through** à travers).

elder [ˈeldər] *a & n* (*of two people*) aîné, -ée (*mf*). ◆**elderly** *a* assez âgé, entre deux âges. ◆**eldest** *a & n* aîné, -ée (*mf*); **his** *or* **her e. brother** l'aîné de ses frères.

elder [ˈeldər] *n* (*tree*) sureau *m*.

elect [ɪ'lekt] *vt Pol* élire (**to** à); **to e. to do** choisir de faire; – **a the president**/*etc* le président/*etc* désigné. ◆**election** *n* élection *f*; **general e.** élections *fpl* législatives; – **a** (*campaign*) électoral; (*day, results*) du scrutin, des élections. ◆**electio'neering** *n* campagne *f* électorale. ◆**elective** *a* (*course*) *Am* facultatif. ◆**electoral** *a* électoral. ◆**electorate** *n* électorat *m*.

electric [ɪ'lektrɪk] *a* électrique; **e. blanket** couverture *f* chauffante; **e. shock** décharge *f* électrique; **e. shock treatment** électrochoc *m*. ◆**electrical** *a* électrique; **e. engineer** ingénieur *m* électricien. ◆**elec'trician** *n* électricien *m*. ◆**elec'tricity** *n* électricité *f*. ◆**electrify** *vt Rail* électrifier; (*excite*) *Fig* électriser. ◆**electrocute** *vt* électrocuter.

electrode [ɪ'lektrəʊd] *n El* électrode *f*.

electron [ɪ'lektrɒn] *n* électron *m*; – *a* (*microscope*) électronique. ◆**elec'tronic** *a* électronique. ◆**elec'tronics** *n* électronique *f*.

elegant [ˈelɪgənt] *a* élégant. ◆**elegance** *n* élégance *f*. ◆**elegantly** *adv* avec élégance, élégamment.

elegy [ˈelədʒɪ] *n* élégie *f*.

element [ˈelɪmənt] *n* (*component, environment*) élément *m*; (*of heater*) résistance *f*; **an e. of truth** un grain *or* une part de vérité; **the human/chance e.** le facteur humain/chance; **in one's e.** dans son élément. ◆**ele'mental** *a* élémentaire. ◆**ele'mentary** *a* élémentaire; (*school*) *Am* primaire; **e. courtesy** la courtoisie la plus élémentaire.

elephant [ˈelɪfənt] *n* éléphant *m*. ◆**elephantine** [elɪ'fæntaɪn] *a* (*large*) éléphantesque; (*clumsy*) gauche.

elevate [ˈelɪveɪt] *vt* élever (**to** à). ◆**ele'vation** *n* élévation *f* (**of** de); (*height*) altitude *f*. ◆**elevator** *n Am* ascenseur *m*.

eleven [ɪ'lev(ə)n] *a & n* onze (*m*). ◆**elevenses** [ɪ'lev(ə)nzɪz] *n Fam* pause-café *f* (*vers onze heures du matin*). ◆**eleventh** *a & n* onzième (*mf*).

elf [elf] *n* (*pl* **elves**) lutin *m*.

elicit [ɪ'lɪsɪt] *vt* tirer, obtenir (**from** de).

elide [ɪ'laɪd] *vt Ling* élider. ◆**elision** *n* élision *f*.

eligible [ˈelɪdʒəb(ə)l] *a* (*for post etc*) admissible (**for** à); (*for political office*) éligible (**for** à); **to be e. for** (*entitled to*) avoir droit à; **an e. young man** (*suitable as husband*) un beau parti. ◆**eligiˈbility** *n* admissibilité *f*; *Pol* éligibilité *f*.

eliminate [ɪˈlɪmɪneɪt] *vt* éliminer (**from** de). ◆**elimiˈnation** *n* élimination *f*.

elite [eɪˈliːt] *n* élite *f* (**of** de).

elk [elk] *n* (*animal*) élan *m*.

ellipse [ɪˈlɪps] *n* *Geom* ellipse *f*. ◆**elliptical** *a* elliptique.

elm [elm] *n* (*tree, wood*) orme *m*.

elocution [eləˈkjuːʃ(ə)n] *n* élocution *f*.

elongate [ˈiːlɒŋgeɪt] *vt* allonger. ◆**elonˈgation** *n* allongement *m*.

elope [ɪˈləʊp] *vi* (*of lovers*) s'enfuir (**with** avec). ◆**—ment** *n* fugue *f* (amoureuse).

eloquent [ˈeləkwənt] *a* éloquent. ◆**eloquence** *n* éloquence *f*.

else [els] *adv* d'autre; **someone e.** quelqu'un d'autre; **everybody e.** tout le monde à part moi, vous *etc*, tous les autres; **nobody/nothing e.** personne/rien d'autre; **something e.** autre chose; **something** *or* **anything e.?** encore quelque chose?; **somewhere e.** ailleurs, autre part; **who e.?** qui encore?, qui d'autre?; **how e.?** de quelle autre façon?; **or e.** ou bien, sinon. ◆**elsewhere** *adv* ailleurs; **e. in the town** dans une autre partie de la ville.

elucidate [ɪˈluːsɪdeɪt] *vt* élucider.

elude [ɪˈluːd] *vt* (*enemy*) échapper à; (*question*) éluder; (*obligation*) se dérober à; (*blow*) esquiver. ◆**elusive** *a* (*enemy, aims*) insaisissable; (*reply*) évasif.

emaciated [ɪˈmeɪsɪeɪtɪd] *a* émacié.

emanate [ˈeməneɪt] *vi* émaner (**from** de).

emancipate [ɪˈmænsɪpeɪt] *vt* (*women*) émanciper. ◆**emanciˈpation** *n* émancipation *f*.

embalm [ɪmˈbɑːm] *vt* (*dead body*) embaumer.

embankment [ɪmˈbæŋkmənt] *n* (*of path etc*) talus *m*; (*of river*) berge *f*.

embargo [ɪmˈbɑːgəʊ] *n* (*pl* **-oes**) embargo *m*.

embark [ɪmˈbɑːk] *vt* embarquer; — *vi* (s')embarquer; **to e. on** (*start*) commencer, entamer; (*launch into*) se lancer dans, s'embarquer dans. ◆**embarˈkation** *n* embarquement *m*.

embarrass [ɪmˈbærəs] *vt* embarrasser, gêner. ◆**—ing** *a* (*question etc*) embarrassant. ◆**—ment** *n* embarras *m*, gêne *f*; (*financial*) embarras *mpl*.

embassy [ˈembəsɪ] *n* ambassade *f*.

embattled [ɪmˈbæt(ə)ld] *a* (*political party, person etc*) assiégé de toutes parts; (*attitude*) belliqueux.

embedded [ɪmˈbedɪd] *a* (*stick, bullet*) enfoncé; (*jewel*) & *Ling* enchâssé; (*in one's memory*) gravé; (*in stone*) scellé.

embellish [ɪmˈbelɪʃ] *vt* embellir. ◆**—ment** *n* embellissement *m*.

embers [ˈembəz] *npl* braise *f*, charbons *mpl* ardents.

embezzl/e [ɪmˈbez(ə)l] *vt* (*money*) détourner. ◆**—ement** *n* détournement *m* de fonds. ◆**—er** *n* escroc *m*, voleur *m*.

embitter [ɪmˈbɪtər] *vt* (*person*) aigrir; (*situation*) envenimer.

emblem [ˈembləm] *n* emblème *m*.

embody [ɪmˈbɒdɪ] *vt* (*express*) exprimer; (*represent*) incarner; (*include*) réunir. ◆**embodiment** *n* incarnation *f* (**of** de).

emboss [ɪmˈbɒs] *vt* (*metal*) emboutir; (*paper*) gaufrer, emboutir. ◆**—ed** *a* en relief.

embrace [ɪmˈbreɪs] *vt* étreindre, embrasser; (*include, adopt*) embrasser; — *vi* s'étreindre, s'embrasser; — *n* étreinte *f*.

embroider [ɪmˈbrɔɪdər] *vt* (*cloth*) broder; (*story, facts*) *Fig* enjoliver. ◆**embroidery** *n* broderie *f*.

embroil [ɪmˈbrɔɪl] *vt* **to e. s.o. in** mêler qn à.

embryo [ˈembrɪəʊ] *n* (*pl* **-os**) embryon *m*. ◆**embryˈonic** *a* *Med* & *Fig* embryonnaire.

emcee [emˈsiː] *n* *Am* présentateur, -trice *mf*.

emend [ɪˈmend] *vt* (*text*) corriger.

emerald [ˈemərəld] *n* émeraude *f*.

emerge [ɪˈmɜːdʒ] *vi* apparaître (**from** de); (*from hole etc*) sortir; (*of truth, from water*) émerger; (*of nation*) naître; **it emerges that** il apparaît que. ◆**emergence** *n* apparition *f*.

emergency [ɪˈmɜːdʒənsɪ] *n* (*case*) urgence *f*; (*crisis*) crise *f*; (*contingency*) éventualité *f*; **in an e.** en cas d'urgence; — *a* (*measure etc*) d'urgence; (*exit, brake*) de secours; (*ward, services*) *Med* des urgences; **e. landing** atterrissage *m* forcé; **e. powers** *Pol* pouvoirs *mpl* extraordinaires.

emery [ˈemərɪ] *a* **e. cloth** toile *f* (d')émeri.

emigrant [ˈemɪgrənt] *n* émigrant, -ante *mf*. ◆**emigrate** *vi* émigrer. ◆**emiˈgration** *n* émigration *f*.

eminent [ˈemɪnənt] *a* éminent. ◆**eminence** *n* distinction *f*; **his E.** *Rel* son Éminence. ◆**eminently** *adv* hautement, remarquablement.

emissary [ˈemɪsərɪ] *n* émissaire *m*.

emit [ɪˈmɪt] *vt* (**-tt-**) (*light, heat etc*) émettre;

(*smell*) dégager. ◆**emission** *n* émission *f*; dégagement *m*.

emotion [ɪˈməʊʃ(ə)n] *n* (*strength of feeling*) émotion *f*; (*joy, love etc*) sentiment *m*. ◆**emotional** *a* (*person, reaction*) émotif; (*story, speech*) émouvant; (*moment*) d'émotion intense; (*state*) *Psy* émotionnel. ◆**emotionally** *adv* (*to say*) avec émotion; **to be e. unstable** avoir des troubles émotifs. ◆**emotive** *a* (*person*) émotif; (*word*) affectif; **an e. issue** une question sensible.

emperor [ˈempərər] *n* empereur *m*.

emphasize [ˈemfəsaɪz] *vt* souligner (**that** que); (*word, fact*) appuyer *or* insister sur, souligner. ◆**emphasis** *n* *Ling* accent *m* (tonique); (*insistence*) insistance *f*; **to lay** *or* **put e. on** mettre l'accent sur. ◆**em'phatic** *a* (*person, refusal*) catégorique; (*forceful*) énergique; **to be e. about** insister sur. ◆**em'phatically** *adv* catégoriquement; énergiquement; **e. no!** absolument pas!

empire [ˈempaɪər] *n* empire *m*.

empirical [emˈpɪrɪk(ə)l] *a* empirique. ◆**empiricism** *n* empirisme *m*.

employ [ɪmˈplɔɪ] *vt* (*person, means*) employer; – *n* **in the e. of** employé par. ◆**employee** [ɪmˈplɔɪiː, emplɔɪˈiː] *n* employé, -ée *mf*. ◆**employer** *n* patron, -onne *mf*. ◆**employment** *n* emploi *m*; **place of e.** lieu *m* de travail; **in the e. of** employé par; **e. agency** bureau *m* de placement.

empower [ɪmˈpaʊər] *vt* autoriser (**to do** à faire).

empress [ˈemprɪs] *n* impératrice *f*.

empt/y [ˈemptɪ] *a* (**-ier, -iest**) vide; (*threat, promise etc*) vain; (*stomach*) creux; **on an e. stomach** à jeun; **to return/etc e.-handed** revenir/etc les mains vides; – *npl* (*bottles*) bouteilles *fpl* vides; – *vt* **to e. (out)** (*box, pocket, liquid etc*) vider; (*vehicle*) décharger; (*objects in box etc*) sortir (**from, out of** de); – *vi* se vider; (*of river*) se jeter (**into** dans). ◆**—iness** *n* vide *m*.

emulate [ˈemjʊleɪt] *vt* imiter. ◆**emu'lation** *n* émulation *f*.

emulsion [ɪˈmʌlʃ(ə)n] *n* (*paint*) peinture *f* (mate); *Phot* émulsion *f*.

enable [ɪˈneɪb(ə)l] *vt* **to e. s.o. to do** permettre à qn de faire.

enact [ɪˈnækt] *vt* (*law*) promulguer; (*part of play*) jouer.

enamel [ɪˈnæm(ə)l] *n* émail *m*; – *a* en émail; – *vt* (**-ll-,** *Am* **-l-**) émailler.

enamoured [ɪˈnæməd] *a* **e. of** (*thing*) séduit par; (*person*) amoureux de.

encamp [ɪnˈkæmp] *vi* camper. ◆**—ment** *n* campement *m*.

encapsulate [ɪnˈkæpsjʊleɪt] *vt* *Fig* résumer.

encase [ɪnˈkeɪs] *vt* recouvrir (**in** de).

enchant [ɪnˈtʃɑːnt] *vt* enchanter. ◆**—ing** *a* enchanteur. ◆**—ment** *n* enchantement *m*.

encircle [ɪnˈsɜːk(ə)l] *vt* entourer; *Mil* encercler. ◆**—ment** *n* encerclement *m*.

enclave [ˈenkleɪv] *n* enclave *f*.

enclos/e [ɪnˈkləʊz] *vt* (*send with letter*) joindre (**in, with** à); (*fence off*) clôturer; **to e. with** (*a fence, wall*) entourer de. ◆**—ed** *a* (*space*) clos; (*cheque etc*) ci-joint; (*market*) couvert. ◆**enclosure** *n* *Com* pièce *f* jointe; (*fence, place*) enceinte *f*.

encompass [ɪnˈkʌmpəs] *vt* (*surround*) entourer; (*include*) inclure.

encore [ˈɒŋkɔːr] *int* & *n* bis (*m*); – *vt* bisser.

encounter [ɪnˈkaʊntər] *vt* rencontrer; – *n* rencontre *f*.

encourage [ɪnˈkʌrɪdʒ] *vt* encourager (**to do** à faire). ◆**—ment** *n* encouragement *m*.

encroach [ɪnˈkrəʊtʃ] *vi* empiéter (**on, upon** sur); **to e. on the land** (*of sea*) gagner du terrain. ◆**—ment** *n* empiétement *m*.

encumber [ɪnˈkʌmbər] *vt* encombrer (**with** de). ◆**encum'brance** *n* embarras *m*.

encyclical [ɪnˈsɪklɪk(ə)l] *n* *Rel* encyclique *f*.

encyclop(a)edia [ɪnsaɪkləˈpiːdɪə] *n* encyclopédie *f*. ◆**encyclop(a)edic** *a* encyclopédique.

end [end] *n* (*of street, object etc*) bout *m*, extrémité *f*; (*of time, meeting, book etc*) fin *f*; (*purpose*) fin *f*, but *m*; **at an e.** (*discussion etc*) fini; (*period*) écoulé; (*patience*) à bout; **in the e.** à la fin; **to come to an e.** prendre fin; **to put an e. to, bring to an e.** mettre fin à; **there's no e. to it** ça n'en finit plus; **no e. of** *Fam* beaucoup de; **six days on e.** six jours d'affilée; **for days on e.** pendant des jours (et des jours); **(standing) on e.** (*box etc*) debout; (*hair*) hérissé; – *a* (*row, house*) dernier; **e. product** *Com* produit *m* fini; *Fig* résultat *m*; – *vt* finir, terminer, achever (**with** par); (*rumour, speculation*) mettre fin à; – *vi* finir, se terminer, s'achever; **to e. in failure** se solder par un échec; **to e. in a point** finir en pointe; **to e. up doing** finir par faire; **to e. up in** (*London etc*) se retrouver à; **he ended up in prison/a doctor** il a fini en prison/par devenir médecin.

endanger [ɪnˈdeɪndʒər] *vt* mettre en danger.

endear [ɪnˈdɪər] *vt* faire aimer *or* apprécier (**to** de); **that's what endears him to me** c'est cela qui me plaît en lui. ◆**—ing** *a* attachant, sympathique. ◆**—ment** *n* parole *f* tendre; **term of e.** terme *m* d'affection.

endeavour [ɪnˈdevər] *vi* s'efforcer (**to do** de faire); *− n* effort *m* (**to do** pour faire).

ending [ˈendɪŋ] *n* fin *f*; (*outcome*) issue *f*; *Ling* terminaison *f*. ◆**endless** *a* (*speech, series etc*) interminable; (*patience*) infini; (*countless*) innombrable. ◆**endlessly** *adv* interminablement.

endive [ˈendɪv, *Am* ˈendaɪv] *n Bot Culin* (*curly*) chicorée *f*; (*smooth*) endive *f*.

endorse [ɪnˈdɔɪs] *vt* (*cheque etc*) endosser; (*action*) approuver; (*claim*) appuyer. ◆**−ment** *n* (*on driving licence*) contravention *f*.

endow [ɪnˈdaʊ] *vt* (*institution*) doter (**with** de); (*chair, hospital bed*) fonder; **endowed with** (*person*) *Fig* doté de. ◆**−ment** *n* dotation *f*; fondation *f*.

endur/e [ɪnˈdjʊər] **1** *vt* (*bear*) supporter (**doing** de faire). **2** *vi* (*last*) durer. ◆**−ing** *a* durable. ◆**−able** *a* supportable. ◆**endurance** *n* endurance *f*, résistance *f*.

enemy [ˈenəmɪ] *n* ennemi, -ie *mf*; *− a* (*army, tank etc*) ennemi.

energy [ˈenədʒɪ] *n* énergie *f*; *− a* (*crisis, resources etc*) énergétique. ◆**ener'getic** *a* énergique; **to feel e.** se sentir en pleine forme. ◆**ener'getically** *adv* énergiquement.

enforc/e [ɪnˈfɔɪs] *vt* (*law*) faire respecter; (*discipline*) imposer (**on** à). ◆**−ed** *a* (*rest, silence etc*) forcé.

engag/e [ɪnˈgeɪdʒ] *vt* (*take on*) engager, prendre; **to e. s.o. in conversation** engager la conversation avec qn; **to e. the clutch** *Aut* embrayer; *− vi* **to e. in** (*launch into*) se lancer dans; (*be involved in*) être mêlé à. ◆**−ed** *a* **1** (*person, toilet*) & *Tel* occupé; **e. in doing** occupé à faire; **to be e. in business**/*etc* être dans les affaires/*etc*. **2** (*betrothed*) fiancé; **to get e.** se fiancer. ◆**−ing** *a* (*smile*) engageant. ◆**−ement** *n* (*agreement to marry*) fiançailles *fpl*; (*meeting*) rendez-vous *m inv*; (*undertaking*) engagement *m*; **to have a prior e.** (*be busy*) être déjà pris, ne pas être libre; **e. ring** bague *f* de fiançailles.

engender [ɪnˈdʒendər] *vt* (*produce*) engendrer.

engine [ˈendʒɪn] *n Aut* moteur *m*; *Rail* locomotive *f*; *Nau* machine *f*; **e. driver** mécanicien *m*.

engineer [endʒɪˈnɪər] **1** *n* ingénieur *m*; (*repairer*) dépanneur *m*; *Rail Am* mécanicien *m*; **civil e.** ingénieur *m* des travaux publics; **mechanical e.** ingénieur *m*

mécanicien. ◆**2** *vt* (*arrange secretly*) machiner. ◆**−ing** *n* ingénierie *f*; (**civil**) **e.** génie *m* civil, travaux *mpl* publics; (**mechanical**) **e.** mécanique *f*; **e. factory** atelier *m* de construction mécanique.

England [ˈɪŋglənd] *n* Angleterre *f*. ◆**English** *a* anglais; **the E. Channel** la Manche; **the E.** les Anglais *mpl*; *− n* (*language*) anglais *m*. ◆**Englishman** *n* (*pl* -men) Anglais *m*. ◆**English-speaking** *a* anglophone. ◆**Englishwoman** *n* (*pl* -women) Anglaise *f*.

engrav/e [ɪnˈgreɪv] *vt* graver. ◆**−ing** *n* gravure *f*. ◆**−er** *n* graveur *m*.

engrossed [ɪnˈgrəʊst] *a* absorbé (**in** par).

engulf [ɪnˈgʌlf] *vt* engloutir.

enhance [ɪnˈhɑːns] *vt* (*beauty etc*) rehausser; (*value*) augmenter.

enigma [ɪˈnɪgmə] *n* énigme *f*. ◆**enig'matic** *a* énigmatique.

enjoy [ɪnˈdʒɔɪ] *vt* aimer (**doing** faire); (*meal*) apprécier; (*income, standard of living etc*) jouir de; **to e. the evening** passer une bonne soirée; **to e. oneself** s'amuser; **to e. being in London**/*etc* se plaire à Londres/*etc*. ◆**−able** *a* agréable. ◆**−ably** *adv* agréablement. ◆**−ment** *n* plaisir *m*.

enlarge [ɪnˈlɑːdʒ] *vt* agrandir; *− vi* s'agrandir; **to e. (up)on** (*say more about*) s'étendre sur. ◆**−ment** *n* agrandissement *m*.

enlighten [ɪnˈlaɪt(ə)n] *vt* éclairer (**s.o. on** *or* **about sth** qn sur qch). ◆**−ing** *a* instructif. ◆**−ment** *n* (*explanations*) éclaircissements *mpl*; **an age of e.** une époque éclairée.

enlist [ɪnˈlɪst] *vi* (*in the army etc*) s'engager; *vt* (*recruit*) engager; (*supporter*) recruter; (*support*) obtenir. ◆**−ment** *n* engagement *m*; recrutement *m*.

enliven [ɪnˈlaɪv(ə)n] *vt* (*meeting, people etc*) égayer, animer.

enmeshed [ɪnˈmeʃt] *a* empêtré (**in** dans).

enmity [ˈenmɪtɪ] *n* inimitié *f* (**between** entre).

enormous [ɪˈnɔːməs] *a* énorme; (*explosion*) terrible; (*success*) fou. ◆**enormity** *n* (*vastness, extent*) énormité *f*; (*atrocity*) atrocité *f*. ◆**enormously** *adv* (*very much*) énormément; (*very*) extrêmement.

enough [ɪˈnʌf] *a* & *n* assez (de); **e. time/ cups**/*etc* assez de temps/de tasses/*etc*; **to have e. to live on** avoir de quoi vivre; **to have e. to drink** avoir assez à boire; **to have had e. of** *Pej* en avoir assez de; **it's e. for me to see that ...** il me suffit de voir que ... ; **that's e.** ça suffit, c'est assez; *− adv* assez, suffisamment (**to** pour); **strangely e., he left** chose curieuse, il est parti.

enquire [ɪn'kwaɪər] *vi* = **inquire.**

enquiry [ɪn'kwaɪərɪ] *n* = **inquiry.**

enrage [ɪn'reɪdʒ] *vt* mettre en rage.

enrapture [ɪn'ræptʃər] *vt* ravir.

enrich [ɪn'rɪtʃ] *vt* enrichir; (*soil*) fertiliser. ◆**—ment** *n* enrichissement *m*.

enrol [ɪn'rəʊl] (*Am* **enroll**) *vi* (**-ll-**) s'inscrire (**in, for** à); – *vt* inscrire. ◆**—ment** *n* inscription *f*; (*people enrolled*) effectif *m*.

ensconced [ɪn'skɒnst] *a* bien installé (**in** dans).

ensemble [ɒn'sɒmb(ə)l] *n* (*clothes*) & *Mus* ensemble *m*.

ensign ['ensən] *n* (*flag*) pavillon *m*; (*rank*) *Am Nau* enseigne *m* de vaisseau.

enslave [ɪn'sleɪv] *vt* asservir.

ensu/e [ɪn'sjuː] *vi* s'ensuivre. ◆**—ing** *a* (*day, year etc*) suivant; (*event*) qui s'ensuit.

ensure [ɪn'ʃʊər] *vt* assurer; **to e. that** (*make sure*) s'assurer que.

entail [ɪn'teɪl] *vt* (*imply, involve*) entraîner, impliquer.

entangle [ɪn'tæŋɡ(ə)l] *vt* emmêler, enchevêtrer; **to get entangled** s'empêtrer. ◆**—ment** *n* enchevêtrement *m*; **an e. with** (*police*) des démêlés *mpl* avec.

enter ['entər] *vt* (*room, vehicle, army etc*) entrer dans; (*road*) s'engager dans; (*university*) s'inscrire à; (*write down*) inscrire (**in** dans, **on** sur); (*in ledger*) porter (**in** sur); **to e. s.o. for** (*exam*) présenter qn à; **to e. a painting/etc in** (*competition*) présenter un tableau/*etc* à; **it didn't e. my head** ça ne m'est pas venu à l'esprit (**that** que); – *vi* entrer; **to e. for** (*race, exam*) s'inscrire pour; **to e. into** (*plans*) entrer dans; (*conversation, relations*) entrer en; **you don't e. into it** tu n'y es pour rien; **to e. into** *or* **upon** (*career*) entrer dans; (*negotiations*) entamer; (*agreement*) conclure.

enterpris/e ['entəpraɪz] *n* (*undertaking, firm*) entreprise *f*; (*spirit*) *Fig* initiative *f*. ◆**—ing** *a* (*person*) plein d'initiative; (*attempt*) hardi.

entertain [entə'teɪn] *vt* amuser, distraire; (*guest*) recevoir; (*idea, possibility*) envisager; (*hope*) chérir; **to e. s.o. to a meal** recevoir qn à dîner; – *vi* (*receive guests*) recevoir. ◆**—ing** *a* amusant. ◆**—er** *n* artiste *mf*. ◆**—ment** *n* amusement *m*, distraction *f*; (*show*) spectacle *m*.

enthral(l) [ɪn'θrɔːl] *vt* (**-ll-**) (*delight*) captiver.

enthuse [ɪn'θjuːz] *vi* **to e. over** *Fam* s'emballer pour. ◆**enthusiasm** *n* enthousiasme *m*. ◆**enthusiast** *n* enthousiaste

mf; **jazz/etc e.** passionné, -ée *mf* du jazz/*etc*. ◆**enthusi'astic** *a* enthousiaste; (*golfer etc*) passionné; **to be e. about** (*hobby*) être passionné de; **he was e. about** *or* **over** (*gift etc*) il a été emballé par; **to get e.** s'emballer (**about** pour). ◆**enthusi-'astically** *adv* avec enthousiasme.

entic/e [ɪn'taɪs] *vt* attirer (par la ruse); **to e. to do** entraîner (par la ruse) à faire. ◆**—ing** *a* séduisant, alléchant. ◆**—ement** *n* (*bait*) attrait *m*.

entire [ɪn'taɪər] *a* entier. ◆**—ly** *adv* tout à fait, entièrement. ◆**entirety** [ɪn'taɪərətɪ] *n* intégralité *f*; **in its e.** en entier.

entitl/e [ɪn'taɪt(ə)l] *vt* **to e. s.o. to do** donner à qn le droit de faire; **to e. s.o. to sth** donner à qn (le) droit à qch; **that entitles me to believe that ...** ça m'autorise à croire que ... . ◆**—ed** *a* (*book*) intitulé; **to be e. to do** avoir le droit de faire; **to be e. to sth** avoir droit à qch. ◆**—ement** *n* **one's e.** son dû.

entity ['entɪtɪ] *n* entité *f*.

entourage ['ɒntʊrɑːʒ] *n* entourage *m*.

entrails ['entreɪlz] *npl* entrailles *fpl*.

entrance 1 ['entrəns] *n* entrée *f* (**to** de); (*to university etc*) admission *f* (**to** à); **e. examination** examen *m* d'entrée. **2** [ɪn'trɑːns] *vt* *Fig* transporter, ravir.

entrant ['entrənt] *n* (*in race*) concurrent, -ente *mf*; (*for exam*) candidat, -ate *mf*.

entreat [ɪn'triːt] *vt* supplier, implorer (**to do** de faire). ◆**entreaty** *n* supplication *f*.

entrée ['ɒntreɪ] *n* *Culin* entrée *f*; (*main dish*) *Am* plat *m* principal.

entrench [ɪn'trentʃ] *vt* **to e. oneself** *Mil* & *Fig* se retrancher.

entrust [ɪn'trʌst] *vt* confier (**to** à); **to e. s.o. with sth** confier qch à qn.

entry ['entrɪ] *n* (*way in, action*) entrée *f*; (*in ledger*) écriture *f*; (*term in dictionary or logbook*) entrée *f*; (*competitor*) *Sp* concurrent, -ente *mf*; (*thing to be judged in competition*) objet *m* (*or* œuvre *f or* projet *m*) soumis à un jury; **e. form** feuille *f* d'inscription; **'no e.'** (*on door etc*) 'entrée interdite'; (*road sign*) 'sens interdit'.

entwine [ɪn'twaɪn] *vt* entrelacer.

enumerate [ɪ'njuːməreɪt] *vt* énumérer. ◆**enume'ration** *n* énumération *f*.

enunciate [ɪ'nʌnsɪeɪt] *vt* (*word*) articuler; (*theory*) énoncer. ◆**enunci'ation** *n* articulation *f*; énonciation *f*.

envelop [ɪn'veləp] *vt* envelopper (**in** fog/mystery/*etc* de brouillard/mystère/*etc*).

envelope ['envələʊp] *n* enveloppe *f*.

envious ['envɪəs] *a* envieux (**of sth** de qch);

e. of s.o. jaloux de qn. ◆**enviable** a enviable. ◆**enviously** adv avec envie.

environment [ɪnˈvaɪərənmənt] n milieu m; (cultural, natural) environnement m. ◆**environ'mental** a du milieu; de l'environnement. ◆**environ'mentalist** n écologiste mf.

envisage [ɪnˈvɪzɪdʒ] vt (imagine) envisager; (foresee) prévoir.

envision [ɪnˈvɪʒ(ə)n] vt Am = **envisage**.

envoy [ˈenvɔɪ] n Pol envoyé, -ée mf.

envy [ˈenvɪ] n envie f; – vt envier (s.o. sth qch à qn).

ephemeral [ɪˈfemərəl] a éphémère.

epic [ˈepɪk] a épique; – n épopée f; (screen) e. film m à grand spectacle.

epidemic [epɪˈdemɪk] n épidémie f; – a épidémique.

epilepsy [ˈepɪlepsɪ] n épilepsie f. ◆**epi'leptic** a & n épileptique (mf).

epilogue [ˈepɪlɒg] n épilogue m.

episode [ˈepɪsəʊd] n épisode m. ◆**episodic** [epɪˈsɒdɪk] a épisodique.

epistle [ɪˈpɪs(ə)l] n épître f.

epitaph [ˈepɪtɑːf] n épitaphe f.

epithet [ˈepɪθet] n épithète f.

epitome [ɪˈpɪtəmɪ] n the e. of l'exemple même de, l'incarnation de. ◆**epitomize** vt incarner.

epoch [ˈiːpɒk] n époque f. ◆**e.-making** a (event) qui fait date.

equal [ˈiːkwəl] a égal (to à); with e. hostility avec la même hostilité; on an e. footing sur un pied d'égalité (with avec); to be e. to égaler; e. to (task, situation) Fig à la hauteur de; – n égal, -ale mf; to treat s.o. as an e. traiter qn en égal or d'égal à égal; he doesn't have his e. il n'a pas son pareil; – vt (-ll-, Am -l-) égaler (in beauty/etc en beauté/etc); equals sign Math signe m d'égalité. ◆**e'quality** n égalité f. ◆**equalize** vt égaliser; – vi Sp égaliser. ◆**equally** adv (to an equal degree, also) également; (to divide) en parts égales; he's e. stupid (just as) il est tout aussi bête.

equanimity [ekwəˈnɪmɪtɪ] n égalité f d'humeur.

equate [ɪˈkweɪt] vt mettre sur le même pied (with que), assimiler (with à).

equation [ɪˈkweɪʒ(ə)n] n Math équation f.

equator [ɪˈkweɪtər] n équateur m; at or on the e. sous l'équateur. ◆**equatorial** [ekwəˈtɔːrɪəl] a équatorial.

equestrian [ɪˈkwestrɪən] a équestre.

equilibrium [iːkwɪˈlɪbrɪəm] n équilibre m.

equinox [ˈiːkwɪnɒks] n équinoxe m.

equip [ɪˈkwɪp] vt (-pp-) équiper (with de);

(well-)equipped with pourvu de; (well-)equipped to do compétent pour faire. ◆—**ment** n équipement m, matériel m.

equity [ˈekwɪtɪ] n (fairness) équité f; pl Com actions fpl. ◆**equitable** a équitable.

equivalent [ɪˈkwɪvələnt] a & n équivalent (m). ◆**equivalence** n équivalence f.

equivocal [ɪˈkwɪvək(ə)l] a équivoque.

era [ˈɪərə, Am ˈerə] n époque f; (historical, geological) ère f.

eradicate [ɪˈrædɪkeɪt] vt supprimer; (evil, prejudice) extirper.

erase [ɪˈreɪz, Am ɪˈreɪs] vt effacer. ◆**eraser** n (rubber) gomme f. ◆**erasure** n rature f.

erect [ɪˈrekt] **1** a (upright) (bien) droit. **2** vt (build) construire; (statue, monument) ériger; (scaffolding) monter; (tent) dresser. ◆**erection** n construction f; érection f; montage m; dressage m.

ermine [ˈɜːmɪn] n (animal, fur) hermine f.

erode [ɪˈrəʊd] vt éroder; (confidence etc) Fig miner, ronger. ◆**erosion** n érosion f.

erotic [ɪˈrɒtɪk] a érotique. ◆**eroticism** n érotisme m.

err [ɜːr] vi (be wrong) se tromper; (sin) pécher.

errand [ˈerənd] n commission f, course f; e. boy garçon m de courses.

erratic [ɪˈrætɪk] a (conduct etc) irrégulier; (person) lunatique.

error [ˈerər] n (mistake) erreur f, faute f; (wrongdoing) erreur f; in e. par erreur. ◆**erroneous** [ɪˈrəʊnɪəs] a erroné.

erudite [ˈeruːdaɪt, Am ˈerjʊdaɪt] a érudit, savant. ◆**eru'dition** n érudition f.

erupt [ɪˈrʌpt] vi (of volcano) entrer en éruption; (of pimples) apparaître; (of war, violence) éclater. ◆**eruption** n (of volcano, pimples, anger) éruption f (of de); (of violence) flambée f.

escalate [ˈeskəleɪt] vi (of war, violence) s'intensifier; (of prices) monter en flèche; – vt intensifier. ◆**esca'lation** n escalade f.

escalator [ˈeskəleɪtər] n escalier m roulant.

escapade [ˈeskəpeɪd] n (prank) frasque f.

escape [ɪˈskeɪp] vi (of gas, animal etc) s'échapper; (of prisoner) s'évader, s'échapper; to e. from (person) échapper à; (place, object) s'échapper de; escaped prisoner évadé, -ée mf; – vt (death) échapper à; (punishment) éviter; that name escapes me ce nom m'échappe; to e. notice passer inaperçu; – n (of gas etc) fuite f; (of person) évasion f, fuite f; to have a lucky or narrow e. l'échapper belle. ◆**escapism** n évasion f (hors de la réalité). ◆**escapist** a (film etc) d'évasion.

eschew [ɪ'stʃuː] vt éviter, fuir.

escort ['eskɔːt] n Mil Nau escorte f; (of woman) cavalier m; – [ɪ'skɔːt] vt escorter.

Eskimo ['eskɪməʊ] n (pl -os) Esquimau, -aude mf; – a esquimau.

esoteric [esəʊ'terɪk] a obscur, ésotérique.

especial [ɪ'speʃəl] a particulier. ◆—ly adv (in particular) particulièrement; (for particular purpose) (tout) exprès; **e. as** d'autant plus que.

espionage ['espɪənɑːʒ] n espionnage m.

esplanade ['espləneɪd] n esplanade f.

espouse [ɪ'spaʊz] vt (a cause) épouser.

espresso [e'spresəʊ] n (pl -os) (café m) express m.

Esq [ɪ'kkwaɪər] abbr (esquire) **J. Smith Esq** (on envelope) Monsieur J. Smith.

essay ['eseɪ] n (attempt) & Liter essai m; Sch rédaction f; Univ dissertation f.

essence ['esəns] n Phil Ch essence f; Culin extrait m, essence f; (main point) essentiel m (of de); **in e.** essentiellement.

essential [ɪ'senʃ(ə)l] a (principal) essentiel; (necessary) indispensable, essentiel; **it's e. that** il est indispensable que (+ sub); – npl **the essentials** l'essentiel m (of de); (of grammar) les éléments mpl. ◆—ly adv essentiellement.

establish [ɪ'stæblɪʃ] vt établir; (state, society) fonder. ◆—ed a (well-)e. (firm) solide; (fact) reconnu; (reputation) établi; **she's (well-)e.** elle a une réputation établie. ◆—ment n (institution, firm) établissement m; **the e. of** l'établissement de; **the E.** les classes fpl dirigeantes.

estate [ɪ'steɪt] n (land) terre(s) f(pl), propriété f; (possessions) Jur fortune f; (of deceased person) succession f; **housing e.** lotissement m; (workers') cité f (ouvrière); **industrial e.** complexe m industriel; **e. agency** agence f immobilière; **e. agent** agent m immobilier; **e. car** break m; **e. tax** Am droits mpl de succession.

esteem [ɪ'stiːm] vt estimer; **highly esteemed** très estimé; – n estime f.

esthetic [es'θetɪk] a Am esthétique.

estimate ['estɪmeɪt] vt (value) estimer, évaluer; (consider) estimer (that que); – ['estɪmət] n (assessment) évaluation f, estimation f; (judgement) évaluation f; (price for work to be done) devis m; **rough e.** chiffre m approximatif. ◆esti'mation n jugement m; (esteem) estime f; **in my e.** à mon avis.

estranged [ɪ'streɪndʒd] a **to become e.** (of couple) se séparer.

estuary ['estjʊərɪ] n estuaire m.

etc [et'setərə] adv etc.

etch [etʃ] vti graver à l'eau forte. ◆—ing n (picture) eau-forte f.

eternal [ɪ'tɜːn(ə)l] a éternel. ◆eternally adv éternellement. ◆eternity n éternité f.

ether ['iːθər] n éther m. ◆e'thereal a éthéré.

ethic ['eθɪk] n éthique f. ◆ethics n (moral standards) moralité f; (study) Phil éthique f ◆ethical a moral, éthique.

Ethiopia [iːθɪ'əʊpɪə] n Éthiopie f. ◆Ethiopian a & n éthiopien, -ienne (mf).

ethnic ['eθnɪk] a ethnique.

ethos ['iːθɒs] n génie m.

etiquette ['etɪket] n (rules) bienséances fpl; (diplomatic) e. protocole m, étiquette f; **professional e.** déontologie f.

etymology [etɪ'mɒlədʒɪ] n étymologie f.

eucalyptus [juːkə'lɪptəs] n (tree) eucalyptus m.

eulogy ['juːlədʒɪ] n panégyrique m, éloge m.

euphemism ['juːfəmɪz(ə)m] n euphémisme m.

euphoria [juː'fɔːrɪə] n euphorie f. ◆euphoric a euphorique.

Euro- ['jʊərəʊ] pref euro-.

Europe ['jʊərəp] n Europe f. ◆Euro'pean a & n européen, -éenne (mf).

euthanasia [juːθə'neɪzɪə] n euthanasie f.

evacuate [ɪ'vækjʊeɪt] vt évacuer. ◆evacu-'ation n évacuation f.

evade [ɪ'veɪd] vt éviter, esquiver; (pursuer, tax) échapper à; (law, question) éluder.

evaluate [ɪ'væljʊeɪt] vt évaluer (at à). ◆evalu'ation n évaluation f.

evangelical [iːvæn'dʒelɪk(ə)l] a Rel évangélique.

evaporat/e [ɪ'væpəreɪt] vi s'évaporer; (of hopes) s'évanouir. ◆—ed a **e. milk** lait m concentré. ◆evapo'ration n évaporation f.

evasion [ɪ'veɪʒ(ə)n] n **e. of** (pursuer etc) fuite f devant; (question) esquive f de; **tax e.** évasion f fiscale. ◆evasive a évasif.

eve [iːv] n **the e. of** la veille de.

even ['iːv(ə)n] **1** a (flat) uni, égal, lisse; (equal) égal; (regular) régulier; (number) pair; **to get e. with** se venger de; **I'll get e. with him (for that)** je lui revaudrai ça; **we're e.** (quits) nous sommes quittes; (in score) nous sommes à égalité; **to break e.** Fin s'y retrouver; – vt **to e. (out or up)** égaliser. **2** adv même; **e. better/more** encore mieux/plus; **e. if or though** même si; **e. so** quand même. ◆—ly adv de manière égale; (regularly) régulièrement. ◆—ness n (of *surface, temper*) égalité f; (*of movement etc*) régularité f. ◆**even-'tempered** a de caractère égal.

evening ['iːvniŋ] n soir m; (*duration of evening, event*) soirée f; **at seven in the e.** à sept heures du soir; **every Tuesday e.** tous les mardis soir; **all e. (long)** toute la soirée; – a (*newspaper etc*) du soir; **e. performance** Th soirée f; **e. dress** tenue f de soirée; (*of woman*) robe f du soir or de soirée.

event [ɪ'vent] n évènement m; Sp épreuve f; **in the e. of death** en cas de décès; **in any e.** en tout cas; **after the e.** après coup. ◆**eventful** a (*journey etc*) mouvementé; (*occasion*) mémorable.

eventual [ɪ'ventʃuəl] a final, définitif. ◆**eventu'ality** n éventualité f. ◆**eventually** adv finalement, à la fin; (*some day or other*) un jour ou l'autre; (*after all*) en fin de compte.

ever ['evər] adv jamais; **has he e. seen it?** l'a-t-il jamais vu?; **more than e.** plus que jamais; **nothing e.** jamais rien; **hardly e.** presque jamais; **e. ready** toujours prêt; **the first e.** le tout premier; **e. since** (*that event etc*) depuis; **e. since then** depuis lors, dès lors; **for e.** (*for always*) pour toujours; (*continually*) sans cesse; **the best son e.** le meilleur fils du monde; **e. so sorry/happy/etc** Fam vraiment désolé/heureux/ etc; **thank you e. so much** Fam merci mille fois; **it's e. such a pity** Fam c'est vraiment dommage; **why e. not?** pourquoi pas donc? ◆**evergreen** n arbre m à feuilles persistantes. ◆**ever'lasting** a éternel. ◆**ever-'more** adv **for e.** à (tout) jamais.

every ['evrɪ] a chaque; **e. child** chaque enfant, tous les enfants; **e. time** chaque fois (**that** que); **e. one** chacun; **e. single one** tous (sans exception); **to have e. confidence in** avoir pleine confiance en; **e. second** or **other day** tous les deux jours; **her e. gesture** ses moindres gestes; **e. bit as big** tout aussi grand (**as** que); **e. so often**, **e. now and then** de temps en temps. ◆**everybody** pron tout le monde; **e. in turn** chacun à son tour. ◆**everyday** a (*happening, life etc*) de tous les jours; (*banal*) banal; **in e. use** d'usage courant. ◆**everyone** pron = everybody. ◆**everyplace** adv Am = everywhere. ◆**everything** pron tout; **e. I have** tout ce que j'ai. ◆**everywhere** adv partout; **e. she goes** où qu'elle aille, partout où elle va.

evict [ɪ'vɪkt] vt expulser (**from** de). ◆**eviction** n expulsion f.

evidence ['evɪdəns] n (*proof*) preuve(s) f(pl); (*testimony*) témoignage m; (*obviousness*) évidence f; **to give e.** témoigner (**against** contre); **e. of** (*wear etc*) des signes mpl de; **in e.** (*noticeable*) (bien) en vue. ◆**evident** a évident (**that** que); **it is e. from ... il apparaît de... (that** que). ◆**evidently** adv (*obviously*) évidemment; (*apparently*) apparemment.

evil ['iːv(ə)l] a (*spell, influence, person*) malfaisant; (*deed, advice, system*) mauvais; (*consequence*) funeste; – n mal m; **to speak e.** dire du mal (**about, of** de).

evince [ɪ'vɪns] vt manifester.

evoke [ɪ'vəuk] vt (*recall, conjure up*) évoquer; (*admiration*) susciter. ◆**evocative** a évocateur.

evolution [iːvə'luːʃ(ə)n] n évolution f. ◆**evolve** vi (*of society, idea etc*) évoluer; (*of plan*) se développer; – vt (*system etc*) développer.

ewe [juː] n brebis f.

ex [eks] n (*former spouse*) Fam ex mf.

ex- [eks] pref ex-; **ex-wife** ex-femme f.

exacerbate [ɪk'sæsəbeɪt] vt (*pain*) exacerber.

exact [ɪg'zækt] **1** a (*accurate, precise etc*) exact; **to be (more) e. about** préciser. **2** vt (*demand*) exiger (**from** de); (*money*) extorquer (**from** à). ◆**—ing** a exigeant. ◆**—ly** adv exactement; **it's 5 o'clock** il est 5 heures juste. ◆**—ness** n exactitude f.

exaggerate [ɪg'zædʒəreɪt] vt exagérer; (*in one's own mind*) s'exagérer; – vi exagérer. ◆**exagge'ration** n exagération f.

exalt [ɪg'zɔːlt] vt (*praise*) exalter. ◆**—ed** a (*position, rank*) élevé. ◆**exal'tation** n exaltation f.

exam [ɪg'zæm] n Univ Sch Fam examen m.

examine [ɪg'zæmɪn] vt examiner; (*accounts, luggage*) vérifier; (*passport*) contrôler; (*orally*) interroger (*témoin, élève*). ◆**exami'nation** n (*inspection*) & Univ Sch examen m; (*of accounts etc*) vérification f; (*of passport*) contrôle m; **class e.** composition f. ◆**examiner** n Sch examinateur, -trice mf.

example [ɪg'zɑːmp(ə)l] n exemple m; **for e.** par exemple; **to set a good/bad e.** donner le bon/mauvais exemple (**to** à); **to make an e. of** punir pour l'exemple.

exasperate [ɪg'zɑːspəreɪt] vt exaspérer; **to get exasperated** s'exaspérer (**at** de). ◆**exaspe'ration** n exaspération f.

excavate ['ekskəveɪt] vt (*dig*) creuser; (*for relics etc*) fouiller; (*uncover*) déterrer. ◆**exca'vation** n Tech creusement m; (*archeological*) fouille f.

exceed [ɪk'siːd] *vt* dépasser, excéder. ◆—**ingly** *adv* extrêmement.

excel [ɪk'sel] *vi* (**-ll-**) exceller (**in sth** en qch, **in doing** à faire); − *vt* surpasser.

Excellency ['eksələnsɪ] *n* (*title*) Excellence *f*.

excellent ['eksələnt] *a* excellent. ◆**excellence** *n* excellence *f*. ◆**excellently** *adv* parfaitement, admirablement.

except [ɪk'sept] *prep* sauf, excepté; **e. for** à part; **e. that** à part le fait que, sauf que; **e. if** sauf si; **to do nothing e. wait** ne rien faire sinon attendre; − *vt* excepter. ◆**exception** *n* exception *f*; **with the e. of** à l'exception de; **to take e. to** (*object to*) désapprouver; (*be hurt by*) s'offenser de. ◆**exceptional** *a* exceptionnel. ◆**exceptionally** *adv* exceptionnellement.

excerpt ['eksɜːpt] *n* (*from film, book etc*) extrait *m*.

excess ['ekses] *n* excès *m*; (*surplus*) Com excédent *m*; **one's excesses** ses excès *mpl*; **to e.** à l'excès; **an e. of** (*details*) un luxe de; − *a* (*weight etc*) excédentaire, en trop; **e. fare** supplément *m* (de billet); **e. luggage** excédent *m* de bagages. ◆**ex'cessive** *a* excessif. ◆**ex'cessively** *adv* (*too, too much*) excessivement; (*very*) extrêmement.

exchange [ɪks'tʃeɪndʒ] *vt* (*addresses, blows etc*) échanger (**for** contre); − *n* échange *m*; Fin change *m*; (*telephone*) **e. central** *m* (téléphonique); **in e.** en échange (**for** de).

Exchequer [ɪks'tʃekər] *n* **Chancellor of the E.** = ministre *m* des Finances.

excise ['eksaɪz] *n* taxe *f* (**on** sur).

excit/e [ɪk'saɪt] *vt* (*agitate, provoke, stimulate*) exciter; (*enthuse*) passionner, exciter. ◆—**ed** *a* excité; (*laughter*) énervé; **to get e.** (*nervous, angry, enthusiastic*) s'exciter; **to be e. about** (*new car, news*) se réjouir de; **to be e. about the holidays** être surexcité à l'idée de partir en vacances. ◆—**ing** *a* (*book, adventure*) passionnant. ◆—**able** *a* excitable. ◆—**edly** *adv* avec agitation; (*to wait, jump about*) dans un état de surexcitation. ◆—**ement** *n* agitation *f*, excitation *f*, fièvre *f*; (*emotion*) vive émotion *f*; (*adventure*) aventure *f*; **great e.** surexcitation *f*.

exclaim [ɪk'skleɪm] *vti* s'exclamer, s'écrier (**that** que). ◆**excla'mation** *n* exclamation *f*; **e. mark** *or* Am **point** point *m* d'exclamation.

exclude [ɪks'kluːd] *vt* exclure (**from** de); (*name from list*) écarter (**from** de). ◆**exclusion** *n* exclusion *f*. ◆**exclusive** *a* (*right, interest, design*) exclusif; (*club, group*) fermé; (*interview*) en exclusivité; **e.**

of wine/*etc* vin/*etc* non compris. ◆**exclusively** *adv* exclusivement.

excommunicate [ekskə'mjuːnɪkeɪt] *vt* excommunier.

excrement ['ekskrəmənt] *n* excrément(s) *m*(*pl*).

excruciating [ɪk'skruːʃɪeɪtɪŋ] *a* insupportable, atroce.

excursion [ɪk'skɜːʃ(ə)n] *n* excursion *f*.

excuse [ɪk'skjuːz] *vt* (*justify, forgive*) excuser (**s.o. for doing** qn d'avoir fait, qn de faire); (*exempt*) dispenser (**from** de); **e. me for asking** permettez-moi de demander; **e. me!** excusez-moi!, pardon!; **you're excused** tu peux t'en aller *or* sortir; − [ɪk'skjuːs] *n* excuse *f*; **it was an e. for** cela a servi de prétexte à.

ex-directory [eksdaɪ'rektərɪ] *a* Tel sur la liste rouge.

execute ['eksɪkjuːt] *vt* (*criminal, order, plan etc*) exécuter. ◆**exe'cution** *n* exécution *f*. ◆**exe'cutioner** *n* bourreau *m*.

executive [ɪg'zekjutɪv] *a* (*power*) exécutif; (*ability*) d'exécution; (*job*) de cadre; (*car, plane*) de direction; − *n* (*person*) cadre *m*; (*board, committee*) bureau *m*; **the e.** Pol l'exécutif *m*; (*senior*) **e.** cadre *m* supérieur; **junior e.** jeune cadre *m*; **business e.** directeur *m* commercial.

exemplary [ɪg'zemplərɪ] *a* exemplaire. ◆**exemplify** *vt* illustrer.

exempt [ɪg'zempt] *a* exempt (**from** de); − *vt* exempter (**from** de). ◆**exemption** *n* exemption *f*.

exercise ['eksəsaɪz] *n* (*of power etc*) & Sch Sp Mil exercice *m*; *pl* Univ Am cérémonies *fpl*; **e. book** cahier *m*; − *vt* exercer; (*troops*) faire faire l'exercice à; (*dog, horse etc*) promener; (*tact, judgement etc*) faire preuve de; (*rights*) faire valoir, exercer; − *vi* (*take exercise*) prendre de l'exercice.

exert [ɪg'zɜːt] *vt* exercer; (*force*) employer; **to e. oneself** (*physically*) se dépenser; **he never exerts himself** (*takes the trouble*) il ne se fatigue jamais; **to e. oneself to do** (*try hard*) s'efforcer de faire. ◆**exertion** *n* effort *m*; (*of force*) emploi *m*.

exhale [eks'heɪl] *vt* (*breathe out*) expirer; (*give off*) exhaler; − *vi* expirer.

exhaust [ɪg'zɔːst] **1** *vt* (*use up, tire*) épuiser; **to become exhausted** s'épuiser. **2** *n* e. (**pipe**) Aut pot *m* *or* tuyau *m* d'échappement. ◆—**ing** *a* épuisant. ◆**exhaustion** *n* épuisement *m*. ◆**exhaustive** *a* (*study etc*) complet; (*research*) approfondi.

exhibit [ɪg'zɪbɪt] *vt* (*put on display*) exposer; (*ticket, courage etc*) montrer; − *n* objet *m* exposé; *Jur* pièce *f* à conviction. ◆**exhi-'bition** *n* exposition *f*; **an e. of** (*display*) une démonstration de; **to make an e. of oneself** se donner en spectacle. ◆**exhi'bitionist** *n* exhibitionniste *mf*. ◆**exhibitor** *n* exposant, -ante *mf*.

exhilarate [ɪgˈzɪlərert] *vt* stimuler; (*of air*) vivifier; (*elate*) rendre fou de joie. ◆**exhila'ration** *n* liesse *f*, joie *f*.

exhort [ɪgˈzɔːt] *vt* exhorter (**to do** à faire, **to sth** à qch).

exhume [eksˈhjuːm] *vt* exhumer.

exile [ˈegzaɪl] *vt* exiler; – *n* (*absence*) exil *m*; (*person*) exilé, -ée *mf*.

exist [ɪgˈzɪst] *vi* exister; (*live*) vivre (**on** de); (**to continue**) **to e.** subsister; **the notion exists that . . .** il existe une notion selon laquelle . . . . ◆**—ing** *a* (*law*) existant; (*circumstances*) actuel. ◆**existence** *n* existence *f*; **to come into e.** être créé; **to be in e.** exister. ◆**exi'stentialism** *n* existentialisme *m*.

exit [ˈeksɪt, ˈegzɪt] *n* (*action*) sortie *f*; (*door, window*) sortie *f*, issue *f*; – *vi Th* sortir.

exodus [ˈeksədəs] *n inv* exode *m*.

exonerate [ɪgˈzɒnəreɪt] *vt* (*from blame*) disculper (**from** de).

exorbitant [ɪgˈzɔːbɪtənt] *a* exorbitant. ◆**—ly** *adv* démesurément.

exorcize [ˈeksɔːsaɪz] *vt* exorciser. ◆**exorcism** *n* exorcisme *m*.

exotic [ɪgˈzɒtɪk] *a* exotique.

expand [ɪkˈspænd] *vt* (*one's fortune, knowledge etc*) étendre; (*trade, ideas*) développer; (*production*) augmenter; (*gas, metal*) dilater; – *vi* s'étendre; se développer; augmenter; se dilater; **to e. on** développer ses idées sur; (*fast or rapidly*) **expanding sector/etc** *Com* secteur/*etc* en (pleine) expansion. ◆**expansion** *n Com Phys Pol* expansion *f*; développement *m*; augmentation *f*. ◆**expansionism** *n* expansionnisme *m*.

expanse [ɪkˈspæns] *n* étendue *f*.

expansive [ɪkˈspænsɪv] *a* expansif. ◆**—ly** *adv* avec effusion.

expatriate [eksˈpætrɪət, *Am* eksˈpeɪtrɪət] *a* & *n* expatrié, -ée (*mf*).

expect [ɪkˈspekt] *vt* (*anticipate*) s'attendre à, attendre, escompter; (*think*) penser (**that** que); (*suppose*) supposer (**that** que); (*await*) attendre; **to e. sth from s.o./sth** attendre qch de qn/qch; **to e. to do** compter faire; **to e. that** (*anticipate*) s'attendre à ce que (+ *sub*); **I e. you to come** (*want*) je te demande de venir; **it was expected** c'était prévu (**that** que); **she's expecting a baby** elle attend un

bébé. ◆**expectancy** *n* attente *f*; **life e.** espérance *f* de vie. ◆**expectant** *a* (*crowd*) qui attend; **e. mother** future mère *f*. ◆**expec'tation** *n* attente *f*; **to come up to s.o.'s expectations** répondre à l'attente de qn.

expedient [ɪksˈpiːdɪənt] *a* avantageux; (*suitable*) opportun; – *n* (*resource*) expédient *m*.

expedite [ˈekspədaɪt] *vt* (*hasten*) accélérer; (*task*) expédier.

expedition [ekspɪˈdɪʃ(ə)n] *n* expédition *f*.

expel [ɪkˈspel] *vt* (-ll-) expulser (**from** de); (*from school*) renvoyer; (*enemy*) chasser.

expend [ɪkˈspend] *vt* (*energy, money*) dépenser; (*resources*) épuiser. ◆**—able** *a* (*object*) remplaçable; (*soldiers*) sacrifiable. ◆**expenditure** *n* (*money spent*) dépenses *fpl*; **an e. of** (*time, money*) une dépense de.

expense [ɪkˈspens] *n* frais *mpl*, dépense *f*; *pl Fin* frais *mpl*; **business/travelling expenses** frais *mpl* généraux/de déplacement; **to go to some e.** faire des frais; **at s.o.'s e.** aux dépens de qn; **an** *or* **one's e. account** une *or* sa note de frais (professionnels).

expensive [ɪkˈspensɪv] *a* (*goods etc*) cher, coûteux; (*hotel etc*) cher; (*tastes*) dispendieux; **to be e.** coûter cher; **an e. mistake** une faute qui coûte cher. ◆**—ly** *adv* à grands frais.

experienc/e [ɪkˈspɪərɪəns] *n* (*knowledge, skill, event*) expérience *f*; **from** *or* **by e.** par expérience; **he's had e. of** (*work etc*) il a déjà fait; (*grief etc*) il a déjà éprouvé; **I've had e. of driving** j'ai déjà conduit; **terrible experiences** de rudes épreuves *fpl*; **unforgettable e.** moment *m* inoubliable; – *vt* (*undergo*) connaître, subir; (*remorse, difficulty*) éprouver; (*joy*) ressentir. ◆**—ed** *a* (*person*) expérimenté; (*eye, ear*) exercé; **to be e. in** s'y connaître en (matière de).

experiment [ɪkˈsperɪmənt] *n* expérience *f*; – [ɪkˈsperɪment] *vi* faire une expérience *or* des expériences; **to e. with sth** *Phys Ch* expérimenter qch. ◆**experi'mental** *a* expérimental; **e. period** période *f* d'expérimentation.

expert [ˈekspɜːt] *n* expert *m* (**on, in** en), spécialiste *mf* (**on, in** de); – *a* expert (**in sth** en qch, **in** *or* **at doing** à faire); (*advice*) d'un expert, d'expert; (*eye*) connaisseur; **e. touch** doigté *m*, grande habileté *f*. ◆**exper'tise** *n* compétence *f* (**in** en). ◆**expertly** *adv* habilement.

expiate [ˈekspɪeɪt] *vt* (*sins*) expier.

expir/e [ɪkˈspaɪər] *vi* expirer. ◆**—ed** *a*

(*ticket, passport etc*) périmé. ◆**expi'ration** *n Am,* ◆**expiry** *n* expiration *f.*

explain [ɪk'spleɪn] *vt* expliquer (**to** à, **that** que); (*reasons*) exposer; (*mystery*) éclaircir; **e. yourself!** explique-toi!; **to e. away** justifier. ◆**—able** *a* explicable. ◆**expla-'nation** *n* explication *f.* ◆**explanatory** *a* explicatif.

expletive [ɪk'spliːtɪv, *Am* 'eksplətɪv] *n* (*oath*) juron *m.*

explicit [ɪk'splɪsɪt] *a* explicite. ◆**—ly** *adv* explicitement.

explode [ɪk'spləʊd] *vi* exploser; **to e. with laughter** *Fig* éclater de rire; – *vt* faire exploser; (*theory*) *Fig* démythifier, discréditer.

exploit 1 [ɪk'splɔɪt] *vt* (*person, land etc*) exploiter. **2** ['eksplɔɪt] *n* (*feat*) exploit *m.* ◆**exploi'tation** *n* exploitation *f.*

explore [ɪk'splɔːr] *vt* explorer; (*possibilities*) examiner. ◆**explo'ration** *n* exploration *f.* ◆**exploratory** *a* d'exploration; (*talks, step etc*) préliminaire, exploratoire; **e. operation** *Med* sondage *m.* ◆**explorer** *n* explorateur, -trice *mf.*

explosion [ɪk'spləʊʒ(ə)n] *n* explosion *f.* ◆**explosive** *a* (*weapon, question*) explosif; (*mixture, gas*) détonant; – *n* explosif *m.*

exponent [ɪk'spəʊnənt] *n* (*of opinion, theory etc*) interprète *m* (**of** de).

export ['ekspɔːt] *n* exportation *f*; – *a* (*goods etc*) d'exportation; – [ɪk'spɔːt] *vt* exporter (**to** vers, **from** de). ◆**expor'tation** *n* exportation *f.* ◆**ex'porter** *n* exportateur, -trice *mf*; (*country*) pays *m* exportateur.

expose [ɪk'spəʊz] *vt* (*leave uncovered, describe*) & *Phot* exposer; (*wire*) dénuder; (*plot, scandal etc*) révéler, dévoiler; (*crook etc*) démasquer; **to e. to** (*subject to*) exposer à; **to e. oneself** *Jur* commettre un attentat à la pudeur. ◆**expo'sition** *n* exposition *f.* ◆**exposure** *n* exposition *f* (**to** à); (*of plot etc*) révélation *f*; (*of house etc*) exposition *f*; *Phot* pose *f*; **to die of e.** mourir de froid.

expound [ɪk'spaʊnd] *vt* (*theory etc*) exposer.

express [ɪk'spres] **1** *vt* exprimer; (*proposition*) énoncer; **to e. oneself** s'exprimer. **2** *a* (*order*) exprès, formel; (*intention*) explicite; (*purpose*) seul; (*letter, delivery*) exprès *inv*; (*train*) rapide, express *inv*; – *adv* (*to send*) par exprès; – *n* (*train*) rapide *m*, express *m inv.* ◆**expression** *n* (*phrase, look etc*) expression *f*; **an e. of** (*gratitude, affection etc*) un témoignage de. ◆**expressive** *a* expressif. ◆**expressly** *adv* expressément. ◆**expressway** *n Am* autoroute *f.*

expulsion [ɪk'spʌlʃ(ə)n] *n* expulsion *f*; (*from school*) renvoi *m.*

expurgate ['ekspəgeɪt] *vt* expurger.

exquisite [ɪk'skwɪzɪt] *a* exquis. ◆**—ly** *adv* d'une façon exquise.

ex-serviceman [eks'sɜːvɪsmən] *n* (*pl* **-men**) ancien combattant *m.*

extant ['ekstənt, ek'stænt] *a* existant.

extend [ɪk'stend] *vt* (*arm, business*) étendre; (*line, visit, meeting*) prolonger (**by** de); (*hand*) tendre (**to s.o.** à qn); (*house*) agrandir; (*knowledge*) élargir; (*time limit*) reculer; (*help, thanks*) offrir (**to** à); **an invitation to** faire une invitation à; – *vi* (*of wall, plain etc*) s'étendre (**to** jusqu'à); (*in time*) se prolonger; **to e. to s.o.** (*of joy etc*) gagner qn. ◆**extension** *n* (*in space*) prolongement *m*; (*in time*) prolongation *f*; (*of powers, measure, meaning, strike*) extension *f*; (*for table, wire*) rallonge *f*; (*to building*) agrandissement(s) *m*(*pl*); (*of telephone*) appareil *m* supplémentaire; (*of office telephone*) poste *m*; **an e.** (**of time**) un délai. ◆**extensive** *a* étendu, vaste; (*repairs, damage*) important; (*use*) courant. ◆**extensively** *adv* (*very much*) beaucoup, considérablement; **e. used** largement répandu.

extent [ɪk'stent] *n* (*scope*) étendue *f*; (*size*) importance *f*; (*degree*) mesure *f*; **to a large/certain e.** dans une large/certaine mesure; **to such an e. that** à tel point que.

extenuating [ɪk'stenjʊeɪtɪŋ] *a* **e. circumstances** circonstances *fpl* atténuantes.

exterior [ɪks'tɪərɪər] *a & n* extérieur (*m*).

exterminate [ɪk'stɜːmɪneɪt] *vt* (*people etc*) exterminer; (*disease*) supprimer; (*evil*) extirper. ◆**extermi'nation** *n* extermination *f*; suppression *f.*

external [ek'stɜːn(ə)l] *a* (*influence, trade etc*) extérieur; **for e. use** (*medicine*) à usage externe; **e. affairs** *Pol* affaires *fpl* étrangères. ◆**—ly** *adv* extérieurement.

extinct [ɪk'stɪŋkt] *a* (*volcano, love*) éteint; (*species, animal*) disparu. ◆**extinction** *n* extinction *f*; disparition *f.*

extinguish [ɪk'stɪŋgwɪʃ] *vt* éteindre. ◆**—er** *n* (*fire*) **e.** extincteur *m.*

extol [ɪk'stəʊl] *vt* (**-ll-**) exalter, louer.

extort [ɪk'stɔːt] *vt* (*money*) extorquer (**from** à); (*consent*) arracher (**from** à). ◆**extortion** *n Jur* extorsion *f* de fonds; **it's** (**sheer**) **e.!** c'est du vol! ◆**extortionate** *a* exorbitant.

extra ['ekstrə] *a* (*additional*) supplémentaire; **one e. glass** un verre de *or* en plus, encore un verre; (**any**) **e. bread?**

encore du pain?; **to be e.** (*spare*) être en trop; (*cost more*) être en supplément; (*of postage*) être en sus; **wine is 3 francs e.** il y a un supplément de 3F pour le vin; **e. care** un soin tout particulier; **e. charge** or **portion** supplément *m*; **e. time** *Fb* prolongation *f*; — *adv* **e. big**/*etc* plus grand/*etc* que d'habitude; — *n* (*perk*) à-côté *m*; *Cin Th* figurant, -ante *mf*; *pl* (*expenses*) frais *mpl* supplémentaires; **an optional e.** (*for car etc*) un accessoire en option.

extra- ['ekstrə] *pref* extra-. ◆**e.-'dry** *a* (*champagne*) brut. ◆**e.-'fine** *a* extra-fin. ◆**e.-'strong** *a* extra-fort.

extract [ɪk'strækt] *vt* extraire (**from** de); (*tooth*) arracher, extraire; (*promise*) arracher, soutirer (**from** à); (*money*) soutirer (**from** à); — ['ekstrækt] *n* (*of book etc*) & *Culin Ch* extrait *m*. ◆**ex'traction** *n* extraction *f*; arrachement *m*; (*descent*) origine *f*.

extra-curricular [ekstrəkə'rɪkjʊlər] *a* (*activities etc*) en dehors des heures de cours, extrascolaire.

extradite ['ekstrədaɪt] *vt* extrader. ◆**extra-'dition** *n* extradition *f*.

extramarital [ekstrə'mærɪt(ə)l] *a* en dehors du mariage, extra-conjugal.

extramural [ekstrə'mjʊərəl] *a* (*studies*) hors faculté.

extraneous [ɪk'streɪnɪəs] *a* (*detail etc*) accessoire.

extraordinary [ɪk'strɔɪdən(ə)rɪ] *a* (*strange, exceptional*) extraordinaire.

extra-special [ekstrə'speʃəl] *a* (*occasion*) très spécial; (*care*) tout particulier.

extravagant [ɪk'strævəgənt] *a* (*behaviour, idea etc*) extravagant; (*claim*) exagéré; (*wasteful with money*) dépensier, prodigue. ◆**extravagance** *n* extravagance *f*; prodigalité *f*; (*thing bought*) folle dépense *f*.

extravaganza [ɪkstrævə'gænzə] *n* *Mus Liter* & *Fig* fantaisie *f*.

extreme [ɪk'striːm] *a* (*exceptional, furthest*) extrême; (*danger, poverty*) très grand; (*praise*) outré; **at the e. end** à l'extrémité; **of e. importance** de première importance; — *n* (*furthest degree*) extrême *m*; **to carry** or **take to extremes** pousser à l'extrême; **extremes of temperature** températures *fpl* extrêmes; **extremes of climate** excès *mpl* du climat. ◆**extremely** *adv* extrêmement. ◆**extremist** *a* & *n* extrémiste (*mf*). ◆**extremity** [ɪk'stremɪtɪ] *n* extrémité *f*.

extricate ['ekstrɪkeɪt] *vt* dégager (**from** de); **to e. oneself from** (*difficulty*) se tirer de.

extrovert ['ekstrəvɜːt] *n* extraverti, -ie *mf*.

exuberant [ɪg'z(j)uːbərənt] *a* exubérant. ◆**exuberance** *n* exubérance *f*.

exude [ɪg'zjuːd] *vt* (*charm, honesty etc*) *Fig* respirer.

exultation [egzʌl'teɪʃ(ə)n] *n* exultation *f*.

eye[1] [aɪ] *n* œil *m* (*pl* yeux); **before my very eyes** sous mes yeux; **to be all eyes** être tout yeux; **as far as the e. can see** à perte de vue; **up to one's eyes in debt** endetté jusqu'au cou; **up to one's eyes in work** débordé de travail; **to have an e. on** (*house, car*) avoir en vue; **to keep an e. on** surveiller; **to make eyes at** *Fam* faire de l'œil à; **to lay** or **set eyes on** voir, apercevoir; **to take one's eyes off s.o./sth** quitter qn/qch des yeux; **to catch the e.** attirer l'œil, accrocher le regard; **keep an e. out!, keep your eyes open!** ouvre l'œil!, sois vigilant!; **we don't see e. to e.** nous n'avons pas le même point de vue; **e. shadow** fard *m* à paupières; **to be an e.-opener for s.o.** *Fam* être une révélation pour qn. ◆**eyeball** *n* globe *m* oculaire. ◆**eyebrow** *n* sourcil *m*. ◆**eye-catching** *a* (*title etc*) accrocheur. ◆**eyeglass** *n* monocle *m*. ◆**eyeglasses** *npl* (*spectacles*) *Am* lunettes *fpl*. ◆**eyelash** *n* cil *m*. ◆**eyelid** *n* paupière *f*. ◆**eyeliner** *n* eye-liner *m*. ◆**eyesight** *n* vue *f*. ◆**eyesore** *n* (*building etc*) horreur *f*. ◆**eyestrain** *n* **to have e.** avoir les yeux qui tirent. ◆**eyewash** *n* (*nonsense*) *Fam* sottises *fpl*. ◆**eyewitness** *n* témoin *m* oculaire.

eye[2] [aɪ] *vt* reluquer, regarder.

F

F, f [ef] *n* F, f *m*.

fable ['feɪb(ə)l] *n* fable *f*.

fabric ['fæbrɪk] *n* (*cloth*) tissu *m*, étoffe *f*; (*of building*) structure *f*; **the f. of society** le tissu social.

fabricate ['fæbrɪkeɪt] *vt* (*invent, make*) fabriquer. ◆**fabri'cation** *n* fabrication *f*.

fabulous ['fæbjʊləs] a (*incredible, legendary*) fabuleux; (*wonderful*) Fam formidable.

façade [fə'saɪd] n Archit & Fig façade f.

face [feɪs] n visage m, figure f; (*expression*) mine f; (*of clock*) cadran m; (*of building*) façade f; (*of cliff*) paroi f; (*of the earth*) surface f; **she laughed in my f.** elle m'a ri au nez; **to show one's f.** se montrer; **f. down(wards)** (*person*) face contre terre; (*thing*) tourné à l'envers; **f. to f.** face à face; **in the f. of** devant; (*despite*) en dépit de; **to save/lose f.** sauver/perdre la face; **to make** *or* **pull faces** faire des grimaces; **to tell s.o. sth to his f.** dire qch à qn tout cru; **f. powder** poudre f de riz; **f. value** (*of stamp etc*) valeur f; **to take sth at f. value** prendre qch au pied de la lettre; – *vt* (*danger, enemy etc*) faire face à; (*accept*) accepter; (*look in the face*) regarder (qn) bien en face; **to f., be facing** (*be opposite*) être en face de; (*of window etc*) donner sur; **faced with** (*prospect, problem*) face à, devant; (*defeat*) menacé par; (*bill*) contraint à payer; **he can't f. leaving** il n'a pas le courage de partir; – *vi* (*of house*) être orienté (**north**/*etc* au nord/*etc*); (*of person*) se tourner (**towards** vers); **to f. up to** (*danger*) faire face à; (*fact*) accepter; **about f.!** Am Mil demi-tour! ◆**facecloth** n gant m de toilette. ◆**facelift** n Med lifting m; (*of building*) ravalement m.

faceless ['feɪsləs] a anonyme.

facet ['fæsɪt] n (*of problem, diamond etc*) facette f.

facetious [fə'siːʃəs] a (*person*) facétieux; (*remark*) plaisant.

facial ['feɪʃ(ə)l] a du visage; Med facial; – n soin m du visage.

facile ['fæsaɪl, Am 'fæs(ə)l] a facile, superficiel.

facilitate [fə'sɪlɪteɪt] vt faciliter. ◆**facility** n (*ease*) facilité f; pl (*possibilities*) facilités fpl; (*for sports*) équipements mpl; (*in harbour, airport etc*) installations fpl; (*means*) moyens mpl, ressources fpl; **special facilities** (*conditions*) conditions fpl spéciales (**for** pour).

facing ['feɪsɪŋ] n (*of dress etc*) parement m.

fact [fækt] n fait m; **as a matter of f., in f.** en fait; **the facts of life** les choses fpl de la vie; **is that a f.?** c'est vrai?; **f. and fiction** le réel et l'imaginaire.

faction ['fækʃ(ə)n] n (*group*) Pol faction f.

factor ['fæktər] n (*element*) facteur m.

factory ['fækt(ə)rɪ] n (*large*) usine f; (*small*) fabrique f; **arms/porcelain f.** manufacture f d'armes/de porcelaine.

factual ['fæktʃʊəl] a objectif, basé sur les faits, factuel; (*error*) de fait.

faculty ['fækəltɪ] n (*aptitude*) & Univ faculté f.

fad [fæd] n (*personal habit*) marotte f; (*fashion*) folie f, mode f (**for** de).

fade [feɪd] vi (*of flower*) se faner; (*of light*) baisser; (*of colour*) passer; (*of fabric*) se décolorer; **to f. (away)** (*of memory, smile*) s'effacer; (*of sound*) s'affaiblir; (*of person*) dépérir; – vt (*fabric*) décolorer.

fag [fæg] n 1 (*cigarette*) Fam clope m, tige f; **f. end** mégot m. 2 (*male homosexual*) Am Sl pédé m.

fagged [fægd] a **f. (out)** (*tired*) Sl claqué.

faggot ['fægət] n 1 Culin boulette f (de viande). 2 (*male homosexual*) Am Sl pédé m.

fail [feɪl] vi (*of person, plan etc*) échouer; (*of business*) faire faillite; (*of light, health, sight*) baisser; (*of memory, strength*) défaillir; (*of brakes*) Aut lâcher; (*run short*) manquer; (*of gas, electricity*) être coupé; (*of engine*) tomber en panne; **to f. in** (*one's duty*) manquer à; (*exam*) échouer à; – vt (*exam*) échouer à; (*candidate*) refuser, recaler; **to f. s.o.** (*let down*) laisser tomber qn, décevoir qn; (*of words*) manquer à qn, faire défaut à qn; **to f. to do** (*omit*) manquer de faire; (*not be able*) ne pas arriver à faire; **I f. to see** je ne vois pas; – n **without f.** à coup sûr, sans faute. ◆**—ed** a (*attempt, poet*) manqué. ◆**—ing** n (*fault*) défaut m; – prep à défaut de; **f. this, f. that** à défaut. ◆**failure** n échec m; (*of business*) faillite f; (*of engine, machine*) panne f; (*of gas etc*) coupure f, panne f; (*person*) raté, -ée mf; **f. to do** (*inability*) incapacité f de faire; **her f. to leave** le fait qu'elle n'est pas partie; **to end in f.** se solder par un échec; **heart f.** arrêt m du cœur.

faint [feɪnt] 1 a (**-er, -est**) léger; (*voice*) faible; (*colour*) pâle; (*idea*) vague; **I haven't the faintest idea** je n'en ai pas la moindre idée. 2 a Med défaillant (**with** de); **to feel f.** se trouver mal, défaillir; – vi s'évanouir (**from** de); **fainting fit** évanouissement m. ◆**—ly** adv (*weakly*) faiblement; (*slightly*) légèrement. ◆**—ness** n légèreté f; faiblesse f. ◆**faint-'hearted** a timoré, timide.

fair¹ [feər] n foire f; (*for charity*) fête f; (*funfair*) fête f foraine; (*larger*) parc m d'attractions. ◆**fairground** n champ m de foire.

fair² [feər] **1** *a* (**-er, -est**) (*equitable*) juste, équitable; (*game, fight*) loyal; **f. (and square)** honnête(ment); **f. play** fair-play *m inv*; **that's not f. play!** ce n'est pas du jeu!; **that's not f. to him** ce n'est pas juste pour lui; **f. enough!** très bien!; — *adv* (*to play*) loyalement. **2** *a* (*rather good*) passable, assez bon; (*amount, warning*) raisonnable; **a f. amount (of)** pas mal (de); **f. copy** copie *f* au propre. **3** *a* (*wind*) favorable; (*weather*) beau. ◆—**ly** *adv* **1** (*to treat*) équitablement; (*to get*) loyalement. **2** (*rather*) assez, plutôt; **f. sure** presque sûr. ◆—**ness¹** *n* justice *f*; (*of decision*) équité *f*; **in all f.** en toute justice. ◆**fair-'minded** *a* impartial. ◆**fair-'sized** *a* assez grand.

fair³ [feər] *a* (*hair, person*) blond; (*complexion, skin*) clair. ◆—**ness²** *n* (*of hair*) blond *m*; (*of skin*) blancheur *f*. ◆**fair-'haired** *a* blond. ◆**fair-'skinned** *a* à la peau claire.

fairy ['feəri] *n* fée *f*; **f. lights** guirlande *f* multicolore; **f. tale** conte *m* de fées.

faith [feiθ] *n* foi *f*; **to have f. in s.o.** avoir confiance en qn; **to put one's f. in** (*justice, medicine etc*) se fier à; **in good/bad f.** de bonne/mauvaise foi; **f. healer** guérisseur, -euse *mf*. ◆**faithful** *a* fidèle. ◆**faithfully** *adv* fidèlement; **yours f.** (*in letter*) Com veuillez agréer l'expression de mes salutations distinguées. ◆**faithfulness** *n* fidélité *f*. ◆**faithless** *a* déloyal, infidèle.

fake [feik] *n* (*painting, document etc*) faux *m*; (*person*) imposteur *m*; — *vt* (*document, signature etc*) falsifier, maquiller; (*election*) truquer; **to f. death** faire semblant d'être mort; — *vi* (*pretend*) faire semblant; — *a* faux; (*election*) truqué.

falcon ['fɔːlkən] *n* faucon *m*.

fall [fɔːl] *n* chute *f*; (*in price, demand etc*) baisse *f*; *pl* (*waterfall*) chutes *fpl* (d'eau); **the f.** *Am* l'automne *m*; — *vi* (*pt* **fell**, *pp* **fallen**) tomber; (*of building*) s'effondrer; **her face fell** *Fig* son visage se rembrunit; **to f. into** tomber dans; (*habit*) *Fig* prendre; **to f. off a bicycle**/*etc* tomber d'une bicyclette/*etc*; **to f. off or down a ladder** tomber (en bas) d'une échelle; **to fall on s.o.** (*of onus*) retomber sur qn; **to f. on a Monday**/*etc* (*of event*) tomber un lundi/*etc*; **to f. over sth** tomber en butant contre qch; **to f. short of** (*expectation*) ne pas répondre à; **to f. short of being** être loin d'être; **to f. victim** devenir victime (**to** de); **to f. asleep** s'endormir; **to f. ill** tomber malade; **to f. due** échoir. ■ **to f. apart** (*of mechanism*) tomber en morceaux; *Fig* se désagréger; **to f. away** (*come off*) se

détacher, tomber; (*of numbers*) diminuer; **to f. back on** (*as last resort*) se rabattre sur; **to f. behind** rester en arrière; (*in work*) prendre du retard; **to f. down** tomber; (*of building*) s'effondrer; **to f. for** *Fam* (*person*) tomber amoureux de; (*trick*) se laisser prendre à; **to f. in** (*collapse*) s'écrouler; **to f. in with** (*tally with*) cadrer avec; (*agree to*) accepter; **to f. off** (*come off*) se détacher, tomber; (*of numbers*) diminuer. ◆**falling-'off** *n* diminution *f*; **to f. out with** (*quarrel with*) se brouiller avec; **to f. over** tomber; (*of table, vase*) se renverser; **to f. through** (*of plan*) tomber à l'eau, échouer. ◆**fallen** *a* tombé; (*angel, woman*) déchu; **f. leaf** feuille *f* morte. ◆**fallout** *n* (*radioactive*) retombées *fpl*.

fallacious [fə'leiʃəs] *a* faux. ◆**fallacy** ['fæləsi] *n* erreur *f*; *Phil* faux raisonnement *m*.

fallible ['fæləb(ə)l] *a* faillible.

fallow ['fæləu] *a* (*land*) en jachère.

false [fɔːls] *a* faux; **a f. bottom** un double fond. ◆**falsehood** *n* mensonge *m*; **truth and f.** le vrai et le faux. ◆**falseness** *n* fausseté *f*. ◆**falsify** *vt* falsifier.

falter ['fɔːltər] *vi* (*of step, resolution*) chanceler; (*of voice, speaker*) hésiter; (*of courage*) vaciller.

fame [feim] *n* renommée *f*; (*glory*) gloire *f*. ◆**famed** *a* renommé.

familiar [fə'miljər] *a* (*task, atmosphere etc*) familier; (*event*) habituel; **f. with s.o.** (*too friendly*) familier avec qn; **to be f. with** (*know*) connaître; **I'm f. with her voice** je connais bien sa voix, sa voix m'est familière; **to make oneself f. with** se familiariser avec; **he looks f. (to me)** je l'ai déjà vu (quelque part). ◆**famili'arity** *n* familiarité *f* (**with** avec); (*of event, sight etc*) caractère *m* familier. ◆**familiarize** *vt* familiariser (**with** avec); **to f. oneself with** se familiariser avec.

family ['fæmili] *n* famille *f*; — *a* (*name, doctor etc*) de famille; (*planning, problem*) familial; (*tree*) généalogique; **f. man** père *m* de famille.

famine ['fæmin] *n* famine *f*.

famished ['fæmiʃt] *a* affamé.

famous ['feiməs] *a* célèbre (**for** par, pour). ◆—**ly** *adv* (*very well*) *Fam* rudement bien.

fan [fæn] **1** *n* (*hand-held*) éventail *m*; (*mechanical*) ventilateur *m*; **f. heater** radiateur *m* soufflant; — *vt* (**-nn-**) (*person etc*) éventer; (*fire, quarrel*) attiser. **2** *n* (*of person*) admirateur, -trice *mf*, fan *m*; *Sp* supporter *m*; **to be a jazz/sports f.** être passionné *or* mordu de jazz/de sport.

fanatic [fə'nætɪk] *n* fanatique *mf*. ◆**fanatical** *a* fanatique. ◆**fanaticism** *n* fanatisme *m*.

fancy ['fænsɪ] **1** *n* (*whim, imagination*) fantaisie *f*; (*liking*) goût *m*; **to take a f. to s.o.** se prendre d'affection pour qn; **I took a f. to it, it took my f.** j'en ai eu envie; **when the f. takes me** quand ça me chante; – *a* (*hat, button etc*) fantaisie *inv*; (*idea*) fantaisiste; (*price*) exorbitant; (*car*) de luxe; (*house, restaurant*) chic; **f. dress** (*costume*) travesti *m*; **f.-dress ball** bal *m* masqué. **2** *vt* (*imagine*) se figurer (**that** que); (*think*) croire (**that** que); (*want*) avoir envie de; (*like*) aimer; **f. that!** tiens (donc)!; **he fancies her** *Fam* elle lui plaît; **to f. oneself as** se prendre pour; **she fancies herself!** elle se prend pour qn! ◆**fancier** *n* **horse/etc f.** amateur *m* de chevaux/*etc*. ◆**fanciful** *a* fantaisiste.

fanfare ['fænfeər] *n* (*of trumpets*) fanfare *f*.

fang [fæŋ] *n* (*of dog etc*) croc *m*; (*of snake*) crochet *m*.

fantastic [fæn'tæstɪk] *a* fantastique; **a f. idea** (*absurd*) une idée aberrante.

fantasy ['fæntəsɪ] *n* (*imagination*) fantaisie *f*; *Psy* fantasme *m*. ◆**fantasize** *vi* fantasmer (**about** sur).

far [fɑːr] *adv* (**farther** *or* **further**, **farthest** *or* **furthest**) (*distance*) loin; **f. bigger/more expensive/etc** (*much*) beaucoup plus grand/plus cher/*etc* (**than** que); **f. more** beaucoup plus; **f. advanced** très avancé; **how f. is it to . . . ?** combien y a-t-il d'ici à . . . ?; **is it f. to . . . ?** sommes-nous, suis-je *etc* loin de . . . ?; **how f. are you going?** jusqu'où vas-tu?; **how f. has he got with?** (*plans, work etc*) où en est-il de?; **so f.** (*time*) jusqu'ici; (*place*) jusque-là; **as f. as** (*place*) jusqu'à; **as f.** *or* **so f. as I know** autant que je sache; **as f.** *or* **so f. as I'm concerned** en ce qui me concerne; **as f. back as 1820** dès 1820; **f. from doing** loin de faire; **f. from it!** loin de là!; **f. away** *or* **off** au loin; **to be (too) f. away** être (trop) loin (**from** de); **f. and wide** partout; **by f.** de loin; **f. into the night** très avant dans la nuit; – *a* (*side, end*) autre; **it's a f. cry from** on est loin de. ◆**faraway** *a* lointain; (*look*) distrait, dans le vague. ◆**far-'fetched** *a* forcé, exagéré. ◆**f.-'flung** *a* (*widespread*) vaste. ◆**f.-'off** *a* lointain. ◆**f.-'reaching** *a* de grande portée. ◆**f.-'sighted** *a* clairvoyant.

farce [fɑːs] *n* farce *f*. ◆**farcical** *a* grotesque, ridicule.

fare [feər] **1** *n* (*price*) prix *m* du billet; (*ticket*) billet *m*; (*taxi passenger*) client, -ente *mf* **2** *n* (*food*) chère *f*, nourriture *f*; **prison f.** régime *m* de prison; **bill of f.** menu *m*. **3** *vi* (*manage*) se débrouiller; **how did she f.?** comment ça s'est passé (pour elle)?

farewell [feə'wel] *n* & *int* adieu (*m*); – *a* (*party etc*) d'adieu.

farm [fɑːm] *n* ferme *f*; – *a* (*worker, produce etc*) agricole; **f. land** terres *fpl* cultivées; – *vt* cultiver; – *vi* être agriculteur. ◆**—ing** *n* agriculture *f*; (*breeding*) élevage *m*; **dairy f.** industrie *f* laitière. ◆**—er** *n* fermier, -ière *mf*, agriculteur *m*. ◆**farmhand** *n* ouvrier, -ière *mf* agricole. ◆**farmhouse** *n* ferme *f*. ◆**farmyard** *n* basse-cour *f*.

farther ['fɑːðər] *adv* plus loin; **nothing is f. from** (*my mind, the truth etc*) rien n'est plus éloigné de; **f. forward** plus avancé; **to get f. away** s'éloigner; – *a* (*end*) autre. ◆**farthest** *a* le plus éloigné; – *adv* le plus loin.

fascinate ['fæsɪneɪt] *vt* fasciner. ◆**fasci'nation** *n* fascination *f*.

fascism ['fæʃɪz(ə)m] *n* fascisme *m*. ◆**fascist** *a* & *n* fasciste (*mf*).

fashion ['fæʃ(ə)n] **1** *n* (*style in clothes etc*) mode *f*; **in f.** à la mode; **out of f.** démodé; **f. designer** (*grand*) couturier *m*; **f. house** maison *f* de couture; **f. show** présentation *f* de collections. **2** *n* (*manner*) façon *f*; (*custom*) habitude *f*; **after a f.** tant bien que mal, plus au moins. **3** *vt* (*make*) façonner. ◆**—able** *a* à la mode; (*place*) chic *inv*; **it's f. to do** il est de bon ton de faire. ◆**—ably** *adv* (*dressed etc*) à la mode.

fast [fɑːst] **1** *a* (**-er, -est**) rapide; **to be f.** (*of clock*) avancer (**by** de); **f. colour** couleur *f* grand teint *inv*; **f. living** vie *f* dissolue; – *adv* (*quickly*) vite; (*firmly*) ferme, bien; **how f.?** à quelle vitesse?; **f. asleep** profondément endormi. **2** *vi* (*go without food*) jeûner; – *n* jeûne *m*.

fasten ['fɑːs(ə)n] *vt* attacher (**to** à); (*door, window*) fermer (bien); **to f. down** *or* **up** attacher; – *vi* (*of dress etc*) s'attacher; (*of door, window*) se fermer. ◆**—er** *n*, ◆**—ing** *n* (*clip*) attache *f*; (*of garment*) fermeture *f*; (*of bag*) fermoir *m*; (*hook*) agrafe *f*.

fastidious [fə'stɪdɪəs] *a* difficile (à contenter), exigeant.

fat [fæt] **1** *n* graisse *f*; (*on meat*) gras *m*; **vegetable f.** huile *f* végétale. **2** *a* (**fatter, fattest**) gras; (*cheek, salary, volume*) gros; **to get f.** grossir; **that's a f. lot of good** *or* **use!** *Iron*

Fam ça va vraiment servir (à quelque chose)! ◆**fathead** *n* imbécile *mf*.

fatal ['feɪt(ə)l] *a* mortel; (*error, blow etc*) *Fig* fatal. ◆**-ly** *adv* (*wounded*) mortellement.

fatality [fə'talɪtɪ] *n* **1** (*person killed*) victime *f*. **2** (*of event*) fatalité *f*.

fate [feɪt] *n* destin *m*, sort *m*; one's f. son sort. ◆**fated** a f. to do destiné à faire; **our meeting/his death/***etc* **was f.** notre rencontre/sa mort/*etc* devait arriver. ◆**fateful** *a* (*important*) fatal, décisif; (*prophetic*) fatidique; (*disastrous*) néfaste.

father ['fɑːðər] *n* père *m*; − *vt* engendrer; (*idea*) *Fig* inventer. ◆**f.-in-law** *n* (*pl* **fathers-in-law**) beau-père *m*. ◆**fatherhood** *n* paternité *f*. ◆**fatherland** *n* patrie *f*. ◆**fatherly** *a* paternel.

fathom ['fæðəm] **1** *n Nau* brasse *f* (= 1,8 m). **2** *vt* to f. (out) (*understand*) comprendre.

fatigue [fə'tiːg] **1** *n* fatigue *f*; − *vt* fatiguer. **2** *n* f. (duty) *Mil* corvée *f*.

fatness ['fætnɪs] *n* corpulence *f*. ◆**fatten** *vt* engraisser. ◆**fattening** *a* qui fait grossir. ◆**fatty** *a* (**-ier, -iest**) (*food*) gras; (*tissue*) *Med* adipeux; − *n* (*person*) *Fam* gros lard *m*.

fatuous ['fætjuəs] *a* stupide.

faucet ['fɔːsɪt] *n* (*tap*) *Am* robinet *m*.

fault [fɔːlt] *n* (*blame*) faute *f*; (*failing, defect*) défaut *m*; (*mistake*) erreur *f*; *Geol* faille *f*; **to find f. (with)** critiquer; **he's at f.** c'est sa faute, il est fautif; **his** *or* **her memory is at f.** sa mémoire lui fait défaut; − *vt* to f. s.o./sth trouver des défauts chez qn/à qch. ◆**f.-finding** *a* critique, chicanier. ◆**faultless** *a* irréprochable. ◆**faulty** *a* (**-ier, -iest**) défectueux.

fauna ['fɔːnə] *n* (*animals*) faune *f*.

favour ['feɪvər] *n* (*approval, advantage*) faveur *f*; (*act of kindness*) service *m*; **to do s.o. a f.** rendre service à qn; **in f.** (*person*) bien vu; (*fashion*) en vogue; **it's in her f. to do** elle a intérêt à faire; **in f. of** (*for the sake of*) au profit de, en faveur de; **to be in f. of** (*support*) être pour, être partisan de; (*prefer*) préférer; − *vt* (*encourage*) favoriser; (*support*) être partisan de; (*prefer*) préférer; **he favoured me with a visit** il a eu la gentillesse de me rendre visite. ◆**-able** *a* favorable (**to** à). ◆**favourite** *a* favori, préféré; − *n* favori, -ite *mf*. ◆**favouritism** *n* favoritisme *m*.

fawn [fɔːn] **1** *n* (*deer*) faon *m*; − *a & n* (*colour*) fauve (*m*). **2** *vi* to f. (up)on flatter, flagorner.

fear [fɪər] *n* crainte *f*, peur *f*; **for f. of** de peur de; **for f. that** de peur que (+ *ne* + *sub*);

there's no f. of his going il ne risque pas d'y aller; **there are fears (that) he might leave** on craint qu'il ne parte; − *vt* craindre; **I f. (that) he might leave** je crains qu'il ne parte; **to f. for** (*one's life etc*) craindre pour. ◆**fearful** *a* (*frightful*) affreux; (*timid*) peureux. ◆**fearless** *a* intrépide. ◆**fearlessness** *n* intrépidité *f*. ◆**fearsome** *a* redoutable.

feasible ['fiːzəb(ə)l] *a* (*practicable*) faisable; (*theory, explanation etc*) plausible. ◆**feasi'bility** *n* possibilité *f* (**of doing** de faire); plausibilité *f*.

feast [fiːst] *n* festin *m*, banquet *m*; *Rel* fête *f*; − *vi* banqueter; **to f. on** (*cakes etc*) se régaler de.

feat [fiːt] *n* exploit *m*, tour *m* de force; **f. of skill** tour *m* d'adresse.

feather ['feðər] **1** *n* plume *f*; **f. duster** plumeau *m*. **2** *vt* to f. one's nest (*enrich oneself*) faire sa pelote.

feature ['fiːtʃər] **1** *n* (*of face, person*) trait *m*; (*of thing, place, machine*) caractéristique *f*; **f. (article)** article *m* de fond; **f. (film)** grand film *m*; **to be a regular f.** (*in newspaper*) paraître régulièrement. **2** *vt* représenter (**as** comme); *Journ Cin* présenter; **a film featuring Chaplin** un film avec Charlot en vedette; − *vi* (*appear*) figurer (**in** dans).

February ['februərɪ] *n* février *m*.

fed [fed] *see* **feed**; − *a* **to be f. up** *Fam* en avoir marre (**with** de).

federal ['fedərəl] *a* fédéral. ◆**federate** *vt* fédérer. ◆**fede'ration** *n* fédération *f*.

fee [fiː] *n* (*price*) prix *m*; (*sum*) somme *f*; **fee(s)** (*professional*) honoraires *mpl*; (*of artist*) cachet *m*; (*for registration*) droits *mpl*; **tuition fees** frais *mpl* de scolarité; **entrance f.** droit *m* d'entrée; **membership fee(s)** cotisation *f*; **f.-paying school** école *f* privée.

feeble ['fiːb(ə)l] *a* (**-er, -est**) faible; (*excuse*) pauvre. ◆**f.-'minded** *a* imbécile.

feed [fiːd] *n* (*food*) nourriture *f*; (*baby's breast feed*) tétée *f*; (*baby's bottle feed*) biberon *m*; − *vt* (*pt & pp* **fed**) donner à manger à, nourrir; (*breast-feed*) allaiter (*un bébé*); (*bottle-feed*) donner le biberon à (*un bébé*); (*machine*) *Fig* alimenter; − *vi* (*eat*) manger; **to f. on** se nourrir de. ◆**-ing** *n* alimentation *f*. ◆**feedback** *n* réaction(s) *f(pl)*.

feel [fiːl] *n* (*touch*) toucher *m*; (*sensation*) sensation *f*; − *vt* (*pt & pp* **felt**) (*be aware of*) sentir; (*experience*) éprouver, ressentir; (*touch*) tâter, palper; (*think*) avoir l'impression (**that** que); **to f. one's way**

avancer à tâtons; – *vi* (*tired, old etc*) se sentir; – **to f. (about)** (*grope*) tâtonner; (*in pocket etc*) fouiller; **it feels hard** c'est dur (au toucher); **I f. sure** je suis sûr (**that** que); **I f. hot/sleepy/hungry** j'ai chaud/sommeil/faim; **she feels better** elle va mieux; **to f. like** (*want*) avoir envie de; **to f. as if** avoir l'impression que; **it feels like cotton** on dirait du coton; **what do you f. about . . . ?** que pensez-vous de . . . ?; **I f. bad about it** ça m'ennuie, ça me fait de la peine; **what does it f. like?** quelle impression ça (te) fait?; **to f. for** (*look for*) chercher; (*pity*) éprouver de la pitié pour; **to f. up to doing** être (assez) en forme pour faire. ◆—**ing** *n* **1** (*emotion, impression*) sentiment *m*; (*physical*) sensation *f*; **a f. for** (*person*) de la sympathie pour; (*music*) une appréciation *f*; **bad f.** animosité *f*. ◆—**er** *n* (*of snail etc*) antenne *f*; **to put out a f.** *Fig* lancer un ballon d'essai.

feet [fiːt] *see* **foot** [1].

feign [feɪn] *vt* feindre, simuler.

feint [feɪnt] *n Mil Boxing* feinte *f*.

feisty ['faɪstɪ] *a* (**-ier, -iest**) (*lively*) *Am Fam* plein d'entrain.

felicitous [fə'lɪsɪtəs] *a* heureux.

feline ['fiːlaɪn] *a* félin.

fell [fel] **1** *see* **fall. 2** *vt* (*tree etc*) abattre.

fellow ['feləʊ] *n* **1** (*man, boy*) garçon *m*, type *m*; **an old f.** un vieux; **poor f.!** pauvre malheureux! **2** (*comrade*) compagnon *m*, compagne *f*; **f. being or man** semblable *m*; **f. countryman, f. countrywoman** compatriote *mf*; **f. passenger** compagnon *m* de voyage, compagne *f* de voyage. **3** (*of society*) membre *m*. ◆**fellowship** *n* camaraderie *f*; (*group*) association *f*; (*membership*) qualité *f* de membre; (*grant*) bourse *f* universitaire.

felony ['felənɪ] *n* crime *m*.

felt[1] [felt] *see* **feel.**

felt[2] [felt] *n* feutre *m*; **f.-tip(ped) pen** crayon *m* feutre.

female ['fiːmeɪl] *a* (*animal etc*) femelle; (*quality, name, voice etc*) féminin; (*vote*) des femmes; **f. student** étudiante *f*; – *n* (*woman*) femme *f*; (*animal*) femelle *f*.

feminine ['femɪnɪn] *a* féminin. ◆**femininity** *n* féminité *f*. ◆**feminist** *a & n* féministe (*mf*).

fenc/e [fens] **1** *n* barrière *f*, clôture *f*; *Sp* obstacle *m*; – *vt* **to f. (in)** clôturer. **2** *vi* (*with sword*) *Sp* faire de l'escrime. **3** *n* (*criminal*) *Fam* receleur, -euse *mf*. ◆—**ing** *n Sp* escrime *f*.

fend [fend] **1** *vi* **to f. for oneself** se débrouil-

ler. **2** *vt* **to f. off** (*blow etc*) parer, éviter. ◆—**er** *n* **1** (*for fire*) garde-feu *m inv*. **2** (*on car*) *Am* aile *f*.

fennel ['fen(ə)l] *n Bot Culin* fenouil *m*.

ferment ['fɜːment] *n* ferment *m*; *Fig* effervescence *f*; – [fə'ment] *vi* fermenter. ◆**fermen'tation** *n* fermentation *f*.

fern [fɜːn] *n* fougère *f*.

ferocious [fə'rəʊʃəs] *a* féroce. ◆**ferocity** *n* férocité *f*.

ferret ['ferɪt] *n* (*animal*) furet *m*; – *vi* **to f. about** (*pry*) fureter; – *vt* **to f. out** dénicher.

Ferris wheel ['ferɪswiːl] *n* (*at funfair*) grande roue *f*.

ferry ['ferɪ] *n* ferry-boat *m*; (*small, for river*) bac *m*; – *vt* transporter.

fertile ['fɜːtaɪl, *Am* 'fɜːt(ə)l] *a* (*land, imagination*) fertile; (*person, creature*) fécond. ◆**fer'tility** *n* fertilité *f*; fécondité *f*. ◆**fertilize** *vt* (*land*) fertiliser; (*egg, animal etc*) féconder. ◆**fertilizer** *n* engrais *m*.

fervent ['fɜːv(ə)nt] *a* fervent. ◆**fervour** *n* ferveur *f*.

fester ['festər] *vi* (*of wound*) suppurer; (*of anger etc*) *Fig* couver.

festival ['festɪv(ə)l] *n Mus Cin* festival *m*; *Rel* fête *f*. ◆**festive** *a* (*atmosphere, clothes*) de fête; (*mood*) joyeux; **f. season** période *f* des fêtes. ◆**fe'stivities** *npl* réjouissances *fpl*, festivités *fpl*.

festoon [fe'stuːn] *vt* **to f. with** orner de.

fetch [fetʃ] *vt* **1** (*person*) amener; (*object*) apporter; **to (go and) f.** aller chercher; **to f. in** rentrer; **to f. out** sortir. **2** (*be sold for*) rapporter (**ten pounds**/*etc* dix livres/*etc*); (*price*) atteindre. ◆—**ing** *a* (*smile etc*) charmant, séduisant.

fête [feɪt] *n* fête *f*; – *vt* fêter.

fetid ['fetɪd] *a* fétide.

fetish ['fetɪʃ] *n* (*magical object*) fétiche *m*; **to make a f. of** *Fig* être obsédé par.

fetter ['fetər] *vt* (*hinder*) entraver.

fettle ['fet(ə)l] *n* **in fine f.** en pleine forme.

fetus ['fiːtəs] *n Am* fœtus *m*.

feud [fjuːd] *n* querelle *f*, dissension *f*.

feudal ['fjuːd(ə)l] *a* féodal.

fever ['fiːvər] *n* fièvre *f*; **to have a f.** (*temperature*) avoir de la fièvre. ◆**feverish** *a* (*person, activity*) fiévreux.

few [fjuː] *a & pron* peu (de); **f. towns**/*etc* peu de villes/*etc*; **a f. towns**/*etc* quelques villes/*etc*; **f. of them** peu d'entre eux; **a f.** quelques-un(e)s (**of** de); **a f. of us** quelques-uns d'entre nous; **one of the f. books** l'un des rares livres; **quite a f., a good f.** bon nombre (de); **a f. more books**/*etc* encore quelques livres/*etc*; **f. and far between** rares (et espacés); **f. came** peu sont venus; **to be f.** être peu nombreux; **every f. days** tous les trois ou quatre jours. ◆**fewer** *a & pron* moins (de) (**than** que); **to be f.** être moins nombreux (**than** que); **no f. than** pas moins de. ◆**fewest** *a & pron* le moins (de).

fiancé(e) [fɪˈɒnseɪ] *n* fiancé, -ée *mf*.

fiasco [fɪˈæskəʊ] *n* (*pl* -os, *Am* -oes) fiasco *m*.

fib [fɪb] *n Fam* blague *f*, bobard *m*; – *vi* (-bb-) *Fam* raconter des blagues. ◆**fibber** *n Fam* blagueur, -euse *mf*.

fibre [ˈfaɪbər] *n* fibre *f*; *Fig* caractère *m*. ◆**fibreglass** *n* fibre *f* de verre.

fickle [ˈfɪk(ə)l] *a* inconstant.

fiction [ˈfɪkʃ(ə)n] *n* fiction *f*; (**works of) f.** romans *mpl*. ◆**fictional** *a*, ◆**fic'titious** *a* fictif.

fiddl/e [ˈfɪd(ə)l] **1** *n* (*violin*) *Fam* violon *m*; – *vi Fam* jouer du violon. **2** *vi Fam* **to f. about** (*waste time*) traînailler, glandouiller; **to f. (about) with** (*watch, pen etc*) tripoter; (*cars etc*) bricoler. **3** *n* (*dishonesty*) *Fam* combine *f*, fraude *f*; – *vi* (*swindle*) *Fam* faire de la fraude; – *vt* (*accounts etc*) *Fam* falsifier. ◆**-ing** *a* (*petty*) insignifiant. ◆**-er** *n* **1** *Fam* joueur, -euse *mf* de violon. **2** (*swindler*) *Sl* combinard, -arde *mf*. ◆**fiddly** *a* (*task*) délicat.

fidelity [fɪˈdelɪtɪ] *n* fidélité *f* (**to** à).

fidget [ˈfɪdʒɪt] *vi* **to f. (about)** gigoter, se trémousser; **to f. (about) with** tripoter; – *n* personne *f* qui ne tient pas en place. ◆**fidgety** *a* agité, remuant.

field [fiːld] *n* champ *m*; *Sp* terrain *m*; (*sphere*) domaine *m*; **to have a f. day** (*a good day*) s'en donner à cœur joie; **f. glasses** jumelles *fpl*; **f. marshal** maréchal *m*.

fiend [fiːnd] *n* démon *m*; **a jazz/etc Fam** un(e) passionné, -ée de jazz/*etc*; (**sex) f.** *Fam* satyre *m*. ◆**fiendish** *a* diabolique.

fierce [fɪəs] *a* (-er, -est) féroce; (*wind, attack*) furieux. ◆**-ness** *n* férocité *f*; fureur *f*.

fiery [ˈfaɪərɪ] *a* (-ier, -iest) (*person, speech*) fougueux; (*sun, eyes*) ardent.

fiesta [fɪˈestə] *n* fiesta *f*.

fifteen [fɪfˈtiːn] *a & n* quinze (*m*). ◆**fifteenth** *a & n* quinzième (*mf*). ◆**fifth** *a & n* cinquième (*mf*); **a f.** un cinquième. ◆**'fiftieth** *a & n* cinquantième (*mf*). ◆**'fifty** *a & n* cinquante (*m*).

fig [fɪg] *n* figue *f*; **f. tree** figuier *m*.

fight [faɪt] *n* bagarre *f*, rixe *f*; *Mil Boxing* combat *m*; (*struggle*) lutte *f*; (*quarrel*) dispute *f*; (*spirit*) combativité *f*; **to put up a (good) f.** bien se défendre; – *vi* (*pt & pp*

fought) se battre (**against** contre); *Mil* se battre, combattre; (*struggle*) lutter; (*quarrel*) se disputer; **to f. back** se défendre; **to f. over sth** se disputer qch; – *vt* se battre avec (**s.o.** qn); (*evil*) lutter contre, combattre; **to f. a battle** livrer bataille; **to f. back** (*tears*) refouler; **to f. off** (*attacker, attack*) repousser; (*illness*) lutter contre; **to f. it out** se bagarrer. ◆**-ing** *n Mil* combat(s) *m(pl)*; – *a* (*person*) combatif; (*troops*) de combat. ◆**-er** *n* combattant, -ante *mf*; *Boxing* boxeur *m*; *Fig* battant *m*, lutteur, -euse *mf*; (*aircraft*) chasseur *m*.

figment [ˈfɪgmənt] *n* **a f. of one's imagination** une création de son esprit.

figurative [ˈfɪgjʊrətɪv] *a* (*meaning*) figuré; (*art*) figuratif. ◆**-ly** *adv* au figuré.

figure[1] [ˈfɪgər, *Am* ˈfɪgjər] *n* **1** (*numeral*) chiffre *m*; (*price*) prix *m*; *pl* (*arithmetic*) calcul *m*. **2** (*shape*) forme *f*; (*outlined shape*) silhouette *f*; (*of woman*) ligne *f*; **she has a nice f.** elle est bien faite. **3** (*diagram*) & *Liter* figure *f*; **a f. of speech** une figure de rhétorique; *Fig* une façon de parler; **f. of eight**, *Am* **f. eight** huit *m*; **f. skating** patinage *m* artistique. **4** (*important person*) figure *f*, personnage *m*. ◆**figurehead** *n Nau* figure *f* de proue; (*person*) *Fig* potiche *f*.

figure[2] [ˈfɪgər, *Am* ˈfɪgjər] **1** *vt* (*imagine*) (s')imaginer; (*guess*) penser (**that** que); **to f. out** arriver à comprendre; (*problem*) résoudre; – *vi* (*make sense*) s'expliquer; **to f. on doing** *Am* compter faire. **2** *vi* (*appear*) figurer (**on** sur).

filament [ˈfɪləmənt] *n* filament *m*.

filch [fɪltʃ] *vt* (*steal*) voler (**from** à).

fil/e [faɪl] **1** *n* (*tool*) lime *f*; – *vt* **to f. (down)** limer. **2** *n* (*folder, information*) dossier *m*; (*loose-leaf*) classeur *m*; (*for card index, computer data*) fichier *m*; – *vt* (*claim, application*) déposer; **to f. (away)** classer. **3** *n* **in single f.** en file; – *vi* **to f. in/out** entrer/sortir à la queue leu leu; **to f. past** (*coffin etc*) défiler devant. ◆**-ing** *n* **f. clerk** documentaliste *mf*; **f. cabinet** classeur *m*. **2** *npl* (*particles*) limaille *f*.

fill [fɪl] *vt* remplir (**with** de); (*tooth*) plomber; (*sail*) gonfler; (*need*) répondre à; **to f. in** (*form*) remplir; (*hole*) combler; (*door*) condamner; **to f. s.o. in on** *Fam* mettre qn au courant de; **to f. up** (*glass etc*) remplir; **to f. up** *or* **out** (*form*) remplir; – *vi* **to f. (up)** se remplir; **to f. out** (*get fatter*) grossir, se remplumer; **to f. up** *Aut* faire le plein; – *n* **to eat one's f.** manger à sa faim; **to have had one's f. of** *Pej* en avoir assez de. ◆**-ing** *a* (*meal etc*) substantiel, nourrissant; – *n* (*in tooth*) plombage *m*; *Culin* garniture *f*; **f. station** poste *m* d'essence. ◆**—er** *n* (*for cracks in wood*) mastic *m*.

fillet ['fɪlɪt, *Am* frɪ'leɪ] *n Culin* filet *m*; – *vt* (*pt & pp* ['fɪ'leɪd]) (*fish*) découper en filets; (*meat*) désosser.

fillip ['fɪlɪp] *n* (*stimulus*) coup *m* de fouet.

filly ['fɪlɪ] *n* (*horse*) pouliche *f.*

film [fɪlm] *n* film *m*; (*layer*) & *Phot* pellicule *f*; – *a* (*festival*) du film; (*studio, technician, critic*) de cinéma; **f. fan** *or* **buff** cinéphile *mf*; **f. library** cinémathèque *f*; **f. star** vedette *f* (de cinéma); – *vt* filmer.

filter ['fɪltər] *n* filtre *m*; (*traffic sign*) flèche *f*; **f. lane** *Aut* couloir *m* (pour tourner); **f. tip** (bout *m*) filtre *m*; **f.-tipped cigarette** cigarette *f* (à bout) filtre; – *vt* filtrer; – *vi* filtrer (**through sth** à travers qch); **to f. through** filtrer.

filth [fɪlθ] *n* saleté *f*; (*obscenities*) *Fig* saletés *fpl*. ◆**filthy** *a* (**-ier, -iest**) (*hands etc*) sale; (*language*) obscène; (*habit*) dégoûtant; **f. weather** un temps infect, un sale temps.

fin [fɪn] *n* (*of fish, seal*) nageoire *f*; (*of shark*) aileron *m*.

final ['faɪn(ə)l] *a* dernier; (*decision*) définitif; (*cause*) final; – *n Sp* finale *f*; *pl Univ* examens *mpl* de dernière année. ◆**finalist** *n Sp* finaliste *mf*. ◆**finalize** *vt* (*plan*) mettre au point; (*date*) fixer (définitivement). ◆**finally** *adv* (*lastly*) enfin, en dernier lieu; (*eventually*) finalement, enfin; (*once and for all*) définitivement.

finale [fɪ'nɑːlɪ] *n Mus* finale *m.*

finance ['faɪnæns] *n* finance *f*; – *a* (*company, page*) financier; – *vt* financer. ◆**fi'nancial** *a* financier; **f. year** année *f* budgétaire. ◆**fi'nancially** *adv* financièrement. ◆**fi'nancier** *n* (grand) financier *m.*

find [faɪnd] *n* (*discovery*) trouvaille *f*; – *vt* (*pt & pp* **found**) trouver; (*sth or s.o. lost*) retrouver; (*difficulty*) éprouver, trouver (**in doing** à faire); **I f. that** je trouve que; **£20 all found** 20 livres logé et nourri; **to f. s.o. guilty** *Jur* prononcer qn coupable; **to f. one's feet** (*settle in*) s'adapter; **to f. oneself** (*to be*) se trouver. ■ **to f. out** *vt* (*information etc*) découvrir; (*person*) démasquer; – *vi* (*enquire*) se renseigner (**about** sur); **to f. out about** (*discover*) découvrir. ◆**—ings** *npl* conclusions *fpl.*

fine¹ [faɪn] *n* (*money*) amende *f*; *Aut* contravention *f*; – *vt* **to f. s.o.** (**£10**/*etc*) infliger une amende (de dix livres/*etc*) à qn.

fine² [faɪn] **1** *a* (**-er, -est**) (*thin, small, not coarse*) fin; (*gold*) pur; (*feeling*) délicat; (*distinction*) subtil; – *adv* (*to cut, write*) menu. **2** *a* (**-er, -est**) (*beautiful*) beau; (*good*) bon; (*excellent*) excellent; **to be f.** (*in good health*) aller bien; – *adv* (*well*) très bien. ◆**—ly** *adv* (*dressed*) magnifiquement; (*chopped*) menu; (*embroidered, ground*) finement.

finery ['faɪnərɪ] *n* (*clothes*) parure *f*, belle toilette *f.*

finesse [fɪ'nes] *n* (*skill, tact*) doigté *m*; (*refinement*) finesse *f.*

finger ['fɪŋgər] *n* doigt *m*; **little f.** auriculaire *m*, petit doigt *m*; **middle f.** majeur *m*; **f. mark** trace *f* de doigt; – *vt* toucher (des doigts), palper. ◆**—ing** *n Mus* doigté *m.* ◆**fingernail** *n* ongle *m.* ◆**fingerprint** *n* empreinte *f* digitale. ◆**fingerstall** *n* doigtier *m.* ◆**fingertip** *n* bout *m* du doigt.

finicky ['fɪnɪkɪ] *a* (*precise*) méticuleux; (*difficult*) difficile (**about** sur).

finish ['fɪnɪʃ] *n* (*end*) fin *f*; *Sp* arrivée *f*; (*of article, car etc*) finition *f*; **paint with a matt f.** peinture *f* mate; – *vt* **to f.** (**off** *or* **up**) finir, terminer; **to f. doing** finir de faire; **to f. s.o. off** (*kill*) achever qn; – *vi* (*of meeting etc*) finir, se terminer; (*of person*) finir, terminer; **to f. first** terminer premier; (*in race*) arriver premier; **to have finished with** (*object*) ne plus avoir besoin de; (*situation, person*) en avoir fini avec; **to f. off** *or* **up** (*of person*) finir, terminer; **to f. up in** (*end up in*) se retrouver à; **to f. up doing** finir par faire; **finishing school** institution *f* pour jeunes filles; **finishing touch** touche *f* finale. ◆**—ed** *a* (*ended, done for*) fini.

finite ['faɪnaɪt] *a* fini.

Finland ['fɪnlənd] *n* Finlande *f.* ◆**Finn** *n* Finlandais, -aise *mf*, Finnois, -oise *mf*. ◆**Finnish** *a* finlandais, finnois; – *n* (*language*) finnois *m.*

fir [fɜːr] *n* (*tree, wood*) sapin *m.*

fire¹ ['faɪər] *n* feu *m*; (*accidental*) incendie *m*; (*electric*) radiateur *m*; **on f.** en feu; (**there's a**) **f.!** au feu!; **f.! f.!** *Mil* feu!; **f. alarm** avertisseur *m* d'incendie; **f. brigade**, *Am* **f. department** pompiers *mpl*; **f. engine** (*vehicle*) voiture *f* de pompiers; (*machine*) pompe *f* à incendie; **f. escape** escalier *m* de secours; **f. station** caserne *f* de pompiers. ◆**firearm** *n* arme *f* à feu. ◆**firebug** *n* pyromane *mf*. ◆**firecracker** *n Am* pétard *m.* ◆**fireguard** *n* garde-feu *m inv.* ◆**fireman** *n* (*pl* **-men**) (sapeur-)pompier *m.* ◆**fireplace** *n* cheminée *f.* ◆**fireproof** *a* (*door*) ignifugé, anti-incendie. ◆**fireside** *n* coin *m* du feu; **f. chair** fauteuil *m.* ◆**firewood** *n* bois *m* de chauffage.

◆**firework** n feu m d'artifice; **a f. display**, fireworks, un feu d'artifice.

fire² ['faɪər] vt (cannon) tirer; (pottery) cuire; (imagination) enflammer; **to f. a gun** tirer un coup de fusil; **to f. questions at** bombarder de questions; **to f. s.o.** (dismiss) Fam renvoyer qn; – vi tirer (**at** sur); **f. away!** Fam vas-y, parle!; **firing squad** peloton m d'exécution; **in** or **Am on the firing line** en butte aux attaques.

firm [fɜːm] **1** n Com maison f, firme f. **2** a (-er, -est) (earth, decision etc) ferme; (strict) ferme (**with** avec); (faith) solide; (character) résolu. ◆**—ly** adv fermement; (to speak) d'une voix ferme. ◆**—ness** n fermeté f; (of faith) solidité f.

first [fɜːst] a premier; **I'll do it f. thing in the morning** je le ferai dès le matin, sans faute; **f. cousin**, -ine mf germain(e); – adv d'abord, premièrement; (for the first time) pour la première fois; **f. of all** tout d'abord; **at f.** d'abord; **to come f.** (in race) arriver premier; (in exam) être le premier; – n premier, -ière mf; Univ = licence f avec mention très bien; **from the f.** dès le début; **f. aid** premiers soins mpl or secours mpl; **f. (gear)** Aut première f. ◆**f.-'class** a (ticket etc) de première (classe); (mail) ordinaire; – adv (to travel) en première. ◆**f.-'hand** a & adv de première main; **to have (had) f.-hand experience of** avoir fait l'expérience personnelle de. ◆**f.-'rate** a excellent. ◆**firstly** adv premièrement.

fiscal ['fɪsk(ə)l] a fiscal.

fish [fɪʃ] n (pl inv or -es [-ɪz]) poisson m; **f. market** marché m aux poissons; **f. bone** arête f; **f. bowl** bocal m; **f. fingers**, Am **f. sticks** Culin bâtonnets mpl de poisson; **f. shop** poissonnerie f; – vi pêcher; **to f. for** (salmon etc) pêcher; (compliment etc) Fig chercher; – vt **to f. out** (from water) repêcher; (from pocket etc) Fig sortir. ◆**—ing** n pêche f; **to go f.** aller à la pêche; **f. net** (of fisherman) filet m (de pêche); (of angler) épuisette f; **f. rod** canne f à pêche. ◆**fisherman** n (pl -men) pêcheur m. ◆**fishmonger** n poissonnier, -ière mf. ◆**fishy** a (-ier, -iest) (smell) de poisson; Fig Pej louche.

fission ['fɪʃ(ə)n] n Phys fission f.

fissure ['fɪʃər] n fissure f.

fist [fɪst] n poing m. ◆**fistful** n poignée f.

fit¹ [fɪt] **1** a (fitter, fittest) (suited) propre, bon (**for** à); (fitting) convenable; (worthy) digne (**for** de); (able) capable (**for** de, **to** de faire); (healthy) en bonne santé; **f. to eat** bon à manger, mangeable; **to see f. to do**

juger à propos de faire; **as you see f.** comme bon vous semble; **f. to drop** Fam prêt à tomber; **to keep f.** se maintenir en forme. **2** vt (-tt-) (of coat etc) aller (bien) à (qn); (match) répondre à; (equal) égaler; **to f. sth on s.o.** (garment) ajuster qch à qn; **to f. sth (on) to sth** (put) poser qch sur qch; (adjust) adapter qch à qch; (fix) fixer qch à qch; **to f. (out** or **up) with** (house, ship etc) équiper de; **to f. (in)** (window) poser; **to f. in** (object) faire entrer; (patient, customer) prendre; **to f. (in) the lock** (of key) aller dans la serrure; – vi (of clothes) aller (bien) (à qn); **this shirt fits (fits me)** cette chemise me va (bien); **to f. (in)** (go in) entrer, aller; (of facts, plans) s'accorder, cadrer (**with** avec); **he doesn't f. in** il ne peut pas s'intégrer; – n **a good f.** (dress etc) à la bonne taille; **a close** or **tight f.** ajusté. ◆**fitted** a (cupboard) encastré; (garment) ajusté; **f. carpet** moquette f; **f. (kitchen) units** éléments mpl de cuisine. ◆**fitting 1** a (suitable) convenable. **2** n (of clothes) essayage m; **f. room** salon m d'essayage; (booth) cabine f d'essayage. **3** npl (in house etc) installations fpl. ◆**fitment** n (furniture) meuble m encastré; (accessory) Tech accessoire m. ◆**fitness** n (of remark etc) à-propos m; (for job) aptitudes fpl (**for** pour); Med santé f. ◆**fitter** n Tech monteur, -euse mf.

fit² [fɪt] n Med & Fig accès m, crise f; **in fits and starts** par à-coups. ◆**fitful** a (sleep) agité.

five [faɪv] a & n cinq (m). ◆**fiver** n Fam billet m de cinq livres.

fix [fɪks] **1** vt (make firm, decide) fixer; (tie with rope) attacher; (mend) réparer; (deal with) arranger; (prepare, cook) Am préparer, faire; (in s.o.'s mind) graver (**in** dans); (conduct fraudulently) Fam truquer; (bribe) Fam acheter; (hopes, ambitions) mettre (**on** en); **to f. s.o.** (punish) Fam régler son compte à qn; **to f. (on)** (lid etc) mettre en place; **to f. up** arranger; **to f. s.o. up with sth** (job etc) procurer qch à qn. **2** n Av Nau position f; (injection) Sl piqûre f; **in a f.** Fam dans le pétrin. ◆**—ed** a (idea, price etc) fixe; (resolution) inébranlable; **how's he f. for . . . ?** Fam (cash etc) a-t-il assez de . . . ?; (tomorrow etc) qu'est-ce qu'il fait pour . . . ? ◆**fixings** npl Culin Am garniture f. ◆**fix'ation** n fixation f. ◆**fixer** n (schemer) Fam combinard, -arde mf. ◆**fixture 1** n Sp match m (prévu). **2** npl (in house) meubles mpl fixes, installations fpl.

fizz [fɪz] *vi* (*of champagne*) pétiller; (*of gas*) siffler. ◆**fizzy** *a* (**-ier, -iest**) pétillant.

fizzle ['fɪz(ə)l] *vi* (*hiss*) siffler; (*of liquid*) pétiller; **to f. out** (*of firework*) rater, faire long feu; (*of plan*) *Fig* tomber à l'eau; (*of custom*) disparaître.

flabbergasted ['flæbəgɑːstɪd] *a Fam* sidéré.

flabby ['flæbɪ] *a* (**-ier, -iest**) (*skin, character, person*) mou, flasque.

flag [flæg] **1** *n* drapeau *m*; *Nau* pavillon *m*; (*for charity*) insigne *m*; **f. stop** *Am* arrêt *m* facultatif; – *vt* (**-gg-**) **to f. down** (*taxi*) faire signe à. **2** *vi* (**-gg-**) (*of plant*) dépérir; (*of conversation*) languir; (*of worker*) fléchir. ◆**flagpole** *n* mât *m*.

flagrant ['fleɪgrənt] *a* flagrant.

flagstone ['flægstəʊn] *n* dalle *f*.

flair [fleər] *n* (*intuition*) flair *m*; **to have a f. for** (*natural talent*) avoir un don pour.

flake [fleɪk] *n* (*of snow etc*) flocon *m*; (*of metal, soap*) paillette *f*; – *vi* **to f. (off)** (*of paint*) s'écailler. ◆**flaky** *a* **f. pastry** pâte *f* feuilletée.

flamboyant [flæm'bɔɪənt] *a* (*person, manner*) extravagant.

flam/e [fleɪm] *n* flamme *f*; **to go up in flames** s'enflammer; – *vi* **to f. (up)** (*of fire, house*) flamber. ◆**-ing** *a* **1** (*sun*) flamboyant. **2** (*damn*) *Fam* fichu.

flamingo [flə'mɪŋgəʊ] *n* (*pl* **-os** *or* **-oes**) (*bird*) flamant *m*.

flammable ['flæməb(ə)l] *a* inflammable.

flan [flæn] *n* tarte *f*.

flank [flæŋk] *n* flanc *m*; – *vt* flanquer (with de).

flannel ['flænəl] *n* (*cloth*) flanelle *f*; (*face*) f. gant *m* de toilette, carré-éponge *m*. ◆**flanne'lette** *n* pilou *m*, finette *f*.

flap [flæp] **1** *vi* (**-pp-**) (*of wings, sail, shutter etc*) battre; – *vt* **to f. its wings** (*of bird*) battre des ailes; – *n* battement *m*. **2** *n* (*of pocket, envelope*) rabat *m*; (*of table*) abattant *m*; (*of door*) battant *m*.

flare [fleər] *n* (*light*) éclat *m*; *Mil* fusée *f* éclairante; (*for runway*) balise *f*; – *vi* (*blaze*) flamber; (*shine*) briller; **to f. up** (*of fire*) s'enflammer; (*of region*) *Fig* s'embraser; (*of war*) éclater; (*get angry*) s'emporter. ◆**f.-up** *n* (*of violence, fire*) flambée *f*; (*of region*) embrasement *m*. ◆**flared** *a* (*skirt*) évasé; (*trousers*) à pattes d'éléphant.

flash [flæʃ] *n* (*of light*) éclat *m*; (*of anger, genius*) éclair *m*; *Phot* flash *m*; **f. of lightning** éclair *m*; **news f.** flash *m*; **in a f.** en un clin d'œil; – *vi* (*shine*) briller; (*on and off*) clignoter; **to f. past** (*rush*) *Fig* passer

comme un éclair; – *vt* (*aim*) diriger (**on, at** sur); (*a light*) projeter; (*a glance*) jeter; **to f. (around)** (*flaunt*) étaler; **to f. one's headlights** faire un appel de phares. ◆**flashback** *n* retour *m* en arrière. ◆**flashlight** *n* lampe *f* électrique *or* de poche; *Phot* flash *m*.

flashy ['flæʃɪ] *a* (**-ier, -iest**) *a* voyant, tape-à-l'œil *inv*.

flask [flɑːsk] *n* thermos® *m* or *f inv*; *Ch* flacon *m*; (*phial*) fiole *f*.

flat¹ [flæt] *a* (**flatter, flattest**) plat; (*tyre, battery*) à plat; (*nose*) aplati; (*beer*) éventé; (*refusal*) net; (*rate, fare*) fixe; (*voice*) *Mus* faux; (*razed to the ground*) rasé; **to put sth (down)** f. mettre qch à plat; **f. (on one's face)** à plat ventre; **to fall f.** *Fig* tomber à plat; **to be f.-footed** avoir les pieds plats; – *adv* (*to say*) carrément; (*to sing*) faux; **f. broke** *Fam* complètement fauché; **in two minutes** f. en deux minutes pile; **f. out** (*to work*) d'arrache-pied; (*to run*) à toute vitesse; – *n* (*of hand*) plat *m*; (*puncture*) *Aut* crevaison *f*; *Mus* bémol *m*. ◆**-ly** *adv* (*to deny etc*) catégoriquement. ◆**-ness** *n* (*of surface*) égalité *f*. ◆**flatten** *vt* (*crops*) coucher; (*town*) raser; **to f. (out)** (*metal etc*) aplatir.

flat² [flæt] *n* (*rooms*) appartement *m*.

flatter ['flætər] *vt* flatter; (*of clothes*) avantager (qn). ◆**-ing** *a* flatteur; (*clothes*) avantageux. ◆**-er** *n* flatteur, -euse *mf*. ◆**flattery** *n* flatterie *f*.

flatulence ['flætjʊləns] *n* **to have f.** avoir des gaz.

flaunt [flɔːnt] *vt* (*show off*) faire étalage de; (*defy*) *Am* narguer, défier.

flautist ['flɔːtɪst] *n* flûtiste *mf*.

flavour ['fleɪvər] *n* (*taste*) goût *m*, saveur *f*; (*of ice cream, sweet etc*) parfum *m*; – *vt* (*food*) assaisonner; (*sauce*) relever; (*ice cream etc*) parfumer (with à). ◆**-ing** *n* assaisonnement *m*; (*in cake*) parfum *m*.

flaw [flɔː] *n* défaut *m*. ◆**flawed** *a* imparfait. ◆**flawless** *a* parfait.

flax [flæks] *n* lin *m*. ◆**flaxen** *a* de lin.

flay [fleɪ] *vt* (*animal*) écorcher; (*criticize*) *Fig* éreinter.

flea [fliː] *n* puce *f*; **f. market** marché *m* aux puces. ◆**fleapit** *n Fam* cinéma *m* miteux.

fleck [flek] *n* (*mark*) petite tache *f*.

fledgling ['fledʒlɪŋ] *n* (*novice*) blanc-bec *m*.

flee [fliː] *vi* (*pt & pp* **fled**) fuir, s'enfuir, se sauver; – *vt* (*place*) s'enfuir de; (*danger etc*) fuir.

fleece [fliːs] **1** *n* (*sheep's coat*) toison *f*. **2** *vt* (*rob*) voler.

fleet [fliːt] *n* (*of ships*) flotte *f*; **a f. of cars** un parc automobile.

fleeting ['fliːtɪŋ] *a* (*visit, moment*) bref; (*beauty*) éphémère.

Flemish ['flemɪʃ] *a* flamand; – *n* (*language*) flamand *m*.

flesh [fleʃ] *n* chair *f*; **her (own) f. and blood** la chair de sa chair; **in the f.** en chair et en os; **f. wound** blessure *f* superficielle. **◆fleshy** *a* (**-ier, -iest**) charnu.

flew [fluː] *see* **fly** [2].

flex [fleks] **1** *vt* (*limb*) fléchir; (*muscle*) faire jouer, bander. **2** *n* (*wire*) fil *m* (souple); (*for telephone*) cordon *m*.

flexible ['fleksɪb(ə)l] *a* flexible, souple. **◆flexi'bility** *n* flexibilité *f*.

flick [flɪk] *vt* donner un petit coup à; **to f. off** (*remove*) enlever (d'une chiquenaude); – *vi* **to f. over** *or* **through** (*pages*) feuilleter; – *n* petit coup *m*; (*with finger*) chiquenaude *f*; **f. knife** couteau *m* à cran d'arrêt.

flicker ['flɪkər] *vi* (*of flame, light*) vaciller; (*of needle*) osciller; – *n* vacillement *m*; **f. of light** lueur *f*.

flier ['flaɪər] *n* **1** (*person*) aviateur, -trice *mf*. **2** (*handbill*) *Am* prospectus *m*, *Pol* tract *m*.

flies [flaɪz] *npl* (*on trousers*) braguette *f*.

flight [flaɪt] *n* **1** (*of bird, aircraft etc*) vol *m*; (*of bullet*) trajectoire *f*; (*of imagination*) élan *m*; (*of stairs*) escalier *m*; **f. deck** cabine *f* de pilotage. **2** (*fleeing*) fuite *f* (**from** de); **to take f.** prendre la fuite.

flighty ['flaɪtɪ] *a* (**-ier, -iest**) inconstant, volage.

flimsy ['flɪmzɪ] *a* (**-ier, -iest**) (*cloth, structure etc*) (trop) léger *or* mince; (*excuse*) mince, frivole.

flinch [flɪntʃ] *vi* (*with pain*) tressaillir; **to f. from** (*duty etc*) se dérober à; **without flinching** (*complaining*) sans broncher.

fling [flɪŋ] **1** *vt* (*pt & pp* **flung**) jeter, lancer; **to f. open** (*door etc*) ouvrir brutalement. **2** *n* **to have one's** *or* **a f.** (*indulge oneself*) s'en donner à cœur joie.

flint [flɪnt] *n* silex *m*; (*for cigarette lighter*) pierre *f*.

flip [flɪp] **1** *vt* (**-pp-**) (*with finger*) donner une chiquenaude à; – *vi* **to f. through** (*book etc*) feuilleter; – *n* chiquenaude *f*; **the f. side** (*of record*) la face deux. **2** *a* (*cheeky*) *Am Fam* effronté.

flip-flops ['flɪpflɒps] *npl* tongs *fpl*.

flippant ['flɪpənt] *a* irrévérencieux; (*off-hand*) désinvolte.

flipper ['flɪpər] *n* (*of seal*) nageoire *f*; (*of swimmer*) palme *f*.

flipping ['flɪpɪŋ] *a Fam* sacré; – *adv Fam* sacrément, bougrement.

flirt [flɜːt] *vi* flirter (**with** avec); – *n* flirteur, -euse *mf*. **◆flir'tation** *n* flirt *m*. **◆flir'tatious** *a* flirteur.

flit [flɪt] *vi* (**-tt-**) (*fly*) voltiger; **to f. in and out** (*of person*) *Fig* entrer et sortir (rapidement).

float [fləʊt] *n Fishing* flotteur *m*; (*in parade*) char *m*; – *vi* flotter (**on** sur); **to f. down the river** descendre la rivière; – *vt* (*boat, currency*) faire flotter; (*loan*) *Com* émettre. **◆—ing** *a* (*wood, debt etc*) flottant; (*population*) instable; (*voters*) indécis.

flock [flɒk] *n* (*of sheep etc*) troupeau *m*; (*of birds*) volée *f*; *Rel Hum* ouailles *fpl*; (*of tourists etc*) foule *f*; – *vi* venir en foule; **to f. round s.o.** s'attrouper autour de qn.

floe [fləʊ] *n* (**ice**) **f.** banquise *f*.

flog [flɒg] *vt* (**-gg-**) **1** (*beat*) flageller. **2** (*sell*) *Sl* vendre. **◆flogging** *n* flagellation *f*.

flood [flʌd] *n* inondation *f*; (*of letters, tears etc*) *Fig* flot *m*, déluge *m*, torrent *m*; – *vt* (*field etc*) inonder (**with** de); (*river*) faire déborder; **to f. (out)** (*house*) inonder; – *vi* (*of building*) être inondé; (*of river*) déborder; (*of people, money*) affluer; **to f. into** (*of tourists etc*) envahir. **◆—ing** *n* inondation *f*. **◆floodgate** *n* (*in water*) vanne *f*.

floodlight ['flʌdlaɪt] *n* projecteur *m*; – *vt* (*pt & pp* **floodlit**) illuminer; **floodlit match** *Sp* (match *m* en) nocturne *m*.

floor [flɔːr] **1** *n* (*ground*) sol *m*; (*wooden etc in building*) plancher *m*; (*storey*) étage *m*; (*dance*) **f.** piste *f* (de danse); **on the f.** par terre; **first f.** premier étage *m*; (*ground floor*) *Am* rez-de-chaussée *m inv*; **f. polish** encaustique *f*; **f. show** spectacle *m* (de cabaret). **2** *vt* (*knock down*) terrasser; (*puzzle*) stupéfier. **◆floorboard** *n* planche *f*.

flop [flɒp] **1** *vi* (**-pp-**) **to f. down** (*collapse*) s'effondrer; **to f. about** s'agiter mollement. **2** *vi* (**-pp-**) *Fam* échouer; (*of play, film etc*) faire un four; – *n Fam* échec *m*, fiasco *m*; *Th Cin* four *m*.

floppy ['flɒpɪ] *a* (**-ier, -iest**) (*soft*) mou; (*clothes*) (trop) large; (*ears*) pendant; **f. disk** (*of computer*) disquette *f*.

flora ['flɔːrə] *n* (*plants*) flore *f*. **◆floral** *a* floral; (*material*) à fleurs.

florid ['flɒrɪd] *a* (*style*) fleuri; (*complexion*) rougeaud, fleuri.

florist ['flɒrɪst] *n* fleuriste *mf*.

floss [flɒs] *n* (**dental**) **f.** fil *m* (de soie) dentaire.

flotilla [flə'tɪlə] *n Nau* flottille *f*.

flounce [flauns] *n* (*frill on dress etc*) volant *m*.

flounder ['flaundər] **1** *vi* (*in water etc*) patauger (avec effort), se débattre; (*in speech*) hésiter, patauger. **2** *n* (*fish*) carrelet *m*.

flour ['flauər] *n* farine *f*.

flourish ['flʌrɪʃ] **1** *vi* (*of person, business, plant etc*) prospérer; (*of the arts*) fleurir. **2** *vt* (*wave*) brandir. **3** *n* (*decoration*) fioriture *f*; *Mus* fanfare *f*. ◆—**ing** *a* prospère, florissant.

flout [flaut] *vt* narguer, braver.

flow [fləu] *vi* couler; (*of current*) El circuler; (*of hair, clothes*) flotter; (*of traffic*) s'écouler; (*of people, money*) affluer; **to f. in** (*of people, money*) affluer; **to f. back** refluer; **to f. into the sea** se jeter dans la mer; – *n* (*of river*) courant *m*; (*of tide*) flux *m*; (*of blood*) & El circulation *f*; (*of traffic, liquid*) écoulement *m*; (*of words*) *Fig* flot *m*. ◆—**ing** *a* (*movement*) gracieux; (*style*) coulant; (*beard*) flottant.

flower ['flauər] *n* fleur *f*; **f. bed** plate-bande *f*; **f. shop** (boutique *f* de) fleuriste *mf*; **f. show** floralies *fpl*; – *vi* fleurir. ◆—**ed** *a* (*dress*) à fleurs. ◆—**ing** *n* floraison *f*; – *a* (*in bloom*) en fleurs; (*with flowers*) à fleurs. ◆**flowery** *a* (*style etc*) fleuri; (*material*) à fleurs.

flown [fləun] *see* **fly 2**.

flu [fluː] *n* (*influenza*) *Fam* grippe *f*.

fluctuate ['flʌktjueɪt] *vi* varier. ◆**fluctu-'ation** *n*(*pl*) (*in prices etc*) fluctuations *fpl* (**in** de).

flue [fluː] *n* (*of chimney*) conduit *m*.

fluent ['fluːənt] *a* (*style*) aisé; **to be f., be a f. speaker** s'exprimer avec facilité; **he's f. in Russian, his Russian is f.** il parle couramment le russe. ◆**fluency** *n* facilité *f*. ◆**fluently** *adv* avec facilité; (*to speak*) *Ling* couramment.

fluff [flʌf] **1** *n* (*down*) duvet *m*; (*of material*) peluche(s) *f*(*pl*); (*on floor*) moutons *mpl*. **2** *vt* (*bungle*) *Fam* rater. ◆**fluffy** *a* (**-ier, -iest**) (*bird etc*) duveteux; (*material*) pelucheux; (*toy*) en peluche; (*hair*) bouffant.

fluid ['fluːɪd] *a* fluide; (*plans*) flexible, non arrêté; – *n* fluide *m*, liquide *m*.

fluke [fluːk] *n Fam* coup *m* de chance; **by a f.** par raccroc.

flummox ['flʌməks] *vt Fam* désorienter, dérouter.

flung [flʌŋ] *see* **fling 1**.

flunk [flʌŋk] *vi* (*in exam*) *Am Fam* être collé; – *vt Am Fam* (*pupil*) coller; (*exam*) être collé à; (*school*) laisser tomber.

flunk(e)y ['flʌŋkɪ] *n Pej* larbin *m*.

fluorescent [fluə'res(ə)nt] *a* fluorescent.

fluoride ['fluəraɪd] *n* (*in water, toothpaste*) fluor *m*.

flurry ['flʌrɪ] *n* **1** (*of activity*) poussée *f*. **2** (*of snow*) rafale *f*.

flush [flʌʃ] **1** *n* (*of blood*) flux *m*; (*blush*) rougeur *f*; (*of youth, beauty*) éclat *m*; (*of victory*) ivresse *f*; – *vi* (*blush*) rougir. **2** *vt* **to f. (out)** (*clean*) nettoyer à grande eau; **to f. the pan** *or* **the toilet** tirer la chasse d'eau; **to f. s.o. out** (*chase away*) faire sortir qn (**from** de). **3** *a* (*level*) de niveau (**with** de); **f. (with money)** *Fam* bourré de fric. ◆—**ed** *a* (*cheeks etc*) rouge; **f. with** (*success*) ivre de.

fluster ['flʌstər] *vt* énerver; **to get flustered** s'énerver.

flute [fluːt] *n* flûte *f*. ◆**flutist** *n Am* flûtiste *mf*.

flutter ['flʌtər] **1** *vi* voltiger; (*of wing*) battre; (*of flag*) flotter (mollement); (*of heart*) palpiter; (*of person*) papillonner; – *vt* **to f. its wings** battre des ailes. **2** *n* **to have a f.** (*bet*) *Fam* parier.

flux [flʌks] *n* changement *m* continuel.

fly 1 [flaɪ] *n* (*insect*) mouche *f*; **f. swatter** (*instrument*) tapette *f*. ◆**flypaper** *n* papier *m* tue-mouches.

fly 2 [flaɪ] *vi* (*pt* **flew**, *pp* **flown**) (*of bird, aircraft etc*) voler; (*of passenger*) aller en avion; (*of time*) passer vite; (*of flag*) flotter; (*flee*) fuir; **to f. away** *or* **off** s'envoler; **to f. out** *Av* partir en avion; (*from room*) sortir à toute vitesse; **I must f.!** il faut que je file!; **to f. at s.o.** (*attack*) sauter sur qn; – *vt* (*aircraft*) piloter; (*passengers*) transporter (par avion); (*airline*) voyager par; (*flag*) arborer; (*kite*) faire voler; **to f. the French flag** battre pavillon français; **to f. across** *or* **over** survoler. ◆—**ing** *n* (*flight*) aviation *f*; **to like f.** aimer l'avion; – *a* (*personnel, saucer etc*) volant; (*visit*) éclair *inv*; **with f. colours** (*to succeed*) haut la main; **a f. start** un très bon départ; **f. time** (*length*) *Av* durée *f* du vol; **ten hours'/etc f. time** dix heures/etc de vol. ◆—**er** *n* = **flier**. ◆**flyby** *n Av Am* défilé *m* aérien. ◆**fly-by-night** *a* (*firm*) véreux. ◆**flyover** *n* (*bridge*) toboggan *m*. ◆**flypast** *n Av* défilé *m* aérien.

fly 3 [flaɪ] *n* (*on trousers*) braguette *f*.

foal [fəul] *n* poulain *m*.

foam [fəum] *n* (*on sea, mouth*) écume *f*; (*on beer*) mousse *f*; **f. rubber** caoutchouc *m* mousse; **f. (rubber) mattress/etc** matelas *m*/etc mousse; – *vi* (*of sea, mouth*) écumer; (*of beer, soap*) mousser.

fob [fɒb] *vt* (-bb-) **to f. sth off on s.o., f. s.o. off with sth**, refiler qch à qn.

focal ['fəʊk(ə)l] *a* focal; **f. point** point *m* central. ◆**focus** *n* foyer *m*; (*of attention, interest*) centre *m*; **in f.** au point; – *vi Phot* mettre au point; (*light*) faire converger; (*efforts, attention*) concentrer (**on** sur); – *vi* (*converge*) converger (**on** sur); **to f. (one's eyes) on** fixer les yeux sur; **to f. on** (*direct one's attention to*) se concentrer sur.

fodder ['fɒdər] *n* fourrage *m*.

foe [fəʊ] *n* ennemi, -ie *mf*.

foetus ['fiːtəs] *n* fœtus *m*.

fog [fɒg] *n* brouillard *m*, brume *f*; – *vt* (-gg-) (*issue*) *Fig* embrouiller. ◆**fogbound** *a* bloqué par le brouillard. ◆**foghorn** *n* corne *f* de brume; (*voice*) *Pej* voix *f* toni-truante. ◆**foglamp** *n* (phare *m*) anti-brouillard *m*. ◆**foggy** *a* (-ier, -iest) (*day*) de brouillard; **it's f.** il fait du brouil-lard; **f. weather** brouillard *m*; **she hasn't the foggiest (idea)** *Fam* elle n'en a pas la moin-dre idée.

fog(e)y ['fəʊgɪ] *n* **old f.** vieille baderne *f*.

foible ['fɔɪb(ə)l] *n* petit défaut *m*.

foil [fɔɪl] **1** *n* feuille *f* de métal; *Culin* papier *m* alu(minium). **2** *n* (*contrasting person*) repoussoir *m*. **3** *vt* (*plans etc*) déjouer.

foist [fɔɪst] *vt* **to f. sth on s.o.** (*fob off*) refiler qch à qn; **to f. oneself on s.o.** s'imposer à qn.

fold[1] [fəʊld] *n* pli *m*; – *vt* plier; (*wrap*) envelopper (**in** dans); **to f. away** or **down** or **up** plier; **to f. back** or **over** replier; **to f. one's arms** (se) croiser les bras; – *vi* (*of chair etc*) se plier; (*of business*) *Fam* s'écrouler; **to f. away** or **down** or **up** (*of chair etc*) se plier; **to f. back** or **over** (*of blanket etc*) se replier. ◆**—ing** *a* (*chair etc*) pliant. ◆**—er** *n* (*file holder*) chemise *f*; (*pamphlet*) dépliant *m*.

fold[2] [fəʊld] *n* (*for sheep*) parc *m* à moutons; *Rel Fig* bercail *m*.

-fold [fəʊld] *suffix* **tenfold** *a* par dix; – *adv* dix fois.

foliage ['fəʊlɪdʒ] *n* feuillage *m*.

folk [fəʊk] **1** *n* gens *mpl* or *fpl*; *pl* gens *mpl* or *fpl*; (*parents*) *Fam* parents *mpl*; **hello folks!** *Fam* salut tout le monde!; **old f. like it** les vieux l'apprécient. **2** *a* (*dance etc*) folklorique; **f. music** (*contemporary*) (musique *f*) folk *m*. ◆**folklore** *n* folklore *m*.

follow ['fɒləʊ] *vt* suivre; (*career*) pour-suivre; **followed by** suivi de; **to f. suit** *Fig* en faire autant; **to f. s.o. around** suivre qn partout; **to f. through** (*idea etc*) poursuivre

jusqu'au bout; **to f. up** (*suggestion, case*) suivre; (*advantage*) exploiter; (*letter*) donner suite à; (*remark*) faire suivre (**with** de); – *vi* **to f. (on)** suivre; **it follows that** il s'ensuit que; **that doesn't f.** ce n'est pas logique. ◆**—ing 1** *a* suivant; – *prep* à la suite de. **2** *n* (*supporters*) partisans *mpl*; **to have a large f.** avoir de nombreux partisans; (*of serial, fashion*) être très suivi. ◆**—er** *n* partisan *m*. ◆**follow-up** *n* suite *f*; (*letter*) rappel *m*.

folly ['fɒlɪ] *n* folie *f*, sottise *f*.

foment [fəʊ'ment] *vt* (*revolt etc*) fomenter.

fond [fɒnd] *a* (-er, -est) (*loving*) tendre, affectueux; (*doting*) indulgent; (*wish, ambi-tion*) naïf; **to be (very) f. of** aimer (beaucoup). ◆**—ly** *adv* tendrement. ◆**—ness** *n* (*for things*) prédilection *f* (**for** pour); (*for people*) affection *f* (**for** pour).

fondle ['fɒnd(ə)l] *vt* caresser.

food [fuːd] *n* nourriture *f*; (*particular substance*) aliment *m*; (*cooking*) cuisine *f*; (*for cats, pigs*) pâtée *f*; (*for plants*) engrais *m*; *pl* (*foodstuffs*) aliments *mpl*; – *a* (*needs etc*) alimentaire; **a fast f. shop** un fast-food; **f. poisoning** intoxication *f* alimentaire; **f. value** valeur *f* nutritive. ◆**foodstuffs** *npl* denrées *fpl* or produits *mpl* alimentaires.

fool [fuːl] *n* imbécile *mf*, idiot, -ote *mf*; **(you) silly f.!** espèce d'imbécile!; **to make a f. of** (*ridicule*) ridiculiser; (*trick*) duper; **to be f. enough to do** être assez stupide pour faire; **to play the f.** faire l'imbécile; – *vt* (*trick*) duper; – *vi* **to f. (about** or **around)** faire l'imbécile; (*waste time*) perdre son temps; **to f. around** (*make love*) *Am Fam* faire l'amour (**with** avec). ◆**foolish** *a* bête, idiot. ◆**foolishly** *adv* bêtement. ◆**fool-ishness** *n* bêtise *f*, sottise *f*. ◆**foolproof** *a* (*scheme etc*) infaillible.

foolhardy ['fuːlhɑːdɪ] *a* téméraire. ◆**fool-hardiness** *n* témérité *f*.

foot[1], *pl* **feet** [fʊt, fiːt] *n* pied *m*; (*of animal*) patte *f*; (*measure*) pied *m* (= 30,48 cm); **at the f. of** (*page, stairs*) au bas de; (*table*) au bout de; **on f.** à pied; **on one's feet** (*stand-ing*) debout; (*recovered*) *Med* sur pied; **f. brake** *Aut* frein *m* au plancher; **f.-and-mouth disease** fièvre *f* aphteuse. ◆**footbridge** *n* passerelle *f*. ◆**foothills** *npl* contreforts *mpl*. ◆**foothold** *n* prise *f* (de pied); *Fig* position *f*; **to gain a f.** pren-dre pied. ◆**footlights** *npl Th* rampe *f*. ◆**footloose** *a* libre de toute attache. ◆**footman** *n* (*pl* -**men**) valet *m* de pied. ◆**footmark** *n* empreinte *f* (de pied). ◆**footnote** *n* note *f* au bas de la page; *Fig* post-scriptum *m*. ◆**footpath** *n* sentier *m*; (*at roadside*) chemin *m* (piétonnier). ◆**footstep** *n* pas *m*; **to follow in s.o.'s footsteps** suivre les traces de qn. ◆**footwear** *n* chaussures *fpl*.

foot² [fʊt] *vt* (*bill*) payer.

football ['fʊtbɔːl] *n* (*game*) football *m*; (*ball*) ballon *m*. ◆**footballer** *n* joueur, -euse *mf* de football.

footing ['fʊtɪŋ] *n* prise *f* (de pied); *Fig* position *f*; **on a war f.** sur le pied de guerre; **on an equal f.** sur un pied d'égalité.

for [fɔr, *unstressed* fər] **1** *prep* pour; (*in exchange for*) contre; (*for a distance of*) pendant; (*in spite of*) malgré; **f. you/me/etc** pour toi/moi/etc; **what f.?** pourquoi?; **what's it f.?** ça sert à quoi?; **f. example** par exemple; **f. love** par amour; **f. sale** à vendre; **to swim f.** (*towards*) nager vers; **a train f.** un train à destination de *or* en direction de; **the road f. London** la route (en direction) de Londres; **fit f. eating** bon à manger; **eager f.** avide de; **to look f.** chercher; **to come f. dinner** venir dîner; **to sell f.** £7 vendre sept livres; **what's the Russian f. 'book'?** comment dit-on 'livre' en russe?; **but f. her** sans elle; **he was away f. a month** (*throughout*) il a été absent pendant un mois; **he won't be back f. a month** il ne sera pas de retour avant un mois; **he's been here f. a month** (*he's still here*) il est ici depuis un mois; **I haven't seen him f. ten years** voilà dix ans que je ne l'ai vu; **it's easy f. her to do it** il lui est facile de le faire; **it's f. you to say** c'est à toi de dire; **f. that to be done** pour que ça soit fait. **2** *conj* (*because*) car.

forage ['fɒrɪdʒ] *vt* **to f.** (**about**) fourrager (*for* pour trouver).

foray ['fɒreɪ] *n* incursion *f*.

forbearance [fɔːˈbeərəns] *n* patience *f*.

forbid [fəˈbɪd] *vt* (*pt* forbad(e), *pp* forbidden, *pres p* forbidding) interdire, défendre (**s.o. to do** à qn de faire); **to f. s.o. sth** interdire *or* défendre qch à qn. ◆**forbidden** *a* (*fruit etc*) défendu; **she is f. to leave** il lui est interdit de partir. ◆**forbidding** *a* menaçant, sinistre.

force [fɔːs] *n* force *f*; **the (armed) forces** *Mil* les forces armées; **by (sheer) f.** de force; **in f.** (*rule*) en vigueur; (*in great numbers*) en grand nombre, en force; – *vt* contraindre, forcer (**to do** à faire); (*impose*) imposer (**on** à); (*push*) pousser; (*lock*) forcer; (*confession*) arracher (**from** à); **to f. back** (*enemy etc*) faire reculer; (*repress*) refouler; **to f. down** (*aircraft*) forcer à atterrir; **to f. out**

faire sortir de force. ◆**forced** *a* forcé (**to do** de faire); **a f. smile** un sourire forcé. ◆**force-feed** *vt* (*pt & pp* f.-fed) nourrir de force. ◆**forceful** *a* énergique, puissant. ◆**forcefully** *adv* avec force, énergiquement. ◆**forcible** *a* de force; (*forceful*) énergique. ◆**forcibly** *adv* (*by force*) de force.

forceps ['fɔːseps] *n* forceps *m*.

ford [fɔːd] *n* gué *m*; – *vt* (*river etc*) passer à gué.

fore [fɔːr] *n* **to come to the f.** se mettre en évidence.

forearm ['fɔːrɑːm] *n* avant-bras *m inv*.

forebod/e [fɔːˈbəʊd] *vt* (*be a warning of*) présager. ◆**—ing** *n* (*feeling*) pressentiment *m*.

forecast ['fɔːkɑːst] *vt* (*pt & pp* forecast) prévoir; – *n* prévision *f*; *Met* prévisions *fpl*; *Sp* pronostic *m*.

forecourt ['fɔːkɔːt] *n* avant-cour *f*; (*of filling station*) aire *f* (de service), devant *m*.

forefathers ['fɔːfɑːðəz] *npl* aïeux *mpl*.

forefinger ['fɔːfɪŋgər] *n* index *m*.

forefront ['fɔːfrʌnt] *n* **in the f. of** au premier rang de.

forego [fɔːˈgəʊ] *vt* (*pp* foregone) renoncer à. ◆**'foregone** *a* **it's a f. conclusion** c'est couru d'avance.

foregoing [fɔːˈgəʊɪŋ] *a* précédent.

foreground ['fɔːgraʊnd] *n* premier plan *m*.

forehead ['fɒrɪd, 'fɔːhed] *n* (*brow*) front *m*.

foreign ['fɒrən] *a* étranger; (*trade*) extérieur; (*travel, correspondent*) à l'étranger; (*produce*) de l'étranger; **F. Minister** ministre *m* des Affaires étrangères. ◆**foreigner** *n* étranger, -ère *mf*.

foreman ['fɔːmən] *n* (*pl* -men) (*worker*) contremaître *m*; (*of jury*) président *m*.

foremost ['fɔːməʊst] **1** *a* principal. **2** *adv* **first and f.** tout d'abord.

forensic [fəˈrensɪk] *a* (*medicine*) légal; (*laboratory*) médico-légal.

forerunner ['fɔːrʌnər] *n* précurseur *m*.

foresee [fɔːˈsiː] *vt* (*pt* foresaw, *pp* foreseen) prévoir. ◆**—able** *a* prévisible.

foreshadow [fɔːˈʃædəʊ] *vt* présager.

foresight ['fɔːsaɪt] *n* prévoyance *f*.

forest ['fɒrɪst] *n* forêt *f*. ◆**forester** *n* (*garde m*) forestier *m*.

forestall [fɔːˈstɔːl] *vt* devancer.

foretaste ['fɔːteɪst] *n* avant-goût *m*.

foretell [fɔːˈtel] *vt* (*pt & pp* foretold) prédire.

forethought ['fɔːθɔːt] *n* prévoyance *f*.

forever [fəˈrevər] *adv* (*for always*) pour toujours; (*continually*) sans cesse.

forewarn [fɔːˈwɔːn] *vt* avertir.

foreword ['fɔːwɜːd] *n* avant-propos *m inv*.

forfeit ['fɔːfɪt] *vt* (*lose*) perdre; − *n* (*penalty*) peine *f*; (*in game*) gage *m*.

forg/e [fɔːdʒ] **1** *vt* (*signature, money*) contrefaire; (*document*) falsifier. **2** *vt* (*friendship, bond*) forger. **3** *vi* **to f. ahead** (*progress*) aller de l'avant. **4** *vt* (*metal*) forger; − *n* forge *f*. ◆**—er** *n* (*of banknotes etc*) faussaire *m*. ◆**forgery** *n* faux *m*, contrefaçon *f*.

forget [fə'get] *vt* (*pt* **forgot**, *pp* **forgotten**, *pres p* **forgetting**) oublier (**to do** de faire); **f. it!** *Fam* (*when thanked*) pas de quoi!; (*it doesn't matter*) peu importe!; **to f. oneself** s'oublier; − *vi* oublier; **to f. about** oublier. ◆**f.-me-not** *n Bot* myosotis *m*. ◆**forgetful** *a* **to be f. (of)** oublier, être oublieux (de). ◆**forgetfulness** *n* manque *m* de mémoire; (*carelessness*) négligence *f*; **in a moment of f.** dans un moment d'oubli.

forgiv/e [fə'gɪv] *vt* (*pt* **forgave**, *pp* **forgiven**) pardonner (**s.o. sth** qch à qn). ◆**—ing** *a* indulgent. ◆**forgiveness** *n* pardon *m*; (*compassion*) clémence *f*.

forgo [fɔː'gəʊ] *vt* (*pp* **forgone**) renoncer à.

fork [fɔːk] *n* **1** (*for eating*) fourchette *f*; (*for garden etc*) fourche *f*. **2** *vi* (*of road*) bifurquer; **to f. left** (*in vehicle*) prendre à gauche; − *n* bifurcation *f*, fourche *f*. **3** *vt* **to f. out** (*money*) *Fam* allonger; − *vi* **to f. out** (*pay*) *Fam* casquer. ◆**—ed** *a* fourchu. ◆**forklift truck** *n* chariot *m* élévateur.

forlorn [fə'lɔːn] *a* (*forsaken*) abandonné; (*unhappy*) triste, affligé.

form [fɔːm] *n* (*shape, type, style*) forme *f*; (*document*) formulaire *m*; *Sch* classe *f*; **it's good f.** c'est ce qui se fait; **in the f. of** en forme de; **a f. of speech** une façon de parler; **on f., in good f.** en (pleine) forme; − *vt* (*group, character etc*) former; (*clay*) façonner; (*habit*) contracter; (*an opinion*) se former; (*constitute*) constituer, former; **to f. part of** faire partie de; − *vi* (*appear*) se former. ◆**for'mation** *n* formation *f*. ◆**formative** *a* formateur.

formal ['fɔːm(ə)l] *a* (*person, tone etc*) cérémonieux; (*stuffy*) *Pej* compassé; (*official*) officiel; (*in due form*) en bonne et due forme; (*denial, structure, logic*) formel; (*resemblance*) extérieur; **f. dress** tenue *f* ou habit *m* de cérémonie; **f. education** éducation *f* scolaire. ◆**for'mality** *n* cérémonie *f*; (*requirement*) formalité *f*. ◆**formally** *adv* (*to declare etc*) officiellement; **f. dressed** en tenue de cérémonie.

format ['fɔːmæt] *n* format *m*.

former ['fɔːmər] **1** *a* (*previous*) ancien; (*situation*) antérieur; **her f. husband** son ex-mari *m*; **in f. days** autrefois. **2** *a* (*of two*) premier; − *pron* **the f.** celui-là, celle-là, le premier, la première. ◆**—ly** *adv* autrefois.

formidable ['fɔːmɪdəb(ə)l] *a* effroyable, terrible.

formula ['fɔːmjʊlə] *n* **1** (*pl* **-as** *or* **-ae** [-iː]) formule *f*. **2** (*pl* **-as**) (*baby's feed*) *Am* mélange *m* lacté. ◆**formulate** *vt* formuler. ◆**formu'lation** *n* formulation *f*.

forsake [fə'seɪk] *vt* (*pt* **forsook**, *pp* **forsaken**) abandonner.

fort [fɔːt] *n Hist Mil* fort *m*; **to hold the f.** (*in s.o.'s absence*) *Fam* prendre la relève.

forte ['fɔːteɪ, *Am* fɔːt] *n* (*strong point*) fort *m*.

forth [fɔːθ] *adv* en avant; **from this day f.** désormais; **and so f.** et ainsi de suite.

forthcoming [fɔːθ'kʌmɪŋ] *a* **1** (*event*) à venir; (*book, film*) qui va sortir; **my f. book** mon prochain livre. **2** (*available*) disponible. **3** (*open*) communicatif; (*helpful*) serviable.

forthright ['fɔːθraɪt] *a* direct, franc.

forthwith [fɔːθ'wɪθ] *adv* sur-le-champ.

fortieth ['fɔːtɪəθ] *a* & *n* quarantième (*mf*).

fortify ['fɔːtɪfaɪ] *vt* (*strengthen*) fortifier; **to f. s.o.** (*of food, drink*) réconforter qn, remonter qn. ◆**fortifi'cation** *n* fortification *f*.

fortitude ['fɔːtɪtjuːd] *n* courage *m* (moral).

fortnight ['fɔːtnaɪt] *n* quinze jours *mpl*, quinzaine *f*. ◆**—ly** *adv* bimensuel; − *adv* tous les quinze jours.

fortress ['fɔːtrɪs] *n* forteresse *f*.

fortuitous [fɔː'tjuːɪtəs] *a* fortuit.

fortunate ['fɔːtʃənɪt] *a* (*choice, event etc*) heureux; **to be f.** (*of person*) avoir de la chance; **it's f. (for her) that** c'est heureux (pour elle) que. ◆**—ly** *adv* heureusement.

fortune ['fɔːtʃuːn] *n* (*wealth*) fortune *f*; (*luck*) chance *f*; (*chance*) sort *m*, hasard *m*, fortune *f*; **to have the good f. to** avoir la chance *ou* le bonheur de; **to tell s.o.'s f.** dire la bonne aventure à qn; **to make one's f.** faire fortune. ◆**f.-teller** *n* diseur, -euse *mf* de bonne aventure.

forty ['fɔːtɪ] *a* & *n* quarante (*m*).

forum ['fɔːrəm] *n* forum *m*.

forward ['fɔːwəd] *adv* **forward(s)** en avant; **to go f.** avancer; **from this time f.** désormais; − *a* (*movement*) en avant; (*gears*) *Aut* avant *inv*; (*child*) *Fig* précoce; (*pert*) effronté; − *n Fb* avant *m*; − *vt* (*letter*) faire suivre; (*goods*) expédier. ◆**—ness** *n* précocité *f*; effronterie *f*. ◆**forward-looking** *a* tourné vers l'avenir.

fossil ['fɒs(ə)l] *n* & *a* fossile (*m*).

foster ['fɒstər] **1** *vt* encourager; (*hope*) nourrir. **2** *vt* (*child*) élever; − *a* (*child, family*) adoptif.

fought [fɔːt] *see* **fight.**

foul [faʊl] **1** *a* (**-er, -est**) infect; (*air*) vicié; (*breath*) fétide; (*language*) grossier; (*action, place*) immonde; **to be f.-mouthed** avoir un langage grossier. **2** *n Sp* coup *m* irrégulier; *Fb* faute *f*; − *a* **f. play** *Sp* jeu *m* irrégulier; *Jur* acte *m* criminel. **3** *vt* **to f. (up)** salir; (*air*) vicier; (*drain*) encrasser; **to f. up** (*life, plans*) *Fam* gâcher. ◆**f.-up** *n* (*in system*) *Fam* raté *m*.

found[1] [faʊnd] *see* **find.**

found[2] [faʊnd] *vt* (*town, opinion etc*) fonder (**on** sur). ◆**—er**[1] *n* fondateur, -trice *mf*. ◆**foun'dation** *n* fondation *f*; (*basis*) *Fig* base *f*, fondement *m*; **without f.** sans fondement; **f. cream** fond *m* de teint.

founder[2] ['faʊndər] *vi* (*of ship*) sombrer.

foundry ['faʊndri] *n* fonderie *f*.

fountain ['faʊntin] *n* fontaine *f*; **f. pen** stylo(-plume) *m*.

four [fɔːr] *a & n* quatre (*m*); **on all fours** à quatre pattes; **the Big F.** *Pol* les quatre Grands; **f.-letter word** = mot *m* de cinq lettres. ◆**fourfold** *a* quadruple; − *adv* au quadruple. ◆**foursome** *n* deux couples *mpl.* ◆**four'teen** *a & n* quatorze (*m*). ◆**fourth** *a & n* quatrième (*mf*).

fowl [faʊl] *n* (*hens*) volaille *f*; **a f.** une volaille.

fox [fɒks] **1** *n* renard *m*. **2** *vt* (*puzzle*) mystifier; (*trick*) tromper. ◆**foxy** *a* (*sly*) rusé, futé.

foxglove ['fɒksglʌv] *n Bot* digitale *f*.

foyer ['fɔɪeɪ] *n Th* foyer *m*; (*in hotel*) hall *m*.

fraction ['frækʃ(ə)n] *n* fraction *f*. ◆**fractionally** *adv* un tout petit peu.

fractious ['frækʃəs] *a* grincheux.

fracture ['fræktʃər] *n* fracture *f*; − *vt* fracturer; **to f. one's leg/***etc* se fracturer la jambe/*etc*; − *vi* se fracturer.

fragile ['frædʒaɪl, *Am* 'frædʒ(ə)l] *a* fragile. ◆**fra'gility** *n* fragilité *f*.

fragment ['frægmənt] *n* fragment *m*, morceau *m*. ◆**frag'mented** *a*, ◆**fragmentary** *a* fragmentaire.

fragrant ['freɪɡrənt] *a* parfumé. ◆**fragrance** *n* parfum *m*.

frail [freɪl] *a* (**-er, -est**) (*person*) frêle, fragile; (*hope, health*) fragile. ◆**frailty** *n* fragilité *f*.

frame [freɪm] **1** *n* (*of person, building*) charpente *f*; (*of picture, bicycle*) cadre *m*; (*of window, car*) châssis *m*; (*of spectacles*) monture *f*; **f. of mind** humeur *f*; − *vt* (*picture*) encadrer; (*proposals etc*) *Fig*

formuler. **2** *vt* **to f. s.o.** *Fam* monter un coup contre qn. ◆**f.-up** *n Fam* coup *m* monté. ◆**framework** *n* structure *f*; **(with)in the f. of** (*context*) dans le cadre de.

franc [fræŋk] *n* franc *m*.

France [frɑːns] *n* France *f*.

franchise ['fræntʃaɪz] *n* **1** *Pol* droit *m* de vote. **2** (*right to sell product*) *Com* franchise *f*.

Franco- ['fræŋkəʊ] *pref* franco-.

frank [fræŋk] **1** *a* (**-er, -est**) (*honest*) franc. **2** *vt* (*letter*) affranchir. ◆**—ly** *adv* franchement. ◆**—ness** *n* franchise *f*.

frankfurter ['fræŋkfɜːtər] *n* saucisse *f* de Francfort.

frantic ['fræntɪk] *a* (*activity, shout*) frénétique; (*rush, desire*) effréné; (*person*) hors de soi; **f. with joy** fou de joie. ◆**frantically** *adv* comme un fou.

fraternal [frə'tɜːn(ə)l] *a* fraternel. ◆**fraternity** *n* (*bond*) fraternité *f*; (*society*) & *Univ Am* confrérie *f*. ◆**fraternize** ['frætənaɪz] *vi* fraterniser (**with** avec).

fraud [frɔːd] *n* **1** *Jur* fraude *f*. **2** (*person*) imposteur *m*. ◆**fraudulent** *a* frauduleux.

fraught [frɔːt] *a* **f. with** plein de, chargé de; **to be f.** (*of situation*) être tendu; (*of person*) *Fam* être contrarié.

fray [freɪ] **1** *vt* (*garment*) effilocher; (*rope*) user; − *vi* s'effilocher; s'user. **2** *n* (*fight*) rixe *f*. ◆**—ed** *a* (*nerves*) *Fig* tendu.

freak [friːk] *n* (*person*) phénomène *m*, monstre *m*; **a jazz/***etc* **f.** *Fam* un(e) fana de jazz/*etc*; − *a* (*result, weather etc*) anormal. ◆**freakish** *a* anormal.

freckle ['frek(ə)l] *n* tache *f* de rousseur. ◆**freckled** *a* couvert de taches de rousseur.

free [friː] *a* (**freer, freest**) (*at liberty, not occupied*) libre; (*gratis*) gratuit; (*lavish*) généreux (**with** de); **to get f.** se libérer; **f. to do** libre de faire; **to let s.o. go f.** relâcher qn; **f. of charge** gratuit; **f. of** (*without*) sans; **f. of s.o.** (*rid of*) débarrassé de qn; **to have a f. hand** *Fig* avoir carte blanche (**to do** pour faire); **f. and easy** décontracté; **f. trade** libre-échange *m*; **f. speech** liberté *f* d'expression; **f. kick** *Fb* coup *m* franc; **f.-range egg** œuf *m* de ferme; − *adv* **f. (of charge)** gratuitement; − *vt* (*pt & pp* **freed**) (*prisoner etc*) libérer; (*trapped person, road*) dégager; (*country*) affranchir, libérer; (*untie*) détacher. ◆**Freefone**® *Tel* = numéro *m* vert. ◆**free-for-'all** *n* mêlée *f* générale. ◆**freehold** *n* propriété *f* foncière libre. ◆**freelance** *a* indépendant; − *n* collaborateur, -trice *mf* indépendant(e). ◆**freeloader** n (*sponger*) *Am* parasite m. ◆**Freemason** n franc-maçon m. ◆**Freemasonry** n franc-maçonnerie f. ◆**freestyle** n *Swimming* nage f libre. ◆**free'thinker** n libre penseur, -euse mf. ◆**freeway** n *Am* autoroute f.

freedom ['friːdəm] n liberté f; f. **from** (*worry, responsibility*) absence f de.

freely ['friːli] adv (*to speak, circulate etc*) librement; (*to give*) libéralement.

freez/e [friːz] vi (*pt froze, pp frozen*) geler; (*of smile*) *Fig* se figer; *Culin* se congeler; **to f. to death** mourir de froid; **to f. up** *or* **over** geler; (*of windscreen*) se givrer; – vt *Culin* congeler, surgeler; (*credits, river*) geler; (*prices, wages*) bloquer; **frozen food** surgelés mpl; – n *Met* gel m; (*of prices etc*) blocage m. ◆**—ing** a (*weather etc*) glacial; (*hands, person*) gelé; **it's f.** on gèle; – n **below f.** au-dessous de zéro. ◆**—er** n (*deep-freeze*) congélateur m; (*in fridge*) freezer m.

freight [freit] n (*goods, price*) fret m; (*transport*) transport m; **f. train** *Am* train m de marchandises; – vt (*ship*) affréter. ◆**—er** n (*ship*) cargo m.

French [frentʃ] a français; (*teacher*) de français; (*embassy*) de France; **F. fries** *Am* frites fpl; **the F.** les Français mpl; – n (*language*) français m. ◆**Frenchman** n (*pl -men*) Français m. ◆**French-speaking** a francophone. ◆**Frenchwoman** n (*pl -women*) Française f.

frenzy ['frenzi] n frénésie f. ◆**frenzied** a (*shouts etc*) frénétique; (*person*) effréné; (*attack*) violent.

frequent ['friːkwənt] a fréquent; **f. visitor** habitué, -ée mf (**to** de); – [fri'kwent] vt fréquenter. ◆**frequency** n fréquence f. ◆**frequently** adv fréquemment.

fresco ['freskəu] n (*pl -oes or -os*) fresque f. **fresh** [freʃ] 1 a (*-er, -est*) frais; (*new*) nouveau; (*impudent*) *Fam* culotté; **to get some f. air** prendre le frais; **f. water** eau f douce. 2 adv **f. from** fraîchement arrivé de; **f. out of, f. from** (*university*) frais émoulu de. ◆**freshen** 1 vi (*of wind*) fraîchir. 2 vi **to f. up** faire un brin de toilette; – vt **to f. up** (*house etc*) retaper; **to f. s.o. up** (*of bath*) rafraîchir qn. ◆**freshener** n **air f.** désodorisant m. ◆**freshman** n (*pl -men*) étudiant, -ante mf de première année. ◆**freshness** n fraîcheur f; (*cheek*) *Fam* culot m.

fret [fret] vi (*-tt-*) (*worry*) se faire du souci, s'en faire; (*of baby*) pleurer. ◆**fretful** a (*baby etc*) grognon.

friar ['fraiər] n frère m, moine m.

friction ['frikʃ(ə)n] n friction f.

Friday ['fraidi] n vendredi m.

fridge [fridʒ] n *Fam* frigo m.

fried [fraid] pt & pp of **fry 1**; – a (*fish etc*) frit; **f. egg** œuf m sur le plat. ◆**frier** n (*pan*) friteuse f.

friend [frend] n ami, -ie mf; (*from school, work*) camarade mf; **to be friends with** être ami avec; **to make friends** se lier (**with** avec). ◆**friendly** a (*-ier, -iest*) amical; (*child, animal*) gentil, affectueux; (*advice*) gentil; **some f. advice** un conseil d'ami; **to be f. with** être ami avec. ◆**friendship** n amitié f.

frieze [friːz] n *Archit* frise f.

frigate ['frigət] n (*ship*) frégate f.

fright [frait] n peur f; (*person, hat etc*) *Fig* *Fam* horreur f; **to have a f.** avoir peur; **to give s.o. a f.** faire peur à qn. ◆**frighten** vt effrayer, faire peur à; **to f. away** *or* **off** (*animal*) effaroucher; (*person*) chasser. ◆**frightened** a effrayé; **to be f.** avoir peur (**of** de). ◆**frightening** a effrayant. ◆**frightful** a affreux. ◆**frightfully** adv (*ugly, late*) affreusement; (*kind, glad*) terriblement.

frigid ['fridʒid] a (*air, greeting etc*) froid; *Psy* frigide.

frill [fril] n *Tex* volant m; pl (*fuss*) *Fig* manières fpl, chichis mpl; (*useless embellishments*) fioritures fpl, superflu m; **no frills** (*spartan*) spartiate.

fringe [frindʒ] 1 n (*of hair, clothes etc*) frange f. 2 n (*of forest*) lisière f; **on the fringe(s) of society** en marge de la société; – a (*group, theatre*) marginal; **f. benefits** avantages mpl divers.

frisk [frisk] 1 vt (*search*) fouiller (au corps). 2 vi **to f.** (**about**) gambader. ◆**frisky** a (*-ier, -iest*) a vif.

fritter ['fritər] 1 vt **to f. away** (*waste*) gaspiller. 2 n *Culin* beignet m.

frivolous ['frivələs] a frivole. ◆**fri'volity** n frivolité f.

frizzy ['frizi] a (*hair*) crépu.

fro [frəu] adv **to go to and f.** aller et venir.

frock [frɔk] n (*dress*) robe f; (*of monk*) froc m.

frog [frɔg] n grenouille f; **a f. in one's throat** *Fig* un chat dans la gorge. ◆**frogman** n (*pl -men*) homme-grenouille m.

frolic ['frɔlik] vi (*pt & pp frolicked*) **to f.** (**about**) gambader; – npl (*capers*) ébats mpl; (*pranks*) gamineries fpl.

from [frɔm, *unstressed* frəm] prep 1 de; **a letter f.** une lettre de; **to suffer f.** souffrir de;

where are you f.? d'où êtes-vous?; **a train f.**
un train en provenance de; **to be ten metres
(away) f. the house** être à dix mètres de la
maison. **2** (*time onwards*) à partir de, dès,
depuis; **f. today (on), as f. today** à partir
d'aujourd'hui, dès aujourd'hui; **f. her childhood** dès *or* depuis son enfance. **3**
(*numbers, prices onwards*) à partir de; **f. five
francs** à partir de cinq francs. **4** (*away
from*) à; **to take/hide/borrow f.** pren-
dre/cacher/emprunter à. **5** (*out of*) dans;
sur; **to take f.** (*box*) prendre dans; (*table*)
prendre sur; **to drink f. a cup/***etc* boire dans
une tasse/*etc*; **to drink (straight) f. the
bottle** boire à (même) la bouteille. **6**
(*according to*) d'après; **f. what I saw** d'après
ce que j'ai vu. **7** (*cause*) par; **f. convic-
tion/habit/***etc* par conviction/habitude/
etc. **8** (*on the part of, on behalf of*) de la part
de; **tell her f. me** dis-lui de ma part.

front [frʌnt] *n* (*of garment, building*) devant
m; (*of boat, car*) avant *m*; (*of crowd*)
premier rang *m*; (*of book*) début *m*; *Mil Pol
Met* front *m*; (*beach*) front *m* de mer;
(*appearance*) *Fig* façade *f*; **in f. (of)** devant;
in f. (*ahead*) en avant; *Sp* en tête; **in the f.**
(*of vehicle*) à l'avant; (*of house*) devant; – *a*
(*tooth etc*) de devant; (*part, wheel, car seat*)
avant *inv*; (*row, page*) premier; (*view*) de
face; **f. door** porte *f* d'entrée; **f. line** *Mil*
front *m*; **f. room** (*lounge*) salon *m*; **f. runner**
Fig favori, -ite *mf*; **f.-wheel drive** (*on vehicle*) traction *f* avant; – *vi* **to f. on to** (*of
windows etc*) donner sur. ◆**frontage** *n*
façade *f*. ◆**frontal** *a* (*attack*) de front.

frontier [ˈfrʌntɪər] *n* frontière *f*; – *a* (*town,
post*) frontière *inv*.

frost [frɒst] *n* gel *m*, gelée *f*; (*frozen drops on
glass, grass etc*) gelée *f* blanche, givre *m*; –
vi **to f. up** (*of windscreen etc*) se givrer.
◆**frostbite** *n* gelure *f*. ◆**frostbitten** *a*
gelé. ◆**frosty** *a* (**-ier, -iest**) glacial;
(*window*) givré; **it's f.** il gèle.

frosted [ˈfrɒstɪd] *a* (*glass*) dépoli.

frosting [ˈfrɒstɪŋ] *n* (*icing*) *Culin* glaçage *m*.

froth [frɒθ] *n* mousse *f*; – *vi* mousser.
◆**frothy** *a* (**-ier, -iest**) (*beer etc*) mousseux.

frown [fraʊn] *n* froncement *m* de sourcils; –
vi froncer les sourcils; **to f. (up)on** *Fig*
désapprouver.

froze, frozen [frəʊz, ˈfrəʊz(ə)n] *see* freeze.

frugal [ˈfruːg(ə)l] *a* (*meal*) frugal; (*thrifty*)
parcimonieux. ◆**-ly** *adv* parcimonieuse-
ment.

fruit [fruːt] *n* fruit *m*; (*some*) **f.** (*one item*) un
fruit; (*more than one*) des fruits; – *a*

(*basket*) à fruits; (*drink*) aux fruits; (*salad*)
de fruits; **f. tree** arbre *m* fruitier. ◆**fruit-
cake** *n* cake *m*. ◆**fruiterer** *n* fruitier, -ière
mf. ◆**fruitful** *a* (*meeting, career etc*) fructueux, fécond. ◆**fruitless** *a* stérile.
◆**fruity** *a* (**-ier, -iest**) *a* fruité, de fruit;
(*joke*) *Fig Fam* corsé.

fruition [fruːˈɪʃ(ə)n] *n* **to come to f.** se
réaliser.

frumpish [ˈfrʌmpɪʃ] *a*, **frumpy** [ˈfrʌmpɪ] *a*
Fam (mal) fagoté.

frustrat/e [frʌˈstreɪt] *vt* (*person*) frustrer;
(*plans*) faire échouer. ◆**-ed** *a* (*mentally,
sexually*) frustré; (*effort*) vain. ◆**-ing** *a*
irritant. ◆**fru'stration** *n* frustration *f*;
(*disappointment*) déception *f*.

fry [fraɪ] **1** *vt* (faire) frire; – *vi* frire. **2** *n* small
f. menu fretin *m*. ◆**-ing** *n* friture *f*; **f. pan**
poêle *f* (à frire). ◆**-er** *n* (*pan*) friteuse *f*.

ft *abbr* (*measure*) = **foot, feet.**

fuddled [ˈfʌd(ə)ld] *a* (*drunk*) gris; (*confused*)
embrouillé.

fuddy-duddy [ˈfʌdɪdʌdɪ] *n* **he's an old
f.-duddy** *Fam* il est vieux jeu.

fudge [fʌdʒ] **1** *n* (*sweet*) caramel *m* mou. **2** *vt*
to f. the issue refuser d'aborder le
problème.

fuel [fjʊəl] *n* combustible *m*; *Aut* carburant
m; **f. (oil)** mazout *m*; – *vt* (**-ll-, *Am* -l-**)
(*stove*) alimenter; (*ship*) ravitailler (en
combustible); (*s.o.'s anger etc*) attiser.

fugitive [ˈfjuːdʒɪtɪv] *n* fugitif, -ive *mf*.

fugue [fjuːg] *n* *Mus* fugue *f*.

fulfil, *Am* **fulfill** [fʊlˈfɪl] *vt* (**-ll-**) (*ambition,
dream*) accomplir, réaliser; (*condition,
duty*) remplir; (*desire*) satisfaire; **to f.
oneself** s'épanouir. ◆**fulfilling** *a* satisfaisant. ◆**fulfilment** *n*, *Am* ◆**fulfillment**
n accomplissement *m*, réalisation *f*; (*feeling*) satisfaction *f*.

full [fʊl] *a* (**-er, -est**) plein (**of** de); (*bus, theatre, meal*) complet; (*life, day*) (bien)
rempli; (*skirt*) ample; (*hour*) entier;
(*member*) à part entière; **the f. price** le prix
fort; **to pay (the) f. fare** payer plein tarif; **to
be f. (up)** (*of person*) *Culin* n'avoir plus
faim; (*of hotel*) être complet; **the f. facts**
tous les faits; **at f. speed** à toute vitesse; **f.
name** (*on form*) nom et prénom; **f. stop**
Gram point *m*; – *adv* **to know f. well** savoir
fort bien; **f. in the face** (*to hit etc*) en pleine
figure; – *n* **in f.** (*text*) intégral; (*to publish,
read*) intégralement; (*to write one's name*)
en toutes lettres; **to the f.** (*completely*) tout
à fait. ◆**fullness** *n* (*of details*) abondance

f; (of dress) ampleur *f.* ◆**fully** *adv* entièrement; *(at least)* au moins.

full-back ['fulbæk] *n Fb* arrière *m.* ◆**f.-'grown** *a* adulte; *(foetus)* arrivé à terme. ◆**f.-'length** *a* *(film)* de long métrage; *(portrait)* en pied; *(dress)* long. ◆**f.-'scale** *a* *(model etc)* grandeur nature *inv*; *(operation etc) Fig* de grande envergure. ◆**f.-'sized** *a* *(model)* grandeur nature *inv.* ◆**f.-'time** *a & adv* à plein temps.

fully-fledged, *Am* **full-fledged** [ful(ɪ)'fledʒd] *a (engineer etc)* diplômé; *(member)* à part entière. ◆**f.-formed** *a (baby etc)* formé. ◆**f.-grown** *a* = **full-grown.**

fulsome ['fulsəm] *a (praise etc)* excessif.

fumble ['fʌmb(ə)l] *vi* to f. *(about) (grope)* tâtonner; *(search)* fouiller (for pour trouver); to f. *(about)* with tripoter.

fume [fjuːm] *vi (give off fumes)* fumer; *(of person) Fig* rager; – *npl* émanations *fpl*; *(from car exhaust)* gaz *m inv.*

fumigate ['fjuːmɪgeɪt] *vt* désinfecter (par fumigation).

fun [fʌn] *n* amusement *m*; to be (good) f. être très amusant; to have (some) f. s'amuser; to make f. of, poke f. at se moquer de; for f., for the f. of it pour le plaisir.

function ['fʌŋkʃ(ə)n] **1** *n (role, duty) & Math* fonction *f*; *(meeting)* réunion *f*; *(ceremony)* cérémonie *f* (publique). **2** *vi (work)* fonctionner. ◆**functional** *a* fonctionnel.

fund [fʌnd] *n (for pension, relief etc) Fin* caisse *f*; *(of knowledge etc) Fig* fond *m*; *pl (money resources)* fonds *mpl*; *(for special purpose)* crédits *mpl*; – *vt (with money)* fournir des fonds *or* des crédits à.

fundamental [fʌndə'ment(ə)l] *a* fondamental; – *npl* principes *mpl* essentiels.

funeral ['fjuːnərəl] *n* enterrement *m*; *(grandiose)* funérailles *fpl*; – *a (service, march)* funèbre; *(expenses, parlour)* funéraire.

funfair ['fʌnfeər] *n* fête *f* foraine; *(larger)* parc *m* d'attractions.

fungus, *pl* **-gi** ['fʌŋgəs, -gaɪ] *n Bot* champignon *m*; *(mould)* moisissure *f.*

funicular [fjuː'nɪkjʊlər] *n* funiculaire *m.*

funk [fʌŋk] *n* to be in a f. *(afraid) Fam* avoir la frousse; *(depressed, sulking) Am Fam* faire la gueule.

funnel ['fʌn(ə)l] *n* **1** *(of ship)* cheminée *f.* **2** *(tube for pouring)* entonnoir *m.*

funny ['fʌnɪ] *a* (**-ier, -iest**) *(amusing)* drôle; *(strange)* bizarre; **a f. idea** une drôle d'idée; there's some f. business going on il y a quelque chose de louche; to feel f. ne pas se

sentir très bien. ◆**funnily** *adv* drôlement; bizarrement; **f. enough** ... chose bizarre ....

fur [fɜːr] **1** *n (of animal)* poil *m*, pelage *m*; *(for wearing etc)* fourrure *f.* **2** *n (in kettle)* dépôt *m* (de tartre); – *vi* (**-rr-**) to f. (up) s'entartrer.

furious ['fjʊərɪəs] *a (violent, angry)* furieux (with, at contre); *(pace, speed)* fou. ◆**—ly** *adv* furieusement; *(to drive, rush)* à une allure folle.

furnace ['fɜːnɪs] *n (forge)* fourneau *m*; *(room etc) Fig* fournaise *f.*

furnish ['fɜːnɪʃ] *vt* **1** *(room)* meubler. **2** *(supply)* fournir (s.o. with sth qch à qn). ◆**—ings** *npl* ameublement *m.*

furniture ['fɜːnɪtʃər] *n* meubles *mpl*; **a piece of f.** un meuble.

furrier ['fʌrɪər] *n* fourreur *m.*

furrow ['fʌrəʊ] *n (on brow) & Agr* sillon *m.*

furry ['fɜːrɪ] *a (animal)* à poil; *(toy)* en peluche.

further ['fɜːðər] **1** *adv & a* = **farther. 2** *adv (more)* davantage, plus; *(besides)* en outre; – *a (additional)* supplémentaire; *(education)* post-scolaire; **f. details** de plus amples détails; **a f. case/etc** *(another)* un autre cas/etc; **without f. delay** sans plus attendre. **3** *vt (cause, research etc)* promouvoir. ◆**furthermore** *adv* en outre. ◆**furthest** *a & adv* = **farthest.**

furtive ['fɜːtɪv] *a* furtif.

fury ['fjʊərɪ] *n (violence, anger)* fureur *f.*

fuse [fjuːz] **1** *vti (melt) Tech* fondre; *Fig* fusionner. **2** *vt* to f. the lights *etc* faire sauter les plombs; – *vi* the lights *etc* have fused les plombs ont sauté; – *n (wire) El* fusible *m*, plomb *m.* **3** *n (of bomb)* amorce *f.* ◆**fused** *a (plug) El* avec fusible incorporé. ◆**fusion** *n (union) & Phys Biol* fusion *f.*

fuselage ['fjuːzəlɑːʒ] *n Av* fuselage *m.*

fuss [fʌs] *n* façons *fpl*, histoires *fpl*, chichis *mpl*; *(noise)* agitation *f*; **what a (lot of) f.!** quelle histoire! to kick up *or* make a f. faire des histoires; to make a f. of être aux petits soins pour; – *vi* faire des chichis; *(worry)* se tracasser (about pour); *(rush about)* s'agiter; to f. over s.o. être aux petits soins pour qn. ◆**fusspot** *n, Am* ◆**fussbudget** *n Fam* enquiquineur, -euse *mf.* ◆**fussy** *a* (**-ier, -iest**) méticuleux; *(difficult)* difficile (about sur).

fusty ['fʌstɪ] *a* (**-ier, -iest**) *(smell)* de renfermé.

futile ['fjuːtaɪl, *Am* 'fjuːt(ə)l] *a* futile, vain. ◆**fu'tility** *n* futilité *f.*

future ['fjuːtʃər] n avenir m; Gram futur m; **in f.** (from now on) à l'avenir; **in the f.** (one day) un jour (futur); − a futur, à venir; (date) ultérieur.

fuzz [fʌz] n **1** (down) Fam duvet m. **2 the f.** (police) Sl les flics mpl. ◆**fuzzy** a (-ier, -iest) (hair) crépu; (picture, idea) flou.

G

G, g [dʒiː] n G, g m. ◆**G.-string** n (cloth) cache-sexe m inv.

gab [gæb] n **to have the gift of the g.** Fam avoir du bagou(t).

gabardine [gæbəˈdiːn] n (material, coat) gabardine f.

gabble ['gæb(ə)l] vi (chatter) jacasser; (indistinctly) bredouiller; − n baragouin m.

gable ['geɪb(ə)l] n Archit pignon m.

gad ['gæd] vi (-dd-) **to g. about** se balader, vadrouiller.

gadget ['gædʒɪt] n gadget m.

Gaelic ['geɪlɪk, 'gælɪk] a & n gaélique (m).

gaffe [gæf] n (blunder) gaffe f, bévue f.

gag [gæg] **1** n (over mouth) bâillon m; − vt (-gg-) (victim, press etc) bâillonner. **2** n (joke) plaisanterie f; Cin Th gag m. **3** vi (-gg-) (choke) Am s'étouffer (**on** avec).

gaggle ['gæg(ə)l] n (of geese) troupeau m.

gaiety ['geɪtɪ] n gaieté f; (of colour) éclat m. ◆**gaily** adv gaiement.

gain [geɪn] vt (obtain, win) gagner; (objective) atteindre; (experience, reputation) acquérir; (popularity) gagner en; **to g. speed/weight** prendre de la vitesse/du poids; − vi (of watch) avancer; **to g. in strength** gagner en force; **to g. on** (catch up with) rattraper; − n (increase) augmentation f (**in** de); (profit) Com bénéfice m, gain m; Fig avantage m. ◆**gainful** a profitable; (employment) rémunéré.

gainsay [geɪn'seɪ] vt (pt & pp gainsaid [-sed]) (person) contredire; (facts) nier.

gait [geɪt] n (walk) démarche f.

gala ['gɑːlə, 'geɪlə] n gala m, fête f; **swimming g.** concours m de natation.

galaxy ['gæləksɪ] n galaxie f.

gale [geɪl] n grand vent m, rafale f (de vent).

gall [gɔːl] **1** n Med bile f; (bitterness) Fig fiel m; (cheek) Fam effronterie f; **g. bladder** vésicule f biliaire. **2** vt (vex) blesser, froisser.

gallant ['gælənt] a (brave) courageux; (splendid) magnifique; (chivalrous) galant. ◆**gallantry** n (bravery) courage m.

galleon ['gælɪən] n (ship) Hist galion m.

gallery ['gælərɪ] n (room etc) galerie f; (for public, press) tribune f; **art g.** (private) galerie f d'art; (public) musée m d'art.

galley ['gælɪ] n (ship) Hist galère f; (kitchen) Nau Av cuisine f.

Gallic ['gælɪk] a (French) français. ◆**gallicism** n (word etc) gallicisme m.

gallivant ['gælɪvænt] vi **to g.** (**about**) Fam courir, vadrouiller.

gallon ['gælən] n gallon m (Br = 4,5 litres; Am = 3,8 litres).

gallop ['gæləp] n galop m; − vi galoper; **to g. away** (rush) Fig partir au galop or en vitesse. ◆**—ing** a (inflation etc) Fig galopant.

gallows ['gæləuz] npl potence f.

gallstone ['gɔːlstəun] n Med calcul m biliaire.

galore [gə'lɔːr] adv à gogo, en abondance.

galoshes [gə'lɒʃɪz] npl (shoes) caoutchoucs mpl.

galvanize ['gælvənaɪz] vt (metal) & Fig galvaniser.

gambit ['gæmbɪt] n **opening g.** Fig manœuvre f stratégique.

gambl/e ['gæmb(ə)l] vi jouer (**on** sur, **with** avec); **to g. on** (count on) miser sur; − vt (wager) jouer; **to g.** (**away**) (lose) perdre (au jeu); − n (bet) & Fig coup m risqué. ◆**—ing** n jeu m. ◆**—er** n joueur, -euse mf.

game [geɪm] **1** n jeu m; (of football, cricket etc) match m; (of tennis, chess, cards) partie f; **to have a g. of** jouer un match de; **games** Sch le sport; **games teacher** professeur m d'éducation physique. **2** n (animals, birds) gibier m; **to be fair g. for** Fig être une proie idéale pour. **3** a (brave) courageux; **g. for** (willing) prêt à. **4** a (leg) estropié; **to have a g. leg** être boiteux. ◆**gamekeeper** n garde-chasse m.

gammon ['gæmən] n (ham) jambon m fumé.

gammy ['gæmɪ] a Fam = game 4.

gamut ['gæmət] n Mus & Fig gamme f.

gang [gæŋ] n bande f; (of workers) équipe f; (of crooks) gang m; − vi **to g. up on** or

against se liguer contre. ◆**gangster** n gangster m.

gangling ['gæŋglɪŋ] a dégingandé.

gangrene ['gæŋgriːn] n gangrène f.

gangway ['gæŋweɪ] n passage m; (in train) couloir m; (in bus, cinema, theatre) allée f; (footbridge) Av Nau passerelle f; g.! dégagez!

gaol [dʒeɪl] n & vt = jail.

gap [gæp] n (empty space) trou m, vide m; (breach) trou m; (in time) intervalle m; (in knowledge) lacune f; the g. between (divergence) l'écart m entre.

gap/e [geɪp] vi (stare) rester or être bouche bée; to g. at regarder bouche bée. ◆—ing a (chasm, wound) béant.

garage ['gærɑː(d)ʒ, 'gærɪdʒ, Am gə'rɑːʒ] n garage m; — vt mettre au garage.

garb [gɑːb] n (clothes) costume m.

garbage ['gɑːbɪdʒ] n ordures fpl; g. can poubelle f; g. collector or man Am éboueur m; g. truck Am camion-benne m.

garble ['gɑːb(ə)l] vt (words etc) déformer, embrouiller.

garden ['gɑːd(ə)n] n jardin m; the gardens (park) le parc; g. centre (store) jardinerie f; (nursery) pépinière f; g. party garden-party f; g. produce produits mpl maraîchers; — vi to be gardening jardiner. ◆—ing n jardinage m. ◆—er n jardinier, -ière mf.

gargle ['gɑːg(ə)l] vi se gargariser; — n gargarisme m.

gargoyle ['gɑːgɔɪl] n Archit gargouille f.

garish ['geərɪʃ, Am 'gærɪʃ] a voyant, criard.

garland ['gɑːlənd] n guirlande f.

garlic ['gɑːlɪk] n ail m; g. sausage saucisson m à l'ail.

garment ['gɑːmənt] n vêtement m.

garnish ['gɑːnɪʃ] vt garnir (with de); — n garniture f.

garret ['gærət] n mansarde f.

garrison ['gærɪsən] n Mil garnison f.

garrulous ['gærələs] a (talkative) loquace.

garter ['gɑːtər] n (round leg) jarretière f; (attached to belt) Am jarretelle f; (for men) fixe-chaussette m.

gas [gæs] 1 n gaz m inv; (gasoline) Am essence f; Med Fam anesthésie f au masque; — a (meter, mask, chamber) à gaz; (pipe) de gaz; (industry) du gaz; (heating) au gaz; g. fire or heater appareil m de chauffage à gaz; g. station Am poste m d'essence; g. stove (portable) réchaud m à gaz; (large) cuisinière f à gaz; — vt (-ss-) (poison) asphyxier; Mil gazer. 2 vi (-ss-) (talk) Fam bavarder; — n for a g. (fun) Am Fam pour rire. ◆**gasbag** n Fam commère

f. ◆**gasman** n (pl -men) employé m du gaz. ◆**gasoline** n Am essence f. ◆**gasworks** n usine f à gaz.

gash [gæʃ] n entaille f; — vt entailler.

gasp [gɑːsp] 1 vi to g. (for breath) haleter; — n halètement m. 2 vi to g. with or in surprise/etc avoir le souffle coupé de surprise/etc; — vt (say gasping) hoqueter; — n a g. of surprise/etc un hoquet de surprise/etc.

gassy ['gæsɪ] a (-ier, -iest) (drink) gazeux.

gastric ['gæstrɪk] a (juices, ulcer) gastrique. ◆**ga'stronomy** n gastronomie f.

gate [geɪt] n (of castle, airport etc) porte f; (at level crossing, field etc) barrière f; (metal) grille f; (in Paris Metro) portillon m. ◆**gateway** n the g. to success/etc le chemin du succès/etc.

gâteau, pl **-eaux** ['gætəʊ, -əʊz] n Culin gros gâteau m à la crème.

gatecrash ['geɪtkræʃ] vti to g. (a party) s'inviter de force (à une réception).

gather ['gæðər] vt (people, objects) rassembler; (pick up) ramasser; (flowers) cueillir; (information) recueillir; (understand) comprendre; (skirt, material) froncer; I g. that ... (infer) je crois comprendre que ...; to g. speed prendre de la vitesse; to g. in (crops, harvest) rentrer; (essays, exam papers) ramasser; to g. up (strength) rassembler; (papers) ramasser; — vi (of people) se rassembler, s'assembler, s'amasser; (of clouds) se former; (of dust) s'accumuler; to g. round s'approcher; to g. round s.o. entourer qn. ◆—ing n (group) réunion f.

gaudy ['gɔːdɪ] a (-ier, -iest) voyant, criard.

gauge [geɪdʒ] n (instrument) jauge f, indicateur m; Rail écartement m; to be a g. of sth Fig permettre de jauger qch; — vt (measure) mesurer; (estimate) évaluer, jauger.

gaunt [gɔːnt] a (thin) décharné.

gauntlet ['gɔːntlɪt] n gant m; to run the g. of Fig essuyer (le feu de).

gauze [gɔːz] n (fabric) gaze f.

gave [geɪv] see give.

gawk [gɔːk] vi to g. (at) regarder bouche bée.

gawp [gɔːp] vi = gawk.

gay [geɪ] a (-er, -est) 1 (cheerful) gai, joyeux; (colour) vif, gai. 2 Fam homo(sexuel), gay inv.

gaze [geɪz] n regard m (fixe); — vi regarder; to g. at regarder (fixement).

gazelle [gə'zel] n (animal) gazelle f.

gazette [gə'zet] n journal m officiel.

GB [dʒiːˈbiː] *abbr* (*Great Britain*) Grande-Bretagne *f*.

GCSE [dʒiːsiːesˈiː] *abbr* (*General Certificate of Secondary Education*) = baccalauréat *m*.

gear [gɪər] **1** *n* matériel *m*, équipement *m*; (*belongings*) affaires *fpl*; (*clothes*) *Fam* vêtements *mpl* (à la mode); (*toothed wheels*) *Tech* engrenage *m*; (*speed*) *Aut* vitesse *f*; **in** g. *Aut* en prise; **not in** g. *Aut* au point mort; g. **lever**, *Am* g. **shift** levier *m* de (changement de) vitesse. **2** *vt* (*adapt*) adapter (**to** à); **geared (up) to do** prêt à faire; **to** g. **oneself up for** se préparer pour. ◆**gearbox** *n* boîte *f* de vitesses.

gee! [dʒiː] *int Am Fam* ça alors!

geese [giːs] *see* **goose**.

geezer [ˈgiːzər] *n Hum Sl* type *m*.

Geiger counter [ˈgaɪɡəkaʊntər] *n* compteur *m* Geiger.

gel [dʒel] *n* (*substance*) gel *m*.

gelatin(e) [ˈdʒelətiːn, *Am* -tən] *n* gélatine *f*.

gelignite [ˈdʒelɪɡnaɪt] *n* dynamite *f* (au nitrate de soude).

gem [dʒem] *n* pierre *f* précieuse; (*person or thing of value*) *Fig* perle *f*; (*error*) *Iron* perle *f*.

Gemini [ˈdʒemɪnaɪ] *n* (*sign*) les Gémeaux *mpl*.

gen [dʒen] *n* (*information*) *Sl* coordonnées *fpl*; – *vi* (-nn-) **to** g. **up on** *Sl* se rancarder sur.

gender [ˈdʒendər] *n Gram* genre *m*; (*of person*) sexe *m*.

gene [dʒiːn] *n Biol* gène *m*.

genealogy [dʒiːnɪˈælədʒɪ] *n* généalogie *f*.

general [ˈdʒenərəl] **1** *a* général; **in** g. en général; **the** g. **public** le (grand) public; **for** g. **use** à l'usage du public; **a** g. **favourite** aimé *or* apprécié de tous; g. **delivery** *Am* poste *f* restante; **to be** g. (*widespread*) être très répandu. **2** *n* (*officer*) *Mil* général *m*. ◆**gene'rality** *n* généralité *f*. ◆**generali-'zation** *n* généralisation *f*. ◆**generalize** *vti* généraliser. ◆**generally** *adv* généralement; g. **speaking** en général, généralement parlant.

generate [ˈdʒenəreɪt] *vt* (*heat*) produire; (*fear, hope etc*) & *Ling* engendrer. ◆**gene-'ration** *n* génération *f*; **the** g. **of** (*heat*) la production de; g. **gap** conflit *m* des générations. ◆**generator** *n El* groupe *m* électrogène, génératrice *f*.

generous [ˈdʒenərəs] *a* généreux (**with** de); (*helping, meal etc*) copieux. ◆**gene'rosity** *n* générosité *f*. ◆**generously** *adv* généreusement; (*to serve s.o.*) copieusement.

genesis [ˈdʒenəsɪs] *n* genèse *f*.

genetic [dʒɪˈnetɪk] *a* génétique. ◆**genetics** *n* génétique *f*.

Geneva [dʒɪˈniːvə] *n* Genève *m or f*.

genial [ˈdʒiːnɪəl] *a* (*kind*) affable; (*cheerful*) jovial.

genie [ˈdʒiːnɪ] *n* (*goblin*) génie *m*.

genital [ˈdʒenɪt(ə)l] *a* génital; – *npl* organes *mpl* génitaux.

genius [ˈdʒiːnɪəs] *n* (*ability, person*) génie *m*; **to have a** g. **for doing/for sth** avoir le génie pour faire/de qch.

genocide [ˈdʒenəsaɪd] *n* génocide *m*.

gent [dʒent] *n Fam* monsieur *m*; **gents' shoes** *Com* chaussures *fpl* pour hommes; **the gents** *Fam* les toilettes *fpl* (pour hommes).

genteel [dʒenˈtiːl] *a Iron* distingué.

gentle [ˈdʒent(ə)l] *a* (-er, -est) (*person, sound, slope etc*) doux; (*hint, reminder*) discret; (*touch*) léger; (*pace*) mesuré; (*exercise, progress*) modéré; (*birth*) noble. ◆**gentleman** *n* (*pl* -men) monsieur *m*; (*well-bred*) gentleman *m*, monsieur *m* bien élevé. ◆**gentlemanly** *a* distingué, bien élevé. ◆**gentleness** *n* douceur *f*. ◆**gently** *adv* doucement; (*to remind*) discrètement; (*smoothly*) en douceur.

genuine [ˈdʒenjuɪn] *a* (*authentic*) véritable, authentique; (*sincere*) sincère, vrai. ◆**—ly** *adv* authentiquement; sincèrement. ◆**—ness** *n* authenticité *f*; sincérité *f*.

geography [dʒɪˈɒɡrəfɪ] *n* géographie *f*. ◆**geo'graphical** *a* géographique.

geology [dʒɪˈɒlədʒɪ] *n* géologie *f*. ◆**geo-'logical** *a* géologique. ◆**geologist** *n* géologue *mf*.

geometry [dʒɪˈɒmɪtrɪ] *n* géométrie *f*. ◆**geo'metric(al)** *a* géométrique.

geranium [dʒɪˈreɪnɪəm] *n Bot* géranium *m*.

geriatric [dʒerɪˈætrɪk] *a* (*hospital*) du troisième âge; g. **ward** service *m* de gériatrie.

germ [dʒɜːm] *n Biol & Fig* germe *m*; *Med* microbe *m*; g. **warfare** guerre *f* bactériologique.

German [ˈdʒɜːmən] *a & n* allemand, -ande (*mf*); G. **measles** *Med* rubéole *f*; G. **shepherd** (*dog*) *Am* berger *m* allemand; – *n* (*language*) allemand *m*. ◆**Ger'manic** *a* germanique.

Germany [ˈdʒɜːmənɪ] *n* Allemagne *f*; **West** G. Allemagne de l'Ouest.

germinate [ˈdʒɜːmɪneɪt] *vi Bot & Fig* germer.

gestation [dʒeˈsteɪʃ(ə)n] *n* gestation *f*.

gesture [ˈdʒestʃər] *n*, geste *m*; – *vi* **to** g. **to**

s.o. **to do** faire signe à qn de faire.
◆**ge'sticulate** vi gesticuler.
get [get] **1** vt (pt & pp **got,** pp Am **gotten,** pres
p **getting**) (obtain) obtenir, avoir; (find)
trouver; (buy) acheter, prendre; (receive)
recevoir, avoir; (catch) attraper, prendre;
(seize) prendre, saisir; (fetch) aller
chercher (qn, qch); (put) mettre; (derive)
tirer (**from** de); (understand) comprendre,
saisir; (prepare) préparer; (lead) mener;
(target) atteindre, avoir; (reputation) se
faire; (annoy) Fam ennuyer; **I have got,** Am
I have gotten j'ai; **to g. s.o. to do sth** faire
faire qch à qn; **to g. sth built/**etc faire
construire/etc qch; **to g. things going** or
started faire démarrer les choses. **2** vi (go)
aller; (arrive) arriver (**to** à); (become)
devenir, se faire; **to g. caught/run over/**etc
se faire prendre/écraser/etc; **to g. married**
se marier; **to g. dressed/washed**
s'habiller/se laver; **where have you got** or
Am **gotten to?** où en es-tu?; **you've got to**
stay (must) tu dois rester; **to g. to do**
(succeed in doing) parvenir à faire; **to g. to**
working se mettre à travailler. ■ **to g. about**
or **(a)round** vi se déplacer; (of news)
circuler; **to g. across** vt (road) traverser;
(person) faire traverser; (message) communiquer; – vi traverser; (of speaker) se
faire comprendre (**to** de); **to g. across to s.o.**
that faire comprendre à qn que; **to g. along**
vi (leave) se sauver; (manage) se débrouiller; (progress) avancer; (be on good terms)
s'entendre (**with** avec); **to g. at** vt (reach)
parvenir à, atteindre; (taunt) s'en prendre
à; **what is he getting at?** où veut-il en
venir?; **to g. away** vi (leave) partir, s'en
aller; (escape) s'échapper; **there's no**
getting away from it il faut le reconnaître,
c'est comme ça. ◆**getaway** n (escape)
fuite f; **to g. back** vt (recover) récupérer;
(replace) remettre; – vi (return) revenir,
retourner; **to g. back at, g. one's own back**
at (punish) se venger de; **g. back!** (move
back) reculez!; **to g. by** vi (pass) passer;
(manage) se débrouiller; **to g. down** vi (go
down) descendre (**from** de); – vt (bring
down) descendre (**from** de); (write) noter;
(depress) Fam déprimer; **to g. down to**
(task, work) se mettre à; **to g. in** vt (bicycle,
washing etc) rentrer; (buy) acheter;
(summon) faire venir; **to g. in a car/**etc
monter dans une voiture/etc; – vi (enter)
entrer; (come home) rentrer; (enter vehicle
or train) monter; (of plane, train) arriver;
(of candidate) Pol être élu; **to g. into** vt
entrer dans; (vehicle, train) monter dans;

(habit) prendre; **to g. into bed/a rage** se
mettre au lit/en colère; **to g. into trouble**
avoir des ennuis; **to g. off** vi (leave) partir;
(from vehicle or train) descendre (**from** de);
(escape) s'en tirer; (finish work) sortir; (be
acquitted) Jur être acquitté; – vt (remove)
enlever; (despatch) expédier; Jur faire
acquitter (qn); **to g. off a chair** se
lever d'une chaise; **to g. off doing** Fam se
dispenser de faire; **to g. on** vt (shoes,
clothes) mettre; (bus, train) monter dans; –
vi (progress) marcher, avancer; (succeed)
réussir; (enter bus or train) monter; (be on good terms)
s'entendre (**with** avec); **how are you getting**
on? comment ça va?; **to g. on to s.o.** (telephone) toucher qn, contacter qn; **to g. on**
with (task) continuer; **to g. out** vi sortir;
(from vehicle or train) descendre (**from,** of
de); **to g. out of** (obligation) échapper à;
(trouble) se tirer de; (habit) perdre; – vt
(remove) enlever; (bring out) sortir (qch),
faire sortir (qn); **to g. over** vt (road) traverser; (obstacle) surmonter; (fence)
franchir; (illness) se remettre de; (surprise)
revenir de; (ideas) communiquer; **let's g. it**
over with finissons-en; – vi (cross) traverser; **to g. round** vt (obstacle) contourner;
(person) entortiller; – vi **to g. round to**
doing en venir à faire; **to g. through** vi
(pass) passer; (finish) finir; (pass exam)
être reçu; **to g. through to s.o.** se faire
comprendre de qn; (on the telephone)
contacter qn; – vt (hole etc) passer par;
(task, meal) venir à bout de; (exam) être
reçu à; **g. me through to your boss** (on the
telephone) passe-moi ton patron; **to g.**
together vi (of people) se rassembler.
◆**g.-together** n réunion f; **to g. up** vi (rise)
se lever (**from** de); **to g. up to** (in book) en
arriver à; (mischief, trouble etc) faire; – vt
(ladder, stairs etc) monter; (party, group)
organiser; **to g. sth up** (bring up) monter
qch. ◆**g.-up** n (clothes) Fam accoutrement
m.
geyser ['giːzər] n **1** (water heater)
chauffe-eau m inv. **2** Geol geyser m.
Ghana ['gɑːnə] n Ghana m.
ghastly ['gɑːstlɪ] a (-ier, -iest) (pale) blême,
pâle; (horrible) affreux.
gherkin ['gɜːkɪn] n cornichon m.
ghetto ['getəʊ] n (pl -os) ghetto m.
ghost [gəʊst] n fantôme m; **not the g. of a**
chance pas l'ombre d'une chance; – a
(story) de fantômes; (ship) fantôme; (town)
mort. ◆—**ly** a spectral.
ghoulish ['guːlɪʃ] a morbide.

giant ['dʒaɪənt] n géant m; – a géant, gigantesque; (steps) de géant; (packet etc) Com géant.

gibberish ['dʒɪbərɪʃ] n baragouin m.

gibe [dʒaɪb] vi railler; **to g. at** railler; – n raillerie f.

giblets ['dʒɪblɪts] npl (of fowl) abats mpl.

giddy ['gɪdɪ] a (-ier, -iest) (heights) vertigineux; **to feel g.** avoir le vertige; **to make g.** donner le vertige à. ◆**giddiness** n vertige m.

gift [gɪft] n cadeau m; (talent) & Jur don m; **g. voucher** chèque-cadeau m. ◆**gifted** a doué (with de, for pour). ◆**giftwrapped** a en paquet-cadeau.

gig [gɪg] n Mus Fam engagement m, séance f.

gigantic [dʒaɪˈgæntɪk] a gigantesque.

giggle ['gɪg(ə)l] vi rire (sottement); – n petit rire m sot; **to have the giggles** avoir le fou rire.

gild [gɪld] vt dorer. ◆**gilt** a doré; – n dorure f.

gills [gɪlz] npl (of fish) ouïes fpl.

gimmick ['gɪmɪk] n (trick, object) truc m.

gin [dʒɪn] n (drink) gin m.

ginger ['dʒɪndʒər] 1 a (hair) roux. 2 n Bot Culin gingembre m; **g. beer** boisson f gazeuse au gingembre. ◆**gingerbread** n pain m d'épice.

gingerly ['dʒɪndʒəlɪ] adv avec précaution.

gipsy ['dʒɪpsɪ] n bohémien, -ienne mf; (Central European) Tsigane mf; – a (music) tsigane.

giraffe [dʒɪˈrɑːf, dʒɪˈræf] n girafe f.

girder ['gɜːdər] n (metal beam) poutre f.

girdle ['gɜːd(ə)l] n (belt) ceinture f; (corset) gaine f.

girl ['gɜːl] n (jeune) fille f; (daughter) fille f; (servant) bonne f; (sweetheart) Fam petite amie f; **English g.** jeune Anglaise f; **g. guide** éclaireuse f. ◆**girlfriend** n amie f; (of boy) petite amie f. ◆**girlish** a de (jeune) fille.

girth [gɜːθ] n (measure) circonférence f; (of waist) tour m.

gist [dʒɪst] n **to get the g. of** comprendre l'essentiel de.

give [gɪv] vt (pt gave, pp given) donner (to à); (help, support) prêter; (gesture, pleasure) faire; (a sigh) pousser; (a look) jeter; (a blow) porter; **g. me York 234** passez-moi le 234 à York; **she doesn't g. a damn** Fam elle s'en fiche; **to g. way** (yield, break) céder (to à); (collapse) s'effondrer; Aut céder la priorité (to à); – n (in fabric etc) élasticité f. ■ **to g. away** vt (prize) distribuer; (money) donner; (facts) révéler; (betray) trahir (qn);

to g. back vt (return) rendre; **to g. in** vi (surrender) céder (to à); – vt (hand in) remettre; **to g. off** vt (smell, heat) dégager; **to g. out** vt distribuer; – vi (of supplies, patience) s'épuiser; (of engine) rendre l'âme; **to g. over** vt (devote) donner, consacrer (to à); **to g. oneself over to** s'adonner à; – vi **g. over!** (stop) Fam arrête!; **to g. up** vi abandonner, renoncer; – vt abandonner, renoncer à; (seat) céder (to à); (prisoner) livrer (to à); (patient) condamner; **to g. up smoking** cesser de fumer. ◆**given** a (fixed) donné; **to be g. to doing** (prone to do) avoir l'habitude de faire; **g. your age** (in view of) étant donné votre âge; **g. that** étant donné que. ◆**giver** n donateur, -trice mf.

glacier ['glæsɪər, Am 'gleɪʃər] n glacier m.

glad [glæd] a (person) content (of, about de). ◆**gladden** vt réjouir. ◆**gladly** adv (willingly) volontiers.

glade [gleɪd] n clairière f.

gladiolus, pl -i [glædɪˈəʊləs, -aɪ] n Bot glaïeul m.

glamour ['glæmər] n (charm) enchantement m; (splendour) éclat m. ◆**glamorize** vt montrer sous un jour séduisant. ◆**glamorous** a séduisant.

glance [glɑːns] 1 n coup m d'œil; – vi jeter un coup d'œil (at à, sur). 2 vt **to g. off sth** (of bullet) ricocher sur qch.

gland [glænd] n glande f. ◆**glandular** a g. fever Med mononucléose f infectieuse.

glar/e [gleər] 1 vi **to g. at s.o.** foudroyer qn (du regard); – n regard m furieux. 2 vi (of sun) briller d'un éclat aveuglant; – n éclat m aveuglant. ◆**—ing** a (sun) aveuglant; (eyes) furieux; (injustice) flagrant; **a g. mistake** une faute grossière.

glass [glɑːs] n verre m; (mirror) miroir m, glace f; pl (spectacles) lunettes fpl; **a pane of g.** une vitre, un carreau; – a (door) vitré; (industry) du verre. ◆**glassful** n (plein) verre m.

glaze [gleɪz] vt (door) vitrer; (pottery) vernisser; (paper) glacer; – n (on pottery) vernis m; (on paper) glacé m. ◆**glazier** n vitrier m.

gleam [gliːm] n lueur f; – vi (re)luire.

glean [gliːn] vt (grain, information etc) glaner.

glee [gliː] n joie f. ◆**gleeful** a joyeux.

glen [glen] n vallon m.

glib [glɪb] a (person) qui a la parole facile; (speech) facile, peu sincère. ◆**—ly** adv (to say) peu sincèrement.

glid/e [glaɪd] vi glisser; (of vehicle) avancer

silencieusement; (*of aircraft, bird*) planer. ◆**—ing** *n Av Sp* vol *m* à voile. ◆**—er** *n Av* planeur *m*.

glimmer ['glɪmər] *vi* luire (faiblement); — *n* (*light, of hope etc*) (faible) lueur *f*.

glimpse [glɪmps] *n* aperçu *m*; **to catch** *or* **get a g. of** entrevoir.

glint [glɪnt] *vi* (*shine with flashes*) briller; — *n* éclair *m*; (*in eye*) étincelle *f*.

glisten ['glɪs(ə)n] *vi* (*of wet surface*) briller; (*of water*) miroiter.

glitter ['glɪtər] *vi* scintiller, briller; — *n* scintillement *m*.

gloat [gləʊt] *vi* jubiler (**over** à la vue de).

globe [gləʊb] *n* globe *m*. ◆**global** *a* (*comprehensive*) global; (*universal*) universel, mondial.

gloom [gluːm] *n* (*darkness*) obscurité *f*; (*sadness*) *Fig* tristesse *f*. ◆**gloomy** *a* (**-ier, -iest**) (*dark, dismal*) sombre, triste; (*sad*) *Fig* triste; (*pessimistic*) pessimiste.

glory ['glɔːrɪ] *n* gloire *f*; **in all one's g.** *Fig* dans toute sa splendeur; **to be in one's g.** (*very happy*) *Fam* être à son affaire; — *vi* to **g. in** se glorifier de. ◆**glorify** *vt* (*praise*) glorifier; **it's a glorified barn**/*etc* ce n'est guère plus qu'une grange/*etc*. ◆**glorious** *a* (*full of glory*) glorieux; (*splendid, enjoyable*) magnifique.

gloss [glɒs] **1** *n* (*shine*) brillant *m*; **g. paint** peinture *f* brillante; **g. finish** brillant *m*. **2** *n* (*note*) glose *f*, commentaire *m*. **3** *vt* to **g. over** (*minimize*) glisser sur; (*conceal*) dissimuler. ◆**glossy** *a* (**-ier, -iest**) brillant; (*paper*) glacé; (*magazine*) de luxe.

glossary ['glɒsərɪ] *n* glossaire *m*.

glove [glʌv] *n* gant *m*; **g. compartment** *Aut* (*shelf*) vide-poches *m inv*; (*enclosed*) boîte *f* à gants. ◆**gloved** *a* **a g. hand** une main gantée.

glow [gləʊ] *vi* (*of sky, fire*) rougeoyer; (*of lamp*) luire; (*of eyes, person*) *Fig* rayonner (**with** de); — *n* rougeoiement *m*; (*of colour*) éclat *m*; (*of lamp*) lueur *f*. ◆**—ing** *a* (*account, terms etc*) très favorable, enthousiaste. ◆**glow-worm** *n* ver *m* luisant.

glucose ['gluːkəʊs] *n* glucose *m*.

glue [gluː] *n* colle *f*; — *vt* coller (**to**, **on** à). ◆**glued** *a* **g. to** (*eyes*) *Fam* fixés *or* rivés sur; **to be g. to** (*television*) *Fam* être cloué devant.

glum [glʌm] *a* (**glummer, glummest**) triste.

glut [glʌt] *vt* (**-tt-**) (*overfill*) rassasier; (*market*) *Com* surcharger (**with** de); — *n* (*of produce, oil etc*) *Com* surplus *m* (**of** de).

glutton ['glʌt(ə)n] *n* glouton, -onne *mf*; **g. for work** bourreau *m* de travail; **g. for**

punishment masochiste *mf*. ◆**gluttony** *n* gloutonnerie *f*.

glycerin(e) ['glɪsərɪn] *n* glycérine *f*.

GMT [dʒiːem'tiː] *abbr* (*Greenwich Mean Time*) GMT.

gnarled [nɑːld] *a* noueux.

gnash [næʃ] *vt* to **g. one's teeth** grincer des dents.

gnat [næt] *n* (*insect*) cousin *m*.

gnaw [nɔː] *vti* to **g. (at)** ronger.

gnome [nəʊm] *n* (*little man*) gnome *m*.

go [gəʊ] **1** *vi* (*3rd person sing pres t* **goes**; *pt* **went**; *pp* **gone**; *pres p* **going**) aller (**to** à, **from** de); (*depart*) partir, s'en aller; (*disappear*) disparaître; (*be sold*) se vendre; (*function*) marcher, fonctionner; (*progress*) aller, marcher; (*become*) devenir; (*be*) être; (*of time*) passer; (*of hearing, strength*) baisser; (*of rope*) céder; (*of fuse*) sauter; (*of material*) s'user; **to go well/badly** (*of event*) se passer bien/mal; **she's going to do** (*is about to, intends to*) elle va faire; **it's all gone** (*finished*) il n'y en a plus; **to go and get** (*fetch*) aller chercher; **to go and see** aller voir; **to go riding/sailing/on a trip**/*etc* faire du cheval/de la voile/un voyage/*etc*; **to let go of** lâcher; **to go to** (*doctor, lawyer etc*) aller voir; **to get things going** faire démarrer les choses; **is there any beer going?** (*available*) y a-t-il de la bière?; **it goes to show that . . .** ça sert à montrer que . . . ; **two hours**/*etc* **to go** (*still left*) encore deux heures/*etc*. **2** *n* (*pl* **goes**) (*energy*) dynamisme *m*; (*attempt*) coup *m*; **to have a go at** (*doing*) **sth** essayer (de faire) qch; **at one go** d'un seul coup; **on the go** en mouvement, actif; **to make a go of** (*make a success of*) réussir. ■ **to go about** *or* **(a)round** *vi* se déplacer; (*of news, rumour*) circuler; **to go about** *vt* (*one's duties etc*) s'occuper de; **to know how to go about it** savoir s'y prendre; **to go across** *vt* traverser; — *vi* (*cross*) traverser; (*go*) aller (**to** à); **to go across to s.o.('s)** faire un saut chez qn; **to go after** *vt* (*follow*) suivre; (*job*) viser; **to go against** *vt* (*of result*) être défavorable à; (*s.o.'s wishes*) aller contre; (*harm*) nuire à; **to go ahead** *vi* aller de l'avant; **to go ahead with** (*plan etc*) poursuivre; **go ahead!** allez-y! ◆**go-ahead** *a* dynamique; — *n* **to get the go-ahead** avoir le feu vert; **to go along** *vi* aller, avancer; **to go along with** (*agree*) être d'accord avec; **to go away** *vi* partir, s'en aller; **to go back** *vi* retourner, revenir; (*in time*) remonter; (*retreat, step back*) reculer; **to go back on** (*promise*) revenir sur; **to go by** *vi* passer; — *vt* (*act according to*) se fonder sur; (*judge from*) juger d'après; (*instruction*) suivre; **to go down** *vi* descendre; (*fall down*) tomber; (*of ship*) couler; (*of sun*) se coucher; (*of storm*) s'apaiser; (*of temperature, price etc*) baisser; (*of tyre*) se dégonfler; **to go down well** (*of speech etc*) être bien reçu; **to go down with** (*illness*) attraper; – *vt* **to go down the stairs/street** descendre l'escalier/la rue; **to go for** *vt* (*fetch*) aller chercher; (*attack*) attaquer; (*like*) *Fam* aimer beaucoup; **to go forward(s)** *vi* avancer; **to go in** *vi* (r)entrer; (*of sun*) se cacher; **to go in for** (*exam*) se présenter à; (*hobby, sport*) faire; (*career*) entrer dans; (*like*) *Fam* aimer beaucoup; – *vt* **to go in a room/etc** entrer dans une pièce/etc; **to go into** *vt* (*room etc*) entrer dans; (*question*) examiner; **to go off** *vi* (*leave*) partir; (*go bad*) se gâter; (*of effect*) passer; (*of alarm*) se déclencher; (*of event*) se passer; – *vt* (*one's food*) perdre le goût de; **to go on** *vi* continuer (*doing* à faire); (*travel*) poursuivre sa route; (*happen*) se passer; (*last*) durer; (*of time*) passer; **to go on at** (*nag*) *Fam* s'en prendre à; **to go on about** *Fam* parler sans cesse de; **to go out** *vi* sortir; (*of light, fire*) s'éteindre; (*of tide*) descendre; (*of newspaper, product*) être distribué (*to* à); (*depart*) partir; **to go out to work** travailler (au dehors); **to go over** *vi* (*go*) aller (*to* à); (*cross over*) traverser; (*to enemy*) passer (*to* à); **to go over to s.o.('s)** faire un saut chez qn; – *vt* examiner; (*speech*) revoir; (*in one's mind*) repasser; (*touch up*) retoucher; (*overhaul*) réviser; (*vehicule, montre*); **to go round** *vi* (*turn*) tourner; (*make a detour*) faire le tour; (*be sufficient*) suffire; **to go round to s.o.('s)** passer chez qn, faire un saut chez qn; **enough to go round** assez pour tout le monde; – *vt* **to go round a corner** tourner un coin; **to go through** *vi* passer; (*of deal*) être conclu; – *vt* (*undergo, endure*) subir; (*examine*) examiner; (*search*) fouiller; (*spend*) dépenser; (*wear out*) user; (*perform*) accomplir; **to go through with** (*carry out*) réaliser, aller jusqu'au bout de; **to go under** *vi* (*of ship, person, firm*) couler; **to go up** *vi* monter; (*explode*) sauter; – *vt* **to go up the stairs/street** monter l'escalier/la rue; **to go without** *vi* se passer de.

goad [gəʊd] *n* aiguillon *m*; – *vt* **to g. (on)** aiguillonner.

goal [gəʊl] *n* but *m*. ◆**goalkeeper** *n Fb* gardien *m* de but, goal *m*. ◆**goalpost** *n Fb* poteau *m* de but.

goat [gəʊt] *n* chèvre *f*; **to get s.o.'s g.** *Fam*

énerver qn. ◆**goa'tee** *n* (*beard*) barbiche *f.*

gobble ['gɒb(ə)l] *vt* **to g. (up)** engloutir, engouffrer.

go-between ['gəʊbɪtwiːn] *n* intermédiaire *mf.*

goblet ['gɒblɪt] *n* verre *m* à pied.

goblin ['gɒblɪn] *n* (*evil spirit*) lutin *m.*

god [gɒd] *n* dieu *m*; **G.** Dieu *m*; **the gods** *Th Fam* le poulailler. ◆**g.-fearing** *a* croyant. ◆**g.-forsaken** *a* (*place*) perdu, misérable. ◆**goddess** *n* déesse *f.* ◆**godly** *a* dévot.

godchild ['gɒdtʃaɪld] *n* (*pl* -**children**) filleul, -eule *mf.* ◆**goddaughter** *n* filleule *f.* ◆**godfather** *n* parrain *m.* ◆**godmother** *n* marraine *f.* ◆**godson** *n* filleul *m.*

goddam(n) ['gɒdæm] *a Am Fam* foutu.

godsend ['gɒdsend] *n* aubaine *f.*

goes [gəʊz] *see* go 1.

goggle ['gɒg(ə)l] **1** *vi* **to g. at** regarder en roulant de gros yeux. **2** *npl* (*spectacles*) lunettes *fpl* (protectrices). ◆**g.-'eyed** *a* aux yeux saillants.

going ['gəʊɪŋ] **1** *n* (*departure*) départ *m*; (*speed*) allure *f*; (*conditions*) conditions *fpl*; **it's hard g.** c'est difficile. **2** *a* **the g. price** le prix pratiqué (**for** pour); **a g. concern** une entreprise qui marche bien. ◆**goings-'on** *npl Pej* activités *fpl.*

go-kart ['gəʊkɑːt] *n Sp* kart *m.*

gold [gəʊld] *n* or *m*; – *a* (*watch etc*) en or; (*coin, dust*) d'or. ◆**golden** *a* (*made of gold*) d'or; (*in colour*) doré, d'or; (*opportunity*) excellent. ◆**goldmine** *n* mine *f* d'or. ◆**gold-'plated** *a* plaqué or. ◆**goldsmith** *n* orfèvre *m.*

goldfinch ['gəʊldfɪntʃ] *n* (*bird*) chardonneret *m.*

goldfish ['gəʊldfɪʃ] *n* poisson *m* rouge.

golf [gɒlf] *n* golf *m.* ◆**golfer** *n* golfeur, -euse *mf.*

golly! ['gɒlɪ] *int* (**by**) **g.!** *Fam* mince (alors)!

gondola ['gɒndələ] *n* (*boat*) gondole *f.* ◆**gondo'lier** *n* gondolier *m.*

gone [gɒn] *see* go 1; – *a* **it's g. two** *Fam* il est plus de deux heures. ◆**goner** *n* **to be a g.** *Sl* être fichu.

gong [gɒŋ] *n* gong *m.*

good [gʊd] *a* (**better, best**) bon; (*kind*) gentil; (*weather*) beau; (*pleasant*) bon, agréable; (*well-behaved*) sage; **be g. enough to . . .** ayez la gentillesse de . . . ; **my g. friend** mon cher ami; **a g. chap** *or* **fellow** un brave type; **g. and strong** bien fort; **a g. (long) walk** une bonne promenade; **very g.!** (*all right*) très bien!; **that's g. of you** c'est gentil de ta part; **to feel g.** se sentir bien;

that isn't g. enough (*bad*) ça ne va pas; (*not sufficient*) ça ne suffit pas; **it's g. for us** ça nous fait du bien; **g. at** (*French etc*) *Sch* bon *or* fort en; **to be g. with** (*children*) savoir s'y prendre avec; **it's a g. thing (that)**... heureusement que ...; **a g. many, a g. deal (of)** beaucoup (de); **as g. as** (*almost*) pratiquement; **g. afternoon**, (*in*) **morning** bonjour; (*on leaving someone*) au revoir; **g. evening** bonsoir; **g. night** bonsoir; (*before going to bed*) bonne nuit; **to make g.** *vi* (*succeed*) réussir; – *vt* (*loss*) compenser; (*damage*) réparer; **G. Friday** Vendredi *m* Saint; – *n* (*virtue*) bien *m*; **for her g.** pour son bien; **there's some g. in him** il a du bon; **it's no g. crying/shouting/etc** ça ne sert à rien de pleurer/crier/*etc*; **that's no g.** (*worthless*) ça ne vaut rien; (*bad*) ça ne va pas; **what's the g.?** à quoi bon?; **for g.** (*to leave, give up etc*) pour de bon.
◆**g.-for-nothing** *a* & *n* propre à rien (*mf*).
◆**g.-'humoured** *a* de bonne humeur.
◆**g.-'looking** *a* beau. ◆**goodness** *n* bonté *f*; **my g.!** mon Dieu! ◆**good'will** *n* bonne volonté *f*; (*zeal*) zèle *m*.

goodbye [gud'bai] *int* & *n* au revoir (*m inv*).

goodly ['gudli] *a* (*size, number*) grand.

goods [gudz] *npl* marchandises *fpl*; (*articles for sale*) articles *mpl*.

gooey ['guːi] *a Fam* gluant, poisseux.

goof [guːf] *vi* **to g. (up)** (*blunder*) *Am* faire une gaffe.

goon [guːn] *n Fam* idiot, -ote *mf*.

goose, *pl* **geese** [guːs, giːs] *n* oie *f*; **g. pimples** *or* **bumps** chair *f* de poule.
◆**gooseflesh** *n* chair *f* de poule.

gooseberry ['guzbəri, *Am* 'guːsberi] *n* groseille *f* à maquereau.

gorge [gɔːdʒ] **1** *n* (*ravine*) gorge *f*. **2** *vt* (*food*) engloutir; **to g. oneself** s'empiffrer (**on** de).

gorgeous ['gɔːdʒəs] *a* magnifique.

gorilla [gə'rilə] *n* gorille *m*.

gormless ['gɔːmləs] *a Fam* stupide.

gorse [gɔːs] *n inv* ajonc(s) *m*(*pl*).

gory ['gɔːri] *a* (**-ier, -iest**) (*bloody*) sanglant; (*details*) *Fig* horrible.

gosh! [gɒʃ] *int Fam* mince (alors)!

go-slow [gəu'sləu] *n* (*strike*) grève *f* perlée.

gospel ['gɒspəl] *n* évangile *m*.

gossip ['gɒsip] *n* (*talk*) bavardage(s) *m*(*pl*); (*malicious*) cancan(s) *m*(*pl*); (*person*) commère *f*; **g. column** *Journ* échos *mpl*; – *vi* bavarder; (*maliciously*) cancaner.
◆**–ing** *a*, ◆**gossipy** *a* bavard, cancanier.

got, gotten [gɒt, 'gɒt(ə)n] *Am* *see* **get.**

Gothic ['gɒθik] *a* & *n* gothique (*m*).

gouge [gaudʒ] *vt* **to g. out** (*eye*) crever.

goulash ['guːlæʃ] *n Culin* goulasch *f*.

gourmet ['guəmei] *n* gourmet *m*.

gout [gaut] *n Med* goutte *f*.

govern ['gʌvən] *vt* (*rule*) gouverner; (*city*) administrer; (*business*) gérer; (*emotion*) maîtriser, gouverner; (*influence*) déterminer; – *vi Pol* gouverner; **governing body** conseil *m* d'administration. ◆**governess** *n* gouvernante *f*. ◆**government** *n* gouvernement *m*; (*local*) administration *f*; – *a* (*department, policy etc*) gouvernemental; (*loan*) d'État. ◆**governor** *n* gouverneur *m*; (*of school*) administrateur, -trice *mf*; (*of prison*) directeur, -trice *mf*.

gown [gaun] *n* (*dress*) robe *f*; (*of judge, lecturer*) toge *f*.

GP [dʒiː'piː] *n abbr* (*general practitioner*) (médecin *m*) généraliste *m*.

GPO [dʒiːpiː'əu] *abbr* (*General Post Office*) = PTT *fpl*.

grab [græb] *vt* (**-bb-**) **to g. (hold of)** saisir, agripper; **to g. sth from s.o.** arracher qch à qn.

grace [greis] **1** *n* (*charm, goodwill etc*) *Rel* grâce *f*; (*extension of time*) délai *m* de grâce; **to say g.** dire le bénédicité. **2** *vt* (*adorn*) orner; (*honour*) honorer (**with** de).
◆**graceful** *a* gracieux. ◆**gracious** *a* (*kind*) aimable, gracieux (**to** envers); (*elegant*) élégant; **good g.!** *Fam* bonté divine!

gradation [grə'deiʃ(ə)n, *Am* grei'deiʃ(ə)n] *n* gradation *f*.

grade [greid] *n* catégorie *f*; *Mil Math* grade *m*; (*of milk*) qualité *f*; (*of eggs*) calibre *m*; (*level*) niveau *m*; (*mark*) *Sch Univ* note *f*; (*class*) *Am Sch* classe *f*; **g. school** *Am* école *f* primaire; **g. crossing** *Am* passage *m* à niveau; – *vt* (*classify*) classer; (*colours etc*) graduer; (*paper*) *Sch Univ* noter.

gradient ['greidiənt] *n* (*slope*) inclinaison *f*.

gradual ['grædʒuəl] *a* progressif, graduel; (*slope*) doux. ◆**–ly** *adv* progressivement, peu à peu.

graduat/e ['grædʒueit] *vi Univ* obtenir son diplôme; *Am Sch* obtenir son baccalauréat; **to g. from** sortir de; – *vt* (*mark with degrees*) graduer; – ['grædʒuət] *n* diplômé, -ée *mf*, licencié, -ée *mf*. ◆**–ed** *a* (*tube etc*) gradué; **to be g.** *Am Sch Univ* = **to graduate** *vi*. ◆**gradu'ation** *n Univ* remise *f* des diplômes.

graffiti [grə'fiːti] *npl* graffiti *mpl*.

graft [grɑːft] *n Med Bot* greffe *f*; – *vt* greffer (**on to** à).

grain [grein] *n* (*seed, particle*) grain *m*;

(*seeds*) grain(s) *m*(*pl*); (*in cloth*) fil *m*; (*in wood*) fibre *f*; (*in leather, paper*) grain *m*; (*of truth*) *Fig* once *f*.

gram(me) [græm] *n* gramme *m*.

grammar ['græmər] *n* grammaire *f*; **g. school** lycée *m*. ◆**gra'mmatical** *a* grammatical.

gramophone ['græməfəʊn] *n* phonographe *m*.

granary ['grænəri] *n* Agr grenier *m*; **g. loaf** pain *m* complet.

grand [grænd] **1** *a* (**-er, -est**) magnifique, grand; (*style*) grandiose; (*concert, duke*) grand; (*piano*) à queue; (*wonderful*) *Fam* magnifique. **2** *n inv Am Sl* mille dollars *mpl*; *Br Sl* mille livres *fpl*. ◆**grandeur** ['grændʒər] *n* magnificence *f*; (*of person, country*) grandeur *f*.

grandchild ['græntʃaɪld] *n* (*pl* **-children**) petit(e)-enfant *mf*. ◆**grand(d)ad** *n Fam* pépé *m*, papi *m*. ◆**granddaughter** *n* petite-fille *f*. ◆**grandfather** *n* grand-père *m*. ◆**grandmother** *n* grand-mère *f*. ◆**grandparents** *npl* grands-parents *mpl*. ◆**grandson** *n* petit-fils *m*.

grandstand ['grændstænd] *n Sp* tribune *f*.

grange [greɪndʒ] *n* (*house*) manoir *m*.

granite ['grænɪt] *n* granit(e) *m*.

granny ['græni] *n Fam* mamie *f*.

grant [grɑːnt] **1** *vt* accorder (**to** à); (*request*) accéder à; (*prayer*) exaucer; (*admit*) admettre (**that** que); **to take for granted** (*event*) considérer comme allant de soi; (*person*) considérer comme faisant partie du décor; **I take (it) for granted that** ... je présume que ... **2** *n* subvention *f*, allocation *f*; *Univ* bourse *f*.

granule ['grænjuːl] *n* granule *m*. ◆**granulated** *a* **g. sugar** sucre *m* cristallisé.

grape [greɪp] *n* grain *m* de raisin; *pl* le raisin, les raisins *mpl*; **to eat grapes** manger du raisin *or* des raisins; **g. harvest** vendange *f*. ◆**grapefruit** *n* pamplemousse *m*. ◆**grapevine** *n* **on the g.** *Fig* par le téléphone arabe.

graph [græf, grɑːf] *n* graphique *m*, courbe *f*; **g. paper** papier *m* millimétré.

graphic ['græfɪk] *a* graphique; (*description*) *Fig* explicite, vivant. ◆**graphically** *adv* (*to describe*) explicitement.

grapple ['græp(ə)l] *vi* **to g. with** (*person, problem etc*) se colleter avec.

grasp [grɑːsp] *vt* (*seize, understand*) saisir; − *n* (*firm hold*) prise *f*; (*understanding*) compréhension *f*; (*knowledge*) connaissance *f*; **to have a strong g.** (*strength of hand*) avoir de la poigne; **within s.o.'s g.**

(*reach*) à la portée de qn. ◆**−ing** *a* (*greedy*) rapace.

grass [grɑːs] *n* herbe *f*; (*lawn*) gazon *m*; **the g. roots** *Pol* la base. ◆**grasshopper** *n* sauterelle *f*. ◆**grassland** *n* prairie *f*. ◆**grassy** *a* herbeux.

grat/e [greɪt] **1** *n* (*for fireplace*) grille *f* de foyer. **2** *vt Culin* râper. **3** *vi* (*of sound*) grincer (**on** sur); **to g. on the ears** écorcher les oreilles; **to g. on s.o.'s nerves** taper sur les nerfs de qn; *Fig* irritant. ◆**−ing 1** *a* (*sound*) grinçant; *Fig* irritant. **2** *n* (*bars*) grille *f*. ◆**−er** *n Culin* râpe *f*.

grateful ['greɪtfʊl] *a* reconnaissant (**to** à, **for** de); (*words, letter*) de remerciement; (*friend, attitude*) plein de reconnaissance; **I'm g. (to you) for your help** je vous suis reconnaissant de votre aide; **I'd be g. if you'd be quieter** j'aimerais bien que tu fasses moins de bruit; **g. thanks** mes sincères remerciements. ◆**−ly** *adv* avec reconnaissance.

gratif/y ['grætɪfaɪ] *vt* (*whim*) satisfaire; **to g. s.o.** faire plaisir à qn. ◆**−ied** *a* très content (**with** *or* **at sth** de qch, **to do** de faire). ◆**−ying** *a* très satisfaisant; **it's g. to ...** ça fait plaisir de .... ◆**gratifi'cation** *n* satisfaction *f*.

gratis ['grætɪs, 'greɪtɪs] *adv* gratis.

gratitude ['grætɪtjuːd] *n* reconnaissance *f*, gratitude *f* (**for** de).

gratuitous [grə'tjuːɪtəs] *a* (*act etc*) gratuit.

gratuity [grə'tjuːɪtɪ] *n* (*tip*) pourboire *m*.

grave¹ [greɪv] *n* tombe *f*; **g. digger** fossoyeur *m*. ◆**gravestone** *n* pierre *f* tombale. ◆**graveyard** *n* cimetière *m*; **auto g.** *Am Fam* cimetière *m* de voitures.

grave² [greɪv] *a* (**-er, -est**) (*serious*) grave. ◆**−ly** *adv* gravement; (*concerned, displeased*) extrêmement.

gravel ['græv(ə)l] *n* gravier *m*.

gravitate ['grævɪteɪt] *vi* **to g. towards** (*be drawn towards*) être attiré vers; (*move towards*) se diriger vers. ◆**gravi'tation** *n* gravitation *f*.

gravity ['grævɪtɪ] *n* **1** (*seriousness*) gravité *f*. **2** *Phys* pesanteur *f*, gravité *f*.

gravy ['greɪvɪ] *n* jus *m* de viande.

gray [greɪ] *Am* = **grey**.

graze [greɪz] **1** *vi* (*of cattle*) paître. **2** *vt* (*scrape*) écorcher; (*touch lightly*) frôler, effleurer; − *n* (*wound*) écorchure *f*.

grease [griːs] *n* graisse *f*; − *vt* graisser. ◆**greaseproof** *a* & *n* **g.** (*paper*) papier *m* sulfurisé. ◆**greasy** *a* (**-ier, -iest**) graisseux; (*hair*) gras; (*road*) glissant.

great [greɪt] *a* (**-er, -est**) grand; (*effort, heat,* *parcel*) gros, grand; (*excellent*) magnifique, merveilleux; **g. at** (*English, tennis etc*) doué pour; **a g. deal** *or* **number (of)**, **a g. many** beaucoup (de); **a g. opinion of** une haute opinion de; **a very g. age** un âge très avancé; **the greatest team**/*etc* (*best*) la meilleure équipe/*etc*; **Greater London** le grand Londres. ◆**g.-'grandfather** *n* arrière-grand-père *m*. ◆**g.-'grandmother** *n* arrière-grand-mère *f*. ◆**greatly** *adv* (*much*) beaucoup; (*very*) très, bien; **I g. prefer** je préfère de beaucoup. ◆**greatness** *n* (*in size, importance*) grandeur *f*; (*in degree*) intensité *f*.

Great Britain [greɪt'brɪt(ə)n] *n* Grande-Bretagne *f*.

Greece [griːs] *n* Grèce *f*. ◆**Greek** *a* grec; − *n* Grec *m*, Greque *f*; (*language*) grec *m*.

greed [griːd] *n* avidité *f* (**for** de); (*for food*) gourmandise *f*. ◆**greed/y** *a* (**-ier, -iest**) avide (**for** de); (*for food*) glouton, gourmand. ◆**—ily** *adv* avidement; (*to eat*) gloutonnement. ◆**—iness** *n* = **greed**.

green [griːn] *a* (**-er, -est**) vert; (*pale*) blême, vert; (*immature*) *Fig* inexpérimenté, naïf; **to turn** *or* **go g.** verdir; **the g. belt** (*land*) la ceinture verte; **the g. light** *Fig* le (feu) vert; **to have g. fingers** *or Am* **a g. thumb** avoir la main verte; **g. with envy** *Fig* vert de jalousie; − *n* (*colour*) vert *m*; (*lawn*) pelouse *f*; (*village square*) place *f* gazonnée; *pl Culin* légumes *mpl* verts. ◆**greenery** *n* (*plants, leaves*) verdure *f*. ◆**greenfly** *n* puceron *m* (des plantes). ◆**greengrocer** *n* marchand, -ande *mf* de légumes. ◆**greenhouse** *n* serre *f*. ◆**greenish** *a* verdâtre. ◆**greenness** *n* (*colour*) vert *m*; (*greenery*) verdure *f*.

greengage ['griːngeɪdʒ] *n* (*plum*) reine-claude *f*.

Greenland ['griːnlənd] *n* Groenland *m*.

greet [griːt] *vt* saluer, accueillir; **to g. s.o.** (*of sight*) s'offrir aux regards de qn. ◆**—ing** *n* salutation *f*; (*welcome*) accueil *m*; *pl* (*for birthday, festival*) vœux *mpl*; **send my greetings to . . .** envoie mon bon souvenir à . . . ; **greetings card** carte *f* de vœux.

gregarious [grɪ'geərɪəs] *a* (*person*) sociable; (*instinct*) grégaire.

gremlin ['gremlɪn] *n Fam* petit diable *m*.

grenade [grə'neɪd] *n* (*bomb*) grenade *f*.

grew [gruː] *see* **grow**.

grey [greɪ] *a* (**-er, -est**) gris; (*outlook*) *Fig* sombre; **to be going g.** grisonner; − *vi* **to be greying** être grisonnant. ◆**g.-'haired** *a* aux cheveux gris. ◆**greyhound** *n* lévrier *m*. ◆**greyish** *a* grisâtre.

grid [grɪd] *n* (*grating*) grille *f*; (*system*) *El* réseau *m*; *Culin* gril *m*. ◆**gridiron** *n Culin* gril *m*.

griddle ['grɪd(ə)l] *n* (*on stove*) plaque *f* à griller.

grief [griːf] *n* chagrin *m*, douleur *f*; **to come to g.** avoir des ennuis; (*of driver, pilot etc*) avoir un accident; (*of plan*) échouer; **good g.!** ciel!, bon sang!

grieve [griːv] *vt* peiner, affliger; − *vi* s'affliger (**over** de); **to g. for s.o.** pleurer qn. ◆**grievance** *n* grief *m*; *pl* (*complaints*) doléances *fpl*.

grievous ['griːvəs] *a* (*serious*) très grave.

grill [grɪl] **1** *n* (*utensil*) gril *m*; (*dish*) grillade *f*; − *vti* griller. **2** *vt* (*question*) *Fam* cuisiner.

grille [grɪl] *n* (*metal bars*) grille *f*; (*radiator*) **g.** *Aut* calandre *f*.

grim [grɪm] *a* (**grimmer, grimmest**) sinistre; (*face*) sévère; (*truth*) brutal; (*bad*) *Fam* (*plutôt*) affreux; **a g. determination** une volonté inflexible. ◆**—ly** *adv* (*to look at*) sévèrement.

grimace ['grɪməs] *n* grimace *f*; − *vi* grimacer.

grime [graɪm] *n* saleté *f*. ◆**grimy** *a* (**-ier, -iest**) sale.

grin [grɪn] *vi* (**-nn-**) avoir un large sourire; (*with pain*) avoir un rictus; − *n* large sourire *m*; (*with pain*) rictus *m*.

grind [graɪnd] **1** *vt* (*pt & pp* **ground**) moudre; (*blade, tool*) aiguiser; (*handle*) tourner; (*oppress*) *Fig* écraser; **to g. one's teeth** grincer des dents; − *vi* **to g. to a halt** s'arrêter (progressivement). **2** *n Fam* corvée *f*, travail *m* long et monotone. ◆**—ing** *a* **g. poverty** la misère noire. ◆**—er** *n* **coffee g.** moulin *m* à café.

grip [grɪp] *vt* (**-pp-**) (*seize*) saisir; (*hold*) tenir serré; (*of story*) *Fig* empoigner (*qn*); **to g. the road** (*of tyres*) adhérer à la route; − *vi* (*of brakes*) mordre; − *n* (*hold*) prise *f*; (*hand clasp*) poigne *f*; **get a g. on yourself!** secoue-toi!; **to get to grips with** (*problem*) s'attaquer à; **in the g. of** en proie à. ◆**gripping** *a* (*book, film etc*) prenant.

gripe [graɪp] *vi* (*complain*) *Sl* rouspéter.

grisly ['grɪzlɪ] *a* (*gruesome*) horrible.

gristle ['grɪs(ə)l] *n Culin* cartilage *m*.

grit [grɪt] **1** *n* (*gravel*) sable *m*; (*gravel*) gravillon *m*; − *vt* (**-tt-**) (*road*) sabler. **2** *n* (*pluck*) *Fam* cran *m*. **3** *vt* (**-tt-**) **to g. one's teeth** serrer les dents.

grizzle ['grɪz(ə)l] *vi Fam* pleurnicher. ◆**grizzly** *a* **1** (*child*) *Fam* pleurnicheur. **2** (*bear*) gris.

groan [grəʊn] *vi* (*with pain*) gémir;

(*complain*) grogner, gémir; − *n* gémissement *m*; grognement *m*.

grocer ['grəʊsər] *n* épicier, -ière *mf*; **grocer's (shop)** épicerie *f*. ◆**grocery** *n* (*shop*) épicerie *f*; *pl* (*food*) épicerie *f*.

grog [grɒg] *n* (*drink*) grog *m*.

groggy ['grɒgɪ] *a* (**-ier, -iest**) (*weak*) faible; (*shaky on one's feet*) pas solide sur les jambes.

groin [grɔɪn] *n* Anat aine *f*.

groom [gruːm] **1** *n* (*bridegroom*) marié *m*. **2** *n* (*for horses*) lad *m*; − *vt* (*horse*) panser; **to g. s.o. for** (*job*) préparer qn pour; **well groomed** (*person*) très soigné.

groove [gruːv] *n* (*for sliding door etc*) rainure *f*; (*in record*) sillon *m*.

grope [grəʊp] *vi* **to g. (about)** tâtonner; **to g. for** chercher à tâtons.

gross [grəʊs] **1** *a* (**-er, -est**) (*coarse*) grossier; (*error*) gros, grossier; (*injustice*) flagrant. **2** *a* (*weight, income*) Com brut; − *vt* faire une recette brute de. **3** *n* (*number*) grosse *f*. ◆**-ly** *adv* grossièrement; (*very*) énormément, extrêmement.

grotesque [grəʊ'tesk] *a* (*ludicrous, strange*) grotesque; (*frightening*) monstrueux.

grotto ['grɒtəʊ] *n* (*pl* **-oes** *or* **-os**) grotte *f*.

grotty ['grɒtɪ] *a* (**-ier, -iest**) *Fam* affreux, moche.

ground¹ [graʊnd] **1** *n* terre *f*, sol *m*; (*area for camping, football etc*) & *Fig* terrain *m*; (*estate*) terres *fpl*; (*earth*) El *Am* terre *f*, masse *f*; (*background*) fond *m*; *pl* (*reasons*) raisons *fpl*, motifs *mpl*; (*gardens*) parc *m*; **on the g.** (*lying etc*) par terre; **to lose g.** perdre du terrain; **g. floor** rez-de-chaussée *m inv*; **g. frost** gelée *f* blanche. **2** *vt* (*aircraft*) bloquer *or* retenir au sol. ◆**-ing** *n* connaissances *fpl* (de fond) (**in** en). ◆**groundless** *a* sans fondement. ◆**groundnut** *n* arachide *f*. ◆**groundsheet** *n* tapis *m* de sol. ◆**groundswell** *n* lame *f* de fond. ◆**groundwork** *n* préparation *f*.

ground² [graʊnd] *see* **grind 1**; − *a* (*coffee*) moulu; − *npl* (**coffee**) **grounds** marc *m* (de café).

group [gruːp] *n* groupe *m*; − *vt* **to g. (together)** grouper; − *vi* se grouper. ◆**-ing** *n* (*group*) groupe *m*.

grouse [graʊs] **1** *n inv* (*bird*) coq *m* de bruyère. **2** *vi* (*complain*) *Fam* rouspéter.

grove [grəʊv] *n* bocage *m*.

grovel ['grɒv(ə)l] *vi* (**-ll-**, *Am* **-l-**) *Pej* ramper, s'aplatir (**to s.o.** devant qn).

grow [grəʊ] *vi* (*pt* **grew**, *pp* **grown**) (*of person*) grandir; (*of plant, hair*) pousser; (*increase*) augmenter, grandir, croître; (*expand*) s'agrandir; **to g. fat(ter)** grossir; **to g. to like** finir par aimer; **to g. into** devenir; **to g. on s.o.** (*of book, music etc*) plaire progressivement à qn; **to g. out of** (*one's clothes*) devenir trop grand pour; (*a habit*) perdre; **to g. up** devenir adulte; **when I g. up** quand je serai grand; − *vt* (*plant, crops*) cultiver, faire pousser; (*beard, hair*) laisser pousser. ◆**-ing** *a* (*child*) qui grandit; (*number*) grandissant. ◆**grown** *a* (*full-grown*) adulte. ◆**grown-up** *n* grande personne *f*, adulte *mf*; − *a* (*ideas etc*) d'adulte. ◆**grower** *n* (*person*) cultivateur, -trice *mf*.

growl [graʊl] *vi* grogner (**at** contre); − *n* grognement *m*.

growth [grəʊθ] *n* croissance *f*; (*increase*) augmentation *f* (**in** de); (*of hair*) pousse *f*; (*beard*) barbe *f*; Med tumeur *f* (**on** à).

grub [grʌb] *n* (*food*) Fam bouffe *f*.

grubby ['grʌbɪ] *a* (**-ier, -iest**) sale.

grudg/e [grʌdʒ] **1** *vt* (*give*) donner à contrecœur; (*reproach*) reprocher (**s.o. sth** qch à qn); **to g. doing** faire à contrecœur. **2** *n* rancune *f*; **to have a g. against** en vouloir à. ◆**-ing** *a* peu généreux. ◆**-ingly** *adv* (*to give etc*) à contrecœur.

gruelling, *Am* **grueling** ['grʊəlɪŋ] *a* (*day, detail etc*) éprouvant, atroce.

gruesome ['gruːsəm] *a* horrible.

gruff [grʌf] *a* (**-er, -est**) (*voice, person*) bourru.

grumble ['grʌmb(ə)l] *vi* (*complain*) grogner (**about, at** contre), se plaindre (**about, at** au sujet de).

grumpy ['grʌmpɪ] *a* (**-ier, -iest**) grincheux.

grunt [grʌnt] *vti* grogner; − *n* grognement *m*.

guarantee [gærən'tiː] *n* garantie *f*; − *vt* garantir (**against** contre); (*vouch for*) se porter garant de; **to g. (s.o.) that** certifier *or* garantir (à qn) que. ◆**guarantor** *n* garant, -ante *mf*.

guard [gɑːd] *n* (*vigilance, group of soldiers etc*) garde *f*; (*individual person*) garde *m*; Rail chef *m* de train; **to keep a g. on** surveiller; **under g.** sous surveillance; **on one's g.** sur ses gardes; **to catch s.o. off his g.** prendre qn au dépourvu; **on g. (duty)** de garde; **to stand g.** monter la garde; − *vt* (*protect*) protéger (**against** contre); (*watch over*) surveiller, garder; − *vi* **to g. against** (*protect oneself*) se prémunir contre; (*prevent*) empêcher; **to g. against doing** se garder de faire. ◆**-ed** *a* (*cautious*) prudent.

◆**guardian** n gardien, -ienne mf; (of child) Jur tuteur, -trice mf.

guerrilla [gə'rılə] n (person) guérillero m; g. **warfare** guérilla f.

guess [ges] n conjecture f; (intuition) intuition f; (estimate) estimation f; **to make a g.** (essayer de) deviner; **an educated** or **informed g.** une conjecture fondée; **at a g.** au jugé, à vue de nez; – vt deviner (**that** que); (estimate) estimer; (suppose) Am supposer (**that** que); (think) Am croire (**that** que); – vi deviner; **I g. (so)** Am je suppose; je crois. ◆**guesswork** n hypothèse f; **by g.** au jugé.

guest [gest] n invité, -ée mf; (in hotel) client, -ente mf; (at meal) convive mf; – a (speaker, singer etc) invité. ◆**guesthouse** n pension f de famille. ◆**guestroom** n chambre f d'ami.

guffaw [gə'fɔː] vi rire bruyamment.

guidance ['gaɪdəns] n (advice) conseils mpl.

guid/e [gaɪd] n (person, book etc) guide m; (indication) indication f; (girl) g. éclaireuse f; **g. dog** chien m d'aveugle; **g. book** guide m; – vt (lead) guider. ◆**—ed** a (missile, rocket) téléguidé; **g. tour** visite f guidée. ◆**—ing** a (principle) directeur. ◆**guidelines** npl lignes fpl directrices, indications fpl à suivre.

guild [gɪld] n association f; Hist corporation f.

guile [gaɪl] n (deceit) ruse f.

guillotine ['gɪlətiːn] n guillotine f; (for paper) massicot m.

guilt [gɪlt] n culpabilité f. ◆**guilty** a (-ier, -iest) coupable; **g. person** coupable mf; **to find s.o. g.** déclarer qn coupable.

guinea pig ['gɪnɪpɪg] n (animal) & Fig cobaye m.

guise [gaɪz] n **under the g. of** sous l'apparence de.

guitar [gɪ'tɑːr] n guitare f. ◆**guitarist** n guitariste mf.

gulf [gʌlf] n (in sea) golfe m; (chasm) gouffre m; **a g. between** Fig un abîme entre.

gull [gʌl] n (bird) mouette f.

gullet ['gʌlɪt] n gosier m.

gullible ['gʌlɪb(ə)l] a crédule.

gully ['gʌlɪ] n (valley) ravine f; (drain) rigole f.

gulp [gʌlp] **1** vt **to g. (down)** avaler (vite); – n (of drink) gorgée f, lampée f; **in** or **at one g.** d'une seule gorgée. **2** vi (with emotion) avoir la gorge serrée; – n serrement m de gorge.

gum¹ [gʌm] n Anat gencive f. ◆**gumboil** n abcès m (dentaire).

gum² [gʌm] **1** n (glue from tree) gomme f; (any glue) colle f; – vt (-mm-) coller. **2** n (for chewing) chewing-gum m.

gumption ['gʌmpʃ(ə)n] n Fam (courage) initiative f; (commonsense) jugeote f.

gun [gʌn] n pistolet m, revolver m; (cannon) canon m; – vt (-nn-) **to g. down** abattre. ◆**gunfight** n échange m de coups de feu. ◆**gunfire** n coups mpl de feu; Mil tir m d'artillerie. ◆**gunman** n (pl -men) bandit m armé. ◆**gunner** n Mil artilleur m. ◆**gunpoint** n **at g.** sous la menace d'un pistolet or d'une arme. ◆**gunpowder** n poudre f à canon. ◆**gunshot** n coup m de feu; **g. wound** blessure f par balle.

gurgle ['gɜːg(ə)l] vi (of water) glouglouter; – n glouglou m.

guru ['gʊruː] n (leader) Fam gourou m.

gush [gʌʃ] vi jaillir (out of de); – n jaillissement m.

gust [gʌst] n (of smoke) bouffée f; **g. (of wind)** rafale f (de vent). ◆**gusty** a (-ier, -iest) (weather) venteux; (day) de vent.

gusto ['gʌstəʊ] n **with g.** avec entrain.

gut [gʌt] **1** n Anat intestin m; (catgut) boyau m; pl Fam (innards) ventre m, tripes fpl; (pluck) cran m, tripes fpl; **he hates your guts** Fam il ne peut pas te sentir. **2** vt (-tt-) (of fire) dévaster.

gutter ['gʌtər] n (on roof) gouttière f; (in street) caniveau m.

guttural ['gʌtərəl] a guttural.

guy [gaɪ] n (fellow) Fam type m.

guzzle ['gʌz(ə)l] vi (eat) bâfrer; – vt (eat) engloutir; (drink) siffler.

gym [dʒɪm] n gym(nastique) f; (gymnasium) gymnase m; **g. shoes** tennis fpl. ◆**gymnasium** n gymnase m. ◆**gymnast** n gymnaste mf. ◆**gymnastics** n gymnastique f.

gynaecology, Am **gynecology** [gaɪnɪ'kɒlədʒɪ] n gynécologie f. ◆**gynaecologist** n, Am ◆**gynecologist** n gynécologue mf.

gypsy ['dʒɪpsɪ] = **gipsy**.

gyrate [dʒaɪ'reɪt] vi tournoyer.

H

H, h [eɪtʃ] *n* H, h, *m*; **H bomb** bombe *f* H.
haberdasher ['hæbədæʃər] *n* mercier, -ière
mf; *(men's outfitter)* Am chemisier *m*.
◆**haberdashery** *n* mercerie *f*; Am
chemiserie *f*.
habit ['hæbɪt] *n* **1** habitude *f*; **to be in/get
into the h. of doing** avoir/prendre
l'habitude de faire; **to make a h. of doing**
avoir pour habitude de faire. **2** *(addiction)*
Med accoutumance *f*; **a h.-forming drug**
une drogue qui crée une accoutumance. **3**
(costume) Rel habit *m*. ◆**ha'bitual** *a*
habituel; *(smoker, drinker etc)* invétéré.
◆**ha'bitually** *adv* habituellement.
habitable ['hæbɪtəb(ə)l] *a* habitable.
◆**habitat** *n* *(of animal, plant)* habitat *m*.
◆**habi'tation** *n* habitation *f*; **fit for h.**
habitable.
hack [hæk] **1** *vt* *(cut)* tailler, hacher. **2** *n* *(old
horse)* rosse *f*; *(hired)* cheval *m* de louage;
h. (writer) *Pej* écrivaillon *m*.
hackney ['hæknɪ] *a* **h. carriage** *Hist* fiacre *m*.
hackneyed ['hæknɪd] *a* *(saying)* rebattu,
banal.
had [hæd] *see* have.
haddock ['hædək] *n* *(fish)* aiglefin *m*;
smoked h. haddock *m*.
haemorrhage ['hemərɪdʒ] *n* Med hémorragie *f*.
haemorrhoids ['hemərɔɪdz] *npl* hémorroïdes *fpl*.
hag [hæg] *n* *(woman)* Pej (vieille) sorcière *f*.
haggard ['hægəd] *a* *(person, face)* hâve,
émacié.
haggl/e ['hæg(ə)l] *vi* marchander; **to h. over**
(thing) marchander; *(price)* débattre,
discuter. ◆**—ing** *n* marchandage *m*.
Hague (The) [ðə'heɪg] *n* La Haye.
ha-ha! [hɑɪ'hɑɪ] *int* *(laughter)* ha, ha!
hail[1] [heɪl] *n* Met & Fig grêle *f*; – *v imp* Met
grêler; **it's hailing** il grêle. ◆**hailstone** *n*
grêlon *m*.
hail[2] [heɪl] **1** *vt* *(greet)* saluer; *(taxi)* héler. **2**
vi **to h. from** *(of person)* être originaire de;
(of ship etc) être en provenance de.
hair [heər] *n* *(on head)* cheveux *mpl*; *(on
body, of animal)* poils *mpl*; **a h.** *(on head)*
un cheveu; *(on body, of animal)* un poil; **by
a hair's breadth** de justesse; **long-/red-/etc**
haired aux cheveux longs/roux/etc; **h.**

cream brillantine *f*; **h. dryer** sèche-cheveux
m inv; **h. spray** (bombe *f* de) laque *f*.
◆**hairbrush** *n* brosse *f* à cheveux.
◆**haircut** *n* coupe *f* de cheveux; **to have a
h.** se faire couper les cheveux. ◆**hairdo** *n*
(pl -dos) *Fam* coiffure *f*. ◆**hairdresser** *n*
coiffeur, -euse *mf*. ◆**hairgrip** *n* pince *f* à
cheveux. ◆**hairnet** *n* résille *f*.
◆**hairpiece** *n* postiche *m*. ◆**hairpin** *n*
épingle *f* à cheveux; **h. bend** *Aut* virage *m*
en épingle à cheveux. ◆**hair-raising** *a* à
faire dresser les cheveux sur la tête.
◆**hair-splitting** *n* ergotage *m*. ◆**hairstyle** *n* coiffure *f*.
hairy ['heərɪ] *a* (-ier, -iest) *(person, animal,
body)* poilu; *(unpleasant, frightening)* Fam
effroyable.
hake [heɪk] *n* *(fish)* colin *m*.
hale [heɪl] *a* **h. and hearty** vigoureux.
half [hɑːf] *n* *(pl* halves) moitié *f*, demi, -ie
mf; *(of match)* Sp mi-temps *f*; **h. (of) the
apple/etc** la moitié de la pomme/etc; **ten
and a h.** dix et demi; **ten and a h. weeks** dix
semaines et demie; **to cut in h.** couper en
deux; **to go halves with** partager les frais
avec; – *a* demi; **h. a day, a h.-day** une
demi-journée; **at h. price** à moitié prix; **h.
man h. beast** mi-homme mi-bête; **h. sleeves**
manches *fpl* mi-longues; – *adv* *(dressed,
full etc)* à demi, à moitié; *(almost)* presque;
h. asleep à moitié endormi; **h. past one** une
heure et demie; **he isn't h. lazy/etc** *Fam* il
est rudement paresseux/etc; **h. as much as**
moitié moins que; **h. as much again** moitié
plus.
half-back ['hɑːfbæk] *n* Fb demi *m*.
◆**h.-'baked** *a* *(idea)* Fam à la manque, à
la noix. ◆**h.-breed** *n*, ◆**h.-caste** *n* Pej
métis, -isse *mf*. ◆**h.-(a-)'dozen** *n*
demi-douzaine *f*. ◆**h.-'hearted** *a* *(person,
manner)* peu enthousiaste; *(effort)* timide.
◆**h.-'hour** *n* demi-heure *f*. ◆**h.-light** *n*
demi-jour *m*. ◆**h.-'mast** *n* **at h.-mast**
(flag) en berne. ◆**h.-'open** *a* entrouvert.
◆**h.-'term** *n* Sch petites vacances *fpl*,
congé *m* de demi-trimestre. ◆**h.-'time** *n*
Sp mi-temps *f*. ◆**half'way** *adv* *(between
places)* à mi-chemin *(between* entre); **to
fill/etc h.** remplir/etc à moitié; **h. through**

(*book*) à la moitié de. ◆**h.-wit** *n*, ◆**h.-'witted** *a* imbécile (*mf*).

halibut ['hælɪbət] *n* (*fish*) flétan *m*.

hall [hɔːl] *n* (*room*) salle *f*; (*house entrance*) entrée *f*, vestibule *m*; (*of hotel*) hall *m*; (*mansion*) manoir *m*; (*for meals*) *Univ* réfectoire *m*; **h. of residence** *Univ* pavillon *m* universitaire; **halls of residence** cité *f* universitaire; **lecture h.** *Univ* amphithéâtre *m*. ◆**hallmark** *n* (*on silver or gold*) poinçon *m*; *Fig* sceau *m*. ◆**hallstand** *n* portemanteau *m*. ◆**hallway** *n* entrée *f*, vestibule *m*.

hallelujah [hælɪ'luːjə] *n* & *int* alléluia (*m*).

hallo! [hə'ləu] *int* (*greeting*) bonjour!; *Tel* allô!; (*surprise*) tiens!

hallow ['hæləu] *vt* sanctifier.

Hallowe'en [hæləu'iːn] *n* la veille de la Toussaint.

hallucination [həluːsɪ'neɪʃ(ə)n] *n* hallucination *f*.

halo ['heɪləu] *n* (*pl* **-oes** *or* **-os**) auréole *f*, halo *m*.

halt [hɔːlt] *n* halte *f*; **to call a h. to** mettre fin à; **to come to a h.** s'arrêter; − *vi* faire halte; − *int Mil* halte! ◆**−ing** *a* (*voice*) hésitant.

halve [hɑːv] *vt* (*time, expense*) réduire de moitié; (*cake, number etc*) diviser en deux.

ham [hæm] *n* **1** jambon *m*; **h. and eggs** œufs *mpl* au jambon. **2** (*actor*) *Th Pej* cabotin, -ine *mf*. ◆**h.-'fisted** *a Fam* maladroit.

hamburger ['hæmbɜːɡər] *n* hamburger *m*.

hamlet ['hæmlɪt] *n* hameau *m*.

hammer ['hæmər] *n* marteau *m*; − *vt* (*metal, table*) marteler; (*nail*) enfoncer (**into** dans); (*defeat*) *Fam* battre à plate(s) couture(s); (*criticize*) *Fam* démolir; **to h. out** (*agreement*) mettre au point; − *vi* frapper (au marteau). ◆**−ing** *n* (*defeat*) *Fam* raclée *f*, défaite *f*.

hammock ['hæmək] *n* hamac *m*.

hamper ['hæmpər] **1** *vt* gêner. **2** *n* (*basket*) panier *m*; (*laundry basket*) *Am* panier à linge.

hamster ['hæmstər] *n* hamster *m*.

hand[1] [hænd] *n* main *f*; **to hold in one's h.** tenir à la main; **by h.** (*to deliver etc*) à la main; **at** *or* **to h.** (*within reach*) sous la main, à portée de la main; (**close**) **at h.** (*person etc*) tout près; (*day etc*) proche; **in h.** (*situation*) bien en main; (*matter*) en question; (*money*) disponible; **on h.** (*ready for use*) disponible; **to have s.o. on one's hands** *Fig* avoir qn sur les bras; **on the right h.** du côté droit (**of** de); **on the one h....** d'une part...; **on the other h....** d'autre part...; **hands up!** (*in attack*) haut les mains!; *Sch* levez la main!; **hands off!** pas touche!, bas les pattes!; **my hands are full** *Fig* je suis très occupé; **to give s.o. a (helping) h.** donner un coup de main à qn; **to get out of h.** (*of person*) devenir impossible; (*of situation*) devenir incontrôlable; **h. in h.** la main dans la main; **h. in h. with** (*together with*) *Fig* de pair avec; **at first h.** de première main; **to win hands down** gagner haut la main; − *a* (*luggage etc*) à main. **2** *n* (*worker*) ouvrier, -ière *mf*; (*of clock*) aiguille *f*; *Cards* jeu *m*; (*writing*) écriture *f*. ◆**handbag** *n* sac *m* à main. ◆**handbook** *n* (*manual*) manuel *m*; (*guide*) guide *m*. ◆**handbrake** *n* frein *m* à main. ◆**handbrush** *n* balayette *f*. ◆**handcuff** *vt* passer les menottes à. ◆**handcuffs** *npl* menottes *fpl*. ◆**hand'made** *a* fait à la main. ◆**hand'picked** *a Fig* trié sur le volet. ◆**handrail** *n* (*on stairs*) rampe *f*. ◆**handshake** *n* poignée *f* de main. ◆**handwriting** *n* écriture *f*. ◆**hand'written** *a* écrit à la main.

hand[2] [hænd] *vt* (*give*) donner (**to** à); **to h. down** (*bring down*) descendre; (*knowledge, heirloom*) transmettre (**to** à); **to h. in** remettre; **to h. out** distribuer; **to h. over** remettre; (*power*) transmettre; **to h. round** (*cakes*) passer. ◆**handout** *n* (*leaflet*) prospectus *m*; (*money*) aumône *f*.

handful ['hændful] *n* (*bunch, group*) poignée *f*; (**quite**) **a h.** (*difficult*) *Fig* difficile.

handicap ['hændɪkæp] *n* (*disadvantage*) & *Sp* handicap *m*; − *vt* (**-pp-**) handicaper. ◆**handicapped** *a* (*disabled*) handicapé.

handicraft ['hændɪkrɑːft] *n* artisanat *m* d'art. ◆**handiwork** *n* artisanat *m* d'art; (*action*) *Fig* ouvrage *m*.

handkerchief ['hæŋkətʃɪf] *n* (*pl* **-fs**) mouchoir *m*; (*for neck*) foulard *m*.

handle ['hænd(ə)l] **1** *n* (*of door*) poignée *f*; (*of knife*) manche *m*; (*of bucket*) anse *f*; (*of saucepan*) queue *f*; (*of pump*) bras *m*. **2** *vt* (*manipulate*) manier; (*touch*) toucher à; (*ship, vehicle*) manœuvrer; (*deal with*) s'occuper de; (*difficult child etc*) s'y prendre avec; − *vi* **to h. well** (*of machine*) être facile à manier.

handlebars ['hænd(ə)lbɑːz] *npl* guidon *m*.

handsome ['hænsəm] *a* (*person, building etc*) beau; (*gift*) généreux; (*profit, sum*) considérable. ◆**−ly** *adv* (*generously*) généreusement.

handy ['hændɪ] *a* (**-ier, -iest**) (*convenient, practical*) commode, pratique; (*skilful*) habile (**at doing** à faire); (*useful*) utile; (*near*) proche, accessible; **to come in h.** se

révéler utile; **to keep h.** avoir sous la main.
◆**handyman** n (pl -men) (DIY enthusiast)
bricoleur m.

hang¹ [hæŋ] **1** vt (pt & pp hung) suspendre
(**on, from** à); (on hook) accrocher (**on, from**
à), suspendre; (wallpaper) poser; (let
dangle) laisser pendre (**from, out of** de); **to
h. with** (decorate with) orner de; **to h. out**
(washing) étendre; (flag) arborer; **to h. up**
(picture etc) accrocher; – vi (dangle)
pendre; (of threat) planer; (of fog, smoke)
flotter; **to h. about** (loiter) traîner, rôder;
(wait) Fam attendre; **to h. down** (dangle)
pendre; (of hair) tomber; **to h. on** (hold out)
résister; (wait) Fam attendre; **to h. on to**
(cling to) ne pas lâcher; (keep) garder; **to h.
out** (of tongue, shirt) pendre; (live) Sl
crécher; **to h. together** (of facts) se tenir; (of
plan) tenir debout; **to h. up** Tel raccrocher.
2 n **to get the h. of sth** Fam arriver à
comprendre qch; **to get the h. of doing** Fam
trouver le truc pour faire. ◆**—ing¹** n
suspension f; – a suspendu (**from** à); (leg,
arm) pendant; **h. on** (wall) accroché à.
◆**hang-glider** n delta-plane® m.
◆**hang-gliding** n vol m libre. ◆**hangnail**
n petites peaux fpl. ◆**hangover** n Fam
gueule f de bois. ◆**hangup** n Fam
complexe m.

hang² [hæŋ] vt (pt & pp hanged) (criminal)
pendre (**for** pour); – vi (of criminal) être
pendu. ◆**—ing²** n Jur pendaison f.
◆**hangman** n (pl -men) bourreau m.

hangar [ˈhæŋər] n Av hangar m.

hanger [ˈhæŋər] n (coat) **h.** cintre m.
◆**hanger-'on** n (pl hangers-on) (person)
Pej parasite m.

hanker [ˈhæŋkər] vi **to h. after** or **for** avoir
envie de. ◆**—ing** n (forte) envie f, (vif)
désir m.

hankie, hanky [ˈhæŋkɪ] n Fam mouchoir m.

hanky-panky [hæŋkɪˈpæŋkɪ] n inv Fam
(deceit) manigances fpl, magouilles fpl;
(sexual behaviour) papouilles fpl, pelotage
m.

haphazard [hæpˈhæzəd] a au hasard, au
petit bonheur; (selection, arrangement)
aléatoire. ◆**—ly** adv au hasard.

hapless [ˈhæplɪs] a Lit infortuné.

happen [ˈhæpən] vi arriver, se passer, se
produire; **to h. to s.o./sth** arriver à qn/qch;
it (so) happens that I know, I h. to know il se
trouve que je le sais; **do you h. to have . . . ?**
est-ce que par hasard vous avez . . . ?;
whatever happens quoi qu'il arrive.
◆**—ing** n événement m.

happy [ˈhæpɪ] a (-ier, -iest) heureux (**to do**

de faire, **about sth** de qch); **I'm not (too** or
very) h. about (doing) it ça ne me plaît pas
beaucoup (de le faire); **H. New Year!**
bonne année!; **H. Christmas!** joyeux Noël!
◆**h.-go-'lucky** a insouciant. ◆**happily**
adv (contentedly) tranquillement; (joy-
ously) joyeusement; (fortunately) heureusement. ◆**happiness** n bonheur m.

harass [ˈhærəs, Am həˈræs] vt harceler.
◆**—ment** n harcèlement m.

harbour [ˈhɑːbər] **1** n port m. **2** vt (shelter)
héberger; (criminal) cacher, abriter; (fear,
secret) nourrir.

hard [hɑːd] a (-er, -est) (not soft, severe) dur;
(difficult) difficile, dur; (study) assidu;
(fact) brutal; (drink) alcoolisé; (water)
calcaire; **h. drinker/worker** gros buveur
m/travailleur m; **a h. frost** une forte gelée;
to be h. on or **to s.o.** être dur avec qn; **to find
it h. to sleep**/etc avoir du mal à dormir/etc;
h. labour Jur travaux mpl forcés; **h. cash**
espèces fpl; **h. core** (group) noyau m; **h. of
hearing** malentendant; **h. up** (broke) Fam
fauché; **to be h. up for** manquer de; – adv
(-er, -est) (to work) dur; (to pull) fort; (to
hit, freeze) dur, fort; (to study) assidûment;
(to think) sérieusement; (to rain) à verse;
(badly) mal; **h. by** tout près; **h. done by**
traité injustement.

hard-and-fast [hɑːdən(d)ˈfɑːst] a (rule)
strict. ◆**'hardback** n livre m relié.
◆**'hardboard** n Isorel® m. ◆**hard-
'boiled** a (egg) dur. ◆**hard-'core** a
(rigid) Pej inflexible. ◆**hard'headed** a
réaliste. ◆**hard'wearing** a résistant.
◆**hard-'working** a travailleur.

harden [ˈhɑːd(ə)n] vti durcir; **to h. oneself to**
s'endurcir à. ◆**—ed** a (criminal) endurci.

hardly [ˈhɑːdlɪ] adv à peine; **he h. talks** il
parle à peine, il ne parle guère; **h. ever**
presque jamais.

hardness [ˈhɑːdnɪs] n dureté f.

hardship [ˈhɑːdʃɪp] n (ordeal) épreuve(s)
f(pl); (deprivation) privation(s) f(pl).

hardware [ˈhɑːdweər] n inv quincaillerie f;
(of computer) & Mil matériel m.

hardy [ˈhɑːdɪ] a (-ier, -iest) (person, plant)
résistant.

hare [heər] n lièvre m. ◆**h.-brained** a
(person) écervelé; (scheme) insensé.

harem [hɑːˈriːm] n harem m.

hark [hɑːk] vi Lit écouter; **to h. back to**
(subject etc) Fam revenir sur.

harm [hɑːm] n (hurt) mal m; (prejudice) tort
m; **he means (us) no h.** il ne nous veut pas
de mal; **she'll come to no h.** il ne lui arrivera
rien; – vt (hurt) faire du mal à; (prejudice)

nuire à, faire du tort à; (*object*) endommager, abîmer. ◆**harmful** *a* nuisible. ◆**harmless** *a* (*person, treatment*) inoffensif; (*hobby, act*) innocent; (*gas, fumes etc*) qui n'est pas nuisible, inoffensif.

harmonica [hɑːˈmɒnɪkə] *n* harmonica *m*.

harmony [ˈhɑːmənɪ] *n* harmonie *f*. ◆**har'monic** *a* & *n* Mus harmonique (*m*). ◆**har'monious** *a* harmonieux. ◆**har'monium** *n* Mus harmonium *m*. ◆**harmonize** *vt* harmoniser; − *vi* s'harmoniser.

harness [ˈhɑːnɪs] *n* (*for horse, baby*) harnais *m*; − *vt* (*horse*) harnacher; (*energy etc*) Fig exploiter.

harp [hɑːp] **1** *n* Mus harpe *f*. **2** *vt* to h. on (**about**) **sth** Fam rabâcher qch. ◆**harpist** *n* harpiste *mf*.

harpoon [hɑːˈpuːn] *n* harpon *m*; − *vt* (*whale*) harponner.

harpsichord [ˈhɑːpsɪkɔːd] *n* Mus clavecin *m*.

harrowing [ˈhærəʊɪŋ] *a* (*tale, memory*) poignant; (*cry, sight*) déchirant.

harsh [hɑːʃ] *a* (**-er, -est**) (*severe*) dur, sévère; (*sound, taste*) âpre; (*surface*) rugueux; (*fabric*) rêche. ◆**−ly** *adv* durement, sévèrement. ◆**−ness** *n* dureté *f*, sévérité *f*; âpreté *f*, rugosité *f*.

harvest [ˈhɑːvɪst] *n* moisson *f*, récolte *f*; (*of people, objects*) Fig ribambelle *f*; − *vt* moissonner, récolter.

has [hæz] *see* have. ◆**has-been** *n* Fam personne *f* finie.

hash [hæʃ] **1** *n* Culin hachis *m*; − *vt* to h. (**up**) hacher. **2** *n* (*mess*) Fam gâchis *m*. **3** *n* (*hashish*) Sl hasch *m*, H *m*.

hashish [ˈhæʃiːʃ] *n* haschisch *m*.

hassle [ˈhæs(ə)l] *n* Fam (*trouble*) histoires *fpl*; (*bother*) mal *m*, peine *f*.

haste [heɪst] *n* hâte *f*; **in h.** à la hâte; **to make h.** se hâter. ◆**hasten** *vi* se hâter (**to do** de faire); − *vt* hâter. ◆**hasty** *a* (**-ier, -iest**) (*sudden*) précipité; (*visit*) rapide; (*decision, work*) hâtif. ◆**hastily** *adv* (*quickly*) en hâte; (*too quickly*) hâtivement.

hat [hæt] *n* chapeau *m*; **that's old h.** Fam (*old-fashioned*) c'est vieux jeu; (*stale*) c'est vieux comme les rues; **to score** or **get a h. trick** Sp réussir trois coups consécutifs.

hatch [hætʃ] **1** *vi* (*of chick, egg*) éclore; − *vt* faire éclore; (*plot*) Fig tramer. **2** *n* (*in kitchen wall*) passe-plats *m inv*.

hatchback [ˈhætʃbæk] *n* (*door*) hayon *m*; (*car*) trois-portes *f inv*, cinq-portes *f inv*.

hatchet [ˈhætʃɪt] *n* hachette *f*.

hate [heɪt] *vt* détester, haïr; **to h. doing** or **to**

do détester faire; **I h. to say it** ça me gêne de le dire; − *n* haine *f*; **pet h.** Fam bête *f* noire. ◆**hateful** *a* haïssable. ◆**hatred** *n* haine *f*.

haughty [ˈhɔːtɪ] *a* (**-ier, -iest**) hautain. ◆**haughtily** *adv* avec hauteur.

haul [hɔːl] **1** *vt* (*pull*) tirer, traîner; (*goods*) camionner. **2** *n* (*fish*) prise *f*; (*of thief*) butin *m*; **a long h.** (*trip*) un long voyage. ◆**haulage** *n* camionnage *m*. ◆**hauler** *n* Am, ◆**haulier** *n* transporteur *m* routier.

haunt [hɔːnt] **1** *vt* hanter. **2** *n* endroit *m* favori; (*of criminal*) repaire *m*. ◆**−ing** *a* (*music, memory*) obsédant.

have [hæv] **1** (*3rd person sing pres t* **has**; *pt* & *pp* **had**; *pres p* **having**) *vt* avoir; (*get*) recevoir, avoir; (*meal, shower etc*) prendre; **he has got, he has** il a; **to h. a walk/ dream/etc** faire une promenade/un rêve/*etc*; **to h. a drink** prendre or boire un verre; **to h. a wash** se laver; **to h. a holiday** (*spend*) passer des vacances; **will you h. . . . ?** (*a cake, some tea etc*) est-ce que tu veux . . . ?; **to let s.o. h. sth** donner qch à qn; **to h. it from s.o. that** tenir de qn que; **he had me by the hair** il me tenait par les cheveux; **I won't h. this** (*allow*) je ne tolérerai pas ça; **you've had it!** Fam tu es fichu!; **to h. on** (*clothes*) porter; **to have sth on** (*be busy*) être pris; **to h. s.o. over** inviter qn chez soi. **2** *v aux* avoir; (*with monter, sortir etc* & *pronominal verbs*) être; **to h. decided/been** avoir décidé/été; **to h. gone** être allé; **to h. cut oneself** s'être coupé; **I've just done it** je viens de le faire; **to h. to do** (*must*) devoir faire; **I've got to go, I h. to go** je dois partir, je suis obligé de partir, il faut que je parte; **I don't h. to go** je ne suis pas obligé de partir; **to h. sth done** (*get sth done*) faire faire qch; **he's had his suitcase brought up** il a fait monter sa valise; **I've had my car stolen** on m'a volé mon auto; **she's had her hair cut** elle s'est fait couper les cheveux; **I've been doing it for months** je le fais depuis des mois; **haven't I?, hasn't she?** *etc* n'est-ce pas?; **no I haven't!** non!; **yes I h.!** si!; **after he had eaten, he left** après avoir mangé, il partit. **3** *npl* **the haves and (the) have-nots** les riches *mpl* et les pauvres *mpl*.

haven [ˈheɪv(ə)n] *n* refuge *m*, havre *m*.

haversack [ˈhævəsæk] *n* (*shoulder bag*) musette *f*.

havoc [ˈhævək] *n* ravages *mpl*.

hawk [hɔːk] **1** *n* (*bird*) & Pol faucon *m*. **2** *vt* (*goods*) colporter. ◆**−er** *n* colporteur, -euse *mf*.

hawthorn [ˈhɔːθɔːn] *n* aubépine *f*.

hay [heɪ] n foin m; **h. fever** rhume m des foins. ◆**haystack** n meule f de foin.

haywire ['heɪwaɪər] a **to go h.** (of machine) se détraquer; (of scheme, plan) mal tourner.

hazard ['hæzəd] n risque m; **health h.** risque m pour la santé; **it's a fire h.** ça risque de provoquer un incendie; – vt (guess, remark etc) hasarder, risquer. ◆**hazardous** a hasardeux.

haze [heɪz] n brume f; **in a h.** (person) Fig dans le brouillard. ◆**hazy** a (-ier, -iest) (weather) brumeux; (sun) voilé; (photo, idea) flou; **I'm h. about my plans** je ne suis pas sûr de mes projets.

hazel ['heɪz(ə)l] n (bush) noisetier m; – a (eyes) noisette inv. ◆**hazelnut** n noisette f.

he [hiː] pron il; (stressed) lui; **he wants** il veut; **he's a happy man** c'est un homme heureux; **if I were he** si j'étais lui; **he and I** lui et moi; – n mâle m; **he-bear** ours m mâle.

head [hed] **1** n (of person, hammer etc) tête f; (of page) haut m; (of bed) chevet m, tête f; (of arrow) pointe f; (of beer) mousse f; (leader) chef m; (subject heading) rubrique f; **h. of hair** chevelure f; **h. cold** rhume m de cerveau; **it didn't enter my h.** ça ne m'est pas venu à l'esprit (that que); **to take it into one's h. to do** se mettre en tête de faire; **the h.** Sch = the headmaster; = the headmistress; **to shout one's h. off** Fam crier à tue-tête; **to have a good h. for business** avoir le sens des affaires; **at the h. of** (in charge of) à la tête de; **at the h. of the table** au haut bout de la table; **at the h. of the list** en tête de liste; **it's above my h.** ça me dépasse; **to keep one's h.** garder son sang-froid; **to go off one's h.** devenir fou; **it's coming to a h.** (of situation) ça devient critique; **heads or tails?** pile ou face?; **per h., a h.** (each) par personne. **2** a principal; (gardener) en chef; **h. waiter** maître m d'hôtel; **h. start** une grosse avance. **3** vt (group, firm) être à la tête de; (list, poll) être en tête de; (vehicle) diriger (towards vers); **to h. the ball** Fb faire une tête; **to h. off** (person) détourner de son chemin; (prevent) empêcher; **to be headed for** Am = to h. for; – vi **to h. for, be heading for** (place) se diriger vers; (ruin etc) Fig aller à. ◆**-ed** a (paper) à en-tête. ◆**-ing** n (of chapter, page etc) titre m; (of subject) rubrique f; (printed on letter etc) en-tête m. ◆**-er** n Fb coup m de tête.

headache ['hedeɪk] n mal m de tête; (difficulty, person) Fig problème m. ◆**head-dress** n (ornamental) coiffe f.

◆**headlamp** n, ◆**headlight** n Aut phare m. ◆**headline** n (of newspaper) manchette f; pl (gros) titres mpl; Rad TV (grands) titres mpl. ◆**headlong** adv (to fall) la tête la première; (to rush) tête baissée. ◆**head-'master** n Sch directeur m; (of lycée) proviseur m. ◆**head'mistress** n Sch directrice f; (of lycée) proviseur m. ◆**head-'on** adv & a (to collide, collision) de plein fouet. ◆**headphones** npl casque m (à écouteurs). ◆**headquarters** npl Com Pol siège m (central); Mil quartier m général. ◆**headrest** n appuie-tête m inv. ◆**headscarf** n (pl -scarves) foulard m. ◆**headstrong** a têtu. ◆**headway** n progrès mpl.

heady ['hedɪ] a (-ier, -iest) (wine etc) capiteux; (action, speech) emporté.

heal [hiːl] vi **to h. (up)** (of wound) se cicatriser; – vt (wound) cicatriser, guérir; (person, sorrow) guérir. ◆**-er** n guérisseur, -euse mf.

health [helθ] n santé f; **h. food** aliment m naturel; **h. food shop** or Am **store** magasin m diététique; **h. resort** station f climatique; **the H. Service** = la Sécurité Sociale. ◆**healthful** a (climate) sain. ◆**healthy** a (-ier, -iest) (person) en bonne santé, sain; (food, attitude etc) sain; (appetite) bon, robuste.

heap [hiːp] n tas m; **heaps of** Fam des tas de; **to have heaps of time** Fam avoir largement le temps; – vt entasser, empiler; **to h. on s.o.** (gifts, praise) couvrir qn de; (work) accabler qn de. ◆**-ed** a **h. spoonful** grosse cuillerée f. ◆**-ing** a **h. spoonful** Am grosse cuillerée f.

hear [hɪər] vt (pt & pp heard [hɜːd]) entendre; (listen to) écouter; (learn) apprendre (that que); **I heard him coming** je l'ai entendu venir; **to h. it said that** entendre dire que; **have you heard the news?** connais-tu la nouvelle?; **I've heard that . . .** on m'a dit que . . . , j'ai appris que . . . ; **to h. out** écouter jusqu'au bout; **h., h.!** bravo!; – vi entendre; (get news) recevoir or avoir des nouvelles (from de); **I've heard of** or **about him** j'ai entendu parler de lui; **she wouldn't h. of it** elle ne voulait pas en entendre parler; **I wouldn't h. of it!** pas question! ◆**-ing** n (sense) ouïe f; Jur audition f; **h. aid** appareil m auditif. ◆**hearsay** n ouï-dire m inv.

hearse [hɜːs] n corbillard m.

heart [hɑːt] n cœur m; pl Cards cœur m; **(off) by h.** par cœur; **to lose h.** perdre courage; **to one's h.'s content** tout son saoul *or* content; **at h.** au fond; **his h. is set on it** il le veut à tout prix, il y tient; **his h. is set on doing it** il veut le faire à tout prix, il tient à le faire; **h. disease** maladie *f* de cœur; **h. attack** crise *f* cardiaque. ◆**heartache** *n* chagrin *m*. ◆**heartbeat** *n* battement *m* de cœur. ◆**heartbreaking** *a* navrant. ◆**heartbroken** *a* navré, au cœur brisé. ◆**heartburn** *n Med* brûlures *fpl* d'estomac. ◆**heartthrob** *n* (*man*) *Fam* idole *f*.

hearten ['hɑːt(ə)n] *vt* encourager. ◆**—ing** *a* encourageant.

hearth [hɑːθ] *n* foyer *m*.

hearty ['hɑːtɪ] *a* (**-ier, -iest**) (*meal, appetite*) gros. ◆**heartily** *adv* (*to eat*) avec appétit; (*to laugh*) de tout son cœur; (*absolutely*) absolument.

heat [hiːt] **1** *n* chaleur *f*; (*of oven*) température *f*; (*heating*) chauffage *m*; **in the h. of** (*argument etc*) dans le feu de; (*the day*) au plus chaud de; **at low h., on a low h.** *Culin* à feu doux; **h. wave** vague *f* de chaleur; *— vti* **to h. (up)** chauffer. **2** *n* (*in race, competition*) éliminatoire *f*; **it was a dead h.** ils sont arrivés ex aequo. ◆**—ed** *a* (*swimming pool*) chauffé; (*argument*) passionné. ◆**—edly** *adv* avec passion. ◆**—ing** *n* chauffage *m*. ◆**—er** *n* radiateur *m*, appareil *m* de chauffage; **water h.** chauffe-eau *m inv*.

heath [hiːθ] *n* (*place, land*) lande *f*.

heathen ['hiːð(ə)n] *a & n* païen, -enne (*mf*).

heather ['heðər] *n* (*plant*) bruyère *f*.

heave [hiːv] *vt* (*lift*) soulever; (*pull*) tirer; (*drag*) traîner; (*throw*) *Fam* lancer; (*a sigh*) pousser; *— vi* (*of stomach, chest*) se soulever; (*retch*) *Fam* avoir des haut-le-cœur; *— n* (*effort*) effort *m* (*pour soulever etc*).

heaven ['hev(ə)n] *n* ciel *m*, paradis *m*; **h. knows when** *Fam* Dieu sait quand; **good heavens!** *Fam* mon Dieu!; **it was h.** *Fam* c'était divin. ◆**—ly** *a* céleste; (*pleasing*) *Fam* divin.

heavy ['hevɪ] *a* (**-ier, -iest**) lourd; (*weight etc*) lourd, pesant; (*work, cold etc*) gros; (*blow*) violent; (*concentration, rain*) fort; (*traffic*) dense; (*smoker, drinker*) grand; (*film, text*) difficile; **a h. day** une journée chargée; **h. casualties** de nombreuses victimes; **to be h. on petrol** *or Am* **gas** *Aut* consommer beaucoup; **it's h. going** c'est difficile. ◆**heavily** *adv* (*to walk, tax etc*) lourdement; (*to breathe*) péniblement; (*to smoke, drink*) beaucoup; (*underlined*) fortement; (*involved*) très; **to rain h.** pleuvoir à verse. ◆**heaviness** *n* pesanteur *f*, lourdeur *f*.

heavyweight *n Boxing* poids *m* lourd; *Fig* personnage *m* important.

Hebrew ['hiːbruː] *a* hébreu (*m only*), hébraïque; *— n* (*language*) hébreu *m*.

heck [hek] *int Fam* zut!; *— n* = **hell** in expressions.

heckl/e ['hek(ə)l] *vt* interpeller, interrompre. ◆**—ing** *n* interpellations *fpl*. ◆**—er** *n* interpellateur, -trice *mf*.

hectic ['hektɪk] *a* (*activity*) fiévreux; (*period*) très agité; (*trip*) mouvementé; **h. life** vie *f* trépidante.

hedge [hedʒ] **1** *n Bot* haie *f*. **2** *vi* (*answer evasively*) ne pas se mouiller, éviter de se compromettre. ◆**hedgerow** *n Bot* haie *f*.

hedgehog ['hedʒhɒg] *n* (*animal*) hérisson *m*.

heed [hiːd] *vt* faire attention à; *— n* **to pay h. to** faire attention à. ◆**—less** *a* **h. of** (*danger etc*) inattentif à.

heel [hiːl] *n* **1** talon *m*; **down at h.,** *Am* **down at the heels** (*shabby*) miteux; **h. bar** cordonnerie *f* express; (*on sign*) 'talon minute'. **2** (*person*) *Am Fam* salaud *m*.

hefty ['heftɪ] *a* (**-ier, -iest**) (*large, heavy*) gros; (*person*) costaud.

heifer ['hefər] *n* (*cow*) génisse *f*.

height [haɪt] *n* hauteur *f*; (*of person*) taille *f*; (*of mountain*) altitude *f*; **the h. of** (*glory, success, fame*) le sommet de, l'apogée *m* de; (*folly, pain*) le comble de; **at the h. of** (*summer, storm*) au cœur de. ◆**heighten** *vt* (*raise*) rehausser; (*tension, interest*) *Fig* augmenter.

heinous ['heɪnəs] *a* (*crime etc*) atroce.

heir [eər] *n* héritier *m*. ◆**heiress** *n* héritière *f*. ◆**heirloom** *n* héritage *m*, bijou *m or* meuble *m* de famille.

heist [haɪst] *n Am Sl* hold-up *m inv*.

held [held] *see* **hold**.

helicopter ['helɪkɒptər] *n* hélicoptère *m*. ◆**heliport** *n* héliport *m*.

hell [hel] *n* enfer *m*; **a h. of a lot** (*very much*) *Fam* énormément, vachement; **a h. of a lot of** (*very many, very much*) *Fam* énormément de; **a h. of a nice guy** *Fam* un type super; **what the h. are you doing?** *Fam* qu'est-ce que tu fous?; **to h. with him** *Fam* qu'il aille se faire voir; **h.!** *Fam* zut!; **to be h.-bent on** *Fam* être acharné à. ◆**hellish** *a* diabolique.

hello! [hə'ləʊ] *int* = **hallo**.

helm [helm] *n Nau* barre *f*.

helmet ['helmɪt] *n* casque *m*.

help [help] *n* aide *f*, secours *m*; (*cleaning woman*) femme *f* de ménage; (*office or shop workers*) employés, -ées *mfpl*; **with the h. of**

(*stick etc*) à l'aide de; **to cry** *or* **shout for h.** crier au secours!; **h.!** au secours!; – *vt* aider (**do, to do** à faire); **to h. s.o. to soup**/*etc* (*serve*) servir du potage/*etc* à qn; **to h. out** aider; **to h. up** aider à monter; **to h. oneself** se servir (**to** de); **I can't h. laughing**/*etc* je ne peux m'empêcher de rire/*etc*; **he can't h. being blind**/*etc* ce n'est pas sa faute s'il est aveugle/*etc*; **it can't be helped** on n'y peut rien; – *vi* **to h. (out)** aider. ◆**—ing** *n* (*serving*) portion *f*. ◆**—er** *n* assistant, -ante *mf*. ◆**helpful** *a* (*useful*) utile; (*obliging*) serviable. ◆**helpless** *a* (*powerless*) impuissant; (*baby*) désarmé; (*disabled*) impotent. ◆**helplessly** *adv* (**to struggle**) en vain.

helter-skelter [heltə'skeltər] **1** *adv* à la débandade. **2** *n* (*slide*) toboggan *m*.

hem [hem] *n* ourlet *m*; – *vt* (**-mm-**) (*garment*) ourler; **to h. in** *Fig* enfermer, cerner.

hemisphere ['hemɪsfɪər] *n* hémisphère *m*.

hemorrhage ['hemərɪdʒ] *n* *Med* hémorragie *f*.

hemorrhoids ['hemərɔɪdz] *npl* hémorroïdes *fpl*.

hemp [hemp] *n* chanvre *m*.

hen [hen] *n* poule *f*; **h. bird** oiseau *m* femelle. ◆**henpecked** *a* (*husband*) harcelé *or* dominé par sa femme.

hence [hens] *adv* **1** (*therefore*) d'où. **2** (*from now*) **ten years**/*etc* **h.** d'ici dix ans/*etc*. ◆**henceforth** *adv* désormais.

henchman ['hentʃmən] *n* (*pl* **-men**) *Pej* acolyte *m*.

hepatitis [hepə'taɪtɪs] *n* hépatite *f*.

her [hɜːr] **1** *pron* la, l'; (*after prep etc*) elle; **(to) h.** (*indirect*) lui; **I see h.** je la vois; **I saw h.** je l'ai vue; **I give (to) h.** je lui donne; **with h.** avec elle. **2** *poss a* son, sa, *pl* ses.

herald ['herəld] *vt* annoncer.

heraldry ['herəldrɪ] *n* héraldique *f*.

herb [hɜːb, *Am* ɜːb] *n* herbe *f*; *pl Culin* fines herbes *fpl*. ◆**herbal** *a* **h. tea** infusion *f* (d'herbes).

Hercules ['hɜːkjʊliːz] *n* (*strong man*) hercule *m*.

herd [hɜːd] *n* troupeau *m*; – *vti* **to h. together** (se) rassembler (en troupeau).

here [hɪər] **1** *adv* ici; (*then*) alors; **h. is, h. are** voici; **h. he is** le voici; **h. she is** la voici; **this man is h.** cet homme-ci; **I won't be h. tomorrow** je ne serai pas là demain; **h. and there** çà et là; **h. you are!** (*take this*) tenez!; **h.'s to you!** (*toast*) à la tienne! **2** *int* (*calling s.o.'s attention*) holà!, écoutez!; (*giving s.o. sth*) tenez! ◆**herea'bouts** *adv* par ici. ◆**here-**

'after *adv* après; (*in book*) ci-après. ◆**here'by** *adv* (*to declare*) par le présent acte. ◆**here'with** *adv* (*with letter*) *Com* ci-joint.

heredity [hɪ'redɪtɪ] *n* hérédité *f*. ◆**hereditary** *a* héréditaire.

heresy ['herəsɪ] *n* hérésie *f*. ◆**heretic** *n* hérétique *mf*. ◆**he'retical** *a* hérétique.

heritage ['herɪtɪdʒ] *n* héritage *m*.

hermetically [hɜː'metɪklɪ] *adv* hermétiquement.

hermit ['hɜːmɪt] *n* solitaire *mf*, ermite *m*.

hernia ['hɜːnɪə] *n* *Med* hernie *f*.

hero ['hɪərəʊ] *n* (*pl* **-oes**) héros *m*. ◆**he'roic** *a* héroïque. ◆**he'roics** *npl Pej* grandiloquence *f*. ◆**heroine** ['herəʊɪn] *n* héroïne *f*. ◆**heroism** ['herəʊɪz(ə)m] *n* héroïsme *m*.

heroin ['herəʊɪn] *n* (*drug*) héroïne *f*.

heron ['herən] *n* (*bird*) héron *m*.

herring ['herɪŋ] *n* hareng *m*; **a red h.** *Fig* une diversion.

hers [hɜːz] *poss pron* le sien, la sienne, *pl* les sien(ne)s; **this hat is h.** ce chapeau est à elle *or* est le sien; **a friend of h.** une amie à elle. ◆**her'self** *pron* elle-même; (*reflexive*) se, s'; (*after prep*) elle; **she cut h.** elle s'est coupée; **she thinks of h.** elle pense à elle.

hesitate ['hezɪteɪt] *vi* hésiter (**over, about** sur; **to do** à faire). ◆**hesitant** *a* hésitant. ◆**hesitantly** *adv* avec hésitation. ◆**hesi-'tation** *n* hésitation *f*.

hessian ['hesɪən] *n* toile *f* de jute.

heterogeneous [het(ə)rəʊ'dʒiːnɪəs] *a* hétérogène.

het up [het'ʌp] *a Fam* énervé.

hew [hjuː] *vt* (*pp* **hewn** *or* **hewed**) tailler.

hexagon ['heksəgən] *n* hexagone *m*. ◆**hex-'agonal** *a* hexagonal.

hey! [heɪ] *int* hé!, holà!

heyday ['heɪdeɪ] *n* (*of person*) apogée *m*, zénith *m*; (*of thing*) âge *m* d'or.

hi! [haɪ] *int Am Fam* salut!

hiatus [haɪ'eɪtəs] *n* (*gap*) hiatus *m*.

hibernate ['haɪbəneɪt] *vi* hiberner. ◆**hiber-'nation** *n* hibernation *f*.

hiccough, hiccup ['hɪkʌp] *n* hoquet *m*; **(the) hiccoughs, (the) hiccups** le hoquet; – *vi* hoqueter.

hick [hɪk] *n* (*peasant*) *Am Sl Pej* plouc *mf*.

hide[1] [haɪd] *vt* (*pt* **hid**, *pp* **hidden**) cacher, dissimuler (**from** à); – *vi* **to h. (away** *or* **out)** se cacher (**from** de). ◆**h.-and-'seek** *n* cache-cache *m inv*. ◆**h.-out** *n* cachette *f*. ◆**hiding** *n* **1 to go into h.** se cacher; **h. place** cachette *f*. **2 a good h.** (*thrashing*) *Fam* une bonne volée *or* correction.

hide² [haɪd] n (skin) peau f.

hideous ['hɪdɪəs] a horrible; (person, sight, crime) hideux. ◆—**ly** adv (badly, very) horriblement.

hierarchy ['haɪərɑːkɪ] n hiérarchie f.

hi-fi ['haɪfaɪ] n hi-fi f inv; (system) chaîne f hi-fi; – a hi-fi inv.

high [haɪ] a (-er, -est) haut; (speed) grand; (price) élevé; (fever) fort, gros; (colour, complexion) vif; (idea, number) grand, élevé; (meat, game) faisandé; (on drugs) Fam défoncé; **to be five metres h.** être haut de cinq mètres, avoir cinq mètres de haut; **it is h. time that** il est grand temps que (+ sub); **h. jump** Sp saut m en hauteur; **h. noon** plein midi m; **h. priest** grand prêtre m; **h. school** Am = collège m d'enseignement secondaire; **h. spirits** entrain m; **h. spot** (of visit, day) point m culminant; (of show) clou m; **h. street** grand-rue f; **h. summer** le cœur de l'été; **h. table** table f d'honneur; **h. and mighty** arrogant; **to leave s.o. h. and dry** Fam laisser qn en plan; – adv **h. (up)** (to fly, throw etc) haut; **to aim h.** viser haut; – n on **h.** en haut; **a new h., an all-time h.** (peak) Fig un nouveau record. ◆—**er** a supérieur (**than** à). ◆—**ly** adv hautement, fortement; (interesting) très; (paid) très bien; (to recommend) chaudement; **to speak h. of** dire beaucoup de bien de; **h. strung** nerveux. ◆—**ness** n H. (title) Altesse f.

highbrow ['haɪbraʊ] a & n intellectuel, -elle (mf).

high-chair ['haɪtʃeər] n chaise f haute. ◆h.-**'class** a (service) de premier ordre; (building) de luxe; (person) raffiné. ◆h.-**'flown** a (language) ampoulé. ◆h.-**'handed** a tyrannique. ◆h.-**'minded** a à l'âme noble. ◆h.-**'pitched** a (sound) aigu. ◆h.-**'powered** a (person) très dynamique. ◆h.-**rise** a **h.-rise flats** tour f. ◆h.-**'speed** a ultra-rapide. ◆h.-**'strung** a Am nerveux. ◆h.-**'up** a (person) haut placé.

highlands ['haɪləndz] npl régions fpl montagneuses.

highlight ['haɪlaɪt] n (of visit, day) point m culminant; (of show) clou m; (in hair) reflet m; – vt souligner.

highroad ['haɪrəʊd] n grand-route f.

highway ['haɪweɪ] n grande route f; Am autoroute f; **public h.** voie f publique; **h. code** code m de la route.

hijack ['haɪdʒæk] vt (aircraft, vehicle) détourner; – n détournement m. ◆—**ing** n (air piracy) piraterie f aérienne; (hijack)

détournement m. ◆—**er** n Av pirate m de l'air.

hik/e [haɪk] **1** n excursion f à pied; – vi marcher à pied. **2** vt (price) Am Fam augmenter; – n Am Fam hausse f. ◆—**er** n excursionniste mf.

hilarious [hɪ'leərɪəs] a (funny) désopilant.

hill [hɪl] n colline f; (small) coteau m; (slope) pente f. ◆**hillbilly** n Am Fam péquenaud, -aude mf. ◆**hillside** n coteau m; **on the h.** à flanc de coteau. ◆**hilly** a (-ier, -iest) accidenté.

hilt [hɪlt] n (of sword) poignée f; **to the h.** Fig au maximum.

him [hɪm] pron le, l'; (after prep etc) lui; (to) **h.** (indirect) lui; **I see h.** je le vois; **I saw h.** je l'ai vu; **I give (to) h.** je lui donne; **with h.** avec lui. ◆**him'self** pron lui-même; (reflexive) se, s'; (after prep) lui; **he cut h.** il s'est coupé; **he thinks of h.** il pense à lui.

hind [haɪnd] a de derrière, postérieur. ◆**hindquarters** npl arrière-train m.

hinder ['hɪndər] vt (obstruct) gêner; (prevent) empêcher (**from doing** de faire). ◆**hindrance** n gêne f.

hindsight ['haɪndsaɪt] n **with h.** rétrospectivement.

Hindu ['hɪnduː] a & n hindou, -oue (mf).

hing/e [hɪndʒ] **1** n (of box, stamp) charnière f; (of door) gond m, charnière f. **2** vi **to h. on** (depend on) dépendre de. ◆—**ed** a à charnière(s).

hint [hɪnt] n indication f; (insinuation) allusion f; (trace) trace f; pl (advice) conseils mpl; **to drop a h.** faire une allusion; – vt laisser entendre (**that** que); – vi **to h. at** faire allusion à.

hip [hɪp] n Anat hanche f.

hippie ['hɪpɪ] n hippie mf.

hippopotamus [hɪpə'pɒtəməs] n hippopotame m.

hire ['haɪər] vt (vehicle etc) louer; (person) engager; **to h. out** donner en location, louer; – n location f; (of boat, horse) louage m; **for h.** à louer; **on h.** en location; **h. purchase** vente f à crédit, location-vente f; **on h. purchase** à crédit.

his [hɪz] **1** poss a son, sa, pl ses. **2** poss pron le sien, la sienne, pl les sien(ne)s; **this hat is h.** ce chapeau est à lui or est le sien; **a friend of h.** un ami à lui.

Hispanic [hɪs'pænɪk] a & n Am hispano-américain, -aine (mf).

hiss [hɪs] vti siffler; – n sifflement m; pl Th sifflets mpl. ◆—**ing** n sifflement(s) m(pl).

history ['hɪstərɪ] n (study, events) histoire f; **it will make h.** or **go down in h.** ça va faire date; **your medical h.** vos antécédents médicaux. ◆**hi'storian** n historien, -ienne mf. ◆**hi'storic(al)** a historique.

histrionic [hɪstrɪˈɒnɪk] a Pej théâtral; – npl attitudes fpl théâtrales.

hit [hɪt] vti (pt & pp hit, pres p hitting) (strike) frapper; (knock against) & Aut heurter; (reach) atteindre; (affect) toucher, affecter; (find) trouver, rencontrer; **to h. the head-lines** Fam faire les gros titres; **to h. back** rendre coup pour coup; (verbally, militarily etc) riposter; **to h. it off** Fam s'entendre bien (with avec); **to h. out (at)** Fam atta-quer; **to h. (up)on** (find) tomber sur; – n (blow) coup m; (success) coup m réussi; Th succès m; **h. (song)** chanson f à succès; **to make a h. with** Fam avoir un succès avec; **h.-and-run driver** chauffard m (qui prend la fuite). ◆**h.-or-'miss** a (chancy, random) aléatoire.

hitch [hɪtʃ] **1** n (snag) anicroche f, os m, problème m. **2** vt (fasten) accrocher (to à). **3** vti **to h. (a lift or a ride)** Fam faire du stop (to jusqu'à). ◆**hitchhike** vi faire de l'auto-stop (to jusqu'à). ◆**hitchhiking** n auto-stop m. ◆**hitchhiker** n auto-stop-peur, -euse mf.

hitherto [hɪðəˈtuː] adv jusqu'ici.

hive [haɪv] **1** n ruche f. **2** vt **to h. off** (industry) dénationaliser.

hoard [hɔːd] n réserve f; (of money) trésor m; – vt amasser. ◆**—ing** n (fence) panneau m d'affichage.

hoarfrost [ˈhɔːfrɒst] n givre m.

hoarse [hɔːs] a (-er, -est) (person, voice) enroué. ◆**—ness** n enrouement m.

hoax [həʊks] n canular m; – vt faire un canular à, mystifier.

hob [hɒb] n (on stove) plaque f chauffante.

hobble [ˈhɒb(ə)l] vi (walk) clopiner.

hobby [ˈhɒbɪ] n passe-temps m inv; **my h.** mon passe-temps favori. ◆**hobbyhorse** n (favourite subject) dada m.

hobnob [ˈhɒbnɒb] vi (-bb-) **to h. with** frayer avec.

hobo [ˈhəʊbəʊ] n (pl -oes or -os) Am vaga-bond m.

hock [hɒk] vt (pawn) Fam mettre au clou; – n **in h.** Fam au clou.

hockey [ˈhɒkɪ] n hockey m; **ice h.** hockey sur glace.

hocus-pocus [həʊkəsˈpəʊkəs] n (talk) charabia m; (deception) tromperie f.

hodgepodge [ˈhɒdʒpɒdʒ] n fatras m.

hoe [həʊ] n binette f, houe f; – vt biner.

hog [hɒg] **1** n (pig) cochon m, porc m; **road h.** Fig chauffard m. **2** n **to go the whole h.**

Fam aller jusqu'au bout. **3** vt (-gg-) Fam monopoliser, garder pour soi.

hoist [hɔɪst] vt hisser; – n Tech palan m.

hold [həʊld] n (grip) prise f; (of ship) cale f; (of aircraft) soute f; **to get h. of** (grab) saisir; (contact) joindre; (find) trouver; **to get a h. of oneself** se maîtriser; – vt (pt & pp held) tenir; (breath, interest, heat, atten-tion) retenir; (a post) occuper; (a record) détenir; (weight) supporter; (possess) posséder; (contain) contenir; (maintain, believe) maintenir (**that** que); (ceremony, mass) célébrer; (keep) garder; **to h. hands** se tenir par la main; **to h. one's own** se débrouiller; (of sick person) se maintenir; **h. the line!** Tel ne quittez pas!; **h. it!** (stay still) ne bouge pas!; **to be held** (of event) avoir lieu; **to h. back** (crowd, tears) contenir; (hide) cacher (from à); **to h. down** (job) occuper; (keep) garder; (person on ground) maintenir au sol; **to h. in** (stomach) rentrer; **to h. off** (enemy) tenir à distance; **to h. on** (keep in place) tenir en place (son chapeau etc); **to h. out** (offer) offrir; (arm) étendre; **to h. over** (postpone) remettre; **to h. together** (nation, group) assurer l'union de; **to h. up** (raise) lever; (support) soutenir; (delay) retarder; (bank) attaquer (à main armée); – vi (of nail, rope) tenir; (of weather) se maintenir; **to h.** (of argu-ment) valoir (for pour); **to h. forth** (talk) Pej disserter; **if the rain holds off** s'il ne pleut pas; **to h. on** (endure) tenir bon; (wait) attendre; **h. on!** Tel ne quittez pas!; **to h. onto** (cling to) tenir bien; (keep) garder; **h. on (tight)!** tenez bon!; **to h. out** (resist) résister; (last) durer. ◆**holdall** n (bag) fourre-tout m inv. ◆**holdup** n (attack) hold-up m inv; (traffic jam) bouchon m; (delay) retard m.

holder [ˈhəʊldər] n (of post, passport) titu-laire mf; (of record, card) détenteur, -trice mf; (container) support m.

holdings [ˈhəʊldɪŋz] npl Fin possessions fpl.

hole [həʊl] n trou m; (town etc) Fam bled m, trou m; (room) Fam baraque f; – vt trouer; – vi **to h. up** (hide) Fam se terrer.

holiday [ˈhɒlɪdeɪ] n (rest) vacances fpl; **holi-day(s)** (from work, school etc) vacances fpl; **a h.** (day off) un congé; **a (public or bank) h.,** Am **a legal h.** un jour férié; **on h.** en vacances; **holidays with pay** congés mpl payés; – a (camp, clothes etc) de vacances; **in h. mood** d'humeur folâtre. ◆**holiday-maker** n vacancier, -ière mf.

holiness [ˈhəʊlɪnəs] n sainteté f.

Holland [ˈhɒlənd] n Hollande f.

hollow ['hɒləʊ] *a* creux; (*victory*) faux; (*promise*) vain; – *n* creux *m*; – *vt* **to h. out** creuser.

holly ['hɒlɪ] *n* houx *m*.

holocaust ['hɒləkɔːst] *n* (*massacre*) holocauste *m*.

holster ['həʊlstər] *n* étui *m* de revolver.

holy ['həʊlɪ] *a* (**-ier, -iest**) saint; (*bread, water*) bénit; (*ground*) sacré.

homage ['hɒmɪdʒ] *n* hommage *m*.

home¹ [həʊm] *n* maison *f*; (*country*) pays *m* (natal); (*for soldiers*) foyer *m*; (**at**) **h.** à la maison, chez soi; **to feel at h.** se sentir à l'aise; **to play at h.** Fb jouer à domicile; **far from h.** loin de chez soi; **a broken h.** un foyer désuni; **a good h.** une bonne famille; **to make one's h. in** s'installer à *or* en; **my h. is here** j'habite ici; – *adv* à la maison, chez soi; **to go** *or* **come h.** rentrer; **to be h.** être rentré; **to drive h.** ramener (*qn*) (en voiture); (*nail*) enfoncer; **to bring sth h. to s.o.** *Fig* faire voir qch à qn; – *a* (*life, pleasures etc*) de famille; *Pol* national; (*cooking, help*) familial; (*visit, match*) à domicile; **h. economics** économie *f* domestique; **h. town** (*birth place*) ville *f* natale; **h. rule** *Pol* autonomie *f*; **H. Office** = ministère *m* de l'Intérieur; **H. Secretary** = ministre *m* de l'Intérieur. ◆**homecoming** *n* retour *m* au foyer. ◆**home'grown** *a Bot* du jardin; *Pol* du pays. ◆**homeland** *n* patrie *f*. ◆**homeloving** *a* casanier. ◆**home'made** *a* (fait à la) maison *inv*. ◆**homework** *n Sch* devoir(s) *m*(*pl*).

home² [həʊm] *vi* **to h. in on** se diriger automatiquement sur.

homeless ['həʊmlɪs] *a* sans abri; – *n* **the h.** les sans-abri *m inv*.

homely ['həʊmlɪ] *a* (**-ier, -iest**) (*simple*) simple; (*comfortable*) accueillant; (*ugly*) *Am* laid.

homesick ['həʊmsɪk] *a* nostalgique; **to be h.** avoir le mal du pays. ◆**—ness** *n* nostalgie *f*, mal *m* du pays.

homeward ['həʊmwəd] *a* (*trip*) de retour; – *adv* **h. bound** sur le chemin de retour.

homey ['həʊmɪ] *a* (**-ier, -iest**) *Am Fam* accueillant.

homicide ['hɒmɪsaɪd] *n* homicide *m*.

homily ['hɒmɪlɪ] *n* homélie *f*.

homogeneous [həʊmə'dʒiːnɪəs] *a* homogène.

homosexual [həʊmə'sekʃʊəl] *a* & *n* homosexuel, -elle (*mf*). ◆**homosexu-'ality** *n* homosexualité *f*.

honest ['ɒnɪst] *a* honnête; (*frank*) franc (**with** avec); (*profit, money*) honnêtement

gagné; **the h. truth** la pure vérité; **to be (quite) h....** pour être franc.... ◆**honesty** *n* honnêteté *f*; franchise *f*; (*of report, text*) exactitude *f*.

honey ['hʌnɪ] *n* miel *m*; (*person*) *Fam* chéri, -ie *mf*. ◆**honeycomb** *n* rayon *m* de miel. ◆**honeymoon** *n* (*occasion*) lune *f* de miel; (*trip*) voyage *m* de noces. ◆**honeysuckle** *n Bot* chèvrefeuille *f*.

honk [hɒŋk] *vi Aut* klaxonner; – *n* coup *m* de klaxon®.

honour ['ɒnər] *n* honneur *m*; **in h. of** en l'honneur de; **an honours degree** *Univ* = une licence; – *vt* honorer (**with** de). ◆**honorary** *a* (*member*) honoraire; (*title*) honorifique. ◆**honourable** *a* honorable.

hood [hʊd] *n* **1** capuchon *m*; (*mask of robber*) cagoule *f*; (*soft car or pram roof*) capote *f*; (*bonnet*) *Aut Am* capot *m*; (*above stove*) hotte *f*. **2** (*hoodlum*) *Am Sl* gangster *m*. ◆**hooded** *a* (*person*) encapuchonné; (*coat*) à capuchon.

hoodlum ['huːdləm] *n Fam* (*hooligan*) voyou *m*; (*gangster*) gangster *m*.

hoodwink ['hʊdwɪŋk] *vt* tromper, duper.

hoof, *pl* **-fs, -ves** [huːf, -fs, -vz] (*Am* [hʊf, -fs, huːvz]) *n* sabot *m*.

hoo-ha ['huːhɑː] *n Fam* tumulte *m*.

hook [hʊk] *n* crochet *m*; (*on clothes*) agrafe *f*; *Fishing* hameçon *m*; **off the h.** (*phone*) décroché; **to let** *or* **get s.o. off the h.** tirer qn d'affaire; – *vt* **to h. (on** *or* **up)** accrocher (**to** à). ◆**-ed** *a* (*nose, beak*) recourbé, crochu; (*end, object*) recourbé; **h. on** *Fam* (*chess etc*) enragé de; (*person*) entiché de; **to be h. on drugs** *Fam* ne plus pouvoir se passer de la drogue. ◆**-er** *n Am Sl* prostituée *f*.

hook(e)y ['hʊkɪ] *n* **to play h.** *Am Fam* faire l'école buissonnière.

hooligan ['huːlɪgən] *n* vandale *m*, voyou *m*. ◆**hooliganism** *n* vandalisme *m*.

hoop [huːp] *n* cerceau *m*; (*of barrel*) cercle *m*.

hoot [huːt] **1** *vi Aut* klaxonner; (*of train*) siffler; (*of owl*) hululer; – *n Aut* coup *m* de klaxon®. **2** *vti* (*jeer*) huer; – *n* huée *f*. ◆**-er** *n Aut* klaxon® *m*; (*of factory*) sirène *f*.

hoover® ['huːvər] *n* aspirateur *m*; – *vt Fam* passer à l'aspirateur.

hop [hɒp] *vi* (**-pp-**) (*of person*) sauter (à cloche-pied); (*of animal*) sauter; (*of bird*) sautiller; **h. in!** (*in car*) montez!; **to h. on a bus** monter dans un autobus; **to h. on a plane** attraper un vol; – *vt* **h. it!** *Fam* fiche le camp!; – *n* (*leap*) saut *m*; *Av* étape *f*.

hope [həʊp] *n* espoir *m*, espérance *f*; – *vi*

espérer; **to h. for** (*desire*) espérer; (*expect*) attendre; **I h. so/not** j'espère que oui/non; – *vt* espérer (**to do** faire, **that** que). ◆**hopeful** *a* (*person*) optimiste, plein d'espoir; (*promising*) prometteur; (*encouraging*) encourageant; **to be h. that** avoir bon espoir que. ◆**hopefully** *adv* avec optimisme; (*one hopes*) on espère (que). ◆**hopeless** *a* désespéré, sans espoir; (*useless, bad*) nul; (*liar*) invétéré. ◆**hopelessly** *adv* sans espoir; (*extremely*) complètement; (*in love*) éperdument.

hops [hɒps] *npl Bot* houblon *m*.

hopscotch ['hɒpskɒtʃ] *n* (*game*) marelle *f*.

horde [hɔːd] *n* horde *f*, foule *f*.

horizon [hə'raɪz(ə)n] *n* horizon *m*; **on the h.** à l'horizon.

horizontal [hɒrɪ'zɒnt(ə)l] *a* horizontal. ◆**-ly** *adv* horizontalement.

hormone ['hɔːməʊn] *n* hormone *f*.

horn [hɔːn] **1** *n* (*of animal*) corne *f*; *Mus* cor *m*; *Aut* klaxon® *m*. **2** *vi* **to h. in** *Am Fam* dire son mot, interrompre.

hornet ['hɔːnɪt] *n* (*insect*) frelon *m*.

horoscope ['hɒrəskəʊp] *n* horoscope *m*.

horror ['hɒrər] *n* horreur *f*; (*little*) **h.** (*child*) *Fam* petit monstre *m*; – *a* (*film etc*) d'épouvante, d'horreur. ◆**ho'rrendous** *a* horrible. ◆**horrible** *a* horrible, affreux. ◆**horribly** *adv* horriblement. ◆**horrid** *a* horrible; (*child*) épouvantable, méchant. ◆**ho'rrific** *a* horrible, horrifiant. ◆**horrify** *vt* horrifier.

hors-d'œuvre [ɔː'dɜːv] *n* hors-d'œuvre *m inv*.

horse [hɔːs] *n* **1** cheval *m*; **to go h. riding** faire du cheval; **h. show** concours *m* hippique. **2 h. chestnut** marron *m* (d'Inde). ◆**horseback** *n* **on h.** à cheval. ◆**horseman** *n* (*pl* **-men**) cavalier *m*. ◆**horseplay** *n* jeux *mpl* brutaux. ◆**horsepower** *n* cheval *m* (vapeur). ◆**horseracing** *n* courses *fpl*. ◆**horseradish** *n* radis *m* noir, raifort *m*. ◆**horseshoe** *n* fer *m* à cheval. ◆**horsewoman** *n* (*pl* **-women**) cavalière *f*.

horticulture ['hɔːtɪkʌltʃər] *n* horticulture *f*. ◆**horti'cultural** *a* horticole.

hose [həʊz] *n* (*tube*) tuyau *m*; – *vt* (*garden etc*) arroser. ◆**hosepipe** *n* tuyau *m*.

hosiery ['həʊzɪərɪ, *Am* 'həʊʒərɪ] *n* bonneterie *f*.

hospice ['hɒspɪs] *n* (*for dying people*) hospice *m* (*pour incurables*).

hospitable [hɒ'spɪtəb(ə)l] *a* hospitalier. ◆**hospitably** *adv* avec hospitalité. ◆**hospi'tality** *n* hospitalité *f*.

hospital ['hɒspɪt(ə)l] *n* hôpital *m*; **in h.,** *Am*

in the h. à l'hôpital; – *a* (*bed etc*) d'hôpital; (*staff, services*) hospitalier. ◆**hospitalize** *vt* hospitaliser.

host [həʊst] *n* **1** (*man who receives guests*) hôte *m*. **2 a h. of** (*many*) une foule de. **3** *Rel* hostie *f*. ◆**hostess** *n* (*in house, aircraft, nightclub*) hôtesse *f*.

hostage ['hɒstɪdʒ] *n* otage *m*; **to take s.o. h.** prendre qn en otage.

hostel ['hɒst(ə)l] *n* foyer *m*; **youth h.** auberge *f* de jeunesse.

hostile ['hɒstaɪl, *Am* 'hɒst(ə)l] *a* hostile (**to, towards** à). ◆**ho'stility** *n* hostilité *f* (**to, towards** envers); *pl Mil* hostilités *fpl*.

hot¹ [hɒt] *a* (**hotter, hottest**) chaud; (*spice*) fort; (*temperament*) passionné; (*news*) *Fam* dernier; (*favourite*) *Sp* grand; **to be** *or* **feel h.** avoir chaud; **it's h.** il fait chaud; **not so h. at** (*good at*) *Fam* pas très calé en; **not so h.** (*bad*) *Fam* pas fameux; **h. dog** (*sausage*) hot-dog *m*. ◆**hotbed** *n Pej* foyer *m* (**of** de). ◆**hot-'blooded** *a* ardent. ◆**hothead** *n* tête *f* brûlée. ◆**hot-'headed** *a* impétueux. ◆**hothouse** *n* serre *f* (chaude). ◆**hotplate** *n* chauffe-plats *m inv*; (*on stove*) plaque *f* chauffante. ◆**hot-'tempered** *a* emporté. ◆**hot-'water bottle** *n* bouillotte *f*.

hot² [hɒt] *vi* (**-tt-**) **to h. up** (*increase*) s'intensifier; (*become dangerous or excited*) chauffer.

hotchpotch ['hɒtʃpɒtʃ] *n* fatras *m*.

hotel [həʊ'tel] *n* hôtel *m*; – *a* (*industry*) hôtelier. ◆**hotelier** [həʊ'telɪeɪ] *n* hôtelier, -ière *mf*.

hotly ['hɒtlɪ] *adv* passionnément.

hound [haʊnd] **1** *n* (*dog*) chien *m* courant. **2** *vt* (*pursue*) poursuivre avec acharnement; (*worry*) harceler.

hour ['aʊər] *n* heure *f*; **half an h., a half-h.** une demi-heure; **a quarter of an h.** un quart d'heure; **paid ten francs an h.** payé dix francs (de) l'heure; **ten miles an h.** dix miles à l'heure; **open all hours** ouvert à toute heure; **h. hand** (*of watch, clock*) petite aiguille *f*. ◆**-ly** *a* (*rate, pay*) horaire; **an h. bus/train/etc** un bus/train/etc toutes les heures; – *adv* toutes les heures; **h. paid, paid h.** payé à l'heure.

house¹, *pl* **-ses** [haʊs, -zɪz] *n* maison *f*; (*audience*) *Th* salle *f*, auditoire *m*; (*performance*) *Th* séance *f*; **the H.** *Pol* la Chambre; **the Houses of Parliament** le Parlement; **at** *or* **to my h.** chez moi; **on the h.** (*free of charge*) aux frais de la maison; **h. prices** prix *mpl* immobiliers. ◆**housebound** *a* confiné chez soi. ◆**house-**

breaking n Jur cambriolage m. ◆**house-broken** a (dog etc) Am propre. ◆**household** n ménage m, maison f, famille f; **h. duties** soins mpl du ménage; **a h. name** un nom très connu. ◆**householder** n (owner) propriétaire mf; (family head) chef m de famille. ◆**housekeeper** n (employee) gouvernante f; (housewife) ménagère f. ◆**housekeeping** n ménage m. ◆**houseman** n (pl -men) interne mf (des hôpitaux). ◆**houseproud** a qui s'occupe méticuleusement de sa maison. ◆**housetrained** a (dog etc) propre. ◆**housewarming** n & a **to have a h.-warming (party)** pendre la crémaillère. ◆**housewife** n (pl -wives) ménagère f. ◆**housework** n (travaux mpl de) ménage m.

hous/e² [hauz] vt loger; (of building) abriter; **it is housed in** (kept) on le garde dans. ◆**—ing** n logement m; (houses) logements mpl; — a (crisis etc) du logement.

hovel ['hɒv(ə)l] n (slum) taudis m.

hover ['hɒvər] vi (of bird, aircraft, danger etc) planer; (of person) rôder, traîner. ◆**hovercraft** n aéroglisseur m.

how [hau] adv comment; **h.'s that?, h. so?, h. come?** Fam comment ça?; **h. kind!** comme c'est gentil!; **h. do you do?** (greeting) bonjour; **h. long/high is . . . ?** quelle est la longueur/hauteur de . . . ?; **h. much?, h. many?** combien?; **h. much time/etc?** combien de temps/etc?; **h. many apples/etc?** combien de pommes/etc?; **h. about a walk?** si on faisait une promenade?; **h. about some coffee?** (si on prenait) du café?; **h. about me?** et moi?

howdy! ['haudɪ] int Am Fam salut!

however [hau'evər] **1** adv **h. big he may be** quelque or si grand qu'il soit; **h. she may do it** de quelque manière qu'elle le fasse; **h. that may be** quoi qu'il en soit. **2** conj cependant.

howl [haul] vi hurler; (of baby) brailler; (of wind) mugir; — n hurlement m; braillement m; mugissement m; (of laughter) éclat m.

howler ['haulər] n (mistake) Fam gaffe f.

HP [eɪtʃ'piː] abbr = **hire purchase.**

hp abbr (horsepower) CV.

HQ [eɪtʃ'kjuː] abbr = **headquarters.**

hub [hʌb] n (of wheel) moyeu m; Fig centre m. ◆**hubcap** n Aut enjoliveur m.

hubbub ['hʌbʌb] n vacarme m.

huckleberry ['hʌk(ə)lbərɪ] n Bot Am myrtille f.

huddle ['hʌd(ə)l] vi **to h. (together)** se blottir (les uns contre les autres).

hue [hjuː] n (colour) teinte f.

huff [hʌf] n **in a h.** (offended) Fam fâché.

hug [hʌg] vt (-gg-) (person) serrer dans ses bras, étreindre; **to h. the kerb/coast** (stay near) serrer le trottoir/la côte; — n (embrace) étreinte f.

huge [hjuːdʒ] a énorme. ◆**—ly** adv énormément. ◆**—ness** n énormité f.

hulk [hʌlk] n (person) lourdaud, -aude mf.

hull [hʌl] n (of ship) coque f.

hullabaloo [hʌləbə'luː] n Fam (noise) vacarme m; (fuss) histoire(s) f(pl).

hullo! ['hʌ'ləu] int = **hallo.**

hum [hʌm] vi (-mm-) (of insect) bourdonner; (of person) fredonner; (of top, radio) ronfler; (of engine) vrombir; — vt (tune) fredonner; — n (of insect) bourdonnement m.

human ['hjuːmən] a humain; **h. being** être m humain; — npl humains mpl. ◆**hu'mane** a (kind) humain. ◆**hu'manely** adv humainement. ◆**humani'tarian** a & n humanitaire (mf). ◆**hu'manity** n (human beings, kindness etc) humanité f. ◆**humanly** adv (possible etc) humainement.

humble ['hʌmb(ə)l] a humble; — vt humilier. ◆**humbly** adv humblement.

humbug ['hʌmbʌg] n (talk) fumisterie f; (person) fumiste mf.

humdrum ['hʌmdrʌm] a monotone.

humid ['hjuːmɪd] a humide. ◆**hu'midify** vt humidifier. ◆**hu'midity** n humidité f.

humiliate [hjuː'mɪlɪeɪt] vt humilier. ◆**humili'ation** n humiliation f. ◆**humility** n humilité f.

humour ['hjuːmər] **1** n (fun) humour m; (temper) humeur f; **to have a sense of h.** avoir le sens de l'humour; **in a good h.** de bonne humeur. **2** vt **to h. s.o.** faire plaisir à qn, ménager qn. ◆**humorist** n humoriste mf. ◆**humorous** a (book etc) humoristique; (person) plein d'humour. ◆**humorously** adv avec humour.

hump [hʌmp] **1** n (lump, mound) bosse f; — vt (one's back) voûter. **2** n **to have the h.** Fam (depression) avoir le cafard; (bad temper) être en rogne. ◆**humpback** a **h. bridge** Aut pont m en dos d'âne.

hunch [hʌntʃ] **1** vt (one's shoulders) voûter. **2** n (idea) Fam intuition f, idée f. ◆**hunchback** n bossu, -ue mf.

hundred ['hʌndrəd] a & n cent (m); **a h. pages** cent pages; **two h. pages** deux cents pages; **hundreds of** des centaines de.

◆**hundredfold** a centuple; – adv au centuple. ◆**hundredth** a & n centième (mf). ◆**hundredweight** n 112 livres (= 50,8 kg); Am 100 livres (= 45,3 kg).

hung [hʌŋ] see hang¹.

Hungary ['hʌŋgəri] n Hongrie f. ◆**Hun'garian** a & n hongrois, -oise (mf); – n (language) hongrois m.

hunger ['hʌŋgər] n faim f. ◆**hungry** a (-ier, -iest) to be or feel h. avoir faim; to go h. souffrir de la faim; to make h. donner faim à; h. for (news etc) avide de. ◆**hungrily** adv avidement.

hunk [hʌŋk] n (gros) morceau m.

hunt [hʌnt] n Sp chasse f; (search) recherche f (for de); – vt Sp chasser; (pursue) poursuivre; (seek) chercher; to h. down (fugitive etc) traquer; to h. out (information etc) dénicher; – vi Sp chasser; to h. for sth (re)chercher qch. ◆**—ing** n Sp chasse f. ◆**—er** n (person) chasseur m.

hurdle ['hɜːd(ə)l] n (fence) Sp haie f; Fig obstacle m.

hurl [hɜːl] vt (throw) jeter, lancer; (abuse) lancer; to h. oneself at s.o. se ruer sur qn.

hurly-burly ['hɜːlɪbɜːlɪ] n tumulte m.

hurray! [hu'reɪ] int hourra!

hurricane ['hʌrɪkən, Am 'hʌrɪkeɪn] n ouragan m.

hurry ['hʌrɪ] n hâte f; in a h. à la hâte, en hâte; to be in a h. être pressé; to be in a h. to do avoir hâte de faire; there's no h. rien ne presse; – vi se dépêcher, se presser (to do de faire); to h. out sortir à la hâte; to h. along or on or up se dépêcher; – vt (person) bousculer, presser; (pace) presser; to h. one's meal manger à toute vitesse; to h. s.o. out faire sortir qn à la hâte. ◆**hurried** a (steps, decision etc) précipité; (travail) fait à la hâte; (visit) éclair inv; to be h. (in a hurry) être pressé.

hurt [hɜːt] vt (pt & pp hurt) (physically) faire du mal à, blesser; (emotionally) faire de la peine à; (offend) blesser; (prejudice, damage) nuire à; to h. s.o.'s feelings blesser qn; his arm hurts (him) son bras lui fait mal; – vi faire mal; – n mal m; – a (injured) blessé. ◆**hurtful** a (remark) blessant.

hurtle ['hɜːt(ə)l] vi to h. along aller à toute vitesse; to h. down dégringoler.

husband ['hʌzbənd] n mari m.

hush [hʌʃ] int chut!; – n silence m; – vt (person) faire taire; (baby) calmer; to h. up (scandal) Fig étouffer. ◆**—ed** a (voice) étouffé; (silence) profond. ◆**hush-hush** a Fam ultra-secret.

husk [hʌsk] n (of rice, grain) enveloppe f.

husky ['hʌskɪ] a (-ier, -iest) (voice) enroué, voilé.

hussy ['hʌsɪ] n Pej friponne f, coquine f.

hustings ['hʌstɪŋz] npl campagne f électorale, élections fpl.

hustle ['hʌs(ə)l] 1 vt (shove, rush) bousculer (qn); – vi (work busily) Am se démener (to get sth pour avoir qch). 2 n h. and bustle agitation f, activité f, tourbillon m.

hut [hʌt] n cabane f, hutte f.

hutch [hʌtʃ] n (for rabbit) clapier m.

hyacinth ['haɪəsɪnθ] n jacinthe f.

hybrid ['haɪbrɪd] a & n hybride (m).

hydrangea [haɪ'dreɪndʒə] n (shrub) hortensia m.

hydrant ['haɪdrənt] n (fire) h. bouche f d'incendie.

hydraulic [haɪ'drɔːlɪk] a hydraulique.

hydroelectric [haɪdrəʊɪ'lektrɪk] a hydroélectrique.

hydrogen ['haɪdrədʒən] n Ch hydrogène m.

hyena [haɪ'iːnə] n (animal) hyène f.

hygiene ['haɪdʒiːn] n hygiène f. ◆**hy'gienic** a hygiénique.

hymn [hɪm] n Rel cantique m, hymne m.

hyper- ['haɪpər] pref hyper-.

hypermarket ['haɪpəmɑːkɪt] n hypermarché m.

hyphen ['haɪf(ə)n] n trait m d'union. ◆**hyphenat/e** vt mettre un trait d'union à. ◆**—ed** a (word) à trait d'union.

hypnosis [hɪp'nəʊsɪs] n hypnose f. ◆**hypnotic** a hypnotique. ◆**'hypnotism** n hypnotisme m. ◆**'hypnotist** n hypnotiseur m. ◆**'hypnotize** vt hypnotiser.

hypochondriac [haɪpə'kɒndrɪæk] n malade mf imaginaire.

hypocrisy [hɪ'pɒkrɪsɪ] n hypocrisie f. ◆**'hypocrite** n hypocrite mf. ◆**hypo'critical** a hypocrite.

hypodermic [haɪpə'dɜːmɪk] a hypodermique.

hypothesis, pl **-eses** [haɪ'pɒθɪsɪs, -ɪsiːz] n hypothèse f. ◆**hypo'thetical** a hypothétique.

hysteria [hɪ'stɪərɪə] n hystérie f. ◆**hysterical** a hystérique; (funny) Fam désopilant; to be or become h. (wildly upset) avoir une crise de nerfs. ◆**hysterically** adv (to cry) sans pouvoir s'arrêter; to laugh h. rire aux larmes. ◆**hysterics** npl (tears etc) crise f de nerfs; (laughter) crise f de rire.

I

I, i [aɪ] *n* I, i *m*.
I [aɪ] *pron* je, j'; (*stressed*) moi; **I want** je
veux; **she and I** elle et moi.
ic/e¹ [aɪs] *n* glace *f*; (*on road*) verglas *m*; **i.
(cream)** glace *f*; **black i.** (*on road*) verglas
m; **i. cube** glaçon *m*; — *vi* **to i.** (**over**) (*of
lake*) geler; (*of windscreen*) givrer. ◆—**ed** *a*
(*tea*) glacé. ◆**iceberg** *n* iceberg *m*
◆**icebox** *n* (*box*) & *Fig* glacière *f*; *Am*
réfrigérateur *m*. ◆**ice-'cold** *a* glacial;
(*drink*) glacé. ◆**ice-skating** *n* patinage *m*
(sur glace). ◆**icicle** *n* glaçon *m*.
ic/e² [aɪs] *vt* (*cake*) glacer. ◆—**ing** *n* (*on
cake etc*) glaçage *m*.
Iceland ['aɪslənd] *n* Islande *f*. ◆**Ice'landic**
a islandais.
icon ['aɪkɒn] *n* *Rel* icône *f*.
icy ['aɪsɪ] *a* (**-ier, -iest**) (*water, hands, room*)
glacé; (*manner, weather*) glacial; (*road etc*)
verglacé.
idea [aɪ'dɪə] *n* idée *f* (**of** de); **I have an i. that
...** j'ai l'impression que ... ; **that's my i.
of rest** c'est ce que j'appelle du repos; **that's
the i.!** *Fam* c'est ça!; **not the slightest** *or*
foggiest i. pas la moindre idée.
ideal [aɪ'dɪəl] *a* idéal; — *n* (*aspiration*) idéal
m; *pl* (*spiritual etc*) idéal *m*. ◆**idealism** *n*
idéalisme *m*. ◆**idealist** *n* idéaliste *mf*.
◆**idea'listic** *a* idéaliste. ◆**idealize** *vt*
idéaliser. ◆**ideally** *adv* idéalement; **i. we
should stay** l'idéal, ce serait de rester *or* que
nous restions.
identical [aɪ'dentɪk(ə)l] *a* identique (**to, with**
à). ◆**identifi'cation** *n* identification *f*; **I
have (some) i.** j'ai une pièce d'identité.
◆**identify** *vt* identifier; **to i.** (**oneself**) **with**
s'identifier avec. ◆**identikit** *n* portrait-
robot *m*. ◆**identity** *n* identité *f*; **i. card**
carte *f* d'identité.
ideology [aɪdɪ'ɒlədʒɪ] *n* idéologie *f*. ◆**ideo-
'logical** *a* idéologique.
idiom ['ɪdɪəm] *n* expression *f* idiomatique;
(*language*) idiome *m*. ◆**idio'matic** *a* idiomatique.
idiosyncrasy [ɪdɪə'sɪŋkrəsɪ] *n* particularité
f.
idiot ['ɪdɪət] *n* idiot, -ote *mf*. ◆**idiocy** *n* idiotie *f*. ◆**idi'otic** *a* idiot, bête. ◆**idi'otically**
adv idiotement.
idle ['aɪd(ə)l] *a* (*unoccupied*) désœuvré, oisif;

(*lazy*) paresseux; (*unemployed*) en
chômage; (*moment*) de loisir; (*machine*) au
repos; (*promise*) vain; (*pleasure, question*)
futile; (*rumour*) sans fondement; — *vi* (*laze
about*) paresser; (*of machine, engine*)
tourner au ralenti; — *vt* **to i. away** (*time*)
gaspiller. ◆—**ness** *n* oisiveté *f*; (*laziness*)
paresse *f*. ◆**idler** *n* paresseux, -euse *mf*.
◆**idly** *adv* paresseusement; (*to suggest,
say*) négligemment.
idol ['aɪd(ə)l] *n* idole *f*. ◆**idolize** *vt* idolâtrer.
idyllic [aɪ'dɪlɪk] *a* idyllique.
i.e. [aɪ'iː] *abbr* (*id est*) c'est-à-dire.
if [ɪf] *conj* si; **if he comes** s'il vient; **even if**
même si; **if so** dans ce cas, si c'est le cas; **if
not for pleasure** sinon pour le plaisir; **if
only I were rich** si seulement j'étais riche; **if
only to look** ne serait-ce que pour regarder;
as if comme si; **as if nothing had happened**
comme si de rien n'était; **as if to say** comme
pour dire; **if necessary** s'il le faut.
igloo ['ɪgluː] *n* igloo *m*.
ignite [ɪg'naɪt] *vt* mettre le feu à; — *vi* prendre feu. ◆**ignition** *n* *Aut* allumage *m*; **to
switch on the i.** mettre le contact.
ignominious [ɪgnə'mɪnɪəs] *a* déshonorant,
ignominieux.
ignoramus [ɪgnə'reɪməs] *n* ignare *mf*.
ignorance ['ɪgnərəns] *n* ignorance *f* (**of** de).
◆**ignorant** *a* ignorant (**of** de). ◆**igno-
rantly** *adv* par ignorance.
ignore [ɪg'nɔːr] *vt* ne prêter aucune attention
à, ne tenir aucun compte de; (*duty*) méconnaître; (*pretend not to recognize*) faire
semblant de ne pas reconnaître.
ilk [ɪlk] *n* **of that i.** (*kind*) de cet acabit.
ill [ɪl] *a* (*sick*) malade; (*bad*) mauvais; **i. will**
malveillance *f*; — *npl* (*misfortunes*) maux
mpl, malheurs *mpl*; — *adv* mal; **to speak i.
of** dire du mal de. ◆**ill-ad'vised** *a*
malavisé, peu judicieux. ◆**ill-'fated** *a*
malheureux. ◆**ill-'gotten** *a* mal acquis.
◆**ill-in'formed** *a* mal renseigné. ◆**ill-
'mannered** *a* mal élevé. ◆**ill-'natured** *a*
(*mean, unkind*) désagréable. ◆**ill-'timed** *a*
inopportun. ◆**ill-'treat** *vt* maltraiter.
illegal [ɪ'liːg(ə)l] *a* illégal. ◆**ille'gality** *n*
illégalité *f*.
illegible [ɪ'ledʒəb(ə)l] *a* illisible.

illegitimate [ɪlɪ'dʒɪtɪmət] *a* (*child, claim*) illégitime. ◆**illegitimacy** *n* illégitimité *f.*

illicit [ɪ'lɪsɪt] *a* illicite.

illiterate [ɪ'lɪtərət] *a* & *n* illettré, -ée (*mf*), analphabète (*mf*). ◆**illiteracy** *n* analphabétisme *m.*

illness ['ɪlnɪs] *n* maladie *f.*

illogical [ɪ'lɒdʒɪk(ə)l] *a* illogique.

illuminate [ɪ'luːmɪneɪt] *vt* (*street, question etc*) éclairer; (*monument etc for special occasion*) illuminer. ◆**illumi'nation** *n* éclairage *m;* illumination *f.*

illusion [ɪ'luːʒ(ə)n] *n* illusion *f* (*about* sur); **I'm not under any i.** je ne me fais aucune illusion (*about* sur, quant à). ◆**illusive** *a,* ◆**illusory** *a* illusoire.

illustrate ['ɪləstreɪt] *vt* (*with pictures, examples*) illustrer (*with* de). ◆**illu'stration** *n* illustration *f.* ◆**i'llustrative** *a* (*example*) explicatif.

illustrious [ɪ'lʌstrɪəs] *a* illustre.

image ['ɪmɪdʒ] *n* image *f;* (*public*) **i.** (*of firm etc*) image *f* de marque; **he's the** (**living** *or* **spitting** *or* **very**) **i. of his brother** c'est (tout) le portrait de son frère. ◆**imagery** *n* images *fpl.*

imagin/e [ɪ'mædʒɪn] *vt* (*picture to oneself*) (s')imaginer, se figurer (*that* que); (*suppose*) imaginer (*that* que); **i. that . . .** imaginez que . . . ; **you're imagining (things)!** tu te fais des illusions! ◆**—ings** *npl* (*dreams*) imaginations *fpl.* ◆**—able** *a* imaginable; **the worst thing i.** le pire que l'on puisse imaginer. ◆**imaginary** *a* imaginaire. ◆**imagi'nation** *n* imagination *f.* ◆**imaginative** *a* plein d'imagination, imaginatif.

imbalance [ɪm'bæləns] *n* déséquilibre *m.*

imbecile ['ɪmbəsiːl, *Am* 'ɪmbəs(ə)l] *a* & *n* imbécile (*mf*). ◆**imbe'cility** *n* imbécillité *f.*

imbibe [ɪm'baɪb] *vt* absorber.

imbued [ɪm'bjuːd] *a* **i. with** (*ideas*) imprégné de; (*feelings*) pénétré de, imbu de.

imitate ['ɪmɪteɪt] *vt* imiter. ◆**imi'tation** *n* imitation *f;* — *a* (*jewels*) artificiel; **i. leather** imitation *f* cuir. ◆**imitative** *a* imitateur. ◆**imitator** *n* imitateur, -trice *mf.*

immaculate [ɪ'mækjʊlət] *a* (*person, appearance, shirt etc*) impeccable.

immaterial [ɪmə'tɪərɪəl] *a* peu important (**to** pour).

immature [ɪmə'tʃʊər] *a* (*fruit*) vert; (*animal*) jeune; (*person*) qui manque de maturité.

immeasurable [ɪ'meʒərəb(ə)l] *a* incommensurable.

immediate [ɪ'miːdɪət] *a* immédiat. ◆**immediacy** *n* caractère *m* immédiat. ◆**immediately** *adv* (*at once*) tout de suite, immédiatement; (*to concern, affect*) directement; — *conj* (*as soon as*) dès que.

immense [ɪ'mens] *a* immense. ◆**immensely** *adv* (*rich etc*) immensément; **to enjoy oneself i.** s'amuser énormément. ◆**immensity** *n* immensité *f.*

immerse [ɪ'mɜːs] *vt* plonger, immerger; **immersed in work** plongé dans le travail. ◆**immersion** *n* immersion *f;* **i. heater** chauffe-eau *m inv* électrique.

immigrate ['ɪmɪɡreɪt] *vi* immigrer. ◆**immigrant** *n* immigrant, -ante *mf;* (*long-established*) immigré, -ée *mf;* — *a* immigré. ◆**immi'gration** *n* immigration *f.*

imminent ['ɪmɪnənt] *a* imminent. ◆**imminence** *n* imminence *f.*

immobile [ɪ'məʊbaɪl, *Am* ɪ'məʊb(ə)l] *a* immobile. ◆**immo'bility** *n* immobilité *f.* ◆**immobilize** *vt* immobiliser.

immoderate [ɪ'mɒdərət] *a* immodéré.

immodest [ɪ'mɒdɪst] *a* impudique.

immoral [ɪ'mɒrəl] *a* immoral. ◆**immo-'rality** *n* immoralité *f.*

immortal [ɪ'mɔːt(ə)l] *a* immortel. ◆**immor-'tality** *n* immortalité *f.* ◆**immortalize** *vt* immortaliser.

immune [ɪ'mjuːn] *a Med & Fig* immunisé (**to, from** contre). ◆**immunity** *n* immunité *f.* ◆**'immunize** *vt* immuniser (**against** contre).

immutable [ɪ'mjuːtəb(ə)l] *a* immuable.

imp [ɪmp] *n* diablotin *m,* lutin *m.*

impact ['ɪmpækt] *n* impact *m* (**on** sur).

impair [ɪm'peər] *vt* détériorer; (*hearing, health*) abîmer.

impale [ɪm'peɪl] *vt* empaler.

impart [ɪm'pɑːt] *vt* communiquer (**to** à).

impartial [ɪm'pɑːʃ(ə)l] *a* impartial. ◆**imparti'ality** *n* impartialité *f.*

impassable [ɪm'pɑːsəb(ə)l] *a* (*road*) impraticable; (*river*) infranchissable.

impasse ['æmpɑːs, *Am* 'ɪmpæs] *n* (*situation*) impasse *f.*

impassioned [ɪm'pæʃ(ə)nd] *a* (*speech etc*) enflammé, passionné.

impassive [ɪm'pæsɪv] *a* impassible. ◆**—ness** *n* impassibilité *f.*

impatient [ɪm'peɪʃ(ə)nt] *a* impatient (**to do** de faire); **i. of** *or* **with** intolérant à l'égard de. ◆**impatience** *n* impatience *f.* ◆**impatiently** *adv* impatiemment.

impeccab/le [ɪm'pekəb(ə)l] *a* impeccable. ◆**—ly** *adv* impeccablement.

impecunious [ɪmpɪˈkjuːnɪəs] *a Hum* sans le sou, impécunieux.

impede [ɪmˈpiːd] *vt* (*hamper*) gêner; **to i. s.o. from doing** (*prevent*) empêcher qn de faire.

impediment [ɪmˈpedɪmənt] *n* obstacle *m*; (*of speech*) défaut *m* d'élocution.

impel [ɪmˈpel] *vt* (-ll-) (*drive*) pousser; (*force*) obliger (**to do** à faire).

impending [ɪmˈpendɪŋ] *a* imminent.

impenetrable [ɪmˈpenɪtrəb(ə)l] *a* (*forest, mystery etc*) impénétrable.

imperative [ɪmˈperətɪv] *a* (*need, tone*) impérieux; (*necessary*) essentiel; **it is i. that you come** il faut absolument que *or* il est indispensable que tu viennes; – *n Gram* impératif *m*.

imperceptible [ɪmpəˈseptəb(ə)l] *a* imperceptible (**to** à).

imperfect [ɪmˈpɜːfɪkt] **1** *a* imparfait; (*goods*) défectueux. **2** *n* (*tense*) *Gram* imparfait *m*. ◆**imper'fection** *n* imperfection *f*.

imperial [ɪmˈpɪərɪəl] *a* impérial; (*majestic*) majestueux; (*measure*) *Br* légal. ◆**imperialism** *n* impérialisme *m*.

imperil [ɪmˈperɪl] *vt* (-ll-, *Am* -l-) mettre en péril.

imperious [ɪmˈpɪərɪəs] *a* impérieux.

impersonal [ɪmˈpɜːsən(ə)l] *a* impersonnel.

impersonate [ɪmˈpɜːsəneɪt] *vt* (*mimic*) imiter; (*pretend to be*) se faire passer pour. ◆**imperso'nation** *n* imitation *f*. ◆**impersonator** *n* imitateur, -trice *mf*.

impertinent [ɪmˈpɜːtɪnənt] *a* impertinent (**to** envers). ◆**impertinence** *n* impertinence *f*. ◆**impertinently** *adv* avec impertinence.

impervious [ɪmˈpɜːvɪəs] *a* imperméable (**to** à).

impetuous [ɪmˈpetjʊəs] *a* impétueux. ◆**impetu'osity** *n* impétuosité *f*.

impetus [ˈɪmpɪtəs] *n* impulsion *f*.

impinge [ɪmˈpɪndʒ] *vi* **to i. on** (*affect*) affecter; (*encroach on*) empiéter sur.

impish [ˈɪmpɪʃ] *a* (*naughty*) espiègle.

implacable [ɪmˈplækəb(ə)l] *a* implacable.

implant [ɪmˈplɑːnt] *vt* (*ideas*) inculquer (**in** à).

implement¹ [ˈɪmplɪmənt] *n* (*tool*) instrument *m*; (*utensil*) *Culin* ustensile *m*; *pl Agr* matériel *m*.

implement² [ˈɪmplɪment] *vt* (*carry out*) mettre en œuvre, exécuter. ◆**implemen'tation** *n* mise *f* en œuvre, exécution *f*.

implicate [ˈɪmplɪkeɪt] *vt* impliquer (**in** dans). ◆**impli'cation** *n* (*consequence, involvement*) implication *f*; (*innuendo*) insinuation *f*; (*impact*) portée *f*; **by i.** implicitement.

implicit [ɪmˈplɪsɪt] *a* (*implied*) implicite;

(*belief, obedience etc*) absolu. ◆**—ly** *adv* implicitement.

implore [ɪmˈplɔːr] *vt* implorer (**s.o. to do** qn de faire).

imply [ɪmˈplaɪ] *vt* (*assume*) impliquer, supposer (**that** que); (*suggest*) laisser entendre (**that** que); (*insinuate*) *Pej* insinuer (**that** que). ◆**implied** *a* implicite.

impolite [ɪmpəˈlaɪt] *a* impoli. ◆**—ness** *n* impolitesse *f*.

import 1 [ɪmˈpɔːt] *vt* (*goods etc*) importer (**from** de); – [ˈɪmpɔːt] *n* (*object, action*) importation *f*. **2** [ˈɪmpɔːt] *n* (*meaning*) sens *m*. ◆**im'porter** *n* importateur, -trice *mf*.

importance [ɪmˈpɔːtəns] *n* importance *f*; **to be of i.** avoir de l'importance; **of no i.** sans importance. ◆**important** *a* (*significant*) important. ◆**importantly** *adv* **more i.** ce qui est plus important.

impose [ɪmˈpəʊz] *vt* imposer (**on** à); (*fine, punishment*) infliger (**on** à); **to i.** (**oneself**) **on s.o.** s'imposer à qn; – *vi* s'imposer. ◆**impo'sition** *n* imposition *f* (**of** de); (*inconvenience*) dérangement *m*.

impossible [ɪmˈpɒsəb(ə)l] *a* impossible (**to do** à faire); **it is i. (for us) to do** il (nous) est impossible de faire; **it is i. that** il est impossible que (+ *sub*); **to make it i. for s.o. to do** mettre qn dans l'impossibilité de faire; – *n* **to do the i.** faire l'impossible. ◆**impossi'bility** *n* impossibilité *f*. ◆**impossibly** *adv* (*late, hard*) incroyablement.

impostor [ɪmˈpɒstər] *n* imposteur *m*.

impotent [ˈɪmpətənt] *a Med* impuissant. ◆**impotence** *n Med* impuissance *f*.

impound [ɪmˈpaʊnd] *vt* (*of police*) saisir, confisquer; (*vehicle*) emmener à la fourrière.

impoverish [ɪmˈpɒvərɪʃ] *vt* appauvrir.

impracticable [ɪmˈpræktɪkəb(ə)l] *a* irréalisable, impraticable.

impractical [ɪmˈpræktɪk(ə)l] *a* peu réaliste.

imprecise [ɪmprɪˈsaɪs] *a* imprécis.

impregnable [ɪmˈpregnəb(ə)l] *a Mil* imprenable; (*argument*) *Fig* inattaquable.

impregnate [ˈɪmpregneɪt] *vt* (*imbue*) imprégner (**with** de); (*fertilize*) féconder.

impresario [ɪmprɪˈsɑːrɪəʊ] *n* (*pl* -os) impresario *m*.

impress [ɪmˈpres] *vt* impressionner (*qn*); (*mark*) imprimer; **to i. sth on s.o.** faire comprendre qch à qn. ◆**impression** *n* impression *f*; **to be under** *or* **have the i. that** avoir l'impression que; **to make a good i. on s.o.** faire une bonne impression à qn. ◆**impressionable** *a* (*person*) impressionnable; (age) où l'on est impressionnable. ◆**impressive** a impressionnant.

imprint [ɪmˈprɪnt] vt imprimer; – [ˈɪmprɪnt] n empreinte f.

imprison [ɪmˈprɪz(ə)n] vt emprisonner. ◆**—ment** n emprisonnement m; **life i.** la prison à vie.

improbable [ɪmˈprɒbəb(ə)l] a improbable; (story, excuse) invraisemblable. ◆**improba'bility** n improbabilité f; invraisemblance f.

impromptu [ɪmˈprɒmptjuː] a & adv impromptu.

improper [ɪmˈprɒpər] a (indecent) inconvenant, indécent; (wrong) incorrect. ◆**impropriety** [ɪmprəˈpraɪətɪ] n inconvenance f; (wrong use) Ling impropriété f.

improve [ɪmˈpruːv] vt améliorer; (mind) cultiver, développer; **to i. one's English** se perfectionner en anglais; **to i. s.o.'s looks** embellir qn; **to i. oneself** se cultiver; – vi s'améliorer; (of business) aller de mieux en mieux, reprendre; **to i. on** (do better than) faire mieux que. ◆**—ment** n amélioration f; (of mind) développement m; (progress) progrès m(pl); **there has been some** or **an i.** il y a du mieux.

improvise [ˈɪmprəvaɪz] vti improviser. ◆**improvi'sation** n improvisation f.

impudent [ˈɪmpjʊdənt] a impudent. ◆**impudence** n impudence f.

impulse [ˈɪmpʌls] n impulsion f; **on i.** sur un coup de tête. ◆**im'pulsive** a (person, act) impulsif, irréfléchi; (remark) irréfléchi. ◆**im'pulsively** adv de manière impulsive.

impunity [ɪmˈpjuːnɪtɪ] n **with i.** impunément.

impure [ɪmˈpjʊər] a impur. ◆**impurity** n impureté f.

in [ɪn] prep **1** dans; **in the box/the school/etc** dans la boîte/l'école/etc; **in an hour('s time)** dans une heure; **in so far as** dans la mesure où. **2** à; **in school** à l'école; **in the garden** dans le jardin, au jardin; **in Paris** à Paris; **in the USA** aux USA; **in Portugal** au Portugal; **in fashion** à la mode; **in pencil** au crayon; **in my opinion** à mon avis. **3** en; **in summer/secret/French** en été/secret/français; **in Spain** en Espagne; **in May** en mai, au mois de mai; **in season** en saison; **in an hour** (during the period of an hour) en une heure; **in doing en** faisant; **dressed in black** habillé en noir; **in all** en tout. **4** de; **in a soft voice** d'une voix douce; **the best in the class** le meilleur de la classe. **5** in **the rain** sous la pluie; **in the morning** le matin; **he hasn't done it in years** ça fait des années qu'il ne l'a pas fait; **in an hour** (at the end of

an hour) au bout d'une heure; **one in ten** un sur dix; **in thousands** par milliers; **in here** ici; **in there** là-dedans. **6** adv **to be in** (home) être là, être à la maison; (of train) être arrivé; (in fashion) être en vogue; (in season) être en saison; (in power) Pol être au pouvoir; **day in day out** jour après jour; **in on** (a secret) au courant de; **we're in for some rain/trouble/etc** on va avoir de la pluie/des ennuis/etc; **it's the in thing** Fam c'est dans le vent. **7** npl **the ins and outs of** les moindres détails de.

inability [ɪnəˈbɪlɪtɪ] n incapacité f (**to do** de faire).

inaccessible [ɪnakˈsesəb(ə)l] a inaccessible.

inaccurate [ɪnˈækjʊrət] a inexact. ◆**inaccuracy** n inexactitude f.

inaction [ɪnˈækʃ(ə)n] n inaction f.

inactive [ɪnˈæktɪv] a inactif; (mind) inerte. ◆**inac'tivity** n inactivité f, inaction f.

inadequate [ɪnˈædɪkwət] a (quantity) insuffisant; (person) pas à la hauteur, insuffisant; (work) médiocre. ◆**inadequacy** n insuffisance f. ◆**inadequately** adv insuffisamment.

inadmissible [ɪnədˈmɪsəb(ə)l] a inadmissible.

inadvertently [ɪnədˈvɜːtəntlɪ] adv par inadvertance.

inadvisable [ɪnədˈvaɪzəb(ə)l] a (action) à déconseiller; **it is i. to** il est déconseillé de.

inane [ɪˈneɪn] a (absurd) inepte.

inanimate [ɪnˈænɪmət] a inanimé.

inappropriate [ɪnəˈprəʊprɪət] a (unsuitable) peu approprié, inadéquat; (untimely) inopportun.

inarticulate [ɪnɑːˈtɪkjʊlət] a (person) incapable de s'exprimer; (sound) inarticulé.

inasmuch as [ɪnəzˈmʌtʃəz] adv (because) vu que; (to the extent that) en ce sens que.

inattentive [ɪnəˈtentɪv] a inattentif (**to** à).

inaudible [ɪnˈɔːdəb(ə)l] a inaudible.

inaugural [ɪˈnɔːgjʊrəl] a inaugural. ◆**inaugurate** vt (policy, building) inaugurer; (official) installer (dans ses fonctions). ◆**inaugu'ration** n inauguration f; investiture f.

inauspicious [ɪnɔːˈspɪʃəs] a peu propice.

inborn [ɪnˈbɔːn] a inné.

inbred [ɪnˈbred] a (quality etc) inné.

Inc abbr (Incorporated) Am Com SA, SARL.

incalculable [ɪnˈkælkjʊləb(ə)l] a incalculable.

incandescent [ɪnkænˈdes(ə)nt] a incandescent.

incapable [ɪnˈkeɪpəb(ə)l] a incapable (of

doing de faire); **i. of** (*pity etc*) inaccessible à.

incapacitate [ɪnkə'pæsɪteɪt] *vt Med* rendre incapable (*de travailler etc*). ◆**incapacity** *n* (*inability*) *Med* incapacité *f*.

incarcerate [ɪn'kɑːsəreɪt] *vt* incarcérer. ◆**incarce'ration** *n* incarcération *f*.

incarnate [ɪn'kɑːnət] *a* incarné; – [ɪn'kɑːneɪt] *vt* incarner. ◆**incar'nation** *n* incarnation *f*.

incendiary [ɪn'sendɪərɪ] *a* (*bomb*) incendiaire.

incense 1 [ɪn'sens] *vt* mettre en colère. **2** ['ɪnsens] *n* (*substance*) encens *m*.

incentive [ɪn'sentɪv] *n* encouragement *m*, motivation *f*; **to give s.o. an i. to work**/*etc* encourager qn à travailler/*etc*.

inception [ɪn'sepʃ(ə)n] *n* début *m*.

incessant [ɪn'ses(ə)nt] *a* incessant. ◆**—ly** *adv* sans cesse.

incest ['ɪnsest] *n* inceste *m*. ◆**in'cestuous** *a* incestueux.

inch [ɪntʃ] *n* pouce *m* (= 2,54 cm); (*loosely*) *Fig* centimètre *m*; **within an i. of** (*success*) à deux doigts de; **i. by i.** petit à petit; – *vti* **to i.** (*one's way*) **forward** avancer petit à petit.

incidence ['ɪnsɪdəns] *n* fréquence *f*.

incident ['ɪnsɪdənt] *n* incident *m*; (*in book, film etc*) épisode *m*.

incidental [ɪnsɪ'dent(ə)l] *a* accessoire, secondaire; (*music*) de fond; **i. expenses** frais *mpl* accessoires. ◆**—ly** *adv* accessoirement; (*by the way*) à propos.

incinerate [ɪn'sɪnəreɪt] *vt* (*refuse, leaves etc*) incinérer. ◆**incinerator** *n* incinérateur *m*.

incipient [ɪn'sɪpɪənt] *a* naissant.

incision [ɪn'sɪʒ(ə)n] *n* incision *f*.

incisive [ɪn'saɪsɪv] *a* incisif.

incisor [ɪn'saɪzər] *n* (*tooth*) incisive *f*.

incite [ɪn'saɪt] *vt* inciter (**to do** à faire). ◆**—ment** *n* incitation *f* (**to do** à faire).

incline 1 [ɪn'klaɪn] *vt* (*tilt, bend*) incliner; **to i. s.o. to do** incliner qn à faire; **to be inclined to do** (*feel a wish to*) être enclin à faire; (*tend to*) avoir tendance à faire; – *vi* **to i. or be inclined towards** (*indulgence etc*) incliner à. **2** ['ɪnklaɪn] *n* (*slope*) inclinaison *f*. ◆**incli'nation** *n* inclination *f*; **to have no i. to do** n'avoir aucune envie de faire.

includ/e [ɪn'kluːd] *vt* (*contain*) comprendre, englober; (*refer to*) s'appliquer à; **my invitation includes you** mon invitation s'adresse aussi à vous; **to be included** être compris; (*on list*) être inclus. ◆**—ing** *prep* y compris; **i. service** service *m* compris. ◆**inclusion** *n* inclusion *f*. ◆**inclusive** *a* inclus; **from the fourth to the tenth of May**

i. du quatre jusqu'au dix mai inclus(ivement); **to be i. of** comprendre; **i. charge** prix *m* global.

incognito [ɪnkɒg'niːtəʊ] *adv* incognito.

incoherent [ɪnkəʊ'hɪərənt] *a* incohérent. ◆**—ly** *adv* sans cohérence.

income ['ɪnkʌm] *n* revenu *m*; **private i.** rentes *fpl*; **i. tax** impôt *m* sur le revenu.

incoming ['ɪnkʌmɪŋ] *a* (*tenant, president*) nouveau; **i. tide** marée *f* montante; **i. calls** *Tel* appels *mpl* de l'extérieur.

incommunicado [ɪnkəmjuːnɪ'kɑːdəʊ] *a* (*tenu*) au secret.

incomparable [ɪn'kɒmpərəb(ə)l] *a* incomparable.

incompatible [ɪnkəm'pætəb(ə)l] *a* incompatible (**with** avec). ◆**incompati'bility** *n* incompatibilité *f*.

incompetent [ɪn'kɒmpɪtənt] *a* incompétent. ◆**incompetence** *n* incompétence *f*.

incomplete [ɪnkəm'pliːt] *a* incomplet.

incomprehensible [ɪnkɒmprɪ'hensəb(ə)l] *a* incompréhensible.

inconceivable [ɪnkən'siːvəb(ə)l] *a* inconcevable.

inconclusive [ɪnkən'kluːsɪv] *a* peu concluant.

incongruous [ɪn'kɒŋgruəs] *a* (*building, colours*) qui jure(nt) (**with** avec); (*remark, attitude*) incongru; (*absurd*) absurde.

inconsequential [ɪnkɒnsɪ'kwenʃ(ə)l] *a* sans importance.

inconsiderate [ɪnkən'sɪdərət] *a* (*action, remark*) irréfléchi, inconsidéré; **to be i.** (*of person*) manquer d'égards (**towards** envers).

inconsistent [ɪnkən'sɪstənt] *a* inconséquent, incohérent; (*reports etc at variance*) contradictoire; **i. with** incompatible avec. ◆**inconsistency** *n* inconséquence *f*, incohérence *f*.

inconsolable [ɪnkən'səʊləb(ə)l] *a* inconsolable.

inconspicuous [ɪnkən'spɪkjuəs] *a* peu en évidence, qui passe inaperçu. ◆**—ly** *adv* discrètement.

incontinent [ɪn'kɒntɪnənt] *a* incontinent.

inconvenient [ɪnkən'viːnɪənt] *a* (*room, situation*) incommode; (*time*) inopportun; **it's i. (for me) to ...** ça me dérange de ...; **that's very i.** c'est très gênant. ◆**inconvenience** *n* (*bother*) dérangement *m*; (*disadvantage*) inconvénient *m*; – *vt* déranger, gêner.

incorporate [ɪn'kɔːpəreɪt] *vt* (*introduce*) incorporer (**into** dans); (*contain*) contenir;

incorporated society *Am* société *f* anonyme, société *f* à responsabilité limitée.
incorrect [ɪnkə'rekt] *a* incorrect, inexact; **you're i.** vous avez tort.
incorrigible [ɪn'kɒrɪdʒəb(ə)l] *a* incorrigible.
incorruptible [ɪnkə'rʌptəb(ə)l] *a* incorruptible.
increas/e [ɪn'kriːs] *vi* augmenter; (*of effort, noise*) s'intensifier; **to i. in weight** prendre du poids; – *vt* augmenter; intensifier; – ['ɪnkriːs] *n* augmentation *f* (**in, of** de); intensification *f* (**in, of** de); **on the i.** en hausse. ◆**—ing** *a* (*amount etc*) croissant. ◆**—ingly** *adv* de plus en plus.
incredib/le [ɪn'kredəb(ə)l] *a* incroyable. ◆**—ly** *adv* incroyablement.
incredulous [ɪn'kredjʊləs] *a* incrédule. ◆**incre'dulity** *n* incrédulité *f*.
increment ['ɪŋkrəmənt] *n* augmentation *f*.
incriminat/e [ɪn'krɪmɪneɪt] *vt* incriminer. ◆**—ing** *a* compromettant.
incubate ['ɪŋkjʊbeɪt] *vt* (*eggs*) couver. ◆**incu'bation** *n* incubation *f*. ◆**incubator** *n* (*for baby, eggs*) couveuse *f*.
inculcate ['ɪnkʌlkeɪt] *vt* inculquer (**in** à).
incumbent [ɪn'kʌmbənt] *a* **it is i. upon him** *or* **her** to il lui incombe de; – *n Rel Pol* titulaire *mf*.
incur [ɪn'kɜːr] *vt* (**-rr-**) (*debt*) contracter; (*expenses*) faire; (*criticism, danger*) s'attirer.
incurable [ɪn'kjʊərəb(ə)l] *a* incurable.
incursion [ɪn'kɜːʃ(ə)n] *n* incursion *f* (**into** dans).
indebted [ɪn'detɪd] *a* **i. to s.o. for sth/for doing sth** redevable à qn de qch/d'avoir fait qch. ◆**—ness** *n* dette *f*.
indecent [ɪn'diːs(ə)nt] *a* (*offensive*) indécent; (*unsuitable*) peu approprié. ◆**indecency** *n* indécence *f*; (*crime*) *Jur* outrage *m* à la pudeur. ◆**indecently** *adv* indécemment.
indecisive [ɪndɪ'saɪsɪv] *a* (*person, answer*) indécis. ◆**indecision** *n*, ◆**indecisiveness** *n* indécision *f*.
indeed [ɪn'diːd] *adv* en effet; **very good/etc i.** vraiment très bon/*etc*; **yes i.!** bien sûr!; **thank you very much i.!** merci mille fois!
indefensible [ɪndɪ'fensəb(ə)l] *a* indéfendable.
indefinable [ɪndɪ'faɪnəb(ə)l] *a* indéfinissable.
indefinite [ɪn'defɪnət] *a* (*feeling, duration etc*) indéfini; (*plan*) mal déterminé. ◆**—ly** *adv* indéfiniment.
indelible [ɪn'deləb(ə)l] *a* (*ink, memory*) indélébile; **i. pencil** crayon *m* à marquer.

indelicate [ɪn'delɪkət] *a* (*coarse*) indélicat.
indemnify [ɪn'demnɪfaɪ] *vt* indemniser (**for** de). ◆**indemnity** *n* indemnité *f*.
indented [ɪn'dentɪd] *a* (*edge*) dentelé, découpé; (*line*) *Typ* renfoncé. ◆**inden'tation** *n* denteloure *f*, découpoure *f*; *Typ* renfoncement *m*.
independent [ɪndɪ'pendənt] *a* indépendant (**of** de); (*opinions, reports*) de sources différentes. ◆**independence** *n* indépendance *f*. ◆**independently** *adv* de façon indépendante; **i. of** indépendamment de.
indescribable [ɪndɪ'skraɪbəb(ə)l] *a* indescriptible.
indestructible [ɪndɪ'strʌktəb(ə)l] *a* indestructible.
indeterminate [ɪndɪ'tɜːmɪnət] *a* indéterminé.
index ['ɪndeks] *n* (*in book etc*) index *m*; (*in library*) catalogue *m*; (*number, sign*) indice *m*; **i. card** fiche *f*; **i. finger** index *m*; – *vt* (*classify*) classer. ◆**i.-'linked** *a Econ* indexé (**to** sur).
India ['ɪndɪə] *n* Inde *f*. ◆**Indian** *a & n* indien, -ienne (*mf*).
indicate ['ɪndɪkeɪt] *vt* indiquer (**that** que); **I was indicating right** *Aut* j'avais mis mon clignotant droit. ◆**indi'cation** *n* (*sign*) indice *m*, indication *f*; (*idea*) idée *f*. ◆**in'dicative** *a* indicatif (**of** de); – *n* (*mood*) *Gram* indicatif *m*. ◆**indicator** *n* (*instrument*) indicateur *m*; (*sign*) indication *f* (**of** de); *Aut* clignotant *m*; (*display board*) tableau *m* (indicateur).
indict [ɪn'daɪt] *vt* inculper (**for** de). ◆**—ment** *n* inculpation *f*.
Indies ['ɪndɪz] *npl* **the West I.** les Antilles *fpl*.
indifferent [ɪn'dɪf(ə)rənt] *a* indifférent (**to** à); (*mediocre*) *Pej* médiocre. ◆**indifference** *n* indifférence *f* (**to** à). ◆**indifferently** *adv* indifféremment.
indigenous [ɪn'dɪdʒɪnəs] *a* indigène.
indigestion [ɪndɪ'dʒestʃ(ə)n] *n* dyspepsie *f*; (**an attack of**) **i.** une indigestion, une crise de foie. ◆**indigestible** *a* indigeste.
indignant [ɪn'dɪgnənt] *a* indigné (**at** de, **with** contre); **to become i.** s'indigner. ◆**indignantly** *adv* avec indignation. ◆**indig'nation** *n* indignation *f*.
indignity [ɪn'dɪgnɪtɪ] *n* indignité *f*.
indigo ['ɪndɪɡəʊ] *n & a* (*colour*) indigo *m & a inv*.
indirect [ɪndaɪ'rekt] *a* indirect. ◆**—ly** *adv* indirectement.
indiscreet [ɪndɪ'skriːt] *a* indiscret. ◆**indiscretion** *n* indiscrétion *f*.
indiscriminate [ɪndɪ'skrɪmɪnət] *a* (*person*)

qui manque de discernement; (*random*) fait, donné *etc* au hasard. ◆**—ly** *adv* (*at random*) au hasard; (*without discrimination*) sans discernement.

indispensable [ɪndɪ'spensəb(ə)l] *a* indispensable (**to** à).

indisposed [ɪndɪ'spəʊzd] *a* (*unwell*) indisposé. ◆**indispo'sition** *n* indisposition *f*.

indisputable [ɪndɪ'spjuːtəb(ə)l] *a* incontestable.

indistinct [ɪndɪ'stɪŋkt] *a* indistinct.

indistinguishable [ɪndɪ'stɪŋgwɪʃəb(ə)l] *a* indifférenciable (**from** de).

individual [ɪndɪ'vɪdʒʊəl] *a* individuel; (*unusual, striking*) singulier, particulier; − *n* (*person*) individu *m*. ◆**individualist** *n* individualiste *mf*. ◆**individua'listic** *a* individualiste. ◆**individu'ality** *n* (*distinctiveness*) individualité *f*. ◆**individually** *adv* (*separately*) individuellement; (*unusually*) de façon (très) personnelle.

indivisible [ɪndɪ'vɪzəb(ə)l] *a* indivisible.

Indo-China [ɪndəʊ'tʃaɪnə] *n* Indochine *f*.

indoctrinate [ɪn'dɒktrɪneɪt] *vt Pej* endoctriner. ◆**indoctri'nation** *n* endoctrinement *m*.

indolent ['ɪndələnt] *a* indolent. ◆**indolence** *n* indolence *f*.

indomitable [ɪn'dɒmɪtəb(ə)l] *a* (*will, energy*) indomptable.

Indonesia [ɪndəʊ'niːʒə] *n* Indonésie *f*.

indoor ['ɪndɔːr] *a* (*games, shoes etc*) d'intérieur; (*swimming pool etc*) couvert. ◆**in'doors** *adv* à l'intérieur; **to go** *or* **come i.** rentrer.

induce [ɪn'djuːs] *vt* (*persuade*) persuader (**to do** de faire); (*cause*) provoquer; **to i. labour** *Med* déclencher le travail. ◆**—ment** *n* encouragement *m* (**to do** à faire).

indulge [ɪn'dʌldʒ] *vt* (*s.o.'s desires*) satisfaire; (*child etc*) gâter, tout passer à; **to i. oneself** se gâter; − *vi* **to i. in** (*action*) s'adonner à; (*ice cream etc*) se permettre. ◆**indulgence** *n* indulgence *f*. ◆**indulgent** *a* indulgent (**to** envers, **with** avec).

industrial [ɪn'dʌstrɪəl] *a* industriel; (*conflict, legislation*) du travail; **i. action** action *f* revendicative; **i. park** *Am* complexe *m* industriel. ◆**industrialist** *n* industriel, -ielle *mf*. ◆**industrialized** *a* industrialisé.

industrious [ɪn'dʌstrɪəs] *a* travailleur.

industry ['ɪndəstrɪ] *n* industrie *f*; (*hard work*) application *f*.

inedible [ɪn'edəb(ə)l] *a* immangeable.

ineffective [ɪnɪ'fektɪv] *a* (*measure etc*) sans effet, inefficace; (*person*) incapable. ◆**—ness** *n* inefficacité *f*.

ineffectual [ɪnɪ'fektʃʊəl] *a* (*measure etc*) inefficace; (*person*) incompétent.

inefficient [ɪnɪ'fɪʃ(ə)nt] *a* (*person, measure etc*) inefficace; (*machine*) peu performant. ◆**inefficiency** *n* inefficacité *f*.

ineligible [ɪn'elɪdʒəb(ə)l] *a* (*candidate*) inéligible; **to be i. for** ne pas avoir droit à.

inept [ɪ'nept] *a* (*foolish*) inepte; (*unskilled*) peu habile (**at sth** à qch); (*incompetent*) incapable, inapte. ◆**ineptitude** *n* (*incapacity*) inaptitude *f*.

inequality [ɪnɪ'kwɒlətɪ] *n* inégalité *f*.

inert [ɪ'nɜːt] *a* inerte. ◆**inertia** [ɪ'nɜːʃə] *n* inertie *f*.

inescapable [ɪnɪ'skeɪpəb(ə)l] *a* inéluctable.

inevitable [ɪn'evɪtəb(ə)l] *a* inévitable. ◆**inevitably** *adv* inévitablement.

inexcusable [ɪnɪk'skjuːzəb(ə)l] *a* inexcusable.

inexhaustible [ɪnɪg'zɔːstəb(ə)l] *a* inépuisable.

inexorable [ɪn'eksərəb(ə)l] *a* inexorable.

inexpensive [ɪnɪk'spensɪv] *a* bon marché *inv*.

inexperience [ɪnɪk'spɪərɪəns] *n* inexpérience *f*. ◆**inexperienced** *a* inexpérimenté.

inexplicable [ɪnɪk'splɪkəb(ə)l] *a* inexplicable.

inexpressible [ɪnɪk'spresəb(ə)l] *a* inexprimable.

inextricable [ɪnɪk'strɪkəb(ə)l] *a* inextricable.

infallible [ɪn'fæləb(ə)l] *a* infaillible. ◆**infalli'bility** *n* infaillibilité *f*.

infamous ['ɪnfəməs] *a* (*evil*) infâme. ◆**infamy** *n* infamie *f*.

infant ['ɪnfənt] *n* (*child*) petit(e) enfant *mf*; (*baby*) nourrisson *m*; **i. school** classes *fpl* préparatoires. ◆**infancy** *n* petite enfance *f*; **to be in its i.** (*of art, technique etc*) en être à ses premiers balbutiements. ◆**infantile** *a* (*illness, reaction etc*) infantile.

infantry ['ɪnfəntrɪ] *n* infanterie *f*.

infatuated [ɪn'fætʃʊeɪtɪd] *a* amoureux; **i. with** (*person*) amoureux de, engoué de; (*sport etc*) engoué de. ◆**infatu'ation** *n* engouement *m* (**for, with** pour).

infect [ɪn'fekt] *vt* (*contaminate*) *Med* infecter; **to become infected** s'infecter; **to i. s.o. with sth** communiquer qch à qn. ◆**infection** *n* infection *f*. ◆**infectious** *a* (*disease*) infectieux, contagieux; (*person, laughter etc*) contagieux.

infer [ɪn'fɜːr] *vt* (**-rr-**) déduire (**from** de, **that** que). ◆**'inference** *n* déduction *f*, conclusion *f*.

inferior [ɪnˈfɪərɪər] a inférieur (**to** à); (*goods, work*) de qualité inférieure; – n (*person*) *Pej* inférieur, -eure *mf*. ◆**inferi'ority** n infériorité *f*.

infernal [ɪnˈfɜːn(ə)l] a infernal. ◆**—ly** adv *Fam* épouvantablement.

inferno [ɪnˈfɜːnəu] n (*pl* -os) (*blaze*) brasier *m*, incendie *m*; (*hell*) enfer *m*.

infertile [ɪnˈfɜːtaɪl, *Am* ɪnˈfɜːt(ə)l] a (*person, land*) stérile.

infest [ɪnˈfest] vt infester (**with** de).

infidelity [ɪnfɪˈdelɪtɪ] n infidélité *f*.

infighting [ˈɪnfaɪtɪŋ] n (*within group*) luttes *fpl* intestines.

infiltrate [ˈɪnfɪltreɪt] vi s'infiltrer (**into** dans); – vt (*group etc*) s'infiltrer dans. ◆**infil-'tration** n infiltration *f*; *Pol* noyautage *m*.

infinite [ˈɪnfɪnɪt] a & n infini (*m*). ◆**infi-nitely** adv infiniment. ◆**in'finity** n *Math Phot* infini *m*; **to i.** *Math* à l'infini.

infinitive [ɪnˈfɪnɪtɪv] n *Gram* infinitif *m*.

infirm [ɪnˈfɜːm] a infirme. ◆**infirmary** n (*sickbay*) infirmerie *f*; (*hospital*) hôpital *m*. ◆**infirmity** n (*disability*) infirmité *f*.

inflame [ɪnˈfleɪm] vt enflammer. ◆**inflammable** a inflammable. ◆**infla'mmation** n *Med* inflammation *f*. ◆**inflammatory** a (*remark*) incendiaire.

inflate [ɪnˈfleɪt] vt (*tyre, prices etc*) gonfler. ◆**inflatable** a gonflable. ◆**inflation** n *Econ* inflation *f*. ◆**inflationary** a *Econ* inflationniste.

inflection [ɪnˈflekʃ(ə)n] n *Gram* flexion *f*; (*of voice*) inflexion *f*.

inflexible [ɪnˈfleksəb(ə)l] a inflexible.

inflexion [ɪnˈflekʃ(ə)n] n = **inflection**.

inflict [ɪnˈflɪkt] vt infliger (**on** à); (*wound*) occasionner (**on** à).

influence [ˈɪnfluəns] n influence *f*; **under the i. of** (*anger, drugs*) sous l'effet de; **under the i. of drink** *or* **alcohol** *Jur* en état d'ébriété; – vt influencer. ◆**influ'ential** a influent.

influenza [ɪnfluˈenzə] n *Med* grippe *f*.

influx [ˈɪnflʌks] n flot *m*, afflux *m*.

info [ˈɪnfəu] n *Sl* tuyaux *mpl*, renseignements *mpl* (**on** sur).

inform [ɪnˈfɔːm] vt informer (**of** de, **that** que); – vi **to i. on** dénoncer. ◆**—ed** a informé; **to keep s.o. i. of** tenir qn au courant de. ◆**informant** n informateur, -trice *mf*. ◆**informative** a instructif. ◆**informer** n (*police*) **i.** indicateur, -trice *mf*.

informal [ɪnˈfɔːm(ə)l] a (*without fuss*) simple, sans façon; (*occasion*) dénué de formalité; (*tone, expression*) familier; (*announcement*) officieux; (*meeting*) non-officiel. ◆**infor-'mality** n simplicité *f*; (*of tone etc*) familiarité *f*. ◆**informally** adv (*without fuss*) sans cérémonie; (*to meet*) officieusement; (*to dress*) simplement.

information [ɪnfəˈmeɪʃ(ə)n] n (*facts*) renseignements *mpl* (**about, on** sur); (*knowledge*) & *Math* information *f*; **a piece of i.** un renseignement, une information; **to get some i.** se renseigner.

infrared [ɪnfrəˈred] a infrarouge.

infrequent [ɪnˈfriːkwənt] a peu fréquent.

infringe [ɪnˈfrɪndʒ] vt (*rule*) contrevenir à; – vi **to i. upon** (*encroach on*) empiéter sur. ◆**—ment** n infraction *f* (**of** à).

infuriat/e [ɪnˈfjuərɪeɪt] vt exaspérer. ◆**—ing** a exaspérant.

infuse [ɪnˈfjuːz] vt (*tea*) (faire) infuser. ◆**infusion** n infusion *f*.

ingenious [ɪnˈdʒiːnɪəs] a ingénieux. ◆**inge'nuity** n ingéniosité *f*.

ingot [ˈɪŋgət] n lingot *m*.

ingrained [ɪnˈgreɪnd] a (*prejudice*) enraciné; **i. dirt** crasse *f*.

ingratiat/e [ɪnˈgreɪʃɪeɪt] vt **to i. oneself with** s'insinuer dans les bonnes grâces de. ◆**—ing** a (*person, smile*) insinuant.

ingratitude [ɪnˈgrætɪtjuːd] n ingratitude *f*.

ingredient [ɪnˈgriːdɪənt] n ingrédient *m*.

ingrown [ɪnˈgrəun] a (*nail*) incarné.

inhabit [ɪnˈhæbɪt] vt habiter. ◆**—able** a habitable. ◆**inhabitant** n habitant, -ante *mf*.

inhale [ɪnˈheɪl] vt aspirer; **to i. the smoke** (*of smoker*) avaler la fumée. ◆**inha'lation** n inhalation *f*. ◆**inhaler** n *Med* inhalateur *m*.

inherent [ɪnˈhɪərənt] a inhérent (**in** à). ◆**—ly** adv intrinsèquement, en soi.

inherit [ɪnˈherɪt] vt hériter (de); (*title*) succéder à. ◆**inheritance** n héritage *m*; (*process*) *Jur* succession *f*; (*cultural*) patrimoine *m*.

inhibit [ɪnˈhɪbɪt] vt (*hinder*) gêner; (*control*) maîtriser; (*prevent*) empêcher (**from** de); **to be inhibited** être inhibé, avoir des inhibitions. ◆**inhi'bition** n inhibition *f*.

inhospitable [ɪnhɒˈspɪtəb(ə)l] a inhospitalier.

inhuman [ɪnˈhjuːmən] a (*not human, cruel*) inhumain. ◆**inhu'mane** a (*not kind*) inhumain. ◆**inhu'manity** n brutalité *f*, cruauté *f*.

inimitable [ɪˈnɪmɪtəb(ə)l] a inimitable.

iniquitous [ɪˈnɪkwɪtəs] a inique. ◆**iniquity** n iniquité *f*.

initial [ɪˈnɪʃ(ə)l] a initial, premier; – n (*letter*) initiale *f*; (*signature*) paraphe *m*; –

vt (**-ll-**, Am **-l-**) parapher. ◆**—ly** adv initialement, au début.

initiate [ɪ'nɪʃɪeɪt] vt (reforms) amorcer; (schemes) inaugurer; **to i. s.o. into** initier qn à; **the initiated** les initiés mpl. ◆**initi'ation** n amorce f; inauguration f; initiation f. ◆**initiator** n initiateur, -trice mf.

initiative [ɪ'nɪʃətɪv] n initiative f.

inject [ɪn'dʒekt] vt injecter (**into** à); (new life etc) Fig insuffler (**into** à). ◆**injection** n Med injection f, piqûre f.

injunction [ɪn'dʒʌŋkʃ(ə)n] n Jur ordonnance f.

injur/e ['ɪndʒər] vt (physically) blesser; (prejudice, damage) nuire à; (one's chances) compromettre; **to i. one's foot**/etc se blesser au pied/etc. ◆**—ed** a blessé; – n **the i.** les blessés mpl. ◆**injury** n (to flesh) blessure f; (fracture) fracture f; (sprain) foulure f; (bruise) contusion f; (wrong) Fig préjudice m.

injurious [ɪn'dʒʊərɪəs] a préjudiciable (**to** à).

injustice [ɪn'dʒʌstɪs] n injustice f.

ink [ɪŋk] n encre f; **Indian i.** encre f de Chine. ◆**inkpot** n, ◆**inkwell** n encrier m. ◆**inky** a couvert d'encre.

inkling ['ɪŋklɪŋ] n (petite) idée f; **to have some** or **an i. of sth** soupçonner qch, avoir une (petite) idée de qch.

inlaid [ɪn'leɪd] a (marble etc) incrusté (**with** de); (wood) marqueté.

inland ['ɪnlənd, 'ɪnlænd] a intérieur; **the I. Revenue** le fisc; – [ɪn'lænd] adv à l'intérieur (des terres).

in-laws ['ɪnlɔːz] npl belle-famille f.

inlet ['ɪnlet] n (of sea) crique f; **i. pipe** tuyau m d'arrivée.

inmate ['ɪnmeɪt] n résident, -ente mf; (of asylum) interné, -ée mf; (of prison) détenu, -ue mf.

inmost ['ɪnməʊst] a le plus profond.

inn [ɪn] n auberge f. ◆**innkeeper** n aubergiste mf.

innards ['ɪnədz] npl Fam entrailles fpl.

innate [ɪ'neɪt] a inné.

inner ['ɪnər] a intérieur; (ear) interne; (feelings) intime, profond; **the i. city** le cœur de la ville; **an i. circle** (group of people) un cercle restreint; **the i. circle** le saint des saints; **i. tube** (of tyre) chambre f à air. ◆**innermost** a le plus profond.

inning ['ɪnɪŋ] n Baseball tour m de batte. ◆**innings** n inv Cricket tour m de batte; **a good i.** Fig une vie longue.

innocent ['ɪnəs(ə)nt] a innocent. ◆**inno-**

cence n innocence f. ◆**innocently** adv innocemment.

innocuous [ɪ'nɒkjʊəs] a inoffensif.

innovate ['ɪnəveɪt] vi innover. ◆**inno-'vation** n innovation f. ◆**innovator** n innovateur, -trice mf.

innuendo [ɪnjʊ'endəʊ] n (pl **-oes** or **-os**) insinuation f.

innumerable [ɪ'njuːmərəb(ə)l] a innombrable.

inoculate [ɪ'nɒkjʊleɪt] vt vacciner (**against** contre). ◆**inocu'lation** n inoculation f.

inoffensive [ɪnə'fensɪv] a inoffensif.

inoperative [ɪn'ɒpərətɪv] a (without effect) inopérant.

inopportune [ɪn'ɒpətjuːn] a inopportun.

inordinate [ɪ'nɔːdɪnət] a excessif. ◆**—ly** adv excessivement.

in-patient ['ɪnpeɪʃ(ə)nt] n malade mf hospitalisé(e).

input ['ɪnpʊt] n (computer operation) entrée f; (data) données fpl; (current) El énergie f.

inquest ['ɪnkwest] n enquête f.

inquir/e [ɪn'kwaɪər] vi se renseigner (**about** sur); **to i. after** s'informer de; **to i. into** examiner, faire une enquête sur; – vt demander; **to i. how to get to** demander le chemin de. ◆**—ing** a (mind, look) curieux. ◆**inquiry** n (question) question f; (request for information) demande f de renseignements; (information) renseignements mpl; Jur enquête f; **to make inquiries** demander des renseignements; (of police) enquêter.

inquisitive [ɪn'kwɪzɪtɪv] a curieux. ◆**inquisitively** adv avec curiosité. ◆**inqui'sition** n (inquiry) & Rel inquisition f.

inroads ['ɪnrəʊdz] npl (attacks) incursions fpl (**into** dans); **to make i. into** (start on) Fig entamer.

insane [ɪn'seɪn] a fou, dément. ◆**insanely** adv comme un fou. ◆**insanity** n folie f, démence f.

insanitary [ɪn'sænɪt(ə)rɪ] a insalubre.

insatiable [ɪn'seɪʃəb(ə)l] a insatiable.

inscribe [ɪn'skraɪb] vt inscrire; (book) dédicacer (**to** à). ◆**inscription** n inscription f; dédicace f.

inscrutable [ɪn'skruːtəb(ə)l] a impénétrable.

insect ['ɪnsekt] n insecte m; – a (powder, spray) insecticide; **i. repellant** crème f anti-insecte. ◆**in'secticide** n insecticide m.

insecure [ɪnsɪ'kjʊər] a (not fixed) peu solide; (furniture, ladder) branlant, bancal; (window) mal fermé; (uncertain) incertain;

(*unsafe*) peu sûr; (*person*) qui manque d'assurance. ◆**insecurity** *n* (*of person, situation*) insécurité *f*.

insemination [ɪnsemɪˈneɪʃ(ə)n] *n Med* insémination *f*.

insensible [ɪnˈsensəb(ə)l] *a Med* inconscient.

insensitive [ɪnˈsensɪtɪv] *a* insensible (**to** à). ◆**insensi'tivity** *n* insensibilité *f*.

inseparable [ɪnˈsep(ə)rəb(ə)l] *a* inséparable (**from** de).

insert [ɪnˈsɜːt] *vt* insérer (**in, into** dans). ◆**insertion** *n* insertion *f*.

inshore [ˈɪnʃɔːr] *a* côtier.

inside [ɪnˈsaɪd] *adv* dedans, à l'intérieur; **come i.!** entrez!; − *prep* à l'intérieur de, dans; (*time*) en moins de; − *n* dedans *m*, intérieur *m*; *pl* (*stomach*) *Fam* ventre *m*; **on the i.** à l'intérieur (**of** de); **i. out** (*coat, socks etc*) à l'envers; (*to know, study etc*) à fond; **to turn everything i. out** *Fig* tout chambouler; − *a* intérieur; (*information*) obtenu à la source; **the i. lane** *Aut* la voie de gauche, *Am* la voie de droite.

insidious [ɪnˈsɪdɪəs] *a* insidieux.

insight [ˈɪnsaɪt] *n* perspicacité *f*; **to give an i. into** (*s.o.'s character*) permettre de comprendre, éclairer; (*question*) donner un aperçu de.

insignia [ɪnˈsɪgnɪə] *npl* (*of important person*) insignes *mpl*.

insignificant [ɪnsɪgˈnɪfɪkənt] *a* insignifiant. ◆**insignificance** *n* insignifiance *f*.

insincere [ɪnsɪnˈsɪər] *a* peu sincère. ◆**insincerity** *n* manque *m* de sincérité.

insinuate [ɪnˈsɪnjʊeɪt] *vt* **1** *Pej* insinuer (**that** que). **2 to i. oneself into** s'insinuer dans. ◆**insinu'ation** *n* insinuation *f*.

insipid [ɪnˈsɪpɪd] *a* insipide.

insist [ɪnˈsɪst] *vi* insister (**on doing** pour faire); **to i. on sth** (*demand*) exiger qch; (*assert*) affirmer qch; − *vt* (*order*) insister (**that** pour que); (*declare firmly*) affirmer (**that** que); **I i. that you come** or **on your coming** j'insiste pour que tu viennes. ◆**insistence** *n* insistance *f*; **her i. on seeing me** l'insistance qu'elle met à vouloir me voir. ◆**insistent** *a* insistant; **I was i.** (**about it**) j'ai été pressant. ◆**insistently** *adv* avec insistance.

insolent [ˈɪnsələnt] *a* insolent. ◆**insolence** *n* insolence *f*. ◆**insolently** *adv* insolemment.

insoluble [ɪnˈsɒljʊb(ə)l] *a* insoluble.

insolvent [ɪnˈsɒlvənt] *a Fin* insolvable.

insomnia [ɪnˈsɒmnɪə] *n* insomnie *f*. ◆**insomniac** *n* insomniaque *mf*.

insomuch as [ɪnsəʊˈmʌtʃəz] *adv* = **inasmuch as.**

inspect [ɪnˈspekt] *vt* inspecter; (*tickets*) contrôler; (*troops*) passer en revue. ◆**inspection** *n* inspection *f*; contrôle *m*; revue *f*. ◆**inspector** *n* inspecteur, -trice *mf*; (*on bus*) contrôleur, -euse *mf*.

inspir/e [ɪnˈspaɪər] *vt* inspirer (**s.o. with sth** qch à qn); **to be inspired to do** avoir l'inspiration de faire. ◆**—ed** *a* inspiré. ◆**—ing** *a* qui inspire. ◆**inspi'ration** *n* inspiration *f*; (*person*) source *f* d'inspiration.

instability [ɪnstəˈbɪlɪtɪ] *n* instabilité *f*.

install [ɪnˈstɔːl] *vt* installer. ◆**insta'llation** *n* installation *f*.

instalment [ɪnˈstɔːlmənt] (*Am* **installment**) *n* (*of money*) acompte *m*, versement *m* (partiel); (*of serial*) épisode *m*; (*of publication*) fascicule *m*; **to buy on the i. plan** *Am* acheter à crédit.

instance [ˈɪnstəns] *n* (*example*) exemple *m*; (*case*) cas *m*; (*occasion*) circonstance *f*; **for i.** par exemple; **in the first i.** en premier lieu.

instant [ˈɪnstənt] *a* immédiat; **i. coffee** café *m* soluble or instantané, nescafé® *m*; **of the 3rd i.** (*in letter*) *Com* du 3 courant; − *n* (*moment*) instant *m*; **this** (**very**) **i.** (*at once*) à l'instant; **the i. that** (*as soon as*) dès que. ◆**instan'taneous** *a* instantané. ◆**instantly** *adv* immédiatement.

instead [ɪnˈsted] *adv* (*as alternative*) au lieu de cela, plutôt; **i. of** au lieu de; **i. of s.o.** à la place de qn; (**of him** or **her**) à sa place.

instep [ˈɪnstep] *n* (*of foot*) cou-de-pied *m*; (*of shoe*) cambrure *f*.

instigate [ˈɪnstɪgeɪt] *vt* provoquer. ◆**insti'gation** *n* instigation *f*. ◆**instigator** *n* instigateur, -trice *mf*.

instil [ɪnˈstɪl] *vt* (**-ll-**) (*idea*) inculquer (**into** à); (*courage*) insuffler (**into** à).

instinct [ˈɪnstɪŋkt] *n* instinct *m*; **by i.** d'instinct. ◆**in'stinctive** *a* instinctif. ◆**in'stinctively** *adv* instinctivement.

institute [ˈɪnstɪtjuːt] **1** *vt* (*rule, practice*) instituer; (*inquiry, proceedings*) *Jur* entamer, intenter. **2** *n* institut *m*. ◆**insti'tution** *n* (*custom, private or charitable organization etc*) institution *f*; (*school, hospital*) établissement *m*; (*home*) *Med* asile *m*. ◆**insti'tutional** *a* institutionnel.

instruct [ɪnˈstrʌkt] *vt* (*teach*) enseigner (**s.o. in sth** qch à qn); **to i. s.o. about sth** (*inform*) instruire qn de qch; **to i. s.o. to do** (*order*) charger qn de faire. ◆**instruction** *n* (*teaching*) instruction *f*; *pl* (*orders*) instructions *fpl*; **instructions** (**for use**) mode *m*

d'emploi. ◆**instructive** a instructif.
◆**instructor** n professeur m; Sp moniteur,
-trice mf; Mil instructeur m; Univ Am
maître-assistant, -ante mf; **driving i.**
moniteur, -trice mf de conduite.

instrument ['ɪnstrʊmənt] n instrument m.
◆**instru'mental** a Mus instrumental; **to
be i. in sth/in doing sth** contribuer à qch/à
faire qch. ◆**instru'mentalist** n Mus
instrumentaliste mf. ◆**instrumen'tation**
n Mus orchestration f.

insubordinate [ɪnsəˈbɔːdɪnət] a indiscipliné. ◆**insubordi'nation** n indiscipline f.

insubstantial [ɪnsəbˈstænʃ(ə)l] a (argument,
evidence) peu solide.

insufferable [ɪnˈsʌfərəb(ə)l] a intolérable.

insufficient [ɪnsəˈfɪʃənt] a insuffisant.
◆**—ly** adv insuffisamment.

insular ['ɪnsjʊlər] a (climate) insulaire;
(views) Pej étroit, borné.

insulate ['ɪnsjʊleɪt] vt (against cold etc) & El
isoler; (against sound) insonoriser; **to i. s.o.
from** Fig protéger qn de; **insulating tape**
chatterton m. ◆**insu'lation** n isolation f;
insonorisation f; (material) isolant m.

insulin ['ɪnsjʊlɪn] n Med insuline f.

insult [ɪnˈsʌlt] vt insulter; − ['ɪnsʌlt] n insulte
f (**to** à).

insuperable [ɪnˈsuːpərəb(ə)l] a insurmontable.

insure [ɪnˈʃʊər] vt 1 (protect against damage
etc) assurer (**against** contre). 2 Am =
ensure. ◆**insurance** n assurance f; **i.
company** compagnie f d'assurances; **i.
policy** police f d'assurance.

insurgent [ɪnˈsɜːdʒənt] a & n insurgé, -ée
(mf).

insurmountable [ɪnsəˈmaʊntəb(ə)l] a
insurmontable.

insurrection [ɪnsəˈrekʃ(ə)n] n insurrection
f.

intact [ɪnˈtækt] a intact.

intake ['ɪnteɪk] n (of food) consommation f;
Sch Univ admissions fpl; Tech admission f.

intangible [ɪnˈtændʒəb(ə)l] a intangible.

integral ['ɪntɪɡrəl] a intégral; **to be an i. part
of** faire partie intégrante de.

integrate ['ɪntɪɡreɪt] vt intégrer (**into** dans);
− vi s'intégrer (**into** dans); (**racially**) **integrated** (school etc) Am où se pratique la
déségrégation raciale. ◆**integration** n
intégration f; (**racial**) **i.** déségrégation f
raciale.

integrity [ɪnˈteɡrɪtɪ] n intégrité f.

intellect ['ɪntɪlekt] n (faculty) intellect m,
intelligence f; (cleverness, person) intelli-

gence f. ◆**inte'llectual** a & n intellectuel,
-elle (mf).

intelligence [ɪnˈtelɪdʒəns] n intelligence f;
Mil renseignements mpl. ◆**intelligent** a
intelligent. ◆**intelligently** adv intelligemment. ◆**intelli'gentsia** n intelligentsia f.

intelligible [ɪnˈtelɪdʒəb(ə)l] a intelligible.
◆**intelligi'bility** n intelligibilité f.

intemperance [ɪnˈtempərəns] n intempérance f.

intend [ɪnˈtend] vt (gift, remark etc) destiner
(**for** à); **to i. to do** avoir l'intention de faire;
I i. you to stay mon intention est que vous
restiez. ◆**—ed** a (deliberate) intentionnel,
voulu; (planned) projeté; **i. to be** (meant)
destiné à être. ◆**intention** n intention f (**of
doing** de faire). ◆**intentional** a intentionnel; **it wasn't i.** ce n'était pas fait exprès.
◆**intentionally** adv intentionnellement,
exprès.

intense [ɪnˈtens] a intense; (interest) vif;
(person) passionné. ◆**intensely** adv intensément; Fig extrêmement. ◆**intensifi-
'cation** n intensification f. ◆**intensify** vt
intensifier; − vi s'intensifier. ◆**intensity** n
intensité f. ◆**intensive** a intensif; **in i.
care** Med en réanimation.

intent [ɪnˈtent] 1 a (look) attentif; **i. on** (task)
absorbé par; **i. on doing** résolu à faire. 2 n
intention f; **to all intents and purposes** en
fait, essentiellement.

inter [ɪnˈtɜːr] vt (**-rr-**) enterrer.

inter- ['ɪntə(r)] pref inter-.

interact [ɪntərˈækt] vi (of ideas etc) être
interdépendants; (of people) agir conjointement; Ch interagir. ◆**interaction** n
interaction f.

intercede [ɪntəˈsiːd] vi intercéder (**with**
auprès de).

intercept [ɪntəˈsept] vt intercepter. ◆**interception** n interception f.

interchange ['ɪntətʃeɪndʒ] n Aut échangeur
m. ◆**inter'changeable** a interchangeable.

intercom ['ɪntəkɒm] n interphone m.

interconnect/ed [ɪntəkəˈnektɪd] a (facts
etc) liés. ◆**—ing** a **i. rooms** pièces fpl
communicantes.

intercontinental [ɪntəkɒntɪˈnent(ə)l] a
intercontinental.

intercourse ['ɪntəkɔːs] n (sexual, social)
rapports mpl.

interdependent [ɪntədɪˈpendənt] a interdépendant; (parts of machine) solidaire.

interest ['ɪnt(ə)rɪst, 'ɪntrəst] n intérêt m; Fin
intérêts mpl; **an i. in** (stake) Com des intérêts dans; **his** or **her i. is** (hobby etc) ce qui

l'intéresse c'est; **to take an i. in** s'intéresser à; **to be of i. to s.o.** intéresser qn; – *vt* intéresser. ◆**—ed** *a* (*involved*) intéressé; (*look*) d'intérêt; **to seem i.** sembler intéressé (**in** par); **to be i. in sth/s.o.** s'intéresser à qch/qn; **I'm i. in doing** ça m'intéresse de faire; **are you i.?** ça vous intéresse? ◆**—ing** *a* intéressant. ◆**—ingly** *adv* **i.** (**enough**), **she . . .** curieusement, elle . . . .

interface ['ɪntəfeɪs] *n Tech* interface *f*.

interfer/e [ɪntə'fɪər] *vi* se mêler des affaires d'autrui; **to i. in** s'ingérer dans; **to i. with** (*upset*) déranger; (*touch*) toucher (à). ◆**—ing** *a* (*person*) importun. ◆**interference** *n* ingérence *f*; *Rad* parasites *mpl*.

interim ['ɪntərɪm] *n* intérim *m*; **in the i.** pendant l'intérim; – *a* (*measure etc*) provisoire; (*post*) intérimaire.

interior [ɪn'tɪərɪər] *a* intérieur; – *n* intérieur *m*; **Department of the I.** *Am* ministère *m* de l'Intérieur.

interjection [ɪntə'dʒek∫(ə)n] *n* interjection *f*.

interlock [ɪntə'lɒk] *vi Tech* s'emboîter.

interloper ['ɪntələupər] *n* intrus, -use *mf*.

interlude ['ɪntəluːd] *n* intervalle *m*; *Th* intermède *m*; *Mus TV* interlude *m*.

intermarry [ɪntə'mærɪ] *vi* se marier (entre eux). ◆**intermarriage** *n* mariage *m* (*entre personnes de races etc différentes*).

intermediary [ɪntə'miːdɪərɪ] *a* & *n* intermédiaire (*mf*).

intermediate [ɪntə'miːdɪət] *a* intermédiaire; (*course*) *Sch* moyen.

interminable [ɪn'tɜːmɪnəb(ə)l] *a* interminable.

intermingle [ɪntə'mɪŋg(ə)l] *vi* se mélanger.

intermission [ɪntə'mɪ∫(ə)n] *n Cin Th* entracte *m*.

intermittent [ɪntə'mɪtənt] *a* intermittent. ◆**—ly** *adv* par intermittence.

intern 1 [ɪn'tɜːn] *vt Pol* interner. **2** ['ɪntɜːn] *n Med Am* interne *mf* (des hôpitaux). ◆**inter'nee** *n* interné, -ée *mf*. ◆**in'ternment** *n Pol* internement *m*.

internal [ɪn'tɜːn(ə)l] *a* interne; (*policy, flight*) intérieur; **i. combustion engine** moteur *m* à explosion; **the I. Revenue Service** *Am* le fisc. ◆**—ly** *adv* intérieurement.

international [ɪntə'næ∫(ə)nəl] *a* international; (*fame, reputation*) mondial; – *n* (*match*) rencontre *f* internationale; (*player*) international *m*. ◆**—ly** *adv* (*renowned etc*) mondialement.

interplanetary [ɪntə'plænɪt(ə)rɪ] *a* interplanétaire.

interplay ['ɪntəpleɪ] *n* interaction *f*, jeu *m*.

interpolate [ɪn'tɜːpəleɪt] *vt* interpoler.

interpret [ɪn'tɜːprɪt] *vt* interpréter; – *vi Ling* faire l'interprète. ◆**interpre'tation** *n* interprétation *f*. ◆**interpreter** *n* interprète *mf*.

interrelated [ɪntərɪ'leɪtɪd] *a* en corrélation. ◆**interrelation** *n* corrélation *f*.

interrogate [ɪn'terəgeɪt] *vt* (*question closely*) interroger. ◆**interro'gation** *n* interrogation *f*; *Jur* interrogatoire *m*. ◆**interrogator** *n* (*questioner*) interrogateur, -trice *mf*.

interrogative [ɪntə'rɒgətɪv] *a* & *n Gram* interrogatif (*m*).

interrupt [ɪntə'rʌpt] *vt* interrompre. ◆**interruption** *n* interruption *f*.

intersect [ɪntə'sekt] *vt* couper; – *vi* s'entrecouper, se couper. ◆**intersection** *n* (*crossroads*) croisement *m*; (*of lines etc*) intersection *f*.

intersperse [ɪntə'spɜːs] *vt* parsemer (**with** de).

intertwine [ɪntə'twaɪn] *vt* entrelacer.

interval ['ɪntəv(ə)l] *n* intervalle *m*; *Th* entracte *m*; **at intervals** (*time*) de temps à autre; (*space*) par intervalles; **bright intervals** *Met* éclaircies *fpl*.

intervene [ɪntə'viːn] *vi* intervenir; (*of event*) survenir; **ten years intervened** dix années s'écoulèrent; **if nothing intervenes** s'il n'arrive rien entre-temps. ◆**intervention** *n* intervention *f*.

interview ['ɪntəvjuː] *n* entrevue *f*, entretien *m* (**with** avec); *Journ TV* interview *f*; **to call for (an) i.** convoquer; – *vt* avoir une entrevue avec; *Journ TV* interviewer. ◆**—er** *n Journ TV* interviewer *m*; *Com Pol* enquêteur, -euse *mf*.

intestine [ɪn'testɪn] *n* intestin *m*.

intimate¹ ['ɪntɪmət] *a* intime; (*friendship*) profond; (*knowledge, analysis*) approfondi. ◆**intimacy** *n* intimité *f*. ◆**intimately** *adv* intimement.

intimate² ['ɪntɪmeɪt] *vt* (*hint*) suggérer (**that** que). ◆**inti'mation** *n* (*announcement*) annonce *f*; (*hint*) suggestion *f*; (*sign*) indication *f*.

intimidate [ɪn'tɪmɪdeɪt] *vt* intimider. ◆**intimi'dation** *n* intimidation *f*.

into ['ɪntuː, *unstressed* 'ɪntə] *prep* **1** dans; **to put i.** mettre dans; **to go i.** (*room, detail*) entrer dans. **2** en; **to translate i.** traduire en; **to change i.** transformer *or* changer en; **to go i. town** aller en ville; **i. pieces** (*to break etc*) en morceaux. **3** **to be i.** yoga/*etc Fam* être à fond dans le yoga/*etc.*

intolerable [ɪn'tɒlərəb(ə)l] *a* intolérable

(**that** que (+ *sub*)). ◆**intolerably** *adv* insupportablement. ◆**intolerance** *n* intolérance *f*. ◆**intolerant** *a* intolérant (**of** de). ◆**intolerantly** *adv* avec intolérance.

intonation [ɪntə'neɪʃ(ə)n] *n Ling* intonation *f*.

intoxicate [ɪn'tɒksɪkeɪt] *vt* enivrer. ◆**intoxicated** *a* ivre. ◆**intoxi'cation** *n* ivresse *f*.

intra- ['ɪntrə] *pref* intra-.

intransigent [ɪn'trænsɪdʒənt] *a* intransigeant. ◆**intransigence** *n* intransigeance *f*.

intransitive [ɪn'trænsɪtɪv] *a* & *n Gram* intransitif (*m*).

intravenous [ɪntrə'viːnəs] *a Med* intraveineux.

intrepid [ɪn'trepɪd] *a* intrépide.

intricate ['ɪntrɪkət] *a* complexe, compliqué. ◆**intricacy** *n* complexité *f*. ◆**intricately** *adv* de façon complexe.

intrigu/e 1 [ɪn'triːg] *vt* (*interest*) intriguer; **I'm intrigued to know** . . . je suis curieux de savoir . . . . **2** ['ɪntriːg] *n* (*plot*) intrigue *f*. ◆**—ing** *a* (*news etc*) curieux.

intrinsic [ɪn'trɪnsɪk] *a* intrinsèque. ◆**intrinsically** *adv* intrinsèquement.

introduce [ɪntrə'djuːs] *vt* (*insert, bring in*) introduire (**into** dans); (*programme, subject*) présenter; **to i. s.o. to s.o.** présenter qn à qn; **to i. s.o. to Dickens/geography/etc** faire découvrir Dickens/la géographie/*etc* à qn. ◆**introduction** *n* introduction *f*; présentation *f*; (*book title*) initiation *f*; **her i. to** (*life abroad etc*) son premier contact avec. ◆**introductory** *a* (*words*) d'introduction; (*speech*) de présentation; (*course*) d'initiation.

introspective [ɪntrə'spektɪv] *a* introspectif. ◆**introspection** *n* introspection *f*.

introvert ['ɪntrəvɜːt] *n* introverti, -ie *mf*.

intrude [ɪn'truːd] *vi* (*of person*) s'imposer (**on s.o.** à qn), déranger (**on s.o.** qn); **to i. on** (*s.o.'s time etc*) abuser de. ◆**intruder** *n* intrus, -use *mf*. ◆**intrusion** *n* intrusion *f* (**into** dans); **forgive my i.** pardonnez-moi de vous avoir dérangé.

intuition [ɪntjuː'ɪʃ(ə)n] *n* intuition *f*. ◆**in'tuitive** *a* intuitif.

inundate ['ɪnʌndeɪt] *vt* inonder (**with** de); **inundated with work** submergé de travail. ◆**inun'dation** *n* inondation *f*.

invad/e [ɪn'veɪd] *vt* envahir; (*privacy*) violer. ◆**—er** *n* envahisseur, -euse *mf*.

invalid¹ ['ɪnvəlɪd] *a* & *n* malade (*mf*); (*through injury*) infirme (*mf*); **i. car** voiture *f* d'infirme.

invalid² [ɪn'vælɪd] *a* non valable. ◆**invalidate** *vt* invalider, annuler.

invaluable [ɪn'væljʊəb(ə)l] *a* (*help etc*) inestimable.

invariab/le [ɪn'veərɪəb(ə)l] *a* invariable. ◆**—ly** *adv* invariablement.

invasion [ɪn'veɪʒ(ə)n] *n* invasion *f*; **i. of s.o.'s privacy** intrusion *f* dans la vie privée de qn.

invective [ɪn'vektɪv] *n* invective *f*.

inveigh [ɪn'veɪ] *vi* **to i. against** invectiver contre.

inveigle [ɪn'veɪg(ə)l] *vt* **to i. s.o. into doing** amener qn à faire par la ruse.

invent [ɪn'vent] *vt* inventer. ◆**invention** *n* invention *f*. ◆**inventive** *a* inventif. ◆**inventiveness** *n* esprit *m* d'invention. ◆**inventor** *n* inventeur, -trice *mf*.

inventory ['ɪnvənt(ə)rɪ] *n* inventaire *m*.

inverse [ɪn'vɜːs] *a* & *n Math* inverse (*m*).

invert [ɪn'vɜːt] *vt* intervertir; **inverted commas** guillemets *mpl*. ◆**inversion** *n* interversion *f*; *Gram Anat etc* inversion *f*.

invest [ɪn'vest] *vt* (*funds*) investir (**in** dans); (*money*) placer, investir; (*time, effort*) consacrer (**in** à); **to i. s.o. with** (*endow*) investir qn de; – *vi* **to i. in** (*project*) placer son argent dans; (*firm*) investir dans; (*house, radio etc*) *Fig* se payer. ◆**investiture** *n* (*of bishop etc*) investiture *f*. ◆**investment** *n* investissement *m*, placement *m*. ◆**investor** *n* (*shareholder*) actionnaire *mf*; (*saver*) épargnant, -ante *mf*.

investigate [ɪn'vestɪgeɪt] *vt* (*examine*) examiner, étudier; (*crime*) enquêter sur. ◆**investi'gation** *n* examen *m*, étude *f*; (*by police*) enquête *f* (**of** sur); (*inquiry*) enquête *f*, investigation *f*. ◆**investigator** *n* (*detective*) enquêteur, -euse *mf*.

inveterate [ɪn'vetərət] *a* invétéré.

invidious [ɪn'vɪdɪəs] *a* qui suscite la jalousie; (*hurtful*) blessant; (*odious*) odieux.

invigilate [ɪn'vɪdʒɪleɪt] *vi* être de surveillance (*à un examen*). ◆**invigilator** *n* surveillant, -ante *mf*.

invigorat/e [ɪn'vɪgəreɪt] *vt* revigorer. ◆**—ing** *a* stimulant.

invincible [ɪn'vɪnsəb(ə)l] *a* invincible.

invisible [ɪn'vɪzəb(ə)l] *a* invisible; **i. ink** encre *f* sympathique.

invit/e [ɪn'vaɪt] *vt* inviter (**to do** à faire); (*ask for*) demander; (*lead to, give occasion for*) appeler; (*trouble*) chercher; **to i. out** inviter (à sortir); **to i. over** inviter (à venir); – ['ɪnvaɪt] *n Fam* invitation *f*. ◆**—ing** *a* engageant, invitant; (*food*) appétissant. ◆**invi'tation** *n* invitation *f*.

invoice ['ɪnvɔɪs] *n* facture *f*; – *vt* facturer.

invoke [ɪn'vəʊk] *vt* invoquer.

involuntar/y [ɪn'vɒləntərɪ] *a* involontaire. ◆—**ily** *adv* involontairement.

involv/e [ɪn'vɒlv] *vt* (*include*) mêler (*qn*) (**in** à), impliquer (*qn*) (**in** dans); (*associate*) associer (*qn*) (**in** à); (*entail*) entraîner; **to i. oneself, get involved** (*commit oneself*) s'engager (**in** dans); **to i. s.o. in expense** entraîner qn à des dépenses; **the job involves going abroad** le poste nécessite des déplacements à l'étranger. ◆—**ed** *a* (*complicated*) compliqué; **the factors/etc i.** (*at stake*) les facteurs/*etc* en jeu; **the person i.** la personne en question; **i. with s.o.** mêlé aux affaires de qn; **personally i.** concerné; **emotionally i. with** amoureux de; **to become i.** (*of police*) intervenir. ◆—**ement** *n* participation *f* (**in** à), implication *f* (**in** dans); (*commitment*) engagement *m* (**in** dans); (*problem*) difficulté *f*; **emotional i.** liaison *f*.

invulnerable [ɪn'vʌln(ə)rəb(ə)l] *a* invulnérable.

inward ['ɪnwəd] *a & adv* (*movement, to move*) vers l'intérieur; – *a* (*inner*) intérieur. ◆**i.-looking** *a* replié sur soi. ◆**inwardly** *adv* (*inside*) à l'intérieur; (*to laugh, curse etc*) intérieurement. ◆**inwards** *adv* vers l'intérieur.

iodine ['aɪədiːn, *Am* 'aɪədaɪn] *n Med* teinture *f* d'iode.

iota [aɪ'əʊtə] *n* (*of truth etc*) grain *m*; (*in text*) iota *m*.

IOU [aɪəʊ'juː] *n abbr* (*I owe you*) reconnaissance *f* de dette.

IQ [aɪ'kjuː] *n abbr* (*intelligence quotient*) QI *m inv*.

Iran [ɪ'rɑːn] *n* Iran *m*. ◆**Iranian** [ɪ'reɪnɪən] *a & n* iranien, -ienne (*mf*).

Iraq [ɪ'rɑːk] *n* Irak *m*. ◆**Iraqi** *a & n* irakien, -ienne (*mf*).

irascible [ɪ'ræsəb(ə)l] *a* irascible.

ire ['aɪər] *n Lit* courroux *m*. ◆**i'rate** *a* furieux.

Ireland ['aɪələnd] *n* Irlande *f*. ◆**Irish** *a* irlandais; – *n* (*language*) irlandais *m*. ◆**Irishman** *n* (*pl* -**men**) Irlandais *m*. ◆**Irishwoman** *n* (*pl* -**women**) Irlandaise *f*.

iris ['aɪərɪs] *n Anat Bot* iris *m*.

irk [ɜːk] *vt* ennuyer. ◆**irksome** *a* ennuyeux.

iron ['aɪən] *n* fer *m*; (*for clothes*) fer *m* (à repasser); **old i., scrap i.** ferraille *f*; **i. and steel industry** sidérurgie *f*; **the I. Curtain** *Pol* le rideau de fer; – *vt* (*clothes*) repasser; **to i. out** (*difficulties*) *Fig* aplanir. ◆—**ing** *n* repassage *m*; **i. board** planche *f* à repasser. ◆**ironmonger** *n* quincailler *m*. ◆**iron-**

mongery *n* quincaillerie *f*. ◆**ironwork** *n* ferronnerie *f*.

irony ['aɪərənɪ] *n* ironie *f*. ◆**i'ronic(al)** *a* ironique.

irradiate [ɪ'reɪdɪeɪt] *vt* irradier.

irrational [ɪ'ræʃən(ə)l] *a* (*act*) irrationnel; (*fear*) irraisonné; (*person*) peu rationnel, illogique.

irreconcilable [ɪrekən'saɪləb(ə)l] *a* irréconciliable, inconciliable; (*views, laws etc*) inconciliable.

irrefutable [ɪrɪ'fjuːtəb(ə)l] *a* irréfutable.

irregular [ɪ'regjʊlər] *a* irrégulier. ◆**irregu-'larity** *n* irrégularité *f*.

irrelevant [ɪ'reləvənt] *a* (*remark*) non pertinent; (*course*) peu utile; **i. to** sans rapport avec; **that's i.** ça n'a rien à voir. ◆**irrelevance** *n* manque *m* de rapport.

irreparable [ɪ'rep(ə)rəb(ə)l] *a* (*harm, loss*) irréparable.

irreplaceable [ɪrɪ'pleɪsəb(ə)l] *a* irremplaçable.

irrepressible [ɪrɪ'presəb(ə)l] *a* (*laughter etc*) irrépressible.

irresistible [ɪrɪ'zɪstəb(ə)l] *a* (*person, charm etc*) irrésistible.

irresolute [ɪ'rezəluːt] *a* irrésolu, indécis.

irrespective of [ɪrɪ'spektɪvəv] *prep* sans tenir compte de.

irresponsible [ɪrɪ'spɒnsəb(ə)l] *a* (*act*) irréfléchi; (*person*) irresponsable.

irretrievable [ɪrɪ'triːvəb(ə)l] *a* irréparable.

irreverent [ɪ'revərənt] *a* irrévérencieux.

irreversible [ɪrɪ'vɜːsəb(ə)l] *a* (*process*) irréversible; (*decision*) irrévocable.

irrevocable [ɪ'revəkəb(ə)l] *a* irrévocable.

irrigate ['ɪrɪgeɪt] *vt* irriguer. ◆**irri'gation** *n* irrigation *f*.

irritat/e ['ɪrɪteɪt] *vt* irriter. ◆—**ing** *a* irritant. ◆**irritable** *a* (*easily annoyed*) irritable. ◆**irritant** *n* irritant *m*. ◆**irri'tation** *n* (*anger*) & *Med* irritation *f*.

is [ɪz] *see* be.

Islam ['ɪzlɑːm] *n* islam *m*. ◆**Islamic** [ɪz'læmɪk] *a* islamique.

island ['aɪlənd] *n* île *f*; **traffic i.** refuge *m*; – *a* insulaire. ◆**islander** *n* insulaire *mf*. ◆**isle** [aɪl] *n* île *f*; **the British Isles** les îles Britanniques.

isolate ['aɪsəleɪt] *vt* isoler (**from** de). ◆**isolated** *a* (*remote, unique*) isolé. ◆**iso'lation** *n* isolement *m*; **in i.** isolément.

Israel ['ɪzreɪl] *n* Israël *m*. ◆**Is'raeli** *a & n* israélien, -ienne (*mf*).

issue ['ɪʃuː] *vt* (*book etc*) publier; (*an order*) donner; (*tickets*) distribuer; (*passport*) délivrer; (*stamps, banknotes*) émettre;

(*warning*) lancer; (*supply*) fournir (**with** de, **to** à); – *vi* **to i. from** (*of smell*) se dégager de; (*stem from*) provenir de; – *n* (*matter*) question *f*; (*problem*) problème *m*; (*outcome*) résultat *m*; (*of text*) publication *f*; (*of stamps etc*) émission *f*; (*newspaper*) numéro *m*; **at i.** (*at stake*) en cause; **to make an i. of** faire toute une affaire de.

isthmus ['ɪsməs] *n Geog* isthme *m*.

it [ɪt] *pron* **1** (*subject*) il, elle; (*object*) le, la, l'; **(to) it** (*indirect object*) lui; **it bites** (*dog*) il mord; **I've done it** je l'ai fait. **2** (*impersonal*) il; **it's snowing** il neige; **it's hot** il fait chaud. **3** (*non specific*) ce, cela, ça; **it's good** c'est bon; **it was pleasant** c'était agréable; **who is it?** qui est-ce?; **that's it!** (*I agree*) c'est ça!; (*it's done*) ça y est!; **to consider it wise to do** juger prudent de faire; **it was Paul who . . .** c'est Paul qui . . . ; **she's got it in her to succeed** elle est capable de réussir; **to have it in for s.o.** en vouloir à qn. **4 of it, from it, about it** en; **in it, to it, at it** y; **on it** dessus; **under it** dessous.

italic [ɪ'tælɪk] *a Typ* italique; – *npl* italique *m*.

Italy ['ɪtəlɪ] *n* Italie *f*. ◆**I'talian** *a* & *n* italien, -ienne (*mf*); – *n* (*language*) italien *m*.

itch [ɪtʃ] *n* démangeaison(s) *f*(*pl*); **to have an i. to do** avoir une envie folle de faire; – *vi* démanger; **his arm itches** son bras le *ou* lui démange; **I'm itching to do** *Fig* ça me démange de faire. ◆**—ing** *n* démangeaison(s) *f*(*pl*). ◆**itchy** *a* **an i. hand** une main qui me démange.

item ['aɪtəm] *n Com Journ* article *m*; (*matter*) question *f*; (*on entertainment programme*) numéro *m*; **a news i.** une information. ◆**itemize** *vt* détailler.

itinerant [aɪ'tɪnərənt] *a* (*musician, actor*) ambulant; (*judge, preacher*) itinérant.

itinerary [aɪ'tɪnərərɪ] *n* itinéraire *m*.

its [ɪts] *poss* a son, sa, *pl* ses. ◆**it'self** *pron* lui-même, elle-même; (*reflexive*) se, s'; **goodness i.** la bonté même; **by i.** tout seul.

IUD [aɪjuː'diː] *n abbr* (*intrauterine device*) stérilet *m*.

ivory ['aɪvərɪ] *n* ivoire *m*.

ivy ['aɪvɪ] *n* lierre *m*.

J

J, j [dʒeɪ] *n* J, j *m*.

jab [dʒæb] *vt* (**-bb-**) (*thrust*) enfoncer (**into** dans); (*prick*) piquer (*qn*) (**with sth** du bout de qch); – *n* coup *m* (sec); (*injection*) *Med Fam* piqûre *f*.

jabber ['dʒæbər] *vi* bavarder, jaser; – *vt* bredouiller. ◆**—ing** *n* bavardage *m*.

jack [dʒæk] **1** *n Aut* cric *m*; – *vt* **to j. up** soulever (*avec un cric*); (*price*) *Fig* augmenter. **2** *n Cards* valet *m*. **3** *vt* **to j. (in)** (*job etc*) *Fam* plaquer. **4** *n* **j. of all trades** homme *m* à tout faire. ◆**j.-in-the-box** *n* diable *m* (à ressort).

jackal ['dʒæk(ə)l] *n* (*animal*) chacal *m*.

jackass ['dʒækæs] *n* (*fool*) idiot, -ote *mf*.

jackdaw ['dʒækdɔː] *n* (*bird*) choucas *m*.

jacket ['dʒækɪt] *n* (*short coat*) veste *f*; (*of man's suit*) veston *m*; (*of woman*) veste *f*, jaquette *f*; (*bulletproof*) gilet *m*; (*dust*) j. (*of book*) jaquette *f*; **in their jackets** (*potatoes*) en robe des champs.

jack-knife ['dʒæknaɪf] **1** *n* couteau *m* de poche. **2** *vi* (*of lorry, truck*) se mettre en travers de la route.

jackpot ['dʒækpɒt] *n* gros lot *m*.

jacks [dʒæks] *npl* (jeu *m* d')osselets *mpl*.

jacuzzi [dʒə'kuːzɪ] *n* (*bath, pool*) jacousi *m*.

jade [dʒeɪd] *n* **1** (*stone*) jade *m*. **2** (*horse*) rosse *f*, canasson *m*.

jaded ['dʒeɪdɪd] *a* blasé.

jagged ['dʒægɪd] *a* déchiqueté.

jaguar ['dʒægjʊər] *n* (*animal*) jaguar *m*.

jail [dʒeɪl] *n* prison *f*; – *vt* emprisonner (**for theft/***etc* pour vol/*etc*); **to j. for life** condamner à perpétuité. ◆**jailbreak** *n* évasion *f* (de prison). ◆**jailer** *n* geôlier, -ière *mf*.

jalopy [dʒə'lɒpɪ] *n* (*car*) *Fam* vieux tacot *m*.

jam [dʒæm] *n* (*traffic*) j. embouteillage *m*; **in a j.** (*trouble*) *Fig Fam* dans le pétrin. **2** *vt* (**-mm-**) (*squeeze, make stuck*) coincer, bloquer; (*gun*) enrayer; (*street, corridor etc*) encombrer; (*building*) envahir; *Rad* brouiller; **to j. sth into** (*pack, cram*) (en)tasser qch dans; (*thrust, put*) enfoncer *or* fourrer qch dans; **to j. on** (*brakes*) bloquer; – *vi* (*get stuck*) se coincer, se bloquer; (*of gun*) s'enrayer; **to j. into** (*of crowd*) s'entasser dans. ◆**jammed** a (*machine etc*) coincé, bloqué; (*street etc*) encombré. ◆**jam-'packed** a (*hall etc*) bourré de monde.

Jamaica [dʒə'meɪkə] n Jamaïque f.

jangl/e ['dʒæŋg(ə)l] vi cliqueter; – n cliquetis m. ◆**—ing** a (*noise*) discordant.

janitor ['dʒænɪtər] n concierge m.

January ['dʒænjʊərɪ] n janvier m.

Japan [dʒə'pæn] n Japon m. ◆**Japa'nese** a & n japonais, -aise (mf); – n (*language*) japonais m.

jar [dʒɑːr] **1** n (*vessel*) pot m; (*large, glass*) bocal m. **2** n (*jolt*) choc m; – vt (-rr-) (*shake*) ébranler. **3** vi (-rr-) (*of noise*) grincer; (*of note*) Mus détonner; (*of colours, words*) jurer (**with** avec); **to j. on** (*s.o.'s nerves*) porter sur; (*s.o.'s ears*) écorcher. ◆**jarring** a (*note*) discordant.

jargon ['dʒɑːgən] n jargon m.

jasmine ['dʒæzmɪn] n Bot jasmin m.

jaundice ['dʒɔːndɪs] n Med jaunisse f. ◆**jaundiced** a (*bitter*) Fig aigri; **to take a j. view** of voir d'un mauvais œil.

jaunt [dʒɔːnt] n (*journey*) balade f.

jaunt/y ['dʒɔːntɪ] a (-ier, -iest) (*carefree*) insouciant; (*cheerful, lively*) allègre; (*hat etc*) coquet, chic. ◆**—ily** adv avec insouciance; allègrement.

javelin ['dʒævlɪn] n javelot m.

jaw [dʒɔː] **1** n Anat mâchoire f. **2** vi (*talk*) Pej Fam papoter; – n **to have a j.** Pej Fam tailler une bavette.

jay [dʒeɪ] n (*bird*) geai m.

jaywalker ['dʒeɪwɔːkər] n piéton m imprudent.

jazz [dʒæz] n jazz m; – vt **to j. up** Fam (*music*) jazzifier; (*enliven*) animer; (*clothes, room*) égayer.

jealous ['dʒeləs] a jaloux (**of** de). ◆**jealousy** n jalousie f.

jeans [dʒiːnz] npl (blue-)jean m.

jeep [dʒiːp] n jeep f.

jeer [dʒɪər] vti **to j. (at)** (*mock*) railler; (*boo*) huer; – n raillerie f; pl (*boos*) huées fpl. ◆**—ing** a railleur; – n railleries fpl; (*of crowd*) huées fpl.

jell [dʒel] vi (*of ideas etc*) Fam prendre tournure.

jello® ['dʒeləʊ] n inv Culin Am gelée f. ◆**jellied** a Culin en gelée. ◆**jelly** n Culin gelée f. ◆**jellyfish** n méduse f.

jeopardy ['dʒepədɪ] n danger m, péril m. ◆**jeopardize** vt mettre en danger or en péril.

jerk [dʒɜːk] **1** vt donner une secousse à (*pour tirer, pousser etc*); – n secousse f, saccade f. **2** n (*person*) Pej Fam pauvre type m;

(*stupid*) j. crétin, -ine mf. ◆**jerk/y** a (-ier, -iest) **1** saccadé. **2** (*stupid*) Am Fam stupide, bête. ◆**—ily** adv par saccades.

jersey ['dʒɜːzɪ] n (*cloth*) jersey m; (*garment*) & Fb maillot m.

Jersey ['dʒɜːzɪ] n Jersey f.

jest [dʒest] n plaisanterie f; **in j.** pour rire; – vi plaisanter. ◆**—er** n Hist bouffon m.

Jesus ['dʒiːzəs] n Jésus m; **J. Christ** Jésus-Christ m.

jet [dʒet] **1** n (*of liquid, steam etc*) jet m. **2** n Av avion m à réaction; – a (*engine*) à réaction; **j. lag** fatigue f (due au décalage horaire). ◆**jet-lagged** a Fam qui souffre du décalage horaire.

jet-black [dʒet'blæk] a noir comme (du) jais, (noir) de jais.

jettison ['dʒetɪs(ə)n] vt Nau jeter à la mer; (*fuel*) Av larguer; Fig abandonner.

jetty ['dʒetɪ] n jetée f; (*landing-place*) embarcadère m.

Jew [dʒuː] n (*man*) Juif m; (*woman*) Juive f. ◆**Jewess** n Juive f. ◆**Jewish** a juif.

jewel ['dʒuːəl] n bijou m; (*in watch*) rubis m. ◆**jewelled** a orné de bijoux. ◆**jeweller** n bijoutier, -ière mf. ◆**jewellery** n, Am ◆**jewelry** n bijoux mpl.

jib [dʒɪb] vi (-bb-) regimber (**at** devant); **to j. at doing** se refuser à faire.

jibe [dʒaɪb] vi & n = gibe.

jiffy ['dʒɪfɪ] n Fam instant m.

jig [dʒɪg] n (*dance, music*) gigue f.

jigsaw ['dʒɪgsɔː] n **j.** (*puzzle*) puzzle m.

jilt [dʒɪlt] vt (*lover*) laisser tomber.

jingle ['dʒɪŋg(ə)l] vi (*of keys, bell etc*) tinter; – vt faire tinter; – n tintement m.

jinx [dʒɪŋks] n (*person, object*) porte-malheur m inv; (*spell, curse*) (mauvais) sort m, poisse f.

jitters ['dʒɪtəz] npl **to have the j.** Fam avoir la frousse. ◆**jittery** a **to be j.** Fam avoir la frousse.

job [dʒɒb] n (*task*) travail m; (*post*) poste m, situation f; (*crime*) Fam coup m; **to have a j. doing** or **to do** (*much trouble*) avoir du mal à faire; **to have the j. of doing** (*unpleasant task*) être obligé de faire; (*for a living etc*) être chargé de faire; **it's a good j. (that)** Fam heureusement que; **that's just the j.** Fam c'est juste ce qu'il faut; **out of a j.** au chômage. ◆**jobcentre** n agence f nationale pour l'emploi. ◆**jobless** a au chômage.

jockey ['dʒɒkɪ] n jockey m; – vi **to j. for** (*position, job*) manœuvrer pour obtenir.

jocular ['dʒɒkjʊlər] a jovial, amusant.

jog [dʒɒg] **1** n (*jolt*) secousse f; (*nudge*) coup

m de coude; – *vt* (-gg-) (*shake*) secouer; (*elbow*) pousser; (*memory*) *Fig* rafraîchir. **2** *vi* (-gg-) **to j. along** (*of vehicle*) cahoter; (*of work*) aller tant bien que mal; (*of person*) faire son petit bonhomme de chemin. **3** *vi* (-gg-) *Sp* faire du jogging. ◆**jogging** *n Sp* jogging *m*.

john [dʒɒn] *n* (*toilet*) *Am Sl* cabinets *mpl*.

join [dʒɔɪn] **1** *vt* (*unite*) joindre, réunir; (*link*) relier; (*wires, pipes*) raccorder; **to j. s.o.** (*catch up with, meet*) rejoindre qn; (*associate oneself with, go with*) se joindre à qn (**in doing** pour faire); **to j. the sea** (*of river*) rejoindre la mer; **to j. hands** se donner la main; **to j. together** *or* **up** (*objects*) joindre; – *vi* (*of roads, rivers etc*) se rejoindre; **to j.** (**together** *or* **up**) (*of objects*) se joindre (**with** à); **to j. in** participer; **to j. in a game** prendre part à un jeu; – *n* raccord *m*, joint *m*. **2** *vt* (*become a member of*) s'inscrire à (*club, parti*); (*army*) s'engager dans; (*queue, line*) se mettre à; – *vi* (*become a member*) devenir membre; **to j. up** *Mil* s'engager.

joiner [ˈdʒɔɪnər] *n* menuisier *m*.

joint [dʒɔɪnt] **1** *n Anat* articulation *f*; *Culin* rôti *m*; *Tech* joint *m*; **out of j.** *Med* démis. **2** *n* (*nightclub etc*) *Sl* boîte *f*. **3** *a* (*account, statement etc*) commun; (*effort*) conjugué; **j. author** coauteur *m*. ◆—**ly** *adv* conjointement.

jok/e [dʒəʊk] *n* plaisanterie *f*; (*trick*) tour *m*; **it's no j.** (*it's unpleasant*) ce n'est pas drôle (**doing** de faire); – *vi* plaisanter (**about** sur). ◆—**er** *n* plaisantin *m*; (*fellow*) *Fam* type *m*; *Cards* joker *m*. ◆—**ingly** *adv* en plaisantant.

jolly [ˈdʒɒlɪ] **1** *a* (-ier, -iest) (*happy*) gai; (*drunk*) *Fam* éméché. **2** *adv* (*very*) *Fam* rudement. ◆**jollifi'cation** *n* (*merry-making*) réjouissances *fpl*. ◆**jollity** *n* jovialité *f*; (*merry-making*) réjouissances *fpl*.

jolt [dʒəʊlt] *vt* **to j. s.o.** (*of vehicle*) cahoter qn; (*shake*) *Fig* secouer qn; – *vi* **to j. (along)** (*of vehicle*) cahoter; – *n* cahot *m*, secousse *f*; (*shock*) *Fig* secousse *f*.

Jordan [ˈdʒɔːd(ə)n] *n* Jordanie *f*.

jostle [ˈdʒɒs(ə)l] *vt* (*push*) bousculer; – *vi* (*push each other*) se bousculer (**for** pour obtenir); **don't j.!** ne bousculez pas!

jot [dʒɒt] *vt* (-tt-) **to j. down** noter. ◆**jotter** *n* (*notepad*) bloc-notes *m*.

journal [ˈdʒɜːn(ə)l] *n* (*periodical*) revue *f*, journal *m*. ◆**journa'lese** *n* jargon *m* journalistique. ◆**journalism** *n* journalisme *m*. ◆**journalist** *n* journaliste *mf*.

journey [ˈdʒɜːnɪ] *n* (*trip*) voyage *m*;

(*distance*) trajet *m*; **to go on a j.** partir en voyage; – *vi* voyager.

jovial [ˈdʒəʊvɪəl] *a* jovial.

joy [dʒɔɪ] *n* joie *f*; *pl* (*of countryside, motherhood etc*) plaisirs *mpl* (**of** de). ◆**joyful** *a*, ◆**joyous** *a* joyeux. ◆**joyride** *n* virée *f* (*dans une voiture volée*).

joystick [ˈdʒɔɪstɪk] *n* (*of aircraft, computer*) manche *m* à balai.

JP [dʒeɪˈpiː] *abbr* = **Justice of the Peace.**

jubilant [ˈdʒuːbɪlənt] *a* **to be j.** jubiler. ◆**jubi'lation** *n* jubilation *f*.

jubilee [ˈdʒuːbɪliː] *n* (**golden**) **j.** jubilé *m*.

Judaism [ˈdʒuːdeɪɪz(ə)m] *n* judaïsme *m*.

judder [ˈdʒʌdər] *vi* (*shake*) vibrer; – *n* vibration *f*.

judg/e [dʒʌdʒ] *n* juge *m*; – *vti* juger; **judging by** à en juger par. ◆—**(e)ment** *n* jugement *m*.

judicial [dʒuːˈdɪʃ(ə)l] *a* judiciaire. ◆**judiciary** *n* magistrature *f*. ◆**judicious** *a* judicieux.

judo [ˈdʒuːdəʊ] *n* judo *m*.

jug [dʒʌg] *n* cruche *f*; (*for milk*) pot *m*.

juggernaut [ˈdʒʌgənɔːt] *n* (*truck*) poids *m* lourd, mastodonte *m*.

juggl/e [ˈdʒʌg(ə)l] *vi* jongler; – *vt* jongler avec. ◆—**er** *n* jongleur, -euse *mf*.

Jugoslavia [juːgəʊˈslɑːvɪə] *n* Yougoslavie *f*. ◆**Jugoslav** *a* & *n* yougoslave (*mf*).

juice [dʒuːs] *n* jus *m*; (*in stomach*) suc *m*. ◆**juicy** *a* (-ier, -iest) (*fruit*) juteux; (*meat*) succulent; (*story*) *Fig* savoureux.

jukebox [ˈdʒuːkbɒks] *n* juke-box *m*.

July [dʒuːˈlaɪ] *n* juillet *m*.

jumble [ˈdʒʌmb(ə)l] *vt* (*objects, facts etc*) brouiller, mélanger; – *n* fouillis *m*; **j. sale** (*used clothes etc*) vente *f* de charité.

jumbo [ˈdʒʌmbəʊ] *a* géant; – *a* & *n* (*pl* -os) **j. (jet)** jumbo-jet *m*, gros-porteur *m*.

jump [dʒʌmp] *n* (*leap*) saut *m*, bond *m*; (*start*) sursaut *m*; (*increase*) hausse *f*; – *vi* sauter (**at** sur); (*start*) sursauter; (*of price, heart*) faire un bond; **to j. about** sautiller; **to j. across sth** traverser qch d'un bond; **to j. to conclusions** tirer des conclusions hâtives; **j. in** *or* **on!** *Aut* montez!; **to j. on** (*bus*) sauter dans; **to j. off** *or* **out** sauter; **to j. off sth, j. out of sth** sauter de qch; **to j. out of the window** sauter par la fenêtre; **to j. up** se lever d'un bond; – *vt* sauter; **to j. the lights** *Aut* griller un feu rouge; **to j. the rails** (*of train*) dérailler; **to j. the queue** resquiller.

jumper [ˈdʒʌmpər] *n* pull(-over) *m*; (*dress*) *Am* robe *f* chasuble.

jumpy [ˈdʒʌmpɪ] *a* (-ier, -iest) nerveux.

junction ['dʒʌŋkʃ(ə)n] *n* (*joining*) jonction *f*; (*crossroads*) carrefour *m*.

juncture ['dʒʌŋktʃər] *n* **at this j.** (*critical point in time*) en ce moment même.

June [dʒuːn] *n* juin *m*.

jungle ['dʒʌŋg(ə)l] *n* jungle *f*.

junior ['dʒuːnɪər] *a* (*younger*) plus jeune; (*in rank, status etc*) subalterne; (*teacher, doctor*) jeune; **to be j. to s.o., be s.o.'s j.** être plus jeune que qn; (*in rank, status*) être au-dessous de qn; **Smith j.** Smith fils *or* junior; **j. school** école *f* primaire; **j. high school** *Am* = collège *m* d'enseignement secondaire; − *n* cadet, -ette *mf*; *Sch* petit, -ite *mf*, petit(e) élève *mf*; *Sp* junior *mf*, cadet, -ette *mf*.

junk [dʒʌŋk] **1** *n* (*objects*) bric-à-brac *m inv*; (*metal*) ferraille *f*; (*goods*) *Pej* camelote *f*; (*film, book etc*) *Pej* idiotie *f*; (*nonsense*) idioties *fpl*; **j. shop** (boutique *f* de) brocanteur *m*. **2** *vt* (*get rid of*) *Am Fam* balancer.

junkie ['dʒʌŋkɪ] *n Fam* drogué, -ée *mf*.

junta ['dʒʌntə] *n Pol* junte *f*.

jurisdiction [dʒuərɪs'dɪkʃ(ə)n] *n* juridiction *f*.

jury ['dʒuərɪ] *n* (*in competition*) & *Jur* jury *m*. ◆**juror** *n Jur* juré *m*.

just [dʒʌst] **1** *adv* (*exactly, slightly*) juste; (*only*) juste, seulement; (*simply*) (tout) simplement; **it's j. as I thought** c'est bien ce que je pensais; **j. at that time** à cet instant

même; **she has/had j. left** elle vient/venait de partir; **I've j. come from** j'arrive de; **I'm j. coming!** j'arrive!; **he'll (only) j. catch the bus** il aura son bus de justesse; **he j. missed it** il l'a manqué de peu; **j. as big/light/etc** tout aussi grand/léger/etc (**as** que); **j. listen!** écoute donc!; **j. a moment!** un instant!; **j. over ten** un peu plus de dix; **j. one** un(e) seul(e) (**of** de); **j. about** (*approximately*) à peu près; (*almost*) presque; **j. about to do** sur le point de faire. **2** *a* (*fair*) juste (**to** envers). ◆**-ly** *adv* avec justice. ◆**-ness** *n* (*of cause etc*) justice *f*.

justice ['dʒʌstɪs] *n* justice *f*; (*judge*) juge *m*; **to do j. to** (*meal*) faire honneur à; **it doesn't do you j.** (*hat, photo*) cela ne vous avantage pas; (*attitude*) cela ne vous fait pas honneur; **J. of the Peace** juge *m* de paix.

justify ['dʒʌstɪfaɪ] *vt* justifier; **to be justified in doing** (*have right*) être en droit de faire; (*have reason*) avoir toutes les bonnes raisons de faire. ◆**justi'fiable** *a* justifiable. ◆**justi'fiably** *adv* légitimement. ◆**justifi'cation** *n* justification *f*.

jut [dʒʌt] *vi* (-tt-) **to j. out** faire saillie; **to j. out over sth** (*overhang*) surplomber qch.

jute [dʒuːt] *n* (*fibre*) jute *m*.

juvenile ['dʒuːvənaɪl] *n* adolescent, -ente *mf*; − *a* (*court, book etc*) pour enfants; (*delinquent*) jeune; (*behaviour*) *Pej* puéril.

juxtapose [dʒʌkstə'pəuz] *vt* juxtaposer. ◆**juxtapo'sition** *n* juxtaposition *f*.

K

K, k [keɪ] *n* K, k *m*.

kaleidoscope [kə'laɪdəskəup] *n* kaléidoscope *m*.

kangaroo [kæŋgə'ruː] *n* kangourou *m*.

kaput [kə'put] *a* (*broken, ruined*) *Sl* fichu.

karate [kə'rɑːtɪ] *n Sp* karaté *m*.

keel [kiːl] *n Nau* quille *f*; − *vi* **to k. over** (*of boat*) chavirer.

keen [kiːn] *a* (*edge, appetite*) aiguisé; (*interest, feeling*) vif; (*mind*) pénétrant; (*wind*) coupant, piquant; (*enthusiastic*) enthousiaste; **a k. sportsman** un passionné de sport; **to be k. to do** *or* **on doing** tenir (beaucoup) à faire; **to be k. on** (*music, sport etc*) être passionné de; **he is k. on her/the idea** elle/l'idée lui plaît beaucoup. ◆**-ly** *adv* (*to work etc*) avec enthousiasme; (*to feel, interest*) vivement. ◆**-ness** *n*

enthousiasme *m*; (*of mind*) pénétration *f*; (*of interest*) intensité *f*; **k. to do** empressement *m* à faire.

keep¹ [kiːp] *vt* (*pt & pp kept*) garder; (*shop, car*) avoir; (*diary, promise*) tenir; (*family*) entretenir; (*rule*) observer, respecter; (*feast day*) célébrer; (*birthday*) fêter; (*detain, delay*) retenir; (*put*) mettre; **to k. (on)** doing (*continue*) continuer à faire; **to k. clean** tenir *or* garder propre; **to k. from** (*conceal*) cacher à; **to k. s.o. from doing** (*prevent*) empêcher qn de faire; **to k. s.o. waiting/working** faire attendre/travailler qn; **to k. sth going** (*engine, machine*) laisser qch en marche; **to k. s.o. in whisky/etc** fournir qn en whisky/etc; **to k. an appointment** se rendre à un rendez-vous; **to k. back** (*withhold, delay*) retenir; (*conceal*) cacher (**from**

à); **to k. down** (*control*) maîtriser; (*restrict*) limiter; (*costs, price*) maintenir bas; **to k. in** empêcher de sortir; (*pupil*) *Sch* consigner; **to k. off** *or* **away** (*person*) éloigner (**from** de); **'k. off the grass'** 'ne pas marcher sur les pelouses'; **k. your hands off!** n'y touche(z) pas!; **to k. on** (*hat, employee*) garder; **to k. out** empêcher d'entrer; **to k. up** (*continue, maintain*) continuer (**doing sth** à faire qch); (*road, building*) entretenir; – *vi* (*continue*) continuer; (*remain*) rester; (*of food*) se garder, se conserver; (*wait*) attendre; **how is he keeping?** comment va-t-il?; **to k. still** rester *or* se tenir tranquille; **to k. from doing** (*refrain*) s'abstenir de faire; **to k. going** (*continue*) continuer; **to k. at it** (*keep doing it*) continuer à le faire; **to k. away** *or* **off** *or* **back** ne pas s'approcher (**from** de); **if the rain keeps off** s'il ne pleut pas; **to k. on at s.o.** harceler qn; **to k. out** rester en dehors (**of** de); **to k. to** (*subject, path*) ne pas s'écarter de; (*room*) garder; **to k. to the left** tenir la gauche; **to k. to oneself** se tenir à l'écart; **to k. up** (*continue*) continuer; (*follow*) suivre; **to k. up with s.o** (*follow*) suivre qn; (*in quality of work etc*) se maintenir à la hauteur de qn; – *n* (*food*) subsistance *f*; **to have one's k.** être logé et nourri; **for keeps** *Fam* pour toujours. ◆**—ing** *n* (*care*) garde *f*; **in k. with** in rapport avec. ◆**—er** *n* gardien, -ienne *mf*.

keep² [kiːp] *n* (*tower*) *Hist* donjon *m*.

keepsake ['kiːpseɪk] *n* (*object*) souvenir *m*.

keg [keg] *n* tonnelet *m*.

kennel ['ken(ə)l] *n* niche *f*; (*for boarding*) chenil *m*.

Kenya ['kiːnjə, 'kenjə] *n* Kenya *m*.

kept [kept] *see* **keep¹**; – *a* **well** *or* **nicely k.** (*house etc*) bien tenu.

kerb [kɜːb] *n* bord *m* du trottoir.

kernel ['kɜːn(ə)l] *n* (*of nut*) amande *f*.

kerosene ['kerəsiːn] *n* (*aviation fuel*) kérosène *m*; (*paraffin*) *Am* pétrole *m* (lampant).

ketchup ['ketʃəp] *n* (*sauce*) ketchup *m*.

kettle ['ket(ə)l] *n* bouilloire *f*; **the k. is boiling** l'eau bout.

key [kiː] *n* clef *f*, clé *f*; (*of piano, typewriter, computer*) touche *f*; – *a* (*industry, post etc*) clef (*f inv*), clé (*f inv*); **k. man** pivot *m*; **k. ring** porte-clefs *m inv*. ◆**keyboard** *n* clavier *m*. ◆**keyhole** *n* trou *m* de (la) serrure. ◆**keynote** *n* (*of speech*) note *f* dominante. ◆**keystone** *n* (*of policy etc*) & *Archit* clef *f* de voûte.

keyed [kiːd] *a* **to be k. up** avoir les nerfs tendus.

khaki ['kɑːkɪ] *a* & *n* kaki *a inv* & *m*.

kibbutz [kɪ'buts] *n* kibboutz *m*.

kick [kɪk] *n* coup *m* de pied; (*of horse*) ruade *f*; **to get a k. out of doing** (*thrill*) *Fam* prendre un malin plaisir à faire; **for kicks** *Pej* *Fam* pour le plaisir; – *vt* donner un coup de pied à; (*of horse*) lancer une ruade à; **to k. back** (*ball*) renvoyer (*du pied*); **to k. down** *or* **in** démolir à coups de pied; **to k. out** (*eject*) *Fam* flanquer dehors; **to k. up** (*fuss, row*) *Fam* faire; – *vi* donner des coups de pied; (*of horse*) ruer; **to k. off** *Fb* donner le coup d'envoi; (*start*) *Fig* démarrer. ◆**k.-off** *n* *Fb* coup *m* d'envoi.

kid [kɪd] **1** *n* (*goat*) chevreau *m*. **2** *n* (*child*) *Fam* gosse *mf*; **his** *or* **her k. brother** *Am* *Fam* son petit frère. **3** *vti* (**-dd-**) (*joke, tease*) *Fam* blaguer; **to k. oneself** se faire des illusions.

kidnap ['kɪdnæp] *vt* (**-pp-**) kidnapper. ◆**kidnapping** *n* enlèvement *m*. ◆**kidnapper** *n* kidnappeur, -euse *mf*.

kidney ['kɪdnɪ] *n* *Anat* rein *m*; *Culin* rognon *m*; **on a k. machine** sous rein artificiel; **k. bean** haricot *m* rouge.

kill [kɪl] *vt* tuer; (*bill*) *Pol* repousser, faire échouer; (*chances*) détruire; (*rumour*) étouffer; (*story*) *Fam* supprimer; (*engine*) *Fam* arrêter; **my feet are killing me** *Fam* je ne sens plus mes pieds, j'ai les pieds en compote; **to k. off** (*person etc*) & *Fig* détruire; – *vi* tuer; – *n* mise *f* à mort; (*prey*) animaux *mpl* tués. ◆**—ing 1** *n* (*of person*) meurtre *m*; (*of group*) massacre *m*; (*of animal*) mise *f* à mort; **to make a k.** *Fin* réussir un beau coup. **2** *a* (*tiring*) *Fam* tuant. ◆**—er** *n* tueur, -euse *mf*. ◆**killjoy** *n* rabat-joie *m inv*.

kiln [kɪln] *n* (*for pottery*) four *m*.

kilo ['kiːləʊ] *n* (*pl* **-os**) kilo *m*. ◆**kilogramme** ['kɪləʊɡræm] *n* kilogramme *m*.

kilometre [kɪ'lɒmɪtər] *n* kilomètre *m*.

kilowatt ['kɪləʊwɒt] *n* kilowatt *m*.

kilt [kɪlt] *n* kilt *m*.

kimono [kɪ'məʊnəʊ] *n* (*pl* **-os**) kimono *m*.

kin [kɪn] *n* (*relatives*) parents *mpl*; **one's next of k.** son plus proche parent.

kind [kaɪnd] **1** *n* (*sort, type*) genre *m*; **a k. of** une sorte *or* une espèce de; **to pay in k.** payer en nature; **what k. of drink/etc is it?** qu'est-ce que c'est comme boisson/*etc*?; **that's the k. of man he is** il est comme ça; **nothing of the k.!** absolument pas!; **k. of worried/sad/etc** (*somewhat*) plutôt inquiet/triste/*etc*; **k. of fascinated** (*as if*) *Fam* comme fasciné; **in a k. of way** d'une certaine façon; **it's the only one of its k.**, **it's one of a k.** c'est unique en son genre; **we are**

two of a k. nous nous ressemblons. **2** *a* (**-er,** **-est**) (*helpful, pleasant*) gentil (**to** avec, pour), bon (**to** pour); **that's k. of you** c'est gentil *or* aimable à vous. ◆**k.-'hearted** *a* qui a bon cœur. ◆**kindly** *adv* avec bonté; **k. wait**/*etc* ayez la bonté d'attendre/*etc*; **not to take k. to sth** ne pas apprécier qch; − *a* (*person*) bienveillant. ◆**kindness** *n* bonté *f*, gentillesse *f*.

kindergarten ['kɪndəgɑːt(ə)n] *n* jardin *m* d'enfants.

kindle ['kɪnd(ə)l] *vt* allumer; − *vi* s'allumer.

kindred ['kɪndrɪd] *n* (*relationship*) parenté *f*; (*relatives*) parents *mpl*. **k. spirit** semblable *mf*, âme *f* sœur.

king [kɪŋ] *n* roi *m*. ◆**k.-size(d)** *a* géant; (*cigarette*) long. ◆**kingdom** *n* royaume *m*; **animal/plant k.** règne *m* animal/végétal. ◆**kingly** *a* royal.

kingfisher ['kɪŋfɪʃər] *n* (*bird*) martin-pêcheur *m*.

kink [kɪŋk] *n* (*in rope*) entortillement *m*.

kinky ['kɪŋkɪ] *a* (**-ier, -iest**) (*person*) *Psy Pej* vicieux; (*clothes etc*) bizarre.

kinship ['kɪnʃɪp] *n* parenté *f*.

kiosk ['kiːɒsk] *n* kiosque *m*; (**telephone**) **k.** cabine *f* (téléphonique).

kip [kɪp] *vi* (**-pp-**) (*sleep*) *Sl* roupiller.

kipper ['kɪpər] *n* (*herring*) kipper *m*.

kiss [kɪs] *n* baiser *m*, bise *f*; **the k. of life** *Med* le bouche-à-bouche; − *vt* (*person*) embrasser; **to k. s.o.'s hand** baiser la main de qn; − *vt* s'embrasser.

kit [kɪt] *n* équipement *m*, matériel *m*; (*set of articles*) trousse *f*; **gym k.** (*belongings*) affaires *fpl* de gym; **tool k.** trousse *f* à outils; (**do-it-yourself**) **k.** kit *m*; **in k. form** en kit; **k. bag** sac *m* (*de soldat etc*); − *vt* (**-tt-**) **to k. out** équiper (**with** de).

kitchen ['kɪtʃɪn] *n* cuisine *f*; **k. cabinet** buffet *m* de cuisine; **k. garden** jardin *m* potager; **k. sink** évier *m*. ◆**kitche'nette** *n* kitchenette *f*, coin-cuisine *m*.

kite [kaɪt] *n* (*toy*) cerf-volant *m*.

kith [kɪθ] *n* **k. and kin** amis *mpl* et parents *mpl*.

kitten ['kɪt(ə)n] *n* chaton *m*, petit chat *m*.

kitty ['kɪtɪ] *n* (*fund*) cagnotte *f*.

km *abbr* (*kilometre*) km.

knack [næk] *n* (*skill*) coup *m* (de main), truc *m* (**of doing** pour faire); **to have a** *or* **the k. of doing** (*aptitude, tendency*) avoir le don de faire.

knackered ['nækəd] *a* (*tired*) *Sl* vanné.

knapsack ['næpsæk] *n* sac *m* à dos.

knead [niːd] *vt* (*dough*) pétrir.

knee [niː] *n* genou *m*; **to go down on one's knees** se mettre à genoux; **k. pad** *Sp* genouillère *f*. ◆**kneecap** *n Anat* rotule *f*. ◆**knees-up** *n Sl* soirée *f* dansante, sauterie *f*.

kneel [niːl] *vi* (*pt & pp* **knelt** *or* **kneeled**) **to k. (down)** s'agenouiller; **to be kneeling (down)** être à genoux.

knell [nel] *n* glas *m*.

knew [njuː] *see* know.

knickers ['nɪkəz] *npl* (*woman's undergarment*) culotte *f*, slip *m*.

knick-knack ['nɪknæk] *n* babiole *f*.

knife [naɪf] *n* (*pl* **knives**) couteau *m*; (*penknife*) canif *m*; − *vt* poignarder.

knight [naɪt] *n Hist & Br Pol* chevalier *m*; *Chess* cavalier *m*; − *vt* (*of monarch*) *Br Pol* faire (*qn*) chevalier. ◆**knighthood** *n* titre *m* de chevalier.

knit [nɪt] *vt* (**-tt-**) tricoter; **to k. together** *Fig* souder; **to k. one's brow** froncer les sourcils; − *vi* tricoter; **to k. (together)** (*of bones*) se souder. ◆**knitting** *n* tricot *m*; **k. needle** aiguille *f* à tricoter. ◆**knitwear** *n* tricots *mpl*.

knob [nɒb] *n* (*on door etc*) bouton *m*; (*on stick*) pommeau *m*; (*of butter*) noix *f*.

knock [nɒk] *vt* (*strike*) frapper; (*collide with*) heurter; (*criticize*) *Fam* critiquer; **to k. one's head on** se cogner la tête contre; **to k. senseless** (*stun*) assommer; **to k. to the ground** jeter à terre; **to k. about** (*ill-treat*) malmener; **to k. back** (*drink, glass etc*) *Fam* s'envoyer (derrière la cravate), siffler; **to k. down** (*vase, pedestrian etc*) renverser; (*house, tree, wall etc*) abattre; (*price*) baisser, casser; **to k. in** (*nail*) enfoncer; **to k. off** (*person, object*) faire tomber (**from** de); (*do quickly*) *Fam* expédier; (*steal*) *Fam* piquer; **to k. £5 off (the price)** baisser le prix de cinq livres, faire cinq livres sur le prix; **to k. out** (*stun*) assommer; (*beat in competition*) éliminer; **to k. oneself out** (*tire*) *Fam* s'esquinter (**doing** à faire); **to k. over** (*pedestrian, vase etc*) renverser; **to k. up** (*meal*) *Fam* préparer à la hâte; − *vi* (*strike*) frapper; **to k. against** *or* **into** (*bump into*) heurter; **to k. about** (*travel*) *Fam* bourlinguer; (*lie around, stand around*) traîner; **to k. off** (*stop work*) *Fam* s'arrêter de travailler; − *n* (*blow*) coup *m*; (*collision*) heurt *m*; **there's a k. at the door** quelqu'un frappe; **I heard a k.** j'ai entendu frapper. ◆**knockdown** *a* **k. price** prix *m* imbattable. ◆**knock-'kneed** *a* cagneux. ◆**knock-out** *n Boxing* knock-out *m*; **to be a k.-out** (*of person, film etc*) *Fam* être formidable.

knocker ['nɒkər] n (for door) marteau m.

knot [nɒt] **1** n (in rope etc) nœud m; – vt (-tt-) nouer. **2** n (unit of speed) Nau nœud m. **◆knotty** a (-ier, -iest) (wood etc) noueux; (problem) Fig épineux.

know [nəʊ] vt (pt **knew**, pp **known**) (facts, language etc) savoir; (person, place etc) connaître; (recognize) reconnaître (**by** à); **to k. that** savoir que; **for all I k.** (autant) que je sache; **I'll let you k.** je te le ferai savoir; **I'll have you k. that** ... sachez que ... ; **to k. (a lot) about** (person, event) en savoir long sur; (cars, sewing etc) s'y connaître en; **I've never known him to complain** je ne l'ai jamais vu se plaindre; **to get to k. (about) sth** apprendre qch; **to get to k. s.o.** (meet) faire la connaissance de qn; – vi savoir; **I k.** je (le) sais; **I wouldn't k.,** I k. nothing about it je n'en sais rien; **I k. about that** je sais ça, je suis au courant; **to k. of** (have heard of) avoir entendu parler de; **do you k.?** (a good tailor etc) connais-tu?; **you (should) k. better than to do that** tu es trop intelligent pour faire ça; **you should have known better** tu aurais dû réfléchir; – n **in the k.** Fam au courant. **◆—ing** a (smile, look) entendu. **◆—ingly** adv (consciously) sciemment. **◆known** a connu; **a k. expert** un expert reconnu; **well k.** (bien) connu (**that** que); **she is k. to be** ... on sait qu'elle est .... **◆know-all** n, Am **◆know-it-all** n je-sais-tout mf inv. **◆know-how** n (skill) compétence f (**to do** pour faire), savoir-faire m inv.

knowledge ['nɒlɪdʒ] n connaissance f (**of** de); (learning) connaissances fpl, savoir m; **to (the best) of my k.** à ma connaissance; **without the k. of** à l'insu de; **to have no k. of** ignorer; **general k.** culture f générale. **◆knowledgeable** a bien informé (**about** sur).

knuckle ['nʌk(ə)l] **1** n articulation f du doigt. **2** vi **to k. down to** (task) Fam s'atteler à; **to k. under** céder.

Koran [kə'rɑːn] n Rel Coran m.

kosher ['kəʊʃər] a Rel kascher inv.

kowtow [kaʊ'taʊ] vi se prosterner (**to** devant).

kudos ['kjuːdɒs] n (glory) gloire f.

L

L, l [el] L, l m.

lab [læb] n Fam labo m. **◆laboratory** [lə'bɒrət(ə)rɪ, Am 'læbrətərɪ] n laboratoire m; **language l.** laboratoire m de langues.

label ['leɪb(ə)l] n étiquette f; – vt (-ll-, Am -l-) (goods, person) étiqueter (**as** comme).

laborious [lə'bɔːrɪəs] a laborieux.

labour ['leɪbər] n (work, childbirth) travail m; (workers) main-d'œuvre f; L. Br Pol les travaillistes mpl; **in l.** Med au travail; – a (market, situation) du travail; (conflict, dispute) ouvrier; (relations) ouvriers-patronat inv; **l. force** main-d'œuvre f; **l. union** Am syndicat m; – vi (toil) peiner; – vt **to l. a point** insister sur un point. **◆—ed** a (style) laborieux. **◆—er** n (on roads etc) manœuvre m; Agr ouvrier m agricole.

laburnum [lə'bɜːnəm] n Bot cytise f.

labyrinth ['læbɪrɪnθ] n labyrinthe m.

lace [leɪs] **1** n (cloth) dentelle f. **2** n (of shoe) lacet m; – vt **to l. (up)** (tie up) lacer. **3** vt (drink) additionner, arroser (**with** de).

lacerate ['læsəreɪt] vt (flesh etc) lacérer.

lack [læk] n manque m; **for l. of** à défaut de; – vt manquer de; – vi **to be lacking** manquer (**in, for** de).

lackey ['lækɪ] n Hist & Fig laquais m.

laconic [lə'kɒnɪk] a laconique.

lacquer ['lækər] n laque f; – vt laquer.

lad [læd] n gars m, garçon m; **when I was a l.** quand j'étais gosse.

ladder ['lædər] n échelle f; (in stocking) maille f filée; – vti (stocking) filer.

laden ['leɪd(ə)n] a chargé (**with** de).

ladle ['leɪd(ə)l] n louche f.

lady ['leɪdɪ] n dame f; **a young l.** une jeune fille; (married) une jeune femme; **the l. of the house** la maîtresse de maison; **Ladies and Gentlemen!** Mesdames, Mesdemoiselles, Messieurs!; **l. doctor** femme f médecin; **l. friend** amie f; **ladies' room** Fig toilettes fpl. **◆l.-in-'waiting** n (pl ladies-in-waiting) dame f d'honneur. **◆ladybird** n, Am **◆ladybug** n coccinelle f. **◆ladylike** a (manner) distingué; **she's (very) l.** elle est très grande dame.

lag [læg] **1** vi (-gg-) **to l. behind** (in progress, work) avoir du retard; (dawdle) traîner; **to l. behind s.o.** avoir du retard sur qn; – n

time l. (*between events*) décalage *m*; (*between countries*) décalage *m* horaire. **2** *vt* (-gg-) (*pipe*) calorifuger.

lager ['lɑːgər] *n* bière *f* blonde.

lagoon [lə'guːn] *n* lagune *f*; (*small, coral*) lagon *m*.

laid [leɪd] *see* **lay²**. ◆**l.-'back** *a Fam* relax.

lain [leɪn] *see* **lie¹**.

lair [leər] *n* tanière *f*.

laity ['leɪtɪ] *n* **the l.** les laïcs *mpl*.

lake [leɪk] *n* lac *m*.

lamb [læm] *n* agneau *m*. ◆**lambswool** *n* laine *f* d'agneau.

lame [leɪm] *a* (-er, -est) (*person, argument*) boiteux; (*excuse*) piètre; **to be l.** boiter. ◆**-ness** *n Med* claudication *f*; (*of excuse*) *Fig* faiblesse *f*.

lament [lə'ment] *n* lamentation *f*; — *vt* **to l. (over)** se lamenter sur. ◆**lamentable** *a* lamentable. ◆**lamen'tation** *n* lamentation *f*.

laminated ['læmɪneɪtɪd] *a* (*metal*) laminé.

lamp [læmp] *n* lampe *f*; (*bulb*) ampoule *f*; *Aut* feu *m*. ◆**lamppost** *n* réverbère *m*. ◆**lampshade** *n* abat-jour *m inv*.

lance [lɑːns] **1** *n* (*weapon*) lance *f*. **2** *vt Med* inciser.

land [lænd] **1** *n* terre *f*; (*country*) pays *m*; (*plot of*) **l.** terrain *m*; **on dry l.** sur la terre ferme; **no man's l.** *Mil & Fig* no man's land *m inv*; — *a* (*flora, transport etc*) terrestre; (*reform, law*) agraire; (*owner, tax*) foncier. **2** *vi* (*of aircraft*) atterrir, se poser; (*of ship*) mouiller, relâcher; (*of passengers*) débarquer; (*of bomb etc*) (re)tomber; **to l. up** (*end up*) se retrouver; — *vt* (*passengers, cargo*) débarquer; (*aircraft*) poser; (*blow*) *Fig* flanquer (**on** à); (*job, prize etc*) *Fam* décrocher; **to l. s.o. in trouble** *Fam* mettre qn dans le pétrin; **to be landed with** *Fam* (*person*) avoir sur les bras; (*fine*) ramasser, écoper de. ◆**-ed** *a* (*owning land*) terrien. ◆**-ing** *n* **1** *Av* atterrissage *m*; *Nau* débarquement *m*; **forced l.** atterrissage *m* forcé; **l. stage** débarcadère *m*. **2** *n* (*at top of stairs*) palier *m*; (*floor*) étage *m*. ◆**landlady** *n* logeuse *f*, propriétaire *f*. ◆**landlocked** *a* sans accès à la mer. ◆**landlord** *n* propriétaire *m*; (*of pub*) patron *m*. ◆**landmark** *n* point *m* de repère. ◆**landslide** *n Geol* glissement *m* de terrain, éboulement *m*; *Pol* raz-de-marée *m inv* électoral.

landscape ['lændskeɪp] *n* paysage *m*.

lane [leɪn] *n* (*in country*) chemin *m*; (*in town*) ruelle *f*; (*division of road*) voie *f*; (*line of traffic*) file *f*; *Av Nau Sp* couloir *m*; **bus l.** couloir *m* (*réservé aux autobus*).

language ['læŋgwɪdʒ] *n* (*faculty, style*) langage *m*; (*national tongue*) langue *f*; **computer l.** langage *m* machine; — *a* (*laboratory*) de langues; (*teacher, studies*) de langue(s).

languid ['læŋgwɪd] *a* languissant. ◆**languish** *vi* languir (**for, after** après).

lank [læŋk] *a* (*hair*) plat et terne.

lanky ['læŋkɪ] *a* (-ier, -iest) dégingandé.

lantern ['læntən] *n* lanterne *f*; **Chinese l.** lampion *m*.

lap [læp] **1** *n* (*of person*) genoux *mpl*; **the l. of luxury** le plus grand luxe. **2** *n Sp* tour *m* (de piste). **3** *vt* (-pp-) **to l. up** (*drink*) laper; (*like very much*) *Fam* adorer; (*believe*) *Fam* gober; — *vi* (*of waves*) clapoter. **4** *vi* (-pp-) **to l. over** (*overlap*) se chevaucher.

lapel [lə'pel] *n* (*of jacket etc*) revers *m*.

lapse [læps] **1** *n* (*fault*) faute *f*; (*weakness*) défaillance *f*; **a l. of memory** un trou de mémoire; **a l. in behaviour** un écart de conduite; — *vi* (*err*) commettre une faute; **to l. into** retomber dans. **2** *n* (*interval*) intervalle *m*; **a l. of time** un intervalle (**between** entre). **3** *vi* (*expire*) se périmer, expirer; (*of subscription*) prendre fin.

larceny ['lɑːsənɪ] *n* vol *m* simple.

lard [lɑːd] *n* saindoux *m*.

larder ['lɑːdər] *n* (*cupboard*) garde-manger *m inv*.

large [lɑːdʒ] *a* (-er, -est) (*in size or extent*) grand; (*in volume, bulkiness*) gros; (*quantity*) grand, important; **to become** *or* **grow** *or* **get l.** grossir, grandir; **to a l. extent** en grande mesure; **at l.** (*of prisoner, animal*) en liberté; (*as a whole*) en général; **by and l.** dans l'ensemble, généralement. ◆**l.-scale** *a* (*reform*) (fait) sur une grande échelle. ◆**largely** *adv* (*to a great extent*) en grande mesure. ◆**largeness** *n* grandeur *f*; grosseur *f*.

largesse [lɑː'ʒes] *n* largesse *f*.

lark [lɑːk] **1** *n* (*bird*) alouette *f*. **2** *n* (*joke*) *Fam* rigolade *f*, blague *f*; — *vi* **to l. about** *Fam* s'amuser.

larva, *pl* **-vae** ['lɑːvə, -viː] *n* (*of insect*) larve *f*.

larynx ['lærɪŋks] *n Anat* larynx *m*. ◆**laryn'gitis** *n Med* laryngite *f*.

lascivious [lə'sɪvɪəs] *a* lascif.

laser ['leɪzər] *n* laser *m*.

lash [læʃ] *n* (*with whip*) coup *m* de fouet; — *vt* (*strike*) fouetter; (*tie*) attacher (**to** à); **the dog lashed its tail** le chien donna un coup de queue; — *vi* **to l. out** (*spend wildly*) *Fam* claquer son argent; **to l. out at** envoyer des coups à; (*abuse*) *Fig* invectiver; (*criticize*) *Fig* fustiger. ◆**—ings** *npl* **l.** of *Culin Fam* des masses de, une montagne de.

lash² [læʃ] *n* (*eyelash*) cil *m*.

lass [læs] *n* jeune fille *f*.

lassitude ['læsitjuːd] *n* lassitude *f*.

lasso [læ'suː] *n* (*pl* -os) lasso *m*; — *vt* attraper au lasso.

last¹ [laːst] *a* dernier; **the l. ten lines** les dix dernières lignes; **l. but one** avant-dernier; **l. night** (*evening*) hier soir; (*during night*) cette nuit; **the day before l.** avant-hier; — *adv* (*lastly*) en dernier lieu, enfin; (*on the last occasion*) (pour) la dernière fois; **to leave l.** sortir le dernier *or* en dernier; — *n* (*person, object*) dernier, -ière *mf*; (*end*) fin *f*; **the l.** of **the beer**/etc (*remainder*) le reste de la bière/etc; **at (long) l.** enfin. ◆**l.-ditch** *a* désespéré. ◆**l.-minute** *a* de dernière minute. ◆**lastly** *adv* en dernier lieu, enfin.

last² [laːst] *vi* durer; **to l. (out)** (*endure, resist*) tenir; (*of money, supplies*) durer; **it lasted me ten years** ça m'a duré *or* fait dix ans. ◆**—ing** *a* durable.

latch [lætʃ] **1** *n* loquet *m*; **the door is on the l.** la porte n'est pas fermée à clef. **2** *vi* **to l. on to** *Fam* (*grab*) s'accrocher à; (*understand*) saisir.

late¹ [leit] *a* (-er, -est) (*not on time*) en retard (**for** à); (*former*) ancien; (*meal, fruit, season, hour*) tardif; (*stage*) avancé; (*edition*) dernier; **to be l.** (*of person, train etc*) être en retard, avoir du retard; **to be l. (in) coming** arriver en retard; **he's an hour l.** il a une heure de retard; **to make s.o. l.** mettre qn en retard; **it's l.** il est tard; **Easter**/etc **is l.** Pâques/etc est tard; **in l. June**/etc fin juin/etc; **a later edition**/etc (*more recent*) une édition/etc plus récente; **the latest edition**/etc (*last*) la dernière édition/etc; **in later life** plus tard dans la vie; **to take a later train** prendre un train plus tard; **at a later date** à une date ultérieure; **the latest date** la date limite; **at the latest** au plus tard; **of l.** dernièrement; — *adv* (*in the day, season etc*) tard; (*not on time*) en retard; **it's getting l.** il se fait tard; **later (on)** plus tard; **not** *or* **no later than** pas plus tard que. ◆**latecomer** *n* retardataire *mf*. ◆**lately** *adv* dernièrement. ◆**lateness** *n* (*of person, train etc*) retard *m*; **constant l.** des retards continuels; **the l. of the hour** l'heure tardive.

late² [leit] *a* **the l. Mr Smith**/etc (*deceased*) feu Monsieur Smith/etc; **our l. friend** notre regretté ami.

latent ['leitənt] *a* latent.

lateral ['lætərəl] *a* latéral.

lathe [leið] *n Tech* tour *m*.

lather ['laːðər] *n* mousse *f*; — *vt* savonner; — *vi* mousser.

Latin ['lætin] *a* latin; **L. America** Amérique *f* latine; **L. American** d'Amérique latine; — *n* (*person*) Latin, -ine *mf*; (*language*) latin *m*.

latitude ['lætitjuːd] *n Geog & Fig* latitude *f*.

latrines [lə'triːnz] *npl* latrines *fpl*.

latter ['lætər] *a* (*later, last-named*) dernier; (*second*) deuxième; — *n* dernier, -ière *mf*; second, -onde *mf*. ◆**—ly** *adv* dernièrement; (*late in life*) sur le tard.

lattice ['lætis] *n* treillis *m*.

laudable ['lɔːdəb(ə)l] *a* louable.

laugh [laːf] *n* rire *m*; **to have a good l.** bien rire; — *vi* rire (**at, about** de); **to l. to oneself** rire en soi-même; — *vt* **to l. off** tourner en plaisanterie. ◆**—ing** *a* riant; **it's no l. matter** il n'y a pas de quoi rire; **to be the l.-stock of** être la risée de. ◆**—able** *a* ridicule. ◆**laughter** *n* rire(s) *m*(*pl*); **to roar with l.** rire aux éclats.

launch [lɔːntʃ] **1** *n* (*motor boat*) vedette *f*; (*pleasure boat*) bateau *m* de plaisance. **2** *vt* (*rocket, boat, fashion etc*) lancer; — *vi* **to l. (out) into** (*begin*) se lancer dans; — *n* lancement *m*. ◆**—ing** *n* lancement *m*.

launder ['lɔːndər] *vt* (*clothes*) blanchir; (*money from drugs etc*) *Fig* blanchir. ◆**—ing** *n* blanchissage *m*. ◆**launde'rette** *n, Am* ◆**laundromat** *n* laverie *f* automatique. ◆**laundry** *n* (*place*) blanchisserie *f*; (*clothes*) linge *m*.

laurel ['lɔrəl] *n Bot* laurier *m*.

lava ['laːvə] *n Geol* lave *f*.

lavatory ['lævətri] *n* cabinets *mpl*.

lavender ['lævindər] *n* lavande *f*.

lavish ['lævɪʃ] *a* prodigue (**with** de); (*helping, meal*) généreux; (*decor, house etc*) somptueux; (*expenditure*) excessif; — *vt* prodiguer (**sth on s.o.** qch à qn). ◆**—ly** *adv* (*to give*) généreusement; (*to furnish*) somptueusement.

law [lɔː] *n* (*rule, rules*) loi *f*; (*study, profession, system*) droit *m*; **court of l., l. court** cour *f* de justice; **l. and order** l'ordre public. ◆**l.-abiding** *a* respectueux des lois. ◆**lawful** *a* (*action*) légal; (*child, wife etc*) légitime. ◆**lawfully** *adv* légalement. ◆**lawless** *a* (*country*) anarchique. ◆**lawlessness** *n* anarchie *f*. ◆**lawsuit** *n* procès *m*.

lawn [lɔːn] *n* pelouse *f*, gazon *m*; **l. mower** tondeuse *f* (à gazon); **l. tennis** tennis *m* (sur gazon).

lawyer ['lɔːjər] *n* (*in court*) avocat *m*; (*author,* *legal expert*) juriste *m*; (*for wills, sales*) notaire *m*.

lax [læks] *a* (*person*) négligent; (*discipline, behaviour*) relâché; **to be l. in doing** faire avec négligence. ◆**laxity** *n*, ◆**laxness** *n* négligence *f*; relâchement *m*.

laxative ['læksətɪv] *n & a Med* laxatif (*m*).

lay¹ [leɪ] *a* (*non-religious*) laïque; (*non-specialized*) d'un profane; **l. person** profane *mf*. ◆**layman** *n* (*pl* -**men**) (*non-specialist*) profane *mf*.

lay² [leɪ] (*pt & pp* **laid**) **1** *vt* (*put down, place*) poser; (*table*) mettre; (*blanket*) étendre (**over** sur); (*trap*) tendre; (*money*) miser (**on** sur); (*accusation*) porter; (*ghost*) exorciser; **to l. a bet** parier; **to l. bare** mettre à nu; **to l. waste** ravager; **to l. s.o. open to** exposer qn à; **to l. one's hands on** mettre la main sur; **to l. a hand** *or* **a finger on s.o.** lever la main sur qn; **to l. down** poser; (*arms*) déposer; (*condition*) (im)poser; **to l. down the law** faire la loi (**to** à); **to l. s.o. off** (*worker*) licencier qn; **to l. on** (*install*) mettre, installer; (*supply*) fournir; **to l. it on (thick)** *Fam* y aller un peu fort; **to l. out** (*garden*) dessiner; (*house*) concevoir; (*prepare*) préparer; (*display*) disposer; (*money*) *Fam* dépenser (**on** pour); **to be laid up** (*in bed*) *Med* être alité; − *vi* **to l. into** *Fam* attaquer; **to l. off** (*stop*) *Fam* arrêter; **to l. off s.o.** (*leave alone*) *Fam* laisser qn tranquille; **l. off!** (*don't touch*) *Fam* pas touche!; **to l. out** *Fam* payer. **2** *vt* (*egg*) pondre; − *vi* (*of bird etc*) pondre. ◆**layabout** *n Fam* fainéant, -ante *mf*. ◆**lay-by** *n* (*pl* -**bys**) *Aut* aire *f* de stationnement *or* de repos. ◆**lay-off** *n* (*of worker*) licenciement *m*. **layout** *n* disposition *f*; *Typ* mise *f* en pages. ◆**lay-over** *n Am* halte *f*.

lay³ [leɪ] *see* **lie¹**.

layer ['leɪər] *n* couche *f*.

laze [leɪz] *vi* **to l. (about** *or* **around**) paresser. ◆**lazy** *a* (-**ier**, -**iest**) (*person etc*) paresseux; (*holiday*) passé à ne rien faire. ◆**lazybones** *n Fam* paresseux, -euse *mf*.

lb *abbr* (*libra*) = **pound** (*weight*).

lead¹ [liːd] *vt* (*pt & pp* **led**) (*conduct*) mener, conduire (**to** à); (*team, government etc*) diriger; (*regiment*) commander; (*life*) mener; **to l. s.o. in/out/etc** faire entrer/sortir/*etc* qn; **to l. s.o. to do** (*induce*) amener qn à faire; **to l. the way** montrer le chemin; **to l. the world** tenir le premier rang mondial; **easily led** influençable; **to l. away** *or* **off** emmener qn; **to l. back** ramener; **to l. on** (*tease*) faire marcher; − *vi* (*of street etc*) mener, conduire (**to** à); (*in match*) mener;

(*in race*) être en tête; (*go ahead*) aller devant; **to l. to** (*result in*) aboutir à; (*cause*) causer, amener; **to l. up to** (*of street*) conduire à, mener à; (*precede*) précéder; (*approach gradually*) en venir à; − *n* (*distance or time ahead*) *Sp* avance *f* (**over** sur); (*example*) exemple *m*, initiative *f*; (*clue*) piste *f*, indice *m*; (*star part*) *Th* rôle *m* principal; (*leash*) laisse *f*; (*wire*) *El* fil *m*; **to take the l.** *Sp* prendre la tête; **to be in the l.** (*in race*) être en tête; (*in match*) mener. ◆**leading** *a* (*main*) principal, (*important*) important; (*front*) de tête; **the l. author** l'auteur principal *or* le plus important; **a l. figure** un personnage marquant; **the l. lady** *Cin* la vedette féminine; **l. article** *Journ* éditorial *m*. ◆**leader** *n* chef *m*; *Pol* dirigeant, -ante *mf*; (*of strike, riot*) meneur, -euse *mf*; (*guide*) guide *m*; (*article*) *Journ* éditorial *m*. ◆**leadership** *n* direction *f*; (*qualities*) qualités *fpl* de chef; (*leaders*) *Pol* dirigeants *mpl*.

lead² [led] *n* (*metal*) plomb *m*; (*of pencil*) mine *f*; **l. pencil** crayon *m* à mine de plomb. ◆**leaden** *a* (*sky*) de plomb.

leaf [liːf] *n* (*pl* **leaves**) *Bot* feuille *f*; (*of book*) feuillet *m*; (*of table*) rallonge *f*. **2** *vi* **to l. through** (*book*) feuilleter. ◆**leaflet** *n* prospectus *m*; (*containing instructions*) notice *f*. ◆**leafy** *a* (-**ier**, -**iest**) (*tree*) feuillu.

league [liːg] *n* **1** (*alliance*) ligue *f*; *Sp* championnat *m*; **in l. with** *Pej* de connivence avec. **2** (*measure*) *Hist* lieue *f*.

leak [liːk] *n* (*in pipe, information etc*) fuite *f*; (*in boat*) voie *f* d'eau; − *vi* (*of liquid, pipe, tap etc*) fuir; (*of ship*) faire eau; **to l. out** (*of information*) *Fig* être divulgué; − *vt* (*liquid*) répandre; (*information*) *Fig* divulguer. ◆**−age** *n* fuite *f*; (*amount lost*) perte *f*. ◆**leaky** *a* (-**ier**, -**iest**) (*a kettle etc*) qui fuit.

lean¹ [liːn] *a* (-**er**, -**est**) (*thin*) maigre; (*year*) difficile. ◆**−ness** *n* maigreur *f*.

lean² [liːn] *vi* (*pt & pp* **leaned** *or* **leant** [lent]) (*of object*) pencher; (*of person*) se pencher; **to l. against/on** (*of person*) s'appuyer contre/sur; **to l. back against** s'adosser à; **to l. on s.o.** (*influence*) *Fam* faire pression sur qn (**to do** pour faire); **to l. forward** *or* **over** (*of person*) se pencher (en avant); **to l. over** (*of object*) pencher; − *vt* appuyer (**against** contre); **to l. one's head on/out of** pencher la tête sur/par. ◆**−ing 1** *a* penché; **l. against** (*resting*) appuyé contre. **2** *npl* tendances *fpl* (**towards** à). ◆**lean-to** *n* (*pl* -**tos**) (*building*) appentis *m*.

leap [liːp] *n* (*jump*) bond *m*, saut *m*; (*change, increase etc*) *Fig* bond *m*; **l. year** année *f* bissextile; **in leaps and bounds** à pas de géant; – *vi* (*pt* & *pp* **leaped** *or* **leapt** [lept]) bondir, sauter; (*of flames*) jaillir; (*of profits*) faire un bond; **to l. to one's feet, l. up** se lever d'un bond. ◆**leapfrog** *n* saute-mouton *m inv.*

learn [lɜːn] *vt* (*pt* & *pp* **learned** *or* **learnt**) apprendre (**that** que); **to l. (how) to do** apprendre à faire; – *vi* apprendre; **to l. about** (*study*) étudier; (*hear about*) apprendre. ◆**—ed** [-ɪd] *a* savant. ◆**—ing** *n* érudition *f*, savoir *m*; (*of language*) apprentissage *m* (**of** de). ◆**—er** *n* débutant, -ante *mf*.

lease [liːs] *n Jur* bail *m*; **a new l. of life** *or Am* **on life** un regain de vie, une nouvelle vie; – *vt* (*house etc*) louer à bail. ◆**leasehold** *n* propriété *f* louée à bail.

leash [liːʃ] *n* laisse *f*; **on a l.** en laisse.

least [liːst] *a* **the l.** (*smallest amount of*) le moins de; (*slightest*) le *or* la moindre; **he has (the) l. talent** il a le moins de talent (**of all** de tous); **the l. effort/noise/***etc* le moindre effort/bruit/*etc*; – *n* **the l.** le moins; **at l.** (*with quantity*) au moins; **at l. that's what she says** du moins c'est ce qu'elle dit; **not in the l.** pas du tout; – *adv* (*to work, eat etc*) le moins; (*with adjective*) le *or* la moins; **l. of all** (*especially not*) surtout pas.

leather ['leðər] *n* cuir *m*; (**wash**) **l.** peau *f* de chamois.

leave [liːv] *n* (*holiday*) congé *m*; (*consent*) & *Mil* permission *f*; **l. of absence** congé *m* exceptionnel; **to take (one's) l. of** prendre congé de. **2** *vt* (*pt* & *pp* **left**) (*allow to remain, forget*) laisser; (*depart from*) quitter; (*room*) sortir de, quitter; **to l. the table** sortir de table; **to l. s.o. in charge of s.o./sth** laisser à qn la garde de qn/qch; **to l. sth with s.o.** (*entrust, give*) laisser qch à qn; **to be left (over)** rester; **there's no hope/bread/***etc* **left** il ne reste plus d'espoir/de pain/*etc*; **l. it to me!** laisse-moi faire!; **I'll l. it (up) to you** je m'en remets à toi; **to l. go (of)** (*release*) lâcher; **to l. behind** laisser; (*surpass*) dépasser; (*in race*) *Sp* distancer; **to l. off** (*lid*) ne pas (re)mettre; **to l. off doing** (*stop*) *Fam* arrêter de faire; **to l. on** (*hat, gloves*) garder; **to l. out** (*forget*) omettre; (*exclude*) exclure; – *vi* (*depart*) partir (**from** de, **for** pour); **to l. off** (*stop*) *Fam* s'arrêter. ◆**leavings** *npl* restes *mpl.*

Lebanon ['lebənən] *n* Liban *m.* ◆**Leba-'nese** *a* & *n* libanais, -aise (*mf*).

lecher ['letʃər] *n* débauché *m.* ◆**lecherous** *a* lubrique, luxurieux.

lectern ['lektən] *n* (*for giving speeches*) pupitre *m*; *Rel* lutrin *m.*

lecture ['lektʃər] **1** *n* (*public speech*) conférence *f*; (*as part of series*) *Univ* cours *m* (magistral); – *vi* faire une conférence *or* un cours; **I l. in chemistry** je suis professeur de chimie. **2** *vt* (*scold*) *Fig* faire la morale à, sermonner; – *n* (*scolding*) sermon *m.* ◆**lecturer** *n* conférencier, -ière *mf*; *Univ* enseignant, -ante *mf.* ◆**lectureship** *n* poste *m* à l'université.

led [led] *see* **lead** [1].

ledge [ledʒ] *n* rebord *m*; (*on mountain*) saillie *f.*

ledger ['ledʒər] *n* *Com* registre *m*, grand livre *m.*

leech [liːtʃ] *n* (*worm, person*) sangsue *f.*

leek [liːk] *n* poireau *m.*

leer [lɪər] *vi* **to l. (at)** lorgner; – *n* regard *m* sournois.

leeway ['liːweɪ] *n* (*freedom*) liberté *f* d'action; (*safety margin*) marge *f* de sécurité.

left [left] *see* **leave** 2; – *a* **l. luggage office** consigne *f.* ◆**leftovers** *npl* restes *mpl.*

left [left] *a* (*side, hand etc*) gauche; – *adv* à gauche; – *n* gauche *f*; **on** *or* **to the l.** à gauche (**of** de). ◆**l.-hand** *a* à *or* de gauche; **on the l.-hand side** à gauche (**of** de). ◆**l.-'handed** *a* (*person*) gaucher. ◆**l.-wing** *a* *Pol* de gauche. ◆**leftist** *n* & *a* *Pol* gauchiste (*mf*).

leg [leg] *n* jambe *f*; (*of bird, dog etc*) patte *f*; (*of lamb*) *Culin* gigot *m*; (*of chicken*) *Culin* cuisse *f*; (*of table*) pied *m*; (*of journey*) étape *f*; **to pull s.o.'s l.** (*make fun of*) mettre qn en boîte; **on its last legs** (*machine etc*) *Fam* prêt à claquer; **to be on one's last legs** *Fam* avoir un pied dans la tombe. ◆**l.-room** *n* place *f* pour les jambes. ◆**leggy** *a* (**-ier**, **-iest**) (*person*) aux longues jambes, tout en jambes.

legacy ['legəsɪ] *n* *Jur* & *Fig* legs *m.*

legal ['liːg(ə)l] *a* (*lawful*) légal; (*mind, affairs, adviser*) juridique; (*aid, error*) judiciaire; **l. expert** juriste *m*; **l. proceedings** procès *m.* ◆**le'gality** *n* légalité *f.* ◆**legalize** *vt* légaliser. ◆**legally** *adv* légalement.

legation [lɪ'geɪʃ(ə)n] *n* *Pol* légation *f.*

legend ['ledʒənd] *n* (*story, inscription etc*) légende *f.* ◆**legendary** *a* légendaire.

leggings ['legɪŋz] *npl* jambières *fpl.*

legible ['ledʒəb(ə)l] *a* lisible. ◆**legi'bility** *n* lisibilité *f.* ◆**legibly** *adv* lisiblement.

legion ['liːdʒən] *n* *Mil* & *Fig* légion *f.*

legislate ['ledʒɪsleɪt] *vi* légiférer. ◆**legis-**

'lation n (laws) législation f; (action) élaboration f des lois; **(piece of) l.** loi f. ◆**legislative** a législatif.

legitimate [lɪ'dʒɪtɪmət] a (reason, child etc) légitime. ◆**legitimacy** n légitimité f.

legless ['legləs] a (drunk) Fam (complètement) bourré.

leisure ['leʒər, Am 'liːʒər] n **l. (time)** loisirs mpl; **l. activities** loisirs mpl; **moment of l.** moment m de loisir; **at (one's) l.** à tête reposée. ◆**—ly** a (walk, occupation) peu fatigant; (meal, life) calme; **at a l. pace, in a l. way** sans se presser.

lemon ['lemən] n citron m; **l. drink, l. squash** citronnade f; **l. tea** thé m au citron. ◆**lemo'nade** n (fizzy) limonade f; (still) Am citronnade f.

lend [lend] vt (pt & pp lent) prêter (to à); (charm, colour etc) Fig donner (to à); **to l. credence to** ajouter foi à. ◆**—ing** n prêt m. ◆**—er** n prêteur, -euse mf.

length [leŋθ] n longueur f; (section of pipe etc) morceau m; (of road) tronçon m; (of cloth) métrage m; (of horse, swimming pool) Sp longueur f; (duration) durée f; **l. of time** temps m; **at l.** (at last) enfin; (at great) **l.** (in detail) dans le détail; (for a long time) longuement; **to go to great lengths** se donner beaucoup de mal (**to do** pour faire). ◆**lengthen** vt allonger; (in time) prolonger. ◆**lengthwise** adv dans le sens de la longueur. ◆**lengthy** a (-ier, -iest) long.

lenient ['liːnɪənt] a indulgent (to envers). ◆**leniency** n indulgence f. ◆**leniently** adv avec indulgence.

lens [lenz] n lentille f; (in spectacles) verre m; Phot objectif m.

Lent [lent] n Rel Carême m.

lentil ['lent(ə)l] n Bot Culin lentille f.

leopard ['lepəd] n léopard m.

leotard ['liːətɑːd] n collant m (de danse).

leper ['lepər] n lépreux, -euse mf. ◆**leprosy** n lèpre f.

lesbian ['lezbɪən] n & a lesbienne (f).

lesion ['liːʒ(ə)n] n Med lésion f.

less [les] a & n moins (de) (**than** que); **l. time/etc** moins de temps/etc; **she has l. (than you)** elle en a moins (que toi); **l. than a kilo/ten/etc** (with quantity, number) moins d'un kilo/de dix/etc; — adv (to sleep, know etc) moins (**than** que); **l. (often)** moins souvent; **l. and l.** de moins en moins; **one l.** un(e) de moins; — prep moins; **l. six francs** moins six francs. ◆**lessen** vti diminuer. ◆**lessening** n diminution f. ◆**lesser** a moindre; — **n the l.** of le or la moindre de.

-less [ləs] suffix sans; **childless** sans enfants.

lesson ['les(ə)n] n leçon f; **an English l.** une leçon or un cours d'anglais; **I have lessons now** j'ai cours maintenant.

lest [lest] conj Lit de peur que (+ ne + sub).

let¹ [let] **1** vt (pt & pp let, pres p letting) (allow) laisser (**s.o. do** qn faire); **to l. s.o. have sth** donner qch à qn; **to l. away** (allow to leave) laisser partir; **to l. down** (lower) baisser; (hair) dénouer; (dress) rallonger; (tyre) dégonfler; **to l. s.o. down** (disappoint) décevoir qn; **don't l. me down** je compte sur toi; **the car l. me down** la voiture est tombée en panne. ◆**letdown** n déception f; **to l. in** (person, dog) faire entrer; (noise, light) laisser entrer; **to l. in the clutch** Aut embrayer; **to l. s.o. in on** Fig mettre qn au courant de; **to l. oneself in for** (expense) se laisser entraîner à; (trouble) s'attirer; **to l. off** (bomb) faire éclater; (firework, gun) faire partir; **to l. s.o. off** laisser partir qn; (not punish) ne pas punir qn; (clear) Jur disculper qn; **to be l. off** with (a fine etc) s'en tirer avec; **to l. s.o. off doing** dispenser qn de faire; **to l. on that** Fam (admit) avouer que; (reveal) dire que; **to l. out** faire or laisser sortir; (prisoner) relâcher; (cry, secret) laisser échapper; (skirt) élargir; **to l. s.o. out (of the house)** ouvrir la porte à qn; **to l. out the clutch** Aut débrayer; — vi ne rien dire, garder la bouche cousue; **to l. up** (of rain, person etc) s'arrêter. ◆**letup** n arrêt m, répit m. **2** v aux **l. us eat/go/etc**, **l.'s eat/go/etc** mangeons/partons/etc; **l.'s go for a stroll** allons nous promener; **l. him come** qu'il vienne.

let² [let] vt (pt & pp let, pres p letting) **to l. (off or out)** (house, room etc) louer. ◆**letting** n (renting) location f.

lethal ['liːθ(ə)l] a mortel; (weapon) meurtrier.

lethargy ['leθədʒɪ] n léthargie f. ◆**le'thargic** a léthargique.

letter ['letər] n (missive, character) lettre f; **man of letters** homme m de lettres; **l. bomb** lettre f piégée; **l. writer** correspondant, -ante mf. ◆**letterbox** n boîte f aux or à lettres. ◆**letterhead** n en-tête m. ◆**lettering** n (letters) lettres fpl; (on tomb) inscription f.

lettuce ['letɪs] n laitue f, salade f.

leuk(a)emia [luː'kiːmɪə] n leucémie f.

level ['lev(ə)l] **1** n niveau m; **on the l.** (speed) en palier; — a (surface) plat, uni; (object on surface) horizontal; (spoonful) ras; (equal in score) à égalité (**with** avec); (in height) au même niveau, à la même hauteur (**with** que); **l. crossing** *Rail* passage *m* à niveau; − *vt* (**-ll-**, *Am* **-l-**) (*surface, differences*) niveler, aplanir; (*plane down*) raboter; (*building*) raser; (*gun*) braquer; (*accusation*) lancer (**at** contre); − *vi* **to l. off** *or* **out** (*stabilize*) *Fig* se stabiliser. **2** *n* **on the l.** *Fam* (*honest*) honnête, franc; (*frankly*) honnêtement, franchement; − *vi* (**-ll-**, *Am* **-l-**) **to l. with** *Fam* être franc avec. ◆**l.-'headed** *a* équilibré.

lever ['liːvər, *Am* 'levər] *n* levier *m*. ◆**leverage** *n* (*power*) influence *f*.

levity ['levɪtɪ] *n* légèreté *f*.

levy ['levɪ] *vt* (*tax, troops*) lever; − *n* (*tax*) impôt *m*.

lewd [luːd] *a* (**-er, -est**) obscène.

liable ['laɪəb(ə)l] *a* **l. to** (*dizziness etc*) sujet à; (*fine, tax*) passible de; **he's l. to do** il est susceptible de faire, il pourrait faire; **l. for** (*responsible*) responsable de. ◆**lia'bility** *n* responsabilité *f* (**for** de); (*disadvantage*) handicap *m*; *pl* (*debts*) dettes *fpl*.

liaise [lɪ'eɪz] *vi* travailler en liaison (**with** avec). ◆**liaison** *n* (*association*) & *Mil* liaison *f*.

liar ['laɪər] *n* menteur, -euse *mf*.

libel ['laɪb(ə)l] *vt* (**-ll-**, *Am* **-l-**) diffamer (par écrit); − *n* diffamation *f*.

liberal ['lɪbərəl] *a* (*open-minded*) & *Pol* libéral; (*generous*) généreux (**with** de); − *n* *Pol* libéral, -ale *mf*. ◆**liberalism** *n* libéralisme *m*.

liberate ['lɪbəreɪt] *vt* libérer. ◆**libe'ration** *n* libération *f*. ◆**liberator** *n* libérateur, -trice *mf*.

liberty ['lɪbətɪ] *n* liberté *f*; **at l. to do** libre de faire; **what a l.!** (*cheek*) *Fam* quel culot!; **to take liberties with s.o.** se permettre des familiarités avec qn.

Libra ['liːbrə] *n* (*sign*) la Balance.

library ['laɪbrərɪ] *n* bibliothèque *f*. ◆**li'brarian** *n* bibliothécaire *mf*.

libretto [lɪ'bretəʊ] *n* (*pl* **-os**) *Mus* livret *m*.

Libya ['lɪbɪə] *n* Libye *f*. ◆**Libyan** *a* & *n* libyen, -enne (*mf*).

lice [laɪs] *see* **louse**.

licence, *Am* **license** ['laɪsəns] *n* **1** permis *m*, autorisation *f*; (*for driving*) permis *m*; *Com* licence *f*; **pilot's l.** brevet *m* de pilote; **l. fee** *Rad TV* redevance *f*; **l. plate/number** *Aut* plaque *f*/numéro *m* d'immatriculation. **2** (*freedom*) licence *f*.

license ['laɪsəns] *vt* accorder une licence à, autoriser; **licensed premises** établissement *m* qui a une licence de débit de boissons.

licit ['lɪsɪt] *a* licite.

lick [lɪk] *vt* lécher; (*defeat*) *Fam* écraser; (*beat physically*) *Fam* rosser; **to be licked** (*by problem etc*) *Fam* être dépassé; − *n* coup *m* de langue; **a l. of paint** un coup de peinture. ◆**—ing** *n* *Fam* (*defeat*) déculottée *f*; (*beating*) rossée *f*.

licorice ['lɪkərɪʃ, -rɪs] *n* *Am* réglisse *f*.

lid [lɪd] *n* **1** (*of box etc*) couvercle *m*. **2** (*of eye*) paupière *f*.

lido ['liːdəʊ] *n* (*pl* **-os**) piscine *f* (découverte).

lie[1] [laɪ] *vi* (*pt* **lay**, *pp* **lain**, *pres p* **lying**) (*in flat position*) s'allonger, s'étendre; (*remain*) rester; (*be*) être; (*in grave*) reposer; **to be lying** (*on the grass etc*) être allongé *or* étendu; **he lay asleep** il dormait; **here lies** (*on tomb*) ci-gît; **the problem lies in** le problème réside dans; **to l. heavy on** (*of meal etc*) & *Fig* peser sur; **to l. low** (*hide*) se cacher; (*be inconspicuous*) se faire tout petit; **to l. about** *or* **around** (*of objects, person*) traîner; **to l. down, to have a l.-down** s'allonger, se coucher; **lying down** (*resting*) allongé, couché; **to l. in, to have a l.-in** *Fam* faire la grasse matinée.

lie[2] [laɪ] *vi* (*pt* & *pp* **lied**, *pres p* **lying**) (*tell lies*) mentir; − *n* mensonge *m*; **to give the l. to** (*show as untrue*) démentir.

lieu [luː] *n* **in l.** *of* au lieu de.

lieutenant [lef'tenənt, *Am* luː'tenənt] *n* lieutenant *m*.

life [laɪf] *n* (*pl* **lives**) vie *f*; (*of battery, machine*) durée *f* (de vie); **to come to l.** (*of street, party etc*) s'animer; **at your time of l.** à ton âge; **loss of l.** perte *f* en vies humaines; **true to l.** conforme à la réalité; **to take one's (own) l.** se donner la mort; **bird l.** les oiseaux *mpl*; − *a* (*cycle, style*) de vie; (*belt, raft*) de sauvetage; (*force*) vital; **l. annuity** rente *f* viagère; **l. blood** *Fig* âme *f*; **l. insurance** assurance-vie *f*; **l. jacket** gilet *m* de sauvetage; **l. peer** pair *m* à vie. ◆**lifeboat** *n* canot *m* de sauvetage. ◆**lifebuoy** *n* bouée *f* de sauvetage. ◆**lifeguard** *n* maître-nageur *m* sauveteur. ◆**lifeless** *a* sans vie. ◆**lifelike** *a* qui semble vivant. ◆**lifelong** *a* de toute sa vie; (*friend*) de toujours. ◆**lifesaving** *n* sauvetage *m*. ◆**lifesize(d)** *a* grandeur nature *inv*. ◆**lifetime** *n* vie *f*; *Fig* éternité *f*; **in my l.** de mon vivant; **a once-in-a-l. experience**/*etc* l'expérience/*etc* de votre vie.

lift [lɪft] *vt* lever; (*sth heavy*) (sou)lever; (*ban, siege*) lever; (*idea etc*) *Fig* voler, prendre (**from** à); **to l. down** *or* **off** (*take down*) descendre (**from** de); **to l. out** (*take out*) sortir; **to l. up** (*arm, eyes*) lever; (*object*) (sou)lever; – *vi* (*of fog*) se lever; **to l. off** (*of space vehicle*) décoller; – *n* (*elevator*) ascenseur *m*; **to give s.o. a l.** emmener *or* accompagner qn (en voiture) (**to** à). ◆**l.-off** *n Av* décollage *m*.

ligament ['lɪgəmənt] *n* ligament *m*.

light¹ [laɪt] **1** *n* lumière *f*; (*daylight*) jour *m*, lumière *f*; (*on vehicle*) feu *m*, (*headlight*) phare *m*; **by the l. of** à la lumière de; **in the l. of** (*considering*) à la lumière de; **in that l.** *Fig* sous ce jour *or* cet éclairage; **against the l.** à contre-jour; **to bring to l.** mettre en lumière; **to come to l.** être découvert; **to throw l. on** (*matter*) éclaircir; **do you have a l.?** (*for cigarette*) est-ce que vous avez du feu?; **to set l. to** mettre le feu à; **leading l.** (*person*) *Fig* phare *m*, sommité *f*, lumière *f*; **l. bulb** ampoule *f* (électrique); – *vt* (*pt & pp* **lit** *or* **lighted**) (*candle etc*) allumer; (*match*) gratter; **to l. (up)** (*room*) éclairer; – *vi* **to l. up** (*of window*) s'allumer. **2** *a* (*bright, not dark*) clair. ◆**—ing** *n El* éclairage *m*; **the l. of** (*candle etc*) l'allumage *m* de. ◆**lighten¹** *vt* (*light up*) éclairer; (*colour, hair*) éclaircir. ◆**lighter** *n* (*for cigarettes etc*) briquet *m*; *Culin* allume-gaz *m inv*. ◆**lighthouse** *n* phare *m*. ◆**lightness¹** *n* clarté *f*.

light² [laɪt] *a* (*in weight, quantity, strength etc*) léger; (*task*) facile; **l. rain** pluie *f* fine; **to travel l.** voyager avec peu de bagages. ◆**l.-'fingered** *a* chapardeur. ◆**l.-'headed** *a* (*giddy, foolish*) étourdi. ◆**l.-'hearted** *a* gai. ◆**lighten²** *vt* (*a load*) alléger. ◆**lightly** *adv* légèrement. ◆**lightness²** *n* légèreté *f*.

light³ [laɪt] *vi* (*pt & pp* **lit** *or* **lighted**) **to l. upon** trouver par hasard.

lightning ['laɪtnɪŋ] *n* (*Met* (*light*) éclair *m*; (*charge*) foudre *f*; (*flash of*) **l.** éclair *m*; – *a* (*speed*) foudroyant; (*visit*) éclair *inv*; **l. conductor** paratonnerre *m*.

lightweight ['laɪtweɪt] *a* (*cloth etc*) léger; (*not serious*) pas sérieux, léger.

like¹ [laɪk] *a* (*alike*) semblable, pareil; – *prep* comme; **l. this** comme ça; **what's he l.?** (*physically, as character*) comment est-il?; **to be** *or* **look l.** ressembler à; **what was the book l.?** comment as-tu trouvé le livre?; **I have one l. it** j'en ai un pareil; – *adv* **nothing l. as big/etc** loin d'être aussi grand/*etc*; – *conj* (*as*) *Fam* comme; **it's l. I say** c'est comme je vous le dis; – *n* . . . **and the l.** . . . et ainsi de suite; **the l. of which we shan't see again** comme on n'en reverra plus; **the likes of you** des gens de ton acabit.

like² [laɪk] *vt* aimer (bien) (**to do, doing** faire); **I l. him** je l'aime bien, il me plaît; **she likes it here** elle se plaît ici; **to l. best** préférer; **I'd l. to come** (*want*) je voudrais (bien) *or* j'aimerais (bien) venir; **I'd l. a kilo of apples** je voudrais un kilo de pommes; **would you l. a cigar?** voulez-vous un cigare?; **if you l.** si vous voulez; (**how**) **would you l. to come?** ça te plairait *or* te dirait de venir?; – *npl* **one's likes** nos goûts *mpl*. ◆**—ing** *n* **a l. for** (*person*) de la sympathie pour; (*thing*) du goût pour; **to my l.** à mon goût. ◆**likeable** *a* sympathique.

likely ['laɪkli] *a* (**-ier, -iest**) (*event, result etc*) probable; (*excuse*) vraisemblable; (*place*) propice; (*candidate*) prometteur; **a l. excuse!** *Iron* belle excuse!; **it's l. (that) she'll come** il est probable qu'elle viendra; **he's l. to come** il viendra probablement; **he's not l. to come** il ne risque pas de venir; – *adv* **very l.** très probablement; **not l.!** pas question! ◆**likelihood** *n* probabilité *f*; **there's little l. that** il y a peu de chances que (+ *sub*).

liken ['laɪkən] *vt* comparer (**to** à).

likeness ['laɪknɪs] *n* ressemblance *f*; **a family l.** un air de famille; **it's a good l.** c'est très ressemblant.

likewise ['laɪkwaɪz] *adv* (*similarly*) de même, pareillement.

lilac ['laɪlək] *n* lilas *m*; – *a* (*colour*) lilas *inv*.

Lilo® ['laɪləʊ] *n* (*pl* -**os**) matelas *m* pneumatique.

lilt [lɪlt] *n Mus* cadence *f*.

lily ['lɪli] *n* lis *m*, lys *m*; **l. of the valley** muguet *m*.

limb [lɪm] *n Anat* membre *m*; **to be out on a l.** *Fig* être le seul de son opinion.

limber ['lɪmbər] *vi* **to l. up** faire des exercices d'assouplissement.

limbo (in) [ɪn'lɪmbəʊ] *adv* (*uncertain, waiting*) dans l'expectative.

lime [laɪm] *n* **1** (*tree*) tilleul *m*. **2** (*substance*) chaux *f*. **3** (*fruit*) lime *f*, citron *m* vert; **l. juice** jus *m* de citron vert.

limelight ['laɪmlaɪt] *n* **in the l.** (*glare of publicity*) en vedette.

limit ['lɪmɪt] *n* limite *f*; (*restriction*) limitation *f* (**of** de); **that's the l.!** *Fam* c'est le comble!; **within limits** dans une certaine limite; – *vt* limiter (**to** à); **to l. oneself to doing** se borner à faire. ◆**—ed** *a* (*restricted*) limité; (*mind*) borné; (*edition*) à tirage limité; **l. company** *Com* société *f* à responsabilité limitée; (**public**) **l. company** (*with shareholders*) société *f* anonyme; **to a**

l. degree jusqu'à un certain point. ◆**limi-
'tation** n limitation f. ◆**limitless** a illimité.

limousine [limə'ziːn] n (car) limousine f;
(airport etc shuttle) Am voiture-navette f.

limp [limp] 1 vi (of person) boiter; (of vehicle
etc) Fig avancer tant bien que mal; − n to
have a l. boiter. 2 a (-er, -est) (soft) mou;
(flabby) flasque; (person, hat) avachi.

limpid ['limpid] a (liquid) Lit limpide.

linchpin ['lintʃpin] n (person) pivot m.

linctus ['liŋktəs] n Med sirop m (contre la
toux).

line[1] [lain] n ligne f; (stroke) trait m, ligne f;
(of poem) vers m; (wrinkle) ride f; (track)
voie f; (rope) corde f; (row) rangée f; (of vehicles) file f; (queue) Am file f, queue f;
(family) lignée f; (business) métier m, rayon
m; (article) Com article m; one's lines (of
actor) son texte m; on the l. Tel (speaking)
au téléphone; (at other end of line) au bout
du fil; to be on the l. (at risk) être en
danger; hold the l.! Tel ne quittez pas!; the
hot l. Tel le téléphone rouge; to stand in l.
Am faire la queue; to step or get out of l.
Fig refuser de se conformer; (misbehave)
faire une incartade; out of l. with (ideas etc)
en désaccord avec; in l. with conforme à;
he's in l. for (promotion etc) il doit recevoir;
to take a hard l. adopter une attitude
ferme; along the same lines (to work, think)
de la même façon; sth along those lines qch
dans ce genre-là; to drop a l. Fam envoyer
un mot (to à); where do we draw the l.? où
fixer les limites?; − vt (paper) régler; (face)
rider; to l. the street (of trees) border la rue;
(of people) faire la haie le long de la rue; to
l. up (children, objects) aligner; (arrange)
organiser; (get ready) préparer; to have sth
lined up (in mind) avoir qch en vue; − vi to
l. up s'aligner; (queue) Am faire la queue.
◆**l.-up** n (row) file f; Pol front m; TV
programme(s) m(pl).

line[2] [lain] vt (clothes) doubler; (pockets)
Fig se remplir. ◆**lining** n (of clothes)
doublure f; (of brakes) garniture f.

lineage ['liniidʒ] n lignée f.

linear ['liniər] a linéaire.

linen ['linin] n (sheets etc) linge m; (material) (toile f de) lin m, fil m.

liner ['lainər] n 1 (ship) paquebot m. 2
(dust)bin l. sac m poubelle.

linesman ['lainzmən] n (pl -men) Fb etc
juge m de touche.

linger ['liŋgər] vi to l. (on) (of person)
s'attarder; (of smell, memory) persister; (of
doubt) subsister. ◆**—ing** a (death) lent.

lingo ['liŋgəu] n (pl -os) Hum Fam jargon m.

linguist ['liŋgwist] n linguiste mf. ◆**lin-
'guistic** a linguistique. ◆**lin'guistics** n
linguistique f.

liniment ['linimənt] n onguent m, pommade
f.

link [liŋk] vt (connect) relier (to à); (relate,
associate) lier (to à); to l. up Tel relier; − vi
to l. up (of roads) se rejoindre; − n (connection) lien m; (of chain) maillon m; (by road,
rail) liaison f. ◆**l.-up** n TV Rad liaison f;
(of spacecraft) jonction f.

lino ['lainəu] n (pl -os) lino m. ◆**linoleum**
[li'nəuliəm] n linoléum m.

linseed ['linsiːd] n l. oil huile f de lin.

lint [lint] n Med tissu m ouaté; (fluff)
peluche(s) f(pl).

lion ['laiən] n lion m; l. cub lionceau m.
◆**lioness** n lionne f.

lip [lip] n Anat lèvre f; (rim) bord m; (cheek)
Sl culot m. ◆**l.-read** vi (pt & pp -read
[red]) lire sur les lèvres. ◆**lipstick** n (material) rouge m à lèvres; (stick) tube m de
rouge.

liqueur [li'kjuər] n liqueur f.

liquid ['likwid] n & a liquide (m). ◆**liquefy**
vt liquéfier; − vi se liquéfier. ◆**liquidizer** n
Culin (for fruit juices) centrifugeuse f; (for
purées etc) robot m, moulinette® f.

liquidate ['likwideit] vt (debt, person)
liquider. ◆**liqui'dation** n liquidation f.

liquor ['likər] n alcool m, spiritueux m; l.
store Am magasin m de vins et de
spiritueux.

liquorice ['likəris, -ris] n réglisse f.

lira, pl **lire** ['liərə, 'liərei] n (currency) lire f.

lisp [lisp] vi zézayer; − n to have a l. zézayer.

list [list] 1 n liste f; − vt (one's possessions
etc) faire la liste de; (names) mettre sur la
liste; (enumerate) énumérer; (catalogue)
cataloguer. 2 vi (of ship) gîter. ◆**—ed** a
(monument etc) classé.

listen ['lisən] vi écouter; to l. to écouter; to l.
(out) for (telephone, person etc) tendre
l'oreille pour, guetter; to l. in (to) Rad
écouter. ◆**—ing** n écoute f (to de). ◆**—er**
n Rad auditeur, -trice mf; to be a good l.
(pay attention) savoir écouter.

listless ['listləs] a apathique, indolent.
◆**—ness** n apathie f.

lit [lit] see **light**[1] 1.

litany ['litəni] n Rel litanies fpl.

literal ['litərəl] a littéral; (not exaggerated)
réel. ◆**—ly** adv littéralement; (really) réellement; he took it l. il l'a pris au pied de la
lettre.

literate ['litərət] a qui sait lire et écrire;

highly l. (*person*) très instruit. ◆**literacy** *n* capacité *f* de lire et d'écrire; (*of country*) degré *m* d'alphabétisation.

literature ['lɪt(ə)rɪtʃər] *n* littérature *f*; (*pamphlets etc*) documentation *f*. ◆**literary** *a* littéraire.

lithe [laɪð] *a* agile, souple.

litigation [lɪtɪ'geɪʃ(ə)n] *n Jur* litige *m*.

litre ['liːtər] *n* litre *m*.

litter ['lɪtər] **1** *n* (*rubbish*) détritus *m*; (*papers*) papiers *mpl*; (*bedding for animals*) litière *f*; (*confusion*) *Fig* fouillis *m*; **l. basket** *or* **bin** boîte *f* à ordures; – *vt* **to l. (with papers** *or* **rubbish)** (*street etc*) laisser traîner des papiers *or* des détritus dans; **a street littered with** une rue jonchée de. **2** *n* (*young animals*) portée *f*.

little ['lɪt(ə)l] **1** *a* (*small*) petit; **the l. ones** les petits. **2** *a & n* (*not much*) peu (de); **l. time/money/***etc* peu de temps/d'argent/ *etc*; **I've l. left** il m'en reste peu; **she eats l.** elle mange peu; **to have l.** to say avoir peu de chose à dire; **as l. as possible** le moins possible; **a l. money/time/***etc* (*some*) un peu d'argent/de temps/*etc*; **I have a l.** (*some*) j'en ai un peu; **the l. that I have** le peu que j'ai; – *adv* (*somewhat, rather*) peu; **a l. heavy/***etc* un peu lourd/*etc*; **to work/***etc* **a l.** travailler un peu; **it's l. better** (*hardly*) ce n'est guère mieux; **l. by l.** peu à peu.

liturgy ['lɪtədʒɪ] *n* liturgie *f*.

live¹ [lɪv] *vi* vivre; (*reside*) habiter, vivre; **where do you l.?** où habitez-vous?; **to l. in Paris** habiter (à) Paris; **to l. off** *or* **on** (*eat*) vivre de; (*sponge on*) *Pej* vivre aux crochets *or* aux dépens de (*qn*); **to l. on** (*of memory etc*) survivre, se perpétuer; **to l. through** (*experience*) vivre; (*survive*) survivre à; **to l. up to** (*one's principles*) vivre selon; (*s.o.'s expectations*) se montrer à la hauteur de; – *vt* (*life*) vivre, mener; (*one's faith etc*) vivre pleinement; **to l. down** faire oublier (avec le temps); **to l. it up** *Fam* mener la grande vie.

live² [laɪv] **1** *a* (*alive, lively*) vivant; (*coal*) ardent; (*bomb*) non explosé; (*ammunition*) réel, de combat; (*wire*) *El* sous tension; (*switch*) *El* mal isolé; (*plugged in*) *El* branché; **a real l. king/***etc* un roi/*etc* en chair et en os. **2** *a & adv Rad TV* en direct; **a l. broadcast** une émission en direct; **a l. audience** le *or* un public; **a l. recording** un enregistrement public.

livelihood ['laɪvlɪhʊd] *n* moyens *mpl* de subsistance; **my l.** mon gagne-pain; **to earn one's** *or* **a l.** gagner sa vie.

livel/y ['laɪvlɪ] *a* (**-ier, -iest**) (*person, style*)

vif, vivant; (*street, story*) vivant; (*interest, mind, colour*) vif; (*day*) mouvementé; (*forceful*) vigoureux; (*conversation, discussion*) animé. ◆**—iness** *n* vivacité *f*.

liven ['laɪv(ə)n] *vt* **to l. up** (*person*) égayer; (*party*) animer; – *vi* **to l. up** (*of person, party*) s'animer.

liver ['lɪvər] *n* foie *m*.

livery ['lɪvərɪ] *n* (*uniform*) livrée *f*.

livestock ['laɪvstɒk] *n* bétail *m*.

livid ['lɪvɪd] *a* (*blue-grey*) livide; (*angry*) *Fig* furieux; **l. with cold** blême de froid.

living ['lɪvɪŋ] **1** *a* (*alive*) vivant; **not a l. soul** (*nobody*) personne, pas âme qui vive; **within l. memory** de mémoire d'homme; **l. or dead** mort ou vif; **the l.** les vivants *mpl*. **2** *n* (*livelihood*) vie *f*; **to make a** *or* **one's l.** gagner sa vie; **to work for a l.** travailler pour vivre; **the cost of l.** le coût de la vie; – *a* (*standard, conditions*) de vie; (*wage*) qui permet de vivre; **l. room** salle *f* de séjour.

lizard ['lɪzəd] *n* lézard *m*.

llama ['lɑːmə] *n* (*animal*) lama *m*.

load [ləʊd] *n* (*object carried, burden*) charge *f*; (*freight*) chargement *m*, charge *f*; (*strain, weight*) poids *m*; **a l. of, loads of** (*people, money etc*) *Fam* un tas de, énormément de; **to take a l. off s.o.'s mind** ôter un grand poids à qn; – *vt* charger; **to l. down** *or* **up** charger (**with** de); – *vi* **to l. (up)** charger la voiture, le navire *etc*. ◆**—ed** *a* (*gun, vehicle etc*) chargé; (*dice*) pipé; (*rich*) *Fam* plein aux as; **a l. question** une question piège; **l. (down) with** (*debts*) accablé de.

loaf [ləʊf] **1** *n* (*pl* **loaves**) pain *m*; **French l.** baguette *f*. **2** *n* **to l. (about)** fainéanter. ◆**—er** *n* fainéant, -ante *mf*.

loam [ləʊm] *n* (*soil*) terreau *m*.

loan [ləʊn] *n* (*money lent*) prêt *m*; (*money borrowed*) emprunt *m*; **on l. from** prêté par; (*out*) **on l.** (*book*) sorti; **may I have the l. of . . . ?** puis-je emprunter . . . ?; – *vt* (*lend*) prêter (**to** à).

loath [ləʊθ] *a* **l. to do** *Lit* peu disposé à faire.

loath/e [ləʊð] *vt* détester (**doing** faire). ◆**—ing** *n* dégoût *m*. ◆**loathsome** *a* détestable.

lobby ['lɒbɪ] **1** *n* (*of hotel*) vestibule *m*, hall *m*; *Th* foyer *m*. **2** *n Pol* groupe *m* de pression, lobby *m*; – *vt* faire pression sur.

lobe [ləʊb] *n Anat* lobe *m*.

lobster ['lɒbstər] *n* homard *m*; (*spiny*) langouste *f*.

local ['ləʊk(ə)l] *a* local; (*of the neighbourhood*) du *or* de quartier; (*regional*) du pays; **are you l.?** êtes-vous du coin *or* d'ici?; **the doctor is l.** le médecin est tout près d'ici; **a l. phone call** (*within town*) une communication urbaine; – *n* (*pub*) *Fam* bistrot *m* du coin, pub *m*; **she's a l.** elle est du coin; **the locals** (*people*) les gens du coin. ◆**lo'cality** *n* (*neighbourhood*) environs *mpl*; (*region*) région *f*; (*place*) lieu *m*; (*site*) emplacement *m*. ◆**localize** *vt* (*confine*) localiser. ◆**locally** *adv* dans les environs, dans le coin; (*around here*) par ici; (*in precise place*) localement.

locate [ləu'keɪt] *vt* (*find*) repérer; (*pain, noise, leak*) localiser; (*situate*) situer; (*build*) construire. ◆**location** *n* (*site*) emplacement *m*; (*act*) repérage *m*; localisation *f*; **on l.** *Cin* en extérieur.

lock [lɒk] **1** *vt* **to l. (up)** fermer à clef; **to l. the wheels** *Aut* bloquer les roues; **to l. s.o. in** enfermer qn; **to l. s.o. in sth** enfermer qn dans qch; **to l. s.o. out** (*accidentally*) enfermer qn dehors; **to l. away** *or* **up** (*prisoner*) enfermer; (*jewels etc*) mettre sous clef, enfermer; – *vi* **to l. (up)** fermer à clef; – *n* (*on door, chest etc*) serrure *f*; (*of gun*) cran *m* de sûreté; (*turning circle*) *Aut* rayon *m* de braquage; **(anti-theft) l.** *Aut* antivol *m*; **under l. and key** sous clef. **2** *n* (*on canal*) écluse *f*. **3** *n* (*of hair*) mèche *f*. ◆**locker** *n* casier *m*; (*for luggage*) *Rail* casier *m* de consigne automatique; (*for clothes*) vestiaire *m* (métallique); **l. room** *Sp Am* vestiaire *m*. ◆**lockout** *n* (*industrial*) lock-out *m inv*. ◆**locksmith** *n* serrurier *m*.

locket ['lɒkɪt] *n* (*jewel*) médaillon *m*.

loco ['ləukəu] *a Sl* cinglé, fou.

locomotion [ləukə'məuʃ(ə)n] *n* locomotion *f*. ◆**locomotive** *n* locomotive *f*.

locum ['ləukəm] *n* (*doctor*) remplaçant, -ante *mf*.

locust ['ləukəst] *n* criquet *m*, sauterelle *f*.

lodg/e [lɒdʒ] **1** *vt* (*person*) loger; (*valuables*) déposer (**with** chez); **to l. a complaint** porter plainte; – *vi* (*of bullet*) se loger (**in** dans); **to be lodging** (*accommodated*) être logé (**with** chez). **2** *n* (*house*) pavillon *m* de gardien *or* de chasse; (*of porter*) loge *f*. ◆—**ing** *n* (*accommodation*) logement *m*; *pl* (*flat*) logement *m*; (*room*) chambre *f*; **in lodgings** en meublé. ◆—**er** *n* (*room and meals*) pensionnaire *mf*; (*room only*) locataire *mf*.

loft [lɒft] *n* (*attic*) grenier *m*.

loft/y ['lɒftɪ] *a* (**-ier**, **-iest**) (*high, noble*) élevé; (*haughty*) hautain. ◆—**iness** *n* hauteur *f*.

log [lɒg] **1** *n* (*tree trunk*) rondin *m*; (*for fire*) bûche *f*, rondin *m*; **l. fire** feu *m* de bois. **2** *vt* (**-gg-**) (*facts*) noter; **to l. (up)** (*distance*) faire, couvrir. ◆**logbook** *n Nau Av* journal *m* de bord.

logarithm ['lɒgərɪðəm] *n* logarithme *m*.

loggerheads (at) [æt'lɒgəhedz] *adv* en désaccord (**with** avec).

logic ['lɒdʒɪk] *n* logique *f*. ◆**logical** *a* logique. ◆**logically** *adv* logiquement.

logistics [lə'dʒɪstɪks] *n* logistique *f*.

logo ['ləugəu] *n* (*pl* **-os**) logo *m*.

loin [lɔɪn] *n* (*meat*) filet *m*.

loins [lɔɪnz] *npl Anat* reins *mpl*.

loiter ['lɔɪtər] *vi* traîner.

loll [lɒl] *vi* (*in armchair etc*) se prélasser.

lollipop ['lɒlɪpɒp] *n* (*sweet on stick*) sucette *f*; (*ice on stick*) esquimau *m*. ◆**lolly** *n Fam* sucette *f*; (*money*) *Sl* fric *m*; **(ice) l.** *Fam* esquimau *m*.

London ['lʌndən] *n* Londres *m or f*; – *a* (*taxi etc*) londonien. ◆**Londoner** *n* Londonien, -ienne *mf*.

lone [ləun] *a* solitaire; **l. wolf** *Fig* solitaire *mf*. ◆**loneliness** *n* solitude *f*. ◆**lonely** *a* (**-ier**, **-iest**) (*road, house, life etc*) solitaire; (*person*) seul, solitaire. ◆**loner** *n* solitaire *mf*. ◆**lonesome** *a* solitaire.

long [lɒŋ] **1** *a* (**-er**, **-est**) long; **to be ten metres l.** être long de dix mètres, avoir dix mètres de long; **to be six weeks l.** durer six semaines; **how l. is...** quelle est la longueur de...?; (*time*) quelle est la durée de...?; **a l. time** longtemps; **in the l. run** à la longue; **a l. face** une grimace; **a l. memory** une bonne mémoire; **l. jump** *Sp* saut *m* en longueur. **2** *adv* (*a long time*) longtemps; **l. before** longtemps avant; **has he been here l.?** il y a longtemps qu'il est ici?, il est ici depuis longtemps?; **how l. (ago)?** (il y a) combien de temps?; **not l. ago** il y a peu de temps; **before l.** sous *or* avant peu; **no longer** ne plus; **she no longer swims** elle ne nage plus; **a bit longer** (*to wait etc*) encore un peu; **I won't be l.** je n'en ai pas pour longtemps; **at the longest** (tout) au plus; **all summer l.** tout l'été; **l. live the queen/**etc vive la reine/etc; **as l. as, so l. as** (*provided that*) pourvu que (+ *sub*); **as l. as I live** tant que je vivrai.

long [lɒŋ] *vi* **to l. for sth** avoir très envie de qch; **to l. for s.o.** languir après qn; **to l. to do** avoir très envie de faire. ◆—**ing** *n* désir *m*, envie *f*.

long-distance [lɒŋ'dɪstəns] *a* (*race*) de fond; (*phone call*) interurbain; (*flight*) long-courrier. ◆**long-drawn-'out** *a* interminable. ◆**long'haired** *a* aux cheveux longs. ◆**longhand** *n* écriture *f* normale. ◆**long-'playing** *a* **l.-playing record** 33 tours *m inv*. ◆**long-range** *a* (*forecast*) à long terme. ◆**long'sighted** *a Med* presbyte. ◆**long'standing** a de longue date. ◆**long'suffering** a très patient. ◆**long-'term** a à long terme. ◆**long-'winded** a (speech, speaker) verbeux.

longevity [lɒnˈdʒevɪtɪ] n longévité f.

longitude [ˈlɒndʒɪtjuːd] n longitude f.

longways [ˈlɒŋweɪz] adv en longueur.

loo [luː] n (toilet) Fam cabinets mpl.

look [lʊk] n regard m; (appearance) air m, allure f; (good) looks la beauté, un beau physique; **to have a l. (at)** jeter un coup d'œil (à), regarder; **to have a l. (for)** chercher; **to have a l. (a)round** regarder; (walk) faire un tour; **let me have a l.** fais voir; **I like the l. of him** il me fait bonne impression, il me plaît; – vti regarder; **to l. s.o. in the face** regarder qn dans les yeux; **to l. tired/happy**/etc (seem) sembler or avoir l'air fatigué/heureux/etc; **to l. pretty/ugly** (be) être joli/laid; **to l. one's age** faire son âge; **l. here!** dites donc!; **you l. like** or as if **you're tired** tu as l'air fatigué, on dirait que tu es fatigué; **it looks like** or as if **she won't leave** elle n'a pas l'air de vouloir partir; **it looks like it!** c'est probable; **to l. like a child** avoir l'air d'un enfant; **to l. like an apple** avoir l'air d'être une pomme; **you l. like my brother** (resemble) tu ressembles à mon frère; **it looks like rain** (to me) il me semble or on dirait qu'il va pleuvoir; **what does he l. like?** (describe him) comment est-il?; **to l. well** or good (of person) avoir bonne mine; **you l. good in that hat**/etc ce chapeau/etc te va très bien; **that looks bad** (action etc) ça fait mauvais effet. ■ **to l. after** vt (deal with) s'occuper de, (patient, baby) soigner; (keep safely) garder (for s.o. pour qn); **to l. after oneself** (keep healthy) faire bien attention à soi; **I can l. after myself** (cope) je suis assez grand pour me débrouiller; **to l. around** vt (visit) visiter; – vi (have a look) regarder; (walk round) faire un tour; **to l. at** vt regarder; (consider) considérer, voir; (check) vérifier; **to l. away** vi détourner les yeux; **to l. back** vi regarder derrière soi; (in time) regarder en arrière; **to l. down** vi baisser les yeux; (from height) regarder en bas; **to l. down on** (consider scornfully) mépriser, regarder de haut; **to l. for** vt (seek) chercher; **to l. forward to** vt (event) attendre avec impatience; **to l. in** vi regarder (à l'intérieur); **to l. in on s.o.** Fam passer voir qn; **to l. into** vt (examine) examiner; (find out about) se renseigner sur; **to l. on** vi regarder; – vt (consider) considérer, voir; **to l. out** vi (be careful) faire attention (for à); **to l. out for** (seek)

chercher; (watch) guetter; **to l. (out) on to** (of window, house etc) donner sur; **to l. over** or **through** vt (examine fully) examiner, regarder de près; (briefly) parcourir; (region, town) parcourir, visiter; **to l. round** vt (visit) visiter; – vi (have a look) regarder; (walk round) faire un tour; (look back) se retourner; **to l. round for** (seek) chercher; **to l. up** vi (of person) lever les yeux; (into the air or sky) regarder en l'air; (improve) s'améliorer; **to l. up to s.o.** Fig respecter qn; – vt (word) chercher; **to l. s.o. up** (visit) passer voir qn. ◆**-looking** suffix pleasant-/tired-/etc l. à l'air agréable/fatigué/etc. ◆**looking-glass** n glace f, miroir m.

lookout [ˈlʊkaʊt] n (soldier) guetteur m; (sailor) vigie f; **l. (post)** poste m de guet; (on ship) vigie f; **to be on the l.** faire le guet; **to be on the l. for** guetter.

loom [luːm] **1** vi **to l. (up)** (of mountain etc) apparaître indistinctement; Fig paraître imminent. **2** n Tex métier m à tisser.

loony [ˈluːnɪ] n & a Sl imbécile (mf).

loop [luːp] n (in river etc) & Av boucle f; (contraceptive device) stérilet m; **to l. the loop** Av boucler la boucle. ◆**loophole** n (in rules) point m faible, lacune f; (way out) échappatoire f.

loose [luːs] a (-er, -est) (screw, belt, knot) desserré; (tooth, stone) branlant; (page) détaché; (animal) libre, (set loose) lâché; (clothes) flottant; (hair) dénoué; (flesh) flasque; (wording, translation) approximatif, vague; (link) vague; (discipline) relâché; (articles) Com en vrac; (cheese, tea etc) Com au poids; (woman) Pej facile; **l. change** petite monnaie f; **l. covers** housses fpl; **l. living** vie f dissolue; **to get l.** (of dog, page) se détacher; **to set** or **turn l.** (dog etc) libérer, lâcher; **he's at l. end** or Am **at l. ends** il ne sait pas trop quoi faire; – n **on the l.** (prisoner etc) en liberté; – vt (animal) lâcher. ◆**loosely** adv (to hang) lâchement; (to hold, tie) sans serrer; (to translate) librement; (to link) vaguement. ◆**loosen** vt (knot, belt, screw) desserrer; (rope) détendre; (grip) relâcher; – vt **to l. up** Sp faire des exercices d'assouplissement. ◆**looseness** n (of screw, machine parts) jeu m.

loot [luːt] n butin m; (money) Sl fric m; – vt piller. ◆**—ing** n pillage m. ◆**—er** n pillard, -arde mf.

lop [lɒp] vt (-pp-) **to l. (off)** couper.

lop-sided [lɒpˈsaɪdɪd] a (crooked) de travers; **to walk l.-sided** (limp) se déhancher.

loquacious [ləʊˈkweɪʃəs] a loquace.

lord [lɔːd] *n* seigneur *m*; (*title*) *Br* lord *m*; **good L.!** *Fam* bon sang!; **oh L.!** *Fam* mince!; **the House of Lords** *Pol* la Chambre des Lords; — *vt* dominer qn. ◆**lordly** *a* digne d'un grand seigneur; (*arrogant*) hautain. ◆**lordship** *n* **Your L.** (*to judge*) Monsieur le juge.

lore [lɔːr] *n* traditions *fpl*.

lorry ['lɒrɪ] *n* camion *m*; (*heavy*) poids *m* lourd; **l. driver** camionneur *m*; **long-distance l. driver** routier *m*.

los/e [luːz] *vt* (*pt & pp* **lost**) perdre; **to get lost** (*of person*) se perdre; **the ticket/etc got lost** on a perdu le billet/etc; **get lost!** *Fam* fiche le camp!; **to l. s.o. sth** faire perdre qch à qn; **to l. interest in** se désintéresser de; **I've lost my bearings** je suis désorienté; **the clock loses six minutes a day** la pendule retarde de six minutes par jour; **to l. one's life** trouver la mort (**in** dans); — *vi* perdre; **to l. out** être perdant; **to l. to** *Sp* être battu par. ◆**—ing** *a* perdant; **a l. battle** *Fig* une bataille perdue d'avance. ◆**—er** *n* perdant, -ante *mf*; (*failure in life*) *Fam* paumé, -ée *mf*; **to be a good l.** être bon *or* beau joueur.

loss [lɒs] *n* perte *f*; **at a l.** (*confused*) perplexe; **to sell at a l.** *Com* vendre à perte; **at a l. to do** incapable de faire. ◆**lost** *a* perdu; **l. property**, *Am* **l. and found** objets *mpl* trouvés.

lot [lɒt] *n* **1** (*destiny*) sort *m*; (*batch, land*) lot *m*; **to draw lots** tirer au sort; **parking l.** *Am* parking *m*; **a bad l.** (*person*) *Fam* un mauvais sujet. **2 the l.** (*everything*) (le) tout; **the l. of you** vous tous; **a l. of, lots of** beaucoup de; **a l.** beaucoup; **quite a l.** pas mal (**of** de); **such a l.** tellement (**of** de), tant (**of** de); **what a l. of flowers/water/etc!** que de fleurs/d'eau/etc!; **what a l.!** quelle quantité!; **what a l. of flowers/etc you have!** que vous avez (beaucoup) de fleurs/etc!

lotion ['ləʊʃ(ə)n] *n* lotion *f*.

lottery ['lɒtərɪ] *n* loterie *f*.

lotto ['lɒtəʊ] *n* (*game*) loto *m*.

loud [laʊd] *a* (**-er**, **-est**) bruyant; (*voice, radio*) fort; (*noise, cry*) grand; (*gaudy*) voyant; — *adv* (*to shout etc*) fort; **out l.** tout haut. ◆**—ly** *adv* (*to speak, laugh etc*) bruyamment, fort; (*to shout*) fort. ◆**—ness** *n* (*of voice etc*) force *f*; (*noise*) bruit *m*. ◆**loud'hailer** *n* mégaphone *m*. ◆**loudmouth** *n* (*person*) *Fam* grande gueule *f*. ◆**loud'speaker** *n* haut-parleur *m*; (*of hi-fi unit*) enceinte *f*.

lounge [laʊndʒ] **1** *n* salon *m*; **l. suit** complet *m* veston. **2** *vi* (*loll*) se prélasser; **to l. about** (*idle*) paresser; (*stroll*) flâner.

louse, *pl* **lice** [laʊs, laɪs] **1** *n* (*insect*) pou *m*. **2** *n* (*person*) *Pej Sl* salaud *m*. **3** *vt* **to l. up** (*mess up*) *Sl* gâcher.

lousy ['laʊzɪ] *a* (**-ier**, **-iest**) (*bad*) *Fam* infect; **l. with** (*crammed, loaded*) *Sl* bourré de.

lout [laʊt] *n* rustre *m*. ◆**loutish** *a* (*attitude*) de rustre.

lov/e [lʌv] *n* amour *m*; *Tennis* zéro *m*; **in l.** amoureux (**with** de); **they're in l.** ils s'aiment; **art is his** *or* **her l.** l'art est sa passion; **yes, my l.** oui mon amour; — *vt* aimer; (*like very much*) adorer, aimer (beaucoup) (**to do, doing** faire); **give him** *or* **her my l.** (*greeting*) dis-lui bien des choses de ma part; **l. affair** liaison *f* (amoureuse). ◆**—ing** *a* affectueux, aimant. ◆**—able** *a* adorable. ◆**—er** *n* (*man*) amant *m*; (*woman*) maîtresse *f*; **a l. of** (*art, music etc*) un amateur de; **a nature l.** un amoureux de la nature. ◆**lovesick** *a* amoureux.

lovely ['lʌvlɪ] *a* (**-ier**, **-iest**) (*pleasing*) agréable, bon; (*excellent*) excellent; (*pretty*) joli; (*charming*) charmant; (*kind*) gentil; **the weather's l.** il fait beau; **l. to see you!** je suis ravi de te voir; **l. and hot/dry/etc** bien chaud/sec/etc.

low[1] [ləʊ] *a* (**-er**, **-est**) bas; (*speed, income, intelligence*) faible; (*opinion, quality*) mauvais; **she's l. on** (*money etc*) elle n'a plus beaucoup de; **to feel l.** (*depressed*) être déprimé; **in a l. voice** à voix basse; **lower** inférieur; — *adv* (**-er**, **-est**) bas; **to turn (down) l.** mettre plus bas; **to run l.** (*of supplies*) s'épuiser; — *n* Met dépression *f*; **to reach a new l.** *or* **an all-time l.** (*of prices etc*) atteindre leur niveau le plus bas. ◆**low-'calorie** (*a diet*) (à) basses calories. ◆**low-'cost** *a* bon marché *inv*. ◆**low-cut** *a* décolleté. ◆**low-down** *a* méprisable. ◆**lowdown** *n* (*facts*) *Fam* tuyaux *mpl*. ◆**low-'fat** *a* (*milk*) écrémé; (*cheese*) de régime. ◆**low-'key** *a* (*discreet*) discret. ◆**lowland(s)** *n* plaine *f*. ◆**low-level** *a* bas. ◆**low-paid** *a* mal payé. ◆**low-'salt** *a* (*food*) à faible teneur en sel.

low[2] [ləʊ] *vi* (*of cattle*) meugler.

lower ['ləʊər] *vt* baisser; **to l. s.o./sth** (*by rope*) descendre qn/qch; **to l. oneself** *Fig* s'abaisser. ◆**—ing** *n* (*drop*) baisse *f*.

lowly ['ləʊlɪ] *a* (**-ier**, **-iest**) humble.

loyal ['lɔɪəl] *a* loyal (**to** envers), fidèle (**to** à). ◆**loyalty** *n* loyauté *f*, fidélité *f*.

lozenge ['lɒzɪndʒ] *n* (*sweet*) *Med* pastille *f*; (*shape*) *Geom* losange *m*.

LP [el'piː] *abbr* = long-playing record.

L-plates ['elpleɪts] *npl Aut* plaques *fpl* d'apprenti conducteur.

Ltd *abbr* (*Limited*) *Com* SARL.

lubricate ['luːbrɪkeɪt] *vt* lubrifier; *Aut* graisser. ◆**lubricant** *n* lubrifiant *m*. ◆**lubri'cation** *n Aut* graissage *m*.

lucid ['luːsɪd] *a* lucide. ◆**lu'cidity** *n* lucidité *f*.

luck [lʌk] *n* (*chance*) chance *f*; (*good fortune*) (bonne) chance *f*, bonheur *m*; (*fate*) hasard *m*, fortune *f*; **bad l.** malchance *f*, malheur *m*; **hard l.!, tough l.!** pas de chance!; **worse l.** (*unfortunately*) malheureusement. ◆**luckily** *adv* heureusement. ◆**lucky** *a* (**-ier, -iest**) (*person*) chanceux, heureux; (*guess, event*) heureux; **to be l.** (*of person*) avoir de la chance (**to do** de faire); **I've had a l. day** j'ai eu de la chance aujourd'hui; **l. charm** porte-bonheur *m inv*; **l. number/etc** chiffre *m/etc* porte-bonheur; **how l.!** quelle chance!

lucrative ['luːkrətɪv] *a* lucratif.

ludicrous ['luːdɪkrəs] *a* ridicule.

ludo ['luːdəʊ] *n* jeu *m* des petits chevaux.

lug [lʌg] *vt* (**-gg-**) (*pull*) traîner; **to l. around** trimbaler.

luggage ['lʌgɪdʒ] *n* bagages *mpl*.

lugubrious [luːˈguːbrɪəs] *a* lugubre.

lukewarm ['luːkwɔːm] *a* tiède.

lull [lʌl] **1** *n* arrêt *m*; (*in storm*) accalmie *f*. **2** *vt* (**-ll-**) apaiser; **to l. to sleep** endormir. ◆**lullaby** ['lʌləbaɪ] *n* berceuse *f*.

lumbago [lʌmˈbeɪgəʊ] *n* lumbago *m*.

lumber[1] ['lʌmbər] *n* (*timber*) bois *m* de charpente; (*junk*) bric-à-brac *m inv*. ◆**lumberjack** *n Am Can* bûcheron *m*. ◆**lumberjacket** *n* blouson *m*. ◆**lumber-room** *n* débarras *m*.

lumber[2] ['lʌmbər] *vt* **to l. s.o. with sth/s.o.** *Fam* coller qch/qn à qn; **he got lumbered with the chore** il s'est appuyé la corvée.

luminous ['luːmɪnəs] *a* (*dial etc*) lumineux.

lump [lʌmp] *n* morceau *m*; (*in soup*) grumeau *m*; (*bump*) bosse *f*; (*swelling*) *Med* grosseur *f*; **l. sum** somme *f* forfaitaire; − *vt* **to l. together** réunir; *Fig Pej* mettre dans le même sac. ◆**lumpy** *a* (**-ier, -iest**) (*soup etc*) grumeleux; (*surface*) bosselé.

lunar ['luːnər] *a* lunaire.

lunatic ['luːnətɪk] *a* fou, dément; − *n* fou *m*, folle *f*. ◆**lunacy** *n* folie *f*, démence *f*.

lunch [lʌntʃ] *n* déjeuner *m*; **to have l.** déjeuner; **l. break, l. hour, l. time** heure *f* du déjeuner; − *vi* déjeuner (**on, off** de). ◆**luncheon** *n* déjeuner *m*; **l. meat** mortadelle *f*, saucisson *m*; **l. voucher** chèque-déjeuner *m*.

lung [lʌŋ] *n* poumon *m*; **l. cancer** cancer *m* du poumon.

lunge [lʌndʒ] *n* coup *m* en avant; − *vi* **to l. at** s.o. se ruer sur qn.

lurch [lɜːtʃ] **1** *vi* (*of person*) tituber; (*of ship*) faire une embardée. **2** *n* **to leave s.o. in the l.** *Fam* laisser qn en plan, laisser tomber qn.

lure [lʊər] *vt* attirer (par la ruse) (**into** dans); − *n* (*attraction*) attrait *m*.

lurid ['lʊərɪd] *a* (*horrifying*) horrible, affreux; (*sensational*) à sensation; (*gaudy*) voyant; (*colour, sunset*) sanglant.

lurk [lɜːk] *vi* (*hide*) se cacher (**in** dans); (*prowl*) rôder; (*of suspicion, fear etc*) persister.

luscious ['lʌʃəs] *a* (*food etc*) appétissant.

lush [lʌʃ] **1** *a* (*vegetation*) luxuriant; (*wealthy*) *Fam* opulent. **2** *n Am Sl* ivrogne *mf*.

lust [lʌst] *n* (*for person, object*) convoitise *f* (**for** de); (*for power, knowledge*) soif *f* (**for** de); − *vi* **to l. after** (*object, person*) convoiter; (*power, knowledge*) avoir soif de.

lustre ['lʌstər] *n* (*gloss*) lustre *m*.

lusty ['lʌstɪ] *a* (**-ier, -iest**) vigoureux.

lute [luːt] *n Mus* luth *m*.

Luxembourg ['lʌksəmbɜːg] *n* Luxembourg *m*.

luxuriant [lʌgˈʒʊərɪənt] *a* luxuriant. ◆**luxuriate** *vi* (*laze about*) paresser (**in bed/etc** au lit/etc).

luxury ['lʌkʃərɪ] *n* luxe *m*; − *a* (*goods, flat etc*) de luxe. ◆**luxurious** [lʌgˈʒʊərɪəs] *a* luxueux.

lying ['laɪɪŋ] *see* **lie**[1,2]; − *n* le mensonge; − *a* (*account*) mensonger; (*person*) menteur.

lynch [lɪntʃ] *vt* lyncher. ◆**−ing** *n* lynchage *m*.

lynx [lɪŋks] *n* (*animal*) lynx *m*.

lyre ['laɪər] *n Mus Hist* lyre *f*.

lyric ['lɪrɪk] *a* lyrique; − *npl* (*of song*) paroles *fpl*. ◆**lyrical** *a* (*effusive*) lyrique. ◆**lyricism** *n* lyrisme *m*.

M

M, m [em] *n* M, m *m*.

m *abbr* **1** (*metre*) mètre *m*. **2** (*mile*) mile *m*.

MA *abbr* = **Master of Arts.**

ma'am [mæm] *n* madame *f*.

mac [mæk] *n* (*raincoat*) *Fam* imper *m*.

macabre [mə'kɑːbrə] *a* macabre.

macaroni [mækə'rəʊnɪ] *n* macaroni(s) *m*(*pl*).

macaroon [mækə'ruːn] *n* (*cake*) macaron *m*.

mace [meɪs] *n* (*staff, rod*) masse *f*.

Machiavellian [mækɪə'velɪən] *a* machiavélique.

machination [mækɪ'neɪʃ(ə)n] *n* machination *f*.

machine [mə'ʃiːn] *n* (*apparatus, car, system etc*) machine *f*. ◆**machinegun** *n* mitrailleuse *f*; – *vt* (**-nn-**) mitrailler. ◆**machinery** *n* (*machines*) machines *fpl*; (*works*) mécanisme *m*; *Fig* rouages *mpl*. ◆**machinist** *n* (*on sewing machine*) piqueur, -euse *mf*.

macho ['mætʃəʊ] *n* (*pl* **-os**) macho *m*; – *a* (*attitude etc*) macho (*f inv*).

mackerel ['mækrəl] *n inv* (*fish*) maquereau *m*.

mackintosh ['mækɪntɒʃ] *n* imperméable *m*.

mad [mæd] *a* (**madder, maddest**) fou; (*dog*) enragé; (*bull*) furieux; **m. (at)** (*angry*) *Fam* furieux (contre); **to be m. (keen) on** *Fam* (*person*) être fou de; (*films etc*) se passionner *or* s'emballer pour; **to drive me m.** to go *Fam* il m'a cassé les pieds pour que j'y aille; **like m.** comme un fou. ◆**maddening** *a* exaspérant. ◆**madhouse** *n* *Fam* maison *f* de fous. ◆**madly** *adv* (*in love, to spend money etc*) follement; (*desperately*) désespérément. ◆**madman** *n* (*pl* **-men**) fou *m*. ◆**madness** *n* folie *f*.

Madagascar [mædə'gæskər] *n* Madagascar *f*.

madam ['mædəm] *n* (*married*) madame *f*; (*unmarried*) mademoiselle *f*.

made [meɪd] *see* **make.**

Madeira [mə'dɪərə] *n* (*wine*) madère *m*.

madonna [mə'dɒnə] *n* *Rel* madone *f*.

maestro ['maɪstrəʊ] *n* (*pl* **-os**) *Mus* maestro *m*.

Mafia ['mæfɪə] *n* maf(f)ia *f*.

magazine [mægə'ziːn] *n* (*periodical*) magazine *m*, revue *f*; (*of gun, camera*) magasin *m*.

maggot ['mægət] *n* ver *m*, asticot *m*. ◆**maggoty** *a* véreux.

magic ['mædʒɪk] *n* magie *f*; – *a* (*word, wand*) magique. ◆**magical** *a* (*evening etc*) magique. ◆**ma'gician** *n* magicien, -ienne *mf*.

magistrate ['mædʒɪstreɪt] *n* magistrat *m*.

magnanimous [mæg'nænɪməs] *a* magnanime.

magnate ['mægneɪt] *n* (*tycoon*) magnat *m*.

magnesium [mæg'niːzɪəm] *n* magnésium *m*.

magnet ['mægnɪt] *n* aimant *m*. ◆**mag'netic** *a* magnétique. ◆**magnetism** *n* magnétisme *m*. ◆**magnetize** *vt* magnétiser.

magnificent [mæg'nɪfɪsənt] *a* magnifique. ◆**magnificence** *n* magnificence *f*. ◆**magnificently** *adv* magnifiquement.

magnify ['mægnɪfaɪ] *vt* (*image*) & *Fig* grossir; (*sound*) amplifier; **magnifying glass** loupe *f*. ◆**magnifi'cation** *n* grossissement *m*; amplification *f*. ◆**magnitude** *n* ampleur *f*.

magnolia [mæg'nəʊlɪə] *n* (*tree*) magnolia *m*.

magpie ['mægpaɪ] *n* (*bird*) pie *f*.

mahogany [mə'hɒgənɪ] *n* acajou *m*.

maid [meɪd] *n* (*servant*) bonne *f*; **old m.** *Pej* vieille fille *f*. ◆**maiden** *n* *Old-fashioned* jeune fille *f*; – *a* (*speech etc*) premier; (*flight*) inaugural; **m. name** nom *m* de jeune fille. ◆**maidenly** *a* virginal.

mail [meɪl] *n* (*system*) poste *f*; (*letters*) courrier *m*; – *a* (*van, bag etc*) postal; **m. order** vente *f* par correspondance; – *vt* mettre à la poste; **mailing list** liste *f* d'adresses. ◆**mailbox** *n* *Am* boîte *f* à *or* aux lettres. ◆**mailman** *n* (*pl* **-men**) *Am* facteur *m*.

maim [meɪm] *vt* mutiler, estropier.

main [meɪn] **1** *a* principal; **the m. thing is to ...** l'essentiel est de ...; **m. line** *Rail* grande ligne *f*; **m. road** grande route *f*; **in the m.** (*mostly*) en gros, dans l'ensemble. **2** *n* water/gas **m.** conduite *f* d'eau/de gaz; **the mains** *El* le secteur; **a mains radio** une radio secteur. ◆**-ly** *adv* principalement, surtout. ◆**mainland** *n* continent *m*. ◆**main-**

stay n (*of family etc*) soutien m; (*of organization, policy*) pilier m. ◆**mainstream** n tendance f dominante.

maintain [meɪn'teɪn] vt (*continue, assert*) maintenir (**that** que); (*vehicle, family etc*) entretenir; (*silence*) garder. ◆**maintenance** n (*of vehicle, road etc*) entretien m; (*of prices, order, position etc*) maintien m; (*alimony*) pension f alimentaire.

maisonette [meɪzə'net] n duplex m.

maize [meɪz] n (*cereal*) maïs m.

majesty ['mædʒəstɪ] n majesté f; **Your M.** (*title*) Votre Majesté. ◆**ma'jestic** a majestueux.

major ['meɪdʒər] **1** a (*main, great*) & *Mus* majeur; **a m. road** une grande route. **2** n *Mil* commandant m. **3** n (*subject*) *Univ Am* dominante f; – vi **to m. in** se spécialiser en. ◆**majo'rette** n (**drum**) m. majorette f.

Majorca [mə'jɔːkə] n Majorque f.

majority [mə'dʒɒrɪtɪ] n majorité f (**of** de); **in the** or **a m.** en majorité, majoritaire; **the m. of people** la plupart des gens; – a (*vote etc*) majoritaire.

make [meɪk] vt (*pt & pp* **made**) faire; (*tool, vehicle etc*) fabriquer; (*decision*) prendre; (*friends, wage*) se faire; (*points*) *Sp* marquer; (*destination*) arriver à; **to m. happy/tired/***etc* rendre heureux/fatigué/*etc*; **he made ten francs on it** *Com* ça lui a rapporté dix francs; **she made the train** (*did not miss*) elle a eu le train; **to m. s.o. do sth** faire faire qch à qn, obliger qn à faire qch; **to m. oneself heard** se faire entendre; **to m. oneself at home** se mettre à l'aise; **to m. ready** préparer; **to m. yellow** jaunir; **she made him her husband** elle en a fait son mari; **to m. do** (*manage*) se débrouiller (**with** avec); **to m. do with** (*be satisfied with*) se contenter de; **to m. it** (*arrive*) arriver; (*succeed*) réussir; (*say*) dire; **I m. it five o'clock** j'ai cinq heures; **what do you m. of it?** qu'en penses-tu?; **I can't m.** anything of it je n'y comprends rien; **to m. a living** gagner sa vie; **you're made (for life)** ton avenir est assuré; **to m. believe** (*pretend*) faire semblant (**that one is** d'être); (n) **it's m.-believe** (*story etc*) c'est pure invention; **to live in a world of m.-believe** se bercer d'illusions; – vi **to m. as if to** (*appear to*) faire mine de; **to m. for** (*go towards*) aller vers; – n (*brand*) marque f; **of French/***etc* **m.** de fabrication française/*etc.* ■ **to m. off** vi (*run away*) se sauver; **to m. out** vt (*see*) distinguer; (*understand*) comprendre; (*decipher*) déchiffrer; (*draw up*) faire (*chèque, liste*); (*claim*) prétendre (**that** que);

you made me out to be silly tu m'as fait passer pour un idiot; – vi (*manage*) *Fam* se débrouiller; **to m. over** vt (*transfer*) céder; (*change*) transformer (**into** en); **to m. up** vt (*story*) inventer; (*put together*) faire (*collection, liste, lit etc*); (*prepare*) préparer; (*form*) former, composer; (*loss*) compenser; (*quantity*) compléter; (*quarrel*) régler; (*one's face*) maquiller; – vi (*of friends*) se réconcilier; **to m. up for** (*loss, damage, fault*) compenser; (*lost time, mistake*) rattraper. ◆**m.-up** n (*of object etc*) constitution f; (*of person*) caractère m; (*for face*) maquillage m. ◆**making** n (*manufacture*) fabrication f; (*of dress*) confection f; **history in the m.** l'histoire en train de se faire; **the makings of** les éléments mpl (essentiels) de; **to have the makings of a pianist/***etc* avoir l'étoffe d'un pianiste/*etc.* ◆**maker** n *Com* fabricant m. ◆**makeshift** n expédient m; – a (*arrangement etc*) de fortune, provisoire.

maladjusted [mælə'dʒʌstɪd] a inadapté.

malaise [mæ'leɪz] n malaise m.

malaria [mə'leərɪə] n malaria f.

Malaysia [mə'leɪzɪə] n Malaysia f.

male [meɪl] a *Biol Bot etc* mâle; (*clothes, sex*) masculin; – n (*man, animal*) mâle m.

malevolent [mə'levələnt] a malveillant. ◆**malevolence** n malveillance f.

malfunction [mæl'fʌŋkʃ(ə)n] n mauvais fonctionnement m; – vi fonctionner mal.

malice ['mælɪs] n méchanceté f; **to bear s.o. m.** vouloir du mal à qn. ◆**ma'licious** a malveillant. ◆**ma'liciously** adv avec malveillance.

malign [mə'laɪn] vt (*slander*) calomnier.

malignant [mə'lɪgnənt] a (*person etc*) malfaisant; **m. tumour** *Med* tumeur f maligne. ◆**malignancy** n *Med* malignité f.

malingerer [mə'lɪŋgərər] n (*pretending illness*) simulateur, -euse mf.

mall [mɔːl] n (*shopping*) **m.** (*covered*) galerie f marchande; (*street*) rue f piétonnière.

malleable ['mælɪəb(ə)l] a malléable.

mallet ['mælɪt] n (*tool*) maillet m.

malnutrition [mælnjuː'trɪʃ(ə)n] n malnutrition f, sous-alimentation f.

malpractice [mæl'præktɪs] n *Med Jur* faute f professionnelle.

malt [mɔːlt] n malt m.

Malta ['mɔːltə] n Malte f. ◆**Mal'tese** a & n maltais, -aise (mf).

mammal ['mæm(ə)l] n mammifère m.

mammoth ['mæməθ] a (*large*) immense; – n (*extinct animal*) mammouth m.

man [mæn] *n* (*pl* **men** [men]) homme *m*; (*player*) *Sp* joueur *m*; (*chess piece*) pièce *f*; **a golf m.** (*enthusiast*) un amateur de golf; **he's a Bristol m.** (*by birth*) il est de Bristol; **to be m. and wife** être mari et femme; **my old m.** *Fam* (*father*) mon père; (*husband*) mon homme; **yes old m.!** *Fam* oui mon vieux!; **the m. in the street** l'homme de la rue; – *vt* (**-nn-**) (*ship*) pourvoir d'un équipage; (*fortress*) armer; (*guns*) servir; (*be on duty at*) être de service à; **manned spacecraft** engin *m* spatial habité. ◆**manhood** *n* (*period*) âge *m* d'homme. ◆**manhunt** *n* chasse *f* à l'homme. ◆**manlike** *a* (*quality*) d'homme viril. ◆**manly** *a* (**-ier, -iest**) viril. ◆**man-'made** *a* artificiel; (*fibre*) synthétique. ◆**manservant** *n* (*pl* **menservants**) domestique *m*. ◆**man-to-'man** *a* & *adv* d'homme à homme.

manacle ['mænɪk(ə)l] *n* menotte *f*.

manag/e ['mænɪdʒ] *vt* (*run*) diriger; (*affairs etc*) *Com* gérer; (*handle*) manier; (*take*) *Fam* prendre; (*eat*) *Fam* manger; (*contribute*) *Fam* donner; **to m. to do** (*succeed*) réussir *or* arriver à faire; (*contrive*) se débrouiller pour faire; **I'll m. it** j'y arriverai; – *vi* (*succeed*) y arriver; (*make do*) se débrouiller (**with** avec); **to m. without sth** se passer de qch. ◆**–ing** *a* **m. director** directeur *m* général; **the m. director** le PDG. ◆**–eable** *a* (*parcel, person etc*) maniable; (*feasible*) faisable. ◆**–ement** *n* direction *f*; (*of property etc*) gestion *f*; (*executive staff*) cadres *mpl*. ◆**–er** *n* directeur *m*; (*of shop, café*) gérant *m*; (*business*) *m.* (*of actor, boxer etc*) manager *m*. ◆**manage'ress** *n* directrice *f*; gérante *f*. ◆**managerial** [mænə'dʒɪərɪəl] *a* directorial; **the m. class** *or* **staff** les cadres *mpl*.

mandarin ['mændərɪn] **1** *n* (*high-ranking official*) haut fonctionnaire *m*; (*in political party*) bonze *m*; (*in university*) *Pej* mandarin *m*. **2** *a* & *n* **m.** (*orange*) mandarine *f*.

mandate ['mændeɪt] *n* mandat *m*. ◆**mandatory** *a* obligatoire.

mane [meɪn] *n* crinière *f*.

maneuver [mə'nuːvər] *n* & *vti Am* = **manoeuvre**.

mangle ['mæŋɡ(ə)l] **1** *n* (*for wringing*) essoreuse *f*; – *vt* (*clothes*) essorer. **2** *vt* (*damage*) mutiler.

mango ['mæŋɡəʊ] *n* (*pl* **-oes** *or* **-os**) (*fruit*) mangue *f*.

mangy ['meɪndʒɪ] *a* (*animal*) galeux.

manhandle [mæn'hænd(ə)l] *vt* maltraiter.

manhole ['mænhəʊl] *n* trou *m* d'homme; **m. cover** plaque *f* d'égout.

mania ['meɪnɪə] *n* manie *f*. ◆**maniac** *n* fou *m*, folle *f*; *Psy Med* maniaque *mf*; **sex m.** obsédé *m* sexuel.

manicure ['mænɪkjʊər] *n* soin *m* des mains; – *vt* (*person*) manucurer; (*s.o.'s nails*) faire. ◆**manicurist** *n* manucure *mf*.

manifest ['mænɪfest] **1** *a* (*plain*) manifeste. **2** *vt* (*show*) manifester.

manifesto [mænɪ'festəʊ] *n* (*pl* **-os** *or* **-oes**) *Pol* manifeste *m*.

manifold ['mænɪfəʊld] *a* multiple.

manipulate [mə'nɪpjʊleɪt] *vt* manœuvrer; (*facts, electors etc*) *Pej* manipuler. ◆**manipu'lation** *n* manœuvre *f*; *Pej* manipulation *f* (**of** de).

mankind [mæn'kaɪnd] *n* (*humanity*) le genre humain.

manner ['mænər] *n* (*way*) manière *f*; (*behaviour*) attitude *f*, comportement *m*; *pl* (*social habits*) manières *fpl*; **in this m.** (*like this*) de cette manière; **all m. of** toutes sortes de. ◆**mannered** *a* (*affected*) maniéré; **well-/bad-m.** bien/mal élevé. ◆**mannerism** *n* *Pej* tic *m*.

manoeuvre [mə'nuːvər] *n* manœuvre *f*; – *vti* manœuvrer. ◆**manoeuvra'bility** *n* (*of vehicle etc*) maniabilité *f*.

manor ['mænər] *n* **m.** (**house**) manoir *m*.

manpower ['mænpaʊər] *n* (*labour*) main-d'œuvre *f*; *Mil* effectifs *mpl*; (*effort*) force *f*.

mansion ['mænʃ(ə)n] *n* hôtel *m* particulier; (*in country*) manoir *m*.

manslaughter ['mænslɔːtər] *n* *Jur* homicide *m* involontaire.

mantelpiece ['mænt(ə)lpiːs] *n* (*shelf*) cheminée *f*.

mantle ['mænt(ə)l] *n* (*cloak*) cape *f*.

manual ['mænjʊəl] **1** *a* (*work etc*) manuel. **2** *n* (*book*) manuel *m*.

manufactur/e [mænjʊ'fæktʃər] *vt* fabriquer; – *n* fabrication *f*. ◆**–er** *n* fabricant *mf*.

manure [mə'njʊər] *n* fumier *m*, engrais *m*.

manuscript ['mænjʊskrɪpt] *n* manuscrit *m*.

many ['menɪ] *a* & *n* beaucoup (**de**); **m. things** beaucoup de choses; **m. came** beaucoup sont venus; **very m., a good** *or* **great m.** un très grand nombre (**de**); (**a good** *or* **great**) **m. of** un (très) grand nombre de; **m. of them** un grand nombre d'entre eux; **m. times, m. a time** bien des fois; **m. kinds** toutes sortes (**de**); **how m.?** combien (**de**)?; **too m.** trop (**de**); **one too m.** un de trop; **there are too m. of them** ils sont trop nombreux; **so m.** tant (**de**); **as m. books/etc**

map 500 Marxism

as autant de livres/*etc* que; **as m. as** (*up to*) jusqu'à.

map [mæp] *n* (*of country etc*) carte *f*; (*plan*) plan *m*; – *vt* (**-pp-**) faire la carte *or* le plan de; **to m. out** (*road*) faire le tracé de; (*one's day etc*) *Fig* organiser.

maple ['meɪp(ə)l] *n* (*tree, wood*) érable *m*.

mar [mɑːr] *vt* (**-rr-**) gâter.

marathon ['mærəθən] *n* marathon *m*.

maraud [mə'rɔːd] *vi* piller. ◆**—ing** *a* pillard. ◆**—er** *n* pillard, -arde *mf*.

marble ['mɑːb(ə)l] *n* (*substance*) marbre *m*; (*toy ball*) bille *f*.

march [mɑːtʃ] *n* *Mil* marche *f*; – *vi* *Mil* marcher (au pas); **in/out/***etc* *Fig* entrer/sortir/*etc* d'un pas décidé; **to m. past** défiler; – *vt* **to m. s.o. off** *or* **away** emmener qn. ◆**m.-past** *n* défilé *m*.

March [mɑːtʃ] *n* mars *m*.

mare [meər] *n* jument *f*.

margarine [mɑːdʒə'riːn] *n* margarine *f*.

margin ['mɑːdʒɪn] *n* (*of page etc*) marge *f*; **by a narrow m.** (*to win*) de justesse. ◆**marginal** *a* marginal; **m. seat** *Pol* siège *m* disputé. ◆**marginally** *adv* très légèrement.

marguerite [mɑːgə'riːt] *n* (*daisy*) marguerite *f*.

marigold ['mærɪgəʊld] *n* (*flower*) souci *m*.

marijuana [mærɪ'wɑːnə] *n* marijuana *f*.

marina [mə'riːnə] *n* marina *f*.

marinate ['mærɪneɪt] *vti* *Culin* mariner.

marine [mə'riːn] **1** *a* (*life, flora etc*) marin. **2** *n* (*soldier*) fusilier *m* marin, *Am* marine *m*.

marionette [mærɪə'net] *n* marionnette *f*.

marital ['mærɪt(ə)l] *a* matrimonial; (*relations*) conjugal; **m. status** situation *f* de famille.

maritime ['mærɪtaɪm] *a* (*province, climate etc*) maritime.

marjoram ['mɑːdʒərəm] *n* (*spice*) marjolaine *f*.

mark[1] [mɑːk] *n* (*symbol*) marque *f*; (*stain, trace*) trace *f*, tache *f*, marque *f*; (*token, sign*) *Fig* signe *m*; (*for exercise etc*) *Sch* note *f*; (*target*) but *m*; (*model*) *Tech* série *f*; **to make one's m.** *Fig* s'imposer; **up to the m.** (*person, work*) à la hauteur; – *vt* marquer; (*exam etc*) *Sch* corriger, noter; (*pay attention to*) faire attention à; **to m. time** *Mil* marquer le pas; *Fig* piétiner; **m. you . . . !** remarquez que . . . !; **to m. down** (*price*) baisser; **to m. off** (*separate*) séparer; (*on list*) cocher; **to m. out** (*area*) délimiter; **to m. s.o. out for** désigner qn pour; **to m. up** (*increase*) augmenter. ◆**—ed** *a* (*noticeable*) marqué. ◆**—edly** [-ɪdlɪ] *adv* visiblement.

◆**—ing(s)** *n*(*pl*) (*on animal etc*) marques *fpl*; (*on road*) signalisation *f* horizontale. ◆**—er** *n* (*flag etc*) marque *f*; (*pen*) feutre *m*, marqueur *m*.

mark[2] [mɑːk] *n* (*currency*) mark *m*.

market ['mɑːkɪt] *n* marché *m*; **on the open m.** en vente libre; **on the black m.** au marché noir; **the Common M.** le Marché commun; **m. value** valeur *f* marchande; **m. price** prix *m* courant; **m. gardener** maraîcher, -ère *mf*; – *vt* (*sell*) vendre; (*launch*) commercialiser. ◆**—ing** *n* marketing *m*, vente *f*. ◆**—able** *a* vendable.

marksman ['mɑːksmən] *n* (*pl* **-men**) tireur *m* d'élite.

marmalade ['mɑːməleɪd] *n* confiture *f* d'oranges.

maroon [mə'ruːn] *a* (*colour*) bordeaux *inv*.

marooned [mə'ruːnd] *a* abandonné; (*in snowstorm etc*) bloqué (**by** par).

marquee [mɑːˈkiː] *n* (*for concerts, garden parties etc*) chapiteau *m*; (*awning*) *Am* marquise *f*.

marquis ['mɑːkwɪs] *n* marquis *m*.

marrow ['mærəʊ] *n* **1** (*of bone*) moelle *f*. **2** (*vegetable*) courge *f*.

marr/y ['mærɪ] *vt* épouser, se marier avec; **to m.** (**off**) (*of priest etc*) marier; – *vi* se marier. ◆**—ied** *a* marié; (*life, state*) conjugal; **m. name** nom *m* de femme mariée; **to get m.** se marier. ◆**marriage** *n* mariage *m*; **to be related by m. to** être parent par alliance de; – *a* (*bond*) conjugal; (*certificate*) de mariage; **m. bureau** agence *f* matrimoniale. ◆**marriageable** *a* en état de se marier.

marsh [mɑːʃ] *n* marais *m*, marécage *m*. ◆**marshland** *n* marécages *mpl*. ◆**marsh-'mallow** *n* *Bot Culin* guimauve *f*.

marshal ['mɑːʃ(ə)l] **1** *n* (*in army*) maréchal *m*; (*in airforce*) général *m*; (*at public event*) membre *m* du service d'ordre; *Jur Am* shérif *m*. **2** *vt* (**-ll-**, *Am* **-l-**) (*gather*) rassembler; (*lead*) mener cérémonieusement.

martial ['mɑːʃ(ə)l] *a* martial; **m. law** loi *f* martiale.

Martian ['mɑːʃ(ə)n] *n* & *a* martien, -ienne (*mf*).

martyr ['mɑːtər] *n* martyr, -yre *mf*; – *vt* *Rel* martyriser. ◆**martyrdom** *n* martyre *m*.

marvel ['mɑːv(ə)l] *n* (*wonder*) merveille *f*; (*miracle*) miracle *m*; – *vi* (**-ll-**, *Am* **-l-**) s'émerveiller (**at** de); – *vt* **to m. that** s'étonner de ce que (+ *sub or indic*). ◆**marvellous** *a* merveilleux.

Marxism ['mɑːksɪz(ə)m] *n* marxisme *m*. ◆**Marxist** *a* & *n* marxiste (*mf*).

marzipan ['mɑːzɪpæn] *n* pâte *f* d'amandes.

mascara [mæˈskɑːrə] *n* mascara *m*.

mascot ['mæskɒt] *n* mascotte *f*.

masculine ['mæskjʊlɪn] *a* masculin. ◆**mascuˈlinity** *n* masculinité *f*.

mash [mæʃ] *n* (*for poultry etc*) pâtée *f*; (*potatoes*) *Culin* purée *f*; − *vt* **to m.** (**up**) (*crush*) & *Culin* écraser; **mashed potatoes** purée *f* (de pommes de terre).

mask [mɑːsk] *n* masque *m*; − *vt* (*cover, hide*) masquer (**from** à).

masochism ['mæsəkɪz(ə)m] *n* masochisme *m*. ◆**masochist** *n* masochiste *mf*. ◆**masoˈchistic** *a* masochiste.

mason ['meɪs(ə)n] *n* maçon *m*. ◆**masonry** *n* maçonnerie *f*.

masquerade [mɑːskəˈreɪd] *n* (*gathering, disguise*) mascarade *f*; − *vi* **to m. as** se faire passer pour.

mass¹ [mæs] *n* masse *f*; **a m. of** (*many*) une multitude de; (*pile*) un tas de, une masse de; **to be a m. of bruises** *Fam* être couvert de bleus; **masses of** *Fam* des masses de; **the masses** (*people*) les masses *fpl*; − *a* (*education*) des masses; (*culture, demonstration*) de masse; (*protests, departure*) en masse; (*production*) en série, en masse; (*hysteria*) collectif; **m. grave** fosse *f* commune; **m. media** mass media *mpl*; − *vi* (*of troops, people*) se masser. ◆**m.-proˈduce** *vt* fabriquer en série.

mass² [mæs] *n Rel* messe *f*.

massacre ['mæsəkər] *n* massacre *m*; − *vt* massacrer.

massage ['mæsɑːʒ] *n* massage *m*; − *vt* masser. ◆**maˈsseur** *n* masseur *m*. ◆**maˈsseuse** *n* masseuse *f*.

massive ['mæsɪv] *a* (*solid*) massif; (*huge*) énorme, considérable. ◆**−ly** *adv* (*to increase, reduce etc*) considérablement.

mast [mɑːst] *n Nau* mât *m*; *Rad TV* pylône *m*.

master ['mɑːstər] *n* maître *m*; (*in secondary school*) professeur *m*; **a m.'s degree** une maîtrise (**in** de); **M. of Arts/Science** (*person*) *Univ* Maître *m* ès lettres/sciences; **m. of ceremonies** (*presenter*) *Am* animateur, -trice *mf*; **m. card** carte *f* maîtresse; **m. stroke** coup *m* de maître; **m. key** passe-partout *m inv*; **old m.** (*painting*) tableau *m* de maître; **I'm my own m.** je ne dépends que de moi; − *vt* (*control*) maîtriser; (*subject, situation*) dominer; **she has mastered Latin** elle possède le latin. ◆**masterly** *a* magistral. ◆**mastery** *n* maîtrise *f* (**of** de).

mastermind ['mɑːstəmaɪnd] *n* (*person*) cerveau *m*; − *vt* organiser.

masterpiece ['mɑːstəpiːs] *n* chef-d'œuvre *m*.

mastic ['mæstɪk] *n* mastic *m* (silicone).

masturbate ['mæstəbeɪt] *vi* se masturber. ◆**masturˈbation** *n* masturbation *f*.

mat [mæt] **1** *n* tapis *m*, natte *f*; (*at door*) paillasson *m*; (**table**) **m.** (*of fabric*) napperon *m*; (*hard*) dessous-de-plat *m inv*; (**place**) **m. set** *m* (de table). **2** *a* (*paint, paper*) mat.

match¹ [mætʃ] *n* allumette *f*; **book of matches** pochette *f* d'allumettes. ◆**matchbox** *n* boîte *f* à allumettes. ◆**matchstick** *n* allumette *f*.

match² [mætʃ] **1** *n* (*game*) *Sp* match *m*; (*equal*) égal, -ale *mf*; (*marriage*) mariage *m*; **to be a good m.** (*of colours, people etc*) être bien assortis; **he's a good m.** (*man to marry*) c'est un bon parti; − *vt* (*clothes*) aller (bien) avec; **to m.** (**up to**) (*equal*) égaler; **to m.** (**up**) (*plates etc*) assortir; **to be well-matched** (*of colours, people etc*) être (bien) assortis, aller (bien) ensemble; − *vi* (*go with each other*) être assortis, aller (bien) ensemble. ◆**−ing** *a* (*dress etc*) assorti.

mate [meɪt] **1** *n* (*friend*) camarade *mf*; (*of animal*) mâle *m*, femelle *f*; **builder's/electrician's/etc m.** aide-maçon/-électricien/*etc m*. **2** *vi* (*of animals*) s'accoupler (**with** avec). **3** *n Chess* mat *m*; − *vt* faire *or* mettre mat.

material [məˈtɪərɪəl] **1** *a* matériel; (*important*) important. **2** *n* (*substance*) matière *f*; (*cloth*) tissu *m*; (*for book*) matériaux *mpl*; **material(s)** (*equipment*) matériel *m*; **building material(s)** matériaux *mpl* de construction. ◆**materialism** *n* matérialisme *m*. ◆**materialist** *n* matérialiste *mf*. ◆**materiaˈlistic** *a* matérialiste. ◆**materialize** *vi* se matérialiser. ◆**materially** *adv* matériellement; (*well-off etc*) sur le plan matériel.

maternal [məˈtɜːn(ə)l] *a* maternel. ◆**maternity** *n* maternité *f*; **m. hospital, m. unit** maternité *f*; − *a* (*clothes*) de grossesse; (*allowance, leave*) de maternité.

mathematical [mæθəˈmætɪk(ə)l] *a* mathématique; **to have a m. brain** être doué pour les maths. ◆**matheˈmatician** *n* mathématicien, -ienne *mf*. ◆**mathematics** *n* mathématiques *fpl*. ◆**maths**, *Am* ◆**math** *n Fam* maths *fpl*.

matinée ['mætɪneɪ] *n Th* matinée *f*.

matriculation [mətrɪkjʊ'leɪʃ(ə)n] *n Univ* inscription *f*.

matrimony ['mætrɪmənɪ] *n* mariage *m*. ◆**matri'monial** *a* matrimonial.

matrix, *pl* **-ices** ['meɪtrɪks, -ɪsiːz] *n Tech* matrice *f*.

matron ['meɪtrən] *n Lit* mère *f* de famille, dame *f* âgée; (*nurse*) infirmière *f* (en) chef. ◆**matronly** *a* (*air etc*) de mère de famille; (*mature*) mûr; (*portly*) corpulent.

matt [mæt] *a* (*paint, paper*) mat.

matted ['mætɪd] *a* **m. hair** cheveux *mpl* emmêlés.

matter[1] ['mætər] *n* matière *f*; (*affair*) affaire *f*, question *f*; (*thing*) chose *f*; **no m.!** (*no importance*) peu importe!; **no m. what she does** quoi qu'elle fasse; **no m. where you go** où que tu ailles; **no m. who you are** qui que vous soyez; **no m. when** quel que soit le moment; **what's the m.?** qu'est-ce qu'il y a?; **what's the m. with you?** qu'est-ce que tu as?; **there's sth the m.** il y a qch qui ne va pas; **there's sth the m. with my leg** j'ai qch à la jambe; **there's nothing the m. with him** il n'a rien; – *vi* (*be important*) importer (**to à**); **it doesn't m. if/when/who/etc** peu importe si/quand/qui/*etc*; **it doesn't m.!** ça ne fait rien!, peu importe! ◆**m.-of-'fact** *a* (*person, manner*) terre à terre; (*voice*) neutre.

matter[2] ['mætər] *n* (*pus*) *Med* pus *m*.

matting ['mætɪŋ] *n* (*material*) nattage *m*; **a piece of m.**, **some m.** une natte.

mattress ['mætrəs] *n* matelas *m*.

mature [mə'tʃʊər] *a* mûr; (*cheese*) fait; – *vt* (*person, plan*) (faire) mûrir; – *vi* mûrir; (*of cheese*) se faire. ◆**maturity** *n* maturité *f*.

maul [mɔːl] *vt* (*of animal*) mutiler; (*person*) *Fig* malmener.

mausoleum [mɔːsə'liːəm] *n* mausolée *m*.

mauve [məʊv] *a & n* (*colour*) mauve (*m*).

maverick ['mævərɪk] *n & a Pol* dissident, -ente (*mf*).

mawkish ['mɔːkɪʃ] *a* d'une sensiblerie excessive, mièvre.

maxim ['mæksɪm] *n* maxime *f*.

maximum ['mæksɪməm] *n* (*pl* **-ima** [-ɪmə] *or* **-imums**) maximum *m*; – *a* maximum (*f inv*), maximal. ◆**maximize** *vt* porter au maximum.

may [meɪ] *v aux* (*pt* **might**) **1** (*possibility*) **he m. come** il peut arriver; **he might come** il pourrait arriver; **I m. or might be wrong** il se peut que je me trompe, je me trompe peut-être; **you m. or might have** tu aurais pu; **I m. or might have forgotten it** je l'ai peut-être oublié; **we m. or might as well go**

nous ferions aussi bien de partir; **she fears I m. or might get lost** elle a peur que je ne me perde. **2** (*permission*) **m. I stay?** puis-je rester?; **m. I?** vous permettez?; **you m. go** tu peux partir. **3** (*wish*) **m. you be happy** (que tu) sois heureux. ◆**maybe** *adv* peut-être.

May [meɪ] *n* mai *m*.

mayhem ['meɪhem] *n* (*chaos*) pagaïe *f*; (*havoc*) ravages *mpl*.

mayonnaise [meɪə'neɪz] *n* mayonnaise *f*.

mayor [meər] *n* (*man, woman*) maire *m*. ◆**mayoress** *n* femme *f* du maire.

maze [meɪz] *n* labyrinthe *m*.

MC [em'siː] *abbr* = master of ceremonies.

me [miː] *pron* me, m'; (*after prep etc*) moi; (**to**) **me** (*indirect*) me, m'; **she knows me** elle me connaît; **he helps me** il m'aide; **he gives** (**to**) **me** il me donne; **with me** avec moi.

meadow ['medəʊ] *n* pré *m*, prairie *f*.

meagre ['miːgər] *a* maigre.

meal [miːl] *n* **1** (*food*) repas *m*. **2** (*flour*) farine *f*.

mealy-mouthed [miːlɪ'maʊðd] *a* mielleux.

mean[1] [miːn] *vt* (*pt & pp* **meant** [ment]) (*signify*) vouloir dire, signifier; (*destine*) destiner (**for** à); (*entail*) entraîner; (*represent*) représenter; (*refer to*) faire allusion à; **to m. to do** (*intend*) avoir l'intention de faire, vouloir faire; **I m. it**, **I m. what I say** je suis sérieux; **to m. sth to s.o.** (*matter*) avoir de l'importance pour qn; **it means sth to me** (*name, face*) ça me dit qch; **I didn't m. to!** je ne l'ai pas fait exprès!; **you were meant to come** vous étiez censé venir. ◆**—ing** *n* sens *m*, signification *f*. ◆**meaningful** *a* significatif. ◆**meaningless** *a* qui n'a pas de sens; (*absurd*) *Fig* insensé.

mean[2] [miːn] *a* (**-er**, **-est**) (*stingy*) avare, mesquin; (*petty*) mesquin; (*nasty*) méchant; (*inferior*) misérable. ◆**—ness** *n* (*greed*) avarice *f*; (*nastiness*) méchanceté *f*.

mean[3] [miːn] *a* (*distance*) moyen; – *n* (*middle position*) milieu *m*; (*average*) *Math* moyenne *f*; **the happy m.** le juste milieu.

meander [mɪ'ændər] *vi* (*of river*) faire des méandres.

means [miːnz] *n(pl)* (*method*) moyen(s) *m(pl)* (**to do, of doing** de faire); (*wealth*) moyens *mpl*; **by m. of** (*stick etc*) au moyen de; (*work, concentration*) à force de; **by all m.!** très certainement!; **by no m.** nullement; **independent** *or* **private m.** fortune *f* personnelle.

meant [ment] *see* **mean**[1].

meantime ['miːntaɪm] *adv & n* (**in the**) **m.** entre-temps. ◆**meanwhile** *adv* entre-temps.

measles ['miːz(ə)lz] *n* rougeole *f*.

measly ['miːzlɪ] *a* (*contemptible*) *Fam* minable.

measur/e ['meʒər] *n* mesure *f*; (*ruler*) règle *f*; **made to m.** fait sur mesure; − *vt* mesurer; (*strength etc*) *Fig* estimer, mesurer; (*adjust, adapt*) adapter (**to** à); **to m. up** mesurer; − *vi* **to m. up to** être à la hauteur de. ◆**—ed** *a* (*careful*) mesuré. ◆**—ement** *n* (*of chest, waist etc*) tour *m*; *pl* (*dimensions*) mesures *fpl*; **your hip m.** ton tour de hanches.

meat [miːt] *n* viande *f*; (*of crab, lobster etc*) chair *f*; *Fig* substance *f*; **m. diet** régime *m* carné. ◆**meaty** *a* (**-ier, -iest**) (*fleshy*) charnu; (*flavour*) de viande; *Fig* substantiel.

mechanic [mɪˈkænɪk] *n* mécanicien, -ienne *mf*. ◆**mechanical** *a* mécanique; (*reply etc*) *Fig* machinal. ◆**mechanics** *n* (*science*) mécanique *f*; *pl* (*workings*) mécanisme *m*. ◆**'mechanism** *n* mécanisme *m*. ◆**'mechanize** *vt* mécaniser.

medal ['med(ə)l] *n* médaille *f*. ◆**me-'dallion** *n* (*ornament, jewel*) médaillon *m*. ◆**medallist** *n* médaillé, -ée *mf*; **to be a gold/silver m.** *Sp* être médaille d'or/ d'argent.

meddle ['med(ə)l] *vi* (*interfere*) se mêler (**in** de); (*tamper*) toucher (**with** à). ◆**meddlesome** *a* qui se mêle de tout.

media ['miːdɪə] *npl* **1** **the (mass) m.** les médias *mpl*. **2** *see* **medium 2**.

mediaeval [medrˈiːv(ə)l] *a* médiéval.

median ['miːdɪən] *a* **m. strip** *Aut Am* bande *f* médiane.

mediate ['miːdɪeɪt] *vi* servir d'intermédiaire (**between** entre). ◆**medi'ation** *n* médiation *f*. ◆**mediator** *n* médiateur, -trice *mf*.

medical ['medɪk(ə)l] *a* médical; (*school, studies*) de médecine; (*student*) en médecine; − *n* (*in school, army*) visite *f* médicale; (*private*) examen *m* médical. ◆**medicated** *a* (*shampoo*) médical. ◆**medi'cation** *n* médicaments *mpl*. ◆**me'dicinal** *a* médicinal. ◆**medicine** *n* médecine *f*; (*substance*) médicament *m*; **m. cabinet, m. chest** pharmacie *f*.

medieval [medrˈiːv(ə)l] *a* médiéval.

mediocre [miːdrˈəʊkər] *a* médiocre. ◆**mediocrity** *n* médiocrité *f*.

meditate ['medɪteɪt] *vi* méditer (**on** sur). ◆**medi'tation** *n* méditation *f*. ◆**meditative** *a* méditatif.

Mediterranean [medɪtəˈreɪnɪən] *a* méditerranéen; − *n* **the M.** la Méditerranée.

medium ['miːdɪəm] **1** *a* (*average, middle*) moyen. **2** *n* (*pl* **media** ['miːdɪə]) *Phys* véhicule *m*; *Biol* milieu *m*; (*for conveying data or publicity*) support *m*; **through the m. of** par l'intermédiaire de; **the happy m.** le juste milieu. **3** *n* (*person*) médium *m*. ◆**m.-sized** *a* de moyen, de taille moyenne.

medley ['medlɪ] *n* mélange *m*; *Mus* pot-pourri *m*.

meek [miːk] *a* (**-er, -est**) doux.

meet [miːt] *vt* (*pt & pp* **met**) (*encounter*) rencontrer; (*see again, join*) retrouver; (*pass in street, road etc*) croiser; (*fetch*) (*aller or venir*) chercher; (*wait for*) attendre; (*debt, enemy, danger*) faire face à; (*need*) combler; (*be introduced to*) faire la connaissance de; **to arrange to m. s.o.** donner rendez-vous à qn; − *vi* (*of people, teams, rivers, looks*) se rencontrer; (*of people by arrangement*) se retrouver; (*be introduced*) se connaître; (*of society*) se réunir; (*of trains, vehicles*) se croiser; **to m. up with** rencontrer; (*by arrangement*) retrouver; **to m. up** se rencontrer; se retrouver; **to m. with** (*accident, problem*) avoir; (*loss, refusal*) essuyer; (*obstacle, difficulty*) rencontrer; **to m. with s.o.** *Am* rencontrer qn; retrouver qn; − *n Sp Am* réunion *f*; **to make a m. with** *Fam* donner rendez-vous à. ◆**—ing** *n* réunion *f*; (*large*) assemblée *f*; (*between two people*) rencontre *f*, (*prearranged*) rendez-vous *m inv*; **in a m.** en conférence.

megalomania [megələʊˈmeɪnɪə] *n* mégalomanie *f*. ◆**megalomaniac** *n* mégalomane *mf*.

megaphone ['megəfəʊn] *n* porte-voix *m inv*.

melancholy ['melənkəlɪ] *n* mélancolie *f*; − *a* mélancolique.

mellow ['meləʊ] *a* (**-er, -est**) (*fruit*) mûr; (*colour, voice, wine*) moelleux; (*character*) mûri par l'expérience; − *vi* (*of person*) s'adoucir.

melodrama ['melədrɑːmə] *n* mélodrame *m*. ◆**melodra'matic** *a* mélodramatique.

melody ['melədɪ] *n* mélodie *f*. ◆**me'lodic** *a* mélodique. ◆**me'lodious** *a* mélodieux.

melon ['melən] *n* (*fruit*) melon *m*.

melt [melt] *vi* fondre; **to m. into** (*merge*) *Fig* se fondre dans; − *vt* (faire) fondre; **to m. down** (*metal object*) fondre; **melting point** point *m* de fusion; **melting pot** *Fig* creuset *m*.

member ['membər] *n* membre *m*; **M. of Parliament** député *m*. ◆**membership** *n* adhésion *f* (**of** à); (*number*) nombre *m* de(s) membres; (*members*) membres *mpl*; **m. (fee)** cotisation *f*.

membrane ['membreɪn] n membrane f.
memento [mə'mentəʊ] n (pl -os or -oes) (object) souvenir m.
memo ['meməʊ] n (pl -os) note f; **m. pad** bloc-notes m. **◆memo'randum** n note f; Pol Com mémorandum m.
memoirs ['memwɑːz] npl (essays) mémoires mpl.
memory ['memərɪ] n mémoire f; (recollection) souvenir m; **to the** or **in m. of** à la mémoire de. **◆memorable** a mémorable. **◆me'morial** a (plaque etc) commémoratif; – n monument m, mémorial m. **◆memorize** vt apprendre par cœur.
men [men] see **man**. **◆menfolk** n Fam hommes mpl.
menac/e ['menɪs] n danger m; (nuisance) Fam plaie f; (threat) menace f; – vt menacer. **◆—ingly** adv (to say) d'un ton menaçant; (to do) d'une manière menaçante.
menagerie [mɪ'nædʒərɪ] n ménagerie f.
mend [mend] vt (repair) réparer; (clothes) raccommoder; **to m. one's ways** se corriger, s'amender; – n raccommodage m; **to be on the m.** (after illness) aller mieux.
menial ['miːnɪəl] a inférieur.
meningitis [menɪn'dʒaɪtɪs] n Med méningite f.
menopause ['menəpɔːz] n ménopause f.
menstruation [menstrʊ'eɪʃ(ə)n] n menstruation f.
mental ['ment(ə)l] a mental; (hospital) psychiatrique; (mad) Sl fou; **m. strain** tension f nerveuse. **◆men'tality** n mentalité f. **◆mentally** adv mentalement; **he's m. handicapped** c'est un handicapé mental; **she's m. ill** c'est une malade mentale.
mention ['menʃ(ə)n] vt mentionner, faire mention de; **not to m.** . . . . sans parler de . . . , sans compter . . . ; **don't m. it!** il n'y a pas de quoi!; **no savings/etc worth mentioning** pratiquement pas d'économies/etc; – n mention f.
mentor ['mentɔː] n (adviser) mentor m.
menu ['menjuː] n menu m.
mercantile ['mɜːkəntaɪl] a (activity etc) commercial; (ship) marchand; (nation) commerçant.
mercenary ['mɜːsɪnərɪ] a n mercenaire (m).
merchandise ['mɜːtʃəndaɪz] n (articles) marchandises fpl; (total stock) marchandise f.
merchant ['mɜːtʃ(ə)nt] n (trader) Fin négociant, -ante mf; **(retail) m.** commerçant m (en détail); **wine m.** négociant, -ante mf en vins; (shopkeeper) marchand m de

vins; – a (vessel, navy) marchand; (seaman) de la marine marchande; **m. bank** banque f de commerce.
mercury ['mɜːkjʊrɪ] n mercure m.
mercy ['mɜːsɪ] n pitié f; Rel miséricorde f; **to beg for m.** demander grâce; **at the m. of** à la merci de; **it's a m. that** . . . (stroke of luck) c'est une chance que . . . . **◆merciful** a miséricordieux. **◆mercifully** adv (fortunately) Fam heureusement. **◆merciless** a impitoyable.
mere [mɪər] a simple; (only) ne . . . que; **she's a m. child** ce n'est qu'une enfant; **it's a m. kilometre** ça ne fait qu'un kilomètre; **by m. chance** par pur hasard; **the m. sight of her** or **him** sa seule vue. **◆—ly** adv (tout) simplement.
merg/e [mɜːdʒ] vi (blend) se mêler (with à); (of roads) se (re)joindre; (of firms) Com fusionner; – vt (unify) Pol unifier; Com fusionner. **◆—er** n Com fusion f.
meridian [mə'rɪdɪən] n méridien m.
meringue [mə'ræŋ] n (cake) meringue f.
merit ['merɪt] n mérite m; **on its merits** (to consider sth etc) objectivement; – vt mériter.
mermaid ['mɜːmeɪd] n (woman) sirène f.
merry ['merɪ] a (-ier, -iest) gai; (drunk) Fam éméché. **◆m.-go-round** n (at funfair etc) manège m. **◆m.-making** n réjouissances fpl. **◆merrily** adv gaiement. **◆merriment** n gaieté f, rires mpl.
mesh [meʃ] n (of net etc) maille f; (fabric) tissu m à mailles; (of intrigue etc) Fig réseau m; (of circumstances) Fig engrenage m; **wire m.** grillage m.
mesmerize ['mezməraɪz] vt hypnotiser.
mess¹ [mes] **1** n (confusion) désordre m, pagaïe f; (muddle) gâchis m; (dirt) saleté f; **in a m.** en désordre; (trouble) Fam dans le pétrin; (pitiful state) dans un triste état; **to make a m. of** (spoil) gâcher. **2** vt **to m. s.o. about** (bother, treat badly) Fam déranger qn, embêter qn; **to m. up** (spoil) gâcher; (dirty) salir; (room) mettre en désordre; – vi **to m. about** (have fun, idle) s'amuser; (play the fool) faire l'idiot; **to m. about with** (fiddle with) s'amuser avec. **◆m.-up** n (disorder) Fam gâchis m. **◆messy** a (-ier, -iest) (untidy) en désordre; (dirty) sale; (confused) Fig embrouillé, confus.
mess² [mes] n Mil mess m inv.
message ['mesɪdʒ] n message m. **◆messenger** n messager, -ère mf; (in office, hotel) coursier, -ière mf.
Messiah [mɪ'saɪə] n Messie m.

Messrs ['mesəz] *npl* **M. Brown** Messieurs *or* MM Brown.

met [met] *see* meet.

metal ['met(ə)l] *n* métal *m*. ◆**me'tallic** *a* métallique; (*paint*) métallisé. ◆**metal-work** *n* (*objects*) ferronnerie *f*; (*study, craft*) travail *m* des métaux.

metamorphosis, *pl* **-oses** [metə'mɔɪfəsɪs, -əsiːz] *n* métamorphose *f*.

metaphor ['metəfər] *n* métaphore *f*. ◆**met-a'phorical** *a* métaphorique.

metaphysical [metə'fɪzɪk(ə)l] *a* métaphysique.

mete [miːt] *vt* **to m. out** (*justice*) rendre; (*punishment*) infliger.

meteor ['miːtɪər] *n* météore *m*. ◆**mete'oric** *a* **m. rise** *Fig* ascension *f* fulgurante. ◆**meteorite** *n* météorite *m*.

meteorological [miːtɪərə'lɒdʒɪk(ə)l] *a* météorologique. ◆**meteo'rology** *n* météorologie *f*.

meter ['miːtər] *n* (*device*) compteur *m*; (*parking*) **m.** parcmètre *m*; **m. maid** *Aut Fam* contractuelle *f*.

method ['meθəd] *n* méthode *f*. ◆**me'thodical** *a* méthodique.

Methodist ['meθədɪst] *a & n Rel* méthodiste (*mf*).

methylated ['meθɪleɪtɪd] *a* **m. spirit(s)** alcool *m* à brûler. ◆**meths** *n Fam* = methylated spirits.

meticulous [mɪ'tɪkjʊləs] *a* méticuleux. ◆**—ness** *n* soin *m* méticuleux.

metre ['miːtər] *n* mètre *m*. ◆**metric** ['metrɪk] *a* métrique.

metropolis [mə'trɒpəlɪs] *n* (*chief city*) métropole *f*. ◆**metro'politan** *a* métropolitain.

mettle ['met(ə)l] *n* courage *m*, fougue *f*.

mew [mjuː] *vi* (*of cat*) miauler.

mews [mjuːz] *n* (*street*) ruelle *f*; **m. flat** appartement *m* chic (*aménagé dans une ancienne écurie*).

Mexico ['meksɪkəʊ] *n* Mexique *m*. ◆**Mexi-can** *a & n* mexicain, -aine (*mf*).

mezzanine ['mezəniːn] *n* **m.** (*floor*) entresol *m*.

miaow [miː'aʊ] *vi* (*of cat*) miauler; — *n* miaulement *m*; — *int* miaou.

mice [maɪs] *see* mouse.

mickey ['mɪkɪ] *n* **to take the m. out of s.o.** *Sl* charrier qn.

micro- ['maɪkrəʊ] *pref* micro-.

microbe ['maɪkrəʊb] *n* microbe *m*.

microchip ['maɪkrəʊtʃɪp] *n* puce *f*.

microcosm ['maɪkrəʊkɒz(ə)m] *n* microcosme *m*.

microfilm ['maɪkrəʊfɪlm] *n* microfilm *m*.

microphone ['maɪkrəfəʊn] *n* microphone *m*.

microscope ['maɪkrəskəʊp] *n* microscope *m*. ◆**micro'scopic** *a* microscopique.

microwave ['maɪkrəʊweɪv] *n* micro-onde *f*; **m. oven** four *m* à micro-ondes.

mid [mɪd] *a* (**in**) **m.-June** (à) la mi-juin; (**in**) **m. morning** au milieu de la matinée; **in m. air** en plein ciel; **to be in one's m.-twenties** avoir environ vingt-cinq ans.

midday [mɪd'deɪ] *n* midi *m*; — *a* de midi.

middle ['mɪd(ə)l] *n* milieu *m*; (*waist*) *Fam* taille *f*; (**right**) **in the m. of** au (beau) milieu de; **in the m. of work** en plein travail; **in the m. of saying/working/etc** en train de dire/travailler/etc; — *a* (*central*) du milieu; (*class, ear, quality*) moyen; (*name*) deuxième. ◆**m.-'aged** *a* d'un certain âge. ◆**m.-'class** *a* bourgeois. ◆**m.-of-the-'road** *a* (*politics, views*) modéré; (*music, tastes*) sage.

middling ['mɪdlɪŋ] *a* moyen, passable.

midge [mɪdʒ] *n* (*fly*) moucheron *m*.

midget ['mɪdʒɪt] *n* nain *m*, naine *f*; — *a* minuscule.

Midlands ['mɪdləndz] *npl* **the M.** les comtés *mpl* du centre de l'Angleterre.

midnight ['mɪdnaɪt] *n* minuit *f*.

midriff ['mɪdrɪf] *n Anat* diaphragme *m*; (*belly*) *Fam* ventre *m*.

midst [mɪdst] *n* **in the m. of** (*middle*) au milieu de; **in our/their m.** parmi nous/eux.

midsummer [mɪd'sʌmər] *n* milieu *m* de l'été; (*solstice*) solstice *m* d'été. ◆**mid-winter** *n* milieu *m* de l'hiver; solstice *m* d'hiver.

midterm ['mɪdtɜːm] *a* **m. holidays** *Sch* petites vacances *fpl*.

midway [mɪd'weɪ] *a & adv* à mi-chemin.

midweek [mɪd'wiːk] *n* milieu *m* de la semaine.

midwife ['mɪdwaɪf] *n* (*pl* **-wives**) sage-femme *f*.

might [maɪt] **1** *see* may. **2** *n* (*strength*) force *f*. ◆**mighty** *a* (**-ier, -iest**) puissant; (*ocean*) vaste; (*very great*) *Fam* sacré; — *adv* (*very*) *Fam* rudement.

migraine ['miːgreɪn, 'maɪgreɪn] *n Med* migraine *f*.

migrate [maɪ'greɪt] *vi* émigrer. ◆**'migrant** *a & n* **m. (worker)** migrant, -ante (*mf*). ◆**migration** *n* migration *f*.

mike [maɪk] *n Fam* micro *m*.

mild [maɪld] *a* (**-er, -est**) (*person, weather, taste etc*) doux; (*beer, punishment*) léger; (*medicine, illness*) bénin; ◆**—ly** *adv* doucement; *(slightly)* légèrement; **to put it m.** pour ne pas dire plus. ◆**—ness** *n* douceur *f*; légèreté *f*; caractère *m* bénin.

mildew ['mɪldjuː] *n (on cheese etc)* moisissure *f*.

mile [maɪl] *n* mile *m*, mille *m* (= *1,6 km)*; *pl (loosely)* = kilomètres *mpl*; **to walk for miles** marcher pendant des kilomètres; **miles better** *(much)* Fam bien mieux. ◆**mileage** *n* = kilométrage *m*; **m. (per gallon)** = consommation *f* aux cent kilomètres. ◆**milestone** *n* = borne *f* kilométrique; *Fig* jalon *m*.

militant ['mɪlɪtənt] *a & n* militant, -ante *(mf)*. ◆**military** *a* militaire; — *n* **the m.** *(soldiers)* les militaires *mpl*; *(army)* l'armée *f*. ◆**militate** *vi (of arguments etc)* militer **(in favour of** pour).

militia [mə'lɪʃə] *n* milice *f*. ◆**militiaman** *n (pl -men)* milicien *m*.

milk [mɪlk] *n* lait *m*; **evaporated m.** lait *m* concentré; — *a (chocolate)* au lait; *(bottle, can)* à lait; *(diet)* lacté; *(produce)* laitier; **m. float** voiture *f* de laitier; **m. shake** milk-shake *m*; — *vt (cow)* traire; *(extract)* *Fig* soutirer **(s.o. of sth** qch à qn); *(exploit)* *Fig* exploiter. ◆**—ing** *n* traite *f*. ◆**milkman** *n (pl -men)* laitier *m*. ◆**milky** *a (-ier, -iest) (diet)* lacté; *(coffee, tea)* au lait; *(colour)* laiteux; **the M. Way** la Voie lactée.

mill [mɪl] **1** *n* moulin *m*; *(factory)* usine *f*; **cotton m.** filature *f* de coton; **paper m.** papeterie *f*; — *vt (grind)* moudre. **2** *vi* **to m. around** *(of crowd)* grouiller. ◆**miller** *n* meunier, -ière *mf*. ◆**millstone** *n (burden)* boulet *m* **(round one's neck** qu'on traîne).

millennium, *pl* **-nia** [mɪ'lenɪəm, -nɪə] *n* millénaire *m*.

millet ['mɪlɪt] *n Bot* millet *m*.

milli- [mɪlɪ] *pref* milli-.

millimetre ['mɪlɪmiːtər] *n* millimètre *m*.

million ['mɪljən] *n* million *m*; **a m. men/etc** un million d'hommes/*etc*; **two m.** deux millions. ◆**millio'naire** *n* millionnaire *mf*. ◆**millionth** *a & n* millionième *(mf)*.

mime [maɪm] *n (actor)* mime *mf*; *(art)* mime *m*; — *vti* mimer.

mimeograph® ['mɪmɪəgræf] *vt* polycopier.

mimic ['mɪmɪk] *vt (-ck-)* imiter; — *n* imitateur, -trice *mf*. ◆**mimicking** *n*, ◆**mimicry** *n* imitation *f*.

mimosa [mɪ'məʊzə] *n Bot* mimosa *m*.

minaret [mɪnə'ret] *n (of mosque)* minaret *m*.

mince [mɪns] *n (meat)* hachis *m* (de viande); *Am* = **mincemeat;** — *vt* hacher; **not to m. matters** *or* **one's words** ne pas mâcher ses

mots. ◆**mincemeat** *n (dried fruit)* mélange *m* de fruits secs. ◆**mincer** *n (machine)* hachoir *m*.

mind [maɪnd] **1** *n* esprit *m*; *(sanity)* raison *f*; *(memory)* mémoire *f*; *(opinion)* avis *m*, idée *f*; *(thought)* pensée *f*; *(head)* tête *f*; **to change one's m.** changer d'avis; **to my m.** à mon avis; **in two minds** *(undecided)* irrésolu; **to make up one's m.** se décider; **to be on s.o.'s m.** *(worry)* préoccuper qn; **out of one's m.** *(mad)* fou; **to bring to m.** *(recall)* rappeler; **to bear** *or* **keep in m.** *(remember)* se souvenir de; **to have in m.** *(person, plan)* avoir en vue; **to have a good m. to do** avoir bien envie de faire. **2** *vti (heed)* faire attention à; *(look after)* garder, s'occuper de; *(noise, dirt etc)* être gêné par; *(one's language)* surveiller; **m. you don't fall** *(beware)* prends garde de ne pas tomber; **m. you do it** n'oublie pas de le faire; **do you m. if?** *(I smoke etc)* ça vous gêne si?; *(I leave, help etc)* ça ne vous fait rien si?; **I don't m. the sun** le soleil ne me gêne pas, je ne suis pas gêné par le soleil; **I don't m.** *(care)* ça m'est égal; **I wouldn't m. a cup of tea** *(would like)* j'aimerais bien une tasse de thé; **I m. that . . .** ça m'ennuie *or* me gêne que . . . ; **never m.!** *(it doesn't matter)* ça ne fait rien!, tant pis!; *(don't worry)* ne vous en faites pas!; **m. (out)!** *(watch out)* attention!; **m. you . . .** remarquez (que) . . . ; **m. your own business!, never you m.!** mêlez-vous de ce qui vous regarde! ◆**—ed** *suffix* **fair-m.** *a* impartial; **like-m.** *a* de même opinion. ◆**—er** *n (for children)* gardien, -ienne *mf*, *(nurse)* nourrice *f*; *(bodyguard)* Fam gorille *m*. ◆**mind-boggling** *a* stupéfiant, qui confond l'imagination. ◆**mindful** *a* **m. of sth/doing** attentif à qch/à faire. ◆**mindless** *a* stupide.

mine¹ [maɪn] *poss pron* le mien, la mienne, *pl* les mien(ne)s; **this hat is m.** ce chapeau est à moi *or* est le mien; **a friend of m.** un ami à moi.

min/e² [maɪn] **1** *n (for coal, gold etc) & Fig* mine *f*; — *vt* **to m. (for)** *(coal etc)* extraire. **2** *n (explosive)* mine *f*; — *vt (beach, bridge etc)* miner. ◆**—ing** *n* exploitation *f* minière; — *a (industry)* minier. ◆**—er** *n* mineur *m*.

mineral ['mɪnərəl] *a & n* minéral *(m)*.

mingle ['mɪŋɡ(ə)l] *vi* se mêler **(with** à); **to m. with** *(socially)* fréquenter.

mingy ['mɪndʒɪ] *a (-ier, -iest) (mean)* Fam radin.

mini- ['mɪnɪ] *pref* mini-.

miniature ['mɪnɪtʃər] *n* miniature *f*; — *a (train etc)* miniature *inv*; *(tiny)* minuscule.

minibus ['mɪnɪbʌs] *n* minibus *m*. ◆**minicab** *n* (radio-)taxi *m*.

minim ['mɪnɪm] *n Mus* blanche *f*.

minimum ['mɪnɪməm] *n* (*pl* **-ima** [-ɪmə] *or* **-ums**) minimum *m*; – *a* minimum (*f inv*), minimal. ◆**minimal** *a* minimal. ◆**minimize** *vt* minimiser.

minister ['mɪnɪstər] *n Pol Rel* ministre *m*. ◆**mini'sterial** *a* ministériel. ◆**ministry** *n* ministère *m*.

mink [mɪŋk] *n* (*animal, fur*) vison *m*.

minor ['maɪnər] *a* (*small*) *Jur Mus* mineur; (*detail, operation*) petit; – *n Jur* mineur, -eure *mf*.

Minorca [mɪ'nɔːkə] *n* Minorque *f*.

minority [maɪ'nɒrɪtɪ] *n* minorité *f*; **in the** *or* **a m.** en minorité, minoritaire; – *a* minoritaire.

mint [mɪnt] **1** *n* (*place*) Hôtel *m* de la Monnaie; **a m.** (**of money**) *Fig* une petite fortune; – *vt* (*money*) frapper; – *a* (*stamp*) neuf; **in m. condition** à l'état neuf. **2** *n Bot Culin* menthe *f*; (*sweet*) pastille *f* de menthe; – *a* à la menthe.

minus ['maɪnəs] *prep Math* moins; (*without*) *Fam* sans; **it's m. ten** (**degrees**) il fait moins dix (degrés); – *n* **m.** (**sign**) (signe *m*) moins *m*.

minute¹ ['mɪnɪt] **1** *n* minute *f*; **this** (**very**) **m.** (*now*) à la minute; **any m.** (**now**) d'une minute à l'autre; **m. hand** (*of clock*) grande aiguille *f*. **2** *npl* (*of meeting*) procès-verbal *m*.

minute² [maɪ'njuːt] *a* (*tiny*) minuscule; (*careful, exact*) minutieux.

minx [mɪŋks] *n* (*girl*) *Pej* diablesse *f*, chipie *f*.

miracle ['mɪrək(ə)l] *n* miracle *m*. ◆**mi'raculous** *a* miraculeux.

mirage ['mɪrɑːʒ] *n* mirage *m*.

mire [maɪər] *n Lit* fange *f*.

mirror ['mɪrər] *n* miroir *m*, glace *f*; *Fig* miroir *m*; (**rear view**) **m.** *Aut* rétroviseur *m*; – *vt* refléter.

mirth [mɜːθ] *n Lit* gaieté *f*, hilarité *f*.

misadventure [mɪsəd'ventʃər] *n* mésaventure *f*.

misanthropist [mɪ'zænθrəpɪst] *n* misanthrope *mf*.

misapprehend [mɪsæprɪ'hend] *vt* mal comprendre. ◆**misapprehension** *n* malentendu *m*.

misappropriate [mɪsə'prəuprɪeɪt] *vt* (*money*) détourner.

misbehave [mɪsbɪ'heɪv] *vi* se conduire mal; (*of child*) faire des sottises.

miscalculate [mɪs'kælkjʊleɪt] *vt* mal calculer; – *vi Fig* se tromper. ◆**miscalcu-'lation** *n* erreur *f* de calcul.

miscarriage [mɪs'kærɪdʒ] *n* **to have a m.** *Med* faire une fausse couche; **m. of justice** erreur *f* judiciaire. ◆**miscarry** *vi Med* faire une fausse couche; (*of plan*) *Fig* échouer.

miscellaneous [mɪsɪ'leɪnɪəs] *a* divers.

mischief ['mɪstʃɪf] *n* espièglerie *f*; (*maliciousness*) méchanceté *f*; **to get into m.** faire des bêtises; **full of m. = mischievous**; **to make m. for** (*trouble*) créer des ennuis à; **to do s.o. a m.** (*harm*) faire mal à qn; **a little m.** (*child*) un petit démon. ◆**mischievous** *a* (*playful, naughty*) espiègle, malicieux; (*malicious*) méchant.

misconception [mɪskən'sepʃ(ə)n] *n* idée *f* fausse.

misconduct [mɪs'kɒndʌkt] *n* mauvaise conduite *f*; *Com* mauvaise gestion *f*.

misconstrue [mɪskən'struː] *vt* mal interpréter.

misdeed [mɪs'diːd] *n* méfait *m*.

misdemeanor [mɪsdɪ'miːnər] *n Jur* délit *m*.

misdirect [mɪsdɪ'rekt] *vt* (*letter*) mal adresser; (*energies*) mal diriger; (*person*) mal renseigner.

miser ['maɪzər] *n* avare *mf*. ◆**—ly** *a* avare.

misery ['mɪzərɪ] *n* (*suffering*) souffrances *fpl*; (*sadness*) tristesse *f*; (*sad person*) *Fam* grincheux, -euse *mf*; *pl* (*troubles*) misères *fpl*; **his life is a m.** il est malheureux. ◆**miserable** *a* (*wretched*) misérable; (*unhappy*) malheureux; (*awful*) affreux; (*derisory*) dérisoire. ◆**miserably** *adv* misérablement; (*to fail*) lamentablement.

misfire [mɪs'faɪər] *vi* (*of engine*) avoir des ratés; (*of plan*) *Fig* rater.

misfit ['mɪsfɪt] *n Pej* inadapté, -ée *mf*.

misfortune [mɪs'fɔːtʃuːn] *n* malheur *m*, infortune *f*.

misgivings [mɪs'gɪvɪŋz] *npl* (*doubts*) doutes *mpl*; (*fears*) craintes *fpl*.

misguided [mɪs'gaɪdɪd] *a* (*action etc*) imprudent; **to be m.** (*of person*) se tromper.

mishandle [mɪs'hænd(ə)l] *vt* (*affair, situation*) traiter avec maladresse; (*person*) s'y prendre mal avec.

mishap ['mɪshæp] *n* (*accident*) mésaventure *f*; (*hitch*) contretemps *m*.

misinform [mɪsɪn'fɔːm] *vt* mal renseigner.

misinterpret [mɪsɪn'tɜːprɪt] *vt* mal interpréter.

misjudge [mɪs'dʒʌdʒ] *vt* (*person, distance etc*) mal juger.

mislay [mɪs'leɪ] *vt* (*pt & pp* **mislaid**) égarer.

mislead [mɪs'liːd] *vt* (*pt & pp* **misled**) tromper. ◆**—ing** *a* trompeur.

mismanage [mɪs'mænɪdʒ] *vt* mal administrer. ◆—**ment** *n* mauvaise administration *f*.

misnomer [mɪs'nəʊmər] *n* (*name*) nom *m* or terme *m* impropre.

misogynist [mɪ'sɒdʒɪnɪst] *n* misogyne *mf*.

misplac/e [mɪs'pleɪs] *vt* (*trust etc*) mal placer; (*lose*) égarer. ◆—**ed** *a* (*remark etc*) déplacé.

misprint ['mɪsprɪnt] *n* faute *f* d'impression, coquille *f*.

mispronounce [mɪsprə'naʊns] *vt* mal prononcer.

misquote [mɪs'kwəʊt] *vt* citer inexactement.

misrepresent [mɪsreprɪ'zent] *vt* présenter sous un faux jour.

miss[1] [mɪs] *vt* (*train, target, opportunity etc*) manquer, rater; (*not see*) ne pas voir; (*not understand*) ne pas comprendre; (*one's youth, deceased person etc*) regretter; (*sth just lost*) remarquer l'absence de; **he misses Paris/her** Paris/elle lui manque; **I m.** you tu me manques; **don't m. seeing this play** (*don't fail to*) ne manque pas de voir cette pièce; **to m. out** (*omit*) sauter; – *vi* manquer, rater; **to m. out** (*lose a chance*) rater l'occasion; **to m. out on** (*opportunity etc*) rater, laisser passer; – *n* coup *m* manqué; **that was** *or* **we had a near m.** on l'a échappé belle; **I'll give it a m.** *Fam* (*not go*) je n'y irai pas; (*not take or drink or eat*) je n'en prendrai pas. ◆—**ing** *a* (*absent*) absent; (*in war, after disaster*) disparu; (*object*) manquant; **there are two cups/students m.** il manque deux tasses/deux étudiants.

miss[2] [mɪs] *n* mademoiselle *f*; **Miss Brown** Mademoiselle *or* Mlle Brown.

misshapen [mɪs'ʃeɪp(ə)n] *a* difforme.

missile ['mɪsaɪl, *Am* 'mɪs(ə)l] *n* (*rocket*) *Mil* missile *m*; (*object thrown*) projectile *m*.

mission ['mɪʃ(ə)n] *n* mission *f*. ◆**missionary** *n* missionnaire *m*.

missive ['mɪsɪv] *n* (*letter*) missive *f*.

misspell [mɪs'spel] *vt* (*pt & pp* -**ed** *or* **misspelt**) mal écrire.

mist [mɪst] *n* (*fog*) brume *f*; (*on glass*) buée *f*; – *vi* **to m. over** *or* **up** s'embuer.

mistake [mɪ'steɪk] *n* erreur *f*, faute *f*; **to make a m.** se tromper, faire (une) erreur; **by m.** par erreur; – *vt* (*pt* **mistook**, *pp* **mistaken**) (*meaning, intention etc*) se tromper sur; **to m. the date/place/etc** se tromper de date/de lieu/*etc*; **you can't m.**, **there's no mistaking** (*his face, my car etc*) il est impossible de ne pas reconnaître; **to m.**

s.o./sth for prendre qn/qch pour. ◆**mistaken** *a* (*idea etc*) erroné; **to be m.** se tromper. ◆**mistakenly** *adv* par erreur.

mister ['mɪstər] *n Fam* monsieur *m*.

mistletoe ['mɪs(ə)ltəʊ] *n Bot* gui *m*.

mistreat [mɪs'triːt] *vt* maltraiter.

mistress ['mɪstrɪs] *n* maîtresse *f*; (*in secondary school*) professeur *m*.

mistrust [mɪs'trʌst] *n* méfiance *f*; – *vt* se méfier de. ◆**mistrustful** *a* méfiant.

misty ['mɪstɪ] *a* (-**ier**, -**iest**) (*foggy*) brumeux; (*glass*) embué.

misunderstand [mɪsʌndə'stænd] *vt* (*pt & pp* -**stood**) mal comprendre. ◆**misunderstanding** *n* (*disagreement*) malentendu *m*; (*mistake*) erreur *f*. ◆**misunderstood** *a* (*person*) incompris.

misuse [mɪs'juːz] *vt* (*word, tool*) mal employer; (*power etc*) abuser de; – [mɪs'juːs] *n* (*of word*) emploi *m* abusif; (*of tool*) usage *m* abusif; (*of power etc*) abus *m*.

mite [maɪt] *n* **1** (*insect*) mite *f*. **2** (*poor*) *m*. (*child*) (*pauvre*) petit, -ite *mf*. **3** **a m.** (*somewhat*) *Fam* un petit peu.

mitigate ['mɪtɪgeɪt] *vt* atténuer.

mitt(en) [mɪt, 'mɪt(ə)n] *n* (*glove*) moufle *f*.

mix [mɪks] *vt* mélanger, mêler; (*cement, cake*) préparer; (*salad*) remuer; **to m. up** mélanger; (*perplex*) embrouiller (*qn*); (*confuse, mistake*) confondre (**with** avec); **to be mixed up with s.o.** (*involved*) être mêlé aux affaires de qn; **to m. up in** (*involve*) mêler à; – *vi* se mêler; (*of colours*) s'allier; **to m. with** (*socially*) fréquenter; **she doesn't m. (in)** elle n'est pas sociable; – *n* (*mixture*) mélange *m*. ◆—**ed** *a* (*school, marriage*) mixte; (*society*) mêlé; (*feelings*) mitigés, mêlés; (*results*) divers; (*nuts, chocolates etc*) assortis; **to be (all) m. up** (*of person*) être désorienté; (*of facts, account etc*) être embrouillé. ◆—**ing** *n* mélange *m*. ◆—**er** *n Culin El* mixe(u)r *m*; (*for mortar*) *Tech* malaxeur *m*; **to be a good m.** (*of person*) être sociable. ◆**mixture** *n* mélange *m*; (*for cough*) sirop *m*. ◆**mix-up** *n Fam* confusion *f*.

mm *abbr* (*millimetre*) mm.

moan [məʊn] *vi* (*groan*) gémir; (*complain*) se plaindre (**to** à, **about** de, **that** que); – *n* gémissement *m*; plainte *f*.

moat [məʊt] *n* douve(s) *f(pl)*.

mob [mɒb] *n* (*crowd*) cohue *f*, foule *f*; (*gang*) bande *f*; **the m.** (*masses*) la populace; (*Mafia*) *Am Sl* la mafia; – *vt* (-**bb**-) assiéger. ◆**mobster** *n Am Sl* gangster *m*.

mobile ['məʊbaɪl, *Am* 'məʊb(ə)l] *a* mobile; (*having a car etc*) *Fam* motorisé; **m. home**

mobil-home m; **m. library** bibliobus m; − n (Am ['məubiːl]) (ornament) mobile m.
◆**mo'bility** n mobilité f. ◆**mobili'zation** n mobilisation f. ◆**mobilize** vti mobiliser.

moccasin ['mɒkəsɪn] n (shoe) mocassin m.

mocha ['məukə] n (coffee) moka m.

mock [mɒk] **1** vt se moquer de; (mimic) singer; − vi se moquer (**at** de). **2** a (false) simulé; (exam) blanc. ◆**—ing** n moquerie f; − a moqueur. ◆**mockery** n (act) moquerie f; (parody) parodie f; **to make a m. of** tourner en ridicule.

mock-up ['mɒkʌp] n (model) maquette f.

mod cons [mɒd'kɒnz] abbr Fam = **modern conveniences**.

mode [məud] n (manner, way) mode m; (fashion, vogue) mode f.

model ['mɒd(ə)l] n (example, person etc) modèle m; (fashion) **m.** mannequin m; (scale) **m.** modèle m (réduit); − a (behaviour, factory etc) modèle; (car, plane) modèle réduit inv; **m. railway** train n miniature; − vt modeler (**on** sur); (hats) présenter (les modèles de); − vi (for fashion) être mannequin; (pose for artist) poser. ◆**modelling** n (of statues etc) modelage m.

moderate[1] ['mɒdərət] a modéré; (in speech) mesuré; (result) passable; − n Pol modéré, -ée mf. ◆**—ly** adv (in moderation) modérément; (averagely) moyennement.

moderate[2] ['mɒdəreɪt] vt (diminish, tone down) modérer. ◆**mode'ration** n modération f; **in m.** avec modération.

modern ['mɒd(ə)n] a moderne; **m. languages** langues fpl vivantes; **m. conveniences** tout le confort moderne.
◆**modernism** n modernisme m. ◆**moderni'zation** n modernisation f. ◆**modernize** vt moderniser.

modest ['mɒdɪst] a modeste. ◆**modesty** n (quality) modestie f; (moderation) modération f; (of salary etc) modicité f.

modicum ['mɒdɪkəm] n **a m. of** un soupçon de, un petit peu de.

modify ['mɒdɪfaɪ] vt (alter) modifier; (tone down) modérer. ◆**modifi'cation** n modification f.

modulate ['mɒdjuleɪt] vt moduler. ◆**modu'lation** n modulation f.

module ['mɒdjuːl] n module m.

mogul ['məug(ə)l] n magnat m, manitou m.

mohair ['məuheər] n mohair m.

moist [mɔɪst] a (-er, -est) humide; (clammy, sticky) moite. ◆**moisten** vt humecter.
◆**moisture** n humidité f; (on glass) buée f.

◆**moisturiz/e** vt (skin) hydrater. ◆**—er** n (cream) crème f hydratante.

molar ['məulər] n (tooth) molaire f.

molasses [mə'læsɪz] n (treacle) Am mélasse f.

mold [məuld] Am = **mould**.

mole [məul] n **1** (on skin) grain m de beauté. **2** (animal, spy) taupe f.

molecule ['mɒlɪkjuːl] n molécule f.

molest [mə'lest] vt (annoy) importuner; (child, woman) Jur attenter à la pudeur de.

mollusc ['mɒləsk] n mollusque m.

mollycoddle ['mɒlɪkɒd(ə)l] vt dorloter.

molt [məult] Am = **moult**.

molten ['məult(ə)n] a (metal) en fusion.

mom [mɒm] n Am Fam maman f.

moment ['məumənt] n moment m, instant m; **this (very) m.** (now) à l'instant; **the m. she leaves** dès qu'elle partira; **any m.** (now) d'un moment or d'un instant à l'autre.
◆**momentarily** (Am [məumən'terɪlɪ]) adv (temporarily) momentanément; (soon) Am tout à l'heure. ◆**momentary** a momentané.

momentous [məu'mentəs] a important.

momentum [məu'mentəm] n (speed) élan m; **to gather** or **gain m.** (of ideas etc) Fig gagner du terrain.

mommy ['mɒmɪ] n Am Fam maman f.

Monaco ['mɒnəkəu] n Monaco f.

monarch ['mɒnək] n monarque m. ◆**monarchy** n monarchie f.

monastery ['mɒnəst(ə)rɪ] n monastère m.

Monday ['mʌndɪ] n lundi m.

monetary ['mʌnɪt(ə)rɪ] a monétaire.

money ['mʌnɪ] n argent m; **paper m.** papier-monnaie m, billets mpl; **to get one's m.'s worth** en avoir pour son argent; **he gets** or **earns good m.** il gagne bien (sa vie); **to be in the m.** Fam rouler sur l'or; **m. order** mandat m. ◆**moneybags** n Pej Fam richard, -arde mf. ◆**moneybox** n tirelire f.
◆**moneychanger** n changeur m.
◆**moneylender** n prêteur, -euse mf sur gages. ◆**moneymaking** a lucratif.
◆**money-spinner** n (source of wealth) Fam mine f d'or.

mongol ['mɒŋg(ə)l] n & a Med mongolien, -ienne (mf).

mongrel ['mʌŋgrəl] n (dog) bâtard m.

monitor ['mɒnɪtər] **1** n (pupil) chef m de classe. **2** n (screen) Tech moniteur m. **3** vt (a broadcast) Rad écouter; (check) Fig contrôler.

monk [mʌŋk] n moine m, religieux m.

monkey ['mʌŋkɪ] n singe m; **little m.** (child) Fam polisson, -onne mf; **m. business** Fam singeries *fpl*; – *vi* to m. about *Fam* faire l'idiot.

mono ['mɒnəʊ] *a* (*record etc*) mono *inv*.

mono- ['mɒnəʊ] *pref* mono-.

monocle ['mɒnək(ə)l] *n* monocle *m*.

monogram ['mɒnəgræm] *n* monogramme *m*.

monologue ['mɒnəlɒg] *n* monologue *m*.

monopoly [mə'nɒpəlɪ] *n* monopole *m*. ◆**monopolize** *vt* monopoliser.

monosyllable ['mɒnəsɪləb(ə)l] *n* monosyllabe *m*. ◆**monosy'llabic** *a* monosyllabique.

monotone ['mɒnətəʊn] *n* in a m. sur un ton monocorde.

monotony [mə'nɒtənɪ] *n* monotonie *f*. ◆**monotonous** *a* monotone.

monsoon [mɒn'suːn] *n* (*wind, rain*) mousson *f*.

monster ['mɒnstər] *n* monstre *m*. ◆**mon'strosity** *n* (*horror*) monstruosité *f*. ◆**monstrous** *a* (*abominable, enormous*) monstrueux.

month [mʌnθ] *n* mois *m*. ◆**monthly** *a* mensuel; m. payment mensualité *f*; – *n* (*periodical*) mensuel *m*; – *adv* (*every month*) mensuellement.

Montreal [mɒntrɪ'ɔːl] *n* Montréal *m or f*.

monument ['mɒnjumənt] *n* monument *m*. ◆**monu'mental** *a* monumental; m. mason marbrier *m*.

moo [muː] *vi* meugler; – *n* meuglement *m*.

mooch [muːtʃ] **1** *vi* to m. around *Fam* flâner. **2** *vt* to m. sth off s.o. (*cadge*) *Am Sl* taper qch à qn.

mood [muːd] *n* (*of person*) humeur *f*; (*of country*) état *m* d'esprit; *Gram* mode *m*; in a good/bad m. de bonne/mauvaise humeur; to be in the m. to do *or* for doing être d'humeur à faire, avoir envie de faire. ◆**moody** *a* (**-ier, -iest**) (*changeable*) d'humeur changeante; (*bad-tempered*) de mauvaise humeur.

moon [muːn] *n* lune *f*; once in a blue m. (*rarely*) *Fam* tous les trente-six du mois; over the m. (*delighted*) *Fam* ravi (about de). ◆**moonlight 1** *n* clair *m* de lune. **2** *vi Fam* travailler au noir. ◆**moonshine** *n* (*talk*) *Fam* balivernes *fpl*.

moor [mʊər] **1** *vt Nau* amarrer; – *vi* mouiller. **2** *n* (*open land*) lande *f*. ◆**—ings** *npl Nau* (*ropes etc*) amarres *fpl*; (*place*) mouillage *m*.

moose [muːs] *n inv* (*animal*) orignac *m*, élan *m*.

moot [muːt] **1** *a* (*point*) discutable. **2** *vt* (*question*) soulever, suggérer.

mop [mɒp] **1** *n* balai *m* (à laver), balai *m* éponge; dish m. lavette *f*; m. of hair tignasse *f*. **2** *vt* (**-pp-**) to m. (up) (*wipe*) essuyer; to m. one's brow s'essuyer le front.

mope [məʊp] *vi* to m. (about) être déprimé, avoir le cafard.

moped ['məʊped] *n* cyclomoteur *m*, mobylette® *f*.

moral ['mɒrəl] *a* moral; – *n* (*of story etc*) morale *f*, *pl* (*standards*) moralité *f*, morale *f*. ◆**morale** [mə'rɑːl, *Am* mə'ræl] *n* moral *m*. ◆**moralist** *n* moraliste *mf*. ◆**mo'rality** *n* (*morals*) moralité *f*. ◆**moralize** *vi* moraliser. ◆**morally** *adv* moralement.

morass [mə'ræs] *n* (*land*) marais *m*; (*mess*) *Fig* bourbier *m*.

moratorium [mɒrə'tɔːrɪəm] *n* moratoire *m*.

morbid ['mɔːbɪd] *a* morbide.

more [mɔːr] *a & n* plus (de) (than que); (*other*) d'autres; m. cars/*etc* plus de voitures/*etc*; he has m. (than you) il en a plus (que toi); a few m. months encore quelques mois, quelques mois de plus; (some) m. tea/*etc* encore du thé/*etc*; (some) m. details d'autres détails; m. than a kilo/ten/*etc* (*with quantity, number*) plus d'un kilo/de dix/*etc*; – *adv* (*tired, rapidly etc*) plus (than que); m. and m. de plus en plus; m. or less plus ou moins; the m. he shouts the m. hoarse he gets plus il crie plus il s'enroue; she hasn't any m. elle n'en a plus. ◆**mo'reover** *adv* de plus, d'ailleurs.

moreish ['mɔːrɪʃ] *a Fam* qui a un goût de revenez-y.

mores ['mɔːreɪz] *npl* mœurs *fpl*.

morgue [mɔːg] *n* (*mortuary*) morgue *f*.

moribund ['mɒrɪbʌnd] *a* moribond.

morning ['mɔːnɪŋ] *n* matin *m*; (*duration of morning*) matinée *f*; in the m. (*every morning*) le matin; (*during the morning*) pendant la matinée; (*tomorrow*) demain matin; at seven in the m. à sept heures du matin; every Tuesday m. tous les mardis matin; in the early m. au petit matin; – *a* du matin, matinal. ◆**mornings** *adv Am* le matin.

Morocco [mə'rɒkəʊ] *n* Maroc *m*. ◆**Moroccan** *a & n* marocain, -aine (*mf*).

moron ['mɔːrɒn] *n* crétin, -ine *mf*.

morose [mə'rəʊs] *a* morose.

morphine ['mɔːfiːn] *n* morphine *f*.

Morse [mɔːs] *n & a* M. (code) morse *m*.

morsel ['mɔːs(ə)l] *n* (*of food*) petite bouchée *f*.

mortal ['mɔːt(ə)l] *a & n* mortel, -elle (*mf*). ◆**mor'tality** *n* (*death rate*) mortalité *f*.

mortar ['mɔːtər] *n* mortier *m*.

mortgage ['mɔːgɪdʒ] n prêt-logement m; − vt (house, future) hypothéquer.

mortician [mɔːˈtɪʃ(ə)n] n Am entrepreneur m de pompes funèbres.

mortify ['mɔːtɪfaɪ] vt mortifier.

mortuary ['mɔːtʃʊərɪ] n morgue f.

mosaic [məʊˈzeɪk] n mosaïque f.

Moscow ['mɒskəʊ, Am 'mɒskaʊ] n Moscou m or f.

Moses ['məʊzɪz] a M. basket couffin m.

Moslem ['mɒzlɪm] a & n musulman, -ane (mf).

mosque [mɒsk] n mosquée f.

mosquito [mɒˈskiːtəʊ] n (pl -oes) moustique m; **m. net** moustiquaire f.

moss [mɒs] n Bot mousse f. ◆**mossy** a moussu.

most [məʊst] a & n **the m.** (greatest in amount etc) le plus (de); **I have (the) m.** j'ai le plus de livres; **I have (the) m.** j'en ai le plus; **m. (of the) books**/etc la plupart des livres/etc; **m. of the cake**/etc la plus grande partie du gâteau/etc; **m. of them** la plupart d'entre eux; **m. of it** la plus grande partie; **at (the very) m.** tout au plus; **to make the m. of** profiter (au maximum) de; − adv (le) plus; (very) fort, très; **the m. beautiful** le plus beau, la plus belle (**in, of** de); **to talk (the) m.** parler le plus; **m. of all** (especially) surtout. ◆**−ly** adv surtout, pour la plupart.

motel [məʊˈtel] n motel m.

moth [mɒθ] n papillon m de nuit; (clothes) m. mite f. ◆**m.-eaten** a mité. ◆**mothball** n boule f de naphtaline.

mother ['mʌðər] n mère f; **M.'s Day** la fête des Mères; **m. tongue** langue f maternelle; − vt (care for) materner. ◆**motherhood** n maternité f. ◆**motherly** a maternel.

mother-in-law ['mʌðərɪnlɔː] n (pl mothers-in-law) belle-mère f. ◆**m.-of-pearl** n (substance) nacre f. ◆**m.-to-'be** n (pl mothers-to-be) future mère f.

motion ['məʊʃ(ə)n] n mouvement m; Pol motion f; **m. picture** film m; − vti **to m. (to) s.o. to do** faire signe à qn de faire. ◆**−less** a immobile.

motive ['məʊtɪv] n motif m (**for, of** de); Jur mobile m (**for** de). ◆**motivate** vt (person, decision etc) motiver. ◆**moti'vation** n motivation f; (incentive) encouragement m.

motley ['mɒtlɪ] a (coloured) bigarré; (collection) hétéroclite.

motor ['məʊtər] n (engine) moteur m; (car) Fam auto f; − a (industry, vehicle etc) automobile; (accident) d'auto; **m. boat** canot m automobile; **m. mechanic** mécanicien-auto m; **m. mower** tondeuse f à moteur; − vi (drive) rouler en auto. ◆**−ing** n Sp automobilisme m; **school of m.** auto-école f. ◆**motorbike** n Fam moto f. ◆**motorcade** n cortège m (officiel) (de voitures). ◆**motorcar** n automobile f. ◆**motorcycle** n moto f, motocyclette f. ◆**motorcyclist** n motocycliste mf. ◆**motorist** n automobiliste mf. ◆**motorized** a motorisé. ◆**motorway** n autoroute f.

mottled ['mɒt(ə)ld] a tacheté.

motto ['mɒtəʊ] n (pl -oes) devise f.

mould [məʊld] **1** n (shape) moule m; − vt (clay etc) mouler; (statue, character) modeler. **2** n (growth, mildew) moisissure f. ◆**mouldy** a (-ier, -iest) moisi; **to go m.** moisir.

moult [məʊlt] vi muer. ◆**−ing** n mue f.

mound [maʊnd] n (of earth) tertre m; (pile) Fig monceau m.

mount [maʊnt] **1** n (mountain) Lit mont m. **2** n (horse) monture f; (frame for photo or slide) cadre m; (stamp hinge) charnière f; − vt (horse, hill, jewel, photo, demonstration etc) monter; (ladder, tree etc) monter sur, grimper à; (stamp) coller (dans un album); − vi (up) (on horse) se mettre en selle. **3** vi (increase) monter; **to m. up** (add up) chiffrer (**to** à); (accumulate) s'accumuler.

mountain ['maʊntɪn] n montagne f; − a (people, life) montagnard. ◆**mountai'neer** n alpiniste mf. ◆**mountai'neering** n alpinisme m. ◆**mountainous** a montagneux.

mourn [mɔːn] vti **to m. (for)** pleurer. ◆**−ing** n deuil m; **in m.** en deuil. ◆**−er** n parent, -ente mf or ami, -ie mf du défunt or de la défunte. ◆**mournful** a triste.

mouse, pl **mice** [maʊs, maɪs] n souris f. ◆**mousetrap** n souricière f.

mousse [muːs] n Culin mousse f.

moustache [məˈstɑːʃ, Am 'mʌstæʃ] n moustache f.

mousy ['maʊsɪ] a (-ier, -iest) (hair) Pej châtain terne; (shy) Fig timide.

mouth [maʊθ] n (pl -s [maʊðz]) bouche f; (of dog, lion etc) gueule f; (of river) embouchure f; (of cave, harbour) entrée f; − [maʊð] vt Pej dire. ◆**mouthful** n (of food) bouchée f; (of liquid) gorgée f. ◆**mouthorgan** n harmonica m. ◆**mouthpiece** n Mus embouchure f; (spokesman) Fig porte-parole m inv. ◆**mouthwash** n bain m de bouche. ◆**mouth-watering** a appétissant.

mov/e [muːv] n mouvement m; (change of

house etc) déménagement *m*; (*change of job*) changement *m* d'emploi; (*transfer of employee*) mutation *f*; (*in game*) coup *m*, (*one's turn*) tour *m*; (*act*) *Fig* démarche *f*; (*step*) pas *m*; (*attempt*) tentative *f*; **to make a m.** (*leave*) se préparer à partir; (*act*) *Fig* passer à l'action; **to get a m. on** *Fam* se dépêcher; **on the m.** en marche; **–** *vt* déplacer, remuer, bouger; (*arm, leg*) remuer; (*crowd*) faire partir; (*put*) mettre; (*transport*) transporter; (*piece in game*) jouer; (*propose*) *Pol* proposer; **to m. s.o.** (*incite*) pousser qn (**to do** à faire); (*emotionally*) émouvoir qn; (*transfer in job*) muter qn; **to m. house** déménager; **to m. sth back** reculer qch; **to m. sth down** descendre qch; **to m. sth forward** avancer qch; **to m. sth over** pousser qch; **–** *vi* bouger, remuer; (*go*) aller (**to** à); (*pass*) passer (**to** à); (*leave*) partir; (*change seats*) changer de place; (*progress*) avancer; (*act*) agir; (*play*) jouer; **to m.** (**out**) (*of house etc*) déménager; **to m. to** (*a new region etc*) aller habiter; **to m. about** se déplacer; (*fidget*) remuer; **to m. along** *or* **forward** *or* **on** avancer; **to m. away** *or* **off** (*go away*) s'éloigner; **to m. back** (*withdraw*) reculer; (*return*) retourner; **to m. in** (*to house*) emménager; **to m. into** (*house*) emménager dans; **m. on!** circulez!; **to m. over** *or* **up** se pousser. ◆**–ing** *a* en mouvement; (*part*) *Tech* mobile; (*stairs*) mécanique; (*touching*) émouvant. ◆**mov(e)able** *a* mobile. ◆**movement** *n* (*action, group etc*) & *Mus* mouvement *m*.

movie ['muːvɪ] *n Fam* film *m*; **the movies** (*cinema*) le cinéma; **m. camera** caméra *f*. ◆**moviegoer** *n* cinéphile *mf*.

mow [məʊ] *vt* (*pp* **mown** *or* **mowed**) (*field*) faucher; **to m. the lawn** tondre le gazon; **to m. down** (*kill etc*) *Fig* faucher. ◆**–er** *n* (**lawn**) **m.** tondeuse *f* (à gazon).

MP [em'piː] *n abbr* (*Member of Parliament*) député *m*.

Mrs ['mɪsɪz] *n* (*married woman*) **Mrs Brown** Madame *or* Mme Brown.

Ms [mɪz] *n* (*married or unmarried woman*) **Ms Brown** Madame *or* Mme Brown.

MSc, *Am* **MS** *abbr* = **Master of Science.**

much [mʌtʃ] *a* & *n* beaucoup (**de**); **not m. time/money/etc** pas beaucoup de temps/d'argent/etc; **not m.** pas beaucoup; **m. of** (*a good deal of*) une bonne partie de; **as m.** (*to do, know etc*) autant que; **as m. wine/etc as** autant de vin/etc que; **as m. as you like** autant que tu veux; **twice as m.** deux fois plus (**de**); **how m.?** combien (**de**)?; **too m.**

trop (**de**); **so m.** tant (**de**), tellement (**de**); **I know/I shall do this m.** je sais/je ferai ceci (**du moins**); **this m. wine** ça de vin; **it's not m. of a garden** ce n'est pas merveilleux comme jardin; **m. the same** presque le même; **–** *adv* **very m.** beaucoup; **not** (**very**) **m.** pas beaucoup; **she doesn't say very m.** elle ne dit pas grand-chose.

muck [mʌk] **1** *n* (*manure*) fumier *m*; (*filth*) *Fig* saleté *f*. **2** *vi* **to m. about** *Fam* (*have fun, idle*) s'amuser; (*play the fool*) faire l'idiot; **to m. about with** *Fam* (*fiddle with*) s'amuser avec; (*alter*) changer (*texte etc*); **to m. in** (*join in*) *Fam* participer, contribuer; **–** *vt* **to m. s.o. about** *Fam* embêter qn, déranger qn; **to m. up** (*spoil*) *Fam* gâcher, ruiner. ◆**m.-up** *n Fam* gâchis *m*. ◆**mucky** *a* (**-ier, -iest**) sale.

mucus ['mjuːkəs] *n* mucosités *fpl*.

mud [mʌd] *n* boue *f*. ◆**muddy** *a* (**-ier, -iest**) (*water*) boueux; (*hands etc*) couvert de boue. ◆**mudguard** *n* garde-boue *m inv*.

muddle ['mʌd(ə)l] *n* (*mess*) désordre *m*; (*mix-up*) confusion *f*; **in a m.** (*room etc*) sens dessus dessous, en désordre; (*person*) désorienté; (*mind, ideas*) embrouillé; **–** *vt* (*person, facts etc*) embrouiller; (*papers*) mélanger; **–** *vi* **to m. through** *Fam* se débrouiller tant bien que mal.

muff [mʌf] *n* (*for hands*) manchon *m*.

muffin ['mʌfɪn] *n* petit pain *m* brioché.

muffl/e ['mʌf(ə)l] *vt* (*noise*) assourdir. ◆**–ed** *a* (*noise*) sourd. ◆**–er** *n* (*scarf*) cache-col *m inv*; *Aut Am* silencieux *m*.

mug [mʌg] **1** *n* grande tasse *f*; (*of metal or plastic*) gobelet *m*; (**beer**) **m.** chope *f*. **2** *n* (*face*) *Sl* gueule *f*; **m. shot** *Pej* photo *f* (d'identité). **3** *n* (*fool*) *Fam* niais, -aise *mf*. **4** *vt* (**-gg-**) (*attack*) agresser. ◆**mugger** *n* agresseur *m*. ◆**mugging** *n* agression *f*.

muggy ['mʌgɪ] *a* (**-ier, -iest**) (*weather*) lourd.

mulberry ['mʌlbərɪ] *n* (*fruit*) mûre *f*.

mule [mjuːl] *n* (*male*) mulet *m*; (*female*) mule *f*.

mull [mʌl] **1** *vt* (*wine*) chauffer. **2** *vi* **to m. over** (*think over*) ruminer.

mullet ['mʌlɪt] *n* (*fish*) mulet *m*; (**red**) **m.** rouget *m*.

multi- ['mʌltɪ] *pref* multi-.

multicoloured ['mʌltɪkʌləd] *a* multicolore.

multifarious [mʌltɪ'feərɪəs] *a* divers.

multimillionaire [mʌltɪmɪljə'neər] *n* milliardaire *mf*.

multinational [mʌltɪ'næʃ(ə)nəl] *n* multinationale *f*.

multiple ['mʌltɪp(ə)l] *a* multiple; – *n Math* multiple *m*. ◆**multipli'cation** *n* multiplication *f*. ◆**multi'plicity** *n* multiplicité *f*. ◆**multiply** *vt* multiplier; – *vi* (*reproduce*) se multiplier.

multistorey [mʌltɪ'stɔːrɪ] (*Am* **multistoried**) *a* à étages.

multitude ['mʌltɪtjuːd] *n* multitude *f*.

mum [mʌm] **1** *n Fam* maman *f*. **2** *a* **to keep m.** garder le silence.

mumble ['mʌmb(ə)l] *vti* marmotter.

mumbo-jumbo [mʌmbəʊ'dʒʌmbəʊ] *n* (*words*) charabia *m*.

mummy ['mʌmɪ] *n* **1** *Fam* maman *f*. **2** (*body*) momie *f*.

mumps [mʌmps] *n* oreillons *mpl*.

munch [mʌntʃ] *vti* (*chew*) mastiquer; **to m. (on)** (*eat*) *Fam* bouffer.

mundane [mʌn'deɪn] *a* banal.

municipal [mjuː'nɪsɪp(ə)l] *a* municipal. ◆**munici'pality** *n* municipalité *f*.

munitions [mjuː'nɪʃ(ə)nz] *npl* munitions *fpl*.

mural ['mjʊərəl] *a* mural; – *n* fresque *f*, peinture *f* murale.

murder ['mɜːdər] *n* meurtre *m*, assassinat *m*; **it's m.** (*dreadful*) *Fam* c'est affreux; – *vt* (*kill*) assassiner; (*spoil*) *Fig* massacrer. ◆**—er** *n* meurtrier, -ière *mf*, assassin *m*. ◆**murderous** *a* meurtrier.

murky ['mɜːkɪ] *a* (-**ier**, -**iest**) obscur; (*water, business, past*) trouble; (*weather*) nuageux.

murmur ['mɜːmər] *n* murmure *m*; (*of traffic*) bourdonnement *m*; – *vti* murmurer.

muscle ['mʌs(ə)l] *n* muscle *m*; – *vi* **to m. in on** (*group*) *Sl* s'introduire par la force à. ◆**muscular** *a* (*tissue etc*) musculaire; (*brawny*) musclé.

muse [mjuːz] *vi* méditer (**on** sur).

museum [mjuː'zɪəm] *n* musée *m*.

mush [mʌʃ] *n* (*soft mass*) bouillie *f*; *Fig* sentimentalité *f*. ◆**mushy** *a* (-**ier**, -**iest**) (*food etc*) en bouillie; *Fig* sentimental.

mushroom ['mʌʃrʊm] **1** *n* champignon *m*. **2** *vi* (*grow*) pousser comme des champignons; (*spread*) se multiplier.

music ['mjuːzɪk] *n* musique *f*; **m. centre** chaîne *f* stéréo compacte; **m. critic** critique *m* musical; **m. hall** music-hall *m*; **m. lover** mélomane *mf*; **canned m.** musique *f* (de fond) enregistrée. ◆**musical** *a* musical; (*instrument*) de musique; **to be (very) m.** être (très) musicien; – *n* (*film, play*) comédie *f* musicale. ◆**mu'sician** *n* musicien, -ienne *mf*.

musk [mʌsk] *n* (*scent*) musc *m*.

Muslim ['mʊzlɪm] *a* & *n* musulman, -ane (*mf*).

muslin ['mʌzlɪn] *n* (*cotton*) mousseline *f*.

mussel ['mʌs(ə)l] *n* (*mollusc*) moule *f*.

must [mʌst] *v aux* **1** (*necessity*) **you m. obey** tu dois obéir, il faut que tu obéisses. **2** (*certainty*) **she m. be clever** elle doit être intelligente; **I m. have seen it** j'ai dû le voir; – *n* **this is a m.** ceci est (absolument) indispensable.

mustache [mʌ'stæʃ] *n Am* moustache *f*.

mustard ['mʌstəd] *n* moutarde *f*.

muster ['mʌstər] *vt* (*gather*) rassembler; (*sum*) réunir; – *vi* se rassembler.

musty ['mʌstɪ] *a* (-**ier**, -**iest**) (*smell*) de moisi; **it smells m., it's m.** ça sent le moisi.

mutation [mjuː'teɪʃ(ə)n] *n Biol* mutation *f*.

mut/e [mjuːt] *a* (*silent*) & *Gram* muet; – *vt* (*sound, colour*) assourdir. ◆**—ed** *a* (*criticism*) voilé.

mutilate ['mjuːtɪleɪt] *vt* mutiler. ◆**muti'lation** *n* mutilation *f*.

mutiny ['mjuːtɪnɪ] *n* mutinerie *f*; – *vi* se mutiner. ◆**mutinous** *a* (*troops*) mutiné.

mutter ['mʌtər] *vti* marmonner.

mutton ['mʌt(ə)n] *n* (*meat*) mouton *m*.

mutual ['mjuːtʃʊəl] *a* (*help, love etc*) mutuel, réciproque; (*common, shared*) commun; **m. fund** *Fin Am* fonds *m* commun de placement. ◆**—ly** *adv* mutuellement.

muzzle ['mʌz(ə)l] *n* (*snout*) museau *m*; (*device*) muselière *f*; (*of gun*) gueule *f*; – *vt* (*animal, press etc*) museler.

my [maɪ] *poss a* mon, ma, *pl* mes. ◆**my'self** *pron* moi-même; (*reflexive*) me, m'; (*after prep*) moi; **I wash m.** je me lave; **I think of m.** je pense à moi.

mystery ['mɪstərɪ] *n* mystère *m*. ◆**my'sterious** *a* mystérieux.

mystic ['mɪstɪk] *a* & *n* mystique (*mf*). ◆**mystical** *a* mystique. ◆**mysticism** *n* mysticisme *m*. ◆**my'stique** *n* (*mystery, power*) mystique *f* (**of** de).

mystify ['mɪstɪfaɪ] *vt* (*bewilder*) laisser perplexe; (*fool*) mystifier. ◆**mystifi'cation** *n* (*bewilderment*) perplexité *f*.

myth [mɪθ] *n* mythe *m*. ◆**mythical** *a* mythique. ◆**mytho'logical** *a* mythologique. ◆**my'thology** *n* mythologie *f*.

N

N, n [en] *n* N, n *m*; **the nth time** la énième fois.

nab [næb] *vt* (**-bb-**) (*catch, arrest*) *Fam* épingler.

nag [næg] *vti* (**-gg-**) (*criticize*) critiquer; **to n. (at) s.o.** (*pester*) harceler *or* embêter qn (**to do** pour qu'il fasse). ◆**nagging** *a* (*doubt, headache*) qui subsiste; – *n* critiques *fpl*.

nail [neɪl] **1** *n* (*of finger, toe*) ongle *m*; – *a* (*polish, file etc*) à ongles. **2** *n* (*metal*) clou *m*; – *vt* clouer; **to n. s.o.** (*nab*) *Fam* épingler qn; **to n. down** (*lid etc*) clouer.

naïve [naɪˈiːv] *a* naïf. ◆**naïveté** *n* naïveté *f*.

naked ['neɪkɪd] *a* (*person*) (tout) nu; (*eye, flame*) nu; **to see with the n. eye** voir à l'œil nu. ◆**—ness** *n* nudité *f*.

name [neɪm] *n* nom *m*; (*reputation*) *Fig* réputation *f*; **my n. is** . . . je m'appelle . . . ; **in the n. of** au nom de; **to put one's n. down for** (*school, course*) s'inscrire à; (*job, house*) demander, faire une demande pour avoir; **to call s.o. names** injurier qn; **first n., given n.** prénom *m*; **last n.** nom *m* de famille; **a good/bad n.** *Fig* une bonne/mauvaise réputation; **n. plate** plaque *f*; – *vt* nommer; (*ship, street*) baptiser; (*designate*) désigner, nommer; (*date, price*) fixer; **he was named after** *or Am* **for** . . . il a reçu le nom de . . . . ◆**—less** *a* sans nom, anonyme. ◆**—ly** *adv* (*that is*) à savoir. ◆**namesake** *n* (*person*) homonyme *m*.

nanny ['nænɪ] *n* nurse *f*, bonne *f* d'enfants; (*grandmother*) *Fam* mamie *f*.

nanny-goat ['nænɪgəʊt] *n* chèvre *f*.

nap [næp] *n* (*sleep*) petit somme *m*; **to have** *or* **take a n.** faire un petit somme; (*after lunch*) faire la sieste; – *vi* (**-pp-**) **to be napping** sommeiller; **to catch napping** *Fig* prendre au dépourvu.

nape [neɪp] *n* **n. (of the neck)** nuque *f*.

napkin ['næpkɪn] *n* (*at table*) serviette *f*; (*for baby*) couche *f*. ◆**nappy** *n* (*for baby*) couche *f*. ◆**nappy-liner** *n* protège-couche *m*.

narcotic [nɑːˈkɒtɪk] *a & n* narcotique (*m*).

narrate [nəˈreɪt] *vt* raconter. ◆**narration** *n*, ◆'**narrative** *n* (*story*) récit *m*, narration *f*; (*art, act*) narration *f*. ◆**narrator** *n* narrateur, -trice *m f*.

narrow ['nærəʊ] *a* (**-er, -est**) étroit; (*major-*

ity) faible, petit; – *vi* (*of path*) se rétrécir; **to n. down** (*of choice etc*) se limiter (**to** à); – *vt* **to n. (down)** (*limit*) limiter. ◆**—ly** *adv* (**to miss etc**) de justesse; (*strictly*) strictement; **he n. escaped** *or* **missed being killed/etc** il a failli être tué/*etc*. ◆**—ness** *n* étroitesse *f*.

narow-minded [nærəʊˈmaɪndɪd] *a* borné. ◆**—ness** *n* étroitesse *f* (d'esprit).

nasal ['neɪz(ə)l] *a* nasal; (*voice*) nasillard.

nasty ['nɑːstɪ] *a* (**-ier, -iest**) (*bad*) mauvais, vilain; (*spiteful*) méchant, désagréable (**to, towards** avec); **a n. mess** *or* **muddle** un gâchis. ◆**nastily** *adv* (*to act*) méchamment; (*to rain*) horriblement. ◆**nastiness** *n* (*malice*) méchanceté *f*; **the n. of the weather/taste/etc** le mauvais temps/goût/*etc*.

nation ['neɪʃ(ə)n] *n* nation *f*; **the United Nations** les Nations Unies. ◆**n.-wide** *a & adv* dans le pays (tout) entier. ◆**national** *a* national; **n. anthem** hymne *m* national; **N. Health Service** = Sécurité *f* Sociale; **n. insurance** = assurances *fpl* sociales; – *n* (*citizen*) ressortissant, -ante *mf*. ◆**nationalist** *n* nationaliste *mf*. ◆**nationa'listic** *a Pej* nationaliste. ◆**natio'nality** *n* nationalité *f*. ◆**nationalize** *vt* nationaliser. ◆**nationally** *adv* (*to travel, be known etc*) dans le pays (tout) entier.

native ['neɪtɪv] *a* (*country*) natal; (*habits, costume*) du pays; (*tribe, plant*) indigène; (*charm, ability*) inné; **n. language** langue *f* maternelle; **to be an English n. speaker** parler l'anglais comme langue maternelle; – *n* (*person*) autochtone *mf*; (*non-European in colony*) indigène *mf*; **to be a n. of** être originaire *or* natif de.

nativity [nəˈtɪvɪtɪ] *n Rel* nativité *f*.

NATO ['neɪtəʊ] *n abbr* (*North Atlantic Treaty Organization*) OTAN *f*.

natter ['nætər] *vi Fam* bavarder; – *n Fam* **to have a n.** bavarder.

natural ['nætʃ(ə)rəl] *a* naturel; (*actor, gardener etc*) né; – *n* **to be a n. for** (*job etc*) *Fam* être celui qu'il faut pour, être fait pour. ◆**naturalist** *n* naturaliste *mf*. ◆**naturally** *adv* (*as normal, of course*) naturellement; (*by nature*) de nature; (*with naturalness*) avec naturel. ◆**naturalness** *n* naturel *m*.

naturalize ['nætʃ(ə)rəlaɪz] vt (person) Pol naturaliser. ◆**naturali'zation** n naturalisation f.

nature ['neɪtʃər] n (natural world, basic quality) nature f; (disposition) naturel m; **by n.** de nature; **n. study** sciences fpl naturelles.

naught [nɔːt] n **1** Math zéro m. **2** (nothing) Lit rien m.

naught/y ['nɔːtɪ] a (-ier, -iest) (child) vilain, malicieux; (joke, story) osé, grivois. ◆—**ily** adv (to behave) mal; (to say) avec malice. ◆—**iness** n mauvaise conduite f.

nausea ['nɔːzɪə] n nausée f. ◆**nauseate** vt écœurer. ◆**nauseous** a (smell etc) nauséabond; **to feel n.** Am (sick) avoir envie de vomir; (disgusted) Fig être écœuré.

nautical ['nɔːtɪk(ə)l] a nautique.

naval ['neɪv(ə)l] a naval; (power, hospital) maritime; (officer) de marine.

nave [neɪv] n (of church) nef f.

navel ['neɪv(ə)l] n Anat nombril m.

navigate ['nævɪgeɪt] vi naviguer; – vt (boat) diriger, piloter; (river) naviguer sur. ◆**navigable** a (river) navigable; (seaworthy) en état de naviguer. ◆**navi'gation** n navigation f. ◆**navigator** n Av navigateur m.

navvy ['nævɪ] n (labourer) terrassier m.

navy ['neɪvɪ] n marine f; – a **n.** (blue) bleu marine inv.

Nazi ['nɑːtsɪ] a & n Pol Hist nazi, -ie (mf).

near [nɪər] adv (-er, -est) près; **quite n., n. at hand** tout près; **to draw n.** (s')approcher (to de); (of date) approcher; **n. to** près de; **to come n. to being killed/etc** faillir être tué/etc; **n. enough** (more or less) Fam plus ou moins; – prep (-er, -est) **n.** (to) près de; **n. the bed** près du lit; **to be n.** (to) **victory/death** frôler la victoire/la mort; **n. the end** vers la fin; **to come n. to s.o.** s'approcher de qn; – a (-er, -est) proche; (likeness) fidèle; **the nearest hospital** l'hôpital le plus proche; **the nearest way** la route la plus directe; **in the n. future** dans un avenir proche; **to the nearest franc** (to calculate) à un franc près; (to round up or down) au franc supérieur or inférieur; **n. side** Aut côté m gauche, Am côté m droit; – vt (approach) approcher de; **nearing completion** près d'être achevé. ◆**near'by** adv tout près; – ['nɪəbaɪ] a proche. ◆**nearness** n (in space, time) proximité f.

nearly ['nɪəlɪ] adv presque; **she (very) n. fell** elle a failli tomber; **not n. as clever/etc** loin d'être aussi intelligent/etc que.

neat [niːt] a (-er, -est) (clothes, work) soigné,

propre, net; (room) ordonné, bien rangé; (style) élégant; (pretty) Fam joli, beau; (pleasant) Fam agréable; **to drink one's whisky/etc n.** prendre son whisky/etc sec. ◆—**ly** adv avec soin; (skilfully) habilement. ◆—**ness** n netteté f; (of room) ordre m.

necessary ['nesɪs(ə)rɪ] a nécessaire; **it's n. to do** il est nécessaire de faire, il faut faire; **to make it n. for s.o. to do** mettre qn dans la nécessité de faire; **to do what's n.** or **the n.** Fam faire le nécessaire (**for** pour); – npl **the necessaries** (food etc) l'indispensable m. ◆**nece'ssarily** adv nécessairement.

necessity [nɪ'sesɪtɪ] n (obligation, need) nécessité f; (poverty) indigence f; **there's no n. for you to do that** tu n'es pas obligé de faire cela; **of n.** nécessairement; **to be a n.** être indispensable; **the (bare) necessities** le (strict) nécessaire. ◆**necessitate** vt nécessiter.

neck¹ [nek] n Anat cou m; (of dress, horse) encolure f; (of bottle) col m; **low n.** (of dress) décolleté m. **n. and n.** Sp à égalité. ◆**necklace** n collier m. ◆**neckline** n encolure f. ◆**necktie** n cravate f.

neck² [nek] vi (kiss etc) Fam se peloter.

nectarine ['nektəriːn] n (fruit) nectarine f, brugnon m.

née [neɪ] adv **n.** Dupont née Dupont.

need [niːd] **1** n (necessity, want, poverty) besoin m; **in n.** dans le besoin; **to be in n. of** avoir besoin de; **there's no n. (for you) to do** tu n'as pas besoin de faire; **if n. be** si besoin est, s'il le faut; – vt avoir besoin de; **you n. it** tu en as besoin, il te le faut; **it needs an army to do, an army is needed to do** il faut une armée pour faire; **this sport needs patience** ce sport demande de la patience; **her hair needs cutting** il faut qu'elle se fasse couper les cheveux. **2** v aux **n. he wait?** est-il obligé d'attendre?, a-t-il besoin d'attendre?; **I needn't have rushed** ce n'était pas la peine de me presser; **I n. hardly say that . . .** je n'ai guère besoin de dire que . . . . ◆**needless** a inutile. ◆**needlessly** adv inutilement. ◆**needy** a (-ier, -iest) a nécessiteux.

needle ['niːd(ə)l] **1** n aiguille f; (of record player) saphir m. **2** vt (irritate) Fam agacer. ◆**needlework** n couture f, travaux mpl d'aiguille; (object) ouvrage m.

negate [nɪ'geɪt] vt (nullify) annuler; (deny) nier. ◆**negation** n (denial) & Gram négation f.

negative ['negətɪv] a négatif; – n Phot négatif m; (word) Gram négation f; (form)

Gram forme *f* négative; **to answer in the n.** répondre par la négative.

neglect [nɪ'glekt] *vt* (*person, health, work etc*) négliger; (*garden, car etc*) ne pas s'occuper de; (*duty*) manquer à; (*rule*) désobéir à, méconnaître; **to n. to do** négliger de faire; – *n* (*of person*) manque *m* de soins (**of** envers); (*of rule*) désobéissance *f* (**of** à); (*of duty*) manquement *m* (**of** à); (*carelessness*) négligence *f*; **in a state of n.** (*garden, house etc*) mal tenu. ◆**neglected** *a* (*appearance, person*) négligé; (*garden, house etc*) mal tenu; **to feel n.** sentir qu'on vous néglige. ◆**neglectful** *a* négligent; **to be n. of** négliger.

negligent ['neglɪdʒənt] *a* négligent. ◆**negligence** *n* négligence *f*. ◆**negligently** *adv* négligemment.

negligible ['neglɪdʒəb(ə)l] *a* négligeable.

negotiate [nɪ'gəʊʃɪeɪt] **1** *vti Fin Pol* négocier. **2** *vt* (*fence, obstacle*) franchir; (*bend*) *Aut* négocier. ◆**negotiable** *a Fin* négociable. ◆**negoti'ation** *n* négociation *f*; **in n. with** en pourparlers avec. ◆**negotiator** *n* négociateur, -trice *mf*.

Negro ['niːgrəʊ] *n* (*pl* -**oes**) (*man*) Noir *m*; (*woman*) Noire *f*; – *a* noir; (*art, sculpture etc*) nègre. ◆**Negress** *n* Noire *f*.

neigh [neɪ] *vi* (*of horse*) hennir; – *n* hennissement *m*.

neighbour ['neɪbər] *n* voisin, -ine *mf*. ◆**neighbourhood** *n* (*neighbours*) voisinage *m*; (*district*) quartier *m*, voisinage *m*; (*region*) région *f*; **in the n. of ten pounds** dans les dix livres. ◆**neighbouring** *a* avoisinant. ◆**neighbourly** *a* (*feeling etc*) de bon voisinage, amical; **they're n.** (**people**) ils sont bons voisins.

neither ['naɪðər, *Am* 'niːðər] *adv* ni; **n. . . . nor** ni . . . ni; **n. you nor me** ni toi ni moi; **he n. sings nor dances** il ne chante ni ne danse; – *conj* (*not either*) (ne) . . . non plus; **n. shall I go** je n'y irai pas non plus; **n. do I, n. can I** *etc* (ni) moi non plus; – *a* **n. boy (came)** aucun des deux garçons (n'est venu); **on n. side** ni d'un côté ni de l'autre; – *pron* **n. (of them)** ni l'un(e) ni l'autre, aucun(e) (des deux).

neo- ['niːəʊ] *pref* néo-.

neon ['niːɒn] *n* (*gas*) néon *m*; – *a* (*lighting etc*) au néon.

nephew ['nevjuː, 'nefjuː] *n* neveu *m*.

nepotism ['nepətɪz(ə)m] *n* népotisme *m*.

nerve [nɜːv] *n* nerf *m*; (*courage*) *Fig* courage *m* (**to do** de faire); (*confidence*) assurance *f*; (*calm*) sang-froid *m*; (*cheek*) *Fam* culot *m* (**to do** de faire); **you get on my nerves** *Fam* tu me portes *or* me tapes sur les nerfs; **to have (an attack of) nerves** (*fear, anxiety*) avoir le trac; **a bundle** *or* **mass** *or* **bag of nerves** (*person*) *Fam* un paquet de nerfs; **to have bad nerves** être nerveux; – *a* (*cell, centre*) nerveux. ◆**n.-racking** *a* éprouvant pour les nerfs. ◆**nervous** *a* (*tense*) & *Anat* nerveux; (*worried*) inquiet (**about** de); **to be** *or* **feel n.** (*ill-at-ease*) se sentir mal à l'aise; (*before exam etc*) avoir le trac. ◆**nervously** *adv* nerveusement; (*worriedly*) avec inquiétude. ◆**nervousness** *n* nervosité *f*; (*fear*) trac *m*. ◆**nervy** *a* (-**ier**, -**iest**) *Fam* (*anxious*) nerveux; (*brash*) *Am* culotté.

nest [nest] *n* nid *m*; **n. egg** (*money saved*) pécule *m*; **n. of tables** table *f* gigogne; – *vi* (*of bird*) (se) nicher.

nestle ['nes(ə)l] *vi* se pelotonner (**up to** contre); **a village nestling in** (*forest, valley etc*) un village niché dans.

net [net] **1** *n* filet *m*; **n. curtain** voilage *m*; – *vt* (**-tt-**) (*fish*) prendre au filet. **2** *a* (*profit, weight etc*) net *inv*; – *vt* (**-tt-**) (*of person, firm etc*) gagner net; **this venture netted him** *or* **her . . . .** cette entreprise lui a rapporté . . . . ◆**netting** *n* (*nets*) filets *mpl*; (*mesh*) mailles *fpl*; (*fabric*) voile *m*; (*wire*) **n.** treillis *m*.

Netherlands (the) [ðə'neðələndz] *npl* les Pays-Bas *mpl*.

nettle ['net(ə)l] *n Bot* ortie *f*.

network ['netwɜːk] *n* réseau *m*.

neurosis, *pl* -**oses** [njʊə'rəʊsɪs, -əʊsiːz] *n* névrose *f*. ◆**neurotic** *a* & *n* névrosé, -ée (*mf*).

neuter ['njuːtər] **1** *a* & *n Gram* neutre (*m*). **2** *vt* (*cat etc*) châtrer.

neutral ['njuːtrəl] *a* neutre; (*policy*) de neutralité; – *n El* neutre *m*; **in n. (gear)** *Aut* au point mort. ◆**neu'trality** *n* neutralité *f*. ◆**neutralize** *vt* neutraliser.

never ['nevər] *adv* **1** (*not ever*) (ne) . . . jamais; **n. lies** elle ne ment jamais; **n. in (all) my life** jamais de ma vie; **n. again** plus jamais. **2** (*certainly not*) *Fam* **I n. did it** je ne l'ai pas fait. ◆**n.-'ending** *a* interminable.

nevertheless [nevəðə'les] *adv* néanmoins, quand même.

new [njuː] *a* (-**er**, -**est**) nouveau; (*brand-new*) neuf; **to be n. to** (*job*) être nouveau dans; (*city*) être un nouveau-venu dans, être fraîchement installé dans; **a n. boy** *Sch* un nouveau; **what's n.?** *Fam* quoi de neuf?; **a n. glass/pen/**etc (*different*) un autre verre/stylo/etc; **to break n. ground** innover; **n. look** style *m* nouveau; **as good as**

n. comme neuf; **a n.-laid egg** un œuf du jour; **a n.-born baby** un nouveau-né, une nouveau-née. ◆**newcomer** *n* nouveau-venu *m*, nouvelle-venue *f*. ◆**new-'fangled** *a Pej* moderne. ◆**new-found** *a* nouveau. ◆**newly** *adv* (*recently*) nouvellement, fraîchement; **the n.-weds** les nouveaux mariés. ◆**newness** *n* (*condition*) état *m* neuf; (*novelty*) nouveauté *f*.

news [njuːz] *n* nouvelle(s) *f(pl)*; *Journ Rad TV* informations *fpl*, actualités *fpl*; **sports/etc n.** (*newspaper column*) chronique *f or* rubrique *f* sportive/*etc*; **a piece of n.**, **some n.** une nouvelle; *Journ Rad TV* une information; **n. headlines** titres *mpl* de l'actualité; **n. flash** flash *m*. ◆**newsagent** *n* marchand, -ande *mf* de journaux. ◆**newsboy** *n* vendeur *m* de journaux. ◆**newscaster** *n* présentateur, -trice *mf*. ◆**newsletter** *n* (*of club, group etc*) bulletin *m*. ◆**newspaper** *n* journal *m*. ◆**newsreader** *n* présentateur, -trice *mf*. ◆**newsreel** *n Cin* actualités *fpl*. ◆**newsworthy** *a* digne de faire l'objet d'un reportage. ◆**newsy** *a* (**-ier, -iest**) *Fam* plein de nouvelles.

newt [njuːt] *n* (*animal*) triton *m*.

New Zealand [njuː'ziːlənd] *n* Nouvelle-Zélande *f*; *– a* néo-zélandais. ◆**New Zealander** *n* Néo-Zélandais, -aise *mf*.

next [nekst] *a* prochain; (*room, house*) d'à-côté, voisin; (*following*) suivant; **n. month** (*in the future*) le mois prochain; **he returned the n. month** (*in the past*) il revint le mois suivant; **the n. day** le lendemain; **the n. morning** le lendemain matin; **within the n. ten days** d'ici (à) dix jours, dans un délai de dix jours; **(by) this time n. week** d'ici (à) la semaine prochaine; **from one year to the n.** d'une année à l'autre; **you're n.** c'est ton tour; **n. (please)!** (au) suivant!; **the n. thing to do is . . .** ce qu'il faut faire ensuite c'est . . . ; **the n. size (up)** la taille au-dessus; **to live/etc n.** door habiter/*etc* à côté (to de); **n.-door neighbour/room** voisin *m*/pièce *f* d'à-côté; *– n* (*in series etc*) suivant, -ante *mf*; *– adv* (*afterwards*) ensuite, après; (*now*) maintenant; **when you come n.** la prochaine fois que tu viendras; **the n. best solution** la seconde solution; *– prep* **n. to** (*beside*) à côté de; **n. to nothing** presque rien.

NHS [eneitʃ'es] *abbr* = **National Health Service**.

nib [nib] *n* (*of pen*) plume *f*, bec *m*.

nibble ['nib(ə)l] *vti* (*eat*) grignoter; (*bite*) mordiller.

nice [naɪs] *a* (**-er, -est**) (*pleasant*) agréable; (*charming*) charmant, gentil; (*good*) bon; (*fine*) beau; (*pretty*) joli; (*kind*) gentil (**to** avec); (*respectable*) bien *inv*; (*subtle*) délicat; **it's n. here** c'est bien ici; **n. and easy/warm/etc** (*very*) bien facile/chaud/*etc*. ◆**n.-'looking** *a* beau, joli. ◆**nicely** *adv* agréablement; (*kindly*) gentiment; (*well*) bien. ◆**niceties** ['naɪsətɪz] *npl* (*pleasant things*) agréments *mpl*; (*subtleties*) subtilités *fpl*.

niche [niːʃ, nɪtʃ] *n* **1** (*recess*) niche *f*. **2** (*job*) (bonne) situation *f*; (*direction*) voie *f*; **to make a n. for oneself** faire son trou.

nick [nik] **1** *n* (*on skin, wood*) entaille *f*; (*in blade, crockery*) brèche *f*. **2** *n* (*prison*) *Sl* taule *f*; *– vt* (*steal, arrest*) *Sl* piquer. **3** *n* **in the n. of time** juste à temps; **in good n.** *Sl* en bon état.

nickel ['nik(ə)l] *n* (*metal*) nickel *m*; (*coin*) *Am* pièce *f* de cinq cents.

nickname ['nikneim] *n* (*informal name*) surnom *m*; (*short form*) diminutif *m*; *– vt* surnommer.

nicotine ['nikətiːn] *n* nicotine *f*.

niece [niːs] *n* nièce *f*.

nifty ['nifti] *a* (**-ier, -iest**) (*stylish*) chic *inv*; (*skilful*) habile; (*fast*) rapide.

Nigeria [naɪ'dʒɪərɪə] *n* Nigéria *m or f*. ◆**Nigerian** *a* & *n* nigérian, -ane (*mf*).

niggardly ['nigədlɪ] *a* (*person*) avare; (*amount*) mesquin.

niggling ['niglɪŋ] *a* (*trifling*) insignifiant; (*irksome*) irritant; (*doubt*) persistant.

night [naɪt] *n* nuit *f*; (*evening*) soir *m*; *Th* soirée *f*; **last n.** (*evening*) hier soir; (*night*) la nuit dernière; **to have an early/late n.** se coucher tôt/tard; **to have a good n.** (*sleep well*) bien dormir; **first n.** *Th* première *f*; *– a* (*work etc*) de nuit; (*life*) nocturne; **n. school** cours *mpl* du soir; **n. watchman** veilleur *m* de nuit. ◆**nightcap** *n* (*drink*) boisson *f* (*alcoolisée ou chaude prise avant de se coucher*). ◆**nightclub** *n* boîte *f* de nuit. ◆**nightdress** *n*, ◆**nightgown** *n*, *Fam* ◆**nightie** *n* (*woman's*) chemise *f* de nuit. ◆**nightfall** *n* **at n.** à la tombée de la nuit. ◆**nightlight** *n* veilleuse *f*. ◆**nighttime** *n* nuit *f*.

nightingale ['naɪtɪŋgeɪl] *n* rossignol *m*.

nightly ['naɪtlɪ] *adv* chaque nuit *or* soir; *– a* de chaque nuit *or* soir.

nil [nil] *n* (*nothing*) & *Sp* zéro *m*; **the risk/result/etc is n.** le risque/résultat/*etc* est nul.

nimble ['nimb(ə)l] *a* (**-er, -est**) agile.

nincompoop ['nɪŋkəmpuːp] *n Fam* imbécile *mf*.

nine [naɪn] *a & n* neuf (*m*). ◆**nine'teen** *a & n* dix-neuf (*m*). ◆**nine'teenth** *a & n* dix-neuvième (*mf*). ◆**ninetieth** *a & n* quatre-vingt-dixième (*mf*). ◆**ninety** *a & n* quatre-vingt-dix (*m*). ◆**ninth** *a & n* neuvième (*mf*); **a n.** un neuvième.

nip [nɪp] **1** *vt* (-pp-) (*pinch, bite*) pincer; **to n. in the bud** *Fig* étouffer dans l'œuf; – *n* pinçon *m*; **there's a n. in the air** ça pince. **2** *vi* (-pp-) (*dash*) **Fam to n. round to s.o.** courir *or* faire un saut chez qn; **to n. in/out** entrer/sortir un instant.

nipper ['nɪpər] *n* (*child*) *Fam* gosse *mf*.

nipple ['nɪp(ə)l] *n* bout *m* de sein, mamelon *m*; (*teat on bottle*) *Am* tétine *f*.

nippy ['nɪpɪ] *a* **1** (-ier, -iest) (*chilly*) frais; **it's n.** (*weather*) ça pince. **2 to be n. (about it)** (*quick*) *Fam* faire vite.

nit [nɪt] *n* **1** (*fool*) *Fam* idiot, -ote *mf*. **2** (*of louse*) lente *f*. ◆**nitwit** *n* (*fool*) *Fam* idiot, -ote *mf*.

nitrogen ['naɪtrədʒən] *n* azote *m*.

nitty-gritty [nɪtɪ'grɪtɪ] *n* **to get down to the n.-gritty** *Fam* en venir au fond du problème.

no [nəʊ] *adv & n* non (*m inv*); **no!** non!; **no more than ten/a kilo/etc** pas plus de dix/d'un kilo/etc; **no more time/etc** plus de temps/etc; **I have no more time** je n'ai plus de temps/etc; **no more than you** pas plus que vous; **you can do no better** tu ne peux pas faire mieux; **the noes** *Pol* les non; – *a* aucun(e); pas de; **I've (got)** *or* **I have no idea** je n'ai aucune idée; **no child came** aucun enfant n'est venu; **I've (got)** *or* **I have no time/etc** je n'ai pas de temps/etc; **of no importance/value/etc** sans importance/valeur/etc; **with no gloves/etc on** sans gants/etc; **there's no knowing . . .** impossible de savoir . . . ; **'no smoking'** 'défense de fumer'; **no way!** *Am Fam* pas question!; **no one = nobody.**

noble ['nəʊb(ə)l] *a* (-er, -est) noble; (*building*) majestueux. ◆**nobleman** *n* (*pl* -men) noble *m*. ◆**noblewoman** *n* (*pl* -women) noble *f*. ◆**no'bility** *n* (*character, class*) noblesse *f*.

nobody ['nəʊbɒdɪ] *pron* (ne) . . . personne; **n. came** personne n'est venu; **he knows n.** il ne connaît personne; **n.!** personne!; – *n* **a n.** une nullité.

nocturnal [nɒk'tɜːn(ə)l] *a* nocturne.

nod [nɒd] **1** *vti* (-dd-) **to n. (one's head)** incliner la tête, faire un signe de tête; – *n* inclination *f or* signe *m* de tête. **2** *vi* (-dd-) **to n. off** (*go to sleep*) s'assoupir.

noise [nɔɪz] *n* bruit *m*; (*of bell, drum*) son *m*; **to make a n.** faire du bruit. ◆**noisily** *adv* bruyamment. ◆**noisy** *a* (-ier, -iest) (*person, street etc*) bruyant.

nomad ['nəʊmæd] *n* nomade *mf*. ◆**no'madic** *a* nomade.

nominal ['nɒmɪn(ə)l] *a* (*value, fee etc*) nominal; (*head, ruler*) de nom.

nominate ['nɒmɪneɪt] *vt Pol* désigner, proposer (**for** candidat à); (*appoint*) désigner, nommer. ◆**nomi'nation** *n* désignation *f or* proposition *f* de candidat; (*appointment*) nomination *f*. ◆**nomi'nee** *n* (*candidate*) candidat *m*.

non- [nɒn] *pref* non-.

nonchalant ['nɒnʃələnt] *a* nonchalant.

noncommissioned [nɒnkə'mɪʃ(ə)nd] *a* **n. officer** *Mil* sous-officier *m*.

non-committal [nɒnkə'mɪt(ə)l] *a* (*answer, person*) évasif.

nonconformist [nɒnkən'fɔːmɪst] *a & n* non-conformiste (*mf*).

nondescript ['nɒndɪskrɪpt] *a* indéfinissable; *Pej* médiocre.

none [nʌn] *pron* aucun(e) *mf*; (*in filling a form*) néant; **n. of them** aucun d'eux; **she has n. (at all)** elle n'en a pas (du tout); **n. (at all) came** pas un(e) seul(e) n'est venu(e); **n. can tell** personne ne peut le dire; **n. of the cake/etc** pas une seule partie du gâteau/etc; **n. of the trees/etc** aucun arbre/etc, aucun des arbres/etc; **n. of it** *or* **this** rien (de ceci); – *adv* **n. too hot/etc** pas tellement chaud/etc; **he's n. the happier/wiser/etc** il n'en est pas plus heureux/sage/etc; **n. the less** néanmoins. ◆**nonethe'less** *adv* néanmoins.

nonentity [nɒ'nentɪtɪ] *n* (*person*) nullité *f*.

non-existent [nɒnɪg'zɪstənt] *a* inexistant.

non-fiction [nɒn'fɪkʃ(ə)n] *n* littérature *f* non-romanesque; (*in library*) ouvrages *mpl* généraux.

non-flammable [nɒn'flæməb(ə)l] *a* ininflammable.

nonplus [nɒn'plʌs] *vt* (-ss-) dérouter.

nonsense ['nɒnsəns] *n* absurdités *fpl*; **that's n.** c'est absurde. ◆**non'sensical** *a* absurde.

non-smoker [nɒn'sməʊkər] *n* (*person*) non-fumeur, -euse *mf*; (*compartment*) *Rail* compartiment *m* non-fumeurs.

non-stick [nɒn'stɪk] *a* (*pan*) anti-adhésif, qui n'attache pas.

non-stop [nɒn'stɒp] *a* sans arrêt; (*train,*

flight) direct; – *adv* (*to work etc*) sans arrêt; (*to fly*) sans escale.

noodles ['nuːd(ə)lz] *npl* nouilles *fpl*; (*in soup*) vermicelle(s) *m*(*pl*).

nook [nuk] *n* coin *m*; **in every n. and cranny** dans tous les coins (et recoins).

noon [nuːn] *n* midi *m*; **at n.** à midi; – *a* (*sun etc*) de midi.

noose [nuːs] *n* (*loop*) nœud *m* coulant; (*of hangman*) corde *f*.

nor [nɔːr] *conj* ni; **neither you n. me** ni toi ni moi; **she neither drinks n. smokes** elle ne fume ni ne boit; **n. do I, n. can I** *etc* (ni) moi non plus; **n. will I (go)** je n'y irai pas non plus.

norm [nɔːm] *n* norme *f*.

normal ['nɔːm(ə)l] *a* normal; – *n* **above n.** au-dessus de la normale. ◆**nor'mality** *n* normalité *f*. ◆**normalize** *vt* normaliser. ◆**normally** *adv* normalement.

Norman ['nɔːmən] *a* normand.

north [nɔːθ] *n* nord *m*; – *a* (*coast*) nord *inv*; (*wind*) du nord; **to be n. of** être au nord de; **N. America/Africa** Amérique *f*/Afrique *f* du Nord; **N. American** *a* & *n* nord-américain, -aine (*mf*); – *adv* au nord, vers le nord. ◆**northbound** *a* (*carriageway*) nord *inv*; (*traffic*) en direction du nord. ◆**north-'east** *n* & *a* nord-est *m* & *a inv*. ◆**northerly** *a* (*point*) nord *inv*; (*direction, wind*) du nord. ◆**northern** *a* (*coast*) nord *inv*; (*town*) du nord; **N. France** le Nord de la France; **N. Europe** Europe *f* du Nord; **N. Ireland** Irlande *f* du Nord. ◆**northerner** *n* habitant, -ante *mf* du Nord. ◆**northward(s)** *a* & *adv* vers le nord. ◆**north-'west** *n* & *a* nord-ouest *m* & *a inv*.

Norway ['nɔːweɪ] *n* Norvège *f*. ◆**Nor'wegian** *a* & *n* norvégien, -ienne (*mf*); – *n* (*language*) norvégien *m*.

nose [nəʊz] *n* nez *m*; **her n. is bleeding** elle saigne du nez; **to turn one's n. up** *Fig* faire le dégoûté (**at** devant); – *vi* **to n. about** (*pry*) *Fam* fouiner. ◆**nosebleed** *n* saignement *m* de nez. ◆**nosedive** *n* *Av* piqué *m*; (*in prices*) chute *f*.

nos(e)y ['nəʊzɪ] *a* (**-ier, -iest**) fouineur, indiscret; **n. parker** fouineur, -euse *mf*.

nosh [nɒʃ] *vi* *Fam* (*eat heavily*) bouffer; (*nibble*) grignoter (entre les repas); – *n* (*food*) *Fam* bouffe *f*.

nostalgia [nɒ'stældʒɪə] *n* nostalgie *f*. ◆**nostalgic** *a* nostalgique.

nostril ['nɒstr(ə)l] *n* (*of person*) narine *f*; (*of horse*) naseau *m*.

not [nɒt] *adv* **1** (ne) . . . pas; **he's n. there, he** isn't there il n'est pas là; **n. yet** pas encore; **why n.?** pourquoi pas?; **n. one reply/etc** pas une seule réponse/*etc*; **n. at all** pas du tout; (*after 'thank you'*) je vous en prie. **2** non; **I think/hope n.** je pense/j'espère que non; **n. guilty** non coupable; **isn't she?, don't you?** *etc* non?

notable ['nəʊtəb(ə)l] *a* (*remarkable*) notable; – *n* (*person*) notable *m*. ◆**notably** *adv* (*noticeably*) notablement; (*particularly*) notamment.

notary ['nəʊtərɪ] *n* notaire *m*.

notation [nəʊ'teɪʃ(ə)n] *n* notation *f*.

notch [nɒtʃ] **1** *n* (*in wood etc*) entaille *f*, encoche *f*; (*in belt, wheel*) cran *m*. **2** *vt* **to n. up** (*a score*) marquer; (*a victory*) enregistrer.

note [nəʊt] *n* (*written comment, tone etc*) & *Mus* note *f*; (*summary, preface*) notice *f*; (*banknote*) billet *m*; (*piano key*) touche *f*; (*message, letter*) petit mot *m*; **to take (a) n. of, make a n. of** prendre note de; **of n.** (*athlete, author etc*) éminent; – *vt* (*take note of*) noter; (*notice*) remarquer, noter; **to n. down** noter. ◆**notebook** *n* carnet *m*; *Sch* cahier *m*; (*pad*) bloc-notes *m*. ◆**notepad** *n* bloc-notes *m*. ◆**notepaper** *n* papier *m* à lettres.

noted ['nəʊtɪd] *a* (*author etc*) éminent; **to be n. for** être connu pour.

noteworthy ['nəʊtwɜːðɪ] *a* notable.

nothing ['nʌθɪŋ] *pron* (ne) . . . rien; **he knows n.** il ne sait rien; **n. to do/eat/etc** rien à faire/manger/*etc*; **n. big/etc** rien de grand/*etc*; **n. much** pas grand-chose; **I've got n. to do with it** je n'y suis pour rien; **I can do n. (about it)** je n'y peux rien; **to come to n.** (*of effort etc*) ne rien donner; **there's n. like it** il n'y a rien de tel; **for n.** (*in vain, free of charge*) pour rien; – *adv* **to look n. like s.o.** ne ressembler nullement à qn; **n. like as large/etc** loin d'être aussi grand/*etc*; – *n* **a (mere) n.** (*person*) une nullité; (*thing*) un rien. ◆**—ness** *n* (*void*) néant *m*.

notice ['nəʊtɪs] *n* (*notification*) avis *m*; *Journ* annonce *f*; (*sign*) pancarte *f*, écriteau *m*; (*poster*) affiche *f*; (*review of film etc*) critique *f*; (*attention*) attention *f*; (*knowledge*) connaissance *f*; (**advance**) **n.** (*of departure etc*) préavis *m*; (**to quit**), **n.** (*of dismissal*) congé *m*; **to give (in) one's n.** (*resignation*) donner sa démission; **to give s.o. n. of** (*inform of*) avertir qn de; **to take n.** faire attention (**of** à); **to bring sth to s.o.'s n.** porter qch à la connaissance de qn; **until further n.** jusqu'à nouvel ordre; **at short n.** à bref délai; **n. board** tableau *m* d'affichage; *– vt* (*perceive*) remarquer (*qn*); (*fact, trick, danger*) s'apercevoir de, remarquer; **I n. that** je m'aperçois que. ◆**—able** *a* visible, perceptible; **that's n.** ça se voit; **she's n.** elle se fait remarquer.

notify ['nəʊtɪfaɪ] *vt* (*inform*) aviser (**s.o. of sth** qn de qch); (*announce*) notifier (**to** à). ◆**notifi'cation** *n* annonce *f*, avis *m*.

notion ['nəʊʃ(ə)n] **1** *n* (*thought*) idée *f*; (*awareness*) notion *f*; **some n. of** (*knowledge*) quelques notions de. **2** *npl* (*sewing articles*) *Am* mercerie *f*.

notorious [nəʊ'tɔːrɪəs] *a* (*event, person etc*) tristement célèbre; (*stupidity, criminal*) notoire. ◆**notoriety** [-ə'raɪətɪ] *n* (triste) notoriété *f*.

notwithstanding [nɒtwɪð'stændɪŋ] *prep* malgré; *– adv* tout de même.

nougat ['nuːɡaɪ] *n* nougat *m*.

nought [nɔːt] *n* *Math* zéro *m*.

noun [naʊn] *n* *Gram* nom *m*.

nourish ['nʌrɪʃ] *vt* nourrir. ◆**—ing** *a* nourrissant. ◆**—ment** *n* nourriture *f*.

novel ['nɒv(ə)l] **1** *n* *Liter* roman *m*. **2** *a* (*new*) nouveau, original. ◆**novelist** *n* romancier, -ière *mf*. ◆**novelty** *n* (*newness, object, idea*) nouveauté *f*.

November [nəʊ'vembər] *n* novembre *m*.

novice ['nɒvɪs] *n* novice *mf* (**at** en).

now [naʊ] *adv* maintenant; **just n., right n.** en ce moment; **I saw her just n.** je l'ai vue à l'instant; **for n.** pour le moment; **even n.** encore maintenant; **from n. on** désormais, à partir de maintenant; **until n., up to n.** jusqu'ici; **before n.** avant; **n. and then** de temps à autre; **n. hot, n. cold** tantôt chaud, tantôt froid; **n. (then)!** bon!, alors!; (*telling s.o. off*) allons!; **n. it happened that . . .** or il advint que . . . ; *– conj* **n. (that)** maintenant que. ◆**nowadays** *adv* aujourd'hui, de nos jours.

noway ['nəʊweɪ] *adv* *Am* nullement.

nowhere ['nəʊweər] *adv* nulle part; **n. else** nulle part ailleurs; **it's n. I know** ce n'est pas un endroit que je connais; **n. near the house** loin de la maison; **n. near enough** loin d'être assez.

nozzle ['nɒz(ə)l] *n* (*of hose*) jet *m*, lance *f* (à eau); (*of syringe, tube*) embout *m*.

nth [enθ] *a* nième.

nuance ['njuːɑːns] *n* (*of meaning, colour etc*) nuance *f*.

nub [nʌb] *n* (*of problem*) cœur *m*.

nuclear ['njuːklɪər] *a* nucléaire; **n. scientist** spécialiste *mf* du nucléaire, atomiste *mf*.

nucleus, *pl* **-clei** ['njuːklɪəs, -klɪaɪ] *n* noyau *m*.

nude [njuːd] *a* nu; *– n* (*female or male figure*) nu *m*; **in the n.** (tout) nu. ◆**nudism** *n* nudisme *m*, naturisme *m*. ◆**nudist** *n* nudiste *mf*, naturiste *mf*; *– a* (*camp*) de nudistes, de naturistes. ◆**nudity** *n* nudité *f*.

nudge [nʌdʒ] *vt* pousser du coude; *– n* coup *m* de coude.

nugget ['nʌɡɪt] *n* (*of gold etc*) pépite *f*.

nuisance ['njuːs(ə)ns] *n* (*annoyance*) embêtement *m*; (*person*) peste *f*; **that's a n.** c'est embêtant; **he's being a n., he's making a n. of himself** il nous embête, il m'embête *etc*.

null [nʌl] *a* **n. (and void)** nul (et non avenu). ◆**nullify** *vt* infirmer.

numb [nʌm] *a* (*stiff*) engourdi; *Fig* paralysé; *– vt* engourdir; *Fig* paralyser.

number ['nʌmbər] *n* nombre *m*; (*of page, house, newspaper etc*) numéro *m*; **a dance/song n.** un numéro de danse/de chant; **a/any n. of** un certain/grand nombre de; **n. plate** (*of vehicle*) plaque *f* d'immatriculation; *– vt* (*page etc*) numéroter; (*amount, count*) compter; **they n. eight** ils sont au nombre de huit. ◆**—ing** *n* numérotage *m*.

numeral ['njuːm(ə)rəl] *n* chiffre *m*; *– a* numéral. ◆**nu'merical** *a* numérique. ◆**numerous** *a* nombreux.

numerate ['njuːm(ə)rət] *a* (*person*) qui sait compter.

nun [nʌn] *n* religieuse *f*.

nurs/e [nɜːs] **1** *n* infirmière *f*; (*nanny*) nurse *f*; (*male*) **n.** infirmier *m*. **2** *vt* (*look after*) soigner; (*cradle*) bercer; (*suckle*) nourrir; (*a grudge etc*) *Fig* nourrir; (*support, encourage*) *Fig* épauler (*qn*). ◆**—ing** *a* (*mother*) qui allaite; (*the sick*) qui soigne; **n. staff** le personnel infirmier; *– n* (*care*) soins *mpl*; (*job*) profession *f* d'infirmière *or* d'infirmier; **n. home** clinique *f*. ◆**nursemaid** *n* bonne *f* d'enfants.

nursery ['nɜːsərɪ] *n* (*room*) chambre *f* d'enfants; (*for plants, trees*) pépinière *f*; (*day*) **n.** (*school etc*) crèche *f*, garderie *f*; **n. rhyme** chanson *f* enfantine; **n. school** école *f* maternelle.

nurture ['nɜːtʃər] *vt* (*educate*) éduquer.

nut¹ [nʌt] *n* (*fruit*) fruit *m* à coque; (*walnut*) noix *f*; (*hazelnut*) noisette *f*; (*peanut*) cacah(o)uète *f*; **Brazil/cashew n.** noix *f* du Brésil/de cajou. ◆**nutcracker(s)** *n*(*pl*) casse-noix *m inv*. ◆**nutshell** *n* coquille *f* de noix; **in a n.** *Fig* en un mot.

nut² [nʌt] *n* **1** (*for bolt*) *Tech* écrou *m*. **2**

(*head*) *Sl* caboche *f*. **3** (*person*) *Sl* cinglé, -ée *mf*; **to be nuts** *Sl* être cinglé. ◆**nutcase** *n* cinglé, -ée *mf*. ◆**nutty** *a* (**-ier, -iest**) *Sl* cinglé.

nutmeg ['nʌtmeg] *n* muscade *f*.

nutritious [njuː'trɪʃəs] *a* nutritif. ◆'**nutri-** **ent** *n* élément *m* nutritif. ◆**nutrition** *n* nutrition *f*.

nylon ['naɪlɒn] *n* nylon *m*; *pl* (*stockings*) bas *mpl* nylon.

nymph [nɪmf] *n* nymphe *f*. ◆**nympho-** '**maniac** *n Pej* nymphomane *f*.

O

O, o [əʊ] *n* O, o *m*.

oaf [əʊf] *n* rustre *m*. ◆**oafish** *a* (*behaviour*) de rustre.

oak [əʊk] *n* (*tree, wood*) chêne *m*.

OAP [əʊeɪ'piː] *n abbr* (*old age pensioner*) retraité, -ée *mf*.

oar [ɔːr] *n* aviron *m*, rame *f*.

oasis, pl oases [əʊ'eɪsɪs, əʊ'eɪsiːz] *n* oasis *f*.

oath [əʊθ] *n* (*pl -s* [əʊðz]) (*promise*) serment *m*; (*profanity*) juron *m*; **to take an o. to do** faire le serment de faire.

oats [əʊts] *npl* avoine *f*. ◆**oatmeal** *n* flocons *mpl* d'avoine.

obedient [ə'biːdɪənt] *a* obéissant. ◆**obe-** **dience** *n* obéissance *f* (**to** à). ◆**obediently** *adv* docilement.

obelisk ['ɒbəlɪsk] *n* (*monument*) obélisque *m*.

obese [əʊ'biːs] *a* obèse. ◆**obesity** *n* obésité *f*.

obey [ə'beɪ] *vt* obéir à; **to be obeyed** être obéi; – *vi* obéir.

obituary [ə'bɪtjʊərɪ] *n* nécrologie *f*.

object¹ ['ɒbdʒɪkt] *n* (*thing*) objet *m*; (*aim*) but *m*, objet *m*; *Gram* complément *m* (d'objet); **with the o. of** dans le but de; **that's no o.** (*no problem*) ça ne pose pas de problème; **price no o.** prix *m* indifférent.

object² [əb'dʒekt] *vi* **to o. to sth/s.o.** désapprouver qch/qn; **I o. to you(r) doing that** ça me gêne que tu fasses ça; **I o.!** je proteste!; **she didn't o. when . . .** elle n'a fait aucune objection quand . . . ; – *vt* **to o. that** objecter que. ◆**objection** *n* objection *f*; **I've got no o.** ça ne me gêne pas, je n'y vois pas d'objection *or* d'inconvénient. ◆**objectionable** *a* très désagréable. ◆**objector** *n* opposant, -ante *mf* (**to** à); **conscientious o.** objecteur *m* de conscience.

objective [əb'dʒektɪv] **1** *a* (*opinion etc*) objectif. **2** *n* (*aim, target*) objectif *m*. ◆**objectively** *adv* objectivement. ◆**ob-** **jec'tivity** *n* objectivité *f*.

obligate ['ɒblɪgeɪt] *vt* contraindre (**to do** à faire). ◆**obli'gation** *n* obligation *f*; (*debt*) dette *f*; **under an o. to do** dans l'obligation de faire; **under an o. to s.o.** redevable à qn (**for** de). ◆o'**bligatory** *a* (*compulsory*) obligatoire; (*imposed by custom*) de rigueur.

oblig/e [ə'blaɪdʒ] *vt* **1** (*compel*) obliger (**s.o. to do** qn à faire); **obliged to do** obligé de faire. **2** (*help*) rendre service à, faire plaisir à; **obliged to s.o.** reconnaissant à qn (**for** de); **much obliged!** merci infiniment! ◆**—ing** *a* (*kind*) obligeant. ◆**—ingly** *adv* obligeamment.

oblique [ə'bliːk] *a* oblique; (*reference*) *Fig* indirect.

obliterate [ə'blɪtəreɪt] *vt* effacer. ◆**oblite-** '**ration** *n* effacement *m*.

oblivion [ə'blɪvɪən] *n* oubli *m*. ◆**oblivious** *a* inconscient (**to, of** de).

oblong ['ɒblɒŋ] *a* (*elongated*) oblong; (*rectangular*) rectangulaire; – *n* rectangle *m*.

obnoxious [əb'nɒkʃəs] *a* odieux; (*smell*) nauséabond.

oboe ['əʊbəʊ] *n Mus* hautbois *m*.

obscene [əb'siːn] *a* obscène. ◆**obscenity** *n* obscénité *f*.

obscure [əb'skjʊər] *a* (*reason, word, actor, life etc*) obscur; – *vt* (*hide*) cacher; (*confuse*) embrouiller, obscurcir. ◆**obscurely** *adv* obscurément. ◆**obscurity** *n* obscurité *f*.

obsequious [əb'siːkwɪəs] *a* obséquieux.

observe [əb'zɜːv] *vt* (*notice, watch, respect*) observer; (*say*) (faire) remarquer (**that** que); **to o. the speed limit** respecter la limitation de vitesse. ◆**observance** *n* (*of rule etc*) observation *f*. ◆**observant** *a* observateur. ◆**obser'vation** *n* (*observing, remark*) observation *f*; (*by police*) surveillance *f*; **under o.** (*hospital patient*) en obser-

vation. ◆**observatory** n observatoire m.
◆**observer** n observateur, -trice mf.

obsess [əb'ses] vt obséder. ◆**obsession** n obsession f; **to have an o. with** or **about** avoir l'obsession de. ◆**obsessive** a (memory, idea) obsédant; (fear) obsessif; (neurotic) Psy obsessionnel; **to be o. about** avoir l'obsession de.

obsolete ['ɒbsəliːt] a (out of date, superseded) désuet, dépassé; (ticket) périmé; (machinery) archaïque. ◆**obso'lescent** a quelque peu désuet; (word) vieilli.

obstacle ['ɒbstək(ə)l] n obstacle m.

obstetrics [əb'stetriks] n Med obstétrique f. ◆**obste'trician** n médecin m accoucheur.

obstinate ['ɒbstɪnət] a (person, resistance etc) obstiné, opiniâtre; (disease, pain) rebelle, opiniâtre. ◆**obstinacy** n obstination f. ◆**obstinately** adv obstinément.

obstreperous [əb'strepərəs] a turbulent.

obstruct [əb'strʌkt] vt (block) boucher; (hinder) entraver; (traffic) entraver, bloquer. ◆**obstruction** n (act, state) & Med Pol Sp obstruction f; (obstacle) obstacle m; (in pipe) bouchon m; (traffic jam) embouteillage m. ◆**obstructive** a to be o. faire de l'obstruction.

obtain [əb'teɪn] 1 vt obtenir. 2 vi (of practice etc) avoir cours. ◆**—able** a (available) disponible; (on sale) en vente.

obtrusive [əb'truːsɪv] a (person) importun; (building etc) trop en évidence.

obtuse [əb'tjuːs] a (angle, mind) obtus.

obviate ['ɒbvɪeɪt] vt (necessity) éviter.

obvious ['ɒbvɪəs] a évident; **he's the o. man to see** c'est évidemment l'homme qu'il faut voir. ◆**—ly** adv (evidently, of course) évidemment; (conspicuously) visiblement.

occasion [ə'keɪʒ(ə)n] 1 n (time, opportunity) occasion f; (event, ceremony) événement m; **on the o. of** à l'occasion de; **on o.** à l'occasion; **on several occasions** à plusieurs reprises or occasions. 2 n (cause) raison f, occasion f; – vt occasionner. ◆**occasional** a (event) qui a lieu de temps en temps; (rain, showers) intermittent; **she drinks the o. whisky** elle boit un whisky de temps en temps. ◆**occasionally** adv de temps en temps; **very o.** très souvent, rarement.

occult [ə'kʌlt] a occulte.

occupy ['ɒkjʊpaɪ] vt (house, time, space, post etc) occuper; **to keep oneself occupied** s'occuper (**doing** à faire). ◆**occupant** n (inhabitant) occupant, -ante mf. ◆**occu-'pation** n (activity) occupation f; (job) emploi m; (trade) métier m; (profession)

profession f; **the o. of** (action) l'occupation f de; **fit for o.** (house) habitable. ◆**occu-'pational** a (hazard) du métier; (disease) du travail. ◆**occupier** n (of house) occupant, -ante mf; Mil occupant m.

occur [ə'kɜːr] vi (-rr-) (happen) avoir lieu; (be found) se rencontrer; (arise) se présenter; **it occurs to me that...** il me vient à l'esprit que...; **the idea occurred to her to...** l'idée lui est venue de.... ◆**occurrence** [ə'kʌrəns] n (event) évènement m; (existence) existence f; (of word) Ling occurrence f.

ocean ['əʊʃ(ə)n] n océan m. ◆**oce'anic** a océanique.

o'clock [ə'klɒk] adv (it's) three o'c./etc (il est) trois heures/etc.

octagon ['ɒktəgən] n octogone m. ◆**oc'tagonal** a octogonal.

octave ['ɒktɪv, 'ɒkteɪv] n Mus octave f.

October [ɒk'təʊbər] n octobre m.

octogenarian [ɒktəʊ'dʒɪneərɪən] n octogénaire mf.

octopus ['ɒktəpəs] n pieuvre f.

odd [ɒd] a 1 (strange) bizarre, curieux; **an o. size** une taille peu courante. 2 (number) impair. 3 (left over) **I have an o. penny** il me reste un penny; **a few o. stamps** quelques timbres (qui restent); **the o. man out, the o. one out** l'exception f; **sixty o.** soixante et quelques; **an o. glove/book/etc** un gant/livre/etc dépareillé. 4 (occasional) qu'on fait, voit etc de temps en temps; **to find the o. mistake** trouver de temps en temps une (petite) erreur; **at o. moments** de temps en temps; **o. jobs** (around house) menus travaux mpl; **o. job man** homme m à tout faire. ◆**oddity** n (person) personne f bizarre; (object) curiosité f; pl (of language, situation) bizarreries fpl. ◆**oddly** adv bizarrement; **o. (enough), he was...** chose curieuse, il était.... ◆**oddment** n Com fin f de série. ◆**oddness** n bizarrerie f.

odds [ɒdz] npl 1 (in betting) cote f; (chances) chances fpl; **we have heavy o. against us** nous avons très peu de chances de réussir. 2 **it makes no o.** (no difference) Fam ça ne fait rien. 3 **at o.** (in disagreement) en désaccord (**with** avec). 4 **o. and ends** des petites choses.

ode [əʊd] n (poem) ode f.

odious ['əʊdɪəs] a détestable, odieux.

odour ['əʊdər] n odeur f. ◆**—less** a inodore.

oecumenical [iːkjuː'menɪk(ə)l] a Rel œcuménique.

of [əv, stressed ɒv] prep de; **of the table** de la

table; **of the boy** du garçon; **of the boys** des garçons; **of a book** d'un livre; **of it, of them** en; **she has a lot of it** *or* **of them** elle en a beaucoup; **a friend of his** un ami à lui; **there are ten of us** nous sommes dix; **that's nice of you** c'est gentil de ta part; **of no value/interest/***etc* sans valeur/intérêt/*etc*; **of late** ces derniers temps; **a man of fifty** un homme de cinquante ans; **the fifth of June** le cinq juin.

off [ɒf] **1** *adv* (*absent*) absent, parti; (*light, gas, radio etc*) éteint, fermé; (*tap*) fermé; (*switched off at mains*) coupé; (*detached*) détaché; (*removed*) enlevé; (*cancelled*) annulé; (*not fit to eat or drink*) mauvais; (*milk, meat*) tourné; **o.** à 2 km (*d'ici or* de là), éloigné de 2 km; **to be** *ou* **go o.** (*leave*) partir; **where are you o. to?** où vas-tu?; **he has his hat o.** il a enlevé son chapeau; **with his, my** *etc* **gloves o.** sans gants; **a day o.** (*holiday*) un jour de congé; **I'm o. today, I have today o.** j'ai congé aujourd'hui; **the strike's o.** il n'y aura pas de grève, la grève est annulée; **5% o.** une réduction de 5%; **on and o., o. and on** (*sometimes*) de temps à autre; **to be better o.** (*wealthier, in a better position*) être mieux. **2** *prep* (*from*) de; (*distant*) éloigné de; **to fall/***etc* **o. the wall/ladder/***etc* tomber/*etc* du mur/de l'échelle/*etc*; **to get o. the bus/***etc* descendre du bus/*etc*; **to take sth o. the table/***etc* prendre qch sur la table/*etc*; **to eat o. a plate** manger dans une assiette; **to keep** *or* **stay o. the grass** ne pas marcher sur les pelouses; **she's o. her food** elle ne mange plus rien; **o. Dover/***etc* Nau au large de Douvres/*etc*; **o. limits** interdit; **the o. side** *Aut* le côté droit, *Am* le côté gauche. ◆**off'beat** *a* excentrique. ◆**off'-'colour** *a* (*ill*) patraque; (*indecent*) scabreux. ◆**off'hand** *a* désinvolte; – *adv* impromptu. ◆**off'handedness** *n* désinvolture *f*. ◆**off-licence** *n* magasin *m* de vins et de spiritueux. ◆**off-'load** *vt* (*vehicle etc*) décharger; **to o.-load sth onto s.o.** (*task etc*) se décharger de qch sur qn. ◆**off-'peak** *a* (*crowds, traffic*) aux heures creuses; (*rate, price*) heures creuses *inv*; **o.-peak hours** heures *fpl* creuses. ◆**off-putting** *a Fam* rebutant. ◆**off'side** *a* to be **o.** *Fb* être hors jeu. ◆**off'stage** *a* & *adv* dans les coulisses. ◆**off-'white** *a* blanc cassé *inv*.

offal ['ɒf(ə)l] *n* Culin abats *mpl*.

offence [ə'fens] *n Jur* délit *m*; **to take o.** s'offenser (**at** de); **to give o.** offenser.

offend [ə'fend] *vt* froisser, offenser; (*eye*) Fig

choquer; **to be offended (at)** se froisser (de), s'offenser (de). ◆**—ing** *a* (*object, remark*) incriminé. ◆**offender** *n Jur* délinquant, -ante *mf*; (*habitual*) récidiviste *mf*.

offensive [ə'fensiv] **1** *a* (*unpleasant*) choquant, repoussant; (*insulting*) insultant, offensant; (*weapon*) offensif. **2** *n Mil* offensive *f*.

offer ['ɒfər] *n* offre *f*; **on (special) o.** Com en promotion, en réclame; **o. of marriage** demande *f* en mariage; – *vt* offrir; (*opinion, remark*) proposer; **to o. to do** offrir *ou* proposer de faire. ◆**—ing** *n* (*gift*) offrande *f*; (*act*) offre *f*; **peace o.** cadeau *m* de réconciliation.

office ['ɒfis] *n* **1** bureau *m*; (*of doctor*) *Am* cabinet *m*; (*of lawyer*) étude *f*; **head o.** siège *m* central; **o. block** immeuble *m* de bureaux; **o. worker** employé, -ée *mf* de bureau. **2** (*post*) fonction *f*; (*duty*) fonctions *fpl*; **to be in o.** (*of party etc*) Pol être au pouvoir. **3** **one's good offices** (*help*) ses bons offices *mpl*.

officer ['ɒfisər] *n* (*in army, navy etc*) officier *m*; (*of company*) Com directeur, -trice *mf*; (*police*) **o.** agent *m* (de police).

official [ə'fiʃ(ə)l] *a* officiel; (*uniform*) réglementaire; – *n* (*person of authority*) officiel *m*; (*civil servant*) fonctionnaire *mf*; (*employee*) employé, -ée *mf*. ◆**officialdom** *n* bureaucratie *f*. ◆**officially** *adv* officiellement. ◆**officiate** *vi* faire fonction d'officiel (**at** à); (*preside*) présider; *Rel* officier.

officious [ə'fiʃəs] *a Pej* empressé.

offing ['ɒfiŋ] *n* **in the o.** en perspective.

offset ['ɒfset, ɒf'set] *vt* (*pt & pp* offset, *pres p* offsetting) (*compensate for*) compenser; (*s.o.'s beauty etc by contrast*) faire ressortir.

offshoot ['ɒfʃuːt] *n* (*of firm*) ramification *f*; (*consequence*) conséquence *f*.

offspring ['ɒfspriŋ] *n* progéniture *f*.

often ['ɒf(t)ən] *adv* souvent; **how o.?** combien de fois?; **how o. do they run?** (*trains, buses etc*) il y en a tous les combien?; **once too o.** une fois de trop; **every so o.** de temps en temps.

ogle ['əʊg(ə)l] *vt Pej* reluquer.

ogre ['əʊgər] *n* ogre *m*.

oh! [əʊ] *int* oh!, ah!; (*pain*) aïe!; **oh yes?** ah oui?, ah bon?

oil [ɔil] *n* (*for machine, in cooking etc*) huile *f*; (*mineral*) pétrole *m*; (*fuel oil*) mazout *m*; **to paint in oils** faire de la peinture à l'huile; – *a* (*industry, product*) pétrolier; (*painting, paints*) à l'huile; **o. lamp** lampe *f* à pétrole *or* à huile; **o. change** *Aut* vidange *f*; – *vt*

graisser, huiler. ◆**oilcan** n burette f.
◆**oilfield** n gisement m pétrolifère. ◆**oil-fired** a au mazout. ◆**oilskin(s)** n(pl)
(garment) ciré m. ◆**oily** a (-ier, -iest)
(substance, skin) huileux; (hands) grais-seux; (food) gras.

ointment ['ɔɪntmənt] n pommade f.

OK [əʊ'keɪ] int (approval, exasperation) ça
va!; (agreement) d'accord!, entendu!, OK!;
– a (satisfactory) bien inv; (unharmed) sain
et sauf; (undamaged) intact; (without
worries) tranquille; **it's OK now** (fixed) ça
marche maintenant; **I'm OK** (healthy) je
vais bien; – adv (to work etc) bien; – vt (pt
& pp **OKed**, pres p **OKing**) approuver.

okay [əʊ'keɪ] = OK.

old [əʊld] a (-er, -est) vieux; (former)
ancien; **how o. is he?** quel âge a-t-il?; **he's
ten years o.** il a dix ans, il est âgé de dix
ans; **he's older than** il est plus âgé que; **an
older son** un fils aîné; **the oldest son** le fils
aîné; **o. enough to do** assez grand pour
faire; **o. enough to marry/vote** en âge de se
marier/de voter; **an o. man** un vieillard, un
vieil homme; **an o. woman** une vieille
(femme); **to get** or **grow old(er)** vieillir; **o.
age** vieillesse f; **the O. Testament** l'Ancien
Testament; **the O. World** l'Ancien Monde;
any o. how Fam n'importe comment; – n
the o. (people) les vieux mpl. ◆**o.-
'fashioned** a (customs etc) d'autrefois;
(idea, attitude) Pej vieux jeu inv; (person)
de la vieille école, Pej vieux jeu inv.
◆**o.-'timer** n (old man) Fam vieillard m.

olden ['əʊld(ə)n] a **in o. days** jadis.

olive ['ɒlɪv] n (fruit) olive f; – a **o. (green)**
(vert) olive inv; **o. oil** huile f d'olive; **o. tree**
olivier m.

Olympic [ə'lɪmpɪk] a olympique.

ombudsman ['ɒmbʊdzmən] n (pl -men)
Pol médiateur m.

omelet(te) ['ɒmlɪt] n omelette f; **cheese/etc
o.** omelette au fromage/etc.

omen ['əʊmən] n augure m. ◆**ominous** a
de mauvais augure; (tone) menaçant;
(noise) sinistre.

omit [əʊ'mɪt] vt (-tt-) omettre (**to do** de
faire). ◆**omission** n omission f.

omni- ['ɒmnɪ] pref omni-. ◆**om'nipotent**
a omnipotent.

on [ɒn] prep **1** (position) sur; **on the chair** sur
la chaise; **to put on** (to) mettre sur; **to look
out on to** donner sur. **2** (concerning, about)
sur; **an article on** un article sur; **to speak** or
talk on Dickens/etc parler de Dickens/etc.
3 (manner, means) à; **on foot** à pied; **on the
blackboard** au tableau; **on the radio** à la

radio; **on the train/plane**/etc dans le
train/avion/etc; **on holiday**, Am **on vacation** en vacances; **to be on** (course) suivre;
(project) travailler à; (salary) toucher;
(team, committee) être membre de, faire
partie de; **to keep** or **stay on** (road, path etc)
suivre; **it's on me!** (I'll pay) Fam c'est moi
qui paie! **4** (time) **on Monday** lundi; **on
Mondays** le lundi; **on May 3rd** le 3 mai; **on
the evening of May 3rd** le 3 mai au soir; **on
my arrival** à mon arrivée. **5** (+ present
participle) en; **on learning that ...** en
apprenant que ...; **on seeing this** en
voyant ceci. **6** adv (ahead) en avant; (in
progress) en cours; (started) commencé;
(lid, brake) mis; (light, radio) allumé; (gas,
tap) ouvert; (machine) en marche; **on (and
on)** sans cesse; **to play**/etc **on** continuer à
jouer/etc; **she has her hat on** elle a mis or
elle porte son chapeau; **he has sth/nothing
on** il est habillé/tout nu; **I've got sth on**
(I'm busy) je suis pris; **the strike's on** la
grève aura lieu; **what's on?** TV qu'y a-t-il à
la télé?; Cin Th qu'est-ce qu'on joue?;
there's a film on on passe un film; **to be on
at s.o.** (pester) Fam être après qn; **I've been
on to him** Tel je l'ai eu au bout du fil; **to be
on to s.o.** (of police etc) être sur la piste de
qn; **from then on** à partir de là. ◆**on-coming** a (vehicle) qui vient en sens
inverse. ◆**on-going** a (project) en cours.

once [wʌns] adv (on one occasion) une fois;
(formerly) autrefois; **o. a month**/etc une
fois par mois/etc; **o. again**, **o. more** encore
une fois; **at o.** (immediately) tout de suite;
all at o. (suddenly) tout à coup; (at the same
time) à la fois; **o. and for all** une fois pour
toutes; – conj une fois que. ◆**o.-over** n **to
give sth the o.-over** (quick look) Fam
regarder qch d'un coup d'œil.

one [wʌn] a **1** un, une; **o. man** un homme; **o.
woman** une femme; **twenty-o.** vingt-et-un.
2 (sole) seul; **my o. (and only) aim** mon seul
(et unique) but. **3** (same) même; **in the o.
bus** dans le même bus; – pron **1** un, une; **do
you want o.?** en veux-tu (un)?; **he's o. of us**
il est des nôtres; **o. of them** l'un d'eux, l'une
d'elles; **a big/small**/etc **o.** un grand/petit/
etc; **this book is o. that I've read** ce livre est
parmi ceux que j'ai lus; **she's o.** (a teacher,
gardener etc) elle l'est; **this o.** celui-ci,
celle-ci; **that o.** celui-là, celle-là; **the o. who**
or **which** celui or celle qui; **it's Paul's o.** Fam
c'est celui de Paul; **it's my o.** Fam c'est à
moi; **another o.** un(e) autre; **I for o.** pour
ma part. **2** (impersonal) on; **o. knows** on
sait; **it helps o.** ça nous or vous aide; **one's**

family sa famille. ◆**one-'armed** *a* (*person*) manchot. ◆**one-'eyed** *a* borgne. ◆**one-'off** *a*, *Am* **one-of-a-'kind** *a Fam* unique, exceptionnel. ◆**one-'sided** *a* (*judgement etc*) partial; (*contest*) inégal; (*decision*) unilatéral. ◆**one-time** *a* (*former*) ancien. ◆**one-'way** *a* (*street*) à sens unique; (*traffic*) en sens unique; (*ticket*) *Am* simple.

oneself [wʌn'self] *pron* soi-même; (*reflexive*) se, s'; **to cut o.** se couper.

onion ['ʌnjən] *n* oignon *m*.

onlooker ['ɒnlʊkər] *n* spectateur, -trice *mf*.

only ['əʊnlɪ] *a* seul; **the o. house**/*etc* la seule maison/*etc*; **the o. one** le seul, la seule; **an o. son** un fils unique; – *adv* seulement, ne . . . que; **I o. have ten, I have ten o.** je n'en ai que dix, j'en ai dix seulement; **if o.** si seulement; **not o.** non seulement; **I have o. just seen it** je viens tout juste de le voir; – *conj* (*but*) *Fam* seulement; **o. I can't** seulement je ne peux pas.

onset ['ɒnset] *n* (*of disease*) début *m*; (*of old age*) approche *m*.

onslaught ['ɒnslɔːt] *n* attaque *f*.

onto ['ɒntʊ] *prep* = **on to**.

onus ['əʊnəs] *n inv* **the o. is on you**/*etc* c'est votre/*etc* responsabilité (**to do** de faire).

onward(s) ['ɒnwəd(z)] *adv* en avant; **from that time o.** à partir de là.

onyx ['ɒnɪks] *n* (*precious stone*) onyx *m*.

ooze [uːz] *vi* **to o. (out)** suinter; – *vt* (*blood etc*) laisser couler.

opal ['əʊp(ə)l] *n* (*precious stone*) opale *f*.

opaque [əʊ'peɪk] *a* opaque; (*unclear*) *Fig* obscur.

open ['əʊpən] *a* ouvert; (*site, view, road*) dégagé; (*car*) décapoté, découvert; (*meeting*) public; (*competition*) ouvert à tous; (*post*) vacant; (*attempt, envy*) manifeste; (*question*) non résolu; (*result*) indécis; (*ticket*) *Av* open *inv*; **wide o.** grand ouvert; **in the o. air** en plein air; **in the o. country** en rase campagne; **the o. spaces** les grands espaces; **it's o. to doubt** c'est douteux; **o. to** (*criticism, attack*) exposé à; (*ideas, suggestions*) ouvert à; **I've got an o. mind on it** je n'ai pas d'opinion arrêtée là-dessus; **to leave o.** (*date*) ne pas préciser; – *n* (**out**) **in the o.** (*outside*) en plein air; **to sleep** (**out**) **in the o.** dormir à la belle étoile; **to bring** (**out**) **into the o.** (*reveal*) divulguer; – *vt* ouvrir; (*conversation*) entamer; (*legs*) écarter; **to o. out** *or* **up** ouvrir; – *vi* (*of flower, eyes etc*) s'ouvrir; (*of shop, office etc*) ouvrir; (*of play*) débuter; (*of film*) sortir; **the door opens** (*is opened*) la porte s'ouvre; (*can open*) la porte ouvre; **to o. on to** (*of window etc*) donner sur; **to o. out** *or* **up** s'ouvrir; **to o. out** (*widen*) s'élargir; **to o. up** (*open a or the door*) ouvrir. ◆**—ing** *n* ouverture *f*; (*of flower*) éclosion *f*; (*career prospect, trade outlet*) débouché *m*; – *a* (*time, speech*) d'ouverture; **o. night** *Th* première *f*. ◆**—ly** *adv* (*not secretly, frankly*) ouvertement; (*publicly*) publiquement. ◆**—ness** *n* (*frankness*) franchise *f*; **o. of mind** ouverture *f* d'esprit.

open-air [əʊpən'eər] *a* (*pool etc*) en plein air. ◆**o.-'heart** *a* (*operation*) *Med* à cœur ouvert. ◆**o.-'necked** *a* (*shirt*) sans cravate. ◆**o.-'plan** *a Archit* sans cloisons.

opera ['ɒprə] *n* opéra *m*; **o. glasses** jumelles *fpl* de théâtre. ◆**ope'ratic** *a* d'opéra. ◆**ope'retta** *n* opérette *f*.

operat/e ['ɒpəreɪt] **1** *vi* (*of machine etc*) fonctionner; (*proceed*) opérer; – *vt* faire fonctionner; (*business*) gérer. **2** *vi* (*of surgeon*) opérer (**on s.o.** qn, **for** de). ◆**—ing** *a* **o. costs** frais *mpl* d'exploitation; **o. theatre**, *Am* **o. room** *Med* salle *f* d'opération; **o. wing** *Med* bloc *m* opératoire. ◆**ope'ration** *n* (*working*) fonctionnement *m*; *Med Mil Math etc* opération *f*; **in o.** (*machine*) en service; (*plan*) *Fig* en vigueur. ◆**ope-'rational** *a* opérationnel. ◆**operative** *a Med* opératoire; (*law, measure etc*) en vigueur; – *n* ouvrier, -ière *mf*. ◆**operator** *n Tel* standardiste *mf*; (*on machine*) opérateur, -trice *mf*; (*criminal*) escroc *m*; **tour o.** organisateur, -trice *mf* de voyages, voyagiste *m*.

opinion [ə'pɪnjən] *n* opinion *f*, avis *m*; **in my o.** à mon avis. ◆**opinionated** *a* dogmatique.

opium ['əʊpɪəm] *n* opium *m*.

opponent [ə'pəʊnənt] *n* adversaire *mf*.

opportune ['ɒpətjuːn] *a* opportun. ◆**oppor'tunism** *n* opportunisme *m*.

opportunity [ɒpə'tjuːnɪtɪ] *n* occasion *f* (**to do** de faire); *pl* (*prospects*) perspectives *fpl*; **equal opportunities** des chances *fpl* égales.

oppos/e [ə'pəʊz] *vt* (*person, measure etc*) s'opposer à; (*law, motion*) *Pol* faire opposition à. ◆**—ed** *a* opposé (**to** à); **as o. to** par opposition à. ◆**—ing** *a* (*team, interests*) opposé. ◆**oppo'sition** *n* opposition *f* (**to** à); **the o.** (*rival camp*) *Fam* l'adversaire *m*.

opposite ['ɒpəzɪt] *a* (*side etc*) opposé; (*house*) d'en face; **one's o. number** (*counterpart*) son homologue *mf*; – *adv* (*to sit etc*) en face; – *prep* **o. (to)** en face de; – *n* **the o.** le contraire, l'opposé *m*.

oppress [ə'pres] *vt* (*tyrannize*) opprimer; (*of heat, anguish*) oppresser; **the oppressed** les opprimés *mpl.* ◆**oppression** *n* oppression *f.* ◆**oppressive** *a* (*ruler etc*) oppressif; (*heat*) oppressant; (*régime*) tyrannique. ◆**oppressor** *n* oppresseur *m.*

opt [ɒpt] *vi* **to o. for** opter pour; **to o. to do** choisir de faire; **to o. out** *Fam* refuser de participer (**of** à). ◆**option** *n* option *f;* (*subject*) *Sch* matière *f* à option; **she has no o.** elle n'a pas le choix. ◆**optional** *a* facultatif; **o. extra** (*on car etc*) option *f,* accessoire *m* en option.

optical ['ɒptik(ə)l] *a* (*glass*) optique; (*illusion, instrument etc*) d'optique. ◆**op'tician** *n* opticien, -ienne *mf.*

optimism ['ɒptimiz(ə)m] *n* optimisme *m.* ◆**optimist** *n* optimiste *mf.* ◆**opti'mistic** *a* optimiste. ◆**opti'mistically** *adv* avec optimisme.

optimum ['ɒptiməm] *a & n* optimum (*m*); **the o. temperature** la température optimum. ◆**optimal** *a* optimal.

opulent ['ɒpjulənt] *a* opulent. ◆**opulence** *n* opulence *f.*

or [ɔːr] *conj* ou; **one or two** un ou deux; **he doesn't drink or smoke** il ne boit ni ne fume; **ten or so** environ dix.

oracle ['ɒrək(ə)l] *n* oracle *m.*

oral ['ɔːrəl] *a* oral; – *n* (*examination*) *Sch* oral *m.*

orange ['ɒrɪndʒ] **1** *n* (*fruit*) orange *f;* – *a* (*drink*) à l'orange; **o. tree** oranger *m.* **2** *a & n* (*colour*) orange *a & m inv.* ◆**orangeade** *n* orangeade *f.*

orang-outang [ɔːræŋuːˈtæŋ] *n* orang-outan(g) *m.*

oration [ɔːˈreɪʃ(ə)n] *n* **funeral o.** oraison *f* funèbre.

oratory ['ɒrətəri] *n* (*words*) *Pej* rhétorique *f.*

orbit ['ɔːbit] *n* (*of planet etc*) & *Fig* orbite *f;* – *vt* (*sun etc*) graviter autour de.

orchard ['ɔːtʃəd] *n* verger *m.*

orchestra ['ɔːkistrə] *n* (*classical*) orchestre *m.* ◆**or'chestral** *a* (*music*) orchestral; (*concert*) symphonique. ◆**orchestrate** *vt* (*organize*) & *Mus* orchestrer.

orchid ['ɔːkid] *n* orchidée *f.*

ordain [ɔːˈdeɪn] *vt* (*priest*) ordonner; **to o. that** décréter que.

ordeal [ɔːˈdiːl] *n* épreuve *f,* supplice *m.*

order ['ɔːdər] *n* (*command, structure, association etc*) ordre *m;* (*purchase*) *Com* commande *f;* **in o.** (*drawer, room etc*) en ordre; (*passport etc*) en règle; **in (numerical) o.** dans l'ordre numérique; **in working o.** en état de marche; **in o. of age** par ordre d'âge; **in o. to do** pour faire; **in o. that** que (+ *sub*); **it's in o. to smoke/*etc*** (*allowed*) il est permis de fumer/*etc*; **out of o.** (*machine*) en panne; (*telephone*) en dérangement; **to make** *or* **place an o.** *Com* passer une commande; **on o.** *Com* commandé; **money o.** mandat *m;* **postal o.** mandat *m* postal; – *vt* (*command*) ordonner (**s.o. to do** à qn de faire); (*meal, goods etc*) commander; (*taxi*) appeler; **to o. s.o. around** commander qn, régenter qn; – *vi* (*in café etc*) commander. ◆**—ly 1** *a* (*tidy*) ordonné; (*mind*) méthodique; (*crowd*) discipliné. **2** *n Mil* planton *m;* (*in hospital*) garçon *m* de salle.

ordinal ['ɔːdinəl] *a* (*number*) ordinal.

ordinary ['ɔːd(ə)nri] *a* (*usual*) ordinaire; (*average*) moyen; (*mediocre*) médiocre, ordinaire; **an o. individual** un simple particulier; **in o. use** d'usage courant; **in the o. course of events** en temps normal; **in the o. way** normalement; **it's out of the o.** ça sort de l'ordinaire.

ordination [ɔːdɪˈneɪʃ(ə)n] *n Rel* ordination *f.*

ordnance ['ɔːdnəns] *n* (*guns*) *Mil* artillerie *f.*

ore [ɔːr] *n* minerai *m.*

organ ['ɔːgən] *n* **1** *Anat & Fig* organe *m.* **2** *Mus* orgue *m,* orgues *fpl;* **barrel o.** orgue *m* de Barbarie. ◆**organist** *n* organiste *mf.*

organic [ɔːˈgænik] *a* organique. ◆**'organism** *n* organisme *m.*

organization [ɔːgənaɪˈzeɪʃ(ə)n] *n* (*arrangement, association*) organisation *f.*

organiz/e ['ɔːgənaɪz] *vt* organiser. ◆**—ed** (*mind, group etc*) organisé. ◆**—er** *n* organisateur, -trice *mf.*

orgasm ['ɔːgæz(ə)m] *n* orgasme *m.*

orgy ['ɔːdʒɪ] *n* orgie *f.*

orient ['ɔːrɪənt] *vt Am* = **orientate.** ◆**orientate** *vt* orienter.

Orient ['ɔːrɪənt] *n* **the O.** l'Orient *m.* ◆**ori'ental** *a & n* oriental, -ale (*mf*).

orifice ['ɒrɪfɪs] *n* orifice *m.*

origin ['ɒrɪdʒɪn] *n* origine *f.*

original [əˈrɪdʒɪn(ə)l] *a* (*first*) premier, originel, primitif; (*novel, unusual*) original; (*sin*) originel; (*copy, version*) original; – *n* (*document etc*) original *m.* ◆**origi'nality** *n* originalité *f.* ◆**originally** *adv* (*at first*) à l'origine; (*in a novel way*) originalement; **she comes o. from** elle est originaire de. ◆**originate** *vi* (*begin*) prendre naissance (**in** dans); **to o. from** (*of idea etc*) émaner de; (*of person*) être originaire de; – *vt* être l'auteur de. ◆**originator** *n* auteur *m* (**of** de).

ornament ['ɔːnəmənt] *n* (*decoration*) orne-

ment *m*; *pl* (*vases etc*) bibelots *mpl*.
◆orna'mental *a* ornemental. ◆orna-men'tation *n* ornementation *f*. ◆or'nate *a* (*style etc*) (très) orné. ◆or'nately *adv* (*decorated etc*) de façon surchargée, à outrance.

orphan ['ɔːf(ə)n] *n* orphelin, -ine *mf*; – *a* orphelin. ◆orphaned *a* orphelin; he was o. by the accident l'accident l'a rendu orphelin. ◆orphanage *n* orphelinat *m*.

orthodox ['ɔːθədɒks] *a* orthodoxe. ◆orthodoxy *n* orthodoxie *f*.

orthop(a)edics [ɔːθə'piːdɪks] *n* orthopédie *f*.

Oscar ['ɒskər] *n* Cin oscar *m*.

oscillate ['ɒsɪleɪt] *vi* osciller.

ostensibly [ɒ'stensɪblɪ] *adv* apparemment, en apparence.

ostentation [ɒsten'teɪʃ(ə)n] *n* ostentation *f*. ◆ostentatious *a* plein d'ostentation, prétentieux.

ostracism ['ɒstrəsɪz(ə)m] *n* ostracisme *m*. ◆ostracize *vt* proscrire, frapper d'ostracisme.

ostrich ['ɒstrɪtʃ] *n* autruche *f*.

other ['ʌðər] *a* autre; o. people d'autres; the o. one l'autre *mf*; I have no o. gloves than these je n'ai pas d'autres gants que ceux-ci; – *pron* autre; (*some*) others d'autres; some do, others don't les uns le font, les autres ne le font pas; none o. than, no o. than nul autre que; – *adv* o. than autrement que. ◆otherwise *adv* autrement; – *a* (*different*) (tout) autre.

otter ['ɒtər] *n* loutre *f*.

ouch! [autʃ] *int* aïe!, ouille!

ought [ɔːt] *v aux* **1** (*obligation, desirability*) you o. to leave tu devrais partir; I o. to have done it j'aurais dû le faire; he said he o. to stay il a dit qu'il devait rester. **2** (*probability*) it o. to be ready ça devrait être prêt.

ounce [auns] *n* (*measure*) & *Fig* once *f* (= 28,35 g).

our [auər] *poss a* notre, *pl* nos. ◆ours *pron* le nôtre, la nôtre, *pl* les nôtres; this book is o. ce livre est à nous *or* est le nôtre; a friend of o. un ami à nous. ◆our'selves *pron* nous-mêmes; (*reflexive & after prep etc*) nous; we wash o. nous nous lavons.

oust [aust] *vt* évincer (**from** de).

out [aut] *adv* (*outside*) dehors; (*not at home etc*) sorti; (*light, fire*) éteint; (*news, secret*) connu; (*flower*) ouvert; (*book*) publié, sorti; (*finished*) fini; to be *or* go o. a lot sortir beaucoup; he's o. in Italy il est (parti) en Italie; o. there là-bas; to have a

day o. sortir pour la journée; **5 km o.** *Nau* à 5 km du rivage; the sun's o. il fait (du) soleil; the tide's o. la marée est basse; you're o. (*wrong*) tu t'es trompé; (*in game etc*) tu es éliminé (**of** de); the trip *or* journey o. l'aller *m*; to be o. to win être résolu à gagner; – *prep* o. of (*outside*) en dehors de; (*danger, breath, reach, water*) hors de; (*without*) sans; o. of pity/love/*etc* par pitié/amour/*etc*; to look/jump/*etc* o. of (*window etc*) regarder/sauter/*etc* par; to drink/take/copy o. of boire/prendre/copier dans; made o. of (*wood etc*) fait en; to make sth o. of a box/rag/*etc* faire qch avec une boîte/un chiffon/*etc*; a page o. of une page de; she's o. of town elle n'est pas en ville; **5 km o. of** (*away from*) à 5 km de; four o. of five quatre sur cinq; o. of the blue de manière inattendue; to feel o. of it *or* of things se sentir hors du coup. ◆'out-and-out *a* (*cheat, liar etc*) achevé; (*believer*) à tout crin. ◆o.-of-'date *a* (*expired*) périmé; (*old-fashioned*) démodé. ◆o.-of-'doors *adv* dehors. ◆o.-of-the-'way *a* (*place*) écarté.

outbid [aut'bɪd] *vt* (*pt & pp* outbid, *pres p* outbidding) to o. s.o. (sur)enchérir sur qn.

outboard ['autbɔːd] *a* o. motor *Nau* moteur *m* hors-bord *inv*.

outbreak ['autbreɪk] *n* (*of war*) début *m*; (*of violence, pimples*) éruption *f*; (*of fever*) accès *m*; (*of hostilities*) ouverture *f*.

outbuilding ['autbɪldɪŋ] *n* (*of mansion, farm*) dépendance *f*.

outburst ['autbɜːst] *n* (*of anger, joy*) explosion *f*; (*of violence*) flambée *f*; (*of laughter*) éclat *m*.

outcast ['autkɑːst] *n* (**social**) o. paria *m*.

outcome ['autkʌm] *n* résultat *m*, issue *f*.

outcry ['autkraɪ] *n* tollé *m*.

outdated [aut'deɪtɪd] *a* démodé.

outdistance [aut'dɪstəns] *vt* distancer.

outdo [aut'duː] *vt* (*pt* outdid, *pp* outdone) surpasser (**in** en).

outdoor ['autdɔːr] *a* (*game*) de plein air; (*pool, life*) en plein air; o. clothes tenue *f* pour sortir. ◆out'doors *adv* dehors.

outer ['autər] *a* extérieur; o. space l'espace *m* (cosmique); the o. suburbs la grande banlieue.

outfit ['autfɪt] *n* équipement *m*; (*kit*) trousse *f*; (*toy*) panoplie *f* (*de pompier, cow-boy etc*); (*clothes*) costume *m*; (*for woman*) toilette *f*; (*group, gang*) *Fam* bande *f*; (*firm*) *Fam* boîte *f*; sports/ski o. tenue *f* de sport/de ski. ◆outfitter *n* chemisier *m*.

outgoing ['autɡəuɪŋ] **1** *a* (*minister etc*)

sortant; *(mail, ship)* en partance. **2** *a (sociable)* liant, ouvert. **3** *npl (expenses)* dépenses *fpl.*

outgrow [aʊt'grəʊ] *vt (pt* **outgrew,** *pp* **outgrown)** *(clothes)* devenir trop grand pour; *(habit)* perdre (en grandissant); **to o. s.o.** *(grow more than)* grandir plus vite que qn.

outhouse ['aʊthaʊs] *n (of mansion, farm)* dépendance *f; (lavatory) Am* cabinets *mpl* extérieurs.

outing ['aʊtɪŋ] *n* sortie *f,* excursion *f.*

outlandish [aʊt'lændɪʃ] *a (weird)* bizarre; *(barbaric)* barbare.

outlast [aʊt'lɑːst] *vt* durer plus longtemps que; *(survive)* survivre à.

outlaw ['aʊtlɔː] *n* hors-la-loi *m inv;* − *vt (ban)* proscrire.

outlay ['aʊtleɪ] *n (money)* dépense(s) *f(pl).*

outlet ['aʊtlet] *n (for liquid, of tunnel etc)* sortie *f; El* prise *f* de courant; *(market for goods) Com* débouché *m; (for feelings, energy)* moyen *m* d'exprimer, exutoire *m;* **retail o.** *Com* point *m* de vente, magasin *m.*

outline ['aʊtlaɪn] *n (shape)* contour *m,* profil *m;* **(rough) o.** *(of article, plan etc)* esquisse *f;* **the broad** *or* **general** *or* **main outline(s)** *(chief features)* les grandes lignes; − *vt (plan, situation)* décrire à grands traits, esquisser; *(book, speech)* résumer; **to be outlined against** *(of tree etc)* se profiler sur.

outlive [aʊt'lɪv] *vt* survivre à.

outlook ['aʊtlʊk] *n inv (for future)* perspective(s) *f(pl); (point of view)* perspective *f* **(on** sur), attitude *f* **(on** à l'égard de); *Met* prévisions *fpl.*

outlying ['aʊtlaɪɪŋ] *a (remote)* isolé; *(neighbourhood)* périphérique.

outmoded [aʊt'məʊdɪd] *a* démodé.

outnumber [aʊt'nʌmbər] *vt* être plus nombreux que.

outpatient ['aʊtpeɪʃ(ə)nt] *n* malade *mf* en consultation externe.

outpost ['aʊtpəʊst] *n* avant-poste *m.*

output ['aʊtpʊt] *n* rendement *m,* production *f; (computer process)* sortie *f; (computer data)* donnée(s) *f(pl)* de sortie.

outrage ['aʊtreɪdʒ] *n* atrocité *f,* crime *m; (indignity)* indignité *f; (scandal)* scandale *m; (indignation)* indignation *f;* **bomb o.** attentat *m* à la bombe; − *vt (morals)* outrager; **outraged by sth** indigné de qch. ◆**out'rageous** *a (atrocious)* atroce; *(shocking)* scandaleux; *(dress, hat etc)* grotesque.

outright ['aʊtraɪt] *adv (completely)* complètement; *(to say, tell)* franchement; *(to be*

killed*)* sur le coup; **to buy o.** *(for cash)* acheter au comptant; − ['aʊtraɪt] *a (complete)* complet; *(lie, folly)* pur; *(refusal, rejection etc)* catégorique, net; *(winner)* incontesté.

outset ['aʊtset] *n* **at the o.** au début; **from the o.** dès le départ.

outside [aʊt'saɪd] *adv* (au) dehors, à l'extérieur; **to go o.** sortir; − *prep* à l'extérieur de, en dehors de; *(beyond) Fig* en dehors de; **o. my room** *or* **door** à la porte de ma chambre; − *n* extérieur *m,* dehors *m;* − ['aʊtsaɪd] *a* extérieur; *(bus or train seat etc)* côté couloir *inv; (maximum) Fig* maximum; **the o. lane** *Aut* la voie de droite, *Am* la voie de gauche; **an o. chance** une faible chance. ◆**out'sider** *n (stranger)* étranger, -ère *mf; Sp* outsider *m.*

outsize ['aʊtsaɪz] *a (clothes)* grande taille *inv.*

outskirts ['aʊtskɜːts] *npl* banlieue *f.*

outsmart [aʊt'smɑːt] *vt* être plus malin que.

outspoken [aʊt'spəʊk(ə)n] *a (frank)* franc.

outstanding [aʊt'stændɪŋ] *a* remarquable, exceptionnel; *(problem, business)* non réglé, en suspens; *(debt)* impayé; **work o.** travail *m* à faire.

outstay [aʊt'steɪ] *vt* **to o. one's welcome** abuser de l'hospitalité de son hôte, s'incruster.

outstretched [aʊt'stretʃt] *a (arm)* tendu.

outstrip [aʊt'strɪp] *vt* **(-pp-)** devancer.

outward ['aʊtwəd] *a (look, movement)* vers l'extérieur; *(sign, appearance)* extérieur; **o. journey** *or* **trip** aller *m.* ◆**outward(s)** *adv* vers l'extérieur.

outweigh [aʊt'weɪ] *vt (be more important than)* l'emporter sur.

outwit [aʊt'wɪt] *vt* **(-tt-)** être plus malin que.

oval ['əʊv(ə)l] *a* & *n* ovale *(m).*

ovary ['əʊvərɪ] *n Anat* ovaire *m.*

ovation [əʊ'veɪʃ(ə)n] *n* **(standing) o.** ovation *f.*

oven ['ʌv(ə)n] *n* four *m; (hot place) Fig* fournaise *f;* **o. glove** gant *m* isolant.

over ['əʊvər] *prep (on)* sur; *(above)* au-dessus de; *(on the other side of)* de l'autre côté de; **bridge o. the river** pont *m* sur le fleuve; **to jump/look/etc o. sth** sauter/regarder/*etc* par-dessus qch; **to fall o. the balcony/etc** tomber du balcon/*etc;* **she fell o. it** elle en est tombée; **o. it** *(on)* dessus; *(above)* au-dessus; *(to jump etc)* par-dessus; **to criticize/etc o. sth** *(about)* critiquer/*etc* à propos de qch; **an advantage o.** un avantage sur *or* par rapport à; **o. the radio** *(on)* à la radio; **o. the phone** au téléphone; **o. the holidays** (*during*) pendant les vacances; **o. ten days** (*more than*) plus de dix jours; **men o. sixty** les hommes de plus de soixante ans; **o. and above** en plus de; **he's o. his flu** (*recovered from*) il est remis de sa grippe; **all o. Spain** (*everywhere in*) dans toute l'Espagne, partout en Espagne; **all o. the carpet** (*everywhere on*) partout sur le tapis; **–** *adv* (*above*) (par-)dessus; (*finished*) fini; (*danger*) passé; (*again*) encore; (*too*) trop; **jump o.!** sautez par-dessus!; **o. here** ici; **o. there** là-bas; **to be** *or* **come** *or* **go o.** (*visit*) passer; **he's o. in Italy** il est (parti) en Italie; **she's o. from Paris** elle est venue de Paris; **all o.** (*everywhere*) partout; **wet all o.** tout mouillé; **it's (all) o.!** (*finished*) c'est fini!; **she's o.** (*fallen*) elle est tombée; **a kilo or o.** (*more*) un kilo ou plus; **I have ten o.** (*left*) il m'en reste dix; **there's some bread o.** il reste du pain; **o. and to.** (*again*) (*often*) à plusieurs reprises; **to start all o.** (*again*) recommencer à zéro; **o. pleased**/*etc* trop content/*etc.* ◆**o.-a'bundant** *a* surabondant. ◆**o.-de'veloped** *a* trop développé. ◆**o.-fa'miliar** *a* trop familier. ◆**o.-in'dulge** *vt* (*one's desires etc*) céder trop facilement à; (*person*) trop gâter. ◆**o.-sub'scribed** *a* (*course*) ayant trop d'inscrits.

overall 1 [əʊvər'ɔːl] *a* (*measurement, length, etc*) total; (*result, effort etc*) global; **–** *adv* globalement. **2** ['əʊvərɔːl] *n* blouse *f* (de travail); *pl* bleus *mpl* de travail.

overawe [əʊvər'ɔː] *vt* intimider.

overbalance [əʊvə'bæləns] *vi* basculer.

overbearing [əʊvə'beərɪŋ] *a* autoritaire.

overboard ['əʊvəbɔːd] *adv* à la mer.

overburden [əʊvə'bɜːd(ə)n] *vt* surcharger.

overcast [əʊvə'kɑːst] *a* (*sky*) couvert.

overcharge [əʊvə'tʃɑːdʒ] *vt* **to o. s.o. for sth** faire payer qch trop cher à qn.

overcoat ['əʊvəkəʊt] *n* pardessus *m*.

overcome [əʊvə'kʌm] *vt* (*pt* **overcame**, *pp* **overcome**) (*enemy, shyness etc*) vaincre; (*disgust, problem*) surmonter; **to be o. by** (*fatigue, grief*) être accablé par; (*fumes, temptation*) succomber à; **he was o. by emotion** l'émotion eut raison de lui.

overcrowded [əʊvə'kraʊdɪd] *a* (*house, country*) surpeuplé; (*bus, train*) bondé. ◆**overcrowding** *n* surpeuplement *m*.

overdo [əʊvə'duː] *vt* (*pt* **overdid**, *pp* **overdone**) exagérer; *Culin* cuire trop; **to o. it** (*exaggerate*) exagérer; (*work too much*) se surmener; *Iron* se fatiguer.

overdose ['əʊvədəʊs] *n* overdose *f*, dose *f* excessive (*de barbituriques etc*).

overdraft ['əʊvədrɑːft] *n* *Fin* découvert *m*. ◆**over'draw** *vt* (*pt* **overdrew**, *pp* **overdrawn**) (*account*) mettre à découvert.

overdress [əʊvə'dres] *vi* s'habiller avec trop de recherche.

overdue [əʊvə'djuː] *a* (*train etc*) en retard; (*debt*) arriéré; (*apology, thanks*) tardif.

overeat [əʊvər'iːt] *vi* manger trop.

overestimate [əʊvər'estɪmeɪt] *vt* surestimer.

overexcited [əʊvərɪk'saɪtɪd] *a* surexcité.

overfeed [əʊvə'fiːd] *vt* (*pt & pp* **overfed**) suralimenter.

overflow 1 ['əʊvəfləʊ] *n* (*outlet*) trop-plein *m*; (*of people, objects*) *Fig* excédent *m*. **2** [əʊvə'fləʊ] *vi* déborder (**with** de); **to be overflowing with** (*of town, shop, house etc*) regorger de (*visiteurs, livres etc*).

overgrown [əʊvə'grəʊn] *a* envahi par la végétation; **o. with** (*weeds etc*) envahi par; **you're an o. schoolgirl** *Fig Pej* tu as la mentalité d'une écolière.

overhang [əʊvə'hæŋ] *vi* (*pt & pp* **overhung**) faire saillie; **–** *vt* surplomber.

overhaul [əʊvə'hɔːl] *vt* (*vehicle, doctrine etc*) réviser; **–** ['əʊvəhɔːl] *n* révision *f*.

overhead [əʊvə'hed] *adv* au-dessus; **–** ['əʊvəhed] **1** *a* (*railway etc*) aérien. **2** *npl* (*expenses*) frais *mpl* généraux.

overhear [əʊvə'hɪər] *vt* (*pt & pp* **overheard**) surprendre, entendre.

overheat [əʊvə'hiːt] *vt* surchauffer; **–** *vi* (*of engine*) chauffer.

overjoyed [əʊvə'dʒɔɪd] *a* ravi, enchanté.

overland ['əʊvəlænd] *a & adv* par voie de terre.

overlap [əʊvə'læp] *vi* (**-pp-**) se chevaucher; **–** *vt* chevaucher; **–** ['əʊvəlæp] *n* chevauchement *m*.

overleaf [əʊvə'liːf] *adv* au verso.

overload [əʊvə'ləʊd] *vt* surcharger.

overlook [əʊvə'lʊk] *vt* **1** (*not notice*) ne pas remarquer; (*forget*) oublier; (*disregard, ignore*) passer sur. **2** (*of window, house etc*) donner sur; (*of tower, fort*) dominer.

overly ['əʊvəlɪ] *adv* excessivement.

overmuch [əʊvə'mʌtʃ] *adv* trop, excessivement.

overnight [əʊvə'naɪt] *adv* (*during the night*) (pendant) la nuit; (*all night*) toute la nuit; (*suddenly*) *Fig* du jour au lendemain; **to stay o.** passer la nuit; **–** ['əʊvənaɪt] *a* (*stay*) d'une nuit; (*clothes*) pour une nuit; (*trip*) de nuit.

overpass ['əʊvəpæs] *n* (*bridge*) *Am* toboggan *m*.

overpopulated [əuvə'pɒpuleitid] *a* surpeuplé.

overpower [əuvə'pauər] *vt* (*physically*) maîtriser; (*defeat*) vaincre; *Fig* accabler. ◆—**ing** *a* (*charm etc*) irrésistible; (*heat etc*) accablant.

overrat/e [əuvə'reit] *vt* surestimer. ◆—**ed** *a* surfait.

overreach [əuvə'riːtʃ] *vt* **to o. oneself** trop entreprendre.

overreact [əuvərɪ'ækt] *vi* réagir excessivement.

overrid/e [əuvə'raid] *vt* (*pt* **overrode,** *pp* **overridden**) (*invalidate*) annuler; (*take no notice of*) passer outre à; (*be more important than*) l'emporter sur. ◆—**ing** *a* (*passion*) prédominant; (*importance*) primordial.

overrule [əuvə'ruːl] *vt* (*reject*) rejeter.

overrun [əuvə'rʌn] *vt* (*pt* **overran,** *pp* **overrun,** *pres p* **overrunning**) **1** (*invade*) envahir. **2** (*go beyond*) aller au-delà de.

overseas [əuvə'siːz] *adv* (*Africa etc*) outre-mer; (*abroad*) à l'étranger; – ['əuvəsiːz] *a* (*visitor, market etc*) d'outre-mer; étranger; (*trade*) extérieur.

overse/e [əuvə'siː] *vt* (*pt* **oversaw,** *pp* **overseen**) surveiller. ◆—**er** ['əuvəsiːər] *n* (*foreman*) contremaître *m*.

overshadow [əuvə'ʃædəu] *vt* (*make less important*) éclipser; (*make gloomy*) assombrir.

overshoot [əuvə'ʃuːt] *vt* (*pt & pp* **overshot**) (*of aircraft*) & *Fig* dépasser.

oversight ['əuvəsait] *n* omission *f*, oubli *m*; (*mistake*) erreur *f*.

oversimplify [əuvə'simplifai] *vti* trop simplifier.

oversize(d) ['əuvəsaiz(d)] *a* trop grand.

oversleep [əuvə'sliːp] *vi* (*pt & pp* **overslept**) dormir trop longtemps, oublier de se réveiller.

overspend [əuvə'spend] *vi* dépenser trop.

overstaffed [əuvə'stɑːft] *a* au personnel pléthorique.

overstay [əuvə'stei] *vt* **to o. one's welcome** abuser de l'hospitalité de son hôte, s'incruster.

overstep [əuvə'step] *vt* (-**pp**-) dépasser.

overt ['əuvɜːt] *a* manifeste.

overtake [əuvə'teik] *vt* (*pt* **overtook,** *pp* **overtaken**) dépasser; (*vehicle*) doubler, dépasser; **overtaken by** (*nightfall, storm*) surpris par; – *vi Aut* doubler, dépasser.

overtax [əuvə'tæks] *vt* **1** (*strength*) excéder; (*brain*) fatiguer. **2** (*taxpayer*) surimposer.

overthrow [əuvə'θrəu] *vt* (*pt* **overthrew,** *pp* **overthrown**) *Pol* renverser; – ['əuvəθrəu] *n* renversement *m*.

overtime ['əuvətaim] *n* heures *fpl* supplémentaires; – *adv* **to work o.** faire des heures supplémentaires.

overtones ['əuvətəunz] *npl Fig* note *f*, nuance *f* (**of** de).

overture ['əuvətjuər] *n Mus & Fig* ouverture *f*.

overturn [əuvə'tɜːn] *vt* (*chair, table etc*) renverser; (*car, boat*) retourner; (*decision etc*) *Fig* annuler; – *vi* (*of car, boat*) se retourner.

overweight [əuvə'weit] *a* **to be o.** (*of suitcase etc*) peser trop; (*of person*) avoir des kilos en trop.

overwhelm [əuvə'welm] *vt* (*of feelings, heat etc*) accabler; (*defeat*) écraser; (*amaze*) bouleverser. ◆—**ed** *a* (*overjoyed*) ravi (**by, with** de); **o. with** (*grief, work etc*) accablé de; (*offers*) submergé par; **o. by** (*kindness, gift etc*) vivement touché par. ◆—**ing** *a* (*heat, grief etc*) accablant; (*majority*) écrasant; (*desire*) irrésistible; (*impression*) dominant. ◆—**ingly** *adv* (*to vote, reject etc*) en masse; (*utterly*) carrément.

overwork [əuvə'wɜːk] *n* surmenage *m*; – *vi* se surmener; – *vt* surmener.

overwrought [əuvə'rɔːt] *a* (*tense*) tendu.

owe [əu] *vt* devoir (**to** à); **I'll o. it (to) you, I'll o. you (for) it** (*money*) je te le devrai; **to o. it to oneself to do** se devoir de faire. ◆**owing 1** *a* (*money etc*) dû, qu'on doit. **2** *prep* **o. to** à cause de.

owl [aul] *n* hibou *m*.

own [əun] **1** *a* propre; **my o. house** ma propre maison; – *pron* **it's my (very) o.** c'est à moi (tout seul); **a house of his o.** sa propre maison, sa maison à lui; **(all) on one's o.** (*alone*) tout seul; **to get one's o. back** prendre sa revanche (**on** sur, **for** de); **to come into one's o.** (*fulfil oneself*) s'épanouir. **2** *vt* (*possess*) posséder; **who owns this ball/etc?** à qui appartient cette balle/etc? **3** *vi* **to o. up** (*confess*) avouer; **to o. up to sth** avouer qch. ◆**owner** *n* propriétaire *mf*. ◆**ownership** *n* possession *f*; **home o.** accession *f* à la propriété; **public o.** *Econ* nationalisation *f*.

ox, *pl* **oxen** [ɒks, 'ɒks(ə)n] *n* bœuf *m*.

oxide ['ɒksaid] *n Ch* oxide *m*. ◆**oxidize** *vi* s'oxyder; – *vt* oxyder.

oxygen ['ɒksidʒ(ə)n] *n* oxygène *m*; – *a* (*mask, tent*) à oxygène.

oyster ['ɔistər] *n* huître *f*.

P

P, p [piː] *n* P, p *m*.

p [piː] *abbr* = **penny, pence**.

pa [pɑɪ] *n* (*father*) *Fam* papa *m*.

pace [peɪs] *n* (*speed*) pas *m*, allure *f*; (*measure*) pas *m*; **to keep p. with** (*follow*) suivre; (*in work, progress*) se maintenir à la hauteur de; – *vi* **to p. up and down** faire les cent pas; – *vt* (*room etc*) arpenter. ◆**pacemaker** *n* (*device*) stimulateur *m* cardiaque.

Pacific [pəˈsɪfɪk] *a* (*coast etc*) pacifique; – *n* **the P.** le Pacifique.

pacify [ˈpæsɪfaɪ] *vt* (*country*) pacifier; (*calm, soothe*) apaiser. ◆**pacifier** *n* (*dummy*) *Am* sucette *f*, tétine *f*. ◆**pacifist** *n* & *a* pacifiste (*mf*).

pack [pæk] **1** *n* (*bundle, packet*) paquet *m*; (*bale*) balle *f*; (*of animal*) charge *f*; (*rucksack*) sac *m* (à dos); *Mil* paquetage *m*; (*of hounds, wolves*) meute *f*; (*of runners*) *Sp* peloton *m*; (*of thieves*) bande *f*; (*of cards*) jeu *m*; (*of lies*) tissu *m*. **2** *vt* (*fill*) remplir (**with** de); (*excessively*) bourrer; (*suitcase*) faire; (*object into box etc*) emballer; (*object into suitcase*) mettre dans sa valise; (*make into package*) empaqueter; **to p. into** (*cram*) entasser dans; (*put*) mettre dans; **to p. away** (*tidy away*) ranger; **to p. (down)** (*compress, crush*) tasser; **to p. off** (*person*) *Fam* expédier; **to p. up** (*put into box*) emballer; (*put into case*) mettre dans sa valise; (*give up*) *Fam* laisser tomber; – *vi* (*fill one's bags*) faire ses valises; **to p. into** (*of people*) s'entasser dans; **to p. in** *or* **up** (*of machine, vehicle*) *Fam* tomber en panne; **to p. up** (*stop*) *Fam* s'arrêter; (*leave*) plier bagage. ◆**—ed** *a* (*bus, cinema etc*) bourré; **p. lunch** panier-repas *m*; **p. out** (*crowded*) *Fam* bourré. ◆**—ing** *n* (*material, action*) emballage *m*; **p. case** caisse *f* d'emballage.

package [ˈpækɪdʒ] *n* paquet *m*; (*computer programs*) progiciel *m*; **p. deal** *Com* contrat *m* global, train *m* de propositions; **p. tour** voyage *m* organisé; – *vt* emballer, empaqueter. ◆**—ing** *n* (*material, action*) emballage *m*.

packet [ˈpækɪt] *n* paquet *m*; (*of sweets*) sachet *m*, paquet *m*; **to make/cost a p.** *Fam* faire/coûter beaucoup d'argent.

pact [pækt] *n* pacte *m*.

pad [pæd] *n* (*wad, plug*) tampon *m*; (*for writing, notes etc*) bloc *m*; (*on leg*) *Sp* jambière *f*; (*on knee*) *Sp* genouillère *f*; (*room*) *Sl* piaule *f*; **launch(ing) p.** rampe *f* de lancement; **ink(ing) p.** tampon *m* encreur; – *vt* (**-dd-**) (*stuff*) rembourrer, matelasser; **to p. out** (*speech, text*) délayer. ◆**padding** *n* rembourrage *m*; (*of speech, text*) délayage *m*.

paddle [ˈpæd(ə)l] **1** *vi* (*splash about*) barboter; (*dip one's feet*) se mouiller les pieds; – *n* **to have a (little) p.** se mouiller les pieds. **2** *n* (*pole*) pagaie *f*; **p. boat, p. steamer** bateau *m* à roues; – *vt* **to p. a canoe** pagayer.

paddock [ˈpædək] *n* enclos *m*; (*at racecourse*) paddock *m*.

paddy [ˈpædɪ] *n* **p. (field)** rizière *f*.

padlock [ˈpædlɒk] *n* (*on door etc*) cadenas *m*; (*on bicycle, moped*) antivol *m*; – *vt* (*door etc*) cadenasser.

p(a)ediatrician [piːdɪəˈtrɪʃ(ə)n] *n* *Med* pédiatre *mf*.

pagan [ˈpeɪɡən] *a* & *n* païen, -enne (*mf*). ◆**paganism** *n* paganisme *m*.

page [peɪdʒ] **1** *n* (*of book etc*) page *f*. **2** *n* **p. (boy)** (*in hotel etc*) chasseur *m*; (*at court*) *Hist* page *m*; – *vt* **to p. s.o.** faire appeler qn.

pageant [ˈpædʒənt] *n* grand spectacle *m* historique. ◆**pageantry** *n* pompe *f*, apparat *m*.

pagoda [pəˈɡəʊdə] *n* pagode *f*.

paid [peɪd] *see* **pay**; – *a* (*assassin etc*) à gages; **to put p. to** (*hopes, plans*) anéantir; **to put p. to s.o.** (*ruin*) couler qn.

pail [peɪl] *n* seau *m*.

pain [peɪn] *n* (*physical*) douleur *f*; (*grief*) peine *f*; *pl* (*efforts*) efforts *mpl*; **to have a p. in one's arm** avoir mal *or* une douleur au bras; **to be in p.** souffrir; **to go to** *or* **take (great) pains to do** (*exert oneself*) se donner du mal à faire; **to go to** *or* **take (great) pains not to do** (*be careful*) prendre bien soin de ne pas faire; **to be a p. (in the neck)** (*of person*) *Fam* être casse-pieds; – *vt* (*grieve*) peiner. ◆**p.-killer** *n* analgésique *m*, calmant *m*. ◆**painful** *a* (*illness, operation*) douloureux; (*arm, leg*) qui fait mal, douloureux; (*distressing*) douloureux, pénible; (*difficult*) pénible; (*bad*) *Fam* affreux. ◆**painless** a sans douleur; (*illness, operation*) indolore; (*easy*) Fam facile. ◆**painstaking** a (*person*) soigneux; (*work*) soigné.

paint [peint] n peinture f; pl (in box, tube) couleurs fpl; − vt (*colour, describe*) peindre; **to p. blue**/*etc* peindre en bleu/*etc*; − vi peindre. ◆**—ing** n (*activity*) peinture f; (*picture*) tableau m, peinture f. ◆**—er** n peintre m. ◆**paintbrush** n pinceau m. ◆**paintwork** n peinture(s) f(pl).

pair [peər] n paire f; (*man and woman*) couple m; **a p. of shorts** un short; **the p. of you** Fam vous deux; − vi **to p. off** (*of people*) former un couple; − vt (*marry*) marier.

pajama(s) [pə'dʒɑːmə(z)] a & npl Am = **pyjama(s)**.

Pakistan [pɑːkɪ'stɑːn] n Pakistan m. ◆**Pakistani** a & n pakistanais, -aise (mf).

pal [pæl] n Fam copain m, copine f; − vi (-ll-) **to p. up** devenir copains; **to p. up with** devenir copain avec.

palace ['pælɪs] n (*building*) palais m. ◆**palatial** [pə'leɪʃ(ə)l] a comme un palais.

palatable ['pælətəb(ə)l] a (*food*) agréable; (*fact, idea etc*) acceptable.

palate ['pælɪt] n Anat palais m.

palaver [pə'lɑːvər] n Fam (*fuss*) histoire(s) f(pl); (*talk*) palabres mpl.

pale [peɪl] a (-er, -est) (*face, colour etc*) pâle; **p. ale** bière f blonde; − vi pâlir. ◆**—ness** n pâleur f.

palette ['pælɪt] n (*of artist*) palette f.

paling ['peɪlɪŋ] n (*fence*) palissade f.

pall [pɔːl] **1** vi devenir insipide or ennuyeux (on pour). **2** n (*of smoke*) voile m.

pallbearer ['pɔːlbeərər] n personne f qui aide à porter un cercueil.

pallid ['pælɪd] a pâle. ◆**pallor** n pâleur f.

pally ['pælɪ] a (-ier, -iest) Fam copain am, copine af (with avec).

palm [pɑːm] **1** n (*of hand*) paume f. **2** n (*symbol*) palme f; **p. (tree)** palmier m; **p. (leaf)** palme f; **P. Sunday** les Rameaux mpl. **3** vt Fam **to p. sth off** (*pass off*) refiler qch (on à), coller qch (on à); **to p. s.o. off on s.o.** coller qn à qn.

palmist ['pɑːmɪst] n chiromancien, -ienne mf. ◆**palmistry** n chiromancie f.

palpable ['pælpəb(ə)l] a (*obvious*) manifeste.

palpitate ['pælpɪteɪt] vi (*of heart*) palpiter. ◆**palpi'tation** n palpitation f.

paltry ['pɔːltrɪ] a (-ier, -iest) misérable, dérisoire.

pamper ['pæmpər] vt dorloter.

pamphlet ['pæmflɪt] n brochure f.

pan [pæn] **1** n casserole f; (*for frying*) poêle f (à frire); (*of lavatory*) cuvette f. **2** vt (-nn-) (*criticize*) Fam éreinter. **3** vi (-nn-) **to p. out** (*succeed*) aboutir.

Pan- [pæn] pref pan-.

panacea [pænə'sɪə] n panacée f.

panache [pə'næʃ] n (*showy manner*) panache m.

pancake ['pænkeɪk] n crêpe f.

pancreas ['pæŋkrɪəs] n Anat pancréas m.

panda ['pændə] n (*animal*) panda m; **P. car** = voiture f pie inv (de la police).

pandemonium [pændɪ'məʊnɪəm] n (*chaos*) chaos m; (*uproar*) tumulte m; (*place*) bazar m.

pander ['pændər] vi **to p. to** (*tastes, fashion etc*) sacrifier à; **to p. to s.o.** or **to s.o.'s desires** se plier aux désirs de qn.

pane [peɪn] n vitre f, carreau m.

panel ['pæn(ə)l] n **1** (*of door etc*) panneau m; (**control**) **p.** Tech El console f; (**instrument**) **p.** Av Aut tableau m de bord. **2** (*of judges*) jury m; (*of experts*) groupe m; (*of candidates*) équipe f; **a p. of guests** des invités; **a p. game** TV Rad un jeu par équipes. ◆**panelled** a (*room etc*) lambrissé. ◆**panelling** n lambris m. ◆**panellist** n TV Rad (*guest*) invité, -ée mf; (*expert*) expert m; (*candidate*) candidat, -ate mf.

pangs [pæŋz] npl **p. of conscience** remords mpl (de conscience); **p. of hunger/death** les affres fpl de la faim/de la mort.

panic ['pænɪk] n panique f; **to get into a p.** paniquer; − vi (-ck-) s'affoler, paniquer. ◆**p.-stricken** a affolé. ◆**panicky** (*person*) a Fam qui s'affole facilement; **to get p.** s'affoler.

panorama [pænə'rɑːmə] n panorama m. ◆**panoramic** a panoramique.

pansy ['pænzɪ] n Bot pensée f.

pant [pænt] vi (*gasp*) haleter.

panther ['pænθər] n (*animal*) panthère f.

panties ['pæntɪz] npl (*female underwear*) slip m.

pantomime ['pæntəmaɪm] n (*show*) spectacle m de Noël.

pantry ['pæntrɪ] n (*larder*) garde-manger m inv; (*storeroom in hotel etc*) office m or f.

pants [pænts] npl (*male underwear*) slip m; (*loose, long*) caleçon m; (*female underwear*) slip m; (*trousers*) Am pantalon m.

pantyhose ['pæntɪhəʊz] n (*tights*) Am collant(s) m(pl).

papacy ['peɪpəsɪ] n papauté f. ◆**papal** a papal.

paper ['peɪpər] n papier m; (*newspaper*) journal m; (*wallpaper*) papier m peint;

(*exam*) épreuve *f* (écrite); (*student's exercise*) *Sch* copie *f*; (*learned article*) exposé *m*, communication *f*; **brown p.** papier *m* d'emballage; **to put down on p.** mettre par écrit; − *a* (*bag etc*) en papier; (*cup, plate*) en carton; **p. clip** trombone *m*; **p. knife** coupe-papier *m inv*; **p. mill** papeterie *f*; **p. shop** marchand *m* de journaux; − *vt* (*room, wall*) tapisser. ◆**paperback** *n* (*book*) livre *m* de poche. ◆**paperboy** *n* livreur *m* de journaux. ◆**paperweight** *n* presse-papiers *m inv*. ◆**paperwork** *n* Com écritures *fpl*; (*red tape*) *Pej* paperasserie *f*.

paprika ['pæprɪkə] *n* paprika *m*.

par [pɑːr] *n* **on a p.** au même niveau (**with** que); **below p.** (*unwell*) *Fam* pas en forme.

para- ['pærə] *pref* para-.

parable ['pærəb(ə)l] *n* (*story*) parabole *f*.

parachute ['pærəʃuːt] *n* parachute *f*; **to drop by p.** (*men, supplies*) parachuter; − *vi* descendre en parachute; − *vt* parachuter. ◆**parachutist** *n* parachutiste *mf*.

parade [pə'reɪd] **1** *n* Mil (*ceremony*) parade *f*; (*procession*) défilé *m*; **fashion p.** défilé *m* de mode *or* de mannequins; **p. ground** Mil terrain *m* de manœuvres; **to make a p.** of faire étalage de; − *vi* Mil défiler; **to p. about** (*walk about*) se balader; − *vt* faire étalage de. **2** *n* (*street*) avenue *f*.

paradise ['pærədaɪs] *n* paradis *m*.

paradox ['pærədɒks] *n* paradoxe *m*. ◆**para'doxically** *adv* paradoxalement.

paraffin ['pærəfɪn] *n* pétrole *m* (lampant); (*wax*) *Am* paraffine *f*; **p. lamp** lampe *f* à pétrole.

paragon ['pærəg(ə)n] *n* **p. of virtue** modèle *m* de vertu.

paragraph ['pærəɡrɑːf] *n* paragraphe *m*; **'new p.'** 'à la ligne'.

parakeet ['pærəkiːt] *n* perruche *f*.

parallel ['pærəlel] *a* (*comparable*) & Math parallèle (**with, to** à); **to run p. to** *or* **with** être parallèle à; − *n* (*comparison*) & Geog parallèle *m*; (*line*) Math parallèle *f*; − *vt* être semblable à.

paralysis [pə'ræləsɪs] *n* paralysie *f*. ◆**'paralyse** *vt* (*Am* **-lyze**) paralyser. ◆**para'lytic** *a* & *n* paralytique (*mf*).

parameter [pə'ræmɪtər] *n* paramètre *m*.

paramount ['pærəmaʊnt] *a* **of p. importance** de la plus haute importance.

paranoia [pærə'nɔɪə] *n* paranoïa *f*. ◆**'paranoid** *a* & *n* paranoïaque (*mf*).

parapet ['pærəpɪt] *n* parapet *m*.

paraphernalia [pærəfə'neɪlɪə] *n* attirail *m*.

paraphrase ['pærəfreɪz] *n* paraphrase *f*; − *vt* paraphraser.

parasite ['pærəsaɪt] *n* (*person, organism*) parasite *m*.

parasol ['pærəsɒl] *n* (*over table, on beach*) parasol *m*; (*lady's*) ombrelle *f*.

paratrooper ['pærətruːpər] *n* Mil parachutiste *m*. ◆**paratroops** *npl* Mil parachutistes *mpl*.

parboil [pɑː'bɔɪl] *vt* Culin faire bouillir à demi.

parcel ['pɑːs(ə)l] **1** *n* colis *m*, paquet *m*; **to be part and p. of** faire partie intégrante de. **2** *vt* (**-ll-**, *Am* **-l-**) **to p. out** (*divide*) partager; **to p. up** faire un paquet de.

parch [pɑːtʃ] *vt* dessécher; **to be parched** (*thirsty*) être assoiffé; **to make parched** (*thirsty*) donner très soif à.

parchment ['pɑːtʃmənt] *n* parchemin *m*.

pardon ['pɑːd(ə)n] *n* pardon *m*; Jur grâce *f*; **general p.** amnistie *f*; **I beg your p.** (*apologize*) je vous prie de m'excuser; (*not hearing*) vous dites?; **p.?** (*not hearing*) comment?; **p. (me)!** (*sorry*) pardon!; − *vt* pardonner (**s.o. for sth** qch à qn); **to p. s.o.** pardonner (à) qn; Jur gracier qn.

pare [peər] *vt* (*trim*) rogner; (*peel*) éplucher; **to p. down** Fig réduire, rogner.

parent ['peərənt] *n* père *m*, mère *f*; **one's parents** ses parent *mpl*, son père et sa mère; **p. firm, p. company** Com maison *f* mère. ◆**parentage** *n* (*origin*) origine *f*. ◆**pa'rental** *a* des parents, parental. ◆**parenthood** *n* paternité *f*, maternité *f*.

parenthesis, *pl* **-eses** [pə'renθəsɪs, -əsiːz] *n* parenthèse *f*.

Paris ['pærɪs] *n* Paris *m or f*. ◆**Parisian** [pə'rɪzɪən, *Am* pə'riːʒən] *a* & *n* parisien, -ienne (*mf*).

parish ['pærɪʃ] *n* Rel paroisse *f*; (*civil*) commune *f*; − *a* (*church, register*) paroissial; **p. council** conseil *m* municipal. ◆**pa'rishioner** *n* paroissien, -ienne *mf*.

parity ['pærɪtɪ] *n* parité *f*.

park [pɑːk] **1** *n* (*garden*) parc *m*. **2** *vt* (*vehicle*) garer; (*put*) Fam mettre, poser; − *vi* Aut se garer; (*remain parked*) stationner. ◆**—ing** *n* stationnement *m*; **'no p.'** 'défense de stationner'; **p. bay** aire *f* de stationnement; **p. lot** *Am* parking *m*; **p. meter** parcmètre *m*; **p. place** endroit *m* pour se garer; **p. ticket** contravention *f*.

parka ['pɑːkə] *n* (*coat*) parka *m*.

parkway ['pɑːkweɪ] *n Am* avenue *f*.

parliament ['pɑːləmənt] *n* parlement *m*; **P.** Br Parlement *m*. ◆**parlia'mentary** *a* parlementaire. ◆**parliamen'tarian** *n* parlementaire *mf* (expérimenté(e)).

parlour ['pɑːlər] *n* (*in mansion*) (petit) salon

m; **ice-cream p.** *Am* salon de glaces; **p. game** jeu *m* de société.

parochial [pə'rəʊkɪəl] *a* (*mentality, quarrel*) *Pej* de clocher; (*person*) *Pej* provincial, borné; *Rel* paroissial.

parody ['pærədɪ] *n* parodie *f*; – *vt* parodier.

parole [pə'rəʊl] *n* **on p.** *Jur* en liberté conditionnelle.

parquet ['pɑːkeɪ] *n* **p. (floor)** parquet *m*.

parrot ['pærət] *n* perroquet *m*; **p. fashion** *Pej* comme un perroquet.

parry ['pærɪ] *vt* (*blow*) parer; (*question*) éluder; – *n* *Sp* parade *f*.

parsimonious [pɑːsɪ'məʊnɪəs] *a* parcimonieux. ◆—**ly** *adv* avec parcimonie.

parsley ['pɑːslɪ] *n* persil *m*.

parsnip ['pɑːsnɪp] *n* panais *m*.

parson ['pɑːs(ə)n] *n* pasteur *m*; **p.'s nose** (*of chicken*) croupion *m*.

part [pɑːt] **1** *n* partie *f*; (*of machine*) pièce *f*; (*of periodical*) livraison *f*; (*of serial*) épisode *m*; (*in play, film, activity*) rôle *m*; (*division*) *Culin* mesure *f*; (*in hair*) *Am* raie *f*; **to take p.** participer (**in** à); **to take s.o.'s p.** (*side*) prendre parti pour qn; **in p.** en partie; **for the most p.** dans l'ensemble; **to be a p. of** faire partie de; **on the p. of** (*on behalf of*) de la part de; **for my p.** pour ma part; **in these parts** dans ces parages; **p. exchange** reprise *f*; **to take in p. exchange** reprendre; **p. owner** copropriétaire *mf*; **p. payment** paiement *m* partiel; – *adv* en partie; **p. American** en partie américain. **2** *vt* (*separate*) séparer; (*crowd*) diviser; **to p. one's hair** se faire une raie; **to p. company with** (*leave*) quitter; – *vi* (*of friends etc*) se quitter; (*of married couple*) se séparer; **to p. with** (*get rid of*) se séparer de. ◆—**ing 1** *n* séparation *f*; – *a* (*gift, words*) d'adieu. **2** *n* (*in hair*) raie *f*.

partake [pɑː'teɪk] *vi* (*pt* **partook**, *pp* **partaken**) **to p. in** participer à; **to p. of** (*meal, food*) prendre, manger.

partial ['pɑːʃəl] *a* partiel; (*biased*) partial (**towards** envers); **to be p. to** (*fond of*) *Fam* avoir un faible pour. ◆**parti'ality** *n* (*bias*) partialité *f*; (*liking*) prédilection *f*.

participate [pɑː'tɪsɪpeɪt] *vi* participer (**in** à). ◆**participant** *n* participant, -ante *mf*. ◆**partici'pation** *n* participation *f*.

participle ['pɑːtɪsɪp(ə)l] *n* participe *m*.

particle ['pɑːtɪk(ə)l] *n* (*of atom, dust, name*) particule *f*; (*of truth*) grain *m*.

particular [pə'tɪkjʊlər] **1** *a* (*specific, special*) particulier; (*fastidious, fussy*) difficile (**about** sur); (*meticulous*) méticuleux; **this p. book** ce livre-ci en particulier; **in p. en**

particulier; **to be p. about** faire très attention à. **2** *n* (*detail*) détail *m*; **s.o.'s particulars** le nom et l'adresse de qn; (*description*) le signalement de qn. ◆—**ly** *adv* particulièrement.

partisan [pɑːtɪ'zæn, *Am* 'pɑːtɪz(ə)n] *n* partisan *m*.

partition [pɑː'tɪʃ(ə)n] **1** *n* (*of room*) cloison *f*; – *vt* **to p. off** cloisonner. **2** *n* (*of country*) *Pol* partition *f*, partage *m*; – *vt* *Pol* partager.

partly ['pɑːtlɪ] *adv* en partie; **p. English p. French** moitié anglais moitié français.

partner ['pɑːtnər] *n* *Com* associé, -ée *mf*; (*lover, spouse*) & *Sp Pol* partenaire *mf*; (*of racing driver etc*) coéquipier, -ière *mf*; (*dancing*) *m* cavalier, -ière *mf*. ◆**partnership** *n* association *f*; **to take into p.** prendre comme associé(e); **in p. with** en association avec.

partridge ['pɑːtrɪdʒ] *n* perdrix *f*.

part-time [pɑːt'taɪm] *a* & *adv* à temps partiel; (*half-time*) à mi-temps.

party ['pɑːtɪ] *n* (*group*) groupe *m*; *Pol* parti *m*; (*in contract, lawsuit*) *Jur* partie *f*; *Mil* détachement *m*; *Tel* correspondant, -ante *mf*; **rescue p.** équipe *f* de sauveteurs or de secours; **third p.** *Jur* tiers *m*; **innocent p.** innocent, -ente *mf*; **to be (a) p. to** (*crime*) être complice de; **p. line** *Tel* ligne *f* partagée; *Pol* ligne *f* du parti; **p. ticket** billet *m* collectif. **2** (*gathering*) réception *f*; (*informal*) surprise-partie *f*; (*for birthday*) fête *f*; **cocktail p.** cocktail *m*; **dinner p.** dîner *m*; **tea p.** thé *m*.

pass [pɑːs] **1** *n* (*entry permit*) laissez-passer *m inv*; (*free ticket*) *Th* billet *m* de faveur; (*season ticket*) carte *f* d'abonnement; (*over mountains*) *Geog* col *m*; *Fb etc* passe *f*; (*in exam*) mention *f* passable (**in French/**etc en français/etc); **to make a p. at** faire des avances à; **p. mark** (*in exam*) moyenne *f*, barre *f* d'admissibilité; **p. key** passe-partout *m inv*. **2** *vi* (*go, come, disappear*) passer (**to** à, **through** par); (*overtake*) *Aut* dépasser; (*in exam*) être reçu (**in French/**etc en français/etc); (*take place*) se passer; **that'll p.** (*be acceptable*) ça ira; **he can p. for thirty** on lui donnerait trente ans; **to p. along** or **through** passer; **to p. away** or **on** (*die*) mourir; **to p. by** passer (à côté); **to p. off** (*happen*) se passer; **to p. on to** (*move on to*) passer à; **to p. out** (*faint*) s'évanouir; – *vt* (*move, spend, give etc*) passer (**to** à); (*go past*) passer devant (*immeuble etc*); (*vehicle*) dépasser; (*exam*) être reçu à; (*candidate*) recevoir; (*judgement, opinion*) prononcer (**on** sur); (*remark*) faire; (*allow*) autoriser; (bill, law) Pol voter; **to p. (by) s.o.** (in street) croiser qn; **to p. by** (building) passer devant; **to p. oneself off as** se faire passer pour; **to p. sth off on** (fob off on) refiler qch à; **to p. on** (message, title, illness etc) transmettre (**to** à); **to p. out** or **round** (hand out) distribuer; **to p. over** (ignore) passer sur, oublier; **to p. round** (cigarettes, sweets etc) faire passer; **to p. up** (chance etc) laisser passer. ◆**—ing** a (vehicle etc) qui passe; (beauty) passager; — n (of visitor, vehicle etc) passage m; (of time) écoulement m; (death) disparition f.

passable ['pɑːsəb(ə)l] a (not bad) passable; (road) praticable; (river) franchissable.

passage ['pæsɪdʒ] n (passing, way through, of text, of speech etc) passage m; (of time) écoulement m; (corridor) couloir m; Nau traversée f, passage m. ◆**passageway** n (way through) passage m; (corridor) couloir m.

passbook ['pɑːsbʊk] n livret m de caisse d'épargne.

passenger ['pæsɪndʒər] n passager, -ère mf; Rail voyageur, -euse mf.

passer-by [pɑːsə'baɪ] n (pl **passers-by**) passant, -ante mf.

passion ['pæʃ(ə)n] n passion f; **to have a p. for** (cars etc) avoir la passion de, adorer. ◆**passionate** a passionné. ◆**passionately** adv passionnément.

passive ['pæsɪv] a (not active) passif; — n Gram passif m. ◆**—ness** n passivité f.

Passover ['pɑːsəʊvər] n Rel Pâque f.

passport ['pɑːspɔːt] n passeport m.

password ['pɑːswɜːd] n mot m de passe.

past [pɑːst] **1** n (time, history) passé m; **in the p.** (formerly) dans le temps; **it's a thing of the p.** ça n'existe plus; — a (gone by) passé; (former) ancien; **these p. months** ces derniers mois; **that's all p.** c'est du passé; **in the p. tense** Gram au passé. **2** prep (in front of) devant; (after) après; (further than) plus loin que; (too old for) Fig trop vieux pour; **p. four o'clock** quatre heures passées, plus de quatre heures; **to be p. fifty** avoir cinquante ans passés; **it's p. belief** c'est incroyable; **I wouldn't put it p. him** ça ne m'étonnerait pas de lui, il en est bien capable; — adv devant; **to go p.** passer.

pasta ['pæstə] n Culin pâtes fpl (alimentaires).

paste [peɪst] **1** n (of meat) pâté m; (of anchovy etc) beurre m; (dough) pâte f. **2** n (glue) colle f (blanche); — vt coller; **to p. up** (notice etc) afficher.

pastel ['pæstəl, Am pæ'stel] n pastel m; — a (shade) pastel inv; (drawing) au pastel.

pasteurized ['pæstəraɪzd] a (milk) pasteurisé.

pastiche [pæ'stiːʃ] n pastiche m.

pastille ['pæstɪl, Am pæ'stiːl] n pastille f.

pastime ['pɑːstaɪm] n passe-temps m inv.

pastor ['pɑːstər] n Rel pasteur m. ◆**pastoral** a pastoral.

pastry ['peɪstrɪ] n (dough) pâte f; (cake) pâtisserie f; **puff p.** pâte f feuilletée. ◆**pastrycook** n pâtissier, -ière mf.

pasture ['pɑːstʃər] n pâturage m.

pasty 1 ['peɪstɪ] a (-ier, -iest) (complexion) terreux. **2** ['pæstɪ] n Culin petit pâté m (en croûte).

pat [pæt] **1** vt (-tt-) (cheek, table etc) tapoter; (animal) caresser; — n petite tape; caresse f. **2** adv **to answer p.** avoir la réponse toute prête; **to know sth off p.** savoir qch sur le bout du doigt.

patch [pætʃ] n (for clothes) pièce f; (over eye) bandeau m; (for bicycle tyre) rustine® f; (of colour) tache f; (of sky) morceau m; (of fog) nappe f; (of ice) plaque f; **a cabbage/etc p.** un carré de choux/etc; **a bad p.** Fig une mauvaise passe; **not to be a p. on** (not as good as) Fam ne pas arriver à la cheville de; — vt **to p. (up)** (clothing) rapiécer; **to p. up** (quarrel) régler; (marriage) replâtrer. ◆**patchwork** n patchwork m. ◆**patchy** a (-ier, -iest) inégal.

patent 1 ['peɪtənt] a patent, manifeste; **p. leather** cuir m verni. **2** ['peɪtənt, 'pætənt] n brevet m (d'invention); — vt (faire) breveter. ◆**—ly** adv manifestement.

paternal [pə'tɜːn(ə)l] a paternel. ◆**paternity** n paternité f.

path [pɑːθ] n (pl **-s** [pɑːðz]) sentier m, chemin m; (in park) allée f; (of river) cours m; (of bullet, planet) trajectoire f. ◆**pathway** n sentier m, chemin m.

pathetic [pə'θetɪk] a pitoyable.

pathology [pə'θɒlədʒɪ] n pathologie f. ◆**patho'logical** a pathologique.

pathos ['peɪθɒs] n pathétique m.

patient ['peɪʃ(ə)nt] **1** a patient. **2** n (in hospital) malade mf, patient, -ente mf; (on doctor's or dentist's list) patient, -ente mf. ◆**patience** n patience f; **to have p.** prendre patience; **to lose p.** perdre patience; **I have no p. with him** il m'impatiente; **to play p.** Cards faire des réussites. ◆**patiently** adv patiemment.

patio ['pætɪəʊ] n (pl **-os**) patio m.

patriarch ['peɪtrɪɑːk] n patriarche m.

patriot ['pætrɪət, 'peɪtrɪət] n patriote mf. ◆**patri'otic** a (views, speech etc) patriotique; (person) patriote. ◆**patriotism** n patriotisme m.

patrol [pə'trəʊl] n patrouille f; **p. boat** patrouilleur m; **police p. car** voiture f de police; **p. wagon** Am fourgon m cellulaire; – vi (**-ll-**) patrouiller; – vt patrouiller dans. ◆**patrolman** n (pl **-men**) Am agent m de police; (repair man) Aut dépanneur m.

patron ['peɪtrən] n (of artist) protecteur, -trice mf; (customer) Com client, -ente mf; (of cinema, theatre) habitué, -ée mf; **p. saint** patron, -onne mf. ◆**patronage** n (support) patronage m; (of the arts) protection f; (custom) Com clientèle f. ◆**patroniz/e** ['pætrənaɪz, Am 'peɪtrənaɪz] vt **1** Com accorder sa clientèle à. **2** (person) Pej traiter avec condescendance. ◆**—ing** a condescendant.

patter ['pætər] **1** n (of footsteps) petit bruit m; (of rain, hail) crépitement m; – vi (of rain, hail) crépiter, tambouriner. **2** n (talk) baratin m.

pattern ['pæt(ə)n] n dessin m, motif m; (paper model for garment) patron m; (fabric sample) échantillon m; Fig modèle m; (plan) plan m; (method) formule f; (of a crime) scénario m. ◆**patterned** a (dress, cloth) à motifs.

paucity ['pɔːsɪtɪ] n pénurie f.

paunch [pɔːntʃ] n panse f, bedon m. ◆**paunchy** a (**-ier, -iest**) bedonnant.

pauper ['pɔːpər] n pauvre mf, indigent, -ente mf.

pause [pɔːz] n pause f; (in conversation) silence m; – vi (stop) faire une pause; (hesitate) hésiter.

pav/e [peɪv] vt paver; **to p. the way for** Fig ouvrir la voie à. ◆**—ing** n (surface) pavage m, dallage m; **p. stone** pavé m. ◆**pavement** n trottoir m; (roadway) Am chaussée f; (stone) pavé m.

pavilion [pə'vɪljən] n (building) pavillon m.

paw [pɔː] **1** n patte f; – vt (of animal) donner des coups de patte à. **2** vt (touch improperly) tripoter.

pawn [pɔːn] **1** n Chess pion m. **2** vt mettre en gage; – n **in p.** en gage. ◆**pawnbroker** n prêteur, -euse mf sur gages. ◆**pawnshop** n mont-de-piété m.

pay [peɪ] n salaire m; (of workman) paie f, salaire m; Mil solde f, paie f; **p. phone** téléphone m public; **p. day** jour m de paie; **p. slip** bulletin m or fiche f de paie; – vt (pt & pp **paid**) (person, sum) payer; (deposit) verser; (yield) Com rapporter; (compliment, attention, visit) faire; **to p. s.o. to do** or **for doing** payer qn pour faire; **to p. s.o. for sth** payer qch à qn; **to p. money into one's account** or **the bank** verser de l'argent sur son compte; **it pays (one) to be cautious** on a intérêt à être prudent; **to p. homage** or **tribute to** rendre hommage à; **to p. back** (creditor, loan etc) rembourser; **I'll p. you back for this!** je te revaudrai ça!; **to p. in** (cheque) verser (**to one's account** sur son compte); **to p. off** (debt, creditor etc) rembourser; (in instalments) rembourser par acomptes; (staff, worker) licencier; **to p. off an old score** or **a grudge** Fig régler un vieux compte; **to p. out** (spend) dépenser; **to p. up** payer; – vi payer; **to p. for sth** payer qch; **to p. a lot (for)** payer cher; **to p. off** (be successful) être payant; **to p. up** payer. ◆**—ing** a (guest) payant; (profitable) rentable. ◆**—able** a (due) payable; **a cheque p. to** un chèque à l'ordre de. ◆**—ment** n paiement m; (of deposit) versement m; (reward) récompense f; **on p. of 20 francs** moyennant 20 francs. ◆**payoff** n Fam (reward) récompense f; (revenge) règlement m de comptes. ◆**payroll** n **to be on the p. of** (firm, factory) être employé par; **to have twenty workers on the p.** employer vingt ouvriers.

pea [piː] n pois m; **garden** or **green peas** petits pois mpl; **p. soup** soupe f aux pois.

peace [piːs] n paix f; **p. of mind** tranquillité f d'esprit; **in p.** en paix; **at p.** en paix (**with** avec); **to have (some) p. and quiet** avoir la paix; **to disturb the p.** troubler l'ordre public; **to hold one's p.** garder le silence. ◆**p.-keeping** a (force) de maintien de la paix; (measure) de pacification. ◆**p.-loving** a pacifique. ◆**peaceable** a paisible, pacifique. ◆**peaceful** a paisible, calme; (coexistence, purpose, demonstration) pacifique. ◆**peacefulness** n paix f.

peach [piːtʃ] n (fruit) pêche f; (tree) pêcher m; – a (colour) pêche inv.

peacock ['piːkɒk] n paon m.

peak [piːk] n (mountain top) sommet m; (mountain itself) pic m; (of cap) visière f; (of fame etc) Fig sommet m, apogée m; **the traffic has reached** or **is at its p.** la circulation est à son maximum; – a (hours, period) de pointe; (demand, production) maximum; – vi (of sales etc) atteindre son maximum. ◆**peaked** a **p. cap** casquette f.

peaky ['piːkɪ] a (**-ier, -iest**) Fam (ill) patraque; (pale) pâlot.

peal [piːl] **1** n (of laughter) éclat m; (of thun-

der) roulement *m*. **2** *n* **p. of bells** carillon *m*; – *vi* **to p. (out)** (*of bells*) carillonner.

peanut ['piːnʌt] *n* cacah(o)uète *f*; (*plant*) arachide *f*; **to earn/etc peanuts** (*little money*) *Fam* gagner/*etc* des clopinettes.

pear [peər] *n* poire *f*; **p. tree** poirier *m*.

pearl [pɜːl] *n* perle *f*; (*mother-of-pearl*) nacre *f*. ◆**pearly** *a* (**-ier, -iest**) (*colour*) nacré.

peasant ['pezənt] *n* & *a* paysan, -anne (*mf*).

peashooter ['piːʃuːtər] *n* sarbacane *f*.

peat [piːt] *n* tourbe *f*.

pebble ['peb(ə)l] *n* (*stone*) caillou *m*; (*on beach*) galet *m*. ◆**pebbly** *a* (*beach*) (couvert) de galets.

pecan ['piːkæn] *n* (*nut*) *Am* pacane *f*.

peck [pek] *vti* **to p. (at)** (*of bird*) picorer (*du pain etc*); (*person*) *Fig* donner un coup de bec à; **to p. at one's food** (*of person*) manger du bout des dents; – *n* coup *m* de bec; (*kiss*) *Fam* bécot *m*.

peckish ['pekiʃ] *a* **to be p.** (*hungry*) *Fam* avoir un petit creux.

peculiar [pɪˈkjuːliər] *a* (*strange*) bizarre; (*characteristic, special*) particulier (**to** à). ◆**peculi'arity** *n* (*feature*) particularité *f*; (*oddity*) bizarrerie *f*. ◆**peculiarly** *adv* bizarrement; (*specially*) particulièrement.

pedal ['ped(ə)l] *n* pédale *f*; **p. boat** pédalo *m*; – *vi* (**-ll-**, *Am* **-l-**) pédaler; – *vt* (*bicycle etc*) actionner les pédales de. ◆**pedalbin** *n* poubelle *f* à pédale.

pedant ['pedənt] *n* pédant, -ante *mf*. ◆**pe'dantic** *a* pédant. ◆**pedantry** *n* pédantisme *m*.

peddl/e ['ped(ə)l] *vt* colporter; (*drugs*) faire le trafic de; – *vi* faire du colportage. ◆**—er** *n Am* (*door-to-door*) colporteur, -euse *mf*; (*in street*) camelot *m*; **drug p.** revendeur, -euse *mf* de drogues.

pedestal ['pedɪst(ə)l] *n Archit & Fig* piédestal *m*.

pedestrian [pəˈdestrɪən] **1** *n* piéton *m*; **p. crossing** passage *m* pour piétons; **p. precinct** zone *f* piétonnière. **2** *a* (*speech, style*) prosaïque. ◆**pedestrianize** *vt* (*street etc*) rendre piétonnier.

pedigree ['pedɪgriː] *n* (*of dog, horse etc*) pedigree *m*; (*of person*) ascendance *f*; – *a* (*dog, horse etc*) de race.

pedlar ['pedlər] *n* (*door-to-door*) colporteur, -euse *mf*; (*in street*) camelot *m*.

pee [piː] *n* **to go for a p.** *Fam* faire pipi.

peek [piːk] *n* coup *m* d'œil (furtif); – *vi* jeter un coup d'œil (furtif) (**at** à).

peel [piːl] *n* (*of vegetable, fruit*) pelure(s) *f(pl)*, épluchure(s) *f(pl)*; (*of orange skin*) écorce *f*; (*in food, drink*) zeste *m*; **a piece of**

p. une pelure, une épluchure; – *vt* (*fruit, vegetable*) peler, éplucher; **to keep one's eyes peeled** *Fam* être vigilant; **to p. off** (*label etc*) décoller; – *vi* (*of sunburnt skin*) peler; (*of paint*) s'écailler; **to p. easily** (*of fruit*) se peler facilement. ◆**—ings** *npl* pelures *fpl*, épluchures *fpl*. ◆**—er** *n* (*knife etc*) éplucheur *m*.

peep [piːp] **1** *n* coup *m* d'œil (furtif); – *vi* **to p. (at)** regarder furtivement; **to p. out** se montrer; **peeping Tom** voyeur, -euse *mf*. **2** *vi* (*of bird*) pépier. ◆**peephole** *n* judas *m*.

peer [pɪər] **1** *n* (*equal*) pair *m*, égal, -ale *mf*; (*noble*) pair *m*. **2** *vi* **to p. (at)** regarder attentivement (*comme pour mieux voir*); **to p. into** (*darkness*) scruter. ◆**peerage** *n* (*rank*) pairie *f*.

peeved [piːvd] *a Fam* irrité.

peevish ['piːvɪʃ] *a* grincheux, irritable.

peg [peg] **1** *n* (*wooden*) *Tech* cheville *f*; (*metal*) *Tech* fiche *f*; (*for tent*) piquet *m*; (*for clothes*) pince *f* (à linge); (*for coat, hat etc*) patère *f*; **to buy off the p.** acheter en prêt-à-porter. **2** *vt* (**-gg-**) (*prices*) stabiliser.

pejorative [pɪˈdʒɒrətɪv] *a* péjoratif.

pekin(g)ese [piːkɪˈniːz] *n* (*dog*) pékinois *m*.

pelican ['pelɪk(ə)n] *n* (*bird*) pélican *m*.

pellet ['pelɪt] *n* (*of paper etc*) boulette *f*; (*for gun*) (grain *m* de) plomb *m*.

pelt [pelt] **1** *n* (*skin*) peau *f*; (*fur*) fourrure *f*. **2** *vt* **to p. s.o. with** (*stones etc*) bombarder qn de. **3** *vi* **it's pelting (down)** (*raining*) il pleut à verse. **4** *vi* **to p. along** (*run, dash*) *Fam* foncer, courir.

pelvis [pelvɪs] *n Anat* bassin *m*.

pen [pen] **1** *n* (*dipped in ink*) porte-plume *m inv*; (*fountain pen*) stylo *m* (à encre *or* à plume); (*ballpoint*) stylo *m* à bille, stylo(-)bille *m*; **to live by one's p.** *Fig* vivre de sa plume; **p. friend, p. pal** correspondant, -ante *mf*; **p. name** pseudonyme *m*; **p. nib** (bec *m* de) plume *f*; **p. pusher** *Pej* gratte-papier *m inv*; – *vt* (**-nn-**) (*write*) écrire. **2** *n* (*enclosure for baby or sheep or cattle*) parc *m*.

penal ['piːn(ə)l] *a* (*law, code etc*) pénal; (*colony*) pénitentiaire. ◆**penalize** *vt Sp Jur* pénaliser (**for** pour); (*handicap*) désavantager.

penalty ['pen(ə)ltɪ] *n Jur* peine *f*; (*fine*) amende *f*; *Sp* pénalisation *f*; *Fb* penalty *m*; *Rugby* pénalité *f*; **to pay the p.** *Fig* subir les conséquences.

penance ['penəns] *n* pénitence *f*.

pence [pens] *see* **penny.**

pencil ['pens(ə)l] *n* crayon *m*; **in p.** au crayon; **p. box** plumier *m*; **p. sharpener**

taille-crayon(s) m inv; − vt (-ll-, Am -l-) crayonner; **to p. in** Fig noter provisoirement.

pendant ['pendənt] n pendentif m; (on earring, chandelier) pendeloque f.

pending ['pendiŋ] **1** a (matter) en suspens. **2** prep (until) en attendant.

pendulum ['pendjuləm] n (of clock) balancier m, pendule m; Fig pendule m.

penetrat/e ['penitreit] vt (substance, mystery etc) percer; (plan, secret etc) découvrir; − vti **to p. (into)** (forest, group etc) pénétrer dans. ◆**—ing** a (mind, cold etc) pénétrant. ◆**pene'tration** n pénétration f.

penguin ['peŋgwin] n manchot m, pingouin m.

penicillin [peni'silin] n pénicilline f.

peninsula [pə'ninsjulə] n presqu'île f, péninsule f. ◆**pensinsular** a péninsulaire.

penis ['piːnis] n pénis m.

penitent ['penitənt] a & n pénitent, -ente (mf). ◆**penitence** n pénitence f.

penitentiary [peni'tenʃəri] n Am prison f (centrale).

penknife ['pennaif] n (pl **-knives**) canif m.

pennant ['penənt] n (flag) flamme f, banderole f.

penny ['peni] n **1** (pl **pennies**) (coin) penny m; Am Can cent m; **I don't have a p.** Fig je n'ai pas le sou. **2** (pl **pence** [pens]) (value, currency) penny m. ◆**p.-pinching** a (miserly) Fam avare. ◆**penniless** a sans le sou.

pension ['penʃ(ə)n] n pension f; **retirement p.** (pension f de) retraite f; (private) retraite f complémentaire; − vt **to p. off** mettre à la retraite. ◆**—able** a (age) de la retraite; (job) qui donne droit à une retraite. ◆**—er** n pensionné, -ée mf; (old age) **p.** retraité, -ée mf.

pensive ['pensiv] a pensif.

pentagon ['pentəgən] n **the P.** Am Pol le Pentagone.

pentathlon [pen'tæθlən] n Sp pentathlon m.

Pentecost ['pentikɒst] n (Whitsun) Am Pentecôte f.

penthouse ['penthaus] n appartement m de luxe (construit sur le toit d'un immeuble).

pent-up ['pent'ʌp] a (feelings) refoulé.

penultimate [pi'nʌltimət] a avant-dernier.

peony ['piəni] n Bot pivoine f.

people ['piːp(ə)l] npl (in general) gens mpl or fpl; (specific persons) personnes fpl; (of region, town) habitants mpl, gens mpl or fpl; **the p.** (citizens) Pol le peuple; **old p.** les personnes fpl âgées; **old people's home**

hospice m de vieillards; (private) maison f de retraite; **two p.** deux personnes; **English p.** les Anglais mpl, le peuple anglais; **a lot of p.** beaucoup de monde or de gens; **p. think that . . .** on pense que . . . ; − n (nation) peuple m; − vt (populate) peupler (**with** de).

pep [pep] n entrain m; **p. talk** Fam petit laïus d'encouragement; − vt (-pp-) **to p. up** (perk up) ragaillardir.

pepper ['pepər] n poivre m; (vegetable) poivron m; − vt poivrer. ◆**peppercorn** n grain m de poivre. ◆**peppermint** n (plant) menthe f poivrée; (sweet) pastille f de menthe. ◆**peppery** a Culin poivré.

per [pɜːr] prep par; **p. annum** par an; **p. head, p. person** par personne; **p. cent** pour cent; **50 pence p. kilo** 50 pence le kilo; **40 km p. hour** 40 km à l'heure. ◆**per'centage** n pourcentage m.

perceive [pə'siːv] vt (see, hear) percevoir; (notice) remarquer (**that** que). ◆**perceptible** a perceptible. ◆**perception** n perception f (**of** de); (intuition) intuition f. ◆**perceptive** a (person) perspicace; (study, remark) pénétrant.

perch [pɜːtʃ] **1** n perchoir m; − vi (of bird) (se) percher; (of person) Fig se percher, se jucher; − vt (put) percher. **2** n (fish) perche f.

percolate ['pɜːkəleit] vi (of liquid) filtrer, passer (**through** par); − vt (coffee) faire dans une cafetière; **percolated coffee** du vrai café. ◆**percolator** n cafetière f; (in café or restaurant) percolateur m.

percussion [pə'kʌʃ(ə)n] n Mus percussion f.

peremptory [pə'remptəri] a péremptoire.

perennial [pə'reniəl] **1** a (complaint, subject etc) perpétuel. **2** a (plant) vivace; − n plante f vivace.

perfect ['pɜːfikt] a parfait; − a & n **p.** (tense) Gram parfait m; − [pə'fekt] vt (book, piece of work etc) parachever, parfaire; (process, technique) mettre au point; (one's French etc) parfaire ses connaissances en. ◆**per'fection** n perfection f; (act) parachèvement m (**of** de); **mise** f au point (**of** de); **to p.** à la perfection. ◆**per'fectionist** n perfectionniste mf. ◆**'perfectly** adv parfaitement.

perfidious [pə'fidiəs] a Lit perfide.

perforate ['pɜːfəreit] vt perforer. ◆**perfo'ration** n perforation f.

perform [pə'fɔːm] vt (task, miracle) accomplir; (a function, one's duty) remplir; (rite) célébrer; (operation) Med pratiquer (on sur); (a play, symphony) jouer; (sonata) interpréter; – vi (play) jouer; (sing) chanter; (dance) danser; (of circus animal) faire un numéro; (function) fonctionner; (behave) se comporter; **you performed very well!** tu as très bien fait! ◆**—ing** a (animal) savant. ◆**perform̂ance** n **1** (show) Th représentation f, séance f; Cin Mus séance f. **2** (of athlete, machine etc) performance f; (of actor, musician etc) interprétation f; (circus act) numéro m; (fuss) Fam histoire(s) f(pl); **the p. of one's duties** l'exercice m de ses fonctions. ◆**performer** n interprète mf (**of** de); (entertainer) artiste mf.

perfume ['pɜːfjuːm] n parfum m; – [pə'fjuːm] vt parfumer.

perfunctory [pə'fʌŋktəri] a (action) superficiel; (smile etc) de commande.

perhaps [pə'hæps] adv peut-être; **p. not** peut-être que non.

peril ['peril] n péril m, danger m; **at your p.** à vos risques et péril. ◆**perilous** a périlleux.

perimeter [pə'rimitər] n périmètre m.

period ['piəriəd] **1** n (length of time, moment in time) période f; (historical) époque f; (time limit) délai m; (lesson) Sch leçon f; (full stop) Gram point m; **in the p. of a month** en l'espace d'un mois; **I refuse, p.!** Am je refuse, un point c'est tout!; – a (furniture etc) d'époque; (costume) de l'époque. **2** n (menstruation) règles fpl. ◆**peri'odic** a périodique. ◆**peri'odical** n (magazine) périodique m. ◆**peri-'odically** adv périodiquement.

periphery [pə'rifəri] n périphérie f. ◆**peripheral** a (question) sans rapport direct (**to** avec); (interest) accessoire; (neighbourhood) périphérique.

periscope ['periskəup] n périscope m.

perish ['perif] vi (die) périr; (of food, substance) se détériorer; **to be perished or perishing** (of person) Fam être frigorifié. ◆**—ing** a (cold, weather) Fam glacial. ◆**—able** a (food) périssable; – npl denrées fpl périssables.

perjure ['pɜːdʒər] vt **to p. oneself** se parjurer. ◆**perjurer** n (person) parjure mf. ◆**perjury** n parjure m; **to commit p.** se parjurer.

perk [pɜːk] **1** vi **to p. up** (buck up) se ragaillardir; – vt **to p. s.o. up** remonter qn, ragaillardir qn. **2** n (advantage) avantage m; (extra profit) à-côté m. ◆**perky** a (-ier, -iest) (cheerful) guilleret, plein d'entrain.

perm [pɜːm] n (of hair) permanente f; – vt **to**

have one's hair permed se faire faire une permanente.

permanent ['pɜːmənənt] a permanent; (address) fixe; **she's p. here** elle est ici à titre permanent. ◆**permanence** n permanence f. ◆**permanently** adv à titre permanent.

permeate ['pɜːmieit] vt (of ideas etc) se répandre dans; **to p. (through)** (of liquid etc) pénétrer. ◆**permeable** a perméable.

permit [pə'mit] vt (-tt-) permettre (**s.o. to do** à qn de faire); **weather permitting** si le temps le permet; – ['pɜːmit] n (licence) permis m; (entrance pass) laissez-passer m inv. ◆**per'missible** a permis. ◆**per-'mission** n permission f, autorisation f (**to do** de faire); **to ask (for)/give p.** demander/donner la permission. ◆**per-'missive** a (trop) tolérant, laxiste. ◆**per-'missiveness** n laxisme m.

permutation [pɜːmjuː'teif(ə)n] n permutation f.

pernicious [pə'nifəs] a (harmful) & Med pernicieux.

pernickety [pə'nikəti] a Fam (precise) pointilleux; (demanding) difficile (**about** sur).

peroxide [pə'rɒksaid] n (bleach) eau f oxygénée; – a (hair, blond) oxygéné.

perpendicular [pɜːpən'dikjulər] a & n perpendiculaire (f).

perpetrate ['pɜːpitreit] vt (crime) perpétrer. ◆**perpetrator** n auteur m.

perpetual [pə'petjuəl] a perpétuel. ◆**perpetually** adv perpétuellement. ◆**perpetuate** vt perpétuer. ◆**perpetuity** [pɜːpi'tjuːti] n perpétuité f.

perplex [pə'pleks] vt rendre perplexe, dérouter. ◆**—ed** a perplexe. ◆**—ing** a déroutant. ◆**perplexity** n perplexité f; (complexity) complexité f.

persecute ['pɜːsikjuːt] vt persécuter. ◆**perse'cution** n persécution f.

persever/e [pɜːsi'viər] vi persévérer (**in** dans). ◆**—ing** a (persistent) persévérant. ◆**perseverance** n persévérance f.

Persian ['pɜːf(ə)n, 'pɜːʒ(ə)n] a (language, cat, carpet) persan; – n (language) persan m.

persist [pə'sist] vi persister (**in doing** à faire, **in sth** dans qch). ◆**persistence** n persistance f. ◆**persistent** a (fever, smell etc) persistant; (person) obstiné; (attempts, noise etc) continuel. ◆**persistently** adv (stubbornly) obstinément; (continually) continuellement.

person ['pɜːs(ə)n] n personne f; **in p.** en personne; **a p. to p. call** Tel une communi-

cation avec préavis. ◆**personable** a
avenant, qui présente bien.
personal ['pɜːsən(ə)l] a personnel; (*application*) en personne; (*hygiene, friend*) intime;
(*life*) privé; (*indiscreet*) indiscret; **p. assistant, p. secretary** secrétaire m particulier,
secrétaire f particulière. ◆**perso'nality** n
(*character, famous person*) personnalité f; **a
television p.** une vedette de la télévision.
◆**personalize** vt personnaliser. ◆**personally** adv personnellement; (*in person*)
en personne.
personify [pəˈsɒnɪfaɪ] vt personnifier.
◆**personifi'cation** n personnification f.
personnel [pɜːsəˈnel] n (*staff*) personnel m;
(*department*) service m du personnel.
perspective [pəˈspektɪv] n (*artistic & viewpoint*) perspective f; **in (its true) p.** Fig sous
son vrai jour.
perspire [pəˈspaɪər] vi transpirer. ◆**perspi'ration** n transpiration f, sueur f.
persuade [pəˈsweɪd] vt persuader (**s.o. to do**
qn de faire). ◆**persuasion** n persuasion f;
Rel religion f. ◆**persuasive** a (*person,
argument etc*) persuasif. ◆**persuasively**
adv de façon persuasive.
pert [pɜːt] a (*impertinent*) impertinent;
(*lively*) gai, plein d'entrain; (*hat etc*)
coquet, chic. ◆**—ly** adv avec impertinence.
pertain [pəˈteɪn] vi **to p. to** (*relate*) se
rapporter à; (*belong*) appartenir à.
pertinent ['pɜːtɪnənt] a pertinent. ◆**—ly** adv
pertinemment.
perturb [pəˈtɜːb] vt troubler, perturber.
Peru [pəˈruː] n Pérou m. ◆**Peruvian** a & n
péruvien, -ienne (mf).
peruse [pəˈruːz] vt lire (attentivement);
(*skim through*) parcourir. ◆**perusal** n
lecture f.
pervade [pəˈveɪd] vt se répandre dans.
◆**pervasive** a qui se répand partout,
envahissant.
perverse [pəˈvɜːs] a (*awkward*) contrariant;
(*obstinate*) entêté; (*wicked*) pervers.
◆**perversion** n perversion f; (*of justice,
truth*) travestissement m. ◆**perversity** n
esprit m de contradiction; (*obstinacy*)
entêtement m; (*wickedness*) perversité f.
pervert [pəˈvɜːt] vt pervertir; (*mind*)
corrompre; (*justice, truth*) travestir; —
['pɜːvɜːt] n perverti, -ie mf.
pesky ['peskɪ] a (**-ier, -iest**) (*troublesome*)
Am Fam embêtant.
pessimism ['pesɪmɪz(ə)m] n pessimisme m.
◆**pessimist** n pessimiste mf. ◆**pessi-
'mistic** a pessimiste. ◆**pessi'mistically**
adv avec pessimisme.

pest [pest] n animal m or insecte m nuisible;
(*person*) Fam casse-pieds mf inv, peste f.
◆**pesticide** n pesticide m.
pester ['pestər] vt (*harass*) harceler (**with
questions** de questions); **to p. s.o. to do
sth/for sth** harceler or tarabuster qn pour
qu'il fasse qch/jusqu'à ce qu'il donne qch.
pet [pet] **1** n animal m (domestique);
(*favourite person*) chouchou, -oute mf; **yes
(my) p.** Fam oui mon chou; **to have** or **keep
a p.** avoir un animal chez soi; – a (*dog etc*)
domestique; (*tiger etc*) apprivoisé; (*favourite*) favori; **p. shop** magasin m d'animaux;
p. hate bête f noire; **p. name** petit nom m
(d'amitié); **p. subject** dada m. **2** vt (**-tt-**)
(*fondle*) caresser; (*sexually*) Fam peloter;
– vi Fam se peloter.
petal ['pet(ə)l] n pétale m.
peter ['piːtər] vi **to p. out** (*run out*) s'épuiser;
(*dry up*) se tarir; (*die out*) mourir; (*disappear*) disparaître.
petite [pəˈtiːt] a (*woman*) petite et mince,
menue.
petition [pəˈtɪʃ(ə)n] n (*signatures*) pétition f;
(*request*) Jur requête f; **p. for divorce**
demande f en divorce; – vt adresser une
pétition or une requête à (**for sth** pour
demander qch).
petrify ['petrɪfaɪ] vt (*frighten*) pétrifier de
terreur.
petrol ['petrəl] n essence f; **I've run out of p.**
je suis tombé en panne d'essence; **p. engine**
moteur m à essence; **p. station** poste m
d'essence, station-service f.
petroleum [pəˈtrəʊlɪəm] n pétrole m.
petticoat ['petɪkəʊt] n jupon m.
petty ['petɪ] a (**-ier, -iest**) (*small*) petit; (*trivial*) insignifiant, menu, petit; (*mean*)
mesquin; **p. cash** Com petite caisse f,
menue monnaie f. ◆**pettiness** n petitesse
f; insignifiance f; mesquinerie f.
petulant ['petjʊlənt] a irritable. ◆**petulance** n irritabilité f.
petunia [pɪˈtjuːnɪə] n Bot pétunia m.
pew [pjuː] n banc m d'église; **take a p.!** Hum
assieds-toi!
pewter ['pjuːtər] n étain m.
phallic ['fælɪk] a phallique.
phantom ['fæntəm] n fantôme m.
pharmacy ['fɑːməsɪ] n pharmacie f.
◆**pharmaceutical** [-'sjuːtɪk(ə)l] a pharmaceutique. ◆**pharmacist** n pharmacien,
-ienne mf.
pharynx ['færɪŋks] n Anat pharynx m.
◆**pharyn'gitis** n Med pharyngite f.
phase [feɪz] n (*stage*) phase f; – vt **to p.**

in/out introduire/supprimer progressivement. ◆**phased** a (changes etc) progressif.
PhD [piːeɪtʃ'diː] n abbr (Doctor of Philosophy) (degree) Univ doctorat m.
pheasant ['fezənt] n (bird) faisan m.
phenomenon, pl **-ena** [fɪ'nɒmɪnən, -ɪnə] n phénomène m. ◆**phenomenal** a phénoménal.
phew! [fjuː] int (relief) ouf!
philanderer [fɪ'lændərər] n coureur m de jupons.
philanthropist [fɪ'lænθrəpɪst] n philanthrope mf. ◆**philan'thropic** a philanthropique.
philately [fɪ'lætəlɪ] n philatélie. ◆**phila'telic** a philatélique. ◆**philatelist** n philatéliste mf.
philharmonic [fɪlə'mɒnɪk] a philharmonique.
Philippines ['fɪlɪpiːnz] npl **the P.** les Philippines fpl.
philistine ['fɪlɪstaɪn] n béotien, -ienne mf, philistin m.
philosophy [fɪ'lɒsəfɪ] n philosophie f. ◆**philosopher** n philosophe mf. ◆**philo'sophical** a philosophique; (stoical, resigned) Fig philosophe. ◆**philo'sophically** adv (to say etc) avec philosophie. ◆**philosophize** vi philosopher.
phlegm [flem] n Med glaires fpl; (calmness) Fig flegme m. ◆**phleg'matic** a flegmatique.
phobia ['fəubɪə] n phobie f.
phone [fəun] n téléphone m; **on the p.** (speaking here) au téléphone; (at other end) au bout du fil; **to be on the p.** (as subscriber) avoir le téléphone; **p. call** coup m de fil or de téléphone; **to make a p. call** téléphoner (to à); **p. book** annuaire m; **p. box, p. booth** cabine f téléphonique; **p. number** numéro m de téléphone; – vt (message) téléphoner (to à); **to p. s.o. (up)** téléphoner à qn; – vi **to p. (up)** téléphoner; **to p. back** rappeler. ◆**phonecard** n télécarte f.
phonetic [fə'netɪk] a phonétique. ◆**phonetics** n (science) phonétique f.
phoney ['fəunɪ] a (-ier, -iest) Fam (jewels, writer etc) faux; (attack, firm) bidon inv; (attitude) fumiste; – n Fam (impostor) imposteur m; (joker, shirker) fumiste mf; **it's a p.** (jewel, coin etc) c'est du faux.
phonograph ['fəunəgræf] n Am électrophone m.
phosphate ['fɒsfeɪt] n Ch phosphate m.
phosphorus ['fɒsfərəs] n Ch phosphore m.
photo ['fəutəu] n (pl **-os**) photo f; **to have one's p. taken** se faire photographier.

◆**photocopier** n (machine) photocopieur m. ◆**photocopy** n photocopie f; – vt photocopier. ◆**photo'genic** a photogénique. ◆**photograph** n photographie f; – vt photographier; – vi **to p. well** être photogénique. ◆**photographer** [fə'tɒgrəfər] n photographe mf. ◆**photo'graphic** a photographique. ◆**photography** [fə'tɒgrəfɪ] n (activity) photographie f. ◆**photostat**® = photocopy.
phras/e [freɪz] n (saying) expression f; (idiom) & Gram locution f; – vt (express) exprimer; (letter) rédiger. ◆**—ing** n (wording) termes mpl. ◆**phrasebook** n (for tourists) manuel m de conversation.
physical ['fɪzɪk(ə)l] a physique; (object, world) matériel; **p. examination** Med examen m médical; **p. education, p. training** éducation f physique. ◆**physically** adv physiquement; **p. impossible** matériellement impossible.
physician [fɪ'zɪʃ(ə)n] n médecin m.
physics ['fɪzɪks] n (science) physique f. ◆**physicist** n physicien, -ienne mf.
physiology [fɪzɪ'ɒlədʒɪ] n physiologie f. ◆**physio'logical** a physiologique.
physiotherapy [fɪzɪəu'θerəpɪ] n kinésithérapie f. ◆**physiotherapist** n kinésithérapeute mf.
physique [fɪ'ziːk] n (appearance) physique m; (constitution) constitution f.
piano [pɪ'ænəu] n (pl **-os**) piano m. ◆**'pianist** n pianiste mf.
piazza [pɪ'ætsə] n (square) place f; (covered) passage m couvert.
picayune [pɪkə'juːn] a (petty) Am Fam mesquin.
pick [pɪk] n (choice) choix m; **the p. of** (best) le meilleur de; **the p. of the bunch** le dessus du panier; **to take one's p.** faire son choix, choisir; – vt (choose) choisir; (flower, fruit etc) cueillir; (hole) faire (**in** dans); (lock) crocheter; **to p. one's nose** se mettre les doigts dans le nez; **to p. one's teeth** se curer les dents; **to p. a fight** chercher la bagarre (**with** avec); **to p. holes in** Fig relever les défauts de; **to p. (off)** (remove) enlever; **to p. out** (choose) choisir; (identify) reconnaître, distinguer; **to p. up** (sth dropped) ramasser; (fallen person or chair) relever; (person into air, weight) soulever; (cold, money) Fig ramasser; (habit, accent, speed) prendre; (fetch, collect) (passer) prendre; (find) trouver; (baby) prendre dans ses bras; (programme etc) Rad capter; (survivor) recueillir; (arrest) arrêter, ramasser; (learn) apprendre; – vi **to p. and choose** choisir

avec soin; **to p. on** (*nag*) harceler; (*blame*) accuser; **why p. on me?** pourquoi moi?; **to p. up** (*improve*) s'améliorer; (*of business, trade*) reprendre; *Med* aller mieux; (*resume*) continuer. ◆**—ing 1** *n* (*choosing*) choix *m* (**of** de); (*of flower, fruit etc*) cueillette *f*. **2** *npl* (*leftovers*) restes *mpl*; *Com* profits *mpl*. ◆**pick-me-up** *n* (*drink*) *Fam* remontant *m*. ◆**pick-up** *n* (*of record player*) (bras *m* de) pick-up *m*; (*person*) *Pej Fam* partenaire *mf* de rencontre; **p.-up** (**truck**) pick-up *m*.

pick(axe) (*Am* **-ax**) ['pɪk(æks)] *n* (*tool*) pioche *f*; **ice pick** pic *m* à glace.

picket ['pɪkɪt] **1** *n* (*striker*) gréviste *mf*; **p. (line)** piquet *m* (de grève); – *vt* (*factory*) installer des piquets de grève aux portes de. **2** *n* (*stake*) piquet *m*.

pickle ['pɪk(ə)l] **1** *n* (*brine*) saumure *f*; (*vinegar*) vinaigre *m*; *pl* (*vegetables*) pickles *mpl*; *Am* concombres *mpl*, cornichons *mpl*; – *vt* mariner. **2** *n* **in a p.** (*trouble*) *Fam* dans le pétrin.

pickpocket ['pɪkpɒkɪt] *n* (*thief*) pickpocket *m*.

picky ['pɪkɪ] *a* (**-ier, -iest**) (*choosey*) *Am* difficile.

picnic ['pɪknɪk] *n* pique-nique *m*; – *vi* (**-ck-**) pique-niquer.

pictorial [pɪk'tɔːrɪəl] *a* (*in pictures*) en images; (*periodical*) illustré.

picture ['pɪktʃər] **1** *n* image *f*; (*painting*) tableau *m*, peinture *f*; (*drawing*) dessin *m*; (*photo*) photo *f*; (*film*) film *m*; (*scene*) *Fig* tableau *m*; **the pictures** *Cin* le cinéma; **to put s.o. in the p.** *Fig* mettre qn au courant; **p. frame** cadre *m*. **2** *vt* (*imagine*) s'imaginer (**that** que); (*remember*) revoir; (*depict*) décrire.

picturesque [pɪktʃə'resk] *a* pittoresque.

piddling ['pɪdlɪŋ] *a* *Pej* dérisoire.

pidgin ['pɪdʒɪn] *n* **p. (English)** pidgin *m*.

pie [paɪ] *n* (*of meat, vegetable*) tourte *f*; (*of fruit*) tarte *f*, tourte *f*; (*compact filling*) pâté *m* en croûte; **cottage p.** hachis *m* Parmentier.

piebald ['paɪbɔːld] *a* pie *inv*.

piece [piːs] *n* morceau *m*; (*of bread, paper, chocolate, etc*) bout *m*, morceau *m*; (*of fabric, machine, game, artillery*) pièce *f*; (*coin*) pièce *f*; **bits and pieces** des petites choses; **in pieces** en morceaux, en pièces; **to smash to pieces** briser en morceaux; **to take to pieces** (*machine etc*) démonter; **to come to pieces** se démonter; **to go to pieces** (*of person*) *Fig* craquer; **a p. of luck/news/**etc une chance/nouvelle/etc; **in**

one p. (*object*) intact; (*person*) indemne; – *vt* **to p. together** (*facts*) reconstituer; (*one's life*) refaire. ◆**piecemeal** *adv* petit à petit; – *a* (*unsystematic*) peu méthodique. ◆**piecework** *n* travail *m* à la tâche *or* à la pièce.

pier [pɪər] *n* (*promenade*) jetée *f*; (*for landing*) appontement *m*.

pierc/e [pɪəs] *vt* percer; (*of cold, sword, bullet*) transpercer (*qn*). ◆**—ing** *a* (*voice, look etc*) perçant; (*wind etc*) glacial.

piety ['paɪətɪ] *n* piété *f*.

piffling ['pɪflɪŋ] *a* *Fam* insignifiant.

pig [pɪg] *n* cochon *m*, porc *m*; (*evil person*) *Pej* cochon *m*; (*glutton*) *Pej* goinfre *m*. ◆**piggish** *a* *Pej* (*dirty*) sale; (*greedy*) goinfre. ◆**piggy** *a* (*greedy*) *Fam* goinfre. ◆**piggybank** *n* tirelire *f* (*en forme de cochon*).

pigeon ['pɪdʒɪn] *n* pigeon *m*. ◆**pigeonhole** *n* casier *m*; – *vt* classer; (*shelve*) mettre en suspens.

piggyback ['pɪgɪbæk] *n* **to give s.o. a p.** porter qn sur le dos.

pigheaded [pɪg'hedɪd] *a* obstiné.

pigment ['pɪgmənt] *n* pigment *m*. ◆**pigmen'tation** *n* pigmentation *f*.

pigsty ['pɪgstaɪ] *n* porcherie *f*.

pigtail ['pɪgteɪl] *n* (*hair*) natte *f*.

pike [paɪk] *n* **1** (*fish*) brochet *m*. **2** (*weapon*) pique *f*.

pilchard ['pɪltʃəd] *n* pilchard *m*, sardine *f*.

pile¹ [paɪl] *n* pile *f*; (*fortune*) *Fam* fortune *f*; **piles of, a p. of** *Fam* beaucoup de, un tas de; – *vt* **to p. (up)** (*stack up*) empiler; – *vi* **to p. into** (*of people*) s'entasser dans; **to p. up** (*accumulate*) s'accumuler, s'amonceler. ◆**p.-up** *n* *Aut* collision *f* en chaîne, carambolage *m*.

pile² [paɪl] *n* (*of carpet*) poils *mpl*.

piles [paɪlz] *npl* *Med* hémorroïdes *fpl*.

pilfer ['pɪlfər] *vt* (*steal*) chaparder (**from s.o.** à qn). ◆**—ing**, *n*, ◆**—age** *n* chapardage *m*.

pilgrim ['pɪlgrɪm] *n* pèlerin *m*. ◆**pilgrimage** *n* pèlerinage *m*.

pill [pɪl] *n* pilule *f*; **to be on the p.** (*of woman*) prendre la pilule; **to go on/off the p.** se mettre à/arrêter la pilule.

pillage ['pɪlɪdʒ] *vti* piller; – *n* pillage *m*.

pillar ['pɪlər] *n* pilier *m*; (*of smoke*) *Fig* colonne *f*. ◆**p.-box** *n* boîte *f* à *or* aux lettres (*située sur le trottoir*).

pillion ['pɪljən] *adv* **to ride p.** (*on motorbike*) monter derrière.

pillory ['pɪlərɪ] *vt* (*ridicule, scorn*) mettre au pilori.

pillow ['pɪləʊ] *n* oreiller *m*. ◆**pillowcase** *n*, ◆**pillowslip** *n* taie *f* d'oreiller.

pilot ['paɪlət] **1** *n* (*of aircraft, ship*) pilote *m*; – *vt* piloter; – *a* **p. light** (*on appliance*) voyant *m*. **2** *a* (*experimental*) (-)pilote; **p. scheme** projet(-)pilote *m*.

pimento [pɪ'mentəʊ] *n* (*pl* -os) piment *m*.

pimp [pɪmp] *n* souteneur *m*.

pimple ['pɪmp(ə)l] *n* bouton *m*. ◆**pimply** *a* (-ier, iest) boutonneux.

pin [pɪn] *n* épingle *f*; (*drawing pin*) punaise *f*; *Tech* goupille *f*, fiche *f*; **to have pins and needles** *Med Fam* avoir des fourmis (**in** dans); **p. money** argent *m* de poche; – *vt* (-nn-) **to p. (on)** (*attach*) épingler (**to** sur, à); (*to wall*) punaiser (**to, on** à); **to p. one's hopes on** mettre tous ses espoirs dans; **to p. on** (**to**) **s.o.** (*crime, action*) accuser qn de; **to p. down** (*immobilize*) immobiliser; (*fix*) fixer; (*enemy*) clouer; **to p. s.o. down** *Fig* forcer qn à préciser ses idées; **to p. up** (*notice*) afficher. ◆**pincushion** *n* pelote *f* (à épingles). ◆**pinhead** *n* tête *f* d'épingle.

pinafore ['pɪnəfɔːr] *n* (*apron*) tablier *m*; (*dress*) robe *f* chasuble.

pinball ['pɪnbɔːl] *a* **p. machine** flipper *m*.

pincers ['pɪnsəz] *npl* tenailles *fpl*.

pinch [pɪntʃ] **1** *n* (*mark*) pinçon *m*; (*of salt*) pincée *f*; **to give s.o. a p.** pincer qn; **at a p.**, *Am* **in a p.** (*if necessary*) au besoin; **to feel the p.** *Fig* souffrir (*du manque d'argent etc*); – *vt* pincer; – *vi* (*of shoes*) faire mal. **2** *vt Fam* (*steal*) piquer (**from** à); (*arrest*) pincer.

pine [paɪn] **1** *n* (*tree, wood*) pin *m*; **p. forest** pinède *f*. **2** *vi* **to p. for** désirer vivement (retrouver), languir après; **to p. away** dépérir.

pineapple ['paɪnæp(ə)l] *n* ananas *m*.

ping [pɪŋ] *n* bruit *m* métallique. ◆**pinger** *n* (*on appliance*) signal *m* sonore.

ping-pong ['pɪŋpɒŋ] *n* ping-pong *m*.

pink [pɪŋk] *a & n* (*colour*) rose (*m*).

pinkie ['pɪŋkɪ] *n Am* petit doigt *m*.

pinnacle ['pɪnək(ə)l] *n* (*highest point*) *Fig* apogée *m*.

pinpoint ['pɪnpɔɪnt] *vt* (*locate*) repérer; (*define*) définir.

pinstripe ['pɪnstraɪp] *a* (*suit*) rayé.

pint [paɪnt] *n* pinte *f* (*Br* = 0,57 litre, *Am* = 0,47 litre); **a p. of beer** = un demi.

pinup ['pɪnʌp] *n* (*girl*) pin-up *f inv*.

pioneer [paɪə'nɪər] *n* pionnier, -ière *mf*; – *vt* (*research, study*) entreprendre pour la première fois.

pious ['paɪəs] *a* (*person, deed*) pieux.

pip [pɪp] **1** *n* (*of fruit*) pépin *m*. **2** *n* (*on uniform*) *Mil* galon *m*, sardine *f*. **3** *npl* **the pips** (*sound*) *Tel* le bip-bip.

pip/e [paɪp] **1** *n* tuyau *m*; (*of smoker*) pipe *f*; (*instrument*) *Mus* pipeau *m*; **the pipes** (*bagpipes*) *Mus* la cornemuse; **(peace) p.** calumet *m* de la paix; **to smoke a p.** fumer la pipe; **p. cleaner** cure-pipe *m*; **p. dream** chimère *f*; – *vt* (*water etc*) transporter par tuyaux *or* par canalisation; **piped music** musique *f* (de fond) enregistrée. **2** *vi* **to p. down** (*shut up*) *Fam* la boucler, se taire. ◆**—ing** *n* (*system of pipes*) canalisations *fpl*, tuyaux *mpl*; **length of p.** tuyau *m*; – *adv* **it's p. hot** (*soup etc*) c'est très chaud. ◆**pipeline** *n* pipeline *m*; **it's in the p.** *Fig* c'est en route.

pirate ['paɪərət] *n* pirate *m*; – *a* (*radio, ship*) pirate. ◆**piracy** *n* piraterie *f*. ◆**pirated** *a* (*book, record etc*) pirate.

Pisces ['paɪsiːz] *npl* (*sign*) les Poissons *mpl*.

pistachio [pɪ'stæʃɪəʊ] *n* (*pl* -os) (*fruit, flavour*) pistache *f*.

pistol ['pɪst(ə)l] *n* pistolet *m*.

piston ['pɪst(ə)n] *n Aut* piston *m*.

pit [pɪt] **1** *n* (*hole*) trou *m*; (*mine*) mine *f*; (*quarry*) carrière *f*; (*of stomach*) creux *m*; *Th* orchestre *m*; *Sp Aut* stand *m* de ravitaillement. **2** *vt* (-tt-) **to p. oneself** *or* **one's wits against** se mesurer à. **3** *n* (*stone of fruit*) *Am* noyau *m*. ◆**pitted** *a* **1** (*face*) grêlé; **p. with rust** piqué de rouille. **2** (*fruit*) *Am* dénoyauté.

pitch¹ [pɪtʃ] **1** *n Sp* terrain *m*; (*in market*) place *f*. **2** *n* (*degree*) degré *m*; (*of voice*) hauteur *f*; *Mus* ton *m*. **3** *vt* (*ball*) lancer; (*camp*) établir; (*tent*) dresser; **a pitched battle** *Mil* une bataille rangée; *Fig* une belle bagarre. **4** *vi* (*of ship*) tanguer. **5** *vi* **to p. in** (*cooperate*) *Fam* se mettre de la partie; **to p. into s.o.** attaquer qn.

pitch² [pɪtʃ] *n* (*tar*) poix *f*. ◆**p.-'black** *a*, ◆**p.-'dark** *a* noir comme dans un four.

pitcher ['pɪtʃər] *n* cruche *f*, broc *m*.

pitchfork ['pɪtʃfɔːk] *n* fourche *f* (à foin).

pitfall ['pɪtfɔːl] *n* (*trap*) piège *m*.

pith [pɪθ] *n* (*of orange*) peau *f* blanche; (*essence*) *Fig* moelle *f*. ◆**pithy** *a* (-ier, -iest) (*remark etc*) piquant et concis.

pitiful ['pɪtɪfəl] *a* pitoyable. ◆**pitiless** *a* impitoyable.

pittance ['pɪtəns] *n* (*income*) revenu *m or* salaire *m* misérable; (*sum*) somme *f* dérisoire.

pitter-patter ['pɪtəpætər] *n* = **patter 1**.

pity ['pɪtɪ] *n* pitié *f*; **(what) a p.!** (quel) dommage!; **it's a p.** c'est dommage (**that**

que (+ *sub*), **to do** de faire); **to have** or **take p. on** avoir pitié de; − *vt* plaindre.
pivot ['pɪvət] *n* pivot *m*; − *vi* pivoter.
pixie ['pɪksɪ] *n* (*fairy*) lutin *m*.
pizza ['piːtsə] *n* pizza *f*.
placard ['plækɑːd] *n* (*notice*) affiche *f*.
placate [plə'keɪt, *Am* 'pleɪkeɪt] *vt* calmer.
place [pleɪs] *n* endroit *m*; (*specific*) lieu *m*; (*house*) maison *f*; (*premises*) locaux *mpl*; (*seat, position, rank*) place *f*; **in the first p.** (*firstly*) en premier lieu; **to take p.** (*happen*) avoir lieu; **market p.** (*square*) place *f* du marché; **at my p., to my p.** *Fam* chez moi; **some p.** (*somewhere*) *Am* quelque part; **no p.** (*nowhere*) *Am* nulle part; **all over the p.** partout; **to lose one's p.** perdre sa place; (*in book etc*) perdre sa page; **p. setting** couvert *m*; **to lay three places** (*at the table*) mettre trois couverts; **to take the p. of** remplacer; **in p. of** à la place de; **out of p.** (*remark, object*) déplacé; (*person*) déplacé; **p. mat** set *m* (de table); − *vt* (*put, situate, invest*) & *Sp* placer; (*an order*) *Com* passer (**with s.o.** à qn); (*remember*) se rappeler; (*identify*) reconnaître. ◆**placing** *n* (*of money*) placement *m*.
placid ['plæsɪd] *a* placide.
plagiarize ['pleɪdʒəraɪz] *vt* plagier. ◆**plagiarism** *n* plagiat *m*.
plague [pleɪg] **1** *n* (*disease*) peste *f*; (*nuisance*) *Fam* plaie *f*. **2** *vt* (*harass, pester*) harceler (**with** de).
plaice [pleɪs] *n* (*fish*) carrelet *m*, plie *f*.
plaid [plæd] *n* (*fabric*) tissu *m* écossais.
plain¹ [pleɪn] **1** *a* (**-er, -est**) (*clear, obvious*) clair; (*outspoken*) franc; (*simple*) simple; (*not patterned*) uni; (*woman, man*) sans beauté; (*sheer*) pur; **in p. clothes** en civil; **to make it p. to s.o.** that faire comprendre à qn que; **p. speaking** franc-parler *m*; − *adv* (*tired etc*) tout bonnement. ◆**−ly** *adv* clairement; franchement. ◆**−ness** *n* clarté *f*; simplicité *f*; manque *m* de beauté.
plain² [pleɪn] *n Geog* plaine *f*.
plaintiff ['pleɪntɪf] *n Jur* plaignant, -ante *mf*.
plait [plæt] *n* tresse *f*, natte *f*; − *vt* tresser, natter.
plan [plæn] *n* projet *m*; (*elaborate*) plan *m*; (*of house, book etc*) & *Pol Econ* plan *m*; **the best p. would be to . . .** le mieux serait de . . . ; **according to p.** comme prévu; **to have no plans** (*be free*) n'avoir rien de prévu; **to change one's plans** (*decide differently*) changer d'idée; **master p.** stratégie *f* d'ensemble; − *vt* (**-nn-**) (*envisage, decide on*) prévoir, projeter; (*organize*) organiser;

(*prepare*) préparer; (*design*) concevoir; *Econ* planifier; **to p. to do** (*intend*) avoir l'intention de faire; **as planned** comme prévu; − *vi* faire des projets; **to p. for** (*rain, disaster*) prévoir. ◆**planning** *n Econ* planification *f*; (*industrial, commercial*) planning *m*; **family p.** planning *m* familial; **town p.** urbanisme *m*. ◆**planner** *n* **town p.** urbaniste *mf*.
plane [pleɪn] *n* **1** (*aircraft*) avion *m*. **2** *Carp* rabot *m*. **3** (*tree*) platane *m*. **4** (*level*) & *Fig* plan *m*.
planet ['plænɪt] *n* planète *f*. ◆**plane- 'tarium** *n* planétarium *m*. ◆**planetary** *a* planétaire.
plank [plæŋk] *n* planche *f*.
plant [plɑːnt] **1** *n* plante *f*; **house p.** plante d'appartement; − *vt* planter (**with** en, de); (*bomb*) *Fig* (dé)poser; **to p. sth on s.o.** (*hide*) cacher qch sur qn. **2** *n* (*machinery*) matériel *m*; (*fixtures*) installation *f*; (*factory*) usine *f*. ◆**plan'tation** *n* (*land, trees etc*) plantation *f*.
plaque [plæk] *n* **1** (*commemorative plate*) plaque *f*. **2** (*on teeth*) plaque *f* dentaire.
plasma ['plæzmə] *n Med* plasma *m*.
plaster ['plɑːstər] *n* (*substance*) plâtre *m*; (*sticking*) **p.** sparadrap *m*; **p. of Paris** plâtre *m* à mouler; **in p.** *Med* dans le plâtre; **p. cast** *Med* plâtre *m*; − *vt* plâtrer; **to p. down** (*hair*) plaquer; **to p. with** (*cover*) couvrir de. ◆**−er** *n* plâtrier *m*.
plastic ['plæstɪk] *a* (*substance, art*) plastique; (*object*) en plastique; **p. explosive** plastic *m*; **p. surgery** chirurgie *f* esthétique; − *n* plastique *m*, matière *f* plastique.
plasticine® ['plæstɪsiːn] *n* pâte *f* à modeler.
plate [pleɪt] *n* (*dish*) assiette *f*; (*metal sheet on door, on vehicle etc*) plaque *f*; (*book illustration*) gravure *f*; (*dental*) dentier *m*; **gold/silver p.** vaisselle *f* d'or/d'argent; **a lot on one's p.** (*work*) *Fig* du pain sur la planche; **p. glass** verre *m* à vitre; − *vt* (*jewellery, metal*) plaquer (**with** de). ◆**plateful** *n* assiettée *f*, assiette *f*.
plateau ['plætəʊ] *n* (*pl* **-s** or **-x**) plateau *m*.
platform ['plætfɔːm] *n* estrade *f*; (*for speaker*) tribune *f*; (*on bus*) & *Pol* plate-forme *f*; *Rail* quai *m*; **p. shoes** chaussures *fpl* à semelles compensées.
platinum ['plætɪnəm] *n* (*metal*) platine *m*; − *a* **p.** or **p.-blond(e) hair** cheveux *mpl* platinés.
platitude ['plætɪtjuːd] *n* platitude *f*.
platonic [plə'tɒnɪk] *a* (*love etc*) platonique.
platoon [plə'tuːn] *n Mil* section *f*.

platter ['plætər] n Culin plat m.

plaudits ['plɔːdɪts] npl applaudissements mpl.

plausible ['plɔːzəb(ə)l] a (argument etc) plausible; (speaker etc) convaincant.

play [pleɪ] n (amusement, looseness) jeu m; Th pièce f (de théâtre), spectacle m; **a p. on words** un jeu de mots; **to come into p.** entrer en jeu; **to call into p.** faire entrer en jeu; − vt (card, part, tune etc) jouer; (game) jouer à; (instrument) jouer de; (match) disputer (with avec); (team, opponent) jouer contre; (record) passer; (radio) faire marcher; **to p. ball with** Fig coopérer avec; **to p. the fool** faire l'idiot; **to p. a part in doing/in sth** contribuer à faire/à qch; **to p. it cool** Fam garder son sang-froid; **to p. back** (tape) réécouter; **to p. down** minimiser; **to p. s.o. up** Fam (of bad back etc) tracasser qn; (of child etc) faire enrager qn; **played out** Fam (tired) épuisé; (idea, method) périmé, vieux jeu inv; − vi jouer (with avec, at à); (of record player, tape recorder) marcher; **what are you playing at?** Fam qu'est-ce que tu fais?; **to p. about or around** jouer, s'amuser; **to p. on** (piano etc) jouer de; (s.o.'s emotions etc) jouer sur; **to p. up** (of child, machine etc) Fam faire des siennes; **to p. up to s.o.** faire de la lèche à qn. ◆**—ing** n jeu m; **p. card** carte f à jouer; **p. field** terrain m de jeu. ◆**—er** n Sp joueur, -euse mf; Th acteur m, actrice f; **clarinette/etc p.** joueur, -euse mf de clarinette/etc; **cassette p.** lecteur m de cassettes.

play-act ['pleɪækt] vi jouer la comédie. ◆**playboy** n playboy m. ◆**playgoer** n amateur m de théâtre. ◆**playground** n Sch cour f de récréation. ◆**playgroup** n = playschool. ◆**playmate** n camarade mf. ◆**playpen** n parc m (pour enfants). ◆**playroom** n (in house) salle f de jeux. ◆**playschool** n garderie f (d'enfants). ◆**plaything** n (person) Fig jouet m. ◆**playtime** n Sch récréation f. ◆**playwright** n dramaturge mf.

playful ['pleɪfəl] a enjoué; (child) joueur. ◆**—ly** adv (to say) en badinant. ◆**—ness** n enjouement m.

plc [piːel'siː] abbr (public limited company) SA.

plea [pliː] n (request) appel m; (excuse) excuse f; **to make a p. of guilty** Jur plaider coupable. ◆**plead** vi Jur plaider; **to p. with s.o. to do** implorer qn de faire; **to p. for** (help etc) implorer; − vt Jur plaider; (as excuse) alléguer. ◆**pleading** n (requests) prières fpl.

pleasant ['plezənt] a agréable; (polite) aimable. ◆**—ly** adv agréablement. ◆**—ness** n (charm) charme m; (of person) amabilité f. ◆**pleasantries** npl (jokes) plaisanteries fpl; (polite remarks) civilités fpl.

pleas/e [pliːz] adv s'il vous plaît, s'il te plaît; **p. sit down** asseyez-vous, je vous prie; **p. do!** bien sûr!, je vous en prie!; **'no smoking p.'** 'prière de ne pas fumer'; − vt plaire à; (satisfy) contenter; **hard to p.** difficile (à contenter), exigeant; **p. yourself!** comme tu veux!; − vi plaire; **do as you p.** fais comme tu veux; **as much or as many as you p.** autant qu'il vous plaira. ◆**—ed** a content (with de, that que (+ sub), to do de faire); **p. to meet you!** enchanté!; **I'd be p. to!** avec plaisir! ◆**—ing** a agréable, plaisant.

pleasure ['pleʒər] n plaisir m; **p. boat** bateau m de plaisance. ◆**pleasurable** a très agréable.

pleat [pliːt] n (fold) pli m; − vt plisser.

plebiscite ['plebɪsɪt, -saɪt] n plébiscite m.

pledge [pledʒ] **1** n (promise) promesse f, engagement m (to do de faire); − vt promettre (to do de faire). **2** n (token, object) gage m; − vt (pawn) engager.

plenty ['plentɪ] n abondance f; **in p.** en abondance; **p. of** beaucoup de; **that's p.** (enough) c'est assez, ça suffit. ◆**plentiful** a abondant.

plethora ['pleθərə] n pléthore f.

pleurisy ['plʊərɪsɪ] n Med pleurésie f.

pliable ['plaɪəb(ə)l] a souple.

pliers ['plaɪəz] npl (tool) pince(s) f(pl).

plight [plaɪt] n (crisis) situation f critique; **(sorry) p.** triste situation f.

plimsoll ['plɪmsəʊl] n chaussure f de tennis, tennis f.

plinth [plɪnθ] n socle m.

plod [plɒd] vi (-dd-) **to p. (along)** avancer or travailler laborieusement; **to p. through** (book) lire laborieusement. ◆**plodding** a (slow) lent; (step) pesant. ◆**plodder** n (steady worker) bûcheur, -euse mf.

plonk [plɒŋk] **1** int (splash) plouf! **2** vt **to p. (down)** (drop) Fam poser (bruyamment). **3** n (wine) Pej Sl pinard m.

plot [plɒt] **1** n (conspiracy) complot m (against contre); Cin Th Liter intrigue f; − vti (-tt-) comploter (to do de faire). **2** n p. (of land) terrain m; (patch in garden) carré m de terre; **building p.** terrain m à bâtir. **3** vt (-tt-) **to p. (out)** déterminer; (graph, diagram) tracer; (one's position) relever. ◆**plotting** n (conspiracies) complots mpl.

plough [plaʊ] n charrue f; − vt labourer; to

p. back into (*money*) *Fig* réinvestir dans; − *vi* labourer; **to p. into** (*crash into*) percuter; **to p. through** (*snow etc*) avancer péniblement dans; (*fence, wall*) défoncer. ◆**ploughman** *n* (*pl* **-men**) laboureur *m*; **p.'s lunch** *Culin* assiette *f* composée (*de crudités et fromage*).

plow [plaʊ] *Am* = **plough**.

ploy [plɔɪ] *n* stratagème *m*.

pluck [plʌk] **1** *n* courage *m*; − *vt* **to p. up courage** s'armer de courage. **2** *vt* (*fowl*) plumer; (*eyebrows*) épiler; (*string*) *Mus* pincer; (*flower*) cueillir. ◆**plucky** *a* (**-ier, -iest**) courageux.

plug [plʌg] **1** *n* (*of cotton wool, wood etc*) tampon *m*, bouchon *m*; (*for sink etc drainage*) bonde *f*; − *vt* (**-gg-**) **to p. (up)** (*stop up*) boucher. **2** *n* *El* fiche *f*, prise *f* (*mâle*); − *vt* (**-gg-**) **to p. in** brancher. **3** *n* *Aut* bougie *f*. **4** *n* (*publicity*) *Fam* battage *m* publicitaire; − *vt* (**-gg-**) *Fam* faire du battage publicitaire pour. **5** *vi* (**-gg-**) **to p. away** (*work*) *Fam* bosser *m*. ◆**plughole** *n* trou *m* (*du lavabo etc*), vidange *f*.

plum [plʌm] *n* prune *f*; **a p. job** *Fam* un travail en or, un bon fromage.

plumage ['pluːmɪdʒ] *n* plumage *m*.

plumb [plʌm] **1** *vt* (*probe, understand*) sonder. **2** *adv* (*crazy etc*) *Am Fam* complètement; **p. in the middle** en plein milieu.

plumber ['plʌmər] *n* plombier *m*. ◆**plumbing** *n* plomberie *f*.

plume [pluːm] *n* (*feather*) plume *f*; (*on hat etc*) plumet *m*; **a p. of smoke** un panache de fumée.

plummet ['plʌmɪt] *vi* (*of aircraft etc*) plonger; (*of prices*) dégringoler.

plump [plʌmp] **1** *a* (**-er, -est**) (*person*) grassouillet; (*arm, chicken*) dodu; (*cushion, cheek*) rebondi. **2** *vi* **to p. for** (*choose*) se décider pour, choisir. ◆**-ness** *n* rondeur *f*.

plunder ['plʌndər] *vt* piller; − *n* (*act*) pillage *m*; (*goods*) butin *m*.

plung/e [plʌndʒ] *vt* (*thrust*) plonger (**into** dans); − *vi* (*dive*) plonger (**into** dans); (*fall*) tomber (**from** de); (*rush*) se lancer; − *n* (*dive*) plongeon *m*; (*fall*) chute *f*; **to take the p.** *Fig* se jeter à l'eau. ◆**-ing** *a* (*neckline*) plongeant. ◆**-er** *n* ventouse *f* (*pour déboucher un tuyau*), débouchoir *m*.

plural ['plʊərəl] *a* (*form*) pluriel; (*noun*) au pluriel; − *n* pluriel *m*; **in the p.** au pluriel.

plus [plʌs] *prep* plus; − *a* (*factor etc*) & *El* positif; **twenty p.** vingt et quelques; − *n* **p.**

(*sign*) *Math* (signe *m*) plus *m*; **it's a p.** c'est un (avantage en) plus.

plush [plʌʃ] *a* (**-er, -est**) (*splendid*) somptueux.

plutonium [pluːˈtəʊnɪəm] *n* plutonium *m*.

ply [plaɪ] **1** *vt* (*trade*) exercer; (*oar, tool*) *Lit* manier. **2** *vi* **to p. between** (*travel*) faire la navette entre. **3** *vt* **to p. s.o. with** (*whisky etc*) faire boire continuellement à qn; (*questions*) bombarder qn de.

p.m. [piːˈem] *adv* (*afternoon*) de l'après-midi; (*evening*) du soir.

PM [piːˈem] *n abbr* (*Prime Minister*) Premier ministre *m*.

pneumatic [njuːˈmætɪk] *a* **p. drill** marteau-piqueur *m*, marteau *m* pneumatique.

pneumonia [njuːˈməʊnɪə] *n* pneumonie *f*.

poach [pəʊtʃ] **1** *vt* (*egg*) pocher. **2** *vi* (*hunt, steal*) braconner; − *vt* (*employee from rival firm*) débaucher, piquer. ◆**-ing** *n* braconnage *m*. ◆**-er** *n* **1** (*person*) braconnier *m*. **2** (*egg*) **p.** pocheuse *f*.

PO Box [piːəʊˈbɒks] *abbr* (*Post Office Box*) BP.

pocket ['pɒkɪt] *n* poche *f*; (*area*) *Fig* petite zone *f*; (*of resistance*) poche *f*, îlot *m*; **I'm $5 out of p.** j'ai perdu 5 dollars; − *a* (*money, book etc*) de poche; − *vt* (*gain, steal*) empocher. ◆**pocketbook** *n* (*notebook*) carnet *m*; (*woman's handbag*) *Am* sac *m* à main. ◆**pocketful** *n* **a p. of** une pleine poche de.

pockmarked ['pɒkmaːkt] *a* (*face*) grêlé.

pod [pɒd] *n* cosse *f*.

podgy ['pɒdʒɪ] *a* (**-ier, -iest**) (*arm etc*) dodu; (*person*) rondelet.

podium ['pəʊdɪəm] *n* podium *m*.

poem ['pəʊɪm] *n* poème *m*. ◆**poet** *n* poète *m*. ◆**po'etic** *a* poétique. ◆**poetry** *n* poésie *f*.

poignant ['pɔɪnjənt] *a* poignant.

point [pɔɪnt] **1** *n* (*of knife etc*) pointe *f*; *pl Rail* aiguillage *m*; (*power*) **p.** *El* prise *f* (de courant). **2** *n* (*dot, position, question, degree, score etc*) point *m*; (*decimal*) virgule *f*; (*meaning*) *Fig* sens *m*; (*importance*) intérêt *m*; (*remark*) remarque *f*; **p. of view** point *m* de vue; **at this p. in time** en ce moment; **on the p. of doing** sur le point de faire; **what's the p.?** à quoi bon? (*of waiting/etc* attendre/*etc*); **there's no p. (in) staying/***etc* ça ne sert à rien de rester/*etc*; **that's not the p.** il ne s'agit pas de ça; **it's beside the p.** c'est à côté de la question; **to the p.** (*relevant*) pertinent; **get to the p.!** au fait!; **to make a p. of doing** prendre garde de faire; **his good**

points ses qualités *fpl; his bad points* ses défauts *mpl.* **3** *vt (aim)* pointer (**at** sur); *(vehicle)* tourner (**towards** vers); **to p. the way** indiquer le chemin (**to** à); *Fig* montrer la voie (**to** à); **to p. one's finger at** indiquer du doit, pointer son doigt vers; **to p. out** *(show)* indiquer; *(mention)* signaler (**that** que); – *vi* **to p. (at** *or* **to s.o.)** indiquer (qn) du doigt; **to p. to, be pointing to** *(show)* indiquer; **to p. east** indiquer l'est; **to be pointing** *(of vehicle)* être tourné (**towards** vers); *(of gun)* être braqué (**at** sur). ◆**—ed** *a* pointu; *(beard)* en pointe; *(remark, criticism)* *Fig* pertinent; *(incisive)* mordant. ◆**—edly** *adv (to the point)* avec pertinence; *(incisively)* d'un ton mordant. ◆**—er** *n (on dial etc)* index *m; (advice)* conseil *m; (clue)* indice *m;* **to be a p. to** *(possible solution etc)* laisser entrevoir. ◆**—less** *a* inutile, futile. ◆**—lessly** *adv* inutilement.

point-blank [pɔɪnt'blæŋk] *adv & a (to shoot, a shot)* à bout portant; *(to refuse, a refusal)* *Fig* (tout) net; *(to request, a request)* de but en blanc.

pois/e [pɔɪz] *n (balance)* équilibre *m; (of body)* port *m; (grace)* grâce *f; (confidence)* assurance *f,* calme *m;* – *vt* tenir en équilibre. ◆**—ed** *a* en équilibre; *(hanging)* suspendu; *(composed)* calme; **p. to attack/etc** *(ready)* prêt à attaquer/etc.

poison ['pɔɪz(ə)n] *n* poison *m; (of snake)* venin *m;* **p. gas** gaz *m* toxique; – *vt* empoisonner; **to p. s.o.'s mind** corrompre qn. ◆**poisoning** *n* empoisonnement *m.* ◆**poisonous** *a (fumes, substance)* toxique; *(snake)* venimeux; *(plant)* vénéneux.

pok/e [pəʊk] *vt (push)* pousser *(avec un bâton etc); (touch)* toucher; *(fire)* tisonner; **to p. sth into** *(put, thrust)* fourrer *or* enfoncer qch dans; **to p. one's finger at** pointer son doigt vers; **to p. one's nose into** fourrer le nez dans; **to p. a hole in** faire un trou dans; **to p. one's head out of the window** passer la tête par la fenêtre; **to p. out s.o.'s eye** crever un œil à qn; – *vi* pousser; **to p. about** *or* **around in** fouiner dans; – *n (jab)* (petit) coup *m; (shove)* poussée *f,* coup *m.* ◆**—er** *n* **1** *(for fire)* tisonnier *m.* **2** *Cards* poker *m.*

poky ['pəʊkɪ] *a (-ier, -iest) (small)* exigu et misérable, rikiki; *(slow) Am* lent.

Poland ['pəʊlənd] *n* Pologne *f.* ◆**Pole** *n* Polonais, -aise *mf.*

polarize ['pəʊləraɪz] *vt* polariser.

pole [pəʊl] *n* **1** *(rod)* perche *f; (fixed)* poteau *m; (for flag)* mât *m.* **2** *Geog* pôle *m;*

North/South P. pôle Nord/Sud. ◆**polar** *a* polaire; **p. bear** ours *m* blanc.

polemic [pə'lemɪk] *n* polémique *f.* ◆**polemical** *a* polémique.

police [pə'liːs] *n* police *f; more or extra* **p.** des renforts *mpl* de police; – *a (inquiry etc)* de la police; *(state, dog)* policier; **p. cadet** agent *m* de police stagiaire; **p. car** voiture *f* de police; **p. force** police *f;* – *vt (city etc)* maintenir l'ordre *or* la paix dans; *(frontier)* contrôler. ◆**policeman** *n (pl* **-men)** agent *m* de police. ◆**policewoman** *n (pl* **-women)** femme-agent *f.*

policy ['pɒlɪsɪ] *n* **1** *Pol Econ etc* politique *f; (individual course of action)* règle *f,* façon *f* d'agir; *pl (ways of governing)* *Pol* politique *f;* **matter of p.** question *f* de principe. **2** *(insurance)* **p.** police *f* (d'assurance); **p. holder** assuré, -ée *mf.*

polio(myelitis) ['pəʊlɪəʊ(maɪə'laɪtɪs)] *n* polio(myélite) *f;* **p. victim** polio *mf.*

polish ['pɒlɪʃ] *vt (floor, table, shoes etc)* cirer; *(metal)* astiquer; *(rough surface)* polir; *(manners) Fig* raffiner; *(style) Fig* polir; **to p. up** *(one's French etc)* travailler; **to p. off** *(food, work etc) Fam* liquider, finir (en vitesse); – *n (for shoes)* cirage *m; (for floor, furniture)* cire *f; (shine)* vernis *m; Fig* raffinement *m; (nail)* **p.** vernis *m* (à ongles); **to give sth a p.** faire briller qch.

Polish ['pəʊlɪʃ] *a* polonais; – *n (language)* polonais *m.*

polite [pə'laɪt] *a* (**-er, -est**) poli (**to, with** avec); **in p. society** dans la bonne société. ◆**—ly** *adv* poliment. ◆**—ness** *n* politesse *f.*

political [pə'lɪtɪk(ə)l] *a* politique. ◆**politician** *n* homme *m or* femme *f* politique. ◆**politicize** *vt* politiser. ◆**'politics** *n* politique *f.*

polka ['pɒlkə, *Am* 'pəʊlkə] *n (dance)* polka *f;* **p. dot** pois *m.*

poll [pəʊl] *n (voting)* scrutin *m,* élection *f; (vote)* vote *m; (turnout)* participation *f* électorale; *(list)* liste *f* électorale; **to go to the polls** aller aux urnes; **(opinion) p.** sondage *m* (d'opinion); **50% of the p.** 50% des votants; – *vt (votes)* obtenir; *(people)* sonder l'opinion de. ◆**—ing** *n (election)* élections *fpl;* **p. booth** isoloir *m;* **p. station** bureau *m* de vote.

pollen ['pɒlən] *n* pollen *m.*

pollute [pə'luːt] *vt* polluer. ◆**pollutant** *n* polluant *m.* ◆**pollution** *n* pollution *f.*

polo ['pəʊləʊ] *n Sp* polo *m;* **p. neck** *(sweater, neckline)* col *m* roulé.

polyester [pɒlɪ'estər] *n* polyester *m.*

Polynesia [pɒlɪ'niːʒə] n Polynésie f.
polytechnic [pɒlɪ'teknɪk] n institut m universitaire de technologie.
polythene ['pɒlɪθiːn] n polyéthylène m; **p. bag** sac m en plastique.
pomegranate ['pɒmɪɡrænɪt] n (fruit) grenade f.
pomp [pɒmp] n pompe f. ◆**pom'posity** n emphase f, solennité f. ◆**pompous** a pompeux.
pompon ['pɒmpɒn] n (ornament) pompon m.
pond [pɒnd] n étang m; (stagnant) mare f; (artificial) bassin m.
ponder ['pɒndər] vt to p. (over) réfléchir à; – vi réfléchir.
ponderous ['pɒndərəs] a (heavy, slow) pesant.
pong [pɒŋ] n Sl mauvaise odeur f; – vi (stink) Sl schlinguer.
pontificate [pɒn'tɪfɪkeɪt] vi (speak) Pej pontifier (**about** sur).
pony ['pəʊnɪ] n poney m. ◆**ponytail** n (hair) queue f de cheval.
poodle ['puːd(ə)l] n caniche m.
poof [pʊf] n (homosexual) Pej Sl pédé m.
pooh! [puː] int bah!; (bad smell) ça pue!
pooh-pooh ['puː'puː] vt (scorn) dédaigner; (dismiss) se moquer de.
pool [puːl] **1** n (puddle) flaque f; (of blood) mare f; (pond) étang m; (for swimming) piscine f. **2** n (of experience, talent) réservoir m; (of advisers etc) équipe f; (of typists) Com pool m; (kitty) cagnotte f; (football) **pools** prognostics mpl (sur les matchs de football); – vt (share) mettre en commun; (combine) unir. **3** n Sp billard m américain.
pooped [puːpt] a (exhausted) Am Fam vanné, crevé.
poor [pʊər] a (-er, -est) (not rich, deserving pity) pauvre; (bad) mauvais; (inferior) médiocre; (meagre) maigre; (weak) faible; **p. thing!** le or la pauvre!; – n **the p.** les pauvres mpl. ◆**-ly** adv (badly) mal; (clothed, furnished) pauvrement. **2** a (ill) malade.
pop¹ [pɒp] **1** int pan! – n (noise) bruit m sec; **to go p.** faire pan; (of champagne bottle) faire pop; – vt (-pp-) (balloon etc) crever; (bottle top, button) faire sauter; – vi (burst) crever; (come off) sauter; (of ears) se déboucher. **2** vt (put) Fam mettre; – vi Fam **to p. in** (go in) entrer (en passant); **to p. off** (leave) partir; **to p. out** sortir (un instant); **to p. over** or **round** faire un saut (to chez); **to p. up** (of person) surgir, réapparaître; (of question etc) surgir.

◆**p.-'eyed** a aux yeux exorbités. ◆**p.-up book** n livre m en relief.
pop² [pɒp] **1** n (music) pop m; – a (concert, singer etc) pop inv. **2** n (father) Am Fam papa m. **3** n (soda) **p.** (drink) Am soda m.
popcorn ['pɒpkɔːn] n pop-corn m.
pope [pəʊp] n pape m; **p.'s nose** (of chicken) croupion m.
poplar ['pɒplər] n (tree, wood) peuplier m.
poppy ['pɒpɪ] n (cultivated) pavot m; (red, wild) coquelicot m.
poppycock ['pɒpɪkɒk] n Fam fadaises fpl.
popsicle® ['pɒpsɪk(ə)l] n (ice lolly) Am esquimau m.
popular ['pɒpjʊlər] a (person, song, vote, science etc) populaire; (fashionable) à la mode; **to be p. with** plaire beaucoup à. ◆**popu'larity** n popularité f (**with** auprès de). ◆**popularize** vt populariser; (science, knowledge) vulgariser. ◆**popularly** adv communément.
populat/e ['pɒpjʊleɪt] vt peupler. ◆**-ed** a peuplé (**with** de). ◆**popu'lation** n population f. ◆**populous** a (crowded) populeux.
porcelain ['pɔːsəlɪn] n porcelaine f.
porch [pɔːtʃ] n porche m; (veranda) Am véranda f.
porcupine ['pɔːkjʊpaɪn] n (animal) porc-épic m.
pore [pɔːr] **1** n (of skin) pore m. **2** vi **to p. over** (book, question etc) etudier de près. ◆**porous** a poreux.
pork [pɔːk] n (meat) porc m; **p. butcher** charcutier, -ière mf.
pornography [pɔː'nɒɡrəfɪ] n (Fam porn) pornographie f. ◆**porno'graphic** a pornographique, porno (f inv).
porpoise ['pɔːpəs] n (sea animal) marsouin m.
porridge ['pɒrɪdʒ] n porridge m; **p. oats** flocons mpl d'avoine.
port [pɔːt] **1** n (harbour) port m; **p. of call** escale f; – a (authorities, installations etc) portuaire. **2** n **p. (side)** (left) Nau Av bâbord m; – a de bâbord. **3** n (wine) porto m.
portable ['pɔːtəb(ə)l] a portatif, portable.
portal ['pɔːt(ə)l] n portail m.
porter ['pɔːtər] n (for luggage) porteur m; (doorman) portier m; (caretaker) concierge m, (of public building) gardien, -ienne mf.
portfolio [pɔːt'fəʊlɪəʊ] n (pl -os) Com Pol portefeuille m.
porthole ['pɔːthəʊl] n Nau Av hublot m.
portico ['pɔːtɪkəʊ] n (pl -oes or -os) Archit portique m; (of house) porche m.
portion ['pɔːʃ(ə)n] n (share, helping) portion

f; (*of train, book etc*) partie *f*; − *vt* **to p. out** répartir.

portly ['pɔːtlɪ] *a* (**-ier, -iest**) corpulent.

portrait ['pɔːtrɪt, 'pɔːtreɪt] *n* portrait *m*; **p. painter** portraitiste *mf*.

portray [pɔː'treɪ] *vt* (*describe*) représenter. ◆**portrayal** *n* portrait *m*, représentation *f*.

Portugal ['pɔːtjʊg(ə)l] *n* Portugal. ◆**Portu-'guese** *a & n inv* portugais, -aise (*mf*); − *n* (*language*) portugais *m*.

pose [pəʊz] **1** *n* (*in art or photography*) & *Fig* pose *f*; − *vi* (*of model etc*) poser (**for** pour); **to p. as a lawyer**/*etc* se faire passer pour un avocat/*etc*. **2** *vt* (*question*) poser. ◆**poser** *n* **1** (*question*) *Fam* colle *f*. **2** = **poseur**. ◆**poseur** [-'zɜːr] *n Pej* poseur, -euse *mf*.

posh [pɒʃ] *a Pej Fam* (*smart*) chic *inv*; (*snobbish*) snob (*f inv*).

position [pə'zɪʃ(ə)n] *n* (*place, posture, opinion etc*) position *f*; (*of building, town*) emplacement *m*, position *f*; (*job, circumstances*) situation *f*; (*customer window in bank etc*) guichet *m*; **in a p. to do** en mesure *or* en position de faire; **in a good p. to do** bien placé pour faire; **in p.** en place, en position; − *vt* (*camera, machine etc*) mettre en position; (*put*) placer.

positive ['pɒzɪtɪv] *a* positif; (*order*) catégorique; (*progress, change*) réel; (*tone*) assuré; (*sure*) sûr, certain (**of** de, **that** que); **a p. genius** *Fam* un vrai génie. ◆**−ly** *adv* (*for certain*) & *El* positivement; (*undeniably*) indéniablement; (*completely*) complètement; (*categorically*) catégoriquement.

possess [pə'zes] *vt* posséder. ◆**possession** *n* possession *f*; **in p. of** en possession de; **to take p. of** prendre possession de. ◆**possessive** *a* (*adjective, person etc*) possessif; − *n Gram* possessif *m*. ◆**possessor** *n* possesseur *m*.

possible ['pɒsəb(ə)l] *a* possible (**to do** à faire); **it is p.** (**for us**) **to do it** il (nous) est possible de le faire; **it is p. that** il est possible que (+ *sub*); **as far as p.** dans la mesure du possible; **if p.** si possible; **as much** *or* **as many as p.** autant que possible; − *n* (*person, object*) *Fam* choix *m* possible. ◆**possi'bility** *n* possibilité; **some p. of** quelques chances *fpl* de; **there's some p. that** il est (tout juste) possible que (+ *sub*); **she has possibilities** elle promet; **it's a distinct p.** c'est bien possible. ◆**possibly** *adv* **1** (*with can, could etc*) **if you p. can** si cela t'est possible; **to do all one p. can** faire tout son possible (**to do** pour faire); **he**

cannot p. stay il ne peut absolument pas rester. **2** (*perhaps*) peut-être.

post[1] [pəʊst] *n* (*postal system*) poste *f*; (*letters*) courrier *m*; **by p.** par la poste; **to catch/miss the p.** avoir/rater la levée; − *a* (*bag, code etc*) postal; **p. office** (*bureau m de*) poste *f*; **P. Office** (*administration*) (service *m* des) postes *fpl*; − *vt* (*put in postbox*) poster, mettre à la poste; (*send*) envoyer; **to keep s.o. posted** *Fig* tenir qn au courant. ◆**postage** *n* tarif *m* (postal), tarifs *mpl* (postaux) (**to** pour); **p. stamp** timbre-poste *m*. ◆**postal** *a* (*district etc*) postal; (*inquiries*) par la poste; (*clerk*) des postes; (*vote*) par correspondance. ◆**postbox** *n* boîte *f* à *or* aux lettres. ◆**postcard** *n* carte *f* postale. ◆**postcode** *n* code *m* postal. ◆**post-'free** *adv*, ◆**post'paid** *adv* franco.

post[2] [pəʊst] *n* (*job, place*) & *Mil* poste *m*; − *vt* (*sentry, guard*) poster; (*employee*) affecter (**to** à). ◆**−ing** *n* (*appointment*) affectation *f*.

post[3] [pəʊst] *n* (*pole*) poteau *m*; (*of bed, door*) montant *m*; **finishing** *or* **winning p.** *Sp* poteau *m* d'arrivée; − *vt* **to p. (up)** (*notice etc*) afficher.

post- [pəʊst] *pref* post-; **p.-1800** après 1800.

postdate [pəʊst'deɪt] *vt* postdater.

poster ['pəʊstər] *n* affiche *f*; (*for decoration*) poster *m*.

posterior [pɒ'stɪərɪər] *n* (*buttocks*) *Hum* postérieur *m*.

posterity [pɒ'sterɪtɪ] *n* postérité *f*.

postgraduate [pəʊst'grædʒʊət] *a* (*studies etc*) *Univ* de troisième cycle; − *n* étudiant, -ante *mf* de troisième cycle.

posthumous ['pɒstjʊməs] *a* posthume. ◆**−ly** *adv* à titre posthume.

postman ['pəʊstmən] *n* (*pl* **-men**) facteur *m*. ◆**postmark** *n* cachet *m* de la poste; − *vt* oblitérer. ◆**postmaster** *n* receveur *m* (des postes).

post-mortem [pəʊst'mɔːtəm] *n* **p.-mortem** (**examination**) autopsie *f* (**on** de).

postpone [pəʊ'spəʊn] *vt* remettre (**for** de), renvoyer (à plus tard). ◆**−ment** *n* remise *f*, renvoi *m*.

postscript ['pəʊstskrɪpt] *n* post-scriptum *m inv*.

postulate ['pɒstjʊleɪt] *vt* postuler.

posture ['pɒstʃər] *n* posture *f*; *Fig* attitude *f*; − *vi* (*for effect*) *Pej* poser.

postwar ['pəʊstwɔːr] *a* d'après-guerre.

posy ['pəʊzɪ] *n* petit bouquet *m* (de fleurs).

pot[1] [pɒt] **1** *n* pot *m*; (*for cooking*) marmite *f*; **pots and pans** casseroles *fpl*; **jam p.** pot *m* à

confiture; **to take p. luck** tenter sa chance;
(*with food*) manger à la fortune du pot; **to
go to p.** *Fam* aller à la ruine; **gone to p.**
(*person, plans etc*) *Fam* fichu; − *vt* (**-tt-**)
mettre en pot. **2** *n* (*marijuana*) *Sl*
marie-jeanne *f*; (*hashish*) *Sl* haschisch *m*.
◆**potted** *a* **1** (*plant*) en pot; (*jam, meat*)
en bocaux. **2** (*version etc*) abrégé,
condensé.

potato [pə'teɪtəʊ] *n* (*pl* **-oes**) pomme *f* de
terre; **p. peeler** (*knife*) couteau *m* à
éplucher, éplucheur *m*; **p. crisps,** *Am* **p.
chips** pommes *fpl* chips.

potbelly ['pɒtbelɪ] *n* bedaine *f*. ◆**potbellied** *a* ventru.

potent ['pəʊtənt] *a* puissant; (*drink*) fort;
(*man*) viril. ◆**potency** *n* puissance *f*; (*of
man*) virilité *f*.

potential [pə'tenʃ(ə)l] *a* (*danger, resources*)
potentiel; (*client, sales*) éventuel; (*leader,
hero etc*) en puissance; − *n* potentiel *m*; *Fig*
(*perspectives fpl* d')avenir *m*; **to have p.**
avoir de l'avenir. ◆**potenti'ality** *n* poten-
tialité *f*; *pl Fig* (perspectives *fpl* d')avenir
m. ◆**potentially** *adv* potentiellement.

pothole ['pɒthəʊl] *n* (*in road*) nid *m* de
poules; (*in rock*) gouffre *m*; (*cave*) caverne
f. ◆**potholing** *n* spéléologie *f*.

potion ['pəʊʃ(ə)n] *n* breuvage *m* magique;
Med potion *f*.

potshot ['pɒtʃɒt] *n* **to take a p.** faire un
carton (**at** sur).

potter ['pɒtər] **1** *n* (*person*) potier *m*. **2** *vi* **to
p. (about)** bricoler. ◆**pottery** *n* (*art*)
poterie *f*; (*objects*) poteries *fpl*; **a piece of p.**
une poterie.

potty ['pɒtɪ] *a* **1** (**-ier, -iest**) (*mad*) *Fam*
toqué. **2** *n* pot *m* (de bébé).

pouch [paʊtʃ] *n* petit sac *m*; (*of kangaroo,
under eyes*) poche *f*; (*for tobacco*) blague *f*.

pouf(fe) [puːf] *n* (*seat*) pouf *m*.

poultice ['pəʊltɪs] *n Med* cataplasme *m*.

poultry ['pəʊltrɪ] *n* volaille *f*. ◆**poulterer** *n*
volailler *m*.

pounce [paʊns] *vi* (*leap*) bondir, sauter (**on**
sur); **to p. on** (*idea*) *Fig* sauter sur; − *n*
bond *m*.

pound [paʊnd] **1** *n* (*weight*) livre *f* (= 453,6
grammes); **p. (sterling)** livre *f* (sterling). **2** *n*
(*for cars, dogs*) fourrière *f*. **3** *vt* (*spices, nuts
etc*) piler; (*meat*) attendrir; (*bombard*) *Mil*
pilonner; **to p. (on)** (*thump*) *Fig* taper sur,
marteler; (*of sea*) battre; − *vi* (*of heart*)
battre à tout rompre; (*walk heavily*)
marcher à pas pesants.

pour [pɔːr] *vt* (*liquid*) verser; (*wax*) couler;
to p. money into investir beaucoup d'argent

dans; **to p. away** *or* **off** (*empty*) vider; **to p.
out** verser; (*empty*) vider; (*feelings*)
épancher (**to** devant); − *vi* **to p. (out)** (*of
liquid*) couler *or* sortir à flots; **to p. in** (*of
liquid, sunshine*) entrer à flots; (*of people,
money*) *Fig* affluer; **to p. out** (*of people*)
sortir en masse (**from** de); (*of smoke*)
s'échapper (**from** de); **it's pouring (down)** il
pleut à verse; **pouring rain** pluie *f* torrentielle.

pout [paʊt] *vti* **to p. (one's lips)** faire la
moue; − *n* moue *f*.

poverty ['pɒvətɪ] *n* pauvreté *f*; (**grinding** *or*
extreme) **p.** misère *f*. ◆**p.-stricken** *a*
(*person*) indigent; (*conditions*) misérable.

powder ['paʊdər] *n* poudre *f*; **p. keg** (*place*)
Fig poudrière *f*; **p. puff** houppette *f*; **p.
room** toilettes *fpl* (*pour dames*); − *vt* (*hair,
skin*) poudrer; **to p. one's face** *or* **nose** se
poudrer. ◆**—ed** *a* (*milk, eggs*) en poudre.
◆**powdery** *a* (*snow*) poudreux; (*face*)
couvert de poudre.

power ['paʊər] *n* (*ability, authority*) pouvoir
m; (*strength, nation*) & *Math Tech* puissance *f*; (*energy*) *Phys Tech* énergie *f*;
(*current*) *El* courant *m*; **he's a p.** within the
firm c'est un homme de poids au sein de
l'entreprise; **in p.** *Pol* au pouvoir; **in one's
p.** en son pouvoir; **the p. of speech** la
faculté de la parole; **p. cut** coupure *f* de
courant; **p. station,** *Am* **p. plant** *El* centrale
f (électrique); − *vt* **to be powered by** être
actionné *or* propulsé par; (*gas, oil etc*)
fonctionnant à. ◆**powerful** *a* puissant.
◆**powerfully** *adv* puissamment. ◆**powerless** *a* impuissant (**to do** à faire).

practicable ['præktɪkəb(ə)l] *a* (*project, road
etc*) praticable.

practical ['præktɪk(ə)l] *a* (*knowledge,
person, tool etc*) pratique; **p. joke** farce *f*.
◆**practi'cality** *n* (*of scheme etc*) aspect *m*
pratique; (*of person*) sens *m* pratique;
(*detail*) détail *m* pratique.

practically ['præktɪk(ə)lɪ] *adv* (*almost*)
pratiquement.

practice ['præktɪs] *n* (*exercise, proceeding*)
pratique *f*; (*habit*) habitude *f*; *Sp*
entraînement *m*; (*rehearsal*) répétition *f*;
(*of profession*) exercice *m* (**of** de); (*clients*)
clientèle *f*; **to put into p.** mettre en
pratique; **in p.** (*in reality*) en pratique; **to be
in p.** (*have skill etc*) être en forme; (*of
doctor, lawyer*) exercer; **to be in general p.**
(*of doctor*) faire de la médecine générale; **to
be out of p.** avoir perdu la pratique. ◆**practis/e** *vt* (*put into practice*) pratiquer; (*medicine, law etc*) exercer; (*flute,*

piano etc) s'exercer à; (*language*) (s'exercer à) parler (**on** avec); (*work at*) travailler; (*do*) faire; – *vi Mus Sp* s'exercer; (*of doctor, lawyer*) exercer; – *n Am* = **practice.** ◆—**ed** *a* (*experienced*) chevronné; (*ear, eye*) exercé. ◆—**ing** *a Rel* pratiquant; (*doctor, lawyer*) exerçant.

practitioner [præk'tɪʃ(ə)nər] *n* praticien, -ienne *mf*; **general p.** (médecin *m*) généraliste *m*.

pragmatic [præg'mætɪk] *a* pragmatique.

prairie(s) ['preərɪ(z)] *n*(*pl*) (*in North America*) Prairies *fpl*.

praise [preɪz] *vt* louer (**for sth** de qch); **to p. s.o. for doing** *or* **having done** louer qn d'avoir fait; – *n* louange(s) *f*(*pl*), éloge(s) *m*(*pl*); **in p. of** à la louange de. ◆**praiseworthy** *a* digne d'éloges.

pram [præm] *n* landau *m*, voiture *f* d'enfant.

prance [prɑːns] *vi* **to p. about** (*of dancer etc*) caracoler; (*strut*) se pavaner; (*go about*) *Fam* se balader.

prank [præŋk] *n* (*trick*) farce *f*, tour *m*; (*escape*) frasque *f*.

prattle ['præt(ə)l] *vi* jacasser.

prawn [prɔːn] *n* crevette *f* (rose), bouquet *m*.

pray [preɪ] *vt Lit* prier (**that** que (+ *sub*), **s.o. to do** qn de faire); – *vi Rel* prier; **to p. (to God) for sth** prier Dieu pour qu'il nous accorde qch. ◆**prayer** [preər] *n* prière *f*.

pre- [priː] *pref* **p.-1800** avant 1800.

preach [priːtʃ] *vti* prêcher; (*sermon*) faire; **to p. to s.o.** *Rel & Fig* prêcher qn. ◆—**ing** *n* prédication *f*. ◆—**er** *n* prédicateur *m*.

preamble [priː'æmb(ə)l] *n* préambule *m*.

prearrange [priːə'reɪndʒ] *vt* arranger à l'avance.

precarious [prɪ'keərɪəs] *a* précaire.

precaution [prɪ'kɔːʃ(ə)n] *n* précaution *f* (**of doing** de faire); **as a p.** par précaution.

preced/e [prɪ'siːd] *vti* précéder; **to p. sth by sth** faire précéder qch de qch. ◆—**ing** *a* précédent.

precedence ['presɪdəns] *n* (*in rank*) préséance *f*; (*importance*) priorité *f*; **to take p. over** avoir la préséance sur; avoir la priorité sur. ◆**precedent** *n* précédent *m*.

precept ['priːsept] *n* précept *m*.

precinct ['priːsɪŋkt] *n* (*of convent etc*) enceinte *f*; (*boundary*) limite *f*; (*of town*) *Am Pol* circonscription *f*; (*for shopping*) zone *f* (piétonnière).

precious ['preʃəs] **1** *a* précieux; **her p. little bike** *Iron* son cher petit vélo. **2** *adv* **p. few, p. little** *Fam* très peu (de).

precipice ['presɪpɪs] *n* (*sheer face*) *Geog* à-pic *m inv*; (*chasm*) *Fig* précipice *m*.

precipitate [prɪ'sɪpɪteɪt] *vt* (*hasten, throw*) & *Ch* précipiter; (*trouble, reaction etc*) provoquer, déclencher. ◆**precipi'tation** *n* (*haste*) & *Ch* précipitation *f*; (*rainfall*) précipitations *fpl*.

précis ['preɪsiː, *pl* 'preɪsiːz] *n inv* précis *m*.

precise [prɪ'saɪs] *a* précis; (*person*) minutieux. ◆—**ly** *adv* (*accurately, exactly*) précisément; **at 3 o'clock p.** à 3 heures précises; **p. nothing** absolument rien. ◆**precision** *n* précision *f*.

preclude [prɪ'kluːd] *vt* (*prevent*) empêcher (**from doing** de faire); (*possibility*) exclure.

precocious [prɪ'kəʊʃəs] *a* (*child etc*) précoce. ◆—**ness** *n* précocité *f*.

preconceived [priːkən'siːvd] *a* préconçu. ◆**preconception** *n* préconception *f*.

precondition [priːkən'dɪʃ(ə)n] *n* préalable *m*.

precursor [priː'kɜːsər] *n* précurseur *m*.

predate [priː'deɪt] *vt* (*precede*) précéder; (*cheque etc*) antidater.

predator ['predətər] *n* (*animal*) prédateur *m*. ◆**predatory** *a* (*animal, person*) rapace.

predecessor ['priːdɪsesər] *n* prédécesseur *m*.

predicament [prɪ'dɪkəmənt] *n* situation *f* fâcheuse.

predict [prɪ'dɪkt] *vt* prédire. ◆**predictable** *a* prévisible. ◆**prediction** *n* prédiction *f*.

predispose [priːdɪ'spəʊz] *vt* prédisposer (**to do** à faire). ◆**predispo'sition** *n* prédisposition *f*.

predominant [prɪ'dɒmɪnənt] *a* prédominant. ◆**predominance** *n* prédominance *f*. ◆**predominantly** *adv* (*almost all*) pour la plupart, en majorité. ◆**predominate** *vi* prédominer (**over** sur).

preeminent [priː'emɪnənt] *a* prééminent.

preempt [priː'empt] *vt* (*decision, plans etc*) devancer.

preen [priːn] *vt* (*feathers*) lisser; **she's preening herself** *Fig* elle se bichonne.

prefab ['priːfæb] *n Fam* maison *f* préfabriquée. ◆**pre'fabricate** *vt* préfabriquer.

preface ['prefɪs] *n* préface *f*; – *vt* (*speech etc*) faire précéder (**with** de).

prefect ['priːfekt] *n Sch* élève *mf* chargé(e) de la discipline; (*French official*) préfet *m*.

prefer [prɪ'fɜːr] *vt* (**-rr-**) préférer (**to** à), aimer mieux (**to que**); **to p. to do** préférer faire, aimer mieux faire; **to p. charges** *Jur* porter plainte (**against** contre). ◆'**preferable** *a* préférable (**to** à). ◆'**preferably** *adv* de préférence. ◆'**preference** *n* préférence *f* (**for** pour); **in p. to** de préférence à. ◆**prefe'rential** *a* préférentiel.

prefix ['priːfɪks] n préfixe m.

pregnant ['pregnənt] a (woman) enceinte; (animal) pleine; **five months p.** enceinte de cinq mois. ◆**pregnancy** n (of woman) grossesse f.

prehistoric [priːhɪ'stɒrɪk] a préhistorique.

prejudge [priː'dʒʌdʒ] vt (question) préjuger de; (person) juger d'avance.

prejudic/e ['predʒədɪs] n (bias) préjugé m, parti m pris; (attitude) préjugés mpl; Jur préjudice m; – vt (person) prévenir (against contre); (success, chances etc) porter préjudice à, nuire à. ◆**—ed** a (idea) partial; **she's p.** elle a des préjugés or un préjugé (**against** contre); (on an issue) elle est de parti pris. ◆**preju'dicial** a Jur préjudiciable.

preliminary [prɪ'lɪmɪnərɪ] a (initial) initial; (speech, inquiry, exam) préliminaire; – npl préliminaires mpl.

prelude ['preljuːd] n prélude m; – vt préluder à.

premarital [priː'mærɪt(ə)l] a avant le mariage.

premature ['premətʃuər, Am priːmə'tʃuər] a prématuré. ◆**—ly** adv prématurément; (born) avant terme.

premeditate [priː'medɪteɪt] vt préméditer. ◆**premedi'tation** n préméditation f.

premier ['premɪər, Am prɪ'mɪər] n Premier ministre m.

première ['premɪeər, Am prɪ'mjeər] n Th Cin première f.

premise ['premɪs] n Phil prémisse f.

premises ['premɪsɪz] npl locaux mpl; **on the p.** sur les lieux; **off the p.** hors des lieux.

premium ['priːmɪəm] n Fin prime f; (insurance) **p.** prime f (d'assurance); **to be at a p.** (rare) être (une) denrée rare, faire prime; **p. bond** bon m à lots.

premonition [premə'nɪʃ(ə)n, Am priːmə'nɪʃ(ə)n] n prémonition f, pressentiment m.

prenatal [priː'neɪt(ə)l] a Am prénatal.

preoccupy [priː'ɒkjupaɪ] vt (worry) préoccuper (**with** de). ◆**preoccu'pation** n préoccupation f; **a p. with** (money etc) une obsession de.

prep [prep] a **p. school** école f primaire privée; Am école f secondaire privée; – n (homework) Sch devoirs mpl.

prepaid [priː'peɪd] a (reply) payé.

prepar/e [prɪ'peər] vt préparer (sth for s.o. qch à qn, s.o. for sth qn à qch); **to p. to do se** préparer à faire; – vi **to p. for** (journey, occasion) faire des préparatifs pour; (get dressed up for) se préparer pour; (exam) préparer. ◆**—ed** a (ready) prêt, disposé (**to**

do à faire); **to be p. for** (expect) s'attendre à. ◆**prepa'ration** n préparation f; pl préparatifs mpl (**for** de). ◆**pre'paratory** a préparatoire; **p. school** = prep school.

preposition [prepə'zɪʃ(ə)n] n préposition f.

prepossessing [priːpə'zesɪŋ] a avenant, sympathique.

preposterous [prɪ'pɒstərəs] a absurde.

prerecorded [priːrɪ'kɔːdɪd] a (message etc) enregistré à l'avance; **p. broadcast** Rad TV émission f en différé.

prerequisite [priː'rekwɪzɪt] n (condition f) préalable m.

prerogative [prɪ'rɒgətɪv] n prérogative f.

Presbyterian [prezbɪ'tɪərɪən] a & n Rel presbytérien, -ienne (mf).

preschool ['priːskuːl] a (age etc) préscolaire.

prescrib/e [prɪ'skraɪb] vt prescrire. ◆**—ed** a (textbook) (inscrit) au programme. ◆**prescription** n (order) prescription f; Med ordonnance f; **on p.** sur ordonnance.

presence ['prezəns] n présence f; **in the p. of** en présence de; **p. of mind** présence f d'esprit.

present[1] ['prezənt] **1** a (not absent) présent (**at** à, **in** dans); **those p.** les personnes présentes. **2** a (year, state etc) présent, actuel; (being considered) présent; (job, house etc) actuel; – n (time) présent m; **for the p.** pour le moment; **at p.** à présent. **3** n (gift) cadeau m. ◆**—ly** adv (soon) tout à l'heure; (now) à présent. ◆**present-'day** a actuel.

present[2] [prɪ'zent] vt (show, introduce, compere etc) présenter (**to** à); (concert etc) donner; (proof) fournir; **to p. s.o. with** (gift) offrir à qn; (prize) remettre à qn. ◆**—able** a présentable. ◆**—er** n présentateur, -trice mf. ◆**presen'tation** n présentation f; (of prize) remise f.

preserve [prɪ'zɜːv] **1** vt (keep, maintain) conserver; (fruit etc) Culin mettre en conserve; **to p. from** (protect) préserver de. **2** n (sphere) domaine m. **3** n & npl (fruit etc) Culin confiture f. ◆**preser'vation** n conservation f. ◆**preservative** n (in food) agent m de conservation. ◆**preserver** n **life p.** Am gilet m de sauvetage.

preside [prɪ'zaɪd] vi présider; **to p. over** or **at** (meeting) présider.

president ['prezɪdənt] n président, -ente mf. ◆**presidency** n présidence f. ◆**presi-'dential** a présidentiel.

press[1] [pres] **1** n (newspapers) presse f; (printing firm) imprimerie f; (printing) **p.** presse f; – a (conference etc) de presse. **2** n

(*machine for trousers, gluing etc*) presse *f*;
(*for making wine*) pressoir *m*.

press² [pres] *vt* (*button, doorbell etc*)
appuyer sur; (*tube, lemon, creditor*)
presser; (*hand*) serrer; (*clothes*) repasser;
(*demand, insist on*) insister sur; (*claim*)
renouveler; **to p. s.o. to do** (*urge*) presser qn
de faire; **to p. down** (*button etc*) appuyer
sur; **to p. charges** *Jur* engager des poursuites (**against** contre); – *vi* (*with finger*)
appuyer (**on** sur); (*of weight*) faire pression
(**on** sur); (*of time*) presser; **to p. for sth** faire
des démarches pour obtenir qch; (*insist*)
insister pour obtenir qch; **to p. on**
(*continue*) continuer (**with sth** qch); – *n* **to
give sth a p.** (*trousers etc*) repasser qch.
◆—**ed** *a* (hard). (*busy*) débordé; **to be
hard p.** (*in difficulties*) être en difficultés; **to
be** (hard) **p. for** (*time, money*) être à court
de. ◆—**ing 1** *a* (*urgent*) pressant. **2** *n* (*ironing*) repassage *m*.

pressgang ['presgæŋ] *vt* **to p. s.o.** faire pression sur qn (**into doing** pour qu'il fasse).
◆**press-stud** *n* (bouton-)pression *f*.
◆**press-up** *n Sp* pompe *f*.

pressure ['preʃər] *n* pression *f*; **the p. of
work** le surmenage; **p. cooker**
cocotte-minute *f*; **p. group** groupe *m* de
pression; **under p.** (*duress*) sous la
contrainte; (*hurriedly, forcibly*) sous pression; – *vt* **to p. s.o.** faire pression sur qn
(**into doing** pour qu'il fasse). ◆**pressurize**
vt Av pressuriser; **to p. s.o.** faire pression
sur qn (**into doing** pour qu'il fasse).

prestige [pre'stiːʒ] *n* prestige *m*.
◆**prestigious** [pre'stɪdʒəs, *Am* -'stiːdʒəs]
a prestigieux.

presume [pri'zjuːm] *vt* (*suppose*) présumer
(**that** que); **to p. to do** se permettre de faire.
◆**presumably** *adv* (*you'll come etc*) je
présume que. ◆**presumption** *n* (*supposition, bold attitude*) présomption *f*.
◆**presumptuous** *a* présomptueux.

presuppose [priːsə'pəʊz] *vt* présupposer
(**that** que).

pretence [pri'tens] *n* feinte *f*; (*claim, affectation*) prétention *f*; (*pretext*) prétexte *m*;
to make a p. of sth/of doing feindre qch/de
faire; **on** *or* **under false pretences** sous des
prétextes fallacieux. ◆**pretend** *vt* (*make
believe*) faire semblant (**to do** de faire, **that**
que); (*claim, maintain*) prétendre (**to do**
faire, **that** que); – *vi* faire semblant; **to p. to**
(*throne, title*) prétendre à.

pretension [pri'tenʃ(ə)n] *n* (*claim, vanity*)
prétention *f*. ◆**pre'tentious** *a* prétentieux.

pretext ['priːtekst] *n* prétexte *m*; **on the p.
of/that** sous prétexte de/que.

pretty ['prɪtɪ] **1** *a* (-**ier**, -**iest**) joli. **2** *adv Fam*
(*rather, quite*) assez; **p. well, p. much, p.
nearly** (*almost*) pratiquement, à peu de
chose près.

prevail [pri'veɪl] *vi* (*be prevalent*) prédominer; (*win*) prévaloir (**against** contre); **to
p. (up)on s.o.** (*persuade*) persuader qn (**to
do** de faire). ◆—**ing** *a* (*most common*)
courant; (*most important*) prédominant;
(*situation*) actuel; (*wind*) dominant.

prevalent ['prevələnt] *a* courant, répandu.
◆**prevalence** *n* fréquence *f*; (*predominance*) prédominance *f*.

prevaricate [pri'værɪkeɪt] *vi* user de
faux-fuyants.

prevent [pri'vent] *vt* empêcher (**from doing**
de faire). ◆**preventable** *a* évitable.
◆**prevention** *n* prévention *f*. ◆**preventive** *a* préventif.

preview ['priːvjuː] *n* (*of film, painting*)
avant-première *f*; (*survey*) *Fig* aperçu *m*.

previous ['priːvɪəs] *a* précédent, antérieur;
(*experience*) préalable; **she's had a p. job**
elle a déjà eu un emploi; **p. to** avant. ◆—**ly**
adv avant, précédemment.

prewar ['priːwɔːr] *a* d'avant-guerre.

prey [preɪ] *n* proie *f*; **to be (a) p. to** être en
proie à; **bird of p.** rapace *m*, oiseau *m* de
proie; – *vi* **to p. on** faire sa proie de; **to p.
on s.o.** *or* **s.o.'s mind** *Fig* tracasser qn.

price [praɪs] *n* (*of object, success etc*) prix *m*;
to pay a high p. for sth payer cher qch; *Fig*
payer chèrement qch; **he wouldn't do it at
any p.** il ne le ferait à aucun prix; – *a*
(*control, war, rise etc*) des prix; **p. list** tarif
m; – *vt* mettre un prix à; **it's priced at £5** ça
coûte cinq livres. ◆**priceless** *a* (*jewel,
help etc*) inestimable; (*amusing*) *Fam*
impayable. ◆**pricey** *a* (-**ier**, -**iest**) *Fam*
coûteux.

prick [prɪk] *vt* piquer (**with** avec); (*burst*)
crever; **to p. up one's ears** dresser l'oreille;
– *n* (*act, mark, pain*) piqûre *f*.

prickle ['prɪk(ə)l] *n* (*of animal*) piquant *m*;
(*of plant*) épine *f*, piquant *m*. ◆**prickly** *a*
(-**ier**, -**iest**) (*plant*) épineux; (*animal*)
hérissé; (*subject*) *Fig* épineux; (*person*) *Fig*
irritable.

pride [praɪd] *n* (*satisfaction*) fierté *f*;
(*self-esteem*) amour-propre *m*, orgueil *m*;
(*arrogance*) orgueil *m*; **to take p. in** (*person,
work etc*) être fier de; (*look after*) prendre
soin de; **to take p. in doing** mettre (toute) sa
fierté à faire; **to be s.o.'s p. and joy** être la
fierté de qn; **to have p. of place** avoir la

place d'honneur; – *vt* **to p. oneself on** s'enorgueillir de.
priest [priːst] *n* prêtre *m*. ◆**priesthood** *n* (*function*) sacerdoce *m*. ◆**priestly** *a* sacerdotal.
prig [prig] *n* hypocrite *mf*, pharisien, -ienne *mf*. ◆**priggish** *a* hypocrite, suffisant.
prim [prim] *a* (**primmer, primmest**) **p. (and proper)** (*affected*) guindé; (*seemly*) convenable; (*neat*) impeccable.
primacy ['praiməsi] *n* primauté *f*.
primary ['praiməri] *a* Sch Pol Geol etc primaire; (*main, basic*) principal, premier; **of p. importance** de première importance; – *n* (*election*) Am primaire *f*. ◆**primarily** [Am prai'merili] *adv* essentiellement.
prime [praim] **1** *a* (*reason etc*) principal; (*importance*) primordial; (*quality, number*) premier; (*meat*) de premier choix; (*example, condition*) excellent, parfait; **P. Minister** Premier ministre *m*. **2** *n* **the p. of life** la force de l'âge. **3** *vt* (*gun, pump*) amorcer; (*surface*) apprêter. ◆**primer** *n* **1** (*book*) Sch premier livre *m*. **2** (*paint*) apprêt *m*.
primeval [prai'miːv(ə)l] *a* primitif.
primitive ['primitiv] *a* (*art, society, conditions etc*) primitif. ◆**–ly** *adv* (*to live*) dans des conditions primitives.
primrose ['primrəuz] *n* Bot primevère *f* (jaune).
prince [prins] *n* prince *m*. ◆**princely** *a* princier. ◆**prin'cess** *n* princesse *f*. ◆**princi'pality** *n* principauté *f*.
principal ['prinsip(ə)l] **1** *a* (*main*) principal. **2** *n* (*of school*) directeur, -trice *mf*. ◆**–ly** *adv* principalement.
principle ['prinsip(ə)l] *n* principe *m*; **in p.** en principe; **on p.** par principe.
print [print] *n* (*of finger, foot etc*) empreinte *f*; (*letters*) caractères *mpl*; (*engraving*) estampe *f*, gravure *f*; (*fabric, textile design*) imprimé *m*; Phot épreuve *f*; (*ink*) encre *m*; **in p.** (*book*) disponible (en librairie); **out of p.** (*book*) épuisé; – *vt* Typ imprimer; Phot tirer; (*write*) écrire en caractères d'imprimerie; **to p. 100 copies of** (*book etc*) tirer à 100 exemplaires; **to p. out** (*of computer*) imprimer. ◆**–ed** *a* imprimé; **matter** *or* **papers** imprimés *mpl*; **to have a book p.** publier un livre. ◆**–ing** *n* (*action*) Typ impression *f*; (*technique, art*) Typ imprimerie *f*; Phot tirage *m*; **p. press** Typ presse *f*. ◆**–able** *a* **not p.** (*word etc*) Fig obscène. ◆**–er** *n* (*person*) imprimeur *m*; (*of computer*) imprimante *f*. ◆**print-out** *n* (*of computer*) sortie *f* sur imprimante.
prior ['praiər] *a* précédent, antérieur; (*expe-

rience) préalable; **p. to sth/to doing** avant qch/de faire.
priority [prai'ɒriti] *n* priorité *f* (**over** sur).
priory ['praiəri] *n* Rel prieuré *m*.
prise [praiz] *vt* **to p. open/off** (*box, lid*) ouvrir/enlever (en faisant levier).
prism ['priz(ə)m] *n* prisme *m*.
prison ['priz(ə)n] *n* prison *f*; **in p.** en prison; – *a* (*system, life etc*) pénitentiaire; (*camp*) de prisonniers; **p. officer** gardien, -ienne *mf* de prison. ◆**prisoner** *n* prisonnier, -ière *mf*; **to take s.o. p.** faire qn prisonnier.
prissy ['prisi] *a* (**-ier, -iest**) bégueule.
pristine ['pristiːn] *a* (*condition*) parfait; (*primitive*) primitif.
privacy ['praivəsi, 'privəsi] *n* intimité *f*, solitude *f*; (*quiet place*) coin *m* retiré; (*secrecy*) secret *m*; **to give s.o. some p.** laisser qn seul. ◆**private** **1** *a* privé; (*lesson, car etc*) particulier; (*confidential*) confidentiel; (*personal*) personnel; (*wedding etc*) intime; **a p. citizen** un simple particulier; **p. detective,** *Fam* **p. investigator,** *Fam* **p. eye** détective *m* privé; **p. parts** parties *fpl* génitales; **p. place** coin *m* retiré; **p. tutor** précepteur *m*; **to be a very p. person** aimer la solitude; – *n* **in p.** (*not publicly*) en privé; (*ceremony*) dans l'intimité. **2** *n* Mil (*simple*) soldat *m*. ◆**privately** *adv* en privé; (*inwardly*) intérieurement; (*personally*) à titre personnel; (*to marry, dine etc*) dans l'intimité; **p. owned** appartenant à un particulier.
privet ['privit] *n* (*bush*) troène *m*.
privilege ['priviliʤ] *n* privilège *m*. ◆**privileged** *a* privilégié; **to be p. to do** avoir le privilège de faire.
privy ['privi] *a* **p. to** (*knowledge etc*) au courant de.
prize[1] [praiz] *n* prix *m*; (*in lottery*) lot *m*; **the first p.** (*in lottery*) le gros lot; – *a* (*essay, animal etc*) primé; **a p. fool/**etc *Fig Hum* un parfait idiot/etc. ◆**p.-giving** *n* distribution *f* des prix. ◆**p.-winner** *n* lauréat, -ate *mf*; (*in lottery*) gagnant, -ante *mf*. ◆**p.-winning** *a* (*essay, animal etc*) primé; (*ticket*) gagnant.
priz/e[2] [praiz] *vt* (*value*) priser. ◆**–ed** *a* (*possession etc*) précieux.
prize[3] [praiz] *vt* = **prise**.
pro [prəu] *n* (*professional*) Fam pro *mf*.
pro- [prəu] *pref* pro-.
probable ['prɒbəb(ə)l] *a* probable (**that** que); (*plausible*) vraisemblable. ◆**proba'bility** *n* probabilité *f*; **in all p.** selon toute probabilité. ◆**probably** *adv* probablement, vraisemblablement.
probation [prə'beiʃ(ə)n] *n* **on p.** Jur en

liberté surveillée, sous contrôle judiciaire; (*in job*) à l'essai; **p. officer** responsable *mf* des délinquants mis en liberté surveillée. ◆**probationary** *a* (*period*) d'essai, *Jur* de liberté surveillée.

prob/e [prəʊb] *n* (*device*) sonde *f*; *Journ* enquête *f* (**into** dans); − *vt* (*investigate*) & *Med* sonder; (*examine*) examiner; − *vi* (*investigate*) faire des recherches; *Pej* fouiner; **to p. into** (*origins etc*) sonder. ◆**—ing** *a* (*question etc*) pénétrant.

problem ['prɒbləm] *n* problème *m*; **he's got a drug/a drink p.** c'est un drogué/un alcoolique; **you've got a smoking p.** tu fumes beaucoup trop; **no p.!** *Am Fam* pas de problème!; **to have a p. doing** avoir du mal à faire; − *a* (*child*) difficile, caractériel. ◆**proble'matic** *a* problématique; **it's p. whether** il est douteux que (+ *sub*).

procedure [prə'siːdʒər] *n* procédure *f*.

proceed [prə'siːd] *vi* (*go*) avancer, aller; (*act*) procéder; (*continue*) continuer; (*of debate*) se poursuivre; **to p. to** (*next question etc*) passer à; **to p. with** (*task etc*) continuer; **to p. to do** (*start*) se mettre à faire. ◆**—ing** *n* (*course of action*) procédé *m*; *pl* (*events*) événements *mpl*; (*meeting*) séance *f*; (*discussions*) débats *mpl*; (*minutes*) actes *mpl*; **to take (legal) proceedings** intenter un procès (**against** contre).

proceeds ['prəʊsiːdz] *npl* (*profits*) produit *m*, bénéfices *mpl*.

process ['prəʊses] **1** *n* (*operation, action*) processus *m*; (*method*) procédé *m* (**for** or **of doing** pour faire); **in p.** (*work etc*) en cours; **in the p. of doing** en train de faire. **2** *vt* (*food, data etc*) traiter; (*examine*) examiner; *Phot* développer; **processed cheese** fromage *m* fondu. ◆**—ing** *n* traitement *m*; *Phot* développement *m*; **data** or **information p.** informatique *f*. ◆**processor** *n* (*in computer*) processeur *m*; **food p.** robot *m* (ménager); **word p.** machine *f* de traitement de texte.

procession [prə'sef(ə)n] *n* cortège *m*, défilé *m*.

proclaim [prə'kleɪm] *vt* proclamer (**that** que); **to p. king** proclamer roi. ◆**procla-'mation** *n* proclamation *f*.

procrastinate [prə'kræstɪneɪt] *vi* temporiser, tergiverser.

procreate ['prəʊkrɪeɪt] *vt* procréer. ◆**pro-cre'ation** *n* procréation *f*.

procure [prə'kjʊər] *vt* obtenir; **to p. sth (for oneself)** se procurer qch; **to p. sth for s.o.** procurer qch à qn.

prod [prɒd] *vti* (**-dd-**) **to p. (at)** pousser (*du coude, avec un bâton etc*); **to p. s.o. into doing** *Fig* pousser qn à faire; − *n* (petit) coup *m*; (*shove*) poussée *f*.

prodigal ['prɒdɪɡ(ə)l] *a* (*son etc*) prodigue.

prodigious [prə'dɪdʒəs] *a* prodigieux.

prodigy ['prɒdɪdʒɪ] *n* prodige *m*; **infant p., child p.** enfant *mf* prodige.

produce [prə'djuːs] *vt* (*manufacture, yield etc*) produire; (*bring out, show*) sortir (*pistolet, mouchoir etc*); (*passport, proof*) présenter; (*profit*) rapporter; (*cause*) provoquer, produire; (*publish*) publier; (*play*) *Th TV* mettre en scène; (*film*) *Cin* produire; *Rad* réaliser; (*baby*) donner naissance à; **oil-producing country** pays *m* producteur de pétrole; − *vi* (*of factory etc*) produire; − ['prɒdjuːs] *n* (*agricultural etc*) produits *mpl*. ◆**pro'ducer** *n* (*of goods*) & *Cin* producteur, -trice *mf*; *Th TV* metteur *m* en scène; *Rad* réalisateur, -trice *mf*.

product ['prɒdʌkt] *n* produit *m*.

production [prə'dʌkʃ(ə)n] *n* production *f*; *Th TV* mise *f* en scène; *Rad* réalisation *f*; **to work on the p. line** travailler à la chaîne. ◆**productive** *a* (*land, meeting, efforts*) productif. ◆**produc'tivity** *n* productivité *f*.

profane [prə'feɪn] *a* (*sacrilegious*) sacrilège; (*secular*) profane; − *vt* (*dishonour*) profaner. ◆**profanities** *npl* (*oaths*) blasphèmes *mpl*.

profess [prə'fes] *vt* professer; **to p. to be** prétendre être. ◆**—ed** *a* (*anarchist etc*) déclaré.

profession [prə'feʃ(ə)n] *n* profession *f*; **by p.** de profession. ◆**professional** *a* professionnel; (*man, woman*) qui exerce une profession libérale; (*army*) de métier; (*diplomat*) de carrière; (*piece of work*) de professionnel; − *n* professionnel, -elle *mf*; (*executive, lawyer etc*) membre *m* des professions libérales. ◆**professionalism** *n* professionnalisme *m*. ◆**professionally** *adv* professionnellement; (*to perform, play*) en professionnel; (*to meet s.o.*) dans le cadre de son travail.

professor [prə'fesər] *n* *Univ* professeur *m* (titulaire d'une chaire). ◆**profe'ssorial** *a* professoral.

proffer ['prɒfər] *vt* offrir.

proficient [prə'fiʃ(ə)nt] *a* compétent (**in** en). ◆**proficiency** *n* compétence *f*.

profile ['prəʊfaɪl] *n* (*of person, object*) profil *m*; **in p.** de profil; **to keep a low p.** *Fig* garder un profil bas. ◆**profiled** *a* **to be p. against** se profiler sur.

profit ['prɒfɪt] *n* profit *m*, bénéfice *m*; **to sell**

at a p. vendre à profit; **p. margin** marge *f* bénéficiaire; **p. motive** recherche *f* du profit; — *vi* **to p. by** *or* **from** tirer profit de. ◆**p.-making** *a* à but lucratif. ◆**profita-'bility** *n Com* rentabilité *f*. ◆**profitable** *a Com* rentable; (*worthwhile*) *Fig* rentable, profitable. ◆**profitably** *adv* avec profit. ◆**profi'teer** *n Pej* profiteur, -euse *mf*; — *vi* *Pej* faire des profits malhonnêtes.

profound [prəˈfaʊnd] *a* (*silence, remark etc*) profond. ◆**profoundly** *adv* profondément. ◆**profundity** *n* profondeur *f*.

profuse [prəˈfjuːs] *a* abondant; **p. in** (*praise etc*) prodigue de. ◆**profusely** *adv* (*to flow, grow*) à profusion; (*to bleed*) abondamment; (*to thank*) avec effusion; **to apologize p.** se répandre en excuses. ◆**profusion** *n* profusion *f*; **in p.** à profusion.

progeny [ˈprɒdʒɪnɪ] *n* progéniture *f*.

program[1] [ˈprəʊɡræm] *n* (*of computer*) programme *m*; — *vt* (**-mm-**) (*computer*) programmer. ◆**programming** *n* programmation *f*. ◆**programmer** *n* (**computer**) **p.** programmeur, -euse *mf*.

programme, *Am* **program**[2] [ˈprəʊɡræm] *n* programme *m*; (*broadcast*) émission *f*; — *vt* (*arrange*) programmer.

progress [ˈprəʊɡres] *n* progrès *m*(*pl*); **to make (good) p.** faire des progrès; (*in walking, driving etc*) bien avancer; **in p.** en cours; — [prəˈɡres] *vi* (*advance, improve*) progresser; (*of story, meeting*) se dérouler. ◆**pro'gression** *n* progression *f*. ◆**pro-'gressive** *a* (*gradual*) progressif; (*party*) *Pol* progressiste; (*firm, ideas*) moderniste. ◆**pro'gressively** *adv* progressivement.

prohibit [prəˈhɪbɪt] *vt* interdire (**s.o. from doing** à qn de faire); **we're prohibited from leaving**/*etc* il nous est interdit de partir/*etc*. ◆**prohi'bition** *n* prohibition *f*. ◆**prohibitive** *a* (*price, measure etc*) prohibitif.

project[1] [ˈprɒdʒekt] *n* (*plan*) projet *m* (**for** sth pour qch; **to do, for doing** pour faire); (*undertaking*) entreprise *f*; (*study*) étude *f*; (**housing**) **p.** (*for workers*) *Am* cité *f* (ouvrière). **2** [prəˈdʒekt] *vt* (*throw, show etc*) projeter; — *vi* (*jut out*) faire saillie. ◆**—ed** *a* (*planned*) prévu. ◆**pro'jection** *n* projection *f*; (*projecting object*) saillie *f*. ◆**pro'jectionist** *n Cin* projectionniste *mf*. ◆**pro'jector** *n Cin* projecteur *m*.

proletarian [prəʊləˈteərɪən] *n* prolétaire *mf*; — *a* (*class*) prolétarien; (*outlook*) de prolétaire. ◆**proletariat** *n* prolétariat *m*.

proliferate [prəˈlɪfəreɪt] *vi* proliférer. ◆**prolife'ration** *n* prolifération *f*.

prolific [prəˈlɪfɪk] *a* prolifique.

prologue [ˈprəʊlɒɡ] *n* prologue *m* (**to** de, à).

prolong [prəˈlɒŋ] *vt* prolonger.

promenade [prɒməˈnɑːd] *n* (*place, walk*) promenade *f*; (*gallery*) *Th* promenoir *m*.

prominent [ˈprɒmɪnənt] *a* (*nose*) proéminent; (*chin, tooth*) saillant; (*striking*) *Fig* frappant, remarquable; (*role*) majeur; (*politician*) marquant; (*conspicuous*) (bien) en vue. ◆**prominence** *n* (*importance*) importance *f*. ◆**prominently** *adv* (*displayed, placed*) bien en vue.

promiscuous [prəˈmɪskjʊəs] *a* (*person*) de mœurs faciles; (*behaviour*) immoral. ◆**promi'scuity** *n* liberté *f* de mœurs; immoralité *f*.

promis/e [ˈprɒmɪs] *n* promesse *f*; **to show great p., be full of p.** (*hope*) être très prometteur; — *vt* promettre (**s.o. sth, sth to s.o.** qch à qn; **to do** de faire; **that** que); — *vi* **I p.!** je te le promets!; **p.?** promis? ◆**—ing** *a* (*start etc*) prometteur; (*person*) qui promet; **that looks p.** ça s'annonce bien.

promote [prəˈməʊt] *vt* (*product, research*) promouvoir; (*good health, awareness*) favoriser; **to p. s.o.** promouvoir qn (**to** à); **promoted (to) manager/general/**etc promu directeur/général/*etc*. ◆**promoter** *n Sp* organisateur, -trice *mf*; (*instigator*) promoteur, -trice *mf*. ◆**promotion** *n* (*of person*) avancement *m*, promotion *f*; (*of sales, research etc*) promotion *f*.

prompt [prɒmpt] **1** *a* (*speedy*) rapide; (*punctual*) à l'heure, ponctuel; **p. to act** prompt à agir; — *adv* **at 8 o'clock p.** à 8 heures pile. **2** *vt* (*urge*) inciter, pousser (**to do** à faire); (*cause*) provoquer. **3** *vt* (*person*) *Th* souffler (son rôle) à. ◆**—ing** *n* (*urging*) incitation *f*. ◆**—er** *n Th* souffleur, -euse *mf*. ◆**—ness** *n* rapidité *f*; (*readiness to act*) promptitude *f*.

prone [prəʊn] *a* **1 p. to sth** (*liable*) prédisposé à qch; **to be p. to do** avoir tendance à faire. **2** (*lying flat*) sur le ventre.

prong [prɒŋ] *n* (*of fork*) dent *f*.

pronoun [ˈprəʊnaʊn] *n Gram* pronom *m*. ◆**pro'nominal** *a* pronominal.

pronounce [prəˈnaʊns] *vt* (*articulate, declare*) prononcer; — *vi* (*articulate*) prononcer; (*give judgment*) se prononcer (**on** sur). ◆**pronouncement** *n* déclaration *f*. ◆**pronunci'ation** *n* prononciation *f*.

pronto [ˈprɒntəʊ] *adv* (*at once*) *Fam* illico.

proof [pruːf] **1** *n* (*evidence*) preuve *f*; (*of book, photo*) épreuve *f*; (*of drink*) teneur *f* en alcool. **2** *a* **p. against** (*material*) à l'épreuve de (*feu, acide etc*). ◆**proof-reader** *n Typ* correcteur, -trice *mf*.

prop [prɒp] **1** *n Archit* support *m*, étai *m*; (*for clothes line*) perche *f*; (*person*) *Fig* soutien *m*; − *vt* (**-pp-**) **to p. up** (*ladder etc*) appuyer (**against** contre); (*one's head*) caler; (*wall*) étayer; (*help*) *Fig* soutenir. **2** *n* **prop(s)** *Th* accessoire(s) *m*(*pl*).

propaganda [prɒpə'gændə] *n* propagande *f*. ◆**propagandist** *n* propagandiste *mf*.

propagate ['prɒpəgeɪt] *vt* propager; − *vi* se propager.

propel [prə'pel] *vt* (**-ll-**) (*drive, hurl*) propulser. ◆**propeller** *n Av Nau* hélice *f*.

propensity [prə'pensɪtɪ] *n* propension *f* (**for** sth à qch, **to do** à faire).

proper ['prɒpər] *a* (*suitable, seemly*) convenable; (*correct*) correct; (*right*) bon; (*real, downright*) véritable; (*noun, meaning*) propre; **in the p. way** comme il faut; **the village**/*etc* **p.** le village/*etc* proprement dit. ◆**−ly** *adv* comme il faut, convenablement, correctement; (*completely*) *Fam* vraiment; **very p.** (*quite rightly*) à juste titre.

property ['prɒpətɪ] **1** *n* (*building etc*) propriété *f*; (*possessions*) biens *mpl*, propriété *f*; − *a* (*crisis, market etc*) immobilier; (*owner, tax*) foncier. **2** *n* (*of substance etc*) propriété *f*. ◆**propertied** *a* possédant.

prophecy ['prɒfɪsɪ] *n* prophétie *f*. ◆**prophesy** [-ɪsaɪ] *vti* prophétiser; **to p. that** prédire que.

prophet ['prɒfɪt] *n* prophète *m*. ◆**prophetic** *a* prophétique.

proponent [prə'pəʊnənt] *n* (*of cause etc*) défenseur *m*, partisan, -ane *mf*.

proportion [prə'pɔːʃ(ə)n] *n* (*ratio*) proportion *f*; (*portion*) partie *f*; (*amount*) pourcentage *m*; *pl* (*size*) proportions *fpl*; **in p.** en proportion (**to** de); **out of p.** hors de proportion (**to** avec); − *vt* proportionner (**to** à); **well** *or* **nicely proportioned** bien proportionné. ◆**proportional** *a*, ◆**proportionate** *a* proportionnel (**to** à).

propose [prə'pəʊz] *vt* (*suggest*) proposer (**to** à, **that** que (+ *sub*)); **to p. to do, p. doing** (*intend*) se proposer de faire; − *vi* faire une demande (en mariage) (**to** à). ◆**proposal** *n* proposition *f*; (*of marriage*) demande *f* (en mariage). ◆**propo'sition** *n* proposition *f*; (*matter*) *Fig* affaire *f*.

propound [prə'paʊnd] *vt* proposer.

proprietor [prə'praɪətər] *n* propriétaire *mf*. ◆**proprietary** *a* (*article*) *Com* de marque déposée; **p. name** marque *f* déposée.

propriety [prə'praɪətɪ] *n* (*behaviour*) bienséance *f*; (*of conduct, remark*) justesse *f*.

propulsion [prə'pʌlʃ(ə)n] *n* propulsion *f*.

pros [prəʊz] *npl* **the p. and cons** le pour et le contre.

prosaic [prəʊ'zeɪɪk] *a* prosaïque.

proscribe [prəʊ'skraɪb] *vt* proscrire.

prose [prəʊz] *n* prose *f*; (*translation*) *Sch* thème *m*.

prosecute ['prɒsɪkjuːt] *vt* poursuivre (en justice) (**for stealing**/*etc* pour vol/*etc*). ◆**prose'cution** *n Jur* poursuites *fpl*; **the p.** (*lawyers*) = le ministère public. ◆**prosecutor** *n* (**public**) **p.** *Jur* procureur *m*.

prospect¹ ['prɒspekt] *n* (*idea, outlook*) perspective *f* (**of doing** de faire); (*possibility*) possibilité *f* (**of sth** de qch); (*future*) **prospects** perspectives *fpl* d'avenir; **it has prospects** c'est prometteur; **she has prospects** elle a de l'avenir. ◆**pro'spective** *a* (*possible*) éventuel; (*future*) futur.

prospect² [prə'spekt] *vt* (*land*) prospecter; − *vi* **to p. for** (*gold etc*) chercher. ◆**−ing** *n* prospection *f*. ◆**prospector** *n* prospecteur, -trice *mf*.

prospectus [prə'spektəs] *n* (*publicity leaflet*) prospectus *m*; *Univ* guide *m* (de l'étudiant).

prosper ['prɒspər] *vi* prospérer. ◆**prosperity** *n* prospérité *f*. ◆**prosperous** *a* (*thriving*) prospère; (*wealthy*) riche, prospère.

prostate ['prɒsteɪt] *n* **p.** (**gland**) *Anat* prostate *f*.

prostitute ['prɒstɪtjuːt] *n* (*woman*) prostituée *f*; − *vt* prostituer. ◆**prosti'tution** *n* prostitution *f*.

prostrate ['prɒstreɪt] *a* (*prone*) sur le ventre; (*worshipper*) prosterné; (*submissive*) soumis; (*exhausted*) prostré; − [prɒ'streɪt] *vt* **to p. oneself** se prosterner (**before** devant).

protagonist [prəʊ'tægənɪst] *n* protagoniste *mf*.

protect [prə'tekt] *vt* protéger (**from** de, **against** contre); (*interests*) sauvegarder. ◆**protection** *n* protection *f*. ◆**protective** *a* (*tone etc*) & *Econ* protecteur; (*screen, clothes etc*) de protection. ◆**protector** *n* protecteur, -trice *mf*.

protein ['prəʊtiːn] *n* protéine *f*.

protest ['prəʊtest] *n* protestation *f* (**against** contre); **under p.** contre son gré; − [prə'test] *vt* protester (**that** que); (*one's innocence*) protester de; − *vi* protester (**against** contre); (*in the streets etc*) *Pol* contester. ◆**−er** *n Pol* contestataire *mf*.

Protestant ['prɒtɪstənt] *a* & *n* protestant,

-ante (*mf*). **◆Protestantism** *n* protestantisme *m*.

protocol ['prəʊtəkɒl] *n* protocole *m*.

prototype ['prəʊtəʊtaɪp] *n* prototype *m*.

protract [prə'trækt] *vt* prolonger.

protractor [prə'træktər] *n* (*instrument*) *Geom* rapporteur *m*.

protrud/e [prə'truːd] *vi* dépasser; (*of balcony, cliff etc*) faire saillie; (*of tooth*) avancer. **◆—ing** *a* saillant; (*of tooth*) qui avance.

proud [praʊd] *a* (**-er**, **-est**) (*honoured, pleased*) fier (**of** de, **to do** de faire); (*arrogant*) orgueilleux. **◆—ly** *adv* fièrement; orgueilleusement.

prove [pruːv] *vt* prouver (**that** que); **to p. oneself** faire ses preuves; – *vi* **to p. (to be) difficult**/*etc* s'avérer difficile/*etc*. **◆proven** *a* (*method etc*) éprouvé.

proverb ['prɒvɜːb] *n* proverbe *m*. **◆pro-'verbial** *a* proverbial.

provid/e [prə'vaɪd] *vt* (*supply*) fournir (**s.o. with sth** qch à qn); (*give*) donner, offrir (**to** à); **to p. s.o. with** (*equip*) pourvoir qn de; **to p. that** *Jur* stipuler que; – *vi* **to p. for s.o.** (*s.o.'s needs*) pourvoir aux besoins de qn; (*s.o.'s future*) assurer l'avenir de qn; **to p. for sth** (*make allowance for*) prévoir qch. **◆—ed** *conj* **p. (that)** pourvu que (+ *sub*). **◆—ing** *conj* **p. (that)** pourvu que (+ *sub*).

providence ['prɒvɪdəns] *n* providence *f*.

provident ['prɒvɪdənt] *a* (*society*) de prévoyance; (*person*) prévoyant.

province ['prɒvɪns] *n* province *f*; *Fig* domaine *m*, compétence *f*; **the provinces** la province; **in the provinces** en province. **◆pro'vincial** *a & n* provincial, -ale (*mf*).

provision [prə'vɪʒ(ə)n] *n* (*supply*) provision *f*; (*clause*) disposition *f*; **the p. of** (*supplying*) la fourniture de; **to make p. for** = **to provide for**.

provisional [prə'vɪʒən(ə)l] *a* provisoire. **◆—ly** *adv* provisoirement.

proviso [prə'vaɪzəʊ] *n* (*pl* -os) stipulation *f*.

provok/e [prə'vəʊk] *vt* (*rouse, challenge*) provoquer (**to do, into doing** à faire); (*annoy*) agacer; (*cause*) provoquer (*accident, reaction etc*). **◆—ing** *a* (*annoying*) agaçant. **◆provo'cation** *n* provocation *f*. **◆provocative** *a* (*person, remark etc*) provocant; (*thought-provoking*) qui donne à penser.

prow [praʊ] *n* *Nau* proue *f*.

prowess ['praʊes] *n* (*bravery*) courage *m*; (*skill*) talent *m*.

prowl [praʊl] *vi* **to p. (around)** rôder; – *n* **to be on the p.** rôder. **◆—er** *n* rôdeur, -euse *mf*.

proximity [prɒk'sɪmɪtɪ] *n* proximité *f*.

proxy ['prɒksɪ] *n* **by p.** par procuration.

prude [pruːd] *n* prude *f*. **◆prudery** *n* pruderie *f*. **◆prudish** *a* prude.

prudent ['pruːdənt] *a* prudent. **◆prudence** *n* prudence *f*. **◆prudently** *adv* prudemment.

prun/e [pruːn] **1** *n* (*dried plum*) pruneau *m*. **2** *vt* (*cut*) *Bot* tailler, élaguer; (*speech etc*) *Fig* élaguer. **◆—ing** *n* *Bot* taille *f*.

pry [praɪ] **1** *vi* être indiscret; **to p. into** (*meddle*) se mêler de; (*s.o.'s reasons etc*) chercher à découvrir. **2** *vt* **to p. open** *Am* forcer (en faisant levier). **◆—ing** *a* indiscret.

PS [piː'es] *abbr* (*postscript*) P.-S.

psalm [sɑːm] *n* psaume *m*.

pseud [sjuːd] *n* *Fam* bêcheur, -euse *mf*.

pseudo- ['sjuːdəʊ] *pref* pseudo-.

pseudonym ['sjuːdənɪm] *n* pseudonyme *m*.

psychiatry [saɪ'kaɪətrɪ] *n* psychiatrie *f*. **◆psychi'atric** *a* psychiatrique. **◆psychiatrist** *n* psychiatre *mf*.

psychic ['saɪkɪk] *a* (méta)psychique; **I'm not p.** *Fam* je ne suis pas devin; – *n* (*person*) médium *m*.

psycho- ['saɪkəʊ] *pref* psycho-. **◆psychoa'nalysis** *n* psychanalyse *f*. **◆psycho-'analyst** *n* psychanalyste *mf*.

psychology [saɪ'kɒlədʒɪ] *n* psychologie *f*. **◆psycho'logical** *a* psychologique. **◆psychologist** *n* psychologue *mf*.

psychopath ['saɪkəʊpæθ] *n* psychopathe *mf*.

psychosis, *pl* **-oses** [saɪ'kəʊsɪs, -əʊsiːz] *n* psychose *f*.

PTO [piːtiː'əʊ] *abbr* (*please turn over*) TSVP.

pub [pʌb] *n* pub *m*.

puberty ['pjuːbətɪ] *n* puberté *f*.

public ['pʌblɪk] *a* public; (*baths, library*) municipal; **to make a p. protest** protester publiquement; **in the p. eye** très en vue; **p. building** édifice *m* public; **p. company** société *f* par actions; **p. corporation** société *f* nationalisée; **p. figure** personnalité *f* connue; **p. house** pub *m*; **p. life** les affaires *fpl* publiques; **to be p.-spirited** avoir le sens civique; – *n* public *m*; **in p.** en public; **a member of the p.** un simple particulier; **the sporting**/*etc* **p.** les amateurs *mpl* de sport/*etc*. **◆—ly** *adv* publiquement; **p. owned** (*nationalized*) *Com* nationalisé.

publican ['pʌblɪk(ə)n] *n* patron, -onne *mf* d'un pub.

publication [pʌblɪˈkeɪʃ(ə)n] n (*publishing, book etc*) publication f.

publicity [pʌbˈlɪsɪtɪ] n publicité f. ◆'**publicize** vt rendre public; (*advertise*) Com faire de la publicité pour.

publish ['pʌblɪʃ] vt publier; (*book*) éditer, publier; **to p. s.o.** éditer qn; '**published weekly**' 'paraît toutes les semaines'. ◆**-ing** n publication f (**of** de); (*profession*) édition f. ◆**-er** n éditeur, -trice mf.

puck [pʌk] n (*in ice hockey*) palet m.

pucker ['pʌkər] vt & to p. (**up**) (*brow, lips*) plisser; – vi **to p.** (**up**) plisser.

pudding ['pʊdɪŋ] n dessert m, gâteau m; (**plum**) **p.** pudding m; **rice p.** riz m au lait.

puddle ['pʌd(ə)l] n flaque f (d'eau).

pudgy ['pʌdʒɪ] a (**-ier, -iest**) = podgy.

puerile ['pjʊəraɪl] a puérile.

puff [pʌf] n (*of smoke*) bouffée f; (*of wind, air*) bouffée f, souffle m; **to have run out of p.** Fam être à bout de souffle; – vi (*blow, pant*) souffler; **to p. at** (*cigar*) tirer sur; – vt (*smoke etc*) souffler (**into** dans); **to p. out** (*cheeks etc*) gonfler. ◆**puffy** a (**-ier, -iest**) (*swollen*) gonflé.

puke [pjuːk] vi (*vomit*) Sl dégueuler.

pukka ['pʌkə] a Fam authentique.

pull [pʊl] n (*attraction*) attraction f; (*force*) force f; (*influence*) influence f; **to give sth a p.** tirer qch; – vt (*draw, tug*) tirer; (*tooth*) arracher; (*stopper*) enlever; (*trigger*) appuyer sur; (*muscle*) se claquer; **to p. apart** or **to bits** or **to pieces** mettre en pièces; **to p. a face** faire la moue; **to (get s.o. to) p. strings** Fig se faire pistonner; – vi (*tug*) tirer; (*go, move*) aller; **to p. at** or **on** tirer (sur). ■ **to p. along** vt (*drag, tug*) traîner (**to** jusqu'à); **to p. away** vt (*move*) éloigner; (*snatch*) arracher (**from** à); – vi Aut démarrer; **to p. away from** s'éloigner de; **to p. back** vi (*withdraw*) Mil se retirer; – vt retirer; (*curtains*) ouvrir; **to p. down** vt (*lower*) baisser; (*knock down*) faire tomber; (*demolish*) démolir, abattre; **to p. in** vt (*rope*) ramener; (*drag into room etc*) faire entrer; (*stomach*) rentrer; (*crowd*) attirer; – vi (*arrive*) Aut arriver; **to p. in** se garer; **to p. into the station** (*of train*) entrer en gare; **to p. off** vt enlever; (*plan, deal*) Fig mener à bien; **to p. it off** Fig réussir son coup; **to p. on** vt (*boots etc*) mettre; **to p. out** vt (*extract*) arracher (**from** à); (*remove*) enlever (**from** de); (*from pocket, bag etc*) tirer, sortir (**from** de); (*troops*) retirer; – vi (*depart*) Aut démarrer; (*move out*) Aut déboîter; **to p. out from** (*negotiations etc*) se retirer de; **to p. over** vt (*drag*) traîner (**to** jusqu'à); (*knock down*) faire tomber; – vi Aut se ranger (sur le côté); **to p. round** vi Med se remettre; **to p. through** vi s'en tirer; **to p. oneself together** vt se ressaisir; **to p. up** vt (*socks, bucket etc*) remonter; (*haul up*) hisser; (*uproot*) arracher; (*stop*) arrêter; – vi Aut s'arrêter. ◆**p.-up** n Sp traction f.

pulley ['pʊlɪ] n poulie f.

pullout ['pʊlaʊt] n (*in newspaper etc*) supplément m détachable.

pullover ['pʊləʊvər] n pull(-over) m.

pulp [pʌlp] n (*of fruit etc*) pulpe f; (*for paper*) pâte f à papier; **in a p.** Fig en bouillie.

pulpit ['pʊlpɪt] n Rel chaire f.

pulsate [pʌlˈseɪt] vi produire des pulsations, battre. ◆**pulsation** n (*heartbeat etc*) pulsation f.

pulse [pʌls] n Med pouls m.

pulverize ['pʌlvəraɪz] vt (*grind, defeat*) pulvériser.

pumice ['pʌmɪs] n **p.** (**stone**) pierre f ponce.

pump [pʌmp] **1** n pompe f; (**petrol**) **p. attendant** pompiste mf; – vt pomper; (*blood*) Med faire circuler; (*money*) Fig injecter (**into** dans); **to p. s.o.** (**for information**) tirer les vers du nez à qn; **to p. in** refouler (*à l'aide d'une pompe*); **to p. out** pomper (**of** de); **to p. air into, p. up** (*tyre*) gonfler; – vi pomper; (*of heart*) battre. **2** n (*for dancing*) escarpin m; (*plimsoll*) tennis f.

pumpkin ['pʌmpkɪn] n potiron m.

pun [pʌn] n calembour m.

punch¹ [pʌntʃ] n (*blow*) coup m de poing; (*force*) Fig punch m; **to pack a p.** Boxing & Fig avoir du punch; **p. line** (*of joke*) astuce f finale; – vt (*person*) donner un coup de poing à; (*ball etc*) frapper d'un coup de poing. ◆**p.-up** n Fam bagarre f.

punch² [pʌntʃ] **1** n (*for tickets*) poinçonneuse f; (*for paper*) perforeuse f; **p. card** carte f perforée; – vt (*ticket*) poinçonner; (*with date*) composter; (*card, paper*) perforer; **to p. a hole in** faire un trou dans; **2** n (*drink*) punch m.

punctilious [pʌŋkˈtɪlɪəs] a pointilleux.

punctual ['pʌŋktʃʊəl] a (*arriving on time*) à l'heure; (*regularly on time*) ponctuel, exact. ◆**punctu'ality** n ponctualité f, exactitude f. ◆**punctually** adv à l'heure; (*habitually*) ponctuellement.

punctuate ['pʌŋktʃʊeɪt] vt ponctuer (**with** de). ◆**punctu'ation** n ponctuation f; **p. mark** signe m de ponctuation.

puncture ['pʌŋktʃər] n (*in tyre*) crevaison f;

to have a p. crever; − *vt* (*burst*) crever; (*pierce*) piquer; − *vi* (*of tyre*) crever.

pundit ['pʌndɪt] *n* expert *m*, ponte *m*.

pungent ['pʌndʒənt] *a* âcre, piquant. ◆**pungency** *n* âcreté *f*.

punish ['pʌnɪʃ] *vt* punir (**for sth** de qch, **for doing** *or* **having done** pour avoir fait); (*treat roughly*) Fig malmener. ◆**—ing** *a* (*tiring*) éreintant. ◆**—able** *a* punissable (**by** de). ◆**—ment** *n* punition *f*, châtiment *m*; **capital p.** peine *f* capitale; **to take a (lot of) p.** (*damage*) Fig en encaisser.

punitive ['pjuːnɪtɪv] *a* (*measure etc*) punitif.

punk [pʌŋk] **1** *n* (*music*) punk *m*; (*fan*) punk *mf*; − *a* punk *inv*. **2** *n* (*hoodlum*) Am Fam voyou *m*.

punt [pʌnt] **1** *n* barque *f* (à fond plat). **2** *vi* (*bet*) Fam parier. ◆**—ing** *n* canotage *m*. ◆**—er** *n* **1** (*gambler*) parieur, -euse *mf*. **2** (*customer*) Sl client, -ente *mf*.

puny ['pjuːnɪ] *a* (*-ier, -iest*) (*sickly*) chétif; (*small*) petit; (*effort*) faible.

pup [pʌp] *n* (*dog*) chiot *m*.

pupil ['pjuːpɪl] *n* **1** (*person*) élève *mf*. **2** (*of eye*) pupille *f*.

puppet ['pʌpɪt] *n* marionnette *f*; − *a* (*government, leader*) fantoche *m*.

puppy ['pʌpɪ] *n* (*dog*) chiot *m*.

purchas/e ['pɜːtʃɪs] *n* (*bought article, buying*) achat *m*; − *vt* acheter (**from s.o.** à qn, **for s.o.** à *or* pour qn). ◆**—er** *n* acheteur, -euse *mf*.

pure [pjʊər] *a* (*-er, -est*) pur. ◆**purely** *adv* purement. ◆**purifi'cation** *n* purification *f*. ◆**purify** *vt* purifier. ◆**purity** *n* pureté *f*.

purée ['pjʊəreɪ] *n* purée *f*.

purgatory ['pɜːgətrɪ] *n* purgatoire *m*.

purge [pɜːdʒ] *n* Pol Med purge *f*; − *vt* (*rid*) purger (**of** de); (*group*) Pol épurer.

purist ['pjʊərɪst] *n* puriste *mf*.

puritan ['pjʊərɪt(ə)n] *n & a* puritain, -aine (*mf*). ◆**puri'tanical** *a* puritain.

purl [pɜːl] *n* (*knitting stitch*) maille *f* à l'envers.

purple ['pɜːp(ə)l] *a & n* violet (*m*); **to go p.** (*with anger*) devenir pourpre; (*with shame*) devenir cramoisi.

purport [pɜːˈpɔːt] *vt* **to p. to be** (*claim*) prétendre être.

purpose ['pɜːpəs] *n* **1** (*aim*) but *m*; **for this p.** dans ce but; **on p.** exprès; **to no p.** inutilement; **to serve no p.** ne servir à rien; **for (the) purposes of** pour les besoins de. **2** (*determination, willpower*) résolution *f*; **to have a sense of p.** être résolu. ◆**p.-'built** *a* construit spécialement. ◆**purposeful** *a* (*determined*) résolu. ◆**purposefully** *adv*

dans un but précis; (*resolutely*) résolument. ◆**purposely** *adv* exprès.

purr [pɜːr] *vi* ronronner; − *n* ronron(nement) *m*.

purse [pɜːs] **1** *n* (*for coins*) porte-monnaie *m inv*; (*handbag*) Am sac *m* à main. **2** *vt* **to p. one's lips** pincer les lèvres.

purser ['pɜːsər] *n* Nau commissaire *m* du bord.

pursue [pəˈsjuː] *vt* (*chase, hound, seek, continue*) poursuivre; (*fame, pleasure*) rechercher; (*course of action*) suivre. ◆**pursuer** *n* poursuivant, -ante *mf*. ◆**pursuit** *n* (*of person, glory etc*) poursuite *f*; (*activity, pastime*) occupation *f*; **to go in p. of** se mettre à la poursuite de.

purveyor [pəˈveɪər] *n* Com fournisseur *m*.

pus [pʌs] *n* pus *m*.

push [pʊʃ] *n* (*shove*) poussée *f*; (*energy*) Fig dynamisme *m*; (*help*) coup *m* de pouce; (*campaign*) campagne *f*; **to give s.o./sth a p.** pousser qn/qch; **to give s.o. the p.** (*dismiss*) Fam flanquer qn à la porte; − *vt* pousser (**to, as far as** jusqu'à); (*product*) Com pousser la vente de; (*drugs*) Fam revendre; **to p. (down)** (*button*) appuyer sur; (*lever*) abaisser; **to p. (forward)** (*views etc*) mettre en avant; **to p. sth into/between** (*thrust*) enfoncer *or* fourrer qch dans/entre; **to p. s.o. into doing** (*urge*) pousser qn à faire; **to p. sth off the table** faire tomber qch de la table (en le poussant); **to p. s.o. off a cliff** pousser qn du haut d'une falaise; **to be pushing forty**/*etc* Fam friser la quarantaine/*etc*; − *vi* pousser; **to p. for** faire pression pour obtenir. ■ **to p. about** *or* **around** *vt* (*bully*) Fam marcher sur les pieds à; **to p. aside** *vt* (*person, objection etc*) écarter; **to p. away** *or* **back** *vt* repousser; (*curtains*) ouvrir; **to p. in** *vi* (*in queue*) Fam resquiller; **to p. off** *vi* (*leave*) Fam filer; **p. off!** Fam fiche le camp!; **to p. on** *vi* continuer (**with** sth qch); (*in journey*) poursuivre sa route; **to p. over** *vt* (*topple*) renverser; **to p. through** *vt* (*law*) faire adopter; − *vti* **to p. (one's way) through** se frayer un chemin (**a crowd**/*etc* à travers une foule/*etc*); **to p. up** *vt* (*lever etc*) relever; (*increase*) Fam augmenter, relever. ◆**pushed** *a* **to be p.** (**for time**) (*rushed, busy*) être très bousculé. ◆**pusher** *n* (*of drugs*) revendeur, -euse *mf* (de drogue).

pushbike ['pʊʃbaɪk] *n* Fam vélo *m*. ◆**push-button** *n* poussoir *m*; − *a* (*radio etc*) à poussoir. ◆**pushchair** *n* poussette *f* (pliante). ◆**pushover** *n* **to be a p.** (*easy*)

Fam être facile, être du gâteau. ◆**push-up** *n Sp Am* pompe *f*.

pushy ['pʊʃɪ] *a* (**-ier, -iest**) *Pej* entreprenant; (*in job*) arriviste.

puss(y) ['pʊs(ɪ)] *n* (*cat*) minet *m*, minou *m*.

put [pʊt] *vt* (*pt & pp* **put**, *pres p* **putting**) mettre; (*savings, money*) placer (**into** dans); (*pressure, mark*) faire (**on** sur); (*problem, argument*) présenter (**to** à); (*question*) poser (**to** à); (*say*) dire; (*estimate*) évaluer (**at** à); **to p. it bluntly** pour parler franc. ■ **to p. across** *vt* (*idea etc*) communiquer (**to** à); **to p. away** *vt* (*in its place*) ranger (*livre, voiture etc*); **to p. s.o. away** (*criminal*) mettre qn en prison; (*insane person*) enfermer qn; **to p. back** *vt* remettre; (*receiver*) *Tel* raccrocher; (*progress, clock*) retarder; **to p. by** *vt* (*money*) mettre de côté; **to p. down** *vt* (*on floor, table etc*) poser; (*passenger*) déposer; (*deposit*) *Fin* verser; (*revolt*) réprimer; (*write down*) inscrire; (*assign*) attribuer (**to** à); (*kill*) faire piquer (*chien etc*); **to p. forward** *vt* (*argument, clock, meeting*) avancer; (*opinion*) exprimer; (*candidate*) proposer (**for** à); **to p. in** *vt* (*insert*) introduire; (*add*) ajouter; (*present*) présenter; (*request, application*) faire; (*enrol*) inscrire (**for** à); (*spend*) passer (*une heure etc*) (**doing** à faire); − *vi* **to p. in for** (*job etc*) faire une demande de; **to p. in at** (*of ship etc*) faire escale à; **to p. off** *vt* (*postpone*) renvoyer (à plus tard); (*passenger*) déposer; (*gas, radio*) fermer; (*dismay*) déconcerter; **to p. s.o. off** (*dissuade*) dissuader qn (**doing** de faire); **to p. s.o. off** (*disgust*) dégoûter qn (**sth** de qch); **to p. s.o. off doing** (*disgust*) ôter à qn l'envie de faire; **to p. on** *vt* (*clothes, shoe etc*) mettre; (*weight, accent*) prendre; (*film*) jouer; (*gas, radio*) mettre, allumer; (*record, cassette*) passer; (*clock*) avancer; **to p. s.o. on** (*tease*) *Am* faire marcher qn; **she p. me on to you** elle m'a donné votre adresse; **p. me on to him!** *Tel* passez-le-moi!; **to p. out** *vt* (*take

outside) sortir; (*arm, leg*) étendre; (*hand*) tendre; (*tongue*) tirer; (*gas, light*) éteindre, fermer; (*inconvenience*) déranger; (*upset*) déconcerter; (*issue*) publier; (*dislocate*) démettre; **to p. through** *vt Tel* passer (**to** à); **to p. together** *vt* (*assemble*) assembler; (*compose*) composer; (*prepare*) préparer; (*collection*) faire; **to p. up** *vi* (*lodge*) descendre (**at a hotel** dans un hôtel); **to p. up with** (*tolerate*) supporter; − *vt* (*lift*) lever; (*window*) remonter; (*tent, statue, barrier, ladder*) dresser; (*flag*) hisser; (*building*) construire; (*umbrella*) ouvrir; (*picture, poster*) mettre; (*price, sales, numbers*) augmenter; (*resistance, plea, suggestion*) offrir; (*candidate*) proposer (**for** à); (*guest*) loger; **p.-up job** *Fam* coup *m* monté. ◆**p.-you-up** *n* canapé-lit *m*, convertible *m*.

putrid ['pjuːtrɪd] *a* putride. ◆**putrify** *vi* se putréfier.

putt [pʌt] *n Golf* putt *m*. ◆**putting** *n Golf* putting *m*; **p. green** green *m*.

putter ['pʌtər] *vi* **to p. around** *Am* bricoler.

putty ['pʌtɪ] *n* (*pour fixer une vitre*) mastic *m*.

puzzl/e ['pʌz(ə)l] *n* mystère *m*, énigme *f*; (*game*) casse-tête *m inv*; (*jigsaw*) puzzle *m*; − *vt* laisser perplexe; **to p. out why/when/** *etc* essayer de comprendre pourquoi/quand/*etc*; − *vi* **to p. over** (*problem, event*) se creuser la tête sur. ◆**−ed** *a* perplexe. ◆**−ing** *a* mystérieux, surprenant.

PVC [piːviːˈsiː] *n* (*plastic*) PVC *m*.

pygmy ['pɪgmɪ] *n* pygmée *m*.

pyjama [pɪˈdʒɑːmə] *a* (*jacket etc*) de pyjama. ◆**pyjamas** *npl* pyjama *m*; **a pair of p.** un pyjama.

pylon ['paɪlən] *n* pylône *m*.

pyramid ['pɪrəmɪd] *n* pyramide *f*.

Pyrenees [pɪrəˈniːz] *npl* **the P.** les Pyrénées *fpl*.

python ['paɪθən] *n* (*snake*) python *m*.

Q

Q, q [kjuː] *n* Q, q *m*.

quack [kwæk] **1** *n* (*of duck*) coin-coin *m inv*. **2** *a & n* **q.** (**doctor**) charlatan *m*.

quad(rangle) ['kwɒd(ræŋg(ə)l)] *n* (*of college*) cour *f*.

quadruped ['kwɒdruped] *n* quadrupède *m*.

quadruple [kwɒˈdruːp(ə)l] *vt* quadrupler.

quadruplets [kwɒˈdruːplɪts] (*Fam* **quads** [kwɒdz]) *npl* quadruplés, -ées *mfpl*.

quaff [kwɒf] *vt* (*drink*) avaler.

quagmire ['kwægmaɪər] *n* bourbier *m*.

quail [kweɪl] *n* (*bird*) caille *f*.

quaint [kweɪnt] *a* (**-er, -est**) (*picturesque*) pittoresque; (*antiquated*) vieillot; (*odd*) bizarre. ◆**—ness** *n* pittoresque *m*; caractère *m* vieillot; bizarrerie *f*.

quake [kweɪk] *vi* trembler (**with** de); *– n Fam* tremblement *m* de terre.

Quaker ['kweɪkər] *n* quaker, -eresse *mf*.

qualification [kwɒlɪfɪ'keɪʃ(ə)n] *n* **1** (*competence*) compétence *f* (**for** pour, **to do** pour faire); (*diploma*) diplôme *m*; *pl* (*requirements*) conditions *fpl* requises. **2** (*reservation*) réserve *f*.

qualify ['kwɒlɪfaɪ] **1** *vt* (*make competent*) & *Sp* qualifier (**for sth** pour qch, **to do** pour faire); *– vi* obtenir son diplôme (**as a doctor**/*etc* de médecin/*etc*); *Sp* se qualifier (**for** pour); **to q. for** (*post*) remplir les conditions requises pour. **2** *vt* (*modify*) faire des réserves à; (*opinion*) nuancer; *Gram* qualifier. ◆**qualified** *a* (*able*) qualifié (**to do** pour faire); (*doctor etc*) diplômé; (*success*) limité; (*opinion*) nuancé; (*support*) conditionnel. ◆**qualifying** *a* (*exam*) d'entrée; **q. round** *Sp* (épreuve *f*) éliminatoire *f*.

quality ['kwɒlɪtɪ] *n* qualité *f*; *– a* (*product*) de qualité. ◆**qualitative** *a* qualitatif.

qualms [kwɑːmz] *npl* (*scruples*) scruples *mpl*; (*anxieties*) inquiétudes *fpl*.

quandary ['kwɒndrɪ] *n* **in a q.** bien embarrassé; **to be in a q. about what to do** ne pas savoir quoi faire.

quantity ['kwɒntɪtɪ] *n* quantité *f*; **in q.** (*to purchase etc*) en grande(s) quantité(s). ◆**quantify** *vt* quantifier. ◆**quantitative** *a* quantitatif.

quarantine ['kwɒrəntiːn] *n Med* quarantaine *f*; *– vt* mettre en quarantaine.

quarrel ['kwɒrəl] *n* querelle *f*, dispute *f*; **to pick a q.** chercher querelle (**with** à qn); *– vi* (**-ll-**, *Am* **-l-**) se disputer, se quereller (**with** avec); **to q. with sth** trouver à redire à qch. ◆**quarrelling** *n*, *Am* ◆**quarreling** *n* (*quarrels*) querelles *fpl*. ◆**quarrelsome** *a* querelleur.

quarry ['kwɒrɪ] *n* **1** (*excavation*) carrière *f*. **2** (*prey*) proie *f*.

quart [kwɔːt] *n* litre *m* (*mesure approximative*) (*Br = 1,14 litres, Am = 0,95 litre*).

quarter ['kwɔːtər] *n* **1** quart *m*; (*of year*) trimestre *m*; (*money*) *Am Can* quart *m* de dollar; (*of moon, fruit*) quartier *m*; **to divide into quarters** diviser en quatre; **q. (of a) pound** quart *m* de livre; **a q. past nine**, *Am* **a q. after nine** neuf heures et *or* un quart; **a q. to nine** neuf heures moins le quart; **from all quarters** de toutes parts. **2** *n* (*district*)

quartier *m*; *pl* (*circles*) milieux *mpl*; (*living*) **quarters** logement(s) *m*(*pl*); *Mil* quartier(s) *m*(*pl*); *– vt* (*troops*) *Mil* cantonner. ◆**—ly** *a* trimestriel; *– adv* trimestriellement; *– n* publication *f* trimestrielle.

quarterfinal [kwɔːtə'faɪn(ə)l] *n Sp* quart *m* de finale.

quartet(te) [kwɔː'tet] *n Mus* quatuor *m*; (**jazz**) **q.** quartette *m*.

quartz [kwɔːts] *n* quartz *m*; *– a* (*clock etc*) à quartz.

quash [kwɒʃ] *vt* (*rebellion etc*) réprimer; (*verdict*) *Jur* casser.

quaver ['kweɪvər] **1** *vi* chevroter; *– n* chevrotement *m*. **2** *n Mus* croche *f*.

quay [kiː] *n Nau* quai *m*. ◆**quayside** *n* **on the q.** sur les quais.

queas/y ['kwiːzɪ] *a* (**-ier, -iest**) **to feel** *or* **be q.** avoir mal au cœur. ◆**—iness** *n* mal *m* au cœur.

Quebec [kwɪ'bek] *n* le Québec.

queen [kwiːn] *n* reine *f*; *Chess Cards* dame *f*; **the q. mother** la reine mère.

queer ['kwɪər] *a* (**-er, -est**) (*odd*) bizarre; (*dubious*) louche; (*ill*) *Fam* patraque; *– n* (*homosexual*) *Pej Fam* pédé *m*.

quell [kwel] *vt* (*revolt etc*) réprimer.

quench [kwentʃ] *vt* (*fire*) éteindre; **to q. one's thirst** se désaltérer.

querulous ['kweruləs] *a* (*complaining*) grognon.

query ['kwɪərɪ] *n* question *f*; (*doubt*) doute *m*; *– vt* mettre en question.

quest [kwest] *n* quête *f* (**for** de); **in q. of** en quête de.

question ['kwestʃ(ə)n] *n* question *f*; **there's some q. of it** il en est question; **there's no q. of it, it's out of the q.** il n'en est pas question, c'est hors de question; **without q.** incontestable(ment); **in q.** en question, dont il s'agit; **q. mark** point *m* d'interrogation; **q. master** *TV Rad* animateur, -trice *mf*; *– vt* interroger (**about** sur); (*doubt*) mettre en question; **to q. whether** douter que (*+ sub*). ◆**—ing** *a* (*look etc*) interrogateur; *– n* interrogation *f*. ◆**—able** *a* douteux. ◆**questio'nnaire** *n* questionnaire *m*.

queue [kjuː] *n* (*of people*) queue *f*; (*of cars*) file *f*; **to stand in a q., form a q.** faire la queue; *– vi* **to q. (up)** faire la queue.

quibbl/e ['kwɪb(ə)l] *vi* ergoter, discuter (**over** sur). ◆**—ing** *n* ergotage *m*.

quiche [kiːʃ] *n* (*tart*) quiche *f*.

quick [kwɪk] **1** *a* (**-er, -est**) rapide; **q. to react** prompt à réagir; **to be q.** faire vite; **to have a q. shave/meal/***etc* se raser/manger/*etc* en vitesse; **to be a q. worker** travailler vite; – *adv* (**-er, -est**) vite; **as q. as a flash** en un clin d'œil. **2** *n* **to cut to the q.** blesser au vif. ◆**q.-'tempered** *a* irascible. ◆**q.-'witted** *a* à l'esprit vif. ◆**quicken** *vt* accélérer; – *vi* s'accélérer. ◆**quickie** *n* (*drink*) *Fam* pot *m* (*pris en vitesse*). ◆**quickly** *adv* vite. ◆**quicksands** *npl* sables *mpl* mouvants.

quid [kwɪd] *n inv Fam* livre *f* (sterling).

quiet [kwaɪət] *a* (**-er, -est**) (*silent, still, peaceful*) tranquille, calme; (*machine, vehicle, temperament*) silencieux; (*gentle*) doux; (*voice*) bas, doux; (*sound*) léger, doux; (*private*) intime; (*colour*) discret; **to be** *or* **keep q.** (*shut up*) se taire; (*make no noise*) ne pas faire de bruit; **q.!** silence!; **to keep q. about sth, keep sth q.** ne pas parler de qch; **on the q.** (*secretly*) *Fam* en cachette; – *vt* = **quieten.** ◆**quieten** *vti* **to q. (down)** (se) calmer. ◆**quietly** *adv* tranquillement; (*gently, not loudly*) doucement; (*silently*) silencieusement; (*secretly*) en cachette; (*discreetly*) discrètement. ◆**quietness** *n* tranquillité *f*.

quill [kwɪl] *n* (*pen*) plume *f* (d'oie).

quilt [kwɪlt] *n* édredon *m*; (**continental**) **q.** couette *f*; – *vt* (*stitch*) piquer; (*pad*) matelasser.

quintessence [kwɪn'tesəns] *n* quintessence *f*.

quintet(te) [kwɪn'tet] *n* quintette *m*.

quintuplets [kwɪn'tjuːplɪts] (*Fam* **quins** [kwɪnz]) *npl* quintuplés, -ées *mfpl*.

quip [kwɪp] *n* (*remark*) boutade *f*; – *vi* (**-pp-**) faire des boutades; – *vt* dire sur le ton de la boutade.

quirk [kwɜːk] *n* bizarrerie *f*; (*of fate*) caprice *m*.

quit [kwɪt] *vt* (*pt & pp* **quit** *or* **quitted,** *pres p* **quitting**) (*leave*) quitter; **to q. doing** arrêter de faire; – *vi* (*give up*) abandonner; (*resign*) démissionner.

quite [kwaɪt] *adv* (*entirely*) tout à fait; (*really*) vraiment; (*rather*) assez; **q. another matter** une tout autre affaire *or* question; **q. a genius** un véritable génie; **q. good** (*not bad*) pas mal (du tout); **q. (so)!** exactement!; **I q. understand** je comprends très bien; **q. a lot** pas mal (**of** de); **q. a (long) time ago** il y a pas mal de temps.

quits [kwɪts] *a* quitte (**with** envers); **to call it q.** en rester là.

quiver [ˈkwɪvər] *vi* frémir (**with** de); (*of voice*) trembler, frémir; (*of flame*) vaciller, trembler.

quiz [kwɪz] *n* (*pl* **quizzes**) (*riddle*) devinette *f*; (*test*) test *m*; **q. (programme)** *TV Rad* jeu(-concours) *m*; – *vt* (**-zz-**) questionner. ◆**quizmaster** *n* *TV Rad* animateur, -trice *mf*.

quizzical [ˈkwɪzɪk(ə)l] *a* (*mocking*) narquois; (*perplexed*) perplexe.

quorum [ˈkwɔːrəm] *n* quorum *m*.

quota [ˈkwəʊtə] *n* quota *m*.

quote [kwəʊt] *vt* citer; (*reference number*) *Com* rappeler; (*price*) indiquer; (*price on Stock Exchange*) coter; – *vi* **to q. from** (*author, book*) citer; – *n Fam* = **quotation; in quotes** entre guillemets. ◆**quo'tation** *n* citation *f*; (*estimate*) *Com* devis *m*; (*on Stock Exchange*) cote *f*; **q. marks** guillemets *mpl*; **in q. marks** entre guillemets.

quotient [ˈkwəʊʃ(ə)nt] *n* quotient *m*.

R

R, r [ɑːr] *n* R, r *m*.

rabbi [ˈræbaɪ] *n* rabbin *m*; **chief r.** grand rabbin.

rabbit [ˈræbɪt] *n* lapin *m*.

rabble [ˈræb(ə)l] *n* (*crowd*) cohue *f*; **the r.** *Pej* la populace.

rabies [ˈreɪbiːz] *n Med* rage *f*. ◆**rabid** [ˈræbɪd] *a* (*dog*) enragé; (*person*) *Fig* fanatique.

raccoon [rəˈkuːn] *n* (*animal*) raton *m* laveur.

rac/e¹ [reɪs] *n Sp & Fig* course *f*; – *vt*

(*horse*) faire courir; (*engine*) emballer; **to r.** (**against** *or* **with**) **s.o.** faire une course avec qn; – *vi* (*run*) courir; (*of engine*) s'emballer; (*of pulse*) battre à tout rompre. ◆**—ing** *n* courses *fpl*; – *a* (*car, bicycle etc*) de course; **r. driver** coureur *m* automobile. ◆**racecourse** *n* champ *m* de courses. ◆**racegoer** *n* turfiste *mf*. ◆**racehorse** *n* cheval *m* de course. ◆**racetrack** *n* piste *f*; (*for horses*) *Am* champ *m* de courses.

race² [reɪs] *n* (*group*) race *f*; – *a* (*prejudice etc*) racial; **r. relations** rapports *mpl* entre

les races. ◆**racial** *a* racial. ◆**racialism** *n*
racisme *m*. ◆**racism** *n* racisme *m*.
◆**racist** *a* & *n* raciste (*mf*).

rack [ræk] **1** *n* (*shelf*) étagère *f*; (*for bottles
etc*) casier *m*; (*for drying dishes*) égouttoir
m; (**luggage**) **r.** (*on bicycle*) porte-bagages *m
inv*; (*on bus, train etc*) filet *m* à bagages;
(**roof**) **r.** (*of car*) galerie *f*. **2** *vt* to **r.** one's
brains se creuser la cervelle. **3** *n* to go to **r.**
and ruin (*of person*) aller à la ruine; (*of
building*) tomber en ruine; (*of health*) se
délabrer.

racket ['rækɪt] *n* **1** (*for tennis etc*) raquette *f*.
2 (*din*) vacarme *m*. **3** (*crime*) racket *m*;
(*scheme*) combine *f*; **the drug(s) r.** le trafic
m de (la) drogue. ◆**racke'teer** *n* racket-
teur *m*. ◆**racke'teering** *n* racket *m*.

racoon [rə'kuːn] *n* (*animal*) raton *m* laveur.

racy ['reɪsɪ] *a* (**-ier, -iest**) piquant; (*suggestive*) osé.

radar ['reɪdɑːr] *n* radar *m*; – *a* (*control, trap
etc*) radar *inv*; **r. operator** radariste *mf*.

radiant ['reɪdɪənt] *a* (*person*) rayonnant
(**with** de), radieux. ◆**radiance** *n* éclat *m*,
rayonnement *m*. ◆**radiantly** *adv* (*to shine*)
avec éclat; **r. happy** rayonnant de joie.

radiate ['reɪdɪeɪt] *vt* (*emit*) dégager; (*joy*) *Fig*
rayonner de; – *vi* (*of heat, lines*) rayonner
(**from** de). ◆**radia'tion** *n* (*of heat etc*)
rayonnement *m* (**of** de); (*radioactivity*)
Phys radiation *f*; (*rays*) irradiation *f*; **r.
sickness** mal *m* des rayons.

radiator ['reɪdɪeɪtər] *n* radiateur *m*.

radical ['rædɪk(ə)l] *a* radical; – *n* (*person*)
Pol radical, -ale *mf*.

radio ['reɪdɪəʊ] *n* (*pl* **-os**) radio *f*; **on the r.** à
la radio; **car r.** autoradio *m*; **r. set** poste *m*
(de) radio; **r. operator** radio *m*; **r. wave**
onde *f* hertzienne; – *vt* (*message*) transmettre (par radio) (**to** à); **to r. s.o.** appeler
qn par radio. ◆**r.-con'trolled** *a* radio-
guidé. ◆**radio'active** *a* radioactif. ◆**ra-
dioac'tivity** *n* radioactivité *f*.

radiographer [reɪdɪ'ɒgrəfər] *n* (*technician*)
radiologue *mf*. ◆**radiography** *n* radiographie *f*. ◆**radiologist** *n* (*doctor*) radiologue *mf*. ◆**radiology** *n* radiologie *f*.

radish ['rædɪʃ] *n* radis *m*.

radius, *pl* **-dii** ['reɪdɪəs, -dɪaɪ] *n* (*of circle*)
rayon *m*; **within a r. of** dans un rayon de.

RAF [ɑɪret'ef] *n abbr* (*Royal Air Force*) armée
f de l'air (britannique).

raffia ['ræfɪə] *n* raphia *m*.

raffle ['ræf(ə)l] *n* tombola *f*.

raft [rɑːft] *n* (*boat*) radeau *m*.

rafter ['rɑːftər] *n* (*beam*) chevron *m*.

rag [ræg] *n* **1** (*old garment*) loque *f*, haillon

m; (*for dusting etc*) chiffon *m*; **in rags**
(*clothes*) en loques; (*person*) en haillons;
r.-and-bone man chiffonnier *m*. **2** (*newspaper*) torchon *m*. **3** (*procession*) *Univ*
carnaval *m* (*au profit d'œuvres de charité*).
◆**ragged** ['rægɪd] *a* (*clothes*) en loques;
(*person*) en haillons; (*edge*) irrégulier.
◆**ragman** *n* (*pl* **-men**) chiffonnier *m*.

ragamuffin ['rægəmʌfɪn] *n* va-nu-pieds *m
inv*.

rag/e [reɪdʒ] *n* rage *f*; (*of sea*) furie *f*; **to fly
into a r.** se mettre en rage; **to be all the r.** (*of
fashion etc*) faire fureur; – *vi* (*be angry*)
rager; (*of storm, battle*) faire rage. ◆**—ing**
a (*storm, fever*) violent; **a r. fire** un grand
incendie; **in a r. temper** furieux.

raid [reɪd] *n Mil* raid *m*; (*by police*) descente
f; (*by thieves*) hold-up *m*; **air r.** raid *m*
aérien, attaque *f* aérienne; – *vt* faire un
raid *or* une descente *or* un hold-up dans;
Av attaquer; (*larder, fridge etc*) *Fam* dévaliser. ◆**raider** *n* (*criminal*) malfaiteur *m*;
pl Mil commando *m*.

rail [reɪl] **1** *n* (*for train*) rail *m*; **by r.** (*to
travel*) par le train; (*to send*) par chemin de
fer; **to go off the rails** (*of train*) dérailler; –
a ferroviaire; (*strike*) des cheminots. **2** *n*
(*rod on balcony*) balustrade *f*; (*on stairs, for
spotlight*) rampe *f*; (*for curtain*) tringle *f*;
(*towel*) **r.** porte-serviettes *m inv*. ◆**railing**
n (*of balcony*) balustrade *f*; *pl* (*fence*) grille
f. ◆**railroad** *n Am* = **railway**; **r. track** voie
f ferrée. ◆**railway** *n* (*system*) chemin *m* de
fer; (*track*) voie *f* ferrée; – *a* (*ticket*) de
chemin de fer; (*network*) ferroviaire; **r. line**
(*route*) ligne *f* de chemin de fer; (*track*) voie
f ferrée; **r. station** gare *f*. ◆**railwayman** *n*
(*pl* **-men**) cheminot *m*.

rain [reɪn] *n* pluie *f*; **in the r.** sous la pluie; **I'll
give you a r. check** (*for invitation*) *Am Fam*
j'accepterai volontiers à une date ultérieure; – *vi* pleuvoir; **to r. (down)** (*of blows,
bullets*) pleuvoir; **it's raining** il pleut.
◆**rainbow** *n* arc-en-ciel *m*. ◆**raincoat** *n*
imper(méable) *m*. ◆**raindrop** *n* goutte *f*
de pluie. ◆**rainfall** *n* (*shower*) chute *f* de
pluie; (*amount*) précipitations *fpl*. ◆**rainstorm** *n* trombe *f* d'eau. ◆**rainwater** *n* eau
f de pluie. ◆**rainy** *a* (**-ier, -iest**) pluvieux;
the r. season la saison des pluies.

raise [reɪz] *vt* (*lift*) lever; (*sth heavy*)
(sou)lever; (*child, animal, voice, statue*)
élever; (*crops*) cultiver; (*salary, price*)
augmenter, relever; (*temperature*) faire
monter; (*question, protest*) soulever; (*taxes,
blockade*) lever; **to r. a smile/a laugh** (*in
others*) faire sourire/rire; **to r. s.o.'s hopes**

faire naître les espérances de qn; **to r. money** réunir des fonds; – *n* (*pay rise*) *Am* augmentation *f* (de salaire).

raisin ['reɪz(ə)n] *n* raison *m* sec.

rake [reɪk] *n* râteau *m*; – *vt* (*garden*) ratisser; (*search*) fouiller dans; **to r. (up)** (*leaves*) ramasser (avec un râteau); **to r. in** (*money*) *Fam* ramasser à la pelle; **to r. up** (*the past*) remuer. ◆**r.-off** *n Fam* pot-de-vin *m*, ristourne *f*.

rally ['rælɪ] *vt* (*unite, win over*) rallier (**to** à); (*one's strength*) *Fig* reprendre; – *vi* se rallier (**to** à); (*recover*) se remettre (**from** de); **to r. round** (*help*) venir en aide (**s.o.** à qn); – *n Mil* ralliement *m*; *Pol* rassemblement *m*; *Sp Aut* rallye *m*.

ram [ræm] **1** *n* (*animal*) bélier *m*. **2** *vt* (-**mm**-) (*ship*) heurter; (*vehicle*) emboutir; **to r. sth into** (*thrust*) enfoncer qch dans.

rambl/e ['ræmb(ə)l] **1** *n* (*hike*) randonnée *f*; – *vi* faire une randonnée *or* des randonnées. **2** *vi* **to r. on** (*talk*) *Pej* discourir. ◆—**ing** **1** *a* (*house*) construit sans plan; (*spread out*) vaste; (*rose etc*) grimpant. **2** *a* (*speech*) décousu; – *npl* divagations *fpl*. ◆—**er** *n* promeneur, -euse *mf*.

ramification [ræmɪfɪ'keɪʃ(ə)n] *n* ramification *f*.

ramp [ræmp] *n* (*slope*) rampe *f*; (*in garage*) *Tech* pont *m* (de graissage); *Av* passerelle *f*; **'r.'** *Aut* 'dénivellation'.

rampage ['ræmpeɪdʒ] *n* **to go on the r.** (*of crowd*) se déchaîner; (*loot*) se livrer au pillage.

rampant ['ræmpənt] *a* **to be r.** (*of crime, disease etc*) sévir.

rampart ['ræmpɑːt] *n* rempart *m*.

ramshackle ['ræmʃæk(ə)l] *a* délabré.

ran [ræn] *see* **run**.

ranch [rɑːntʃ] *n Am* ranch *m*; **r. house** maison *f* genre bungalow (sur sous-sol).

rancid ['rænsɪd] *a* rance.

rancour ['ræŋkər] *n* rancœur *f*.

random ['rændəm] *n* **at r.** au hasard; – *a* (*choice*) fait au hasard; (*sample*) prélevé au hasard; (*pattern*) irrégulier.

randy ['rændɪ] *a* (-**ier**, -**iest**) *Fam* sensuel, lascif.

rang [ræŋ] *see* **ring**[2].

range [reɪndʒ] **1** *n* (*of gun, voice etc*) portée *f*; (*of aircraft, ship*) rayon *m* d'action; (*series*) gamme *f*; (*choice*) choix *m*; (*of prices*) éventail *m*; (*of voice*) *Mus* étendue *f*; (*of temperature*) variations *fpl*; (*sphere*) *Fig* champ *m*, étendue *f*; – *vi* (*vary*) varier; (*extend*) s'étendre; (*roam*) errer, rôder. **2** *n* (*of mountains*) chaîne *f*; (*grassland*) *Am*

prairie *f*. **3** *n* (*stove*) *Am* cuisinière *f*. **4** *n* (*shooting or rifle*) **r.** (*at funfair*) stand *m* de tir; (*outdoors*) champ *m* de tir.

ranger ['reɪndʒər] *n* (*forest*) **r.** *Am* garde *m* forestier.

rank [ræŋk] **1** *n* (*position, class*) rang *m*; (*grade*) *Mil* grade *m*, rang *m*; **the r. and file** (*workers etc*) *Pol* la base; **the ranks** (*men in army, numbers*) les rangs *mpl* (of de); **taxi r.** station *f* de taxi; – *vti* **to r. among** compter parmi. **2** *a* (-**er**, -**est**) (*smell*) fétide; (*vegetation*) luxuriant; *Fig* absolu.

rankle ['ræŋk(ə)l] *vi* **it rankles (with me)** je l'ai sur le cœur.

ransack ['rænsæk] *vt* (*search*) fouiller; (*plunder*) saccager.

ransom ['ræns(ə)m] *n* rançon *f*; **to hold to r.** rançonner; – *vt* (*redeem*) racheter.

rant [rænt] *vi* **to r. (and rave)** tempêter (**at** contre).

rap [ræp] *n* petit coup *m* sec; – *vi* (-**pp**-) frapper (**at** à); – *vt* **to r. s.o. over the knuckles** taper sur les doigts de qn.

rapacious [rə'peɪʃəs] *a* (*greedy*) rapace.

rape [reɪp] *vt* violer; – *n* viol *m*. ◆**rapist** *n* violeur *m*.

rapid ['ræpɪd] **1** *a* rapide. **2** *n & npl* (*of river*) rapide(s) *m(pl)*. ◆**ra'pidity** *n* rapidité *f*. ◆**rapidly** *adv* rapidement.

rapport [ræ'pɔːr] *n* (*understanding*) rapport *m*.

rapt [ræpt] *a* (*attention*) profond.

rapture ['ræptʃər] *n* extase *f*; **to go into raptures** s'extasier (**about** sur). ◆**rapturous** *a* (*welcome, applause*) enthousiaste.

rare [reər] *a* (-**er**, -**est**) rare; (*meat*) *Culin* saignant; (*first-rate*) *Fam* fameux; **it's r. for her to do it** il est rare qu'elle le fasse. ◆—**ly** *adv* rarement. ◆—**ness** *n* rareté *f*. ◆**rarity** *n* (*quality, object*) rareté *f*.

rarefied ['reərɪfaɪd] *a* raréfié.

raring ['reərɪŋ] *a* **r. to start**/*etc* impatient de commencer/*etc*.

rascal ['rɑːsk(ə)l] *n* coquin, -ine *mf*. ◆**rascally** *a* (*child etc*) coquin; (*habit, trick etc*) de coquin.

rash [ræʃ] **1** *n Med* éruption *f*. **2** *a* (-**er**, -**est**) irréfléchi. ◆—**ly** *adv* sans réfléchir. ◆—**ness** *n* irréflexion *f*.

rasher ['ræʃər] *n* tranche *f* de lard.

rasp [rɑːsp] *n* (*file*) râpe *f*.

raspberry ['rɑːzbərɪ] *n* (*fruit*) framboise *f*; (*bush*) framboisier *m*.

rasping ['rɑːspɪŋ] *a* (*voice*) âpre.

rat [ræt] **1** *n* rat *m*; **r. poison** mort-aux-rats *f*; **the r. race** *Fig* la course au bifteck, la jungle. **2** *vi* (-**tt**-) **to r. on** (*desert*) lâcher;

(*denounce*) cafarder sur; (*promise etc*) manquer à.

rate [reɪt] **1** *n* (*percentage, level*) taux *m*; (*speed*) vitesse *f*; (*price*) tarif *m*; *pl* (*on housing*) impôts *mpl* locaux; **insurance rates** primes *fpl* d'assurance; **r. of flow** débit *m*; **postage** *or* **postal r.** tarif *m* postal; **at the r. of** à une vitesse de; (*amount*) à raison de; **at this r.** (*slow speed*) à ce train-là; **at any r.** en tout cas; **the success r.** (*chances*) les chances *fpl* de succès; (*candidates*) le pourcentage de reçus. **2** *vt* (*evaluate*) évaluer; (*regard*) considérer (**as** comme); (*deserve*) mériter; **to r. highly** apprécier (beaucoup); **to be highly rated** être très apprécié. ◆**rateable** *a* **r. value** valeur *f* locative nette. ◆**ratepayer** *n* contribuable *mf*.

rather ['rɑːðər] *adv* (*preferably, fairly*) plutôt; **I'd r. stay** j'aimerais mieux *or* je préférerais rester (**than** que); **I'd r. you came** je préférerais que vous veniez; **r. than leave**/*etc* plutôt que de partir/*etc*; **r. more tired**/*etc* un peu plus fatigué/*etc* (**than** que); **it's r. nice** c'est bien.

ratify ['rætɪfaɪ] *vt* ratifier. ◆**ratifiˈcation** *n* ratification *f*.

rating ['reɪtɪŋ] *n* (*classification*) classement *m*; (*wage etc level*) indice *m*; **credit r.** *Fin* réputation *f* de solvabilité; **the ratings** *TV* l'indice *m* d'écoute.

ratio ['reɪʃɪəʊ] *n* (*pl* -**os**) proportion *f*.

ration ['ræʃ(ə)n, *Am* 'reɪʃ(ə)n] *n* ration *f*; *pl* (*food*) vivres *mpl*; – *vt* rationner; **I was rationed to** . . . ma ration était . . . .

rational ['ræʃən(ə)l] *a* (*method, thought etc*) rationnel; (*person*) raisonnable. ◆**rationalize** *vt* (*organize*) rationaliser; (*explain*) justifier. ◆**rationally** *adv* raisonnablement.

rattle ['ræt(ə)l] **1** *n* (*baby's toy*) hochet *m*; (*of sports fan*) crécelle *f*. **2** *n* petit bruit *m* (sec); cliquetis *m*; crépitement *m*; – *vi* faire du bruit; (*of bottles*) cliqueter; (*of gunfire*) crépiter; (*of window*) trembler; – *vt* (*shake*) agiter; (*window*) faire trembler; (*keys*) faire cliqueter. **3** *vt* **to r. s.o.** (*make nervous*) *Fam* ébranler qn; **to r. off** (*poem etc*) *Fam* débiter (à toute vitesse). ◆**rattlesnake** *n* serpent *m* à sonnette.

ratty ['rætɪ] *a* (-**ier**, -**iest**) **1** (*shabby*) *Am Fam* minable. **2** **to get r.** (*annoyed*) *Fam* prendre la mouche.

raucous ['rɔːkəs] *a* rauque.

raunchy ['rɔːntʃɪ] *a* (-**ier**, -**iest**) (*joke etc*) *Am Fam* grivois.

ravage ['rævɪdʒ] *vt* ravager; – *npl* ravages *mpl*.

rav/e [reɪv] *vi* (*talk nonsense*) divaguer; (*rage*) tempêter (**at** contre); **to r. about** (*enthuse*) ne pas se tarir d'éloges sur; – *a* **r. review** *Fam* critique *f* dithyrambique. ◆**—ing** *a* **to be r. mad** être fou furieux; – *npl* (*wild talk*) divagations *fpl*.

raven ['reɪv(ə)n] *n* corbeau *m*.

ravenous ['rævənəs] *a* vorace; **I'm r.** *Fam* j'ai une faim de loup.

ravine [rə'viːn] *n* ravin *m*.

ravioli [rævɪ'əʊlɪ] *n* ravioli *mpl*.

ravish ['rævɪʃ] *vt* (*rape*) *Lit* violenter. ◆**—ing** *a* (*beautiful*) ravissant. ◆**—ingly** *adv* **r. beautiful** d'une beauté ravissante.

raw [rɔː] *a* (-**er**, -**est**) (*vegetable etc*) cru; (*sugar*) brut; (*immature*) inexpérimenté; (*wound*) à vif; (*skin*) écorché; (*weather*) rigoureux; **r. edge** bord *m* coupé; **r. material** matière *f* première; **to get a r. deal** *Fam* être mal traité.

Rawlplug® ['rɔːlplʌg] *n* cheville *f*, tampon *m*.

ray [reɪ] *n* (*of light, sun etc*) & *Phys* rayon *m*; (*of hope*) *Fig* lueur *f*.

raze [reɪz] *vt* **to r. (to the ground)** (*destroy*) raser.

razor ['reɪzər] *n* rasoir *m*.

re [riː] *prep Com* en référence à.

re- [riː] *pref* ré-, re-, r-.

reach [riːtʃ] *vt* (*place, aim etc*) atteindre, arriver à; (*gain access to*) accéder à; (*of letter*) parvenir à (qn); (*contact*) joindre (qn); **to r. s.o. (over) sth** (*hand over*) passer qch à qn; **to r. out** (*one's arm*) (é)tendre; – *vi* (*extend*) s'étendre (**to** à); (*of voice*) porter; **to r. (out)** (é)tendre le bras (**for** pour prendre); – *n* portée *f*; *Boxing* allonge *f*; **within r. of** à portée de; (*near*) à proximité de; **within easy r.** (*object*) à portée de main; (*shops*) facilement accessible.

react [rɪ'ækt] *vi* réagir. ◆**reaction** *n* réaction *f*. ◆**reactionary** *a* & *n* réactionnaire (*mf*).

reactor [rɪ'æktər] *n* réacteur *m*.

read [riːd] *vt* (*pt & pp* **read** [red]) lire; (*study*) *Univ* faire des études de; (*meter*) relever; (*of instrument*) indiquer; **to r. back** *or* **over** relire; **to r. out** lire (à haute voix); **to r. through** (*skim*) parcourir; **to r. up (on)** (*study*) étudier; – *vi* lire; **to r. well** (*of text*) se lire bien; **to r. to s.o.** faire la lecture à qn; **to r. about** (*s.o., sth*) lire qch sur; **to r. for** (*degree*) *Univ* préparer; – *n* **to have a r.** *Fam* faire un peu de lecture; **this book's a**

good r. *Fam* ce livre est agréable à lire. ◆**—ing** *n* lecture *f*; (*of meter*) relevé *m*; (*by instrument*) indication *f*; (*variant*) variante *f*; *— a* (*room*) de lecture; **r. matter** choses *fpl* à lire; **r. lamp** lampe *f* de bureau *or* de chevet. ◆**—able** *a* lisible. ◆**—er** *n* lecteur, -trice *mf*; (*book*) livre *m* de lecture. ◆**readership** *n* lecteurs *mpl*, public *m*.

readdress [riːəˈdres] *vt* (*letter*) faire suivre.

readjust [riːəˈdʒʌst] *vt* (*instrument*) régler; (*salary*) réajuster; *— vi* se réadapter (**to** à). ◆**—ment** *n* réglage *m*; réajustement *m*; réadaptation *f*.

readily [ˈredɪlɪ] *adv* (*willingly*) volontiers; (*easily*) facilement. ◆**readiness** *n* empressement *m* (**to do** à faire); **in r. for** prêt pour.

ready [ˈredɪ] *a* (-ier, -iest) prêt (**to do** à faire, **for sth** à *or* pour qch); (*quick*) *Fig* prompt (**to do** à faire); **to get sth r.** préparer qch; **to get r.** se préparer (**for sth** à qch, **to do** à faire); **r. cash, r. money** argent *m* liquide; *— n* at the r. *Fam* tout prêt. ◆**r.-'cooked** *a* tout cuit. ◆**r.-'made** *a* tout fait; **r.-made clothes** prêt-à-porter *m inv*.

real [rɪəl] *a* vrai, véritable; (*life, world etc*) réel; **it's the r. thing** *Fam* c'est du vrai de vrai; **r. estate** *Am* immobilier *m*; *— adv Fam* vraiment; **r. stupid** vraiment bête; *— n* **for r.** *Fam* pour de vrai. ◆**realism** *n* réalisme *m*. ◆**realist** *n* réaliste *mf*. ◆**rea-'listic** *a* réaliste. ◆**rea'listically** *adv* avec réalisme.

reality [rɪˈælətɪ] *n* réalité *f*; **in r.** en réalité.

realize [ˈrɪəlaɪz] *vt* **1** (*know*) se rendre compte de, réaliser; (*understand*) comprendre (**that** que); **to r. that** (*know*) se rendre compte que. **2** (*carry out, convert into cash*) réaliser; (*price*) atteindre. ◆**reali'zation** *n* **1** (*prise f de*) conscience *f*. **2** (*of aim, assets*) réalisation *f*.

really [ˈrɪəlɪ] *adv* vraiment; **is it r. true?** est-ce bien vrai?

realm [relm] *n* (*kingdom*) royaume *m*; (*of dreams etc*) *Fig* monde *m*.

realtor [ˈrɪəltər] *n Am* agent *m* immobilier.

reap [riːp] *vt* (*field, crop*) moissonner; *Fig* récolter.

reappear [riːəˈpɪər] *vi* réapparaître.

reappraisal [riːəˈpreɪz(ə)l] *n* réévaluation *f*.

rear [rɪər] **1** *n* (*back part*) arrière *m*; (*of column*) queue *f*; **in** *or* **at the r.** à l'arrière (*of* de); **from the r.** par derrière; *— a* arrière *inv*, de derrière; **r.-view mirror** rétroviseur *m*. **2** *vt* (*family, animals etc*) élever; (*one's head*) relever. **3** *vi* **to r. (up)** (*of horse*) se cabrer. ◆**rearguard** *n* arrière-garde *f*.

rearrange [riːəˈreɪndʒ] *vt* réarranger.

reason [ˈriːz(ə)n] *n* (*cause, sense*) raison *f*; **the r. for/why** *or* **that . . .** la raison de/pour laquelle . . . ; **for no r.** sans raison; **that stands to r.** cela va sans dire, c'est logique; **within r.** avec modération; **to do everything within r. to . . .** faire tout ce qu'il est raisonnable de faire pour . . . ; **to have every r. to believe/***etc* avoir tout lieu de croire/*etc*; *— vi* raisonner; **to r. with s.o.** raisonner qn; *— vt* **to r. that** calculer que. ◆**—ing** *n* raisonnement *m*. ◆**—able** *a* raisonnable. ◆**—ably** *adv* raisonnablement; (*fairly, rather*) assez; **r. fit** en assez bonne forme.

reassur/e [riːəˈʃuər] *vt* rassurer. ◆**—ing** *a* rassurant. ◆**reassurance** *n* réconfort *m*.

reawaken [riːəˈweɪk(ə)n] *vt* (*interest etc*) réveiller. ◆**—ing** *n* réveil *m*.

rebate [ˈriːbeɪt] *n* (*discount on purchase*) ristourne *f*; (*refund*) remboursement *m* (partiel).

rebel [ˈreb(ə)l] *a* & *n* rebelle (*mf*); *—* [rɪˈbel] *vi* (-ll-) se rebeller (**against** contre). ◆**re'bellion** *n* rébellion *f*. ◆**re'bellious** *a* rebelle.

rebirth [ˈriːbɜːθ] *n* renaissance *f*.

rebound [rɪˈbaʊnd] *vi* (*of ball*) rebondir; (*of stone*) ricocher; (*of lies, action etc*) *Fig* retomber (**on** sur); *—* [ˈriːbaʊnd] *n* rebond *m*; ricochet *m*; **on the r.** (*to marry s.o. etc*) par dépit.

rebuff [rɪˈbʌf] *vt* repousser; *— n* rebuffade *f*.

rebuild [riːˈbɪld] *vt* (*pt* & *pp* **rebuilt**) reconstruire.

rebuke [rɪˈbjuːk] *vt* réprimander; *— n* réprimande *f*.

rebuttal [rɪˈbʌt(ə)l] *n* réfutation *f*.

recalcitrant [rɪˈkælsɪtrənt] *a* récalcitrant.

recall [rɪˈkɔːl] *vt* (*call back*) rappeler; (*remember*) se rappeler (**that** que, **doing** avoir fait); **to r. sth to s.o.** rappeler qch à qn; *— n* rappel *m*; **beyond r.** irrévocable.

recant [rɪˈkænt] *vi* se rétracter.

recap [riːˈkæp] *vti* (-pp-) récapituler; *— n* récapitulation *f*. ◆**reca'pitulate** *vti* récapituler. ◆**recapitu'lation** *n* récapitulation *f*.

recapture [riːˈkæptʃər] *vt* (*prisoner etc*) reprendre; (*rediscover*) retrouver; (*recreate*) recréer; *— n* (*of prisoner*) arrestation *f*.

reced/e [rɪˈsiːd] *vi* (*into the distance*) s'éloigner; (*of floods*) baisser. ◆**—ing** *a* (*forehead*) fuyant; **his hair(line) is r.** son front se dégarnit.

receipt [rɪˈsiːt] *n* (*for payment*) reçu *m* (**for** de); (*for letter, parcel*) récépissé *m*, accusé *m* de réception; *pl* (*takings*) recettes *fpl*; **to acknowledge r.** accuser réception (**of** de); **on r. of** dès réception de.

receiv/e [rɪ'siːv] *vt* recevoir; (*stolen goods*) *Jur* receler. ◆**—ing** *n Jur* recel *m*. ◆**—er** *n Tel* combiné *m*; *Rad* récepteur *m*; (*of stolen goods*) *Jur* receleur, -euse *mf*; **to pick up** *or* **lift the r.** *Tel* décrocher.

recent ['riːsənt] *a* récent; **in r. months** ces mois-ci. ◆**—ly** *adv* récemment; **as r. as** pas plus tard que.

receptacle [rɪ'septək(ə)l] *n* récipient *m*.

reception [rɪ'sepʃ(ə)n] *n* (*receiving, welcome, party etc*) & *Rad* réception *f*; **r. desk** réception *f*; **r. room** salle *f* de séjour. ◆**receptionist** *n* réceptionniste *mf*. ◆**receptive** *a* réceptif (**to an idea**/*etc* à une idée/*etc*); **r. to s.o.** compréhensif envers qn.

recess [rɪ'ses, 'riːses] *n* **1** (*holiday*) vacances *fpl*; *Sch Am* récréation *f*. **2** (*alcove*) renfoncement *m*; (*nook*) & *Fig* recoin *m*.

recession [rɪ'seʃ(ə)n] *n Econ* récession *f*.

recharge [riː'tʃɑːdʒ] *vt* (*battery*) recharger.

recipe ['resɪpɪ] *n Culin* & *Fig* recette *f* (**for** de).

recipient [rɪ'sɪpɪənt] *n* (*of award, honour*) récipiendaire *m*.

reciprocal [rɪ'sɪprək(ə)l] *a* réciproque. ◆**reciprocate** *vt* (*compliment*) retourner; (*gesture*) faire à son tour; — *vi* (*do the same*) en faire autant.

recital [rɪ'saɪt(ə)l] *n Mus* récital *m*.

recite [rɪ'saɪt] *vt* (*poem etc*) réciter; (*list*) énumérer. ◆**reci'tation** *n* récitation *f*.

reckless ['rekləs] *a* (*rash*) imprudent. ◆**—ly** *adv* imprudemment.

reckon ['rek(ə)n] *vt* (*count*) compter; (*calculate*) calculer; (*consider*) considérer; (*think*) *Fam* penser (**that** que); — *vi* compter; calculer; **to r. with** (*take into account*) compter avec; (*deal with*) avoir affaire à; **to r. on/without** compter sur/sans; **to r. on doing** *Fam* compter *or* penser faire. ◆**—ing** *n* calcul(s) *m*(*pl*).

reclaim [rɪ'kleɪm] *vt* **1** (*land*) mettre en valeur; (*from sea*) assécher. **2** (*ask for back*) réclamer; (*luggage at airport*) récupérer.

reclin/e [rɪ'klaɪn] *vi* (*of person*) être allongé; (*of head*) être appuyé; — *vt* (*head*) appuyer (**on** sur). ◆**—ing** *a* (*seat*) à dossier inclinable *or* réglable.

recluse [rɪ'kluːs] *n* reclus, -use *mf*.

recognize ['rekəgnaɪz] *vt* reconnaître (**by** à, **that** que). ◆**recog'nition** *n* reconnaissance *f*; **to change beyond** *or* **out of all r.** devenir méconnaissable; **to gain r.** être reconnu. ◆**recognizable** *a* reconnaissable.

recoil [rɪ'kɔɪl] *vi* reculer (**from doing** à l'idée de faire).

recollect [rekə'lekt] *vt* se souvenir de; **to r. that** se souvenir que; — *vi* se souvenir. ◆**recollection** *n* souvenir *m*.

recommend [rekə'mend] *vt* (*praise, support, advise*) recommander (**to** à, **for** pour); **to r. s.o. to do** recommander à qn de faire. ◆**recommen'dation** *n* recommandation *f*.

recompense ['rekəmpens] *vt* (*reward*) récompenser; — *n* récompense *f*.

reconcile ['rekənsaɪl] *vt* (*person*) réconcilier (**with, to** avec); (*opinion*) concilier (**with** avec); **to r. oneself to sth** se résigner à qch. ◆**reconcili'ation** *n* réconciliation *f*.

reconditioned [riːkən'dɪʃ(ə)nd] *a* (*engine*) refait (à neuf).

reconnaissance [rɪ'kɒnɪsəns] *n Mil* reconnaissance *f*. ◆**reconnoitre** [rekə'nɔɪtər] *vt Mil* reconnaître.

reconsider [riːkən'sɪdər] *vt* reconsidérer; — *vi* revenir sur sa décision.

reconstruct [riːkən'strʌkt] *vt* (*crime*) reconstituer.

record 1 ['rekɔːd] *n* (*disc*) disque *m*; **r. library** discothèque *f*; **r. player** électrophone *m*. **2** *n Sp* & *Fig* record *m*; — *a* (*attendance, time etc*) record *inv*. **3** *n* (*report*) rapport *m*; (*register*) registre *m*; (*recording on tape etc*) enregistrement *m*; (*mention*) mention *f*; (*note*) note *f*; (*background*) antécédents *mpl*; (*case history*) dossier *m*; (*police*) **r.** casier *m* judiciaire; (*public*) **records** archives *fpl*; **to make** *or* **keep a r. of** noter; **on r.** (*fact, event*) attesté; **off the r.** à titre confidentiel; **their safety r.** leurs résultats *mpl* en matière de sécurité. **4** [rɪ'kɔːd] *vt* (*on tape, in register etc*) enregistrer; (*in diary*) noter; (*relate*) rapporter (**that** que); — *vi* (*on tape etc*) enregistrer. ◆**—ed** *a* enregistré; (*prerecorded*) *TV* en différé; (*fact*) attesté; **letter sent (by) r. delivery** = lettre *f* avec avis de réception. ◆**—ing** *n* enregistrement *m*. ◆**—er** *n Mus* flûte *f* à bec; (*tape*) **r.** magnétophone *m*.

recount 1 [rɪ'kaʊnt] *vt* (*relate*) raconter. **2** ['riːkaʊnt] *n Pol* nouveau dépouillement *m* du scrutin.

recoup [rɪ'kuːp] *vt* (*loss*) récupérer.

recourse ['riːkɔːs] *n* recours *m*; **to have r. to** avoir recours à.

recover [rɪ'kʌvər] **1** *vt* (*get back*) retrouver, récupérer. **2** *vi* (*from shock etc*) se remettre; (*get better*) *Med* se remettre (**from** de); (*of* *economy, country*) se redresser; (*of currency*) remonter. ◆**recovery** n **1** *Econ* redressement m. **2 the r. of sth** (*getting back*) la récupération de qch.

recreate [riːkrɪˈeɪt] vt recréer.

recreation [rekrɪˈeɪʃ(ə)n] n récréation f. ◆**recreational** a (*activity etc*) de loisir.

recrimination [rɪkrɪmɪˈneɪʃ(ə)n] n *Jur* contre-accusation f.

recruit [rɪˈkruːt] n recrue f; – vt recruter; **to r. s.o. to do** (*persuade*) *Fig* embaucher qn pour faire. ◆**recruitment** n recrutement m.

rectangle [ˈrektæŋg(ə)l] n rectangle m. ◆**recˈtangular** a rectangulaire.

rectify [ˈrektɪfaɪ] vt rectifier. ◆**rectifiˈcation** n rectification f.

rector [ˈrektər] n *Rel* curé m; *Univ* président m.

recuperate [rɪˈkuːpəreɪt] vi récupérer (ses forces); – vt récupérer.

recur [rɪˈkɜːr] vi (**-rr-**) (*of theme*) revenir; (*of event*) se reproduire; (*of illness*) réapparaître. ◆**recurrence** [rɪˈkʌrəns] n répétition f; (*of illness*) réapparition f. ◆**recurrent** a fréquent.

recycle [riːˈsaɪk(ə)l] vt (*material*) recycler.

red [red] a (**redder, reddest**) rouge; (*hair*) roux; **to turn** *or* **go r.** rougir; **r. light** (*traffic light*) feu m rouge; **R. Cross** Croix-Rouge f; **R. Indian** Peau-Rouge mf; (*colour*) rouge m; **R.** (*person*) *Pol* rouge mf; **in the r.** (*firm, account*) en déficit; (*person*) à découvert. ◆**r.-ˈfaced** a *Fig* rouge de confusion. ◆**r.-ˈhanded** adv **caught r.-handed** pris en flagrant délit. ◆**r.-ˈhot** a brûlant. ◆**redden** vti rougir. ◆**reddish** a rougeâtre; (*hair*) carotte. ◆**redness** n rougeur f; (*of hair*) rousseur f.

redcurrant [redˈkʌrənt] n groseille f.

redecorate [riːˈdekəreɪt] vt (*room etc*) refaire; – vi refaire la peinture et les papiers.

redeem [rɪˈdiːm] vt (*restore to favour, free, pay off*) racheter; (*convert into cash*) réaliser; **redeeming feature** point m favorable. ◆**redemption** n rachat m; réalisation f; *Rel* rédemption f.

redeploy [riːdɪˈplɔɪ] vt (*staff*) réorganiser; (*troops*) redéployer.

redhead [ˈredhed] n roux m, rousse f.

redirect [riːdaɪˈrekt] vt (*mail*) faire suivre.

redo [riːˈduː] vt (*pt* **redid**, *pp* **redone**) refaire.

redress [rɪˈdres] n **to seek r.** demander réparation (**for** à).

reduce [rɪˈdjuːs] vt réduire (**to** à, **by** de); (*temperature*) faire baisser; **at a reduced**

price (*ticket*) à prix réduit; (*goods*) au rabais. ◆**reduction** n réduction f; (*of temperature*) baisse f; (*discount*) rabais m.

redundant [rɪˈdʌndənt] a (*not needed*) superflu, de trop; **to make r.** (*workers*) mettre en chômage, licencier. ◆**redundancy** n (*of workers*) licenciement m; **r. pay(ment)** indemnité f de licenciement.

re-echo [riːˈekəʊ] vi résonner; – vt (*sound*) répercuter; *Fig* répéter.

reed [riːd] n **1** *Bot* roseau m. **2** *Mus* anche f; – a (*instrument*) à anche.

re-educate [riːˈedjʊkeɪt] vt (*criminal, limb*) rééduquer.

reef [riːf] n récif m, écueil m.

reek [riːk] vi puer; **to r. of** (*smell*) & *Fig* puer; – n puanteur f.

reel [riːl] **1** n (*of thread, film*) bobine f; (*film itself*) *Cin* bande f; (*of hose*) dévidoir m; (*for fishing line*) moulinet m. **2** vi (*stagger*) chanceler; (*of mind*) chavirer; (*of head*) tourner. **3** vt **to r. off** (*rattle off*) débiter (à toute vitesse).

re-elect [riːɪˈlekt] vt réélire.

re-entry [riːˈentrɪ] n (*of spacecraft*) rentrée f.

re-establish [riːɪˈstæblɪʃ] vt rétablir.

ref [ref] n *Sp Fam* arbitre m.

refectory [rɪˈfektərɪ] n réfectoire m.

refer [rɪˈfɜːr] vi (**-rr-**) **to r. to** (*allude to*) faire allusion à; (*speak of*) parler de; (*apply to*) s'appliquer à; (*consult*) se reporter à; – vt **to r. sth to** (*submit*) soumettre qch à; **to r. s.o. to** (*office, article etc*) renvoyer qn à. ◆**refeˈree** n *Sp* arbitre m; (*for job etc*) répondant, -ante mf; – vt *Sp* arbitrer. ◆**ˈreference** n (*in book, recommendation*) référence f; (*allusion*) allusion f (**to** à); (*mention*) mention f (**to** de); (*connection*) rapport m (**to** avec); **in** *or* **with r. to** concernant; *Com* suite à; **terms of r.** (*of person, investigating body*) compétence f; (*of law*) étendue f; **r. book** livre m de référence.

referendum [refəˈrendəm] n référendum m.

refill [riːˈfɪl] vt remplir (à nouveau); (*lighter, pen etc*) recharger; – [ˈriːfɪl] n recharge f; **a r.** (*drink*) *Fam* un autre verre.

refine [rɪˈfaɪn] vt (*oil, sugar, manners*) raffiner; (*metal, ore*) affiner; (*technique, machine*) perfectionner; – vi **to r. upon** raffiner sur. ◆**refinement** n (*of person*) raffinement m; (*of sugar, oil*) raffinage m; (*of technique*) perfectionnement m; pl (*improvements*) *Tech* améliorations fpl. ◆**refinery** n raffinerie f.

refit [riːˈfɪt] vt (**-tt-**) (*ship*) remettre en état.

reflate [riːˈfleɪt] vt (*economy*) relancer.

reflect [rɪ'flekt] **1** vt (light) & Fig refléter; (of mirror) réfléchir, refléter; **to r. sth on s.o.** (credit, honour) faire rejaillir qch sur qn; – vi **to r. on s.o., be reflected on s.o.** (rebound) rejaillir sur qn. **2** vi (think) réfléchir (**on** à); – vt **to r. that** penser que. ◆**reflection** n **1** (thought, criticism) réflexion (**on** sur); **on r.** tout bien réfléchi. **2** (image) & Fig reflet m; (reflecting) réflexion f (**of** de). ◆**reflector** n réflecteur m. ◆**reflexion** n = reflection. ◆**reflexive** a (verb) Gram réfléchi.

reflex ['riːfleks] n & a réflexe (m); **r. action** réflexe m.

refloat [riː'fləʊt] vt (ship) & Com renflouer.

reform [rɪ'fɔːm] n réforme f; – vt réformer; (person, conduct) corriger; – vi (of person) se réformer. ◆**—er** n réformateur, -trice mf.

refrain [rɪ'freɪn] **1** vi s'abstenir (**from doing** de faire). **2** n Mus & Fig refrain m.

refresh [rɪ'freʃ] vt (of bath, drink) rafraîchir; (of sleep, rest) délasser; **to r. oneself** (drink) se rafraîchir; **to r. one's memory** se rafraîchir la mémoire. ◆**—ing** a rafraîchissant; (sleep) réparateur; (pleasant) agréable; (original) nouveau. ◆**—er** a (course) de recyclage. ◆**—ments** npl (drinks) rafraîchissements mpl; (snacks) collation f.

refrigerate [rɪ'frɪdʒəreɪt] vt réfrigérer. ◆**refrigerator** n réfrigérateur m.

refuel [riː'fjʊəl] vi (-ll-, Am -l-) Av se ravitailler; – vt Av ravitailler.

refuge ['refjuːdʒ] n refuge m; **to take r.** se réfugier (**in** dans). ◆**refu'gee** n réfugié, -ée mf.

refund [rɪ'fʌnd] vt rembourser; – ['riːfʌnd] n remboursement m.

refurbish [riː'fɜːbɪʃ] vt remettre à neuf.

refuse¹ [rɪ'fjuːz] vt refuser (**s.o. sth** qch à qn, **to do** de faire); – vi refuser. ◆**refusal** n refus m.

refuse² ['refjuːs] n (rubbish) ordures fpl, détritus m; (waste materials) déchets mpl; **r. collector** éboueur m; **r. dump** dépôt m d'ordures.

refute [rɪ'fjuːt] vt réfuter.

regain [rɪ'geɪn] vt (favour, lost ground) regagner; (strength) récupérer, retrouver, reprendre; (health, sight) retrouver; (consciousness) reprendre.

regal ['riːg(ə)l] a royal, majestueux.

regalia [rɪ'geɪlɪə] npl insignes mpl (royaux).

regard [rɪ'gɑːd] vt (consider) considérer, regarder; (concern) regarder; **as regards** en ce qui concerne; – n considération f (**for** pour); **to have (a) great r. for** avoir de l'estime pour; **without r. to** sans égard

pour; **with r. to** en ce qui concerne; **to give** or **send one's regards to** (greetings) faire ses hommages à. ◆**—ing** prep en ce qui concerne. ◆**—less 1** a **r. of** sans tenir compte de. **2** adv (all the same) Fam quand même.

regatta [rɪ'gætə] n régates fpl.

regency ['riːdʒənsɪ] n régence f.

regenerate [rɪ'dʒenəreɪt] vt régénérer.

reggae ['regeɪ] n (music) reggae m; – a (group etc) reggae inv.

régime [reɪ'ʒiːm] n Pol régime m.

regiment ['redʒɪmənt] n régiment m. ◆**regi'mental** a régimentaire, du régiment. ◆**regimen'tation** n discipline f excessive.

region ['riːdʒ(ə)n] n région f; **in the r. of** (about) Fig environ; **in the r. of £500** dans les 500 livres. ◆**regional** a régional.

register ['redʒɪstər] n registre m; Sch cahier m d'appel; **electoral r.** liste f électorale; – vt (record, note) enregistrer; (birth, death) déclarer; (vehicle) immatriculer; (express) exprimer; (indicate) indiquer; (letter) recommander; (realize) Fam réaliser; – vi (enrol) s'inscrire; (in hotel) signer le registre; **it hasn't registered (with me)** Fam je n'ai pas encore réalisé ça. ◆**—ed** a (member) inscrit; (letter) recommandé; **r. trademark** marque f déposée. ◆**regi'strar** n officier m de l'état civil; Univ secrétaire m général. ◆**regi'stration** n enregistrement m; (enrolment) inscription f; **r. (number)** Aut numéro m d'immatriculation; **r. document** Aut = carte f grise. ◆**registry** a & n **r. (office)** bureau m de l'état civil.

regress [rɪ'gres] vi régresser.

regret [rɪ'gret] vt (-tt-) regretter (**doing, to do** de faire; **that** que (+ sub)); **I r. to hear that . . .** je suis désolé d'apprendre que . . . ; – n regret m. ◆**regretfully** adv **r., I . . .** à mon grand regret, je . . . . ◆**regrettable** a regrettable (**that** que (+ sub)). ◆**regrettably** adv malheureusement; (poor, ill etc) fâcheusement.

regroup [riː'gruːp] vi se regrouper; – vt regrouper.

regular ['regjʊlər] a (steady, even) régulier; (surface) uni; (usual) habituel; (price, size) normal; (reader, listener) fidèle; (staff) permanent; (fool, slave etc) Fam vrai; **a r. guy** Am Fam un chic type; – n (in bar etc) habitué, -ée mf; Mil régulier m. ◆**regu'larity** n régularité f. ◆**regularly** adv régulièrement.

regulate ['regjʊleɪt] vt régler. ◆**regu-**

'lation 1 *n* (*rule*) règlement *m*; – *a* (*uniform etc*) réglementaire. **2** *n* (*regulating*) réglage *m*.

rehabilitate [riːhəˈbɪlɪteɪt] *vt* (*in public esteem*) réhabiliter; (*wounded soldier etc*) réadapter.

rehash [riːˈhæʃ] *vt* (*text*) *Pej* remanier; *Culin* réchauffer; – [ˈriːhæʃ] *n* **a r.** *Culin* & *Fig* du réchauffé.

rehearse [rɪˈhɜːs] *vt* *Th* répéter; (*prepare*) *Fig* préparer; – *vi* *Th* répéter. ◆**rehearsal** *n* *Th* répétition *f*.

reign [reɪn] *n* règne *m*; **in** or **during the r. of** sous le règne de; – *vi* régner (**over** sur).

reimburse [riːɪmˈbɜːs] *vt* rembourser (**for** de). ◆—**ment** *n* remboursement *m*.

rein [reɪn] *n* **reins** rênes *fpl*; **to give free r. to** *Fig* donner libre cours à.

reindeer [ˈreɪndɪər] *n inv* renne *m*.

reinforce [riːɪnˈfɔːs] *vt* renforcer (**with** de); **reinforced concrete** béton *m* armé. ◆—**ment** *n* renforcement *m* (**of** de); *pl* *Mil* renforts *mpl*.

reinstate [riːɪnˈsteɪt] *vt* réintégrer. ◆—**ment** *n* réintégration *f*.

reissue [riːˈɪʃuː] *vt* (*book*) rééditer.

reiterate [riːˈɪtəreɪt] *vt* (*say again*) réitérer.

reject [rɪˈdʒekt] *vt* (*refuse to accept*) rejeter; (*as useless*) refuser; – [ˈriːdʒekt] *n* *Com* article *m* de rebut; – *a* (*article*) de deuxième choix; **r. shop** solderie *f*. ◆**re'jection** *n* rejet *m*; (*of candidate etc*) refus *m*.

rejoic/e [rɪˈdʒɔɪs] *vi* se réjouir (**over** or **at sth** de qch, **in doing** de faire). ◆—**ing(s)** *n*(*pl*) réjouissance(s) *f*(*pl*).

rejoin [rɪˈdʒɔɪn] **1** *vt* (*join up with*) rejoindre. **2** *vi* (*retort*) répliquer.

rejuvenate [rɪˈdʒuːvəneɪt] *vt* rajeunir.

rekindle [riːˈkɪnd(ə)l] *vt* rallumer.

relapse [ˈriːlæps] *n* *Med* rechute *f*; – *vi* *Med* rechuter; **to r. into** *Fig* retomber dans.

relat/e [rɪˈleɪt] **1** *vt* (*narrate*) raconter (**that** que); (*report*) rapporter (**that** que). **2** *vt* (*connect*) établir un rapport entre (*faits etc*); **to r. sth to** (*link*) rattacher qch à; – *vi* **to r. to** (*apply to*) se rapporter à; (*get on with*) communiquer or s'entendre avec. ◆—**ed** *a* (*linked*) lié (**to** à); (*languages, styles*) apparentés; **to be r. to** (*by family*) être parent de.

relation [rɪˈleɪʃ(ə)n] *n* (*relative*) parent, -ente *mf*; (*relationship*) rapport *m*, relation *f* (**between** entre, **with** avec); **what r. are you to him?** quel est ton lien de parenté avec lui?; **international**/*etc* **relations** relations *fpl* internationales/*etc*. ◆**relationship** *n* (*kinship*) lien(s) *m*(*pl*) de parenté; (*rela-*

tions) relations *fpl*, rapports *mpl*; (*connection*) rapport *m*; **in r. to** relativement à.

relative [ˈrelətɪv] *n* (*person*) parent, -ente *mf*; – *a* relatif (**to** à); (*respective*) respectif; **r. to** (*compared to*) relativement à; **to be r. to** (*depend on*) être fonction de. ◆**relatively** *adv* relativement.

relax [rɪˈlæks] **1** *vt* (*person, mind*) détendre; – *vi* se détendre; **r.!** (*calm down*) *Fam* du calme! **2** *vt* (*grip, pressure etc*) relâcher; (*restrictions, principles, control*) assouplir. ◆—**ed** *a* (*person, atmosphere*) décontracté, détendu. ◆—**ing** *a* (*bath etc*) délassant. ◆**rela'xation** *n* **1** (*rest, recreation*) détente *f*; (*of body*) décontraction *f*. **2** (*of grip etc*) relâchement *m*; (*of restrictions etc*) assouplissement *m*.

relay [ˈriːleɪ] *n* relais *m*; **r. race** course *f* de relais; – *vt* (*message etc*) *Rad* retransmettre, *Fig* transmettre (**to** à).

release [rɪˈliːs] *vt* (*free*) libérer (**from** de); (*bomb, s.o.'s hand*) lâcher; (*spring*) déclencher; (*brake*) desserrer; (*film, record*) sortir; (*news, facts*) publier; (*smoke, trapped person*) dégager; (*tension*) éliminer; – *n* libération *f*; (*of film, book*) sortie *f* (**of** de); (*record*) nouveau disque *m*; (*film*) nouveau film *m*; (*relief*) *Fig* délivrance *f*; *Psy* défoulement *m*; **press r.** communiqué *m* de presse; **to be on general r.** (*of film*) passer dans toutes les salles.

relegate [ˈrelɪgeɪt] *vt* reléguer (**to** à).

relent [rɪˈlent] *vi* (*be swayed*) se laisser fléchir; (*change one's mind*) revenir sur sa décision. ◆—**less** *a* implacable.

relevant [ˈreləvənt] *a* (*apt*) pertinent (**to** à); (*fitting*) approprié; (*useful*) utile; (*significant*) important; **that's not r.** ça n'a rien à voir. ◆**relevance** *n* pertinence *f* (**to** à); (*significance*) intérêt *m*; (*connection*) rapport *m* (**to** avec).

reliable [rɪˈlaɪəb(ə)l] *a* (*person, information, firm*) sérieux, sûr, fiable; (*machine*) fiable. ◆**relia'bility** *n* (*of person*) sérieux *m*, fiabilité *f*; (*of machine, information, firm*) fiabilité *f*. ◆**reliably** *adv* **to be r. informed that** apprendre de source sûre que.

reliance [rɪˈlaɪəns] *n* (*trust*) confiance *f* (**on** en); (*dependence*) dépendance *f* (**on** de). ◆**reliant** *a* **to be r. on** (*dependent*) dépendre de; (*trusting*) avoir confiance en.

relic [ˈrelɪk] *n* relique *f*; *pl* (*of the past*) vestiges *mpl*.

relief [rɪˈliːf] *n* (*from pain etc*) soulagement *m* (**from** à); (*help, supplies*) secours *m*; (*in art*) & *Geog* relief *m*; **tax r.** dégrèvement *m*; **to be on r.** *Am* recevoir l'aide sociale; – *a* (*train etc*) supplémentaire; (*work etc*) de secours; **r. road** route *f* de délestage. ◆**relieve** *vt* (*pain etc*) soulager; (*boredom*) dissiper; (*situation*) remédier à; (*take over from*) relayer (*qn*); (*help*) secourir, soulager; **to r. s.o. of** (*rid*) débarrasser qn de; **to r. s.o. of his post** relever qn de ses fonctions; **to r. congestion in** *Aut* décongestionner; **to r. oneself** (*go to the lavatory*) *Hum Fam* se soulager.

religion [rɪˈlɪdʒ(ə)n] *n* religion *f*. ◆**religious** *a* religieux; (*war, book*) de religion. ◆**religiously** *adv* religieusement.

relinquish [rɪˈlɪŋkwɪʃ] *vt* (*give up*) abandonner; (*let go*) lâcher.

relish [ˈrelɪʃ] *n* (*liking, taste*) goût *m* (*for* pour); (*pleasure*) plaisir *m*; (*seasoning*) assaisonnement *m*; **to eat with r.** manger de bon appétit; − *vt* (*food etc*) savourer; (*like*) aimer (*doing* faire).

relocate [riːləʊˈkeɪt] *vi* (*move to new place*) déménager; **to r. in** *or* **to** s'installer à.

reluctant [rɪˈlʌktənt] *a* (*greeting, gift, promise*) accordé à contrecœur; **to be r. to do** être peu disposé à faire; **a r. teacher**/*etc* un professeur/*etc* malgré lui. ◆**reluctance** *n* répugnance *f* (*to do* à faire). ◆**reluctantly** *adv* à contrecœur.

rely [rɪˈlaɪ] *vi* **to r. on** (*count on*) compter sur; (*be dependent upon*) dépendre de.

remain [rɪˈmeɪn] **1** *vi* rester. **2** *npl* restes *mpl*; **mortal r.** dépouille *f* mortelle. ◆**—ing** *a* qui reste(nt). ◆**remainder** *n* **1** reste *m*; **the r.** (*remaining people*) les autres *mfpl*; **the r. of the girls** les autres filles. **2** (*book*) invendu *m* soldé.

remand [rɪˈmɑːnd] *vt* **to r. (in custody)** *Jur* placer en détention préventive; − *n* **on r.** en détention préventive.

remark [rɪˈmɑːk] *n* remarque *f*; − *vt* (*faire*) remarquer (*that* que); − *vi* **to r. on** faire des remarques sur. ◆**—able** *a* remarquable (*for* par). ◆**—ably** *adv* remarquablement.

remarry [riːˈmærɪ] *vi* se remarier.

remedial [rɪˈmiːdɪəl] *a* (*class*) *Sch* de rattrapage; (*measure*) de redressement; (*treatment*) *Med* thérapeutique.

remedy [ˈremɪdɪ] *vt* remédier à; − *n* remède *m* (*for* contre, à, de).

remember [rɪˈmembər] *vt* se souvenir de, se rappeler; (*commemorate*) commémorer; **to r. that/doing** se rappeler que/d'avoir fait; **to r. to do** (*not forget to do*) penser à faire; **r. me to your mother!** rappelle-moi à son bon souvenir!; − *vi* se souvenir, se rappeler. ◆**remembrance** *n* (*memory*) souvenir *m*; **in r. of** en souvenir de.

remind [rɪˈmaɪnd] *vt* rappeler (**s.o. of sth** qch à qn, **s.o. that** à qn que); **to r. s.o. to do** penser à qn à faire; **that** *or* **which reminds me!** à propos! ◆**—er** *n* (*of event & letter*) rappel *m*; (*note to do sth*) pense-bête *m*; **it's a r. (for him** *or* **her) that . . .** c'est pour lui rappeler que. . . .

reminisce [remɪˈnɪs] *vi* raconter *or* se rappeler ses souvenirs (**about** de). ◆**reminiscences** *npl* réminiscences *fpl*. ◆**reminiscent** *a* **r. of** qui rappelle.

remiss [rɪˈmɪs] *a* négligent.

remit [rɪˈmɪt] *vt* (**-tt-**) (*money*) envoyer. ◆**remission** *n Jur* remise *f* (de peine); *Med Rel* rémission *f*. ◆**remittance** *n* (*sum*) paiement *m*.

remnant [ˈremnənt] *n* (*remaining part*) reste *m*; (*trace*) vestige *m*; (*of fabric*) coupon *m*; (*oddment*) fin *f* de série.

remodel [riːˈmɒd(ə)l] *vt* (**-ll-**, *Am* **-l-**) remodeler.

remonstrate [ˈremənstreɪt] *vi* **to r. with s.o.** faire des remontrances à.

remorse [rɪˈmɔːs] *n* remords *m*(*pl*) (*for* pour); **without r.** sans pitié. ◆**—less** *a* implacable. ◆**—lessly** *adv* (*to hit etc*) implacablement.

remote [rɪˈməʊt] *a* (**-er, -est**) **1** (*far-off*) lointain, éloigné; (*isolated*) isolé; (*aloof*) distant; **r. from** loin de; **r. control** télécommande *f*. **2** (*slight*) petit, vague; **not the remotest idea** pas la moindre idée. ◆**—ly** *adv* (*slightly*) vaguement, un peu; (*situated*) au loin; **not r. aware**/*etc* nullement conscient/*etc*. ◆**—ness** *n* éloignement *m*; isolement *m*; *Fig* attitude *f* distante.

remould [ˈriːməʊld] *n* pneu *m* rechapé.

remove [rɪˈmuːv] *vt* (*clothes, stain etc*) enlever (**from s.o.** à qn, **from sth** de qch); (*withdraw*) retirer; (*lead away*) emmener (**to** à); (*furniture*) déménager; (*obstacle, threat, word*) supprimer; (*fear, doubt*) dissiper; (*employee*) renvoyer; (**far**) **removed from** loin de. ◆**removable** *a* (*lining etc*) amovible. ◆**removal** *n* enlèvement *m*; déménagement *m*; suppression *f*; **r. man** déménageur *m*; **r. van** camion *m* de déménagement. ◆**remover** *n* (*for make-up*) démaquillant *m*; (*for nail polish*) dissolvant *m*; (*for paint*) décapant *m*; (*for stains*) détachant *m*.

remunerate [rɪˈmjuːnəreɪt] *vt* rémunérer. ◆**remune′ration** *n* rémunération *f*.

renaissance [rəˈneɪsəns] *n* (*in art etc*) renaissance *f*.

rename [riːˈneɪm] *vt* (*street etc*) rebaptiser.

render [ˈrendər] *vt* (*give, make*) rendre; *Mus*

interpréter; (*help*) prêter. ◆—**ing** *n* *Mus*
interprétation *f*; (*translation*) traduction *f*.
rendez-vous ['rɒndɪvuː, *pl* -vuːz] *n inv*
rendez-vous *m inv*.
renegade ['renɪɡeɪd] *n* renégat, -ate *mf*.
reneg(u)e [rɪ'niːɡ] *vi* **to r. on** (*promise etc*)
revenir sur.
renew [rɪ'njuː] *vt* renouveler; (*resume*)
reprendre; (*library book*) renouveler le prêt
de. ◆—**ed** *a* (*efforts*) renouvelés; (*attempt*)
nouveau; **with r. vigour**/*etc* avec un regain
de vigueur/*etc*. ◆**renewable** *a* renouvelable. ◆**renewal** *n* renouvellement *m*;
(*resumption*) reprise *f*; (*of strength etc*)
regain *m*.
renounce [rɪ'naʊns] *vt* (*give up*) renoncer à;
(*disown*) renier.
renovate ['renəveɪt] *vt* (*house*) rénover,
restaurer; (*painting*) restaurer. ◆**reno-
'vation** *n* rénovation *f*; restauration *f*.
renown [rɪ'naʊn] *n* renommée *f*.
◆**renowned** *a* renommé (**for** pour).
rent [rent] *n* loyer *m*; (*of television*) (prix *m*
de) location *f*; **r. collector** encaisseur *m* de
loyers; – *vt* louer; **to r. out** louer; – *vi* (*of
house etc*) se louer. ◆**r.-'free** *adv* sans
payer de loyer; – *a* gratuit. ◆**rental** *n* (*of
television*) (prix *m* de) location *f*; (*of telephone*) abonnement *m*.
renunciation [rɪnʌnsɪ'eɪʃ(ə)n] *n* (*giving up*)
renonciation *f* (**of** à); (*disowning*) reniement *m* (**of** de).
reopen [riː'əʊpən] *vti* rouvrir. ◆—**ing** *n*
réouverture *f*.
reorganize [riː'ɔːɡənaɪz] *vt* réorganiser.
rep [rep] *n Fam* représentant, -ante *mf* de
commerce.
repaid [riː'peɪd] *see* **repay**.
repair [rɪ'peər] *vt* réparer; – *n* réparation *f*;
beyond r. irréparable; **in good/bad r.** en
bon/mauvais état; **'road under r.'** *Aut*
'travaux'; **r. man** réparateur *m*; **r. woman**
réparatrice *f*.
reparation [repə'reɪʃ(ə)n] *n* réparation *f* (**for**
de); *pl Mil Hist* réparations *fpl*.
repartee [repɑː'tiː] *n* (*sharp reply*) repartie *f*.
repatriate [riː'pætrɪeɪt] *vt* rapatrier.
repay [riː'peɪ] *vt* (*pt & pp* **repaid**) (*pay back*)
rembourser; (*kindness*) payer de retour;
(*reward*) récompenser (**for** de). ◆—**ment** *n*
remboursement *m*; récompense *f*.
repeal [rɪ'piːl] *vt* (*law*) abroger; – *n* abroga-
tion *f*.
repeat [rɪ'piːt] *vt* répéter (**that** que); (*promise, threat*) réitérer; (*class*) *Sch* redoubler;
to r. oneself *or* **itself** se répéter; – *vi*
répéter; **to r. on s.o.** (*of food*) *Fam* revenir à

qn; – *n TV Rad* rediffusion *f*; – *a* (*performance*) deuxième. ◆—**ed** *a* répété;
(*efforts*) renouvelés. ◆—**edly** *adv* à
maintes reprises.
repel [rɪ'pel] *vt* (-ll-) repousser. ◆**repellent**
a repoussant; **insect r.** insectifuge *m*.
repent [rɪ'pent] *vi* se repentir (**of** de).
◆**repentance** *n* repentir *m*. ◆**repentant**
a repentant.
repercussion [riːpə'kʌʃ(ə)n] *n* répercussion
f.
repertoire ['repətwɑː] *n Th & Fig* répertoire *m*. ◆**repertory** *n Th & Fig* répertoire
m; **r. (theatre)** théâtre *m* de répertoire.
repetition [repɪ'tɪʃ(ə)n] *n* répétition *f*.
◆**repetitious** *a*, ◆**re'petitive** *a* (*speech
etc*) répétitif.
replace [rɪ'pleɪs] *vt* (*take the place of*)
remplacer (**by, with** par); (*put back*) remettre, replacer; (*receiver*) *Tel* raccrocher.
◆—**ment** *n* remplacement *m* (**of** de);
(*person*) remplaçant, -ante *mf*; (*machine
part*) pièce *f* de rechange.
replay ['riːpleɪ] *n Sp* match *m* rejoué;
(instant *or* **action) r.** *TV* répétition *f* immé-
diate (au ralenti).
replenish [rɪ'plenɪʃ] *vt* (*refill*) remplir (de
nouveau) (**with** de); (*renew*) renouveler.
replete [rɪ'pliːt] *a* **r. with** rempli de; **r. (with
food)** rassasié.
replica ['replɪkə] *n* copie *f* exacte.
reply [rɪ'plaɪ] *vti* répondre; – *n* réponse *f*; **in
r.** en réponse (**to** à).
report [rɪ'pɔːt] *n* (*account*) rapport *m*; (*of
meeting*) compte rendu *m*; *Journ TV Rad*
reportage *m*; *Pol* enquête *f*; *Sch Met* bulletin *m*; (*rumour*) rumeur *f*; (*of gun*) détonation *f*; – *vt* (*give account of*) rapporter,
rendre compte de; (*announce*) annoncer
(**that** que); (*notify*) signaler (**to** à);
(*denounce*) dénoncer (**to** à); (*event*) *Journ*
faire un reportage sur; – *vi* faire un
rapport *or Journ* un reportage (**on** sur); (*go*)
se présenter (**to** à, **to s.o.** chez qn, **for work**
au travail). ◆—**ed** *a* (*speech*) *Gram* indirect; **it is r. that** on dit que; **r. missing** porté
disparu. ◆—**edly** *adv* à ce qu'on dit.
◆—**ing** *n Journ* reportage *m*. ◆—**er** *n*
reporter *m*.
repose [rɪ'pəʊz] *n Lit* repos *m*.
repossess [riːpə'zes] *vt Jur* reprendre
possession de.
reprehensible [reprɪ'hensəb(ə)l] *a* répréhensible.
represent [reprɪ'zent] *vt* représenter.
◆**represen'tation** *n* représentation *f*; *pl*
(*complaints*) remontrances *fpl*. ◆**repre-**

sentative a représentatif (**of** de); − n représentant, -ante mf; *Pol Am* député m.

repress [rɪ'pres] vt réprimer; (*feeling*) refouler. ◆**repressive** a répressif.

reprieve [rɪ'priːv] n *Jur* sursis m; *Fig* répit m, sursis m; − vt accorder un sursis or *Fig* un répit à.

reprimand ['reprɪmɑːnd] n réprimande f; − vt réprimander.

reprint ['riːprɪnt] n (*reissue*) réimpression f; − vt réimprimer.

reprisal [rɪ'praɪz(ə)l] n **reprisals** représailles fpl; **in r. for** en représailles de.

reproach [rɪ'prəʊtʃ] n (*blame*) reproche m; (*shame*) honte f; **beyond r.** sans reproche; − vt reprocher (**s.o. for sth** qch à qn). ◆**reproachful** a réprobateur. ◆**reproachfully** adv d'un ton or d'un air réprobateur.

reproduce [riːprə'djuːs] vt reproduire; − vi *Biol Bot* se reproduire. ◆**reproduction** n (*of sound etc*) & *Biol Bot* reproduction f. ◆**reproductive** a reproducteur.

reptile ['reptaɪl] n reptile m.

republic [rɪ'pʌblɪk] n république f. ◆**republican** a & n républicain, -aine (*mf*).

repudiate [rɪ'pjuːdɪeɪt] vt (*offer*) repousser; (*accusation*) rejeter; (*spouse, idea*) répudier.

repugnant [rɪ'pʌgnənt] a répugnant; **he's r. to me** il me répugne. ◆**repugnance** n répugnance f (**for** pour).

repulse [rɪ'pʌls] vt repousser. ◆**repulsion** n répulsion f. ◆**repulsive** a repoussant.

reputable ['repjʊtəb(ə)l] a de bonne réputation. ◆**re'pute** n réputation f; **of r.** de bonne réputation. ◆**re'puted** a réputé (**to be** pour être). ◆**re'putedly** adv à ce qu'on dit.

reputation [repjʊ'teɪʃ(ə)n] n réputation f; **to have a r. for frankness/etc** avoir la réputation d'être franc/etc.

request [rɪ'kwest] n demande f (**for** de); **on r.** sur demande; **on s.o.'s r.** à la demande de qn; **by popular r.** à la demande générale; **r. stop** (*for bus*) arrêt m facultatif; − vt demander (**from** or **of s.o.** à qn, **s.o. to do** à qn de faire).

requiem ['rekwɪəm] n requiem m inv.

requir/e [rɪ'kwaɪər] vt (*necessitate*) demander; (*demand*) exiger; (*of person*) avoir besoin de (*qch, qn*); (*staff*) rechercher; **to r. sth of s.o.** (*order*) exiger qch de qn; **to r. s.o. to do** exiger de qn qu'il fasse; (*ask*) demander à qn de faire; **if required** s'il le faut. ◆**—ed** a requis, exigé. ◆**—ement** n

(*need*) exigence f; (*condition*) condition f (requise).

requisite ['rekwɪzɪt] **1** a nécessaire. **2** n (*for travel etc*) article m; **toilet requisites** articles mpl or nécessaire m de toilette.

requisition [rekwɪ'zɪʃ(ə)n] vt réquisitionner; − n réquisition f.

reroute [riː'ruːt] vt (*aircraft etc*) dérouter.

rerun ['riːrʌn] n *Cin* reprise f; *TV* rediffusion f.

resale ['riːseɪl] n revente f.

resat [riː'sæt] see **resit**.

rescind [rɪ'sɪnd] vt *Jur* annuler; (*law*) abroger.

rescu/e ['reskjuː] vt (*save*) sauver; (*set free*) délivrer (**from** de); − n (*action*) sauvetage m (**of** de); (*help, troops etc*) secours mpl; **to go/etc to s.o.'s r.** aller/etc au secours de qn; **to the r.** à la rescousse; − a (*team, operation*) de sauvetage. ◆**—er** n sauveteur m.

research [rɪ'sɜːtʃ] n recherches fpl (**on, into** sur); **some r.** de la recherche; **a piece of r.** (*work*) un travail de recherche; − vi faire des recherches (**on, into** sur). ◆**—er** n chercheur, -euse mf.

resemble [rɪ'zemb(ə)l] vt ressembler à. ◆**resemblance** n ressemblance f (**to** avec).

resent [rɪ'zent] vt (*anger*) s'indigner de, ne pas aimer; (*bitterness*) éprouver de l'amertume à l'égard de; **I r. that** ça m'indigne. ◆**resentful** a **to be r.** éprouver de l'amertume. ◆**resentment** n amertume f, ressentiment m.

reserv/e [rɪ'zɜːv] **1** vt (*room, decision etc*) réserver; (*right*) se réserver; (*one's strength*) ménager; − n (*reticence*) réserve f. **2** n (*stock, land*) réserve f; **r.** (*player*) *Sp* remplaçant, -ante mf; **the r.** *Mil* la réserve; **the reserves** (*troops*) *Mil* les réserves fpl; **nature r.** réserve f naturelle; **in r.** en réserve; **r. tank** *Av Aut* réservoir m de secours. ◆**—ed** a (*person, room*) réservé. ◆**reser'vation** n **1** (*doubt etc*) réserve f; (*booking*) réservation f. **2** (*land*) *Am* réserve f; **central r.** (*on road*) terre-plein m.

reservoir ['rezəvwɑːr] n réservoir m.

resettle [riː'set(ə)l] vt (*refugees*) implanter.

reshape [riː'ʃeɪp] vt (*industry etc*) réorganiser.

reshuffle [riː'ʃʌf(ə)l] n (**cabinet**) **r.** *Pol* remaniement m (ministériel); − vt *Pol* remanier.

reside [rɪ'zaɪd] vi résider. ◆**'residence** n (*home*) résidence f; (*of students*) foyer m; **in r.** (*doctor*) sur place; (*students on campus*) sur le campus, (*in halls of residence*) rentrés. ◆**'resident** n habitant, -ante mf; (of hotel) pensionnaire mf; (foreigner) résident, -ente mf; – a résidant, qui habite sur place; (population) fixe; (correspondent) permanent; **to be r. in London** résider à Londres. ◆**resi'dential** a (neighbourhood) résidentiel.

residue ['rezidjuː] n résidu m. ◆**re'sidual** a résiduel.

resign [ri'zain] vt (right, claim) abandonner; **to r. (from) one's job** démissionner; **to r. oneself to sth/to doing** se résigner à qch/à faire; – vi démissionner (**from** de). ◆**—ed** a résigné. ◆**resig'nation** n (from job) démission f; (attitude) résignation f.

resilient [ri'ziliənt] a élastique; (person) Fig résistant. ◆**resilience** n élasticité f; Fig résistance f.

resin ['rezin] n résine f.

resist [ri'zist] vt (attack etc) résister à; **to r. doing sth** s'empêcher de faire qch; **she can't r. cakes** elle ne peut pas résister devant les gâteaux; **he can't r. her** (indulgence) il ne peut rien lui refuser; (charm) il ne peut pas résister à son charme; – vi résister. ◆**resistance** n résistance f (**to** à). ◆**resistant** a résistant (**to** à); **r. to** Med rebelle à.

resit [riː'sit] vt (pt & pp resat, pres p resitting) (exam) repasser.

resolute ['rezəluːt] a résolu. ◆**—ly** adv résolument. ◆**reso'lution** n résolution f.

resolve [ri'zɒlv] vt résoudre (**to do** de faire, **that** que); – n résolution f. ◆**—ed** a résolu (**to do** à faire).

resonant ['rezənənt] a (voice) résonnant; **to be r. with** résonner de. ◆**resonance** n résonance f.

resort [ri'zɔːt] **1** n (recourse) recours m (**to** à); **as a last r.** en dernier ressort; – vi **to r. to s.o.** avoir recours à qn; **to r. to doing** en venir à faire; **to r. to drink** se rabattre sur la boisson. **2** n (holiday) r. station f de vacances; **seaside/ski r.** station f balnéaire/de ski.

resound [ri'zaʊnd] vi résonner (**with** de); Fig avoir du retentissement. ◆**—ing** a (success, noise) retentissant.

resource [ri'sɔːs, ri'zɔːs] n (expedient, recourse) ressource f; pl (wealth etc) ressources fpl. ◆**resourceful** a (person, scheme) ingénieux. ◆**resourcefulness** n ingéniosité f, ressource f.

respect [ri'spekt] n respect m (**for** pour, de); (aspect) égard m; **in r. of, with r. to** en ce qui concerne; **with all due r.** sans vouloir vous vexer; – vt respecter. ◆**respecta'bility** n

respectabilité f. ◆**respectable** a (honourable, sizeable) respectable; (satisfying) honnête; (clothes, behaviour) convenable. ◆**respectably** adv (to dress etc) convenablement; (rather well) passablement. ◆**respectful** a respectueux (**to** envers, **of** de). ◆**respectfully** adv respectueusement.

respective [ri'spektiv] a respectif. ◆**—ly** adv respectivement.

respiration [respi'reiʃ(ə)n] n respiration f.

respite ['respait] n répit m.

respond [ri'spɒnd] vi répondre (**to** à); **to r. to treatment** Med réagir positivement au traitement. ◆**response** n réponse f; **in p.** to en réponse à.

responsible [ri'spɒnsəb(ə)l] a responsable (**for** de, **to s.o.** devant qn); (job) à responsabilités; **who's r. for...?** qui est (le) responsable de...? ◆**responsi'bility** n responsabilité f. ◆**responsibly** adv de façon responsable.

responsive [ri'spɒnsiv] a (reacting) qui réagit bien; (alert) éveillé; (attentive) qui fait attention; **r. to** (kindness) sensible à; (suggestion) réceptif à. ◆**—ness** n (bonne) réaction f.

rest [rest] n (repose) repos m; (support) support m; **to have** or **take a r.** se reposer; **to set** or **put s.o.'s mind at r.** tranquilliser qn; **to come to r.** (of ball etc) s'immobiliser; (of bird, eyes) se poser (**on** sur); **r. home** maison f de repos; **r. room** Am toilettes fpl; – vi (relax) se reposer; (be buried) reposer; **to r. on** (of roof, argument) reposer sur; **I won't r. till** je n'aurai de repos que (+ sub); **to be resting on** (of hand etc) être posé sur; **a resting place** un lieu de repos; – vt (eyes etc) reposer; (horse etc) laisser reposer; (lean) poser, appuyer (**on** sur); (base) fonder. ◆**restful** a reposant.

rest [rest] n (remainder) reste m (**of** de); **the r.** (others) les autres mfpl; **the r. of the men**/etc les autres hommes/etc; – vi (remain) **it rests with you to do** il vous incombe de faire; **r. assured** soyez assuré (**that** que).

restaurant ['restərɒnt] n restaurant m.

restitution [resti'tjuːʃ(ə)n] n (for damage) Jur réparation f; **to make r. of** restituer.

restive ['restiv] a (person, horse) rétif.

restless ['restləs] a agité. ◆**—ly** adv avec agitation. ◆**—ness** n agitation f.

restore [ri'stɔːr] vt (give back) rendre (**to** à); (order, right) Jur rétablir; (building, painting) restaurer; (to life or power) ramener (qn) (**to** à).

restrain [rɪ'streɪn] vt (person, emotions) retenir, maîtriser; (crowd) contenir; (limit) limiter; **to r. s.o. from doing** retenir qn de faire; **to r. oneself** se maîtriser. ◆—**ed** a (feelings) contenu; (tone) mesuré. ◆**restraint** n (moderation) retenue f, mesure f; (restriction) contrainte f.

restrict [rɪ'strɪkt] vt limiter, restreindre (**to** à). ◆—**ed** a (space, use) restreint; (sale) contrôlé. ◆**restriction** n restriction f, limitation f. ◆**restrictive** a restrictif.

result [rɪ'zʌlt] n (outcome, success) résultat m; **as a r.** en conséquence; **as a r. of** par suite de; – vi résulter (**from** de); **to r. in** aboutir à.

resume [rɪ'zjuːm] vti (begin or take again) reprendre; **to r. doing** se remettre à faire. ◆**resumption** n reprise f.

résumé ['rezjuːmeɪ] n (summary) résumé m; Am curriculum vitae m inv.

resurface [riː'sɜːfɪs] vt (road) refaire le revêtement de.

resurgence [rɪ'sɜːdʒəns] n réapparition f.

resurrect [rezə'rekt] vt (custom, hero) Pej ressusciter. ◆**resurrection** n résurrection f.

resuscitate [rɪ'sʌsɪteɪt] vt Med réanimer.

retail ['riːteɪl] n (vente f au) détail m; – a (price, shop etc) de détail; – vi se vendre (au détail); – vt vendre (au détail), détailler; – adv (to sell) au détail. ◆—**er** n détaillant, -ante mf.

retain [rɪ'teɪn] vt (hold back, remember) retenir; (freshness, hope etc) conserver. ◆**retainer** n (fee) avance f, acompte m. ◆**retention** n (memory) mémoire f. ◆**retentive** a (memory) fidèle.

retaliate [rɪ'tælɪeɪt] vi riposter (**against s.o.** contre qn, **against an attack** à une attaque). ◆**retali'ation** n riposte f, représailles fpl; **in r. for** en représailles de.

retarded [rɪ'tɑːdɪd] a (mentally) r. arriéré.

retch [retʃ] vi avoir un or des haut-le-cœur.

rethink [riː'θɪŋk] vt (pt & pp rethought) repenser.

reticent ['retɪsənt] a réticent. ◆**reticence** n réticence f.

retina ['retɪnə] n Anat rétine f.

retir/e [rɪ'taɪər] 1 vi (from work) prendre sa retraite; – vt mettre à la retraite. 2 vi (withdraw) se retirer (**from, to** à); (go to bed) aller se coucher. ◆—**ed** a (having stopped working) retraité. ◆—**ing** a 1 (age) de la retraite. 2 (reserved) réservé. ◆**retirement** n retraite f; **r. age** âge m de la retraite.

retort [rɪ'tɔːt] vt rétorquer; – n réplique f.

retrace [riː'treɪs] vt (past event) se

remémorer, reconstituer; **to r. one's steps** revenir sur ses pas, rebrousser chemin.

retract [rɪ'trækt] vt (statement etc) rétracter; – vi (of person) se rétracter. ◆**retraction** n (of statement) rétractation f.

retrain [riː'treɪn] vi se recycler; – vt recycler. ◆—**ing** n recyclage m.

retread ['riːtred] n pneu m rechapé.

retreat [rɪ'triːt] n (withdrawal) retraite f; (place) refuge m; – vi se retirer (**from** de); Mil battre en retraite.

retrial [riː'traɪəl] n Jur nouveau procès m.

retribution [retrɪ'bjuːʃ(ə)n] n châtiment m.

retrieve [rɪ'triːv] vt (recover) récupérer; (rescue) sauver (**from** de); (loss, error) réparer; (honour) rétablir. ◆**retrieval** n récupération f; **information r.** recherche f documentaire. ◆**retriever** n (dog) chien m d'arrêt.

retro- ['retrəʊ] pref rétro-. ◆**retro'active** a rétroactif.

retrograde ['retrəgreɪd] a rétrograde.

retrospect ['retrəspekt] n **in r.** rétrospectivement. ◆**retro'spective 1** a (law, effect) rétroactif. **2** n (of film director, artist) rétrospective f.

return [rɪ'tɜːn] vi (come back) revenir; (go back) retourner; (go back home) rentrer; **to r. to** (subject) revenir à; – vt (give back) rendre; (put back) remettre; (bring back) & Fin rapporter; (send back) renvoyer; (greeting) répondre à; (candidate) Pol élire; – n retour m; (yield) Fin rapport m; pl (profits) Fin bénéfices mpl; **the r. to school** la rentrée (des classes); **r. (ticket)** (billet m d')aller et retour m; **tax r.** déclaration f de revenus; **many happy returns (of the day)!** bon anniversaire!; **in r.** (exchange) en échange (**for** de); – a (trip, flight etc) (de) retour; **r. match** match m retour. ◆—**able** a (bottle) consigné.

reunion [riː'juːnɪən] n réunion f. ◆**reu'nite** vt réunir.

rev [rev] n Aut Fam tour m; **r. counter** compte-tours m inv; – vt (-vv-) **to r. (up)** (engine) Fam faire ronfler.

revamp [riː'væmp] vt (method, play etc) Fam remanier.

reveal [rɪ'viːl] vt (make known) révéler (**that** que); (make visible) laisser voir. ◆—**ing** a (sign etc) révélateur.

revel ['rev(ə)l] vi (-ll-) faire la fête; **to r. in sth** se délecter de qch. ◆**revelling** n, ◆**revelry** n festivités fpl. ◆**reveller** n noceur, -euse mf.

revenge [rɪ'vendʒ] n vengeance f; Sp revanche f; **to have** or **get one's r.** se venger (on s.o. de qn, **on s.o. for sth** de qch sur qn); **in r.** pour se venger; – *vt* venger.

revenue ['revənjuː] *n* revenu *m*.

reverberate [rɪ'vɜːbəreɪt] *vi* (*of sound*) se répercuter.

revere [rɪ'vɪər] *vt* révérer. ◆**'reverence** *n* révérence *f*. ◆**'reverend** *a* (*father*) Rel révérend; – *n* **R. Smith** (*Anglican*) le révérend Smith; (*Catholic*) l'abbé *m* Smith; (*Jewish*) le rabbin Smith. ◆**'reverent** *a* respectueux.

reverse [rɪ'vɜːs] *a* contraire; (*order, image*) inverse; **r. side** (*of coin etc*) revers *m*; (*of paper*) verso *m*; – *n* contraire *m*; (*of coin, fabric etc*) revers *m*; (*of paper*) verso *m*; **in r. (gear)** *Aut* en marche arrière; – *vt* (*situation*) renverser; (*order, policy*) inverser; (*decision*) annuler; (*bucket etc*) retourner; **to r. the charges** *Tel* téléphoner en PCV; – *vti* **to r. (the car)** faire marche arrière; **to r. in/out** rentrer/sortir en marche arrière; **reversing light** phare *m* de recul. ◆**reversal** *n* renversement *m*; (*of policy, situation, opinion*) revirement *m*; (*of fortune*) revers *m*. ◆**reversible** *a* (*fabric etc*) réversible.

revert [rɪ'vɜːt] *vi* **to r. to** revenir à.

review [rɪ'vjuː] **1** *vt* (*troops, one's life*) passer en revue; (*situation*) réexaminer; (*book*) faire la critique de; – *n* revue *f*; (*of book*) critique *f*. **2** *n* (*magazine*) revue *f*. ◆**—er** *n* critique *m*.

revile [rɪ'vaɪl] *vt* injurier.

revise [rɪ'vaɪz] *vt* (*opinion, notes, text*) réviser; – *vi* (*for exam*) réviser (**for** pour). ◆**revision** *n* révision *f*.

revitalize [riː'vaɪt(ə)laɪz] *vt* revitaliser.

revive [rɪ'vaɪv] *vt* (*unconscious person, memory, conversation*) ranimer; (*dying person*) réanimer; (*custom, plan, fashion*) ressusciter; (*hope, interest*) faire renaître; – *vi* (*of unconscious person*) reprendre connaissance; (*of country, dying person*) ressusciter; (*of hope, interest*) renaître. ◆**revival** *n* (*of custom, business, play*) reprise *f*; (*of country*) essor *m*; (*of faith, fashion, theatre*) renouveau *m*.

revoke [rɪ'vəuk] *vt* (*decision*) annuler; (*contract*) Jur révoquer.

revolt [rɪ'vəult] *n* révolte *f*; – *vt* (*disgust*) révolter; – *vi* (*rebel*) se révolter (**against** contre). ◆**—ing** *a* dégoûtant; (*injustice*) révoltant.

revolution [revə'luːʃ(ə)n] *n* révolution *f*. ◆**revolutionary** *a* & *n* révolutionnaire (*mf*). ◆**revolutionize** *vt* révolutionner.

revolv/e [rɪ'vɒlv] *vi* tourner (**around** autour

de). ◆**—ing** **r. chair** fauteuil *m* pivotant; **r. door(s)** (*porte f à*) tambour *m*.

revolver [rɪ'vɒlvər] *n* revolver *m*.

revue [rɪ'vjuː] *n* (*satirical*) Th revue *f*.

revulsion [rɪ'vʌlʃ(ə)n] *n* **1** (*disgust*) dégoût *m*. **2** (*change*) revirement *m*.

reward [rɪ'wɔːd] *n* récompense *f* (**for** de); – *vt* récompenser (**s.o. for sth** qn de *or* pour qch). ◆**—ing** *a* qui (en) vaut la peine; (*satisfying*) satisfaisant; (*financially*) rémunérateur.

rewind [riː'waɪnd] *vt* (*pt & pp* **rewound**) (*tape*) réembobiner.

rewire [riː'waɪər] *vt* (*house*) refaire l'installation électrique de.

rewrite [riː'raɪt] *vt* (*pt* **rewrote**, *pp* **rewritten**) récrire; (*edit*) réécrire.

rhapsody ['ræpsədɪ] *n* rhapsodie *f*.

rhetoric ['retərɪk] *n* rhétorique *f*. ◆**rhe-'torical** *a* (*question*) de pure forme.

rheumatism ['ruːmətɪz(ə)m] *n* Med rhumatisme *m*; **to have r.** avoir des rhumatismes. ◆**rheu'matic** *a* (*pain*) rhumatismal; (*person*) rhumatisant.

rhinoceros [raɪ'nɒsərəs] *n* rhinocéros *m*.

rhubarb ['ruːbɑːb] *n* rhubarbe *f*.

rhyme [raɪm] *n* rime *f*; (*poem*) vers *mpl*; – *vi* rimer.

rhythm ['rɪð(ə)m] *n* rythme *m*. ◆**rhythmic(al)** *a* rythmique.

rib [rɪb] *n* Anat côte *f*.

ribald ['rɪb(ə)ld] *a* Lit grivois.

ribbon ['rɪbən] *n* ruban *m*; **to tear to ribbons** mettre en lambeaux.

rice [raɪs] *n* riz *m*. ◆**ricefield** *n* rizière *f*.

rich [rɪtʃ] *a* (**-er, -est**) riche (**in** en); (*profits*) gros; – *n* **the r.** les riches *mpl*. ◆**riches** *npl* richesses *fpl*. ◆**richly** *adv* (*dressed, illustrated etc*) richement; (*deserved*) amplement. ◆**richness** *n* richesse *f*.

rick [rɪk] *vt* **to r. one's back** se tordre le dos.

rickety ['rɪkɪtɪ] *a* (*furniture*) branlant.

ricochet ['rɪkəʃeɪ] *vi* ricocher; – *n* ricochet *m*.

rid [rɪd] *vt* (*pt & pp* **rid**, *pres p* **ridding**) débarrasser (**of** de); **to get r. of, r. oneself of** se débarrasser de. ◆**riddance** *n* **good r.!** Fam bon débarras!

ridden ['rɪd(ə)n] *see* ride.

-ridden ['rɪd(ə)n] *suffix* **debt-r.** criblé de dettes; **disease-r.** en proie à la maladie.

riddle ['rɪd(ə)l] **1** *n* (*puzzle*) énigme *f*. **2** *vt* cribler (**with** de); **riddled with** (*bullets, holes, mistakes*) criblé de; (*criminals*) plein de; (*corruption*) en proie à.

rid/e [raɪd] *n* (*on bicycle, by car etc*) promenade *f*; (*distance*) trajet *m*; (*in taxi*) course *f*; (*on merry-go-round*) tour *m*; **to go for a (car) r.** faire une promenade (en voiture); **to give s.o. a r.** *Aut* emmener qn en voiture; **to have a r. on** (*bicycle*) monter sur; **to take s.o. for a r.** (*deceive*) *Fam* mener qn en bateau; − *vi* (*pt* **rode**, *pp* **ridden**) aller (à bicyclette, à moto, à cheval *etc*) (**to** à); (*on horse*) *Sp* monter (à cheval); **to be riding in a car** être en voiture; **to r. up** (*of skirt*) remonter; − *vt* (*a particular horse*) monter; (*distance*) faire (à cheval *etc*); **to r. a horse or horses** (*go riding*) *Sp* monter à cheval; **I was riding (on) a bike/donkey** j'étais à bicyclette/à dos d'âne; **to know how to r. a bike** savoir faire de la bicyclette; **to r. a bike to** aller à bicyclette à; **may I r. your bike?** puis-je monter sur ta bicyclette?; **to r. s.o.** (*annoy*) *Am Fam* harceler qn. ◆**—ing** *n* (*horse*) **r.** équitation *f*; **r. boots** bottes *fpl* de cheval. ◆**—er** *n* **1** (*on horse*) cavalier, -ière *mf*; (*cyclist*) cycliste *mf*. **2** (*to document*) *Jur* annexe *f*.

ridge [rɪdʒ] *n* (*of roof, mountain*) arête *f*, crête *f*.

ridicule ['rɪdɪkjuːl] *n* ridicule *m*; **to hold up to r.** tourner en ridicule; **object of r.** objet *m* de risée; − *vt* tourner en ridicule, ridiculiser. ◆**ri'diculous** *a* ridicule.

rife [raɪf] *a* (*widespread*) répandu.

riffraff ['rɪfræf] *n* racaille *f*.

rifle ['raɪf(ə)l] **1** *n* fusil *m*, carabine *f*. **2** *vt* (*drawers, pockets etc*) vider.

rift [rɪft] *n* (*crack*) fissure *f*; (*in party*) *Pol* scission *f*; (*disagreement*) désaccord *m*.

rig [rɪg] **1** *n* (*oil*) **r.** derrick *m*; (*at sea*) plate-forme *f* pétrolière. **2** *vt* (*-gg-*) (*result, election etc*) *Pej* truquer; **to r. up** (*equipment*) installer; (*meeting etc*) *Fam* arranger. **3** *vt* (*dress*) *Fam* habiller. ◆**r.-out** *n Fam* tenue *f*.

right¹ [raɪt] **1** *a* (*correct*) bon, exact, juste; (*fair*) juste; (*angle*) droit; **to be r.** (*of person*) avoir raison (**to do** de faire); **it's the r. road** c'est la bonne route, c'est bien la route; **the r. time** l'heure exacte; **the clock's r.** la pendule est à l'heure; **at the r. time** au bon moment; **he's the r. man** c'est l'homme qu'il faut; **the r. thing to do** la meilleure chose à faire; **it's not r. to steal** ce n'est pas bien de voler; **it doesn't look r.** ça ne va pas; **to put r.** (*error*) rectifier; (*fix*) arranger; **to put s.o. r.** (*inform*) éclairer qn, détromper qn; **r.!** bien!; **that's r.** c'est ça, c'est bien, c'est exact; − *adv* (*straight*) (tout) droit; (*completely*) tout à fait; (*correctly*) juste; (*well*) bien; **she did r.** elle a bien fait; **r. round** tout autour (**sth** de qch);

r. behind juste derrière; **r. here** ici même; **r. away, r. now** tout de suite; **R. Honourable** *Pol* Très Honorable; − *n* **to be in the r.** avoir raison; **r. and wrong** le bien et le mal; − *vt* (*error, wrong, car*) redresser. **2** all **r.** *a* (*satisfactory*) bien *inv*; (*unharmed*) sain et sauf; (*undamaged*) intact; (*without worries*) tranquille; **it's all r.** ça va; **it's all r. now** (*fixed*) ça marche maintenant; **I'm all r.** (*healthy*) je vais bien, ça va; − *adv* (*well*) bien; **all r.!, r. you are!** (*yes*) d'accord!; **I got your letter all r.** j'ai bien reçu ta lettre. ◆**rightly** *adv* bien, correctement; (*justifiably*) à juste titre; **r. or wrongly** à tort ou à raison.

right² [raɪt] *a* (*hand, side etc*) droit; − *adv* à droite; − *n* droite *f*; **on** *or* **to the r.** à droite (**of** de). ◆**r.-hand** *a* à *or* de droite; **on the r.-hand side** à droite (**of** de); **r.-hand man** bras *m* droit. ◆**r.-'handed** *a* (*person*) droitier. ◆**r.-wing** *a Pol* de droite.

right³ [raɪt] *n* (*claim, entitlement*) droit *m* (**to do** de faire); **to have a r. to sth** avoir droit à qch; **he's famous in his own r.** il est lui-même célèbre; **r. of way** *Aut* priorité *f*; **human rights** les droits de l'homme.

righteous ['raɪtʃəs] *a* (*person*) vertueux; (*cause, indignation*) juste.

rightful ['raɪtfəl] *a* légitime. ◆**—ly** *adv* légitimement.

rigid ['rɪdʒɪd] *a* rigide. ◆**ri'gidity** *n* rigidité *f*. ◆**rigidly** *adv* (*opposed*) rigoureusement (**to** à).

rigmarole ['rɪgmərəʊl] *n* (*process*) procédure *f* compliquée.

rigour ['rɪgər] *n* rigueur *f*. ◆**rigorous** *a* rigoureux.

rile [raɪl] *vt* (*annoy*) *Fam* agacer.

rim [rɪm] *n* (*of cup etc*) bord *m*; (*of wheel*) jante *f*.

rind [raɪnd] *n* (*of cheese*) croûte *f*; (*of melon, lemon*) écorce *f*; (*of bacon*) couenne *f*.

ring¹ [rɪŋ] *n* anneau *m*; (*on finger*) anneau *m*, (*with stone*) bague *f*; (*of people, chairs*) cercle *m*; (*of smoke, for napkin*) rond *m*; (*gang*) bande *f*; (*at circus*) piste *f*; *Boxing* ring *m*; (*burner on stove*) brûleur *m*; **diamond r.** bague *f* de diamants; **to have rings under one's eyes** avoir les yeux cernés; **r. road** route *f* de ceinture; (*motorway*) périphérique *m*; − *vt* **to r.** (*round*) (*surround*) entourer (**with** de); (*item on list etc*) entourer d'un cercle. ◆**ringleader** *n Pej* (*of gang*) chef *m* de bande; (*of rebellion etc*) meneur, -euse *mf*.

ring² [rɪŋ] *n* (*sound*) sonnerie *f*; **there's a r. on sonne**; **to give s.o. a r.** (*phone call*) passer un coup de fil à qn; **a r. of** (*truth*) *Fig* l'accent *m* de; – *vi* (*pt* **rang,** *pp* **rung**) (*of bell, person etc*) sonner; (*of sound, words*) retentir; **to r. (up)** *Tel* téléphoner; **to r. back** *Tel* rappeler; **to r. for s.o.** sonner qn; **to r. off** *Tel* raccrocher; **to r. out** (*of bell*) sonner; (*of sound*) retentir; – *vt* sonner; **to r. s.o. (up)** *Tel* téléphoner à qn; **to r. s.o. back** *Tel* rappeler qn; **to r. the bell** sonner; **to r. the doorbell** sonner à la porte; **that rings a bell** *Fam* ça me rappelle quelque chose; **to r. in** (*the New Year*) carillonner. ◆—**ing** *a* **r. tone** *Tel* tonalité *f*; – *n* (*of bell*) sonnerie *f*; **a r. in one's ears** un bourdonnement dans les oreilles.

ringlet ['rɪŋlɪt] *n* (*curl*) anglaise *f*.

rink [rɪŋk] *n* (*ice-skating*) patinoire *f*; (*roller-skating*) skating *m*.

rinse [rɪns] *vt* rincer; **to r. one's hands** se passer les mains à l'eau; (*remove soap*) se rincer les mains; **to r. out** rincer; – *n* rinçage *m*; (*hair colouring*) shampooing *m* colorant; **to give sth a r.** rincer qch.

riot ['raɪət] *n* (*uprising*) émeute *f*; (*demonstration*) manifestation *f* violente; **a r. of colour** *Fig* une orgie de couleurs; **to run r.** (*of crowd*) se déchaîner; **the r. police** = les CRS *mpl*; – *vi* (*rise up*) faire une émeute; (*fight*) se bagarrer. ◆—**ing** *n* émeutes *fpl*; bagarres *fpl*. ◆—**er** *n* émeutier, -ière *mf*; (*demonstrator*) manifestant, -ante *mf* violent(e). ◆**riotous** *a* (*crowd etc*) tapageur; **r. living** vie *f* dissolue.

rip [rɪp] *vt* (-**pp**-) déchirer; **to r. off** *or* **out** arracher; **to r. off** *Fam* (*deceive*) rouler; (*steal*) *Am* voler; **to r. up** déchirer; – *vi* (*of fabric*) se déchirer; – *n* déchirure *f*; **it's a r.-off** *Fam* c'est du vol organisé.

ripe [raɪp] *a* (-**er,** -**est**) mûr; (*cheese*) fait. ◆**ripen** *vti* mûrir. ◆**ripeness** *n* maturité *f*.

ripple ['rɪp(ə)l] *n* (*on water*) ride *f*; (*of laughter*) *Fig* cascade *f*; – *vi* (*of water*) se rider.

ris/e [raɪz] *vi* (*pt* **rose,** *pp* **risen**) (*get up from chair or bed*) se lever; (*of temperature, balloon, price etc*) monter, s'élever; (*in society*) s'élever; (*of hope*) grandir; (*of sun, curtain, wind*) se lever; (*of dough*) lever; **to r. in price** augmenter de prix; **to r. to the surface** remonter à la surface; **the river rises in . . .** le fleuve prend sa source dans . . . ; **to r. (up)** (*rebel*) se soulever (*against* contre); **to r. to power** accéder au pouvoir; **to r. from the dead** ressusciter; – *n* (*of sun, curtain*) lever *m*; (*in pressure, price etc*) hausse *f* (**in** de); (*in river*) crue *f*; (*of leader*) *Fig* ascension *f*; (*of industry, technology*)

essor *m*; (*to power*) accession *f*; (*slope in ground*) éminence *f*; (*pay*) **r.** augmentation *f* (de salaire); **to give r. to** donner lieu à. ◆—**ing** *n* (*of curtain*) lever *m*; (*of river*) crue *f*; (*revolt*) soulèvement *m*; – *a* (*sun*) levant; (*number*) croissant; (*tide*) montant; (*artist etc*) d'avenir; **the r. generation** la nouvelle génération; **r. prices** la hausse des prix. ◆—**er** *n* **early r.** lève-tôt *mf inv*; **late r.** lève-tard *mf inv*.

risk [rɪsk] *n* risque *m* (**of doing** de faire); **at r.** (*person*) en danger; (*job*) menacé; **at your own r.** à tes risques et périls; – *vt* (*one's life, an accident etc*) risquer; **she won't r. leaving** (*take the risk*) elle ne se risquera pas à partir; **let's r. it** risquons le coup. ◆**riski-ness** *n* risques *mpl*. ◆**risky** *a* (-**ier,** -**iest**) (*full of risk*) risqué.

rissole ['rɪsəʊl] *n Culin* croquette *f*.

rite [raɪt] *n* rite *m*; **the last rites** *Rel* les derniers sacrements *mpl*. ◆**ritual** *a & n* rituel (*m*).

ritzy ['rɪtsɪ] *a* (-**ier,** -**iest**) *Fam* luxueux, classe *inv*.

rival ['raɪv(ə)l] *a* (*firm etc*) rival; (*forces, claim etc*) opposé; – *n* rival, -ale *mf*; – *vt* (-**ll**-, *Am* -**l**-) (*compete with*) rivaliser avec (**in** de); (*equal*) égaler (**in** en). ◆**rivalry** *n* rivalité *f* (**between** entre).

river ['rɪvər] *n* (*small*) rivière *f*; (*major, flowing into sea*) & *Fig* fleuve *m*; **the R. Thames** la Tamise; – *a* (*port etc*) fluvial; **r. bank** rive *f*. ◆**riverside** *a & n* (**by the**) **r.** au bord de l'eau.

rivet ['rɪvɪt] *n* (*pin*) rivet *m*; – *vt* riveter; (*eyes*) *Fig* fixer. ◆—**ing** *a* (*story etc*) fascinant.

Riviera [rɪvɪ'eərə] *n* **the (French) R.** la Côte d'Azur.

road [rəʊd] *n* route *f* (**to** qui va à); (*small*) chemin *m*; (*in town*) rue *f*; (*roadway*) chaussée *f*; (*path*) *Fig* voie *f*, chemin *m*, route *f* (**to** de); **the Paris r.** la route de Paris; **across** *or* **over the r.** (*building etc*) en face; **by r.** par la route; **get out of the r.!** ne reste pas sur la chaussée!; – *a* (*map, safety*) routier; (*accident*) de la route; (*sense*) de la conduite; **r. hog** *Fam* chauffard *m*; **r. sign** panneau *m* (routier *or* de signalisation); **r. works** travaux *mpl*. ◆**roadblock** *n* barrage *m* routier. ◆**roadside** *a & n* (**by the**) **r.** au bord de la route. ◆**roadway** *n* chaussée *f*. ◆**roadworthy** *a* (*vehicle*) en état de marche.

roam [rəʊm] *vt* parcourir; – *vi* errer, rôder; **to r. (about) the streets** (*of child etc*) traîner dans les rues.

roar [rɔːr] *vi* hurler; (*of lion, wind, engine*) rugir; (*of thunder*) gronder; **to r. with laughter** éclater de rire; **to r. past** (*of truck etc*) passer dans un bruit de tonnerre; – *vt* **to r. (out)** hurler; – *n* hurlement *m*; rugissement *m*; grondement *m*. ◆—**ing** *n* = roar *n*; – *a* **a r. fire** une belle flambée; **a r. success** un succès fou; **to do a r. trade** vendre beaucoup (**in** de).

roast [rəʊst] *vt* rôtir; (*coffee*) griller; – *vi* (*of meat*) rôtir; **we're roasting here** *Fam* on rôtit ici; – *n* (*meat*) rôti *m*; – *a* (*chicken etc*) rôti; **r. beef** rosbif *m*.

rob [rɒb] *vt* (**-bb-**) (*person*) voler; (*bank, house*) dévaliser; **to r. s.o. of sth** voler qch à qn; (*deprive*) priver qn de qch. ◆**robber** *n* voleur, -euse *mf*. ◆**robbery** *n* vol *m*; **it's daylight r.!** c'est du vol organisé; **armed r.** vol *m* à main armée.

robe [rəʊb] *n* (*of priest, judge etc*) robe *f*; (*dressing gown*) peignoir *m*.

robin ['rɒbɪn] *n* (*bird*) rouge-gorge *m*.

robot ['rəʊbɒt] *n* robot *m*.

robust [rəʊ'bʌst] *a* robuste.

rock¹ [rɒk] **1** *vt* (*baby, boat*) bercer, balancer; (*cradle, branch*) secouer; (*violently*) secouer; – *vi* (*sway*) se balancer; (*of building, ground*) trembler. **2** *n Mus* rock *m*. ◆—**ing** *n* (*horse, chair*) à bascule. ◆**rocky¹** *a* (**-ier, -iest**) (*furniture etc*) branlant.

rock² [rɒk] *n* (*substance*) roche *f*; (*boulder, rock face*) rocher *m*; (*stone*) *Am* pierre *f*; **a stick of r.** (*sweet*) un bâton de sucre d'orge; **r. face** paroi *f* rocheuse; **on the rocks** (*whisky*) avec des glaçons; (*marriage*) en pleine débâcle. ◆**r.-'bottom** *n* point *m* le plus bas; – *a* (*prices*) les plus bas, très bas. ◆**r.-climbing** *n* varappe *f*. ◆**rockery** *n* (*in garden*) rocaille *f*. ◆**rocky²** *a* (**-ier, -iest**) (*road*) rocailleux; (*hill*) rocheux.

rocket ['rɒkɪt] *n* fusée *f*; – *vi* (*of prices*) *Fig* monter en flèche.

rod [rɒd] *n* (*wooden*) baguette *f*; (*metal*) tige *f*; (*of curtain*) tringle *f*; (*for fishing*) canne *f* à pêche.

rode [rəʊd] *see* ride.

rodent ['rəʊdənt] *n* (*animal*) rongeur *m*.

rodeo ['rəʊdɪəʊ] *n* (*pl* -os) *Am* rodéo *m*.

roe [rəʊ] *n* **1** (*eggs*) œufs *mpl* de poisson. **2 r.** (*deer*) chevreuil *m*.

rogue [rəʊg] *n* (*dishonest*) crapule *f*; (*mischievous*) coquin, -ine *mf*. ◆**roguish** *a* (*smile etc*) coquin.

role [rəʊl] *n* rôle *m*.

roll [rəʊl] *n* (*of paper, film etc*) rouleau *m*; (*of bread*) petit pain *m*; (*of fat, flesh*) bourrelet *m*; (*of drum, thunder*) roulement *m*; (*of ship*) roulis *m*; (*list*) liste *f*; **to have a r. call** faire l'appel; **r. neck** (*neckline, sweater*) col *m* roulé; – *vi* (*of ball, ship etc*) rouler; (*of person, animal*) se rouler; **to be rolling in money** *or* **in it** *Fam* rouler sur l'or; **r. on tonight!** *Fam* vivement ce soir!; **to r. in** *Fam* (*flow in*) affluer; (*of person*) s'amener; **to r. over** (*many times*) se rouler; (*once*) se retourner; **to r. up** (*arrive*) *Fam* s'amener; **to r. (up) into a ball** (*of animal*) se rouler en boule; – *vt* rouler; **to r. down** (*blind*) baisser; (*slope*) descendre (en roulant); **to r. on** (*paint, stocking*) mettre; **to r. out** (*dough*) étaler; **to r. up** (*map, cloth*) rouler; (*sleeve, trousers*) retrousser. ◆—**ing** *a* (*ground, gait*) onduleux; **r. pin** rouleau *m* à pâtisserie. ◆—**er** *n* (*for hair, painting etc*) rouleau *m*; **r. coaster** (*at funfair*) montagnes *fpl* russes. ◆**roller-skate** *n* patin *m* à roulettes; – *vi* faire du patin à roulettes.

rollicking ['rɒlɪkɪŋ] *a* joyeux (et bruyant).

roly-poly [rəʊlɪ'pəʊlɪ] *a Fam* grassouillet.

Roman ['rəʊmən] **1** *a* & *n* romain, -aine *mf*. **2 R. Catholic** *a* & *n* catholique (*mf*).

romance [rəʊ'mæns] **1** *n* (*story*) histoire *f* or roman *m* d'amour; (*love*) amour *m*; (*affair*) aventure *f* amoureuse; (*charm*) poésie *f*. **2** *a* **R. language** langue *f* romane. ◆**romantic** *a* (*of love, tenderness etc*) romantique; (*fanciful, imaginary*) romanesque; – *n* (*person*) romantique *mf*. ◆**romantically** *adv* (*to behave*) de façon romantique. ◆**romanticism** *n* romantisme *m*.

Romania [rəʊ'meɪnɪə] *n* Roumanie *f*. ◆**Romanian** *a* & *n* roumain, -aine *mf*; – *n* (*language*) roumain *m*.

romp [rɒmp] *vi* s'ébattre (bruyamment); **to r. through** (*exam*) *Fig* avoir les doigts dans le nez; – *n* ébats *mpl*.

rompers ['rɒmpəz] *npl* (*for baby*) barboteuse *f*.

roof [ruːf] *n* (*of building, vehicle*) toit *m*; (*of tunnel, cave*) plafond *m*; **r. of the mouth** voûte *f* du palais; **r. rack** (*of car*) galerie *f*. ◆—**ing** *n* toiture *f*. ◆**rooftop** *n* toit *m*.

rook [rʊk] *n* **1** (*bird*) corneille *f*. **2** *Chess* tour *f*.

rookie ['rʊkɪ] *n* (*new recruit*) *Mil Fam* bleu *m*.

room [ruːm, rʊm] *n* **1** (*in house etc*) pièce *f*; (*bedroom*) chambre *f*; (*large, public*) salle *f*; **one's rooms** son appartement *m*; **in rooms** en meublé; **men's r., ladies' r.** *Am* toilettes *fpl*. **2** (*space*) place *f* (**for** pour); (*some*) **r.** de la place; **there's r. for doubt** le doute est permis; **no r. for** doubt aucun doute possible. ◆**rooming house** n Am maison f de rapport. ◆**roommate** n camarade mf de chambre. ◆**roomy** a (-ier, -iest) spacieux; (clothes) ample.

roost [ruːst] vi (of bird) percher; – n perchoir m.

rooster ['ruːstər] n coq m.

root [ruːt] **1** n (of plant, person etc) & Math racine f; Fig cause f, origine f; **to pull up by the root(s)** déraciner; **to take r.** (of plant) & Fig prendre racine; **to put down (new) roots** Fig s'enraciner; **r. cause** cause f première; – vt **to r. out** (destroy) extirper. **2** vi (of plant cutting) s'enraciner; **to r. about for** fouiller pour trouver. **3** vi **to r. for** (cheer, support) Fam encourager. ◆**—ed** a **deeply r.** bien enraciné (**in** dans); **r. to the spot** (immobile) cloué sur place. ◆**—less** a sans racines.

rope [rəʊp] n corde f; Nau cordage m; **to know the ropes** Fam être au courant; – vt (tie) lier; **to r. s.o. in** (force to help) Fam embrigader qn (**to do** pour faire); **to r. off** séparer (par une corde).

rop(e)y ['rəʊpɪ] a (-ier, -iest) Fam (thing) minable; (person) patraque.

rosary ['rəʊzərɪ] n Rel chapelet m.

rose¹ [rəʊz] n **1** (flower) rose f; (colour) rose m; **r. bush** rosier m. **2** (of watering can) pomme f. ◆**ro'sette** n Sp cocarde f; (rose-shaped) rosette f. ◆**rosy** a (-ier, -iest) (pink) rose; (future) Fig tout en rose.

rose² [rəʊz] see **rise**.

rosé ['rəʊzeɪ] n (wine) rosé m.

rosemary ['rəʊzmərɪ] n Bot Culin romarin m.

roster ['rɒstər] n (duty) **r.** liste f (de service).

rostrum ['rɒstrəm] n tribune f; Sp podium m.

rot [rɒt] n pourriture f; (nonsense) Fam inepties fpl; – vti (-tt-) **to r.** (**away**) pourrir.

rota ['rəʊtə] n liste f (de service).

rotate [rəʊ'teɪt] vi tourner; – vt faire tourner; (crops) alterner. ◆**'rotary** a rotatif; **r. airer** (washing line) séchoir m parapluie; – n (roundabout) Aut Am sens m giratoire. ◆**rotation** n rotation f; **in r.** à tour de rôle.

rote [rəʊt] n **by r.** machinalement.

rotten ['rɒt(ə)n] a (decayed, corrupt) pourri; (bad) Fam moche; (filthy) Fam sale; **to feel r.** (ill) être mal fichu. ◆**rottenness** n pourriture f. ◆**rotting** a (meat, fruit etc) qui pourrit.

rotund [rəʊ'tʌnd] a (round) rond; (plump) rondelet.

rouble ['ruːb(ə)l] n (currency) rouble m.

rouge [ruːʒ] n rouge m (à joues).

rough¹ [rʌf] a (-er, -est) (surface, task, manners) rude; (ground) inégal, accidenté; (rocky) rocailleux; (plank, bark) rugueux; (sound) âpre, rude; (coarse) grossier; (brutal) brutal; (weather, neighbourhood) mauvais; (sea) agité; (justice) sommaire; (diamond) brut; **a r. child** (unruly) un enfant dur; **to feel r.** (ill) Fam être mal fichu; **r. and ready** (conditions, solution) grossier (mais adéquat); – adv (to sleep, live) à la dure; (to play) brutalement; – n (violent man) Fam voyou m; – vt **to r. it** Fam vivre à la dure; **to r. up** (hair) ébouriffer; (person) Fam malmener. ◆**r.-and- 'tumble** n (fight) mêlée f; (of s.o.'s life) remue-ménage m inv. ◆**roughen** vt rendre rude. ◆**roughly¹** adv (not gently) rudement; (coarsely) grossièrement; (brutally) brutalement. ◆**roughness** n rudesse f; inégalité f; grossièreté f; brutalité f.

rough² [rʌf] a (-er, -est) (calculation, figure, terms etc) approximatif; **r. copy, r. draft** brouillon m; **r. paper** du papier brouillon; **r. guess, r. estimate** approximation f; **a r. plan** l'ébauche f d'un projet; – vt **to r. out** (plan) ébaucher. ◆**—ly²** adv (approximately) à peu (de choses) près.

roughage ['rʌfɪdʒ] n (in food) fibres fpl (alimentaires).

roulette [ruː'let] n roulette f.

round [raʊnd] **1** adv autour; **all r., right r.** tout autour; **to go r. to s.o.** passer chez qn; **to ask r.** inviter chez soi; **he'll be r.** il passera; **r. here** par ici; **the long way r.** le chemin le plus long; – prep autour de; **r. about** (house etc) autour de; (approximately) environ; **r. (about) midday** vers midi; **to go r.** (world) faire le tour de; (corner) tourner. **2** a (-er, -est) rond; **a r. trip** Am un (voyage) aller et retour. **3** n (slice) Culin tranche f; Sp Pol manche f; (of golf) partie f; Boxing round m; (of talks) série f; (of drinks, visits) tournée f; **one's round(s)** (of milkman etc) sa tournée; (of doctor) ses visites fpl; (of policeman) sa ronde; **delivery r.** livraisons fpl, tournée f; **r. of applause** salve f d'applaudissements; **r. of ammunition** cartouche f, balle f; – vt **to r. a corner** (in car) prendre un virage; **to r. off** (finish) terminer; **to r. up** (gather) rassembler; (figure) arrondir au chiffre supérieur. ◆**r.-'shouldered** a voûté, aux épaules rondes. ◆**rounded** a arrondi. ◆**rounders** npl Sp sorte de baseball. ◆**roundness** n rondeur f. ◆**roundup** n (of criminals) rafle f.

roundabout ['raʊndəbaʊt] **1** *a* indirect, détourné. **2** *n* (*at funfair*) manège *m*; (*junction*) *Aut* rond-point *m* (à sens giratoire).

rous/e [raʊz] *vt* éveiller; **roused (to anger)** en colère; **to r. to action** inciter à agir. ◆—**ing** *a* (*welcome*) enthousiaste; (*speech*) vibrant; (*music*) allègre.

rout [raʊt] *n* (*defeat*) déen déroute *f*; – *vt* mettre route.

route 1 [ruːt] *n* itinéraire *m*; (*of aircraft*) route *f*; **sea r.** route *f* maritime; **bus r.** ligne *f* d'autobus; – *vt* (*train etc*) fixer l'itinéraire de. **2** [raʊt] *n* (*delivery round*) *Am* tournée *f*.

routine [ruːˈtiːn] *n* routine *f*; **one's daily r.** (*in office etc*) son travail journalier; **the daily r.** (*monotony*) le train-train quotidien; – *a* (*inquiry, work etc*) de routine; *Pej* routinier.

rov/e [rəʊv] *vi* errer; – *vt* parcourir. ◆—**ing** *a* (*life*) nomade; (*ambassador*) itinérant.

row¹ [rəʊ] **1** *n* (*line*) rang *m*, rangée *f*; (*of cars*) file *f*; **two days in a r.** deux jours de suite *or* d'affilée. **2** *vi* (*in boat*) ramer; – *vt* (*boat*) faire aller à la rame; (*person*) transporter en canot; – *n* **to go for a r.** canoter; **r. boat** *Am* bateau *m* à rames.◆—**ing** *n* canotage *m*; *Sp* aviron *m*; **r. boat** bateau *m* à rames.

row² [raʊ] *n Fam* (*noise*) vacarme *m*; (*quarrel*) querelle *f*; – *vi Fam* se quereller (**with** avec).

rowdy ['raʊdɪ] *a* (**-ier, -iest**) chahuteur (et brutal); – *n* (*person*) *Fam* voyou *m*.

royal ['rɔɪəl] *a* royal; – *npl* **the royals** *Fam* la famille royale. ◆**royalist** *a* & *n* royaliste (*mf*). ◆**royally** *adv* (*to treat*) royalement. ◆**royalty 1** (*persons*) personnages *mpl* royaux. **2** *npl* (*from book*) droits *mpl* d'auteur; (*on oil, from patent*) royalties *fpl*.

rub [rʌb] *vt* (**-bb-**) frotter; (*polish*) astiquer; **to r. shoulders with** *Fig* coudoyer, côtoyer; **to r. away** (*mark*) effacer; (*tears*) essuyer; **to r. down** (*person*) frictionner; (*wood, with sandpaper*) poncer; **to r. in** (*cream*) *Med* faire pénétrer (en massant); **to r. it in** *Pej Fam* retourner le couteau dans la plaie; **to r. off** *or* **out** (*mark*) effacer; **rubbing alcohol** *Am* alcool *m* à 90°; – *vi* frotter; **to r. off** (*of mark*) partir; (*of manners etc*) déteindre (**on s.o.** sur qn); – *n* (*massage*) friction *f*; **to give sth a r.** frotter qch; (*polish*) astiquer qch.

rubber ['rʌbər] *n* (*substance*) caoutchouc *m*; (*eraser*) gomme *f*; (*contraceptive*) *Am Sl* capote *f*; **r. stamp** tampon *m*. ◆**r.-'stamp** *vt Pej* approuver (sans discuter). ◆**rubbery** *a* caoutchouteux.

rubbish ['rʌbɪʃ] **1** *n* (*refuse*) ordures *fpl*, détritus *mpl*; (*waste*) déchets *mpl*; (*junk*) saleté(s) *f*(*pl*); (*nonsense*) *Fig* absurdités *fpl*; **that's r.** (*absurd*) c'est absurde; (*worthless*) ça ne vaut rien; **r. bin** poubelle *f*; **r. dump** dépôt *m* d'ordures, décharge *f* (publique); (*in garden*) tas *m* d'ordures. **2** *vt* **to r. s.o./sth** (*criticize*) *Fam* dénigrer qn/qch. ◆**rubbishy** *a* (*book etc*) sans valeur; (*goods*) de mauvaise qualité.

rubble ['rʌb(ə)l] *n* décombres *mpl*.

ruble ['ruːb(ə)l] *n* (*currency*) rouble *m*.

ruby ['ruːbɪ] *n* (*gem*) rubis *m*.

rucksack ['rʌksæk] *n* sac *m* à dos.

ruckus ['rʌkəs] *n* (*uproar*) *Fam* chahut *m*.

rudder ['rʌdər] *n* gouvernail *m*.

ruddy [rʌdɪ] *a* (**-ier, -iest**) **1** (*complexion*) coloré. **2** (*bloody*) *Sl* fichu.

rude [ruːd] *a* (**-er, -est**) (*impolite*) impoli (**to** envers); (*coarse*) grossier; (*indecent*) indécent, obscène; (*shock*) violent. ◆—**ly** *adv* impoliment; grossièrement. ◆—**ness** *n* impolitesse *f*; grossièreté *f*.

rudiments ['ruːdɪmənts] *npl* rudiments *mpl*. ◆**rudi'mentary** *a* rudimentaire.

ruffian ['rʌfɪən] *n* voyou *m*.

ruffle ['rʌf(ə)l] **1** *vt* (*hair*) ébouriffer; (*water*) troubler; **to r. s.o.** (*offend*) froisser qn. **2** *n* (*frill*) ruche *f*.

rug [rʌg] *n* carpette *f*, petit tapis *m*; (*over knees*) plaid *m*; (*bedside*) **r.** descente *f* de lit.

rugby ['rʌgbɪ] *n* **r. (football)** rugby *m*. ◆**rugger** *n Fam* rugby *m*.

rugged ['rʌgɪd] *a* (*surface*) rugueux, rude; (*terrain, coast*) accidenté; (*person, features, manners*) rude; (*determination*) *Fig* farouche.

ruin ['ruːɪn] *n* (*destruction, rubble, building etc*) ruine *f*; **in ruins** (*building*) en ruine; – *vt* (*health, country, person etc*) ruiner; (*clothes*) abîmer; (*spoil*) gâter. ◆—**ed** *a* (*person, country etc*) ruiné; (*building*) en ruine. ◆**ruinous** *a* ruineux.

rul/e [ruːl] **1** *n* (*principle*) règle *f*; (*regulation*) règlement *m*; (*custom*) coutume *f*; (*authority*) autorité *f*; *Pol* gouvernement *m*; **against the rules** contraire à la règle; **as a (general) r.** en règle générale; **it's the** *or* **a r. that** il est de règle que (+ *sub*); – *vt* (*country*) *Pol* gouverner; (*decide*) *Jur Sp* décider (**that** que); **to r. s.o.** (*dominate*) mener qn; **to r. out** (*exclude*) exclure; – *vi* (*of monarch*) régner (**over** sur); (*of judge*) statuer (**against** contre, **on** sur). **2** *n* (*for measuring*) règle *f*. ◆—**ed** *a* (*paper*) réglé, ligné. ◆—**ing** *a* (*passion*) dominant;

(*class*) dirigeant; (*party*) *Pol* au pouvoir; − *n Jur Sp* décision *f*. ◆**ruler** *n* **1** (*of country*) *Pol* dirigeant, -ante *mf*; (*sovereign*) souverain, -aine *mf*. **2** (*measure*) règle *f*.

rum [rʌm] *n* rhum *m*.

Rumania [ruːˈmeɪnɪə] *see* **Romania**.

rumble [ˈrʌmb(ə)l] *vi* (*of train, thunder, gun*) gronder; (*of stomach*) gargouiller; − *n* grondement *m*; gargouillement *m*.

ruminate [ˈruːmɪneɪt] *vi* **to r. over** (*scheme etc*) ruminer.

rummage [ˈrʌmɪdʒ] *vi* **to r. (about)** farfouiller; **r. sale** (*used clothes etc*) *Am* vente *f* de charité.

rumour [ˈruːmər] *n* rumeur *f*, bruit *m*. ◆**rumoured** *a* **it is r. that** on dit que.

rump [rʌmp] *n* (*of horse*) croupe *f*; (*of fowl*) croupion *m*; **r. steak** rumsteck *m*.

rumple [ˈrʌmp(ə)l] *vt* (*clothes*) chiffonner.

run [rʌn] *n* (*running*) course *f*; (*outing*) tour *m*; (*journey*) parcours *m*, trajet *m*; (*series*) série *f*; (*period*) période *f*; *Cards* suite *f*; (*rush*) ruée *f* (on sur); (*trend*) tendance *f*; (*for skiing*) piste *f*; (*in cricket*) point *m*; **to go for a r.** courir, faire une course à pied; **on the r.** (*prisoner etc*) en fuite; **to have the r. of** (*house etc*) avoir à sa disposition; **in the long r.** avec le temps, à la longue; **the runs** *Med Fam* la diarrhée; − *vi* (*pt* ran, *pp* run, *pres p* running) courir; (*flee*) fuir; (*of curtain*) glisser; (*of river, nose, pen, tap*) couler; (*of colour in washing*) déteindre; (*of ink*) baver; (*melt*) fondre; (*of play, film*) se jouer; (*of contract*) être valide; (*last*) durer; (*pass*) passer; (*function*) marcher; (*tick over*) *Aut* tourner; (*of stocking*) filer; **to r. down/in/etc** descendre/entrer/etc en courant; **to r. for president** être candidat à la présidence; **to r. with blood** ruisseler de sang; **to r. between** (*of bus*) faire le service entre; **to go running** *Sp* faire du jogging; **the road runs to . . .** la route va à . . . ; **the river runs into the sea** le fleuve se jette dans la mer; **it runs into a hundred pounds** ça va chercher dans les cent livres; **it runs in the family** ça tient de famille; − *vt* (*race, risk*) courir; (*horse*) faire courir; (*temperature, errand*) faire; (*blockade*) forcer; (*machine*) faire fonctionner; (*engine*) *Aut* faire tourner; (*drive*) *Aut* conduire; (*furniture, goods*) transporter (**to** à); (*business, country etc*) diriger; (*courses, events*) organiser; (*film, play*) présenter; (*house*) tenir; (*article*) publier (on sur); (*bath*) faire couler; **to r. one's hand over** passer la main sur; **to r. one's eye over** jeter un coup d'œil à *or* sur; **to r. its course** (*of illness etc*) suivre son

cours; **to r. 5 km** *Sp* faire 5 km de course à pied; **to r. a car** avoir une voiture. ■ **to r. about** *vi* courir çà et là; (*gallivant*) se balader; **to r. across** *vt* (*meet*) tomber sur; **to r. along** *vi* **r. along!** filez!; **to r. away** *vi* (*flee*) s'enfuir, se sauver (**from** de); **to r. back** *vt* (*person*) *Aut* ramener (**to** à); **to r. down** *vt* (*pedestrian*) *Aut* renverser; (*belittle*) dénigrer; (*restrict*) limiter peu à peu. ◆**r.-ʹdown** *a* (*weak, tired*) *Med* à plat; (*district etc*) miteux; **to r. in** *vt* (*vehicle*) roder; **to r. in** (*of police*) *Fam* arrêter qn; **to r. into** *vt* (*meet*) tomber sur; (*crash into*) *Aut* percuter; **to r. into debt** s'endetter; **to r. off** *vt* (*print*) tirer; − *vi* (*flee*) s'enfuir; **to r. out** *vi* (*of stocks*) s'épuiser; (*of lease*) expirer; (*of time*) manquer; **to r. out of** (*time, money*) manquer de; **we've r. out of coffee** on n'a plus de café; − *vt* **to r. s.o. out of** (*chase*) chasser qn de; **to r. over** *vi* (*of liquid*) déborder; − *vt* (*kill pedestrian*) *Aut* écraser; (*knock down pedestrian*) *Aut* renverser; (*notes, text*) revoir; **to r. round** *vt* (*surround*) entourer; **to r. through** *vt* (*recap*) revoir; **to r. up** *vt* (*bill, debts*) laisser s'accumuler. ◆**r.-up** *n* **the r.-up to** (*elections etc*) la période qui précède. ◆**running** *n* course *f*; (*of machine*) fonctionnement *m*; (*of firm, country*) direction *f*; **to be in/out of the r.** être/ne plus être dans la course; − *a* (*commentary*) suivi; (*battle*) continuel; **r. water** eau *f* courante; **six days/etc r.** six jours/etc de suite; **r. costs** (*of factory*) frais *mpl* d'exploitation; (*of car*) dépenses *fpl* courantes. ◆**runner** *n Sp etc* coureur *m*; **r. bean** haricot *m* (grimpant). ◆**runner-ʹup** *n Sp* second, -onde *mf*. ◆**runny** *a* (-ier, -iest) *a* liquide; (*nose*) qui coule.

runaway [ˈrʌnəweɪ] *n* fugitif, -ive *mf*; − *a* (*car, horse*) emballé; (*lorry*) fou; (*wedding*) clandestin; (*victory*) qu'on remporte haut la main; (*inflation*) galopant.

rung[1] [rʌŋ] *n* (*of ladder*) barreau *m*.

rung[2] [rʌŋ] *see* **ring**[2].

run-of-the-mill [rʌnəvðəˈmɪl] *a* ordinaire.

runway [ˈrʌnweɪ] *n Av* piste *f*.

rupture [ˈrʌptʃər] *n Med* hernie *f*; **the r. of** (*breaking*) la rupture de; − *vt* rompre; **to r. oneself** se donner une hernie.

rural [ˈrʊərəl] *a* rural.

ruse [ruːz] *n* (*trick*) ruse *f*.

rush[1] [rʌʃ] *vi* (*move fast, throw oneself*) se précipiter, se ruer (**at** sur, **towards** vers); (*of blood*) affluer (**to** à); (*hurry*) se dépêcher (**to do** de faire); (*of vehicle*) foncer; **to r. out** partir en vitesse; − *vt* (*attack*) *Mil* foncer sur; **to r. s.o.** bousculer qn; **to r. s.o. to hospital** transporter qn d'urgence à l'hôpital; **to r. (through) sth** (*job, meal, order etc*) faire, manger, envoyer *etc* qch en vitesse; **to be rushed into** (*decision, answer etc*) être forcé à prendre, donner *etc*; – *n* ruée *f* (**for** vers, **on** sur); (*confusion*) bousculade *f*; (*hurry*) hâte *f*; (*of orders*) avalanche *f*; **to be in a r.** être pressé (**to do** de faire); **to leave/etc in a r.** partir/*etc* en vitesse; **the gold r.** la ruée vers l'or; **the r. hour** l'heure *f* d'affluence; **a r. job** un travail d'urgence.

rush² [rʌʃ] *n* (*plant*) jonc *m*.

rusk [rʌsk] *n* biscotte *f*.

russet ['rʌsɪt] *a* roux, roussâtre.

Russia ['rʌʃə] *n* Russie *f*. ◆**Russian** *a* & *n* russe (*mf*); – *n* (*language*) russe *m*.

rust [rʌst] *n* rouille *f*; – *vi* (se) rouiller. ◆**rustproof** *a* inoxydable. ◆**rusty** *a* (-ier, -iest) (*metal, athlete, memory etc*) rouillé.

rustic ['rʌstɪk] *a* rustique.

rustle ['rʌs(ə)l] **1** *vi* (*of leaves*) bruire; (*of skirt*) froufrouter; – *n* bruissement *m*; frou-frou *m*. **2** *vt* **to r. up** *Fam* (*prepare*) préparer; (*find*) trouver.

rut [rʌt] *n* ornière *f*; **to be in a r.** *Fig* être encroûté.

rutabaga [ruːtəˈbeɪɡə] *n* (*swede*) *Am* rutabaga *m*.

ruthless ['ruːθləs] *a* (*attack, person etc*) impitoyable, cruel; (*in taking decisions*) très ferme. ◆**—ness** *n* cruauté *f*.

rye [raɪ] *n* seigle *m*; **r. bread** pain *m* de

S

S, s [es] *n* S, s *m*.

Sabbath ['sæbəθ] *n* (*Jewish*) sabbat *m*; (*Christian*) dimanche *m*. ◆**sa'bbatical** *a* (*year etc*) *Univ* sabbatique.

sabotage ['sæbətɑːʒ] *n* sabotage *m*; – *vt* saboter. ◆**saboteur** [-'tɜːr] *n* saboteur, -euse *mf*.

sabre ['seɪbər] *n* (*sword*) sabre *m*.

saccharin ['sækərɪn] *n* saccharine *f*.

sachet ['sæʃeɪ] *n* (*of lavender etc*) sachet *m*; (*of shampoo*) dosette *f*.

sack [sæk] **1** *n* (*bag*) sac *m*. **2** *vt* (*dismiss*) *Fam* virer, renvoyer; – *n Fam* **to get the s.** se faire virer; **to give s.o. the s.** virer qn. **3** *vt* (*town etc*) saccager, mettre à sac. ◆**—ing** **1** (*cloth*) toile *f* à sac. **2** (*dismissal*) *Fam* renvoi *m*.

sacrament ['sækrəmənt] *n Rel* sacrement *m*.

sacred ['seɪkrɪd] *a* (*holy*) sacré.

sacrifice ['sækrɪfaɪs] *n* sacrifice *m*; – *vt* sacrifier (**to** à, **for sth/s.o.** pour qch/qn).

sacrilege ['sækrɪlɪdʒ] *n* sacrilège *m*. ◆**sacri'legious** *a* sacrilège.

sacrosanct ['sækrəʊsæŋkt] *a Iron* sacro-saint.

sad [sæd] *a* (**sadder, saddest**) triste. ◆**sadden** *vt* attrister. ◆**sadly** *adv* tristement; (*unfortunately*) malheureusement; (*very*) très. ◆**sadness** *n* tristesse *f*.

saddle ['sæd(ə)l] *n* selle *f*; **to be in the s.** (*in control*) *Fig* tenir les rênes; – *vt* (*horse*) seller; **to s. s.o. with** (*chore, person*) *Fam* coller à qn.

sadism ['seɪdɪz(ə)m] *n* sadisme *m*. ◆**sadist** *n* sadique *mf*. ◆**sa'distic** *a* sadique.

sae [eseɪˈiː] *abbr* = **stamped addressed envelope.**

safari [səˈfɑːrɪ] *n* safari *m*; **to be** *or* **go on s.** faire un safari.

safe¹ [seɪf] *a* (**-er, -est**) (*person*) en sécurité; (*equipment, toy, animal*) sans danger; (*place, investment, method*) sûr; (*bridge, ladder*) solide; (*prudent*) prudent; (*winner*) assuré, garanti; **s. (and sound)** sain et sauf; **it's s. to go out** on peut sortir sans danger; **the safest thing (to do) is** . . . le plus sûr est de . . . ; **s. from** à l'abri de; **to be on the s. side** pour plus de sûreté; **in s. hands** en mains sûres; **s. journey!** bon voyage! ◆**s.-'conduct** *n* sauf-conduit *m*. ◆**safe-'keeping** *n* **for s.** à garder en sécurité. ◆**safely** *adv* (*without mishap*) sans accident; (*securely*) en sûreté; (*without risk*) sans risque, sans danger. ◆**safety** *n* sécurité *f*; (*solidity*) solidité *f*; (*salvation*) salut *m*; – *a* (*belt, device, screen, margin*) de sécurité; (*pin, razor, chain, valve*) de sûreté; **s. precaution** mesure *f* de sécurité.

safe² [seɪf] *n* (*for money etc*) coffre-fort *m*.

safeguard ['seɪfɡɑːd] *n* sauvegarde *f* (**against** contre); – *vt* sauvegarder.

saffron ['sæfrən] n safran m.

sag [sæg] vi (-gg-) (of roof, ground) s'affaisser; (of cheeks) pendre; (of prices, knees) fléchir. ◆**sagging** a (roof, breasts) affaissé.

saga ['sɑːgə] n Liter saga f; (bad sequence of events) Fig feuilleton m.

sage [seɪdʒ] n 1 Bot Culin sauge f. 2 (wise man) sage m.

Sagittarius [sædʒɪ'teərɪəs] n (sign) le Sagittaire.

sago ['seɪgəʊ] n (cereal) sagou m.

Sahara [sə'hɑːrə] n the S. (desert) le Sahara.

said [sed] see say.

sail [seɪl] vi (navigate) naviguer; (leave) partir; Sp faire de la voile; (glide) Fig glisser; **to s. into port** entrer au port; **to s. round** (world, island etc) faire le tour de en bateau; **to s. through** (exam etc) Fig réussir haut la main; — vt (boat) piloter; (seas) parcourir; — n voile f; (trip) tour m en bateau; **to set s.** (of boat) partir (**for** à destination de). ◆**—ing** n navigation f; Sp voile f; (departure) départ m; (crossing) traversée f; **s. boat** voilier m. ◆**sailboard** n planche f (à voile). ◆**sailboat** n Am voilier m. ◆**sailor** n marin m, matelot m.

saint [seɪnt] n saint m, sainte f; **S. John** saint Jean; **s.'s day** Rel fête f (de saint). ◆**saintly** a (-ier, -iest) saint.

sake [seɪk] n **for my/your s.** pour moi/toi; **for your father's s.** pour (l'amour de) ton père; (just) **for the s. of eating/**etc simplement pour manger/etc; **for heaven's** or **God's s.** pour l'amour de Dieu.

salacious [sə'leɪʃəs] a obscène.

salad ['sæləd] n (dish of vegetables, fruit etc) salade f; **s. bowl** saladier m; **s. cream** mayonnaise f; **s. dressing** vinaigrette f.

salamander ['sæləmændər] n (lizard) salamandre f.

salami [sə'lɑːmɪ] n salami m.

salary ['sælərɪ] n (professional) traitement m; (wage) salaire m. ◆**salaried** a (person) qui perçoit un traitement.

sale [seɪl] n vente f; **sale(s)** (at reduced prices) Com soldes mpl; **in a** or **the s.**, Am **on s.** (cheaply) en solde; **on s.** (available) en vente; (up) **for s.** à vendre; **to put up for s.** mettre en vente; **s. price** Com prix m de solde; **sales check** or **slip** Am reçu m. ◆**saleable** a Com vendable. ◆**sales-clerk** n Am vendeur, -euse mf. ◆**salesman** n (pl -men) (in shop) vendeur m; (travelling) s. représentant m (de commerce). ◆**saleswoman** n (pl -women) vendeuse f; représentante f (de commerce).

salient ['seɪlɪənt] a (point, fact) marquant.

saliva [sə'laɪvə] n salive f. ◆**'salivate** vi saliver.

sallow ['sæləʊ] a (-er, -est) jaunâtre.

sally ['sælɪ] n Mil sortie f; — vi **to s. forth** sortir allégrement.

salmon ['sæmən] n saumon m.

salmonella [sælmə'nelə] n (poisoning) salmonellose f.

salon ['sælɒn] n **beauty/hairdressing s.** salon m de beauté/de coiffure.

saloon [sə'luːn] n Nau salon m; (car) berline f; (bar) Am bar m; **s. bar** (of pub) salle f chic.

salt [sɔːlt] n sel m; **bath salts** sels mpl de bain; — a (water, beef etc) salé; (mine) de sel; **s. free** sans sel; — vt saler. ◆**saltcellar** n, Am ◆**saltshaker** n salière f. ◆**salty** a (-ier, -iest) a salé.

salubrious [sə'luːbrɪəs] a salubre.

salutary ['sæljʊtərɪ] a salutaire.

salute [sə'luːt] n Mil salut m; (of guns) salve f; — vt (greet) & Mil saluer; — vi Mil faire un salut.

salvage ['sælvɪdʒ] n sauvetage m (of de); récupération f (of de); (saved goods) objets mpl sauvés; — vt (save) sauver (from de); (old iron etc to be used again) récupérer.

salvation [sæl'veɪʃ(ə)n] n salut m.

same [seɪm] a même; **the (very) s. house as** (exactement) la même maison que; — pron **the s.** le même, la même; **the s. (thing)** la même chose; **it's all the s. to me** ça m'est égal; **all** or **just the s.** tout de même; **to do the s.** en faire autant. ◆**—ness** n identité f; Pej monotonie f.

sampl/e ['sɑːmp(ə)l] n échantillon m; (of blood) prélèvement m; — vt (wine, cheese etc) déguster, goûter; (product, recipe etc) essayer; (army life etc) goûter de. ◆**—ing** n (of wine) dégustation f.

sanatorium [sænə'tɔːrɪəm] n sanatorium m.

sanctify ['sæŋktɪfaɪ] vt sanctifier. ◆**sanctity** n sainteté f. ◆**sanctuary** n Rel sanctuaire m; (refuge) & Pol asile m; (for animals) réserve f.

sanctimonious [sæŋktɪ'məʊnɪəs] a (person, manner) tartuffe.

sanction ['sæŋkʃ(ə)n] n (approval, punishment) sanction f; — vt (approve) sanctionner.

sand [sænd] n sable m; **the sands** (beach) la plage; — vt (road) sabler; **to s. (down)** (wood etc) poncer. ◆**sandbag** n sac m de sable. ◆**sandcastle** n château m de sable. ◆**sander** n (machine) ponceuse f. ◆**sandpaper** n papier m de verre; — vt

poncer. ◆**sandstone** n (*rock*) grès m.
◆**sandy** a (-ier, -iest) (*beach*) de sable;
(*road, ground*) sablonneux; (*water*)
sableux. 2 (*hair*) blond roux inv.

sandal ['sænd(ə)l] n sandale f.

sandwich ['sænwidʒ] 1 n sandwich m;
cheese/*etc* s. sandwich au fromage/*etc*. 2 vt
to s. (in) (*fit in*) intercaler; **sandwiched in
between** (*caught*) coincé entre.

sane [sein] a (-er, -est) (*person*) sain
(d'esprit); (*idea, attitude*) raisonnable.

sang [sæŋ] see sing.

sanguine ['sæŋgwin] a (*hopeful*) optimiste.

sanitarium [sæni'teəriəm] n Am sanatorium
m.

sanitary ['sænitəri] a (*fittings, conditions*)
sanitaire; (*clean*) hygiénique. ◆**sani-
'tation** n hygiène f (publique); (*plumbing
etc*) installations fpl sanitaires.

sanity ['sæniti] n santé f mentale; (*reason*)
raison f.

sank [sæŋk] see sink².

Santa Claus ['sæntəklɔːz] n le père Noël.

sap [sæp] 1 n Bot & Fig sève f. 2 vt (-pp-)
(*weaken*) miner (*énergie etc*).

sapphire ['sæfaiər] n (*jewel, needle*) saphir
m.

sarcasm ['sɑːkæz(ə)m] n sarcasme m.
◆**sar'castic** a sarcastique.

sardine [sɑː'diːn] n sardine f.

Sardinia [sɑː'diniə] n Sardaigne f.

sardonic [sɑː'dɒnik] a sardonique.

sash [sæʃ] n 1 (*on dress*) ceinture f; (*of
mayor etc*) écharpe f. 2 s. window fenêtre f à
guillotine.

sat [sæt] see sit.

Satan ['seit(ə)n] n Satan m. ◆**sa'tanic** a
satanique.

satchel ['sætʃ(ə)l] n cartable m.

satellite ['sætəlait] n satellite m; **s.** (*country*)
Pol pays m satellite.

satiate ['seiʃieit] vt rassasier.

satin ['sætin] n satin m.

satire ['sætaiər] n satire f (on contre).
◆**sa'tirical** a satirique. ◆**satirist** n
écrivain m satirique. ◆**satirize** vt faire la
satire de.

satisfaction [sætis'fækʃ(ə)n] n satisfaction
f. ◆**satis'factory** a satisfaisant. ◆**'satisfy**
vt satisfaire; (*persuade, convince*)
persuader (**that** que); (*demand, condition*)
satisfaire à; **to s. oneself as to/that**
s'assurer de/que; **satisfied with** satisfait de;
– vi donner satisfaction. ◆**'satisfying** a
satisfaisant; (*food, meal*) substantiel.

satsuma [sæt'suːmə] n (*fruit*) mandarine f.

saturate ['sætʃəreit] vt (*fill*) saturer (**with**
de); (*soak*) tremper. ◆**satu'ration** n saturation f.

Saturday ['sætədi] n samedi m.

sauce [sɔːs] n 1 sauce f; **tomato s.** sauce
tomate; **s. boat** saucière f. 2 (*cheek*) Fam
toupet m. ◆**saucy** a (-ier, -iest) (*cheeky*)
impertinent; (*smart*) Fam coquet.

saucepan ['sɔːspən] n casserole f.

saucer ['sɔːsər] n soucoupe f.

Saudi Arabia [saudiə'reibiə, Am sɔːdiə-
'reibiə] n Arabie f Séoudite.

sauna ['sɔːnə] n sauna m.

saunter ['sɔːntər] vi flâner.

sausage ['sɒsidʒ] n (*cooked, for cooking*)
saucisse f; (*precooked, dried*) saucisson m.

sauté ['səutei] a Culin sauté.

savage ['sævidʒ] a (*primitive*) sauvage;
(*fierce*) féroce; (*brutal, cruel*) brutal, sauvage; – n (*brute*) sauvage mf; – vt (*of
animal, critic etc*) attaquer (férocement).
◆**savagery** n (*cruelty*) sauvagerie f.

sav/e [seiv] 1 vt sauver (**from** de); (*keep*)
garder, réserver; (*money, time*) économiser,
épargner; (*stamps*) collectionner; (*prevent*)
empêcher (**from** de); (*problems, trouble*)
éviter; **that will s. him or her (the bother of)
going** ça lui évitera d'y aller; **to s. up**
(*money*) économiser; – vi **to s. (up)** faire
des économies (**for sth, to buy sth** pour
(s')acheter qch); – n Fb arrêt m. 2 prep
(*except*) sauf. ◆—**ing** n (*of time, money*)
économie f, épargne f (**of** de); (*rescue*)
sauvetage m; (*thrifty habit*) l'épargne f; pl
(*money*) économies fpl; **savings bank** caisse
f d'épargne. ◆**saviour** n sauveur m.

saveloy ['sævələi] n cervelas m.

savour ['seivər] n (*taste, interest*) saveur f; –
vt savourer. ◆**savoury** a (*tasty*)
savoureux; (*not sweet*) Culin salé; **not very
s.** (*neighbourhood*) Fig peu recommandable.

saw¹ [sɔː] n scie f; – vt (pt sawed, pp sawn or
sawed) scier; **to s. off** scier; **a sawn-off** or
Am **sawed-off shotgun** un fusil à canon scié.
◆**sawdust** n sciure f. ◆**sawmill** n scierie
f.

saw² [sɔː] see see¹.

saxophone ['sæksəfəun] n saxophone m.

say [sei] vt (pt & pp said [sed]) dire (**to** à, **that**
que); (*prayer*) faire, dire; (*of dial etc*)
marquer; **to s. again** répéter; **it is said that
. . .** on dit que . . . ; **what do you s. to a
walk?** que dirais-tu d'une promenade?;
(let's) s. tomorrow disons demain; **to s. the
least** c'est le moins que l'on puisse dire; **to
s. nothing of . . .** sans parler de . . . ; **that's
to s.** c'est-à-dire; – vi dire; **you don't s.!**

Fam sans blague!; **I s.!** dites donc!; **s.!** *Am Fam* dis donc!; − *n* **to have one's s.** dire ce que l'on a à dire, s'exprimer; **to have a lot of s.** avoir beaucoup d'influence; **to have no s.** ne pas avoir voix au chapitre (**in** pour). ◆**—ing** *n* proverbe *m*.

scab [skæb] *n* **1** *Med* croûte *f*. **2** (*blackleg*) *Fam* jaune *m*.

scaffold ['skæfəld] *n* échafaudage *m*; (*gallows*) échafaud *m*. ◆**—ing** *n* échafaudage *m*.

scald [skɔːld] *vt* (*burn, cleanse*) ébouillanter; (*sterilize*) stériliser; − *n* brûlure *f*.

scale [skeɪl] **1** *n* (*of map, wages etc*) échelle *f*; (*of numbers*) série *f*; *Mus* gamme *f*; **on a small/large s.** sur une petite/grande échelle; − *a* (*drawing*) à l'échelle; **s. model** modèle *m* réduit; − *vt* **to s. down** réduire (proportionnellement). **2** *n* (*on fish*) écaille *f*; (*dead skin*) *Med* squame *f*; (*on teeth*) tartre *m*; − *vt* (*teeth*) détartrer. **3** *vt* (*wall*) escalader.

scales [skeɪlz] *npl* (*for weighing*) balance *f*; (**bathroom**) **s.** pèse-personne *m*; (**baby**) **s.** pèse-bébé *m*.

scallion ['skæljən] *n* (*onion*) *Am* ciboule *f*.

scallop ['skɒləp] *n* coquille *f* Saint-Jacques.

scalp [skælp] *n* *Med* cuir *m* chevelu; − *vt* (*cut off too much hair from*) *Fig Hum* tondre (*qn*).

scalpel ['skælp(ə)l] *n* bistouri *m*, scalpel *m*.

scam [skæm] *n* (*swindle*) *Am Fam* escroquerie *f*.

scamp [skæmp] *n* coquin, -ine *mf*.

scamper ['skæmpər] *vi* **to s. off** *or* **away** détaler.

scampi ['skæmpɪ] *npl* gambas *fpl*.

scan [skæn] **1** *vt* (**-nn-**) (*look at briefly*) parcourir (des yeux); (*scrutinize*) scruter; (*poetry*) scander; (*of radar*) balayer. **2** *n* **to have a s.** (*of pregnant woman*) passer une échographie.

scandal ['skænd(ə)l] *n* (*disgrace*) scandale *m*; (*gossip*) médisances *fpl*; **to cause a s.** (*of film, book etc*) causer un scandale; (*of attitude, conduct*) faire (du) scandale. ◆**scandalize** *vt* scandaliser. ◆**scandalous** *a* scandaleux.

Scandinavia [skændɪ'neɪvɪə] *n* Scandinavie *f*. ◆**Scandinavian** *a & n* scandinave (*mf*).

scanner ['skænər] *n* (*device*) *Med* scanner *m*.

scant [skænt] *a* (*meal, amount*) insuffisant; **s. attention/regard** peu d'attention/de cas. ◆**scantily** *adv* insuffisamment; **s. dressed** à peine vêtu. ◆**scanty** *a* (**-ier, -iest**) insuffisant; (*bikini*) minuscule.

scapegoat ['skeɪpgəʊt] *n* bouc *m* émissaire.

scar [skɑːr] *n* cicatrice *f*; − *vt* (**-rr-**) marquer d'une cicatrice; *Fig* marquer.

scarce [skeəs] *a* (**-er, -est**) (*food, people, book etc*) rare; **to make oneself s.** se tenir à l'écart. ◆**scarcely** *adv* à peine. ◆**scarceness** *n*, ◆**scarcity** *n* (*shortage*) pénurie *f*; (*rarity*) rareté *f*.

scare [skeər] *n* peur *f*; **to give s.o. a s.** faire peur à qn; **bomb s.** alerte *f* à la bombe; − *vt* faire peur à; **to s. off** (*person*) faire fuir; (*animal*) effaroucher. ◆**scared** *a* effrayé; **to be s. (stiff)** avoir (très) peur. ◆**scarecrow** *n* épouvantail *m*. ◆**scaremonger** *n* alarmiste *mf*. ◆**scary** *a* (**-ier, -iest**) *Fam* qui fait peur.

scarf [skɑːf] *n* (*pl* **scarves**) (*long*) écharpe *f*; (*square, for women*) foulard *m*.

scarlet ['skɑːlət] *a* écarlate; **s. fever** scarlatine *f*.

scathing ['skeɪðɪŋ] *a* (*remark etc*) acerbe; **to be s. about** critiquer de façon acerbe.

scatter ['skætər] *vt* (*disperse*) disperser (*foule, nuages etc*); (*dot or throw about*) éparpiller; (*spread*) répandre; − *vi* (*of crowd*) se disperser. ◆**—ing** *n* **a s. of houses/etc** quelques maisons/etc dispersées. ◆**scatterbrain** *n* écervelé, -ée *mf*. ◆**scatty** *a* (**-ier, -iest**) *Fam* écervelé, farfelu.

scaveng/e ['skævɪndʒ] *vi* fouiller dans les ordures (**for** pour trouver). ◆**—er** *n* *Pej* clochard, -arde *mf* (qui fait les poubelles).

scenario [sɪ'nɑːrɪəʊ] *n* (*pl* **-os**) *Cin & Fig* scénario *m*.

scene [siːn] *n* (*setting, fuss*) & *Th* scène *f*; (*of crime, accident etc*) lieu *m*; (*situation*) situation *f*; (*incident*) incident *m*; (*view*) vue *f*; **behind the scenes** *Th & Fig* dans les coulisses; **on the s.** sur les lieux; **to make** *or* **create a s.** faire une scène (à qn). ◆**scenery** *n* paysage *m*, décor *m*; *Th* décor(s) *m*(*pl*). ◆**scenic** *a* (*beauty etc*) pittoresque.

scent [sent] *n* (*fragrance, perfume*) parfum *m*; (*animal's track*) & *Fig* piste *f*; − *vt* parfumer (**with** de); (*smell, sense*) flairer.

sceptic ['skeptɪk] *a & n* sceptique (*mf*). ◆**sceptical** *a* sceptique. ◆**scepticism** *n* scepticisme *m*.

sceptre ['septər] *n* sceptre *m*.

schedul/e ['ʃedjuːl, *Am* 'skedjʊl] *n* (*of work etc*) programme *m*; (*timetable*) horaire *m*; (*list*) liste *f*; **to be behind s.** (*of person, train*) avoir du retard; **to be on s.** (*on time*) être à l'heure; (*up to date*) être à jour; **ahead of s.** en avance; **according to s.** comme prévu; −

scheme 588 scout

vt (*plan*) prévoir; (*event*) fixer le programme *or* l'horaire de. ◆**—ed** *a* (*planned*) prévu; (*service, flight*) régulier; **she's s. to leave at 8** elle doit partir à 8 h.

schem/e [skiːm] *n* plan *m* (**to do** pour faire); (*idea*) idée *f*; (*dishonest trick*) combine *f*, manœuvre *f*; (*arrangement*) arrangement *m*; *– vi* manœuvrer. ◆**—ing** *a* intrigant; *– npl Pej* machinations *fpl.* ◆**—er** *n* intrigant, -ante *mf.*

schizophrenic [skɪtsəʊ'frenɪk] *a* & *n* schizophrène (*mf*).

scholar ['skɒlər] *n* érudit, -ite *mf*; (*specialist*) spécialiste *mf*; (*grant holder*) boursier, -ière *mf.* ◆**scholarly** *a* érudit. ◆**scholarship** *n* érudition *f*; (*grant*) bourse *f* (d'études). ◆**scho'lastic** *a* scolaire.

school [skuːl] *n* école *f*; (*teaching, lessons*) classe *f*; *Univ Am* faculté *f*; (*within university*) institut *m*, département *m*; **in** *or* **at s.** à l'école; **secondary s.,** *Am* **high s.** collège *m*, lycée *m*; **public s.** école *f* privée; *Am* école publique; **s. of motoring** auto-école *f*; **summer s.** cours *mpl* d'été *or* de vacances; *– a* (*year, equipment etc*) scolaire; (*hours*) de classe; **s. fees** frais *mpl* de scolarité. ◆**—ing** *n* (*learning*) instruction *f*; (*attendance*) scolarité *f*. ◆**schoolboy** *n* écolier *m.* ◆**schooldays** *npl* années *fpl* d'école. ◆**schoolgirl** *n* écolière *f.* ◆**schoolhouse** *n* école *f.* ◆**school-'leaver** *n* jeune *mf* qui a terminé ses études secondaires. ◆**schoolmaster** *n* (*primary*) instituteur *m*; (*secondary*) professeur *m.* ◆**schoolmate** *n* camarade *mf* de classe. ◆**schoolmistress** *n* institutrice *f*; professeur *m.* ◆**schoolteacher** *n* (*primary*) instituteur, -trice *mf*; (*secondary*) professeur *m.*

schooner ['skuːnər] *n Nau* goélette *f.*

science ['saɪəns] *n* science *f*; **to study s.** étudier les sciences; *– a* (*subject*) scientifique; (*teacher*) de sciences; **s. fiction** science-fiction *f.* ◆**scien'tific** *a* scientifique. ◆**scientist** *n* scientifique *mf.*

scintillating ['sɪntɪleɪtɪŋ] *a* (*conversation, wit*) brillant.

scissors ['sɪzəz] *npl* ciseaux *mpl*; **a pair of s.** une paire de ciseaux.

sclerosis [sklɪ'rəʊsɪs] *n Med* sclérose *f*; **multiple s.** sclérose en plaques.

scoff [skɒf] **1** *vt* **to s. at** se moquer de. **2** *vti* (*eat*) *Fam* bouffer.

scold [skəʊld] *vt* gronder, réprimander (**for doing** pour avoir fait). ◆**—ing** *n* réprimande *f.*

scone [skəʊn, skɒn] *n* petit pain *m* au lait.

scoop [skuːp] *n* (*shovel*) pelle *f* (à main);

(*spoon-shaped*) *Culin* cuiller *f*; *Journ* exclusivité *f*; **at one s.** d'un seul coup; *– vt* (*prizes*) rafler; **to s. out** (*hollow out*) (è)vider; **to s. up** ramasser (avec une pelle *or* une cuiller).

scoot [skuːt] *vi* (*rush, leave*) *Fam* filer.

scooter ['skuːtər] *n* (*child's*) trottinette *f*; (*motorcycle*) scooter *m.*

scope [skəʊp] *n* (*range*) étendue *f*; (*of mind*) envergure *f*; (*competence*) compétence(s) *f(pl)*; (*limits*) limites *fpl*; **s. for sth/for doing** (*opportunity*) des possibilités *fpl* de qch/de faire; **the s. of one's activity** le champ de ses activités.

scorch [skɔːtʃ] *vt* (*linen, grass etc*) roussir; *– n s.* (*mark*) brûlure *f* légère. ◆**—ing** *a* (*day*) torride; (*sun, sand*) brûlant. ◆**—er** *n Fam* journée *f* torride.

score[1] [skɔːr] *n Sp* score *m*; *Cards* marque *f*; *Mus* partition *f*; (*of film*) musique *f*; **to settle** *Fig* un compte à régler; **on that s.** (*in that respect*) à cet égard; *– vt* (*point, goal*) marquer; (*exam mark*) avoir; (*success*) remporter; *Mus* orchestrer; *– vi* marquer un point *or* un but; (*keep score*) marquer les points. ◆**scoreboard** *n Sp* tableau *m* d'affichage. ◆**scorer** *n Sp* marqueur *m.*

score[2] [skɔːr] *n* (*twenty*) vingt; **a s. of** une vingtaine de; **scores of** *Fig* un grand nombre de.

score[3] [skɔːr] *vt* (*cut*) rayer; (*paper*) marquer.

scorn [skɔːn] *vt* mépriser; *– n* mépris *m.* ◆**scornful** *a* méprisant; **to be s. of** mépriser. ◆**scornfully** *adv* avec mépris.

Scorpio ['skɔːpɪəʊ] *n* (*sign*) le Scorpion.

scorpion ['skɔːpɪən] *n* scorpion *m.*

Scot [skɒt] *n* Écossais, -aise *mf.* ◆**Scotland** *n* Écosse *f.* ◆**Scotsman** *n* (*pl* **-men**) Écossais *m.* ◆**Scotswoman** *n* (*pl* **-women**) Écossaise *f.* ◆**Scottish** *a* écossais.

scotch [skɒtʃ] **1** *a* **s. tape**® *Am* scotch® *m.* **2** *vt* (*rumour*) étouffer; (*attempt*) faire échouer.

Scotch [skɒtʃ] *n* (*whisky*) scotch *m.*

scot-free [skɒt'friː] *adv* sans être puni.

scoundrel ['skaʊndr(ə)l] *n* vaurien *m.*

scour ['skaʊər] *vt* (*pan*) récurer; (*streets etc*) *Fig* parcourir (**for** à la recherche de). ◆**—er** *n* tampon *m* à récurer.

scourge [skɜːdʒ] *n* fléau *m.*

scout [skaʊt] *n* (*soldier*) éclaireur *m*; **(boy) s.** scout *m*, éclaireur *m*; **girl s.** *Am* éclaireuse *f*; **s. camp** camp *m* scout. **2** *vi* **to**

s. round for (*look for*) chercher. ◆**—ing** *n* scoutisme *m*.

scowl [skaʊl] *vi* se renfrogner; **to s. at s.o.** regarder qn d'un air mauvais. ◆**—ing** *a* renfrogné.

scraggy ['skrægɪ] *a* (**-ier, -iest**) (*bony*) osseux, maigrichon; (*unkempt*) débraillé.

scram [skræm] *vi* (**-mm-**) *Fam* filer.

scramble ['skræmb(ə)l] **1** *vi* **to s. for** se ruer vers; **to s. up** (*climb*) grimper; **to s. through** traverser avec difficulté; − *n* ruée *f* (**for** vers). **2** *vt* (*egg, message*) brouiller.

scrap [skræp] **1** *n* (*piece*) petit morceau *m* (**of** de); (*of information, news*) fragment *m*; *pl* (*food*) restes *mpl*; **not a s. of** (*truth etc*) pas un brin de; **s. paper** (*papier m*) brouillon *m*. **2** *n* (*metal*) ferraille *f*; **to sell for s.** vendre à la casse; − *a* (*yard, heap*) de ferraille; **s. dealer, s. merchant** marchand *m* de ferraille; **s. iron** ferraille *f*; **on the s. heap** *Fig* au rebut; − *vt* (**-pp-**) envoyer à la ferraille; (*unwanted object, idea, plan*) *Fig* mettre au rancart. **3** *n* (*fight*) *Fam* bagarre *f*. ◆**scrapbook** *n* album *m* (*pour collages etc*).

scrap/e [skreɪp] *vt* racler, gratter; (*skin*) *Med* érafler; **to s. away** *or* **off** (*mud etc*) racler; **to s. together** (*money, people*) réunir (difficilement); − *vi* **to s. against** frotter contre; **to s. along** *Fig* se débrouiller; **to s. through** (*in exam*) réussir de justesse; − *n* raclement *m*; éraflure *f*; **to get into a s.** *Fam* s'attirer des ennuis. ◆**—ings** *npl* raclures *fpl*. ◆**—er** *n* racloir *m*.

scratch [skrætʃ] *n* (*mark, injury*) éraflure *f*; (*on glass*) rayure *f*; **to have a s.** (*scratch oneself*) *Fam* se gratter; **to start from s.** (re)partir de zéro; **to be/come up to s.** être/se montrer à la hauteur; − *vt* (*to relieve an itch*) gratter; (*skin, wall etc*) érafler; (*glass*) rayer; (*with claw*) griffer; (*one's name*) graver (**on** sur); − *vi* (*relieve an itch*) se gratter; (*of cat etc*) griffer; (*of pen*) gratter, accrocher.

scrawl [skrɔːl] *vt* griffonner; − *n* griffouillis *m*.

scrawny ['skrɔːnɪ] *a* (**-ier, -iest**) (*bony*) osseux, maigrichon.

scream [skriːm] *vti* crier, hurler; **to s. at s.o.** crier après qn; **to s. with pain/etc** hurler de douleur/etc; − *n* cri *m* (perçant).

screech [skriːtʃ] *vi* crier, hurler; (*of brakes*) hurler; − *n* cri *m*; hurlement *m*.

screen [skriːn] **1** *n* écran *m*; *Fig* masque *m*; (*folding*) s. paravent *m*. **2** *vt* (*hide*) cacher (**from s.o.** à qn); (*protect*) protéger (**from** de); (*a film*) projeter; (*visitors, documents*) filtrer; (*for cancer etc*) *Med* faire subir un test de dépistage à (*qn*) (**for** pour). ◆**—ing** *n* (*of film*) projection *f*; (*selection*) tri *m*; (*medical examination*) (test *m* de) dépistage *m*. ◆**screenplay** *n Cin* scénario *m*.

screw [skruː] *n* vis *f*; − *vt* visser (**to** à); **to s. down** *or* **on** visser; **to s. off** dévisser; **to s. up** (*paper*) chiffonner; (*eyes*) plisser; (*mess up*) *Sl* gâcher; **to s. one's face up** grimacer. ◆**screwball** *n* & *a Am Fam* cinglé, -ée (*mf*). ◆**screwdriver** *n* tournevis *m*. ◆**screwy** *a* (**-ier, -iest**) (*idea, person etc*) farfelu.

scribble ['skrɪb(ə)l] *vti* griffonner; − *n* griffonnage *m*.

scribe [skraɪb] *n* scribe *m*.

scrimmage ['skrɪmɪdʒ] *n Fb Am* mêlée *f*.

script [skrɪpt] *n* (*of film*) scénario *m*; (*of play*) texte *m*; (*in exam*) copie *f*. ◆**scriptwriter** *n Cin* scénariste *mf*, dialoguiste *mf*; *TV Rad* dialoguiste *mf*.

Scripture ['skrɪptʃər] *n Rel* Écriture *f* (sainte).

scroll [skrəʊl] *n* rouleau *m* (de parchemin); (*book*) manuscrit *m*.

scrooge [skruːdʒ] *n* (*miser*) harpagon *m*.

scroung/e [skraʊndʒ] *vt* (*meal*) se faire payer (**off** *or* **from s.o.** par qn); (*steal*) piquer (**off** *or* **from s.o.** à qn); **to s. money off** *or* **from** taper; − *vi* vivre en parasite; (*beg*) quémander; **to s. around for** *Pej* chercher. ◆**—er** *n* parasite *m*.

scrub [skrʌb] **1** *vt* (**-bb-**) frotter, nettoyer (à la brosse); (*pan*) récurer; (*cancel*) *Fig* annuler; **to s. out** (*erase*) *Fig* effacer; − *vi* (*scrub floors*) frotter les planchers; **scrubbing brush** brosse *f* dure; − *n* **to give sth a s.** frotter qch; **s. brush** *Am* brosse *f* dure. **2** *n* (*land*) broussailles *fpl*.

scruff [skrʌf] *n* **1 by the s. of the neck** par la peau du cou. **2** (*person*) *Fam* individu *m* débraillé. ◆**scruffy** *a* (**-ier, -iest**) (*untidy*) négligé; (*dirty*) malpropre.

scrum [skrʌm] *n Rugby* mêlée *f*.

scrumptious ['skrʌmpʃəs] *a Fam* super bon, succulent.

scruple ['skruːp(ə)l] *n* scrupule *m*. ◆**scrupulous** *a* scrupuleux. ◆**scrupulously** *adv* (*conscientiously*) scrupuleusement; (*completely*) absolument.

scrutinize ['skruːtɪnaɪz] *vt* scruter. ◆**scrutiny** *n* examen *m* minutieux.

scuba ['skjuːbə, *Am* 'skuːbə] *n* scaphandre *m* autonome; **s. diving** la plongée sous-marine.

scuff [skʌf] *vt* **to s. (up)** (*scrape*) érafler.

scuffle ['skʌf(ə)l] *n* bagarre *f*.

scullery ['skʌlərɪ] *n* arrière-cuisine *f.*

sculpt [skʌlpt] *vti* sculpter. ◆**sculptor** *n* sculpteur *m.* ◆**sculpture** *n* (*art, object*) sculpture *f;* – *vti* sculpter.

scum [skʌm] *n* 1 (*on liquid*) écume *f.* 2 *Pej* (*people*) racaille *f;* (*person*) salaud *m;* **the s. of** (*society etc*) la lie de.

scupper ['skʌpər] *vt* (*plan*) *Fam* saboter.

scurf [skɜːf] *n* pellicules *fpl.*

scurrilous ['skʌrɪləs] *a* (*criticism, attack*) haineux, violent et grossier.

scurry ['skʌrɪ] *vi* (*rush*) se précipiter, courir; **to s. off** décamper.

scuttle ['skʌt(ə)l] 1 *vt* (*ship*) saborder. 2 *vi* **to s. off** filer.

scythe [saɪð] *n* faux *f.*

sea [siː] *n* mer *f;* (**out**) **at s.** en mer; **by s.** par mer; **by** *or* **beside the s.** au bord de la mer; **to be all at s.** *Fig* nager complètement; – *a* (*level, breeze*) de la mer; (*water, fish*) de mer; (*air, salt*) marin; (*battle, power*) naval; (*route*) maritime; **s. bed, s. floor** fond *m* de la mer; **s. lion** (*animal*) otarie *f.* ◆**seaboard** *n* littoral *m.* ◆**seafarer** *n* marin *m.* ◆**seafood** *n* fruits *mpl* de mer. ◆**seafront** *n* front *m* de mer. ◆**seagull** *n* mouette *f.* ◆**seaman** *n* (*pl* -**men**) marin *m.* ◆**seaplane** *n* hydravion *m.* ◆**seaport** *n* port *m* de mer. ◆**seashell** *n* coquillage *m.* ◆**seashore** *n* bord *m* de la mer. ◆**seasick** *a* **to be s.** avoir le mal de mer. ◆**seasickness** *n* mal *m* de mer. ◆**seaside** *n* bord *m* de la mer; – *a* (*town, holiday*) au bord de la mer. ◆**seaway** *n* route *f* maritime. ◆**seaweed** *n* algue(s) *f(pl).* ◆**seaworthy** *a* (*ship*) en état de naviguer.

seal [siːl] 1 *n* (*animal*) phoque *m.* 2 *n* (*mark, design*) sceau *m;* (*on letter*) cachet *m* (*de cire*); (*putty for sealing*) joint *m;* – *vt* (*document, container*) sceller; (*with wax*) cacheter; (*stick down*) coller; (*with putty*) boucher; (*s.o.'s fate*) *Fig* décider de; **to s. off** (*room etc*) interdire l'accès de; **to s. off a house/district** (*of police, troops*) boucler une maison/un quartier.

seam [siːm] *n* (*in cloth etc*) couture *f;* (*of coal, quartz etc*) veine *f.*

seamy ['siːmɪ] *a* (-**ier, -iest**) **the s. side** le côté peu reluisant (**of** de).

séance ['seɪɑːns] *n* séance *f* de spiritisme.

search [sɜːtʃ] *n* (*quest*) recherche *f* (**for** de); (*of person, place*) fouille *f;* **in s. of** à la recherche de; **s. party** équipe *f* de secours; – *vt* (*person, place*) fouiller (**for** pour trouver); (*study*) examiner (*documents etc*); **to s. (through) one's papers/***etc* **for sth** chercher qch dans ses papiers/*etc;* – *vi* chercher; **to s. for sth** chercher qch. ◆—**ing** *a* (*look*) pénétrant; (*examination*) minutieux. ◆**searchlight** *n* projecteur *m.*

season ['siːz(ə)n] 1 *n* saison *f;* **the festive s.** la période des fêtes; **in the peak s.**, **in (the) high s.** en pleine *or* haute saison; **in the low** *or* **off s.** en basse saison; **a Truffaut s.** *Cin* une rétrospective Truffaut; **s. ticket** carte *f* d'abonnement. 2 *vt* (*food*) assaisonner; **highly seasoned** (*dish*) relevé. ◆—**ed** *a* (*worker*) expérimenté; (*soldier*) aguerri. ◆—**ing** *n* *Culin* assaisonnement *m.* ◆**seasonable** *a* (*weather*) de saison. ◆**seasonal** *a* saisonnier.

seat [siːt] *n* (*for sitting, centre*) & *Pol* siège *m;* (*on train, bus*) banquette *f;* (*in) Cin Th* fauteuil *m;* (*place*) place *f;* (*of trousers*) fond *m;* **to take** *or* **have a s.** s'asseoir; **in the hot s.** (*in difficult position*) *Fig* sur la sellette; **s. belt** ceinture *f* de sécurité; – *vt* (*at table*) placer (*qn*); (*on one's lap*) asseoir (*qn*); **the room seats 50** la salle a 50 places (*assises*); **be seated!** asseyez-vous! ◆—**ed** *a* (*sitting*) assis. ◆—**ing** *n* **s.** (*room*) (*seats*) places *fpl* assises; **the s. arrangements** la disposition des places; **s. capacity** nombre *m* de places assises. ◆—**er** *a* & *n* **two-s.** (*car*) voiture *f* à deux places.

secateurs [sekə'tɜːz] *npl* sécateur *m.*

secede [sɪ'siːd] *vi* faire sécession. ◆**secession** *n* sécession *f.*

secluded [sɪ'kluːdɪd] *a* (*remote*) isolé. ◆**seclusion** *n* solitude *f.*

second[1] ['sekənd] *a* deuxième, second; **every s. week** une semaine sur deux; **in s. (gear)** *Aut* en seconde; **s. to none** sans pareil; **s. in command** second *m;* *Mil* commandant *m* en second; – *adv* (*to say*) deuxièmement; **to come s.** *Sp* se classer deuxième; **the s. biggest** le deuxième en ordre de grandeur; **the s. richest country** le deuxième pays le plus riche; **my s. best** (*choice*) mon deuxième choix; – *n* (*person, object*) deuxième *mf,* second, -onde *mf;* **Louis the S.** Louis Deux; *pl* (*goods*) *Com* articles *mpl* de second choix; – *vt* (*motion*) appuyer. ◆**s.-'class** *a* (*product*) de qualité inférieure; (*ticket*) *Rail* de seconde (*classe*); (*mail*) non urgent. ◆**s.-'rate** *a* médiocre. ◆**secondly** *adv* deuxièmement.

second[2] ['sekənd] *n* (*unit of time*) seconde *f;* **s. hand** (*of clock, watch*) trotteuse *f.*

second[3] [sɪ'kɒnd] *vt* (*employee*) détacher (**to** à). ◆—**ment** *n* détachement *m;* **on s.** en (*position de*) détachement (**to** à).

secondary ['sekəndərɪ] *a* secondaire.

secondhand [sekənd'hænd] 1 *a* & *adv* (*not*

new) d'occasion. **2** *a* (*report, news*) de seconde main.

secret ['siːkrɪt] *a* secret; − *n* secret *m*; **in s.** en secret; **an open s.** le secret de Polichinelle. ◆**secrecy** *n* (*discretion, silence*) secret *m*; **in s.** en secret. ◆**secretive** *a* (*person*) cachottier; (*organization*) qui a le goût du secret; **to be s. about** faire un mystère de; (*organization*) être très discret sur. ◆**secretively** *adv* en catimini.

secretary ['sekrət(ə)rɪ] *n* secrétaire *mf*; **Foreign S., Am S. of State** = ministre *m* des Affaires étrangères. ◆**secre'tarial** *a* (*work*) de secrétaire, de secrétariat; (*school*) de secrétariat. ◆**secre'tariat** *n* (*in international organization*) secrétariat *m*.

secrete [sɪ'kriːt] *vt Med Biol* sécréter. ◆**sec'retion** *n* sécrétion *f*.

sect [sekt] *n* secte *f*. ◆**sec'tarian** *a* & *n Pej* sectaire (*mf*).

section ['sekʃ(ə)n] *n* (*of road, book, wood etc*) section *f*; (*of town, country*) partie *f*; (*of machine, furniture*) élément *m*; (*department*) section *f*; (*in store*) rayon *m*; **the sports/etc s.** (*of newspaper*) la page des sports/etc; − *vt* **to s. off** (*separate*) séparer.

sector ['sektər] *n* secteur *m*.

secular ['sekjulər] *a* (*teaching etc*) laïque; (*music, art*) profane.

secure [sɪ'kjuər] **1** *a* (*person, valuables*) en sûreté, en sécurité; (*in one's mind*) tranquille; (*place*) sûr; (*solid, firm*) solide; (*door, window*) bien fermé; (*certain*) assuré; **s. from** à l'abri de; (*emotionally*) s. sécurisé; − *vt* (*fasten*) attacher; (*window etc*) bien fermer; (*success, future etc*) assurer; **to s. against** protéger de. **2** *vt* (*obtain*) procurer (*sth for s.o.* qch à qn); **to s. sth** (*for oneself*) se procurer qch. ◆**securely** *adv* (*firmly*) solidement; (*safely*) en sûreté. ◆**security** *n* sécurité *f*; (*for loan, bail*) caution *f*; **s. firm** société *f* de surveillance; **s. guard** agent *m* de sécurité; (*transferring money*) convoyeur *m* de fonds.

sedan [sɪ'dæn] *n* (*saloon*) *Aut Am* berline *f*.

sedate [sɪ'deɪt] **1** *a* calme. **2** *vt* mettre sous calmants. ◆**sedation** *n* **under s.** sous calmants. ◆'**sedative** *n* calmant *m*.

sedentary ['sedəntərɪ] *a* sédentaire.

sediment ['sedɪmənt] *n* sédiment *m*.

sedition [sə'dɪʃ(ə)n] *n* sédition *f*. ◆**seditious** *a* séditieux.

seduce [sɪ'djuːs] *vt* séduire. ◆**seducer** *n* séducteur, -trice *mf*. ◆**seduction** *n* séduc-

tion *f*. ◆**seductive** *a* (*person, offer*) séduisant.

see[1] [siː] *vti* (*pt* **saw**, *pp* **seen**) voir; **we'll s. on** verra (bien); **I s.!** je vois!; **I can s.** (*clearly*) j'y vois clair; **I saw him run(ning)** je l'ai vu courir; **to s. reason** entendre raison; **to s. the joke** comprendre la plaisanterie; **s. who it is** va voir qui c'est; **s. you (later)!** à tout à l'heure!; **s. you (soon)!** à bientôt!; **to s. about** (*deal with*) s'occuper de; (*consider*) songer à; **to s. in the New Year** fêter la Nouvelle Année; **to s. s.o. off** accompagner qn (*à la gare etc*); **to s. s.o. out** raccompagner qn; **to s. through** (*task*) mener à bonne fin; **to s. s.o. through** (*be enough for*) suffire à qn; **to s. through s.o.** deviner le jeu de qn; **to s. to** (*deal with*) s'occuper de; (*mend*) réparer; **to s. (to it) that** (*attend*) veiller à ce que (+ *sub*); (*check*) s'assurer que; **to s. s.o. to** (*accompany*) raccompagner qn à. ◆**s.-through** *a* (*dress etc*) transparent.

see[2] [siː] *n* (*of bishop*) siège *m* (épiscopal).

seed [siːd] *n Agr* graine *f*; (*in grape*) pépin *m*; (*source*) *Fig* germe *m*; *Tennis* tête *f* de série; **seed(s)** (*for sowing*) *Agr* graines *fpl*; **to go to s.** (*of lettuce etc*) monter en graine. ◆**seedbed** *n Bot* semis *m*; (*of rebellion etc*) *Fig* foyer *m* (**of** de). ◆**seedling** *n* (*plant*) semis *m*.

seedy ['siːdɪ] *a* (**-ier, -iest**) miteux. ◆**seediness** *n* aspect *m* miteux.

seeing ['siːɪŋ] *conj* **s. (that)** vu que.

seek [siːk] *vt* (*pt* & *pp* **sought**) chercher (**to do** à faire); (*ask for*) demander (**from** à); **to s.** (*after*) rechercher; **to s. out** aller trouver.

seem [siːm] *vi* sembler (**to do** faire); **it seems that** ... (*impression*) il semble que ... (+ *sub or indic*); (*rumour*) il paraît que ... ; **it seems to me that** ... il me semble que ... .; **we s. to know each other** il me semble qu'on se connaît; **I can't s. to do it** je n'arrive pas à le faire. ◆**-ing** *a* apparent. ◆**-ingly** *adv* apparemment.

seemly ['siːmlɪ] *a* convenable.

seen [siːn] *see* **see**[1].

seep [siːp] *vi* (*ooze*) suinter; **to s. into** s'infiltrer dans. ◆**-age** *n* suintement *m*; infiltration(s) *f(pl)* (**into** dans); (*leak*) fuite *f*.

seesaw ['siːsɔː] *n* (jeu *m* de) bascule *f*.

seethe [siːð] *vi* **to s. with anger** bouillir de colère; **to s. with people** grouiller de monde.

segment ['segmənt] *n* segment *m*; (*of orange*) quartier *m*.

segregate ['segrɪgeɪt] *vt* séparer; (**racially**)

segregated (*school*) où se pratique la ségrégation raciale. ◆**segre'gation** *n* ségrégation *f*.

seize [siːz] **1** *vt* saisir; (*power, land*) s'emparer de; – *vi* **to s. on** (*offer etc*) saisir. **2** *vi* **to s. up** (*of engine*) (se) gripper. ◆**seizure** [-ʒər] *n* (*of goods etc*) saisie *f*; *Mil* prise *f*; *Med* crise *f*.

seldom ['seldəm] *adv* rarement.

select [sɪ'lekt] *vt* choisir (**from** parmi); (*candidates, pupils etc*) & *Sp* sélectionner; – *a* (*chosen*) choisi; (*exclusive*) sélect, chic *inv*. ◆**selection** *n* sélection *f*. ◆**selective** *a* (*memory, recruitment etc*) sélectif; (*person*) qui opère un choix; (*choosey*) difficile.

self [self] *n* (*pl* **selves**) **the s.** *Phil* le moi; **he's back to his old s.** *Fam* il est redevenu lui-même. ◆**s.-a'ssurance** *n* assurance *f*. ◆**s.-a'ssured** *a* sûr de soi. ◆**s.-'catering** *a* où l'on fait la cuisine soi-même. ◆**s.-'centred** *a* égocentrique. ◆**s.-'cleaning** *a* (*oven*) autonettoyant. ◆**s.-con'fessed** *a* (*liar*) de son propre aveu. ◆**s.-'confident** *a* sûr de soi. ◆**s.-'conscious** *a* gêné. ◆**s.-'consciousness** *n* gêne *f*. ◆**s.-con'tained** *a* (*flat*) indépendant. ◆**s.-con'trol** *n* maîtrise *f* de soi. ◆**s.-de'feating** *a* qui a un effet contraire à celui qui est recherché. ◆**s.-de'fence** *n* *Jur* légitime défense *f*. ◆**s.-de'nial** *n* abnégation *f*. ◆**s.-determi'nation** *n* autodétermination *f*. ◆**s.-'discipline** *n* autodiscipline *f*. ◆**s.-em'ployed** *a* qui travaille à son compte. ◆**s.-es'teem** *n* amour-propre *m*. ◆**s.-'evident** *a* évident, qui va de soi. ◆**s.-ex'planatory** *a* qui tombe sous le sens, qui se passe d'explication. ◆**s.-'governing** *a* autonome. ◆**s.-im'portant** *a* suffisant. ◆**s.-in'dulgent** *a* qui ne se refuse rien. ◆**s.-'interest** *n* intérêt *m* (personnel). ◆**s.-o'pinionated** *a* entêté. ◆**s.-'pity** *n* **to feel s.-pity** s'apitoyer sur son propre sort. ◆**s.-'portrait** *n* autoportrait *m*. ◆**s.-po'ssessed** *a* assuré. ◆**s.-raising** *or Am* **s.-rising 'flour** *n* farine *f* à levure. ◆**s.-re'liant** *a* indépendant. ◆**s.-re'spect** *n* amour-propre *m*. ◆**s.-re'specting** *a* qui se respecte. ◆**s.-'righteous** *a* pharisaïque. ◆**s.-'sacrifice** *n* abnégation *f*. ◆**s.-'satisfied** *a* content de soi. ◆**s.-'service** *n* & *a* libre-service (*m inv*). ◆**s.-'styled** *a* soi-disant. ◆**s.-su'fficient** *a* indépendant, qui a son indépendance. ◆**s.-su'p-**

porting *a* financièrement indépendant. ◆**s.-'taught** *a* autodidacte.

selfish ['selfɪʃ] *a* égoïste; (*motive*) intéressé. ◆**selfless** *a* désintéressé. ◆**selfishness** *n* égoïsme *m*.

selfsame ['selfseɪm] *a* même.

sell [sel] *vt* (*pt & pp* **sold**) vendre; (*idea etc*) *Fig* faire accepter; **she sold me it for twenty pounds** elle me l'a vendu vingt livres; **to s. back** revendre; **to s. off** liquider; **to have** *or* **be sold out of** (*cheese etc*) n'avoir plus de; **this book is sold out** ce livre est épuisé; – *vi* se vendre; (*of idea etc*) *Fig* être accepté; **to s. up** vendre sa maison; *Com* vendre son affaire; **selling price** prix *m* de vente. ◆**seller** *n* vendeur, -euse *mf*. ◆**sellout** *n* **1** (*betrayal*) trahison *f*. **2 it was a s.** *Th Cin* tous les billets ont été vendus.

sellotape® ['seləteɪp] *n* scotch® *m*; – *vt* scotcher.

semantic [sɪ'mæntɪk] *a* sémantique. ◆**semantics** *n* sémantique *f*.

semaphore ['seməfɔːr] *n* (*device*) *Rail Nau* sémaphore *m*; (*system*) signaux *mpl* à bras.

semblance ['sembləns] *n* semblant *m*.

semen ['siːmən] *n* sperme *m*.

semester [sɪ'mestər] *n* *Univ* semestre *m*.

semi- ['semɪ] *pref* demi-, semi-. ◆**semiauto'matic** *a* semi-automatique. ◆**semibreve** [-briːv] *n* *Mus* ronde *f*. ◆**semicircle** *n* demi-cercle *m*. ◆**semi'circular** *a* semi-circulaire. ◆**semi'colon** *n* point-virgule *m*. ◆**semi-'conscious** *a* à demi conscient. ◆**semide'tached** *a* **s. house** maison *f* jumelle. ◆**semi'final** *n* *Sp* demi-finale *f*.

seminar ['semɪnɑːr] *n* *Univ* séminaire *m*.

seminary ['semɪnərɪ] *n* *Rel* séminaire *m*.

Semite ['siːmaɪt, *Am* 'semaɪt] *n* Sémite *mf*. ◆**Se'mitic** *a* sémite; (*language*) sémitique.

semolina [seməˈliːnə] *n* semoule *f*.

senate ['senɪt] *n* *Pol* sénat *m*. ◆**senator** *n* *Pol* sénateur *m*.

send [send] *vt* (*pt & pp* **sent**) envoyer (**to** à); **to s. s.o. for sth/s.o.** envoyer qn chercher qch/qn; **to s. s.o. crazy** *or* **mad** rendre qn fou; **to s. s.o. packing** *Fam* envoyer promener qn; **to s. away** *or* **off** envoyer (**to** à); (*dismiss*) renvoyer; **to s. back** renvoyer; **to s. in** (*form*) envoyer; (*person*) faire entrer; **to s. on** (*letter, luggage*) faire suivre; **to s. out** (*invitation etc*) envoyer; (*heat*) émettre; (*from room etc*) faire sortir (qn); **to s. up** (*balloon, rocket*) lancer; (*price, luggage*) faire monter; (*mock*) *Fam* parodier; – *vi* **to s. away** *or* **off for** commander (par courrier); **to s. for** (*doctor etc*) faire venir, envoyer chercher; **to s. (out) for** (*meal, groceries*) envoyer chercher. ◆**s.-off** *n* **to give s.o. a s.-off** *Fam* faire des adieux chaleureux à qn. ◆**s.-up** *n Fam* parodie *f*. ◆**sender** *n* expéditeur, -trice *mf*.

senile ['siːnaɪl] *a* gâteux, sénile. ◆**se'nility** *n* gâtisme *m*, sénilité *f*.

senior ['siːnɪər] *a* (*older*) plus âgé; (*position, executive, rank*) supérieur; (*teacher, partner*) principal; **to be s. to s.o.,** **be s.o.'s s.** être plus âgé que qn; (*in rank*) être au-dessus de qn; **Brown s.** Brown père; **s. citizen** personne *f* âgée; **s. year** *Sch Univ Am* dernière année *f*; – *n* aîné, -ée *mf*; *Sch* grand, -ande *mf*; *Sch Univ Am* étudiant, -ante *mf* de dernière année; *Sp* senior *mf*. ◆**seni'ority** *n* priorité *f* d'âge; (*in service*) ancienneté *f*; (*in rank*) supériorité *f*.

sensation [sen'seɪʃ(ə)n] *n* sensation *f*. ◆**sensational** *a* (*event*) qui fait sensation; (*newspaper, film*) à sensation; (*terrific*) *Fam* sensationnel.

sense [sens] *n* (*faculty, awareness, meaning*) sens *m*; **a s. of hearing** (le sens de) l'ouïe *f*; **to have (good) s.** avoir du bon sens; **a s. of** (*physical*) une sensation de (*chaleur etc*); (*mental*) un sentiment de (*honte etc*); **a s. of humour/direction** le sens de l'humour/de l'orientation; **a s. of time** la notion de l'heure; **to bring s.o. to his senses** ramener qn à la raison; **to make s.** (*of story, action etc*) avoir du sens; **to make s. of** comprendre; – *vt* sentir (intuitivement) (**that** que); (*have a foreboding of*) pressentir. ◆**—less** *a* (*stupid, meaningless*) insensé; (*unconscious*) sans connaissance. ◆**—lessness** *n* stupidité *f*.

sensibility [sensɪ'bɪlətɪ] *n* sensibilité *f*; *pl* (*touchiness*) susceptibilité *f*.

sensible ['sensəb(ə)l] *a* (*wise*) raisonnable, sensé; (*clothes*) pratique.

sensitive ['sensɪtɪv] *a* (*responsive, painful*) sensible (**to** à); (*delicate*) délicat (*peau, question etc*); (*touchy*) susceptible (**about** à propos de). ◆**sensi'tivity** *n* sensibilité *f*; (*touchiness*) susceptibilité *f*.

sensory ['sensərɪ] *a* sensoriel.

sensual ['senʃʊəl] *a* (*bodily, sexual*) sensuel. ◆**sensu'ality** *n* sensualité *f*. ◆**sensuous** *a* (*pleasing, refined*) sensuel. ◆**sensuously** *adv* avec sensualité. ◆**sensuousness** *n* sensualité *f*.

sent [sent] *see* **send**.

sentence ['sentəns] **1** *n Gram* phrase *f*. **2** *n Jur* condamnation *f*; (*punishment*) peine *f*;

to pass s. prononcer une condamnation (**on** s.o. contre qn); **to serve a s.** purger une peine; – *vt Jur* prononcer une condamnation contre; **to s. to** condamner à.

sentiment ['sentɪmənt] *n* sentiment *m*. ◆**senti'mental** *a* sentimental. ◆**sentimen'tality** *n* sentimentalité *f*.

sentry ['sentrɪ] *n* sentinelle *f*; **s. box** guérite *f*.

separate ['sepərət] *a* (*distinct*) séparé; (*independent*) indépendant; (*different*) différent; (*individual*) particulier; – ['sepəreɪt] *vt* séparer (**from** de); – *vi* se séparer (**from** de). ◆**'separately** *adv* séparément. ◆**sepa'ration** *n* séparation *f*.

separates ['sepərəts] *npl* (*garments*) coordonnés *mpl*.

September [sep'tembər] *n* septembre *m*.

septic ['septɪk] *a* (*wound*) infecté; **s. tank** fosse *f* septique.

sequel ['siːkw(ə)l] *n* suite *f*.

sequence ['siːkwəns] *n* (*order*) ordre *m*; (*series*) succession *f*; *Mus Cards* séquence *f*; **film s.** séquence de film; **in s.** dans l'ordre, successivement.

sequin ['siːkwɪn] *n* paillette *f*.

serenade [serə'neɪd] *n* sérénade *f*; – *vt* donner une *or* la sérénade à.

serene [sə'riːn] *a* serein. ◆**serenity** *n* sérénité *f*.

sergeant ['saːdʒənt] *n Mil* sergent *m*; (*in police force*) brigadier *m*.

serial ['sɪərɪəl] *n* (*story, film*) feuilleton *m*; **s. number** (*of banknote, TV set etc*) numéro de série. ◆**serialize** *vt* publier en feuilleton; *TV Rad* adapter en feuilleton.

series ['sɪəriːz] *n inv* série *f*; (*book collection*) collection *f*.

serious ['sɪərɪəs] *a* sérieux; (*illness, mistake, tone*) grave, sérieux; (*damage*) important. ◆**—ly** *adv* sérieusement; (*ill, damaged*) gravement; **to take s.** prendre au sérieux. ◆**—ness** *n* sérieux *m*; (*of illness etc*) gravité *f*; (*of damage*) importance *f*; **in all s.** sérieusement.

sermon ['saːmən] *n* sermon *m*.

serpent ['saːpənt] *n* serpent *m*.

serrated [sə'reɪtɪd] *a* (*knife*) à dents (de scie).

serum ['sɪərəm] *n* sérum *m*.

servant ['saːvənt] *n* (*in house etc*) domestique *mf*; (*person who serves*) serviteur *m*; **public s.** fonctionnaire *mf*.

serve [saːv] *vt* servir (**to s.o.** à qn, **s.o. with sth** qch à qn); (*of train, bus etc*) desservir (*un village, un quartier etc*); (*supply*) *El* alimenter; (*apprenticeship*) faire; (*summons*) *Jur* remettre (**on** à); **it serves its**

purpose ça fait l'affaire; **(it) serves you right!** *Fam* ça t'apprendra!; **to s. up** *or* **out** servir; − *vi* servir **(as de)**; **to s. on** (*jury, committee*) être membre de; **to s. to show**/*etc* servir à montrer/*etc*; − *n Tennis* service *m*.

servic/e ['sɜːvɪs] *n* (*serving*) & *Mil Rel Tennis* service *m*; (*machine or vehicle repair*) révision *f*; **to be of s.** être utile à, rendre service à; **the (armed) services** les forces *fpl* armées; **s. (charge)** (*tip*) service *m*; **s. department** (*workshop*) atelier *m*; **s. area** (*on motorway*) aire *f* de service; **s. station** station-service *f*; − *vt* (*machine, vehicle*) réviser. **◆—ing** *n Tech Aut* révision *f*. **◆serviceable** *a* (*usable*) utilisable; (*useful*) commode; (*durable*) solide. **◆serviceman** *n* (*pl* **-men**) *n* militaire *m*.

serviette [sɜːvɪ'et] *n* serviette *f* (de table).

servile ['sɜːvaɪl] *a* servile.

session ['seʃ(ə)n] *n* séance *f*; *Jur Pol* session *f*, séance *f*; *Univ* année *f* or trimestre *m* universitaire; *Univ Am* semestre *m* universitaire.

set [set] **1** *n* (*of keys, needles, tools*) jeu *m*; (*of stamps, numbers*) série *f*; (*of people*) groupe *m*; (*of facts*) & *Math* ensemble *m*; (*of books*) collection *f*; (*of plates*) service *m*; (*of tyres*) train *m*; (*kit*) trousse *f*; (*stage*) *Th Cin* plateau *m*; (*scenery*) *Th Cin* décor *m*, scène *f*; (*hairstyle*) mise *f* en plis; *Tennis* set *m*; **television s.** téléviseur *m*; **radio s.** poste *m* de radio; **tea s.** service *m* à thé; **chess s.** (*box*) jeu *m* d'échecs; **a s. of teeth** une rangée de dents, une denture; **the skiing/racing s.** le monde du ski/des courses. **2** *a* (*time etc*) fixe; (*lunch*) à prix fixe; (*book etc*) *Sch* au programme; (*speech*) préparé à l'avance; (*in one's habits*) régulier; (*situated*) situé; **s. phrase** expression *f* consacrée; **a s. purpose** un but déterminé; **the s. menu** le plat du jour; **dead s. against** absolument opposé à; **s. on doing** résolu à faire; **to be s. on sth** vouloir qch à tout prix; **all s.** (*ready*) prêt **(to do** pour faire); **to be s. back from** (*of house etc*) être en retrait de (*route etc*). **3** *vt* (*pt & pp* **set**, *pres p.* **setting**) (*put*) mettre, poser; (*date, limit etc*) fixer; (*record*) *Sp* établir; (*adjust*) *Tech* régler; (*arm etc in plaster*) *Med* plâtrer; (*task*) donner (**for s.o.** à qn); (*problem*) poser; (*diamond*) monter; (*precedent*) créer; **to have one's hair s.** se faire faire une mise en plis; **to s.** (*loose*) (*dog*) lâcher (**on** contre); **to s. s.o.** (**off**) **crying**/*etc* faire pleurer/*etc* qn; **to s. back** (*in time*) retarder; (*cost*) *Fam* coûter; **to s.**

down déposer; **to s. off** (*bomb*) faire exploser; (*activity, mechanism*) déclencher; (*complexion, beauty*) rehausser; **to s. out** (*display, explain*) exposer (**to** à); (*arrange*) disposer; **to s. up** (*furniture*) installer; (*statue, tent*) dresser; (*school*) fonder; (*government*) établir; (*business*) créer; (*inquiry*) ouvrir; **to s. s.o. up in business** lancer qn dans les affaires; − *vi* (*of sun*) se coucher; (*of jelly*) prendre; (*of bone*) *Med* se ressouder; **to s. about** (*job*) se mettre à; **to s. about doing** se mettre à faire; **to s. in** (*start*) commencer; (*arise*) surgir; **to s. off** *or* **out** (*leave*) partir; **to s. out do do** entreprendre de faire; **to s. up in business** monter une affaire; **to s. upon** (*attack*) attaquer (*qn*). **◆setting** *n* (*surroundings*) cadre *m*; (*of sun*) coucher *m*; (*of diamond*) monture *f*. **◆setter** *n* chien *m* couchant.

setback ['setbæk] *n* revers *m*; *Med* rechute *f*.

setsquare ['setskweər] *n Math* équerre *f*.

settee [se'tiː] *n* canapé *m*.

settle ['set(ə)l] *vt* (*decide, arrange, pay*) régler; (*date*) fixer; (*place in position*) placer; (*person*) installer (*dans son lit etc*); (*nerves*) calmer; (*land*) coloniser; **let's s. things** arrangeons les choses; **that's (all) settled** (*decided*) c'est décidé; − *vi* (*live*) s'installer, s'établir; (*of dust*) se déposer; (*of bird*) se poser; (*of snow*) tenir; **to s. (down) into** (*armchair*) s'installer dans; (*job*) s'habituer à; **to s. (up) with s.o.** régler qn; **to s. for** se contenter de, accepter; **to s. down** (*in chair or house*) s'installer; (*of nerves*) se calmer; (*in one's lifestyle*) se ranger; (*marry*) se caser; **to s. down to** (*get used to*) s'habituer à; (*work, task*) se mettre à. **◆settled** *a* (*weather, period*) stable; (*habits*) régulier. **◆settlement** *n* (*of account etc*) règlement *m*; (*agreement*) accord *m*; (*colony*) colonie *f*. **◆settler** *n* colon *m*.

set-to [set'tuː] *n* (*quarrel*) *Fam* prise *f* de bec.

setup ['setʌp] *n Fam* situation *f*.

seven ['sev(ə)n] *a & n* sept (*m*). **◆seven'teen** *a & n* dix-sept (*m*). **◆seven'teenth** *a & n* dix-septième (*mf*). **◆seventh** *a & n* septième (*mf*). **◆seventieth** *a & n* soixante-dixième (*mf*). **◆seventy** *a & n* soixante-dix (*m*); **s.-one** soixante et onze.

sever ['sevər] *vt* sectionner, couper; (*relations*) *Fig* rompre. **◆severing** *n*, **◆severance** *n* (*of relations*) rupture *f*.

several ['sev(ə)rəl] *a & pron* plusieurs (**of** d'entre).

severe [sə'vɪər] *a* (*judge, tone etc*) sévère; (*winter, training*) rigoureux; (*test*) dur; (*injury*) grave; (*blow, pain*) violent; (*cold, frost*) intense; (*overwork*) excessif; **a s. cold** *Med* un gros rhume; **s. to** *or* **with s.o.** sévère envers qn. ◆**severely** *adv* sévèrement; (*wounded*) gravement. ◆**se'verity** *n* sévérité *f*; rigueur *f*; gravité *f*; violence *f*.

sew [səʊ] *vti* (*pt* sewed, *pp* sewn [səʊn] *or* sewed) coudre; **to s. on** (*button*) (re)coudre; **to s. up** (*tear*) (re)coudre. ◆—**ing** *n* couture *f*; **s. machine** machine *f* à coudre.

sewage ['suːɪdʒ] *n* eaux *fpl* usées *or* d'égout. ◆**sewer** *n* égout *m*.

sewn [səʊn] *see* **sew.**

sex [seks] *n* (*gender, sexuality*) sexe *m*; (*activity*) relations *fpl* sexuelles; **the opposite s.** l'autre sexe; **to have s. with** coucher avec; – *a* (*education, act etc*) sexuel; **s. maniac** obsédé, -ée *mf* sexuel(le). ◆**sexist** *a* & *n* sexiste (*mf*). ◆**sexual** *a* sexuel. ◆**sexu'ality** *n* sexualité *f*. ◆**sexy** *a* (-ier, -iest) (*book, garment, person*) sexy *inv*; (*aroused*) qui a envie (de faire l'amour).

sextet [sek'stet] *n* sextuor *m*.

sh! [ʃ] *int* chut!

shabby ['ʃæbɪ] *a* (-ier, -iest) (*town, room etc*) miteux; (*person*) pauvrement vêtu; (*mean*) *Fig* mesquin. ◆**shabbily** *adv* (*dressed*) pauvrement. ◆**shabbiness** *n* aspect *m* miteux; mesquinerie *f*.

shack [ʃæk] **1** *n* cabane *f*. **2** *vi* **to s. up with** *Pej Fam* se coller avec.

shackles ['ʃæk(ə)lz] *npl* chaînes *fpl*.

shade [ʃeɪd] *n* ombre *f*; (*of colour*) ton *m*, nuance *f*; (*of opinion, meaning*) nuance *f*; (*of lamp*) abat-jour *m inv*; (*blind*) store *m*; **in the s.** à l'ombre; **a s.** *faster/taller/etc* (*slightly*) un rien plus vite/plus grand/*etc*; – *vt* (*of tree*) ombrager; (*protect*) abriter (**from** de); **to s. in** (*drawing*) ombrer. ◆**shady** *a* (-ier, -iest) (*place*) ombragé; (*person etc*) *Fig* louche.

shadow ['ʃædəʊ] **1** *n* ombre *f*. **2** *a* (*cabinet*) *Pol* fantôme. **3** *vt* **to s. s.o.** (*follow*) filer qn. ◆**shadowy** *a* (-ier, -iest) (*form etc*) obscur, vague.

shaft [ʃɑːft] *n* **1** (*of tool*) manche *m*; (*in machine*) arbre *m*; **s. of light** trait *m* de lumière. **2** (*of mine*) puits *m*; (*of lift*) cage *f*.

shaggy ['ʃægɪ] *a* (-ier, -iest) (*hair, beard*) broussailleux; (*dog etc*) à longs poils.

shake [ʃeɪk] *vt* (*pt* shook, *pp* shaken) (*move up and down*) secouer; (*bottle*) agiter; (*belief, resolution etc*) *Fig* ébranler; (*upset*) bouleverser, secouer; **to s. the windows** (*of shock*) ébranler les vitres; **to s. one's head**

(*say no*) secouer la tête; **to s. hands with** serrer la main à; **we shook hands** nous nous sommes serré la main; **to s. off** (*dust etc*) secouer; (*cough, infection, pursuer*) *Fig* se débarrasser de; **to s. s.o. up** (*disturb, rouse*) secouer qn; **to s. sth out of sth** (*remove*) secouer qch de qch; **s. yourself out of it!** secoue-toi!; – *vi* trembler (**with** de); – *n* secousse *f*; **to give sth a s.** secouer qch; **with a s. of his** *or* **her head** en secouant la tête; **in two shakes** (*soon*) *Fam* dans une minute. ◆**s.-up** *n Fig* réorganisation *f*.

shaky [ʃeɪkɪ] *a* (-ier, -iest) (*trembling*) tremblant; (*ladder etc*) branlant; (*memory, health*) chancelant; (*on one's legs, in a language*) mal assuré.

shall [ʃæl, *unstressed* ʃəl] *v aux* **1** (*future*) **I s. come, I'll come** je viendrai; **we s. not come, we shan't come** nous ne viendrons pas. **2** (*question*) **s. I leave?** veux-tu que je parte?; **s. we leave?** on part? **3** (*order*) **he s. do it if I order it** il devra le faire si je l'ordonne.

shallot [ʃə'lɒt] *n* (*onion*) échalote *f*.

shallow ['ʃæləʊ] *a* (-er, -est) peu profond; *Fig Pej* superficiel; – *npl* (*of river*) bas-fond *m*. ◆—**ness** *n* manque *m* de profondeur; *Fig Pej* caractère *m* superficiel.

sham [ʃæm] *n* (*pretence*) comédie *f*, feinte *f*; (*person*) imposteur *m*; (*jewels*) imitation *f*; – *a* (*false*) faux; (*illness, emotion*) feint; – *vt* (-mm-) feindre.

shambles ['ʃæmb(ə)lz] *n* désordre *m*, pagaïe *f*; **to be a s.** être en pagaïe; **to make a s. of** gâcher.

shame [ʃeɪm] *n* (*feeling, disgrace*) honte *f*; **it's a s.** c'est dommage (**to do** de faire); **it's a s. (that)** c'est dommage que (+ *sub*); **what a s.!** (quel) dommage!; **to put to s.** faire honte à; – *vt* (*disgrace, make ashamed*) faire honte à. ◆**shamefaced** *a* honteux; (*bashful*) timide. ◆**shameful** *a* honteux. ◆**shamefully** *adv* honteusement. ◆**shameless** *a* (*brazen*) effronté; (*indecent*) impudique.

shammy ['ʃæmɪ] *n* **s. (leather)** *Fam* peau *f* de chamois.

shampoo [ʃæm'puː] *n* shampooing *m*; – *vt* (*carpet*) shampooiner; **to s. s.o.'s hair** faire un shampooing à qn.

shandy ['ʃændɪ] *n* (*beer*) panaché *m*.

shan't [ʃɑːnt] = **shall not.**

shanty[1] ['ʃæntɪ] *n* (*hut*) baraque *f*. ◆**shantytown** *n* bidonville *f*.

shanty[2] ['ʃæntɪ] *n* **sea s.** chanson *f* de marins.

shap/e [ʃeɪp] *n* forme *f*; **in (good) s.** (*fit*) en forme; **to be in good/bad s.** (*of vehicle,* *house etc*) être en bon/mauvais état; (*of business*) marcher bien/mal; **to take s.** prendre forme; **in the s. of a pear** en forme de poire; – *vt* (*fashion*) façonner (**into** en); (*one's life*) *Fig* déterminer; – *vi* **to s. up** (*of plans*) prendre (bonne) tournure, s'annoncer bien; (*of pupil, wrongdoer*) s'y mettre, s'appliquer; (*of patient*) faire des progrès. ◆**—ed** *suffix* **pear-s.**/*etc* en forme de poire/*etc*. ◆**shapeless** *a* informe. ◆**shapely** *a* (**-ier, -iest**) (*woman, legs*) bien tourné.

share [ʃeər] *n* part *f* (**of,** in de); (*in company*) *Fin* action *f*; **one's (fair) s.** sa part de; **to do one's (fair) s.** fournir sa part d'efforts; **stocks and shares** *Fin* valeurs *fpl* (boursières); – *vt* (*meal, joy, opinion etc*) partager (**with** avec); (*characteristic*) avoir en commun; **to s. out** (*distribute*) partager; – *vi* **to s. (in)** partager. ◆**shareholder** *n* *Fin* actionnaire *mf*.

shark [ʃɑːk] *n* (*fish*) & *Fig* requin *m*.

sharp [ʃɑːp] **1** *a* (**-er, -est**) (*knife, blade etc*) tranchant; (*pointed*) pointu; (*point, voice*) aigu; (*pace, mind*) vif; (*pain*) aigu, vif; (*change, bend*) brusque; (*taste*) piquant; (*words, wind, tone*) âpre; (*eyesight, cry*) perçant; (*distinct*) net; (*lawyer etc*) *Pej* peu scrupuleux; **s. practice** *Pej* procédé(s) *m(pl)* malhonnête(s); – *adv* (*to stop*) net; **five o'clock**/*etc* cinq heures/*etc* pile; **s. right/left** tout de suite à droite/à gauche. **2** *n* *Mus* dièse *m*. ◆**sharpen** *vt* (*knife*) aiguiser; (*pencil*) tailler. ◆**sharpener** *n* (*for pencils*) taille-crayon(s) *m inv*; (*for blades*) aiguisoir *m*. ◆**sharply** *adv* (*suddenly*) brusquement; (*harshly*) vivement; (*clearly*) nettement. ◆**sharpness** *n* (*of blade*) tranchant *m*; (*of picture*) netteté *f*. ◆**sharpshooter** *n* tireur *m* d'élite.

shatter [ˈʃætər] *vt* (*smash*) fracasser; (*glass*) faire voler en éclats; (*career, health*) briser; (*person, hopes*) anéantir; – *vi* (*smash*) se fracasser; (*of glass*) voler en éclats. ◆**—ed** *a* (*exhausted*) anéanti. ◆**—ing** *a* (*defeat*) accablant; (*news, experience*) bouleversant.

shav/e [ʃeɪv] *vt* (*person, head*) raser; **to s. off one's beard**/*etc* se raser la barbe/*etc*; – *vi* se raser; – *n* **to have a s.** se raser, se faire la barbe; **to have a close s.** *Fig Fam* l'échapper belle. ◆**—ing** *n* rasage *m*; (*strip of wood*) copeau *m*; **s. brush** blaireau *m*; **s. cream, s. foam** crème *f* à raser. ◆**shaven** *a* rasé (de près). ◆**shaver** *n* rasoir *m* électrique.

shawl [ʃɔːl] *n* châle *m*.

she [ʃiː] *pron* elle; **s. wants** elle veut; **she's a**

happy woman c'est une femme heureuse; **if I were s.** si j'étais elle; – *n* femelle *f*; **s.-bear** ourse *f*.

sheaf [ʃiːf] *n* (*pl* **sheaves**) (*of corn*) gerbe *f*.

shear [ʃiər] *vt* tondre; – *npl* cisaille(s) *f(pl)*; **pruning shears** sécateur *m*. ◆**—ing** *n* tonte *f*.

sheath [ʃiːθ] *n* (*pl* **-s** [ʃiːðz]) (*container*) gaine *f*, fourreau *m*; (*contraceptive*) préservatif *m*.

shed [ʃed] **1** *n* (*in garden etc*) remise *f*; (*for goods or machines*) hangar *m*. **2** *vt* (*pt & pp* **shed,** *pres p* **shedding**) (*tears, warmth etc*) répandre; (*lose*) perdre; (*get rid of*) se défaire de; (*clothes*) enlever; **to s. light on** *Fig* éclairer.

sheen [ʃiːn] *n* lustre *m*.

sheep [ʃiːp] *n inv* mouton *m*. ◆**sheepdog** *n* chien *m* de berger. ◆**sheepskin** *n* peau *f* de mouton.

sheepish [ˈʃiːpɪʃ] *a* penaud. ◆**—ly** *adv* d'un air penaud.

sheer [ʃiər] **1** *a* (*luck, madness etc*) pur; (*impossibility etc*) absolu; **it's s. hard work** ça demande du travail; **by s. determination/hard work** à force de détermination/de travail. **2** *a* (*cliff*) à pic; – *adv* (*to rise*) à pic. **3** *a* (*fabric*) très fin.

sheet [ʃiːt] *n* (*on bed*) drap *m*; (*of paper, wood etc*) feuille *f*; (*of glass, ice*) plaque *f*; (*dust cover*) housse *f*; (*canvas*) bâche *f*; **s. metal** tôle *f*.

sheikh [ʃeɪk] *n* scheik *m*, cheik *m*.

shelf [ʃelf] *n* (*pl* **shelves**) rayon *m*, étagère *f*; (*in shop*) rayon *m*; (*of cliff*) saillie *f*; **to be (left) on the s.** (*not married*) *Fam* être toujours célibataire.

shell [ʃel] **1** *n* coquille *f*; (*of tortoise*) carapace *f*; (*seashell*) coquillage *m*; (*of peas*) cosse *f*; (*of building*) carcasse *f*; – *vt* (*peas*) écosser; (*nut, shrimp*) décortiquer. **2** *n* (*explosive*) *Mil* obus *m*; – *vt* (*town etc*) *Mil* bombarder. ◆**—ing** *n* *Mil* bombardement *m*. ◆**shellfish** *n inv* *Culin* (*oysters etc*) fruits *mpl* de mer.

shelter [ˈʃeltər] *n* (*place, protection*) abri *m*; **to take s.** se mettre à l'abri (**from** de); **to seek s.** chercher un abri; – *vt* abriter (**from** de); (*criminal*) protéger; – *vi* s'abriter. ◆**—ed** *a* (*place*) abrité; (*life*) très protégé.

shelve [ʃelv] *vt* (*postpone*) laisser en suspens.

shelving [ˈʃelvɪŋ] *n* (*shelves*) rayonnage(s) *m(pl)*; **s. unit** (*set of shelves*) étagère *f*.

shepherd [ˈʃepəd] **1** *n* berger *m*; **s.'s pie** hachis *m* Parmentier. **2** *vt* **to s. in** faire

entrer; **to s. s.o. around** piloter qn.
◆**shepherdess** *n* bergère *f*.

sherbet ['ʃɜːbət] *n* (*powder*) poudre *f*
acidulée; (*water ice*) *Am* sorbet *m*.

sheriff ['ʃerɪf] *n Am* shérif *m*.

sherry ['ʃerɪ] *n* xérès *m*, sherry *m*.

shh! [ʃ] *int* chut!

shield [ʃiːld] *n* bouclier *m*; (*on coat of arms*)
écu *m*; (*screen*) *Tech* écran *m*; – *vt* protéger
(*from* de).

shift [ʃɪft] *n* (*change*) changement *m* (*of, in*
de); (*period of work*) poste *m*; (*workers*)
équipe *f*; **gear s.** *Aut Am* levier *m* de vitesse;
s. work travail *m* en équipe; – *vt* (*move*)
déplacer, bouger; (*limb*) bouger;
(*employee*) muter (*to* à); (*scenery*) *Th*
changer; (*blame*) rejeter (*on to* sur); **to s.
places** changer de place; **to s. gear(s)** *Aut
Am* changer de vitesse; – *vi* bouger; (*of
heavy object*) se déplacer; (*of views*)
changer; (*pass*) passer (*to* à); (*go*) aller (*to*
à); **to s. to** (*new town*) déménager à; **to s.
along** avancer; **to s. over** *or* **up** se pousser.
◆**—ing** *a* (*views*) changeant.

shiftless ['ʃɪftləs] *a* velléitaire, paresseux.

shifty ['ʃɪftɪ] *a* (**-ier, -iest**) (*sly*) sournois;
(*dubious*) louche.

shilling ['ʃɪlɪŋ] *n* shilling *m*.

shilly-shally ['ʃɪlɪʃælɪ] *vi* hésiter, tergiverser.

shimmer ['ʃɪmər] *vi* chatoyer, miroiter; – *n*
chatoiement *m*, miroitement *m*.

shin [ʃɪn] *n* tibia *m*; **s. pad** *n Sp* jambière *f*.

shindig ['ʃɪndɪg] *n Fam* réunion *f* bruyante.

shin/e [ʃaɪn] *vi* (*pt & pp* **shone** [ʃɒn, *Am*
ʃəʊn]) briller; **s. with** (*happiness etc*)
rayonner de; – *vt* (*polish*) faire briller; **to s.
a light** *or* **a torch** éclairer (*on* sth qch); – *n*
éclat *m*; (*on shoes, cloth*) brillant *m*.
◆**—ing** *a* (*bright, polished*) brillant; **a shining example of** un bel exemple de. ◆**shiny**
a (**-ier, -iest**) (*bright, polished*) brillant;
(*clothes, through wear*) lustré.

shingle ['ʃɪŋ(ə)l] *n* (*on beach*) galets *mpl*;
(*on roof*) bardeau *m*.

shingles ['ʃɪŋ(ə)lz] *n Med* zona *m*.

ship [ʃɪp] *n* navire *m*, bateau *m*; **by s.** en
bateau; **s. owner** armateur *m*; – *vt* (**-pp-**)
(*send*) expédier; (*transport*) transporter;
(*load up*) embarquer (*on to* sur). ◆**shipping** *n* (*traffic*) navigation *f*; (*ships*) navires
mpl; – *a* (*agent*) maritime; **s. line** compagnie *f* de navigation. ◆**shipbuilding** *n*
construction *f* navale. ◆**shipmate** *n*
camarade *m* de bord. ◆**shipment** *n*
(*goods*) chargement *m*, cargaison *f*.
◆**shipshape** *a & adv* en ordre. ◆**ship-
wreck** *n* naufrage *m*. ◆**shipwrecked** *a*

naufragé; **to be s.** faire naufrage. ◆**shipyard** *n* chantier *m* naval.

shirk [ʃɜːk] *vt* (*duty*) se dérober à; (*work*)
éviter de faire; – *vi* tirer au flanc. ◆**—er** *n*
tire-au-flanc *m inv*.

shirt [ʃɜːt] *n* chemise *f*; (*of woman*) chemisier
m. ◆**shirtfront** *n* plastron *m*. ◆**shirtsleeves** *npl* **in** (*one's*) **s.** en bras de
chemise.

shiver ['ʃɪvər] *vi* frissonner (*with* de); – *n*
frisson *m*.

shoal [ʃəʊl] *n* (*of fish*) banc *m*.

shock [ʃɒk] *n* (*moral blow*) choc *m*; (*impact*)
& *Med* choc *m*; (*of explosion*) secousse *f*;
(**electric**) **s.** décharge *f* (électrique) (*from*
sth en touchant qch); **a feeling of s.** un
sentiment d'horreur; **suffering from s.,
in a state of s.** en état de choc; **to come as
a s. to s.o.** stupéfier qn; – *a* (*tactics,
wave*) de choc; (*effect, image etc*) -choc
inv; **s. absorber** amortisseur *m*; – *vt*
(*offend*) choquer; (*surprise*) stupéfier; (*disgust*) dégoûter. ◆**—ing** *a* affreux; (*outrageous*) scandaleux; (*indecent*) choquant.
◆**—ingly** *adv* affreusement. ◆**—er** *n* **to be
a s.** *Fam* être affreux *or* horrible. ◆**shockproof** *a* résistant au choc.

shoddy ['ʃɒdɪ] *a* (**-ier, -iest**) (*goods etc*) de
mauvaise qualité. ◆**shoddily** *adv* (*made,
done*) mal.

shoe [ʃuː] *n* chaussure *f*, soulier *m*; (*for
horse*) fer *m*; (*Aut*) sabot *m* (de frein); **in your
shoes** *Fig* à ta place; **s. polish** cirage *m*; – *vt*
(*pt & pp* **shod**) (*horse*) ferrer. ◆**shoehorn**
n chausse-pied *m*. ◆**shoelace** *n* lacet *m*.
◆**shoemaker** *n* fabricant *m* de chaussures; (*cobbler*) cordonnier *m*. ◆**shoe-
string** *n* **on a s.** *Fig* avec peu d'argent (en
poche).

shone [ʃɒn, *Am* ʃəʊn] *see* **shine**.

shoo [ʃuː] *vt* **to s.** (**away**) chasser; – *int*
ouste!

shook [ʃʊk] *see* **shake**.

shoot[1] [ʃuːt] *vt* (*pt & pp* **shot**) (*kill*) tuer
(d'un coup de feu), abattre; (*wound*)
blesser (d'un coup de feu); (*execute*) fusiller; (*hunt*) chasser; (*gun*) tirer un coup de;
(*bullet*) tirer; (*missile, glance, questions*)
lancer (*at* à); (*film*) tourner; (*person*) *Phot*
prendre; **to s. down** (*aircraft*) abattre; – *vi*
(*with gun, bow etc*) tirer (*at* sur); **to s.
ahead/off** avancer/partir à toute vitesse; **to
s. up** (*grow*) pousser vite; (*rise, spurt*) jaillir;
(*of price*) monter en flèche. ◆**—ing** *n*
(*gunfire, execution*) fusillade *f*; (*shots*)
coups *mpl* de feu; (*murder*) meurtre *m*; (*of*

film) tournage *m*; (*hunting*) chasse *f*.
◆**shoot-out** *n Fam* fusillade *f*.
shoot² [ʃuːt] *n* (*on plant*) pousse *f*.

shop [ʃɒp] **1** *n* magasin *m*; (*small*) boutique *f*; (*workshop*) atelier *m*; **at the baker's s.** à la boulangerie, chez le boulanger; **s. assistant** vendeur, -euse *mf*; **s. floor** (*workers*) ouvriers *mpl*; **s. steward** délégué, -ée *mf* syndical(e); **s. window** vitrine *f*; – *vi* (**-pp-**) faire ses courses (**at** chez); **to s. around** comparer les prix. **2** *vt* (**-pp-**) **to s. s.o.** *Fam* dénoncer qn (*à la police etc*). ◆**shopping** *n* (*goods*) achats *mpl*; **to go s.** faire des courses; **to do one's s.** faire ses courses; – *a* (*street, district*) commerçant; (*bag*) à provisions; **s. centre** centre *m* commercial. ◆**shopper** *n* (*buyer*) acheteur, -euse *mf*; (*customer*) client, -ente *mf*; (*bag*) sac *m* à provisions.

shopkeeper [ʃɒpkiːpər] *n* commerçant, -ante *mf*. ◆**shoplifter** *n* voleur, -euse *mf* à l'étalage. ◆**shoplifting** *n* vol *m* à l'étalage. ◆**shopsoiled** *a, Am* ◆**shopworn** *a* abîmé.

shore [ʃɔːr] **1** *n* (*of sea, lake*) rivage *m*; (*coast*) côte *f*, bord *m* de (la) mer; (*beach*) plage *f*; **on s.** (*passenger*) *Nau* à terre. **2** *vt* **to s. up** (*prop up*) étayer.

shorn [ʃɔːn] *a* (*head*) tondu; **s. of** (*stripped of*) *Lit* dénué de.

short [ʃɔːt] *a* (**-er, -est**) court; (*person, distance*) petit; (*syllable*) bref; (*curt, impatient*) brusque; **a s. time** *or* **while ago** il y a peu de temps; **s. cut** raccourci *m*; **to be s. of money/time** être à court d'argent/de temps; **we're s. of ten men** il nous manque dix hommes; **money/time is s.** l'argent/le temps manque; **not far s. of** pas loin de; **s. of** (*except*) sauf; **to be s. for** (*of name*) être l'abréviation *or* le diminutif de; **in s.** bref; **s. circuit** *El* court-circuit *m*; **s. list** liste *f* de candidats choisis; – *adv* **to cut s.** (*visit etc*) abréger; (*person*) couper la parole à; **to go** *or* **get** *or* **run s.** of manquer de; **to get** *or* **run s.** manquer; **to stop s.** s'arrêter net; – *n El* court-circuit *m*; (**a pair of**) **shorts** un short. ◆**shorten** *vt* (*visit, line, dress etc*) raccourcir. ◆**shortly** *adv* (*soon*) bientôt; **s. after** peu après. ◆**shortness** *n* (*of person*) petitesse *f*; (*of hair, stick, legs*) manque *m* de longueur.

shortage [ʃɔːtɪdʒ] *n* manque *m*, pénurie *f*; (*crisis*) crise *f*.

shortbread [ʃɔːtbred] *n* sablé *m*. ◆**short-'change** *vt* (*buyer*) ne pas rendre juste à. ◆**short-'circuit** *vt El & Fig* court-circuiter. ◆**shortcoming** *n* défaut *m*.

◆**shortfall** *n* manque *m*. ◆**shorthand** *n* sténo *f*; **s. typist** sténodactylo *f*. ◆**short-'handed** *a* à court de personnel. ◆**short-'lived** *a* éphémère. ◆**short'sighted** *a* myope; *Fig* imprévoyant. ◆**short-'sightedness** *n* myopie *f*; imprévoyance *f*. ◆**short-'sleeved** *a* à manches courtes. ◆**short-'staffed** *a* à court de personnel. ◆**short-'term** *a* à court terme.

shortening [ʃɔːt(ə)nɪŋ] *n Culin* matière *f* grasse.

shot [ʃɒt] *see* **shoot¹**; – *n* coup *m*; (*bullet*) balle *f*; *Cin Phot* prise *f* de vues; (*injection*) *Med* piqûre *f*; **a good s.** (*person*) un bon tireur; **to have a s. at (doing) sth** essayer de faire qch; **a long s.** (*attempt*) un coup à tenter; **big s.** *Fam* gros bonnet *m*; **like a s.** (*at once*) tout de suite; **to be s. of** (*rid of*) *Fam* être débarrassé de. ◆**shotgun** *n* fusil *m* de chasse.

should [ʃʊd, *unstressed* ʃəd] *v aux* **1** (= *ought to*) **you s. do it** vous devriez le faire; **I s. have stayed** j'aurais dû rester; **that s. be Pauline** ça doit être Pauline. **2** (= *would*) **I s. like to** j'aimerais bien; **it's strange she s. say no** il est étrange qu'elle dise non. **3** (*possibility*) **if he s. come** s'il vient; **s. I be free** si je suis libre.

shoulder [ʃəʊldər] **1** *n* épaule *f*; **to have round shoulders** avoir le dos voûté, être voûté; (**hard**) **s.** (*of motorway*) accotement *m* stabilisé; **s. bag** sac *m* à bandoulière; **s. blade** omoplate *f*; **s.-length hair** cheveux *mpl* mi-longs. **2** *vt* (*responsibility*) endosser, assumer.

shout [ʃaʊt] *n* cri *m*; **to give s.o. a s.** appeler qn; – *vi* **to s.** (**out**) crier; **to s. to** *or* **at s.o. to do** crier à qn de faire; **to s. at s.o.** (*scold*) crier après qn; – *vt* **to s.** (**out**) (*insult etc*) crier; **to s. down** (*speaker*) huer. ◆—**ing** *n* (*shouts*) cris *mpl*.

shove [ʃʌv] *n* poussée *f*; **to give a s. (to)** pousser; – *vt* pousser; (*put*) *Fam* fourrer; **to s. sth into** (*thrust*) enfoncer *or* fourrer qch dans; **to s. s.o. around** *Fam* régenter qn; – *vi* pousser; **to s. off** (*leave*) *Fam* ficher le camp, filer; **to s. over** (*move over*) *Fam* se pousser.

shovel [ʃʌv(ə)l] *n* pelle *f*; – *vt* (**-ll-**, *Am* **-l-**) (*grain etc*) pelleter; **to s. up** *or* **away** (*remove*) enlever à la pelle; **to s. sth into** (*thrust*) *Fam* fourrer qch dans.

show [ʃəʊ] *n* (*of joy, force*) démonstration *f* (**of** de); (*semblance*) semblant *m* (**of** de); (*ostentation*) parade *f*; (*sight*) & *Th* spectacle *m*; (*performance*) *Cin* séance *f*; (*exhibition*) exposition *f*; **the Boat/Motor S.** le

Salon de la Navigation/de l'Automobile; **horse** s. concours *m* hippique; **to give a good s.** *Sp Mus Th* jouer bien; **good s.!** bravo!; **(just) for s.** pour l'effet; **on s.** (*painting etc*) exposé; **s. business** le monde du spectacle; **s. flat** appartement *m* témoin; – *vt* (*pt* **showed**, *pp* **shown**) montrer (**to** à, **that** que); (*exhibit*) exposer; (*film*) passer, donner; (*indicate*) indiquer, montrer; **to s. s.o. to the door** reconduire qn; **it (just) goes to s. that...** ça (dé)montre (bien) que...; **I'll s.** him *or* her! *Fam* je lui apprendrai!; – *vi* (*be visible*) se voir; (*of film*) passer; '**now showing**' *Cin* 'à l'affiche' (**at** à). ■ **to s. (a)round** *vt* faire visiter; **he** *or* **she was shown (a)round the house** on lui a fait visiter la maison; **to s. in** *vt* faire entrer; **to s. off** *vt Pej* étaler; (*highlight*) faire valoir; – *vi Pej* crâner. ◆**s.-off** *n Pej* crâneur, -euse *mf*; **to s. out** *vt* (*visitor*) reconduire; **to s. up** *vt* (*fault*) faire ressortir; (*humiliate*) faire honte à; – *vi* ressortir (**against** sur); (*of error*) être visible; (*of person*) *Fam* arriver, s'amener. ◆**showing** *n* (*of film*) projection *f* (**of** de); (*performance*) *Cin* séance *f*; (*of team, player*) performance *f*.

showcase ['ʃəʊkeɪs] *n* vitrine *f*. ◆**showdown** *n* confrontation *f*, conflit *m*. ◆**showgirl** *n* (*in chorus etc*) girl *f*. ◆**showjumping** *n Sp* jumping *m*. ◆**showmanship** *n* art *m* de la mise en scène. ◆**showpiece** *n* modèle *m* du genre. ◆**showroom** *n* (*for cars etc*) salle *f* d'exposition.

shower ['ʃaʊər] *n* (*of rain*) averse *f*; (*of blows*) déluge *m*; (*bath*) douche *f*; (*party*) *Am* réception *f* (*pour la remise de cadeaux*); – *vt* **to s. s.o. with** (*gifts, abuse*) couvrir qn de. ◆**showery** *a* pluvieux.

shown [ʃəʊn] *see* **show**.

showy ['ʃəʊɪ] *a* (**-ier, -iest**) (*colour, hat*) voyant; (*person*) prétentieux.

shrank [ʃræŋk] *see* **shrink 1**.

shrapnel ['ʃræpn(ə)l] *n* éclats *mpl* d'obus.

shred [ʃred] *n* lambeau *m*; (*of truth*) *Fig* grain *m*; **not a s. of evidence** pas la moindre preuve; – *vt* (**-dd-**) mettre en lambeaux; (*cabbage, carrots*) râper. ◆**shredder** *n* *Culin* râpe *f*.

shrew [ʃruː] *n* (*woman*) *Pej* mégère *f*.

shrewd [ʃruːd] *a* (**-er, -est**) (*person, plan*) astucieux. ◆**—ly** *adv* astucieusement. ◆**—ness** *n* astuce *f*.

shriek [ʃriːk] *n* cri *m* (aigu); – *vti* crier; **to s. with pain/laughter** hurler de douleur/de rire.

shrift [ʃrɪft] *n* **to get short s.** être traité sans ménagement.

shrill [ʃrɪl] *a* (**-er, -est**) aigu, strident.

shrimp [ʃrɪmp] *n* crevette *f*; (*person*) *Pej* nabot, -ote *mf*; (*child*) *Pej* puce *f*.

shrine [ʃraɪn] *n* lieu *m* saint; (*tomb*) châsse *f*.

shrink [ʃrɪŋk] **1** *vi* (*pt* **shrank**, *pp* **shrunk** *or* **shrunken**) (*of clothes*) rétrécir; (*of aging person*) se tasser; (*of amount, audience etc*) diminuer; **to s. from** reculer devant (**doing** l'idée de faire); – *vt* rétrécir. **2** *n* (*person*) *Am Hum* psy(chiatre) *m*. ◆**—age** *n* rétrécissement *m*; diminution *f*.

shrivel ['ʃrɪv(ə)l] *vi* (**-ll-**, *Am* **-l-**) **to s. (up)** se ratatiner; – *vt* **to s. (up)** ratatiner.

shroud [ʃraʊd] *n* linceul *m*; (*of mystery*) *Fig* voile *m*; – *vt* **shrouded in mist** enseveli *or* enveloppé sous la brume; **shrouded in mystery** enveloppé de mystère.

Shrove Tuesday [ʃrəʊv'tjuːzdɪ] *n* Mardi *m* gras.

shrub [ʃrʌb] *n* arbrisseau *m*.

shrug [ʃrʌg] *vt* (**-gg-**) **to s. one's shoulders** hausser les épaules; **to s. off** (*dismiss*) écarter (dédaigneusement); – *n* haussement *m* d'épaules.

shrunk(en) ['ʃrʌŋk(ən)] *see* **shrink 1**.

shudder ['ʃʌdər] *vi* frémir (**with** de); (*of machine etc*) vibrer; – *n* frémissement *m*; vibration *f*.

shuffle ['ʃʌf(ə)l] **1** *vti* **to s. (one's feet)** traîner les pieds. **2** *vt* (*cards*) battre.

shun [ʃʌn] *vt* (**-nn-**) fuir, éviter; **to s. doing** éviter de faire.

shunt [ʃʌnt] *vt* (*train, conversation*) aiguiller (**on** to sur); **we were shunted (to and fro)** *Fam* on nous a baladés (**from** office **to** office/*etc* de bureau en bureau/*etc*).

shush! [ʃʊʃ] *int* chut!

shut [ʃʌt] *vt* (*pt* & *pp* **shut**, *pp* **shutting**) fermer; **to s. one's finger in** (*door etc*) se prendre le doigt dans; **to s. away** *or* **in** (*lock away or in*) enfermer; **to s. down** fermer; **to s. off** fermer; (*engine*) arrêter; (*isolate*) isoler; **to s. out** (*light*) empêcher d'entrer; (*view*) boucher; (*exclude*) exclure (**of, from** de); **to s. s.o. out** (*lock out accidentally*) enfermer qn dehors; **to s. up** fermer; (*lock up*) enfermer (*personne, objet précieux etc*); (*silence*) *Fam* faire taire; – *vi* (*of door etc*) se fermer; (*of shop, museum etc*) fermer; **the door doesn't s.** la porte ne ferme pas; **to s. down** fermer (définitivement); **to s. up** (*be quiet*) *Fam* se taire. ◆**shutdown** *n* fermeture *f*.

shutter ['ʃʌtər] *n* volet *m*; (*of camera*) obturateur *m*.

shuttle ['ʃʌt(ə)l] n (bus, spacecraft etc) navette f; (in vehicle etc) transporter. ◆**shuttlecock** n (in badminton) volant m.

shy [ʃaɪ] a (-er, -est) timide; **to be s.** of doing avoir peur de faire; – vi **to s. away** reculer (**from s.o.** devant qn, **from doing** à l'idée de faire). ◆**—ness** n timidité f.

Siamese [saɪəˈmiːz] a siamois; **S. twins** frères mpl siamois, sœurs fpl siamoises.

sibling ['sɪblɪŋ] n frère m, sœur f.

Sicily ['sɪsɪlɪ] n Sicile f.

sick [sɪk] a (-er, -est) (ill) malade; (mind) malsain; (humour) noir; (cruel) sadique; **to be s.** (vomit) vomir; **to be off** or **away s.** be on s. leave être en congé de maladie; **to feel s.** avoir mal au cœur; **to be s. (and tired) of** Fam il m'écœure; – n **the s.** les malades mpl; – vi (vomit) Fam vomir; – vt **to s. sth up** Fam vomir qch. ◆**sickbay** n infirmerie f. ◆**sickbed** n lit m de malade. ◆**sickly** a (-ier, -iest) maladif; (pale, faint) pâle; (taste) écœurant. ◆**sickness** n maladie f; (vomiting) vomissement(s) m(pl); **motion s.** Aut mal m de la route.

sicken ['sɪkən] 1 vt écœurer. 2 vi **to be sickening for** (illness) couver. ◆**—ing** a écœurant.

side [saɪd] n côté m; (of hill, animal) flanc m; (of road, river) bord m; (of beef) quartier m; (of question) aspect m; (of character) facette f, aspect m; Sp équipe f; Pol parti m; **the right s.** (of fabric) l'endroit m; **the wrong s.** (of fabric) l'envers m; **by the s. of** (nearby) à côté de; **at** or **by my s.** à côté de moi, à mes côtés; **s. by s.** l'un à côté de l'autre; **to move to one s.** s'écarter; **on this s.** de ce côté; **on the other s.** de l'autre côté; **the other s.** TV Fam l'autre chaîne f; **on the big**/etc **s.** Fam plutôt grand/etc; **to take sides with** se ranger du côté de; **on our s.** de notre côté, avec nous; **on the s.** Fam (secretly) en catimini; (to make money) en plus; – a (lateral) latéral; (effect, issue) secondaire; (glance, view) de côté; (street) transversal; – vi **to s. with** se ranger du côté de. ◆**-sided** suffix **ten-s.** à dix côtés. ◆**sideboard 1** n buffet m. **2** npl (hair) pattes fpl. ◆**sideburns** npl (hair) Am pattes fpl. ◆**sidecar** n side-car m. ◆**sidekick** n Fam associé, -ée mf. ◆**sidelight** n Aut feu m de position. ◆**sideline** n activité f secondaire. ◆**sidesaddle** adv (to ride) en amazone. ◆**sidestep** vt (-pp-) éviter. ◆**sidetrack** vt **to get sidetracked** s'écarter du sujet. ◆**sidewalk** n Am trottoir m. ◆**sideways** adv & a de côté.

siding ['saɪdɪŋ] n Rail voie f de garage.

sidle ['saɪd(ə)l] vi **to s. up to s.o.** s'approcher furtivement de qn.

siege [siːdʒ] n Mil siège m.

siesta [sɪˈestə] n sieste f.

sieve [sɪv] n tamis m; (for liquids) Culin passoire f; – vt tamiser. ◆**sift** vt tamiser; **to s. out** (truth) Fig dégager; – vi **to s. through** (papers etc) examiner (à la loupe).

sigh [saɪ] n soupir m; – vti soupirer.

sight [saɪt] n vue f; (spectacle) spectacle m; (on gun) mire f; **to lose s.** of perdre de vue; **to catch s.** of apercevoir; **to come into s.** apparaître; **at first s.** à première vue; **by s.** de vue; **on** or **at s.** à vue; **in s.** (target, end, date etc) en vue; **keep out of s.!** ne te montre pas!; **he hates the s.** of me il ne peut pas me voir; **it's a lovely s.** c'est beau à voir; **the (tourist) sights** les attractions fpl touristiques; **to set one's sights on** (job etc) viser; **a s. longer**/etc Fam bien plus long/etc; vt (land) apercevoir. ◆**—ed** a qui voit, clairvoyant. ◆**—ing** n **to make a s.** of voir. ◆**sightseer** n touriste mf. ◆**sightseeing** n tourisme m.

sightly ['saɪtlɪ] a **not very s.** laid.

sign [saɪn] 1 n signe m; (notice) panneau m; (over shop, inn) enseigne f; **no s.** of aucune trace de; **to use s. language** parler par signes. **2** vt (put signature to) signer; **to s. away** or **over** céder (**to** à); **to s. on** or **up** (worker, soldier) engager; – vi signer; **to s. for** (letter) signer le reçu de; **to s. in** signer le registre; **to s. off** dire au revoir; **to s. on** (on the dole) s'inscrire au chômage; **to s. on** or **up** (of soldier, worker) s'engager; (for course) s'inscrire. ◆**signpost** n poteau m indicateur; – vt flécher.

signal ['sɪgnəl] n signal m; **traffic signals** feux mpl de circulation; **s. box,** Am **s. tower** Rail poste m d'aiguillage; – vt (-ll-, Am -l-) (message) communiquer (**to** à); (arrival etc) signaler (**to** à); – vi faire des signaux; **to s. (to) s.o. to do** faire signe à qn de faire. ◆**signalman** n (pl -men) Rail aiguilleur m.

signature ['sɪgnətʃər] n signature f; **s. tune** indicatif m (musical). ◆**signatory** n signataire mf.

signet ring ['sɪgnɪtrɪŋ] n chevalière f.

significant [sɪgˈnɪfɪkənt] a (meaningful) significatif; (important, large) important. ◆**significance** n (meaning) signification f; (importance) importance f. ◆**significantly** adv (appreciably) sensiblement; **s.,**

he . . . fait significatif, il . . . . ◆**'signify** vt (*mean*) signifier (**that** que); (*make known*) indiquer, signifier (**to** à).

silence ['saɪləns] n silence m; **in s.** en silence; – vt faire taire. ◆**silencer** n (*on car, gun*) silencieux m. ◆**silent** a silencieux; (*film, anger*) muet; **to keep** or **be s.** garder le silence (**about** sur). ◆**silently** adv silencieusement.

silhouette [sɪluː'et] n silhouette f. ◆**silhouetted** a **to be s. against** se profiler contre.

silicon ['sɪlɪkən] n silicium m; **s. chip** puce f de silicium. ◆**silicone** ['sɪlɪkən] n silicone f.

silk [sɪlk] n soie f. ◆**silky** a (-ier, -iest) soyeux.

sill [sɪl] n (*of window etc*) rebord m.

silly ['sɪlɪ] a (-ier, -iest) idiot, bête; **to do sth s.** faire une bêtise; **s. fool, Fam s. billy** idiot, -ote mf; – adv (*to act, behave*) bêtement.

silo ['saɪləʊ] n (pl -os) silo m.

silt [sɪlt] n vase f.

silver ['sɪlvər] n argent m; (*silverware*) argenterie f; **£5 in s.** 5 livres en pièces d'argent; – a (*spoon etc*) en argent, d'argent; (*hair, colour*) argenté; **s. jubilee** vingt-cinquième anniversaire m (d'un événement); **s. paper** papier m d'argent; **s. plate** argenterie f. ◆**s.-'plated** a plaqué argent. ◆**silversmith** n orfèvre m. ◆**silverware** n argenterie f. ◆**silvery** a (*colour*) argenté.

similar ['sɪmɪlər] a semblable (**to** à). ◆**simi-'larity** n ressemblance f (**between** entre, **to** avec). ◆**similarly** adv de la même façon; (*likewise*) de même.

simile ['sɪmɪlɪ] n Liter comparaison f.

simmer ['sɪmər] vi Culin mijoter, cuire à feu doux; (*of water*) frémir; (*of revolt, hatred etc*) couver; **to s. with** (*rage*) bouillir de; **to s. down** (*calm down*) Fam se calmer; – vt faire cuire à feu doux; (*water*) laisser frémir.

simper ['sɪmpər] vi minauder.

simple ['sɪmp(ə)l] a (-er, -est) (*plain, uncomplicated, basic etc*) simple. ◆**s.-'minded** a simple d'esprit. ◆**s.-'mindedness** n simplicité f d'esprit. ◆**simpleton** n nigaud, -aude mf. ◆**sim'plicity** n simplicité f. ◆**simplifi'cation** n simplification f. ◆**simplify** vt simplifier. ◆**sim'plistic** a simpliste. ◆**simply** adv (*plainly, merely*) simplement; (*absolutely*) absolument.

simulate ['sɪmjʊleɪt] vt simuler.

simultaneous [sɪməl'teɪnɪəs, Am saɪməl-'teɪnɪəs] a simultané. ◆—**ly** adv simultanément.

sin [sɪn] n péché m; – vi (-nn-) pécher.

since [sɪns] **1** prep (*in time*) depuis; **s. my departure** depuis mon départ; – conj depuis que; **s. she's been here** depuis qu'elle est ici; **it's a year s. I saw him** ça fait un an que je ne l'ai pas vu; – adv (*ever*) **s.** depuis. **2** conj (*because*) puisque.

sincere [sɪn'sɪər] a sincère. ◆**sincerely** adv sincèrement; **yours s.** (*in letter*) Com veuillez croire à mes sentiments dévoués. ◆**sin'cerity** n sincérité f.

sinew ['sɪnjuː] n Anat tendon m.

sinful ['sɪnfəl] a (*guilt-provoking*) coupable; (*shocking*) scandaleux; **he's s.** c'est un pécheur; **that's s.** c'est un péché.

sing [sɪŋ] vti (pt **sang**, pp **sung**) chanter; **to s. up** chanter plus fort. ◆—**ing** n (*of bird & musical technique*) chant m; (*way of singing*) façon f de chanter; – a (*lesson, teacher*) de chant. ◆—**er** n chanteur, -euse mf.

singe [sɪndʒ] vt (*cloth*) roussir; (*hair*) brûler; **to s. s.o.'s hair** (*at hairdresser's*) faire un brûlage à qn.

single ['sɪŋg(ə)l] a (*only one*) seul; (*room, bed*) pour une personne; (*unmarried*) célibataire; **s. ticket** billet m simple; **every s. day** tous les jours sans exception; **s. party** Pol parti m unique; – n (*ticket*) aller m (simple); (*record*) 45 tours m inv; pl Tennis simples mpl; **singles bar** bar m pour célibataires; – vt **to s. out** (*choose*) choisir. ◆**s.-'breasted** a (*jacket*) droit. ◆**s.-'decker** n (*bus*) autobus m sans impériale. ◆**s.-'handed** a sans aide. ◆**s.-'minded** a (*person*) résolu, qui n'a qu'une idée en tête. ◆**singly** adv (*one by on*) un à un.

singlet ['sɪŋglɪt] n (*garment*) maillot m de corps.

singsong ['sɪŋsɒŋ] n **to get together for a s.** se réunir pour chanter.

singular ['sɪŋgjʊlər] **1** a (*unusual*) singulier. **2** a Gram (*form*) singulier; (*noun*) au singulier; – n Gram singulier m; **in the s.** au singulier.

sinister ['sɪnɪstər] a sinistre.

sink¹ [sɪŋk] n (*in kitchen*) évier m; (*washbasin*) lavabo m.

sink² [sɪŋk] vi (pt **sank**, pp **sunk**) (*of ship, person etc*) couler; (*of sun, price, water level*) baisser; (*collapse, subside*) s'affaisser; **to s. (down) into** (*mud etc*) s'enfoncer dans; (*armchair etc*) s'affaler dans; **to s. in** (*of ink etc*) pénétrer; (*of fact etc*) Fam rentrer (dans le crâne); **has that sunk in?** *Fam* as-tu compris ça?; − *vt* (*ship*) couler; (*well*) creuser; **to s. into** (*thrust*) enfoncer dans; (*money*) *Com* investir dans; **a sinking feeling** un serrement de cœur.

sinner ['sɪnər] *n* pécheur *m*, pécheresse *f*.

sinuous ['sɪnjuəs] *a* sinueux.

sinus [saɪnəs] *n Anat* sinus *m inv*.

sip [sɪp] *vi* (-**pp**-) boire à petites gorgées; − *n* (*mouthful*) petite gorgée *f*; (*drop*) goutte *f*.

siphon ['saɪfən] *n* siphon *m*; − *vt* **to s. off** (*petrol*) siphonner; (*money*) *Fig* détourner.

sir [sɜːr] *n* monsieur *m*; **S. Walter Raleigh** (*title*) sir Walter Raleigh.

siren ['saɪərən] *n* (*of factory etc*) sirène *f*.

sirloin ['sɜːlɔɪn] *n* (*steak*) faux-filet *m*; (*joint*) aloyau *m*.

sissy ['sɪsɪ] *n* (*boy, man*) *Fam* femmelette *f*.

sister ['sɪstər] *n* sœur *f*; (*nurse*) infirmière *f* en chef. ◆**s.-in-law** *n* (*pl* **sisters-in-law**) belle-sœur *f*. ◆**sisterly** *a* fraternel.

sit [sɪt] *vi* (*pp & pp* **sat**, *pres p* **sitting**) s'asseoir; (*for artist*) poser (**for** pour); (*remain*) rester; (*of assembly etc*) siéger, être en séance; **to be sitting** (*of person, cat etc*) être assis; (*of bird*) être perché; **she sat** *or* **was sitting reading** elle était assise à lire; **to s. around** (*do nothing*) ne rien faire; **to s. back** (*in chair*) se caler; (*rest*) se reposer; (*do nothing*) ne rien faire; **to s. down** s'asseoir; **s.-down strike** grève *f* sur le tas; **to s. in on** (*lecture etc*) assister à; **to s. on** (*jury etc*) être membre de; (*fact etc*) *Fam* garder pour soi; **to s. through** *or* **out** (*film etc*) rester jusqu'au bout de; **to s. up** (*straight*) s'asseoir (bien droit); **to s. up waiting for s.o.** (*at night*) ne pas se coucher en attendant qn; − *vt* **to s. s.o. (down)** asseoir qn; **to s. (for)** (*exam*) se présenter à; **to s. out** (*event, dance*) ne pas prendre part à. ◆**sitting** *n* séance *f*; (*for one's portrait*) séance *f* de pose; (*in restaurant*) service *m*; − *a* (*committee etc*) en séance; **s. duck** *Fam* victime *f* facile; **s. tenant** locataire *mf* en possession des lieux. ◆**sitting room** *n* salon *m*.

site [saɪt] *n* emplacement *m*; (*archaeological*) site *m*; (*building*) **s.** chantier *m*; **launching s.** aire *f* de lancement; − *vt* (*building*) placer.

sit-in ['sɪtɪn] *n Pol* sit-in *m inv*.

sitter ['sɪtər] *n* (*for child*) baby-sitter *mf*.

situate ['sɪtʃʊeɪt] *vt* situer; **to be situated** être situé. ◆**situ'ation** *n* situation *f*.

six [sɪks] *a & n* six (*m*). ◆**six'teen** *a & n* seize (*m*). ◆**six'teenth** *a & n* seizième (*mf*). ◆**sixth** *a & n* sixième (*mf*); (**lower**) **s.**

form *Sch* = classe *f* de première; (**upper**) **s. form** *Sch* = classe *f* terminale; **a s.** (*fraction*) un sixième. ◆**sixtieth** *a & n* soixantième (*mf*). ◆**sixty** *a & n* soixante (*m*).

size [saɪz] **1** *n* (*of person, animal, garment etc*) taille *f*; (*measurements*) dimensions *fpl*; (*of egg, packet*) grosseur *f*; (*of book*) grandeur *f*, format *m*; (*of problem, town, damage*) importance *f*, étendue *f*; (*of sum*) montant *m*, importance *f*; (*of shoes, gloves*) pointure *f*; (*of shirt*) encolure *f*; **hip/chest s.** tour *m* de hanches/de poitrine; **it's the s. of . . .** c'est grand comme . . . **2** *n* (*glue*) colle *f*. **3** *vt* **to s. up** (*person*) jauger; (*situation*) évaluer. ◆**sizeable** *a* assez grand *or* gros.

sizzl/e ['sɪz(ə)l] *vi* grésiller. ◆**—ing** *a* **s.** (**hot**) brûlant.

skat/e¹ [skeɪt] *n* patin *m*; − *vi* patiner. ◆**—ing** *n* patinage *m*; **to go s.** faire du patinage; **s. rink** (*ice*) patinoire *f*; (*roller*) skating *m*. ◆**skateboard** *n* skateboard *m*. ◆**skater** *n* patineur, -euse *mf*.

skate² [skeɪt] *n* (*fish*) raie *f*.

skedaddle [skɪ'dæd(ə)l] *vi Fam* déguerpir.

skein [skeɪn] *n* (*of yarn*) écheveau *m*.

skeleton ['skelɪt(ə)n] *n* squelette *m*; − *a* (*crew, staff*) (réduit au) minimum; **s. key** passe-partout *m inv*.

skeptic ['skeptɪk] *Am* = **sceptic**.

sketch [sketʃ] *n* (*drawing*) croquis *m*, esquisse *f*; *Th* sketch *m*; **a rough s. of** (*plan*) *Fig* une esquisse de; − *vt* **to s. (out)** (*view, idea etc*) esquisser; **to s. in** (*details*) ajouter; − *vi* faire un *or* des croquis. ◆**sketchy** *a* (-**ier**, -**iest**) incomplet, superficiel.

skew [skjuː] *n* **on the s.** de travers.

skewer ['skjuər] *n* (*for meat etc*) broche *f*; (*for kebab*) brochette *f*.

ski [skiː] *n* (*pl* **skis**) ski *m*; **s. lift** télésiège *m*; **s. pants** fuseau *m*; **s. run** piste *f* de ski; **s. tow** téléski *m*; − *vi* (*pt* **skied** [skiːd], *pres p* **skiing**) faire du ski. ◆**—ing** *n Sp* ski *m*; − *a* (*school, clothes*) de ski. ◆**—er** *n* skieur, -euse *mf*.

skid [skɪd] **1** *vi* (-**dd**-) *Aut* déraper; **to s. into** déraper et heurter; − *n* dérapage *m*. **2** **a s. row** *Am* quartier *m* de clochards *or* de squats.

skill [skɪl] *n* habileté *f*, adresse *f* (**at** à); (*technique*) technique *f*; **one's skills** (*aptitudes*) ses compétences *fpl*. ◆**skilful** *a, Am* ◆**skillful** *a* habile (**at doing** à faire, **at sth** à qch). ◆**skilled** *a* habile (**at doing** à faire, **at sth** à qch); (*worker*) qualifié; (*work*) de spécialiste, de professionnel.

skillet ['skɪlɪt] *n Am* poêle *f* (à frire).

skim [skɪm] **1** *vt* (-**mm**-) (*milk*) écrémer;

(*soup*) écumer. **2** *vti* (**-mm-**) **to s. (over)**
(*surface*) effleurer; **to s. through** (*book*)
parcourir.

skimp [skɪmp] *vi* (*on fabric, food etc*) lésiner
(**on** sur). ◆**skimpy** *a* (**-ier, -iest**) (*clothes*)
étriqué; (*meal*) insuffisant.

skin [skɪn] *n* peau *f*; **he has thick s.** *Fig* c'est
un dur; **s. diving** plongée *f* sous-marine; **s.
test** cuti-(réaction) *f*; – *vt* (**-nn-**) (*animal*)
écorcher; (*fruit*) peler. ◆**s.-'deep** *a*
superficiel. ◆**s.-'tight** *a* moulant, collant.

skinflint ['skɪnflɪnt] *n* avare *mf*.

skinhead ['skɪnhed] *n* skinhead *m*, jeune
voyou *m*.

skinny ['skɪnɪ] *a* (**-ier, -iest**) maigre.

skint [skɪnt] *a* (*penniless*) *Fam* fauché.

skip¹ [skɪp] **1** *vi* (**-pp-**) (*jump*) sauter; (*hop
about*) sautiller; (*with rope*) sauter à la
corde; **to s. off** (*leave*) *Fam* filer; **skipping
rope** corde *f* à sauter; – *n* petit saut *m*. **2** *vt*
(**-pp-**) (*omit, miss*) sauter; **to s. classes**
sécher les cours; **s. it!** (*forget it*) *Fam* laisse
tomber!

skip² [skɪp] *n* (*container for debris*) benne *f*.

skipper ['skɪpər] *n Nau Sp* capitaine *m*.

skirmish ['skɜːmɪʃ] *n* accrochage *m*.

skirt [skɜːt] **1** *n* jupe *f*. **2** *vt* **to s. round**
contourner; **skirting board** (*on wall*)
plinthe *f*.

skit [skɪt] *n Th* pièce *f* satirique; **a s. on** une
parodie de.

skittle ['skɪt(ə)l] *n* quille *f*; *pl* (*game*) jeu *m*
de quilles.

skiv/e [skaɪv] *vi* (*skirk*) *Fam* tirer au flanc;
to s. off (*slip away*) *Fam* se défiler. ◆**—er** *n*
Fam tire-au-flanc *m inv*.

skivvy ['skɪvɪ] *n Pej Fam* bonne *f* à tout
faire, bon(n)iche *f*.

skulk [skʌlk] *vi* rôder (furtivement).

skull [skʌl] *n* crâne *m*. ◆**skullcap** *n* calotte
f.

skunk [skʌŋk] *n* (*animal*) mouffette *f*;
(*person*) *Pej* salaud *m*.

sky [skaɪ] *n* ciel *m*. ◆**skydiving** *n* parachutisme *m* (en chute libre). ◆**sky-'high** *a*
(*prices*) exorbitant. ◆**skylight** *n* lucarne *f*.
◆**skyline** *n* (*outline of buildings*) ligne *f*
d'horizon. ◆**skyrocket** *vi* (*of prices*) *Fam*
monter en flèche. ◆**skyscraper** *n*
gratte-ciel *m inv*.

slab [slæb] *n* (*of concrete etc*) bloc *m*; (*thin,
flat*) plaque *f*; (*of chocolate*) tablette *f*,
plaque *f*; (*paving stone*) dalle *f*.

slack [slæk] *a* (**-er, -est**) (*knot, spring*) lâche;
(*discipline, security*) relâché; (*trade,
grip*) faible, mou; (*negligent*) négligent;
(*worker, student*) peu sérieux; **s. periods**

(*weeks etc*) périodes *fpl* creuses; (*hours*)
heures *fpl* creuses; **to be s.** (*of rope*) avoir du
mou; – *vi* **to s. off** (*in effort*) se relâcher.
◆**slacken** *vi* **to s. (off)** (*in effort*) se
relâcher; (*of production, speed, zeal*)
diminuer; – *vt* **to s. (off)** (*rope*) relâcher;
(*pace, effort*) ralentir. ◆**slacker** *n*
(*person*) *Fam* flemmard, -arde *mf*.
◆**slackly** *adv* (*loosely*) lâchement.
◆**slackness** *n* négligence *f*; (*of discipline*)
relâchement *m*; (*of rope*) mou *m*; *Com* stagnation *f*.

slacks [slæks] *npl* pantalon *m*.

slag [slæg] *n* (*immoral woman*) *Sl* salope *f*,
traînée *f*.

slagheap ['slæghiːp] *n* terril *m*.

slake [sleɪk] *vt* (*thirst*) *Lit* étancher.

slalom ['slɑːləm] *n Sp* slalom *m*.

slam [slæm] **1** *vt* (**-mm-**) (*door, lid*) claquer;
(*hit*) frapper violemment; **to s. (down)** (*put
down*) poser violemment; **to s. on the
brakes** écraser le frein, freiner à bloc; – *vi*
(*of door*) claquer; – *n* claquement *m*. **2** *vt*
(**-mm-**) (*criticize*) *Fam* critiquer (avec virulence).

slander ['slɑːndər] *n* diffamation *f*,
calomnie *f*; – *vt* diffamer, calomnier.

slang [slæŋ] *n* argot *m*; – *a* (*word etc*)
d'argot, argotique. ◆**slanging match** *n*
Fam engueulade *f*.

slant [slɑːnt] *n* inclinaison *f*; (*point of view*)
Fig angle *m* (**on** sur); (*bias*) *Fig* parti-pris
m; **on a s.** penché; (*roof*) en pente; – *vi* (*of
writing*) pencher; (*of roof*) être en pente; –
vt (*writing*) faire pencher; (*news*) *Fig*
présenter de façon partiale. ◆**—ed** *a*,
◆**—ing** *a* penché; (*roof*) en pente.

slap [slæp] **1** *n* tape *f*, claque *f*; (*on face*) gifle
f; – *vt* (**-pp-**) donner une tape à; **to s. s.o.'s
face** gifler qn; **to s. s.o.'s bottom** donner
une fessée à qn. **2** *vt* (**-pp-**) (*put*) mettre,
flanquer; **to s. on** (*apply*) appliquer à la
va-vite; (*add*) ajouter. **3** *adv* **s. in the middle**
Fam en plein milieu. ◆**slapdash** *a*
(*person*) négligent; (*task*) fait à la va-vite;
– *adv* à la va-vite. ◆**slaphappy** *a Fam*
(*carefree*) insouciant; (*negligent*) négligent.
◆**slapstick** *a & n s.* (*comedy*) grosse farce
f. ◆**slap-up 'meal** *n Fam* gueuleton *m*.

slash [slæʃ] **1** *vt* (*cut with blade etc*) entailler,
tailler; (*sever*) trancher; – *n* entaille *f*,
taillade *f*. **2** *vt* (*reduce*) réduire radicalement; (*prices*) *Com* écraser.

slat [slæt] *n* (*in blind*) lamelle *f*.

slate [sleɪt] *n* ardoise *f*. **2** *vt* (*book etc*) *Fam*
critiquer, démolir.

slaughter ['slɔːtər] *vt* (*people*) massacrer;

(*animal*) abattre; − *n* massacre *m*; abattage *m*. ◆**slaughterhouse** *n* abattoir *m*.

Slav [slɑ:v] *a* & *n* slave (*mf*). ◆**Sla'vonic** *a* (*language*) slave.

slave [sleɪv] *n* esclave *mf*; **the s. trade** *Hist* la traite des noirs; **s. driver** *Fig Pej* négrier *m*; − *vi* **to s. (away)** se crever (au travail), bosser comme une bête; **to s. away doing** s'escrimer à faire. ◆**slavery** *n* esclavage *m*. ◆**slavish** *a* servile.

slaver ['slævər] *vi* (*dribble*) baver (**over** sur); − *n* bave *f*.

slay [sleɪ] *vt* (*pt* **slew**, *pp* **slain**) *Lit* tuer.

sleazy ['sli:zɪ] *a* (**-ier, -iest**) *Fam* sordide, immonde.

sledge [sledʒ] (*Am* **sled** [sled]) *n* luge *f*; (*horse-drawn*) traîneau *m*.

sledgehammer ['sledʒhæmər] *n* masse *f*.

sleek [sli:k] *a* (**-er, -est**) lisse, brillant; (*manner*) onctueux.

sleep [sli:p] *n* sommeil *m*; **to have a s., get some s.** dormir; **to send to s.** endormir; **to go** *or* **get to s.** s'endormir; **to go to s.** (*of arm, foot*) *Fam* s'engourdir; − *vi* (*pt* & *pp* **slept**) dormir; (*spend the night*) coucher; **s. tight** *or* **well!** dors bien!; **I'll s. on it** *Fig* je déciderai demain, la nuit portera conseil; − *vt* **this room sleeps six** on peut coucher *or* loger six personnes dans cette chambre; **to s. it off** *Fam*, **s. off a hangover** cuver son vin. ◆**-ing** *a* (*asleep*) endormi; **s. bag** sac *m* de couchage; **s. car** wagon-lit *m*; **s. pill** somnifère *m*; **s. quarters** chambre(s) *f*(*pl*), dortoir *m*. ◆**sleeper** *n* **1 to be a light/sound s.** avoir le sommeil léger/ lourd. **2** *Rail* (*on track*) traverse *f*; (*berth*) couchette *f*; (*train*) train *m* couchettes. ◆**sleepiness** *n* torpeur *f*. ◆**sleepless** *a* (*hours*) sans sommeil; (*night*) d'insomnie. ◆**sleepwalker** *n* somnambule *mf*. ◆**sleepwalking** *n* somnambulisme *m*. ◆**sleepy** *a* (**-ier, -iest**) (*town, voice*) endormi; **to be s.** (*of person*) avoir sommeil.

sleet [sli:t] *n* neige *f* fondue; (*sheet of ice*) *Am* verglas *m*; − *vi* **it's sleeting** il tombe de la neige fondue.

sleeve [sli:v] *n* (*of shirt etc*) manche *f*; (*of record*) pochette *f*; **up one's s.** (*surprise, idea etc*) *Fig* en réserve; **long-/short-sleeved** à manches longues/courtes.

sleigh [sleɪ] *n* traîneau *m*.

sleight [slaɪt] *n* **s. of hand** prestidigitation *f*.

slender ['slendər] *a* (*person*) mince, svelte; (*neck, hand*) fin; (*feeble, small*) *Fig* faible.

slept [slept] *see* **sleep**.

sleuth [slu:θ] *n* (*detective*) *Hum* (fin) limier *m*.

slew [slu:] *n* **a s. of** *Am Fam* un tas de, une tapée de.

slice [slaɪs] *n* tranche *f*; (*portion*) *Fig* partie *f*, part *f*; − *vt* **to s. (up)** couper (en tranches); **to s. off** (*cut off*) couper.

slick [slɪk] **1** *a* (**-er, -est**) (*glib*) qui a la parole facile; (*manner*) mielleux; (*cunning*) astucieux; (*smooth, slippery*) lisse. **2** *n* **oil s.** nappe *f* de pétrole; (*large*) marée *f* noire.

slid/e [slaɪd] *n* (*act*) glissade *f*; (*in value etc*) *Fig* baisse *f*; (*in playground*) toboggan *m*; (*on ice*) glissoire *f*; (*for hair*) barrette *f*; *Phot* diapositive *f*; (*of microscope*) lamelle *f*, lame *f*; **s. rule** règle *f* à calcul; − *vi* (*pt* & *pp* **slid**) glisser; **to s. into** (*room etc*) se glisser dans; − *vt* (*letter etc*) glisser (**into** dans); (*table etc*) faire glisser. ◆**-ing** *a* (*door, panel*) à glissière; (*roof*) ouvrant; **s. scale** *Com* échelle *f* mobile.

slight [slaɪt] **1** *a* (**-er, -est**) (*slim*) mince; (*frail*) frêle; (*intelligence*) faible; **the slightest thing** la moindre chose; **not in the slightest** pas le moins du monde. **2** *vt* (*offend*) offenser; (*ignore*) bouder; − *n* affront *m* (**on** à). ◆**-ly** *adv* légèrement, un peu; **s. built** fluet.

slim [slɪm] *a* (**slimmer, slimmest**) mince; − *vi* (**-mm-**) maigrir. ◆**slimming** *a* (*diet*) amaigrissant; (*food*) qui ne fait pas grossir. ◆**slimness** *n* minceur *f*.

slime [slaɪm] *n* boue *f* (visqueuse); (*of snail*) bave *f*. ◆**slimy** *a* (**-ier, -iest**) (*muddy*) boueux; (*sticky, smarmy*) visqueux.

sling [slɪŋ] **1** *n* (*weapon*) fronde *f*; (*toy*) lance-pierres *m inv*; (*for arm*) *Med* écharpe *f*; **in a s.** en écharpe. **2** *vt* (*pt* & *pp* **slung**) (*throw*) jeter, lancer; (*hang*) suspendre; **to s. away** *or* **out** (*throw out*) *Fam* balancer. ◆**slingshot** *n* *Am* lance-pierres *m inv*.

slip [slɪp] **1** *n* (*mistake*) erreur *f*; (*woman's undergarment*) combinaison *f*; (*of paper for filing*) fiche *f*; **a s. of paper** (*bit*) un bout de papier; **a s. (of the tongue)** un lapsus; **to give s.o. the s.** fausser compagnie à qn; **s. road** *Aut* bretelle *f*. **2** *vi* (**-pp-**) glisser; **to s. into** (*go, slip*) se glisser dans; (*habit*) prendre; (*garment*) mettre; **to let s.** (*chance, oath, secret*) laisser échapper; **to s. through** (*crowd*) se faufiler parmi; **to s. along** *or* **over** to faire un saut chez; **to s. away** (*escape*) s'esquiver; **to s. back/in** retourner/entrer furtivement; **to s. out** sortir furtivement; (*pop out*) sortir (un instant); (*of secret*) s'éventer; **to s. past** (*guards*) passer sans être vu de; **to s. up** (*make a* *mistake*) *Fam* gaffer; − *vt* (*slide*) glisser (**to à**, **into** dans); **it slipped his** *or* **her notice** ça lui a échappé; **it slipped his** *or* **her mind** ça lui est sorti de l'esprit; **to s. off** (*garment etc*) enlever; **to s. on** (*garment etc*) mettre. ◆**s.-up** *n Fam* gaffe *f*, erreur *f*.

slipcover ['slɪpkʌvər] *n Am* housse *f*.

slipper ['slɪpər] *n* pantoufle *f*.

slippery ['slɪpərɪ] *a* glissant.

slipshod ['slɪpʃɒd] *a* (*negligent*) négligent; (*slovenly*) négligé.

slit [slɪt] *n* (*opening*) fente *f*; (*cut*) coupure *f*; − *vt* (*pt & pp* **slit**, *pres p* **slitting**) (*cut*) couper; (*tear*) déchirer; **to s. open** (*sack*) éventrer.

slither ['slɪðər] *vi* glisser; (*of snake*) se couler.

sliver ['slɪvər] *n* (*of apple etc*) lichette *f*; (*of wood*) éclat *m*.

slob [slɒb] *n Fam* malotru *m*, goujat *m*.

slobber ['slɒbər] *vi* (*of dog etc*) baver (**over** sur); − *n* bave *f*.

slog [slɒg] **1** *n* **a** (**hard**) **s.** (*effort*) un gros effort; (*work*) un travail dur; − *vi* (**-gg-**) **to s.** (**away**) bosser, trimer. **2** *vt* (**-gg-**) (*hit*) donner un grand coup à.

slogan ['sləʊgən] *n* slogan *m*.

slop [slɒp] *n* **slops** eaux *fpl* sales; − *vi* (**-pp-**) **to s.** (**over**) (*spill*) se répandre; − *vt* répandre.

slop/e [sləʊp] *n* pente *f*; (*of mountain*) flanc *m*; (*slant*) inclinaison *f*; − *vi* être en pente; (*of handwriting*) pencher; **to s. down** descendre en pente. ◆**—ing** *a* en pente; (*handwriting*) penché.

sloppy ['slɒpɪ] *a* (**-ier, -iest**) (*work, appearance*) négligé; (*person*) négligent; (*mawkish*) sentimental; (*wet*) détrempé; (*watery*) liquide.

slosh [slɒʃ] *vt* (*pour*) *Fam* répandre. ◆**—ed** *a* (*drunk*) *Fam* bourré.

slot [slɒt] *n* (*slit*) fente *f*; (*groove*) rainure *f*; (*in programme*) *Rad TV* créneau *m*; **s. machine** (*vending*) distributeur *m* automatique; (*gambling*) machine *f* à sous; − *vt* (**-tt-**) (*insert*) insérer (**into** dans); − *vi* s'insérer (**into** dans).

sloth [sləʊθ] *n Lit* paresse *f*.

slouch [slaʊtʃ] **1** *vi* ne pas se tenir droit; (*have stoop*) avoir le dos voûté; (*in chair*) se vautrer (**in** dans); **slouching over** (*desk etc*) penché sur; − *n* mauvaise tenue *f*; **with a s.** (*to walk*) en se tenant mal; **the dos voûté. 2** *n Fam* (*person*) lourdaud, -aude *mf*; (*lazy*) paresseux, -euse *mf*.

slovenly ['slʌvənlɪ] *a* négligé. ◆**slovenli-**

-ness *n* (*of dress*) négligé *m*; (*carelessness*) négligence *f*.

slow [sləʊ] *a* (**-er, -est**) lent; (*business*) calme; (*party, event*) ennuyeux; **at (a) s. speed** à vitesse réduite; **to be a s. walker** marcher lentement; **to be s.** (*of clock, watch*) retarder; **to be five minutes s.** retarder de cinq minutes; **to be s. to act** *or* **in acting** être lent à agir; **in s. motion** au ralenti; − *adv* lentement; − *vt* **to s. down** *or* **up** ralentir; (*delay*) retarder; − *vi* **to s. down** *or* **up** ralentir. ◆**—ly** *adv* lentement; (*bit by bit*) peu à peu. ◆**—ness** *n* lenteur *f*.

slowcoach ['sləʊkəʊtʃ] *n Fam* lambin, -ine *mf*. ◆**slow-down** *n* ralentissement *m*; **s.-down** (*strike*) *Am* grève *f* perlée. ◆**slow-'moving** *a* (*vehicle etc*) lent. ◆**slowpoke** *n Am Fam* lambin, -ine *mf*.

sludge [slʌdʒ] *n* gadoue *f*.

slue [sluː] *n Am Fam* = **slew**.

slug [slʌg] **1** *n* (*mollusc*) limace *f*. **2** *n* (*bullet*) *Am Sl* pruneau *m*. **3** *vt* (**-gg-**) (*hit*) *Am Fam* frapper; − *n* coup *m*, marron *m*.

sluggish ['slʌgɪʃ] *a* lent, mou.

sluice [sluːs] *n* **s. (gate)** vanne *f*.

slum [slʌm] *n* (*house*) taudis *m*; **the slums** les quartiers *mpl* pauvres; − *a* (*district*) pauvre; − *vt* (**-mm-**) **to s. it** *Fam* manger de la vache enragée. ◆**slummy** *a* (**-ier, -iest**) sordide, pauvre.

slumber ['slʌmbər] *n Lit* sommeil *m*.

slump [slʌmp] *n* baisse *f* soudaine (**in** de); (*in prices*) effondrement *m*; *Econ* crise *f*; − *vi* (*decrease*) baisser; (*of prices*) s'effondrer; **to s. into** (*armchair etc*) s'affaisser dans.

slung [slʌŋ] *see* **sling 2**.

slur [slɜːr] **1** *vt* (**-rr-**) prononcer indistinctement; **to s. one's words** manger ses mots. **2** *n* **to cast a s. on** (*reputation etc*) porter atteinte à. ◆**slurred** *a* (*speech*) indistinct.

slush [slʌʃ] *n* (*snow*) neige *f* fondue; (*mud*) gadoue *f*. ◆**slushy** *a* (**-ier, -iest**) (*road*) couvert de neige fondue.

slut [slʌt] *n Pej* (*immoral*) salope *f*, traînée *f*; (*untidy*) souillon *f*.

sly [slaɪ] *a* (**-er, -est**) (*deceitful*) sournois; (*crafty*) rusé; − *n* **on the s.** en cachette. ◆**—ly** *adv* sournoisement; (*in secret*) en cachette.

smack [smæk] **1** *n* claque *f*; gifle *f*; fessée *f*; − *vt* donner une claque à; **to s. s.o.'s face** gifler qn; **to s. s.o.('s bottom)** donner une fessée à qn. **2** *adv* **s. in the middle** *Fam* en plein milieu. **3** *vi* **to s.** (*be suggestive of*) avoir des relents de. ◆**—ing** *n* fessée *f*.

small [smɔːl] *a* (**-er, -est**) petit; **in the s. hours** au petit matin; **s. talk** menus propos *mpl*; — *adv* (*to cut, chop*) menu; — *n* **the s. of the back** le creux *m* des reins. ◆**—ness** *n* petitesse *f*. ◆**smallholding** *n* petite ferme *f*. ◆**small-scale** *a Fig* peu important. ◆**small-time** *a* (*crook, dealer etc*) petit, sans grande envergure.

smallpox ['smɔːlpɒks] *n* petite vérole *f*.

smarmy ['smɑːmɪ] *a* (**-ier, -iest**) *Pej Fam* visqueux, obséquieux.

smart¹ [smɑːt] *a* (**-er, -est**) (*in appearance*) élégant; (*astute*) astucieux; (*clever*) intelligent; (*quick*) rapide; **s. aleck** *Fam* je-sais-tout *mf inv*. ◆**smarten** *vt* **to s. up** (*room etc*) embellir; — *vti* **to s. (oneself) up** (*make oneself spruce*) se faire beau, s'arranger. ◆**smartly** *adv* élégamment; (*quickly*) vite; (*astutely*) astucieusement. ◆**smartness** *n* élégance *f*.

smart² [smɑːt] *vi* (*sting*) brûler, faire mal.

smash [smæʃ] *vt* (*break*) briser; (*shatter*) fracasser; (*enemy*) écraser; (*record*) pulvériser; **to s. s.o.'s face (in)** *Fam* casser la gueule à qn; **to s. down** *or* **in** (*door*) fracasser; **to s. up** (*car*) esquinter; (*room*) démolir; — *vi* se briser; **to s. into** (*of car*) se fracasser contre; — *n* (*noise*) fracas *m*; (*blow*) coup *m*; (*accident*) collision *f*; **s. hit** *Fam* succès *m* fou. ◆**s.-up** *n* collision *f*.

smashing ['smæʃɪŋ] *a* (*wonderful*) *Fam* formidable. ◆**smasher** *n* **to be a (real) s.** *Fam* être formidable.

smattering ['smætərɪŋ] *n* **a s. of** (*French etc*) quelques notions *fpl* de.

smear [smɪər] *vt* (*coat*) enduire (**with** de); (*stain*) tacher (**with** de); (*smudge*) faire une trace sur; — *n* (*mark*) trace *f*; (*stain*) tache *f*; *Med* frottis *m*; **a s. on** (*attack*) *Fig* une atteinte à; **s. campaign** campagne *f* de diffamation.

smell [smel] *n* odeur *f*; (*sense of*) **s.** odorat *m*; — *vt* (*pt & pp* **smelled** *or* **smelt**) sentir; (*of animal*) flairer; — *vi* (*stink*) sentir (mauvais); (*have smell*) avoir une odeur; **to s. of smoke**/*etc* sentir la fumée/*etc*; **smelling salts** sels *mpl*. ◆**smelly** *a* (**-ier, -iest**) **to be s.** sentir (mauvais).

smelt¹ [smelt] *see* **smell**.

smelt² [smelt] *vt* (*ore*) fondre; **smelting works** fonderie *f*.

smidgen ['smɪdʒən] *n* **a s.** (*a little*) *Am Fam* un brin (**of** de).

smil/e [smaɪl] *n* sourire *m*; — *vi* sourire (**at s.o.** à qn, **at sth** de qch). ◆**—ing** *a* souriant.

smirk [smɜːk] *n* (*smug*) sourire *m* suffisant; (*scornful*) sourire *m* goguenard.

smith [smɪθ] *n* (*blacksmith*) forgeron *m*.

smithereens [smɪðə'riːnz] *npl* **to smash to s.** briser en mille morceaux.

smitten ['smɪt(ə)n] *a* **s. with** *Hum* (*desire, remorse*) pris de; (*in love with*) épris de.

smock [smɒk] *n* blouse *f*.

smog [smɒg] *n* brouillard *m* épais, smog *m*.

smoke [sməʊk] *n* fumée *f*; **to have a s.** fumer une cigarette *etc*; — *vt* (*cigarette, salmon etc*) fumer; **to s. out** (*room etc*) enfumer; — *vi* fumer; **'no smoking'** 'défense de fumer'; **smoking compartment** *Rail* compartiment *m* fumeurs. ◆**smokeless** *a* **s. fuel** combustible *m* non polluant. ◆**smoker** *n* fumeur, -euse *mf*; *Rail* compartiment *m* fumeurs. ◆**smoky** *a* (**-ier, -iest**) (*air*) enfumé; (*wall*) noirci de fumée; **it's s. here** il y a de la fumée ici.

smooth [smuːð] *a* (**-er, -est**) (*surface, skin etc*) lisse; (*road*) à la surface égale; (*movement*) régulier, sans à-coups; (*flight*) agréable; (*cream, manners*) onctueux; (*person*) doucereux; (*sea*) calme; **the s. running** la bonne marche (**of** de); — *vt* **to s. down** *or* **out** lisser; **to s. out** *or* **over** (*problems etc*) *Fig* aplanir. ◆**—ly** *adv* (*to land, pass off*) en douceur. ◆**—ness** *n* aspect *m* lisse; (*of road*) surface *f* égale.

smother ['smʌðər] *vt* (*stifle*) étouffer; **to s. with** (*kisses etc*) *Fig* couvrir de.

smoulder ['sməʊldər] *vi* (*of fire, passion etc*) couver.

smudge [smʌdʒ] *n* tache *f*, bavure *f*; — *vt* (*paper etc*) faire des taches sur, salir.

smug [smʌg] *a* (**smugger, smuggest**) (*smile etc*) béat; (*person*) content de soi, suffisant. ◆**—ly** *adv* avec suffisance.

smuggl/e ['smʌg(ə)l] *vt* passer (en fraude); **smuggled goods** contrebande *f*. ◆**—ing** *n* contrebande *f*. ◆**—er** *n* contrebandier, -ière *mf*.

smut [smʌt] *n inv* (*obscenity*) saleté(s) *f*(*pl*). ◆**smutty** *a* (**-ier, -iest**) (*joke etc*) cochon.

snack [snæk] *n* casse-croûte *m inv*; **s. bar** snack(-bar) *m*.

snafu [snæ'fuː] *n Sl* embrouillamini *m*.

snag [snæg] *n* **1** (*hitch*) inconvénient *m*, os *m*. **2** (*in cloth*) accroc *m*.

snail [sneɪl] *n* escargot *m*; **at a s.'s pace** comme une tortue.

snake [sneɪk] *n* (*reptile*) serpent *m*; — *vi* (*of river*) serpenter.

snap [snæp] **1** *vt* (**-pp-**) casser (avec un bruit sec); (*fingers, whip*) faire claquer; **to s. up a bargain** sauter sur une occasion; — *vi* se casser net; (*of whip*) claquer; (*of person*) *Fig* parler sèchement (**at** à); **s. out of it!** *Fam* secoue-toi!; — *n* claquement *m*, bruit m sec; *Phot* photo f; (*fastener*) *Am* bouton-pression m; **cold s.** *Met* coup m de froid. **2** a soudain, brusque; **to make a s. decision** décider sans réfléchir. ◆**snapshot** n photo f, instantané m.

snappy ['snæpɪ] a (**-ier, -iest**) (*pace*) vif; **make it s.!** *Fam* dépêche-toi!

snare [sneər] n piège m.

snarl [snɑːl] vi gronder (en montrant les dents); – n grondement m. ◆**s.-up** n *Aut Fam* embouteillage m.

snatch [snætʃ] vt saisir (*d'un geste vif*); (*some rest etc*) *Fig* (réussir à) prendre; **to s. sth from s.o.** arracher qch à qn; – n (*theft*) vol m (à l'arraché).

snatches ['snætʃɪz] npl (*bits*) fragments mpl (of de).

snazzy ['snæzɪ] a (**-ier, -iest**) *Fam* (*flashy*) tapageur; (*smart*) élégant.

sneak [sniːk] **1** vi **to s. in/out** entrer/sortir furtivement; **to s. off** s'esquiver; – a (*attack, visit*) furtif. **2** n (*telltale*) *Sch Fam* rapporteur, -euse mf; – vi **to s. on** *Sch Fam* dénoncer. ◆**sneaking** a (*suspicion*) vague; (*desire*) secret. ◆**sneaky** a (**-ier, -iest**) (*sly*) *Fam* sournois.

sneaker ['sniːkər] n (*shoe*) tennis f.

sneer [snɪər] n ricanement m; – vi ricaner; **to s. at** se moquer de.

sneeze [sniːz] n éternuement m; – vi éternuer.

snicker ['snɪkər] n & vi *Am* = snigger.

snide [snaɪd] a (*remark etc*) sarcastique.

sniff [snɪf] n reniflement m; – vt renifler; (*of dog*) flairer, renifler; **to s. out** (*bargain*) *Fig* renifler; – vi **to s. (at)** renifler. ◆**sniffle** vi renifler; – n **a s., the sniffles** *Fam* un petit rhume.

snigger ['snɪgər] n (petit) ricanement m; – vi ricaner. ◆**-ing** n ricanement(s) m(pl).

snip [snɪp] n (*piece*) petit bout m (coupé); (*bargain*) *Fam* bonne affaire f; **to make a s.** couper; – vt (**-pp-**) couper.

sniper ['snaɪpər] n *Mil* tireur m embusqué.

snippet ['snɪpɪt] n (*of conversation etc*) bribe f.

snivel ['snɪv(ə)l] vi (**-ll-**, *Am* **-l-**) pleurnicher. ◆**snivelling** a pleurnicheur.

snob [snɒb] n snob mf. ◆**snobbery** n snobisme m. ◆**snobbish** a snob inv.

snook [snuːk] n **to cock a s.** faire un pied de nez (at à).

snooker ['snuːkər] n snooker m, *sorte de jeu de billard*.

snoop [snuːp] vi fourrer son nez partout; **to s. on s.o.** (*spy on*) espionner qn.

snooty ['snuːtɪ] a (**-ier, -iest**) *Fam* snob inv.

snooze [snuːz] n petit somme m; – vi faire un petit somme.

snor/e [snɔːr] vi ronfler; – n ronflement m. ◆**-ing** n ronflements mpl.

snorkel ['snɔːk(ə)l] n *Sp Nau* tuba m.

snort [snɔːt] vi (*grunt*) grogner; (*sniff*) renifler; (*of horse*) renâcler; – n (*grunt*) grognement m.

snot [snɒt] n *Pej Fam* morve f. ◆**snotty** a (**-ier, -iest**) *Fam* (*nose*) qui coule; (*child*) morveux. ◆**snotty-nosed** a *Fam* morveux.

snout [snaʊt] n museau m.

snow [snəʊ] n neige f; – vi neiger; – vt **to be snowed in** être bloqué par la neige; **to be s. under with** (*work etc*) être submergé de. ◆**snowball** n boule f de neige; – vi (*increase*) faire boule de neige. ◆**snowbound** a bloqué par la neige. ◆**snow-capped** a (*mountain*) enneigé. ◆**snowdrift** n congère f. ◆**snowdrop** n *Bot* perce-neige m or f inv. ◆**snowfall** n chute f de neige. ◆**snowflake** n flocon m de neige. ◆**snowman** n (pl **-men**) bonhomme m de neige. ◆**snowmobile** n motoneige f. ◆**snowplough** n, *Am* ◆**snowplow** n chasse-neige m inv. ◆**snowstorm** n tempête f de neige. ◆**snowy** a (**-ier, -iest**) (*weather, hills, day etc*) neigeux.

snub [snʌb] **1** n rebuffade f; – vt (**-bb-**) (*offer etc*) rejeter; **to s. s.o.** snober qn. **2** a (*nose*) retroussé.

snuff [snʌf] **1** n tabac m à priser. **2** vt **to s. (out)** (*candle*) moucher. ◆**snuffbox** n tabatière f.

snuffle ['snʌf(ə)l] vi & n = sniffle.

snug [snʌg] a (**snugger, snuggest**) (*house etc*) confortable, douillet; (*garment*) bien ajusté; **we're s.** (*in chair etc*) on est bien; **s. in bed** bien au chaud dans son lit.

snuggle ['snʌg(ə)l] vi **to s. up to** se pelotonner contre.

so [səʊ] **1** adv (*to such a degree*) si, tellement (that que); (*thus*) ainsi, comme ça; **so that** (*purpose*) pour que (+ sub); (*result*) si bien que; **so as to do** pour faire; **I think so** je le pense, je pense que oui; **do so!** faites-le!; **if so** si oui; **is that so?** c'est vrai?; **so am I, so do I** etc moi aussi; **so much** (*to work etc*) tant, tellement (that que); **so much courage/etc** tant or tellement de courage/etc (that que); **so many** tant, tellement; **so many books/etc** tant or tellement de livres/etc (that que); **so very fast/etc** vraiment si vite/etc; **ten or so** environ dix; **so long!** *Fam* au revoir!; **and so on** et ainsi de suite. **2** *conj* (*therefore*) donc; (*in that case*) alors; **so what?** et alors? ◆**So-and-so** *n* **Mr So-and-so** Monsieur Un tel. ◆**so-'called** *a* soi-disant *inv.* ◆**so-so** *a Fam* comme ci comme ça.

soak [səʊk] *vt* (*drench*) tremper; (*washing, food*) faire tremper; **to s. up** absorber; – *vi* (*of washing etc*) tremper; **to s. in** (*of liquid*) s'infiltrer; – *n* **to give sth a s.** faire tremper qch. ◆**—ed** *a* **s. (through)** trempé (jusqu'aux os). ◆**—ing** *n* & *adv* **s. (wet)** trempé; – *n* trempage *m*.

soap [səʊp] *n* savon *m*; **s. opera** téléroman *m*; **s. powder** lessive *f*; – *vt* savonner. ◆**soapflakes** *npl* savon *m* en paillettes. ◆**soapsuds** *npl* mousse *f* de savon. ◆**soapy** *a* (**-ier, -iest**) *a* savonneux.

soar [sɔːr] *vi* (*of bird etc*) s'élever; (*of price*) monter (en flèche); (*of hope*) Fig grandir.

sob [sɒb] *n* sanglot *m*; – *vi* (**-bb-**) sangloter. ◆**sobbing** *n* (*sobs*) sanglots *mpl*.

sober ['səʊbər] **1** *a* **he's s.** (*not drunk*) il n'est pas ivre; – *vti* **to s. up** dessoûler. **2** *a* (*serious*) sérieux, sensé; (*meal, style*) sobre. ◆**—ly** *adv* sobrement.

soccer ['sɒkər] *n* football *m*.

sociable ['səʊʃəb(ə)l] *a* (*person*) sociable; (*evening*) amical. ◆**sociably** *adv* (*to act, reply*) aimablement.

social ['səʊʃəl] *a* social; (*life, gathering*) mondain; **s. club** foyer *m*; **s. science(s)** sciences *fpl* humaines; **s. security** (*aid*) aide *f* sociale; (*retirement pension*) *Am* pension *f* de retraite; **s. services** = sécurité *f* sociale; **s. worker** assistant *m* social; – *n* (*gathering*) réunion *f* (amicale). ◆**socialism** *n* socialisme *m*. ◆**socialist** *a* & *n* socialiste (*mf*). ◆**socialite** *n* mondain, -aine *mf*. ◆**socialize** *vi* (*mix*) se mêler aux autres; (*talk*) bavarder (**with** avec). ◆**socially** *adv* socialement; (*to meet s.o., behave*) en société.

society [sə'saɪətɪ] *n* (*community, club, companionship etc*) société *f*; *Univ Sch* club *m*; – *a* (*wedding etc*) mondain.

sociology [səʊsɪ'ɒlədʒɪ] *n* sociologie *f*. ◆**socio'logical** *a* sociologique. ◆**sociologist** *n* sociologue *mf*.

sock [sɒk] **1** *n* chaussette *f*. **2** *vt* (*hit*) *Sl* flanquer un marron à.

socket ['sɒkɪt] *n* (*of bone*) cavité *f*; (*of eye*) orbite *f*; (*power point*) *El* prise *f* de courant; (*of lamp*) douille *f*.

sod [sɒd] *n* (*turf*) *Am* gazon *m*.

soda ['səʊdə] *n* **1** *Ch* soude *f*; **washing s.** cristaux *mpl* de soude. **2** (*water*) eau *f* de Seltz; **s. (pop)** *Am* soda *m*.

sodden ['sɒd(ə)n] *a* (*ground*) détrempé.

sodium ['səʊdɪəm] *n Ch* sodium *m*.

sofa ['səʊfə] *n* canapé *m*, divan *m*; **s. bed** canapé-lit *m*.

soft [sɒft] *a* (**-er, -est**) (*smooth, gentle, supple*) doux; (*butter, ground, snow*) mou; (*wood, heart, paste, colour*) tendre; (*flabby*) flasque, mou; (*easy*) facile; (*indulgent*) indulgent; (*cowardly*) Fam poltron; (*stupid*) Fam ramolli; **it's too s.** (*radio etc*) ce n'est pas assez fort; **s. drink** boisson *f* non alcoolisée. ◆**s.-'boiled** *a* (*egg*) à la coque. ◆**soften** ['sɒf(ə)n] *vt* (*object*) ramollir; (*voice, pain, colour*) adoucir; – *vi* se ramollir; s'adoucir. ◆**softie** *n Fam* sentimental, -ale *mf*; (*weakling*) mauviette *f*. ◆**softly** *adv* doucement. ◆**softness** *n* douceur *f*; (*of butter, ground, snow*) mollesse *f*.

software ['sɒftweər] *n inv* (*of computer*) logiciel *m*.

soggy ['sɒgɪ] *a* (**-ier, -iest**) (*ground*) détrempé; (*biscuit, bread*) ramolli.

soil [sɔɪl] **1** *n* (*earth*) sol *m*, terre *f*. **2** *vt* (*dirty*) salir; – *vi* se salir.

solar ['səʊlər] *a* solaire.

sold [səʊld] *see* sell.

solder ['sɒldər, *Am* 'sɒdər] *vt* souder; – *n* soudure *f*.

soldier ['səʊldʒər] **1** *n* soldat *m*, militaire *m*. **2** *vi* **to s. on** persévérer.

sole [səʊl] **1** *n* (*of shoe*) semelle *f*; (*of foot*) plante *f*; – *vt* ressemeler. **2** *a* (*only*) seul, unique; (*rights, representative*) *Com* exclusif. **3** *n* (*fish*) sole *f*. ◆**—ly** *adv* uniquement; **you're s. to blame** tu es seul coupable.

solemn ['sɒləm] *a* (*formal*) solennel; (*serious*) grave. ◆**so'lemnity** *n* solennité *f*; gravité *f* ◆**solemnly** *adv* (*to promise*) solennellement; (*to say*) gravement.

solicit [sə'lɪsɪt] *vt* (*seek*) solliciter; – *vi* (*of prostitute*) racoler. ◆**solicitor** *n* (*for wills etc*) notaire *m*.

solid ['sɒlɪd] *a* (*car, character, meal etc*) & *Ch* solide; (*wall, line, ball*) plein; (*gold, rock*) massif; (*crowd, mass*) compact; **frozen s.** entièrement gelé; **ten days s.** dix jours d'affilée; – *n Ch* solide *m*; *pl Culin* aliments *mpl* solides. ◆**so'lidify** *vi* se solidifier. ◆**so'lidity** *n* solidité *f*. ◆**solidly** *adv* (*built etc*) solidement; (*to support, vote*) en masse.

solidarity [sɒlɪ'dærətɪ] *n* solidarité *f* (**with** avec).

soliloquy [sə'lɪləkwɪ] *n* monologue *m*.

solitary ['sɒlɪtərɪ] *a* (*lonely, alone*) solitaire;

(*only*) seul; **s. confinement** *Jur* isolement *m* (cellulaire). ◆**solitude** *n* solitude *f*.

solo ['səʊləʊ] *n* (*pl* **-os**) *Mus* solo *m*; – *a* solo *inv*; – *adv Mus* en solo; (*to fly*) en solitaire. ◆**soloist** *n Mus* soliste *mf*.

solstice ['sɒlstɪs] *n* solstice *m*.

soluble ['sɒljʊb(ə)l] *a* (*substance, problem*) soluble.

solution [sə'luːʃ(ə)n] *n* (*to problem etc*) & *Ch* solution *f* (**to** de).

solv/e [sɒlv] *vt* (*problem etc*) résoudre. ◆**—able** *a* soluble.

solvent ['sɒlvənt] **1** *a* (*financially*) solvable. **2** *n Ch* (dis)solvant *m*. ◆**solvency** *n Fin* solvabilté *f*.

sombre ['sɒmbər] *a* sombre, triste.

some [sʌm] *a* **1** (*amount, number*) **s. wine** du vin; **s. glue** de la colle; **s. water** de l'eau; **s. dogs** des chiens; **s. pretty flowers** de jolies fleurs. **2** (*unspecified*) un, une; **s. man (or other)** un homme (quelconque); **s. charm** (*a certain amount of*) un certain charme; **s. other way** quelque autre *or* une autre moyen; **that's s. book!** *Fam* ça, c'est un livre! **3** (*a few*) quelques, certains; (*a little*) un peu de; – *pron* **1** (*number*) quelques-un(e)s, certain(e)s (**of** de, d'entre). **2** (*a certain quantity*) en; **I want s.** j'en veux; **do you have s.?** en as-tu?; **s. of it is over** il en reste un peu *or* une partie; – *adv* (*about*) quelque; **s. ten years** quelque dix ans.

somebody ['sʌmbədɪ] *pron* = **someone**. ◆**someday** *adv* un jour. ◆**somehow** *adv* (*in some way*) d'une manière ou d'une autre; (*for some reason*) on ne sait pourquoi. ◆**someone** *pron* quelqu'un; **at s.'s house** chez qn; **s. small**/*etc* quelqu'un de petit/*etc*. ◆**someplace** *adv Am* quelque part. ◆**something** *pron* quelque chose; **s. awful**/*etc* quelque chose d'affreux/*etc*; **s. of a liar**/*etc* un peu menteur/*etc*; – *adv* **she plays s. like . . .** elle joue un peu comme . . . ; **it was s. awful** c'était vraiment affreux. ◆**sometime 1** *adv* un jour; **s. in May**/*etc* au cours du mois de mai/*etc*; **s. before his departure** avant son départ. **2** *a* (*former*) ancien. ◆**sometimes** *adv* quelquefois, parfois. ◆**somewhat** *adv* quelque peu, assez. ◆**somewhere** *adv* quelque part; **s. about fifteen** (*approximately*) environ quinze.

somersault ['sʌməsɔːlt] *n* culbute *f*; (*in air*) saut *m* périlleux; – *vi* faire la *or* une culbute.

son [sʌn] *n* fils *m*. ◆**s.-in-law** *n* (*pl* **sons-in-law**) beau-fils *m*, gendre *m*.

sonar ['səʊnɑːr] *n* sonar *m*.

sonata [sə'nɑːtə] *n Mus* sonate *f*.

song [sɒŋ] *n* chanson *f*; (*of bird*) chant *m*. ◆**songbook** *n* recueil *m* de chansons.

sonic ['sɒnɪk] *a* **s. boom** bang *m* (supersonique).

sonnet ['sɒnɪt] *n* (*poem*) sonnet *m*.

soon [suːn] *adv* (**-er, -est**) (*in a short time*) bientôt; (*quickly*) vite; (*early*) tôt; **s. after** peu après; **as s. as she leaves** aussitôt qu'elle partira; **no sooner had he spoken than** à peine avait-il parlé que; **I'd sooner leave** je préférerais partir; **I'd just as s. leave** j'aimerais autant partir; **sooner or later** tôt ou tard.

soot [sʊt] *n* suie *f*. ◆**sooty** *a* (**-ier, -iest**) couvert de suie.

sooth/e [suːð] *vt* (*pain, nerves*) calmer; *Fig* rassurer. ◆**—ing** *a* (*ointment, words*) calmant.

sophisticated [sə'fɪstɪkeɪtɪd] *a* (*person, taste*) raffiné; (*machine, method, beauty*) sophistiqué.

sophomore ['sɒfəmɔːr] *n Am* étudiant, -ante *mf* de seconde année.

soporific [sɒpə'rɪfɪk] *a* (*substance, speech etc*) soporifique.

sopping ['sɒpɪŋ] *a* & *adv* **s. (wet)** trempé.

soppy ['sɒpɪ] *a* (**-ier, -iest**) *Fam* (*silly*) idiot, bête; (*sentimental*) sentimental.

soprano [sə'prɑːnəʊ] *n* (*pl* **-os**) *Mus* (*singer*) soprano *mf*; (*voice*) soprano *m*.

sorbet ['sɔːbeɪ] *n* (*water ice*) sorbet *m*.

sorcerer ['sɔːsərər] *n* sorcier *m*.

sordid ['sɔːdɪd] *a* (*act, street etc*) sordide.

sore [sɔːr] *a* (**-er, -est**) (*painful*) douloureux; (*angry*) *Am* fâché (**at** contre); **a s. point** *Fig* un sujet délicat; **she has a s. thumb** elle a mal au pouce; **he's still s.** *Med* il a encore mal; – *n Med* plaie *f*. ◆**—ly** *adv* (*tempted, regretted*) très; **s. needed** dont on a grand besoin. ◆**—ness** *n* (*pain*) douleur *f*.

sorrow ['sɒrəʊ] *n* chagrin *m*, peine *f*. ◆**sorrowful** *a* triste.

sorry ['sɒrɪ] *a* (**-ier, -iest**) (*sight, state etc*) triste; **to be s.** (*regret*) être désolé, regretter (**to do** de faire); **I'm s. she can't come** je regrette qu'elle ne puisse pas venir; **I'm s. about the delay** je m'excuse pour ce retard; **s.!** pardon!; **to say s.** demander pardon (**to** à); **to feel** *or* **be s. for** plaindre.

sort [sɔːt] *n* **1** genre *m*, espèce *f*, sorte *f*; **a s. of** une sorte *or* espèce de; **a good s.** (*person*) *Fam* un brave type; **s. of sad**/*etc* plutôt triste/*etc*. **2** *vt* (*letters*) trier; (*classify, select*) trier; (*separate*) séparer (**from** de); (*arrange*) arranger; (*tidy*) ranger; (*problem*) régler; **to s. s.o. out** (*punish*) *Fam* faire voir à qn; − *vi* **to s. through** (*letters etc*) trier; **sorting office** centre *m* de tri. ◆**—er** *n* (*person*) trieur, -euse *mf*.

soufflé ['suːfleɪ] *n Culin* soufflé *m*.

sought [sɔːt] *see* **seek**.

soul [səʊl] *n* âme *f*; **not a living s.** (*nobody*) personne, pas âme qui vive; **a good s.** *Fig* un brave type; **s. mate** âme *f* sœur. ◆**s.-destroying** *a* abrutissant. ◆**s.-searching** *n* examen *m* de conscience.

sound¹ [saʊnd] *n* son *m*; (*noise*) bruit *m*; **I don't like the s. of it** ça ne me plaît pas du tout; − *a* (*wave, film*) sonore; (*engineer*) du son; **s. archives** phonothèque *f*; **s. barrier** mur *m* du son; **s. effects** bruitage *m*; − *vt* (*bell, alarm etc*) sonner; (*bugle*) sonner de; (*letter*) *Gram* prononcer; **to s. one's horn** *Aut* klaxonner; − *vi* retentir, sonner; (*seem*) sembler; **to s. like** sembler être; (*resemble*) ressembler à; **it sounds like** *or* **as if** il semble que (+ *sub or indic*); **to s. off about** *Pej* (*boast*) se vanter de; (*complain*) rouspéter à propos de. ◆**soundproof** *a* insonorisé; − *vt* insonoriser. ◆**soundtrack** *n* (*of film etc*) bande *f* sonore.

sound² [saʊnd] *a* (**-er, -est**) (*healthy*) sain; (*sturdy, reliable*) solide; (*instinct*) sûr; (*advice*) sensé; (*beating, sense*) bon; − *adv* **s. asleep** profondément endormi. ◆**—ly** *adv* (*asleep*) profondément; (*reasoned*) solidement; (*beaten*) complètement. ◆**—ness** *n* (*of mind*) santé *f*; (*of argument*) solidité *f*.

sound³ [saʊnd] *vt* (*test, measure*) sonder; **to s. s.o. out** sonder qn (**about** sur).

soup [suːp] *n* soupe *f*, potage *m*; **in the s.** (*in trouble*) *Fam* dans le pétrin.

sour ['saʊər] *a* (**-er, -est**) aigre; **to turn s.** (*of wine*) s'aigrir; (*of milk*) tourner; (*of friendship*) se détériorer; (*of conversation*) tourner au vinaigre; − *vi* (*of temper*) s'aigrir.

source [sɔːs] *n* (*origin*) source *f*; **s. of energy** source d'énergie.

south [saʊθ] *n* sud *m*; − *a* (*coast*) sud *inv*; (*wind*) du sud; **to be s. of** être au sud de; **S. America/Africa** Amérique *f*/Afrique *f* du Sud; **S. American** *a* & *n* sud-américain, -aine (*mf*); **S. African** *a* & *n* sud-africain, -aine (*mf*); − *adv* au sud, vers le sud. ◆**southbound** *a* (*carriageway*) sud *inv*; (*traffic*) en direction du sud. ◆**south-'east** *n* & *a* sud-est *m* & *a* inv. ◆**southerly** ['sʌðəlɪ] *a* (*point*) sud *inv*; (*direction, wind*) du sud. ◆**southern** ['sʌðən] *a* (*town*) du sud; (*coast*) sud *inv*; **S. Italy** le Sud de

l'Italie; **S. Africa** Afrique *f* australe. ◆**southerner** ['sʌðənər] *n* habitant, -ante *mf* du Sud. ◆**southward(s)** *a* & *adv* vers le sud. ◆**south-'west** *n* & *a* sud-ouest *m* & *a* inv.

souvenir [suːvə'nɪər] *n* (*object*) souvenir *m*.

sovereign ['sɒvrɪn] *n* souverain, -aine *mf*; − *a* (*State, authority*) souverain; (*rights*) de souveraineté. ◆**sovereignty** *n* souveraineté *f*.

Soviet ['səʊvɪət] *a* soviétique; **the S. Union** l'Union *f* soviétique.

sow¹ [saʊ] *n* (*pig*) truie *f*.

sow² [səʊ] *vt* (*pt* **sowed**, *pp* **sowed** *or* **sown**) (*seeds, doubt etc*) semer; (*land*) ensemencer (**with** de).

soya ['sɔɪə] *n* **s. (bean)** graine *f* de soja. ◆**soybean** *n Am* graine *f* de soja.

sozzled ['sɒz(ə)ld] *a* (*drunk*) *Sl* bourré.

spa [spɑː] *n* (*town*) station *f* thermale; (*spring*) source *f* minérale.

space [speɪs] *n* (*gap, emptiness*) espace *m*; (*period*) période *f*; **blank s.** espace *m*, blanc *m*; **(outer)** l'espace (cosmique); **to take up s.** (*room*) prendre de la place; **in the s. of** en l'espace de; **s. heater** (*electric*) radiateur *m*; − *a* (*voyage etc*) spatial; − *vt* **to s. out** espacer; **double/single spacing** (*on typewriter*) double/simple interligne *m*. ◆**spaceman** *n* (*pl* **-men**) astronaute *m*. ◆**spaceship** *n*, ◆**spacecraft** *n inv* engin *m* spatial. ◆**spacesuit** *n* scaphandre *m* (de cosmonaute).

spacious ['speɪʃəs] *a* spacieux, grand. ◆**—ness** *n* grandeur *f*.

spade [speɪd] *n* **1** (*for garden*) bêche *f*; (*of child*) pelle *f*. **2** *Cards* pique *m*. ◆**spadework** *n Fig* travail *m* préparatoire; (*around problem or case*) débroussaillage *m*.

spaghetti [spə'getɪ] *n* spaghetti(s) *mpl*.

Spain [speɪn] *n* Espagne *f*.

span [spæn] *n* (*of arch*) portée *f*; (*of wings*) envergure *f*; (*of life*) *Fig* durée *f*; − *vt* (**-nn-**) (*of bridge etc*) enjamber (*rivière etc*); *Fig* couvrir, embrasser.

Spaniard ['spænjəd] *n* Espagnol, -ole *mf*. ◆**Spanish** *a* espagnol; − *n* (*language*) espagnol *m*. ◆**Spanish-A'merican** *a* hispano-américain.

spaniel ['spænjəl] *n* épagneul *m*.

spank [spæŋk] *vt* fesser, donner une fessée à; − *n* **to give s.o. a s.** fesser qn. ◆**—ing** *n* fessée *f*.

spanner ['spænər] *n* (*tool*) clé *f* (à écrous); **adjustable s.** clé *f* à molette.

spar/e¹ [speər] **1** *a* (*extra, surplus*) de *or* en

trop; (*clothes, tyre*) de rechange; (*wheel*) de secours; (*available*) disponible; (*bed, room*) d'ami; **s. time** loisirs *mpl*; − *n* **s. (part)** *Tech Aut* pièce *f* détachée. **2** *vt* (*do without*) se passer de; (*s.o.'s life*) épargner; (*efforts, s.o.'s feelings*) ménager; **to s. s.o.** (*not kill*) épargner qn; (*grief, details etc*) épargner à qn; (*time*) accorder à qn; (*money*) donner à qn; **I can't s. the time** je n'ai pas le temps; **five to s.** cinq de trop. ◆—**ing** *a* (*use*) modéré; **to be s. with** (*butter etc*) ménager.
spare² [speər] *a* (*lean*) maigre.
spark [spɑːk] **1** *n* étincelle *f*. **2** *vt* **to s. off** (*cause*) provoquer. ◆**spark(ing) plug** *n Aut* bougie *f*.
sparkl/e ['spɑːk(ə)l] *vi* étinceler, scintiller; − *n* éclat *m*. ◆—**ing** *a* (*wine, water*) pétillant.
sparrow ['spærəʊ] *n* moineau *m*.
sparse [spɑːs] *a* clairsemé. ◆—**ly** *adv* (*populated etc*) peu.
spartan ['spɑːtən] *a* spartiate, austère.
spasm ['spæzəm] *n* (*of muscle*) spasme *m*; (*of coughing etc*) *Fig* accès *m*. ◆**spas-'modic** *a* (*pain etc*) spasmodique; *Fig* irrégulier.
spastic ['spæstɪk] *n* handicapé, -ée *mf* moteur.
spat [spæt] *see* **spit 1.**
spate [speɪt] *n* **a s. of** (*orders etc*) une avalanche de.
spatter ['spætər] *vt* (*clothes, person etc*) éclabousser (**with** de); − *vi* **to s. over s.o.** (*of mud etc*) éclabousser qn.
spatula ['spætjʊlə] *n* spatule *f*.
spawn [spɔːn] *n* (*of fish etc*) frai *m*; − *vi* frayer; − *vt* pondre; *Fig* engendrer.
speak [spiːk] *vi* (*pt* **spoke**, *pp* **spoken**) parler; (*formally, in assembly*) prendre la parole; **so to s.** pour ainsi dire; **that speaks for itself** c'est évident; **to s. of** être du bien de; **nothing to s. of** pas grand-chose; **Bob speaking** *Tel* Bob à l'appareil; **that's spoken for** c'est pris or réservé; **to s. out** or **up** (*boldly*) parler (franchement); **to s. up** (*more loudly*) parler plus fort; − *vt* (*language*) parler; (*say*) dire; **to s. one's mind** dire ce que l'on pense. ◆—**ing** *n* **public s.** art *m* oratoire; − *a* **to be on s. terms with** parler à; **English-/French-speaking** anglophone/francophone. ◆—**er** *n* (*public*) orateur *m*; (*in dialogue*) interlocuteur, -trice *mf*; (*loudspeaker*) El haut-parleur *m*; (*of hi-fi*) enceinte *f*; **to be a Spanish/a bad/etc s.** parler espagnol/mal/*etc*.
spear [spɪər] *n* lance *f*. ◆**spearhead** *vt*

(*attack*) être le fer de lance de; (*campaign*) mener.
spearmint ['spɪəmɪnt] *n Bot* menthe *f* (verte); − *a* à la menthe; (*chewing-gum*) mentholé.
spec [spek] *n* **on s.** (*as a gamble*) *Fam* à tout hasard.
special ['speʃ(ə)l] *a* spécial; (*care, attention*) (tout) particulier; (*measures*) Pol extraordinaire; (*favourite*) préféré; **by s. delivery** (*letter etc*) par exprès; − *n* **today's s.** (*in restaurant*) le plat du jour. ◆**specialist** *n* spécialiste *mf* (**in** de); − *a* (*dictionary, knowledge*) technique, spécialisé. ◆**speci'ality** *n* spécialité *f*. ◆**specialize** *vi* se spécialiser (**in** dans). ◆**specialized** *a* spécialisé. ◆**specially** *adv* (*specifically*) spécialement; (*on purpose*) (tout) spécialement. ◆**specialty** *n Am* spécialité *f*.
species ['spiːʃiːz] *n inv* espèce *f*.
specific [spə'sɪfɪk] *a* précis, explicite; *Phys Ch* spécifique. ◆**specifically** *adv* (*expressly*) expressément; (*exactly*) précisément.
specify ['spesɪfaɪ] *vt* spécifier (**that** que). ◆**specifi'cation** *n* spécification *f*; *pl* (*of car, machine etc*) caractéristiques *fpl*.
specimen ['spesɪmɪn] *n* (*example, person*) spécimen *m*; (*of blood*) prélèvement *m*; (*of urine*) échantillon *m*; **s. signature** spécimen *m* de signature; **s. copy** (*of book etc*) spécimen *m*.
specious ['spiːʃəs] *a* spécieux.
speck [spek] *n* (*stain*) petite tache *f*; (*of dust*) grain *m*; (*dot*) point *m*.
speckled ['spek(ə)ld] *a* tacheté.
specs [speks] *npl Fam* lunettes *fpl*.
spectacle ['spektək(ə)l] **1** *n* (*sight*) spectacle *m*. **2** *npl* (*glasses*) lunettes *fpl*. ◆**spec-'tacular** *a* spectaculaire. ◆**spec'tator** *n Sp etc* spectateur, -trice *mf*.
spectre ['spektər] *n* (*menacing image*) spectre *m* (**of** de).
spectrum, *pl* **-tra** ['spektrəm, -trə] *n Phys* spectre *m*; (*range*) *Fig* gamme *f*.
speculate ['spekjʊleɪt] *vi Fin Phil* spéculer; **to s. about** (*s.o.'s motives etc*) s'interroger sur; − *vt* **to s. that** (*guess*) conjecturer que. ◆**specu'lation** *n Fin Phil* spéculation *f*; (*guessing*) conjectures *fpl* (**about** sur). ◆**speculator** *n* spéculateur, -trice *mf*. ◆**speculative** *a Fin Phil* spéculatif; **that's s.** (*guesswork*) c'est très (très) hypothétique.
sped [sped] *see* **speed 1.**
speech [spiːtʃ] *n* (*talk, address*) & *Gram* discours *m* (**on** sur); (*faculty*) parole *f*;

(*diction*) élocution *f*; (*of group*) langage *m*; **a short s.** une allocution *f*; **freedom of s.** liberté *f* d'expression; **part of s.** *Gram* catégorie *f* grammaticale. ◆**—less** *a* muet (**with de**).

speed [spiːd] **1** *n* (*rate of movement*) vitesse *f*; (*swiftness*) rapidité *f*; **s. limit** *Aut* limitation *f* de vitesse; **–** *vt* (*pt & pp* **sped**) **to s. up** accélérer; **–** *vi* **to s. up** (*of person*) aller plus vite; (*of pace*) s'accélérer; **to s. past** passer à toute vitesse (**sth** devant qch). **2** *vi* (*pt & pp* **speeded**) (*drive too fast*) aller trop vite. ◆**—ing** *n Jur* excès *m* de vitesse. ◆**speedboat** *n* vedette *f*. ◆**spee'dometer** *n Aut* compteur *m* (de vitesse). ◆**speedway** *n Sp* piste *f* de vitesse pour motos; *Sp Aut Am* autodrome *m*.

speed/y ['spiːdɪ] *a* (**-ier, -iest**) rapide. ◆**—ily** *adv* rapidement.

spell [spel] *n* (*magic*) charme *m*, sortilège *m*; (*curse*) sort *m*; *Fig* charme *m*; **under a s.** envoûté. ◆**spellbound** *a* (*audience etc*) captivé.

spell [spel] *n* (*period*) (courte) période *f*; (*moment, while*) moment *m*; **s. of duty** tour *m* de service.

spell [spel] *vt* (*pt & pp* **spelled** *or* **spelt**) (*write*) écrire; (*say aloud*) épeler; (*of letters*) former (*mot*); (*mean*) *Fig* signifier; **to be able to s.** savoir l'orthographe; **how is it spelt?** comment cela s'écrit-il?; **to s. out** (*aloud*) épeler; *Fig* expliquer très clairement. ◆**—ing** *n* orthographe *f*.

spend [spend] **1** *vt* (*pt & pp* **spent**) (*money*) dépenser (**on** pour); **–** *vi* dépenser. **2** *vt* (*pt & pp* **spent**) (*time, holiday etc*) passer (**on sth** sur qch, **doing** à faire); (*energy, care etc*) consacrer (**on sth** à qch, **doing** à faire). ◆**—ing** *n* dépenses *fpl*; **–** *a* (*money*) de poche. ◆**—er** *n* **to be a big s.** dépenser beaucoup. ◆**spendthrift** *n* **to be a s.** être dépensier.

spent [spent] *see* **spend**; **–** *a* (*used*) utilisé; (*energy*) épuisé.

sperm [spɜːm] *n* (*pl* **sperm** *or* **sperms**) sperme *m*.

spew [spjuː] *vt* vomir.

sphere [sfɪər] *n* (*of influence, action etc*) & *Geom Pol* sphère *f*; (*of music, poetry etc*) domaine *m*; **the social s.** le domaine social. ◆**spherical** ['sferɪk(ə)l] *a* sphérique.

sphinx [sfɪŋks] *n* sphinx *m*.

spice [spaɪs] *n Culin* épice *f*; (*interest etc*) *Fig* piment *m*; **–** *vt* épicer. ◆**spicy** *a* (**-ier, -iest**) épicé; (*story*) *Fig* pimenté.

spick-and-span [spɪkən'spæn] *a* (*clean*) impeccable.

spider ['spaɪdər] *n* araignée *f*.

spiel [ʃpiːl] *n Fam* baratin *m*.

spike [spaɪk] *n* (*of metal*) pointe *f*; **–** *vt* (*pierce*) transpercer. ◆**spiky** *a* (**-ier, -iest**) *a* garni de pointes.

spill [spɪl] *vt* (*pt & pp* **spilled** *or* **spilt**) (*liquid*) répandre, renverser (**on, over** sur); **to s. the beans** *Fam* vendre la mèche; **–** *vi* **to s. (out)** se répandre; **to s. over** déborder.

spin [spɪn] *n* (*motion*) tour *m*; (*car ride*) petit tour *m*; (*on washing machine*) essorage *m*; **s. dryer** essoreuse *f*; **–** *vt* (*pt & pp* **spun**, *pres p* **spinning**) (*web, yarn, wool etc*) filer (**into** en); (*wheel, top*) faire tourner; (*washing*) essorer; (*story*) *Fig* débiter; **to s. out** (*speech etc*) faire durer; **–** *vi* (*of spinner, spider*) filer; **to s. (round)** (*of dancer, top, planet etc*) tourner; (*of head, room*) *Fig* tourner; (*of vehicle*) faire un tête-à-queue. ◆**spinning** *n* (*by hand*) filage *m*; (*process*) *Tech* filature *f*; **s. top** toupie *f*; **s. wheel** rouet *m*. ◆**spin-'dry** *vt* essorer. ◆**spin-off** *n* avantage *m* inattendu; (*of process, book etc*) dérivé *m*.

spinach ['spɪnɪdʒ] *n* (*plant*) épinard *m*; (*leaves*) *Culin* épinards *mpl*.

spindle ['spɪnd(ə)l] *n Tex* fuseau *m*. ◆**spindly** *a* (**-ier, -iest**) (*legs, arms*) grêle.

spine [spaɪn] *n Anat* colonne *f* vertébrale; (*spike of animal or plant*) épine *f*. ◆**spinal** *a* (*column*) vertébral; **s. cord** moelle *f* épinière. ◆**spineless** *a Fig* mou, faible.

spinster ['spɪnstər] *n* célibataire *f*; *Pej* vieille fille *f*.

spiral ['spaɪərəl] **1** *n* spirale *f*; **–** *a* en spirale; (*staircase*) en colimaçon. **2** *vi* (**-ll-**, *Am* **-l-**) (*of prices*) monter en flèche.

spire [spaɪər] *n* (*of church*) flèche *f*.

spirit ['spɪrɪt] **1** *n* (*soul, ghost etc*) esprit *m*; (*courage*) *Fig* courage *m*, vigueur *f*; *pl* (*drink*) alcool *m*, spiritueux *mpl*; **spirit(s)** (*morale*) moral *m*; *Ch* alcool *m*; **in good spirits** de bonne humeur; **the right s.** l'attitude *f* qu'il faut; **–** *a* (*lamp*) à alcool; **s. level** niveau *m* à bulle (d'air). **2** *vt* **to s. away** (*person*) faire disparaître mystérieusement; (*steal*) *Hum* subtiliser. ◆**—ed** *a* (*person, remark*) fougueux; (*campaign*) vigoureux.

spiritual ['spɪrɪtʃʊəl] *a Phil Rel* spirituel; **–** *n* (**Negro**) *n* (negro-)spiritual *m*. ◆**spiritualism** *n* spiritisme *m*. ◆**spiritualist** *n* spirite *mf*.

spit [spɪt] **1** *n* crachat *m*; **–** *vi* (*pt & pp* **spat** *or* **spit**, *pres p* **spitting**) cracher; (*splutter*) *Fig* crépiter; **–** *vt* cracher; **to s. out** (re)cracher; **the spitting image of s.o.** le portrait (tout craché) de qn. **2** *n* (*for meat*) broche *f*.

spite [spaɪt] **1** *n* in s. of malgré; **in s. of the fact that** (*although*) bien que (+ *sub*). **2** *n* (*dislike*) rancune *f*; − *vt* (*annoy*) contrarier. ◆**spiteful** *a* méchant. ◆**spitefully** *adv* méchamment.

spittle ['spɪt(ə)l] *n* salive *f*, crachat(s) *m*(*pl*).

splash [splæʃ] *vt* (*spatter*) éclabousser (**with** de, **over** sur); (*spill*) répandre; − *vi* (*of mud, ink etc*) faire des éclaboussures; (*of waves*) clapoter, déferler; **to s. over sth/s.o.** éclabousser qch/qn; **to s. (about)** (*in river, mud*) patauger; (*in bath*) barboter; **to s. out** (*spend money*) *Fam* claquer de l'argent; − *n* (*splashing*) éclaboussement *m*; (*of colour*) *Fig* tache *f*; **s. (mark)** éclaboussure *f*; **s.!** plouf!

spleen [spliːn] *n Anat* rate *f*.

splendid ['splendɪd] *a* (*wonderful, rich, beautiful*) splendide. ◆**splendour** *n* splendeur *f*.

splint [splɪnt] *n Med* éclisse *f*.

splinter ['splɪntər] *n* (*of wood etc*) éclat *m*; (*in finger*) écharde *f*; **s. group** *Pol* groupe *m* dissident.

split [splɪt] *n* fente *f*; (*tear*) déchirure *f*; (*of couple*) rupture *f*; *Pol* scission *f*; **to do the splits** (*in gymnastics*) faire le grand écart; **one's s.** (*share*) *Fam* sa part; − *a* **a s. second** une fraction de seconde; − *vt* (*pt & pp* **split**, *pres p* **splitting**) (*break apart*) fendre; (*tear*) déchirer; **to s. (up)** (*group*) diviser; (*money, work*) partager (**between** entre); **to s. one's head open** s'ouvrir la tête; **to s. one's sides (laughing)** se tordre (de rire); **to s. hairs** *Fig* couper les cheveux en quatre; **s.-level apartment** duplex *m*; − *vi* se fendre; (*tear*) se déchirer; **to s. (up)** (*of group*) éclater; (*of couple*) rompre, se séparer; **to s. off** (*become loose*) se détacher (**from** de); **to s. up** (*of crowd*) se disperser. ◆**splitting** *a* (*headache*) atroce. ◆**split-up** *n* (*of couple*) rupture *f*.

splodge [splɒdʒ] *n*, **splotch** [splɒtʃ] *n* (*mark*) tache *f*.

splurge [splɜːdʒ] *vi* (*spend money*) *Fam* claquer de l'argent.

splutter ['splʌtər] *vi* (*of sparks, fat*) crépiter; (*stammer*) bredouiller.

spoil [spɔɪl] *vt* (*pt & pp* **spoilt** *or* **spoiled**) (*pamper, make unpleasant or less good*) gâter; (*damage, ruin*) abîmer; (*pleasure, life*) gâcher, gâter. ◆**spoilsport** *n* rabat-joie *m inv*.

spoils [spɔɪlz] *npl* (*rewards*) butin *m*.

spoke[1] [spəʊk] *n* (*of wheel*) rayon *m*.

spoke[2] [spəʊk] *see* **speak.** ◆**spoken** *see* **speak;** − *a* (*language etc*) parlé; **softly s.** (*person*) à la voix douce. ◆**spokesman** *n* (*pl* **-men**) porte-parole *m inv* (**for, of** de).

sponge [spʌndʒ] **1** *n* éponge *f*; **s. bag** trousse *f* de toilette; **s. cake** gâteau *m* de Savoie; − *vt* **to s. down/off** laver/enlever à l'éponge. **2** *vi* **to s. off** *or* **on s.o.** *Fam* vivre aux crochets de qn; − *vt* **to s. sth off s.o.** *Fam* taper qn de qch. ◆**sponger** *n Fam* parasite *m*. ◆**spongy** *a* (**-ier, -iest**) spongieux.

sponsor ['spɒnsər] *n* (*of appeal, advertiser etc*) personne *f* assurant le patronage (**of** de); (*for membership*) parrain *m*, marraine *f*; *Jur* garant, -ante *mf*; *Sp* sponsor *m*; − *vt* (*appeal etc*) patronner; (*member, firm*) parrainer. ◆**sponsorship** *n* patronage *m*; parrainage *m*.

spontaneous [spɒn'teɪnɪəs] *a* spontané. ◆**spontaneity** [spɒntə'neɪɪtɪ] *n* spontanéité *f*. ◆**spontaneously** *adv* spontanément.

spoof [spuːf] *n Fam* parodie *f* (**on** de).

spooky ['spuːkɪ] *a* (**-ier, -iest**) *Fam* qui donne le frisson.

spool [spuːl] *n* bobine *f*.

spoon [spuːn] *n* cuiller *f*. ◆**spoonfeed** *vt* (*pt & pp* **spoonfed**) (*help*) *Fig* mâcher le travail à. ◆**spoonful** *n* cuillerée *f*.

sporadic [spə'rædɪk] *a* sporadique; **s. fighting** échauffourées *fpl*. ◆**sporadically** *adv* sporadiquement.

sport [spɔːt] **1** *n* sport *m*; **a (good) s.** (*person*) *Fam* un chic type; **to play s.** *or Am* **sports** faire du sport; **sports club** club *m* sportif; **sports car/jacket** voiture *f*/veste *f* de sport; **sports results** résultats *mpl* sportifs. **2** *vt* (*wear*) arborer. ◆**—ing** *a* (*conduct, attitude, person etc*) sportif; **that's s. of you** *Fig* c'est chic de ta part. ◆**sportsman** *n* (*pl* **-men**) sportif *m*. ◆**sportsmanlike** *a* sportif. ◆**sportsmanship** *n* sportivité *f*. ◆**sportswear** *n* vêtements *mpl* de sport. ◆**sportswoman** *n* (*pl* **-women**) sportive *f*. ◆**sporty** *a* (**-ier, -iest**) sportif.

spot[1] [spɒt] *n* (*stain, mark*) tache *f*; (*dot*) point *m*; (*polka dot*) pois *m*; (*pimple*) bouton *m*; (*place*) endroit *m*, coin *m*; (*act*) *Th* numéro *m*; (*drop*) goutte *f*; **a s. of** (*bit*) *Fam* un peu de; **a soft s. for** un faible pour; **on the s.** sur place, sur les lieux; (*at once*) sur le coup; **in a (tight) s.** (*difficulty*) dans le pétrin; (**accident**) **black s.** *Aut* point *m* noir; **s. cash** argent *m* comptant; **s. check** contrôle *m* au hasard *or* l'improviste. ◆**spotless** *a* (*clean*) impeccable. ◆**spot-**

lessly *adv* s. **clean** impeccable. ◆**spotlight** *n* (*lamp*) *Th* projecteur *m*; (*for photography etc*) spot *m*; **in the s.** *Th* sous le feu des projecteurs. ◆**spot·'on** *a* *Fam* tout à fait exact. ◆**spotted** *a* (*fur*) tacheté; (*dress etc*) à pois; (*stained*) taché. ◆**spotty** *a* (-ier, -iest) **1** (*face etc*) boutonneux. **2** (*patchy*) *Am* inégal.

spot² [spɒt] *vt* (-tt-) (*notice*) apercevoir, remarquer.

spouse [spaʊs, spaʊz] *n* époux *m*, épouse *f*.

spout [spaʊt] **1** *n* (*of jug etc*) bec *m*; **up the s.** (*hope etc*) *Sl* fichu. **2** *vi* to s. (**out**) jaillir. **3** *vt* (*say*) *Pej* débiter.

sprain [spreɪn] *n* entorse *f*, foulure *f*; **to s. one's ankle/wrist** se fouler la cheville/le poignet.

sprang [spræŋ] *see* spring¹.

sprawl [sprɔːl] *vi* (*of town, person*) s'étaler; **to be sprawling** être étalé; – *n* **the urban s.** les banlieues *fpl* tentaculaires. ◆**—ing** *a* (*city*) tentaculaire.

spray [spreɪ] **1** *n* (*water drops*) (nuage *m* de) gouttelettes *fpl*; (*from sea*) embruns *mpl*; (*can, device*) bombe *f*, vaporisateur *m*; **hair s.** laque *f* à cheveux; – *vt* (*liquid, surface*) vaporiser; (*crops, plant*) arroser, traiter; (*car etc*) peindre à la bombe. **2** *n* (*of flowers*) petit bouquet *m*.

spread [spred] *vt* (*pt & pp* spread) (*stretch, open out*) étendre; (*legs, fingers*) écarter; (*strew*) répandre, étaler (**over** sur); (*paint, payment, cards, visits*) étaler; (*people*) disperser; (*fear, news*) répandre; (*illness*) propager; **to s. out** étendre; écarter; étaler; – *vi* (*of fire, town, fog*) s'étendre; (*of news, fear*) se répandre; **to s. out** (*of people*) se disperser; – *n* (*of fire, illness, ideas*) propagation *f*; (*of wealth*) répartition *f*; (*paste*) *Culin* pâte *f* (à tartiner); (*meal*) festin *m*; **cheese s.** fromage *m* à tartiner. ◆**s.-'eagled** *a* bras et jambes écartés.

spree [spriː] *n* **to go on a spending s.** faire des achats extravagants.

sprig [sprɪg] *n* (*branch of heather etc*) brin *m*; (*of parsley*) bouquet *m*.

sprightli/y ['spraɪtlɪ] *a* (-ier, -iest) alerte. ◆**—iness** *n* vivacité *f*.

spring¹ [sprɪŋ] *n* (*metal device*) ressort *m*; (*leap*) bond *m*; – *vi* (*pt* sprang, *pp* sprung) (*leap*) bondir; **to s. to mind** venir à l'esprit; **to s. into action** passer à l'action; **to s. from** (*stem from*) provenir de; **to s. up** (*appear*) surgir; – *vt* (*news*) annoncer brusquement (**on** à); (*surprise*) faire (**on** à); **to s. a leak** (*of boat*) commencer à faire eau. ◆**spring-**

board *n* tremplin *m*. ◆**springy** *a* (-ier, -iest) élastique.

spring² [sprɪŋ] *n* (*season*) printemps *m*; **in (the) s.** au printemps; **s. onion** ciboule *f*. ◆**s.-'cleaning** *n* nettoyage *m* de printemps. ◆**springlike** *a* printanier. ◆**springtime** *n* printemps *m*.

spring³ [sprɪŋ] *n* (*of water*) source *f*; **s. water** eau *f* de source.

sprinkl/e ['sprɪŋk(ə)l] *vt* (*sand etc*) répandre (**on, over** sur); **to s. with water, s. water on** asperger d'eau, arroser; **to s. with** (*sugar, salt, flour*) saupoudrer de. ◆**—ing** *n* **a s. of** (*a few*) quelques. ◆**—er** *n* (*in garden*) arroseur *m*.

sprint [sprɪnt] *n* *Sp* sprint *m*; – *vi* sprinter. ◆**—er** *n* sprinter *m*, sprinteuse *f*.

sprite [spraɪt] *n* (*fairy*) lutin *m*.

sprout [spraʊt] **1** *vi* (*of seed, bulb etc*) germer, pousser; **to s. up** (*grow*) pousser vite; (*appear*) surgir; – *vt* (*leaves*) pousser; (*beard*) *Fig* laisser pousser. **2** *n* (**Brussels**) **s.** chou *m* de Bruxelles.

spruce [spruːs] *a* (-er, -est) (*neat*) pimpant, net; – *vt* **to s. oneself up** se faire beau.

sprung [sprʌŋ] *see* spring¹; – *a* (*mattress, seat*) à ressorts.

spry [spraɪ] *a* (**spryer, spryest**) (*old person etc*) alerte.

spud [spʌd] *n* (*potato*) *Fam* patate *f*.

spun [spʌn] *see* spin.

spur [spɜːr] *n* (*of horse rider etc*) éperon *m*; (*stimulus*) *Fig* aiguillon *m*; **on the s. of the moment** sur un coup de tête; – *vt* (-rr-) **to s. (on)** (*urge on*) éperonner.

spurious ['spjʊərɪəs] *a* faux.

spurn [spɜːn] *vt* rejeter (avec mépris).

spurt [spɜːt] *vi* (*gush out*) jaillir; (*rush*) foncer; **to s. out** jaillir; – *n* jaillissement *m*; (*of energy*) sursaut *m*; **to put on a s.** (*rush*) foncer.

spy [spaɪ] *n* espion, -onne *mf*; – *a* (*story etc*) d'espionnage; **s. hole** (*peephole*) judas *m*; **s. ring** réseau *m* d'espionnage; – *vi* espionner; **to s. on s.o.** espionner qn; – *vt* (*notice*) *Lit* apercevoir. ◆**—ing** *n* espionnage *m*.

squabbl/e ['skwɒb(ə)l] *vi* se chamailler (**over** à propos de); – *n* chamaillerie *f*. ◆**—ing** *n* chamailleries *fpl*.

squad [skwɒd] *n* (*group*) & *Mil* escouade *f*; (*team*) *Sp* équipe *f*; **s. car** voiture *f* de police.

squadron ['skwɒdrən] *n* *Mil* escadron *m*; *Nau Av* escadrille *f*.

squalid ['skwɒlɪd] *a* sordide. ◆**squalor** *n* conditions *fpl* sordides.

squall [skwɔːl] *n* (*of wind*) rafale *f*.

squander ['skwɒndər] vt (money, time etc) gaspiller (**on** en).

square ['skweər] n carré m; (on chessboard, graph paper) case f; (in town) place f; (drawing implement) Tech équerre f; **to be back to s. one** repartir à zéro; – a carré; (in order, settled) Fig en ordre; (honest) honnête; (meal) solide; (all) s. (quits) quitte (with envers); – vt (settle) mettre en ordre, régler; (arrange) arranger; Math carrer; (reconcile) faire cadrer; – vi (tally) cadrer (with avec); **to s. up to** faire face à. ◆**—ly** adv (honestly) honnêtement; (exactly) tout à fait; **s. in the face** bien en face.

squash [skwɒʃ] **1** vt (crush) écraser; (squeeze) serrer; – n **lemon/orange s.** (concentrated) sirop m de citron/d'orange; (diluted) citronnade f/orangeade f. **2** n (game) squash m. **3** n (vegetable) Am courge f. ◆**squashy** a (-ier, -iest) (soft) mou.

squat [skwɒt] **1** a (short and thick) trapu. **2** vi (-tt-) **to s. (down)** s'accroupir. **3** n (house) squat m. ◆**squatting** a accroupi. ◆**squatter** n squatter m.

squawk [skwɔːk] vi pousser des cris rauques; – n cri m rauque.

squeak [skwiːk] vi (of door) grincer; (of shoe) craquer; (of mouse) faire couic; – n grincement m; craquement m; couic m. ◆**squeaky** a (-ier, -iest) (door) grinçant; (shoe) qui craque.

squeal [skwiːl] vi pousser des cris aigus; (of tyres) crisser; – n cri m aigu; crissement m. **2** vi **to s. on s.o.** (inform on) Fam balancer qn.

squeamish ['skwiːmɪʃ] a bien délicat, facilement dégoûté.

squeegee ['skwiːdʒiː] n raclette f (à vitres).

squeez/e [skwiːz] vt (press) presser; (hand, arm) serrer; **to s. sth out of s.o.** (information) soutirer qch à qn; **to s. sth into** faire rentrer qch dans; **to s. (out)** (extract) exprimer (**from** de); – vi **to s. through/into/**etc (force oneself) se glisser par/dans/ etc; – n pression f; **to give sth a s.** presser qch; **it's a tight s.** il y a peu de place; **credit s.** Fin restrictions fpl de crédit. ◆**—er** n **lemon s.** presse-citron m inv.

squelch [skweltʃ] **1** vi patauger (en faisant floc-floc). **2** vt (silence) Fam réduire au silence.

squid [skwɪd] n (mollusc) calmar m.

squiggle ['skwɪg(ə)l] n ligne f onduleuse, gribouillis m.

squint [skwɪnt] n Med strabisme m; **to have a s.** loucher; – vi loucher; (in the sunlight etc) plisser les yeux.

squire ['skwaɪər] n propriétaire m terrien.

squirm [skwɜːm] vi (wriggle) se tortiller; **to s. in pain** se tordre de douleur.

squirrel ['skwɪrəl, Am 'skwɜːrəl] n écureuil m.

squirt [skwɜːt] **1** vt (liquid) faire gicler; – n giclée f, jet m. **2** n **little s.** (person) Fam petit morveux m.

stab [stæb] vt (-bb-) (with knife etc) poignarder; – n coup m (de couteau or de poignard). ◆**stabbing** n **there was a s.** quelqu'un a été poignardé; – a (pain) lancinant.

stable[1] ['steɪb(ə)l] a (-er, -est) stable; **mentally s.** (person) bien équilibré. ◆**sta-'bility** n stabilité f; **mental s.** équilibre m. ◆**stabilize** vt stabiliser; – vi se stabiliser. ◆**stabilizer** n stabilisateur m.

stable[2] ['steɪb(ə)l] n écurie f; **s. boy** lad m.

stack [stæk] **1** n (heap) tas m; **stacks of** (lots of) Fam un or des tas de; – vt **to s. (up)** entasser. **2** npl (in library) réserve f.

stadium ['steɪdɪəm] n Sp stade m.

staff [stɑːf] **1** n personnel m; Sch professeurs mpl; Mil état-major m; **s. meeting** Sch Univ conseil m des professeurs; **s. room** Sch Univ salle f des professeurs; – vt pourvoir en personnel. **2** n (stick) Lit bâton m.

stag [stæg] n cerf m; **s. party** réunion f entre hommes.

stage[1] [steɪdʒ] n (platform) Th scène f; **the s.** (profession) le théâtre; **on s.** sur (la) scène; **s. door** entrée f des artistes; **s. fright** le trac; – vt (play) Th monter; Fig organiser, effectuer; **it was staged** (not real) c'était un coup monté. ◆**s.-hand** n machiniste m. ◆**s.-manager** n régisseur m.

stage[2] [steɪdʒ] n (phase) stade m, étape f; (of journey) étape f; (of track, road) section f; **in (easy) stages** par étapes; **at an early s.** au début.

stagecoach ['steɪdʒkəʊtʃ] n Hist diligence f.

stagger ['stægər] **1** vi (reel) chanceler. **2** vt (holidays etc) étaler, échelonner. **3** vt **to s. s.o.** (shock, amaze) stupéfier qn. ◆**—ing** a stupéfiant.

stagnant ['stægnənt] a stagnant. ◆**stag-'nate** vi stagner. ◆**stag'nation** n stagnation f.

staid [steɪd] a posé, sérieux.

stain [steɪn] **1** vt (mark, dirty) tacher (with

de); − *n* tache *f*. **2** *vt* (*colour*) teinter (*du bois*); **stained glass window** vitrail *m*; − *n* (*colouring for wood*) teinture *f*. ◆—**less** *a* (*steel*) inoxydable; **s.-steel** knife/*etc* couteau *m*/*etc* inoxydable.

stair [steər] *n* a s. (*step*) une marche; **the stairs** (*staircase*) l'escalier *m*; − *a* (*carpet etc*) d'escalier. ◆**staircase** *n*, ◆**stairway** *n* escalier *m*.

stake [steɪk] **1** *n* (*post*) pieu *m*; (*for plant*) tuteur *m*; *Hist* bûcher *m*; − *vt* **to s. (out)** (*land*) jalonner, délimiter; **to s. one's claim to** revendiquer. **2** *n* (*betting*) enjeu *m*; (*investment*) *Fin* investissement *m*; (*interest*) *Fin* intérêts *mpl*; **at s.** en jeu; − *vt* (*bet*) jouer (**on** sur).

stale [steɪl] *a* (**-er, -est**) (*food*) pas frais; (*bread*) rassis; (*beer*) éventé; (*air*) vicié; (*smell*) de renfermé; (*news*) *Fig* vieux; (*joke*) usé, vieux; (*artist*) manquant d'invention. ◆—**ness** *n* (*of food*) manque *m* de fraîcheur.

stalemate ['steɪlmeɪt] *n* *Chess* pat *m*; *Fig* impasse *f*.

stalk [stɔːk] **1** *n* (*of plant*) tige *f*, queue *f*; (*of fruit*) queue *f*. **2** *vt* (*animal, criminal*) traquer. **3** *vi* **to s. out** (*walk*) partir avec raideur *or* en marchant à grands pas.

stall [stɔːl] **1** *n* (*in market*) étal *m*, éventaire *m*; (*for newspapers, flowers*) kiosque *m*; (*in stable*) stalle *f*; **the stalls** *Cin* l'orchestre *m*. **2** *vti* *Aut* caler. **3** *vi* **to s. (for time)** chercher à gagner du temps.

stallion ['stæljən] *n* (*horse*) étalon *m*.

stalwart ['stɔːlwət] *a* (*supporter*) brave, fidèle; − *n* (*follower*) fidèle *mf*.

stamina ['stæmɪnə] *n* vigueur *f*, résistance *f*.

stammer ['stæmər] *vti* bégayer; − *n* bégaiement *m*; **to have a s.** être bègue.

stamp [stæmp] **1** *n* (*for postage, implement*) timbre *m*; (*mark*) cachet *m*, timbre *m*; **the s. of** *Fig* la marque de; **men of your s.** les hommes de votre trempe; **s. collecting** philatélie *f*; − *vt* (*mark*) tamponner, timbrer; (*letter*) timbrer; (*metal*) estamper; **to s. sth on sth** (*affix*) apposer qch sur qch; **to s. out** (*rebellion, evil*) écraser; (*disease*) supprimer; **stamped addressed envelope** enveloppe *f* timbrée à votre adresse. **2** *vti* **to s. (one's feet)** taper *or* frapper des pieds; **stamping ground** *Fam* lieu *m* favori.

stampede [stæm'piːd] *n* fuite *f* précipitée; (*rush*) ruée *f*; − *vi* fuir en désordre; (*rush*) se ruer.

stance [stɑːns] *n* position *f*.

stand [stænd] *n* (*position*) position *f*; (*support*) support *m*; (*at exhibition*) stand *m*; (*for spectators*) *Sp* tribune *f*; (*witness*) **s.** *Jur Am* barre *f*; **to make a s., take one's s.** prendre position (**against** contre); **news/flower s.** (*in street*) kiosque *m* à journaux/à fleurs; **hat s.** porte-chapeaux *m inv*; **music s.** pupitre *m* à musique; − *vt* (*pt & pp* **stood**) (*pain, journey, person etc*) supporter; **to s. (up)** (*put straight*) mettre (debout); **to s. s.o. sth** (*pay for*) payer qch à qn; **to s. a chance** avoir une chance; **to s. s.o. up** *Fam* poser un lapin à qn; − *vi* être *or* se tenir (debout); (*rise*) se lever; (*remain*) rester (debout); (*be situated*) se trouver; (*be*) être; (*of object, argument*) reposer (**on** sur); **to leave to s.** (*liquid*) laisser reposer; **to s. to lose** risquer de perdre; **to s. around** (*in street etc*) traîner; **to s. aside** s'écarter; **to s. back** reculer; **to s. by** (*do nothing*) rester là (sans rien faire); (*be ready*) être prêt (**à partir** *or* **à intervenir**); (*one's opinion etc*) s'en tenir à; (*friend etc*) rester fidèle à; **to s. down** (*withdraw*) se désister; **to s. for** (*represent*) représenter; *Pol* être candidat à; (*put up with*) supporter; **to s. in for** (*replace*) remplacer; **to s. out** (*be visible or conspicuous*) ressortir (**against** sur); **to s. over s.o.** (*watch closely*) surveiller qn; **to s. up** (*rise*) se lever; **to s. up for** (*defend*) défendre; **to s. up to** (*resist*) résister à. ◆—**ing** *a* debout *inv*; (*committee, offer, army*) permanent; **s. room** places *fpl* debout; **s. joke** plaisanterie *f* classique; − *n* (*reputation*) réputation *f*; (*social, professional*) rang *m*; (*financial*) situation *f*; **of six years' s.** (*duration*) qui dure depuis six ans; **of long s.** de longue date. ◆**standby** *n* (*pl* **-bys**) **on s.** prêt à partir *or* à intervenir; − *a* (*battery etc*) de réserve; (*ticket*) *Av* sans garantie. ◆**stand-in** *n* remplaçant, -ante *mf* (**for** de); *Th* doublure *f* (**for** de).

standard ['stændəd] **1** *n* (*norm*) norme *f*, critère *m*; (*level*) niveau *m*; (*of weight, gold*) étalon *m*; *pl* (*morals*) principes *mpl*; **s. of living** niveau *m* de vie; **to be** *or* **come up to s.** (*of person*) être à la hauteur; (*of work etc*) être au niveau; − *a* (*average*) ordinaire, courant; (*model, size*) *Com* standard *inv*; (*weight*) étalon *inv*; (*dictionary, book*) classique; **s. lamp** lampadaire *m*. **2** *n* (*flag*) étendard *m*. ◆**standardize** *vt* standardiser.

stand-offish [stænd'ɒfɪʃ] *a* (*person*) distant, froid.

standpoint ['stændpɔɪnt] *n* point *m* de vue.

standstill ['stændstɪl] *n* **to bring to a s.** immobiliser; **to come to a s.** s'immobiliser;

at a s. immobile; (*industry, negotiations*) paralysé.

stank [stæŋk] *see* **stink**.

stanza ['stænzə] *n* strophe *f*.

stapl/e ['steɪp(ə)l] **1** *a* (*basic*) de base; **s. food** *or* **diet** nourriture *f* de base. **2** *n* (*for paper etc*) agrafe *f*; – *vt* agrafer. ◆—**er** *n* (*for paper etc*) agrafeuse *f*.

star [stɑːr] *n* étoile *f*; (*person*) *Cin* vedette *f*; **shooting s.** étoile *f* filante; **s. part** rôle *m* principal; **the Stars and Stripes, the S.-Spangled Banner** *Am* la bannière étoilée; **two-s.** (**petrol**) de l'ordinaire *m*; **four-s.** (**petrol**) du super; – *vi* (**-rr-**) (*of actor*) être la vedette (**in** de); – *vt* (*of film*) avoir pour vedette. ◆**stardom** *n* célébrité *f*. ◆**starfish** *n* étoile *f* de mer. ◆**starlit** *a* (*night*) étoilé.

starboard ['stɑːbəd] *n Nau Av* tribord *m*.

starch [stɑːtʃ] *n* (*for stiffening*) amidon *m*; *pl* (*foods*) féculents *mpl*; – *vt* amidonner. ◆**starchy** *a* (**-ier, -iest**) (*food*) féculent; (*formal*) *Fig* guindé.

stare [steər] *n* regard *m* (fixe); – *vi* **to s. at** fixer (du regard); – *vt* **to s. s.o. in the face** dévisager qn.

stark [stɑːk] *a* (**-er, -est**) (*place*) désolé; (*austere*) austère; (*fact, reality*) brutal; **the s. truth** la vérité toute nue; – *adv* **s. naked** complètement nu. ◆**starkers** *a Sl* complètement nu, à poil.

starling ['stɑːlɪŋ] *n* étourneau *m*.

starry ['stɑːrɪ] *a* (**-ier, -iest**) (*sky*) étoilé. ◆**s.-'eyed** *a* (*naïve*) ingénu, naïf.

start[1] [stɑːt] *n* commencement *m*, début *m*; (*of race*) départ *m*; (*lead*) *Sp & Fig* avance *f* (**on** sur); **to make a s.** commencer; **for a s.** pour commencer; **from the s.** dès le début; – *vt* commencer; (*bottle*) entamer, commencer; (*fashion*) lancer; **to s. a war** provoquer une guerre; **to s. a fire** (*in grate*) allumer un feu; (*accidentally*) provoquer un incendie; **to s. s.o.** (**off**) **on** (*career*) lancer qn dans; **to s.** (**up**) (*engine, vehicle*) mettre en marche; **to s. doing** *or* **to do** commencer *or* se mettre à faire; – *vi* commencer (**with sth** par qch, **by doing** par faire); **to s. on sth** commencer qch; **to s.** (**up**) commencer; (*of vehicle*) démarrer; **to s.** (**off** *or* **out**) (*leave*) partir (**for** pour); (*in job*) débuter; **to s. back** (*return*) repartir; **to s. with** (*firstly*) pour commencer. ◆—**ing** *n* (*point, line*) de départ; **s. post** *Sp* ligne *f* de départ; **s. from** à partir de. ◆—**er** *n* (*runner*) partant *m*; (*official*) *Sp* starter *m*; (*device*) *Aut* démarreur *m*; *pl Culin*

hors-d'œuvre *m inv*; **for starters** (*first*) pour commencer.

start[2] [stɑːt] *vi* (*be startled, jump*) sursauter; – *n* sursaut *m*; **to give s.o. a s.** faire sursauter qn.

startle ['stɑːt(ə)l] *vt* (*make jump*) faire sursauter; (*alarm*) *Fig* alarmer; (*surprise*) surprendre.

starve [stɑːv] *vi* (*die*) mourir de faim; (*suffer*) souffrir de la faim; **I'm starving** *Fig* je meurs de faim; – *vt* (*kill*) laisser mourir de faim; (*make suffer*) faire souffrir de la faim; (*deprive*) *Fig* priver (**of** de). ◆**star-'vation** *n* faim *f*; – *a* (*wage, ration*) de famine; **on a s. diet** à la diète.

stash [stæʃ] *vt* **to s. away** (*hide*) cacher; (*save up*) mettre de côté.

state[1] [steɪt] **1** *n* (*condition*) état *m*; (*pomp*) apparat *m*; **not in a** (**fit**) **s. to, in no** (**fit**) **s. to** hors d'état de; **to lie in s.** (*of body*) être exposé. **2** *n* **S.** (*nation etc*) État *m*; **the States** *Geog Fam* les États-Unis *mpl*; – *a* (*secret, document*) d'État; (*control, security*) de l'État; (*school, education*) public; **s. visit** voyage *m* officiel; **S. Department** *Pol Am* Département *m* d'État. ◆**stateless** *a* apatride; **s. person** apatride *mf*. ◆**state-'owned** *a* étatisé. ◆**statesman** *n* (*pl* **-men**) homme *m* d'État. ◆**statesman-ship** *n* diplomatie *f*.

state[2] [steɪt] *vt* déclarer (**that** que); (*opinion*) formuler; (*problem*) exposer; (*time, date*) fixer. ◆**statement** *n* déclaration *f*; *Jur* déposition *f*; **bank s., s. of account** *Fin* relevé *m* de compte.

stately ['steɪtlɪ] *a* (**-ier, -iest**) majestueux; **s. home** château *m*.

static ['stætɪk] *a* statique; – *n* (*noise*) *Rad* parasites *mpl*.

station ['steɪʃ(ə)n] *n Rail* gare *f*; (*underground*) station *f*; (*position*) & *Mil* poste *m*; (*social*) rang *m*; (**police**) **s.** commissariat *m* *or* poste *m* (de police); **space/observation/radio/***etc* **s.** station *f* spatiale/d'observation/de radio/*etc*; **bus** *or* **coach s.** gare *f* routière; **s. wagon** *Aut Am* break *m*; – *vt* (*position*) placer, poster. ◆**stationmaster** *n Rail* chef *m* de gare.

stationary ['steɪʃ(ə)nərɪ] *a* (*motionless*) stationnaire; (*vehicle*) à l'arrêt.

stationer ['steɪʃ(ə)nər] *n* papetier, -ière *mf*; **s.'s** (**shop**) papeterie *f*. ◆**stationery** *n* (*paper*) papier *m*; (*articles*) papeterie *f*.

statistic [stə'tɪstɪk] *n* (*fact*) statistique *f*; *pl* (*science*) la statistique. ◆**statistical** *a* statistique.

statue [ˈstætʃuɪ] n statue f. ◆**statu'esque** a (beauty etc) sculptural.

stature [ˈstætʃər] n stature f.

status [ˈsteɪtəs] n (position) situation f; Jur statut m; (prestige) standing m, prestige m; **s. symbol** marque f de standing; **s. quo** statu quo m inv.

statute [ˈstætʃuɪt] n (law) loi f; pl (of club, institution) statuts mpl. ◆**statutory** a (right etc) statutaire; **s. holiday** fête f légale.

staunch [stɔɪntʃ] a (-er, -est) loyal, fidèle. ◆**—ly** adv loyalement.

stave [steɪv] 1 vt to **s. off** (danger, disaster) conjurer; (hunger) tromper. 2 n Mus portée f.

stay [steɪ] 1 n (visit) séjour m; — vi (remain) rester; (reside) loger; (visit) séjourner; to **s. put** ne pas bouger; to **s. with** (plan, idea) ne pas lâcher; to **s. away** (keep one's distance) ne pas s'approcher (from de); to **s. away from** (school, meeting etc) ne pas aller à; to **s. in** (at home) rester à la maison; (of nail, tooth etc) tenir; to **s. out** (outside) rester dehors; (not come home) ne pas rentrer; to **s. out of sth** (not interfere in) ne pas se mêler de qch; (avoid) éviter qch; to **s. up** (at night) ne pas se coucher; (of fence etc) tenir; to **s. up late** se coucher tard; **staying power** endurance f. 2 vt (hunger) tromper. ◆**s.-at-home** n & a Pej casanier, -ière (mf).

St Bernard [sənt'bɜɪnəd, Am seɪntbə'naɪd] n (dog) saint-bernard m.

stead [sted] n to **stand s.o. in good s.** être bien utile à qn; **in s.o.'s s.** à la place de qn.

steadfast [ˈstedfaɪst] a (intention etc) ferme.

steady [ˈstedɪ] a (-ier, -iest) (firm, stable) stable; (hand) sûr, assuré; (progress, speed, demand) régulier, constant; (nerves) solide; (staid) sérieux; **a s. boyfriend** un petit ami; **s. (on one's feet)** solide sur ses jambes; — adv to **go s. with** Fam sortir avec; — vt (chair etc) maintenir (en place); (hand) assurer; (nerves) calmer; (wedge, prop up) caler; to **s. oneself** (stop oneself falling) reprendre son aplomb. ◆**steadily** adv (to walk) d'un pas assuré; (regularly) régulièrement; (gradually) progressivement; (continuously) sans arrêt. ◆**steadiness** n stabilité f; régularité f.

steak [steɪk] n steak m, bifteck m. ◆**steakhouse** n grill(-room) m.

steal [stiɪl] vti (pt **stole**, pp **stolen**) voler (from s.o. à qn).

steal [stiɪl] vi (pt **stole**, pp **stolen**) to **s. in/out** entrer/sortir furtivement. ◆**stealth**

[stelθ] n **by s.** furtivement. ◆**stealthy** a (-ier, -iest) furtif.

steam [stiɪm] n vapeur f; (on glass) buée f; to **let off s.** (unwind) Fam se défouler, décompresser; **s. engine/iron** locomotive f/fer m à vapeur; — vt Culin cuire à la vapeur; to **get steamed up** (of glass) se couvrir de buée; Fig Fam s'énerver; — vi (of kettle etc) fumer; to **s. up** (of glass) se couvrir de buée. ◆**steamer** n, ◆**steamship** n (bateau m à) vapeur m; (liner) paquebot m. ◆**steamroller** n rouleau m compresseur. ◆**steamy** a (-ier, -iest) humide; (window) embué; (love affair etc) brûlant.

steel [stiɪl] 1 n acier m; **s. industry** sidérurgie f. 2 vt to **s. oneself** s'endurcir (against contre). ◆**steelworks** n aciérie f.

steep [stiɪp] 1 a (-er, -est) (stairs, slope etc) raide; (hill) escarpé; (price) Fig excessif. 2 vt (soak) tremper (in dans); **steeped in** Fig imprégné de. ◆**—ly** adv (to rise) en pente raide, (of prices) Fig excessivement.

steeple [ˈstiɪp(ə)l] n clocher m.

steeplechase [ˈstiɪp(ə)ltʃeɪs] n (race) steeple(-chase) m.

steer [stɪər] vt (vehicle, person) diriger, piloter; (ship) diriger, gouverner; — vi (of person) Nau tenir le gouvernail, gouverner; to **s. towards** faire route vers; to **s. clear of** éviter. ◆**—ing** n Aut direction f; **s. wheel** volant m.

stem [stem] 1 n (of plant etc) tige f; (of glass) pied m. 2 vt (-mm-) to **s. (the flow of)** (stop) arrêter, contenir. 3 vi (-mm-) to **s. from** provenir de.

stench [stentʃ] n puanteur f.

stencil [ˈstens(ə)l] n (metal, plastic) pochoir m; (paper, for typing) stencil m; — vt (-ll-, Am -l-) (notes etc) polycopier.

stenographer [stə'nɒɡrəfər] n Am sténodactylo f.

step [step] n (movement, sound) pas m; (stair) marche f; (on train, bus) marchepied m; (doorstep) pas m de la porte; (action) Fig mesure f; **(flight of) steps** (indoors) escalier m; (outdoors) perron m; **(pair of) steps** (ladder) escabeau m; **s. by s.** pas à pas; to **keep in s.** marcher au pas; **in s. with** Fig en accord avec; — vi (-pp-) (walk) marcher (on sur); **s. this way!** (venez) par ici!; to **s. aside** s'écarter; to **s. back** reculer; to **s. down** descendre (from de); (withdraw) Fig se retirer; to **s. forward** faire un pas en avant; to **s. in** entrer; (intervene) Fig intervenir; to **s. into** (car etc) monter dans; to **s. off** (chair etc) descendre de; to **s. out of** (car etc) descendre de; **to s. over** (*obstacle*) enjamber; − *vt* **to s. up** (*increase*) augmenter, intensifier; (*speed up*) activer. ◆**stepladder** *n* escabeau *m*. ◆**stepping-stone** *n* *Fig* tremplin *m* (**to** pour arriver à).

stepbrother ['stepbrʌðər] *n* demi-frère *m*. ◆**stepdaughter** *n* belle-fille *f*. ◆**stepfather** *n* beau-père *m*. ◆**stepmother** *n* belle-mère *f*. ◆**stepsister** *n* demi-sœur *f*. ◆**stepson** *n* beau-fils *m*.

stereo ['sterɪəʊ] *n* (*pl* **-os**) (*sound*) stéréo(phonie) *f*; (*record player*) chaîne *f* (stéréo *inv*); − *a* (*record etc*) stéréo *inv*; (*broadcast*) en stéréo. ◆**stereo'phonic** *a* stéréophonique.

stereotype ['sterɪətaɪp] *n* stéréotype *m*. ◆**stereotyped** *a* stéréotypé.

sterile ['sterail, *Am* 'sterəl] *a* stérile. ◆**ste'rility** *n* stérilité *f*. ◆**sterili'zation** *n* stérilisation *f*. ◆**sterilize** *vt* stériliser.

sterling ['stɜːlɪŋ] *n* (*currency*) livre(s) *f(pl)* sterling *inv*; − *a* (*pound*) sterling *inv*; (*silver*) fin; (*quality, person*) *Fig* sûr.

stern [stɜːn] **1** *a* (**-er, -est**) sévère. **2** *n* (*of ship*) arrière *m*.

stethoscope ['steθəskəʊp] *n* stéthoscope *m*.

stetson ['stetsən] *n* *Am* chapeau *m* à larges bords.

stevedore ['stiːvədɔːr] *n* docker *m*.

stew [stjuː] *n* ragoût *m*; **in a s.** *Fig* dans le pétrin; **s. pan, s. pot** cocotte *f*; − *vt* (*meat*) faire *or* cuire en ragoût; (*fruit*) faire cuire; **stewed fruit** compote *f*; − *vi* cuire. ◆**—ing** *a* (*pears etc*) à cuire.

steward ['stjuːəd] *n* *Av Nau* steward *m*; (*in college, club etc*) intendant *m* (*préposé au ravitaillement*); **shop s.** délégué, -ée *mf* syndical(e). ◆**stewar'dess** *n* *Av* hôtesse *f*.

stick¹ [stɪk] *n* (*piece of wood, chalk, dynamite*) bâton *m*; (*branch*) branche *f*; (*for walking*) canne *f*; **the sticks** *Pej Fam* la campagne, la cambrousse; **to give s.o. some s.** (*scold*) *Fam* engueuler qn.

stick² [stɪk] *vt* (*pt & pp* **stuck**) (*glue*) coller; (*put*) *Fam* mettre, planter; (*tolerate*) *Fam* supporter; **to s. sth into** (*thrust*) planter *or* enfoncer qch dans; **to s. down** (*envelope*) coller; (*put down*) *Fam* poser; **to s. on** (*stamp*) coller; (*hat etc*) mettre, planter; **to s. out** (*tongue*) tirer; (*head*) *Fam* sortir; **to s. it out** (*resist*) *Fam* tenir le coup; **to s. up** (*notice*) afficher; (*hand*) *Fam* lever; − *vi* coller, adhérer (**to** à); (*of food in pan*) attacher; (*remain*) *Fam* rester; (*of drawer etc*) être bloqué *or* coincé; **to s. by s.o.** rester fidèle à qn; **to s. to the facts** (*confine oneself to*) s'en tenir aux faits; **to s. around** *Fam* rester dans les parages; **to s. out** (*of petticoat etc*) dépasser; (*of tooth*) avancer; **to s. up for** (*defend*) défendre; **sticking plaster** sparadrap *m*. ◆**sticker** *n* (*label*) autocollant *m*. ◆**stick-on** *a* (*label*) adhésif. ◆**stick-up** *n* *Fam* hold-up *m* *inv*.

stickler ['stɪklər] *n* **a s. for** (*rules, discipline, details*) intransigeant sur.

sticky ['stɪkɪ] *a* (**-ier, -iest**) collant, poisseux; (*label*) adhésif; (*problem*) *Fig* difficile.

stiff [stɪf] *a* (**-er, -est**) raide; (*joint, leg etc*) ankylosé; (*brush, paste*) dur; (*person*) *Fig* froid, guindé; (*difficult*) difficile; (*price*) élevé; (*whisky*) bien tassé; **to have a s. neck** avoir le torticolis; **to feel s.** être courbaturé; **to be bored s.** *Fam* s'ennuyer à mourir; **frozen s.** *Fam* complètement gelé. ◆**stiffen** *vt* raidir; − *vi* se raidir. ◆**stiffly** *adv* (*coldly*) *Fig* froidement. ◆**stiffness** *n* raideur *f*; (*hardness*) dureté *f*.

stifle ['staɪf(ə)l] *vt* (*feeling, person etc*) étouffer; − *vi* **it's stifling** on étouffe.

stigma ['stɪgmə] *n* (*moral stain*) flétrissure *f*. ◆**stigmatize** *vt* (*denounce*) stigmatiser.

stile [staɪl] *n* (*between fields etc*) échalier *m*.

stiletto [stɪ'letəʊ] *a* **s. heel** talon *m* aiguille.

still¹ [stɪl] *adv* encore, toujours; (*even*) encore; (*nevertheless*) tout de même; **better s., s. better** encore mieux.

still² [stɪl] *a* (**-er, -est**) (*motionless*) immobile; (*calm*) calme, tranquille; (*drink*) non gazeux; **to keep** *or* **lie** *or* **stand s.** rester tranquille; **s. life** nature *f* morte; − *n* (*of night*) silence *m*; *Cin* photo *f*. ◆**stillborn** *a* mort-né. ◆**stillness** *n* immobilité *f*; calme *m*.

still³ [stɪl] *n* (*for making alcohol*) alambic *m*.

stilt [stɪlt] *n* (*pole*) échasse *f*.

stilted ['stɪltɪd] *a* guindé.

stimulate ['stɪmjʊleɪt] *vt* stimuler. ◆**stimulant** *n* *Med* stimulant *m*. ◆**stimu'lation** *n* stimulation *f*. ◆**stimulus**, *pl* **-li** [-laɪ] *n* (*encouragement*) stimulant *m*; (*physiological*) stimulus *m*.

sting [stɪŋ] *vt* (*pt & pp* **stung**) (*of insect, ointment, wind etc*) piquer; (*of remark*) *Fig* blesser; − *vi* piquer; − *n* piqûre *f*; (*insect's organ*) dard *m*. ◆**—ing** *a* (*pain, remark*) cuisant.

sting/y ['stɪndʒɪ] *a* (**-ier, -iest**) avare, mesquin; **s. with** (*money, praise*) avare de; (*food, wine*) mesquin sur. ◆**—iness** *n* avarice *f*.

stink [stɪŋk] *n* puanteur *f*; **to cause** *or* **make a s.** (*trouble*) *Fam* faire du foin; − *vi* (*pt* **stank** *or* **stunk**, *pp* **stunk**) puer; (*of book, film etc*)

Fam être infect; **to s. of smoke**/*etc* empester la fumée/*etc*; — *vt* **to s. out** (*room etc*) empester. ◆**—ing** *a Fam* infect, sale. ◆**—er** *n Fam* (*person*) sale type *m*; (*question, task etc*) vacherie *f*.

stint [stɪnt] **1** *n* (*share*) part *f* de travail; (*period*) période *f* de travail. **2** *vi* **to s. on** lésiner sur.

stipend ['staɪpend] *n Rel* traitement *n*.

stipulate ['stɪpjʊleɪt] *vt* stipuler (**that** que). ◆**stipu'lation** *n* stipulation *f*.

stir [stɜr] *n* agitation *f*; **to give sth a s.** remuer qch; **to cause a s.** *Fig* faire du bruit; — *vt* (**-rr-**) (*coffee, leaves etc*) remuer; (*excite*) *Fig* exciter; (*incite*) inciter (**to do** à faire); **to s. oneself** (*make an effort*) se secouer; **to s. up** (*trouble*) provoquer; (*memory*) réveiller; — *vi* remuer, bouger. ◆**stirring** *a* (*speech etc*) excitant, émouvant.

stirrup ['stɪrəp] *n* étrier *m*.

stitch [stɪtʃ] *n* point *m*; (*in knitting*) maille *f*; *Med* point *m* de suture; **a s.** (**in one's side**) (*pain*) un point de côté; **to be in stitches** *Fam* se tordre (de rire); — *vt* **to s.** (**up**) (*sew up*) coudre; *Med* suturer.

stoat [stəʊt] *n* (*animal*) hermine *f*.

stock [stɒk] *n* (*supply*) provision *f*, stock *m*, réserve *f*; (*of knowledge, jokes*) fonds *m*, mine *f*; *Fin* valeurs *fpl*, titres *mpl*; (*descent, family*) souche *f*; (*soup*) bouillon *m*; (*cattle*) bétail *m*; **the stocks** *Hist* le pilori; **in s.** (*goods*) en magasin, disponible; **out of s.** (*goods*) épuisé, non disponible; **to take s.** *Fig* faire le point (**of** de); **s. reply**/**size** réponse *f*/taille *f* courante; **s. phrase** expression *f* toute faite; **the S. Exchange** or **Market** la Bourse; — *vt* (*sell*) vendre; (*keep in store*) stocker; **to s.** (**up**) (*shop, larder*) approvisionner; **well-stocked** bien approvisionné; — *vi* **to s. up** s'approvisionner (**with** de, en). ◆**stockbroker** *n* agent *m* de change. ◆**stockcar** *n* stock-car *m*. ◆**stockholder** *n Fin* actionnaire *mf*. ◆**stockist** *n* dépositaire *mf*, stockiste *m*. ◆**stockpile** *vt* stocker, amasser. ◆**stockroom** *n* réserve *f*, magasin *m*. ◆**stocktaking** *n Com* inventaire *m*.

stocking ['stɒkɪŋ] *n* (*garment*) bas *m*.

stocky ['stɒkɪ] *a* (**-ier, -iest**) trapu.

stodge [stɒdʒ] *n* (*food*) *Fam* étouffe-chrétien *m inv*. ◆**stodgy** *a* (**-ier, -iest**) *Fam* lourd, indigeste; (*person, style*) compassé.

stoic ['stəʊɪk] *a* & *n* stoïque (*mf*). ◆**stoical** *a* stoïque. ◆**stoicism** *n* stoïcisme *m*.

stoke [stəʊk] *vt* (*fire*) entretenir; (*engine*) chauffer. ◆**—er** *n Rail* chauffeur *m*.

stole[1] [stəʊl] *n* (*shawl*) étole *f*.

stole[2], **stolen** [stəʊl, 'stəʊl(ə)n] *see* **steal**[1,2].

stolid ['stɒlɪd] *a* (*manner, person*) impassible.

stomach ['stʌmək] **1** *n Anat* estomac *m*; (*abdomen*) ventre *m*; — *vt* (*put up with*) *Fig* supporter. ◆**stomachache** *n* mal *m* de ventre; **to have a s.** avoir mal au ventre.

stone [stəʊn] *n* pierre *f*; (*pebble*) caillou *m*; (*in fruit*) noyau *m*; (*in kidney*) *Med* calcul *m*; (*weight*) = 6,348 kg; **a stone's throw away** *Fig* à deux pas d'ici; — *vt* lancer des pierres sur, lapider; (*fruit*) dénoyauter. ◆**stonemason** *n* tailleur *m* de pierre, maçon *m*. ◆**stony** *a* **1** (**-ier, -iest**) (*path etc*) pierreux, caillouteux. **2 s. broke** (*penniless*) *Sl* fauché.

stone- [stəʊn] *pref* complètement. ◆**s.-'broke** *a Am Sl* fauché. ◆**s.-'cold** *a* complètement froid. ◆**s.-'dead** *a* raide mort. ◆**s.-'deaf** *a* sourd comme un pot.

stoned [stəʊnd] *a* (*high on drugs*) *Fam* camé.

stooge [stuːdʒ] *n* (*actor*) comparse *mf*; (*flunkey*) *Pej* larbin *m*; (*dupe*) *Pej* pigeon *m*.

stood [stʊd] *see* **stand**.

stool [stuːl] *n* tabouret *m*.

stoop [stuːp] **1** *n* **to have a s.** être voûté; — *vi* se baisser; **to s. to doing**/**to sth** *Fig* s'abaisser à faire/à qch. **2** *n* (*in front of house*) *Am* perron *m*.

stop [stɒp] *n* (*place, halt*) arrêt *m*, halte *f*; *Av Nau* escale *f*; *Gram* point *m*; **bus s.** arrêt *m* d'autobus; **to put a s. to** mettre fin à; **to bring to a s.** arrêter; **to come to a s.** s'arrêter; **without a s.** sans arrêt; **s. light** (*on vehicle*) stop *m*; **s. sign** (*road sign*) stop *m*; — *vt* (**-pp-**) arrêter; (*end*) mettre fin à; (*prevent*) empêcher (**from doing** de faire); (*cheque*) faire opposition à; **to s. up** (*sink, pipe, leak etc*) boucher; — *vi* s'arrêter; (*of pain, conversation etc*) cesser; (*stay*) rester; **to s. eating**/*etc* s'arrêter de manger/*etc*; **to s. snowing**/*etc* cesser de neiger/*etc*; **to s. by** passer (**s.o.'s** chez qn); **to s. off** or **over** (*on journey*) s'arrêter. ◆**stoppage** *n* arrêt *m*; (*in pay*) retenue *f*; (*in work*) arrêt *m* de travail; (*strike*) débrayage *m*; (*blockage*) obstruction *f*. ◆**stopper** *n* bouchon *m*.

stopcock ['stɒpkɒk] *n* robinet *m* d'arrêt. ◆**stopgap** *n* bouche-trou *m*; — *a* intérimaire. ◆**stopoff** *n* ◆**stopover** *n* halte *f*. ◆**stopwatch** *n* chronomètre *m*.

store [stɔɪr] n (supply) provision f; (of information, jokes etc) Fig fonds m; (depot, warehouse) entrepôt m; (shop) grand magasin m, Am magasin m; (computer memory) mémoire f; **to have sth in s. for s.o.** (surprise) réserver qch à qn; **to keep in s.** garder en réserve; **to set great s. by** attacher une grande importance à; – vt **to s. (up)** (in warehouse etc) emmagasiner; (for future use) mettre en réserve; **to s. (away)** (furniture) entreposer. ◆**storage** n emmagasinage m; (for future use) mise f en réserve; **s. space** or **room** espace m de rangement. ◆**storekeeper** n magasinier m; (shopkeeper) Am commerçant, -ante mf. ◆**storeroom** n réserve f.

storey ['stɔɪrɪ] n étage m.

stork [stɔɪk] n cigogne f.

storm [stɔɪm] **1** n (weather) & Fig tempête f; (thunderstorm) orage m; **s. cloud** nuage m orageux. **2** vt (attack) Mil prendre d'assaut. **3** vi **to s. out** (angrily) sortir comme une furie. ◆**stormy** a (-ier, -iest) (weather, meeting etc) orageux; (wind) d'orage.

story ['stɔɪrɪ] n **1** histoire f; (newspaper article) article m; **s. (line)** Cin Th intrigue f; **short s.** Liter nouvelle f, conte m; **fairy s.** conte m de fées. **2** (storey) Am étage m. ◆**storyteller** n conteur, -euse mf; (liar) Fam menteur, -euse mf.

stout [staʊt] **1** a (-er, -est) (person) gros, corpulent; (stick, volume) gros, épais; (shoes) solide. **2** n (beer) bière f brune. ◆**-ness** n corpulence f.

stove [stəʊv] n (for cooking) cuisinière f; (solid fuel) fourneau m; (small) réchaud m; (for heating) poêle m.

stow [stəʊ] **1** vt (cargo) arrimer; **to s. away** (put away) ranger. **2** vi **to s. away** Nau voyager clandestinement. ◆**stowaway** n Nau passager, -ère mf clandestin(e).

straddle ['stræd(ə)l] vt (chair, fence) se mettre or être à califourchon sur; (step over, span) enjamber; (line in road) Aut chevaucher.

straggl/e ['stræg(ə)l] vi (stretch) s'étendre (en désordre); (trail) traîner (en désordre); **to s. in** entrer par petits groupes. ◆**-er** n traînard, -arde mf.

straight [streɪt] a (-er, -est) droit; (hair) raide; (route) direct; (tidy) en ordre; (frank) franc; (refusal) net; (actor, role) sérieux; **I want to get this s.** comprenons-nous bien; **to keep a s. face** garder son sérieux; **to put** or **set s.** (tidy) ranger; – n **the s.** Sp la ligne droite; – adv (to walk etc) droit; (directly) tout droit, directe-

ment; (to drink gin, whisky etc) sec; **s. away** (at once) tout de suite; **s. out, s. off** sans hésiter; **s. opposite** juste en face; **s. ahead** or **on** (to walk etc) tout droit; **s. ahead** (to look) droit devant soi. ◆**straighta'way** adv tout de suite. ◆**straighten** vt (up) redresser; (tie, room) arranger; **to s. things out** Fig arranger les choses. ◆**straight-'forward** a (frank) franc; (easy) simple.

strain [streɪn] **1** n (tension) f; (tiredness) fatigue f; (stress) Med tension f nerveuse; (effort) effort m; – vt (rope, wire) tendre excessivement; (muscle) Med froisser; (ankle, wrist) fouler; (eyes) fatiguer; (voice) forcer; Fig mettre à l'épreuve; **to s. one's ears** (to hear) tendre l'oreille; **to s. oneself** (hurt oneself) se faire mal; (tire oneself) se fatiguer; – vi fournir un effort (**to do** pour faire). **2** vt (soup etc) passer; (vegetables) égoutter. **3** n (breed) lignée f; (of virus) souche f; (streak) tendance f. **4** npl Mus accents mpl (**of** de). ◆**—ed** a (relations) tendu; (laugh) forcé; (ankle, wrist) foulé. ◆**—er** n passoire f.

strait [streɪt] **1** n & npl Geog détroit m. **2** npl **in financial straits** dans l'embarras. ◆**straitjacket** n camisole f de force. ◆**strait'laced** a collet monté inv.

strand [strænd] n (of wool etc) brin m; (of hair) mèche f; (of story) Fig fil m.

stranded ['strændɪd] a (person, vehicle) en rade.

strange [streɪndʒ] a (-er, -est) (odd) étrange, bizarre; (unknown) inconnu; (new) nouveau; **to feel s.** (in a new place) se sentir dépaysé. ◆**strangely** adv étrangement; **s. (enough) she ...** chose étrange, elle .... ◆**strangeness** n étrangeté f. ◆**stranger** n (unknown) inconnu, -ue mf; (outsider) étranger, -ère mf; **he's a s. here** il n'est pas d'ici; **she's a s. to me** elle m'est inconnue.

strangle ['stræŋg(ə)l] vt étrangler. ◆**strangler** n étrangleur, -euse mf. ◆**stranglehold** n emprise f totale (**on** sur).

strap [stræp] n courroie f, sangle f; (on dress) bretelle f; (on watch) bracelet m; (on sandal) lanière f; – vt (-pp-) **to s. (down** or **in)** attacher (avec une courroie).

strapping ['stræpɪŋ] a (well-built) robuste.

stratagem ['strætədʒəm] n stratagème m.

strategy ['strætədʒɪ] n stratégie f. ◆**stra-'tegic** a stratégique.

stratum, pl **-ta** ['strɑːtəm, -tə] n couche f.

straw [strɔː] n paille f; **a (drinking) s.** une paille; **that's the last s.!** c'est le comble!

strawberry ['strɔːbərɪ] n fraise f; – a

(*flavour, ice cream*) à la fraise; (*jam*) de fraises; (*tart*) aux fraises.

stray [streɪ] *a* (*lost*) perdu; **a s. car**/*etc* une voiture/*etc* isolée; **a few s. cars**/*etc* quelques rares voitures/*etc*; − *n* animal *m* perdu; − *vi* s'égarer; **to s. from** (*subject, path*) s'écarter de.

streak [striːk] *n* (*line*) raie *f*; (*of light*) filet *m*; (*of colour*) strie *f*; (*trace*) Fig trace *f*; (*tendency*) tendance *f*; **grey**/*etc* **streaks** (*in hair*) mèches *fpl* grises/*etc*; **a mad s.** une tendance à la folie; **my literary s.** ma fibre littéraire. ◆**streaked** *a* (*marked*) strié, zébré; (*stained*) taché (**with** de). ◆**streaky** *a* (**-ier, -iest**) strié; (*bacon*) pas trop maigre.

stream [striːm] *n* (*brook*) ruisseau *m*; (*current*) courant *m*; (*flow*) & Fig flot *m*; Sch classe *f* (de niveau); − *vi* ruisseler (**with** de); **to s. in** (*of sunlight, people etc*) Fig entrer à flots.

streamer ['striːmər] *n* (*paper*) serpentin *m*; (*banner*) banderole *f*.

streamlin/e ['striːmlaɪn] *vt* (*work, method etc*) rationaliser. ◆**−ed** *a* (*shape*) aérodynamique.

street [striːt] *n* rue *f*; **s. door** porte *f* d'entrée; **s. lamp, s. light** réverbère *m*; **s. map, s. plan** plan *m* des rues; **up my s.** Fig Fam dans mes cordes; **streets ahead** Fam très en avance (**of** sur). ◆**streetcar** *n* (*tram*) Am tramway *m*.

strength [streŋθ] *n* force *f*; (*health, energy*) forces *fpl*; (*of wood, fabric*) solidité *f*; **on the s. of** Fig en vertu de; **in full s.** au (grand) complet. ◆**strengthen** *vt* (*building, position etc*) renforcer, consolider; (*body, soul, limb*) fortifier.

strenuous ['strenjuəs] *a* (*effort etc*) vigoureux, énergique; (*work*) ardu; (*active*) actif; (*tiring*) fatigant. ◆**−ly** *adv* énergiquement.

strep [strep] *a* **s. throat** Med Am angine *f*.

stress [stres] *n* (*pressure*) pression *f*; Med Psy tension *f* (nerveuse), stress *m*; (*emphasis*) & Gram accent *m*; Tech tension *f*; **under s.** Med Psy sous pression, stressé; − *vt* insister sur; (*word*) accentuer; **to s. that** souligner que. ◆**stressful** *a* stressant.

stretch [stretʃ] *vt* (*rope, neck*) tendre; (*shoe, rubber*) étirer; (*meaning*) Fig forcer; **to s. (out)** (*arm, leg*) étendre, allonger; **to s. (out) one's arm** (*reach out*) tendre le bras (**to take** pour prendre); **to s. one's legs** Fig se dégourdir les jambes; **to s. s.o.** Fig exiger un effort de qn; **to be (fully) stretched** (*of budget etc*) être tiré au maximum; **to s. out** (*visit*) prolonger; − *vi* (*of person, elastic*)

s'étirer; (*of influence etc*) s'étendre; **to s. (out)** (*of rope, plain*) s'étendre; − *n* (*area, duration*) étendue *f*; (*of road*) tronçon *m*, partie *f*; (*route, trip*) trajet *m*; **at a s.** d'une (seule) traite; **ten**/*etc* **hours at a s.** dix/*etc* heures d'affilée; **s. socks**/*etc* chaussettes *fpl*/*etc* extensibles; **s. nylon** nylon *m* stretch *inv.* ◆**stretchmarks** *npl* (*on body*) vergetures *fpl*.

stretcher ['stretʃər] *n* brancard *m*.

strew [struː] *vt* (*pt* **strewed**, *pp* **strewed** *or* **strewn**) (*scatter*) répandre; **strewn with** (*covered*) jonché de.

stricken ['strɪk(ə)n] *a* **s. with** (*illness*) atteint de; (*panic*) frappé de.

strict [strɪkt] *a* (**-er, -est**) (*severe, absolute*) strict. ◆**−ly** *adv* strictement; **s. forbidden** formellement interdit. ◆**−ness** *n* sévérité *f*.

stride [straɪd] *n* (*grand*) pas *m*, enjambée *f*; **to make great strides** Fig faire de grands progrès; − *vi* (*pt* **strode**) **to s. across** *or* **over** enjamber; **to s. up and down a room** arpenter une pièce.

strident ['straɪdənt] *a* strident.

strife [straɪf] *n inv* conflit(s) *m(pl)*.

strik/e [straɪk] **1** *n* (*attack*) Mil raid *m* (aérien); (*of oil etc*) découverte *f*; − *vt* (*pt* & *pp* **struck**) (*hit, impress*) frapper; (*collide with*) heurter; (*beat*) battre; (*a blow*) donner; (*a match*) frotter; (*gold, problem*) trouver; (*coin*) frapper; (*of clock*) sonner; **to s. a bargain** conclure un accord; **to s. a balance** trouver l'équilibre; **to s. (off)** (*from list*) rayer (**from** de); **to be struck off** (*of doctor*) être radié; **it strikes me as**/**that** il me semble être/que; **how did it s. you?** quelle impression ça t'a fait?; **to s. down** (*illness etc*) terrasser (*qn*); **to s. up a friendship** lier amitié (**with** avec); − *vi* **to s. (at)** (*attack*) attaquer; **to s. back** (*retaliate*) riposter; **to s. out** donner des coups. **2** *n* (*of workers*) grève *f*; **to go (out) on s.** se mettre en grève (**for** pour obtenir, **against** pour protester contre); − *vi* (*pt* & *pp* **struck**) (*of workers*) faire grève. ◆**−ing** *a* (*impressive*) frappant. ◆**−ingly** *adv* (*beautiful etc*) extraordinairement. ◆**−er** *n* gréviste *mf*; Fb buteur *m*.

string [strɪŋ] *n* ficelle *f*; (*of anorak, apron*) cordon *m*; (*of violin, racket etc*) corde *f*; (*of pearls, beads*) rang *m*; (*of onions, insults*) chapelet *m*; (*of people, vehicles*) file *f*; (*of questions etc*) série *f*; **to pull strings** Fig faire jouer ses relations; − *a* (*instrument, quartet*) Mus à cordes; **s. bean** haricot *m* vert; − *vt* (*pt* & *pp* **strung**) (*beads*) enfiler; **to s. up**

(*hang up*) suspendre; − *vi* **to s. along (with)** *Fam* suivre. ◆**—ed** *a* (*instrument*) *Mus* à cordes. ◆**stringy** *a* (**-ier, -iest**) (*meat etc*) filandreux.

stringent ['strɪndʒ(ə)nt] *a* rigoureux. ◆**stringency** *n* rigueur *f*.

strip [strɪp] **1** *n* (*piece*) bande *f*; (*of water*) bras *m*; (**thin**) **s.** (*of metal etc*) lamelle *f*; **landing s.** piste *f* or terrain *m* d'atterrissage; **s. cartoon, comic s.** bande *f* dessinée. **2** *vt* (**-pp-**) (*undress*) déshabiller; (*bed*) défaire; (*deprive*) dépouiller (**of** de); **to s. (down)** (*machine*) démonter; **to s. off** (*remove*) enlever; − *vi* **to s. (off)** (*undress*) se déshabiller. ◆**stripper** *n* (*woman*) stripteaseuse *f*; (*paint*) décapant *m*. ◆**strip-'tease** *n* strip-tease *m*.

stripe [straɪp] *n* rayure *f*; *Mil* galon *m*. ◆**striped** *a* rayé (**with** de). ◆**stripy** *a* rayé.

strive [straɪv] *vi* (*pt* **strove**, *pp* **striven**) s'efforcer (**to do** de faire, **for** d'obtenir).

strode [strəud] *see* **stride.**

stroke [strəuk] *n* (*movement*) coup *m*; (*of pen, genius*) trait *m*; (*of brush*) touche *f*; (*on clock*) coup *m*; (*caress*) caresse *f*; *Med* coup *m* de sang; (*swimming style*) nage *f*; **at a s.** d'un coup; **a s. of luck** un coup de chance; **you haven't done a s. (of work)** tu n'as rien fait; **heat s.** (*sunstroke*) insolation *f*; **four-s. engine** moteur *m* à quatre temps; − *vt* (*beard, cat etc*) caresser.

stroll [strəul] *n* promenade *f*; − *vi* se promener, flâner; **to s. in**/*etc* entrer/*etc* sans se presser. ◆**—ing** *a* (*musician etc*) ambulant.

stroller ['strəulər] *n* (*pushchair*) *Am* poussette *f*.

strong [strɒŋ] *a* (**-er, -est**) fort; (*shoes, nerves*) solide; (*interest*) vif; (*measures*) énergique; (*supporter*) ardent; **sixty s.** au nombre de soixante; − *adv* **to be going s.** aller toujours bien. ◆**—ly** *adv* (*to protest, defend*) énergiquement; (*to desire, advise, remind*) fortement; (*to feel*) profondément; **s. built** solide. ◆**strongarm** *a* brutal. ◆**strongbox** *n* coffre-fort *m*. ◆**stronghold** *n* bastion *m*. ◆**strong-'willed** *a* résolu.

strove [strəuv] *see* **strive.**

struck [strʌk] *see* **strike 1,2.**

structure ['strʌktʃər] *n* structure *f*; (*of building*) armature *f*; (*building itself*) construction *f*. ◆**structural** *a* structural; (*fault*) *Archit* de construction.

struggle ['strʌg(ə)l] *n* (*fight*) lutte *f* (**to do** pour faire); (*effort*) effort *m*; **to put up a s.** résister; **to have a s. doing** or **to do** avoir du mal à faire; − *vi* (*fight*) lutter, se battre (**with** avec); (*resist*) résister; (*thrash about wildly*) se débattre; **to s. to do** (*try hard*) s'efforcer de faire; **to s. out of** sortir péniblement de; **to s. along** or **on** se débrouiller; **a struggling lawyer**/*etc* un avocat/*etc* qui a du mal à débuter.

strum [strʌm] *vt* (**-mm-**) (*guitar etc*) gratter de.

strung [strʌŋ] *see* **string**; − *a* **s. out** (*things, people*) espacés; (*washing*) étendu.

strut [strʌt] **1** *vi* (**-tt-**) **to s. (about** or **around)** se pavaner. **2** *n* (*support*) *Tech* étai *m*.

stub [stʌb] **1** *n* (*of pencil, cigarette etc*) bout *m*; (*counterfoil of cheque etc*) talon *m*; − *vt* (**-bb-**) **to s. out** (*cigarette*) écraser. **2** *vt* (**-bb-**) **to s. one's toe** se cogner le doigt de pied (**on, against** contre).

stubble ['stʌb(ə)l] *n* barbe *f* de plusieurs jours.

stubborn ['stʌbən] *a* (*person*) entêté, opiniâtre; (*cough, efforts, manner etc*) opiniâtre. ◆**—ly** *adv* opiniâtrement. ◆**—ness** *n* entêtement *m*; opiniâtreté *f*.

stubby ['stʌbɪ] *a* (**-ier, -iest**) (*finger etc*) gros et court, épais; (*person*) trapu.

stuck [stʌk] *see* **stick**²; − *a* (*caught, jammed*) coincé; **s. in bed**/**indoors** cloué au lit/chez soi; **to be s.** (*unable to do sth*) ne pas savoir quoi faire; **I'm s. (for an answer)** je ne sais que répondre; **to be s. with sth./s.o.** se farcir qch/qn. ◆**s.-'up** *a Fam* prétentieux, snob *inv*.

stud [stʌd] *n* **1** (*nail*) clou *m* (à grosse tête); (*for collar*) bouton *m* de col. **2** (*farm*) haras *m*; (*horses*) écurie *f*; (*stallion*) étalon *m*; (*virile man*) *Sl* mâle *m*. ◆**studded** *a* (*boots, tyres*) clouté; **s. with** (*covered*) *Fig* constellé de, parsemé de.

student ['stjuːdənt] *n* *Univ* étudiant, -ante *mf*; *Sch Am* élève *mf*; **music**/*etc* **s.** étudiant, -ante en musique/*etc*; − *a* (*life, protest*) étudiant; (*restaurant, residence, grant*) universitaire.

studio ['stjuːdɪəu] *n* (*pl* **-os**) (*of painter etc*) & *Cin TV* studio *m*; **s. flat** or *Am* **apartment** studio *m*.

studious ['stjuːdɪəs] *a* (*person*) studieux. ◆**—ly** *adv* (*carefully*) avec soin. ◆**—ness** *n* application *f*.

study ['stʌdɪ] *n* étude *f*; (*office*) bureau *m*; − *vt* (*learn, observe*) étudier; − *vi* étudier; **to s. to be a doctor**/*etc* faire des études pour devenir médecin/*etc*; **to s. for** (*exam*) préparer. ◆**studied** *a* (*deliberate*) étudié.

stuff [stʌf] **1** *n* (*thing*) truc *m*, chose *f*;

(*substance*) substance *f*; (*things*) trucs *mpl*, choses *fpl*; (*possessions*) affaires *fpl*; (*nonsense*) sottises *fpl*; **this s.'s good, it's good s.** c'est bon (ça). **2** *vt* (*chair, cushion etc*) rembourrer (**with** avec); (*animal*) empailler; (*cram, fill*) bourrer (**with** de); (*put, thrust*) fourrer (**into** dans); (*chicken etc*) Culin farcir; **to s. (up)** (*hole etc*) colmater; **my nose is stuffed (up)** j'ai le nez bouché. ◆**—ing** *n* (*padding*) bourre *f*; Culin farce *f*.

stuffy ['stʌfɪ] *a* (**-ier, -iest**) (*room etc*) mal aéré; (*formal*) Fig compassé; (*old-fashioned*) vieux jeu *inv*; **it smells s.** ça sent le renfermé.

stumble ['stʌmb(ə)l] *vi* trébucher (**over** sur, **against** contre); **to s. across** *or* **on** (*find*) tomber sur; **stumbling block** pierre *f* d'achoppement.

stump [stʌmp] *n* (*of tree*) souche *f*; (*of limb*) moignon *m*; (*of pencil*) bout *m*; Cricket piquet *m*.

stumped [stʌmpt] *a* **to be s. by sth** (*baffled*) ne pas savoir que penser de qch.

stun [stʌn] *vt* (**-nn-**) (*daze*) étourdir; (*animal*) assommer; (*amaze*) Fig stupéfier. ◆**stunned** *a* Fig stupéfait (**by** par). ◆**stunning** *a* (*blow*) étourdissant; (*news*) stupéfiant; (*terrific*) Fam sensationnel.

stung [stʌŋ] *see* sting.

stunk [stʌŋk] *see* stink.

stunt [stʌnt] **1** *n* (*feat*) tour *m* (de force); Cin cascade *f*; (*ruse, trick*) truc *m*; **s. man** Cin cascadeur *m*; **s. woman** Cin cascadeuse *f*. **2** *vt* (*growth*) retarder. ◆**—ed** *a* (*person*) rabougri.

stupefy ['stjuːpɪfaɪ] *vt* (*of drink etc*) abrutir; (*amaze*) Fig stupéfier.

stupendous [stjuːˈpendəs] *a* prodigieux.

stupid ['stjuːpɪd] *a* stupide, bête; **a s. thing** une sottise; **s. fool, s. idiot** idiot, -ote *mf*. ◆**stu'pidity** *n* stupidité *f*. ◆**stupidly** *adv* stupidement, bêtement.

stupor ['stjuːpər] *n* (*daze*) stupeur *f*.

sturdy ['stɜːdɪ] *a* (**-ier, -iest**) (*person, shoe etc*) robuste. ◆**sturdiness** *n* robustesse *f*.

sturgeon ['stɜːdʒ(ə)n] *n* (*fish*) esturgeon *m*.

stutter ['stʌtər] *n* bégaiement *m*; **to have a s.** être bègue; *— vi* bégayer.

sty [staɪ] *n* (*pigsty*) porcherie *f*.

sty(e) [staɪ] *n* (*on eye*) orgelet *m*.

style [staɪl] *n* style *m*; (*fashion*) mode *f*; (*design of dress etc*) modèle *m*; (*of hair*) coiffure *f*; (*sort*) genre *m*; **to have s.** avoir de la classe; **in s.** (*in superior manner*) de la meilleure façon possible; (*to live, travel*) dans le luxe; *— vt* (*design*) créer; **he styles**

himself . . . *Pej* il se fait appeler . . . ; **to s. s.o.'s hair** coiffer qn. ◆**styling** *n* (*cutting of hair*) coupe *f*. ◆**stylish** *a* chic, élégant. ◆**stylishly** *adv* élégamment. ◆**stylist** *n* (*hair*) **s.** coiffeur, -euse *mf*. ◆**sty'listic** *a* de style, stylistique. ◆**stylized** *a* stylisé.

stylus ['staɪləs] *n* (*of record player*) pointe *f* de lecture.

suave [swɑːv] *a* (**-er, -est**) (*urbane*) courtois; *Pej* doucereux.

sub- [sʌb] *pref* sous-, sub-.

subconscious [sʌbˈkɒnʃəs] *a* & *n* subconscient (*m*). ◆**—ly** *adv* inconsciemment.

subcontract [sʌbkənˈtrækt] *vt* sous-traiter. ◆**subcontractor** *n* sous-traitant *m*.

subdivide [sʌbdɪˈvaɪd] *vt* subdiviser (**into** en). ◆**subdivision** *n* subdivision *f*.

subdu/e [səbˈdjuː] *vt* (*country*) asservir; (*feelings*) maîtriser. ◆**—ed** *a* (*light*) atténué; (*voice*) bas; (*reaction*) faible; (*person*) qui manque d'entrain.

subheading ['sʌbhedɪŋ] *n* sous-titre *m*.

subject¹ ['sʌbdʒɪkt] *n* **1** (*matter*) & Gram sujet *m*; *Sch Univ* matière *f*; **s. matter** (*topic*) sujet *m*; (*content*) contenu *m*. **2** (*citizen*) ressortissant, -ante *mf*; (*of monarch, monarchy*) sujet, -ette *mf*; (*person in experiment*) sujet *m*.

subject² ['sʌbdʒekt] *a* (*tribe etc*) soumis; **s. to** (*prone to*) sujet à (*maladie etc*); (*ruled by*) soumis à (*loi, règle etc*); (*conditional upon*) sous réserve de; **prices are s. to change** les prix peuvent être modifiés; *—* [səbˈdʒekt] *vt* soumettre (**to** à); (*expose*) exposer (**to** à). ◆**sub'jection** *n* soumission *f* (**to** à).

subjective [səbˈdʒektɪv] *a* subjectif. ◆**—ly** *adv* subjectivement. ◆**subjec'tivity** *n* subjectivité *f*.

subjugate ['sʌbdʒʊgeɪt] *vt* subjuguer.

subjunctive [səbˈdʒʌŋktɪv] *n* Gram subjonctif *m*.

sublet [sʌbˈlet] *vt* (*pt* & *pp* **sublet**, *pres p* **subletting**) sous-louer.

sublimate ['sʌblɪmeɪt] *vt* Psy sublimer.

sublime [səˈblaɪm] *a* sublime; (*indifference, stupidity*) suprême; *— n* sublime *m*.

submachine-gun [sʌbməˈʃiːngʌn] *n* mitraillette *f*.

submarine ['sʌbməriːn] *n* sous-marin *m*.

submerge [səbˈmɜːdʒ] *vt* (*flood, overwhelm*) submerger; (*immerse*) immerger (**in** dans); *— vi* (*of submarine*) s'immerger.

submit [səbˈmɪt] *vt* (**-tt-**) soumettre (**to** à); **to s. that** (*suggest*) suggérer que; *— vi* se soumettre (**to** à). ◆**submission** *n* soumission *f* (**to** à). ◆**submissive** *a* soumis. ◆**submissively** *adv* avec soumission.

subnormal [sʌb'nɔːm(ə)l] *a* au-dessous de la normale; (*mentally*) arriéré.

subordinate [sə'bɔːdinət] *a* subalterne; *Gram* subordonné; – *n* subordonné, -ée *mf*; – [sə'bɔːdineit] *vt* subordonner (**to** à). ◆**subordi'nation** *n* subordination *f* (**to** à).

subpoena [səb'piːnə] *vt Jur* citer; – *n Jur* citation *f*.

subscribe [səb'skraib] *vt* (*money*) donner (**to** à); – *vi* cotiser; **to s. to** (*take out subscription*) s'abonner à (*journal etc*); (*be a subscriber*) être abonné à (*journal etc*); (*fund, idea*) souscrire à. ◆**subscriber** *n Journ Tel* abonné, -ée *mf*. ◆**subscription** *n* (*to newspaper etc*) abonnement *m*; (*to fund, idea*) & *Fin* souscription *f*; (*to club etc*) cotisation *f*.

subsequent ['sʌbsikwənt] *a* postérieur (**to** à); **our s. problems** les problèmes que nous avons eus par la suite; **s. to** (*as a result of*) consécutif à. ◆**—ly** *adv* par la suite.

subservient [səb'sɜːviənt] *a* obséquieux; **to be s. to** (*a slave to*) être asservi à.

subside [səb'said] *vi* (*of building, land*) s'affaisser; (*of wind, flood*) baisser. ◆**'subsidence** *n* affaissement *m*.

subsidiary [səb'sidiəri] *a* accessoire; (*subject*) *Univ* secondaire; – *n* (*company*) *Com* filiale *f*.

subsidize ['sʌbsidaiz] *vt* subventionner. ◆**subsidy** *n* subvention *f*.

subsist [səb'sist] *vi* (*of person, doubts etc*) subsister. ◆**subsistence** *n* subsistance *f*.

substance ['sʌbstəns] *n* substance *f*; (*firmness*) solidité *f*; **a man of s.** un homme riche. ◆**substantial** [səb'stænʃ(ə)l] *a* important, considérable; (*meal*) substantiel. ◆**sub'stantially** *adv* considérablement, beaucoup; **s. true**/*etc* (*to a great extent*) en grande partie vrai/*etc*; **s. different** très différent.

substandard [sʌb'stændəd] *a* de qualité inférieure.

substantiate [səb'stænʃieit] *vt* prouver, justifier.

substitute ['sʌbstitjuːt] *n* (*thing*) produit *m* de remplacement; (*person*) remplaçant, -ante *mf* (**for** de); **there's no s. for . . .** rien ne peut remplacer . . . ; – *vt* substituer (**for** à); – *vi* **to s. for** remplacer; (*deputize for in job*) se substituer à. ◆**substi'tution** *n* substitution *f*.

subtitle ['sʌbtait(ə)l] *n* sous-titre *m*; – *vt* sous-titrer.

subtle ['sʌt(ə)l] *a* (-**er**, -**est**) subtil. ◆**sub-**

tlety *n* subtilité *f*. ◆**subtly** *adv* subtilement. .

subtotal [sʌb'təut(ə)l] *n* total *m* partiel, sous-total *m*.

subtract [səb'trækt] *vt* soustraire (**from** de). ◆**subtraction** *n* soustraction *f*.

suburb ['sʌbɜːb] *n* banlieue *f*; **the suburbs** la banlieue; **in the suburbs** en banlieue. ◆**su'burban** *a* (*train*) de banlieue; (*accent*) de la banlieue. ◆**su'burbia** *n* la banlieue.

subversive [səb'vɜːsiv] *a* subversif. ◆**subversion** *n* subversion *f*. ◆**subvert** *vt* (*system etc*) bouleverser; (*person*) corrompre.

subway ['sʌbwei] *n* passage *m* souterrain; *Rail Am* métro *m*.

succeed [sək'siːd] **1** *vi* réussir (**in doing** à faire, **in sth** dans qch). **2** *vt* **to s. s.o.** (*follow*) succéder à qn; – *vi* **to s. to the throne** succéder à la couronne. ◆**—ing** *a* (*in past*) suivant; (*in future*) futur; (*consecutive*) consécutif.

success [sək'ses] *n* succès *m*, réussite *f*; **to make a s. of sth** réussir qch; **he was a s.** il a eu du succès; **his** *or* **her s. in the exam** sa réussite à l'examen; **s. story** réussite *f* complète *or* exemplaire. ◆**successful** *a* (*venture etc*) couronné de succès, réussi; (*outcome*) heureux; (*candidate in exam*) admis, reçu; (*in election*) élu; (*writer, film etc*) à succès; **to be s.** réussir (**in** dans, **in an exam** à un examen, **in doing** à faire). ◆**successfully** *adv* avec succès.

succession [sək'seʃ(ə)n] *n* succesion *f*; **in s.** successivement; **ten days in s.** dix jours consécutifs; **in rapid s.** coup sur coup. ◆**successive** *a* successif; **ten s. days** dix jours consécutifs. ◆**successor** *n* successeur *m* (**of, to** de).

succinct [sək'siŋkt] *a* succinct.

succulent ['sʌkjulənt] *a* succulent.

succumb [sə'kʌm] *vi* (*yield*) succomber (**to** à).

such [sʌtʃ] *a* tel; **s. a car**/*etc* une telle voiture/*etc*; **s. happiness**/*etc* (*so much*) tant *or* tellement de bonheur/*etc*; **there's no s. thing** ça n'existe pas; **I said no s. thing** je n'ai rien dit de tel; **s. as** comme, tel que; **s. and s.** tel ou tel; – *adv* (*so very*) si; (*in comparisons*) aussi; **a kind woman as you** une femme aussi gentille que vous; **s. long trips** de si longs voyages; **s. a large helping** une si grosse portion; – *pron* **happiness**/*etc* **as s.** le bonheur/*etc* en tant que tel; **s. was**

my idea telle était mon idée. ◆**suchlike** *n* . . . **and s.** *Fam* . . . et autres.

suck [sʌk] *vt* sucer; (*of baby*) téter (*lait, biberon etc*); **to s. (up)** (*with straw, pump*) aspirer; **to s. up** *or* **in** (*absorb*) absorber; − *vi* (*of baby*) téter; **to s. at** sucer. ◆**—er** *n* **1** (*fool*) *Fam* pigeon *m*, dupe *f*. **2** (*pad*) ventouse *f*.

suckle ['sʌk(ə)l] *vt* (*of woman*) allaiter; (*of baby*) téter.

suction ['sʌkʃ(ə)n] *n* succion *f*; **s. disc, s. pad** ventouse *f*.

Sudan [suːdɑːn] *n* Soudan *m*.

sudden ['sʌd(ə)n] *a* soudain, subit; **all of a s.** tout à coup. ◆**—ly** *adv* subitement. ◆**—ness** *n* soudaineté *f*.

suds [sʌdz] *npl* mousse *f* de savon.

sue [suː] *vt* poursuivre (en justice); − *vi* engager des poursuites (judiciaires).

suede [sweɪd] *n* daim *m*; − *a* de daim.

suet ['suːɪt] *n* graisse *f* de rognon.

suffer ['sʌfər] *vi* souffrir (**from de**); **to s. from pimples/the flu** avoir des boutons/la grippe; **your work**/*etc* **will s.** ton travail/*etc* s'en ressentira; − *vt* (*attack, loss etc*) subir; (*pain*) ressentir; (*tolerate*) souffrir. ◆**—ing** *n* souffrance(s) *f(pl)*. ◆**—er** *n* *Med* malade *mf*; (*from misfortune*) victime *f*.

suffice [sə'faɪs] *vi* suffire.

sufficient [sə'fɪʃ(ə)nt] *a* (*quantity, number*) suffisant; **s. money**/*etc* (*enough*) suffisamment d'argent/*etc*; **to have s.** en avoir suffisamment. ◆**—ly** *adv* suffisamment.

suffix ['sʌfɪks] *n* *Gram* suffixe *m*.

suffocate ['sʌfəkeɪt] *vti* étouffer, suffoquer. ◆**suffo'cation** *n* (*of industry, mind etc*) & *Med* étouffement *m*, asphyxie *f*.

suffrage ['sʌfrɪdʒ] *n* (*right to vote*) *Pol* suffrage *m*.

suffused [sə'fjuːzd] *a* **s. with** (*light, tears*) baigné de.

sugar ['ʃugər] *n* sucre *m*; − *a* (*cane, tongs*) à sucre; (*industry*) sucrier; **s. bowl** sucrier *m*; − *vt* sucrer. ◆**sugary** *a* (*taste, tone*) sucré.

suggest [sə'dʒest] *vt* (*propose*) suggérer, proposer (**to à, that que** (+ *sub*)); (*evoke, imply*) suggérer; (*hint*) *Pej* insinuer. ◆**suggestion** *n* suggestion *f*, proposition *f*; (*evocation*) suggestion *f*; *Pej* insinuation *f*. ◆**suggestive** *a* suggestif; **to be s. of** suggérer.

suicide ['suːɪsaɪd] *n* suicide *m*; **to commit s.** se suicider. ◆**sui'cidal** *a* suicidaire.

suit [suːt] **1** *n* (*man's*) complet *m*, costume *m*; (*woman's*) tailleur *m*; (*of pilot, diver etc*) combinaison *f*. **2** *n* (*lawsuit*) *Jur* procès *m*. **3** *n* *Cards* couleur *f*. **4** *vt* (*satisfy, be appropri-*

ate to) convenir à; (*of dress, colour etc*) aller (bien) à; (*adapt*) adapter (**to** à); **it suits me to stay** ça m'arrange de rester; **s. yourself!** comme tu voudras!; **suited to** (*made for*) fait pour; (*appropriate to*) approprié à; **well suited** (*couple etc*) bien assorti. ◆**suita-'bility** *n* (*of remark etc*) à-propos *m*; (*of person*) aptitudes *fpl* (**for** pour); **I'm not sure of the s. of it** (*date etc*) je ne sais pas si ça convient. ◆**suitable** *a* qui convient (**for** à); (*dress, colour*) qui va (bien); (*example*) approprié; (*socially*) convenable. ◆**suitably** *adv* convenablement.

suitcase ['suːtkeɪs] *n* valise *f*.

suite [swiːt] *n* (*rooms*) suite *f*; (*furniture*) mobilier *m*; **bedroom s.** (*furniture*) chambre *f* à coucher.

suitor ['suːtər] *n* soupirant *m*.

sulfur ['sʌlfər] *n* *Am* soufre *m*.

sulk [sʌlk] *vi* bouder. ◆**sulky** *a* (-ier, -iest) boudeur.

sullen ['sʌlən] *a* maussade. ◆**—ly** *adv* d'un air maussade.

sully ['sʌlɪ] *vt* *Lit* souiller.

sulphur ['sʌlfər] *n* soufre *m*.

sultan ['sʌltən] *n* sultan *m*.

sultana [sʌl'tɑːnə] *n* raisin *m* de Smyrne.

sultry ['sʌltrɪ] *a* (-ier, -iest) (*heat*) étouffant; *Fig* sensuel.

sum [sʌm] **1** *n* (*amount, total*) somme *f*; *Math* calcul *m*; *pl* (*arithmetic*) le calcul; **s. total** résultat *m*. **2** *vt* (-mm-) **to s. up** (*facts etc*) récapituler, résumer; (*text*) résumer; (*situation*) évaluer; (*person*) jauger; − *vi* **to s. up** récapituler. ◆**summing-'up** *n* (*pl* summings-up) résumé *m*.

summarize ['sʌməraɪz] *vt* résumer. ◆**summary** *n* résumé *m*; − *a* (*brief*) sommaire.

summer ['sʌmər] *n* été *m*; **in (the) s.** en été; **Indian s.** été indien *or* de la Saint-Martin; − *a* d'été; **s. holidays** grandes vacances *fpl*. ◆**summerhouse** *n* pavillon *m* (de gardien). ◆**summertime** *n* été *m*; **in (the) s.** en été. ◆**summery** *a* (*weather etc*) estival; (*dress*) d'été.

summit ['sʌmɪt] *n* (*of mountain, power etc*) sommet *m*; **s. conference/meeting** *Pol* conférence *f*/rencontre *f* au sommet.

summon ['sʌmən] *vt* (*call*) appeler; (*meeting, s.o. to meeting*) convoquer (**to** à); **to s. s.o. to do** sommer qn de faire; **to s. up** (*courage, strength*) rassembler.

summons ['sʌmənz] *n* *Jur* assignation *f*; − *vt* *Jur* assigner.

sumptuous ['sʌmptʃuəs] *a* somptueux. ◆**—ness** *n* somptuosité *f*.

sun [sʌn] *n* soleil *m*; **in the s.** au soleil; **the**

sun's shining il fait (du) soleil; – *a* (*cream, filter etc*) solaire; **s. lounge** solarium *m*; – *vt* (**-nn-**) **to s. oneself** se chauffer au soleil. ◆**sunbaked** *a* brûlé par le soleil. ◆**sunbathe** *vi* prendre un bain de soleil. ◆**sunbeam** *n* rayon *m* de soleil. ◆**sunburn** *n* (*tan*) bronzage *m*; *Med* coup *m* de soleil. ◆**sunburnt** *a* bronzé; *Med* brûlé par le soleil. ◆**sundial** *n* cadran *m* solaire. ◆**sundown** *n* coucher *m* du soleil. ◆**sundrenched** *a* brûlé par le soleil. ◆**sunflower** *n* tournesol *m*. ◆**sunglasses** *npl* lunettes *fpl* de soleil. ◆**sunlamp** *n* lampe *f* à rayons ultraviolets. ◆**sunlight** *n* (lumière *f* du) soleil *m*. ◆**sunlit** *a* ensoleillé. ◆**sunrise** *n* lever *m* du soleil. ◆**sunroof** *n Aut* toit *m* ouvrant. ◆**sunset** *n* coucher *m* du soleil. ◆**sunshade** *n* (*on table*) parasol *m*; (*portable*) ombrelle *f*. ◆**sunshine** *n* soleil *m*. ◆**sunstroke** *n* insolation *f*. ◆**suntan** *n* bronzage *m*; – *a* (*lotion, oil*) solaire. ◆**suntanned** *a* bronzé. ◆**sunup** *n Am* lever *m* du soleil.

sundae ['sʌndeɪ] *n* glace *f* aux fruits.

Sunday ['sʌndɪ] *n* dimanche *m*.

sundry ['sʌndrɪ] *a* divers; **all and s.** tout le monde; – *npl Com* articles *mpl* divers.

sung [sʌŋ] *see* sing.

sunk [sʌŋk] *see* sink²; – *a* **I'm s.** *Fam* je suis fichu. ◆**sunken** *a* (*rock etc*) submergé; (*eyes*) cave.

sunny ['sʌnɪ] *a* (-ier, -iest) ensoleillé; **it's s.** il fait (du) soleil; **s. period** *Met* éclaircie *f*.

super ['suːpər] *a Fam* sensationnel.

super- ['suːpər] *pref* super-.

superannuation [suːpərænjuˈeɪʃ(ə)n] *n* (*amount*) cotisations *fpl* (pour la) retraite.

superb [suːˈpɜːb] *a* superbe.

supercilious [suːpəˈsɪlɪəs] *a* hautain.

superficial [suːpəˈfɪʃ(ə)l] *a* superficiel. ◆**-ly** *adv* superficiellement.

superfluous [suːˈpɜːflʊəs] *a* superflu.

superhuman [suːpəˈhjuːmən] *a* surhumain.

superimpose [suːpərɪmˈpəʊz] *vt* superposer (**on** à).

superintendent [suːpərɪnˈtendənt] *n* directeur, -trice *mf*; (*police*) **s.** commissaire *m* (de police).

superior [suːˈpɪərɪər] *a* supérieur (**to** à); (*goods*) de qualité supérieure; – *n* (*person*) supérieur, -eure *mf*. ◆**superi'ority** *n* supériorité *f*.

superlative [suːˈpɜːlətɪv] *a* sans pareil; – *a & n Gram* superlatif (*m*).

superman ['suːpəmæn] *n* (*pl* -men) surhomme *m*.

supermarket ['suːpəmɑːkɪt] *n* supermarché *m*.

supernatural [suːpəˈnætʃ(ə)rəl] *a & n* surnaturel (*m*).

superpower ['suːpəpaʊər] *n Pol* superpuissance *f*.

supersede [suːpəˈsiːd] *vt* remplacer, supplanter.

supersonic [suːpəˈsɒnɪk] *a* supersonique.

superstition [suːpəˈstɪʃ(ə)n] *n* superstition *f*. ◆**superstitious** *a* superstitieux.

supertanker ['suːpətæŋkər] *n* pétrolier *m* géant.

supervise ['suːpəvaɪz] *vt* (*person, work*) surveiller; (*office, research*) diriger. ◆**super'vision** *n* surveillance *f*; direction *f*. ◆**supervisor** *n* surveillant, -ante *mf* (*in office*) chef *m* de service; (*shop*) chef *m* de rayon. ◆**super'visory** *a* (*post*) de surveillant(e).

supper ['sʌpər] *n* dîner *m*; (*late-night*) souper *m*.

supple ['sʌp(ə)l] *a* souple. ◆**-ness** *n* souplesse *f*.

supplement ['sʌplɪmənt] *n* (*addition*) & *Journ* supplément *m* (**to** à); – ['sʌplɪment] *vt* compléter; **to s. one's income** arrondir ses fins de mois. ◆**supple'mentary** *a* supplémentaire.

supply [səˈplaɪ] *vt* (*provide*) fournir; (*feed*) alimenter (**with** en); (*equip*) équiper, pourvoir (**with** de); **to s. s.o. with sth, s. sth to s.o.** (*facts etc*) fournir qch à qn; – *n* (*stock*) provision *f*, réserve *f*; (*equipment*) matériel *m*; **the s. of** (*act*) la fourniture de; **the s. of gas/electricity to** l'alimentation *f* en gaz/électricité de; (*food*) **supplies** vivres *mpl*; (*office*) **supplies** fournitures *fpl* (de bureau); **s. and demand** l'offre *f* et la demande; **to be in short s.** manquer; – *a* (*ship, train*) ravitailleur; **s. teacher** suppléant, -ante *mf*. ◆**-ing** *n* (*provision*) fourniture *f*; (*feeding*) alimentation *f*. ◆**supplier** *n Com* fournisseur *m*.

support [səˈpɔːt] *vt* (*bear weight of*) soutenir, supporter; (*help, encourage*) soutenir, appuyer; (*theory, idea*) appuyer; (*be in favour of*) être en faveur de; (*family, wife etc*) assurer la subsistance de; (*endure*) supporter; – *n* (*help, encouragement*) appui *m*, soutien *m*; *Tech* support *m*; **means of s.** moyens *mpl* de subsistance; **in s. of** en faveur de; (*evidence, theory*) à l'appui de. ◆**-ing** *a* (*role*) *Th Cin* secondaire; (*actor*) qui a un rôle secondaire. ◆**supporter** *n* partisan, -ane *mf*; *Fb* supporter *m*. ◆**sup-portive** *a* to be s. prêter son appui (**of, to** à).

suppos/e [sə'pəuz] *vti* supposer (**that** que); **I'm supposed to work** *or* **be working** (*ought*) je suis censé travailler; **he's s. to be rich** on le dit riche; **I s. (so)** je pense; **I don't s. so, I s. not** je ne pense pas; **you're tired, I s.** vous êtes fatigué, je suppose; **s.** *or* **supposing we go** (*suggestion*) si nous partions; **s.** *or* **supposing (that) you're right** supposons que tu aies raison. ◆**—ed** *a* soi-disant. ◆**—edly** [-ɪdlɪ] *adv* soi-disant. ◆**suppo-'sition** *n* supposition *f*.

suppository [sə'pɒzɪtərɪ] *n* Med supposi-toire *m*.

suppress [sə'pres] *vt* (*put an end to*) supprimer; (*feelings*) réprimer; (*scandal, yawn etc*) étouffer. ◆**suppression** *n* suppression *f*; répression *f*. ◆**suppressor** *n El* dispositif *m* antiparasite.

supreme [suː'priːm] *a* suprême. ◆**supremacy** *n* suprématie *f* (**over** sur).

supremo [suː'priːməu] *n* (*pl* -os) *Fam* grand chef *m*.

surcharge ['sɜːtʃɑːdʒ] *n* (*extra charge*) supplément *m*; (*on stamp*) surcharge *f*; (*tax*) surtaxe *f*.

sure [ʃuər] *a* (-er, -est) sûr (**of** de, **that** que); **she's s. to accept** il est sûr qu'elle acceptera; **it's s. to snow** il va sûrement neiger; **to make s. of** s'assurer de; **for s.** à coup sûr, pour sûr; **s.!**, *Fam* **s. thing!** bien sûr!; **s. enough** (*in effect*) en effet; **it s. is cold** *Am* il fait vraiment froid; **be s. to do it!** ne manquez pas de le faire! ◆**surefire** *a* infaillible. ◆**surely** *adv* (*certainly*) sûre-ment; **s. he didn't refuse?** (*I think, I hope*) il n'a tout de même pas refusé.

surety ['ʃuərətɪ] *n* caution *f*.

surf [sɜːf] *n* (*foam*) ressac *m*. ◆**surfboard** *n* planche *f* (de surf). ◆**surfing** *n Sp* surf *m*.

surface ['sɜːfɪs] *n* surface *f*; **s. area** superficie *f*; **s. mail** courrier *m* par voie(s) de surface; **on the s.** (*to all appearances*) *Fig* en apparence; — *vt* (*road*) revêtir; — *vi* (*of swimmer etc*) remonter à la surface; (*of ideas, person etc*) *Fam* apparaître.

surfeit ['sɜːfɪt] *n* (*excess*) excès *m* (**of** de).

surge [sɜːdʒ] *n* (*of sea, enthusiasm*) vague *f*; (*rise*) montée *f*; — *vi* (*of crowd, hatred*) déferler; (*rise*) monter; **to s. forward** se lancer en avant.

surgeon ['sɜːdʒ(ə)n] *n* chirurgien *m*. ◆**surgery** *n* (*science*) chirurgie *f*; (*doctor's office*) cabinet *m*; (*sitting, period*) consulta-tion *f*; **to undergo s.** subir une intervention.

◆**surgical** *a* chirurgical; (*appliance*) orthopédique; **s. spirit** alcool *m* à 90°.

surly ['sɜːlɪ] *a* (-ier, -iest) bourru. ◆**surli-ness** *n* air *m* bourru.

surmise [sə'maɪz] *vt* conjecturer (**that** que).

surmount [sə'maunt] *vt* (*overcome, be on top of*) surmonter.

surname ['sɜːneɪm] *n* nom *m* de famille.

surpass [sə'pɑːs] *vt* surpasser (**in** en).

surplus ['sɜːpləs] *n* surplus *m*; — *a* (*goods*) en surplus; **some s. material**/*etc* (*left over*) un surplus de tissu/*etc*; **s. stock** surplus *mpl*.

surpris/e [sə'praɪz] *n* surprise *f*; **to give s.o. a s.** faire une surprise à qn; **to take s.o. by s.** prendre qn au dépourvu; — *a* (*visit, result etc*) inattendu; — *vt* (*astonish*) étonner, surprendre; (*come upon*) surprendre. ◆**—ed** *a* surpris (**that** que (+ *sub*), **at** sth de qch, **at seeing**/*etc* de voir/*etc*); **I'm s. at his** *or* **her stupidity** sa bêtise m'étonne *or* me surprend. ◆**—ing** *a* surprenant. ◆**—ingly** *adv* étonnamment; **s.** (**enough**) **he . . .** chose étonnante, il . . . .

surrealistic [sərɪə'lɪstɪk] *a* (*strange*) *Fig* surréaliste.

surrender [sə'rendər] **1** *vi* (*give oneself up*) se rendre (**to** à); **to s. to** (*police*) se livrer à; — *n Mil* reddition *f*, capitulation *f*. **2** *vt* (*hand over*) remettre, rendre (**to** à); (*right, claim*) renoncer à.

surreptitious [sʌrəp'tɪʃəs] *a* subreptice.

surrogate ['sʌrəgət] *n* substitut *m*; **s. mother** mère *f* porteuse.

surround [sə'raund] *vt* entourer (**with** de); *Mil* encercler; **surrounded by** entouré de. ◆**—ing** *a* environnant. ◆**—ings** *npl* environs *mpl*; (*setting*) cadre *m*.

surveillance [sɜː'veɪləns] *n* (*of prisoner etc*) surveillance *f*.

survey [sə'veɪ] *vt* (*look at*) regarder; (*review*) passer en revue; (*house etc*) inspecter; (*land*) arpenter; — ['sɜːveɪ] *n* (*investigation*) enquête *f*; (*of house etc*) inspection *f*; (*of opinion*) sondage *m*; **a (general) s. of** une vue générale de. ◆**sur'veying** *n* arpentage *m*. ◆**sur'veyor** *n* (arpenteur *m*) géomètre *m*; (*of house etc*) expert *m*.

survive [sə'vaɪv] *vi* (*of person, custom etc*) survivre; — *vt* survivre à. ◆**survival** *n* (*act*) survie *f*; (*relic*) vestige *m*. ◆**survivor** *n* survivant, -ante *mf*.

susceptible [sə'septəb(ə)l] *a* (*sensitive*) sensible (**to** à); **s. to colds**/*etc* (*prone to*) prédisposé aux rhumes/*etc*. ◆**suscepti-'bility** *n* sensibilité *f*; prédisposition *f*; *pl* susceptibilité *f*.

suspect ['sʌspekt] n & a suspect, -ecte (mf); – [sə'spekt] vt soupçonner (**that** que, **of sth** de qch, **of doing** d'avoir fait); (think questionable) suspecter, douter de; **yes, I s.** oui, j'imagine.

suspend [sə'spend] vt 1 (hang) suspendre (**from** à). 2 (stop, postpone, dismiss) suspendre; (passport etc) retirer (provisoirement); (pupil) Sch renvoyer; **suspended sentence** Jur condamnation f avec sursis. ◆**suspender** n (for stocking) jarretelle f; pl (braces) Am bretelles fpl; **s. belt** porte-jarretelles m inv. ◆**suspension** n 1 (stopping) suspension f; (of passport etc) retrait m (provisoire). 2 (of vehicle etc) suspension f; **s. bridge** pont m suspendu.

suspense [sə'spens] n attente f (angoissée); (in film, book etc) suspense m; **in s.** (person, matter) en suspens.

suspicion [sə'spiʃ(ə)n] n soupçon m; **to arouse s.** éveiller les soupçons; **with s.** (distrust) avec méfiance; **under s.** considéré comme suspect. ◆**suspicious** a (person) soupçonneux, méfiant; (behaviour) suspect; **s.(-looking)** (suspect) suspect; **to be s. of** or **about** (distrust) se méfier de. ◆**suspiciously** adv (to behave etc) d'une manière suspecte; (to consider etc) avec méfiance.

sustain [sə'stein] vt (effort, theory) soutenir; (weight) supporter; (with food) nourrir; (life) maintenir; (damage, attack) subir; (injury) recevoir. ◆**sustenance** n (food) nourriture f; (quality) valeur f nutritive.

swab [swɒb] n (pad) Med tampon m; (specimen) Med prélèvement m.

swagger ['swægər] vi (walk) parader; – n démarche f fanfaronne.

swallow ['swɒləʊ] 1 vt avaler; **to s. down** or **up** avaler; **to s. up** Fig engloutir; – vi avaler. 2 n (bird) hirondelle f.

swam [swæm] see **swim**.

swamp [swɒmp] n marais m, marécage m; – vt (flood, overwhelm) submerger (**with** de). ◆**swampy** a (-ier, -iest) marécageux.

swan [swɒn] n cygne m.

swank [swæŋk] vi (show off) Fam crâner, fanfaronner.

swap [swɒp] n échange m; pl (stamps etc) doubles mpl; – vt (-pp-) échanger (**for** contre); **to s. seats** changer de place; – vi échanger.

swarm [swɔːm] n (of bees, people etc) essaim m; – vi (of streets, insects, people etc) fourmiller (**with** de); **to s. in** (of people) entrer en foule.

swarthy ['swɔːðɪ] a (-ier, -iest) (dark) basané.

swastika ['swɒstɪkə] n (Nazi emblem) croix f gammée.

swat [swɒt] vt (-tt-) (fly etc) écraser.

sway [sweɪ] vi se balancer, osciller; – vt balancer; Fig influencer; – n balancement m; Fig influence f.

swear ['sweər] vt (pt **swore**, pp **sworn**) jurer (**to do** de faire, **that** que); **to s. an oath** prêter serment; **to s. s.o. to secrecy** faire jurer le silence à qn; **sworn enemies** ennemis mpl jurés; – vi (take an oath) jurer (**to sth** de qch); (curse) jurer, pester (**at** contre); **she swears by this lotion** elle ne jure que par cette lotion. ◆**swearword** n gros mot m, juron m.

sweat [swet] n sueur f; **s. shirt** sweat-shirt m; – vi (of person, wall etc) suer (**with** de); – vt **to s. out** (cold) Med se débarrasser de (en transpirant). ◆**sweater** n (garment) pull m. ◆**sweaty** a (-ier, -iest) (shirt etc) plein de sueur; (hand) moite; (person) (tout) en sueur, (tout) en nage.

swede [swiːd] n (vegetable) rutabaga m.

Swede [swiːd] n Suédois, -oise mf. ◆**Sweden** n Suède f. ◆**Swedish** a suédois; – n (language) suédois m.

sweep [swiːp] n coup m de balai; (movement) Fig (large) mouvement m; (curve) courbe f; **to make a clean s.** (removal) faire table rase (**of** de); (victory) remporter une victoire totale; – vt (pt & pp **swept**) (with broom) balayer; (chimney) ramoner; (river) draguer; **to s. away** or **out** or **up** balayer; **to s. away** or **along** (carry off) emporter; **to s. aside** (dismiss) écarter; – vi **to s. (up)** balayer; **to s. in** (of person) Fig entrer rapidement or majestueusement; **to s. through** (of fear etc) saisir (groupe etc); (of disease etc) ravager (pays etc). ◆**—ing** a (gesture) large; (change) radical; (statement) trop général. ◆**sweepstake** n (lottery) sweepstake m.

sweet [swiːt] a (-er, -est) (not sour) doux; (agreeable) agréable, doux; (tea, coffee etc) sucré; (person, house, kitchen) mignon, gentil; **to have a s. tooth** aimer les sucreries; **to be s.-smelling** sentir bon; **s. corn** maïs m; **s. pea** Bot pois m de senteur; **s. potato** patate f douce; **s. shop** confiserie f; **s. talk** Fam cajoleries fpl, douceurs fpl; – n (candy) bonbon m; (dessert) dessert m; **my s.!** (darling) mon ange! ◆**sweeten** vt (tea etc) sucrer; Fig adoucir. ◆**sweetener** n saccharine f. ◆**sweetie** n (darling) Fam chéri, -ie mf. ◆**sweetly** adv (kindly) gentiment; (*softly*) doucement. ◆**sweetness** *n* douceur *f*; (*taste*) goût *m* sucré.

sweetbread ['swiːtbred] *n* ris *m* de veau *or* d'agneau.

sweetheart ['swiːthɑːt] *n* (*lover*) ami, -ie *mf*; **my s.!** (*darling*) mon ange!

swell [swel] **1** *n* (*of sea*) houle *f*. **2** *a* (*very good*) *Am Fam* formidable. **3** *vi* (*pt* swelled, *pp* swollen *or* swelled) se gonfler; (*of river, numbers*) grossir; **to s. (up)** *Med* enfler, gonfler; − *vt* (*river, numbers*) grossir. ◆**—ing** *n Med* enflure *f*.

swelter ['sweltər] *vi* étouffer. ◆**—ing** *a* étouffant; **it's s.** on étouffe.

swept [swept] *see* **sweep**.

swerve [swɜːv] *vi* (*while running etc*) faire un écart; (*of vehicle*) faire une embardée.

swift [swift] **1** *a* (**-er, -est**) rapide; **s. to act** prompt à agir. **2** *n* (*bird*) martinet *m*. ◆**—ly** *adv* rapidement. ◆**—ness** *n* rapidité *f*.

swig [swig] *n* (*of beer etc*) lampée *f*.

swill [swil] *vt* **to s. (out** *or* **down)** laver (à grande eau).

swim [swim] *n* baignade *f*; **to go for a s.** se baigner; − *vi* (*pt* swam, *pp* swum, *pres p* swimming) nager; *Sp* faire de la natation; (*of head, room*) *Fig* tourner; **to go swimming** aller nager; **to s. away** se sauver (à la nage); − *vt* (*river*) traverser à la nage; (*length, crawl etc*) nager. ◆**swimming** *n* natation *f*; **s. costume** maillot *m* de bain; **s. pool, s. baths** piscine *f*; **s. trunks** slip *m or* caleçon *m* de bain. ◆**swimmer** *n* nageur, -euse *mf*. ◆**swimsuit** *n* maillot *m* de bain.

swindl/e ['swind(ə)l] *n* escroquerie *f*; − *vt* escroquer; **to s. s.o. out of money** escroquer de l'argent à qn. ◆**—er** *n* escroc *m*.

swine [swain] *n inv* (*person*) *Pej* salaud *m*.

swing [swiŋ] *n* (*seat*) balançoire *f*; (*movement*) balancement *m*; (*of pendulum*) oscillation *f*; (*in opinion*) revirement *m*; (*rhythm*) rythme *m*; **to be in full s.** battre son plein; **to be in the s. of things** *Fam* être dans le bain; **s. door** porte *f* de saloon; − *vi* (*pt & pp* swung) (*sway*) se balancer; (*of pendulum*) osciller; (*turn*) virer; **to s. round** (*turn suddenly*) virer, tourner; (*of person*) se retourner (vivement); (*of vehicle in collision etc*) faire un tête-à-queue; **to s. into action** passer à l'action; − *vt* (*arms etc*) balancer; (*axe*) brandir; (*influence*) *Fam* influencer; **to s. round** (*car etc*) faire tourner. ◆**—ing** *a Fam* (*trendy*) dans le vent; (*lively*) plein de vie; (*music*) entraînant.

swingeing ['swindʒiŋ] *a* **s. cuts** des réductions *fpl* draconiennes.

swipe [swaip] *vt Fam* (*hit*) frapper dur; (*steal*) piquer (**from s.o.** à qn); − *n Fam* grand coup *m*.

swirl [swɜːl] *n* tourbillon *m*; − *vi* tourbillonner.

swish [swiʃ] **1** *a* (*posh*) *Fam* rupin, chic. **2** *vi* (*of whip etc*) siffler; (*of fabric*) froufrouter; − *n* sifflement *m*; froufrou *m*.

Swiss [swis] *a* suisse; − *n inv* Suisse *m*, Suissesse *f*; **the S.** les Suisses *mpl*.

switch [switʃ] *n El* bouton *m* (électrique), interrupteur *m*; (*change*) changement *m* (**in** de); (*reversal*) revirement *m* (**in** de); − *vt* (*money, employee etc*) transférer (**to** à); (*affection, support*) reporter (**to** sur, **from** de); (*exchange*) échanger (**for** contre); **to s. buses/etc** changer de bus/*etc*; **to s. places** *or* **seats** changer de place; **to s. off** (*lamp, gas, radio etc*) éteindre; (*engine*) arrêter; **to s. itself off** (*of heating etc*) s'éteindre tout seul; **to s. on** (*lamp, gas, radio etc*) mettre, allumer; (*engine*) mettre en marche; − *vi* **to s. (over)** to passer à; **to s. off** (*switch off light, radio etc*) éteindre; **to s. on** (*switch on light, radio etc*) allumer. ◆**switchback** *n* (*at funfair*) montagnes *fpl* russes. ◆**switchblade** *n Am* couteau *m* à cran d'arrêt. ◆**switchboard** *n Tel* standard *m*; **s. operator** standardiste *mf*.

Switzerland ['switsələnd] *n* Suisse *f*.

swivel ['swiv(ə)l] *vi* (**-ll-**, *Am* **-l-**) **to s. (round)** (*of chair etc*) pivoter; − *a* **s. chair** fauteuil *m* pivotant.

swollen ['swəʊl(ə)n] *see* **swell 3**; − *a* (*leg etc*) enflé.

swoon [swuːn] *vi Lit* se pâmer.

swoop [swuːp] **1** *vi* **to s. (down) on** (*of bird*) fondre sur. **2** *n* (*of police*) descente *f*; − *vi* faire une descente (**on** dans).

swop [swɒp] *n*, *vt & vi* = **swap**.

sword [sɔːd] *n* épée *f*. ◆**swordfish** *n* espadon *m*.

swore, sworn [swɔːr, swɔːn] *see* **swear**.

swot [swɒt] *vti* (**-tt-**) (*study*) *Fam* potasser; **to s. (up) for** (*exam*), **to s. up on** (*subject*) *Fam* potasser; − *n Pej Fam* bûcheur, -euse *mf*.

swum [swʌm] *see* **swim**.

swung [swʌŋ] *see* **swing**.

sycamore ['sikəmɔːr] *n* (*maple*) sycomore *m*; (*plane*) *Am* platane *m*.

sycophant ['sikəfænt] *n* flagorneur, -euse *mf*.

syllable ['siləb(ə)l] *n* syllabe *f*.

syllabus ['siləbəs] *n Sch Univ* programme *m*.

symbol ['simb(ə)l] *n* symbole *m*. ◆**sym-**

'**bolic** *a* symbolique. ◆**symbolism** *n* symbolisme *m*. ◆**symbolize** *vt* symboliser.

symmetry ['sɪmətrɪ] *n* symétrie *f*. ◆**sy'mmetrical** *a* symétrique.

sympathy ['sɪmpəθɪ] *n* (*pity*) compassion *f*; (*understanding*) compréhension *f*; (*condolences*) condoléances *fpl*; (*solidarity*) solidarité *f* (**for** avec); **to be in s. with** (*workers in dispute*) être du côté de; (*s.o.'s opinion etc*) comprendre, être en accord avec. ◆**sympa'thetic** *a* (*showing pity*) compatissant; (*understanding*) compréhensif; **s. to** (*favourable*) bien disposé à l'égard de. ◆**sympa'thetically** *adv* avec compassion; avec compréhension. ◆**sympathize** *vi* **I s. (with you)** (*pity*) je compatis (à votre sort); (*understanding*) je vous comprends. ◆**sympathizer** *n* *Pol* sympathisant, -ante *mf*.

symphony ['sɪmfənɪ] *n* symphonie *f*; − *a* (*orchestra, concert*) symphonique. ◆**sym'phonic** *a* symphonique.

symposium [sɪm'pəʊzɪəm] *n* symposium *m*.

symptom ['sɪmptəm] *n* symptôme *m*. ◆**sympto'matic** *a* symptomatique (**of** de).

synagogue ['sɪnəgɒg] *n* synagogue *f*.

synchronize ['sɪŋkrənaɪz] *vt* synchroniser.

syndicate ['sɪndɪkət] *n* (*of businessmen, criminals*) syndicat *m*.

syndrome ['sɪndrəʊm] *n* *Med & Fig* syndrome *m*.

synod ['sɪnəd] *n* *Rel* synode *m*.

synonym ['sɪnənɪm] *n* synonyme *m*. ◆**sy'nonymous** *a* synonyme (**with** de).

synopsis, *pl* **-opses** [sɪ'nɒpsɪs, -ɒpsiːz] *n* résumé *m*, synopsis *m*; (*of film*) synopsis *m*.

syntax ['sɪntæks] *n* *Gram* syntaxe *f*.

synthesis, *pl* **-theses** ['sɪnθəsɪs, -θəsiːz] *n* synthèse *f*.

synthetic [sɪn'θetɪk] *a* synthétique.

syphilis ['sɪfɪlɪs] *n* syphilis *f*.

Syria ['sɪrɪə] *n* Syrie *f*. ◆**Syrian** *a & n* syrien, -ienne (*mf*).

syringe [sɪ'rɪndʒ] *n* seringue *f*.

syrup ['sɪrəp] *n* sirop *m*; (**golden**) **s.** (*treacle*) mélasse *f* (raffinée). ◆**syrupy** *a* sirupeux.

system ['sɪstəm] *n* (*structure, plan, network etc*) & *Anat* système *m*; (*human body*) organisme *m*; (*order*) méthode *f*; **systems analyst** analyste-programmeur *mf*. ◆**syste'matic** *a* systématique. ◆**syste'matically** *adv* systématiquement.

T

T, t [tiː] *n* T, t *m*. ◆**T-junction** *n* *Aut* intersection *f* en T. ◆**T-shirt** *n* tee-shirt *m*, T-shirt *m*.

ta! [tɑː] *int Sl* merci!

tab [tæb] *n* (*label*) étiquette *f*; (*tongue*) patte *f*; (*loop*) attache *f*; (*bill*) *Am* addition *f*; **to keep tabs on** *Fam* surveiller (de près).

tabby ['tæbɪ] *a* **t. cat** chat, chatte *mf* tigré(e).

table¹ ['teɪb(ə)l] *n* **1** (*furniture*) table *f*; **bedside/card/operating t.** table de nuit/de jeu/d'opération; **to lay** *or* **set/clear the t.** mettre/débarrasser la table; (**sitting) at the t.** à table; **t. top** dessus *m* de table. **2** (*list*) table *f*; **t. of contents** table des matières. ◆**tablecloth** *n* nappe *f*. ◆**tablemat** *n* (*of fabric*) napperon *m*; (*hard*) dessous-de-plat *m inv*. ◆**tablespoon** *n* = cuiller *f* à soupe. ◆**tablespoonful** *n* = cuillerée *f* à soupe.

table² ['teɪb(ə)l] *vt* (*motion etc*) *Pol* présenter; (*postpone*) *Am* ajourner.

tablet ['tæblɪt] *n* **1** (*pill*) *Med* comprimé *m*. **2** (*inscribed stone*) plaque *f*.

tabloid ['tæblɔɪd] *n* (*newspaper*) quotidien *m* populaire.

taboo [tə'buː] *a & n* tabou (*m*).

tabulator ['tæbjʊleɪtər] *n* (*of typewriter*) tabulateur *m*.

tacit ['tæsɪt] *a* tacite. ◆**—ly** *adv* tacitement.

taciturn ['tæsɪtɜːn] *a* taciturne.

tack [tæk] **1** *n* (*nail*) semence *f*; (*thumbtack*) *Am* punaise *f*; **to get down to brass tacks** *Fig* en venir aux faits; − *vt* **to t. (down)** clouer. **2** *n* (*stitch*) *Tex* point *m* de bâti; − *vt* **to t. (down** *or* **on)** bâtir; **to t. on** (*add*) *Fig* (r)ajouter. **3** *vi* (*of ship*) louvoyer; − *n* (*course of action*) *Fig* voie *f*.

tackle ['tæk(ə)l] **1** *n* (*gear*) matériel *m*, équipement *m*. **2** *vt* (*task, problem etc*) s'attaquer à; (*thief etc*) saisir; *Sp* plaquer; − *n* *Sp* plaquage *m*.

tacky ['tækɪ] *a* (**-ier, -iest**) **1** (*wet, sticky*) collant, pas sec. **2** (*clothes, attitude etc*) *Am Fam* moche.

tact [tækt] *n* tact *m*. ◆**tactful** *a* (*remark etc*) plein de tact, diplomatique; **she's t.** elle a du tact. ◆**tactfully** *adv* avec tact. ◆**tactless** *a* qui manque de tact. ◆**tactlessly** *adv* sans tact.

tactic ['tæktɪk] *n* a t. une tactique; **tactics** la tactique. ◆**tactical** *a* tactique.

tactile ['tæktaɪl] *a* tactile.

tadpole ['tædpəʊl] *n* têtard *m*.

taffy ['tæfɪ] *n* (*toffee*) *Am* caramel *m* (*dur*).

tag [tæg] **1** *n* (*label*) étiquette *f*; (*end piece*) bout *m*; – *vt* (**-gg-**) **to t. on** (*add*) *Fam* rajouter (**to** à). **2** *vi* (**-gg-**) **to t. along** (*follow*) suivre.

Tahiti [tɑːˈhiːtɪ] *n* Tahiti *m*.

tail [teɪl] **1** *n* (*of animal*) queue *f*; (*of shirt*) pan *m*; *pl* (*outfit*) habit *m*, queue-de-pie *f*; **t. end** fin *f*, bout *m*; **heads or tails?** pile ou face? **2** *vt* (*follow*) suivre, filer. **3** *vi* **to t. off** (*lessen*) diminuer. ◆**tailback** *n* (*of traffic*) bouchon *m*. ◆**taillight** *n Aut Am* feu *m* arrière *inv*.

tailor ['teɪlər] *n* (*person*) tailleur *m*; – *vt* (*garment*) façonner; *Fig* adapter (**to, to suit** à). ◆**t.-'made** *a* à fait sur mesure; **t.-made for** (*specially designed*) conçu pour; (*suited*) fait pour.

tainted ['teɪntɪd] *a* (*air*) pollué; (*food*) gâté; *Fig* souillé.

take [teɪk] *vt* (*pt* **took**, *pp* **taken**) prendre; (*choice*) faire; (*prize*) remporter; (*exam*) passer; (*contain*) contenir; *Math* soustraire (**from** de); (*tolerate*) supporter; (*bring*) apporter (*qch*) (**to** à), (*person*) amener (**to** à), (*person by car*) conduire (**to** à); (*escort*) accompagner (**to** à); (*lead away*) emmener (*of road*) mener (*qn*); **to t. sth to s.o.** (ap)porter qch à qn; **to t. s.o. (out) to** (*theatre etc*) emmener qn à; **to t. sth with one** emporter qch; **to t. over** *or* **round** *or* **along** (*object*) apporter; (*person*) amener; **to t. s.o. home** (*on foot, by car etc*) ramener qn; **it takes an army/courage/***etc* (*requires*) il faut une armée/du courage/*etc* (**to do** pour faire); **I took an hour to do it** *or* **over it** j'ai mis une heure à le faire, ça m'a pris une heure pour le faire; **I t. it that** je présume que; – *n Cin* prise *f* de vue(s); – *vi* (*of fire*) prendre. ◆**to t. after** *vi* (*be like*) ressembler à; **to t. apart** *vt* (*machine*) démonter; **to t. away** *vt* (*thing*) emporter; (*person*) emmener; (*remove*) enlever (**from** à); *Math* soustraire (**from** de). ◆**t.-away** *a* (*meal*) à emporter; – *n* café *m or* restaurant *m* qui fait des plats à emporter; (*meal*) plat *m* à emporter; **to t. back** *vt* (*return*) rapporter; (*statement*) retirer; **to t. down** *vt* (*object*) descendre; (*notes*) prendre; **to t. in** *vt* (*chair, car etc*) rentrer; (*orphan*) recueil-

lir; (*skirt*) reprendre; (*include*) englober; (*distance*) couvrir; (*understand*) comprendre; (*deceive*) *Fam* rouler; **to t. off** *vt* (*remove*) enlever; (*train, bus*) supprimer; (*lead away*) emmener; (*mimic*) imiter; *Math* déduire (**from** de); – *vi* (*of aircraft*) décoller. ◆**takeoff** *n* (*of aircraft*) décollage *m*; **to t. on** *vt* (*work, employee, passenger, shape*) prendre; **to t. out** *vt* (*from pocket etc*) sortir; (*stain*) enlever; (*tooth*) arracher; (*licence, insurance*) prendre; **to t. it out on** *Fam* passer sa colère sur. ◆**t.-out** *a & n Am* = **t.-away**; **to t. over** *vt* (*be responsible for the running of*) prendre la direction de; (*overrun*) envahir; (*buy out*) *Com* racheter (*compagnie*); **to t. over s.o.'s job** remplacer qn; – *vi Mil Pol* prendre le pouvoir; (*relieve*) prendre la relève (**from** de); (*succeed*) prendre la succession (**from** de). ◆**t.-over** *n Com* rachat *m*; *Pol* prise *f* de pouvoir; **to t. round** *vt* (*distribute*) distribuer; (*visitor*) faire visiter; **to t. to** *vi* **to t. to doing** se mettre à faire; **I didn't t. to him/it** il/ça ne m'a pas plu; **to t. up** *vt* (*carry up*) monter; (*hem*) raccourcir; (*continue*) reprendre; (*occupy*) prendre; (*hobby*) se mettre à; – *vi* **to t. up with** se lier avec. ◆**taken** *a* (*seat*) pris; (*impressed*) impressionné (**with**, **by** par); **to be t. ill** tomber malade. ◆**taking** *n* (*capture*) *Mil* prise *f*; *pl* (*money*) *Com* recette *f*.

talcum ['tælkəm] *a* **t. powder** talc *m*.

tale [teɪl] *n* (*story*) conte *m*; (*account, report*) récit *m*; (*lie*) histoire *f*; **to tell tales** rapporter (**on** sur).

talent ['tælənt] *n* talent *m*; (*talented people*) talents *mpl*; **to have a t. for** avoir du talent pour. ◆**talented** *a* doué, talentueux.

talk [tɔːk] *n* (*words*) propos *mpl*; (*gossip*) bavardage(s) *m*(*pl*); (*conversation*) conversation *f* (**about** à propos de); (*interview*) entretien *m*; (*lecture*) exposé *m* (**on** sur); (*informal*) causerie *f* (**on** sur); *pl* (*negotiations*) pourparlers *mpl*; **to have a t. with** parler avec; **there's t. of** on parle de; – *vi* parler (**to** à; **with** avec; **about, of** de); (*chat*) bavarder; **to t. s.o. into doing/out of doing** persuader qn de faire/de ne pas faire; **to t. over** discuter (de); **to t. s.o. round** persuader qn. ◆**—ing** *a* (*film*) parlant; **to give s.o. a talking-to** *Fam* passer un savon à qn. ◆**talkative** *a* bavard. ◆**talker** *n* causeur, -euse *mf*; **she's a good t.** elle parle bien.

tall [tɔːl] *a* (**-er, -est**) (*person*) grand; (*tree,* *house etc*) haut; **how t. are you?** combien mesures-tu?; **a t. story** *Fig* une histoire invraisemblable *or* à dormir debout. ◆**tallboy** *n* grande commode *f*. ◆**tallness** *n* (*of person*) grande taille *f*; (*of building etc*) hauteur *f*.

tally ['tælɪ] *vi* correspondre (**with** à).

tambourine [tæmbə'riːn] *n* tambourin *m*.

tame [teɪm] *a* (**-er, -est**) (*animal, bird*) apprivoisé; (*person*) *Fig* docile; (*book, play*) fade. − *vt* (*animal, bird*) apprivoiser; (*lion, passion*) dompter.

tamper ['tæmpər] *vi* **to t. with** (*lock, car etc*) toucher à; (*text*) altérer.

tampon ['tæmpɒn] *n* tampon *m* hygiénique.

tan [tæn] **1** *n* (*suntan*) bronzage *m*; − *vti* (**-nn-**) bronzer. **2** *a* (*colour*) marron clair *inv*. **3** *vt* (**-nn-**) (*hide*) tanner.

tandem ['tændəm] *n* **1** (*bicycle*) tandem *m*. **2 in t.** (*to work etc*) en tandem.

tang [tæŋ] *n* (*taste*) saveur *f* piquante; (*smell*) odeur *f* piquante. ◆**tangy** *a* (**-ier, -iest**) piquant.

tangerine [tændʒə'riːn] *n* mandarine *f*.

tangible ['tændʒəb(ə)l] *a* tangible.

tangl/e ['tæŋg(ə)l] *n* enchevêtrement *m*; **to get into a t.** (*of rope*) s'enchevêtrer; (*of hair*) s'emmêler; (*of person*) *Fig* se mettre dans une situation pas possible. ◆**−ed** *a* enchevêtré; (*hair*) emmêlé; **to get t. =** **to get into a tangle**.

tank [tæŋk] *n* **1** (*for storage of water, fuel etc*) réservoir *m*; (*vat*) cuve *f*; (**fish**) t. aquarium *m*. **2** (*vehicle*) *Mil* char *m*, tank *m*.

tankard ['tæŋkəd] *n* (*beer mug*) chope *f*.

tanker ['tæŋkər] *n* (*truck*) *Aut* camion-citerne *m*; (**oil**) t. (*ship*) pétrolier *m*.

tantalizing ['tæntəlaɪzɪŋ] *a* (*irrésistiblement*) tentant. ◆**−ly** *adv* d'une manière tentante.

tantamount ['tæntəmaʊnt] *a* **it's t. to** cela équivaut à.

tantrum ['tæntrəm] *n* accès *m* de colère.

tap [tæp] **1** *n* (*for water*) robinet *m*; **on t.** *Fig* disponible. **2** *vti* (**-pp-**) frapper légèrement, tapoter; − *n* petit coup *m*; **t. dancing** claquettes *fpl*. **3** *vt* (*phone*) placer sur table d'écoute. **4** *vt* (**-pp-**) (*resources*) exploiter.

tape [teɪp] **1** *n* ruban *m*; (**sticky**) **t.** ruban adhésif; **t. measure** mètre *m* (à) ruban; − *vt* (*stick*) coller (*avec du ruban adhésif*). **2** *n* (*for sound recording*) bande *f* (*magnétique*); (**video**) **t.** bande (vidéo); **t. recorder** magnétophone *m*; − *vt* enregistrer.

taper ['teɪpər] **1** *vi* (*of fingers etc*) s'effiler; **to t. off** *Fig* diminuer. **2** *n* (*candle*) *Rel* cierge

m. ◆**−ed** *a*, ◆**−ing** *a* (*fingers*) fuselé; (*trousers*) à bas étroits.

tapestry ['tæpəstrɪ] *n* tapisserie *f*.

tapioca [tæpɪ'əʊkə] *n* tapioca *m*.

tar [tɑːr] *n* goudron *m*; − *vt* (**-rr-**) goudronner.

tardy ['tɑːdɪ] *a* (**-ier, -iest**) (*belated*) tardif; (*slow*) lent.

target ['tɑːgɪt] *n* cible *f*; *Fig* objectif *m*; **t. date** date *f* fixée; − *vt* (*aim*) *Fig* destiner (**at** à); (*aim at*) *Fig* viser.

tariff ['tærɪf] *n* (*tax*) tarif *m* douanier; (*prices*) tarif *m*.

tarmac ['tɑːmæk] *n* macadam *m* (*goudronné*); (*runway*) piste *f*.

tarnish ['tɑːnɪʃ] *vt* ternir.

tarpaulin [tɑː'pɔːlɪn] *n* bâche *f* (*goudronnée*).

tarragon ['tærəgən] *n* *Bot Culin* estragon *m*.

tarry ['tærɪ] *vi* (*remain*) *Lit* rester.

tart [tɑːt] **1** *n* (*pie*) tarte *f*. **2** *a* (**-er, -est**) (*taste, remark*) aigre. **3** *n* (*prostitute*) *Pej Fam* poule *f*. **4** *vt* **to t. up** *Pej Fam* (*decorate*) embellir; (*dress*) attifer. ◆**−ness** *n* aigreur *f*.

tartan ['tɑːt(ə)n] *n* tartan *m*; − *a* écossais.

tartar ['tɑːtər] **1** *n* (*on teeth*) tartre *m*. **2 t. sauce** sauce *f* tartare.

task [tɑːsk] *n* tâche *f*; **to take to t.** prendre à partie; **t. force** *Mil* détachement *m* spécial; *Pol* commission *f* spéciale.

tassel ['tæs(ə)l] *n* (*on clothes etc*) gland *m*.

taste [teɪst] *n* goût *m*; **to get a t. for** prendre goût à; **in good/bad t.** de bon/mauvais goût; **to have a t. of** goûter; goûter à; goûter de; − *vt* (*eat, enjoy*) goûter; (*try, sample*) goûter à; (*make out the taste of*) sentir (le goût de); (*experience*) goûter de; − *vi* **to t. of** *or* **like** avoir un goût de; **to t. delicious/etc** avoir un goût délicieux/etc; **how does it t.?** comment le trouves-tu?; − *a* **t. bud** papille *f* gustative. ◆**tasteful** *a* de bon goût. ◆**tastefully** *adv* avec goût. ◆**tasteless** *a* (*food etc*) sans goût; (*joke etc*) *Fig* de mauvais goût. ◆**tasty** *a* (**-ier, -iest**) savoureux.

tat [tæt] *see* **tit 2**.

ta-ta! [tæ'tɑː] *int Sl* au revoir!

tattered ['tætəd] *a* (*clothes*) en lambeaux; (*person*) déguenillé. ◆**tatters** *npl* **in t.** en lambeaux.

tattoo [tæ'tuː] **1** *n* (*pl* **-oos**) (*on body*) tatouage *m*; − *vt* tatouer. **2** *n* (*pl* **-oos**) *Mil* spectacle *m* militaire.

tatty ['tætɪ] *a* (**-ier, -iest**) (*clothes etc*) *Fam* miteux.

taught [tɔːt] *see* **teach**.

taunt [tɔːnt] vt railler; − n raillerie f. ◆—**ing** a railleur.

Taurus ['tɔːrəs] n (sign) le Taureau.

taut [tɔːt] a (rope, person etc) tendu.

tavern ['tævən] n taverne f.

tawdry ['tɔːdrɪ] a (-ier, -iest) Pej tape-à-l'œil inv.

tawny ['tɔːnɪ] a (colour) fauve; (port) ambré.

tax¹ [tæks] n taxe f, impôt m; (income) t. impôts mpl (sur le revenu); − a fiscal; t. **collector** percepteur m; t. **relief** dégrèvement m (d'impôt); − vt (person, goods) imposer. ◆**taxable** a imposable. ◆**tax-'ation** n (act) imposition f; (taxes) impôts mpl. ◆**tax-free** a exempt d'impôts. ◆**taxman** n (pl -men) Fam percepteur m. ◆**taxpayer** n contribuable mf.

tax² [tæks] vt (patience etc) mettre à l'épreuve; (tire) fatiguer. ◆—**ing** a (journey etc) éprouvant.

taxi ['tæksɪ] **1** n taxi m; t. **cab** taxi m; t. **rank**, Am t. **stand** station f de taxis. **2** vi (of aircraft) rouler au sol.

tea [tiː] n thé m; (snack) goûter m; high t. goûter m (dînatoire); to have t. prendre le thé; (afternoon snack) goûter; t. **break** pause-thé f; t. **chest** caisse f (à thé); t. **cloth** (for drying dishes) torchon m; t. **set** service m à thé; t. **towel** torchon m. ◆**teabag** n sachet m de thé. ◆**teacup** n tasse f à thé. ◆**tealeaf** n (pl -leaves) feuille f de thé. ◆**teapot** n théière f. ◆**tearoom** n salon m de thé. ◆**teaspoon** n petite cuiller f. ◆**teaspoonful** n cuillerée f à café. ◆**teatime** n l'heure f du thé.

teach [tiːtʃ] vt (pt & pp taught) apprendre (s.o. sth qch à qn, that que); (in school etc) enseigner (s.o. sth qch à qn); to t. s.o. (how) to do apprendre à qn à faire; to t. **school** Am enseigner; to t. **oneself** sth apprendre qch tout seul; − vi enseigner. ◆—**ing** n enseignement m; − a (staff) enseignant; (method, material) pédagogique; t. **profession** enseignement m; (teachers) enseignants mpl; t. **qualification** diplôme m permettant d'enseigner. ◆—**er** n professeur m; (in primary school) instituteur, -trice mf.

teak [tiːk] n (wood) teck m.

team [tiːm] n Sp équipe f; (of oxen) attelage m; t. **mate** coéquipier, -ière mf; − vi to t. **up** faire équipe (with avec). ◆**teamster** n Am routier m. ◆**teamwork** n collaboration f.

tear¹ [teər] n déchirure f; − vt (pt tore, pp torn) (rip) déchirer; (snatch) arracher (from s.o. à qn); torn between Fig tiraillé entre; to t. **down** (house etc) démolir; to t. **away** or off

or out (forcefully) arracher; (stub, receipt, stamp etc) détacher; to t. **up** déchirer; − vi (of cloth etc) se déchirer. **2** vi (pt tore, pp torn) to t. **along** (rush) aller à toute vitesse.

tear² [tɪər] n larme f; in tears en larmes; close to or near (to) tears au bord des larmes. ◆**tearful** a (eyes, voice) larmoyant; (person) en larmes. ◆**tearfully** adv en pleurant. ◆**teargas** n gaz m lacrymogène.

tearaway ['teərəweɪ] n Fam petit voyou m.

teas/e [tiːz] vt taquiner; (harshly) tourmenter; − n (person) taquin, -ine f. ◆—**ing** a (remark etc) taquin. ◆—**er** n **1** (person) taquin, -ine mf. **2** (question) Fam colle f.

teat [tiːt] n (of bottle, animal) tétine f.

technical ['teknɪk(ə)l] a technique. ◆**techni'cality** n (detail) détail m technique. ◆**technically** adv techniquement; Fig théoriquement. ◆**tech'nician** n technicien, -ienne m. ◆**tech'nique** n technique f. ◆**technocrat** n technocrate m. ◆**techno'logical** a technologique. ◆**tech'nology** n technologie f.

teddy ['tedɪ] n t. (bear) nounours m (en peluche).

tedious ['tiːdɪəs] a fastidieux. ◆**tediousness** n, ◆**tedium** n ennui m.

teem [tiːm] vi **1** (swarm) grouiller (with de). **2** to t. (with rain) pleuvoir à torrents. ◆—**ing** a **1** (crowd, street etc) grouillant. **2** t. **rain** pluie f torrentielle.

teenage ['tiːneɪdʒ] a (person, behaviour) adolescent; (fashion) pour adolescents. ◆**teenager** n adolescent, -ente mf. ◆**teens** npl in one's t. adolescent.

teeny (weeny) ['tiːnɪ('wiːnɪ)] a (tiny) Fam minuscule.

tee-shirt ['tiːʃɜːt] n tee-shirt m.

teeter ['tiːtər] vi chanceler.

teeth [tiːθ] see tooth. ◆**teeth/e** [tiːð] vi faire ses dents. ◆—**ing** n dentition f; t. **ring** anneau m de dentition; t. **troubles** Fig difficultés fpl de mise en route.

teetotal [tiː'təʊt(ə)l] a, ◆**teetotaller** n (personne f) qui ne boit pas d'alcool.

tele- ['telɪ] pref télé-.

telecommunications [telɪkəmjuːnɪ'keɪʃ(ə)nz] npl télécommunications fpl.

telegram ['telɪɡræm] n télégramme m.

telegraph ['telɪɡrɑːf] n télégraphe m; − a (wire etc) télégraphique; t. **pole** poteau m télégraphique.

telepathy [tə'lepəθɪ] n télépathie f.

telephone ['telɪfəʊn] n téléphone m; on the t. (speaking) au téléphone; − a (call, line etc) téléphonique; (directory) du téléphone; (*number*) de téléphone; **t. booth, t. box** cabine *f* téléphonique; – *vi* téléphoner; – *vt* (*message*) téléphoner (**to** à); **to t. s.o.** téléphoner à qn. ◆**te'lephonist** *n* téléphoniste *mf*.

teleprinter ['telɪprɪntər] *n* téléscripteur *m*.

telescope ['telɪskəup] *n* télescope *m*. ◆**tele'scopic** *a* (*pictures, aerial, umbrella*) télescopique.

teletypewriter [telɪ'taɪpraɪtər] *n Am* téléscripteur *m*.

televise ['telɪvaɪz] *vt* téléviser. ◆**tele-'vision** *n* télévision *f*; **on (the) t.** à la télévision; **to watch (the) t.** regarder la télévision; – *a* (*programme etc*) de télévision; (*serial, report*) télévisé.

telex ['teleks] *n* (*service, message*) télex *m*; – *vt* envoyer par télex.

tell [tel] *vt* (*pt & pp* **told**) dire (**s.o. sth** qch à qn, **that** que); (*story*) raconter; (*future*) prédire; (*distinguish*) distinguer (**from** de); (*know*) savoir; **to t. s.o. to do** dire à qn de faire; **to know how to t. the time** savoir lire l'heure; **to t. the difference** voir la différence (**between** entre); **to t. off** (*scold*) *Fam* gronder; – *vi* dire; (*have an effect*) avoir un effet; (*know*) savoir; **to t. of** *or* **about sth** parler de qch; **to t. on s.o.** *Fam* rapporter sur qn. ◆**—ing** *a* (*smile etc*) révélateur; (*blow*) efficace. ◆**telltale** *n Fam* rapporteur, -euse *mf*.

teller ['telər] *n* (*bank*) **t.** caissier, -ière *mf*.

telly ['telɪ] *n Fam* télé *f*.

temerity [tə'merɪtɪ] *n* témérité *f*.

temp [temp] *n* (*secretary etc*) *Fam* intérimaire *mf*.

temper ['tempər] **1** *n* (*mood, nature*) humeur *f*; (*anger*) colère *f*; **to lose one's t.** se mettre en colère; **in a bad t.** de mauvaise humeur; **to have a (bad** *or* **an awful) t.** avoir un caractère de cochon. **2** *vt* (*steel*) tremper; *Fig* tempérer.

temperament ['temp(ə)rəmənt] *n* tempérament *m*. ◆**tempera'mental** *a* (*person, machine etc*) capricieux; (*inborn*) inné.

temperance ['temp(ə)rəns] *n* (*in drink*) tempérance *f*.

temperate ['tempərət] *a* (*climate etc*) tempéré.

temperature ['temp(ə)rətʃər] *n* température *f*; **to have a t.** *Med* avoir *or* faire de la température.

tempest ['tempɪst] *n Lit* tempête *f*. ◆**tem-'pestuous** *a* (*meeting etc*) orageux.

template ['templət] *n* (*of plastic, metal etc*) *Tex* patron *m*; *Math* trace-courbes *m inv*.

temple ['temp(ə)l] *n* **1** *Rel* temple *m*. **2** *Anat* tempe *f*.

tempo ['tempəu] *n* (*pl* **-os**) tempo *m*.

temporal ['temp(ə)rəl] *a* temporel.

temporary ['temp(ə)rərɪ] *a* provisoire; (*job, worker*) temporaire; (*secretary*) intérimaire.

tempt [tempt] *vt* tenter; **tempted to do** tenté de faire; **to t. s.o. to do** persuader qn de faire. ◆**—ing** *a* tentant. ◆**—ingly** *adv* d'une manière tentante. ◆**temp'tation** *n* tentation *f*.

ten [ten] *a & n* dix (*m*). ◆**tenfold** *a* **t. increase** augmentation *f* par dix; – *adv* **to increase t.** (se) multiplier par dix.

tenable ['tenəb(ə)l] *a* (*argument*) défendable; (*post*) qui peut être occupé.

tenacious [tə'neɪʃəs] *a* tenace. ◆**tenacity** *n* ténacité *f*.

tenant ['tenənt] *n* locataire *nmf*. ◆**tenancy** *n* (*lease*) location *f*; (*period*) occupation *f*.

tend [tend] **1** *vt* (*look after*) s'occuper de. **2** *vi* **to t. to do** avoir tendance à faire; **to t. towards** incliner vers. ◆**tendency** *n* tendance *f* (**to do** à faire).

tendentious [ten'denʃəs] *a Pej* tendancieux.

tender¹ ['tendər] *a* (*delicate, soft, loving*) tendre; (*painful, sore*) sensible. ◆**—ly** *adv* tendrement. ◆**—ness** *n* tendresse *f*; (*soreness*) sensibilité *f*; (*of meat*) tendreté *f*.

tender² ['tendər] **1** *vt* (*offer*) offrir; **to t. one's resignation** donner sa démission. **2** *n* **to be legal t.** (*of money*) avoir cours. **3** *n* (*for services etc*) *Com* soumission *f* (**for** pour).

tendon ['tendən] *n Anat* tendon *m*.

tenement ['tenəmənt] *n* immeuble *m* (de rapport) (*Am* dans un quartier pauvre).

tenet ['tenɪt] *n* principe *m*.

tenner ['tenər] *n Fam* billet *m* de dix livres.

tennis ['tenɪs] *n* tennis *m*; **table t.** tennis de table; **t. court** court *m* (de tennis), tennis *m*.

tenor ['tenər] *n* **1** (*sense, course*) sens *m* général. **2** *Mus* ténor *m*.

tenpin ['tenpɪn] *a* **t. bowling** bowling *m*. ◆**tenpins** *n Am* bowling *m*.

tense [tens] **1** *a* (**-er, -est**) (*person, muscle, situation*) tendu; – *vt* tendre, crisper; – *vi* **to t. (up)** (*of person, face*) se crisper. **2** *n Gram* temps *m*. ◆**tenseness** *n* tension *f*. ◆**tension** *n* tension *f*.

tent [tent] *n* tente *f*.

tentacle ['tentək(ə)l] *n* tentacule *m*.

tentative ['tentətɪv] *a* (*not definite*) provisoire; (*hesitant*) timide. ◆**—ly** *adv* provisoirement; timidement.

tenterhooks ['tentəhuks] *npl* **on t.** (*anxious*) sur des charbons ardents.

tenth [tenθ] *a* & *n* dixième (*mf*); **a t.** un dixième.

tenuous ['tenjuəs] *a* (*link, suspicion etc*) ténu.

tenure ['tenjər] *n* (*in job*) période *f* de jouissance; (*job security*) *Am* titularisation *f*.

tepid ['tepɪd] *a* (*liquid*) & *Fig* tiède.

term [tɜːm] *n* (*word, limit*) terme *m*; (*period*) période *f*; *Sch Univ* trimestre *m*; (*semester*) *Am* semestre *m*; *pl* (*conditions*) conditions *fpl*; (*prices*) *Com* prix *mpl*; **t. (of office)** *Pol* mandat *m*; **easy terms** *Fin* facilités *fpl* de paiement; **on good/bad terms** en bons/mauvais termes (**with s.o.** avec qn); **to be on close terms** être intime (**with** avec); **in terms of** (*speaking of*) sur le plan de; **in real terms** dans la pratique; **to come to terms with** (*person*) tomber d'accord avec; (*situation etc*) *Fig* faire face à; **in the long/short t.** à long/court terme; **at (full) t.** (*baby*) à terme; – *vt* (*name, call*) appeler.

terminal ['tɜːmɪn(ə)l] **1** *n* (*of computer*) terminal *m*; *El* borne *f*; (**air**) **t.** aérogare *f*; (**oil**) **t.** terminal *m* (pétrolier). **2** *a* (*patient, illness*) incurable; (*stage*) terminal. ◆**—ly** *adv* **t. ill** (*patient*) incurable.

terminate ['tɜːmɪneɪt] *vt* mettre fin à; (*contract*) résilier; (*pregnancy*) interrompre; – *vi* se terminer. ◆**termi'nation** *n* fin *f*; résiliation *f*; interruption *f*.

terminology [tɜːmɪ'nɒlədʒɪ] *n* terminologie *f*.

terminus ['tɜːmɪnəs] *n* terminus *m*.

termite ['tɜːmaɪt] *n* (*insect*) termite *m*.

terrace ['terɪs] *n* terrace *f*; (*houses*) maisons *fpl* en bande; **the terraces** *Sp* les gradins *mpl*. ◆**terraced** *a* **t. house** maison *f* attenante aux maisons voisines.

terracota [terə'kɒtə] *n* terre *f* cuite.

terrain [tə'reɪn] *n Mil Geol* terrain *m*.

terrestrial [tə'restrɪəl] *a* terrestre.

terrible ['terəb(ə)l] *a* affreux, terrible. ◆**terribly** *adv* (*badly*) affreusement; (*very*) terriblement.

terrier ['terɪər] *n* (*dog*) terrier *m*.

terrific [tə'rɪfɪk] *a Fam* (*extreme*) terrible; (*excellent*) formidable, terrible. ◆**terrifically** *adv Fam* (*extremely*) terriblement; (*extremely well*) terriblement bien.

terrify ['terɪfaɪ] *vt* terrifier; **to be terrified of** avoir très peur de. ◆**—ing** *a* terrifiant. ◆**—ingly** *adv* épouvantablement.

territory ['terɪtərɪ] *n* territoire *m*. ◆**terri'torial** *a* territorial.

terror ['terər] *n* terreur *f*; (*child*) *Fam* polisson, -onne *mf*. ◆**terrorism** *n* terrorisme

m. ◆**terrorist** *n* & *a* terroriste (*mf*). ◆**terrorize** *vt* terroriser.

terry(cloth) ['terɪ(klɒθ)] *n* tissu-éponge *m*.

terse [tɜːs] *a* laconique.

tertiary ['tɜːʃərɪ] *a* tertiaire.

Terylene® ['terəliːn] *n* tergal® *m*.

test [test] *vt* (*try*) essayer; (*examine*) examiner; (*analyse*) analyser; (*product, intelligence*) tester; (*pupil*) *Sch* faire subir une interrogation à; (*nerves, courage etc*) *Fig* éprouver; – *n* (*trial*) test *m*, essai *m*; examen *m*; analyse *f*; *Sch* interrogation *f*, test *m*; (*of courage etc*) *Fig* épreuve *f*; **driving t.** (examen *m* du) permis *m* de conduire; – *a* (*pilot, flight*) d'essai; **t. case** *Jur* affaire-test *f*; **t. match** *Sp* match *m* international; **t. tube** éprouvette *f*; **t. tube baby** bébé *m* éprouvette.

testament ['testəmənt] *n* testament *m*; (*proof, tribute*) témoignage *m*; **Old/New T.** *Rel* Ancien/Nouveau Testament.

testicle ['testɪk(ə)l] *n Anat* testicule *m*.

testify ['testɪfaɪ] *vi Jur* témoigner (**against** contre); **to t. to sth** (*of person, event etc*) témoigner de qch; – *vt* **to t. that** *Jur* témoigner que. ◆**testi'monial** *n* références *fpl*, recommandation *f*. ◆**testimony** *n* témoignage *m*.

testy ['testɪ] *a* (**-ier, -iest**) irritable.

tetanus ['tetənəs] *n Med* tétanos *m*.

tête-à-tête [teɪtɑː'teɪt] *n* tête-à-tête *m inv*.

tether ['teðər] **1** *vt* (*fasten*) attacher. **2** *n* **at the end of one's t.** à bout de nerfs.

text [tekst] *n* texte *m*. ◆**textbook** *n* manuel *m*.

textile ['tekstaɪl] *a* & *n* textile (*m*).

texture ['tekstʃər] *n* (*of fabric, cake etc*) texture *f*; (*of paper, wood*) grain *m*.

Thames [temz] *n* **the T.** la Tamise *f*.

than [ðən, *stressed* ðæn] *conj* **1** que; **happier t.** plus heureux que; **he has more t. you** il en a plus que toi; **fewer oranges t. plums** moins d'oranges que de prunes. **2** (*with numbers*) de; **more t. six** plus de six.

thank [θæŋk] *vt* remercier (**for sth** de qch, **for doing** d'avoir fait); **t. you** merci (**for sth** pour *ou* de qch, **for doing** d'avoir fait); **no, t. you** (non) merci; **t. God, t. heavens, t. goodness** Dieu merci; – *npl* remerciements *mpl*; **thanks to** (*because of*) grâce à; (**many**) **thanks!** merci (beaucoup)! ◆**thankful** *a* reconnaissant (**for** de); **t. that** bien heureux que (+ *sub*). ◆**thankfully** *adv* (*gratefully*) avec reconnaissance; (*happily*) heureusement. ◆**thankless** *a* ingrat. ◆**Thanks'giving** *n* **T. (day)** (*holiday*) *Am* jour *m* d'action de grâce(s).

that [ðət, *stressed* ðæt] **1** *conj* que; **to say t.** dire que. **2** *rel pron* (*subject*) qui; (*object*) que; **the boy t. left** le garçon qui est parti; **the book t. I read** le livre que j'ai lu; **the carpet t. I put it on** (*with prep*) le tapis sur lequel je l'ai mis; **the house t. she told me about** la maison dont elle m'a parlé; **the day/morning t. she arrived** le jour/matin où elle est arrivée. **3** *dem a* (*pl see* those) ce, cet (*before vowel or mute h*), cette; (*opposed to 'this'*) ... + -là; **t. day** ce jour; ce jour-là; **t. girl** cette fille; cette fille-là. **4** *dem pron* (*pl see* those) ça, cela; ce; **t. (one)** celui-là *m*, celle-là *f*; **give me t.** donne-moi ça *or* cela; **I prefer t. (one)** je préfère celui-là; **before t.** avant ça *or* cela; **t.'s right** c'est juste; **who's t.?** qui est-ce?; **t.'s the house** c'est la maison; **what do you mean by t.?** qu'entends-tu par là; **t. is (to say)** ... c'est-à-dire .... **5** *adv* (*so*) *Fam* si; **not t. good** pas si bon; **t. high** (*pointing*) haut comme ça; **t. much** (*to cost, earn etc*) (au)tant que ça.

thatch [θætʃ] *n* chaume *m*. ◆**thatched** *a* (*roof*) de chaume; **t. cottage** chaumière *f*.

thaw [θɔː] *n* dégel *m*; – *vi* dégeler; (*of snow*) fondre; **it's thawing** *Met* ça dégèle; **to t. (out)** (*of person*) *Fig* se dégeler; – *vt* (*ice*) dégeler, faire fondre; (*food*) faire dégeler; (*snow*) faire fondre.

the [ðə, *before vowel* ði, *stressed* ðiː] *def art* le, l', la, *pl* les; **t. roof** le toit; **t. man** l'homme; **t. moon** la lune; **t. orange** l'orange; **t. boxes** les boîtes; **the smallest** le plus petit; **of t., from t.** du, de l', de la, *pl* des; **to t., at t.** au, à l', à la, *pl* aux; **Elizabeth t. Second** Élisabeth deux; **all t. better** d'autant mieux.

theatre ['θɪətər] *n* (*place, art*) & *Mil* théâtre *m*. ◆**theatregoer** *n* amateur *m* de théâtre. ◆**the'atrical** *a* théâtral; **t. company** troupe *f* de théâtre.

theft [θeft] *n* vol *m*.

their [ðeər] *poss a* leur, *pl* leurs; **t. house** leur maison *f*. ◆**theirs** [ðeəz] *poss pron* le leur, la leur, *pl* les leurs; **this book is t.** ce livre est à eux *or* est le leur; **a friend of t.** un ami à eux.

them [ðəm, *stressed* ðem] *pron* les; (*after prep etc*) eux *mpl*, elles *fpl*; **(to) t.** (*indirect*) leur; **I see t.** je les vois; **I give (to) t.** je leur donne; **with t.** avec eux, avec elles; **ten of t.** dix d'entre eux, dix d'entre elles; **all of t.** tous, toutes. ◆**them'selves** *pron* eux-mêmes *mpl*, elles-mêmes *fpl*; (*reflexive*) se, s'; (*after prep etc*) eux *mpl*, elles *fpl*;

they wash t. ils se lavent, elles se lavent; **they think of t.** ils pensent à eux, elles pensent à elles.

theme [θiːm] *n* thème *m*; **t. song** *or* **tune** *Cin TV* chanson *f* principale.

then [ðen] **1** *adv* (*at that time*) alors, à ce moment-là; (*next*) ensuite, puis; **from t. on** dès lors; **before t.** avant cela; **until t.** jusque-là, jusqu'alors; – **a the t. mayor/***etc* le maire/*etc* d'alors. **2** *conj* (*therefore*) donc, alors.

theology [θɪ'ɒlədʒɪ] *n* théologie *f*. ◆**theo'logical** *a* théologique. ◆**theo'logian** *n* théologien *m*.

theorem ['θɪərəm] *n* théorème *m*.

theory ['θɪərɪ] *n* théorie *f*; **in t.** en théorie. ◆**theo'retical** *a* théorique. ◆**theo'retically** *adv* théoriquement. ◆**theorist** *n* théoricien, -ienne *mf*.

therapy ['θerəpɪ] *n* thérapeutique *f*. ◆**ther-a'peutic** *a* thérapeutique.

there [ðeər] *adv* là; (*down or over*) t. là-bas; **on t.** là-dessus; **she'll be t.** elle sera là, elle y sera; **t. is, t. are** il y a; (*pointing*) voilà; **t. he is** le voilà; **t. she is** la voilà; **t. they are** les voilà; **that man t.** cet homme-là; **t. (you are)!** (*take this*) tenez!; **t., (t.,) don't cry!** allons, allons, ne pleure pas! ◆**therea-'bout(s)** *adv* par là; (*in amount*) à peu près. ◆**there'after** *adv* après cela. ◆**thereby** *adv* de ce fait. ◆**therefore** *adv* donc. ◆**thereu'pon** *adv* sur ce.

thermal ['θɜːm(ə)l] *a* (*energy, unit*) thermique; (*springs*) thermal; (*underwear*) tribo-électrique, en thermolactyl®.

thermometer [θə'mɒmɪtər] *n* thermomètre *m*.

thermonuclear [θɜːməʊ'njuːklɪər] *a* thermonucléaire.

Thermos® ['θɜːməs] *n* **T. (flask)** thermos® *m or f*.

thermostat ['θɜːməstæt] *n* thermostat *m*.

thesaurus [θɪ'sɔːrəs] *n* dictionnaire *m* de synonymes.

these [ðiːz] **1** *dem a* (*sing see* this) ces; (*opposed to 'those'*) ... + -ci; **t. men** ces hommes; ces hommes-ci. **2** *dem pron* (*sing see* this) **t. (ones)** ceux-ci *mpl*, celles-ci *fpl*; **t. are my friends** ce sont mes amis.

thesis, *pl* **theses** ['θiːsɪs, 'θiːsiːz] *n* thèse *f*.

they [ðeɪ] *pron* **1** ils *mpl*, elles *fpl*; (*stressed*) eux *mpl*, elles *fpl*; **t. go** ils vont, elles vont; **t. are doctors** ce sont des médecins. **2** (*people in general*) on, *t.* say on dit.

thick [θɪk] *a* (-er, -est) épais; (*stupid*) *Fam* lourd; **to be t.** (*of friends*) *Fam* être très liés; – *adv* (*to grow*) dru; (*to spread*) en couche épaisse; – *n* **in the t. of** (*battle etc*) au plus

gros de. ◆**thicken** vt épaissir; – vi
s'épaissir. ◆**thickly** adv (to grow, fall) dru;
(to spread) en couche épaisse; (populated,
wooded) très. ◆**thickness** n épaisseur f.

thicket ['θɪkɪt] n (trees) fourré m.

thickset [θɪk'set] a (person) trapu. ◆**thick-
skinned** a (person) dur, peu sensible.

thief [θiːf] n (pl thieves) voleur, -euse mf.
◆**thiev/e** vti voler. ◆—**ing** a voleur; – n
vol m.

thigh [θaɪ] n cuisse f. ◆**thighbone** n fémur
m.

thimble ['θɪmb(ə)l] n dé m (à coudre).

thin [θɪn] a (**thinner, thinnest**) (slice, paper
etc) mince; (person, leg) maigre, mince;
(soup) peu épais; (hair, audience) clairsemé; (powder) fin; (excuse, profit) Fig
maigre, mince; – adv (to spread) en couche
mince; – vt (**-nn-**) **to t.** (**down**) (paint etc)
délayer; – vi **to t. out** (of crowd, mist)
s'éclaircir. ◆—**ly** adv (to spread) en couche
mince; (populated, wooded) peu;
(disguised) à peine. ◆—**ness** n minceur f;
maigreur f.

thing [θɪŋ] n chose f; **one's things** (belongings, clothes) ses affaires fpl; **it's a funny t.**
c'est drôle; **poor little t.!** pauvre petit!;
that's (just) the t. voilà (exactement) ce
qu'il faut; **how are things?,** Fam **how's
things?** comment (ça) va?; **I'll think things
over** j'y réfléchirai; **for one t. . . . , and for
another t.** d'abord . . . et ensuite; **tea things**
(set) service m à thé; (dishes) vaisselle f.
◆**thingummy** n Fam truc m, machin m.

think [θɪŋk] vi (pt & pp **thought**) penser
(**about, of** à); **to t.** (**carefully**) réfléchir
(**about, of** à); **to t. of doing** penser or songer
à faire; **to t. highly of, t. a lot of** penser
beaucoup de bien de; **she doesn't t. much of
it** ça ne lui dit pas grand-chose; **to t. better
of it** se raviser; **I can't t. of it** je n'arrive pas
à m'en souvenir; – vt penser (**that** que); **I t.
so** je pense or crois que oui; **what do you t.
of him?** que penses-tu de lui?; **I thought it
difficult** je l'ai trouvé difficile; **to t. out** or
through (reply etc) réfléchir à,
peser; **to t. over** réfléchir à; **to t. up** (invent)
inventer, avoir l'idée de; – n **to have a t.**
Fam réfléchir (**about** à); – a **t. tank** comité
m d'experts. ◆—**ing** a (person) intelligent;
– n (opinion) opinion f; **to my t.** à mon avis.
◆—**er** n penseur, -euse mf.

thin-skinned [θɪn'skɪnd] a (person) susceptible.

third [θɜːd] a troisième; **t. person** or **party**
tiers m; **t.-party insurance** assurance f au
tiers; **T. World** Tiers-Monde m; – n

troisième mf; **a t.** (fraction) un tiers; – adv
(in race) troisième. ◆—**ly** adv troisièmement.

third-class [θɜːd'klɑːs] a de troisième
classe. ◆**t.-rate** a (très) inférieur.

thirst [θɜːst] n soif f (**for** de). ◆**thirsty** a
(**-ier, -iest**) a **to be** or **feel t.** avoir soif; **to
make t.** donner soif à; **t. for** (power etc) Fig
assoiffé de.

thirteen [θɜː'tiːn] a & n treize (m).
◆**thirteenth** a & n treizième (mf).
◆'**thirtieth** a & n trentième (mf).
◆'**thirty** a & n trente (m).

this [ðɪs] **1** dem a (pl see **these**) ce, cet (before
vowel or mute h), cette; (opposed to 'that')
. . . + -ci; **t. book** ce livre; ce livre-ci; **t.
man** cet homme; cet homme-ci; **t. photo**
cette photo; cette photo-ci. **2** dem pron (pl
see **these**) ceci; ce; **t.** (**one**) celui-ci m,
celle-ci f; **give me t.** donne-moi ceci; **I
prefer t.** (**one**) je préfère celui-ci; **before t.**
avant ceci; **who's t.?** qui est-ce?; **t. is Paul**
c'est Paul; **t. is the house** voici la maison. **3**
adv (so) Fam si; **t. high** (pointing) haut
comme ceci; **t. far** (until now) jusqu'ici.

thistle ['θɪs(ə)l] n chardon m.

thorn [θɔːn] n épine f. ◆**thorny** a (**-ier,
-iest**) (bush, problem etc) épineux.

thorough ['θʌrə] a (painstaking, careful)
minutieux, consciencieux; (knowledge,
examination) approfondi; (rogue, liar)
fieffé; (disaster) complet; **to give sth a t.
washing** laver qch à fond. ◆—**ly** adv
(completely) tout à fait; (painstakingly)
avec minutie; (to know, clean, wash) à fond.
◆—**ness** n minutie f; (depth) profondeur
f.

thoroughbred ['θʌrəbred] n (horse)
pur-sang m inv.

thoroughfare ['θʌrəfeər] n (street) rue f; '**no
t.**' 'passage interdit'.

those [ðəʊz] **1** dem a (sing see **that**) ces;
(opposed to 'these') . . . + -là; **t. men** ces
hommes; ces hommes-là. **2** dem pron (sing
see **that**) **t.** (**ones**) ceux-là mpl, celles-là fpl;
t. are my friends ce sont mes amis.

though [ðəʊ] **1** conj (even) **t.** bien que (+
sub); **as t.** comme si; **strange t. it may seem**
si étrange que cela puisse paraître. **2** adv
(nevertheless) cependant, quand même.

thought [θɔːt] see **think**; – n pensée f; (idea)
idée f, penseé f; (careful) **t.** réflexion f; **without** (a) **t. for** sans penser à; **to have second
thoughts** changer d'avis; **on second
thoughts,** Am **on second t.** à la réflexion.
◆**thoughtful** a (pensive) pensif; (serious)
sérieux; (considerate, kind) gentil, préve-

nant. ◆**thoughtfully** adv (*considerately*) gentiment. ◆**thoughtfulness** n gentillesse f, prévenance f. ◆**thoughtless** a (*towards others*) désinvolte; (*careless*) étourdi. ◆**thoughtlessly** adv (*carelessly*) étourdiment; (*inconsiderately*) avec désinvolture.

thousand ['θaʊzənd] a & n mille a & n inv; **a t. pages** mille pages; **two t. pages** deux mille pages; **thousands of** des milliers de.

thrash [θræʃ] **1** vt **to t. s.o.** rouer qn de coups; (*defeat*) écraser qn; **to t. out** (*plan etc*) élaborer (à force de discussions). **2** vi **to t. about** (*struggle*) se débattre. ◆**—ing** n (*beating*) correction f.

thread [θred] n (*yarn*) & Fig fil m; (*of screw*) pas m; — vt (*needle, beads*) enfiler; **to t. one's way** Fig se faufiler (**through the crowd**/*etc* parmi la foule/*etc*). ◆**threadbare** a élimé, râpé.

threat [θret] n menace f (to à). ◆**threaten** vi menacer; — vt menacer (**to do** de faire, **with sth** de qch). ◆**threatening** a menaçant. ◆**threateningly** adv (*to say*) d'un ton menaçant.

three [θriː] a & n trois (m); **t.-piece suite** canapé m et deux fauteuils. ◆**threefold** a triple; — adv **to increase t.** tripler. ◆**three-'wheeler** n (*tricycle*) tricycle m; (*car*) voiture f à trois roues.

thresh [θreʃ] vt Agr battre.

threshold ['θreʃhəʊld] n seuil m.

threw [θruː] see **throw.**

thrift [θrɪft] n (*virtue*) économie f. ◆**thrifty** a (**-ier, -iest**) économe.

thrill [θrɪl] n émotion f, frisson m; **to get a t. out of doing** prendre plaisir à faire; — vt (*delight*) réjouir; (*excite*) faire frissonner. ◆**—ed** a ravi (**with sth** de qch, **to do or** faire). ◆**—ing** a passionnant. ◆**—er** n film m or roman m à suspense.

thriv/e [θraɪv] vi (*of business, person, plant etc*) prospérer; **he or she thrives on hard work** le travail lui profite. ◆**—ing** a prospère, florissant.

throat [θrəʊt] n gorge f; **to have a sore t.** avoir mal à la gorge. ◆**throaty** a (*voice*) rauque; (*person*) à la voix rauque.

throb [θrɒb] vi (**-bb-**) (*of heart*) palpiter; (*of engine*) vrombir; Fig vibrer; **my finger is throbbing** mon doigt me fait des élancements; — n palpitation f; vrombissement m; élancement m.

throes [θrəʊz] npl **in the t. of** au milieu de; (*illness, crisis*) en proie à; **in the t. of doing** en train de faire.

thrombosis [θrɒm'bəʊsɪs] n (*coronary*) Med infarctus m.

throne [θrəʊn] n trône m.

throng [θrɒŋ] n foule f; — vi (*rush*) affluer; — vt (*street, station etc*) se presser dans; **thronged with people** noir de monde.

throttle ['θrɒt(ə)l] **1** n Aut accélérateur m. **2** vt (*strangle*) étrangler.

through [θruː] prep (*place*) à travers; (*time*) pendant; (*means*) par; (*thanks to*) grâce à; **to go** or **get t.** (*forest etc*) traverser; (*hole etc*) passer par; **t. the window/door** par la fenêtre/porte; **to speak t. one's nose** parler du nez; **Tuesday t. Saturday** Am de mardi à samedi; — adv à travers; **to go t.** (*cross*) traverser; (*pass*) passer; **to let t.** laisser passer; **all** or **right t.** (*to the end*) jusqu'au bout; **French t. and t.** français jusqu'au bout des ongles; **to be t.** (*finished*) Am Fam avoir fini; **we're t.** Am Fam c'est fini entre nous; **I'm t. with the book** Am Fam je n'ai plus besoin du livre; **to put you t. (to him)** Tel je vous le passe; — a (*train, traffic, ticket*) direct; **'no t. road'** (*no exit*) 'voie sans issue'. ◆**through'out** prep **t. the neighbourhood**/*etc* dans tout le quartier/*etc*; **t. the day**/*etc* (*time*) pendant toute la journée/*etc*; — adv (*everywhere*) partout; (*all the time*) tout le temps. ◆**throughway** n Am autoroute f.

throw [θrəʊ] n (*of stone etc*) jet m; Sp lancer m; (*of dice*) coup m; (*turn*) tour m; — vt (pt **threw**, pp **thrown**) jeter (**to, at** à); (*stone, ball*) lancer, jeter; (*hurl*) projeter; (*of horse*) désarçonner (qn); (*party, reception*) donner; (*baffle*) Fam dérouter; **to t. away** (*discard*) jeter; (*ruin, waste*) Fig gâcher; **to t. back** (*ball*) renvoyer (**to** à); (*one's head*) rejeter en arrière; **to t. in** (*include as extra*) Fam donner en prime; **to t. off** (*get rid of*) se débarrasser de; **to t. out** (*discard*) jeter; (*suggestion*) repousser; (*expel*) mettre (qn) à la porte; (*distort*) fausser (*calcul etc*); **to t. over** abandonner; **to t. up** (*job*) Fam laisser tomber; — vi **to t. up** (*vomit*) Sl dégobiller. ◆**throwaway** a (*disposable*) à jeter, jetable.

thrush [θrʌʃ] n (*bird*) grive f.

thrust [θrʌst] n (*push*) poussée f; (*stab*) coup m; (*of argument*) poids m; (*dynamism*) allant m; — vt (pt & pp **thrust**) (*push*) pousser; (*put*) mettre (**into** dans); **to t. sth into sth** (*stick, knife, pin*) enfoncer qch dans qch; **to t. sth/s.o. upon s.o.** Fig imposer qch/qn à qn.

thud [θʌd] n bruit m sourd.

thug [θʌg] n voyou m.

thumb [θʌm] *n* pouce *m*; **with a t. index** (*book*) à onglets; – *vt* **to t. (through)** (*book etc*) feuilleter; **to t. a lift** or **a ride** *Fam* faire du stop. ◆**thumbtack** *n Am* punaise *f*.

thump [θʌmp] *vt* (*person*) frapper, cogner sur; (*table*) taper sur; **to t. one's head** (*on door etc*) se cogner la tête (**on** contre); – *vi* frapper, cogner (**on** sur); (*of heart*) battre à grands coups; – *n* (grand) coup *m*; (*noise*) bruit *m* sourd. ◆**—ing** *a* (*huge, great*) *Fam* énorme.

thunder ['θʌndər] *n* tonnerre *m*; – *vi* (*of weather, person, guns*) tonner; **it's thundering** *Met* il tonne; **to t. past** passer (vite) dans un bruit de tonnerre. ◆**thunderbolt** *n* (*event*) *Fig* coup *m* de tonnerre. ◆**thunderclap** *n* coup *m* de tonnerre. ◆**thunderstorm** *n* orage *m*. ◆**thunderstruck** *a* abasourdi.

Thursday ['θɜːzdɪ] *n* jeudi *m*.

thus [ðʌs] *adv* ainsi.

thwart [θwɔːt] *vt* (*plan, person*) contrecarrer.

thyme [taɪm] *n Bot Culin* thym *m*.

thyroid ['θaɪrɔɪd] *a* & *n Anat* thyroïde (*f*).

tiara [tɪ'ɑːrə] *n* (*of woman*) diadème *m*.

tic [tɪk] *n* (*in face, limbs*) tic *m*.

tick [tɪk] **1** *n* (*of clock*) tic-tac *m*; – *vi* faire tic-tac; **to t. over** (*of engine, factory, business*) tourner au ralenti. **2** *n* (*on list*) coche *f*, trait *m*; – *vt* **to t. (off)** cocher; **to t. off** (*reprimand*) *Fam* passer un savon à. **3** *n* (*moment*) *Fam* instant *m*. **4** *n* (*insect*) tique *f*. **5** *adv* **on t.** (*on credit*) *Fam* à crédit. ◆**—ing** *n* (*of clock*) tic-tac *m*; **to give s.o. a t.-off** *Fam* passer un savon à qn.

ticket ['tɪkɪt] *n* billet *m*; (*for tube, bus, cloakroom*) ticket *m*; (*for library*) carte *f*; (*fine*) *Aut Fam* contravention *f*, contredanse *f*; *Pol Am* liste *f*; (*price*) **t.** étiquette *f*; **t. collector** contrôleur, -euse *mf*; **t. holder** personne *f* munie d'un billet; **t. office** guichet *m*.

tickle ['tɪk(ə)l] *vt* chatouiller; (*amuse*) *Fig* amuser; – *n* chatouillement *m*. ◆**ticklish** *a* (*person*) chatouilleux; (*fabric*) qui chatouille; (*problem*) *Fig* délicat.

tidbit ['tɪdbɪt] *n* (*food*) *Am* bon morceau *m*.

tiddlywinks ['tɪdlɪwɪŋks] *n* jeu *m* de puce.

tide [taɪd] **1** *n* marée *f*; **against the t.** *Nau* & *Fig* à contre-courant; **the rising t. of discontent** le mécontentement grandissant. **2** *vt* **to t. s.o. over** (*help out*) dépanner qn. ◆**tidal** *a* (*river*) qui a une marée; **t. wave** raz-de-marée *m inv*; (*in public opinion etc*) *Fig* vague *f* de fond. ◆**tidemark** *n Fig Hum* ligne *f* de crasse.

tidings ['taɪdɪŋz] *npl Lit* nouvelles *fpl*.

tidy ['taɪdɪ] *a* (**-ier, -iest**) (*place, toys etc*) bien rangé; (*clothes, looks*) soigné; (*methodical*) ordonné; (*amount, sum*) *Fam* joli, bon; **to make t.** ranger; – *vt* **to t. (up** or **away)** ranger; **to t. oneself (up)** s'arranger; **to t. out** (*cupboard etc*) vider; – *vi* **to t. up** ranger. ◆**tidily** *adv* avec soin. ◆**tidiness** *n* (bon) ordre *m*; (*care*) soin *m*.

tie [taɪ] *n* (*string, strap etc*) & *Fig* lien *m*, attache *f*; (*necktie*) cravate *f*; (*sleeper*) *Rail Am* traverse *f*; *Sp* égalité *f* de points; (*match*) match *m* nul; – *vt* (*fasten*) attacher, lier (**to** à); (*a knot*) faire (**in** à); (*shoe*) lacer; (*link*) lier (**to** à); **to t. down** attacher; **to t. s.o. down to** (*date, place etc*) obliger qn à accepter; **to t. up** attacher; (*money*) *Fig* immobiliser; **to be tied up** (*linked*) être lié (**with** avec); (*busy*) *Fam* être occupé; – *vi Sp* finir à égalité de points; *Fb* faire match nul; (*in race*) être ex aequo; **to t. in with** (*tally with*) se rapporter à. ◆**t.-up** *n* (*link*) lien *m*; (*traffic jam*) *Am Fam* bouchon *m*.

tier [tɪər] *n* (*seats*) *Sp Th* gradin *m*; (*of cake*) étage *m*.

tiff [tɪf] *n* petite querelle *f*.

tiger ['taɪgər] *n* tigre *m*. ◆**tigress** *n* tigresse *f*.

tight [taɪt] *a* (**-er, -est**) (*rope etc*) raide; (*closely-fitting clothing*) ajusté, (*fitting too closely*) (trop) étroit, (trop) serré; (*drawer, lid*) dur; (*control*) strict; (*schedule, credit*) serré; (*drunk*) *Fam* gris; (*with money*) *Fam* avare; **a t. spot** or **corner** *Fam* une situation difficile; **it's a t. squeeze** il y a juste la place; – *adv* (*to hold, shut, sleep*) bien; (*to squeeze*) fort; **to sit t.** ne pas bouger. ◆**tighten** *vt* **to t. (up)** (*rope*) tendre; (*bolt etc*) (res)serrer; (*security*) *Fig* renforcer; – *vi* **to t. up on** se montrer plus strict à l'égard de. ◆**tightly** *adv* (*to hold*) bien; (*to squeeze*) fort; **t. knit** (*close*) très uni. ◆**tightness** *n* (*of garment*) étroitesse *f*; (*of control*) rigueur *f*; (*of rope*) tension *f*.

tight-fitting [taɪt'fɪtɪŋ] *a* (*garment*) ajusté. ◆**tightfisted** *a* avare. ◆**'tightrope** *n* corde *f* raide. ◆**'tightwad** *n* (*miser*) *Am Fam* grippe-sou *m*.

tights [taɪts] *npl* (*garment*) collant *m*; (*for dancer etc*) justaucorps *m*.

til/e [taɪl] *n* (*on roof*) tuile *f*; (*on wall or floor*) carreau *m*; – *vt* (*wall, floor*) carreler. ◆**—ed** *a* (*roof*) de tuiles; (*wall, floor*) carrelé.

till [tɪl] **1** *prep* & *conj* = **until**. **2** *n* (*for money*) caisse *f* (enregistreuse). **3** *vt* (*land*) *Agr* cultiver.

tilt [tɪlt] *vti* pencher; − *n* inclinaison *f*; **(at) full t.** à toute vitesse.

timber ['tɪmbər] *n* bois *m* (de construction); (*trees*) arbres *mpl*; − *a* de or en bois. ◆**timberyard** *n* entrepôt *m* de bois.

time [taɪm] *n* temps *m*; (*point in time*) moment *m*; (*epoch*) époque *f*; (*on clock*) heure *f*; (*occasion*) fois *f*; *Mus* mesure *f*; **in (the course of) t., with (the passage of) t.** avec le temps; **some of the t.** (*not always*) une partie du temps; **most of the t.** la plupart du temps; **in a year's t.** dans un an; **a long t.** longtemps; **a short t.** peu de temps, un petit moment; **full-t.** à plein temps; **part-t.** à temps partiel; **to have a good** or **a nice t.** (*fun*) s'amuser (bien); **to have a hard t. doing** avoir du mal à faire; **t. off** du temps libre; **in no t. (at all)** en un rien de temps; **(just) in t.** (*to arrive*) à temps (**for sth** pour qch, **to do** pour faire); **in my t.** (*formerly*) de mon temps; **from t. to t.** de temps en temps; **what t. is it?** quelle heure est-il?; **the right** or **exact t.** l'heure *f* exacte; **on t.** à l'heure; **at the same t.** en même temps (**as** que); (*simultaneously*) à la fois; **for the t. being** pour le moment; **at the t.** à ce moment-là; **at the present t.** à l'heure actuelle; **at times** par moments, parfois; **at one t.** à un moment donné; **this t. tomorrow** demain à cette heure-ci; **(the) next t. you come** la prochaine fois que tu viendras; **(the) last t.** la dernière fois; **one at a t.** un à un; **t. and again** maintes fois; **ten times** ten dix fois dix; **t. bomb** bombe *f* à retardement; **t. lag** décalage *m*; **t. limit** délai *m*; **t. zone** fuseau *m* horaire; − *vt* (*sportsman, worker etc*) chronométrer; (*programme, operation*) minuter; (*choose the time of*) choisir le moment de; (*to plan*) prévoir. ◆**timing** *n* chronométrage *m*; minutage *m*; (*judgement of artist etc*) rythme *m*; **the t. of** (*time*) le moment choisi pour. ◆**time-consuming** *a* qui prend du temps. ◆**time-honoured** *a* consacré (par l'usage).

timeless ['taɪmləs] *a* éternel.

timely ['taɪmlɪ] *a* à propos. ◆**timeliness** *n* à-propos *m*.

timer ['taɪmər] *n* Culin minuteur *m*, compte-minutes *m inv*; (*sand-filled*) sablier *m*; (*on machine*) minuteur *m*; (*to control lighting*) minuterie *f*.

timetable ['taɪmteɪb(ə)l] *n* horaire *m*; (*in school*) emploi *m* du temps.

timid ['tɪmɪd] *a* (*shy*) timide; (*fearful*) timoré. ◆−**ly** *adv* timidement.

tin [tɪn] *n* étain *m*; (*tinplate*) fer-blanc *m*; (*can*) boîte *f*; (*for baking*) moule *m*; **t. can** boîte *f* (en fer-blanc); **t. opener** ouvre-boîtes *m inv*; **t. soldier** soldat *m* de plomb. ◆**tinfoil** *n* papier *m* d'aluminium, papier alu. ◆**tinned** *a* en boîte. ◆**tinplate** *n* fer-blanc *m*.

tinge [tɪndʒ] *n* teinte *f*. ◆**tinged** *a* **t. with** (*pink etc*) teinté de; (*jealousy etc*) Fig empreint de.

tingle ['tɪŋg(ə)l] *vi* picoter; **it's tingling** ça me picote. ◆**tingly** *a* (*feeling*) de picotement.

tinker ['tɪŋkər] *vi* **to t.** (**about**) with bricoler.

tinkle ['tɪŋk(ə)l] *vi* tinter; − *n* tintement *m*; **to give s.o. a t.** (*phone s.o.*) Fam passer un coup de fil à qn.

tinny ['tɪnɪ] *a* (**-ier, -iest**) (*sound*) métallique; (*vehicle, machine*) de mauvaise qualité.

tinsel ['tɪns(ə)l] *n* clinquant *m*, guirlandes *fpl* de Noël.

tint [tɪnt] *n* teinte *f*; (*for hair*) shampooing *m* colorant; − *vt* (*paper, glass*) teinter.

tiny ['taɪnɪ] *a* (**-ier, -iest**) tout petit.

tip [tɪp] **1** *n* (*end*) bout *m*; (*pointed*) pointe *f*. **2** *n* (*money*) pourboire *m*; − *vt* (**-pp-**) donner un pourboire à. **3** *n* (*advice*) conseil *m*; (*information*) & *Sp* tuyau *m*; **to get a t.-off** se faire tuyauter; − *vt* (**-pp-**) **to t. a horse**/*etc* donner un cheval/*etc* gagnant; **to t. off** (*police*) prévenir. **4** *n* (*for rubbish*) décharge *f*; − *vt* (**-pp-**) **to t.** (**up** *or* **over**) (*tilt*) incliner, pencher; (*overturn*) faire basculer; **to t.** (**out**) (*liquid, load*) déverser (**into** dans); − *vi* **to t.** (**up** *or* **over**) (*tilt*) pencher; (*overturn*) basculer.

tipped [tɪpt] *a* **t. cigarette** cigarette *f* (à bout) filtre.

tipple ['tɪp(ə)l] *vi* (*drink*) Fam picoler.

tipsy ['tɪpsɪ] *a* (**-ier, -iest**) (*drunk*) gai, pompette.

tiptoe ['tɪptəʊ] *n* **on t.** sur la pointe des pieds; − *vi* marcher sur la pointe des pieds.

tiptop ['tɪptɒp] *a* Fam excellent.

tirade [taɪ'reɪd] *n* diatribe *f*.

tir/e[1] ['taɪər] *vt* fatiguer; **to t. out** (*exhaust*) épuiser; − *vi* se fatiguer. ◆−**ed** *a* fatigué; **to be t. of sth/s.o./doing** en avoir assez de qch/de qn/de faire; **to get t. of doing** se lasser de faire. ◆−**ing** *a* fatigant. ◆**tiredness** *n* fatigue *f*. ◆**tireless** *a* infatigable. ◆**tiresome** *a* ennuyeux.

tire[2] ['taɪər] *n Am* pneu *m*.

tissue ['tɪʃuː] *n Biol* tissu *m*; (*handkerchief*) mouchoir *m* en papier, kleenex® *m*; **t. (paper)** papier *m* de soie.

tit [tɪt] *n* **1** (*bird*) mésange *f*. **2 to give t. for tat** rendre coup pour coup.

titbit ['tɪtbɪt] *n* (*food*) bon morceau *m*.

titillate ['tɪtɪleɪt] *vt* exciter.

titl/e ['taɪt(ə)l] *n* (*name, claim*) & *Sp* titre *m*;
t. deed titre *m* de propriété; **t. role** *Th Cin*
rôle *m* principal; – *vt* (*film*) intituler, titrer.
◆**—ed** *a* (*person*) titré.

titter ['tɪtər] *vi* rire bêtement.

tittle-tattle ['tɪt(ə)ltæt(ə)l] *n Fam* commé-
rages *mpl*.

to [tə, *stressed* tuː] **1** *prep* à; (*towards*) vers;
(*of feelings, attitude*) envers; (*right up to*)
jusqu'à; (*of*) de; **give it to him** *or* **her**
donne-le-lui; **to town** en ville; **to France** en
France; **to Portugal** au Portugal; **to the**
butcher('s)/*etc* chez le boucher/*etc*; **the**
road to la route de; **the train to** le train
pour; **well-disposed to** bien disposé envers;
kind to gentil envers *or* avec *or* pour; **from**
bad to worse de mal en pis; **ten to one**
(*proportion*) dix contre un; **it's ten**
(**minutes**) **to one** il est une heure moins dix;
one person to a room une personne par
chambre; **to say/to remember**/*etc* (*with*
inf) dire/se souvenir/*etc*; **she tried to** elle a
essayé; **wife**/*etc*-**to-be** future femme *f*/*etc*.
2 *adv* **to push to** (*door*) fermer; **to go** *or* **walk**
to and fro aller et venir. ◆**to-do** [tə'duː] *n*
(*fuss*) *Fam* histoire *f*.

toad [təʊd] *n* crapaud *m*.

toadstool ['təʊdstuːl] *n* champignon *m*
(vénéneux).

toast [təʊst] **1** *n Culin* pain *m* grillé, toast *m*;
– *vt* (*bread*) (faire) griller. **2** *n* (*drink*) toast
m; – *vt* (*person*) porter un toast à; (*success,*
event) arroser. ◆**toaster** *n* grille-pain *m*
inv.

tobacco [tə'bækəʊ] *n* (*pl* **-os**) tabac *m*.
◆**tobacconist** *n* buraliste *mf*; **t., tobacco-**
nist's (shop) (bureau *m* de) tabac *m*.

toboggan [tə'bɒgən] *n* luge *f*, toboggan *m*.

today [tə'deɪ] *adv* & *n* aujourd'hui (*m*).

toddle ['tɒd(ə)l] *vi* **to t. off** (*leave*) *Hum Fam*
se sauver.

toddler ['tɒdlər] *n* petit(e) enfant *mf*.

toddy ['tɒdɪ] *n* (*hot*) **t.** grog *m*.

toe [təʊ] **1** *n* orteil *m*; **on one's toes** *Fig* vigilant. **2** *vt* **to t. the line** se conformer; **to t. the**
party line respecter la ligne du parti.
◆**toenail** *n* ongle *m* du pied.

toffee ['tɒfɪ] *n* (*sweet*) caramel *m* (*dur*); **t.**
apple pomme *f* d'amour.

together [tə'geðər] *adv* ensemble; (*at the*
same time) en même temps; **t. with** avec.
◆**—ness** *n* (*of group*) camaraderie *f*; (*of*
husband and wife) intimité *f*.

togs [tɒgz] *npl* (*clothes*) *Sl* nippes *fpl*.

toil [tɔɪl] *n* labeur *m*; – *vi* travailler dur.

toilet ['tɔɪlɪt] *n* (*room*) toilettes *fpl*, cabinets

mpl; (*bowl, seat*) cuvette *f or* siège *m* des
cabinets; **to go to the t.** aller aux toilettes;
– *a* (*articles*) de toilette; **t. paper** papier *m*
hygiénique; **t. roll** rouleau *m* de papier
hygiénique; **t. water** (*perfume*) eau *f* de
toilette. ◆**toiletries** *npl* articles *mpl* de
toilette.

token ['təʊkən] *n* (*symbol, sign*) témoignage
m; (*metal disc*) jeton *m*; (*voucher*) bon *m*;
gift t. chèque-cadeau *m*; **book t.**
chèque-livre *m*; **record t.** chèque-disque *m*;
– *a* symbolique.

told [təʊld] *see* **tell**; – *adv* **all t.** (*taken*
together) en tout.

tolerable ['tɒlərəb(ə)l] *a* (*bearable*) toléra-
ble; (*fairly good*) passable. ◆**tolerably**
adv (*fairly, fairly well*) passablement.
◆**tolerance** *n* tolérance *f*. ◆**tolerant** *a*
tolérant (**of** à l'égard de). ◆**tolerantly** *adv*
avec tolérance. ◆**tolerate** *vt* tolérer.

toll [təʊl] **1** *n* péage *m*; – *a* (*road*) à péage. **2**
n **the death t.** le nombre de morts, le bilan
en vies humaines; **to take a heavy t.** (*of acci-*
dent etc) faire beaucoup de victimes. **3** *vi*
(*of bell*) sonner. ◆**tollfree** *a* **t. number** *Tel*
Am numéro *m* vert.

tomato [tə'mɑːtəʊ, *Am* tə'meɪtəʊ] *n* (*pl*
-oes) tomate *f*.

tomb [tuːm] *n* tombeau *m*. ◆**tombstone** *n*
pierre *f* tombale.

tomboy ['tɒmbɔɪ] *n* (*girl*) garçon *m* manqué.

tomcat ['tɒmkæt] *n* matou *m*.

tome [təʊm] *n* (*book*) tome *m*.

tomfoolery [tɒm'fuːlərɪ] *n* niaiserie(s) *f(pl)*.

tomorrow [tə'mɒrəʊ] *adv* & *n* demain (*m*);
t. morning/evening demain matin/soir; **the**
day after t. après-demain.

ton [tʌn] *n* tonne *f* (*Br* = 1016 *kg, Am* =
907 *kg*); **metric t.** tonne *f* (= 1000 *kg*); **tons**
of (*lots of*) *Fam* des tonnes de.

tone [təʊn] *n* ton *m*; (*of radio, telephone*)
tonalité *f*; **in that t.** sur ce ton; **to set the t.**
donner le ton; **she's t.-deaf** elle n'a pas
d'oreille; – *vt* **to t. down** atténuer; **to t. up**
(*muscles, skin*) tonifier; – *vi* **to t. in**
s'harmoniser (**with** avec).

tongs [tɒŋz] *npl* pinces *fpl*; (*for sugar*) pince
f; (*curling*) **t.** fer *m* à friser.

tongue [tʌŋ] *n* langue *f*; **t. in cheek**
ironique(ment). ◆**t.-tied** *a* muet (et gêné).

tonic ['tɒnɪk] *a* & *n* tonique (*m*); **gin and t.**
gin-tonic *m*.

tonight [tə'naɪt] *adv* & *n* (*this evening*) ce soir
(*m*); (*during the night*) cette nuit (*f*).

tonne [tʌn] *n* (*metric*) tonne *f*. ◆**tonnage** *n*
tonnage *m*.

tonsil ['tɒns(ə)l] *n* amygdale *f*. ◆**tonsi'l-**

lectomy n opération f des amygdales.
◆**tonsillitis** [tɒnsə'laɪtəs] n **to have t.** avoir une angine.

too [tuː] adv **1** (excessively) trop; **t. tired to play** trop fatigué pour jouer; **t. hard to solve** trop difficile à résoudre; **it's only t. true** ce n'est que trop vrai. **2** (also) aussi; (moreover) en plus.

took [tʊk] see **take**.

tool [tuːl] n outil m; **t. bag, t. kit** trousse f à outils.

toot [tuːt] vti **to t. (the horn)** Aut klaxonner.

tooth, pl **teeth** [tuːθ, tiːθ] n dent f; **front t.** dent de devant; **back t.** molaire f; **milk/wisdom t.** dent de lait/de sagesse; **t. decay** carie f dentaire; **to have a sweet t.** aimer les sucreries; **long in the t.** (old) Hum chenu, vieux. ◆**toothache** n mal m de dents. ◆**toothbrush** n brosse f à dents. ◆**toothcomb** n peigne m fin. ◆**toothpaste** n dentifrice m. ◆**toothpick** n cure-dent m.

top[1] [tɒp] n (of mountain, tower, tree) sommet m; (of wall, dress, ladder, page) haut m; (of box, table, surface) dessus m; (of list) tête f; (of water) surface f; (of car) toit m; (of bottle, tube) bouchon m; (bottle cap) capsule f; (of saucepan) couvercle m; (of pen) capuchon m; **pyjama t.** veste f de pyjama; **(at the) t. of the class** le premier de la classe; **on t. of** sur; (in addition to) Fig en plus de; **on t.** (in bus etc) en haut; **from t. to bottom** de fond en comble; **the big t.** (circus) le chapiteau; – a (drawer, shelf) du haut, premier; (step, layer, storey) dernier; (upper) supérieur; (in rank, exam) premier; (chief) principal; (best) meilleur; (great, distinguished) éminent; (maximum) maximum; **in t. gear** Aut en quatrième vitesse; **at t. speed** à toute vitesse; **t. hat** (chapeau m) haut-de-forme m. ◆**t.-'flight** a Fam excellent. ◆**t.-'heavy** a trop lourd du haut. ◆**t.-level** a (talks etc) au sommet. ◆**t.-'notch** a Fam excellent. ◆**t.-'ranking** a (official) haut placé. ◆**t.-'secret** a ultra-secret.

top[2] [tɒp] vt (-pp-) (exceed) dépasser; **to t. up** (glass etc) remplir (de nouveau); (coffee, oil etc) rajouter; **and to t. it all** . . . et pour comble . . . ; **topped with** Culin nappé de.

top[3] [tɒp] n (toy) toupie f.

topaz ['təʊpæz] n (gem) topaze f.

topic ['tɒpɪk] n sujet m. ◆**topical** a d'actualité. ◆**topi'cality** n actualité f.

topless ['tɒpləs] a (woman) aux seins nus.

topography [tə'pɒgrəfɪ] n topographie f.

topple ['tɒp(ə)l] vi **to t. (over)** tomber; – vt **to t. (over)** faire tomber.

topsy-turvy [tɒpsɪ'tɜːvɪ] a & adv sens dessus dessous.

torch [tɔːtʃ] n (burning) torche f, flambeau m; (electric) lampe f électrique. ◆**torchlight** n & a **by t.** à la lumière des flambeaux; **t. procession** retraite f aux flambeaux.

tore [tɔːr] see **tear**[1].

torment [tɔː'ment] vt (make suffer) tourmenter; (annoy) agacer; – ['tɔːment] n tourment m.

tornado [tɔː'neɪdəʊ] n (pl -oes) tornade f.

torpedo [tɔː'piːdəʊ] n (pl -oes) torpille f; **t. boat** torpilleur m; – vt torpiller.

torrent ['tɒrənt] n torrent m. ◆**torrential** [tə'renʃ(ə)l] a torrentiel.

torrid ['tɒrɪd] a (love affair etc) brûlant, passionné; (climate, weather) torride.

torso ['tɔːsəʊ] n (pl -os) torse m.

tortoise ['tɔːtəs] n tortue f. ◆**tortoiseshell** a (comb etc) en écaille; (spectacles) à monture d'écaille.

tortuous ['tɔːtʃʊəs] a tortueux.

tortur/e ['tɔːtʃər] n torture f; – vt torturer. ◆**-er** n tortionnaire m.

Tory ['tɔːrɪ] n tory m; – a tory inv.

toss [tɒs] vt (throw) jeter, lancer (**to** à); **to t. s.o. (about)** (of boat, vehicle) ballotter qn, faire tressauter qn; **to t. a coin** jouer à pile ou à face; **to t. back** (one's head) rejeter en arrière; – vi **to t. (about), t. and turn** (in one's sleep etc) se tourner et se retourner; **we'll t. (up) for it, we'll t. up** on va jouer à pile ou à face; – n **with a t. of the head** d'un mouvement brusque de la tête. ◆**t.-up** n **it's a t.-up whether he leaves or stays** Sl il y a autant de chances pour qu'il parte ou pour qu'il reste.

tot [tɒt] **1** n (tiny) **t.** petit(e) enfant mf. **2** vt (-tt-) **to t. up** (total) Fam additionner.

total ['təʊt(ə)l] a total; **the t. sales** le total des ventes; – n total m; **in t.** au total; – vt (-ll-, Am -l-) (of debt, invoice) s'élever à; **to t. (up)** (find the total of) totaliser; **that totals $9** ça fait neuf dollars en tout. ◆**—ly** adv totalement.

totalitarian [təʊtælɪ'teərɪən] a Pol totalitaire.

tote [təʊt] **1** n Sp Fam pari m mutuel. **2** vt (gun) porter.

totter ['tɒtər] vi chanceler.

touch [tʌtʃ] n (contact) contact m, toucher m; (sense) toucher m; (of painter) & Fb Rugby touche f; **a t. of** (small amount) un petit peu de, un soupçon de; **the finishing**

touches la dernière touche; **in t. with** (*person*) en contact avec; (*events*) au courant de; **to be out of t. with** ne plus être en contact avec; (*events*) ne plus être au courant de; **to get in t.** se mettre en contact (**with** avec); **we lost t.** on s'est perdu de vue; − *vt* toucher; (*lay a finger on, tamper with, eat*) toucher à; (*move emotionally*) toucher; (*equal*) Fig égaler; **to t. up** retoucher; **I don't t. the stuff** (*beer etc*) je n'en bois jamais; − *vi* (*of lines, ends etc*) se toucher; **don't t.!** n'y *or* ne touche pas!; **he's always touching** c'est un touche-à-tout; **to t. down** (*of aircraft*) atterrir; **to t. on** (*subject*) toucher à. ◆**─ed** *a* (*emotionally*) touché (by dc); (*crazy*) Fam cinglé. ◆**─ing** *a* (*story etc*) touchant. ◆**touch-and-'go** *a* (*uncertain*) Fam douteux. ◆**touchdown** *n* Av atterrissage *m*. ◆**touchline** *n* Fb Rugby (ligne *f* de) touche *f*.

touchy ['tʌtʃi] *a* (**-ier, -iest**) (*sensitive*) susceptible (**about** à propos de).

tough [tʌf] *a* (**-er, -est**) (*hard*) dur; (*meat, businessman*) coriace; (*sturdy*) solide; (*strong*) fort; (*relentless*) acharné; (*difficult*) difficile, dur; **t. guy** dur *m*; **t. luck!** Fam pas de chance!, quelle déveine!; − *n* (*tough guy*) Fam dur *m*. ◆**toughen** *vt* (*body, person*) endurcir; (*reinforce*) renforcer. ◆**toughness** *n* dureté *f*; solidité *f*; force *f*.

toupee ['tuːpei] *n* postiche *m*.

tour [tuər] *n* (*journey*) voyage *m*; (*visit*) visite *f*; (*by artist, team etc*) tournée *f*; (*on bicycle, on foot*) randonnée *f*; **on t.** en voyage; en tournée; **a t. of** (*France*) un voyage en; une tournée en; une randonnée en; − *vt* visiter; (*of artist etc*) être en tournée en *or* dans *etc*. ◆**─ing** *n* tourisme *m*; **to go t.** faire du tourisme. ◆**tourism** *n* tourisme *m*. ◆**tourist** *n* touriste *mf*; − *a* touristique; (*class*) touriste *inv*; **t. office** syndicat *m* d'initiative. ◆**touristy** *a* Pej Fam (trop) touristique.

tournament ['tuənəmənt] *n* Sp & Hist tournoi *m*.

tousled ['tauz(ə)ld] *a* (*hair*) ébouriffé.

tout [taut] *vi* racoler; **to t. for** (*customers*) racoler; − *n* racoleur, -euse *mf*; **ticket t.** revendeur, -euse *mf* (en fraude) de billets.

tow [təu] *vt* (*car, boat*) remorquer; (*caravan, trailer*) tracter; **to t. away** (*vehicle*) Jur emmener à la fourrière; − *n* '**on t.**' 'en remorque'; **t. truck** (*breakdown lorry*) Am dépanneuse *f*. ◆**towpath** *n* chemin *m* de halage. ◆**towrope** *n* (câble *m* de) remorque *f*.

toward(s) [tə'wɔːd(z), Am tɔːd(z)] *prep* vers;

(*of feelings*) envers; **money t.** de l'argent pour (acheter).

towel ['tauəl] *n* serviette *f* (de toilette); (*for dishes*) torchon *m*; **t. rail** porte-serviettes *m inv*. ◆**towelling** *n*, Am ◆**toweling** *n* tissu-éponge *m*; (**kitchen**) **t.** Am essuie-tout *m inv*.

tower ['tauər] *n* tour *f*; **t. block** tour *f*, immeuble *m*; **ivory t.** Fig tour *f* d'ivoire; − *vi* **to t. above** *or* **over** dominer. ◆**─ing** *a* très haut.

town [taun] *n* ville *f*; **in t., (in)to t.** en ville; **out of t.** en province; **country t.** bourg *m*; **t. centre** centre-ville *m*; **t. clerk** secrétaire *mf* de mairie; **t. council** conseil *m* municipal; **t. hall** mairie *f*; **t. planner** urbaniste *mf*; **t. planning** urbanisme *m*. ◆**township** *n* (*in South Africa*) commune *f* (noire).

toxic ['tɒksik] *a* toxique. ◆**toxin** *n* toxine *f*.

toy [tɔi] *n* jouet *m*; **soft t.** (jouet *m* en) peluche *f*; − *a* (*gun*) d'enfant; (*house, car, train*) miniature; − *vi* **to t. with** jouer avec. ◆**toyshop** *n* magasin *m* de jouets.

trac/e [treis] *n* trace *f* (**of** de); **to vanish** *or* **disappear without (a) t.** disparaître sans laisser de traces; − *vt* (*draw*) tracer; (*with tracing paper*) (dé)calquer; (*locate*) retrouver (la trace de), dépister; (*follow*) suivre (la piste de) (**to** à); (*relate*) retracer; **to t. (back) to** (*one's family*) faire remonter jusqu'à. ◆**─ing** *n* (*drawing*) calque *m*; **t. paper** papier-calque *m inv*.

track [træk] *n* trace *f*, (*of bullet, rocket*) trajectoire *f*; (*of person, animal, tape recorder*) & Sp piste *f*; (*of record*) plage *f*; Rail voie *f*; (*path*) piste *f*, chemin *m*; Sch Am classe *f* (de niveau); **to keep t. of** suivre; **to lose t. of** (*friend*) perdre de vue; (*argument*) perdre le fil de; **to make tracks** Fam se sauver; **the right t.** la bonne voie *or* piste; **t. event** Sp épreuve *f* sur piste; **t. record** (*of person, firm etc*) Fig antécédents *mpl*; − *vt* **to t. (down)** (*locate*) retrouver, dépister; (*pursue*) traquer. ◆**─er** *a* **t. dog** chien *m* policier. ◆**tracksuit** *n* Sp survêtement *m*.

tract [trækt] *n* (*stretch of land*) étendue *f*.

traction ['trækʃ(ə)n] *n* Tech traction *f*.

tractor ['træktər] *n* tracteur *m*.

trade [treid] *n* commerce *m*; (*job*) métier *m*; (*exchange*) échange *m*; − *a* (*fair, balance, route*) commercial; (*price*) de (demi-)gros; (*secret*) de fabrication; (*barrier*) douanier; **t. union** syndicat *m*; **t. unionist** syndicaliste *mf*; − *vi* faire du commerce (**with** avec); **to t. in** (*sugar etc*) faire le commerce de; − *vt* (*exchange*) échanger (**for** contre); **to t. sth in** (*old article*) faire reprendre qch. ◆**t.-in** *n*

Com reprise *f*. ◆**t.-off** *n* échange *m*.
◆**trading** *n* commerce *m*; − *a* (*activity, port etc*) commercial; (*nation*) commerçant; **t. estate** zone *f* industrielle. ◆**trader** *n* commerçant, -ante *mf*; (*street*) **t.** vendeur, -euse *mf* de rue. ◆**tradesman** *n* (*pl* -men) commerçant *m*.

trademark ['treɪdmɑːk] *n* marque *f* de fabrique; (**registered**) **t.** marque déposée.

tradition [trə'dɪʃ(ə)n] *n* tradition *f*. ◆**tra-'ditional** *a* traditionnel. ◆**traditionally** *adv* traditionnellement.

traffic ['træfɪk] **1** *n* (*on road*) circulation *f*; *Av Nau Rail* trafic *m*; **busy** *or* **heavy t.** beaucoup de circulation; **heavy t.** (*vehicles*) poids *mpl* lourds; **t. circle** *Am* rond-point *m*; **t. cone** cône *m* de chantier; **t. jam** embouteillage *m*; **t. lights** feux *mpl* (de signalisation); (*when red*) feu *m* rouge; **t. sign** panneau *m* de signalisation. **2** *n* (*trade*) *Pej* trafic *m* (**in** de); − *vi* (**-ck-**) trafiquer (**in** de). ◆**trafficker** *n Pej* trafiquant, -ante *mf*.

tragedy ['trædʒədɪ] *n Th & Fig* tragédie *f*. ◆**tragic** *a* tragique. ◆**tragically** *adv* tragiquement.

trail [treɪl] *n* (*of powder, smoke, blood etc*) traînée *f*; (*track*) piste *f*, trace *f*; (*path*) sentier *m*; **in its t.** (*wake*) dans son sillage; − *vt* (*drag*) traîner; (*caravan*) tracter; (*follow*) suivre (la piste de); − *vi* (*on the ground etc*) traîner; (*of plant*) ramper; **to t. behind** (*lag behind*) traîner. ◆**—er** *n* **1** *Aut* remorque *f*; *Am* caravane *f*. **2** *Cin* bande *f* annonce.

train [treɪn] **1** *n* (*engine, transport, game*) train *m*; (*underground*) rame *f*; (*procession*) *Fig* file *f*; (*of events*) suite *f*; (*of dress*) traîne *f*; **my t. of thought** le fil de ma pensée; **t. set** train *m* électrique. **2** *vt* (*teach, develop*) former (**to do** à faire); *Sp* entraîner; (*animal, child*) dresser (**to do** à faire); (*ear*) exercer; **to t. oneself to do** s'entraîner à faire; **to t. sth on** (*aim*) braquer qch sur; − *vi* recevoir une formation (**as a doctor**/*etc* de médecin/*etc*); *Sp* s'entraîner. ◆**—ed** *a* (*having professional skill*) qualifié; (*nurse etc*) diplômé; (*animal*) dressé; (*ear*) exercé. ◆**—ing** *n* formation *f*; *Sp* entraînement *m*; (*of animal*) dressage *m*; **to be in t.** *Sp* s'entraîner; (**teachers'**) **t. college** école *f* normale. ◆**trai'nee** *n & a* stagiaire *mf*. ◆**trainer** *n* (*of athlete, racehorse*) entraîneur *m*; (*of dog, lion etc*) dresseur *m*; (*running shoe*) jogging *m*, chaussure *f* de sport.

traipse [treɪps] *vi Fam* (*tiredly*) traîner les pieds; **to t.** (**about**) (*wander*) se balader.

trait [treɪt] *n* (*of character*) trait *m*.

traitor ['treɪtər] *n* traître *m*.

trajectory [trə'dʒektərɪ] *n* trajectoire *f*.

tram [træm] *n* tram(way) *m*.

tramp [træmp] **1** *n* (*vagrant*) clochard, -arde *mf*; (*woman*) *Pej Am* traînée *f*. **2** *vi* (*walk*) marcher d'un pas lourd; (*hike*) marcher à pied; − *vt* (*streets etc*) parcourir; − *n* (*sound*) pas lourds *mpl*; (*hike*) randonnée *f*.

trample ['træmp(ə)l] *vti* **to t. sth** (*underfoot*), **t. on sth** piétiner qch.

trampoline [træmpə'liːn] *n* trampoline *m*.

trance [trɑːns] *n* **in a t.** (*mystic*) en transe.

tranquil ['træŋkwɪl] *a* tranquille. ◆**tran-'quillity** *n* tranquillité *f*. ◆**tranquillizer** *n Med* tranquillisant *m*.

trans- [træns, trænz] *pref* trans-.

transact [træn'zækt] *vt* (*business*) traiter. ◆**transaction** *n* (*in bank etc*) opération *f*; (*on Stock Market*) transaction *f*; **the t. of** (*business*) la conduite de.

transatlantic [trænzət'læntɪk] *a* transatlantique.

transcend [træn'send] *vt* transcender. ◆**transcendent** *a* transcendant.

transcribe [træn'skraɪb] *vt* transcrire. ◆**'transcript** *n* (*document*) transcription *f*. ◆**transcription** *n* transcription *f*.

transfer [træns'fɜːr] *vt* (**-rr-**) (*person, goods etc*) transférer (**to** à); (*power*) *Pol* faire passer (**to** à); **to t. the charges** téléphoner en PCV; − *vi* être transféré (**to** à); − ['trænsfɜːr] *n* transfert *m* (**to** à); (*of power*) *Pol* passation *f*; (*image*) décalcomanie *f*; **bank** *or* **credit t.** virement *m* (bancaire). ◆**trans'ferable** *a* **not t.** (*on ticket*) strictement personnel.

transform [træns'fɔːm] *vt* transformer (**into** en). ◆**transfor'mation** *n* transformation *f*. ◆**transformer** *n El* transformateur *m*.

transfusion [træns'fjuːʒ(ə)n] *n* (**blood**) **t.** transfusion *f* (sanguine).

transient ['trænzɪənt] *a* (*ephemeral*) transitoire.

transistor [træn'zɪstər] *n* (*device*) transistor *m*; **t.** (**radio**) transistor *m*.

transit ['trænzɪt] *n* transit *m*; **in t.** en transit.

transition [træn'zɪʃ(ə)n] *n* transition *f*. ◆**transitional** *a* de transition, transitoire.

transitive ['trænzɪtɪv] *a Gram* transitif.

transitory ['trænzɪtərɪ] *a* transitoire.

translate [træns'leɪt] *vt* traduire (**from** de, **into** en). ◆**translation** *n* traduction *f*; (*into mother tongue*) *Sch* version *f*; (*from mother tongue*) *Sch* thème *m*. ◆**translator** *n* traducteur, -trice *mf*.

transmit [trænz'mɪt] *vt* (**-tt-**) (*send, pass*)

transmettre; − *vti* (*broadcast*) émettre. ◆**transmission** *n* transmission *f*; (*broadcast*) émission *f*. ◆**transmitter** *n* Rad TV émetteur *m*.

transparent [træns'pærənt] *a* transparent. ◆**transparency** *n* transparence *f*; (*slide*) Phot diapositive *f*.

transpire [træn'spaɪər] *vi* (*of secret etc*) s'ébruiter; (*happen*) Fam arriver; **it transpired that . . .** il s'est avéré que . . . .

transplant [træns'plɑːnt] *vt* (*plant*) transplanter; (*organ*) Med greffer, transplanter; − ['trænsplɑːnt] *n* Med greffe *f*, transplantation *f*.

transport [træn'spɔːt] *vt* transporter; − ['trænspɔːt] *n* transport *m*; **public t.** les transports en commun; **do you have a t.?** es-tu motorisé?; **t. café** routier *m*. ◆**transpor'tation** *n* transport *m*.

transpose [træns'pəʊz] *vt* transposer.

transvestite [trænz'vestaɪt] *n* travesti *m*.

trap [træp] *n* piège *m*; (*mouth*) Pej Sl gueule *f*; **t. door** trappe *f*; − *vt* (*-pp-*) (*snare*) prendre (au piège); (*jam, corner*) coincer, bloquer; (*cut off by snow etc*) bloquer (**by** par); **to t. one's finger** se coincer le doigt. ◆**trapper** *n* (*hunter*) trappeur *m*.

trapeze [trə'piːz] *n* (*in circus*) trapèze *m*; **t. artist** trapéziste *mf*.

trappings ['træpɪŋz] *npl* signes *mpl* extérieurs.

trash [træʃ] *n* (*nonsense*) sottises *fpl*; (*junk*) saleté(s) *f*(*pl*); (*waste*) Am ordures *fpl*; (*riffraff*) Am racaille *f*. ◆**trashcan** *n* Am poubelle *f*. ◆**trashy** *a* (**-ier, -iest**) (*book etc*) moche, sans valeur; (*goods*) de camelote.

trauma ['trɔːmə, 'traʊmə] *n* (*shock*) traumatisme *m*. ◆**trau'matic** *a* traumatisant. ◆**traumatize** *vt* traumatiser.

travel ['trævəl] *vi* (**-ll-,** Am **-l-**) voyager; (*move*) aller, se déplacer; − *vt* (*country, distance, road*) parcourir; − *n* & *npl* voyages *mpl*; **on one's travels** en voyage; − *a* (*agency, book*) de voyages; **t. brochure** dépliant *m* touristique. ◆**travelled** *a* **to be well** *or* **widely t.** avoir beaucoup voyagé. ◆**travelling** *n* voyages *mpl*; − *a* (*bag etc*) de voyage; (*expenses*) de déplacement; (*circus, musician*) ambulant. ◆**traveller** *n* voyageur, -euse *mf*; **traveller's cheque,** Am **traveler's check** chèque *m* de voyage. ◆**travelogue** *n*, Am ◆**travelog** *n* (*book*) récit *m* de voyages. ◆**travelsickness** *n* (*in car*) mal *m* de la route; (*in aircraft*) mal de l'air.

travesty ['trævəstɪ] *n* parodie *f*.

travolator ['trævəleɪtər] *n* trottoir *m* roulant.

trawler ['trɔːlər] *n* (*ship*) chalutier *m*.

tray [treɪ] *n* plateau *m*; (*for office correspondence etc*) corbeille *f*.

treacherous ['tretʃ(ə)rəs] *a* (*person, action, road, journey etc*) traître. ◆**treacherously** *adv* traîtreusement; (*dangerously*) dangereusement. ◆**treachery** *n* traîtrise *f*.

treacle ['triːk(ə)l] *n* mélasse *f*.

tread [tred] *vi* (*pt* **trod,** *pp* **trodden**) (*walk*) marcher (**on** sur); (*proceed*) Fig avancer; − *vt* (*path*) parcourir; (*soil*) Fig fouler; **to t. sth into a carpet** étaler qch (avec les pieds) sur un tapis; − *n* (*step*) pas *m*; (*of tyre*) chape *f*. ◆**treadmill** *n* Pej Fig routine *f*.

treason ['triːz(ə)n] *n* trahison *f*.

treasure ['treʒər] *n* trésor *m*; **a real t.** (*person*) Fig une vraie perle; **t. hunt** chasse *f* au trésor; − *vt* (*value*) tenir à, priser; (*keep*) conserver (précieusement). ◆**treasurer** *n* trésorier, -ière *mf*. ◆**Treasury** *n* **the T.** Pol = le ministère des Finances.

treat [triːt] **1** *vt* (*person, product etc*) & Med traiter; (*consider*) considérer (**as** comme); **to t. with care** prendre soin de; **to t. s.o. to sth** offrir qch à qn. **2** *n* (*pleasure*) plaisir *m* (spécial); (*present*) cadeau-surprise *m*; (*meal*) régal *m*; **it was a t. (for me) to do it** ça m'a fait plaisir de le faire. ◆**treatment** *n* (*behaviour*) & Med traitement *m*; **his t. of her** la façon dont il la traite; **rough t.** mauvais traitements *mpl*.

treatise ['triːtɪz] *n* (*book*) traité *m* (**on** de).

treaty ['triːtɪ] *n* Pol traité *m*.

treble ['treb(ə)l] *a* triple; − *vti* tripler; − *n* le triple; **it's t. the price** c'est le triple du prix.

tree [triː] *n* arbre *m*; **Christmas t.** sapin *m* de Noël; **family t.** arbre *m* généalogique. ◆**t.-lined** *a* bordé d'arbres. ◆**t.-top** *n* cime *f* (d'un arbre). ◆**t.-trunk** *n* tronc *m* d'arbre.

trek [trek] *vi* (**-kk-**) cheminer *or* voyager (péniblement); Sp marcher à pied; (*go*) Fam traîner; − *n* voyage *m* (pénible); Sp randonnée *f*; (*distance*) Fam tirée *f*.

trellis ['trelɪs] *n* treillage *m*.

tremble ['tremb(ə)l] *vi* trembler (**with** de). ◆**tremor** *n* tremblement *m*; (**earth) t.** secousse *f* (sismique).

tremendous [trə'mendəs] *a* (*huge*) énorme; (*dreadful*) terrible; (*wonderful*) formidable, terrible. ◆**—ly** *adv* terriblement.

trench [trentʃ] *n* tranchée *f*.

trend [trend] *n* tendance *f* (**towards** à); **the t.** (*fashion*) la mode; **to set a** *or* **the t.** donner le ton, lancer une *or* la mode. ◆**trendy** *a* (-ier, -iest) (*person, clothes, topic etc*) *Fam* à la mode, dans le vent.

trepidation [trepɪ'deɪʃ(ə)n] *n* inquiétude *f.*

trespass ['trespəs] *vi* s'introduire sans autorisation (**on**, **upon** dans); '**no trespassing**' 'entrée interdite'.

tresses ['tresɪz] *npl Lit* chevelure *f.*

trestle ['tres(ə)l] *n* tréteau *m.*

trial ['traɪəl] *n Jur* procès *m*; (*test*) essai *m*; (*ordeal*) épreuve *f*; **t. of strength** épreuve de force; **to go** *or* **be on t.**, **stand t.** passer en jugement; **to put s.o. on t.** juger qn; **by t. and error** par tâtonnements; – *a* (*period, flight etc*) d'essai; (*offer*) à l'essai; **t. run** (*of new product etc*) période *f* d'essai.

triangle ['traɪæŋg(ə)l] *n* triangle *m*; (*setsquare*) *Math Am* équerre *f.* ◆**tri-'angular** *a* triangulaire.

tribe [traɪb] *n* tribu *f.* ◆**tribal** *a* tribal.

tribulations [trɪbjʊ'leɪʃ(ə)nz] *npl* (**trials and**) **t.** tribulations *fpl.*

tribunal [traɪ'bjuːn(ə)l] *n* commission *f*, tribunal *m*; *Mil* tribunal *m.*

tributary ['trɪbjʊtərɪ] *n* affluent *m.*

tribute ['trɪbjuːt] *n* hommage *m*, tribut *m*; **to pay t.** to rendre hommage à.

trick [trɪk] *n* (*joke, deception* & *of conjurer etc*) tour *m*; (*ruse*) astuce *f*; (*habit*) manie *f*; **to play a t. on s.o.** jouer un tour à qn; **card t.** tour *m* de cartes; **that will do the t.** *Fam* ça fera l'affaire; **t. photo** photo *f* truquée; **t. question** question-piège *f*; – *vt* (*deceive*) tromper, attraper; **to t. s.o. into doing sth** amener qn à faire qch par la ruse. ◆**trickery** *n* ruse *f.* ◆**tricky** *a* (-ier, -iest) (*problem etc*) difficile, délicat; (*person*) rusé.

trickle ['trɪk(ə)l] *n* (*of liquid*) filet *m*; **a t. of** (*letters, people etc*) *Fig* un petit nombre de; – *vi* (*flow*) dégouliner, couler (lentement); **to t. in** (*of letters, people etc*) *Fig* arriver en petit nombre.

tricycle ['traɪsɪk(ə)l] *n* tricycle *m.*

trier ['traɪər] *n* **to be a t.** être persévérant.

trifl/e ['traɪf(ə)l] *n* (*article, money*) bagatelle *f*, (*dessert*) diplomate *m*; – *adv* **a t. small/too much/etc** un tantinet petit/trop/etc; – *vi* **to t. with** (*s.o.'s feelings*) jouer avec; (*person*) plaisanter avec. ◆—**ing** *a* insignifiant.

trigger ['trɪgər] *n* (*of gun*) gâchette *f*; – *vt* **to t. (off)** (*start, cause*) déclencher.

trilogy ['trɪlədʒɪ] *n* trilogie *f.*

trim [trɪm] **1** *a* (**trimmer**, **trimmest**) (*neat*) soigné, net; (*slim*) svelte; – *n* **in t.** (*fit*) en (bonne) forme. **2** *n* (*cut*) légère coupe *f*; (*haircut*) coupe *f* de rafraîchissement; **to**

have a t. se faire rafraîchir les cheveux; – *vt* (-mm-) couper (légèrement); (*finger nail, edge*) rogner; (*hair*) rafraîchir. **3** *n* (*on garment*) garniture *f*; (*on car*) garnitures *fpl*; – *vt* (-mm-) **to t. with** (*lace etc*) orner de. ◆**trimmings** *npl* garniture(s) *f(pl)*; (*extras*) *Fig* accessoires *mpl.*

Trinity ['trɪnɪtɪ] *n* **the T.** (*union*) *Rel* la Trinité.

trinket ['trɪŋkɪt] *n* colifichet *m.*

trio ['triːəʊ] *n* (*pl* **-os**) (*group*) & *Mus* trio *m.*

trip [trɪp] **1** *n* (*journey*) voyage *m*; (*outing*) excursion *f*; **to take a t. to** (*cinema, shops etc*) aller à. **2** *n* (*stumble*) faux pas *m*; – *vi* (-pp-) **to t. (over** *or* **up)** trébucher; **to t. over sth** trébucher contre qch; – *vt* **to t. s.o. up** faire trébucher qn. **3** *vi* (-pp-) (*walk gently*) marcher d'un pas léger. ◆**tripper** *n* **day t.** excursionniste *mf.*

tripe [traɪp] *n Culin* tripes *fpl*; (*nonsense*) *Fam* bêtises *fpl.*

triple ['trɪp(ə)l] *a* triple; – *vti* tripler. ◆**triplets** *npl* (*children*) triplés, -ées *mfpl.*

triplicate ['trɪplɪkət] *n* **in t.** en trois exemplaires.

tripod ['traɪpɒd] *n* trépied *m.*

trite [traɪt] *a* banal. ◆—**ness** *n* banalité *f.*

triumph ['traɪʌmf] *n* triomphe *m* (**over** sur); – *vi* triompher (**over** de). ◆**tri'umphal** *a* triomphal. ◆**tri'umphant** *a* (*team, army, gesture*) triomphant; (*success, welcome, return*) triomphal. ◆**tri'umphantly** *adv* triomphalement.

trivia ['trɪvɪə] *npl* vétilles *fpl.* ◆**trivial** *a* (*unimportant*) insignifiant; (*trite*) banal. ◆**trivi'ality** *n* insignifiance *f*; banalité *f*; *pl* banalités *fpl.*

trod, trodden [trɒd, 'trɒd(ə)n] *see* **tread.**

trolley ['trɒlɪ] *n* (*for luggage*) chariot *m*; (*for shopping*) poussette *f* (de marché); (*in supermarket*) caddie® *m*; (*trolleybus*) trolley *m*; (**tea**) **t. table** *f* roulante; (*for tea urn*) chariot *m*; **t. (car)** *Am* tramway *m.* ◆**trolleybus** *n* trolleybus *m.*

trombone [trɒm'bəʊn] *n Mus* trombone *m.*

troop [truːp] *n* bande *f*; *Mil* troupe *f*; **the troops** (*army, soldiers*) les troupes, la troupe; – *vi* **to t. in/out/etc** entrer/sortir/etc en masse. ◆—**ing** *n* **t. the colour** le salut du drapeau. ◆—**er** *n* (*state*) **t.** *Am* membre *m* de la police montée.

trophy ['trəʊfɪ] *n* trophée *m.*

tropic ['trɒpɪk] *n* tropique *m.* ◆**tropical** *a* tropical.

trot [trɒt] *n* (*of horse*) trot *m*; **on the t.** (*one after another*) *Fam* de suite; – *vi* (-tt-) trotter; **to t. off** or **along** (leave) Hum Fam se sauver; − vt **to t. out** (say) Fam débiter.

troubl/e ['trʌb(ə)l] n (difficulty) ennui(s) m(pl); (bother, effort) peine f, mal m; **trouble(s)** (social unrest etc) & Med troubles mpl; **to be in t.** avoir des ennuis; **to get into t.** s'attirer des ennuis (with avec); **the t. (with you) is . . .** l'ennui (avec toi) c'est que . . . ; **to go to the t. of doing, take the t. to do** se donner la peine or le mal de faire; **I didn't put her to any t.** je ne l'ai pas dérangée; **to find the t.** trouver le problème; **a spot of t.** un petit problème; **a t. spot** Pol un point chaud; − vt (inconvenience) déranger, ennuyer; (worry, annoy) ennuyer; (hurt) faire mal à; (grieve) peiner; **to t. to do** se donner la peine de faire; − vi **to t. (oneself)** se déranger. ◆**—ed** a (worried) inquiet; (period) agité. ◆**trouble-free** a (machine, vehicle) qui ne tombe jamais en panne, fiable. ◆**troublemaker** n fauteur m de troubles. ◆**troubleshooter** n Tech dépanneur m, expert m; Pol conciliateur, -trice mf.

troublesome ['trʌb(ə)ls(ə)m] a ennuyeux, gênant; (leg etc) qui fait mal.

trough [trɒf] n (for drinking) abreuvoir m; (for feeding) auge f; **t. of low pressure** Met dépression f.

trounce [traʊns] vt (defeat) écraser.

troupe [truːp] n Th troupe f.

trousers ['traʊzəz] npl pantalon m; **a pair of t., some t.** un pantalon; **(short) t.** culottes fpl courtes.

trousseau ['truːsəʊ] n (of bride) trousseau m.

trout [traʊt] n truite f.

trowel ['traʊəl] n (for cement or plaster) truelle f; (for plants) déplantoir m.

truant ['truːənt] n (pupil, shirker) absentéiste mf; **to play t.** faire l'école buissonnière. ◆**truancy** n Sch absentéisme m scolaire.

truce [truːs] n Mil trêve f.

truck [trʌk] n **1** (lorry) camion m; Rail wagon m plat; **t. driver** camionneur m; (long-distance) routier m; **t. stop** (restaurant) routier m. **2 t. farmer** Am maraîcher, -ère mf. ◆**trucker** n Am (haulier) transporteur m routier; (driver) camionneur m, routier m.

truculent ['trʌkjʊlənt] a agressif.

trudge [trʌdʒ] vi marcher d'un pas pesant.

true [truː] a (-er, -est) vrai; (accurate) exact; (genuine) vrai, véritable; **t. to** (person, promise etc) fidèle à; **t. to life** conforme à la réalité; **to come t.** se réaliser; **to hold t.** (of argument etc) valoir (for pour); **too t.!** Fam

ah, ça oui! ◆**truly** adv vraiment; (faithfully) fidèlement; **well and t.** bel et bien.

truffle ['trʌf(ə)l] n (mushroom) truffe f.

truism ['truːɪz(ə)m] n lapalissade f.

trump [trʌmp] **1** n Cards atout m; **t. card** (advantage) Fig atout m. **2** vt **to t. up** (charge, reason) inventer.

trumpet ['trʌmpɪt] n trompette f; **t. player** trompettiste mf.

truncate [trʌŋ'keɪt] vt tronquer.

truncheon ['trʌntʃ(ə)n] n matraque f.

trundle ['trʌnd(ə)l] vti **to t. along** rouler bruyamment.

trunk [trʌŋk] n (of tree, body) tronc m; (of elephant) trompe f; (case) malle f; (of vehicle) Am coffre m; pl (for swimming) slip m or caleçon m de bain; **t. call** Tel communication f interurbaine; **t. road** route f nationale.

truss [trʌs] vt **to t. (up)** (prisoner) ligoter.

trust [trʌst] n (faith) confiance f (in en); (group) Fin trust m; Jur fidéicommis m; **to take on t.** accepter de confiance; − vt (person, judgement) avoir confiance en, se fier à; (instinct, promise) se fier à; **to t. s.o. with sth, t. sth to s.o.** confier qch à qn; **to t. s.o. to do** (rely on, expect) compter sur qn pour faire; **I t. that** (hope) j'espère que; − vi **to t. in s.o.** se fier à qn; **to t. to luck** or **chance** se fier au hasard. ◆**—ed** a (friend, method etc) éprouvé. ◆**—ing** a confiant. ◆**trus'tee** n (of school) administrateur -trice mf. ◆**trustworthy** a sûr, digne de confiance.

truth [truːθ] n (pl -s [truːðz]) vérité f; **there's some t. in . . .** il y a du vrai dans . . . . ◆**truthful** a (statement etc) véridique, vrai; (person) sincère. ◆**truthfully** adv sincèrement.

try [traɪ] **1** vt essayer (**to do, doing** de faire); (s.o.'s patience etc) mettre à l'épreuve; **to t. one's hand at** s'essayer à; **to t. one's luck** tenter sa chance; **to t. (out)** (car, method etc) essayer; (employee etc) mettre à l'essai; **to t. on** (clothes, shoes) essayer; − vi essayer (for sth d'obtenir qch); **to t. hard** faire un gros effort; **t. and come!** essaie de venir!; − n (attempt) & Rugby essai m; **to have a t.** essayer; **at (the) first t.** du premier coup. **2** vt (person) Jur juger (**for theft**/etc pour vol/etc). ◆**—ing** a pénible, éprouvant.

tsar [zɑːr] n tsar m.

tub [tʌb] n (for washing clothes etc) baquet m; (bath) baignoire f; (for ice cream etc) pot m.

tuba ['tjuːbə] n Mus tuba m.

tubby ['tʌbɪ] a (-ier, -iest) Fam dodu.

tube [tjuːb] *n* tube *m*; *Rail Fam* métro *m*; *(of tyre)* chambre *f* à air. ◆**tubing** *n (tubes)* tubes *mpl*. ◆**tubular** *a* tubulaire.

tuberculosis [tjuːbɜːkjuˈləʊsɪs] *n* tuberculose *f*.

tuck [tʌk] **1** *n (fold in garment)* rempli *m*; – *vt (put)* mettre; **to t. away** ranger; *(hide)* cacher; **to t. in** *(shirt)* rentrer; *(person in bed, a blanket)* border; **to t. up** *(skirt)* remonter. **2** *vi* **to t. in** *(eat) Fam* manger; **to t. into** *(meal) Fam* attaquer; – *n* **t. shop** *Sch* boutique *f* à provisions.

Tuesday [ˈtjuːzdɪ] *n* mardi *m*.

tuft [tʌft] *n (of hair, grass)* touffe *f*.

tug [tʌg] **1** *vt* (**-gg-**) *(pull)* tirer; – *vi* tirer (**at, on** sur); – *n* **to give sth a t.** tirer (sur) qch. **2** *n (boat)* remorqueur *m*.

tuition [tjuːˈɪʃ(ə)n] *n (teaching)* enseignement *m*; *(lessons)* leçons *fpl*; *(fee)* frais *mpl* de scolarité.

tulip [ˈtjuːlɪp] *n* tulipe *f*.

tumble [ˈtʌmb(ə)l] *vi* **to t. (over)** *(fall)* dégringoler; *(backwards)* tomber à la renverse; **to t. to sth** *(understand) Sl* réaliser qch; – *n (fall)* dégringolade *f*. **t. drier** sèche-linge *m inv*.

tumbledown [ˈtʌmb(ə)ldaʊn] *a* délabré.

tumbler [ˈtʌmblər] *n (drinking glass)* gobelet *m*.

tummy [ˈtʌmɪ] *n Fam* ventre *m*.

tumour [ˈtjuːmər] *n* tumeur *f*.

tumult [ˈtjuːmʌlt] *n* tumulte *m*. ◆**tu'multuous** *a* tumultueux.

tuna [ˈtjuːnə] *n* **t. (fish)** thon *m*.

tun/e [tjuːn] *n (melody)* air *m*; **to be** *or* **sing in t./out of t.** chanter juste/faux; **in t.** *(instrument)* accordé; **out of t.** *(instrument)* désaccordé; **in t. with** *(harmony) Fig* en accord avec; **to the t. of £50** d'un montant de 50 livres, dans les 50 livres; – *vt* **to t. (up)** *Mus* accorder; *Aut* régler; – *vi* **to t. in (to)** *Rad TV* se mettre à l'écoute (de), écouter. ◆**—ing** *n Aut* réglage *m*; **t. fork** *Mus* diapason *m*. ◆**tuneful** *a* mélodieux.

tunic [ˈtjuːnɪk] *n* tunique *f*.

Tunisia [tjuːˈnɪzɪə] *n* Tunisie *f*. ◆**Tunisian** *a* & *n* tunisien, -ienne *(mf)*.

tunnel [ˈtʌn(ə)l] *n* tunnel *m*; *(in mine)* galerie *f*; – *vi* (**-ll-**, *Am* **-l-**) percer un tunnel *(into* dans).

turban [ˈtɜːbən] *n* turban *m*.

turbine [ˈtɜːbaɪn, *Am* ˈtɜːbɪn] *n* turbine *f*.

turbulence [ˈtɜːbjʊləns] *n Phys Av* turbulences *fpl*.

turbulent [ˈtɜːbjʊlənt] *a (person etc)* turbulent.

tureen [tjʊˈriːn, təˈriːn] *n (soup)* **t.** soupière *f*.

turf [tɜːf] **1** *n (grass)* gazon *m*; **the t.** *Sp* le turf; **t. accountant** bookmaker *m*. **2** *vt* **to t. out** *(get rid of) Fam* jeter dehors.

turgid [ˈtɜːdʒɪd] *a (style, language)* boursouflé.

turkey [ˈtɜːkɪ] *n* dindon *m*, dinde *f*; *(as food)* dinde *f*.

Turkey [ˈtɜːkɪ] *n* Turquie *f*. ◆**Turk** *n* Turc *m*, Turque *f*. ◆**Turkish** *a* turc; **T. delight** *(sweet)* loukoum *m*; – *n (language)* turc *m*.

turmoil [ˈtɜːmɔɪl] *n* confusion *f*, trouble *m*; **in t.** en ébullition.

turn [tɜːn] *n (movement, action & in game etc)* tour *m*; *(in road)* tournant *m*; *(of events, mind)* tournure *f*; *Med* crise *f*; *Psy* choc *m*; *(act) Th* numéro *m*; **t. of phrase** tour *m or* tournure *f* (de phrase); **to take turns** se relayer; **in t.** à tour de rôle; **by turns** tour à tour; **in (one's) t.** à son tour; **it's your t. to play** c'est à toi de jouer; **to do s.o. a good t.** rendre service à qn; **the t. of the century** le début du siècle; – *vt* tourner; *(mechanically)* faire tourner; *(mattress, pancake)* retourner; **to turn s.o./sth into** *(change)* changer *or* transformer qn/qch en; **to t. sth red/yellow** rougir/jaunir qch; **to t. sth on s.o.** *(aim)* braquer qch sur qn; **she's turned twenty** elle a vingt ans passés; **it's turned seven** il est sept heures passées; **it turns my stomach** cela me soulève le cœur; – *vi (of wheel, driver etc)* tourner; *(turn head or body)* se (re)tourner *(towards* vers); *(become)* devenir; **to t. to** *(question, adviser etc)* se tourner vers; **to t. against** se retourner contre; **to t. into** *(change)* se changer *or* se transformer en. ■ **to t. around** *vi (of person)* se retourner; **to t. away** *vt (avert)* détourner (**from** de); *(refuse)* renvoyer *(qn)*; – *vi (stop facing)* détourner les yeux, se détourner; **to t. back** *vt (bed sheet, corner of page)* replier; *(person)* renvoyer; *(clock)* reculer (**to** jusqu'à); – *vi (return)* retourner (sur ses pas); **to t. down** *vt (fold down)* rabattre; *(gas, radio etc)* baisser; *(refuse)* refuser *(qn, offre etc)*; **to t. in** *vt (hand in)* rendre (**to** à); *(prisoner etc) Fam* livrer (à la police); – *vi (go to bed) Fam* se coucher; **to t. off** *vt (light, radio etc)* éteindre; *(tap)* fermer; *(machine)* arrêter; – *vi (in vehicle)* tourner; **to t. on** *vt (light, radio etc)* mettre, allumer; *(tap)* ouvrir; *(machine)* mettre en marche; **to t. s.o. on** *(sexually) Fam* exciter qn; – *vi* **to t. out** *vt (light)* éteindre; *(contents of box etc)* vider (**from** de); *(produce)* produire; – *vi (of crowds)* venir; *(happen)* se passer; **it turns out that** il s'avère que; **she turned out to be ...** elle s'est révélée être ...; **to t. over** vt (*page*) tourner; − vi (*of vehicle, person etc*) se retourner; (*of car engine*) tourner au ralenti; **to t. round** vt (*head, object*) tourner; (*vehicle*) faire faire demi-tour à; − vi (*of person*) se retourner; **to t. up** vt (*radio, light etc*) mettre plus fort; (*collar*) remonter; (*unearth, find*) déterrer; **a turned-up nose** un nez retroussé; − vi (*arrive*) arriver; (*be found*) être (re)trouvé. ◆**turning** n (*street*) petite rue f; (*bend in road*) tournant m; **t. circle** Aut rayon m de braquage; **t. point** (*in time*) tournant m. ◆**turner** n (*workman*) tourneur m.

turncoat ['tɜːnkəʊt] n renégat, -ate mf. ◆**turn-off** n (*in road*) embranchement m. ◆**turnout** n (*people*) assistance f; (*at polls*) participation f. ◆**turnover** n (*money*) Com chiffre m d'affaires; (*of stock*) Com rotation f; **staff t.** (*starting and leaving*) la rotation du personnel; **apple t.** chausson m (aux pommes). ◆**turnup** n (*on trousers*) revers m.

turnip ['tɜːnɪp] n navet m.

turnpike ['tɜːnpaɪk] n Am autoroute f à péage.

turnstile ['tɜːnstaɪl] n (*gate*) tourniquet m.

turntable ['tɜːnteɪb(ə)l] n (*of record player*) platine f.

turpentine ['tɜːpəntaɪn] (*Fam* **turps** [tɜːps]) n térébenthine f.

turquoise ['tɜːkwɔɪz] a turquoise inv.

turret ['tʌrɪt] n tourelle f.

turtle ['tɜːt(ə)l] n tortue f de mer; Am tortue f. ◆**turtleneck** a (*sweater*) à col roulé; − n col m roulé.

tusk [tʌsk] n (*of elephant*) défense f.

tussle ['tʌs(ə)l] n bagarre f.

tutor ['tjuːtər] n précepteur, -trice mf; Univ directeur, -trice mf d'études; Univ Am assistant, -ante mf; − vt donner des cours particuliers à. ◆**tu'torial** n Univ travaux mpl dirigés.

tut-tut! [tʌt'tʌt] int allons donc!

tuxedo [tʌk'siːdəʊ] n (pl **-os**) Am smoking m.

TV [tiː'viː] n télé f.

twaddle ['twɒd(ə)l] n fadaises fpl.

twang [twæŋ] n son m vibrant; (**nasal**) **t.** nasillement m; − vi (*of wire etc*) vibrer.

twee [twiː] a (*fussy*) maniéré.

tweed [twiːd] n tweed m.

tweezers ['twiːzəz] npl pince f (à épiler).

twelve [twelv] a & n douze (m). ◆**twelfth** a & n douzième (mf).

twenty ['twentɪ] a & n vingt (m). ◆**twentieth** a & n vingtième (mf).

twerp [twɜːp] n Sl crétin, -ine mf.

twice [twaɪs] adv deux fois; **t. as heavy/etc** deux fois plus lourd/etc; **t. a month/etc, t. monthly/etc** deux fois par mois/etc.

twiddle ['twɪd(ə)l] vti **to t. (with) sth** (*pencil, knob etc*) tripoter qch; **to t. one's thumbs** se tourner les pouces.

twig [twɪg] **1** n (*of branch*) brindille f. **2** vti (-gg-) (*understand*) Sl piger.

twilight ['twaɪlaɪt] n crépuscule m; − a crépusculaire.

twin [twɪn] n jumeau m, jumelle f; **identical t.** vrai jumeau; **t. brother** frère m jumeau; **t. beds** lits mpl jumeaux; **t. town** ville f jumelée; − vt (-nn-) (*town*) jumeler. ◆**twinning** n jumelage m.

twine [twaɪn] **1** n (*string*) ficelle f. **2** vi (*twist*) s'enlacer (**round** autour de).

twinge [twɪndʒ] n a **t. (of pain)** un élancement; **a t. of remorse** un pincement de remords.

twinkle ['twɪŋk(ə)l] vi (*of star*) scintiller; (*of eye*) pétiller; − n scintillement m; pétillement m.

twirl [twɜːl] vi tournoyer; − vt faire tournoyer; (*moustache*) tortiller.

twist [twɪst] vt (*wine, arm etc*) tordre; (*roll round*) enrouler; (*weave together*) entortiller; (*knob*) tourner; (*truth etc*) Fig déformer; **to t. s.o.'s arm** Fig forcer la main à qn; − vi (*wind*) s'entortiller (**round sth** autour de qch); (*of road, river*) serpenter; − n torsion f; (*turn*) tour m; (*in rope*) entortillement m; (*bend in road*) tournant m; (*in story*) coup m de théâtre; (*in event*) tournure f; (*of lemon*) zeste m; **a road full of twists** une route qui fait des zigzags. ◆**—ed** a (*ankle, wire, mind*) tordu. ◆**—er** n **tongue t.** mot m or expression f imprononçable.

twit [twɪt] n Fam idiot, -ote mf.

twitch [twɪtʃ] **1** n (*nervous*) tic m; − vi (*of person*) avoir un tic; (*of muscle*) se convulser. **2** n (*jerk*) secousse f.

twitter ['twɪtər] vi (*of bird*) pépier.

two [tuː] a & n deux (m). ◆**t.-cycle** n Am = **t.-stroke**. ◆**t.-'faced** a Fig hypocrite. ◆**t.-'legged** a bipède. ◆**t.-piece** n (*garment*) deux-pièces m inv. ◆**t.-'seater** n Aut voiture f à deux places. ◆**t.-stroke** n **t.-stroke (engine)** deux-temps m inv. ◆**t.-way** a (*traffic*) dans les deux sens; **t.-way radio** émetteur-récepteur m.

twofold ['tuːfəʊld] *a* double; – *adv* **to increase t.** doubler.

twosome ['tuːsəm] *n* couple *m*.

tycoon [taɪ'kuːn] *n* magnat *m*.

type¹ [taɪp] *n* **1** (*example, person*) type *m*; (*sort*) genre *m*, sorte *f*, type *m*; **blood t.** groupe *m* sanguin. **2** (*print*) Typ caractères *mpl*; **in large t.** en gros caractères. ◆**typesetter** *n* compositeur, trice *mf*.

typ/e² [taɪp] *vti* (*write*) taper (à la machine). ◆—**ing** *n* dactylo(graphie) *f*; **a page of t.** une page dactylographiée; **t. error** faute *f* de frappe. ◆**typewriter** *n* machine *f* à écrire. ◆**typewritten** *a* dactylographié. ◆**typist** *n* dactylo *f*.

typhoid ['taɪfɔɪd] *n* **t. (fever)** Med typhoïde *f*.

typhoon [taɪ'fuːn] *n* Met typhon *m*.

typical ['tɪpɪk(ə)l] *a* typique (**of** de); (*customary*) habituel; **that's t. (of him)!** c'est bien lui! ◆**typically** *adv* typiquement; (*as usual*) comme d'habitude. ◆**typify** *vt* être typique de; (*symbolize*) représenter.

tyranny ['tɪrənɪ] *n* tyrannie *f*. ◆**ty'rannical** *a* tyrannique. ◆**tyrant** ['taɪərənt] *n* tyran *m*.

tyre ['taɪər] *n* pneu *m*.

U

U, u [juː] *n* U, u *m*. ◆**U-turn** *n* Aut demi-tour *m*; Fig Pej volte-face *f inv*.

ubiquitous [juː'bɪkwɪtəs] *a* omniprésent.

udder ['ʌdər] *n* (*of cow etc*) pis *m*.

ugh! [ɜː(h)] *int* pouah!

ugly ['ʌglɪ] *a* (**-ier, -iest**) laid, vilain. ◆**ugliness** *n* laideur *f*.

UK [juː'keɪ] *abbr* = **United Kingdom.**

ulcer ['ʌlsər] *n* ulcère *m*.

ulterior [ʌl'tɪərɪər] *a* **u. motive** arrière-pensée *f*.

ultimate ['ʌltɪmət] *a* (*final, last*) ultime; (*definitive*) définitif; (*basic*) fondamental; (*authority*) suprême. ◆—**ly** *adv* (*finally*) à la fin; (*fundamentally*) en fin de compte; (*subsequently*) à une date ultérieure.

ultimatum [ʌltɪ'meɪtəm] *n* ultimatum *m*.

ultra- ['ʌltrə] *pref* ultra-.

ultramodern [ʌltrə'mɒdən] *a* ultra-moderne.

ultraviolet [ʌltrə'vaɪələt] *a* ultraviolet.

umbilical [ʌm'bɪlɪk(ə)l] *a* **u. cord** cordon *m* ombilical.

umbrage ['ʌmbrɪdʒ] *n* **to take u.** se froisser (**at** de).

umbrella [ʌm'brelə] *n* parapluie *m*; **u. stand** porte-parapluies *m inv*.

umpire ['ʌmpaɪər] *n* Sp arbitre *m*; – *vt* arbitrer.

umpteen [ʌmp'tiːn] *a* (*many*) Fam je ne sais combien de. ◆**umpteenth** *a* Fam énième.

un- [ʌn] *pref* in-, peu, non, sans.

UN [juː'en] *abbr* = **United Nations.**

unabashed [ʌnə'bæʃt] *a* nullement déconcerté.

unabated [ʌnə'beɪtɪd] *a* aussi fort qu'avant.

unable [ʌn'eɪb(ə)l] *a* **to be u. to do** être incapable de faire; **he's u. to swim** il ne sait pas nager.

unabridged [ʌnə'brɪdʒd] *a* intégral.

unacceptable [ʌnək'septəb(ə)l] *a* inacceptable.

unaccompanied [ʌnə'kʌmpənɪd] *a* (*person*) non accompagné; (*singing*) sans accompagnement.

unaccountab/le [ʌnə'kaʊntəb(ə)l] *a* inexplicable. ◆—**ly** *adv* inexplicablement.

unaccounted [ʌnə'kaʊntɪd] *a* **to be (still) u. for** rester introuvable.

unaccustomed [ʌnə'kʌstəmd] *a* inaccoutumé; **to be u. to sth/to doing** ne pas être habitué à qch/à faire.

unadulterated [ʌnə'dʌltəreɪtɪd] *a* pur.

unaided [ʌn'eɪdɪd] *a* sans aide.

unanimity [juːnə'nɪmɪtɪ] *n* unanimité *f*. ◆**u'nanimous** *a* unanime. ◆**u'nanimously** *adv* à l'unanimité.

unappetizing [ʌn'æpɪtaɪzɪŋ] *a* peu appétissant.

unapproachable [ʌnə'prəʊtʃəb(ə)l] *a* (*person*) inabordable.

unarmed [ʌn'ɑːmd] *a* (*person*) non armé; (*combat*) à mains nues.

unashamed [ʌnə'ʃeɪmd] *a* éhonté; **she's u. about it** elle n'en a pas honte. ◆—**ly** [-ɪdlɪ] *adv* sans vergogne.

unassailable [ʌnə'seɪləb(ə)l] *a* (*argument, reputation*) inattaquable.

unassuming [ʌnə'sjuːmɪŋ] *a* modeste.

unattached [ʌnə'tætʃt] *a* (*independent, not married*) libre.

unattainable [ʌnə'teɪnəb(ə)l] *a* inaccessible.

unattended [ʌnə'tendɪd] _a_ sans surveillance.

unattractive [ʌnə'træktɪv] _a_ (_idea, appearance etc_) peu attrayant; (_character_) peu sympathique; (_ugly_) laid.

unauthorized [ʌn'ɔːθəraɪzd] _a_ non autorisé.

unavailable [ʌnə'veɪləb(ə)l] _a_ (_person, funds_) indisponible; (_article_) Com épuisé.

unavoidab/le [ʌnə'vɔɪdəb(ə)l] _a_ inévitable. ◆**—ly** _adv_ inévitablement; (_delayed_) pour une raison indépendante de sa volonté.

unaware [ʌnə'weər] _a_ to be u. of ignorer; **to be u. that** ignorer que. ◆**unawares** _adv_ to catch s.o. u. prendre qn au dépourvu.

unbalanced [ʌn'bælənst] _a_ (_mind, person_) déséquilibré.

unbearab/le [ʌn'beərəb(ə)l] _a_ insupportable. ◆**—ly** _adv_ insupportablement.

unbeatable [ʌn'biːtəb(ə)l] _a_ imbattable. ◆**unbeaten** _a_ (_player_) invaincu; (_record_) non battu.

unbeknown(st) [ʌnbɪ'nəʊn(st)] _a_ u. to à l'insu de.

unbelievable [ʌnbɪ'liːvəb(ə)l] _a_ incroyable. ◆**unbelieving** _a_ incrédule.

unbend [ʌn'bend] _vi_ (_pt & pp_ unbent) (_relax_) se détendre. ◆**—ing** _a_ inflexible.

unbias(s)ed [ʌn'baɪəst] _a_ impartial.

unblock [ʌn'blɒk] _vt_ (_sink etc_) déboucher.

unborn [ʌn'bɔːn] _a_ (_child_) à naître.

unbounded [ʌn'baʊndɪd] _a_ illimité.

unbreakable [ʌn'breɪkəb(ə)l] _a_ incassable. ◆**unbroken** _a_ (_continuous_) continu; (_intact_) intact; (_record_) non battu.

unbridled [ʌn'braɪd(ə)ld] _a_ Fig débridé.

unburden [ʌn'bɜːd(ə)n] _vt_ to u. oneself Fig s'épancher (to auprès de, avec).

unbutton [ʌn'bʌt(ə)n] _vt_ déboutonner.

uncalled-for [ʌn'kɔːldfɔːr] _a_ déplacé, injustifié.

uncanny [ʌn'kænɪ] _a_ (-ier, -iest) étrange, mystérieux.

unceasing [ʌn'siːsɪŋ] _a_ incessant. ◆**—ly** _adv_ sans cesse.

unceremoniously [ʌnserɪ'məʊnɪəslɪ] _adv_ (_to treat_) sans ménagement; (_to show out_) brusquement.

uncertain [ʌn'sɜːt(ə)n] _a_ incertain (about, of de); **it's** or **he's u.** whether or that il n'est pas certain que (+ _sub_). ◆**uncertainty** _n_ incertitude _f_.

unchanged [ʌn'tʃeɪndʒd] _a_ inchangé. ◆**unchanging** _a_ immuable.

uncharitable [ʌn'tʃærɪtəb(ə)l] _a_ peu charitable.

unchecked [ʌn'tʃekt] _adv_ sans opposition.

uncivil [ʌn'sɪv(ə)l] _a_ impoli, incivil.

uncivilized [ʌn'sɪvɪlaɪzd] _a_ barbare.

uncle ['ʌŋk(ə)l] _n_ oncle _m_.

unclear [ʌn'klɪər] _a_ (_meaning_) qui n'est pas clair; (_result_) incertain; **it's u. whether . . .** on ne sait pas très bien si . . . .

uncomfortable [ʌn'kʌmftəb(ə)l] _a_ (_house, chair etc_) inconfortable; (_heat, experience_) désagréable; (_feeling_) troublant; **she is** or **feels u.** (_uneasy_) elle est mal à l'aise.

uncommon [ʌn'kɒmən] _a_ rare. ◆**—ly** _adv_ (_very_) extraordinairement; **not u.** (_fairly often_) assez souvent.

uncommunicative [ʌnkə'mjuːnɪkətɪv] _a_ peu communicatif.

uncomplicated [ʌn'kɒmplɪkeɪtɪd] _a_ simple.

uncompromising [ʌn'kɒmprəmaɪzɪŋ] _a_ intransigeant.

unconcerned [ʌnkən'sɜːnd] _a_ (_not anxious_) imperturbable; (_indifferent_) indifférent (by, with à).

unconditional [ʌnkən'dɪʃ(ə)nəl] _a_ inconditionnel; (_surrender_) sans condition.

unconfirmed [ʌnkən'fɜːmd] _a_ non confirmé.

uncongenial [ʌnkən'dʒiːnɪəl] _a_ peu agréable; (_person_) antipathique.

unconnected [ʌnkə'nektɪd] _a_ (_events, facts etc_) sans rapport (with avec).

unconscious [ʌn'kɒnʃəs] _a_ Med sans connaissance; (_desire_) inconscient; **u. of** (_unaware of_) inconscient de; – _n_ Psy inconscient _m_. ◆**—ly** _adv_ inconsciemment.

uncontrollable [ʌnkən'trəʊləb(ə)l] _a_ (_emotion, laughter_) irrépressible.

unconventional [ʌnkən'venʃ(ə)nəl] _a_ peu conventionnel.

unconvinced [ʌnkən'vɪnst] _a_ to be or **remain u.** ne pas être convaincu (of de). ◆**unconvincing** _a_ peu convaincant.

uncooperative [ʌnkəʊ'ɒp(ə)rətɪv] _a_ peu coopératif.

uncork [ʌn'kɔːk] _vt_ (_bottle_) déboucher.

uncouple [ʌn'kʌp(ə)l] _vt_ (_carriages_) Rail dételer.

uncouth [ʌn'kuːθ] _a_ grossier.

uncover [ʌn'kʌvər] _vt_ (_saucepan, conspiracy etc_) découvrir.

unctuous ['ʌŋktʃʊəs] _a_ (_insincere_) onctueux.

uncut [ʌn'kʌt] _a_ (_film, play_) intégral; (_diamond_) brut.

undamaged [ʌn'dæmɪdʒd] _a_ (_goods_) en bon état.

undaunted [ʌn'dɔːntɪd] _a_ nullement découragé.

undecided [ʌndɪ'saɪdɪd] _a_ (_person_) indécis

(about sur); **I'm u.** whether to do it or not je n'ai pas décidé si je le ferai ou non.
undefeated [ʌndɪ'fiːtɪd] *a* invaincu.
undeniable [ʌndɪ'naɪəb(ə)l] *a* incontestable.
under ['ʌndər] *prep* sous; (*less than*) moins de; (*according to*) selon; **children u. nine** les enfants de moins de *or* enfants au-dessous de neuf ans; **u. the circumstances** dans les circonstances; **u. there** là-dessous; **u. it** dessous; **u. (the command of) s.o.** sous les ordres de qn; **u. age** mineur; **u. discussion/repair** en discussion/réparation; **u. way** (*in progress*) en cours; (*on the way*) en route; **to be u. the impression that** avoir l'impression que; – *adv* au-dessous.
under- ['ʌndər] *pref* sous-.
undercarriage ['ʌndəkærɪdʒ] *n* (*of aircraft*) train *m* d'atterrissage.
undercharge [ʌndə'tʃɑːdʒ] *vt* **I undercharged him (for it)** je ne (le) lui ai pas fait payer assez.
underclothes ['ʌndəkləʊðz] *npl* sous-vêtements *mpl*.
undercoat ['ʌndəkəʊt] *n* (*of paint*) couche *f* de fond.
undercooked [ʌndə'kʊkt] *a* pas assez cuit.
undercover [ʌndə'kʌvər] *a* (*agent, operation*) secret.
undercurrent ['ʌndəkʌrənt] *n* (*in sea*) courant *m* (sous-marin); **an u. of** *Fig* un courant profond de.
undercut [ʌndə'kʌt] *vt* (*pt & pp* undercut, *pres p* undercutting) *Com* vendre moins cher que.
underdeveloped [ʌndədɪ'veləpt] *a* (*country*) sous-développé.
underdog ['ʌndədɒg] *n* (*politically, socially*) opprimé, -ée *mf*; (*likely loser*) perdant, -ante *mf* probable.
underdone [ʌndə'dʌn] *a Culin* pas assez cuit; (*steak*) saignant.
underestimate [ʌndər'estɪmeɪt] *vt* sous-estimer.
underfed [ʌndə'fed] *a* sous-alimenté.
underfoot [ʌndə'fʊt] *adv* sous les pieds.
undergo [ʌndə'gəʊ] *vt* (*pt* underwent, *pp* undergone) subir.
undergraduate [ʌndə'grædʒʊət] *n* étudiant, -ante *mf* (qui prépare la licence).
underground ['ʌndəgraʊnd] *a* souterrain; (*secret*) *Fig* clandestin; – *n Rail* métro *m*; (*organization*) *Pol* résistance *f*; – [ʌndə'graʊnd] *adv* sous terre; **to go u.** (*of fugitive etc*) *Fig* passer dans la clandestinité.
undergrowth ['ʌndəgrəʊθ] *n* sous-bois *m inv*.

underhand [ʌndə'hænd] *a* (*dishonest*) sournois.
underlie [ʌndə'laɪ] *vt* (*pt* underlay, *pp* underlain, *pres p* underlying) sous-tendre.
◆**underlying** *a* (*basic*) fondamental; (*hidden*) profond.
underline [ʌndə'laɪn] *vt* (*text, idea etc*) souligner.
undermanned [ʌndə'mænd] *a* (*office etc*) à court de personnel.
undermine [ʌndə'maɪn] *vt* (*building, strength, society etc*) miner, saper.
underneath [ʌndə'niːθ] *prep* sous; – *adv* (en) dessous; **the book u.** le livre d'en dessous; – *n* dessous *m*.
undernourished [ʌndə'nʌrɪʃt] *a* sous-alimenté.
underpants ['ʌndəpænts] *npl* (*male underwear*) slip *m*; (*loose, long*) caleçon *m*.
underpass ['ʌndəpɑːs] *n* (*for cars or pedestrians*) passage *m* souterrain.
underpay [ʌndə'peɪ] *vt* sous-payer.
◆**underpaid** *a* sous-payé.
underpriced [ʌndə'praɪst] *a* **it's u.** le prix est trop bas, c'est bradé.
underprivileged [ʌndə'prɪvɪlɪdʒd] *a* défavorisé.
underrate [ʌndə'reɪt] *vt* sous-estimer.
undershirt ['ʌndəʃɜːt] *n Am* tricot *m* or maillot *m* de corps.
underside ['ʌndəsaɪd] *n* dessous *m*.
undersigned ['ʌndəsaɪnd] *a* soussigné; **I the u.** je soussigné(e).
undersized [ʌndə'saɪzd] *a* trop petit.
underskirt ['ʌndəskɜːt] *n* jupon *m*.
understaffed [ʌndə'stɑːft] *a* à court de personnel.
understand [ʌndə'stænd] *vti* (*pt & pp* understood) comprendre; **u. that** (*hear*) je crois comprendre que, il paraît que; **I've been given to u. that** on m'a fait comprendre que. ◆**—ing** *n* (*act, faculty*) compréhension *f*; (*agreement*) accord *m*, entente *f*; (*sympathy*) entente *f*; **on the u. that** à condition que (+ *sub*); – *a* (*person*) compréhensif. ◆**understood** *a* (*agreed*) entendu; (*implied*) sous-entendu. ◆**understandable** *a* compréhensible. ◆**understandably** *adv* naturellement.
understatement ['ʌndəsteɪtmənt] *n* euphémisme *m*.
understudy ['ʌndəstʌdɪ] *n Th* doublure *f*.
undertak/e [ʌndə'teɪk] *vt* (*pt* undertook, *pp* undertaken) (*task*) entreprendre; (*responsibility*) assumer; **to u. to do** se charger de faire. ◆**—ing** *n* (*task*) entreprise *f*; (*prom-*

ise) promesse *f*; **to give an u.** promettre (**that** que).

undertaker ['ʌndəteɪkər] *n* entrepreneur *m* de pompes funèbres.

undertone ['ʌndətəʊn] *n* **in an u.** à mi-voix; **an u. of** (*criticism, sadness etc*) *Fig* une note de.

undervalue [ʌndə'væljuː] *vt* sous-évaluer; **it's undervalued at ten pounds** ça vaut plus que dix livres.

underwater [ʌndə'wɔːtər] *a* sous-marin; − *adv* sous l'eau.

underwear ['ʌndəweər] *n* sous-vêtements *mpl.*

underweight [ʌndə'weɪt] *a* (*person*) qui ne pèse pas assez; (*goods*) d'un poids insuffisant.

underworld ['ʌndəwɜːld] *n* **the u.** (*criminals*) le milieu, la pègre.

undesirable [ʌndɪ'zaɪərəb(ə)l] *a* peu souhaitable (**that** que (+ *sub*)); (*person*) indésirable; − *n* (*person*) indésirable *mf.*

undetected [ʌndɪ'tektɪd] *a* non découvert; **to go u.** passer inaperçu.

undies ['ʌndɪz] *npl* (*female underwear*) *Fam* dessous *mpl.*

undignified [ʌn'dɪɡnɪfaɪd] *a* qui manque de dignité.

undisciplined [ʌn'dɪsɪplɪnd] *a* indiscipliné.

undiscovered [ʌndɪ'skʌvəd] *a* **to remain u.** ne pas être découvert.

undisputed [ʌndɪ'spjuːtɪd] *a* incontesté.

undistinguished [ʌndɪ'stɪŋɡwɪʃt] *a* médiocre.

undivided [ʌndɪ'vaɪdɪd] *a* **my u. attention** toute mon attention.

undo [ʌn'duː] *vt* (*pt* **undid**, *pp* **undone**) défaire; (*bound person, hands*) détacher, délier; (*a wrong*) réparer. ◆**—ing** *n* (*downfall*) perte *f*, ruine *f*. ◆**undone** *a* **to leave u.** (*work etc*) ne pas faire; **to come u.** (*of knot etc*) se défaire.

undoubted [ʌn'daʊtɪd] *a* indubitable. ◆**—ly** *adv* indubitablement.

undreamt-of [ʌn'dremtɒv] *a* insoupçonné.

undress [ʌn'dres] *vi* se déshabiller; − *vt* déshabiller; **to get undressed** se déshabiller.

undue [ʌn'djuː] *a* excessif. ◆**unduly** *adv* excessivement.

undulating ['ʌndjʊleɪtɪŋ] *a* (*movement*) onduleux; (*countryside*) vallonné.

undying [ʌn'daɪɪŋ] *a* éternel.

unearned [ʌn'ɜːnd] *a* **u. income** rentes *fpl.*

unearth [ʌn'ɜːθ] *vt* (*from ground*) déterrer; (*discover*) *Fig* dénicher, déterrer.

unearthly [ʌn'ɜːθlɪ] *a* sinistre, mystérieux; **u. hour** *Fam* heure *f* indue.

uneasy [ʌn'iːzɪ] *a* (*peace, situation*) précaire; (*silence*) gêné; **to be** or **feel u.** (*ill at ease*) être mal à l'aise, être gêné; (*worried*) être inquiet.

uneconomic(al) [ʌniːkə'nɒmɪk((ə)l)] *a* peu économique.

uneducated [ʌn'edʒʊkeɪtɪd] *a* (*person*) inculte; (*accent*) populaire.

unemployed [ʌnɪm'plɔɪd] *a* sans travail, en chômage; − *n* **the u.** les chômeurs *mpl.* ◆**unemployment** *n* chômage *m.*

unending [ʌn'endɪŋ] *a* interminable.

unenthusiastic [ʌnɪnθjuːzɪ'æstɪk] *a* peu enthousiaste.

unenviable [ʌn'envɪəb(ə)l] *a* peu enviable.

unequal [ʌn'iːkwəl] *a* inégal; **to be u. to** (*task*) ne pas être à la hauteur de. ◆**unequalled** *a* (*incomparable*) inégalé.

unequivocal [ʌnɪ'kwɪvək(ə)l] *a* sans équivoque.

unerring [ʌn'ɜːrɪŋ] *a* infaillible.

unethical [ʌn'eθɪk(ə)l] *a* immoral.

uneven [ʌn'iːv(ə)n] *a* inégal.

uneventful [ʌnɪ'ventfəl] *a* (*journey, life etc*) sans histoires.

unexceptionable [ʌnɪk'sepʃ(ə)nəb(ə)l] *a* irréprochable.

unexpected [ʌnɪk'spektɪd] *a* inattendu. ◆**—ly** *adv* à l'improviste; (*suddenly*) subitement; (*unusually*) exceptionnellement.

unexplained [ʌnɪk'spleɪnd] *a* inexpliqué.

unfailing [ʌn'feɪlɪŋ] *a* (*optimism, courage, support etc*) inébranlable; (*supply*) inépuisable.

unfair [ʌn'feər] *a* injuste (**to s.o.** envers qn); (*competition*) déloyal. ◆**—ly** *adv* injustement. ◆**—ness** *n* injustice *f.*

unfaithful [ʌn'feɪθfəl] *a* infidèle (**to** à).

unfamiliar [ʌnfə'mɪlɪər] *a* inconnu, peu familier; **to be u. with** ne pas connaître.

unfashionable [ʌn'fæʃ(ə)nəb(ə)l] *a* (*subject etc*) démodé; (*district etc*) peu chic *inv*, ringard; **it's u. to do** il n'est pas de bon ton de faire.

unfasten [ʌn'fɑːs(ə)n] *vt* défaire.

unfavourable [ʌn'feɪv(ə)rəb(ə)l] *a* défavorable.

unfeeling [ʌn'fiːlɪŋ] *a* insensible.

unfinished [ʌn'fɪnɪʃt] *a* inachevé; **to have some u. business** avoir une affaire à régler.

unfit [ʌn'fɪt] *a* (*unwell*) mal fichu; (*unsuited*) inapte (**for sth** à qch, **to do** à faire); (*unworthy*) indigne (**for sth** de qch, **to do** de faire);

to be u. to do (*incapable*) ne pas être en état de faire.

unflagging [ʌnˈflægɪŋ] *a* (*zeal*) inlassable; (*interest*) soutenu.

unflappable [ʌnˈflæpəb(ə)l] *a Fam* imperturbable.

unflattering [ʌnˈflæt(ə)rɪŋ] *a* peu flatteur.

unflinching [ʌnˈflɪntʃɪŋ] *a* (*fearless*) intrépide.

unfold [ʌnˈfəʊld] *vt* déplier; (*wings*) déployer; (*ideas, plan*) *Fig* exposer; – *vi* (*of story, view*) se dérouler.

unforeseeable [ʌnfɔːˈsiːəb(ə)l] *a* imprévisible. ◆**unforeseen** *a* imprévu.

unforgettable [ʌnfəˈgetəb(ə)l] *a* inoubliable.

unforgivable [ʌnfəˈgɪvəb(ə)l] *a* impardonnable.

unfortunate [ʌnˈfɔːtʃ(ə)nət] *a* malheureux; (*event*) fâcheux; **you were u.** tu n'as pas eu de chance. ◆**—ly** *adv* malheureusement.

unfounded [ʌnˈfaʊndɪd] *a* (*rumour etc*) sans fondement.

unfriendly [ʌnˈfrendlɪ] *a* peu amical, froid. ◆**unfriendliness** *n* froideur *f*.

unfulfilled [ʌnfʊlˈfɪld] *a* (*desire*) insatisfait; (*plan*) non réalisé; (*condition*) non rempli.

unfurl [ʌnˈfɜːl] *vt* (*flag etc*) déployer.

unfurnished [ʌnˈfɜːnɪʃt] *a* non meublé.

ungainly [ʌnˈgeɪnlɪ] *a* (*clumsy*) gauche.

ungodly [ʌnˈgɒdlɪ] *a* impie; **u. hour** *Fam* heure *f* indue.

ungrammatical [ʌngrəˈmætɪk(ə)l] *a* non grammatical.

ungrateful [ʌnˈgreɪtfəl] *a* ingrat.

unguarded [ʌnˈgɑːdɪd] *a* **in an u. moment** dans un moment d'inattention.

unhappy [ʌnˈhæpɪ] *a* (**-ier, -iest**) (*sad*) malheureux, triste; (*worried*) inquiet; **u. with** (*not pleased*) mécontent de; **he's u. about doing it** ça le dérange de le faire. ◆**unhappily** *adv* (*unfortunately*) malheureusement. ◆**unhappiness** *n* tristesse *f*.

unharmed [ʌnˈhɑːmd] *a* indemne, sain et sauf.

unhealthy [ʌnˈhelθɪ] *a* (**-ier, -iest**) (*person*) en mauvaise santé; (*climate, place, job*) malsain; (*lungs*) malade.

unheard-of [ʌnˈhɜːdɒv] *a* (*unprecedented*) inouï.

unheeded [ʌnˈhiːdɪd] *a* **it went u.** on n'en a pas tenu compte.

unhelpful [ʌnˈhelpfəl] *a* (*person*) peu obligeant *or* serviable; (*advice*) peu utile.

unhinge [ʌnˈhɪndʒ] *vt* (*person, mind*) déséquilibrer.

unholy [ʌnˈhəʊlɪ] *a* (**-ier, -iest**) impie; (*din*) *Fam* de tous les diables.

unhook [ʌnˈhʊk] *vt* (*picture, curtain*) décrocher; (*dress*) dégrafer.

unhoped-for [ʌnˈhəʊptfɔːr] *a* inespéré.

unhurried [ʌnˈhʌrɪd] *a* (*movement*) lent; (*stroll, journey*) fait sans hâte.

unhurt [ʌnˈhɜːt] *a* indemne, sain et sauf.

unhygienic [ʌnhaɪˈdʒiːnɪk] *a* pas très hygiénique.

unicorn [ˈjuːnɪkɔːn] *n* licorne *f*.

uniform [ˈjuːnɪfɔːm] **1** *n* uniforme *m*. **2** *a* (*regular*) uniforme; (*temperature*) constant. ◆**uniformed** *a* en uniforme. ◆**uni-'formity** *n* uniformité *f*. ◆**uniformly** *adv* uniformément.

unify [ˈjuːnɪfaɪ] *vt* unifier. ◆**unifi'cation** *n* unification *f*.

unilateral [juːnɪˈlæt(ə)rəl] *a* unilatéral.

unimaginable [ʌnɪˈmædʒɪnəb(ə)l] *a* inimaginable. ◆**unimaginative** *a* (*person, plan etc*) qui manque d'imagination.

unimpaired [ʌnɪmˈpeəd] *a* intact.

unimportant [ʌnɪmˈpɔːtənt] *a* peu important.

uninhabitable [ʌnɪnˈhæbɪtəb(ə)l] *a* inhabitable. ◆**uninhabited** *a* inhabité.

uninhibited [ʌnɪnˈhɪbɪtɪd] *a* (*person*) sans complexes.

uninitiated [ʌnɪˈnɪʃɪeɪtɪd] *n* **the u.** les profanes *mpl*, les non-initiés.

uninjured [ʌnˈɪndʒəd] *a* indemne.

uninspiring [ʌnɪnˈspaɪərɪŋ] *a* (*subject etc*) pas très inspirant.

unintelligible [ʌnɪnˈtelɪdʒəb(ə)l] *a* inintelligible.

unintentional [ʌnɪnˈtenʃ(ə)nəl] *a* involontaire.

uninterested [ʌnˈɪntrɪstɪd] *a* indifférent (**in** à). ◆**uninteresting** *a* (*book etc*) inintéressant; (*person*) fastidieux.

uninterrupted [ʌnɪntəˈrʌptɪd] *a* ininterrompu.

uninvited [ʌnɪnˈvaɪtɪd] *a* (*to arrive*) sans invitation. ◆**uninviting** *a* peu attrayant.

union [ˈjuːnɪən] *n* union *f*; (*trade union*) syndicat *m*; – *a* syndical; (**trade**) **u. member** syndiqué, -ée *mf*; **U. Jack** drapeau *m* britannique. ◆**unionist** *n* **trade u.** syndicaliste *mf*. ◆**unionize** *vt* syndiquer.

unique [juːˈniːk] *a* unique. ◆**—ly** *adv* exceptionnellement.

unisex [ˈjuːnɪseks] *a* (*clothes etc*) unisexe *inv*.

unison [ˈjuːnɪs(ə)n] *n* **in u.** à l'unisson (**with** de).

unit [ˈjuːnɪt] *n* unité *f*; (*of furniture etc*) élément *m*; (*system*) bloc *m*; (*group, team*) groupe *m*; **u. trust** *Fin* fonds *m* commun de placement.

unite [juːˈnaɪt] *vt* unir; (*country, party*) unifier; **United Kingdom** Royaume-Uni *m*; **United Nations** (Organisation *f* des) Nations unies *fpl*; **United States (of America)** États-Unis *mpl* (d'Amérique); – *vi* s'unir. ◆**unity** *n* (*cohesion*) unité *f*; (*harmony*) *Fig* harmonie *f*.

universal [juːnɪˈvɜːs(ə)l] *a* universel. ◆**–ly** *adv* universellement.

universe [ˈjuːnɪvɜːs] *n* univers *m*.

university [juːnɪˈvɜːsɪtɪ] *n* université *f*; **at u.** à l'université; – *a* universitaire; (*student, teacher*) d'université.

unjust [ʌnˈdʒʌst] *a* injuste.

unjustified [ʌnˈdʒʌstɪfaɪd] *a* injustifié.

unkempt [ʌnˈkempt] *a* (*appearance*) négligé; (*hair*) mal peigné.

unkind [ʌnˈkaɪnd] *a* peu aimable (**to s.o.** avec qn); (*nasty*) méchant (**to s.o.** avec qn). ◆**–ly** *adv* méchamment.

unknowingly [ʌnˈnəʊɪŋlɪ] *adv* inconsciemment.

unknown [ʌnˈnəʊn] *a* inconnu; **u. to me, he'd left** il était parti, ce que j'ignorais; – *n* (*person*) inconnu, -ue *mf*; **the u.** *Phil* l'inconnu *m*; **u. (quantity)** *Math* & *Fig* inconnue *f*.

unlawful [ʌnˈlɔːfəl] *a* illégal.

unleaded [ʌnˈledɪd] *a* (*gasoline*) *Am* sans plomb.

unleash [ʌnˈliːʃ] *vt* (*force etc*) déchaîner.

unless [ʌnˈles] *conj* à moins que; **u. she comes** à moins qu'elle ne vienne; **u. you work harder, you'll fail** à moins de travailler plus dur, vous échouerez.

unlike [ʌnˈlaɪk] *a* différent; – *prep* **u. me, she . . .** à la différence de moi *or* contrairement à moi, elle . . . ; **he's very u. his father** il n'est pas du tout comme son père; **that's u. him** ça ne lui ressemble pas.

unlikely [ʌnˈlaɪklɪ] *a* improbable; (*implausible*) invraisemblable; **she's u. to win** il est peu probable qu'elle gagne. ◆**unlikelihood** *n* improbabilité *f*.

unlimited [ʌnˈlɪmɪtɪd] *a* illimité.

unlisted [ʌnˈlɪstɪd] *a* (*phone number*) *Am* qui ne figure pas à l'annuaire.

unload [ʌnˈləʊd] *vt* décharger.

unlock [ʌnˈlɒk] *vt* ouvrir (*avec une clef*).

unlucky [ʌnˈlʌkɪ] *a* (**-ier, -iest**) (*person*) malchanceux; (*colour, number etc*) qui porte malheur; **you're u.** tu n'as pas de chance. ◆**unluckily** *adv* malheureusement.

unmade [ʌnˈmeɪd] *a* (*bed*) défait.

unmanageable [ʌnˈmænɪdʒəb(ə)l] *a* (*child*) difficile; (*hair*) difficile à coiffer; (*packet, size*) peu maniable.

unmanned [ʌnˈmænd] *a* (*ship*) sans équipage; (*spacecraft*) inhabité.

unmarked [ʌnˈmɑːkt] *a* (*not blemished*) sans marque; **u. police car** voiture *f* banalisée.

unmarried [ʌnˈmærɪd] *a* célibataire.

unmask [ʌnˈmɑːsk] *vt* démasquer.

unmentionable [ʌnˈmenʃ(ə)nəb(ə)l] *a* dont il ne faut pas parler; (*unpleasant*) innommable.

unmercifully [ʌnˈmɜːsɪf(ə)lɪ] *adv* sans pitié.

unmistakable [ʌnmɪˈsteɪkəb(ə)l] *a* (*obvious*) indubitable; (*face, voice etc*) facilement reconnaissable.

unmitigated [ʌnˈmɪtɪgeɪtɪd] *a* (*disaster*) absolu; (*folly*) pur.

unmoved [ʌnˈmuːvd] *a* **to be u.** (*feel no emotion*) ne pas être ému (**by par**); (*be unconcerned*) être indifférent (**by** à).

unnatural [ʌnˈnætʃ(ə)rəl] *a* (*not normal*) pas naturel; (*crime*) contre nature; (*affected*) qui manque de naturel. ◆**–ly** **not u.** naturellement.

unnecessary [ʌnˈnesəs(ə)rɪ] *a* inutile; (*superfluous*) superflu.

unnerve [ʌnˈnɜːv] *vt* désarçonner, déconcerter.

unnoticed [ʌnˈnəʊtɪst] *a* inaperçu.

unobstructed [ʌnəbˈstrʌktɪd] *a* (*road, view*) dégagé.

unobtainable [ʌnəbˈteɪnəb(ə)l] *a* impossible à obtenir.

unobtrusive [ʌnəbˈtruːsɪv] *a* discret.

unoccupied [ʌnˈɒkjupaɪd] *a* (*person, house*) inoccupé; (*seat*) libre.

unofficial [ʌnəˈfɪʃ(ə)l] *a* officieux; (*visit*) privé; (*strike*) sauvage. ◆**–ly** *adv* à titre officieux.

unorthodox [ʌnˈɔːθədɒks] *a* peu orthodoxe.

unpack [ʌnˈpæk] *vt* (*case*) défaire; (*goods, belongings, contents*) déballer; **to u. a comb/etc from** sortir un peigne/*etc* de; – *vi* défaire sa valise; (*take out goods*) déballer.

unpaid [ʌnˈpeɪd] *a* (*bill, sum*) impayé; (*work, worker*) bénévole; (*leave*) non payé.

unpalatable [ʌnˈpælətəb(ə)l] *a* désagréable, déplaisant.

unparalleled [ʌnˈpærəleld] *a* sans égal.

unperturbed [ʌnpəˈtɜːbd] *a* nullement déconcerté.

unplanned [ʌnˈplænd] *a* (*visit, baby etc*) imprévu.

unpleasant [ʌnˈplezənt] *a* désagréable (**to s.o.** avec qn). ◆**–ness** *n* caractère *m* désagréable (**of** de); (*quarrel*) petite querelle *f*.

unplug [ʌn'plʌg] *vt* (**-gg-**) *El* débrancher; (*unblock*) déboucher.

unpopular [ʌn'pɒpjʊlər] *a* impopulaire; **to be u. with** ne pas plaire à.

unprecedented [ʌn'presidentid] *a* sans précédent.

unpredictable [ʌnprɪ'dɪktəb(ə)l] *a* imprévisible; (*weather*) indécis.

unprepared [ʌnprɪ'peəd] *a* non préparé; (*speech*) improvisé; **to be u. for** (*not expect*) ne pas s'attendre à.

unprepossessing [ʌnpriːpə'zesɪŋ] *a* peu avenant.

unpretentious [ʌnprɪ'tenʃəs] *a* sans prétention.

unprincipled [ʌn'prɪnsɪp(ə)ld] *a* sans scrupules.

unprofessional [ʌnprə'feʃ(ə)nəl] *a* (*unethical*) contraire aux règles de sa profession.

unpublished [ʌn'pʌblɪʃt] *a* (*text, writer*) inédit.

unpunished [ʌn'pʌnɪʃt] *a* **to go u.** rester impuni.

unqualified [ʌn'kwɒlɪfaɪd] *a* **1** (*teacher etc*) non diplômé; **he's u. to do** il n'est pas qualifié pour faire. **2** (*support*) sans réserve; (*success, rogue*) parfait.

unquestionab/le [ʌn'kwestʃ(ə)nəb(ə)l] *a* incontestable. ◆**—ly** *adv* incontestablement.

unravel [ʌn'ræv(ə)l] *vt* (**-ll-**, *Am* **-l-**) (*threads etc*) démêler; (*mystery*) *Fig* éclaircir.

unreal [ʌn'rɪəl] *a* irréel. ◆**unrea'listic** *a* peu réaliste.

unreasonable [ʌn'riːz(ə)nəb(ə)l] *a* qui n'est pas raisonnable; (*price*) excessif.

unrecognizable [ʌnrekəg'naɪzəb(ə)l] *a* méconnaissable.

unrelated [ʌnrɪ'leɪtɪd] *a* (*facts etc*) sans rapport (**to** avec); **we're u.** il n'y a aucun lien de parenté entre nous.

unrelenting [ʌnrɪ'lentɪŋ] *a* (*person*) implacable; (*effort*) acharné.

unreliable [ʌnrɪ'laɪəb(ə)l] *a* (*person*) peu sérieux, peu sûr; (*machine*) peu fiable.

unrelieved [ʌnrɪ'liːvd] *a* (*constant*) constant; (*colour*) uniforme.

unremarkable [ʌnrɪ'mɑːkəb(ə)l] *a* médiocre.

unrepeatable [ʌnrɪ'piːtəb(ə)l] *a* (*offer*) unique.

unrepentant [ʌnrɪ'pentənt] *a* impénitent.

unreservedly [ʌnrɪ'zɜːvɪdlɪ] *adv* sans réserve.

unrest [ʌn'rest] *n* troubles *mpl*, agitation *f*.

unrestricted [ʌnrɪ'strɪktɪd] *a* illimité; (*access*) libre.

unrewarding [ʌnrɪ'wɔːdɪŋ] *a* ingrat; (*financially*) peu rémunérateur.

unripe [ʌn'raɪp] *a* (*fruit*) vert, pas mûr.

unroll [ʌn'rəʊl] *vt* dérouler; – *vi* se dérouler.

unruffled [ʌn'rʌf(ə)ld] *a* (*person*) calme.

unruly [ʌn'ruːlɪ] *a* (**-ier, -iest**) indiscipliné.

unsafe [ʌn'seɪf] *a* (*place, machine etc*) dangereux; (*person*) en danger.

unsaid [ʌn'sed] *a* **to leave sth u.** passer qch sous silence.

unsaleable [ʌn'seɪləb(ə)l] *a* invendable.

unsatisfactory [ʌnsætɪs'fækt(ə)rɪ] *a* peu satisfaisant. ◆**un'satisfied** *a* insatisfait; **u. with** peu satisfait de.

unsavoury [ʌn'seɪv(ə)rɪ] *a* (*person, place etc*) répugnant.

unscathed [ʌn'skeɪðd] *a* indemne.

unscrew [ʌn'skruː] *vt* dévisser.

unscrupulous [ʌn'skruːpjʊləs] *a* (*person, act*) peu scrupuleux.

unseemly [ʌn'siːmlɪ] *a* inconvenant.

unseen [ʌn'siːn] **1** *a* inaperçu. **2** *n* (*translation*) *Sch* version *f*.

unselfish [ʌn'selfɪʃ] *a* (*person, motive etc*) désintéressé.

unsettl/e [ʌn'set(ə)l] *vt* (*person*) troubler. ◆**—ed** *a* (*weather, situation*) instable; (*in one's mind*) troublé; (*in a job*) mal à l'aise.

unshakeable [ʌn'ʃeɪkəb(ə)l] *a* (*person, faith*) inébranlable.

unshaven [ʌn'ʃeɪv(ə)n] *a* pas rasé.

unsightly [ʌn'saɪtlɪ] *a* laid, disgracieux.

unskilled [ʌn'skɪld] *a* inexpert; (*work*) de manœuvre; **u. worker** manœuvre *m*, ouvrier, -ière *mf* non qualifié(e).

unsociable [ʌn'səʊʃəb(ə)l] *a* insociable.

unsocial [ʌn'səʊʃəl] *a* **to work u. hours** travailler en dehors des heures de bureau.

unsolved [ʌn'sɒlvd] *a* (*problem*) non résolu; (*mystery*) inexpliqué; (*crime*) dont l'auteur n'est pas connu.

unsophisticated [ʌnsə'fɪstɪkeɪtɪd] *a* simple.

unsound [ʌn'saʊnd] *a* (*construction etc*) peu solide; (*method*) peu sûr; (*decision*) peu judicieux; **he is of u. mind** il n'a pas toute sa raison.

unspeakable [ʌn'spiːkəb(ə)l] *a* (*horrible*) innommable.

unspecified [ʌn'spesɪfaɪd] *a* indéterminé.

unsporting [ʌn'spɔːtɪŋ] *a* déloyal.

unstable [ʌn'steɪb(ə)l] *a* instable.

unsteady [ʌn'stedɪ] *a* (*hand, voice, step etc*) mal assuré; (*table, ladder etc*) instable. ◆**unsteadily** *adv* (*to walk*) d'un pas mal assuré.

unstinting [ʌn'stɪntɪŋ] a (generosity) sans bornes.

unstoppable [ʌn'stɒpəb(ə)l] a qu'on ne peut (pas) arrêter.

unstuck [ʌn'stʌk] a **to come u.** (of stamp etc) se décoller; (fail) Fam se planter.

unsuccessful [ʌnsək'sesfəl] a (attempt etc) infructueux; (outcome, candidate) malheureux; (application) non retenu; **to be u.** ne pas réussir (**in doing** à faire); (of book, artist) ne pas avoir de succès. ◆—**ly** adv en vain, sans succès.

unsuitable [ʌn'suːtəb(ə)l] a qui ne convient pas (**for** à); (example) peu approprié; (manners, clothes) peu convenable. ◆**unsuited** a **u. to** impropre à; **they're u.** ils ne sont pas compatibles.

unsure [ʌn'ʃʊər] a incertain (**of, about** de).

unsuspecting [ʌnsə'spektɪŋ] a qui ne se doute de rien.

unswerving [ʌn'swɜːvɪŋ] a (loyalty etc) inébranlable.

unsympathetic [ʌnsɪmpə'θetɪk] a incompréhensif; **u. to** indifférent à.

untangle [ʌn'tæŋg(ə)l] vt (rope etc) démêler.

untapped [ʌn'tæpt] a inexploité.

untenable [ʌn'tenəb(ə)l] a (position) intenable.

unthinkable [ʌn'θɪŋkəb(ə)l] a impensable, inconcevable.

untidy [ʌn'taɪdɪ] a (-ier, -iest) (appearance, hair) peu soigné; (room) en désordre; (unmethodical) désordonné. ◆**untidily** adv sans soin.

untie [ʌn'taɪ] vt (person, hands) détacher; (knot, parcel) défaire.

until [ʌn'tɪl] prep jusqu'à; **u. then** jusque-là; **not u. tomorrow/etc** (in the future) pas avant demain/etc; **I didn't come u. Monday** (in the past) je ne suis venu que lundi; – conj **u. she comes** jusqu'à ce qu'elle vienne, en attendant qu'elle vienne; **do nothing u. I come** (before) ne fais rien avant que j'arrive.

untimely [ʌn'taɪmlɪ] a inopportun; (death) prématuré.

untiring [ʌn'taɪ(ə)rɪŋ] a infatigable.

untold [ʌn'təʊld] a (quantity, wealth) incalculable.

untoward [ʌntə'wɔːd] a malencontreux.

untranslatable [ʌntræn'leɪtəb(ə)l] a intraduisible.

untroubled [ʌn'trʌb(ə)ld] a (calm) calme.

untrue [ʌn'truː] a faux. ◆**untruth** n contre-vérité f. ◆**untruthful** a (person) menteur; (statement) mensonger.

unused 1 [ʌn'juːzd] a (new) neuf; (not in use) inutilisé. **2** [ʌn'juːst] a **u. to sth/to doing** peu habitué à qch/à faire.

unusual [ʌn'juːʒʊəl] a exceptionnel, rare; (strange) étrange. ◆—**ly** adv exceptionnellement.

unveil [ʌn'veɪl] vt dévoiler. ◆—**ing** n (ceremony) inauguration f.

unwanted [ʌn'wɒntɪd] a (useless) superflu, dont on n'a pas besoin; (child) non désiré.

unwarranted [ʌn'wɒrəntɪd] a injustifié.

unwavering [ʌn'weɪv(ə)rɪŋ] a (belief etc) inébranlable.

unwelcome [ʌn'welkəm] a (news, fact) fâcheux; (gift, visit) inopportun; (person) importun.

unwell [ʌn'wel] a indisposé.

unwieldy [ʌn'wiːldɪ] a (package etc) encombrant.

unwilling [ʌn'wɪlɪŋ] a **he's u. to do** il ne neut pas faire, il est peu disposé à faire. ◆—**ly** adv à contrecœur.

unwind [ʌn'waɪnd] **1** vt (thread etc) dérouler; – vi se dérouler. **2** vi (relax) Fam décompresser.

unwise [ʌn'waɪz] a imprudent. ◆—**ly** adv imprudemment.

unwitting [ʌn'wɪtɪŋ] a involontaire. ◆—**ly** adv involontairement.

unworkable [ʌn'wɜːkəb(ə)l] a (idea etc) impraticable.

unworthy [ʌn'wɜːðɪ] a indigne (**of** de).

unwrap [ʌn'ræp] vt (-pp-) ouvrir, défaire.

unwritten [ʌn'rɪt(ə)n] a (agreement) verbal, tacite.

unyielding [ʌn'jiːldɪŋ] a (person) inflexible.

unzip [ʌn'zɪp] vt (-pp-) ouvrir (la fermeture éclair® de).

up [ʌp] adv en haut; (in the air) en l'air; (of sun, hand) levé; (out of bed) levé, debout; (of road) en travaux; (of building) construit; (finished) fini; **to come** or **go up** monter; **to be up** (of price, level etc) être monté (**by** de); **up there** là-haut; **up above** au-dessus; **up on** (roof etc) sur; **further** or **higher up** plus haut; **up to** (as far as) jusqu'à; (task) Fig à la hauteur de; **to be up to doing** (capable) être de taille à faire; (in a position to) être à même de faire; **it's up to you to do it** c'est à toi de le faire; **it's up to you** ça dépend de toi; **where are you up to?** (in book etc) où en es-tu?; **what are you up to?** Fam que fais-tu?; **what's up?** (what's the matter?) Fam qu'est-ce qu'il y a?; **time's up** c'est l'heure; **halfway up** (on hill etc) à mi-chemin; **to walk up and down** marcher de long en large; **to be well up in** (versed in) Fam s'y connaître en; **to be up against**

(confront) être confronté à; **up (with) the workers**/etc! Fam vive(nt) les travailleurs/etc!; − prep (a hill) en haut de; (a tree) dans; (a ladder) sur; **to go up** (hill, stairs) monter; **to live up the street** habiter plus loin dans la rue; − npl **to have ups and downs** avoir des hauts et des bas; − vt (-pp-) (increase) Fam augmenter. ◆**up-and-'coming** a plein d'avenir. ◆**upbeat** a (cheerful) Am Fam optimiste. ◆**upbringing** n éducation f. ◆**upcoming** a Am imminent. ◆**up'date** vt mettre à jour. ◆**up'grade** vt (job) revaloriser; (person) promouvoir. ◆**up'hill 1** adv **to go u.** monter. **2** ['ʌphɪl] a (struggle, task) pénible. ◆**up'hold** vt (pt & pp upheld) maintenir. ◆**upkeep** n entretien m. ◆**uplift** [ʌp'lɪft] vt élever; − ['ʌplɪft] n élévation f spirituelle. ◆**upmarket** a Com haut de gamme. ◆**upright 1** a & adv (erect) droit; − n (post) montant m. **2** a (honest) droit. ◆**uprising** n insurrection f. ◆**up'root** vt (plant, person) déraciner. ◆**upside 'down** adv à l'envers; **to turn u. down** (room, plans etc) Fig chambouler. ◆**up'stairs** adv en haut; **to go u.** monter (l'escalier); − ['ʌpsteəz] a (people, room) du dessus. ◆**up'stream** adv en amont. ◆**upsurge** n (of interest) recrudescence f; (of anger) accès m. ◆**uptake** n **to be quick on the u.** comprendre vite. ◆**up'tight** a Fam (tense) crispé; (angry) en colère. ◆**up-to-'date** a moderne; (information) à jour; (well-informed) au courant (on de). ◆**upturn** n (improvement) amélioration f (in de); (rise) hausse f (in de). ◆**up'turned** a (nose) retroussé. ◆**upward** a (movement) ascendant; (path) qui monte; (trend) à la hausse. ◆**upwards** adv vers le haut; **from five francs u.** à partir de cinq francs; **u. of fifty** cinquante et plus.

upheaval [ʌp'hiːv(ə)l] n bouleversement m.
upholster [ʌp'həʊlstər] vt (pad) rembourrer; (cover) recouvrir. ◆**upholsterer** n tapissier m. ◆**upholstery** n (activity) réfection f de sièges; (in car) sièges mpl.
upon [ə'pɒn] prep sur.
upper ['ʌpər] 1 a supérieur; **u. class** aristocratie f; **to have**/**get the u. hand** avoir/prendre le dessus. **2** n (of shoe) empeigne f, dessus m. ◆**u.-'class** a aristocratique. ◆**uppermost** a (highest) le plus haut; **to be u.** (on top) être en dessus.
uproar ['ʌprɔːr] n tumulte m.
upset [ʌp'set] vt (pt & pp upset, pres p upsetting) (knock over) renverser; (plans, stomach, routine etc) déranger; **to u. s.o.** (grieve)

peiner qn; (offend) vexer qn; (annoy) contrarier qn; − a vexé; contrarié; (stomach) dérangé; − ['ʌpset] n (in plans etc) dérangement m (in de); (grief) peine f; **to have a stomach u.** avoir l'estomac dérangé.
upshot ['ʌpʃɒt] n résultat m.
upstart ['ʌpstɑːt] n Pej parvenu, -ue mf.
uranium [jʊ'reɪnɪəm] n uranium m.
urban ['ɜːbən] a urbain.
urbane [ɜː'beɪn] a courtois, urbain.
urchin ['ɜːtʃɪn] n polisson, -onne mf.
urge [ɜːdʒ] vt **to u. s.o. to do** (advise) conseiller vivement à qn de faire; **to u. on** (person, team) encourager; − n forte envie f, besoin m.
urgency ['ɜːdʒənsɪ] n urgence f; (of request, tone) insistance f. ◆**urgent** a urgent, pressant; (tone) insistant; (letter) urgent. ◆**urgently** adv d'urgence; (insistently) avec insistance.
urinal [jʊ'raɪn(ə)l] n urinoir m.
urine ['jʊ(ə)rɪn] n urine f. ◆**urinate** vi uriner.
urn [ɜːn] n urne f; (for coffee or tea) fontaine f.
us [əs, stressed ʌs] pron nous; **(to) us** (indirect) nous; **she sees us** elle nous voit; **he gives (to) us** il nous donne; **with us** avec nous; **all of us** nous tous; **let's** or **let us eat!** mangeons!
US [juːes] abbr = United States.
USA [juːesˈeɪ] abbr = United States of America.
usage ['juːsɪdʒ] n (custom) & Ling usage m.
use [juːs] n usage m, emploi m; (way of using) emploi m; **to have the u. of** avoir l'usage de; **to make u. of** se servir de; **in u.** en usage; **out of u.** hors d'usage; **ready for u.** prêt à l'emploi; **to be of u.** servir, être utile; **it's no u. crying**/etc ça ne sert à rien de pleurer/etc; **what's the u. of worrying**/etc? à quoi bon s'inquiéter/etc?, à quoi ça sert de s'inquiéter/etc?; **I have no u. for it** je n'en ai pas l'usage, qu'est-ce que je ferais de ça?; **he's no u.** (hopeless) il est nul; − [juːz] vt se servir de, utiliser, employer (**as** comme; **to do, for doing** pour faire); **it's used to do** or **for doing** ça sert à faire; **it's used as** ça sert de; **I u. it to clean** je m'en sers pour nettoyer, ça me sert à nettoyer; **to u.** (up) (fuel etc) consommer; (supplies) épuiser; (money) dépenser. ◆**used 1** [juːzd] a (second-hand) d'occasion; (stamp) oblitéré. **2** [juːst] v aux **I u. to do** avant, je faisais; − a **u. to sth/to doing** (accustomed) habitué à qch/à faire; **to get u. to** s'habituer à. ◆**useful** ['juːsfəl] a utile; **to**

come in u. être utile; **to make oneself u.** se rendre utile. ◆**usefulness** *n* utilité *f*.
◆**useless** ['juːsləs] *a* inutile; (*unusable*) inutilisable; (*person*) nul, incompétent.
◆**user** ['juːzər] *n* (*of road, dictionary etc*) usager *m*; (*of machine*) utilisateur, -trice *mf*.

usher ['ʌʃər] *n* (*in church or theatre*) placeur *m*; (*in law court*) huissier *m*; – *vt* **to u. in** faire entrer; (*period etc*) Fig inaugurer. ◆**ushe'rette** *n* Cin ouvreuse *f*.

USSR [juːsesɑːr] *n abbr* (*Union of Soviet Socialist Republics*) URSS *f*.

usual ['juːʒuəl] *a* habituel, normal; **as u.** comme d'habitude; **it's her u. practice** c'est son habitude; – *n* **the u.** (*food, excuse etc*) Fam la même chose que d'habitude. ◆**—ly** *adv* d'habitude.

usurer ['juːʒərər] *n* usurier, -ière *mf*.

usurp [juːzɜːp] *vt* usurper.

utensil [juːtens(ə)l] *n* ustensile *m*.

uterus ['juːt(ə)rəs] *n* Anat utérus *m*.

utilitarian [juːtɪlɪ'teərɪən] *a* utilitaire. ◆**u'tility** *n* (*public*) **u.** service *m* public; – *a* (*goods vehicle*) utilitaire.

utilize ['juːtɪlaɪz] *vt* utiliser. ◆**utili'zation** *n* utilisation *f*.

utmost ['ʌtməʊst] *a* **the u. ease/etc** (*greatest*) la plus grande facilité/etc; **the u. danger/limit/etc** (*extreme*) un danger/une limite/etc extrême; – *n* **to do one's u.** faire tout son possible (**to do** pour faire).

utopia [juːtəʊpɪə] *n* (*perfect state*) utopie *f*. ◆**utopian** *a* utopique.

utter ['ʌtər] **1** *a* complet, total; (*folly*) pur; (*idiot*) parfait; **it's u. nonsense** c'est complètement absurde. **2** *vt* (*say, express*) proférer; (*a cry, sigh*) pousser. ◆**utterance** *n* (*remark etc*) déclaration *f*; **to give u. to** exprimer. ◆**utterly** *adv* complètement.

V

V, v [viː] *n* V, v *m*. ◆**V.-neck(ed)** *a* (*pullover etc*) à col en V.

vacant ['veɪkənt] *a* (*post*) vacant; (*room, seat*) libre; (*look*) vague, dans le vide. ◆**vacancy** *n* (*post*) poste *m* vacant; (*room*) chambre *f* disponible; '**no vacancies**' (*in hotel*) 'complet'. ◆**vacantly** *adv* **to gaze v.** regarder dans le vide.

vacate [və'keɪt, Am 'veɪkeɪt] *vt* quitter.

vacation [veɪ'keɪʃ(ə)n] *n Am* vacances *fpl*; **on v.** en vacances. ◆**—er** *n Am* vacancier, -ière *mf*.

vaccinate ['væksɪneɪt] *vt* vacciner. ◆**vacci'nation** *n* vaccination *f*. ◆**vaccine** [-iːn] *n* vaccin *m*.

vacillate ['væsɪleɪt] *vi* (*hesitate*) hésiter.

vacuum ['vækjʊ(ə)m] *n* vide *m*; **v. cleaner** aspirateur *m*; **v. flask** thermos® *m or f*; – *vt* (*carpet etc*) passer à l'aspirateur. ◆**v.-packed** *a* emballé sous vide.

vagabond ['vægəbɒnd] *n* vagabond, -onde *mf*.

vagary ['veɪgərɪ] *n* caprice *m*.

vagina [və'dʒaɪnə] *n* vagin *m*.

vagrant ['veɪgrənt] *n Jur* vagabond, -onde *mf*.

vague [veɪg] *a* (**-er, -est**) vague; (*memory, outline, photo*) flou; **the vaguest idea** la moindre idée; **he was v.** (**about it**) il est resté vague. ◆**—ly** *adv* vaguement.

vain [veɪn] *a* (**-er, -est**) **1** (*attempt, hope*) vain; **in v.** en vain; **his or her efforts were in v.** ses efforts ont été inutiles. **2** (*conceited*) vaniteux. ◆**—ly** *adv* (*in vain*) vainement.

valentine ['væləntaɪn] *n* (*card*) carte *f* de la Saint-Valentin.

valet ['væleɪ, 'væleɪ] *n* valet *m* de chambre.

valiant ['vælɪənt] *a* courageux. ◆**valour** *n* bravoure *f*.

valid ['vælɪd] *a* (*ticket, motive etc*) valable. ◆**validate** *vt* valider. ◆**va'lidity** *n* validité *f*; (*of argument*) justesse *f*.

valley ['vælɪ] *n* vallée *f*.

valuable ['væljʊəb(ə)l] *a* (*object*) de (grande) valeur; (*help, time etc*) Fig précieux; – *npl* objets *mpl* de valeur.

value ['væljuː] *n* valeur *f*; **to be of great/little v.** (*of object*) valoir cher/peu (cher); **it's good v.** c'est très avantageux; **v. added tax** taxe *f* à la valeur ajoutée; – *vt* (*appraise*) évaluer; (*appreciate*) attacher de la valeur à. ◆**valu'ation** *n* évaluation *f*; (*by expert*) expertise *f*. ◆**valuer** *n* expert *m*.

valve [vælv] *n* (*of machine*) soupape *f*; (*in radio*) lampe *f*; (*of tyre*) valve *f*; (*of heart*) valvule *f*.

vampire ['væmpaɪər] *n* vampire *m*.

van [væn] *n* (*small*) camionnette *f*; (*large*) camion *m*; Rail fourgon *m*.

vandal ['vænd(ə)l] *n* vandale *mf*. ◆**vandal-**

ism n vandalisme m. ◆**vandalize** vt saccager, détériorer.

vanguard ['væŋɡɑːd] n (of army, progress etc) avant-garde f.

vanilla [və'nɪlə] n vanille f; – a (ice cream) à la vanille.

vanish ['vænɪʃ] vi disparaître.

vanity ['vænɪtɪ] n vanité f; **v. case** vanity m inv.

vanquish ['væŋkwɪʃ] vt vaincre.

vantage point ['vɑːntɪdʒpɔɪnt] n (place, point of view) (bon) point m de vue.

vapour ['veɪpər] n vapeur f; (on glass) buée f.

variable ['veərɪəb(ə)l] a variable. ◆**variance** n at v. en désaccord (**with** avec). ◆**variant** a différent; – n variante f. ◆**vari'ation** n variation f.

varicose ['værɪkəʊs] a **v. veins** varices fpl.

variety [və'raɪətɪ] n **1** (diversity) variété f; **a v. of opinions/reasons/**etc (many) diverses opinions/raisons/etc; **a v. of** (articles) Com une gamme de. **2** Th variétés fpl; **v. show** spectacle m de variétés.

various ['veərɪəs] a divers. ◆—**ly** adv diversement.

varnish ['vɑːnɪʃ] vt vernir; – n vernis m.

vary ['veərɪ] vti varier (**from** de). ◆**varied** a varié. ◆**varying** a variable.

vase [vɑːz, Am veɪs] n vase m.

Vaseline® ['væsəliːn] n vaseline f.

vast [vɑːst] a vaste, immense. ◆—**ly** adv (very) infiniment, extrêmement. ◆—**ness** n immensité f.

vat [væt] n cuve f.

VAT [viːtiː, væt] n abbr (value added tax) TVA f.

Vatican ['vætɪkən] n Vatican m.

vaudeville ['vɔːdəvɪl] n Th Am variétés fpl.

vault [vɔːlt] **1** n (cellar) cave f; (tomb) caveau m; (in bank) chambre f forte, coffres mpl; (roof) voûte f. **2** vti (jump) sauter.

veal [viːl] n (meat) veau m.

veer [vɪər] vi (of wind) tourner; (of car, road) virer; **to v. off the road** quitter la route.

vegan ['viːɡən] n végétaliste mf.

vegetable ['vedʒtəb(ə)l] n légume m; – a (kingdom, oil) végétal; **v. garden** (jardin m) potager m. ◆**vege'tarian** a & n végétarien, -ienne (mf). ◆**vege'tation** n végétation f.

vegetate ['vedʒɪteɪt] vi (of person) Pej végéter.

vehement ['vɪəmənt] a (feeling, speech) véhément; (attack) violent. ◆—**ly** adv avec véhémence; violemment.

vehicle ['viːɪk(ə)l] n véhicule m; **heavy goods v.** (lorry) poids m lourd.

veil [veɪl] n (covering) & Fig voile m; – vt (face, truth etc) voiler.

vein [veɪn] n (in body or rock) veine f; (in leaf) nervure f; (mood) Fig esprit m.

vellum ['veləm] n (paper, skin) vélin m.

velocity [və'lɒsɪtɪ] n vélocité f.

velvet ['velvɪt] n velours m; – a de velours. ◆**velvety** a velouté.

vendetta [ven'detə] n vendetta f.

vending machine ['vendɪŋməʃiːn] n distributeur m automatique.

vendor ['vendər] n vendeur, -euse mf.

veneer [və'nɪər] n (wood) placage m; (appearance) Fig vernis m.

venerable ['ven(ə)rəb(ə)l] a vénérable. ◆**venerate** vt vénérer.

venereal [və'nɪərɪəl] a (disease etc) vénérien.

venetian [və'niːʃ(ə)n] a **v. blind** store m vénitien.

vengeance ['vendʒəns] n vengeance f; **with a v.** (to work, study etc) furieusement; (to rain, catch up etc) pour de bon.

venison ['venɪs(ə)n] n venaison f.

venom ['venəm] n (substance) & Fig venin m. ◆**venomous** a (speech, snake etc) venimeux.

vent [vent] **1** n (hole) orifice m; (for air) bouche f d'aération; (in jacket) fente f. **2** n **to give v. to** (feeling etc) donner libre cours à; – vt (anger) décharger (**on** sur).

ventilate ['ventɪleɪt] vt ventiler. ◆**venti-'lation** n ventilation f. ◆**ventilator** n (in wall etc) ventilateur m.

ventriloquist [ven'trɪləkwɪst] n ventriloque mf.

venture ['ventʃər] n entreprise f (risquée); **my v. into** mon incursion f dans; – vt (opinion, fortune) hasarder; **to v. to do** (dare) oser faire; – vi s'aventurer, se risquer (**into** dans).

venue ['venjuː] n lieu m de rencontre or de rendez-vous.

veranda(h) [və'rændə] n véranda f.

verb [vɜːb] n verbe m. ◆**verbal** a (promise, skill etc) verbal. ◆**verbatim** [vɜː'beɪtɪm] a & adv mot pour mot.

verbose [vɜː'bəʊs] a (wordy) verbeux.

verdict ['vɜːdɪkt] n verdict m.

verdigris ['vɜːdɪɡrɪs] n vert-de-gris m inv.

verge [vɜːdʒ] n (of road) accotement m, bord m; **on the v. of** Fig (ruin, tears etc) au bord de; (discovery) à la veille de; **on the v. of doing** sur le point de faire; – vi **to v. on** friser, frôler; (of colour) tirer sur.

verger ['vɜːdʒər] n Rel bedeau m.

verify ['verɪfaɪ] *vt* vérifier. ◆**verifi'cation** *n* vérification *f*.

veritable ['verɪtəb(ə)l] *a* véritable.

vermicelli [vɜːmɪ'selɪ] *n Culin* vermicelle(s) *m(pl)*.

vermin ['vɜːmɪn] *n* (*animals*) animaux *mpl* nuisibles; (*insects, people*) vermine *f*.

vermouth ['vɜːməθ] *n* vermouth *m*.

vernacular [və'nækjʊlər] *n* (*of region*) dialecte *m*.

versatile ['vɜːsətaɪl, *Am* 'vɜːsət(ə)l] *a* (*mind*) souple; (*material, tool, computer*) polyvalent; **he's v.** il a des talents variés, il est polyvalent. ◆**versa'tility** *n* souplesse *f*; **his v.** la variété de ses talents.

verse [vɜːs] *n* (*stanza*) strophe *f*; (*poetry*) vers *mpl*; (*of Bible*) verset *m*.

versed [vɜːst] *a* (**well**) **v. in** versé dans.

version ['vɜːʃ(ə)n] *n* version *f*.

versus ['vɜːsəs] *prep* contre.

vertebra, *pl* **-ae** ['vɜːtɪbrə, -iː] *n* vertèbre *f*.

vertical ['vɜːtɪk(ə)l] *a* vertical; – *n* verticale *f*. ◆**—ly** *adv* verticalement.

vertigo ['vɜːtɪɡəʊ] *n* (*fear of falling*) vertige *m*.

verve [vɜːv] *n* fougue *f*.

very ['verɪ] **1** *adv* très; **I'm v. hot** j'ai très chaud; **v. much** beaucoup; **the v. first** le tout premier; **at the v. least/most** tout au moins/plus; **at the v. latest** au plus tard. **2** *a* (*actual*) même; **his** *or* **her v. brother** son frère même; **at the v. end** (*of play etc*) tout à la fin; **to the v. end** jusqu'au bout.

vespers ['vespəz] *npl Rel* vêpres *fpl*.

vessel ['ves(ə)l] *n Anat Bot Nau* vaisseau *m*; (*receptacle*) récipient *m*.

vest [vest] *n* tricot *m* or maillot *m* de corps; (*woman's*) chemise *f* (américaine); (*waistcoat*) *Am* gilet *m*.

vested ['vestɪd] *a* **v. interests** *Com* droits *mpl* acquis; **she's got a v. interest in** *Fig* elle est directement intéressée dans.

vestige ['vestɪdʒ] *n* vestige *m*; **not a v. of truth/good sense** pas un grain de vérité/de bon sens.

vestry ['vestrɪ] *n* sacristie *f*.

vet [vet] **1** *n* vétérinaire *mf*. **2** *vt* (**-tt-**) (*document*) examiner de près; (*candidate*) se renseigner à fond sur. ◆**veteri'narian** *n Am* vétérinaire *mf*. ◆**veterinary** *a* vétérinaire; **v. surgeon** vétérinaire *m*.

veteran ['vet(ə)rən] *n* vétéran *m*; (*war*) **v.** ancien combattant *m*; – *a* **v. golfer/etc** golfeur/etc expérimenté.

veto ['viːtəʊ] *n* (*pl* -**oes**) (*refusal*) veto *m* inv; (*power*) droit *m* de veto; – *vt* mettre *or* opposer son veto à.

vex [veks] *vt* contrarier, fâcher; **vexed question** question *f* controversée.

via ['vaɪə] *prep* via, par.

viable ['vaɪəb(ə)l] *a* (*baby, firm, plan etc*) viable. ◆**via'bility** *n* viabilité *f*.

viaduct ['vaɪədʌkt] *n* viaduc *m*.

vibrate [vaɪ'breɪt] *vi* vibrer. ◆**'vibrant** *a* vibrant. ◆**vibration** *n* vibration *f*. ◆**vibrator** *n* vibromasseur *m*.

vicar ['vɪkər] *n* (*in Church of England*) pasteur *m*. ◆**vicarage** *n* presbytère *m*.

vicarious [vɪ'keərɪəs] *a* (*emotion*) ressenti indirectement. ◆**—ly** *adv* (*to experience*) indirectement.

vice [vaɪs] *n* **1** (*depravity*) vice *m*; (*fault*) défaut *m*; **v. squad** brigade *f* des mœurs. **2** (*tool*) étau *m*.

vice- [vaɪs] *pref* vice-. ◆**v.-'chancellor** *n Univ* président *m*.

vice versa [vaɪs(ɪ)'vɜːsə] *adv* vice versa.

vicinity [və'sɪnɪtɪ] *n* environs *mpl*; **in the v. of** (*place, amount*) aux environs de.

vicious ['vɪʃəs] *a* (*spiteful*) méchant; (*violent*) brutal; **v. circle** cercle *m* vicieux. ◆**—ly** *adv* méchamment; brutalement. ◆**—ness** *n* méchanceté *f*; brutalité *f*.

vicissitudes [vɪ'sɪsɪtjuːdz] *npl* vicissitudes *fpl*.

victim ['vɪktɪm] *n* victime *f*; **to be the v. of** être victime de. ◆**victimize** *vt* persécuter. ◆**victimi'zation** *n* persécution *f*.

Victorian [vɪk'tɔːrɪən] *a & n* victorien, -ienne (*mf*).

victory ['vɪktərɪ] *n* victoire *f*. ◆**victor** *n* vainqueur *m*. ◆**vic'torious** *a* victorieux.

video ['vɪdɪəʊ] *a* vidéo *inv*; – *n* **v.** (*cassette*) vidéocassette *f*; **v.** (*recorder*) magnétoscope *m*; **on v.** sur cassette; **to make a v. of** faire une cassette de; – *vt* (*programme etc*) enregistrer au magnétoscope. ◆**videotape** *n* bande *f* vidéo.

vie [vaɪ] *vi* (*pres p* **vying**) rivaliser (**with** avec).

Vietnam [vjet'næm, *Am* -'nɑːm] *n* Viêt-nam *m*. ◆**Vietna'mese** *a & n* vietnamien, -ienne (*mf*).

view [vjuː] *n* vue *f*; **to come into v.** apparaître; **in full v. of everyone** à la vue de tous; **in my v.** (*opinion*) à mon avis; **on v.** (*exhibit*) exposé; **in v. of** (*considering*) étant donné (**the fact that** que); **with a v. to doing** afin de faire; – *vt* (*regard*) considérer; (*house*) visiter. ◆**—er** *n* **1** *TV* téléspectateur, -trice *mf*. **2** (*for slides*) visionneuse *f*. ◆**viewfinder** *n Phot* viseur *m*. ◆**viewpoint** *n* point *m* de vue.

vigil ['vɪdʒɪl] n veille f; (over sick person or corpse) veillée f.

vigilant ['vɪdʒɪlənt] a vigilant. ◆**vigilance** n vigilance f.

vigilante [vɪdʒɪ'læntɪ] n Pej membre m d'une milice privée.

vigour ['vɪgər] n vigueur f. ◆**vigorous** a (person, speech etc) vigoureux.

vile [vaɪl] a (-er, -est) (base) infâme, vil; (unpleasant) abominable.

vilify ['vɪlɪfaɪ] vt diffamer.

villa ['vɪlə] n (in country) grande maison f de campagne.

village ['vɪlɪdʒ] n village m. ◆**villager** n villageois, -oise mf.

villain ['vɪlən] n scélérat, -ate mf; (in story or play) traître m. ◆**villainy** n infamie f.

vindicate ['vɪndɪkeɪt] vt justifier. ◆**vindi-'cation** n justification f.

vindictive [vɪn'dɪktɪv] a vindicatif, rancunier.

vine [vaɪn] n (grapevine) vigne f; v. grower viticulteur m. ◆**vineyard** ['vɪnjəd] n vignoble m.

vinegar ['vɪnɪgər] n vinaigre m.

vintage ['vɪntɪdʒ] **1** n (year) année f. **2** a (wine) de grand cru; (car) d'époque; (film) classique; (good) Fig bon; v. Shaw/etc du meilleur Shaw/etc.

vinyl ['vaɪnəl] n vinyle m.

viola [vɪ'əʊlə] n (instrument) Mus alto m.

violate ['vaɪəleɪt] vt violer. ◆**vio'lation** n violation f.

violence ['vaɪələns] n violence f. ◆**violent** a violent; **a v.** dislike une aversion vive. ◆**violently** adv violemment; **to be v. sick** (vomit) vomir.

violet ['vaɪələt] **1** a & n (colour) violet (m). **2** n (plant) violette f.

violin [vaɪə'lɪn] n violon m; – a (concerto etc) pour violon. ◆**violinist** n violoniste mf.

VIP [vi:aɪ'pi:] n abbr (very important person) personnage m de marque.

viper ['vaɪpər] n vipère f.

virgin ['vɜːdʒɪn] n vierge f; **to be a v.** (of woman, man) être vierge; – a (woman, snow etc) vierge. ◆**vir'ginity** n virginité f.

Virgo ['vɜːgəʊ] n (sign) la Vierge.

virile ['vɪraɪl, Am 'vɪrəl] a viril. ◆**vi'rility** n virilité f.

virtual ['vɜːtʃʊəl] a it was a v. failure/etc ce fut en fait un échec/etc. ◆**—ly** adv (in fact) en fait; (almost) pratiquement.

virtue ['vɜːtʃuː] n **1** (goodness, chastity) vertu f; (advantage) mérite m, avantage m. **2** by or in v. of en raison de. ◆**virtuous** a vertueux.

virtuoso, pl **-si** [vɜːtʃʊ'əʊsəʊ, -siː] n virtuose mf. ◆**virtuosity** [-'ɒsɪtɪ] n virtuosité f.

virulent ['vɪrʊlənt] a virulent. ◆**virulence** n virulence f.

virus ['vaɪ(ə)rəs] n virus m.

visa ['viːzə] n visa m.

vis-à-vis [viːzɑːˈviː] prep vis-à-vis de.

viscount ['vaɪkaʊnt] n vicomte m. ◆**viscountess** n vicomtesse f.

viscous ['vɪskəs] a visqueux.

vise [vaɪs] n (tool) Am étau m.

visible ['vɪzəb(ə)l] a visible. ◆**visi'bility** n visibilité f. ◆**visibly** adv visiblement.

vision ['vɪʒ(ə)n] n vision f; **a man/a woman of v.** Fig un homme/une femme qui voit loin. ◆**visionary** a & n visionnaire (mf).

visit ['vɪzɪt] n (call, tour) visite f; (stay) séjour m; – vt (place) visiter; **to visit s.o.** (call on) rendre visite à qn; (stay with) faire un séjour chez qn; – vi être en visite (Am with chez). ◆**—ing** a (card, hours) de visite. ◆**visitor** n visiteur, -euse mf; (guest) invité, -ée mf; (in hotel) client, -ente mf.

visor ['vaɪzər] n (of helmet) visière f.

vista ['vɪstə] n (view of place etc) vue f; (of future) Fig perspective f.

visual ['vɪʒʊəl] a visuel; **v. aid** (in teaching) support m visuel. ◆**visualize** vt (imagine) se représenter; (foresee) envisager.

vital ['vaɪt(ə)l] a vital; **of v. importance** d'importance capitale; **v. statistics** (of woman) Fam mensurations fpl. ◆**—ly** adv extrêmement.

vitality [vaɪ'tælɪtɪ] n vitalité f.

vitamin ['vɪtəmɪn, Am 'vaɪtəmɪn] n vitamine f.

vitriol ['vɪtrɪəl] n Ch Fig vitriol m. ◆**vitri-'olic** a (attack, speech etc) au vitriol.

vivacious [vɪ'veɪʃəs] a plein d'entrain.

vivid ['vɪvɪd] a (imagination, recollection etc) vif; (description) vivant. ◆**—ly** adv (to describe) de façon vivante; **to remember sth v.** avoir un vif souvenir de qch.

vivisection [vɪvɪ'sekʃ(ə)n] n vivisection f.

vocabulary [və'kæbjʊlərɪ] n vocabulaire m.

vocal ['vəʊk(ə)l] a (cords, music) vocal; (outspoken, noisy, critical) qui se fait entendre. ◆**vocalist** n chanteur, -euse mf.

vocation [vəʊ'keɪʃ(ə)n] n vocation f. ◆**vocational** a professionnel.

vociferous [və'sɪf(ə)rəs] a bruyant.

vodka ['vɒdkə] n vodka f.

vogue [vəʊg] n vogue f; **in v.** en vogue.

voice [vɔɪs] n voix f; **at the top of one's v.** à

tue-tête; – vt (feeling, opinion etc) formuler, exprimer.

void [vɔɪd] **1** n vide m; – a v. of (lacking in) dépourvu de. **2** a (not valid) Jur nul.

volatile ['vɒlətaɪl, Am 'vɒlət(ə)l] a (person) versatile, changeant; (situation) explosif.

volcano [vɒl'keɪnəʊ] n (pl -oes) volcan m. ◆**volcanic** [-'kænɪk] a volcanique.

volition [və'lɪʃ(ə)n] n of one's own v. de son propre gré.

volley ['vɒlɪ] n (of blows) volée f; (gunfire) salve f; (of insults) Fig bordée f. ◆**volleyball** n Sp volley(-ball) m.

volt [vəʊlt] n El volt m. ◆**voltage** n voltage m.

volume ['vɒljuːm] n (book, capacity, loudness) volume m. ◆**voluminous** [və'luːmɪnəs] a volumineux.

voluntary ['vɒlənt(ə)rɪ] a volontaire; (unpaid) bénévole. ◆**voluntarily** [Am vɒlən'terɪlɪ] adv volontairement; bénévolement. ◆**volun'teer** n volontaire mf; – vi se proposer (for sth pour qch, to do pour faire); Mil s'engager comme volontaire (for dans); – vt offrir (spontanément).

voluptuous [və'lʌptʃʊəs] a voluptueux, sensuel.

vomit ['vɒmɪt] vti vomir; – n (matter) vomi m.

voracious [və'reɪʃəs] a (appetite, reader etc) vorace.

vot/e [vəʊt] n vote m; (right to vote) droit m de vote; **to win votes** gagner des voix; **v. of censure** or **no confidence** motion f de censure; **v. of thanks** discours m de remerciement; – vt (bill, funds etc) voter; (person) élire; – vi voter; **to v. Conservative** voter conservateur or pour les conservateurs. ◆**–ing** n vote m (of de); (polling) scrutin m. ◆**–er** n Pol électeur, -trice mf.

vouch [vaʊtʃ] vi **to v. for** répondre de.

voucher ['vaʊtʃər] n (for meals etc) bon m, chèque m.

vow [vaʊ] n vœu m; – vt (obedience etc) jurer (to à); **to v. to do** jurer de faire, faire le vœu de faire.

vowel ['vaʊəl] n voyelle f.

voyage ['vɔɪdʒ] n voyage m (par mer).

vulgar ['vʌlgər] a vulgaire. ◆**vul'garity** n vulgarité f.

vulnerable ['vʌln(ə)rəb(ə)l] a vulnérable. ◆**vulnera'bility** n vulnérabilité f.

vulture ['vʌltʃər] n vautour m.

W

W, w ['dʌb(ə)ljuː] n W, w m.

wacky ['wækɪ] a (-ier, -iest) Am Fam farfelu.

wad [wɒd] n (of banknotes, papers etc) liasse f; (of cotton wool, cloth) tampon m.

waddle ['wɒd(ə)l] vi se dandiner.

wade [weɪd] vi **to w. through** (mud, water etc) patauger dans; (book etc) Fig venir péniblement à bout de; **I'm wading through this book** j'avance péniblement dans ce livre.

wafer ['weɪfər] n (biscuit) gaufrette f; Rel hostie f.

waffle ['wɒf(ə)l] **1** n (talk) Fam verbiage m, blabla m; – vi Fam parler pour ne rien dire, blablater. **2** n (cake) gaufre f.

waft [wɒft] vi (of smell etc) flotter.

wag [wæg] **1** vt (-gg-) (tail, finger) agiter, remuer; – vi remuer; **tongues are wagging** Pej on en jase, les langues vont bon train. **2** n (joker) farceur, -euse mf.

wage [weɪdʒ] **1** n wage(s) salaire m, paie f; **w. claim** or **demand** revendication f salariale; **w. earner** salarié, -ée mf; (breadwin-

ner) soutien m de famille; **w. freeze** blocage m des salaires; **w. increase** or **rise** augmentation f de salaire. **2** vt (campaign) mener; **to w. war** faire la guerre (on à).

wager ['weɪdʒər] n pari m; – vt parier (that que).

waggle ['wæg(ə)l] vti remuer.

wag(g)on ['wægən] n (cart) chariot m; Rail wagon m (de marchandises); **on the w.** (abstinent) Fam au régime sec.

waif [weɪf] n enfant mf abandonné(e).

wail [weɪl] vi (cry out, complain) gémir; (of siren) hurler; – n gémissement m; (of siren) hurlement m.

waist [weɪst] n taille f; **stripped to the w.** nu jusqu'à la ceinture. ◆**waistband** n (part of garment) ceinture f. ◆**waistcoat** ['weɪskəʊt] n gilet m. ◆**waistline** n taille f.

wait [weɪt] **1** n attente f; **to lie in w. (for)** guetter; – vi attendre; **to w. for** attendre; **w. until I've gone, w. for me to go** attends que je sois parti; **to keep s.o. waiting** faire attendre qn; **w. and see!** attends voir!; **I can't w.**

to do it j'ai hâte de le faire; **to w. about (for)** attendre; **to w. behind** rester; **to w. up** veiller; **to w. up for s.o.** attendre le retour de qn avant de se coucher. **2** vi (serve) **to w. at table** servir à table; **to w. on s.o.** servir qn. ◆**—ing** n attente f; **'no w.'** Aut 'arrêt interdit'; – a w. list/room liste f/salle f d'attente. ◆**waiter** n garçon m (de café), serveur m; **w.!** garçon! ◆**waitress** n serveuse f; **w.!** mademoiselle!

waive [weɪv] vt renoncer à, abandonner.

wake¹ [weɪk] vi (pt **woke**, pp **woken**) **to w. (up)** se réveiller; **to w. up to** (fact etc) Fig prendre conscience de; – vt **to w. (up)** réveiller; **to spend one's waking hours working**/etc passer ses journées à travailler/etc. ◆**waken** vt éveiller, réveiller; – vi s'éveiller, se réveiller.

wake² [weɪk] n (of ship) & Fig sillage m; **in the w. of** Fig dans le sillage de, à la suite de.

Wales [weɪlz] n pays m de Galles.

walk [wɔːk] n promenade f; (short) (petit) tour m; (gait) démarche f; (pace) marche f, pas m; (path) allée f, chemin m; **to go for a w.** faire une promenade; (shorter) faire un (petit) tour; **to take for a w.** (child etc) emmener se promener; (baby, dog) promener; **five minutes' w.** (away) à cinq minutes à pied; **walks of life** Fig conditions sociales fpl; – vi marcher; (stroll) se promener; (go on foot) aller à pied; **w.!** (don't run) ne cours pas!; **to w. away or off** s'éloigner, partir (**from** de); **to w. away or off with** (steal) Fam faucher; **to w. in** entrer; **to w. into** (tree etc) rentrer dans; (trap) tomber dans; **to w. out** (leave) partir; (of workers) se mettre en grève; **to w. out on s.o.** (desert) Fam laisser tomber qn; **to w. over** (go up to) s'approcher de; – vt (distance) faire à pied; (streets) (par)courir; (take for a walk) promener (bébé, chien); **to w. s.o. to** (station etc) accompagner qn à. ◆**—ing** n marche f (à pied); – a **a w. corpse/dictionary** (person) Fig un cadavre/dictionnaire ambulant; **at a w. pace** au pas; **w. stick** canne f. ◆**walker** n marcheur, -euse mf; (for pleasure) promeneur, -euse mf. ◆**walkout** n (strike) grève f surprise; (from meeting) départ m (en signe de protestation). ◆**walkover** n (in contest etc) victoire f facile. ◆**walkway** n moving w. trottoir m roulant.

walkie-talkie [wɔːkɪˈtɔːkɪ] n talkie-walkie m.

Walkman® [ˈwɔːkmən] n (pl **Walkmans**) baladeur m.

wall [wɔːl] n mur m; (of cabin, tunnel, stomach etc) paroi f; (of ice) Fig muraille f; (of smoke) Fig rideau m; **to go to the w.** (of firm) Fig faire faillite; – a mural; – vt **to w. up** (door etc) murer; **walled city** ville f fortifiée. ◆**wallflower** n Bot giroflée f; **to be a w.** (at dance) faire tapisserie. ◆**wallpaper** n papier m peint; – vt tapisser. ◆**wall-to-wall 'carpet(ing)** n moquette f.

wallet [ˈwɒlɪt] n portefeuille m.

wallop [ˈwɒləp] vt (hit) Fam taper sur; – n (blow) Fam grand coup m.

wallow [ˈwɒləʊ] vi **to w. in** (mud, vice etc) se vautrer dans.

wally [ˈwɒlɪ] n (idiot) Fam andouille f, imbécile mf.

walnut [ˈwɔːlnʌt] n (nut) noix f; (tree, wood) noyer m.

walrus [ˈwɔːlrəs] n (animal) morse m.

waltz [wɔːls, Am wɒlts] n valse f; – vi valser.

wan [wɒn] a (pale) Lit pâle.

wand [wɒnd] n baguette f (magique).

wander [ˈwɒndər] vi (of thoughts) vagabonder; **to w. (about or around)** (roam) errer, vagabonder; (stroll) flâner; **to w. from or off** (path, subject) s'écarter de; **to w. off** (go away) s'éloigner; **my mind's wandering** je suis distrait; – vt **to w. the streets** errer dans les rues. ◆**—ing** a (life, tribe) vagabond, nomade; – npl vagabondages mpl. ◆**—er** n vagabond, -onde mf.

wane [weɪn] vi (of moon, fame, strength etc) décroître; – n **to be on the w.** décroître, être en déclin.

wangle [ˈwæŋg(ə)l] vt Fam (obtain) se débrouiller pour obtenir; (avoiding payment) carotter (**from** à).

want [wɒnt] vt vouloir (**to do** faire); (ask for) demander; (need) avoir besoin de; **I w. him to go** je veux qu'il parte; **you w. to try** (should) tu devrais essayer; **you're wanted on the phone** on vous demande au téléphone; – vi **not to w. for** (not lack) ne pas manquer de; – n (lack) manque m (**of** de); (poverty) besoin m; **for w. of** par manque de; **for w. of money/time** faute d'argent/de temps; **for w. of anything better** faute de mieux; **your wants** (needs) tes besoins mpl. ◆**—ed** a (man, criminal) recherché par la police; **to feel w.** sentir qu'on vous aime. ◆**—ing** a (inadequate) insuffisant; **to be w.** manquer (**in** de).

wanton [ˈwɒntən] a (gratuitous) gratuit; (immoral) impudique.

war [wɔːr] n guerre f; **at w.** en guerre (**with** avec); **to go to w.** entrer en guerre (**with** avec); **to declare w.** déclarer la guerre (**on** à); – a (wound, criminal etc) de guerre; **w.**

memorial monument *m* aux morts. ◆**warfare** *n* guerre *f.* ◆**warhead** *n* (*of missile*) ogive *f.* ◆**warlike** *a* guerrier. ◆**warmonger** *n* fauteur *m* de guerre. ◆**warpath** *n* to be on the w. (*angry*) *Fam* être d'humeur massacrante. ◆**warring** *a* (*countries etc*) en guerre; (*ideologies etc*) *Fig* en conflit. ◆**warship** *n* navire *m* de guerre. ◆**wartime** *n* in w. en temps de guerre.

warble ['wɔːb(ə)l] *vi* (*of bird*) gazouiller.

ward¹ [wɔːd] *n* **1** (*in hospital*) salle *f.* **2** (*child*) *Jur* pupille *mf.* **3** (*electoral division*) circonscription *f* électorale.

ward² [wɔːd] *vt* to w. off (*blow, anger*) détourner; (*danger*) éviter.

warden ['wɔːd(ə)n] *n* (*of institution, Am of prison*) directeur, -trice *mf;* (*of park*) gardien, -ienne *mf;* (*traffic*) w. contractuel, -elle *mf.*

warder ['wɔːdər] *n* gardien *m* (de prison).

wardrobe ['wɔːdrəub] *n* (*cupboard*) penderie *f;* (*clothes*) garde-robe *f.*

warehouse, *pl* **-ses** ['weəhaus, -zɪz] *n* entrepôt *m.*

wares [weəz] *npl* marchandises *fpl.*

warily ['weərɪlɪ] *adv* avec précaution.

warm [wɔːm] *a* (**-er, -est**) chaud, (*iron, oven*) moyen; (*welcome, thanks etc*) chaleureux; **to be** *or* **feel w.** avoir chaud; **it's (nice and) w.** (*of weather*) il fait (agréablement) chaud; **to get w.** (*of person, room etc*) se réchauffer; (*of food, water*) chauffer; – *vt* **to w. (up)** (*person, food etc*) réchauffer; – *vi* **to w. up** (*of person, room, engine*) se réchauffer; (*of food, water*) chauffer; (*of discussion*) s'échauffer; **to w. to s.o.** *Fig* se prendre de sympathie pour qn. ◆**warm-'hearted** *a* chaleureux. ◆**warmly** *adv* (*to wrap up*) chaudement; (*to welcome, thank etc*) chaleureusement. ◆**warmth** *n* chaleur *f.*

warn [wɔːn] *vt* avertir, prévenir (**that** que); **to w. s.o. against** *or* **off sth** mettre qn en garde contre qch; **to w. s.o. against doing** conseiller à qn de ne pas faire. ◆**-ing** *n* avertissement *m;* (*advance notice*) (pré)avis *m; Met* avis *m;* (*alarm*) alerte *f;* **without w.** sans prévenir; **a note** *or* **word of w.** une mise en garde; **w. light** (*on appliance etc*) voyant *m* lumineux; **hazard w. lights** *Aut* feux *mpl* de détresse.

warp [wɔːp] **1** *vt* (*wood etc*) voiler; (*judgment, person etc*) *Fig* pervertir; **a warped mind** un esprit tordu; **a warped account** un récit déformé; – *vi* se voiler. **2** *n Tex* chaîne *f.*

warrant ['wɒrənt] **1** *n Jur* mandat *m;* **a w. for**

your arrest un mandat d'arrêt contre vous. **2** *vt* (*justify*) justifier; **I w. you that . . .** (*declare confidently*) je t'assure que . . . . ◆**warranty** *n Com* garantie *f.*

warren ['wɒrən] *n* (**rabbit**) w. garenne *f.*

warrior ['wɒrɪər] *n* guerrier, -ière *mf.*

wart [wɔːt] *n* verrue *f.*

wary ['weərɪ] *a* (**-ier, -iest**) prudent; **to be w. of s.o./sth** se méfier de qn/qch; **to be w. of doing** hésiter beaucoup à faire.

was [wɒz, *stressed* wɒz] *see* **be.**

wash [wɒʃ] *n* (*clothes*) lessive *f;* (*of ship*) sillage *m;* **to have a w.** se laver; **to give sth a w.** laver qch; **to do the w.** faire la lessive; **in the w.** à la lessive; – *vt* laver; (*flow over*) baigner; **to w. one's hands** se laver les mains (*Fig of sth* de qch). **to w. (away)** (*of sea etc*) emporter (*qch, qn*); **to w. away** *or* **off** *or* **out** (*stain*) faire partir (en lavant); **to w. down** (*vehicle, deck*) laver à grande eau; (*food*) arroser (**with** de); **to w. out** (*bowl etc*) laver; – *vi* se laver; (*do the dishes*) laver la vaisselle; **to w. away** *or* **off** *or* **out** (*of stain*) partir (au lavage); **to w. up** (*do the dishes*) faire la vaisselle; (*have a wash*) *Am* se laver. ◆**washed-'out** *a* (*tired*) lessivé. ◆**washed-'up** *a* (**all**) **w.-up** (*person, plan*) *Sl* fichu. ◆**washable** *a* lavable. ◆**washbasin** *n* lavabo *m.* ◆**washcloth** *n Am* gant *m* de toilette. ◆**washout** *n Sl* (*event etc*) fiasco *m;* (*person*) nullité *f.* ◆**washroom** *n Am* toilettes *fpl.*

washer ['wɒʃər] *n* (*ring*) rondelle *f,* joint *m.*

washing ['wɒʃɪŋ] *n* (*act*) lavage *m;* (*clothes*) lessive *f,* linge *m;* **to do the w.** faire la lessive; **w. line** corde *f* à linge; **w. machine** machine *f* à laver; **w. powder** lessive *f.* ◆**w.-'up** *n* vaisselle *f;* **to do the w.-up** faire la vaisselle; **w.-up liquid** produit *m* pour la vaisselle.

wasp [wɒsp] *n* guêpe *f.*

wast/e [weɪst] *n* gaspillage *m;* (*of time*) perte *f;* (*rubbish*) déchets *mpl; pl* (*land*) étendue *f* déserte; **w. disposal unit** broyeur *m* d'ordures; – *a* **w. material** *or* **products** déchets *mpl;* **w. land** (*uncultivated*) terres *fpl* incultes; (*in town*) terrain *m* vague; **w. paper** vieux papiers *mpl;* **w. pipe** tuyau *m* d'évacuation; – *vt* (*money, food etc*) gaspiller; (*time, opportunity*) perdre; **to w. one's time on frivolities/*etc*** gaspiller son temps en frivolités/*etc,* perdre son temps à des frivolités/*etc;* **to w. one's life** gâcher sa vie; – *vi* **to w. away** dépérir. ◆**-ed** *a* (*effort*) inutile; (*body etc*) émacié. ◆**wastage** *n* gaspillage *m;* (*losses*) pertes *fpl; some* w. (*of goods, staff etc*) du déchet. ◆**wastebin** *n* (*in kitchen*) poubelle *f*. ◆**wastepaper basket** *n* corbeille *f* (à papier).

wasteful ['weɪstfəl] *a* (*person*) gaspilleur; (*process*) peu économique.

watch [wɒtʃ] **1** *n* (*small clock*) montre *f*. **2** *n* (*over suspect, baby etc*) surveillance *f*; *Nau* quart *m*; **to keep (a) w.** *on or* **over** surveiller; **to keep w.** faire le guet; **to be on the w. (for)** guetter; – *vt* regarder; (*observe*) observer; (*suspect, baby etc*) surveiller; (*be careful of*) faire attention à; – *vi* regarder; **to w. (out) for** (*be on the lookout for*) guetter; **to w. out** (*take care*) faire attention (**for** à); **w. out!** attention!; **to w. over** surveiller. ◆**watchdog** *n* chien *m* de garde. ◆**watchmaker** *n* horloger, -ère *mf*. ◆**watchman** *n* (*pl* **-men**) **night w.** veilleur *m* de nuit. ◆**watchstrap** *n* bracelet *m* de montre. ◆**watchtower** *n* tour *f* de guet.

watchful ['wɒtʃfəl] *a* vigilant.

water ['wɔːtər] *n* eau *f*; **by w.** en bateau; **under w.** (*road, field etc*) inondé; (*to swim*) sous l'eau; **at high w.** à marée haute; **it doesn't hold w.** (*of theory etc*) *Fig* ça ne tient pas debout; **in hot w.** *Fig* dans le pétrin; **w. cannon** lance *f* à eau; **w. ice** sorbet *m*; **w. lily** nénuphar *m*; **w. pistol** pistolet *m* à eau; **w. polo** *Sp* water-polo *m*; **w. power** énergie *f* hydraulique; **w. rates** taxes *fpl* sur l'eau; **w. skiing** ski *m* nautique; **w. tank** réservoir *m* d'eau; **w. tower** château *m* d'eau; – *vt* (*plant etc*) arroser; **to w. down** (*wine etc*) couper (d'eau); (*text etc*) édulcorer; – *vi* (*of eyes*) larmoyer; **it makes his** *or* **her mouth w.** ça lui fait venir l'eau à la bouche. ◆**—ing** *n* (*of plant etc*) arrosage *m*; **w. can** arrosoir *m*. ◆**watery** *a* (*colour*) délavé; (*soup*) *Pej* trop liquide; (*eyes*) larmoyant; **w. tea** *or* **coffee** de la lavasse.

watercolour ['wɔːtəkʌlər] *n* (*picture*) aquarelle *f*; (*paint*) couleur *f* pour aquarelle. ◆**watercress** *n* cresson *m* (de fontaine). ◆**waterfall** *n* chute *f* d'eau. ◆**waterhole** *n* (*in desert*) point *m* d'eau. ◆**waterline** *n* (*on ship*) ligne *f* de flottaison. ◆**waterlogged** *a* délavé. ◆**watermark** *n* (*in paper*) filigrane *m*. ◆**watermelon** *n* pastèque *f*. ◆**waterproof** *a* (*material*) imperméable. ◆**watershed** *n* (*turning point*) tournant *m* (décisif). ◆**watertight** *a* (*container etc*) étanche. ◆**waterway** *n* voie *f* navigable. ◆**waterworks** *n* (*place*) station *f* hydraulique.

watt [wɒt] *n El* watt *m*.

wave [weɪv] *n* (*of sea*) & *Fig* vague *f*; (*in hair*) ondulation *f*; *Rad* onde *f*; (*sign*) signe *m* (de la main); **long/medium/short w.** *Rad* ondes *fpl* longues/moyennes/courtes; – *vi* (*with hand*) faire signe (de la main); (*of flag*) flotter; **to w. to** (*greet*) saluer de la main; – *vt* (*arm, flag etc*) agiter; (*hair*) onduler; **to w. s.o. on** faire signe à qn d'avancer; **to w. aside** (*objection etc*) écarter. ◆**waveband** *n Rad* bande *f* de fréquence. ◆**wavelength** *n Rad* & *Fig* longueur *f* d'ondes.

waver ['weɪvər] *vi* (*of flame, person etc*) vaciller.

wavy ['weɪvɪ] *a* (**-ier, -iest**) (*line*) onduleux; (*hair*) ondulé.

wax [wæks] **1** *n* cire *f*; (*for ski*) fart *m*; – *vt* cirer; (*ski*) farter; (*car*) lustrer; – *a* (*candle, doll etc*) de cire; **w. paper** *Culin Am* papier *m* paraffiné. **2** *vi* (*of moon*) croître. **3** *vi* **to w. lyrical/merry** (*become*) se faire lyrique/gai. ◆**waxworks** *npl* (*place*) musée *m* de cire; (*dummies*) figures *fpl* de cire.

way [weɪ] **1** *n* (*path, road*) chemin *m* (**to** de); (*direction*) sens *m*, direction *f*; (*distance*) distance *f*; **all the w., the whole w.** (*to talk etc*) pendant tout le chemin; **this w.** par ici; **that way** par là; **which w.?** par où?; **to lose one's w.** se perdre; **I'm on my w.** (*coming*) j'arrive; (*going*) je pars; **he made his w. out/home** il est sorti/rentré; **the w. there** l'aller *m*; **the w. back** le retour; **the w. in** l'entrée *f*; **the w. out** la sortie; **a w. out of** (*problem etc*) *Fig* une solution à; **the w. is clear** *Fig* la voie est libre; **across the w.** en face; **on the w.** en route (**to** pour); **by w. of** (*via*) par; (*as*) *Fig* comme; **out of the w.** (*isolated*) isolé; **to go out of one's w. to do** se donner du mal pour faire; **by the w ....** *Fig* à propos ...; **to be** *or* **stand in the w.** barrer le passage; **she's in my w.** (*hindrance*) *Fig* elle me gêne; **to get out of the w., make w.** s'écarter; **to give w.** céder; *Aut* céder le passage *or* la priorité; **a long w.** (*away or* **off**) très loin; **it's the wrong w. up** c'est dans le mauvais sens; **do it the other w. round** fais le contraire; **to get under w.** (*of campaign etc*) démarrer; – *adv* (*behind etc*) très loin; **w. ahead** très en avance (**of** sur). **2** *n* (*manner*) façon *f*; (*means*) moyen *m*; (*condition*) état *m*; (*habit*) habitude *f*; (*particular*) égard *m*; **one's ways** (*behaviour*) ses manières *fpl*; **to get one's own w.** obtenir ce qu'on veut; **(in) this w.** de cette façon; **in a way** (*to some extent*) dans un certain sens; **w. of life** façon *f* de vivre, mode *m* de vie; **no w.!** (*certainly not*) *Fam* pas question! ◆**wayfarer** *n* voyageur, -euse *mf*. ◆**way-'out** *a Fam* extraordinaire. ◆**wayside** n by the w. au bord de la route.

waylay [wer'leɪ] vt (pt & pp -**laid**) (attack) attaquer par surprise; (stop) Fig arrêter au passage.

wayward ['weɪwəd] a rebelle, capricieux.

WC [dʌb(ə)lju:'siː] n w-c mpl, waters mpl.

we [wiː] pron nous; **we go** nous allons; **we teachers** nous autres professeurs; **we never know** (indefinite) on ne sait jamais.

weak [wiːk] a (-er, -est) faible; (tea, coffee) léger; (health, stomach) fragile. ◆**w.-'willed** a faible. ◆**weaken** vt affaiblir; — vi faiblir. ◆**weakling** n (in body) mauviette f; (in character) faible mf. ◆**weakly** adv faiblement. ◆**weakness** n faiblesse f; (of health, stomach) fragilité f; (fault) point m faible; **a w. for** (liking) un faible pour.

weal [wiːl] n (wound on skin) marque f, zébrure f.

wealth [welθ] n (money, natural resources) richesse(s) f(pl); **a w. of** (abundance) Fig une profusion de. ◆**wealthy** a (-ier, -iest) riche; — n the w. les riches mpl.

wean [wiːn] vt (baby) sevrer.

weapon ['wepən] n arme f. ◆**weaponry** n armements mpl.

wear [weər] **1** vt (pt wore, pp worn) (have on body) porter; (look, smile) avoir; (put on) mettre; **to have nothing to w.** n'avoir rien à se mettre; — n men's/sports w. vêtements mpl pour hommes/de sport; **evening w.** tenue f de soirée. **2** vt (pt wore, pp worn) to w. (away or down or out) (material, patience etc) user; **to w. s.o. out** (exhaust) épuiser qn; **to w. oneself out** s'épuiser (doing à faire); — vi (last) faire de l'usage, durer; **to w. (out)** (of clothes etc) s'user; **to w. off** (of colour, pain etc) passer, disparaître; **to w. on** (of time) passer; **to w. out** (of patience) s'épuiser; — n (use) usage m; w. (and tear) usure f. ◆**-ing** a (tiring) épuisant. ◆**-er** n the w. of (hat, glasses etc) la personne qui porte.

weary ['wɪərɪ] a (-ier, -iest) (tired) fatigué, las (of doing de faire); (tiring) fatigant; (look, smile) las; — vi to w. of se lasser de. ◆**wearily** adv avec lassitude. ◆**weariness** n lassitude f.

weasel ['wiːz(ə)l] n belette f.

weather ['weðər] n temps m; what's the w. like? quel temps fait-il?; in (the) hot w. par temps chaud; under the w. (not well) Fig patraque; — a (chart etc) météorologique. w. forecast, w. report prèvisions fpl météorologiques, météo f; w. vane girouette f; —

vt (storm, hurricane) essuyer; (crisis) Fig surmonter. ◆**weather-beaten** a (face, person) tanné, hâlé. ◆**weathercock** n girouette f. ◆**weatherman** n (pl -men) TV Rad Fam monsieur m météo.

weav/e [wiːv] vt (pt wove, pp woven) (cloth, plot) tisser; (basket, garland) tresser; — vi Tex tisser; **to w. in and out of** (crowd, cars etc) Fig se faufiler entre; — n (style) tissage m. ◆**-ing** n tissage m. ◆**-er** n tisserand, -ande mf.

web [web] n (of spider) toile f; (of lies) Fig tissu m. ◆**webbed** a (foot) palmé. ◆**webbing** n (in chair) sangles fpl.

wed [wed] vt (-dd-) (marry) épouser; (qualities etc) Fig allier (to à); — vi se marier. ◆**wedded** a (bliss, life) conjugal. ◆**wedding** n mariage m; golden/silver w. noces fpl d'or/d'argent; — a (cake) de noces; (anniversary, present) de mariage; (dress) de mariée; **his** or **her w. day** le jour de son mariage; w. ring, Am w. band alliance f. ◆**wedlock** n born out of w. illégitime.

wedge [wedʒ] n (for splitting) coin m; (under wheel, table etc) cale f; w. heel (of shoe) semelle f compensée; — vt (wheel, table etc) caler; (push) enfoncer (into dans); wedged (in) between (caught, trapped) coincé entre.

Wednesday ['wenzdɪ] n mercredi m.

wee [wiː] a (tiny) Fam tout petit.

weed [wiːd] n (plant) mauvaise herbe f; (weak person) Fam mauviette f; w. killer désherbant m; — vti désherber; — vt to w. out Fig éliminer (from de). ◆**weedy** a (-ier, -iest) (person) Fam maigre et chétif.

week [wiːk] n semaine f; the w. before last pas la semaine dernière, celle d'avant; the w. after next pas la semaine prochaine, celle d'après; tomorrow w., a w. tomorrow demain en huit. ◆**weekday** n jour m de semaine. ◆**week'end** n week-end m; at or on or over the w. ce week-end, pendant le week-end. ◆**weekly** a hebdomadaire; — adv toutes les semaines; — n (magazine) hebdomadaire m.

weep [wiːp] vi (pt pp wept) pleurer; (of wound) suinter; **to w. for s.o.** pleurer qn; — vt (tears) pleurer; weeping willow saule m pleureur.

weft [weft] n Tex trame f.

weigh [weɪ] vt peser; **to w. down** (with load etc) surcharger (with de); (bend) faire plier; **to w. up** (goods, chances etc) peser; — vi peser; **it's weighing on my mind** ça me tracasse; **to w. down on s.o.** (of worries etc) accabler qn. ◆**weighing-machine** n balance f.

weight [weɪt] n poids m; **to put on w.** grossir; **to lose w.** maigrir; **to carry w.** (of argument etc) Fig avoir du poids (**with** pour); **to pull one's w.** (do one's share) Fig faire sa part du travail; **w. lifter** haltérophile mf; **w. lifting** haltérophilie f; − vt **to w.** (**down**) (light object) maintenir avec un poids; **to w. down with** (overload) surcharger de. ◆**weightlessness** n apesanteur f. ◆**weighty** a (-ier, -iest) lourd; (argument, subject) Fig de poids.

weighting ['weɪtɪŋ] n (on salary) indemnité f de résidence.

weir [wɪər] n (across river) barrage m.

weird [wɪəd] a (-er, -est) (odd) bizarre; (eerie) mystérieux.

welcome ['welkəm] a (pleasant) agréable; (timely) opportun; **to be w.** (of person, people) être le bienvenu or la bienvenue or les bienvenu(e)s; **w.!** soyez le bienvenu or la bienvenue or les bienvenu(e)s!; **to make s.o. (feel) w.** faire bon accueil à qn; **you're w.!** (after 'thank you') il n'y a pas de quoi!; **w. to do** (free) libre de faire; **you're w. to (take or use) my bike** mon vélo est à ta disposition; **you're w. to it!** Iron grand bien vous fasse!; − n accueil m; **to extend a w. to** (greet) souhaiter la bienvenue à; − vt accueillir; (warmly) faire bon accueil à; (be glad of) se réjouir de; **I w. you!** je vous souhaite la bienvenue! ◆**welcoming** a (smile etc) accueillant; (speech, words) d'accueil.

weld [weld] vt **to w.** (**together**) souder; (groups etc) Fig unir; − n (joint) soudure f. ◆**−ing** n soudure f. ◆**−er** n soudeur m.

welfare ['welfeər] n (physical, material) bien-être m; (spiritual) santé f; (public aid) aide f sociale; **public w.** (good) le bien public; **the w. state** (in Great Britain) l'État-providence m; **w. work** assistance f sociale.

well¹ [wel] **1** n (for water) puits m; (of stairs, lift) cage f; (oil) **w.** puits de pétrole. **2** vi **to w. up** (rise) monter.

well² [wel] adv (**better, best**) bien; **to do w.** (succeed) réussir; **you'd do w. to refuse** tu ferais bien de refuser; **w. done!** bravo!; **I, you, she** etc **might (just) as w. have left** il valait mieux partir, autant valait partir; **it's just as w. that** (lucky) heureusement que . . . ; **as w.** (also) aussi; **as w. as** aussi bien que; **as w. as two cats, he has . . .** en plus de deux chats, il a . . . ; − a bien inv; **she's w.** (healthy) elle va bien; **not a w. man** un

homme malade; **to get w.** se remettre; **that's all very w., but . . .** tout ça c'est très joli, mais . . . ; − int eh bien!; **w., w.!** (surprise) tiens, tiens!; **enormous, w., quite big** énorme, enfin, assez grand.

well-behaved [welbɪ'heɪvd] a sage. ◆**w.-'being** n bien-être m. ◆**w.-'built** a (person, car) solide. ◆**w.-'founded** a bien fondé. ◆**w.-'heeled** a (rich) Fam nanti. ◆**w.-in'formed** a (person, newspaper) bien informé. ◆**w.-'known** a (bien) connu. ◆**w.-'meaning** a bien intentionné. ◆**w.-nigh** adv presque. ◆**w.-'off** a aisé, riche. ◆**w.-'read** a instruit. ◆**w.-'spoken** a (person) qui a un accent cultivé, qui parle bien. ◆**w.-'thought-of** a hautement considéré. ◆**w.-'timed** a opportun. ◆**w.-to-'do** a aisé, riche. ◆**w.-'tried** a (method) éprouvé. ◆**w.-'trodden** a (path) battu. ◆**w.-wishers** npl admirateurs, -trices mfpl. ◆**w.-'worn** a (clothes, carpet) usagé.

wellington ['welɪŋtən] n botte f de caoutchouc.

welsh [welʃ] vi **to w. on** (debt, promise) ne pas honorer.

Welsh [welʃ] a gallois; **W. rabbit** Culin toast m au fromage; − n (language) gallois m. ◆**Welshman** n (pl -men) Gallois m. ◆**Welshwoman** n (pl -women) Galloise f.

wench [wentʃ] n Hum jeune fille f.

wend [wend] vt **to w. one's way** s'acheminer (to vers).

went [went] see **go 1.**

wept [wept] see **weep.**

were [wər, stressed wɜːr] see **be.**

werewolf ['weəwulf] n (pl -wolves) loup-garou m.

west [west] n ouest m; − a (coast) ouest inv; (wind) d'ouest; **W. Africa** Afrique f occidentale; **W. Indian** a & n antillais, -aise (mf); **the W. Indies** les Antilles fpl; − adv à l'ouest, vers l'ouest. ◆**westbound** a (carriageway) ouest inv; (traffic) en direction de l'ouest. ◆**westerly** a (point) ouest inv; (direction) de l'ouest; (wind) d'ouest. ◆**western** a (coast) ouest inv; (culture) Pol occidental; **W. Europe** Europe f de l'Ouest; − n (film) western m. ◆**westerner** n habitant, -ante mf de l'Ouest; Pol occidental, -ale mf. ◆**westernize** vt occidentaliser. ◆**westward(s)** a & adv vers l'ouest.

wet [wet] a (**wetter, wettest**) mouillé; (damp, rainy) humide; (day, month) de pluie; **w. paint/ink** peinture f/encre f fraîche; **w. through** trempé; **to get w.** se mouiller; **it's w.** (raining) il pleut; **he's w.** (weak-willed)

Fam c'est une lavette; **w. blanket** *Fig* rabat-joie *m inv*; **w. nurse** nourrice *f*; **w. suit** combinaison *f* de plongée; – *n* the w. (*rain*) la pluie; (*damp*) l'humidité *f*; – *vt* (**-tt-**) mouiller. ◆**—ness** *n* humidité *f*.

whack [wæk] *n* (*blow*) grand coup *m*; – *vt* donner un grand coup à. ◆**—ed** *a* w. (**out**) (*tired*) *Fam* claqué. ◆**—ing** *a* (*big*) *Fam* énorme.

whale [weɪl] *n* baleine *f*. ◆**whaling** *n* pêche *f* à la baleine.

wham! [wæm] *int* vlan!

wharf [wɔːf] *n* (*pl* **wharfs** *or* **wharves**) (*for ships*) quai *m*.

what [wɒt] **1** *a* quel, quelle, *pl* quel(le)s; **w. book?** quel livre?; **w. one?** *Fam* lequel?, laquelle?; **w. a fool**/*etc*! quel idiot/*etc*!; **I know w. book it is** je sais quel livre c'est; **w. (little) she has** le peu qu'elle a. **2** *pron* (*in questions*) qu'est-ce qui; (*object*) (qu'est-ce) que; (*after prep*) quoi; **w.'s happening?** qu'est-ce qui se passe?; **w. does he do?** qu'est-ce qu'il fait?, que fait-il?; **w. is it?** qu'est-ce que c'est?; **w.'s that book?** quel est ce livre?; **w.!** (*surprise*) quoi!, comment!; **w.'s it called?** comment ça s'appelle?; **w. for?** pourquoi?; **w. about me**/*etc*? et moi/*etc*?; **w. about leaving**/*etc*? si on partait/*etc*? **3** *pron* (*indirect, relative*) ce qui; (*object*) ce que; **I know w. will happen/w. she'll do** je sais ce qui arrivera/ce qu'elle fera; **w. happens is . . .** ce qui arrive c'est que . . . ; **w. I need** ce dont j'ai besoin. ◆**what'ever** *a* **w. (the) mistake**/*etc* (*no matter what*) quelle que soit l'erreur/*etc*; **of w. size** de n'importe quelle taille; **no chance w.** pas la moindre chance; **nothing w.** rien du tout; – *pron* (*no matter what*) quoi que (+ *sub*); **w. happens** quoi qu'il arrive; **w. you do** quoi que tu fasses; **w. is important** tout ce qui est important; **w. you want** tout ce que tu veux. ◆**what's-it** *n* (*thing*) *Fam* machin *m*. ◆**whatso'ever** *a* & *pron* = **whatever**.

wheat [wiːt] *n* blé *m*, froment. *m*. ◆**wheatgerm** *n* germes *mpl* de blé.

wheedle ['wiːd(ə)l] *vt* **to w. s.o.** enjôler qn (**into doing** pour qu'il fasse); **to w. sth out of s.o.** obtenir qch de qn par la flatterie.

wheel [wiːl] **1** *n* roue *f*; **at the w.** *Aut* au volant; *Nau* au gouvernail; – *vt* (*push*) pousser; – *vi* (*turn*) tourner. **2** *vi* **to w. and deal** *Fam* faire des combines. ◆**wheelbarrow** *n* brouette *f*. ◆**wheelchair** *n* fauteuil *m* roulant.

wheeze [wiːz] **1** *vi* respirer bruyamment. **2** *n* (*scheme*) *Fam* combine *f*. ◆**wheezy** *a* (**-ier, -iest**) poussif.

whelk [welk] *n* (*mollusc*) buccin *m*.

when [wen] *adv* quand; – *conj* quand, lorsque; (*whereas*) alors que; **I've finished** quand j'aurai fini; **w. I saw him** *or* **w. I'd seen him, I left** après l'avoir vu, je suis parti; **the day/moment w.** le jour/moment où; **I talked about w. . . .** j'ai parlé de l'époque où . . . . ◆**when'ever** *conj* (*at whatever time*) quand; (*each time that*) chaque fois que.

where [weər] *adv* où; **w. are you from?** d'où êtes-vous?; – *conj* où; (*whereas*) alors que; **that's w. you'll find it** c'est là que tu le trouveras; **I found it w. she'd left it** je l'ai trouvé là où elle l'avait laissé; **I went to w. he was** je suis allé à l'endroit où il était. ◆**whereabouts** *adv* où (*donc*); – *n* his **w.** l'endroit *m* où il est. ◆**where'as** *conj* alors que. ◆**where'by** *adv* par quoi. ◆**where'upon** *adv* sur quoi. ◆**wher-'ever** *conj* **w. you go** (*everywhere*) partout où tu iras, où que tu ailles; **I'll go w. you like** (*anywhere*) j'irai (là) où vous voudrez.

whet [wet] *vt* (**-tt-**) (*appetite, desire etc*) aiguiser.

whether ['weðər] *conj* si; **I don't know w. to leave** je ne sais pas si je dois partir; **w. she does it or not** qu'elle le fasse ou non; **w. now or tomorrow** que ce soit maintenant ou demain; **it's doubtful w.** il est douteux que (+ *sub*).

which [wɪtʃ] **1** *a* (*in questions etc*) quel, quelle, *pl* quel(le)s; **w. hat?** quel chapeau?; **in w. case** auquel cas. **2** *rel pron* qui; (*object*) que; (*after prep*) lequel, laquelle, *pl* lesquel(le)s; **the house w. is . . .** la maison qui est . . . ; **the book w. I like** le livre que j'aime; **the film of w. . . .** le film dont *or* duquel . . . ; **she's ill, w. is sad** elle est malade, ce qui est triste; **he lies, w. I don't like** il ment, ce que je n'aime pas; **after w.** (*whereupon*) après quoi. **3** *pron* **w. (one)** (*in questions*) lequel, laquelle, *pl* lesquel(le)s; **w. (one) of us?** lequel *or* laquelle d'entre nous?; **w. (ones) are the best of the books** quels sont les meilleurs de ces livres? **4** *pron* **w. (one)** (*the one that*) celui qui, celle qui, *pl* ceux qui, celles qui; (*object*) celui que *etc*; **show me w. (one) is red** montrez-moi celui *or* celle qui est rouge; **I know w. (ones) you want** je sais ceux *or* celles que vous désirez. ◆**which'ever** *a* & *pron* **w. book/etc** *or* **w. of the books/etc you buy** quel que soit le livre/*etc* que tu achètes; **take w. books** *or* **w. of the books interest you** prenez les livres qui vous intéressent; **take w. (one) you like** prends celui *or* celle que tu veux; **w. (ones) remain** ceux *or* celles qui restent.

whiff [wɪf] *n* (*puff*) bouffée *f*; (*smell*) odeur *f*.

while [waɪl] *conj* (*when*) pendant que; (*although*) bien que (+ *sub*); (*as long as*) tant que; (*whereas*) tandis que; **w. doing** (*in the course of*) en faisant; − *n* a w. un moment, quelque temps; **all the w.** tout le temps; − *vt* **to w. away** (*time*) passer. ◆**whilst** [waɪlst] *conj* = **while**.

whim [wɪm] *n* caprice *m*.

whimper ['wɪmpər] *vi* (*of dog, person*) gémir faiblement; (*snivel*) *Pej* pleurnicher; − *n* faible gémissement *m*; **without a w.** (*complaint*) *Fig* sans se plaindre.

whimsical ['wɪmzɪk(ə)l] *a* (*look, idea*) bizarre; (*person*) fantasque, capricieux.

whine [waɪn] *vi* gémir; (*complain*) *Fig* se plaindre; − *n* gémissement *m*; plainte *f*.

whip [wɪp] *n* fouet *m*; − *vt* (**-pp-**) (*person, cream etc*) fouetter; (*defeat*) *Fam* dérouiller; **to w. off** (*take off*) enlever brusquement; **to w. out** (*from pocket etc*) sortir brusquement (**from** de); **to w. up** (*interest*) susciter; (*meal*) *Fam* préparer rapidement; − *vi* (*move*) aller à toute vitesse; **to w. round to s.o.'s** faire un saut chez qn. ◆**whip-round** *n Fam* collecte *f*.

whirl [wɜːl] *vi* tourbillonner, tournoyer; − *vt* faire tourbillonner; − *n* tourbillon *m*. ◆**whirlpool** *n* tourbillon *m*; **w. bath** *Am* bain *m* à remous. ◆**whirlwind** *n* tourbillon *m* (de vent).

whirr [wɜːr] *vi* (*of engine*) vrombir; (*of top*) ronronner.

whisk [wɪsk] **1** *n Culin* fouet *m*; − *vt* fouetter. **2** *vt* **to w. away** *or* **off** (*tablecloth etc*) enlever rapidement; (*person*) emmener rapidement; (*chase away*) chasser.

whiskers ['wɪskəz] *npl* (*of animal*) moustaches *fpl*; (*beard*) barbe *f*; (*moustache*) moustache *f*; (*side*) w. favoris *mpl*.

whisky, *Am* **whiskey** ['wɪskɪ] *n* whisky *m*.

whisper ['wɪspər] *vti* chuchoter; **w. to me!** chuchote à mon oreille!; − *n* chuchotement *m*; (*rumour*) *Fig* rumeur *f*, bruit *m*.

whistle ['wɪs(ə)l] *n* sifflement *m*; (*object*) sifflet *m*; **to blow** *or* **give a w.** siffler; − *vti* siffler; **to w. at** (*girl*) siffler; **to w. for** (*dog, taxi*) siffler.

Whit [wɪt] *a* **W. Sunday** dimanche *m* de Pentecôte.

white [waɪt] *a* (**-er, -est**) blanc; **to go** *or* **turn w.** blanchir; **w. coffee** café *m* au lait; **w. elephant** *Fig* objet *m or* projet *m etc* inutile;

w. lie pieux mensonge *m*; **w. man** blanc *m*; **w. woman** blanche *f*; − *n* (*colour, of egg, of eye*) blanc *m*; (*person*) blanc *m*, blanche *f*. ◆**white-collar 'worker** *n* employé, -ée *mf* de bureau. ◆**whiten** *vti* blanchir. ◆**whiteness** *n* blancheur *f*. ◆**whitewash** *n* (*for walls etc*) blanc *m* de chaux; − *vt* blanchir à la chaux; (*person*) *Fig* blanchir; (*faults*) justifier.

whiting ['waɪtɪŋ] *n* (*fish*) merlan *m*.

Whitsun ['wɪts(ə)n] *n* la Pentecôte.

whittle ['wɪt(ə)l] *vt* **to w. down** (*wood*) tailler; (*price etc*) *Fig* rogner.

whizz [wɪz] **1** *vi* (*rush*) aller à toute vitesse; **to w. past** passer à toute vitesse; **to w. through the air** fendre l'air. **2** *a* **w. kid** *Fam* petit prodige *m*.

who [huː] *pron* qui; **w. did it?** qui (est-ce qui) a fait ça?; **the woman w.** la femme qui; **w. did you see** tu as vu qui? ◆**who'ever** *pron* (*no matter who*) qui que ce soit qui; (*object*) qui que ce soit que; **w. has travelled** (*anyone who*) quiconque a *or* celui qui a voyagé; **w. you are** qui que vous soyez; **this man, w. he is** cet homme, quel qu'il soit; **w. did that?** qui donc a fait ça?

whodunit [huː'dʌnɪt] *n* (*detective story*) *Fam* polar *m*.

whole [həʊl] *a* entier; (*intact*) intact; **the w. time** tout le temps; **the w. apple** toute la pomme, la pomme (tout) entière; **the w. truth** toute la vérité; **the w. world** le monde entier; **the w. lot** le tout; **to swallow sth w.** avaler qch tout rond; − *n* (*unit*) tout *m*; (*total*) totalité *f*; **the w. of the village** le village (tout) entier, tout le village; **the w. of the night** toute la nuit; **on the w., as a w.** dans l'ensemble. ◆**whole-'hearted** *a*, ◆**whole-'heartedly** *adv* sans réserve. ◆**wholemeal** *a*, *Am* ◆**wholewheat** *a* (*bread*) complet. ◆**wholly** *adv* entièrement.

wholesale ['həʊlseɪl] *n Com* gros *m*; − *a* (*firm*) de gros; (*destruction etc*) *Fig* en masse; − *adv* (*in bulk*) en gros; (*to buy or sell one article*) au prix de gros; (*to destroy etc*) *Fig* en masse. ◆**wholesaler** *n* grossiste *mf*.

wholesome ['həʊlsəm] *a* (*food, climate etc*) sain.

whom [huːm] *pron* (*object*) que; (*in questions and after prep*) qui; **w. did she see?** qui a-t-elle vu?; **the man w. you know** l'homme que tu connais; **with w.** avec qui; **of w.** dont.

whooping cough ['huːpɪŋkɒf] *n* coqueluche *f*.

whoops! [wʊps] *int* (*apology etc*) oups!
whopping ['wɒpɪŋ] *a* (*big*) *Fam* énorme.
◆**whopper** *n Fam* chose *f* énorme.
whore [hɔːr] *n* (*prostitute*) putain *f*.
whose [huːz] *poss pron & a* à qui, de qui; **w. book is this?, w. is this book?** à qui est ce livre?; **w. daughter are you?** de qui es-tu la fille?; **the woman w. book I have** la femme dont *or* de qui j'ai le livre; **the man w. mother I spoke to** l'homme à la mère de qui j'ai parlé.
why [waɪ] **1** *adv* pourquoi; **w. not?** pourquoi pas?; − *conj* **the reason w. they . . .** la raison pour laquelle ils . . . ; − *npl* **the whys and wherefores** le pourquoi et le comment. **2** *int* (*surprise*) eh bien!, tiens!
wick [wɪk] *n* (*of candle, lamp*) mèche *f*.
wicked ['wɪkɪd] *a* (*evil*) méchant, vilain; (*mischievous*) malicieux. ◆**−ly** *adv* méchamment; malicieusement. ◆**−ness** *n* méchanceté *f*.
wicker ['wɪkər] *n* osier *m*; − *a* (*chair etc*) en osier, d'osier. ◆**wickerwork** *n* (*objects*) vannerie *f*.
wicket ['wɪkɪt] *n* (*cricket stumps*) guichet *m*.
wide [waɪd] *a* (**-er, -est**) large; (*desert, ocean*) vaste; (*choice, knowledge, variety*) grand; **to be three metres w.** avoir trois mètres de large; − *adv* (*to fall, shoot*) loin du but; (*to open*) tout grand. ◆**wide-'awake** *a* (*alert, not sleeping*) éveillé. ◆**widely** *adv* (*to broadcast, spread*) largement; (*to travel*) beaucoup; **w. different** très différent; **it's w. thought** *or* **believed that . . .** on pense généralement que . . . . ◆**widen** *vt* élargir; − *vi* s'élargir. ◆**wideness** *n* largeur *f*.
widespread ['waɪdspred] *a* (très) répandu.
widow ['wɪdəʊ] *n* veuve *f*. ◆**widowed** *a* (*man*) veuf; (*woman*) veuve; **to be w.** (*become a widower or widow*) devenir veuf *or* veuve. ◆**widower** *n* veuf *m*.
width [wɪdθ] *n* largeur *f*.
wield [wiːld] *vt* (*handle*) manier; (*brandish*) brandir; (*power*) *Fig* exercer.
wife [waɪf] *n* (*pl* **wives**) femme *f*, épouse *f*.
wig [wɪg] *n* perruque *f*.
wiggle ['wɪg(ə)l] *vt* agiter; **to w. one's hips** tortiller des hanches; − *vi* (*of worm etc*) se tortiller; (*of tail*) remuer.
wild [waɪld] *a* (**-er, -est**) (*animal, flower, region etc*) sauvage; (*enthusiasm, sea*) déchaîné; (*idea, life*) fou; (*look*) farouche; (*angry*) furieux (**with** contre); **w. with** (*joy, anger etc*) fou de; **I'm not w. about it** (*plan etc*) *Fam* ça ne m'emballe pas; **to be w. about s.o.** (*very fond of*) être dingue de qn; **to grow w.** (*of plant*) pousser à l'état sau-

vage; **to run w.** (*of animals*) courir en liberté; (*of crowd*) se déchaîner; **the W. West** *Am* le Far West; − *npl* régions *fpl* sauvages. ◆**wildcat 'strike** *n* grève *f* sauvage. ◆**wild-'goose chase** *n* fausse piste *f*. ◆**wildlife** *n* animaux *mpl* sauvages, faune *f*.
wilderness ['wɪldənəs] *n* désert *m*.
wildly ['waɪldlɪ] *adv* (*madly*) follement; (*violently*) violemment.
wile [waɪl] *n* ruse *f*, artifice *m*.
wilful ['wɪlfəl] *a* (*Am* **willful**) (*intentional, obstinate*) volontaire. ◆**−ly** *adv* volontairement.
will[1] [wɪl] *v aux* **he will come, he'll come** (*future tense*) il viendra (**won't he?** n'est-ce pas?); **you will not come, you won't come** tu ne viendras pas (**will you?** n'est-ce pas?); **w. you have a tea?** veux-tu prendre un thé?; **w. you be quiet!** veux-tu taire!; **I w.!** (*yes*) oui!; **it won't open** ça ne s'ouvre pas, ça ne veut pas s'ouvrir.
will[2] [wɪl] **1** *vt* (*wish, intend*) vouloir (**that** que (+ *sub*)); **to w. oneself to do** faire un effort de volonté pour faire; − *n* volonté *f*; **against one's w.** à contrecœur; **at w.** (*to depart etc*) quand on veut; (*to choose*) à volonté. **2** *n* (*legal document*) testament *m*. ◆**willpower** *n* volonté *f*.
willing ['wɪlɪŋ] *a* (*helper, worker*) de bonne volonté; (*help etc*) spontané; **to be w. to do** être disposé *or* prêt à faire, vouloir bien faire; − *n* **to show w.** faire preuve de bonne volonté. ◆**−ly** *adv* (*with pleasure*) volontiers; (*voluntarily*) volontairement. ◆**−ness** *n* (*goodwill*) bonne volonté *f*; **his** *or* **her w. to do** (*enthusiasm*) son empressement *m* à faire.
willow ['wɪləʊ] *n* (*tree, wood*) saule *m*. ◆**willowy** *a* (*person*) svelte.
willy-nilly [wɪlɪ'nɪlɪ] *adv* bon gré mal gré, de gré ou de force.
wilt [wɪlt] *vi* (*of plant*) dépérir; (*of enthusiasm etc*) *Fig* décliner.
wily [waɪlɪ] *a* (**-ier, -iest**) rusé.
wimp [wɪmp] *n* (*weakling*) *Fam* mauviette *f*.
win [wɪn] *n* (*victory*) victoire *f*; − *vi* (*pt & pp* **won**, *pres p* **winning**) gagner; − *vt* (*money, race etc*) gagner; (*victory, prize*) remporter; (*fame*) acquérir; (*friends*) se faire; **to w. s.o. over** gagner qn (**to** à). ◆**winning** *a* (*number, horse etc*) gagnant; (*team*) victorieux; (*goal*) décisif; (*smile*) engageant; − *npl* gains *mpl*.
wince [wɪns] *vi* (*flinch*) tressaillir; (*pull a face*) grimacer; **without wincing** sans sourciller.

winch [wɪntʃ] n treuil m; − vt to w. (up) hisser au treuil.

wind [wɪnd] n vent m; (breath) souffle m; **to have w.** Med avoir des gaz; **to get w. of** Fig avoir vent de; **in the w.** Fig dans l'air; **w. instrument** Mus instrument m à vent; − vt **to w. s.o.** (of blow etc) couper le souffle à qn. ◆**windbreak** n (fence, trees) brise-vent m inv. ◆**windcheater** n, Am ◆**windbreaker** n blouson m, coupe-vent m inv. ◆**windfall** n (piece of fruit) fruit m abattu par le vent; (unexpected money) Fig aubaine f. ◆**windmill** n moulin m à vent. ◆**windpipe** n Anat trachée f. ◆**windscreen** n, Am ◆**windshield** n Aut pare-brise m inv; **w. wiper** essuie-glace m inv. ◆**windsurfing** n **to go w.** faire de la planche à voile. ◆**windswept** a (street etc) balayé par les vents. ◆**windy** a (-ier, -iest) venteux, venté; **it's w.** (of weather) il y a du vent.

wind [waɪnd] vt (pt & pp wound) (roll) enrouler; **to w. (up)** (clock) remonter; **to w. up** (meeting) terminer; (firm) liquider; − vi (of river, road) serpenter; **to w. down** (relax) se détendre; **to w. up** (end up) finir (doing par faire); **to w. up with sth** se retrouver avec qch. ◆**—ing** a (road etc) sinueux; (staircase) tournant. ◆**—er** n (of watch) remontoir m.

window ['wɪndəʊ] n fenêtre f; (pane) vitre f, carreau m; (in vehicle or train) vitre f; (in shop) vitrine f; (counter) guichet m; **French w.** porte-fenêtre f; **w. box** jardinière f; **w. cleaner** or Am **washer** laveur, -euse mf de carreaux; **w. dresser** étalagiste mf; **w. ledge** = **windowsill**; **to go w. shopping** faire du lèche-vitrines. ◆**windowpane** n vitre f, carreau m. ◆**windowsill** n (inside) appui m de (la) fenêtre; (outside) rebord m de (la) fenêtre.

wine [waɪn] n vin m; − a (bottle, cask) à vin; **w. cellar** cave f (à vin); **w. grower** viticulteur m; **w. list** carte f des vins; **w. taster** dégustateur, -trice mf de vins; **w. tasting** dégustation f de vins; **w. waiter** sommelier m; − vt **to w. and dine s.o.** offrir à dîner et à boire à qn. ◆**wineglass** n verre m à vin. ◆**wine-growing** a viticole.

wing [wɪŋ] n aile f; **the wings** Th les coulisses fpl; **under one's w.** Fig sous son aile. ◆**winged** a ailé. ◆**winger** n Sp ailier m. ◆**wingspan** n envergure f.

wink [wɪŋk] vi faire un clin d'œil (**at, to** à); (of light) clignoter; − n clin m d'œil.

winkle ['wɪŋk(ə)l] n (sea animal) bigorneau m.

winner ['wɪnər] n (of contest etc) gagnant, -ante mf; (of argument, fight) vainqueur m; **that idea/etc is a w.** Fam c'est une idée/etc en or.

winter ['wɪntər] n hiver m; − a d'hiver; **in (the) w.** en hiver. ◆**wintertime** n hiver m. ◆**wintry** a hivernal.

wip/e [waɪp] vt essuyer; **to w. one's feet/hands** s'essuyer les pieds/les mains; **to w. away** or **off** or **up** (liquid) essuyer; **to w. out** (clean) essuyer; (erase) effacer; (destroy) anéantir; − vi **to w. up** (dry the dishes) essuyer la vaisselle; − n coup m de torchon or d'éponge. ◆**—er** n Aut essuie-glace m inv.

wir/e ['waɪər] n fil m; (telegram) télégramme m; **w. netting** grillage m; − vt **to w. (up)** (house) El faire l'installation électrique de; **to w. s.o.** (telegraph) télégraphier à qn. ◆**—ing** n El installation f électrique. ◆**wirecutters** npl pince f coupante.

wireless ['waɪələs] n (set) TSF f, radio f; **by w.** (to send a message) par sans-fil.

wiry ['waɪərɪ] a (-ier, -iest) maigre et nerveux.

wisdom ['wɪzdəm] n sagesse f.

wise [waɪz] a (-er, -est) (prudent) sage, prudent; (learned) savant; **to put s.o. w./be w. to** Fam mettre qn/être au courant de; **w. guy** Fam gros malin m. ◆**wisecrack** n Fam (joke) astuce f; (sarcastic remark) sarcasme m. ◆**wisely** adv prudemment.

-wise [waɪz] suffix (with regard to) money/etc-wise question argent/etc.

wish [wɪʃ] vt souhaiter, vouloir (**to do** faire); **I w. (that) you could help me/could have helped me** je voudrais que/j'aurais voulu que vous m'aidiez; **I w. I hadn't done that** je regrette d'avoir fait ça; **if you w.** si tu veux; **I w. you well** or **luck** je vous souhaite bonne chance; **I wished him** or **her (a) happy birthday** je lui ai souhaité bon anniversaire; **I w. I could** si seulement je pouvais; − vi **to w. for sth** souhaiter qch; − n (specific) souhait m, vœu m; (general) désir m; **the w. for sth/to do** le désir de qch/de faire; **best wishes** (on greeting card) meilleurs vœux mpl; (in letter) amitiés fpl, bien amicalement; **send him** or **her my best wishes** fais-lui mes amitiés. ◆**wishbone** n bréchet m. ◆**wishful** a **it's w. thinking (on your part)** tu te fais des illusions, tu prends tes désirs pour la réalité.

wishy-washy ['wɪʃɪwɒʃɪ] a (taste, colour) fade.

wisp [wɪsp] n (of smoke) volute f; (of hair)

fine mèche *f*; **a (mere) w. of a girl** une fillette toute menue.

wisteria [wɪ'stɪərɪə] *n Bot* glycine *f*.

wistful ['wɪstfəl] *a* mélancolique et rêveur. ◆**—ly** *adv* avec mélancolie.

wit [wɪt] *n* **1** (*humour*) esprit *m*; (*person*) homme *m or* femme *f* d'esprit. **2 wit(s)** (*intelligence*) intelligence *f* (**to do** de faire); **to be at one's wits'** *or* **wit's end** ne plus savoir que faire.

witch [wɪtʃ] *n* sorcière *f*. ◆**witchcraft** *n* sorcellerie *f*. ◆**witch-hunt** *n Pol* chasse *f* aux sorcières.

with [wɪð] *prep* **1** avec; **come w. me** viens avec moi; **w. no hat** sans chapeau; **I'll be right w. you** je suis à vous dans une minute; **I'm w. you** (*I understand*) *Fam* je te suis; **w. it** (*up-to-date*) *Fam* dans le vent. **2** (*at the house, flat etc of*) chez; **she's staying w. me** elle loge chez moi; **it's a habit w. me** c'est une habitude chez moi. **3** (*cause*) de; **to jump w. joy** sauter de joie. **4** (*instrument, means*) avec, de; **to write w. a pen** écrire avec un stylo; **to fill w.** remplir de; **satisfied w.** satisfait de; **w. my own eyes** de mes propres yeux. **5** (*description*) à; **w. blue eyes** aux yeux bleus. **6** (*despite*) malgré.

withdraw [wɪð'drɔː] *vt* (*pt* withdrew, *pp* withdrawn) retirer (**from** de); **—** *vi* se retirer (**from** de). ◆**withdrawn** *a* (*person*) renfermé. ◆**withdrawal** *n* retrait *m*; **to suffer from w. symptoms** (*of drug addict etc*) être en manque.

wither ['wɪðər] *vi* (*of plant etc*) se flétrir; **—** *vt* flétrir. ◆**—ed** *a* (*limb*) atrophié. ◆**—ing** *a* (*look*) foudroyant; (*remark*) cinglant.

withhold [wɪð'həʊld] *vt* (*pt & pp* withheld) (*help, permission etc*) refuser (**from** à); (*decision*) différer; (*money*) retenir (**from** de); (*information etc*) cacher (**from** à).

within [wɪ'ðɪn] *adv* à l'intérieur; **—** *prep* (*place, container etc*) à l'intérieur de, dans; **w. a kilometre of** à moins d'un kilomètre de; **w. a month** (*to return etc*) avant un mois; (*to finish sth*) en moins d'un mois; (*to pay*) sous un mois; **w. my means** dans les limites de mes moyens; **w. sight** en vue.

without [wɪ'ðaʊt] *prep* sans; **w. a tie**/*etc* sans cravate/*etc*; **w. doing** sans faire.

withstand [wɪð'stænd] *vt* (*pt & pp* withstood) résister à.

witness ['wɪtnɪs] *n* (*person*) témoin *m*; (*evidence*) *Jur* témoignage *m*; **to bear w. to** témoigner de; **—** *vt* être (le) témoin de, voir; (*document*) signer (pour attester l'authenticité de).

witty ['wɪtɪ] *a* (**-ier, -iest**) spirituel. ◆**witti-**

cism *n* bon mot *m*, mot *m* d'esprit. ◆**wittiness** *n* esprit *m*.

wives [waɪvz] *see* wife.

wizard ['wɪzəd] *n* magicien *m*; (*genius*) *Fig* génie *m*, as *m*.

wizened ['wɪz(ə)nd] *a* ratatiné.

wobble ['wɒb(ə)l] *vi* (*of chair etc*) branler, boiter; (*of cyclist, pile etc*) osciller; (*of jelly, leg*) trembler; (*of wheel*) tourner de façon irrégulière. ◆**wobbly** *a* (*table etc*) bancal, boiteux; **to be w. = to wobble**.

woe [wəʊ] *n* malheur *m*. ◆**woeful** *a* triste.

woke, woken [wəʊk, 'wəʊkən] *see* wake¹.

wolf [wʊlf] **1** *n* (*pl* wolves) loup *m*; **w. whistle** sifflement *m* admiratif. **2** *vt* **to w. (down)** (*food*) engloutir.

woman, *pl* **women** ['wʊmən, 'wɪmɪn] *n* femme *f*; **she's a London w.** c'est une Londonienne; **w. doctor** femme *f* médecin; **women drivers** les femmes *fpl* au volant; **w. friend** amie *f*; **w. teacher** professeur *m* femme; **women's** (*attitudes, clothes etc*) féminin. ◆**womanhood** *n* (*quality*) féminité *f*; **to reach w.** devenir femme. ◆**womanizer** *n Pej* coureur *m* (de femmes *or* de jupons). ◆**womanly** *a* féminin.

womb [wuːm] *n* utérus *m*.

women ['wɪmɪn] *see* woman.

won [wʌn] *see* win.

wonder ['wʌndər] **1** *n* (*marvel*) merveille *f*, miracle *m*; (*sense, feeling*) émerveillement *m*; **in w.** (*to watch etc*) émerveillé; (**it's**) **no w.** ce n'est pas étonnant (**that** que (+ *sub*)); **—** *vi* (*marvel*) s'étonner (**at** de); **—** *vt* **I w. that** je *or* ça m'étonne que (+ *sub*). **2** *vt* (*ask oneself*) se demander (**if** si, **why** pourquoi); **—** *vi* (*reflect*) songer (**about** à). ◆**wonderful** *a* (*excellent, astonishing*) merveilleux. ◆**wonderfully** *adv* (*beautiful, hot etc*) merveilleusement; (*to do, work etc*) à merveille.

wonky ['wɒŋkɪ] *a* (**-ier, -iest**) *Fam* (*table etc*) bancal; (*hat, picture*) de travers.

won't [wəʊnt] = will not.

woo [wuː] *vt* (*woman*) faire la cour à, courtiser; (*try to please*) *Fig* chercher à plaire à.

wood [wʊd] *n* (*material, forest*) bois *m*. ◆**woodcut** *n* gravure *f* sur bois. ◆**wooded** *a* (*valley etc*) boisé. ◆**wooden** *a* de *or* en bois; (*manner, dancer etc*) *Fig* raide. ◆**woodland** *n* région *f* boisée. ◆**woodpecker** *n* (*bird*) pic *m*. ◆**woodwind** *n* (*instruments*) *Mus* bois *mpl*. ◆**woodwork** *n* (*craft, objects*) menuiserie *f*. ◆**woodworm** *n* (*larvae*) vers *mpl* (du bois); **it has w.** c'est vermoulu. ◆**woody** *a*

(**-ier, -iest**) (*hill etc*) boisé; (*stem etc*) ligneux.

wool [wʊl] *n* laine *f*; – *a* de laine; (*industry*) lainier. ◆**woollen** *a* de laine; (*industry*) lainier; – *npl* (*garments*) lainages *mpl*. ◆**woolly** *a* (**-ier, -iest**) laineux; (*unclear*) *Fig* nébuleux; – *n* (*garment*) *Fam* lainage *m*.

word [wɜːd] *n* mot *m*; (*spoken*) parole *f*, mot *m*; (*promise*) parole *f*; (*command*) ordre *m*; *pl* (*of song etc*) paroles *fpl*; **by w. of mouth** de vive voix; **to have a w. with s.o.** (*speak to*) parler à qn; (*advise, lecture*) avoir un mot avec qn; **in other words** autrement dit; **I have no w. from** (*news*) je suis sans nouvelles de; **to send w. that . . .** faire savoir que . . . ; **to leave w. that . . .** dire que . . . ; **the last w. in** (*latest development*) le dernier cri en matière de; **w. processing** traitement *m* de texte; – *vt* (*express*) rédiger, formuler. ◆**wording** *n* termes *mpl*. ◆**wordy** *a* (**-ier, -iest**) verbeux.

wore [wɔːr] *see* **wear 1,2.**

work [wɜːk] *n* travail *m*; (*product*) & *Liter* œuvre *f*, ouvrage *m*; (*building or repair work*) travaux *mpl*; **to be at w.** travailler; **farm w.** travaux *mpl* agricoles; **out of w.** au *or* en chômage; **a day off w.** un jour de congé *or* de repos; **he's off w.** il n'est pas allé travailler; **the works** (*mechanism*) le mécanisme; **a gas works** (*factory*) une usine à gaz; **w. force** main-d'œuvre *f*; **a heavy w. load** beaucoup de travail; – *vi* travailler; (*of machine etc*) marcher, fonctionner; (*of drug*) agir; **to w. on** (*book etc*) travailler à; (*principle*) se baser sur; **to w. at** *or* **on sth** (*improve*) travailler qch; **to w. loose** (*of knot, screw*) se desserrer; (*of tooth*) se mettre à branler; **to w. towards** (*result, agreement, aim*) travailler à; **to w. out** (*succeed*) marcher; (*train*) *Sp* s'entraîner; **it works out at £5** ça fait cinq livres; **it works up to** (*climax*) ça tend vers; **to w. up to sth** (*in speech etc*) en venir à qch; – *vt* (*person*) faire travailler; (*machine*) faire marcher; (*mine*) exploiter; (*miracle*) faire; (*metal, wood etc*) travailler; **to get worked up** s'exciter; **to w. in** (*reference, bolt*) introduire; **to w. off** (*debt*) payer en travaillant; (*excess fat*) se débarrasser de (par l'exercice); (*anger*) passer, assouvir; **to w. out** (*solve*) résoudre; (*calculate*) calculer; (*scheme, plan*) élaborer; **to w. up an appetite** s'ouvrir l'appétit; **to w. up enthusiasm** s'enthousiasmer; **to w. one's way up** (*rise socially etc*) faire du chemin. ◆**working** *a* (*day, clothes etc*) de travail; (*population*) actif; **Monday's a w. day** on travaille le lundi, lundi est un jour ouvré; **w. class** class *f* ouvrière; **in w. order** en état de marche; – *npl* (*mechanism*) mécanisme *m*. ◆**workable** *a* (*plan*) praticable. ◆**worker** *n* travailleur, -euse *mf*; (*manual*) ouvrier, -ière *mf*; (*employee, clerk*) employé, -ée *mf*; **blue-collar w.** col *m* bleu.

workaholic [wɜːkə'hɒlɪk] *n* *Fam* bourreau *m* de travail. ◆**'workbench** *n* établi *m*. ◆**working-'class** *a* ouvrier. ◆**'workman** *n* (*pl* **-men**) ouvrier *m*. ◆**'workmanship** *n* maîtrise *f*, travail *m*. ◆**'workmate** *n* camarade *mf* de travail. ◆**'workout** *n* *Sp* (*séance f*) d'entraînement *m*. ◆**'workroom** *n* salle *f* de travail. ◆**'workshop** *n* atelier *m*. ◆**'work-shy** *a* peu enclin au travail. ◆**work-to-'rule** *n* grève *f* du zèle.

world [wɜːld] *n* monde *m*; **all over the w.** dans le monde entier; **the richest/etc in the world** le *or* la plus riche/etc du monde; **a w. of** (*a lot of*) énormément de; **to think the w. of** penser énormément de bien de; **why in the w. . . . ?** pourquoi diable . . . ?; **out of this w.** (*wonderful*) *Fam* formidable; – *a* (*war etc*) mondial; (*champion, cup, record*) du monde. ◆**world-'famous** *a* de renommée mondiale. ◆**worldly** *a* (*pleasures*) de ce monde; (*person*) qui a l'expérience du monde. ◆**world'wide** *a* universel.

worm [wɜːm] **1** *n* ver *m*. **2** *vt* **to w. one's way into** s'insinuer dans; **to w. sth out of s.o.** soutirer qch à qn. ◆**worm-eaten** *a* (*wood*) vermoulu; (*fruit*) véreux.

worn [wɔːn] *see* **wear 1,2;** – *a* (*tyre etc*) usé. ◆**worn-'out** *a* (*object*) complètement usé; (*person*) épuisé.

worry ['wʌrɪ] *n* souci *m*; – *vi* s'inquiéter (**about sth** de qch, **about s.o.** pour qn); – *vt* inquiéter; **to be worried** être inquiet; **to be worried sick** se ronger les sangs. ◆**—ing** *a* (*news etc*) inquiétant. ◆**worrier** *n* anxieux, -euse *mf*. ◆**worryguts** *n*, *Am* ◆**worrywart** *n* *Fam* anxieux, -euse *mf*.

worse [wɜːs] *a* pire, plus mauvais (**than** que); **to get w.** se détériorer; **he's getting w.** (*in health*) il va de plus en plus mal; (*in behaviour*) il se conduit de plus en plus mal; – *adv* plus mal (**than** que); **I could do w.** je pourrais faire pire; **to hate/etc w. than** détester/etc plus que; **to be w. off** (*financially*) aller moins bien financièrement; – *n* **there's w. (to come)** il y a pire encore; **a change for the w.** une détérioration. ◆**worsen** *vti* empirer.

worship ['wɜːʃɪp] *n* culte *m*; **his W. the Mayor** Monsieur le Maire; – *vt* (**-pp-**)

(*person*) & *Rel* adorer; (*money etc*) *Pej* avoir le culte de; − *vi Rel* faire ses dévotions (**at** à). ◆**worshipper** *n* adorateur, -trice *mf*; (*in church*) fidèle *mf*.

worst [wɜːst] *a* pire, plus mauvais; − *adv* (**the**) **w.** le plus mal; **to come off w.** (*in struggle etc*) avoir le dessous; − *n* **the w.** (**one**) (*object, person*) le *or* la pire, le *or* la plus mauvais(e); **the w.** (**thing**) **is that** . . . le pire c'est que . . . ; **at** (**the**) **w.** au pis aller; **at its w.** (*crisis*) à son plus mauvais point *or* moment; **to get the w. of it** (*in struggle etc*) avoir le dessous; **the w. is yet to come** on n'a pas encore vu le pire.

worsted [ˈwʊstɪd] *n* laine *f* peignée.

worth [wɜːθ] *n* valeur *f*; **to buy 50 pence w. of chocolates** acheter pour cinquante pence de chocolats; − *a* **to be w.** valoir; **how much** *or* **what is it w.?** ça vaut combien?; **the film's w. seeing** le film vaut la peine *or* le coup d'être vu; **it's w.** (**one's**) **while** ça (en) vaut la peine *or* le coup; **it's w.** (**while**) **waiting** ça vaut la peine d'attendre. ◆**worthless** *a* qui ne vaut rien. ◆**worth'while** *a* (*book, film etc*) qui vaut la peine d'être lu, vu *etc*; (*activity*) qui (en) vaut la peine; (*contribution, plan*) valable; (*cause*) louable; (*satisfying*) qui donne des satisfactions.

worthy [ˈwɜːðɪ] *a* (**-ier, -iest**) digne (**of** de); (*laudable*) louable; − *n* (*person*) notable *m*.

would [wʊd, *unstressed* wəd] *v aux* **I w. stay, I'd stay** (*conditional tense*) je resterais; **he w. have done it** il l'aurait fait; **w. you help me, please?** voulez-vous m'aider, s'il vous plaît?; **w. you like some tea?** voudriez-vous (prendre) du thé?; **I w. see her every day** (*used to*) je la voyais chaque jour. ◆**would-be** *a* (*musician etc*) soi-disant.

wound¹ [wuːnd] *vt* (*hurt*) blesser; **the wounded** les blessés *mpl*; − *n* blessure *f*.

wound² [waʊnd] *see* **wind**².

wove, woven [wəʊv, ˈwəʊv(ə)n] *see* **weave**.

wow! [waʊ] *int Fam* (c'est) formidable!

wrangle [ˈræŋg(ə)l] *n* dispute *f*; − *vi* se disputer.

wrap [ræp] *vt* (**-pp-**) **to w.** (**up**) envelopper; **to w.** (**oneself**) **up** (*dress warmly*) se couvrir; **wrapped up in** (*engrossed*) *Fig* absorbé par; − *n* (*shawl*) châle *m*; (*cape*) pèlerine *f*; **plastic w.** *Am* scel-o-frais® *m*. ◆**wrapping** *n* (*action, material*) emballage *m*; **w. paper** papier *m* d'emballage. ◆**wrapper** *n* (*of sweet*) papier *m*; (*of book*) jaquette *f*.

wrath [rɒθ] *n Lit* courroux *m*.

wreak [riːk] *vt* **to w. vengeance on** se venger de; **to w. havoc on** ravager.

wreath [riːθ] *n* (*pl* **-s** [riːðz]) (*on head, for funeral*) couronne *f*.

wreck [rek] *n* (*ship*) épave *f*; (*sinking*) naufrage *m*; (*train etc*) train *m etc* accidenté; (*person*) épave *f* (humaine); **to be a nervous w.** être à bout de nerfs; − *vt* détruire; (*ship*) provoquer le naufrage de; (*career, hopes etc*) *Fig* briser, détruire. ◆**−age** *n* (*fragments*) débris *mpl*. ◆**−er** *n* (*breakdown truck*) *Am* dépanneuse *f*.

wren [ren] *n* (*bird*) roitelet *m*.

wrench [rentʃ] *vt* (*tug at*) tirer sur; (*twist*) tordre; **to w. sth from s.o.** arracher qch à qn; − *n* mouvement *m* de torsion; (*tool*) clé *f* (à écrous), *Am* clé *f* à mollette; (*distress*) *Fig* déchirement *m*.

wrest [rest] *vt* **to w. sth from s.o.** arracher qch à qn.

wrestl/e [ˈres(ə)l] *vi* lutter (**with s.o.** contre qn); **to w. with** (*problem etc*) *Fig* se débattre avec. ◆**−ing** *n Sp* lutte *f*; (**all-in**) **w.** catch *m*. ◆**−er** *n* lutteur, -euse *mf*; catcheur, -euse *mf*.

wretch [retʃ] *n* (*unfortunate person*) malheureux, -euse *mf*; (*rascal*) misérable *mf*. ◆**wretched** [-ɪd] *a* (*poor, pitiful*) misérable; (*dreadful*) affreux; (*annoying*) maudit.

wriggle [ˈrɪg(ə)l] *vi* **to w.** (**about**) se tortiller; (*of fish*) frétiller; **to w. out of** (*difficulty, task etc*) esquiver; − *vt* (*fingers, toes*) tortiller.

wring [rɪŋ] *vt* (*pt & pp* **wrung**) (*neck*) tordre; **to w.** (**out**) (*clothes*) essorer; (*water*) faire sortir; **to w. sth out of s.o.** *Fig* arracher qch à qn; **wringing wet** (*trempé*) à tordre.

wrinkle [ˈrɪŋk(ə)l] *n* (*on skin*) ride *f*; (*in cloth or paper*) pli *m*; − *vt* (*skin*) rider; (*cloth, paper*) plisser; − *vi* se rider; faire des plis.

wrist [rɪst] *n* poignet *m*. ◆**wristwatch** *n* montre-bracelet *f*.

writ [rɪt] *n* acte *m* judiciaire; **to issue a w. against s.o.** assigner qn (en justice).

write [raɪt] *vt* (*pt* **wrote**, *pp* **written**) écrire; **to w. down** noter; **to w. off** (*debt*) passer aux profits et pertes; **to w. out** écrire; (*copy*) recopier; **to w. up** (*from notes*) rédiger; (*diary, notes*) mettre à jour; − *vi* écrire; **to w. away** *or* **off** *or* **up for** (*details etc*) écrire pour demander; **to w. back** répondre; **to w. in** *Rad TV* écrire (**for information/***etc* pour demander des renseignements/*etc*). ◆**w.-off** *n* **a** (**complete**) **w.-off** (*car*) une véritable épave. ◆**w.-up** *n* (*report*) *Journ* compte rendu *m*. ◆**writing** *n* (*handwriting*) écriture *f*; (*literature*) littérature *f*; **to put** (**down**) **in w.** mettre par écrit; **some w.** (*on page*) quelque chose d'écrit; **his** *or* **her**

writing(s) (*works*) ses écrits *mpl*; **w. desk** secrétaire *m*; **w. pad** bloc *m* de papier à lettres; **w. paper** papier *m* à lettres. ◆**writer** *n* auteur *m* (**of** de); (*literary*) écrivain *m*.

writhe [raɪð] *vi* (*in pain etc*) se tordre.

written [ˈrɪt(ə)n] *see* write.

wrong [rɒŋ] *a* (*sum, idea etc*) faux, erroné; (*direction, time etc*) mauvais; (*unfair*) injuste; **to be w.** (*of person*) avoir tort (**to do** de faire); (*mistaken*) se tromper; **it's w. to swear**/*etc* (*morally*) c'est mal de jurer/*etc*; **it's the w. road** ce n'est pas la bonne route; **you're the w. man** (*for job etc*) tu n'es pas l'homme qu'il faut; **the clock's w.** la pendule n'est pas à l'heure; **something's w.** quelque chose ne va pas; **something's w. with the phone** le téléphone ne marche pas bien; **something's w. with her arm** elle a quelque chose au bras; **nothing's w.** tout va bien; **what's w. with you?** qu'est-ce que tu as?; **the w. way round** *or* **up** à l'envers; – *adv* mal; **to go w.** (*err*) se tromper; (*of plan*) mal tourner; (*of vehicle, machine*) tomber en panne; – *n* (*injustice*) injustice *f*; (*evil*) mal *m*; **to be in the w.** avoir tort; **right and w.** le bien et le mal; – *vt* faire (du) tort à. ◆**wrongdoer** *n* (*criminal*) malfaiteur *m*. ◆**wrongful** *a* injustifié; (*arrest*) arbitraire. ◆**wrongfully** *adv* à tort. ◆**wrongly** *adv* incorrectement; (*to inform, translate*) mal; (*to suspect etc*) à tort.

wrote [rəʊt] *see* write.

wrought [rɔːt] *a* **w. iron** fer *m* forgé. ◆**w.-'iron** *a* en fer forgé.

wrung [rʌŋ] *see* wring.

wry [raɪ] *a* (**wryer, wryest**) (*comment*) ironique; (*smile*) forcé; **to pull a w. face** grimacer.

X

X, x [eks] *n* X, x *m*. ◆**X-ray** *n* (*beam*) rayon *m* X; (*photo*) radio(graphie) *f*; **to have an X-ray** passer une radio; **X-ray examination** examen *m* radioscopique; – *vt* radiographier.

xenophobia [zenəˈfəʊbɪə] *n* xénophobie *f*.

Xerox® [ˈzɪərɒks] *n* photocopie *f*; – *vt* photocopier.

Xmas [ˈkrɪsməs] *n* *Fam* Noël *m*.

xylophone [ˈzaɪləfəʊn] *n* xylophone *m*.

Y

Y, y [waɪ] *n* Y, y *m*.

yacht [jɒt] *n* yacht *m*. ◆**-ing** *n* yachting *m*.

yank [jæŋk] *vt* *Fam* tirer d'un coup sec; **to y. off** *or* **out** arracher; – *n* coup *m* sec.

Yank(ee) [ˈjæŋk(ɪ)] *n* *Fam* Ricain, -aine *mf*, *Pej* Amerloque *mf*.

yap [jæp] *vi* (**-pp-**) (*of dog*) japper; (*jabber*) *Fam* jacasser.

yard [jɑːd] *n* **1** (*of house etc*) cour *f*; (*for storage*) dépôt *m*, chantier *m*; (*garden*) *Am* jardin *m* (*à l'arrière de la maison*); **builder's y.** chantier *m* de construction. **2** (*measure*) yard *m* (= 91,44 cm). ◆**yardstick** *n* (*criterion*) mesure *f*.

yarn [jɑːn] *n* **1** (*thread*) fil *m*. **2** (*tale*) *Fam* longue histoire *f*.

yawn [jɔːn] *vi* bâiller; – *n* bâillement *m*. ◆**-ing** *a* (*gulf etc*) béant.

yeah [jeə] *adv* (*yes*) *Fam* ouais.

year [jɪər] *n* an *m*, année *f*; (*of wine*) année *f*; **school/tax**/*etc* **y.** année *f* scolaire/fiscale/*etc*; **this y.** cette année; **in the y. 1990** en (l'an) 1990; **he's ten years old** il a dix ans; **New Y.** Nouvel An, Nouvelle Année; **New Year's Day** le jour de l'An; **New Year's Eve** la Saint-Sylvestre. ◆**yearbook** *n* annuaire *m*. ◆**yearly** *a* annuel; – *adv* annuellement.

yearn [jɜːn] *vi* **to y. for s.o.** languir après qn; **to y. for sth** avoir très envie de qch; **to y. to do** avoir très envie de faire. ◆**-ing** *n* grande envie *f* (**for** de, **to do** de faire); (*nostalgia*) nostalgie *f*.

yeast [jiːst] *n* levure *f*.

yell [jel] *vti* **to y. (out)** hurler; **to y. at s.o.** (*scold*) crier après qn; – *n* hurlement *m*.

yellow ['jeləʊ] **1** *a* & *n* (*colour*) jaune (*m*); – *vi* jaunir. **2** *a* (*cowardly*) *Fam* froussard. ◆**yellowish** *a* jaunâtre.

yelp [jelp] *vi* (*of dog*) japper; – *n* jappement *m*.

yen [jen] *n* (*desire*) grande envie *f* (**for** de, **to do** de faire).

yes [jes] *adv* oui; (*contradicting negative question*) si; – *n* oui *m inv*.

yesterday ['jestədɪ] *adv* & *n* hier (*m*); **y. morning/evening** hier matin/soir; **the day before y.** avant-hier.

yet [jet] **1** *adv* encore; (*already*) déjà; **she hasn't come (as) y.** elle n'est pas encore venue; **has he come y.?** est-il déjà arrivé?; **the best y.** le meilleur jusqu'ici; **y. more complicated** (*even more*) encore plus compliqué; **not (just) y.**, **not y. awhile** pas pour l'instant. **2** *conj* (*nevertheless*) pourtant.

yew [juː] *n* (*tree, wood*) if *m*.

Yiddish ['jɪdɪʃ] *n* & *a* yiddish (*m*).

yield [jiːld] *n* rendement *m*; (*profit*) rapport *m*; – *vt* (*produce*) produire, rendre; (*profit*) rapporter; (*give up*) céder (**to** à); – *vi* (*surrender, give way*) céder (**to** à); (*of tree, land etc*) rendre; **'y.'** (*road sign*) *Am* 'cédez la priorité'.

yob(bo) ['jɒb(əʊ)] *n* (*pl* **yob(bo)s**) *Sl* loubar(d) *m*.

yoga ['jəʊgə] *n* yoga *m*.

yog(h)urt ['jɒgət, *Am* 'jəʊgɜːt] *n* yaourt *m*.

yoke [jəʊk] *n* (*for oxen*) & *Fig* joug *m*.

yokel ['jəʊk(ə)l] *n Pej* plouc *m*.

yolk [jəʊk] *n* jaune *m* (d'œuf).

yonder ['jɒndər] *adv Lit* là-bas.

you [juː] *pron* **1** (*polite form singular*) vous; (*familiar form singular*) tu; (*polite and familiar form plural*) vous; (*object*) vous; te, t'; *pl* vous; (*after prep & stressed*) vous; toi; *pl* vous; **(to) y.** (*indirect*) vous; te, t'; *pl* vous; **y. are** vous êtes; tu es; **I see y.** je vous vois; je te vois; **I give it to y.** je vous le donne; je te le donne; **with y.** avec vous; avec toi; **y. teachers** vous autres professeurs; **y. idiot!** espèce d'imbécile! **2** (*indefinite*) on; (*object*) vous; te, t'; *pl* vous; **y. never know** on ne sait jamais.

young [jʌŋ] *a* (**-er, -est**) jeune; **my young(er) brother** mon (frère) cadet; **his** *or* **her youngest brother** le cadet de ses frères; **the youngest son** le cadet; – *n* (*of animals*) petits *mpl*; (*people*) les jeunes *mpl*. ◆**young-looking** *a* qui a l'air jeune. ◆**youngster** *n* jeune *mf*.

your [jɔːr] *poss a* (*polite form singular, polite and familiar form plural*) votre, *pl* vos; (*familiar form singular*) ton, ta, *pl* tes; (*one's*) son, sa, *pl* ses. ◆**yours** *poss pron* le vôtre, la vôtre, *pl* les vôtres; (*familiar form singular*) le tien, la tienne, *pl* les tien(ne)s; **this book is y.** ce livre est à vous *or* est le vôtre; ce livre est à toi *or* est le tien; **a friend of y.** un ami à vous; un ami à toi. ◆**your-'self** *pron* (*polite form*) vous-même; (*familiar form*) toi-même; (*reflexive*) vous; te, t'; (*after prep*) vous; toi; **you wash y.** vous vous lavez; tu te laves. ◆**your-'selves** *pron pl* vous-mêmes; (*reflexive & after prep*) vous.

youth [juːθ] *n* (*pl* **-s** [juːðz]) (*age, young people*) jeunesse *f*; (*young man*) jeune *m*; **y. club** maison *f* des jeunes. ◆**youthful** *a* (*person*) jeune; (*quality, smile etc*) juvénile, jeune. ◆**youthfulness** *n* jeunesse *f*.

yoyo ['jəʊjəʊ] *n* (*pl* **-os**) yo-yo *m inv*.

yucky ['jʌkɪ] *a Sl* dégueulasse.

Yugoslav ['juːgəʊslɑːv] *a* & *n* yougoslave (*mf*). ◆**Yugo'slavia** *n* Yougoslavie *f*.

yummy ['jʌmɪ] *a* (**-ier, -iest**) *Sl* délicieux.

yuppie ['jʌpɪ] *n* jeune cadre *m* ambitieux, jeune loup *m*, NAP *mf*.

Z

Z, z [zed, *Am* ziː] *n* Z, z *m*.

zany ['zeɪnɪ] *a* (**-ier, -iest**) farfelu.

zeal [ziːl] *n* zèle *m*. ◆**zealous** ['zeləs] *a* zélé. ◆**zealously** *adv* avec zèle.

zebra ['ziːbrə, 'zebrə] *n* zèbre *m*; **z. crossing** passage *m* pour piétons.

zenith ['zenɪθ] *n* zénith *m*.

zero ['zɪərəʊ] *n* (*pl* **-os**) zéro *m*; **z. hour** *Mil* & *Fig* l'heure H.

zest [zest] *n* **1** (*gusto*) entrain *m*; (*spice*) *Fig* piquant *m*; **z. for living** appétit *m* de vivre. **2** (*of lemon, orange*) zeste *m*.

zigzag ['zɪgzæg] *n* zigzag *m*; – *a* & *adv* en zigzag; – *vi* (**-gg-**) zigzaguer.

zinc [zɪŋk] *n* (*metal*) zinc *m*.

zip [zɪp] **1** *n* **z. (fastener)** fermeture *f* éclair®; – *vt* (**-pp-**) **to z. (up)** fermer (avec une fermeture éclair®). **2** *n* (*vigour*) *Fam* entrain *m*; – *vi* (**-pp-**) (*go quickly*) aller comme l'éclair. **3** *a* **z. code** *Am* code *m* postal. ◆**zipper** *n* *Am* fermeture *f* éclair®.

zit [zɪt] *n* (*pimple*) *Am Fam* bouton *m*.

zither ['zɪðər] *n* cithare *f*.

zodiac ['zəʊdɪæk] *n* zodiaque *m*.

zombie ['zɒmbɪ] *n* (*spiritless person*) *Fam* robot *m*, zombie *m*.

zone [zəʊn] *n* zone *f*; (*division of city*) secteur *m*.

zoo [zuː] *n* zoo *m*. ◆**zoological** [zuːə-ˈlɒdʒɪk(ə)l] *a* zoologique. ◆**zoology** [zuːˈɒlədʒɪ] *n* zoologie *f*.

zoom [zuːm] **1** *vi* (*rush*) se précipiter; **to z. past** passer comme un éclair. **2** *n* **z. lens** zoom *m*; – *vi* **to z. in** *Cin* faire un zoom, zoomer (**on** sur).

zucchini [zuːˈkiːnɪ] *n* (*pl* **-ni** *or* **-nis**) *Am* courgette *f*.

zwieback ['zwiːbæk] *n* (*rusk*) *Am* biscotte *f*.